Equal Employment Opportunity Commission

DOCUMENT AND REFERENCE TEXT
An Index to Minority Group Employment Information

Prepared by the Research Division of
The Institute of Labor and Industrial Relations
The University of Michigan-Wayne State University

[Produced under contract with
The Equal Employment Opportunity Commission-1967]

ACKNOWLEDGMENTS

The Document and Reference Text (DART) is the product of many individuals' efforts, both in the Equal Employment Opportunity Commission and the Institute of Labor and Industrial Relations of The University of Michigan - Wayne State University. In addition, many persons in public and private agencies and in universities responded generously to requests for materials relating to minority group employment.

In the Institute of Labor and Industrial Relations the following individuals were integrally involved in the DART project: Louis A. Ferman and J.A. Miller provided general and editorial supervision; Elizabeth R. Kolasky worked in every phase of the project, organizing and supervising major parts of the editorial work; Carol Borut initiated and directed the early phases of the acquisitions program; Kirsten Kingdon edited the bibliography in preparation for coding; and Jeffry Piker, Charles Jennings, and Charles Betsey aided in the collection and preparation of materials for the DART.

Consultation services for the DART project were provided by Gloria L. Dardarian and Robert E. Booth, both of the Library Science Department, Wayne State University.

At the Equal Employment Opportunity Commission, the following individuals were responsible for obtaining Commission approval of funds for this contract and provided technical guidance in the planning and preparation of the DART:

Charles B. Markham -- Director, Office of Research and Reports

Phyllis A. Wallace -- Acting Chief, Technical Studies

William H. Enneis -- Staff Psychologist

CONTENTS

Introduction and User's Guide

In January 1967, the Institute of Labor and Industrial Relations, The University of Michigan-Wayne State University, entered into an agreement with the Equal Employment Opportunity Commission for the preparation of an index to literature relating to employment and employment-related problems of major categories of minority workers covered under Title VII of the Civil Rights Act of 1964. The following points identify the essential features of this project.

A literature search of published and unpublished materials was conducted on five categories of workers -- Negro Americans, Spanish-speaking Americans (including Puerto Rican and Mexican Americans), American Indians, Oriental Americans, and women. Items relating to the Negro and employment were catalogued for the period 1940-1966. For the other categories of workers, materials produced between 1956-1966 were catalogued. A few documents produced in early 1967 were included as they came to the attention of the project staff, but no systematic search was made for materials bearing 1967 publication dates. In addition, attention was paid to materials relating to employment discrimination due to religious affiliation, with special reference to Jewish workers.

The literature search employed two basic methods. First, general and specialized library collections were examined for references to minority group employment. More than two hundred different periodicals were surveyed. Second, written requests were directed to various organizations and individuals for their assistance in locating documents and bibliographic references to materials on minority group employment. The overall response was gratifying; the only problem encountered was a lack of control over incoming information. In most cases, it was impossible to determine whether the lack of reply indicated there was no available information or whether there was simply no response to the written request.

The Document and Reference Text (DART) is the end product of this search. The DART is a computer-generated literature index based on the full title Key-Word-In-Context (KWIC) indexing system. KWIC indexing involves the development of a vocabulary of index terms by isolating keywords in the titles of articles or books to be indexed. In some cases additional keywords taken from abstracts or from the text of a document can be used to supplement words which appear in titles and further describe the document being indexed. These supplementary words are called "enrichment terms." Enrichment terms have been added to keywords drawn from titles where (1) the title was considered misleading or not revealing as to content, and (2) the project staff had access to information which provided for the selection of additional key descriptors. More detailed information about the KWIC format follows in the User's Guide.

USER'S GUIDE

Document Code

Each bibliographic entry included in the DART has been assigned a document identification code. This code is an important part of the index, and the user should understand its composition. The following are typical document identification codes:

CSHANLW63724
ISTEISX64373
NEDUCTS64721
NWACHDX65720

Each entry has been assigned a document identification code according to the following system:

1. The first letter refers to a specific minority group or a composite grouping with which the document is concerned. In the DART nine initial letters are used. Their references are:

I	Documents refer specifically to	American Indians
J		Jewish Americans
M		Mexican Americans
N		Negroes
O		Orientals
P		Puerto Ricans
W		women
C	Documents refer to more than on specific minority group, e.g., Negroes and Puerto Ricans; Negro women	
G	Documents refer to general problems involving minority group employment, e.g., provisions of Title VII of the Civil Rights Act of 1964	

2.   The six letters which follow the initial letter (C<u>SHANLW</u>63724) refer to the first four letters of the author's last name (CS<u>HAN</u>LW63724), the first letter of the author's first name (CSHAN<u>L</u>W63724), and the author's middle initial (CSHANL<u>W</u>63724). For documents having more than one author, only the name and initials of the first author are used in constructing the document identification code. When an author's last name has less than four letters, or the author's middle initial is not supplied, the letter X has been inserted to maintain the line length of the code (e.g., MAY<u>X</u>). In cases of institutional authorships, the same rules have been applied with few modifications. For example, in one of the preceding document identification code illustrations (NEDUCT64721), the Education Testing Service represents an institutional author and the letters EDUCTS in the code designate this authorship.

3.   The first two numbers following the author designation refer to the year of publication (CSHANLW<u>63</u>724; NWACHDX<u>65</u>720). In cases of documents bearing no publication date, the letters <u>ND</u> have been used.

4.   The last three numbers (CSHANLW64<u>724</u>) are accession numbers assigned to entries by the project staff and have no user relevance.

<u>Abbreviations and Punctuation Marks</u>

The computer program used in preparing the DART KWIC-Index necessitated the development of several conventions affecting the use of abbreviations and punctuation marks.

Abbreviations used in the DART are listed alphabetically with their full English equivalents in Appendix A. (See Contents)

Alterations in conventional punctuation marks for purposes of computer processing include the following:

1.   A single hyphen between two letters <u>within</u> a word is used as a substitute for the apostrophe. When an apostrophe appears at the end of the word, however, it has been omitted.

2.   A single hyphen <u>between two words</u> is used to join those words in a compound, or conceptual, sense for purposes of indexing. For example, Title VII appears in the index as TITLE-VII, Mexican American as MEXICAN-AMERICAN, technological change as TECHNOLOGICAL-CHANGE, etc. These compound forms represent keywords developed for user convenience.

3.　　All quotation marks or italicizations in the original citations have been omitted.

4.　　The comma is used both normally and as a substitute for the semi-colon.

5.　　The period is used normally and as a substitute for the colon, the exclamation mark, and the question mark.

Keyword Index

Document citations are arranged alphabetically by keyword. The keywords appear in bold face on the left side of the page, as seen in the following example. Any given citation will appear as an entry under each of its keywords. If, for example, a citation contains the keywords EQUAL-EMPLOYMENT-OPPORTUNITY, DISCRIMINATION, and PRACTICES, then that citation will appear in full under each of these keywords with its assigned document code. Within the citation, the keyword being referenced will be in bold print.

```
EQUAL-EMPLOYMENT-OPP
    WHAT THE SUPERVISOR SHOULD KNOW ABOUT THE EQUAL-EMPLOYMENT-OPPORTUNITY LAW.                          GAHEREX65804

    PARTIAL INVENTORY OF ON-GOING RESEARCH IN EQUAL-EMPLOYMENT-OPPORTUNITIES.                             GANDEBR67589

    MANAGEMENT GUIDE. EQUAL-EMPLOYMENT-OPPORTUNITY.                                                       GASSOIC63407

    AN ASSESSMENT OF THE SUITABILITY OF THE FACETED STRUCTURE OF THE WRU EDUCATION THESAURUS AS A FRAMEWORK
    FOR PREPARATION OF A THESAURUS OF EQUAL-EMPLOYMENT-OPPORTUNITY TERMS.                                 GBARHGC66162

    6. TEST TECHNOLOGY AND EQUAL-EMPLOYMENT-OPPORTUNITY.                                                  GBAYRAG66428

    EQUAL-EMPLOYMENT-OPPORTUNITY UNDER CIVIL-RIGHTS-ACT OF 1964.                                          GBERGRK64437

    EQUAL-EMPLOYMENT-OPPORTUNITY AND EXECUTIVE ORDER 10925.                                               GBIRNOX62451

    THE QUESTS FOR ECONOMIC STABILITY AND EQUAL-EMPLOYMENT-OPPORTUNITY.                                   GBRIMAF66475

    A SPECIAL REPORT -- THE EQUAL-EMPLOYMENT-OPPORTUNITY LAW, TITLE-VII OF THE CIVIL-RIGHTS-ACT OF 1964.  GBURENAND495
```

In the example, the keyword is truncated at 20 spaces. This is true for all keywords with more than 20 letters (including hyphens). In all cases there will be a sufficient number of letters of the keyword to enable the reader to ascertain which keyword is being referenced.

Bibliography

The bibliography is divided into nine sections, according to the initial letters of the document identification codes. (See preceding section on Document Code) The three parts of the bibliographic entry are author, title (including enrichment terms, if these have been added), and source. Each of these is illustrated by the following example:

NHOLL JH65560   HOLLAND   JH ──①   *EDUCATIONAL TESTING SERVICE
②──►PREPARATION OF THE NEGRO COLLEGE GRADUATE FOR BUSINESS.
③──►/EMPLOYMENT─SELECTION/
④──►SELECTING AND TRAINING NEGROES FOR MANAGERIAL POSITIONS.   ⑤
      EDUCATIONAL TESTING SERVICE. PRINCETON, NEW JERSEY. 1965.
      PP 23-34.

    1.   Author's last name, followed by the first letter of the author's first name and middle initial if supplied. In cases of institutional authorships, the full name or an abbreviation is given.

    2.   Title of document. Titles longer than one line will have the second and any additional lines indented two spaces.

    3.   Keywords enclosed by slashes /   / are enrichment terms. These terms are NOT a part of the original document titles.

    4.   Source of document.

    5.   Names of organizations preceded by an asterisk are "supplementary index" terms and have been used to compile the Institutional Sponsors List. (See Contents) Organizations so identified are key sponsors or producers of information relating to minority group employment. In the DART they are selectively identified.

Author Index

The Author Index is arranged alphabetically by author (whether individual, corporate, primary or secondary) and the code numbers of all the entries by that author which appear in the index.

Institutional Sponsors Index

The Institutional Sponsors Index is arranged alphabetically by name of organization and the code numbers of all the entries identified with the particular organization which appear in the index.

List of Keywords

All keywords used in the index appear in this alphabetical listing. Keywords include selected important words from the titles of documents and enrichment terms purposely assigned to some documents.

When using the List of Keywords, it is important to note that certain words with variant forms may be separated in the listing because of the alphabetizing technique used in computer processing. For example, the words COED and CO-ED both appear in the index, as do RESURVEY and RE-SURVEY, but in neither case are they listed consecutively. Thus, the user must be sensitive to words having variant forms.

List of Suppressed Words

Words in document titles that do not appear as index terms can be found in the List of Suppressed Words. This list can assist the user in avoiding fruitless searches for words that have been prevented from indexing.

Conducting a Search

The user's access to relevant documents is provided through the List of Keywords and the Keyword Index itself. The List of Suppressed Words aids the user in eliminating certain words as a starting point.

If the List of Keywords is used as the starting point for a search, the user should select from the List those keywords which best describe his subject interests. Then, by referring to the Keyword Index under each of the selected keywords, he will find a list of relevant citations. Although the user may find it easier to browse first in the List of Suppressed Words or the List of Keywords, he may, of course, use the Keyword Index directly.

The user should remember that KWIC indexes do not provide cross-references, and he must establish his own list of "see" and "see also" references. For example, if a user is interested in documents relating to fair employment legislation, relevant citations may be found under the keywords TITLE-VII, CIVIL-RIGHTS-ACT, LEGIS-LATION, and LAW. A user should also search the antonymic form of a given keyword, e.g., EMPLOYMENT and UNEMPLOYMENT. The normal redundancy of alphabetical listing will aid the user in his search by listing in close proximity such related keywords as EMPLOYEE, EMPLOYER, and EMPLOYMENT. When a relevant citation is located, the user may wish to expand his search by using all or some portion of the keywords assigned to that citation.

The easiest way to find all papers by a given author is to consult the Author Index, and using the document codes listed, locate the complete references in the Bibliography.

Keyword Index

ABC
ABC REPORT 1964. /COLLEGE EDUCATION/

NDARTCX64309

ABILITY
ON SPECIAL-TRAINING-UNIT PERFORMANCE AS AN INDEX OF NEGRO **ABILITY**.

NERICRW46339

THE UPPER LIMIT OF **ABILITY** AMONG AMERICAN NEGROES.

NJENKMD48607

ABOLISH
SUGGESTED LANGUAGE FOR A STATE ACT TO **ABOLISH** DISCRIMINATORY WAGE RATES BASED ON SEX.

WUSDLAB64218

ABSENT
THE **ABSENT** FATHER HAUNTS THE NEGRO FAMILY.

NLINCCE65694

ABSENTEEISM
ABSENTEEISM AMONG WOMEN WORKERS IN INDUSTRY.

WISAMVX62876

WHAT ABOUT WOMEN-S **ABSENTEEISM** AND LABOR TURNOVER.

WUSDLAB65225

ABSORPTION
THE PREDICTION AND EXPLANATION OF ECONOMIC **ABSORPTION** AMONG MEXICAN-AMERICANS, NEGROES, AND ANGLOS IN A NORTHERN INDUSTRIAL COMMUNITY.

CSHANLW63120

THE ECONOMIC **ABSORPTION** AND CULTURAL INTEGRATION OF IMMIGRANT MEXICAN-AMERICAN AND NEGRO WORKERS.

CSHANLW64124

THE ECONOMIC **ABSORPTION** OF IN-MIGRANT LABORERS IN A NORTHERN INDUSTRIAL COMMUNITY. /MEXICAN-AMERICAN NEGRO/

CSHANLW64486

THE PREDICTION OF ECONOMIC **ABSORPTION** AND CULTURAL INTEGRATION AMONG MEXICAN-AMERICANS, NEGROES, AND ANGLOS IN A NORTHERN INDUSTRIAL COMMUNITY.

CSHANLW66123

ECONOMIC **ABSORPTION** AND CULTURAL INTEGRATION OF THE URBAN NEWCOMER. /NEGRO MEXICAN-AMERICAN/

CUVIOIP65277

THE ECONOMIC **ABSORPTION** OF NAVAHO INDIAN MIGRANTS IN DENVER, COLORADO.

IWEPPRS65684

ABSTRACT
STATISTICAL **ABSTRACT** OF THE UNITED STATES. 1964. /DEMOGRAPHY/

CUSBURC64380

ABUNDANCE
POLITICAL NECESSITIES OF **ABUNDANCE**. /GUARANTEED-INCOME/

GTHEORX64610

THE POLITICAL NECESSITIES OF **ABUNDANCE**. /GUARANTEED-INCOME/

GTHEORX64968

UN-MET NEED IN A LAND OF **ABUNDANCE**.

NEPSTLA63337

ABUSES
URBAN JOB DISCRIMINATION. **ABUSES** AND REDRESS.

GRICOLX66237

ACADEMIC
SOCIAL-STRATIFICATION AND **ACADEMIC** ACHIEVEMENT. /NEGRO ORIENTAL/

CWILSAB63325

SOME NON-INTELLECTUAL CORRELATES OF **ACADEMIC** ACHIEVEMENT AMONG MEXICAN-AMERICAN SECONDARY SCHOOL STUDENTS.

MGILLLJ62401

A COMPARISON OF THE **ACADEMIC** ACHIEVEMENTS OF WHITE AND NEGRO HIGH SCHOOL GRADUATES. /EDUCATION/

NBULLHA50132

THE RELATION OF RACIAL SEGREGATION IN EARLY SCHOOLING TO THE LEVEL OF ASPIRATION AND **ACADEMIC** ACHIEVEMENT OF NEGRO STUDENTS IN A NORTHERN HIGH SCHOOL.

NSAINJN62137

ACADEMIC WOMEN. /OCCUPATIONS/

WBERNJX64638

THE PRESENT SITUATION IN THE **ACADEMIC** WORLD OF WOMEN TRAINED IN ENGINEERING. /OCCUPATIONS/

WBERNJX65639

THE **ACADEMIC** MARKET PLACE. /OCCUPATIONS/

WCAPLTX58679

ACADEMIC WOMAN. /OCCUPATIONS/

WECKERE59746

ACADEMIC WOMEN. /OCCUPATIONS/

WELLMMX65749

THE COMPARATIVE **ACADEMIC** ACHIEVEMENT OF WOMEN FORTY YEARS OF AGE AND OVER AND WOMEN EIGHTEEN TO TWENTY FIVE.

WHALFIT61814

THE COMPARATIVE **ACADEMIC** ACHIEVEMENT OF YOUNG AND OLD. /TRAINING/

WHALFIT62813

WOMEN ON COLLEGE AND UNIVERSITY FACULTIES. A HISTORICAL SURVEY AND A STUDY OF THEIR PRESENT **ACADEMIC** STATUS. /OCCUPATIONS/

WPOLLLA65063

RELATIONSHIP BETWEEN THE EDUCATIONAL GOALS AND THE **ACADEMIC** PERFORMANCE OF WOMEN. A CONFIRMATION.

WWEITHX59260

ACCEPTANCE
TRADE UNION COMPLIANCE WITH PRESIDENTIAL DIRECTIVES, MEMBERSHIP **ACCEPTANCE**, SENIORITY, ETC.

NCOOPJX64294

COMMUNITY RESISTANCE TO AND **ACCEPTANCE** OF DESEGREGATION.

NKILLLM65651

THE RELATIONSHIP OF PARENTAL IDENTIFICATION TO SEX ROLE **ACCEPTANCE** IN MARRIED, SINGLE, CAREER AND NON-CAREER WOMEN. /WORK-WOMEN-ROLE/

WBREYCH64654

ACCESS
ACCULTURATION, **ACCESS** AND ALCOHOL IN A TRI-ETHNIC COMMUNITY.

MGRAVTD67214

OBJECTIVE **ACCESS** IN THE OPPORTUNITY STRUCTURE. THE ASSESSMENT OF THREE ETHNIC GROUPS WITH RESPECT TO QUANTIFIED SOCIAL STRUCTURAL VARIABLES.

MRENDGX63461

LAST MAN IN. RACIAL **ACCESS** TO UNIONS.

NGREESX59451

ACCESS OF GIRLS AND WOMEN TO EDUCATION IN RURAL AREAS. A COMPARATIVE STUDY.

WUNESCO64166

ACCIDENTAL
I STATEMENT BEFORE THE HOUSE POST OFFICE AND CIVIL SERVICE SUBCOMMITTEE ON POSTAL OPERATIONS, II DISCRIMINATION. PLANNED AND **ACCIDENTAL**. /TESTING/

GENNEWH67928

THE **ACCIDENTAL** CENTURY. /TECHNOLOGICAL-CHANGE/

GHARRMX65597

ACCOMODATION
COMPILATION OF LAWS AGAINST DISCRIMINATION, EMPLOYMENT, EDUCATIONAL INSTITUTIONS, PLACES OF PUBLIC **ACCOMODATION**. PUBLIC HOUSING, PUBLICLY ASSISTED HOUSING, PRIVATE HOUSING. /MASSACHUSETTS/

GMASSCAND963

ACCOMODATION BETWEEN NEGRO AND WHITE EMPLOYEES IN A WEST COAST AIRCRAFT INDUSTRY, 1942-1944.

ACCOMODATION   (CONTINUATION)   NREEDBA47045
    /CASE-STUDY/

    PUERTO-RICANS IN PHILADELPHIA. MIGRATION AND **ACCOMODATION**. /PENNSYLVANIA/   PKOSSJD65822

    PATTERNS OF SOCIAL **ACCOMODATION** OF THE MIGRANT PUERTO-RICAN IN THE AMERICAN SOCIAL STRUCTURE. PSEDAEX58850

ACCOMODATIONS
    EXPLANATION AND DIGEST OF THE 1966 KENTUCKY CIVIL-RIGHTS-ACT COVERING EMPLOYMENT AND PUBLIC   GKENTCHND844
    ACCOMODATIONS. ENACTED JANUARY 27 1966, EFFECTIVE JULY 1 1966.

    LAWS AGAINST DISCRIMINATION. EMPLOYMENT, PUBLIC **ACCOMODATIONS**, HOUSING. /OHIO/   GOHIOCR65125

ACCREDITED
    ATTITUDES TOWARD WOMEN COLLEGE TEACHERS IN INSTITUTIONS OF HIGHER EDUCATION **ACCREDITED** BY THE NORTH   WBERWHD62475
    CENTRAL ASSOCIATION.

ACCULTURATION
    THEORY, METHOD AND FINDINGS IN THE STUDY OF **ACCULTURATION**. A REVIEW. /MEXICAN-AMERICAN NEGRO/   CPETECX65989

    THE ASSIMILATION AND **ACCULTURATION** OF MIGRANTS TO URBAN AREAS. /MEXICAN-AMERICAN NEGRO/   CSHANLW63484

    ACCULTURATION, SELF-IDENTIFICATION, AND PERSONALITY ADJUSTMENT.   ICHANNA65543

    HEALTH PRACTICES AND EDUCATIONAL ASPIRATIONS AS INDICATORS OF **ACCULTURATION** AND SOCIAL-CLASS AMONG THE   IKUPFHJ62216
    EASTERN CHEROKEE. /NORTH-CAROLINA/

    TODAY -- **ACCULTURATION**.   IMAYHMP62589

    THE CULTURE AND **ACCULTURATION** OF THE DELAWARE INDIANS.   INEWCWW56600

    THE **ACCULTURATION** OF AMERICAN-INDIANS.   IVOGTEZ57678

    SOME PROBLEMS IN THE **ACCULTURATION** OF MEXICAN LABORERS TO A FACTORY.   MALBEPM64356

    ACCULTURATION, ACCESS AND ALCOHOL IN A TRI-ETHNIC COMMUNITY.   MGRAVTD67214

    A STUDY OF THE **ACCULTURATION** AND SOCIAL ASPIRATIONS OF SIXTY JUNIOR HIGH SCHOOL STUDENTS FROM THE MEXICAN   MJONEBM62421
    ETHNIC GROUP.

    ACCULTURATION AND NEGRO BLUE-COLLAR WORKERS.   NSTAMRX64171

    CONTRASTIVE **ACCULTURATION** OF CALIFORNIA JAPANESE. COMPARATIVE APPROACH TO THE STUDY OF IMMIGRANTS.   OBEFUHX65701

    THE VALIDATION OF **ACCULTURATION**. A CONDITION TO ETHNIC ASSIMILATION.   OBROOLX55708

    THE PUERTO-RICAN COMMUNITY IN AMERICA. RAPID **ACCULTURATION**.   PBOWALX62889

ACCULTURIZATION
    COMPARISON OF MEXICANS, NEGROES AND WHITES WITH RESPECT TO OCCUPATIONAL HISTORY, RURAL-URBAN RESIDENCE   CGOLDVX60494
    HISTORY AND **ACCULTURIZATION** WITHIN THE INSTITUTIONAL STRUCTURE OF LANSING, MICHIGAN.

ACCUSED
    LARGE CORPORATIONS **ACCUSED** OF DISCRIMINATION AGAINST JEWS IN MANAGEMENT, EXECUTIVE CAPACITIES BY   JWORLOX64773
    AMERICAN-JEWISH-COMMITTEE.

ACHIEVEMENT
    SOCIAL-STRATIFICATION AND ACADEMIC **ACHIEVEMENT**. /NEGRO ORIENTAL/   CWILSAB63325

    MINORITY-GROUP AND CLASS STATUS AS RELATED TO SOCIAL AND PERSONALITY FACTORS IN SCHOLASTIC **ACHIEVEMENT**.   GDEUTMP60640

    RACE, ETHNICITY, AND THE **ACHIEVEMENT** SYNDROME.   GROSEBC59252

    MANPOWER PROGRAMS. THEIR CONTRIBUTION TO THE **ACHIEVEMENT** OF EQUAL-OPPORTUNITY MANPOWER ADMINISTRATION.   GWHITHC65558

    THE EFFECT OF RESIDENTIAL SEGREGATION UPON EDUCATIONAL **ACHIEVEMENT** AND ASPIRATIONS.   GWILSAB60567

    ANOMIE AND **ACHIEVEMENT** MOTIVATION. A STUDY OF PERSONALITY DEVELOPMENT WITHIN CULTURAL DISORGANIZATION.   IKERCAC59018

    SOME NON-INTELLECTUAL CORRELATES OF ACADEMIC **ACHIEVEMENT** AMONG MEXICAN-AMERICAN SECONDARY SCHOOL   MGILLLJ62401
    STUDENTS.

    SOME DIFFERENCES IN FACTORS RELATED TO EDUCATIONAL **ACHIEVEMENT** OF TWO MEXICAN-AMERICAN GROUPS.   MMONTPX60443

    SPANISH-SPEAKING AND ENGLISH SPEAKING CHILDREN IN SOUTHWEST TEXAS. A COMPARATIVE STUDY OF INTELLIGENCE,   MRATLYX60460
    SOCIO-ECONOMIC STATUS, AND **ACHIEVEMENT**.

    TOWARD EQUALITY. BALTIMORE-S PROGRESS-REPORT. A CHRONICLE OF PROGRESS SINCE WORLD-WAR-II TOWARD THE   NBALTUL58048
    ACHIEVEMENT OF EQUAL-RIGHTS AND OPPORTUNITIES FOR NEGROES IN MARYLAND 1946-1958.

    EDUCATIONAL **ACHIEVEMENT** AND JOB-OPPORTUNITIES. A VICIOUS CIRCLE.   NBLALHM58084

    OPERATION **ACHIEVEMENT**. /NEW-YORK EMPLOYMENT/   NCALVIJ63176

    INFORMAL FACTORS IN CAREER **ACHIEVEMENT**.   NDALTMX51247

    FAMILY AND **ACHIEVEMENT**. A PROPOSAL TO STUDY THE EFFECT OF FAMILY SOCIALIZATION ON ACHIEVEMENT AND   NEPPSEG65334
    PERFORMANCE AMONG URBAN NEGRO AMERICANS.

    FAMILY AND ACHIEVEMENT. A PROPOSAL TO STUDY THE EFFECT OF FAMILY SOCIALIZATION ON **ACHIEVEMENT** AND   NEPPSEG65334
    PERFORMANCE AMONG URBAN NEGRO AMERICANS.

    COMMUNITY FACTORS AFFECTING MOTIVATION AND **ACHIEVEMENT** IN A DECADE OF DECISION. /EDUCATION/   NGRANLB62441

    ACHIEVEMENT MOTIVATION CHARACTERISTICS OF NEGRO COLLEGE FRESHMEN.   NHARREC59492

    WORKING AT IMPROVING THE MOTIVATIONAL AND **ACHIEVEMENT** LEVELS OF THE DEPRIVED.   NHARREC63367

    INTELLIGENCE AND EDUCATIONAL **ACHIEVEMENT** OF A MATCHED SAMPLE OF WHITE AND NEGRO STUDENTS.   NMCQURX60730

    ACHIEVEMENT OF MALE HIGH SCHOOL DROPOUTS AND GRADUATES IN ALABAMA VOCATIONAL SCHOOLS.   NMILLGJ65791

    SOME CORRELATES OF HIGH NEED FOR **ACHIEVEMENT** AMONG URBAN NORTHERN NEGROES.   NNUTTRL46951

    THE RELATION OF RACIAL SEGREGATION IN EARLY SCHOOLING TO THE LEVEL OF ASPIRATION AND ACADEMIC **ACHIEVEMENT**   NSAINJN62137
    OF NEGRO STUDENTS IN A NORTHERN HIGH SCHOOL.

    ACHIEVEMENT, CULTURE AND PERSONALITY. THE CASE OF THE JAPANESE-AMERICANS.   OCAUDWX61711

ACHIEVEMENT   (CONTINUATION)

THE **ACHIEVEMENT** MOTIVE IN WOMEN. A STUDY OF THE IMPLICATIONS FOR CAREER DEVELOPMENT.

WBARURX66453

THE COMPARATIVE ACADEMIC **ACHIEVEMENT** OF WOMEN FORTY YEARS OF AGE AND OVER AND WOMEN EIGHTEEN TO TWENTY FIVE.

WHALFIT61814

THE COMPARATIVE ACADEMIC **ACHIEVEMENT** OF YOUNG AND OLD. /TRAINING/

WHALFIT62813

ACHIEVEMENTS

A COMPARISON OF THE ACADEMIC **ACHIEVEMENTS** OF WHITE AND NEGRO HIGH SCHOOL GRADUATES. /EDUCATION/

NBULLHA50132

NEGROES IN FIVE NEW-YORK CITIES. A STUDY OF PROBLEMS, **ACHIEVEMENTS** AND TRENDS. /RACE-RELATIONS/

NGRIEES58455

FAMILY PATTERNS, **ACHIEVEMENTS**, AND ASPIRATIONS OF URBAN NEGROES.

NLYSTMH61718

SIGNIFICANT **ACHIEVEMENTS** OF NEGROES IN EDUCATION 1907-1947. /OCCUPATIONS/

NWHITMJ48249

ACHIEVING

CRITICAL PROBLEMS IN **ACHIEVING** EQUAL-EMPLOYMENT-OPPORTUNITY.

GLOCKHC66906

THE ROLE OF MANPOWER POLICY IN **ACHIEVING** AGGREGATE GOALS. /EMPLOYMENT INCOME/

GTHURLC66640

ACT

GUIDE TO LAWFUL AND UNLAWFUL PRE-EMPLOYMENT INQUIRIES BY EMPLOYERS, EMPLOYMENT-AGENCIES, AND LABOR ORGANIZATIONS UNDER THE CALIFORNIA FAIR-EMPLOYMENT-PRACTICE **ACT**, LABOR CODE, SECTIONS 1410-1432.

GCALDIR60527

FAIR-EMPLOYMENT-PRACTICE **ACT**...FEPC RULES AND REGULATIONS... GUIDE TO PRE-EMPLOYMENT INQUIRIES. /CALIFORNIA/

GCALFEP61533

COMMISSION ENFORCEMENT OF STATE LAWS AGAINST DISCRIMINATION. A COMPARATIVE ANALYSIS OF THE KANSAS **ACT**.

GDYSORB65657

FAIR-EMPLOYMENT-PRACTICES **ACT**, STATE LAWS GRANTING EQUAL RIGHTS, PRIVILEGES, ETC.

GELWAEX58662

FAIR-EMPLOYMENT-PRACTICES **ACT** AND REGULATION 30. /HAWAII/

GHAWADL64766

QUESTIONING APPLICANTS FOR EMPLOYMENT, A GUIDE FOR APPLICATION FORMS AND INTERVIEWS UNDER THE HAWAII FAIR-EMPLOYMENT-PRACTICES **ACT**.

GHAWADL64767

FAIR-EMPLOYMENT-PRACTICE **ACT** OF ILLINOIS.

GILLIFEND795

YOUTH EMPLOYMENT **ACT**.

GLEVISA63898

CALIFORNIA FAIR-EMPLOYMENT-PRACTICE **ACT**.

GMERCMA59975

MINNESOTA STATE **ACT** AGAINST DISCRIMINATION, AS APPROVED BY THE MINNESOTA LEGISLATURE, APRIL 1961. /LEGISLATION/

GMINNSCND010

LEGAL RULINGS INTERPRETING THE PROVISIONS OF THE PENNSYLVANIA FAIR-EMPLOYMENT-PRACTICE **ACT**.

GPENNFE58153

THE NEW FEDERAL FAIR-EMPLOYMENT-PRACTICES **ACT** -- COMPARISON WITH STATE LAW AND AN ANALYSIS OF RELEVANT STATE EXPERIENCES. /MISSOURI/

GROBEPC64239

MASSACHUSETTS FAIR-EMPLOYMENT-PRACTICE **ACT** OF 1946.

GUSDLAB46075

EQUAL-EMPLOYMENT-OPPORTUNITY **ACT** OF 1962. REPORT TO ACCOMPANY HR 10144.

GUSHOUR62340

EQUAL-EMPLOYMENT-OPPORTUNITY **ACT** OF 1963, REPORT TO ACCOMPANY HR 405.

GUSHOUR63341

FEDERAL EQUALITY OF OPPORTUNITY IN EMPLOYMENT **ACT**.

GUSSENA52350

UNITED STATES HAS STANDING UNDER INTERSTATE COMMERCE **ACT** AND COMMERCE CLAUSE TO ENJOIN SEGREGATIVE PRACTICES OF CITY. /LEGISLATION/

NHARVLR64500

RAILWAY LABOR **ACT** -- DENIAL OF UNION MEMBERSHIP TO NEGROES.

NMINNLR58800

RACE DISCRIMINATION AND THE NLRA **ACT**. THE BRAVE NEW WORLD OF MIRANDA. /LEGISLATION/

NSOVEMI63169

ON THE JOB, WOMEN **ACT** MUCH LIKE MEN. /OCCUPATIONS/

WBUSIWX63667

SUGGESTED LANGUAGE FOR A STATE **ACT** TO ABOLISH DISCRIMINATORY WAGE RATES BASED ON SEX.

WUSDLAB64218

THE NURSING SHORTAGE AND THE NURSE TRAINING **ACT** OF 1964. /MANPOWER/

WYETTDX66246

ACTION

ACTION FOR EMPLOYMENT. A DEMONSTRATION NEIGHBORHOOD MANPOWER PROJECT.

GALLCTO66361

LABOR UNIONS IN **ACTION**, A STUDY OF THE MAINSPRINGS OF UNIONISM.

GBARBJX48421

TRADE UNION LEADERSHIP COUNCIL --EXPERIMENT IN COMMUNITY **ACTION**. /DETROIT MICHIGAN/

GBATTRX63426

ECONOMIC EQUALITY AND GOVERNMENT **ACTION**.

GBERLAA66222

ANTI-DISCRIMINATION LAWS IN **ACTION** IN NEW-JERSEY. A LAW-SOCIOLOGY STUDY.

GBLUMAW65459

ACTION PROGRAMS FOR FEPC ADVISORY COMMITTEES. /CALIFORNIA/

GCALFEP66528

POSITIVE **ACTION** ON UNEMPLOYMENT.

GCASSFH63562

POVERTY IN NEW-YORK CITY. FACTS FOR PLANNING COMMUNITY **ACTION**.

GCOMCCN64210

MINORITY PROGRAM CALLS FOR COMMUNITY **ACTION**.

GCRAICE65619

JOB OPPORTUNITIES FROM FEPC **ACTION**.

GHOWDEX65785

IMPLEMENTING AFFIRMATIVE **ACTION** WITH AIR-FORCE CONTRACTORS.

GHUNTHX63789

THE COMMUNITY **ACTION** AGENCY-S ROLE IN COMPREHENSIVE MANPOWER PROGRAMS -- PLANNING AND PROBLEMS.

GKANERD66863

MISSOURI LOCAL GOVERNMENT **ACTION** IN THE AREA OF HUMAN-RIGHTS.

GMISSCH63022

FINDINGS OF FACT, CONCLUSIONS AND **ACTION** OF THE COMMISSION ON HUMAN-RELATIONS IN RE. INVESTIGATIVE PUBLIC HEARINGS INTO ALLEGED DISCRIMINATORY PRACTICE BY THE HOTEL AND RESTAURANT INDUSTRY IN PHILADELPHIA. /PENNSYLVANIA/

GPHILCH61176

TITLE-VII. RELATIONSHIP AND EFFECT ON STATE **ACTION**. /LEGISLATION/

GPURDJW66209

STATE EXECUTIVE AUTHORITY TO PROMOTE CIVIL-RIGHTS. AN **ACTION** PROGRAM FOR THE 1960-S.

GSILAJX63310

A TIME FOR **ACTION**. PROCEEDINGS OF THE NATIONAL CONFERENCE ON EQUAL-EMPLOYMENT-OPPORTUNITY, 1962.

ACTION   (CONTINUATION)
/MILITARY/   GUSDARM62193

   DOCUMENTARY HISTORY OF THE FOX PROJECT, 1948-1959. A PROGRAM IN **ACTION** ANTHROPOLOGY.   INETTRM60599

   NEGRO UNIONISTS ORGANIZE FOR **ACTION**.   NBUSIWX60157

   AFL-CIO COUNCIL GETS NEGRO DEMAND FOR MORE **ACTION** ON BIAS IN UNIONS.   NBUSIWX61144

   MINORITY PROGRAM CALLS FOR COMMUNITY **ACTION**.   NCRAICE65240

   NAACP LABOR MANUAL. A GUIDE TO **ACTION**.   NHILLHX58531

   IDEOLOGY AND INTERESTS. THE DETERMINANTS OF UNION **ACTION**.   NKORNWA53659

   FACTS FOR **ACTION**. /LOUISVILLE KENTUCKY/   NLOUIHR66716

   THE NEGRO FAMILY. THE CASE FOR NATIONAL **ACTION**.   NMOYNDP65862

   TRADE UNION LEADERSHIP COUNCIL. EXPERIMENT IN COMMUNITY **ACTION**.   NNEWXUT63088

   RACIAL DISCRIMINATION IN EMPLOYMENT. PROPOSALS FOR CORRECTIVE **ACTION**.   NPOLLDX63006

   COUNSELING GIRLS AND WOMEN. AWARENESS. ANALYSIS. **ACTION**.   WBERRJX66642

   COMMUNITY WOMEN-S GROUPS TAKE **ACTION**. /HOUSEHOLD-WORKERS/   WBUFFDX66661

   ACTION FOR EQUAL-PAY.   WUSDLAB64183

ACTIONS
REPORT AND SUMMARY OF THE AIR FORCE ON **ACTIONS** TAKEN BY LOCKHEED AIRCRAFT CORPORATION AT THE AIR FORCE
PLANT NO 6 IN MARIETTA, GEORGIA. /INDUSTRY/   NPRESCD61013

ACTIVE
EMPLOYMENT COUNSELING AS AN INTEGRAL PART OF AN **ACTIVE** LABOR-MARKET POLICY.   GEHRLRA65791

   AN **ACTIVE** EMPLOYER MANPOWER POLICY.   GLIVEER66567

   PRELIMINARY REPORT ON SURVEY OF **ACTIVE** APPRENTICES. /CALIFORNIA/   MCALDIR62376

   NEGRO AMERICAN LABOR COUNCIL IS **ACTIVE** IN NEW-YORK STATE.   NBROOTR61119

ACTIVITIES
SUPPLEMENTARY **ACTIVITIES** FOR STATE GOVERNMENTS SEEKING TO ELIMINATE DISCRIMINATION.   GROUTFB64264

ANNUAL REPORT OF THE SECRETARY OF HEALTH, EDUCATION, AND WELFARE TO THE CONGRESS ON TRAINING **ACTIVITIES**
UNDER THE MANPOWER-DEVELOPMENT-AND-TRAINING-ACT, 1965.   GUSDHEW66978

A SURVEY OF THE ECONOMIC AND CULTURAL CONDITIONS OF THE NEGRO POPULATION OF LOUISVILLE, KENTUCKY AND A
REVIEW OF THE PROGRAM AND **ACTIVITIES** OF THE LOUISVILLE URBAN-LEAGUE. JANUARY-FEBRUARY, 1948.   NNATLUL48903

STUDY OF ECONOMIC AND CULTURAL **ACTIVITIES** IN THE WARREN AREA AS THEY RELATE TO MINORITY PEOPLE. /OHIO/   NWARRUL64986

A STUDY OF JOB MOTIVATIONS, **ACTIVITIES**, AND SATISFACTIONS OF PRESENT AND PROSPECTIVE WOMEN COLLEGE
FACULTY MEMBERS. /OCCUPATIONS/   WCOOKWX60252

ACTIVITY
SOCIAL INTEGRATION, ATTITUDES AND UNION **ACTIVITY**.   GDEANLR54944

   REPORT ON INDIAN FARM LABOR **ACTIVITY**.   IUSDLAB66668

ACTS
FAIR-EMPLOYMENT-PRACTICE **ACTS** AND THE COURTS.   GBERNYX64448

   STATE FAIR-EMPLOMENT LAWS AND THEIR ADMINISTRATION. TEXTS, FEDERAL-STATE COOPERATION, PROHIBITED **ACTS**.   GBURENA64497

   BRIEF SUMMARY OF STATE LAWS AGAINST DISCRIMINATION IN PRIVATE EMPLOYMENT. FAIR-EMPLOYMENT-PRACTICE **ACTS**.   GUSDLAB63439

   A STUDY OF STATE AND LOCAL LEGISLATIVE AND ADMINISTRATIVE **ACTS** DESIGNED TO MEET PROBLEMS OF HUMAN-RIGHTS.   GWISCLR52573

ADAPTATION
THE **ADAPTATION** OF LABOR RESOURCES TO CHANGING NEEDS. /MOBILITY/   GLESTRA66532

   MOBILITY AND WORKER **ADAPTATION** TO ECONOMIC CHANGE IN THE US.   GTRAVHX63836

   THE MIGRATION AND **ADAPTATION** OF AMERICAN INDIANS TO LOS-ANGELES. /CALIFORNIA/   IPRICJA67608

   AMERICAN-INDIANS IN LOS-ANGELES. A STUDY OF **ADAPTATION** TO A CITY. /CALIFORNIA/   IUVCALA66675

   ADAPTATION OF PAPAGO WORKERS TO OFF-RESERVATION OCCUPATIONS.   IWADDJX66680

   KINSHIP AS A FACTOR AFFECTING CANTONESE ECONOMIC **ADAPTATION** IN THE UNITED STATES.   OBARNML66698

ADAPTATIONS
EXCLUSIONS AND **ADAPTATIONS**. A RE-EVALUATION OF THE CULTURE-OF-POVERTY THEME.   NCOHERXND221

ADC
FACTS ON **ADC** IN NORTH-CAROLINA. /NEGRO AMERICAN-INDIAN/   CNORTCS59934

   NEGRO **ADC** MOTHERS LOOK FOR WORK. /WOMEN/   CWILLJJ58324

   THE POVERTY-DEPENDENCY SYNDROME OF THE **ADC** FEMALE-BASED NEGRO FAMILY.   NSTROFL64074

ADDICT
NEGRO **ADDICT** OCCUPATIONAL HISTORY.   NBATEWM66880

ADDRESS
ADDRESS TO COMMUNITY RELATIONS SERVICE STAFF TRAINING SESSION, JANUARY 12, 1967, ON JOBS NOW. /NEGRO
PUERTO-RICAN YOUTH/   CCOLEBX67918

   THE NEGRO WOMAN AT WORK. **ADDRESS** TO CONFERENCE ON THE NEGRO WOMAN IN THE USA.   CKEYSMD65646

   ADDRESS BEFORE THE CIVIL-RIGHTS CONFERENCE.   GWIRTWW65571

   ADDRESS AT THE CONVOCATION OF THE NAACP LEGAL DEFENSE AND EDUCATIONAL FUND. /LEGISLATION/   GWIRTWW66570

   ADDRESS. /DISCRIMINATION AFFIRMATIVE-ACTION/   NWIRTWX66236

   ADDRESS TO CONFERENCE ON EDUCATION AND JOB OPPORTUNITIES FOR WOMEN RETURNING TO THE LABOR-MARKET.   WDOUTAX62741

ADDRESS (CONTINUATION)

ADDRESS BEFORE LEAGUE-OF-WOMEN-VOTERS, JANUARY 7, 1965. /WORK-WOMAN-ROLE/   WFOWLGH65766

THE NATION-S WORKING MOTHERS AND THE NEED FOR DAY CARE. **ADDRESS.** /EMPLOYMENT-CONDITIONS/   WKEYSMD65897

ADDRESSES

DISCRIMINATION AND NATIJNAL WELFARE. A SERIES OF **ADDRESSES** AND DISCUSSIONS.   NMACIRM49731

ADEQUACY

NEGRO EDUCATION IN AMERICA. ITS **ADEQUACY**, PROBLEMS AND NEEDS.   NCLIFVA62215

CRITERIA FOR ASSESSING FEASIBILITY OF MOTHERS EMPLOYMENT AND **ADEQUACY** OF CHILD CARE PLANS.   WUSDHEW66173

ADJUDICATION

EFFECT OF SCHOOL ASSIGNMENT LAWS ON FEDERAL **ADJUDICATION** OF INTEGRATION CONTROVERSIES.   NCOLULR57224

ADJUSTING

METHODS OF **ADJUSTING** TO AUTOMATION AND TECHNOLOGICAL-CHANGE. /INDUSTRY/   GBOKXDX64737

ADJUSTING TO CHANGE. /TECHNOLOGICAL-CHANGE/   GNATLCT66850

ADJUSTMENT

OCCUPATIONAL AND RESIDENTIAL **ADJUSTMENT** OF RURAL MIGRANTS. /NEGRO MEXICAN-AMERICAN/   CSHANLW61119

THE URBAN **ADJUSTMENT** OF IMMIGRANTS. THE RELATIONSHIP OF EDUCATION TO OCCUPATIONAL AND TOTAL FAMILY INCOME. /NEGRO MEXICAN-AMERICAN/   CSHANLW63122

MEASURING THE **ADJUSTMENT** OF IMMIGRANT LABORERS. /MEXICAN-AMERICAN NEGRO/   CSHANLW63487

URBAN **ADJUSTMENT** AND ITS RELATIONSHIP TO THE SOCIAL ANTECEDENTS OF IMMIGRANT WORKERS. /NEGRO MEXICAN-AMERICAN/   CSHANLW65121

JOB **ADJUSTMENT** PROBLEMS OF DELINQUENT MINORITY-GROUP YOUTH.   GAMOSWE64874

ATTITUDE TOWARD OCCUPATIONAL CHANGE AS AN INDICATOR OF PROSPECTS FOR **ADJUSTMENT.**   GDUNKJE64653

LABOUR-FORCE **ADJUSTMENT** OF WORKERS AFFECTED BY TECHNOLOGICAL-CHANGE.   GGOODRC64622

INCOME, RESOURCES, AND **ADJUSTMENT** POTENTIALS AMONG RURAL FAMILIES IN NORTH AND WEST FLORIDA.   GREUSLA62388

ACCULTURATION, SELF-IDENTIFICATION, AND PERSONALITY **ADJUSTMENT.**   ICHANNA65543

CORRELATES OF **ADJUSTMENT** AMONG AMERICAN-INDIANS IN AN URBAN ENVIRONMENT.   IMARTHW64588

INDIANS OF THE MISSOURI-BASIN -- CULTURAL FACTORS IN THEIR SOCIAL AND ECONOMIC **ADJUSTMENT.**   IREIFBX58610

THE DISPLACED PERSON AND THE SOCIAL AGENCY. A STUDY OF THE CASEWORK PROCESS AND ITS RELATION TO IMMIGRANT **ADJUSTMENT.**   JCRYSDX58714

RESOURCE USE AND **ADJUSTMENT.** RURAL FAMILIES IN THE CENTRAL LOUISIANA MIXED FARMING AREA.   NBOLTBX61396

THE ASSESSMENT OF **ADJUSTMENT** OF AGED NEGRO WOMEN IN A SOUTHERN CITY.   NHIMEJX62072

THE SOCIO-ECONOMIC **ADJUSTMENT** OF THE NEGRO IN SEATTLE BETWEEN 1940 AND 1950. /WASHINGTON/   NKENNTH54273

THE URBAN-LEAGUE AND THE VOCATIONAL GUIDANCE AND **ADJUSTMENT** OF NEGRO YOUTH.   NNICHLE52922

MIGRATION AND **ADJUSTMENT** EXPERIENCES OF RURAL WORKERS IN INDIANAPOLIS. /INDIANA/   NSMITED53143

THE **ADJUSTMENT** OF NEGROES IN A NORTHERN INDUSTRIAL COMMUNITY.   NZIMMBG62360

SOME CANTONESE-AMERICAN PROBLEMS OF STATUS **ADJUSTMENT.**   OBARNML58699

THE **ADJUSTMENT** OF PUERTO-RICANS IN NEW-YORK-CITY.   PFITZJP59801

THE ECONOMIC AND SOCIAL **ADJUSTMENT** OF LOW-INCOME FEMALE-HEADED FAMILIES.   WBERNSE65458

VOCATIONAL INTERESTS AND OCCUPATIONAL **ADJUSTMENT** OF COLLEGE WOMEN.   WWARRPA59222

ADJUSTMENTS

SEMINARS ON PRIVATE **ADJUSTMENTS** TO AUTOMATION AND TECHNOLOGICAL-CHANGE.   GPRESCL64772

FARM LABOR **ADJUSTMENTS** TO CHANGING TECHNOLOGY.   GTOLLGS67974

PERSONAL AND ENVIRONMENTAL OBSTACLES TO PRODUCTION **ADJUSTMENTS** ON SOUTH-CAROLINA PIEDMONT AREA FARMS.   NTAYLCC58411

ADL

ADL AT WORK. THE CRUMBLING WALLS. /EMPLOYMENT DISCRIMINATION/   JADLBXX63688

ADL REPORTS ON SOCIAL, EMPLOYMENT, EDUCATIONAL AND HOUSING DISCRIMINATION.   JANTIDL57690

ADMINISTRATION

STATE FAIR-EMPLOMENT LAWS AND THEIR **ADMINISTRATION.** TEXTS, FEDERAL-STATE COOPERATION, PROHIBITED ACTS.   GBURENA64497

SOME GENERAL OBSERVATIONS ON THE **ADMINISTRATION** OF STATE FAIR-EMPLOYMENT-PRACTICE LAWS.   GGIRARA64721

APPROACHES TO INCOME IMPROVEMENT. EXPERIENCES OF FAMILIES RECEIVING PRODUCTION LOANS UNDER THE FARMERS HOME **ADMINISTRATION.**   GHENDWE59422

DEVELOPMENT AND **ADMINISTRATION** OF THE NEW-YORK STATE LAW AGAINST DISCRIMINATION.   GHIGBJX67143

MANPOWER PROGRAMS. THEIR CONTRIBUTION TO THE ACHIEVEMENT OF EQUAL-OPPORTUNITY MANPOWER **ADMINISTRATION.**   GWHITHC65558

JEWS IN COLLEGE AND UNIVERSITY **ADMINISTRATION.**   JAMERJC66693

RACIAL DISCRIMINATION IN THE FEDERAL SERVICE. A STUDY IN THE SOCIOLOGY OF **ADMINISTRATION.**   NBRADWC53106

THE NEGRO IN SCHOOL **ADMINISTRATION.**   NOVERXX61967

THE CIVIL-RIGHTS PROGRAMS OF THE KENNEDY **ADMINISTRATION.**   NSULLDF64190

WORKING RULES FOR ASSURING NONDISCRIMINATION IN HOSPITAL **ADMINISTRATION.**   NYALELJ64660

ADMINISTRATIVE

FEPC. AN **ADMINISTRATIVE** STUDY OF SELECTED STATE AND LOCAL PROGRAMS.   GALFOAL54869

THE RIGHT TO EQUAL TREATMENT. **ADMINISTRATIVE** ENFORCEMENT OF ANTIDISCRIMINATION LEGISLATION.   GBAMBMA61416

MANPOWER DEVELOPMENT TRAINING. TOTAL NUMBER OF NEW ENROLLEES DURING THE MONTH BY RACE AND OCCUPATION

ADMINISTRATIVE   (CONTINUATION)
STATEWIDE AND BY ADMINISTRATIVE AREA, SEPTEMBER, 1966, OCTOBER, 1966. /CALIFORNIA/   GCALDEM66518

  ADMINISTRATIVE LAW -- HUMAN-RELATIONS COMMISSIONS, PENNSYLVANIA LAW AND DISCRIMINATORY EMPLOYMENT
  PRACTICE.   GTEMPLQ63349

  A STUDY OF STATE AND LOCAL LEGISLATIVE AND ADMINISTRATIVE ACTS DESIGNED TO MEET PROBLEMS OF HUMAN-RIGHTS.   GWISCLR52573

  CIVIL-RIGHTS POLICY IN THE FEDERAL SYSTEM. PROPOSALS FOR A BETTER USE OF ADMINISTRATIVE PROCESS.   GWITHJX65575

ADMINISTRATORS
SURVEY OF SALARIES AND PERSONNEL PRACTICES FOR TEACHERS AND ADMINISTRATORS IN NURSING EDUCATIONAL
PROGRAMS, DECEMBER 1965.   WAMERNA66612

ADMISSION
INEQUALITY OF OPPORTUNITY IN HIGHER EDUCATION. A STUDY OF MINORITY GROUP AND RELATED BARRIERS TO COLLEGE
ADMISSION.   GBERKDS48446

  ADMISSION OF WOMEN TO MEDICAL SCHOOL.   WWULSJH66278

ADOLESCENCE
ADOLESCENCE. CULTURAL DEPRIVATION, POVERTY, AND THE DROPOUT.   GHUNTOE66939

ADOLESCENT
A COMPARATIVE STUDY OF THE OCCUPATIONAL INTERESTS OF NEGRO AND WHITE ADOLESCENT BOYS.   NCONNSM65471

  PROBLEMS AND NEEDS OF NEGRO ADOLESCENT WORKERS.   NGRANLB40980

  STUDY OF ADOLESCENT GIRLS. /ASPIRATIONS/   WDOUVEX57742

  COUNSELING ADOLESCENT GIRLS IN THE 1960-S.   WHAVIRJ65833

ADOLESCENTS
SEX DIFFERENCES IN OCCUPATIONAL CHOICE PATTERNS AMONG ADOLESCENTS. /ASPIRATIONS WOMEN NEGRO/   CSPREJX62999

  CHIPPEWA ADOLESCENTS. A CHANGING GENERATION.   IMILLFC64590

  ADOLESCENTS NEED JOBS.   ITHOMHX61629

ADULT
FORMAL OCCUPATIONAL TRAINING OF ADULT WORKERS. ITS EXTENT, NATURE, AND USE.   GBEDEMX64448

  ADULT AND YOUTH EMPLOYMENT PROJECT, AUGUST-SEPTEMBER 1965.   GHEALDV65646

  ADULT AND YOUTH EMPLOYMENT PROJECT, APRIL-MAY 1965.   GHEALDV65647

  THE RELATIONSHIP OF THE SOCIAL-STRUCTURE OF AN INDIAN COMMUNITY TO ADULT AND JUVENILE-DELINQUENCY.
  /POVERTY ECONOMIC-STATUS/   IMINNMS63218

  PROCEEDINGS OF THE CONFERENCE ON EDUCATION FOR ADULT MIGRANT WORKERS. /TEXAS/   MTEXACM62498

  WORKING WITH STUDENTS INSIDE AND OUTSIDE THE CLASSROOM IN ADULT BASIC EDUCATION PROGRAMS.   NBRAZWF64285

  PROBLEMS FOR ADULT EDUCATION RELATED TO ACQUIRING CAPABILITIES FOR WORK.   NGOLDFH63430

  FATHER-ABSENCE AND NEGRO ADULT PERSONALITY. A RESEARCH NOTE.   NPETTTFND990

  ROLE CONCEPTION AS A PREDICTOR OF ADULT FEMALE ROLES. /WORK-WOMAN-ROLE/   WANGRSS66619

  A SURVEY OF SPECIAL EDUCATIONAL PROGRAMS FOR ADULT WOMEN IN UNIVERSITY EXTENSION DIVISIONS AND EVENING
  COLLEGES AS OF SPRING 1965.   WLORIRK66942

  UNIVERSITY PROGRAMS OF CONTINUING EDUCATION FOR THE ADULT WOMAN.   WTINKAH64156

ADULT-EDUCATION
JOB TRAINING THROUGH ADULT-EDUCATION.   NBLUMAA67098

ADULTS
EMPLOYMENT, EDUCATION AND MARRIAGE OF YOUNG NEGRO ADULTS.   NCOXXOC41934

ADVANCEMENT
THE PROSPECT FOR ADVANCEMENT IN BUSINESS OF THE MARRIED WOMAN COLLEGE GRADUATE. /OCCUPATIONS/   WBECKEL64632

ADVANCES
ECONOMIC ADVANCES OF THE AMERICAN NEGRO.   NGERSGX65082

  NEGROES. BIG ADVANCES IN JOBS, WEALTH, STATUS.   NUSNEWR58271

ADVENTURE
THE NEGRO-S ADVENTURE IN GENERAL BUSINESS.   NOAKXVV49952

ADVISORS
HEALTH, EDUCATION, AND WELFARE ASPECTS OF THE ECONOMIC REPORT OF THE PRESENT AND ANNUAL REPORT OF THE
COUNCIL OF ECONOMIC ADVISORS.   GUSDHEW66711

ADVISORY
REPORT OF THE CALIFORNIA STATE ADVISORY COMMITTEE TO THE UNITED STATES COMMISSION ON CIVIL-RIGHTS ON
CALIFORNIA-S PROGRAM FOR EQUAL-OPPORTUNITY IN APPRENTICESHIP.   GBECKWL62432

  ACTION PROGRAMS FOR FEPC ADVISORY COMMITTEES. /CALIFORNIA/   GCALFEP66528

  PLANS-FOR-PROGRESS. A FIRST YEAR REPORT BY THE PLANS FOR PROGRESS ADVISORY COUNCIL.   GPRESCD64112

  THE NATIONAL CONFERENCE AND THE REPORTS OF THE STATE ADVISORY COMMITTEES TO THE U.S. COMMISSION ON
  CIVIL-RIGHTS, 1959.   GUSCOMC60405

  REPORTS ON APPRENTICESHIP, NINE STATE ADVISORY COMMITTEES. /CALIFORNIA FLORIDA MARYLAND CONNECTICUT
  WASHINGTON-DC NEW-JERSEY NEW-YORK TENNESSEE WISCONSIN/   GUSCCMC64407

  STATEMENT TO THE NEW-YORK STATE ADVISORY COMMITTEE TO THE US COMMISSION ON CIVIL-RIGHTS, MAY 23, 1966.
  /EMPLOYMENT LEGISLATION/   NPOLIEX66004

  REPORT OF THE CALIFORNIA ADVISORY COMMISSION ON THE STATUS OF WOMEN. /FEP EMPLOYMENT-CONDITIONS
  DISCRIMINATION MIGRANTS/   WCALACW67673

AFDC
CIVIL-RIGHTS AND THE REHABILITATION OF AFDC CLIENTS.   GSETSLX64296

AFFIRMATIVE
IMPLEMENTING AFFIRMATIVE ACTION WITH AIR-FORCE CONTRACTORS.   GHUNTHX63789

AFFIRMATIVE   (CONTINUATION)
OUTREACH -- THE **AFFIRMATIVE** APPROACH. /EMPLOYMENT SES/   NFRANWH66698

AFFIRMATIVE-ACTION
THE **AFFIRMATIVE-ACTION** CONCEPT OF EQUAL-EMPLOYMENT-OPPORTUNITY.   GPRICWS65688

EQUAL-EMPLOYMENT-OPPORTUNITY TRAINING, A PROGRAM FOR **AFFIRMATIVE-ACTION**.   GUSCISC63384

A LOOK AT THE FEPC-S **AFFIRMATIVE-ACTION** PROGRAM.   GYABRSX65588

ADDRESS. /DISCRIMINATION **AFFIRMATIVE-ACTION**/   NWIRTWX66236

AFFIRMATIVE-ACTIONS
AFFIRMATIVE-ACTIONS IN EMPLOYMENT. A SPECIAL FEPC REPORT. /CALIFORNIA/   GCALFEP65529

AFFLUENCE
POVERTY AMID **AFFLUENCE**.   GFISHLX66682

CHALLENGE TO **AFFLUENCE**. /UNEMPLOYMENT/   GMYRDGX63035

POVERTY, **AFFLUENCE** AND OPPORTUNITY.   GORNAOA64140

POVERTY AMID **AFFLUENCE**.   GORNAOA66320

POVERTY IN **AFFLUENCE**.   GWILLRE65665

AFL
THE **AFL** FIGHTS BIGOTRY. /UNION/   GJEWILCND824

AFL-CIO
AFL-CIO COUNCIL GETS NEGRO DEMAND FOR MORE ACTION ON BIAS IN UNIONS.   NBUSIWX61144

TRADE UNIONS PRACTICES AND THE NEGRO WORKER -- THE ESTABLISHMENT AND IMPLEMENTATION OF **AFL-CIO**
ANTI-DISCRIMINATION POLICY.   NDAVINF60312

NAACP AND THE **AFL-CIO**. AN OVERVIEW. /UNION/   NGROSJA62461

RACISM WITHIN ORGANIZED LABOR. A REPORT OF THE FIVE YEARS OF THE **AFL-CIO**, 1955-1960. /UNION/   NHILLHX60542

THE **AFL-CIO** AND THE NEGRO. /UNION/   NHUTCJXND590

POLICY RESOLUTION ADOPTED BY **AFL-CIO** 6TH CONSTITUTIONAL CONVENTION, SAN FRANCISCO, DEC 1965. /EEO/   WAFLCIO65617

AGE
EMPLOYMENT AND PERSONAL CHARACTERISTICS. EMPLOYMENT BY **AGE**, RACE, NATIVITY, EDUCATION, MARITAL-STATUS,
HOUSEHOLD RELATIONSHIPS, ETC. /DEMOGRAPHY/   CUSBURC53372

NONWHITE POPULATION BY RACE. NEGROES, INDIANS, JAPANESE, CHINESE, FILIPINOS. BY **AGE**, SEX, MARITAL-STATUS,
EDUCATION. EMPLOYMENT-STATUS, OCCUPATIONAL-STATUS, INCOME, ETC. /DEMOGRAPHY/   CUSBURC53378

NONWHITE POPULATION BY RACE. NEGROES, INDIANS, JAPANESE,CHINESE, FILIPINOS. BY **AGE**, SEX,
MARITAL-STATUS,EDUCATION, EMPLOYMENT-STATUS, OCCUPATIONAL-STATUS, INCOME, ETC. /DEMOGRAPHY/   CUSBURC63176

OCCUPATIONAL CHARACTERISTICS. DATA ON **AGE**, RACE, EDUCATION, WORK EXPERIENCE, INCOME, ETC. FOR WORKERS IN
EACH OCCUPATION.   CUSBURC63177

EMPLOYMENT OF SCHOOL **AGE** YOUTH, OCTOBER 1965.   GBOGAFA66918

NET MIGRATION OF THE POPULATION, 1950-60, BY **AGE**, SEX, AND COLOR. VOL II, ANALYTICAL GROUPINGS OF
COUNTIES. /INCOME/   GBOWLGK65434

POTENTIAL SUPPLY AND REPLACEMENT OF RURAL MALES OF LABOR-FORCE **AGE**, 1960-70.   GBOWLGK66430

AGE AND INCOME-DISTRIBUTION. /DEMOGRAPHY/   GBRADDS65679

EMPLOYMENT AND INCOME BY **AGE**, SEX, COLOR AND RESIDENCE. /DETROIT MICHIGAN/   GDETRCC63948

MORTALITY BY OCCUPATION AND INDUSTRY AMONG MEN 20 TO 64 YEARS OF **AGE**. UNITED STATES, 1950. /DEMOGRAPHY/   GGURALX62748

THE ASSOCIATION OF INCOME AND EDUCATION FOR MALES, BY REGION, RACE, AND **AGE**.   GLASSRL65998

MOST NOTORIOUS VICTORY. MAN IN AN **AGE** OF AUTOMATION.   GSELIBB66841

THE NAVAJO IN THE MACHINE **AGE**. HUMAN RESOURCES ARE IMPORTANT TOO.   INAPIAX58594

ARAPAHOE INDIAN TRAINS FOR SPACE **AGE**.   IUSDLAB66960

HIDDEN UNEMPLOYMENT 1953-62. A QUANTITATIVE ANALYSIS BY **AGE** AND SEX.   NDERNTX66264

THE RACIAL PRACTICES OF ORGANIZED LABOR -- IN THE **AGE** OF GOMPERS AND AFTER. /UNION/   NHILLHX65541

INDUSTRY COMES OF **AGE** IN THE SOUTH.   NNOLAEW53926

THE NEGRO COMES OF **AGE** IN INDUSTRY.   NWEAVRC43301

AGE OF COMPLETION OF CHILDBEARING AND ITS RELATION TO THE PARTICIPATION OF WOMEN IN THE LABOR-FORCE.
UNITED STATES 1910-1955.   WDAYXLH57725

THE COMPARATIVE ACADEMIC ACHIEVEMENT OF WOMEN FORTY YEARS OF **AGE** AND OVER AND WOMEN EIGHTEEN TO TWENTY
FIVE.   WHALFIT61814

AGE AND MARITAL-STATUS AND THEIR RELATIONSHIP TO SUCCESS IN PRACTICAL NURSING. /OCCUPATIONS/   WMEADLX63967

WOMEN HOUSEHOLD WORKERS COVERED BY OLD **AGE**, SURVIVORS, AND DISABILITY INSURANCE.   WPOLIEJ65285

WHAT ABOUT WOMANPOWER IN THE SPACE **AGE**.   WSTEIER62134

LABOR-FORCE SENSITIVITY TO EMPLOYMENT BY **AGE**, SEX.   WTELLAX65714

AGED
LABOR-FORCE PARTICIPATION OF YOUNG PERSONS **AGED** 14-24.   GFEARRXND929

PLANNING CONSTRUCTIVE ECONOMIC OPPORTUNITIES FOR THE JEWISH **AGED**.   JBARSIX59700

COORDINATED PLANNING FOR ECONOMIC OPPORTUNTIES FOR JEWISH **AGED**.   JRABIDX59751

THE ASSESSMENT OF ADJUSTMENT OF **AGED** NEGRO WOMEN IN A SOUTHERN CITY.   NHIMEJX62072

THE **AGED** NEGRO AND HIS INCOME.   NORSHMX64960

AGED **(CONTINUATION)**
THE CHANGING NUMBER AND DISTRIBUTION OF THE AGED NEGRO POPULATION OF THE UNITED STATES. /DEMOGRAPHY/   NSMITLT58145

A MEMORANDUM ON THE MOTIVATIONS OF MIDDLE AGED WOMEN IN THE LOWER EDUCATIONAL BRACKETS TO RETURN TO WORK. /ASPIRATIONS/   WJEWIVA61880

THE MIDDLE AGED WOMAN AND THE LABOR-MARKET.   WJEWIVA62881

A PILOT STUDY OF THE MOTIVATIONS AND PROBLEMS OF MIDDLE AGED HOMEMAKERS IN LOWER SOCIO-ECONOMIC GROUPS IN SEEKING EMPLOYMENT. /ASPIRATIONS/   WJEWIVA62883

AGENCIES
REPORT ON TWENTY STATE ANTI-DISCRIMINATION AGENCIES AND THE LAWS THEY ADMINISTER.   GAMERJD61387

A FIVE-STATE SURVEY OF DISCRIMINATION BY COMMERCIAL EMPLOYMENT AGENCIES.   GAMERJD63386

CENTRAL ROLE OF INTERGROUP AGENCIES IN THE LABOR-MARKET. CHANGING RESEARCH AND PERSONNEL REQUIREMENTS.   GHOPEJX61780

GOVERNMENTAL FAIR-EMPLOYMENT AGENCIES. AN APPRAISAL OF FEDERAL, STATE, AND MUNICIPAL EFFORTS TO END JOB DISCRIMINATION.   GNORGPH62120

THE CALIFORNIA FEPC. STEPCHILD OF THE STATE AGENCIES.   GSTANLR65333

SUMMARY FACT SHEETS FOR STATE PUBLIC AGENCIES WITH JURISDICTION OVER DISCRIMINATION IN EMPLOYMENT.   GUSCCMC65416

FEDERAL AGENCIES WITH PRIMARY CIVIL-RIGHTS RESPONSIBILITIES.   GUSDLAB65447

CESEGREGATION OF SOCIAL AGENCIES IN THE SOUTH.   NGOLDJX65427

NEGRO EMPLOYMENT IN KENTUCKY STATE AGENCIES.   NKENTCH66643

EQUAL-EMPLOYMENT-OPPORTUNITIES IN MISSOURI STATE AGENCIES. A SURVEY OF NEGRO EMPLOYMENT, SPRING-SUMMER 1963.   NMISSCH64801

MINORITY-GROUP STUDY, JUNE 1963. NEGRO AND TOTAL EMPLOYMENT IN SELECTED AGENCIES.   NPRESCD63010

CHARACTERISTICS OF NEGRO EMPLOYMENT IN FEDERAL AGENCIES IN ATLANTA, GEORGIA.   NPRESCP60016

COMBATING DISCRIMINATION IN THE EMPLOYMENT OF NEGROES IN WAR INDUSTRIES AND GOVERNMENT AGENCIES.   NRAMSLA43128

EQUAL-OPPORTUNITY IN FARM PROGRAMS -- AN APPRAISAL OF SERVICES RENDERED BY AGENCIES OF THE UNITED STATES DEPARTMENT OF AGRICULTURE.   NUSCOMC65232

EXPERIENCES OF NEGRO HIGH SCHOOL GIRLS WITH DOMESTIC PLACEMENT AGENCIES. /HOUSEHOLD-WORKERS/   WRUSSRD62135

AGENCY
EQUAL-EMPLOYMENT-OPPORTUNITY IN THE DEFENSE SUPPLY AGENCY.   GDEFESA64631

HOPI INDIAN AGENCY.   IUSOINT64651

THE DISPLACED PERSON AND THE SOCIAL AGENCY. A STUDY OF THE CASEWORK PROCESS AND ITS RELATION TO IMMIGRANT ADJUSTMENT.   JCRYSDX58714

AGENCY-S
THE COMMUNITY ACTION AGENCY-S ROLE IN COMPREHENSIVE MANPOWER PROGRAMS -- PLANNING AND PROBLEMS.   GKANERD66863

AGES
RURAL-FARM MALES ENTERING AND LEAVING WORKING AGES, 1940-50 AND 1950-60. REPLACEMENT RATIOS AND RATES. /OCCUPATIONS/   GBOWLGK56433

AGGREGATE
STRUCTURAL UNEMPLOYMENT AND AGGREGATE DEMAND.   GGILPEG66632

POVERTY, AGGREGATE DEMAND, AND ECONOMIC STRUCTURE.   GKERSJA66941

THE ROLE OF MANPOWER POLICY IN ACHIEVING AGGREGATE GOALS. /EMPLOYMENT INCOME/   GTHURLC66640

AGGRESSIVE
AGGRESSIVE RECRUITMENT AND THE PUBLIC SERVICE.   GGREGGX61071

AGING
SENIOR CITIZENS AND HOW THEY LIVE. AN ANALYSIS OF 1960 CENSUS DATA. PART II. THE AGING NONWHITE AND HIS HOUSING. /ECONOMIC-STATUS/   GUSHHFX63321

THE AGING NEGRO. SOME IMPLICATIONS FOR SOCIAL-WELFARE SERVICES.   NBEATWM60066

AGRICULTURAL
IMPLICATIONS OF THE RECENT CENSUSES FOR PROFESSIONAL AGRICULTURAL WORKERS. /OCCUPATIONS/   GBEALCL61412

A SOCIAL PROFILE OF AGRICULTURAL MIGRATORY PEOPLE IN COLORADO. /MIGRANT-WORKERS/   GCOLOSD59919

SOME REGIONAL DIFFERENCES IN WAGES OF AGRICULTURAL WORKERS. /MIGRANT-WORKERS/   GMAITST60436

MARYLAND TB -- VD HEALTH PROGRAM AMONG AGRICULTURAL MIGRANTS.   GMARYSD65958

THE ROLE OF AGRICULTURAL TECHNOLOGY IN SOUTHERN SOCIAL CHANGE.   GRAPEAX46037

INCOMES OF MIGRATORY AGRICULTURAL WORKERS.   GTEXAAE60350

SELECTED REFERENCES ON DOMESTIC MIGRATORY AGRICULTURAL WORKERS, THEIR FAMILIES, PROBLEMS, AND PROGRAMS, 1955-1960.   GUSDLAB61495

MAJOR AGRICULTURAL MIGRANT LABOR DEMAND AREAS.   GUSDLAB61509

HOUSING FOR MIGRANT AGRICULTURAL WORKERS. LABOR CAMP STANDARDS.   GUSDLAB62508

AGRICULTURAL WORKERS AND WORKMEN-S COMPENSATION. /MIGRANT-WORKERS/   GUSDLAB64506

COVERAGE OF AGRICULTURAL WORKERS UNDER STATE AND FEDERAL LAWS. /MIGRANT-WORKERS/   GUSDLAB64507

A HISTORY OF THE INTERRELATIONSHIPS BETWEEN IMPORTED MEXICAN LABOR, DOMESTIC MIGRANTS, AND THE TEXAS AGRICULTURAL ECONOMY.   MGRAVRP60405

MIGRATORY AGRICULTURAL WORKERS IN THE UNITED STATES.   MJORGJM60422

HOUSING DEFICIENCIES OF AGRICULTURAL WORKERS AND OTHER LOW INCOME GROUPS.   MMCMIOX62434

INCOMES OF MIGRATORY AGRICULTURAL WORKERS.   MMETZWH60439

AGRICULTURAL   (CONTINUATION)
INFORMATION CONCERNING ENTRY OF MEXICAN **AGRICULTURAL** WORKERS INTO THE UNITED STATES.   MUSDLAB59335

CHANGING PATTERNS IN **AGRICULTURAL** PRODUCTIONS, WEST-VIRGINIA, 1920-1950. /OCCUPATIONS/   NANGLRA54254

NO HARVEST FOR THE REAPER. THE STORY OF THE MIGRATORY **AGRICULTURAL** WORKER IN THE UNITED STATES.   NHILLHX59534

THE EFFECT OF A CHANGING **AGRICULTURAL** PATTERN ON NEGRO FARMERS OF SOUTH-CAROLINA.   NHURSRL56253

AGRICULTURAL SEASONAL LABORERS OF COLORADO AND CALIFORNIA. /MIGRANT-WORKERS/   NKARRCHN0636

NEGROES IN THE CALIFORNIA **AGRICULTURAL** LABOR-FORCE.   NRECOCW59042

AN ANALYSIS OF SELECTIVE FACTORS INFLUENCING FARM INCOME IN HALE COUNTY, AS A BASIS FOR ESTABLISHING A
MORE EFFECTIVE VOCATIONAL **AGRICULTURAL** PROGRAM. /ALABAMA/   NSALTDR52347

LAND TENURE IN THE SOUTHERN REGION. PROCEEDINGS OF PROFESSIONAL **AGRICULTURAL** WORKERS TENTH ANNUAL
CONFERENCE.   NTUSKIX51218

THE PHYSICAL GEOGRAPHY OF THE PALOUSE REGION, WASHINGTON AND IDAHO, AND ITS RELATION TO THE **AGRICULTURAL**
ECCNCMY.   OSHROCR58762

HOW TO HIRE **AGRICULTURAL** WORKERS FROM PUERTO-RICO.   PPUERRDN0788

CONCERN FOR **AGRICULTURAL** MIGRANTS IN MARYLAND.   PUVMAXX64856

EARNINGS AND HOURS OF WOMEN **AGRICULTURAL** WORKERS.   WCALDIR64268

AGRICULTURE
LABOR UNIONISM IN AMERICAN **AGRICULTURE**. /NEGRO MEXICAN-AMERICAN ORIENTAL/   CJAMISM45005

UNITED STATES CENSUS OF **AGRICULTURE**. COLOR, RACE, AND TENURE OF FARM OPERATOR. GENERAL REPORT, VOLUME II.
/DEMOGRAPHY/   CUSBURC59382

EFFECT OF MECHANIZATION ON EMPLOYMENT OF MIGRATORY LABOR IN **AGRICULTURE** AND FOOD PROCESSING.
/MIGRANT-WORKERS/   GDELASE59946

THE FARM WORKER IN A CHANGING **AGRICULTURE**. PART I IN A SERIES ON TECHNOLOGICAL-CHANGE AND FARM LABOR USE,
KERN-COUNTY, CALIFORNIA, 1961.   GMETZWH64387

THE LOW-INCOME PROBLEM IN **AGRICULTURE**.   GMOOREJ64030

THE MEXICAN IMMIGRANT WORKER IN SOUTHWESTERN **AGRICULTURE**.   MTHOMAN56501

THE DETERMINATION OF CERTAIN MAJOR FACTORS AFFECTING THE NEGRO VETERAN IN THE ON-THE-JOB TRAINING PROGRAM
IN VOCATIONAL **AGRICULTURE** IN THE STATE OF ALABAMA AS A BASIS FOR PLANNING A MORE EFFECTIVE PROGRAM.   NBATTEF49338

THE NEGRO IN AMERICAN **AGRICULTURE**.   NBEALCL66063

THE NEGRO-S CHANGING PLACE IN SOUTHERN **AGRICULTURE**.   NCHRIDE58206

THE CHANGING STATUS OF THE NEGRO IN SOUTHERN **AGRICULTURE**.   NJONELW50623

FACTORS AFFECTING FARM PLACEMENT OF NEGRO VOCATIONAL **AGRICULTURE** STUDENTS IN ALABAMA.   NMCQUFT45348

THE NEGRO IN SOUTHERN **AGRICULTURE**.   NPERLVX53982

REFLECTIONS ON POVERTY WITHIN **AGRICULTURE**.   NSCHUTW50144

OCCUPATIONAL ESTABLISHMENT OF FORMER STUDENTS OF VOCATIONAL **AGRICULTURE** IN MONTGOMERY TRAINING SCHOOL
AREA. /ALABAMA/   NSCOTCDND346

EQUAL-OPPORTUNITY IN FARM PROGRAMS -- AN APPRAISAL OF SERVICES RENDERED BY AGENCIES OF THE UNITED STATES
DEPARTMENT OF **AGRICULTURE**.   NUSCOMC65232

THE EVOLVING LOW-INCOME PROBLEM IN **AGRICULTURE**. /ECONOMIC-STATUS/   WWELCFJ60227

AID
TRAINING **AID**. CULTURAL DIFFERENCES, TRAINING IN NONDISCRIMINATION, READING ASSIGNMENTS. /EMPLOYMENT
MEXICAN-AMERICAN NEGRO/   CCALDSW65447

IN **AID** OF THE UNEMPLOYED.   GBECKJX64878

PROGRAMS TO **AID** THE UNEMPLOYED IN THE 1960-S.   GBECKJX65430

FEDERAL **AID** TO DEPRESSED AREAS. AN EVALUATION OF THE AREA-REDEVELOPMENT-ADMINISTRATION.   GLEVISA64896

PROGRAMS IN **AID** OF THE POOR.   GLEVISA65601

PROGRAMS IN **AID** OF THE POOR. /ANTI-POVERTY/   GLEVISA66729

AID-TO-DEPENDENT-CHI
A STUDY TO DETERMINE THE EMPLOYMENT POTENTIAL OF MOTHERS RECEIVING **AID-TO-DEPENDENT-CHILDREN** ASSISTANCE. WBROODJ64656

AIDING
AIDING NEGRO BUSINESSMEN. SMALL BUSINESS OPPORTUNITIES CORPORATION, PHILADELPHIA. /PENNSYLVANIA/   NBUSIWX64143

AIDS
PROGRAM **AIDS** FOR VOCATIONAL OPPORTUNITY PROGRAM.   NNATLUL49895

RESOURCES FOR THE EMPLOYMENT OF MATURE WOMEN AND/OR THEIR CONTINUING EDUCATION. A SELECTED BIBLIOGRAPHY
AND **AIDS**.   WBERNML66746

AIR
CIVIL-RIGHTS IN **AIR** TRANSPORTATION AND GOVERNMENT INITIATIVE.   GDIXORX63644

REPORT AND SUMMARY OF THE **AIR** FORCE ON ACTIONS TAKEN BY LOCKHEED AIRCRAFT CORPORATION AT THE AIR FORCE
PLANT NO 6 IN MARIETTA, GEORGIA. /INDUSTRY/   NPRESCD61013

REPORT AND SUMMARY OF THE **AIR** FORCE ON ACTIONS TAKEN BY LOCKHEED AIRCRAFT CORPORATION AT THE AIR FORCE
PLANT NO 6 IN MARIETTA, GEORGIA. /INDUSTRY/   NPRESCD61013

AIR-FORCE
IMPLEMENTING AFFIRMATIVE ACTION WITH **AIR-FORCE** CONTRACTORS.   GHUNTHX63789

AIRCRAFT
CARRYING OUT A PLAN FOR JOB INTEGRATION AND DOING IT -- IN THE HEART OF GEORGIA -- WITHOUT A SINGLE
UNPLEASANT INCIDENT. THAT-S THE EXPERIENCE OF LOCKHEED **AIRCRAFT** CORPORATION AT ITS MARIETTA PLANT.

AIRCRAFT   (CONTINUATION)
/INDUSTRY/   NBUSIWX63148

    REPORT AND SUMMARY OF THE AIR FORCE ON ACTIONS TAKEN BY LOCKHEED AIRCRAFT CORPORATION AT THE AIR FORCE
    PLANT NO 6 IN MARIETTA, GEORGIA. /INDUSTRY/   NPRESCD61013

    ACCOMODATION BETWEEN NEGRO AND WHITE EMPLOYEES IN A WEST COAST AIRCRAFT INDUSTRY, 1942-1944.
    /CASE-STUDY/   NREEDBA47045

    NEGRO EMPLOYMENT IN THE AIRCRAFT INDUSTRY.   NWEAVRC45302

AIRLINE
    STATE FAIR-EMPLOYMENT-PRACTICE LEGISLATION UNCONSTITUTIONALLY BURDENS INTERSTATE COMMERCE WHEN APPLIED TO
    INTERSTATE AIRLINE.   NHARVLR62499

AIRPLANE
    NEGRO EMPLOYMENT IN AIRPLANE PLANTS. /INDUSTRY/   NUSDLAB43827

AKRON
    SENIORITY IN THE AKRON RUBBER INDUSTRY.   NUSDLAB44841

ALABAMA
    INCOME, EDUCATION AND UNEMPLOYMENT IN NEIGHBORHOODS. BIRMINGHAM, ALABAMA. /DEMOGRAPHY/   CUSDLAB63453

    ECONOMIC-TRENDS IN EXTENSION WORK WITH NEGRO FARMERS IN ALABAMA, 1936-1948.   GGAINRL48341

    THE DETERMINATION OF CERTAIN MAJOR FACTORS AFFECTING THE NEGRO VETERAN IN THE ON-THE-JOB TRAINING PROGRAM
    IN VOCATIONAL AGRICULTURE IN THE STATE OF ALABAMA AS A BASIS FOR PLANNING A MORE EFFECTIVE PROGRAM. NBATTEF49338

    THE ORIGIN AND DEVELOPMENT OF THE NEGRO VISITING TEACHER IN ALABAMA. /OCCUPATIONS/   NBOATRF49345

    FACTORS AFFECTING THE PRESENT FARMING PROGRAMS OF ONE HUNDRED NEGRO FARMS IN THE PATRONAGE AREA OF THE
    MACON COUNTY TRAINING SCHOOL, IN ALABAMA, WITH EMPHASIS FOR IMPROVEMENT.   NBRONCA51337

    VOCATIONAL CHOICES OF NEGRO HIGH SCHOOL STUDENTS IN MACON COUNTY, ALABAMA, AND THEIR RELATIONSHIP TO
    BASIC OCCUPATIONAL ACTIVITES OF THE SCHOOL COMMUNITIES. /ASPIRATIONS/   NCHAPEJ49351

    THE EVALUATION OF PRACTICES CARRIED ON BY TWO HUNDRED NEGRO FARMERS IN THE PRODUCTION OF COTTON IN MACON
    COUNTY, ALABAMA.   NGOLDSM48350

    NEGRO EMPLOYMENT IN THE BIRMINGHAM METROPOLITAN AREA. /ALABAMA CASE-STUDY/   NHAWLLT55502

    AN ECONOMIC ANALYSIS OF SPECIFIED INCORPORATED AND UNINCORPORATED FARMERS COOPERATIVE ASSOCIATIONS
    OPERATED BY NEGRO FARMERS IN ALABAMA.   NLIGHMB53340

    FACTORS AFFECTING FARM PLACEMENT OF NEGRO VOCATIONAL AGRICULTURE STUDENTS IN ALABAMA.   NMCQUFT45348

    ACHIEVEMENT OF MALE HIGH SCHOOL DROPOUTS AND GRADUATES IN ALABAMA VOCATIONAL SCHOOLS.   NMILLGJ65791

    HEARINGS --TRI-CITIES AREA OF ALABAMA.   NNATILR58875

    THE NEGRO AND UNIONISM IN THE BIRMINGHAM, ALABAMA IRON AND STEEL INDUSTRY.   NNORTHR43941

    BOYCOTT IN BIRMINGHAM. /ALABAMA/   NOSBOGR62460

    NEGRO EMPLOYMENT IN BIRMINGHAM. THREE CASES. /ALABAMA/   NROWARL67091

    AN ANALYSIS OF SELECTIVE FACTORS INFLUENCING FARM INCOME IN HALE COUNTY, AS A BASIS FOR ESTABLISHING A
    MORE EFFECTIVE VOCATIONAL AGRICULTURAL PROGRAM. /ALABAMA/   NSALTDR52347

    OCCUPATIONAL ESTABLISHMENT OF FORMER STUDENTS OF VOCATIONAL AGRICULTURE IN MONTGOMERY TRAINING SCHOOL
    AREA. /ALABAMA/   NSCOTCDND346

    A STUDY OF FARM MANAGEMENT PRACTICES ON 100 NEGRO FARMS IN MACON COUNTY, ALABAMA, 1949.   NSHAWBJ50339

    THE INFLUENCE OF TUSKEGEE-INSTITUTE ON THE HEALTH, EDUCATIONAL, ECONOMIC, AND POLITICAL ASPECTS OF THE
    NEGRO POPULATION OF MACON COUNTY, ALABAMA.   NSHIEAR51342

    THE GENERAL CONDITION OF THE ALABAMA NEGRO.   NSNCCXX65187

ALBANY
    RACE-RELATIONS IN THE ALBANY TROY AREA. A PROFILE FOR 1957. /NEW-YORK/   NGRIEES57503

ALBION
    SURVEY OF ALBION, MICHIGAN.   NMICCRC64772

ALBUQUERQUE
    REPORT OF INDIAN RECRUITMENT AND TRAINING MEETING AT ALBUQUERQUE, NEW-MEXICO, ON DECEMBER 6, 1966. IUSDLAB66321

ALCOHOL
    ACCULTURATION, ACCESS AND ALCOHOL IN A TRI-ETHNIC COMMUNITY.   MGRAVTD67214

ALCORN-COUNTY
    THE RURAL WORKING HOMEMAKER. ALCORN-COUNTY, MISSISSIPPI. /WORK-FAMILY-CONFLICT/   WBRYAES61660

ALIENATION
    VALUE ORIENTATION, ROLE CONFLICT, AND ALIENATION FROM WORK. A CROSS-CULTURAL STUDY.   MZURCLA65520

    NOTE ON NEGRO ALIENATION.   NGORDDX65976

ALLEGED
    FINDINGS OF FACT, CONCLUSIONS AND ACTION OF THE COMMISSION ON HUMAN-RELATIONS IN RE. INVESTIGATIVE PUBLIC
    HEARINGS INTO ALLEGED DISCRIMINATORY PRACTICE BY THE HOTEL AND RESTAURANT INDUSTRY IN PHILADELPHIA.
    /PENNSYLVANIA/   GPHILCH61176

ALLEGING
    COMPLAINTS ALLEGING DISCRIMINATION BECAUSE OF PUERTO-RICAN NATIONAL ORIGIN, JULY 1, 1945-SEPTEMBER 1,
    1958.   PNEWYSA58836

ALLIANCE
    THE ROOTS OF THE NEGRO-UNION ALLIANCE. /UNION/   NMARSRX66746

    DEVELOPMENTS IN THE NEGRO-LABOR ALLIANCE. /UNION/   NSTROEK56185

ALONE
    EMPLOYMENT BY MERIT ALONE.   GBOWMGW61466

ALUMNAE
    WORK MOTIVATION OF COLLEGE ALUMNAE. FIVE-YEAR FOLLOWUP.   WEYDELD67223

ALUMNAE   (CONTINUATION)
    FIFTEEN YEARS AFTER COLLEGE -- A STUDY OF **ALUMNAE** OF THE CLASS OF 1945.   WUSDLAB62193

AMBITION
    BACKGROUND AND **AMBITION** OF MALE MEXICAN-AMERICAN HIGH SCHOOL SENIORS IN LOS-ANGELES. /CALIFORNIA/   MHELLCS63414

    SOME COMPARISONS AMONG NEGRO-WHITE COLLEGE STUDENTS. SOCIAL **AMBITION** AND ESTIMATED SOCIAL MOBILITY.   NHARREE66786

AMBITIONS
    AMBITIONS EDUCATION IMPROVEMENT PROJECT UNDER WAY IN SOUTH.   GAMERCE64370

    AMBITIONS OF MEXICAN-AMERICAN YOUTH -- GOALS AND MEANS OF MOBILITY OF HIGH SCHOOL SENIORS.   MHELLCS64413

    SOME ASPECTS OF WOMEN-S **AMBITIONS**.   WTURNRH64162

AMBIVALENCE
    THE ROOTS OF **AMBIVALENCE** IN AMERICAN WOMEN. /WORK-FAMILY-CONFLICT/   WROSSASND133

    AMBIVALENCE IN AMERICAN WOMEN. /WORK-FAMILY-CONFLICT/   WROSSAS66090

AMENDED
    RULES AND REGULATIONS OF THE PRESIDENT-S COMMITTEE ON EQUAL-EMPLOYMENT-OPPORTUNITY AS **AMENDED**.   GBURENA63496

    GOVERNMENT CONTRACT EMPLOYMENT. RULES AND REGULATIONS... EFFECTIVE JULY 22, 1961, AS **AMENDED** SEPTEMBER 7,
    1963.   GPRESCD63110

AMENDMENT
    FREEDOM OF CHOICE IN PERSONAL SERVICE OCCUPATIONS. 13TH **AMENDMENT** LIMITATIONS ON ANTIDISCRIMINATION
    LEGISLATION.   GAVINAX64410

AMENDMENTS
    THE CONSTITUTIONAL RIGHT TO MEMBERSHIP IN A LABOR UNION -- FIFTH AND FOURTEENTH **AMENDMENTS**.   NELLIGH59330

    AMENDMENTS TO THE TAFT-HARTLEY. A REJECTION OF RACIAL DISCRIMINATION. /LEGISLATION/   NOSHAJB54964

AMERICAN-INDIAN
    MEETING TODAYS CHALLENGE FOR EMPLOYMENT. /**AMERICAN-INDIAN** NEGRO MEXICAN-AMERICAN/   CARIZSE65403

    THE ECONOMY AND THE MINORITY POOR. /NEGRO **AMERICAN-INDIAN** MEXICAN-AMERICAN PUERTO-RICAN/   CBATCAB66879

    APACHE, NAVAHO, AND SPANIARD. /MEXICAN-AMERICAN **AMERICAN-INDIAN**/   CFORBJX60561

    FAMILY STRUCTURE AND SCHOOL PERFORMANCE. A COMPARATIVE STUDY OF STUDENTS FROM THREE ETHNIC BACKGROUNDS IN
    AN INTEGRATED SCHOOL. /MEXICAN-AMERICAN **AMERICAN-INDIAN**/   CGRIFJX65407

    CULTURAL DIFFERENCES IN AMERICAN ETHNIC GROUPS. BIBLIOGRAPHY. /**AMERICAN-INDIAN** NEGRO SPANISH-AMERICAN/   CLIBRCX64899

    CHANGING PATTERNS OF PREJUDICE. /NEGRO PUERTO-RICAN ORIENTAL **AMERICAN-INDIAN**/   CMARRAJ62055

    FACTS ON ADC IN NORTH-CAROLINA. /NEGRO **AMERICAN-INDIAN**/   CNORTCS59934

    NEW PROBLEM OF LARGE SCALE UNEMPLOYABILITY. /NEGRO MEXICAN-AMERICAN **AMERICAN-INDIAN**/   CROSEAM64553

    MINORITY-GROUPS IN NEVADA. /NEGRO **AMERICAN-INDIAN**/   CRUSCER66807

    SOCIO-ECONOMIC DIFFERENTIALS AMONG NONWHITE RACES. /NEGRO ORIENTAL **AMERICAN-INDIAN**/   CSCHMCF65107

    THE TRAINING OF MIGRANT FARM WORKERS. A FOLLOW-UP STUDY OF TWO EXPERIMENTAL AND DEMONSTRATION PROGRAMS
    UNDER THE MANPOWER-DEVELOPMENT-AND-TRAINING-ACT. /MEXICAN-AMERICAN **AMERICAN-INDIAN**/   CUNIVOD66054

    POVERTY IN THE UNITED STATES, HEARINGS. /**AMERICAN-INDIAN** NEGRO PUERTO-RICAN EMPLOYMENT/   CUSHOUR64346

    THE VOICE OF THE **AMERICAN-INDIAN**. DECLARATION OF INDIAN PURPOSE.   IAMERIC61524

    THE DEMOGRAPHY OF THE **AMERICAN-INDIAN**.   IHADLJN57569

    SOCIAL SURVEY OF **AMERICAN-INDIAN** URBAN INTEGRATION.   IHIRAJXND444

    REFERENCE ENCYCLOPEDIA ON THE **AMERICAN-INDIAN**.   IKLEIBA67899

    THE WAR AGAINST POVERTY -- THE **AMERICAN-INDIAN**.   INASHPX64597

    BROKEN PEACE PIPES. A 400 YEAR HISTORY OF THE **AMERICAN-INDIAN**.   IPEITIM64604

    QUESTIONS REGARDING **AMERICAN-INDIAN** CRIMINALITY.   ISTEWOX64302

    LAW AND THE **AMERICAN-INDIAN**.   IUSCOMC65636

    SOCIAL SECURITY AND THE **AMERICAN-INDIAN**.   IUSDHEW60639

    OPERATION BOOTSTRAP FOR THE **AMERICAN-INDIAN**.   IUSHOUR59669

    WHY NO INTEGRATION FOR THE **AMERICAN-INDIAN**.   IUSNEWR62672

    FORMAL EDUCATION IN AN **AMERICAN-INDIAN** COMMUNITY.   IWAXXML64683

AMERICAN-INDIANS
    AMERICAN-INDIANS. NEGLECTED MINORITY. /ECONOMIC-STATUS/   IDENNLB66547

    COMPARATIVE STUDIES OF NORTH **AMERICAN-INDIANS**.   IDRIVHE57954

    EDUCATION AMONG **AMERICAN-INDIANS**. INDIVIDUAL AND CULTURAL ASPECTS.   IHAVIRJ57574

    AMERICAN-INDIANS AND THEIR ECONOMIC DEVELOPMENT.   IHUMAOX61820

    TERMINATION OF FEDERAL SUPERVISION. DISINTEGRATION AND THE **AMERICAN-INDIANS**.   ILAFAOX57075

    CORRELATES OF ADJUSTMENT AMONG **AMERICAN-INDIANS** IN AN URBAN ENVIRONMENT.   IMARTHW64588

    HANDBOOK OF **AMERICAN-INDIANS** NORTH OF MEXICO.   ISMITIB59619

    EDUCATION AMONG **AMERICAN-INDIANS**. INSTITUTIONAL ASPECTS.   ITHOMHX57630

    AMERICAN-INDIANS SEEK NEW OPPORTUNITIES.   IUSDINTND665

    AMERICAN-INDIANS AND THE FEDERAL GOVERNMENT.   IUSDINT65640

    ANSWERS TO QUESTIONS ABOUT **AMERICAN-INDIANS**.   IUSDINT65642

AMERICAN-INDIANS   (CONTINUATION)
    VOCATIONAL TRAINING PROGRAMS FCR AMERICAN-INDIANS.   IUSDLAB64009

    WHERE THE REAL POVERTY IS. PLIGHT OF AMERICAN-INDIANS.   IUSNEWR66671

    AMERICAN-INDIANS IN LOS-ANGELES. A STUDY OF ADAPTATICN TO A CITY. /CALIFCRNIA/   IUVCALA66675

    AMERICAN-INDIANS AND THEIR ECONOMIC DEVELOPMENT.   IVOGEFW61677

    THE ACCULTURATION OF AMERICAN-INDIANS.   IVOGTEZ57678

    AMERICAN-INDIANS AND WHITE PEOPLE.   IWAXXRH61224

AMERICAN-JEWISH-COMM
    LARGE CCRPORATIONS ACCUSED OF DISCRIMINATION AGAINST JEWS IN MANAGEMENT, EXECUTIVE CAPACITIES BY
    AMERICAN-JEWISH-COMMITTEE.   JWORLOX64773

AMERICANIZATION
    A SURVEY OF THE PROBLEMS INVOLVED IN THE AMERICANIZATION OF THE MEXICAN-AMERICAN.   MREYEIX57463

AMERICANS
    SPANISH-SPEAKING AMERICANS. MEXICANS AND PUERTO-RICANS IN THE UNITED STATES.   CBLAIBX59366

    PREJUDICE TOWARD MEXICAN AND NEGRO AMERICANS. A COMPARISON.   CPINKAX63458

    THE INTEGRATION OF AMERICANS OF MEXICAN, PUERTO-RICAN, AND ORIENTAL DESCENT.   CYINGJM56519

    THE INVISIBLE AMERICANS. /PCVERTY UNEMPLOYMENT/   GBAGDBH63754

    EXPANDING APPRENTICESHIP FOR ALL AMERICANS.   GHENNJF63770

    A FAIR CHANCE FOR ALL AMERICANS.   GNATLCL54041

    THE INTEGRATION OF AMERICANS OF INDIAN DESCENT.   IDOZIEP57077

    INDIANS AND OTHER AMERICANS, TWO WAYS OF LIFE MEET.   IFEYXHE59558

    FAMILY AND ACHIEVEMENT. A PROPOSAL TO STUDY THE EFFECT OF FAMILY SOCIALIZATION ON ACHIEVEMENT AND
    PERFORMANCE AMONG URBAN NEGRO AMERICANS.   NEPPSEG65334

    YOUNG NEGRO TALENT. SURVEY OF THE EXPERIENCES AND EXPECTATIONS OF NEGRO AMERICANS WHO GRADUATED FROM
    COLLEGE IN 1961.   NFICHJH64867

    STUDIES IN THE HIGHER EDUCATION OF NEGRO AMERICANS.   NJOURNE66627

    THE WASTED AMERICANS. /POVERTY/   NMAYXEX64760

    OUR ORIENTAL AMERICANS.   ORITTXX65758

ANALYSIS
    NEGROES AND MEXICAN-AMERICANS IN SOUTH AND EAST LOS-ANGELES. AN ANALYSIS OF A SPECIAL US CENSUS SURVEY OF
    NOVEMBER 1965. /CALIFORNIA/   CCALDIR66168

    UNDER-ACHIEVEMENT AMONG MINORITY-GROUP STUDENTS. AN ANALYSIS AND A PROPOSAL. /YOUTH NEGRO
    MEXICAN-AMERICAN PUERTO-RICAN/   CHOBACW63555

    ANALYSIS OF CITY ORDINANCES AGAINST RACIAL AND RELIGIOUS DISCRIMINATION IN EMPLOYMENT.   GAMERJCND380

    FEDERAL CIVIL-RIGHTS-ACT OF 1960. SUMMARY AND ANALYSIS.   GAMERJD60385

    THE CIVIL-RIGHTS AND CIVIL-LIBERTIES DECISIONS OF THE US SUPREME COURT FOR THE 1962-63 TERM. A SUMMARY
    AND ANALYSIS.   GAMERJD63384

    HUMAN CAPITAL. A THEORETICAL AND EMPIRICAL ANALYSIS WITH SPECIAL REFERENCE TO EDUCATION.   GBECKGS64700

    REVIEW AND ANALYSIS OF CITY CERTIFICATIONS AND APPOINTMENTS. /BERKELEY CALIFORNIA/   GBERKCM64444

    A BENEFIT-COST ANALYSIS OF THE ECONOMIC EFFECTIVENESS OF RETRAINING THE UNEMPLOYED.   GBORUME64142

    THE CIVIL-RIGHTS-ACT OF 1964. WHAT IT MEANS -- TO EMPLOYERS, BUSINESSMEN, UNIONS, EMPLOYEES,
    MINORITY-GROUPS. TEXT, ANALYSIS, LEGISLATIVE HISTORY.   GBUREON64492

    A SUMMARY ANALYSIS OF FIVE YEARS OF CLAIMS EXPERIENCE BY THE MICHIGAN
    FAIR-EMPLOYMENT-PRACTICES-COMMISSION, FEBRUARY, 1961.   GCOUSFR61612

    A SUMMARY ANALYSIS OF SIX YEARS OF CLAIMS EXPERIENCE BY THE MICHIGAN FAIR-EMPLOYMENT
    PRACTICES-COMMISSION, FEBRUARY 1962.   GCOUSFR62613

    AN ANALYSIS OF THE EXPERIENCED HIRED FARM WORKING FORCE, 1948-1957. /SKILLS/   GCOWHJD60423

    REPORT ON AND ANALYSIS OF SECOND CENSUS OF CITY EMPLOYEES TO DETERMINE BASES FOR FUTURE PERSONNEL
    CEVELOPMENTS. /DETROIT MICHIGAN/   GDETRCC66639

    EDUCATION AND OCCUPATIONAL MOBILITY. A REGRESSION ANALYSIS.   GDUNCOD63652

    COMMISSION ENFORCEMENT OF STATE LAWS AGAINST DISCRIMINATION. A COMPARATIVE ANALYSIS OF THE KANSAS ACT.   GDYSORB65657

    COMPARATIVE ANALYSIS OF STATE FAIR-EMPLOYMENT-PRACTICES LAWS.   GHARTPX62762

    REPORT OF FINDINGS AND RECOMMENDATIONS RESULTING FROM AN ANALYSIS OF THE EMPLOYMENT PRACTICES IN THE
    VARICUS CEPARTMENTS OF THE CITY OF LOS-ANGELES. /CALIFORNIA/   GLOSAOC63917

    AN ANALYSIS OF THE EFFECTIVENESS OF THE NEW-YORK STATE LAW AGAINST DISCRIMINATION.   GMARPAW53940

    SURVEY AND ANALYSIS OF NON-WHITE EMPLOYMENT BY THE CITY OF MINNEAPOLIS. /MINNESOTA/   GMINLMH65002

    AN ANALYSIS OF STATE FEPC LEGISLATION.   GMORGCA57031

    WHITE UNEMPLOYMENT IN THE UNITED STATES, 1947-1958, AN ANALYSIS OF TRENDS.   GNEWYSA58089

    RETRAINING UNDER THE MANPOWER-DEVELOPMENT-ACT. A COST-BENEFIT ANALYSIS.   GPAGEDA64775

    THE NEW FEDERAL FAIR-EMPLOYMENT-PRACTICES ACT -- COMPARISON WITH STATE LAW AND AN ANALYSIS OF RELEVANT
    STATE EXPERIENCES. /MISSOURI/   GROBEPC64239

    RACIAL AND ETHNIC EMPLOYMENT PATTERN SURVEY OF THE CITY AND COUNTY OF SAN-FRANCISCO GOVERNMENT.
    DEPARTMENTAL ANALYSIS. /CALIFORNIA/   GSANFHR65264

    A BENEFIT-COST ANALYSIS OF MANPOWER RETRAINING.   GSOMEGJ64157

ANALYSIS   (CONTINUATION)
SENIOR CITIZENS AND HOW THEY LIVE. AN **ANALYSIS** OF 1960 CENSUS DATA. PART II. THE AGING NONWHITE AND HIS HOUSING. /ECONOMIC-STATUS/   GUSHHFX63321

A QUANTITATIVE **ANALYSIS** OF WHITE-NONWHITE INCOME DIFFERENTIALS IN THE US IN 1939.   GZEMAMX55594

ANALYSIS OF MALE NAVAHO STUDENTS PERCEPTIONS OF OCCUPATIONAL OPPORTUNITIES AND THEIR ATTITUDES TOWARD DEVELOPMENT OF SKILLS AND TRAITS NECESSARY FOR OCCUPATIONAL COMPETENCE.   IDESPCW65548

AN **ANALYSIS** OF CURRENT PATTERNS IN HUMAN RESOURCE DEVELOPMENT IN SAN-ANTONIO, TEXAS.   MDAVIHW66387

ANALYSIS OF POPULATION CHANGES IN NEW-MEXICO COUNTIES.   MPIERGK61457

AN **ANALYSIS** OF THE MEXICAN-AMERICAN MIGRANT LABOR FORCE IN THE STOCKBRIDGE AREA. /MICHIGAN/   MRODRFX66464

THE EDUCATION OF THE SPANISH-SPEAKING IN THE SOUTHWEST -- AN **ANALYSIS** OF THE 1960 CENSUS MATERIALS. MSAMOJX63469

AN ECONOMICAL AND HISTORICAL **ANALYSIS** OF THE CAUSES OF VARIATION AMONG NORTHERN STANDARD METROPOLITAN AREAS IN PRODUCTIVITY OF NEGRO MEN IN 1949.   NBATCAB61060

ANALYSIS OF THE TECHNIQUES OF RACIAL INTEGRATION IN THREE MANUFACTURING FIRMS. /INDUSTRY/   NCAMPFX54178

DESEGREGATION. A PSYCHOLOGICAL **ANALYSIS**.   NCOOKSW57234

HIDDEN UNEMPLOYMENT 1953-62. A QUANTITATIVE **ANALYSIS** BY AGE AND SEX.   NDERNTX66264

FORTUNE PRESS **ANALYSIS**, NEGROES. /EMPLOYMENT/   NFORTUN45052

APPRENTICES, SKILLED CRAFTSMEN AND THE NEGRO. AN **ANALYSIS**.   NHILLHX60525

THE NEGRO WAGE-EARNER AND APPRENTICESHIP TRAINING PROGRAMS. A CRITICAL **ANALYSIS** WITH RECOMMENDATIONS. NHILLHX60532

TWENTY YEARS OF STATE FAIR-EMPLOYMENT-PRACTICE COMMISSIONS. A CRITICAL **ANALYSIS** WITH RECOMMENDATIONS. NHILLHX64550

EQUALITY OF EMPLOYMENT OPPORTUNITY. A PROCESS **ANALYSIS** OF UNION INITIATIVE.   NHOPEJX60569

AN **ANALYSIS** OF THE IMPLEMENTATION OF THE UAW-CIO-S FAIR PRACTICES AND ANTI-DISCRIMINATION POLICIES IN SELECTED CHICAGO LOCALS. /UNION/   NJONEJE51883

AN ECONOMIC **ANALYSIS** OF SPECIFIED INCORPORATED AND UNINCORPORATED FARMERS COOPERATIVE ASSOCIATIONS OPERATED BY NEGRO FARMERS IN ALABAMA.   NLIGHMB53340

A SOCIOLOGICAL **ANALYSIS** OF A BI-RACIAL LOCAL LABOR UNION.   NMERCJJ56768

AN HISTORICAL SURVEY AND **ANALYSIS** OF THE PROGRESS OF NEGROES IN PUBLIC-SERVICE 1932-1952.   NOLIVLW56955

AN **ANALYSIS** OF SELECTIVE FACTORS INFLUENCING FARM INCOME IN HALE COUNTY, AS A BASIS FOR ESTABLISHING A MORE EFFECTIVE VOCATIONAL AGRICULTURAL PROGRAM. /ALABAMA/   NSALTDR52347

AN **ANALYSIS** OF UNEMPLOYED PUERTO-RICAN MIGRANTS IN NEW-YORK CITY.   PREMEGN58847

AN INVERTED FACTOR **ANALYSIS** OF PERSONALITY DIFFERENCES BETWEEN CAREER AND HOMEMAKING-ORIENTED WOMEN. /ASPIRATIONS/   WAVILDL64316

COUNSELING GIRLS AND WOMEN. AWARENESS. **ANALYSIS**. ACTION.   WBERRJX66642

MARRIED WOMEN IN THE LABOR-FORCE -- AN ECONOMIC **ANALYSIS**.   WCAINGG66672

AN **ANALYSIS** OF FACTORS INFLUENCING MARRIED WOMEN-S ACTUAL OR PLANNED WORK PARTICIPATION.   WWELLMW61261

ANALYTICAL
NET MIGRATION OF THE POPULATION, 1950-60, BY AGE, SEX, AND COLOR. VOL II, **ANALYTICAL** GROUPINGS OF COUNTIES. /INCOME/   GBOWLGK65434

ANCESTRY
EQUAL-RIGHTS UNDER THE LAW. PROVIDING FOR EQUAL TREATMENT FOR ALL CITIZENS REGARDLESS OF RACE, RELIGION, COLOR, NATIONAL ORIGIN OR **ANCESTRY**. /CALIFORNIA/   GCALAGO60511

CALIFORNIANS OF JAPANESE, CHINESE, FILIPINO **ANCESTRY**.   OCALDIR65709

ANGLO
POVERTY IN THE SOUTHWEST. A COMPARATIVE STUDY OF MEXICAN-AMERICAN, NONWHITE AND **ANGLO** FAMILIES. /NEGRO/ CMITTFG66777

CONTRASTS BETWEEN SPANISH FOLK AND **ANGLO** URBAN CULTURAL VALUES. /EDUCATION ASPIRATIONS/   MVALDBX64449

ANGLO-AMERIANS
THE MUTUAL IMAGES AND EXPECTATIONS OF **ANGLO-AMERIANS** AND MEXICAN-AMERICANS.   MSIMMOG61490

ANGLO-CAUCASIANS
THE URBAN REALITY. A COMPARATIVE STUDY OF THE SOCIO-ECONOMIC SITUATION OF MEXICAN-AMERICANS, NEGROES AND **ANGLO-CAUCASIANS** IN LOS-ANGELES COUNTY. /CALIFORNIA/   CLOSACH65708

ANGLOS
THE PREDICTION AND EXPLANATION OF ECONOMIC ABSORPTION AMONG MEXICAN-AMERICANS, NEGROES, AND **ANGLOS** IN A NORTHERN INDUSTRIAL COMMUNITY.   CSHANLW63120

THE PREDICTION OF ECONOMIC ABSORPTION AND CULTURAL INTEGRATION AMONG MEXICAN-AMERICANS, NEGROES, AND **ANGLOS** IN A NORTHERN INDUSTRIAL COMMUNITY.   CSHANLW66123

ANN-ARBOR
HUMAN-RELATIONS IN **ANN-ARBOR**, A COMMUNITY PROFILE.   NPIKEJX67101

ANNOTATED
INTEGRATION IN BUSINESS AND INDUSTRY. A SELECTED. **ANNOTATED** BIBLIOGRAPHY.   GAMERJC64383

COUNSELOR-S GUIDE TO OCCUPATIONAL AND OTHER MANPOWER INFORMATION. AN **ANNOTATED** BIBLIOGRAPHY.   GLAFADP65782

SCHOOL DROPOUTS. A COMMENTARY AND **ANNOTATED** BIBLIOGRAPHY.   GMILLSM64071

MASTER **ANNOTATED** BIBLIOGRAPHY OF PAPERS OF MOBILIZATION-FOR-YOUTH. PUBLISHED, UNPUBLISHED AND PRESENTED AT CONFERENCES.   GMOBIFY65025

SELECTED **ANNOTATED** REFERENCES ON FAIR-EMPLOYMENT-PRACTICES LEGISLATION.   GNELSRJ52055

A SURVEY OF CURRENT LITERATURE ON AUTOMATION AND OTHER TECHNOLOGICAL-CHANGES. A SELECTED **ANNOTATED** BIBLIOGRAPHY.   GUSDLAB64825

UNEMPLOYMENT AND RETRAINING. AN **ANNOTATED** BIBLIOGRAPHY OF RESEARCH.   GUSDLAB65503

ANNOTATED   (CONTINUATION)
MATERIALS RELATING TO THE EDUCATION OF SPANISH-SPEAKING PEOPLE IN THE UNITED STATES, AN ANNOTATED
BIBLIOGRAPHY.   MSANCGI59478

ANNOTATIONS
THE EDUCATION OF WOMEN AND GIRLS IN A CHANGING SOCIETY. A SELECTED BIBLIOGRAPHY WITH ANNOTATIONS.   WWIGNTX65267

ANNUAL
ANNUAL FARM LABOR REPORT, 1965, CALIFORNIA DEPARTMENT OF EMPLOYMENT, FARM LABOR SERVICE. /NEGRO
MEXICAN-AMERICAN WOMEN/   CCALDEM66906

NJ ANTI-DISCRIMINATION LAW. FIRST ANNUAL REPORT. /NEW-JERSEY/   GLABOLR46871

NY ANTI-DISCRIMINATION LAW. 1946 ANNUAL REPORT. /NEW-YORK/   GLABOLR46872

REPORT ON SECOND ANNUAL SPRING CONFERENCE ON CIVIL-RIGHTS OF NEW-JERSEY COMMISSION-ON-CIVIL-RIGHTS, APRIL
23, 1966.   GNEWJCC66056

COMMISSIONS FOR HUMAN RIGHTS, 15TH ANNUAL CONFERENCE, PROCEEDINGS.   GPENNHR63166

SECOND ANNUAL REPORT, THE PRESIDENT-S COMMITTEE ON GOVERNMENT CONTRACTS.   GPRESCH55124

FOURTH ANNUAL REPORT ON EQUAL JOB OPPORTUNITY, 1956-1957, PRESIDENT-S COMMITTEE ON GOVERNMENT CONTRACTS. GPRESCH57122

FIRST ANNUAL REPORT, PRESIDENT-S COMMITTEE ON GOVERNMENT EMPLOYMENT POLICY, APRIL 30 1956.   GPRESCP56193

SECOND ANNUAL REPORT, PRESIDENT-S COMMITTEE ON GOVERNMENT EMPLOYMENT POLICY, 1957.   GPRESCP57194

THIRD ANNUAL REPORT, PRESIDENT-S COMMITTEE ON GOVERNMENT EMPLOYMENT POLICY, 1958.   GPRESCP58195

FOURTH ANNUAL REPORT, PRESIDENT-S COMMITTEE CN GOVERNMENT EMPLOYMENT POLICY.   GPRESCP59196

HEALTH, EDUCATION, AND WELFARE ASPECTS OF THE ECONOMIC REPORT OF THE PRESENT AND ANNUAL REPORT OF THE
COUNCIL OF ECONOMIC ADVISORS.   GUSDHEW66711

ANNUAL REPORT OF THE SECRETARY OF HEALTH, EDUCATION, AND WELFARE TO THE CONGRESS ON TRAINING ACTIVITIES
UNDER THE MANPOWER-DEVELOPMENT-AND-TRAINING-ACT, 1965.   GUSDHEW66978

ANNUAL REPORTS OF US DEPARTMENT OF THE INTERIOR.   IUSDINTND666

CLEVELAND-S ANNUAL JOB CENTER FOR COLLEGE GRADUATES.   NCOCKHW65218

NATIONAL NEGRO LABOR COUNCIL, THIRD ANNUAL CONVENTION. /UNION/   NPERRPX54987

ANNUAL FAMILY AND OCCUPATIONAL EARNINGS OF RESIDENTS OF TWO NEGRO HOUSING PROJECTS IN ATLANTA 1937-1944.
/GEORGIA/   NRITTAL45062

LAND TENURE IN THE SOUTHERN REGION. PROCEEDINGS OF PROFESSIONAL AGRICULTURAL WORKERS TENTH ANNUAL
CONFERENCE.   NTUSKIX51218

ANNUAL FARM LABOR REPORT. /NEW-JERSEY/   PNEWJSE63831

3RD ANNUAL WOMEN-S CONFERENCE, PROCEEDINGS.   WUVUTXX66254

ANOMIA
URBANISM, RACE, AND ANOMIA.   GKILLLX62853

ANOMIE
ANOMIE AND ACHIEVEMENT MOTIVATION. A STUDY OF PERSONALITY DEVELOPMENT WITHIN CULTURAL DISORGANIZATION. IKERCAC59018

SOME CORRELATES OF ANOMIE AMONG RURAL NEGROES.   NLEWICE66688

ANSWER
AUTOMATION AND JOBLESSNESS. IS RETRAINING THE ANSWER.   GGLAZWX62866

FEPC. HOW TO ANSWER ITS CRITICS.   GRABKSX58213

JOBS FOR NEGROES. ONE COMPANY-S ANSWER. /CASE-STUDY INDUSTRY/   NBUSIMX64142

ANSWERS
QUESTIONS AND ANSWERS ABOUT EMPLOYMENT ON MERIT.   GAMERFC50379

ISSUES AND ANSWERS. /EEO/   GJOHNMW65827

SOME QUESTIONS AND ANSWERS ON THE CIVIL-RIGHTS BILL.   GLEADCCND888

QUESTIONS AND ANSWERS ABOUT PERMANENT FAIR-EMPLOYMENT-PRACTICES COMMISSIONS.   GNORTMT45124

42 QUESTIONS AND ANSWERS ABOUT FAIR-EMPLOYMENT-PRACTICES.   GOREGBLND138

SOME QUESTIONS AND ANSWERS ON THE NON-DISCRIMINATION POLICY OF THE FEDERAL GOVERNMENT.   GPRESCP55199

ANSWERS TO QUESTIONS ABOUT AMERICAN-INDIANS.   IUSDINT65642

RACE RELATIONS. QUESTIONS AND ANSWERS FOR PERSONNEL MEN.   NSHOSAX64132

ANTECEDENTS
URBAN ADJUSTMENT AND ITS RELATIONSHIP TO THE SOCIAL ANTECEDENTS OF IMMIGRANT WORKERS. /NEGRO
MEXICAN-AMERICAN/   CSHANLW65121

ANTHROPOLOGICAL
SOME CULTURAL AND ANTHROPOLOGICAL ASPECTS OF ENGLISH AS A SECOND LANGUAGE.   MRUBEAJ66468

SOME CHANGING ROLES OF WOMEN IN SUBURBIA. A SOCIAL ANTHROPOLOGICAL CASE STUDY. /WORK-FAMILY-CONFLICT/ WSCOFNE60109

ANTHROPOLOGY
DOCUMENTARY HISTORY OF THE FCX PROJECT, 1948-1959. A PROGRAM IN ACTION ANTHROPOLOGY.   INETTRM60599

ANTI
THE RACIAL ISSUE AS AN ANTI UNION TOOL AND THE NATIONAL-LABOR-RELATIONS-BOARD.   NSACHRX63888

ANTI-BIAS
CPI -- CHEMICAL PROCESS INDUSTRIES -- TAKES LEAD IN ANTI-BIAS DRIVE. /INDUSTRY/   NCHEMWX61199

ANTI-DISCRIMINATION
REPORT ON TWENTY STATE ANTI-DISCRIMINATION AGENCIES AND THE LAWS THEY ADMINISTER.   GAMERJD61387

ANTI-DISCRIMINATION LAWS IN ACTION IN NEW-JERSEY. A LAW-SOCIOLOGY STUDY.   GBLUMAW65459

ANTI-DISCRIMINATION (CONTINUATION)
ANTI-DISCRIMINATION LEGISLATION IN THE AMERICAN STATES.   GGRAVWB48734

NJ ANTI-DISCRIMINATION LAW. FIRST ANNUAL REPORT. /NEW-JERSEY/   GLABOLR46871

NY ANTI-DISCRIMINATION LAW. 1946 ANNUAL REPORT. /NEW-YORK/   GLABOLR46872

DISCRIMINATION IN EMPLOYMENT. FEDERAL AND STATE PRACTICES IN ANTI-DISCRIMINATION.   GLEITRD49892

LAW AND EQUAL-OPPORTUNITY. ANTI-DISCRIMINATION LAW IN MASSACHUSETTS.   GMAYHLH63970

EVERYBODY-S BUSINESS. A SUMMARY CF NEW-YORK STATE ANTI-DISCRIMINATION LAWS AND HOW TO USE THEM.   GNATLFC46048

ANTI-DISCRIMINATION PACT SIGNED IN PHILADELPHIA. /PENNSYLVANIA/   GPUBLWX63207

ANTI-DISCRIMINATION CLAUSES REVISITED.   GWORTMS65585

TRADE UNIONS PRACTICES AND THE NEGRO WORKER -- THE ESTABLISHMENT AND IMPLEMENTATION OF AFL-CIO
ANTI-DISCRIMINATION POLICY.   NDAVINF60312

AN ANALYSIS OF THE IMPLEMENTATION OF THE UAW-CIO-S FAIR PRACTICES AND ANTI-DISCRIMINATION POLICIES IN
SELECTED CHICAGO LOCALS. /UNION/   NJONEJE51883

ANTI-DISCRIMINATION LEGISLATION IN 1947.   NUSDLAB47810

ANTI-DISCRIMINATION LEGISLATION.   NUSDLAB48149

ANTI-DISCRIMINATION IN INDUSTRY.   NYOUNCE45358

ANTI-DISCRIMINATORY
RACE-RELATIONS AND ANTI-DISCRIMINATORY LEGISLATION.   GBURMJH51500

SURVEY OF STATE ANTI-DISCRIMINATORY LAWS.   GLABOLR44877

ANTI-JAPANESE
THE POLITICS OF PREJUDICE. THE ANTI-JAPANESE MOVEMENT IN CALIFORNIA AND THE STRUGGLE FOR JAPANESE
EXCLUSION.   ODANIRX61716

ANTI-LABOR
THE ANTI-LABOR FRONT. /UNION/   NBERNVH43555

ANTI-NEPOTISM
ANTI-NEPOTISM RULES IN AMERICAN COLLEGES AND UNIVERSITIES -- THEIR EFFECT ON THE FACULTY EMPLOYMENT OF
WOMEN.   WDOLAEF60951

ANTI-POVERTY
THE FEDERAL ANTI-POVERTY PROGRAM AND SOME IMPLICATIONS OF SUBPROFESSIONAL TRAINING.   GGORDJE65135

IMPLICATIONS OF THE ANTI-POVERTY PROGRAM FOR EDUCATION AND EMPLOYMENT.   GLEVILA65781

PROGRAMS IN AID OF THE POOR. /ANTI-POVERTY/   GLEVISA66729

THE ROLE OF EMPLOYMENT POLICY. /ANTI-POVERTY/   GMINSHX65655

THE NEW ANTI-POVERTY IDEOLOGY AND THE NEGRO.   NRIESFX65060

POVERTY. /SOUTH ANTI-POVERTY/   NULMXAX66712

ANTIDISCRIMINATION
ANTIDISCRIMINATION LEGISLATION AS AN INFRINGEMENT OF FREEDOM OF CHOICE.   GAVINAX60409

FREEDOM OF CHOICE IN PERSONAL SERVICE OCCUPATIONS. 13TH AMENDMENT LIMITATIONS ON ANTIDISCRIMINATION
LEGISLATION.   GAVINAX64410

THE RIGHT TO EQUAL TREATMENT. ADMINISTRATIVE ENFORCEMENT OF ANTIDISCRIMINATION LEGISLATION.   GBAMBMA61416

THE CONSCIENCE OF THE GOVERNMENT. /ANTIDISCRIMINATION/   GBERNBI62447

THE RIGHTS AND RESPONSIBILITY OF UNION MEMBERS. /ANTIDISCRIMINATION/   GGOLDAX58974

CITY PROBLEMS OF 1963. /ANTIDISCRIMINATION/   GKENNJF63842

THE POLITICS OF ANTIDISCRIMINATION LEGISLATION.   GLOCKDX65146

ANTIDISCRIMINATION PROVISIONS IN MAJOR CONTRACTS, 1961.   GLUDELE62923

ANTIDISCRIMINATION IN EMPLOYMENT.   GUSSENA54330

MOVING AHEAD. AIMS AND METHODS. /CIVIL-RIGHTS ANTIDISCRIMINATION/   GWOFFHX62577

THE INCIDENCE OF ANTIDISCRIMINATION CLAUSES IN UNION CONTRACTS.   GWORTMS65681

ANXIETY
EFFECTS OF ANXIETY, THREAT, AND RACIAL ENVIRONMENT ON TASK PERFORMANCE OF NEGRO COLLEGE STUDENTS.   NKATZIX63640

APACHE
APACHE, NAVAHO, AND SPANIARD. /MEXICAN-AMERICAN AMERICAN-INDIAN/   CFORBJX60561

SAN-CARLOS APACHE WAGE LABOR.   IADAMWX57522

DEVELOPMENT OF THE SAN-CARLOS APACHE CATTLE INDUSTRY. /CALIFORNIA/   IGETTHT58563

NEEDS AND RESOURCES OF THE JICARILLA APACHE INDIAN TRIBE.   ISTANRI58623

THE RELATIONSHIP BETWEEN UNEARNED INCOME AND INDIVIDUAL PRODUCTIVE EFFORT ON THE JICARILLA APACHE INDIAN
RESERVATION.   IWILSHC61687

JICARILLA APACHE POLITICAL AND ECONOMIC STRUCTURES.   IWILSHC64235

APPEALS
APPEALS FROM DISCRIMINATION IN FEDERAL EMPLOYMENT. A CASE-STUDY.   NSHOSAX63131

APPLICANT
UTILIZING OUR MANPOWER RESOURCES. SPECIAL APPLICANT GROUPS.   GUSDLAB63665

THE UNITED STATES EMPLOYMENT SERVICE AND THE NEGRO WORK APPLICANT.   NUSWAMC44276

APPLICANTS
CHARACTERISTICS OF RETRAINING APPLICANTS. /CALIFORNIA NEGRO MEXICAN-AMERICAN WOMEN/   CCALDEM66166

APPLICANTS   (CONTINUATION)
EVALUATING JOB APPLICANTS WITH POLICE RECORDS.   /CALIFORNIA/   GCALFEP66532

FAIR-EMPLOYMENT-PRACTICES EQUAL GOOD EMPLOYMENT PRACTICES. GUIDELINES FOR TESTING AND SELECTING MINORITY   GCALFEP66540
JOB APPLICANTS.   /CALIFORNIA/

QUESTICNING APPLICANTS FOR EMPLOYMENT. A GUIDE FOR APPLICATION FORMS AND INTERVIEWS UNDER THE HAWAII   GHAWADL64767
FAIR-EMPLOYMENT-PRACTICES ACT.

TESTING MINORITY-GROUP APPLICANTS.   GKETCWA66942

MANAGEMENT-S CONCERN WITH RECENT CIVIL-RIGHTS LEGISLATION AFFECTING MANAGEMENT-S OBLIGATIONS TO HIS   GKOPPRW65858
EMPLOYEES AND APPLICANTS FOR EMPLOYMENT, MAINLY IN THE STATE OF NEW-YORK.

TESTING MINORITY-GROUP APPLICANTS FOR EMPLOYMENT.   GLOCKHC65907

3 CURRENT PROBLEMS IN TEST PERFORMANCE OF JOB APPLICANTS.   GLOPEFM66909

PROBLEMS, RESEARCH, AND RECOMMENDATIONS IN THE EMPLOYMENT TESTING OF MINORITY-GROUP APPLICANTS.   GNEWCMR66163

TESTING OF MINORITY-GROUP APPLICANTS FOR EMPLOYMENT.   GWALLPX66539

PLACEMENT OF NON-ENGLISH SPEAKING APPLICANTS.   GWATSMMND544

PLACEMENT EXPERIENCES OF APPLICANTS TO A PRIVATE EMPLOYMENT-AGENCY.   NANTIDL55901

DIFFERENTIAL SELECTION AMONG APPLICANTS FROM DIFFERENT SOCIO-ECONOMIC AND ETHNIC BACKGROUNDS.   NBARRRS65056

INTEREST PATTERN FAKING BY FEMALE JOB APPLICANTS. /ASPIRATIONS/   WBECKJA63633

APPLICATION
ELIMINATION OF RACE DISCRIMINATION IN THE APPLICATION BLANK.   GDARTCX47626

QUESTICNING APPLICANTS FOR EMPLOYMENT, A GUIDE FOR APPLICATION FORMS AND INTERVIEWS UNDER THE HAWAII   GHAWADL64767
FAIR-EMPLOYMENT-PRACTICES ACT.

APPLIES
EPISODE I. ARTHUR BROWN APPLIES FOR A JOB. /DISCRIMINATION/   NLAWSEX45035

APPLY
JEWS NEED NOT APPLY. /DISCRIMINATION EMPLOYMENT/   JWEISAX58770

APPOINTMENT
RACE, NATIONALITY, AND RELIGION -- THEIR RELATIONSHIP TO APPOINTMENT POLICIES AND CASEWORK.   GHAGEDJ57752

APPOINTMENTS
REVIEW AND ANALYSIS OF CITY CERTIFICATIONS AND APPOINTMENTS. /BERKELEY CALIFORNIA/   GBERKCM64444

A PRELIMINARY REPORT ON MEDICAL STAFF APPOINTMENTS HELD BY NEGRO PHYSICIANS AT PREDOMINANTLY WHITE   NCHICCO60201
HOSPITALS. /CHICAGO ILLINOIS/

INTEGRATION ON HOSPITAL APPOINTMENTS AND IN HOSPITAL CARE. /CHICAGO ILLINOIS/   NCHICUL58202

APPRAISAL
SELF APPRAISAL FOR MERIT PROMOTION. A RESEARCH MANUAL.   GBOWMGW63467

GOVERNMENTAL FAIR-EMPLOYMENT AGENCIES. AN APPRAISAL OF FEDERAL, STATE, AND MUNICIPAL EFFORTS TO END JOB   GNORGPH62120
DISCRIMINATION.

REVIEW APPRAISAL. KLAMATH INDIAN ASSETS.   IUSSENA59674

NEGROES AND GOVERNMENTAL SERVICES. AN APPRAISAL.   NBOYDWM46252

EQUAL-OPPORTUNITY IN FARM PROGRAMS -- AN APPRAISAL OF SERVICES RENDERED BY AGENCIES OF THE UNITED STATES   NUSCOMC65232
DEPARTMENT OF AGRICULTURE.

A CRITICAL APPRAISAL OF PROFESSION TRAINING OF NEGRO TEACHERS IN OKTIBBEHA COUNTY MISSISSIPPI.   NWILLMM50234

APPRENTICE
APPRENTICE PROGRAMS.   GPRESCD64106

MANAGEMENT, RACIAL DISCRIMINATION AND APPRENTICE TRAINING   NKOVAIX64663

APPRENTICES
JOINT STAND REJECTS RACIAL QUOTAS FOR PLUMBING APPRENTICES.   GAIRCHR63867

RECENT TRENDS IN THE TEST SELECTION OF APPRENTICES.   GMOTLAW53033

ETHNIC SURVEY OF APPRENTICES. /CALIFORNIA/   GWEBBEB65546

PRELIMINARY REPORT ON SURVEY OF ACTIVE APPRENTICES. /CALIFORNIA/   MCALDIR62376

APPRENTICES, SKILLED CRAFTSMEN AND THE NEGRO. AN ANALYSIS.   NHILLHX60525

APPRENTICESHIP
REPORT OF THE CALIFORNIA STATE ADVISORY COMMITTEE TO THE UNITED STATES COMMISSION ON CIVIL-RIGHTS ON   GBECKWL62432
CALIFORNIA-S PROGRAM FOR EQUAL-OPPORTUNITY IN APPRENTICESHIP.

APPRENTICESHIP AND TESTS, FEP SUMMARY OF LATEST DEVELOPMENTS.   GBUREON65491

A COMPILATION OF STATISTICAL DATA, CHARTS AND OTHER RESOURCE MATERIAL FOR CONFERENCE PARTICIPANTS.   GCALCNA60516
/APPRENTICESHIP CALIFORNIA YOUTH/

THE CALIFORNIA PLAN FOR EQUAL-OPPORTUNITY IN APPRENTICESHIP FOR MINORITY-GROUPS.   GCALDIR63523

EQUAL-OPPORTUNITY IN APPRENTICESHIP AND TRAINING -- THE CALIFORNIA PROGRAM.   GCALDIR65524

STATISTICS ON APPRENTICESHIP AND THEIR LIMITATIONS.   GGROOPX64745

EXPANDING APPRENTICESHIP FOR ALL AMERICANS.   GHENNJF63770

GUIDANCE, TRAINING AND APPRENTICESHIP FACTORS AFFECTING MINORITY-GROUPS.   GNATLAM60037

APPRENTICESHIP. AN EVALUATION OF THE NEED.   GSTRAGX65715

HOUSING, EMPLOYMENT OPPORTUNITIES AND APPRENTICESHIP TRAINING, REPORT. /NEW-JERSEY/   GUSCOMC63404

REPORTS ON APPRENTICESHIP, NINE STATE ADVISORY COMMITTEES. /CALIFORNIA FLORIDA MARYLAND CONNECTICUT

APPRENTICESHIP (CONTINUATION)
WASHINGTON-DC NEW-JERSEY NEW-YORK TENNESSEE WISCONSIN/   GUSCOMC64407

EQUAL-OPPORTUNITY IN **APPRENTICESHIP** PROGRAMS.   GUSHOUR61343

APPRENTICESHIP TRAINING IN NEW-YORK. OPENINGS IN 1963.   GWORKDL63582

THE WDL **APPRENTICESHIP** TRAINING PROGRAM. REPORT OF A YEAR-S EXPERIMENT.   GWORKDL65584

MAKING **APPRENTICESHIP** WORK.   NAMERFX66014

THE NEGRO WAGE-EARNER AND **APPRENTICESHIP** TRAINING PROGRAMS. A CRITICAL ANALYSIS WITH RECOMMENDATIONS.   NHILLHX60532

RACIAL DISCRIMINATION IN THE NATION-S **APPRENTICESHIP** TRAINING PROGRAM.   NHILLHX62539

APPRENTICESHIP TRAINING PROGRAMS AND RACIAL DISCRIMINATION.   NKOVAIX65024

NEGRO PARTICIPATION IN **APPRENTICESHIP** PROGRAMS.   NMARSRX66327

NEGRO PARTICIPATION IN **APPRENTICESHIP** PROGRAMS.   NMARSRX67118

APPRENTICESHIP AND TRAINING OPPORTUNITIES FOR NEGRO YOUTHS IN SELECTED URBAN-LEAGUE CITIES.   NNATLUL61885

PUBLIC POLICY AND DISCRIMINATION IN **APPRENTICESHIP**.   NSTRAGX65182

THE NEGRO WAGE-EARNER AND **APPRENTICESHIP** TRAINING PROGRAMS.   NUSDLAB60249

APPRENTICESHIPS
THE NEGRO AND **APPRENTICESHIPS**.   NKURSHX65669

NEGROES IN **APPRENTICESHIPS**, NEW-YORK STATE.   NUSDLAB60830

APPROACH
REPORT OF INDUSTRY AND LABOR-MANAGEMENT CLINICS. IMPLEMENTATION OF EMPLOYMENT IN MERIT PROGRAMS IN NON
FEPC STATES BY DIRECT **APPROACH** TO TOP MANAGEMENT.   GFISKUR51684

A METHODOLOGICAL **APPROACH** TO IDENTIFICATION AND CLASSIFICATION OF CERTAIN TYPES OF INACTIVE WORK-SEEKERS.
/UNEMPLOYMENT LABOR-MARKET/   GLIEBEE65569

THE COMMUNITY **APPROACH**. /EEO/   GMATTEG64967

THE AMERICAN LOWER-CLASSES. A TYPOLOGICAL **APPROACH**.   GMILLSM64727

ETHNIC STRATIFICATION. A COMPARATIVE **APPROACH**.   GSHIBTX65303

TRAINING FOR TOMORROW-S SCIENTISTS AND TECHNICIANS. A COMMUNITY **APPROACH** TO A COMMUNITY NEED.   NFINLOE60356

OUTREACH -- THE AFFIRMATIVE **APPROACH**. /EMPLOYMENT SES/   NFRANWH66698

OCCUPATIONAL CHOICE. AN **APPROACH** TO A GENERAL THEORY.   NGINZEX51410

EQUALITY OF OPPORTUNITY. A UNION **APPROACH** TO FAIR EMPLOYMENT.   NHOPEJX56570

FUTURE OCCUPATIONAL DIFFERENCES BETWEEN THE RACES. A MARKOV **APPROACH**.   NLEWISX66693

ATLANTA-S SEGREGATED **APPROACH** TO INTEGRATED EMPLOYMENT. /GEORGIA/   NTHOMHX62205

THE ROLE OF CIVIL-RIGHTS ORGANIZATIONS. A MARSHALL PLAN **APPROACH**.   NTUCKSX66209

CONTRASTIVE ACCULTURATION OF CALIFORNIA JAPANESE. COMPARATIVE **APPROACH** TO THE STUDY OF IMMIGRANTS.   OBEFUHX65701

A FUNCTIONAL **APPROACH** TO THE GAINFUL EMPLOYMENT OF MARRIED WOMEN.   WHACKHM61812

APPROACHES
APPROACHES TO INCOME IMPROVEMENT. EXPERIENCES OF FAMILIES RECEIVING PRODUCTION LOANS UNDER THE FARMERS
HOME ADMINISTRATION.   GHENDWE59422

SOME SUGGESTED **APPROACHES** FOR TEST DEVELOPMENT AND MEASUREMENT.   GKRUGRE66863

PROBLEMS AND **APPROACHES** IN INTEGRATING MINORITY-GROUP WORK FORCES.   GSPERBJ53330

APPROACHES TO THE SCHOOL DROPOUT PROBLEM.   GSULLNV65653

WHAT ARE SOME INDUSTRIAL RELATIONS **APPROACHES** TO INTEGRATION.   NHOMAHL63564

SOCIAL TRENDS IN AMERICA AND STRATEGIC **APPROACHES** TO THE NEGRO PROBLEM.   NMYRDGX48871

NEW **APPROACHES** TO COUNSELING GIRLS IN THE 1960-S.   WMIDWRP65209

APTITUDE
APTITUDE TESTING, TRAINING, AND EMPLOYEE DEVELOPMENT, WITH A SECTION ON THE EMPLOYMENT OF
MINORITY-GROUPS.   GAMERMA49389

NEW DIRECTIONS IN US EMPLOYMENT-SERVICE **APTITUDE** TEST RESEARCH.   GDVORBJ65656

THE VALIDITY OF OCCUPATIONAL **APTITUDE** TESTS.   GGHISEE66788

RACE, **APTITUDE** AND VOCATIONAL INTERESTS.   NCHANNN65191

TEST BIAS. VALIDITY OF THE SCHOLASTIC **APTITUDE** TEST FOR NEGRO AND WHITE STUDENTS IN INTEGRATED COLLEGES.   NCLEATA66923

POST-HIGH SCHOOL PLANS FOR SENIOR GIRLS IN RELATION TO SCHOLASTIC **APTITUDE**. /ASPIRATIONS/   WMILLRX61983

BACKGROUND FACTORS AND COLLEGE GOING PLANS AMONG HIGH **APTITUDE** PUBLIC HIGH SCHOOL SENIORS. /ASPIRATIONS/   WSTICGX56141

APTITUDES
A SURVEY OF WOMEN-S **APTITUDES** FOR ARMY JOBS. /MILITARY/   WFUCHEF63772

ARAPAHOE
ARAPAHOE INDIAN TRAINS FOR SPACE AGE.   IUSDLAB66960

AREA
CHARACTERISTICS, RESOURCES, AND INCOMES OF RURAL HOUSEHOLDS, PIEDMONT **AREA**, SOUTH-CAROLINA.   GBURCTA62408

MANPOWER RESOURCES OF THE SAN-FRANCISCO OAKLAND BAY **AREA** 1960-1970. /CALIFORNIA/   GCALDEM63520

MEDICAL SERVICE JOB OPPORTUNITIES 1964-66, SAN-FRANCISCO BAY **AREA**. /CALIFORNIA/   GCALDEM64521

HOTEL AND RESTAURANT JOB OPPORTUNITIES, SAN-FRANCISCO BAY **AREA**, 1964-1966. /CALIFORNIA/   GCALDEM65517

AREA   (CONTINUATION)

MANPOWER DEVELOPMENT TRAINING. TOTAL NUMBER OF NEW ENROLLEES DURING THE MONTH BY RACE AND OCCUPATION
STATEWIDE AND BY ADMINISTRATIVE AREA, SEPTEMBER, 1966, OCTOBER, 1966. /CALIFORNIA/   GCALDEM66518

SAN-MATEO AREA MINORITY JOB SURVEY. /CALIFORNIA/   GCALFEP65542

REPORT OF THE DIAGNOSTIC SURVEY OF TENANT HOUSEHOLDS IN THE WEST SIDE URBAN-RENEWAL AREA OF
NEW-YORK-CITY.   GGREEAI65474

STUDY OF OCCUPATIONAL CHARACTERISTICS OF NON-WHITES IN THE EAST BATON-ROUGE AREA. /LOUISIANA/   GHARRWRND760

BAY AREA CONFERENCE ON FULL-EMPLOYMENT. /SAN-FRANCISCO CALIFORNIA/   GHIRSFI64776

HIRING PROCEDURES AND SELECTION STANDARDS IN THE SAN-FRANCISCO BAY AREA. /CALIFORNIA/   GMALMTF55934

A STUDY OF UNEMPLOYMENT, TRAINING AND PLACEMENT PATTERNS IN THE MUSKEGON AREA. /MICHIGAN/   GMICFEA57979

MISSOURI LOCAL GOVERNMENT ACTION IN THE AREA OF HUMAN-RIGHTS.   GMISSCH63022

THE NEXT STEPS TOWARD EQUALITY OF OPPORTUNITY IN THE SYRACUSE METROPOLITAN AREA. REPORT OF THE SYRACUSE
CONFERENCE ON HUMAN RIGHTS AND HOUSING, JULY 2-3 1962. /NEW-YORK/   GNEWYSB62103

FAIR EMPLOYMENT SURVEY OF THE WESTCHESTER AREA. /PENNSYLVANIA/   GPENNHR65163

PSYCHOLOGICAL TESTS AND FAIR EMPLOYMENT. A STUDY OF EMPLOYMENT TESTING IN THE SAN-FRANCISCO BAY AREA.
/CALIFORNIA/   GRUSHJT66268

MEETING THE MANPOWER PROBLEMS OF. I. AREA RECEVELOPMENT, II. AUTOMATION.   GUSDLAB62708

JOB OPPORTUNITIES FOR MINORITIES IN THE SEATTLE AREA. /WASHINGTON/   GUVWAIL48532

RELOCATED AMERICAN INDIANS IN THE SAN-FRANCISCO BAY AREA. SOCIAL INTERACTION AND INDIAN IDENTITY.
/CALIFORNIA/   IALBOJX64523

RELOCATEES FROM GALLUP AREA TO THE DENVER FIELD EMPLOYMENT ASSISTANCE OFFICE. /COLORADO/   IGRAVTDND438

FAMILY COMPOSITION AND CHARACTERISTICS OF AN ECONOMICALLY DEPRIVED CROSS-CULTURAL ROCKY-MOUNTAIN AREA. MANDRWH66359

THE MEXICAN IN THE NORTHERN URBAN AREA. A COMPARISON OF TWO GENERATIONS.   MGOLDNX59403

AN ANALYSIS OF THE MEXICAN-AMERICAN MIGRANT LABOR FORCE IN THE STOCKBRIDGE AREA. /MICHIGAN/   MRODRFX66464

INCOME AND RELATED CHARACTERISTICS OF RURAL HOUSEHOLDS IN THE CENTRAL LOUISIANA MIXED FARMING AREA. NBOLTBX60398

RESOURCE USE AND ADJUSTMENT. RURAL FAMILIES IN THE CENTRAL LOUISIANA MIXED FARMING AREA.   NBOLTBX61396

FARM INCOME PREDICTIONS FOR SMALL FARMS IN THE CENTRAL LOUISIANA MIXED FARMING AREA.   NBOLTBX62399

FACTORS AFFECTING THE PRESENT FARMING PROGRAMS OF ONE HUNDRED NEGRO FARMS IN THE PATRONAGE AREA OF THE
MACON COUNTY TRAINING SCHOOL, IN ALABAMA, WITH EMPHASIS FOR IMPROVEMENT.   NBRONCA51337

THE ECONOMIC-STATUS OF NEGROES IN THE SAN-FRANCISCO OAKLAND BAY AREA. A REPORT BASED ON THE 1960 CENSUS
OF POPULATION. /CALIFORNIA/   NCALFES63172

SOCIO-ECONOMIC CLASS AND AREA AS CORRELATES OF ILLEGAL BEHAVIOR AMONG JUVENILES.   NCLARJP62209

SOCIAL-DEPENDENCY IN THE SAN-FRANCISCO BAY AREA. TODAY AND TOMORROW. /CALIFORNIA/   NGREEMX63449

RACE-RELATIONS IN THE ALBANY TROY AREA. A PROFILE FOR 1957. /NEW-YORK/   NGRIEES57503

NEGRO EMPLOYMENT IN THE BIRMINGHAM METROPOLITAN AREA. /ALABAMA CASE-STUDY/   NHAWLLT55502

RACIAL DISCRIMINATION IN EMPLOYMENT IN THE CINNCINATI AREA. /OHIO/   NKUHNAX62668

LABOR AND TECHNOLOGY ON SELECTED COTTON PLANTATIONS IN THE DELTA AREA OF MISSISSIPPI, 1953-1957. NLERANL59404

PLANTATION ORGANIZATION AND THE RESIDENT LABOR-FORCE, DELTA AREA, MISSISSIPPI.   NLERANL60403

NEGRO FARM LABOR IN THE DELTA AREA OF MISSISSIPPI. SUPPLY AND UTILIZATION.   NLERANL61416

PROPOSALS FOR THE IMPROVEMENT OF HUMAN RELATIONS IN THE LOS-ANGELES METROPOLITAN AREA. /EMPLOYMENT
CALIFORNIA/   NLOSACC65365

POSTWAR STATUS OF NEGRO WORKERS IN SAN-FRANCISCO AREA. /CALIFORNIA/   NMCENDX50721

A STUDY OF EMPLOYMENT AND TRAINING PATTERNS IN THE LANSING AREA. /MICHIGAN/   NMICFEP58778

EMPLOYMENT AS IT RELATES TO NEGROES IN THE MILWAUKEE INDUSTRIAL AREA. /WISCONSIN/   NMILWUL48793

HEARINGS --TRI-CITIES AREA OF ALABAMA.   NNATILR58875

MINORITY-GROUPS AND INTERGROUP RELATIONS IN THE SAN-FRANCISCO BAY AREA. /CALIFORNIA/   NRECOCW63043

SOCIAL AND CULTURAL CHANGE IN THE PLANTATION AREA.   NRUBIMX54297

OCCUPATIONAL ESTABLISHMENT OF FORMER STUDENTS OF VOCATIONAL AGRICULTURE IN MONTGOMERY TRAINING SCHOOL
AREA. /ALABAMA/   NSCOTCDND346

PERSONAL AND ENVIRONMENTAL OBSTACLES TO PRODUCTION ADJUSTMENTS ON SOUTH-CAROLINA PIEDMONT AREA FARMS. NTAYLCC58411

NEGRO EMPLOYMENT IN THREE COMPANIES IN THE NEW-ORLEANS AREA. /CASE-STUDY LOUISIANA/   NUSDLAB55828

STUDY OF ECONOMIC AND CULTURAL ACTIVITIES IN THE WARREN AREA AS THEY RELATE TO MINORITY PEOPLE. /OHIO/ NWARRUL64986

NEGRO EMPLOYMENT PRACTICES IN THE CHATTANOOGA AREA. /TENNESSEE/   NWESSWH55314

THREE COMPANIES -- NEW-ORLEANS AREA. /CASE-STUDY LOUISIANA/   NWISSHW55332

POPULATIONS OF NEW-YORK STATE. REPORT NO 2. THE PUERTO-RICAN POPULATION OF THE NEW-YORK-CITY AREA. PNEWYCO62838

AREA-REDEVELOPMENT-A
FEDERAL AID TO DEPRESSED AREAS. AN EVALUATION OF THE AREA-REDEVELOPMENT-ADMINISTRATION.   GLEVISA64896

AREAS
FACTORS AFFECTING EDUCATIONAL-ATTAINMENT IN DEPRESSED URBAN AREAS. /NEGRO PUERTO-RICAN/   CGOLDML63426

THE ASSIMILATION AND ACCULTURATION OF MIGRANTS TO URBAN AREAS. /MEXICAN-AMERICAN NEGRO/   CSHANLW63484

MOBILITY FOR METROPOLITAN AREAS.   CUSBURC63173

AREAS   (CONTINUATION)
    MOBILITY FOR STATES AND STATE ECONOMIC AREAS. /DEMOGRAPHY/   CUSBURC63174

    RECENT POPULATION TRENDS IN THE UNITED STATES WITH EMPHASIS ON RURAL AREAS. /EDUCATION/   GBEALCL63426

    POVERTY IN RURAL AREAS OF THE UNITED STATES.   GBIRDAR64450

    OBSTACLES TO DESEGREGATION IN AMERICA-S URBAN AREAS.   GGRIEGX64743

    AREAS OF COMMISSION CONCERN. /KANSAS-CITY MISSOURI/   GKANCIC62840

    FEDERAL AID TO DEPRESSED AREAS. AN EVALUATION OF THE AREA-REDEVELOPMENT-ADMINISTRATION.   GLEVISA64896

    RESOURCES AND INCOMES OF RURAL FAMILIES IN THE COASTAL PLAIN AREAS OF GEORGIA.   GMCARWC59392

    SOCIAL DYNAMITE. THE REPORT OF THE CONFERENCE ON UNEMPLOYED, OUT-OF-SCHOOL YOUTH IN URBAN AREAS, MAY
    24-26, 1961.   GNATLCC61039

    EDUCATION IN DEPRESSED AREAS.   GPASSHA63724

    RACIAL CHANGES IN METROPOLITAN AREAS, 1950-1960. /DEMOGRAPHY/   GSCHNLF63288

    MAJOR AGRICULTURAL MIGRANT LABOR DEMAND AREAS.   GUSDLAB61509

    INDIANS IN RURAL AND RESERVATION AREAS. /CALIFORNIA/   ICALACI66542

    ECONOMIC BASE STUDY OF SAN-ANTONIO AND TWENTY-SEVEN COUNTY AREAS. /TEXAS/   MSANACP64476

    SELF RADIUS AND GOALS OF YOUTH IN DIFFERENT URBAN AREAS.   MSHERCW61489

    OCCUPATION-PATTERNS OF SPANISH-AMERICANS IN SELECTED AREAS OF TEXAS.   MSKRARL62494

    MEXICAN-AMERICAN AND TOTAL EMPLOYMENT IN SELECTED STATES AND STANDARD METROPOLITAN STATISTICAL AREAS.   MUSCISC63504

    MIGRATION AND OPPORTUNITY. A STUDY OF STANDARD METROPOLITAN AREAS IN THE UNITED-STATES.   NBALATR63047

    AN ECONOMICAL AND HISTORICAL ANALYSIS OF THE CAUSES OF VARIATION AMONG NORTHERN STANDARD METROPOLITAN
    AREAS IN PRODUCTIVITY OF NEGRO MEN IN 1949.   NBATCAB61060

    ATTITUDE TOWARD JOB-MOBILITY AMONG HOUSEHOLD HEADS IN LOW-INCOME AREAS OF THE RURAL SOUTH.   NDUNKJX64300

    AREAS OF RESEARCH IN RACE-RELATIONS.   NFRAZEF58376

    TO STEM THIS TIDE, A SURVEY OF RACIAL TENSION AREAS IN THE U.S.   NJOHNCS43617

    THE EFFECT OF THE GHETTO ON THE DISTRIBUTION AND LEVEL OF NONWHITE EMPLOYMENT IN URBAN AREAS.   NKAINJF64631

    RACIAL CHANGES IN METROPOLITAN AREAS, 1950-1960. /DEMOGRAPHY MIGRATION/   NSCHNLF65109

    THE CHANGING COLOR COMPOSITION OF METROPOLITAN AREAS. /DEMOGRAPHY/   NSHARHX62125

    POVERTY AREAS OF OUR MAJOR CITIES. THE EMPLOYMENT SITUATION OF NEGRO AND WHITE WORKERS IN METROPOLITAN
    AREAS COMPARED IN A SPECIAL LABOR-FORCE REPORT.   NWETZJR66114

    POVERTY AREAS OF OUR MAJOR CITIES. THE EMPLOYMENT SITUATION OF NEGRO AND WHITE WORKERS IN METROPOLITAN
    AREAS COMPARED IN A SPECIAL LABOR-FORCE REPORT.   NWETZJR66114

    THE FEMALE LABOR-FORCE IN METROPOLITAN AREAS. AN INTERNATIONAL COMPARISON.   WCOLLAX62697

    INVESTIGATION OF DIFFERENCES IN OCCUPATIONAL-PREFERENCES, STEREOTYPIC THINKING, AND PSYCHOLOGICAL NEEDS
    AMONG UNDERGRADUATE WOMEN STUDENTS IN SELECTED CURRICULAR AREAS. /ASPIRATIONS/   WKITTRE60313

    PROBLEM AREAS IN TRAINING FOR AUTOMATED WORK. /TECHNOLOGICAL-CHANGE/   WLIPSOX64936

    ACCESS OF GIRLS AND WOMEN TO EDUCATION IN RURAL AREAS. A COMPARATIVE STUDY.   WUNESCO64166

ARIZONA
    FINAL REPORT. EXPERIMENTAL AND DEMONSTRATION ON-JOB-TRAINING PROJECT. /MIGRANT-WORKERS MEXICAN-AMERICAN
    NEGRO ARIZONA/   CSKILTO66324

    INCOME, EDUCATION AND UNEMPLOYMENT IN NEIGHBORHOODS. PHOENIX, ARIZONA. /DEMOGRAPHY/   CUSDLAB63480

    SUB-EMPLOYMENT IN THE SLUMS OF PHOENIX. /ARIZONA/   GUSDLAB66513

    ARIZONA RESERVATIONS ECONOMICS. SURVEY REPORT.   IARIZCI63528

    MANPOWER SERVICES TO ARIZONA INDIANS. /SES/   IARIZSE66912

    THE CHANGING ROLE OF THE INDIAN IN ARIZONA.   IKELLWH58577

    FARMERS, WORKERS, AND MACHINES. TECHNOLOGICAL AND SOCIAL-CHANGE IN FARM INDUSTRIES OF ARIZONA.   MPADFHX65450

ARIZONA-S
    ARIZONA-S EXPERIENCE UNDER THE CIVIL-RIGHTS-ACT.   GCRAICE66620

ARKANSAS
    TWO PLANTS -- LITTLE-ROCK. /CASE-STUDY INDUSTRY ARKANSAS/   NECKAEW55319

ARMED
    INTEGRATION IN THE ARMED SERVICES. /MILITARY/   NEVANJC56340

    RACIAL INTEGRATION IN THE ARMED FORCES. /MILITARY/   NMOSKCC66855

    INTEGRATION IN THE ARMED SERVICES. A PROGRESS REPORT. /MILITARY/   NUSDDEF55195

    INTEGRATION AND THE NEGRO OFFICER IN THE ARMED FORCES OF THE UNITED STATES OF AMERICA. /MILITARY/   NUSDDEF62240

    SEGREGATION IN THE ARMED FORCES. /MILITARY/   NUSDLAB44151

    THE NEGRO IN THE ARMED FORCES. /MILITARY/   NWEILFD47309

ARMY
    THE NEGRO IN THE US ARMY. /MILITARY/   NDWYERJ53312

    THE NEGRO IN THE ARMY TODAY. /MILITARY/   NHASTWH42466

    THE NEGRO POLICY OF THE AMERICAN ARMY SINCE WORLD-WAR-II. /MILITARY/   NREDDLD53044

    WHAT THE NEGRO THINKS OF THE ARMY. /MILITARY/   NWHITWX42465

ARMY   (CONTINUATION)
A SURVEY OF WOMEN-S APTITUDES FOR ARMY JOBS. /MILITARY/   WFUCHEF63772

ARRANGEMENTS
WORKING MOTHERS AND THEIR ARRANGEMENTS FOR CARE OF THEIR CHILDREN. /EMPLOYMENT-CONDITIONS/   WLAJEHC59922

CHILD CARE ARRANGEMENTS OF FULLTIME WORKING MOTHERS. /EMPLOYMENT-CONDITIONS/   WUSDHEW59171

CHILD CARE ARRANGEMENTS OF THE NATION-S WORKING MOTHERS. A PRELIMINARY REPORT.   WUSDHEW65172

ARREST
EMPLOYABILITY AND THE JUVENILE ARREST RECORD.   GSPAREV66839

ARROWHEAD
LAKE ARROWHEAD CONFERENCE ON EQUAL-EMPLOYMENT-OPPORTUNITY, OCTOBER 22-24, 1963 -- RECORD OF PROCEEDINGS.
LOS-ANGELES, CALIFORNIA.   GUSFEDE63513

REPORT OF ARROWHEAD REGIONAL CONFERENCE ON THE STATUS OF WOMEN IN NORTHERN MINNESOTA.   WARRORC66216

ARTS
LIBERAL ARTS WOMEN GRADUATES, CLASS OF 1958. /WORK-WOMEN-ROLE/   WLICHMW59933

ASPIRATION
SOME EDUCATIONAL IMPLICATIONS OF THE INFLUENCE OF REJECTION ON ASPIRATION LEVELS OF MINORITY-GROUP
CHILDREN.   GGOFFRM54366

THE OUTLOOK OF WORKING CLASS YOUTH. /DROP-OUT ASPIRATION/   GMILLSM62570

SOCIAL-STATUS AND EDUCATIONAL AND OCCUPATIONAL ASPIRATION.   GSEWEWH57297

OCCUPATIONAL AND EDUCATIONAL LEVELS OF ASPIRATION OF MEXICAN-AMERICAN YOUTH.   MDEHOAX61388

LEVELS OF ASPIRATION OF MEXICAN-AMERICANS IN EL-PASO SCHOOLS. /TEXAS/   MNALLFX59447

MOTIVATION AND ASPIRATION IN THE NEGRO COLLEGE.   NGURIPX66352

ASPIRATION LEVELS OF NEGRO DELINQUENT, DEPENDENT, AND PUBLIC SCHOOL BOYS.   NMITCLE57804

THE RELATION OF RACIAL SEGREGATION IN EARLY SCHOOLING TO THE LEVEL OF ASPIRATION AND ACADEMIC ACHIEVEMENT
OF NEGRO STUDENTS IN A NORTHERN HIGH SCHOOL.   NSAINJN62137

RACIAL AND FAMILY EXPERIENCE CORRELATES OF MOBILITY ASPIRATION.   NSMITHP62144

POST GRADUATION ROLE PREFERENCE OF SENIOR WOMEN IN COLLEGE. /ASPIRATION/   WCHRIHX56690

ROLE CONCEPTION AND CAREER ASPIRATION. A STUDY OF IDENTITY IN NURSING.   WCORWRG61707

ASPIRATIONS
THE IMMIGRANT. VALUE ORIENTATIONS AND VOCATIONAL ASPIRATIONS. /NEGRO MEXICAN-AMERICAN/   CPETECL64988

SEX DIFFERENCES IN OCCUPATIONAL CHOICE PATTERNS AMONG ADOLESCENTS. /ASPIRATIONS WOMEN NEGRO/   CSPREJX62999

BACKGROUND FACTORS RELATING TO COLLEGE PLANS AND COLLEGE ENROLLMENT AMONG PUBLIC HIGH SCHOOL STUDENTS.
/ASPIRATIONS/   GEDUCTS57959

RURAL-URBAN DIFFERENCES IN ASPIRATIONS.   GMIDDRX59573

ECONOMIC FACTORS INFLUENCING EDUCATIONAL-ATTAINMENTS AND ASPIRATIONS OF FARM YOUTH.   GMOOREJ64386

RESIDENTIAL SEGREGATION OF SOCIAL-CLASSES AND ASPIRATIONS OF HIGH SCHOOL BOYS.   GWILSAB59568

THE EFFECT OF RESIDENTIAL SEGREGATION UPON EDUCATIONAL ACHIEVEMENT AND ASPIRATIONS.   GWILSAB60567

LEVEL OF OCCUPATIONAL ASPIRATIONS AMONG MONTANA INDIANS IN GRADE AND HIGH SCHOOL.   IDOUGGV60550

HEALTH PRACTICES AND EDUCATIONAL ASPIRATIONS AS INDICATORS OF ACCULTURATION AND SOCIAL-CLASS AMONG THE
EASTERN CHEROKEE. /NORTH-CAROLINA/   IKUPFHJ62216

THE SOCIAL ASPIRATIONS OF A SELECTED GROUP OF SPANISH NAME PEOPLE IN LAREDO, TEXAS.   MGUERIX59409

CLASS AS AN EXPLANATION OF ETHNIC DIFFERENCES IN MOBILITY ASPIRATIONS -- THE CASE OF MEXICAN-AMERICANS. MHELLCS65415

A STUDY OF THE ACCULTURATION AND SOCIAL ASPIRATIONS OF SIXTY JUNIOR HIGH SCHOOL STUDENTS FROM THE MEXICAN
ETHNIC GROUP.   MJONEBM62421

CONTRASTS BETWEEN SPANISH FOLK AND ANGLO URBAN CULTURAL VALUES. /EDUCATION ASPIRATIONS/   MVALDBX64449

SOCIAL FACTORS IN OCCUPATIONAL AND EDUCATIONAL ASPIRATIONS OF NEGRO AND WHITE STUDENTS.   NADDIOP61002

OCCUPATIONAL ASPIRATIONS OF LOWER-CLASS NEGRO AND WHITE YOUTH.   NANTOAX59027

EGO DEVELOPMENT AMONG SEGREGATED NEGRO CHILDREN. /ASPIRATIONS/   NAUSUDP65036

LOWER-CLASS NEGRO MOTHERS ASPIRATIONS FOR THEIR CHILDREN.   NBELLRR65074

CLASS AND FAMILY INFLUENCES ON STUDENT ASPIRATIONS.   NBENNWS64574

RACE AND SOCIAL-CLASS AS SEPARATE FACTORS RELATED TO SOCIAL ENVIRONMENT. /ASPIRATIONS/   NBLOORX63096

A COMPARISON OF THE VOCATIONAL ASPIRATIONS OF PAIRED SIXTH-GRADE WHITE AND NEGRO CHILDREN WHO ATTEND
SEGREGATED SCHOOLS.   NBROWRG65895

A COMPARISON OF THE SOCIAL CHARACTERISTICS AND EDUCATIONAL ASPIRATIONS OF NORTHERN, LOWER-CLASS, NEGRO
PARENTS WHO ACCEPTED AND DECLINED AN OPPORTUNITY FOR INTEGRATED EDUCATION FOR THEIR CHILDREN.   NCAGLLT66904

VOCATIONAL CHOICES OF NEGRO HIGH SCHOOL STUDENTS IN MACON COUNTY, ALABAMA, AND THEIR RELATIONSHIP TO
BASIC OCCUPATIONAL ACTIVITES OF THE SCHOOL COMMUNITIES. /ASPIRATIONS/   NCHAPEJ49351

LIBERALISM AND THE NEGRO. /ASPIRATIONS/   NCOMMXX64467

WHY SHOULD NEGROES WORK. /ASPIRATIONS/   NDIZAJE66015

I Q PERFORMANCE, EDUCATIONAL AND OCCUPATIONAL ASPIRATIONS OF YOUTH IN A SOUTHERN CITY -- A RACIAL
COMPARISON.   NGEISPX62397

ASPIRATIONS OF NEGRO AND WHITE STUDENTS.   NGISTNP63419

SOCIAL-CLASS CONSTRAINTS ON THE OCCUPATIONAL ASPIRATIONS OF STUDENTS ATTENDING SOME PREDOMINANTLY NEGRO

THE EDUCATIONAL AND OCCUPATIONAL **ASPIRATIONS** AND PLANS OF NEGRO AND WHITE MALE ELEMENTARY SCHOOL STUDENTS.   NGURIPX66467

SOCIAL-STATUS AND **ASPIRATIONS** IN PHILADELPHIA-S NEGRO POPULATION.   /PENNSYLVANIA/   NHOLLRG59562

VOCATIONAL **ASPIRATIONS** OF NEGRO YOUTH IN CALIFORNIA.   NKLEIRJ62655

A PILOT STUDY OF PERSONALITY FACTORS RELATED TO OCCUPATIONAL **ASPIRATIONS** OF NEGRO COLLEGE STUDENTS.   NLAWRPF50368

NEGRO AND WHITE CHILDREN-S PLANS FOR THEIR FUTURES. /**ASPIRATIONS**/   NLITTLW66697

FAMILY PATTERNS, ACHIEVEMENTS, AND **ASPIRATIONS** OF URBAN NEGROES.   NLOTTAJ63487

AT WORK IN NORTH-CAROLINA TODAY. 48 CASE-REPORTS ON NORTH-CAROLINA NEGROES NOW EMPLOYED OR PREPARING THEMSELVES FOR EMPLOYMENT...THEIR EDUCATION, JOB QUALIFICATIONS, AND CAREER **ASPIRATIONS**.   NLYSTMH61718

RETREATISM AND OCCUPATIONAL **ASPIRATIONS** AMONG WHITE AND NEGRO HIGH SCHOOL SENIORS.   NNORTCGND933

THE EFFECT OF SEGREGATION ON THE **ASPIRATIONS** OF NEGRO YOUTH.   NPOWEEC61009

SOME ASPECTS OF VOCATIONAL **ASPIRATIONS** AND VALUE ORIENTATION AMONG NEGRO BOYS IN THE LOWER SOCIO-ECONOMIC CLASSES.   NSAINJN66136

WHY THEY DON-T WANT TO WORK. /**ASPIRATIONS**/   NSCHMWX63139

EMPLOYMENT EXPERIENCES OF NEGRO PHILADELPHIANS. A DESCRIPTIVE STUDY OF THE EMPLOYMENT EXPERIENCES, PERCEPTIONS, AND **ASPIRATIONS** OF SELECTED PHILADELPHIA WHITES AND NON-WHITES.   NSCHWMX64022

NEGRO WORKER LIFTS HIS SIGHTS. /**ASPIRATIONS**/   NSIEGAI59718

ENHANCING THE OCCUPATIONAL OUTLOOK AND VOCATIONAL **ASPIRATIONS** OF SOUTHERN SECONDARY YOUTH. A CONFERENCE OF SECONDARY SCHOOL PRINCIPALS AND COUNSELORS.   NTHOMJA46202

OCCUPATIONAL **ASPIRATIONS** OF NEGRO MALE HIGH SCHOOL STUDENTS.   NUSDLAB65334

WALK IN DIGNITY. /**ASPIRATIONS**/   NUZELOX61278

COMPARATIVE STUDY OF SOCIO-ECONOMIC AND SOCIAL-PSYCHOLOGICAL DETERMINANTS OF EDUCATIONAL AND OCCUPATIONAL **ASPIRATIONS** OF NEGRO AND WHITE COLLEGE SENIORS.   NWARRDX64314

AFTER HIGH SCHOOL WHAT...HIGHLIGHTS OF A STUDY OF CAREER PLANS OF NEGRO AND WHITE RURAL YOUTH IN THREE FLORIDA COUNTIES. /**ASPIRATIONS**/   NWHITRM59319

OCCUPATIONAL PLANS AND **ASPIRATIONS**. PUERTO-RICAN AND AMERICAN HIGH SCHOOL SENIORS COMPARED.   NYOUMEG65390

WHY DO BRIGHT GIRLS NOT TAKE STIFF COURSES. /**ASPIRATIONS**/   PSILVRM63100

THE ROLE OUTLOOK OF EDUCATED WOMEN. /**ASPIRATIONS**/   WALBJMH61603

AN INVERTED FACTOR ANALYSIS OF PERSONALITY DIFFERENCES BETWEEN CAREER AND HOMEMAKING-ORIENTED WOMEN. /**ASPIRATIONS**/   WANGRSS64484

INTEREST PATTERN FAKING BY FEMALE JOB APPLICANTS. /**ASPIRATIONS**/   WAVILDL64316

CONTINUING EDUCATION OF WOMEN. NEEDS, **ASPIRATIONS**, AND PLANS.   WBECKJA63633

CHANGES IN CAREER **ASPIRATIONS**.   WBERRJX63641

GREAT **ASPIRATIONS**.   WCOLECX69695

FACTORS INFLUENCING WOMEN-S DECISIONS ABOUT HIGHER EDUCATION. /**ASPIRATIONS**/   WDAVIJA64724

SEX AS A FACTOR IN THE DETERMINATION OF EDUCATIONAL CHOICE. /**ASPIRATIONS**/   WDAVIOD59716

STUDY OF ADOLESCENT GIRLS. /**ASPIRATIONS**/   WDOLEAA64737

WHAT EVERY ABLE WOMAN SHOULD KNOW. /WORK-PATTERN **ASPIRATIONS**/   WDOUVEX57742

ROLE EXPECTATIONS OF YOUNG WOMEN REGARDING MARRIAGE AND A CAREER. /**ASPIRATIONS** WORK-FAMILY-CONFLICT/   WDREWEM61743

WORK VALUES AND BACKGROUND FACTORS AS PREDICTORS OF WOMEN-S DESIRE TO WORK. /**ASPIRATIONS**/   WEMPELT58751

CAREER DECISIONS AND PROFESSIONAL EXPECTATIONS OF NURSING-STUDENTS. /**ASPIRATIONS**/   WEYDELD62754

SOME INTELLECTUAL ATTRIBUTES AND EDUCATIONAL INTERESTS OF UNIVERSITY WOMEN IN VARIOUS MAJORS. /**ASPIRATIONS**/   WFOXXDJ61767

ATTITUDES OF WOMEN REGARDING GAINFUL EMPLOYMENT OF MARRIED WOMEN. /**ASPIRATIONS**/   WGENTLX60790

PRACTITIONERS AND NON-PRACTITIONERS IN A GROUP OF WOMEN PHYSICIANS. /**ASPIRATIONS**/   WGLENHM59789

COLLEGE WOMEN-S IDENTIFICATIONS WITH THEIR FATHERS IN RELATION TO VOCATIONAL INTEREST PATTERNS. /**ASPIRATIONS**/   WGLICRX65791

SOCIAL ROLE EXPECTATION. MOTIVATIONAL VARIABLE IN GIRLS. /**ASPIRATIONS**/   WHALLWJ63815

A COMMENTARY ON THE MOTIVATION AND EDUCATION OF COLLEGE WOMEN. /**ASPIRATIONS**/   WHANSDE64821

THE MOTIVATION OF COLLEGE WOMEN TODAY. A CLOSER LOOK. /**ASPIRATIONS**/   WHEISPX62837

THE MOTIVATION OF COLLEGE WOMEN TODAY. THE CULTURAL SETTING. /**ASPIRATIONS**/   WHEISPX62839

THE DECISION TO WORK. /**ASPIRATIONS**/   WHEISPX63840

INTEREST AND PERSONALITY CORRELATES OF CAREER-MOTIVATED AND HOMEMAKING-MOTIVATED COLLEGE WOMEN. /**ASPIRATIONS**/   WHOFFLW63847

A MEMORANDUM ON THE MOTIVATIONS OF MIDDLE AGED WOMEN IN THE LOWER EDUCATIONAL BRACKETS TO RETURN TO WORK. /**ASPIRATIONS**/   WHOYTDP58850

IN QUEST OF WIDER HORIZONS. THE WOMAN AFTER FORTY THINKS ABOUT A JOB. /**ASPIRATIONS**/   WJEWIVA61880

A PILOT STUDY OF THE MOTIVATIONS AND PROBLEMS OF MIDDLE AGED HOMEMAKERS IN LOWER SOCIO-ECONOMIC GROUPS IN SEEKING EMPLOYMENT. /**ASPIRATIONS**/   WJEWIVA62882

INVESTIGATION OF DIFFERENCES IN OCCUPATIONAL PREFERENCES, STEREOTYPIC THINKING, AND PSYCHOLOGICAL NEEDS   WJEWIVA62883

ASPIRATIONS (CONTINUATION)
AMONG UNDERGRADUATE WOMEN STUDENTS IN SELECTED CURRICULAR AREAS. /ASPIRATIONS/   WKITTRE60313

THE IMPACT OF CULTURAL CHANGE ON WOMEN-S POSITION. /BLUE-COLLAR **ASPIRATIONS**/   WKONOGX66913

CHANGES IN SELECTED PERSONALITY CHARACTERISTICS AND PERSISTENCE IN THE CAREER CHOICES OF WOMEN ASSOCIATED WITH A FOUR YEAR COLLEGE EDUCATION AT ONE OF THE COLLEGES OF THE CITY UNIVERSITY OF NEW-YORK. /ASPIRATIONS/   WLEINMX64925

A QUESTIONNAIRE PORTRAIT OF THE FRESHMAN COED. AFTER COLLEGE WHAT. /ASPIRATIONS/   WLLOYBJ66938

KNOWLEDGE AND INTERESTS CONCERNING SIXTEEN OCCUPATIONS AMONG ELEMENTARY AND SECONDARY SCHOOL STUDENTS. /ASPIRATIONS/   WMELSRC63968

POST-HIGH SCHOOL PLANS FOR SENIOR GIRLS IN RELATION TO SCHOLASTIC APTITUDE. /ASPIRATIONS/   WMILLRX61983

INTEREST PROFILES OF UNIVERSITY WOMEN. /ASPIRATIONS/   WMITCED57986

PSYCHOLOGICAL AND SOCIOLOGICAL FACTORS IN PREDICTION OF CAREER PATTERNS OF WOMEN. /ASPIRATIONS/   WMULVMC61080

PSYCHOLOGICAL AND SOCIOLOGICAL FACTORS IN PREDICTION OF CAREER PATTERNS FOR WOMEN. /ASPIRATIONS/   WMULVMC63006

WHAT EDUCATED WOMEN WANT. /ASPIRATIONS/   WNEWSXX66029

FAMILIAL CORRELATES OF ORIENTATION TOWARD FUTURE EMPLOYMENT AMONG COLLEGE WOMEN. /ASPIRATIONS/   WSIEGAX63572

OCCUPATIONAL CHOICE AMONG CAREER ORIENTED COLLEGE WOMEN. /ASPIRATIONS/   WSIMPRL61115

OCCUPATIONAL PLANNING BY YOUNG WOMEN, A STUDY OF OCCUPATIONAL EXPERIENCES, **ASPIRATIONS**, ATTITUDES, AND PLANS OF COLLEGE AND HIGH SCHOOL GIRLS.   WSLOCWL56116

COMMITMENT TO WORK. /ASPIRATIONS/   WSOBCMG63126

BACKGROUND FACTORS AND COLLEGE GOING PLANS AMONG HIGH APTITUDE PUBLIC HIGH SCHOOL SENIORS. /ASPIRATIONS/   WSTICGX56141

POSITION CHOICES AND CAREERS. ELEMENTS OF A THEORY. /ASPIRATIONS/   WTIEDDV58154

IS IT VIVA LA DIFFERENCE. /ASPIRATIONS/   WTURNRH66161

ASSEMBLY
MIGRATORY LABOR IN COLORADO. REPORT TO THE COLORADO GENERAL **ASSEMBLY**.   MCOLOLC62383

STATEMENT BEFORE CALIFORNIA LEGISLATURE **ASSEMBLY**, INTERIM SUBCOMMITTEE ON ECONOMIC OPPORTUNITY ON BEHALF OF CHINATOWN-NORTH BEACH DISTRICT COUNCIL.   OWONGLJ64771

ASSESSING
CRITERIA FOR **ASSESSING** FEASIBILITY OF MOTHERS EMPLOYMENT AND ADEQUACY OF CHILD CARE PLANS.   WUSDHEW66173

ASSESSMENT
THE IMPLICATIONS OF THE CIVIL-RIGHTS-ACT OF 1964 FOR PSYCHOLOGICAL **ASSESSMENT** IN INDUSTRY. /TESTING/   GASHXPX66405

AN **ASSESSMENT** OF THE SUITABILITY OF THE FACETED STRUCTURE OF THE WRU EDUCATION THESAURUS AS A FRAMEWORK FOR PREPARATION OF A THESAURUS OF EQUAL-EMPLOYMENT-OPPORTUNITY TERMS.   GBARHGC66162

OBJECTIVE ACCESS IN THE OPPORTUNITY STRUCTURE. THE **ASSESSMENT** OF THREE ETHNIC GROUPS WITH RESPECT TO QUANTIFIED SOCIAL STRUCTURAL VARIABLES.   MRENOGX63461

THE **ASSESSMENT** OF ADJUSTMENT OF AGED NEGRO WOMEN IN A SOUTHERN CITY.   NHIMEJX62072

SHORTAGE OR SURPLUS. AN **ASSESSMENT** OF BOSTON WOMANPOWER IN INDUSTRY, GOVERNMENT, AND RESEARCH. JUNE 7-8, 1963. /MASSACHUSETTS/   WUSDLAB66217

ASSETS
REVIEW APPRAISAL. KLAMATH INDIAN **ASSETS**.   IUSSENA59674

ASSIGNMENT
EFFECT OF SCHOOL **ASSIGNMENT** LAWS ON FEDERAL ADJUDICATION OF INTEGRATION CONTROVERSIES.   NCOLULR57224

CIVIL-RIGHTS -- RACIAL DISCRIMINATION IN TEACHER HIRING AND **ASSIGNMENT** FORBIDDEN.   NKELLPL66734

DISCRIMINATION IN THE HIRING AND **ASSIGNMENT** OF NEGRO TEACHERS IN PUBLIC SCHOOL SYSTEMS.   NMICLRX66068

PART-TIME **ASSIGNMENT** OF WOMEN IN TEACHING. /OCCUPATIONS/   WSAMPJX65099

ASSIGNMENTS
TRAINING AID. CULTURAL DIFFERENCES, TRAINING IN NONDISCRIMINATION, READING **ASSIGNMENTS**. /EMPLOYMENT MEXICAN-AMERICAN NEGRO/   CCALDSW65447

ASSIMILATION
THE **ASSIMILATION** AND ACCULTURATION OF MIGRANTS TO URBAN AREAS. /MEXICAN-AMERICAN NEGRO/   CSHANLW63484

ASSIMILATION IN AMERICAN LIFE. THE ROLE OF RACE, RELIGION, AND NATIONAL ORIGINS.   GGORDMM64729

SPECIAL **ASSIMILATION** PROBLEMS OF UNDERPRIVILEGED IMMIGRANTS TO PHILADELPHIA. /PENNSYLVANIA/   GPENNEL62502

ASSIMILATION OF THE SPOKANE INDIANS. /WASHINGTON/   IROYXPX61612

THE MEASUREMENT OF **ASSIMILATION**. THE SPOKANE INDIANS. /WASHINGTON/   IROYXPX66613

ASSIMILATION OF THE SPOKANE INDIANS. /WASHINGTON/   ISTONCX62626

OBSTACLES TO **ASSIMILATION** OF THE MEXICAN-AMERICAN IN THE UNITED STATES.   MBEALRL60362

NATURALIZATION AND **ASSIMILATION** PRONENESS OF CALIFORNIA IMMIGRANT POPULATIONS.   MKRASWX63425

GATEKEEPERS IN THE PROCESS OF **ASSIMILATION**.   MKURTNR66270

WHEN THE MIGRANT LABORER SETTLES DOWN -- A REPORT OF THE FINDINGS OF A PROJECT ON VALUE **ASSIMILATION** OF IMMIGRANT LABORERS.   MPETECL64454

OCCUPATIONAL **ASSIMILATION** AS A COMPETITIVE PROCESS.   NHODGRW65556

MIGRATION, MOBILITY, AND THE **ASSIMILATION** OF THE NEGRO.   NTAEUIB58363

THE VALIDATION OF ACCULTURATION. A CONDITION TO ETHNIC **ASSIMILATION**.   OBROOLX55708

ASSIMILATION OF CHINESE IN AMERICA. CHANGES IN ORIENTATION AND SOCIAL PERCEPTIONS.   OFONGSL65722

ASSIMILATION OR PLURALISM.   OKITADX65734

ASSIST
WE MUST **ASSIST** OUR INDIAN BROTHERS TO HELP THEMSELVES.   IBOTTRV56540

ASSISTANCE
PUBLIC WELFARE. POVERTY -- PREVENTION OR PERPETUATION. A STUDY OF THE STATE DEPARTMENT OF PUBLIC
ASSISTANCE OF THE STATE OF WASHINGTON.   GGREEAI64479

TRAINING OF PUBLIC **ASSISTANCE** RECIPIENTS UNDER THE MDTA.   GROSORG66258

PUBLIC **ASSISTANCE** RECIPIENTS IN NEW-YORK STATE, JANUARY-FEBRUARY 1957.   GSNYDEM58114

PROGRESS IN EMPLOYMENT **ASSISTANCE**.   IDAVIRC62546

RELOCATEES FROM GALLUP AREA TO THE DENVER FIELD EMPLOYMENT **ASSISTANCE** OFFICE. /COLORADO/   IGRAVTDND438

EMPLOYMENT **ASSISTANCE** REFERENCE BIBLIOGRAPHY.   IUSDINTND452

EMPLOYMENT **ASSISTANCE** PROGRAM.   IUSDINT64647

A FOLLOWUP STUDY OF 1963 RECIPIENTS OF THE SERVICES OF THE EMPLOYMENT **ASSISTANCE** PROGRAM,
BUREAU-OF-INDIAN-AFFAIRS.   IUSDINT66650

SOME CHARACTERISTICS OF PUBLIC **ASSISTANCE** CASES IN NEW-YORK CITY, AUGUST, 1959.   PNEWYDW60835

A STUDY TO DETERMINE THE EMPLOYMENT POTENTIAL OF MOTHERS RECEIVING AID-TO-DEPENDENT-CHILDREN **ASSISTANCE**.   WBROODJ64656

ASSISTANTS
NEGROES AS TEACHING **ASSISTANTS** IN SOME PUBLICLY SUPPORTED UNIVERSITIES. /OCCUPATIONS/   NDANIWG62248

ASSISTED
COMPILATION OF LAWS AGAINST DISCRIMINATION, EMPLOYMENT, EDUCATIONAL INSTITUTIONS, PLACES OF PUBLIC
ACCOMODATION, PUBLIC HOUSING, PUBLICLY **ASSISTED** HOUSING, PRIVATE HOUSING. /MASSACHUSETTS/   GMASSCAND963

ASSOCIATION
MEMORANDUM OF UNDERSTANDING BETWEEN CALIFORNIA STATE FAIR- EMPLOYMENT-PRACTICE-COMMISSION AND
BANK-OF-AMERICA NATIONAL TRUST AND SAVINGS **ASSOCIATION**.   GCALFEPND537

THE **ASSOCIATION** OF INCOME AND EDUCATION FOR MALES, BY REGION, RACE, AND AGE.   GLASSRL65998

THE NATIONAL TECHNICAL **ASSOCIATION**. /OCCUPATIONS/   NEVANJC43258

ATTITUDES TOWARD WOMEN COLLEGE TEACHERS IN INSTITUTIONS OF HIGHER EDUCATION ACCREDITED BY THE NORTH
CENTRAL **ASSOCIATION**.   WBERWHD62475

REPORT OF THE EXPLORATORY STATISTICAL SURVEY OF THE EDUCATIONAL-ATTAINMENT, NUMBER, AND AVAILABILITY OF
THE MEMBERSHIP OF THE AMERICAN **ASSOCIATION** OF UNIVERSITY WOMEN FOR TEACHING IN THE FIELDS OF SCIENCE AND
MATHEMATICS. /OCCUPATIONS/   WDOLAEF57735

SPEECH ABOUT JOB OPPORTUNITIES FOR GIRLS BEFORE THE MARYLAND STATE PERSONNEL AND GUIDANCE **ASSOCIATION**.   WTERLRX64148

ASSOCIATIONS
AN ECONOMIC ANALYSIS OF SPECIFIED INCORPORATED AND UNINCORPORATED FARMERS COOPERATIVE **ASSOCIATIONS**
OPERATED BY NEGRO FARMERS IN ALABAMA.   NLIGHMB53340

ASTD
PROGRESS IN WATTS -- THE LOS-ANGELES **ASTD** COMMUNITY AFFAIRS PROGRAM. /CALIFORNIA/   NTRAIAD66580

ATASCOSA-COUNTY
OCCUPATIONAL CHANGE AMONG SPANISH-AMERICANS IN **ATASCOSA-COUNTY** AND SAN-ANTONIO, TEXAS.   MSKRARL66492

ATLANTA
INCOME, EDUCATION AND UNEMPLOYMENT IN NEIGHBORHOODS. **ATLANTA**, GEORGIA. /DEMOGRAPHY/   CUSDLAB63451

CHARACTERISTICS OF NEGRO EMPLOYMENT IN FEDERAL AGENCIES IN **ATLANTA**, GEORGIA.   NPRESCP60016

ANNUAL FAMILY AND OCCUPATIONAL EARNINGS OF RESIDENTS OF TWO NEGRO HOUSING PROJECTS IN **ATLANTA** 1937-1944.
/GEORGIA/   NRITTAL45062

ATLANTA -- THE NEGRO AND EMPLOYMENT OPPORTUNITIES IN THE SOUTH, THE THIRD OF A SERIES OF EMPLOYMENT
STUDIES IN SOUTHERN CITIES. /GEORGIA/   NSOUTRC62155

PLANS-FOR-PROGRESS. **ATLANTA** SURVEY. /GEORGIA/   NSOUTRC63163

ATLANTA-S
ATLANTA-S SEGREGATED APPROACH TO INTEGRATED EMPLOYMENT. /GEORGIA/   NTHOMHX62205

ATLANTIC
REPORTS OF THE MEETINGS OF THE COMMITTEE OF OFFICIALS ON MIGRATORY FARM LABOR OF THE **ATLANTIC** SEABOARD
STATES. /MIGRANT-WORKERS/   GCOUNSG58932

MIGRATORY FARM WORKERS IN THE **ATLANTIC** COAST STREAM. I. CHANGES IN NEW-YORK, 1953 AND 1957.   GLARSOF60406

MIGRATORY FARM WORKERS IN THE **ATLANTIC** COAST STREAM.   GMETZWH55426

MIGRATORY FARM WORKERS IN THE **ATLANTIC** COAST STREAM. WESTERN NEW-YORK, JUNE 1953.   GMOTHJR54405

MIGRATORY FARM WORKERS IN THE **ATLANTIC** COAST STREAM, II. EDUCATION OF NEW-YORK WORKERS AND THEIR
CHILDREN, 1953 AND 1957.   GSHAREF60427

ATLANTIC-CITY
LABOR-S CIVIL-RIGHTS STAND REAFFIRMED AT **ATLANTIC-CITY**.   NAMERFX58013

ATOMIC-ENERGY-COMMIS
NONDISCRIMINATION IN FEDERALLY-ASSISTED PROGRAMS OF THE DEPARTMENT-OF-THE-TREASURY,
DEPARTMENT-OF-DEFENSE, **ATOMIC-ENERGY-COMMISSION**, CIVIL-AERONAUTICS-BOARD, FEDERAL-AVIATION-AGENCY,
VETERANS-ADMINISTRATION.   GFEDERX64673

ATTACKS
AMERICAN LABOR **ATTACKS** ITS OWN SEGREGATION PROBLEM. /UNION/   NCHASWX58194

ATTAINMENT
EDUCATIONAL **ATTAINMENT** OF WORKERS, MARCH 1964.   GJOHNDF65784

SCHOOL ATTENDANCE AND **ATTAINMENT**. FUNCTION AND DYSFUNCTION OF SCHOOL AND FAMILY SOCIAL SYSTEMS.
/EMPLOYMENT DROP-OUT/   NBERTAL62882

THE EFFECT OF LOW EDUCATIONAL **ATTAINMENT** ON INCOMES. A COMPARATIVE STUDY OF SELECTED ETHNIC GROUPS.   OFOGEWX66721

ATTENDANCE
SCHOOL **ATTENDANCE** AND ATTAINMENT. FUNCTION AND DYSFUNCTION OF SCHOOL AND FAMILY SOCIAL SYSTEMS.

ATTENDANCE   (CONTINUATION)
/EMPLOYMENT DROP-OUT/   NBERTAL62882

   THE RELATIONSHIP BETWEEN MECHANIZATION OF COTTON PRODUCTION AND **ATTENDANCE** AND ENROLLMENT IN THE RURAL
   SCHOOLS OF COAHOMA COUNTY, MISSISSIPPI.   NMCLABF51349

   FACTORS ASSOCIATED WITH GRADUATE SCHOOL **ATTENDANCE** AND ROLE DEFINITION OF THE WOMAN DOCTORAL CANDIDATES
   AT THE PENNSYLVANIA STATE UNIVERSITY. /OCCUPATIONS/   WFIELJC61763

ATTENDING
   SOCIAL-CLASS CONSTRAINTS ON THE OCCUPATIONAL ASPIRATIONS OF STUDENTS **ATTENDING** SOME PREDOMINANTLY NEGRO
   COLLEGES.   NGURIPX66467

   SOME CHARACTERISTICS OF STUDENTS FROM POVERTY BACKGROUNDS **ATTENDING** PREDOMINANTLY NEGRO COLLEGES IN THE
   DEEP SOUTH.   NGURIPX66468

ATTITUDE
   ATTITUDE TOWARD OCCUPATIONAL CHANGE AS AN INDICATOR OF PROSPECTS FOR ADJUSTMENT.   GDUNKJE64653

   ATTITUDE TOWARD JOB-MOBILITY AMONG HOUSEHOLD HEADS IN LOW-INCOME AREAS OF THE RURAL SOUTH.   NDUNKJX64300

   THE STATE-EMPLOYMENT-SERVICE AND THE **ATTITUDE** OF UNEMPLOYABLE DROPOUTS.   NHARRIE66991

   MARITAL DISAGREEMENT IN WORKING WIFE MARRIAGES AS A FUNCTION OF HUSBAND-S **ATTITUDE** TOWARDS WIFE-S
   EMPLOYMENT. /WORK-FAMILY-CONFLICT/   WGIANAX57779

ATTITUDES
   THE CHILD-REARING **ATTITUDES** OF DISADVANTAGED NEGRO MOTHERS AND SOME EDUCATIONAL IMPLICATIONS.   CRADINX65031

   EMPLOYMENT OPPORTUNITIES FOR HIGH SCHOOL DROPOUTS, A STUDY OF EMPLOYERS PRACTICES, NEEDS AND **ATTITUDES** IN
   THE DISTRICT OF COLUMBIA. /WASHINGTON-DC/   GBURESS57499

   SOCIAL INTEGRATION, **ATTITUDES** AND UNION ACTIVITY.   GDEANLR54944

   MANAGEMENT AND MINORITY GROUPS, A STUDY OF **ATTITUDES** AND PRACTICES IN HIRING AND UPGRADING.   GMARKPI57085

   MOBILITY, METHODS OF JOB SEARCH, **ATTITUDES**, AND MOTIVATION OF DISPLACED WORKERS.   GSHEPHL64621

   WORK HISTORY, **ATTITUDES**, AND INCOME OF THE UNEMPLOYED.   GSTEIRL63838

   ANALYSIS OF MALE NAVAHO STUDENTS PERCEPTIONS OF OCCUPATIONAL OPPORTUNITIES AND THEIR **ATTITUDES** TOWARD
   DEVELOPMENT OF SKILLS AND TRAITS NECESSARY FOR OCCUPATIONAL COMPETENCE.   IDESPCW65548

   RACIAL **ATTITUDES** AND THE EMPLOYMENT OF NEGROES.   NBULLHA51133

   MINORITY-GROUP **ATTITUDES** OF NEGROES AND IMPLICATIONS FOR GUIDANCE.   NENGLWH57333

   EFFECTS OF ON-THE-JOB EXPERIENCE WITH NEGROES UPON RACIAL **ATTITUDES** OF WHITE WORKERS IN UNION SHOPS.   NGUNDRH50466

   ATTITUDES OF WHITE DEPARTMENT STORE EMPLOYEES TOWARD NEGRO CO-WORKERS.   /CASE-STUDY/   NHARDJX52482

   A STUDY OF OCCUPATIONAL **ATTITUDES**.   NHARREC53493

   OCCUPATIONAL MOBILITY AND **ATTITUDES** TOWARD NEGROES.   NHODGRWND355

   ATTITUDES TOWARD DESEGREGATION.   NHYMAHH56591

   THE IMPORTANCE OF CONTACT IN DETERMINING **ATTITUDES** TOWARD NEGROES.   NMACKBK48488

   SOME **ATTITUDES** TOWARD EMPLOYING NEGROES AS TEACHERS IN A NORTHERN UNIVERSITY.   NMARCFL48054

   SOUTHERN RACIAL **ATTITUDES**, CONFLICT, AWARENESS AND POLITICAL CHANGE.   NMATTDR62758

   ATTITUDES TOWARD ETHNIC FARM WORKERS IN COACHELLA-VALLEY. /CALIFORNIA/   NMCOOEC55719

   ATTITUDES TOWARD SOCIAL MOBILITY AS REVEALED BY SAMPLES OF NEGRO AND WHITE BOYS.   NMONTJB58809

   RACE, ECONOMIC **ATTITUDES**, AND BEHAVIOR.   NMORGJX62850

   OCCUPATIONAL **ATTITUDES** OF NEGRO WORKERS.   NRICHEX43056

   THE IMPACT OF MILITARY SERVICE UPON THE RACIAL **ATTITUDES** OF NEGRO SERVICEMEN IN WORLD-WAR II.   NROBEHW53065

   THE INFLUENCE OF A BORDER CITY UNION ON THE RACE **ATTITUDES** OF ITS MEMBERS.   NROSEAW53293

   MANAGEMENT AND MINORITY-GROUPS, A STUDY OF **ATTITUDES** AND PRACTICES IN HIRING AND UPGRADING.   NROSEBX59080

   SURVEY OF NEGRO **ATTITUDES** TOWARD LAW.   NZEITLX65359

   NOTES ON MIGRATION AND WORKERS **ATTITUDES** TOWARD IT.   PGREGPX61857

   A STUDY OF ELEMENTARY SCHOOL TEACHER-S **ATTITUDES** TOWARD THE WOMAN PRINCIPAL AND TOWARD ELEMENTARY
   PRINCIPALSHIP AS A CAREER. /DISCRIMINATION/   WBARTAK58629

   ATTITUDES TOWARD WOMEN COLLEGE TEACHERS IN INSTITUTIONS OF HIGHER EDUCATION ACCREDITED BY THE NORTH
   CENTRAL ASSOCIATION.   WBERWHD62475

   AN EXPLORATORY STUDY OF EMPLOYERS **ATTITUDES** TOWARD WORKING MOTHERS.   WCONYJE61704

   EMPLOYERS **ATTITUDES** TOWARD WORKING MOTHERS.   WCONYJE63703

   THE ROLE OF THE EDUCATED WOMAN, AN EMPIRICAL STUDY OF THE **ATTITUDES** OF A GROUP OF COLLEGE WOMEN.
   /WORK-WOMAN-ROLE/   WFREEMB65770

   ATTITUDES OF WOMEN REGARDING GAINFUL EMPLOYMENT OF MARRIED WOMEN. /ASPIRATIONS/   WGLENHM59789

   ATTITUDES OF COLLEGE STUDENTS TOWARD EMPLOYMENT AMONG MARRIED WOMEN. /WORK-FAMILY-CONFLICT/   WHEWEVH64482

   ATTITUDES TOWARD CAREER AND MARRIAGE AND THE DEVELOPMENT OF LIFE STYLES IN YOUNG WOMEN.
   /WORK-FAMILY-CONFLICT/   WMATTEX64962

   SOME **ATTITUDES** AND OPINIONS OF EMPLOYED WOMEN.   WRAMSGV63132

   OCCUPATIONAL PLANNING BY YOUNG WOMEN, A STUDY OF OCCUPATIONAL EXPERIENCES, ASPIRATIONS, **ATTITUDES**, AND
   PLANS OF COLLEGE AND HIGH SCHOOL GIRLS.   WSLOCWL56116

   WOMEN-S **ATTITUDES** TOWARD CAREERS.   WSTEIAX59137

ATTITUDINAL
   SOCIAL AND **ATTITUDINAL** CHARACTERISTICS OF SPANISH-SPEAKING MIGRANT AND EX-MIGRANT WORKERS IN THE

ATTITUDINAL   (CONTINUATION)
   SOUTHWEST.   MULIBHX66503

   MATERNAL EMPLOYMENT. SITUATIONAL AND **ATTITUDINAL** VARIABLES. /WORK-FAMILY-CONFLICT/   WBRIEDX61655

ATTRIBUTES
   SOME INTELLECTUAL **ATTRIBUTES** AND EDUCATIONAL INTERESTS OF UNIVERSITY WOMEN IN VARIOUS MAJORS.
   /ASPIRATIONS/   WGENTLX60790

AUDIT
   AUDIT OF NEGRO VETERANS AND SERVICEMEN. 1960. /PUBLIC-EMPLOYMENT/   NAMERVC60019

   THE 1960 **AUDIT** OF NEGRO VETERANS AND SERVICEMAN.   /MILITARY/   NFELDJA61350

AUSTIN
   A CASE-STUDY OF LATIN-AMERICAN UNIONIZATION IN **AUSTIN**, TEXAS.   MPARISF64452

AUTHORITARIANISM
   EFFECTS OF WHITE **AUTHORITARIANISM** IN BI-RACIAL WORK GROUPS.   NKATZIX60639

AUTHORITY
   OPINION CONCERNING THE SCOPE AND **AUTHORITY** OF THE JURISDICTION THAT MAY BE GRANTED TO CITY OR COUNTY
   HUMAN-RELATIONS-COMMISSIONS IN THE FIELDS OF EMPLOYMENT AND HOUSING. /CALIFORNIA/   GCALAGO63512

   REPORT OF INQUIRY CONCERNING CHARGES OF DISCRIMINATING PRACTICES IN THE NEW-YORK STATE THRUWAY **AUTHORITY**.   GNEWYSB64104

   DIVISION OF **AUTHORITY** UNDER TITLE-VII OF THE CIVIL-RIGHTS-ACT OF 1964. A PRELIMINARY STUDY IN
   FEDERAL-STATE INTERAGENCY RELATIONS.   GROSESJ66254

   STATE EXECUTIVE **AUTHORITY** TO PROMOTE CIVIL-RIGHTS. AN ACTION PROGRAM FOR THE 1960-S.   GSILAJX63310

   EMPLOYMENT-TRENDS AMONG CALIFORNIA YOUTH **AUTHORITY** WARDS ON PAROLE. 1948-62.   MCALDYA63378

   EMPLOYMENT AND EMPLOYABILITY AMONG CALIFORNIA YOUTH **AUTHORITY** WARDS. A SURVEY.   MSECKJP62483

AUTO
   STUDY SHOWS FEW JEWS HAVE TOP JOBS IN **AUTO** INDUSTRY.   JNATIJM63748

   NEGRO LABOR IN THE **AUTO** INDUSTRY.   NBAILLH43045

   VOCATIONAL GRADUATES IN **AUTO** MECHANICS. A FOLLOW-UP STUDY OF NEGRO AND WHITE YOUTH. /OCCUPATIONS/   NLEVEBX66036

AUTOMATED
   PROBLEM AREAS IN TRAINING FOR **AUTOMATED** WORK. /TECHNOLOGICAL-CHANGE/   WLIPSOX64936

AUTOMATING
   SOME PROPOSALS FOR GOVERNMENT POLICY IN AN **AUTOMATING** SOCIETY.   GGANSHJ65696

AUTOMATION
   LABOR LOOKS AT **AUTOMATION**.   GAFLCIOND863

   AUTOMATION AND PUBLIC WELFARE.   GAMERPW64798

   AUTOMATION, PRODUCTIVITY AND MANPOWER PROBLEMS.   GBOKXDX64736

   METHODS OF ADJUSTING TO **AUTOMATION** AND TECHNOLOGICAL-CHANGE. /INDUSTRY/   GBOKXDX64737

   AUTOMATION AND ECONOMIC PROGRESS. A SUMMARY OF THE REPORT OF THE NATIONAL COMMISSION ON TECHNOLOGY,
   AUTOMATION, AND ECONOMIC PROGRESS.   GBOWEHR66748

   AUTOMATION AND ECONOMIC PROGRESS. A SUMMARY OF THE REPORT OF THE NATIONAL COMMISSION ON TECHNOLOGY,
   AUTOMATION, AND ECONOMIC PROGRESS.   GBOWEHR66748

   THE ECONOMICS OF **AUTOMATION**.   GBRONYX57921

   REPORT TO THE GOVERNOR AND THE LEGISLATURE OF THE COMMISSION ON MANPOWER, **AUTOMATION** AND TECHNOLOGY,
   1964. /CALIFORNIA/   GCALCMA65515

   PUBLIC WELFARE, **AUTOMATION**, AND EXPERIMENTAL MANPOWER PROGRAMS.   GCONFAP63545

   SEMINAR ON MANPOWER POLICY AND PROGRAM. LABOR LOOKS AT **AUTOMATION** AND CIVIL-RIGHTS.   GCONWJT65496

   AUTOMATION. THE IMPACT ON JOBS AND PEOPLE.   GCOONRB64871

   SEMINAR ON MANPOWER POLICY AND PROGRAM -- **AUTOMATION**, SKILL, AND MANPOWER PREDICTIONS.   GCROSER66148

   AUTOMATION AND TECHNOLOGICAL-CHANGE.   GDUNLJT62698

   AUTOMATION AND JOBLESSNESS. IS RETRAINING THE ANSWER.   GGLAZWX62866

   AUTOMATION. NATIONWIDE STUDIES IN THE US.   GGREELX64614

   AUTOMATION.   GKILLCC62861

   AUTOMATION, JOBS, AND MANPOWER.   GKILLCC63755

   JOBS, MEN AND MACHINES. PROBLEMS OF **AUTOMATION**.   GMARKCX64949

   THE STRUCTURE OF UNEMPLOYMENT AND **AUTOMATION**.   GNAVIPX57007

   THE EFFECTS OF **AUTOMATION** ON OCCUPATIONS AND WORKERS IN PENNSYLVANIA.   GPENNSE65641

   AUTOMATION IMPLICATIONS FOR THE FUTURE.   GPHILMX62616

   SEMINARS ON PRIVATE ADJUSTMENTS TO **AUTOMATION** AND TECHNOLOGICAL-CHANGE.   GPRESCL64772

   AUTOMATION, MANPOWER, AND EDUCATION.   GROSEJM66008

   THE MANPOWER PROBLEMS OF **AUTOMATION**.   GSALNEX65769

   ON THEORIES OF **AUTOMATION**. A POLEMIC AGAINST DANIEL BELL AND OTHERS. /UNEMPLOYMENT/   GSELIBB66609

   MOST NOTORIOUS VICTORY. MAN IN AN AGE OF **AUTOMATION**.   GSELIBB66841

   MEETING THE MANPOWER PROBLEMS OF. I. AREA REDEVELOPMENT. II. **AUTOMATION**.   GUSDLAB62708

   IMPLICATIONS OF **AUTOMATION** AND OTHER TECHNOLOGICAL DEVELOPMENTS, A SELECTED BIBLIOGRAPHY.   GUSDLAB63450

   CONSOLIDATED INVENTORY OF DEPARTMENT OF LABOR RESEARCH ON **AUTOMATION** AND TECHNOLOGICAL-CHANGE.   GUSDLAB64619

AUTOMATION   (CONTINUATION)
A SURVEY OF CURRENT LITERATURE ON **AUTOMATION** AND OTHER TECHNOLOGICAL-CHANGES. A SELECTED ANNOTATED
BIBLIOGRAPHY.   GUSDLAB64825

MANPOWER IMPLICATIONS OF **AUTOMATION**.   GUSDLAB65608

IMPACT OF **AUTOMATION** ON EMPLOYMENT.   GUSHOUR61985

AUTOMATION AND UNEMPLOYMENT.   GWARDRX62821

EFFECTS OF **AUTOMATION** ON THE POSITION OF NEGROES IN A SOUTHERN INDUSTRIAL PLANT.   NHARTJW64495

AUTOMATION AND THE RETRAINING OF NEGRO WORKERS.   NNATLUL62886

THE REAL NEWS ABOUT **AUTOMATION**.   NSILBCE65035

IMPACT OF OFFICE **AUTOMATION** IN THE INTERNAL REVENUE SERVICE. A STUDY OF THE MANPOWER IMPLICATIONS DURING
THE FIRST STAGES OF THE CHANGEOVER. /ECONOMIC-STATUS/   NUSDLAB63198

AUTOMATION AND THE NEGRO. WILL WE SURVIVE.   NWILSCE65326

THE INTERMINGLED REVOLUTIONS -- THE NEGRO AND **AUTOMATION**.   NYOUNWM64299

AUTOMATION IN THE OFFICE. /TECHNOLOGICAL-CHANGE/   WHOOSIR61848

AUTOMATION AND EMPLOYMENT. /TECHNOLOGICAL-CHANGE/   WKREPJX64916

OFFICE WORK AND **AUTOMATION**. /TECHNOLOGICAL-CHANGE/   WLEVIHS56929

MANPOWER IMPLICATIONS OF **AUTOMATION**.   WORGAEC64045

AUTOMATION AND EMPLOYMENT OPPORTUNITIES FOR OFFICE WORKERS. THE EFFECT OF ELECTRONIC COMPUTERS ON
EMPLOYMENT OF CLERICAL WORKERS, WITH A SPECIAL REPORT ON PROGRAMMERS.   WPASCWX58178

OFFICE **AUTOMATION** AND WHITE-COLLAR EMPLOYMENT.   WSMITGM59122

AUTOMATION AND THE WHITE-COLLAR WORKER.   WSTIEJX57142

AUTOMOBILE
EMPLOYMENT OF JEWISH PERSONNEL IN THE **AUTOMOBILE** INDUSTRY. /DISCRIMINATION/   JRIGHXX63756

SENIORITY IN THE **AUTOMOBILE** INDUSTRY.   NUSDLAB44842

AUTOMOBILE-WORKERS
THE NEGRO **AUTOMOBILE-WORKERS**. /OCCUPATIONS/   NBAILLH43043

AVAILABILITY
REPORT OF THE EXPLORATORY STATISTICAL SURVEY OF THE EDUCATIONAL-ATTAINMENT, NUMBER, AND **AVAILABILITY** OF
THE MEMBERSHIP OF THE AMERICAN ASSOCIATION OF UNIVERSITY WOMEN FOR TEACHING IN THE FIELDS OF SCIENCE AND
MATHEMATICS. /OCCUPATIONS/   WOOLAEF57735

BACK-TO-WORK
THE GREAT **BACK-TO-WORK** MOVEMENT. /WORK-FAMILY-CONFLICT/   WBELLDX56635

BACKGROUND
MIGRATORY-LABOR IN THE WEST. **BACKGROUND** INFORMATION FOR THE WESTERN INTERSTATE CONFERENCE ON MIGRATORY
LABOR. /MIGRANT-WORKERS/   GCOUNSG60931

BACKGROUND FACTORS RELATING TO COLLEGE PLANS AND COLLEGE ENROLLMENT AMONG PUBLIC HIGH SCHOOL STUDENTS.
/ASPIRATIONS/   GEDUCTS57959

THE CHANGING ECONOMIC **BACKGROUND** OF AMERICAN RACE-RELATIONS.   GROSEAW50288

REACTION TO MEXICAN-AMERICANS, A **BACKGROUND** PAPER.   MCABRYA65372

MEXICAN-AMERICANS, A **BACKGROUND** PAPER.   MGUZMRX65411

BACKGROUND AND AMBITION OF MALE MEXICAN-AMERICAN HIGH SCHOOL SENIORS IN LOS-ANGELES. /CALIFORNIA/   MHELLCS63414

THE PROBLEM OF CULTURAL BIAS IN SELECTION. I. **BACKGROUND** AND LITERATURE. /TESTING/   NCAMPJT65179

THE SOCIO-ECONOMIC **BACKGROUND** OF NEGRO HEALTH STATUS.   NJOHNCS49616

NEGLECTED TALENTS. **BACKGROUND** AND PROSPECTS OF NEGRO COLLEGE GRADUATES.   NNATLOR66880

THE **BACKGROUND** OF THE 1947 COLLEGE STUDENT. /LABOR-MARKET/   NQUARBX47257

THE PROBLEM OF CULTURAL BIAS IN SELECTION. II. ETHNIC **BACKGROUND** AND TEST PERFORMANCE.   NROBES065068

WORK VALUES AND **BACKGROUND** FACTORS AS PREDICTORS OF WOMEN-S DESIRE TO WORK. /ASPIRATIONS/   WEYDELD62754

BACKGROUND FACTORS AND COLLEGE GOING PLANS AMONG HIGH APTITUDE PUBLIC HIGH SCHOOL SENIORS. /ASPIRATIONS/ WSTICGX56141

BACKGROUND FACTS ON WOMEN WORKERS IN THE UNITED STATES.   WUSDLAB66638

BACKGROUNDS
FAMILY STRUCTURE AND SCHOOL PERFORMANCE. A COMPARATIVE STUDY OF STUDENTS FROM THREE ETHNIC **BACKGROUNDS** IN
AN INTEGRATED SCHOOL. /MEXICAN-AMERICAN AMERICAN-INDIAN/   CGRIFJX65407

DIFFERENTIAL SELECTION AMONG APPLICANTS FROM DIFFERENT SOCIO-ECONOMIC AND ETHNIC **BACKGROUNDS**.   NBARRRS65056

SOME CHARACTERISTICS OF STUDENTS FROM POVERTY **BACKGROUNDS** ATTENDING PREDOMINANTLY NEGRO COLLEGES IN THE
DEEP SOUTH.   NGURIPX66468

BAILEYS
BAILEYS REPORT ON SEMINOLES.   IBAILAL57531

BAKING
THE EMPLOYMENT OF NEGROES AS DRIVER SALESMEN IN THE **BAKING** INDUSTRY.   NNEWYSA60919

BALANCED
THE **BALANCED** ETHNIC WORK GROUP.   GSCOTWW61290

BALTIMORE
INCOME, EDUCATION AND UNEMPLOYMENT IN NEIGHBORHOODS. **BALTIMORE**, MARYLAND. /DEMOGRAPHY/   CUSDLAB63452

THE EMPLOYMENT SITUATION OF WHITE AND NEGRO YOUTH IN THE CITY OF **BALTIMORE**. INITIAL EXPERIENCES IN THE
LABOR-MARKET. /MARYLAND/   NJOHNHU63735

BALTIMORE   (CONTINUATION)
   THE EMPLOYMENT SITUATION OF WHITE AND NEGRO YOUTH IN THE CITY OF **BALTIMORE**. /MARYLAND/   NLEVEBX63684

BALTIMORE-S
   TOWARD EQUALITY, **BALTIMORE**-S PROGRESS-REPORT. A CHRONICLE OF PROGRESS SINCE WORLD-WAR-II TOWARD THE
   ACHIEVEMENT OF EQUAL-RIGHTS AND OPPORTUNITIES FOR NEGROES IN MARYLAND 1946-1958.   NBALTUL58048

   TOWARD EQUALITY, **BALTIMORE**-S PROGRESS-REPORT, 1962 SUPPLEMENT. /MARYLAND/   NBALTUL62049

BAN
   UNION **BAN** ON NEGROES UPHELD.   NUSNEWR57209

BANK
   BANK BARRIERS /DISCRIMINATICN/   GANTIDL61393

   BANK OF AMERICA EMPLOYMENT PRACTICES. FIRST REPORT BY CALIFORNIA FEPC.   GCALFEP64530

BANK-OF-AMERICA
   MEMORANDUM OF UNDERSTANDING BETWEEN CALIFORNIA STATE FAIR- EMPLOYMENT-PRACTICE-COMMISSION AND
   BANK-OF-AMERICA NATIONAL TRUST AND SAVINGS ASSOCIATION.   GCALFEPND537

BANKING
   PATTERNS OF DISCRIMINATION IN THE FINANCIAL INSTITUTIONS OF THE DISTRICT-OF-COLUMBIA. THE **BANKING**,
   SAVINGS AND LOAN, AND INSURANCE INDUSTRIES.   GDISTCC66642

   THE **BANKING** INDUSTRY. VERIFIED COMPLAINTS AND INFORMAL INVESTIGATIONS. /NEW-YORK/   GNEWYSA58076

   PATTERNS OF EXCLUSION FROM THE EXECUTIVE-SUITE. COMMERCIAL **BANKING**.   JAMERJC66696

   INSURANCE, **BANKING**, PUBLIC UTILITIES. /DISCRIMINATION EMPLOYMENT/   JSIMOBX58763

   WOMEN IN **BANKING**. /OCCUPATIONS/   WGILDGN59783

BANKS
   REPORT OF 1961 - 1962 SURVEY OF PHILADELPHIA **BANKS** AND ATTACHED COMPOSITE TABULATION OF NON-WHITES.
   /PENNSYLVANIA/   GPHILCH62180

   THE MUTUAL SAVINGS **BANKS** OF NEW-YORK-CITY. /DISCRIMINATION/   JAMERJC65694

   THE MUTUAL SAVINGS **BANKS** OF NEW-YORK-CITY. A FOLLOW-UP REPORT ON THE EXCLUSION OF JEWS AT TOP-MANAGEMENT
   AND POLICY-MAKING LEVELS.   JAMERJC66695

   REPORT OF THE 1961-1962 SURVEY OF PHILADELPHIA **BANKS**. /PENNSYLVANIA/   NPHILCH62995

BAR
   UNIONS BEFORE THE **BAR**. HISTORICAL TRIALS SHOWING THE EVOLUTION OF LABOR RIGHTS IN THE US.   GLIEBEX50901

   HOW MANY CONTRACTS **BAR** DISCRIMINATION IN EMPLOYMENT.   GWORTMS64586

BARGAINING
   DISCRIMINATION BY LABOR UNIONS IN THE EXERCISE OF STATUTORY **BARGAINING** POWERS.   GDODDEM45646

   DISCRIMINATION IN UNION MEMBERSHIP. DENIAL OF DUE PROCESS UNDER FEDERAL COLLECTIVE **BARGAINING**
   LEGISLATION.   GPRESSB58126

   THE NEGRO REVOLUTION AND THE LAW OF COLLECTIVE **BARGAINING**.   NGOULWB65437

BARRIER
   NEGRO DIALECT, THE LAST **BARRIER** TO INTEGRATION.   NGREEGC63447

BARRIERS
   BREAKING THE **BARRIERS** OF OCCUPATIONAL ISOLATION. A REPORT ON UPGRADING LOW-SKILL, LOW-WAGE WORKERS.
   /NEGRO PUERTO-RICAN/   CPROJAX66237

   BANK **BARRIERS** /DISCRIMINATICN/   GANTIDL61393

   INEQUALITY OF OPPORTUNITY IN HIGHER EDUCATION. A STUDY OF MINORITY GROUP AND RELATED **BARRIERS** TO COLLEGE
   ADMISSION.   GBERKDS48446

   ETHNIC AND RACE **BARRIERS**.   GKAHLJA57831

   THE MENOMINEE TERMINATION CRISIS. **BARRIERS** IN THE WAY OF A RAPID CULTURAL TRANSITION.   IAMESDW59525

   BARRIERS. PATTERNS OF DISCRIMINATION AGAINST JEWS.   JBELTNC58702

   BARRIERS IN HIGHER EDUCATION.   JEPSTBR58718

   REMOVING JOB **BARRIERS**.   NABRACX57510

   BARRIERS TO NEGRO WAR EMPLOYMENT.   NGRANLB42440

   THE WORKING WOMAN. **BARRIERS** IN EMPLOYMENT. /DISCRIMINATION/   WHARREX64827

   BARRIERS TO THE CAREER CHOICE OF ENGINEERING, MEDICINE, OR SCIENCE AMONG AMERICAN WOMEN. /OCCUPATIONS/   WROSSAS65091

BARRIO
   THE **BARRIO**. /EDUCATION INCCME/   MARIARX66360

BASE
   ECONOMIC **BASE** STUDY OF SAN-ANTONIO AND TWENTY-SEVEN COUNTY AREAS. /TEXAS/   MSANACP64476

BASES
   REPORT ON AND ANALYSIS OF SECOND CENSUS OF CITY EMPLOYEES TO DETERMINE **BASES** FOR FUTURE PERSONNEL
   DEVELOPMENTS. /DETROIT MICHIGAN/   GDETRCC66639

BASIC
   BASIC ISSUES AFFECTING YOUTH EMPLOYMENT.   GFREEMK64005

   SOME **BASIC** CONSTITUTIONAL RIGHTS OF ECONOMIC SIGNIFICANCE.   GHALERX51754

   SUPERVISOR DEVELOPMENT PROGRAM, **BASIC** COURSE, NONDISCRIMINATION POLICY. /MILITARY/   GUSDARM56192

   US GOVERNMENT POLICY TOWARD AMERICAN INDIANS. A FEW **BASIC** FACTS.   IELLIMB57554

   BASIC NEEDS OF INDIAN PEOPLE.   IUSDINT57643

   BASIC NEEDS OF SPANISH-AMERICAN FARM FAMILIES IN NEW-MEXICO.   MGRISGXND408

   WORKING WITH STUDENTS INSIDE AND OUTSIDE THE CLASSROOM IN ADULT **BASIC** EDUCATION PROGRAMS.   NBRAZWF64285

BASIC   (CONTINUATION)
    VOCATIONAL CHOICES OF NEGRO HIGH SCHOOL STUDENTS IN MACON COUNTY, ALABAMA, AND THEIR RELATIONSHIP TO
    BASIC OCCUPATIONAL ACTIVITES OF THE SCHOOL COMMUNITIES. /ASPIRATIONS/   NCHAPEJ49351

    THREE BASIC THEMES IN MEXICAN AND PUERTO-RICAN FAMILIES.   PTRENRD58800

BATON-ROUGE
    STUDY OF OCCUPATIONAL CHARACTERISTICS OF NON-WHITES IN THE EAST BATON-ROUGE AREA. /LOUISIANA/ GHARRWRND760

BATTLE
    THE CALIFORNIA FARM WORKER. STILL IN DUBIOUS BATTLE. /MIGRANT-WORKERS UNION/   GMEISDX60461

    THE BATTLE AGAINST UNEMPLOYMENT.   GOKUNAX65133

    THE VOCATIONAL GUIDANCE AND EDUCATION OF NEGROES. THE NEGRO AND THE BATTLE OF PRODUCTION.   NWILKDA42233

BATTLE-AXES
    THE CASE OF THE BATTLE-AXES. /EMPLOYMENT/   WWALSCM57266

BATTLEFRONT
    MISSISSIPPI. BATTLEFRONT FOR LABOR. /UNION/   NBARTBX65057

BAY
    MANPOWER RESOURCES OF THE SAN-FRANCISCO OAKLAND BAY AREA 1960-1970. /CALIFORNIA/   GCALDEM63520

    MEDICAL SERVICE JOB OPPORTUNITIES 1964-66, SAN-FRANCISCO BAY AREA. /CALIFORNIA/   GCALDEM64521

    HOTEL AND RESTAURANT JOB OPPORTUNITIES, SAN-FRANCISCO BAY AREA, 1964-1966. /CALIFORNIA/   GCALDEM65517

    BAY AREA CONFERENCE ON FULL-EMPLOYMENT. /SAN-FRANCISCO CALIFORNIA/   GHIRSFI64776

    HIRING PROCEDURES AND SELECTION STANDARDS IN THE SAN-FRANCISCO BAY AREA. /CALIFORNIA/   GMA_MTF55934

    PSYCHOLOGICAL TESTS AND FAIR EMPLOYMENT. A STUDY OF EMPLOYMENT TESTING IN THE SAN-FRANCISCO BAY AREA.
    /CALIFORNIA/   GRUSHJT66268

    RELOCATED AMERICAN INDIANS IN THE SAN-FRANCISCO BAY AREA. SOCIAL INTERACTION AND INDIAN IDENTITY.
    /CALIFORNIA/   IALBOJX64523

    THE ECONOMIC-STATUS OF NEGROES IN THE SAN-FRANCISCO OAKLAND BAY AREA. A REPORT BASED ON THE 1960 CENSUS
    OF POPULATION. /CALIFORNIA/   NCALFES63172

    SOCIAL-DEPENDENCY IN THE SAN-FRANCISCO BAY AREA. TODAY AND TOMORROW. /CALIFORNIA/   NGREEMX63449

    MINORITY-GROUPS AND INTERGROUP RELATIONS IN THE SAN-FRANCISCO BAY AREA. /CALIFORNIA/   NRECOCW63043

BEET
    SUGAR BEET LABOR IN NORTHERN COLORADO. /MIGRANT-WORKERS/   GDAVIIF58939

BEHAVIOR
    RACE. INDIVIDUAL AND COLLECTIVE BEHAVIOR.   GTHOMET58356

    DIFFERENCES IN DROPOUT AND OTHER SCHOOL BEHAVIOR BETWEEN TWO GROUPS OF TENTH GRADE BOYS IN AN URBAN HIGH
    SCHOOL.   MMUNORF57446

    SOCIO-ECONOMIC CLASS AND AREA AS CORRELATES OF ILLEGAL BEHAVIOR AMONG JUVENILES.   NCLARJP62209

    GOAL-ORIENTATIONS AND ILLEGAL BEHAVIOR AMONG JUVENILES.   NCLARJP63208

    BEHAVIOR AND PRODUCTIVITY IN BI-RACIAL WORK GROUPS.   NKATZIX58638

    RACE. ECONOMIC ATTITUDES. AND BEHAVIOR.   NMORGJX62850

    THE JOB HUNT. JOB SEEKING BEHAVIOR OF UNEMPLOYED WORKERS IN A LOCAL ECONOMY.   NSHEPHL66128

    THE DEVELOPMENT OF BEHAVIOR AND PERSONALITY. /WORK-WOMEN-ROLE/   WANDEJE60614

    WHAT ASPECTS OF CHILD BEHAVIOR SHOULD BE STUDIED IN RELATION TO MATERNAL EMPLOYMENT.   WHARTRE61829

BELATED
    REASONS FOR BELATED EDUCATION. A STUDY OF THE PLIGHT OF THE OLDER NEGRO TEACHERS. /OCCUPATIONS/ NCUNNGE58244

BELT
    GROWING UP IN THE BLACK BELT. NEGRO YOUTH IN THE RURAL SOUTH.   NJOHNCS41611

BENEFIT
    BENEFIT POLICIES IN RELATION TO RECRUITMENT OF OLDER WORKERS, HANDICAPPED, AND MINORITY GROUPS. GBARRGJ51425

    MATERNITY BENEFIT PROVISIONS FOR EMPLOYED WOMEN. /EMPLOYMENT-CONDITIONS/   WUSDLAB60206

    FRINGE BENEFIT PROVISIONS FROM STATE MINIMUM WAGE LAWS AND ORDERS, SEPTEMBER 1, 1966.
    /EMPLOYMENT-CONDITIONS/   WUSDLAB66195

BENEFIT-COST
    A BENEFIT-COST ANALYSIS OF THE ECONOMIC EFFECTIVENESS OF RETRAINING THE UNEMPLOYED.   GBORUME64142

    A BENEFIT-COST ANALYSIS OF MANPOWER RETRAINING.   GSOMEGJ64157

BENEFITS
    MONEY BENEFITS OF EDUCATION BY SEX AND RACE IN NEW-YORK STATE, 1956.   GGREEWX61741

    OCCUPATIONAL BENEFITS TO WHITES FROM THE SUBORDINATION OF NEGROES. /DISCRIMINATION/   NGLENND63423

BERKELEY
    REVIEW AND ANALYSIS OF CITY CERTIFICATIONS AND APPOINTMENTS. /BERKELEY CALIFORNIA/   GBERKCM64444

    WASTED MANPOWER -- BERKELEY CHALLENGE AND OPPORTUNITY. WORKSHOP COSPONSORED WITH THE BERKELEY UNIFIED
    SCHOOL-DISTRICT MARCH 15-16, 1963. /CALIFORNIA/   NKENNVD63642

    WASTED MANPOWER -- BERKELEY CHALLENGE AND OPPORTUNITY. WORKSHOP COSPONSORED WITH THE BERKELEY UNIFIED
    SCHOOL-DISTRICT MARCH 15-16, 1963. /CALIFORNIA/   NKENNVD63642

BI-RACIAL
    BEHAVIOR AND PRODUCTIVITY IN BI-RACIAL WORK GROUPS.   NKATZIX58638

    EFFECTS OF WHITE AUTHORITARIANISM IN BI-RACIAL WORK GROUPS.   NKATZIX60639

    A SOCIOLOGICAL ANALYSIS OF A BI-RACIAL LOCAL LABOR UNION.   NMERCJJ56768

BI-RACIAL   (CONTINUATION)
    MANAGEMENT POLICIES AND BI-RACIAL INTEGRATION IN INDUSTRY.   NMOHRFT54806

    BI-RACIAL COOPERATION IN PLACEMENT OF NEGROES.   NUSDLAB42811

BIAS
    INTERIM REPORT TO THE MAYOR CN ITS INQUIRY INTO CHARGES OF RACIAL BIAS IN THE CITY BUILDING AND
    CONSTRUCTION INDUSTRY.   /NEW-YORK NEGRO PUERTO-RICAN/   CNEWYC064917

    UNIONS URGED TO FOLLOW THROUGH ON PLEDGES TO COMBAT JOB BIAS.   GAFLCI063365

    JOB BIAS IN L A. /LOS-ANGELES CALIFORNIA/   GANTIDL57397

    HOW WELL CAN UNIONS KEEP PLEDGE ON BIAS.   GBUSIWX62505

    AN INVESTIGATION OF ITEM BIAS. /TESTING/   GCLEATA66924

    THE CONGRESSIONAL HEARINGS AND ISSUES IN PSYCHOLOGICAL TESTING. INVASIONS OF PRIVACY AND TEST BIAS. GGORDJEND934

    POSSIBLE SOLUTIONS TO THE PROBLEM OF CULTURAL BIAS IN TESTS.   GKRUGRE64946

    US PLAN TO BREAK CYCLE OF BIAS AND POVERTY.   GRICHEX66235

    UNION BIAS.   NBUSIWX54879

    AFL-CIO COUNCIL GETS NEGRO DEMAND FOR MORE ACTION ON BIAS IN UNIONS.   NBUSIWX61144

    NLRB CRACKS DOWN ON UNION BIAS.   NBUSIWX64887

    THE PROBLEM OF CULTURAL BIAS IN SELECTION. I. BACKGROUND AND LITERATURE. /TESTING/   NCAMPJT65179

    TEST BIAS. VALIDITY OF THE SCHOLASTIC APTITUDE TEST FOR NEGRO AND WHITE STUDENTS IN INTEGRATED COLLEGES. NCLEATA66923

    BIAS IN UNIONS.   NFORTXX57373

    THE PROBLEMS OF CULTURAL BIAS IN SELECTION, POSSIBLE SOLUTION TO THE PROBLEM OF CULTURAL BIAS IN TESTS. NKRUGRE64731

    THE PROBLEMS OF CULTURAL BIAS IN SELECTION, POSSIBLE SOLUTION TO THE PROBLEM OF CULTURAL BIAS IN TESTS. NKRUGRE64731

    INTER-AGENCY POLICY ON RACIAL BIAS.   NLABORR43029

    THE PROBLEM OF CULTURAL BIAS IN SELECTION. II. ETHNIC BACKGROUND AND TEST PERFORMANCE.   NROBESO65068

BIBLIOGRAPHY
    CULTURAL DIFFERENCES IN AMERICAN ETHNIC GROUPS. BIBLIOGRAPHY. /AMERICAN-INDIAN NEGRO SPANISH-AMERICAN/ CLIBRCX64899

    SELECTED BIBLIOGRAPHY FOR DISADVANTAGED YOUTH.   /NEGRO PUERTO-RICAN/   CUSDHEWND855

    STATE FAIR-EMPLOYMENT-PRACTICES-COMMISSIONS -- A SELECTED BIBLIOGRAPHY.   GAMERCR46373

    INTEGRATION IN BUSINESS AND INDUSTRY. A SELECTED, ANNOTATED BIBLIOGRAPHY.   GAMERJC64383

    ECONOMIC AND SOCIAL DEPRIVATIONS. ITS EFFECTS ON CHILDREN AND FAMILIES IN THE UNITED STATES -- A SELECTED
    BIBLIOGRAPHY.   GCHILCX64571

    JOB AND CAREER DEVELOPMENT FOR THE POOR...THE HUMAN SERVICES. INCLUDES BIBLIOGRAPHY.   GGOLDGS66360

    COUNSELOR-S GUIDE TO OCCUPATIONAL AND OTHER MANPOWER INFORMATION. AN ANNOTATED BIBLIOGRAPHY.   GLAFADP65782

    SCHOOL DROPOUTS. A COMMENTARY AND ANNOTATED BIBLIOGRAPHY.   GMILLSM64071

    MASTER ANNOTATED BIBLIOGRAPHY CF PAPERS OF MOBILIZATION-FOR-YOUTH. PUBLISHED, UNPUBLISHED AND PRESENTED
    AT CCNFERENCES.   GMOBIFY65025

    A SELECTIVE BIBLIOGRAPHY ON DISCRIMINATION IN HOUSING AND EMPLOYMENT.   GNEWYLF60075

    BIBLIOGRAPHY ON VOLUNTARY FAIR-EMPLOYMENT PROGRAMS.   GUSCOMC65392

    BIBLIOGRAPHY ON EQUAL-EMPLOYMENT-OPPORTUNITY.   GUSCOMC66393

    SELECTED BIBLIOGRAPHY ON STATE FAIR-EMPLOYMENT-PRACTICE COMMISSIONS.   GUSCOMC66414

    IMPLICATIONS OF AUTOMATION AND OTHER TECHNOLOGICAL DEVELOPMENTS, A SELECTED BIBLIOGRAPHY.   GUSDLAB63450

    A SURVEY OF CURRENT LITERATURE ON AUTOMATION AND OTHER TECHNOLOGICAL-CHANGES. A SELECTED ANNOTATED
    BIBLIOGRAPHY.   GUSDLAB64825

    UNEMPLOYMENT AND RETRAINING. AN ANNOTATED BIBLIOGRAPHY OF RESEARCH.   GUSDLAB65503

    EMPLOYMENT ASSISTANCE REFERENCE BIBLIOGRAPHY.   IUSDINTND452

    MATERIALS RELATING TO THE EDUCATION OF SPANISH-SPEAKING PEOPLE IN THE UNITED STATES, AN ANNOTATED
    BIBLIOGRAPHY.   MSANCGI59478

    A SELECTIVE BIBLIOGRAPHY OF CALIFORNIA LABOR HISTORY.   MSLOBMX64495

    MEXICAN-AMERICAN STUDY PROJECT. ADVANCE REPORT 3, BIBLIOGRAPHY.   MUVCALM66510

    A BIBLIOGRAPHY OF CIVIL-RIGHTS AND CIVIL-LIBERTIES. /EMPLOYMENT UNION   MILITARY/   NBRODAD62117

    THE NEGRO AMERICAN. A BIBLIOGRAPHY.   NMILLEW66129

    RACIAL DISCRIMINATION IN EMPLOYMENT. BIBLIOGRAPHY.   NNORGPH62931

    VOCATICNAL GUIDANCE BIBLIOGRAPHY.   NTANNAX40199

    BIBLIOGRAPHY ON THE ECONOMIC-STATUS OF THE NEGRO.   NUSDLAB65254

    BIBLIOGRAPHY ON THE PUERTO-RICAN. HIS CULTURE AND SOCIETY.   PMOBIFYND024

    RESOURCES FOR THE EMPLOYMENT OF MATURE WOMEN AND/OR THEIR CONTINUING EDUCATION. A SELECTED BIBLIOGRAPHY
    AND AIDS.   WBERNML66746

    THE CHANGING ROLE OF COLLEGE WOMEN. A BIBLIOGRAPHY. /WORK-WOMAN-ROLE/   WSCHWJX62106

    BIBLIOGRAPHY ON AMERICAN WOMEN WORKERS.   WUSDLAB66201

    THE EDUCATION OF WOMEN AND GIRLS IN A CHANGING SOCIETY. A SELECTED BIBLIOGRAPHY WITH ANNOTATIONS. WWIGNTX65267

BICULTURATION
BICULTURATION OF MESQUAKIE TEENAGE BOYS.   IPOLGSX60605

BIDS
THE NEGRO BIDS FOR UNION POWER.   NBRUNDX60128

BIGOTRY
THE AFL FIGHTS BIGOTRY.   /UNION/   GJEWILCND824

BILL
THE CONTROVERSY OVER THE EQUAL-EMPLOYMENT-OPPORTUNITY PROVISIONS OF THE CIVIL-RIGHTS BILL. PRO AND CON.   GCONGDX64594

SOME QUESTIONS AND ANSWERS ON THE CIVIL-RIGHTS BILL.   GLEADCCND888

A MODEL STATE FAIR-EMPLOYMENT-PRACTICE BILL.   GNAACNL45036

BRIEF SUBMITTED IN SUPPORT OF SENATE BILL NO 984, A BILL TO PROHIBIT DISCRIMINATION IN EMPLOYMENT....   GTUTTCH47368

BRIEF SUBMITTED IN SUPPORT OF SENATE BILL NO 984, A BILL TO PROHIBIT DISCRIMINATION IN EMPLOYMENT....   GTUTTCH47368

BILLS
MIGRATORY LABOR BILLS.   GUSSENA63305

BIOLOGICAL
CAREERS FOR WOMEN IN BIOLOGICAL SCIENCES.   /OCCUPATIONS/   WMURPMC60009

BIOSCIENTISTS
INFORMAL COMMUNICATION AMONG BIOSCIENTISTS. /EMPLOYMENT-CONDITIONS/   WBERNJX63643

BIRMINGHAM
INCOME, EDUCATION AND UNEMPLOYMENT IN NEIGHBORHOODS. BIRMINGHAM, ALABAMA. /DEMOGRAPHY/   CUSDLAB63453

NEGRO EMPLOYMENT IN THE BIRMINGHAM METROPOLITAN AREA. /ALABAMA CASE-STUDY/   NHAWLLT55502

THE NEGRO AND UNIONISM IN THE BIRMINGHAM, ALABAMA IRON AND STEEL INDUSTRY.   NNORTHR43941

BOYCOTT IN BIRMINGHAM. /ALABAMA/   NOSBOGR62460

NEGRO EMPLOYMENT IN BIRMINGHAM. THREE CASES. /ALABAMA/   NROWARL67091

BIRTH
STATE OF BIRTH. /DEMOGRAPHY/   CUSBURC63185

PUERTO-RICANS IN THE UNITED STATES. SOCIAL AND ECONOMIC DATA FOR PERSONS OF PUERTO-RICAN BIRTH AND
PARENTAGE. /DEMOGRAPHY/   PUSBURC63182

BISHOP-S
COMPREHENSIVE REPORT OF THE OFFICE OF THE BISHOP-S COMMITTEE FOR MIGRANT-WORKERS.   MNATLCBND082

BISMARK
MINUTES OF INDIAN EMPLOYMENT MEETING HELD NOVEMBER 29-30, 1966 IN BISMARK, NORTH-DAKOTA. ·   IUSDLAB66322

BLACK
PROFILE IN BLACK AND WHITE. DISCRIMINATION AND INEQUALITY OF OPPORTUNITY.   GNATLULNDO85

AMERICAN INDIANS, WHITE AND BLACK. THE PHENOMENON OF TRANSCULTURATION.   IHALLAI63571

CONFRONTATION. BLACK AND WHITE. /CIVIL-RIGHTS/   NBENNLX65881

EDUCATE THE BLACK ONE TOO.   NBLAIGE66081

ECONOMIC PROGRESS IN BLACK AND WHITE.   NBRIMAF66114

BLACK METROPOLIS. A STUDY OF NEGRO LIFE IN A NORTHERN CITY.   NDRAKSC45291

BLACK BOURGEOISIE. THE RISE OF A MIDDLE-CLASS IN THE UNITED STATES.   NFRAZEF57371

GROWING UP IN THE BLACK BELT. NEGRO YOUTH IN THE RURAL SOUTH.   NJOHNCS41611

DIXIE IN BLACK AND WHITE. /UNION/   NMEZEAG47492

BLACK ODYSSEY. THE STORY OF THE NEGRO IN AMERICA.   NOTTLRX45966

BLACK FAMILIES AND THE WHITE HOUSE.   NRAINLX66033

THE BLACK MAN-S BURDEN. /DISCRIMINATION ECONOMIC-STATUS/   NREDDJS43546

CRISIS IN BLACK AND WHITE.   NSILBCE65135

BLACKFEET
THE BLACKFEET.   IEWERJC58557

LIFE ON THE BLACKFEET INDIAN RESERVATION TODAY.   IMUSEPI57593

BLACKLAND
INCOMES OF RURAL FAMILIES IN THE BLACKLAND PRAIRIES.   GADKIWG63410

BLANK
ELIMINATION OF RACE DISCRIMINATION IN THE APPLICATION BLANK.   GDARTCX47626

BLIND
IS LABOR COLOR BLIND. /UNION/   NFLEIHX59359

BLINDNESS
FAREWELL TO COLOR BLINDNESS.   NBECKWL65069

BLOCK
EAST-HARLEM BLOCK COMMUNITY DEVELOPMENT PROGRAM. /NEW-YORK/   PBORDDXND781

BLS
THE BLS STUDY OF NURSES SALARIES AND EMPLOYMENT CONDITIONS.   WAMERJN57378

BLUE-COLLAR
ACCULTURATION AND NEGRO BLUE-COLLAR WORKERS.   NSTAMRX64171

CAREERS AS CONCERNS OF BLUE-COLLAR GIRLS. /OCCUPATIONS/   WDAVIEX64721

THE IMPACT OF CULTURAL CHANGE ON WOMEN-S POSITION. /BLUE-COLLAR ASPIRATIONS/   WKONOGX66913

BLUE-COLLAR   (CONTINUATION)
TESTIMONY. PUBLIC HEARING. WOMEN IN PUBLIC AND PRIVATE EMPLOYMENT, CALIFORNIA. /BLUE-COLLAR
EMPLOYMENT-CONDITIONS/   WMENGVX66969

SPEAKING FOR THE WORKING CLASS WIFE.   /BLUE-COLLAR/   WSEXTPC62299

BLUEPRINT
YOUTH IN THE GHETTO. A STUDY OF THE CONSEQUENCES OF POWERLESSNESS AND A BLUEPRINT FOR CHANGE.   /NEW-YORK/   NHARLYO64485

BLUEPRINT FOR TALENT. SEARCHING AMERICA-S HIDDEN MANPOWER.   NPLAURL57003

BNA
TEXTS OF RULES AND REGULATIONS OF PRESIDENT-S COMMITTEE ON EQUAL-EMPLOYMENT-OPPORTUNITY RELATING TO
OBLIGATIONS OF GOVERNMENT CONTRACTORS AND SUBCONTRACTORS, EFFECTIVE JULY 22, 1961. A BNA SPECIAL REPORT.   GBURENA61498

BOARD
EQUAL-OPPORTUNITIES PLAN STRESSED IN STATE PERSONNEL BOARD DOCUMENT. /CALIFORNIA/   GCALSEM64548

ETHNIC CENSUS OF EXAMINATION COMPETITORS, JAN-JUNE 1965, CALIFORNIA STATE PERSONNEL BOARD.   GCALSPB65551

REPORT OF THE SPECIAL COMMITTEE ON NONDISCRIMINATION OF THE BOARD OF PUBLIC EDUCATION, PHILADELPHIA.
/PENNSYLVANIA/   GPHILBE64172

DISCRIMINATION AND THE NLRB. THE SCOPE OF THE BOARD POWER UNDER SECTIONS 8A3 AND 8B2.   GUVCHLR64212

WAR LABOR BOARD DECISION ON WAGES OF NEGROES.   NUSDLAB43848

BOILERMAKERS
NEGRO STATUS IN THE BOILERMAKERS UNION.   NMARSTX44753

BOOK
PROBLEMS OF YOUTH. A FACT BOOK. /EMPLOYMENT/   GUSLIBC64823

THE AMERICAN NEGRO REFERENCE BOOK.   NDAVIJP66260

1961 COMMISSION ON CIVIL-RIGHTS REPORT BOOK 3. EMPLOYMENT.   NUSCOMC61231

HEALTH MANPOWER SOURCE BOOK. SECTION 2. NURSING PERSONNEL.   WUSDHEW66177

BOOM
BEHIND LOS-ANGELES. JOB-LESS NEGROES AND THE BOOM. /UNEMPLOYMENT CALIFORNIA/   NMOYNDP65860

BOOTSTRAP
OPERATION BOOTSTRAP FOR THE AMERICAN-INDIAN.   IUSHOUR59669

BORDER
THE INFLUENCE OF A BORDER CITY UNION ON THE RACE ATTITUDES OF ITS MEMBERS.   NROSEAW53293

BOSS
FAIR PLAY STARTS WITH THE BOSS. /EMPLOYMENT DISCRIMINATION/   GNIXORM56117

BOSSES
WOMEN AS BOSSES. /OCCUPATIONS/   WHAMMKX56817

BOSTON
INCOME, EDUCATION AND UNEMPLOYMENT IN NEIGHBORHOODS. BOSTON, MASSACHUSETTS. /DEMOGRAPHY/   CUSDLAB63454

SUB-EMPLOYMENT IN THE SLUMS OF BOSTON. /MASSACHUSETTS/   GUSDLAB66518

THE NEGRO IN BOSTON. /MASSACHUSETTS/   NEDWARM61327

THE VOICE OF THE GHETTO. A REPORT ON TWO BOSTON NEIGHBORHOOD MEETINGS. /MASSACHUSETTS/   NUSCOMC67149

SHORTAGE OR SURPLUS. AN ASSESSMENT OF BOSTON WOMANPOWER IN INDUSTRY, GOVERNMENT, AND RESEARCH. JUNE 7-8,
1963. /MASSACHUSETTS/   WUSDLAB66217

THE NEXT STEP -- A GUIDE TO PART-TIME OPPORTUNITIES IN GREATER BOSTON FOR THE EDUCATED WOMAN.
/MASSACHUSETTS/   WWHITMS64266

BOURGEOISIE
BLACK BOURGEOISIE. THE RISE OF A MIDDLE-CLASS IN THE UNITED STATES.   NFRAZEF57371

BOYCOTT
BOYCOTT IN BIRMINGHAM. /ALABAMA/   NOSBOGR62460

BOYS
RESIDENTIAL SEGREGATION OF SOCIAL-CLASSES AND ASPIRATIONS OF HIGH SCHOOL BOYS.   GWILSAB59568

BICULTURATION OF MESQUAKIE TEENAGE BOYS.   IPOLGSX60605

DIFFERENCES IN DROPOUT AND OTHER SCHOOL BEHAVIOR BETWEEN TWO GROUPS OF TENTH GRADE BOYS IN AN URBAN HIGH
SCHOOL.   MMUNORF57446

A COMPARATIVE STUDY OF THE OCCUPATIONAL INTERESTS OF NEGRO AND WHITE ADOLESCENT BOYS.   NCONNSM65471

ASPIRATION LEVELS OF NEGRO DELINQUENT, DEPENDENT, AND PUBLIC SCHOOL BOYS.   NMITCLE57804

ATTITUDES TOWARD SOCIAL MOBILITY AS REVEALED BY SAMPLES OF NEGRO AND WHITE BOYS.   NMONTJB58809

SOME ASPECTS OF VOCATIONAL ASPIRATIONS AND VALUE ORIENTATION AMONG NEGRO BOYS IN THE LOWER SOCIO-ECONOMIC
CLASSES.   NSCHMWX63139

BRACERO
MERCHANTS OF LABOR. THE MEXICAN BRACERO STORY.   MGALAEX66397

BRACERO IN CALIFORNIA.   MGILMNR62402

VANISHING BRACERO.   MMCBRJG63433

TERMINATION OF THE BRACERO PROGRAM. SOME EFFECTS ON FARM LABOR AND MIGRANT HOUSING NEEDS.   MMCELRC65385

TEXAS AND THE BRACERO PROGRAM.   MSCRUOM63482

THE BRACERO STORY.   MSOTOAX59370

BRACEROS
NO DICE FOR BRACEROS.   MTURNWX65166

BRACKETS
A MEMORANDUM ON THE MOTIVATIONS OF MIDDLE AGED WOMEN IN THE LOWER EDUCATIONAL BRACKETS TO RETURN TO WORK.

BRACKETS (CONTINUATION)
/ASPIRATIONS/   WJEWIVA61880

BRAVE
RACE DISCRIMINATION AND THE NLRA ACT. THE BRAVE NEW WORLD OF MIRANDA. /LEGISLATION/   NSOVEMI63169

BREAKDOWN
IS THERE A BREAKDOWN OF THE NEGRO FAMILY.   NHERZEX66521

BREAKTHROUGH
BREAKTHROUGH ON THE COLOR FRONT. /MILITARY/   NNICHLX54920

BREWERIES
A STUDY OF THE EMPLOYMENT OPPORTUNITIES FOR NEGROES IN BREWERIES OF THE UNITED STATES. /INDUSTRY/   NKERNJH51897

BREWERY
DISCRIMINATION IN THE HIRING HALL. A CASE-STUDY OF PRESSURES TO PROMOTE INTEGRATION IN NEW-YORK-S BREWERY
INDUSTRY.   NLANGGE59670

BRIEF
BRIEF SUBMITTED IN SUPPORT OF SENATE BILL NO 984, A BILL TO PROHIBIT DISCRIMINATION IN EMPLOYMENT....   GTUTTCH47368

BRIEF SUMMARY OF STATE LAWS AGAINST DISCRIMINATION IN PRIVATE EMPLOYMENT. FAIR-EMPLOYMENT-PRACTICE ACTS.   GUSDLAB63439

A BRIEF SURVEY OF HIGHER EDUCATION FOR NEGROES.   NSTOKMS64180

BRIGHT
WHY DO BRIGHT GIRLS NOT TAKE STIFF COURSES. /ASPIRATIONS/   WALBJMH61603

BRONX
INCOME. EDUCATION AND UNEMPLOYMENT IN NEIGHBORHOODS. NEW-YORK-CITY -- THE BRONX. /DEMOGRAPHY/   CUSDLAB63472

BROOKLYN
INCOME. EDUCATION AND UNEMPLOYMENT IN NEIGHBORHOODS. NEW-YORK-CITY -- BROOKLYN. /DEMOGRAPHY/   CUSDLAB63471

BROOME-COUNTY
RACE-RELATIONS IN BROOME-COUNTY, A PROFILE FOR 1958. /NEW-YORK/   NGRIEES58456

BROTHERHOOD
THE BROTHERHOOD OF SLEEPING CAR PORTERS. /UNION/   NBRAZBR46108

BROTHERS
WE MUST ASSIST OUR INDIAN BROTHERS TO HELP THEMSELVES.   IBOTTRV56540

WE CALL ALL MEN BROTHERS. /UNION/   NMEANGX57763

BRUNSWICK
BRUNSWICK. /GEORGIA/   NWATTPX64293

BUFFALO
INCOME. EDUCATION AND UNEMPLOYMENT IN NEIGHBORHOODS. BUFFALO, NEW-YORK. /DEMOGRAPHY/   CUSDLAB63455

SUPPLEMENTARY REPORT ON PUERTO-RICANS IN BUFFALO. /NEW-YORK/   PIMSETP62820

BUILD
RACE PROBLEMS BUILD UP FOR UNIONS.   NBUSIWX58880

BUILDING
INTERIM REPORT TO THE MAYOR ON ITS INQUIRY INTO CHARGES OF RACIAL BIAS IN THE CITY BUILDING AND
CONSTRUCTION INDUSTRY. /NEW-YORK NEGRO PUERTO-RICAN/   CNEWYC064917

RACIAL DISCRIMINATION IN THE CINCINNATI BUILDING TRADES. A COMPREHENSIVE REPORT AND RECOMMENDATIONS.
/OHIO/   GOHIOCR64129

A SURVEY OF DISCRIMINATION IN THE BUILDING TRADES INDUSTRY, NEW-YORK CITY.   GSHAUDF63300

JIM CROW IN BUILDING UNIONS.   NLIFEMX66493

NEGRO WORKERS IN THE BUILDING TRADES IN SELECTED CITIES. NORFOLK, VIRGINIA. /INDUSTRY/   NNATLUL46894

NEGRO WORKERS IN THE BUILDING TRADES IN CERTAIN CITIES.   NNATLUL47904

NEGROES AND THE BUILDING TRADES UNION.   NNATLUL57902

RACIAL DISCRIMINATION IN THE CINCINNATI BUILDING TRADES. REPORT AND RECOMMENDATIONS. /OHIO/   NOHIOCR66605

A SURVEY OF DISCRIMINATION IN THE BUILDING TRADES INDUSTRY. NEW-YORK CITY.   NSHAUDX63126

BULLETIN
RESEARCH BULLETIN ON INTERGROUP-RELATIONS. /EEO/   GSMITCX62319

BURDEN
THE BURDEN OF POVERTY.   MMITTFG66442

THE BLACK MAN-S BURDEN. /DISCRIMINATION ECONOMIC-STATUS/   NREDDJS43546

THE BURDEN OF SOUTHERN HISTORY.   NWOODCV60061

BURDENS
STATE FAIR-EMPLOYMENT-PRACTICE LEGISLATION UNCONSTITUTIONALLY BURDENS INTERSTATE COMMERCE WHEN APPLIED TO
INTERSTATE AIRLINE.   NHARVLR62499

BUREAU
BUREAU OF MIGRANT-LABOR REPORT. /NEW-JERSEY NEGRO PUERTO-RICAN/   CNEWJDL61907

THE MEASUREMENT AND INTERPRETATION OF JOB VACANCIES. A CONFERENCE REPORT OF THE NATIONAL BUREAU OF
ECONOMIC RESEARCH. /LABOR-MARKET/   GNATLBE66611

THE INDIAN BUREAU AND THE WAR-ON-POVERTY.   INASHPX64134

THE BUREAU OF INDIAN AFFAIRS VOLUNTARY RELOCATION SERVICES.   IUSDINT60644

BUREAU-OF-INDIAN-AFF
REGIONAL ORGANIZATION. BUREAU-OF-INDIAN-AFFAIRS.   ITAYLTW57627

A FOLLOWUP STUDY OF 1963 RECIPIENTS OF THE SERVICES OF THE EMPLOYMENT ASSISTANCE PROGRAM,
BUREAU-OF-INDIAN-AFFAIRS.   IUSDINT66650

THE ROLE OF THE BUREAU-OF-INDIAN-AFFAIRS SINCE 1933.   IZIMMWX57248

BUSINESS

> EQUAL JOB OPPORTUNITY IS GOOD BUSINESS. GAMERJC54381

> INTEGRATION IN BUSINESS AND INDUSTRY. A SELECTED, ANNOTATED BIBLIOGRAPHY. GAMERJC64383

> IMPLICATIONS FOR BUSINESS OF THE CIVIL-RIGHTS-ACT OF 1964. GBENEDX65434

> THE NEW CIVIL-RIGHTS LAW AND YOUR BUSINESS. GBERGNJ64438

> BUSINESS WIDENS ITS HIRING RANGE. GBUSIWX65502

> THE FEDERAL MANAGER-S ROLE IN DEMOCRACY-S UNFINISHED BUSINESS. GCLINRX61577

> INTERGROUP RELATIONS WITHIN BUSINESS AND INDUSTRY. GGENECC49713

> HOW RACE-RELATIONS AFFECT YOUR BUSINESS. GKHEETW63850

> MANPOWER PROBLEMS AND THE BUSINESS COMMUNITY. GKRUGDHND865

> EVERYBODY-S BUSINESS. A SUMMARY OF NEW-YORK STATE ANTI-DISCRIMINATION LAWS AND HOW TO USE THEM. GNATLFC46048

> THE CIVIL-RIGHTS-ACT. IMPLICATIONS FOR BUSINESS. GNEWYCA64068

> BUSINESS -- NEXT TARGET FOR INTEGRATION. /INDUSTRY/ GPERRJX63170

> FAIR-EMPLOYMENT IS GOOD BUSINESS. EXAMPLES OF FAIR PRACTICES FOR TITLE-VII OF THE CIVIL-RIGHTS-ACT OF 1964. GPOTOII65188

> MERIT EMPLOYMENT -- UNFINISHED BUSINESS. GPURYMJ62210

> THE PRICE BUSINESS PAYS. /INDUSTRY DISCRIMINATION/ GROPEEX49245

> BIG BUSINESS FAILS AMERICA. /INDUSTRY/ GSCRESX63292

> INDUSTRY-S UNFINISHED BUSINESS. /CASE-STUDY/ GSOUTSE50324

> TASK FORCE FOR EQUAL-OPPORTUNITY IN BUSINESS. GUSDCOM65432

> FRANCHISE COMPANY DATA FOR EQUAL-OPPORTUNITY IN BUSINESS. GUSDCOM66431

> THE MANAGEMENT OF RACIAL INTEGRATION IN BUSINESS. A SPECIAL REPORT TO MANAGEMENT. NALEXRD64868

> NEW BUSINESS WAYS IN THE SOUTH. NBUSIWX61158

> MORE RACE PRESSURE ON BUSINESS. NBUSIWX62153

> AIDING NEGRO BUSINESSMEN. SMALL BUSINESS OPPORTUNITIES CORPORATION, PHILADELPHIA. /PENNSYLVANIA/ NBUSIWX64143

> THE MANAGEMENT OF RACIAL INTEGRATION IN BUSINESS. NDORIGF64282

> PROBLEMS AND OPPORTUNITIES CONFRONTING NEGROES IN THE FIELD OF BUSINESS. REPORT ON THE NATIONAL CONFERENCE ON SMALL BUSINESS. /OCCUPATIONS/ NFITZNH63358

> PROBLEMS AND OPPORTUNITIES CONFRONTING NEGROES IN THE FIELD OF BUSINESS. REPORT ON THE NATIONAL CONFERENCE ON SMALL BUSINESS. /OCCUPATIONS/ NFITZNH63358

> THE NEGRO CHALLENGE TO THE BUSINESS COMMUNITY. /INDUSTRY/ NGINZEX64408

> FAIR EMPLOYMENT IS GOOD BUSINESS AT G FOX OF HARTFORD. /CASE-STUDY CONNECTICUT/ NGREEMX48448

> PREPARATION OF THE NEGRO COLLEGE GRADUATE FOR BUSINESS. /EMPLOYMENT-SELECTION/ NHOLLJH65560

> THE NEGRO IN AMERICAN BUSINESS. THE CONFLICT BETWEEN SEPARATISM AND INTEGRATION. NKINZRH50654

> WHAT SHOULD THE BUSINESS RESPONSE BE TO THE NEGRO REVOLUTION. A PUBLIC RELATIONS PROGRAM FOR DEALING WITH MINORITY-GROUPS. NLANGJF65671

> PRIVATE BUSINESS AND EDUCATION IN THE SOUTH. NMILLHH60780

> BUSINESS AND CIVIL-RIGHTS. NMITCJP64295

> EMPLOYMENT ON MERIT. THE CONTINUING CHALLENGE TO BUSINESS. NEGRO-S ECONOMIC LOT. NMORRJJ57854

> THE NEGRO-S ADVENTURE IN GENERAL BUSINESS. NOAKXVV49952

> NEGRO BUSINESS AND BUSINESS EDUCATION. THEIR PRESENT AND PROSPECTIVE DEVELOPMENT. NPIERJA47998

> NEGRO BUSINESS AND BUSINESS EDUCATION. THEIR PRESENT AND PROSPECTIVE DEVELOPMENT. NPIERJA47998

> NEGROES IN THE WORK GROUP. HOW 33 BUSINESS AND INDUSTRIAL FIRMS OFFERED EQUAL-EMPLOYMENT-OPPORTUNITIES TO ALL. NSEIDJX50114

> MORE SALARIED POSITIONS ARE OPENED TO NEGROES BY BUSINESS AND INDUSTRY HERE. /NEW-YORK/ NSTETDX63154

> THE POST-WAR OUTLOOK FOR NEGROES IN SMALL BUSINESS, THE ENGINEERING AND THE TECHNICAL VOCATIONS. NWALKJO46580

> THE PLACEMENT OF NEGRO COLLEGE GRADUATES IN BUSINESS ORGANIZATIONS. NWHITEW64321

> THE OPPORTUNITIES FOR BUSINESS OWNERSHIP AMONG NEGROES. NWHITWL66231

> THE NEGRO-S PARTICIPATION IN AMERICAN BUSINESS. NYOUNHB63347

> REBUILDING CITIES. THE EFFECTS OF DISPLACEMENT AND RELOCATION ON SMALL BUSINESS. NZIMMBG64247

> THE PROSPECT FOR ADVANCEMENT IN BUSINESS OF THE MARRIED WOMAN COLLEGE GRADUATE. /OCCUPATIONS/ WBECKEL64632

> BACK FROM THE HOME TO BUSINESS. /WORK-FAMILY-CONFLICT/ WBUSIWX61666

> CAREER OPPORTUNITIES FOR WOMEN IN BUSINESS. /OCCUPATIONS/ WKINGAG63904

> WOMEN ARE TRAINING FOR BUSINESS. /OCCUPATIONS/ WMARSEM62956

> UNFINISHED BUSINESS. CONTINUING EDUCATION FOR WOMEN. WRAUSEX61076

> A STUDY OF WOMEN IN OFFICE MANAGEMENT POSITIONS WITH IMPLICATIONS FOR BUSINESS EDUCATION. /OCCUPATIONS/ WRUSHEM57096

> SALARIED WOMEN IN UPPER LEVEL POSITIONS IN KANSAS BUSINESS FIRMS. WSTOCFT59143

> TODAY-S BUSINESS WOMAN. HER CHARACTERISTICS, HER NEED FOR FURTHER EDUCATION, HER FUTURE IN MANAGEMENT.

35

BUSINESS (CONTINUATION)
/OCCUPATIONS/   WTHOMMH63152

   MANAGING WOMEN EMPLOYEES IN SMALL BUSINESS.   WUSSMBA62248

BUSINESS-MAN
A NEGRO BUSINESS-MAN SPEAKS HIS MIND.   NFULLSB63390

BUSINESSES
THE CENSUS OF NEGRO-OWNED BUSINESSES. /PHILADELPHIA PENNSYLVANIA OCCUPATIONS/   NDREXIT64295

BUSINESSMAN
SOUTH-S RACE DISPUTES INVOLVE BUSINESSMAN.   NBUSIWX60162

   THE NEGRO BUSINESSMAN. IN SEARCH OF A TRADITION. /OCCUPATIONS/   NFOLEEP66369

   THE CIVIL-RIGHTS REVOLUTION AND THE BUSINESSMAN.   NMCKERB64723

   THE BUSINESSMAN AND THE NEGRO. /INDUSTRY/   NSILBCE63133

BUSINESSMEN
THE CIVIL-RIGHTS-ACT OF 1964. WHAT IT MEANS -- TO EMPLOYERS, BUSINESSMEN, UNIONS, EMPLOYEES,
MINORITY-GROUPS. TEXT, ANALYSIS, LEGISLATIVE HISTORY.   GBUREON64492

   WHAT MASSIVE RESISTANCE COSTS NORFOLK AND ITS BUSINESSMEN. /VIRGINIA/   NBUSIWX58165

   AIDING NEGRO BUSINESSMEN. SMALL BUSINESS OPPORTUNITIES CORPORATION, PHILADELPHIA. /PENNSYLVANIA/   NBUSIWX64143

   NEGRO BUSINESSMEN OF NEW-ORLEANS.   NFORTXX49054

   NEGRO UNEMPLOYMENT -- WHAT CITY BUSINESSMEN ARE DOING ABOUT IT.   NSCHMJC64108

CALIFORNIA
TESTIMONY. PUBLIC HEARING. WOMEN IN PUBLIC AND PRIVATE EMPLOYMENT, CALIFORNIA. /MEXICAN-AMERICAN/   CARYWSX66621

   REPORT TO GOVERNOR EDMUND G BROWN. SECOND ETHNIC SURVEY OF EMPLOYMENT AND PROMOTION IN STATE GOVERNMENT.
/CALIFORNIA NEGRO MEXICAN-AMERICAN/   CBECKWL65070

   CHARACTERISTICS OF RETRAINING APPLICANTS. /CALIFORNIA NEGRO MEXICAN-AMERICAN WOMEN/   CCALDEM66166

   ANNUAL FARM LABOR REPORT, 1965. CALIFORNIA DEPARTMENT OF EMPLOYMENT, FARM LABOR SERVICE. /NEGRO
MEXICAN-AMERICAN WOMEN/   CCALDEM66906

   REPORT ON OAKLAND SCHOOLS. AN INVESTIGATION UNDER SECTION 1421 OF THE CALIFORNIA LABOR CODE OF THE
OAKLAND UNIFIED SCHOOL DISTRICT 1962-1963. /NEGRO ORIENTAL MEXICAN-AMERICAN/   CCALDIR63710

   NEGROES AND MEXICAN-AMERICANS IN SOUTH AND EAST LOS-ANGELES. AN ANALYSIS OF A SPECIAL US CENSUS SURVEY OF
NOVEMBER 1965. /CALIFORNIA/   CCALDIR66168

   NEGROES AND MEXICAN-AMERICANS IN THE CALIFORNIA STATE GOVERNMENT, A COOPERATIVE PROJECT.   CCALOGB65171

   RACIAL CHARACTERISTICS. MDTA TRAINEES, SAN-FRANCISCO. /CALIFORNIA NEGRO MEXICAN-AMERICAN/   CELTCEX63332

   THE URBAN REALITY. A COMPARATIVE STUDY OF THE SOCIO-ECONOMIC SITUATION OF MEXICAN-AMERICANS, NEGROES AND
ANGLO-CAUCASIANS IN LOS-ANGELES COUNTY. /CALIFORNIA/   CLOSACH65708

   FARM MECHANIZATION AND LABOR STABILIZATION. PART II IN A SERIES ON TECHNOLOGICAL-CHANGE AND FARM LABOR
USE, KERN COUNTY, CALIFORNIA, 1961. /NEGRO MEXICAN-AMERICAN/   CMETZWH65389

   INCOME, EDUCATION AND UNEMPLOYMENT IN NEIGHBORHOODS. OAKLAND, CALIFORNIA. /DEMOGRAPHY/   CUSDLAB63476

   INCOME, EDUCATION AND UNEMPLOYMENT IN NEIGHBORHOODS. SAN-DIEGO, CALIFORNIA. /DEMOGRAPHY/   CUSDLAB63483

   INCOME, EDUCATION AND UNEMPLOYMENT IN NEIGHBORHOODS. SAN-FRANCISCO, CALIFORNIA. /DEMOGRAPHY/   CUSDLAB63484

   INCOME, EDUCATION AND UNEMPLOYMENT IN NEIGHBORHOODS. LOS-ANGELES, CALIFORNIA. /DEMOGRAPHY/   CUSDLAB63565

   HARD-CORE UNEMPLOYMENT AND POVERTY IN LOS-ANGELES. /CALIFORNIA NEGRO MEXICAN-AMERICAN/   CUVCAIIND524

   REPORT. EVALUATION STUDY OF YOUTH TRAINING AND EMPLOYMENT PROJECT, EAST LOS-ANGELES. /NEGRO
MEXICAN-AMERICAN CALIFORNIA/   CWEINJL64310

   JOB BIAS IN L A. /LOS-ANGELES CALIFORNIA/   GANTIDL57397

   A CIVIL-RIGHTS INVENTORY OF SAN-FRANCISCO. PART I, EMPLOYMENT. /CALIFORNIA/   GBABOIX58606

   SAN FRANCISCO-S PLAN FOR DEMOCRATIC RACIAL-RELATIONS. /CALIFORNIA/   GBAYXAC43427

   REPORT OF THE CALIFORNIA STATE ADVISORY COMMITTEE TO THE UNITED STATES COMMISSION ON CIVIL-RIGHTS ON
CALIFORNIA-S PROGRAM FOR EQUAL-OPPORTUNITY IN APPRENTICESHIP.   GBECKWL62432

   SECOND ETHNIC SURVEY OF EMPLOYMENT AND PROMOTION IN STATE GOVERNMENT. /CALIFORNIA/   GBECKWL65433

   REVIEW AND ANALYSIS OF CITY CERTIFICATIONS AND APPOINTMENTS. /BERKELEY CALIFORNIA/   GBERKCM64444

   SOME PROBLEMS IN MINORITY-GROUP EDUCATION IN THE LOS-ANGELES PUBLIC SCHOOLS. /CALIFORNIA/   GBULLPX63489

   EQUAL-RIGHTS UNDER THE LAW. PROVIDING FOR EQUAL TREATMENT FOR ALL CITIZENS REGARDLESS OF RACE, RELIGION,
COLOR, NATIONAL ORIGIN OR ANCESTRY. /CALIFORNIA/   GCALAGO60511

   OPINION CONCERNING THE SCOPE AND AUTHORITY OF THE JURISDICTION THAT MAY BE GRANTED TO CITY OR COUNTY
HUMAN-RELATIONS-COMMISSIONS IN THE FIELDS OF EMPLOYMENT AND HOUSING. /CALIFORNIA/   GCALAGO63512

   HEARING OF THE SUBCOMMITTEE ON ECONOMIC DEVELOPMENT, EDITED TRANSCRIPT, JANUARY 28 AND 29, 1964.
/CALIFORNIA FEP/   GCALAIW64510

   TOWARD EQUAL-EMPLOYMENT-OPPORTUNITY. /CALIFORNIA/   GCALBOE64513

   REPORT TO THE GOVERNOR AND THE LEGISLATURE OF THE COMMISSION ON MANPOWER, AUTOMATION AND TECHNOLOGY,
1964. /CALIFORNIA/   GCALCMA65515

   A COMPILATION OF STATISTICAL DATA, CHARTS AND OTHER RESOURCE MATERIAL FOR CONFERENCE PARTICIPANTS.
/APPRENTICESHIP CALIFORNIA YOUTH/   GCALCNA60516

   MANPOWER RESOURCES OF THE SAN-FRANCISCO OAKLAND BAY AREA 1960-1970. /CALIFORNIA/   GCALDEM63520

   MEDICAL SERVICE JOB OPPORTUNITIES 1964-66, SAN-FRANCISCO BAY AREA. /CALIFORNIA/   GCALDEM64521

   HOTEL AND RESTAURANT JOB OPPORTUNITIES, SAN-FRANCISCO BAY AREA, 1964-1966. /CALIFORNIA/   GCALDEM65517

CALIFORNIA   (CONTINUATION)
MANPOWER DEVELOPMENT TRAINING. TOTAL NUMBER OF NEW ENROLLEES DURING THE MONTH BY RACE AND OCCUPATION STATEWIDE AND BY ADMINISTRATIVE AREA, SEPTEMBER, 1966, OCTOBER, 1966. /CALIFORNIA/   GCALDEM66518

HEALTH OF MIGRANTS. /CALIFORNIA/   GCALDIR60522

GUIDE TO LAWFUL AND UNLAWFUL PRE-EMPLOYMENT INQUIRIES BY EMPLOYERS, EMPLOYMENT-AGENCIES, AND LABOR ORGANIZATIONS UNDER THE CALIFORNIA FAIR-EMPLOYMENT-PRACTICE ACT, LABOR CODE, SECTIONS 1410-1432.   GCALDIR60527

THE CALIFORNIA PLAN FOR EQUAL-OPPORTUNITY IN APPRENTICESHIP FOR MINORITY-GROUPS.   GCALDIR63523

FUNCTIONS AND RESPONSIBILITIES OF FEPC. /CALIFORNIA/   GCALDIR63526

EQUAL-OPPORTUNITY IN APPRENTICESHIP AND TRAINING -- THE CALIFORNIA PROGRAM.   GCALDIR65524

EMPLOYMENT PRACTICES, CITY OF PASADENA, AN INVESTIGATION UNDER SECTION 1421 OF THE CALIFORNIA LABOR CODE 1963-1965.   GCALFEPND531

MEMORANDUM OF UNDERSTANDING BETWEEN CALIFORNIA STATE FAIR- EMPLOYMENT-PRACTICE-COMMISSION AND BANK-OF-AMERICA NATIONAL TRUST AND SAVINGS ASSOCIATION.   GCALFEPND537

COMMUNITY SURVEY. LONG BEACH, CALIFORNIA.   GCALFEPND541

FAIR-EMPLOYMENT-PRACTICE ACT...FEPC RULES AND REGULATIONS... GUIDE TO PRE-EMPLOYMENT INQUIRIES. /CALIFORNIA/   GCALFEP61533

PROMOTING EQUAL JOB OPPORTUNITY, A GUIDE FOR EMPLOYERS. /CALIFORNIA/   GCALFEP63538

STATEMENT ON SURVEYS AND STATISTICS AS TO RACIAL AND ETHNIC COMPOSITION OF WORK-FORCE OR UNION MEMBERSHIP. /CALIFORNIA/   GCALFEP63539

BANK OF AMERICA EMPLOYMENT PRACTICES. FIRST REPORT BY CALIFORNIA FEPC.   GCALFEP64530

LOS-ANGELES CITY SCHOOLS. AN INVESTIGATION OF EMPLOYMENT PRACTICES. /CALIFORNIA/   GCALFEP64536

AFFIRMATIVE-ACTIONS IN EMPLOYMENT. A SPECIAL FEPC REPORT. /CALIFORNIA/   GCALFEP65529

SAN-MATEO AREA MINORITY JOB SURVEY. /CALIFORNIA/   GCALFEP65542

ACTION PROGRAMS FOR FEPC ADVISORY COMMITTEES. /CALIFORNIA/   GCALFEP66528

EVALUATING JOB APPLICANTS WITH POLICE RECORDS. /CALIFORNIA/   GCALFEP66532

FAIR-EMPLOYMENT-PRACTICES EQUAL GOOD EMPLOYMENT PRACTICES. GUIDELINES FOR TESTING AND SELECTING MINORITY JOB APPLICANTS. /CALIFORNIA/   GCALFEP66540

LABOR AND CIVIL-RIGHTS. /CALIFORNIA UNION/   GCALLFX59544

LABOR AND CIVIL-RIGHTS 1964. /CALIFORNIA UNION/   GCALLFX64545

GOVENOR-S CODE OF FAIR PRACTICE /CALIFORNIA/   GCALOGB63546

EQUAL-OPPORTUNITIES PLAN STRESSED IN STATE PERSONNEL BOARD DOCUMENT. /CALIFORNIA/   GCALSEM64548

SCHOOL. MINORITIES AND EQUAL-RIGHTS, SELECTED MATERIAL. /CALIFORNIA/   GCALSLIND549

ETHNIC CENSUS OF EXAMINATION COMPETITORS, JAN-JUNE 1965, CALIFORNIA STATE PERSONNEL BOARD.   GCALSPB65551

ETHNIC CENSUS OF EXAMINATION COMPETITORS, JULY-DEC 1965, CALIFORNIA STATE-PERSONNEL-BOARD.   GCALSPB65552

THE ITINERANT FARM LABOR PROJECT REPORT. /MIGRANT-WORKERS CALIFORNIA/   GCALVRS60553

A SUMMARY REPORT OF PRACTICES AND PROGRAMS DESIGNED TO REDUCE THE NUMBER OF DROPOUTS IN THE HIGH SCHOOLS OF LOS-ANGELES COUNTY. /CALIFORNIA/   GDELMDT66147

CALIFORNIA LOCAL GOVERNMENT AND INTEGRATION.   GFORDJA63695

BAY AREA CONFERENCE ON FULL-EMPLOYMENT. /SAN-FRANCISCO CALIFORNIA/   GHIRSFI64776

SURVEY OF MINORITY-GROUP EMPLOYMENT AND PATIENT CARE IN PRIVATE HOSPITAL FACILITIES IN LOS-ANGELES COUNTY. /CALIFORNIA/   GLOSACCND914

TESTIMONY OF HUMAN RELATIONS. /LOS-ANGELES CALIFORNIA/   GLOSACCND915

REPORTS ON THE PATTERN OF EMPLOYMENT OF MINORTY-GROUP PERSONS IN DEPARTMENT OF COUNTY GOVERNMENT.LOS-ANGELES CALIFORNIA/   GLOSACC62913

PROPOSED POLICY REGARDING STATISTICS ON EMPLOYMENT. /LOS-ANGELES CALIFORNIA/   GLOSACC64912

REPORT OF FINDINGS AND RECOMMENDATIONS RESULTING FROM AN ANALYSIS OF THE EMPLOYMENT PRACTICES IN THE VARIOUS DEPARTMENTS OF THE CITY OF LOS-ANGELES. /CALIFORNIA/   GLOSAOC63917

HIRING PROCEDURES AND SELECTION STANDARDS IN THE SAN-FRANCISCO BAY AREA. /CALIFORNIA/   GMALMTF55934

THE CALIFORNIA FARM WORKER. STILL IN DUBIOUS BATTLE. /MIGRANT-WORKERS UNION/   GMEISDX60461

CALIFORNIA FAIR-EMPLOYMENT-PRACTICE ACT.   GMERCMA59975

ETHNIC SURVEY OF EMPLOYMENT IN STATE GOVERNMENT. /CALIFORNIA/   GMESPFA63977

THE FARM WORKER IN A CHANGING AGRICULTURE. PART I IN A SERIES ON TECHNOLOGICAL-CHANGE AND FARM LABOR USE, KERN-COUNTY, CALIFORNIA, 1961.   GMETZWH64387

A HUMAN-RELATIONS PROGRAM FOR SAN-FRANCISCO. /CALIFORNIA/   GMITCJP64277

THE PATTERN OF DEPENDENT POVERTY IN CALIFORNIA.   GRAABEX64120

TESTIMONY TO THE SUBCOMMITTEE ON RACE-RELATIONS AND URBAN PROBLEMS. /SES CALIFORNIA/   GREDMWX64221

THE SAN-FRANCISCO NON-WHITE POPULATION 1950-1960. /CALIFORNIA/   GROSETXND250

GRAPE WORKERS WIN NEW GAINS. /MIGRANT-WORKERS UNION CALIFORNIA/   GROSSLX66557

PSYCHOLOGICAL TESTS AND FAIR EMPLOYMENT. A STUDY OF EMPLOYMENT TESTING IN THE SAN-FRANCISCO BAY AREA. /CALIFORNIA/   GRUSHJT66268

DIMENSIONS IN DISCRIMINATION, A PRELIMINARY SURVEY OF SAN-DIEGO-S COMMUNITY PROBLEMS OF DISCRIMINATION PART II. /CALIFORNIA/   GSANDLW65274

CALIFORNIA   (CONTINUATION)
FINAL REPORT OF SAN-FRANCISCO **CALIFORNIA** COMMISSION ON EQUAL-EMPLOYMENT-OPPORTUNITY.   GSANFCE60275

RACIAL AND ETHNIC EMPLOYMENT PATTERN SURVEY OF THE CITY AND COUNTY OF SAN-FRANCISCO GOVERNMENT.
DEPARTMENTAL ANALYSIS. /CALIFORNIA/   GSANFHR65264

THE **CALIFORNIA** FEPC. STEPCHILD OF THE STATE AGENCIES.   GSTANLR65333

THE **CALIFORNIA** FAIR-EMPLOYMENT-PRACTICES-COMMISSION. ITS HISTORY, ACCOMPLISHMENTS, AND LIMITATIONS.   GTOBRMC63361

CALIFORNIA FEPC.   GTOBRMC65360

US COMMISSION-ON-CIVIL-RIGHTS, HEARINGS. LOS-ANGELES AND SAN-FRANCISCO, **CALIFORNIA**. JANUARY 25-26, 1960,
JANUARY 27-28, 1960.   GUSCOMC60400

REPORTS ON APPRENTICESHIP, NINE STATE ADVISORY COMMITTEES. /CALIFORNIA FLORIDA MARYLAND CONNECTICUT
WASHINGTON-DC NEW-JERSEY NEW-YORK TENNESSEE WISCONSIN/   GUSCCMC64407

MINORITY WORKER HIRING AND REFERRAL IN SAN-FRANCISCO. /CALIFORNIA/   GUSDLAB58076

SUB-EMPLOYMENT IN THE SLUMS OF LOS-ANGELES. /CALIFORNIA/   GUSDLAB66514

SUB-EMPLOYMENT IN THE SLUMS OF SAN-FRANCISCO. /CALIFORNIA/   GUSDLAB66519

SUB-EMPLOYMENT IN THE SLUMS OF OAKLAND. /CALIFORNIA/   GUSDLAB66521

LAKE ARROWHEAD CONFERENCE ON EQUAL-EMPLOYMENT-OPPORTUNITY, OCTOBER 22-24, 1963 -- RECORD OF PROCEEDINGS.
LOS-ANGELES, **CALIFORNIA**.   GUSFEDE63513

ETHNIC SURVEY OF APPRENTICES. /CALIFORNIA/   GWEBBEB65546

EMPLOYMENT PRACTICES, CITY OF SAN-DIEGO, 1963-1964. /CALIFORNIA/   GZOOKOX64596

RELOCATED AMERICAN INDIANS IN THE SAN-FRANCISCO BAY AREA. SOCIAL INTERACTION AND INDIAN IDENTITY.
 /CALIFORNIA/   IALBOJX64523

INDIANS IN RURAL AND RESERVATION AREAS. /CALIFORNIA/   ICALACI66542

AMERICAN INDIANS IN **CALIFORNIA**. POPULATION, EDUCATION, EMPLOYMENT, INCOME.   ICALDIR65541

DEVELOPMENT OF THE SAN-CARLOS APACHE CATTLE INDUSTRY. /CALIFORNIA/   IGETTHT58563

THE SAN-CARLOS INDIAN CATTLE INDUSTRY. /CALIFORNIA/   IGETTHT63564

A CENSUS OF INDIANS IN LOS-ANGELES. /CALIFORNIA/   IPRICJA67606

THE MIGRATION AND ADAPTATION OF AMERICAN INDIANS TO LOS-ANGELES. /CALIFORNIA/   IPRICJA67608

INDIANS OF **CALIFORNIA**, PAST AND PRESENT.   IQUINFX60609

SAN-FRANCISCO RELOCATEES. /CALIFORNIA/   ITAXXSXND441

AMERICAN-INDIANS IN LOS-ANGELES. A STUDY OF ADAPTATION TO A CITY. /CALIFORNIA/   IUVCALA66675

A REPORT ON THE JEWISH POPULATION OF LOS-ANGELES. /CALIFORNIA/   JMASAGX59746

GLIMPSES OF JEWISH LIFE IN SAN-FRANCISCO. /CALIFORNIA/   JZARCMM64776

TRANSCRIPT OF PROCEEDINGS OF THE INTERIM SUBCOMMITTEE ON SPECIAL EMPLOYMENT PROBLEMS. /CALIFORNIA/   MCALAIC64374

PRELIMINARY REPORT ON SURVEY OF ACTIVE APPRENTICES. /CALIFORNIA/   MCALDIR62376

EMPLOYMENT-TRENDS AMONG **CALIFORNIA** YOUTH AUTHORITY WARDS ON PAROLE. 1948-62.   MCALDYA63378

DOMESTIC AND IMPORTED WORKERS IN THE HARVEST LABOR-MARKET, SANTA-CLARA COUNTY, **CALIFORNIA**, 1954.   MFULLVX56396

BRACERO IN **CALIFORNIA**.   MGILMNR62402

BACKGROUND AND AMBITION OF MALE MEXICAN-AMERICAN HIGH SCHOOL SENIORS IN LOS-ANGELES. /CALIFORNIA/   MHELLCS63414

NATURALIZATION AND ASSIMILATION PRONENESS OF **CALIFORNIA** IMMIGRANT POPULATIONS.   MKRASWX63425

SOME NOTES ON THE MEXICAN POPULATION OF LOS-ANGELES COUNTY. /CALIFORNIA/   MLOSACDND431

MEXICAN-AMERICAN FAMILIES. LOS-ANGELES COUNTY. /CALIFORNIA/   MMCNAPH57435

STATEMENT ON EMPLOYMENT PROBLEMS OF MEXICAN-AMERICANS IN **CALIFORNIA**.   MMORADX63445

MEXICAN-AMERICANS IN THE LOS-ANGELES REGION. /CALIFORNIA/   MORTIMX62449

THE EFFECTS OF IMPORTED MEXICAN FARM LABOR IN A **CALIFORNIA** COUNTY.   MROONJF61465

EMPLOYMENT AND EMPLOYABILITY AMONG **CALIFORNIA** YOUTH AUTHORITY WARDS. A SURVEY.   MSECKJP62483

A SELECTIVE BIBLIOGRAPHY OF **CALIFORNIA** LABOR HISTORY.   MSLOBMX64495

SUMMARY REPORT OF THE STUDY OF DROP-OUTS IN THE THREE SENIOR HIGH SCHOOLS, COMPTON UNION HIGH SCHOOL
DISTRICT. /CALIFORNIA/   MWHITNX60517

HOW UNIONS ARE SIGNING THEM UP. /MIGRANT-WORKERS CALIFORNIA/   MWINGWX66536

REPORT FROM LOS-ANGELES. /CALIFORNIA/   NBUGGJA66131

FIGHTING POVERTY. THE VIEW FROM WATTS. /LOS-ANGELES CALIFORNIA/   NBULLPX66135

INTERIM REPORT ON OAKLAND SCHOOLS. /CALIFORNIA/   NCALFEP66169

THE ECONOMIC-STATUS OF NEGROES IN THE SAN-FRANCISCO OAKLAND BAY AREA. A REPORT BASED ON THE 1960 CENSUS
OF POPULATION. /CALIFORNIA/   NCALFES63172

ETHNIC CENSUS OF EXAMINATION COMPETITORS. REPORT OF EXAMINATIONS GIVEN JULY THROUGH DECEMBER, 1965,
SUMMARY. /TESTING CALIFORNIA/   NCALFPB66173

SOME PRACTICAL STUDIES IN PUBLIC TRANSPORTATION. /EMPLOYMENT-CONDITIONS WATTS LOS-ANGELES CALIFORNIA/   NCARLJX65593

TESTIMONY BEFORE STATE SENATE FACT FINDING SUBCOMMITTEE ON RACE-RELATIONS AND URBAN PROBLEMS, FINAL
HEARING, JANUARY 20 1965. /CALIFORNIA FEPC/   NGRAHCX65439

SOCIAL-DEPENDENCY IN THE SAN-FRANCISCO BAY AREA. TODAY AND TOMORROW. /CALIFORNIA/   NGREEMX63449

CALIFORNIA   (CONTINUATION)
   THE NEGRO WAR WORKER IN SAN-FRANCISCO.   /CALIFORNIA/   NJOHNCS44612

   AGRICULTURAL SEASONAL LABORERS OF COLORADO AND CALIFORNIA. /MIGRANT-WORKERS/   NKARRCHND636

   WASTED MANPOWER -- BERKELEY CHALLENGE AND OPPORTUNITY. WORKSHOP COSPONSORED WITH THE BERKELEY UNIFIED
   SCHOOL-DISTRICT MARCH 15-16, 1963. /CALIFORNIA/   NKENNVD63642

   VOCATIONAL ASPIRATIONS OF NEGRO YOUTH IN CALIFORNIA.   NLAWRPF50368

   THE NEGRO IN LOS-ANGELES COUNTY. /CALIFORNIA/   NLOSACC63709

   PROPOSALS FOR THE IMPROVEMENT OF HUMAN RELATIONS IN THE LOS-ANGELES METROPOLITAN AREA. /EMPLOYMENT
   CALIFORNIA/   NLOSACC65365

   ATTITUDES TOWARD ETHNIC FARM WORKERS IN COACHELLA-VALLEY. /CALIFORNIA/   NMCDOEC55719

   POSTWAR STATUS OF NEGRO WORKERS IN SAN-FRANCISCO AREA. /CALIFORNIA/   NMCENDX50721

   BEHIND LOS-ANGELES. JOB-LESS NEGROES AND THE BOOM. /UNEMPLOYMENT CALIFORNIA/   NMOYNDP65860

   WATTS ONE YEAR LATER. /TRAINING CALIFORNIA LOS-ANGELES/   NPAGEDX66970

   THE NEGRO ISSUE IN CALIFORNIA.   NRECOCW48041

   NEGROES IN THE CALIFORNIA AGRICULTURAL LABOR-FORCE.   NRECOCW59042

   MINORITY-GROUPS AND INTERGROUP RELATIONS IN THE SAN-FRANCISCO BAY AREA. /CALIFORNIA/   NRECOCW63043

   SOME LESSONS FROM WATTS. /LOS-ANGELES CALIFORNIA/   NRUSTBX66098

   THE WATTS MANIFESTO AND THE MCCONE REPORT. /LOS-ANGELES CALIFORNIA/   NRUSTBX66099

   THE MAYOR AND THE FIRE CHIEF. THE FIGHT OVER INTEGRATING THE LOS-ANGELES FIRE DEPARTMENT. /CALIFORNIA
   CASE-STUDY/   NSHERFP59130

   PROGRESS IN WATTS -- THE LOS-ANGELES ASTD COMMUNITY AFFAIRS PROGRAM. /CALIFORNIA/   NTRAIAD66580

   MINORITY-GROUPS IN CALIFORNIA.   NUSDLAB66826

   PREJUDICE IS NOT THE WHOLE STORY. EXAMINATION OF THREE CASES OF NEGRO UPGRADING IN TRACTION COMPANIES IN
   PHILADELPHIA, LOS-ANGELES AND CHICAGO. /PENNSYLVANIA CALIFORNIA ILLINOIS/   NWECKJE45308

   CONTRASTIVE ACCULTURATION OF CALIFORNIA JAPANESE. COMPARATIVE APPROACH TO THE STUDY OF IMMIGRANTS.   OBEFUHX65701

   THE POLITICS OF PREJUDICE. THE ANTI-JAPANESE MOVEMENT IN CALIFORNIA AND THE STRUGGLE FOR JAPANESE
   EXCLUSION.   ODANIRX61716

   THE SETTLEMENT OF MERCED-COUNTY, CALIFORNIA.   OGRAHJC57728

   STATEMENT BEFORE CALIFORNIA SENATE SUB-COMMITTEE ON RACE-RELATIONS AND URBAN PROBLEMS.   OLCWXHW64745

   STATEMENT BEFORE CALIFORNIA LEGISLATURE ASSEMBLY, INTERIM SUBCOMMITTEE ON ECONOMIC OPPORTUNITY ON BEHALF
   OF CHINATOWN-NORTH BEACH DISTRICT COUNCIL.   OWONGLJ64771

   TESTIMONY. PUBLIC HEARING. WOMEN IN PUBLIC AND PRIVATE EMPLOYMENT, CALIFORNIA. /DISCRIMINATION EEOC/   WBALEHX66625

   TESTIMONY. PUBLIC HEARING. WOMEN IN PUBLIC AND PRIVATE EMPLOYMENT, CALIFORNIA. /EMPLOYMENT-CONDITIONS/   WBECHCX66631

   STATEMENT. PUBLIC HEARING. WOMEN IN PUBLIC AND PRIVATE EMPLOYMENT, CALIFORNIA. /FEP
   EMPLOYMENT-CONDITIONS DISCRIMINATION/   WBELAJX66634

   STATEMENT. PUBLIC HEARING. WOMEN IN PUBLIC AND PRIVATE EMPLOYMENT, CALIFORNIA. /FEP
   EMPLOYMENT-CONDITIONS DISCRIMINATION/   WBENNSJ66637

   TESTIMONY. PUBLIC HEARING, WOMEN IN PUBLIC AND PRIVATE EDUCATION, CALIFORNIA. /FEP
   EMPLOYMENT-CONDITIONS DISCRIMINATION MIGRANT-WORKERS/   WBLOCHX66649

   TESTIMONY. PUBLIC HEARING, WOMAN IN PUBLIC AND PRIVATE EMPLOYMENT, CALIFORNIA. /DISCRIMINATION/   WBROWAX66657

   TESTIMONY PRESENTED AT PUBLIC HEARING, APRIL 28, 1966. SAN-FRANCISCO, CALIFORNIA. /FEP
   EMPLOYMENT-CONDITIONS DISCRIMINATION MIGRANTS/   WCALACW62676

   TESTIMONY PRESENTED AT PUBLIC HEARING, APRIL 29, 1966. SAN-FRANCISCO, CALIFORNIA. /FEP
   EMPLOYMENT-CONDITIONS CHILDREN/   WCALACW66677

   REPORT OF THE CALIFORNIA ADVISORY COMMISSION ON THE STATUS OF WOMEN. /FEP EMPLOYMENT-CONDITIONS
   DISCRIMINATION MIGRANTS/   WCALACW67673

   CALIFORNIA WOMANPOWER.   WCALDIR66267

   WOMAN WORKERS IN CALIFORNIA, 1949-SEPTEMBER 1966.   WCALDIR67269

   WOMEN WORKERS IN CALIFORNIA. JANUARY 1949-AUGUST 1964.   WCALIDL64678

   TESTIMONY. PUBLIC HEARING. WOMEN IN PUBLIC AND PRIVATE EMPLOYMENT, CALIFORNIA. /EMPLOYMENT-CONDITIONS/   WCHANHD66687

   TESTIMONY. PUBLIC HEARING. WOMEN IN PUBLIC AND PRIVATE EMPLOYMENT, CALIFORNIA. /FEP
   EMPLOYMENT-CONDITIONS DISCRIMINATION MIGRANTS/   WCLIFFG66692

   TESTIMONY. PUBLIC HEARING. WOMEN IN PUBLIC AND PRIVATE EMPLOYMENT, CALIFORNIA. /DISCRIMINATION/   WCOLLNX66696

   TESTIMONY. PUBLIC HEARING. WOMEN IN PUBLIC AND PRIVATE EMPLOYMENT, CALIFORNIA. /EMPLOYMENT-CONDITIONS/   WCOMPBX66702

   TESTIMONY. PUBLIC HEARING. WOMEN IN PUBLIC AND PRIVATE EMPLOYMENT, CALIFORNIA. /TRAINING/   WCUMMGX66711

   TESTIMONY. PUBLIC HEARING. WOMEN IN PUBLIC AND PRIVATE EMPLOYMENT, CALIFORNIA. /EMPLOYMENT-CONDITIONS/   WDIBRJX66732

   TESTIMONY. PUBLIC HEARING. WOMAN IN PUBLIC AND PRIVATE EMPLOYMENT, CALIFORNIA. /DISCRIMINATION/   WDORAMX66739

   TESTIMONY. PUBLIC HEARING. WOMEN IN PUBLIC AND PRIVATE EMPLOYMENT, CALIFORNIA. /EMPLOYMENT-CONDITIONS/   WEVANSX66753

   TESTIMONY. PUBLIC HEARING. WOMEN IN PUBLIC AND PRIVATE EMPLOYMENT, CALIFORNIA. /EMPLOYMENT-CONDITIONS/   WFEINBX66760

   TESTIMONY. PUBLIC HEARING. WOMEN IN PUBLIC AND PRIVATE EMPLOYMENT, CALIFORNIA. /DISCRIMINATION/   WFOOTJX66765

   TESTIMONY. PUBLIC HEARING. WOMEN IN PUBLIC AND PRIVATE EMPLOYMENT, CALIFORNIA. /EMPLOYMENT-CONDITIONS/   WGABELX66773

   TESTIMONY. PUBLIC HEARING. WOMEN IN PUBLIC AND PRIVATE EMPLOYMENT, CALIFORNIA. /DISCRIMINATION/   WGEIGPX66776

CALIFORNIA   (CONTINUATION)
TESTIMONY, PUBLIC HEARING, WOMEN IN PUBLIC AND PRIVATE EMPLOYMENT, **CALIFORNIA**. /DEMOGRAPHY/   WGERSMX66777

TESTIMONY, PUBLIC HEARING, WOMEN IN PUBLIC AND PRIVATE EMPLOYMENT, **CALIFORNIA**. /EMPLOYMENT-CONDITIONS/   WGILBRX66780

TESTIMONY, PUBLIC HEARING, WOMEN IN PUBLIC AND PRIVATE EMPLOYMENT, **CALIFORNIA**. /EMPLOYMENT-CONDITIONS/   WGLENEM66788

TESTIMONY, PUBLIC HEARING, WOMEN IN PUBLIC AND PRIVATE EMPLOYMENT, **CALIFORNIA**. /DISCRIMINATION
WORK-FAMILY-CONFLICT/   WGUPTRC66808

TESTIMONY, PUBLIC HEARING, WOMEN IN PUBLIC AND PRIVATE EMPLOYMENT, **CALIFORNIA**. /EMPLOYMENT-CONDITIONS/   WGUPTRC66809

TESTIMONY, PUBLIC HEARING, WOMEN IN PUBLIC AND PRIVATE EMPLOYMENT, **CALIFORNIA**. /EMPLOYMENT-CONDITIONS/   WHEALWX66836

TESTIMONY, PUBLIC HEARING, WOMEN IN PUBLIC AND PRIVATE EMPLOYMENT, **CALIFORNIA**. /DISCRIMINATION/   WHILLHX66844

TESTIMONY, PUBLIC HEARING, WOMEN IN PUBLIC AND PRIVATE EMPLOYMENT, **CALIFORNIA**. /MOTA EEO/   WINGRLX66859

STATEMENT, PUBLIC HEARING, WOMEN IN PUBLIC AND PRIVATE EMPLOYMENT, **CALIFORNIA**. /EMPLOYMENT-CONDITIONS
MIGRANT-WORKERS/   WKAUFDX66886

TESTIMONY, PUBLIC HEARING, WOMEN IN PUBLIC AND PRIVATE EMPLOYMENT, **CALIFORNIA**. /EMPLOYMENT-CONDITIONS/   WKELLET66888

STATEMENT, PUBLIC HEARING, WOMEN IN PUBLIC AND PRIVATE EMPLOYMENT, **CALIFORNIA**. /EMPLOYMENT-CONDITIONS/   WKENNVX66890

STATEMENT, PUBLIC HEARING, WOMEN IN PUBLIC AND PRIVATE EMPLOYMENT, **CALIFORNIA**. /EMPLOYMENT-CONDITIONS/   WKNIGTF66911

TESTIMONY, PUBLIC HEARING, WOMEN IN PUBLIC AND PRIVATE EMPLOYMENT, **CALIFORNIA**. /FEP MIGRANT-WORKERS
EMPLOYMENT-CONDITIONS/   WLLOYMX66940

TESTIMONY, PUBLIC HEARING, WOMEN IN PUBLIC AND PRIVATE EMPLOYMENT, **CALIFORNIA**. /FEP   EMPLOYMENT
CONDITIONS/   WLOWEDX66943

TESTIMONY, PUBLIC HEARING, WOMEN IN PUBLIC AND PRIVATE EMPLOYMENT, **CALIFORNIA**. /EMPLOYMENT-CONDITIONS/   WMACKJW66950

TESTIMONY, PUBLIC HEARING, WOMEN IN PUBLIC AND PRIVATE EMPLOYMENT, **CALIFORNIA**. /OCCUPATIONS
EMPLOYMENT-CONDITIONS/   WMCLALX66947

TESTIMONY, PUBLIC HEARING, WOMEN IN PUBLIC AND PRIVATE EMPLOYMENT, **CALIFORNIA**. /BLUE-COLLAR
EMPLOYMENT-CONDITIONS/   WMENGVX66969

STATEMENT, PUBLIC HEARING, WOMEN IN PUBLIC AND PRIVATE EMPLOYMENT, **CALIFORNIA**. /FEP
EMPLOYMENT-CONDITIONS MIGRANT-WORKERS/   WMILLJJ66979

TESTIMONY, PUBLIC HEARING, WOMEN IN PUBLIC AND PRIVATE EMPLOYMENT, **CALIFORNIA**. /EMPLOYMENT-CONDITIONS/   WMILLKL66980

TESTIMONY, PUBLIC HEARING, WOMEN IN PUBLIC AND PRIVATE EMPLOYMENT, **CALIFORNIA**. /EMPLOYMENT-CONDITIONS/   WMORAMX66995

TESTIMONY, PUBLIC HEARING, WOMEN IN PUBLIC AND PRIVATE EMPLOYMENT, **CALIFORNIA**.   WMOTHWA66001

TESTIMONY, PUBLIC HEARING, WOMEN IN PUBLIC AND PRIVATE EMPLOYMENT, **CALIFORNIA**. /EMPLOYMENT-CONDITIONS/   WMYRIRX66013

TESTIMONY, PUBLIC HEARING, WOMEN IN PUBLIC AND PRIVATE EMPLOYMENT, **CALIFORNIA**. /EMPLOYMENT-CONDITIONS/   WPALMGX66047

TESTIMONY, PUBLIC HEARING, WOMEN IN PUBLIC AND PRIVATE EMPLOYMENT, **CALIFORNIA**. /FEP
EMPLOYMENT-CONDITIONS MIGRANT-WORKERS/   WPEEVMX66052

TESTIMONY, PUBLIC HEARING, WOMEN IN PUBLIC AND PRIVATE EMPLOYMENT, **CALIFORNIA**. /EMPLOYMENT-CONDITIONS/   WRILEEX66081

TESTIMONY, PUBLIC HEARING, WOMEN IN PUBLIC AND PRIVATE EMPLOYMENT, **CALIFORNIA**. /FEP
EMPLOYMENT-CONDITIONS/   WSCHRPX66104

TESTIMONY, PUBLIC HEARING, WOMEN IN PUBLIC AND PRIVATE EMPLOYMENT, **CALIFORNIA**. /EMPLOYMENT-CONDITIONS/   WSHEAHX66112

TESTIMONY, PUBLIC HEARING, WOMEN IN PUBLIC AND PRIVATE EMPLOYMENT, **CALIFORNIA**. /FEP
EMPLOYMENT-CONDITIONS DISCRIMINATION/   WSMITWH66123

TESTIMONY, PUBLIC HEARING, WOMEN IN PUBLIC AND PRIVATE EMPLOYMENT, **CALIFORNIA**. /FEP
EMPLOYMENT-CONDITIONS DISCRIMINATION MIGRANT-WORKERS/   WSPENNX66129

TESTIMONY, PUBLIC HEARING, WOMEN IN PUBLIC AND PRIVATE EMPLOYMENT, **CALIFORNIA**. /LABOR-MARKET/   WSTEPRX66138

TESTIMONY, PUBLIC HEARING, WOMEN IN PUBLIC AND PRIVATE EMPLOYMENT, **CALIFORNIA**. /FEPC/   WSTERAX66140

TESTIMONY, PUBLIC HEARING, WOMEN IN PUBLIC AND PRIVATE EMPLOYMENT, **CALIFORNIA**. /EMPLOYMENT-CONDITIONS/   WTHOMDX66151

TESTIMONY, PUBLIC HEARING, WOMEN IN PUBLIC AND PRIVATE EMPLOYMENT, **CALIFORNIA**. /EMPLOYMENT-CONDITIONS
DISCRIMINATION/   WTHOMGX66149

STATEMENT, PUBLIC HEARING, WOMEN IN PUBLIC AND PRIVATE EMPLOYMENT, **CALIFORNIA**. /FEP
EMPLOYMENT-CONDITIONS DISCRIMINATION/   WVAILLX66256

TESTIMONY, PUBLIC HEARING, WOMEN IN PUBLIC AND PRIVATE EMPLOYMENT, **CALIFORNIA**. /EMPLOYMENT-CONDITIONS
MIGRANT-WORKERS/   WWEBEJX66258

TESTIMONY, PUBLIC HEARING, WOMEN IN PUBLIC AND PRIVATE EMPLOYMENT, **CALIFORNIA**. /FEP
EMPLOYMENT-CONDITIONS MIGRANT-WORKERS/   WWOMEIX66273

TESTIMONY, PUBLIC HEARING, WOMEN IN PUBLIC AND PRIVATE EMPLOYMENT, **CALIFORNIA**. /EMPLOYMENT-CONDITIONS/   WWOODWX66276

CALIFORNIA-S
REPORT OF THE CALIFORNIA STATE ADVISORY COMMITTEE TO THE UNITED STATES COMMISSION ON CIVIL-RIGHTS ON
CALIFORNIA-S PROGRAM FOR EQUAL-OPPORTUNITY IN APPRENTICESHIP.   GBECKWL62432

CALIFORNIA-S MINORITY-GROUPS PROGRAM.   GWOODMJ64581

CALIFORNIA-S FARM LABOR PROBLEMS. /MIGRANT-WORKERS/   MCALSSE63380

CALIFORNIA-S FRUIT AND VEGETABLE CANNING INDUSTRY. AN ECONOMIC STUDY.   OBENJMP61704

CALIFORNIANS
CALIFORNIANS OF SPANISH SURNAME. POPULATION, EMPLOYMENT, INCOME, EDUCATION.   MCALDIR64377

NEGRO **CALIFORNIANS**, POPULATION, EMPLOYMENT, INCOME, EDUCATION.   NCALDIR63167

CALIFORNIANS OF JAPANESE, CHINESE, FILIPINO ANCESTRY.   OCALDIR65709

CALVERT
EMPLOYMENT OF NEGRO MANPOWER IN **CALVERT** COUNTY, MARYLAND.   NLERANL60401

CALVERT   (CONTINUATION)
INCOME. EMPLOYMENT STATUS AND CHANGE IN **CALVERT** COUNTY, MARYLAND.   NROHRWC58400

CAMDEN
THE MINORITY-GROUP WORKER IN **CAMDEN** COUNTY. /NEW-JERSEY/   GBOGITX54057

CAMP
OAK GLEN -- A TRAINING **CAMP** FOR UNEMPLOYED YOUTH. /NEGRO MEXICAN-AMERICAN/   CUSDLAB66323

HOUSING FOR MIGRANT AGRICULTURAL WORKERS. LABOR **CAMP** STANDARDS.   GUSDLAB62508

CAMPAIGN
CIVIL-RIGHTS. 1960-63. THE NEGRO **CAMPAIGN** TO WIN EQUAL RIGHTS AND OPPORTUNITIES IN THE UNITED STATES.   NFACTOF64341

CAMPAIGNS
WHY DROPOUT **CAMPAIGNS** FAIL.   GBARDBX66533

THE DYNAMICS OF STATE **CAMPAIGNS** FOR FAIR-EMPLOYMENT-PRACTICES LEGISLATION.   GUVCHCE50211

EMPLOYEE CHOICE AND SOME PROBLEMS OF RACE AND REMEDIES IN REPRESENTATION **CAMPAIGNS**.   NYALELJ63599

CAMPS
AMERICA-S CONCENTRATION **CAMPS**. THE FACTS ABOUT OUR INDIAN RESERVATIONS TODAY.   IEMBRCB56555

CAMPUS
FIRST CATALYST ON **CAMPUS** CONFERENCE. PROCEEDINGS. /WORK-WOMEN-ROLE/   WCATAXX64683

CANDIDATES
FACTORS ASSOCIATED WITH GRADUATE SCHOOL ATTENDANCE AND ROLE DEFINITION OF THE WOMAN DOCTORAL **CANDIDATES**
AT THE PENNSYLVANIA STATE UNIVERSITY. /OCCUPATIONS/   WFIELJC61763

CANNING
CALIFORNIA-S FRUIT AND VEGETABLE **CANNING** INDUSTRY. AN ECONOMIC STUDY.   OBENJMP61704

CANTONESE
KINSHIP AS A FACTOR AFFECTING **CANTONESE** ECONOMIC ADAPTATION IN THE UNITED STATES.   OBARNML66698

CANTONESE-AMERICAN
SOME **CANTONESE-AMERICAN** PROBLEMS OF STATUS ADJUSTMENT.   OBARNML58699

CAPABILITIES
PROBLEMS FOR ADULT EDUCATION RELATED TO ACQUIRING **CAPABILITIES** FOR WORK.   NGOLDFH63430

CAPACITIES
LARGE CORPORATIONS ACCUSED OF DISCRIMINATION AGAINST JEWS IN MANAGEMENT. EXECUTIVE **CAPACITIES** BY
AMERICAN-JEWISH-COMMITTEE.   JWORLOX64773

CAPITAL
HUMAN **CAPITAL**. A THEORETICAL AND EMPIRICAL ANALYSIS WITH SPECIAL REFERENCE TO EDUCATION.   GBECKGS64700

HUMAN **CAPITAL** AS A SOUTHERN RESOURCE.   GCOLBMR63994

HUMAN **CAPITAL** IN SOUTHERN DEVELOPMENT 1939-1963.   GCOLBMR65793

FAIR-EMPLOYMENT IN THE NATION-S **CAPITAL**. A STUDY OF PROGRESS AND DILEMMA. /WASHINGTON-DC/   GSAWYDA62279

AMERICAN INDIAN **CAPITAL** CONFERENCE ON POVERTY. MAY 9-12, 1964. FINDINGS.   IAMERIN64087

NEXT IT-S A MIXED POLICE FORCE. INTEGRATIONISTS LATEST GOAL IN NATION-S **CAPITAL**. /WASHINGTON-DC/   NUSNEWR57274

CAPITOL
THE PRACTICES OF CRAFT UNIONS IN WASHINGTON-DC WITH RESPECT TO MINORITY GROUPS IN CIVIL-RIGHTS IN THE
NATION-S **CAPITOL**.   GSEGABD59294

CAR
THE BROTHERHOOD OF SLEEPING **CAR** PORTERS. /UNION/   NBRAZBR46108

CARDERS
MEXICAN GREEN **CARDERS**. PRELIMINARY REPORT.   MGALLLX62399

CARE
SURVEY OF MINORITY-GROUP EMPLOYMENT AND PATIENT **CARE** IN PRIVATE HOSPITAL FACILITIES IN LOS-ANGELES
COUNTY. /CALIFORNIA/   GLOSACCND914

INTEGRATION ON HOSPITAL APPOINTMENTS AND IN HOSPITAL **CARE**. /CHICAGO ILLINOIS/   NCHICUL58202

DAY **CARE** SERVICES. FORM AND SUBSTANCE. /EMPLOYMENT-CONDITIONS/   WHOFFGL61846

PART-TIME **CARE**. THE DAY-CARE PROBLEM. /EMPLOYMENT-CONDITIONS/   WHOSLEM64540

CHILD **CARE** FACILITIES FOR WOMEN WORKERS. /EMPLOYMENT-CONDITIONS/   WINTELR58864

DAY **CARE** IN A CHANGING ECONOMY. /EMPLOYMENT-CONDITIONS/   WKEYSMD64894

THE NATION-S WORKING MOTHERS AND THE NEED FOR DAY **CARE**. ADDRESS. /EMPLOYMENT-CONDITIONS/   WKEYSMD65897

WORKING MOTHERS AND THEIR ARRANGEMENTS FOR **CARE** OF THEIR CHILDREN. /EMPLOYMENT-CONDITIONS/   WLAJEHC59922

CHILD **CARE** ARRANGEMENTS OF FULLTIME WORKING MOTHERS. /EMPLOYMENT-CONDITIONS/   WUSDHEW59171

CHILD **CARE** ARRANGEMENTS OF THE NATION-S WORKING MOTHERS. A PRELIMINARY REPORT.   WUSDHEW65172

CRITERIA FOR ASSESSING FEASIBILITY OF MOTHERS EMPLOYMENT AND ADEQUACY OF CHILD **CARE** PLANS.   WUSDHEW66173

CAREER
JOB AND **CAREER** DEVELOPMENT FOR THE POOR...THE HUMAN SERVICES. INCLUDES BIBLIOGRAPHY.   GGOLDGS66360

PLACEMENT AND **CAREER** COUNSELING AT PREDOMINANTLY NEGRO COLLEGES.   NBEAUAG66067

A **CAREER** BREAK FOR NON-WHITES.   NBUSIWX60147

INFORMAL FACTORS IN **CAREER** ACHIEVEMENT.   NDALTMX51247

CAREER PREPARATION AND EXPECTATIONS OF NEGRO COLLEGE STUDENTS.   NFICHJH66789

OCCUPATIONAL CHOICE AND THE TEACHING **CAREER**.   NGUBAEG59463

THE **CAREER** PATTERNS OF NEGRO LAWYERS IN LOUISIANA. /OCCUPATIONS/   NGUILBM60465

CAREER   (CONTINUATION)
AT WORK IN NORTH-CAROLINA TODAY. 48 CASE-REPORTS ON NORTH-CAROLINA NEGROES NOW EMPLOYED OR PREPARING
THEMSELVES FOR EMPLOYMENT...THEIR EDUCATION, JOB QUALIFICATIONS, AND CAREER ASPIRATIONS.   NNORTCGND933

NEGRO CAREER EXPECTATIONS.   NSEXTPX63117

CAREER PATTERNS OF TEACHERS IN NEGRO COLLEGES.   NTHOMDC58204

AFTER HIGH SCHOOL WHAT...HIGHLIGHTS OF A STUDY OF CAREER PLANS OF NEGRO AND WHITE RURAL YOUTH IN THREE
FLORIDA COUNTIES. /ASPIRATIONS/   NYOUMEG65390

SOCIAL ORIGINS AND CAREER PREPARATION AMONG FILIPINOS IN AMERICAN UNIVERSITIES.   OBELTAG61703

MEDICINE AS A CAREER FOR WOMEN. /OCCUPATIONS/   WAMERMW65607

AN INVERTED FACTOR ANALYSIS OF PERSONALITY DIFFERENCES BETWEEN CAREER AND HOMEMAKING-ORIENTED WOMEN.
/ASPIRATIONS/   WAVILDL64316

A STUDY OF ELEMENTARY SCHOOL TEACHER-S ATTITUDES TOWARD THE WOMAN PRINCIPAL AND TOWARD ELEMENTARY
PRINCIPALSHIP AS A CAREER. /DISCRIMINATION/   WBARTAK58629

THE ACHIEVEMENT MOTIVE IN WOMEN. A STUDY OF THE IMPLICATIONS FOR CAREER DEVELOPMENT.   WBARURX66453

THE RELATIONSHIP OF PARENTAL IDENTIFICATION TO SEX ROLE ACCEPTANCE IN MARRIED, SINGLE, CAREER AND
NON-CAREER WOMEN. /WORK-WOMEN-ROLE/   WBREYCH64654

CAREER GUIDANCE FOR GIRLS. /COUNSELING/   WCALDED60445

MODERN AMERICAN CAREER WOMEN. /OCCUPATIONS/   WCLYMEX59693

CHANGES IN CAREER ASPIRATIONS.   WCOLECX69695

ROLE CONCEPTION AND CAREER ASPIRATION. A STUDY OF IDENTITY IN NURSING.   WCORWRG61707

SOCIAL FACTORS WHICH AFFECT CAREER CHOICE IN PSYCHIATRIC NURSING.   WDOUGAM61740

ROLE EXPECTATIONS OF YOUNG WOMEN REGARDING MARRIAGE AND A CAREER. /ASPIRATIONS WORK-FAMILY-CONFLICT/   WEMPELT58751

CAREER DECISIONS AND PROFESSIONAL EXPECTATIONS OF NURSING-STUDENTS. /ASPIRATIONS/   WFOXXDJ61767

CAREER OPPORTUNITIES FOR WOMEN IN BUSINESS. /OCCUPATIONS/   WKINGAG63904

CHANGES IN SELECTED PERSONALITY CHARACTERISTICS AND PERSISTENCE IN THE CAREER CHOICES OF WOMEN ASSOCIATED
WITH A FOUR YEAR COLLEGE EDUCATION AT ONE OF THE COLLEGES OF THE CITY UNIVERSITY OF NEW-YORK.
/ASPIRATIONS/   WLEINMX64925

LIFE INSURANCE SELLING AS A CAREER FOR WOMEN. /OCCUPATIONS/   WLEITSF61926

FROM KITCHEN TO CAREER. /WORK-FAMILY-CONFLICT/   WLEWIAB65930

MARRIAGE AND CAREER CONFLICTS IN GIRLS AND YOUNG WOMEN. /WORK-FAMILY-CONFLICT/   WMATTEX60961

THE COUNSELOR AND GIRLS CAREER DEVELOPMENT. /COUNSELING/   WMATTEX63960

ATTITUDES TOWARD CAREER AND MARRIAGE AND THE DEVELOPMENT OF LIFE STYLES IN YOUNG WOMEN.
/WORK-FAMILY-CONFLICT/   WMATTEX64962

PERCEPTIONS OF ROLE CONFLICTS AND SELF CONFLICTS AMONG CAREER AND NON-CAREER COLLEGE EDUCATED WOMEN.
/WORK-FAMILY-CONFLICT/   WMORGDD62996

PSYCHOLOGICAL AND SOCIOLOGICAL FACTORS IN PREDICTION OF CAREER PATTERNS OF WOMEN. /ASPIRATIONS/   WMULVMC61080

PSYCHOLOGICAL AND SOCIOLOGICAL FACTORS IN PREDICTION OF CAREER PATTERNS FOR WOMEN. /ASPIRATIONS/   WMULVMC63006

REALITIES. EDUCATIONAL, ECONOMIC, LEGAL AND PERSONAL NEEDS OF CAREER WOMEN.   WPARKRX66049

CLIMBING A CAREER PYRAMID -- IN SKIRTS. /OCCUPATIONS/   WROEXAV64086

BARRIERS TO THE CAREER CHOICE OF ENGINEERING, MEDICINE, OR SCIENCE AMONG AMERICAN WOMEN. /OCCUPATIONS/   WROSSAS65091

SECOND CAREER. /WORK-FAMILY-CONFLICT NEW-YORK/   WSCHWJX60108

OCCUPATIONAL CHOICE AMONG CAREER ORIENTED COLLEGE WOMEN. /ASPIRATIONS/   WSIMPRL61115

CAREER DEVELOPMENT OF WOMEN. SOME PROPOSITIONS.   WTIEDDV59153

WORLD OF WORK CONFERENCE ON CAREER AND JOB OPPORTUNITIES, WASHINGTON, DC, JULY 1962.   WUSDLAB64242

EXPLODING THE MYTHS. EXPANDING EMPLOYMENT OPPORTUNITIES FOR CAREER WOMEN.   WUVCAEC66249

SOME CORRELATES OF HOMEMAKING VS CAREER PREFERENCE AMONG COLLEGE HOME ECONOMICS STUDENTS.
/WORK-FAMILY-CONFLICT/   WVETTLX64257

INTEREST AND VALUES OF CAREER AND HOME MAKING ORIENTED WOMEN.   WWAGMMX66761

THE COLLEGE GIRL LOOKS AHEAD TO HER CAREER OPPORTUNITIES.   WZAPOMW56280

CAREER-MARRIAGE
THE RELATIONSHIP OF SELECTED VARIABLES TO CAREER-MARRIAGE PLANS OF UNIVERSITY FRESHMAN WOMEN.
/WORK-FAMILY-CONFLICT/   WZISSCX62284

CAREER-MOTIVATED
INTEREST AND PERSONALITY CORRELATES OF CAREER-MOTIVATED AND HOMEMAKING-MOTIVATED COLLEGE WOMEN.
/ASPIRATIONS/   WHOYTDP58850

CAREER-SEEKING
IN SEARCH OF A FUTURE. A STUDY OF CAREER-SEEKING EXPERIENCES OF SELECTED NEGRO HIGH SCHOOL GRADUATES IN
WASHINGTON-DC WHICH WAS AN EFFORT TO PROVIDE KNOWLEDGE HELPFUL IN SOLVING ONE OF THE MOST CRITICAL
PROBLEMS FACING URBAN AMERICA TODAY.   NGRIEES63454

CAREERS
NEW CAREERS FOR THE POOR.   GPEARAX65099

AN EXPERIMENT IN RETRAINING UNEMPLOYED MEN FOR PRACTICAL NURSING CAREERS.   GPEIMSC66139

CAREERS FOR YOUTH.   MMEXIEC63441

CAREERS FOR NEGROES ON NEWSPAPERS. /OCCUPATIONS/   NAMERNG66018

CAREERS   (CONTINUATION)
    NEW OPPORTUNITIES FOR NEGROES...IN EDUCATION...IN CAREERS.   NCHANTX63190

    PROFITABLE CAREERS -- WITHOUT COLLEGE.   NEBONXX59318

    CAREERS FOR WOMEN IN SCIENCE. /OCCUPATIONS/   WBARBMS58627

    THE INTERRUPTION AND RESUMPTION OF WOMEN-S CAREERS.   WBARURX66457

    CAREERS AS CONCERNS OF BLUE-COLLAR GIRLS. /OCCUPATIONS/   WDAVIEX64721

    MARRIAGE AND CAREERS FOR GIRLS. /WORK-FAMILY-CONFLICT/   WGARFSH57774

    CAREERS FOR WOMEN IN RETAILING. /OCCUPATIONS/   WGROSSB59807

    EXECUTIVE CAREERS FOR WOMEN. /OCCUPATIONS/   WMAULFX61065

    CAREERS FOR WOMEN IN BIOLOGICAL SCIENCES. /OCCUPATIONS/   WMURPMC60009

    WOMEN IN SCIENTIFIC CAREERS. /OCCUPATIONS/   WNATLSF61022

    CAREERS AFTER FORTY. /WORK-FAMILY-CONFLICT/   WNIEMJX58033

    CAREERS FOR WOMEN AFTER MARRIAGE AND CHILDREN. /WORK-FAMILY-CONFLICT/   WONEIBP65043

    WOMEN-S ATTITUDES TOWARD CAREERS.   WSTEIAX59137

    HIGH SCHOOL GUIDANCE COUNSELOR-S PERCEPTIONS OF SELECTED CAREERS FOR WOMEN COLLEGE GRADUATES.   WSWOPMR63146

    POSITION CHOICES AND CAREERS. ELEMENTS OF A THEORY. /ASPIRATIONS/   WTIEDDV58154

    FEDERAL CAREERS FOR WOMEN.   WUSCISC61167

    GOVERNMENT CAREERS FOR WOMEN -- A STUDY.   WUSDLAB57198

CAROLINAS
    NEW HOPE FOR RURAL DIXIE. FIRMS IN CAROLINAS CREATE JOBS FOR NEGROES.   NEBONXX64317

    1966 EMPLOYMENT SURVEY IN THE TEXTILE INDUSTRY OF THE CAROLINAS.   NWALLPA66591

CARRIERS
    COMMON CARRIERS AND THE STATE FEPC.   GKOVAIX63025

CASE
    THE DISCRIMINATION CASE. /NEGRO PUERTO-RICAN SES/   CCOHEHX65917

    FEPC -- A CASE HISTORY IN PARLIAMENTARY MANEUVER.   GMASLWX46959

    PROGRESS WITHOUT FEDERAL COMPULSION. ARGUING THE CASE FOR COMPROMISE METHODS.   GNORTHR52122

    THE CASE FOR AN INCOME-GUARANTEE.   GTOBIJX66973

    A COMPANY CASE HISTORY. /INDUSTRY EEO/   GWITTHW64576

    THE DETRIBALIZATION OF THE NARRAGANSETT INDIANS. A CASE STUDY.   IBOISEX56886

    PERCEIVED OPPORTUNITIES, EXPECTATIONS, AND THE DECISION TO REMAIN ON RELOCATION. THE CASE OF THE NAVAHO
    INDIAN MIGRANT TO DENVER, COLORADO.   IGRAVTD65567

    CLASS AS AN EXPLANATION OF ETHNIC DIFFERENCES IN MOBILITY ASPIRATIONS -- THE CASE OF MEXICAN-AMERICANS. MHELLCS65415

    POVERTY. THE SPECIAL CASE OF THE NEGRO.   NBATCAB65061

    THE MOTOROLA CASE. /TESTING/   NFRENRL65385

    THE CASE AGAINST TOKENISM.   NKINGML62144

    THE NEGRO FAMILY. THE CASE FOR NATIONAL ACTION.   NMOYNDP65862

    NEGROES IN A WAR INDUSTRY. THE CASE OF SHIPBUILDING.   NNORTHR43942

    RACIAL DISCRIMINATION AND THE NLRB. THE HUGHES TOOL CASE, PART ONE.   NVIRGLR64017

    RACIAL DISCRIMINATION AND THE NLRB. THE HUGHES TOOL CASE, PART TWO.   NVIRGLR64018

    ACHIEVEMENT, CULTURE AND PERSONALITY. THE CASE OF THE JAPANESE-AMERICANS.   OCAUDWX61711

    THE CASE FOR THE WORKING MOTHER.   WCOTTDW65708

    DIGEST OF CASE STUDIES ON CONTINUITIES AND DISCONTINUITIES IN THE EMPLOYMENT-EDUCATION-FAMILY PATTERNS OF
    WOMEN-S LIVES.   WDELAPJ60224

    PANEL DISCUSSION. THE CASE FOR AND AGAINST THE EMPLOYMENT OF WOMEN. /OCCUPATIONS/   WHARRTW65824

    THE CASE AGAINST FULL-TIME MOTHERHOOD. /EMPLOYMENT/   WROSSAS65092

    SOME CHANGING ROLES OF WOMEN IN SUBURBIA. A SOCIAL ANTHROPOLOGICAL CASE STUDY. /WORK-FAMILY-CONFLICT/   WSCOFNE60109

    THE FEMALE LABOR-FORCE. A CASE STUDY IN THE INTERPRETATION OF HISTORICAL STATISTICS.   WSMUTRW60124

    THE CASE OF THE BATTLE-AXES. /EMPLOYMENT/   WWALSCM57266

CASE-REPORTS
    AT WORK IN INDUSTRY TODAY. 50 CASE-REPORTS ON NEGROES AT WORK.   NGENEEX64398

    AT WORK IN NORTH-CAROLINA TODAY. 48 CASE-REPORTS ON NORTH-CAROLINA NEGROES NOW EMPLOYED OR PREPARING
    THEMSELVES FOR EMPLOYMENT...THEIR EDUCATION, JOB QUALIFICATIONS, AND CAREER ASPIRATIONS.   NNORTCGND933

CASE-STUDIES
    PROGRESS TOWARD INTEGRATION. FOUR CASE-STUDIES. /EMPLOYMENT FEPC NEW-YORK/   NBACKSX59040

    NEGRO HIRING -- SOME CASE-STUDIES. /INDUSTRY/   NBAMBJJ49050

    CASE-STUDIES IN URBAN-LEAGUE METHODS.   NCOLUUL59227

CASE-STUDY
    EQUAL-OPPORTUNITIES BY LAW. A CASE-STUDY.   GDUNNDD63654

    INDUSTRY-S UNFINISHED BUSINESS. /CASE-STUDY/   GSOUTSE50324

CASE-STUDY (CONTINUATION)
A **CASE-STUDY** OF LATIN-AMERICAN UNIONIZATION IN AUSTIN, TEXAS.   MPARISF64452

  NEGRO PLATFORM WORKERS. /INDUSTRY **CASE-STUDY**/   NAMERCR45011

  NEGRO UNEMPLOYMENT. A **CASE-STUDY**.   NBAROHX63054

  CASE-STUDY OF A RIOT THE PHILADELPHIA STORY. /PENNSYLVANIA/   NBERSLE66078

  NEGRO UNEMPLOYMENT. A **CASE-STUDY**.   NBROWHX63894

  JOBS FOR NEGROES. ONE COMPANY-S ANSWER. /**CASE-STUDY** INDUSTRY/   NBUSIMX64142

  TWO PLANTS -- LITTLE-ROCK. /**CASE-STUDY** INDUSTRY ARKANSAS/   NECKAEW55319

  MONTHLY SUMMARY OF EVENTS AND TRENDS IN RACE-RELATIONS. /CINCINNATI OHIO **CASE-STUDY** UNION/   NFISKUX44357

  FAIR EMPLOYMENT IS GOOD BUSINESS AT G FOX OF HARTFORD. /**CASE-STUDY** CONNECTICUT/   NGREEMX48448

  ATTITUDES OF WHITE DEPARTMENT STORE EMPLOYEES TOWARD NEGRO CO-WORKERS. /**CASE-STUDY**/   NHARDJX52482

  NEGRO EMPLOYMENT IN THE BIRMINGHAM METROPOLITAN AREA. /ALABAMA **CASE-STUDY**/   NHAWLLT55502

  THE SELF-SURVEY OF THE PACKINGHOUSE UNION. A TECHNIQUE FOR EFFECTING CHANGE. /**CASE-STUDY**/   NHOPEJX53574

  NEGRO EMPLOYMENT IN THREE SOUTHERN PLANTS OF INTERNATIONAL HARVESTER COMPANY. /**CASE-STUDY**/   NHOPEJX55572

  DISCRIMINATION IN THE HIRING HALL. A **CASE-STUDY** OF PRESSURES TO PROMOTE INTEGRATION IN NEW-YORK-S BREWERY
  INDUSTRY.   NLANGGE59670

  RACIAL DIFFERENCES IN MIGRATION AND JOB-SEARCH. A **CASE-STUDY**.   NLURIMX66712

  SOME FACTORS INFLUENCING THE UPGRADING OF NEGROES IN THE SOUTHERN PETROLEUM REFINING INDUSTRY.
  /**CASE-STUDY**/   NMARSRX63748

  LOUISVILLE. SPECIAL REPORT. /**CASE-STUDY** KENTUCKY/   NMUSEBX64868

  MEMPHIS. SPECIAL REPORT. /**CASE-STUDY**/   NMUSEBX64869

  THE INTRODUCTION OF NEGROES INTO WHITE DEPARTMENTS. /**CASE-STUDY** INDUSTRY/   NPALMER55972

  ACCOMODATION BETWEEN NEGRO AND WHITE EMPLOYEES IN A WEST COAST AIRCRAFT INDUSTRY, 1942-1944.
  /**CASE-STUDY**/   NREEDBA47045

  ADMINISTERING CHANGES. A **CASE-STUDY** OF HUMAN-RELATIONS IN A FACTORY.   NRONKHC52129

  THE MAYOR AND THE FIRE CHIEF. THE FIGHT OVER INTEGRATING THE LOS-ANGELES FIRE DEPARTMENT. /CALIFORNIA
  CASE-STUDY/   NSHERFP59130

  APPEALS FROM DISCRIMINATION IN FEDERAL EMPLOYMENT. A **CASE-STUDY**.   NSHOSAX63131

  JOBS FOR NEGROES. SOME NORTH-SOUTH PLANT STUDIES. /**CASE-STUDY**/   NSTEEEH53174

  INTERNATIONAL-HARVESTER-S NON-DISCRIMINATION POLICY. /**CASE-STUDY**/   NUSDLAB54822

  NEGRO EMPLOYMENT IN THREE COMPANIES IN THE NEW-ORLEANS AREA. /**CASE-STUDY** LOUISIANA/   NUSDLAB55828

  PLAN FOR EQUAL-JOB-OPPORTUNITY AT LOCKHEED-AIRCRAFT-CORP. /INDUSTRY **CASE-STUDY**/   NUSDLAB61838

  THE EMPLOYED POOR. A **CASE-STUDY**. /WASHINGTON-DC/   NWILLCV65989

  THREE COMPANIES — NEW-ORLEANS AREA. /**CASE-STUDY** LOUISIANA/   NWISSHW55332

  PART-TIME WORKING MOTHERS -- A **CASE-STUDY**.   WWORTNB60245

CASES
PROCESSING EMPLOYMENT DISCRIMINATION **CASES**. /LEGISLATION/   GBLUMAW67117

  CASES ARE PEOPLE. AN INTERPRETATION OF THE PENNSYLVANIA FAIR-EMPLOYMENT-PRACTICE LAW.   GSHIREM58304

  NEGRO EMPLOYMENT IN BIRMINGHAM. THREE **CASES**. /ALABAMA/   NROWARL67091

  PREJUDICE IS NOT THE WHOLE STORY. EXAMINATION OF THREE **CASES** OF NEGRO UPGRADING IN TRACTION COMPANIES IN
  PHILADELPHIA, LOS-ANGELES AND CHICAGO. /PENNSYLVANIA CALIFORNIA ILLINOIS/   NWECKJE45308

  SOME CHARACTERISTICS OF PUBLIC ASSISTANCE **CASES** IN NEW-YORK CITY, AUGUST, 1959.   PNEWYDW60835

CASEWORK
RACE, NATIONALITY, AND RELIGION -- THEIR RELATIONSHIP TO APPOINTMENT POLICIES AND **CASEWORK**.   GHAGEDJ57752

  THE DISPLACED PERSON AND THE SOCIAL AGENCY. A STUDY OF THE **CASEWORK** PROCESS AND ITS RELATION TO IMMIGRANT
  ADJUSTMENT.   JCRYSDX58714

CASTE
CASTE, ECONOMY, AND VIOLENCE.   NDAVIAX45938

  CASTE AND CLASS IN A SOUTHERN TOWN.   NDOLLJX49281

  SOCIAL CLASS AND COLOR **CASTE** IN AMERICA.   NWARNWL62292

CASUALTIES
THE NEW NEGRO **CASUALTIES**. /OCCUPATIONS TEACHERS/   NARISJM65029

CATALYST
FIRST **CATALYST** ON CAMPUS CONFERENCE, PROCEEDINGS. /WORK-WOMEN-ROLE/   WCATAXX64683

CATEGORIES
NEGRO EMPLOYMENT IN THE FEDERAL GOVERNMENT BY CIVIL SERVICE REGION, STATE AND PAY **CATEGORIES**, JUNE 1962.   NPRESCD62012

CATTLE
DEVELOPMENT OF THE SAN-CARLOS APACHE **CATTLE** INDUSTRY. /CALIFORNIA/   IGETTHT58563

  THE SAN-CARLOS INDIAN **CATTLE** INDUSTRY. /CALIFORNIA/   IGETTHT63564

CAUSES
THE **CAUSES** OF POVERTY.   GTHURLC67972

  AN ECONOMICAL AND HISTORICAL ANALYSIS OF THE **CAUSES** OF VARIATION AMONG NORTHERN STANDARD METROPOLITAN

CAUSES (CONTINUATION)
AREAS IN PRODUCTIVITY OF NEGRO MEN IN 1949.   NBATCAB61060

HARD-CORE UNEMPLOYMENT IN DETROIT. **CAUSES** AND REMEDIES. /MICHIGAN/   NWACHHMND289

LONG-RANGE **CAUSES** AND CONSEQUENCES OF THE EMPLOYMENT OF MARRIED WOMEN.   WBLOORO65884

CENSUS
NEGROES AND MEXICAN-AMERICANS IN SOUTH AND EAST LOS-ANGELES. AN ANALYSIS OF A SPECIAL US **CENSUS** SURVEY OF
NOVEMBER 1965. /CALIFORNIA/   CCALDIR66168

UNITED STATES **CENSUS** OF AGRICULTURE. COLOR, RACE, AND TENURE OF FARM OPERATOR. GENERAL REPORT, VOLUME II.
/DEMOGRAPHY/   CUSBURC59382

GENERAL SOCIAL AND ECONOMIC CHARACTERISTICS. SUMMARY, US **CENSUS** OF 1960. /DEMOGRAPHY/   CUSBURC62374

CURRENT POPULATION REPORTS -- SPECIAL **CENSUS** OF CLEVELAND, OHIO. /DEMOGRAPHY/   CUSBURC65379

ETHNIC **CENSUS** OF EXAMINATION COMPETITORS, JAN-JUNE 1965, CALIFORNIA STATE PERSONNEL BOARD.   GCALSPB65551

ETHNIC **CENSUS** OF EXAMINATION COMPETITORS, JULY-DEC 1965, CALIFORNIA STATE-PERSONNEL-BOARD.   GCALSPB65552

REPORT ON AND ANALYSIS OF SECOND **CENSUS** OF CITY EMPLOYEES TO DETERMINE BASES FOR FUTURE PERSONNEL
DEVELOPMENTS. /DETROIT MICHIGAN/   GDETRCC66639

SENIOR CITIZENS AND HOW THEY LIVE. AN ANALYSIS OF 1960 **CENSUS** DATA. PART II. THE AGING NONWHITE AND HIS
HOUSING. /ECONOMIC-STATUS/   GUSHHFX63321

A **CENSUS** OF INDIANS IN LOS-ANGELES. /CALIFORNIA/   IPRICJA67606

POPULATION AND INCOME **CENSUS**. WIND-RIVER RESERVATION, WYOMING.   IUSDINT60655

THE EDUCATION OF THE SPANISH-SPEAKING IN THE SOUTHWEST -- AN ANALYSIS OF THE 1960 **CENSUS** MATERIALS.   MSAMCJX63469

THE ECONOMIC-STATUS OF NEGROES IN THE SAN-FRANCISCO OAKLAND BAY AREA. A REPORT BASED ON THE 1960 **CENSUS**
OF POPULATION. /CALIFORNIA/   NCALFES63172

ETHNIC **CENSUS** OF EXAMINATION COMPETITORS. REPORT OF EXAMINATIONS GIVEN JULY THROUGH DECEMBER, 1965,
SUMMARY. /TESTING CALIFORNIA/   NCALFPB66173

THE **CENSUS** OF NEGRO-OWNED BUSINESSES. /PHILADELPHIA PENNSYLVANIA OCCUPATIONS/   NDREXIT64295

THE UNEMPLOYMENT RATE AND GRADE LEVEL RELATIONSHIP IN CHICAGO AS REVEALED IN THE 1960 **CENSUS**. /ILLINOIS/   NHARGAJ65990

PHILADELPHIA-S PUERTO-RICAN POPULATION, WITH 1960 **CENSUS** DATA. /PENNSYLVANIA/   PPITTCH64844

CENSUS OF POPULATION. 1960, PUERTO-RICANS IN THE UNITED STATES.   PUSBURC63854

CENSUSES
IMPLICATIONS OF THE RECENT **CENSUSES** FOR PROFESSIONAL AGRICULTURAL WORKERS. /OCCUPATIONS/   GBEALCL61412

CENTER
STORM **CENTER** OF THE FIGHT -- FEPC.   GCONGDX50597

CLEVELAND-S ANNUAL JOB **CENTER** FOR COLLEGE GRADUATES.   NCOCKHW65218

EQUAL-EMPLOYMENT-OPPORTUNITY IN THE SUBURBAN SHOPPING **CENTER**. FACT OR FICTION. /MICHIGAN/   NMICFEP63777

CENTRAL
CENTRAL ROLE OF INTERGROUP AGENCIES IN THE LABOR-MARKET. CHANGING RESEARCH AND PERSONNEL REQUIREMENTS.   GHOPEJX61780

INCOME AND RELATED CHARACTERISTICS OF RURAL HOUSEHOLDS IN THE **CENTRAL** LOUISIANA MIXED FARMING AREA.   NBOLTBX60398

RESOURCE USE AND ADJUSTMENT. RURAL FAMILIES IN THE **CENTRAL** LOUISIANA MIXED FARMING AREA.   NBOLTBX61396

FARM INCOME PREDICTIONS FOR SMALL FARMS IN THE **CENTRAL** LOUISIANA MIXED FARMING AREA.   NBOLTBX62399

THE OCCUPATIONAL SITUATION OF **CENTRAL** HARLEM YOUTH.   NHOUSLX65577

ATTITUDES TOWARD WOMEN COLLEGE TEACHERS IN INSTITUTIONS OF HIGHER EDUCATION ACCREDITED BY THE NORTH
CENTRAL ASSOCIATION.   WBERWHD62475

CENTURY
THE ACCIDENTAL **CENTURY**. /TECHNOLOGICAL-CHANGE/   GHARRMX65597

FREEDOM TO THE FREE. **CENTURY** OF EMANCIPATION, 1863-1963.   GUSCOMC63398

A **CENTURY** OF CHANGE. NEGROES IN THE US ECONOMY, 1860-1960. /OCCUPATIONAL-PATTERNS/   NHAYEMX62506

THE PROGRESS OF THE NEGRO AFTER A **CENTURY** OF EMANCIPATION.   NLOGARW63046

A **CENTURY** OF STRUGGLE.   NPROGXX62059

ASSURING FREEDOM TO THE FREE. A **CENTURY** OF EMANCIPATION IN THE USA.   NROSEAM64290

WOMEN PHYSICIANS IN THE TWENTY-FIRST **CENTURY**. /OCCUPATIONS/   WFAYXMX66758

WOMAN-S **CENTURY** OF PROGRESS. IS IT TO END IN REGRESSION. /WORK-WOMAN-ROLE/   WMCKARC58946

A **CENTURY** OF HIGHER EDUCATION FOR AMERICAN WOMEN.   WNEWCMX59027

CERTIFICATIONS
REVIEW AND ANALYSIS OF CITY **CERTIFICATIONS** AND APPOINTMENTS. /BERKELEY CALIFORNIA/   GBERKCM64444

CHALLENGE
MEETING TODAYS **CHALLENGE** FOR EMPLOYMENT. /AMERICAN-INDIAN NEGRO MEXICAN-AMERICAN/   CARIZSE65403

EQUAL-EMPLOYMENT-OPPORTUNITY. A **CHALLENGE** TO THE EMPLOYMENT SERVICE.   GCASSFH66561

CIVIL-RIGHTS -- A NATIONAL **CHALLENGE**.   GHANNJA61988

CHALLENGE TO AFFLUENCE. /UNEMPLOYMENT/   GMYRDGX63035

CIVIL-RIGHTS. THE FACTS AND THE **CHALLENGE**.   GSLAIDX64316

MANPOWER. THE **CHALLENGE** OF THE 1960-S.   GUSDLAB60488

THE NEGRO **CHALLENGE** TO THE BUSINESS COMMUNITY. /INDUSTRY/   NGINZEX64408

CHALLENGE   (CONTINUATION)
A CHALLENGE TO NEGRO LEADERSHIP.   NJOHNJG60618

WASTED MANPOWER -- BERKELEY CHALLENGE AND OPPORTUNITY. WORKSHOP COSPONSORED WITH THE BERKELEY UNIFIED
SCHOOL-DISTRICT MARCH 15-16, 1963.   /CALIFORNIA/   NKENNVD63642

EMPLOYMENT ON MERIT. THE CONTINUING CHALLENGE TO BUSINESS, NEGRO-S ECONOMIC LOT.   NMORRJJ57854

THE NEW CHALLENGE TO LIBERALISM.   NTYLEGX63539

EDUCATION-S CHALLENGE TO AMERICAN NEGRO YOUTH.   NWOLFDP62336

THE SOCIAL REVOLUTION. CHALLENGE TO THE NATION. /CIVIL-RIGHTS/   NYOUNWM63600

THE CHALLENGE TO WOMEN.   /WORK-WOMAN-ROLE/   WFARBSM66755

CHALLENGES
MANPOWER DEVELOPMENT. CHARGES AND CHALLENGES. /TECHNOLOGICAL-CHANGE TRAINING/   GBOLIAC65528

CHANGES AND CHALLENGES IN THE 60-S. / INTEGRATION TECHNOLOGICAL-CHANGE   TEACHER/   NBRAGEW63312

CHALLENGES TO DEMOCRACY. /ECONOMY/   NWEAVRC63298

CHALLENGING
NEGRO MARKET. GROWING, CHANGING, CHALLENGING.   NBLACLE63493

CHAMPAIGN-URBANA
THE EMPLOYABILITY OF THE CHAMPAIGN-URBANA, ILLINOIS, NEGRO.   NBEAKJR64062

A STUDY OF THE NEGRO COMMUNITY IN CHAMPAIGN-URBANA, ILLINOIS.   NBINDAM61079

CHANCE
A FAIR CHANCE FOR ALL AMERICANS.   GNATLCL54041

WHAT NURSES NEED IS A CHANCE TO GROW. /OCCUPATIONAL-STATUS/   WGINSEX62786

SECOND CHANCE. NEW EDUCATION FOR WOMEN.   WRAUSEX62075

WOMAN-S DESTINY -- CHOICE OR CHANCE. REPORT OF CONFERENCE AT THE UNIVERSITY OF WASHINGTON, NOVEMBER
21-22, 1963.   WUSDLAB65233

CHANCES
PERCEIVED LIFE CHANCES IN THE OPPORTUNITY STRUCTURE. A STUDY OF A TRI-ETHNIC HIGH SCHOOL. MGUERCX62410

CHANGE
AMERICA-S POOR. REALITY AND CHANGE. /RETRAINING SKILLS UNEMPLOYMENT/   GAMERFX66674

ATTITUDE TOWARD OCCUPATIONAL CHANGE AS AN INDICATOR OF PROSPECTS FOR ADJUSTMENT.   GDUNKJE64653

TECHNOLOGY AND SOCIAL CHANGE.   GGINZEX64972

TWENTY YEARS OF ECONOMIC AND INDUSTRIAL CHANGE. /TECHNOLOGICAL-CHANGE EMPLOYMENT/   GGORDRA65675

CONTINUITY AND CHANGE IN SOUTHERN MIGRATION. /DEMOGRAPHY/   GHAMICH65757

DEMOGRAPHIC CHANGE AND RACIAL GHETTOS. THE CRISIS OF AMERICAN CITIES.   GHILLHX66691

POPULATION CHANGE AND POVERTY REDUCTION, 1947-1975.   GLAMPRJ66882

POPULATION CHANGE AND THE SUPPLY OF LABOR.   GLEBESX60276

CYBERNATION AND SOCIAL CHANGE. /TECHNOLOGICAL-CHANGE/   GMICADN64673

ADJUSTING TO CHANGE. /TECHNOLOGICAL-CHANGE/   GNATLCT66850

THE ROLE OF AGRICULTURAL TECHNOLOGY IN SOUTHERN SOCIAL CHANGE.   GRAPEAX46037

MOBILITY AND WORKER ADAPTATION TO ECONOMIC CHANGE IN THE US.   GTRAVHX63836

SEMINAR ON MANPOWER POLICY AND PROGRAM. CYBERNATION AND SOCIAL CHANGE.   GUSDLAB64982

THE AMERICAN INDIAN, PERSPECTIVES FOR STUDY OF SOCIAL CHANGE.   IEGGAFR66552

CHANGE AND RESISTANCE IN AN ISOLATED NAVAHO COMMUNITY.   ISHEPMX64618

PERSPECTIVES IN AMERICAN INDIAN CULTURE CHANGE.   ISPICEH61621

MENOMINEE WOMEN AND CULTURE CHANGE.   ISPINLS62622

OCCUPATIONAL CHANGE AMONG SPANISH-AMERICANS IN ATASCOSA-COUNTY AND SAN-ANTONIO, TEXAS.   MSKRARL66492

FACTORY FOLKWAYS. A STUDY OF INSTITUTIONAL STRUCTURE AND CHANGE.   NELLSJS52331

A CLIMATE OF CHANGE. THE NEW-HAVEN STORY. /CONNECTICUT/   NFARRGR65344

YOUTH IN THE GHETTO. A STUDY OF THE CONSEQUENCES OF POWERLESSNESS AND A BLUEPRINT FOR CHANGE. /NEW-YORK/   NHARLYO64485

A CENTURY OF CHANGE. NEGROES IN THE US ECONOMY, 1860-1960. /OCCUPATIONAL-PATTERNS/   NHAYEMX62506

A SOCIOLOGICAL INTERPRETATION OF SOCIAL CHANGE IN THE SOUTH.   NHEBERX46508

STATE LAWS AND THE NEGRO. SOCIAL CHANGE AND THE IMPACT OF LAW.   NHILLHX65545

THE ROLE OF LAW IN SECURING EQUAL-EMPLOYMENT-OPPORTUNITY. LEGAL POWERS AND SOCIAL CHANGE. NHILLHX66544

THE SELF-SURVEY OF THE PACKINGHOUSE UNION. A TECHNIQUE FOR EFFECTING CHANGE. /CASE-STUDY/ NHOPEJX53574

SOUTHERN RACIAL ATTITUDES. CONFLICT, AWARENESS AND POLITICAL CHANGE.   NMATTDR62758

THE SOUTH IN CONTINUITY AND CHANGE.   NMCKIJC65726

DEMOGRAPHIC ASPECTS OF CONTEMPORARY CHANGE. /SOUTH/   NPARRCH63975

THE IMPACT OF SOCIO-ECONOMIC CHANGE ON RACIAL GROUPS IN A RURAL SETTING.   NPELLRJ62981

INCOME, EMPLOYMENT STATUS AND CHANGE IN CALVERT COUNTY, MARYLAND.   NROHRWC58400

SOCIAL CHANGE AND THE NEGRO PROBLEM.   NROSEAM64296

CHANGE   (CONTINUATION)
THE AMERICAN NEGRO PROBLEM IN THE CONTEXT OF SOCIAL CHANGE.   NROSEAM65289

SOCIAL AND CULTURAL CHANGE IN THE PLANTATION AREA.   NRUBIMX54297

DEMOGRAPHIC AND ECONOMIC CHANGE IN THE SOUTH, 1940-1960.   NSPENJJ63716

HOUGH, CLEVELAND, OHIO -- A STUDY OF SOCIAL LIFE AND CHANGE.   NSUSSMB59192

CHANGE IN THE STATUS OF THE NEGRO IN AMERICAN SOCIETY.   NWALKHJ57291

DESEGREGATION IN AMERICAN SOCIETY. THE RECORD OF A GENERATION OF CHANGE.   NYINGJM63345

THE PUERTO-RICAN WORKER CONFRONTS THE COMPLEX URBAN SOCIETY -- A PRESCRIPTION FOR CHANGE.   PCARDLA67874

MIGRANTS AND CULTURE CHANGE.   PPAULIX55843

CHANGE AND CHOICE FOR THE COLLEGE WOMAN. /WORK-WOMAN-ROLE/   WAAUWJX62601

VALUE CHANGE IN COLLEGE WOMEN. /WORK-WOMEN-ROLE/   WBROWDR62658

THE IMPACT OF CULTURAL CHANGE ON WOMEN-S POSITION. /BLUE-COLLAR ASPIRATIONS/   WKONOGX66913
CHANGES
CHANGES IN THE LABOR-FORCE PARTICIPATION OF THE OLDER WORKER.   GHAUSPM54764

MIGRATORY FARM WORKERS IN THE ATLANTIC COAST STREAM. I. CHANGES IN NEW-YORK, 1953 AND 1957.   GLARSOF60406

GEOGRAPHIC CHANGES IN US EMPLOYMENT FROM 1950 TO 1960.   GMANOSP63855

CHANGES IN THE NUMBER AND COMPOSITION OF THE POOR. /DEMOGRAPHY/   GMILLHP65656

RACIAL CHANGES IN METROPOLITAN AREAS, 1950-1960. /DEMOGRAPHY/   GSCHNLF63288

MIGRATORY WORKERS IN NEW-YORK, CHANGES, 1953, 1957, AND 1958.   GSHAREF59428

PROJECTED CHANGES IN THE OCCUPATIONAL STRUCTURE OF THE LABOR-FORCE. IMPLICATIONS FOR PUBLIC WELFARE.   GSIFFHX64105

INDIAN AFFAIRS, A STUDY OF THE CHANGES IN POLICY OF THE UNITED STATES TOWARD INDIANS.   ITYLESL64634

ANALYSIS OF POPULATION CHANGES IN NEW-MEXICO COUNTIES.   MPIERGK61457

CHANGES IN PUBLIC AND PRIVATE LANGUAGE AMONG SPANISH-SPEAKING MIGRANTS TO AN INDUSTRIAL CITY.   MSCHETJ65481

CHANGES AND CHALLENGES IN THE 60-S. /INTEGRATION TECHNOLOGICAL-CHANGE TEACHER/   NBRAGEW63312

CHANGES IN NONWHITE EMPLOYMENT 1960-1966.   NCAMPJT66010

CHANGES IN OCCUPATIONS AS THEY AFFECT THE NEGRO.   NEDWAGF64323

CHANGES IN THE AMERICAN OCCUPATIONAL-STRUCTURE AND OCCUPATIONAL GAINS OF NEGROES DURING THE 1940-S.   NGLENND62422

SOME CHANGES IN THE RELATIVE STATUS OF AMERICAN NON-WHITES, 1940 TO 1960. /INCOME OCCUPATIONAL-STATUS
EDUCATION/   NGLENND63421

PERSONNEL PRACTICES AND WARTIME CHANGES. /EMPLOYMENT/   NHAASFJ46548

CHANGES IN THE SOCIAL STRATIFICATION OF THE SOUTH.   NHEBERX56507

EDUCATIONAL CHANGES AFFECTING AMERICAN NEGROES.   NLOGARW64704

ADMINISTERING CHANGES. A CASE-STUDY OF HUMAN-RELATIONS IN A FACTORY.   NRONKHO52129

RACIAL CHANGES IN METROPOLITAN AREAS, 1950-1960. /DEMOGRAPHY MIGRATION/   NSCHNLF65109

CHANGES IN THE CONTEMPORARY SOUTH.   NSINDAX64141

ASSIMILATION OF CHINESE IN AMERICA. CHANGES IN ORIENTATION AND SOCIAL PERCEPTIONS.   OFONGSL65722

CHINESE IMMIGRATION AND POPULATION CHANGES SINCE 1940.   OLEEXRX57740

CHANGES IN CAREER ASPIRATIONS.   WCOLECX69695

SOME IMPLICATIONS ON CURRENT CHANGES IN SEX ROLE PATTERNS. /WORK-WOMAN-ROLE/   WHARTRE60828

CHANGES IN SELECTED PERSONALITY CHARACTERISTICS AND PERSISTENCE IN THE CAREER CHOICES OF WOMEN ASSOCIATED
WITH A FOUR YEAR COLLEGE EDUCATION AT ONE OF THE COLLEGES OF THE CITY UNIVERSITY OF NEW-YORK.
/ASPIRATIONS/   WLEINMX64925
CHANGING
THE NEWCOMERS. NEGROES AND PUERTO-RICANS IN A CHANGING METROPOLIS   CHANDOX59481

CHANGING PATTERNS OF PREJUDICE. /NEGRO PUERTO-RICAN ORIENTAL AMERICAN-INDIAN/   CMARRAJ62055

THE CHANGING STATUS OF NEGRO WOMEN WORKERS.   CUSDLAB64072

JOBS, WAGES AND CHANGING TECHNOLOGY.   GARONRL65747

THE AMERICAN LABOR-FORCE. ITS GROWTH AND CHANGING COMPOSITION. /DEMOGRAPHY/   GBANCGX58417

CHANGING COMPOSITION OF THE AMERICAN WORK-FORCE.   GCOOPSX59928

COUNSELOR-S VIEWS ON CHANGING MANAGEMENT POLICIES.   GCOXXTX63618

CHANGING EMPHASIS IN OCCUPATIONAL TEST DEVELOPMENT.   GDVORBJ65650

THE ROLE OF THE UNITED STATES EMPLOYMENT-SERVICE IN A CHANGING ECONOMY.   GHABEWX64649

CENTRAL ROLE OF INTERGROUP AGENCIES IN THE LABOR-MARKET. CHANGING RESEARCH AND PERSONNEL REQUIREMENTS.   GHOPEJX61780

THE ADAPTATION OF LABOR RESOURCES TO CHANGING NEEDS. /MOBILITY/   GLESTRA66532

THE LABOR-FORCE UNDER CHANGING INCOME AND EMPLOYMENT.   GLONGCX58047

THE FARM WORKER IN A CHANGING AGRICULTURE. PART I IN A SERIES ON TECHNOLOGICAL-CHANGE AND FARM LABOR USE,
KERN-COUNTY, CALIFORNIA, 1961.   GMETZWH64387

JOBS, 1960-1970. THE CHANGING PATTERN. /EMPLOYMENT-TRENDS/   GNEWYSE60108

THE **CHANGING** ECONOMIC BACKGROUND OF AMERICAN RACE-RELATIONS.   GROSEAW50288

CHANGING PATTERNS IN EMPLOYMENT OF NONWHITE WORKERS.   GRUSSJL66269

THE **CHANGING** STRUCTURE OF UNEMPLOYMENT. AN ECONOMETRIC STUDY.   GTHURLC65970

FARM LABOR ADJUSTMENTS TO **CHANGING** TECHNOLOGY.   GTOLLGS67974

EDUCATION FOR A **CHANGING** WORLD OF WORK. /YOUTH/   GUSDHEW63834

THE **CHANGING** PATTERN IN EMPLOYMENT. /EQUAL-EMPLOYMENT-OPPORTUNITY/   GWALLLM63520

WELFARE CRITERIA AND **CHANGING** TASTES.   GWECKRS62987

SOME PROBLEMS INVOLVED IN THE **CHANGING** STATUS OF THE AMERICAN INDIAN.   IBARNML56534

THE ROLE OF WOMEN IN A **CHANGING** NAVAHO SOCIETY.   IHAMALS57985

THE **CHANGING** ROLE OF THE INDIAN IN ARIZONA.   IKELLWH58577

CHIPPEWA ADOLESCENTS. A **CHANGING** GENERATION.   IMILLFC64590

OUR **CHANGING** ELITE COLLEGES. /EDUCATION/   JBLOOLX60705

CHANGING PATTERNS IN AGRICULTURAL PRODUCTIONS, WEST-VIRGINIA, 1920-1950. /OCCUPATIONS/   NANGLRA54254

NEGRO MARKET. GROWING, **CHANGING**, CHALLENGING.   NBLACLE63493

THE PERSONNEL JOB IN A **CHANGING** WORLD. /INDUSTRY/   NBLOOJW64093

THE NEGRO-S **CHANGING** PLACE IN SOUTHERN AGRICULTURE.   NCHRIDE58206

SOUTHERN ECONOMIC DEVELOPMENT AS REVEALED BY THE **CHANGING** STRUCTURE OF EMPLOYMENT.   NDUNNES62309

THE **CHANGING** ECONOMIC STATUS OF THE MISSISSIPPI NEGRO.   NEATHBJ64314

EDUCATIONAL IMPERATIVE. THE NEGRO IN THE **CHANGING** SOUTH.   NGOLDFH63429

CHANGING OCCUPATIONAL-STATUS OF NEGRO EDUCATION.   NHARENX62483

CHANGING STRUCTURES OF WHITE-NEGRO RELATIONS IN THE SOUTH.   NHIMEJS51552

CHANGING SOCIAL-ROLES IN THE NEW SOUTH.   NHIMEJS62998

EQUAL-EMPLOYMENT-OPPORTUNITY. **CHANGING** PROBLEMS, CHANGING TECHNIQUES.   NHOPEJX63568

EQUAL-EMPLOYMENT-OPPORTUNITY. CHANGING PROBLEMS, **CHANGING** TECHNIQUES.   NHOPEJX63568

THE EFFECT OF A **CHANGING** AGRICULTURAL PATTERN ON NEGRO FARMERS OF SOUTH-CAROLINA.   NHURSRL56253

THE **CHANGING** STATUS OF THE NEGRO IN SOUTHERN AGRICULTURE.   NJONELW50623

CHANGING PATTERNS OF NEGRO EMPLOYMENT. /OCCUPATIONAL-PATTERNS/   NKIFEAX64649

NEGROES IN A **CHANGING** LABOR-MARKET. /UNEMPLOYMENT/   NKILLCC67653

THE **CHANGING** NEGRO FAMILY.   NLEWIHX60690

THE PLACE OF THE NEGRO FARMER IN THE **CHANGING** ECONOMY OF THE COTTON SOUTH.   NNEALEE50905

LABOR-FORCE AND DEMOGRAPHIC FACTORS AFFECTING THE **CHANGING** RELATIVE STATUS OF THE AMERICAN NEGRO.
1940-1950.   NPHILWM57997

CHANGING EMPLOYMENT PATTERNS OF NEGROES, 1920-1950.   NPRESHB62125

CHANGING CHARACTERISTICS OF THE NEGRO POPULATION.   NPRICDO65018

THE **CHANGING** COLOR COMPOSITION OF METROPOLITAN AREAS. /DEMOGRAPHY/   NSHARHX62125

THE **CHANGING** OCCUPATIONAL STRUCTURE OF THE SOUTH.   NSIMPRL65140

THE **CHANGING** NUMBER AND DISTRIBUTION OF THE AGED NEGRO POPULATION OF THE UNITED STATES. /DEMOGRAPHY/   NSMITLT58145

THE **CHANGING** CHARACTER OF NEGRO MIGRATION. /DEMOGRAPHY/   NTAEUKE65194

CHANGING EMPLOYMENT PRACTICES IN THE CONSTRUCTION INDUSTRY. EXPERIENCE REPORT 102.   NUSCONM65233

THE **CHANGING** STRUCTURE OF THE AMERICAN CITY AND THE NEGRO.   NWEAVRC64299

AMERICAN WOMEN. THE **CHANGING** IMAGE. /WORK-WOMEN-ROLE/   WCASSBB62682

THE **CHANGING** STATUS OF WOMEN.   WCHICRC62689

REVOLUTION WITHOUT IDEOLOGY. THE **CHANGING** PLACE OF WOMEN IN AMERICA. /WORK-WOMEN-ROLE/   WDEGLCN64727

COUNSELING IMPLICATIONS OF WOMAN-S **CHANGING** ROLE.   WGASSGZ59775

THE **CHANGING** PATTERNS OF WOMEN-S WORK. SOME PSYCHOLOGICAL CORRELATES.   WGINZEX58784

CHANGING PATTERNS IN WOMEN-S LIVES IN 1960. /WORK-WOMAN-ROLE/   WHAWKAL60834

CHANGING VALUES IN COLLEGE. /WORK-WOMAN-ROLE/   WJACOPE57877

THE **CHANGING** STATUS OF THE SOUTHERN WOMAN. /WORK-WOMAN-ROLE/   WJOHNGG65884

DAY CARE IN A **CHANGING** ECONOMY. /EMPLOYMENT-CONDITIONS/   WKEYSMD64894

CHANGING REALITIES IN WOMEN-S LIVES. /WORK-WOMAN-ROLE/   WKEYSMD65893

WOMEN-S **CHANGING** ROLE IN THE US EMPLOYMENT MARKET.   WMUNTEE56007

WOMEN-S **CHANGING** ROLES THROUGH THE LIFE CYCLE.   WNEUGBL59025

THE FEMALE LABOR-FORCE IN THE UNITED STATES. FACTORS GOVERNING ITS GROWTH AND **CHANGING** COMPOSITION.   WOPPEVK66096

THE **CHANGING** ROLE OF COLLEGE WOMEN. A BIBLIOGRAPHY. /WORK-WOMAN-ROLE/   WSCHWJX62106

SOME **CHANGING** ROLES OF WOMEN IN SUBURBIA. A SOCIAL ANTHROPOLOGICAL CASE STUDY. /WORK-FAMILY-CONFLICT/   WSCOFNE60109

CHANGING   (CONTINUATION)

THE CHANGING WOMAN WORKER. A STUDY OF THE FEMALE LABOR-FORCE IN NEW-JERSEY AND IN THE NATION FROM 1940 TO 1958.
WSMITGM60120

UNIONS AND THE CHANGING STATUS OF WOMEN WORKERS.
WUSDLABND224

THE CHANGING ROLE OF WOMEN IN OUR CHANGING SOCIETY.
WUSDLAB62253

THE CHANGING ROLE OF WOMEN IN OUR CHANGING SOCIETY.
WUSDLAB62253

WOMEN TELEPHONE WORKERS AND CHANGING TECHNOLOGY.
WUSDLAB63239

WISCONSIN GOVERNOR-S CONFERENCE ON THE CHANGING STATUS OF WOMEN, JAN 31-FEB 1 1964.
WUSDLAB65232

CHANGING CULTURAL CONCEPTS IN WOMEN-S LIVES. /WORK-WOMAN-ROLE/
WUSEERH64255

HOW WOMEN-S ROLE IN US IS CHANGING.
WUSNEWR66245

THE EDUCATION OF WOMEN AND GIRLS IN A CHANGING SOCIETY. A SELECTED BIBLIOGRAPHY WITH ANNOTATIONS.
WWIGNTX65267

CHANGING PROFILE OF THE NATION-S WORK-FORCE.
WWIRTWW63271

CHARACTER

THE CHANGING CHARACTER OF NEGRO MIGRATION. /DEMOGRAPHY/
NTAEUKE65194

CHARACTERISTICS

CHARACTERISTICS OF RETRAINING APPLICANTS. /CALIFORNIA NEGRO MEXICAN-AMERICAN WOMEN/
CCALDEM66166

RACIAL CHARACTERISTICS, MDTA TRAINEES, SAN-FRANCISCO. /CALIFORNIA NEGRO MEXICAN-AMERICAN/
CELTOEX63332

ECONOMIC, SOCIAL, AND DEMOGRAPHIC CHARACTERISTICS OF SPANISH-AMERICAN WAGE WORKERS ON US FARMS. /PUERTO-RICAN MEXICAN-AMERICAN/
CFRIERE63805

EMPLOYMENT AND PERSONAL CHARACTERISTICS. EMPLOYMENT BY AGE, RACE, NATIVITY, EDUCATION, MARITAL-STATUS, HOUSEHOLD RELATIONSHIPS, ETC. /DEMOGRAPHY/
CUSBURC53372

GENERAL SOCIAL AND ECONOMIC CHARACTERISTICS. SUMMARY, US CENSUS OF 1960. /DEMOGRAPHY/
CUSBURC62374

CHARACTERISTICS OF PROFESSIONAL WORKERS. /DEMOGRAPHY/
CUSBURC63167

CHARACTERISTICS OF TEACHERS. /DEMOGRAPHY/
CUSBURC63168

EMPLOYMENT-STATUS AND WORK CHARACTERISTICS. STATISTICS ON THE RELATION BETWEEN EMPLOYMENT AND SOCIAL AND ECONOMIC CHARACTERISTICS. /DEMOGRAPHY/
CUSBURC63170

EMPLOYMENT-STATUS AND WORK CHARACTERISTICS. STATISTICS ON THE RELATION BETWEEN EMPLOYMENT AND SOCIAL AND ECONOMIC CHARACTERISTICS. /DEMOGRAPHY/
CUSBURC63170

OCCUPATIONAL CHARACTERISTICS. DATA ON AGE, RACE, EDUCATION, WORK EXPERIENCE, INCOME, ETC. FOR WORKERS IN EACH OCCUPATION.
CUSBURC63177

PERSONS BY FAMILY CHARACTERISTICS. FAMILY MEMBERS BY SOCIAL, ECONOMIC AND HOUSING CHARACTERISTICS OF FAMILIES. /DEMOGRAPHY/
CUSBURC63180

PERSONS BY FAMILY CHARACTERISTICS. FAMILY MEMBERS BY SOCIAL, ECONOMIC AND HOUSING CHARACTERISTICS OF FAMILIES. /DEMOGRAPHY/
CUSBURC63180

POPULATION AND LABOR-FORCE CHARACTERISTICS OF FIVE SOUTHEASTERN PENNSYLVANIA COUNTIES.
GANDEBXND391

CHARACTERISTICS OF THE U.S. POPULATION BY FARM AND NON-FARM ORIGIN.
GBEALCL64423

CHARACTERISTICS OF THE POPULATION OF HIRED FARMWORKER HOUSEHOLDS. /ECONOMIC-STATUS/
GBOWLGK65424

CHARACTERISTICS, RESOURCES, AND INCOMES OF RURAL HOUSEHOLDS, PIEDMONT AREA, SOUTH-CAROLINA.
GBURCTA62408

CHARACTERISTICS OF SCHOOL DROPOUTS AND HIGH SCHOOL GRADUATES, FARM AND NONFARM, 1960.
GCOWHJD64419

THE EMPLOYED POOR. THEIR CHARACTERISTICS AND OCCUPATIONS.
GCUMMLD65623

STUDY OF OCCUPATIONAL CHARACTERISTICS OF NON-WHITES IN THE EAST BATON-ROUGE AREA. /LOUISIANA/
GHARRWRND760

ILLINOIS JOB SEEKERS SURVEY. EDUCATION, SKILLS, LENGTH OF UNEMPLOYMENT, AND PERSONAL CHARACTERISTICS.
GILLIDI62004

CHARACTERISTICS OF FARM WORKERS AS RELATED TO STABILIZATION OF THE WORK FORCE. /MIGRANT-WORKERS/
GMETZWH62504

MARITAL AND FAMILY CHARACTERISTICS OF WORKERS, MARCH 1963.
GPERRVC64168

THE SOCIO-ECONOMIC AND PHYSICAL CHARACTERISTICS OF THE VARIOUS NEIGHBORHOODS IN PUEBLO. /COLORADO/
GPUEBRP65459

RESOURCE CHARACTERISTICS AND UTILIZATION AND LEVEL OF LIVING ITEMS, RURAL HOUSEHOLDS, NORTH AND WEST FLORIDA, 1956.
GREUSLA60391

FAMILY INCOME AND RELATED CHARACTERISTICS AMONG LOW-INCOME COUNTIES AND STATES.
GRODDAL64241

FAMILY CHARACTERISTICS OF WORKERS, 1959.
GSCHIJX60283

MARITAL AND FAMILY CHARACTERISTICS OF WORKERS, MARCH 1960.
GSCHIJX61284

MARITAL AND FAMILY CHARACTERISTICS OF WORKERS, MARCH 1961.
GSCHIJX62285

MARITAL AND FAMILY CHARACTERISTICS OF WORKERS, MARCH 1962.
GSCHIJX63286

CHARACTERISTICS OF THE POPULATION OF HIRED FARMWORKER HOUSEHOLDS.
GUSDAGR65422

FAMILY CHARACTERISTICS OF THE LONG TERM UNEMPLOYED. A REPORT ON A STUDY OF CLAIMANTS UNDER THE TEMPORARY EXTENDED UNEMPLOYMENT COMPENSATION PROGRAM, 1961-2.
GUSDLAB61445

CHARACTERISTICS OF 6000 WHITE AND NONWHITE PERSONS ENROLLED IN MANPOWER-DEVELOPMENT-AND-TRAINING-ACT TRAINING.
GUSDLAB63197

FAMILY CHARACTERISTICS OF THE LONG-TERM UNEMPLOYED.
GUSDLAB63762

MARITAL AND FAMILY CHARACTERISTICS OF WORKERS, MARCH 1964.
GUSDLAB64201

UTE INDIAN SURVEY -- PRELIMINARY REPORT, SOCIAL AND ECONOMIC CHARACTERISTICS.
IBRIGYUND442

POPULATION CHARACTERISTICS, LIVING CONDITIONS AND INCOME OF INDIAN FAMILIES, NORTHERN-CHEYENNE RESERVATION, JULY, 1961.
IUSDINT63656

CHARACTERISTICS   (CONTINUATION)
  POPULATION CHARACTERISTICS, LIVING CONDITIONS, AND INCOME OF INDIAN FAMILIES, FORT-PECK RESERVATION,
  1951-1961.   IUSDINT63657

  POPULATION CHARACTERISTICS, LIVING CONDITIONS AND INCOMES OF INDIAN FAMILIES, FORT-BELKNAP RESERVATION. IUSDINT63658

  POPULATION CHARACTERISTICS, LIVING CONDITIONS AND INCOMES OF INDIAN FAMILIES, ROCKY-BAY-S RESERVATION.   IUSDINT63659

  SOCIAL CHARACTERISTICS OF AMERICAN JEWS.   JGLAZNX60726

  DEMOGRAPHIC CHARACTERISTICS OF AMERICAN JEWS.   JGOLDNX62727

  FAMILY COMPOSITION AND CHARACTERISTICS OF AN ECONOMICALLY DEPRIVED CROSS-CULTURAL ROCKY-MOUNTAIN AREA.   MANDRWH66359

  DEMOGRAPHIC CHARACTERISTICS.   MBARRDN66701

  ECONOMIC, SOCIAL AND DEMOGRAPHIC CHARACTERISTICS OF SPANISH-AMERICAN WAGE WORKERS ON US FARMS.   MFRIERE63394

  SOME CHARACTERISTICS OF SPANISH-NAME TEXANS AND FOREIGN LATIN-AMERICANS IN TEXAS HIGHER EDUCATION.   MRENNRR57462

  SOCIAL AND ATTITUDINAL CHARACTERISTICS OF SPANISH-SPEAKING MIGRANT AND EX-MIGRANT WORKERS IN THE
  SOUTHWEST.   MULIBHX66503

  THE CHARACTERISTICS OF THE SUPPLY OF NEGROES FOR PROFESSIONAL OCCUPATIONS.   NANDERW65024

  SOME DEMOGRAPHIC CHARACTERISTICS OF RURAL YOUTH.   NBEEGJA63072

  INCOME AND RELATED CHARACTERISTICS OF RURAL HOUSEHOLDS IN THE CENTRAL LOUISIANA MIXED FARMING AREA.   NBOLTBX60398

  A COMPARISON OF THE SOCIAL CHARACTERISTICS AND EDUCATIONAL ASPIRATIONS OF NORTHERN, LOWER-CLASS, NEGRO
  PARENTS WHO ACCEPTED AND DECLINED AN OPPORTUNITY FOR INTEGRATED EDUCATION FOR THEIR CHILDREN.   NCAGLLT66904

  CHARACTERISTICS OF THE LOWER-BLUE-COLLAR CLASS.SOCIO-ECONOMIC/   NCOHEAK63219

  SOME PERSONALITY CHARACTERISTICS OF SOUTHERN NEGRO STUDENTS.   NGROSMM57462

  SOME CHARACTERISTICS OF STUDENTS FROM POVERTY BACKGROUNDS ATTENDING PREDOMINANTLY NEGRO COLLEGES IN THE
  DEEP SOUTH.   NGURIPX66468

  ACHIEVEMENT MOTIVATION CHARACTERISTICS OF NEGRO COLLEGE FRESHMEN.   NHARREC59492

  DIFFERENTIAL CHARACTERISTICS OF SUPERIOR AND UNSELECTED NEGRO COLLEGE STUDENTS.   NJENKMD48608

  CHARACTERISTICS OF THE AMERICAN NEGRO.   NKLINOX44656

  A REPORT ON THE CHARACTERISTICS OF MICHIGAN-S NON-WHITE POPULATION.   NMICCRC65773

  CHARACTERISTICS OF NEGRO COLLEGE CHIEF LIBRARIANS. /OCCUPATIONS/   NPOLLFM64005

  CHARACTERISTICS OF NEGRO EMPLOYMENT IN FEDERAL AGENCIES IN ATLANTA, GEORGIA.   NPRESCP60016

  CHANGING CHARACTERISTICS OF THE NEGRO POPULATION.   NPRICDO65018

  SOCIAL CHARACTERISTICS OF HIGH SCHOOL SENIORS IN URBAN NEGRO HIGH SCHOOLS IN TWO STATES.   NSMITBF56147

  PERSONAL AND ON-THE-JOB CHARACTERISTICS RELATED TO NEGRO PERCEPTIONS OF DISCRIMINATION.   NSOLDHX56152

  DEMOGRAPHIC CHARACTERISTICS OF THE NEGRO POPULATION IN THE UNITED STATES.   NVALIPX63279

  SOME CHARACTERISTICS OF PUBLIC ASSISTANCE CASES IN NEW-YORK CITY, AUGUST, 1959.   PNEWYDW60835

  CHARACTERISTICS OF POPULATION AND LABOR IN NEW-YORK STATE, 1956 AND 1957. PUERTO-RICANS IN NEW-YORK CITY. PNEWYSE60839

  RELATIONS AMONG MATERNAL EMPLOYMENT INDICES AND DEVELOPMENTAL CHARACTERISTICS OF CHILDREN.
  /WORK-FAMILY-CONFLICT/   WBURCLG61665

  A SURVEY OF THE SOCIAL AND OCCUPATIONAL CHARACTERISTICS OF A METROPOLITAN NURSE. COMPLEMENT.
  /OCCUPATIONAL-DISTRIBUTION/   WDEUTIX56730

  A SURVEY OF THE SOCIAL AND OCCUPATIONAL CHARACTERISTICS OF A METROPOLITAN NURSE COMPLEMENT.   WDEUTIX57369

  CHANGES IN SELECTED PERSONALITY CHARACTERISTICS AND PERSISTENCE IN THE CAREER CHOICES OF WOMEN ASSOCIATED
  WITH A FOUR YEAR COLLEGE EDUCATION AT ONE OF THE COLLEGES OF THE CITY UNIVERSITY OF NEW-YORK.
  /ASPIRATIONS/   WLEINMX64925

  CHARACTERISTICS OF WOMEN-S COLLEGE STUDENTS.   WROWEFB64095

  TODAY-S BUSINESS WOMAN. HER CHARACTERISTICS, HER NEED FOR FURTHER EDUCATION, HER FUTURE IN MANAGEMENT.
  /OCCUPATIONS/   WTHOMMH63152

  FAMILY CHARACTERISTICS OF WORKING WIVES.   WUSBURC59169

  EMPLOYMENT AND CHARACTERISTICS OF WOMEN ENGINEERS. /OCCUPATIONS/   WUSDLAB56989

CHARGES
  INTERIM REPORT TO THE MAYOR ON ITS INQUIRY INTO CHARGES OF RACIAL BIAS IN THE CITY BUILDING AND
  CONSTRUCTION INDUSTRY. /NEW-YORK NEGRO PUERTO-RICAN/   CNEWYCO64917

  MANPOWER DEVELOPMENT. CHARGES AND CHALLENGES. /TECHNOLOGICAL-CHANGE TRAINING/   GBOLIAC65528

  INVESTIGATION OF CHARGES OF DISCRIMINATORY PRACTICES IN THE NEW-YORK STATE-EMPLOYMENT-SERVICE.   GNEWYSA59083

  REPORT OF INQUIRY CONCERNING CHARGES OF DISCRIMINATING PRACTICES IN THE NEW-YORK STATE THRUWAY AUTHORITY. GNEWYSB64104

  A COMPARISON OF TUITION-AND-FEE CHARGES IN NEGRO INSTITUTIONS WITH CHARGES IN INSTITUTIONS OF THE
  SOUTHEAST AND OF THE NATION. 1962-1963. /EDUCATION/   NDAMILX64127

  A COMPARISON OF TUITION-AND-FEE CHARGES IN NEGRO INSTITUTIONS WITH CHARGES IN INSTITUTIONS OF THE
  SOUTHEAST AND OF THE NATION. 1962-1963. /EDUCATION/   NDAMILX64127

CHARLOTTE
  WORKERS WANTED. A STUDY OF EMPLOYERS HIRING POLICIES, PREFERENCES, AND PRACTICES IN NEW-HAVEN AND
  CHARLOTTE. /CONNECTICUT NORTH-CAROLINA/   NNOLAEW49928

  CHARLOTTE. /NORTH-CAROLINA/   NWATTPX64294

CHARTS
  A COMPILATION OF STATISTICAL DATA, CHARTS AND OTHER RESOURCE MATERIAL FOR CONFERENCE PARTICIPANTS.

CHARTS   (CONTINUATION)
    /APPRENTICESHIP CALIFORNIA YOUTH/   GCALCNA60516

CHATTANOOGA
    THE NEGRO AND EMPLOYMENT-OPPORTUNITIES IN THE SOUTH. CHATTANOOGA REGION. /TENNESSEE/   NCHATCC62197

    CHATTANOOGA -- THE NEGRO AND EMPLOYMENT OPPORTUNITIES IN THE SOUTH, THE SECOND OF A SERIES OF EMPLOYMENT
    STUDIES IN SOUTHERN CITIES. /TENNESSEE/   NSOUTRC62156

    NEGRO EMPLOYMENT PRACTICES IN THE CHATTANOOGA AREA. /TENNESSEE/   NWESSWH55314

CHAUVINISM
    LEFT SECTARIANISM IN THE FIGHT FOR NEGRO RIGHTS AND AGAINST WHITE CHAUVINISM.   NFOSTWZ53375

CHEMICAL
    CPI -- CHEMICAL PROCESS INDUSTRIES -- TAKES LEAD IN ANTI-BIAS DRIVE. /INDUSTRY/   NCHEMWX61199

CHEMISTS
    EMPLOYMENT OF WOMEN CHEMISTS IN INDUSTRIAL LABORATORIES. /OCCUPATIONS/   WPARRJB65050

CHEROKEE
    SYMPOSIUM ON CHEROKEE AND INDIAN CULTURE.   IFENTWN61620

    HEALTH PRACTICES AND EDUCATIONAL ASPIRATIONS AS INDICATORS OF ACCULTURATION AND SOCIAL-CLASS AMONG THE
    EASTERN CHEROKEE. /NORTH-CAROLINA/   IKUPFHJ62216

CHEROKEES
    CHEROKEES AT THE CROSSROADS.   IGULIJX60568

CHICAGO
    INCOME. EDUCATION AND UNEMPLOYMENT IN NEIGHBORHOODS. CHICAGO, ILLINOIS. /DEMOGRAPHY/   CUSDLAB63456

    FINAL REPORT ON JOBS II PROJECT. /CHICAGO ILLINOIS/   GCHICBC65319

    HUMAN-RELATIONS NEWS OF CHICAGO. /ILLINOIS/   GCHICHR59565

    YOUR CIVIL-RIGHTS. /CHICAGO ILLINOIS/   GCHICHR62568

    MERIT EMPLOYMENT IN CHICAGO. /ILLINOIS/   GCHICMC56566

    1964 MANPOWER SURVEY. /CHICAGO ILLINOIS/   GCOMIEF64592

    ORGANIZING THE UNEMPLOYED. THE CHICAGO PROJECT. /ILLINOIS/   GFLACRX64964

    A REPORT ON EMPLOYMENT OF NONWHITES IN CHICAGO. /ILLINOIS/   GILLICH55792

    LABOR AND CIVIL-RIGHTS IN CHICAGO. /ILLINOIS UNION/   GWESTJX66551

    THE NEGRO WORKER IN THE CHICAGO JOB-MARKET. /ILLINOIS/   NBAROHX66055

    CHICAGO STARTS MOVING ON EQUAL JOB QUESTION. /ILLINOIS/   NBUSIWX64298

    A PRELIMINARY REPORT ON MEDICAL STAFF APPOINTMENTS HELD BY NEGRO PHYSICIANS AT PREDOMINANTLY WHITE
    HOSPITALS. /CHICAGO ILLINOIS/   NCHICCO60201

    TWO YEAR REPORT ON THE YOUTH GUIDANCE PROJECT. 1958-1959. /CHICAGO   ILLINOIS/   NCHICULND203

    INTEGRATION ON HOSPITAL APPOINTMENTS AND IN HOSPITAL CARE. /CHICAGO ILLINOIS/   NCHICUL58202

    THE NEGRO POPULATION OF CHICAGO. A STUDY OF RESIDENTIAL SUCCESSION. /ILLINOIS OCCUPATIONAL-PATTERNS/ NDUNCOD57306

    THE NEGRO FAMILY IN CHICAGO. /ILLINOIS/   NFRAZEF64380

    RECENT MIGRATION TO CHICAGO. /LABOR-FORCE ILLINOIS/   NFREERX50967

    THE UNEMPLOYMENT RATE AND GRADE LEVEL RELATIONSHIP IN CHICAGO AS REVEALED IN THE 1960 CENSUS. /ILLINOIS/   NHARGAJ65990

    AN ANALYSIS OF THE IMPLEMENTATION OF THE UAW-CIO-S FAIR PRACTICES AND ANTI-DISCRIMINATION POLICIES IN
    SELECTED CHICAGO LOCALS. /UNION/   NJONEJE51883

    THE NEGRO AS AN IMMIGRANT GROUP. RECENT TRENDS IN RACIAL AND ETHNIC SEGREGATION IN CHICAGO. /ILLINOIS/ NTAEUKE64196

    PREJUDICE IS NOT THE WHOLE STORY. EXAMINATION OF THREE CASES OF NEGRO UPGRADING IN TRACTION COMPANIES IN
    PHILADELPHIA. LOS-ANGELES AND CHICAGO. /PENNSYLVANIA CALIFORNIA ILLINOIS/   NWECKJE45308

CHILD
    THE MINORITY CHILD AND THE SCHOOLS.   GBULLPX62488

    THE WORLD OF THE MIGRANT CHILD.   GSUTTEX57344

    CHILD REARING AMONG LOW-INCOME FAMILIES. /ECONOMIC-STATUS/   NLEWIHX61040

    WHAT ASPECTS OF CHILD BEHAVIOR SHOULD BE STUDIED IN RELATION TO MATERNAL EMPLOYMENT.   WHARTRE61829

    CHILD CARE FACILITIES FOR WOMEN WORKERS. /EMPLOYMENT-CONDITIONS/   WINTELR58864

    CHILD CARE ARRANGEMENTS OF FULLTIME WORKING MOTHERS. /EMPLOYMENT-CONDITIONS/   WUSDHEW59171

    CHILD CARE ARRANGEMENTS OF THE NATION-S WORKING MOTHERS. A PRELIMINARY REPORT.   WUSDHEW65172

    CRITERIA FOR ASSESSING FEASIBILITY OF MOTHERS EMPLOYMENT AND ADEQUACY OF CHILD CARE PLANS.   WUSDHEW66173

CHILD-REARING
    THE CHILD-REARING ATTITUDES OF DISADVANTAGED NEGRO MOTHERS AND SOME EDUCATIONAL IMPLICATIONS.   CRADINX65031

CHILDBEARING
    AGE OF COMPLETION OF CHILDBEARING AND ITS RELATION TO THE PARTICIPATION OF WOMEN IN THE LABOR-FORCE.
    UNITED STATES 1910-1955.   WDAYXLH57725

CHILDREN
    SPANISH-SPEAKING CHILDREN. /MEXICAN-AMERICAN PUERTO-RICAN EDUCATION/   CBURMJH60287

    THE NATION-S CHILDREN. VOL I. THE FAMILY AND SOCIAL-CHANGE. VOL II. DEVELOPMENT AND EDUCATION. VOL III.
    PROBLEMS AND PROSPECTS. /NEGRO PUERTO-RICAN MEXICAN-AMERICAN WOMEN/   CGINZEX60720

    ECONOMIC AND SOCIAL DEPRIVATIONS. ITS EFFECTS ON CHILDREN AND FAMILIES IN THE UNITED STATES -- A SELECTED
    BIBLIOGRAPHY.   GCHILCX64571

    WHAT MIGRANT FARM CHILDREN LEARN.   GCOLERX66133

CHILDREN   (CONTINUATION)
SOME CONSIDERATIONS AS TO THE CONTRIBUTIONS OF SOCIAL, PERSONALITY, AND RACIAL FACTORS TO SCHOOL
RETARDATION IN MINORITY-GROUP **CHILDREN**.   GDEUTMP56641

SOME EDUCATIONAL IMPLICATIONS OF THE INFLUENCE OF REJECTION ON ASPIRATION LEVELS OF MINORITY-GROUP
CHILDREN.   GGOFFRM54366

AN EXPERIMENT IN VOCATIONAL EDUCATION FOR **CHILDREN** OF MIGRATORY FARM WORKERS, JULY-AUGUST 1956.   GNATLCRND046

CHILDREN OF THE POOR.   GORSHMX63141

FACTORS ASSOCIATED WITH SCHOOL DROPOUTS AND JUVENILE-DELINQUENCY AMONG LOWER-CLASS **CHILDREN**.   GPALMFX63671

MIGRATORY FARM WORKERS IN THE ATLANTIC COAST STREAM, II. EDUCATION OF NEW-YORK WORKERS AND THEIR
CHILDREN, 1953 AND 1957.   GSHAREF60427

CHILDREN AND YOUTH IN THE 1960-S.   GWHITHC60559

CHILDREN OF THE GILDED GHETTO. CONFLICT RESOLUTION OF THREE GENERATIONS OF AMERICAN JEWS.
/OCCUPATIONAL-PATTERNS/   JKRAMJR61736

EDUCATING MIGRANT **CHILDREN** IN COLORADO.   MCOLOSD61384

SPANISH-SPEAKING AND ENGLISH SPEAKING **CHILDREN** IN SOUTHWEST TEXAS. A COMPARATIVE STUDY OF INTELLIGENCE,
SOCIO-ECONOMIC STATUS, AND ACHIEVEMENT.   MRATLYX60460

EGO DEVELOPMENT AMONG SEGREGATED NEGRO **CHILDREN**. /ASPIRATIONS/   NAUSUDP65036

LOWER-CLASS NEGRO MOTHERS ASPIRATIONS FOR THEIR **CHILDREN**.   NBELLRR65074

CHILDREN AND INCOME IN NEGRO FAMILIES.   NBERNEH46077

A COMPARISON OF THE VOCATIONAL ASPIRATIONS OF PAIRED SIXTH-GRADE WHITE AND NEGRO **CHILDREN** WHO ATTEND
SEGREGATED SCHOOLS.   NBROWRG65895

A COMPARISON OF THE SOCIAL CHARACTERISTICS AND EDUCATIONAL ASPIRATIONS OF NORTHERN, LOWER-CLASS, NEGRO
PARENTS WHO ACCEPTED AND DECLINED AN OPPORTUNITY FOR INTEGRATED EDUCATION FOR THEIR **CHILDREN**.   NCAGLLT66904

PROBLEMS AND NEEDS OF NEGRO **CHILDREN** AND YOUTH RESULTING FROM FAMILY DISORGANIZATION.   NFRAZEF50382

THE VOCATIONAL PREFERENCE OF NEGRO **CHILDREN**.   NGRAYSW44446

A STUDY OF PROFESSIONAL PREPARATION OF NEGRO TEACHERS OF EXCEPTIONAL **CHILDREN** IN NORTH-CAROLINA COUNTY
AND CITY PUBLIC SCHOOLS.   NKNIGOB65023

THE HOPES OF NEGRO WORKERS FOR THEIR **CHILDREN**.   NPURCTV64022

THE RELATIONSHIP BETWEEN TEST INTELLIGENCE OF THIRD GRADE NEGRO **CHILDREN** AND THE OCCUPATIONS OF THEIR
PARENTS.   NROBIML47070

THE CULTURE OF UNEMPLOYMENT. SOME NOTES ON NEGRO **CHILDREN**.   NSCHWMX64110

SOCIAL SECURITY PROGRAM STATISTICS RELATING TO NONWHITE FAMILIES AND **CHILDREN**.   NUSDHEW58241

SOME SOCIOLOGICAL ASPECTS OF VOCATIONAL GUIDANCE OF NEGRO **CHILDREN**.   NYOUNMN44348

RELATIONS AMONG MATERNAL EMPLOYMENT INDICES AND DEVELOPMENTAL CHARACTERISTICS OF **CHILDREN**.
/WORK-FAMILY-CONFLICT/   WBURCLG61665

TESTIMONY PRESENTED AT PUBLIC HEARING, APRIL 29, 1966. SAN-FRANCISCO, CALIFORNIA. /FEP
EMPLOYMENT-CONDITIONS **CHILDREN**/   WCALACW66677

WORK, WOMEN, AND **CHILDREN**. /WORK-FAMILY-CONFLICT/   WDAVIHX60715

WORKING MOTHERS AND MALADJUSTED **CHILDREN**.   WHANDHX57818

CHILDREN OF WORKING MOTHERS, 1960.   WHERZEX64123

WORKING MOTHERS AND THEIR ARRANGEMENTS FOR CARE OF THEIR **CHILDREN**. /EMPLOYMENT-CONDITIONS/   WLAJEHC59922

CHILDREN AND WORKING MOTHERS.   WMACCEE58949

CAREERS FOR WOMEN AFTER MARRIAGE AND **CHILDREN**. /WORK-FAMILY-CONFLICT/   WONEIBP65043

CHILDREN-S
NEGRO AND WHITE **CHILDREN-S** PLANS FOR THEIR FUTURES. /ASPIRATIONS/   NLOTTAJ63487

CHINA-TOWN
CHINESE PEOPLE AND **CHINA-TOWN** IN NEW-YORK CITY.   OWUXXCT58772

CHINATOWN-NORTH
STATEMENT BEFORE CALIFORNIA LEGISLATURE ASSEMBLY, INTERIM SUBCOMMITTEE ON ECONOMIC OPPORTUNITY ON BEHALF
OF **CHINATOWN-NORTH** BEACH DISTRICT COUNCIL.   OWONGLJ64771

CHINESE
NONWHITE POPULATION BY RACE. NEGROES, INDIANS, JAPANESE, **CHINESE**, FILIPINOS. BY AGE, SEX, MARITAL-STATUS,
EDUCATION, EMPLOYMENT-STATUS, OCCUPATIONAL-STATUS, INCOME, ETC. /DEMOGRAPHY/   CUSBURC53378

NONWHITE POPULATION BY RACE. NEGROES, INDIANS, JAPANESE,**CHINESE**, FILIPINOS. BY AGE, SEX,
MARITAL-STATUS,EDUCATION, EMPLOYMENT-STATUS, OCCUPATIONAL-STATUS, INCOME, ETC. /DEMOGRAPHY/   CUSBURC63176

CALIFORNIANS OF JAPANESE, **CHINESE**, FILIPINO ANCESTRY.   OCALDIR65709

ASSIMILATION OF **CHINESE** IN AMERICA. CHANGES IN ORIENTATION AND SOCIAL PERCEPTIONS.   OFONGSL65722

CHINESE IN AMERICAN LIFE. SOME ASPECTS OF THEIR HISTORY, STATUS, PROBLEMS AND CONTRIBUTIONS.   OKUNGSW62737

THE **CHINESE** IN THE UNITED STATES OF AMERICA.   OLEEXRH60741

CHINESE IMMIGRATION AND POPULATION CHANGES SINCE 1940.   OLEEXRX57740

CHINESE PEOPLE AND CHINA-TOWN IN NEW-YORK CITY.   OWUXXCT58772

CHIPPEWA
THE EMPLOYABILITY OF **CHIPPEWA** INDIANS AND POOR WHITES.   ILIEBLX66041

CHIPPEWA ADOLESCENTS. A CHANGING GENERATION.   IMILLFC64590

CHOICE
SEX DIFFERENCES IN OCCUPATIONAL **CHOICE** PATTERNS AMONG ADOLESCENTS. /ASPIRATIONS WOMEN NEGRO/   CSPREJX62999

CHOICE   (CONTINUATION)
ANTIDISCRIMINATION LEGISLATION AS AN INFRINGEMENT OF FREEDOM OF **CHOICE**.   GAVINAX60409

FREEDOM OF **CHOICE** IN PERSONAL SERVICE OCCUPATIONS. 13TH AMENDMENT LIMITATIONS ON ANTIDISCRIMINATION
LEGISLATION.   GAVINAX64410

CURRICULUM **CHOICE** IN THE NEGRO COLLEGE.   NBRAZWF60109

OCCUPATIONAL **CHOICE** IN THE NEGRO COLLEGE.   NBRAZWF60112

OCCUPATIONAL **CHOICE**. AN APPROACH TO A GENERAL THEORY.   NGINZEX51410

OCCUPATIONAL **CHOICE** AND THE TEACHING CAREER.   NGUBAEG59463

EMPLOYEE **CHOICE** AND SOME PROBLEMS OF RACE AND REMEDIES IN REPRESENTATION CAMPAIGNS.   NYALELJ63599

CHANGE AND **CHOICE** FOR THE COLLEGE WOMAN. /WORK-WOMAN-ROLE/   WAAUWJX62601

LIFE GOALS AND VOCATIONAL **CHOICE**. /WORK-WOMAN-ROLE/   WASTIAW64620

NOTES ON THE ROLE OF **CHOICE** IN THE PSYCHOLOGY OF PROFESSIONAL WOMEN. /OCCUPATIONS/   WBAILLX64623

SEX AS A FACTOR IN THE DETERMINATION OF EDUCATIONAL **CHOICE**. /ASPIRATIONS/   WDOLEAA64737

SOCIAL FACTORS WHICH AFFECT CAREER **CHOICE** IN PSYCHIATRIC NURSING.   WDOUGAM61740

BARRIERS TO THE CAREER **CHOICE** OF ENGINEERING, MEDICINE, OR SCIENCE AMONG AMERICAN WOMEN. /OCCUPATIONS/   WROSSAS65091

OCCUPATIONAL **CHOICE** AMONG CAREER ORIENTED COLLEGE WOMEN. /ASPIRATIONS/   WSIMPRL61115

WOMAN-S DESTINY -- **CHOICE** OR CHANCE. REPORT OF CONFERENCE AT THE UNIVERSITY OF WASHINGTON, NOVEMBER
21-22, 1963.   WUSDLAB65233

CHOICES
SOME SOCIOLOGICAL ROOTS OF VOCATIONAL **CHOICES**.   GYOUNME46593

VOCATIONAL **CHOICES** OF NEGRO HIGH SCHOOL STUDENTS IN MACON COUNTY, ALABAMA, AND THEIR RELATIONSHIP TO
BASIC OCCUPATIONAL ACTIVITES OF THE SCHOOL COMMUNITIES. /ASPIRATIONS/   NCHAPEJ49351

OCCUPATIONAL **CHOICES** OF NEGRO HIGH SCHOOL SENIORS IN TEXAS.   NTURNBA57165

CHANGES IN SELECTED PERSONALITY CHARACTERISTICS AND PERSISTENCE IN THE CAREER **CHOICES** OF WOMEN ASSOCIATED
WITH A FOUR YEAR COLLEGE EDUCATION AT ONE OF THE COLLEGES OF THE CITY UNIVERSITY OF NEW-YORK.
/ASPIRATIONS/   WLEINMX64925

POSITION **CHOICES** AND CAREERS. ELEMENTS OF A THEORY. /ASPIRATIONS/   WTIEDDV58154

CHRONICLE
TOWARD EQUALITY, BALTIMORE-S PROGRESS-REPORT. A **CHRONICLE** OF PROGRESS SINCE WORLD-WAR-II TOWARD THE
ACHIEVEMENT OF EQUAL-RIGHTS AND OPPORTUNITIES FOR NEGROES IN MARYLAND 1946-1958.   NBALTUL58048

A **CHRONICLE** OF RACE-RELATIONS -- THE UNITED STATES, NORTH AND SOUTH.   NDUBOWE41298

A **CHRONICLE** OF RACE-RELATIONS, FEPC.   NDUBOWE43297

CIGAR
NEGRO WOMEN IN THE CLOTHING, **CIGAR** AND LAUNDRY INDUSTRIES OF PHILADELPHIA, 1960.   CPORTRP43103

CINCINNATI
INCOME, EDUCATION AND UNEMPLOYMENT IN NEIGHBORHOODS. **CINCINNATI**, OHIO. /DEMOGRAPHY/   CUSDLAB63457

RACIAL DISCRIMINATION IN THE **CINCINNATI** BUILDING TRADES. A COMPREHENSIVE REPORT AND RECOMMENDATIONS.
/OHIO/   GOHIOCR64129

MONTHLY SUMMARY OF EVENTS AND TRENDS IN RACE-RELATIONS. /**CINCINNATI** OHIO CASE-STUDY UNION/   NFISKUX44357

RACIAL DISCRIMINATION IN THE **CINCINNATI** BUILDING TRADES. REPORT AND RECOMMENDATIONS. /OHIO/   NOHIOCR66605

CINNCINATI
RACIAL DISCRIMINATION IN EMPLOYMENT IN THE **CINNCINATI** AREA. /OHIO/   NKUHNAX62668

CIO
THE ROLE OF THE NEGRO IN THE ORGANIZATION OF THE **CIO**. /UNION/   NCOOPJE56235

THE **CIO** AND THE NEGRO IN THE SOUTH. /UNION/   NMASOJR45323

TO WIN THESE RIGHTS. A PERSONAL STORY OF THE **CIO** IN THE SOUTH. /UNION/   NMASOJR52324

CITIES
THE SCHOOL DROPOUT PROBLEM IN MAJOR **CITIES** OF NEW-YORK STATE. ROCHESTER -- PART I. /NEGRO PUERTO-RICAN/   CNEWYSD62090

FAIR-EMPLOYMENT-PRACTICES LEGISLATION OF EIGHT STATES AND TWO **CITIES**.   GBERGMX51441

DEMOGRAPHIC CHANGE AND RACIAL GHETTOS. THE CRISIS OF AMERICAN **CITIES**.   GHILLHX66691

A TALE OF 22 **CITIES**. TITLE-VII OF THE CIVIL-RIGHTS-ACT OF 1964.   GKOTHCA65732

ETHNIC PATTERNS IN AMERICAN **CITIES**.   GLIEBSX63904

POVERTY IN THE **CITIES**.   GORNAOA67138

MUNICIPAL HUMAN-RELATIONS COMMISSION. A SURVEY OF PROGRAMS IN SELECTED **CITIES** OF THE UNITED STATES.   GRICHCM63236

A SHARPER LOOK AT UNEMPLOYMENT IN US **CITIES**, AND SLUMS.   GUSDLAB66520

NEGROES IN FIVE NEW-YORK **CITIES**. A STUDY OF PROBLEMS, ACHIEVEMENTS AND TRENDS. /RACE-RELATIONS/   NGRIEES58455

EXPERIMENTAL AND DEMONSTRATION MANPOWER PROJECT FOR THE RECRUITMENT, TRAINING, PLACEMENT AND FOLLOW-UP OF
RURAL UNEMPLOYED WORKERS IN TEN NORTH FLORIDA **CITIES**. FINAL REPORT. /PARTICIPANTS/   NJACKTA66597

THE BIG **CITIES** BIG PROBLEM. /GHETTO EMPLOYMENT/   NKAINJF66630

NEGRO WORKERS IN THE BUILDING TRADES IN SELECTED **CITIES**. NORFOLK, VIRGINIA. /INDUSTRY/   NNATLUL46894

NEGRO WORKERS IN THE BUILDING TRADES IN CERTAIN **CITIES**.   NNATLUL47904

APPRENTICESHIP AND TRAINING OPPORTUNITIES FOR NEGRO YOUTHS IN SELECTED URBAN-LEAGUE **CITIES**.   NNATLUL61885

SURVEY OF UNEMPLOYMENT IN SELECTED URBAN-LEAGUE **CITIES**.   NNATLUL61898

CITIES   (CONTINUATION)
NONWHITE MIGRANTS TO AND FROM SELECTED CITIES.   NPRICD048019

HOUSTON -- THE NEGRO AND EMPLOYMENT OPPORTUNITIES IN THE SOUTH, THE FIRST OF A SERIES OF EMPLOYMENT
STUDIES IN SOUTHERN CITIES. /TEXAS/   NSOUTRC61161

ATLANTA -- THE NEGRO AND EMPLOYMENT OPPORTUNITIES IN THE SOUTH, THE THIRD OF A SERIES OF EMPLOYMENT
STUDIES IN SOUTHERN CITIES. /GEORGIA/   NSOUTRC62155

CHATTANOOGA -- THE NEGRO AND EMPLOYMENT OPPORTUNITIES IN THE SOUTH, THE SECOND OF A SERIES OF EMPLOYMENT
STUDIES IN SOUTHERN CITIES. /TENNESSEE/   NSOUTRC62156

SOUTHERN CITIES EMPLOYING NEGRO POLICEMEN -- INCLUDING NORTH-CAROLINA CITIES OVER 15,000 POPULATION.   NSTEEDL46173

SOUTHERN CITIES EMPLOYING NEGRO POLICEMEN -- INCLUDING NORTH-CAROLINA CITIES OVER 15,000 POPULATION.   NSTEEDL46173

NEGROES IN CITIES. /DEMOGRAPHY SEGREGATION/   NTAEUKE65197

THE RELATIVE POSITION OF THE NEGRO MALE IN THE LABOR-FORCE OF LARGE AMERICAN CITIES.   NTURNRH51217

POVERTY AREAS OF OUR MAJOR CITIES. THE EMPLOYMENT SITUATION OF NEGRO AND WHITE WORKERS IN METROPOLITAN
AREAS COMPARED IN A SPECIAL LABOR-FORCE REPORT.   NWETZJR66114

REBUILDING CITIES. THE EFFECTS OF DISPLACEMENT AND RELOCATION ON SMALL BUSINESS.   NZIMMBG64247

CITIZENS
EQUAL-RIGHTS UNDER THE LAW. PROVIDING FOR EQUAL TREATMENT FOR ALL CITIZENS REGARDLESS OF RACE, RELIGION,
COLOR, NATIONAL ORIGIN OR ANCESTRY. /CALIFORNIA/   GCALAGO60511

LOCAL CONTRACTS AND SUB-CONTRACTS. THE ROLES OF CITY GOVERNMENT AND PRIVATE CITIZENS GROUPS.   GJONEMX64829

SENIOR CITIZENS AND HOW THEY LIVE. AN ANALYSIS OF 1960 CENSUS DATA. PART II. THE AGING NONWHITE AND HIS
HOUSING. /ECONOMIC-STATUS/   GUSHHFX63321

A PROGRAM FOR INDIAN CITIZENS. A SUMMARY REPORT.   IFUNDFT61562

CITY
ETHNIC SURVEY OF MUNICIPAL-EMPLOYEES, A REPORT ON THE NUMBER AND DISTRIBUTION OF NEGROES AND
PUERTO-RICANS AND OTHER EMPLOYEES BY THE CITY OF NEW-YORK.   CNEWYCO64916

INTERIM REPORT TO THE MAYOR ON ITS INQUIRY INTO CHARGES OF RACIAL BIAS IN THE CITY BUILDING AND
CONSTRUCTION INDUSTRY. /NEW-YORK NEGRO PUERTO-RICAN/   CNEWYCO64917

ANALYSIS OF CITY ORDINANCES AGAINST RACIAL AND RELIGIOUS DISCRIMINATION IN EMPLOYMENT.   GAMERJCND380

REVIEW AND ANALYSIS OF CITY CERTIFICATIONS AND APPOINTMENTS. /BERKELEY CALIFORNIA/   GBERKCM64444

OPINION CONCERNING THE SCOPE AND AUTHORITY OF THE JURISDICTION THAT MAY BE GRANTED TO CITY OR COUNTY
HUMAN-RELATIONS-COMMISSIONS IN THE FIELDS OF EMPLOYMENT AND HOUSING. /CALIFORNIA/   GCALAGO63512

EMPLOYMENT PRACTICES. CITY OF PASADENA, AN INVESTIGATION UNDER SECTION 1421 OF THE CALIFORNIA LABOR CODE
1963-1965.   GCALFEPND531

LOS-ANGELES CITY SCHOOLS. AN INVESTIGATION OF EMPLOYMENT PRACTICES. /CALIFORNIA/   GCALFEP64536

POVERTY IN NEW-YORK CITY. FACTS FOR PLANNING COMMUNITY ACTION.   GCOMCCN64210

REPORT ON AND ANALYSIS OF SECOND CENSUS OF CITY EMPLOYEES TO DETERMINE BASES FOR FUTURE PERSONNEL
DEVELOPMENTS. /DETROIT MICHIGAN/   GDETRCC66639

A STUDY OF FAIR-EMPLOYMENT-PRACTICES OF THE CITY GOVERNMENT. /GRAND-RAPIDS MICHIGAN/   GGRANRH66733

THE CITY GOVERNMENT AND MINORITY-GROUPS.   GINTECM63816

LOCAL CONTRACTS AND SUB-CONTRACTS. THE ROLES OF CITY GOVERNMENT AND PRIVATE CITIZENS GROUPS.   GJONEMX64829

CITY PROBLEMS OF 1963. /ANTIDISCRIMINATION/   GKENNJF63842

REPORT OF FINDINGS AND RECOMMENDATIONS RESULTING FROM AN ANALYSIS OF THE EMPLOYMENT PRACTICES IN THE
VARIOUS DEPARTMENTS OF THE CITY OF LOS-ANGELES. /CALIFORNIA/   GLOSAOC63917

SURVEY AND ANALYSIS OF NON-WHITE EMPLOYMENT BY THE CITY OF MINNEAPOLIS. /MINNESOTA/   GMINLMH65002

THE POOR IN CITY AND SUBURB. 1964.   GORSHMX66282

A SPECIAL REPORT. CITY CONTRACT COMPLIANCE. PROGRESS IN 1963. /PHILADELPHIA PENNSYLVANIA/   GPHILCH64179

RACIAL AND ETHNIC EMPLOYMENT PATTERN SURVEY OF THE CITY AND COUNTY OF SAN-FRANCISCO GOVERNMENT.
DEPARTMENTAL ANALYSIS. /CALIFORNIA/   GSANFHR65264

A SURVEY OF DISCRIMINATION IN THE BUILDING TRADES INDUSTRY, NEW-YORK CITY.   GSHAUDF63300

YOUTH IN NEW-YORK CITY. OUT OF SCHOOL AND OUT OF WORK.   GVCGAAS62074

CITY EMPLOYMENT SURVEY. PERCENTAGE OF MINORITY-GROUP EMPLOYEES BY DEPARTMENT. /YONKERS NEW-YORK/   GYONKCC66592

EMPLOYMENT PRACTICES, CITY OF SAN-DIEGO, 1963-1964. /CALIFORNIA/   GZOOKDX64596

INDIAN RELOCATION. PROBLEMS OF DEPENDENCY AND MANAGEMENT IN THE CITY.   IABLOJX65085

AMERICAN-INDIANS IN LOS-ANGELES. A STUDY OF ADAPTATION TO A CITY. /CALIFORNIA/   IUVCALA66675

JEWS IN AND OUT OF NEW-YORK CITY. /ECONOMIC-STATUS/   JLAZRBX61034

ACROSS THE TRACKS. MEXICAN-AMERICANS IN A TEXAS CITY.   MRUBEAJ66466

CHANGES IN PUBLIC AND PRIVATE LANGUAGE AMONG SPANISH-SPEAKING MIGRANTS TO AN INDUSTRIAL CITY.   MSCHETJ65481

BLACK METROPOLIS. A STUDY OF NEGRO LIFE IN A NORTHERN CITY.   NDRAKSC45291

I Q PERFORMANCE, EDUCATIONAL AND OCCUPATIONAL ASPIRATIONS OF YOUTH IN A SOUTHERN CITY -- A RACIAL
COMPARISON.   NGEISPX62397

UNITED STATES HAS STANDING UNDER INTERSTATE COMMERCE ACT AND COMMERCE CLAUSE TO ENJOIN SEGREGATIVE
PRACTICES OF CITY. /LEGISLATION/   NHARVLR64500

NEW-YORK CITY COMMISSION ON HUMAN RIGHTS, CONSTRUCTION TRADES HEARING, TESTIMONY. /INDUSTRY/   NHILLHX66546

THE ASSESSMENT OF ADJUSTMENT OF AGED NEGRO WOMEN IN A SOUTHERN CITY.   NHIMEJX62072

CITY   (CONTINUATION)
THE EMPLOYMENT SITUATION OF WHITE AND NEGRO YOUTH IN THE CITY OF BALTIMORE. INITIAL EXPERIENCES IN THE
LABOR-MARKET. /MARYLAND/   NJOHNHU63735

A STUDY OF PROFESSIONAL PREPARATION OF NEGRO TEACHERS OF EXCEPTIONAL CHILDREN IN NORTH-CAROLINA COUNTY
AND CITY PUBLIC SCHOOLS.   NKNIGOB65023

THE EMPLOYMENT SITUATION OF WHITE AND NEGRO YOUTH IN THE CITY OF BALTIMORE. /MARYLAND/   NLEVEBX63684

THE NEGRO-S JOURNEY TO THE CITY -- PART I.   NNEWMDK65908

THE NEGRO-S JOURNEY TO THE CITY -- PART II.   NNEWMDK65909

OPINION BY HONORABLE BENJAMIN LENCHER. CITY OF PITTSBURGH VS PLUMBERS LOCAL UNION NO 27. /PENNSYLVANIA/   NPITTLJ65001

THE INFLUENCE OF A BORDER CITY UNION ON THE RACE ATTITUDES OF ITS MEMBERS.   NROSEAW53293

NEGRO UNEMPLOYMENT -- WHAT CITY BUSINESSMEN ARE DOING ABOUT IT.   NSCHMJC64108

A SURVEY OF DISCRIMINATION IN THE BUILDING TRADES INDUSTRY. NEW-YORK CITY.   NSHAUDX63126

THE CITY AND THE NEGRO.   NSILBCE62134

CITY CONTRACTORS AND FAIR-EMPLOYMENT. EXPERIENCE REPORT 103.   NUSCONM66234

NEGROES IN NEW-YORK CITY. OCCUPATIONAL DISTRIBUTION.   NUSDLAB49831

THE CHANGING STRUCTURE OF THE AMERICAN CITY AND THE NEGRO.   NWEAVRC64299

CHINESE PEOPLE AND CHINA-TOWN IN NEW-YORK CITY.   OWUXXCT58772

80 PUERTO-RICAN FAMILIES IN NEW-YORK CITY.   PBERLBB58780

THE IMPACT OF PUERTO-RICAN MIGRATION ON GOVERNMENTAL SERVICES IN NEW-YORK CITY.   PDWORMB57797

IMPLICATIONS OF PUERTO-RICAN MIGRATION TO THE CONTINENT OUTSIDE NEW-YORK CITY.   PGERNAC56808

LABOR UNIONS AND PUERTO-RICAN MEMBERS IN NEW-YORK CITY.   PGRAYLX63027

PUERTO-RICAN INTEGRATION IN THE SKIRT INDUSTRY IN NEW-YORK CITY.   PHELFBH59481

PLACING PUERTO-RICAN WORKERS IN THE NEW-YORK CITY LABOR-MARKET.   PMONTHX60830

SOME CHARACTERISTICS OF PUBLIC ASSISTANCE CASES IN NEW-YORK CITY, AUGUST, 1959.   PNEWYDW60835

PUERTO-RICAN EMPLOYMENT IN NEW-YORK CITY HOTELS. /OCCUPATIONS/   PNEWYSA58837

CHARACTERISTICS OF POPULATION AND LABOR IN NEW-YORK STATE, 1956 AND 1957. PUERTO-RICANS IN NEW-YORK CITY.   PNEWYSE60839

AN ANALYSIS OF UNEMPLOYED PUERTO-RICAN MIGRANTS IN NEW-YORK CITY.   PREMEGN58847

ISLAND IN THE CITY. THE WORLD OF SPANISH HARLEM.   PWAKEDX59858

CHANGES IN SELECTED PERSONALITY CHARACTERISTICS AND PERSISTENCE IN THE CAREER CHOICES OF WOMEN ASSOCIATED
WITH A FOUR YEAR COLLEGE EDUCATION AT ONE OF THE COLLEGES OF THE CITY UNIVERSITY OF NEW-YORK.
/ASPIRATIONS/   WLEINMX64925

CITY-S
DEVELOPING NEW-YORK CITY-S HUMAN RESOURCES. VOL 1. /NEGRO PUERTO-RICAN/   CINSTOP66034

CIVIC
THE PREPARATION OF DISADVANTAGED YOUTH FOR EMPLOYMENT AND CIVIC RESPONSIBILITIES.   NPERRJX64985

CIVIL
I STATEMENT BEFORE THE HOUSE POST OFFICE AND CIVIL SERVICE SUBCOMMITTEE ON POSTAL OPERATIONS, II
DISCRIMINATION. PLANNED AND ACCIDENTAL. /TESTING/   GENNEWH67928

A CIVIL RIGHTS INVENTORY OF SAN FRANCISCO. PART I. /UNION/   NBABOIX58893

NEGRO EMPLOYMENT IN THE FEDERAL GOVERNMENT BY CIVIL SERVICE REGION, STATE AND PAY CATEGORIES, JUNE 1962.   NPRESCD62012

REPORT OF THE COMMITTEE ON CIVIL AND POLITICAL RIGHTS.   WPRESCO63065

CIVIL-AERONAUTICS-BO
NONDISCRIMINATION IN FEDERALLY-ASSISTED PROGRAMS OF THE DEPARTMENT-OF-THE-TREASURY,
DEPARTMENT-OF-DEFENSE, ATOMIC-ENERGY-COMMISSION, CIVIL-AERONAUTICS-BOARD, FEDERAL-AVIATION-AGENCY,
VETERANS-ADMINISTRATION.   GFEDERX64673

CIVIL-LIBERTIES
THE CIVIL-RIGHTS AND CIVIL-LIBERTIES DECISIONS OF THE US SUPREME COURT FOR THE 1962-63 TERM. A SUMMARY
AND ANALYSIS.   GAMERJD63384

SECURITY. CIVIL-LIBERTIES AND UNIONS.   GFLEIHX57686

A BIBLIOGRAPHY OF CIVIL-RIGHTS AND CIVIL-LIBERTIES. /EMPLOYMENT UNION   MILITARY/   NBROOAD62117

CIVIL-RIGHTS
THE PUSH OF AN ELBOW. CIVIL-RIGHTS AND OUR SPANISH-SPEAKING MINORITY. /MEXICAN-AMERICAN PUERTO-RICAN/   CBURMJH60371

CIVIL-RIGHTS IN 1956.   GABRACX56861

PARLEY ON CIVIL-RIGHTS.   GAMERFX57873

CIVIL-RIGHTS RESOLUTION.   GAMERFX59872

CIVIL-RIGHTS IN THE UNITED STATES, 1953.   GAMERJC53388

THE CIVIL-RIGHTS AND CIVIL-LIBERTIES DECISIONS OF THE US SUPREME COURT FOR THE 1962-63 TERM. A SUMMARY
AND ANALYSIS.   GAMERJD63384

A CIVIL-RIGHTS INVENTORY OF SAN-FRANCISCO. PART I. EMPLOYMENT. /CALIFORNIA/   GBABOIX58606

WHERE THE STATES STAND IN CIVIL-RIGHTS.   GBARNRX62423

REPORT OF THE CALIFORNIA STATE ADVISORY COMMITTEE TO THE UNITED STATES COMMISSION ON CIVIL-RIGHTS ON
CALIFORNIA-S PROGRAM FOR EQUAL-OPPORTUNITY IN APPRENTICESHIP.   GBECKWL62432

COMPENSATING EMPLOYEES UNDER THE NEW CIVIL-RIGHTS LAW.   GBENGEJ65436

THE NEW CIVIL-RIGHTS LAW AND YOUR BUSINESS.   GBERGNJ64438

STATE CIVIL-RIGHTS STATUTES. SOME PROPOSALS.   GBONFAE64463

LABOR AND CIVIL-RIGHTS. /CALIFORNIA UNION/   GCALLFX59544

LABOR AND CIVIL-RIGHTS 1964. /CALIFORNIA UNION/   GCALLFX64545

YOUR CIVIL-RIGHTS. /CHICAGO ILLINOIS/   GCHICHR62568

THE CONTROVERSY OVER THE EQUAL-EMPLOYMENT-OPPORTUNITY PROVISIONS OF THE CIVIL-RIGHTS BILL. PRO AND CON.   GCONGDX64594

SEMINAR ON MANPOWER POLICY AND PROGRAM. LABOR LOOKS AT AUTOMATION AND CIVIL-RIGHTS.   GCONWJT65496

ECONOMICS AND THE CIVIL-RIGHTS CRISIS.   GDERNTX64947

CIVIL-RIGHTS IN AIR TRANSPORTATION AND GOVERNMENT INITIATIVE.   GDIXCRX63644

CIVIL-RIGHTS IN THE 88TH CONGRESS, FIRST SESSION, 1963.   GEDELHX63658

CIVIL-RIGHTS. EMPLOYMENT OPPORTUNITY, AND ECONOMIC GROWTH.   GFEILJG65677

LABOR AND THE CIVIL-RIGHTS REVOLUTION. /UNICN/   GFLEIHX60685

PROGRESS IN CIVIL-RIGHTS TO 1964. /EEO/   GFLEIHX65106

CIVIL-RIGHTS AND THE LIMITS CF LAW.   GFREUPA64700

LABOR LOOKS AT THE CRISES IN CIVIL-RIGHTS. /UNION/   GGOLDHX58975

CIVIL-RIGHTS -- A NATIONAL CHALLENGE.   GHANNJA61988

RIGHT-TO-WORK-LAWS AND CIVIL-RIGHTS. /UNION/   GHERLAK64771

CIVIL-RIGHTS IN INDIANA.   GINDICRND804

CIVIL-RIGHTS PROBLEMS IN PERSONNEL AND LABOR-RELATIONS.   GKAMMTX65832

THE CONSTITUTION AND CIVIL-RIGHTS.   GKONVMR47856

A CENTURY-OF CIVIL-RIGHTS.   GKONVMR61477

MANAGEMENT-S CONCERN WITH RECENT CIVIL-RIGHTS LEGISLATION AFFECTING MANAGEMENT-S OBLIGATIONS TO HIS
EMPLOYEES AND APPLICANTS FCR EMPLOYMENT, MAINLY IN THE STATE OF NEW-YORK.   GKOPPRW65858

SOME QUESTIONS AND ANSWERS ON THE CIVIL-RIGHTS BILL.   GLEADCCND888

SOLVING AN AMERICAN DILEMMA. THE ROLE OF THE FEPC OFFICIAL, A COMPARATIVE STUDY OF STATE CIVIL-RIGHTS
COMMISSIONS.   GLLOYKM64317

THE ENFORCEMENT OF CIVIL-RIGHTS. /DISCRIMINATION/   GMARSBX62942

CIVIL-RIGHTS AND EMPLOYMENT, SELECTED REFERENCES.   GMICSUSND984

THE PEOPLE TAKE THE LEAD. A RECORD OF PROGRESS IN CIVIL-RIGHTS, 1948-1957.   GNATLLS57049

THE PECPLE TAKE THE LEAD. A RECORD OF PROGRESS IN CIVIL-RIGHTS, 1954-1963.   GNATLLS63050

REPORT ON SECOND ANNUAL SPRING CONFERENCE CN CIVIL-RIGHTS OF NEW-JERSEY COMMISSION-ON-CIVIL-RIGHTS, APRIL
23, 1966.   GNEWJCC66056

STATEMENT TO THE COMMITTEE ON LEGISLATION IN SUPPORT OF AN EFFECTIVE FEDERAL FEP LAW AND OTHER VITAL
CIVIL-RIGHTS LEGISLATION.   GOLIVWX60134

A GUIDE TO GOVERNMENT OFFICIALS. /CIVIL-RIGHTS/   GOREGBLND135

HOW THE NEW CIVIL-RIGHTS LAW AFFECTS YOUR EMPLOYMENT PRACTICES.   GPRENHI64104

THE 1964 CIVIL-RIGHTS LAW, A HARD LOOK.   GRACHCXND212

CIVIL-RIGHTS AND LIBERTIES AND LABOR UNIONS.   GRAUHJL57217

OPERATING UNDER THE CIVIL-RIGHTS LAW.   GRESEIA64222

EQUALITY OF JOB OPPORTUNITY AND CIVIL-RIGHTS.   GREUTWP60223

CIVIL-RIGHTS ORDINANCES.   GRHYNCS63234

THE QUEST FOR THE DREAM. THE DEVELOPMENT OF CIVIL-RIGHTS AND HUMAN-RELATIONS IN MODERN AMERICA.   GROCHJP63057

THE PRACTICES OF CRAFT UNIONS IN WASHINGTON-CC WITH RESPECT TO MINURITY GROUPS IN CIVIL-RIGHTS IN THE
NATICN-S CAPITOL.   GSEGABD59294

CIVIL-RIGHTS AND THE REHABILITATION OF AFDC CLIENTS.   GSETSLX64296

STATE EXECUTIVE AUTHORITY TO PROMOTE CIVIL-RIGHTS. AN ACTION PROGRAM FOR THE 1960-S.   GSILAJX63310

CIVIL-RIGHTS. THE FACTS AND THE CHALLENGE.   GSLAIDX64316

THE NATIONAL CONFERENCE AND THE REPORTS OF THE STATE ADVISORY COMMITTEES TO THE U.S. COMMISSION ON
CIVIL-RIGHTS. 1959.   GUSCOMC60405

A REPORT TO THE US COMMISSION ON CIVIL-RIGHTS. /MISSOURI/   GUSCOMC63406

REPORT ON FLORIDA OF THE US COMMISSION ON CIVIL-RIGHTS.   GUSCCMC63409

FEDERAL AGENCIES WITH PRIMARY CIVIL-RIGHTS RESPONSIBILITIES.   GUSDLAB65447

LABOR AND CIVIL-RIGHTS IN CHICAGO. /ILLINOIS UNION/   GWESTJX66551

ADDRESS BEFORE THE CIVIL-RIGHTS CONFERENCE.   GWIRTWW65571

CIVIL-RIGHTS POLICY IN THE FEDERAL SYSTEM. PROPOSALS FOR A BETTER USE OF ADMINISTRATIVE PROCESS.   GWITHJX65575

MOVING AHEAD. AIMS AND METHODS. /CIVIL-RIGHTS ANTIDISCRIMINATION/   GWOFFHX62577

CIVIL-RIGHTS AND JEWISH INSTITUTIONS.   JPILCJX64749

CIVIL-RIGHTS   (CONTINUATION)
   MEXICAN-AMERICANS AND CIVIL-RIGHTS.   MALMAAS64357

      THE CIVIL-RIGHTS SITUATION OF MEXICAN-AMERICANS AND SPANISH-AMERICANS.   MBURMJH61370

      THE CIVIL-RIGHTS FIGHT. A LOOK AT THE LEGISLATIVE RECORD.   NAFLCIO60005

      LABOR-S CIVIL-RIGHTS STAND REAFFIRMED AT ATLANTIC-CITY.   NAMERFX58013

      THE NEGRO VANGUARD. /CIVIL-RIGHTS/   NBARDRX59878

      CONFRONTATION. BLACK AND WHITE. /CIVIL-RIGHTS/   NBENNLX65881

      A BIBLIOGRAPHY OF CIVIL-RIGHTS AND CIVIL-LIBERTIES. /EMPLOYMENT UNION   MILITARY/   NBROOAD62117

      WE SHALL OVERCOME. /CIVIL-RIGHTS/   NDORMMX64953

      CIVIL-RIGHTS. 1960-63. THE NEGRO CAMPAIGN TO WIN EQUAL RIGHTS AND OPPORTUNITIES IN THE UNITED STATES.   NFACTOF64341

      THE FEDERAL EXECUTIVE AND CIVIL-RIGHTS. 1961-1965.   NFLEMHC66362

      THE DECADE OF HOPE. /CIVIL-RIGHTS ECONOMIC/   NFORECX51371

      BEYOND CIVIL-RIGHTS.   NHENTNX65026

      EDUCATION AND CIVIL-RIGHTS IN 1965.   NJOURNE65625

      CIVIL-RIGHTS PROBLEMS IN PERSONNEL AND LABOR-RELATIONS.   NKAMOTCND633

      CIVIL-RIGHTS -- RACIAL DISCRIMINATION IN TEACHER HIRING AND ASSIGNMENT FORBIDDEN.   NKELLPL66734

      WHY WE CAN-T WAIT. /CIVIL-RIGHTS EQUAL-OPPORTUNITY/   NKINGML64022

      THE CIVIL-RIGHTS MOVEMENT AND EMPLOYMENT.   NMCKERB64722

      THE CIVIL-RIGHTS REVOLUTION AND THE BUSINESSMAN.   NMCKERB64723

      CIVIL-RIGHTS STRATEGIES FOR NEGRO EMPLOYMENT.   NMEIEAX67764

      BUSINESS AND CIVIL-RIGHTS.   NMITCJP64295

      NEGRO YOUTH -- EDUCATION, EMPLOYMENT, AND CIVIL-RIGHTS.   NPEARAX64980

      STATEMENT TO THE NEW-YORK STATE ADVISORY COMMITTEE TO THE US COMMISSION ON CIVIL-RIGHTS, MAY 23, 1966.
        /EMPLOYMENT LEGISLATION/   NPOLIEX66004

      TODAY-S CIVIL-RIGHTS REVOLUTION.   NRANDAP63035

      CIVIL-RIGHTS. THE LAW AND THE UNIONS.   NRASKAH64038

      GOVERNOR-S CIVIL-RIGHTS TASK FORCE. REPORT. /RHODE-ISLAND/   NRHODIC64051

      CIVIL-RIGHTS AT THE CROSSROADS.   NRUSTBX66097

      SOCIAL-CLASS FACTORS UNDERLYING THE CIVIL-RIGHTS MOVEMENT.   NSCOTJW66112

      CIVIL-RIGHTS. EMPLOYMENT, AND THE SOCIAL STATUS OF AMERICAN NEGROES.   NSHEPHL66129

      THE FEDERAL EXECUTIVE AND CIVIL-RIGHTS.   NSOUTRC61160

      EXECUTIVE SUPPORT OF CIVIL-RIGHTS.   NSOUTRC62159

      CIVIL-RIGHTS AND THE NORTHERN GHETTO.   NSTUDOT64188

      THE CIVIL-RIGHTS PROGRAMS OF THE KENNEDY ADMINISTRATION.   NSULLDF64190

      THE ROLE OF CIVIL-RIGHTS ORGANIZATIONS. A MARSHALL PLAN APPROACH.   NTUCKSX66209

      1961 COMMISSION ON CIVIL-RIGHTS REPORT BOOK 3. EMPLOYMENT.   NUSCOMC61231

      URBAN-RENEWAL AND CIVIL-RIGHTS.   NWINTSB64329

      THE SOCIAL REVOLUTION. CHALLENGE TO THE NATION. /CIVIL-RIGHTS/   NYOUNWM63600

      CIVIL-RIGHTS -- DISCRIMINATION IN LABOR UNIONS.   NYOUNWM64349

CIVIL-RIGHTS-ACT
   FEDERAL CIVIL-RIGHTS-ACT OF 1960. SUMMARY AND ANALYSIS.   GAMERJD60385

      THE IMPLICATIONS OF THE CIVIL-RIGHTS-ACT OF 1964 FOR PSYCHOLOGICAL ASSESSMENT IN INDUSTRY. /TESTING/   GASHXPX66405

      IMPLICATIONS FOR BUSINESS OF THE CIVIL-RIGHTS-ACT OF 1964.   GBENEDX65434

      COVERAGE UNDER TITLE-VII OF THE CIVIL-RIGHTS-ACT.   GBENEMC66435

      EQUAL-EMPLOYMENT-OPPORTUNITY UNDER CIVIL-RIGHTS-ACT OF 1964.   GBERGRK64437

      EMPLOYMENT DISCRIMINATION. STATE FEPC LAWS AND THE IMPACT OF OF TITLE-VII OF THE CIVIL-RIGHTS-ACT OF
      1964.   GBRYEGL65896

      A SPECIAL REPORT -- THE EQUAL-EMPLOYMENT-OPPORTUNITY LAW, TITLE-VII OF THE CIVIL-RIGHTS-ACT OF 1964.   GBURENANC495

      THE CIVIL-RIGHTS-ACT OF 1964. WHAT IT MEANS -- TO EMPLOYERS, BUSINESSMEN, UNIONS, EMPLOYEES,
      MINORITY-GROUPS. TEXT. ANALYSIS. LEGISLATIVE HISTORY.   GBUREON64492

      CIVIL-RIGHTS-ACT OF 1964. WITH EXPLANATION -- PUBLIC LAW 88-352 -- AS APPROVED BY THE PRESIDENT ON JULY
      2. 1964.   GCOMMCH64588

      FAIR-EMPLOYMENT-PRACTICES UNDER THE CIVIL-RIGHTS-ACT OF 1964.   GCOMMCH64590

      ARIZONA-S EXPERIENCE UNDER THE CIVIL-RIGHTS-ACT.   GCRAICE66620

      UNION RACIAL DISCRIMINATION -- RECENT DEVELOPMENTS BEFORE THE NLRB AND THEIR IMPLICATIONS UNDER TITLE-VII
      OF THE CIVIL-RIGHTS-ACT OF 1964.   GGEORLJ65714

      OKLAHOMA GEARS FOR THE CIVIL-RIGHTS-ACT.   GJELTMM66823

      EXPLANATION AND DIGEST OF THE 1966 KENTUCKY CIVIL-RIGHTS-ACT COVERING EMPLOYMENT AND PUBLIC

CIVIL-RIGHTS-ACT   (CONTINUATION)
ACCOMODATIONS. ENACTED JANUARY 27 1966, EFFECTIVE JULY 1 1966.   GKENTCHN0844

A TALE OF 22 CITIES. TITLE-VII OF THE CIVIL-RIGHTS-ACT OF 1964.   GKOTHCA65732

EMPLOYMENT DISCRIMINATION. STATE FAIR-EMPLOYMENT-PRACTICES LAWS AND THE IMPACT OF TITLE-VII OF THE
CIVIL-RIGHTS-ACT OF 1964.   GLAWXRD65885

THE CIVIL-RIGHTS-ACT, IMPLICATIONS FOR BUSINESS.   GNEWYCA64068

THE CIVIL-RIGHTS-ACT OF 1964 -- SOURCE AND SCOPE OF CONGRESSIONAL POWER.   GNORTUL65672

FAIR-EMPLOYMENT IS GOOD BUSINESS. EXAMPLES OF FAIR PRACTICES FOR TITLE-VII OF THE CIVIL-RIGHTS-ACT OF
1964.   GPOTOII65188

DIVISION OF AUTHORITY UNDER TITLE-VII OF THE CIVIL-RIGHTS-ACT OF 1964. A PRELIMINARY STUDY IN
FEDERAL-STATE INTERAGENCY RELATIONS.   GROSESJ66254

UNION-S DUTY OF FAIR REPRESENTATION AND THE CIVIL-RIGHTS-ACT OF 1964.   GSHERHL65302

ENFORCEMENT OF FAIR-EMPLOYMENT UNDER THE CIVIL-RIGHTS-ACT OF 1964.   GUVCHLR64213

REGIONAL CONFERENCES ON IMPLEMENTING THE CIVIL-RIGHTS-ACT.   NFREYMX66386

EMPLOYMENT SECURITY, SENIORITY AND RACE. THE ROLE OF TITLE-VII OF THE CIVIL-RIGHTS-ACT OF 1964.   NGOULWB67864

TITLE-VII. EQUAL-EMPLOYMENT SECTION. CIVIL-RIGHTS-ACT OF 1964. THE WAR-AGAINST-POVERTY.   NHILLHX65549

THE CIVIL-RIGHTS-ACT OF 1964. RACIAL DISCRIMINATION BY LABOR UNIONS.   NSAINJL66138

THE CIVIL-RIGHTS-ACT.   NUSDLAB64147

CLASSIFICATION ON THE BASIS OF SEX AND THE 1964 CIVIL-RIGHTS-ACT.   WIOWALR65102

SEX AND THE CIVIL-RIGHTS-ACT.   /LEGISLATION/   WUHLXGX66200

WOMEN AND THE EQUAL-EMPLOYMENT PROVISIONS OF THE CIVIL-RIGHTS-ACT.   WUSDLAB65234

CIVIL-SERVICE
EMPLOYMENT IN CIVIL-SERVICE OF MINORITY-GROUPS. /DETROIT MICHIGAN/   GDETRCC63638

CIVIL-SERVICE TESTING AND JOB DISCRIMINATION.   GGORDJE66281

FURNISHING EQUAL-OPPORTUNITY FOR MINORITIES IN CIVIL-SERVICE.   GGREGGX62070

CIVILIAN
CIVILIAN PERSONNEL -- NONDISCRIMINATION IN EMPLOYMENT. /MILITARY/   GUSDAIR62189

READJUSTMENTS OF VETERANS TO CIVILIAN LIFE.   NUSDLAB46839

CLAIMANTS
FAMILY CHARACTERISTICS OF THE LONG TERM UNEMPLOYED. A REPORT ON A STUDY OF CLAIMANTS UNDER THE TEMPORARY
EXTENDED UNEMPLOYMENT COMPENSATION PROGRAM, 1961-2.   GUSDLAB61445

CLAIMS
A SUMMARY ANALYSIS OF FIVE YEARS OF CLAIMS EXPERIENCE BY THE MICHIGAN
FAIR-EMPLOYMENT-PRACTICES-COMMISSION, FEBRUARY, 1961.   GCCUSFR61612

A SUMMARY ANALYSIS OF SIX YEARS OF CLAIMS EXPERIENCE BY THE MICHIGAN FAIR-EMPLOYMENT
PRACTICES-COMMISSION, FEBRUARY 1962.   GCOUSFR62613

CLARK
THE MANPOWER REVOLUTION. ITS POLICY CONSEQUENCES. EXCERPTS FROM SENATE HEARINGS BEFORE THE CLARK
SUBCOMMITTEE.   GMANGGL66217

CLASH
NO MORE COUSIN TOMS. THE CLASH BETWEEN THE UNIONS AND THE NEGROES.   NJACOPX63602

CLASS
CLASS DIFFERENCES IN THE SOCIALIZATION PRACTICES OF NEGRO MOTHERS.   CKAMICKN0632

MINORITY-GROUP AND CLASS STATUS AS RELATED TO SOCIAL AND PERSONALITY FACTORS IN SCHOLASTIC ACHIEVEMENT.   GDEUTMP60640

THE OUTLOOK OF WORKING CLASS YOUTH. /DROP-OUT ASPIRATION/   GMILLSM62570

TEST PERFORMANCE IN RELATION TO ETHNIC GROUP AND SOCIAL CLASS.   GROBES063683

CLASS AS AN EXPLANATION OF ETHNIC DIFFERENCES IN MOBILITY ASPIRATIONS -- THE CASE OF MEXICAN-AMERICANS.   MHELLCS65415

CLASS CONSCIOUSNESS AND SOCIAL MOBILITY IN A MEXICAN-AMERICAN COMMUNITY.   MPENAFX63453

CLASS AND FAMILY INFLUENCES ON STUDENT ASPIRATIONS.   NBENNWS64574

SOCIO-ECONOMIC CLASS AND AREA AS CORRELATES OF ILLEGAL BEHAVIOR AMONG JUVENILES.   NCLARJP62209

COLOR, CLASS, PERSONALITY, AND JUVENILE DELINQUENCY.   NCLARKB59210

CHARACTERISTICS OF THE LOWER-BLUE-COLLAR CLASS.SOCIO-ECONOMIC/   NCOHEAK63219

THE NEGRO MIDDLE CLASS IS RIGHT IN THE MIDDLE. /ECONOMIC-STATUS/   NCORDDX66030

CASTE AND CLASS IN A SOUTHERN TOWN.   NDOLLJX49281

ETHNIC AND CLASS PREFERENCES AMONG COLLEGE NEGROES.   NEBOIAX60315

THE NEGRO PROFESSIONAL CLASS. /OCCUPATIONAL-PATTERNS/   NEDWAGF59324

EDUCABILITY AND REHABILITATION. THE FUTURE OF THE WELFARE CLASS.   NHESSRD64523

CULTURE, CLASS AND FAMILY LIFE AMONG LOW-INCOME NEGROES.   NLEWIHX67691

THE NEGRO LEADERSHIP CLASS.   NTHOMOC63713

SOCIAL CLASS AND COLOR CASTE IN AMERICA.   NWARNWL62292

LIBERAL ARTS WOMEN GRADUATES, CLASS OF 1958. /WORK-WOMEN-ROLE/   WLICHMW59933

SPEAKING FOR THE WORKING CLASS WIFE. /BLUE-COLLAR/   WSEXTPC62299

CLASS (CONTINUATION)
FIRST JOBS OF COLLEGE WOMEN -- REPORT ON WOMEN GRADUATES, **CLASS** OF 1957.   WUSDLAB59194

FIFTEEN YEARS AFTER COLLEGE -- A STUDY OF ALUMNAE OF THE **CLASS** OF 1945.   WUSDLAB62193

COLLEGE WOMEN SEVEN YEARS AFTER GRADUATION -- RESURVEY OF WOMEN GRADUATES **CLASS** OF 1957.   WUSDLAB66185

CLASSES
LABOR AND LABORING **CLASSES**.   NBLOOGF50095

SOME ASPECTS OF VOCATIONAL ASPIRATIONS AND VALUE ORIENTATION AMONG NEGRO BOYS IN THE LOWER SOCIO-ECONOMIC
CLASSES.   NSCHMWX63139

CLASSIFICATION
A METHODOLOGICAL APPROACH TO IDENTIFICATION AND **CLASSIFICATION** OF CERTAIN TYPES OF INACTIVE WORK-SEEKERS.
/UNEMPLOYMENT LABOR-MARKET/   GLIEBEE65569

CLASSIFICATION ON THE BASIS OF SEX AND THE 1964 CIVIL-RIGHTS-ACT.   WICWALR65102

CLASSROOM
WORKING WITH STUDENTS INSIDE AND OUTSIDE THE **CLASSROOM** IN ADULT BASIC EDUCATION PROGRAMS.   NBRAZWF64285

CLAUSE
THE NONDISCRIMINATION **CLAUSE** IN GOVERNMENT CONTRACTS.   GPASLRS57148

UNITED STATES HAS STANDING UNDER INTERSTATE COMMERCE ACT AND COMMERCE **CLAUSE** TO ENJOIN SEGREGATIVE
PRACTICES OF CITY. /LEGISLATION/   NHARVLR64500

NON-DISCRIMINATION **CLAUSE** IN GOVERNMENT CONTRACTS IS MANDATORY.   NUSDLAB43833

CLAUSES
ANTI-DISCRIMINATION **CLAUSES** REVISITED.   GWORTMS65585

THE INCIDENCE OF ANTIDISCRIMINATION **CLAUSES** IN UNION CONTRACTS.   GWORTMS65681

CLEAR
THE IMPLICATIONS OF PROJECT **CLEAR**. /DESEGREGATION/   NFORMPB55372

CLERICAL
AUTOMATION AND EMPLOYMENT OPPORTUNITIES FOR OFFICE WORKERS. THE EFFECT OF ELECTRONIC COMPUTERS ON
EMPLOYMENT OF **CLERICAL** WORKERS, WITH A SPECIAL REPORT ON PROGRAMMERS.   WPASCWX58178

CLERICAL OCCUPATIONS FOR WOMEN -- TODAY AND TOMORROW. /OCCUPATIONS/   WUSDLAB64188

CLERKS
THE RETAIL **CLERKS**. /TECHNOLOGICAL-CHANGE/   WHARRMX62823

CLEVELAND
CURRENT POPULATION REPORTS -- SPECIAL CENSUS OF **CLEVELAND**, OHIO. /DEMOGRAPHY/   CUSBURC65379

INCOME, EDUCATION AND UNEMPLOYMENT IN NEIGHBORHOODS. **CLEVELAND**, OHIO. /DEMOGRAPHY/   CUSDLAB63458

SUB-EMPLOYMENT IN THE SLUMS OF **CLEVELAND**. /OHIO/   GUSDLAB66516

THE NEGRO IN **CLEVELAND**, 1950-1963. /OHIO/   NCLEVUL64916

HOUGH, **CLEVELAND**, OHIO -- A STUDY OF SOCIAL LIFE AND CHANGE.   NSUSSMB59192

CLEVELAND-S
CLEVELAND-S ANNUAL JOB CENTER FOR COLLEGE GRADUATES.   NCOCKHW65218

CLIENTS
CIVIL-RIGHTS AND THE REHABILITATION OF AFDC **CLIENTS**.   GSETSLX64296

THE NEGRO LAWYER AND HIS **CLIENTS**. /OCCUPATIONS/   NHALEWH52476

CLINICS
REPORT OF INDUSTRY AND LABOR-MANAGEMENT **CLINICS**. IMPLEMENTATION OF EMPLOYMENT IN MERIT PROGRAMS IN NON
FEPC STATES BY DIRECT APPROACH TO TOP MANAGEMENT.   GFISKUR51684

CLOTHING
NEGRO WOMEN IN THE **CLOTHING**, CIGAR AND LAUNDRY INDUSTRIES OF PHILADELPHIA, 1960.   CPORTRP43103

CO-ED
INITIATION INTO A WOMAN-S PROFESSION. IDENTITY PROBLEMS IN THE STATUS TRANSITION OF **CO-ED** TO STUDENT
NURSE.   WDAVIFX66723

CO-WORKERS
ATTITUDES OF WHITE DEPARTMENT STORE EMPLOYEES TOWARD NEGRO **CO-WORKERS**. /CASE-STUDY/   NHARDJX52482

COACHELLA-VALLEY
ATTITUDES TOWARD ETHNIC FARM WORKERS IN **COACHELLA-VALLEY**. /CALIFORNIA/   NMCDOEC55719

COAHOMA
THE RELATIONSHIP BETWEEN MECHANIZATION OF COTTON PRODUCTION AND ATTENDANCE AND ENROLLMENT IN THE RURAL
SCHOOLS OF **COAHOMA** COUNTY, MISSISSIPPI.   NMCLABF51349

COAL
RACE RELATIONSHIP IN THE POCAHONTAS **COAL** FIELD.   NMINARD52794

COAST
MIGRATORY FARM WORKERS IN THE ATLANTIC **COAST** STREAM. I. CHANGES IN NEW-YORK, 1953 AND 1957.   GLARSOF60406

MIGRATORY FARM WORKERS IN THE ATLANTIC **COAST** STREAM.   GMETZWH55426

MIGRATORY FARM WORKERS IN THE ATLANTIC **COAST** STREAM. WESTERN NEW-YORK, JUNE 1953.   GMOTHJR54405

MIGRATORY FARM WORKERS IN THE ATLANTIC **COAST** STREAM. II. EDUCATION OF NEW-YORK WORKERS AND THEIR
CHILDREN. 1953 AND 1957.   GSHAREF60427

INDIANS OF THE NORTHWEST **COAST**.   IDOUCPX63549

ACCOMODATION BETWEEN NEGRO AND WHITE EMPLOYEES IN A WEST **COAST** AIRCRAFT INDUSTRY, 1942-1944.
/CASE-STUDY/   NREEDBA47045

COASTAL
RESOURCES AND INCOMES OF RURAL FAMILIES IN THE **COASTAL** PLAIN AREAS OF GEORGIA.   GMCARWC59392

CODE
REPORT ON OAKLAND SCHOOLS. AN INVESTIGATION UNDER SECTION 1421 OF THE CALIFORNIA LABOR **CODE** OF THE

CODE (CONTINUATION)
OAKLAND UNIFIED SCHOOL DISTRICT 1962-1963. /NEGRO ORIENTAL MEXICAN-AMERICAN/   CCALDIR63710

GUIDE TO LAWFUL AND UNLAWFUL PRE-EMPLOYMENT INQUIRIES BY EMPLOYERS, EMPLOYMENT-AGENCIES, AND LABOR
ORGANIZATIONS UNDER THE CALIFORNIA FAIR-EMPLOYMENT-PRACTICE ACT, LABOR **CODE**, SECTIONS 1410-1432.   GCALDIR60527

EMPLOYMENT PRACTICES. CITY OF PASADENA, AN INVESTIGATION UNDER SECTION 1421 OF THE CALIFORNIA LABOR **CODE**
1963-1965.   GCALFEPND531

GOVENOR-S **CODE** OF FAIR PRACTICE /CALIFORNIA/   GCALOGB63546

COED
A QUESTIONNAIRE PORTRAIT OF THE FRESHMAN **COED**. AFTER COLLEGE WHAT. /ASPIRATIONS/   WLLOYBJ66938

COLLAR
WHITE **COLLAR** EMPLOYMENT. TRENDS AND STRUCTURE.   GBANYCA61420

COLLECTION
MATERIALS **COLLECTION** ON WOMEN.   WSMITCLND118

COLLECTIONS
SPECIAL WOMEN-S **COLLECTIONS** IN US LIBRARIES.   WBELLMS59636

COLLECTIVE
DISCRIMINATION IN UNION MEMBERSHIP. DENIAL OF DUE PROCESS UNDER FEDERAL **COLLECTIVE** BARGAINING
LEGISLATION.   GPRESSB58126

RACE. INDIVIDUAL AND **COLLECTIVE** BEHAVIOR.   GTHOMET58356

THE NEGRO REVOLUTION AND THE LAW OF **COLLECTIVE** BARGAINING.   NGOULWB65437

COLLECTIVE-BARGAININ
A GUIDE TO INDUSTRIAL-RELATIONS IN THE UNITED STATES. EQUAL JOB OPPORTUNITY UNDER **COLLECTIVE-BARGAINING**.   GUSDLAB58449

RECENT **COLLECTIVE-BARGAINING** AND TECHNOLOGICAL-CHANGE.   NDAVILM64942

COLLEGE
THE VALUES OF NEGRO WOMEN **COLLEGE** STUDENTS.   CEAGLOW45313

A NOTE ON THE VALUES OF SOUTHERN **COLLEGE** WOMEN, WHITE AND NEGRO.   CGRAYSW47445

THE NEGRO **COLLEGE** WOMAN.   CNOBLJL54924

THE NEGRO WOMAN **COLLEGE** GRADUATE.   CNOBLJL55925

INEQUALITY OF OPPORTUNITY IN HIGHER EDUCATION. A STUDY OF MINORITY GROUP AND RELATED BARRIERS TO **COLLEGE**
ADMISSION.   GBERKDS48446

HOW TO RECRUIT MINORITY-GROUP **COLLEGE** GRADUATES, ITS PROBLEMS, ITS TECHNIQUES, ITS SOURCES, ITS
OPPORTUNITIES.   GCALVRX63555

EDUCATIONAL STATUS, **COLLEGE** PLANS, AND OCCUPATIONAL-STATUS OF FARM AND NONFARM YOUTHS. OCTOBER 1959.   GCOWHJD61427

BACKGROUND FACTORS RELATING TO **COLLEGE** PLANS AND COLLEGE ENROLLMENT AMONG PUBLIC HIGH SCHOOL STUDENTS.
/ASPIRATIONS/   GEDUCTS57959

BACKGROUND FACTORS RELATING TO COLLEGE PLANS AND **COLLEGE** ENROLLMENT AMONG PUBLIC HIGH SCHOOL STUDENTS.
/ASPIRATIONS/   GEDUCTS57959

SURVEY OF OHIO **COLLEGE** AND UNIVERSITY PLACEMENT OFFICES WITH REGARD TO JOB PLACEMENT OF MINORITY
STUDENTS.   GOHIOCR62132

PROJECTIONS OF SCHOOL AND **COLLEGE** ENROLLMENT IN THE UNITED STATES TO 1985. /DEMOGRAPHY/   GUSBURC66160

JEWS IN **COLLEGE** AND UNIVERSITY ADMINISTRATION.   JAMERJC66693

THE JEWISH **COLLEGE** STUDENT.   JSHOSRJ57761

CURRICULUM CHOICE IN THE NEGRO **COLLEGE**.   NBRAZWF60109

OCCUPATIONAL CHOICE IN THE NEGRO **COLLEGE**.   NBRAZWF60112

THE NEGRO GRADUATE, 1950-1960. /**COLLEGE** EDUCATION/   NBROWAX60125

THE NEGRO **COLLEGE** STUDENT. SOME FACTS AND SOME CONCERNS.   NCLARKB64307

CLEVELAND-S ANNUAL JOB CENTER FOR **COLLEGE** GRADUATES.   NCOCKHW65218

EDUCATION AND MARGINALITY. A STUDY OF THE NEGRO **COLLEGE** GRADUATE.   NCUTHMV49936

ABC REPORT 1964. /**COLLEGE** EDUCATION/   NDARTCX64309

A STUDY OF JOB-OPPORTUNITIES IN THE STATE OF FLORIDA FOR NEGRO **COLLEGE** GRADUATES.   NDECKPM60261

ETHNIC AND CLASS PREFERENCES AMONG **COLLEGE** NEGROES.   NEBOIAX60315

PROFITABLE CAREERS -- WITHOUT **COLLEGE**.   NEBONXX59318

RELATION OF MOTHER-S EMPLOYMENT TO INTELLECTUAL PERFORMANCE OF NEGRO **COLLEGE** STUDENTS.   NEPPSEG64336

YOUNG NEGRO TALENT. SURVEY OF THE EXPERIENCES AND EXPECTATIONS OF NEGRO AMERICANS WHO GRADUATED FROM
COLLEGE IN 1961.   NFICHJH64867

CAREER PREPARATION AND EXPECTATIONS OF NEGRO **COLLEGE** STUDENTS.   NFICHJH66789

MOTIVATION AND ASPIRATION IN THE NEGRO **COLLEGE**.   NGURIPX66352

ACHIEVEMENT MOTIVATION CHARACTERISTICS OF NEGRO **COLLEGE** FRESHMEN.   NHARREC59492

SOME COMPARISONS AMONG NEGRO-WHITE **COLLEGE** STUDENTS. SOCIAL AMBITION AND ESTIMATED SOCIAL MOBILITY.   NHARREE66786

THE RIGHT TO KNOWLEDGE. /**COLLEGE** EDUCATION/   NHEALHX64306

PREPARATION OF THE NEGRO **COLLEGE** GRADUATE FOR BUSINESS. /EMPLOYMENT-SELECTION/   NHOLLJH65560

COLLEGE, COLOR, AND EMPLOYMENT. RACIAL DIFFERENTIALS IN POSTGRADUATE EMPLOYMENT AMONG 1964 GRADUATES OF
LOUISIANA COLLEGES.   NHUSOCF66328

DIFFERENTIAL CHARACTERISTICS OF SUPERIOR AND UNSELECTED NEGRO **COLLEGE** STUDENTS.   NJENKMD48608

COLLEGE   (CONTINUATION)
    EFFECTS OF ANXIETY, THREAT, AND RACIAL ENVIRONMENT ON TASK PERFORMANCE OF NEGRO **COLLEGE** STUDENTS.   NKATZIX63640

    A PILOT STUDY OF PERSONALITY FACTORS RELATED TO OCCUPATIONAL ASPIRATIONS OF NEGRO **COLLEGE** STUDENTS.   NLITTLW66697

    TEACHER SUPPLY AND DEMAND IN THE NEGRO **COLLEGE**.   NLLOYRG54045

    YOU NEED TO SEE IT TO BELIEVE IT. REPORT OF THE 1963 SUMMER STUDY-SKILLS PROGRAMS. /COLLEGE EDUCATION/   NMARTWD63303

    RECRUITING NEGRO **COLLEGE** GRADUATES.   NNATLIC64231

    NEGLECTED TALENTS. BACKGROUND AND PROSPECTS OF NEGRO **COLLEGE** GRADUATES.   NNATLOR66880

    CHARACTERISTICS OF NEGRO **COLLEGE** CHIEF LIBRARIANS. /OCCUPATIONS/   NPOLLFM64005

    THE BACKGROUND OF THE 1947 **COLLEGE** STUDENT. /LABOR-MARKET/   NQUARBX47257

    NEGRO AMERICAN **COLLEGE** YOUTH-S OUTLOOK ON THE FUTURE.   NROBES057067

    REVOLUTION IN EVOLUTION. /COLLEGE RECRUITMENT/   NSCOTFG66111

    SECRETARY-S CONFERENCE WITH **COLLEGE** PRESIDENTS AND EXECUTIVES. /EDUCATION EMPLOYMENT/   NUSDLAB63301

    THE ROLE OF THE NEGRO **COLLEGE**.   NWEAVEK44297

    THE PLACEMENT OF NEGRO **COLLEGE** GRADUATES IN BUSINESS ORGANIZATIONS.   NWHITEW64321

    COMPARATIVE STUDY OF SOCIO-ECONOMIC AND SOCIAL-PSYCHOLOGICAL DETERMINANTS OF EDUCATIONAL AND OCCUPATIONAL
    ASPIRATIONS OF NEGRO AND WHITE **COLLEGE** SENIORS.   NWHITRM59319

    CHANGE AND CHOICE FOR THE **COLLEGE** WOMAN. /WORK-WOMAN-ROLE/   WAAUWJX62601

    THE PROSPECT FOR ADVANCEMENT IN BUSINESS OF THE MARRIED WOMAN **COLLEGE** GRADUATE. /OCCUPATIONS/   WBECKEL64632

    ATTITUDES TOWARD WOMEN **COLLEGE** TEACHERS IN INSTITUTIONS OF HIGHER EDUCATION ACCREDITED BY THE NORTH
    CENTRAL ASSOCIATION.   WBERWHD62475

    THE **COLLEGE** AND THE CONTINUING EDUCATION OF WOMEN.   WBLACGW63648

    VALUE CHANGE IN **COLLEGE** WOMEN. /WORK-WOMEN-ROLE/   WBROWDR62658

    POST GRADUATION ROLE PREFERENCE OF SENIOR WOMEN IN **COLLEGE**. /ASPIRATION/   WCHRIHX56690

    A SOURCE FOR **COLLEGE** FACULTIES. /OCCUPATIONS/   WCLAYFL62691

    A STUDY OF JOB MOTIVATIONS, ACTIVITIES, AND SATISFACTIONS OF PRESENT AND PROSPECTIVE WOMEN **COLLEGE**
    FACULTY MEMBERS. /OCCUPATIONS/   WCOOKWX60252

    THE POST-PARENTAL PHASE IN THE LIFE CYCLE OF 50 **COLLEGE** EDUCATED WOMEN. /WORK-FAMILY-CONFLICT/   WDAVIIX60717

    WORK MOTIVATION OF **COLLEGE** ALUMNAE. FIVE-YEAR FOLLOWUP.   WEYDELD67223

    THE ROLE OF THE EDUCATED WOMAN. AN EMPIRICAL STUDY OF THE ATTITUDES OF A GROUP OF **COLLEGE** WOMEN.
     /WORK-WOMAN-ROLE/   WFREEMB65770

    THE EFFECT OF THE SOCIAL CONTEXT IN THE VOCATIONAL COUNSELING OF **COLLEGE** WOMEN.   WGURIMG63810

    COLLEGE WOMEN-S IDENTIFICATIONS WITH THEIR FATHERS IN RELATION TO VOCATIONAL INTEREST PATTERNS.
     /ASPIRATIONS/   WHALLWJ63815

    TECHNICAL EDUCATION IN THE JUNIOR **COLLEGE**.   WHARRNC64825

    IMPLICATIONS FROM RECENT RESEARCH ON **COLLEGE** STUDENTS. /MANPOWER/   WHEISPX59838

    A COMMENTARY ON THE MOTIVATION AND EDUCATION OF **COLLEGE** WOMEN. /ASPIRATIONS/   WHEISPX62837

    THE MOTIVATION OF **COLLEGE** WOMEN TODAY. A CLOSER LOOK. /ASPIRATIONS/   WHEISPX62839

    THE MOTIVATION OF **COLLEGE** WOMEN TODAY. THE CULTURAL SETTING. /ASPIRATIONS/   WHEISPX63840

    ATTITUDES OF **COLLEGE** STUDENTS TOWARD EMPLOYMENT AMONG MARRIED WOMEN. /WORK-FAMILY-CONFLICT/   WHEWEVH64482

    INTEREST AND PERSONALITY CORRELATES OF CAREER-MOTIVATED AND HOMEMAKING-MOTIVATED **COLLEGE** WOMEN.
     /ASPIRATIONS/   WHOYTDP58850

    RETENTION AND WITHDRAWAL OF **COLLEGE** STUDENTS. /DROP-OUT/   WIFFERE57854

    STUDY OF JOB OPPORTUNITIES FOR WOMEN **COLLEGE** GRADUATES. /OCCUPATIONS/   WINTEAP58861

    PARTICIPATION IN PART-TIME WORK BY WOMEN **COLLEGE** STUDENTS.   WISAALE57875

    CHANGING VALUES IN **COLLEGE**. /WORK-WOMAN-ROLE/   WJACOPE57877

    CHANGES IN SELECTED PERSONALITY CHARACTERISTICS AND PERSISTENCE IN THE CAREER CHOICES OF WOMEN ASSOCIATED
    WITH A FOUR YEAR **COLLEGE** EDUCATION AT ONE OF THE COLLEGES OF THE CITY UNIVERSITY OF NEW-YORK.
     /ASPIRATIONS/   WLEINMX64925

    TODAY-S WOMEN **COLLEGE** GRADUATES. /WORK-WOMEN-ROLE/   WLEOPAK59927

    A QUESTIONNAIRE PORTRAIT OF THE FRESHMAN COED. AFTER **COLLEGE** WHAT. /ASPIRATIONS/   WLLOYBJ66938

    RUTGERS -- THE STATE UNIVERSITY. FORD FOUNDATION PROGRAM FOR THE RETRAINING IN MATHEMATICS OF **COLLEGE**
    GRADUATE WOMEN. /TRAINING/   WMARTHM63957

    PERCEPTIONS OF ROLE CONFLICTS AND SELF CONFLICTS AMONG CAREER AND NON-CAREER **COLLEGE** EDUCATED WOMEN.
    /WORK-FAMILY-CONFLICT/   WMORGDO62996

    WOMEN GRADUATES OF COOPERATIVE WORK-STUDY PROGRAMS ON THE **COLLEGE** LEVEL. /SKILLS/   WMOSBWB57999

    NEW HORIZONS FOR **COLLEGE** WOMEN. /WORK-WOMEN-ROLE/   WMULLLC60005

    TEACHING. OPPORTUNITIES FOR WOMEN **COLLEGE** GRADUATES.   WNATLEA64019

    EFFECTIVE **COLLEGE** RECRUITING. /TECHNOLOGICAL-CHANGE/   WODIOGS61042

    WOMEN ON **COLLEGE** AND UNIVERSITY FACULTIES. A HISTORICAL SURVEY AND A STUDY OF THEIR PRESENT ACADEMIC
    STATUS. /OCCUPATIONS/   WPOLLLA65063

    NEW SOURCES OF **COLLEGE** TEACHERS. /OCCUPATIONS/   WRILESB61287

COLLEGE   (CONTINUATION)
    CHARACTERISTICS OF WOMEN-S COLLEGE STUDENTS.   WROWEFB64095

    REPORT -- 1965-66 -- RETRAINING PROGRAM IN MATHEMATICS AND SCIENCE FOR COLLEGE GRADUATE WOMEN.   WRUTGMR66098

    IS COLLEGE EDUCATION WASTED ON WOMEN.   WSANFNX57102

    THE AMERICAN COLLEGE. /WOMAN-WORK-ROLE/   WSANFNX62101

    THE CHANGING ROLE OF COLLEGE WOMEN. A BIBLIOGRAPHY. /WORK-WOMAN-ROLE/   WSCHWJX62106

    FIVE THOUSAND WOMEN COLLEGE GRADUATES REPORT.   WSHOSRX56113

    FAMILIAL CORRELATES OF ORIENTATION TOWARD FUTURE EMPLOYMENT AMONG COLLEGE WOMEN. /ASPIRATIONS/   WSIEGAX63572

    OCCUPATIONAL CHOICE AMONG CAREER ORIENTED COLLEGE WOMEN. /ASPIRATIONS/   WSIMPRL61115

    OCCUPATIONAL PLANNING BY YOUNG WOMEN, A STUDY OF OCCUPATIONAL EXPERIENCES, ASPIRATIONS, ATTITUDES, AND
    PLANS OF COLLEGE AND HIGH SCHOOL GIRLS.   WSLOCWL56116

    BACKGROUND FACTORS AND COLLEGE GOING PLANS AMONG HIGH APTITUDE PUBLIC HIGH SCHOOL SENIORS. /ASPIRATIONS/   WSTICGX56141

    JOB OPPORTUNITIES FOR WOMEN COLLEGE GRADUATES.   WSWERSX64145

    ROOM AT THE TOP FOR COLLEGE WOMEN.   WSWERSX64767

    HIGH SCHOOL GUIDANCE COUNSELOR-S PERCEPTIONS OF SELECTED CAREERS FOR WOMEN COLLEGE GRADUATES.   WSWOPMR63146

    WOMEN IN COLLEGE AND UNIVERSITY TEACHING. /OCCUPATIONS/   WTOTAJV65159

    EMPLOYMENT OF JUNE 1955 WOMEN COLLEGE GRADUATES.   WUSDLAB56990

    FIRST JOBS OF COLLEGE WOMEN -- REPORT ON WOMEN GRADUATES. CLASS OF 1957.   WUSDLAB59194

    FIFTEEN YEARS AFTER COLLEGE -- A STUDY OF ALUMNAE OF THE CLASS OF 1945.   WUSDLAB62193

    JOB HORIZONS FOR COLLEGE WOMEN IN THE 1960-S.   WUSDLAB64202

    COLLEGE WOMEN SEVEN YEARS AFTER GRADUATION -- RESURVEY OF WOMEN GRADUATES CLASS OF 1957.   WUSDLAB66185

    SOME CORRELATES OF HOMEMAKING VS CAREER PREFERENCE AMONG COLLEGE HOME ECONOMICS STUDENTS.
    /WORK-FAMILY-CONFLICT/   WVETTLX64257

    VOCATIONAL INTERESTS AND OCCUPATIONAL ADJUSTMENT OF COLLEGE WOMEN.   WWARRPA59222

    THE COLLEGE GIRL LOOKS AHEAD TO HER CAREER OPPORTUNITIES.   WZAPOMW56280

    COLLEGE WOMEN AND EMPLOYMENT.   WZAPOMW59281

COLLEGE-EDUCATED
    A NEW LIFE PATTERN FOR THE COLLEGE-EDUCATED WOMAN. /WORK-FAMILY-CONFLICT/   WSTEIER65133

COLLEGE-TRAINED
    WHY COLLEGE-TRAINED MOTHERS WORK.   WROSSJE65770

COLLEGES
    OUR CHANGING ELITE COLLEGES. /EDUCATION/   JBLOOLX60705

    PLACEMENT AND CAREER COUNSELING AT PREDOMINANTLY NEGRO COLLEGES.   NBEAUAG66067

    THE NEGRO STUDENT AT INTEGRATED COLLEGES.   NCLARKB63214

    TEST BIAS. VALIDITY OF THE SCHOLASTIC APTITUDE TEST FOR NEGRO AND WHITE STUDENTS IN INTEGRATED COLLEGES.   NCLEATA66923

    SOCIAL-CLASS CONSTRAINTS ON THE OCCUPATIONAL ASPIRATIONS OF STUDENTS ATTENDING SOME PREDOMINANTLY NEGRO
    COLLEGES.   NGURIPX66467

    SOME CHARACTERISTICS OF STUDENTS FROM POVERTY BACKGROUNDS ATTENDING PREDOMINANTLY NEGRO COLLEGES IN THE
    DEEP SOUTH.   NGURIPX66468

    COLLEGE. COLOR, AND EMPLOYMENT. RACIAL DIFFERENTIALS IN POSTGRADUATE EMPLOYMENT AMONG 1964 GRADUATES OF
    LOUISIANA COLLEGES.   NHUSOCF66328

    NEGRO COLLEGES. LONG IGNORED, SOUTHERN SCHOOLS NOW COURTED BY MAJOR UNIVERSITIES AND FOUNDATIONS.   NLANGEX64304

    THE PREDOMINANTLY NEGRO COLLEGES AND UNIVERSITIES IN TRANSITION.   NMCGREJ65720

    THE UTILIZATION OF NEGRO TEACHERS IN THE COLLEGES OF NEW-YORK STATE.   NMOSSJA60857

    A STUDY OF THE POTENTIAL SUPPLY OF NEGRO TEACHERS FOR THE COLLEGES OF NEW-YORK STATE.   NMOSSJA61858

    THE MARKET FOR NEGRO EDUCATORS IN COLLEGES AND UNIVERSITIES OUTSIDE THE SOUTH.   NRCSEHM61076

    LIBRARY RESOURCES AND SERVICES IN WHITE AND NEGRO COLLEGES. /EDUCATION/   NSAMOTX65128

    CAREER PATTERNS OF TEACHERS IN NEGRO COLLEGES.   NTHOMOC58204

    FACULTY EDUCATION AND INCOME IN NEGRO AND WHITE COLLEGES.   NUSDLAB65819

    ANTI-NEPOTISM RULES IN AMERICAN COLLEGES AND UNIVERSITIES -- THEIR EFFECT ON THE FACULTY EMPLOYMENT OF
    WOMEN.   WDOLAEF60951

    CHANGES IN SELECTED PERSONALITY CHARACTERISTICS AND PERSISTENCE IN THE CAREER CHOICES OF WOMEN ASSOCIATED
    WITH A FOUR YEAR COLLEGE EDUCATION AT ONE OF THE COLLEGES OF THE CITY UNIVERSITY OF NEW-YORK.
    /ASPIRATIONS/   WLEINMX64925

    A SURVEY OF SPECIAL EDUCATIONAL PROGRAMS FOR ADULT WOMEN IN UNIVERSITY EXTENSION DIVISIONS AND EVENING
    COLLEGES AS OF SPRING 1965.   WLORIRK66942

COLOR
    UNITED STATES CENSUS OF AGRICULTURE. COLOR, RACE, AND TENURE OF FARM OPERATOR. GENERAL REPORT, VOLUME II.
    /DEMOGRAPHY/   CUSBURC59382

    OCCUPATIONS BY EARNINGS AND EDUCATION. STATISTICS FOR MEN 18-64 YEARS OLD, BY COLOR, IN SELECTED
    OCCUPATIONS. /DEMOGRAPHY/   CUSBURC63178

    NET MIGRATION OF THE POPULATION, 1950-60, BY AGE, SEX, AND COLOR. VOL II, ANALYTICAL GROUPINGS OF
    COUNTIES. /INCOME/   GBOWLGK65434

COLOR   (CONTINUATION)
EQUAL-RIGHTS UNDER THE LAW. PROVIDING FOR EQUAL TREATMENT FOR ALL CITIZENS REGARDLESS OF RACE, RELIGION,   GCALAGO60511
COLOR, NATIONAL ORIGIN OR ANCESTRY. /CALIFORNIA/

LABOR-FORCE PROJECTIONS BY COLOR. 1970-1980.   GCOOPSX66604

EMPLOYMENT AND INCOME BY AGE, SEX, COLOR AND RESIDENCE. /DETROIT MICHIGAN/   GDETRCC63948

STATES LAWS ON RACE AND COLOR.   GMURRPX50034

RULINGS ON PRE-EMPLOYMENT INQUIRIES RELATING TO RACE, CREED, COLOR OR NATIONAL ORIGIN UNDER THE NEW-YORK   GNEWYSBND106
STATE LAW AGAINST DISCRIMINATION.

JOBS WITHOUT CREED OR COLOR.   GRAUSWX45583

FAREWELL TO COLOR BLINDNESS.   NBECKWL65069

THE FUTURE OF THE COLOR LINE. /SOUTH/   NBLUMHX65327

JOBS AND THE COLOR LINE.   NCHILRR57205

COLOR, CLASS, PERSONALITY, AND JUVENILE DELINQUENCY.   NCLARKB59210

IS LABOR COLOR BLIND. /UNION/   NFLEIHX59359

COLLEGE, COLOR, AND EMPLOYMENT. RACIAL DIFFERENTIALS IN POSTGRADUATE EMPLOYMENT AMONG 1964 GRADUATES OF   NHUSOCF66328
LOUISIANA COLLEGES.

JOBS AND COLOR. NEGRO EMPLOYMENT IN TENNESSEE STATE GOVERNMENT.   NLONGHH62706

WORK AND COLOR. /UNION/   NMASOLR52063

THE DESIGNATION OF RACE OR COLOR ON FORMS.   NMINOAX66795

BREAKTHROUGH ON THE COLOR FRONT. /MILITARY/   NNICHLX54920

THE TREND SINCE 1944 ON THE COLOR LINE IN INDUSTRY.   NOPINRC51959

THE CHANGING COLOR COMPOSITION OF METROPOLITAN AREAS. /DEMOGRAPHY/   NSHARHX62125

SEGREGATION. A COLOR PATTERN FROM THE PAST -- OUR STRUGGLE TO WIPE IT OUT.   NSURVGX47191

COLOR, RACE AND TENURE OF FARM OPERATORS.   NUSBURC62225

SOCIAL CLASS AND COLOR CASTE IN AMERICA.   NWARNWL62292

SOUTHERN RACE PROGRESS. THE WAVERING COLOR LINE.   NWOOFTJ57340

COLORADO
INCOME, EDUCATION AND UNEMPLOYMENT IN NEIGHBORHOODS. DENVER, COLORADO. /DEMOGRAPHY/   CUSDLAB63460

HUMAN-RELATIONS IN COLORADO. 1858-1959.   GATKIJA61408

A SOCIAL PROFILE OF AGRICULTURAL MIGRATORY PEOPLE IN COLORADO. /MIGRANT-WORKERS/   GCOLOSD59919

SUGAR BEET LABOR IN NORTHERN COLORADO. /MIGRANT-WORKERS/   GDAVIIF58939

PLANT INSPECTION SURVEY BY MANAGEMENT -- MINORITY-GROUP INTEGRATION. /COLORADO/   GDENNGHND632

THE SOCIO-ECONOMIC AND PHYSICAL CHARACTERISTICS OF THE VARIOUS NEIGHBORHOODS IN PUEBLO. /COLORADO/   GPUEBRP65459

RELOCATEES FROM GALLUP AREA TO THE DENVER FIELD EMPLOYMENT ASSISTANCE OFFICE. /COLORADO/   IGRAVTDND438

A STUDY OF NAVAHO URBAN RELOCATION IN DENVER COLORADO.   IGRAVTD64566

PERCEIVED OPPORTUNITIES, EXPECTATIONS, AND THE DECISION TO REMAIN ON RELOCATION. THE CASE OF THE NAVAHO   IGRAVTD65567
INDIAN MIGRANT TO DENVER, COLORADO.

VALUES, EXPECTATIONS AND RELOCATION. THE NAVAHO MIGRANT TO DENVER. /COLORADO/   IGRAVTD66146

THE ECONOMIC ABSORPTION OF NAVAHO INDIAN MIGRANTS IN DENVER, COLORADO.   IWEPPRS65684

MIGRATORY LABOR IN COLORADO.   MCOLOLC60382

MIGRATORY LABOR IN COLORADO. REPORT TO THE COLORADO GENERAL ASSEMBLY.   MCOLOLC62383

MIGRATORY LABOR IN COLORADO. REPORT TO THE COLORADO GENERAL ASSEMBLY.   MCOLCLC62383

EDUCATING MIGRANT CHILDREN IN COLORADO.   MCOLOSD61384

AGRICULTURAL SEASONAL LABORERS OF COLORADO AND CALIFORNIA. /MIGRANT-WORKERS/   NKARRCHND636

COLORED
DISCRIMINATION IN RATE OF COMPENSATION BETWEEN COLORED AND WHITE TEACHERS HELD UNCONSTITUTIONAL.   NHARVLR40497

THE USE OF COLORED PERSONS IN SKILLED OCCUPATIONS.   NOCONWB41094

OCCUPATIONAL DISTRIBUTION OF EMPLOYED COLORED WORKERS OF MARYLAND.   NUSDLAB40834

COLUMBIA
EMPLOYMENT OPPORTUNITIES FOR HIGH SCHOOL DROPOUTS. A STUDY OF EMPLOYERS PRACTICES, NEEDS AND ATTITUDES IN   GBURESS57499
THE DISTRICT OF COLUMBIA. /WASHINGTON-DC/

MEDICAL SOCIETY OF THE DISTRICT OF COLUMBIA TO ADMIT NEGRO PHYSICIANS. /OCCUPATIONS/   NJOURNM52628

COLVILLE
HUMAN RESOURCES SURVEY OF THE COLVILLE CONFEDERATE TRIBES.   IBLOOJA59538

COMBATING
COMBATING DISCRIMINATION IN EMPLOYMENT.   GBULLPX61523

COMBATING DISCRIMINATION IN EMPLOYMENT IN NEW-YORK STATE.   GRACKFX49215

COMBATING DISCRIMINATION IN THE EMPLOYMENT OF NEGROES IN WAR INDUSTRIES AND GOVERNMENT AGENCIES.   NRAMSLA43128

COMMENT
VOCATIONAL TRAINING TO IMPROVE JOB OPPORTUNITIES FOR MINORITY-GROUPS. COMMENT.   GFINEMX64681

DISCRIMINATION AND THE OCCUPATIONAL PROGRESS OF NEGROES. A COMMENT.   NBECKGS62068

COMMENT   (CONTINUATION)
EDITORIAL **COMMENT**. FEPC HEARINGS REDUCE RACE PROBLEM TO LOWEST TERMS -- EQUAL-ECONOMIC-OPPORTUNITY.   NTHOMCH43160

COMMENTARY
SCHOOL DROPOUTS. A **COMMENTARY** AND ANNOTATED BIBLIOGRAPHY.   GMILLSM64071

A **COMMENTARY** ON THE MOTIVATION AND EDUCATION OF COLLEGE WOMEN. /ASPIRATIONS/   WHEISPX62837

COMMENTS
COMMENTS ON EQUAL-EMPLOYMENT-OPPORTUNITIES. PROBLEMS AND PROSPECTS.   GMCKERB65930

TITLE-VII. COVERAGE AND **COMMENTS**. /LEGISLATION/   GSCHMCT66287

COMMENTS ON MANAGEMENT PROBLEMS.   NNATLIC43921

MATHEMATICS RETRAINING PROGRAM. NOTES AND **COMMENTS**, APRIL 1964, 1965, 1966. /TRAINING/   WRUTGMR64097

COMMERCE
STATE FAIR-EMPLOYMENT-PRACTICE LEGISLATION UNCONSTITUTIONALLY BURDENS INTERSTATE **COMMERCE** WHEN APPLIED TO
INTERSTATE AIRLINE.   NHARVLR62499

UNITED STATES HAS STANDING UNDER INTERSTATE **COMMERCE** ACT AND COMMERCE CLAUSE TO ENJOIN SEGREGATIVE
PRACTICES OF CITY. /LEGISLATION/   NHARVLR64500

UNITED STATES HAS STANDING UNDER INTERSTATE COMMERCE ACT AND **COMMERCE** CLAUSE TO ENJOIN SEGREGATIVE
PRACTICES OF CITY. /LEGISLATION/   NHARVLR64500

COMMERCIAL
A FIVE-STATE SURVEY OF DISCRIMINATION BY **COMMERCIAL** EMPLOYMENT AGENCIES.   GAMERJD63386

PATTERNS OF EXCLUSION FROM THE EXECUTIVE-SUITE. **COMMERCIAL** BANKING.   JAMERJC66696

COMMISSION
REPORT OF THE CALIFORNIA STATE ADVISORY COMMITTEE TO THE UNITED STATES **COMMISSION** ON CIVIL-RIGHTS ON
CALIFORNIA-S PROGRAM FOR EQUAL-OPPORTUNITY IN APPRENTICESHIP.   GBECKWL62432

AUTOMATION AND ECONOMIC PROGRESS. A SUMMARY OF THE REPORT OF THE NATIONAL **COMMISSION** ON TECHNOLOGY,
AUTOMATION, AND ECONOMIC PROGRESS.   GBOWEHR66748

REPORT TO THE GOVERNOR AND THE LEGISLATURE OF THE **COMMISSION** ON MANPOWER, AUTOMATION AND TECHNOLOGY,
1964. /CALIFORNIA/   GCALCMA65515

COMMISSION ENFORCEMENT OF STATE LAWS AGAINST DISCRIMINATION. A COMPARATIVE ANALYSIS OF THE KANSAS ACT.   GDYSORB65657

AREAS OF **COMMISSION** CONCERN. /KANSAS-CITY MISSOURI/   GKANCIC62840

PROVING DISCRIMINATION AT THE **COMMISSION** LEVEL.   GLAMBWH66857

THE NEW-YORK STATE **COMMISSION** AGAINST DISCRIMINATION. A NEW TECHNIQUE FOR AN OLD PROBLEM.   GNEWYSA47107

THE INSURANCE INDUSTRY -- VERIFIED COMPLAINTS AND INFORMAL INVESTIGATIONS HANDLED BY THE NEW-YORK STATE
COMMISSION AGAINST DISCRIMINATION, JULY 1 1945-SEPTEMBER 15, 1958.   GNEWYSA58082

FINDINGS OF FACT, CONCLUSIONS AND ACTION OF THE **COMMISSION** ON HUMAN-RELATIONS IN RE. INVESTIGATIVE PUBLIC
HEARINGS INTO ALLEGED DISCRIMINATORY PRACTICE BY THE HOTEL AND RESTAURANT INDUSTRY IN PHILADELPHIA.
/PENNSYLVANIA/   GPHILCH61176

MUNICIPAL HUMAN-RELATIONS **COMMISSION**. A SURVEY OF PROGRAMS IN SELECTED CITIES OF THE UNITED STATES.   GRICHCH63236

FINAL REPORT OF SAN-FRANCISCO CALIFORNIA **COMMISSION** ON EQUAL-EMPLOYMENT-OPPORTUNITY.   GSANFCE60275

THE NATIONAL CONFERENCE AND THE REPORTS OF THE STATE ADVISORY COMMITTEES TO THE U.S. **COMMISSION** ON
CIVIL-RIGHTS. 1959.   GUSCCMC60405

A REPORT TO THE US **COMMISSION** ON CIVIL-RIGHTS. /MISSOURI/   GUSCCMC63406

REPORT ON FLORIDA OF THE US **COMMISSION** ON CIVIL-RIGHTS.   GUSCCMC63409

FINAL REPORT. US **COMMISSION** ON FAIR-EMPLOYMENT-PRACTICES, JUNE 28, 1946.   GUSCOMF47417

DIGEST OF LEGAL INTERPRETATIONS ISSUED OR ADOPTED BY THE **COMMISSION** OCTOBER 9, 1965 THROUGH DECEMBER 31,
1965.   GUSEEOC66509

FINAL REPORT. EMPLOYMENT AND TRAINING, REPORT FOR GOVERNOR-S **COMMISSION**.   NBULLPX65483

NEW-YORK CITY **COMMISSION** ON HUMAN RIGHTS, CONSTRUCTION TRADES HEARING, TESTIMONY. /INDUSTRY/   NHILLHX66546

REPORT OF THE **COMMISSION** ON THE EMPLOYMENT PROBLEMS OF NEGROES TO GOVERNOR SALTONSTALL. /MASSACHUSETTS/   NMASSCE42757

COMMISSION ON MANPOWER UTILIZATION REPORTS.   NNATLAI55872

STATEMENT TO THE NEW-YORK STATE ADVISORY COMMITTEE TO THE US **COMMISSION** ON CIVIL-RIGHTS, MAY 23, 1966.
/EMPLOYMENT LEGISLATION/   NPOLIEX66004

1961 **COMMISSION** ON CIVIL-RIGHTS REPORT BOOK 3. EMPLOYMENT.   NUSCCMC61231

REPORT OF THE CALIFORNIA ADVISORY **COMMISSION** ON THE STATUS OF WOMEN. /FEP EMPLOYMENT-CONDITIONS
DISCRIMINATION MIGRANTS/   WCALACW67673

REPORT ON THE MISSOURI **COMMISSION** ON THE STATUS OF WOMEN. /WORK-WOMEN-ROLE/   WCOLUMX64700

PROGRESS OF THE **COMMISSION** ON THE STATUS OF WOMAN. /WORK-WOMAN-ROLE/   WELLIKX63748

FIRST REPORT. IOWA GOVERNOR-S **COMMISSION** ON THE STATUS OF WOMEN. /EMPLOYMENT-CONDITIONS/   WIOWAGC64796

REPORT OF PRESIDENT-S **COMMISSION** ON STATUS OF WOMEN.   WPRESCO63993

WISCONSIN WOMEN. REPORT OF THE WISCONSIN GOVERNOR-S **COMMISSION** ON THE STATUS OF WOMEN.   WWISXGC65272

COMMISSION-AGAINST-D
RHODE-ISLAND **COMMISSION-AGAINST-DISCRIMINATION**, RULES OF PRACTICE AND PROCEDURE.   GRHODICND232

COMMISSION-ON-CIVIL-
REPORT ON SECOND ANNUAL SPRING CONFERENCE ON CIVIL-RIGHTS OF NEW-JERSEY **COMMISSION-ON-CIVIL**-RIGHTS, APRIL
23. 1966.   GNEWJCC66056

US **COMMISSION-ON-CIVIL**-RIGHTS. HEARINGS. LOS-ANGELES AND SAN-FRANCISCO, CALIFORNIA. JANUARY 25-26, 1960,
JANUARY 27-28, 1960.   GUSCCMC60400

COMMISSION-ON-CIVIL- (CONTINUATION)
EMPLOYMENT. 1961 US **COMMISSION-ON-CIVIL**-RIGHTS REPORT, VOLUME 3.   GUSCOMC61395

   US **COMMISSION-ON-CIVIL**-RIGHTS, HEARINGS. DETROIT, MICHIGAN. DEC 14-15 1960.   GUSCOMC61399

   US **COMMISSION-ON-CIVIL**-RIGHTS, HEARINGS. NEW-ORLEANS, LOUISIANA. SEPTEMBER 27-28, 1960, MAY 5-6, 1961. GUSCOMC61403

   US **COMMISSION-ON-CIVIL**-RIGHTS, HEARINGS. MEMPHIS, TENNESSEE. JUNE 25-26, 1962.   GUSCOMC62401

   US **COMMISSION-ON-CIVIL**-RIGHTS, HEARINGS. NEWARK, NEW-JERSEY. SEPTEMBER 11-12, 1962.   GUSCOMC62402

COMMISSIONER
   INDIAN AFFAIRS 1964, A PROGRESS REPORT FROM THE **COMMISSIONER** OF INDIAN AFFAIRS.   IUSDINT64652

COMMISSIONS
   POLICIES AND PRACTICES OF DISCRIMINATION **COMMISSIONS**. /FEPC/   GCARTEA56559

   SOLVING AN AMERICAN DILEMMA. THE ROLE OF THE FEPC OFFICIAL, A COMPARATIVE STUDY OF STATE CIVIL-RIGHTS
   COMMISSIONS.   GLLOYKM64317

   QUESTIONS AND ANSWERS ABOUT PERMANENT FAIR-EMPLOYMENT-PRACTICES **COMMISSIONS**.   GNORTMT45124

   COMMISSIONS FOR HUMAN RIGHTS, 15TH ANNUAL CONFERENCE, PROCEEDINGS.   GPENNHR63166

   ADMINISTRATIVE LAW -- HUMAN-RELATIONS **COMMISSIONS**, PENNSYLVANIA LAW AND DISCRIMINATORY EMPLOYMENT
   PRACTICE.   GTEMPLQ63349

   SELECTED BIBLIOGRAPHY ON STATE FAIR-EMPLOYMENT-PRACTICE **COMMISSIONS**.   GUSCOMC66414

   TWENTY YEARS OF STATE FAIR-EMPLOYMENT-PRACTICE **COMMISSIONS**. A CRITICAL ANALYSIS WITH RECOMMENDATIONS.   NHILLHX64550

   THE EXPERIENCE OF STATE FAIR-EMPLOYMENT **COMMISSIONS**. A COMPARATIVE STUDY.   NSUTIAX65343

   PROGRESS AND PROSPECTS. THE REPORT OF THE SECOND NATIONAL CONFERENCE OF GOVERNORS **COMMISSIONS** ON THE
   STATUS OF WOMEN. /EMPLOYMENT-CONDITIONS/   WGOVECS65798

   GOVERNORS **COMMISSIONS** ON THE STATUS OF WOMEN.   WUSDLAB64199

COMMITMENT
   THE **COMMITMENT** REQUIRED OF A WOMAN ENTERING A SCIENTIFIC PROFESSION. /OCCUPATIONS/   WBETTBX65645

   COMMITMENT TO WORK. /ASPIRATIONS/   WSOBOMG63126

COMMITTEE
   REPORT OF THE CALIFORNIA STATE ADVISORY **COMMITTEE** TO THE UNITED STATES COMMISSION ON CIVIL-RIGHTS ON
   CALIFORNIA-S PROGRAM FOR EQUAL-OPPORTUNITY IN APPRENTICESHIP.   GBECKWL62432

   TEXTS OF RULES AND REGULATIONS OF PRESIDENT-S **COMMITTEE** ON EQUAL-EMPLOYMENT-OPPORTUNITY RELATING TO
   OBLIGATIONS OF GOVERNMENT CONTRACTORS AND SUBCONTRACTORS, EFFECTIVE JULY 22, 1961. A BNA SPECIAL REPORT.   GBURENA61498

   RULES AND REGULATIONS OF THE PRESIDENT-S **COMMITTEE** ON EQUAL-EMPLOYMENT-OPPORTUNITY AS AMENDED.   GBURENA63496

   REPORTS OF THE MEETINGS OF THE **COMMITTEE** OF OFFICIALS ON MIGRATORY FARM LABOR OF THE ATLANTIC SEABOARD
   STATES. /MIGRANT-WORKERS/   GCOUNSG58932

   REPORT AND RECOMMENDATIONS OF DELAWARE **COMMITTEE** ON MIGRATORY LABOR. /MIGRANT-WORKERS/   GDELACM58945

   AN EQUAL-OPPORTUNITIES **COMMITTEE** AT WORK IN TEXAS.   GDESHEA66633

   THE FIRST NINE MONTHS. REPORT OF THE PRESIDENT-S **COMMITTEE** ON EQUAL-EMPLOYMENT-OPPORTUNITY.   GFEDEBJ62672

   THE JOB AHEAD FOR THE PRESIDENT-S **COMMITTEE** ON EQUAL-EMPLOYMENT-OPPORTUNITY.   GHOLLJR61999

   REPORT ON THE STRUCTURE AND OPERATIONS OF THE PRESIDENT-S **COMMITTEE** ON EQUAL-EMPLOYMENT-OPPORTUNITY.   GKHEETW62852

   REPORT OF NEW-YORK STATE JOINT LEGISLATIVE **COMMITTEE** ON MIGRANT-LABOR.   GNEWYSLND115

   MIGRATORY LABOR IN OHIO, A REPORT BY THE GOVERNOR-S **COMMITTEE**, AUGUST 1962.   GOHIOGC62095

   STATEMENT TO THE **COMMITTEE** ON LEGISLATION IN SUPPORT OF AN EFFECTIVE FEDERAL FEP LAW AND OTHER VITAL
   CIVIL-RIGHTS LEGISLATION.   GOLIVWX60134

   REPORT OF THE SPECIAL **COMMITTEE** ON NONDISCRIMINATION OF THE BOARD OF PUBLIC EDUCATION, PHILADELPHIA.
   /PENNSYLVANIA/   GPHILBE64172

   THE AMERICAN DREAM...EQUAL OPPORTUNITY, A REPORT ON THE COMMUNITY LEADER-S CONFERENCE SPONSORED BY
   PRESIDENT-S **COMMITTEE** ON EQUAL-EMPLOYMENT-OPPORTUNITY, MAY 19, 1962.   GPRESCD62105

   THE FIRST NINE MONTHS -- SPECIAL YEAR-END REPORT, APRIL 7, 1961-JANUARY 15, 1962, PRESIDENT-S **COMMITTEE**
   ON EQUAL-EMPLOYMENT-OPPORTUNITY.   GPRESCD62108

   REPORT TO THE PRESIDENT, NOVEMBER 26, 1963 BY THE PRESIDENT-S **COMMITTEE** ON EQUAL-EMPLOYMENT-OPPORTUNITY. GPRESCD64114

   FIRST REPORT, PRESIDENT-S **COMMITTEE** ON GOVERNMENT CONTRACTS.   GPRESCH54120

   SECOND ANNUAL REPORT, THE PRESIDENT-S **COMMITTEE** ON GOVERNMENT CONTRACTS.   GPRESCH55124

   FOURTH ANNUAL REPORT ON EQUAL JOB OPPORTUNITY, 1956-1957, PRESIDENT-S **COMMITTEE** ON GOVERNMENT CONTRACTS. GPRESCH57122

   FIVE YEARS OF PROGRESS, 1953-1958, A REPORT TO PRESIDENT EISENHOWER BY THE PRESIDENT-S **COMMITTEE** ON
   GOVERNMENT CONTRACTS.   GPRESCH58121

   PATTERN FOR PROGRESS, SEVENTH REPORT, FINAL REPORT TO PRESIDENT EISENHOWER FROM THE **COMMITTEE** ON
   GOVERNMENT CONTRACTS.   GPRESCH60123

   FIRST ANNUAL REPORT, PRESIDENT-S **COMMITTEE** ON GOVERNMENT EMPLOYMENT POLICY, APRIL 30 1956.   GPRESCP56193

   SECOND ANNUAL REPORT, PRESIDENT-S **COMMITTEE** ON GOVERNMENT EMPLOYMENT POLICY, 1957.   GPRESCP57194

   THIRD ANNUAL REPORT, PRESIDENT-S **COMMITTEE** ON GOVERNMENT EMPLOYMENT POLICY, 1958.   GPRESCP58195

   FOURTH ANNUAL REPORT, PRESIDENT-S **COMMITTEE** ON GOVERNMENT EMPLOYMENT POLICY.   GPRESCP59196

   PRESIDENT-S **COMMITTEE** ON EQUAL-EMPLOYMENT-OPPORTUNITY.   GTAYLHX62348

   PROCEEDINGS OF THE 50TH ANNIVERSARY OBSERVANCE OF THE AMERICAN JEWISH **COMMITTEE**. APRIL 10-14, 1957. THE
   PURSUIT OF EQUALITY AT HOME AND ABROAD. /ECONOMIC-OPPORTUNITY/   JAMERJC58692

   COMPREHENSIVE REPORT OF THE OFFICE OF THE BISHOP-S **COMMITTEE** FOR MIGRANT-WORKERS.   MNATLCBND082

COMMITTEE   (CONTINUATION)
PLACEMENT SERVICE OF THE AMERICAN FRIENDS SERVICE **COMMITTEE**. A TECHNIQUE IN RACE-RELATIONS.   NLOESFS46703

REPORT OF THE **COMMITTEE** ON UNFAIR EMPLOYMENT PRACTICES.   NNEBRLC51906

STATEMENT TO THE NEW-YORK STATE ADVISORY **COMMITTEE** TO THE US COMMISSION ON CIVIL-RIGHTS, MAY 23, 1966.
/EMPLOYMENT LEGISLATION/   NPOLIEX66004

NEW-YORK WOMEN. A REPORT AND RECOMMENDATIONS FROM THE NEW-YORK GOVERNOR-S **COMMITTEE** ON THE EDUCATION AND
EMPLOYMENT OF WOMEN.   WNEWYGW64799

REPORT OF THE **COMMITTEE** ON CIVIL AND POLITICAL RIGHTS.   WPRESCO63065

REPORT OF THE **COMMITTEE** ON EDUCATION. /EQUAL-OPPORTUNITY COUNSELING/   WPRESCO63066

REPORT OF THE **COMMITTEE** ON FEDERAL EMPLOYMENT.   WPRESCO63067

REPORT OF THE **COMMITTEE** ON PRIVATE EMPLOYMENT, 1963.   WPRESCO63068

REPORT OF THE **COMMITTEE** ON PROTECTIVE LABOR LEGISLATION, 1963.   WPRESCC63069

REPORT OF THE **COMMITTEE** ON SOCIAL INSURANCE AND TAXES, 1963.   WPRESCO63070

COMMITTEES
ACTION PROGRAMS FOR FEPC ADVISORY **COMMITTEES**. /CALIFORNIA/   GCALFEP66528

HANDBOOK FOR LOCAL UNION FAIR PRACTICES **COMMITTEES**. REVISED EDITION.   GUAWXFPND369

THE NATIONAL CONFERENCE AND THE REPORTS OF THE STATE ADVISORY **COMMITTEES** TO THE U.S. COMMISSION ON
CIVIL-RIGHTS, 1959.   GUSCOMC60405

REPORTS ON APPRENTICESHIP, NINE STATE ADVISORY **COMMITTEES**. /CALIFORNIA FLORIDA MARYLAND CONNECTICUT
WASHINGTON-DC NEW-JERSEY NEW-YORK TENNESSEE WISCONSIN/   GUSCOMC64407

COMMUNICATION
INFORMAL **COMMUNICATION** AMONG BIOSCIENTISTS. /EMPLOYMENT-CONDITIONS/   WBERNJX63643

COMMUNICATIONS
COMMUNICATIONS EMPLOYEES AND GOOD SERVICE. /NEW-YORK/   GNEWYSA54077

COMMUNITIES
SCHOOL AND EARLY EMPLOYMENT EXPERIENCE OF YOUTH. A REPORT ON SEVEN **COMMUNITIES**, 1952-57.   GUSDLAB60494

VISITS MADE TO 20 INDIAN **COMMUNITIES**.   IHETZTX58575

KLAMATH INDIANS IN TWO NON-INDIAN **COMMUNITIES**. KLAMATH-FALLS AND EUGENE-SPRINGFIELD. /OREGON/   ILIVIMG59582

VOCATIONAL CHOICES OF NEGRO HIGH SCHOOL STUDENTS IN MACON COUNTY, ALABAMA, AND THEIR RELATIONSHIP TO
BASIC OCCUPATIONAL ACTIVITES OF THE SCHOOL **COMMUNITIES**. /ASPIRATIONS/   NCHAPEJ49351

NEGRO LEADERSHIP IN RURAL GEORGIA **COMMUNITIES**. OCCUPATIONAL AND SOCIAL ASPECTS.   NEDWAVA42328

COMMUNITY
ADDRESS TO **COMMUNITY** RELATIONS SERVICE STAFF TRAINING SESSION, JANUARY 12, 1967, ON JOBS NOW. /NEGRO
PUERTO-RICAN YOUTH/   CCOLEBX67918

THE PREDICTION AND EXPLANATION OF ECONOMIC ABSORPTION AMONG MEXICAN-AMERICANS, NEGROES, AND ANGLOS IN A
NORTHERN INDUSTRIAL **COMMUNITY**.   CSHANLW63120

THE ECONOMIC ABSORPTION OF IN-MIGRANT LABORERS IN A NORTHERN INDUSTRIAL **COMMUNITY**. /MEXICAN-AMERICAN
NEGRO/   CSHANLW64486

THE PREDICTION OF ECONOMIC ABSORPTION AND CULTURAL INTEGRATION AMONG MEXICAN-AMERICANS, NEGROES, AND
ANGLOS IN A NORTHERN INDUSTRIAL **COMMUNITY**.   CSHANLW66123

TRADE UNION LEADERSHIP COUNCIL --EXPERIMENT IN **COMMUNITY** ACTION. /DETROIT MICHIGAN/   GBATTRX63426

RURAL INDUSTRIALIZATION IN A LOUISIANA **COMMUNITY**. /ECONOMIC-STATUS OCCUPATIONS/   GBERTAL59393

COMMUNITY SURVEY. LONG BEACH, CALIFORNIA.   GCALFEPND541

POVERTY IN NEW-YORK CITY. FACTS FOR PLANNING **COMMUNITY** ACTION.   GCOMCCN64210

THE **COMMUNITY** LOOKS AT MIGRANT LABOR. /MIGRANT-WORKERS/   GCONSLO59926

MINORITY PROGRAM CALLS FOR **COMMUNITY** ACTION.   GCRAICE65619

THE **COMMUNITY** ACTION AGENCY-S ROLE IN COMPREHENSIVE MANPOWER PROGRAMS -- PLANNING AND PROBLEMS.   GKANERD66863

MANPOWER PROBLEMS AND THE BUSINESS **COMMUNITY**.   GKRUGOHND865

COMMUNITY VALUES IN EDUCATION AND OCCUPATIONAL SELECTION. A STUDY OF YOUTH IN EMMITSBURG, MARYLAND.   GLEONRC64894

THE **COMMUNITY** APPROACH. /EEO/   GMATTEG64967

THE AMERICAN DREAM...EQUAL OPPORTUNITY, A REPORT ON THE **COMMUNITY** LEADER-S CONFERENCE SPONSORED BY
PRESIDENT-S COMMITTEE ON EQUAL-EMPLOYMENT-OPPORTUNITY, MAY 19, 1962.   GPRESCD62105

REGIONAL **COMMUNITY** LEADERS CONFERENCE ON EQUAL-EMPLOYMENT-OPPORTUNITY, PROCEEDINGS.   GPRESCD64113

DIMENSIONS IN DISCRIMINATION, A PRELIMINARY SURVEY OF SAN-DIEGO-S **COMMUNITY** PROBLEMS OF DISCRIMINATION
PART II. /CALIFORNIA/   GSANDLW65274

THE RELATIONSHIP OF THE SOCIAL-STRUCTURE OF AN INDIAN **COMMUNITY** TO ADULT AND JUVENILE-DELINQUENCY.
/POVERTY ECONOMIC-STATUS/   IMINNMS63218

FRUITLAND, NEW-MEXICO. A NAVAHO **COMMUNITY** IN TRANSITION.   ISASATT60615

CHANGE AND RESISTANCE IN AN ISOLATED NAVAHO **COMMUNITY**.   ISHEPMX64618

POVERTY, **COMMUNITY** AND POWER. /ECONOMIC-STATUS/   IWARRCX65668

FORMAL EDUCATION IN AN AMERICAN-INDIAN **COMMUNITY**.   IWAXXML64683

A PLANNED **COMMUNITY** FOR MIGRATORY FARM WORKERS.   MFEERAB62392

ACCULTURATION, ACCESS AND ALCOHOL IN A TRI-ETHNIC **COMMUNITY**.   MGRAVTD67214

CLASS CONSCIOUSNESS AND SOCIAL MOBILITY IN A MEXICAN-AMERICAN **COMMUNITY**.   MPENAFX63453

COMMUNITY   (CONTINUATION)
  A STUDY OF THE NEGRO **COMMUNITY** IN CHAMPAIGN-URBANA, ILLINOIS.   NBINDAM61079

  SECURING SKILLS NEEDED FOR SUCCESS. **COMMUNITY** JOB TRAINING FOR NEGROES.   NBLUMAA66099

  HARLEM, A **COMMUNITY** IN TRANSITION.   NCLARJH64309

  MINORITY PROGRAM CALLS FOR **COMMUNITY** ACTION.   NCRAICE65240

  SCHOOL-DESEGREGATION AND NEW INDUSTRY. THE SOUTHERN **COMMUNITY** LEADERS VIEWPOINT.   NCROMRX63243

  TRAINING FOR TOMORROW-S SCIENTISTS AND TECHNICIANS. A **COMMUNITY** APPROACH TO A COMMUNITY NEED.   NFINLOE60356

  TRAINING FOR TOMORROW-S SCIENTISTS AND TECHNICIANS. A COMMUNITY APPROACH TO A **COMMUNITY** NEED.   NFINLOE60356

  AN INSIGHT INTO STRUCTURAL UNEMPLOYMENT -- THE EXPERIENCE OF A MINORITY GROUP IN A PROSPEROUS **COMMUNITY**.   NGERSWJ65634

  THE NEGRO CHALLENGE TO THE BUSINESS **COMMUNITY**. /INDUSTRY/   NGINZEX64408

  COMMUNITY FACTORS AFFECTING MOTIVATION AND ACHIEVEMENT IN A DECADE OF DECISION. /EDUCATION/   NGRANLB62441

  UNIONS AND THE NEGRO **COMMUNITY**.   NHILLHX64997

  JACKSONVILLE LOOKS AT ITS NEGRO **COMMUNITY**. /FLORIDA/   NJACKCC46598

  COMMUNITY RESISTANCE TO AND ACCEPTANCE OF DESEGREGATION.   NKILLLM65651

  DESEGREGATION, INTEGRATION, AND THE NEGRO **COMMUNITY**.   NLEWIHX56073

  BRICKS WITHOUT STRAW. STUDIES OF **COMMUNITY** UNEMPLOYMENT PROBLEMS, THE NEGROES DILEMMA. /LOUISVILLE
  KENTUCKY/   NLOUIHR64715

  UNIONS AND THE NEGRO **COMMUNITY**.   NMARSRX64061

  NILES **COMMUNITY** SELF SURVEY. /MICHIGAN/   NMICCRC65771

  INTER-RACIAL PLANNING FOR **COMMUNITY** ORGANIZATION... EMPLOYMENT PROBLEMS OF THE NEGRO.   NNATLUL44900

  TRADE UNION LEADERSHIP COUNCIL. EXPERIMENT IN **COMMUNITY** ACTION.   NNEWXUT63088

  HUMAN-RELATIONS IN ANN-ARBOR. A **COMMUNITY** PROFILE.   NPIKEJX67101

  MIGRATION PATTERNS OF NEGROES FROM A RURAL NORTHEASTERN MISSISSIPPI **COMMUNITY**. /DEMOGRAPHY/   NRUBIMX60094

  DESEGREGATION. A **COMMUNITY** DESIGN. /PHILADELPHIA PENNSYLVANIA/   NSCHEGX61104

  THE NEGRO **COMMUNITY** AND THE DEVELOPMENT OF NEGRO POTENTIAL.   NSMUTRW57146

  OCCUPATIONAL PRESTIGE IN A NEGRO **COMMUNITY**.   NSOLZRX61153

  ECONOMIC STRUCTURE OF THE HARLEM **COMMUNITY**. /NEW-YORK/   NSTEVHR64177

  PROGRESS IN WATTS -- THE LOS-ANGELES ASTD **COMMUNITY** AFFAIRS PROGRAM. /CALIFORNIA/   NTRAIAD66580

  A REPORT ON **COMMUNITY** FACTORS IN NASHVILLE RELATED TO THE NEGRO IN MEDICINE. /TENNESSEE/   NVALIPX56281

  NEGRO FAMILIES IN RURAL WISCONSIN. A STUDY OF THEIR **COMMUNITY** LIFE.   NWISCGC59331

  THE ADJUSTMENT OF NEGROES IN A NORTHERN INDUSTRIAL **COMMUNITY**.   NZIMMBG62360

  EAST-HARLEM BLOCK **COMMUNITY** DEVELOPMENT PROGRAM. /NEW-YORK/   PBORDDXND781

  THE PUERTO-RICAN **COMMUNITY** IN AMERICA. RAPID ACCULTURATION.   PBOWALX62889

  SCHOOL AND **COMMUNITY** COURSE. THE LOWER STATUS PUERTO-RICAN FAMILY.   PBRAMJX63784

  COMMUNITY WOMEN-S GROUPS TAKE ACTION. /HOUSEHOLD-WORKERS/   WBUFFDX66661

COMMUNITY-ACTION
  GUIDELINES FOR **COMMUNITY-ACTION**.   NNATLUL65889

COMPANIES
  LIFE INSURANCE **COMPANIES**. /DISCRIMINATION/   GANTIDL62398

  EMPLOYMENT IN INSURANCE **COMPANIES**. /DISCRIMINATION/   JRIGHXX59755

  THE NEGRO AND EQUAL-EMPLOYMENT-OPPORTUNITIES. A REVIEW OF MANAGEMENT EXPERIENCES IN TWENTY **COMPANIES**.   NFERMLA66790

  HIRING NEGROES FOR BETTER JOBS. EXPERIENCE OF LEADING **COMPANIES**. /INDUSTRY/   NOPINRC64957

  NEGRO EMPLOYMENT IN THREE **COMPANIES** IN THE NEW-ORLEANS AREA. /CASE-STUDY LOUISIANA/   NUSDLAB55828

  PREJUDICE IS NOT THE WHOLE STORY. EXAMINATION OF THREE CASES OF NEGRO UPGRADING IN TRACTION **COMPANIES** IN
  PHILADELPHIA, LOS-ANGELES AND CHICAGO. /PENNSYLVANIA CALIFORNIA ILLINOIS/   NWECKJE45308

  THREE **COMPANIES** -- NEW-ORLEANS AREA. /CASE-STUDY LOUISIANA/   NWISSHW55332

COMPANY
  DEVELOPING FAIR-EMPLOYMENT PROGRAMS. A PROGRAM FOR THE SMALLER **COMPANY**.   GJENSJJ66785

  IMPACT OF **COMPANY** POLICY UPON DISCRIMINATION.   GLONDJX54908

  FRANCHISE **COMPANY** DATA FOR EQUAL-OPPORTUNITY IN BUSINESS.   GUSDCOM66431

  A **COMPANY** CASE HISTORY. /INDUSTRY EEO/   GWITTHW64576

  MORE ROOM AT THE TOP. **COMPANY** EXPERIENCE IN EMPLOYING NEGROES IN PROFESSIONAL AND MANAGEMENT JOBS.
  /INDUSTRY/   NBIRDCX63080

  COMPANY EXPERIENCE WITH NEGRO EMPLOYMENT. /INDUSTRY/   NHABBSX66472

  NEGRO EMPLOYMENT IN THREE SOUTHERN PLANTS OF INTERNATIONAL HARVESTER **COMPANY**. /CASE-STUDY/   NHOPEJX55572

  EQUAL-EMPLOYMENT-OPPORTUNITY. **COMPANY** POLICIES AND EXPERIENCE.   NMILLGW64070

  COMPANY EXPERIENCE WITH THE EMPLOYMENT OF NEGROES. /INDUSTRY/   NPRINUI54020

COMPANY-S
  JOBS FOR NEGROES. ONE **COMPANY-S** ANSWER. /CASE-STUDY INDUSTRY/   NBUSIMX64142

COMPARATIVE
THE EFFECT OF LOW EDUCATIONAL-ATTAINMENT ON INCOMES. A COMPARATIVE STUDY OF SELECTED ETHNIC GROUPS.
/NEGRO MEXICAN-AMERICAN/   CFOGEWX66367

FAMILY STRUCTURE AND SCHOOL PERFORMANCE. A COMPARATIVE STUDY OF STUDENTS FROM THREE ETHNIC BACKGROUNDS IN
AN INTEGRATED SCHOOL. /MEXICAN-AMERICAN AMERICAN-INDIAN/   CGRIFJX65407

THE URBAN REALITY. A COMPARATIVE STUDY OF THE SOCIO-ECONOMIC SITUATION OF MEXICAN-AMERICANS, NEGROES AND
ANGLO-CAUCASIANS IN LOS-ANGELES COUNTY. /CALIFORNIA/   CLOSACH65708

POVERTY IN THE SOUTHWEST. A COMPARATIVE STUDY OF MEXICAN-AMERICAN, NONWHITE AND ANGLO FAMILIES. /NEGRO/   CMITTFG66777

COMMISSION ENFORCEMENT OF STATE LAWS AGAINST DISCRIMINATION. A COMPARATIVE ANALYSIS OF THE KANSAS ACT.   GDYSORB65657

COMPARATIVE ANALYSIS OF STATE FAIR-EMPLOYMENT-PRACTICES LAWS.   GHARTPX62762

SOLVING AN AMERICAN DILEMMA. THE ROLE OF THE FEPC OFFICIAL. A COMPARATIVE STUDY OF STATE CIVIL-RIGHTS
COMMISSIONS.   GLLOYKM64317

ETHNIC STRATIFICATION. A COMPARATIVE APPROACH.   GSHIBTX65303

COMPARATIVE STUDIES OF NORTH AMERICAN-INDIANS.   IDRIVHE57954

SPANISH-SPEAKING AND ENGLISH SPEAKING CHILDREN IN SOUTHWEST TEXAS. A COMPARATIVE STUDY OF INTELLIGENCE,
SOCIO-ECONOMIC STATUS, AND ACHIEVEMENT.   MRATLYX60460

A COMPARATIVE STUDY OF THE OCCUPATIONAL INTERESTS OF NEGRO AND WHITE ADOLESCENT BOYS.   NCONNSM65471

COMPARATIVE PSYCHOLOGICAL STUDIES OF NEGROES AND WHITES IN THE UNITED STATES.   NDREGRM60292

THE EXPERIENCE OF STATE FAIR-EMPLOYMENT COMMISSIONS. A COMPARATIVE STUDY.   NSUTIAX65343

COMPARATIVE STUDY OF SOCIO-ECONOMIC AND SOCIAL-PSYCHOLOGICAL DETERMINANTS OF EDUCATIONAL AND OCCUPATIONAL
ASPIRATIONS OF NEGRO AND WHITE COLLEGE SENIORS.   NWHITRM59319

CONTRASTIVE ACCULTURATION OF CALIFORNIA JAPANESE. COMPARATIVE APPROACH TO THE STUDY OF IMMIGRANTS. OBEFUHX65701

THE EFFECT OF LOW EDUCATIONAL ATTAINMENT ON INCOMES. A COMPARATIVE STUDY OF SELECTED ETHNIC GROUPS. OFOGEWX66721

A COMPARATIVE STUDY OF TOP LEVEL MALE AND FEMALE EXECUTIVES IN HARRIS-COUNTY. /TEXAS OCCUPATIONS/   WDOLLPA65738

THE COMPARATIVE ACADEMIC ACHIEVEMENT OF WOMEN FORTY YEARS OF AGE AND OVER AND WOMEN EIGHTEEN TO TWENTY
FIVE.   WHALFIT61814

THE COMPARATIVE ACADEMIC ACHIEVEMENT OF YOUNG AND OLD. /TRAINING/   WHALFIT62813

ACCESS OF GIRLS AND WOMEN TO EDUCATION IN RURAL AREAS. A COMPARATIVE STUDY.   WUNESCO64166

COMPARED
POVERTY AREAS OF OUR MAJOR CITIES. THE EMPLOYMENT SITUATION OF NEGRO AND WHITE WORKERS IN METROPOLITAN
AREAS COMPARED IN A SPECIAL LABOR-FORCE REPORT.   NWETZJR66114

OCCUPATIONAL PLANS AND ASPIRATIONS. PUERTO-RICAN AND AMERICAN HIGH SCHOOL SENIORS COMPARED.   PSILVRM63100

COMPARISON
COMPARISON OF MEXICANS, NEGROES AND WHITES WITH RESPECT TO OCCUPATIONAL HISTORY, RURAL-URBAN RESIDENCE
HISTORY AND ACCULTURIZATION WITHIN THE INSTITUTIONAL STRUCTURE OF LANSING, MICHIGAN.   CGOLDVX60494

PREJUDICE TOWARD MEXICAN AND NEGRO AMERICANS. A COMPARISON.   CPINKAX63458

THE NEW FEDERAL FAIR-EMPLOYMENT-PRACTICES ACT -- COMPARISON WITH STATE LAW AND AN ANALYSIS OF RELEVANT
STATE EXPERIENCES. /MISSOURI/   GROBEPC64239

A COMPARISON OF MAJOR UNITED STATES RELIGIOUS GROUPS. /ECONOMIC-STATUS/   JLAZRBX61033

THE MEXICAN IN THE NORTHERN URBAN AREA. A COMPARISON OF TWO GENERATIONS.   MGOLDNX59403

A COMPARISON OF THE VOCATIONAL ASPIRATIONS OF PAIRED SIXTH-GRADE WHITE AND NEGRO CHILDREN WHO ATTEND
SEGREGATED SCHOOLS.   NBROWRG65895

A COMPARISON OF THE ACADEMIC ACHIEVEMENTS OF WHITE AND NEGRO HIGH SCHOOL GRADUATES. /EDUCATION/   NBULLHA50132

A COMPARISON OF THE SOCIAL CHARACTERISTICS AND EDUCATIONAL ASPIRATIONS OF NORTHERN, LOWER-CLASS, NEGRO
PARENTS WHO ACCEPTED AND DECLINED AN OPPORTUNITY FOR INTEGRATED EDUCATION FOR THEIR CHILDREN.   NCAGLLT66904

A COMPARISON OF TUITION-AND-FEE CHARGES IN NEGRO INSTITUTIONS WITH CHARGES IN INSTITUTIONS OF THE
SOUTHEAST AND OF THE NATION. 1962-1963. /EDUCATION/   NDAMILX64127

I Q PERFORMANCE, EDUCATIONAL AND OCCUPATIONAL ASPIRATIONS OF YOUTH IN A SOUTHERN CITY -- A RACIAL
COMPARISON.   NGEISPX62397

A COMPARISON OF THE OCCUPATIONS OF THE FIRST AND SECOND GENERATION PUERTO-RICANS IN THE MAINLAND
LABOR-MARKET, AND HOW THE WORK OF THE NEW-YORK STATE DEPARTMENT OF LABORFFECTS PUERTO-RICANS.   PRAUSCX61846

THE FEMALE LABOR-FORCE IN METROPOLITAN AREAS. AN INTERNATIONAL COMPARISON.   WCOLLAX62697

A COMPARISON OF THE MALE-FEMALE ROLES IN ENGINEERING. /OCCUPATION/   WROBISS63083

COMPARISONS
MIGRATORY WORKERS IN NEW-YORK STATE, 1959 AND COMPARISONS WITH 1953, 1957, AND 1958.   GWHYTDR60407

RECENT RESEARCH IN PSYCHOLOGICAL COMPARISONS OF NEGROES AND WHITES IN THE UNITED STATES.   NDREGRM65293

SOME COMPARISONS AMONG NEGRO-WHITE COLLEGE STUDENTS. SOCIAL AMBITION AND ESTIMATED SOCIAL MOBILITY. NHARREE66786

COMPENSATING
COMPENSATING EMPLOYEES UNDER THE NEW CIVIL-RIGHTS LAW.   GBENGEJ65436

COMPENSATION
FAMILY CHARACTERISTICS OF THE LONG TERM UNEMPLOYED. A REPORT ON A STUDY OF CLAIMANTS UNDER THE TEMPORARY
EXTENDED UNEMPLOYMENT COMPENSATION PROGRAM, 1961-2.   GUSDLAB61445

AGRICULTURAL WORKERS AND WORKMEN-S COMPENSATION. /MIGRANT-WORKERS/   GUSDLAB64506

DISCRIMINATION IN RATE OF COMPENSATION BETWEEN COLORED AND WHITE TEACHERS HELD UNCONSTITUTIONAL.   NHARVLR40497

COMPENSATORY
THE ETHICS OF COMPENSATORY JUSTICE.PREFERENTIAL-TREATMENT/   GLICHRX64900

COMPENSATORY-EDUCATI
THE CIRCLE OF FUTILITY. /COMPENSATORY-EDUCATION POLICY-RECOMMENDATIONS/   NSCHRPX64125

COMPETENCE
ANALYSIS OF MALE NAVAHO STUDENTS PERCEPTIONS OF OCCUPATIONAL OPPORTUNITIES AND THEIR ATTITUDES TOWARD
DEVELOPMENT OF SKILLS AND TRAITS NECESSARY FOR OCCUPATIONAL **COMPETENCE**.   IDESPCW65548

COMPETING
RACIAL DISCRIMINATION ON THE JOBSITE. **COMPETING** THEORIES AND COMPETING FORUMS.   NMEYEBI65210

RACIAL DISCRIMINATION ON THE JOBSITE. COMPETING THEORIES AND **COMPETING** FORUMS.   NMEYEBI65210

COMPETITIVE
OCCUPATIONAL ASSIMILATION AS A **COMPETITIVE** PROCESS.   NHODGRW65556

COMPETITORS
ETHNIC CENSUS OF EXAMINATION **COMPETITORS**, JAN-JUNE 1965, CALIFORNIA STATE PERSONNEL BOARD.   GCALSPB65551

ETHNIC CENSUS OF EXAMINATION **COMPETITORS**, JULY-DEC 1965, CALIFORNIA STATE-PERSONNEL-BOARD.   GCALSPB65552

ETHNIC CENSUS OF EXAMINATION **COMPETITORS**. REPORT OF EXAMINATIONS GIVEN JULY THROUGH DECEMBER, 1965,
SUMMARY. /TESTING CALIFORNIA/   NCALFPB66173

COMPILATION
A **COMPILATION** OF STATISTICAL DATA, CHARTS AND OTHER RESOURCE MATERIAL FOR CONFERENCE PARTICIPANTS.
/APPRENTICESHIP CALIFORNIA YOUTH/   GCALCNA60516

COMPILATION OF LAWS AGAINST DISCRIMINATION, EMPLOYMENT, EDUCATIONAL INSTITUTIONS, PLACES OF PUBLIC
ACCOMODATION, PUBLIC HOUSING, PUBLICLY ASSISTED HOUSING, PRIVATE HOUSING. /MASSACHUSETTS/   GMASSCAND963

COMPILATION OF LAWS AGAINST DISCRIMINATION, A REFERENCE MANUAL.   GNEWYSA48078

COMPILED
INTERRACIAL HUMAN RELATIONS IN MANAGEMENT, A **COMPILED** REPORT PRESENTED ORALLY...JANUARY 17 1951.   GMCKEIX51926

COMPLAINT
TITLE-VII. **COMPLAINT** PROCEDURES AND REMEDIES. /LEGISLATION/   GWALKRW66538

COMPLAINTS
THE BANKING INDUSTRY. VERIFIED **COMPLAINTS** AND INFORMAL INVESTIGATIONS. /NEW-YORK/   GNEWYSA58076

THE INSURANCE INDUSTRY -- VERIFIED **COMPLAINTS** AND INFORMAL INVESTIGATIONS HANDLED BY THE NEW-YORK STATE
COMMISSION AGAINST DISCRIMINATION, JULY 1 1945-SEPTEMBER 15, 1958.   GNEWYSA58082

COMPLAINTS ALLEGING DISCRIMINATION BECAUSE OF PUERTO-RICAN NATIONAL ORIGIN, JULY 1, 1945-SEPTEMBER 1,
1958.   PNEWYSA58836

COMPLIANCE
A SPECIAL REPORT. CITY CONTRACT **COMPLIANCE**. PROGRESS IN 1963. /PHILADELPHIA PENNSYLVANIA/   GPHILCH64179

GUIDE FOR INVESTIGATIONS AND **COMPLIANCE** REVIEWS IN EQUAL-EMPLOYMENT-OPPORTUNITY.   GPRESCD62109

COMPLIANCE GUIDE, RECOMMENDATIONS FOR OBTAINING COMPLIANCE WITH THE NONDISCRIMINATION PROVISIONS IN
GOVERNMENT CONTRACTS.   GPRESCH58119

COMPLIANCE GUIDE, RECOMMENDATIONS FOR OBTAINING **COMPLIANCE** WITH THE NONDISCRIMINATION PROVISIONS IN
GOVERNMENT CONTRACTS.   GPRESCH58119

TRADE UNION **COMPLIANCE** WITH PRESIDENTIAL DIRECTIVES, MEMBERSHIP ACCEPTANCE, SENIORITY, ETC.   NCOOPJX64294

MANAGEMENT **COMPLIANCE** WITH PRESIDENTIAL DIRECTIVES.   NLAWRRG64296

COMPOSITE
REPORT OF 1961 - 1962 SURVEY OF PHILADELPHIA BANKS AND ATTACHED **COMPOSITE** TABULATION OF NON-WHITES.
/PENNSYLVANIA/   GPHILCH62180

COMPOSITION
THE AMERICAN LABOR-FORCE. ITS GROWTH AND CHANGING **COMPOSITION**. /DEMOGRAPHY/   GBANCGX58417

THE **COMPOSITION** OF NET MIGRATION AMONG COUNTIES IN THE UNITED STATES, 1950-60.   GBOWLGK66414

STATEMENT ON SURVEYS AND STATISTICS AS TO RACIAL AND ETHNIC **COMPOSITION** OF WORK-FORCE OR UNION
MEMBERSHIP. /CALIFORNIA/   GCALFEP63539

CHANGING **COMPOSITION** OF THE AMERICAN WORK-FORCE.   GCOOPSX59928

CHANGES IN THE NUMBER AND **COMPOSITION** OF THE POOR. /DEMOGRAPHY/   GMILLHP65656

FAMILY **COMPOSITION** AND CHARACTERISTICS OF AN ECONOMICALLY DEPRIVED CROSS-CULTURAL ROCKY-MOUNTAIN AREA. MANDRWH66359

NEW-MEXICO COUNTY INDUSTRIAL **COMPOSITION** AND LEVELS OF LIVING.   MSANDAD63479

POPULATION DISTRIBUTION AND **COMPOSITION** IN THE NEW SOUTH.   NBOGUDJ54102

THE CHANGING COLOR **COMPOSITION** OF METROPOLITAN AREAS. /DEMOGRAPHY/   NSHARHX62125

THE FEMALE LABOR-FORCE IN THE UNITED STATES. FACTORS GOVERNING ITS GROWTH AND CHANGING **COMPOSITION**.   WOPPEVK66096

COMPREHENSIVE
THE COMMUNITY ACTION AGENCY-S ROLE IN **COMPREHENSIVE** MANPOWER PROGRAMS -- PLANNING AND PROBLEMS.   GKANERD66863

FEDERAL LEGISLATION FOR A **COMPREHENSIVE** PROGRAM ON YOUTH EMPLOYMENT.   GNIXORA66847

RACIAL DISCRIMINATION IN THE CINCINNATI BUILDING TRADES. A **COMPREHENSIVE** REPORT AND RECOMMENDATIONS.
/OHIO/   GOHIOCR64129

TOWARDS FULL EMPLOYMENT. PROPOSALS FOR A **COMPREHENSIVE** EMPLOYMENT AND MANPOWER POLICY IN THE UNITED
STATES.   GUSSENA64332

COMPREHENSIVE REPORT OF THE OFFICE OF THE BISHOP-S COMMITTEE FOR MIGRANT-WORKERS.   MNATLCBND0082

COMPROMISE
PROGRESS WITHOUT FEDERAL COMPULSION. ARGUING THE CASE FOR **COMPROMISE** METHODS.   GNORTHR52122

SEGREGATION DEAL. NEW-ORLEANS REGION FEPC PERMITS **COMPROMISE**. /LOUISIANA/   NBUSIWX45161

COMPTON
SUMMARY REPORT OF THE STUDY OF DROP-OUTS IN THE THREE SENIOR HIGH SCHOOLS, **COMPTON** UNION HIGH SCHOOL

COMPTON (CONTINUATION)
DISTRICT. /CALIFORNIA/   MWHITNX60517

COMPULSION
PROGRESS WITHOUT FEDERAL **COMPULSION**. ARGUING THE CASE FOR COMPROMISE METHODS.   GNORTHR52122

COMPUTER
THE **COMPUTER** AND THE AMERICAN ECONOMY.   GMANGGL66526

WHEN THE **COMPUTER** TAKES OVER THE OFFICE. /TECHNOLOGICAL-CHANGE/   WHOOSIR60000

COMPUTERS
AUTOMATION AND EMPLOYMENT OPPORTUNITIES FOR OFFICE WORKERS. THE EFFECT OF ELECTRONIC **COMPUTERS** ON
EMPLOYMENT OF CLERICAL WORKERS. WITH A SPECIAL REPORT ON PROGRAMMERS.   WPASCWX58178

CONCENTRATION
AMERICA-S **CONCENTRATION** CAMPS. THE FACTS ABOUT OUR INDIAN RESERVATIONS TODAY.   IEMBRCB56555

THE **CONCENTRATION** OF SPANISH-SURNAME POPULATION IN THE FIVE SOUTHWESTERN STATES.   MUSCCMC62505

CONCEPT
THE AFFIRMATIVE-ACTION **CONCEPT** OF EQUAL-EMPLOYMENT-OPPORTUNITY.   GPRICWS65688

POWER AS A PRIMARY **CONCEPT** IN THE STUDY OF MINORITIES.   GSCHERA56058

THE **CONCEPT** OF POVERTY. /ECONOMIC-OPPORTUNITY/   GUSCHAC65186

CONCEPT OF THE FEMININE ROLE. /WORK-WOMAN-ROLE/   WSTEIAX63135

CONCEPTION
ROLE **CONCEPTION** AS A PREDICTOR OF ADULT FEMALE ROLES. /WORK-WOMAN-ROLE/   WANGRSS66619

ROLE **CONCEPTION** AND CAREER ASPIRATION. A STUDY OF IDENTITY IN NURSING.   WCORWRG61707

CONCEPTS
CHANGING CULTURAL **CONCEPTS** IN WOMEN-S LIVES. /WORK-WOMAN-ROLE/   WUSEERH64255

CONCEPTUAL
MANPOWER PROJECTIONS. SOME **CONCEPTUAL** PROBLEMS AND RESEARCH NEEDS. /EMPLOYMENT-TRENDS/   GSWERSX66535

CONCERN
AREAS OF COMMISSION **CONCERN**. /KANSAS-CITY MISSOURI/   GKANCIC62840

MANAGEMENT-S **CONCERN** WITH RECENT CIVIL-RIGHTS LEGISLATION AFFECTING MANAGEMENT-S OBLIGATIONS TO HIS
EMPLOYEES AND APPLICANTS FOR EMPLOYMENT. MAINLY IN THE STATE OF NEW-YORK.   GKOPPRW65858

MAJOR POLITICAL ISSUES WHICH DIRECTLY **CONCERN** NEGROES.   NMILLJE48250

CONCERN FOR AGRICULTURAL MIGRANTS IN MARYLAND.   PUVMAXX64856

CONCERNS
THE NEGRO COLLEGE STUDENT. SOME FACTS AND SOME **CONCERNS**.   NCLARKB64307

CAREERS AS **CONCERNS** OF BLUE-COLLAR GIRLS. /OCCUPATIONS/   WDAVIEX64721

CONCILIATION
PATTERNS OF **CONCILIATION** UNDER THE NEW-YORK STATE LAW AGAINST DISCRIMINATION.   GNEWXYL51100

CONCLUSIONS
THE ROLE OF THE SECONDARY SCHOOLS IN THE PREPARATION OF YOUTH FOR EMPLOYMENT. SUMMARY, **CONCLUSIONS**. AND
RECOMMENDATIONS.   GKAUFJJ67963

FINDINGS OF FACT, **CONCLUSIONS** AND ACTION OF THE COMMISSION ON HUMAN-RELATIONS IN RE. INVESTIGATIVE PUBLIC
HEARINGS INTO ALLEGED DISCRIMINATORY PRACTICE BY THE HOTEL AND RESTAURANT INDUSTRY IN PHILADELPHIA.
/PENNSYLVANIA/   GPHILCH61176

CONCLUSIONS AND RECOMMENDATIONS. FIRST CONFERENCE ON MIGRANT-LABOR.   GTEXACO59351

INTELLIGENCE IN THE UNITED STATES. A SURVEY -- WITH **CONCLUSIONS** FOR MANPOWER UTILIZATION IN EDUCATION AND
EMPLOYMENT.   NMINEJB57796

CONDITION
THE GENERAL **CONDITION** OF THE ALABAMA NEGRO.   NSNCCXX65187

THE VALIDATION OF ACCULTURATION. A **CONDITION** TO ETHNIC ASSIMILATION.   OBROOLX55708

CONDITIONS
CONDITIONS FOR MIGRANTS -- A NATIONAL DISGRACE.   GSCHWLX66556

ECONOMY AND **CONDITIONS** OF THE FORT-HALL INDIAN RESERVATION.   INYBRNX64603

POPULATION CHARACTERISTICS. LIVING **CONDITIONS** AND INCOME OF INDIAN FAMILIES, NORTHERN-CHEYENNE
RESERVATION. JULY, 1961.   IUSDINT63656

POPULATION CHARACTERISTICS. LIVING **CONDITIONS**, AND INCOME OF INDIAN FAMILIES, FORT-PECK RESERVATION,
1951-1961.   IUSDINT63657

POPULATION CHARACTERISTICS. LIVING **CONDITIONS** AND INCOMES OF INDIAN FAMILIES, FORT-BELKNAP RESERVATION.   IUSDINT63658

POPULATION CHARACTERISTICS. LIVING **CONDITIONS** AND INCOMES OF INDIAN FAMILIES, ROCKY-BAY-S RESERVATION.   IUSDINT63659

WHAT ARE THE PSYCHOLOGICAL EFFECTS OF SEGREGATION UNDER **CONDITIONS** OF EQUAL FACILITIES.   NCHEIIX49198

THE GENERAL **CONDITIONS** OF MISSISSIPPI NEGROES.   NCOUNFO63929

NAACP VIEWS **CONDITIONS**.   NGUSCKI63469

SUMMARY OF A SURVEY OF SOCIAL AND ECONOMIC **CONDITIONS** IN MORRIS COUNTY NEW-JERSEY AS THEY AFFECT THE
NEGRO.   NKERNJH57645

A SURVEY OF THE ECONOMIC AND CULTURAL **CONDITIONS** OF THE NEGRO POPULATION OF LOUISVILLE, KENTUCKY AND A
REVIEW OF THE PROGRAM AND ACTIVITIES OF THE LOUISVILLE URBAN-LEAGUE. JANUARY-FEBRUARY, 1948.   NNATLUL48903

NOTES ON THE **CONDITIONS** OF NEGROES. /EDUCATION DISCRIMINATION/   NSTREGX45463

THE NEGRO IN THE WEST. SOME FACTS RELATING TO SOCIAL AND ECONOMIC **CONDITIONS**. NO 1. THE NEGRO WORKER.   NUSDLABND256

IMPROVED **CONDITIONS** FOR NEGROES IN LOUISVILLE. /KENTUCKY/   NUSDLAB45820

CONDITIONS   (CONTINUATION)
THE BLS STUDY OF NURSES SALARIES AND EMPLOYMENT **CONDITIONS**.   WAMERJN57378

EMPLOYMENT AND **CONDITIONS** OF WORK OF NURSES.   WINTELO60862

THE SHORTAGE OF NURSES AND **CONDITIONS** OF WORK IN NURSING. /OCCUPATIONS/   WKRUSMX58920

TESTIMONY, PUBLIC HEARING, WOMEN IN PUBLIC AND PRIVATE EMPLOYMENT, CALIFORNIA. /FEP   EMPLOYMENT
 CONDITIONS/   WLOWEDX66943

CONFERENCE
THE NEGRO WOMAN AT WORK. ADDRESS TO **CONFERENCE** ON THE NEGRO WOMAN IN THE USA.   CKEYSMD65646

CONFERENCE ISSUE -- TOWARD EQUAL-OPPORTUNITY IN EMPLOYMENT.   GBUFFLR64484

A COMPILATION OF STATISTICAL DATA, CHARTS AND OTHER RESOURCE MATERIAL FOR **CONFERENCE** PARTICIPANTS.
 /APPRENTICESHIP CALIFORNIA YOUTH/   GCALCNA60516

MINORITY-GROUPS **CONFERENCE** ON EQUAL-EMPLOYMENT-OPPORTUNITIES.   GCHURRX55572

MIGRATORY-LABOR IN THE WEST. BACKGROUND INFORMATION FOR THE WESTERN INTERSTATE **CONFERENCE** ON MIGRATORY
LABOR. /MIGRANT-WORKERS/   GCOUNSG60931

CONFERENCE ON UNSKILLED WORKERS IN THE LABOR-FORCE. PROBLEMS AND PROSPECTS.   GGITLAL66134

A **CONFERENCE** ON UNEMPLOYMENT.   GGORDMS63727

LONG-TERM MANPOWER PROJECTIONS. PROCEEDINGS OF A **CONFERENCE** CONDUCTED BY THE RESEARCH PROGRAM ON
UNEMPLOYMENT AND THE AMERICAN ECONOMY.   GGORDRA65613

BAY AREA **CONFERENCE** ON FULL-EMPLOYMENT. /SAN-FRANCISCO CALIFORNIA/   GHIRSFI64776

REMARKS AT THE PLANS-FOR-PROGRESS **CONFERENCE**.   GHUMPHH65788

LAKE-ARROWHEAD **CONFERENCE** ON EQUAL-EMPLOYMENT-OPPORTUNITY.   GLOSAFEND916

PROCEEDINGS OF **CONFERENCE** ON EDUCATION FOR OPPORTUNITY, OPPORTUNITY FOR EDUCATION.   GMICFEP61982

THE MEASUREMENT AND INTERPRETATION OF JOB VACANCIES. A **CONFERENCE** REPORT OF THE NATIONAL BUREAU OF
ECONOMIC RESEARCH.   /LABOR-MARKET/   GNATLBE66611

SOCIAL DYNAMITE. THE REPORT OF THE **CONFERENCE** ON UNEMPLOYED, OUT-OF-SCHOOL YOUTH IN URBAN AREAS, MAY
24-26, 1961.   GNATLCC61039

DIGEST OF FINDINGS FROM A WORKING **CONFERENCE** OF LOCAL COUNCILS. /FEPC/   GNATLCS45045

PROCEEDINGS OF THE NATIONAL-SHARECROPPERS-FUND **CONFERENCE** ON MIGRATORY LABOR AND LOW-INCOME FARMERS.
NOVEMBER 13 1957.   GNATLSF57299

REPORT ON SECOND ANNUAL SPRING **CONFERENCE** ON CIVIL-RIGHTS OF NEW-JERSEY COMMISSION-ON-CIVIL-RIGHTS, APRIL
23, 1966.   GNEWJCC66056

THE NEXT STEPS TOWARD EQUALITY OF OPPORTUNITY IN THE SYRACUSE METROPOLITAN AREA. REPORT OF THE SYRACUSE
CONFERENCE ON HUMAN RIGHTS AND HOUSING, JULY 2-3 1962. /NEW-YORK/   GNEWYSB62103

COMMISSIONS FOR HUMAN RIGHTS, 15TH ANNUAL **CONFERENCE**, PROCEEDINGS.   GPENNHR63166

CONFERENCE ON EQUAL-EMPLOYMENT-OPPORTUNITY.   GPOTTGX65189

THE AMERICAN DREAM...EQUAL OPPORTUNITY, A REPORT ON THE COMMUNITY LEADER-S **CONFERENCE** SPONSORED BY
PRESIDENT-S COMMITTEE ON EQUAL-EMPLOYMENT-OPPORTUNITY, MAY 19, 1962.   GPRESCD62105

REGIONAL COMMUNITY LEADERS **CONFERENCE** ON EQUAL-EMPLOYMENT-OPPORTUNITY, PROCEEDINGS.   GPRESCD64113

CONCLUSIONS AND RECOMMENDATIONS, FIRST **CONFERENCE** ON MIGRANT-LABOR.   GTEXACO59351

THE NATIONAL **CONFERENCE** AND THE REPORTS OF THE STATE ADVISORY COMMITTEES TO THE U.S. COMMISSION ON
CIVIL-RIGHTS, 1959.   GUSCOMC60405

A TIME FOR ACTION. PROCEEDINGS OF THE NATIONAL **CONFERENCE** ON EQUAL-EMPLOYMENT-OPPORTUNITY, 1962.
 /MILITARY/   GUSDARM62193

CONFERENCE ON EQUAL JOB OPPORTUNITY.   GUSDLAB56027

MIGRATORY FARM LABOR **CONFERENCE**, PROCEEDINGS.   GUSDLAB57359

CONFERENCE ON EQUAL-EMPLOYMENT-OPPORTUNITY.   GUSDLAB65026

CONFERENCE ON EQUAL-EMPLOYMENT-OPPORTUNITY, AUGUST 16, 1961.   GUSDSTA61507

LAKE ARROWHEAD **CONFERENCE** ON EQUAL-EMPLOYMENT-OPPORTUNITY, OCTOBER 22-24, 1963 -- RECORD OF PROCEEDINGS.
LOS-ANGELES, CALIFORNIA.   GUSFEDE63513

ADDRESS BEFORE THE CIVIL-RIGHTS **CONFERENCE**.   GWIRTWW65571

AMERICAN INDIAN CAPITAL **CONFERENCE** ON POVERTY, MAY 9-12, 1964. FINDINGS.   IAMERIN64087

NATIONAL **CONFERENCE** ON MANPOWER PROGRAMS FOR INDIANS. SUMMATION.   IKRUGDH67811

PROCEEDINGS OF THE **CONFERENCE** ON INDIAN TRIBES AND TREATIES.   IUVMNCC56676

PROCEEDINGS OF EMPLOYMENT OPPORTUNITIES EDUCATIONAL **CONFERENCE**.   MCOUNMA62930

PROCEEDINGS OF THE **CONFERENCE** ON EDUCATION FOR ADULT MIGRANT WORKERS. /TEXAS/   MTEXACM62498

PROBLEMS AND OPPORTUNITIES CONFRONTING NEGROES IN THE FIELD OF BUSINESS, REPORT ON THE NATIONAL
CONFERENCE ON SMALL BUSINESS. /OCCUPATIONS/   NFITZNH63358

CONFERENCE ON EQUAL JOB OPPORTUNITY.   NMCKIGB56725

LAND TENURE IN THE SOUTHERN REGION. PROCEEDINGS OF PROFESSIONAL AGRICULTURAL WORKERS TENTH ANNUAL
CONFERENCE.   NTUSKIX51218

CONFERENCE ON PROBLEMS IN EMPLOYMENT CONFRONTING NEGROES IN NEW-JERSEY, OCTOBER 18 1962.   NUSDLAB62242

SECRETARY-S **CONFERENCE** WITH COLLEGE PRESIDENTS AND EXECUTIVES. /EDUCATION EMPLOYMENT/   NUSDLAB63301

ENHANCING THE OCCUPATIONAL OUTLOOK AND VOCATIONAL ASPIRATIONS OF SOUTHERN SECONDARY YOUTH. A **CONFERENCE**

CONFERENCE   (CONTINUATION)
OF SECONDARY SCHOOL PRINCIPALS AND COUNSELORS.   NUSDLAB65334

CONFERENCE ON EQUAL-EMPLOYMENT-OPPORTUNITY.   NUSDLAB65813

SUMMARY REPORT. EQUAL-EMPLOYMENT-OPPORTUNITY CONFERENCE.   NUSNAAS63267

PROBLEMS OF WORKING WOMEN. SUMMARY REPORT OF A CONFERENCE.   WAFLCIO61618

REPORT OF ARROWHEAD REGIONAL CONFERENCE ON THE STATUS OF WOMEN IN NORTHERN MINNESOTA.   WARRORC66216

FIRST CATALYST ON CAMPUS CONFERENCE, PROCEEDINGS. /WORK-WOMEN-ROLE/   WCATAXX64683

REPORT ON THE FIRST CONFERENCE ON THE STATUS OF WOMEN. /WORK-WOMEN-ROLE/   WCOLUMX64699

ADDRESS TO CONFERENCE ON EDUCATION AND JOB OPPORTUNITIES FOR WOMEN RETURNING TO THE LABOR-MARKET. WDOUTAX62741

PROGRESS AND PROSPECTS. THE REPORT OF THE SECOND NATIONAL CONFERENCE OF GOVERNORS COMMISSIONS ON THE
STATUS OF WOMEN.   /EMPLOYMENT-CONDITIONS/   WGOVECS65798

CONFERENCE ON EMPLOYMENT PROBLEMS OF WORKING WOMEN.   WIOWAGC64797

A CONFERENCE TO ENLIST THE PARTICIPATION OF 50 INSTITUTIONS OF HIGHER EDUCATION IN SPECIFIC R AND D
PROGRAMS TO PREPARE WOMEN FOR PRODUCTIVE EMPLOYMENT.   WLLOYBJ64937

CONFERENCE ON WOMEN IN THE UPPER PENINSULA ECONOMY. REPORT. /MICHIGAN/   WMICOLA64976

REPORT OF CONFERENCE ON EMPLOYMENT PROBLEMS OF WORKING WOMEN.   WSTATUI63131

WORLD OF WORK CONFERENCE ON CAREER AND JOB OPPORTUNITIES, WASHINGTON, DC, JULY 1962.   WUSDLAB64242

WISCONSIN GOVERNOR-S CONFERENCE ON THE CHANGING STATUS OF WOMEN, JAN 31-FEB 1 1964.   WUSDLAB65232

WOMAN-S DESTINY -- CHOICE OR CHANCE. REPORT CF CONFERENCE AT THE UNIVERSITY OF WASHINGTON, NOVEMBER
21-22, 1963.   WUSDLAB65233

3RD ANNUAL WOMEN-S CONFERENCE. PROCEEDINGS.   WUVUTXX66254

CONFERENCES
MASTER ANNOTATED BIBLIOGRAPHY OF PAPERS OF MOBILIZATION-FOR-YOUTH. PUBLISHED, UNPUBLISHED AND PRESENTED
AT CONFERENCES.   GMOBIFY65025

REGIONAL CONFERENCES ON IMPLEMENTING THE CIVIL-RIGHTS-ACT.   NFREYMX66386

TO FULFILL THESE RIGHTS. SUMMARY REPORT OF PRE-WHITE-HOUSE CONFERENCES.   WYWCAXX66079

CONFLICT
MINORITIES AND THE AMERICAN PROMISE. THE CONFLICT OF PRINCIPLE AND PRACTICE.   GCOLESG54580

CHILDREN OF THE GILDED GHETTO. CONFLICT RESOLUTION OF THREE GENERATIONS OF AMERICAN JEWS.
/OCCUPATIONAL-PATTERNS/   JKRAMJR61736

VALUE ORIENTATION, ROLE CONFLICT, AND ALIENATION FROM WORK. A CROSS-CULTURAL STUDY.   MZURCLA65520

RECENT EFFECTS OF RACIAL CONFLICT ON SOUTHERN INDUSTRIAL DEVELOPMENT.   NHILLHX59543

THE NATURAL HISTORY OF SOCIAL CONFLICT AND WHITE-NEGRO RELATIONS.   NHIMEJS49553

THE NEGRO IN AMERICAN BUSINESS. THE CONFLICT BETWEEN SEPARATISM AND INTEGRATION.   NKINZRH50654

CONFLICT RESPONSE. DETROIT NEGROES FACE UNEMPLOYMENT. /MICHIGAN/   NLEGGJC59678

SOUTHERN RACIAL ATTITUDES. CONFLICT, AWARENESS AND POLITICAL CHANGE.   NMATTDR62758

THE FEMALE PHYSICIAN IN PUBLIC HEALTH. CONFLICT AND RECONCILIATION OF THE SEX AND PROFESSIONAL ROLES.
/OCCUPATIONS/   WKOSAJX64915

CONFLICTING
PROSPECTS FOR EQUAL-EMPLOYMENT. CONFLICTING PORTENTS.   NMARSRX65744

CONFLICTS
MARRIAGE AND CAREER CONFLICTS IN GIRLS AND YOUNG WOMEN. /WORK-FAMILY-CONFLICT/   WMATTEX60961

PERCEPTIONS OF ROLE CONFLICTS AND SELF CONFLICTS AMONG CAREER AND NON-CAREER COLLEGE EDUCATED WOMEN.
/WORK-FAMILY-CONFLICT/   WMORGDD62996

PERCEPTIONS OF ROLE CONFLICTS AND SELF CONFLICTS AMONG CAREER AND NON-CAREER COLLEGE EDUCATED WOMEN.
/WORK-FAMILY-CONFLICT/   WMORGDD62996

WISCONSIN FAIR-EMPLOYMENT-PRACTICES DIVISION INQUIRY INTO THE CONFLICTS BETWEEN STATE PROTECTIVE LABOR
LEGISLATION AND STATE AND FEDERAL LAWS PROHIBITING DISCRIMINATION BASED ON SEX. /EMPLOYMENT-CONDITIONS/ WUAWXWC65165

CONFRONTATION
THE EMERGING RURAL SOUTH. A REGION UNDER CONFRONTATION BY MASS SOCIETY.   GBERTAL66140

CONFRONTATION. BLACK AND WHITE. /CIVIL-RIGHTS/   NBENNLX65881

CONFRONTING
PROBLEMS AND OPPORTUNITIES CONFRONTING NEGROES IN THE FIELD OF BUSINESS. REPORT ON THE NATIONAL
CONFERENCE ON SMALL BUSINESS. /OCCUPATIONS/   NFITZNH63358

CONFERENCE ON PROBLEMS IN EMPLOYMENT CONFRONTING NEGROES IN NEW-JERSEY, OCTOBER 18 1962.   NUSDLAB62242

CONGRESS
SHOULD CONGRESS PASS A LAW PROHIBITING EMPLOYMENT DISCRIMINATION.   GCONGDX45596

CONGRESS AND THE JOHNSON POVERTY PROGRAM.   GCONGDX66356

CIVIL-RIGHTS IN THE 88TH CONGRESS, FIRST SESSION, 1963.   GEDELHX63658

STATEMENT ON BEHALF OF AMERICAN JEWISH CONGRESS ON DISCRIMINATION IN EMPLOYMENT.   GMASLWX61961

THE OUTLOOK FOR A NEW FEPC. THE 80TH CONGRESS AND JOB DISCRIMINATION.   GROSSMX47261

ANNUAL REPORT OF THE SECRETARY OF HEALTH, EDUCATION, AND WELFARE TO THE CONGRESS ON TRAINING ACTIVITIES
UNDER THE MANPOWER-DEVELOPMENT-AND-TRAINING-ACT, 1965.   GUSDHEW66978

THE NEGRO CONGRESS.   NRANDAP40576

CONGRESS-OF-RACIAL-E
THE CONGRESS-OF-RACIAL-EQUALITY AND ITS STRATEGY.   NRICHMX65055

CONGRESSIONAL
THE CONGRESSIONAL HEARINGS AND ISSUES IN PSYCHOLOGICAL TESTING. INVASIONS OF PRIVACY AND TEST BIAS.   GGORDJEND934

THE CIVIL-RIGHTS-ACT OF 1964 -- SOURCE AND SCOPE OF CONGRESSIONAL POWER.   GNORTUL65672

CONNECTICUT
EXTRAVAGANT INJUSTICE. DISCRIMINATION IN INDUSTRY. /CONNECTICUT/   GROPEEXND243

MINORITY-GROUP INTEGRATION BY LABOR AND MANAGEMENT. A STUDY OF THE EMPLOYMENT PRACTICES OF THE LARGER
EMPLOYERS. AND THE MEMBERSHIP PRACTICES OF THE LARGER LABOR UNIONS WITH RESPECT TO RACE, RELIGION, AND
NATIONAL ORIGIN. CONNECTICUT, 1951.   GSTETHG53598

REPORTS ON APPRENTICESHIP, NINE STATE ADVISORY COMMITTEES. /CALIFORNIA FLORIDA MARYLAND CONNECTICUT
WASHINGTON-DC NEW-JERSEY NEW-YORK TENNESSEE WISCONSIN/   GUSCCMC64407

A CLIMATE OF CHANGE. THE NEW-HAVEN STORY. /CONNECTICUT/   NFARRGR65344

FAIR EMPLOYMENT IS GOOD BUSINESS AT G FOX OF HARTFORD. /CASE-STUDY CONNECTICUT/   NGREEMX48448

NEGRO AND WHITE IN A CONNECTICUT TOWN.   NLEEXFF61674

WORKERS WANTED. A STUDY OF EMPLOYERS HIRING POLICIES, PREFERENCES, AND PRACTICES IN NEW-HAVEN AND
CHARLOTTE. /CONNECTICUT NORTH-CAROLINA/   NNOLAEW49928

A SURVEY OF NEW-HAVEN-S NEWCOMERS. THE PUERTO-RICANS. /CONNECTICUT/   PDONCDX59796

CONQUEST
CYBERNATION. THE SILENT CONQUEST. /TECHNOLOGICAL-CHANGE/   GMICADN62978

THE ULTIMATE CONQUEST OF NEGRO ECONOMIC INEQUALITY.   NCALLEX64175

CONSCIENCE
THE CONSCIENCE OF THE GOVERNMENT. /ANTIDISCRIMINATION/   GBERNBI62447

CONSCIOUSNESS
CLASS CONSCIOUSNESS AND SOCIAL MOBILITY IN A MEXICAN-AMERICAN COMMUNITY.   MPENAFX63453

ECONOMIC INSECURITY AND WORKING-CLASS CONSCIOUSNESS.   NLEGGJC64677

CONSEQUENCES
THE MANPOWER REVOLUTION. ITS POLICY CONSEQUENCES. EXCERPTS FROM SENATE HEARINGS BEFORE THE CLARK
SUBCOMMITTEE.   GMANGGL66217

CONSEQUENCES OF DISCRIMINATORY UNION MEMBERSHIP POLICY.   GWESTRL53019

YOUTH IN THE GHETTO. A STUDY OF THE CONSEQUENCES OF POWERLESSNESS AND A BLUEPRINT FOR CHANGE. /NEW-YORK/   NHARLYC64485

ECONOMIC AND SOCIAL CONSEQUENCES OF RACIAL DISCRIMINATORY PRACTICES.   NUNITNX63224

SOME ECONOMIC CONSEQUENCES OF THE PUERTO-RICAN MIGRATION INTO PERTH-AMBOY, 1949-1954. /NEW-JERSEY/   PGOLUFX55812

LONG-RANGE CAUSES AND CONSEQUENCES OF THE EMPLOYMENT OF MARRIED WOMEN.   WBLOORO65884

CONSOLIDATED
CONSOLIDATED INVENTORY OF DEPARTMENT OF LABOR RESEARCH ON LABOR-FORCE EMPLOYMENT AND UNEMPLOYMENT.   GUSDLAB64441

CONSOLIDATED INVENTORY OF DEPARTMENT OF LABOR RESEARCH ON AUTOMATION AND TECHNOLOGICAL-CHANGE.   GUSDLAB64619

CONSTITUTION
THE CONSTITUTION AND JOB DISCRIMINATION.   GCOUNVX64608

THE CONSTITUTION AND CIVIL-RIGHTS.   GKONVMR47856

THE CONSTITUTION AND THE LABOR UNION.   GWELLHX61549

CONSTITUTIONAL
THE FEDERAL INTEREST IN EMPLOYMENT DISCRIMINATION. HEREIN THE CONSTITUTIONAL SCOPE OF EXECUTIVE POWER TO
WITHOLD APPROPRIATE FUNDS.   GFERGCC64679

SOME BASIC CONSTITUTIONAL RIGHTS OF ECONOMIC SIGNIFICANCE.   GHALERX51754

THE CONSTITUTIONAL RIGHT TO MEMBERSHIP IN A LABOR UNION -- FIFTH AND FOURTEENTH AMENDMENTS.   NELLIGH59330

POLICY RESOLUTION ADOPTED BY AFL-CIO 6TH CONSTITUTIONAL CONVENTION, SAN FRANCISCO, DEC 1965. /EEO/   WAFLCIO65617

CONSTRAINTS
CONSTRAINTS ON ECONOMIC PROGRESS ON THE ROSEBUD SIOUX INDIAN RESERVATION.   IEICHCK60553

SOCIAL-CLASS CONSTRAINTS ON THE OCCUPATIONAL ASPIRATIONS OF STUDENTS ATTENDING SOME PREDOMINANTLY NEGRO
COLLEGES.   NGURIPX66467

CONSTRUCTION
INTERIM REPORT TO THE MAYOR ON ITS INQUIRY INTO CHARGES OF RACIAL BIAS IN THE CITY BUILDING AND
CONSTRUCTION INDUSTRY. /NEW-YORK NEGRO PUERTO-RICAN/   CNEWYCO64917

NEW SQUEEZE ON CONSTRUCTION. /UNION/   NBROOTX66631

NEW-YORK CITY COMMISSION ON HUMAN RIGHTS, CONSTRUCTION TRADES HEARING, TESTIMONY. /INDUSTRY/   NHILLHX66546

EMPLOYMENT DISTRIBUTION STUDY OF THE CONSTRUCTION INDUSTRY IN MICHIGAN.   NMICCRC66606

CHANGING EMPLOYMENT PRACTICES IN THE CONSTRUCTION INDUSTRY. EXPERIENCE REPORT 102.   NUSCONM65233

CONSULTANTS
MEXICAN FARM LABOR CONSULTANTS REPORT.   MUSDLAB59508

CONSULTATIONS
PRIVATE-HOUSEHOLD EMPLOYMENT -- SUMMARY OF FIRST AND SECOND CONSULTATIONS. /HOUSEHOLD-WORKERS/   WUSDLAB64212

CONSUMER
THE POOR PAY MORE. CONSUMER PRACTICES OF LOW-INCOME FAMILIES.   GCAPLDX63310

CONSUMER EXPENDITURES AND INCOME WITH EMPHASIS ON LOW-INCOME FAMILIES.   GUSDLAB64833

CONSUMPTION
CONSUMPTION, WORK, AND POVERTY.   GORSHMX65959

CONSUMPTION   (CONTINUATION)
  LABOR SUPPLY, FAMILY INCOME, AND CONSUMPTION.   WMINCJX60985

CONTACT
  THE IMPORTANCE OF CONTACT IN DETERMINING ATTITUDES TOWARD NEGROES.   NMACKBK48488

CONTEMPORARY
  THE VANISHING SERVANT AND THE CONTEMPORARY STATUS-SYSTEM OF THE AMERICAN SOUTH.   NANDEAX53022

  THE ROLE OF THE NEGRO IN THE HEALING PROFESSIONS IN CONTEMPORARY AMERICA. /OCCUPATIONS/   NMCPHEL55728

  DEMOGRAPHIC ASPECTS OF CONTEMPORARY CHANGE. /SOUTH/   NPARRCH63975

  CHANGES IN THE CONTEMPORARY SOUTH.   NSINDAX64141

CONTEXT
  THE AMERICAN NEGRO PROBLEM IN THE CONTEXT OF SOCIAL CHANGE.   NROSEAM65289

  THE EFFECT OF THE SOCIAL CONTEXT IN THE VOCATIONAL COUNSELING OF COLLEGE WOMEN.   WGURIMG63810

CONTINUING
  NEGRO VERSUS WHITE INTELLIGENCE. A CONTINUING CONTROVERSY.   NMCCOWM58062

  EMPLOYMENT ON MERIT. THE CONTINUING CHALLENGE TO BUSINESS, NEGRO-S ECONOMIC LOT.   NMORRJJ57854

  CONTINUING EDUCATION -- FOCUS ON COUNSELING AND TRAINING.   WAAUWFX65616

  RESOURCES FOR THE EMPLOYMENT OF MATURE WOMEN AND/OR THEIR CONTINUING EDUCATION. A SELECTED BIBLIOGRAPHY
  AND AIDS.   WBERNML66746

  UNIVERSITY OF KANSAS-CITY PROJECT FOR CONTINUING EDUCATION OF WOMEN.   WBERRJX63640

  CONTINUING EDUCATION OF WOMEN. NEEDS, ASPIRATIONS, AND PLANS.   WBERRJX63641

  THE COLLEGE AND THE CONTINUING EDUCATION OF WOMEN.   WBLACGW63648

  CONTINUING EDUCATION FOR WOMEN.   WBUNTMI61664

  RESEARCH REPORT. SURVEY OF CONTINUING EDUCATION PROGRAMS.   WFIELBX64762

  PILOT PROJECTS FOR CONTINUING EDUCATION FOR WOMEN.   WMERRMH63972

  REPORT ON UNDERGRADUATE COUNSELING AND CONTINUING EDUCATION AND GUIDANCE FOR MATURE WOMAN.   WNICOHG64032

  UNFINISHED BUSINESS. CONTINUING EDUCATION FOR WOMEN.   WRAUSEX61076

  MINNESOTA PLAN FOR WOMEN-S CONTINUING EDUCATION. A PROGRESS REPORT.   WSENDVL61298

  THE CONTINUING LEARNER. /EDUCATION/   WSOLODX64128

  UNIVERSITY PROGRAMS OF CONTINUING EDUCATION FOR THE ADULT WOMAN.   WTINKAH64156

  WHY CONTINUING EDUCATION PROGRAMS FOR WOMEN.   WUSDLAB63229

  CONTINUING EDUCATION FOR WOMEN.   WUVCHCF61686

CONTINUITIES
  DIGEST OF CASE STUDIES ON CONTINUITIES AND DISCONTINUITIES IN THE EMPLOYMENT-EDUCATION-FAMILY PATTERNS OF
  WOMEN-S LIVES.   WDELAPJ60224

  SOME CONTINUITIES AND DISCONTINUITIES IN THE EDUCATION OF WOMEN. /WORK-FAMILY-CONFLICT/   WRIESDX56079

CONTRACT
  A SPECIAL REPORT, CITY CONTRACT COMPLIANCE. PROGRESS IN 1963. /PHILADELPHIA PENNSYLVANIA/   GPHILCH64179

  GOVERNMENT CONTRACT EMPLOYMENT. RULES AND REGULATIONS... EFFECTIVE JULY 22, 1961, AS AMENDED SEPTEMBER 7,
  1963.   GPRESCD63110

  ENFORCEMENT OF NONDISCRIMINATION REQUIREMENTS FOR GOVERNMENT CONTRACT WORK.   GSPECWH63329

CONTRACTOR
  CONTRACTOR GROUP HITS REVISED EQUAL EMPLOYMENT STANDARDS.   GAIRCHR63866

CONTRACTORS
  TEXTS OF RULES AND REGULATIONS OF PRESIDENT-S COMMITTEE ON EQUAL-EMPLOYMENT-OPPORTUNITY RELATING TO
  OBLIGATIONS OF GOVERNMENT CONTRACTORS AND SUBCONTRACTORS, EFFECTIVE JULY 22, 1961. A BNA SPECIAL REPORT.   GBURENA61498

  IMPLEMENTING AFFIRMATIVE ACTION WITH AIR-FORCE CONTRACTORS.   GHUNTHX63789

  EQUAL-EMPLOYMENT-OPPORTUNITY GUIDE FOR DEPARTMENT OF THE NAVY CONTRACTORS.   GUSDDEF64433

  CITY CONTRACTORS AND FAIR-EMPLOYMENT. EXPERIENCE REPORT 103.   NUSCONM66234

CONTRACTS
  STATE AND LOCAL CONTRACTS AND SUBCONTRACTS.   GCONWJE64599

  LOCAL CONTRACTS AND SUB-CONTRACTS. THE ROLES OF CITY GOVERNMENT AND PRIVATE CITIZENS GROUPS.   GJONEMX64829

  ANTIDISCRIMINATION PROVISIONS IN MAJOR CONTRACTS, 1961.   GLUDELE62923

  GOVERNMENT CONTRACTS AND SOCIAL CONTROL. A PRELIMINARY INQUIRY.   GMILLAS55985

  GOVERNMENT CONTRACTS AND FAIR-EMPLOYMENT-PRACTICES.   GNORGPH64119

  THE NONDISCRIMINATION CLAUSE IN GOVERNMENT CONTRACTS.   GPASLRS57148

  FIELD MANUAL ON EQUAL-EMPLOYMENT-OPPORTUNITY UNDER GOVERNMENT CONTRACTS.   GPRESCD65107

  FIRST REPORT. PRESIDENT-S COMMITTEE ON GOVERNMENT CONTRACTS.   GPRESCH54120

  SECOND ANNUAL REPORT. THE PRESIDENT-S COMMITTEE ON GOVERNMENT CONTRACTS.   GPRESCH55124

  FOURTH ANNUAL REPORT ON EQUAL JOB OPPORTUNITY, 1956-1957, PRESIDENT-S COMMITTEE ON GOVERNMENT CONTRACTS.   GPRESCH57122

  COMPLIANCE GUIDE. RECOMMENDATIONS FOR OBTAINING COMPLIANCE WITH THE NONDISCRIMINATION PROVISIONS IN
  GOVERNMENT CONTRACTS.   GPRESCH58119

  FIVE YEARS OF PROGRESS, 1953-1958, A REPORT TO PRESIDENT EISENHOWER BY THE PRESIDENT-S COMMITTEE ON

CONTRACTS   (CONTINUATION)
GOVERNMENT CONTRACTS.   GPRESCH58121

PATTERN FOR PROGRESS. SEVENTH REPORT. FINAL REPORT TO PRESIDENT EISENHOWER FROM THE COMMITTEE ON
GOVERNMENT CONTRACTS.   GPRESCH60123

HOW MANY CONTRACTS BAR DISCRIMINATION IN EMPLOYMENT.   GWORTMS64586

THE INCIDENCE OF ANTIDISCRIMINATION CLAUSES IN UNION CONTRACTS.   GWORTMS65681

NON-DISCRIMINATION CLAUSE IN GOVERNMENT CONTRACTS IS MANDATORY.   NUSDLAB43833

CONTRASTS
CONTRASTS BETWEEN SPANISH FOLK AND ANGLO URBAN CULTURAL VALUES. /EDUCATION ASPIRATIONS/   MVALDBX64449

RACIAL CONTRASTS IN INCOME.   NHARPRM60487

CONTRIBUTION
MANPOWER PROGRAMS. THEIR CONTRIBUTION TO THE ACHIEVEMENT OF EQUAL-OPPORTUNITY MANPOWER ADMINISTRATION.   GWHITHC65558

CONTRIBUTIONS
ONE AMERICA. THE HISTORY, CONTRIBUTIONS, AND PRESENT PROBLEMS OF OUR RACIAL AND NATIONAL MINORITIES.   GBROWFJ45477

SOME CONSIDERATIONS AS TO THE CONTRIBUTIONS OF SOCIAL, PERSONALITY, AND RACIAL FACTORS TO SCHOOL
RETARDATION IN MINORITY-GROUP CHILDREN.   GDEUTMP56641

CHINESE IN AMERICAN LIFE. SOME ASPECTS OF THEIR HISTORY, STATUS, PROBLEMS AND CONTRIBUTIONS.   OKUNGSW62737

CONTROL
GOVERNMENT CONTRACTS AND SOCIAL CONTROL. A PRELIMINARY INQUIRY.   GMILLAS55985

THE NEGRO UNION OFFICIAL. A STUDY OF SPONSORSHIP AND CONTROL.   NKORNWA52661

UNION STRUCTURE AND PUBLIC POLICY. THE CONTROL OF UNION RACIAL PRACTICES.   NMARSRX63752

A PROPOSAL FOR THE PREVENTION AND CONTROL OF DELINQUENCY BY EXPANDING OPPORTUNITIES.   NMOBIFY62263

CONTROLS
EQUALITY BY STATUTES -- LEGAL CONTROLS OVER GROUP DISCRIMINATION.   GBERGMX52440

CONTROVERSIAL
I AM A CONTROVERSIAL DENTIST. /OCCUPATIONS/   NREEDET62046

CONTROVERSIES
EFFECT OF SCHOOL ASSIGNMENT LAWS ON FEDERAL ADJUDICATION OF INTEGRATION CONTROVERSIES.   NCOLULR57224

CONTROVERSY
THE GREAT EMPLOYMENT CONTROVERSY. /TECHNOLOGICAL-CHANGE/   GBUCKWX62875

THE CONTROVERSY OVER THE EQUAL-EMPLOYMENT-OPPORTUNITY PROVISIONS OF THE CIVIL-RIGHTS BILL. PRO AND CON. GCONGDX64594

NEGRO VERSUS WHITE INTELLIGENCE. A CONTINUING CONTROVERSY.   NMCCOWM58062

THE CONTROVERSY OVER EQUAL-RIGHTS FOR NEGROES.   NOPINRC56956

NEGRO AMERICAN INTELLIGENCE. A NEW LOOK AT AN OLD CONTROVERSY.   NPETTTF63063

CONVENTION
VIGOROUS RIGHTS EFFORTS PLEDGED BY CONVENTION.   GAMERFX59577

NATIONAL NEGRO LABOR COUNCIL. THIRD ANNUAL CONVENTION. /UNION/   NPERRPX54987

POLICY RESOLUTION ADOPTED BY AFL-CIO 6TH CONSTITUTIONAL CONVENTION, SAN FRANCISCO, DEC 1965. /EEO/   WAFLCIC65617

COOPERATION
STATE FAIR-EMPLOMENT LAWS AND THEIR ADMINISTRATION. TEXTS, FEDERAL-STATE COOPERATION, PROHIBITED ACTS. GBURENA64497

BI-RACIAL COOPERATION IN PLACEMENT OF NEGROES.   NUSDLAB42811

COOPERATIVE
NEGROES AND MEXICAN-AMERICANS IN THE CALIFORNIA STATE GOVERNMENT, A COOPERATIVE PROJECT.   CCALOGB65171

COOPERATIVE EXTENSION SERVICE WORK WITH LOW-INCOME FAMILIES.   IUSDAGR63638

PLACING INDIANS WHO LIVE ON RESERVATIONS. A COOPERATIVE PROGRAM.   IUSDLAB59667

AN ECONOMIC ANALYSIS OF SPECIFIED INCORPORATED AND UNINCORPORATED FARMERS COOPERATIVE ASSOCIATIONS
OPERATED BY NEGRO FARMERS IN ALABAMA.   NLIGHMB53340

WOMEN GRADUATES OF COOPERATIVE WORK-STUDY PROGRAMS ON THE COLLEGE LEVEL. /SKILLS/   WMOSBWB57999

COOPERATIVES
COOPERATIVES, CREDIT UNIONS, AND POOR PEOPLE.   NSOUTRC66524

COORDINATED
COORDINATED PLANNING FOR ECONOMIC OPPORTUNTIES FOR JEWISH AGED.   JRABIDX59751

MEETING THE PSYCHOLOGICAL CRISES OF NEGRO YOUTH THROUGH A COORDINATED GUIDANCE SERVICE.   NBRAZWF58111

COORDINATION
COORDINATION AMONG FEDERAL MANPOWER PROGRAMS.   GROBSRT66721

COORDINATION OF MANPOWER PROGRAMS.   GTAYLHC66967

CORPORATE
CORPORATE HIRING POLICIES AND THE NEGRO. /INDUSTRY/   NNEWSXX64911

CORPORATION
THE CORPORATION AND TITLE-VII.   GVIOTVH66113

LIBERTY IN THE BIG CORPORATION.   GWESTAF61557

CARRYING OUT A PLAN FOR JOB INTEGRATION AND DOING IT -- IN THE HEART OF GEORGIA -- WITHOUT A SINGLE
UNPLEASANT INCIDENT. THAT'S THE EXPERIENCE OF LOCKHEED AIRCRAFT CORPORATION AT ITS MARIETTA PLANT.
/INDUSTRY/   NBUSIWX63148

AIDING NEGRO BUSINESSMEN. SMALL BUSINESS OPPORTUNITIES CORPORATION, PHILADELPHIA. /PENNSYLVANIA/   NBUSIWX64143

REPORT AND SUMMARY OF THE AIR FORCE ON ACTIONS TAKEN BY LOCKHEED AIRCRAFT CORPORATION AT THE AIR FORCE

CORPORATION   (CONTINUATION)
    PLANT NO 6 IN MARIETTA, GEORGIA. /INDUSTRY/   NPRESCD61013

CORPORATIONS
    LARGE **CORPORATIONS** ACCUSED OF DISCRIMINATION AGAINST JEWS IN MANAGEMENT, EXECUTIVE CAPACITIES BY
    AMERICAN-JEWISH-COMMITTEE.   JWORLOX64773

    DO **CORPORATIONS** HAVE A SOCIAL DUTY. /INDUSTRY/   NHACKAX63475

CORRECTIVE
    RACIAL DISCRIMINATION IN EMPLOYMENT. PROPOSALS FOR **CORRECTIVE** ACTION.   NPOLLDX63006

CORRELATES
    IDENTIFICATION AND MODIFICATION OF THE SOCIAL-PSYCHOLOGICAL **CORRELATES** OF ECONOMIC DEPENDENCY. PROJECT
    FINAL REPORT.   GKIMMPR66137

    CORRELATES OF ADJUSTMENT AMONG AMERICAN-INDIANS IN AN URBAN ENVIRONMENT.   IMARTHW64588

    SOME NON-INTELLECTUAL **CORRELATES** OF ACADEMIC ACHIEVEMENT AMONG MEXICAN-AMERICAN SECONDARY SCHOOL
    STUDENTS.   MGILLLJ62401

    CORRELATES OF SOUTHERN NEGRO PERSONALITY.   NBRAZWF64496

    SOCIO-ECONOMIC CLASS AND AREA AS **CORRELATES** OF ILLEGAL BEHAVIOR AMONG JUVENILES. NCLARJP62209

    SOME **CORRELATES** OF ANOMIE AMONG RURAL NEGROES.   NLEWICE66688

    SOME **CORRELATES** OF HIGH NEED FOR ACHIEVEMENT AMONG URBAN NORTHERN NEGROES.   NNUTTRL46951

    RACIAL AND FAMILY EXPERIENCE **CORRELATES** OF MOBILITY ASPIRATION.   NSMITHP62144

    THE CHANGING PATTERNS OF WOMEN-S WORK. SOME PSYCHOLOGICAL **CORRELATES**.   WGINZEX58784

    INTEREST AND PERSONALITY **CORRELATES** OF CAREER-MOTIVATED AND HOMEMAKING-MOTIVATED COLLEGE WOMEN.
    /ASPIRATIONS/   WHOYTDP58850

    FAMILIAL **CORRELATES** OF ORIENTATION TOWARD FUTURE EMPLOYMENT AMONG COLLEGE WOMEN. /ASPIRATIONS/   WSIEGAX63572

    CORRELATES OF PRESENT AND FUTURE WORK STATUS OF MARRIED WOMEN.   WSOBOMB60125

    SOME **CORRELATES** OF HOMEMAKING VS CAREER PREFERENCE AMONG COLLEGE HOME ECONOMICS STUDENTS.
    /WORK-FAMILY-CONFLICT/   WVETTLX64257

CORRELATIONS
    CORRELATIONS BETWEEN INCOME AND LABOR-FORCE PARTICIPATION BY RACE.   NDORNSM56283

COST
    THE **COST** OF RETRAINING THE HARD-CORE UNEMPLOYED.   GBORUME65745

    THE HIGH **COST** OF DISCRIMINATION. THE WASTE IN MANPOWER, MORALE, AND PRODUCTIVITY COSTS AMERICAN INDUSTRY
    30 BILLION DOLLARS A YEAR.   GROPEEX63244

    MANPOWER TRAINING, SOME **COST** DIMENSIONS.   GYOUNSX67144

    ON THE **COST** OF BEING A NEGRO. /INCOME EDUCATION/   NSIEGPM65146

COST-BENEFIT
    RETRAINING UNDER THE MANPOWER-DEVELOPMENT-ACT. A **COST-BENEFIT** ANALYSIS.   GPAGEDA64775

COSTS
    ECONOMIC **COSTS** OF RACIAL DISCRIMINATION IN EMPLOYMENT.   GCOUNEA62205

    THE HIGH COST OF DISCRIMINATION. THE WASTE IN MANPOWER, MORALE, AND PRODUCTIVITY **COSTS** AMERICAN INDUSTRY
    30 BILLION DOLLARS A YEAR.   GROPEEX63244

    RETRAINING. AN EVALUATION OF GAINS AND **COSTS**.   GSOMEGG65717

    WHAT MASSIVE RESISTANCE **COSTS** NORFOLK AND ITS BUSINESSMEN. /VIRGINIA/   NBUSIWX58165

    PREJUDICE **COSTS** TOO MUCH.   NSHISBX56538

COTTON
    THE EVALUATION OF PRACTICES CARRIED ON BY TWO HUNDRED NEGRO FARMERS IN THE PRODUCTION OF **COTTON** IN MACON
    COUNTY, ALABAMA.   NGCLDSM48350

    LABOR AND TECHNOLOGY ON SELECTED **COTTON** PLANTATIONS IN THE DELTA AREA OF MISSISSIPPI, 1953-1957.   NLERANL59404

    THE RELATIONSHIP BETWEEN MECHANIZATION OF **COTTON** PRODUCTION AND ATTENDANCE AND ENROLLMENT IN THE RURAL
    SCHOOLS OF COAHOMA COUNTY, MISSISSIPPI.   NMCLABF51349

    THE PLACE OF THE NEGRO FARMER IN THE CHANGING ECONOMY OF THE **COTTON** SOUTH.   NNEALEE50905

    THE NEW REVOLUTION IN THE **COTTON** ECONOMY.   NSTREJH57184

COTTON-PICKER
    THE MECHANICAL **COTTON-PICKER**, NEGRO MIGRATION, AND THE INTEGRATION MOVEMENT.   NDILLHCND274

COUNCIL
    TRADE UNION LEADERSHIP **COUNCIL** --EXPERIMENT IN COMMUNITY ACTION. /DETROIT MICHIGAN/   GBATTRX63426

    PLANS-FOR-PROGRESS. A FIRST YEAR REPORT BY THE PLANS FOR PROGRESS ADVISORY **COUNCIL**.   GPRESCD64112

    HEALTH, EDUCATION, AND WELFARE ASPECTS OF THE ECONOMIC REPORT OF THE PRESENT AND ANNUAL REPORT OF THE
    COUNCIL OF ECONOMIC ADVISORS.   GUSDHEW66711

    NEGRO AMERICAN LABOR **COUNCIL** IS ACTIVE IN NEW-YORK STATE.   NBROOTR61119

    AFL-CIO **COUNCIL** GETS NEGRO DEMAND FOR MORE ACTION ON BIAS IN UNIONS.   NBUSIWX61144

    TRADE UNION LEADERSHIP **COUNCIL**. EXPERIMENT IN COMMUNITY ACTION.   NNEWXUT63088

    NATIONAL NEGRO LABOR **COUNCIL**, THIRD ANNUAL CONVENTION. /UNION/   NPERRPX54987

    STATEMENT BEFORE CALIFORNIA LEGISLATURE ASSEMBLY, INTERIM SUBCOMMITTEE ON ECONOMIC OPPORTUNITY ON BEHALF
    OF CHINATOWN-NORTH BEACH DISTRICT **COUNCIL**.   OWONGLJ64771

COUNCILS
    DIGEST OF FINDINGS FROM A WORKING CONFERENCE OF LOCAL **COUNCILS**. /FEPC/   GNATLCS45045

COUNSELING

COUNSELING MINORITY-GROUP YOUTH. DEVELOPING THE EXPERIENCE OF EQUALITY THROUGH EDUCATION.   GBRIGWA62473

EMPLOYMENT COUNSELING AS AN INTEGRAL PART OF AN ACTIVE LABOR-MARKET POLICY.   GEHRLRA65791

TECHNOLOGICAL-CHANGE AND VOCATIONAL COUNSELING.   GSAMLJX64843

PLACEMENT AND CAREER COUNSELING AT PREDOMINANTLY NEGRO COLLEGES.   NBEAUAG66067

NEGROES. VOCATIONAL GUIDANCE AND COUNSELING IN THE SOUTHERN FIELD.   NEDWAGL47325

COUNSELING NEGRO STUDENTS. AN EDUCATIONAL DILEMMA.   NPHILWB59996

CONTINUING EDUCATION -- FOCUS ON COUNSELING AND TRAINING.   WAAUWFX65616

COUNSELING GIRLS AND WOMEN. AWARENESS. ANALYSIS. ACTION.   WBERRJX66642

CAREER GUIDANCE FOR GIRLS. /COUNSELING/   WCALDED60445

COUNSELING THE MATURE WOMAN.   WDOLAEF66733

COUNSELING IMPLICATIONS OF WOMAN-S CHANGING ROLE.   WGASSGZ59775

THE EFFECT OF THE SOCIAL CONTEXT IN THE VOCATIONAL COUNSELING OF COLLEGE WOMEN.   WGURIMG63810

COUNSELING ADOLESCENT GIRLS IN THE 1960-S.   WHAVIRJ65833

COUNSELING OF GIRLS AND MATURE WOMEN.   WHEDGJN64994

VOCATIONAL GUIDANCE AND TRAINING OF GIRLS AND WOMEN. /COUNSELING/   WINTELO64863

COUNSELORS AND GIRLS. /COUNSELING/   WLEWIEC65931

THE COUNSELOR AND GIRLS CAREER DEVELOPMENT. /COUNSELING/   WMATTEX63960

COUNSELING GIRLS TOWARD NEW PERSPECTIVES.   WMIDDAR65190

NEW APPROACHES TO COUNSELING GIRLS IN THE 1960-S.   WMIDWRP65209

REPORT ON UNDERGRADUATE COUNSELING AND CONTINUING EDUCATION AND GUIDANCE FOR MATURE WOMAN.   WNICOHG64032

REPORT OF THE COMMITTEE ON EDUCATION. /EQUAL-OPPORTUNITY COUNSELING/   WPRESCO63066

COUNSELING GIRLS IN THE SIXTIES.   WSIMPAX66114

COUNSELING TODAY-S GIRLS FOR TOMORROW-S WOMANHOOD.   WWESTEM65210

COUNSELLING

COUNSELLING SERVICES.   ITHOMBXND439

COUNSELOR

THE SCHOOL COUNSELOR AT WORK ON OCCUPATIONAL DISCRIMINATION.   GDIXALX46643

THE COUNSELOR AND THE NEGRO STUDENT.   NCHAPAA66192

THE ROLE OF THE COUNSELOR IN THE GUIDANCE OF NEGRO STUDENTS.   NTRUEDL60208

THE COUNSELOR AND GIRLS CAREER DEVELOPMENT. /COUNSELING/   WMATTEX63960

WHEN WILL THE EDUCATIONAL NEEDS OF WOMEN BE MET. SOME QUESTIONS FOR THE COUNSELOR.   WNEUMRR63026

COUNSELOR-S

COUNSELOR-S VIEWS ON CHANGING MANAGEMENT POLICIES.   GCOXXTX63618

COUNSELOR-S GUIDE TO OCCUPATIONAL AND OTHER MANPOWER INFORMATION. AN ANNOTATED BIBLIOGRAPHY.   GLAFADP65782

HIGH SCHOOL GUIDANCE COUNSELOR-S PERCEPTIONS OF SELECTED CAREERS FOR WOMEN COLLEGE GRADUATES.   WSWOPMR63146

COUNSELORS

UNFAIR EMPLOYMENT PRACTICES AS VIEWED BY PRIVATE EMPLOYMENT COUNSELORS.   GKEENVX52015

ENHANCING THE OCCUPATIONAL OUTLOOK AND VOCATIONAL ASPIRATIONS OF SOUTHERN SECONDARY YOUTH. A CONFERENCE
OF SECONDARY SCHOOL PRINCIPALS AND COUNSELORS.   NUSDLAB65334

COUNSELORS AND GIRLS. /COUNSELING/   WLEWIEC65931

NONTRADITIONALLY TRAINED WOMEN AS MENTAL HEALTH COUNSELORS/PSYCHOTHERAPISTS.   WMAGOTM66779

IMPLICATIONS OF TWO PILOT PROJECTS IN TRAINING MATURE WOMEN AS COUNSELORS.   WRIOCMJ65082

COUNTIES

POPULATION AND LABOR-FORCE CHARACTERISTICS OF FIVE SOUTHEASTERN PENNSYLVANIA COUNTIES.   GANDEBXND391

NET MIGRATION OF THE POPULATION, 1950-60, BY AGE, SEX, AND COLOR. VOL II, ANALYTICAL GROUPINGS OF
COUNTIES. /INCOME/   GBOWLGK65434

THE COMPOSITION OF NET MIGRATION AMONG COUNTIES IN THE UNITED STATES, 1950-60.   GBOWLGK66414

FAMILY INCOME AND RELATED CHARACTERISTICS AMONG LOW-INCOME COUNTIES AND STATES.   GRODOAL64241

LEVELS OF LIVING OF SPANISH-AMERICAN RURAL AND URBAN FAMILIES IN TWO SOUTH TEXAS COUNTIES.   MCLEMHM63381

OCCUPATIONAL-PATTERNS OF RURAL AND URBAN SPANISH-AMERICANS IN TWO SOUTH TEXAS COUNTIES.   MCOTHML66385

INCOMES OF RURAL AND URBAN SPANISH-AMERICANS IN TWO SOUTH TEXAS COUNTIES.   MDICKBE65389

ANALYSIS OF POPULATION CHANGES IN NEW-MEXICO COUNTIES.   MPIERGK61457

AFTER HIGH SCHOOL WHAT...HIGHLIGHTS OF A STUDY OF CAREER PLANS OF NEGRO AND WHITE RURAL YOUTH IN THREE
FLORIDA COUNTIES. /ASPIRATIONS/   NYOUMEG65390

FINAL REPORT. EXPERIMENTAL AND DEMONSTRATION MANPOWER PROJECT FOR THE RECRUITMENT, TRAINING, PLACEMENT
AND FOLLOW-UP OF RURAL UNEMPLOYED WORKERS IN TEN NORTH FLORIDA COUNTIES.   WFLORMP66326

COUNTY

THE URBAN REALITY. A COMPARATIVE STUDY OF THE SOCIO-ECONOMIC SITUATION OF MEXICAN-AMERICANS, NEGROES AND
ANGLO-CAUCASIANS IN LOS-ANGELES COUNTY. /CALIFORNIA/   CLOSACH65708

FARM MECHANIZATION AND LABOR STABILIZATION. PART II IN A SERIES ON TECHNOLOGICAL-CHANGE AND FARM LABOR

COUNTY   (CONTINUATION)
LSE, KERN COUNTY, CALIFORNIA, 1961. /NEGRO MEXICAN-AMERICAN/   CMETZWH65389

THE MINORITY-GROUP WORKER IN CAMDEN COUNTY. /NEW-JERSEY/   GBOGITX54057

OPINION CONCERNING THE SCOPE AND AUTHORITY OF THE JURISDICTION THAT MAY BE GRANTED TO CITY OR COUNTY
HUMAN-RELATIONS-COMMISSIONS IN THE FIELDS OF EMPLOYMENT AND HOUSING. /CALIFORNIA/   GCALAG063512

A SUMMARY REPORT OF PRACTICES AND PROGRAMS DESIGNED TO REDUCE THE NUMBER OF DROPOUTS IN THE HIGH SCHOOLS
OF LOS-ANGELES COUNTY. /CALIFORNIA/   GDELMOT66147

SURVEY OF MINORITY-GROUP EMPLOYMENT AND PATIENT CARE IN PRIVATE HOSPITAL FACILITIES IN LOS-ANGELES
COUNTY. /CALIFORNIA/   GLOSACCND914

REPORTS ON THE PATTERN OF EMPLOYMENT OF MINORTY-GROUP PERSONS IN DEPARTMENT OF COUNTY
GOVERNMENT.LOS-ANGELES CALIFORNIA/   GLOSACC62913

RACIAL AND ETHNIC EMPLOYMENT PATTERN SURVEY OF THE CITY AND COUNTY OF SAN-FRANCISCO GOVERNMENT.
CEPARTMENTAL ANALYSIS. /CALIFORNIA/   GSANFHR65264

DOMESTIC AND IMPORTED WORKERS IN THE HARVEST LABOR-MARKET, SANTA-CLARA COUNTY, CALIFORNIA, 1954. MFULLVX56396

SOME NCTES ON THE MEXICAN POPULATION OF LOS-ANGELES COUNTY. /CALIFORNIA/   MLOSACDND431

MEXICAN-AMERICAN FAMILIES. LOS-ANGELES COUNTY. /CALIFORNIA/   MMCNAPH57435

THE EFFECTS OF IMPORTED MEXICAN FARM LABOR IN A CALIFORNIA COUNTY.   MROONJF61465

FCONOMIC BASE STUDY OF SAN-ANTONIO AND TWENTY-SEVEN COUNTY AREAS. /TEXAS/   MSANACP64476

NEW-MEXICO COUNTY INDUSTRIAL COMPOSITION AND LEVELS OF LIVING.   MSANDAD63479

FACTORS AFFECTING THE PRESENT FARMING PROGRAMS OF ONE HUNDRED NEGRO FARMS IN THE PATRONAGE AREA OF THE
MACON COUNTY TRAINING SCHOOL, IN ALABAMA, WITH EMPHASIS FOR IMPROVEMENT.   NBRONCA51337

VOCATIONAL CHOICES OF NEGRO HIGH SCHOOL STUDENTS IN MACON COUNTY, ALABAMA, AND THEIR RELATIONSHIP TO
PASIC CCCUPATIONAL ACTIVITES OF THE SCHOOL CCMMUNITIES. /ASPIRATIONS/   NCHAPEJ49351

THE EVALUATION OF PRACTICES CARRIED ON BY TWO HUNDRED NEGRO FARMERS IN THE PRODUCTION OF COTTON IN MACON
COUNTY, ALABAMA.   NGOLDSM48350

SUMMARY OF A SURVEY OF SOCIAL AND ECONOMIC CONDITIONS IN MORRIS COUNTY NEW-JERSEY AS THEY AFFECT THE
NEGRO.   NKERNJH57645

A STUDY OF PROFESSIONAL PREPARATION OF NEGRO TEACHERS OF EXCEPTIONAL CHILDREN IN NORTH-CAROLINA COUNTY
AND CITY PUBLIC SCHOOLS.   NKNIG0B65023

EMPLOYMENT OF NEGRO MANPOWER IN CALVERT COUNTY, MARYLAND.   NLERANL60401

THE NEGRO IN LOS-ANGELES COUNTY. /CALIFORNIA/   NLOSACC63709.

THE RELATIONSHIP BETWEEN MECHANIZATION OF COTTON PRODUCTION AND ATTENDANCE AND ENROLLMENT IN THE RURAL
SCHOOLS OF COAHOMA COUNTY, MISSISSIPPI.   NMCLABF51349

INCCME. EMPLOYMENT STATUS ANC CHANGE IN CALVERT COUNTY, MARYLAND.   NROHRWC58400

AN ANALYSIS OF SELECTIVE FACTORS INFLUENCING FARM INCOME IN HALE COUNTY, AS A BASIS FOR ESTABLISHING A
MORE EFFECTIVE VOCATIONAL AGRICULTURAL PROGRAM. /ALABAMA/   NSALTOR52347

A STUDY OF FARM MANAGEMENT PRACTICES ON 100 NEGRO FARMS IN MACON COUNTY, ALABAMA, 1949.   NSHAWBJ50339

THE INFLUENCE OF TUSKEGEE-INSTITUTE ON THE HEALTH, EDUCATIONAL, ECONOMIC, AND POLITICAL ASPECTS OF THE
NEGRO POPULATION OF MACON COUNTY, ALABAMA.   NSHIEAR51342

A CRITICAL APPRAISAL OF PROFESSION TRAINING OF NEGRO TEACHERS IN OKTIBBEHA COUNTY MISSISSIPPI.   NWILLMM50234

COURSE
SUPERVISOR DEVELOPMENT PROGRAM, BASIC COURSE, NONDISCRIMINATION POLICY. /MILITARY/   GUSDARM56192

SCHOOL AND COMMUNITY COURSE. THE LOWER STATUS PUERTO-RICAN FAMILY.   PBRAMJX63784

COURSES
WHY DO BRIGHT GIRLS NOT TAKE STIFF COURSES. /ASPIRATIONS/   WALBJMH61603

COURT
THE CIVIL-RIGHTS AND CIVIL-LIBERTIES DECISIONS OF THE US SUPREME COURT FOR THE 1962-63 TERM. A SUMMARY
ANC ANALYSIS.   GAMERJD63384

SOME RECENT UNITED STATES SUPREME COURT DECISIONS AFFECTING THE RIGHTS OF NEGRO WORKERS.   NCHICCA47914

COURTS
FAIR-EMPLOYMENT-PRACTICE ACTS AND THE COURTS.   GBERNYX64448

COVERAGE
COVERAGE UNDER TITLE-VII OF THE CIVIL-RIGHTS-ACT.   GBENEMC66435

TITLE-VII. COVERAGE AND COMMENTS. /LEGISLATION/   GSCHMCT66287

COVERAGE OF AGRICULTURAL WORKERS UNDER STATE AND FEDERAL LAWS. /MIGRANT-WORKERS/   GUSDLAB64507

COVERED
WOMEN HOUSEHOLD WORKERS COVERED BY OLD AGE, SURVIVORS, AND DISABILITY INSURANCE.   WPOLIEJ65285

CPA
THE STATUS OF THE NEGRO CPA IN THE UNITED STATES. /OCCUPATIONS/   NHARRLJ62494

CPI
CPI -- CHEMICAL PROCESS INDUSTRIES -- TAKES LEAD IN ANTI-BIAS DRIVE. /INDUSTRY/   NCHEMWX61199

CRAFT
THE PRACTICES OF CRAFT UNIONS IN WASHINGTON-DC WITH RESPECT TO MINORITY GROUPS IN CIVIL-RIGHTS IN THE
NATICN-S CAPITOL.   GSEGABD59294

DISCRIMINATION IN CRAFT UNIONS.   GYABRSM65587

CRAFT UNIONS. A LINK IN THE CIRCLE OF NEGRO DISCRIMINATION.   NBLOCHC57088

CRAFT UNIONS AND THE NEGRO IN HISTORICAL PERSPECTIVE.   NBLOCHD58087

CRAFT   (CONTINUATION)
     STATUS OF NEGROES IN **CRAFT** UNIONS...PITTSBURGH LABOR-MARKET. /PENNSYLVANIA/   NPITTMC65002

CRAFTSMEN
     OPPORTUNITIES-INDUSTRIALIZATION-CENTER. **CRAFTSMEN** WITH CONFIDENCE. /TRAINING/   GSULLLH66220

     APPRENTICES, SKILLED **CRAFTSMEN** AND THE NEGRO. AN ANALYSIS.   NHILLHX60525

CREATION
     THE ROLE OF JOB **CREATION** PROGRAMS. /MANPOWER/   GMANGGL65728

CREDIT
     COOPERATIVES, **CREDIT** UNIONS, AND POOR PEOPLE.   NSOUTRC66524

CREED
     RULINGS ON PRE-EMPLOYMENT INQUIRIES RELATING TO RACE, **CREED**, COLOR OR NATIONAL ORIGIN UNDER THE NEW-YORK
     STATE LAW AGAINST DISCRIMINATION.   GNEWYSBND106

     JOBS WITHOUT **CREED** OR COLOR.   GRAUSWX45583

CREWS
     MIGRANT **CREWS** IN EASTERN MARYLAND.   GSHOSAL65306

CRIME
     PUNISHMENT WITHOUT **CRIME**. WHAT YOU CAN DO ABOUT PREJUDICE. /DISCRIMINATION/   GFINESA49962

CRIMINALITY
     QUESTIONS REGARDING AMERICAN-INDIAN **CRIMINALITY**.   ISTEWOX64302

CRISES
     LABOR LOOKS AT THE **CRISES** IN CIVIL-RIGHTS. /UNION/   GGOLDHX58975

     MEETING THE PSYCHOLOGICAL **CRISES** OF NEGRO YOUTH THROUGH A COORDINATED GUIDANCE SERVICE.   NBRAZWF58111

CRISIS
     THE COMING **CRISIS**. YOUTH WITHOUT WORK.   GAMERFX63375

     ECONOMICS AND THE CIVIL-RIGHTS **CRISIS**.   GDERNTX64947

     DEMOGRAPHIC CHANGE AND RACIAL GHETTOS. THE **CRISIS** OF AMERICAN CITIES.   GHILLHX66691

     A MIGRANT LABOR **CRISIS** IN IMMOKALEE. /FLORIDA/   GSOWDWT59328

     THE MENOMINEE TERMINATION **CRISIS**. BARRIERS IN THE WAY OF A RAPID CULTURAL TRANSITION.   IAMESDW59525

     RACIAL **CRISIS** IN AMERICA.   NKILLLM64652

     ECONOMIC **CRISIS** AND EXPECTATIONS OF VIOLENCE. A STUDY OF UNEMPLOYED NEGROES .   NLEGGJC64679

     AMERICAN ENTERPRISE AND THE RACIAL **CRISIS**.   NROBIJX63069

     CRISIS IN BLACK AND WHITE.   NSILBCE65135

     THE DEEPENING **CRISIS** IN METROPOLIS.   NSILBCE65136

CRITERIA
     WELFARE **CRITERIA** AND CHANGING TASTES.   GWECKRS62987

     POVERTY AND THE **CRITERIA** FOR PUBLIC EXPENDITURES.   GWOLOHX65990

     CRITERIA FOR ASSESSING FEASIBILITY OF MOTHERS EMPLOYMENT AND ADEQUACY OF CHILD CARE PLANS.   WUSDHEW66173

CRITICAL
     CRITICAL ISSUES IN EMPLOYMENT POLICY. A REPORT. /UNEMPLOYMENT/   GHARBFH66476

     CRITICAL PROBLEMS IN ACHIEVING EQUAL-EMPLOYMENT-OPPORTUNITY.   GLOCKHC66906

     PSYCHOLOGICAL TESTING IN INDUSTRY. A **CRITICAL** EVALUATION.   GSTANES64635

     IN SEARCH OF A FUTURE. A STUDY OF CAREER-SEEKING EXPERIENCES OF SELECTED NEGRO HIGH SCHOOL GRADUATES IN
     WASHINGTON-DC WHICH WAS AN EFFORT TO PROVIDE KNOWLEDGE HELPFUL IN SOLVING ONE OF THE MOST **CRITICAL**
     PROBLEMS FACING URBAN AMERICA TODAY.   NGRIEES63454

     THE NEGRO WAGE-EARNER AND APPRENTICESHIP TRAINING PROGRAMS. A **CRITICAL** ANALYSIS WITH RECOMMENDATIONS.   NHILLHX60532

     TWENTY YEARS OF STATE FAIR-EMPLOYMENT-PRACTICE COMMISSIONS. A **CRITICAL** ANALYSIS WITH RECOMMENDATIONS.   NHILLHX64550

     A **CRITICAL** SUMMARY. THE NEGRO ON THE HOME FRONT IN WORLD-WARS I AND II.   NREIDID43048

     A **CRITICAL** APPRAISAL OF PROFESSION TRAINING OF NEGRO TEACHERS IN OKTIBBEHA COUNTY MISSISSIPPI.   NWILLMM50234

CRITICS
     FEPC. HOW TO ANSWER ITS **CRITICS**.   GRABKSX58213

CROSS-CULTURAL
     FAMILY COMPOSITION AND CHARACTERISTICS OF AN ECONOMICALLY DEPRIVED **CROSS-CULTURAL** ROCKY-MOUNTAIN AREA.   MANDRWH66359

     VALUE ORIENTATION, ROLE CONFLICT, AND ALIENATION FROM WORK. A **CROSS-CULTURAL** STUDY.   MZURCLA65520

CROSSROADS
     PROGRESS OR POVERTY. THE US AT THE **CROSSROADS**.   GKEYSLH64862

     CHEROKEES AT THE **CROSSROADS**.   IGULIJX60568

     MEXICAN-AMERICAN YOUTH. FORGOTTEN YOUTH AT THE **CROSSROADS**.   MHELLCS66416

     CIVIL-RIGHTS AT THE **CROSSROADS**.   NRUSTBX66097

CROW
     JIM **CROW** IN BUILDING UNIONS.   NLIFEMX66493

     JANE **CROW** AND THE LAW. SEX DISCRIMINATION AND TITLE-VII.   WMURRPX65010

CULTURAL
     TRAINING AID. **CULTURAL** DIFFERENCES. TRAINING IN NONDISCRIMINATION, READING ASSIGNMENTS. /EMPLOYMENT
     MEXICAN-AMERICAN NEGRO/   CCALDSW65447

     CULTURAL DIFFERENCES IN AMERICAN ETHNIC GROUPS. BIBLIOGRAPHY. /AMERICAN-INDIAN NEGRO SPANISH-AMERICAN/   CLIBRCX64899

CULTURAL   (CONTINUATION)
    THE ECONOMIC ABSORPTION AND **CULTURAL** INTEGRATION OF IMMIGRANT MEXICAN-AMERICAN AND NEGRO WORKERS.   CSHANLW64124

    CULTURAL AND RELATED RESTRAINTS AND MEANS OF OVERCOMING THEM. /MEXICAN-AMERICAN NEGRO INTEGRATION/   CSHANLW65485

    THE PREDICTION OF ECONOMIC ABSORPTION AND **CULTURAL** INTEGRATION AMONG MEXICAN-AMERICANS, NEGROES, AND
    ANGLOS IN A NORTHERN INDUSTRIAL COMMUNITY.   CSHANLW66123

    ECCNCMIC ABSORPTION AND **CULTURAL** INTEGRATION OF THE URBAN NEWCOMER. /NEGRO MEXICAN-AMERICAN/   CUVIOIP65277

    ADOLESCENCE. **CULTURAL** DEPRIVATION, POVERTY, AND THE DROPOUT.   GHUNTDE66939

    POSSIBLE SOLUTIONS TO THE PROBLEM OF **CULTURAL** BIAS IN TESTS.   GKRUGRE64946

    RACIAL AND **CULTURAL** MINORITIES.   GSIMPGE65314

    THE MENOMINEE TERMINATION CRISIS. BARRIERS IN THE WAY OF A RAPID **CULTURAL** TRANSITION.   IAMESDW59525

    EDUCATION AMONG AMERICAN-INDIANS. INDIVIDUAL AND **CULTURAL** ASPECTS.   IHAVIRJ57574

    SOCIAL AND **CULTURAL** CONSIDERATIONS IN THE DEVELOPMENT OF MANPOWER PROGRAMS FOR INDIANS.   IKELLWH67579

    ANCMIE AND ACHIEVEMENT MOTIVATION. A STUDY OF PERSONALITY DEVELOPMENT WITHIN **CULTURAL** DISORGANIZATION.   IKERCAC59018

    THE INDIAN TRIBES OF THE US. ETHNIC AND **CULTURAL** SURVIVAL.   IMCNIDX61586

    INDIANS OF THE MISSOURI-BASIN -- **CULTURAL** FACTORS IN THEIR SOCIAL AND ECONOMIC ADJUSTMENT.   IREIFBX58610

    CULTURAL AND ECONOMIC-STATUS OF THE SIOUX PEOPLE.   IUSDINT64645

    A **CULTURAL** MINORITY IMPROVES ITSELF.   MATKIJA61361

    MEXICAN **CULTURAL** PATTERNS.   MIMMASM57420

    SOME **CULTURAL** AND ANTHROPOLOGICAL ASPECTS OF ENGLISH AS A SECOND LANGUAGE.   MRUBEAJ66468

    IMPLICATIONS OF **CULTURAL** VALUES IN EDUCATION.   MVALDBX64448

    CONTRASTS BETWEEN SPANISH FOLK AND ANGLO URBAN **CULTURAL** VALUES. /EDUCATION ASPIRATIONS/   MVALDBX64449

    A REVIEW OF THE ECONOMIC AND **CULTURAL** PROBLEMS OF WICHITA, KANSAS.   NBANNWM65051

    THE PROBLEM OF **CULTURAL** BIAS IN SELECTION. I. BACKGROUND AND LITERATURE. /TESTING/   NCAMPJT65179

    SOME WCRK-RELATED **CULTURAL** DEPRIVATICNS OF LOWER-CLASS NEGRO YOUTHS.   NHIMEJS64554

    THE PROBLEMS OF **CULTURAL** BIAS IN SELECTION, POSSIBLE SOLUTION TO THE PROBLEM OF CULTURAL BIAS IN TESTS.   NKRUGRE64731

    THE PROBLEMS OF **CULTURAL** BIAS IN SELECTION, POSSIBLE SOLUTION TO THE PROBLEM OF **CULTURAL** BIAS IN TESTS.   NKRUGRE64731

    CULTURAL EXPOSURE AND RACE AS VARIABLES IN PREDICTING TRAINING AND JOB SUCCESS. /TESTING/   NLOCKHCND700

    THE NEGRO WORKER-S **CULTURAL** AND OCCUPATIONAL LIMITATIONS.   NMCPICM61729

    A SURVEY OF THE ECONOMIC AND **CULTURAL** CONDITIONS OF THE NEGRO POPULATION OF LOUISVILLE, KENTUCKY AND A
    REVIEW OF THE PROGRAM AND ACTIVITIES OF THE LOUISVILLE URBAN-LEAGUE. JANUARY-FEBRUARY, 1948.   NNATLUL48903

    THE PROBLEM OF **CULTURAL** BIAS IN SELECTION. II. ETHNIC BACKGROUND AND TEST PERFORMANCE.   NROBESC65068

    SOCIAL AND **CULTURAL** CHANGE IN THE PLANTATION AREA.   NRUBIMX54297

    STUDY OF ECONOMIC AND **CULTURAL** ACTIVITIES IN THE WARREN AREA AS THEY RELATE TO MINORITY PEOPLE. /OHIO/   NWARRUL64986

    CULTURAL VALUES AND THE PUERTO-RICAN.   PMONSJX57828

    THE MOTIVATION OF COLLEGE WOMEN TODAY. THE **CULTURAL** SETTING. /ASPIRATIONS/   WHEISPX63840

    THE IMPACT OF **CULTURAL** CHANGE ON WOMEN-S POSITION. /BLUE-COLLAR ASPIRATIONS/   WKONOGX66913

    CHANGING **CULTURAL** CONCEPTS IN WOMEN-S LIVES. /WORK-WOMAN-ROLE/   WUSEERH64255

CULTURAL-BACKGROUND
    THE **CULTURAL-BACKGROUND** CF SCUTHERN NEGROES.   NFRAZEF57378

CULTURALLY
    TESTING OF **CULTURALLY** DIFFERENT GROUPS.   GCAMPJX64093

    TEACHERS OF **CULTURALLY** DISADVANTAGED AMERICAN YOUTH.   NROUSRX63310

CULTURE
    THE **CULTURE** OF THE SLUM.   GDAVIAX63132

    THE PRESENT STATUS OF THE **CULTURE** FAIR TESTING MOVEMENT.   GLAMBNM64880

    THESE CUR PEOPLE. MINORITIES IN AMERICAN **CULTURE**.   GSCHERA49281

    SYMPCSIUM ON CHEROKEE AND INDIAN **CULTURE**.   IFENTWN61620

    THE **CULTURE** AND ACCULTURATION OF THE DELAWARE INDIANS.   INEWCWW56600

    PERSPECTIVES IN AMERICAN INDIAN **CULTURE** CHANGE.   ISPICEH61621

    MENOMINEE WOMEN AND **CULTURE** CHANGE.   ISPINLS62622

    A STUDY CF AMERICAN AND MEXICAN-AMERICAN **CULTURE** VALUES AND THEIR SIGNIFICANCE IN EDUCATION.   MCABRYA63373

    NEGRO TEEN-AGE **CULTURE**.   NHIMEJX61071

    A HISTORICAL REVIEW OF THE IMPACT OF SOCIAL AND ECONOMIC STRUCTURE ON NEGRO **CULTURE** AND HOW IT INFLUENCES
    FAMILY LIVING.   NJACKJX64596

    CULTURE. CLASS AND FAMILY LIFE AMONG LOW-INCCME NEGROES.   NLEWIHX67691

    THE **CULTURE** OF UNEMPLOYMENT. SOME NOTES ON NEGRO CHILDREN.   NSCHWMX64110

    ACHIEVEMENT, **CULTURE** AND PERSONALITY. THE CASE OF THE JAPANESE-AMERICANS.   OCAUDWX61711

    THE **CULTURE** OF POVERTY.   PLEWIOX66824

CULTURE   (CONTINUATION)
LA VIDA. A PUERTO-RICAN FAMILY IN THE **CULTURE** OF POVERTY -- SAN-JUAN AND NEW-YORK.   PLEWIOX66825

BIBLIOGRAPHY ON THE PUERTO-RICAN. HIS **CULTURE** AND SOCIETY.   PMOBIFYND024

PUERTO-RICAN **CULTURE**.   PORTIRX62841

MIGRANTS AND **CULTURE** CHANGE.   PPAULIX55843

CULTURE-OF-POVERTY
EXCLUSIONS AND ADAPTATIONS. A RE-EVALUATION OF THE **CULTURE-OF-POVERTY** THEME.   NCOHERXND221

CULTURES
FACTORS AFFECTING EMPLOYEE SELECTION IN TWO **CULTURES**. /DISCRIMINATION/   GTRIAHC63083

CUMBERLANDS
NIGHT COMES TO THE **CUMBERLANDS**. /ECONOMIC-STATUS/   NCAUDHM62911

CURRENT
CURRENT POPULATION REPORTS -- SPECIAL CENSUS OF CLEVELAND, OHIO. /DEMOGRAPHY/   CUSBURC65379

CURRENT DATA ON NONWHITE WOMEN WORKERS. /NEGRO/   CUSDLAB65261

THE **CURRENT** SITUATION OF THE HIRED FARM LABOR-FORCE.   GBOWLGK67920

4. **CURRENT** PROBLEMS IN TEST PERFORMANCE OF JOB-APPLICANTS.   GDUGARD66651

CURRENT INTERNATIONAL UNION POLICIES AFFECTING MINORITIES AND THEIR IMPLEMENTATION.   GHOPEJX49781

CURRENT MINORITY POLICIES AND THEIR IMPLEMENTATION IN INTERNATIONAL UNIONS.   GHOPEJX51782

3 **CURRENT** PROBLEMS IN TEST PERFORMANCE OF JOB APPLICANTS.   GLOPEFM66909

CURRENT MANPOWER PROBLEMS. AN INTRODUCTORY SURVEY.   GSTURAF64837

A SURVEY OF **CURRENT** LITERATURE ON AUTOMATION AND OTHER TECHNOLOGICAL-CHANGES. A SELECTED ANNOTATED
BIBLIOGRAPHY.   GUSDLAB64825

AN ANALYSIS OF **CURRENT** PATTERNS IN HUMAN RESOURCE DEVELOPMENT IN SAN-ANTONIO, TEXAS.   MDAVIHW66387

THE AMERICAN NEGRO AND THE **CURRENT** SCENE.   NJONEJAND738

SOME IMPLICATIONS ON **CURRENT** CHANGES IN SEX ROLE PATTERNS. /WORK-WOMAN-ROLE/   WHARTRE60828

SUMMARY OF **CURRENT** RESEARCH ON WOMEN-S ROLES.   WNOBLJL59035

CURRICULAR
INVESTIGATION OF DIFFERENCES IN OCCUPATIONAL PREFERENCES, STEREOTYPIC THINKING, AND PSYCHOLOGICAL NEEDS
AMONG UNDERGRADUATE WOMEN STUDENTS IN SELECTED **CURRICULAR** AREAS. /ASPIRATIONS/   WKITTRE60313

CURRICULUM
CURRICULUM CHOICE IN THE NEGRO COLLEGE.   NBRAZWF60109

CUSTOMER
CUSTOMER REACTIONS TO THE INTEGRATION OF NEGRO SALES PERSONNEL.   NSAENGX50101

CUSTOMERS
PICKETING BY NEGROES TO OBTAIN EMPLOYMENT IN PROPORTION TO NEGRO **CUSTOMERS** HELD UNLAWFUL.   NHARVLR49498

CYBERNATION
CYBERNATION AND JOB SECURITY. /UNEMPLOYMENT/   GMANGGL66529

CYBERNATION. THE SILENT CONQUEST. /TECHNOLOGICAL-CHANGE/   GMICADN62978

CYBERNATION AND SOCIAL CHANGE. /TECHNOLOGICAL-CHANGE/   GMICADN64673

SEMINAR ON MANPOWER POLICY AND PROGRAM. **CYBERNATION** AND SOCIAL CHANGE.   GUSDLAB64982

CYCLE
US PLAN TO BREAK **CYCLE** OF BIAS AND POVERTY.   GRICHEX66235

THE POST-PARENTAL PHASE IN THE LIFE **CYCLE** OF 50 COLLEGE EDUCATED WOMEN. /WORK-FAMILY-CONFLICT/   WDAVIIX60717

WOMEN-S CHANGING ROLES THROUGH THE LIFE **CYCLE**.   WNEUGBL59025

DAKOTA
THE URBANIZATION OF THE **DAKOTA** INDIANS.   IWHITRX59686

DALLAS
INCOME, EDUCATION AND UNEMPLOYMENT IN NEIGHBORHOODS. **DALLAS**, TEXAS. /DEMOGRAPHY/   CUSDLAB63459

DATA
RACIAL DISTRIBUTION OF SELECTED UNEMPLOYMENT INSURANCE AND EMPLOYMENT SERVICE **DATA**. JULY-DECEMBER 1966.
/NEGRO MEXICAN-AMERICAN/   CCALDEM67907

OCCUPATIONAL CHARACTERISTICS. **DATA** ON AGE, RACE, EDUCATION, WORK EXPERIENCE, INCOME, ETC. FOR WORKERS IN
EACH OCCUPATION.   CUSBURC63177

PERSONS OF SPANISH-SURNAME. SOCIAL AND ECONOMIC **DATA** FOR WHITE PERSONS OF SPANISH SURNAME IN 5
SOUTHWESTERN STATES. /DEMOGRAPHY/   CUSBURC63181

CURRENT **DATA** ON NONWHITE WOMEN WORKERS. /NEGRO/   CUSDLAB65261

THE HIRED FARM WORKING FORCE OF 1963 WITH SUPPLEMENTARY **DATA** FOR 1962. /ECONOMIC-STATUS/   GBOWLGK65432

A COMPILATION OF STATISTICAL **DATA**, CHARTS AND OTHER RESOURCE MATERIAL FOR CONFERENCE PARTICIPANTS.
/APPRENTICESHIP CALIFORNIA YOUTH/   GCALCNA60516

OCCUPATIONAL EMPLOYMENT STATISTICS, SOURCES AND **DATA**.   GGREEHX66627

FRANCHISE COMPANY **DATA** FOR EQUAL-OPPORTUNITY IN BUSINESS.   GUSDCOM66431

SENIOR CITIZENS AND HOW THEY LIVE. AN ANALYSIS OF 1960 CENSUS **DATA**. PART II. THE AGING NONWHITE AND HIS
HOUSING. /ECONOMIC-STATUS/   GUSHHFX63321

RELATIVE INCOME OF NEGRO MEN. SOME RECENT **DATA**.   NFEINRX66349

PHILADELPHIA-S PUERTO-RICAN POPULATION, WITH 1960 CENSUS **DATA**. /PENNSYLVANIA/   PPITTCH64844

DATA (CONTINUATION)
PUERTO-RICANS IN THE UNITED STATES. SOCIAL AND ECONOMIC **DATA** FOR PERSONS OF PUERTO-RICAN BIRTH AND
PARENTAGE. /DEMOGRAPHY/   PUSBURC63182

DAY
A NEW **DAY** FOR THE AMERICAN INDIAN.   IHUMPHH66003

THE PRESENT **DAY** DISTRIBUTION OF UNITED STATES INDIANS.   ITAXXSX56628

DAY CARE SERVICES: FORM AND SUBSTANCE. /EMPLOYMENT-CONDITIONS/   WHOFFGL61846

DAY CARE IN A CHANGING ECONOMY. /EMPLOYMENT-CONDITIONS/   WKEYSMD64894

THE NATION-S WORKING MOTHERS AND THE NEED FOR **DAY** CARE. ADDRESS. /EMPLOYMENT-CONDITIONS/   WKEYSMD65897

DAY-CARE
PART-TIME CARE. THE **DAY-CARE** PROBLEM. /EMPLOYMENT-CONDITIONS/   WHOSLEM64540

DEBATE
THE MANPOWER REVOLUTION -- A CALL FOR **DEBATE**.   GKIRSGC64860

PREFERENTIAL-HIRING FOR NEGROES. A **DEBATE**.   NAMERCX63010

DECADES
INCOMES AND DEPENDENCY IN THE COMING **DECADES**.   GDAVIMX64870

EDUCATION FOR THE COMING **DECADES**.   ITHOMHX61631

DECAY
THE ILGWU TODAY -- THE **DECAY** OF A LABOR UNION.   NHILLHX62528

DECERTIFIES
NLRB **DECERTIFIES** RACIALLY SEGREGATED UNION LOCALS.   NCHECDX64890

DECISION
PERCEIVED OPPORTUNITIES, EXPECTATIONS, AND THE **DECISION** TO REMAIN ON RELOCATION. THE CASE OF THE NAVAHO
INDIAN MIGRANT TO DENVER, COLORADO.   IGRAVTD65567

COMMUNITY FACTORS AFFECTING MOTIVATION AND ACHIEVEMENT IN A DECADE OF **DECISION**. /EDUCATION/   NGRANLB62441

WAR LABOR BOARD **DECISION** ON WAGES OF NEGROES.   NUSDLAB43848

THE **DECISION** TO WORK. /ASPIRATIONS/   WHOFFLW63847

DECISION-MAKING
PREJUDICE AND **DECISION-MAKING**. /EMPLOYMENT DISCRIMINATION/   GDAILCA66926

DECISIONS
THE CIVIL-RIGHTS AND CIVIL-LIBERTIES **DECISIONS** OF THE US SUPREME COURT FOR THE 1962-63 TERM. A SUMMARY
AND ANALYSIS.   GAMERJD63384

THE LAWFULNESS OF THE SEGREGATION **DECISIONS**.   GBLACCX60452

FACTORS IN WORKERS **DECISIONS** TO FOREGO RETRAINING UNDER THE MANPOWER-DEVELOPMENT-AND-RETRAINING-ACT.   NBRAZWF64318

SOME RECENT UNITED STATES SUPREME COURT **DECISIONS** AFFECTING THE RIGHTS OF NEGRO WORKERS.   NCHICCA47914

FACTORS INFLUENCING WOMEN-S **DECISIONS** ABOUT HIGHER EDUCATION. /ASPIRATIONS/   WDAVIOD59716

CAREER **DECISIONS** AND PROFESSIONAL EXPECTATIONS OF NURSING-STUDENTS. /ASPIRATIONS/   WFOXXDJ61767

DECLARATION
THE VOICE OF THE AMERICAN-INDIAN. **DECLARATION** OF INDIAN PURPOSE.   IAMERIC61524

DECLINE
DECLINE IN THE RELATIVE INCOME OF NEGRO MEN.   NBATCAB64058

DEFENSE
EQUAL-EMPLOYMENT-OPPORTUNITY IN THE **DEFENSE** SUPPLY AGENCY.   GDEFESA64631

MINORITIES IN **DEFENSE**.   GUSOFPM42519

ADDRESS AT THE CONVOCATION OF THE NAACP LEGAL **DEFENSE** AND EDUCATIONAL FUND. /LEGISLATION/   GWIRTWW66570

IN **DEFENSE** OF THE NEGRO FAMILY.   NRIESFX66059

EMPLOYER SPECIFICATIONS FOR **DEFENSE** WORKERS.   NUSDLAB41244

NEGRO WORKERS AND THE NATIONAL **DEFENSE** PROGRAM.   NUSDLAB41253

NEGRO PARTICIPATION IN **DEFENSE** WORK.   NUSDLAB41829

DEFENSE INDUSTRIES AND THE NEGRO.   NWEAVRC42552

DEGREE
SOCIAL WORK **DEGREE** PROGRESS REPORT. /TRAINING/   WNYUYUG66031

DELANO
HUELGA. THE FIRST 100 DAYS OF THE GREAT **DELANO** STRIKE. /UNION/   MNELSEX66028

TALES OF THE **DELANO** REVOLUTION.   MVALDLX66512

DELAWARE
REPORT AND RECOMMENDATIONS OF **DELAWARE** COMMITTEE ON MIGRATORY LABOR. /MIGRANT-WORKERS/   GDELACM58945

MIGRATORY LABOR IN **DELAWARE**.   GWELFCD56548

THE CULTURE AND ACCULTURATION OF THE **DELAWARE** INDIANS.   INEWCWW56600

DELINQUENCY
LOWER-CLASS **DELINQUENCY** AND WORK PROGRAMS.   GMARTJM66854

STUDY OF SOCIO-CULTURAL FACTORS THAT INHIBIT OR ENCOURAGE **DELINQUENCY** AMONG MEXICAN-AMERICANS.   MLOSARW58432

COLOR, CLASS, PERSONALITY, AND JUVENILE **DELINQUENCY**.   NCLARKB59210

A PROPOSAL FOR THE PREVENTION AND CONTROL OF **DELINQUENCY** BY EXPANDING OPPORTUNITIES.   NMOBIFY62263

DELINQUENT
JOB ADJUSTMENT PROBLEMS OF **DELINQUENT** MINORITY-GROUP YOUTH.   GAMOSWE64874

DELINQUENT (CONTINUATION)

ASPIRATION LEVELS OF NEGRO **DELINQUENT**, DEPENDENT, AND PUBLIC SCHOOL BOYS.   NMITCLE57804

THE DROPOUT AND THE **DELINQUENT**. PROMISING PRACTICES GLEANED FROM A YEAR OF STUDY.   NSCHRDX63141

DELTA

LABOR AND TECHNOLOGY ON SELECTED COTTON PLANTATIONS IN THE **DELTA** AREA OF MISSISSIPPI, 1953-1957.   NLERANL59404

PLANTATION ORGANIZATION AND THE RESIDENT LABOR-FORCE, **DELTA** AREA, MISSISSIPPI.   NLERANL60403

NEGRO FARM LABOR IN THE **DELTA** AREA OF MISSISSIPPI. SUPPLY AND UTILIZATION.   NLERANL61416

DEMAND

STRUCTURAL UNEMPLOYMENT AND AGGREGATE **DEMAND**.   GGILPEG66632

POVERTY, AGGREGATE **DEMAND**, AND ECONOMIC STRUCTURE.   GKERSJA66941

MAJOR AGRICULTURAL MIGRANT LABOR **DEMAND** AREAS.   GUSDLAB61509

AFL-CIO COUNCIL GETS NEGRO **DEMAND** FOR MORE ACTION ON BIAS IN UNIONS.   NBUSIWX61144

TEACHER SUPPLY AND **DEMAND** IN THE NEGRO COLLEGE.   NLLOYRG54045

THE **DEMAND** FOR EQUAL-RIGHTS.   NSCHEGX64103

THE INTERACTION OF **DEMAND** AND SUPPLY AND ITS EFFECT ON THE FEMALE LABOR-FORCE IN THE UNITED STATES.   WOPPEVK66289

HELP WANTED -- FEMALE. A STUDY OF **DEMAND** AND SUPPLY IN A LOCAL JOB MARKET FOR WOMEN. /MANPOWER/   WSMITGM64121

DEMOCRACY

DEMOCRACY ON THE JOB.   GINDUBX51811

THE PRACTICE OF RACIAL **DEMOCRACY**.   GNATLIC65593

LABOR-S ROLE. **DEMOCRACY** ON THE JOB. /UNION/   GSLAIDX66317

UNION **DEMOCRACY** AND FAIR REPRESENTATION. FEDERAL RESPONSIBILITY IN A FEDERAL SYSTEM.   GWELLHX58550

THE TROUBLESOME PRESENCE. AMERICAN **DEMOCRACY** AND THE NEGRO.   NGINZEX64414

CHALLENGES TO **DEMOCRACY**. /ECONOMY/   NWEAVRC63298

THE PRACTICE OF RACIAL **DEMOCRACY**.   NYOUNWM65000

DEMOCRACY-S

THE FEDERAL MANAGER-S ROLE IN **DEMOCRACY-S** UNFINISHED BUSINESS.   GCLINRX61577

DEMOCRATIC

SAN FRANCISCO-S PLAN FOR **DEMOCRATIC** RACIAL-RELATIONS. /CALIFORNIA/   GBAYXAC43427

MANPOWER POLICIES FOR A **DEMOCRATIC** SOCIETY.   GDAVIHX65629

DEMOGRAPHIC

ECONOMIC, SOCIAL, AND **DEMOGRAPHIC** CHARACTERISTICS OF SPANISH-AMERICAN WAGE WORKERS ON US FARMS. /PUERTO-RICAN MEXICAN-AMERICAN/   CFRIERE63805

SOME **DEMOGRAPHIC** ASPECTS OF POVERTY IN THE UNITED STATES.   GDAVIKX65663

DEMOGRAPHIC CHANGE AND RACIAL GHETTOS. THE CRISIS OF AMERICAN CITIES.   GHILLHX66691

DEMOGRAPHIC CHARACTERISTICS OF AMERICAN JEWS.   JGOLDNX62727

DEMOGRAPHIC AND SOCIAL ASPECTS.   JSHERBC64759

DEMOGRAPHIC CHARACTERISTICS.   MBARRDN66701

ECONOMIC, SOCIAL AND **DEMOGRAPHIC** CHARACTERISTICS OF SPANISH-AMERICAN WAGE WORKERS ON US FARMS.   MFRIERE63394

SOME **DEMOGRAPHIC** CHARACTERISTICS OF RURAL YOUTH.   NBEEGJA63072

DEMOGRAPHIC FACTORS IN THE INTEGRATION OF THE NEGRO.   NHAUSPM65501

DEMOGRAPHIC AND SOCIAL FACTORS IN THE POVERTY OF THE NEGRO.   NHAUSPM66992

SOME TENDENCIES IN **DEMOGRAPHIC** TRENDS IN MARYLAND, 1950-1956.   NJACKEG57070

DEMOGRAPHIC ASPECTS OF CONTEMPORARY CHANGE. /SOUTH/   NPARRCH63975

LABOR-FORCE AND **DEMOGRAPHIC** FACTORS AFFECTING THE CHANGING RELATIVE STATUS OF THE AMERICAN NEGRO, 1940-1950.   NPHILWM57997

DEMOGRAPHIC AND ECONOMIC CHANGE IN THE SOUTH, 1940-1960.   NSPENJJ63716

THE EMPLOYMENT OF NEGROES. SOME **DEMOGRAPHIC** CONSIDERATIONS.   NUSDLAB66245

DEMOGRAPHIC CHARACTERISTICS OF THE NEGRO POPULATION IN THE UNITED STATES.   NVALIPX63279

WORLD-S WORKING POPULATION. SOME **DEMOGRAPHIC** ASPECTS.   WINTELR56871

DEMOGRAPHY

EMPLOYMENT AND PERSONAL CHARACTERISTICS. EMPLOYMENT BY AGE, RACE, NATIVITY, EDUCATION, MARITAL-STATUS, HOUSEHOLD RELATIONSHIPS, ETC. /DEMOGRAPHY/   CUSBURC53372

NONWHITE POPULATION BY RACE. NEGROES, INDIANS, JAPANESE, CHINESE, FILIPINOS. BY AGE, SEX, MARITAL-STATUS, EDUCATION, EMPLOYMENT-STATUS, OCCUPATIONAL-STATUS, INCOME, ETC. /DEMOGRAPHY/   CUSBURC53378

EMPLOYMENT OF WHITE AND NON-WHITE PERSONS, 1955. /DEMOGRAPHY/   CUSBURC56373

UNITED STATES CENSUS OF AGRICULTURE. COLOR, RACE, AND TENURE OF FARM OPERATOR. GENERAL REPORT, VOLUME II. /DEMOGRAPHY/   CUSBURC59382

GENERAL SOCIAL AND ECONOMIC CHARACTERISTICS. SUMMARY, US CENSUS OF 1960. /DEMOGRAPHY/   CUSBURC62374

CHARACTERISTICS OF PROFESSIONAL WORKERS. /DEMOGRAPHY/   CUSBURC63167

CHARACTERISTICS OF TEACHERS. /DEMOGRAPHY/   CUSBURC63168

EDUCATIONAL-ATTAINMENT. /DEMOGRAPHY/   CUSBURC63169

EMPLOYMENT-STATUS AND WORK CHARACTERISTICS. STATISTICS ON THE RELATION BETWEEN EMPLOYMENT AND SOCIAL AND ECONOMIC CHARACTERISTICS. /DEMOGRAPHY/   CUSBURC63170

INCOME OF THE ELDERLY POPULATION. /DEMOGRAPHY/   CUSBURC63171

LIFETIME AND RECENT MIGRATION. /DEMOGRAPHY/   CUSBURC63172

MOBILITY FOR STATES AND STATE ECONOMIC AREAS. /DEMOGRAPHY/   CUSBURC63174

NATIVITY AND PARENTAGE. /DEMOGRAPHY/   CUSBURC63175

NONWHITE POPULATION BY RACE. NEGROES, INDIANS, JAPANESE,CHINESE, FILIPINOS. BY AGE, SEX, MARITAL-STATUS,EDUCATION, EMPLOYMENT-STATUS, OCCUPATIONAL-STATUS, INCOME, ETC. /DEMOGRAPHY/   CUSBURC63176

OCCUPATIONS BY EARNINGS AND EDUCATION. STATISTICS FOR MEN 18-64 YEARS OLD, BY COLOR, IN SELECTED OCCUPATIONS. /DEMOGRAPHY/   CUSBURC63178

OCCUPATION BY INDUSTRY. /DEMOGRAPHY/   CUSBURC63179

PERSONS BY FAMILY CHARACTERISTICS. FAMILY MEMBERS BY SOCIAL, ECONOMIC AND HOUSING CHARACTERISTICS OF FAMILIES. /DEMOGRAPHY/   CUSBURC63180

PERSONS OF SPANISH-SURNAME. SOCIAL AND ECONOMIC DATA FOR WHITE PERSONS OF SPANISH SURNAME IN 5 SOUTHWESTERN STATES. /DEMOGRAPHY/   CUSBURC63181

SCHOOL ENROLLMENT. /DEMOGRAPHY/   CUSBURC63183

SOURCES AND STRUCTURE OF FAMILY INCOME. /DEMOGRAPHY/   CUSBURC63184

STATE OF BIRTH. /DEMOGRAPHY/   CUSBURC63185

TRENDS IN THE INCOME OF FAMILIES AND PERSONS IN THE UNITED STATES. 1947-1960. /DEMOGRAPHY/   CUSBURC63381

NEGRO POPULATION. MARCH 1964. /WOMEN DEMOGRAPHY/   CUSBURC64376

STATISTICAL ABSTRACT OF THE UNITED STATES. 1964. /DEMOGRAPHY/   CUSBURC64380

INCOME IN 1964 OF FAMILIES AND PERSONS IN THE UNITED STATES. /DEMOGRAPHY/   CUSBURC65375

NEGRO POPULATION. MARCH 1965. /WOMEN DEMOGRAPHY/   CUSBURC65377

CURRENT POPULATION REPORTS -- SPECIAL CENSUS OF CLEVELAND, OHIO. /DEMOGRAPHY/   CUSBURC65379

INCOME, EDUCATION AND UNEMPLOYMENT IN NEIGHBORHOODS. ATLANTA, GEORGIA. /DEMOGRAPHY/   CUSDLAB63451

INCOME, EDUCATION AND UNEMPLOYMENT IN NEIGHBORHOODS. BALTIMORE, MARYLAND. /DEMOGRAPHY/   CUSDLAB63452

INCOME, EDUCATION AND UNEMPLOYMENT IN NEIGHBORHOODS. BIRMINGHAM, ALABAMA. /DEMOGRAPHY/   CUSDLAB63453

INCOME, EDUCATION AND UNEMPLOYMENT IN NEIGHBORHOODS. BOSTON, MASSACHUSETTS. /DEMOGRAPHY/   CUSDLAB63454

INCOME, EDUCATION AND UNEMPLOYMENT IN NEIGHBORHOODS. BUFFALO, NEW-YORK. /DEMOGRAPHY/   CUSDLAB63455

INCOME, EDUCATION AND UNEMPLOYMENT IN NEIGHBORHOODS. CHICAGO, ILLINOIS. /DEMOGRAPHY/   CUSDLAB63456

INCOME, EDUCATION AND UNEMPLOYMENT IN NEIGHBORHOODS. CINCINNATI, OHIO. /DEMOGRAPHY/   CUSDLAB63457

INCOME, EDUCATION AND UNEMPLOYMENT IN NEIGHBORHOODS. CLEVELAND, OHIO. /DEMOGRAPHY/   CUSDLAB63458

INCOME, EDUCATION AND UNEMPLOYMENT IN NEIGHBORHOODS. DALLAS, TEXAS. /DEMOGRAPHY/   CUSDLAB63459

INCOME, EDUCATION AND UNEMPLOYMENT IN NEIGHBORHOODS. DENVER, COLORADO. /DEMOGRAPHY/   CUSDLAB63460

INCOME, EDUCATION AND UNEMPLOYMENT IN NEIGHBORHOODS. DETROIT, MICHIGAN. /DEMOGRAPHY/   CUSDLAB63461

INCOME, EDUCATION AND UNEMPLOYMENT IN NEIGHBORHOODS. HOUSTON, TEXAS. /DEMOGRAPHY/   CUSDLAB63462

INCOME, EDUCATION AND UNEMPLOYMENT IN NEIGHBORHOODS. INDIANAPOLIS, INDIANA. /DEMOGRAPHY/   CUSDLAB63463

INCOME, EDUCATION AND UNEMPLOYMENT IN NEIGHBORHOODS. KANSAS-CITY, MISSOURI. /DEMOGRAPHY/   CUSDLAB63464

INCOME, EDUCATION AND UNEMPLOYMENT IN NEIGHBORHOODS. MEMPHIS, TENNESSEE. /DEMOGRAPHY/   CUSDLAB63466

INCOME, EDUCATION AND UNEMPLOYMENT IN NEIGHBORHOODS. MILWAUKEE, WISCONSIN. /DEMOGRAPHY/   CUSDLAB63467

INCOME, EDUCATION AND UNEMPLOYMENT IN NEIGHBORHOODS. MINNEAPOLIS -- ST-PAUL, MINNESOTA. /DEMOGRAPHY/   CUSDLAB63468

INCOME, EDUCATION AND UNEMPLOYMENT IN NEIGHBORHOODS. NEW-ORLEANS, LOUISIANA. /DEMOGRAPHY/   CUSDLAB63469

INCOME, EDUCATION AND UNEMPLOYMENT IN NEIGHBORHOODS. NEWARK, NEW-JERSEY. /DEMOGRAPHY/   CUSDLAB63470

INCOME, EDUCATION AND UNEMPLOYMENT IN NEIGHBORHOODS. NEW-YORK-CITY -- BROOKLYN. /DEMOGRAPHY/   CUSDLAB63471

INCOME, EDUCATION AND UNEMPLOYMENT IN NEIGHBORHOODS. NEW-YORK-CITY -- THE BRONX. /DEMOGRAPHY/   CUSDLAB63472

INCOME, EDUCATION AND UNEMPLOYMENT IN NEIGHBORHOODS. NEW-YORK-CITY -- MANHATTAN. /DEMOGRAPHY/   CUSDLAB63473

INCOME, EDUCATION AND UNEMPLOYMENT IN NEIGHBORHOODS. NEW-YORK-CITY -- QUEENS. /DEMOGRAPHY/   CUSDLAB63474

INCOME, EDUCATION AND UNEMPLOYMENT IN NEIGHBORHOODS. NEW-YORK-CITY -- STATEN-ISLAND. /DEMOGRAPHY/   CUSDLAB63475

INCOME, EDUCATION AND UNEMPLOYMENT IN NEIGHBORHOODS. OAKLAND, CALIFORNIA. /DEMOGRAPHY/   CUSDLAB63476

INCOME, EDUCATION AND UNEMPLOYMENT IN NEIGHBORHOODS. OKLAHOMA-CITY, OKLAHOMA. /DEMOGRAPHY/   CUSDLAB63477

INCOME, EDUCATION AND UNEMPLOYMENT IN NEIGHBORHOODS. PHILADELPHIA, PENNSYLVANIA. /DEMOGRAPHY/   CUSDLAB63478

INCOME, EDUCATION AND UNEMPLOYMENT IN NEIGHBORHOODS. PITTSBURGH, PENNSYLVANIA. /DEMOGRAPHY/   CUSDLAB63479

INCOME, EDUCATION AND UNEMPLOYMENT IN NEIGHBORHOODS. PHOENIX, ARIZONA. /DEMOGRAPHY/   CUSDLAB63480

INCOME, EDUCATION AND UNEMPLOYMENT IN NEIGHBORHOODS. ST-LOUIS, MISSOURI. /DEMOGRAPHY/   CUSDLAB63481

INCOME, EDUCATION AND UNEMPLOYMENT IN NEIGHBORHOODS. SAN-ANTONIO, TEXAS. /DEMOGRAPHY/   CUSDLAB63482

INCOME, EDUCATION AND UNEMPLOYMENT IN NEIGHBORHOODS. SAN-DIEGO, CALIFORNIA. /DEMOGRAPHY/   CUSDLAB63483

INCOME, EDUCATION AND UNEMPLOYMENT IN NEIGHBORHOODS. SAN-FRANCISCO, CALIFORNIA. /DEMOGRAPHY/   CUSDLAB63484

DEMOGRAPHY   (CONTINUATION)
INCOME, EDUCATION AND UNEMPLOYMENT IN NEIGHBORHOODS. SEATTLE, WASHINGTON. /DEMOGRAPHY/   CUSDLAB63485

INCOME, EDUCATION AND UNEMPLOYMENT IN NEIGHBORHOODS. TAMPA, ST-PETERSBURG FLORIDA. /DEMOGRAPHY/   CUSDLAB63486

INCOME, EDUCATION AND UNEMPLOYMENT IN NEIGHBORHOODS. WASHINGTON-DC. /DEMOGRAPHY/   CUSDLAB63487

INCOME, EDUCATION AND UNEMPLOYMENT IN NEIGHBORHOODS. LOS-ANGELES, CALIFORNIA. /DEMOGRAPHY/   CUSDLAB63565

THE AMERICAN LABOR-FORCE. ITS GROWTH AND CHANGING COMPOSITION. /DEMOGRAPHY/   GBANCGX58417

AGE AND INCOME-DISTRIBUTION. /DEMOGRAPHY/   GBRADDS65679

MORTALITY BY OCCUPATION AND INDUSTRY AMONG MEN 20 TO 64 YEARS OF AGE. UNITED STATES, 1950. /DEMOGRAPHY/   GGURALX62748

CONTINUITY AND CHANGE IN SOUTHERN MIGRATION. /DEMOGRAPHY/   GHAMICH65757

CHANGES IN THE NUMBER AND COMPOSITION OF THE POOR. /DEMOGRAPHY/   GMILLHP65656

INCOME-DISTRIBUTION IN THE UNITED STATES. /DEMOGRAPHY/   GMILLHP66778

RACIAL CHANGES IN METROPOLITAN AREAS, 1950-1960. /DEMOGRAPHY/   GSCHNLF63288

LOW-INCOME FAMILIES AND UNRELATED INDIVIDUALS IN THE UNITED STATES. 1964. /DEMOGRAPHY/   GUSBURC65151

MOBILITY OF THE POPULATION OF THE UNITED STATES, JANUARY 1, 1950 TO FEBRUARY 1, 1965. /DEMOGRAPHY/   GUSBURC65161

MOBILITY OF THE POPUFATION FC THE UNITED STATES, MARCH 1964 TO MARCH 1965. /DEMOGRAPHY/   GUSBURC66158

POPULATION OF THE UNITED STATES BY METROPOLITAN AND NONMETROPOLITAN RESIDENCE. /DEMOGRAPHY/   GUSBURC66159

PROJECTIONS OF SCHOOL AND COLLEGE ENROLLMENT IN THE UNITED STATES TO 1985. /DEMOGRAPHY/   GUSBURC66160

THE DEMOGRAPHY OF THE AMERICAN-INDIAN.   IHADLJN57569

MODERN KLAMATH. DEMOGRAPHY AND ECONOMY.   ISTERTX65625

INDIAN HEALTH HIGHLIGHTS. /DEMOGRAPHY/   IUSDHEW66813

INDIANS. /DEMOGRAPHY/   IUSDINT66654

SOME ASPECTS OF JEWISH DEMOGRAPHY.   JANTOAX58697

JEWISH POPULATION IN THE UNITED STATES, 1960. /DEMOGRAPHY/   JCHENAX61712

JEWISH POPULATION IN THE UNITED STATES, 1961. /DEMOGRAPHY/   JCHENAX62713

DISTRIBUTION OF NEGRO POPULATION IN THE UNITED STATES. /DEMOGRAPHY/   NCALEWC56069

THE NEGRO LEAVES THE SOUTH. /DEMOGRAPHY MIGRATION/   NHAMICH64479

MIGRATION PATTERNS OF NEGROES FROM A RURAL NORTHEASTERN MISSISSIPPI COMMUNITY. /DEMOGRAPHY/   NRUBIMX60094

RACIAL CHANGES IN METROPOLITAN AREAS, 1950-1960. /DEMOGRAPHY MIGRATION/   NSCHNLF65109

THE CHANGING COLOR COMPOSITION OF METROPOLITAN AREAS. /DEMOGRAPHY/   NSHARHX62125

THE CHANGING NUMBER AND DISTRIBUTION OF THE AGED NEGRO POPULATION OF THE UNITED STATES. /DEMOGRAPHY/   NSMITLT58145

THE CHANGING CHARACTER OF NEGRO MIGRATION. /DEMOGRAPHY/   NTAEUKE65194

NEGROES IN CITIES. /DEMOGRAPHY SEGREGATION/   NTAEUKE65197

THE NEGRO POPULATION IN THE UNITED STATES. /DEMOGRAPHY/   NTAEUKE65198

THE NEGRO POPULATION IN DULUTH MINNESOTA, 1950. /DEMOGRAPHY/   NTURBGX52210

NEGRO-WHITE DIFFERENTIALS IN GEOGRAPHIC MOBILITY, 1964, 1965. /DEMOGRAPHY/   NUSDCOM64194

PUERTO-RICANS IN THE UNITED STATES. SOCIAL AND ECONOMIC DATA FOR PERSONS OF PUERTO-RICAN BIRTH AND
PARENTAGE. /DEMOGRAPHY/   PUSBURC63182

TESTIMONY. PUBLIC HEARING, WOMEN IN PUBLIC AND PRIVATE EMPLOYMENT, CALIFORNIA. /DEMOGRAPHY/   WGERSMX66777

DEMONSTRATION
SECRETARIAL TRAINING WITH SPEECH IMPROVEMENT. AN EXPERIMENTAL AND DEMONSTRATION PROJECT. /NEGRO WOMEN/   CSAINMD66320

FINAL REPORT. EXPERIMENTAL AND DEMONSTRATION ON-JOB-TRAINING PROJECT. /MIGRANT-WORKERS MEXICAN-AMERICAN
NEGRO ARIZONA/   CSKILTO66324

THE TRAINING OF MIGRANT FARM WORKERS. A FOLLOW-UP STUDY OF TWO EXPERIMENTAL AND DEMONSTRATION PROGRAMS
UNDER THE MANPOWER-DEVELOPMENT-AND-TRAINING-ACT. /MEXICAN-AMERICAN AMERICAN-INDIAN/   CUNIVOD66054

ACTION FOR EMPLOYMENT. A DEMONSTRATION NEIGHBORHOOD MANPOWER PROJECT.   GALLCTO66361

A DEMONSTRATION PROJECT DESIGNED TO TEST THE LIFE-STYLE AND THE GROWTH POTENTIAL OF URBAN DROPOUTS FROM
DISADVANTAGED HOMES.   GCLEAMP66130

BRIDGE TO EMPLOYMENT. DEMONSTRATION MANPOWER PROGRAMS.   GUSDLAB63442

EXPERIMENTAL AND DEMONSTRATION MANPOWER PROJECT FOR THE RECRUITMENT, TRAINING, PLACEMENT AND FOLLOW-UP OF
RURAL UNEMPLOYED WORKERS IN TEN NORTH FLORIDA CITIES. FINAL REPORT. /PARTICIPANTS/   NJACKTA66597

FINAL REPORT. EXPERIMENTAL AND DEMONSTRATION MANPOWER PROJECT FOR THE RECRUITMENT, TRAINING, PLACEMENT
AND FOLLOW-UP OF RURAL UNEMPLOYED WORKERS IN TEN NORTH FLORIDA COUNTIES.   WFLORMP66326

DEMONSTRATIONAL
DEMONSTRATIONAL FEATURES OF THE TUSKEGEE-INSTITUTE. RETRAINING PROJECT.   NTUSKIX65766

DENTAL
THE NEGRO IN DENTAL EDUCATION.   NDUMMCO59302

DENTIST
I AM A CONTROVERSIAL DENTIST. /OCCUPATIONS/   NREEDET62046

DENTISTS
SURVEY OF EMPLOYMENT-CONDITIONS OF NURSES EMPLOYED BY PHYSICIANS AND/OR DENTISTS, JULY 1964.   WAMERNA65610

DENVER
INCOME, EDUCATION AND UNEMPLOYMENT IN NEIGHBORHOODS. DENVER, COLORADO. /DEMOGRAPHY/   CUSDLAB63460

DENVER   (CONTINUATION)
RELOCATEES FROM GALLUP AREA TO THE **DENVER** FIELD EMPLOYMENT ASSISTANCE OFFICE. /COLORADO/   IGRAVTDND438

A STUDY OF NAVAHO URBAN RELOCATION IN **DENVER** COLORADO.   IGRAVTD64566

PERCEIVED OPPORTUNITIES, EXPECTATIONS, AND THE DECISION TO REMAIN ON RELOCATION. THE CASE OF THE NAVAHO
INDIAN MIGRANT TO **DENVER**, COLORADO.   IGRAVTD65567

VALUES, EXPECTATIONS AND RELOCATION. THE NAVAHO MIGRANT TO **DENVER**. /COLORADO/   IGRAVTD66146

THE ECONOMIC ABSORPTION OF NAVAHO INDIAN MIGRANTS IN **DENVER**, COLORADO.   IWEPPRS65684

DEPARTMENT
ANNUAL FARM LABOR REPORT, 1965, CALIFORNIA **DEPARTMENT** OF EMPLOYMENT, FARM LABOR SERVICE. /NEGRO
MEXICAN-AMERICAN WOMEN/   CCALDEM66906

MANPOWER IMPLICATIONS OF TECHNOLOGICAL-CHANGE. RESEARCH FINDINGS OF THE US **DEPARTMENT** OF LABOR.   GBRANSX63876

PUBLIC WELFARE. POVERTY -- PREVENTION OR PERPETUATION. A STUDY OF THE STATE **DEPARTMENT** OF PUBLIC
ASSISTANCE OF THE STATE CF WASHINGTON.   GGREEAI64479

REPORTS ON THE PATTERN OF EMPLOYMENT OF MINORTY-GROUP PERSONS IN **DEPARTMENT** CF COUNTY
GOVERNMENT.LOS-ANGELES CALIFORNIA/   GLOSACC62913

SPECIAL REPORT, AN INVESTIGATION OF THE PERSONNEL POLICIES AND PRACTICES OF THE MICHIGAN STATE HIGHWAY
DEPARTMENT, MARCH 1961.   GMICFEP61983

EMPLOYMENT IN **DEPARTMENT** STORES. /NEW-YORK/   GNEWYSA58079

HEALTH WORK AMONG MIGRANTS IN 1958 BY THE NEW-JERSEY STATE **DEPARTMENT** OF HEALTH.   GSHEPAC59301

HOW **DEPARTMENT** X ELIMINATED SEGREGATION.   GUSCISC49388

EQUAL-EMPLOYMENT-OPPORTUNITY GUIDE FOR **DEPARTMENT** OF THE NAVY CONTRACTORS.   GUSDDEF64433

CONSOLIDATED INVENTORY OF **DEPARTMENT** OF LABOR RESEARCH ON LABOR-FORCE EMPLOYMENT AND UNEMPLOYMENT.   GUSDLAB64441

CONSOLIDATED INVENTORY OF **DEPARTMENT** OF LABOR RESEARCH ON AUTOMATION AND TECHNOLOGICAL-CHANGE.   GUSDLAB64619

EQUAL-EMPLOYMENT-OPPORTJNITY IN THE US POST OFFICE **DEPARTMENT**. A SUPPLEMENTAL REPORT TO THE POSTMASTER
GENERAL.   GUSPODA63516

CITY EMPLOYMENT SURVEY. PERCENTAGE OF MINORITY-GROUP EMPLOYEES BY **DEPARTMENT**. /YONKERS NEW-YORK/   GYONKCC66592

ANNUAL REPORTS OF US **DEPARTMENT** OF THE INTERIOR.   IUSDINTND666

STUDY OF DETROIT POLICE **DEPARTMENT** PERSONNEL PRACTICES. /MICHIGAN OCCUPATIONS/   NDETRCC63267

ATTITUDES OF WHITE **DEPARTMENT** STORE EMPLOYEES TOWARD NEGRO CO-WORKERS. /CASE-STUDY/   NHARDJX52482

US **DEPARTMENT** OF LABOR, PUBLIC HEARING, TESTIMONY. /MIGRANT-WORKERS/   NHILLHX63548

INTEGRATION OF NEGROES IN **DEPARTMENT** STORES.   NNATLUL46891

THE MAYOR AND THE FIRE CHIEF. THE FIGHT OVER INTEGRATING THE LOS-ANGELES FIRE **DEPARTMENT**. /CALIFORNIA
CASE-STUDY/   NSHERFP59130

EQUAL-OPPORTUNITY IN FARM PROGRAMS -- AN APPRAISAL OF SERVICES RENDERED BY AGENCIES OF THE UNITED STATES
DEPARTMENT OF AGRICULTURE.   NUSCOMC65232

REPORTS OF PUERTO-RICO **DEPARTMENT** OF LABOR, MIGRATION DIVISION ON PLACEMENT.   PPUERRDND791

A COMPARISON OF THE OCCUPATIONS OF THE FIRST AND SECOND GENERATION PUERTO-RICANS IN THE MAINLAND
LABOR-MARKET, AND HOW THE WORK OF THE NEW-YORK STATE **DEPARTMENT** OF LABORFFECTS PUERTO-RICANS.   PRAUSCX61846

DEPARTMENT-OF-DEFENS
NONDISCRIMINATION IN FEDERALLY-ASSISTED PROGRAMS OF THE DEPARTMENT-OF-THE-TREASURY,
DEPARTMENT-OF-DEFENSE, ATOMIC-ENERGY-COMMISSION, CIVIL-AERONAUTICS-BOARD, FEDERAL-AVIATION-AGENCY,
VETERANS-ADMINISTRATION.   GFEDERX64673

DEPARTMENT-OF-THE-TR
NONDISCRIMINATION IN FEDERALLY-ASSISTED PROGRAMS OF THE **DEPARTMENT-OF-THE-TREASURY**,
DEPARTMENT-OF-DEFENSE, ATOMIC-ENERGY-COMMISSION, CIVIL-AERONAUTICS-BOARD, FEDERAL-AVIATION-AGENCY,
VETERANS-ADMINISTRATION.   GFEDERX64673

DEPARTMENTAL
RACIAL AND ETHNIC EMPLOYMENT PATTERN SURVEY OF THE CITY AND COUNTY OF SAN-FRANCISCO GOVERNMENT.
DEPARTMENTAL ANALYSIS. /CALIFORNIA/   GSANFHR65264

DEPARTMENTS
REPORT OF FINDINGS AND RECOMMENDATIONS RESULTING FROM AN ANALYSIS OF THE EMPLOYMENT PRACTICES IN THE
VARIOUS **DEPARTMENTS** OF THE CITY OF LOS-ANGELES. /CALIFORNIA/   GLOSAOC63917

THE INTRODUCTION OF NEGROES INTO WHITE **DEPARTMENTS**. /CASE-STUDY INDUSTRY/   NPALMER55972

DEPENDENCY
A NATIONAL PROGRAM FOR THE IMPROVEMENT OF WELFARE SERVICES AND THE REDUCTION OF WELFARE **DEPENDENCY**.   GCOHENE65664

INCOMES AND **DEPENDENCY** IN THE COMING DECADES.   GDAVIMX64870

IDENTIFICATION AND MODIFICATION OF THE SOCIAL-PSYCHOLOGICAL CORRELATES OF ECONOMIC **DEPENDENCY**. PROJECT
FINAL REPORT.   GKIMMPR66137

INDIAN RELOCATION. PROBLEMS OF **DEPENDENCY** AND MANAGEMENT IN THE CITY.   IABLOJX65085

DEPENDENT
THE PATTERN OF **DEPENDENT** POVERTY IN CALIFORNIA.   GRAABEX64120

ASPIRATION LEVELS OF NEGRO DELINQUENT, **DEPENDENT**, AND PUBLIC SCHOOL BOYS.   NMITCLE57804

DEPRESSED
FACTORS AFFECTING EDUCATIONAL-ATTAINMENT IN **DEPRESSED** URBAN AREAS. /NEGRO PUERTO-RICAN/   CGOLDML63426

FEDERAL AID TO **DEPRESSED** AREAS. AN EVALUATION OF THE AREA-REDEVELOPMENT-ADMINISTRATION.   GLEVISA64896

EDUCATION IN **DEPRESSED** AREAS.   GPASSHA63724

DEPRIVATION
POVERTY AND **DEPRIVATION** IN THE UNITED STATES. THE PLIGHT OF TWO-FIFTHS OF A NATION.   GCONFOE62873

DEPRIVATION   (CONTINUATION)
ADOLESCENCE. CULTURAL DEPRIVATION, POVERTY, AND THE DROPOUT.   GHUNTOE66939

ECONOMIC DEPRIVATION AND EXTREMISM. A STUDY OF UNEMPLOYED NEGROES.   NLEGGJC61680

DEPRIVATIONS
ECONOMIC AND SOCIAL DEPRIVATIONS. ITS EFFECTS ON CHILDREN AND FAMILIES IN THE UNITED STATES -- A SELECTED
BIBLIOGRAPHY.   GCHILCX64571

SOME WORK-RELATED CULTURAL DEPRIVATIONS OF LOWER-CLASS NEGRO YOUTHS.   NHIMEJS64554

DEPRIVED
EDUCATION OF THE DEPRIVED AND SEGREGATED.   GBANKSC65419

FAMILY COMPOSITION AND CHARACTERISTICS OF AN ECONOMICALLY DEPRIVED CROSS-CULTURAL ROCKY-MOUNTAIN AREA.   MANDRWH66359

WORKING AT IMPROVING THE MOTIVATIONAL AND ACHIEVEMENT LEVELS OF THE DEPRIVED.   NHARREC63367

DES-MOINES
EMPLOYMENT REVIEW. /DES-MOINES IOWA/   GDESMCH65635

EMPLOYMENT SURVEY OF DES-MOINES FIRMS. /IOWA/   NDESMCH65265

DESCENT
THE INTEGRATION OF AMERICANS OF MEXICAN, PUERTO-RICAN, AND ORIENTAL DESCENT.   CYINGJM56519

THE INTEGRATION OF AMERICANS OF INDIAN DESCENT.   IDOZIEP57077

THE AMERICAN OF MEXICAN DESCENT.   MSANCGI61477

DESEGREGATION
RACIAL DESEGREGATION AND INTEGRATION.   GANNAOA56578

OBSTACLES TO DESEGREGATION IN AMERICA-S URBAN AREAS.   GGRIEGX64743

SEGREGATION AND DESEGREGATION. A DIGEST OF RECENT RESEARCH.   GTUMIMM57164

DESEGREGATION AND THE ECONOMIC FUTURE OF THE NEGRO MIDDLE-CLASS.   NBRIMAF65890

RACIAL DESEGREGATION IN THE PUBLIC SERVICE, WITH PARTICULAR REFERENCE TO THE US GOVERNMENT.   NBROWVJ54127

ON DESEGREGATION AND MATTERS SOCIOLOGICAL. /ECONOMIC-STATUS/   NCAMPEQ61909

DESEGREGATION. A PSYCHOLOGICAL ANALYSIS.   NCOOKSW57234

DESEGREGATION AND THE EMPLOYMENT OF NEGRO TEACHERS. /OCCUPATIONS/   NDODDHH55950

DUAL PARTS OF DESEGREGATION. LEGISLATION TO EDUCATE AND TRAIN NEGROES FOR BETTER JOBS.   NDUSCJX63311

THE NEGRO TEACHER AND DESEGREGATION.   NDWYERJ57956

THE IMPLICATIONS OF PROJECT CLEAR. /DESEGREGATION/   NFORMPB55372

THE NEGRO MIDDLE-CLASS AND DESEGREGATION.   NFRAZEF57381

DESEGREGATION OF SOCIAL AGENCIES IN THE SOUTH.   NGOLDJX65427

ATTITUDES TOWARD DESEGREGATION.   NHYMAHH56591

REVIEW OF EVIDENCE RELATING TO EFFECTS OF DESEGREGATION ON THE INTELLECTUAL PERFORMANCE OF NEGROES.   NKATZIX64637

COMMUNITY RESISTANCE TO AND ACCEPTANCE OF DESEGREGATION.   NKILLLM65651

LEGAL EDUCATION. DESEGREGATION IN LAW SCHOOLS.   NLEFLRA57676

DESEGREGATION, INTEGRATION, AND THE NEGRO COMMUNITY.   NLEWIHX56073

URBAN DESEGREGATION.   NNORTLK65950

DESEGREGATION. A COMMUNITY DESIGN. /PHILADELPHIA PENNSYLVANIA/   NSCHEGX61104

DESEGREGATION AND INTEGRATION IN SOCIAL WORK.   NSIMOSM56262

DESEGREGATION IN HIGHER EDUCATION.   NSOUTRC63157

SCHOOL DESEGREGATION IN 1966. THE SLOW UNDOING.   NSOUTRC66150

DESEGREGATION. SOME PROPOSITIONS AND RESEARCH SUGGESTIONS.   NSUCHEA58189

THE QUEST FOR IDENTITY AND STATUS. FACETS OF THE DESEGREGATION PROCESS IN THE UPPER MIDWEST.
/ECONOMIC-STATUS/   NTILLJA61161

DESEGREGATION IN AMERICAN SOCIETY. THE RECORD OF A GENERATION OF CHANGE.   NYINGJM63345

DESERT
THE AMERICAN INDIAN. GHETTOS IN THE DESERT.   ISTEISX64373

DESIGN
DESEGREGATION. A COMMUNITY DESIGN. /PHILADELPHIA PENNSYLVANIA/   NSCHEGX61104

DESIGNATION
THE DESIGNATION OF RACE OR COLOR ON FORMS.   NMINDAX66795

DESIGNED
A DEMONSTRATION PROJECT DESIGNED TO TEST THE LIFE-STYLE AND THE GROWTH POTENTIAL OF URBAN DROPOUTS FROM
DISADVANTAGED HOMES.   GCLEAMP66130

A SUMMARY REPORT OF PRACTICES AND PROGRAMS DESIGNED TO REDUCE THE NUMBER OF DROPOUTS IN THE HIGH SCHOOLS
OF LOS-ANGELES COUNTY. /CALIFORNIA/   GDELMOT66147

A STUDY OF STATE AND LOCAL LEGISLATIVE AND ADMINISTRATIVE ACTS DESIGNED TO MEET PROBLEMS OF HUMAN-RIGHTS.   GWISCLR52573

DETERMINANTS
SOME DETERMINANTS OF LOW FAMILY INCOME.   GCREADX61621

IDEOLOGY AND INTERESTS. THE DETERMINANTS OF UNION ACTION.   NKCRNWA53659

EMPLOYMENT GAINS AND THE DETERMINANTS OF THE OCCUPATIONAL DISTRIBUTION OF NEGROES.   NTHURLC67971

DETERMINANTS   (CONTINUATION)
    COMPARATIVE STUDY OF SOCIO-ECONOMIC AND SOCIAL-PSYCHOLOGICAL **DETERMINANTS** OF EDUCATIONAL AND OCCUPATIONAL
    ASPIRATIONS OF NEGRO AND WHITE COLLEGE SENIORS.   NWHITRM59319

DETERMINATION
    THE **DETERMINATION** OF CERTAIN MAJOR FACTORS AFFECTING THE NEGRO VETERAN IN THE ON-THE-JOB TRAINING PROGRAM
    IN VOCATIONAL AGRICULTURE IN THE STATE OF ALABAMA AS A BASIS FOR PLANNING A MORE EFFECTIVE PROGRAM.   NBATTEF49338

    SEX AS A FACTOR IN THE **DETERMINATION** OF EDUCATIONAL CHOICE. /ASPIRATIONS/   WDOLEAA64737

DETERMINE
    REPORT ON AND ANALYSIS OF SECOND CENSUS OF CITY EMPLOYEES TO **DETERMINE** BASES FOR FUTURE PERSONNEL
    DEVELOPMENTS. /DETROIT MICHIGAN/   GDETRCC66639

    A STUDY TO **DETERMINE** THE EMPLOYMENT POTENTIAL OF MOTHERS RECEIVING AID-TO-DEPENDENT-CHILDREN ASSISTANCE. WBROODJ64656

    SOME FACTORS WHICH **DETERMINE** THE DISTRIBUTION OF THE FEMALE WORK-FORCE. /LABOR-FORCE/   WJCUROI62883

DETERMINING
    THE IMPORTANCE OF CONTACT IN **DETERMINING** ATTITUDES TOWARD NEGROES.   NMACKBK48488

    FACTORS **DETERMINING** THE LABOR-FORCE PARTICIPATION OF MARRIED WOMEN.   WMAHOTA61951

DETRIBALIZATION
    THE **DETRIBALIZATION** OF THE NARRAGANSETT INDIANS. A CASE STUDY.   IBOISEX56886

DETROIT
    INCOME, EDUCATION AND UNEMPLOYMENT IN NEIGHBORHOODS. **DETROIT**, MICHIGAN. /DEMOGRAPHY/   CUSDLAB63461

    TRADE UNION LEADERSHIP COUNCIL --EXPERIMENT IN COMMUNITY ACTION. /**DETROIT** MICHIGAN/   GBATTRX63426

    EMPLOYMENT IN CIVIL-SERVICE OF MINORITY-GROUPS. /**DETROIT** MICHIGAN/   GDETRCC63638

    EMPLOYMENT AND INCOME BY AGE, SEX, COLOR AND RESIDENCE. /**DETROIT** MICHIGAN/   GDETRCC63948

    REPORT ON AND ANALYSIS OF SECOND CENSUS OF CITY EMPLOYEES TO DETERMINE BASES FOR FUTURE PERSONNEL
    DEVELOPMENTS. /**DETROIT** MICHIGAN/   GDETRCC66639

    HOME INTERVIEW STUDY OF LOW-INCOME HOUSEHOLDS IN **DETROIT**, MICHIGAN.   GGREEAI65472

    STUDY OF SERVICES TO DEAL WITH POVERTY IN **DETROIT**, MICHIGAN.   GGREEAI65480

    US COMMISSION-ON-CIVIL-RIGHTS, HEARINGS. **DETROIT**, MICHIGAN. DEC 14-15 1960.   GUSCOMC61399

    DETROIT FEELS BRUNT OF NEGRO PRESSURE. /MICHIGAN/   NBUSIWX63149

    STUDY OF **DETROIT** POLICE DEPARTMENT PERSONNEL PRACTICES. /MICHIGAN OCCUPATIONS/   NDETRCC63267

    CONFLICT RESPONSE. **DETROIT** NEGROES FACE UNEMPLOYMENT. /MICHIGAN/   NLEGGJC59678

    HARD-CORE UNEMPLOYMENT IN **DETROIT**. CAUSES AND REMEDIES. /MICHIGAN/   NWACHHMND289

DETROIT-S
    DETROIT-S INSURED UNEMPLOYED AND EMPLOYABLE WELFARE RECIPIENTS. /MICHIGAN/   GWICKED63561

    DETROIT-S OLD HABIT. /EMPLOYMENT DISCRIMINATION/   JFORSAX63723

DEVELOPING
    DEVELOPING NEW-YORK CITY-S HUMAN RESOURCES. VOL 1. /NEGRO PUERTO-RICAN/   CINSTOP66034

    COUNSELING MINORITY-GROUP YOUTH. **DEVELOPING** THE EXPERIENCE OF EQUALITY THROUGH EDUCATION.   GBRIGWA62473

    DEVELOPING FAIR-EMPLOYMENT PROGRAMS. A PROGRAM FOR THE SMALLER COMPANY.   GJENSJJ66785

    DEVELOPING FAIR-EMPLOYMENT PROGRAMS. GUIDELINES FOR SELECTION.   GLOCKHC66780

DEVELOPMENT
    THE NATION-S CHILDREN. VOL I. THE FAMILY AND SOCIAL-CHANGE. VOL II. **DEVELOPMENT** AND EDUCATION. VOL III.
    PROBLEMS AND PROSPECTS. /NEGRO PUERTO-RICAN MEXICAN-AMERICAN WOMEN/   CGINZEX60720

    AN EXPERIMENT IN MANPOWER **DEVELOPMENT**. /TRAINING MISSISSIPPI NEGRO WOMEN/   CSELFHO66325

    MANPOWER **DEVELOPMENT** PROGRAMS FOR FARM PEOPLE.   GALLECC67910

    APTITUDE TESTING, TRAINING, AND EMPLOYEE **DEVELOPMENT**, WITH A SECTION ON THE EMPLOYMENT OF
    MINORITY-GROUPS.   GAMERMA49389

    MANPOWER RETRAINING IN THE SOUTH-S RURAL POPULATION -- AN OPPORTUNITY FOR **DEVELOPMENT**.   GBACHFT63413

    MANPOWER **DEVELOPMENT**. CHARGES AND CHALLENGES. /TECHNOLOGICAL-CHANGE TRAINING/   GBOLIAC65528

    FAIR-EMPLOYMENT LEGISLATION IN NEW-YORK STATE. ITS HISTORY, **DEVELOPMENT**, AND SUGGESTED USE ELSEWHERE. GBRADPX46247

    HEARING OF THE SUBCOMMITTEE ON ECONOMIC **DEVELOPMENT**, EDITED TRANSCRIPT, JANUARY 28 AND 29, 1964.
    /CALIFORNIA FEP/   GCALAIW64510

    MANPOWER **DEVELOPMENT** TRAINING. TOTAL NUMBER OF NEW ENROLLEES DURING THE MONTH BY RACE AND OCCUPATION
    STATEWIDE AND BY ADMINISTRATIVE AREA, SEPTEMBER, 1966, OCTOBER, 1966. /CALIFORNIA/   GCALDEM66518

    HUMAN CAPITAL IN SOUTHERN **DEVELOPMENT** 1939-1963.   GCOLBMR65793

    CHANGING EMPHASIS IN OCCUPATIONAL TEST **DEVELOPMENT**.   GDVORBJ65650

    TRAINING AND **DEVELOPMENT**.   GFUGAGR64704

    JOB AND CAREER **DEVELOPMENT** FOR THE POOR...THE HUMAN SERVICES. INCLUDES BIBLIOGRAPHY.   GGOLDGS66360

    DEVELOPMENT OF TRAINING INCENTIVES FOR THE YOUTH OF MINORITY-GROUPS. /ECONOMIC-STATUS/   GGRANLB57979

    ESSAYS IN SOUTHERN ECONOMIC **DEVELOPMENT**.   GGREEMX64450

    SOME GENERAL ASPECTS OF RECENT REGIONAL **DEVELOPMENT**. /SOUTH/   GHENDJM64142

    DEVELOPMENT AND ADMINISTRATION OF THE NEW-YORK STATE LAW AGAINST DISCRIMINATION.   GHIGBJX67143

    SOME SUGGESTED APPROACHES FOR TEST **DEVELOPMENT** AND MEASUREMENT.   GKRUGRE66863

    FAIR-EMPLOYMENT-PRACTICES LEGISLATION. A SUMMARY OF ITS HISTORY AND **DEVELOPMENT** WITH STATEMENTS ON BOTH

DEVELOPMENT (CONTINUATION)
SIDES.   GMITCJA52016

THE QUEST FOR THE DREAM. THE **DEVELOPMENT** OF CIVIL-RIGHTS AND HUMAN-RELATIONS IN MODERN AMERICA.   GROCHJP63057

SUPERVISOR **DEVELOPMENT** PROGRAM. BASIC COURSE. NONDISCRIMINATION POLICY. /MILITARY/   GUSDARM56192

MANPOWER **DEVELOPMENT** AND TRAINING.   GUSDHEW65763

SOCIAL **DEVELOPMENT**. KEY TO THE GREAT SOCIETY. /SOCIO-ECONOMIC WELFARE/   GUSDHEW66639

HEALTH AND ECONOMIC **DEVELOPMENT**.   IBAUMLX64535

ANALYSIS OF MALE NAVAHO STUDENTS PERCEPTIONS OF OCCUPATIONAL OPPORTUNITIES AND THEIR ATTITUDES TOWARD   IDESPCW65548
DEVELOPMENT OF SKILLS AND TRAITS NECESSARY FOR OCCUPATIONAL COMPETENCE.

DEVELOPMENT OF THE SAN-CARLOS APACHE CATTLE INDUSTRY. /CALIFORNIA/   IGETTHT58563

AMERICAN-INDIANS AND THEIR ECONOMIC **DEVELOPMENT**.   IHUMAOX61820

SOCIAL AND CULTURAL CONSIDERATIONS IN THE **DEVELOPMENT** OF MANPOWER PROGRAMS FOR INDIANS.   IKELLWH67579

ANOMIE AND ACHIEVEMENT MOTIVATION. A STUDY OF PERSONALITY **DEVELOPMENT** WITHIN CULTURAL DISORGANIZATION. IKERCAC59018

THE ECONOMIC **DEVELOPMENT** AND URBANIZATION OF THE NAVAJO INDIAN RESERVATION.   ISELLCL62616

AN EVALUATION OF THE 10-YEAR **DEVELOPMENT** PROGRAM OF THE UTE TRIBE OF THE UINTAH AND OURAY RESERVATION, IUSDINT58648
UTAH.

INDIAN INDUSTRIAL **DEVELOPMENT** PROGRAM. A NEW INDUSTRIAL OPPORTUNITY.   IUSDINT64653

AMERICAN-INDIANS AND THEIR ECONOMIC **DEVELOPMENT**.   IVOGEFW61677

AN ANALYSIS OF CURRENT PATTERNS IN HUMAN RESOURCE **DEVELOPMENT** IN SAN-ANTONIO, TEXAS.   MDAVIHW66387

EGO **DEVELOPMENT** AMONG SEGREGATED NEGRO CHILDREN. /ASPIRATIONS/   NAUSUDP65036

THE FRENCH AND THE NON-FRENCH IN LOUISIANA. A STUDY OF THE RELEVANCE OF ETHNIC FACTORS IN RURAL   NBERTAL65394
DEVELOPMENT. /ECONOMIC-STATUS/

THE ORIGIN AND **DEVELOPMENT** OF THE NEGRO VISITING TEACHER IN ALABAMA. /OCCUPATIONS/   NBOATRF49345

CERTAIN ASPECTS OF THE ECONOMIC **DEVELOPMENT** OF THE AMERICAN NEGRO 1864-1960.   NDUMOAL45303

RECENT SOUTHERN ECONOMIC **DEVELOPMENT**.   NDUNNES62308

SOUTHERN ECONOMIC **DEVELOPMENT** AS REVEALED BY THE CHANGING STRUCTURE OF EMPLOYMENT.   NDUNNES62309

GRANTS AND PROJECTS RELATED TO THE **DEVELOPMENT** OF THE AMERICAN NEGRO. ALL FISCAL YEARS THROUGH JUNE 10, NFORDFX66133
1966.

RECENT EFFECTS OF RACIAL CONFLICT ON SOUTHERN INDUSTRIAL **DEVELOPMENT**.   NHILLHX59543

PLANNING THE END OF THE AMERICAN GHETTO. A PROGRAM OF ECONOMIC **DEVELOPMENT** FOR EQUAL-RIGHTS.   NHILLHX66538

NEGRO BUSINESS AND BUSINESS EDUCATION. THEIR PRESENT AND PROSPECTIVE **DEVELOPMENT**.   NPIERJA47998

THE NEGRO IN THE INDUSTRIAL **DEVELOPMENT** OF THE SOUTH.   NRABOSH53029

THE NEGRO COMMUNITY AND THE **DEVELOPMENT** OF NEGRO POTENTIAL.   NSMUTRW57146

NEGRO ENTREPRENEURSHIP IN SOUTHERN ECONOMIC **DEVELOPMENT**.   NYOUNHB64346

EAST-HARLEM BLOCK COMMUNITY **DEVELOPMENT** PROGRAM. /NEW-YORK/   PBORODXND781

THE **DEVELOPMENT** OF BEHAVIOR AND PERSONALITY. /WORK-WOMEN-ROLE/   WANDEJE60614

THE ACHIEVEMENT MOTIVE IN WOMEN. A STUDY OF THE IMPLICATIONS FOR CAREER **DEVELOPMENT**.   WBARURX66453

FEMALE LABOR-FORCE PARTICIPATION AND ECONOMIC **DEVELOPMENT**.   WHABESX58811

THE COUNSELOR AND GIRLS CAREER **DEVELOPMENT**. /COUNSELING/   WMATTEX63960

ATTITUDES TOWARD CAREER AND MARRIAGE AND THE **DEVELOPMENT** OF LIFE STYLES IN YOUNG WOMEN.   WMATTEX64962
/WORK-FAMILY-CONFLICT/

CAREER **DEVELOPMENT** OF WOMEN. SOME PROPOSITIONS.   WTIEDDV59153

DEVELOPMENTAL
RELATIONS AMONG MATERNAL EMPLOYMENT INDICES AND **DEVELOPMENTAL** CHARACTERISTICS OF CHILDREN.   WBURCLG61665
/WORK-FAMILY-CONFLICT/

DEVELOPMENTS
APPRENTICESHIP AND TESTS. FEP SUMMARY OF LATEST **DEVELOPMENTS**.   GBUREON65491

REPORT ON AND ANALYSIS OF SECOND CENSUS OF CITY EMPLOYEES TO DETERMINE BASES FOR FUTURE PERSONNEL   GDETRCC66639
DEVELOPMENTS. /DETROIT MICHIGAN/

UNION RACIAL DISCRIMINATION -- RECENT **DEVELOPMENTS** BEFORE THE NLRB AND THEIR IMPLICATIONS UNDER TITLE-VII GGEORLJ65714
OF THE CIVIL-RIGHTS-ACT OF 1964.

IMPLICATIONS OF AUTOMATION AND OTHER TECHNOLOGICAL **DEVELOPMENTS**. A SELECTED BIBLIOGRAPHY.   GUSDLAB63450

LABOR-FORCE **DEVELOPMENTS** FOR WHITE AND NONWHITE WORKERS,954-1964.   GUSDLAB64110

OCCUPATIONAL **DEVELOPMENTS**. SHORTAGES OF SKILLED TECHNICAL MANPOWER HIGHEST IN RECENT YEARS.   GUSDLAB65561

FARM LABOR **DEVELOPMENTS** -- EMPLOYMENT AND WAGE SUPPLEMENT.   GUSDLAB66446

RECENT **DEVELOPMENTS** IN RACE-RELATIONS AND ORGANIZED LABOR.   NHENDVW66213

DEVELOPMENTS IN THE NEGRO-LABOR ALLIANCE. /UNION/   NSTROEK56185

DIAGNOSTIC
REPORT OF THE **DIAGNOSTIC** SURVEY OF TENANT HOUSEHOLDS IN THE WEST SIDE URBAN-RENEWAL AREA OF   GGREEAI65474
NEW-YORK-CITY.

DIALECT
NEGRO **DIALECT**. THE LAST BARRIER TO INTEGRATION.   NGREEGC63447

DIETICIANS
OPPORTUNITIES FOR NEGRO WOMEN AS DIETICIANS. /OCCUPATIONS/   CUSDLAB43837

DIFFERENCES
TRAINING AID. CULTURAL DIFFERENCES, TRAINING IN NONDISCRIMINATION, READING ASSIGNMENTS. /EMPLOYMENT
MEXICAN-AMERICAN NEGRO/   CCALDSW65447

CLASS DIFFERENCES IN THE SOCIALIZATION PRACTICES OF NEGRO MOTHERS.   CKAMICKND632

CULTURAL DIFFERENCES IN AMERICAN ETHNIC GROUPS. BIBLIOGRAPHY. /AMERICAN-INDIAN NEGRO SPANISH-AMERICAN/   CLIBRCX64899

SEX DIFFERENCES IN OCCUPATIONAL CHOICE PATTERNS AMONG ADOLESCENTS. /ASPIRATIONS WOMEN NEGRO/   CSPREJX62999

SOCIOECONOMIC DIFFERENCES BETWEEN WHITE AND NONWHITE FARM POPULATIONS IN THE SOUTH.   GCOWHJD64616

SOME REGIONAL DIFFERENCES IN WAGES OF AGRICULTURAL WORKERS. /MIGRANT-WORKERS/   GMAITST60436

RURAL-URBAN DIFFERENCES IN ASPIRATIONS.   GMIDDRX59573

CLASS AS AN EXPLANATION OF ETHNIC DIFFERENCES IN MOBILITY ASPIRATIONS -- THE CASE OF MEXICAN-AMERICANS.   MHELLCS65415

SOME DIFFERENCES IN FACTORS RELATED TO EDUCATIONAL ACHIEVEMENT OF TWO MEXICAN-AMERICAN GROUPS.   MMONTPX60443

DIFFERENCES IN DROPOUT AND OTHER SCHOOL BEHAVIOR BETWEEN TWO GROUPS OF TENTH GRADE BOYS IN AN URBAN HIGH
SCHOOL.   MMUNORF57446

AMERICAN NEGRO AND IMMIGRANT EXPERIENCES. SIMILARITIES AND DIFFERENCES.   NAPPEJJ66805

SOCIAL INFLUENCES IN NEGRO-WHITE INTELLIGENCE DIFFERENCES.   NDEUTMX64268

THE MEANINGFULNESS OF NEGRO-WHITE DIFFERENCES IN INTELLIGENCE TEST PERFORMANCE.   NHICKRA66740

NEGRO-WHITE DIFFERENCES ON THE MMPI. /TESTING/   NHOKAJE60559

RACIAL DIFFERENCES AND THE FUTURE. /INTELLIGENCE EQUAL-OPPORTUNITY/   NINGLDJ64067

NEGRO-WHITE DIFFERENCES IN INTELLIGENCE TEST PERFORMANCE.   NKLINOX63657

FUTURE OCCUPATIONAL DIFFERENCES BETWEEN THE RACES. A MARKOV APPROACH.   NLEWISX66693

RACIAL DIFFERENCES IN MIGRATION AND JOB-SEARCH. A CASE-STUDY.   NLURIMX66712

NEGRO-WHITE DIFFERENCES IN GEOGRAPHIC MOBILITY.   NMUELEX66864

RACIAL DIFFERENCES IN INTELLIGENCE.   NPLOTLX59064

A NOTE ON RACIAL DIFFERENCES IN JOB VALUES AND DESIRES.   NSINGSL56142

EMPLOYMENT INTEGRATION AND WAGE DIFFERENCES IN A SOUTHERN PLANT.   NWEINRX59311

AN INVERTED FACTOR ANALYSIS OF PERSONALITY DIFFERENCES BETWEEN CAREER AND HOMEMAKING-ORIENTED WOMEN.
/ASPIRATIONS/   WAVILDL64316

INVESTIGATION OF DIFFERENCES IN OCCUPATIONAL PREFERENCES, STEREOTYPIC THINKING, AND PSYCHOLOGICAL NEEDS
AMONG UNDERGRADUATE WOMEN STUDENTS IN SELECTED CURRICULAR AREAS. /ASPIRATIONS/   WKITTRE60313

PAY DIFFERENCES BETWEEN MEN AND WOMEN. /DISCRIMINATION/   WSANBHX64100

WOMEN WORKERS IN 1960. GEOGRAPHICAL DIFFERENCES.   WUSDLAB62241

DIFFERENT
TESTING OF CULTURALLY DIFFERENT GROUPS.   GCAMPJX64093

SELF RADIUS AND GOALS OF YOUTH IN DIFFERENT URBAN AREAS.   MSHERCW61489

DIFFERENTIAL SELECTION AMONG APPLICANTS FROM DIFFERENT SOCIO-ECONOMIC AND ETHNIC BACKGROUNDS.   NBARRRS65056

PSYCHOLOGICAL PROBLEMS OF WOMEN IN DIFFERENT SOCIAL ROLES. /WORK-WOMAN-ROLE/   WJAHOMX55879

DIFFERENTIAL
THE WHITE-NON-WHITE UNEMPLOYMENT DIFFERENTIAL.   GGILMHJ63436

UNIONISM, MIGRATION, AND THE MALE NONWHITE-WHITE UNEMPLOYMENT DIFFERENTIAL.   GRAPPLA66216

DIFFERENTIAL SELECTION AMONG APPLICANTS FROM DIFFERENT SOCIO-ECONOMIC AND ETHNIC BACKGROUNDS.   NBARRRS65056

THE ANATOMY OF THE NEGRO-WHITE INCOME DIFFERENTIAL.   NGALLLE65391

DIFFERENTIAL CHARACTERISTICS OF SUPERIOR AND UNSELECTED NEGRO COLLEGE STUDENTS.   NJENKMD48608

DIFFERENTIALS
SOCIO-ECONOMIC DIFFERENTIALS AMONG NONWHITE RACES. /NEGRO ORIENTAL AMERICAN-INDIAN/   CSCHMCF65107

DISCRIMINATION AND THE WHITE -- NONWHITE UNEMPLOYMENT DIFFERENTIALS.   GGILMHJ63716

HIGHLIGHTS OF WHITE-NONWHITE DIFFERENTIALS.   GHUYCEE65790

WHITE-NONWHITE DIFFERENTIALS IN HEALTH, EDUCATION, AND WELFARE.   GUSDHEW65435

A QUANTITATIVE ANALYSIS OF WHITE-NONWHITE INCOME DIFFERENTIALS IN THE US IN 1939.   GZEMAMX55594

DIFFERENTIALS IN THE INCIDENCE OF POVERTY IN TEXAS. /ECONOMIC-STATUS/   MUPHAWK66533

COLLEGE, COLOR, AND EMPLOYMENT. RACIAL DIFFERENTIALS IN POSTGRADUATE EMPLOYMENT AMONG 1964 GRADUATES OF
LOUISIANA COLLEGES.   NHUSOCF66328

NEGRO-WHITE DIFFERENTIALS IN GEOGRAPHIC MOBILITY, 1964, 1965. /DEMOGRAPHY/   NUSDCOM64194

DIFFERENTIATION
URBAN DIFFERENTIATION. PROBLEMS AND PROSPECTS.   GMCELDX65051

RESIDENTIAL SEGREGATION AND SOCIAL DIFFERENTIATION.   NDUNCOD59305

OCCUPATIONAL DIFFERENTIATION OF NEGROES AND WHITES IN THE UNITED STATES.   NGIBBJP65401

DIGEST
EXPLANATION AND DIGEST OF THE 1966 KENTUCKY CIVIL-RIGHTS-ACT COVERING EMPLOYMENT AND PUBLIC
ACCOMODATIONS. ENACTED JANUARY 27 1966, EFFECTIVE JULY 1 1966.   GKENTCHND844

DIGEST   (CONTINUATION)
DIGEST OF FINDINGS FROM A WORKING CONFERENCE OF LOCAL COUNCILS. /FEPC/   GNATLCS45045

SEGREGATION AND DESEGREGATION. A **DIGEST** OF RECENT RESEARCH.   GTUMIMM57164

DIGEST OF LEGAL INTERPRETATIONS ISSUED OR ADOPTED BY THE COMMISSION OCTOBER 9, 1965 THROUGH DECEMBER 31,   GUSEEOC66509
1965.

DIGEST OF CASE STUDIES ON CONTINUITIES AND DISCONTINUITIES IN THE EMPLOYMENT-EDUCATION-FAMILY PATTERNS OF   WDELAPJ60224
WOMEN-S LIVES.

DIGEST OF STATE LEGISLATION OF SPECIAL INTEREST TO WOMEN WORKERS.   WUSDLABND191

DILEMMA
SOLVING AN AMERICAN **DILEMMA**. THE ROLE OF THE FEPC OFFICIAL, A COMPARATIVE STUDY OF STATE CIVIL-RIGHTS   GLLOYKM64317
COMMISSIONS.

FAIR-EMPLOYMENT IN THE NATION-S CAPITAL. A STUDY OF PROGRESS AND **DILEMMA**. /WASHINGTON-DC/   GSAWYDA62279

THE **DILEMMA** OF THE NEGRO PROFESSIONAL.   NBACKKX64039

BRICKS WITHOUT STRAW. STUDIES OF COMMUNITY UNEMPLOYMENT PROBLEMS, THE NEGROES **DILEMMA**.   /LOUISVILLE   NLOUIHR64715
KENTUCKY/

AN AMERICAN **DILEMMA**.   NMYRDGX44870

COUNSELING NEGRO STUDENTS. AN EDUCATIONAL **DILEMMA**.   NPHILWB59996

THE MODERN MOTHER-S **DILEMMA**. /WORK-FAMILY-CONFLICT/   WGRUESM57984

THE WOMEN PHYSICIANS **DILEMMA**. /OCCUPATIONS/   WWILLJJ66269

DILEMMAS
DILEMMAS OF URBAN AMERICA.   GWEAVRC66707

CARK GHETTO. **DILEMMAS** OF SOCIAL POWER.   NCLARKB65211

ETHNIC STATUS AND OCCUPATIONAL **DILEMMAS**.   NVOLLHM66287

DIMENSION
POWER AS A **DIMENSION** OF EDUCATION.   GDODSDW62647

DIMENSIONS
DIMENSIONS OF THE FARM LABOR PROBLEM.   GBISHCE67915

UNEMPLOYMENT IN THE UNITED STATES. QUANTITATIVE **DIMENSIONS**.   GBOWEWG65464

THE **DIMENSIONS** OF POVERTY.   GMILLHP65952

DIMENSIONS IN DISCRIMINATION. A PRELIMINARY SURVEY OF SAN-DIEGO-S COMMUNITY PROBLEMS OF DISCRIMINATION   GSANDLW65274
PART II. /CALIFORNIA/

MANPOWER TRAINING. SOME COST **DIMENSIONS**.   GYOUNSX67144

ECONOMIC **DIMENSIONS** IN RACE-RELATIONS.   NHENDVW61511

ECONOMIC **DIMENSIONS**. /SOUTH INCOME TECHNOLOGY/   NHENDVW63514

DIRECTIONS
NEW DIRECTIONS IN US EMPLOYMENT-SERVICE APTITUDE TEST RESEARCH.   GDVORBJ65656

DIRECTIVES
TRADE UNION COMPLIANCE WITH PRESIDENTIAL **DIRECTIVES**. MEMBERSHIP ACCEPTANCE, SENIORITY, ETC.   NCOOPJX64294

MANAGEMENT COMPLIANCE WITH PRESIDENTIAL **DIRECTIVES**.   NLAWRRG64296

DIRECTORY
TRADE AND INDUSTRIAL EDUCATION FOR GIRLS AND WOMEN. A **DIRECTORY** OF TRAINING PROGRAMS.   WUSDHEW60175

DISABILITY
WOMEN HOUSEHOLD WORKERS COVERED BY OLD AGE, SURVIVORS, AND **DISABILITY** INSURANCE.   WPOLIEJ65285

DISADVANTAGED
OPPORTUNITIES IN NURSING FOR **DISADVANTAGED** YOUTH. /WOMEN NEGRO OCCUPATIONS/   CFRAKFX66375

THE CHILD-REARING ATTITUDES OF **DISADVANTAGED** NEGRO MOTHERS AND SOME EDUCATIONAL IMPLICATIONS.   CRADINX65031

SELECTED BIBLIOGRAPHY FOR **DISADVANTAGED** YOUTH. /NEGRO PUERTO-RICAN/   CUSDHEWND855

DISADVANTAGED STUDENTS AND DISCRIMINATION.   GCLARKB60574

A DEMONSTRATION PROJECT DESIGNED TO TEST THE LIFE-STYLE AND THE GROWTH POTENTIAL OF URBAN DROPOUTS FROM   GCLEAMP66130
DISADVANTAGED HOMES.

TESTING THE **DISADVANTAGED**.   GCULHMM65651

TRAINING **DISADVANTAGED** GROUPS UNDER THE MANPOWER-DEVELOPMENT-TRAINING-ACT.   GHELPCW63501

THE NEW ROLE OF THE EMPLOYMENT SERVICE IN SERVING THE **DISADVANTAGED**. /SES/   GLEVILA66599

EDUCATION AND THE **DISADVANTAGED** AMERICAN.   GNATLEA62126

SUMMARY OF PROCEEDINGS. WORKSHOP ON THE IMPACT OF A TIGHTENING LABOR-MARKET ON THE EMPLOYABILITY AND   GNEWYUC66116
EMPLOYMENT OF **DISADVANTAGED** YOUTH.

THE **DISADVANTAGED** POOR. EDUCATION AND EMPLOYMENT.   GUSCHAC66187

DISADVANTAGED YOUTH -- RECOGNIZING THE PROBLEM.   NAMOSWE64331

THE PREPARATION OF **DISADVANTAGED** YOUTH FOR EMPLOYMENT AND CIVIC RESPONSIBILITIES.   NPERRJX64985

TEACHERS OF CULTURALLY **DISADVANTAGED** AMERICAN YOUTH.   NROUSRX63310

JOB GUIDANCE AND THE **DISADVANTAGED**.   NSAITCX64308

WHO ARE THE **DISADVANTAGED** GIRLS 16-21 YEARS OLD.   WUSDLAB64228

DISADVANTAGES
LEGAL **DISADVANTAGES** OF MIGRATORY WORKERS.   GGIVERA65695

DISCONTINUITIES
DIGEST OF CASE STUDIES ON CONTINUITIES AND **DISCONTINUITIES** IN THE EMPLOYMENT-EDUCATION-FAMILY PATTERNS OF WOMEN-S LIVES.   WDELAPJ60224

SOME CONTINUITIES AND **DISCONTINUITIES** IN THE EDUCATION OF WOMEN.   /WORK-FAMILY-CONFLICT/   WRIESDX56079

DISCRIMINATING
REPORT OF INQUIRY CONCERNING CHARGES OF **DISCRIMINATING** PRACTICES IN THE NEW-YORK STATE THRUWAY AUTHORITY.   GNEWYSB64104

DISCRIMINATION
IMPLICATIONS OF THE STUDIES. /DISCRIMINATION LOW-INCOME NEGRO PUERTO-RICAN POLICY-RECOMMENDATIONS/   CABRACX59001

THE **DISCRIMINATION** CASE. /NEGRO PUERTO-RICAN SES/   CCOHEHX65917

REGISTRIES AND INTERGROUP RELATIONS. /NEGRO WOMEN **DISCRIMINATION**/   CKASUMX59013

LAST HIRED -- FIRST FIRED. /DISCRIMINATION/   GABRACX58361

ANALYSIS OF CITY ORDINANCES AGAINST RACIAL AND RELIGIOUS **DISCRIMINATION** IN EMPLOYMENT.   GAMERJCND380

A FIVE-STATE SURVEY OF **DISCRIMINATION** BY COMMERCIAL EMPLOYMENT AGENCIES.   GAMERJD63386

LIFE INSURANCE. THE PATIENT IMPROVES. /DISCRIMINATION/   GANTIDL59399

BANK BARRIERS /DISCRIMINATION/   GANTIDL61393

LIFE INSURANCE COMPANIES. /DISCRIMINATION/   GANTIDL62398

DISCRIMINATION AND LOW INCOMES.   GANTOAX59401

THE SOCIAL MEANING OF **DISCRIMINATION**.   GANTCAX60400

DISCRIMINATION -- THE LAW OF THE LAND VERSUS THE LAW OF THE LAND.   GAPRUVJ63402

WEAPONS AGAINST **DISCRIMINATION** IN PUBLIC OFFICE.   GAVINAX62411

THE ECONOMICS OF **DISCRIMINATION**.   GBECKGS57429

THE SUPREME-COURT AND GROUP **DISCRIMINATION** SINCE 1937.   GBERGMX49443

EQUALITY BY STATUTES -- LEGAL CONTROLS OVER GROUP **DISCRIMINATION**.   GBERGMX52440

DISCRIMINATION, UNIONS, AND TITLE-VII.   GBLAKGR64453

OCCUPATIONAL **DISCRIMINATION**. SOME THEORETICAL PROPOSITIONS.   GBLALHM62454

RECOGNITION OF **DISCRIMINATION** -- A SOLUTION.   GBLOCHD58456

THE INDIVIDUAL RIGHT TO ELIMINATE EMPLOYMENT **DISCRIMINATION** BY LITIGATION.   GBLUMAW66566

PROCESSING EMPLOYMENT **DISCRIMINATION** CASES. /LEGISLATION/   GBLUMAW67117

THE ROLE OF LEGISLATION IN ELIMINATING RACIAL **DISCRIMINATION**.   GBONFAE65462

BUCK STOPS HERE. /DISCRIMINATION/   GBRAVHX59471

EMPLOYMENT **DISCRIMINATION**. STATE FEPC LAWS AND THE IMPACT OF OF TITLE-VII OF THE CIVIL-RIGHTS-ACT OF 1964.   GBRYEGL65896

COMBATING **DISCRIMINATION** IN EMPLOYMENT.   GBULLPX61523

THE OPERATION OF THE NEW-JERSEY LAW AGAINST **DISCRIMINATION**.   GBUSTJL49507

DISCRIMINATION AND FAIR-EMPLOYMENT-PRACTICES LAWS.   GCALDWF65699

POLICIES AND PRACTICES OF **DISCRIMINATION** COMMISSIONS. /FEPC/   GCARTEA56559

THE NLRB AND RACIAL **DISCRIMINATION**. /LEGISLATION/   GCARTRX65560

DISADVANTAGED STUDENTS AND **DISCRIMINATION**.   GCLARKB60574

THE PEOPLE VS. **DISCRIMINATION**. THE FEPC FIGHT INITIATES A NEW EPOCH.   GCOHEFS46579

SHOULD CONGRESS PASS A LAW PROHIBITING EMPLOYMENT **DISCRIMINATION**.   GCONGDX45596

ECONOMIC COSTS OF RACIAL **DISCRIMINATION** IN EMPLOYMENT.   GCOUNEA62205

POTENTIAL ECONOMIC GAINS FROM ELIMINATING **DISCRIMINATION**.   GCOUNEA66204

THE CONSTITUTION AND JOB **DISCRIMINATION**.   GCOUNVX64608

DISCRIMINATION AND THE LAW.   GCOUNVX65609

DISCRIMINATION IN EMPLOYMENT.   GCOUNVX65610

A STUDY OF PATTERNS OF **DISCRIMINATION** IN EMPLOYMENT FOR THE EQUAL-EMPLOYMENT-OPPORTUNITY-COMMISSION, WASHINGTON-DC.   GCOUSFR66478

PREJUDICE AND DECISION-MAKING. /EMPLOYMENT DISCRIMINATION/   GDAILCA66926

ELIMINATION OF RACE **DISCRIMINATION** IN THE APPLICATION BLANK.   GDARTCX47626

PATTERNS OF **DISCRIMINATION** IN THE FINANCIAL INSTITUTIONS OF THE DISTRICT-OF-COLUMBIA. THE BANKING, SAVINGS AND LOAN, AND INSURANCE INDUSTRIES.   GDISTCC66642

THE SCHOOL COUNSELOR AT WORK ON OCCUPATIONAL **DISCRIMINATION**.   GDIXALX46643

DISCRIMINATION BY LABOR UNIONS IN THE EXERCISE OF STATUTORY BARGAINING POWERS.   GDODDEM45646

COMMISSION ENFORCEMENT OF STATE LAWS AGAINST **DISCRIMINATION**. A COMPARATIVE ANALYSIS OF THE KANSAS ACT.   GDYSORB65657

THE MYRDALIAN HYPOTHESES. RANK ORDER OF **DISCRIMINATION**.   GEDMUER44495

I STATEMENT BEFORE THE HOUSE POST OFFICE AND CIVIL SERVICE SUBCOMMITTEE ON POSTAL OPERATIONS, II **DISCRIMINATION**. PLANNED AND ACCIDENTAL. /TESTING/   GENNEWH67928

HOW THE PRESIDENT IS WINNING THE WAR ON **DISCRIMINATION**.   GFACTMA56670

EQUAL-EMPLOYMENT-OPPORTUNITY. /DISCRIMINATION/   GFEILJG62675

DISCRIMINATION   (CONTINUATION)

THE FEDERAL INTEREST IN EMPLCYMENT DISCRIMINATION. HEREIN THE CONSTITUTIONAL SCOPE OF EXECUTIVE POWER TO WITHOLD APPROPRIATE FUNDS.   GFERGCC64679

DISCRIMINATION IN EMPLOYMENT.   GFERMIX60680

PUNISHMENT WITHOUT CRIME. WHAT YOU CAN DO ABCUT PREJUDICE. /DISCRIMINATION/   GFINESA49962

UNION RACIAL DISCRIMINATION -- RECENT DEVELOPMENTS BEFORE THE NLRB AND THEIR IMPLICATIONS UNDER TITLE-VII OF THE CIVIL-RIGHTS-ACT OF 1964.   GGEORLJ65714

DISCRIMINATION AND THE WHITE -- NONWHITE UNEMPLOYMENT DIFFERENTIALS.   GGILMHJ63716

ECONCMIC DISCRIMINATION AND UNEMPLOYMENT.   GGILMHJ65717

PARNASSUS RESTRICTED. JJB DISCRIMINATION IN THE PROFESSIONS.   GGOLDMH46724

CIVIL-SERVICE TESTING AND JOB DISCRIMINATION.   GGORDJE66281

SCHOCLING, DISCRIMINATION. AND JOBS.   GHENNJF63278

THE FAIR REPRESENTATION DOCTRINE. AN EFFECTIVE WEAPON AGAINST UNION RACIAL DISCRIMINATION.   GHERRNM64772

DEVELOPMENT AND ADMINISTRATICN OF THE NEW-YORK STATE LAW AGAINST DISCRIMINATION.   GHIGBJX67143

NEW-YORK STATE-S PROGRAM AGAINST DISCRIMINATION IN EMPLOYMENT. THE WORK OF THE NEW-YORKEW-YORK STATE-COMMISSION-AGAINST-DISCRIMINATION.   GINDUBX57812

DISCRIMINATION IN THE FIELD CF EMPLOYMENT AND OCCUPATION.   GINTELC58817

LEGISLATION AGAINST RACIAL OR RELIGIOUS DISCRIMINATION IN EMPLOYMENT, NEW-YORK.   GIVESLM52819

DISCRIMINATION WITHOUT PREJUDICE. A STUDY OF PROMOTION PRACTICES IN INDUSTRY.   GKAHNRL64733

RACIAL DISCRIMINATION IN UNICNS.   GKAHNSD65011

LABOR LAW -- UNICN MEMBERSHIP DENIED ON THE BASIS OF RACIAL DISCRIMINATION. /WISCONSIN LEGISLATION/   GKAUFET58014

RACIAL DISCRIMINATION IN EMPLOYMENT AND THE FEDERAL LAW.   GKOVAIX58026

THE ECCNOMICS OF DISCRIMINATION.   GKRUEA063862

DISCRIMINATION AND FAIR-EMPLCYMENT-PRACTICES.   GLABOLJ65819

ENFORCEMENT OF NEW-YORK LAW AGAINST DISCRIMINATION.   GLABCRR51879

PROVING DISCRIMINATION AT THE COMMISSION LEVEL.   GLAMBWH66857

EMPLOYMENT DISCRIMINATION. STATE FAIR-EMPLOYMENT-PRACTICES LAWS AND THE IMPACT UF TITLE-VII OF THE CIVIL-RIGHTS-ACT OF 1964.   GLAWXRD65885

LEGISLATION OUTLAWING RACIAL DISCRIMINATION IN EMPLOYMENT.   GLAWYGR45886

DISCRIMINATION IN EMPLOYMENT. FEDERAL AND STATE PRACTICES IN ANTI-DISCRIMINATION.   GLEITRD49892

STATE LAWS AGAINST DISCRIMINATION.   GLESKTX61895

IMPACT OF COMPANY POLICY UPON DISCRIMINATION.   GLONDJX54908

DISCRIMINATION AND NATIONAL WELFARE.   GMACIRM49025

RACIAL AND RELIGIOUS DISCRIMINATION IN EMPLOYMENT AND THE ROLE OF THE NLRB.   GMALOWH61935

AN ANALYSIS OF THE EFFECTIVENESS OF THE NEW-YORK STATE LAW AGAINST DISCRIMINATION.   GMARPAW53940

THE ENFORCEMENT OF CIVIL-RIGHTS. /DISCRIMINATION/   GMARSBX62942

STATEMENT ON BEHALF OF AMERICAN JEWISH CONGRESS ON DISCRIMINATION IN EMPLOYMENT.   GMASLWX61961

COMPILATION OF LAWS AGAINST DISCRIMINATION. EMPLOYMENT, EDUCATIONAL INSTITUTIONS, PLACES OF PUBLIC ACCOMOCATICN. PUBLIC HOJSING, PUBLICLY ASSISTED HOUSING, PRIVATE HOUSING. /MASSACHUSETTS/   GMASSCAND963

DISCRIMINATION IN EMPLOYMENT.   GMCNIRK48932

DISCRIMINATION IN EMPLOYMENT.   GMENCWX62974

MINNESCTA STATE ACT AGAINST DISCRIMINATION, AS APPROVED BY THE MINNESOTA LEGISLATURE, APRIL 1961. /LEGISLATION/   GMINNSCND010

PROFILE IN BLACK AND WHITE. DISCRIMINATION AND INEQUALITY OF OPPORTUNITY.   GNATLULND085

PATTERNS OF CONCILIATION UNDER THE NEW-YORK STATE LAW AGAINST DISCRIMINATION.   GNEWXYL51100

A SELECTIVE BIBLIOGRAPHY ON DISCRIMINATION IN HOUSING AND EMPLOYMENT.   GNEWYLF60075

THE NEW-YORK STATE COMMISSION AGAINST DISCRIMINATION. A NEW TECHNIQUE FOR AN OLD PROBLEM.   GNEWYSA47107

COMPILATION OF LAWS AGAINST DISCRIMINATION. A REFERENCE MANUAL.   GNEWYSA48078

THE INSURANCE INDUSTRY -- VERIFIED COMPLAINTS AND INFORMAL INVESTIGATIONS HANDLED BY THE NEW-YORK STATE COMMISSION AGAINST DISCRIMINATION, JULY 1 1945-SEPTEMBER 15, 1958.   GNEWYSA58082

RULINGS ON PRE-EMPLOYMENT INQUIRIES RELATING TO RACE, CREED, COLOR OR NATIONAL ORIGIN UNDER THE NEW-YORK STATE LAW AGAINST DISCRIMINATION.   GNEWYSBND106

FAIR PLAY STARTS WITH THE BOSS. /EMPLOYMENT DISCRIMINATION/   GNIXCRM56117

GOVERNMENTAL FAIR-EMPLCYMENT AGENCIES. AN APPRAISAL CF FEDERAL, STATE, AND MUNICIPAL EFFORTS TO END JOB DISCRIMINATION.   GNORGPH62120

RACIAL DISCRIMINATION IN THE CINCINNATI BUILDING TRADES. A COMPREHENSIVE REPORT AND RECOMMENDATIONS. /CHIO/   GOHICCR64129

LAWS AGAINST DISCRIMINATION. EMPLOYMENT, PUBLIC ACCOMODATICNS, HOUSING. /OHIO/   GOHIOCR65125

PATTERNS OF DISCRIMINATION IN THE GLASS AND MACHINE TOOL INDUSTRIES IN OHIO.   GOHICCR66126

PATTERNS OF DISCRIMINATION IN THE GLASS INDUSTRY IN OHIO.   GOHIOCR66127

PATTERNS OF DISCRIMINATION IN THE MACHINE TOOL INDUSTRY IN OHIO.   GOHICCR66128

DISCRIMINATION IN URBAN EMPLOYMENT.   GPALMEN47145

DISCRIMINATION IN HOUSING ANC EMPLOYMENT. WHAT TYPE OF PROBLEM IS IT.   GPEDDWX64150

INCCME-DISTRIBUTION AS A FACTOR IN REGIONAL GROWTH, WITH SPECIAL REFERENCE TO THE SOUTHEAST UNITED
STATES. /DISCRIMINATION/   GPHILEW65773

DISCRIMINATION IN UNION MEMBERSHIP. DENIAL OF DUE PROCESS UNDER FEDERAL COLLECTIVE BARGAINING
LEGISLATION.   GPRESSB58126

ENFORCEMENT OF LAWS AGAINST DISCRIMINATION IN EMPLOYMENT.   GRABKSX64211

COMBATING DISCRIMINATION IN EMPLOYMENT IN NEW-YORK STATE.   GRACKFX49215

THE INTERRELATIONSHIPS JF DISCRIMINATION IN EMPLOYMENT, IN EDUCATION, AND IN HOUSING.   GRAVIMJ61219

URBAN JOB DISCRIMINATION. ABUSES AND REDRESS.   GRICOLX66237

EXTRAVAGANT INJUSTICE. DISCRIMINATION IN INDUSTRY. /CONNECTICUT/   GROPEEXND243

THE PRICE BUSINESS PAYS.   /INDUSTRY DISCRIMINATION/   GROPEEX49245

THE HIGH COST OF DISCRIMINATION. THE WASTE IN MANPOWER, MORALE, AND PRODUCTIVITY COSTS AMERICAN INDUSTRY
30 BILLION DOLLARS A YEAR.   GROPEEX63244

THE LAW AND RACIAL DISCRIMINATION IN EMPLOYMENT.   GROSESJ65255

THE CUTLOOK FOR A NEW FEPC. THE 80TH CONGRESS AND JOB DISCRIMINATION.   GROSSMX47261

SUPPLEMENTARY ACTIVITIES FOR STATE GOVERNMENTS SEEKING TO ELIMINATE DISCRIMINATION.   GROUTFB64264

THE INFLUENCE OF DISCRIMINATION ON MINORITY-GROUP MEMBERS IN ITS RELATION TO ATTEMPTS TO COMBAT
CISCRIMINATION.   GSAENGX48273

THE INFLUENCE OF DISCRIMINATION ON MINORITY-GROUP MEMBERS IN ITS RELATION TO ATTEMPTS TO COMBAT
DISCRIMINATION.   GSAENGX48273

CIMENSIONS IN DISCRIMINATION, A PRELIMINARY SURVEY OF SAN-DIEGO-S COMMUNITY PROBLEMS OF DISCRIMINATION
PART II. /CALIFORNIA/   GSANDLW65274

DIMENSIONS IN DISCRIMINATION, A PRELIMINARY SURVEY OF SAN-DIEGO-S COMMUNITY PROBLEMS OF DISCRIMINATION
PART II. /CALIFORNIA/   GSANDLW65274

A SURVEY OF DISCRIMINATION IN THE BUILDING TRADES INDUSTRY, NEW-YORK CITY.   GSHAUDF63300

LEGAL SANCTIONS AGAINST JOB DISCRIMINATION.   GSIMOCK46311

LEGAL RESTRAINTS ON RACIAL DISCRIMINATION IN EMPLOYMENT.   GSOVEMI66326

TAILORING THE TECHNIQUES TO ELIMINATE AND PREVENT EMPLOYMENT DISCRIMINATION.   GSPITHX64331

STATE LEGISLATION IN LABOR-RELATIONS AND DISCRIMINATION IN EMPLOYMENT, 1945.   GSPITRS45332

AN ALTERNATIVE THEORY OF ECONOMIC DISCRIMINATION.   GTHURLC67969

FACTORS AFFECTING EMPLOYEE SELECTION IN TWO CULTURES. /DISCRIMINATION/   GTRIAHC63083

LAW OF DISCRIMINATION IN THE EMPLOYMENT OF NONWHITES.   GTURNRH52366

DISCRIMINATION AND LIVELIHOOD.   GTUSSJE63367

BRIEF SUBMITTED IN SUPPORT OF SENATE BILL NO 984, A BILL TO PRCHIBIT DISCRIMINATION IN EMPLOYMENT....   GTUTTCH47368

UAW CUTLAWS DISCRIMINATION. /UNION/   GUAWXIU56370

SUMMARY FACT SHEETS FOR STATE PUBLIC AGENCIES WITH JURISDICTION OVER DISCRIMINATION IN EMPLOYMENT.   GUSCCMC65416

FIRST YEAR UNDER NEW-YORK LAW AGAINST DISCRIMINATION.   GUSDLAB47074

BRIEF SUMMARY OF STATE LAWS AGAINST DISCRIMINATION IN PRIVATE EMPLOYMENT. FAIR-EMPLOYMENT-PRACTICE ACTS.   GUSDLAB63439

DISCRIMINATION AND FULL UTILIZATION CF MANPOWER RESOURCES, 1952.   GUSSENA52347

DISCRIMINATION AND THE NLRB. THE SCOPE OF THE BOARD POWER UNDER SECTIONS 8A3 AND 8B2.   GUVCHLR64212

DISCRIMINATION...AN ECONOMIC WASTE.   GWACHWWND536

MEMBERSHIP DISCRIMINATION IN LABOR UNIONS.   GWASHLR64541

FOSTWAR EMPLOYMENT DISCRIMINATION.   GWEISAJ47547

FEDERAL REMEDIES FOR RACIAL DISCRIMINATION BY LABOR UNIONS.   GWEISLX62597

FINAL REPORT. PATTERNS OF DISCRIMINATION STUDY -- WISCONSIN.   GWISCIC66587

HOW MANY CONTRACTS BAR DISCRIMINATION IN EMPLOYMENT.   GWORTMS64586

DISCRIMINATION IN CRAFT UNIONS.   GYABRSM65587

ADL AT WORK. THE CRUMBLING WALLS. /EMPLOYMENT DISCRIMINATION/   JADLBXX63688

JEWISH LAW GRADUATE. /EMPLOYMENT DISCRIMINATION/   JADLBXX64689

THE MUTUAL SAVINGS BANKS OF NEW-YORK-CITY. /DISCRIMINATION/   JAMERJC65694

ADL REPORTS ON SOCIAL, EMPLOYMENT, EDUCATIONAL AND HCUSING DISCRIMINATION.   JANTIOL57690

BARRIERS. PATTERNS OF DISCRIMINATION AGAINST JEWS.   JBELTNC58702

WHO SHALL BE OUR DOCTORS. /CCCUPATIONS DISCRIMINATION/   JBLOOLX57706

MECICAL SCHOOL QUOTAS. /EDUCATION DISCRIMINATION/   JBRAVHX58707

SOME OF MY BEST FRIENDS... /EMPLOYMENT DISCRIMINATION/   JEPSTBRND719

DETROIT-S OLD HABIT. /EMPLOYMENT DISCRIMINATION/   JFORSAX63723

DISCRIMINATION   (CONTINUATION)
    STATE LAWS AGAINST DISCRIMINATION IN EDUCATION.   JHARTPX58730

    EQUAL RIGHTS FOR THE SATURDAY SABBATH OBSERVER. /EMPLOYMENT DISCRIMINATION/   JHARTPX63729

    EMPLOYMENT DISCRIMINATION -- PART I.   JRIGHXX57753

    EMPLOYMENT DISCRIMINATION -- PART II.   JRIGHXX57754

    EMPLOYMENT IN INSURANCE COMPANIES. /DISCRIMINATION/   JRIGHXX59755

    EMPLOYMENT OF JEWISH PERSONNEL IN THE AUTOMOBILE INDUSTRY. /DISCRIMINATION/   JRIGHXX63756

    JEWISH LAW STUDENT AND NEW-YORK JOBS. /EMPLOYMENT DISCRIMINATION/   JRIGHXX64757

    INSURANCE, BANKING, PUBLIC UTILITIES. /DISCRIMINATION EMPLOYMENT/   JSIMCBX58763

    JEWS NEED NOT APPLY. /DISCRIMINATION EMPLOYMENT/   JWEISAX58770

    LARGE CORPORATIONS ACCUSED OF DISCRIMINATION AGAINST JEWS IN MANAGEMENT, EXECUTIVE CAPACITIES BY
    AMERICAN-JEWISH-COMMITTEE.   JWORLOX64773

    DISCRIMINATION AND THE OCCUPATIONAL PROGRESS OF NEGROES. A COMMENT.   NBECKGS62068

    RACIAL EQUALITY AND THE LAW. THE ROLE OF LAW IN THE REDUCTION OF DISCRIMINATION IN THE UNITED-STATES.   NBERGMX54076

    ECONOMIC DISCRIMINATION AND NEGRO INCREASES.   NBLALHM56083

    PERCENT NONWHITE AND DISCRIMINATION IN THE SOUTH.   NBLALHM57085

    URBANIZATION AND DISCRIMINATION IN THE SOUTH.   NBLALHM59086

    THE CIRCLE OF DISCRIMINATION AGAINST NEGROES.   NBLOCHD55082

    CRAFT UNIONS. A LINK IN THE CIRCLE OF NEGRO DISCRIMINATION.   NBLOCHD57088

    DISCRIMINATION AGAINST THE NEGRO IN EMPLOYMENT IN NEW-YORK, 1920-1963.   NBLOCHD65089

    SOME EFFECTS OF DISCRIMINATION IN EMPLOYMENT.   NBLOCHD66092

    DISCRIMINATION WITHOUT PREJUDICE. /INDUSTRY/   NBLOORO55094

    RACIAL DISCRIMINATION IN THE FEDERAL SERVICE. A STUDY IN THE SOCIOLOGY OF ADMINISTRATION.   NBRADWC53106

    UNION FIGHTS DISCRIMINATION.   NBUSIWX51164

    THE PSYCHOLOGY OF THE NEGRO UNDER DISCRIMINATION.   NCAYTHR51187

    RACIAL DISCRIMINATION BY A UNION AGAINST EMPLOYEES IT DOES NOT REPRESENT. /LEGISLATION/   NCOLULR52226

    RACIAL DISCRIMINATION AND THE DUTY OF FAIR REPRESENTATION. /LEGISLATION/   NCOLULR65225

    JIM-CROW AMERICA. /DISCRIMINATION/   NCONREX47233

    DISCRIMINATION 1963. /OCCUPATIONAL-STATUS/   NFINLOX63355

    UNIONS AND DISCRIMINATION.   NFLEIHX59360

    DISCRIMINATION, A NOTICE TO INDUSTRY.   NFORTXX55051

    REVOLT IN THE SOUTH. /UNION DISCRIMINATION/   NFORTXX56881

    NEGRO-S REAL PROBLEM. /DISCRIMINATION/   NGISSIX65418

    OCCUPATIONAL BENEFITS TO WHITES FROM THE SUBORDINATION OF NEGROES. /DISCRIMINATION/   NGLENND63423

    RACIAL DISCRIMINATION IN AMERICAN LABOR UNIONS.   NGUHAME65464

    RACIAL DISCRIMINATION BY UNIONS.   NHALLGD57987

    DISCRIMINATION IN RATE OF COMPENSATION BETWEEN COLORED AND WHITE TEACHERS HELD UNCONSTITUTIONAL.   NHARVLR40497

    PATTERNS OF EMPLOYMENT DISCRIMINATION.   NHILLHX62537

    RACIAL DISCRIMINATION IN THE NATION-S APPRENTICESHIP TRAINING PROGRAM.   NHILLHX62539

    THE PATTERN OF JOB DISCRIMINATION AGAINST NEGROES.   NHILLHX65536

    RACIAL INEQUALITY IN EMPLOYMENT. THE PATTERNS OF DISCRIMINATION.   NHILLHX65540

    EFFORTS TO ELIMINATE RACIAL DISCRIMINATION IN INDUSTRY -- WITH PARTICULAR REFERENCE TO THE SOUTH.   NHOPEJX54566

    DISCRIMINATION -- USA. /EEO/   NJAVIJK60006

    THE PROBLEMS OF RACIAL DISCRIMINATION IN UNION MEMBERSHIP.   NJENKHX47605

    CIVIL-RIGHTS -- RACIAL DISCRIMINATION IN TEACHER HIRING AND ASSIGNMENT FORBIDDEN.   NKELLPL66734

    DISCRIMINATION IN AMERICA TODAY.   NKENNJF63016

    MANAGEMENT, RACIAL DISCRIMINATION AND APPRENTICE TRAINING   NKOVAIX64663

    APPRENTICESHIP TRAINING PROGRAMS AND RACIAL DISCRIMINATION.   NKOVAIX65024

    THE ECONOMICS OF DISCRIMINATION.   NKRUEAO63666

    RACIAL DISCRIMINATION IN EMPLOYMENT IN THE CINNCINATI AREA. /OHIO/   NKUHNAX62668

    UNION HELD GUILTY OF RACE DISCRIMINATION.   NLABORR45027

    DISCRIMINATION IN THE HIRING HALL. A CASE-STUDY OF PRESSURES TO PROMOTE INTEGRATION IN NEW-YORK-S BREWERY
    INDUSTRY.   NLANGGE59670

    EPISODE I. ARTHUR BROWN APPLIES FOR A JOB. /DISCRIMINATION/   NLAWSEX45035

    DISCRIMINATION IN EMPLOYMENT.   NLEITRO49681

    PATTERNS OF DISCRIMINATION STUDY -- LOUISVILLE HUMAN-RELATIONS-COMMISSION. /KENTUCKY/   NLOUIHR66582

DISCRIMINATION   (CONTINUATION)
RACIAL DISCRIMINATION AND THE FEDERAL LAW. A PROBLEM IN NULLIFICATION.   NLUSKLX63713

DISCRIMINATION AND NATIONAL WELFARE. A SERIES OF ADDRESSES AND DISCUSSIONS.   NMACIRM49731

RACIAL DISCRIMINATION ON THE JOBSITE. COMPETING THEORIES AND COMPETING FORUMS.   NMEYEBI65210

DISCRIMINATION IN THE HIRING AND ASSIGNMENT OF NEGRO TEACHERS IN PUBLIC SCHOOL SYSTEMS.   NMICLRX66068

INDUSTRIAL DISCRIMINATION -- THE SKELETON IN EVERYONE-S CLOSET.   NMIHLLF62779

RACIAL DISCRIMINATION AND PRIVATE EDUCATION.   NMILLAS57069

THE NATIONAL-LABOR-RELATIONS ACT-AND RACIAL DISCRIMINATION. /LEGISLATION/   NMOLIRL66807

RACIAL DISCRIMINATION IN EMPLOYMENT. BIBLIOGRAPHY.   NNORGPH62931

RACE DISCRIMINATION IN UNIONS.   NNORTHR45946

RACE DISCRIMINATION IN TRADE UNIONS. RECORD AND OUTLOOK.   NNORTHR46945

DISCRIMINATION AND THE TRADE UNIONS.   NNORTHR49936

RACIAL DISCRIMINATION IN THE CINCINNATI BUILDING TRADES. REPORT AND RECOMMENDATIONS.   /OHIO/   NOHIOCR66605

AMENDMENTS TO THE TAFT-HARTLEY. A REJECTION OF RACIAL DISCRIMINATION. /LEGISLATION/   NOSHAJB54964

DISCRIMINATION IN URBAN EMPLOYMENT.   NPALMEN47971

THE PRICE WE PAY FOR DISCRIMINATION. /SOUTH ECONOMY/   NPATTBX64979

RACIAL DISCRIMINATION IN EMPLOYMENT. PROPOSALS FOR CORRECTIVE ACTION.   NPCLLDX63006

RACIAL DISCRIMINATION IN UNION MEMBERSHIP.   NPROMHJ59127

COMBATING DISCRIMINATION IN THE EMPLOYMENT OF NEGROES IN WAR INDUSTRIES AND GOVERNMENT AGENCIES.   NRAMSLA43128

DISCRIMINATION AND THE OCCUPATIONAL PROGRESS OF NEGROES.   NRAYAEX61040

THE BLACK MAN-S BURDEN. /DISCRIMINATION ECONOMIC-STATUS/   NREDDJS43546

DISCRIMINATION IN INDUSTRY.   NROPEEX52073

RACE PREJUDICE AND DISCRIMINATION. READINGS IN INTERGROUP RELATIONS IN THE US.   NROSEAM51075

THE LAW AND RACIAL DISCRIMINATION IN EMPLOYMENT.   NROSESJ67078

THE CIVIL-RIGHTS-ACT OF 1964. RACIAL DISCRIMINATION BY LABOR UNIONS.   NSAINJL66138

THE NORTH AMERICAN NEGRO. /DISCRIMINATION/   NSANCLA42537

A SURVEY OF DISCRIMINATION IN THE BUILDING TRADES INDUSTRY. NEW-YORK CITY.   NSHAUDX63126

APPEALS FROM DISCRIMINATION IN FEDERAL EMPLOYMENT. A CASE-STUDY.   NSHOSAX63131

DISCRIMINATION AND LOW-INCOMES.   NSLAIDX61021

PERSONAL AND ON-THE-JOB CHARACTERISTICS RELATED TO NEGRO PERCEPTIONS OF DISCRIMINATION.   NSOLDHX56152

DISCRIMINATION IN HIGHER EDUCATION.   NSOUTCD51166

THE NATIONAL-LABOR-RELATIONS-ACT AND RACIAL DISCRIMINATION. /LEGISLATION/   NSOVEMI62168

RACE DISCRIMINATION AND THE NLRA ACT. THE BRAVE NEW WORLD OF MIRANDA. /LEGISLATION/   NSOVEMI63169

PUBLIC POLICY AND DISCRIMINATION IN APPRENTICESHIP.   NSTRAGX65182

NOTES ON THE CONDITIONS OF NEGROES. /EDUCATION DISCRIMINATION/   NSTREGX45463

RACIAL DISCRIMINATION IN UNIONS.   NTEMPLQ65200

DISCRIMINATION AGAINST NEGROES.   NTHOMPX43203

FOCI OF DISCRIMINATION IN THE EMPLOYMENT OF NONWHITES.   NTURNRH52212

A SELECTED LIST OF REFERENCES RELATING TO DISCRIMINATION AND SEGREGATION IN EDUCATION, 1949 TO JUNE 1955.   NTUSKIX55220

EVERYBODY SEEMED TO LIKE CHARLIE. /DISCRIMINATION/   NULMEAX65223

LEGISLATION AGAINST DISCRIMINATION IN EMPLOYMENT.   NUSDLAB45825

SIX MONTHS OPERATION OF NEW-YORK LAW AGAINST DISCRIMINATION.   NUSDLAB46843

TWO STATE REPORT ON JOB DISCRIMINATION. /NEW-YORK NEW-JERSEY/   NUSDLAB58844

UNION PROGRAM FOR ELIMINATING DISCRIMINATION.   NUSDLAB63846

RACIAL DISCRIMINATION AND THE NLRB. THE HUGHES TOOL CASE, PART ONE.   NVIRGLR64017

RACIAL DISCRIMINATION AND THE NLRB. THE HUGHES TOOL CASE, PART TWO.   NVIRGLR64018

THE NEGRO AND DISCRIMINATION IN EMPLOYMENT.   NWACHDD65288

ADDRESS. /DISCRIMINATION AFFIRMATIVE-ACTION/   NWIRTWX66236

WHAT PRICE PREJUDICE -- ON THE ECONOMICS OF DISCRIMINATION.   NYOUNWM63356

CIVIL-RIGHTS -- DISCRIMINATION IN LABOR UNIONS.   NYOUNWM64349

DISCRIMINATION AGAINST PUERTO-RICANS.   PGARCAX58806

COMPLAINTS ALLEGING DISCRIMINATION BECAUSE OF PUERTO-RICAN NATIONAL ORIGIN, JULY 1, 1945-SEPTEMBER 1,
1958.   PNEWYSA58836

TESTIMONY. PUBLIC HEARING. WOMEN IN PUBLIC AND PRIVATE EMPLOYMENT, CALIFORNIA. /DISCRIMINATION EEOC/   WBALEHX66625

A STUDY OF ELEMENTARY SCHOOL TEACHER-S ATTITUDES TOWARD THE WOMAN PRINCIPAL AND TOWARD ELEMENTARY
PRINCIPALSHIP AS A CAREER.   /DISCRIMINATION/   WBARTAK58629

DISCRIMINATION   (CONTINUATION)
STATEMENT, PUBLIC HEARING, WOMEN IN PUBLIC AND PRIVATE EMPLOYMENT, CALIFORNIA.   /FEP
EMPLOYMENT-CONDITIONS DISCRIMINATION/   WBELAJX66634

STATEMENT, PUBLIC HEARING, WOMEN IN PUBLIC AND PRIVATE EMPLOYMENT, CALIFORNIA.   /FEP
EMPLOYMENT-CONDITIONS DISCRIMINATION/   WBENNSJ66637

TESTIMONY, PUBLIC HEARING, WOMEN IN PUBLIC AND PRIVATE EDUCATION, CALIFORNIA.   /FEP
EMPLOYMENT-CONDITIONS DISCRIMINATION MIGRANT-WORKERS/   WBLOCHX66649

TESTIMONY, PUBLIC HEARING, WOMAN IN PUBLIC AND PRIVATE EMPLOYMENT, CALIFORNIA.   /DISCRIMINATION/   WBROWAX66657

TESTIMONY PRESENTED AT PUBLIC HEARING, MARCH 31 -- APRIL 1, 1966.   /FEP EMPLOYMENT-CONDITIONS
DISCRIMINATION MIGRANTS/   WCALACW62675

TESTIMONY PRESENTED AT PUBLIC HEARING, APRIL 28, 1966. SAN-FRANCISCO, CALIFORNIA.   /FEP
EMPLOYMENT-CONDITIONS DISCRIMINATION MIGRANTS/   WCALACW62676

TESTIMONY PRESENTED AT PUBLIC HEARING, FEBRUARY 24-25, 1966. /FEP EMPLOYMENT-CONDITIONS DISCRIMINATION
MIGRANTS/   WCALACW66674

REPORT OF THE CALIFORNIA ADVISORY COMMISSION ON THE STATUS OF WOMEN. /FEP EMPLOYMENT-CONDITIONS
DISCRIMINATION MIGRANTS/   WCALACW67673

TESTIMONY, PUBLIC HEARING, WOMEN IN PUBLIC AND PRIVATE EMPLOYMENT, CALIFORNIA.   /FEP
EMPLOYMENT-CONDITIONS DISCRIMINATION MIGRANTS/   WCLIFFG66692

TESTIMONY, PUBLIC HEARING, WOMEN IN PUBLIC AND PRIVATE EMPLOYMENT, CALIFORNIA.   /DISCRIMINATION/   WCOLLNX66696

EQUAL PAY FOR WOMEN. /DISCRIMINATION/   WCOMMXX63701

TESTIMONY, PUBLIC HEARING, WOMAN IN PUBLIC AND PRIVATE EMPLOYMENT, CALIFORNIA.   /DISCRIMINATION/   WDORAMX66739

TESTIMONY, PUBLIC HEARING, WOMEN IN PUBLIC AND PRIVATE EMPLOYMENT, CALIFORNIA.   /DISCRIMINATION/   WFOOTJX66765

TESTIMONY, PUBLIC HEARING, WOMEN IN PUBLIC AND PRIVATE EMPLOYMENT, CALIFORNIA.   /DISCRIMINATION/   WGEIGPX66776

NOTES ON WOMEN IN INDUSTRY -- PRESENTED AT AMERICAN PSYCHOLOGICAL SYMPOSIUM, SEPT 1963. /DISCRIMINATION/   WGILMBV63970

TESTIMONY, PUBLIC HEARING, WOMEN IN PUBLIC AND PRIVATE EMPLOYMENT, CALIFORNIA. /DISCRIMINATION
WORK-FAMILY-CONFLICT/   WGUPTRC66808

THE WORKING WOMAN. BARRIERS IN EMPLOYMENT.   /DISCRIMINATION/   WHARREX64827

THE STATUS OF WOMEN. /DISCRIMINATION/   WHERZNK60377

TESTIMONY, PUBLIC HEARING, WOMEN IN PUBLIC AND PRIVATE EMPLOYMENT, CALIFORNIA. /DISCRIMINATION/   WHILLHX66844

DISCRIMINATION IN EMPLOYMENT OR OCCUPATION ON THE BASIS OF MARITAL-STATUS.   WINTELR62865

WOMAN AT WORK -- A STUDY IN PREJUDICE. /DISCRIMINATION/   WMARMJX66954

JANE CROW AND THE LAW. SEX DISCRIMINATION AND TITLE-VII.   WMURRPX65010

PAY DIFFERENCES BETWEEN MEN AND WOMEN. /DISCRIMINATION/   WSANBHX64100

TESTIMONY, PUBLIC HEARING, WOMEN IN PUBLIC AND PRIVATE EMPLOYMENT, CALIFORNIA.   /FEP
EMPLOYMENT-CONDITIONS DISCRIMINATION/   WSMITWH66123

TESTIMONY, PUBLIC HEARING, WOMEN IN PUBLIC AND PRIVATE EMPLOYMENT, CALIFORNIA.   /FEP
EMPLOYMENT-CONDITIONS DISCRIMINATION MIGRANT-WORKERS/   WSPENNX66129

TESTIMONY, PUBLIC HEARING, WOMEN IN PUBLIC AND PRIVATE EMPLOYMENT, CALIFORNIA. /EMPLOYMENT-CONDITIONS
DISCRIMINATION/   WTHOMGX66149

WISCONSIN FAIR-EMPLOYMENT-PRACTICES DIVISION INQUIRY INTO THE CONFLICTS BETWEEN STATE PROTECTIVE LABOR
LEGISLATION AND STATE AND FEDERAL LAWS PROHIBITING DISCRIMINATION BASED ON SEX. /EMPLOYMENT-CONDITIONS/   WUAWXWD65165

LAWS ON SEX DISCRIMINATION IN EMPLOYMENT.   WUSDLAB66K05

STATEMENT, PUBLIC HEARING, WOMEN IN PUBLIC AND PRIVATE EMPLOYMENT, CALIFORNIA.   /FEP
EMPLOYMENT-CONDITIONS DISCRIMINATION/   WVAILLX66256

A LOOK AT THE OTHER WOMAN. /RACE DISCRIMINATION/   WWALDSX65017

IS DISCRIMINATION AGAINST TALENTED WOMEN NECESSARY.   WWARNCF61220

DISCRIMINATORY
DISCRIMINATORY ASPECTS OF THE LABOR MARKET OF THE 60-S.   GBUCKLF

DISCRIMINATORY PROMOTION SYSTEMS.   GDOERPB67115

LOCAL REGULATION OF DISCRIMINATORY EMPLOYMENT PRACTICES.   GELSOAX47661

EMPLOYMENT TESTS AND DISCRIMINATORY HIRING.   GGUIORM66747

INVESTIGATION OF CHARGES OF DISCRIMINATORY PRACTICES IN THE NEW-YORK STATE-EMPLOYMENT-SERVICE.   GNEWYSA59083

FINDINGS OF FACT, CONCLUSIONS AND ACTION OF THE COMMISSION ON HUMAN-RELATIONS IN RE. INVESTIGATIVE PUBLIC
HEARINGS INTO ALLEGED DISCRIMINATORY PRACTICE BY THE HOTEL AND RESTAURANT INDUSTRY IN PHILADELPHIA.
/PENNSYLVANIA/   GPHILCH61176

ADMINISTRATIVE LAW -- HUMAN-RELATIONS COMMISSIONS, PENNSYLVANIA LAW AND DISCRIMINATORY EMPLOYMENT
PRACTICE.   GTEMPLQ63349

CONSEQUENCES OF DISCRIMINATORY UNION MEMBERSHIP POLICY.   GWESTRL53019

THE PROPOSED LEGISLATIVE DEATH KNELL OF PRIVATE DISCRIMINATORY EMPLOYMENT PRACTICES.   GWILSAX45566

THE JEWISH LAW STUDENT AND NEW-YORK JOBS -- DISCRIMINATORY EFFECTS IN LAW FIRM HIRING PRACTICES.
/OCCUPATIONS/   JYALELJ64774

DISCRIMINATORY ASPECTS OF THE LABOR MARKET OF THE 60-S.   NBUCKLF61130

ECONOMIC AND SOCIAL CONSEQUENCES OF RACIAL DISCRIMINATORY PRACTICES.   NUNITNX63224

SUGGESTED LANGUAGE FOR A STATE ACT TO ABOLISH DISCRIMINATORY WAGE RATES BASED ON SEX.   WUSDLAB64218

DISCUSSION
DISCUSSION ON EQUAL-EMPLOYMENT-OPPORTUNITIES.   GPOLIEX65102

DISCUSSION   (CONTINUATION)
PANEL DISCUSSION. THE COMMITTMENT REQUIRED OF A WOMAN ENTERING A SCIENTIFIC PROFESSION. /OCCUPATIONS/   WBUNTMI65663

DISCUSSION. WOMEN IN MEDICINE. /OCCUPATIONS/   WGRIFAM65803

PANEL DISCUSSION. THE CASE FOR AND AGAINST THE EMPLOYMENT OF WOMEN. /OCCUPATIONS/   WHARRTW65824

DISCUSSIONS
DISCRIMINATION AND NATIONAL WELFARE. A SERIES OF ADDRESSES AND DISCUSSIONS.   NMACIRM49731

DISINTEGRATION
TERMINATION OF FEDERAL SUPERVISION. DISINTEGRATION AND THE AMERICAN-INDIANS.   ILAFAOX57075

DISORGANIZATION
ANOMIE AND ACHIEVEMENT MOTIVATION. A STUDY OF PERSONALITY DEVELOPMENT WITHIN CULTURAL DISORGANIZATION.   IKERCAC59018

PROBLEMS AND NEEDS OF NEGRO CHILDREN AND YOUTH RESULTING FROM FAMILY DISORGANIZATION.   NFRAZEF50382

DISPLACED
MOBILITY. METHODS OF JOB SEARCH, ATTITUDES, AND MOTIVATION OF DISPLACED WORKERS.   GSHEPHL64621

RELOCATION OF THE DISPLACED WORKER.   IMETZWX63081

THE DISPLACED PERSON AND THE SOCIAL AGENCY. A STUDY OF THE CASEWORK PROCESS AND ITS RELATION TO IMMIGRANT
ADJUSTMENT.   JCRYSDX58714

DISPLACED TEACHERS. /OCCUPATIONS/   NCOMMXX65229

DISPLACEMENT
REBUILDING CITIES. THE EFFECTS OF DISPLACEMENT AND RELOCATION ON SMALL BUSINESS.   NZIMMBG64247

DISPOSSESSED
THE DISPOSSESSED.   GFORTXX40459

DISPUTES
SOUTH-S RACE DISPUTES INVOLVE BUSINESSMAN.   NBUSIWX60162

DISTANCE
DISTANCE OF MIGRATION AND SOCIO-ECONOMIC STATUS OF MIGRANTS.   NROSEAM58291

DISTINGUISH
SOME FACTORS WHICH DISTINGUISH DROP-OUTS FROM HIGH SCHOOL GRADUATES.   NGRAGWL49978

DISTRIBUTION
RACIAL DISTRIBUTION OF SELECTED UNEMPLOYMENT INSURANCE AND EMPLOYMENT SERVICE DATA. JULY-DECEMBER 1966.
/NEGRO MEXICAN-AMERICAN/   CCALDEM67907

ETHNIC SURVEY OF MUNICIPAL-EMPLOYEES. A REPORT ON THE NUMBER AND DISTRIBUTION OF NEGROES AND
PUERTO-RICANS AND OTHER EMPLOYEES BY THE CITY OF NEW-YORK.   CNEWYCO64916

POVERTY IN TEXAS. THE DISTRIBUTION OF LOW-INCOME FAMILIES.   GKUVLWP65867

THE PRESENT DAY DISTRIBUTION OF UNITED STATES INDIANS.   ITAXXSX56628

DISTRIBUTION OF SPANISH-NAME PEOPLE IN THE SOUTHWEST. TABLES AND MAP.   MHOLLSX56417

POPULATION DISTRIBUTION AND COMPOSITION IN THE NEW SOUTH.   NBOGUDJ54102

DISTRIBUTION OF NEGRO POPULATION IN THE UNITED STATES. /DEMOGRAPHY/   NCALEWC56069

RESIDENTIAL DISTRIBUTION AND OCCUPATIONAL-STRATIFICATION.   NDUNCOC55307

THE EFFECT OF THE GHETTO ON THE DISTRIBUTION AND LEVEL OF NONWHITE EMPLOYMENT IN URBAN AREAS.   NKAINJF64631

EMPLOYMENT DISTRIBUTION STUDY OF THE CONSTRUCTION INDUSTRY IN MICHIGAN.   NMICCRC66606

THE CHANGING NUMBER AND DISTRIBUTION OF THE AGED NEGRO POPULATION OF THE UNITED STATES. /DEMOGRAPHY/   NSMITLT58145

EMPLOYMENT GAINS AND THE DETERMINANTS OF THE OCCUPATIONAL DISTRIBUTION OF NEGROES.   NTHURLC67971

OCCUPATIONAL DISTRIBUTION OF EMPLOYED COLORED WORKERS OF MARYLAND.   NUSDLAB40834

OCCUPATIONAL DISTRIBUTION OF NEGROES IN 1940.   NUSDLAB44835

NEGROES IN NEW-YORK CITY. OCCUPATIONAL DISTRIBUTION.   NUSDLAB49831

SOME FACTORS WHICH DETERMINE THE DISTRIBUTION OF THE FEMALE WORK-FORCE. /LABOR-FORCE/   WJOUROI62883

LABOR-FORCE PARTICIPATION RATES AND PERCENT DISTRIBUTION OF MOTHERS WITH HUSBAND PRESENT.   WUSDLAB64204

DISTRICT
REPORT ON OAKLAND SCHOOLS. AN INVESTIGATION UNDER SECTION 1421 OF THE CALIFORNIA LABOR CODE OF THE
OAKLAND UNIFIED SCHOOL DISTRICT 1962-1963. /NEGRO ORIENTAL MEXICAN-AMERICAN/   CCALDIR63710

EMPLOYMENT OPPORTUNITIES FOR HIGH SCHOOL DROPOUTS. A STUDY OF EMPLOYERS PRACTICES, NEEDS AND ATTITUDES IN
THE DISTRICT OF COLUMBIA. /WASHINGTON-DC/   GBURESS57499

EMPLOYMENT PRACTICES OF THE PHILADELPHIA SCHOOL DISTRICT. /PENNSYLVANIA/   GPENNHR62162

SUMMARY REPORT OF THE STUDY OF DROP-OUTS IN THE THREE SENIOR HIGH SCHOOLS, COMPTON UNION HIGH SCHOOL
DISTRICT. /CALIFORNIA/   MWHITNX60517

MEDICAL SOCIETY OF THE DISTRICT OF COLUMBIA TO ADMIT NEGRO PHYSICIANS. /OCCUPATIONS/   NJOURNM52628

STATEMENT BEFORE CALIFORNIA LEGISLATURE ASSEMBLY, INTERIM SUBCOMMITTEE ON ECONOMIC OPPORTUNITY ON BEHALF
OF CHINATOWN-NORTH BEACH DISTRICT COUNCIL.   OWONGLJ64771

DISTRICT-OF-COLUMBIA
PATTERNS OF DISCRIMINATION IN THE FINANCIAL INSTITUTIONS OF THE DISTRICT-OF-COLUMBIA. THE BANKING,
SAVINGS AND LOAN, AND INSURANCE INDUSTRIES.   GDISTCC66642

DIVISION
DIVISION OF AUTHORITY UNDER TITLE-VII OF THE CIVIL-RIGHTS-ACT OF 1964. A PRELIMINARY STUDY IN
FEDERAL-STATE INTERAGENCY RELATIONS.   GROSESJ66254

LABOR-NEGRO DIVISION WIDENS. /UNION/   NBUSIWX60152

REPORTS OF PUERTO-RICO DEPARTMENT OF LABOR, MIGRATION DIVISION ON PLACEMENT.   PPUERRCND791

DIVISION   (CONTINUATION)
THE MIGRATION **DIVISION** -- POLICY, FUNCTIONS, OBJECTIVES.   PPUERRD57789

WISCONSIN FAIR-EMPLOYMENT-PRACTICES **DIVISION** INQUIRY INTO THE CONFLICTS BETWEEN STATE PROTECTIVE LABOR
LEGISLATION AND STATE AND FEDERAL LAWS PROHIBITING DISCRIMINATION BASED ON SEX. /EMPLOYMENT-CONDITIONS/   WUAWXWD65165

DIVISION-OF-LABOR
SOUTHERN POVERTY AND THE RACIAL **DIVISION-OF-LABOR**.   NDEWEDX62271

DIVISIONS
A SURVEY OF SPECIAL EDUCATIONAL PROGRAMS FOR ADULT WOMEN IN UNIVERSITY EXTENSION **DIVISIONS** AND EVENING
COLLEGES AS OF SPRING 1965.   WLORIRK66942

DIXIE
NEW HOPE FOR RURAL **DIXIE**. FIRMS IN CAROLINAS CREATE JOBS FOR NEGROES.   NEBONXX64317

DIXIE IN BLACK AND WHITE. /UNION/   NMEZEAG47492

DOCTORAL
FACTORS ASSOCIATED WITH GRADUATE SCHOOL ATTENDANCE AND ROLE DEFINITION OF THE WOMAN **DOCTORAL** CANDIDATES
AT THE PENNSYLVANIA STATE UNIVERSITY. /OCCUPATIONS/   WFIELJC61763

MATURE WOMEN IN **DOCTORAL** PROGRAMS. /OCCUPATIONS/   WRANDKS65073

DOCTORS
WHO SHALL BE OUR **DOCTORS**. /OCCUPATIONS DISCRIMINATION/   JBLOOLX57706

DOCTRINE
THE FAIR REPRESENTATION **DOCTRINE**. AN EFFECTIVE WEAPON AGAINST UNION RACIAL DISCRIMINATION.   GHERRNM64772

DOCUMENT
EQUAL-OPPORTUNITIES PLAN STRESSED IN STATE PERSONNEL BOARD **DOCUMENT**. /CALIFORNIA/   GCALSEM64548

DOCUMENTARY
DOCUMENTARY HISTORY OF THE FCX PROJECT, 1948-1959. A PROGRAM IN ACTION ANTHROPOLOGY.   INETTRM60599

DOGMA
PREJUDICE AND ECONOMIC **DOGMA**.   GROUCJX55263

DOLLARS
THE HIGH COST OF DISCRIMINATION. THE WASTE IN MANPOWER, MORALE, AND PRODUCTIVITY COSTS AMERICAN INDUSTRY
30 BILLION **DOLLARS** A YEAR.   GROPEEX63244

DOMESTIC
SELECTED REFERENCES ON **DOMESTIC** MIGRATORY AGRICULTURAL WORKERS, THEIR FAMILIES, PROBLEMS, AND PROGRAMS,
1955-1960.   GUSDLAB61495

DOMESTIC AND IMPORTED WORKERS IN THE HARVEST LABOR-MARKET, SANTA-CLARA COUNTY, CALIFORNIA, 1954.   MFULLVX56396

A HISTORY OF THE INTERRELATIONSHIPS BETWEEN IMPORTED MEXICAN LABOR, **DOMESTIC** MIGRANTS, AND THE TEXAS
AGRICULTURAL ECONOMY.   MGRAVRP60405

EXPERIENCES OF NEGRO HIGH SCHOOL GIRLS WITH **DOMESTIC** PLACEMENT AGENCIES. /HOUSEHOLD-WORKERS/   WRUSSRD62135

DOMESTIC-SERVANTS
THE EMPLOYMENT OF NEGRO WOMEN AS **DOMESTIC-SERVANTS** IN NEW-ORLEANS. /LOUISIANA/   CGILMHX44403

DOMESTIC-SERVICE
DOMESTIC-SERVICE AND THE NEGRO.   NCHAPDX64193

DREAM
THE AMERICAN **DREAM**...EQUAL OPPORTUNITY, A REPORT ON THE COMMUNITY LEADER-S CONFERENCE SPONSORED BY
PRESIDENT-S COMMITTEE ON EQUAL-EMPLOYMENT-OPPORTUNITY, MAY 19, 1962.   GPRESCD62105

THE QUEST FOR THE **DREAM**. THE DEVELOPMENT OF CIVIL-RIGHTS AND HUMAN-RELATIONS IN MODERN AMERICA.   GROCHJP63057

THE AMERICAN **DREAM** AND THE NEGRO.   NDRAKSC63288

THE NEGRO-S MIDDLE-CLASS **DREAM**.   NLINCCE64695

THE AMERICAN **DREAM**...EQUAL OPPORTUNITY.   NPRESCD62014

DRIVE
THE NEGRO **DRIVE** FOR JOBS.   NBUSIWX63154

CPI -- CHEMICAL PROCESS INDUSTRIES -- TAKES LEAD IN ANTI-BIAS **DRIVE**. /INDUSTRY/   NCHEMWX61199

MANAGEMENTS GUIDELINES FOR MEETING THE NEGRO **DRIVE** FOR JOB EQUALITY. /INDUSTRY/.   NOPINRC63958

DRIVER
THE EMPLOYMENT OF NEGROES AS **DRIVER** SALESMEN IN THE BAKING INDUSTRY.   NNEWYSA60919

DRIVES
LABOR **DRIVES** TO CLOSE THE SOUTH-S OPEN-SHOP. /UNION/   NRONYVX65072

DROP-OUT
THE OUTLOOK OF WORKING CLASS YOUTH. /DROP-OUT ASPIRATION/   GMILLSM62570

TODAY-S **DROP-OUT** -- TOMORROW-S PROBLEMS.   IUSDINT59662

MEXICAN-AMERICANS IN URBAN PUBLIC HIGH SCHOOLS. AN EXPLORATION OF THE **DROP-OUT** PROGRAM.   MSHELPM59488

SCHOOL ATTENDANCE AND ATTAINMENT, FUNCTION AND DYSFUNCTION OF SCHOOL AND FAMILY SOCIAL SYSTEMS.
/EMPLOYMENT **DROP-OUT**/   NBERTAL62882

RETENTION AND WITHDRAWAL OF COLLEGE STUDENTS. /DROP-OUT/   WIFFERE57854

DROP-OUTS
SUMMARY REPORT OF THE STUDY OF **DROP-OUTS** IN THE THREE SENIOR HIGH SCHOOLS, COMPTON UNION HIGH SCHOOL
DISTRICT. /CALIFORNIA/   MWHITNX60517

SOME FACTORS WHICH DISTINGUISH **DROP-OUTS** FROM HIGH SCHOOL GRADUATES.   NGRAGWL49978

DROP-OUTS FROM SCHOOLS OF NURSING. THE EFFECT OF SELF- AND ROLE PERCEPTION.   WKIBRAK58902

DROPOUT
THE SCHOOL **DROPOUT** PROBLEM IN MAJOR CITIES OF NEW-YORK STATE. ROCHESTER -- PART I. /NEGRO PUERTO-RICAN/   CNEWYSD62090

WHY **DROPOUT** CAMPAIGNS FAIL.   GBARDBX66533

DROPOUT (CONTINUATION)

REALITIES OF THE JOB-MARKET FOR THE HIGH SCHOOL DROPOUT.   GBIENHX64111

SCHOOL DROPOUT RATES AMONG FARM AND NONFARM YOUTH 1950 AND 1960.   GCOWHJD63421

ADOLESCENCE. CULTURAL DEPRIVATION, POVERTY, AND THE DROPOUT.   GHUNTOE66939

APPROACHES TO THE SCHOOL DROPOUT PROBLEM.   GSULLNV65653

DIFFERENCES IN DROPOUT AND OTHER SCHOOL BEHAVIOR BETWEEN TWO GROUPS OF TENTH GRADE BOYS IN AN URBAN HIGH
SCHOOL.   MMUNORF57446

TWO PROJECTS FOR DROPOUT YOUTH.   NJEWIEA64609

THE SCHOOL DROPOUT IN LOUISIANA 1963-1964.   NLOUISD64714

THE DROPOUT AND THE DELINQUENT. PROMISING PRACTICES GLEANED FROM A YEAR OF STUDY.   NSCHRDX63141

DROPOUTS

EMPLOYMENT OF HIGH SCHOOL GRADUATES AND DROPOUTS IN 1964.   GBOGAFA65750

EMPLOYMENT OPPORTUNITIES FOR HIGH SCHOOL DROPOUTS. A STUDY OF EMPLOYERS PRACTICES, NEEDS AND ATTITUDES IN
THE DISTRICT OF COLUMBIA. /WASHINGTON-DC/   GBURESS57499

UNTAPPED GOOD. THE REHABILITATION OF SCHOOL DROPOUTS.   GCHANNM66803

A DEMONSTRATION PROJECT DESIGNED TO TEST THE LIFE-STYLE AND THE GROWTH POTENTIAL OF URBAN DROPOUTS FROM
DISADVANTAGED HOMES.   GCLEAMP66130

CHARACTERISTICS OF SCHOOL DROPOUTS AND HIGH SCHOOL GRADUATES, FARM AND NONFARM, 1960.   GCOWHJD64419

A SUMMARY REPORT OF PRACTICES AND PROGRAMS DESIGNED TO REDUCE THE NUMBER OF DROPOUTS IN THE HIGH SCHOOLS
OF LOS-ANGELES COUNTY. /CALIFORNIA/   GDELMDT66147

DROPOUTS. A POLITICAL PROBLEM. /EMPLOYMENT/   GMILLSM62354

SCHOOL DROPOUTS. A COMMENTARY AND ANNOTATED BIBLIOGRAPHY.   GMILLSM64071

SCHOOL FAILURES AND DROPOUTS.   GNEISEG63054

FACTORS ASSOCIATED WITH SCHOOL DROPOUTS AND JUVENILE-DELINQUENCY AMONG LOWER-CLASS CHILDREN.   GPALMFX63671

EMPLOYMENT OF HIGH SCHOOL GRADUATES AND DROPOUTS IN 1962.   GSCHIJX63282

PROGRAMS FOR HIGH SCHOOL DROPOUTS. EXPERIENCE REPORT 101.   GUSCONF64976

DROPOUTS -- SELECTED REFERENCES.   GUSDHEW64764

EMPLOYMENT OF HIGH SCHOOL GRADUATES AND DROPOUTS IN 1965.   GUSDLAB66073

WARRIOR DROPOUTS. /YOUTH/   IWAXXRH67812

DROPOUTS TO NOWHERE.   NBARKNX62053

DROPOUTS AND THE RATE OF UNEMPLOYMENT. /YOUTH/   NDUNCBX65304

THE STATE-EMPLOYMENT-SERVICE AND THE ATTITUDE OF UNEMPLOYABLE DROPOUTS.   NHARRIE66991

HIGH SCHOOL GRADUATES AND DROPOUTS -- A NEW LOOK AT A PERSISTENT PROBLEM.   NLIVIAH58044

ACHIEVEMENT OF MALE HIGH SCHOOL DROPOUTS AND GRADUATES IN ALABAMA VOCATIONAL SCHOOLS.   NMILLGJ65791

AN EMPIRICAL STUDY OF HIGH SCHOOL DROPOUTS IN REGARD TO TEN POSSIBLY RELATED FACTORS.   NTHOMRJ54159

SCHOOL DROPOUTS. THE FEMALE SPECIES.   WSCHRDX62105

DUE

DISCRIMINATION IN UNION MEMBERSHIP. DENIAL OF DUE PROCESS UNDER FEDERAL COLLECTIVE BARGAINING
LEGISLATION.   GPRESSB58126

DULUTH

THE NEGRO POPULATION IN DULUTH MINNESOTA, 1950. /DEMOGRAPHY/   NTURBGX52210

DURHAM

THE NEGRO TOBACCO WORKER AND HIS UNION IN DURHAM, NORTH-CAROLINA.   NRICEJD41053

DUTIES

UNION RIGHTS AND UNION DUTIES.   NSEIDJI43115

DUTY

THE DUTY OF FAIR REPRESENTATION.   GCOXXAX57617

UNION-S DUTY OF FAIR REPRESENTATION AND THE CIVIL-RIGHTS-ACT OF 1964.   GSHERHL65302

RACIAL DISCRIMINATION AND THE DUTY OF FAIR REPRESENTATION. /LEGISLATION/   NCOLULR65225

DO CORPORATIONS HAVE A SOCIAL DUTY. /INDUSTRY/   NHACKAX63475

DYNAMICS

THE DYNAMICS OF STATE CAMPAIGNS FOR FAIR-EMPLOYMENT-PRACTICES LEGISLATION.   GUVCHCE50211

EARNING

A WOMAN-S GUIDE TO EARNING A GOOD LIVING.   WWINTEX61270

EARNINGS

OCCUPATIONS BY EARNINGS AND EDUCATION. STATISTICS FOR MEN 18-64 YEARS OLD, BY COLOR, IN SELECTED
OCCUPATIONS. /DEMOGRAPHY/   CUSBURC63178

EDUCATION, SKILL LEVEL, AND EARNINGS OF THE HIRED FARM WORKING FORCE OF 1961.   GCOWHJD63420

EMPLOYMENT AND EARNINGS OF MIGRANT FARM WORKERS IN NEW-YORK STATE.   GNEWYSE60110

NATIONAL EMPLOYMENT, SKILLS, AND EARNINGS OF FARM LABOR.   GSCHUTW67964

EMPLOYMENT AND EARNINGS.   GUSDLABND444

EMPLOYMENT AND EARNINGS STATISTICS FOR THE UNITED STATES, 1909-1966.   GUSDLAB66832

ANNUAL FAMILY AND OCCUPATIONAL EARNINGS OF RESIDENTS OF TWO NEGRO HOUSING PROJECTS IN ATLANTA 1937-1944.

EARNINGS   (CONTINUATION)
  /GEORGIA/   NRITTAL45062

  EARNINGS AND HOURS OF WOMEN AGRICULTURAL WORKERS.   WCALDIR64268

  EARNINGS IN THE WOMEN-S AND MISSES COAT AND SUIT INDUSTRY.   WUSDLAB57988

  NURSES AND OTHER HOSPITAL PERSONNEL -- THEIR EARNINGS AND EMPLOYMENT-CONDITIONS.   WUSDLAB61211

  WOMEN-S EARNINGS IN LOW-INCOME FAMILIES.   WUSDLAB66236

EAST
  NEGROES AND MEXICAN-AMERICANS IN SOUTH AND EAST LOS-ANGELES. AN ANALYSIS OF A SPECIAL US CENSUS SURVEY OF
  NOVEMBER 1965. /CALIFORNIA/   CCALDIR66168

  REPORT. EVALUATION STUDY OF YOUTH TRAINING AND EMPLOYMENT PROJECT, EAST LOS-ANGELES. /NEGRO
  MEXICAN-AMERICAN CALIFORNIA/   CWEINJL64310

  STUDY OF OCCUPATIONAL CHARACTERISTICS OF NON-WHITES IN THE EAST BATON-ROUGE AREA. /LOUISIANA/   GHARRWRND760

  WESTERNERS FROM THE EAST. ORIENTAL IMMIGRANTS REAPPRAISED.   ODANIRX66084

EAST-HARLEM
  EAST-HARLEM BLOCK COMMUNITY DEVELOPMENT PROGRAM. /NEW-YORK/   PBORDDXND781

EAST-HARLEM-YOUTH-EM
  THE STORY OF EAST-HARLEM-YOUTH-EMPLOYMENT-SERVICE, INC.   PEASTHY64799

EASTERN
  MIGRANT CREWS IN EASTERN MARYLAND.   GSHOSAL65306

  HEALTH PRACTICES AND EDUCATIONAL ASPIRATIONS AS INDICATORS OF ACCULTURATION AND SOCIAL-CLASS AMONG THE
  EASTERN CHEROKEE. /NORTH-CAROLINA/   IKUPFHJ62216

ECOLOGICAL
  THE ATTRACTIVENESS OF THE SOUTH TO WHITES AND NONWHITES. AN ECOLOGICAL STUDY.   GHEERDM63769

ECONOMETRIC
  THE CHANGING STRUCTURE OF UNEMPLOYMENT. AN ECONOMETRIC STUDY.   GTHURLC65970

  WORKING WIVES. AN ECONOMETRIC STUDY.   WROSERX58089

ECONOMIC
  ECONOMIC, SOCIAL, AND DEMOGRAPHIC CHARACTERISTICS OF SPANISH-AMERICAN WAGE WORKERS ON US FARMS.
  /PUERTO-RICAN MEXICAN-AMERICAN/   CFRIERE63805

  ECONOMIC GROWTH AND EMPLOYMENT OPPORTUNITIES FOR MINORITIES. /NEGRO WOMEN/   CHIESDL64775

  THE PREDICTION AND EXPLANATION OF ECONOMIC ABSORPTION AMONG MEXICAN-AMERICANS, NEGROES, AND ANGLOS IN A
  NORTHERN INDUSTRIAL COMMUNITY.   CSHANLW63120

  THE ECONOMIC ABSORPTION AND CULTURAL INTEGRATION OF IMMIGRANT MEXICAN-AMERICAN AND NEGRO WORKERS. CSHANLW64124

  THE ECONOMIC ABSORPTION OF IN-MIGRANT LABORERS IN A NORTHERN INDUSTRIAL COMMUNITY. /MEXICAN-AMERICAN
  NEGRO/   CSHANLW64486

  THE PREDICTION OF ECONOMIC ABSORPTION AND CULTURAL INTEGRATION AMONG MEXICAN-AMERICANS, NEGROES, AND
  ANGLOS IN A NORTHERN INDUSTRIAL COMMUNITY.   CSHANLW66123

  GENERAL SOCIAL AND ECONOMIC CHARACTERISTICS. SUMMARY, US CENSUS OF 1960. /DEMOGRAPHY/   CUSBURC62374

  EMPLOYMENT-STATUS AND WORK CHARACTERISTICS. STATISTICS ON THE RELATION BETWEEN EMPLOYMENT AND SOCIAL AND
  ECONOMIC CHARACTERISTICS. /DEMOGRAPHY/   CUSBURC63170

  MOBILITY FOR STATES AND STATE ECONOMIC AREAS. /DEMOGRAPHY/   CUSBURC63174

  PERSONS BY FAMILY CHARACTERISTICS. FAMILY MEMBERS BY SOCIAL, ECONOMIC AND HOUSING CHARACTERISTICS OF
  FAMILIES. /DEMOGRAPHY/   CUSBURC63180

  PERSONS OF SPANISH-SURNAME. SOCIAL AND ECONOMIC DATA FOR WHITE PERSONS OF SPANISH SURNAME IN 5
  SOUTHWESTERN STATES. /DEMOGRAPHY/   CUSBURC63181

  ECONOMIC ABSORPTION AND CULTURAL INTEGRATION OF THE URBAN NEWCOMER. /NEGRO MEXICAN-AMERICAN/   CUVIOIP65277

  POLICIES FOR THE PROMOTION OF ECONOMIC GROWTH.   GACKLGX66680

  TRICKLING DOWN. THE RELATIONSHIP BETWEEN ECONOMIC GROWTH AND THE EXTENT OF POVERTY AMONG AMERICAN
  FAMILIES.   GANDEWH64392

  ECONOMIC EQUALITY AND GOVERNMENT ACTION.   GBERLAA66222

  A BENEFIT-COST ANALYSIS OF THE ECONOMIC EFFECTIVENESS OF RETRAINING THE UNEMPLOYED.   GBORUME64142

  THE ECONOMIC EFFECTIVENESS OF RETRAINING THE UNEMPLOYED.   GBORUME66919

  AUTOMATION AND ECONOMIC PROGRESS. A SUMMARY OF THE REPORT OF THE NATIONAL COMMISSION ON TECHNOLOGY,
  AUTOMATION, AND ECONOMIC PROGRESS.   GBOWEHR66748

  AUTOMATION AND ECONOMIC PROGRESS. A SUMMARY OF THE REPORT OF THE NATIONAL COMMISSION ON TECHNOLOGY,
  AUTOMATION, AND ECONOMIC PROGRESS.   GBOWEHR66748

  MIGRATION PATTERNS OF THE RURAL-FARM POPULATION. THIRTEEN ECONOMIC REGIONS OF THE UNITED STATES,
  1940-1950.   GBOWLGK57415

  EFFECTS ON ECONOMIC GROWTH OF THE EMPLOYMENT SHIFT TO SERVICE INDUSTRIES.   GBRADME64797

  THE QUESTS FOR ECONOMIC STABILITY AND EQUAL-EMPLOYMENT-OPPORTUNITY.   GBRIMAF66475

  HEARING OF THE SUBCOMMITTEE ON ECONOMIC DEVELOPMENT. EDITED TRANSCRIPT, JANUARY 28 AND 29, 1964.
  /CALIFORNIA FEP/   GCALAIW64510

  ECONOMIC AND SOCIAL DEPRIVATIONS. ITS EFFECTS ON CHILDREN AND FAMILIES IN THE UNITED STATES -- A SELECTED
  BIBLIOGRAPHY.   GCHILCX64571

  ECONOMIC MANPOWER AND SOCIAL-WELFARE.   GCLAGEX65794

  ECONOMIC REPORTS OF THE PRESIDENT.   GCOUNEAND239

  ECONOMIC COSTS OF RACIAL DISCRIMINATION IN EMPLOYMENT.   GCOUNEA62205

ECONOMIC   (CONTINUATION)
POTENTIAL ECONOMIC GAINS FROM ELIMINATING DISCRIMINATION.   GCOUNEA66204

CIVIL-RIGHTS, EMPLOYMENT OPPORTUNITY, AND ECONOMIC GROWTH.   GFEILJG65677

ECONOMIC DISCRIMINATION AND UNEMPLOYMENT.   GGILMHJ65717

TWENTY YEARS OF ECONOMIC AND INDUSTRIAL CHANGE. /TECHNOLOGICAL-CHANGE EMPLOYMENT/   GGORDRA65675

ESSAYS IN SOUTHERN ECONOMIC DEVELOPMENT.   GGREEMX64450

SOME BASIC CONSTITUTIONAL RIGHTS OF ECONOMIC SIGNIFICANCE.   GHALERX51754

ECONOMIC GROWTH, EQUAL-OPPORTUNITY, RESEARCH, JOINT EFFORT, EMPLOYMENT.   GILLIGC63798

POVERTY, AGGREGATE DEMAND, AND ECONOMIC STRUCTURE.   GKERSJA66941

IDENTIFICATION AND MODIFICATION OF THE SOCIAL-PSYCHOLOGICAL CORRELATES OF ECONOMIC DEPENDENCY. PROJECT
FINAL REPORT.   GKIMMPR66137

THE EFFECT OF STATE FAIR-EMPLOYMENT LEGISLATION ON THE ECONOMIC POSITION OF NONWHITE MALES.   GLANDWM66883

ETHNIC AND ECONOMIC MINORITIES. UNION-S FUTURE OR UNRECRUITABLE.   GMARSRX63945

ECONOMIC FACTORS INFLUENCING EDUCATIONAL-ATTAINMENTS AND ASPIRATIONS OF FARM YOUTH.   GMOOREJ64386

THE MEASUREMENT AND INTERPRETATION OF JOB VACANCIES. A CONFERENCE REPORT OF THE NATIONAL BUREAU OF
ECONOMIC RESEARCH. /LABOR-MARKET/   GNATLBE66611

EQUAL ECONOMIC OPPORTUNITY. A REPORT.   GPRESCG53117

ECONOMIC EXPANSION AND PERSISTING UNEMPLOYMENT. AN OVERVIEW.   GREESAX66722

THE CHANGING ECONOMIC BACKGROUND OF AMERICAN RACE-RELATIONS.   GROSEAW50288

PREJUDICE AND ECONOMIC DOGMA.   GROUCJX55263

THE ECONOMIC VALUE OF EDUCATION.   GSCHUTW63895

VOCATIONAL-TECHNICAL EDUCATION AND ECONOMIC SECURITY.   GSWANJC66155

THE GUARANTEED-INCOME. NEXT STEP IN ECONOMIC REVOLUTION.   GTHEORX66626

THE ECONOMIC SITUATION OF NATIONAL MINORITIES IN THE UNITED STATES OF AMERICA.   GTHOMJA47354

AN ALTERNATIVE THEORY OF ECONOMIC DISCRIMINATION.   GTHURLC67969

MOBILITY AND WORKER ADAPTATION TO ECONOMIC CHANGE IN THE US.   GTRAVHX63836

ECONOMIC, POLITICAL AND PSYCHOLOGICAL ASPECTS OF EMPLOYMENT.   GUPHOWH64528

TESTIMONY BEFORE SUBCOMMITTEE ON ECONOMIC STATISTICS, MAY 17, 1965.   GUSCONG65421

HEALTH, EDUCATION, AND WELFARE ASPECTS OF THE ECONOMIC REPORT OF THE PRESENT AND ANNUAL REPORT OF THE
COUNCIL OF ECONOMIC ADVISORS.   GUSDHEW66711

HEALTH, EDUCATION, AND WELFARE ASPECTS OF THE ECONOMIC REPORT OF THE PRESENT AND ANNUAL REPORT OF THE
COUNCIL OF ECONOMIC ADVISORS.   GUSDHEW66711

DISCRIMINATION...AN ECONOMIC WASTE.   GWACHWWND536

HEALTH AND ECONOMIC DEVELOPMENT.   IBAUMLX64535

BETTER ECONOMIC OPPORTUNITY FOR INDIANS.   IBECKJX66536

UTE INDIAN SURVEY -- PRELIMINARY REPORT, SOCIAL AND ECONOMIC CHARACTERISTICS.   IBRIGYUND442

CONSTRAINTS ON ECONOMIC PROGRESS ON THE ROSEBUD SIOUX INDIAN RESERVATION.   IEICHCK60553

AMERICAN-INDIANS AND THEIR ECONOMIC DEVELOPMENT.   IHUMAOX61820

THE ECONOMIC BASIS OF INDIAN LIFE. /INCOME LABOR-FORCE/   IKELLWH57076

INDIANS OF THE MISSOURI-BASIN -- CULTURAL FACTORS IN THEIR SOCIAL AND ECONOMIC ADJUSTMENT.   IREIFBX58610

THE ECONOMIC DEVELOPMENT AND URBANIZATION OF THE NAVAJO INDIAN RESERVATION.   ISELLCL62616

SOCIAL AND ECONOMIC SURVEY OF POTAWATOMIE JURISDICTION.   IUSDINT57660

YOU ASKED ABOUT THE NAVAJO. EDUCATION, HEALTH, AND ECONOMIC PROBLEMS OF THE NAVAJO.   IUSDINT57664

AMERICAN-INDIANS AND THEIR ECONOMIC DEVELOPMENT.   IVOGEFW61677

THE ECONOMIC ABSORPTION OF NAVAHO INDIAN MIGRANTS IN DENVER, COLORADO.   IWEPPRS65684

ECONOMIC FACTORS IN NAVAHO URBAN RELOCATION.   IWEPPRS65685

JICARILLA APACHE POLITICAL AND ECONOMIC STRUCTURES.   IWILSHC64235

PLANNING CONSTRUCTIVE ECONOMIC OPPORTUNITIES FOR THE JEWISH AGED.   JBARSIX59700

ON THE ECONOMIC SCENE.   JDAVIHX58717

ECONOMIC STRUCTURE AND THE LIFE OF THE JEWS.   JKUZNSX60738

JEWISH ECONOMIC PROSPECTS IN 1965.   JPUCKWX65750

COORDINATED PLANNING FOR ECONOMIC OPPORTUNTIES FOR JEWISH AGED.   JRABIDX59751

ECONOMIC, SOCIAL AND DEMOGRAPHIC CHARACTERISTICS OF SPANISH-AMERICAN WAGE WORKERS ON US FARMS. MFRIERE63394

ECONOMIC BASE STUDY OF SAN-ANTONIO AND TWENTY-SEVEN COUNTY AREAS. /TEXAS/   MSANACP64476

A REVIEW OF THE ECONOMIC AND CULTURAL PROBLEMS OF WICHITA, KANSAS.   NBANNWM65051

ECONOMIC FORCES SERVING THE ENDS OF THE NEGRO PROTEST. /UNEMPLOYMENT/   NBATCAB65059

ECONOMIC DISCRIMINATION AND NEGRO INCREASES.   NBLALHM56083

ECCNOMIC   (CONTINUATION)
    THE RELATICNSHIP OF JUVENILE-DELINQUENCY, RACE, AND ECONOMIC STATUS.   NBLUEJT48097

    ECONOMIC TRENDS IN THE NEGRO MARKET. /ECONOMIC-STATUS/   NBRIMAF64891

    CESEGREGATION ANC THE ECONOMIC FUTURE OF THE NEGRO MIDDLE-CLASS.   NBRIMAF65890

    ECONOMIC PROGRESS IN BLACK AND WHITE.   NBRIMAF66114

    THE ULTIMATE CONQUEST OF NEGRO ECONOMIC INEQUALITY.   NCALLEX64175

    SOCIAL AND ECONOMIC IMPLICATIONS OF INTEGRATING IN THE PUBLIC SCHOOLS.   NCLARKB65213

    THE SOURCES OF ECONOMIC GROWTH IN THE UNITED-STATES AND THE ALTERNATIVE BEFORE US.   /LABOR-FORCE
    ECGNOMY/   NDENIEF62262

    THE NEGRO FAMILY-S SEARCH FOR ECONOMIC SECURITY.   NDOUGJH64285

    THE SOCIAL AND ECONOMIC STATLS OF THE NEGRO IN THE UNITED STATES.   NDRAKSC65289

    CERTAIN ASPECTS OF THE ECONOMIC DEVELOPMENT OF THE AMERICAN NEGRO 1864-1960.   NDUMOAL45303

    RECENT SOUTHERN ECONOMIC DEVELOPMENT.   NDUNNES62308

    SOUTHERN ECONOMIC DEVELOPMENT AS REVEALED BY THE CHANGING STRUCTURE OF EMPLOYMENT.   NDUNNES62309

    THE CHANGING ECONOMIC STATUS OF THE MISSISSIPPI NEGRO.   NEATHBJ64314

    AN ECONOMIC AND SOCIAL PROFILE OF THE NEGRO AMERICAN.   NFEINRX65347

    THE DECADE OF HOPE. /CIVIL-RIGHTS ECONOMIC/   NFORECX51371

    ECONOMIC ADVANCES OF THE AMERICAN NEGRO.   NGERSGX65082

    THE NEGRO AND ECONOMIC OPPORTUNITY.   NGRANLB41443

    THE ECONOMIC IMBALANCE. AN INQUIRY INTO THE ECONOMIC-STATUS OF NEGROES IN THE UNITED STATES, 1935-1960,
    WITH IMPLICATIONS FOR NEGRO EDUCATION.   NHENDVW60512

    ECONOMIC DIMENSICNS IN RACE-RELATIONS.   NHENDVW61511

    ECONOMIC OPPORTUNITY AND NEGRO EDUCATION.   NHENDVW62513

    ECONOMIC DIMENSIONS. /SOUTH INCOME TECHNOLOGY/   NHENDVW63514

    PLANNING THE END OF THE AMERICAN GHETTO. A PROGRAM OF ECONOMIC DEVELOPMENT FOR EQUAL-RIGHTS.   NHILLHX66538

    A MANAGEMENT PERSPECTIVE TOWARD NEGRO ECONOMIC PRESSURES.   NHOFFHX65558

    THE NEGRO-S NEW ECONOMIC LIFE.   NHUGHEJ56583

    A HISTCRICAL REVIEW OF THE IMPACT OF SOCIAL AND ECONOMIC STRUCTURE ON NEGRO CULTURE AND HOW IT INFLUENCES
    FAMILY LIVING.   NJACKJX64596

    SUMMARY OF A SURVEY OF SOCIAL AND ECONOMIC CCNDITIONS IN MORRIS COUNTY NEW-JERSEY AS THEY AFFECT THE
    NEGRO.   NKERNJH57645

    ECONOMIC STATUS OF NONWHITE WORKERS, 1955-62.   NKESSMA63019

    ECONOMIC DEPRIVATION AND EXTREMISM. A STUDY OF UNEMPLOYED NEGRCES.   NLEGGJC61680

    ECONOMIC INSECURITY AND WORKING-CLASS CONSCICUSNESS.   NLEGGJC64677

    ECONOMIC CRISIS AND EXPECTATIONS OF VIOLENCE. A STUDY OF UNEMPLOYED NEGROES .   NLEGGJC64679

    AN ECONOMIC ANALYSIS OF SPECIFIED INCORPORATED AND UNINCORPORATED FARMERS COOPERATIVE ASSOCIATIONS
    OPERATED BY NEGRC FARMERS IN ALABAMA.   NLIGHMB53340

    LIFETIME INCOME AND ECONOMIC GROWTH.   NMILLHP65782

    ECONOMIC INEQUALITY.   NMILLSM65789

    RACE, ECONOMIC ATTITUDES, AND BEHAVIOR.   NMORGJX62850

    EMPLOYMENT ON MERIT. THE CONTINUING CHALLENGE TO BUSINESS, NEGRO-S ECONOMIC LOT.   NMORRJJ57854

    A SURVEY OF THE ECONOMIC AND CULTURAL CONDITIONS OF THE NEGRO POPULATION OF LOUISVILLE, KENTUCKY AND A
    REVIEW OF THE PROGRAM AND ACTIVITIES OF THE LOUISVILLE URBAN-LEAGUE. JANUARY-FEBRUARY, 1948.   NNATLUL48903

    ECONOMIC AND SOCIAL STATUS OF THE NEGRO IN THE UNITED STATES.   NNATLUL62083

    ECONOMIC AND SOCIAL STATUS OF THE NEGRO IN THE UNITED STATES.   NORSHMX61961

    NEGROES IN THE UNITED STATES. THEIR EMPLOYMENT AND ECONOMIC STATUS.   NRINGHH53061

    THE INFLUENCE OF TUSKEGEE-INSTITUTE ON THE HEALTH, ECUCATIONAL, ECONOMIC, AND POLITICAL ASPECTS OF THE
    NEGRC POPULATION OF MACON COUNTY, ALABAMA.   NSHIEAR51342

    ECONOMIC VALUE OF THE NEGRO TO THE SOUTH. PAST, PRESENT, AND POTENTIAL.   NSOUTRC45158

    DEMCGRAPHIC AND ECONOMIC CHANGE IN THE SOUTH, 1940-1960.   NSPENJJ63716

    ECONOMIC STRUCTURE OF THE HARLEM COMMUNITY. /NEW-YORK/   NSTEVHR64177

    CN IMPROVING THE ECONOMIC STATUS OF THE NEGRO.   NTOBIJX65206

    ECONOMIC AND SOCIAL CONSEQUENCES OF RACIAL DISCRIMINATORY PRACTICES.   NUNITNX63224

    THE NEGRO IN THE WEST. SOME FACTS RELATING TO SOCIAL AND ECONOMIC CONDITIONS. NO 1. THE NEGRO WORKER.   NUSDLABND256

    THE ECONOMIC SITUATION OF NEGROES IN THE UNITED STATES.   NUSDLAB62243

    THE NEGROES IN THE UNITED STATES. THEIR ECONOMIC AND SOCIAL SITUATION.   NUSDLAB66257

    EMPLOYMENT AND THE ECONOMIC STATUS OF NEGROES IN THE UNITED STATES.   NUSSENA52333

    EMPLOYMENT AND ECONOMIC STATUS OF NEGROES IN THE US.   NUSSENA54275

    SOCIAL AND ECONOMIC IMPLICATIONS OF MIGRATION FOR THE NEGRO IN THE PRESENT SOCIAL ORDER.   NVALIPX42261

ECONOMIC   (CONTINUATION)
STUDY OF ECONOMIC AND CULTURAL ACTIVITIES IN THE WARREN AREA AS THEY RELATE TO MINORITY PEOPLE. /OHIO/   NWARRUL64986

NEGRO ENTREPRENEURSHIP IN SOUTHERN ECONOMIC DEVELOPMENT.   NYOUNHB64346

KINSHIP AS A FACTOR AFFECTING CANTONESE ECONOMIC ADAPTATION IN THE UNITED STATES.   OBARNML66698

CALIFORNIA-S FRUIT AND VEGETABLE CANNING INDUSTRY. AN ECONOMIC STUDY.   OBENJMP61704

STATEMENT BEFORE CALIFORNIA LEGISLATURE ASSEMBLY, INTERIM SUBCOMMITTEE ON ECONOMIC OPPORTUNITY ON BEHALF
OF CHINATOWN-NORTH BEACH DISTRICT COUNCIL.   OWONGLJ64771

SOME ECONOMIC ASPECTS OF PUERTO-RICAN MIGRATION TO THE UNITED STATES.   PFLEIBM61804

SOME ECONOMIC ASPECTS OF PUERTO-RICAN MIGRATION TO THE UNITED STATES.   PFLEIBM63803

SOME ECONOMIC CONSEQUENCES OF THE PUERTO-RICAN MIGRATION INTO PERTH-AMBOY, 1949-1954. /NEW-JERSEY/   PGOLUFX55812

PUERTO-RICANS IN THE UNITED STATES. SOCIAL AND ECONOMIC DATA FOR PERSONS OF PUERTO-RICAN BIRTH AND
PARENTAGE. /DEMOGRAPHY/   PUSBURC63182

THE ECONOMIC AND SOCIAL ADJUSTMENT OF LOW-INCOME FEMALE-HEADED FAMILIES.   WBERNSE65458

MARRIED WOMEN IN THE LABOR-FORCE -- AN ECONOMIC ANALYSIS.   WCAINGG66672

THE WORKING WIFE AND HER FAMILY-S ECONOMIC POSITION.   WCARRMS62681

FEMALE LABOR-FORCE PARTICIPATION AND ECONOMIC DEVELOPMENT.   WHABESX58811

ECONOMIC ROLE OF WOMEN 45-65. /WORK-WOMAN-ROLE/   WKYRKHX56921

NURSING-S ECONOMIC PLIGHT. /ECONOMIC-STATUS/   WMOSEEX65000

ROLE OF WOMEN IN AMERICAN ECONOMIC LIFE.   WNORRLW56036

REALITIES. EDUCATIONAL, ECONOMIC, LEGAL AND PERSONAL NEEDS OF CAREER WOMEN.   WPARKRX66049

ECONOMIC-GROWTH
EDUCATION, MANPOWER AND ECONOMIC-GROWTH.   GHARBFH64741

ECONOMIC-OPPORTUNITY
THE CONCEPT OF POVERTY. /ECONOMIC-OPPORTUNITY/   GUSCHAC65186

ECONOMIC-OPPORTUNITY-ACT OF 1964.   GUSSENA64348

PROCEEDINGS OF THE 50TH ANNIVERSARY OBSERVANCE OF THE AMERICAN JEWISH COMMITTEE. APRIL 10-14, 1957. THE
PURSUIT OF EQUALITY AT HOME AND ABROAD. /ECONOMIC-OPPORTUNITY/   JAMERJC58692

WHAT THE ECONOMIC-OPPORTUNITY-ACT MEANS TO THE NEGRO.   NWOLFDP65337

ECONOMIC-STATUS
RURAL INDUSTRIALIZATION IN A LOUISIANA COMMUNITY. /ECONOMIC-STATUS OCCUPATIONS/   GBERTAL59393

CHARACTERISTICS OF THE POPULATION OF HIRED FARMWORKER HOUSEHOLDS. /ECONOMIC-STATUS/   GBOWLGK65424

THE HIRED FARM WORKING FORCE OF 1963 WITH SUPPLEMENTARY DATA FOR 1962. /ECONOMIC-STATUS/   GBOWLGK65432

THE HIRED FARM WORKING FORCE OF 1958. /ECONOMIC-STATUS/   GCOWHJD59430

URBAN AND RURAL LEVELS OF LIVING. 1960. /ECONOMIC-STATUS/   GCOWHJD65425

THE HIRED FARM WORKING FORCE OF 1960. /ECONOMIC-STATUS/   GFRIERE62431

DEVELOPMENT OF TRAINING INCENTIVES FOR THE YOUTH OF MINORITY-GROUPS. /ECONOMIC-STATUS/   GGRANLB57979

ECONOMIC-STATUS OF NON-WHITE WORKERS, 1955-1962. /OCCUPATIONAL-DISTRIBUTION/   GKESSMA63848

MIGRANTS. /ECONOMIC-STATUS/   GKURTAX60866

MINORITY-GROUPS AND ECONOMIC-STATUS IN NEW-YORK STATE.   GLANGGE59884

THE HIRED FARM WORKING FORCE OF 1956. /ECONOMIC-STATUS/   GMAITST58428

THE HIRED FARM WORKING FORCE OF 1957. /ECONOMIC-STATUS/   GMAITST59429

SENIOR CITIZENS AND HOW THEY LIVE. AN ANALYSIS OF 1960 CENSUS DATA. PART II. THE AGING NONWHITE AND HIS
HOUSING. /ECONOMIC-STATUS/   GUSHHFX63321

AMERICAN-INDIANS. NEGLECTED MINORITY. /ECONOMIC-STATUS/   IDENNLB66547

THE RELATIONSHIP OF THE SOCIAL-STRUCTURE OF AN INDIAN COMMUNITY TO ADULT AND JUVENILE-DELINQUENCY.
/POVERTY ECONOMIC-STATUS/   IMINNMS63218

CULTURAL AND ECONOMIC-STATUS OF THE SIOUX PEOPLE.   IUSDINT64645

POVERTY. COMMUNITY AND POWER. /ECONOMIC-STATUS/   IWARRCX65668

A COMPARISON OF MAJOR UNITED STATES RELIGIOUS GROUPS. /ECONOMIC-STATUS/   JLAZRBX61033

JEWS IN AND OUT OF NEW-YORK CITY. /ECONOMIC-STATUS/   JLAZRBX61034

ECONOMIC-STATUS.   JREICNX64752

DIFFERENTIALS IN THE INCIDENCE OF POVERTY IN TEXAS. /ECONOMIC-STATUS/   MUPHAWK66533

IN THE MIDST OF PLENTY. THE POOR IN AMERICA. /ECONOMIC-STATUS/   NBAGDBH64877

THE NEGRO MATRIARCHY. /WOMEN ECONOMIC-STATUS/   NBATTMX65313

THE FRENCH AND THE NON-FRENCH IN LOUISIANA. A STUDY OF THE RELEVANCE OF ETHNIC FACTORS IN RURAL
DEVELOPMENT. /ECONOMIC-STATUS/   NBERTAL65394

ECONOMIC TRENDS IN THE NEGRO MARKET. /ECONOMIC-STATUS/   NBRIMAF64891

NON-SEGREGATION, OR QUALITY IN SCHOOLS OF THE DEEP SOUTH. /ECONOMIC-STATUS/   NBRITNX54892

GRADUATE AND PROFESSIONAL EDUCATION IN NEGRO INSTITUTIONS. /ECONOMIC-STATUS/   NBROWAX58893

THE ECONOMIC-STATUS OF NEGROES IN THE SAN-FRANCISCO OAKLAND BAY AREA. A REPORT BASED ON THE 1960 CENSUS

ECONOMIC-STATUS   (CONTINUATION)
    OF POPULATION. /CALIFORNIA/   NCALFES63172

    ON DESEGREGATION AND MATTERS SOCIOLOGICAL. /ECONOMIC-STATUS/   NCAMPEQ61909

    NIGHT COMES TO THE CUMBERLANDS. /ECONOMIC-STATUS/   NCAUDHM62911

    THE NEGRO MIDDLE CLASS IS RIGHT IN THE MIDDLE. /ECONOMIC-STATUS/   NCORDDX66030

    THE NEGRO AMERICAN. /EMPLOYMENT INCOME ECONOMIC-STATUS/   NDAEDXX65246

    GOALS IN THE WAR ON POVERTY. /ECONOMIC-STATUS/   NECKSOX66957

    THE NEGRO MIGRATION. /ECONOMIC-STATUS/   NGRIEGXND982

    EQUALITY IN AMERICA. /ECONOMIC-STATUS/   NGRIMAP64983

    THE ECONOMIC IMBALANCE. AN INQUIRY INTO THE ECONOMIC-STATUS OF NEGROES IN THE UNITED STATES, 1935-1960,
    WITH IMPLICATIONS FOR NEGRO EDUCATION.   NHENDVW60512

    THE ECONOMIC-STATUS OF NEGROES. IN THE NATION AND IN THE SOUTH.   NHENDVW63515

    NEGRO MINORITY. /ECONOMIC-STATUS/   NJOHNCS42550

    INTO THE MAINSTREAM. /RACE-RELATIONS SOUTH ECONOMIC-STATUS/   NJOHNCS47007

    CHILD REARING AMONG LOW-INCOME FAMILIES. /ECONOMIC-STATUS/   NLEWIHX61040

    RECENT TRENDS IN THE ECONOMIC-STATUS OF NEGROES.   NMILLHP63785

    ECONOMIC-STATUS OF THE NEGRO.   NNEWMDKND957

    TRENDS IN THE ECONOMIC-STATUS OF THE NEGRO PEOPLE. /OCCUPATIONAL-PATTERNS/   NPERLVX52983

    THE BLACK MAN-S BURDEN. /DISCRIMINATION ECONOMIC-STATUS/   NREDDJS43546

    THE QUEST FOR IDENTITY AND STATUS. FACETS OF THE DESEGREGATION PROCESS IN THE UPPER MIDWEST.
    /ECONOMIC-STATUS/   NTILLJA61161

    IMPACT OF OFFICE AUTOMATION IN THE INTERNAL REVENUE SERVICE. A STUDY OF THE MANPOWER IMPLICATIONS DURING
    THE FIRST STAGES OF THE CHANGEOVER. /ECONOMIC-STATUS/   NUSDLAB63198

    BIBLIOGRAPHY ON THE ECONOMIC-STATUS OF THE NEGRO.   NUSDLAB65254

    PROFESSIONAL STANDARDS AND ECONOMIC-STATUS OF NURSES IN THE UNITED STATES.   WKRUGDH60917

    NURSING-S ECONOMIC PLIGHT. /ECONOMIC-STATUS/   WMOSEEX65000

    NSA-S PROFESSIONAL STATUS SURVEY, 1964. /ECONOMIC-STATUS/   WNATLSA65023

    THE EVOLVING LOW-INCOME PROBLEM IN AGRICULTURE. /ECONOMIC-STATUS/   WWELCFJ60227

ECONOMIC-TRENDS
    ECONOMIC-TRENDS IN EXTENSION WORK WITH NEGRO FARMERS IN ALABAMA, 1936-1948.   GGAINRL48341

ECONOMICAL
    AN ECONOMICAL AND HISTORICAL ANALYSIS OF THE CAUSES OF VARIATION AMONG NORTHERN STANDARD METROPOLITAN
    AREAS IN PRODUCTIVITY OF NEGRO MEN IN 1949.   NBATCAB61060

ECONOMICALLY
    FAMILY COMPOSITION AND CHARACTERISTICS OF AN ECONOMICALLY DEPRIVED CROSS-CULTURAL ROCKY-MOUNTAIN AREA.   MANDRWH66359

ECONOMICS
    THE ECONOMICS OF POVERTY.   GBATCAB66751

    THE ECONOMICS OF DISCRIMINATION.   GBECKGS57429

    ECONOMICS OF LABOR-RELATIONS. /EQUAL-OPPORTUNITY/   GBLOOGF65885

    THE ECONOMICS OF AUTOMATION.   GBRONYX57921

    ECONOMICS AND THE CIVIL-RIGHTS CRISIS.   GDERNTX64947

    INTRODUCTION TO ECONOMICS OF GROWTH, UNEMPLOYMENT, AND INFLATION.   GHERMHX64938

    THE ECONOMICS OF DISCRIMINATION.   GKRUEAO63862

    MEN WITHOUT WORK, THE ECONOMICS OF UNEMPLOYMENT.   GLEBESX65891

    ECONOMICS IN THE SOUTH.   GMITCBX57017

    THE ECONOMICS OF POVERTY. AN AMERICAN PARADOX.   GWEISBA65666

    ARIZONA RESERVATIONS ECONOMICS. SURVEY REPORT.   IARIZCI63528

    WAR ECONOMICS AND NEGRO LABOR.   NDAVIFG42260

    THE ECONOMICS OF SEGREGATION.   NDILLWP58275

    THE ECONOMICS OF RACISM.   NHARRMX61490

    ECONOMICS FOR THE MINORITY. /POVERTY/   NHARRMX65488

    THE ECONOMICS OF PROTEST.   NHARRMX67489

    PREJUDICE. SUPERSTITION, AND ECONOMICS.   NHOWERW56582

    THE ECONOMICS OF EQUALITY.   NKAHNTX64629

    THE ECONOMICS OF DISCRIMINATION.   NKRUEAO63666

    THE ECONOMICS OF THE NEGRO PROBLEM.   NSILBCE64137

    WHAT PRICE PREJUDICE -- ON THE ECONOMICS OF DISCRIMINATION.   NYOUNWM63356

    SOME CORRELATES OF HOMEMAKING VS CAREER PREFERENCE AMONG COLLEGE HOME ECONOMICS STUDENTS.
    /WORK-FAMILY-CONFLICT/   WVETTLX64257

ECONOMIST-S
    INVESTING IN POOR PEOPLE. AN ECONOMIST-S VIEW.   GSCHUTW65842

ECONOMY
    THE ECONOMY AND THE MINORITY POOR. /NEGRO AMERICAN-INDIAN MEXICAN-AMERICAN PUERTO-RICAN/   CBATCAB66879

    SIGNIFICANT TRENDS IN THE NEW-YORK STATE ECONOMY, WITH SPECIAL REFERENCE TO MINORITY-GROUPS.
    /PUERTO-RICAN NEGRO/   CRUSSVR59482

    UNEMPLOYMENT IN A PROSPEROUS ECONOMY. A REPORT OF THE PRINCETON-MANPOWER-SYMPOSIUM.   GBOWEWG65749

    UNEMPLOYMENT AND AMERICAN ECONOMY.   GGORDRA64526

    LONG-TERM MANPOWER PROJECTIONS. PROCEEDINGS OF A CONFERENCE CONDUCTED BY THE RESEARCH PROGRAM ON
    UNEMPLOYMENT AND THE AMERICAN ECONOMY.   GGORDRA65613

    THE ROLE OF THE UNITED STATES EMPLOYMENT-SERVICE IN A CHANGING ECONOMY.   GHABEWX64649

    MANPOWER POLICY, POVERTY AND THE STATE OF THE ECONOMY.   GKERSJA66733

    WEALTH AND POWER IN AMERICA. /ECONOMY POVERTY/   GKOLKGX62690

    THE MIGRATORY WORKER IN THE FARM ECONOMY.   GLEVILA61357

    THE COMPUTER AND THE AMERICAN ECONOMY.   GMANGGL66526

    EFFECTS ON THE ECONOMY. /EEC/   GMILLGW64986

    TECHNOLOGY AND THE AMERICAN ECONOMY.   GNATLCT66602

    THE STRATEGY AND POLITICAL ECONOMY OF THE WAR-AGAINST-POVERTY.   GORNAOA64958

    HUMAN RESOURCES IN THE URBAN ECONOMY. PART II -- THE LABOR FORCE PERFORMANCE OF MINORITY-GROUPS.   GPERLMX63169

    RURAL PEOPLE IN THE AMERICAN ECONOMY.   GUSDAGR66507

    ECONOMY AND CONDITIONS OF THE FORT-HALL INDIAN RESERVATION.   INYBRNX64603

    MODERN KLAMATH. DEMOGRAPHY AND ECONOMY.   ISTERTX65625

    THE FOX PROJECT. /ECONOMY/   ITAXXSX58157

    A HISTORY OF THE INTERRELATIONSHIPS BETWEEN IMPORTED MEXICAN LABOR, DOMESTIC MIGRANTS, AND THE TEXAS
    AGRICULTURAL ECONOMY.   MGRAVRP60405

    THE NEGRO IN THE NATIONAL ECONOMY.   NBRIMAF66115

    A MORE PRODUCTIVE ROLE FOR THE NEGRO IN THE SOUTH-S ECONOMY.   NCHALWE64912

    CASTE, ECONOMY, AND VIOLENCE.   NDAVIAX45938

    THE SOURCES OF ECONOMIC GROWTH IN THE UNITED-STATES AND THE ALTERNATIVE BEFORE US. /LABOR-FORCE
    ECONOMY/   NDENIEF62262

    A CENTURY OF CHANGE. NEGROES IN THE US ECONOMY, 1860-1960. /OCCUPATIONAL-PATTERNS/   NHAYEMX62506

    THE NEGRO IN OUR ECONOMY.   NHUGHWH48587

    THE EFFECT OF THE WAR ECONOMY ON THE SOUTH. HOW MOBILIZATION WILL AFFECT POSITION OF THE NEGRO.   NJACKJX51595

    THE PLACE OF THE NEGRO FARMER IN THE CHANGING ECONOMY OF THE COTTON SOUTH.   NNEALEE50905

    THE PRICE WE PAY FOR DISCRIMINATION. /SOUTH ECONOMY/   NPATTBX64979

    UNEMPLOYMENT AND THE AMERICAN ECONOMY. RESEARCH PROGRAM ON UNEMPLOYMENT.   NROSSAM63259

    THE NEGRO IN THE AMERICAN ECONOMY.   NROSSAM67082

    THE JOB HUNT. JOB SEEKING BEHAVIOR OF UNEMPLOYED WORKERS IN A LOCAL ECONOMY.   NSHEPHL66128

    THE NEGRO IN THE ST-LOUIS ECONOMY. /MISSOURI/   NSOBEIX54178

    THE NEW REVOLUTION IN THE COTTON ECONOMY.   NSTREJH57184

    CHALLENGES TO DEMOCRACY. /ECONOMY/   NWEAVRC63298

    THE PHYSICAL GEOGRAPHY OF THE PALOUSE REGION, WASHINGTON AND IDAHO, AND ITS RELATION TO THE AGRICULTURAL
    ECONOMY.   OSHROCR58762

    DAY CARE IN A CHANGING ECONOMY. /EMPLOYMENT-CONDITIONS/   WKEYSMD64894

    CONFERENCE ON WOMEN IN THE UPPER PENINSULA ECONOMY. REPORT. /MICHIGAN/   WMICDLA64976

EDUCABILITY
    EDUCABILITY AND REHABILITATION. THE FUTURE OF THE WELFARE CLASS.   NHESSRD64523

EDUCATE
    EDUCATE THE BLACK ONE TOO.   NBLAIGE66081

    DUAL PARTS OF DESEGREGATION. LEGISLATION TO EDUCATE AND TRAIN NEGROES FOR BETTER JOBS.   NDUSCJX63311

EDUCATED
    THE ROLE OUTLOOK OF EDUCATED WOMEN. /ASPIRATIONS/   WANGRSS64484

    A HUGE WASTE. EDUCATED WOMANPOWER.   WBUNTMI61900

    THE POST-PARENTAL PHASE IN THE LIFE CYCLE OF 50 COLLEGE EDUCATED WOMEN. /WORK-FAMILY-CONFLICT/   WDAVIIX60717

    EDUCATED WOMEN -- A MIDCENTURY EVALUATION. /WORK-WOMAN-ROLE/   WDOLAEF56734

    THE ROLE OF THE EDUCATED WOMAN. AN EMPIRICAL STUDY OF THE ATTITUDES OF A GROUP OF COLLEGE WOMEN.
    /WORK-WOMAN-ROLE/   WFREEMB65770

    LIFE STYLES OF EDUCATED WOMEN. /WORK-FAMILY-CONFLICT/   WGINZEX66785

    THE ROLE OF THE EDUCATED WOMAN. /WORK-WOMAN-ROLE/   WJONECX64009

    PERCEPTIONS OF ROLE CONFLICTS AND SELF CONFLICTS AMONG CAREER AND NON-CAREER COLLEGE EDUCATED WOMEN.
    /WORK-FAMILY-CONFLICT/   WMORGDD62996

    WHAT EDUCATED WOMEN WANT. /ASPIRATIONS/   WNEWSXX66029

EDUCATED   (CONTINUATION)
    NEEDS AND OPPORTUNITIES IN OUR SOCIETY FOR THE **EDUCATED** WOMAN.   WPETEEX63054

    THE NEXT STEP -- A GUIDE TO PART-TIME OPPORTUNITIES IN GREATER BOSTON FOR THE **EDUCATED** WOMAN.
      /MASSACHUSETTS/   WWHITMS64266

EDUCATING
    EDUCATING MIGRANT CHILDREN IN COLORADO.   MCOLOSD61384

    EDUCATING THE AMERICAN NEGRO.   NCLIFVA66227

    ON **EDUCATING** WOMEN HIGHLY. /WORK-WOMEN-ROLE/   WCORMML67706

    WHAT-S THE USE OF **EDUCATING** WOMEN. /WORK-WOMAN-ROLE/   WEDDYED63747

    NEEDED. UNIQUE PATTERNS FOR **EDUCATING** WOMEN. /WORK-WOMEN-ROLE/   WIRISLD62874

    EDUCATING TOMORROW-S WOMEN.   WSENDVL64110

EDUCATION
    SPANISH-SPEAKING CHILDREN. /MEXICAN-AMERICAN PUERTO-RICAN **EDUCATION**/   CBURMJH60287

    THE NATION-S CHILDREN. VOL I. THE FAMILY AND SOCIAL-CHANGE. VOL II. DEVELOPMENT AND **EDUCATION**. VOL III.
    PROBLEMS AND PROSPECTS. /NEGRO PUERTO-RICAN MEXICAN-AMERICAN WOMEN/   CGINZEX60720

    THE URBAN ADJUSTMENT OF IMMIGRANTS. THE RELATIONSHIP OF **EDUCATION** TO OCCUPATIONAL AND TOTAL FAMILY
    INCOME. /NEGRO MEXICAN-AMERICAN/   CSHANLW63122

    EMPLOYMENT AND PERSONAL CHARACTERISTICS. EMPLOYMENT BY AGE, RACE, NATIVITY, **EDUCATION**, MARITAL-STATUS,
    HOUSEHOLD RELATIONSHIPS, ETC. /DEMOGRAPHY/   CUSBURC53372

    NONWHITE POPULATION BY RACE. NEGROES, INDIANS, JAPANESE, CHINESE, FILIPINOS. BY AGE, SEX, MARITAL-STATUS,
    EDUCATION. EMPLOYMENT-STATUS, OCCUPATIONAL-STATUS, INCOME, ETC. /DEMOGRAPHY/   CUSBURC53378

    NONWHITE POPULATION BY RACE. NEGROES, INDIANS, JAPANESE,CHINESE, FILIPINOS. BY AGE, SEX,
    MARITAL-STATUS,**EDUCATION**, EMPLOYMENT-STATUS, OCCUPATIONAL-STATUS, INCOME, ETC. /DEMOGRAPHY/   CUSBURC63176

    OCCUPATIONAL CHARACTERISTICS. DATA ON AGE, RACE, **EDUCATION**, WORK EXPERIENCE, INCOME; ETC. FOR WORKERS IN
    EACH OCCUPATION.   CUSBURC63177

    OCCUPATIONS BY EARNINGS AND **EDUCATION**. STATISTICS FOR MEN 18-64 YEARS OLD, BY COLOR, IN SELECTED
    OCCUPATIONS. /DEMOGRAPHY/   CUSBURC63178

    INCOME, **EDUCATION** AND UNEMPLOYMENT IN NEIGHBORHOODS. ATLANTA, GEORGIA. /DEMOGRAPHY/   CUSDLAB63451

    INCOME, **EDUCATION** AND UNEMPLOYMENT IN NEIGHBORHOODS. BALTIMORE, MARYLAND. /DEMOGRAPHY/   CUSDLAB63452

    INCOME, **EDUCATION** AND UNEMPLOYMENT IN NEIGHBORHOODS. BIRMINGHAM, ALABAMA. /DEMOGRAPHY/   CUSDLAB63453

    INCOME, **EDUCATION** AND UNEMPLOYMENT IN NEIGHBORHOODS. BOSTON, MASSACHUSETTS. /DEMOGRAPHY/   CUSDLAB63454

    INCOME, **EDUCATION** AND UNEMPLOYMENT IN NEIGHBORHOODS. BUFFALO, NEW-YORK. /DEMOGRAPHY/   CUSDLAB63455

    INCOME, **EDUCATION** AND UNEMPLOYMENT IN NEIGHBORHOODS. CHICAGO, ILLINOIS. /DEMOGRAPHY/   CUSDLAB63456

    INCOME, **EDUCATION** AND UNEMPLOYMENT IN NEIGHBORHOODS. CINCINNATI, OHIO. /DEMOGRAPHY/   CUSDLAB63457

    INCOME, **EDUCATION** AND UNEMPLOYMENT IN NEIGHBORHOODS. CLEVELAND, OHIO. /DEMOGRAPHY/   CUSDLAB63458

    INCOME, **EDUCATION** AND UNEMPLOYMENT IN NEIGHBORHOODS. DALLAS, TEXAS. /DEMOGRAPHY/   CUSDLAB63459

    INCOME, **EDUCATION** AND UNEMPLOYMENT IN NEIGHBORHOODS. DENVER, COLORADO. /DEMOGRAPHY/   CUSDLAB63460

    INCOME, **EDUCATION** AND UNEMPLOYMENT IN NEIGHBORHOODS. DETROIT, MICHIGAN. /DEMOGRAPHY/   CUSDLAB63461

    INCOME, **EDUCATION** AND UNEMPLOYMENT IN NEIGHBORHOODS. HOUSTON, TEXAS. /DEMOGRAPHY/   CUSDLAB63462

    INCOME, **EDUCATION** AND UNEMPLOYMENT IN NEIGHBORHOODS. INDIANAPOLIS, INDIANA. /DEMOGRAPHY/   CUSDLAB63463

    INCOME, **EDUCATION** AND UNEMPLOYMENT IN NEIGHBORHOODS. KANSAS-CITY, MISSOURI. /DEMOGRAPHY/   CUSDLAB63464

    INCOME, **EDUCATION** AND UNEMPLOYMENT IN NEIGHBORHOODS. MEMPHIS, TENNESSEE. /DEMOGRAPHY/   CUSDLAB63466

    INCOME, **EDUCATION** AND UNEMPLOYMENT IN NEIGHBORHOODS. MILWAUKEE, WISCONSIN. /DEMOGRAPHY/   CUSDLAB63467

    INCOME, **EDUCATION** AND UNEMPLOYMENT IN NEIGHBORHOODS. MINNEAPOLIS -- ST-PAUL, MINNESOTA. /DEMOGRAPHY/ CUSDLAB63468

    INCOME, **EDUCATION** AND UNEMPLOYMENT IN NEIGHBORHOODS. NEW-ORLEANS, LOUISIANA. /DEMOGRAPHY/   CUSDLAB63469

    INCOME, **EDUCATION** AND UNEMPLOYMENT IN NEIGHBORHOODS. NEWARK, NEW-JERSEY. /DEMOGRAPHY/   CUSDLAB63470

    INCOME, **EDUCATION** AND UNEMPLOYMENT IN NEIGHBORHOODS. NEW-YORK-CITY -- BROOKLYN. /DEMOGRAPHY/   CUSDLAB63471

    INCOME, **EDUCATION** AND UNEMPLOYMENT IN NEIGHBORHOODS. NEW-YORK-CITY -- THE BRONX. /DEMOGRAPHY/   CUSDLAB63472

    INCOME, **EDUCATION** AND UNEMPLOYMENT IN NEIGHBORHOODS. NEW-YORK-CITY -- MANHATTAN. /DEMOGRAPHY/   CUSDLAB63473

    INCOME, **EDUCATION** AND UNEMPLOYMENT IN NEIGHBORHOODS. NEW-YORK-CITY -- QUEENS. /DEMOGRAPHY/   CUSDLAB63474

    INCOME, **EDUCATION** AND UNEMPLOYMENT IN NEIGHBORHOODS. NEW-YORK-CITY -- STATEN-ISLAND. /DEMOGRAPHY/   CUSDLAB63475

    INCOME, **EDUCATION** AND UNEMPLOYMENT IN NEIGHBORHOODS. OAKLAND, CALIFORNIA. /DEMOGRAPHY/   CUSDLAB63476

    INCOME, **EDUCATION** AND UNEMPLOYMENT IN NEIGHBORHOODS. OKLAHOMA-CITY, OKLAHOMA. /DEMOGRAPHY/   CUSDLAB63477

    INCOME, **EDUCATION** AND UNEMPLOYMENT IN NEIGHBORHOODS. PHILADELPHIA, PENNSYLVANIA. /DEMOGRAPHY/   CUSDLAB63478

    INCOME, **EDUCATION** AND UNEMPLOYMENT IN NEIGHBORHOODS. PITTSBURGH, PENNSYLVANIA. /DEMOGRAPHY/   CUSDLAB63479

    INCOME, **EDUCATION** AND UNEMPLOYMENT IN NEIGHBORHOODS. PHOENIX, ARIZONA. /DEMOGRAPHY/   CUSDLAB63480

    INCOME, **EDUCATION** AND UNEMPLOYMENT IN NEIGHBORHOODS. ST-LOUIS, MISSOURI. /DEMOGRAPHY/   CUSDLAB63481

    INCOME, **EDUCATION** AND UNEMPLOYMENT IN NEIGHBORHOODS. SAN-ANTONIO, TEXAS. /DEMOGRAPHY/   CUSDLAB63482

    INCOME, **EDUCATION** AND UNEMPLOYMENT IN NEIGHBORHOODS. SAN-DIEGO, CALIFORNIA. /DEMOGRAPHY/   CUSDLAB63483

    INCOME, **EDUCATION** AND UNEMPLOYMENT IN NEIGHBORHOODS. SAN-FRANCISCO, CALIFORNIA. /DEMOGRAPHY/   CUSDLAB63484

INCOME, EDUCATION AND UNEMPLOYMENT IN NEIGHBORHOODS. SEATTLE, WASHINGTON. /DEMOGRAPHY/   CUSDLAB63485

INCOME, EDUCATION AND UNEMPLOYMENT IN NEIGHBORHOODS. TAMPA, ST-PETERSBURG FLORIDA. /DEMOGRAPHY/   CUSDLAB63486

INCOME, EDUCATION AND UNEMPLOYMENT IN NEIGHBORHOODS. WASHINGTON-DC. /DEMOGRAPHY/   CUSDLAB63487

INCOME, EDUCATION AND UNEMPLOYMENT IN NEIGHBORHOODS. LOS-ANGELES, CALIFORNIA. /DEMOGRAPHY/   CUSDLAB63565

AMBITIONS EDUCATION IMPROVEMENT PROJECT UNDER WAY IN SOUTH.   GAMERCE64370

EDUCATION OF THE DEPRIVED AND SEGREGATED.   GBANKSC65419

AN ASSESSMENT OF THE SUITABILITY OF THE FACETED STRUCTURE OF THE WRU EDUCATION THESAURUS AS A FRAMEWORK
FOR PREPARATION OF A THESAURUS OF EQUAL-EMPLOYMENT-OPPORTUNITY TERMS.   GBARHGC66162

RECENT POPULATION TRENDS IN THE UNITED STATES WITH EMPHASIS ON RURAL AREAS. /EDUCATION/   GBEALCL63426

HUMAN CAPITAL. A THEORETICAL AND EMPIRICAL ANALYSIS WITH SPECIAL REFERENCE TO EDUCATION.   GBECKGS64700

INEQUALITY OF OPPORTUNITY IN HIGHER EDUCATION. A STUDY OF MINORITY GROUP AND RELATED BARRIERS TO COLLEGE
ADMISSION.   GBERKDS48446

COUNSELING MINORITY-GROUP YOUTH. DEVELOPING THE EXPERIENCE OF EQUALITY THROUGH EDUCATION.   GBRIGWA62473

APPROACHING EQUALITY OF OPPORTUNITY IN HIGHER EDUCATION.   GBROWFJ55476

SOME PROBLEMS IN MINORITY-GROUP EDUCATION IN THE LOS-ANGELES PUBLIC SCHOOLS. /CALIFORNIA/   GBULLPX63489

EDUCATION OF THE MINORITY POOR -- THE KEY TO THE WAR-ON-POVERTY.   GCLARKB66915

RAISING LOW-INCOMES THROUGH IMPROVED EDUCATION.   GCOMIED65591

EDUCATION, SKILL LEVEL, AND EARNINGS OF THE HIRED FARM WORKING FORCE OF 1961.   GCOWHJD63420

THE RISING LEVELS OF EDUCATION AMONG YOUNG WORKERS.   GCOWHJD65933

POWER AS A DIMENSION OF EDUCATION.   GOODSDW62647

EDUCATION AND OCCUPATIONAL MOBILITY. A REGRESSION ANALYSIS.   GDUNCOD63652

MONEY BENEFITS OF EDUCATION BY SEX AND RACE IN NEW-YORK STATE, 1956.   GGREEWX61741

SELECTED STATE PROGRAMS IN MIGRANT EDUCATION.   GHANEGE64004

EDUCATION, MANPOWER AND ECONOMIC-GROWTH.   GHARBFH64741

ILLINOIS JOB SEEKERS SURVEY. EDUCATION, SKILLS, LENGTH OF UNEMPLOYMENT, AND PERSONAL CHARACTERISTICS. GILLIDI62004

THE ASSOCIATION OF INCOME AND EDUCATION FOR MALES, BY REGION, RACE, AND AGE.   GLASSRL65998

PROSPECTS FOR EDUCATION AND EMPLOYMENT.   GLEAGWVND890

COMMUNITY VALUES IN EDUCATION AND OCCUPATIONAL SELECTION. A STUDY OF YOUTH IN EMMITSBURG, MARYLAND.   GLEONRC64894

IMPLICATIONS OF THE ANTI-POVERTY PROGRAM FOR EDUCATION AND EMPLOYMENT.   GLEVILA65781

PROCEEDINGS OF CONFERENCE ON EDUCATION FOR OPPORTUNITY, OPPORTUNITY FOR EDUCATION.   GMICFEP61982

PROCEEDINGS OF CONFERENCE ON EDUCATION FOR OPPORTUNITY, OPPORTUNITY FOR EDUCATION.   GMICFEP61982

AN EXPERIMENT IN VOCATIONAL EDUCATION FOR CHILDREN OF MIGRATORY FARM WORKERS, JULY-AUGUST 1956.   GNATLCRND046

MANPOWER AND EDUCATION.   GNATLEA56047

EDUCATION AND THE DISADVANTAGED AMERICAN.   GNATLEA62126

EDUCATION IN DEPRESSED AREAS.   GPASSHA63724

REPORT OF THE SPECIAL COMMITTEE ON NONDISCRIMINATION OF THE BOARD OF PUBLIC EDUCATION, PHILADELPHIA.
/PENNSYLVANIA/   GPHILBE64172

THE INTERRELATIONSHIPS OF DISCRIMINATION IN EMPLOYMENT, IN EDUCATION, AND IN HOUSING.   GRAVIMJ61219

AUTOMATION, MANPOWER, AND EDUCATION.   GROSEJM66008

THE ECONOMIC VALUE OF EDUCATION.   GSCHUTW63895

EDUCATION AND INCOME. INEQUALITIES IN OUR PUBLIC SCHOOLS.   GSEXTPX61298

MIGRATORY FARM WORKERS IN THE ATLANTIC COAST STREAM, II. EDUCATION OF NEW-YORK WORKERS AND THEIR
CHILDREN, 1953 AND 1957.   GSHAREF60427

FAIR-EMPLOYMENT-PRACTICE IN NEW-YORK. LAW, EDUCATION GO HAND IN HAND.   GSULLJD50340

VOCATIONAL-TECHNICAL EDUCATION AND ECONOMIC SECURITY.   GSWANJC66155

THE DISADVANTAGED POOR. EDUCATION AND EMPLOYMENT.   GUSCHAC66187

SELECTED STATE PROGRAMS IN MIGRANT EDUCATION.   GUSDHEW63505

EDUCATION FOR A CHANGING WORLD OF WORK. /YOUTH/   GUSDHEW63834

EDUCATION AND TRAINING, THE BRIDGE BETWEEN MAN AND HIS WORK.   GUSDHEW65156

WHITE-NONWHITE DIFFERENTIALS IN HEALTH, EDUCATION, AND WELFARE.   GUSDHEW65435

THE YOUTH WE HAVEN-T SERVED. /EDUCATION TRAINING/   GUSDHEW66002

HEALTH, EDUCATION, AND WELFARE ASPECTS OF THE ECONOMIC REPORT OF THE PRESENT AND ANNUAL REPORT OF THE
COUNCIL OF ECONOMIC ADVISORS.   GUSDHEW66711

ANNUAL REPORT OF THE SECRETARY OF HEALTH, EDUCATION, AND WELFARE TO THE CONGRESS ON TRAINING ACTIVITIES
UNDER THE MANPOWER-DEVELOPMENT-AND-TRAINING-ACT, 1965.   GUSDHEW66978

YOUTH. THE NATION-S RICHEST RESOURCE. THEIR EDUCATION AND EMPLOYMENT NEEDS.   GUSINCC53514

AMERICAN INDIANS IN CALIFORNIA. POPULATION, EDUCATION, EMPLOYMENT, INCOME.   ICALDIR65541

EDUCATION   (CONTINUATION)
  DOORWAY TOWARD THE LIGHT. THE STORY OF THE SPECIAL NAVAJO EDUCATION PROGRAM.   ICOOMLM62646

  EDUCATION AMONG AMERICAN-INDIANS. INDIVIDUAL AND CULTURAL ASPECTS.   IHAVIRJ57574

  HIGHER EDUCATION OF SOUTHWESTERN INDIANS WITH REFERENCE TO SUCCESS AND FAILURE.   IMCGRGD62584

  RELOCATION RIDDLES. /MOBILITY EDUCATION/   ITAYLFX65560

  EDUCATION AMONG AMERICAN-INDIANS. INSTITUTIONAL ASPECTS.   ITHOMHX57630

  EDUCATION FOR THE COMING DECADES.   ITHOMHX61631

  STATISTICS CONCERNING INDIAN EDUCATION. FISCAL YEAR 1956.   IUSDINT56661

  YOU ASKED ABOUT THE NAVAJO. EDUCATION. HEALTH, AND ECONOMIC PROBLEMS OF THE NAVAJO.   IUSDINT57664

  FORMAL EDUCATION IN AN AMERICAN-INDIAN COMMUNITY.   IWAXXML64683

  OUR CHANGING ELITE COLLEGES. /EDUCATION/   JBLOOLX60705

  MEDICAL SCHOOL QUOTAS. /EDUCATION DISCRIMINATION/   JBRAVHX58707

  BARRIERS IN HIGHER EDUCATION.   JEPSTBR58718

  STATE LAWS AGAINST DISCRIMINATION IN EDUCATION.   JHARTPX58730

  THE BARRIO. /EDUCATION INCOME/   MARIARX66360

  A STUDY OF AMERICAN AND MEXICAN-AMERICAN CULTURE VALUES AND THEIR SIGNIFICANCE IN EDUCATION.   MCABRYA63373

  CALIFORNIANS OF SPANISH SURNAME. POPULATION, EMPLOYMENT, INCOME, EDUCATION.   MCALDIR64377

  REPORT BY MEXICAN-AMERICAN LEADERS. EDUCATION, EMPLOYMENT, ETC.   MCALDIR64379

  EDUCATION AND INCOME OF MEXICAN-AMERICANS IN THE SOUTHWEST.   MFOGEWX65393

  TEXAS MIGRANTS PROGRAM. /TRAINING EDUCATION/   MMACNBL67335

  MINORITY-GROUPS AND THEIR EDUCATION IN HAY-COUNTY, TEXAS.   MMEADBS59438

  SOME CHARACTERISTICS OF SPANISH-NAME TEXANS AND FOREIGN LATIN-AMERICANS IN TEXAS HIGHER EDUCATION. MRENNRR57462

  THE EDUCATION OF THE SPANISH-SPEAKING IN THE SOUTHWEST -- AN ANALYSIS OF THE 1960 CENSUS MATERIALS. MSAMOJX63469

  MATERIALS RELATING TO THE EDUCATION OF SPANISH-SPEAKING PEOPLE IN THE UNITED STATES, AN ANNOTATED
  BIBLIOGRAPHY.   MSANCGI59478

  PROCEEDINGS OF THE CONFERENCE ON EDUCATION FOR ADULT MIGRANT WORKERS. /TEXAS/   MTEXACM62498

  IMPLICATIONS OF CULTURAL VALUES IN EDUCATION.   MVALDBX64448

  CONTRASTS BETWEEN SPANISH FOLK AND ANGLO URBAN CULTURAL VALUES. /EDUCATION ASPIRATIONS/   MVALDBX64449

  NEGRO YOUTH AND EMPLOYMENT OPPORTUNITIES. /UNEMPLOYMENT EDUCATION/   NAMOSWE63021

  WASTED TALENT. /EDUCATION/   NBONDHM60888

  WORKING WITH STUDENTS INSIDE AND OUTSIDE THE CLASSROOM IN ADULT BASIC EDUCATION PROGRAMS.   NBRAZWF64285

  TRANSFORMATION OF THE NEGRO-AMERICAN. /EDUCATION EMPLOYMENT INCOME/   NBROOLX65123

  GRADUATE AND PROFESSIONAL EDUCATION IN NEGRO INSTITUTIONS. /ECONOMIC-STATUS/   NBROWAX58893

  THE NEGRO GRADUATE, 1950-1960. /COLLEGE EDUCATION/   NBROWAX60125

  A COMPARISON OF THE ACADEMIC ACHIEVEMENTS OF WHITE AND NEGRO HIGH SCHOOL GRADUATES. /EDUCATION/ NBULLHA50132

  A COMPARISON OF THE SOCIAL CHARACTERISTICS AND EDUCATIONAL ASPIRATIONS OF NORTHERN, LOWER-CLASS, NEGRO
  PARENTS WHO ACCEPTED AND DECLINED AN OPPORTUNITY FOR INTEGRATED EDUCATION FOR THEIR CHILDREN.   NCAGLLT66904

  NEGRO CALIFORNIANS. POPULATION, EMPLOYMENT, INCOME, EDUCATION.   NCALDIR63167

  EDUCATION OF NEGRO LEADERS. INFLUENCES AFFECTING GRADUATE AND PROFESSIONAL STUDIES.   NCALIAX49174

  NEW OPPORTUNITIES FOR NEGROES...IN EDUCATION...IN CAREERS.   NCHANTX63190

  GRADUATE EDUCATION, PUBLIC SERVICE, AND THE NEGRO.   NCIKIWI66207

  NEGRO EDUCATION IN AMERICA. ITS ADEQUACY, PROBLEMS AND NEEDS.   NCLIFVA62215

  THE NEGRO AND EDUCATION.   NCOHEEE63220

  EMPLOYMENT, EDUCATION AND MARRIAGE OF YOUNG NEGRO ADULTS.   NCOXXOC41934

  REASONS FOR BELATED EDUCATION. A STUDY OF THE PLIGHT OF THE OLDER NEGRO TEACHERS. /OCCUPATIONS/ NCUNNGE58244

  INTEGRATION IN PROFESSIONAL EDUCATION. THE STORY OF PERKINS, SOUTHERN METHODIST UNIVERSITY. /VOCATIONS/ NCUNNMX56579

  EDUCATION AND MARGINALITY. A STUDY OF THE NEGRO COLLEGE GRADUATE.   NCUTHMV49936

  A COMPARISON OF TUITION-AND-FEE CHARGES IN NEGRO INSTITUTIONS WITH CHARGES IN INSTITUTIONS OF THE
  SOUTHEAST AND OF THE NATION. 1962-1963. /EDUCATION/   NDAMILX64127

  ABC REPORT 1964. /COLLEGE EDUCATION/   NDARTCX64309

  THE PROGRESS OF THE NEGRO IN HIGHER EDUCATION. 1950-1960.   NDODDHH63278

  THE NEGRO IN DENTAL EDUCATION.   NDUMMC059302

  THE HIGHER EDUCATION OF NEGROES IN THE UNITED STATES.   NEELLWC55329

  THE SEARCH FOR NEGRO MEDICAL STUDENTS. /EDUCATION/   NFALLAG63343

  THE NEGRO POTENTIAL. /EMPLOYMENT INCOME EDUCATION/   NGINZEX56409

  SOME CHANGES IN THE RELATIVE STATUS OF AMERICAN NON-WHITES, 1940 TO 1960. /INCOME OCCUPATIONAL-STATUS
  EDUCATION/   NGLENND63421

PROBLEMS FOR ADULT EDUCATION RELATED TO ACQUIRING CAPABILITIES FOR WORK.   NGOLDFH63430

COMMUNITY FACTORS AFFECTING MOTIVATION AND ACHIEVEMENT IN A DECADE OF DECISION. /EDUCATION/   NGRANLB62441

CHANGING OCCUPATIONAL-STATUS OF NEGRO EDUCATION.   NHARENX62483

HIGHER EDUCATION FOR THE NEGRO.   NHARLBW65486

THE RIGHT TO KNOWLEDGE. /COLLEGE EDUCATION/   NHEALHX64306

THE ECONOMIC IMBALANCE. AN INQUIRY INTO THE ECONOMIC-STATUS OF NEGROES IN THE UNITED STATES, 1935-1960,
WITH IMPLICATIONS FOR NEGRO EDUCATION.   NHENDVW60512

ECONOMIC OPPORTUNITY AND NEGRO EDUCATION.   NHENDVW62513

THE NEGRO AND HIGHER EDUCATION.   NHOLLJX65305

INTELLECTUALLY SUPERIOR NEGRO YOUTH. THEIR PROBLEMS AND NEEDS. /EDUCATION/   NJENKMD50606

NEXT STEPS IN EDUCATION IN THE SOUTH.   NJOHNCS54614

NEGRO YOUTH IN THE SOUTH. /EDUCATION EMPLOYMENT/   NJONELW60010

EDUCATION AND CIVIL-RIGHTS IN 1965.   NJOURNE65625

STUDIES IN THE HIGHER EDUCATION OF NEGRO AMERICANS.   NJOURNE66627

NEGRO JOBS AND EDUCATION.   NKUEBJX63315

LEGAL EDUCATION. DESEGREGATION IN LAW SCHOOLS.   NLEFLRA57676

HIGHER EDUCATION FOR NEGROES. A TOUGH SITUATION.   NLEWIHX49692

YOU NEED TO SEE IT TO BELIEVE IT. REPORT OF THE 1963 SUMMER STUDY-SKILLS PROGRAMS. /COLLEGE EDUCATION/   NMARTWD63303

RACIAL DISCRIMINATION AND PRIVATE EDUCATION.   NMILLAS57069

PRIVATE BUSINESS AND EDUCATION IN THE SOUTH.   NMILLHH60780

INTELLIGENCE IN THE UNITED STATES. A SURVEY -- WITH CONCLUSIONS FOR MANPOWER UTILIZATION IN EDUCATION AND
EMPLOYMENT.   NMINEJB57796

EDUCATION AND RACE.   NNATLUL66888

AT WORK IN NORTH-CAROLINA TODAY. 48 CASE-REPORTS ON NORTH-CAROLINA NEGROES NOW EMPLOYED OR PREPARING
THEMSELVES FOR EMPLOYMENT...THEIR EDUCATION, JOB QUALIFICATIONS, AND CAREER ASPIRATIONS.   NNORTCGND933

NEGRO YOUTH -- EDUCATION, EMPLOYMENT, AND CIVIL-RIGHTS.   NPEARAX64980

NEGRO BUSINESS AND BUSINESS EDUCATION. THEIR PRESENT AND PROSPECTIVE DEVELOPMENT.   NPIERJA47998

GRADUATE EDUCATION OF NEGRO PSYCHOLOGISTS.   NRICHTW56057

NEGRO EDUCATION -- FOR WHAT.   NROBEGX61063

LIBRARY RESOURCES AND SERVICES IN WHITE AND NEGRO COLLEGES. /EDUCATION/   NSAMCTX65128

ON THE COST OF BEING A NEGRO. /INCOME EDUCATION/   NSIEGPM65146

DISCRIMINATION IN HIGHER EDUCATION.   NSOUTCD51166

DESEGREGATION IN HIGHER EDUCATION.   NSOUTRC63157

A BRIEF SURVEY OF HIGHER EDUCATION FOR NEGROES.   NSTOKMS64180

NOTES ON THE CONDITIONS OF NEGROES. /EDUCATION DISCRIMINATION/   NSTREGX45463

SOCIALIZATION. RACE AND THE AMERICAN HIGH SCHOOL. /EDUCATION/   NTENHWP65201

NEGRO JOB STATUS AND EDUCATION.   NTURNRH53213

A SELECTED LIST OF REFERENCES RELATING TO DISCRIMINATION AND SEGREGATION IN EDUCATION, 1949 TO JUNE 1955.   NTUSKIX55220

EQUAL PROTECTION OF THE LAWS IN PUBLIC HIGHER EDUCATION.   NUSCCMC60302

VOCATIONAL EDUCATION FOR NEGRO YOUTH IN TEXAS.   NUSDLAB49847

SECRETARY-S CONFERENCE WITH COLLEGE PRESIDENTS AND EXECUTIVES. /EDUCATION EMPLOYMENT/   NUSDLAB63301

FACULTY EDUCATION AND INCOME IN NEGRO AND WHITE COLLEGES.   NUSDLAB65819

SUMMARY OF RESEARCH DURING 1964 RELATED TO THE NEGRO AND NEGRO EDUCATION.   NWESTEX66315

SIGNIFICANT ACHIEVEMENTS OF NEGROES IN EDUCATION 1907-1947. /OCCUPATIONS/   NWHITMJ48249

THE VOCATIONAL GUIDANCE AND EDUCATION OF NEGROES. THE NEGRO AND THE BATTLE OF PRODUCTION.   NWILKOA42233

WHY JUAN CAN-T READ. /YOUTH EDUCATION/   PARNORX62778

WOMEN-S EDUCATION.   WAAUWEFND274

CONTINUING EDUCATION -- FOCUS ON COUNSELING AND TRAINING.   WAAUWFX65616

THE EDUCATION OF WOMEN -- INFORMATION AND RESEARCH NOTES.   WAMERCEND605

RESOURCES FOR THE EMPLOYMENT OF MATURE WOMEN AND/OR THEIR CONTINUING EDUCATION. A SELECTED BIBLIOGRAPHY
AND AIDS.   WBERNML66746

UNIVERSITY OF KANSAS-CITY PROJECT FOR CONTINUING EDUCATION OF WOMEN.   WBERRJX63640

CONTINUING EDUCATION OF WOMEN. NEEDS, ASPIRATIONS, AND PLANS.   WBERRJX63641

ATTITUDES TOWARD WOMEN COLLEGE TEACHERS IN INSTITUTIONS OF HIGHER EDUCATION ACCREDITED BY THE NORTH
CENTRAL ASSOCIATION.   WBERWHC62475

THE COLLEGE AND THE CONTINUING EDUCATION OF WOMEN.   WBLACGW63648

TESTIMONY. PUBLIC HEARING. WOMEN IN PUBLIC AND PRIVATE EDUCATION, CALIFORNIA. /FEP

EDUCATION   (CONTINUATION)
    EMPLOYMENT-CONDITIONS DISCRIMINATION MIGRANT-WORKERS/   WBLOCHX66649

    CONTINUING EDUCATION FOR WOMEN.   WBUNTMI61664

    EDUCATION AND MANPOWER.   WDAVIHX60941

    EDUCATION OF WOMEN -- SIGNS FOR THE FUTURE.   WDAVIOD57044

    FACTORS INFLUENCING WOMEN-S DECISIONS ABOUT HIGHER EDUCATION. /ASPIRATIONS/   WDAVIOD59716

    THE EDUCATION OF WOMEN -- SIGNS FOR THE FUTURE.   WDAVIOD59937

    EDUCATION AND A WOMAN-S LIFE. /WORK-WOMAN-ROLE/   WDENNLE63729

    HIGHER EDUCATION FOR WOMEN. TIME FOR REAPPRAISAL.   WDOOLAEF63952

    ADDRESS TO CONFERENCE ON EDUCATION AND JOB OPPORTUNITIES FOR WOMEN RETURNING TO THE LABOR-MARKET.   WDOUTAX62741

    RESEARCH REPORT. SURVEY OF CONTINUING EDUCATION PROGRAMS.   WFIELBX64762

    FANTASY, FACT AND THE FUTURE...A REVIEW OF THE STATUS OF WOMEN AND POSSIBLE IMPLICATIONS FOR WOMEN-S
    EDUCATION AND ROLE IN THE NEXT DECADE.   WFITZLE63963

    WOMEN AND HIGHER EDUCATION WITH SPECIAL REFERENCE TO THE UNIVERSITY OF WISCONSIN.   WFREDEB62768

    A TURNING TO TAKE NEXT -- ALTERNATIVE GOALS IN THE EDUCATION OF WOMEN. /WORK-WOMAN-ROLE/   WGOLDFH65792

    WHO GOES TO GRADUATE SCHOOL. /EDUCATION/   WGROPGL59805

    TECHNICAL EDUCATION IN THE JUNIOR COLLEGE.   WHARRNC64825

    A COMMENTARY ON THE MOTIVATION AND EDUCATION OF COLLEGE WOMEN. /ASPIRATIONS/   WHEISPX62837

    CHANGES IN SELECTED PERSONALITY CHARACTERISTICS AND PERSISTENCE IN THE CAREER CHOICES OF WOMEN ASSOCIATED
    WITH A FOUR YEAR COLLEGE EDUCATION AT ONE OF THE COLLEGES OF THE CITY UNIVERSITY OF NEW-YORK.
    /ASPIRATIONS/   WLEINMX64925

    VOCATIONAL EDUCATION AND FEDERAL POLICY.   WLEVISA63039

    A CONFERENCE TO ENLIST THE PARTICIPATION OF 50 INSTITUTIONS OF HIGHER EDUCATION IN SPECIFIC R AND D
    PROGRAMS TO PREPARE WOMEN FOR PRODUCTIVE EMPLOYMENT.   WLLOYBJ64937

    WOMEN-S STATUS -- WOMEN TODAY AND THEIR EDUCATION.   WLLOYEX56941

    WOMEN IN EDUCATION. /OCCUPATIONS/   WMASOVC62958

    PILOT PROJECTS FOR CONTINUING EDUCATION FOR WOMEN.   WMERRMH63972

    EDUCATION AND A WOMAN-S LIFE.   WMONSKJ63987

    A CENTURY OF HIGHER EDUCATION FOR AMERICAN WOMEN.   WNEWCMX59027

    WOMEN-S EDUCATION. FACTS, FINDINGS, AND APPARENT TRENDS.   WNEWCMX64028

    NEW-YORK WOMEN. A REPORT AND RECOMMENDATIONS FROM THE NEW-YORK GOVERNOR-S COMMITTEE ON THE EDUCATION AND
    EMPLOYMENT OF WOMEN.   WNEWYGW64799

    REPORT ON UNDERGRADUATE COUNSELING AND CONTINUING EDUCATION AND GUIDANCE FOR MATURE WOMAN.   WNICOHG64032

    THE IMPACT OF EDUCATION.   WPETEEX63053

    REPORT OF THE COMMITTEE ON EDUCATION. /EQUAL-OPPORTUNITY COUNSELING/   WPRESCO63066

    SEX AND EQUAL-OPPORTUNITY IN HIGHER EDUCATION.   WPUNKHH61071

    GRADUATE EDUCATION FOR WOMEN. THE RADCLIFFE PHD.   WRADCCX56072

    UNFINISHED BUSINESS. CONTINUING EDUCATION FOR WOMEN.   WRAUSEX61076

    SECOND CHANCE. NEW EDUCATION FOR WOMEN.   WRAUSEX62075

    SOME CONTINUITIES AND DISCONTINUITIES IN THE EDUCATION OF WOMEN. /WORK-FAMILY-CONFLICT/   WRIESDX56079

    WOMEN. THEIR ORBITS AND THEIR EDUCATION. /WORK-FAMILY-CONFLICT/   WRIESDX58080

    A STUDY OF WOMEN IN OFFICE MANAGEMENT POSITIONS WITH IMPLICATIONS FOR BUSINESS EDUCATION. /OCCUPATIONS/   WRUSHEM57096

    IS COLLEGE EDUCATION WASTED ON WOMEN.   WSANFNX57102

    UNIVERSITY OF MINNESOTA -- THE MINNESOTA PLAN. /EDUCATION/   WSCHLVX63103

    MINNESOTA PLAN FOR WOMEN-S CONTINUING EDUCATION. A PROGRESS REPORT.   WSENDVL61298

    THE CONTINUING LEARNER. /EDUCATION/   WSOLODX64128

    TODAY-S BUSINESS WOMAN. HER CHARACTERISTICS, HER NEED FOR FURTHER EDUCATION, HER FUTURE IN MANAGEMENT.
    /OCCUPATIONS/   WTHOMMH63152

    UNIVERSITY PROGRAMS OF CONTINUING EDUCATION FOR THE ADULT WOMAN.   WTINKAH64156

    ACCESS OF GIRLS AND WOMEN TO EDUCATION IN RURAL AREAS. A COMPARATIVE STUDY.   WUNESCO64166

    TRADE AND INDUSTRIAL EDUCATION FOR GIRLS AND WOMEN. A DIRECTORY OF TRAINING PROGRAMS.   WUSDHEW60175

    WHY CONTINUING EDUCATION PROGRAMS FOR WOMEN.   WUSDLAB63229

    THE FUROR OVER WOMEN-S EDUCATION.   WUSEERH63215

    REPORT ON PROGRESS IN 1965 ON THE STATUS OF WOMEN. /EDUCATION EMPLOYMENT-CONDITIONS/   WUSINCS65860

    CONTINUING EDUCATION FOR WOMEN.   WUVCHCF61686

    OPPORTUNITIES FOR WOMEN THROUGH EDUCATION.   WUVMICC65251

    THE EDUCATION OF WOMEN AND GIRLS IN A CHANGING SOCIETY. A SELECTED BIBLIOGRAPHY WITH ANNOTATIONS.   WWIGNTX65267

EDUCATION-S
    EDUCATION-S CHALLENGE TO AMERICAN NEGRO YOUTH.   NWOLFDP62336

EDUCATIONAL
THE CHILD-REARING ATTITUDES OF DISADVANTAGED NEGRO MOTHERS AND SOME EDUCATIONAL IMPLICATIONS.   CRADINX65031

EDUCATIONAL STATUS, COLLEGE PLANS, AND OCCUPATIONAL-STATUS OF FARM AND NONFARM YOUTHS. OCTOBER 1959.   GCOWHJD61427

EDUCATIONAL ASPECTS OF FAIR-EMPLOYMENT-PRACTICES-COMMISION LAWS.   GFLEMJG50687

SOME EDUCATIONAL IMPLICATIONS OF THE INFLUENCE OF REJECTION ON ASPIRATION LEVELS OF MINORITY-GROUP
CHILDREN.   GGOFFRM54366

EDUCATIONAL ATTAINMENT OF WORKERS, MARCH 1964.   GJOHNDF65784

EQUALITY OF EDUCATIONAL OPPORTUNITY.   GLIEBMX59902

COMPILATION OF LAWS AGAINST DISCRIMINATION, EMPLOYMENT, EDUCATIONAL INSTITUTIONS, PLACES OF PUBLIC
ACCOMODATION, PUBLIC HOUSING, PUBLICLY ASSISTED HOUSING, PRIVATE HOUSING. /MASSACHUSETTS/   GMASSCAND963

EDUCATIONAL IMPLICATIONS OF TECHNOLOGICAL-CHANGE.   GNATLCO66898

THE EDUCATIONAL STATUS OF A MINORITY. /MIGRANT-WORKERS/   GSAMOJX63501

SOCIAL-STATUS AND EDUCATIONAL AND OCCUPATIONAL ASPIRATION.   GSEWEWH57297

SOME NEW EVIDENCE ON EDUCATIONAL SELECTIVITY IN MIGRATION FROM THE SOUTH.   GSUVAEM65345

THE EFFECT OF RESIDENTIAL SEGREGATION UPON EDUCATIONAL ACHIEVEMENT AND ASPIRATIONS.   GWILSAB60567

ADDRESS AT THE CONVOCATION OF THE NAACP LEGAL DEFENSE AND EDUCATIONAL FUND. /LEGISLATION/   GWIRTWW66570

HEALTH PRACTICES AND EDUCATIONAL ASPIRATIONS AS INDICATORS OF ACCULTURATION AND SOCIAL-CLASS AMONG THE
EASTERN CHEROKEE. /NORTH-CAROLINA/   IKUPFHJ62216

ADL REPORTS ON SOCIAL, EMPLOYMENT, EDUCATIONAL AND HOUSING DISCRIMINATION.   JANTIDL57690

ON THE EDUCATIONAL SCENE.   JGALLBG58724

PROCEEDINGS OF EMPLOYMENT OPPORTUNITIES EDUCATIONAL CONFERENCE.   MCOUNMA62930

OCCUPATIONAL AND EDUCATIONAL LEVELS OF ASPIRATION OF MEXICAN-AMERICAN YOUTH.   MDEHCAX61388

SOME DIFFERENCES IN FACTORS RELATED TO EDUCATIONAL ACHIEVEMENT OF TWO MEXICAN-AMERICAN GROUPS.   MMONTPX60443

EDUCATIONAL STATUS OF A MINORITY.   MSAMOJX63470

SPANISH-AMERICANS RAISING EDUCATIONAL SIGHTS.   MSKRARL65493

THE EDUCATIONAL OUTLOOK FOR NONWHITES IN FLORIDA.   NABRAAA66141

SOCIAL FACTORS IN OCCUPATIONAL AND EDUCATIONAL ASPIRATIONS OF NEGRO AND WHITE STUDENTS.   NADDIDP61002

EDUCATIONAL ACHIEVEMENT AND JOB-OPPORTUNITIES. A VICIOUS CIRCLE.   NBLALHM58084

A COMPARISON OF THE SOCIAL CHARACTERISTICS AND EDUCATIONAL ASPIRATIONS OF NORTHERN, LOWER-CLASS, NEGRO
PARENTS WHO ACCEPTED AND DECLINED AN OPPORTUNITY FOR INTEGRATED EDUCATION FOR THEIR CHILDREN.   NCAGLLT66904

EQUALITY OF EDUCATIONAL OPPORTUNITY.   NCOLEJS66223

EDUCATIONAL PATTERNS IN SOUTHERN MIGRATION.   NFEINRX65348

I Q PERFORMANCE, EDUCATIONAL AND OCCUPATIONAL ASPIRATIONS OF YOUTH IN A SOUTHERN CITY -- A RACIAL
COMPARISON.   NGEISPX62397

EQUAL EDUCATIONAL OPPORTUNITY. ANOTHER ASPECT.   NGIOVPC64279

EDUCATIONAL IMPERATIVE. THE NEGRO IN THE CHANGING SOUTH.   NGOLDFH63429

EDUCATIONAL SELECTIVITY OF NET MIGRATION FROM THE SOUTH.   NHAMICH59986

THE EDUCATIONAL AND OCCUPATIONAL ASPIRATIONS AND PLANS OF NEGRO AND WHITE MALE ELEMENTARY SCHOOL
STUDENTS.   NHOLLRG59562

EDUCATIONAL CHANGES AFFECTING AMERICAN NEGROES.   NLOGARW64704

INTELLIGENCE AND EDUCATIONAL ACHIEVEMENT OF A MATCHED SAMPLE OF WHITE AND NEGRO STUDENTS.   NMCQURX60730

NO LONGER SUPERFLUOUS -- THE EDUCATIONAL REHABILITATION OF THE HARD-CORE UNEMPLOYED.   NPALLNJ65332

COUNSELING NEGRO STUDENTS. AN EDUCATIONAL DILEMMA.   NPHILWB59996

THE INFLUENCE OF TUSKEGEE-INSTITUTE ON THE HEALTH, EDUCATIONAL, ECONOMIC, AND POLITICAL ASPECTS OF THE
NEGRO POPULATION OF MACON COUNTY, ALABAMA.   NSHIEAR51342

COMPARATIVE STUDY OF SOCIO-ECONOMIC AND SOCIAL-PSYCHOLOGICAL DETERMINANTS OF EDUCATIONAL AND OCCUPATIONAL
ASPIRATIONS OF NEGRO AND WHITE COLLEGE SENIORS.   NWHITRM59319

THE EFFECT OF LOW EDUCATIONAL ATTAINMENT ON INCOMES. A COMPARATIVE STUDY OF SELECTED ETHNIC GROUPS.   OFOGEWX66721

SURVEY OF SALARIES AND PERSONNEL PRACTICES FOR TEACHERS AND ADMINISTRATORS IN NURSING EDUCATIONAL
PROGRAMS, DECEMBER 1965.   WAMERNA66612

SEX AS A FACTOR IN THE DETERMINATION OF EDUCATIONAL CHOICE. /ASPIRATIONS/   WDOLEAA64737

SOME INTELLECTUAL ATTRIBUTES AND EDUCATIONAL INTERESTS OF UNIVERSITY WOMEN IN VARIOUS MAJORS.
/ASPIRATIONS/   WGENTLX60790

A MEMORANDUM ON THE MOTIVATIONS OF MIDDLE AGED WOMEN IN THE LOWER EDUCATIONAL BRACKETS TO RETURN TO WORK.
/ASPIRATIONS/   WJEWIVA61880

A SURVEY OF SPECIAL EDUCATIONAL PROGRAMS FOR ADULT WOMEN IN UNIVERSITY EXTENSION DIVISIONS AND EVENING
COLLEGES AS OF SPRING 1965.   WLORIRK66942

WANTED. MORE WOMEN IN EDUCATIONAL LEADERSHIP. /OCCUPATIONS/   WNATLCO65016

WHEN WILL THE EDUCATIONAL NEEDS OF WOMEN BE MET. SOME QUESTIONS FOR THE COUNSELOR.   WNEUMRR63026

REALITIES. EDUCATIONAL, ECONOMIC, LEGAL AND PERSONAL NEEDS OF CAREER WOMEN.   WPARKRX66049

RELATIONSHIP BETWEEN THE EDUCATIONAL GOALS AND THE ACADEMIC PERFORMANCE OF WOMEN. A CONFIRMATION.   WWEITHX59260

EDUCATIONAL-ATTAINME
    THE EFFECT OF LOW EDUCATIONAL-ATTAINMENT ON INCOMES. A COMPARATIVE STUDY OF SELECTED ETHNIC GROUPS.
    /NEGRO MEXICAN-AMERICAN/   CFOGEWX66367

    FACTORS AFFECTING EDUCATIONAL-ATTAINMENT IN DEPRESSED URBAN AREAS. /NEGRO PUERTO-RICAN/   CGOLDML63426

    EDUCATIONAL-ATTAINMENT. /DEMOGRAPHY/   CUSBURC63169

    EDUCATIONAL-ATTAINMENT OF THE WORK FORCE.   GHAMMHR66145

    EDUCATIONAL-ATTAINMENT OF WORKERS, MARCH, 1962.   GJOHNDF63828

    ECONOMIC FACTORS INFLUENCING EDUCATIONAL-ATTAINMENTS AND ASPIRATIONS OF FARM YOUTH.   GMOOREJ64386

    EDUCATIONAL-ATTAINMENT. MARCH 1964.   GUSBURC65152

    EDUCATIONAL-ATTAINMENT AND LABOR-FORCE PARTICIPATION.   WBOWEWGND652

    REPORT OF THE EXPLORATORY STATISTICAL SURVEY OF THE EDUCATIONAL-ATTAINMENT, NUMBER, AND AVAILABILITY OF
    THE MEMBERSHIP OF THE AMERICAN ASSOCIATION OF UNIVERSITY WOMEN FOR TEACHING IN THE FIELDS OF SCIENCE AND
    MATHEMATICS. /OCCUPATIONS/   WDOLAEF57735

    TRENDS IN EDUCATIONAL-ATTAINMENT OF WOMEN.   WUSDLAB65222

    TRENDS IN EDUCATIONAL-ATTAINMENT OF WOMEN.   WUSDLAB67806

EDUCATORS
    THE MARKET FOR NEGRO EDUCATORS IN COLLEGES AND UNIVERSITIES OUTSIDE THE SOUTH.   NROSEHM61076

EEO
    PROGRESS IN CIVIL-RIGHTS TO 1964. /EEO/   GFLEIHX65106

    ISSUES AND ANSWERS. /EEO/   GJOHNMW65827

    THE COMMUNITY APPROACH. /EEO/   GMATTEG64967

    WHAT INDUSTRY CAN DO. /EEO/   GMAYFHX64969

    EFFECTS ON THE ECONOMY. /EEO/   GMILLGW64986

    SELF-ANALYSIS QUESTIONNAIRE. /EEO INDUSTRY/   GPRESCD63115

    FOUNDATION FOR THE GREAT SOCIETY. /EEO/   GROOSFD66242

    RESEARCH BULLETIN ON INTERGROUP-RELATIONS. /EEO/   GSMITCX62319

    MILWAUKEE. A FAIR DEAL. /WISCONSIN EEO/   GWINTEL66569

    A COMPANY CASE HISTORY. /INDUSTRY EEO/   GWITTHW64576

    OPENING THE DOOR TO EMPLOYMENT. /EEO/   NGEORCH64399

    DISCRIMINATION -- USA. /EEO/   NJAVIJK60006

    TO FULFILL THESE RIGHTS. REPORT ON THE WHITE-HOUSE-CONFERENCE. /EEO/   NWATTPX66545

    POLICY RESOLUTION ADOPTED BY AFL-CIO 6TH CONSTITUTIONAL CONVENTION, SAN FRANCISCO, DEC 1965. /EEO/   WAFLCIO65617

    MINORITY REPORT. /EEO/   WDAVICX63718

    TESTIMONY. PUBLIC HEARING. WOMEN IN PUBLIC AND PRIVATE EMPLOYMENT, CALIFORNIA. /MDTA EEO/   WINGRLX66859

    WOMEN IN THE UAW. /EEO/   WUAWXCC66163

EEOC
    TESTIMONY. PUBLIC HEARING. WOMEN IN PUBLIC AND PRIVATE EMPLOYMENT, CALIFORNIA. /DISCRIMINATION EEOC/   WBALEHX66625

EFFECT
    THE EFFECT OF LOW EDUCATIONAL-ATTAINMENT ON INCOMES. A COMPARATIVE STUDY OF SELECTED ETHNIC GROUPS.
    /NEGRO MEXICAN-AMERICAN/   CFOGEWX66367

    EFFECT OF MECHANIZATION ON EMPLOYMENT OF MIGRATORY LABOR IN AGRICULTURE AND FOOD PROCESSING.
    /MIGRANT-WORKERS/   GDELASE59946

    UNEMPLOYMENT. ITS SCOPE, MEASUREMENT, AND EFFECT ON POVERTY.   GFERGRH65012

    TITLE-VII. RELATIONSHIP AND EFFECT ON THE NATIONAL-LABOR- RELATIONS-BOARD. /LEGISLATION/   GFUCHRS66702

    THE EFFECT OF STATE FAIR-EMPLOYMENT LEGISLATION ON THE ECONOMIC POSITION OF NONWHITE MALES.   GLANDWM66883

    TITLE-VII. RELATIONSHIP AND EFFECT ON EXECUTIVE ORDER 11246. /LEGISLATION/   GMANNRD66937

    TITLE-VII. RELATIONSHIP AND EFFECT ON STATE ACTION. /LEGISLATION/   GPURDJW66209

    THE EFFECT OF RESIDENTIAL SEGREGATION UPON EDUCATIONAL ACHIEVEMENT AND ASPIRATIONS.   GWILSAB60567

    EFFECT OF SCHOOL ASSIGNMENT LAWS ON FEDERAL ADJUDICATION OF INTEGRATION CONTROVERSIES.   NCOLULR57224

    FAMILY AND ACHIEVEMENT. A PROPOSAL TO STUDY THE EFFECT OF FAMILY SOCIALIZATION ON ACHIEVEMENT AND
    PERFORMANCE AMONG URBAN NEGRO AMERICANS.   NEPPSEG65334

    THE EFFECT OF A CHANGING AGRICULTURAL PATTERN ON NEGRO FARMERS OF SOUTH-CAROLINA.   NHURSRL56253

    THE EFFECT OF THE WAR ECONOMY ON THE SOUTH. HOW MOBILIZATION WILL AFFECT POSITION OF THE NEGRO.   NJACKJX51595

    THE EFFECT OF THE GHETTO ON THE DISTRIBUTION AND LEVEL OF NONWHITE EMPLOYMENT IN URBAN AREAS.   NKAINJF64631

    THE EFFECT OF SPECIAL INSTRUCTION UPON TEST PERFORMANCE OF HIGH SCHOOL STUDENTS IN TENNESSEE.   NROBESO66961

    THE EFFECT OF SEGREGATION ON THE ASPIRATIONS OF NEGRO YOUTH.   NSAINJN66136

    THE EFFECT OF LOW EDUCATIONAL ATTAINMENT ON INCOMES. A COMPARATIVE STUDY OF SELECTED ETHNIC GROUPS.   OFOGEWX66721

    ANTI-NEPOTISM RULES IN AMERICAN COLLEGES AND UNIVERSITIES -- THEIR EFFECT ON THE FACULTY EMPLOYMENT OF
    WOMEN.   WDOLAEF60951

    THE EFFECT OF THE SOCIAL CONTEXT IN THE VOCATIONAL COUNSELING OF COLLEGE WOMEN.   WGURIMG63810

    DROP-OUTS FROM SCHOOLS OF NURSING. THE EFFECT OF SELF- AND ROLE PERCEPTION.   WKIBRAK58902

EFFECT   (CONTINUATION)
    THE INTERACTION OF DEMAND AND SUPPLY AND ITS EFFECT ON THE FEMALE LABOR-FORCE IN THE UNITED STATES.   WOPPEVK66289

    AUTOMATION AND EMPLOYMENT OPPORTUNITIES FOR OFFICE WORKERS. THE EFFECT OF ELECTRONIC COMPUTERS ON
    EMPLOYMENT OF CLERICAL WORKERS, WITH A SPECIAL REPORT ON PROGRAMMERS.   WPASCWX58178

    EQUAL-PAY FOR WOMEN. ITS EFFECT.   WUSNEWR64244

EFFECTIVENESS
    A BENEFIT-COST ANALYSIS OF THE ECONOMIC EFFECTIVENESS OF RETRAINING THE UNEMPLOYED.   GBORUME64142

    THE ECONOMIC EFFECTIVENESS OF RETRAINING THE UNEMPLOYED.   GBORUME66919

    AN ANALYSIS OF THE EFFECTIVENESS OF THE NEW-YORK STATE LAW AGAINST DISCRIMINATION.   GMARPAW53940

EFFECTS
    EFFECTS ON ECONOMIC GROWTH OF THE EMPLOYMENT SHIFT TO SERVICE INDUSTRIES.   GBRADME64797

    ECONOMIC AND SOCIAL DEPRIVATIONS. ITS EFFECTS ON CHILDREN AND FAMILIES IN THE UNITED STATES -- A SELECTED
    BIBLIOGRAPHY.   GCHILCX64571

    EFFECTS OF TECHNOLOGICAL-CHANGE ON OCCUPATIONAL EMPLOYMENT PATTERNS IN THE UNITED STATES.   GCLAGEX64625

    EFFECTS OF TECHNOLOGICAL-CHANGE ON THE NATURE OF JOBS.   GLEVILA64623

    EFFECTS ON THE ECONOMY. /EEO/   GMILLGW64986

    THE EFFECTS OF AUTOMATION ON OCCUPATIONS AND WORKERS IN PENNSYLVANIA.   GPENNSE65641

    THE EFFECTS OF INDUSTRIALIZATION ON RURAL LOUISIANA. A STUDY OF PLANT EMPLOYEES.   GPRICPH58395

    THE JEWISH LAW STUDENT AND NEW-YORK JOBS -- DISCRIMINATORY EFFECTS IN LAW FIRM HIRING PRACTICES.
    /OCCUPATIONS/   JYALELJ64774

    TERMINATION OF THE BRACERO PROGRAM. SOME EFFECTS ON FARM LABOR AND MIGRANT HOUSING NEEDS.   MMCELRC65385

    THE EFFECTS OF IMPORTED MEXICAN FARM LABOR IN A CALIFORNIA COUNTY.   MROONJF61465

    SOME EFFECTS OF DISCRIMINATION IN EMPLOYMENT.   NBLOCHD66092

    WHAT ARE THE PSYCHOLOGICAL EFFECTS OF SEGREGATION UNDER CONDITIONS OF EQUAL FACILITIES.   NCHEIIX49198

    EFFECTS OF UNEMPLOYMENT ON WHITE AND NEGRO PRISON-ADMISSIONS IN LOUISIANA.   NDOBBDA58277

    EFFECTS OF ON-THE-JOB EXPERIENCE WITH NEGROES UPON RACIAL ATTITUDES OF WHITE WORKERS IN UNION SHOPS.   NGUNDRH50466

    EFFECTS OF AUTOMATION ON THE POSITION OF NEGROES IN A SOUTHERN INDUSTRIAL PLANT.   NHARTJW64495

    A STUDY OF THE EFFECTS OF EFFORTS TO IMPROVE EMPLOYMENT-OPPORTUNITIES OF NEGROES ON THE UTILIZATION OF
    NEGRO WORKERS.   NHARTJW64496

    RECENT EFFECTS OF RACIAL CONFLICT ON SOUTHERN INDUSTRIAL DEVELOPMENT.   NHILLHX59543

    EFFECTS OF WHITE AUTHORITARIANISM IN BI-RACIAL WORK GROUPS.   NKATZIX60639

    EFFECTS OF ANXIETY, THREAT, AND RACIAL ENVIRONMENT ON TASK PERFORMANCE OF NEGRO COLLEGE STUDENTS.   NKATZIX63640

    REVIEW OF EVIDENCE RELATING TO EFFECTS OF DESEGREGATION ON THE INTELLECTUAL PERFORMANCE OF NEGROES.   NKATZIX64637

    THE EFFECTS OF SOUTHERN WHITE WORKERS ON RACE-RELATIONS IN NORTHERN PLANTS.   NKILLLM52650

    FAIR-EMPLOYMENT-PRACTICE LAWS -- EXPERIENCE, EFFECTS, PROSPECTS.   NNORGPH67929

    REBUILDING CITIES. THE EFFECTS OF DISPLACEMENT AND RELOCATION ON SMALL BUSINESS.   NZIMMBG64247

    EMPLOYMENT EFFECTS OF STATE MINIMUM WAGES FOR WOMEN.   WPETEJX59059

EGO
    EGO DEVELOPMENT AMONG SEGREGATED NEGRO CHILDREN. /ASPIRATIONS/   NAUSUDP65036

EISENHOWER
    FIVE YEARS OF PROGRESS, 1953-1958, A REPORT TO PRESIDENT EISENHOWER BY THE PRESIDENT-S COMMITTEE ON
    GOVERNMENT CONTRACTS.   GPRESCH58121

    PATTERN FOR PROGRESS, SEVENTH REPORT. FINAL REPORT TO PRESIDENT EISENHOWER FROM THE COMMITTEE ON
    GOVERNMENT CONTRACTS.   GPRESCH60123

EL-PASO
    LEVELS OF ASPIRATION OF MEXICAN-AMERICANS IN EL-PASO SCHOOLS. /TEXAS/   MNALLFX59447

ELAN
    THE JEWISH ELAN.   JWELLSX60571

ELDERLY
    INCOME OF THE ELDERLY POPULATION. /DEMOGRAPHY/   CUSBURC63171

ELECTRIC
    TECHNICAL REPORT NUMBER 2. EMPLOYMENT PRACTICES OF SELECTED MISSOURI PUBLIC UTILITIES. NATURAL GAS AND
    ELECTRIC.   GMILLRX66021

ELECTRONIC
    AUTOMATION AND EMPLOYMENT OPPORTUNITIES FOR OFFICE WORKERS. THE EFFECT OF ELECTRONIC COMPUTERS ON
    EMPLOYMENT OF CLERICAL WORKERS, WITH A SPECIAL REPORT ON PROGRAMMERS.   WPASCWX58178

ELEMENTARY
    THE EDUCATIONAL AND OCCUPATIONAL ASPIRATIONS AND PLANS OF NEGRO AND WHITE MALE ELEMENTARY SCHOOL
    STUDENTS.   NHOLLRG59562

    A STUDY OF ELEMENTARY SCHOOL TEACHER-S ATTITUDES TOWARD THE WOMAN PRINCIPAL AND TOWARD ELEMENTARY
    PRINCIPALSHIP AS A CAREER. /DISCRIMINATION/   WBARTAK58629

    A STUDY OF ELEMENTARY SCHOOL TEACHER-S ATTITUDES TOWARD THE WOMAN PRINCIPAL AND TOWARD ELEMENTARY
    PRINCIPALSHIP AS A CAREER. /DISCRIMINATION/   WBARTAK58629

    KNOWLEDGE AND INTERESTS CONCERNING SIXTEEN OCCUPATIONS AMONG ELEMENTARY AND SECONDARY SCHOOL STUDENTS.
    /ASPIRATIONS/   WMELSRC63968

ELIMINATE
    THE INDIVIDUAL RIGHT TO ELIMINATE EMPLOYMENT DISCRIMINATION BY LITIGATION.   GBLUMAW66566

ELIMINATE   (CONTINUATION)
SUPPLEMENTARY ACTIVITIES FOR STATE GOVERNMENTS SEEKING TO **ELIMINATE** DISCRIMINATION.   GROUTFB64264

TAILORING THE TECHNIQUES TO **ELIMINATE** AND PREVENT EMPLOYMENT DISCRIMINATION.   GSPITHX64331

EFFORTS TO **ELIMINATE** RACIAL DISCRIMINATION IN INDUSTRY -- WITH PARTICULAR REFERENCE TO THE SOUTH.   NHOPEJX54566

ELIMINATED
HOW DEPARTMENT X **ELIMINATED** SEGREGATION.   GUSCISC49388

ELIMINATING
THE ROLE OF LEGISLATION IN **ELIMINATING** RACIAL DISCRIMINATION.   GBONFAE65462

POTENTIAL ECONOMIC GAINS FROM **ELIMINATING** DISCRIMINATION.   GCOUNEA66204

UNION PROGRAM FOR **ELIMINATING** DISCRIMINATION.   NUSDLAB63846

ELIMINATION
THE **ELIMINATION** OF POVERTY. A PRIMARY GOAL OF PUBLIC POLICY.   GCOHEWJ64925

ELIMINATION OF RACE DISCRIMINATION IN THE APPLICATION BLANK.   GDARTCX47626

FACTORS INVOLVED IN STUDENT **ELIMINATION** FROM HIGH SCHOOL.   NMOORPL54079

ELITE
OUR CHANGING **ELITE** COLLEGES. /EDUCATION/   JBLOOLX60705

ELMIRA
NEGRO AND WHITE YOUTH IN **ELMIRA**. /NEW-YORK/   NANTOAX59026

EMANCIPATION
LABOR AND THE **EMANCIPATION** PROCLAMATION. /UNION/   GKRONJL65861

FREEDOM TO THE FREE. CENTURY OF **EMANCIPATION**, 1863-1963.   GUSCOMC63398

SOCIOLOGY OF **EMANCIPATION**.   NCOLLHX65491

THE PROGRESS OF THE NEGRO AFTER A CENTURY OF **EMANCIPATION**.   NLOGARW63046

ASSURING FREEDOM TO THE FREE. A CENTURY OF **EMANCIPATION** IN THE USA.   NROSEAM64290

WOMEN. **EMANCIPATION** IS STILL TO COME. /WORK-FAMILY-CONFLICT/   WBETTBX64646

EMMITSBURG
COMMUNITY VALUES IN EDUCATION AND OCCUPATIONAL SELECTION. A STUDY OF YOUTH IN **EMMITSBURG**, MARYLAND.   GLEONRC64894

EMPIRICAL
HUMAN CAPITAL. A THEORETICAL AND **EMPIRICAL** ANALYSIS WITH SPECIAL REFERENCE TO EDUCATION.   GBECKGS64700

AN **EMPIRICAL** STUDY OF HIGH SCHOOL DROPOUTS IN REGARD TO TEN POSSIBLY RELATED FACTORS.   NTHOMRJ54159

THE ROLE OF THE EDUCATED WOMAN. AN **EMPIRICAL** STUDY OF THE ATTITUDES OF A GROUP OF COLLEGE WOMEN.
/WORK-WOMAN-ROLE/   WFREEMB65770

EMPLOYABILITY
MARGINAL **EMPLOYABILITY**.   GFURFPH62705

INCREASING **EMPLOYABILITY** OF YOUTH. THE ROLE OF WORK TRAINING.   GMOEDMX66852

SUMMARY OF PROCEEDINGS. WORKSHOP ON THE IMPACT OF A TIGHTENING LABOR-MARKET ON THE **EMPLOYABILITY** AND
EMPLOYMENT OF DISADVANTAGED YOUTH.   GNEWYUC66116

EMPLOYABILITY AND THE JUVENILE ARREST RECORD.   GSPAREV66839

THE **EMPLOYABILITY** OF CHIPPEWA INDIANS AND POOR WHITES.   ILIEBLX66041

EMPLOYMENT AND **EMPLOYABILITY** AMONG CALIFORNIA YOUTH AUTHORITY WARDS. A SURVEY.   MSECKJP62483

THE **EMPLOYABILITY** OF THE CHAMPAIGN-URBANA, ILLINOIS, NEGRO.   NBEAKJR64062

EMPLOYABLE
DETROIT-S INSURED UNEMPLOYED AND **EMPLOYABLE** WELFARE RECIPIENTS. /MICHIGAN/   GWICKED63561

INSURED UNEMPLOYED AND **EMPLOYABLE** WELFARE RECIPIENTS.   GWICKEX63637

EMPLOYED
THE **EMPLOYED** POOR. THEIR CHARACTERISTICS AND OCCUPATIONS.   GCUMMLD65623

COUNTING THE **EMPLOYED** AND THE UNEMPLOYED.   GWOLFSL63578

AT WORK IN NORTH-CAROLINA TODAY. 48 CASE-REPORTS ON NORTH-CAROLINA NEGROES NOW **EMPLOYED** OR PREPARING
THEMSELVES FOR EMPLOYMENT...THEIR EDUCATION, JOB QUALIFICATIONS, AND CAREER ASPIRATIONS.   NNORTCGND933

OCCUPATIONAL DISTRIBUTION OF **EMPLOYED** COLORED WORKERS OF MARYLAND.   NUSDLAB40834

SPECIAL REPORT. A SURVEY OF NEGROES **EMPLOYED** BY THE STATE OF WEST-VIRGINIA.   NVIRGHR64318

THE **EMPLOYED** POOR. A CASE-STUDY. /WASHINGTON-DC/   NWILLCV65989

SURVEY OF EMPLOYMENT-CONDITIONS OF NURSES **EMPLOYED** BY PHYSICIANS AND/OR DENTISTS, JULY 1964.   WAMERNA65610

THE **EMPLOYED** MOTHER IN AMERICA.   WNYEXFI63040

SOME ATTITUDES AND OPINIONS OF **EMPLOYED** WOMEN.   WRAMSGV63132

MANAGEMENT PROBLEMS OF HOMEMAKERS **EMPLOYED** OUTSIDE THE HOME. /WORK-FAMILY-CONFLICT/   WUSDHEW61174

MATERNITY BENEFIT PROVISIONS FOR **EMPLOYED** WOMEN. /EMPLOYMENT-CONDITIONS/   WUSDLAB60206

EMPLOYEE
APTITUDE TESTING, TRAINING, AND **EMPLOYEE** DEVELOPMENT, WITH A SECTION ON THE EMPLOYMENT OF
MINORITY-GROUPS.   GAMERMA49389

TRENDS IN **EMPLOYEE** TESTING.   GHABBSX65112

FACTORS AFFECTING **EMPLOYEE** SELECTION IN TWO CULTURES. /DISCRIMINATION/   GTRIAHC63083

THE NEGRO AS AN **EMPLOYEE**. /INDUSTRY/   NHABBSX65474

EMPLOYEE   (CONTINUATION)
  EMPLOYEE CHOICE AND SOME PROBLEMS OF RACE AND REMEDIES IN REPRESENTATION CAMPAIGNS.   NYALELJ63599

EMPLOYEES
  ETHNIC SURVEY OF MUNICIPAL-EMPLOYEES. A REPORT ON THE NUMBER AND DISTRIBUTION OF NEGROES AND
  PUERTO-RICANS AND OTHER EMPLOYEES BY THE CITY OF NEW-YORK.   CNEWYCO64916

  COMPENSATING EMPLOYEES UNDER THE NEW CIVIL-RIGHTS LAW.   GBENGEJ65436

  THE CIVIL-RIGHTS-ACT OF 1964. WHAT IT MEANS -- TO EMPLOYERS, BUSINESSMEN, UNIONS, EMPLOYEES,
  MINORITY-GROUPS. TEXT, ANALYSIS, LEGISLATIVE HISTORY.   GBUREON64492

  REPORT ON AND ANALYSIS OF SECOND CENSUS OF CITY EMPLOYEES TO DETERMINE BASES FOR FUTURE PERSONNEL
  DEVELOPMENTS. /DETROIT MICHIGAN/   GDETRCC66639

  REPORT OF THE SURVEY OF EMPLOYEES OF THE STATE OF INDIANA, SEPTEMBER 1961.   GINDICR61806

  PROTECTING RIGHTS OF MINORITY EMPLOYEES.   GKINGRL60854

  MANAGEMENT-S CONCERN WITH RECENT CIVIL-RIGHTS LEGISLATION AFFECTING MANAGEMENT-S OBLIGATIONS TO HIS
  EMPLOYEES AND APPLICANTS FOR EMPLOYMENT, MAINLY IN THE STATE OF NEW-YORK.   GKOPPRW65858

  COMMUNICATIONS EMPLOYEES AND GOOD SERVICE. /NEW-YORK/   GNEWYSA54077

  SECOND SURVEY OF NON-WHITE EMPLOYEES IN STATE GOVERNMENT IN PENNSYLVANIA.   GPENNHR65167

  THE EFFECTS OF INDUSTRIALIZATION ON RURAL LOUISIANA. A STUDY OF PLANT EMPLOYEES.   GPRICPH58395

  SURVEY OF NON-WHITE EMPLOYEES IN STATE GOVERNMENT. /PENNSYLVANIA/   GSTRUJW63338

  CITY EMPLOYMENT SURVEY. PERCENTAGE OF MINORITY-GROUP EMPLOYEES BY DEPARTMENT. /YONKERS NEW-YORK/   GYONKCC66592

  RACIAL DISCRIMINATION BY A UNION AGAINST EMPLOYEES IT DOES NOT REPRESENT. /LEGISLATION/   NCOLULR52226

  ATTITUDES OF WHITE DEPARTMENT STORE EMPLOYEES TOWARD NEGRO CO-WORKERS. /CASE-STUDY/   NHARDJX52482

  REPRESENTATION OF NEGROES AND WHITES AS EMPLOYEES IN THE FEDERAL PRISON SYSTEM.   NMORGGD62849

  A FIVE-CITY SURVEY OF NEGRO-AMERICAN EMPLOYEES OF THE FEDERAL GOVERNMENT.   NPRESCP57017

  ACCOMODATION BETWEEN NEGRO AND WHITE EMPLOYEES IN A WEST COAST AIRCRAFT INDUSTRY, 1942-1944.
  /CASE-STUDY/   NREEDBA47045

  WOMEN AS GOVERNMENT EMPLOYEES. /OCCUPATIONS/   WBUSIWX63669

  WOMEN EMPLOYEES IN MANUFACTURING BY INDUSTRY, JANUARY, 1959.   WEMPLAE59752

  OCCUPATIONS AND SALARIES OF WOMEN FEDERAL EMPLOYEES.   WUSDLAB57992

  MANAGING WOMEN EMPLOYEES IN SMALL BUSINESS.   WUSSMBA62248

EMPLOYER
  AN ACTIVE EMPLOYER MANPOWER POLICY.   GLIVEER66567

  THE ROLE OF THE EMPLOYER IN MANPOWER POLICY. /INDUSTRY/   GMYERCA66527

  EMPLOYER SPECIFICATIONS FOR DEFENSE WORKERS.   NUSDLAB41244

EMPLOYERS
  THE SUBSTANCE OF AMERICAN FAIR-EMPLOYMENT-PRACTICES LEGISLATION. I. EMPLOYERS.   GBONFAE67137

  THE CIVIL-RIGHTS-ACT OF 1964. WHAT IT MEANS -- TO EMPLOYERS, BUSINESSMEN, UNIONS, EMPLOYEES,
  MINORITY-GROUPS. TEXT, ANALYSIS, LEGISLATIVE HISTORY.   GBUREON64492

  EMPLOYMENT OPPORTUNITIES FOR HIGH SCHOOL DROPOUTS. A STUDY OF EMPLOYERS PRACTICES, NEEDS AND ATTITUDES IN
  THE DISTRICT OF COLUMBIA. /WASHINGTON-DC/   GBURESS57499

  GUIDE TO LAWFUL AND UNLAWFUL PRE-EMPLOYMENT INQUIRIES BY EMPLOYERS, EMPLOYMENT-AGENCIES, AND LABOR
  ORGANIZATIONS UNDER THE CALIFORNIA FAIR-EMPLOYMENT-PRACTICE ACT, LABOR CODE, SECTIONS 1410-1432.   GCALDIR60527

  PROMOTING EQUAL JOB OPPORTUNITY, A GUIDE FOR EMPLOYERS. /CALIFORNIA/   GCALFEP63538

  SUMMARY OF RULES, REGULATIONS, AND LAWS THAT AFFECT SEASONAL FARM WORKERS AND THEIR EMPLOYERS IN NEW-YORK
  STATE. /MIGRANT-WORKERS/   GNEWYSJND113

  GUIDE TO EMPLOYERS, EMPLOYMENT-AGENCIES AND LABOR UNIONS DEFINING PROPER AND IMPROPER PRE-EMPLOYMENT
  INQUIRIES. /PENNSYLVANIA/   GPENNHRND164

  EMPLOYERS GUIDE TO EQUAL-EMPLOYMENT-OPPORTUNITY.   GSCHEGX66280

  MINORITY-GROUP INTEGRATION BY LABOR AND MANAGEMENT. A STUDY OF THE EMPLOYMENT PRACTICES OF THE LARGER
  EMPLOYERS, AND THE MEMBERSHIP PRACTICES OF THE LARGER LABOR UNIONS WITH RESPECT TO RACE, RELIGION, AND
  NATIONAL ORIGIN. CONNECTICUT, 1951.   GSTETHG53598

  WORKERS WANTED. A STUDY OF EMPLOYERS HIRING POLICIES, PREFERENCES, AND PRACTICES IN NEW-HAVEN AND
  CHARLOTTE. /CONNECTICUT NORTH-CAROLINA/   NNOLAEW49928

  JOB RIGHTS FOR NEGROES -- PRESSURE ON EMPLOYERS.   NUSNEWR66270

  WHITE EMPLOYERS AND NEGRO WORKERS.   NWILSLX43327

  AN EXPLORATORY STUDY OF EMPLOYERS ATTITUDES TOWARD WORKING MOTHERS.   WCONYJE61704

  EMPLOYERS ATTITUDES TOWARD WORKING MOTHERS.   WCONYJE63703

  A NATIONAL INQUIRY OF PRIVATE HOUSEHOLD-EMPLOYEES AND EMPLOYERS.   WNATLCH66014

EMPLOYING
  EMPLOYING MINORITIES SUCCESSFULLY.   GAMERFC48378

  MORE ROOM AT THE TOP. COMPANY EXPERIENCE IN EMPLOYING NEGROES IN PROFESSIONAL AND MANAGEMENT JOBS.
  /INDUSTRY/   NBIRDCX63080

  OFFICIAL ADVICE ON EMPLOYING NEGROES.   NLABORR42030

  SOME ATTITUDES TOWARD EMPLOYING NEGROES AS TEACHERS IN A NORTHERN UNIVERSITY.   NMARCFL48054

  EMPLOYING THE NEGRO IN AMERICAN INDUSTRY   NNORGPH59932

EMPLOYING   (CONTINUATION)
    SOUTHERN CITIES EMPLOYING NEGRO POLICEMEN -- INCLUDING NORTH-CAROLINA CITIES OVER 15,000 POPULATION.   NSTEEDL46173

EMPLOYMENT
    MEETING TODAYS CHALLENGE FOR EMPLOYMENT. /AMERICAN-INDIAN NEGRO MEXICAN-AMERICAN/   CARIZSE65403

    TESTIMONY, PUBLIC HEARING, WOMEN IN PUBLIC AND PRIVATE EMPLOYMENT, CALIFORNIA. /MEXICAN-AMERICAN/   CARYWSX66621

    REPORT TO GOVERNOR EDMUND G BROWN. SECOND ETHNIC SURVEY OF EMPLOYMENT AND PROMOTION IN STATE GOVERNMENT.
    /CALIFORNIA NEGRO MEXICAN-AMERICAN/   CBECKWL65070

    HUMAN-RESOURCE PROBLEMS OF THE COMING DECADE. /EMPLOYMENT NEGRO MEXICAN-AMERICAN/   CBULLPX66136

    ANNUAL FARM LABOR REPORT. 1965. CALIFORNIA DEPARTMENT OF EMPLOYMENT, FARM LABOR SERVICE. /NEGRO
    MEXICAN-AMERICAN WOMEN/   CCALDEM66906

    RACIAL DISTRIBUTION OF SELECTED UNEMPLOYMENT INSURANCE AND EMPLOYMENT SERVICE DATA. JULY-DECEMBER 1966.
    /NEGRO MEXICAN-AMERICAN/   CCALDEM67907

    TRAINING AID. CULTURAL DIFFERENCES, TRAINING IN NONDISCRIMINATION, READING ASSIGNMENTS. /EMPLOYMENT
    MEXICAN-AMERICAN NEGRO/   CCALDSW65447

    THE EMPLOYMENT OF NEGRO WOMEN AS DOMESTIC-SERVANTS IN NEW-ORLEANS. /LOUISIANA/   CGILMHX44403

    ECONOMIC GROWTH AND EMPLOYMENT OPPORTUNITIES FOR MINORITIES. /NEGRO WOMEN/   CHIESDL64775

    EMPLOYMENT AND PERSONAL CHARACTERISTICS. EMPLOYMENT BY AGE, RACE, NATIVITY, EDUCATION, MARITAL-STATUS,
    HOUSEHOLD RELATIONSHIPS, ETC. /DEMOGRAPHY/   CUSBURC53372

    EMPLOYMENT AND PERSONAL CHARACTERISTICS. EMPLOYMENT BY AGE, RACE, NATIVITY, EDUCATION, MARITAL-STATUS,
    HOUSEHOLD RELATIONSHIPS, ETC. /DEMOGRAPHY/   CUSBURC53372

    EMPLOYMENT OF WHITE AND NON-WHITE PERSONS. 1955. /DEMOGRAPHY/   CUSBURC56373

    EMPLOYMENT-STATUS AND WORK CHARACTERISTICS. STATISTICS ON THE RELATION BETWEEN EMPLOYMENT AND SOCIAL AND
    ECONOMIC CHARACTERISTICS. /DEMOGRAPHY/   CUSBURC63170

    POVERTY IN THE UNITED STATES, HEARINGS. /AMERICAN-INDIAN NEGRO PUERTO-RICAN EMPLOYMENT/   CUSHOUR64346

    REPORT. EVALUATION STUDY OF YOUTH TRAINING AND EMPLOYMENT PROJECT, EAST LOS-ANGELES. /NEGRO
    MEXICAN-AMERICAN CALIFORNIA/   CWEINJL64310

    CONTRACTOR GROUP HITS REVISED EQUAL EMPLOYMENT STANDARDS.   GAIRCHR63866

    ACTION FOR EMPLOYMENT. A DEMONSTRATION NEIGHBORHOOD MANPOWER PROJECT.   GALLCTO66361

    INTERINDUSTRY EMPLOYMENT REQUIREMENTS.   GALTEJX65369

    QUESTIONS AND ANSWERS ABOUT EMPLOYMENT ON MERIT.   GAMERFC50379

    ANALYSIS OF CITY ORDINANCES AGAINST RACIAL AND RELIGIOUS DISCRIMINATION IN EMPLOYMENT.   GAMERJCND380

    A FIVE-STATE SURVEY OF DISCRIMINATION BY COMMERCIAL EMPLOYMENT AGENCIES.   GAMERJD63386

    APTITUDE TESTING, TRAINING, AND EMPLOYEE DEVELOPMENT, WITH A SECTION ON THE EMPLOYMENT OF
    MINORITY-GROUPS.   GAMERMA49389

    RACE, EMPLOYMENT TESTS, AND EQUAL-OPPORTUNITY.   GASHXPX65406

    A CIVIL-RIGHTS INVENTORY OF SAN-FRANCISCO. PART I, EMPLOYMENT. /CALIFORNIA/   GBABOIX58606

    WHITE COLLAR EMPLOYMENT. TRENDS AND STRUCTURE.   GBANYCA61420

    SECOND ETHNIC SURVEY OF EMPLOYMENT AND PROMOTION IN STATE GOVERNMENT. /CALIFORNIA/   GBECKWL65433

    YOUTH EMPLOYMENT PROGRAMS IN PERSPECTIVE.   GBENJJG65006

    THE INDIVIDUAL RIGHT TO ELIMINATE EMPLOYMENT DISCRIMINATION BY LITIGATION.   GBLUMAW66566

    PROCESSING EMPLOYMENT DISCRIMINATION CASES. /LEGISLATION/   GBLUMAW67117

    EMPLOYMENT OF HIGH SCHOOL GRADUATES AND DROPOUTS IN 1964.   GBOGAFA65750

    EMPLOYMENT OF SCHOOL AGE YOUTH, OCTOBER 1965.   GBOGAFA66918

    EMPLOYMENT BY MERIT ALONE.   GBOWMGW61466

    EFFECTS ON ECONOMIC GROWTH OF THE EMPLOYMENT SHIFT TO SERVICE INDUSTRIES.   GBRADME64797

    EMPLOYMENT DISCRIMINATION. STATE FEPC LAWS AND THE IMPACT OF OF TITLE-VII OF THE CIVIL-RIGHTS-ACT OF
    1964.   GBRYEGL65896

    NONWHITE EMPLOYMENT IN THE UNITED STATES.   GBUCKLF63479

    THE GREAT EMPLOYMENT CONTROVERSY. /TECHNOLOGICAL-CHANGE/   GBUCKWX62875

    CONFERENCE ISSUE -- TOWARD EQUAL-OPPORTUNITY IN EMPLOYMENT.   GBUFFLR64484

    MERIT EMPLOYMENT. NON-DISCRIMINATION IN INDUSTRY.   GBULLPX60897

    COMBATING DISCRIMINATION IN EMPLOYMENT.   GBULLPX61523

    EQUAL-OPPORTUNITY IN EMPLOYMENT.   GBULLPX66486

    EMPLOYMENT OPPORTUNITIES FOR HIGH SCHOOL DROPOUTS, A STUDY OF EMPLOYERS PRACTICES, NEEDS AND ATTITUDES IN
    THE DISTRICT OF COLUMBIA. /WASHINGTON-DC/   GBURESS57499

    STATE LAWS DEALING WITH NON-DISCRIMINATION IN EMPLOYMENT.   GBUTCGT63508

    OPINION CONCERNING THE SCOPE AND AUTHORITY OF THE JURISDICTION THAT MAY BE GRANTED TO CITY OR COUNTY
    HUMAN-RELATIONS-COMMISSIONS IN THE FIELDS OF EMPLOYMENT AND HOUSING. /CALIFORNIA/   GCALAGO63512

    EMPLOYMENT PRACTICES, CITY OF PASADENA, AN INVESTIGATION UNDER SECTION 1421 OF THE CALIFORNIA LABOR CODE
    1963-1965.   GCALFEPND531

    BANK OF AMERICA EMPLOYMENT PRACTICES. FIRST REPORT BY CALIFORNIA FEPC.   GCALFEP64530

    LOS-ANGELES CITY SCHOOLS. AN INVESTIGATION OF EMPLOYMENT PRACTICES. /CALIFORNIA/   GCALFEP64536

EMPLOYMENT   (CONTINUATION)
AFFIRMATIVE-ACTIONS IN EMPLOYMENT. A SPECIAL FEPC REPORT. /CALIFORNIA/   GCALFEP65529

FAIR-EMPLOYMENT-PRACTICES EQUAL GOOD EMPLOYMENT PRACTICES. GUIDELINES FOR TESTING AND SELECTING MINORITY
JOB APPLICANTS. /CALIFORNIA/   GCALFEP66540

EQUAL-EMPLOYMENT-OPPORTUNITY. A CHALLENGE TO THE EMPLOYMENT SERVICE.   GCASSFH66561

FAIR PRACTICE IN EMPLOYMENT.   GCHALFK48563

MERIT EMPLOYMENT IN CHICAGO. /ILLINOIS/   GCHICMC56566

EFFECTS OF TECHNOLOGICAL-CHANGE ON OCCUPATIONAL EMPLOYMENT PATTERNS IN THE UNITED STATES.   GCLAGEX64625

EMPLOYMENT PRACTICE GUIDE.   GCOMMCH65589

SHOULD CONGRESS PASS A LAW PROHIBITING EMPLOYMENT DISCRIMINATION.   GCONGDX45596

EMPLOYMENT OF JUNE 1959 HIGH SCHOOL GRADUATES, OCTOBER 1959.   GCOOPSX60601

ECONOMIC COSTS OF RACIAL DISCRIMINATION IN EMPLOYMENT.   GCOUNEA62205

DISCRIMINATION IN EMPLOYMENT.   GCOUNVX65610

A STUDY OF PATTERNS OF DISCRIMINATION IN EMPLOYMENT FOR THE EQUAL-EMPLOYMENT-OPPORTUNITY-COMMISSION,
WASHINGTON-DC.   GCOUSFR66478

PREJUDICE AND DECISION-MAKING. /EMPLOYMENT DISCRIMINATION/   GDAILCA66926

EFFECT OF MECHANIZATION ON EMPLOYMENT OF MIGRATORY LABOR IN AGRICULTURE AND FOOD PROCESSING.
/MIGRANT-WORKERS/   GDELASE59946

EMPLOYMENT REVIEW. /DES-MOINES IOWA/   GDESMCH65635

EMPLOYMENT IN CIVIL-SERVICE OF MINORITY-GROUPS. /DETROIT MICHIGAN/   GDETRCC63638

EMPLOYMENT AND INCOME BY AGE, SEX, COLOR AND RESIDENCE. /DETROIT MICHIGAN/   GDETRCC63948

EMPLOYMENT COUNSELING AS AN INTEGRAL PART OF AN ACTIVE LABOR-MARKET POLICY.   GEHRLRA65791

LOCAL REGULATION OF DISCRIMINATORY EMPLOYMENT PRACTICES.   GELSCAX47661

CIVIL-RIGHTS. EMPLOYMENT OPPORTUNITY, AND ECONOMIC GROWTH.   GFEILJG65677

THE FEDERAL INTEREST IN EMPLOYMENT DISCRIMINATION. HEREIN THE CONSTITUTIONAL SCOPE OF EXECUTIVE POWER TO
WITHOLD APPROPRIATE FUNDS.   GFERGCC64679

DISCRIMINATION IN EMPLOYMENT.   GFERMIX60680

POLICIES AFFECTING INCOME-DISTRIBUTION. /EMPLOYMENT INCOME-MAINTENANCE/   GFERNFL65662

REPORT OF INDUSTRY AND LABOR-MANAGEMENT CLINICS. IMPLEMENTATION OF EMPLOYMENT IN MERIT PROGRAMS IN NON
FEPC STATES BY DIRECT APPROACH TO TOP MANAGEMENT.   GFISKUR51684

EQUAL-OPPORTUNITY IN EMPLOYMENT.   GFOLSFM54693

GUIDE TO MERIT EMPLOYMENT. A RESTATEMENT OF INDUSTRY PRINCIPLES AND PRACTICES.   GFOODECND694

EMPLOYMENT PRACTICES, FAIR AND UNFAIR.   GFORDJA65450

BASIC ISSUES AFFECTING YOUTH EMPLOYMENT.   GFREEMK64005

RACIAL INTEGRATION IN EMPLOYMENT.   GGIBSHX54969

NONDISCRIMINATION IN EMPLOYMENT. EXECUTIVE-ORDER 10925.   GGINSGJ61718

US MANPOWER AND EMPLOYMENT POLICY. A REVIEW ESSAY.   GGORDMS65728

TWENTY YEARS OF ECONOMIC AND INDUSTRIAL CHANGE. /TECHNOLOGICAL-CHANGE EMPLOYMENT/   GGORDRA65675

A PUBLIC EMPLOYMENT PROGRAM FOR THE UNEMPLOYED POOR.   GGREEAI65473

OCCUPATIONAL EMPLOYMENT STATISTICS. SOURCES AND DATA.   GGREEHX66627

TECHNOLOGICAL-CHANGE, PRODUCTIVITY, AND EMPLOYMENT IN THE UNITED STATES.   GGREELX64739

EMPLOYMENT TESTS AND DISCRIMINATORY HIRING.   GGUIORM66747

CRITICAL ISSUES IN EMPLOYMENT POLICY. A REPORT. /UNEMPLOYMENT/   GHARBFH66476

QUESTIONING APPLICANTS FOR EMPLOYMENT. A GUIDE FOR APPLICATION FORMS AND INTERVIEWS UNDER THE HAWAII
FAIR-EMPLOYMENT-PRACTICES ACT.   GHAWADL64767

ADULT AND YOUTH EMPLOYMENT PROJECT, AUGUST-SEPTEMBER 1965.   GHEALDV65646

ADULT AND YOUTH EMPLOYMENT PROJECT, APRIL-MAY 1965.   GHEALDV65647

MINORITY-GROUPS. EMPLOYMENT PROBLEMS, REFERENCES.   GHESLMR63773

WARTIME EMPLOYMENT PATTERNS OF NONWHITES AND FEMALE WORKERS IN SOUTHERN INDUSTRY.   GHOPEJX46485

EMPLOYMENT PROBLEMS OF RACIAL MINORITIES.   GHOPEJX61002

FAIR PRACTICE IN EMPLOYMENT.   GHUDDFP46786

WAR-ON-POVERTY. /EMPLOYMENT TRAINING/   GHUMPHH64739

A REPORT ON EMPLOYMENT OF NONWHITES IN CHICAGO. /ILLINOIS/   GILLICH55792

A STUDY OF MERIT EMPLOYMENT IN 100 ILLINOIS FIRMS.   GILLICH56794

ECONOMIC GROWTH. EQUAL-OPPORTUNITY. RESEARCH. JOINT EFFORT. EMPLOYMENT.   GILLIGC63798

SPECIAL REPORT ON EMPLOYMENT OPPORTUNITIES IN ILLINOIS.   GILLIIR48801

HERE-S HOW MERIT EMPLOYMENT PROGRAMS WORK. A REPORT ON PROGRESS AND PROBLEMS IN THE EMPLOYMENT OF
MINORITY-GROUP MEMBERS.   GILLISC56803

HERE-S HOW MERIT EMPLOYMENT PROGRAMS WORK. A REPORT ON PROGRESS AND PROBLEMS IN THE EMPLOYMENT OF

  GILLISC56803

NEW-YORK STATE-S PROGRAM AGAINST DISCRIMINATION IN EMPLOYMENT. THE WORK OF THE NEW-YORKEW-YORK
STATE-COMMISSION-AGAINST-DISCRIMINATION.   GINDUBX57812

PART IV. EMPLOYMENT PROBLEMS OF RACIAL MINORITIES.   GINDURR61813

DISCRIMINATION IN THE FIELD CF EMPLOYMENT AND OCCUPATION.   GINTELC58817

LEGISLATION AGAINST RACIAL OR RELIGIOUS DISCRIMINATION IN EMPLOYMENT. NEW-YORK.   GIVESLM52819

THE ROLE OF THE SECONDARY SCHOOLS IN THE PREPARATION OF YOUTH FOR EMPLOYMENT.   GKAUFJJ67940

THE ROLE OF THE SECONDARY SCHOOLS IN THE PREPARATION OF YOUTH FOR EMPLOYMENT. SUMMARY, CONCLUSIONS. AND
RECOMMENDATIONS.   GKAUFJJ67963

UNFAIR EMPLOYMENT PRACTICES AS VIEWED BY PRIVATE EMPLOYMENT COUNSELORS.   GKEENVX52015

UNFAIR EMPLOYMENT PRACTICES AS VIEWED BY PRIVATE EMPLOYMENT COUNSELORS.   GKEENVX52015

EXPLANATION AND DIGEST JF THE 1966 KENTUCKY CIVIL-RIGHTS-ACT CCVERING EMPLOYMENT AND PUBLIC
ACCOMODATIONS, ENACTED JANUARY 27 1966, EFFECTIVE JULY 1 1966.   GKENTCHND844

PSYCHOLOGICAL TESTING FOR EFFECTIVE EMPLOYMENT PRACTICES AND EQUAL JOB OPPORTUNITIES. GKETCWA65849

MANAGEMENT-S CONCERN WITH RECENT CIVIL-RIGHTS LEGISLATION AFFECTING MANAGEMENT-S OBLIGATIONS TO HIS
EMPLOYEES AND APPLICANTS FOR EMPLOYMENT. MAINLY IN THE STATE OF NEW-YORK.   GKOPPRW65858

RACIAL DISCRIMINATION IN EMPLOYMENT AND THE FEDERAL LAW.   GKOVAIX58026

EMPLOYMENT PROBLEMS OF YOUTH AND MANPOWER PRCGRAMS.   GKRUGDH66864

EMPLOYMENT DISCRIMINATION. STATE FAIR-EMPLOYMENT-PRACTICES LAWS AND THE IMPACT OF TITLE-VII OF THE
CIVIL-RIGHTS-ACT OF 1964.   GLAWXRD65885

LEGISLATION OUTLAWING RACIAL DISCRIMINATION IN EMPLOYMENT.   GLAWYGR45886

PRCSPECTS FOR EDUCATION AND EMPLOYMENT.   GLEAGWVND890

DISCRIMINATION IN EMPLOYMENT. FEDERAL AND STATE PRACTICES IN ANTI-DISCRIMINATION.   GLEITRD49892

WE BELIEVE IN EMPLOYMENT ON MERIT, BUT...   GLELAWC63893

IMPLICATIONS OF THE ANTI-POVERTY PROGRAM FOR EDUCATION AND EMPLOYMENT.   GLEVILA65781

THE NEW ROLE OF THE EMPLOYMENT SERVICE IN SERVING THE DISADVANTAGED. /SES/   GLEVILA66599

YOUTH EMPLOYMENT ACT.   GLEVISA63898

TESTING MINORITY-GROUP APPLICANTS FOR EMPLOYMENT.   GLOCKHC65907

THE LABOR-FORCE UNDER CHANGING INCOME AND EMPLOYMENT.   GLONGCX58047

SURVEY OF MINORITY-GROUP EMPLOYMENT AND PATIENT CARE IN PRIVATE HOSPITAL FACILITIES IN LOS-ANGELES
COUNTY. /CALIFORNIA/   GLOSACCND914

REPORTS ON THE PATTERN OF EMPLOYMENT OF MINORTY-GROUP PERSONS IN DEPARTMENT OF COUNTY
GOVERNMENT.LOS-ANGELES CALIFORNIA/   GLOSACC62913

PROPOSED POLICY REGARDING STATISTICS ON EMPLOYMENT. /LOS-ANGELES CALIFORNIA/   GLOSACC64912

REPORT OF FINDINGS AND RECOMMENDATIONS RESULTING FROM AN ANALYSIS OF THE EMPLOYMENT PRACTICES IN THE
VARICUS DEPARTMENTS OF THE CITY CF LOS-ANGELES. /CALIFORNIA/   GLOSAOC63917

THE REALITY OF EQUAL-OPPCRTUNITY IN FEDERAL EMPLOYMENT.   GMACYJW66933

RACIAL AND RELIGIOUS DISCRIMINATION IN EMPLOYMENT ANC THE ROLE OF THE NLRB.   GMALOWH61935

GECGRAPHIC CHANGES IN US EMPLOYMENT FROM 1950 TO 1960.   GMANOSP63855

STATEMENT ON BEHALF OF AMERICAN JEWISH CONGRESS ON DISCRIMINATION IN EMPLOYMENT.   GMASLWX61961

COMPILATION OF LAWS AGAINST DISCRIMINATION. EMPLOYMENT, EDUCATIONAL INSTITUTIONS, PLACES OF PUBLIC
ACCOMODATICN, PUBLIC HOUSING, PUBLICLY ASSISTED HOUSING, PRIVATE HOUSING. /MASSACHUSETTS/ GMASSCAND963

DISCRIMINATION IN EMPLOYMENT.   GMCNIRK48932

DISCRIMINATION IN EMPLOYMENT.   GMENCWX62974

LABOR-FORCE AND EMPLOYMENT, 1960-62.   GMEREJL63067

ETHNIC SURVEY OF EMPLOYMENT IN STATE GOVERNMENT. /CALIFURNIA/   GMESPFA63977

MERIT EMPLOYMENT IN MICHIGAN. A PICTORIAL REPORT.   GMICFEP63981

CIVIL-RIGHTS AND EMPLOYMENT. SELECTED REFERENCES.   GMICSUSND984

TECHNICAL REPORT NUMBER 1. EMPLOYMENT PRACTICES IN THE HOTEL, MOTEL AND RESTAURANT INDUSTRY OF MISSOURI. GMILLRX66020

TECHNICAL REPORT NUMBER 2. EMPLOYMENT PRACTICES OF SELECTED MISSOURI PUBLIC UTILITIES. NATURAL GAS AND
ELECTRIC.   GMILLRX66021

CROPCUTS. A POLITICAL PRCBLEM. /EMPLOYMENT/   GMILLSM62354

SURVEY AND ANALYSIS OF NON-WHITE EMPLOYMENT BY THE CITY OF MINNEAPOLIS. /MINNESOTA/ GMINLMH65002

THE ROLE OF EMPLOYMENT POLICY. /ANTI-POVERTY/   GMINSHX65655

THE OUTLOOK FOR TECHNOLOGICAL-CHANGE AND EMPLOYMENT.   GNATLCO66897

THE EMPLOYMENT IMPACT OF TECHNOLOGICAL-CHANGE.   GNATLCT66849

PROBLEMS. RESEARCH. AND RECOMMENDATIONS IN THE EMPLOYMENT TESTING OF MINORITY-GROUP APPLICANTS. GNEWCMR66163

REPORT OF A PRELIMINARY STUDY OF EMPLOYMENT PRACTICES INVOLVING MINORITY-GRJUP WORKERS, ESSEX-COUNTY.
NEW-JERSEY.   GNEWJDE46059

REPORT ON A SURVEY OF EMPLOYMENT POLICIES AND HIRING PRACTICES INVOLVING MINORITY-GROUPS IN HUDON-COUNTY,

REPORT ON A SURVEY OF EMPLOYMENT POLICIES AND PRACTICES INVOLVING MINORITY-GROUPS IN MIDDLESEX-COUNTY,
NEW-JERSEY.   GNEWJDE52061

A SELECTIVE BIBLIOGRAPHY ON DISCRIMINATION IN HOUSING AND EMPLOYMENT.   GNEWYLF60075

MANAGEMENT AND MERIT EMPLOYMENT.   GNEWYSAND084

EMPLOYMENT IN DEPARTMENT STORES. /NEW-YORK/   GNEWYSA58079

EMPLOYMENT IN THE HOTEL INDUSTRY. /NEW-YORK/   GNEWYSA58081

RAILROAC. EMPLOYMENT IN THE NEW-YORK AND NEW-JERSEY.   GNEWYSA58101

REPORT ON EMPLOYMENT AND IMAGE OF MINORITY-GROUPS ON TELEVISION.   GNEWYSB63105

EMPLOYMENT AND EARNINGS OF MIGRANT FARM WORKERS IN NEW-YORK STATE.   GNEWYSE60110

SUMMARY OF PROCEEDINGS. WORKSHOP ON THE IMPACT OF A TIGHTENING LABOR-MARKET ON THE EMPLOYABILITY AND
EMPLOYMENT OF DISADVANTAGED YOUTH.   GNEWYUC66116

FEDERAL LEGISLATION FOR A COMPREHENSIVE PROGRAM ON YOUTH EMPLOYMENT.   GNIXORA66847

FAIR PLAY STARTS WITH THE BOSS. /EMPLOYMENT DISCRIMINATION/   GNIXORM56117

SURVEY OF EMPLOYMENT IN STATE GOVERNMENT. /NORTH-CAROLINA/   GNORTCG64121

LAWS AGAINST DISCRIMINATION. EMPLOYMENT, PUBLIC ACCOMODATIONS, HOUSING. /OHIO/   GOHICCR65125

RULES CN EMPLOYMENT INQUIRIES.   GOREGBLND139

DISCRIMINATION IN URBAN EMPLOYMENT.   GPALMEN47145

DISCRIMINATION IN HOUSING AND EMPLOYMENT. WHAT TYPE OF PROBLEM IS IT.   GPEDDWX64150

EMPLOYMENT PRACTICES IN PENNSYLVANIA.   GPENNGC53159

EMPLOYMENT PRACTICES OF THE PHILADELPHIA SCHOOL DISTRICT. /PENNSYLVANIA/   GPENNHR62162

FAIR EMPLOYMENT SURVEY OF THE WESTCHESTER AREA. /PENNSYLVANIA/   GPENNHR65163

REPORT OF PROGRESS IN THE INTEGRATION OF HOTEL AND RESTAURANT EMPLOYMENT, APRIL 1961 TO MARCH 1962.
/PHILADELPHIA PENNSYLVANIA/   GPHILCH62178

A PILOT STUDY OF THE EMPLOYMENT EXPERIENCES OF HIGH SCHOOL GRADUATES.   GPHILCH65177

INSURING FULL EMPLOYMENT.   GPIERJH64846

FEDERAL PROCUREMENT AND EQUAL-OPPORTUNITY EMPLOYMENT.   GPOWETX64190

HOW THE NEW CIVIL-RIGHTS LAW AFFECTS YOUR EMPLOYMENT PRACTICES.   GPRENHI64104

GOVERNMENT CONTRACT EMPLOYMENT. RULES AND REGULATIONS... EFFECTIVE JULY 22, 1961, AS AMENDED SEPTEMBER 7,
1963.   GPRESCD63110

STUDY OF MINORITY-GROUP EMPLOYMENT IN THE FEDERAL GOVERNMENT.   GPRESCC64116

HUMAN-RELATIONS IN FEDERAL EMPLOYMENT.   GPRESCP55197

THE POLICY OF NON-DISCRIMINATION IN EMPLOYMENT IN THE FEDERAL GOVERNMENT.   GPRESCP55198

FIRST ANNUAL REPORT. PRESIDENT-S COMMITTEE ON GOVERNMENT EMPLOYMENT POLICY, APRIL 30 1956.   GPRESCP56193

SECOND ANNUAL REPORT. PRESIDENT-S COMMITTEE ON GOVERNMENT EMPLOYMENT POLICY, 1957.   GPRESCP57194

THIRD ANNUAL REPORT. PRESIDENT-S COMMITTEE ON GOVERNMENT EMPLOYMENT POLICY, 1958.   GPRESCP58195

FOURTH ANNUAL REPORT. PRESIDENT-S COMMITTEE ON GOVERNMENT EMPLOYMENT POLICY.   GPRESCP59196

TRENDS IN THE EMPLOYMENT OF NEGRO-AMERICANS IN UPPER-LEVEL WHITE-COLLAR POSITIONS OF THE FEDERAL
GOVERNMENT.   GPRESCP60200

MERIT EMPLOYMENT -- UNFINISHED BUSINESS.   GPURYMJ62210

ENFORCEMENT OF LAWS AGAINST DISCRIMINATION IN EMPLOYMENT.   GRABKSX64211

COMBATING DISCRIMINATION IN EMPLOYMENT IN NEW-YORK STATE.   GRACKFX49215

THE INTERRELATIONSHIPS OF DISCRIMINATION IN EMPLOYMENT, IN EDUCATION, AND IN HOUSING.   GRAVIMJ61219

THE LAW AND RACIAL DISCRIMINATION IN EMPLOYMENT.   GROSESJ65255

EMPLOYMENT POLICY AND THE LABOR-MARKET.   GROSSAM65720

THE ROLE OF GOVERNMENT IN PROMOTING FULL EMPLOYMENT.   GROSSAM66084

PSYCHOLOGICAL TESTS AND FAIR EMPLOYMENT. A STUDY OF EMPLOYMENT TESTING IN THE SAN-FRANCISCO BAY AREA.
/CALIFORNIA/   GRUSHJT66268

PSYCHOLOGICAL TESTS AND FAIR EMPLOYMENT. A STUDY OF EMPLOYMENT TESTING IN THE SAN-FRANCISCO BAY AREA.
/CALIFORNIA/   GRUSHJT66268

CHANGING PATTERNS IN EMPLOYMENT OF NONWHITE WORKERS.   GRUSSJL66269

FARM AND NON-FARM EMPLOYMENT OPPORTUNITIES FOR LOW-INCOME FARM FAMILIES.   GRUTTVW59270

GEOGRAPHIC MOBILITY AND EMPLOYMENT STATUS, MARCH 1962-MARCH 1963.   GSABESX64271

ESTIMATED NEED FOR SKILLED-WORKERS, 1965-75. /EMPLOYMENT/   GSALTAF66534

RACIAL AND ETHNIC EMPLOYMENT PATTERN SURVEY OF THE CITY AND COUNTY OF SAN-FRANCISCO GOVERNMENT.
DEPARTMENTAL ANALYSIS. /CALIFORNIA/   GSANFHR65264

EMPLOYMENT OF HIGH SCHOOL GRADUATES AND DROPOUTS IN 1962.   GSCHIJX63282

NATIONAL EMPLOYMENT, SKILLS, AND EARNINGS OF FARM LABOR.   GSCHUTW67964

SELECTED LIST OF REFERENCES ON MINORITY-GROUP EMPLOYMENT IN THE PUBLIC SERVICE.   GSIMPDX64312

EMPLOYMENT POLICY PROBLEMS IN A MULTIRACIAL SOCIETY.   GSIMPGE62313

A POLICY FOR FULL EMPLOYMENT.   GSOLORX62323

LEGAL RESTRAINTS ON RACIAL DISCRIMINATION IN EMPLOYMENT.   GSOVEMI66326

TAILORING THE TECHNIQUES TO ELIMINATE AND PREVENT EMPLOYMENT DISCRIMINATION.   GSPITHX64331

STATE LEGISLATION IN LABOR-RELATIONS AND DISCRIMINATION IN EMPLOYMENT, 1945.   GSPITRS45332

MINORITY-GROUP INTEGRATION BY LABOR AND MANAGEMENT. A STUDY OF THE EMPLOYMENT PRACTICES OF THE LARGER
EMPLOYERS, AND THE MEMBERSHIP PRACTICES OF THE LARGER LABOR UNIONS WITH RESPECT TO RACE, RELIGION, AND
NATIONAL ORIGIN. CONNECTICUT, 1951.   GSTETHG53598

ADMINISTRATIVE LAW -- HUMAN-RELATIONS COMMISSIONS, PENNSYLVANIA LAW AND DISCRIMINATORY EMPLOYMENT
PRACTICE.   GTEMPLQ63349

EMPLOYMENT PROGRAM FOR MINORITY-GROUPS.   GTHAMME50353

THE ROLE OF MANPOWER POLICY IN ACHIEVING AGGREGATE GOALS. /EMPLOYMENT INCOME/   GTHURLC66640

EMPLOYMENT SURVEY. /TULSA OKLAHOMA/   GTULSCR66364

LAW OF DISCRIMINATION IN THE EMPLOYMENT OF NONWHITES.   GTURNRH52366

BRIEF SUBMITTED IN SUPPORT OF SENATE BILL NO 984, A BILL TO PROHIBIT DISCRIMINATION IN EMPLOYMENT....   GTUTTCH47368

ECONOMIC, POLITICAL AND PSYCHOLOGICAL ASPECTS OF EMPLOYMENT.   GUPHOWH64528

JOBS TARGET -- EMPLOYMENT.   GUSCHACND383

THE DISADVANTAGED POOR. EDUCATION AND EMPLOYMENT.   GUSCHAC66187

STUDY OF MINORITY GROUP EMPLOYMENT IN THE FEDERAL GOVERNMENT, 1966.   GUSCISC66767

EMPLOYMENT, 1961 US COMMISSION-ON-CIVIL-RIGHTS REPORT, VOLUME 3.   GUSCOMC61395

HOUSING, EMPLOYMENT OPPORTUNITIES AND APPRENTICESHIP TRAINING, REPORT. /NEW-JERSEY/   GUSCCMC63404

REPORT ON WASHINGTON-DC. EMPLOYMENT.   GUSCOMC63412

REPORT ON MARYLAND. EMPLOYMENT.   GUSCOMC64411

SUMMARY FACT SHEETS FOR STATE PUBLIC AGENCIES WITH JURISDICTION OVER DISCRIMINATION IN EMPLOYMENT.   GUSCCMC65416

REPORT ON EMPLOYMENT PROBLEMS OF NONWHITE YOUTH IN MICHIGAN.   GUSCOMC66408

EMPLOYMENT AND UNEMPLOYMENT.   GUSCONG62977

RECENT TRENDS IN PUBLIC EMPLOYMENT.   GUSCONMND419

EXPANDING EMPLOYMENT OPPORTUNITIES IN NEWARK. EXPERIENCE REPORT 101. /NEW-JERSEY/   GUSCONM65418

RECRUITING MINORITIES FOR PUBLIC EMPLOYMENT. EXPERIENCE REPORT 105.   GUSCONM66420

CIVILIAN PERSONNEL -- NONDISCRIMINATION IN EMPLOYMENT. /MILITARY/   GUSDAIR62189

EMPLOYMENT AND EARNINGS.   GUSDLABND444

SCHOOL AND EARLY EMPLOYMENT EXPERIENCE OF YOUTH. A REPORT ON SEVEN COMMUNITIES, 1952-57.   GUSDLAB60494

BRIEF SUMMARY OF STATE LAWS AGAINST DISCRIMINATION IN PRIVATE EMPLOYMENT. FAIR-EMPLOYMENT-PRACTICE ACTS. GUSDLAB63439

BRIDGE TO EMPLOYMENT. DEMONSTRATION MANPOWER PROGRAMS.   GUSDLAB63442

STUDY OF MINORITY-GROUP EMPLOYMENT IN THE FEDERAL GOVERNMENT.   GUSDLAB63500

INDUSTRY EMPLOYMENT GROWTH SINCE WORLD WAR II.   GUSDLAB63831

CONSOLIDATED INVENTORY OF DEPARTMENT OF LABOR RESEARCH ON LABOR-FORCE EMPLOYMENT AND UNEMPLOYMENT.   GUSDLAB64441

EMPLOYMENT OF HIGH SCHOOL GRADUATES AND DROPOUTS IN 1965.   GUSDLAB66073

FARM LABOR DEVELOPMENTS -- EMPLOYMENT AND WAGE SUPPLEMENT.   GUSDLAB66446

EMPLOYMENT SERVICE TASK FORCE REPORT. /MANPOWER SES/   GUSDLAB66559

TECHNOLOGICAL TRENDS IN MAJOR AMERICAN INDUSTRIES. /EMPLOYMENT/   GUSDLAB66637

EMPLOYMENT AND EARNINGS STATISTICS FOR THE UNITED STATES, 1909-1966.   GUSDLAB66832

GUIDELINES ON EMPLOYMENT TESTING PROCEDURES.   GUSEEOC66510

IMPACT OF AUTOMATION ON EMPLOYMENT.   GUSHOUR61985

YOUTH, THE NATION-S RICHEST RESOURCE. THEIR EDUCATION AND EMPLOYMENT NEEDS.   GUSINCC53514

PROBLEMS OF YOUTH. A FACT BOOK. /EMPLOYMENT/   GUSLIBC64823

FEDERAL EQUALITY OF OPPORTUNITY IN EMPLOYMENT ACT.   GUSSENA52350

ANTIDISCRIMINATION IN EMPLOYMENT.   GUSSENA54330

VOLUNTARY FARM EMPLOYMENT SERVICE. /MIGRANT-WORKERS/   GUSSENA64306

TOWARDS FULL EMPLOYMENT. PROPOSALS FOR A COMPREHENSIVE EMPLOYMENT AND MANPOWER POLICY IN THE UNITED
STATES.   GUSSENA64332

TOWARDS FULL EMPLOYMENT. PROPOSALS FOR A COMPREHENSIVE EMPLOYMENT AND MANPOWER POLICY IN THE UNITED
STATES.   GUSSENA64332

SELECTED READINGS IN EMPLOYMENT AND MANPOWER.   GUSSENA64334

THE CHANGING PATTERN IN EMPLOYMENT. /EQUAL-EMPLOYMENT-OPPORTUNITY/   GWALLLM63520

TESTING OF MINORITY-GROUP APPLICANTS FOR EMPLOYMENT.   GWALLPX66539

EMPLOYMENT   (CONTINUATION)

A STUDY OF EMPLOYMENT PATTERNS IN THE GENERAL MERCHANDISE GROUP RETAIL STORES IN NEW-YORK-CITY.   GWATKDC66588

EMPLOYMENT INTEGRATION AND RACIAL WAGE DIFFERENCE IN A SOUTHERN PLANT.   GWEINRX59988

POSTWAR EMPLOYMENT DISCRIMINATION.   GWEISAJ47547

THE PROPOSED LEGISLATIVE DEATH KNELL OF PRIVATE DISCRIMINATORY EMPLOYMENT PRACTICES.   GWILSAX45566

EMPLOYMENT AND UNEMPLOYMENT IN THE UNITED STATES.   GWOFLSX64759

LABOR LOOKS AT EQUAL RIGHTS IN EMPLOYMENT. /UNION/   GWOLLJA64579

HOW MANY CONTRACTS BAR DISCRIMINATION IN EMPLOYMENT.   GWORTMS64586

CITY EMPLOYMENT SURVEY. PERCENTAGE OF MINORITY-GROUP EMPLOYEES BY DEPARTMENT. /YONKERS NEW-YORK/   GYONKCC66592

EMPLOYMENT PRACTICES. CITY OF SAN-DIEGO, 1963-1964. /CALIFORNIA/   GZOOKDX64596

PROBLEMS OF NAVAJO MALE GRADUATES OF INTERMOUNTAIN SCHOOL DURING THEIR FIRST YEAR OF EMPLOYMENT.   IBAKEJE59533

TOWARD A NEW ERA FOR AMERICAN INDIANS. /EMPLOYMENT/   IBENNRL66451

AMERICAN INDIANS IN CALIFORNIA. POPULATION, EDUCATION, EMPLOYMENT, INCOME.   ICALDIR65541

PROGRESS IN EMPLOYMENT ASSISTANCE.   IDAVIRC62546

RELOCATEES FROM GALLUP AREA TO THE DENVER FIELD EMPLOYMENT ASSISTANCE OFFICE. /COLORADO/   IGRAVTDND438

EMPLOYMENT ASSISTANCE REFERENCE BIBLIOGRAPHY.   IUSDINTND452

EMPLOYMENT ASSISTANCE PROGRAM.   IUSDINT64647

A FOLLOWUP STUDY OF 1963 RECIPIENTS OF THE SERVICES OF THE EMPLOYMENT ASSISTANCE PROGRAM,
BUREAU-OF-INDIAN-AFFAIRS.   IUSDINT66650

MINUTES OF INDIAN EMPLOYMENT MEETING HELD NOVEMBER 29-30, 1966 IN BISMARK, NORTH-DAKOTA.   IUSDLAB66322

ADL AT WORK. THE CRUMBLING WALLS. /EMPLOYMENT DISCRIMINATION/   JADLBXX63688

JEWISH LAW GRADUATE. /EMPLOYMENT DISCRIMINATION/   JADLBXX64689

ADL REPORTS ON SOCIAL, EMPLOYMENT, EDUCATIONAL AND HOUSING DISCRIMINATION.   JANTIDL57690

SOME OF MY BEST FRIENDS... /EMPLOYMENT DISCRIMINATION/   JEPSTBRND719

DETROIT-S OLD HABIT. /EMPLOYMENT DISCRIMINATION/   JFORSAX63723

EQUAL RIGHTS FOR THE SATURDAY SABBATH OBSERVER. /EMPLOYMENT DISCRIMINATION/   JHARTPX63729

EMPLOYMENT DISCRIMINATION -- PART I.   JRIGHXX57753

EMPLOYMENT DISCRIMINATION -- PART II.   JRIGHXX57754

EMPLOYMENT IN INSURANCE COMPANIES. /DISCRIMINATION/   JRIGHXX59755

EMPLOYMENT OF JEWISH PERSONNEL IN THE AUTOMOBILE INDUSTRY. /DISCRIMINATION/   JRIGHXX63756

JEWISH LAW STUDENT AND NEW-YORK JOBS. /EMPLOYMENT DISCRIMINATION/   JRIGHXX64757

INSURANCE, BANKING, PUBLIC UTILITIES. /DISCRIMINATION EMPLOYMENT/   JSIMCBX58763

JEWS NEED NOT APPLY. /DISCRIMINATION EMPLOYMENT/   JWEISAX58770

MERRILL-TRUST-FUND TO IMPROVE THE EMPLOYMENT OPPORTUNITIES OF THE MIGRANT FARM WORKERS OF MEXICAN ORIGIN.   MBISHCS62365

EMPLOYMENT PROBLEMS OF THE MEXICAN-AMERICAN.   MBULLPX64369

TRANSCRIPT OF PROCEEDINGS OF THE INTERIM SUBCOMMITTEE ON SPECIAL EMPLOYMENT PROBLEMS. /CALIFORNIA/   MCALAIC64374

CALIFORNIANS OF SPANISH SURNAME. POPULATION, EMPLOYMENT, INCOME, EDUCATION.   MCALDIR64377

REPORT BY MEXICAN-AMERICAN LEADERS. EDUCATION, EMPLOYMENT, ETC.   MCALDIR64379

PROCEEDINGS OF EMPLOYMENT OPPORTUNITIES EDUCATIONAL CONFERENCE.   MCOUNMA62930

STATEMENT ON EMPLOYMENT PROBLEMS OF MEXICAN-AMERICANS IN CALIFORNIA.   MMORADX63445

EMPLOYMENT AND EMPLOYABILITY AMONG CALIFORNIA YOUTH AUTHORITY WARDS. A SURVEY.   MSECKJP62483

MEXICAN-AMERICAN AND TOTAL EMPLOYMENT IN SELECTED STATES AND STANDARD METROPOLITAN STATISTICAL AREAS.   MUSCISC63504

VALUE ORIENTATIONS OF YOUNG MEXICAN-AMERICAN MALES AS REFLECTED IN THEIR WORK PATTERNS AND EMPLOYMENT
PREFERENCES.   MWADDJC62513

EMPLOYMENT PROBLEMS OF THE MEXICAN-AMERICAN.   MWOODMJ64518

EMPLOYMENT PROBLEMS OF MEXICAN-AMERICANS.   MWOODMJ65446

NEGRO YOUTH AND EMPLOYMENT OPPORTUNITIES. /UNEMPLOYMENT EDUCATION/   NAMOSWE63021

EMPLOYMENT OF NEGROES IN THE FEDERAL-GOVERNMENT.   NANDEBE65023

THE NEGROES PROGRESS TOWARD EMPLOYMENT EQUALITY.   NAUGUTX58034

PROGRESS TOWARD INTEGRATION. FOUR CASE-STUDIES. /EMPLOYMENT FEPC NEW-YORK/   NBACKSX59040

RACE-RELATIONS IN AN INDUSTRIAL SOCIETY. /EMPLOYMENT GRIEVANCE-PROCEDURES/   NBACOEF63041

NEGRO EMPLOYMENT IN FEDERAL-GOVERNMENT.   NBAERMF61042

EMPLOYMENT AND INCOME OF NEGRO WORKERS. 1940-1952.   NBEDEMS53071

SCHOOL ATTENDANCE AND ATTAINMENT. FUNCTION AND DYSFUNCTION OF SCHOOL AND FAMILY SOCIAL SYSTEMS.
/EMPLOYMENT DROP-OUT/   NBERTAL62882

THE EMPLOYMENT OF THE NEW-YORK NEGRO IN RETROSPECT.   NBLOCHD59090

DISCRIMINATION AGAINST THE NEGRO IN EMPLOYMENT IN NEW-YORK, 1920-1963.   NBLOCHD65089

SOME EFFECTS OF DISCRIMINATICN IN EMPLOYMENT.   NBLOCHD66092

A BIBLIOGRAPHY OF CIVIL-RIGHTS AND CIVIL-LIBERTIES. /EMPLOYMENT UNION   MILITARY/   NBROOAD62117

TRANSFORMATION OF THE NEGRO-AMERICAN. /EDUCATION EMPLOYMENT INCOME/   NBROCLX65123

WHEN WILL AMERICA-S NEGROES CATCH UP. /EMPLOYMENT/   NBROOLX65124

MANAGING YOUR MANPOWER. NEGRC EMPLOYMENT PROBLEM.   NBROOTR63118

WAR INDUSTRY EMPLOYMENT FOR NEGROES IN MARYLAND.   NBRYSWO43129

RACIAL ATTITUDES AND THE EMPLOYMENT OF NEGROES.   NBULLHA51133

EMPLOYMENT AND TRAINING, THE MCCONE-REPORT -- SIX MONTHS LATER.   NBULLPXND134

FINAL REPORT. EMPLOYMENT AND TRAINING, REPORT FOR GOVERNOR-S COMMISSION.   NBULLPX65483

SUMMARY OF MAJOR POINTS, TALK ON EMPLOYMENT, MCCONE-COMMISSION SERIES.   NBULLPX66898

THE NEGRO-S FORCE IN MARKETPLACE. /EMPLOYMENT/   NBUSIWX62156

NEGRC CALIFORNIANS. POPULATICN, EMPLOYMENT, INCOME, EDUCATION.   NCALDIR63167

OPERATION ACHIEVEMENT. /NEW-YORK EMPLOYMENT/   NCALVIJ63176

CHANGES IN NONWHITE EMPLOYMENT 1960-1966.   NCAMPJT66010

EMPLOYMENT OPPORTUNITY FOR NASHVILLE NEGROES. /TENNESSEE/   NCOMUCE60230

EMPLOYMENT, EDUCATION AND MARRIAGE OF YOUNG NEGRO ADULTS.   NCOXXOC41934

THE NEGRO AMERICAN. /EMPLOYMENT INCOME ECONOMIC-STATUS/   NDAEDXX65246

THE RELATIVE EMPLOYMENT AND INCOME OF AMERICAN NEGROES.   NDANIWG63249

NEGRO EMPLOYMENT IN THE FEDERAL GOVERNMENT.   NDAVIJA45259

POSTWAR EMPLOYMENT AND THE NEGRO WORKER.   NDAVIJA46258

NEGRO EMPLOYMENT. A PROGRESS REPORT.   NDAVIJA52256

TVA ANC NEGRO EMPLOYMENT. /TENNESSEE/   NDAVIJH55253

EMPLOYMENT SURVEY OF DES-MOINES FIRMS. /IOWA/   NDESMCH65265

NEGRO EMPLOYMENT IN SOUTHERN INDUSTRY.   NDEWEDX52270

FOUR STUDIES OF NEGRO EMPLOYMENT IN THE UPPER SOUTH.   NDEWEDX55269

OCCUPATIONAL SHIFTS IN NEGRO EMPLOYMENT.   NOIAMDE65273

NEGRC EMPLOYMENT OPPORTUNITIES DURING AND AFTER THE WAR.   NDGDDAE45949

CESEGREGATION AND THE EMPLOYMENT OF NEGRO TEACHERS. /OCCUPATIONS/   NDODDHH55950

SOUTHERN ECONOMIC DEVELOPMENT AS REVEALED BY THE CHANGING STRUCTURE OF EMPLOYMENT.   NDUVNES62309

NEGRO EMPLOYMENT PROBLEM.   NDUNSRA63310

RELATICN OF MOTHER-S EMPLOYMENT TO INTELLECTUAL PERFCRMANCE OF NEGRO COLLEGE STUDENTS.   NEPPSEG64336

THE NEGROES WHO DO NOT WANT TO END SEGREGATICN. /EMPLOYMENT/   NFAGGHL55255

A NEW LOOK AT EMPLOYMENT.   NFEILJG63346

NEGRC EMPLOYMENT IN MIAMI. /FLORIDA/   NFLURCO62366

FORTUNE PRESS ANALYSIS. NEGROES. /EMPLOYMENT/   NFORTUN45052

THE DEEP SOUTH LOOKS UP. /PCVERTY EMPLOYMENT/   NFORTXX43050

OUTREACH -- THE AFFIRMATIVE APPROACH. /EMPLOYMENT SES/   NFRANWH66698

OPENING THE DOOR TO EMPLOYMENT. /EEO/   NGEORCH64399

RACIAL INTEGRATION IN EMPLOYMENT -- FINDINGS IN TWO KANSAS-CITY HOSPITALS.   NGIBSHX54402

THE NEGRO POTENTIAL. /EMPLOYMENT INCOME EDUCATION/   NGINZEX56409

EMPLOYMENT PATTERNS OF NEGRO MEN AND WOMEN.   NGINZEX66416

THE WAR-TIME EMPLOYMENT OF NEGROES IN THE FEDERAL-GOVERNMENT.   NGOLICL45432

EMPLOYMENT SECURITY, SENIORITY AND RACE. THE ROLE OF TITLE-VII OF THE CIVIL-RIGHTS-ACT OF 1964. NGOULWB67864

BARRIERS TO NEGRO WAR EMPLOYMENT.   NGRANLB42440

FAIR EMPLOYMENT IS GOOD BUSINESS AT G FOX OF HARTFORD. /CASE-STUDY CONNECTICUT/   NGREEMX48448

PERSCNNEL PRACTICES AND WARTIME CHANGES. /EMPLOYMENT/   NHAASFJ46548

CHIEF EXECUTIVES VIEW NEGRO EMPLOYMENT. /INDUSTRY/   NHABBSX65471

COMPANY EXPERIENCE WITH NEGRC EMPLOYMENT. /INDUSTRY/   NHABBSX66472

NEW-YORK-S NONDISCRIMINATION EMPLOYMENT POLICY.   NHARRCV65491

PICKETING BY NEGROES TO OBTAIN EMPLOYMENT IN PROPORTION TO NEGRO CUSTOMERS HELD UNLAWFUL.   NHARVLR49498

NEGRO EMPLOYMENT IN THE BIRMINGHAM METROPOLITAN AREA. /ALABAMA CASE-STUCY/   NHAWLLT55502

NEGROES IN THE GOVERNMENT EMPLOYMENT.   NHENDEW43510

EMPLOYMENT OPPORTUNITIES FOR NASHVILLE NEGROES. /TENNESSEE/   NHENDVW60516

PATTERNS OF EMPLOYMENT DISCRIMINATION.   NHILLHX62537

RACIAL INEQUALITY IN EMPLOYMENT. THE PATTERNS OF DISCRIMINATION.   NHILLHX65540

THE EMPLOYMENT OF NEGROES IN THE US BY MAJOR OCCUPATION AND INDUSTRY.   NHOPEJX53567

NEGRO EMPLOYMENT IN THREE SOUTHERN PLANTS OF INTERNATIONAL HARVESTER COMPANY. /CASE-STUDY/   NHOPEJX55572

EQUALITY OF OPPORTUNITY. A UNION APPROACH TO FAIR EMPLOYMENT.   NHOPEJX56570

EQUALITY OF EMPLOYMENT OPPORTUNITY. A PROCESS ANALYSIS OF UNION INITIATIVE.   NHOPEJX60569

COLLEGE, COLOR, AND EMPLOYMENT. RACIAL DIFFERENTIALS IN POSTGRADUATE EMPLOYMENT AMONG 1964 GRADUATES OF
LOUISIANA COLLEGES.   NHUSOCF66328

COLLEGE, COLOR, AND EMPLOYMENT. RACIAL DIFFERENTIALS IN POSTGRADUATE EMPLOYMENT AMONG 1964 GRADUATES OF
LOUISIANA COLLEGES.   NHUSOCF66328

THE EMPLOYMENT SITUATION OF WHITE AND NEGRO YOUTH IN THE CITY OF BALTIMORE. INITIAL EXPERIENCES IN THE
LABOR-MARKET. /MARYLAND/   NJCHNHU63735

NEGRO YOUTH IN THE SOUTH. /EDUCATION EMPLOYMENT/   NJONELW60010

THE EFFECT OF THE GHETTO ON THE DISTRIBUTION AND LEVEL OF NONWHITE EMPLOYMENT IN URBAN AREAS.   NKAINJF64631

THE BIG CITIES BIG PROBLEM. /GHETTO EMPLOYMENT/   NKAINJF66630

POSITION PAPER ON EMPLOYMENT INTEGRATION.   NKELLKP64641

STATEMENT AND TESTIMONY ON FEDERAL ROLE IN URBAN AFFAIRS. /EMPLOYMENT GHETTO/   NKENNRF66017

NEGRO EMPLOYMENT IN KENTUCKY STATE AGENCIES.   NKENTCH66643

EMPLOYMENT PROBLEMS OF THE OLDER NEGRO WORKER.   NKERNJH50644

A STUDY OF THE EMPLOYMENT OPPORTUNITIES FOR NEGROES IN BREWERIES OF THE UNITED STATES. /INDUSTRY/ NKERNJH51897

CHANGING PATTERNS OF NEGRO EMPLOYMENT. /OCCUPATIONAL-PATTERNS/   NKIFEAX64649

THE NEGRO IN FEDERAL EMPLOYMENT. THE QUEST FOR EQUAL-OPPORTUNITY.   NKRISSX67143

RACIAL DISCRIMINATION IN EMPLOYMENT IN THE CINNCINATI AREA. /OHIO/   NKUHNAX62668

THE EMPLOYMENT OF NEGROES IN PUBLIC WELFARE IN ELEVEN SOUTHERN STATES, 1936-1949. /OCCUPATIONS/   NLARKJR52672

DISCRIMINATION IN EMPLOYMENT.   NLEITRD49681

EMPLOYMENT OF NEGRO MANPOWER IN CALVERT COUNTY, MARYLAND.   NLERANL60401

THE EMPLOYMENT SITUATION OF WHITE AND NEGRO YOUTH IN THE CITY OF BALTIMORE. /MARYLAND/   NLEVEBX63684

PROMOTING EQUAL-EMPLOYMENT THROUGH THE PUBLIC EMPLOYMENT SERVICE.   NLEVILX62686

JOBS AND COLOR. NEGRO EMPLOYMENT IN TENNESSEE STATE GOVERNMENT.   NLONGHH62706

STRICTLY SPEAKING. /EMPLOYMENT/   NLONGMX62048

PROPOSALS FOR THE IMPROVEMENT OF HUMAN RELATIONS IN THE LOS-ANGELES METROPOLITAN AREA. /EMPLOYMENT
CALIFORNIA/   NLOSACC65365

REPORT OF THE COMMISSION ON THE EMPLOYMENT PROBLEMS OF NEGROES TO GOVERNOR SALTONSTALL. /MASSACHUSETTS/   NMASSCE42757

HOSPITAL EMPLOYMENT STUDY.   NMCGCDJ66583

THE CIVIL-RIGHTS MOVEMENT AND EMPLOYMENT.   NMCKERB64722

CIVIL-RIGHTS STRATEGIES FOR NEGRO EMPLOYMENT.   NMEIEAX67764

EMPLOYMENT DISTRIBUTION STUDY OF THE CONSTRUCTION INDUSTRY IN MICHIGAN.   NMICCRC66606

A STUDY OF NON-WHITE EMPLOYMENT IN THE STATE SERVICE. /MICHIGAN/   NMICCSC64775

A FOLLOW-UP STUDY OF NON-WHITE EMPLOYMENT IN THE STATE SERVICE. /MICHIGAN/   NMICCSC65774

A STUDY OF EMPLOYMENT AND TRAINING PATTERNS IN THE LANSING AREA. /MICHIGAN/   NMICFEP58778

THE JOB GAP. /EMPLOYMENT/   NMILLHP66630

EMPLOYMENT AS IT RELATES TO NEGROES IN THE MILWAUKEE INDUSTRIAL AREA. /WISCONSIN/   NMILWUL48793

INTELLIGENCE IN THE UNITED STATES, A SURVEY -- WITH CONCLUSIONS FOR MANPOWER UTILIZATION IN EDUCATION AND
EMPLOYMENT.   NMINEJB57796

EQUAL-EMPLOYMENT-OPPORTUNITIES IN MISSOURI STATE AGENCIES. A SURVEY OF NEGRO EMPLOYMENT, SPRING-SUMMER
1963.   NMISSCH64801

EMPLOYMENT ON MERIT. THE CONTINUING CHALLENGE TO BUSINESS. NEGRO-S ECONOMIC LOT.   NMORRJJ57854

THE NEGRO AND EMPLOYMENT OPPORTUNITIES IN THE SOUTH.   NMOSSJA62856

EMPLOYMENT, INCOME, AND THE ORDEAL OF THE NEGRO FAMILY.   NMOYNDP65861

PROBLEMS AND PROSPECTS OF THE NEGRO MOVEMENT. /EMPLOYMENT/   NMURPRJ66866

GOALS IN NEGRO EMPLOYMENT. /INDUSTRY/   NNATLIC65874

SELECTED STUDIES OF NEGRO EMPLOYMENT IN THE SOUTH.   NNATLPA55881

INTER-RACIAL PLANNING FOR COMMUNITY ORGANIZATION... EMPLOYMENT PROBLEMS OF THE NEGRO.   NNATLUL44900

REPORT OF THE COMMITTEE ON UNFAIR EMPLOYMENT PRACTICES.   NNEBRLC51906

THE EMPLOYMENT OF NEGROES AS DRIVER SALESMEN IN THE BAKING INDUSTRY.   NNEWYSA60919

RACIAL DISCRIMINATION IN EMPLOYMENT. BIBLIOGRAPHY.   NNORGPH62931

AT WORK IN NORTH-CAROLINA TODAY. 48 CASE-REPORTS ON NORTH-CAROLINA NEGROES NOW EMPLOYED OR PREPARING
THEMSELVES FOR EMPLOYMENT...THEIR EDUCATION, JOB QUALIFICATIONS, AND CAREER ASPIRATIONS.   NNORTCGND933

EMPLOYMENT IN STATE GOVERNMENT. /NORTH-CAROLINA/   NNORTCG66092

UNIONS AND NEGRO EMPLOYMENT.   NNORTHR46947

THE NEGRO AND EMPLOYMENT OPPORTUNITY. PROBLEMS AND PRACTICES.   NNORTHR65949

INDUSTRY-S RACIAL EMPLOYMENT POLICIES.   NNORTHR67938

NEGRO EMPLOYMENT IN THE TEXTILE INDUSTRIES OF NORTH AND SOUTH-CAROLINA. /NORTH-CAROLINA/   NOSBUDD66963

EMPLOYMENT SECURITY AND THE NEGRO.   NOXLELA40969

DISCRIMINATION IN URBAN EMPLOYMENT.   NPALMEN47971

NEGRO YOUTH -- EDUCATION, EMPLOYMENT, AND CIVIL-RIGHTS.   NPEARAX64980

THE PREPARATION OF DISADVANTAGED YOUTH FOR EMPLOYMENT AND CIVIC RESPONSIBILITIES.   NPERRJX64985

THE NEGRO REVOLUTION AND EMPLOYMENT.   NPOLIEX64219

STATEMENT TO THE NEW-YORK STATE ADVISORY COMMITTEE TO THE US COMMISSION ON CIVIL-RIGHTS, MAY 23, 1966.
/EMPLOYMENT LEGISLATION/   NPOLIEX66004

RACIAL DISCRIMINATION IN EMPLOYMENT. PROPOSALS FOR CORRECTIVE ACTION.   NPOLLDX63006

NEGRO AND TOTAL EMPLOYMENT BY GRADE AND SALARY GROUPS, JUNE 1961 AND JUNE 1962.   NPRESCD62011

NEGRO EMPLOYMENT IN THE FEDERAL GOVERNMENT BY CIVIL SERVICE REGION, STATE AND PAY CATEGORIES, JUNE 1962. NPRESCD62012

MINORITY-GROUP STUDY, JUNE 1963. NEGRO AND TOTAL EMPLOYMENT IN SELECTED AGENCIES.   NPRESCD63010

CHARACTERISTICS OF NEGRO EMPLOYMENT IN FEDERAL AGENCIES IN ATLANTA, GEORGIA.   NPRESCP60016

CHANGING EMPLOYMENT PATTERNS OF NEGROES, 1920-1950.   NPRESHB62125

COMPANY EXPERIENCE WITH THE EMPLOYMENT OF NEGROES. /INDUSTRY/   NPRINUI54020

MANAGEMENT SOCIAL RESPONSIBILITY AND RACIAL EMPLOYMENT IN THE MEAT-PACKING INDUSTRY.   NPURCTV67123

NO TIME FOR TRAGIC IRONIES. /EMPLOYMENT TECHNOLOGICAL-CHANGE/   NPURYMT63027

PROBLEMS AND TRENDS IN JOB-DEVELOPMENT AND EMPLOYMENT PROGRAMS.   NPURYMT63028

COMBATING DISCRIMINATION IN THE EMPLOYMENT OF NEGROES IN WAR INDUSTRIES AND GOVERNMENT AGENCIES.   NRAMSLA43128

NEGROES IN THE UNITED STATES. THEIR EMPLOYMENT AND ECONOMIC STATUS.   NRINGHH53061

WASTE OF MANPOWER -- RACE AND EMPLOYMENT IN A SOUTHERN STATE.   NROBEGX62064

INCOME, EMPLOYMENT STATUS AND CHANGE IN CALVERT COUNTY, MARYLAND.   NROHRWC58400

TOWARD FAIR EMPLOYMENT. A REVIEW.   NROSERX65130

THE LAW AND RACIAL DISCRIMINATION IN EMPLOYMENT.   NROSESJ67078

EMPLOYMENT OF TEENAGERS, JUNE 1966.   NROSSAM66081

EMPLOYMENT, RACE AND POVERTY.   NROSSAM67086

A REVIEW OF RESEARCH ON THE NEGRO AND EMPLOYMENT IN THE SOUTH.   NROWARL65703

NEGRO EMPLOYMENT IN BIRMINGHAM. THREE CASES. /ALABAMA/   NROWARL67091

NEGRO POLICE EMPLOYMENT IN THE URBAN SOUTH.   NRUDWEM61134

NEGRO LABOR IN THE SOUTHERN CRYSTAL BALL. /EMPLOYMENT/   NRUTHKX49100

NEGRO EMPLOYMENT.   NSHAFHB59118

CIVIL-RIGHTS, EMPLOYMENT, AND THE SOCIAL STATUS OF AMERICAN NEGROES.   NSHEPHL66129

APPEALS FROM DISCRIMINATION IN FEDERAL EMPLOYMENT. A CASE-STUDY.   NSHOSAX63131

EMPLOYMENT EXPERIENCES OF NEGRO PHILADELPHIANS. A DESCRIPTIVE STUDY OF THE EMPLOYMENT EXPERIENCES,
PERCEPTIONS, AND ASPIRATIONS OF SELECTED PHILADELPHIA WHITES AND NON-WHITES.   NSIEGAI59718

EMPLOYMENT EXPERIENCES OF NEGRO PHILADELPHIANS. A DESCRIPTIVE STUDY OF THE EMPLOYMENT EXPERIENCES,
PERCEPTIONS, AND ASPIRATIONS OF SELECTED PHILADELPHIA WHITES AND NON-WHITES.   NSIEGAI59718

HOUSTON -- THE NEGRO AND EMPLOYMENT OPPORTUNITIES IN THE SOUTH, THE FIRST OF A SERIES OF EMPLOYMENT
STUDIES IN SOUTHERN CITIES. /TEXAS/   NSOUTRC61161

HOUSTON -- THE NEGRO AND EMPLOYMENT OPPORTUNITIES IN THE SOUTH, THE FIRST OF A SERIES OF EMPLOYMENT
STUDIES IN SOUTHERN CITIES. /TEXAS/   NSOUTRC61161

THE NEGRO AND EMPLOYMENT OPPORTUNITIES IN THE SOUTH.   NSOUTRC62151

ATLANTA -- THE NEGRO AND EMPLOYMENT OPPORTUNITIES IN THE SOUTH, THE THIRD OF A SERIES OF EMPLOYMENT
STUDIES IN SOUTHERN CITIES. /GEORGIA/   NSOUTRC62155

ATLANTA -- THE NEGRO AND EMPLOYMENT OPPORTUNITIES IN THE SOUTH, THE THIRD OF A SERIES OF EMPLOYMENT
STUDIES IN SOUTHERN CITIES. /GEORGIA/   NSOUTRC62155

CHATTANOOGA -- THE NEGRO AND EMPLOYMENT OPPORTUNITIES IN THE SOUTH, THE SECOND OF A SERIES OF EMPLOYMENT
STUDIES IN SOUTHERN CITIES. /TENNESSEE/   NSOUTRC62156

CHATTANOOGA -- THE NEGRO AND EMPLOYMENT OPPORTUNITIES IN THE SOUTH, THE SECOND OF A SERIES OF EMPLOYMENT
STUDIES IN SOUTHERN CITIES. /TENNESSEE/   NSOUTRC62156

RACIAL WORK AND NEGRO WASTE IN SOUTHERN EMPLOYMENT.   NSOUTRC62300

ATLANTA-S SEGREGATED APPROACH TO INTEGRATED EMPLOYMENT. /GEORGIA/   NTHOMHX62205

EMPLOYMENT GAINS AND THE DETERMINANTS OF THE OCCUPATIONAL DISTRIBUTION OF NEGROES.   NTHURLC67971

FULL EMPLOYMENT AND THE NEGRO WORKER.   NTOWNWS45162

FOCI OF DISCRIMINATION IN THE EMPLOYMENT OF NONWHITES.   NTURNRH52212

STUDY OF MINORITY-GROUP EMPLOYMENT IN THE FEDERAL-GOVERNMENT, 1963.   NUSCISC63228

STUDY OF MINORITY-GROUP EMPLOYMENT IN THE FEDERAL GOVERNMENT, 1965.   NUSCISC65229

1961 COMMISSION ON CIVIL-RIGHTS REPORT BOOK 3. EMPLOYMENT.   NUSCOMC61231

CHANGING EMPLOYMENT PRACTICES IN THE CONSTRUCTION INDUSTRY. EXPERIENCE REPORT 102.   NUSCONM65233

PUBLIC EMPLOYMENT IN SAVANNAH, GEORGIA. EXPERIENCE REPORT 104.   NUSCONM66235

EMPLOYMENT PROBLEMS OF NEGROES IN MICHIGAN.   NUSDLAB41816

EMPLOYMENT OF NEGROES BY FEDERAL-GOVERNMENT.   NUSDLAB43818

NEGRO EMPLOYMENT IN AIRPLANE PLANTS. /INDUSTRY/   NUSDLAB43827

LEGISLATION AGAINST DISCRIMINATION IN EMPLOYMENT.   NUSDLAB45825

NEGRO EMPLOYMENT IN THREE COMPANIES IN THE NEW-ORLEANS AREA. /CASE-STUDY LOUISIANA/   NUSDLAB55828

CONFERENCE ON PROBLEMS IN EMPLOYMENT CONFRONTING NEGROES IN NEW-JERSEY, OCTOBER 18 1962.   NUSDLAB62242

EMPLOYMENT IN METROPOLITAN WASHINGTON. /WASHINGTON-DC/   NUSDLAB63260

SECRETARY-S CONFERENCE WITH COLLEGE PRESIDENTS AND EXECUTIVES. /EDUCATION EMPLOYMENT/   NUSDLAB63301

EMPLOYMENT OF NEGROES BY GOVERNMENT-CONTRACTORS.   NUSDLAB64814

NEGRO EMPLOYMENT IN 1965.   NUSDLAB65247

EMPLOYMENT OF NEGROES IN THE FEDERAL-GOVERNMENT, JUNE 1964.   NUSDLAB65815

THE EMPLOYMENT SITUATION.   NUSDLAB66206

THE EMPLOYMENT OF NEGROES. SOME DEMOGRAPHIC CONSIDERATIONS.   NUSDLAB66245

EMPLOYMENT AND THE ECONOMIC STATUS OF NEGROES IN THE UNITED STATES.   NUSSENA52333

EMPLOYMENT AND ECONOMIC STATUS OF NEGROES IN THE US.   NUSSENA54275

THE UNITED STATES EMPLOYMENT SERVICE AND THE NEGRO WORK APPLICANT.   NUSWAMC44276

THE NEGRO AND DISCRIMINATION IN EMPLOYMENT.   NWACHOD65288

1966 EMPLOYMENT SURVEY IN THE TEXTILE INDUSTRY OF THE CAROLINAS.   NWALLPA66591

THE EMPLOYMENT OF THE NEGRO IN WAR INDUSTRIES.   NWEAVRC43225

EMPLOYMENT OF NEGROES IN UNITED STATES WAR INDUSTRIES.   NWEAVRC44300

NEGRO EMPLOYMENT IN THE AIRCRAFT INDUSTRY.   NWEAVRC45302

EMPLOYMENT INTEGRATION AND WAGE DIFFERENCES IN A SOUTHERN PLANT.   NWEINRX59311

NEGRO EMPLOYMENT PRACTICES IN THE CHATTANOOGA AREA. /TENNESSEE/   NWESSWH55314

A SURVEY OF EMPLOYMENT OPPORTUNITIES AS THEY RELATE TO THE NEGRO IN NEW-ROCHELLE, NEW-YORK, 1955.   NWESTCU55316

POVERTY AREAS OF OUR MAJOR CITIES. THE EMPLOYMENT SITUATION OF NEGRO AND WHITE WORKERS IN METROPOLITAN
AREAS COMPARED IN A SPECIAL LABOR-FORCE REPORT.   NWETZJR66114

WAR AND POSTWAR TRENDS IN EMPLOYMENT OF NEGROES.   NWOLFSL45335

POSTWAR TRENDS IN NEGRO EMPLOYMENT.   NWOLFSL47334

EMPLOYMENT AND WAGES IN THE US.   NWOYTWS53343

THE IMPACT OF PUERTO-RICAN MIGRATION TO THE UNITED STATES. /EMPLOYMENT/   PFLEIBM63437

PUERTO-RICAN EMPLOYMENT IN NEW-YORK CITY HOTELS. /OCCUPATIONS/   PNEWYSA58837

THE BLS STUDY OF NURSES SALARIES AND EMPLOYMENT CONDITIONS.   WAMERJN57378

TESTIMONY, PUBLIC HEARING. WOMEN IN PUBLIC AND PRIVATE EMPLOYMENT, CALIFORNIA. /DISCRIMINATION EEOC/   WBALEHX66625

TESTIMONY. PUBLIC HEARING. WOMEN IN PUBLIC AND PRIVATE EMPLOYMENT, CALIFORNIA. /EMPLOYMENT-CONDITIONS/   WBECHCX66631

STATEMENT. PUBLIC HEARING. WOMEN IN PUBLIC AND PRIVATE EMPLOYMENT, CALIFORNIA. /FEP
EMPLOYMENT-CONDITIONS DISCRIMINATION/   WBELAJX66634

STATEMENT. PUBLIC HEARING. WOMEN IN PUBLIC AND PRIVATE EMPLOYMENT, CALIFORNIA. /FEP
EMPLOYMENT-CONDITIONS DISCRIMINATION/   WBENNSJ66637

RESOURCES FOR THE EMPLOYMENT OF MATURE WOMEN AND/OR THEIR CONTINUING EDUCATION. A SELECTED BIBLIOGRAPHY
AND AIDS.   WBERNML66746

LONG-RANGE CAUSES AND CONSEQUENCES OF THE EMPLOYMENT OF MARRIED WOMEN.   WBLOORO65884

MATERNAL EMPLOYMENT. SITUATIONAL AND ATTITUDINAL VARIABLES. /WORK-FAMILY-CONFLICT/   WBRIEDX61655

A STUDY TO DETERMINE THE EMPLOYMENT POTENTIAL OF MOTHERS RECEIVING AID-TO-DEPENDENT-CHILDREN ASSISTANCE. WBROODJ64656

TESTIMONY, PUBLIC HEARING. WOMAN IN PUBLIC AND PRIVATE EMPLOYMENT, CALIFORNIA. /DISCRIMINATION/   WBROWAX66657

RELATIONS AMONG MATERNAL EMPLOYMENT INDICES AND DEVELOPMENTAL CHARACTERISTICS OF CHILDREN.
/WORK-FAMILY-CONFLICT/   WBURCLG61665

TESTIMONY, PUBLIC HEARING. WOMEN IN PUBLIC AND PRIVATE EMPLOYMENT, CALIFORNIA. /EMPLOYMENT-CONDITIONS/   WCHANHD66687

TESTIMONY, PUBLIC HEARING. WOMEN IN PUBLIC AND PRIVATE EMPLOYMENT, CALIFORNIA. /FEP
EMPLOYMENT-CONDITIONS DISCRIMINATION MIGRANTS/   WCLIFFG66692

TESTIMONY, PUBLIC HEARING. WOMEN IN PUBLIC AND PRIVATE EMPLOYMENT, CALIFORNIA. /DISCRIMINATION/   WCOLLNX66696

TESTIMONY, PUBLIC HEARING. WOMEN IN PUBLIC AND PRIVATE EMPLOYMENT, CALIFORNIA. /EMPLOYMENT-CONDITIONS/   WCOMPBX66702

OPPORTUNITIES AND REQUIREMENTS FOR INITIAL EMPLOYMENT OF SCHOOL LEAVERS. WITH EMPHASIS ON OFFICE AND
RETAIL JOBS. /EMPLOYMENT-SELECTION/   WCOOKFS66705

TESTIMONY, PUBLIC HEARING. WOMEN IN PUBLIC AND PRIVATE EMPLOYMENT, CALIFORNIA. /TRAINING/   WCUMMGX66711

STATUS IMPLICATIONS OF THE **EMPLOYMENT** OF MARRIED WOMEN IN THE UNITED STATES.   WOAYXLH61726

TESTIMCNY, PUBLIC HEARING, WOMEN IN PUBLIC AND PRIVATE **EMPLOYMENT**, CALIFORNIA. /EMPLOYMENT-CONDITIONS/   WDIBRJX66732

ANTI-NEPOTISM RULES IN AMERICAN COLLEGES AND UNIVERSITIES -- THEIR EFFECT ON THE FACULTY **EMPLOYMENT** OF
WOMEN.   WDOLAEF60951

TESTIMCNY, PUBLIC HEARING, WOMAN IN PUBLIC AND PRIVATE **EMPLOYMENT**, CALIFORNIA. /DISCRIMINATION/   WDORAMX66739

TESTIMCNY, PUBLIC HEARING, WOMEN IN PUBLIC AND PRIVATE **EMPLOYMENT**, CALIFORNIA. /EMPLOYMENT-CONDITIONS/   WEVANSX66753

TESTIMCNY, PUBLIC HEARING, WOMEN IN PUBLIC AND PRIVATE **EMPLOYMENT**, CALIFORNIA. /EMPLOYMENT-CONDITIONS/   WFEINBX66760

EMPLOYMENT PROBLEMS OF WORKING WOMEN.   WFLAGJJ63130

TESTIMCNY, PUBLIC HEARING, WOMEN IN PUBLIC AND PRIVATE **EMPLOYMENT**, CALIFORNIA. /DISCRIMINATION/   WFOOTJX66765

TESTIMCNY, PUBLIC HEARING, WOMEN IN PUBLIC AND PRIVATE **EMPLOYMENT**, CALIFORNIA. /EMPLOYMENT-CONDITIONS/   WGABELX66773

TESTIMCNY, PUBLIC HEARING, WOMEN IN PUBLIC AND PRIVATE **EMPLOYMENT**, CALIFORNIA. /DISCRIMINATION/   WGEIGPX66776

TESTIMCNY, PUBLIC HEARING, WOMEN IN PUBLIC AND PRIVATE **EMPLOYMENT**, CALIFORNIA. /DEMOGRAPHY/   WGERSMX66777

MARITAL CISAGREEMENT IN WORKING WIFE MARRIAGES AS A FUNCTION OF HUSBAND-S ATTITUDE TOWARDS WIFE-S
EMPLOYMENT. /WORK-FAMILY-CONFLICT/   WGIANAX57779

TESTIMCNY, PUBLIC HEARING, WOMEN IN PUBLIC AND PRIVATE **EMPLOYMENT**, CALIFORNIA. /EMPLOYMENT-CONDITIONS/   WGILBRX66780

TESTIMCNY, PUBLIC HEARING, WOMEN IN PUBLIC AND PRIVATE **EMPLOYMENT**, CALIFORNIA. /EMPLOYMENT-CONDITIONS/   WGLENEM66788

ATTITUDES OF WOMEN REGARDING GAINFUL **EMPLOYMENT** OF MARRIED WOMEN. /ASPIRATIONS/   WGLENHM59789

TESTIMCNY, PUBLIC HEARING, WOMEN IN PUBLIC AND PRIVATE **EMPLOYMENT**, CALIFORNIA. /DISCRIMINATION
WORK-FAMILY-CONFLICT/   WGUPTRC66808

TESTIMCNY, PUBLIC HEARING, WOMEN IN PUBLIC AND PRIVATE **EMPLOYMENT**, CALIFORNIA. /EMPLOYMENT-CONDITIONS/   WGUPTRC66809

A FUNCTIONAL APPROACH TO THE GAINFUL **EMPLOYMENT** OF MARRIED WOMEN.   WHACKHM61812

THE WORKING WOMAN. BARRIERS IN **EMPLOYMENT**. /DISCRIMINATION/   WHARREX64827

PANEL DISCUSSION. THE CASE FOR AND AGAINST THE **EMPLOYMENT** OF WOMEN. /OCCUPATIONS/   WHARRTW65824

WHAT ASPECTS OF CHILD BEHAVIOR SHOULD BE STUDIED IN RELATION TO MATERNAL **EMPLOYMENT**.   WHARTRE61829

TESTIMONY, PUBLIC HEARING, WOMEN IN PUBLIC AND PRIVATE **EMPLOYMENT**, CALIFORNIA. /EMPLOYMENT-CONDITIONS/   WHEALWX66836

ATTITUDES CF COLLEGE STUDENTS TOWARD **EMPLOYMENT** AMONG MARRIED WOMEN. /WORK-FAMILY-CONFLICT/   WHEWEVH64482

TESTIMCNY, PUBLIC HEARING, WOMEN IN PUBLIC AND PRIVATE **EMPLOYMENT**, CALIFORNIA. /DISCRIMINATION/   WHILLHX66844

TESTIMCNY, PUBLIC HEARING, WOMEN IN PUBLIC AND PRIVATE **EMPLOYMENT**, CALIFORNIA. /MDTA EEO/   WINGRLX66859

EMPLOYMENT AND CONDITIONS OF WORK OF NURSES.   WINTELO60862

PART-TIME **EMPLOYMENT** FOR WOMEN WITH FAMILY RESPONSIBILITIES. /WORK-FAMILY-CONFLICT/   WINTELR57867

DISCRIMINATION IN **EMPLOYMENT** OR OCCUPATION ON THE BASIS OF MARITAL-STATUS.   WINTELR62865

CONFERENCE ON **EMPLOYMENT** PROBLEMS OF WORKING WOMEN.   WIOWAGC64797

A PILOT STUDY OF THE MOTIVATIONS AND PROBLEMS OF MIDDLE AGED HOMEMAKERS IN LOWER SOCIO-ECONOMIC GROUPS IN
SEEKING **EMPLOYMENT**. /ASPIRATIONS/   WJEWIVA62883

STATEMENT, PUBLIC HEARING, WOMEN IN PUBLIC AND PRIVATE **EMPLOYMENT**, CALIFORNIA. /EMPLOYMENT-CONDITIONS
MIGRANT-WORKERS/   WKAUFDX66886

TESTIMCNY, PUBLIC HEARING, WOMEN IN PUBLIC AND PRIVATE **EMPLOYMENT**, CALIFORNIA. /EMPLOYMENT-CONDITIONS/   WKELLET66888

STATEMENT, PUBLIC HEARING, WOMEN IN PUBLIC AND PRIVATE **EMPLOYMENT**, CALIFORNIA. /EMPLOYMENT-CONDITIONS/   WKENNVX66890

TRENDS IN WOMEN-S **EMPLOYMENT**.   WKEYSMD65644

STATEMENT, PUBLIC HEARING, WOMEN IN PUBLIC AND PRIVATE **EMPLOYMENT**, CALIFORNIA. /EMPLOYMENT-CONDITIONS/   WKNIGTF66911

AUTOMATION AND **EMPLOYMENT**. /TECHNOLOGICAL-CHANGE/   WKREPJX64916

A CONFERENCE TO ENLIST THE PARTICIPATION OF 50 INSTITUTIONS OF HIGHER EDUCATION IN SPECIFIC R AND D
PROGRAMS TO PREPARE WOMEN FOR PRODUCTIVE **EMPLOYMENT**.   WLLOYBJ64937

TESTIMCNY, PUBLIC HEARING, WOMEN IN PUBLIC AND PRIVATE **EMPLOYMENT**, CALIFORNIA. /FEP MIGRANT-WORKERS
EMPLOYMENT-CONDITIONS/   WLLOYMX66940

TESTIMCNY, PUBLIC HEARING, WOMEN IN PUBLIC AND PRIVATE **EMPLOYMENT**, CALIFORNIA. /FEP EMPLOYMENT
CONDITIONS/   WLOWEDX66943

TESTIMCNY, PUBLIC HEARING, WOMEN IN PUBLIC AND PRIVATE EMPLOYMENT, CALIFORNIA. /FEP **EMPLOYMENT**
CONDITIONS/   WLOWEDX66943

TESTIMONY, PUBLIC HEARING, WOMEN IN PUBLIC AND PRIVATE **EMPLOYMENT**, CALIFORNIA. /EMPLOYMENT-CONDITIONS/   WMACKJW66950

TESTIMCNY, PUBLIC HEARING, WOMEN IN PUBLIC AND PRIVATE **EMPLOYMENT**, CALIFORNIA. /OCCUPATIONS
EMPLOYMENT-CONDITIONS/   WMCLALX66947

TESTIMCNY, PUBLIC HEARING, WOMEN IN PUBLIC AND PRIVATE **EMPLOYMENT**, CALIFORNIA. /BLUE-COLLAR
EMPLOYMENT-CONDITIONS/   WMENGVX66969

STATEMENT, PUBLIC HEARING, WOMEN IN PUBLIC AND PRIVATE **EMPLOYMENT**, CALIFORNIA. /FEP
EMPLOYMENT-CONDITIONS MIGRANT-WORKERS/   WMILLJJ66979

TESTIMCNY, PUBLIC HEARING, WOMEN IN PUBLIC AND PRIVATE **EMPLOYMENT**, CALIFORNIA. /EMPLOYMENT-CONDITIONS/   WMILLKL66980

TESTIMCNY, PUBLIC HEARING, WOMEN IN PUBLIC AND PRIVATE **EMPLOYMENT**, CALIFORNIA. /EMPLOYMENT-CONDITIONS/   WMORAMX66995

RAISING THE STATUS OF HOUSEHOLD **EMPLOYMENT**. /HOUSEHOLD-WORKERS/   WMORRMM66998

TESTIMCNY, PUBLIC HEARING, WOMEN IN PUBLIC AND PRIVATE **EMPLOYMENT**, CALIFORNIA.   WMOTHWA66001

EMPLOYMENT (CONTINUATION)

WOMEN-S CHANGING ROLE IN THE US **EMPLOYMENT** MARKET.   WMUNTEE56007

TESTIMONY, PUBLIC HEARING, WOMEN IN PUBLIC AND PRIVATE **EMPLOYMENT**, CALIFORNIA. /EMPLOYMENT-CONDITIONS/   WMYRIRX66013

NEW-YORK WOMEN. A REPORT AND RECOMMENDATIONS FROM THE NEW-YORK GOVERNOR-S COMMITTEE ON THE EDUCATION AND
EMPLOYMENT OF WOMEN.   WNEWYGW64799

TESTIMONY, PUBLIC HEARING, WOMEN IN PUBLIC AND PRIVATE **EMPLOYMENT**, CALIFORNIA. /EMPLOYMENT-CONDITIONS/   WPALMGX66047

EMPLOYMENT OF WOMEN CHEMISTS IN INDUSTRIAL LABORATORIES. /OCCUPATIONS/   WPARRJB65050

AUTOMATION AND **EMPLOYMENT** OPPORTUNITIES FOR OFFICE WORKERS. THE EFFECT OF ELECTRONIC COMPUTERS ON
EMPLOYMENT OF CLERICAL WORKERS, WITH A SPECIAL REPORT ON PROGRAMMERS.   WPASCWX58178

AUTOMATION AND EMPLOYMENT OPPORTUNITIES FOR OFFICE WORKERS. THE EFFECT OF ELECTRONIC COMPUTERS ON
EMPLOYMENT OF CLERICAL WORKERS, WITH A SPECIAL REPORT ON PROGRAMMERS.   WPASCWX58178

TESTIMONY, PUBLIC HEARING, WOMEN IN PUBLIC AND PRIVATE **EMPLOYMENT**, CALIFORNIA. /FEP
EMPLOYMENT-CONDITIONS MIGRANT-WORKERS/   WPEEVMX66052

TRAINING. KEY TO **EMPLOYMENT**.   WPETEEX62057

EMPLOYMENT EFFECTS OF STATE MINIMUM WAGES FOR WOMEN.   WPETEJX59059

SOME IMPLICATIONS OF THE **EMPLOYMENT** PATTERNS OF WOMEN UNDER SOCIAL-SECURITY.   WPOLIEJ59454

REPORT OF THE COMMITTEE ON FEDERAL **EMPLOYMENT**.   WPRESCO63067

REPORT OF THE COMMITTEE ON PRIVATE **EMPLOYMENT**, 1963.   WPRESCO63068

TESTIMONY, PUBLIC HEARING, WOMEN IN PUBLIC AND PRIVATE **EMPLOYMENT**, CALIFORNIA. /EMPLOYMENT-CONDITIONS/   WRILEEX66081

THE **EMPLOYMENT** OF STUDENTS, OCTOBER 1961.   WROSECX62087

THE CASE AGAINST FULL-TIME MOTHERHOOD. /EMPLOYMENT/   WROSSAS65092

TESTIMONY, PUBLIC HEARING, WOMEN IN PUBLIC AND PRIVATE **EMPLOYMENT**, CALIFORNIA. /FEP
EMPLOYMENT-CONDITIONS/   WSCHRPX66104

PART-TIME **EMPLOYMENT**.   WSCHWJX64107

TESTIMONY, PUBLIC HEARING, WOMEN IN PUBLIC AND PRIVATE **EMPLOYMENT**, CALIFORNIA. /EMPLOYMENT-CONDITIONS/   WSHEAHX66112

FAMILIAL CORRELATES OF ORIENTATION TOWARD FUTURE **EMPLOYMENT** AMONG COLLEGE WOMEN. /ASPIRATIONS/   WSIEGAX63572

OFFICE AUTOMATION AND WHITE-COLLAR **EMPLOYMENT**.   WSMITGM59122

TESTIMONY, PUBLIC HEARING, WOMEN IN PUBLIC AND PRIVATE **EMPLOYMENT**, CALIFORNIA. /FEP
EMPLOYMENT-CONDITIONS DISCRIMINATION/   WSMITWH66123

TESTIMONY, PUBLIC HEARING, WOMEN IN PUBLIC AND PRIVATE **EMPLOYMENT**, CALIFORNIA. /FEP
EMPLOYMENT-CONDITIONS DISCRIMINATION MIGRANT-WORKERS/   WSPENNX66129

REPORT OF CONFERENCE ON **EMPLOYMENT** PROBLEMS OF WORKING WOMEN.   WSTATUI63131

TESTIMONY, PUBLIC HEARING, WOMEN IN PUBLIC AND PRIVATE **EMPLOYMENT**, CALIFORNIA. /LABOR-MARKET/   WSTEPRX66138

TESTIMONY, PUBLIC HEARING, WOMEN IN PUBLIC AND PRIVATE **EMPLOYMENT**, CALIFORNIA. /FEPC/   WSTERAX66140

LABOR-FORCE SENSITIVITY TO **EMPLOYMENT** BY AGE, SEX.   WTELLAX65714

TESTIMONY, PUBLIC HEARING, WOMEN IN PUBLIC AND PRIVATE **EMPLOYMENT**, CALIFORNIA. /EMPLOYMENT-CONDITIONS/   WTHOMDX66151

TESTIMONY, PUBLIC HEARING, WOMEN IN PUBLIC AND PRIVATE **EMPLOYMENT**, CALIFORNIA. /EMPLOYMENT-CONDITIONS
DISCRIMINATION/   WTHOMGX66149

FEDERAL **EMPLOYMENT** OF WOMEN.   WUSCISC66483

CRITERIA FOR ASSESSING FEASIBILITY OF MOTHERS **EMPLOYMENT** AND ADEQUACY OF CHILD CARE PLANS.   WUSDHEW66173

EMPLOYMENT AND CHARACTERISTICS OF WOMEN ENGINEERS. /OCCUPATIONS/   WUSDLAB56989

EMPLOYMENT OF JUNE 1955 WOMEN COLLEGE GRADUATES.   WUSDLAB56990

PART-TIME **EMPLOYMENT** FOR WOMEN.   WUSDLAB60213

EMPLOYMENT PROBLEMS OF WOMEN.   WUSDLAB62189

PRIVATE-HOUSEHOLD **EMPLOYMENT** -- SUMMARY OF FIRST AND SECOND CONSULTATIONS. /HOUSEHOLD-WORKERS/   WUSDLAB64212

LAWS ON SEX DISCRIMINATION IN **EMPLOYMENT**.   WUSDLAB66K05

EXPLODING THE MYTHS. EXPANDING **EMPLOYMENT** OPPORTUNITIES FOR CAREER WOMEN.   WUVCAEC66249

NEW PATTERNS OF **EMPLOYMENT**.   WUVMICC66685

STATEMENT, PUBLIC HEARING, WOMEN IN PUBLIC AND PRIVATE **EMPLOYMENT**, CALIFORNIA. /FEP
EMPLOYMENT-CONDITIONS DISCRIMINATION/   WVAILLX66256

THE CASE OF THE BATTLE-AXES. /EMPLOYMENT/   WWALSCM57266

TESTIMONY, PUBLIC HEARING, WOMEN IN PUBLIC AND PRIVATE **EMPLOYMENT**, CALIFORNIA. /EMPLOYMENT-CONDITIONS
MIGRANT-WORKERS/   WWEBEJX66258

WOMEN IN THE AMERICAN LABOR-FORCE. **EMPLOYMENT** AND UNEMPLOYMENT.   WWILCRX60268

TESTIMONY, PUBLIC HEARING, WOMEN IN PUBLIC AND PRIVATE **EMPLOYMENT**, CALIFORNIA. /FEP
EMPLOYMENT-CONDITIONS MIGRANT-WORKERS/   WWOMEIX66273

TESTIMONY, PUBLIC HEARING, WOMEN IN PUBLIC AND PRIVATE **EMPLOYMENT**, CALIFORNIA. /EMPLOYMENT-CONDITIONS/   WWOODWX66276

COLLEGE WOMEN AND **EMPLOYMENT**.   WZAPOMW59281

EMPLOYMENT-AGENCIES

THE SUBSTANCE OF AMERICAN FAIR-EMPLOYMENT-PRACTICES LEGISLATION. II. **EMPLOYMENT-AGENCIES**, LABOR
ORGANIZATIONS, AND OTHERS.   GBONFAE67136

GUIDE TO LAWFUL AND UNLAWFUL PRE-EMPLOYMENT INQUIRIES BY EMPLOYERS, **EMPLOYMENT-AGENCIES**, AND LABOR

EMPLOYMENT-AGENCIES (CONTINUATION)
ORGANIZATIONS UNDER THE CALIFORNIA FAIR-EMPLOYMENT-PRACTICE ACT, LABOR CODE, SECTIONS 1410-1432.   GCALDIR60527

    GUIDE TO EMPLOYERS, EMPLOYMENT-AGENCIES AND LABOR UNIONS DEFINING PROPER AND IMPROPER PRE-EMPLOYMENT
INQUIRIES. /PENNSYLVANIA/   GPENNHRND164

EMPLOYMENT-AGENCY
PLACEMENT EXPERIENCES OF APPLICANTS TO A PRIVATE EMPLOYMENT-AGENCY.   NANTIDL55901

    BRINGING BETTER JOBS TO NEGRCES.   /EMPLOYMENT-AGENCY/   NBUSIWX62146

EMPLOYMENT-CONDITION
THE HEALTH OF THE MIGRANT-WORKER. /EMPLOYMENT-CONDITIONS/   GLINDJR66603

    SOME PRACTICAL STUDIES IN PUBLIC TRANSPORTATION. /EMPLOYMENT-CONDITIONS WATTS LOS-ANGELES CALIFORNIA/   NCARLJX55593

    SURVEY OF EMPLOYMENT-CONDITIONS OF NURSES EMPLOYED BY PHYSICIANS AND/OR DENTISTS, JULY 1964.   WAMERNA65610

    SURVEY OF SALARIES AND EMPLOYMENT-CONDITIONS IN NONFEDERAL PSYCHIATRIC HOSPITALS.   WAMERNA65611

    TESTIMONY, PUBLIC HEARING, WCMEN IN PUBLIC AND PRIVATE EMPLOYMENT, CALIFORNIA. /EMPLOYMENT-CONDITIONS/   WBECHCX66631

    STATEMENT, PUBLIC HEARING, WCMEN IN PUBLIC AND PRIVATE EMPLOYMENT, CALIFORNIA. /FEP
EMPLOYMENT-CONDITIONS DISCRIMINATION/   WBELAJX66634

    STATEMENT, PUBLIC HEARING, WCMEN IN PUBLIC AND PRIVATE EMPLOYMENT, CALIFORNIA. /FEP
EMPLOYMENT-CONDITIONS DISCRIMINATION/   WBENNSJ66637

    INFORMAL COMMUNICATION AMONG BIOSCIENTISTS. /EMPLOYMENT-CONDITIONS/   WBERNJX63643

    TESTIMONY, PUBLIC HEARING, WCMEN IN PUBLIC AND PRIVATE EDUCATION, CALIFORNIA. /FEP
EMPLOYMENT-CONDITIONS DISCRIMINATION MIGRANT-WORKERS/   WBLOCHX66649

    TESTIMONY PRESENTED AT PUBLIC HEARING, MARCH 31 -- APRIL 1, 1966. /FEP EMPLOYMENT-CONDITIONS
DISCRIMINATION MIGRANTS/   WCALACW62675

    TESTIMONY PRESENTED AT PUBLIC HEARING, APRIL 28, 1966. SAN-FRANCISCO, CALIFORNIA. /FEP
EMPLOYMENT-CONDITIONS DISCRIMINATION MIGRANTS/   WCALACW62676

    TESTIMONY PRESENTED AT PUBLIC HEARING, FEBRUARY 24-25, 1966. /FEP EMPLOYMENT-CONDITIONS DISCRIMINATION
MIGRANTS/   WCALACW66674

    TESTIMONY PRESENTED AT PUBLIC HEARING, APRIL 29, 1966. SAN-FRANCISCO, CALIFORNIA. /FEP
EMPLOYMENT-CONDITIONS CHILDREN/   WCALACW66677

REPORT OF THE CALIFORNIA ADVISORY COMMISSION ON THE STATUS OF WOMEN. /FEP EMPLOYMENT-CONDITIONS
DISCRIMINATION MIGRANTS/   WCALACW67673

    TESTIMONY, PUBLIC HEARING, WCMEN IN PUBLIC AND PRIVATE EMPLOYMENT, CALIFORNIA. /EMPLOYMENT-CONDITIONS/   WCHANHD66687

    TESTIMONY, PUBLIC HEARING, WCMEN IN PUBLIC AND PRIVATE EMPLOYMENT, CALIFORNIA. /FEP
EMPLOYMENT-CONDITIONS DISCRIMINATION MIGRANTS/   WCLIFFG66692

    TESTIMONY, PUBLIC HEARING, WCMEN IN PUBLIC AND PRIVATE EMPLOYMENT, CALIFORNIA. /EMPLOYMENT-CONDITIONS/   WCOMPBX66702

    STATEMENT ON STATE LAWS. /EMPLOYMENT-CONDITIONS/   WDAVICX65720

    TESTIMONY, PUBLIC HEARING, WCMEN IN PUBLIC AND PRIVATE EMPLOYMENT, CALIFORNIA. /EMPLOYMENT-CONDITIONS/   WDIBRJX66732

    TESTIMONY, PUBLIC HEARING, WCMEN IN PUBLIC AND PRIVATE EMPLOYMENT, CALIFORNIA. /EMPLOYMENT-CONDITIONS/   WEVANSX66753

    TESTIMONY, PUBLIC HEARING, WCMEN IN PUBLIC AND PRIVATE EMPLOYMENT, CALIFORNIA. /EMPLOYMENT-CONDITIONS/   WFEINBX66760

    TESTIMONY, PUBLIC HEARING, WCMEN IN PUBLIC AND PRIVATE EMPLOYMENT, CALIFORNIA. /EMPLOYMENT-CONDITIONS/   WGABELX66773

    TESTIMONY, PUBLIC HEARING, WCMEN IN PUBLIC AND PRIVATE EMPLOYMENT, CALIFORNIA. /EMPLOYMENT-CONDITIONS/   WGILBRX66780

    TESTIMONY, PUBLIC HEARING, WCMEN IN PUBLIC AND PRIVATE EMPLOYMENT, CALIFORNIA. /EMPLOYMENT-CONDITIONS/   WGLENEM66788

PROGRESS AND PROSPECTS. THE REPORT OF THE SECOND NATIONAL CONFERENCE OF GOVERNORS COMMISSIONS ON THE
STATUS OF WOMEN. /EMPLOYMENT-CONDITIONS/   WGOVECS65798

    PROGRESS AND PROSPECTS. /EMPLOYMENT-CONDITIONS/   WGOVECS66215

    TESTIMONY, PUBLIC HEARING, WCMEN IN PUBLIC AND PRIVATE EMPLOYMENT, CALIFORNIA. /EMPLOYMENT-CONDITIONS/   WGUPTRC66809

    TESTIMONY, PUBLIC HEARING, WCMEN IN PUBLIC AND PRIVATE EMPLOYMENT, CALIFORNIA. /EMPLOYMENT-CONDITIONS/   WHEALWX66836

    DAY CARE SERVICES. FORM AND SUBSTANCE. /EMPLOYMENT-CONDITIONS/   WHOFFGL61846

    PART-TIME CARE. THE DAY-CARE PROBLEM. /EMPLOYMENT-CONDITIONS/   WHOSLEM64540

    CHILD CARE FACILITIES FOR WOMEN WORKERS. /EMPLOYMENT-CONDITIONS/   WINTELR58864

    FIRST REPORT. IOWA GOVERNOR-S COMMISSION ON THE STATUS OF WOMEN. /EMPLOYMENT-CONDITIONS/   WIOWAGC64796

    STATEMENT, PUBLIC HEARING, WCMEN IN PUBLIC AND PRIVATE EMPLOYMENT, CALIFORNIA. /EMPLOYMENT-CONDITIONS
MIGRANT-WORKERS/   WKAUFDX66386

    TESTIMONY, PUBLIC HEARING, WCMEN IN PUBLIC AND PRIVATE EMPLOYMENT, CALIFORNIA. /EMPLOYMENT-CONDITIONS/   WKELLET66888

    STATEMENT, PUBLIC HEARING, WCMEN IN PUBLIC AND PRIVATE EMPLOYMENT, CALIFORNIA. /EMPLOYMENT-CONDITIONS/   WKENNVX66890

    DAY CARE IN A CHANGING ECONOMY. /EMPLOYMENT-CONDITIONS/   WKEYSMD64894

    THE NATION-S WORKING MOTHERS AND THE NEED FOR DAY CARE. ADDRESS. /EMPLOYMENT-CONDITIONS/   WKEYSMD65897

    STATEMENT, PUBLIC HEARING, WCMEN IN PUBLIC AND PRIVATE EMPLOYMENT, CALIFORNIA. /EMPLOYMENT-CONDITIONS/   WKNIGTF66911

    WORKING MOTHERS AND THEIR ARRANGEMENTS FOR CARE OF THEIR CHILDREN. /EMPLOYMENT-CONDITIONS/   WLAJEHC59922

    TESTIMONY, PUBLIC HEARING, WOMEN IN PUBLIC AND PRIVATE EMPLOYMENT, CALIFORNIA. /FEP MIGRANT-WORKERS
EMPLOYMENT-CONDITIONS/   WLLOYMX66940

    TESTIMONY, PUBLIC HEARING, WCMEN IN PUBLIC AND PRIVATE EMPLOYMENT, CALIFORNIA. /EMPLOYMENT-CONDITIONS/   WMACKJW66950

    TESTIMONY, PUBLIC HEARING, WCMEN IN PUBLIC AND PRIVATE EMPLOYMENT, CALIFORNIA. /OCCUPATIONS
EMPLOYMENT-CONDITIONS/   WMCLALX66947

EMPLOYMENT-CONDITION (CONTINUATION)
TESTIMONY, PUBLIC HEARING, WOMEN IN PUBLIC AND PRIVATE EMPLOYMENT, CALIFORNIA. /BLUE-COLLAR
EMPLOYMENT-CONDITIONS/   WMENGVX66969

STATEMENT, PUBLIC HEARING, WOMEN IN PUBLIC AND PRIVATE EMPLOYMENT, CALIFORNIA. /FEP
EMPLOYMENT-CONDITIONS MIGRANT-WORKERS/   WMILLJJ66979

TESTIMONY, PUBLIC HEARING, WOMEN IN PUBLIC AND PRIVATE EMPLOYMENT, CALIFORNIA. /EMPLOYMENT-CONDITIONS/   WMILLKL66980

TESTIMONY, PUBLIC HEARING, WOMEN IN PUBLIC AND PRIVATE EMPLOYMENT, CALIFORNIA. /EMPLOYMENT-CONDITIONS/   WMORAMX66995

TESTIMONY, PUBLIC HEARING, WOMEN IN PUBLIC AND PRIVATE EMPLOYMENT, CALIFORNIA. /EMPLOYMENT-CONDITIONS/   WMYRIRX66013

TESTIMONY, PUBLIC HEARING, WOMEN IN PUBLIC AND PRIVATE EMPLOYMENT, CALIFORNIA. /EMPLOYMENT-CONDITIONS/   WPALMGX66047

TESTIMONY, PUBLIC HEARING, WOMEN IN PUBLIC AND PRIVATE EMPLOYMENT, CALIFORNIA. /FEP
EMPLOYMENT-CONDITIONS MIGRANT-WORKERS/   WPEEVMX66052

TESTIMONY, PUBLIC HEARING, WOMEN IN PUBLIC AND PRIVATE EMPLOYMENT, CALIFORNIA. /EMPLOYMENT-CONDITIONS/   WRILEEX66081

TESTIMONY, PUBLIC HEARING, WOMEN IN PUBLIC AND PRIVATE EMPLOYMENT, CALIFORNIA. /FEP
EMPLOYMENT-CONDITIONS/   WSCHRPX66104

TESTIMONY, PUBLIC HEARING, WOMEN IN PUBLIC AND PRIVATE EMPLOYMENT, CALIFORNIA. /EMPLOYMENT-CONDITIONS/   WSHEAHX66112

TESTIMONY, PUBLIC HEARING, WOMEN IN PUBLIC AND PRIVATE EMPLOYMENT, CALIFORNIA. /FEP
EMPLOYMENT-CONDITIONS DISCRIMINATION/   WSMITWH66123

TESTIMONY, PUBLIC HEARING, WOMEN IN PUBLIC AND PRIVATE EMPLOYMENT, CALIFORNIA. /FEP
EMPLOYMENT-CONDITIONS DISCRIMINATION MIGRANT-WORKERS/   WSPENNX66129

TESTIMONY, PUBLIC HEARING, WOMEN IN PUBLIC AND PRIVATE EMPLOYMENT, CALIFORNIA. /EMPLOYMENT-CONDITIONS/   WTHOMDX66151

TESTIMONY, PUBLIC HEARING, WOMEN IN PUBLIC AND PRIVATE EMPLOYMENT, CALIFORNIA. /EMPLOYMENT-CONDITIONS
DISCRIMINATION/   WTHOMGX66149

WISCONSIN FAIR-EMPLOYMENT-PRACTICES DIVISION INQUIRY INTO THE CONFLICTS BETWEEN STATE PROTECTIVE LABOR
LEGISLATION AND STATE AND FEDERAL LAWS PROHIBITING DISCRIMINATION BASED ON SEX. /EMPLOYMENT-CONDITIONS/   WUAWXWD65165

STATEMENT ON WEIGHT LIFTING, HOURS, SENIORITY LAWS AND WOMEN. /EMPLOYMENT-CONDITIONS/   WUAWXWD66164

CHILD CARE ARRANGEMENTS OF FULLTIME WORKING MOTHERS. /EMPLOYMENT-CONDITIONS/   WUSDHEW59171

MATERNITY BENEFIT PROVISIONS FOR EMPLOYED WOMEN. /EMPLOYMENT-CONDITIONS/   WUSDLAB60206

NURSES AND OTHER HOSPITAL PERSONNEL -- THEIR EARNINGS AND EMPLOYMENT-CONDITIONS.   WUSDLAB61211

FRINGE BENEFIT PROVISIONS FROM STATE MINIMUM WAGE LAWS AND ORDERS, SEPTEMBER 1, 1966.
/EMPLOYMENT-CONDITIONS/   WUSDLAB66195

REPORT ON PROGRESS IN 1965 ON THE STATUS OF WOMEN. /EDUCATION EMPLOYMENT-CONDITIONS/   WUSINCS65860

STATEMENT, PUBLIC HEARING, WOMEN IN PUBLIC AND PRIVATE EMPLOYMENT, CALIFORNIA. /FEP
EMPLOYMENT-CONDITIONS DISCRIMINATION/   WVAILLX66256

TESTIMONY, PUBLIC HEARING, WOMEN IN PUBLIC AND PRIVATE EMPLOYMENT, CALIFORNIA. /EMPLOYMENT-CONDITIONS
MIGRANT-WORKERS/   WWEBEJX66258

TESTIMONY, PUBLIC HEARING, WOMEN IN PUBLIC AND PRIVATE EMPLOYMENT, CALIFORNIA. /FEP
EMPLOYMENT-CONDITIONS MIGRANT-WORKERS/   WWOMEIX66273

TESTIMONY, PUBLIC HEARING, WOMEN IN PUBLIC AND PRIVATE EMPLOYMENT, CALIFORNIA. /EMPLOYMENT-CONDITIONS/   WWOODWX66276

EMPLOYMENT-EDUCATION
DIGEST OF CASE STUDIES ON CONTINUITIES AND DISCONTINUITIES IN THE EMPLOYMENT-EDUCATION-FAMILY PATTERNS OF
WOMEN-S LIVES.   WDELAPJ60224

EMPLOYMENT-OPPORTUNI
THE NEGRO AND EMPLOYMENT-OPPORTUNITIES IN THE SOUTH. CHATTANOOGA REGION. /TENNESSEE/   NCHATCC62197

A STUDY OF THE EFFECTS OF EFFORTS TO IMPROVE EMPLOYMENT-OPPORTUNITIES OF NEGROES ON THE UTILIZATION OF
NEGRO WORKERS.   NHARTJW64496

EMPLOYMENT-PRACTICE-
MEMORANDUM OF UNDERSTANDING BETWEEN CALIFORNIA STATE FAIR- EMPLOYMENT-PRACTICE-COMMISSION AND
BANK-OF-AMERICA NATIONAL TRUST AND SAVINGS ASSOCIATION.   GCALFEPND537

EMPLOYMENT-PRACTICES
EMPLOYMENT-PRACTICES IN THE PERFORMING-ARTS.   GUSHOUR63337

EMPLOYMENT-SELECTION
THE NEGRO SALARIED WORKER. /EMPLOYMENT-SELECTION/   NGOURJC65438

PREPARATION OF THE NEGRO COLLEGE GRADUATE FOR BUSINESS. /EMPLOYMENT-SELECTION/   NHOLLJH65560

TAPPING THE NEGRO POTENTIAL. /INDUSTRY EMPLOYMENT-SELECTION PROMOTION/   NJOHNTX65621

OPPORTUNITIES AND REQUIREMENTS FOR INITIAL EMPLOYMENT OF SCHOOL LEAVERS. WITH EMPHASIS ON OFFICE AND
RETAIL JOBS. /EMPLOYMENT-SELECTION/   WCOOKFS66705

EMPLOYMENT-SERVICE
NEW DIRECTIONS IN US EMPLOYMENT-SERVICE APTITUDE TEST RESEARCH.   GDVORBJ65656

EQUAL-EMPLOYMENT-OPPORTUNITY -- AN EMPLOYMENT-SERVICE RESPONSIBILITY.   GFANTAX64671

THE ROLE OF THE UNITED STATES EMPLOYMENT-SERVICE IN A CHANGING ECONOMY.   GHABEWX64649

EMPLOYMENT-STATUS
NONWHITE POPULATION BY RACE. NEGROES, INDIANS, JAPANESE, CHINESE, FILIPINOS. BY AGE, SEX, MARITAL-STATUS,
EDUCATION, EMPLOYMENT-STATUS, OCCUPATIONAL-STATUS, INCOME, ETC. /DEMOGRAPHY/   CUSBURC53378

EMPLOYMENT-STATUS AND WORK CHARACTERISTICS. STATISTICS ON THE RELATION BETWEEN EMPLOYMENT AND SOCIAL AND
ECONOMIC CHARACTERISTICS. /DEMOGRAPHY/   CUSBURC63170

NONWHITE POPULATION BY RACE. NEGROES, INDIANS, JAPANESE,CHINESE, FILIPINOS. BY AGE, SEX,
MARITAL-STATUS,EDUCATION, EMPLOYMENT-STATUS, OCCUPATIONAL-STATUS, INCOME, ETC. /DEMOGRAPHY/   CUSBURC63176

EMPLOYMENT-TRENDS
THE OUTLOOK FOR THE LABOR-FORCE AT MID-DECADE. /EMPLOYMENT-TRENDS/   GCOOPSX64743

EMPLOYMENT-TRENDS   (CONTINUATION)
JOBS, 1960-1970. THE CHANGING PATTERN. /EMPLOYMENT-TRENDS/   GNEWYSE60108

MANPOWER PROJECTIONS. SOME CONCEPTUAL PROBLEMS AND RESEARCH NEEDS. /EMPLOYMENT-TRENDS/   GSWERSX66535

EMPLOYMENT-TRENDS AMONG CALIFORNIA YOUTH AUTHORITY WARDS ON PAROLE. 1948-62.   MCALDYA63378

NEGRO EMPLOYMENT-TRENDS IN THE SOUTH.   NAMERFX53015

RECENT SOUTHERN INDUSTRIALIZATION AND ITS IMPLICATIONS FOR NEGROES LIVING IN THE SOUTH.
/EMPLOYMENT-TRENDS/   NCHICCA53204

ENCYCLOPEDIA
REFERENCE ENCYCLOPEDIA ON THE AMERICAN-INDIAN.   IKLEIBA67899

END
THE WEIGHT OF THE POOR -- A STRATEGY TO END POVERTY. /GUARANTEED-INCOME/   GCLOWRX66525

GOVERNMENTAL FAIR-EMPLOYMENT AGENCIES. AN APPRAISAL OF FEDERAL, STATE, AND MUNICIPAL EFFORTS TO END JOB
DISCRIMINATION.   GNORGPH62120

THE NEGROES WHO DO NOT WANT TO END SEGREGATION. /EMPLOYMENT/   NFAGGHL55255

PLANNING THE END OF THE AMERICAN GHETTO. A PROGRAM OF ECONOMIC DEVELOPMENT FOR EQUAL-RIGHTS.   NHILLHX66538

WOMAN-S CENTURY OF PROGRESS. IS IT TO END IN REGRESSION. /WORK-WOMAN-ROLE/   WMCKARC58946

ENDS
ENDS AND MEANS IN THE WAR-ON-POVERTY.   GLAMPRJ66881

ECONOMIC FORCES SERVING THE ENDS OF THE NEGRO PROTEST. /UNEMPLOYMENT/   NBATCAB65059

ENFORCEMENT
THE RIGHT TO EQUAL TREATMENT. ADMINISTRATIVE ENFORCEMENT OF ANTIDISCRIMINATION LEGISLATION.   GBAMBMA61416

COMMISSION ENFORCEMENT OF STATE LAWS AGAINST DISCRIMINATION. A COMPARATIVE ANALYSIS OF THE KANSAS ACT.   GDYSORB65657

ENFORCEMENT OF NEW-YORK LAW AGAINST DISCRIMINATION.   GLABORR51879

THE ENFORCEMENT OF CIVIL-RIGHTS. /DISCRIMINATION/   GMARSBX62942

ENFORCEMENT OF THE FEDERAL EQUAL-OPPORTUNITY LAW.   GMARSBX64943

FEP LEGISLATION AND ENFORCEMENT IN THE US.   GMEANJE66971

ENFORCEMENT OF LAWS AGAINST DISCRIMINATION IN EMPLOYMENT.   GRABKSX64211

ENFORCEMENT OF NONDISCRIMINATION REQUIREMENTS FOR GOVERNMENT CONTRACT WORK.   GSPECWH63329

ENFORCEMENT OF FAIR-EMPLOYMENT UNDER THE CIVIL-RIGHTS-ACT OF 1964.   GUVCHLR64213

ENGINEERING
OPPORTUNITIES FOR NEGROES IN ENGINEERING. /OCCUPATIONS/   NKIEHRX58648

OPPORTUNITIES FOR NEGROES IN ENGINEERING -- A SECOND REPORT. /OCCUPATIONS/   NKIEHRX64333

THE POST-WAR OUTLOOK FOR NEGROES IN SMALL BUSINESS, THE ENGINEERING AND THE TECHNICAL VOCATIONS.   NWALKJO46580

ENGINEERING TALENT IN SHORT SUPPLY. /OCCUPATIONS/   WAMONRX62613

THE PRESENT SITUATION IN THE ACADEMIC WORLD OF WOMEN TRAINED IN ENGINEERING. /OCCUPATIONS/   WBERNJX65639

ENHANCING THE ROLE OF WOMEN IN SCIENCE, ENGINEERING, AND THE SOCIAL SCIENCES. /OCCUPATIONS/   WKILLJR65903

WOMEN AND THE SCIENTIFIC PROFESSIONS. THE MIT SYMPOSIUM ON AMERICAN WOMEN IN SCIENCE AND ENGINEERING.
/OCCUPATIONS/   WMATTJA65963

A COMPARISON OF THE MALE-FEMALE ROLES IN ENGINEERING. /OCCUPATION/   WROBISS63083

BARRIERS TO THE CAREER CHOICE OF ENGINEERING, MEDICINE, OR SCIENCE AMONG AMERICAN WOMEN. /OCCUPATIONS/   WROSSAS65091

WOMEN IN PROFESSIONAL ENGINEERING. /OCCUPATIONS/   WSOCIOW62127

THE ROLE OF WOMEN IN PROFESSIONAL ENGINEERING. /OCCUPATIONS/   WTORPWG62157

ENGINEERS
STUDY OF THE SHORTAGE AND SALARIES OF SCIENTISTS AND ENGINEERS.   GUSSENA54353

NEGRO ENGINEERS AND STUDENTS REPORT ON THEIR PROFESSION. /OCCUPATIONS/   NKIEHRX58647

THE PRESENT SITUATION OF WOMAN SCIENTISTS AND ENGINEERS IN INDUSTRY AND GOVERNMENT. /OCCUPATIONS/   WBOLTRH65650

EMPLOYMENT AND CHARACTERISTICS OF WOMEN ENGINEERS. /OCCUPATIONS/   WUSDLAB56989

STATISTICS ON WOMEN PROFESSIONAL ENGINEERS. /OCCUPATIONS/   WWEBBJR66226

ENGLISH
SPANISH-SPEAKING AND ENGLISH SPEAKING CHILDREN IN SOUTHWEST TEXAS. A COMPARATIVE STUDY OF INTELLIGENCE,
SOCIO-ECONOMIC STATUS, AND ACHIEVEMENT.   MRATLYX60460

SOME CULTURAL AND ANTHROPOLOGICAL ASPECTS OF ENGLISH AS A SECOND LANGUAGE.   MRUBEAJ66468

ENJOIN
UNITED STATES HAS STANDING UNDER INTERSTATE COMMERCE ACT AND COMMERCE CLAUSE TO ENJOIN SEGREGATIVE
PRACTICES OF CITY. /LEGISLATION/   NHARVLR64500

ENROLLED
CHARACTERISTICS OF 6000 WHITE AND NONWHITE PERSONS ENROLLED IN MANPOWER-DEVELOPMENT-AND-TRAINING-ACT
TRAINING.   GUSDLAB63197

ENROLLEES
MANPOWER DEVELOPMENT TRAINING. TOTAL NUMBER OF NEW ENROLLEES DURING THE MONTH BY RACE AND OCCUPATION
STATEWIDE AND BY ADMINISTRATIVE AREA, SEPTEMBER, 1966, OCTOBER, 1966. /CALIFORNIA/   GCALDEM66518

ENROLLMENT
SCHOOL ENROLLMENT. /DEMOGRAPHY/   CUSBURC63183

BACKGROUND FACTORS RELATING TO COLLEGE PLANS AND COLLEGE ENROLLMENT AMONG PUBLIC HIGH SCHOOL STUDENTS.

ENROLLMENT   (CONTINUATION)
/ASPIRATIONS/   GEDUCTS57959

PROJECTIONS OF SCHOOL AND COLLEGE ENROLLMENT IN THE UNITED STATES TO 1985.   /DEMOGRAPHY/   GUSBURC66160

THE RELATIONSHIP BETWEEN MECHANIZATION OF COTTON PRODUCTION AND ATTENDANCE AND ENROLLMENT IN THE RURAL
SCHOOLS OF COAHOMA COUNTY, MISSISSIPPI.   NMCLABF51349

ENTERING
RURAL-FARM MALES ENTERING AND LEAVING WORKING AGES, 1940-50 AND 1950-60. REPLACEMENT RATIOS AND RATES.
/OCCUPATIONS/   GBOWLGK56433

THE COMMITMENT REQUIRED OF A WOMAN ENTERING A SCIENTIFIC PROFESSION. /OCCUPATIONS/   WBETTBX65645

PANEL DISCUSSION. THE COMMITTMENT REQUIRED OF A WOMAN ENTERING A SCIENTIFIC PROFESSION. /OCCUPATIONS/ WBUNTMI65663

ENTERING THE LABOR-FORCE.   WGOLDBX64794

ENTERPRISE
JOBS FOR THE HARD-TO-EMPLOY IN PRIVATE ENTERPRISE.   GCASSFH66744

MINORITY IN THE ENTERPRISE.   GFOLEAS52692

PUBLIC POLICY, PRIVATE ENTERPRISE AND THE REDUCTION OF POVERTY.   GLONGNE65121

AMERICAN ENTERPRISE AND THE RACIAL CRISIS.   NROBIJX63069

ENTREPRENEUR
THE NEGRO ENTREPRENEUR.   NWHITWL66320

ENTREPRENEURSHIP
NEGRO ENTREPRENEURSHIP IN SOUTHERN ECONOMIC DEVELOPMENT.   NYOUNHB64346

ENTRY
INFORMATION CONCERNING ENTRY OF MEXICAN AGRICULTURAL WORKERS INTO THE UNITED STATES.   MUSDLAB59335

RACIAL FACTORS INFLUENCING ENTRY TO THE SKILLED TRADES. /UNION/   NMARSRX63745

ENVIRONMENT
CORRELATES OF ADJUSTMENT AMONG AMERICAN-INDIANS IN AN URBAN ENVIRONMENT.   IMARTHW64588

RACE AND SOCIAL-CLASS AS SEPARATE FACTORS RELATED TO SOCIAL ENVIRONMENT. /ASPIRATIONS/   NBLOORX63096

EFFECTS OF ANXIETY, THREAT, AND RACIAL ENVIRONMENT ON TASK PERFORMANCE OF NEGRO COLLEGE STUDENTS.   NKATZIX63640

ENVIRONMENTAL
PERSONAL AND ENVIRONMENTAL OBSTACLES TO PRODUCTION ADJUSTMENTS ON SOUTH-CAROLINA PIEDMONT AREA FARMS. NTAYLCC58411

EQUAL
CONTRACTOR GROUP HITS REVISED EQUAL EMPLOYMENT STANDARDS.   GAIRCHR63866

EQUAL RIGHTS FOR ALL.   GAMERFX66376

EQUAL JOB OPPORTUNITY IS GOOD BUSINESS.   GAMERJC54381

THE RIGHT TO EQUAL TREATMENT. ADMINISTRATIVE ENFORCEMENT OF ANTIDISCRIMINATION LEGISLATION.   GBAMBMA61416

EQUAL-RIGHTS UNDER THE LAW. PROVIDING FOR EQUAL TREATMENT FOR ALL CITIZENS REGARDLESS OF RACE, RELIGION,
COLOR, NATIONAL ORIGIN OR ANCESTRY. /CALIFORNIA/   GCALAGO60511

PROMOTING EQUAL JOB OPPORTUNITY, A GUIDE FOR EMPLOYERS. /CALIFORNIA/   GCALFEP63538

FAIR-EMPLOYMENT-PRACTICES EQUAL GOOD EMPLOYMENT PRACTICES. GUIDELINES FOR TESTING AND SELECTING MINORITY
JOB APPLICANTS. /CALIFORNIA/   GCALFEP66540

FAIR-EMPLOYMENT-PRACTICES ACT. STATE LAWS GRANTING EQUAL RIGHTS, PRIVILEGES, ETC.   GELWAEX58662

IMPROVING INDUSTRIAL RACE-RELATIONS -- PART I. EQUAL JOB OPPORTUNITY -- SLOGAN OR REALITY.   GFLEMHC63363

PSYCHOLOGICAL TESTING FOR EFFECTIVE EMPLOYMENT PRACTICES AND EQUAL JOB OPPORTUNITIES.   GKETCWA65849

EQUAL RIGHTS -- HERE AND NOW.   GMEANGX63972

THE AMERICAN DREAM...EQUAL OPPORTUNITY, A REPORT ON THE COMMUNITY LEADER-S CONFERENCE SPONSORED BY
PRESIDENT-S COMMITTEE ON EQUAL-EMPLOYMENT-OPPORTUNITY, MAY 19, 1962.   GPRESCD62105

EQUAL ECONOMIC OPPORTUNITY. A REPORT.   GPRESCG53117

EQUAL JOB OPPORTUNITY AS SET FORTH IN EXECUTIVE ORDERS 10479 AND 10557.   GPRESCH56191

FOURTH ANNUAL REPORT ON EQUAL JOB OPPORTUNITY, 1956-1957, PRESIDENT-S COMMITTEE ON GOVERNMENT CONTRACTS. GPRESCH57122

EQUAL UNDER LAW.   GTENBJX65148

EQUAL PROTECTION OF THE LAWS IN NORTH-CAROLINA.   GUSCOMC62397

CONFERENCE ON EQUAL JOB OPPORTUNITY.   GUSDLAB56027

A GUIDE TO INDUSTRIAL-RELATIONS IN THE UNITED STATES. EQUAL JOB OPPORTUNITY UNDER COLLECTIVE-BARGAINING. GUSDLAB58449

LABOR LOOKS AT EQUAL RIGHTS IN EMPLOYMENT. /UNION/   GWOLLJA64579

EQUAL RIGHTS FOR THE SATURDAY SABBATH OBSERVER. /EMPLOYMENT DISCRIMINATION/   JHARTPX63729

CHICAGO STARTS MOVING ON EQUAL JOB QUESTION. /ILLINOIS/   NBUSIWX64298

WHAT ARE THE PSYCHOLOGICAL EFFECTS OF SEGREGATION UNDER CONDITIONS OF EQUAL FACILITIES.   NCHEIIX49198

CIVIL-RIGHTS, 1960-63. THE NEGRO CAMPAIGN TO WIN EQUAL RIGHTS AND OPPORTUNITIES IN THE UNITED STATES. NFACTOF64341

THE STRUGGLE OF NEGRO TEACHERS IN FLORIDA FOR EQUAL SALARIES. /OCCUPATIONS/   NFERGML49961

EQUAL EDUCATIONAL OPPORTUNITY. ANOTHER ASPECT.   NGIOVPC64279

EQUAL JUSTICE IN AN UNEQUAL WORLD. EQUALITY FOR THE NEGRO -- THE PROBLEM OF SPECIAL TREATMENT.   NKAPLJX66645

CONFERENCE ON EQUAL JOB OPPORTUNITY.   NMCKIGB56725

EQUAL OPPORTUNITY AND EQUAL PAY.   NNORTHR64937

EQUAL   (CONTINUATION)
    EQUAL OPPORTUNITY AND EQUAL PAY.   NNORTHR64937

    THE AMERICAN DREAM...EQUAL OPPORTUNITY.   NPRESCD62014

    EQUAL PROTECTION OF THE LAWS IN PUBLIC HIGHER EDUCATION.   NUSCCMC60302

    TO BE EQUAL.   NYOUNWM64353

    EQUAL PAY FOR WOMEN.   /DISCRIMINATION/   WCOMMXX63701

    EQUAL-PAY FOR EQUAL WORK.   WUSHOUR62020

EQUAL-ECONOMIC-OPPOR
    EDITORIAL COMMENT. FEPC HEARINGS REDUCE RACE PROBLEM TO LOWEST TERMS -- EQUAL-ECONOMIC-OPPORTUNITY.   NTHOMCH43160

EQUAL-EMPLOYMENT
    EQUAL-EMPLOYMENT.   GKARTWX67215

    THE INDUSTRIAL PSYCHOLOGIST. SELECTION AND EQUAL-EMPLOYMENT OPPORTUNITY.   GPARRJA66147

    PROMOTION SYSTEMS AND EQUAL-EMPLOYMENT OPPORTUNITY.   NDOERPB66280

    TITLE-VII. EQUAL-EMPLOYMENT SECTION. CIVIL-RIGHTS-ACT OF 1964. THE WAR-AGAINST-POVERTY.   NHILLHX65549

    PROMOTING EQUAL-EMPLOYMENT THROUGH THE PUBLIC EMPLOYMENT SERVICE.   NLEVILX62686

    PROSPECTS FOR EQUAL-EMPLOYMENT. CONFLICTING PORTENTS.   NMARSRX65744

    SPECIAL ISSUE ON EQUAL-EMPLOYMENT.   NUSGESA63266

    WOMEN AND THE EQUAL-EMPLOYMENT PROVISIONS OF THE CIVIL-RIGHTS-ACT.   WUSDLAB65234

EQUAL-EMPLOYMENT-ACT
    EQUAL-EMPLOYMENT-ACT OF 1966.   GBUREON66493

EQUAL-EMPLOYMENT-OPP
    WHAT THE SUPERVISOR SHOULD KNOW ABOUT THE EQUAL-EMPLOYMENT-OPPORTUNITY LAW.   GAHEREX65804

    PARTIAL INVENTORY OF ON-GOING RESEARCH IN EQUAL-EMPLOYMENT-OPPORTUNITIES.   GANDEBR67589

    MANAGEMENT GUIDE. EQUAL-EMPLOYMENT-OPPORTUNITY.   GASSOIC63407

    AN ASSESSMENT OF THE SUITABILITY OF THE FACETED STRUCTURE OF THE WRU EDUCATION THESAURUS AS A FRAMEWORK
    FOR PREPARATION OF A THESAURUS OF EQUAL-EMPLOYMENT-OPPORTUNITY TERMS.   GBARHGC66162

    6. TEST TECHNOLOGY AND EQUAL-EMPLOYMENT-OPPORTUNITY.   GBAYRAG66428

    EQUAL-EMPLOYMENT-OPPORTUNITY UNDER CIVIL-RIGHTS-ACT OF 1964.   GBERGRK64437

    EQUAL-EMPLOYMENT-OPPORTUNITY AND EXECUTIVE ORDER 10925.   GBIRNOX62451

    THE QUESTS FOR ECONOMIC STABILITY AND EQUAL-EMPLOYMENT-OPPORTUNITY.   GBRIMAF66475

    A SPECIAL REPORT -- THE EQUAL-EMPLOYMENT-OPPORTUNITY LAW, TITLE-VII OF THE CIVIL-RIGHTS-ACT OF 1964.   GBURENAND495

    TEXTS OF RULES AND REGULATIONS OF PRESIDENT-S COMMITTEE ON EQUAL-EMPLOYMENT-OPPORTUNITY RELATING TO
    OBLIGATIONS OF GOVERNMENT CONTRACTORS AND SUBCONTRACTORS, EFFECTIVE JULY 22, 1961. A BNA SPECIAL REPORT.   GBURENA61498

    RULES AND REGULATIONS OF THE PRESIDENT-S COMMITTEE ON EQUAL-EMPLOYMENT-OPPORTUNITY AS AMENDED.   GBURENA63496

    TOWARD EQUAL-EMPLOYMENT-OPPORTUNITY.   /CALIFORNIA/   GCALBOE64513

    EQUAL-EMPLOYMENT-OPPORTUNITY. A CHALLENGE TO THE EMPLOYMENT SERVICE.   GCASSFH66561

    MINORITY-GROUPS CONFERENCE ON EQUAL-EMPLOYMENT-OPPORTUNITIES.   GCHURRX55572

    THE CONTROVERSY OVER THE EQUAL-EMPLOYMENT-OPPORTUNITY PROVISIONS OF THE CIVIL-RIGHTS-BILL. PRO AND CON.   GCONGDX64594

    THE ROLE OF LAW IN EQUAL-EMPLOYMENT-OPPORTUNITY.   GCOOKFC66600

    A STUDY OF PATTERNS OF DISCRIMINATION IN EMPLOYMENT FOR THE EQUAL-EMPLOYMENT-OPPORTUNITY-COMMISSION,
    WASHINGTON-DC.   GCOUSFR66478

    A COMMON GOAL -- EQUAL-EMPLOYMENT-OPPORTUNITY.   GDAVIWG65629

    EQUAL-EMPLOYMENT-OPPORTUNITY IN THE DEFENSE SUPPLY AGENCY.   GDEFESA64631

    EQUAL-EMPLOYMENT-OPPORTUNITY.   GDONACX64648

    EQUAL-EMPLOYMENT-OPPORTUNITIES TODAY.   GDUNNAA62655

    EQUAL-EMPLOYMENT-OPPORTUNITY -- AN EMPLOYMENT-SERVICE RESPONSIBILITY.   GFANTAX64671

    THE FIRST NINE MONTHS. REPORT OF THE PRESIDENT-S COMMITTEE ON EQUAL-EMPLOYMENT-OPPORTUNITY.   GFEDEBJ62672

    EQUAL-EMPLOYMENT-OPPORTUNITY.   /DISCRIMINATION/   GFEILJG62675

    NOW. MASSACHUSETTS PLAN FOR EQUAL-EMPLOYMENT-OPPORTUNITY.   GGCULJX63732

    THE JOB AHEAD FOR THE PRESIDENT-S COMMITTEE ON EQUAL-EMPLOYMENT-OPPORTUNITY.   GHOLLJR61999

    REPORT ON THE STRUCTURE AND OPERATIONS OF THE PRESIDENT-S COMMITTEE ON EQUAL-EMPLOYMENT-OPPORTUNITY.   GKHEETW62852

    CRITICAL PROBLEMS IN ACHIEVING EQUAL-EMPLOYMENT-OPPORTUNITY.   GLOCKHC66906

    LAKE-ARROWHEAD CONFERENCE ON EQUAL-EMPLOYMENT-OPPORTUNITY.   GLOSAFEND916

    EQUAL-EMPLOYMENT-OPPORTUNITIES. PROBLEMS AND PROSPECTS.   GMARSRX65056

    EQUAL-EMPLOYMENT-OPPORTUNITY. SHOULD HIRING STANDARDS BE RELAXED.   GMAYFHX64968

    COMMENTS ON EQUAL-EMPLOYMENT-OPPORTUNITIES. PROBLEMS AND PROSPECTS.   GMCKERB65930

    REMARKS ON EQUAL-EMPLOYMENT-OPPORTUNITIES.   GMCKERB65931

    DISCUSSION ON EQUAL-EMPLOYMENT-OPPORTUNITIES.   GPOLIEX65102

    CONFERENCE ON EQUAL-EMPLOYMENT-OPPORTUNITY.   GPOTTGX65189

EQUAL-EMPLOYMENT-OPP (CONTINUATION)
THE AMERICAN DREAM...EQUAL OPPORTUNITY, A REPORT ON THE COMMUNITY LEADER-S CONFERENCE SPONSORED BY
PRESIDENT-S COMMITTEE ON **EQUAL-EMPLOYMENT-OPPORTUNITY**, MAY 19, 1962.   GPRESCD62105

THE FIRST NINE MONTHS -- SPECIAL YEAR-END REPORT, APRIL 7, 1961-JANUARY 15, 1962, PRESIDENT-S COMMITTEE
ON **EQUAL-EMPLOYMENT-OPPORTUNITY**.   GPRESCD62108

GUIDE FOR INVESTIGATIONS AND COMPLIANCE REVIEWS IN **EQUAL-EMPLOYMENT-OPPORTUNITY**.   GPRESCD62109

REGIONAL COMMUNITY LEADERS CONFERENCE ON **EQUAL-EMPLOYMENT-OPPORTUNITY**, PROCEEDINGS.   GPRESCD64113

REPORT TO THE PRESIDENT, NOVEMBER 26, 1963 BY THE PRESIDENT-S COMMITTEE ON **EQUAL-EMPLOYMENT-OPPORTUNITY**. GPRESCD64114

FIELD MANUAL ON **EQUAL-EMPLOYMENT-OPPORTUNITY** UNDER GOVERNMENT CONTRACTS.   GPRESCD65107

THE AFFIRMATIVE-ACTION CONCEPT OF **EQUAL-EMPLOYMENT-OPPORTUNITY**.   GPRICWS65688

FINAL REPORT OF SAN-FRANCISCO CALIFORNIA COMMISSION ON **EQUAL-EMPLOYMENT-OPPORTUNITY**.   GSANFCE60275

EMPLOYERS GUIDE TO **EQUAL-EMPLOYMENT-OPPORTUNITY**.   GSCHEGX66280

EQUAL-EMPLOYMENT-OPPORTUNITY.   GSNOWCX65683

EQUAL-EMPLOYMENT-OPPORTUNITY.   GTAYLHX62347

PRESIDENT-S COMMITTEE ON **EQUAL-EMPLOYMENT-OPPORTUNITY**.   GTAYLHX62348

EQUAL-EMPLOYMENT-OPPORTUNITY TRAINING, A PROGRAM FOR AFFIRMATIVE-ACTION.   GUSCISC63384

BIBLIOGRAPHY ON **EQUAL-EMPLOYMENT-OPPORTUNITY**.   GUSCOMC66393

EQUAL-EMPLOYMENT-OPPORTUNITY UNDER FEDERAL LAW.   GUSCOMC66396

A TIME FOR ACTION, PROCEEDINGS OF THE NATIONAL CONFERENCE ON **EQUAL-EMPLOYMENT-OPPORTUNITY**, 1962.
/MILITARY/   GUSDARM62193

EQUAL-EMPLOYMENT-OPPORTUNITY GUIDE FOR DEPARTMENT OF THE NAVY CONTRACTORS.   GUSDDEF64433

CONFERENCE ON **EQUAL-EMPLOYMENT-OPPORTUNITY**.   GUSDLAB65026

CONFERENCE ON **EQUAL-EMPLOYMENT-OPPORTUNITY**, AUGUST 16, 1961.   GUSDSTA61507

LAKE ARROWHEAD CONFERENCE ON **EQUAL-EMPLOYMENT-OPPORTUNITY**, OCTOBER 22-24, 1963 -- RECORD OF PROCEEDINGS.
LOS-ANGELES, CALIFORNIA.   GUSFEDE63513

EQUAL-EMPLOYMENT-OPPORTUNITY ACT OF 1962, REPORT TO ACCOMPANY HR 10144.   GUSHOUR62340

EQUAL-EMPLOYMENT-OPPORTUNITY, PARTS I AND II.   GUSHOUR62342

EQUAL-EMPLOYMENT-OPPORTUNITY.   GUSHOUR63338

EQUAL-EMPLOYMENT-OPPORTUNITY ACT OF 1963, REPORT TO ACCOMPANY HR 405.   GUSHOUR63341

EQUAL-EMPLOYMENT-OPPORTUNITY 1965.   GUSHOUR65339

EQUAL-EMPLOYMENT-OPPORTUNITY IN THE US POST OFFICE DEPARTMENT, A SUPPLEMENTAL REPORT TO THE POSTMASTER
GENERAL.   GUSPODA63516

EQUAL-EMPLOYMENT-OPPORTUNITY.   GUSSENA63349

THE CHANGING PATTERN IN EMPLOYMENT. /**EQUAL-EMPLOYMENT-OPPORTUNITY**/   GWALLLM63520

EQUAL-EMPLOYMENT-OPPORTUNITIES.   NCASSFH66185

PROMOTIONS SYSTEMS AND **EQUAL-EMPLOYMENT-OPPORTUNITY**.   NDOERPB66279

THE NEGRO AND **EQUAL-EMPLOYMENT-OPPORTUNITIES**. A REVIEW OF MANAGEMENT EXPERIENCES IN TWENTY COMPANIES. NFERMLA66790

EQUAL-EMPLOYMENT-OPPORTUNITY, HEARING, TESTIMONY.   NHILLHX62547

THE ROLE OF LAW IN SECURING **EQUAL-EMPLOYMENT-OPPORTUNITY**. LEGAL POWERS AND SOCIAL CHANGE.   NHILLHX66544

EQUAL-EMPLOYMENT-OPPORTUNITY. CHANGING PROBLEMS, CHANGING TECHNIQUES.   NHOPEJX63568

GOVERNMENT AND **EQUAL-EMPLOYMENT-OPPORTUNITY**.   NKRISSX67665

MANPOWER SERVICES FOR **EQUAL-EMPLOYMENT-OPPORTUNITY**.   NLEVILX64685

SURVEY OF **EQUAL-EMPLOYMENT-OPPORTUNITIES** IN NEW-JERSEY INVESTOR-OWNED PUBLIC UTILITIES.   NLEVIMJ66607

FINAL REPORT. **EQUAL-EMPLOYMENT-OPPORTUNITY** IN THE TRANSPORTATION INDUSTRY. /MASSACHUSETTS/   NMASSCA66964

EQUAL-EMPLOYMENT-OPPORTUNITY IN THE SUBURBAN SHOPPING CENTER. FACT OR FICTION. /MICHIGAN/   NMICFEP63777

EQUAL-EMPLOYMENT-OPPORTUNITY. COMPANY POLICIES AND EXPERIENCE.   NMILLGW64070

EQUAL-EMPLOYMENT-OPPORTUNITIES IN MISSOURI STATE AGENCIES. A SURVEY OF NEGRO EMPLOYMENT, SPRING-SUMMER
1963.   NMISSCH64801

NEGROES IN THE WORK GROUP. HOW 33 BUSINESS AND INDUSTRIAL FIRMS OFFERED **EQUAL-EMPLOYMENT-OPPORTUNITIES** TO
ALL.   NSEIDJX50114

CONFERENCE ON **EQUAL-EMPLOYMENT-OPPORTUNITY**.   NUSDLAB65813

SUMMARY REPORT. **EQUAL-EMPLOYMENT-OPPORTUNITY** CONFERENCE.   NUSNAAS63267

EQUAL-EMPLOYMENT-POL
EQUAL-EMPLOYMENT-POLICIES.   GUSDHEW63434

EQUAL-JOB-OPPORTUNIT
PLAN FOR **EQUAL-JOB-OPPORTUNITY** AT LOCKHEED-AIRCRAFT-CORP. /INDUSTRY CASE-STUDY/   NUSDLAB61838

EQUAL-JOB-RIGHTS
EQUAL-JOB-RIGHTS.   GBUSIWX61502

EQUAL-OPPORTUNITIES
EQUAL-OPPORTUNITIES PLAN STRESSED IN STATE PERSONNEL BOARD DOCUMENT. /CALIFORNIA/   GCALSEM64548

AN **EQUAL-OPPORTUNITIES** COMMITTEE AT WORK IN TEXAS.   GDESHEA66633

EQUAL-OPPORTUNITIES (CONTINUATION)
EQUAL-OPPORTUNITIES BY LAW. A CASE-STUDY.   GDUNNDD63654

THE NEGRO RECORD IN EQUAL-OPPORTUNITIES.   NGRANLB58596

EQUAL-OPPORTUNITY
RACE, EMPLOYMENT TESTS, AND EQUAL-OPPORTUNITY.   GASHXPX65406

REPORT OF THE CALIFORNIA STATE ADVISORY COMMITTEE TO THE UNITED STATES COMMISSION ON CIVIL-RIGHTS ON
CALIFORNIA-S PROGRAM FOR EQUAL-OPPORTUNITY IN APPRENTICESHIP.   GBECKWL62432

ECONOMICS OF LABOR-RELATIONS. /EQUAL-OPPORTUNITY/   GBLOOGF65885

CONFERENCE ISSUE -- TOWARD EQUAL-OPPORTUNITY IN EMPLOYMENT.   GBUFFLR64484

EQUAL-OPPORTUNITY IN EMPLOYMENT.   GBULLPX66486

THE CALIFORNIA PLAN FOR EQUAL-OPPORTUNITY IN APPRENTICESHIP FOR MINORITY-GROUPS.   GCALDIR63523

EQUAL-OPPORTUNITY IN APPRENTICESHIP AND TRAINING -- THE CALIFORNIA PROGRAM.   GCALDIR65524

EQUAL-OPPORTUNITY IN EMPLOYMENT.   GFOLSFM54693

FURNISHING EQUAL-OPPORTUNITY FOR MINORITIES IN CIVIL-SERVICE.   GGREGGX62070

ECONOMIC GROWTH, EQUAL-OPPORTUNITY, RESEARCH, JOINT EFFORT. EMPLOYMENT.   GILLIGC63798

THE REALITY OF EQUAL-OPPORTUNITY IN FEDERAL EMPLOYMENT.   GMACYJW66933

ENFORCEMENT OF THE FEDERAL EQUAL-OPPORTUNITY LAW.   GMARSBX64943

LAW AND EQUAL-OPPORTUNITY. ANTI-DISCRIMINATION LAW IN MASSACHUSETTS.   GMAYHLH63970

FEDERAL PROCUREMENT AND EQUAL-OPPORTUNITY EMPLOYMENT.   GPOWETX64190

EQUAL-OPPORTUNITY UNDER THE MERIT SYSTEM.   GROSEHS66253

REPORT OF TWIN-CITIES EQUAL-OPPORTUNITY REVIEW. /MINNEAPOLIS ST-PAUL MINNESOTA/   GUSCISC64131

TASK FORCE FOR EQUAL-OPPORTUNITY IN BUSINESS.   GUSDCOM65432

FRANCHISE COMPANY DATA FOR EQUAL-OPPORTUNITY IN BUSINESS.   GUSDCOM66431

EQUAL-OPPORTUNITY IN APPRENTICESHIP PROGRAMS.   GUSHOUR61343

MANPOWER PROGRAMS. THEIR CONTRIBUTION TO THE ACHIEVEMENT OF EQUAL-OPPORTUNITY MANPOWER ADMINISTRATION.   GWHITHC65558

ON THE SOCIAL SCENE. /EQUAL-OPPORTUNITY/   JLEEXAM58739

THE RIGHT TO EQUAL-OPPORTUNITY.   MGLICLB66694

RACIAL DIFFERENCES AND THE FUTURE. /INTELLIGENCE EQUAL-OPPORTUNITY/   NINGLDJ64067

WHY WE CAN-T WAIT. /CIVIL-RIGHTS EQUAL-OPPORTUNITY/   NKINGML64022

THE NEGRO IN FEDERAL EMPLOYMENT. THE QUEST FOR EQUAL-OPPORTUNITY.   NKRISSX67143

THE FIGHT FOR EQUAL-OPPORTUNITY.   NMANGMX63736

LIFELINE TO EQUAL-OPPORTUNITY.   NNATLUL64892

EQUAL-OPPORTUNITY IN FARM PROGRAMS -- AN APPRAISAL OF SERVICES RENDERED BY AGENCIES OF THE UNITED STATES
DEPARTMENT OF AGRICULTURE.   NUSCOMC65232

TOWARD EQUAL-OPPORTUNITY.   NWIRTWW63330

EQUAL-OPPORTUNITY AND EQUAL-PAY.   WNORTHR64037

REPORT OF THE COMMITTEE ON EDUCATION. /EQUAL-OPPORTUNITY COUNSELING/   WPKESCO63066

SEX AND EQUAL-OPPORTUNITY IN HIGHER EDUCATION.   WPUNKHH61071

EQUAL-PAY
EQUAL-PAY FOR WHITE AND NEGRO TEACHERS. /OCCUPATIONS/   NUSDLAB41817

EQUAL-OPPORTUNITY AND EQUAL-PAY.   WNORTHR64037

ACTION FOR EQUAL-PAY.   WUSDLAB64183

WHAT THE EQUAL-PAY PRINCIPLE MEANS TO WOMEN.   WUSDLAB64227

GETTING THE FACTS ON EQUAL-PAY.   WUSDLAB66197

WHY STATE EQUAL-PAY LAWS.   WUSDLAB66230

EQUAL-PAY FOR EQUAL WORK.   WUSHCUR62020

EQUAL-PAY FOR WOMEN. ITS EFFECT.   WUSNEWR64244

EQUAL-PAY-ACT
EQUAL-PAY-ACT OF 1963.   WUSDLAB63991

EQUAL-RIGHTS
EQUAL-RIGHTS UNDER THE LAW. PROVIDING FOR EQUAL TREATMENT FOR ALL CITIZENS REGARDLESS OF RACE, RELIGION,
COLOR, NATIONAL ORIGIN OR ANCESTRY. /CALIFORNIA/   GCALAGO60511

SCHOOL, MINORITIES AND EQUAL-RIGHTS, SELECTED MATERIAL. /CALIFORNIA/   GCALSLIND549

TOWARD EQUALITY, BALTIMORE-S PROGRESS-REPORT, A CHRONICLE OF PROGRESS SINCE WORLD-WAR-II TOWARD THE
ACHIEVEMENT OF EQUAL-RIGHTS AND OPPORTUNITIES FOR NEGROES IN MARYLAND 1946-1958.   NBALTUL58048

PLANNING THE END OF THE AMERICAN GHETTO. A PROGRAM OF ECONOMIC DEVELOPMENT FOR EQUAL-RIGHTS.   NHILLHX66538

THE CONTROVERSY OVER EQUAL-RIGHTS FOR NEGROES.   NOPINRC56956

THE DEMAND FOR EQUAL-RIGHTS.   NSCHEGX64103

EQUALITY
EQUALITY BY STATUTES -- LEGAL CONTROLS OVER GROUP DISCRIMINATION.   GBERGMX52440

EQUALITY (CONTINUATION)
RACIAL **EQUALITY** AND THE LAW.   GBERGMX54442

ECONOMIC **EQUALITY** AND GOVERNMENT ACTION.   GBERLAA66222

COUNSELING MINORITY-GROUP YOUTH. DEVELOPING THE EXPERIENCE OF **EQUALITY** THROUGH EDUCATION.   GBRIGWA62473

APPROACHING **EQUALITY** OF OPPORTUNITY IN HIGHER EDUCATION.   GBROWFJ55476

EQUALITY OF EDUCATIONAL OPPORTUNITY.   GLIEBMX59902

EQUALITY IN OUR TIME. WHAT WE SAID, AND WHAT WE DID NOT SAY.   GLOWESH63921

THE NEXT STEPS TOWARD **EQUALITY** OF OPPORTUNITY IN THE SYRACUSE METROPOLITAN AREA. REPORT OF THE SYRACUSE
CONFERENCE ON HUMAN RIGHTS AND HOUSING, JULY 2-3 1962. /NEW-YORK/   GNEWYSB62103

EQUALITY OF JOB OPPORTUNITY AND CIVIL-RIGHTS.   GREUTWP60223

GIVING REALITY TO THE PROMISE OF **EQUALITY**.   GROBIJB64240

INTRODUCTION. THE STRUGGLE FOR **EQUALITY** AND ITS IMPACT ON INDUSTRIAL-RELATIONS.   GSTEIBX64335

FEDERAL **EQUALITY** OF OPPORTUNITY IN EMPLOYMENT ACT.   GUSSENA52350

PROCEEDINGS OF THE 50TH ANNIVERSARY OBSERVANCE OF THE AMERICAN JEWISH COMMITTEE. APRIL 10-14, 1957. THE
PURSUIT OF **EQUALITY** AT HOME AND ABROAD. /ECONOMIC-OPPORTUNITY/   JAMERJC58692

EQUALITY OF OPPORTUNITY.   JKLINOX58735

STRUGGLE FOR **EQUALITY**. SYMPOSIUM.   JMCLABX64747

IS **EQUALITY** UNFAIR. NEGRO-S PLEA FOR PREFERENTIAL-TREATMENT.   NAMERXX63008

THE NEGROES PROGRESS TOWARD EMPLOYMENT **EQUALITY**.   NAUGUTX58034

TOWARD **EQUALITY**. BALTIMORE-S PROGRESS-REPORT, A CHRONICLE OF PROGRESS SINCE WORLD-WAR-II TOWARD THE
ACHIEVEMENT OF EQUAL-RIGHTS AND OPPORTUNITIES FOR NEGROES IN MARYLAND 1946-1958.   NBALTUL58048

TOWARD **EQUALITY**. BALTIMORE-S PROGRESS-REPORT, 1962 SUPPLEMENT. /MARYLAND/   NBALTUL62049

RACIAL **EQUALITY** AND THE LAW. THE ROLE OF LAW IN THE REDUCTION OF DISCRIMINATION IN THE UNITED-STATES.   NBERGMX54076

THE LIMITED POTENTIAL FOR NEGRO-WHITE JOB **EQUALITY**.   NCHALWE65188

EQUALITY OF EDUCATIONAL OPPORTUNITY.   NCOLEJS66223

THE ROLE OF WHITE RESISTANCE AND FACILITATION IN THE NEGRO STRUGGLE FOR **EQUALITY**.   NGLENND65676

EQUALITY AND BEYOND. /RESIDENTIAL-SEGREGATION/   NGRIEGX66459

EQUALITY IN AMERICA. /ECONOMIC-STATUS/   NGRIMAP64983

THE NEW **EQUALITY**.   NHENTNX64518

EQUALITY OF OPPORTUNITY. A UNION APPROACH TO FAIR EMPLOYMENT.   NHOPEJX56570

EQUALITY OF EMPLOYMENT OPPORTUNITY. A PROCESS ANALYSIS OF UNION INITIATIVE.   NHOPEJX60569

THE ECONOMICS OF **EQUALITY**.   NKAHNTX64629

EQUAL JUSTICE IN AN UNEQUAL WORLD. **EQUALITY** FOR THE NEGRO -- THE PROBLEM OF SPECIAL TREATMENT.   NKAPLJX66645

USES OF LAW IN THE STRUGGLE FOR **EQUALITY**.   NMASLWX55756

PROSPERITY THROUGH **EQUALITY**.   NMILLLX63788

MANAGEMENTS GUIDELINES FOR MEETING THE NEGRO DRIVE FOR JOB **EQUALITY**. /INDUSTRY/.   NOPINRC63958

ARE NEGROES READY FOR **EQUALITY**.   NROWACT60090

INTRODUCTION. THE STRUGGLE FOR **EQUALITY** AND ITS IMPACT ON INDUSTRIAL-RELATIONS.   NSTEIBX64300

THE MEANING OF **EQUALITY**.   WNEUBMX66024

EQUALITY BETWEEN THE SEXES. AN IMMODEST PROPOSAL. /WORK-WOMEN-ROLE/   WROSSAS64132

EQUALIZATION
EFFORTS OF NEGRO TEACHERS IN THE SOUTHERN STATES TO OBTAIN **EQUALIZATION** OF SALARIES.   NJONEER48343

ESSAY
US MANPOWER AND EMPLOYMENT POLICY. A REVIEW **ESSAY**.   GGORDMS65728

ESSAYS
ESSAYS IN SOUTHERN ECONOMIC DEVELOPMENT.   GGREEMX64450

ESSAYS IN AMERICAN JEWISH HISTORY.   JMARCJR58326

ESSEX-COUNTY
REPORT OF A PRELIMINARY STUDY OF EMPLOYMENT PRACTICES INVOLVING MINORITY-GROUP WORKERS, **ESSEX-COUNTY**,
NEW-JERSEY.   GNEWJDE46059

ESTABLISHMENT
TRADE UNIONS PRACTICES AND THE NEGRO WORKER -- THE **ESTABLISHMENT** AND IMPLEMENTATION OF AFL-CIO
ANTI-DISCRIMINATION POLICY.   NDAVINF60312

OCCUPATIONAL **ESTABLISHMENT** OF FORMER STUDENTS OF VOCATIONAL AGRICULTURE IN MONTGOMERY TRAINING SCHOOL
AREA. /ALABAMA/   NSCOTCDND346

ESTIMATED
ESTIMATED NEED FOR SKILLED-WORKERS, 1965-75. /EMPLOYMENT/   GSALTAF66534

SOME COMPARISONS AMONG NEGRO-WHITE COLLEGE STUDENTS. SOCIAL AMBITION AND **ESTIMATED** SOCIAL MOBILITY.   NHARREE66786

ESTIMATES
HOW ACCURATE ARE **ESTIMATES** OF STATE AND LOCAL UNEMPLOYMENT.   GULLMJX63975

ETHICS
THE **ETHICS** OF COMPENSATORY JUSTICE.PREFERENTIAL-TREATMENT/   GLICHRX64900

ETHNIC

REPORT TO GOVERNOR EDMUND G BROWN. SECOND ETHNIC SURVEY OF EMPLOYMENT AND PROMOTION IN STATE GOVERNMENT. /CALIFORNIA NEGRO MEXICAN-AMERICAN/   CBECKWL65070

THE EFFECT OF LOW EDUCATIONAL-ATTAINMENT ON INCOMES. A COMPARATIVE STUDY OF SELECTED ETHNIC GROUPS. /NEGRO MEXICAN-AMERICAN/   CFOGEWX66367

FAMILY STRUCTURE AND SCHOOL PERFORMANCE. A COMPARATIVE STUDY OF STUDENTS FROM THREE ETHNIC BACKGROUNDS IN AN INTEGRATED SCHOOL. /MEXICAN-AMERICAN AMERICAN-INDIAN/   CGRIFJX65407

CULTURAL DIFFERENCES IN AMERICAN ETHNIC GROUPS. BIBLIOGRAPHY. /AMERICAN-INDIAN NEGRO SPANISH-AMERICAN/   CLIBRCX64899

ETHNIC SURVEY OF MUNICIPAL-EMPLOYEES. A REPORT ON THE NUMBER AND DISTRIBUTION OF NEGROES AND PUERTO-RICANS AND OTHER EMPLOYEES BY THE CITY OF NEW-YORK.   CNEWYCC64916

SECOND ETHNIC SURVEY OF EMPLOYMENT AND PROMOTION IN STATE GOVERNMENT. /CALIFORNIA/   GBECKWL65433

RACE AND ETHNIC RELATIONS.   GBERRBX65449

ORGANIZED LABOR AND THE INTEGRATION OF ETHNIC GROUPS. /UNION/   GBLOCHD58455

STATEMENT ON SURVEYS AND STATISTICS AS TO RACIAL AND ETHNIC COMPOSITION OF WORK-FORCE OR UNION MEMBERSHIP. /CALIFORNIA/   GCALFEP63539

ETHNIC CENSUS OF EXAMINATION COMPETITORS, JAN-JUNE 1965, CALIFORNIA STATE PERSONNEL BOARD.   GCALSPB65551

ETHNIC CENSUS OF EXAMINATION COMPETITORS, JULY-DEC 1965, CALIFORNIA STATE-PERSONNEL-BOARD.   GCALSPB65552

QUERIES CONCERNING INDUSTRY AND SOCIETY GROWING OUT OF STUDY OF ETHNIC RELATIONS IN INDUSTRY.   GHUGHEC59787

ETHNIC AND RACE BARRIERS.   GKAHLJA57831

ETHNIC GROUPS AND THE PRACTICE OF MEDICINE. /OCCUPATIONS/   GLIEBSX58042

ETHNIC PATTERNS IN AMERICAN CITIES.   GLIEBSX63904

ETHNIC AND ECONOMIC MINORITIES. UNION-S FUTURE OR UNRECRUITABLE.   GMARSRX63945

ETHNIC RELATIONS IN THE UNITED STATES.   GMCDOEC53050

ETHNIC SURVEY OF EMPLOYMENT IN STATE GOVERNMENT. /CALIFORNIA/   GMESPFA63977

TEST PERFORMANCE IN RELATION TO ETHNIC GROUP AND SOCIAL CLASS.   GROBESO63683

THEY AND WE. RACIAL AND ETHNIC RELATIONS IN THE UNITED STATES.   GROSEPI64251

RACIAL AND ETHNIC EMPLOYMENT PATTERN SURVEY OF THE CITY AND COUNTY OF SAN-FRANCISCO GOVERNMENT. DEPARTMENTAL ANALYSIS. /CALIFORNIA/   GSANFHR65264

THE BALANCED ETHNIC WORK GROUP.   GSCOTWW61290

RACIAL AND ETHNIC RELATIONS. SELECTED READINGS.   GSEGABE66154

ETHNIC STRATIFICATION. A COMPARATIVE APPROACH.   GSHIBTX65303

AMERICAN MINORITY RELATIONS. THE SOCIOLOGY OF RACE AND ETHNIC GROUPS.   GVANDJW63535

ETHNIC SURVEY OF APPRENTICES. /CALIFORNIA/   GWEBBEB65546

THE INDIAN TRIBES OF THE US. ETHNIC AND CULTURAL SURVIVAL.   IMCNIDX61586

A JEW WITHIN AMERICAN SOCIETY -- A STUDY IN ETHNIC INDIVIDUALITY.   JSHERCB61311

CLASS AS AN EXPLANATION OF ETHNIC DIFFERENCES IN MOBILITY ASPIRATIONS — THE CASE OF MEXICAN-AMERICANS.   MHELLCS65415

A STUDY OF THE ACCULTURATION AND SOCIAL ASPIRATIONS OF SIXTY JUNIOR HIGH SCHOOL STUDENTS FROM THE MEXICAN ETHNIC GROUP.   MJONEBM62421

OBJECTIVE ACCESS IN THE OPPORTUNITY STRUCTURE. THE ASSESSMENT OF THREE ETHNIC GROUPS WITH RESPECT TO QUANTIFIED SOCIAL STRUCTURAL VARIABLES.   MRENDGX63461

DIFFERENTIAL SELECTION AMONG APPLICANTS FROM DIFFERENT SOCIO-ECONOMIC AND ETHNIC BACKGROUNDS.   NBARRRS65056

THE FRENCH AND THE NON-FRENCH IN LOUISIANA. A STUDY OF THE RELEVANCE OF ETHNIC FACTORS IN RURAL DEVELOPMENT. /ECONOMIC-STATUS/   NBERTAL65394

ETHNIC CENSUS OF EXAMINATION COMPETITORS. REPORT OF EXAMINATIONS GIVEN JULY THROUGH DECEMBER, 1965, SUMMARY. /TESTING CALIFORNIA/   NCALFPB66173

ETHNIC AND CLASS PREFERENCES AMONG COLLEGE NEGROES.   NEBOIAX60315

ETHNIC FAMILY PATTERNS. THE NEGRO FAMILY IN THE UNITED STATES.   NFRAZEF48379

SITUATIONAL PRESSURES AND FUNCTIONAL ROLE OF THE ETHNIC LABOR LEADERS. /UNION/   NGREESX53453

ATTITUDES TOWARD ETHNIC FARM WORKERS IN COACHELLA-VALLEY. /CALIFORNIA/   NMCDOEC55719

STATUS POSITION, MOBILITY, AND ETHNIC IDENTIFICATION OF THE NEGRO.   NPARKSX64973

THE PROBLEM OF CULTURAL BIAS IN SELECTION. II. ETHNIC BACKGROUND AND TEST PERFORMANCE.   NROBESO65068

THE NEGRO AS AN IMMIGRANT GROUP. RECENT TRENDS IN RACIAL AND ETHNIC SEGREGATION IN CHICAGO. /ILLINOIS/   NTAEUKE64196

ETHNIC STATUS AND OCCUPATIONAL DILEMMAS.   NVOLLHM66287

THE VALIDATION OF ACCULTURATION. A CONDITION TO ETHNIC ASSIMILATION.   OBROOLX55708

THE EFFECT OF LOW EDUCATIONAL ATTAINMENT ON INCOMES. A COMPARATIVE STUDY OF SELECTED ETHNIC GROUPS.   OFOGEWX66721

ETHNIC-GROUP

THE OLD-TIMERS AND THE NEWCOMERS. ETHNIC-GROUP RELATIONS IN A NEEDLE TRADE UNION.   NHERBWX53519

ETHNICALLY

INTERPERSONAL RELATIONS IN ETHNICALLY MIXED SMALL WORK GROUPS.   GSCOTWW59291

ETHNICITY

RACE, ETHNICITY, AND THE ACHIEVEMENT SYNDROME.   GROSEBC59252

ETHNICS

THE ETHNICS OF EXECUTIVE SELECTION.   JWARDLB65769

ETHNOMICS
ETHNOMICS -- NEGRO MUST BE FULL PARTICIPANT IN MARKET PLACE.   NBUNKHC65122

EUGENE-SPRINGFIELD
KLAMATH INDIANS IN TWO NON-INDIAN COMMUNITIES. KLAMATH-FALLS AND **EUGENE-SPRINGFIELD**. /OREGON/   ILIVIMG59582

EVALUATED
THE STATUS OF JOBS AND OCCUPATIONS AS **EVALUATED** BY AN URBAN NEGRO SAMPLE.   NBROWMC55126

EVALUATING
EVALUATING JOB APPLICANTS WITH POLICE RECORDS. /CALIFORNIA/   GCALFEP66532

EVALUATION
THE **EVALUATION** OF WORK BY FEMALES, 1940-1950. /WOMEN NEGRO/   CDORNSM56284

REPORT. **EVALUATION** STUDY OF YOUTH TRAINING AND EMPLOYMENT PROJECT, EAST LOS-ANGELES. /NEGRO
MEXICAN-AMERICAN CALIFORNIA/   CWEINJL64310

EVALUATION OF STATE FAIR-EMPLOYMENT-PRACTICES-COMMISSIONS. EXPERIENCES AND FORECASTS.   GAMERCR49371

FEDERAL AID TO DEPRESSED AREAS. AN **EVALUATION** OF THE AREA-REDEVELOPMENT-ADMINISTRATION.   GLEVISA64896

EVALUATION AND SKILL TRAINING OF OUT-OF-SCHOOL, HARD-CORE UNEMPLOYED YOUTH FOR TRAINING AND PLACEMENT.   GSMITAE65140

RETRAINING, AN **EVALUATION** OF GAINS AND COSTS.   GSOMEGG65717

PSYCHOLOGICAL TESTING IN INDUSTRY. A CRITICAL **EVALUATION**.   GSTANES64635

APPRENTICESHIP. AN **EVALUATION** OF THE NEED.   GSTRAGX65715

PAPAGO INDIANS, **EVALUATION** OF OPPORTUNITIES FOR PERMANENT RELOCATION.   IFITZKXND440

AN **EVALUATION** OF THE 10-YEAR DEVELOPMENT PROGRAM OF THE UTE TRIBE OF THE UINTAH AND OURAY RESERVATION,
UTAH.   IUSDINT58648

THE **EVALUATION** OF PRACTICES CARRIED ON BY TWO HUNDRED NEGRO FARMERS IN THE PRODUCTION OF COTTON IN MACON
COUNTY, ALABAMA.   NGCLDSM48350

RACE AND INTELLIGENCE. AN **EVALUATION**.   NTUMIMM63065

EDUCATED WOMEN -- A MIDCENTURY **EVALUATION**. /WORK-WOMAN-ROLE/   WDOLAEF56734

EVENTS
MONTHLY SUMMARY OF **EVENTS** AND TRENDS IN RACE-RELATIONS. /CINCINNATI OHIO CASE-STUDY UNION/   NFISKUX44357

RECENT **EVENTS** IN NEGRO UNION RELATIONSHIPS.   NWEAVRC44306

EVIDENCE
THE **EVIDENCE** OF PERSISTENT UNEMPLOYMENT.   GINDURR59814

SOME NEW **EVIDENCE** ON EDUCATIONAL SELECTIVITY IN MIGRATION FROM THE SOUTH.   GSUVAEM65345

REVIEW OF **EVIDENCE** RELATING TO EFFECTS OF DESEGREGATION ON THE INTELLECTUAL PERFORMANCE OF NEGROES. NKATZIX64637

EVOLUTION
UNIONS BEFORE THE BAR. HISTORICAL TRIALS SHOWING THE **EVOLUTION** OF LABOR RIGHTS IN THE US.   GLIEBEX50901

THE **EVOLUTION** OF AMERICAN LAW VIS-A-VIS THE AMERICAN NEGRO.   NGARDHX63395

REVOLUTION IN **EVOLUTION**. /COLLEGE RECRUITMENT/   NSCOTFG66111

EX-MIGRANT
SOCIAL AND ATTITUDINAL CHARACTERISTICS OF SPANISH-SPEAKING MIGRANT AND **EX-MIGRANT** WORKERS IN THE
SOUTHWEST.   MULIBHX66503

EXAMINATION
ETHNIC CENSUS OF **EXAMINATION** COMPETITORS, JAN-JUNE 1965, CALIFORNIA STATE PERSONNEL BOARD.   GCALSPB65551

ETHNIC CENSUS OF **EXAMINATION** COMPETITORS, JULY-DEC 1965, CALIFORNIA STATE-PERSONNEL-BOARD.   GCALSPB65552

EXAMINATION OF THE WAR-ON-POVERTY PROGRAM.   GUSHOUR65824

ETHNIC CENSUS OF **EXAMINATION** COMPETITORS. REPORT OF EXAMINATIONS GIVEN JULY THROUGH DECEMBER, 1965,
SUMMARY. /TESTING CALIFORNIA/   NCALFPB66173

SOCIAL-STRUCTURE AND THE NEGRO REVOLT. AN **EXAMINATION** OF SOME HYPOTHESES. /SOCIO-ECONOMIC/   NGESCJA64400

PREJUDICE IS NOT THE WHOLE STORY. **EXAMINATION** OF THREE CASES OF NEGRO UPGRADING IN TRACTION COMPANIES IN
PHILADELPHIA, LOS-ANGELES AND CHICAGO. /PENNSYLVANIA CALIFORNIA ILLINOIS/   NWECKJE45308

EXAMINATIONS
ETHNIC CENSUS OF EXAMINATION COMPETITORS. REPORT OF **EXAMINATIONS** GIVEN JULY THROUGH DECEMBER, 1965,
SUMMARY. /TESTING CALIFORNIA/   NCALFPB66173

EXAMPLES
FAIR-EMPLOYMENT IS GOOD BUSINESS. **EXAMPLES** OF FAIR PRACTICES FOR TITLE-VII OF THE CIVIL-RIGHTS-ACT OF
1964.   GPOTCII65188

EXCERPTS
THE MANPOWER REVOLUTION. ITS POLICY CONSEQUENCES. **EXCERPTS** FROM SENATE HEARINGS BEFORE THE CLARK
SUBCOMMITTEE.   GMANGGL66217

EXCHANGE
NEGROES AND THE LABOR MOVEMENT -- AN **EXCHANGE**.   NLIPSSM62043

EXCLUSION
THE MUTUAL SAVINGS BANKS OF NEW-YORK-CITY. A FOLLOW-UP REPORT ON THE **EXCLUSION** OF JEWS AT TOP-MANAGEMENT
AND POLICY-MAKING LEVELS.   JAMERJC66695

PATTERNS OF **EXCLUSION** FROM THE EXECUTIVE-SUITE. COMMERCIAL BANKING.   JAMERJC66696

THE POLITICS OF PREJUDICE. THE ANTI-JAPANESE MOVEMENT IN CALIFORNIA AND THE STRUGGLE FOR JAPANESE
EXCLUSION.   ODANIRX61716

EXCLUSIONS
EXCLUSIONS AND ADAPTATIONS. A RE-EVALUATION OF THE CULTURE-OF-POVERTY THEME.   NCOHERXND221

EXECUTIVE
EQUAL-EMPLOYMENT-OPPORTUNITY AND **EXECUTIVE** ORDER 10925.   GBIRNOX62451

EXECUTIVE (CONTINUATION)

THE FEDERAL INTEREST IN EMPLOYMENT DISCRIMINATION. HEREIN THE CONSTITUTIONAL SCOPE OF **EXECUTIVE** POWER TO WITHOLD APPROPRIATE FUNDS.   GFERGCC64679

TITLE-VII. RELATIONSHIP AND EFFECT ON **EXECUTIVE** ORDER 11246. /LEGISLATION/   GMANNRD66937

EQUAL JOB OPPORTUNITY AS SET FORTH IN **EXECUTIVE** ORDERS 10479 AND 10557.   GPRESCH56191

STATE **EXECUTIVE** AUTHORITY TO PROMOTE CIVIL-RIGHTS. AN ACTION PROGRAM FOR THE 1960-S.   GSILAJX63310

THE ETHNICS OF **EXECUTIVE** SELECTION.   JWARDLB65769

LARGE CORPORATIONS ACCUSED OF DISCRIMINATION AGAINST JEWS IN MANAGEMENT. **EXECUTIVE** CAPACITIES BY AMERICAN-JEWISH-COMMITTEE.   JWORLOX64773

THE FEDERAL **EXECUTIVE** AND CIVIL-RIGHTS. 1961-1965.   NFLEMHC66362

THE FEDERAL **EXECUTIVE** AND CIVIL-RIGHTS.   NSOUTRC61160

EXECUTIVE SUPPORT OF CIVIL-RIGHTS.   NSOUTRC62159

PETTICOATS RUSTLE ON **EXECUTIVE** LADDER. /OCCUPATIONS/   WBUSIWX62668

THE WOMAN **EXECUTIVE**. /OCCUPATIONS/   WCUSSMX58712

WOMEN IN **EXECUTIVE** POSTS. /OCCUPATIONS/   WGIVEJN60787

EXECUTIVE CAREERS FOR WOMEN. /OCCUPATIONS/   WMAULFX61065

EXECUTIVE-ORDER

NONDISCRIMINATION IN EMPLOYMENT. **EXECUTIVE-ORDER** 10925.   GGINSGJ61718

EXECUTIVE-SUITE

HARVARD LOOKS AT THE **EXECUTIVE-SUITE**.   JAMERJC60691

PATTERNS OF EXCLUSION FROM THE **EXECUTIVE-SUITE**. COMMERCIAL BANKING.   JAMERJC66696

EXECUTIVES

CHIEF **EXECUTIVES** VIEW NEGRO EMPLOYMENT. /INDUSTRY/   NHABBSX65471

SECRETARY-S CONFERENCE WITH COLLEGE PRESIDENTS AND **EXECUTIVES**. /EDUCATION EMPLOYMENT/   NUSDLAB63301

ARE WOMEN **EXECUTIVES** PEOPLE. /OCCUPATIONS/   WBOWMGW65653

A COMPARATIVE STUDY OF TOP LEVEL MALE AND FEMALE **EXECUTIVES** IN HARRIS-COUNTY. /TEXAS OCCUPATIONS/   WDOLLPA65738

WOMEN AS **EXECUTIVES** AND MANAGERS. /OCCUPATIONS/   WMAHRAH65953

WOMEN **EXECUTIVES**. FACT AND FANCY. /OCCUPATIONS/   WSLOTCT58117

WOMEN **EXECUTIVES** IN THE FEDERAL-GOVERNMENT. /OCCUPATIONS/   WWARNWL62993

EXPANDED

EXPANDED UTILIZATION OF MINORITY-GROUP WORKERS.   GGRAYCJ51736

EXPANDING

EXPANDING APPRENTICESHIP FOR ALL AMERICANS.   GHENNJF63770

EXPANDING EMPLOYMENT OPPORTUNITIES IN NEWARK. EXPERIENCE REPORT 101. /NEW-JERSEY/   GUSCONM65418

EXPANDING NEGRO OPPORTUNITIES. /OCCUPATIONAL-STATUS/   NGINZEX60404

A PROPOSAL FOR THE PREVENTION AND CONTROL OF DELINQUENCY BY **EXPANDING** OPPORTUNITIES.   NMOBIFY62263

EXPLODING THE MYTHS. **EXPANDING** EMPLOYMENT OPPORTUNITIES FOR CAREER WOMEN.   WUVCAEC66249

EXPANDS

THE URBAN-LEAGUE **EXPANDS** OPPORTUNITIES.   NYOUNWM66355

EXPANSION

ECONOMIC **EXPANSION** AND PERSISTING UNEMPLOYMENT. AN OVERVIEW.   GREESAX66722

EXPECTATION

SOCIAL ROLE **EXPECTATION**. MOTIVATIONAL VARIABLE IN GIRLS. /ASPIRATIONS/   WHANSDE64821

EXPECTATIONS

PERCEIVED OPPORTUNITIES. **EXPECTATIONS**, AND THE DECISION TO REMAIN ON RELOCATION. THE CASE OF THE NAVAHO INDIAN MIGRANT TO DENVER, COLORADO.   IGRAVTD65567

VALUES. **EXPECTATIONS** AND RELOCATION. THE NAVAHO MIGRANT TO DENVER. /COLORADO/   IGRAVTD66146

THE MUTUAL IMAGES AND **EXPECTATIONS** OF ANGLO-AMERICANS AND MEXICAN-AMERICANS.   MSIMMOG61490

YOUNG NEGRO TALENT. SURVEY OF THE EXPERIENCES AND **EXPECTATIONS** OF NEGRO AMERICANS WHO GRADUATED FROM COLLEGE IN 1961.   NFICHJH64867

CAREER PREPARATION AND **EXPECTATIONS** OF NEGRO COLLEGE STUDENTS.   NFICHJH66789

ECONOMIC CRISIS AND **EXPECTATIONS** OF VIOLENCE. A STUDY OF UNEMPLOYED NEGROES .   NLEGGJC64679

NEGRO CAREER **EXPECTATIONS**.   NSEXTPX63117

ROLE **EXPECTATIONS** OF YOUNG WOMEN REGARDING MARRIAGE AND A CAREER. /ASPIRATIONS WORK-FAMILY-CONFLICT/   WEMPELT58751

CAREER DECISIONS AND PROFESSIONAL **EXPECTATIONS** OF NURSING-STUDENTS. /ASPIRATIONS/   WFOXXDJ61767

EXPECTED-CASES

THE **EXPECTED-CASES** METHOD APPLIED TO THE NON-WHITE MALE LABOR-FORCE.   NTURNRH49211

EXPENDITURES

FAMILY INCOME AND **EXPENDITURES**.   GUSDLAB49028

CONSUMER **EXPENDITURES** AND INCOME WITH EMPHASIS ON LOW-INCOME FAMILIES.   GUSDLAB64833

POVERTY AND THE CRITERIA FOR PUBLIC **EXPENDITURES**.   GWOLOHX65990

EXPENSES

JOB-RELATED **EXPENSES** OF THE WORKING-MOTHERS.   WADDILK63862

EXPERIENCE
OCCUPATIONAL CHARACTERISTICS, DATA ON AGE, RACE, EDUCATION, WORK EXPERIENCE, INCOME, ETC. FOR WORKERS IN
EACH OCCUPATION.   CUSBURC63177

PUVERTY ON THE LOWER-EAST-SIDE. SELECTED ASPECTS OF THE MOBILIZATION-FOR-YOUTH EXPERIENCE.   GBARRSX64130

WORK EXPERIENCE OF THE POPULATION IN 1965.   GBCGAFA66138

COUNSELING MINORITY-GROUP YOUTH. DEVELOPING THE EXPERIENCE OF EQUALITY THROUGH EDUCATION.   GBRIGWA62473

WORK EXPERIENCE OF THE POPULATION IN 1959.   GCOOPSX60603

A SUMMARY ANALYSIS OF FIVE YEARS OF CLAIMS EXPERIENCE BY THE MICHIGAN
FAIR-EMPLOYMENT-PRACTICES-COMMISSION, FEBRUARY, 1961.   GCOUSFR61612

A SUMMARY ANALYSIS OF SIX YEARS OF CLAIMS EXPERIENCE BY THE MICHIGAN FAIR-EMPLOYMENT
PRACTICES-COMMISSION, FEBRUARY 1962.   GCOUSFR62613

ARIZCNA-S EXPERIENCE UNDER THE CIVIL-RIGHTS-ACT.   GCRAICE66620

PART I. THE NEW-ENGLAND EXPERIENCE RETRAINING THE UNEMPLOYED.   GFEDERB62930

PROVING GROUND FOR FAIR-EMPLOYMENT. SOME LESSONS FROM NEW-YORK STATE-S EXPERIENCE.   GNORTHR47123

WORK EXPERIENCE OF THE POPULATION IN 1960.   GROSECX60257

WORK EXPERIENCE OF THE POPULATION IN 1962.   GSABESX64272

PROGRAMS FOR HIGH SCHOOL DROPOUTS. EXPERIENCE REPORT 101.   GUSCONF64976

EXPANDING EMPLOYMENT OPPORTUNITIES IN NEWARK. EXPERIENCE REPORT 101. /NEW-JERSEY/   GUSCONM65418

RECRUITING MINORITIES FOR PUBLIC EMPLOYMENT. EXPERIENCE REPORT 105.   GUSCONM66420

SCHOOL AND EARLY EMPLOYMENT EXPERIENCE OF YOUTH. A REPORT ON SEVEN COMMUNITIES, 1952-57.   GUSDLAB60494

MORE ROOM AT THE TOP. COMPANY EXPERIENCE IN EMPLOYING NEGROES IN PROFESSIONAL AND MANAGEMENT JOBS.
/INDUSTRY/   NBIRDCX63080

CARRYING OUT A PLAN FOR JOB INTEGRATION AND COING IT -- IN THE HEART OF GEORGIA -- WITHOUT A SINGLE
UNPLEASANT INCIDENT. THAT-S THE EXPERIENCE OF LOCKHEED AIRCRAFT CORPORATION AT ITS MARIETTA PLANT.
/INDUSTRY/   NBUSIWX63148

AN INSIGHT INTO STRUCTURAL UNEMPLOYMENT -- THE EXPERIENCE OF A MINORITY GROUP IN A PROSPEROUS COMMUNITY.   NGERSWJ65634

EFFECTS OF ON-THE-JOB EXPERIENCE WITH NEGROES UPON RACIAL ATTITUDES OF WHITE WORKERS IN UNION SHOPS. NGUNDRH50466

COMPANY EXPERIENCE WITH NEGRO EMPLOYMENT. /INDUSTRY/   NHABBSX66472

EQUAL-EMPLOYMENT-OPPORTUNITY. COMPANY POLICIES AND EXPERIENCE.   NMILLGW64070

FAIR-EMPLOYMENT-PRACTICE LAWS -- EXPERIENCE, EFFECTS, PROSPECTS.   NNORGPH67929

HIRING NEGROES FOR BETTER JOBS. EXPERIENCE OF LEADING COMPANIES. /INDUSTRY/   NOPINRC64957

COMPANY EXPERIENCE WITH THE EMPLOYMENT OF NEGROES. /INDUSTRY/   NPRINUI54020

RACIAL AND FAMILY EXPERIENCE CORRELATES OF MOBILITY ASPIRATION.   NSMITHP62144

THE EXPERIENCE OF STATE FAIR-EMPLOYMENT COMMISSIONS. A COMPARATIVE STUDY.   NSUTIAX65343

CHANGING EMPLOYMENT PRACTICES IN THE CONSTRUCTION INDUSTRY. EXPERIENCE REPORT 102.   NUSCONM65233

CITY CONTRACTORS AND FAIR-EMPLOYMENT. EXPERIENCE REPORT 103.   NUSCONM66234

PUBLIC EMPLOYMENT IN SAVANNAH, GEORGIA. EXPERIENCE REPORT 104.   NUSCONM66235

EXPERIENCED
AN ANALYSIS OF THE EXPERIENCED HIRED FARM WORKING FORCE, 1948-1957. /SKILLS/   GCCWHJC60423

EXPERIENCES
EVALUATION OF STATE FAIR-EMPLOYMENT-PRACTICES-COMMISSIONS. EXPERIENCES AND FORECASTS.   GAMERCR49371

APPROACHES TO INCOME IMPROVEMENT. EXPERIENCES OF FAMILIES RECEIVING PRODUCTION LOANS UNDER THE FARMERS
HOME ADMINISTRATION.   GHENDWE59422

THE INDUSTRIAL SETTING. PROBLEMS AND EXPERIENCES. /TESTING/   GLOPEFM65910

A PILOT STUDY OF THE EMPLOYMENT EXPERIENCES OF HIGH SCHOOL GRADUATES.   GPHILCH65177

THE NEW FEDERAL FAIR-EMPLOYMENT-PRACTICES ACT -- COMPARISON WITH STATE LAW AND AN ANALYSIS OF RELEVANT
STATE EXPERIENCES. /MISSOURI/   GROBEPC64239

PLACEMENT EXPERIENCES OF APPLICANTS TO A PRIVATE EMPLOYMENT-AGENCY.   NANTIOL55901

AMERICAN NEGRO AND IMMIGRANT EXPERIENCES. SIMILARITIES AND DIFFERENCES.   NAPPEJJ66805

FAIR-EMPLOYMENT-PRACTICES-COMMISSION EXPERIENCES WITH PSYCHOLOGICAL TESTING.   NASHXPX65031

CN-THE-JOB EXPERIENCES OF NEGRO MANAGERS.   NBLANJW64917

THE NEGRO AND EQUAL-EMPLOYMENT-OPPORTUNITIES. A REVIEW OF MANAGEMENT EXPERIENCES IN TWENTY COMPANIES. NFERMLA66790

YOUNG NEGRO TALENT. SURVEY OF THE EXPERIENCES AND EXPECTATIONS OF NEGRO AMERICANS WHO GRADUATED FROM
COLLEGE IN 1961.   NFICHJH64867

IN SEARCH OF A FUTURE. A STUDY OF CAREER-SEEKING EXPERIENCES OF SELECTED NEGRO HIGH SCHOOL GRADUATES IN
WASHINGTON-DC WHICH WAS AN EFFORT TO PROVIDE KNOWLEDGE HELPFUL IN SOLVING ONE OF THE MOST CRITICAL
PROBLEMS FACING URBAN AMERICA TODAY.   NGRIEES63454

THE EMPLOYMENT SITUATION OF WHITE AND NEGRO YOUTH IN THE CITY OF BALTIMORE. INITIAL EXPERIENCES IN THE
LABOR-MARKET. /MARYLAND/   NJOHNHU63735

EMPLOYMENT EXPERIENCES OF NEGRO PHILADELPHIANS. A DESCRIPTIVE STUDY OF THE EMPLOYMENT EXPERIENCES,
PERCEPTIONS, AND ASPIRATIONS OF SELECTED PHILADELPHIA WHITES AND NON-WHITES.   NSIEGAI59718

EMPLOYMENT EXPERIENCES OF NEGRO PHILADELPHIANS. A DESCRIPTIVE STUDY OF THE EMPLOYMENT EXPERIENCES,
PERCEPTIONS, AND ASPIRATIONS OF SELECTED PHILADELPHIA WHITES AND NON-WHITES.   NSIEGAI59718

EXPERIENCES   (CONTINUATION)
MIGRATION AND ADJUSTMENT **EXPERIENCES** OF RURAL WORKERS IN INDIANAPOLIS. /INDIANA/   NSMITED53143

   EXPERIENCES OF NEGRO HIGH SCHOOL GIRLS WITH DOMESTIC PLACEMENT AGENCIES. /HOUSEHOLD-WORKERS/   WRUSSRD62135

   OCCUPATIONAL PLANNING BY YOUNG WOMEN. A STUDY OF OCCUPATIONAL **EXPERIENCES**, ASPIRATIONS, ATTITUDES, AND
   PLANS OF COLLEGE AND HIGH SCHOOL GIRLS.   WSLOCWL56116

EXPERIMENT
AN **EXPERIMENT** TO TEST THREE MAJOR ISSUES OF WORK PROGRAM METHODOLOGY WITHIN MOBILIZATION-FOR-YOUTH-S
INTEGRATED SERVICES TO OUT-OF-SCHOOL UNEMPLOYED YOUTH. /NEGRO PUERTO-RICAN/   CMOBIFY66024

   AN **EXPERIMENT** IN MANPOWER DEVELOPMENT. /TRAINING MISSISSIPPI NEGRO WOMEN/   CSELFHO66325

   AN **EXPERIMENT** IN VOCATIONAL EDUCATION FOR CHILDREN OF MIGRATORY FARM WORKERS, JULY-AUGUST 1956.   GNATLCRNCO46

   AN **EXPERIMENT** IN RETRAINING UNEMPLOYED MEN FOR PRACTICAL NURSING CAREERS.   GPEIMSC66139

   INDUSTRY-S **EXPERIMENT** TOWARDS INTEGRATION OF MINORITIES INTO INDUSTRY.   GRUBIAX46265

   THE WDL APPRENTICESHIP TRAINING PROGRAM. REPORT OF A YEAR-S **EXPERIMENT**.   GWCRKDL65584

   TRADE UNION LEADERSHIP COUNCIL. **EXPERIMENT** IN COMMUNITY ACTION.   NNEWXUT63088

   AN INDUSTRIAL **EXPERIMENT** TOWARDS INTEGRATION OF MINORITIES INTO INDUSTRY.   NRUBIAX46093

   RESOURCE UNITS IN THE TEACHING OF OCCUPATIONS -- AN **EXPERIMENT** IN GUIDANCE OF PUERTO-RICAN TEENAGERS. PNEWYCC56834

EXPERIMENTAL
SECRETARIAL TRAINING WITH SPEECH IMPROVEMENT. AN **EXPERIMENTAL** AND DEMONSTRATION PROJECT. /NEGRO WOMEN/ CSAINMD66320

   FINAL REPORT. **EXPERIMENTAL** AND DEMONSTRATION ON-JOB-TRAINING PROJECT. /MIGRANT-WORKERS MEXICAN-AMERICAN
   NEGRO ARIZONA/   CSKILTC66324

   THE TRAINING OF MIGRANT FARM WORKERS. A FOLLOW-UP STUDY OF TWO **EXPERIMENTAL** AND DEMONSTRATION PROGRAMS
   UNDER THE MANPOWER-DEVELOPMENT-AND-TRAINING-ACT. /MEXICAN-AMERICAN AMERICAN-INDIAN/   CUNIVOC66054

   PUBLIC WELFARE, AUTOMATION, AND **EXPERIMENTAL** MANPOWER PROGRAMS.   GCCNFAP63545

   EXPERIMENTAL AND DEMONSTRATION MANPOWER PROJECT FOR THE RECRUITMENT, TRAINING, PLACEMENT AND FOLLOW-UP OF
   RURAL UNEMPLOYED WORKERS IN TEN NORTH FLORIDA CITIES. FINAL REPORT. /PARTICIPANTS/   NJACKTA66597

   EXPERIMENTAL FEATURES OF THE TUSKEGEE-INSTITUTE RETRAINING PROJECT.   NTUSKIX65765

   THE MENTALITIES OF NEGRO AND WHITE WORKERS. AN **EXPERIMENTAL** SCHOOL-S INTERPRETATION OF NEGRO TRADE
   UNIONISM.   NVALIPX49280

   FINAL REPORT. **EXPERIMENTAL** AND DEMONSTRATION MANPOWER PROJECT FOR THE RECRUITMENT, TRAINING, PLACEMENT
   AND FOLLOW-UP OF RURAL UNEMPLOYED WORKERS IN TEN NORTH FLORIDA COUNTIES.   WFLORMP66326

EXPLORATION
MEXICAN-AMERICANS IN URBAN PUBLIC HIGH SCHOOLS. AN **EXPLORATION** OF THE DROP-OUT PROGRAM.   MSHELPM59488

EXPLORATORY
AN **EXPLORATORY** STUDY OF EMPLOYERS ATTITUDES TOWARD WORKING MOTHERS.   WCONYJE61704

   REPORT OF THE **EXPLORATORY** STATISTICAL SURVEY OF THE EDUCATIONAL-ATTAINMENT, NUMBER, AND AVAILABILITY OF
   THE MEMBERSHIP OF THE AMERICAN ASSOCIATION OF UNIVERSITY WOMEN FOR TEACHING IN THE FIELDS OF SCIENCE AND
   MATHEMATICS. /OCCUPATIONS/   WOOLAEF57735

EXPOSURE
CULTURAL **EXPOSURE** AND RACE AS VARIABLES IN PREDICTING TRAINING AND JOB SUCCESS. /TESTING/   NLOCKHCND700

EXTREMISM
ECONOMIC DEPRIVATION AND **EXTREMISM**. A STUDY OF UNEMPLOYED NEGROES.   NLEGGJC61680

FACETED
AN ASSESSMENT OF THE SUITABILITY OF THE **FACETED** STRUCTURE OF THE WRU EDUCATION THESAURUS AS A FRAMEWORK
FOR PREPARATION OF A THESAURUS OF EQUAL-EMPLOYMENT-OPPORTUNITY TERMS.   GBARHGC66162

FACETS
THE QUEST FOR IDENTITY AND STATUS. **FACETS** OF THE DESEGREGATION PROCESS IN THE UPPER MIDWEST.
/ECONOMIC-STATUS/   NTILLJA61161

FACILITATION
THE ROLE OF WHITE RESISTANCE AND **FACILITATION** IN THE NEGRO STRUGGLE FOR EQUALITY.   NGLENND65676

FACILITATIVE
FACILITATIVE AND INHIBITIVE FACTORS IN TRAINING PROGRAM RECRUITMENT AMONG RURAL NEGROES.   NMARSCP65738

FACILITIES
SURVEY OF MINORITY-GROUP EMPLOYMENT AND PATIENT CARE IN PRIVATE HOSPITAL **FACILITIES** IN LOS-ANGELES
COUNTY. /CALIFORNIA/   GLOSACCND914

   WHAT ARE THE PSYCHOLOGICAL EFFECTS OF SEGREGATION UNDER CONDITIONS OF EQUAL **FACILITIES**.   NCHEIIX49198

   CHILD CARE **FACILITIES** FOR WOMEN WORKERS. /EMPLOYMENT-CONDITIONS/   WINTELR58864

FACT
FINDINGS OF **FACT**, CONCLUSIONS AND ACTION OF THE COMMISSION ON HUMAN-RELATIONS IN RE. INVESTIGATIVE PUBLIC
HEARINGS INTO ALLEGED DISCRIMINATORY PRACTICE BY THE HOTEL AND RESTAURANT INDUSTRY IN PHILADELPHIA.
/PENNSYLVANIA/   GPHILCH61176

   SUMMARY **FACT** SHEETS FOR STATE PUBLIC AGENCIES WITH JURISDICTION OVER DISCRIMINATION IN EMPLOYMENT.   GUSCOMC65416

   PROBLEMS OF YOUTH. A **FACT** BOOK. /EMPLOYMENT/   GUSLIBC64823

   TESTIMONY BEFORE STATE SENATE **FACT** FINDING SUBCOMMITTEE ON RACE-RELATIONS AND URBAN PROBLEMS, FINAL
   HEARING, JANUARY 20 1963. /CALIFORNIA FEPC/   NGRAHCX65439

   THE ILGWU -- **FACT** AND FICTION. /UNION/   NHILLHX63527

   EQUAL-EMPLOYMENT-OPPORTUNITY IN THE SUBURBAN SHOPPING CENTER. **FACT** OR FICTION. /MICHIGAN/   NMICFEP63777

   FANTASY, **FACT** AND THE FUTURE...A REVIEW OF THE STATUS OF WOMEN AND POSSIBLE IMPLICATIONS FOR WOMEN-S
   EDUCATION AND ROLE IN THE NEXT DECADE.   WFITZLE63963

   WOMEN EXECUTIVES. **FACT** AND FANCY. /OCCUPATIONS/   WSLOTCT58117

WOMEN PRIVATE HOUSEHOLD-WORKERS **FACT** SHEET.   WUSDLAB66238

FACTOR
INCOME-DISTRIBUTION AS A **FACTOR** IN REGIONAL GROWTH, WITH SPECIAL REFERENCE TO THE SOUTHEAST UNITED
STATES. /DISCRIMINATION/   GPHILEW65773

UNDERSTANDING THE HUMAN **FACTOR**, THE KEY TO SUPERVISORY SUCCESS.   GPRESCP59201

KINSHIP AS A **FACTOR** AFFECTING CANTONESE ECONOMIC ADAPTATION IN THE UNITED STATES.   OBARNML66698

AN INVERTED **FACTOR** ANALYSIS OF PERSONALITY DIFFERENCES BETWEEN CAREER AND HOMEMAKING-ORIENTED WOMEN.
/ASPIRATIONS/   WAVILDL64316

SEX AS A **FACTOR** IN THE DETERMINATION OF EDUCATIONAL CHOICE. /ASPIRATIONS/   WDOLEAA64737

FACTORS
FACTORS AFFECTING EDUCATIONAL-ATTAINMENT IN DEPRESSED URBAN AREAS. /NEGRO PUERTO-RICAN/   CGOLDML63426

SOME CONSIDERATIONS AS TO THE CONTRIBUTIONS OF SOCIAL, PERSONALITY, AND RACIAL **FACTORS** TO SCHOOL
RETARDATION IN MINORITY-GROUP CHILDREN.   GDEUTMP56641

MINORITY-GROUP AND CLASS STATUS AS RELATED TO SOCIAL AND PERSONALITY **FACTORS** IN SCHOLASTIC ACHIEVEMENT.   GDEUTMP60640

BACKGROUND **FACTORS** RELATING TO COLLEGE PLANS AND COLLEGE ENROLLMENT AMONG PUBLIC HIGH SCHOOL STUDENTS.
/ASPIRATIONS/   GEDUCTS57959

ECONOMIC **FACTORS** INFLUENCING EDUCATIONAL-ATTAINMENTS AND ASPIRATIONS OF FARM YOUTH.   GMOOREJ64386

GUIDANCE, TRAINING AND APPRENTICESHIP **FACTORS** AFFECTING MINORITY-GROUPS.   GNATLAM60037

FACTORS ASSOCIATED WITH SCHOOL DROPOUTS AND JUVENILE-DELINQUENCY AMONG LOWER-CLASS CHILDREN.   GPALMFX63671

FACTORS AFFECTING EMPLOYEE SELECTION IN TWO CULTURES. /DISCRIMINATION/   GTRIAHC63083

THE PACE OF TECHNOLOGICAL-CHANGE AND THE **FACTORS** AFFECTING IT.   GWOLFSL64624

INDIANS OF THE MISSOURI-BASIN -- CULTURAL **FACTORS** IN THEIR SOCIAL AND ECONOMIC ADJUSTMENT.   IREIFBX58610

ECONOMIC **FACTORS** IN NAVAHO URBAN RELOCATION.   IWEPPRS65685

STUDY OF SOCIO-CULTURAL **FACTORS** THAT INHIBIT OR ENCOURAGE DELINQUENCY AMONG MEXICAN-AMERICANS.   MLOSARW58432

SOME DIFFERENCES IN **FACTORS** RELATED TO EDUCATIONAL ACHIEVEMENT OF TWO MEXICAN-AMERICAN GROUPS.   MMONTPX60443

SOCIAL **FACTORS** IN OCCUPATIONAL AND EDUCATIONAL ASPIRATIONS OF NEGRO AND WHITE STUDENTS.   NADDIDP61002

THE DETERMINATION OF CERTAIN MAJOR **FACTORS** AFFECTING THE NEGRO VETERAN IN THE ON-THE-JOB TRAINING PROGRAM
IN VOCATIONAL AGRICULTURE IN THE STATE OF ALABAMA AS A BASIS FOR PLANNING A MORE EFFECTIVE PROGRAM.   NBATTEF49338

THE FRENCH AND THE NON-FRENCH IN LOUISIANA. A STUDY OF THE RELEVANCE OF ETHNIC **FACTORS** IN RURAL
DEVELOPMENT. /ECONOMIC-STATUS/   NBERTAL65394

RACE AND SOCIAL-CLASS AS SEPARATE **FACTORS** RELATED TO SOCIAL ENVIRONMENT. /ASPIRATIONS/   NBLOORX63096

FACTORS IN WORKERS DECISIONS TO FOREGO RETRAINING UNDER THE MANPOWER-DEVELOPMENT-AND-RETRAINING-ACT.   NBRAZWF64318

FACTORS AFFECTING THE PRESENT FARMING PROGRAMS OF ONE HUNDRED NEGRO FARMS IN THE PATRONAGE AREA OF THE
MACON COUNTY TRAINING SCHOOL, IN ALABAMA, WITH EMPHASIS FOR IMPROVEMENT.   NBRONCA51337

INFORMAL **FACTORS** IN CAREER ACHIEVEMENT.   NDALTMX51247

SOME **FACTORS** WHICH DISTINGUISH DROP-OUTS FROM HIGH SCHOOL GRADUATES.   NGRAGWL49978

COMMUNITY **FACTORS** AFFECTING MOTIVATION AND ACHIEVEMENT IN A DECADE OF DECISION. /EDUCATION/   NGRANLB62441

DEMOGRAPHIC **FACTORS** IN THE INTEGRATION OF THE NEGRO.   NHAUSPM65501

DEMOGRAPHIC AND SOCIAL **FACTORS** IN THE POVERTY OF THE NEGRO.   NHAUSPM66992

A PILOT STUDY OF PERSONALITY **FACTORS** RELATED TO OCCUPATIONAL ASPIRATIONS OF NEGRO COLLEGE STUDENTS.   NLITTLW66697

FACILITATIVE AND INHIBITIVE **FACTORS** IN TRAINING PROGRAM RECRUITMENT AMONG RURAL NEGROES.   NMARSCP65738

SOME **FACTORS** INFLUENCING THE GROWTH OF UNIONS IN THE SOUTH.   NMARSRX60060

SOME **FACTORS** INFLUENCING UNION RACIAL PRACTICES.   NMARSRX62747

RACIAL **FACTORS** INFLUENCING ENTRY TO THE SKILLED TRADES. /UNION/   NMARSRX63745

SOME **FACTORS** INFLUENCING THE UPGRADING OF NEGROES IN THE SOUTHERN PETROLEUM REFINING INDUSTRY.
/CASE-STUDY/   NMARSRX63748

FACTORS AFFECTING FARM PLACEMENT OF NEGRO VOCATIONAL AGRICULTURE STUDENTS IN ALABAMA.   NMCQUFT45348

FACTORS INVOLVED IN STUDENT ELIMINATION FROM HIGH SCHOOL.   NMOORPL54079

LABOR-FORCE AND DEMOGRAPHIC **FACTORS** AFFECTING THE CHANGING RELATIVE STATUS OF THE AMERICAN NEGRO.
1940-1950.   NPHILWM57997

AN ANALYSIS OF SELECTIVE **FACTORS** INFLUENCING FARM INCOME IN HALE COUNTY, AS A BASIS FOR ESTABLISHING A
MORE EFFECTIVE VOCATIONAL AGRICULTURAL PROGRAM. /ALABAMA/   NSALTDR52347

SOCIAL-CLASS **FACTORS** UNDERLYING THE CIVIL-RIGHTS MOVEMENT.   NSCOTJW66112

AN EMPIRICAL STUDY OF HIGH SCHOOL DROPOUTS IN REGARD TO TEN POSSIBLY RELATED **FACTORS**.   NTHOMRJ54159

A REPORT ON COMMUNITY **FACTORS** IN NASHVILLE RELATED TO THE NEGRO IN MEDICINE. /TENNESSEE/   NVALIPX56281

FACTORS INFLUENCING WOMEN-S DECISIONS ABOUT HIGHER EDUCATION. /ASPIRATIONS/   WDAVIOD59716

SOCIAL **FACTORS** WHICH AFFECT CAREER CHOICE IN PSYCHIATRIC NURSING.   WDOUGAM61740

WORK VALUES AND BACKGROUND **FACTORS** AS PREDICTORS OF WOMEN-S DESIRE TO WORK. /ASPIRATIONS/   WEYDELD62754

FACTORS ASSOCIATED WITH GRADUATE SCHOOL ATTENDANCE AND ROLE DEFINITION OF THE WOMAN DOCTORAL CANDIDATES
AT THE PENNSYLVANIA STATE UNIVERSITY. /OCCUPATIONS/   WFIELJC61763

SOME **FACTORS** WHICH DETERMINE THE DISTRIBUTION OF THE FEMALE WORK-FORCE. /LABOR-FORCE/   WJOUROI62883

FACTORS (CONTINUATION)
FACTORS DETERMINING THE LABOR-FORCE PARTICIPATION OF MARRIED WOMEN.   WMAHOTA61951

PSYCHOLOGICAL AND SOCIOLOGICAL **FACTORS** IN PREDICTION OF CAREER PATTERNS OF WOMEN. /ASPIRATIONS/   WMULVMC61080

PSYCHOLOGICAL AND SOCIOLOGICAL **FACTORS** IN PREDICTION OF CAREER PATTERNS FOR WOMEN. /ASPIRATIONS/   WMULVMC63006

THE FEMALE LABOR-FORCE IN THE UNITED STATES. **FACTORS** GOVERNING ITS GROWTH AND CHANGING COMPOSITION.   WOPPEVK66096

BACKGROUND **FACTORS** AND COLLEGE GOING PLANS AMONG HIGH APTITUDE PUBLIC HIGH SCHOOL SENIORS. /ASPIRATIONS/   WSTICGX56141

AN ANALYSIS OF **FACTORS** INFLUENCING MARRIED WOMEN-S ACTUAL OR PLANNED WORK PARTICIPATION.   WWELLMW61261

FACTORY
SOME PROBLEMS IN THE ACCULTURATION OF MEXICAN LABORERS TO A **FACTORY**.   MALBEPM64356

FACTORY FOLKWAYS. A STUDY OF INSTITUTIONAL STRUCTURE AND CHANGE.   NELLSJS52331

ADMINISTERING CHANGES. A CASE-STUDY OF HUMAN-RELATIONS IN A **FACTORY**.   NRONKHO52129

FACTS
FACTS ON ADC IN NORTH-CAROLINA. /NEGRO   AMERICAN-INDIAN/   CNORTCS59934

POVERTY IN NEW-YORK CITY. **FACTS** FOR PLANNING COMMUNITY ACTION.   GCOMCCN64210

FACTS ON THE MANY FACES OF POVERTY.   GNATLUL65084

CIVIL-RIGHTS. THE **FACTS** AND THE CHALLENGE.   GSLAIDX64316

US GOVERNMENT POLICY TOWARD AMERICAN INDIANS. A FEW BASIC **FACTS**.   IELLIMB57554

AMERICA-S CONCENTRATION CAMPS. THE **FACTS** ABOUT OUR INDIAN RESERVATIONS TODAY.   IEMBRCB56555

NEGRO PROGRESS. WHAT THE **FACTS** SHOW.   NBREIGX52113

THE NEGRO COLLEGE STUDENT. SOME **FACTS** AND SOME CONCERNS.   NCLARKB64307

FACTS FOR ACTION. /LOUISVILLE   KENTUCKY/   NLOUIHR66716

THE **FACTS** ON NEGRO PHYSICIANS. /OCCUPATIONS/   NMENZRX49766

THE NEGRO IN THE WEST. SOME **FACTS** RELATING TO SOCIAL AND ECONOMIC CONDITIONS. NO 1. THE NEGRO WORKER.   NUSDLABND256

A SUMMARY IN **FACTS** AND FIGURES.   PPUERRDND792

FACTS ABOUT NURSING.   WAMERNA66608

THE **FACTS**, THE HOPES, AND THE POSSIBILITIES. /WORK-WOMAN-ROLE/   WBANNMC63626

FACING THE **FACTS** ABOUT WOMEN-S LIVES TODAY. /WORK-WOMAN-ROLE/   WKEYSMD65895

THESE ARE THE **FACTS**. /HOUSEHOLD-WORKERS/   WNATLCH66015

WOMEN-S EDUCATION. **FACTS**, FINDINGS, AND APPARENT TRENDS.   WNEWCMX64028

WOMEN AT WORK. 1. THE **FACTS** AND WHY WOMEN WORK. 2. THE SIGNIFICANCE.   WQUINFX62992

GETTING THE **FACTS** ON EQUAL-PAY.   WUSDLAB66197

BACKGROUND **FACTS** ON WOMEN WORKERS IN THE UNITED STATES.   WUSDLAB66638

WOMEN-S WORK. **FACTS**, FINDINGS, AND APPARENT TRENDS.   WZAPOMW64283

FACULTIES
A SOURCE FOR COLLEGE **FACULTIES**. /OCCUPATIONS/   WCLAYFL62691

WOMEN ON COLLEGE AND UNIVERSITY **FACULTIES**. A HISTORICAL SURVEY AND A STUDY OF THEIR PRESENT ACADEMIC
STATUS. /OCCUPATIONS/   WPOLLLA65063

FACULTY
FACULTY EDUCATION AND INCOME IN NEGRO AND WHITE COLLEGES.   NUSDLAB65819

A STUDY OF JOB MOTIVATIONS, ACTIVITIES, AND SATISFACTIONS OF PRESENT AND PROSPECTIVE WOMEN COLLEGE
FACULTY MEMBERS. /OCCUPATIONS/   WCOOKWX60252

ANTI-NEPOTISM RULES IN AMERICAN COLLEGES AND UNIVERSITIES -- THEIR EFFECT ON THE **FACULTY** EMPLOYMENT OF
WOMEN.   WDOLAEF60951

FAILURE
A STUDY OF THE REASONS FOR **FAILURE** ON THE JOB OF SOME GRADUATES OF INTERMOUNTAIN SCHOOL.   IFISHLX60560

HIGHER EDUCATION OF SOUTHWESTERN INDIANS WITH REFERENCE TO SUCCESS AND **FAILURE**.   IMCGRGD62584

FAILURES
SCHOOL **FAILURES** AND DROPOUTS.   GNEISEG63054

FAIR
GOVENOR-S CODE OF **FAIR** PRACTICE /CALIFORNIA/   GCALOGB63546

FAIR PRACTICE IN EMPLOYMENT.   GCHALFK48563

THE DUTY OF **FAIR** REPRESENTATION.   GCOXXAX57617

EMPLOYMENT PRACTICES, **FAIR** AND UNFAIR.   GFORDJA65450

THE **FAIR** REPRESENTATION DOCTRINE. AN EFFECTIVE WEAPON AGAINST UNION RACIAL DISCRIMINATION.   GHERRNM64772

FAIR PRACTICE IN EMPLOYMENT.   GHUDDFP46786

THE PRESENT STATUS OF THE CULTURE **FAIR** TESTING MOVEMENT.   GLAMBNM64880

A **FAIR** CHANCE FOR ALL AMERICANS.   GNATLCL54041

FAIR PLAY STARTS WITH THE BOSS. /EMPLOYMENT   DISCRIMINATION/   GNIXORM56117

FAIR EMPLOYMENT SURVEY OF THE WESTCHESTER AREA. /PENNSYLVANIA/   GPENNHR65163

FAIR-EMPLOYMENT IS GOOD BUSINESS. EXAMPLES OF **FAIR** PRACTICES FOR TITLE-VII OF THE CIVIL-RIGHTS-ACT OF

FAIR   (CONTINUATION)
    1964.   GPOTOII65188

    PSYCHOLOGICAL TESTS AND FAIR EMPLOYMENT. A STUDY OF EMPLOYMENT TESTING IN THE SAN-FRANCISCO BAY AREA.
    /CALIFORNIA/   GRUSHJT66268

    UNION-S DUTY OF FAIR REPRESENTATION AND THE CIVIL-RIGHTS-ACT OF 1964.   GSHERHL65302

    HANDBOOK FOR LOCAL UNION FAIR PRACTICES COMMITTEES. REVISED EDITION.   GUAWXFPND369

    UNION DEMOCRACY AND FAIR REPRESENTATION. FEDERAL RESPONSIBILITY IN A FEDERAL SYSTEM.   GWELLHX58550

    MILWAUKEE. A FAIR DEAL. /WISCONSIN EEO/   GWINTEL66569

    RACIAL DISCRIMINATION AND THE DUTY OF FAIR REPRESENTATION. /LEGISLATION/   NCOLULR65225

    FAIR EMPLOYMENT IS GOOD BUSINESS AT G FOX OF HARTFORD. /CASE-STUDY CONNECTICUT/   NGREEMX48448

    EQUALITY OF OPPORTUNITY, A UNION APPROACH TO FAIR EMPLOYMENT.   NHOPEJX56570

    AN ANALYSIS OF THE IMPLEMENTATION OF THE UAW-CIO-S FAIR PRACTICES AND ANTI-DISCRIMINATION POLICIES IN
    SELECTED CHICAGO LOCALS.   /UNION/   NJONEJE51883

    TOWARD FAIR EMPLOYMENT. A REVIEW.   NROSERX65130

FAIR-EMPLOYERS
    STATES AS FAIR-EMPLOYERS.   GGROVHE61744

FAIR-EMPLOYMENT
    FAIR-EMPLOYMENT LEGISLATION IN NEW-YORK STATE. ITS HISTORY, DEVELOPMENT, AND SUGGESTED USE ELSEWHERE.   GBRADPX46247

    A SUMMARY ANALYSIS OF SIX YEARS OF CLAIMS EXPERIENCE BY THE MICHIGAN FAIR-EMPLOYMENT
    PRACTICES-COMMISSION, FEBRUARY 1962.   GCOUSFR62613

    THE HISTORICAL ROOTS OF FAIR-EMPLOYMENT.   GFLEMJG46688

    DEVELOPING FAIR-EMPLOYMENT PROGRAMS. A PROGRAM FOR THE SMALLER COMPANY.   GJENSJJ66785

    THE EFFECT OF STATE FAIR-EMPLOYMENT LEGISLATION ON THE ECONOMIC POSITION OF NONWHITE MALES.   GLANDWM66883

    DEVELOPING FAIR-EMPLOYMENT PROGRAMS. GUIDELINES FOR SELECTION.   GLOCKHC66780

    FAIR-EMPLOYMENT STATE BY STATE.   GMASLWX45960

    FAIR-EMPLOYMENT IN MASSACHUSETTS, PART I.   GMCKEES52927

    FAIR-EMPLOYMENT IN MASSACHUSETTS, PART II.   GMCKEES52928

    NATIONAL POLITICS OF FAIR-EMPLOYMENT.   GMCKEEX52950

    IMPLEMENTATION OF THE FEDERAL FAIR-EMPLOYMENT POLICY.   GNATLAI49038

    GOVERNMENTAL FAIR-EMPLOYMENT AGENCIES. AN APPRAISAL OF FEDERAL, STATE, AND MUNICIPAL EFFORTS TO END JOB
    DISCRIMINATION.   GNORGPH62120

    TOWARD FAIR-EMPLOYMENT.   GNORGPH64091

    MUNICIPAL FAIR-EMPLOYMENT ORDINANCES AS A VALID EXERCISE OF THE POLICE POWER.   GNORTDL64093

    PROVING GROUND FOR FAIR-EMPLOYMENT. SOME LESSONS FROM NEW-YORK STATE-S EXPERIENCE.   GNORTHR47123

    FAIR-EMPLOYMENT IS GOOD BUSINESS. EXAMPLES OF FAIR PRACTICES FOR TITLE-VII OF THE CIVIL-RIGHTS-ACT OF
    1964.   GPOTOII65188

    FAIR-EMPLOYMENT IN THE NATION-S CAPITAL. A STUDY OF PROGRESS AND DILEMMA. /WASHINGTON-DC/   GSAWYDA62279

    LABOR AND FAIR-EMPLOYMENT PRACTICE. /UNION/   GSLAIDX67840

    FAIR-EMPLOYMENT WORKS -- TOOLS FOR HUMAN-RELATIONS.   GTHOMJA51355

    FAIR-EMPLOYMENT IN THE FEDERAL SERVICE.   GUSCISC51385

    FAIR-EMPLOYMENT IN THE FEDERAL SERVICE, A PROGRESS REPORT ON CONSTRUCTIVE STEPS.   GUSCISC52386

    BIBLIOGRAPHY ON VOLUNTARY FAIR-EMPLOYMENT PROGRAMS.   GUSCOMC65392

    ENFORCEMENT OF FAIR-EMPLOYMENT UNDER THE CIVIL-RIGHTS-ACT OF 1964.   GUVCHLR64213

    FAIR-EMPLOYMENT AND YOUTH. ISI SE PUEDE -- IT CAN BE DONE. RE YOUTH AND OPPORTUNITIES.   MWEBBEB66516

    THE EXPERIENCE OF STATE FAIR-EMPLOYMENT COMMISSIONS. A COMPARATIVE STUDY.   NSUTIAX65343

    CITY CONTRACTORS AND FAIR-EMPLOYMENT. EXPERIENCE REPORT 103.   NUSCONM66234

FAIR-EMPLOYMENT-PRAC
    STATE FAIR-EMPLOYMENT-PRACTICES-COMMISSIONS -- A SELECTED BIBLIOGRAPHY.   GAMERCR46373

    STATE FAIR-EMPLOYMENT-PRACTICES-COMMISSION -- WHAT THE PEOPLE SAY.   GAMERCR47374

    EVALUATION OF STATE FAIR-EMPLOYMENT-PRACTICES-COMMISSIONS. EXPERIENCES AND FORECASTS.   GAMERCR49371

    YOUR RIGHTS UNDER FAIR-EMPLOYMENT-PRACTICE LAWS.   GAMERJC60382

    FAIR-EMPLOYMENT-PRACTICES LEGISLATION OF EIGHT STATES AND TWO CITIES.   GBERGMX51441

    FAIR-EMPLOYMENT-PRACTICE ACTS AND THE COURTS.   GBERNYX64448

    THE SUBSTANCE OF AMERICAN FAIR-EMPLOYMENT-PRACTICES LEGISLATION. II. EMPLOYMENT-AGENCIES, LABOR
    ORGANIZATIONS, AND OTHERS.   GBONFAE67136

    THE SUBSTANCE OF AMERICAN FAIR-EMPLOYMENT-PRACTICES LEGISLATION. I. EMPLOYERS. GBONFAE67137

     FAIR-EMPLOYMENT-PRACTICES.   GBURENA65494

    GUIDE TO LAWFUL AND UNLAWFUL PRE-EMPLOYMENT INQUIRIES BY EMPLOYERS, EMPLOYMENT-AGENCIES, AND LABOR
    ORGANIZATIONS UNDER THE CALIFORNIA FAIR-EMPLOYMENT-PRACTICE ACT, LABOR CODE, SECTIONS 1410-1432.   GCALDIR60527

    DISCRIMINATION AND FAIR-EMPLOYMENT-PRACTICES LAWS.   GCALDWF65699

FAIR-EMPLOYMENT-PRACTICE ACT...FEPC RULES AND REGULATIONS... GUIDE TO PRE-EMPLOYMENT INQUIRIES.
/CALIFORNIA/ GCALFEP61533

FAIR-EMPLOYMENT-PRACTICES EQUAL GOOD EMPLOYMENT PRACTICES. GUIDELINES FOR TESTING AND SELECTING MINORITY
JOB APPLICANTS. /CALIFORNIA/ GCALFEP66540

FAIR-EMPLOYMENT-PRACTICES UNDER THE CIVIL-RIGHTS-ACT OF 1964. GCOMMCH64590

A SUMMARY ANALYSIS OF FIVE YEARS OF CLAIMS EXPERIENCE BY THE MICHIGAN
FAIR-EMPLOYMENT-PRACTICES-COMMISSION, FEBRUARY, 1961. GCOUSFR61612

FAIR-EMPLOYMENT-PRACTICE-COMMISSION GUIDE TO UNLAWFUL PRE-EMPLOYMENT INQUIRIES. GCURRRO60889

STATE ORGANIZATION FOR FAIR-EMPLOYMENT-PRACTICES. GDUFFJX44522

FAIR-EMPLOYMENT-PRACTICES ACT. STATE LAWS GRANTING EQUAL RIGHTS, PRIVILEGES, ETC. GELWAEX58662

EDUCATIONAL ASPECTS OF FAIR-EMPLOYMENT-PRACTICES-COMMISION LAWS. GFLEMJG50687

FAIR-EMPLOYMENT-PRACTICES IN THE PUBLIC SERVICE. GFRIELL62701

SOME GENERAL OBSERVATIONS ON THE ADMINISTRATION OF STATE FAIR-EMPLOYMENT-PRACTICE LAWS. GGIRARA64721

A STUDY OF FAIR-EMPLOYMENT-PRACTICES OF THE CITY GOVERNMENT. /GRAND-RAPIDS MICHIGAN/ GGRANRH66733

GUIDELINES FOR INITIATING FAIR-EMPLOYMENT-PRACTICES. GHAGAJJ63751

FAIR-EMPLOYMENT-PRACTICES AND THE LAW. GHARTPX58763

COMPARATIVE ANALYSIS OF STATE FAIR-EMPLOYMENT-PRACTICES LAWS. GHARTPX62762

FAIR-EMPLOYMENT-PRACTICES ACT AND REGULATION 30. /HAWAII/ GHAWADL64766

QUESTIONING APPLICANTS FOR EMPLOYMENT, A GUIDE FOR APPLICATION FORMS AND INTERVIEWS UNDER THE HAWAII
FAIR-EMPLOYMENT-PRACTICES ACT. GHAWADL64767

FAIR-EMPLOYMENT-PRACTICE ACT OF ILLINOIS. GILLIFEND795

STATE FAIR-EMPLOYMENT-PRACTICE LAWS. REPORT PERSUANT TO PROPOSAL 400. GILLILC57802

FAIR-EMPLOYMENT-PRACTICE-COMMISSION MOVEMENT IN PERSPECTIVE. GKESSLC56846

GUIDE TO FAIR-EMPLOYMENT-PRACTICES. GKHEETW64851

DISCRIMINATION AND FAIR-EMPLOYMENT-PRACTICES. GLABOLJ65819

EMPLOYMENT DISCRIMINATION. STATE FAIR-EMPLOYMENT-PRACTICES LAWS AND THE IMPACT OF TITLE-VII OF THE
CIVIL-RIGHTS-ACT OF 1964. GLAWXRD65885

FAIR-EMPLOYMENT-PRACTICES LEGISLATION. GMEINRG57066

FAIR-EMPLOYMENT-PRACTICES. GMELLML50973

CALIFORNIA FAIR-EMPLOYMENT-PRACTICE ACT. GMERCMA59975

FAIR-EMPLOYMENT-PRACTICES LEGISLATION, A SUMMARY OF ITS HISTORY AND DEVELOPMENT WITH STATEMENTS ON BOTH
SIDES. GMITCJA52016

A MODEL STATE FAIR-EMPLOYMENT-PRACTICE BILL. GNAACNL45036

YOUR RIGHTS... UNDER STATE AND LOCAL FAIR-EMPLOYMENT-PRACTICES LAWS. GNATLLS55051

MUNICIPAL FAIR-EMPLOYMENT-PRACTICES IN NEBRASKA. GNEBRLR62086

SELECTED ANNOTATED REFERENCES ON FAIR-EMPLOYMENT-PRACTICES LEGISLATION. GNELSRJ52055

REPORT WITH RECOMMENDATIONS ON THE SUBJECT OF FEDERAL FAIR-EMPLOYMENT-PRACTICES LEGISLATION. GNEWYCB53069

GOVERNMENT CONTRACTS AND FAIR-EMPLOYMENT-PRACTICES. GNORGPH64119

QUESTIONS AND ANSWERS ABOUT PERMANENT FAIR-EMPLOYMENT-PRACTICES COMMISSIONS. GNORTMT45124

42 QUESTIONS AND ANSWERS ABOUT FAIR-EMPLOYMENT-PRACTICES. GOREGBLND138

LEGAL RULINGS INTERPRETING THE PROVISIONS OF THE PENNSYLVANIA FAIR-EMPLOYMENT-PRACTICE ACT. GPENNFE58153

PROGRESS IN FAIR-EMPLOYMENT-PRACTICES. GRIGHXX59238

THE NEW FEDERAL FAIR-EMPLOYMENT-PRACTICES ACT -- COMPARISON WITH STATE LAW AND AN ANALYSIS OF RELEVANT
STATE EXPERIENCES. /MISSOURI/ GROBEPC64239

PERSONNEL SELECTION TESTS AND FAIR-EMPLOYMENT-PRACTICES. GSEASHX51293

CASES ARE PEOPLE. AN INTERPRETATION OF THE PENNSYLVANIA FAIR-EMPLOYMENT-PRACTICE LAW. GSHIREM58304

FAIR-EMPLOYMENT-PRACTICE IN NEW-YORK. LAW, EDUCATION GO HAND IN HAND. GSULLJD50340

LABOR UNIONS AND FAIR-EMPLOYMENT-PRACTICES LEGISLATION. GTIMBEX54357

THE CALIFORNIA FAIR-EMPLOYMENT-PRACTICES-COMMISSION. ITS HISTORY, ACCOMPLISHMENTS, AND LIMITATIONS. GTOBRMC63361

THE JOB AHEAD IN FAIR-EMPLOYMENT-PRACTICES. GUNITCC62322

SELECTED BIBLIOGRAPHY ON STATE FAIR-EMPLOYMENT-PRACTICE COMMISSIONS. GUSCOMC66414

FINAL REPORT. US COMMISSION ON FAIR-EMPLOYMENT-PRACTICES, JUNE 28, 1946. GUSCOMF47417

PROGRESS TOWARD FAIR-EMPLOYMENT-PRACTICES. GUSDLAB45078

MASSACHUSETTS FAIR-EMPLOYMENT-PRACTICE ACT OF 1946. GUSDLAB46075

BRIEF SUMMARY OF STATE LAWS AGAINST DISCRIMINATION IN PRIVATE EMPLOYMENT. FAIR-EMPLOYMENT-PRACTICE ACTS. GUSDLAB63439

HIRING AND PROMOTION SYSTEMS UNDER FAIR-EMPLOYMENT-PRACTICES LEGISLATION. GUSDLAB67116

FIRST REPORT. US FAIR-EMPLOYMENT-PRACTICE-COMMITTEE. GUSFEPC45512

FINAL REPORT. US FAIR-EMPLOYMENT-PRACTICE-COMMITTEE. GUSFEPC47511

FAIR-EMPLOYMENT-PRAC (CONTINUATION)
THE DYNAMICS OF STATE CAMPAIGNS FOR **FAIR-EMPLOYMENT-PRACTICES** LEGISLATION.   GUVCHCE50211

THE ILLINOIS **FAIR-EMPLOYMENT-PRACTICES-ACT**.   GWIGGCH65598

YOUR RIGHTS UNDER **FAIR-EMPLOYMENT-PRACTICE** LAWS.   /UNION LEGISLATION/   NAFLCIO60004

FAIR-EMPLOYMENT-PRACTICES-COMMISSION EXPERIENCES WITH PSYCHOLOGICAL TESTING.   NASHXPX65031

STATE **FAIR-EMPLOYMENT-PRACTICE** LEGISLATION UNCONSTITUTIONALLY BURDENS INTERSTATE COMMERCE WHEN APPLIED TO
INTERSTATE AIRLINE.   NHARVLR62499

TWENTY YEARS OF STATE **FAIR-EMPLOYMENT-PRACTICE** COMMISSIONS. A CRITICAL ANALYSIS WITH RECOMMENDATIONS.   NHILLHX64550

THE NEGRO-S FUTURE THROUGH **FAIR-EMPLOYMENT-PRACTICES**.   NHODGEN62557

HAVE **FAIR-EMPLOYMENT-PRACTICES-COMMISSION** LAWS INCREASED OPPORTUNITIES FOR NEGROES.   NLETTHA50683

FAIR-EMPLOYMENT-PRACTICE LAWS -- EXPERIENCE, EFFECTS, PROSPECTS.   NNORGPH67929

FAIR-EMPLOYMENT-PRACTICES LEGISLATION.   NPARKRX48974

WISCONSIN **FAIR-EMPLOYMENT-PRACTICES** DIVISION INQUIRY INTO THE CONFLICTS BETWEEN STATE PROTECTIVE LABOR
LEGISLATION AND STATE AND FEDERAL LAWS PROHIBITING DISCRIMINATION BASED ON SEX.   /EMPLOYMENT-CONDITIONS/   WUAWXWC65165

FALLACIES
THE **FALLACIES** OF PERSONALITY TESTING.   GWHYTWH54560

FAMILIAL
FAMILIAL CORRELATES OF ORIENTATION TOWARD FUTURE EMPLOYMENT AMONG COLLEGE WOMEN.   /ASPIRATIONS/   WSIEGAX63572

FAMILIES
POVERTY IN THE SOUTHWEST. A COMPARATIVE STUDY OF MEXICAN-AMERICAN, NONWHITE AND ANGLO **FAMILIES**.   /NEGRO/   CMITTFG66777

PERSONS BY FAMILY CHARACTERISTICS. FAMILY MEMBERS BY SOCIAL, ECONOMIC AND HOUSING CHARACTERISTICS OF
FAMILIES. /DEMOGRAPHY/   CUSBURC63180

TRENDS IN THE INCOME OF **FAMILIES** AND PERSONS IN THE UNITED STATES. 1947-1960.   /DEMOGRAPHY/   CUSBURC63381

INCOME IN 1964 OF **FAMILIES** AND PERSONS IN THE UNITED STATES. /DEMOGRAPHY/   CUSBURC65375

INCOMES OF RURAL **FAMILIES** IN THE BLACKLAND PRAIRIES.   GADKIWG63410

TRICKLING DOWN. THE RELATIONSHIP BETWEEN ECONOMIC GROWTH AND THE EXTENT OF POVERTY AMONG AMERICAN
FAMILIES.   GANDEWH64392

THE POOR PAY MORE. CONSUMER PRACTICES OF LOW-INCOME **FAMILIES**.   GCAPLDX63310

ECONOMIC AND SOCIAL DEPRIVATIONS. ITS EFFECTS ON CHILDREN AND **FAMILIES** IN THE UNITED STATES -- A SELECTED
BIBLIOGRAPHY.   GCHILCX64571

LOW-INCOME **FAMILIES** AND MEASURES OF INCOME INEQUALITY.   GGOLDSF62725

APPROACHES TO INCOME IMPROVEMENT. EXPERIENCES OF **FAMILIES** RECEIVING PRODUCTION LOANS UNDER THE FARMERS
HOME ADMINISTRATION.   GHENDWE59422

POVERTY IN TEXAS. THE DISTRIBUTION OF LOW-INCOME **FAMILIES**.   GKUVLWP65867

RESOURCES AND INCOMES OF RURAL **FAMILIES** IN THE COASTAL PLAIN AREAS OF GEORGIA.   GMCARWC59392

INCOME, RESOURCES, AND ADJUSTMENT POTENTIALS AMONG RURAL **FAMILIES** IN NORTH AND WEST FLORIDA.   GREUSLA62388

FARM AND NON-FARM EMPLOYMENT OPPORTUNITIES FOR LOW-INCOME FARM **FAMILIES**.   GRUTTVW59270

INCOMES OF RURAL **FAMILIES** IN NORTHEAST TEXAS.   GSOUTJH59325

LOW-INCOME **FAMILIES** AND UNRELATED INDIVIDUALS IN THE UNITED STATES. 1964.   /DEMOGRAPHY/   GUSBURC65151

SELECTED REFERENCES ON MIGRATORY WORKERS AND THEIR **FAMILIES**. PROBLEMS AND PROGRAMS.   GUSDLAB56204

PROGRAMS OF NATIONAL ORGANIZATIONS FOR MIGRANT FARM WORKERS AND THEIR **FAMILIES**.   GUSDLAB61202

SELECTED REFERENCES ON DOMESTIC MIGRATORY AGRICULTURAL WORKERS, THEIR **FAMILIES**, PROBLEMS, AND PROGRAMS,
1955-1960.   GUSDLAB61495

CONSUMER EXPENDITURES AND INCOME WITH EMPHASIS ON LOW-INCOME **FAMILIES**.   GUSDLAB64833

COOPERATIVE EXTENSION SERVICE WORK WITH LOW-INCOME **FAMILIES**.   IUSDAGR63638

POPULATION CHARACTERISTICS, LIVING CONDITIONS AND INCOME OF INDIAN **FAMILIES**, NORTHERN-CHEYENNE
RESERVATION. JULY, 1961.   IUSDINT63656

POPULATION CHARACTERISTICS, LIVING CONDITIONS, AND INCOME OF INDIAN **FAMILIES**, FORT-PECK RESERVATION,
1951-1961.   IUSDINT63657

POPULATION CHARACTERISTICS, LIVING CONDITIONS AND INCOMES OF INDIAN **FAMILIES**, FORT-BELKNAP RESERVATION.   IUSDINT63658

POPULATION CHARACTERISTICS, LIVING CONDITIONS AND INCOMES OF INDIAN **FAMILIES**, ROCKY-BAY-S RESERVATION.   IUSDINT63659

LEVELS OF LIVING OF SPANISH-AMERICAN RURAL AND URBAN **FAMILIES** IN TWO SOUTH TEXAS COUNTIES.   MCLEMHM63381

BASIC NEEDS OF SPANISH-AMERICAN FARM **FAMILIES** IN NEW-MEXICO.   MGRISGXND408

MEXICAN-AMERICAN **FAMILIES**. LOS-ANGELES COUNTY.   /CALIFORNIA/   MMCNAPH57435

POVERTY AMONG SPANISH-AMERICANS IN TEXAS. LOW-INCOME **FAMILIES** IN A MINORITY-GROUP.   MUPHAWK66511

CHILDREN AND INCOME IN NEGRO **FAMILIES**.   NBERNEH46077

RESOURCE USE AND ADJUSTMENT. RURAL **FAMILIES** IN THE CENTRAL LOUISIANA MIXED FARMING AREA.   NBOLTBX61396

CHILD REARING AMONG LOW-INCOME **FAMILIES**.   /ECONOMIC-STATUS/   NLEWIHX61040

BLACK **FAMILIES** AND THE WHITE HOUSE.   NRAINLX66033

SOCIAL SECURITY PROGRAM STATISTICS RELATING TO NONWHITE **FAMILIES** AND CHILDREN.   NUSDHEW58241

NEGRO **FAMILIES** IN RURAL WISCONSIN. A STUDY OF THEIR COMMUNITY LIFE.   NWISCGC59331

FAMILIES (CONTINUATION)
80 PUERTO-RICAN **FAMILIES** IN NEW-YORK CITY.   PBERLBB58780

THREE BASIC THEMES IN MEXICAN AND PUERTO-RICAN **FAMILIES**.   PTRENRD58800

THE ECONOMIC AND SOCIAL ADJUSTMENT OF LOW-INCOME FEMALE-HEADED **FAMILIES**.   WBERNSE65458

WOMEN-S EARNINGS IN LOW-INCOME **FAMILIES**.   WUSDLAB66236

FAMILY
THE NATION-S CHILDREN. VOL I. THE **FAMILY** AND SOCIAL-CHANGE. VOL II. DEVELOPMENT AND EDUCATION. VOL III.
PROBLEMS AND PROSPECTS. /NEGRO PUERTO-RICAN MEXICAN-AMERICAN WOMEN/   CGINZEX60720

FAMILY STRUCTURE AND SCHOOL PERFORMANCE. A COMPARATIVE STUDY OF STUDENTS FROM THREE ETHNIC BACKGROUNDS IN
AN INTEGRATED SCHOOL. /MEXICAN-AMERICAN AMERICAN-INDIAN/   CGRIFJX65407

THE URBAN ADJUSTMENT OF IMMIGRANTS. THE RELATIONSHIP OF EDUCATION TO OCCUPATIONAL AND TOTAL **FAMILY**
INCOME. /NEGRO MEXICAN-AMERICAN/   CSHANLW63122

PERSONS BY **FAMILY** CHARACTERISTICS. FAMILY MEMBERS BY SOCIAL, ECONOMIC AND HOUSING CHARACTERISTICS OF
FAMILIES. /DEMOGRAPHY/   CUSBURC63180

PERSONS BY FAMILY CHARACTERISTICS. **FAMILY** MEMBERS BY SOCIAL, ECONOMIC AND HOUSING CHARACTERISTICS OF
FAMILIES. /DEMOGRAPHY/   CUSBURC63180

SOURCES AND STRUCTURE OF **FAMILY** INCOME. /DEMOGRAPHY/   CUSBURC63184

SOME DETERMINANTS OF LOW **FAMILY** INCOME.   GCREADX61621

MARITAL AND **FAMILY** CHARACTERISTICS OF WORKERS, MARCH 1963.   GPERRVC64168

FAMILY INCOME AND RELATED CHARACTERISTICS AMONG LOW-INCOME COUNTIES AND STATES.   GRODOAL64241

FAMILY CHARACTERISTICS OF WORKERS, 1959.   GSCHIJX60283

MARITAL AND **FAMILY** CHARACTERISTICS OF WORKERS, MARCH 1960.   GSCHIJX61284

MARITAL AND **FAMILY** CHARACTERISTICS OF WORKERS, MARCH 1961.   GSCHIJX62285

MARITAL AND **FAMILY** CHARACTERISTICS OF WORKERS, MARCH 1962.   GSCHIJX63286

FAMILY INCOME AND EXPENDITURES.   GUSDLAB49028

FAMILY INCOME STATISTICS.   GUSDLAB49029

FAMILY CHARACTERISTICS OF THE LONG TERM UNEMPLOYED. A REPORT ON A STUDY OF CLAIMANTS UNDER THE TEMPORARY
EXTENDED UNEMPLOYMENT COMPENSATION PROGRAM, 1961-2.   GUSDLAB61445

FAMILY CHARACTERISTICS OF THE LONG-TERM UNEMPLOYED.   GUSDLAB63762

MARITAL AND **FAMILY** CHARACTERISTICS OF WORKERS, MARCH 1964.   GUSDLAB64201

FAMILY PLAN AND REHABILITATION PROGRAMS, STANDING-ROCK RESERVATION.   IUSDINT64649

FAMILY COMPOSITION AND CHARACTERISTICS OF AN ECONOMICALLY DEPRIVED CROSS-CULTURAL ROCKY-MOUNTAIN AREA.   MANDRWH66359

FAMILY ORGANIZATION IN FIVE TYPES OF MIGRATORY WAGE LABOR.   MSOLIML61496

CLASS AND **FAMILY** INFLUENCES ON STUDENT ASPIRATIONS.   NBENNWS64574

SCHOOL ATTENDANCE AND ATTAINMENT. FUNCTION AND DYSFUNCTION OF SCHOOL AND **FAMILY** SOCIAL SYSTEMS.
/EMPLOYMENT DROP-OUT/   NBERTAL62882

NEGRO **FAMILY** LIFE IN AMERICA.   NBILLAX65499

THE NEGRO **FAMILY** AND THE MOYNIHAN-REPORT.   NCARPLX66184

THE URBAN NEGRO **FAMILY**.   NDOUGJH66286

FAMILY AND ACHIEVEMENT. A PROPOSAL TO STUDY THE EFFECT OF FAMILY SOCIALIZATION ON ACHIEVEMENT AND
PERFORMANCE AMONG URBAN NEGRO AMERICANS.   NEPPSEG65334

FAMILY AND ACHIEVEMENT. A PROPOSAL TO STUDY THE EFFECT OF **FAMILY** SOCIALIZATION ON ACHIEVEMENT AND
PERFORMANCE AMONG URBAN NEGRO AMERICANS.   NEPPSEG65334

ETHNIC **FAMILY** PATTERNS. THE NEGRO FAMILY IN THE UNITED STATES.   NFRAZEF48379

ETHNIC **FAMILY** PATTERNS. THE NEGRO **FAMILY** IN THE UNITED STATES.   NFRAZEF48379

PROBLEMS AND NEEDS OF NEGRO CHILDREN AND YOUTH RESULTING FROM **FAMILY** DISORGANIZATION.   NFRAZEF50382

THE NEGRO **FAMILY** IN CHICAGO. /ILLINOIS/   NFRAZEF64380

IS THERE A BREAKDOWN OF THE NEGRO **FAMILY**.   NHERZEX66521

A HISTORICAL REVIEW OF THE IMPACT OF SOCIAL AND ECONOMIC STRUCTURE ON NEGRO CULTURE AND HOW IT INFLUENCES
FAMILY LIVING.   NJACKJX64596

THE CHANGING NEGRO **FAMILY**.   NLEWIHX60690

CULTURE, CLASS AND **FAMILY** LIFE AMONG LOW-INCOME NEGROES.   NLEWIHX67691

THE ABSENT FATHER HAUNTS THE NEGRO **FAMILY**.   NLINCCE65694

FAMILY PATTERNS, ACHIEVEMENTS, AND ASPIRATIONS OF URBAN NEGROES.   NLYSTMH61718

EMPLOYMENT, INCOME, AND THE ORDEAL OF THE NEGRO **FAMILY**.   NMOYNDP65861

THE NEGRO **FAMILY**. THE CASE FOR NATIONAL ACTION.   NMOYNDP65862

CRUCIBLE OF IDENTITY. THE NEGRO LOWER-CLASS **FAMILY**.   NRAINLX66032

IN DEFENSE OF THE NEGRO **FAMILY**.   NRIESFX66059

ANNUAL **FAMILY** AND OCCUPATIONAL EARNINGS OF RESIDENTS OF TWO NEGRO HOUSING PROJECTS IN ATLANTA 1937-1944.
/GEORGIA/   NRITTAL45062

RACIAL AND **FAMILY** EXPERIENCE CORRELATES OF MOBILITY ASPIRATION.   NSMITHP62144

FAMILY   (CONTINUATION)
    THE POVERTY-DEPENDENCY SYNDROME OF THE ADC FEMALE-BASED NEGRO FAMILY.   NSTROFL64074

    THE LOWER STATUS PUERTO-RICAN FAMILY.   PBRAMJX62783

    SCHOOL AND COMMUNITY COURSE. THE LOWER STATUS PUERTO-RICAN FAMILY.   PBRAMJX63784

    LA VIDA. A PUERTO-RICAN FAMILY IN THE CULTURE OF POVERTY -- SAN-JUAN AND NEW-YORK.   PLEWIOX66825

    PART-TIME EMPLOYMENT FOR WOMEN WITH FAMILY RESPONSIBILITIES. /WORK-FAMILY-CONFLICT/   WINTELR57867

    LABOR SUPPLY, FAMILY INCOME, AND CONSUMPTION.   WMINCJX60985

    MARRIAGE, FAMILY, AND SOCIETY. A READER. /WORK-FAMILY-CONFLICT/   WRODMHX65084

    FAMILY CHARACTERISTICS OF WORKING WIVES.   WUSBURC59169

FAMILY-S
    THE NEGRO FAMILY-S SEARCH FOR ECONOMIC SECURITY.   NDOUGJH64285

    THE WORKING WIFE AND HER FAMILY-S ECONOMIC POSITION.   WCARRMS62681

FARM
    ANNUAL FARM LABOR REPORT, 1965, CALIFORNIA DEPARTMENT OF EMPLOYMENT, FARM LABOR SERVICE. /NEGRO
    MEXICAN-AMERICAN WOMEN/   CCALDEM66906

    ANNUAL FARM LABOR REPORT, 1965, CALIFORNIA DEPARTMENT OF EMPLOYMENT, FARM LABOR SERVICE. /NEGRO
    MEXICAN-AMERICAN WOMEN/   CCALDEM66906

    FARM MECHANIZATION AND LABOR STABILIZATION. PART II IN A SERIES ON TECHNOLOGICAL-CHANGE AND FARM LABOR
    USE, KERN COUNTY, CALIFORNIA, 1961. /NEGRO MEXICAN-AMERICAN/   CMETZWH65389

    FARM MECHANIZATION AND LABOR STABILIZATION. PART II IN A SERIES ON TECHNOLOGICAL-CHANGE AND FARM LABOR
    USE, KERN COUNTY, CALIFORNIA, 1961. /NEGRO MEXICAN-AMERICAN/   CMETZWH65389

    THE TRAINING OF MIGRANT FARM WORKERS. A FOLLOW-UP STUDY OF TWO EXPERIMENTAL AND DEMONSTRATION PROGRAMS
    UNDER THE MANPOWER-DEVELOPMENT-AND-TRAINING-ACT. /MEXICAN-AMERICAN AMERICAN-INDIAN/   CUNIVOD66054

    UNITED STATES CENSUS OF AGRICULTURE. COLOR, RACE, AND TENURE OF FARM OPERATOR. GENERAL REPORT, VOLUME II.
    /DEMOGRAPHY/   CUSBURC59382

    MANPOWER DEVELOPMENT PROGRAMS FOR FARM PEOPLE.   GALLECC67910

    CHARACTERISTICS OF THE U.S. POPULATION BY FARM AND NON-FARM ORIGIN.   GBEALCL64423

    DIMENSIONS OF THE FARM LABOR PROBLEM.   GBISHCE67915

    FARM LABOR IN THE UNITED STATES.   GBISHCE67916

    THE HIRED FARM WORKING FORCE OF 1963 WITH SUPPLEMENTARY DATA FOR 1962. /ECONOMIC-STATUS/   GBOWLGK65432

    THE CURRENT SITUATION OF THE HIRED FARM LABOR-FORCE.   GBOWLGK67920

    THE ITINERANT FARM LABOR PROJECT REPORT. /MIGRANT-WORKERS CALIFORNIA/   GCALVRS60553

    WHAT MIGRANT FARM CHILDREN LEARN.   GCOLERX66133

    FRUSTRATION ON THE FARM. /MEXICAN-AMERICAN ORIENTAL UNION/   GCORTJC57372

    REPORTS OF THE MEETINGS OF THE COMMITTEE OF OFFICIALS ON MIGRATORY FARM LABOR OF THE ATLANTIC SEABOARD
    STATES. /MIGRANT-WORKERS/   GCOUNSG58932

    THE HIRED FARM WORKING FORCE OF 1958. /ECONOMIC-STATUS/   GCOWHJD59430

    AN ANALYSIS OF THE EXPERIENCED HIRED FARM WORKING FORCE, 1948-1957. /SKILLS/   GCOWHJD60423

    EDUCATIONAL STATUS, COLLEGE PLANS, AND OCCUPATIONAL-STATUS OF FARM AND NONFARM YOUTHS. OCTOBER 1959.   GCOWHJD61427

    EDUCATION, SKILL LEVEL, AND EARNINGS OF THE HIRED FARM WORKING FORCE OF 1961.   GCOWHJD63420

    SCHOOL DROPOUT RATES AMONG FARM AND NONFARM YOUTH 1950 AND 1960.   GCOWHJD63421

    CHARACTERISTICS OF SCHOOL DROPOUTS AND HIGH SCHOOL GRADUATES, FARM AND NONFARM, 1960.   GCOWHJD64419

    SOCIOECONOMIC DIFFERENCES BETWEEN WHITE AND NONWHITE FARM POPULATIONS IN THE SOUTH.   GCOWHJD64616

    THE HIRED FARM WORKING FORCE OF 1960. /ECONOMIC-STATUS/   GFRIERE62431

    FARM MANPOWER POLICY.   GFULLVX67931

    TODAY-S REALITIES IN THE FARM LABOR-MARKET.   GGOODRC65726

    OCCUPATIONAL MOBILITY FROM THE FARM LABOR-FORCE.   GHATHOE67936

    MIGRATORY FARM WORKERS IN THE ATLANTIC COAST STREAM. I. CHANGES IN NEW-YORK, 1953 AND 1957.   GLARSOF60406

    THE MIGRATORY WORKER IN THE FARM ECONOMY.   GLEVILA61357

    THE HIRED FARM WORKING FORCE OF 1956. /ECONOMIC-STATUS/   GMAITST58428

    THE HIRED FARM WORKING FORCE OF 1957. /ECONOMIC-STATUS/   GMAITST59429

    THE HIRED FARM WORKING FORCE OF 1958.   GMAITST61384

    THE CALIFORNIA FARM WORKER. STILL IN DUBIOUS BATTLE. /MIGRANT-WORKERS UNION/   GMEISOX60461

    MIGRATORY FARM WORKERS IN THE ATLANTIC COAST STREAM.   GMETZWH55426

    CHARACTERISTICS OF FARM WORKERS AS RELATED TO STABILIZATION OF THE WORK FORCE. /MIGRANT-WORKERS/   GMETZWH62504

    THE FARM WORKER IN A CHANGING AGRICULTURE. PART I IN A SERIES ON TECHNOLOGICAL-CHANGE AND FARM LABOR USE,
    KERN-COUNTY, CALIFORNIA, 1961.   GMETZWH64387

    THE FARM WORKER IN A CHANGING AGRICULTURE. PART I IN A SERIES ON TECHNOLOGICAL-CHANGE AND FARM LABOR USE,
    KERN-COUNTY, CALIFORNIA, 1961.   GMETZWH64387

    THE STRUCTURE OF THE FARM LABOR-MARKET AND MIGRATION PATTERNS.   GMIREWX57499

    ECONOMIC FACTORS INFLUENCING EDUCATIONAL-ATTAINMENTS AND ASPIRATIONS OF FARM YOUTH.   GMOOREJ64386

FARM   (CONTINUATION)
MIGRATORY **FARM** WORKERS IN THE ATLANTIC COAST STREAM. WESTERN NEW-YORK, JUNE 1953.   GMOTHJR54405

AN EXPERIMENT IN VOCATIONAL EDUCATION FOR CHILDREN OF MIGRATORY **FARM** WORKERS, JULY-AUGUST 1956.   GNATLCRND046

MIGRANT **FARM** LABOR IN NEW-YORK.   GNEWYSE58109

EMPLOYMENT AND EARNINGS OF MIGRANT **FARM** WORKERS IN NEW-YORK STATE.   GNEWYSE60110

SUMMARY OF RULES, REGULATIONS, AND LAWS THAT AFFECT SEASONAL **FARM** WORKERS AND THEIR EMPLOYERS IN NEW-YORK
STATE. /MIGRANT-WORKERS/   GNEWYSJND113

MIGRANT **FARM** LABOR IN NEW-YORK STATE.   GNEWYSJ63112

A HELPING HAND. SEASONAL **FARM** LABOR IN NEW-YORK STATE. /MIGRANT-WORKERS/   GNEWYSX63087

THE MOVEMENT OF LABOR BETWEEN **FARM** AND NONFARM JOBS.   GPERKBX66150

FARM AND NON-FARM EMPLOYMENT OPPORTUNITIES FOR LOW-INCOME **FARM** FAMILIES.   GRUTTVW59270

FARM AND NON-FARM EMPLOYMENT OPPORTUNITIES FOR LOW-INCOME FARM FAMILIES.   GRUTTVW59270

NATIONAL EMPLOYMENT, SKILLS, AND EARNINGS OF **FARM** LABOR.   GSCHUTW67964

MIGRATORY **FARM** WORKERS IN THE ATLANTIC COAST STREAM, II. EDUCATION OF NEW-YORK WORKERS AND THEIR
CHILDREN. 1953 AND 1957.   GSHAREF60427

MIGRATION OF THE TEXAS **FARM** POPULATION.   GSKRARL57315

TEXAS GROWERS AND WORKERS ON THE **FARM**, LOWER RIO-GRANDE VALLEY.   GTEXAEC59352

FARM LABOR ADJUSTMENTS TO CHANGING TECHNOLOGY.   GTOLLGS67974

MIGRATORY **FARM** WORKERS IN THE MID-CONTINENT STREAMS.   GUSDAGR60425

THE HIRED **FARM** WORKING FORCE OF 1964. A STATISTICAL REPORT.   GUSDAGR65424

NONWHITE **FARM** OPERATORS IN THE UNITED STATES.   GUSDLAB41077

MIGRATORY **FARM** LABOR CONFERENCE, PROCEEDINGS.   GUSDLAB57359

PROGRAMS OF NATIONAL ORGANIZATIONS FOR MIGRANT **FARM** WORKERS AND THEIR FAMILIES.   GUSDLAB61202

FARM LABOR-MARKET IN TRANSITION.   GUSDLAB62991

FARM LABOR DEVELOPMENTS -- EMPLOYMENT AND WAGE SUPPLEMENT.   GUSDLAB66446

VOLUNTARY **FARM** EMPLOYMENT SERVICE. /MIGRANT-WORKERS/   GUSSENA64306

THE HARVEST OF DESPAIR. THE MIGRANT **FARM** WORKER.   GWRIGOX65604

REPORT ON INDIAN **FARM** LABOR ACTIVITY.   IUSDLAB66668

MERRILL-TRUST-FUND TO IMPROVE THE EMPLOYMENT OPPORTUNITIES OF THE MIGRANT **FARM** WORKERS OF MEXICAN ORIGIN.   MBISHCS62365

CALIFORNIA-S **FARM** LABOR PROBLEMS. /MIGRANT-WORKERS/   MCALSSE63380

A PLANNED COMMUNITY FOR MIGRATORY **FARM** WORKERS.   MFEERAB62392

BASIC NEEDS OF SPANISH-AMERICAN **FARM** FAMILIES IN NEW-MEXICO.   MGRISGXND408

TERMINATION OF THE BRACERO PROGRAM. SOME EFFECTS ON **FARM** LABOR AND MIGRANT HOUSING NEEDS.   MMCELRC65385

FARMERS, WORKERS, AND MACHINES. TECHNOLOGICAL AND SOCIAL-CHANGE IN **FARM** INDUSTRIES OF ARIZONA.   MPADFHX65450

THE MEXICAN **FARM** LABOR SUPPLY PROGRAM -- ITS FRIENDS AND FOES.   MPFEIDG63456

THE EFFECTS OF IMPORTED MEXICAN **FARM** LABOR IN A CALIFORNIA COUNTY.   MROONJF61465

MEXICAN **FARM** LABOR CONSULTANTS REPORT.   MUSDLAB59508

FARM LABOR.   MUSHOUR58509

MEXICAN **FARM** LABOR PROGRAM.   MUSHOUR63984

NEGRO **FARM** OPERATORS. NUMBER, LOCATION AND RECENT TRENDS.   NBEALCL58064

FARM INCOME PREDICTIONS FOR SMALL FARMS IN THE CENTRAL LOUISIANA MIXED FARMING AREA.   NBOLTBX62399

NEGRO **FARM** LABOR IN THE DELTA AREA OF MISSISSIPPI. SUPPLY AND UTILIZATION.   NLERANL61416

ATTITUDES TOWARD ETHNIC **FARM** WORKERS IN COACHELLA-VALLEY. /CALIFORNIA/   NMCDOEC55719

FACTORS AFFECTING **FARM** PLACEMENT OF NEGRO VOCATIONAL AGRICULTURE STUDENTS IN ALABAMA.   NMCQUFT45348

AN ANALYSIS OF SELECTIVE FACTORS INFLUENCING **FARM** INCOME IN HALE COUNTY, AS A BASIS FOR ESTABLISHING A
MORE EFFECTIVE VOCATIONAL AGRICULTURAL PROGRAM. /ALABAMA/   NSALTDR52347

OUR WELFARE STATE AND THE WELFARE OF **FARM** PEOPLE.   NSCHUTW64143

A STUDY OF **FARM** MANAGEMENT PRACTICES ON 100 NEGRO FARMS IN MACON COUNTY, ALABAMA, 1949.   NSHAWBJ50339

COLOR, RACE AND TENURE OF **FARM** OPERATORS.   NUSBURC62225

EQUAL-OPPORTUNITY IN **FARM** PROGRAMS -- AN APPRAISAL OF SERVICES RENDERED BY AGENCIES OF THE UNITED STATES
DEPARTMENT OF AGRICULTURE.   NUSCOMC65232

PUERTO-RICAN **FARM** WORKERS IN NEW-JERSEY.   PAINERO59777

LABOR MANAGEMENT ON THE **FARM**.   PGARDSC58807

ANNUAL **FARM** LABOR REPORT. /NEW-JERSEY/   PNEWJSE63831

FARMER
THE PLACE OF THE NEGRO **FARMER** IN THE CHANGING ECONOMY OF THE COTTON SOUTH.   NNEALEE50905

THE AMERICAN **FARMER**. /OCCUPATIONS/   NPOPURB63007

THE DISAPPEARING NEGRO **FARMER** OF FLORIDA, 1920-1950.   NSMITCU56364

FARMERS

ECCNOMIC-TRENDS IN EXTENSION WORK WITH NEGRO **FARMERS** IN ALABAMA, 1936-1948. GGAINRL48341

APPROACHES TO INCOME IMPROVEMENT. EXPERIENCES OF FAMILIES RECEIVING PRODUCTION LOANS UNDER THE **FARMERS** HOME ADMINISTRATION. GHENDWE59422

PROCEEDINGS OF THE NATIONAL-SHARECROPPERS-FUND CONFERENCE ON MIGRATORY LABOR AND LOW-INCOME **FARMERS**. NOVEMBER 13 1957. GNATLSF57299

FARMERS, WORKERS, AND MACHINES. TECHNOLOGICAL AND SOCIAL-CHANGE IN FARM INDUSTRIES OF ARIZONA. MPADFHX65450

THE EVALUATION OF PRACTICES CARRIED ON BY TWO HUNDRED NEGRO **FARMERS** IN THE PRODUCTION OF COTTON IN MACON COUNTY, ALABAMA. NGOLDSM48350

THE EFFECT OF A CHANGING AGRICULTURAL PATTERN ON NEGRO **FARMERS** OF SOUTH-CAROLINA. NHURSRL56253

AN ECONOMIC ANALYSIS OF SPECIFIED INCORPORATED AND UNINCORPORATED **FARMERS** COOPERATIVE ASSOCIATIONS OPERATED BY NEGRO FARMERS IN ALABAMA. NLIGHMB53340

AN ECONOMIC ANALYSIS OF SPECIFIED INCORPORATED AND UNINCORPORATED FARMERS COOPERATIVE ASSOCIATIONS OPERATED BY NEGRO **FARMERS** IN ALABAMA. NLIGHMB53340

A STUDY OF NEGRO **FARMERS** IN SOUTH-CAROLINA. NSOUTRC62165

MIGRANTS POSE PROBLEMS FOR NEW-JERSEY **FARMERS** WHO NEED THEM. PCUNNJT57793

FARMING

INCOME AND RELATED CHARACTERISTICS OF RURAL HOUSEHOLDS IN THE CENTRAL LOUISIANA MIXED **FARMING** AREA. NBOLTBX60398

RESOURCE USE AND ADJUSTMENT. RURAL FAMILIES IN THE CENTRAL LOUISIANA MIXED **FARMING** AREA. NBOLTBX61396

FARM INCOME PREDICTIONS FOR SMALL FARMS IN THE CENTRAL LOUISIANA MIXED **FARMING** AREA. NBOLTBX62399

FACTORS AFFECTING THE PRESENT **FARMING** PROGRAMS OF ONE HUNDRED NEGRO FARMS IN THE PATRONAGE AREA OF THE MACON COUNTY TRAINING SCHOOL, IN ALABAMA, WITH EMPHASIS FOR IMPROVEMENT. NBRONCA51337

FARMS

ECCNCMIC, SOCIAL, AND DEMOGRAPHIC CHARACTERISTICS OF SPANISH-AMERICAN WAGE WORKERS ON US **FARMS**. /PUERTO-RICAN MEXICAN-AMERICAN/ CFRIERE63805

FCONOMIC, SOCIAL AND DEMOGRAPHIC CHARACTERISTICS OF SPANISH-AMERICAN WAGE WORKERS ON US **FARMS**. MFRIERE63394

FARM INCOME PREDICTIONS FOR SMALL **FARMS** IN THE CENTRAL LOUISIANA MIXED FARMING AREA. NBOLTBX62399

FACTORS AFFECTING THE PRESENT FARMING PROGRAMS OF ONE HUNDRED NEGRO **FARMS** IN THE PATRONAGE AREA OF THE MACON COUNTY TRAINING SCHOOL, IN ALABAMA, WITH EMPHASIS FOR IMPROVEMENT. NBRONCA51337

A STUDY OF FARM MANAGEMENT PRACTICES ON 100 NEGRO **FARMS** IN MACON COUNTY, ALABAMA, 1949. NSHAWBJ50339

PERSONAL AND ENVIRONMENTAL OBSTACLES TO PRODUCTION ADJUSTMENTS ON SOUTH-CAROLINA PIEDMONT AREA **FARMS**. NTAYLCC58411

FARMWORKER

CHARACTERISTICS OF THE POPULATION OF HIRED **FARMWORKER** HOUSEHOLDS. /ECONOMIC-STATUS/ GBOWLGK65424

CHARACTERISTICS OF THE POPULATION OF HIRED **FARMWORKER** HOUSEHOLDS. GUSDAGR65422

FARMWORKERS

THE TENURE STATUS OF **FARMWORKERS** IN THE UNITED STATES. GMAIEFH60417

MIGRATORY **FARMWORKERS** IN THE MIDCONTINENT STREAM. GMETZWH60440

FATHER

THE ABSENT **FATHER** HAUNTS THE NEGRO FAMILY. NLINCCE65694

FATHER-ABSENCE

FATHER-ABSENCE AND NEGRO ADULT PERSONALITY. A RESEARCH NOTE. NPETTTFND990

FATHERS

COLLEGE WOMEN-S IDENTIFICATIONS WITH THEIR **FATHERS** IN RELATION TO VOCATIONAL INTEREST PATTERNS. /ASPIRATIONS/ WHALLWJ63815

FEDERAL

FEDERAL CIVIL-RIGHTS-ACT OF 1960. SUMMARY AND ANALYSIS. GAMERJD60385

THE PRESENT STATUS AND PROGRAMS OF FEPC. **FEDERAL**, STATE, AND MUNICIPAL. GBRAZBR51472

THE **FEDERAL** MANAGER-S ROLE IN DEMOCRACY-S UNFINISHED BUSINESS. GCLINRX61577

THE **FEDERAL** INTEREST IN EMPLOYMENT DISCRIMINATION. HEREIN THE CONSTITUTIONAL SCOPE OF EXECUTIVE POWER TO WITHOLD APPROPRIATE FUNDS. GFERGCC64679

THE **FEDERAL** ANTI-POVERTY PROGRAM AND SOME IMPLICATIONS OF SUBPROFESSIONAL TRAINING. GGORDJE65135

FEPC LEGISLATION IN THE UNITED STATES. **FEDERAL**, STATE, MUNICIPAL. GGRAVWB51735

RACIAL DISCRIMINATION IN EMPLOYMENT AND THE **FEDERAL** LAW. GKOVAIX58026

DISCRIMINATION IN EMPLOYMENT. **FEDERAL** AND STATE PRACTICES IN ANTI-DISCRIMINATION. GLEITRD49892

FEDERAL AID TO DEPRESSED AREAS. AN EVALUATION OF THE AREA-REDEVELOPMENT-ADMINISTRATION. GLEVISA64896

FEDERAL MANPOWER POLICIES AND PROGRAMS TO COMBAT UNEMPLOYMENT. GLEVISA64897

THE REALITY OF EQUAL-OPPORTUNITY IN **FEDERAL** EMPLOYMENT. GMACYJW66933

ENFORCEMENT OF THE **FEDERAL** EQUAL-OPPORTUNITY LAW. GMARSBX64943

IMPLEMENTATION OF THE **FEDERAL** FAIR-EMPLOYMENT POLICY. GNATLAI49038

REPORT WITH RECOMMENDATIONS CN THE SUBJECT OF **FEDERAL** FAIR-EMPLOYMENT-PRACTICES LEGISLATION. GNEWYCB53069

FEDERAL LEGISLATION FOR A COMPREHENSIVE PROGRAM ON YOUTH EMPLOYMENT. GNIXORA66847

GOVERNMENTAL FAIR-EMPLOYMENT AGENCIES. AN APPRAISAL OF **FEDERAL**, STATE, AND MUNICIPAL EFFORTS TO END JOB DISCRIMINATION. GNORGPH62120

PROGRESS WITHOUT **FEDERAL** COMPULSION. ARGUING THE CASE FOR COMPROMISE METHODS. GNORTHR52122

STATEMENT TO THE COMMITTEE ON LEGISLATION IN SUPPORT OF AN EFFECTIVE **FEDERAL** FEP LAW AND OTHER VITAL

CIVIL-RIGHTS LEGISLATION.   GOLIVWX60134

FEDERAL PROCUREMENT AND EQUAL-OPPORTUNITY EMPLOYMENT.   GPOWETX64190

STUDY OF MINORITY-GROUP EMPLOYMENT IN THE FEDERAL GOVERNMENT.   GPRESCD64116

HUMAN-RELATIONS IN FEDERAL EMPLOYMENT.   GPRESCP55197

THE POLICY OF NON-DISCRIMINATION IN EMPLOYMENT IN THE FEDERAL GOVERNMENT.   GPRESCP55198

SOME QUESTIONS AND ANSWERS ON THE NON-DISCRIMINATION POLICY OF THE FEDERAL GOVERNMENT.   GPRESCP55199

TRENDS IN THE EMPLOYMENT OF NEGRO-AMERICANS IN UPPER-LEVEL WHITE-COLLAR POSITIONS OF THE FEDERAL
GOVERNMENT.   GPRESCP60200

DISCRIMINATION IN UNION MEMBERSHIP. DENIAL OF DUE PROCESS UNDER FEDERAL COLLECTIVE BARGAINING
LEGISLATION.   GPRESSB58126

THE NEW FEDERAL FAIR-EMPLOYMENT-PRACTICES ACT -- COMPARISON WITH STATE LAW AND AN ANALYSIS OF RELEVANT
STATE EXPERIENCES.   /MISSOURI/   GROBEPC64239

COORDINATION AMONG FEDERAL MANPOWER PROGRAMS.   GROBSRT66721

FAIR-EMPLOYMENT IN THE FEDERAL SERVICE.   GUSCISC51385

FAIR-EMPLOYMENT IN THE FEDERAL SERVICE. A PROGRESS REPORT ON CONSTRUCTIVE STEPS.   GUSCISC52386

STUDY OF MINORITY GROUP EMPLOYMENT IN THE FEDERAL GOVERNMENT, 1966.   GUSCISC66767

EQUAL-EMPLOYMENT-OPPORTUNITY UNDER FEDERAL LAW.   GUSCOMC66396

STUDY OF MINORITY-GROUP EMPLOYMENT IN THE FEDERAL GOVERNMENT.   GUSDLAB63500

COVERAGE OF AGRICULTURAL WORKERS UNDER STATE AND FEDERAL LAWS.   /MIGRANT-WORKERS/   GUSDLAB64507

FEDERAL AGENCIES WITH PRIMARY CIVIL-RIGHTS RESPONSIBILITIES.   GUSDLAB65447

FEDERAL EQUALITY OF OPPORTUNITY IN EMPLOYMENT ACT.   GUSSENA52350

FEDERAL ROLE IN URBAN AFFAIRS.   GUSSENA66351

THE FEDERAL NONDISCRIMINATION POLICY IN THE VETERANS-ADMINISTRATION.   GUSVETA59521

FEDERAL REMEDIES FOR RACIAL DISCRIMINATION BY LABOR UNIONS.   GWEISLX62597

UNION DEMOCRACY AND FAIR REPRESENTATION. FEDERAL RESPONSIBILITY IN A FEDERAL SYSTEM.   GWELLHX58550

UNION DEMOCRACY AND FAIR REPRESENTATION. FEDERAL RESPONSIBILITY IN A FEDERAL SYSTEM.   GWELLHX58550

CIVIL-RIGHTS POLICY IN THE FEDERAL SYSTEM. PROPOSALS FOR A BETTER USE OF ADMINISTRATIVE PROCESS. GWITHJX65575

TERMINATION OF FEDERAL SUPERVISION. DISINTEGRATION AND THE AMERICAN-INDIANS.   ILAFAOX57075

FEDERAL INDIAN POLICY AS IT AFFECTS LOCAL INDIAN AFFAIRS.   IMCKIFX64086

INDIANS ON FEDERAL RESERVATIONS IN THE US.   IUSDHEW58196

AMERICAN-INDIANS AND THE FEDERAL GOVERNMENT.   IUSDINT65640

RACIAL DISCRIMINATION IN THE FEDERAL SERVICE. A STUDY IN THE SOCIOLOGY OF ADMINISTRATION.   NBRADWC53106

EFFECT OF SCHOOL ASSIGNMENT LAWS ON FEDERAL ADJUDICATION OF INTEGRATION CONTROVERSIES.   NCOLULR57224

NEGRO EMPLOYMENT IN THE FEDERAL GOVERNMENT.   NDAVIJA45259

NONDISCRIMINATION IN THE FEDERAL SERVICES.   NDAVIJA46257

THE FEDERAL EXECUTIVE AND CIVIL-RIGHTS. 1961-1965.   NFLEMHC66362

STATEMENT AND TESTIMONY ON FEDERAL ROLE IN URBAN AFFAIRS. /EMPLOYMENT GHETTO/   NKENNRF66017

THE NEGRO IN FEDERAL EMPLOYMENT. THE QUEST FOR EQUAL-OPPORTUNITY.   NKRISSX67143

RACIAL DISCRIMINATION AND THE FEDERAL LAW. A PROBLEM IN NULLIFICATION.   NLUSKLX63713

REPRESENTATION OF NEGROES AND WHITES AS EMPLOYEES IN THE FEDERAL PRISON SYSTEM.   NMORGGD62849

NEGRO EMPLOYMENT IN THE FEDERAL GOVERNMENT BY CIVIL SERVICE REGION, STATE AND PAY CATEGORIES, JUNE 1962. NPRESCD62012

A FIVE-CITY SURVEY OF NEGRO-AMERICAN EMPLOYEES OF THE FEDERAL GOVERNMENT.   NPRESCP57017

CHARACTERISTICS OF NEGRO EMPLOYMENT IN FEDERAL AGENCIES IN ATLANTA, GEORGIA.   NPRESCP60016

APPEALS FROM DISCRIMINATION IN FEDERAL EMPLOYMENT. A CASE-STUDY.   NSHOSAX63131

THE FEDERAL EXECUTIVE AND CIVIL-RIGHTS.   NSOUTRC61160

STUDY OF MINORITY-GROUP EMPLOYMENT IN THE FEDERAL GOVERNMENT, 1965.   NUSCISC65229

VOCATIONAL EDUCATION AND FEDERAL POLICY.   WLEVISA63039

REPORT OF THE COMMITTEE ON FEDERAL EMPLOYMENT.   WPRESCO63067

WISCONSIN FAIR-EMPLOYMENT-PRACTICES DIVISION INQUIRY INTO THE CONFLICTS BETWEEN STATE PROTECTIVE LABOR
LEGISLATION AND STATE AND FEDERAL LAWS PROHIBITING DISCRIMINATION BASED ON SEX. /EMPLOYMENT-CONDITIONS/ WUAWXWD65165

FEDERAL CAREERS FOR WOMEN.   WUSCISC61167

OCCUPATIONS AND SALARIES OF WOMEN IN THE FEDERAL SERVICE.   WUSCISC62168

FEDERAL EMPLOYMENT OF WOMEN.   WUSCISC66483

OCCUPATIONS AND SALARIES OF WOMEN FEDERAL EMPLOYEES.   WUSDLAB57992

GREAT STRIDES MADE IN JOBS FOR WOMEN IN FEDERAL SERVICE.   WUSDLAB62041

WOMEN IN FEDERAL SERVICE. 1939-59.   WWIRTWW62181

FEDERAL-AVIATION-AGE
NONDISCRIMINATION IN FEDERALLY-ASSISTED PROGRAMS OF THE DEPARTMENT-OF-THE-TREASURY,
DEPARTMENT-OF-DEFENSE, ATOMIC-ENERGY-COMMISSION, CIVIL-AERONAUTICS-BOARD, **FEDERAL-AVIATION-AGENCY**,
VETERANS-ADMINISTRATION.   GFEDERX64673

FEDERAL-EMPLOYMENT
GRAPHIC PRESENTATION OF **FEDERAL-EMPLOYMENT**.   GUSCISC61387

FEDERAL-GOVERNMENT
EMPLOYMENT OF NEGROES IN THE **FEDERAL-GOVERNMENT**.   NANDEBE65023

NEGRO EMPLOYMENT IN **FEDERAL-GOVERNMENT**.   NBAERMF61042

THE WAR-TIME EMPLOYMENT OF NEGROES IN THE **FEDERAL-GOVERNMENT**.   NGOLICL45432

THE NEGRO **FEDERAL-GOVERNMENT** WORKER.   NHAYELJ42504

THE NEGRO IN THE **FEDERAL-GOVERNMENT**.   NHOPEJX63576

STUDY OF MINORITY-GROUP EMPLOYMENT IN THE **FEDERAL-GOVERNMENT**, 1963.   NUSCISC63228

EMPLOYMENT OF NEGROES BY **FEDERAL-GOVERNMENT**.   NUSDLAB43818

EMPLOYMENT OF NEGROES IN THE **FEDERAL-GOVERNMENT**, JUNE 1964.   NUSDLAB65815

WOMEN EXECUTIVES IN THE **FEDERAL-GOVERNMENT**. /OCCUPATIONS/   WWARNWL62993

FEDERAL-SERVICE
INTERGROUP RELATIONS IN THE **FEDERAL-SERVICE** .   GDOUGJH61649

FEDERAL-SERVICES
NONDISCRIMINATION IN THE **FEDERAL-SERVICES**.   GDAVIJA46628

FEDERAL-STATE
STATE FAIR-EMPLOMENT LAWS AND THEIR ADMINISTRATION. TEXTS, **FEDERAL-STATE** COOPERATION, PROHIBITED ACTS.   GBURENA64497

DIVISION OF AUTHORITY UNDER TITLE-VII OF THE CIVIL-RIGHTS-ACT OF 1964. A PRELIMINARY STUDY IN
FEDERAL-STATE INTERAGENCY RELATIONS.   GROSESJ66254

FEDERALLY-ASSISTED
NONDISCRIMINATION IN **FEDERALLY-ASSISTED** PROGRAMS OF THE DEPARTMENT-OF-THE-TREASURY,
DEPARTMENT-OF-DEFENSE, ATOMIC-ENERGY-COMMISSION, CIVIL-AERONAUTICS-BOARD, FEDERAL-AVIATION-AGENCY,
VETERANS-ADMINISTRATION.   GFEDERX64673

FEMALE
THE NON-WHITE **FEMALE** IN THE LABOR-FORCE. /WOMEN NEGRO/   CTURNRH51214

WARTIME EMPLOYMENT PATTERNS OF NONWHITES AND **FEMALE** WORKERS IN SOUTHERN INDUSTRY.   GHOPEJX46485

ROLE CONCEPTION AS A PREDICTOR OF ADULT **FEMALE** ROLES. /WORK-WOMAN-ROLE/   WANGRSS66619

INTEREST PATTERN FAKING BY **FEMALE** JOB APPLICANTS. /ASPIRATIONS/   WBECKJA63633

GROWING UP **FEMALE**. /WORK-WOMAN-ROLE/   WBETTBX62883

THE **FEMALE** LABOR-FORCE IN METROPOLITAN AREAS. AN INTERNATIONAL COMPARISON.   WCOLLAX62697

A COMPARATIVE STUDY OF TOP LEVEL MALE AND **FEMALE** EXECUTIVES IN HARRIS-COUNTY. /TEXAS OCCUPATIONS/   WDOLLPA65738

FEMALE LABOR-FORCE PARTICIPATION AND ECONOMIC DEVELOPMENT.   WHABESX58811

REPORT ON THE SURVEY OF **FEMALE** PHYSICIANS GRADUATING FROM MEDICAL SCHOOL BETWEEN 1925 AND 1940.
/OCCUPATIONS/   WHANNFX58819

SPECIAL SUPPLEMENT ON THE AMERICAN **FEMALE**. /WORK-WOMAN-ROLE/   WHARPXX62822

SOME FACTORS WHICH DETERMINE THE DISTRIBUTION OF THE **FEMALE** WORK-FORCE. /LABOR-FORCE/   WJOUROI62883

FEMALE LABOR-FORCE MOBILITY AND ITS SIMULATION.   WKORBJX63435

THE **FEMALE** PHYSICIAN IN PUBLIC HEALTH. CONFLICT AND RECONCILIATION OF THE SEX AND PROFESSIONAL ROLES.
/OCCUPATIONS/   WKOSAJX64915

THE **FEMALE** LABOR-FORCE IN THE UNITED STATES. FACTORS GOVERNING ITS GROWTH AND CHANGING COMPOSITION.   WOPPEVK66096

THE INTERACTION OF DEMAND AND SUPPLY AND ITS EFFECT ON THE **FEMALE** LABOR-FORCE IN THE UNITED STATES.   WOPPEVK66289

SCHOOL DROPOUTS. THE **FEMALE** SPECIES.   WSCHRDX62105

THE CHANGING WOMAN WORKER. A STUDY OF THE **FEMALE** LABOR-FORCE IN NEW-JERSEY AND IN THE NATION FROM 1940 TO
1958.   WSMITGM60120

HELP WANTED -- **FEMALE**. A STUDY OF DEMAND AND SUPPLY IN A LOCAL JOB MARKET FOR WOMEN. /MANPOWER/   WSMITGM64121

THE **FEMALE** LABOR-FORCE. A CASE STUDY IN THE INTERPRETATION OF HISTORICAL STATISTICS.   WSMUTRW60124

THE MARRIED **FEMALE** SCHOOL TEACHER. A CONTINUED STUDY. /WORK-FAMILY-CONFLICT/   WSTEPCM60139

FEMALE-BASED
THE POVERTY-DEPENDENCY SYNDROME OF THE ADC **FEMALE-BASED** NEGRO FAMILY.   NSTROFL64074

FEMALE-HEADED
THE ECONOMIC AND SOCIAL ADJUSTMENT OF LOW-INCOME **FEMALE-HEADED** FAMILIES.   WBERNSE65458

FEMALES
THE EVALUATION OF WORK BY **FEMALES**, 1940-1950. /WOMEN NEGRO/   CDORNSM56284

FEMININE
CONCEPT OF THE **FEMININE** ROLE. /WORK-WOMAN-ROLE/   WSTEIAX63135

FEP
APPRENTICESHIP AND TESTS, **FEP** SUMMARY OF LATEST DEVELOPMENTS.   GBUREON65491

HEARING OF THE SUBCOMMITTEE ON ECONOMIC DEVELOPMENT, EDITED TRANSCRIPT, JANUARY 28 AND 29, 1964.
/CALIFORNIA **FEP**/   GCALAIW64510

FEP LEGISLATION AND ENFORCEMENT IN THE US.   GMEANJE66971

STATEMENT TO THE COMMITTEE ON LEGISLATION IN SUPPORT OF AN EFFECTIVE FEDERAL FEP LAW AND OTHER VITAL

FEP (CONTINUATION)
CIVIL-RIGHTS LEGISLATION.   GOLIVWX60134

   STATEMENT. PUBLIC HEARING, WCMEN IN PUBLIC AND PRIVATE EMPLOYMENT, CALIFORNIA. /FEP
   EMPLOYMENT-CONDITIONS DISCRIMINATION/   WBELAJX66634

   STATEMENT. PUBLIC HEARING. WCMEN IN PUBLIC AND PRIVATE EMPLOYMENT, CALIFORNIA. /FEP
   EMPLOYMENT-CONDITIONS DISCRIMINATION/   WBENNSJ66637

   TESTIMONY. PUBLIC HEARING, WOMEN IN PUBLIC AND PRIVATE EDUCATION, CALIFORNIA. /FEP
   EMPLOYMENT-CONDITIONS DISCRIMINATION MIGRANT-WORKERS/   WBLOCHX66649

   TESTIMCNY PRESENTED AT PUBLIC HEARING, MARCH 31 -- APRIL 1, 1966. /FEP EMPLOYMENT-CONDITIONS
   DISCRIMINATION MIGRANTS/   WCALACW62675

   TESTIMCNY PRESENTED AT PUBLIC HEARING, APRIL 28, 1966. SAN-FRANCISCO, CALIFORNIA. /FEP
   EMPLOYMENT-CONDITIONS DISCRIMINATION MIGRANTS/   WCALACW62676

   TESTIMCNY PRESENTED AT PUBLIC HEARING, FEBRUARY 24-25, 1966. /FEP EMPLOYMENT-CONDITIONS DISCRIMINATION
   MIGRANTS/   WCALACW66674

   TESTIMCNY PRESENTED AT PUBLIC HEARING, APRIL 29, 1966. SAN-FRANCISCO, CALIFORNIA. /FEP
   EMPLOYMENT-CONDITIONS CHILDREN/   WCALACW66677

   REPORT OF THE CALIFORNIA ADVISORY COMMISSION ON THE STATUS OF WOMEN. /FEP EMPLOYMENT-CONDITIONS
   DISCRIMINATION MIGRANTS/   WCALACW67673

   TESTIMCNY. PUBLIC HEARING, WCMEN IN PUBLIC AND PRIVATE EMPLOYMENT, CALIFORNIA. /FEP
   EMPLOYMENT-CONDITIONS DISCRIMINATION MIGRANTS/   WCLIFFG66692

   TESTIMCNY. PUBLIC HEARING, WCMEN IN PUBLIC AND PRIVATE EMPLOYMENT, CALIFORNIA. /FEP MIGRANT-WORKERS
   EMPLOYMENT-CONDITIONS/   WLLOYMX66940

   TESTIMCNY. PUBLIC HEARING, WOMEN IN PUBLIC AND PRIVATE EMPLOYMENT, CALIFORNIA. /FEP EMPLOYMENT
   CCNDITIONS/   WLOWEDX66943

   STATEMENT. PUBLIC HEARING, WCMEN IN PUBLIC AND PRIVATE EMPLOYMENT, CALIFORNIA. /FEP
   EMPLOYMENT-CONDITIONS MIGRANT-WORKERS/   WMILLJJ66979

   TESTIMCNY. PUBLIC HEARING, WCMEN IN PUBLIC AND PRIVATE EMPLOYMENT, CALIFORNIA. /FEP
   EMPLOYMENT-CONDITIONS MIGRANT-WORKERS/   WPEEVMX66052

   TESTIMCNY. PUBLIC HEARING, WCMEN IN PUBLIC AND PRIVATE EMPLOYMENT, CALIFORNIA. /FEP
   EMPLOYMENT-CONDITIONS/   WSCHRPX66104

   TESTIMCNY. PUBLIC HEARING, WCMEN IN PUBLIC AND PRIVATE EMPLOYMENT, CALIFORNIA. /FEP
   EMPLOYMENT-CONDITIONS DISCRIMINATION/   WSMITWH66123

   TESTIMCNY. PUBLIC HEARING, WOMEN IN PUBLIC AND PRIVATE EMPLOYMENT, CALIFORNIA. /FEP
   EMPLOYMENT-CONDITIONS DISCRIMINATION MIGRANT-WORKERS/   WSPENNX66129

   STATEMENT. PUBLIC HEARING, WCMEN IN PUBLIC AND PRIVATE EMPLOYMENT, CALIFORNIA. /FEP
   EMPLOYMENT-CONDITIONS DISCRIMINATION/   WVAILLX66256

   TESTIMCNY. PUBLIC HEARING, WCMEN IN PUBLIC AND PRIVATE EMPLOYMENT, CALIFORNIA. /FEP
   EMPLCYMENT-CONDITIONS MIGRANT-WORKERS/   WWOMEIX66273

FEPC
   FEPC. AN ADMINISTRATIVE STUDY OF SELECTED STATE AND LOCAL PROGRAMS.   GALFOAL54869

   REPORTS ON THE WCRK OF THE FEPC IN NEW-JERSEY AND NEW-YORK.   GAMERCR46372

   AFTER FEPC -- WHAT.   GBECKWL62431

   THE PRESENT STATUS AND PROGRAMS OF FEPC. FEDERAL, STATE, AND MUNICIPAL.   GBRAZBR51472

   EMPLOYMENT DISCRIMINATION. STATE FEPC LAWS AND THE IMPACT OF OF TITLE-VII OF THE CIVIL-RIGHTS-ACT OF
   1964.   GBRYEGL65896

   FUNCTICNS AND RESPONSIBILITIES OF FEPC. /CALIFORNIA/   GCALDIR63526

   FAIR-EMPLOYMENT-PRACTICE ACT...FEPC RULES AND REGULATIONS... GUIDE TO PRE-EMPLOYMENT INQUIRIES.
   /CALIFORNIA/   GCALFEP61533

   BANK OF AMERICA EMPLOYMENT PRACTICES. FIRST REPORT BY CALIFORNIA FEPC.   GCALFEP64530

   AFFIRMATIVE-ACTIONS IN EMPLOYMENT. A SPECIAL FEPC REPORT. /CALIFORNIA/   GCALFEP65529

   ACTICN PROGRAMS FOR FEPC ADVISORY COMMITTEES. /CALIFORNIA/   GCALFEP66528

   POLICIES AND PRACTICES OF DISCRIMINATION COMMISSIONS. /FEPC/   GCARTEA56559

   OUTLOOK REGARDING STATE FEPC LEGISLATION.   GCOBBCW46578

   THE PEOPLE VS. DISCRIMINATION. THE FEPC FIGHT INITIATES A NEW EPOCH.   GCOHEFS46579

   STCRM CENTER OF THE FIGHT -- FEPC.   GCONGDX50597

   FEPC -- HINDSIGHT AND FORESIGHT.   GFEILJG64676

   REPORT OF INDUSTRY AND LABOR-MANAGEMENT CLINICS. IMPLEMENTATION OF EMPLOYMENT IN MERIT PROGRAMS IN NON
   FEPC STATES BY DIRECT APPROACH TO TOP MANAGEMENT.   GFISKUR51684

   FEPC. NEW-YORK VERSION.   GFORTXX50696

   FEPC -- HOW IT WORKS IN SEVEN STATES.   GFURNJC52706

   FEPC LEGISLATION IN THE UNITED STATES, FEDERAL, STATE, MUNICIPAL.   GGRAVWB51735

   JOB CPPORTUNITIES FROM FEPC ACTION.   GHOWDEX65785

   NLRB -- FEPC.   GJEFFAX63822

   THE FOES OF THE FEPC.   GJOHNGW50825

   THE SOCIAL POLITICS OF FEPC. A STUDY IN REFORM PRESSURE MOVEMENTS.   GKESSLC48847

   A REVIEW OF STATE FEPC LAWS.   GKOVAIX58860

FEPC   (CONTINUATION)
COMMCN CARRIERS ANC THE STATE FEPC.   GKOVAIX63025

FEPC. REPORT ON OPERATIONS.   GLABOLR45870

OPERATION UNDER STATE FEPC LAWS.   GLABOLR45873

PRINCIPLES ESTABLISHED BY THE FEPC.   GLABCLR45874

RAILROADS BEFORE THE FEPC.   GLAWYGR45887

SOLVING AN AMERICAN DILEMMA. THE ROLE OF THE FEPC OFFICIAL, A COMPARATIVE STUDY OF STATE CIVIL-RIGHTS
COMMISSIONS.   GLLOYKM64317

FEPC RALLY.   GMARTRG46947

FEPC -- A CASE HISTORY IN PARLIAMENTARY MANEUVER.   GMASLWX46959

FOUR YEARS ON THE JOB IN MICHIGAN. /FEPC/   GMICFEP60980

FEPC IN ILLINOIS. FOUR STORMY YEARS.   GMINSJX65012

AN ANALYSIS OF STATE FEPC LEGISLATION.   GMORGCA57031

FEPC REFERENCE MANUAL.   GNATLCJ48040

DIGEST OF FINDINGS FROM A WORKING CONFERENCE OF LOCAL COUNCILS. /FEPC/   GNATLCS45045

FEPC. HOW TO ANSWER ITS CRITICS.   GRABKSX58213

FEPC IN THE STATES. A PROGRESS REPORT.   GRORTJX58246

THE OUTLOOK FOR A NEW FEPC. THE 80TH CONGRESS AND JOB DISCRIMINATION.   GROSSMX47261

ALL MANNER OF MEN. /FEPC/   GROSSMX48260

RACE, JOBS, AND POLITICS. THE STORY OF FEPC.   GRUCHLX53266

FREEDOM TO WORK. /FEPC LEGISLATION/   GSMITSX55320

THE CALIFORNIA FEPC. STEPCHILD OF THE STATE AGENCIES.   GSTANLR65333

MUNICIPAL FEPC IN MINNEAPOLIS. /MINNESOTA/   GSURVXX47341

CALIFORNIA FEPC.   GTOBRMC65360

FEPC -- SOME PRACTICAL CONSIDERATIONS.   GTOWEJX64362

PROGRESS TOWARD INTEGRATION. FOUR CASE-STUDIES. /EMPLOYMENT FEPC NEW-YORK/   NBACKSX59040

SEGREGATION DEAL. NEW-ORLEANS REGION FEPC PERMITS COMPROMISE. /LOUISIANA/   NBUSIWX45161

A CHRONICLE OF RACE-RELATIONS, FEPC.   NDUBOWE43297

WHEN NEGROES MARCH. THE MARCH-ON-WASHINGTON-MOVEMENT IN THE ORGANIZATIONAL POLITICS FOR FEPC.   NGARFHX59396

TESTIMCNY BEFORE STATE SENATE FACT FINDING SUBCOMMITTEE ON RACE-RELATIONS AND URBAN PROBLEMS, FINAL
HEARING, JANUARY 20 1965. /CALIFORNIA FEPC/   NGRAHCX65439

EDITORIAL COMMENT. FEPC HEARINGS REDUCE RACE PROBLEM TO LOWEST TERMS -- EQUAL-ECONOMIC-OPPORTUNITY.   NTHOMCH43160

TESTIMCNY. PUBLIC HEARING, WOMEN IN PUBLIC AND PRIVATE EMPLOYMENT, CALIFORNIA. /FEPC/   WSTERAX66140

FEPC-S
A LOOK AT THE FEPC-S AFFIRMATIVE-ACTION PROGRAM.   GYABRSX65588

FIELD
DISCRIMINATION IN THE FIELD OF EMPLOYMENT AND OCCUPATION.   GINTELC58817

FIELD MANUAL ON EQUAL-EMPLOYMENT-OPPORTUNITY UNDER GOVERNMENT CONTRACTS.   GPRESCD65107

RELOCATEES FROM GALLUP AREA TO THE DENVER FIELD EMPLOYMENT ASSISTANCE OFFICE. /COLORADO/   IGRAVTDND438

NEGROES. VOCATIONAL GUIDANCE AND COUNSELING IN THE SOUTHERN FIELD.   NEDWAGL47325

PROBLEMS AND OPPORTUNITIES CONFRONTING NEGROES IN THE FIELD OF BUSINESS, REPORT ON THE NATIONAL
CONFERENCE ON SMALL BUSINESS. /OCCUPATIONS/   NFITZNH63358

RACE RELATIONSHIP IN THE POCAHONTAS COAL FIELD.   NMINARD52794

FIELDS
OPINION CONCERNING THE SCOPE AND AUTHORITY OF THE JURISDICTION THAT MAY BE GRANTED TO CITY OR COUNTY
HUMAN-RELATIONS-COMMISSIONS IN THE FIELDS OF EMPLOYMENT AND HOUSING. /CALIFORNIA/   GCALAGO63512

STRANGERS IN OUR FIELDS. /MIGRANT-WORKERS/   MGALAEX56400

REPORT OF THE EXPLORATORY STATISTICAL SURVEY OF THE EDUCATIONAL-ATTAINMENT, NUMBER, AND AVAILABILITY OF
THE MEMBERSHIP OF THE AMERICAN ASSOCIATION OF UNIVERSITY WOMEN FOR TEACHING IN THE FIELDS OF SCIENCE AND
MATHEMATICS. /OCCUPATIONS/   WOOLAEF57735

FIGHT
THE PEOPLE VS. DISCRIMINATION. THE FEPC FIGHT INITIATES A NEW EPOCH.   GCOHEFS46579

STORM CENTER OF THE FIGHT -- FEPC.   GCONGDX50597

HOW WELL DOES TV FIGHT PREJUDICE.   GTUCKJN56363

THE CIVIL-RIGHTS FIGHT. A LOOK AT THE LEGISLATIVE RECORD.   NAFLCIO60005

LEFT SECTARIANISM IN THE FIGHT FOR NEGRO RIGHTS AND AGAINST WHITE CHAUVINISM.   NFOSTWZ53375

THE FIGHT FOR EQUAL-OPPORTUNITY.   NMANGMX63736

THE MAYOR AND THE FIRE CHIEF. THE FIGHT OVER INTEGRATING THE LOS-ANGELES FIRE DEPARTMENT. /CALIFORNIA
CASE-STUDY/   NSHERFP59130

FIGHTING
FIGHTING POVERTY. THE VIEW FROM WATTS. /LOS-ANGELES CALIFORNIA/   NBULLPX66135

FIGHTS
THE AFL FIGHTS BIGOTRY. /UNION/   GJEWILCND824

UNION FIGHTS DISCRIMINATION.   NBUSIWX51164

SOUTHERN LABOR FIGHTS BACK. /UNION/   NGOOGGX48434

THE UAW FIGHTS RACE PREJUDICE. /UNION/   NHOWEIX49581

FILIPINO
CALIFORNIANS OF JAPANESE, CHINESE, FILIPINO ANCESTRY.   OCALDIR65709

FILIPINOS
NONWHITE POPULATION BY RACE. NEGROES, INDIANS, JAPANESE, CHINESE, FILIPINOS. BY AGE, SEX, MARITAL-STATUS,
EDUCATION, EMPLOYMENT-STATUS, OCCUPATIONAL-STATUS, INCOME, ETC. /DEMOGRAPHY/   CUSBURC53378

NONWHITE POPULATION BY RACE. NEGROES, INDIANS, JAPANESE, CHINESE, FILIPINOS. BY AGE, SEX,
MARITAL-STATUS, EDUCATION, EMPLOYMENT-STATUS, OCCUPATIONAL-STATUS, INCOME, ETC. /DEMOGRAPHY/   CUSBURC63176

SOCIAL ORIGINS AND CAREER PREPARATION AMONG FILIPINOS IN AMERICAN UNIVERSITIES.   OBELTAG61703

FINANCIAL
PATTERNS OF DISCRIMINATION IN THE FINANCIAL INSTITUTIONS OF THE DISTRICT-OF-COLUMBIA. THE BANKING,
SAVINGS AND LOAN, AND INSURANCE INDUSTRIES.   GDISTCC66642

FINDINGS
THEORY, METHOD AND FINDINGS IN THE STUDY OF ACCULTURATION. A REVIEW. /MEXICAN-AMERICAN NEGRO/   CPETECX65989

MANPOWER IMPLICATIONS OF TECHNOLOGICAL-CHANGE. RESEARCH FINDINGS OF THE US DEPARTMENT OF LABOR.   GBRANSX63876

REPORT OF FINDINGS AND RECOMMENDATIONS RESULTING FROM AN ANALYSIS OF THE EMPLOYMENT PRACTICES IN THE
VARIOUS DEPARTMENTS OF THE CITY OF LOS-ANGELES. /CALIFORNIA/   GLOSAOC63917

DIGEST OF FINDINGS FROM A WORKING CONFERENCE OF LOCAL COUNCILS. /FEPC/   GNATLCS45045

FINDINGS OF FACT, CONCLUSIONS AND ACTION OF THE COMMISSION ON HUMAN-RELATIONS IN RE. INVESTIGATIVE PUBLIC
HEARINGS INTO ALLEGED DISCRIMINATORY PRACTICE BY THE HOTEL AND RESTAURANT INDUSTRY IN PHILADELPHIA.
/PENNSYLVANIA/   GPHILCH61176

AMERICAN INDIAN CAPITAL CONFERENCE ON POVERTY. MAY 9-12, 1964. FINDINGS.   IAMERIN64087

WHEN THE MIGRANT LABORER SETTLES DOWN -- A REPORT OF THE FINDINGS OF A PROJECT ON VALUE ASSIMILATION OF
IMMIGRANT LABORERS.   MPETECL64454

RACIAL INTEGRATION IN EMPLOYMENT -- FINDINGS IN TWO KANSAS-CITY HOSPITALS.   NGIBSHX54402

WOMEN-S EDUCATION. FACTS, FINDINGS, AND APPARENT TRENDS.   WNEWCMX64028

WOMEN-S WORK. FACTS, FINDINGS, AND APPARENT TRENDS.   WZAPOMW64283

FIRED
LAST HIRED -- FIRST FIRED. /DISCRIMINATION/   GABRACX58361

LAST HIRED. FIRST FIRED. THOUGH NEGRO WORKERS HAVE MADE IMPRESSIVE GAINS THEY MIGHT BE FIRST TO FEEL THE
BITE OF RECESSION.   NNORTHR49940

FIRM
THE JEWISH LAW STUDENT AND NEW-YORK JOBS -- DISCRIMINATORY EFFECTS IN LAW FIRM HIRING PRACTICES.
/OCCUPATIONS/   JYALELJ64774

FIRMS
A STUDY OF MERIT EMPLOYMENT IN 100 ILLINOIS FIRMS.   GILLICH56794

ANALYSIS OF THE TECHNIQUES OF RACIAL INTEGRATION IN THREE MANUFACTURING FIRMS. /INDUSTRY/   NCAMPFX54178

EMPLOYMENT SURVEY OF DES-MOINES FIRMS. /IOWA/   NDESMCH65265

NEW HOPE FOR RURAL DIXIE. FIRMS IN CAROLINAS CREATE JOBS FOR NEGROES.   NEBONXX64317

NEGROES IN THE WORK GROUP. HOW 33 BUSINESS AND INDUSTRIAL FIRMS OFFERED EQUAL-EMPLOYMENT-OPPORTUNITIES TO
ALL.   NSEIDJX50114

SALARIED WOMEN IN UPPER LEVEL POSITIONS IN KANSAS BUSINESS FIRMS.   WSTOCFT59143

FISCAL
STATISTICS CONCERNING INDIAN EDUCATION, FISCAL YEAR 1956.   IUSDINT56661

GRANTS AND PROJECTS RELATED TO THE DEVELOPMENT OF THE AMERICAN NEGRO. ALL FISCAL YEARS THROUGH JUNE 10,
1966.   NFORDFX66133

FLORIDA
INCOME, EDUCATION AND UNEMPLOYMENT IN NEIGHBORHOODS. TAMPA, ST-PETERSBURG FLORIDA. /DEMOGRAPHY/   CUSDLAB63486

RESOURCE CHARACTERISTICS AND UTILIZATION AND LEVEL OF LIVING ITEMS, RURAL HOUSEHOLDS, NORTH AND WEST
FLORIDA, 1956.   GREUSLA60391

INCOME, RESOURCES, AND ADJUSTMENT POTENTIALS AMONG RURAL FAMILIES IN NORTH AND WEST FLORIDA.   GREUSLA62388

THE IMMOKALEE STORY. /MIGRANT-WORKERS FLORIDA/   GSOWDWT58327

A MIGRANT LABOR CRISIS IN IMMOKALEE. /FLORIDA/   GSOWDWT59328

REPORT ON FLORIDA OF THE US COMMISSION ON CIVIL-RIGHTS.   GUSCOMC63409

REPORTS ON APPRENTICESHIP, NINE STATE ADVISORY COMMITTEES. /CALIFORNIA FLORIDA MARYLAND CONNECTICUT
WASHINGTON-DC NEW-JERSEY NEW-YORK TENNESSEE WISCONSIN/   GUSCOMC64407

THE PRESENT STATUS OF THE FLORIDA SEMINOLE INDIANS.   IPEITIM59284

THE EDUCATIONAL OUTLOOK FOR NONWHITES IN FLORIDA.   NABRAAA66141

A STUDY OF JOB-OPPORTUNITIES IN THE STATE OF FLORIDA FOR NEGRO COLLEGE GRADUATES.   NDECKPM60261

THE STRUGGLE OF NEGRO TEACHERS IN FLORIDA FOR EQUAL SALARIES. /OCCUPATIONS/   NFERGML49961

NEGRO EMPLOYMENT IN MIAMI. /FLORIDA/   NFLORCC62366

JACKSONVILLE LOOKS AT ITS NEGRO COMMUNITY. /FLORIDA/   NJACKCC46598

FLORIDA   (CONTINUATION)
EXPERIMENTAL AND DEMONSTRATION MANPOWER PROJECT FOR THE RECRUITMENT, TRAINING, PLACEMENT AND FOLLOW-UP OF
RURAL UNEMPLOYED WORKERS IN TEN NORTH FLORIDA CITIES. FINAL REPORT. /PARTICIPANTS/   NJACKTA66597

THE DISAPPEARING NEGRO FARMER OF FLORIDA, 1920-1950.   NSMITCU56364

AFTER HIGH SCHOOL WHAT...HIGHLIGHTS OF A STUDY OF CAREER PLANS OF NEGRO AND WHITE RURAL YOUTH IN THREE
FLORIDA COUNTIES. /ASPIRATIONS/   NYOUMEG65390

FINAL REPORT. EXPERIMENTAL AND DEMONSTRATION MANPOWER PROJECT FOR THE RECRUITMENT, TRAINING, PLACEMENT
AND FOLLOW-UP OF RURAL UNEMPLOYED WORKERS IN TEN NORTH FLORIDA COUNTIES.   WFLORMP66326

FOLK
CONTRASTS BETWEEN SPANISH FOLK AND ANGLO URBAN CULTURAL VALUES. /EDUCATION ASPIRATIONS/   MVALDBX64449

FOLKWAYS
FACTORY FOLKWAYS. A STUDY OF INSTITUTIONAL STRUCTURE AND CHANGE.   NELLSJS52331

FOLLOW-UP
THE TRAINING OF MIGRANT FARM WORKERS. A FOLLOW-UP STUDY OF TWO EXPERIMENTAL AND DEMONSTRATION PROGRAMS
UNDER THE MANPOWER-DEVELOPMENT-AND-TRAINING-ACT. /MEXICAN-AMERICAN AMERICAN-INDIAN/   CUNIVOD66054

THE MUTUAL SAVINGS BANKS OF NEW-YORK-CITY. A FOLLOW-UP REPORT ON THE EXCLUSION OF JEWS AT TOP-MANAGEMENT
AND POLICY-MAKING LEVELS.   JAMERJC66695

EXPERIMENTAL AND DEMONSTRATION MANPOWER PROJECT FOR THE RECRUITMENT, TRAINING, PLACEMENT AND FOLLOW-UP OF
RURAL UNEMPLOYED WORKERS IN TEN NORTH FLORIDA CITIES. FINAL REPORT. /PARTICIPANTS/   NJACKTA66597

VOCATIONAL GRADUATES IN AUTO MECHANICS. A FOLLOW-UP STUDY OF NEGRO AND WHITE YOUTH. /OCCUPATIONS/   NLEVEBX66036

A FOLLOW-UP STUDY OF NON-WHITE EMPLOYMENT IN THE STATE SERVICE. /MICHIGAN/   NMICCSC65774

FINAL REPORT. EXPERIMENTAL AND DEMONSTRATION MANPOWER PROJECT FOR THE RECRUITMENT, TRAINING, PLACEMENT
AND FOLLOW-UP OF RURAL UNEMPLOYED WORKERS IN TEN NORTH FLORIDA COUNTIES.   WFLORMP66326

FOLLOWUP
A FOLLOWUP STUDY OF 1963 RECIPIENTS OF THE SERVICES OF THE EMPLOYMENT ASSISTANCE PROGRAM,
BUREAU-OF-INDIAN-AFFAIRS.   IUSDINT66650

WORK MOTIVATION OF COLLEGE ALUMNAE. FIVE-YEAR FOLLOWUP.   WEYDELD67223

FOOD
EFFECT OF MECHANIZATION ON EMPLOYMENT OF MIGRATORY LABOR IN AGRICULTURE AND FOOD PROCESSING.
/MIGRANT-WORKERS/   GDELASE59946

FORCE
PROJECTIONS TO 1975. THE GROWTH AND STRUCTURE OF THE LABOR FORCE.   GBAKESS65702

THE HIRED FARM WORKING FORCE OF 1963 WITH SUPPLEMENTARY DATA FOR 1962. /ECONOMIC-STATUS/   GBOWLGK65432

THE HIRED FARM WORKING FORCE OF 1958. /ECONOMIC-STATUS/   GCOWHJD59430

AN ANALYSIS OF THE EXPERIENCED HIRED FARM WORKING FORCE, 1948-1957. /SKILLS/   GCOWHJD60423

EDUCATION, SKILL LEVEL, AND EARNINGS OF THE HIRED FARM WORKING FORCE OF 1961.   GCOWHJD63420

THE HIRED FARM WORKING FORCE OF 1960. /ECONOMIC-STATUS/   GFRIERE62431

EDUCATIONAL-ATTAINMENT OF THE WORK FORCE.   GHAMMHR66145

THE POOR IN THE WORK FORCE. /LABOR-FORCE/   GLEVISA66038

THE HIRED FARM WORKING FORCE OF 1956. /ECONOMIC-STATUS/   GMAITST58428

THE HIRED FARM WORKING FORCE OF 1957. /ECONOMIC-STATUS/   GMAITST59429

THE HIRED FARM WORKING FORCE OF 1958.   GMAITST61384

CHARACTERISTICS OF FARM WORKERS AS RELATED TO STABILIZATION OF THE WORK FORCE. /MIGRANT-WORKERS/   GMETZWH62504

HUMAN RESOURCES IN THE URBAN ECONOMY. PART II -- THE LABOR FORCE PERFORMANCE OF MINORITY-GROUPS.   GPERLMX63169

THE HIRED FARM WORKING FORCE OF 1964. A STATISTICAL REPORT.   GUSDAGR65424

TASK FORCE FOR EQUAL-OPPORTUNITY IN BUSINESS.   GUSDCOM65432

THE SKILLED WORK FORCE OF THE UNITED STATES.   GUSDLAB55498

EMPLOYMENT SERVICE TASK FORCE REPORT. /MANPOWER SES/   GUSDLAB66559

REPORT TO THE SECRETARY OF THE INTERIOR BY THE TASK FORCE ON INDIAN AFFAIRS.   IUSDINT61641

AN ANALYSIS OF THE MEXICAN-AMERICAN MIGRANT LABOR FORCE IN THE STOCKBRIDGE AREA. /MICHIGAN/   MRODRFX66464

THE NEGRO-S FORCE IN MARKETPLACE. /EMPLOYMENT/   NBUSIWX62156

A PILOT STUDY OF AN INTEGRATED WORK FORCE.   NCOUSFR58611

INTEGRATING THE WORK FORCE.   NINDURP66593

REPORT AND SUMMARY OF THE AIR FORCE ON ACTIONS TAKEN BY LOCKHEED AIRCRAFT CORPORATION AT THE AIR FORCE
PLANT NO 6 IN MARIETTA, GEORGIA. /INDUSTRY/   NPRESCD61013

REPORT AND SUMMARY OF THE AIR FORCE ON ACTIONS TAKEN BY LOCKHEED AIRCRAFT CORPORATION AT THE AIR FORCE
PLANT NO 6 IN MARIETTA, GEORGIA. /INDUSTRY/   NPRESCD61013

GOVERNOR-S CIVIL-RIGHTS TASK FORCE. REPORT. /RHODE-ISLAND/   NRHODIC64051

NEXT IT-S A MIXED POLICE FORCE. INTEGRATIONISTS LATEST GOAL IN NATION-S CAPITAL. /WASHINGTON-DC/   NUSNEWR57274

NEGROES ON THE SALES FORCE. THE QUIET INTEGRATION.   NVOGLAJ64286

FORCED
FORCED HIRING OF NEGROES.   NUSNEWR63207

FORCES
LABOR-S TASK FORCES. /UNION/   GSLAIDX64318

PROBLEMS AND APPROACHES IN INTEGRATING MINORITY-GROUP WORK FORCES.   GSPERBJ53330

FORCES   (CONTINUATION)
ECONOMIC FORCES SERVING THE ENDS OF THE NEGRO PROTEST. /UNEMPLOYMENT/   NBATCAB65059

RACIAL INTEGRATION IN THE ARMED FORCES. /MILITARY/   NMOSKCC66855

INTEGRATION AND THE NEGRO OFFICER IN THE ARMED FORCES OF THE UNITED STATES OF AMERICA. /MILITARY/   NUSODEF62240

SEGREGATION IN THE ARMED FORCES. /MILITARY/   NUSDLAB44151

THE NEGRO IN THE ARMED FORCES. /MILITARY/   NWEILFD47309

MISSISSIPPI WORKERS. WHERE THEY COME FROM AND HOW THEY PERFORM. A STUDY OF WORKING FORCES IN SELECTED
MISSISSIPPI INDUSTRIAL PLANTS.   NWOFFBM55333

FORD
RUTGERS -- THE STATE UNIVERSITY. FORD FOUNDATION PROGRAM FOR THE RETRAINING IN MATHEMATICS OF COLLEGE
GRADUATE WOMEN. /TRAINING/   WMARTHM63957

FORECASTS
EVALUATION OF STATE FAIR-EMPLOYMENT-PRACTICES-COMMISSIONS. EXPERIENCES AND FORECASTS.   GAMERCR49371

FOREIGN
SOME CHARACTERISTICS OF SPANISH-NAME TEXANS AND FOREIGN LATIN-AMERICANS IN TEXAS HIGHER EDUCATION.   MRENNRR57462

FORMAL
FORMAL OCCUPATIONAL TRAINING OF ADULT WORKERS. ITS EXTENT, NATURE, AND USE.   GBEDEMX64448

FORMAL EDUCATION IN AN AMERICAN-INDIAN COMMUNITY.   IWAXXML64683

FORMS
QUESTIONING APPLICANTS FOR EMPLOYMENT. A GUIDE FOR APPLICATION FORMS AND INTERVIEWS UNDER THE HAWAII
FAIR-EMPLOYMENT-PRACTICES ACT.   GHAWADL64767

THE DESIGNATION OF RACE OR COLOR ON FORMS.   NMINCAX66795

FORT-BELKNAP
POPULATION CHARACTERISTICS, LIVING CONDITIONS AND INCOMES OF INDIAN FAMILIES, FORT-BELKNAP RESERVATION. IUSDINT63658

FORT-HALL
HUMAN RESOURCES, RELATIONS AND PROBLEMS ON THE FORT-HALL INDIAN RESERVATION.   IHARMHC61572

ECONOMY AND CONDITIONS OF THE FORT-HALL INDIAN RESERVATION.   INYBRNX64603

FORT-PECK
POPULATION CHARACTERISTICS, LIVING CONDITIONS, AND INCOME OF INDIAN FAMILIES, FORT-PECK RESERVATION,
1951-1961.   IUSDINT63657

FORTUNE
FORTUNE PRESS ANALYSIS. NEGROES. /EMPLOYMENT/   NFORTUN45052

FORUMS
RACIAL DISCRIMINATION ON THE JOBSITE. COMPETING THEORIES AND COMPETING FORUMS.   NMEYEBI65210

FOUNDATION
FOUNDATION FOR THE GREAT SOCIETY. /EEO/   GROOSFD66242

RUTGERS -- THE STATE UNIVERSITY. FORD FOUNDATION PROGRAM FOR THE RETRAINING IN MATHEMATICS OF COLLEGE
GRADUATE WOMEN. /TRAINING/   WMARTHM63957

FOUNDATIONS
THE FOUNDATIONS OF THE WAR-ON-POVERTY.   GGALLLE65932

NEGRO COLLEGES. LONG IGNORED. SOUTHERN SCHOOLS NOW COURTED BY MAJOR UNIVERSITIES AND FOUNDATIONS.   NLANGEX64304

FOUNDATIONS OF RACISM IN AMERICAN LIFE.   NODELJH64953

FOX
DOCUMENTARY HISTORY OF THE FOX PROJECT, 1948-1959. A PROGRAM IN ACTION ANTHROPOLOGY.   INETTRM60599

THE FOX PROJECT. /ECONOMY/   ITAXXSX58157

FAIR EMPLOYMENT IS GOOD BUSINESS AT G FOX OF HARTFORD. /CASE-STUDY CONNECTICUT/   NGREEMX48448

FRANCHISE
FRANCHISE COMPANY DATA FOR EQUAL-OPPORTUNITY IN BUSINESS.   GUSDCOM66431

FREEDOM
ANTIDISCRIMINATION LEGISLATION AS AN INFRINGEMENT OF FREEDOM OF CHOICE.   GAVINAX60409

FREEDOM OF CHOICE IN PERSONAL SERVICE OCCUPATIONS. 13TH AMENDMENT LIMITATIONS ON ANTIDISCRIMINATION
LEGISLATION.   GAVINAX64410

FREEDOM TO WORK. /FEPC LEGISLATION/   GSMITSX55320

FREEDOM TO THE FREE. CENTURY OF EMANCIPATION, 1863-1963.   GUSCOMC63398

FREEDOM TO SERVE. /MILITARY/   NPRESCE50015

ASSURING FREEDOM TO THE FREE. A CENTURY OF EMANCIPATION IN THE USA.   NROSEAM64290

FRENCH
THE FRENCH AND THE NON-FRENCH IN LOUISIANA. A STUDY OF THE RELEVANCE OF ETHNIC FACTORS IN RURAL
DEVELOPMENT. /ECONOMIC-STATUS/   NBERTAL65394

FRESHMAN
HIGH SCHOOL FRESHMAN AND SENIORS VIEW THE ROLE OF WOMEN IN MODERN SOCIETY. /WORK-FAMILY-CONFLICT/   WKERNKK65892

A QUESTIONNAIRE PORTRAIT OF THE FRESHMAN COED. AFTER COLLEGE WHAT. /ASPIRATIONS/   WLLOYBJ66938

THE RELATIONSHIP OF SELECTED VARIABLES TO CAREER-MARRIAGE PLANS OF UNIVERSITY FRESHMAN WOMEN.
/WORK-FAMILY-CONFLICT/   WZISSCX62284

FRESHMEN
ACHIEVEMENT MOTIVATION CHARACTERISTICS OF NEGRO COLLEGE FRESHMEN.   NHARREC59492

FRESHMEN INTERVIEW WORKING WIVES.   WMAYXEE59964

A STUDY OF THE LIFE PLANNING OF 550 FRESHMEN WOMEN AT PURDUE UNIVERSITY. /WORK-FAMILY-CONFLICT/   WZISSCX64285

FRINGE
  FRINGE BENEFIT PROVISIONS FROM STATE MINIMUM WAGE LAWS AND ORDERS, SEPTEMBER 1, 1966.
  /EMPLOYMENT-CONDITIONS/   WUSDLAB66195

FRONTIER
  NO FRONTIER TO LEARNING. THE MEXICAN STUDENT IN THE UNITED STATES.   MBEALRL57364

FRONTIERS
  RACE-RELATIONS FRONTIERS IN HAWAII.   GLINDAW61744

FRUIT
  CALIFORNIA-S FRUIT AND VEGETABLE CANNING INDUSTRY. AN ECONOMIC STUDY.   OBENJMP61704

FRUITLAND
  FRUITLAND. NEW-MEXICO. A NAVAHO COMMUNITY IN TRANSITION.   ISASATT60615

FRUSTRATION
  FRUSTRATION ON THE FARM. /MEXICAN-AMERICAN ORIENTAL UNION/   GCORTJC57372

  THE HARLEM RIOT. A STUDY IN MASS FRUSTRATION.   NOLANHX43954

FULL
  INSURING FULL EMPLOYMENT.   GPIERJH64846

  THE ROLE OF GOVERNMENT IN PROMOTING FULL EMPLOYMENT.   GROSSAM66084

  A POLICY FOR FULL EMPLOYMENT.   GSOLORX62323

  DISCRIMINATION AND FULL UTILIZATION OF MANPOWER RESOURCES, 1952.   GUSSENA52347

  TOWARDS FULL EMPLOYMENT. PROPOSALS FOR A COMPREHENSIVE EMPLOYMENT AND MANPOWER POLICY IN THE UNITED
  STATES.   GUSSENA64332

  ETHNOMICS -- NEGRO MUST BE FULL PARTICIPANT IN MARKET PLACE.   NBUNKHC65122

  FULL EMPLOYMENT AND THE NEGRO WORKER.   NTOWNWS45162

  FULL PARTNERSHIP FOR WOMEN -- WHAT STILL NEEDS TO BE DONE.   WVITAIX63218

FULL-EMPLOYMENT
  BAY AREA CONFERENCE ON FULL-EMPLOYMENT. /SAN-FRANCISCO CALIFORNIA/   GHIRSFI64776

FULL-TIME
  UNEMPLOYMENT AMONG FULL-TIME AND PART-TIME WORKERS.   GSTEIRL64336

  THE CASE AGAINST FULL-TIME MOTHERHOOD. /EMPLOYMENT/   WROSSAS65092

FULLTIME
  CHILD CARE ARRANGEMENTS OF FULLTIME WORKING MOTHERS. /EMPLOYMENT-CONDITIONS/   WUSDHEW59171

FUNCTION
  SCHOOL ATTENDANCE AND ATTAINMENT. FUNCTION AND DYSFUNCTION OF SCHOOL AND FAMILY SOCIAL SYSTEMS.
  /EMPLOYMENT DROP-OUT/   NBERTAL62882

  MARITAL DISAGREEMENT IN WORKING WIFE MARRIAGES AS A FUNCTION OF HUSBAND-S ATTITUDE TOWARDS WIFE-S
  EMPLOYMENT. /WORK-FAMILY-CONFLICT/   WGIANAX57779

FUNDS
  THE FEDERAL INTEREST IN EMPLOYMENT DISCRIMINATION. HEREIN THE CONSTITUTIONAL SCOPE OF EXECUTIVE POWER TO
  WITHOLD APPROPRIATE FUNDS.   GFERGCC64679

FUTURE
  REPORT ON AND ANALYSIS OF SECOND CENSUS OF CITY EMPLOYEES TO DETERMINE BASES FOR FUTURE PERSONNEL
  DEVELOPMENTS. /DETROIT MICHIGAN/   GDETRCC66639

  ETHNIC AND ECONOMIC MINORITIES. UNION-S FUTURE OR UNRECRUITABLE.   GMARSRX63945

  AUTOMATION IMPLICATIONS FOR THE FUTURE.   GPHILMX62616

  TRAINING NAVAJOES FOR THE FUTURE.   ILINDVX64581

  THE FUTURE OF THE COLOR LINE. /SOUTH/   NBLUMHX65327

  DESEGREGATION AND THE ECONOMIC FUTURE OF THE NEGRO MIDDLE-CLASS.   NBRIMAF65890

  IN SEARCH OF A FUTURE. A STUDY OF CAREER-SEEKING EXPERIENCES OF SELECTED NEGRO HIGH SCHOOL GRADUATES IN
  WASHINGTON-DC WHICH WAS AN EFFORT TO PROVIDE KNOWLEDGE HELPFUL IN SOLVING ONE OF THE MOST CRITICAL
  PROBLEMS FACING URBAN AMERICA TODAY.   NGRIEES63454

  EDUCABILITY AND REHABILITATION. THE FUTURE OF THE WELFARE CLASS.   NHESSRD64523

  THE NEGRO-S FUTURE THROUGH FAIR-EMPLOYMENT-PRACTICES.   NHODGEN62557

  RACIAL DIFFERENCES AND THE FUTURE. /INTELLIGENCE EQUAL-OPPORTUNITY/   NINGLDJ64067

  FUTURE OCCUPATIONAL DIFFERENCES BETWEEN THE RACES. A MARKOV APPROACH.   NLEWISX66693

  NEGRO AMERICAN COLLEGE YOUTH-S OUTLOOK ON THE FUTURE.   NROBES057067

  INSTITUTIONAL GUIDANCE FACES THE FUTURE.   NSCALEE57272

  FOCUS ON THE FUTURE FOR WOMEN. /WORK-WOMEN-ROLE/   WCRONDH56709

  EDUCATION OF WOMEN -- SIGNS FOR THE FUTURE.   WDAVI0D57044

  THE EDUCATION OF WOMEN -- SIGNS FOR THE FUTURE.   WDAVI0D59937

  FANTASY. FACT AND THE FUTURE...A REVIEW OF THE STATUS OF WOMEN AND POSSIBLE IMPLICATIONS FOR WOMEN-S
  EDUCATION AND ROLE IN THE NEXT DECADE.   WFITZLE63963

  FAMILIAL CORRELATES OF ORIENTATION TOWARD FUTURE EMPLOYMENT AMONG COLLEGE WOMEN. /ASPIRATIONS/ WSIEGAX63572

  CORRELATES OF PRESENT AND FUTURE WORK STATUS OF MARRIED WOMEN.   WSOBOMB60125

  TODAY-S BUSINESS WOMAN. HER CHARACTERISTICS, HER NEED FOR FURTHER EDUCATION. HER FUTURE IN MANAGEMENT.
  /OCCUPATIONS/   WTHOMMH63152

  EVERYBODY-S TALKING ABOUT TRAINED WORKERS FOR THE FUTURE.   WUSDLAB63243

FUTURE   (CONTINUATION)
    FUTURE JOBS FOR HIGH SCHOOL GIRLS.   WUSDLAB65196

FUTURES
    NEGRO AND WHITE CHILDREN-S PLANS FOR THEIR FUTURES. /ASPIRATIONS/   NLOTTAJ63487

GAINFUL
    ATTITUDES OF WOMEN REGARDING GAINFUL EMPLOYMENT OF MARRIED WOMEN. /ASPIRATIONS/   WGLENHM59789

    A FUNCTIONAL APPROACH TO THE GAINFUL EMPLOYMENT OF MARRIED WOMEN.   WHACKHM61812

GAINS
    POTENTIAL ECONOMIC GAINS FROM ELIMINATING DISCRIMINATION.   GCOUNEA66204

    GRAPE WORKERS WIN NEW GAINS. /MIGRANT-WORKERS UNION CALIFORNIA/   GROSSLX66557

    RETRAINING. AN EVALUATION OF GAINS AND COSTS.   GSOMEGG65717

    JOBS FOR NEGROES -- THE GAINS, THE PROBLEMS, AND THE NEW HIRING LAW. /TITLE-VII/   NBUSIWX65151

    NEGRO SUBORDINATION AND WHITE GAINS. /INCOME OCCUPATIONAL-STATUS/   NCUTRPX65245

    CHANGES IN THE AMERICAN OCCUPATIONAL-STRUCTURE AND OCCUPATIONAL GAINS OF NEGROES DURING THE 1940-S.   NGLENND62422

    LAST HIRED. FIRST FIRED. THOUGH NEGRO WORKERS HAVE MADE IMPRESSIVE GAINS THEY MIGHT BE FIRST TO FEEL THE
    BITE OF RECESSION.   NNORTHR49940

    EMPLOYMENT GAINS AND THE DETERMINANTS OF THE OCCUPATIONAL DISTRIBUTION OF NEGROES.   NTHURLC67971

GALLUP
    RELOCATEES FROM GALLUP AREA TO THE DENVER FIELD EMPLOYMENT ASSISTANCE OFFICE. /COLORADO/   IGRAVTDND438

GAP
    IS THE INCOME GAP CLOSED. NO.   NMILLHP62781

    THE JOB GAP. /EMPLOYMENT/   NMILLHP66630

    CLOSING THE GAP. /OCCUPATIONS/   WGILBLM65781

GARMENT
    INVESTIGATION OF THE GARMENT INDUSTRY.   GUSHOUR62344

    LIFE AMONG THE GARMENT WORKERS.   PBRAEPX58782

    PUERTO-RICAN INTEGRATION IN A GARMENT UNION LOCAL.   PHELFRB57815

GAS
    TECHNICAL REPORT NUMBER 2. EMPLOYMENT PRACTICES OF SELECTED MISSOURI PUBLIC UTILITIES. NATURAL GAS AND
    ELECTRIC.   GMILLRX66021

GATEKEEPERS
    GATEKEEPERS IN THE PROCESS OF ASSIMILATION.   MKURTNR66270

GENERATION
    THE NEW LOST GENERATION. JOBLESS YOUTH.   GHARRMX64759

    CHIPPEWA ADOLESCENTS. A CHANGING GENERATION.   IMILLFC64590

    THE NEXT GENERATION. /YOUTH/   NMICHDX65770

    DESEGREGATION IN AMERICAN SOCIETY. THE RECORD OF A GENERATION OF CHANGE.   NYINGJM63345

    A COMPARISON OF THE OCCUPATIONS OF THE FIRST AND SECOND GENERATION PUERTO-RICANS IN THE MAINLAND
    LABOR-MARKET. AND HOW THE WORK OF THE NEW-YORK STATE DEPARTMENT OF LABORFFECTS PUERTO-RICANS.   PRAUSCX61846

GENERATIONS
    CHILDREN OF THE GILDED GHETTO. CONFLICT RESOLUTION OF THREE GENERATIONS OF AMERICAN JEWS.
    /OCCUPATIONAL-PATTERNS/   JKRAMJR61736

    THE MEXICAN IN THE NORTHERN URBAN AREA. A COMPARISON OF TWO GENERATIONS.   MGOLDNX59403

GEOGRAPHIC
    GEOGRAPHIC CHANGES IN US EMPLOYMENT FROM 1950 TO 1960.   GMANOSP63855

    GEOGRAPHIC MOBILITY AND EMPLOYMENT STATUS, MARCH 1962-MARCH 1963.   GSABESX64271

    NEGRO-WHITE DIFFERENCES IN GEOGRAPHIC MOBILITY.   NMUELEX66864

    NEGRO-WHITE DIFFERENTIALS IN GEOGRAPHIC MOBILITY. 1964, 1965. /DEMOGRAPHY/   NUSDCOM64194

GEOGRAPHICAL
    WOMEN WORKERS IN 1960. GEOGRAPHICAL DIFFERENCES.   WUSDLAB62241

GEOGRAPHY
    THE PHYSICAL GEOGRAPHY OF THE PALOUSE REGION, WASHINGTON AND IDAHO, AND ITS RELATION TO THE AGRICULTURAL
    ECONOMY.   OSHROCR58762

GEORGIA
    INCOME, EDUCATION AND UNEMPLOYMENT IN NEIGHBORHOODS. ATLANTA, GEORGIA. /DEMOGRAPHY/   CUSDLAB63451

    RESOURCES AND INCOMES OF RURAL FAMILIES IN THE COASTAL PLAIN AREAS OF GEORGIA.   GMCARWC59392

    BILLION-DOLLAR PRIZE SPURS INTEGRATION. /INDUSTRY GEORGIA/   NBUSIWX61145

    CARRYING OUT A PLAN FOR JOB INTEGRATION AND DOING IT -- IN THE HEART OF GEORGIA -- WITHOUT A SINGLE
    UNPLEASANT INCIDENT. THAT-S THE EXPERIENCE OF LOCKHEED AIRCRAFT CORPORATION AT ITS MARIETTA PLANT.
    /INDUSTRY/   NBUSIWX63148

    NEGRO LEADERSHIP IN RURAL GEORGIA COMMUNITIES. OCCUPATIONAL AND SOCIAL ASPECTS.   NEDWAVA42328

    REPORT AND SUMMARY OF THE AIR FORCE ON ACTIONS TAKEN BY LOCKHEED AIRCRAFT CORPORATION AT THE AIR FORCE
    PLANT NO 6 IN MARIETTA, GEORGIA. /INDUSTRY/   NPRESCD61013

    CHARACTERISTICS OF NEGRO EMPLOYMENT IN FEDERAL AGENCIES IN ATLANTA, GEORGIA.   NPRESCP60016

    ANNUAL FAMILY AND OCCUPATIONAL EARNINGS OF RESIDENTS OF TWO NEGRO HOUSING PROJECTS IN ATLANTA 1937-1944.
    /GEORGIA/   NRITTAL45062

    ATLANTA -- THE NEGRO AND EMPLOYMENT OPPORTUNITIES IN THE SOUTH, THE THIRD OF A SERIES OF EMPLOYMENT

GEORGIA (CONTINUATION)
    STUDIES IN SOUTHERN CITIES. /GEORGIA/   NSOUTRC62155

    PLANS-FOR-PROGRESS. ATLANTA SURVEY. /GEORGIA/   NSOUTRC63163

    ATLANTA-S SEGREGATED APPROACH TO INTEGRATED EMPLOYMENT. /GEORGIA/   NTHOMHX62205

    PUBLIC EMPLOYMENT IN SAVANNAH, GEORGIA. EXPERIENCE REPORT 104.   NUSCONM66235

    BRUNSWICK. /GEORGIA/   NWATTPX64293

GHETTO
    THE SPIRIT OF THE GHETTO. STUDIES OF THE JEWISH QUARTER OF NEW-YORK.   JHAPGHX65989

    CHILDREN OF THE GILDED GHETTO. CONFLICT RESOLUTION OF THREE GENERATIONS OF AMERICAN JEWS.
    /OCCUPATIONAL-PATTERNS/   JKRAMJR61736

    POVERTY IN THE GHETTO.   NBULLPX65138

    CARK GHETTO. DILEMMAS OF SOCIAL POWER.   NCLARKB65211

    YOUTH IN THE GHETTO. A STUDY OF THE CONSEQUENCES OF POWERLESSNESS AND A BLUEPRINT FOR CHANGE. /NEW-YORK/ NHARLYO64485

    PLANNING THE END OF THE AMERICAN GHETTO. A PROGRAM OF ECONOMIC DEVELOPMENT FOR EQUAL-RIGHTS.   NHILLHX66538

    THE EFFECT OF THE GHETTO ON THE DISTRIBUTION AND LEVEL OF NONWHITE EMPLOYMENT IN URBAN AREAS.   NKAINJF64631

    THE BIG CITIES BIG PROBLEM. /GHETTO EMPLOYMENT/   NKAINJF66630

    STATEMENT AND TESTIMONY ON FEDERAL ROLE IN URBAN AFFAIRS. /EMPLOYMENT GHETTO/   NKENNRF66017

    FROM PLANTATION TO GHETTO. AN INTERPRETIVE HISTORY OF AMERICAN NEGROES.   NMEIEAX66765

    THE NEGRO GHETTO. PROBLEMS AND ALTERNATIVES.   NMORRRL65852

    MAN IN METROPOLIS. /RESIDENTIAL-SEGREGATION GHETTO/   NSCHILB65106

    CIVIL-RIGHTS AND THE NORTHERN GHETTO.   NSTUDOT64188

    THE VOICE OF THE GHETTO. A REPORT ON TWO BOSTON NEIGHBORHOOD MEETINGS. /MASSACHUSETTS/   NUSCOMC67149

    THE NEGRO GHETTO.   NWEAVRC48303

GHETTOS
    DEMOGRAPHIC CHANGE AND RACIAL GHETTOS. THE CRISIS OF AMERICAN CITIES.   GHILLHX66691

    THE AMERICAN INDIAN. GHETTOS IN THE DESERT.   ISTEISX64373

    RIOTS. GHETTOS AND THE NEGRO REVOLT.   NSOSKWX67154

GI
    SUMMARY JUSTICE — THE NEGRO GI IN KOREA. /MILITARY/   NMARSTX51755

GIFTED
    GIFTED WOMEN IN THE TRADE UNIONS. /OCCUPATIONS/   WHILLBX62845

GIRL
    THE NEGRO GIRL AND POVERTY. /WOMEN/   CYOUNMB65636

    THAT GIRL IN THE OFFICE. /OCCUPATIONS/   WKNIGRX61910

    THE COLLEGE GIRL LOOKS AHEAD TO HER CAREER OPPORTUNITIES.   WZAPOMW56280

GIRLS
    WHY DO BRIGHT GIRLS NOT TAKE STIFF COURSES. /ASPIRATIONS/   WALBJMH61603

    COUNSELING GIRLS AND WOMEN. AWARENESS. ANALYSIS. ACTION.   WBERRJX66642

    CAREER GUIDANCE FOR GIRLS. /COUNSELING/   WCALDED60445

    CAREERS AS CONCERNS OF BLUE-COLLAR GIRLS. /OCCUPATIONS/   WDAVIEX64721

    STUDY OF ADOLESCENT GIRLS. /ASPIRATIONS/   WDOUVEX57742

    MARRIAGE AND CAREERS FOR GIRLS. /WORK-FAMILY-CONFLICT/   WGARFSH57774

    SOCIAL ROLE EXPECTATION. MOTIVATIONAL VARIABLE IN GIRLS. /ASPIRATIONS/   WHANSDE64821

    WOMAN-S ROLES. HOW GIRLS SEE THEM. /WORK-WOMAN-ROLE/   WHARTRE62830

    COUNSELING ADOLESCENT GIRLS IN THE 1960-S.   WHAVIRJ65833

    COUNSELING OF GIRLS AND MATURE WOMEN.   WHEDGJN64994

    VOCATIONAL GUIDANCE AND TRAINING OF GIRLS AND WOMEN. /COUNSELING/   WINTELO64863

    COUNSELORS AND GIRLS. /COUNSELING/   WLEWIEC65931

    MARRIAGE AND CAREER CONFLICTS IN GIRLS AND YOUNG WOMEN. /WORK-FAMILY-CONFLICT/   WMATTEX60961

    THE COUNSELOR AND GIRLS CAREER DEVELOPMENT. /COUNSELING/   WMATTEX63960

    COUNSELING GIRLS TOWARD NEW PERSPECTIVES.   WMIDDAR65190

    NEW APPROACHES TO COUNSELING GIRLS IN THE 1960-S.   WMIDWRP65209

    POST-HIGH SCHOOL PLANS FOR SENIOR GIRLS IN RELATION TO SCHOLASTIC APTITUDE. /ASPIRATIONS/   WMILLRX61983

    EXPERIENCES OF NEGRO HIGH SCHOOL GIRLS WITH DOMESTIC PLACEMENT AGENCIES. /HOUSEHOLD-WORKERS/   WRUSSRD62135

    COUNSELING GIRLS IN THE SIXTIES.   WSIMPAX66114

    OCCUPATIONAL PLANNING BY YOUNG WOMEN, A STUDY OF OCCUPATIONAL EXPERIENCES, ASPIRATIONS, ATTITUDES, AND
    PLANS OF COLLEGE AND HIGH SCHOOL GIRLS.   WSLOCWL56116

    SPEECH ABOUT JOB OPPORTUNITIES FOR GIRLS BEFORE THE MARYLAND STATE PERSONNEL AND GUIDANCE ASSOCIATION.   WTERLRX64148

    ACCESS OF GIRLS AND WOMEN TO EDUCATION IN RURAL AREAS. A COMPARATIVE STUDY.   WUNESCO64166

GIRLS   (CONTINUATION)
TRADE AND INDUSTRIAL EDUCATION FOR GIRLS AND WOMEN. A DIRECTORY OF TRAINING PROGRAMS.   WUSDHEW60175

TRAINING OPPORTUNITIES FOR WOMEN AND GIRLS.   WUSDLAB60221

WHO ARE THE DISADVANTAGED GIRLS 16-21 YEARS OLD.   WUSDLAB64228

FUTURE JOBS FOR HIGH SCHOOL GIRLS.   WUSDLAB65196

TRAINING WOMEN AND GIRLS FOR WORK.   WWELLJA60262

WOMEN AND GIRLS IN THE LABOR-MARKET TODAY AND TOMORROW.   WWELLJA63263

COUNSELING TODAY-S GIRLS FOR TOMORROW-S WOMANHOOD.   WWESTEM65210

THE EDUCATION OF WOMEN AND GIRLS IN A CHANGING SOCIETY. A SELECTED BIBLIOGRAPHY WITH ANNOTATIONS.   WWIGNTX65267

GLASS
PATTERNS OF DISCRIMINATION IN THE GLASS AND MACHINE TOOL INDUSTRIES IN OHIO.   GOHIOCR66126

PATTERNS OF DISCRIMINATION IN THE GLASS INDUSTRY IN OHIO.   GOHIOCR66127

GOAL
THE ELIMINATION OF POVERTY. A PRIMARY GOAL OF PUBLIC POLICY.   GCOHEWJ64925

A COMMON GOAL -- EQUAL-EMPLOYMENT-OPPORTUNITY.   GDAVIWG65629

NEXT IT-S A MIXED POLICE FORCE. INTEGRATIONISTS LATEST GOAL IN NATION-S CAPITAL. /WASHINGTON-DC/   NUSNEWR57274

GOAL-ORIENTATIONS
GOAL-ORIENTATIONS AND ILLEGAL BEHAVIOR AMONG JUVENILES.   NCLARJP63208

GOALS
THE ROLE OF MANPOWER POLICY IN ACHIEVING AGGREGATE GOALS. /EMPLOYMENT INCOME/   GTHURLC66640

AMBITIONS OF MEXICAN-AMERICAN YOUTH -- GOALS AND MEANS OF MOBILITY OF HIGH SCHOOL SENIORS.   MHELLCS64413

SELF RADIUS AND GOALS OF YOUTH IN DIFFERENT URBAN AREAS.   MSHERCW61489

GOALS IN THE WAR ON POVERTY. /ECONOMIC-STATUS/   NECKSOX66957

GOALS IN NEGRO EMPLOYMENT. /INDUSTRY/   NNATLIC65874

LIFE GOALS AND VOCATIONAL CHOICE. /WORK-WOMAN-ROLE/   WASTIAW64620

A TURNING TO TAKE NEXT -- ALTERNATIVE GOALS IN THE EDUCATION OF WOMEN. /WORK-WOMAN-ROLE/   WGOLDFH65792

GOALS -- A WAY TO FULLER UTILIZATION.   WKEYSMD66896

RELATIONSHIP BETWEEN THE EDUCATIONAL GOALS AND THE ACADEMIC PERFORMANCE OF WOMEN. A CONFIRMATION.   WWEITHX59260

GOMPERS
THE RACIAL PRACTICES OF ORGANIZED LABOR -- IN THE AGE OF GOMPERS AND AFTER. /UNION/   NHILLHX65541

GOVERNMENT
REPORT TO GOVERNOR EDMUND G BROWN. SECOND ETHNIC SURVEY OF EMPLOYMENT AND PROMOTION IN STATE GOVERNMENT.
/CALIFORNIA NEGRO MEXICAN-AMERICAN/   CBECKWL65070

NEGROES AND MEXICAN-AMERICANS IN THE CALIFORNIA STATE GOVERNMENT, A COOPERATIVE PROJECT.   CCALOGB65171

SECOND ETHNIC SURVEY OF EMPLOYMENT AND PROMOTION IN STATE GOVERNMENT. /CALIFORNIA/   GBECKWL65433

ECONOMIC EQUALITY AND GOVERNMENT ACTION.   GBERLAA66222

THE CONSCIENCE OF THE GOVERNMENT. /ANTIDISCRIMINATION/   GBERNBI62447

TEXTS OF RULES AND REGULATIONS OF PRESIDENT-S COMMITTEE ON EQUAL-EMPLOYMENT-OPPORTUNITY RELATING TO
OBLIGATIONS OF GOVERNMENT CONTRACTORS AND SUBCONTRACTORS, EFFECTIVE JULY 22, 1961. A BNA SPECIAL REPORT.   GBURENA61498

CIVIL-RIGHTS IN AIR TRANSPORTATION AND GOVERNMENT INITIATIVE.   GDIXORX63644

CALIFORNIA LOCAL GOVERNMENT AND INTEGRATION.   GFORDJA63695

SOME PROPOSALS FOR GOVERNMENT POLICY IN AN AUTOMATING SOCIETY.   GGANSHJ65696

THE ROLE OF GOVERNMENT. /TECHNOLOGICAL-CHANGE/   GGOLDAX62865

A STUDY OF FAIR-EMPLOYMENT-PRACTICES OF THE CITY GOVERNMENT. /GRAND-RAPIDS MICHIGAN/   GGRANRH66733

GOVERNMENT REGULATION OF UNION POLICIES.   GHICKRX66774

THE CITY GOVERNMENT AND MINORITY-GROUPS.   GINTECM63816

LOCAL CONTRACTS AND SUB-CONTRACTS. THE ROLES OF CITY GOVERNMENT AND PRIVATE CITIZENS GROUPS.   GJONEMX64829

REPORTS ON THE PATTERN OF EMPLOYMENT OF MINORTY-GROUP PERSONS IN DEPARTMENT OF COUNTY
GOVERNMENT.LOS-ANGELES CALIFORNIA/   GLOSACC62913

ETHNIC SURVEY OF EMPLOYMENT IN STATE GOVERNMENT. /CALIFORNIA/   GMESPFA63977

GOVERNMENT CONTRACTS AND SOCIAL CONTROL. A PRELIMINARY INQUIRY.   GMILLAS55985

MISSOURI LOCAL GOVERNMENT ACTION IN THE AREA OF HUMAN-RIGHTS.   GMISSCH63022

GOVERNMENT AND MANPOWER. /POLICY-RECOMMENDATIONS/   GNATLMC64956

GOVERNMENT CONTRACTS AND FAIR-EMPLOYMENT-PRACTICES.   GNORGPH64119

SURVEY OF EMPLOYMENT IN STATE GOVERNMENT. /NORTH-CAROLINA/   GNORTCG64121

A GUIDE TO GOVERNMENT OFFICIALS. /CIVIL-RIGHTS/   GOREGBLND135

THE NONDISCRIMINATION CLAUSE IN GOVERNMENT CONTRACTS.   GPASLRS57148

SECOND SURVEY OF NON-WHITE EMPLOYEES IN STATE GOVERNMENT IN PENNSYLVANIA.   GPENNHR65167

GOVERNMENT CONTRACT EMPLOYMENT. RULES AND REGULATIONS... EFFECTIVE JULY 22, 1961, AS AMENDED SEPTEMBER 7,
1963.   GPRESCD63110

GOVERNMENT   (CONTINUATION)
STUDY OF MINORITY-GROUP EMPLOYMENT IN THE FEDERAL GOVERNMENT.   GPRESCD64116

FIELD MANUAL ON EQUAL-EMPLOYMENT-OPPORTUNITY UNDER GOVERNMENT CONTRACTS.   GPRESCD65107

FIRST REPORT, PRESIDENT-S COMMITTEE ON GOVERNMENT CONTRACTS.   GPRESCH54120

SECOND ANNUAL REPORT, THE PRESIDENT-S COMMITTEE ON GOVERNMENT CONTRACTS.   GPRESCH55124

FOURTH ANNUAL REPORT ON EQUAL JOB OPPORTUNITY, 1956-1957, PRESIDENT-S COMMITTEE ON GOVERNMENT CONTRACTS.   GPRESCH57122

COMPLIANCE GUIDE, RECOMMENDATIONS FOR OBTAINING COMPLIANCE WITH THE NONDISCRIMINATION PROVISIONS IN
GOVERNMENT CONTRACTS.   GPRESCH58119

FIVE YEARS OF PROGRESS, 1953-1958, A REPORT TO PRESIDENT EISENHOWER BY THE PRESIDENT-S COMMITTEE ON
GOVERNMENT CONTRACTS.   GPRESCH58121

PATTERN FOR PROGRESS, SEVENTH REPORT, FINAL REPORT TO PRESIDENT EISENHOWER FROM THE COMMITTEE ON
GOVERNMENT CONTRACTS.   GPRESCH60123

THE POLICY OF NON-DISCRIMINATION IN EMPLOYMENT IN THE FEDERAL GOVERNMENT.   GPRESCP55198

SOME QUESTIONS AND ANSWERS ON THE NON-DISCRIMINATION POLICY OF THE FEDERAL GOVERNMENT.   GPRESCP55199

FIRST ANNUAL REPORT, PRESIDENT-S COMMITTEE ON GOVERNMENT EMPLOYMENT POLICY, APRIL 30 1956.   GPRESCP56193

SECOND ANNUAL REPORT, PRESIDENT-S COMMITTEE ON GOVERNMENT EMPLOYMENT POLICY, 1957.   GPRESCP57194

THIRD ANNUAL REPORT, PRESIDENT-S COMMITTEE ON GOVERNMENT EMPLOYMENT POLICY, 1958.   GPRESCP58195

FOURTH ANNUAL REPORT, PRESIDENT-S COMMITTEE ON GOVERNMENT EMPLOYMENT POLICY.   GPRESCP59196

TRENDS IN THE EMPLOYMENT OF NEGRO-AMERICANS IN UPPER-LEVEL WHITE-COLLAR POSITIONS OF THE FEDERAL
GOVERNMENT.   GPRESCP60200

THE ROLE OF GOVERNMENT IN PROMOTING FULL EMPLOYMENT.   GROSSAM66084

RACIAL AND ETHNIC EMPLOYMENT PATTERN SURVEY OF THE CITY AND COUNTY OF SAN-FRANCISCO GOVERNMENT.
DEPARTMENTAL ANALYSIS. /CALIFORNIA/   GSANFHR65264

ENFORCEMENT OF NONDISCRIMINATION REQUIREMENTS FOR GOVERNMENT CONTRACT WORK.   GSPECWH63329

SURVEY OF NON-WHITE EMPLOYEES IN STATE GOVERNMENT. /PENNSYLVANIA/   GSTRUJW63338

STUDY OF MINORITY GROUP EMPLOYMENT IN THE FEDERAL GOVERNMENT, 1966.   GUSCISC66767

STUDY OF MINORITY-GROUP EMPLOYMENT IN THE FEDERAL GOVERNMENT.   GUSDLAB63500

US GOVERNMENT POLICY TOWARD AMERICAN INDIANS. A FEW BASIC FACTS.   IELLIMB57554

LIVELIHOOD AND TRIBAL GOVERNMENT ON THE KLAMATH INDIAN RESERVATION.   ISTERTX61624

AMERICAN-INDIANS AND THE FEDERAL GOVERNMENT.   IUSDINT65640

RACIAL DESEGREGATION IN THE PUBLIC SERVICE, WITH PARTICULAR REFERENCE TO THE US GOVERNMENT.   NBROWVJ54127

NEGRO EMPLOYMENT IN THE FEDERAL GOVERNMENT.   NDAVIJA45259

NEGROES IN THE GOVERNMENT EMPLOYMENT.   NHENDEW43510

WHAT THE GOVERNMENT REQUIRES OF MANAGEMENT AND UNIONS.   NHORTRX64291

GOVERNMENT AND EQUAL-EMPLOYMENT-OPPORTUNITY.   NKRISSX67665

JOBS AND COLOR. NEGRO EMPLOYMENT IN TENNESSEE STATE GOVERNMENT.   NLONGHH62706

EMPLOYMENT IN STATE GOVERNMENT. /NORTH-CAROLINA/   NNORTCG66092

NEGRO EMPLOYMENT IN THE FEDERAL GOVERNMENT BY CIVIL SERVICE REGION, STATE AND PAY CATEGORIES, JUNE 1962.   NPRESCD62012

A FIVE-CITY SURVEY OF NEGRO-AMERICAN EMPLOYEES OF THE FEDERAL GOVERNMENT.   NPRESCP57017

COMBATING DISCRIMINATION IN THE EMPLOYMENT OF NEGROES IN WAR INDUSTRIES AND GOVERNMENT AGENCIES.   NRAMSLA43128

STUDY OF MINORITY-GROUP EMPLOYMENT IN THE FEDERAL GOVERNMENT, 1965.   NUSCISC65229

NON-DISCRIMINATION CLAUSE IN GOVERNMENT CONTRACTS IS MANDATORY.   NUSDLAB43833

FOR NEGROES. MORE AND BETTER JOBS IN GOVERNMENT.   NUSNEWR62268

THE PRESENT SITUATION OF WOMAN SCIENTISTS AND ENGINEERS IN INDUSTRY AND GOVERNMENT. /OCCUPATIONS/   WBOLTRH65650

WOMEN AS GOVERNMENT EMPLOYEES. /OCCUPATIONS/   WBUSIWX63669

GOVERNMENT CAREERS FOR WOMEN -- A STUDY.   WUSDLAB57198

SHORTAGE OR SURPLUS. AN ASSESSMENT OF BOSTON WOMANPOWER IN INDUSTRY, GOVERNMENT, AND RESEARCH. JUNE 7-8,
1963. /MASSACHUSETTS/   WUSDLAB66217

GOVERNMENT-CONTRACTO
EMPLOYMENT OF NEGROES BY GOVERNMENT-CONTRACTORS.   NUSDLAB64814

GOVERNMENT-SPONSORED
THE ROLE OF GOVERNMENT-SPONSORED TRAINING AND RETRAINING PROGRAMS.   GALLECC65758

IMPLICATIONS OF GOVERNMENT-SPONSORED TRAINING PROGRAMS. /TECHNOLOGICAL-CHANGE/   GWALSJP64620

GOVERNMENTAL
GOVERNMENTAL FAIR-EMPLOYMENT AGENCIES. AN APPRAISAL OF FEDERAL, STATE, AND MUNICIPAL EFFORTS TO END JOB
DISCRIMINATION.   GNORGPH62120

NEGROES AND GOVERNMENTAL SERVICES. AN APPRAISAL.   NBOYDWM46252

THE IMPACT OF PUERTO-RICAN MIGRATION ON GOVERNMENTAL SERVICES IN NEW-YORK CITY.   PDWORMB57797

GOVERNMENTS
SUPPLEMENTARY ACTIVITIES FOR STATE GOVERNMENTS SEEKING TO ELIMINATE DISCRIMINATION.   GROUTFB64264

GOVERNOR
REPORT TO GOVERNOR EDMUND G BROWN. SECOND ETHNIC SURVEY OF EMPLOYMENT AND PROMOTION IN STATE GOVERNMENT.

GOVERNOR   (CONTINUATION)
/CALIFORNIA NEGRO   MEXICAN-AMERICAN/   CBECKWL65070

   REPORT TO THE GOVERNOR AND THE LEGISLATURE OF THE COMMISSION ON MANPOWER, AUTOMATION AND TECHNOLOGY,
   1964. /CALIFORNIA/   GCALCMA65515

   REPORT OF THE COMMISSION ON THE EMPLOYMENT PROBLEMS OF NEGROES TO GOVERNOR SALTONSTALL. /MASSACHUSETTS/   NMASSCE42757

GOVERNOR-S
   MIGRATORY LABOR IN OHIO. A REPORT BY THE GOVERNOR-S COMMITTEE, AUGUST 1962.   GOHIOGC62095

   FINAL REPORT. EMPLOYMENT AND TRAINING, REPORT FOR GOVERNOR-S COMMISSION.   NBULLPX65483

   GOVERNOR-S CIVIL-RIGHTS TASK FORCE. REPORT. /RHODE-ISLAND/   NRHODIC64051

   FIRST REPORT, IOWA GOVERNOR-S COMMISSION ON THE STATUS OF WOMEN. /EMPLOYMENT-CONDITIONS/   WIOWAGC64796

   NEW-YORK WOMEN. A REPORT AND RECOMMENDATIONS FROM THE NEW-YORK GOVERNOR-S COMMITTEE ON THE EDUCATION AND
   EMPLOYMENT OF WOMEN.   WNEWYGW64799

   WISCONSIN GOVERNOR-S CONFERENCE ON THE CHANGING STATUS OF WOMEN, JAN 31-FEB 1 1964.   WUSDLAB65232

   WISCONSIN WOMEN. REPORT OF THE WISCONSIN GOVERNOR-S COMMISSION ON THE STATUS OF WOMEN.   WWISXGC65272

GOVERNORS
   PROGRESS AND PROSPECTS. THE REPORT OF THE SECOND NATIONAL CONFERENCE OF GOVERNORS COMMISSIONS ON THE
   STATUS OF WOMEN. /EMPLOYMENT-CONDITIONS/   WGOVECS65798

   GOVERNORS COMMISSIONS ON THE STATUS OF WOMEN.   WUSDLAB64199

GRADE
   LEVEL OF OCCUPATIONAL ASPIRATIONS AMONG MONTANA INDIANS IN GRADE AND HIGH SCHOOL.   IDOUGGV60550

   DIFFERENCES IN DROPOUT AND OTHER SCHOOL BEHAVIOR BETWEEN TWO GROUPS OF TENTH GRADE BOYS IN AN URBAN HIGH
   SCHOOL.   MMUNORF57446

   A STUDY OF THE OCCUPATIONAL AWARENESS OF A SELECTED GROUP OF NINTH GRADE NEGRO STUDENTS.   NAMOSWE60020

   THE UNEMPLOYMENT RATE AND GRADE LEVEL RELATIONSHIP IN CHICAGO AS REVEALED IN THE 1960 CENSUS. /ILLINOIS/   NHARGAJ65990

   NEGRO AND TOTAL EMPLOYMENT BY GRADE AND SALARY GROUPS, JUNE 1961 AND JUNE 1962.   NPRESCD62011

   THE RELATIONSHIP BETWEEN TEST INTELLIGENCE OF THIRD GRADE NEGRO CHILDREN AND THE OCCUPATIONS OF THEIR
   PARENTS.   NROBIML47070

GRADS
   INDUSTRY RUSHES FOR NEGRO GRADS.   NBUSIWX64297

GRADUATE
   THE NEGRO WOMAN COLLEGE GRADUATE.   CNOBLJL55925

   JEWISH LAW GRADUATE. /EMPLOYMENT DISCRIMINATION/   JADLBXX64689

   GRADUATE AND PROFESSIONAL EDUCATION IN NEGRO INSTITUTIONS. /ECONOMIC-STATUS/   NBROWAX58893

   THE NEGRO GRADUATE, 1950-1960. /COLLEGE EDUCATION/   NBROWAX60125

   EDUCATION OF NEGRO LEADERS. INFLUENCES AFFECTING GRADUATE AND PROFESSIONAL STUDIES.   NCALIAX49174

   GRADUATE EDUCATION, PUBLIC SERVICE, AND THE NEGRO.   NCIKIWI66207

   EDUCATION AND MARGINALITY. A STUDY OF THE NEGRO COLLEGE GRADUATE.   NCUTHMV49936

   PREPARATION OF THE NEGRO COLLEGE GRADUATE FOR BUSINESS. /EMPLOYMENT-SELECTION/   NHOLLJH65560

   GRADUATE EDUCATION OF NEGRO PSYCHOLOGISTS.   NRICHTW56057

   THE PROSPECT FOR ADVANCEMENT IN BUSINESS OF THE MARRIED WOMAN COLLEGE GRADUATE. /OCCUPATIONS/   WBECKEL64632

   FACTORS ASSOCIATED WITH GRADUATE SCHOOL ATTENDANCE AND ROLE DEFINITION OF THE WOMAN DOCTORAL CANDIDATES
   AT THE PENNSYLVANIA STATE UNIVERSITY. /OCCUPATIONS/   WFIELJC61763

   WHO GOES TO GRADUATE SCHOOL. /EDUCATION/   WGROPGL59805

   RUTGERS -- THE STATE UNIVERSITY. FORD FOUNDATION PROGRAM FOR THE RETRAINING IN MATHEMATICS OF COLLEGE
   GRADUATE WOMEN. /TRAINING/   WMARTHM63957

   GRADUATE EDUCATION FOR WOMEN. THE RADCLIFFE PHD.   WRADCCX56072

   REPORT -- 1965-66 -- RETRAINING PROGRAM IN MATHEMATICS AND SCIENCE FOR COLLEGE GRADUATE WOMEN.   WRUTGMR66098

GRADUATED
   YOUNG NEGRO TALENT. SURVEY OF THE EXPERIENCES AND EXPECTATIONS OF NEGRO AMERICANS WHO GRADUATED FROM
   COLLEGE IN 1961.   NFICHJH64867

GRADUATES
   EMPLOYMENT OF HIGH SCHOOL GRADUATES AND DROPOUTS IN 1964.   GBOGAFA65750

   HOW TO RECRUIT MINORITY-GROUP COLLEGE GRADUATES, ITS PROBLEMS, ITS TECHNIQUES, ITS SOURCES, ITS
   OPPORTUNITIES.   GCALVRX63555

   EMPLOYMENT OF JUNE 1959 HIGH SCHOOL GRADUATES, OCTOBER 1959.   GCOOPSX60601

   CHARACTERISTICS OF SCHOOL DROPOUTS AND HIGH SCHOOL GRADUATES, FARM AND NONFARM, 1960.   GCOWHJD64419

   A PILOT STUDY OF THE EMPLOYMENT EXPERIENCES OF HIGH SCHOOL GRADUATES.   GPHILCH65177

   GRADUATES OF THE NORFOLK PROJECT ONE YEAR LATER. /MDTA TRAINING/   GQUINPA65771

   EMPLOYMENT OF HIGH SCHOOL GRADUATES AND DROPOUTS IN 1962.   GSCHIJX63282

   EMPLOYMENT OF HIGH SCHOOL GRADUATES AND DROPOUTS IN 1965.   GUSDLAB66073

   PROBLEMS OF NAVAJO MALE GRADUATES OF INTERMOUNTAIN SCHOOL DURING THEIR FIRST YEAR OF EMPLOYMENT.   IBAKEJE59533

   A STUDY OF THE REASONS FOR FAILURE ON THE JOB OF SOME GRADUATES OF INTERMOUNTAIN SCHOOL.   IFISHLX60560

   A COMPARISON OF THE ACADEMIC ACHIEVEMENTS OF WHITE AND NEGRO HIGH SCHOOL GRADUATES. /EDUCATION/   NBULLHA50132

GRADUATES   (CONTINUATION)
CLEVELAND-S ANNUAL JOB CENTER FOR COLLEGE GRADUATES.   NCOCKHW65218

A STUDY OF JOB-OPPORTUNITIES IN THE STATE OF FLORIDA FOR NEGRO COLLEGE GRADUATES.   NDECKPM60261

SOME FACTORS WHICH DISTINGUISH DROP-OUTS FROM HIGH SCHOOL GRADUATES.   NGRAGWL49978

IN SEARCH OF A FUTURE. A STUDY OF CAREER-SEEKING EXPERIENCES OF SELECTED NEGRO HIGH SCHOOL GRADUATES IN
WASHINGTON-DC WHICH WAS AN EFFORT TO PROVIDE KNOWLEDGE HELPFUL IN SOLVING ONE OF THE MOST CRITICAL
PROBLEMS FACING URBAN AMERICA TODAY.   NGRIEES63454

COLLEGE, COLOR, AND EMPLOYMENT. RACIAL DIFFERENTIALS IN POSTGRADUATE EMPLOYMENT AMONG 1964 GRADUATES OF
LOUISIANA COLLEGES.   NHUSOCF66328

VOCATIONAL GRADUATES IN AUTO MECHANICS. A FOLLOW-UP STUDY OF NEGRO AND WHITE YOUTH. /OCCUPATIONS/   NLEVEBX66036

HIGH SCHOOL GRADUATES AND DROPOUTS -- A NEW LOOK AT A PERSISTENT PROBLEM.   NLIVIAH58044

ACHIEVEMENT OF MALE HIGH SCHOOL DROPOUTS AND GRADUATES IN ALABAMA VOCATIONAL SCHOOLS.   NMILLGJ65791

RECRUITING NEGRO COLLEGE GRADUATES.   NNATLIC64231

NEGLECTED TALENTS. BACKGROUND AND PROSPECTS OF NEGRO COLLEGE GRADUATES.   NNATLOR66880

THE PLACEMENT OF NEGRO COLLEGE GRADUATES IN BUSINESS ORGANIZATIONS.   NWHITEW64321

STUDY OF JOB OPPORTUNITIES FOR WOMEN COLLEGE GRADUATES. /OCCUPATIONS/   WINTEAP58861

TODAY-S WOMEN COLLEGE GRADUATES. /WORK-WOMEN-ROLE/   WLEOPAK59927

LIBERAL ARTS WOMEN GRADUATES, CLASS OF 1958. /WORK-WOMEN-ROLE/   WLICHMW59933

WOMEN GRADUATES OF COOPERATIVE WORK-STUDY PROGRAMS ON THE COLLEGE LEVEL. /SKILLS/   WMOSBWB57999

TEACHING. OPPORTUNITIES FOR WOMEN COLLEGE GRADUATES.   WNATLEA64019

FIVE THOUSAND WOMEN COLLEGE GRADUATES REPORT.   WSHOSRX56113

JOB OPPORTUNITIES FOR WOMEN COLLEGE GRADUATES.   WSWERSX64145

HIGH SCHOOL GUIDANCE COUNSELOR-S PERCEPTIONS OF SELECTED CAREERS FOR WOMEN COLLEGE GRADUATES.   WSWOPMR63146

EMPLOYMENT OF JUNE 1955 WOMEN COLLEGE GRADUATES.   WUSDLAB56990

FIRST JOBS OF COLLEGE WOMEN -- REPORT ON WOMEN GRADUATES, CLASS OF 1957.   WUSDLAB59194

COLLEGE WOMEN SEVEN YEARS AFTER GRADUATION -- RESURVEY OF WOMEN GRADUATES CLASS OF 1957.   WUSDLAB66185

GRADUATING
SURVEY OF WOMEN PHYSICIANS GRADUATING FROM MEDICAL SCHOOL, 1925-1940. /OCCUPATIONS/   WDYKMRA57745

REPORT ON THE SURVEY OF FEMALE PHYSICIANS GRADUATING FROM MEDICAL SCHOOL BETWEEN 1925 AND 1940.
/OCCUPATIONS/   WHANNFX58819

GRADUATION
POST GRADUATION ROLE PREFERENCE OF SENIOR WOMEN IN COLLEGE. /ASPIRATION/   WCHRIHX56690

COLLEGE WOMEN SEVEN YEARS AFTER GRADUATION -- RESURVEY OF WOMEN GRADUATES CLASS OF 1957.   WUSDLAB66185

GRAND-RAPIDS
A STUDY OF FAIR-EMPLOYMENT-PRACTICES OF THE CITY GOVERNMENT. /GRAND-RAPIDS MICHIGAN/   GGRANRH66733

GRANTS
GRANTS AND PROJECTS RELATED TO THE DEVELOPMENT OF THE AMERICAN NEGRO. ALL FISCAL YEARS THROUGH JUNE 10,
1966.   NFORDFX66133

GRAPE
GRAPE WORKERS WIN NEW GAINS. /MIGRANT-WORKERS UNION CALIFORNIA/   GROSSLX66557

GREAT-SOCIETY
COORDINATING THE GREAT-SOCIETY.   GBAILSK66913

GRIEVANCE-PROCEDURES
RACE-RELATIONS IN AN INDUSTRIAL SOCIETY. /EMPLOYMENT GRIEVANCE-PROCEDURES/   NBACOEF63041

GROUP
CONTRACTOR GROUP HITS REVISED EQUAL EMPLOYMENT STANDARDS.   GAIRCHR63866

CONTROLLING GROUP PREJUDICE.   GANNAOA46547

THE SUPREME-COURT AND GROUP DISCRIMINATION SINCE 1937.   GBERGMX49443

EQUALITY BY STATUTES -- LEGAL CONTROLS OVER GROUP DISCRIMINATION.   GBERGMX52440

INEQUALITY OF OPPORTUNITY IN HIGHER EDUCATION. A STUDY OF MINORITY GROUP AND RELATED BARRIERS TO COLLEGE
ADMISSION.   GBERKDS48446

TEST PERFORMANCE IN RELATION TO ETHNIC GROUP AND SOCIAL CLASS.   GRCBES063683

THE BALANCED ETHNIC WORK GROUP.   GSCOTWW61290

STUDY OF MINORITY GROUP EMPLOYMENT IN THE FEDERAL GOVERNMENT, 1966.   GUSCISC66767

A STUDY OF EMPLOYMENT PATTERNS IN THE GENERAL MERCHANDISE GROUP RETAIL STORES IN NEW-YORK-CITY.   GWATKDO66588

NARRAGANSETT SURVIVAL. A STUDY OF GROUP PERSISTENCE THROUGH ADAPTED TRAITS.   IBOISEX59887

THE JEWS. SOCIAL PATTERNS OF AN AMERICAN GROUP.   JSKLAMX58149

THE SOCIAL ASPIRATIONS OF A SELECTED GROUP OF SPANISH NAME PEOPLE IN LAREDO, TEXAS.   MGUERIX59409

A STUDY OF THE ACCULTURATION AND SOCIAL ASPIRATIONS OF SIXTY JUNIOR HIGH SCHOOL STUDENTS FROM THE MEXICAN
ETHNIC GROUP.   MJONEBM62421

THE MIGRANT PROBLEM AND PRESSURE GROUP POLITICS.   MTCMARD61502

A STUDY OF THE OCCUPATIONAL AWARENESS OF A SELECTED GROUP OF NINTH GRADE NEGRO STUDENTS.   NAMOSWE60020

AN INSIGHT INTO STRUCTURAL UNEMPLOYMENT -- THE EXPERIENCE OF A MINORITY GROUP IN A PROSPEROUS COMMUNITY. NGERSWJ65634

GROUP   (CONTINUATION)
   NEGROES IN THE WORK GROUP. HOW 33 BUSINESS AND INDUSTRIAL FIRMS OFFERED EQUAL-EMPLOYMENT-OPPORTUNITIES TO
ALL.   NSEIDJX50114

   IS THE NEGRO AN IMMIGRANT GROUP.   NTAEUKE63195

   THE NEGRO AS AN IMMIGRANT GROUP. RECENT TRENDS IN RACIAL AND ETHNIC SEGREGATION IN CHICAGO. /ILLINOIS/   NTAEUKE64196

   THE ROLE OF THE EDUCATED WOMAN. AN EMPIRICAL STUDY OF THE ATTITUDES OF A GROUP OF COLLEGE WOMEN.
/WORK-WOMAN-ROLE/   WFREEMB65770

   PRACTITIONERS AND NON-PRACTITIONERS IN A GROUP OF WOMEN PHYSICIANS. /ASPIRATIONS/   WGLICRX65791

GROUPINGS
   NET MIGRATION OF THE POPULATION, 1950-60, BY AGE, SEX, AND COLOR. VOL II, ANALYTICAL GROUPINGS OF
COUNTIES. /INCOME/   GBOWLGK65434

GROUPS
   THE EFFECT OF LOW EDUCATIONAL-ATTAINMENT ON INCOMES. A COMPARATIVE STUDY OF SELECTED ETHNIC GROUPS.
/NEGRO MEXICAN-AMERICAN/   CFOGEWX66367

   CULTURAL DIFFERENCES IN AMERICAN ETHNIC GROUPS. BIBLIOGRAPHY. /AMERICAN-INDIAN NEGRO SPANISH-AMERICAN/   CLIBRCX64899

   BENEFIT POLICIES IN RELATION TO RECRUITMENT OF OLDER WORKERS, HANDICAPPED, AND MINORITY GROUPS.   GBARRGJ51425

   ORGANIZED LABOR AND THE INTEGRATION OF ETHNIC GROUPS. /UNION/   GBLOCHD58455

   ORGANIZED LABOR AND MINORITY GROUPS. /UNION/   GBLUEJT47457

   TESTING OF CULTURALLY DIFFERENT GROUPS.   GCAMPJX64093

   THE POSITION OF RACIAL GROUPS IN OCCUPATIONAL STRUCTURES.   GGLICCE47722

   TRAINING DISADVANTAGED GROUPS UNDER THE MANPOWER-DEVELOPMENT-TRAINING-ACT.   GHELPCW63501

   LOCAL CONTRACTS AND SUB-CONTRACTS. THE ROLES OF CITY GOVERNMENT AND PRIVATE CITIZENS GROUPS. GJONEMX64829

   ETHNIC GROUPS AND THE PRACTICE OF MEDICINE. /OCCUPATIONS/   GLIEBSX58042

   MANAGEMENT AND MINORITY GROUPS. A STUDY OF ATTITUDES AND PRACTICES IN HIRING AND UPGRADING.   GMARKPI57085

   INTERPERSONAL RELATIONS IN ETHNICALLY MIXED SMALL WORK GROUPS.   GSCOTWW59291

   THE PRACTICES OF CRAFT UNIONS IN WASHINGTON-DC WITH RESPECT TO MINORITY GROUPS IN CIVIL-RIGHTS IN THE
NATION-S CAPITOL.   GSEGABD59294

   UTILIZING OUR MANPOWER RESOURCES. SPECIAL APPLICANT GROUPS.   GUSOLAB63665

   AMERICAN MINORITY RELATIONS. THE SOCIOLOGY OF RACE AND ETHNIC GROUPS.   GVANDJW63535

   THE MINORITY NEWCOMER IN OPEN AND CLOSED GROUPS.   GZILLRC59595

   A COMPARISON OF MAJOR UNITED STATES RELIGIOUS GROUPS. /ECONOMIC-STATUS/   JLAZRBX61033

   HOUSING DEFICIENCIES OF AGRICULTURAL WORKERS AND OTHER LOW INCOME GROUPS.   MMCMIOX62434

   SOME DIFFERENCES IN FACTORS RELATED TO EDUCATIONAL ACHIEVEMENT OF TWO MEXICAN-AMERICAN GROUPS. MMONTPX60443

   DIFFERENCES IN DROPOUT AND OTHER SCHOOL BEHAVIOR BETWEEN TWO GROUPS OF TENTH GRADE BOYS IN AN URBAN HIGH
SCHOOL.   MMUNORF57446

   OBJECTIVE ACCESS IN THE OPPORTUNITY STRUCTURE. THE ASSESSMENT OF THREE ETHNIC GROUPS WITH RESPECT TO
QUANTIFIED SOCIAL STRUCTURAL VARIABLES.   MRENDGX63461

   THE KNITTING OF RACIAL GROUPS IN INDUSTRY.   NHUGHEC46584

   BEHAVIOR AND PRODUCTIVITY IN BI-RACIAL WORK GROUPS.   NKATZIX58638

   EFFECTS OF WHITE AUTHORITARIANISM IN BI-RACIAL WORK GROUPS.   NKATZIX60639

   THE IMPACT OF SOCIO-ECONOMIC CHANGE ON RACIAL GROUPS IN A RURAL SETTING.   NPELLRJ62981

   NEGRO AND TOTAL EMPLOYMENT BY GRADE AND SALARY GROUPS, JUNE 1961 AND JUNE 1962.   NPRESCD62011

   THE EFFECT OF LOW EDUCATIONAL ATTAINMENT ON INCOMES. A COMPARATIVE STUDY OF SELECTED ETHNIC GROUPS.   OFOGEWX66721

   COMMUNITY WOMEN-S GROUPS TAKE ACTION. /HOUSEHOLD-WORKERS/   WBUFFDX66661

   A PILOT STUDY OF THE MOTIVATIONS AND PROBLEMS OF MIDDLE AGED HOMEMAKERS IN LOWER SOCIO-ECONOMIC GROUPS IN
SEEKING EMPLOYMENT. /ASPIRATIONS/   WJEWIVA62883

GROWERS
   TEXAS GROWERS AND WORKERS ON THE FARM, LOWER RIO-GRANDE VALLEY.   GTEXAEC59352

GROWING
   QUERIES CONCERNING INDUSTRY AND SOCIETY GROWING OUT OF STUDY OF ETHNIC RELATIONS IN INDUSTRY. GHUGHEC59787

   GROWING UP NEGRO.   NAMERCX63009

   NEGRO MARKET. GROWING, CHANGING, CHALLENGING.   NBLACLE63493

   GROWING UP IN THE BLACK BELT. NEGRO YOUTH IN THE RURAL SOUTH.   NJOHNCS41611

   UNIONS FEEL GROWING PRESSURE TO TAKE MORE NEGROES.   NUSNEWR64292

   GROWING UP FEMALE. /WORK-WOMAN-ROLE/   WBETTBX62883

GROWTH
   ECONOMIC GROWTH AND EMPLOYMENT OPPORTUNITIES FOR MINORITIES. /NEGRO WOMEN/   CHIESDL64775

   POLICIES FOR THE PROMOTION OF ECONOMIC GROWTH.   GACKLGX66680

   TRICKLING DOWN. THE RELATIONSHIP BETWEEN ECONOMIC GROWTH AND THE EXTENT OF POVERTY AMONG AMERICAN
FAMILIES.   GANDEWH64392

   PROJECTIONS TO 1975. THE GROWTH AND STRUCTURE OF THE LABOR FORCE.   GBAKESS65702

   THE AMERICAN LABOR-FORCE. ITS GROWTH AND CHANGING COMPOSITION. /DEMOGRAPHY/   GBANCGX58417

GROWTH   (CONTINUATION)
EFFECTS ON ECONOMIC GROWTH OF THE EMPLOYMENT SHIFT TO SERVICE INDUSTRIES.   GBRADME64797

A DEMONSTRATION PROJECT DESIGNED TO TEST THE LIFE-STYLE AND THE GROWTH POTENTIAL OF URBAN DROPOUTS FROM
DISADVANTAGED HOMES.   GCLEAMP66130

CIVIL-RIGHTS. EMPLOYMENT OPPORTUNITY, AND ECONOMIC GROWTH.   GFEILJG65677

INTRODUCTION TO ECONOMICS OF GROWTH, UNEMPLOYMENT, AND INFLATION.   GHERMHX64938

ECONOMIC GROWTH. EQUAL-OPPORTUNITY, RESEARCH, JOINT EFFORT. EMPLOYMENT.   GILLIGC63798

INCOME-DISTRIBUTION AS A FACTOR IN REGIONAL GROWTH, WITH SPECIAL REFERENCE TO THE SOUTHEAST UNITED
STATES. /DISCRIMINATION/   GPHILEW65773

INDUSTRY EMPLOYMENT GROWTH SINCE WORLD WAR II.   GUSDLAB63831

THE SOURCES OF ECONOMIC GROWTH IN THE UNITED-STATES AND THE ALTERNATIVE BEFORE US.   /LABOR-FORCE
ECONOMY/   NDENIEF62262

SOME FACTORS INFLUENCING THE GROWTH OF UNIONS IN THE SOUTH.   NMARSRX60060

LIFETIME INCOME AND ECONOMIC GROWTH.   NMILLHP65782

THE FEMALE LABOR-FORCE IN THE UNITED STATES. FACTORS GOVERNING ITS GROWTH AND CHANGING COMPOSITION.   WOPPEVK66096

GUARANTEED-INCOME
THE GUARANTEED-INCOME.   GAMERCX66756

THE WEIGHT OF THE POOR -- A STRATEGY TO END POVERTY. /GUARANTEED-INCOME/   GCLOWRX66525

INCOME WITHOUT WORK. /GUARANTEED-INCOME/   GHAZLHX66523

FOR A GUARANTEED-INCOME.   GREAGMD64845

GUARANTEED-INCOME PLAN.   GSHAFHB66801

FREE MEN AND FREE MARKETS. /TECHNOLOGICAL-CHANGE GUARANTEED-INCOME/   GTHEORX63682

POLITICAL NECESSITIES OF ABUNDANCE. /GUARANTEED-INCOME/   GTHEORX64610

THE POLITICAL NECESSITIES OF ABUNDANCE. /GUARANTEED-INCOME/   GTHEORX64968

THE GUARANTEED-INCOME. NEXT STEP IN ECONOMIC REVOLUTION.   GTHEORX66626

GUARD
THE NEGRO AND THE NATIONAL GUARD. /MILITARY/   NNEWTIG62915

GUIDANCE
GUIDANCE. TRAINING AND APPRENTICESHIP FACTORS AFFECTING MINORITY-GROUPS.   GNATLAM60037

FROM SCHOOL TO JOB. GUIDANCE FOR MINORITY YOUTH.   GTANNAX63156

VOCATIONAL GUIDANCE FOR MINORITY YOUTH.   NBABOIX59038

MEETING THE PSYCHOLOGICAL CRISES OF NEGRO YOUTH THROUGH A COORDINATED GUIDANCE SERVICE.   NBRAZWF58111

TWO YEAR REPORT ON THE YOUTH GUIDANCE PROJECT, 1958-1959. /CHICAGO   ILLINOIS/   NCHICULND203

NEGROES. VOCATIONAL GUIDANCE AND COUNSELING IN THE SOUTHERN FIELD.   NEDWAGL47325

MINORITY-GROUP ATTITUDES OF NEGROES AND IMPLICATIONS FOR GUIDANCE.   NENGLWH57333

THE GUIDANCE OF NEGRO YOUTH.   NGINZEX67417

GUIDANCE AND MINORITY YOUTH.   NLONGHH62705

THE URBAN-LEAGUE AND THE VOCATIONAL GUIDANCE AND ADJUSTMENT OF NEGRO YOUTH.   NNICHLE52922

UPDATING GUIDANCE AND PERSONNEL PRACTICES.   NROUSRJ62089

JOB GUIDANCE AND THE DISADVANTAGED.   NSAITCX64308

INSTITUTIONAL GUIDANCE FACES THE FUTURE.   NSCALEE57272

VOCATIONAL GUIDANCE BIBLIOGRAPHY.   NTANNAX40199

THE ROLE OF THE COUNSELOR IN THE GUIDANCE OF NEGRO STUDENTS.   NTRUEDL60208

THE VOCATIONAL GUIDANCE AND EDUCATION OF NEGROES. THE NEGRO AND THE BATTLE OF PRODUCTION.   NWILKDA42233

SOME SOCIOLOGICAL ASPECTS OF VOCATIONAL GUIDANCE OF NEGRO CHILDREN.   NYOUNMN44348

RESOURCE UNITS IN THE TEACHING OF OCCUPATIONS -- AN EXPERIMENT IN GUIDANCE OF PUERTO-RICAN TEENAGERS.   PNEWYCC56834

CAREER GUIDANCE FOR GIRLS. /COUNSELING/   WCALDED60445

VOCATIONAL GUIDANCE AND TRAINING OF GIRLS AND WOMEN. /COUNSELING/   WINTELO64863

REPORT ON UNDERGRADUATE COUNSELING AND CONTINUING EDUCATION AND GUIDANCE FOR MATURE WOMAN.   WNICOHG64032

HIGH SCHOOL GUIDANCE COUNSELOR-S PERCEPTIONS OF SELECTED CAREERS FOR WOMEN COLLEGE GRADUATES.   WSWOPMR63146

SPEECH ABOUT JOB OPPORTUNITIES FOR GIRLS BEFORE THE MARYLAND STATE PERSONNEL AND GUIDANCE ASSOCIATION.   WTERLRX64148

GUIDE
MANAGEMENT GUIDE. EQUAL-EMPLOYMENT-OPPORTUNITY.   GASSOIC63407

GUIDE TO LAWFUL AND UNLAWFUL PRE-EMPLOYMENT INQUIRIES BY EMPLOYERS, EMPLOYMENT-AGENCIES, AND LABOR
ORGANIZATIONS UNDER THE CALIFORNIA FAIR-EMPLOYMENT-PRACTICE ACT, LABOR CODE, SECTIONS 1410-1432.   GCALDIR60527

FAIR-EMPLOYMENT-PRACTICE ACT...FEPC RULES AND REGULATIONS... GUIDE TO PRE-EMPLOYMENT INQUIRIES.
/CALIFORNIA/   GCALFEP61533

PROMOTING EQUAL JOB OPPORTUNITY, A GUIDE FOR EMPLOYERS. /CALIFORNIA/   GCALFEP63538

EMPLOYMENT PRACTICE GUIDE.   GCOMMCH65589

FAIR-EMPLOYMENT-PRACTICE-COMMISSION GUIDE TO UNLAWFUL PRE-EMPLOYMENT INQUIRIES.   GCURRRO60889

GUIDE   (CONTINUATION)
GUIDE TO MERIT EMPLOYMENT. A RESTATEMENT OF INDUSTRY PRINCIPLES AND PRACTICES.   GFOODECND694

QUESTIONING APPLICANTS FOR EMPLOYMENT, A GUIDE FOR APPLICATION FORMS AND INTERVIEWS UNDER THE HAWAII
FAIR-EMPLOYMENT-PRACTICES ACT.   GHAWADL64767

GUIDE TO FAIR-EMPLOYMENT-PRACTICES.   GKHEETW64851

COUNSELOR-S GUIDE TO OCCUPATIONAL AND OTHER MANPOWER INFORMATION. AN ANNOTATED BIBLIOGRAPHY.   GLAFADP65782

A GUIDE TO GOVERNMENT OFFICIALS.   /CIVIL-RIGHTS/   GOREGBLND135

GUIDE TO EMPLOYERS, EMPLOYMENT-AGENCIES AND LABOR UNIONS DEFINING PROPER AND IMPROPER PRE-EMPLOYMENT
INQUIRIES. /PENNSYLVANIA/   GPENNHRND164

GUIDE FOR INVESTIGATIONS AND COMPLIANCE REVIEWS IN EQUAL-EMPLOYMENT-OPPORTUNITY.   GPRESCD62109

COMPLIANCE GUIDE. RECOMMENDATIONS FOR OBTAINING COMPLIANCE WITH THE NONDISCRIMINATION PROVISIONS IN
GOVERNMENT CONTRACTS.   GPRESCH58119

EMPLOYERS GUIDE TO EQUAL-EMPLOYMENT-OPPORTUNITY.   GSCHEGX66280

EQUAL-EMPLOYMENT-OPPORTUNITY GUIDE FOR DEPARTMENT OF THE NAVY CONTRACTORS.   GUSODEF64433

A GUIDE TO INDUSTRIAL-RELATIONS IN THE UNITED STATES. EQUAL JOB OPPORTUNITY UNDER COLLECTIVE-BARGAINING.   GUSDLAB58449

NAACP LABOR MANUAL. A GUIDE TO ACTION.   NHILLHX58531

THE NEGRO IN THE US. A RESEARCH GUIDE.   NWELSEK65304

THE NEXT STEP -- A GUIDE TO PART-TIME OPPORTUNITIES IN GREATER BOSTON FOR THE EDUCATED WOMAN.
/MASSACHUSETTS/   WWHITMS64266

A WOMAN-S GUIDE TO EARNING A GOOD LIVING.   WWINTEX61270

GUIDELINES
FAIR-EMPLOYMENT-PRACTICES EQUAL GOOD EMPLOYMENT PRACTICES. GUIDELINES FOR TESTING AND SELECTING MINORITY
JOB APPLICANTS.   /CALIFORNIA/   GCALFEP66540

GUIDELINES FOR INITIATING FAIR-EMPLOYMENT-PRACTICES.   GHAGAJJ63751

DEVELOPING FAIR-EMPLOYMENT PROGRAMS. GUIDELINES FOR SELECTION.   GLOCKHC66780

GUIDELINES ON EMPLOYMENT TESTING PROCEDURES.   GUSEEOC66510

GUIDELINES FOR COMMUNITY-ACTION.   NNATLUL65889

MANAGEMENTS GUIDELINES FOR MEETING THE NEGRO DRIVE FOR JOB EQUALITY.   /INDUSTRY/.   NOPINRC63958

GUIDES
SOME GUIDES FOR SUPERVISING WOMEN WORKERS.   WGRANLJ63800

GUIDING
GUIDING CREATIVE TALENT.   /WORK-WOMAN-ROLE/   WTORREP62158

GUILTY
UNION HELD GUILTY OF RACE DISCRIMINATION.   NLABORR45027

HALE
AN ANALYSIS OF SELECTIVE FACTORS INFLUENCING FARM INCOME IN HALE COUNTY, AS A BASIS FOR ESTABLISHING A
MORE EFFECTIVE VOCATIONAL AGRICULTURAL PROGRAM.   /ALABAMA/   NSALTDR52347

HANDBOOK
HANDBOOK FOR LOCAL UNION FAIR PRACTICES COMMITTEES. REVISED EDITION.   GUAWXFPND369

HANDBOOK OF AMERICAN-INDIANS NORTH OF MEXICO.   ISMITIB59619

1965 HANDBOOK ON WOMEN WORKERS.   WUSDLAB66200

HANDICAPPED
BENEFIT POLICIES IN RELATION TO RECRUITMENT OF OLDER WORKERS, HANDICAPPED, AND MINORITY GROUPS.   GBARRGJ51425

HARD-CORE
HARD-CORE UNEMPLOYMENT AND POVERTY IN LOS-ANGELES. /CALIFORNIA   NEGRO   MEXICAN-AMERICAN/   CUVCAIND524

THE COST OF RETRAINING THE HARD-CORE UNEMPLOYED.   GBORUME65745

TRAINING THE HARD-CORE UNEMPLOYED.   GBROOLB64795

EVALUATION AND SKILL TRAINING OF OUT-OF-SCHOOL, HARD-CORE UNEMPLOYED YOUTH FOR TRAINING AND PLACEMENT.   GSMITAE65140

HELP FOR THE HARD-CORE UNEMPLOYED.   /TRAINING/   NMILLJN66787

NO LONGER SUPERFLUOUS -- THE EDUCATIONAL REHABILITATION OF THE HARD-CORE UNEMPLOYED.   NPALLNJ65332

HARD-CORE UNEMPLOYMENT IN DETROIT. CAUSES AND REMEDIES. /MICHIGAN/   NWACHHMND289

HARD-TO-EMPLOY
JOBS FOR THE HARD-TO-EMPLOY IN PRIVATE ENTERPRISE.   GCASSFH66744

HARLEM
HARLEM. A COMMUNITY IN TRANSITION.   NCLARJH64309

THE POOR OF HARLEM. SOCIAL FUNCTIONING OF THE UNDERCLASS.   NGORDJX65435

THE OCCUPATIONAL SITUATION OF CENTRAL HARLEM YOUTH.   NHOUSLX65577

THE HARLEM RIOT. A STUDY IN MASS FRUSTRATION.   NOLANHX43954

ECONOMIC STRUCTURE OF THE HARLEM COMMUNITY.   /NEW-YORK/   NSTEVHR64177

REPORT FROM A SPANISH HARLEM FORTRESS.   PHAYMRX64153

SPANISH HARLEM. AN ANATOMY OF POVERTY.   PSEXTPC65853

ISLAND IN THE CITY. THE WORLD OF SPANISH HARLEM.   PWAKEDX59858

HARRIS-COUNTY
A COMPARATIVE STUDY OF TOP LEVEL MALE AND FEMALE EXECUTIVES IN HARRIS-COUNTY.   /TEXAS   OCCUPATIONS/   WDOLLPA65738

HARTFORD
    FAIR EMPLOYMENT IS GOOD BUSINESS AT G FOX OF HARTFORD. /CASE-STUDY CONNECTICUT/   NGREEMX48448

HARVARD
    HARVARD LOOKS AT THE EXECUTIVE-SUITE.   JAMERJC60691

HARVEST
    STILL THE HARVEST OF SHAME. /MIGRANT-WORKERS/   GBENNFX64500

    THE HARVEST OF DESPAIR. THE MIGRANT FARM WORKER.   GWRIGDX65604

    DOMESTIC AND IMPORTED WORKERS IN THE HARVEST LABOR-MARKET, SANTA-CLARA COUNTY, CALIFORNIA, 1954.   MFULLVX56396

    NO HARVEST FOR THE REAPER. THE STORY OF THE MIGRATORY AGRICULTURAL WORKER IN THE UNITED STATES.   NHILLHX59534

HARVESTER
    NEGRO EMPLOYMENT IN THREE SOUTHERN PLANTS OF INTERNATIONAL HARVESTER COMPANY. /CASE-STUDY/   NHOPEJX55572

HARVESTERS
    THE HARVESTERS. THE STORY OF THE MIGRANT PEOPLE.   GSHOTLR61684

HATE
    RACE HATE. NEWEST UNION-BUSTING WEAPON IN THE SOUTH.   NCAREJB58181

HAWAII
    FAIR-EMPLOYMENT-PRACTICES ACT AND REGULATION 30. /HAWAII/   GHAWADL64766

    QUESTIONING APPLICANTS FOR EMPLOYMENT, A GUIDE FOR APPLICATION FORMS AND INTERVIEWS UNDER THE HAWAII
    FAIR-EMPLOYMENT-PRACTICES ACT.   GHAWADL64767

    RACE-RELATIONS FRONTIERS IN HAWAII.   GLINDAW61744

HAY-COUNTY
    MINORITY-GROUPS AND THEIR EDUCATION IN HAY-COUNTY, TEXAS.   MMEADBS59438

HEALING
    THE ROLE OF THE NEGRO IN THE HEALING PROFESSIONS IN CONTEMPORARY AMERICA. /OCCUPATIONS/   NMCPHEL55728

HEALTH
    HEALTH OF MIGRANTS. /CALIFORNIA/   GCALDIR60522

    THE HEALTH OF THE MIGRANT-WORKER. /EMPLOYMENT-CONDITIONS/   GLINDJR66603

    MARYLAND TB -- VD HEALTH PROGRAM AMONG AGRICULTURAL MIGRANTS.   GMARYSD65958

    HEALTH PROBLEMS OF MIGRANT-LABOR.   GMIREMX59013

    HEALTH WORK AMONG MIGRANTS IN 1958 BY THE NEW-JERSEY STATE DEPARTMENT OF HEALTH.   GSHEPAC59301

    HEALTH WORK AMONG MIGRANTS IN 1958 BY THE NEW-JERSEY STATE DEPARTMENT OF HEALTH.   GSHEPAC59301

    WHITE-NONWHITE DIFFERENTIALS IN HEALTH, EDUCATION, AND WELFARE.   GUSDHEW65435

    HEALTH, EDUCATION, AND WELFARE ASPECTS OF THE ECONOMIC REPORT OF THE PRESENT AND ANNUAL REPORT OF THE
    COUNCIL OF ECONOMIC ADVISORS.   GUSDHEW66711

    ANNUAL REPORT OF THE SECRETARY OF HEALTH, EDUCATION, AND WELFARE TO THE CONGRESS ON TRAINING ACTIVITIES
    UNDER THE MANPOWER-DEVELOPMENT-AND-TRAINING-ACT, 1965.   GUSDHEW66978

    HEALTH AND ECONOMIC DEVELOPMENT.   IBAUMLX64535

    HEALTH PRACTICES AND EDUCATIONAL ASPIRATIONS AS INDICATORS OF ACCULTURATION AND SOCIAL-CLASS AMONG THE
    EASTERN CHEROKEE. /NORTH-CAROLINA/   IKUPFHJ62216

    INDIAN HEALTH HIGHLIGHTS. /DEMOGRAPHY/   IUSDHEW66813

    YOU ASKED ABOUT THE NAVAJO. EDUCATION, HEALTH, AND ECONOMIC PROBLEMS OF THE NAVAJO.   IUSDINT57664

    INDIAN POVERTY AND INDIAN HEALTH.   IWAGNCJ64681

    A STUDY OF THE MENTAL HEALTH PROBLEMS OF MEXICAN-AMERICAN RESIDENTS. /TEXAS/   MTEXASD61500

    THE SOCIO-ECONOMIC BACKGROUND OF NEGRO HEALTH STATUS.   NJCHNCS49616

    THE INFLUENCE OF TUSKEGEE-INSTITUTE ON THE HEALTH, EDUCATIONAL, ECONOMIC, AND POLITICAL ASPECTS OF THE
    NEGRO POPULATION OF MACON COUNTY, ALABAMA.   NSHIEAR51342

    THE FEMALE PHYSICIAN IN PUBLIC HEALTH. CONFLICT AND RECONCILIATION OF THE SEX AND PROFESSIONAL ROLES.
    /OCCUPATIONS/   WKOSAJX64915

    NONTRADITIONALLY TRAINED WOMEN AS MENTAL HEALTH COUNSELORS/PSYCHOTHERAPISTS.   WMAGOTM66779

    WOMEN IN INDUSTRY -- PATTERNS OF WOMEN-S WORK AND OCCUPATIONAL HEALTH AND SAFETY. /OCCUPATIONS/   WSPIRES60301

    THE HEALTH OF WOMEN WHO WORK.   WUSDHEW65170

    HEALTH MANPOWER SOURCE BOOK. SECTION 2. NURSING PERSONNEL.   WUSDHEW66177

HEALTH-STATUS
    LONGEVITY AND HEALTH-STATUS OF THE NEGRO AMERICAN.   NGOLDMS63431

HEARING
    TESTIMONY, PUBLIC HEARING, WOMEN IN PUBLIC AND PRIVATE EMPLOYMENT, CALIFORNIA. /MEXICAN-AMERICAN/   CARYWSX66621

    HEARING OF THE SUBCOMMITTEE ON ECONOMIC DEVELOPMENT, EDITED TRANSCRIPT, JANUARY 28 AND 29, 1964.
    /CALIFORNIA FEP/   GCALAIW64510

    HEARING.   IUSCONG60637

    TESTIMONY BEFORE STATE SENATE FACT FINDING SUBCOMMITTEE ON RACE-RELATIONS AND URBAN PROBLEMS, FINAL
    HEARING, JANUARY 20 1965. /CALIFORNIA FEPC/   NGRAHCX65439

    EQUAL-EMPLOYMENT-OPPORTUNITY, HEARING, TESTIMONY.   NHILLHX62547

    US DEPARTMENT OF LABOR, PUBLIC HEARING, TESTIMONY. /MIGRANT-WORKERS/   NHILLHX63548

    NEW-YORK CITY COMMISSION ON HUMAN RIGHTS, CONSTRUCTION TRADES HEARING, TESTIMONY. /INDUSTRY/   NHILLHX66546

    HEARING BEFORE THE AD HOC SUBCOMMITTEE ON THE WAR-ON-POVERTY PROGRAM.   NYOUNWM64350

HEARING   (CONTINUATION)

TESTIMCNY, PUBLIC HEARING, WCMEN IN PUBLIC AND PRIVATE EMPLOYMENT, CALIFORNIA. /DISCRIMINATION EEOC/   WBALEHX66625

TESTIMCNY, PUBLIC HEARING, WCMEN IN PUBLIC AND PRIVATE EMPLOYMENT, CALIFORNIA. /EMPLOYMENT-CONDITIONS/   WBECHCX66631

STATEMENT, PUBLIC HEARING, WCMEN IN PUBLIC AND PRIVATE EMPLOYMENT, CALIFORNIA. /FEP
EMPLOYMENT-CONDITIONS DISCRIMINATION/   WBELAJX66634

STATEMENT, PUBLIC HEARING, WCMEN IN PUBLIC AND PRIVATE EMPLOYMENT, CALIFORNIA. /FEP
EMPLOYMENT-CONDITIONS DISCRIMINATION/   WBENNSJ66637

TESTIMCNY, PUBLIC HEARING, WCMEN IN PUBLIC AND PRIVATE EDUCATION, CALIFORNIA. /FEP
EMPLOYMENT-CONDITIONS DISCRIMINATION MIGRANT-WORKERS/   WBLOCHX66649

TESTIMONY, PUBLIC HEARING, WCMAN IN PUBLIC AND PRIVATE EMPLOYMENT, CALIFORNIA. /DISCRIMINATION/   WBROWAX66657

TESTIMCNY PRESENTED AT PUBLIC HEARING, MARCH 31 -- APRIL 1, 1966. /FEP EMPLOYMENT-CONDITIONS
DISCRIMINATION MIGRANTS/   WCALACW62675

TESTIMCNY PRESENTED AT PUBLIC HEARING, APRIL 28, 1966. SAN-FRANCISCO, CALIFORNIA. /FEP
EMPLCYMENT-CONDITIONS DISCRIMINATION MIGRANTS/   WCALACW62676

TESTIMONY PRESENTED AT PUBLIC HEARING, FEBRUARY 24-25, 1966. /FEP EMPLOYMENT-CONDITIONS DISCRIMINATION
MIGRANTS/   WCALACW66674

TESTIMCNY PRESENTED AT PUBLIC HEARING, APRIL 29, 1966. SAN-FRANCISCO, CALIFORNIA. /FEP
EMPLOYMENT-CONDITIONS CHILDREN/   WCALACW66677

TESTIMONY, PUBLIC HEARING, WCMEN IN PUBLIC AND PRIVATE EMPLOYMENT, CALIFORNIA. /EMPLOYMENT-CONDITIONS/   WCHANHD66687

TESTIMCNY, PUBLIC HEARING, WCMEN IN PUBLIC AND PRIVATE EMPLOYMENT, CALIFORNIA. /FEP
EMPLOYMENT-CONDITIONS DISCRIMINATION MIGRANTS/   WCLIFFG66692

TESTIMCNY, PUBLIC HEARING, WCMEN IN PUBLIC AND PRIVATE EMPLOYMENT, CALIFORNIA. /DISCRIMINATION/   WCOLLNX66696

TESTIMCNY, PUBLIC HEARING, WCMEN IN PUBLIC AND PRIVATE EMPLOYMENT, CALIFORNIA. /EMPLOYMENT-CONDITIONS/   WCOMPBX66702

TESTIMCNY, PUBLIC HEARING, WCMEN IN PUBLIC AND PRIVATE EMPLOYMENT, CALIFORNIA. /TRAINING/   WCUMMGX66711

TESTIMCNY, PUBLIC HEARING, WCMEN IN PUBLIC AND PRIVATE EMPLOYMENT, CALIFORNIA. /EMPLOYMENT-CONDITIONS/   WDIBRJX66732

TESTIMCNY, PUBLIC HEARING, WCMAN IN PUBLIC AND PRIVATE EMPLOYMENT, CALIFORNIA. /DISCRIMINATION/   WDORAMX66739

TESTIMCNY, PUBLIC HEARING, WCMEN IN PUBLIC AND PRIVATE EMPLOYMENT, CALIFORNIA. /EMPLOYMENT-CONDITIONS/   WEVANSX66753

TESTIMCNY, PUBLIC HEARING, WCMEN IN PUBLIC AND PRIVATE EMPLOYMENT, CALIFORNIA. /EMPLOYMENT-CONDITIONS/   WFEINBX66760

TESTIMCNY, PUBLIC HEARING, WCMEN IN PUBLIC AND PRIVATE EMPLOYMENT, CALIFORNIA. /DISCRIMINATION/   WFOOTJX66765

TESTIMCNY, PUBLIC HEARING, WCMEN IN PUBLIC AND PRIVATE EMPLOYMENT, CALIFORNIA. /EMPLOYMENT-CONDITIONS/   WGABELX66773

TESTIMCNY, PUBLIC HEARING, WCMEN IN PUBLIC AND PRIVATE EMPLOYMENT, CALIFORNIA. /DISCRIMINATION/   WGEIGPX66776

TESTIMCNY, PUBLIC HEARING, WCMEN IN PUBLIC AND PRIVATE EMPLOYMENT, CALIFORNIA. /DEMOGRAPHY/   WGERSMX66777

TESTIMCNY, PUBLIC HEARING, WCMEN IN PUBLIC AND PRIVATE EMPLOYMENT, CALIFORNIA. /EMPLOYMENT-CONDITIONS/   WGILBRX66780

TESTIMCNY, PUBLIC HEARING, WCMEN IN PUBLIC AND PRIVATE EMPLOYMENT, CALIFORNIA. /EMPLOYMENT-CONDITIONS/   WGLENEM66788

TESTIMCNY, PUBLIC HEARING, WCMEN IN PUBLIC AND PRIVATE EMPLOYMENT, CALIFORNIA. /DISCRIMINATION
WORK-FAMILY-CONFLICT/   WGUPTRC66808

TESTIMCNY, PUBLIC HEARING, WOMEN IN PUBLIC AND PRIVATE EMPLOYMENT, CALIFORNIA. /EMPLOYMENT-CONDITIONS/   WGUPTRC66809

TESTIMCNY, PUBLIC HEARING, WCMEN IN PUBLIC AND PRIVATE EMPLOYMENT, CALIFCRNIA. /EMPLOYMENT-CONDITIONS/   WHEALWX66836

TESTIMCNY, PUBLIC HEARING, WCMEN IN PUBLIC AND PRIVATE EMPLOYMENT, CALIFORNIA. /DISCRIMINATION/   WHILLHX66844

TESTIMCNY, PUBLIC HEARING, WCMEN IN PUBLIC AND PRIVATE EMPLOYMENT, CALIFORNIA. /MOTA EEO/   WINGRLX66859

STATEMENT, PUBLIC HEARING, WCMEN IN PUBLIC AND PRIVATE EMPLOYMENT, CALIFORNIA. /EMPLOYMENT-CONDITIONS
MIGRANT-WORKERS/   WKAUFDX66886

TESTIMCNY, PUBLIC HEARING, WCMEN IN PUBLIC AND PRIVATE EMPLOYMENT, CALIFORNIA. /EMPLOYMENT-CONDITIONS/   WKELLET66888

STATEMENT, PUBLIC HEARING, WCMEN IN PUBLIC AND PRIVATE EMPLOYMENT, CALIFORNIA. /EMPLOYMENT-CONDITIONS/   WKENNVX66890

STATEMENT, PUBLIC HEARING, WCMEN IN PUBLIC AND PRIVATE EMPLOYMENT, CALIFORNIA. /EMPLOYMENT-CONDITIONS/   WKNIGTF66911

TESTIMCNY, PUBLIC HEARING, WCMEN IN PUBLIC AND PRIVATE EMPLOYMENT, CALIFORNIA. /FEP MIGRANT-WORKERS
EMPLOYMENT-CONDITIONS/   WLLOYMX66940

TESTIMCNY, PUBLIC HEARING, WCMEN IN PUBLIC AND PRIVATE EMPLOYMENT, CALIFCRNIA. /FEP EMPLOYMENT
CCNDITICNS/   WLCWEDX66943

TESTIMCNY, PUBLIC HEARING, WCMEN IN PUBLIC AND PRIVATE EMPLOYMENT, CALIFORNIA. /EMPLOYMENT-CONDITIONS/   WMACKJW66950

TESTIMCNY, PUBLIC HEARING, WCMEN IN PUBLIC AND PRIVATE EMPLOYMENT, CALIFCRNIA. /OCCUPATIONS
EMPLOYMENT-CONDITIONS/   WMCLALX66947

TESTIMONY, PUBLIC HEARING, WCMEN IN PUBLIC AND PRIVATE EMPLOYMENT, CALIFORNIA. /BLUE-COLLAR
EMPLOYMENT-CCNDITIONS/   WMENGVX66969

STATEMENT, PUBLIC HEARING, WCMEN IN PUBLIC AND PRIVATE EMPLOYMENT, CALIFORNIA. /FEP
EMPLOYMENT-CONDITIONS MIGRANT-WORKERS/   WMILLJJ66979

TESTIMCNY, PUBLIC HEARING, WCMEN IN PUBLIC AND PRIVATE EMPLOYMENT, CALIFCRNIA. /EMPLOYMENT-CONDITIONS/   WMILLKL66980

TESTIMCNY, PUBLIC HEARING, WCMEN IN PUBLIC AND PRIVATE EMPLOYMENT, CALIFCRNIA. /EMPLOYMENT-CONDITIONS/   WMORAMX66995

TESTIMCNY, PUBLIC HEARING, WCMEN IN PUBLIC AND PRIVATE EMPLOYMENT, CALIFORNIA.   WMOTHWA66001

TESTIMCNY, PUBLIC HEARING, WCMEN IN PUBLIC AND PRIVATE EMPLOYMENT, CALIFCRNIA. /EMPLOYMENT-CONDITIONS/   WMYRIRX66013

TESTIMCNY, PUBLIC HEARING, WCMEN IN PUBLIC AND PRIVATE EMPLOYMENT, CALIFCRNIA. /EMPLOYMENT-CONDITIONS/   WPALMGX66047

TESTIMCNY, PUBLIC HEARING, WOMEN IN PUBLIC AND PRIVATE EMPLOYMENT, CALIFORNIA. /FEP
EMPLOYMENT-CONDITIONS MIGRANT-WORKERS/   WPEEVMX66052

HEARING   (CONTINUATION)
TESTIMONY. PUBLIC HEARING. WOMEN IN PUBLIC AND PRIVATE EMPLOYMENT, CALIFORNIA. /EMPLOYMENT-CONDITIONS/   WRILEEX66081

TESTIMONY. PUBLIC HEARING. WOMEN IN PUBLIC AND PRIVATE EMPLOYMENT, CALIFORNIA. /FEP
EMPLOYMENT-CONDITIONS/   WSCHRPX66104

TESTIMONY. PUBLIC HEARING. WOMEN IN PUBLIC AND PRIVATE EMPLOYMENT, CALIFORNIA. /EMPLOYMENT-CONDITIONS/   WSHEAHX66112

TESTIMONY. PUBLIC HEARING. WOMEN IN PUBLIC AND PRIVATE EMPLOYMENT, CALIFORNIA. /FEP
EMPLOYMENT-CONDITIONS DISCRIMINATION/   WSMITWH66123

TESTIMONY. PUBLIC HEARING. WOMEN IN PUBLIC AND PRIVATE EMPLOYMENT, CALIFORNIA. /FEP
EMPLOYMENT-CONDITIONS DISCRIMINATION MIGRANT-WORKERS/   WSPENNX66129

TESTIMONY. PUBLIC HEARING. WOMEN IN PUBLIC AND PRIVATE EMPLOYMENT, CALIFORNIA. /LABOR-MARKET/   WSTEPRX66138

TESTIMONY. PUBLIC HEARING. WOMEN IN PUBLIC AND PRIVATE EMPLOYMENT, CALIFORNIA. /FEPC/   WSTERAX66140

TESTIMONY. PUBLIC HEARING. WOMEN IN PUBLIC AND PRIVATE EMPLOYMENT, CALIFORNIA. /EMPLOYMENT-CONDITIONS/   WTHOMDX66151

TESTIMONY. PUBLIC HEARING. WOMEN IN PUBLIC AND PRIVATE EMPLOYMENT, CALIFORNIA. /EMPLOYMENT-CONDITIONS
DISCRIMINATION/   WTHOMGX66149

STATEMENT. PUBLIC HEARING. WOMEN IN PUBLIC AND PRIVATE EMPLOYMENT, CALIFORNIA. /FEP
EMPLOYMENT-CONDITIONS DISCRIMINATION/   WVAILLX66256

TESTIMONY. PUBLIC HEARING. WOMEN IN PUBLIC AND PRIVATE EMPLOYMENT, CALIFORNIA. /EMPLOYMENT-CONDITIONS
MIGRANT-WORKERS/   WWEBEJX66258

TESTIMONY. PUBLIC HEARING. WOMEN IN PUBLIC AND PRIVATE EMPLOYMENT, CALIFORNIA. /FEP
EMPLOYMENT-CONDITIONS MIGRANT-WORKERS/   WWOMEIX66273

TESTIMONY. PUBLIC HEARING. WOMEN IN PUBLIC AND PRIVATE EMPLOYMENT, CALIFORNIA. /EMPLOYMENT-CONDITIONS/   WWOODWX66276

HEARINGS
POVERTY IN THE UNITED STATES. HEARINGS. /AMERICAN-INDIAN NEGRO PUERTO-RICAN EMPLOYMENT/   CUSHOUR64346

THE CONGRESSIONAL HEARINGS AND ISSUES IN PSYCHOLOGICAL TESTING. INVASIONS OF PRIVACY AND TEST BIAS.   GGORDJEND934

THE MANPOWER REVOLUTION. ITS POLICY CONSEQUENCES. EXCERPTS FROM SENATE HEARINGS BEFORE THE CLARK
SUBCOMMITTEE.   GMANGGL66217

SUMMARY OF TESTIMONY -- HOTEL RESTAURANT HEARINGS, APPENDIX A. /PHILADELPHIA PENNSYLVANIA/   GPHILCH60181

FINDINGS OF FACT. CONCLUSIONS AND ACTION OF THE COMMISSION ON HUMAN-RELATIONS IN RE. INVESTIGATIVE PUBLIC
HEARINGS INTO ALLEGED DISCRIMINATORY PRACTICE BY THE HOTEL AND RESTAURANT INDUSTRY IN PHILADELPHIA.
/PENNSYLVANIA/   GPHILCH61176

US COMMISSION-ON-CIVIL-RIGHTS. HEARINGS. LOS-ANGELES AND SAN-FRANCISCO, CALIFORNIA. JANUARY 25-26, 1960,
JANUARY 27-28, 1960.   GUSCCMC60400

US COMMISSION-ON-CIVIL-RIGHTS. HEARINGS. DETROIT, MICHIGAN. DEC 14-15 1960.   GUSCOMC61399

US COMMISSION-ON-CIVIL-RIGHTS. HEARINGS. NEW-ORLEANS, LOUISIANA. SEPTEMBER 27-28, 1960, MAY 5-6, 1961.   GUSCOMC61403

US COMMISSION-ON-CIVIL-RIGHTS. HEARINGS. MEMPHIS, TENNESSEE. JUNE 25-26, 1962.   GUSCOMC62401

US COMMISSION-ON-CIVIL-RIGHTS. HEARINGS. NEWARK, NEW-JERSEY. SEPTEMBER 11-12, 1962.   GUSCOMC62402

HEARINGS RELATING TO THE TRAINING AND UTILIZATION OF THE MANPOWER RESOURCES OF THE NATION.   GUSSENA63618

HEARINGS --TRI-CITIES AREA OF ALABAMA.   NNATILR58875

EDITORIAL COMMENT. FEPC HEARINGS REDUCE RACE PROBLEM TO LOWEST TERMS -- EQUAL-ECONOMIC-OPPORTUNITY.   NTHOMCH43160

HERITAGE
THEIR HERITAGE -- POVERTY.   MARAGMX66358

HIDDEN
HIDDEN UNEMPLOYMENT 1953-62. A QUANTITATIVE ANALYSIS BY AGE AND SEX.   NDERNTX66264

BLUEPRINT FOR TALENT. SEARCHING AMERICA-S HIDDEN MANPOWER.   NPLAURL57003

HIGH
REALITIES OF THE JOB-MARKET FOR THE HIGH SCHOOL DROPOUT.   GBIENHX64111

EMPLOYMENT OF HIGH SCHOOL GRADUATES AND DROPOUTS IN 1964.   GBOGAFA65750

EMPLOYMENT OPPORTUNITIES FOR HIGH SCHOOL DROPOUTS. A STUDY OF EMPLOYERS PRACTICES, NEEDS AND ATTITUDES IN
THE DISTRICT OF COLUMBIA. /WASHINGTON-DC/   GBURESS57499

EMPLOYMENT OF JUNE 1959 HIGH SCHOOL GRADUATES, OCTOBER 1959.   GCOOPSX60601

CHARACTERISTICS OF SCHOOL DROPOUTS AND HIGH SCHOOL GRADUATES, FARM AND NONFARM, 1960.   GCOWHJD64419

A SUMMARY REPORT OF PRACTICES AND PROGRAMS DESIGNED TO REDUCE THE NUMBER OF DROPOUTS IN THE HIGH SCHOOLS
OF LOS-ANGELES COUNTY. /CALIFORNIA/   GDELMOT66147

BACKGROUND FACTORS RELATING TO COLLEGE PLANS AND COLLEGE ENROLLMENT AMONG PUBLIC HIGH SCHOOL STUDENTS.
/ASPIRATIONS/   GEDUCTS57959

A PILOT STUDY OF THE EMPLOYMENT EXPERIENCES OF HIGH SCHOOL GRADUATES.   GPHILCH65177

THE HIGH COST OF DISCRIMINATION. THE WASTE IN MANPOWER, MORALE, AND PRODUCTIVITY COSTS AMERICAN INDUSTRY
30 BILLION DOLLARS A YEAR.   GROPEEX63244

EMPLOYMENT OF HIGH SCHOOL GRADUATES AND DROPOUTS IN 1962.   GSCHIJX63282

PROGRAMS FOR HIGH SCHOOL DROPOUTS. EXPERIENCE REPORT 101.   GUSCCNF64976

EMPLOYMENT OF HIGH SCHOOL GRADUATES AND DROPOUTS IN 1965.   GUSDLAB66073

RESIDENTIAL SEGREGATION OF SOCIAL-CLASSES AND ASPIRATIONS OF HIGH SCHOOL BOYS.   GWILSAB59568

MOHAWKS. ROUND TRIP TO THE HIGH STEEL.   IBLUMRX65539

LEVEL OF OCCUPATIONAL ASPIRATIONS AMONG MONTANA INDIANS IN GRADE AND HIGH SCHOOL.   IDOUGGV60550

PERCEIVED LIFE CHANCES IN THE OPPORTUNITY STRUCTURE. A STUDY OF A TRI-ETHNIC HIGH SCHOOL.   MGUERCX62410

HIGH   (CONTINUATION)
BACKGROUND AND AMBITION OF MALE MEXICAN-AMERICAN HIGH SCHOOL SENIORS IN LOS-ANGELES. /CALIFORNIA/   MHELLCS63414

AMBITIONS OF MEXICAN-AMERICAN YOUTH — GOALS AND MEANS OF MOBILITY OF HIGH SCHOOL SENIORS.   MHELLCS64413

A STUDY OF THE ACCULTURATION AND SOCIAL ASPIRATIONS OF SIXTY JUNIOR HIGH SCHOOL STUDENTS FROM THE MEXICAN
ETHNIC GROUP.   MJONEBM62421

DIFFERENCES IN DROPOUT AND OTHER SCHOOL BEHAVIOR BETWEEN TWO GROUPS OF TENTH GRADE BOYS IN AN URBAN HIGH
SCHOOL.   MMUNORF57446

MEXICAN-AMERICANS IN URBAN PUBLIC HIGH SCHOOLS. AN EXPLORATION OF THE DROP-OUT PROGRAM.   MSHELPM59488

SUMMARY REPORT OF THE STUDY OF DROP-OUTS IN THE THREE SENIOR HIGH SCHOOLS, COMPTON UNION HIGH SCHOOL
DISTRICT. /CALIFORNIA/   MWHITNX60517

SUMMARY REPORT OF THE STUDY OF DROP-OUTS IN THE THREE SENIOR HIGH SCHOOLS, COMPTON UNION HIGH SCHOOL
DISTRICT. /CALIFORNIA/   MWHITNX60517

A COMPARISON OF THE ACADEMIC ACHIEVEMENTS OF WHITE AND NEGRO HIGH SCHOOL GRADUATES. /EDUCATION/   NBULLHA50132

VOCATIONAL CHOICES OF NEGRO HIGH SCHOOL STUDENTS IN MACON COUNTY, ALABAMA, AND THEIR RELATIONSHIP TO
BASIC OCCUPATIONAL ACTIVITES OF THE SCHOOL COMMUNITIES. /ASPIRATIONS/   NCHAPEJ49351

SOME FACTORS WHICH DISTINGUISH DROP-OUTS FROM HIGH SCHOOL GRADUATES.   NGRAGWL49978

IN SEARCH OF A FUTURE. A STUDY OF CAREER-SEEKING EXPERIENCES OF SELECTED NEGRO HIGH SCHOOL GRADUATES IN
WASHINGTON-DC WHICH WAS AN EFFORT TO PROVIDE KNOWLEDGE HELPFUL IN SOLVING ONE OF THE MOST CRITICAL
PROBLEMS FACING URBAN AMERICA TODAY.   NGRIEES63454

HIGH SCHOOL GRADUATES AND DROPOUTS -- A NEW LOOK AT A PERSISTENT PROBLEM.   NLIVIAH58044

ACHIEVEMENT OF MALE HIGH SCHOOL DROPOUTS AND GRADUATES IN ALABAMA VOCATIONAL SCHOOLS.   NMILLGJ65791

FACTORS INVOLVED IN STUDENT ELIMINATION FROM HIGH SCHOOL.   NMGORPL54079

SOME CORRELATES OF HIGH NEED FOR ACHIEVEMENT AMONG URBAN NORTHERN NEGROES.   NNUTTRL46951

RETREATISM AND OCCUPATIONAL ASPIRATIONS AMONG WHITE AND NEGRO HIGH SCHOOL SENIORS.   NPOWEEC61009

THE EFFECT OF SPECIAL INSTRUCTION UPON TEST PERFORMANCE OF HIGH SCHOOL STUDENTS IN TENNESSEE.   NROBESO66961

THE RELATION OF RACIAL SEGREGATION IN EARLY SCHOOLING TO THE LEVEL OF ASPIRATION AND ACADEMIC ACHIEVEMENT
OF NEGRO STUDENTS IN A NORTHERN HIGH SCHOOL.   NSAINJN62137

SOCIAL CHARACTERISTICS OF HIGH SCHOOL SENIORS IN URBAN NEGRO HIGH SCHOOLS IN TWO STATES.   NSMITBF56147

SOCIAL CHARACTERISTICS OF HIGH SCHOOL SENIORS IN URBAN NEGRO HIGH SCHOOLS IN TWO STATES.   NSMITBF56147

SOCIALIZATION. RACE AND THE AMERICAN HIGH SCHOOL. /EDUCATION/   NTENHWP65201

AN EMPIRICAL STUDY OF HIGH SCHOOL DROPOUTS IN REGARD TO TEN POSSIBLY RELATED FACTORS.   NTHOMRJ54159

OCCUPATIONAL CHOICES OF NEGRO HIGH SCHOOL SENIORS IN TEXAS.   NTURNBA57165

OCCUPATIONAL ASPIRATIONS OF NEGRO MALE HIGH SCHOOL STUDENTS.   NUZELOX61278

AFTER HIGH SCHOOL WHAT...HIGHLIGHTS OF A STUDY OF CAREER PLANS OF NEGRO AND WHITE RURAL YOUTH IN THREE
FLORIDA COUNTIES. /ASPIRATIONS/   NYOUMEG65390

OCCUPATIONAL PLANS AND ASPIRATIONS. PUERTO-RICAN AND AMERICAN HIGH SCHOOL SENIORS COMPARED.   PSILVRM63100

SEX-ROLE AND PROFESSIONALISM. A STUDY OF HIGH SCHOOL TEACHERS. /OCCUPATIONS/   WCOLCJX63698

HIGH SCHOOL FRESHMAN AND SENIORS VIEW THE ROLE OF WOMEN IN MODERN SOCIETY. /WORK-FAMILY-CONFLICT/   WKERNKK65892

EXPERIENCES OF NEGRO HIGH SCHOOL GIRLS WITH DOMESTIC PLACEMENT AGENCIES. /HOUSEHOLD-WORKERS/   WRUSSRO62135

OCCUPATIONAL PLANNING BY YOUNG WOMEN. A STUDY OF OCCUPATIONAL EXPERIENCES, ASPIRATIONS, ATTITUDES, AND
PLANS OF COLLEGE AND HIGH SCHOOL GIRLS.   WSLOCWL56116

BACKGROUND FACTORS AND COLLEGE GOING PLANS AMONG HIGH APTITUDE PUBLIC HIGH SCHOOL SENIORS. /ASPIRATIONS/   WSTICGX56141

BACKGROUND FACTORS AND COLLEGE GOING PLANS AMONG HIGH APTITUDE PUBLIC HIGH SCHOOL SENIORS. /ASPIRATIONS/   WSTICGX56141

HIGH SCHOOL GUIDANCE COUNSELOR-S PERCEPTIONS OF SELECTED CAREERS FOR WOMEN COLLEGE GRADUATES.   WSWOPMR63146

FUTURE JOBS FOR HIGH SCHOOL GIRLS.   WUSDLA865196

THE MOTIVATION FOR WOMEN TO WORK IN HIGH LEVEL PROFESSIONAL POSITIONS.   WWALTDE62314

HIGHER
INEQUALITY OF OPPORTUNITY IN HIGHER EDUCATION. A STUDY OF MINORITY GROUP AND RELATED BARRIERS TO COLLEGE
ADMISSION.   GBERKDS48446

APPROACHING EQUALITY OF OPPORTUNITY IN HIGHER EDUCATION.   GBROWFJ55476

HIGHER EDUCATION OF SOUTHWESTERN INDIANS WITH REFERENCE TO SUCCESS AND FAILURE.   IMCGRGD62584

BARRIERS IN HIGHER EDUCATION.   JEPSTBR58718

SOME CHARACTERISTICS OF SPANISH-NAME TEXANS AND FOREIGN LATIN-AMERICANS IN TEXAS HIGHER EDUCATION.   MRENNRR57462

THE PROGRESS OF THE NEGRO IN HIGHER EDUCATION. 1950-1960.   NDODDHH63278

THE HIGHER EDUCATION OF NEGROES IN THE UNITED STATES.   NEELLWC55329

HIGHER EDUCATION FOR THE NEGRO.   NHARLBW65486

THE NEGRO AND HIGHER EDUCATION.   NHOLLJX65305

STUDIES IN THE HIGHER EDUCATION OF NEGRO AMERICANS.   NJOURNE66627

HIGHER EDUCATION FOR NEGROES. A TOUGH SITUATION.   NLEWIHX49692

DISCRIMINATION IN HIGHER EDUCATION.   NSOUTCD51166

DESEGREGATION IN HIGHER EDUCATION.   NSOUTRC63157

HIGHER   (CONTINUATION)
A BRIEF SURVEY OF HIGHER EDUCATION FOR NEGROES.   NSTOKMS64180

EQUAL PROTECTION OF THE LAWS IN PUBLIC HIGHER EDUCATION.   NUSCOMC60302

ATTITUDES TOWARD WOMEN COLLEGE TEACHERS IN INSTITUTIONS OF HIGHER EDUCATION ACCREDITED BY THE NORTH
CENTRAL ASSOCIATION.   WBERWHD62475

FACTORS INFLUENCING WOMEN-S DECISIONS ABOUT HIGHER EDUCATION. /ASPIRATICNS/   WDAVIOD59716

HIGHER EDUCATION FOR WOMEN. TIME FOR REAPPRAISAL.   WOOLAEF63952

WOMEN AND HIGHER EDUCATION WITH SPECIAL REFERENCE TO THE UNIVERSITY OF WISCONSIN.   WFREDEB62768

A CONFERENCE TO ENLIST THE PARTICIPATION OF 50 INSTITUTIONS OF HIGHER EDUCATION IN SPECIFIC R AND D
PROGRAMS TO PREPARE WOMEN FOR PRODUCTIVE EMPLOYMENT.   WLLOYBJ64937

A CENTURY OF HIGHER EDUCATION FOR AMERICAN WOMEN.   WNEWCMX59027

SEX AND EQUAL-OPPORTUNITY IN HIGHER EDUCATION.   WPUNKHH61071

HIGHEST
OCCUPATIONAL DEVELOPMENTS. SHORTAGES OF SKILLED TECHNICAL MANPOWER HIGHEST IN RECENT YEARS.   GUSDLAB65561

HIGHLIGHTS
HIGHLIGHTS OF WHITE-NONWHITE DIFFERENTIALS.   GHUYCEE65790

INDIAN HEALTH HIGHLIGHTS. /DEMOGRAPHY/   IUSDHEW66813

AFTER HIGH SCHOOL WHAT...HIGHLIGHTS OF A STUDY OF CAREER PLANS OF NEGRO AND WHITE RURAL YOUTH IN THREE
FLORIDA COUNTIES. /ASPIRATICNS/   NYOUMEG65390

HIGHWAY
SPECIAL REPORT. AN INVESTIGATION OF THE PERSONNEL POLICIES AND PRACTICES OF THE MICHIGAN STATE HIGHWAY
DEPARTMENT. MARCH 1961.   GMICFEP61983

HINDSIGHT
FEPC -- HINDSIGHT AND FORESIGHT.   GFEILJG64676

HIRE
HOW TO HIRE AGRICULTURAL WORKERS FROM PUERTO-RICO.   PPUERRDND788

HIRED
LAST HIRED -- FIRST FIRED. /DISCRIMINATION/   GABRACX58361

CHARACTERISTICS OF THE POPULATION OF HIRED FARMWORKER HOUSEHOLDS. /ECONCMIC-STATUS/   GBOWLGK65424

THE HIRED FARM WORKING FORCE OF 1963 WITH SUPPLEMENTARY DATA FOR 1962. /ECONOMIC-STATUS/   GBOWLGK65432

THE CURRENT SITUATION OF THE HIRED FARM LABOR-FORCE.   GBOWLGK67920

THE HIRED FARM WORKING FORCE OF 1958. /ECONOMIC-STATUS/   GCOWHJD59430

AN ANALYSIS OF THE EXPERIENCED HIRED FARM WORKING FORCE, 1948-1957. /SKILLS/   GCOWHJD60423

EDUCATION, SKILL LEVEL, AND EARNINGS OF THE HIRED FARM WORKING FORCE OF 1961.   GCOWHJD63420

THE HIRED FARM WORKING FORCE OF 1960. /ECONOMIC-STATUS/   GFRIERE62431

THE HIRED FARM WORKING FORCE OF 1956. /ECONCMIC-STATUS/   GMAITST58428

THE HIRED FARM WORKING FORCE OF 1957. /ECONCMIC-STATUS/   GMAITST59429

THE HIRED FARM WORKING FORCE OF 1958.   GMAITST61384

CHARACTERISTICS OF THE POPULATION OF HIRED FARMWORKER HOUSEHOLDS.   GUSDAGR65422

THE HIRED FARM WORKING FORCE OF 1964. A STATISTICAL REPORT.   GUSDAGR65424

LAST HIRED. FIRST FIRED. THOUGH NEGRO WORKERS HAVE MADE IMPRESSIVE GAINS THEY MIGHT BE FIRST TO FEEL THE
BITE OF RECESSION.   NNORTHR49940

HIRING
BUSINESS WIDENS ITS HIRING RANGE.   GBUSIWX65502

EMPLOYMENT TESTS AND DISCRIMINATORY HIRING.   GGUIORM66747

HIRING PROCEDURES AND SELECTION STANDARDS IN THE SAN-FRANCISCO BAY AREA. /CALIFORNIA/   GMALMTF55934

MANAGEMENT AND MINORITY GROUPS. A STUDY OF ATTITUDES AND PRACTICES IN HIRING AND UPGRADING.   GMARKPI57085

EQUAL-EMPLOYMENT-OPPORTUNITY. SHOULD HIRING STANDARDS BE RELAXED.   GMAYFHX64968

REPORT ON A SURVEY OF EMPLOYMENT POLICIES AND HIRING PRACTICES INVOLVING MINORITY-GROUPS IN HUDON-COUNTY,
NEW-JERSEY.   GNEWJDE51060

MINORITY WORKER HIRING AND REFERRAL IN SAN-FRANCISCO. /CALIFORNIA/   GUSDLAB58076

HIRING AND PROMOTION SYSTEMS UNDER FAIR-EMPLOYMENT-PRACTICES LEGISLATION.   GUSDLAB67116

LABOR WEEK. RULES ON HIRING, PROMOTING -- QUESTIONS ANSWERED.   GUSNEWR66518

THE JEWISH LAW STUDENT AND NEW-YORK JOBS -- DISCRIMINATORY EFFECTS IN LAW FIRM HIRING PRACTICES.
/CCCUPATIONS/   JYALELJ64774

NEGRO HIRING -- SOME CASE-STUDIES. /INDUSTRY/   NBAMBJJ49050

HIRING TESTS WAIT FOR THE SCCRE. MYART VS MOTOROLA.   NBUSIWX65150

JOBS FOR NEGROES -- THE GAINS, THE PROBLEMS, AND THE NEW HIRING LAW. /TITLE-VII/   NBUSIWX65151

HIRING NEGRO WORKERS. /INDUSTRY/   NHABBSX64473

CIVIL-RIGHTS -- RACIAL DISCRIMINATION IN TEACHER HIRING AND ASSIGNMENT FORBIDDEN.   NKELLPL66734

DISCRIMINATION IN THE HIRING HALL. A CASE-STUDY OF PRESSURES TO PROMOTE INTEGRATION IN NEW-YORK-S BREWERY
INDUSTRY.   NLANGGE59670

DISCRIMINATION IN THE HIRING AND ASSIGNMENT OF NEGRO TEACHERS IN PUBLIC SCHOOL SYSTEMS.   NMICLRX66068

HIRING   (CONTINUATION)
    CORPORATE HIRING POLICIES AND THE NEGRO. /INDUSTRY/   NNEWSXX64911

    WORKERS WANTED. A STUDY OF EMPLOYERS HIRING POLICIES, PREFERENCES, AND PRACTICES IN NEW-HAVEN AND
    CHARLOTTE. /CONNECTICUT NORTH-CAROLINA/   NNOLAEW49928

    HIRING NEGROES FOR BETTER JOBS. EXPERIENCE OF LEADING COMPANIES. /INDUSTRY/   NOPINRC64957

    MANAGEMENT AND MINORITY-GROUPS. A STUDY OF ATTITUDES AND PRACTICES IN HIRING AND UPGRADING.   NROSEBX59080

    FORCED HIRING OF NEGROES.   NUSNEWR63207

    NEW PUSH FOR HIRING OF NEGROES.   NUSNEWR66273

HISTORICAL
    THE HISTORICAL ROOTS OF FAIR-EMPLOYMENT.   GFLEMJG46688

    UNIONS BEFORE THE BAR. HISTORICAL TRIALS SHOWING THE EVOLUTION OF LABOR RIGHTS IN THE US.   GLIEBEX50901

    AN ECONOMICAL AND HISTORICAL ANALYSIS OF THE CAUSES OF VARIATION AMONG NORTHERN STANDARD METROPOLITAN
    AREAS IN PRODUCTIVITY OF NEGRO MEN IN 1949.   NBATCAB61060

    CRAFT UNIONS AND THE NEGRO IN HISTORICAL PERSPECTIVE.   NBLOCHC58087

    A HISTORICAL REVIEW OF THE IMPACT OF SOCIAL AND ECONOMIC STRUCTURE ON NEGRO CULTURE AND HOW IT INFLUENCES
    FAMILY LIVING.   NJACKJX64596

    AN HISTORICAL SURVEY AND ANALYSIS OF THE PROGRESS OF NEGROES IN PUBLIC-SERVICE 1932-1952.   NOLIVLW56955

    WOMEN ON COLLEGE AND UNIVERSITY FACULTIES. A HISTORICAL SURVEY AND A STUDY OF THEIR PRESENT ACADEMIC
    STATUS. /OCCUPATIONS/   WPOLLLA65063

    THE FEMALE LABOR-FORCE. A CASE STUDY IN THE INTERPRETATION OF HISTORICAL STATISTICS.   WSMUTRW60124

HISTORY
    COMPARISON OF MEXICANS, NEGROES AND WHITES WITH RESPECT TO OCCUPATIONAL HISTORY, RURAL-URBAN RESIDENCE
    HISTORY AND ACCULTURIZATION WITHIN THE INSTITUTIONAL STRUCTURE OF LANSING, MICHIGAN.   CGOLDVX60494

    COMPARISON OF MEXICANS, NEGROES AND WHITES WITH RESPECT TO OCCUPATIONAL HISTORY, RURAL-URBAN RESIDENCE
    HISTORY AND ACCULTURIZATION WITHIN THE INSTITUTIONAL STRUCTURE OF LANSING, MICHIGAN.   CGOLDVX60494

    FAIR-EMPLOYMENT LEGISLATION IN NEW-YORK STATE. ITS HISTORY, DEVELOPMENT, AND SUGGESTED USE ELSEWHERE.   GBRADPX46247

    ONE AMERICA. THE HISTORY, CONTRIBUTIONS, AND PRESENT PROBLEMS OF OUR RACIAL AND NATIONAL MINORITIES.   GBROWFJ45477

    THE CIVIL-RIGHTS-ACT OF 1964. WHAT IT MEANS -- TO EMPLOYERS, BUSINESSMEN, UNIONS, EMPLOYEES,
    MINORITY-GROUPS. TEXT, ANALYSIS, LEGISLATIVE HISTORY.   GBUREON64492

    FEPC -- A CASE HISTORY IN PARLIAMENTARY MANEUVER.   GMASLWX46959

    FAIR-EMPLOYMENT-PRACTICES LEGISLATION, A SUMMARY OF ITS HISTORY AND DEVELOPMENT WITH STATEMENTS ON BOTH
    SIDES.   GMITCJA52016

    WORK HISTORY, ATTITUDES, AND INCOME OF THE UNEMPLOYED.   GSTEIRL63838

    THE CALIFORNIA FAIR-EMPLOYMENT-PRACTICES-COMMISSION. ITS HISTORY, ACCOMPLISHMENTS, AND LIMITATIONS.   GTOBRMC63361

    TITLE-VII. LEGISLATIVE HISTORY.   GVAASFJ66534

    A COMPANY CASE HISTORY. /INDUSTRY EEO/   GWITTHW64576

    DOCUMENTARY HISTORY OF THE FCX PROJECT, 1948-1959. A PROGRAM IN ACTION ANTHROPOLOGY.   INETTRM60599

    BROKEN PEACE PIPES. A 400 YEAR HISTORY OF THE AMERICAN-INDIAN.   IPEITIM64604

    ESSAYS IN AMERICAN JEWISH HISTORY.   JMARCJR58326

    A DECISIVE PATTERN IN AMERICAN JEWISH HISTORY.   JRIVIEX58325

    A HISTORY OF THE INTERRELATIONSHIPS BETWEEN IMPORTED MEXICAN LABOR, DOMESTIC MIGRANTS, AND THE TEXAS
    AGRICULTURAL ECONOMY.   MGRAVRP60405

    A SELECTIVE BIBLIOGRAPHY OF CALIFORNIA LABOR HISTORY.   MSLOBMX64495

    NEGRO ADDICT OCCUPATIONAL HISTORY.   NBATEWM66880

    LABOR IN AMERICA, A HISTORY.   NDULLFR49301

    HISTORY OF THE LABOR MOVEMENT IN THE UNITED STATES. /UNION/   NFONEPS47370

    HISTORY OF RACIAL SEGREGATION IN THE UNITED STATES.   NFRANJH56060

    THE NATURAL HISTORY OF SOCIAL CONFLICT AND WHITE-NEGRO RELATIONS.   NHIMEJS49553

    FROM PLANTATION TO GHETTO. AN INTERPRETIVE HISTORY OF AMERICAN NEGROES.   NMEIEAX66765

    ORGANIZED LABOR IN AMERICAN HISTORY. /UNION/   NTAFTPX64158

    THE BURDEN OF SOUTHERN HISTORY.   NWOODCV60061

    CHINESE IN AMERICAN LIFE. SOME ASPECTS OF THEIR HISTORY, STATUS, PROBLEMS AND CONTRIBUTIONS.   OKUNGSW62737

HOLDING
    JOB HOLDING AMONG NEGRO YOUTH.   NCAPLNX66013

HOME
    HOME INTERVIEW STUDY OF LOW-INCOME HOUSEHOLDS IN DETROIT, MICHIGAN.   GGREEAI65472

    APPROACHES TO INCOME IMPROVEMENT. EXPERIENCES OF FAMILIES RECEIVING PRODUCTION LOANS UNDER THE FARMERS
    HOME ADMINISTRATION.   GHENDWE59422

    PROCEEDINGS OF THE 50TH ANNIVERSARY OBSERVANCE OF THE AMERICAN JEWISH COMMITTEE. APRIL 10-14, 1957. THE
    PURSUIT OF EQUALITY AT HOME AND ABROAD. /ECONOMIC-OPPORTUNITY/   JAMERJC58692

    A CRITICAL SUMMARY. THE NEGRO ON THE HOME FRONT IN WORLD-WARS I AND II.   NREIDID43048

    BACK FROM THE HOME TO BUSINESS. /WORK-FAMILY-CONFLICT/   WBUSIWX61666

    MANAGEMENT PROBLEMS OF HOMEMAKERS EMPLOYED OUTSIDE THE HOME. /WORK-FAMILY-CONFLICT/   WUSOHEW61174

HOME   (CONTINUATION)
    SOME CORRELATES OF HOMEMAKING VS CAREER PREFERENCE AMONG COLLEGE HOME ECONOMICS STUDENTS.
    /WORK-FAMILY-CONFLICT/   WVETTLX64257

    INTEREST AND VALUES OF CAREER AND HOME MAKING ORIENTED WOMEN.   WWAGMMX66761

HOMEMAKER
    THE RURAL WORKING HOMEMAKER. ALCORN-COUNTY, MISSISSIPPI. /WORK-FAMILY-CONFLICT/   WBRYAES61660

    THE HOMEMAKER AND THE WORKING WIFE. /WORK-FAMILY-CONFLICT/   WKOMAMX62912

HOMEMAKERS
    A PILOT STUDY OF THE MOTIVATIONS AND PROBLEMS OF MIDDLE AGED HOMEMAKERS IN LOWER SOCIO-ECONOMIC GROUPS IN
    SEEKING EMPLOYMENT. /ASPIRATIONS/   WJEWIVA62883

    MANAGEMENT PROBLEMS OF HOMEMAKERS EMPLOYED OUTSIDE THE HOME. /WORK-FAMILY-CONFLICT/   WUSDHEW61174

HOMEMAKING
    SOME CORRELATES OF HOMEMAKING VS CAREER PREFERENCE AMONG COLLEGE HOME ECONOMICS STUDENTS.
    /WORK-FAMILY-CONFLICT/   WVETTLX64257

HOMEMAKING-MOTIVATED
    INTEREST AND PERSONALITY CORRELATES OF CAREER-MOTIVATED AND HOMEMAKING-MOTIVATED COLLEGE WOMEN.
    /ASPIRATIONS/   WHOYTDP58850

HOMEMAKING-ORIENTED
    AN INVERTED FACTOR ANALYSIS OF PERSONALITY DIFFERENCES BETWEEN CAREER AND HOMEMAKING-ORIENTED WOMEN.
    /ASPIRATIONS/   WAVILDL64316

HOMES
    A DEMONSTRATION PROJECT DESIGNED TO TEST THE LIFE-STYLE AND THE GROWTH POTENTIAL OF URBAN DROPOUTS FROM
    DISADVANTAGED HOMES.   GCLEAMP66130

HOPE
    NEW HOPE FOR RURAL DIXIE. FIRMS IN CAROLINAS CREATE JOBS FOR NEGROES.   NEBONXX64317

    THE DECADE OF HOPE. /CIVIL-RIGHTS ECONOMIC/   NFORECX51371

HOPES
    THE HOPES OF NEGRO WORKERS FOR THEIR CHILDREN.   NPURCTV64022

    THE FACTS, THE HOPES, AND THE POSSIBILITIES. /WORK-WOMAN-ROLE/   WBANNMC63626

HOPI
    THE HOPI WAY.   ITHOMLX65632

    HOPI INDIAN AGENCY.   IUSDINT64651

HORIZONS
    WIDER HORIZONS FOR NEGRO WORKERS.   NRICHCX64058

    IN QUEST OF WIDER HORIZONS. THE WOMAN AFTER FORTY THINKS ABOUT A JOB. /ASPIRATIONS/   WJEWIVA62882

    NEW HORIZONS FOR WOMEN. /WORK-WOMAN-ROLE/   WKEYSMD64898

    NEW HORIZONS FOR COLLEGE WOMEN. /WORK-WOMEN-ROLE/   WMULLLC60005

    JOB HORIZONS FOR COLLEGE WOMEN IN THE 1960-S.   WUSDLAB64202

HOSPITAL
    SURVEY OF MINORITY-GROUP EMPLOYMENT AND PATIENT CARE IN PRIVATE HOSPITAL FACILITIES IN LOS-ANGELES
    COUNTY. /CALIFORNIA/   GLOSACCND914

    INTEGRATION ON HOSPITAL APPOINTMENTS AND IN HOSPITAL CARE. /CHICAGO ILLINOIS/   NCHICUL58202

    INTEGRATION ON HOSPITAL APPOINTMENTS AND IN HOSPITAL CARE. /CHICAGO ILLINOIS/   NCHICUL58202

    HOSPITAL EMPLOYMENT STUDY.   NMCGODJ66583

    WORKING RULES FOR ASSURING NONDISCRIMINATION IN HOSPITAL ADMINISTRATION.   NYALELJ64600

    NURSES AND OTHER HOSPITAL PERSONNEL -- THEIR EARNINGS AND EMPLOYMENT-CONDITIONS.   WUSDLAB61211

HOSPITALS
    NEGRO NURSES IN HOSPITALS. /WOMEN NEGRO/   CGOLDXX60374

    MINORITY-GROUP INTEGRATION IN HOSPITALS.   NBABOIX61037

    A PRELIMINARY REPORT ON MEDICAL STAFF APPOINTMENTS HELD BY NEGRO PHYSICIANS AT PREDOMINANTLY WHITE
    HOSPITALS. /CHICAGO ILLINOIS/   NCHICCO60201

    RACIAL INTEGRATION IN EMPLOYMENT -- FINDINGS IN TWO KANSAS-CITY HOSPITALS.   NGIBSHX54402

    SURVEY OF SALARIES AND EMPLOYMENT-CONDITIONS IN NONFEDERAL PSYCHIATRIC HOSPITALS.   WAMERNA65611

HOTEL
    HOTEL AND RESTAURANT JOB OPPORTUNITIES, SAN-FRANCISCO BAY AREA, 1964-1966. /CALIFORNIA/   GCALDEM65517

    TECHNICAL REPORT NUMBER 1, EMPLOYMENT PRACTICES IN THE HOTEL, MOTEL AND RESTAURANT INDUSTRY OF MISSOURI. GMILLRX66020

    EMPLOYMENT IN THE HOTEL INDUSTRY. /NEW-YORK/   GNEWYSA58081

    SUMMARY OF TESTIMONY -- HOTEL RESTAURANT HEARINGS, APPENDIX A. /PHILADELPHIA PENNSYLVANIA/   GPHILCH60181

    FINDINGS OF FACT, CONCLUSIONS AND ACTION OF THE COMMISSION ON HUMAN-RELATIONS IN RE. INVESTIGATIVE PUBLIC
    HEARINGS INTO ALLEGED DISCRIMINATORY PRACTICE BY THE HOTEL AND RESTAURANT INDUSTRY IN PHILADELPHIA.
    /PENNSYLVANIA/   GPHILCH61176

    REPORT OF PROGRESS IN THE INTEGRATION OF HOTEL AND RESTAURANT EMPLOYMENT, APRIL 1961 TO MARCH 1962.
    /PHILADELPHIA PENNSYLVANIA/   GPHILCH62178

HOTELS
    PUERTO-RICAN EMPLOYMENT IN NEW-YORK CITY HOTELS. /OCCUPATIONS/   PNEWYSA58837

HOUGH
    HOUGH. CLEVELAND, OHIO -- A STUDY OF SOCIAL LIFE AND CHANGE.   NSUSSMB59192

HOURS
    EARNINGS AND HOURS OF WOMEN AGRICULTURAL WORKERS.   WCALDIR64268

HOURS   (CONTINUATION)
WOMEN WORKERS. WORKING HOURS AND SERVICES.   WKLEIVX65908

STATEMENT ON WEIGHT LIFTING, HOURS, SENIORITY LAWS AND WOMEN. /EMPLOYMENT-CONDITIONS/   WUAWXWC66164

HOUSE
I STATEMENT BEFORE THE HOUSE POST OFFICE AND CIVIL SERVICE SUBCOMMITTEE ON POSTAL OPERATIONS, II
DISCRIMINATION. PLANNED AND ACCIDENTAL. /TESTING/   GENNEWH67928

BLACK FAMILIES AND THE WHITE HOUSE.   NRAINLX66033

THE MOTHER WHO WORKS OUTSIDE THE HOUSE.   WWEINVX61259

HOUSEHOLD
EMPLOYMENT AND PERSONAL CHARACTERISTICS. EMPLOYMENT BY AGE, RACE, NATIVITY, EDUCATION, MARITAL-STATUS,
HOUSEHOLD RELATIONSHIPS, ETC. /DEMOGRAPHY/   CUSBURC53372

ATTITUDE TOWARD JOB-MOBILITY AMONG HOUSEHOLD HEADS IN LOW-INCOME AREAS OF THE RURAL SOUTH.   NDUNKJX64300

THE WORKING-WIFE HOUSEHOLD. PARTS 1 AND 2.   WLINOFX66117

RAISING THE STATUS OF HOUSEHOLD EMPLOYMENT. /HOUSEHOLD-WORKERS/   WMORRMM66998

WOMEN HOUSEHOLD WORKERS COVERED BY OLD AGE, SURVIVORS, AND DISABILITY INSURANCE.   WPOLIEJ65285

TO IMPROVE THE STATUS OF PRIVATE HOUSEHOLD WORK. /HOUSEHOLD-WORKERS/   WUSDLAB65220

HOUSEHOLD-EMPLOYEES
A NATIONAL INQUIRY OF PRIVATE HOUSEHOLD-EMPLOYEES AND EMPLOYERS.   WNATLCH66014

HOUSEHOLD-WORKERS
COMMUNITY WOMEN-S GROUPS TAKE ACTION. /HOUSEHOLD-WORKERS/   WBUFFDX66661

RAISING THE STATUS OF HOUSEHOLD EMPLOYMENT. /HOUSEHOLD-WORKERS/   WMORRMM66998

THESE ARE THE FACTS. /HOUSEHOLD-WORKERS/   WNATLCH66015

EXPERIENCES OF NEGRO HIGH SCHOOL GIRLS WITH DOMESTIC PLACEMENT AGENCIES. /HOUSEHOLD-WORKERS/   WRUSSRD62135

PRIVATE-HOUSEHOLD EMPLOYMENT -- SUMMARY OF FIRST AND SECOND CONSULTATIONS. /HOUSEHOLD-WORKERS/   WUSDLAB64212

TO IMPROVE THE STATUS OF PRIVATE HOUSEHOLD WORK. /HOUSEHOLD-WORKERS/   WUSDLAB65220

WOMEN PRIVATE HOUSEHOLD-WORKERS FACT SHEET.   WUSDLAB66238

HOUSEHOLDS
CHARACTERISTICS OF THE POPULATION OF HIRED FARMWORKER HOUSEHOLDS. /ECONOMIC-STATUS/   GBOWLGK65424

CHARACTERISTICS, RESOURCES, AND INCOMES OF RURAL HOUSEHOLDS, PIEDMONT AREA, SOUTH-CAROLINA.   GBURCTA62408

HOME INTERVIEW STUDY OF LOW-INCOME HOUSEHOLDS IN DETROIT, MICHIGAN.   GGREEAI65472

REPORT OF THE DIAGNOSTIC SURVEY OF TENANT HOUSEHOLDS IN THE WEST SIDE URBAN-RENEWAL AREA OF
NEW-YORK-CITY.   GGREEAI65474

RESOURCE CHARACTERISTICS AND UTILIZATION AND LEVEL OF LIVING ITEMS, RURAL HOUSEHOLDS, NORTH AND WEST
FLORIDA, 1956.   GREUSLA60391

CHARACTERISTICS OF THE POPULATION OF HIRED FARMWORKER HOUSEHOLDS.   GUSDAGR65422

INCOME AND RELATED CHARACTERISTICS OF RURAL HOUSEHOLDS IN THE CENTRAL LOUISIANA MIXED FARMING AREA.   NBOLTBX60398

HOUSEWIFE
TRAPPED HOUSEWIFE. /WORK-FAMILY-CONFLICT/   WGRAYHX62801

HOUSING
PERSONS BY FAMILY CHARACTERISTICS. FAMILY MEMBERS BY SOCIAL, ECONOMIC AND HOUSING CHARACTERISTICS OF
FAMILIES. /DEMOGRAPHY/   CUSBURC63180

OPINION CONCERNING THE SCOPE AND AUTHORITY OF THE JURISDICTION THAT MAY BE GRANTED TO CITY OR COUNTY
HUMAN-RELATIONS-COMMISSIONS IN THE FIELDS OF EMPLOYMENT AND HOUSING. /CALIFORNIA/   GCALAGO63512

THE HOUSING PROBLEM OF THE MIGRANT-WORKER IN MARYLAND.   GMARYSD59956

COMPILATION OF LAWS AGAINST DISCRIMINATION, EMPLOYMENT, EDUCATIONAL INSTITUTIONS, PLACES OF PUBLIC
ACCOMODATION, PUBLIC HOUSING, PUBLICLY ASSISTED HOUSING, PRIVATE HOUSING. /MASSACHUSETTS/   GMASSCAND963

COMPILATION OF LAWS AGAINST DISCRIMINATION, EMPLOYMENT, EDUCATIONAL INSTITUTIONS, PLACES OF PUBLIC
ACCOMODATION, PUBLIC HOUSING, PUBLICLY ASSISTED HOUSING, PRIVATE HOUSING. /MASSACHUSETTS/   GMASSCAND963

COMPILATION OF LAWS AGAINST DISCRIMINATION, EMPLOYMENT, EDUCATIONAL INSTITUTIONS, PLACES OF PUBLIC
ACCOMODATION, PUBLIC HOUSING, PUBLICLY ASSISTED HOUSING, PRIVATE HOUSING. /MASSACHUSETTS/   GMASSCAND963

A SELECTIVE BIBLIOGRAPHY ON DISCRIMINATION IN HOUSING AND EMPLOYMENT.   GNEWYLF60075

THE NEXT STEPS TOWARD EQUALITY OF OPPORTUNITY IN THE SYRACUSE METROPOLITAN AREA. REPORT OF THE SYRACUSE
CONFERENCE ON HUMAN RIGHTS AND HOUSING, JULY 2-3 1962. /NEW-YORK/   GNEWYSB62103

LAWS AGAINST DISCRIMINATION. EMPLOYMENT, PUBLIC ACCOMODATIONS, HOUSING. /OHIO/   GOHIOCR65125

DISCRIMINATION IN HOUSING AND EMPLOYMENT. WHAT TYPE OF PROBLEM IS IT.   GPEDOWX64150

THE INTERRELATIONSHIPS OF DISCRIMINATION IN EMPLOYMENT, IN EDUCATION, AND IN HOUSING.   GRAVIMJ61219

HOUSING, EMPLOYMENT OPPORTUNITIES AND APPRENTICESHIP TRAINING, REPORT. /NEW-JERSEY/   GUSCOMC63404

HOUSING FOR MIGRANT AGRICULTURAL WORKERS. LABOR CAMP STANDARDS.   GUSDLAB62508

SENIOR CITIZENS AND HOW THEY LIVE. AN ANALYSIS OF 1960 CENSUS DATA. PART II. THE AGING NONWHITE AND HIS
HOUSING. /ECONOMIC-STATUS/   GUSHHFX63321

ADL REPORTS ON SOCIAL, EMPLOYMENT, EDUCATIONAL AND HOUSING DISCRIMINATION.   JANTIDL57690

TERMINATION OF THE BRACERO PROGRAM. SOME EFFECTS ON FARM LABOR AND MIGRANT HOUSING NEEDS.   MMCELRC65385

HOUSING DEFICIENCIES OF AGRICULTURAL WORKERS AND OTHER LOW INCOME GROUPS.   MMCMIOX62434

ANNUAL FAMILY AND OCCUPATIONAL EARNINGS OF RESIDENTS OF TWO NEGRO HOUSING PROJECTS IN ATLANTA 1937-1944.

HOUSING   (CONTINUATION)
  /GEORGIA/   NRITTAL45062

HOUSTON
  INCOME, EDUCATION AND UNEMPLOYMENT IN NEIGHBORHOODS. HOUSTON, TEXAS. /DEMOGRAPHY/   CUSDLA863462

  RECENT MIGRATION OF YOUNG MALES INTO HOUSTON, TEXAS.   MWAGODW57515

  HOUSTON -- THE NEGRO AND EMPLOYMENT OPPORTUNITIES IN THE SOUTH, THE FIRST OF A SERIES OF EMPLOYMENT
  STUDIES IN SOUTHERN CITIES. /TEXAS/   NSOUTRC61161

HUDON-COUNTY
  REPORT ON A SURVEY OF EMPLOYMENT POLICIES AND HIRING PRACTICES INVOLVING MINORITY-GROUPS IN HUDON-COUNTY,
  NEW-JERSEY.   GNEWJDE51060

HUELGA
  HUELGA. THE FIRST 100 DAYS OF THE GREAT DELANO STRIKE. /UNION/   MNELSEX66028

HUGE
  A HUGE WASTE. EDUCATED WOMANPOWER.   WBUNTMI61900

HUGHES
  RACIAL DISCRIMINATION AND THE NLRB. THE HUGHES TOOL CASE, PART ONE.   NVIRGLR64017

  RACIAL DISCRIMINATION AND THE NLRB. THE HUGHES TOOL CASE, PART TWO.   NVIRGLR64018

HUI-CH-IAO
  THE HUI-CH-IAO IN THE UNITED STATES OF AMERICA.   OLEEXRH58742

HUMAN
  DEVELOPING NEW-YORK CITY-S HUMAN RESOURCES. VOL 1. /NEGRO PUERTO-RICAN/   CINSTOP66034

  HUMAN CAPITAL. A THEORETICAL AND EMPIRICAL ANALYSIS WITH SPECIAL REFERENCE TO EDUCATION.   GBECKGS64700

  HUMAN CAPITAL AS A SOUTHERN RESOURCE.   GCOLBMR63994

  HUMAN CAPITAL IN SOUTHERN DEVELOPMENT 1939-1963.   GCOLBMR65793

  JOB AND CAREER DEVELOPMENT FCR THE POOR...THE HUMAN SERVICES. INCLUDES BIBLIOGRAPHY.   GGOLDGS66360

  TESTIMONY OF HUMAN RELATIONS. /LOS-ANGELES CALIFORNIA/   GLOSACCN0915

  INTERRACIAL HUMAN RELATIONS IN MANAGEMENT, A COMPILED REPORT PRESENTED ORALLY...JANUARY 17 1951. GMCKEIX51926

  THE NEXT STEPS TOWARD EQUALITY OF OPPORTUNITY IN THE SYRACUSE METROPOLITAN AREA. REPORT OF THE SYRACUSE
  CONFERENCE ON HUMAN RIGHTS AND HOUSING, JULY 2-3 1962. /NEW-YORK/   GNEWYSB62103

  COMMISSIONS FOR HUMAN RIGHTS, 15TH ANNUAL CONFERENCE, PROCEEDINGS.   GPENNHR63166

  HUMAN RESOURCES IN THE URBAN ECONOMY. PART II -- THE LABOR FORCE PERFORMANCE OF MINORITY-GROUPS. GPERLMX63169

  UNDERSTANDING THE HUMAN FACTOR, THE KEY TO SUPERVISORY SUCCESS.   GPRESCP59201

  IMPROVING INDUSTRIAL RACE-RELATIONS -- PART 2, HUMAN PROBLEMS IN IMPROVING INDUSTRIAL RACE-RELATIONS. GSHOSAB63307

  HUMAN RESOURCES SURVEY OF THE COLVILLE CONFEDERATE TRIBES.   IBLOOJA59538

  HUMAN RESOURCES, RELATIONS AND PROBLEMS ON THE FORT-HALL INDIAN RESERVATION.   IHARMHC61572

  THE NAVAJO IN THE MACHINE AGE. HUMAN RESOURCES ARE IMPORTANT TOO.   INAPIAX58594

  AN ANALYSIS OF CURRENT PATTERNS IN HUMAN RESOURCE DEVELOPMENT IN SAN-ANTONIO, TEXAS.   MDAVIHW66387

  NEW-YORK CITY COMMISSION ON HUMAN RIGHTS, CONSTRUCTION TRADES HEARING, TESTIMONY. /INDUSTRY/ NHILLHX66546

  PROPOSALS FOR THE IMPROVEMENT CF HUMAN RELATIONS IN THE LOS-ANGELES METROPOLITAN AREA. /EMPLOYMENT
  CALIFORNIA/   NLOSACC65365

  CF HUMAN RESOURCES AND THE SOUTH.   NROSSJX50088

  ALL THESE PEOPLE. THE NATION-S HUMAN RESOURCES IN THE SOUTH.   NVANCRB45282

  RELEASING HUMAN POTENTIAL.   PEASTHP61798

HUMAN-RELATIONS
  HUMAN-RELATIONS IN COLORADO. 1858-1959.   GATKIJA61408

  HUMAN-RELATIONS NEWS OF CHICAGO. /ILLINOIS/   GCHICHR59565

  HUMAN-RELATIONS IN INDUSTRY.   GGARDBB55707

  A HUMAN-RELATIONS PROGRAM FOR SAN-FRANCISCO. /CALIFORNIA/   GMITCJP64277

  FINDINGS OF FACT, CONCLUSIONS AND ACTION OF THE COMMISSION ON HUMAN-RELATIONS IN RE. INVESTIGATIVE PUBLIC
  HEARINGS INTO ALLEGED DISCRIMINATORY PRACTICE BY THE HOTEL AND RESTAURANT INDUSTRY IN PHILADELPHIA.
  /PENNSYLVANIA/   GPHILCH61176

  HUMAN-RELATIONS IN FEDERAL EMPLOYMENT.   GPRESCP55197

  MUNICIPAL HUMAN-RELATIONS COMMISSION, A SURVEY OF PROGRAMS IN SELECTED CITIES OF THE UNITED STATES. GRICHCM63236

  THE QUEST FOR THE DREAM. THE DEVELOPMENT OF CIVIL-RIGHTS AND HUMAN-RELATIONS IN MODERN AMERICA. GROCHJP63057

  ADMINISTRATIVE LAW -- HUMAN-RELATIONS COMMISSIONS, PENNSYLVANIA LAW AND DISCRIMINATORY EMPLOYMENT
  PRACTICE.   GTEMPLQ63349

  FAIR-EMPLOYMENT WORKS -- TOOLS FOR HUMAN-RELATIONS.   GTHOMJA51355

  HUMAN-RELATIONS IN ANN-ARBOR, A COMMUNITY PROFILE.   NPIKEJX67101

  ADMINISTERING CHANGES. A CASE-STUDY OF HUMAN-RELATIONS IN A FACTORY.   NRONKHO52129

HUMAN-RELATIONS-COMM
  OPINION CONCERNING THE SCOPE AND AUTHORITY OF THE JURISDICTION THAT MAY BE GRANTED TO CITY OR COUNTY
  HUMAN-RELATIONS-COMMISSIONS IN THE FIELDS OF EMPLOYMENT AND HOUSING. /CALIFORNIA/   GCALAGO63512

  LAWS ADMINISTERED BY THE PENNSYLVANIA HUMAN-RELATIONS-COMMISSION.   GPENNHRND165

  PATTERNS OF DISCRIMINATION STUDY -- LOUISVILLE HUMAN-RELATIONS-COMMISSION. /KENTUCKY/   NLOUIHR66582

HUMAN-RESOURCE
    HUMAN-RESOURCE PROBLEMS OF THE COMING DECADE. /EMPLOYMENT NEGRO MEXICAN-AMERICAN/   CBULLPX66136

HUMAN-RESOURCES
    HUMAN-RESOURCES, THE WEALTH OF A NATION. /YOUTH/   NGINZEX58405

HUMAN-RIGHTS
    1963 REPORT OF PROGRESS IN HUMAN-RIGHTS.   GALASSC63366

    INDUSTRY AND HUMAN-RIGHTS.   GANTIDL63396

    MISSOURI LOCAL GOVERNMENT ACTION IN THE AREA OF HUMAN-RIGHTS.   GMISSCH63022

    A STUDY OF STATE AND LOCAL LEGISLATIVE AND ADMINISTRATIVE ACTS DESIGNED TO MEET PROBLEMS OF HUMAN-RIGHTS.   GWISCLR52573

    STUDY OF HUMAN-RIGHTS IN MISSOURI.   NMISSCH60802

HUNT
    THE JOB HUNT. JOB SEEKING BEHAVIOR OF UNEMPLOYED WORKERS IN A LOCAL ECONOMY.   NSHEPHL66128

HUSBAND
    LABOR-FORCE PARTICIPATION RATES AND PERCENT DISTRIBUTION OF MOTHERS WITH HUSBAND PRESENT.   WUSDLAB64204

HUSBAND-S
    MARITAL DISAGREEMENT IN WORKING WIFE MARRIAGES AS A FUNCTION OF HUSBAND-S ATTITUDE TOWARDS WIFE-S
    EMPLOYMENT. /WORK-FAMILY-CONFLICT/   WGIANAX57779

HYPOTHESES
    THE MYRDALIAN HYPOTHESES. RANK ORDER OF DISCRIMINATION.   GEDMUER44495

    SOCIAL-STRUCTURE AND THE NEGRO REVOLT. AN EXAMINATION OF SOME HYPOTHESES. /SOCIO-ECONOMIC/   NGESCJA64400

HYPOTHESIS
    NEGRO INTELLIGENCE AND SELECTIVE MIGRATION. A PHILADELPHIA TEST OF THE KLINEBERG HYPOTHESIS.
    /PENNSYLVANIA/   NLEEXES51673

IDAHO
    THE PHYSICAL GEOGRAPHY OF THE PALOUSE REGION, WASHINGTON AND IDAHO, AND ITS RELATION TO THE AGRICULTURAL
    ECONOMY.   OSHROCR58762

IDENTIFICATION
    IDENTIFICATION AND MODIFICATION OF THE SOCIAL-PSYCHOLOGICAL CORRELATES OF ECONOMIC DEPENDENCY. PROJECT
    FINAL REPORT.   GKIMMPR66137

    A METHODOLOGICAL APPROACH TO IDENTIFICATION AND CLASSIFICATION OF CERTAIN TYPES OF INACTIVE WORK-SEEKERS.
    /UNEMPLOYMENT LABOR-MARKET/   GLIEBEE65569

    STATUS POSITION, MOBILITY, AND ETHNIC IDENTIFICATION OF THE NEGRO.   NPARKSX64973

    NEGRO MALE IDENTIFICATION PROBLEMS.   NWOROIX62341

    THE RELATIONSHIP OF PARENTAL IDENTIFICATION TO SEX ROLE ACCEPTANCE IN MARRIED, SINGLE, CAREER AND
    NON-CAREER WOMEN. /WORK-WOMEN-ROLE/   WBREYCH64654

IDENTIFICATIONS
    COLLEGE WOMEN-S IDENTIFICATIONS WITH THEIR FATHERS IN RELATION TO VOCATIONAL INTEREST PATTERNS.
    /ASPIRATIONS/   WHALLWJ63815

IDENTITY
    RELOCATED AMERICAN INDIANS IN THE SAN-FRANCISCO BAY AREA. SOCIAL INTERACTION AND INDIAN IDENTITY.
    /CALIFORNIA/   IALBOJX64523

    MEMORANDUM ON IDENTITY AND NEGRO YOUTH.   NERIKEX64338

    CRUCIBLE OF IDENTITY. THE NEGRO LOWER-CLASS FAMILY.   NRAINLX66032

    THE QUEST FOR IDENTITY AND STATUS. FACETS OF THE DESEGREGATION PROCESS IN THE UPPER MIDWEST.
    /ECONOMIC-STATUS/   NTILLJA61161

    ROLE CONCEPTION AND CAREER ASPIRATION. A STUDY OF IDENTITY IN NURSING.   WCORWRG61707

    INITIATION INTO A WOMAN-S PROFESSION. IDENTITY PROBLEMS IN THE STATUS TRANSITION OF CO-ED TO STUDENT
    NURSE.   WDAVIFX66723

    THE IDENTITY OF MODERN WOMAN. /WORK-WOMAN-ROLE/   WKRECHS65381

IDEOLOGY
    IDEOLOGY AND INTERESTS. THE DETERMINANTS OF UNION ACTION.   NKORNWA53659

    THE NEW ANTI-POVERTY IDEOLOGY AND THE NEGRO.   NRIESFX65060

    REVOLUTION WITHOUT IDEOLOGY. THE CHANGING PLACE OF WOMEN IN AMERICA. /WORK-WOMEN-ROLE/   WDEGLCN64727

ILGWU
    THE RACIAL PRACTICES OF THE ILGWU -- A REPLY.   GMARSRX64059

    THE ILGWU TODAY -- THE DECAY OF A LABOR UNION.   NHILLHX62528

    THE ILGWU -- FACT AND FICTION. /UNION/   NHILLHX63527

    THE TRUTH ABOUT THE ILGWU. /UNION/   NTYLEGX62222

ILLEGAL
    SOCIO-ECONOMIC CLASS AND AREA AS CORRELATES OF ILLEGAL BEHAVIOR AMONG JUVENILES.   NCLARJP62209

    GOAL-ORIENTATIONS AND ILLEGAL BEHAVIOR AMONG JUVENILES.   NCLARJP63208

ILLINOIS
    INCOME, EDUCATION AND UNEMPLOYMENT IN NEIGHBORHOODS. CHICAGO, ILLINOIS. /DEMOGRAPHY/   CUSDLAB63456

    FINAL REPORT ON JOBS II PROJECT. /CHICAGO ILLINOIS/   GCHICBC65319

    HUMAN-RELATIONS NEWS OF CHICAGO. /ILLINOIS/   GCHICHR59565

    YOUR CIVIL-RIGHTS. /CHICAGO ILLINOIS/   GCHICHR62568

    MERIT EMPLOYMENT IN CHICAGO. /ILLINOIS/   GCHICMC56566

    1964 MANPOWER SURVEY. /CHICAGO ILLINOIS/   GCOMIEF64592

ILLINOIS   (CONTINUATION)
    ORGANIZING THE UNEMPLOYED. THE CHICAGO PROJECT. /ILLINOIS/   GFLACRX64964

    A REPORT ON EMPLOYMENT OF NONWHITES IN CHICAGO. /ILLINOIS/   GILLICH55792

    A STUDY OF MERIT EMPLOYMENT IN 100 ILLINOIS FIRMS.   GILLICH56794

    THE STATUS OF THE NONWHITE LABOR-FORCE IN ILLINOIS AND THE NATION.   GILLICH57793

    NONWHITE POPULATION IN ILLINOIS, 1950-1960.   GILLICH61791

    ILLINOIS JOB SEEKERS SURVEY. EDUCATION, SKILLS, LENGTH OF UNEMPLOYMENT, AND PERSONAL CHARACTERISTICS.   GILLIDI62004

    FAIR-EMPLOYMENT-PRACTICE ACT OF ILLINOIS.   GILLIFEND795

    ILLINOIS JOB SEEKER-S SURVEY.   GILLIGC62799

    SPECIAL REPORT ON EMPLOYMENT OPPORTUNITIES IN ILLINOIS.   GILLIIR48801

    FEPC IN ILLINOIS. FOUR STORMY YEARS.   GMINSJX65012

    LABOR AND CIVIL-RIGHTS IN CHICAGO. /ILLINOIS UNION/   GWESTJX66551

    THE ILLINOIS FAIR-EMPLOYMENT-PRACTICES-ACT.   GWIGGCH65598

    THE NEGRO WORKER IN THE CHICAGO JOB-MARKET. /ILLINOIS/   NBAROHX66055

    THE EMPLOYABILITY OF THE CHAMPAIGN-URBANA, ILLINOIS, NEGRO.   NBEAKJR64062

    A STUDY OF THE NEGRO COMMUNITY IN CHAMPAIGN-URBANA, ILLINOIS.   NBINDAM61079

    CHICAGO STARTS MOVING ON EQUAL JOB QUESTION. /ILLINOIS/   NBUSIWX64298

    A PRELIMINARY REPORT ON MEDICAL STAFF APPOINTMENTS HELD BY NEGRO PHYSICIANS AT PREDOMINANTLY WHITE
    HOSPITALS. /CHICAGO ILLINOIS/   NCHICCO60201

    TWO YEAR REPORT ON THE YOUTH GUIDANCE PROJECT, 1958-1959. /CHICAGO   ILLINOIS/   NCHICULND203

    INTEGRATION ON HOSPITAL APPOINTMENTS AND IN HOSPITAL CARE. /CHICAGO ILLINOIS/   NCHICUL58202

    THE NEGRO POPULATION OF CHICAGO. A STUDY OF RESIDENTIAL SUCCESSION. /ILLINOIS OCCUPATIONAL-PATTERNS/   NDUNCOD57306

    THE NEGRO FAMILY IN CHICAGO. /ILLINOIS/   NFRAZEF64380

    RECENT MIGRATION TO CHICAGO. /LABOR-FORCE ILLINOIS/   NFREERX50967

    THE UNEMPLOYMENT RATE AND GRADE LEVEL RELATIONSHIP IN CHICAGO AS REVEALED IN THE 1960 CENSUS. /ILLINOIS/   NHARGAJ65990

    THE NEGRO AS AN IMMIGRANT GROUP. RECENT TRENDS IN RACIAL AND ETHNIC SEGREGATION IN CHICAGO. /ILLINOIS/   NTAEUKE64196

    PREJUDICE IS NOT THE WHOLE STORY. EXAMINATION OF THREE CASES OF NEGRO UPGRADING IN TRACTION COMPANIES IN
    PHILADELPHIA, LOS-ANGELES AND CHICAGO. /PENNSYLVANIA CALIFORNIA ILLINOIS/   NWECKJE45308

    WOMEN WORKERS IN ILLINOIS.   WILLIBE64330

IMAGE
    REPORT ON EMPLOYMENT AND IMAGE OF MINORITY-GROUPS ON TELEVISION.   GNEWYSB63105

    AMERICAN WOMEN. THE CHANGING IMAGE. /WORK-WOMEN-ROLE/   WCASSBB62682

    AN AMERICAN ANACHRONISM. THE IMAGE OF WOMEN AND WORK. /WORK-WOMAN-ROLE/   WKENNKX64891

IMAGES
    THE MUTUAL IMAGES AND EXPECTATIONS OF ANGLO-AMERIANS AND MEXICAN-AMERICANS.   MSIMMOG61490

IMAGINATION
    RACE-RELATIONS AND THE SOCIOLOGICAL IMAGINATION.   NHUGHEC63585

IMBALANCE
    TRAINING FOR MINORITY-GROUPS. PROBLEMS OF RACIAL IMBALANCE AND SEGREGATION.   NFUSFDR66014

    THE ECONOMIC IMBALANCE. AN INQUIRY INTO THE ECONOMIC-STATUS OF NEGROES IN THE UNITED STATES, 1935-1960,
    WITH IMPLICATIONS FOR NEGRO EDUCATION.   NHENDVW60512

IMBALANCES
    MANPOWER PROGRAM IMPLICATIONS OF SKILL IMBALANCES. /TRAINING/   GCASSFH66565

IMMIGRANT
    THE IMMIGRANT. VALUE ORIENTATIONS AND VOCATIONAL ASPIRATIONS. /NEGRO MEXICAN-AMERICAN/   CPETECL64988

    MEASURING THE ADJUSTMENT OF IMMIGRANT LABORERS. /MEXICAN-AMERICAN NEGRO/   CSHANLW63487

    THE ECONOMIC ABSORPTION AND CULTURAL INTEGRATION OF IMMIGRANT MEXICAN-AMERICAN AND NEGRO WORKERS.   CSHANLW64124

    URBAN ADJUSTMENT AND ITS RELATIONSHIP TO THE SOCIAL ANTECEDENTS OF IMMIGRANT WORKERS. /NEGRO
    MEXICAN-AMERICAN/   CSHANLW65121

    THE DISPLACED PERSON AND THE SOCIAL AGENCY. A STUDY OF THE CASEWORK PROCESS AND ITS RELATION TO IMMIGRANT
    ADJUSTMENT.   JCRYSDX58714

    NATURALIZATION AND ASSIMILATION PRONENESS OF CALIFORNIA IMMIGRANT POPULATIONS.   MKRASWX63425

    WHEN THE MIGRANT LABORER SETTLES DOWN -- A REPORT OF THE FINDINGS OF A PROJECT ON VALUE ASSIMILATION OF
    IMMIGRANT LABORERS.   MPETECL64454

    THE MEXICAN IMMIGRANT WORKER IN SOUTHWESTERN AGRICULTURE.   MTHOMAN56501

    AMERICAN NEGRO AND IMMIGRANT EXPERIENCES. SIMILARITIES AND DIFFERENCES.   NAPPEJJ66805

    IS THE NEGRO AN IMMIGRANT GROUP.   NTAEUKE63195

    THE NEGRO AS AN IMMIGRANT GROUP. RECENT TRENDS IN RACIAL AND ETHNIC SEGREGATION IN CHICAGO. /ILLINOIS/   NTAEUKE64196

IMMIGRANTS
    THE URBAN ADJUSTMENT OF IMMIGRANTS. THE RELATIONSHIP OF EDUCATION TO OCCUPATIONAL AND TOTAL FAMILY
    INCOME. /NEGRO MEXICAN-AMERICAN/   CSHANLW63122

    SPECIAL ASSIMILATION PROBLEMS OF UNDERPRIVILEGED IMMIGRANTS TO PHILADELPHIA. /PENNSYLVANIA/   GPENNEL62502

IMMIGRANTS   (CONTINUATION)
   CONTRASTIVE ACCULTURATION OF CALIFORNIA JAPANESE. COMPARATIVE APPROACH TO THE STUDY OF IMMIGRANTS.   OBEFUHX65701

   WESTERNERS FROM THE EAST. ORIENTAL IMMIGRANTS REAPPRAISED.   ODANIRX66084

   THE JAPANESE SOCIAL STRUCTURE AND THE SOURCE OF MENTAL STRAINS OF JAPANESE IMMIGRANTS IN THE US.   OIGAXMX57732

IMMIGRATION
   JEWISH AND ITALIAN IMMIGRATION AND SUBSEQUENT STATUS MOBILITY.   JSTROFL58764

   MEXICAN IMMIGRATION TO THE UNITED STATES. THE RECORD AND ITS IMPLICATIONS.   MGREBLX66406

   CHINESE IMMIGRATION AND POPULATION CHANGES SINCE 1940.   OLEEXRX57740

IMMOKALEE
   THE IMMOKALEE STORY. /MIGRANT-WORKERS FLORIDA/   GSOWDWT58327

   A MIGRANT LABOR CRISIS IN IMMOKALEE. /FLORIDA/   GSOWDWT59328

IMPACT
   EMPLOYMENT DISCRIMINATION. STATE FEPC LAWS AND THE IMPACT OF OF TITLE-VII OF THE CIVIL-RIGHTS-ACT OF
   1964.   GBRYEGL65896

   AUTOMATION. THE IMPACT ON JOBS AND PEOPLE.   GCOONRB64871

   THE IMPACT OF TECHNOLOGICAL-CHANGE.   GHABEWX63615

   EMPLOYMENT DISCRIMINATION. STATE FAIR-EMPLOYMENT-PRACTICES LAWS AND THE IMPACT OF TITLE-VII OF THE
   CIVIL-RIGHTS-ACT OF 1964.   GLAWXRD65885

   IMPACT OF COMPANY POLICY UPON DISCRIMINATION.   GLONDJX54908

   STATEMENTS RELATING TO THE IMPACT OF TECHNOLOGICAL-CHANGE. /INDUSTRY/   GNATLCT66848

   THE EMPLOYMENT IMPACT OF TECHNOLOGICAL-CHANGE.   GNATLCT66849

   SUMMARY OF PROCEEDINGS. WORKSHOP ON THE IMPACT OF A TIGHTENING LABOR-MARKET ON THE EMPLOYABILITY AND
   EMPLOYMENT OF DISADVANTAGED YOUTH.   GNEWYUC66116

   INTRODUCTION. THE STRUGGLE FOR EQUALITY AND ITS IMPACT ON INDUSTRIAL-RELATIONS.   GSTEIBX64335

   IMPACT OF AUTOMATION ON EMPLOYMENT.   GUSHOUR61985

   STATE LAWS AND THE NEGRO. SOCIAL CHANGE AND THE IMPACT OF LAW.   NHILLHX65545

   A HISTORICAL REVIEW OF THE IMPACT OF SOCIAL AND ECONOMIC STRUCTURE ON NEGRO CULTURE AND HOW IT INFLUENCES
   FAMILY LIVING.   NJACKJX64596

   THE IMPACT OF SOCIO-ECONOMIC CHANGE ON RACIAL GROUPS IN A RURAL SETTING.   NPELLRJ62981

   THE IMPACT OF MILITARY SERVICE UPON THE RACIAL ATTITUDES OF NEGRO SERVICEMEN IN WORLD-WAR II.   NROBEHW53065

   INTRODUCTION. THE STRUGGLE FOR EQUALITY AND ITS IMPACT ON INDUSTRIAL-RELATIONS.   NSTEIBX64300

   IMPACT OF OFFICE AUTOMATION IN THE INTERNAL REVENUE SERVICE. A STUDY OF THE MANPOWER IMPLICATIONS DURING
   THE FIRST STAGES OF THE CHANGEOVER. /ECONOMIC-STATUS/   NUSDLAB63198

   IMPACT OF THE RACE ISSUE ON UNIONS IN THE SOUTH.   NUSNEWR56208

   THE IMPACT OF RACE-RELATIONS ON INDUSTRIAL RELATIONS IN THE SOUTH.   NWHEEJH64230

   IMPACT ON THE INDIVIDUAL. /SOCIAL-CHANGE SOUTH/   NWRIGSJ63344

   THE IMPACT OF PUERTO-RICAN MIGRATION ON GOVERNMENTAL SERVICES IN NEW-YORK CITY.   PDWORMB57797

   THE IMPACT OF PUERTO-RICAN MIGRATION TO THE UNITED STATES. /EMPLOYMENT/   PFLEIBM63437

   THE IMPACT OF CULTURAL CHANGE ON WOMEN-S POSITION. /BLUE-COLLAR ASPIRATIONS/   WKONOGX66913

   THE IMPACT OF EDUCATION.   WPETEEX63053

IMPLEMENTATION
   REPORT OF INDUSTRY AND LABOR-MANAGEMENT CLINICS. IMPLEMENTATION OF EMPLOYMENT IN MERIT PROGRAMS IN NON
   FEPC STATES BY DIRECT APPROACH TO TOP MANAGEMENT.   GFISKUR51684

   CURRENT INTERNATIONAL UNION POLICIES AFFECTING MINORITIES AND THEIR IMPLEMENTATION.   GHOPEJX49781

   CURRENT MINORITY POLICIES AND THEIR IMPLEMENTATION IN INTERNATIONAL UNIONS.   GHOPEJX51782

   IMPLEMENTATION OF THE FEDERAL FAIR-EMPLOYMENT POLICY.   GNATLAI49038

   TRADE UNIONS PRACTICES AND THE NEGRO WORKER -- THE ESTABLISHMENT AND IMPLEMENTATION OF AFL-CIO
   ANTI-DISCRIMINATION POLICY.   NDAVINF60312

   AN ANALYSIS OF THE IMPLEMENTATION OF THE UAW-CIO-S FAIR PRACTICES AND ANTI-DISCRIMINATION POLICIES IN
   SELECTED CHICAGO LOCALS. /UNION/   NJONEJE51883

IMPLEMENTING
   IMPLEMENTING AFFIRMATIVE ACTION WITH AIR-FORCE CONTRACTORS.   GHUNTHX63789

   REGIONAL CONFERENCES ON IMPLEMENTING THE CIVIL-RIGHTS-ACT.   NFREYMX66386

IMPLICATIONS
   IMPLICATIONS OF THE STUDIES. /DISCRIMINATION LOW-INCOME NEGRO PUERTO-RICAN POLICY-RECOMMENDATIONS/   CABRACX59001

   THE CHILD-REARING ATTITUDES OF DISADVANTAGED NEGRO MOTHERS AND SOME EDUCATIONAL IMPLICATIONS.   CRADINX65031

   THE IMPLICATIONS OF THE CIVIL-RIGHTS-ACT OF 1964 FOR PSYCHOLOGICAL ASSESSMENT IN INDUSTRY. /TESTING/   GASHXPX66405

   IMPLICATIONS OF THE RECENT CENSUSES FOR PROFESSIONAL AGRICULTURAL WORKERS. /OCCUPATIONS/   GBEALCL61412

   IMPLICATIONS FOR BUSINESS OF THE CIVIL-RIGHTS-ACT OF 1964.   GBENEDX65434

   MANPOWER IMPLICATIONS OF TECHNOLOGICAL-CHANGE. RESEARCH FINDINGS OF THE US DEPARTMENT OF LABOR.   GBRANSX63876

   MANPOWER PROGRAM IMPLICATIONS OF SKILL IMBALANCES. /TRAINING/   GCASSFH66565

   UNION RACIAL DISCRIMINATION -- RECENT DEVELOPMENTS BEFORE THE NLRB AND THEIR IMPLICATIONS UNDER TITLE-VII

IMPLICATIONS   (CONTINUATION)
OF THE CIVIL-RIGHTS-ACT OF 1964.   GGEORLJ65714

SOME EDUCATIONAL **IMPLICATIONS** OF THE INFLUENCE OF REJECTION ON ASPIRATION LEVELS OF MINORITY-GROUP
CHILDREN.   GGOFFRM54366

THE FEDERAL ANTI-POVERTY PROGRAM AND SOME **IMPLICATIONS** OF SUBPROFESSIONAL TRAINING.   GGORDJE65135

IMPLICATIONS OF THE ANTI-POVERTY PROGRAM FOR EDUCATION AND EMPLOYMENT.   GLEVILA65781

EDUCATIONAL **IMPLICATIONS** OF TECHNOLOGICAL-CHANGE.   GNATLCO66898

THE CIVIL-RIGHTS-ACT. **IMPLICATIONS** FOR BUSINESS.   GNEWYCA64068

AUTOMATION **IMPLICATIONS** FOR THE FUTURE.   GPHILMX62616

PROJECTED CHANGES IN THE OCCUPATIONAL STRUCTURE OF THE LABOR-FORCE. **IMPLICATIONS** FOR PUBLIC WELFARE.   GSIFFHX64105

IMPLICATIONS OF AUTOMATION AND OTHER TECHNOLOGICAL DEVELOPMENTS, A SELECTED BIBLIOGRAPHY.   GUSDLAB63450

MANPOWER **IMPLICATIONS** OF AUTOMATION.   GUSDLAB65608

IMPLICATIONS OF GOVERNMENT-SPONSORED TRAINING PROGRAMS. /TECHNOLOGICAL-CHANGE/   GWALSJP64620

MEXICAN IMMIGRATION TO THE UNITED STATES. THE RECORD AND ITS **IMPLICATIONS**.   MGREBLX66406

SPANISH-AMERICANS OF THE SOUTHWEST. LIFE-STYLE PATTERNS AND THEIR **IMPLICATIONS**.   MHAYDRG66114

IMPLICATIONS OF CULTURAL VALUES IN EDUCATION.   MVALDBX64448

THE AGING NEGRO. SOME **IMPLICATIONS** FOR SOCIAL-WELFARE SERVICES.   NBEATWM60066

RECENT SOUTHERN INDUSTRIALIZATION AND ITS **IMPLICATIONS** FOR NEGROES LIVING IN THE SOUTH.
/EMPLOYMENT-TRENDS/   NCHICCA53204

SOCIAL AND ECONOMIC **IMPLICATIONS** OF INTEGRATING IN THE PUBLIC SCHOOLS.   NCLARKB65213

MINORITY-GROUP ATTITUDES OF NEGROES AND **IMPLICATIONS** FOR GUIDANCE.   NENGLWH57333

THE **IMPLICATIONS** OF PROJECT CLEAR. /DESEGREGATION/   NFORMPB55372

THE ECONOMIC IMBALANCE. AN INQUIRY INTO THE ECONOMIC-STATUS OF NEGROES IN THE UNITED STATES, 1935-1960,
WITH **IMPLICATIONS** FOR NEGRO EDUCATION.   NHENDVW60512

IMPACT OF OFFICE AUTOMATION IN THE INTERNAL REVENUE SERVICE. A STUDY OF THE MANPOWER **IMPLICATIONS** DURING
THE FIRST STAGES OF THE CHANGEOVER. /ECONOMIC-STATUS/   NUSDLAB63198

SOCIAL AND ECONOMIC **IMPLICATIONS** OF MIGRATION FOR THE NEGRO IN THE PRESENT SOCIAL ORDER.   NVALIPX42261

IMPLICATIONS OF PUERTO-RICAN MIGRATION TO THE CONTINENT OUTSIDE NEW-YORK CITY.   PGERNAC56808

IMPLICATIONS OF POPULATION REDISTRIBUTION.   PSENICX57851

THE ACHIEVEMENT MOTIVE IN WOMEN. A STUDY OF THE **IMPLICATIONS** FOR CAREER DEVELOPMENT.   WBARURX66453

STATUS **IMPLICATIONS** OF THE EMPLOYMENT OF MARRIED WOMEN IN THE UNITED STATES.   WDAYXLH61726

FANTASY, FACT AND THE FUTURE...A REVIEW OF THE STATUS OF WOMEN AND POSSIBLE **IMPLICATIONS** FOR WOMEN-S
EDUCATION AND ROLE IN THE NEXT DECADE.   WFITZLE63963

COUNSELING **IMPLICATIONS** OF WOMAN-S CHANGING ROLE.   WGASSGZ59775

SOME **IMPLICATIONS** ON CURRENT CHANGES IN SEX ROLE PATTERNS. /WORK-WOMAN-ROLE/   WHARTRE60828

IMPLICATIONS FROM RECENT RESEARCH ON COLLEGE STUDENTS. /MANPOWER/   WHEISPX59838

MANPOWER **IMPLICATIONS** OF AUTOMATION.   WORGAEC64045

SOME **IMPLICATIONS** OF THE EMPLOYMENT PATTERNS OF WOMEN UNDER SOCIAL-SECURITY.   WPOLIEJ59454

IMPLICATIONS OF TWO PILOT PROJECTS IN TRAINING MATURE WOMEN AS COUNSELORS.   WRIOCMJ65082

A STUDY OF WOMEN IN OFFICE MANAGEMENT POSITIONS WITH **IMPLICATIONS** FOR BUSINESS EDUCATION. /OCCUPATIONS/   WRUSHEM57096

IMPORTED
DOMESTIC AND **IMPORTED** WORKERS IN THE HARVEST LABOR-MARKET, SANTA-CLARA COUNTY, CALIFORNIA, 1954.   MFULLVX56396

A HISTORY OF THE INTERRELATIONSHIPS BETWEEN **IMPORTED** MEXICAN LABOR, DOMESTIC MIGRANTS, AND THE TEXAS
AGRICULTURAL ECONOMY.   MGRAVRP60405

THE EFFECTS OF **IMPORTED** MEXICAN FARM LABOR IN A CALIFORNIA COUNTY.   MROONJF61465

IMPROVE
VOCATIONAL TRAINING TO **IMPROVE** JOB OPPORTUNITIES FOR MINORITY-GROUPS. COMMENT.   GFINEMX64681

VOCATIONAL-TRAINING TO **IMPROVE** JOB OPPORTUNITIES FOR MINORITY-GROUPS.   GWALSJP64540

MERRILL-TRUST-FUND TO **IMPROVE** THE EMPLOYMENT OPPORTUNITIES OF THE MIGRANT FARM WORKERS OF MEXICAN ORIGIN.   MBISHCS62365

A STUDY OF THE EFFECTS OF EFFORTS TO **IMPROVE** EMPLOYMENT-OPPORTUNITIES OF NEGROES ON THE UTILIZATION OF
NEGRO WORKERS.   NHARTJW64496

TO **IMPROVE** THE STATUS OF PRIVATE HOUSEHOLD WORK. /HOUSEHOLD-WORKERS/   WUSDLAB65220

IMPROVED
RAISING LOW-INCOMES THROUGH **IMPROVED** EDUCATION.   GCOMIED65591

IMPROVED CONDITIONS FOR NEGROES IN LOUISVILLE. /KENTUCKY/   NUSDLAB45820

IMPROVEMENT
SECRETARIAL TRAINING WITH SPEECH **IMPROVEMENT**. AN EXPERIMENTAL AND DEMONSTRATION PROJECT. /NEGRO WOMEN/   CSAINMD66320

AMBITIONS EDUCATION **IMPROVEMENT** PROJECT UNDER WAY IN SOUTH.   GAMERCE64370

A NATIONAL PROGRAM FOR THE **IMPROVEMENT** OF WELFARE SERVICES AND THE REDUCTION OF WELFARE DEPENDENCY.   GCOHENE65664

APPROACHES TO INCOME **IMPROVEMENT**. EXPERIENCES OF FAMILIES RECEIVING PRODUCTION LOANS UNDER THE FARMERS
HOME ADMINISTRATION.   GHENDWE59422

IMPROVEMENT   (CONTINUATION)
    FACTORS AFFECTING THE PRESENT FARMING PROGRAMS OF ONE HUNDRED NEGRO FARMS IN THE PATRONAGE AREA OF THE
    MACON COUNTY TRAINING SCHOOL, IN ALABAMA, WITH EMPHASIS FOR **IMPROVEMENT**.   NBRONCA51337

    PROPOSALS FOR THE **IMPROVEMENT** OF HUMAN RELATIONS IN THE LOS-ANGELES METROPOLITAN AREA.   /EMPLOYMENT
    CALIFORNIA/   NLOSACC65365

IMPROVES
    LIFE INSURANCE. THE PATIENT **IMPROVES**.   /DISCRIMINATION/   GANTIDL59399

    A CULTURAL MINORITY **IMPROVES** ITSELF.   MATKIJA61361

IMPROVING
    IMPROVING INDUSTRIAL RACE-RELATIONS -- PART I. EQUAL JOB OPPORTUNITY -- SLOGAN OR REALITY.   GFLEMHC63363

    IMPROVING THE WORK SKILLS OF THE NATION.   GNATLMC55052

    IMPROVING INDUSTRIAL RACE-RELATIONS -- PART 2, HUMAN PROBLEMS IN **IMPROVING** INDUSTRIAL RACE-RELATIONS.   GSHOSAB63307

    IMPROVING INDUSTRIAL RACE-RELATIONS -- PART 2, HUMAN PROBLEMS IN IMPROVING INDUSTRIAL RACE-RELATIONS.   GSHOSAB63307

    WORKING AT **IMPROVING** THE MOTIVATIONAL AND ACHIEVEMENT LEVELS OF THE DEPRIVED.   NHARREC63367

    ON **IMPROVING** THE ECONOMIC STATUS OF THE NEGRO.   NTOBIJX65206

IMPUTATIONS
    SOCIAL MOBILITY AND **IMPUTATIONS** OF WITCHCRAFT IN A MEXICAN-AMERICAN NEIGHBORHOOD OF TEXAS.   MRUBEAJ66467

IN-MIGRANT
    THE ECONOMIC ABSORPTION OF **IN-MIGRANT** LABORERS IN A NORTHERN INDUSTRIAL COMMUNITY.   /MEXICAN-AMERICAN
    NEGRO/   CSHANLW64486

INACTIVE
    A METHODOLOGICAL APPROACH TO IDENTIFICATION AND CLASSIFICATION OF CERTAIN TYPES OF **INACTIVE** WORK-SEEKERS.
    /UNEMPLOYMENT LABOR-MARKET/   GLIEBEE65569

    INACTIVE NURSES. AN UNTAPPED RECRUITMENT SOURCE.   WBARKAE65628

INCENTIVES
    DEVELOPMENT OF TRAINING **INCENTIVES** FOR THE YOUTH OF MINORITY-GROUPS.   /ECONOMIC-STATUS/   GGRANLB57979

INCIDENCE
    THE **INCIDENCE** OF ANTIDISCRIMINATION CLAUSES IN UNION CONTRACTS.   GWORTMS65681

    DIFFERENTIALS IN THE **INCIDENCE** OF POVERTY IN TEXAS. /ECONOMIC-STATUS/   MUPHAWK66533

INCOME
    THE URBAN ADJUSTMENT OF IMMIGRANTS. THE RELATIONSHIP OF EDUCATION TO OCCUPATIONAL AND TOTAL FAMILY
    INCOME. /NEGRO MEXICAN-AMERICAN/   CSHANLW63122

    NONWHITE POPULATION BY RACE. NEGROES, INDIANS, JAPANESE, CHINESE, FILIPINOS. BY AGE, SEX, MARITAL-STATUS,
    EDUCATION. EMPLOYMENT-STATUS, OCCUPATIONAL-STATUS, **INCOME**, ETC. /DEMOGRAPHY/   CUSBURC53378

    INCOME OF THE ELDERLY POPULATION.   /DEMOGRAPHY/   CUSBURC63171

    NONWHITE POPULATION BY RACE. NEGROES, INDIANS, JAPANESE,CHINESE, FILIPINOS. BY AGE, SEX,
    MARITAL-STATUS,EDUCATION, EMPLOYMENT-STATUS, OCCUPATIONAL-STATUS, **INCOME**, ETC. /DEMOGRAPHY/   CUSBURC63176

    OCCUPATIONAL CHARACTERISTICS. DATA ON AGE, RACE, EDUCATION, WORK EXPERIENCE, **INCOME**, ETC. FOR WORKERS IN
    EACH OCCUPATION.   CUSBURC63177

    SOURCES AND STRUCTURE OF FAMILY **INCOME**.   /DEMOGRAPHY/   CUSBURC63184

    TRENDS IN THE **INCOME** OF FAMILIES AND PERSONS IN THE UNITED STATES. 1947-1960.   /DEMOGRAPHY/   CUSBURC63381

    INCOME IN 1964 OF FAMILIES AND PERSONS IN THE UNITED STATES. /DEMOGRAPHY/   CUSBURC65375

    INCOME, EDUCATION AND UNEMPLOYMENT IN NEIGHBORHOODS. ATLANTA, GEORGIA. /DEMOGRAPHY/   CUSDLAB63451

    INCOME, EDUCATION AND UNEMPLOYMENT IN NEIGHBORHOODS. BALTIMORE, MARYLAND. /DEMOGRAPHY/   CUSDLAB63452

    INCOME, EDUCATION AND UNEMPLOYMENT IN NEIGHBORHOODS. BIRMINGHAM, ALABAMA. /DEMOGRAPHY/   CUSDLAB63453

    INCOME, EDUCATION AND UNEMPLOYMENT IN NEIGHBORHOODS. BOSTON, MASSACHUSETTS. /DEMOGRAPHY/   CUSDLAB63454

    INCOME, EDUCATION AND UNEMPLOYMENT IN NEIGHBORHOODS. BUFFALO, NEW-YORK. /DEMOGRAPHY/   CUSDLAB63455

    INCOME, EDUCATION AND UNEMPLOYMENT IN NEIGHBORHOODS. CHICAGO, ILLINOIS. /DEMOGRAPHY/   CUSDLAB63456

    INCOME, EDUCATION AND UNEMPLOYMENT IN NEIGHBORHOODS. CINCINNATI, OHIO. /DEMOGRAPHY/   CUSDLAB63457

    INCOME, EDUCATION AND UNEMPLOYMENT IN NEIGHBORHOODS. CLEVELAND, OHIO. /DEMOGRAPHY/   CUSDLAB63458

    INCOME, EDUCATION AND UNEMPLOYMENT IN NEIGHBORHOODS. DALLAS, TEXAS. /DEMOGRAPHY/   CUSDLAB63459

    INCOME, EDUCATION AND UNEMPLOYMENT IN NEIGHBORHOODS. DENVER, COLORADO. /DEMOGRAPHY/   CUSDLAB63460

    INCOME, EDUCATION AND UNEMPLOYMENT IN NEIGHBORHOODS. DETROIT, MICHIGAN. /DEMOGRAPHY/   CUSDLAB63461

    INCOME, EDUCATION AND UNEMPLOYMENT IN NEIGHBORHOODS. HOUSTON, TEXAS. /DEMOGRAPHY/   CUSDLAB63462

    INCOME, EDUCATION AND UNEMPLOYMENT IN NEIGHBORHOODS. INDIANAPOLIS, INDIANA. /DEMOGRAPHY/   CUSDLAB63463

    INCOME, EDUCATION AND UNEMPLOYMENT IN NEIGHBORHOODS. KANSAS-CITY, MISSOURI. /DEMOGRAPHY/   CUSDLAB63464

    INCOME, EDUCATION AND UNEMPLOYMENT IN NEIGHBORHOODS. MEMPHIS, TENNESSEE. /DEMOGRAPHY/   CUSDLAB63466

    INCOME, EDUCATION AND UNEMPLOYMENT IN NEIGHBORHOODS. MILWAUKEE, WISCONSIN. /DEMOGRAPHY/   CUSDLAB63467

    INCOME, EDUCATION AND UNEMPLOYMENT IN NEIGHBORHOODS. MINNEAPOLIS -- ST-PAUL, MINNESOTA. /DEMOGRAPHY/   CUSDLAB63468

    INCOME, EDUCATION AND UNEMPLOYMENT IN NEIGHBORHOODS. NEW-ORLEANS, LOUISIANA. /DEMOGRAPHY/   CUSDLAB63469

    INCOME, EDUCATION AND UNEMPLOYMENT IN NEIGHBORHOODS. NEWARK, NEW-JERSEY. /DEMOGRAPHY/   CUSDLAB63470

    INCOME, EDUCATION AND UNEMPLOYMENT IN NEIGHBORHOODS. NEW-YORK-CITY -- BROOKLYN. /DEMOGRAPHY/   CUSDLAB63471

    INCOME, EDUCATION AND UNEMPLOYMENT IN NEIGHBORHOODS. NEW-YORK-CITY -- THE BRONX. /DEMOGRAPHY/   CUSDLAB63472

INCOME, EDUCATION AND UNEMPLOYMENT IN NEIGHBORHOODS. NEW-YORK-CITY -- MANHATTAN. /DEMOGRAPHY/	CUSDLAB63473
INCOME, EDUCATION AND UNEMPLOYMENT IN NEIGHBORHOODS. NEW-YORK-CITY -- QUEENS. /DEMOGRAPHY/	CUSDLAB63474
INCOME, EDUCATION AND UNEMPLOYMENT IN NEIGHBORHOODS. NEW-YORK-CITY -- STATEN-ISLAND. /DEMOGRAPHY/	CUSDLAB63475
INCOME, EDUCATION AND UNEMPLOYMENT IN NEIGHBORHOODS. OAKLAND, CALIFORNIA. /DEMOGRAPHY/	CUSDLAB63476
INCOME, EDUCATION AND UNEMPLOYMENT IN NEIGHBORHOODS. OKLAHOMA-CITY, OKLAHOMA. /DEMOGRAPHY/	CUSDLAB63477
INCOME, EDUCATION AND UNEMPLOYMENT IN NEIGHBORHOODS. PHILADELPHIA, PENNSYLVANIA. /DEMOGRAPHY/	CUSDLAB63478
INCOME, EDUCATION AND UNEMPLOYMENT IN NEIGHBORHOODS. PITTSBURGH, PENNSYLVANIA. /DEMOGRAPHY/	CUSDLAB63479
INCOME, EDUCATION AND UNEMPLOYMENT IN NEIGHBORHOODS. PHOENIX, ARIZONA. /DEMOGRAPHY/	CUSDLAB63480
INCOME, EDUCATION AND UNEMPLOYMENT IN NEIGHBORHOODS. ST-LOUIS, MISSOURI. /DEMOGRAPHY/	CUSDLAB63481
INCOME, EDUCATION AND UNEMPLOYMENT IN NEIGHBORHOODS. SAN-ANTONIO, TEXAS. /DEMOGRAPHY/	CUSDLAB63482
INCOME, EDUCATION AND UNEMPLOYMENT IN NEIGHBORHOODS. SAN-DIEGO, CALIFORNIA. /DEMOGRAPHY/	CUSDLAB63483
INCOME, EDUCATION AND UNEMPLOYMENT IN NEIGHBORHOODS. SAN-FRANCISCO, CALIFORNIA. /DEMOGRAPHY/	CUSDLAB63484
INCOME, EDUCATION AND UNEMPLOYMENT IN NEIGHBORHOODS. SEATTLE, WASHINGTON. /DEMOGRAPHY/	CUSDLAB63485
INCOME, EDUCATION AND UNEMPLOYMENT IN NEIGHBORHOODS. TAMPA, ST-PETERSBURG FLORIDA. /DEMOGRAPHY/	CUSDLAB63486
INCOME, EDUCATION AND UNEMPLOYMENT IN NEIGHBORHOODS. WASHINGTON-DC. /DEMOGRAPHY/	CUSDLAB63487
INCOME, EDUCATION AND UNEMPLOYMENT IN NEIGHBORHOODS. LOS-ANGELES, CALIFORNIA. /DEMOGRAPHY/	CUSDLAB63565
NET MIGRATION OF THE POPULATION, 1950-60, BY AGE, SEX, AND COLOR. VOL II, ANALYTICAL GROUPINGS OF COUNTIES. /INCOME/	GBOWLGK65434
SOME DETERMINANTS OF LOW FAMILY INCOME.	GCREADX61621
EMPLOYMENT AND INCOME BY AGE, SEX, COLOR AND RESIDENCE. /DETROIT MICHIGAN/	GDETRCC63948
LOW-INCOME FAMILIES AND MEASURES OF INCOME INEQUALITY.	GGOLDSF62725
INCOME WITHOUT WORK. /GUARANTEED-INCOME/	GHAZLHX66523
APPROACHES TO INCOME IMPROVEMENT. EXPERIENCES OF FAMILIES RECEIVING PRODUCTION LOANS UNDER THE FARMERS HOME ADMINISTRATION.	GHENDWE59422
THE ASSOCIATION OF INCOME AND EDUCATION FOR MALES, BY REGION, RACE, AND AGE.	GLASSRL65998
THE LABOR-FORCE UNDER CHANGING INCOME AND EMPLOYMENT.	GLONGCX58047
INCOME OF THE AMERICAN PEOPLE.	GMILLHP55988
INCOME AND WELFARE IN THE UNITED STATES.	GMORGJN62032
INCOME, RESOURCES, AND ADJUSTMENT POTENTIALS AMONG RURAL FAMILIES IN NORTH AND WEST FLORIDA.	GREUSLA62388
FAMILY INCOME AND RELATED CHARACTERISTICS AMONG LOW-INCOME COUNTIES AND STATES.	GRODOAL64241
EDUCATION AND INCOME. INEQUALITIES IN OUR PUBLIC SCHOOLS.	GSEXTPX61298
WORK HISTORY, ATTITUDES, AND INCOME OF THE UNEMPLOYED.	GSTEIRL63838
THE ROLE OF MANPOWER POLICY IN ACHIEVING AGGREGATE GOALS. /EMPLOYMENT INCOME/	GTHURLC66640
FAMILY INCOME AND EXPENDITURES.	GUSDLAB49028
FAMILY INCOME STATISTICS.	GUSDLAB49029
CONSUMER EXPENDITURES AND INCOME WITH EMPHASIS ON LOW-INCOME FAMILIES.	GUSDLAB64833
A QUANTITATIVE ANALYSIS OF WHITE-NONWHITE INCOME DIFFERENTIALS IN THE US IN 1939.	GZEMAMX55594
AMERICAN INDIANS IN CALIFORNIA. POPULATION, EDUCATION, EMPLOYMENT, INCOME.	ICALDIR65541
THE ECONOMIC BASIS OF INDIAN LIFE. /INCOME LABOR-FORCE/	IKELLWH57076
POPULATION AND INCOME CENSUS. WIND-RIVER RESERVATION, WYOMING.	IUSDINT60655
POPULATION CHARACTERISTICS, LIVING CONDITIONS AND INCOME OF INDIAN FAMILIES, NORTHERN-CHEYENNE RESERVATION, JULY, 1961.	IUSDINT63656
POPULATION CHARACTERISTICS, LIVING CONDITIONS, AND INCOME OF INDIAN FAMILIES, FORT-PECK RESERVATION, 1951-1961.	IUSDINT63657
THE RELATIONSHIP BETWEEN UNEARNED INCOME AND INDIVIDUAL PRODUCTIVE EFFORT ON THE JICARILLA APACHE INDIAN RESERVATION.	IWILSHC61687
THE BARRIO. /EDUCATION INCOME/	MARIARX66360
CALIFORNIANS OF SPANISH SURNAME. POPULATION, EMPLOYMENT, INCOME, EDUCATION.	MCALDIR64377
EDUCATION AND INCOME OF MEXICAN-AMERICANS IN THE SOUTHWEST.	MFOGEWX65393
HOUSING DEFICIENCIES OF AGRICULTURAL WORKERS AND OTHER LOW INCOME GROUPS.	MMCMIOX62434
DECLINE IN THE RELATIVE INCOME OF NEGRO MEN.	NBATCAB64058
EMPLOYMENT AND INCOME OF NEGRO WORKERS. 1940-1952.	NBEDEMS53071
CHILDREN AND INCOME IN NEGRO FAMILIES.	NBERNEH46077
INCOME AND RELATED CHARACTERISTICS OF RURAL HOUSEHOLDS IN THE CENTRAL LOUISIANA MIXED FARMING AREA.	NBOLTBX60398
FARM INCOME PREDICTIONS FOR SMALL FARMS IN THE CENTRAL LOUISIANA MIXED FARMING AREA.	NBOLTBX62399
TRANSFORMATION OF THE NEGRO-AMERICAN. /EDUCATION EMPLOYMENT INCOME/	NBROOLX65123
NEGRO CALIFORNIANS. POPULATION, EMPLOYMENT, INCOME, EDUCATION.	NCALDIR63167

INCOME (CONTINUATION)
NEGRO SUBORDINATION AND WHITE GAINS. /INCOME OCCUPATIONAL-STATUS/ NCUTRPX65245

THE NEGRC AMERICAN. /EMPLOYMENT INCOME ECCNOMIC-STATUS/ NDAEDXX65246

THE RELATIVE EMPLOYMENT AND INCOME OF AMERICAN NEGROES. NDANIWG63249

CORRELATIONS BETWEEN INCOME AND LABOR-FORCE PARTICIPATION BY RACE. NDORNSM56283

RELATIVE INCOME OF NEGRO MEN. SOME RECENT CATA. NFEINRX66349

THE ANATCMY OF THE NEGRO-WHITE INCOME DIFFERENTIAL. NGALLLE65391

THE NEGRO POTENTIAL. /EMPLOYMENT INCOME ECUCATION/ NGINZEX56409

SOME CHANGES IN THE RELATIVE STATUS OF AMERICAN NON-WHITES, 1940 TO 1960. /INCOME OCCUPATIONAL-STATUS
ECUCATICN/ NGLENND63421

RACIAL CONTRASTS IN INCOME. NHARPRM60487

BEYOND PCVERTY OF INCOME. NHENDGX67214

ECCNCMIC DIMENSIONS. /SOUTH INCOME TECHNOLOGY/ NHENDVW63514

IS THE INCOME GAP CLOSED. NO. NMILLHP62781

RICH MAN. POOR MAN. /INCOME/ NMILLHP64784

LIFETIME INCOME AND ECONOMIC GROWTH. NMILLHP65782

EMPLCYMENT, INCOME, AND THE CRDEAL OF THE NEGRO FAMILY. NMOYNDP65861

THE AGED NEGRO AND HIS INCOME. NORSHMX64960

INCOME, EMPLOYMENT STATJS AND CHANGE IN CALVERT COUNTY, MARYLAND. NRCHRWC58400

AN ANALYSIS OF SELECTIVE FACTORS INFLUENCING FARM INCOME IN HALE COUNTY, AS A BASIS FOR ESTABLISHING A
MORE EFFECTIVE VOCATIONAL AGRICULTURAL PROGRAM. /ALABAMA/ NSALTDR52347

CN THE COST OF BEING A NEGRO. /INCOME EDUCATION/ NSIEGPM65146

FACULTY EDUCATION AND INCOME IN NEGRO AND WHITE COLLEGES. NUSDLAB65819

LABOR SUPPLY, FAMILY INCOME, AND CONSUMPTION. WMINCJX60985

INCOME-DISTRIBUTION
AGE ANC INCOME-DISTRIBUTION. /DEMOGRAPHY/ GBRADDS65679

POLICIES AFFECTING INCOME-DISTRIBUTION. /EMPLOYMENT INCOME-MAINTENANCE/ GFERNFL65662

INCOME-DISTRIBUTION AND POVERTY. GLAMPRJ65658

INCOME-DISTRIBUTION IN THE UNITED STATES. /CEMOGRAPHY/ GMILLHP66778

INCOME-DISTRIBUTION AS A FACTOR IN REGIONAL GROWTH, WITH SPECIAL REFERENCE TO THE SOUTHEAST UNITED
STATES. /DISCRIMINATION/ GPHILEW65773

INCOME-GUARANTEE
THE CASE FOR AN INCOME-GUARANTEE. GTOBIJX66973

INCOME-MAINTENANCE
POLICIES AFFECTING INCOME-DISTRIBUTION. /EMPLOYMENT INCOME-MAINTENANCE/ GFERNFL65662

POVERTY AND INCOME-MAINTENANCE FOR THE UNEMPLOYED. GGORDMS65661

UNEMPLOYMENT INSURANCE AND MANPOWER POLICY. /INCOME-MAINTENANCE/ GKRUGDH65628

HELPING THE LONG-TERM UNEMPLOYED. /INCOME-MAINTENANCE TRAINING/ GUSDLAB62221

INCOMES
THE EFFECT OF LOW EDUCATIONAL-ATTAINMENT ON INCOMES. A COMPARATIVE STUDY OF SELECTED ETHNIC GROUPS.
/NEGRO MEXICAN-AMERICAN/ CFOGEWX66367

INCOMES OF RURAL FAMILIES IN THE BLACKLAND PRAIRIES. GADKIWG63410

DISCRIMINATION AND LOW INCOMES. GANTOAX59401

CHARACTERISTICS, RESOURCES, AND INCOMES OF RURAL HOUSEHOLDS, PIEDMONT AREA, SOUTH-CAROLINA. GBURCTA62408

INCOMES AND DEPENDENCY IN THE COMING DECADES. GDAVIMX64870

RESOURCES AND INCOMES OF RURAL FAMILIES IN THE COASTAL PLAIN AREAS OF GEORGIA. GMCARWC59392

INCOMES OF RURAL FAMILIES IN NORTHEAST TEXAS. GSOUTJH59325

INCOMES OF MIGRATORY AGRICULTURAL WORKERS. GTEXAAE60350

POPULATION CHARACTERISTICS, LIVING CONDITIONS AND INCOMES OF INDIAN FAMILIES, FORT-BELKNAP RESERVATION. IUSDINT63658

POPULATICN CHARACTERISTICS, LIVING CCNDITIONS AND INCOMES OF INDIAN FAMILIES, ROCKY-BAY-S RESERVATION. IUSDINT63659

INCOMES OF RURAL AND URBAN SPANISH-AMERICANS IN TWO SOUTH TEXAS COUNTIES. MDICKBE65389

INCOMES OF MIGRATORY AGRICULTURAL WORKERS. MMETZWH60439

THE EFFECT OF LOW EDUCATIONAL ATTAINMENT ON INCOMES. A COMPARATIVE STUDY OF SELECTED ETHNIC GROUPS. OFOGEWX66721

INCREASED
HAVE FAIR-EMPLOYMENT-PRACTICES-COMMISSION LAWS INCREASED OPPORTUNITIES FOR NEGROES. NLETTHA50683

INCREASED INDUSTRIAL PLACEMENTS OF WORKERS. NUSDLAB41821

INCREASES
ECCNCMIC DISCRIMINATION AND NEGRO INCREASES. NBLALHM56083

INCREASING
INCREASING EMPLOYABILITY OF YOUTH. THE ROLE OF WORK TRAINING. GMOEDMX66852

INCREASING STRUCTURAL UNEMPLOYMENT RE-EXAMINED. GSTOIVX66001

RESERVATION, JULY, 1961.   IUSDINT63656

POPULATION CHARACTERISTICS, LIVING CONDITIONS, AND INCOME OF **INDIAN** FAMILIES, FORT-PECK RESERVATION, 1951-1961.   IUSDINT63657

POPULATION CHARACTERISTICS, LIVING CONDITIONS AND INCOMES OF **INDIAN** FAMILIES, FORT-BELKNAP RESERVATION.   IUSDINT63658

POPULATION CHARACTERISTICS, LIVING CONDITIONS AND INCOMES OF **INDIAN** FAMILIES, ROCKY-BAY-S RESERVATION.   IUSDINT63659

HOPI **INDIAN** AGENCY.   IUSDINT64651

INDIAN AFFAIRS 1964, A PROGRESS REPORT FROM THE COMMISSIONER OF INDIAN AFFAIRS.   IUSDINT64652

INCIAN AFFAIRS 1964, A PROGRESS REPORT FROM THE COMMISSIONER OF **INDIAN** AFFAIRS.   IUSDINT64652

INDIAN INDUSTRIAL DEVELOPMENT PROGRAM. A NEW INDUSTRIAL OPPORTUNITY.   IUSDINT64653

REPORT OF **INDIAN** RECRUITMENT AND TRAINING MEETING AT ALBUQUERQUE, NEW-MEXICO, ON DECEMBER 6, 1966.   IUSDLAB66321

MINUTES OF **INDIAN** EMPLOYMENT MEETING HELD NOVEMBER 29-30, 1966 IN BISMARK, NORTH-DAKOTA.   IUSDLAB66322

REPORT ON **INDIAN** FARM LABOR ACTIVITY.   IUSDLAB66668

ARAPAHOE **INDIAN** TRAINS FOR SPACE AGE.   IUSDLAB66960

INDIAN UNEMPLOYMENT SURVEY, JULY 1963.   IUSHOUR63670

KLAMATH **INDIAN** TRIBE.   IUSSENA56673

REVIEW APPRAISAL. KLAMATH **INDIAN** ASSETS.   IUSSENA59674

PROCEEDINGS OF THE CONFERENCE ON **INDIAN** TRIBES AND TREATIES.   IUVMNCC56676

INDIAN POVERTY AND INDIAN HEALTH.   IWAGNCJ64681

INCIAN POVERTY AND **INDIAN** HEALTH.   IWAGNCJ64681

THE **INDIAN** AND THE WHITE MAN.   IWASHWE64682

THE ECONOMIC ABSORPTION OF NAVAHO **INDIAN** MIGRANTS IN DENVER, COLORADO.   IWEPPRS65684

THE RELATIONSHIP BETWEEN UNEARNED INCOME AND INDIVIDUAL PRODUCTIVE EFFORT ON THE JICARILLA APACHE **INDIAN** RESERVATION.   IWILSHC61687

INDIANA
INCOME, EDUCATION AND UNEMPLOYMENT IN NEIGHBORHOODS. INDIANAPOLIS, **INDIANA**. /DEMOGRAPHY/   CUSDLAB63463

CIVIL-RIGHTS IN **INDIANA**.   GINDICRND804

REPORT OF THE SURVEY OF EMPLOYEES OF THE STATE OF **INDIANA**, SEPTEMBER 1961.   GINDICR61806

MIGRATION AND ADJUSTMENT EXPERIENCES OF RURAL WORKERS IN INDIANAPOLIS. /**INDIANA**/   NSMITED53143

INDIANAPOLIS
INCOME, EDUCATION AND UNEMPLOYMENT IN NEIGHBORHOODS. **INDIANAPOLIS**, INDIANA. /DEMOGRAPHY/   CUSDLAB63463

MIGRATION AND ADJUSTMENT EXPERIENCES OF RURAL WORKERS IN **INDIANAPOLIS**. /INDIANA/   NSMITED53143

INDIANS
NONWHITE POPULATION BY RACE. NEGROES, **INDIANS**, JAPANESE, CHINESE, FILIPINOS. BY AGE, SEX, MARITAL-STATUS, EDUCATION, EMPLOYMENT-STATUS, OCCUPATIONAL-STATUS, INCOME, ETC. /DEMOGRAPHY/   CUSBURC53378

NONWHITE POPULATION BY RACE. NEGROES, **INDIANS**, JAPANESE,CHINESE, FILIPINOS. BY AGE, SEX, MARITAL-STATUS,EDUCATION, EMPLOYMENT-STATUS, OCCUPATIONAL-STATUS, INCOME, ETC. /DEMOGRAPHY/   CUSBURC63176

RELOCATED AMERICAN **INDIANS** IN THE SAN-FRANCISCO BAY AREA. SOCIAL INTERACTION AND INDIAN IDENTITY. /CALIFORNIA/   IALBOJX64523

MANPOWER SERVICES TO ARIZONA **INDIANS**. /SES/   IARIZSE66912

INDIANS OF THE SOUTHWEST.   IATKIMJ63529

THE **INDIANS** IN MODERN AMERICA.   IBAIRDA56532

BETTER ECONOMIC OPPORTUNITY FOR **INDIANS**.   IBECKJX66536

TOWARD A NEW ERA FOR AMERICAN **INDIANS**. /EMPLOYMENT/   IBENNRL66451

THE DETRIBALIZATION OF THE NARRAGANSETT **INDIANS**. A CASE STUDY.   IBOISEX56886

INDIANS IN RURAL AND RESERVATION AREAS. /CALIFORNIA/   ICALAC166542

AMERICAN **INDIANS** IN CALIFORNIA. POPULATION, EDUCATION, EMPLOYMENT, INCOME.   ICALDIR65541

INDIANS OF THE NORTHWEST COAST.   IDOUCPX63549

LEVEL OF OCCUPATIONAL ASPIRATIONS AMONG MONTANA **INDIANS** IN GRADE AND HIGH SCHOOL.   IDOUGGV60550

US GOVERNMENT POLICY TOWARD AMERICAN **INDIANS**. A FEW BASIC FACTS.   IELLIMB57554

SELECTED REFERENCES ON THE PLAINS **INDIANS**.   IEWERJC60816

INDIANS AND OTHER AMERICANS. TWO WAYS OF LIFE MEET.   IFEYXHE59558

PAPAGO **INDIANS**. EVALUATION OF OPPORTUNITIES FOR PERMANENT RELOCATION.   IFITZKXND440

AMERICAN **INDIANS**.   IHAGAWT61570

AMERICAN **INDIANS**, WHITE AND BLACK. THE PHENOMENON OF TRANSCULTURATION.   IHALLAI63571

THE URBANIZATION OF THE YANKTON **INDIANS**.   IHURTWR66576

SOCIAL AND CULTURAL CONSIDERATIONS IN THE DEVELOPMENT OF MANPOWER PROGRAMS FOR **INDIANS**.   IKELLWH67579

NATIONAL CONFERENCE ON MANPOWER PROGRAMS FOR **INDIANS**. SUMMATION.   IKRUGDH67811

THE EMPLOYABILITY OF CHIPPEWA **INDIANS** AND POOR WHITES.   ILIEBLX66041

INDIANS   (CONTINUATION)
    INDIANS WORK AT THEIR OWN SKI RESORT. /NEW-MEXICO/   ILINDVX66580

    KLAMATH INDIANS IN TWO NON-INDIAN COMMUNITIES. KLAMATH-FALLS AND EUGENE-SPRINGFIELD. /OREGON/   ILIVIMG59582

    HIGHER EDUCATION OF SOUTHWESTERN INDIANS WITH REFERENCE TO SUCCESS AND FAILURE.   IMCGRGD62584

    THE INDIANS AND THE GREAT SOCIETY. REMARKS.   IMONDWX66591

    THE NEW TRAIL FOR AMERICAN INDIANS.   INASHPX62596

    THE CULTURE AND ACCULTURATION OF THE DELAWARE INDIANS.   INEWCWW56600

    THE PRESENT STATUS OF THE FLORIDA SEMINOLE INDIANS.   IPEITIM59284

    THE LUISENO INDIANS IN 1965.   IPRICJA65607

    A CENSUS OF INDIANS IN LOS-ANGELES. /CALIFORNIA/   IPRICJA67606

    THE MIGRATION AND ADAPTATION OF AMERICAN INDIANS TO LOS-ANGELES. /CALIFORNIA/   IPRICJA67608

    INDIANS OF CALIFORNIA, PAST AND PRESENT.   IQUINFX60609

    INDIANS OF THE MISSOURI-BASIN -- CULTURAL FACTORS IN THEIR SOCIAL AND ECONOMIC ADJUSTMENT.   IREIFBX58610

    INDIANS OF DU LAC.   IROYXEP59611

    ASSIMILATION OF THE SPOKANE INDIANS. /WASHINGTON/   IROYXPX61612

    THE MEASUREMENT OF ASSIMILATION. THE SPOKANE INDIANS. /WASHINGTON/   IROYXPX66613

    ASSIMILATION OF THE SPOKANE INDIANS. /WASHINGTON/   ISTONCX62626

    THE PRESENT DAY DISTRIBUTION OF UNITED STATES INDIANS.   ITAXXSX56628

    INDIAN AFFAIRS. A STUDY OF THE CHANGES IN POLICY OF THE UNITED STATES TOWARD INDIANS.   ITYLESL64634

    INDIANS ON FEDERAL RESERVATIONS IN THE US.   IUSDHEW58196

    INDIANS. /DEMOGRAPHY/   IUSDINT66654

    PLACING INDIANS WHO LIVE ON RESERVATIONS. A COOPERATIVE PROGRAM.   IUSDLAB59667

    THE URBANIZATION OF THE DAKOTA INDIANS.   IWHITRX59686

INDICATOR
    ATTITUDE TOWARD OCCUPATIONAL CHANGE AS AN INDICATOR OF PROSPECTS FOR ADJUSTMENT.   GDUNKJE64653

INDICATORS
    SELECTED MANPOWER INDICATORS FOR STATES.   GUSDLAB65826

    HEALTH PRACTICES AND EDUCATIONAL ASPIRATIONS AS INDICATORS OF ACCULTURATION AND SOCIAL-CLASS AMONG THE
    EASTERN CHEROKEE. /NORTH-CAROLINA/   IKUPFHJ62216

INDICES
    RELATIONS AMONG MATERNAL EMPLOYMENT INDICES AND DEVELOPMENTAL CHARACTERISTICS OF CHILDREN.
    /WORK-FAMILY-CONFLICT/   WBURCLG61665

INDIVIDUAL
    THE INDIVIDUAL RIGHT TO ELIMINATE EMPLOYMENT DISCRIMINATION BY LITIGATION.   GBLUMAW66566

    RACE. INDIVIDUAL AND COLLECTIVE BEHAVIOR.   GTHOMET58356

    EDUCATION AMONG AMERICAN-INDIANS. INDIVIDUAL AND CULTURAL ASPECTS.   IHAVIRJ57574

    THE RELATIONSHIP BETWEEN UNEARNED INCOME AND INDIVIDUAL PRODUCTIVE EFFORT ON THE JICARILLA APACHE INDIAN
    RESERVATION.   IWILSHC61687

    IMPACT ON THE INDIVIDUAL. /SOCIAL-CHANGE   SOUTH/   NWRIGSJ63344

INDIVIDUALITY
    A JEW WITHIN AMERICAN SOCIETY -- A STUDY IN ETHNIC INDIVIDUALITY.   JSHERCB61311

INDIVIDUALS
    LOW-INCOME FAMILIES AND UNRELATED INDIVIDUALS IN THE UNITED STATES. 1964. /DEMOGRAPHY/   GUSBURC65151

INDUSTRIAL
    THE PREDICTION AND EXPLANATION OF ECONOMIC ABSORPTION AMONG MEXICAN-AMERICANS, NEGROES, AND ANGLOS IN A
    NORTHERN INDUSTRIAL COMMUNITY.   CSHANLW63120

    THE ECONOMIC ABSORPTION OF IN-MIGRANT LABORERS IN A NORTHERN INDUSTRIAL COMMUNITY. /MEXICAN-AMERICAN
    NEGRO/   CSHANLW64486

    THE PREDICTION OF ECONOMIC ABSORPTION AND CULTURAL INTEGRATION AMONG MEXICAN-AMERICANS, NEGROES, AND
    ANGLOS IN A NORTHERN INDUSTRIAL COMMUNITY.   CSHANLW66123

    IMPROVING INDUSTRIAL RACE-RELATIONS -- PART I. EQUAL JOB OPPORTUNITY -- SLOGAN OR REALITY.   GFLEMHC63363

    TWENTY YEARS OF ECONOMIC AND INDUSTRIAL CHANGE. /TECHNOLOGICAL-CHANGE EMPLOYMENT/   GGORDRA65675

    THE INDUSTRIAL SETTING. PROBLEMS AND EXPERIENCES. /TESTING/   GLOPEFM65910

    THE INDUSTRIAL PSYCHOLOGIST. SELECTION AND EQUAL-EMPLOYMENT OPPORTUNITY.   GPARRJA66147

    IMPROVING INDUSTRIAL RACE-RELATIONS -- PART 2, HUMAN PROBLEMS IN IMPROVING INDUSTRIAL RACE-RELATIONS. GSHOSAB63307

    IMPROVING INDUSTRIAL RACE-RELATIONS -- PART 2, HUMAN PROBLEMS IN IMPROVING INDUSTRIAL RACE-RELATIONS. GSHOSAB63307

    AMERICA-S INDUSTRIAL AND OCCUPATIONAL MANPOWER REQUIREMENTS, 1964-75.   GUSDLAB66437

    CAN SEGREGATION SURVIVE IN AN INDUSTRIAL SOCIETY.   GYINGJM58590

    INDIAN INDUSTRIAL DEVELOPMENT PROGRAM. A NEW INDUSTRIAL OPPORTUNITY.   IUSDINT64653

    INDIAN INDUSTRIAL DEVELOPMENT PROGRAM. A NEW INDUSTRIAL OPPORTUNITY.   IUSDINT64653

    NEW-MEXICO COUNTY INDUSTRIAL COMPOSITION AND LEVELS OF LIVING.   MSANDAD63479

    CHANGES IN PUBLIC AND PRIVATE LANGUAGE AMONG SPANISH-SPEAKING MIGRANTS TO AN INDUSTRIAL CITY.   MSCHETJ65481

INDUSTRIAL   (CONTINUATION)
   RACE-RELATIONS IN AN INDUSTRIAL SOCIETY. /EMPLOYMENT GRIEVANCE-PROCEDURES/   NBACOEF63041

   EFFECTS OF AUTOMATION ON THE POSITION OF NEGROES IN A SOUTHERN INDUSTRIAL PLANT.   NHARTJW64495

   RECENT EFFECTS OF RACIAL CONFLICT ON SOUTHERN INDUSTRIAL DEVELOPMENT.   NHILLHX59543

   WHAT ARE SOME INDUSTRIAL RELATIONS APPROACHES TO INTEGRATION.   NHCMAHL63564

   INDUSTRIAL INTEGRATION OF NEGROES. THE UPGRADING PROCESS.   NHOPEJX52571

   THE POST-WAR INDUSTRIAL OUTLOOK FOR NEGROES.   NHOWAUG44579

   RACE-RELATIONS IN INDUSTRIAL RELATIONS.   NHUGHEC46586

   SOCIAL-MOBILITY IN INDUSTRIAL SOCIETY.   NLIPSSM59696

   INDUSTRIAL DISCRIMINATION -- THE SKELETON IN EVERYONE-S CLOSET.   NMIHLLF62779

   EMPLOYMENT AS IT RELATES TO NEGROES IN THE MILWAUKEE INDUSTRIAL AREA. /WISCONSIN/   NMILWUL48793

   THE INDUSTRIAL INTEGRATION OF THE NEGRO.   NPATTTH63978

   THE NEGRO IN THE INDUSTRIAL DEVELOPMENT OF THE SOUTH.   NRABOSH53029

   AN INDUSTRIAL EXPERIMENT TOWARDS INTEGRATION OF MINORITIES INTO INDUSTRY.   NRUBIAX46093

   NEGROES IN THE WORK GROUP. HOW 33 BUSINESS AND INDUSTRIAL FIRMS OFFERED EQUAL-EMPLOYMENT-OPPORTUNITIES TO
   ALL.   NSEIDJX50114

   INCREASED INDUSTRIAL PLACEMENTS OF WORKERS.   NUSDLAB41821

   THE IMPACT OF RACE-RELATIONS ON INDUSTRIAL RELATIONS IN THE SOUTH.   NWHEEJH64230

   MISSISSIPPI WORKERS. WHERE THEY COME FROM AND HOW THEY PERFORM. A STUDY OF WORKING FORCES IN SELECTED
   MISSISSIPPI INDUSTRIAL PLANTS.   NWOFFBM55333

   THE ADJUSTMENT OF NEGROES IN A NORTHERN INDUSTRIAL COMMUNITY.   NZIMMBG62360

   EMPLOYMENT OF WOMEN CHEMISTS IN INDUSTRIAL LABORATORIES. /OCCUPATIONS/   WPARRJB65050

   WHAT THE INDUSTRIAL PSYCHOLOGIST MUST KNOW ABOUT TODAY-S AND TOMORROW-S WOMAN.   WPERLEX63100

   TRADE AND INDUSTRIAL EDUCATION FOR GIRLS AND WOMEN. A DIRECTORY OF TRAINING PROGRAMS.   WUSDHEW60175

INDUSTRIAL-RELATIONS
   INTRODUCTION. THE STRUGGLE FOR EQUALITY AND ITS IMPACT ON INDUSTRIAL-RELATIONS.   GSTEIBX64335

   A GUIDE TO INDUSTRIAL-RELATIONS IN THE UNITED STATES. EQUAL JOB OPPORTUNITY UNDER COLLECTIVE-BARGAINING.   GUSDLAB58449

   INTRODUCTION. THE STRUGGLE FOR EQUALITY AND ITS IMPACT ON INDUSTRIAL-RELATIONS.   NSTEIBX64300

INDUSTRIALIZATION
   RURAL INDUSTRIALIZATION IN A LOUISIANA COMMUNITY. /ECONOMIC-STATUS OCCUPATIONS/   GBERTAL59393

   RURAL INDUSTRIALIZATION. A SUMMARY OF FIVE STUDIES. /UNEMPLOYMENT OCCUPATIONS/   GMAITST61383

   THE EFFECTS OF INDUSTRIALIZATION ON RURAL LOUISIANA. A STUDY OF PLANT EMPLOYEES.   GPRICPH58395

   INDUSTRIALIZATION AND RACE-RELATIONS.   NBLUMHX65100

   RECENT SOUTHERN INDUSTRIALIZATION AND ITS IMPLICATIONS FOR NEGROES LIVING IN THE SOUTH.
   /EMPLOYMENT-TRENDS/   NCHICCA53204

   INDUSTRIALIZATION AND RACE-RELATIONS.   NHUNTGX65588

   INDUSTRIALIZATION AND RACE-RELATIONS IN THE SOUTHERN US.   NMARSRX65739

INDUSTRIES
   NEGRO WOMEN IN THE CLOTHING, CIGAR AND LAUNDRY INDUSTRIES OF PHILADELPHIA, 1960.   CPORTRP43103

   EFFECTS ON ECONOMIC GROWTH OF THE EMPLOYMENT SHIFT TO SERVICE INDUSTRIES.   GBRADME64797

   PATTERNS OF DISCRIMINATION IN THE FINANCIAL INSTITUTIONS OF THE DISTRICT-OF-COLUMBIA. THE BANKING,
   SAVINGS AND LOAN, AND INSURANCE INDUSTRIES.   GDISTCC66642

   PATTERNS OF DISCRIMINATION IN THE GLASS AND MACHINE TOOL INDUSTRIES IN OHIO.   GOHICCR66126

   TECHNOLOGICAL TRENDS IN 36 MAJOR AMERICAN INDUSTRIES.   GUSDLAB64802

   TECHNOLOGICAL TRENDS IN MAJOR AMERICAN INDUSTRIES. /EMPLOYMENT/   GUSDLAB66637

   FARMERS, WORKERS, AND MACHINES. TECHNOLOGICAL AND SOCIAL-CHANGE IN FARM INDUSTRIES OF ARIZONA.   MPADFHX65450

   CPI -- CHEMICAL PROCESS INDUSTRIES -- TAKES LEAD IN ANTI-BIAS DRIVE. /INDUSTRY/   NCHEMWX61199

   HOW MANAGEMENT CAN INTEGRATE NEGROES IN WAR INDUSTRIES.   NDAVIJA42255

   NEGROES AND THE SERVICE INDUSTRIES. /OCCUPATIONS/   NDIAMDE64272

   NEGRO EMPLOYMENT IN THE TEXTILE INDUSTRIES OF NORTH AND SOUTH-CAROLINA. /NORTH-CAROLINA/   NOSBUDD66963

   COMBATING DISCRIMINATION IN THE EMPLOYMENT OF NEGROES IN WAR INDUSTRIES AND GOVERNMENT AGENCIES.   NRAMSLA43128

   DEFENSE INDUSTRIES AND THE NEGRO.   NWEAVRC42552

   THE EMPLOYMENT OF THE NEGRO IN WAR INDUSTRIES.   NWEAVRC43225

   EMPLOYMENT OF NEGROES IN UNITED STATES WAR INDUSTRIES.   NWEAVRC44300

INDUSTRY
   SENIORITY AND POSTWAR JOBS. RUBBER INDUSTRY. /NEGRO WOMEN/   CLABORR44028

   INTERIM REPORT TO THE MAYOR ON ITS INQUIRY INTO CHARGES OF RACIAL BIAS IN THE CITY BUILDING AND
   CONSTRUCTION INDUSTRY. /NEW-YORK NEGRO PUERTO-RICAN/   CNEWYCO64917

   OCCUPATION BY INDUSTRY. /DEMOGRAPHY/   CUSBURC63179

   THE USE OF PSYCHOLOGICAL TESTS IN INDUSTRY.   GALBRLE63368

INTEGRATION IN BUSINESS AND **INDUSTRY**. A SELECTED, ANNOTATED BIBLIOGRAPHY.	GAMERJC64383
INDUSTRY AND HUMAN-RIGHTS.	GANTIDL63396
THE IMPLICATIONS OF THE CIVIL-RIGHTS-ACT OF 1964 FOR PSYCHOLOGICAL ASSESSMENT IN **INDUSTRY**. /TESTING/	GASHXPX66405
METHODS OF ADJUSTING TO AUTOMATION AND TECHNOLOGICAL-CHANGE. /**INDUSTRY**/	GBOKXOX64737
MERIT EMPLOYMENT. NON-DISCRIMINATION IN **INDUSTRY**.	GBULLPX60897
REPORT OF **INDUSTRY** AND LABOR-MANAGEMENT CLINICS. IMPLEMENTATION OF EMPLOYMENT IN MERIT PROGRAMS IN NON FEPC STATES BY DIRECT APPROACH TO TOP MANAGEMENT.	GFISKUR51684
GUIDE TO MERIT EMPLOYMENT. A RESTATEMENT OF **INDUSTRY** PRINCIPLES AND PRACTICES.	GFOODECND694
PSYCHOLOGICAL TESTING. SOME PROBLEMS AND SOLUTIONS. /**INDUSTRY**/	GFRENWL66101
HUMAN-RELATIONS IN **INDUSTRY**.	GGAROBB55707
INTERGROUP RELATIONS WITHIN BUSINESS AND **INDUSTRY**.	GGENECC49713
MORTALITY BY OCCUPATION AND **INDUSTRY** AMONG MEN 20 TO 64 YEARS OF AGE. UNITED STATES, 1950. /DEMOGRAPHY/	GGURALX62748
WARTIME EMPLOYMENT PATTERNS OF NONWHITES AND FEMALE WORKERS IN SOUTHERN **INDUSTRY**.	GHOPEJX46485
QUERIES CONCERNING **INDUSTRY** AND SOCIETY GROWING OUT OF STUDY OF ETHNIC RELATIONS IN INDUSTRY.	GHUGHEC59787
QUERIES CONCERNING INDUSTRY AND SOCIETY GROWING OUT OF STUDY OF ETHNIC RELATIONS IN **INDUSTRY**.	GHUGHEC59787
DISCRIMINATION WITHOUT PREJUDICE. A STUDY OF PROMOTION PRACTICES IN **INDUSTRY**.	GKAHNRL64733
HOW INTEGRATION IS WORKING OUT IN **INDUSTRY**.	GMANARX56936
WHAT **INDUSTRY** CAN DO. /EEO/	GMAYFHX64969
MINORITY-GROUP WORKERS IN **INDUSTRY**.	GMEYESM56058
TECHNICAL REPORT NUMBER 1. EMPLOYMENT PRACTICES IN THE HOTEL, MOTEL AND RESTAURANT **INDUSTRY** OF MISSOURI.	GMILLRX66020
THE ROLE OF THE EMPLOYER IN MANPOWER POLICY. /**INDUSTRY**/	GMYERCA66527
INTER-GROUP RELATIONS WITHIN LABOR AND **INDUSTRY**.	GNATLCL49042
STATEMENTS RELATING TO THE IMPACT OF TECHNOLOGICAL-CHANGE. /**INDUSTRY**/	GNATLCT66848
MANPOWER UNLIMITED. /**INDUSTRY** INTEGRATION/	GNEWYSA57086
THE BANKING **INDUSTRY**. VERIFIED COMPLAINTS AND INFORMAL INVESTIGATIONS. /NEW-YORK/	GNEWYSA58076
EMPLOYMENT IN THE HOTEL **INDUSTRY**. /NEW-YORK/	GNEWYSA58081
THE INSURANCE **INDUSTRY** -- VERIFIED COMPLAINTS AND INFORMAL INVESTIGATIONS HANDLED BY THE NEW-YORK STATE COMMISSION AGAINST DISCRIMINATION, JULY 1 1945-SEPTEMBER 15, 1958.	GNEWYSA58082
PATTERNS OF DISCRIMINATION IN THE GLASS **INDUSTRY** IN OHIO.	GOHIOCR66127
PATTERNS OF DISCRIMINATION IN THE MACHINE TOOL **INDUSTRY** IN OHIO.	GOHIOCR66128
BUSINESS -- NEXT TARGET FOR INTEGRATION. /**INDUSTRY**/	GPERRJX63170
FINDINGS OF FACT, CONCLUSIONS AND ACTION OF THE COMMISSION ON HUMAN-RELATIONS IN RE. INVESTIGATIVE PUBLIC HEARINGS INTO ALLEGED DISCRIMINATORY PRACTICE BY THE HOTEL AND RESTAURANT **INDUSTRY** IN PHILADELPHIA. /PENNSYLVANIA/	GPHILCH61176
SELF-ANALYSIS QUESTIONNAIRE. /EEO **INDUSTRY**/	GPRESCC63115
EXTRAVAGANT INJUSTICE. DISCRIMINATION IN **INDUSTRY**. /CONNECTICUT/	GROPEEXND243
THE PRICE BUSINESS PAYS. /**INDUSTRY** DISCRIMINATION/	GROPEEX49245
THE HIGH COST OF DISCRIMINATION. THE WASTE IN MANPOWER, MORALE, AND PRODUCTIVITY COSTS AMERICAN **INDUSTRY** 30 BILLION DOLLARS A YEAR.	GRCPEEX63244
THEY DID IT IN ST-LOUIS. /**INDUSTRY** INTEGRATION MISSOURI/	GROSSMX47262
INDUSTRY-S EXPERIMENT TOWARDS INTEGRATION OF MINORITIES INTO **INDUSTRY**.	GRUBIAX46265
BIG BUSINESS FAILS AMERICA. /**INDUSTRY**/	GSCRESX63292
A SURVEY OF DISCRIMINATION IN THE BUILDING TRADES **INDUSTRY**, NEW-YORK CITY.	GSHAUDF63300
MANPOWER NEEDS BY **INDUSTRY** TO 1975.	GSTAMHX65768
PSYCHOLOGICAL TESTING IN **INDUSTRY**. A CRITICAL EVALUATION.	GSTANES64635
TOLERANCE IN **INDUSTRY**. THE RECORD.	GTURNHC50365
INDUSTRY EMPLOYMENT GROWTH SINCE WORLD WAR II.	GUSOLAB63831
INVESTIGATION OF THE GARMENT INDUSTRY.	GUSHOUR62344
WESTERN-ELECTRIC AND ITS PLAN-FOR-PROGRESS. A THREE YEAR REPORT. /**INDUSTRY**/	GWESTEC64553
A COMPANY CASE HISTORY. /**INDUSTRY** EEO/	GWITTHW64576
DEVELOPMENT OF THE SAN-CARLOS APACHE CATTLE **INDUSTRY**. /CALIFORNIA/	IGETTHT58563
THE SAN-CARLOS INDIAN CATTLE **INDUSTRY**. /CALIFORNIA/	IGETTHT63564
STUDY SHOWS FEW JEWS HAVE TOP JOBS IN AUTO **INDUSTRY**.	JNATIJM63748
EMPLOYMENT OF JEWISH PERSONNEL IN THE AUTOMOBILE **INDUSTRY**. /DISCRIMINATION/	JRIGHXX63756
NEGRO PLATFORM WORKERS. /**INDUSTRY** CASE-STUDY/	NAMERCR45011
THE NEGRO WORKER. /**INDUSTRY**/	NAMERMA42017
NEGRO LABOR IN THE AUTO **INDUSTRY**.	NBAILLH43045

NEGRC HIRING -- SOME CASE-STUDIES. /INDUSTRY/   NBAMBJJ49050

MORE ROOM AT THE TOP. COMPANY EXPERIENCE IN EMPLOYING NEGROES IN PROFESSIONAL AND MANAGEMENT JOBS.
  /INDUSTRY/   NBIRDCX63080

THE PERSONNEL JOB IN A CHANGING WORLD. /INDUSTRY/   NBLOCJW64093

DISCRIMINATION WITHOUT PREJUDICE. /INDUSTRY/   NBLOORO55094

WAR INDUSTRY EMPLOYMENT FOR NEGROES IN MARYLAND.   NBRYSWO43129

JOBS FOR NEGROES. ONE COMPANY-S ANSWER. /CASE-STUDY INDUSTRY/   NBUSIMX64142

BILLION-DOLLAR PRIZE SPURS INTEGRATION. /INDUSTRY   GEORGIA/   NBUSIWX61145

CARRYING OUT A PLAN FOR JOB INTEGRATION AND DOING IT -- IN THE HEART OF GEORGIA -- WITHOUT A SINGLE
UNPLEASANT INCIDENT. THAT-S THE EXPERIENCE OF LOCKHEED AIRCRAFT CORPORATION AT ITS MARIETTA PLANT.
  /INDUSTRY/   NBUSIWX63148

INDUSTRY RUSHES FOR NEGRO GRADS.   NBUSIWX64297

ANALYSIS OF THE TECHNIQUES OF RACIAL INTEGRATION IN THREE MANUFACTURING FIRMS. /INDUSTRY/   NCAMPFX54178

CPI -- CHEMICAL PROCESS INDUSTRIES -- TAKES LEAD IN ANTI-BIAS DRIVE. /INDUSTRY/   NCHEMWX61199

THEY MAKE OPPORTUNITY KNOCK. /INDUSTRY   URBAN-LEAGUE/   NCHEMWX63200

SCHOOL-DESEGREGATION AND NEW INDUSTRY. THE SOUTHERN COMMUNITY LEADERS VIEWPOINT.   NCROMRX63243

NEGRC EMPLOYMENT IN SOUTHERN INDUSTRY.   NDEWEDX52270

TWO PLANTS -- LITTLE-ROCK. /CASE-STUDY INDUSTRY ARKANSAS/   NECKAEW55319

INDUSTRY AND RACE IN THE SOUTHERN US.   NEDMCMS65321

THE TECHNIQUE OF INTRODUCING NEGROES INTO THE PLANT. /INDUSTRY/   NFELDHX42351

DISCRIMINATION. A NOTICE TO INDUSTRY.   NFORTXX55051

AT WORK IN INDUSTRY TODAY. 50 CASE-REPORTS ON NEGROES AT WORK.   NGENEEX64398

THE NEGRO CHALLENGE TO THE BUSINESS COMMUNITY. /INDUSTRY/   NGINZEX64408

HIRING NEGRO WORKERS. /INDUSTRY/   NHABBSX64473

CHIEF EXECUTIVES VIEW NEGRO EMPLOYMENT. /INDUSTRY/   NHABBSX65471

THE NEGRO AS AN EMPLOYEE. /INDUSTRY/   NHABBSX65474

COMPANY EXPERIENCE WITH NEGRO EMPLOYMENT. /INDUSTRY/   NHABBSX66472

CO CORPORATIONS HAVE A SOCIAL DUTY. /INDUSTRY/   NHACKAX63475

THE USE OF NEGRO LABOR IN SOUTHERN INDUSTRY. /OCCUPATIONAL-PATTERNS/   NHALLDE53477

THE NEGRO WORKER IN INDUSTRY.   NHILLHX57533

NEW-YORK CITY COMMISSION ON HUMAN RIGHTS, CONSTRUCTION TRADES HEARING, TESTIMONY. /INDUSTRY/   NHILLHX66546

THE EMPLOYMENT OF NEGROES IN THE US BY MAJOR OCCUPATION AND INDUSTRY.   NHOPEJX53567

EFFORTS TO ELIMINATE RACIAL DISCRIMINATION IN INDUSTRY -- WITH PARTICULAR REFERENCE TO THE SOUTH.   NHOPEJX54566

THE KNITTING OF RACIAL GROUPS IN INDUSTRY.   NHUGHEC46584

TAPPING THE NEGRO POTENTIAL. /INDUSTRY EMPLOYMENT-SELECTION PROMOTION/   NJOHNTX65621

INDUSTRY ON TRIAL. /PREFERENTIAL-TREATMENT/   NKAPPLX63635

A STUDY OF THE EMPLOYMENT OPPORTUNITIES FOR NEGROES IN BREWERIES OF THE UNITED STATES. /INDUSTRY/   NKERNJH51897

DISCRIMINATION IN THE HIRING HALL. A CASE-STUDY OF PRESSURES TC PROMOTE INTEGRATION IN NEW-YORK-S BREWERY
INDUSTRY.   NLANGGE59670

HOW INTEGRATION IS WORKING OUT IN INDUSTRY. THE NEGRO WORKER.   NMANARX56734

SOME FACTORS INFLUENCING THE UPGRADING OF NEGROES IN THE SOUTHERN PETROLEUM REFINING INDUSTRY.
  /CASE-STUDY/   NMARSRX63748

FINAL REPORT. EQUAL-EMPLOYMENT-OPPORTUNITY IN THE TRANSPORTATION INDUSTRY. /MASSACHUSETTS/   NMASSCA66964

EMPLOYMENT DISTRIBUTION STUDY OF THE CONSTRUCTION INDUSTRY IN MICHIGAN.   NMICCRC66606

SOLVING RACIAL PROBLEMS IN YOUR PLANT. /INDUSTRY/   NMODEIX45805

MANAGEMENT POLICIES AND BI-RACIAL INTEGRATION IN INDUSTRY.   NMOHRFT54806

AMERICAN NEGROES -- A WASTED RESOURCE. /INDUSTRY/   NMORRJJ57853

GOALS IN NEGRO EMPLOYMENT. /INDUSTRY/   NNATLIC65874

NEGRC WORKERS IN THE BUILDING TRADES IN SELECTED CITIES. NORFOLK, VIRGINIA. /INDUSTRY/   NNATLUL46894

CORPORATE HIRING POLICIES AND THE NEGRO. /INDUSTRY/   NNEWSXX64911

THE EMPLOYMENT OF NEGROES AS DRIVER SALESMEN IN THE BAKING INDUSTRY.   NNEWYSA60919

INDUSTRY COMES OF AGE IN THE SOUTH.   NNOLAEW53926

EMPLOYING THE NEGRO IN AMERICAN INDUSTRY   NNORGPH59932

THE NEGRO AND UNIONISM IN THE BIRMINGHAM, ALABAMA IRCN AND STEEL INDUSTRY.   NNORTHR43941

NEGRCES IN A WAR INDUSTRY. THE CASE OF SHIPBUILDING.   NNORTHR43942

THE TREND SINCE 1944 ON THE COLOR LINE IN INDUSTRY.   NOPINRC51959

MANAGEMENTS GUIDELINES FOR MEETING THE NEGRO DRIVE FOR JOB EQUALITY. /INDUSTRY/.   NOPINRC63958

INDUSTRY   (CONTINUATION)
HIRING NEGROES FOR BETTER JOBS. EXPERIENCE OF LEADING COMPANIES. /INDUSTRY/   NOPINRC64957

A STUDY OF THE LONGSHORE INDUSTRY IN NEW-ORLEANS WITH EMPHASIS ON NEGRO LONGSHOREMEN. /LOUISIANA/   NORTICF56962

INTEGRATION IN INDUSTRY.   NOWENJA61968

THE INTRODUCTION OF NEGROES INTO WHITE DEPARTMENTS. /CASE-STUDY INDUSTRY/   NPALMER55972

REPORT AND SUMMARY OF THE AIR FORCE ON ACTIONS TAKEN BY LOCKHEED AIRCRAFT CORPORATION AT THE AIR FORCE
PLANT NO 6 IN MARIETTA, GEORGIA. /INDUSTRY/   NPRESCD61013

COMPANY EXPERIENCE WITH THE EMPLOYMENT OF NEGROES. /INDUSTRY/   NPRINUI54020

MANAGEMENT VERSUS JIM-CROW. /INDUSTRY/   NPURCTV62023

MANAGEMENT SOCIAL RESPONSIBILITY AND RACIAL EMPLOYMENT IN THE MEAT-PACKING INDUSTRY.   NPURCTV67123

ACCOMOCATION BETWEEN NEGRO AND WHITE EMPLOYEES IN A WEST COAST AIRCRAFT INDUSTRY, 1942-1944.
/CASE-STUDY/   NREEDBA47045

DISCRIMINATION IN INDUSTRY.   NROPEEX52073

THE NEGRO IN INDUSTRY.   NROSERX53077

AN INDUSTRIAL EXPERIMENT TOWARDS INTEGRATION OF MINORITIES INTO INDUSTRY.   NRUBIAX46093

A SURVEY OF DISCRIMINATION IN THE BUILDING TRADES INDUSTRY. NEW-YORK CITY.   NSHAUDX63126

THE BUSINESSMAN AND THE NEGRO. /INDUSTRY/   NSILBCE63133

MORE SALARIED POSITIONS ARE OPENED TO NEGROES BY BUSINESS AND INDUSTRY HERE. /NEW-YORK/   NSTETDX63154

CHANGING EMPLOYMENT PRACTICES IN THE CONSTRUCTION INDUSTRY. EXPERIENCE REPORT 102.   NUSCONM65233

NEGRO EMPLOYMENT IN AIRPLANE PLANTS. /INDUSTRY/   NUSDLAB43827

SENIORITY IN THE AKRON RUBBER INDUSTRY.   NUSDLAB44841

SENIORITY IN THE AUTOMOBILE INDUSTRY.   NUSDLAB44842

PLAN FOR EQUAL-JOB-OPPORTUNITY AT LOCKHEED-AIRCRAFT-CORP. /INDUSTRY CASE-STUDY/   NUSDLAB61838

1966 EMPLOYMENT SURVEY IN THE TEXTILE INDUSTRY OF THE CAROLINAS.   NWALLPA66591

THE NEGRO COMES OF AGE IN INDUSTRY.   NWEAVRC43301

NEGRO EMPLOYMENT IN THE AIRCRAFT INDUSTRY.   NWEAVRC45302

ANTI-DISCRIMINATION IN INDUSTRY.   NYOUNCE45358

INTEGRATION IN INDUSTRY.   NYOUNWM64351

CALIFORNIA-S FRUIT AND VEGETABLE CANNING INDUSTRY. AN ECONOMIC STUDY.   OBENJMP61704

PUERTO-RICAN INTEGRATION IN THE SKIRT INDUSTRY IN NEW-YORK CITY.   PHELFBH59481

LET-S PUT WOMEN IN THEIR PLACE. /INDUSTRY/   WALBEGS61602

THE PRESENT SITUATION OF WOMAN SCIENTISTS AND ENGINEERS IN INDUSTRY AND GOVERNMENT. /OCCUPATIONS/   WBOLTRH65650

WOMEN EMPLOYEES IN MANUFACTURING BY INDUSTRY, JANUARY, 1959.   WEMPLAE59752

WOMEN IN INDUSTRY. /OCCUPATIONS/   WGILBLM62782

NOTES ON WOMEN IN INDUSTRY -- PRESENTED AT AMERICAN PSYCHOLOGICAL SYMPOSIUM, SEPT 1963. /DISCRIMINATION/   WGILMBV63970

ABSENTEEISM AMONG WOMEN WORKERS IN INDUSTRY.   WISAMVX62876

WOMEN MATHEMATICIANS IN INDUSTRY. /OCCUPATIONS/   WSENDVL64111

WOMEN IN INDUSTRY -- PATTERNS OF WOMEN-S WORK AND OCCUPATIONAL HEALTH AND SAFETY. /OCCUPATIONS/   WSPIRES60301

EARNINGS IN THE WOMEN-S AND MISSES COAT AND SUIT INDUSTRY.   WUSDLAB57988

SHORTAGE OR SURPLUS. AN ASSESSMENT OF BOSTON WOMANPOWER IN INDUSTRY, GOVERNMENT, AND RESEARCH. JUNE 7-8,
1963. /MASSACHUSETTS/   WUSDLAB66217

INDUSTRY-S
INDUSTRY-S EXPERIMENT TOWARDS INTEGRATION OF MINORITIES INTO INDUSTRY.   GRUBIAX46265

INDUSTRY-S UNFINISHED BUSINESS. /CASE-STUDY/   GSOUTSE50324

INDUSTRY-S MOST UNDERDEVELOPED RESOURCE.   NNATLUL64890

INDUSTRY-S RACIAL EMPLOYMENT POLICIES.   NNORTHR67938

INEQUALITIES
EDUCATION AND INCOME. INEQUALITIES IN OUR PUBLIC SCHOOLS.   GSEXTPX61298

THE PROBLEM OF SELF-IMPOSED INEQUALITIES.   GWATTWW66223

PROGRESS IN INTERRACIAL RELATIONSHIPS. INEQUALITIES FOR NEGROES.   NLEWIES43689

INEQUALITY
INEQUALITY OF OPPORTUNITY IN HIGHER EDUCATION. A STUDY OF MINORITY GROUP AND RELATED BARRIERS TO COLLEGE
ADMISSION.   GBERKDS48446

LOW-INCOME FAMILIES AND MEASURES OF INCOME INEQUALITY.   GGOLDSF62725

PROFILE IN BLACK AND WHITE. DISCRIMINATION AND INEQUALITY OF OPPORTUNITY.   GNATLULND085

THE ULTIMATE CONQUEST OF NEGRO ECONOMIC INEQUALITY.   NCALLEX64175

RACIAL INEQUALITY IN EMPLOYMENT. THE PATTERNS OF DISCRIMINATION.   NHILLHX65540

ECONOMIC INEQUALITY.   NMILLSM65789

OCCUPATIONAL PATTERNS OF INEQUALITY.   NTURNRH54216

INFLATION
INTRODUCTION TO ECONOMICS OF GROWTH, UNEMPLOYMENT, AND **INFLATION**.   GHERMHX64938

INFLUENCE
SOME EDUCATIONAL IMPLICATIONS OF THE **INFLUENCE** OF REJECTION ON ASPIRATION LEVELS OF MINORITY-GROUP
CHILDREN.   GGOFFRM54366

THE **INFLUENCE** OF DISCRIMINATION ON MINORITY-GROUP MEMBERS IN ITS RELATION TO ATTEMPTS TO COMBAT
DISCRIMINATION.   GSAENGX48273

THE **INFLUENCE** OF A BORDER CITY UNION ON THE RACE ATTITUDES OF ITS MEMBERS.   NROSEAW53293

THE **INFLUENCE** OF TUSKEGEE-INSTITUTE ON THE HEALTH, EDUCATIONAL, ECONOMIC, AND POLITICAL ASPECTS OF THE
NEGRO POPULATION OF MACON COUNTY, ALABAMA.   NSHIEAR51342

INFLUENCES
CLASS AND FAMILY **INFLUENCES** ON STUDENT ASPIRATIONS.   NBENNWS64574

EDUCATION OF NEGRO LEADERS. **INFLUENCES** AFFECTING GRADUATE AND PROFESSIONAL STUDIES.   NCALIAX49174

SOCIAL **INFLUENCES** IN NEGRO-WHITE INTELLIGENCE DIFFERENCES.   NDEUTMX64268

A HISTORICAL REVIEW OF THE IMPACT OF SOCIAL AND ECONOMIC STRUCTURE ON NEGRO CULTURE AND HOW IT **INFLUENCES**
FAMILY LIVING.   NJACKJX64596

INFLUENCING
ECONOMIC FACTORS **INFLUENCING** EDUCATIONAL-ATTAINMENTS AND ASPIRATIONS OF FARM YOUTH.   GMOOREJ64386

SOME FACTORS **INFLUENCING** THE GROWTH OF UNIONS IN THE SOUTH.   NMARSRX60060

SOME FACTORS **INFLUENCING** UNION RACIAL PRACTICES.   NMARSRX62747

RACIAL FACTORS **INFLUENCING** ENTRY TO THE SKILLED TRADES. /UNION/   NMARSRX63745

SOME FACTORS **INFLUENCING** THE UPGRADING OF NEGROES IN THE SOUTHERN PETROLEUM REFINING INDUSTRY.
/CASE-STUDY/   NMARSRX63748

AN ANALYSIS OF SELECTIVE FACTORS **INFLUENCING** FARM INCOME IN HALE COUNTY, AS A BASIS FOR ESTABLISHING A
MORE EFFECTIVE VOCATIONAL AGRICULTURAL PROGRAM. /ALABAMA/   NSALTDR52347

FACTORS **INFLUENCING** WOMEN-S DECISIONS ABOUT HIGHER EDUCATION. /ASPIRATIONS/   WDAVIOD59716

AN ANALYSIS OF FACTORS **INFLUENCING** MARRIED WOMEN-S ACTUAL OR PLANNED WORK PARTICIPATION.   WWELLMW61261

INFORMATION
MIGRATORY-LABOR IN THE WEST. BACKGROUND **INFORMATION** FOR THE WESTERN INTERSTATE CONFERENCE ON MIGRATORY
LABOR. /MIGRANT-WORKERS/   GCOUNSG60931

COUNSELOR-S GUIDE TO OCCUPATIONAL AND OTHER MANPOWER **INFORMATION**. AN ANNOTATED BIBLIOGRAPHY.   GLAFADP65782

INFORMATION NETWORKS IN LABOR-MARKETS.   GREESAX65119

INFORMATION CONCERNING ENTRY OF MEXICAN AGRICULTURAL WORKERS INTO THE UNITED STATES.   MUSDLAB59335

THE EDUCATION OF WOMEN -- **INFORMATION** AND RESEARCH NOTES.   WAMERCEND605

INFRINGEMENT
ANTIDISCRIMINATION LEGISLATION AS AN **INFRINGEMENT** OF FREEDOM OF CHOICE.   GAVINAX60409

INHIBIT
STUDY OF SOCIO-CULTURAL FACTORS THAT **INHIBIT** OR ENCOURAGE DELINQUENCY AMONG MEXICAN-AMERICANS.   MLOSARW58432

INHIBITIVE
FACILITATIVE AND **INHIBITIVE** FACTORS IN TRAINING PROGRAM RECRUITMENT AMONG RURAL NEGROES.   NMARSCP65738

INITIATIVE
CIVIL-RIGHTS IN AIR TRANSPORTATION AND GOVERNMENT **INITIATIVE**.   GDIXORX63644

EQUALITY OF EMPLOYMENT OPPORTUNITY. A PROCESS ANALYSIS OF UNION **INITIATIVE**.   NHOPEJX60569

INJUSTICE
EXTRAVAGANT **INJUSTICE**. DISCRIMINATION IN INDUSTRY. /CONNECTICUT/   GROPEEXND243

INQUIRIES
GUIDE TO LAWFUL AND UNLAWFUL PRE-EMPLOYMENT **INQUIRIES** BY EMPLOYERS, EMPLOYMENT-AGENCIES, AND LABOR
ORGANIZATIONS UNDER THE CALIFORNIA FAIR-EMPLOYMENT-PRACTICE ACT, LABOR CODE, SECTIONS 1410-1432.   GCALDIR60527

FAIR-EMPLOYMENT-PRACTICE ACT...FEPC RULES AND REGULATIONS... GUIDE TO PRE-EMPLOYMENT **INQUIRIES**.
/CALIFORNIA/   GCALFEP61533

FAIR-EMPLOYMENT-PRACTICE-COMMISSION GUIDE TO UNLAWFUL PRE-EMPLOYMENT **INQUIRIES**.   GCURRRO60889

RULINGS ON PRE-EMPLOYMENT **INQUIRIES** RELATING TO RACE, CREED, COLOR OR NATIONAL ORIGIN UNDER THE NEW-YORK
STATE LAW AGAINST DISCRIMINATION.   GNEWYSBND106

RULES ON EMPLOYMENT **INQUIRIES**.   GOREGBLND139

GUIDE TO EMPLOYERS, EMPLOYMENT-AGENCIES AND LABOR UNIONS DEFINING PROPER AND IMPROPER PRE-EMPLOYMENT
INQUIRIES. /PENNSYLVANIA/   GPENNHRND164

INQUIRY
INTERIM REPORT TO THE MAYOR ON ITS **INQUIRY** INTO CHARGES OF RACIAL BIAS IN THE CITY BUILDING AND
CONSTRUCTION INDUSTRY. /NEW-YORK NEGRO PUERTO-RICAN/   CNEWYCO64917

GOVERNMENT CONTRACTS AND SOCIAL CONTROL. A PRELIMINARY **INQUIRY**.   GMILLAS55985

REPORT OF **INQUIRY** CONCERNING CHARGES OF DISCRIMINATING PRACTICES IN THE NEW-YORK STATE THRUWAY AUTHORITY.   GNEWYSB64104

THE ECONOMIC IMBALANCE. AN **INQUIRY** INTO THE ECONOMIC-STATUS OF NEGROES IN THE UNITED STATES, 1935-1960,
WITH IMPLICATIONS FOR NEGRO EDUCATION.   NHENDVW60512

A NATIONAL **INQUIRY** OF PRIVATE HOUSEHOLD-EMPLOYEES AND EMPLOYERS.   WNATLCH66014

WISCONSIN FAIR-EMPLOYMENT-PRACTICES DIVISION **INQUIRY** INTO THE CONFLICTS BETWEEN STATE PROTECTIVE LABOR
LEGISLATION AND STATE AND FEDERAL LAWS PROHIBITING DISCRIMINATION BASED ON SEX. /EMPLOYMENT-CONDITIONS/   WUAWXWD65165

INSECURITY
SLUMS AND SOCIAL **INSECURITY**.   GSCHOAL65122

INSECURITY   (CONTINUATION)
ECONOMIC INSECURITY AND WORKING-CLASS CONSCIOUSNESS.   NLEGGJC64677

INSIGHT
AN INSIGHT INTO STRUCTURAL UNEMPLOYMENT -- THE EXPERIENCE OF A MINORITY GROUP IN A PROSPEROUS COMMUNITY.   NGERSWJ65634

INSPECTION
PLANT INSPECTION SURVEY BY MANAGEMENT -- MINORITY-GROUP INTEGRATION. /COLORADO/   GDENNGHND632

INSTITUTE
RADCLIFFE INSTITUTE FOR INDEPENDENT STUDY. /TRAINING/   WSMITCX63119

INSTITUTIONAL
COMPARISON OF MEXICANS, NEGROES AND WHITES WITH RESPECT TO OCCUPATIONAL HISTORY, RURAL-URBAN RESIDENCE
HISTORY AND ACCULTURIZATION WITHIN THE INSTITUTIONAL STRUCTURE OF LANSING, MICHIGAN.   CGOLDVX60494

MDTA INSTITUTIONAL TRAINING OF NONWHITES.   GMARSJX66944

EDUCATION AMONG AMERICAN-INDIANS. INSTITUTIONAL ASPECTS.   ITHOMHX57630

FACTORY FOLKWAYS. A STUDY OF INSTITUTIONAL STRUCTURE AND CHANGE.   NELLSJS52331

INSTITUTIONAL GUIDANCE FACES THE FUTURE.   NSCALEE57272

INSTITUTIONS
PATTERNS OF DISCRIMINATION IN THE FINANCIAL INSTITUTIONS OF THE DISTRICT-OF-COLUMBIA. THE BANKING,
SAVINGS AND LOAN, AND INSURANCE INDUSTRIES.   GDISTCC66642

COMPILATION OF LAWS AGAINST DISCRIMINATION, EMPLOYMENT, EDUCATIONAL INSTITUTIONS, PLACES OF PUBLIC
ACCOMODATION. PUBLIC HOUSING, PUBLICLY ASSISTED HOUSING, PRIVATE HOUSING. /MASSACHUSETTS/   GMASSCAND963

CIVIL-RIGHTS AND JEWISH INSTITUTIONS.   JPILCJX64749

GRADUATE AND PROFESSIONAL EDUCATION IN NEGRO INSTITUTIONS. /ECONOMIC-STATUS/   NBROWAX58893

A COMPARISON OF TUITION-AND-FEE CHARGES IN NEGRO INSTITUTIONS WITH CHARGES IN INSTITUTIONS OF THE
SOUTHEAST AND OF THE NATION. 1962-1963. /EDUCATION/   NDAMILX64127

A COMPARISON OF TUITION-AND-FEE CHARGES IN NEGRO INSTITUTIONS WITH CHARGES IN INSTITUTIONS OF THE
SOUTHEAST AND OF THE NATION. 1962-1963. /EDUCATION/   NDAMILX64127

ATTITUDES TOWARD WOMEN COLLEGE TEACHERS IN INSTITUTIONS OF HIGHER EDUCATION ACCREDITED BY THE NORTH
CENTRAL ASSOCIATION.   WBERWHD62475

A CONFERENCE TO ENLIST THE PARTICIPATION OF 50 INSTITUTIONS OF HIGHER EDUCATION IN SPECIFIC R AND D
PROGRAMS TO PREPARE WOMEN FOR PRODUCTIVE EMPLOYMENT.   WLLOYBJ64937

INSTRUCTION
THE EFFECT OF SPECIAL INSTRUCTION UPON TEST PERFORMANCE OF HIGH SCHOOL STUDENTS IN TENNESSEE.   NROBESO66961

INSURANCE
RACIAL DISTRIBUTION OF SELECTED UNEMPLOYMENT INSURANCE AND EMPLOYMENT SERVICE DATA. JULY-DECEMBER 1966.
/NEGRO MEXICAN-AMERICAN/   CCALDEM67907

LIFE INSURANCE. THE PATIENT IMPROVES. /DISCRIMINATION/   GANTIDL59399

LIFE INSURANCE COMPANIES. /DISCRIMINATION/   GANTIDL62398

PATTERNS OF DISCRIMINATION IN THE FINANCIAL INSTITUTIONS OF THE DISTRICT-OF-COLUMBIA. THE BANKING,
SAVINGS AND LOAN, AND INSURANCE INDUSTRIES.   GDISTCC66642

UNEMPLOYMENT INSURANCE AND MANPOWER POLICY. /INCOME-MAINTENANCE/   GKRUGDH65628

THE INSURANCE INDUSTRY -- VERIFIED COMPLAINTS AND INFORMAL INVESTIGATIONS HANDLED BY THE NEW-YORK STATE
COMMISSION AGAINST DISCRIMINATION, JULY 1 1945-SEPTEMBER 15, 1958.   GNEWYSA58082

EMPLOYMENT IN INSURANCE COMPANIES. /DISCRIMINATION/   JRIGHXX59755

INSURANCE, BANKING, PUBLIC UTILITIES. /DISCRIMINATION EMPLOYMENT/   JSIMOBX58763

LIFE INSURANCE SELLING AS A CAREER FOR WOMEN. /OCCUPATIONS/   WLEITSF61926

WOMEN HOUSEHOLD WORKERS COVERED BY OLD AGE, SURVIVORS, AND DISABILITY INSURANCE.   WPOLIEJ65285

REPORT OF THE COMMITTEE ON SOCIAL INSURANCE AND TAXES, 1963.   WPRESCO63070

INSURED
DETROIT-S INSURED UNEMPLOYED AND EMPLOYABLE WELFARE RECIPIENTS. /MICHIGAN/   GWICKED63561

INSURED UNEMPLOYED AND EMPLOYABLE WELFARE RECIPIENTS.   GWICKEX63637

INSURING
INSURING FULL EMPLOYMENT.   GPIERJH64846

INTEGRATE
HOW MANAGEMENT CAN INTEGRATE NEGROES IN WAR INDUSTRIES.   NDAVIJA42255

INTEGRATED
FAMILY STRUCTURE AND SCHOOL PERFORMANCE. A COMPARATIVE STUDY OF STUDENTS FROM THREE ETHNIC BACKGROUNDS IN
AN INTEGRATED SCHOOL. /MEXICAN-AMERICAN AMERICAN-INDIAN/   CGRIFJX65407

AN EXPERIMENT TO TEST THREE MAJOR ISSUES OF WORK PROGRAM METHODOLOGY WITHIN MOBILIZATION-FOR-YOUTH-S
INTEGRATED SERVICES TO OUT-OF-SCHOOL UNEMPLOYED YOUTH. /NEGRO PUERTO-RICAN/   CMOBIFY66024

AN INTEGRATED POSITIVE MANPOWER POLICY.   GBAKKEW65753

THE INTEGRATED WORK-FORCE. WHERE ARE WE NOW.   GMULFRH66116

A COMPARISON OF THE SOCIAL CHARACTERISTICS AND EDUCATIONAL ASPIRATIONS OF NORTHERN, LOWER-CLASS, NEGRO
PARENTS WHO ACCEPTED AND DECLINED AN OPPORTUNITY FOR INTEGRATED EDUCATION FOR THEIR CHILDREN.   NCAGLLT66904

THE NEGRO STUDENT AT INTEGRATED COLLEGES.   NCLARKB63214

TEST BIAS. VALIDITY OF THE SCHOLASTIC APTITUDE TEST FOR NEGRO AND WHITE STUDENTS IN INTEGRATED COLLEGES.   NCLEATA66923

A PILOT STUDY OF AN INTEGRATED WORK FORCE.   NCOUSFR58611

THE NEGRO INTEGRATED.   NFALCNS45342

INTEGRATED   (CONTINUATION)
ATLANTA-S SEGREGATED APPROACH TO **INTEGRATED** EMPLOYMENT. /GEORGIA/   NTHOMHX62205

INTEGRATING
ISSUES AND PROBLEMS IN **INTEGRATING** NEEDED SUPPORTIVE SERVICES IN NEIGHBORHOOD-YOUTH-CORPS PROJECTS.   GBATTMX66131

PROBLEMS AND APPROACHES IN **INTEGRATING** MINORITY-GROUP WORK FORCES.   GSPERBJ53330

INTEGRATING THE NEGRO TEACHER OUT OF A JOB. /OCCUPATIONS/   NCARTBX65999

SOCIAL AND ECONOMIC IMPLICATIONS OF **INTEGRATING** IN THE PUBLIC SCHOOLS.   NCLARKB65213

INTEGRATING THE WORK FORCE.   NINDURP66593

THE MAYOR AND THE FIRE CHIEF. THE FIGHT OVER **INTEGRATING** THE LOS-ANGELES FIRE DEPARTMENT. /CALIFORNIA
CASE-STUDY/   NSHERFP59130

INTEGRATION
INTEGRATION IN PROFESSIONAL NURSING. /OCCUPATIONS NEGRO WOMEN/   CCARNME62183

THE ECONOMIC ABSORPTION AND CULTURAL **INTEGRATION** OF IMMIGRANT MEXICAN-AMERICAN AND NEGRO WORKERS.   CSHANLW64124

CULTURAL AND RELATED RESTRAINTS AND MEANS OF OVERCOMING THEM. /MEXICAN-AMERICAN NEGRO **INTEGRATION**/   CSHANLW65485

THE PREDICTION OF ECONOMIC ABSORPTION AND CULTURAL **INTEGRATION** AMONG MEXICAN-AMERICANS, NEGROES, AND
ANGLOS IN A NORTHERN INDUSTRIAL COMMUNITY.   CSHANLW66123

ECONOMIC ABSORPTION AND CULTURAL **INTEGRATION** OF THE URBAN NEWCOMER. /NEGRO MEXICAN-AMERICAN/   CUVIOIP65277

THE **INTEGRATION** OF AMERICANS OF MEXICAN, PUERTO-RICAN, AND ORIENTAL DESCENT.   CYINGJM56519

STRENGTHENING THE **INTEGRATION** OF MINORITY-GROUPS. THE PROBLEM IS TACKLED AS A UNION PROBLEM.   GALGOME52107

INTEGRATION IN BUSINESS AND INDUSTRY. A SELECTED, ANNOTATED BIBLIOGRAPHY.   GAMERJC64383

RACIAL DESEGREGATION AND **INTEGRATION**.   GANNAOA56578

ORGANIZED LABOR AND THE **INTEGRATION** OF ETHNIC GROUPS. /UNION/   GBLOCHD58455

SOCIAL **INTEGRATION**, ATTITUDES AND UNION ACTIVITY.   GDEANLR54944

PLANT INSPECTION SURVEY BY MANAGEMENT -- MINORITY-GROUP **INTEGRATION**. /COLORADO/   GDENNGHND632

CALIFORNIA LOCAL GOVERNMENT AND **INTEGRATION**.   GFORDJA63695

RACIAL **INTEGRATION** IN EMPLOYMENT.   GGIBSHX54969

HOW **INTEGRATION** IS WORKING OUT IN INDUSTRY.   GMANARX56936

MINORITY-GROUPS. SEGREGATION AND **INTEGRATION**.   GNATLCN55044

MANPOWER UNLIMITED. /INDUSTRY **INTEGRATION**/   GNEWYSA57086

BUSINESS -- NEXT TARGET FOR **INTEGRATION**. /INDUSTRY/   GPERRJX63170

REPORT OF PROGRESS IN THE **INTEGRATION** OF HOTEL AND RESTAURANT EMPLOYMENT, APRIL 1961 TO MARCH 1962.
/PHILADELPHIA PENNSYLVANIA/   GPHILCH62178

THEY DID IT IN ST-LOUIS. /INDUSTRY **INTEGRATION** MISSOURI/   GROSSMX47262

INDUSTRY-S EXPERIMENT TOWARDS **INTEGRATION** OF MINORITIES INTO INDUSTRY.   GRUBIAX46265

MINORITY-GROUP **INTEGRATION** BY LABOR AND MANAGEMENT. A STUDY OF THE EMPLOYMENT PRACTICES OF THE LARGER
EMPLOYERS, AND THE MEMBERSHIP PRACTICES OF THE LARGER LABOR UNIONS WITH RESPECT TO RACE, RELIGION, AND
NATIONAL ORIGIN, CONNECTICUT, 1951.   GSTETHG53598

PRINCETON-S LESSON. SCHOOL **INTEGRATION** IS NOT ENOUGH. /NEW-JERSEY/   GSTREPX64337

EMPLOYMENT **INTEGRATION** AND RACIAL WAGE DIFFERENCE IN A SOUTHERN PLANT.   GWEINRX59988

THE **INTEGRATION** OF AMERICANS OF INDIAN DESCENT.   IDOZIEP57077

SOCIAL SURVEY OF AMERICAN-INDIAN URBAN **INTEGRATION**.   IHIRAJXND444

WHY NO **INTEGRATION** FOR THE AMERICAN-INDIAN.   IUSNEWR62672

INTEGRATION OF MINORITIES.   MLANDRX60426

THE MANAGEMENT OF RACIAL **INTEGRATION** IN BUSINESS, A SPECIAL REPORT TO MANAGEMENT.   NALEXRD64868

MINORITY-GROUP **INTEGRATION** IN HOSPITALS.   NBABOIX61037

PROGRESS TOWARD **INTEGRATION**. FOUR CASE-STUDIES. /EMPLOYMENT FEPC NEW-YORK/   NBACKSX59040

CHANGES AND CHALLENGES IN THE 60-S. /**INTEGRATION** TECHNOLOGICAL-CHANGE TEACHER/   NBRAGEW63312

BILLION-DOLLAR PRIZE SPURS **INTEGRATION**. /INDUSTRY GEORGIA/   NBUSIWX61145

CARRYING OUT A PLAN FOR JOB **INTEGRATION** AND DOING IT -- IN THE HEART OF GEORGIA -- WITHOUT A SINGLE
UNPLEASANT INCIDENT. THAT-S THE EXPERIENCE OF LOCKHEED AIRCRAFT CORPORATION AT ITS MARIETTA PLANT.
/INDUSTRY/   NBUSIWX63148

ANALYSIS OF THE TECHNIQUES OF RACIAL **INTEGRATION** IN THREE MANUFACTURING FIRMS. /INDUSTRY/   NCAMPFX54178

INTEGRATION ON HOSPITAL APPOINTMENTS AND IN HOSPITAL CARE. /CHICAGO ILLINOIS/   NCHICUL58202

EFFECT OF SCHOOL ASSIGNMENT LAWS ON FEDERAL ADJUDICATION OF **INTEGRATION** CONTROVERSIES.   NCOLULR57224

NEGRO TEACHERS. MARTYRS TO **INTEGRATION**. /OCCUPATIONS/   NCOXXOC53935

INTEGRATION IN PROFESSIONAL EDUCATION. THE STORY OF PERKINS, SOUTHERN METHODIST UNIVERSITY. /VOCATIONS/ NCUVNMX56579

THE MECHANICAL COTTON-PICKER, NEGRO MIGRATION, AND THE **INTEGRATION** MOVEMENT.   NDILLHCND274

THE MANAGEMENT OF RACIAL **INTEGRATION** IN BUSINESS.   NDORIGF64282

INTEGRATION IN THE ARMED SERVICES. /MILITARY/   NEVANJC56340

THE RELUCTANT SOUTH. /**INTEGRATION**/   NFICHJH59464

INTEGRATION   (CONTINUATION)
       THE INTEGRATION OF THE NEGRO INTO AMERICAN SOCIETY.   NFRAZEF51578

       RACIAL INTEGRATION IN EMPLOYMENT -- FINDINGS IN TWO KANSAS-CITY HOSPITALS.   NGIBSHX54402

       NEGRO DIALECT. THE LAST BARRIER TO INTEGRATION.   NGREEGC63447

       DEMOGRAPHIC FACTORS IN THE INTEGRATION OF THE NEGRO.   NHAUSPM65501

       WHAT ARE SOME INDUSTRIAL RELATIONS APPROACHES TO INTEGRATION.   NHOMAHL63564

       INDUSTRIAL INTEGRATION OF NEGROES. THE UPGRADING PROCESS.   NHOPEJX52571

       THE NEXT STEP. TEACHER INTEGRATION.   NJANSPA66603

       POSITION PAPER ON EMPLOYMENT INTEGRATION.   NKELLKP64641

       THE NEGRO IN AMERICAN BUSINESS. THE CONFLICT BETWEEN SEPARATISM AND INTEGRATION.   NKINZRH50654

       DISCRIMINATION IN THE HIRING HALL. A CASE-STUDY OF PRESSURES TO PROMOTE INTEGRATION IN NEW-YORK-S BREWERY
       INDUSTRY.   NLANGGE59670

       DESEGREGATION. INTEGRATION, AND THE NEGRO COMMUNITY.   NLEWIHX56073

       INTEGRATION NORTH AND SOUTH.   NLOTHOX56710

       HOW INTEGRATION IS WORKING OUT IN INDUSTRY. THE NEGRO WORKER.   NMANARX56734

       MANAGEMENT POLICIES AND BI-RACIAL INTEGRATION IN INDUSTRY.   NMOHRFT54806

       RACIAL INTEGRATION IN THE ARMED FORCES. /MILITARY/   NMOSKCC66855

       INTEGRATION OF NEGROES IN DEPARTMENT STORES.   NNATLUL46891

       INTEGRATION IN THE WORK-FORCE. WHY AND HOW.   NNATLUL55901

       INTEGRATION IN INDUSTRY.   NOWENJA61968

       THE INDUSTRIAL INTEGRATION OF THE NEGRO.   NPATTTH63978

       AN INDUSTRIAL EXPERIMENT TOWARDS INTEGRATION OF MINORITIES INTO INDUSTRY.   NRUBIAX46093

       CUSTOMER REACTIONS TO THE INTEGRATION OF NEGRO SALES PERSONNEL.   NSAENGX50101

       DESEGREGATION AND INTEGRATION IN SOCIAL WORK.   NSIMOSM56262

       SOUTHERN UNIONS AND THE INTEGRATION ISSUE.   NTREWHL56207

       INTEGRATION IN THE ARMED SERVICES. A PROGRESS REPORT. /MILITARY/   NUSDDEF55195

       INTEGRATION AND THE NEGRO OFFICER IN THE ARMED FORCES OF THE UNITED STATES OF AMERICA. /MILITARY/   NUSDDEF62240

       NEGROES ON THE SALES FORCE. THE QUIET INTEGRATION.   NVOGLAJ64286

       EMPLOYMENT INTEGRATION AND WAGE DIFFERENCES IN A SOUTHERN PLANT.   NWEINRX59311

       INTEGRATION IN INDUSTRY.   NYOUNWM64351

       THE INTEGRATION OF PUERTO-RICANS.   PFITZJP55802

       PUERTO-RICAN INTEGRATION IN THE SKIRT INDUSTRY IN NEW-YORK CITY.   PHELFBH59481

       PUERTO-RICAN INTEGRATION IN A GARMENT UNION LOCAL.   PHELFRB57815

INTEGRATIONISTS
       NEXT IT-S A MIXED POLICE FORCE. INTEGRATIONISTS LATEST GOAL IN NATION-S CAPITAL. /WASHINGTON-DC/   NUSNEWR57274

INTELLECTUAL
       RELATION OF MOTHER-S EMPLOYMENT TO INTELLECTUAL PERFORMANCE OF NEGRO COLLEGE STUDENTS.   NEPPSEG64336

       REVIEW OF EVIDENCE RELATING TO EFFECTS OF DESEGREGATION ON THE INTELLECTUAL PERFORMANCE OF NEGROES.   NKATZIX64637

       SOME INTELLECTUAL ATTRIBUTES AND EDUCATIONAL INTERESTS OF UNIVERSITY WOMEN IN VARIOUS MAJORS.
       /ASPIRATIONS/   WGENTLX60790

INTELLECTUALLY
       INTELLECTUALLY SUPERIOR NEGRO YOUTH. THEIR PROBLEMS AND NEEDS. /EDUCATION/   NJENKMC50606

INTELLIGENCE
       SPANISH-SPEAKING AND ENGLISH SPEAKING CHILDREN IN SOUTHWEST TEXAS. A COMPARATIVE STUDY OF INTELLIGENCE,
       SOCIO-ECONOMIC STATUS, AND ACHIEVEMENT.   MRATLYX60460

       INTELLIGENCE OF THE AMERICAN NEGRO.   NANTIOL63911

       SOCIAL INFLUENCES IN NEGRO-WHITE INTELLIGENCE DIFFERENCES.   NDEUTMX64268

       THE MEANINGFULNESS OF NEGRO-WHITE DIFFERENCES IN INTELLIGENCE TEST PERFORMANCE.   NHICKRA66740

       RACIAL DIFFERENCES AND THE FUTURE. /INTELLIGENCE EQUAL-OPPORTUNITY/   NINGLDJ64067

       NEGRO-WHITE DIFFERENCES IN INTELLIGENCE TEST PERFORMANCE.   NKLINOX63657

       NEGRO INTELLIGENCE AND SELECTIVE MIGRATION. A PHILADELPHIA TEST OF THE KLINEBERG HYPOTHESIS.
       /PENNSYLVANIA/   NLEEXES51673

       NEGRO VERSUS WHITE INTELLIGENCE. A CONTINUING CONTROVERSY.   NMCCOWM58062

       INTELLIGENCE AND EDUCATIONAL ACHIEVEMENT OF A MATCHED SAMPLE OF WHITE AND NEGRO STUDENTS.   NMCQURX60730

       INTELLIGENCE IN THE UNITED STATES, A SURVEY -- WITH CONCLUSIONS FOR MANPOWER UTILIZATION IN EDUCATION AND
       EMPLOYMENT.   NMINEJB57796

       THE INTELLIGENCE OF AMERICAN NEGROES.   NNORTRD56935

       NEGRO AMERICAN INTELLIGENCE. A NEW LOOK AT AN OLD CONTROVERSY.   NPETTTF63063

       RACIAL DIFFERENCES IN INTELLIGENCE.   NPLOTLX59064

       THE RELATIONSHIP BETWEEN TEST INTELLIGENCE OF THIRD GRADE NEGRO CHILDREN AND THE OCCUPATIONS OF THEIR

INTELLIGENCE   (CONTINUATION)
   PARENTS.   NROBIML47070

   THE TESTING OF NEGRO **INTELLIGENCE**.   NSHUEAX66145

   RACE AND **INTELLIGENCE**. AN EVALUATION.   NTUMIMM63065

INTER-AGENCY
   INTER-AGENCY POLICY ON RACIAL BIAS.   NLABORR43029

INTER-GROUP
   INTER-GROUP RELATIONS WITHIN LABOR AND INDUSTRY.   GNATLCL49042

INTER-INDUSTRY
   INTER-INDUSTRY LABOR MOBILITY AMONG MEN, 1957-60.   NGALLLE66392

INTER-RACIAL
   DEALING WITH **INTER-RACIAL** TENSIONS ON LOCAL UNION GRASS ROOTS BASIS.   NANDEEC50894

   INTER-RACIAL PLANNING FOR COMMUNITY ORGANIZATION... EMPLOYMENT PROBLEMS OF THE NEGRO.   NNATLUL44900

INTERACTION
   RELOCATED AMERICAN INDIANS IN THE SAN-FRANCISCO BAY AREA. SOCIAL **INTERACTION** AND INDIAN IDENTITY.
   /CALIFORNIA/   IALBOJX64523

   THE **INTERACTION** OF DEMAND AND SUPPLY AND ITS EFFECT ON THE FEMALE LABOR-FORCE IN THE UNITED STATES.   WOPPEVK66289

INTERAGENCY
   DIVISION OF AUTHORITY UNDER TITLE-VII OF THE CIVIL-RIGHTS-ACT OF 1964. A PRELIMINARY STUDY IN
   FEDERAL-STATE **INTERAGENCY** RELATIONS.   GROSESJ66254

INTEREST
   THE FEDERAL **INTEREST** IN EMPLOYMENT DISCRIMINATION. HEREIN THE CONSTITUTIONAL SCOPE OF EXECUTIVE POWER TO
   WITHOLD APPROPRIATE FUNDS.   GFERGCC64679

   MINORITY RIGHTS AND THE PUBLIC **INTEREST**.   GLUSKLX42924

   LABOR AND THE PUBLIC **INTEREST**. /UNION/   GWIRTWW64572

   INTEREST PATTERN FAKING BY FEMALE JOB APPLICANTS. /ASPIRATIONS/   WBECKJA63633

   COLLEGE WOMEN-S IDENTIFICATIONS WITH THEIR FATHERS IN RELATION TO VOCATIONAL **INTEREST** PATTERNS.
   /ASPIRATIONS/   WHALLWJ63815

   INTEREST AND PERSONALITY CORRELATES OF CAREER-MOTIVATED AND HOMEMAKING-MOTIVATED COLLEGE WOMEN.
   /ASPIRATIONS/   WHOYTDP58850

   INTEREST PROFILES OF UNIVERSITY WOMEN. /ASPIRATIONS/   WMITCED57986

   DIGEST OF STATE LEGISLATION OF SPECIAL **INTEREST** TO WOMEN WORKERS.   WUSDLABND191

   INTEREST AND VALUES OF CAREER AND HOME MAKING ORIENTED WOMEN.   WWAGMMX66761

INTERESTS
   RACE, APTITUDE AND VOCATIONAL **INTERESTS**.   NCHANNN65191

   A COMPARATIVE STUDY OF THE OCCUPATIONAL **INTERESTS** OF NEGRO AND WHITE ADOLESCENT BOYS.   NCONASM65471

   IDEOLOGY AND **INTERESTS**. THE DETERMINANTS OF UNION ACTION.   NKORNWA53659

   INTERESTS OF NEGROES AND WHITES.   NSTROEK52186

   SOME INTELLECTUAL ATTRIBUTES AND EDUCATIONAL **INTERESTS** OF UNIVERSITY WOMEN IN VARIOUS MAJORS.
   /ASPIRATIONS/   WGENTLX60790

   KNOWLEDGE AND **INTERESTS** CONCERNING SIXTEEN OCCUPATIONS AMONG ELEMENTARY AND SECONDARY SCHOOL STUDENTS.
   /ASPIRATIONS/   WMELSRC63968

   VOCATIONAL **INTERESTS** AND OCCUPATIONAL ADJUSTMENT OF COLLEGE WOMEN.   WWARRPA59222

INTERGROUP
   REGISTRIES AND **INTERGROUP** RELATIONS. /NEGRO WOMEN DISCRIMINATION/   CKASUMX59013

   AMERICAN MINORITIES. A TEXTBOOK OF READINGS IN **INTERGROUP** RELATIONS.   GBARRML57424

   MANUAL OF **INTERGROUP** RELATIONS.   GDEANJP55630

   INTERGROUP RELATIONS IN THE FEDERAL-SERVICE .   GDOUGJH61649

   INTERGROUP RELATIONS WITHIN BUSINESS AND INDUSTRY.   GGENECC49713

   CENTRAL ROLE OF **INTERGROUP** AGENCIES IN THE LABOR-MARKET. CHANGING RESEARCH AND PERSONNEL REQUIREMENTS.   GHOPEJX61780

   SITUATIONAL PATTERNING AND **INTERGROUP** RELATIONS.   GKOHNML56145

   THE REDUCTION OF **INTERGROUP** TENSIONS.   GWILLRM47564

   MINORITY-GROUPS AND **INTERGROUP** RELATIONS IN THE SAN-FRANCISCO BAY AREA. /CALIFORNIA/   NRECOCW63043

   RACE PREJUDICE AND DISCRIMINATION. READINGS IN **INTERGROUP** RELATIONS IN THE US.   NROSEAM51075

INTERGROUP-RELATIONS
   RESEARCH BULLETIN ON **INTERGROUP-RELATIONS**. /EEO/   GSMITCX62319

INTERIM
   INTERIM REPORT TO THE MAYOR ON ITS INQUIRY INTO CHARGES OF RACIAL BIAS IN THE CITY BUILDING AND
   CONSTRUCTION INDUSTRY. /NEW-YORK NEGRO PUERTO-RICAN/   CNEWYCO64917

   INTERIM REVISED PROJECTIONS OF US LABOR-FORCE, 1965-1975.   GCOOPSX62602

   TRANSCRIPT OF PROCEEDINGS OF THE **INTERIM** SUBCOMMITTEE ON SPECIAL EMPLOYMENT PROBLEMS. /CALIFORNIA/   MCALAIC64374

   INTERIM REPORT ON OAKLAND SCHOOLS. /CALIFORNIA/   NCALFEP66169

   STATEMENT BEFORE CALIFORNIA LEGISLATURE ASSEMBLY, **INTERIM** SUBCOMMITTEE ON ECONOMIC OPPORTUNITY ON BEHALF
   OF CHINATOWN-NORTH BEACH DISTRICT COUNCIL.   OWONGLJ64771

INTERINDUSTRY
   INTERINDUSTRY EMPLOYMENT REQUIREMENTS.   GALTEJX65369

INTERIOR
ANNUAL REPORTS OF US DEPARTMENT OF THE **INTERIOR**.   IUSDINTND666

REPORT TO THE SECRETARY OF THE **INTERIOR** BY THE TASK FORCE ON INDIAN AFFAIRS.   IUSDINT61641

INTERMOUNTAIN
PROBLEMS OF NAVAJO MALE GRADUATES OF **INTERMOUNTAIN** SCHOOL DURING THEIR FIRST YEAR OF EMPLOYMENT.   IBAKEJE59533

A STUDY OF THE REASONS FOR FAILURE ON THE JOB OF SOME GRADUATES OF **INTERMOUNTAIN** SCHOOL.   IFISHLX60560

INTERNATIONAL
CURRENT **INTERNATIONAL** UNION POLICIES AFFECTING MINORITIES AND THEIR IMPLEMENTATION.   GHOPEJX49781

CURRENT MINORITY POLICIES AND THEIR IMPLEMENTATION IN **INTERNATIONAL** UNIONS.   GHOPEJX51782

MEMBERSHIP POLICIES OF **INTERNATIONAL** UNIONS AS THEY AFFECT NEGRO WORKERS.   NGRANLB41442

NEGRO EMPLOYMENT IN THREE SOUTHERN PLANTS OF **INTERNATIONAL** HARVESTER COMPANY. /CASE-STUDY/   NHOPEJX55572

RECENT TRENDS OF MEMBERSHIP OF **INTERNATIONAL** UNIONS AS THEY AFFECT NEGRO WORKERS.   NJOHNRA44620

THE FEMALE LABOR-FORCE IN METROPOLITAN AREAS. AN **INTERNATIONAL** COMPARISON.   WCOLLAX62697

INTERNATIONAL-HARVES
INTERNATIONAL-HARVESTER-S NON-DISCRIMINATION POLICY. /CASE-STUDY/   NUSDLAB54822

INTERPERSONAL
INTERPERSONAL RELATIONS IN ETHNICALLY MIXED SMALL WORK GROUPS.   GSCOTWW59291

INTERPRETATION
THE MEASUREMENT AND **INTERPRETATION** OF JOB VACANCIES. A CONFERENCE REPORT OF THE NATIONAL BUREAU OF
ECONOMIC RESEARCH. /LABOR-MARKET/   GNATLBE66611

CASES ARE PEOPLE. AN **INTERPRETATION** OF THE PENNSYLVANIA FAIR-EMPLOYMENT-PRACTICE LAW.   GSHIREM58304

A SOCIOLOGICAL **INTERPRETATION** OF SOCIAL CHANGE IN THE SOUTH.   NHEBERX46508

THE MENTALITIES OF NEGRO AND WHITE WORKERS. AN EXPERIMENTAL SCHOOL-S **INTERPRETATION** OF NEGRO TRADE
UNIONISM.   NVALIPX49280

THE FEMALE LABOR-FORCE. A CASE STUDY IN THE **INTERPRETATION** OF HISTORICAL STATISTICS.   WSMUTRW60124

INTERPRETATIONS
DIGEST OF LEGAL **INTERPRETATIONS** ISSUED OR ADOPTED BY THE COMMISSION OCTOBER 9, 1965 THROUGH DECEMBER 31,
1965.   GUSEEOC66509

INTERPRETING
LEGAL RULINGS **INTERPRETING** THE PROVISIONS OF THE PENNSYLVANIA FAIR-EMPLOYMENT-PRACTICE ACT.   GPENNFE58153

INTERPRETIVE
FROM PLANTATION TO GHETTO. AN **INTERPRETIVE** HISTORY OF AMERICAN NEGROES.   NMEIEAX66765

INTERRACIAL
INTERRACIAL HUMAN RELATIONS IN MANAGEMENT. A COMPILED REPORT PRESENTED ORALLY..:JANUARY 17 1951.   GMCKEIX51926

PROGRESS IN **INTERRACIAL** RELATIONSHIPS. INEQUALITIES FOR NEGROES.   NLEWIES43689

INTERRELATIONSHIPS
THE **INTERRELATIONSHIPS** OF DISCRIMINATION IN EMPLOYMENT, IN EDUCATION, AND IN HOUSING.   GRAVIMJ61219

A HISTORY OF THE **INTERRELATIONSHIPS** BETWEEN IMPORTED MEXICAN LABOR, DOMESTIC MIGRANTS, AND THE TEXAS
AGRICULTURAL ECONOMY.   MGRAVRP60405

INTERSTATE
THE MIGRANT LABOR PROBLEM -- ITS STATE AND **INTERSTATE** ASPECTS. /NEGRO   MEXICAN-AMERICAN/   CPALEHA63098

MIGRATORY-LABOR IN THE WEST. BACKGROUND INFORMATION FOR THE WESTERN **INTERSTATE** CONFERENCE ON MIGRATORY
LABOR. /MIGRANT-WORKERS/   GCOUNSG60931

STATE FAIR-EMPLOYMENT-PRACTICE LEGISLATION UNCONSTITUTIONALLY BURDENS **INTERSTATE** COMMERCE WHEN APPLIED TO
INTERSTATE AIRLINE.   NHARVLR62499

STATE FAIR-EMPLOYMENT-PRACTICE LEGISLATION UNCONSTITUTIONALLY BURDENS INTERSTATE COMMERCE WHEN APPLIED TO
INTERSTATE AIRLINE.   NHARVLR62499

UNITED STATES HAS STANDING UNDER **INTERSTATE** COMMERCE ACT AND COMMERCE CLAUSE TO ENJOIN SEGREGATIVE
PRACTICES OF CITY. /LEGISLATION/   NHARVLR64500

INTERVENTION
THE **INTERVENTION** OF THE UNION IN THE PLANT.   NSEXTBX53116

INTERVIEW
HOME **INTERVIEW** STUDY OF LOW-INCOME HOUSEHOLDS IN DETROIT, MICHIGAN.   GGREEAI65472

FRESHMEN **INTERVIEW** WORKING WIVES.   WMAYXEE59964

INTERVIEWS
QUESTIONING APPLICANTS FOR EMPLOYMENT. A GUIDE FOR APPLICATION FORMS AND **INTERVIEWS** UNDER THE HAWAII
FAIR-EMPLOYMENT-PRACTICES ACT.   GHAWADL64767

INTRA-PLANT
INTRA-PLANT MOBILITY OF NEGRO AND WHITE WORKERS.   NGARBAP65394

INTRODUCTION
INTRODUCTION TO ECONOMICS OF GROWTH, UNEMPLOYMENT, AND INFLATION.   GHERMHX64938

INTRODUCTION. THE STRUGGLE FOR EQUALITY AND ITS IMPACT ON INDUSTRIAL-RELATIONS.   GSTEIBX64335

THE **INTRODUCTION** OF NEGROES INTO WHITE DEPARTMENTS. /CASE-STUDY INDUSTRY/   NPALMER55972

INTRODUCTION. THE STRUGGLE FOR EQUALITY AND ITS IMPACT ON INDUSTRIAL-RELATIONS.   NSTEIBX64300

INVASIONS
THE CONGRESSIONAL HEARINGS AND ISSUES IN PSYCHOLOGICAL TESTING. **INVASIONS** OF PRIVACY AND TEST BIAS.   GGORDJEND934

INVENTORY
PARTIAL **INVENTORY** OF ON-GOING RESEARCH IN EQUAL-EMPLOYMENT-OPPORTUNITIES.   GANDEBR67589

A CIVIL-RIGHTS **INVENTORY** OF SAN-FRANCISCO. PART I. EMPLOYMENT. /CALIFORNIA/   GBABOIX58606

INVENTORY   (CONTINUATION)
    CONSOLIDATED **INVENTORY** OF DEPARTMENT OF LABOR RESEARCH ON LABOR-FORCE EMPLOYMENT AND UNEMPLOYMENT.   GUSDLAB64441

    CONSOLIDATED **INVENTORY** OF DEPARTMENT OF LABOR RESEARCH ON AUTOMATION AND TECHNOLOGICAL-CHANGE.   GUSDLAB64619

    A CIVIL RIGHTS **INVENTORY** OF SAN FRANCISCO. PART I.   /UNION/   NBABOIX58893

INVESTIGATION
    REPORT ON OAKLAND SCHOOLS. AN **INVESTIGATION** UNDER SECTION 1421 OF THE CALIFORNIA LABOR CODE OF THE
    OAKLAND UNIFIED SCHOOL DISTRICT 1962-1963.   /NEGRO ORIENTAL MEXICAN-AMERICAN/   CCALDIR63710

    EMPLOYMENT PRACTICES. CITY OF PASADENA, AN **INVESTIGATION** UNDER SECTION 1421 OF THE CALIFORNIA LABOR CODE
    1963-1965.   GCALFEPND531

    LOS-ANGELES CITY SCHOOLS. AN **INVESTIGATION** OF EMPLOYMENT PRACTICES.   /CALIFORNIA/   GCALFEP64536

    AN **INVESTIGATION** OF ITEM BIAS.   /TESTING/   GCLEATA66924

    SPECIAL REPORT. AN **INVESTIGATION** OF THE PERSONNEL POLICIES AND PRACTICES OF THE MICHIGAN STATE HIGHWAY
    DEPARTMENT. MARCH 1961.   GMICFEP61983

    INVESTIGATION OF CHARGES OF DISCRIMINATORY PRACTICES IN THE NEW-YORK STATE-EMPLOYMENT-SERVICE.   GNEWYSA59083

    INVESTIGATION OF THE GARMENT INDUSTRY.   GUSHOUR62344

    INVESTIGATION OF DIFFERENCES IN OCCUPATIONAL PREFERENCES, STEREOTYPIC THINKING, AND PSYCHOLOGICAL NEEDS
    AMONG UNDERGRADUATE WOMEN STUDENTS IN SELECTED CURRICULAR AREAS. /ASPIRATIONS/   WKITTRE60313

INVESTIGATIONS
    THE BANKING INDUSTRY. VERIFIED COMPLAINTS AND INFORMAL **INVESTIGATIONS**.   /NEW-YORK/   GNEWYSA58076

    THE INSURANCE INDUSTRY -- VERIFIED COMPLAINTS AND INFORMAL **INVESTIGATIONS** HANDLED BY THE NEW-YORK STATE
    COMMISSION AGAINST DISCRIMINATION, JULY 1 1945-SEPTEMBER 15, 1958.   GNEWYSA58082

    GUIDE FOR **INVESTIGATIONS** AND COMPLIANCE REVIEWS IN EQUAL-EMPLOYMENT-OPPORTUNITY.   GPRESCD62109

INVESTIGATIVE
    FINDINGS OF FACT, CONCLUSIONS AND ACTION OF THE COMMISSION ON HUMAN-RELATIONS IN RE. **INVESTIGATIVE** PUBLIC
    HEARINGS INTO ALLEGED DISCRIMINATORY PRACTICE BY THE HOTEL AND RESTAURANT INDUSTRY IN PHILADELPHIA.
    /PENNSYLVANIA/   GPHILCH61176

INVESTING
    INVESTING IN POOR PEOPLE. AN ECONOMIST-S VIEW.   GSCHUTW65842

INVESTOR-OWNED
    SURVEY OF EQUAL-EMPLOYMENT-OPPORTUNITIES IN NEW-JERSEY **INVESTOR-OWNED** PUBLIC UTILITIES.   NLEVIMJ66607

IOWA
    EMPLOYMENT REVIEW.   /DES-MOINES **IOWA**/   GDESMCH65635

    EMPLOYMENT SURVEY OF DES-MOINES FIRMS.   /**IOWA**/   NDESMCH65265

    FIRST REPORT. **IOWA** GOVERNOR-S COMMISSION ON THE STATUS OF WOMEN.   /EMPLOYMENT-CONDITIONS/   WIOWAGC64796

IRON
    THE NEGRO AND UNIONISM IN THE BIRMINGHAM, ALABAMA **IRON** AND STEEL INDUSTRY.   NNORTHR43941

IRREGULARITIES
    LABOR-MANAGEMENT **IRREGULARITIES**.   GUSHOUR61345

ISOLATED
    CHANGE AND RESISTANCE IN AN **ISOLATED** NAVAHO COMMUNITY.   ISHEPMX64618

ISOLATION
    BREAKING THE BARRIERS OF OCCUPATIONAL **ISOLATION**, A REPORT ON UPGRADING LOW-SKILL, LOW-WAGE WORKERS.
    /NEGRO PUERTO-RICAN/   CPROJAX66237

ISSUE
    CONFERENCE **ISSUE** -- TOWARD EQUAL-OPPORTUNITY IN EMPLOYMENT.   GBUFFLR64484

    POVERTY AS A PUBLIC **ISSUE**.   GSELIBB65686

    RACE **ISSUE** AND UNIONS IN THE SOUTH.   NBUSIWX56160

    THE RACIAL **ISSUE**.   NFRAZEF47384

    THE NEGRO **ISSUE** IN CALIFORNIA.   NRECOCW48041

    THE RACIAL **ISSUE** AS AN ANTI UNION TOOL AND THE NATIONAL-LABOR-RELATIONS-BOARD.   NSACHRX63888

    SOUTHERN UNIONS AND THE INTEGRATION **ISSUE**.   NTREWHL56207

    SPECIAL **ISSUE** ON EQUAL-EMPLOYMENT.   NUSGESA63266

    IMPACT OF THE RACE **ISSUE** ON UNIONS IN THE SOUTH.   NUSNEWR56208

ISSUES
    AN EXPERIMENT TO TEST THREE MAJOR **ISSUES** OF WORK PROGRAM METHODOLOGY WITHIN MOBILIZATION-FOR-YOUTH-S
    INTEGRATED SERVICES TO OUT-OF-SCHOOL UNEMPLOYED YOUTH. /NEGRO PUERTO-RICAN/   CMOBIFY66024

    ISSUES AND PROBLEMS IN INTEGRATING NEEDED SUPPORTIVE SERVICES IN NEIGHBORHOOD-YOUTH-CORPS PROJECTS.   GBATTMX66131

    BASIC **ISSUES** AFFECTING YOUTH EMPLOYMENT.   GFREEMK64005

    THE CONGRESSIONAL HEARINGS AND **ISSUES** IN PSYCHOLOGICAL TESTING. INVASIONS OF PRIVACY AND TEST BIAS.   GGORDJEND934

    SOME **ISSUES** IN KNOWING THE UNEMPLOYED.   GGURSOR64749

    CRITICAL **ISSUES** IN EMPLOYMENT POLICY, A REPORT. /UNEMPLOYMENT/   GHARBFH66476

    ISSUES AND ANSWERS. /EEO/   GJOHNMW65827

    MAJOR POLITICAL **ISSUES** WHICH DIRECTLY CONCERN NEGROES.   NMILLJE48250

    WOMEN TODAY. TRENDS AND **ISSUES** IN THE UNITED STATES. /WORK-WOMAN-ROLE/   WYWCAXX63078

ITALIAN
    JEWISH AND **ITALIAN** IMMIGRATION AND SUBSEQUENT STATUS MOBILITY.   JSTROFL58764

ITINERANT
  THE **ITINERANT** FARM LABOR PROJECT REPORT. /MIGRANT-WORKERS CALIFORNIA/   GCALVRS60553

JACKSONVILLE
  JACKSONVILLE LOOKS AT ITS NEGRO COMMUNITY. /FLORIDA/   NJACKCC46598

JAPANESE
  NONWHITE POPULATION BY RACE. NEGROES, INDIANS, **JAPANESE**, CHINESE, FILIPINOS. BY AGE, SEX, MARITAL-STATUS,
  EDUCATION, EMPLOYMENT-STATUS, OCCUPATIONAL-STATUS, INCOME, ETC. /DEMOGRAPHY/   CUSBURC53378

  NONWHITE POPULATION BY RACE. NEGROES, INDIANS, **JAPANESE**,CHINESE, FILIPINOS. BY AGE, SEX,
  MARITAL-STATUS,EDUCATION, EMPLOYMENT-STATUS, OCCUPATIONAL-STATUS, INCOME, ETC. /DEMOGRAPHY/   CUSBURC63176

  CONTRASTIVE ACCULTURATION OF CALIFORNIA **JAPANESE**. COMPARATIVE APPROACH TO THE STUDY OF IMMIGRANTS.   OBEFUHX65701

  CALIFORNIANS OF **JAPANESE**, CHINESE, FILIPINO ANCESTRY.   OCALDIR65709

  THE POLITICS OF PREJUDICE. THE ANTI-JAPANESE MOVEMENT IN CALIFORNIA AND THE STRUGGLE FOR **JAPANESE**
  EXCLUSION.   ODANIRX61716

  THE **JAPANESE** SOCIAL STRUCTURE AND THE SOURCE OF MENTAL STRAINS OF JAPANESE IMMIGRANTS IN THE US.   OIGAXMX57732

  THE **JAPANESE** SOCIAL STRUCTURE AND THE SOURCE OF MENTAL STRAINS OF **JAPANESE** IMMIGRANTS IN THE US.   OIGAXMX57732

  THE **JAPANESE** AMERICAN.   OTHOMDS56765

JAPANESE-AMERICANS
  ACHIEVEMENT, CULTURE AND PERSONALITY. THE CASE OF THE **JAPANESE-AMERICANS**.   OCAUDWX61711

JEOPARDY
  DOUBLE **JEOPARDY** -- THE OLDER NEGRO IN AMERICA TODAY.   NNATLUL64887

JEW
  A **JEW** WITHIN AMERICAN SOCIETY -- A STUDY IN ETHNIC INDIVIDUALITY.   JSHERCB61311

JEWISH
  STATEMENT ON BEHALF OF AMERICAN **JEWISH** CONGRESS ON DISCRIMINATION IN EMPLOYMENT.   GMASLWX61961

  JEWISH LAW GRADUATE. /EMPLOYMENT DISCRIMINATION/   JADLBXX64689

  PROCEEDINGS OF THE 50TH ANNIVERSARY OBSERVANCE OF THE AMERICAN **JEWISH** COMMITTEE. APRIL 10-14, 1957. THE
  PURSUIT OF EQUALITY AT HOME AND ABROAD. /ECONOMIC-OPPORTUNITY/   JAMERJC58692

  SOME ASPECTS OF **JEWISH** DEMOGRAPHY.   JANTOAX58697

  PLANNING CONSTRUCTIVE ECONOMIC OPPORTUNITIES FOR THE **JEWISH** AGED.   JBARSIX59700

  JEWISH POPULATION IN THE UNITED STATES, 1960. /DEMOGRAPHY/   JCHENAX61712

  JEWISH POPULATION IN THE UNITED STATES, 1961. /DEMOGRAPHY/   JCHENAX62713

  AMERICAN **JEWISH** YEARBOOK.   JFINEMXND720

  THE SPIRIT OF THE GHETTO. STUDIES OF THE **JEWISH** QUARTER OF NEW-YORK.   JHAPGHX65989

  ESSAYS IN AMERICAN **JEWISH** HISTORY.   JMARCJR58326

  A REPORT ON THE **JEWISH** POPULATION OF LOS-ANGELES. /CALIFORNIA/   JMASAGX59746

  CIVIL-RIGHTS AND **JEWISH** INSTITUTIONS.   JPILCJX64749

  JEWISH ECONOMIC PROSPECTS IN 1965.   JPUCKWX65750

  COORDINATED PLANNING FOR ECONOMIC OPPORTUNTIES FOR **JEWISH** AGED.   JRABIDX59751

  EMPLOYMENT OF **JEWISH** PERSONNEL IN THE AUTOMOBILE INDUSTRY. /DISCRIMINATION/   JRIGHXX63756

  JEWISH LAW STUDENT AND NEW-YORK JOBS. /EMPLOYMENT DISCRIMINATION/   JRIGHXX64757

  A DECISIVE PATTERN IN AMERICAN **JEWISH** HISTORY.   JRIVIEX58325

  THE **JEWISH** COLLEGE STUDENT.   JSHOSRJ57761

  JEWISH AND ITALIAN IMMIGRATION AND SUBSEQUENT STATUS MOBILITY.   JSTROFL58764

  LEGACY OF THE **JEWISH** LABOR MOVEMENT.   JTYLEGX65766

  THE **JEWISH** ELAN.   JWELLSX60571

  THE **JEWISH** LAW STUDENT AND NEW-YORK JOBS -- DISCRIMINATORY EFFECTS IN LAW FIRM HIRING PRACTICES.
  /OCCUPATIONS/   JYALELJ64774

  JEWISH LAW STUDENT AND NEW-YORK JOBS.   JYOUNJX65775

  GLIMPSES OF **JEWISH** LIFE IN SAN-FRANCISCO. /CALIFORNIA/   JZARCMM64776

  NEGRO MILITANTS, **JEWISH** LIBERALS, AND THE UNIONS.   NBROOTR61121

JEWS
  JEWS IN COLLEGE AND UNIVERSITY ADMINISTRATION.   JAMERJC66693

  THE MUTUAL SAVINGS BANKS OF NEW-YORK-CITY. A FOLLOW-UP REPORT ON THE EXCLUSION OF **JEWS** AT TOP-MANAGEMENT
  AND POLICY-MAKING LEVELS.   JAMERJC66695

  BARRIERS. PATTERNS OF DISCRIMINATION AGAINST **JEWS**.   JBELTNC58702

  SOCIAL CHARACTERISTICS OF AMERICAN **JEWS**.   JGLAZNX60726

  THE **JEWS**.   JGLAZNX63725

  DEMOGRAPHIC CHARACTERISTICS OF AMERICAN **JEWS**.   JGOLDNX62727

  CHILDREN OF THE GILDED GHETTO. CONFLICT RESOLUTION OF THREE GENERATIONS OF AMERICAN **JEWS**.
  /OCCUPATIONAL-PATTERNS/   JKRAMJR61736

  ECONOMIC STRUCTURE AND THE LIFE OF THE **JEWS**.   JKUZNSX60738

  JEWS IN AND OUT OF NEW-YORK CITY. /ECONOMIC-STATUS/   JLAZRBX61034

JEWS (CONTINUATION)

STUDY SHOWS FEW **JEWS** HAVE TOP JOBS IN AUTO INDUSTRY.   JNATIJM63748

THE **JEWS**. SOCIAL PATTERNS OF AN AMERICAN GROUP.   JSKLAMX58149

JEWS NEED NOT APPLY. /DISCRIMINATION EMPLOYMENT/   JWEISAX58770

LARGE CORPORATIONS ACCUSED OF DISCRIMINATION AGAINST **JEWS** IN MANAGEMENT, EXECUTIVE CAPACITIES BY
AMERICAN-JEWISH-COMMITTEE.   JWORLOX64773

JICARILLA

NEEDS AND RESOURCES OF THE **JICARILLA** APACHE INDIAN TRIBE.   ISTANRI58623

THE RELATIONSHIP BETWEEN UNEARNED INCOME AND INDIVIDUAL PRODUCTIVE EFFORT ON THE **JICARILLA** APACHE INDIAN
RESERVATION.   IWILSHC61687

JICARILLA APACHE POLITICAL AND ECONOMIC STRUCTURES.   IWILSHC64235

JIM-CROW

JIM-CROW AMERICA. /DISCRIMINATION/   NCONREX47233

MANAGEMENT VERSUS **JIM-CROW**. /INDUSTRY/   NPURCTV62023

JOB

UNIONS URGED TO FOLLOW THROUGH ON PLEDGES TO COMBAT **JOB** BIAS.   GAFLCIO63365

EQUAL **JOB** OPPORTUNITY IS GOOD BUSINESS.   GAMERJC54381

JOB ADJUSTMENT PROBLEMS OF DELINQUENT MINORITY-GROUP YOUTH.   GAMOSWE64874

JOB BIAS IN L A. /LOS-ANGELES CALIFORNIA/   GANTIDL57397

MEDICAL SERVICE **JOB** OPPORTUNITIES 1964-66, SAN-FRANCISCO BAY AREA. /CALIFORNIA/   GCALDEM64521

HOTEL AND RESTAURANT **JOB** OPPORTUNITIES, SAN-FRANCISCO BAY AREA, 1964-1966. /CALIFORNIA/ GCALDEM65517

PROMOTING EQUAL **JOB** OPPORTUNITY. A GUIDE FOR EMPLOYERS. /CALIFORNIA/   GCALFEP63538

SAN-MATEO AREA MINORITY **JOB** SURVEY. /CALIFORNIA/   GCALFEP65542

EVALUATING **JOB** APPLICANTS WITH POLICE RECORDS. /CALIFORNIA/   GCALFEP66532

FAIR-EMPLOYMENT-PRACTICES EQUAL GOOD EMPLOYMENT PRACTICES. GUIDELINES FOR TESTING AND SELECTING MINORITY
JOB APPLICANTS. /CALIFORNIA/   GCALFEP66540

THE CONSTITUTION AND **JOB** DISCRIMINATION.   GCOUNVX64608

VOCATIONAL TRAINING TO IMPROVE **JOB** OPPORTUNITIES FOR MINORITY-GROUPS. COMMENT.   GFINEMX64681

IMPROVING INDUSTRIAL RACE-RELATIONS -- PART I. EQUAL **JOB** OPPORTUNITY -- SLOGAN OR REALITY. GFLEMHC63363

ARE **JOB** TESTS RELIABLE.   GFUERJS65703

JOB AND CAREER DEVELOPMENT FOR THE POOR...THE HUMAN SERVICES. INCLUDES BIBLIOGRAPHY.   GGOLDGS66360

PARNASSUS RESTRICTED. **JOB** DISCRIMINATION IN THE PROFESSIONS.   GGOLDMH46724

CIVIL-SERVICE TESTING AND **JOB** DISCRIMINATION.   GGORDJE66281

JOB TENURE OF AMERICAN WORKERS.   GHAMEHR63755

THE **JOB** AHEAD FOR THE PRESIDENT-S COMMITTEE ON EQUAL-EMPLOYMENT-OPPORTUNITY.   GHOLLJR61999

JOB OPPORTUNITIES FROM FEPC ACTION.   GHOWDEX65785

ILLINOIS **JOB** SEEKERS SURVEY. EDUCATION, SKILLS, LENGTH OF UNEMPLOYMENT, AND PERSONAL CHARACTERISTICS. GILLIDI62004

ILLINOIS **JOB** SEEKER-S SURVEY.   GILLIGC62799

DEMOCRACY ON THE **JOB**.   GINDUBX51811

PSYCHOLOGICAL TESTING FOR EFFECTIVE EMPLOYMENT PRACTICES AND EQUAL **JOB** OPPORTUNITIES.   GKETCWA65849

3 CURRENT PROBLEMS IN TEST PERFORMANCE OF **JOB** APPLICANTS.   GLCPEFM66909

THE ROLE OF **JOB** CREATION PROGRAMS. /MANPOWER/   GMANGGL65728

CYBERNATION AND **JOB** SECURITY. /UNEMPLOYMENT/   GMANGGL66529

JOB OPPORTUNITIES AND POVERTY.   GMEANGC65674

TESTS AND THE REQUIREMENTS OF THE **JOB**.   GMETZJH65119

FOUR YEARS ON THE **JOB** IN MICHIGAN. /FEPC/   GMICFEP60980

THE MEASUREMENT AND INTERPRETATION OF **JOB** VACANCIES. A CONFERENCE REPORT OF THE NATIONAL BUREAU OF
ECONOMIC RESEARCH. /LABOR-MARKET/   GNATLBE66611

GOVERNMENTAL FAIR-EMPLOYMENT AGENCIES. AN APPRAISAL OF FEDERAL, STATE, AND MUNICIPAL EFFORTS TO END **JOB**
DISCRIMINATION.   GNORGPH62120

SURVEY OF OHIO COLLEGE AND UNIVERSITY PLACEMENT OFFICES WITH REGARD TO **JOB** PLACEMENT OF MINORITY
STUDENTS.   GOHIOCR62132

EQUAL **JOB** OPPORTUNITY AS SET FORTH IN EXECUTIVE ORDERS 10479 AND 10557.   GPRESCH56191

FOURTH ANNUAL REPORT ON EQUAL **JOB** OPPORTUNITY, 1956-1957, PRESIDENT-S COMMITTEE ON GOVERNMENT CONTRACTS. GPRESCH57122

EQUALITY OF **JOB** OPPORTUNITY AND CIVIL-RIGHTS.   GREUTWP60223

URBAN **JOB** DISCRIMINATION. ABUSES AND REDRESS.   GRICOLX66237

THE OUTLOOK FOR A NEW FEPC. THE 80TH CONGRESS AND **JOB** DISCRIMINATION.   GROSSMX47261

MOBILITY, METHODS OF **JOB** SEARCH, ATTITUDES, AND MOTIVATION OF DISPLACED WORKERS.   GSHEPHL64621

LEGAL SANCTIONS AGAINST **JOB** DISCRIMINATION.   GSIMOCK46311

LABOR-S ROLE. DEMOCRACY ON THE **JOB**. /UNION/   GSLAIDX66317

FROM SCHOOL TO JOB. GUIDANCE FOR MINORITY YOUTH.   GTANNAX63156

THE JOB AHEAD IN FAIR-EMPLOYMENT-PRACTICES.   GUNITCC62322

CONFERENCE ON EQUAL JOB OPPORTUNITY.   GUSDLAB56027

A GUIDE TO INDUSTRIAL-RELATIONS IN THE UNITED STATES. EQUAL JOB OPPORTUNITY UNDER COLLECTIVE-BARGAINING.   GUSDLAB58449

JOB OPPORTUNITIES FOR MINORITIES IN THE SEATTLE AREA. /WASHINGTON/   GUVWAIL48532

VOCATIONAL-TRAINING TO IMPROVE JOB OPPORTUNITIES FOR MINORITY-GROUPS.   GWALSJP64540

A STUDY OF THE REASONS FOR FAILURE ON THE JOB OF SOME GRADUATES OF INTERMOUNTAIN SCHOOL.   IFISHLX60560

REMOVING JOB BARRIERS.   NABRACX57510

THE PERSONNEL JOB IN A CHANGING WORLD. /INDUSTRY/   NBLOOJW64093

SECURING SKILLS NEEDED FOR SUCCESS. COMMUNITY JOB TRAINING FOR NEGROES.   NBLUMAA66099

JOB TRAINING THROUGH ADULT-EDUCATION.   NBLUMAA67098

CARRYING OUT A PLAN FOR JOB INTEGRATION AND DOING IT -- IN THE HEART OF GEORGIA -- WITHOUT A SINGLE
UNPLEASANT INCIDENT. THAT-S THE EXPERIENCE OF LOCKHEED AIRCRAFT CORPORATION AT ITS MARIETTA PLANT.
/INDUSTRY/   NBUSIWX63148

CHICAGO STARTS MOVING ON EQUAL JOB QUESTION. /ILLINOIS/   NBUSIWX64298

JOB HOLDING AMONG NEGRO YOUTH.   NCAPLNX66013

INTEGRATING THE NEGRO TEACHER OUT OF A JOB. /OCCUPATIONS/   NCARTBX65999

RESEARCH ON NEGRO JOB SUCCESS.   NCHALWE62189

THE LIMITED POTENTIAL FOR NEGRO-WHITE JOB EQUALITY.   NCHALWE65188

JOB QUOTAS AND THE MERIT SYSTEM.   NCHASET63195

CLEVELAND-S ANNUAL JOB CENTER FOR COLLEGE GRADUATES.   NCOCKHW65218

JOB OUTLOOK FOR YOUTH.   NEBONXX63316

THE PATTERN OF JOB DISCRIMINATION AGAINST NEGROES.   NHILLHX65536

EPISODE I. ARTHUR BROWN APPLIES FOR A JOB. /DISCRIMINATION/   NLAWSEX45035

CULTURAL EXPOSURE AND RACE AS VARIABLES IN PREDICTING TRAINING AND JOB SUCCESS. /TESTING/   NLOCKHCND700

CONFERENCE ON EQUAL JOB OPPORTUNITY.   NMCKIGB56725

THE JOB GAP. /EMPLOYMENT/   NMILLHP66630

NEGRO-S SEARCH FOR A BETTER JOB.   NNEWSXX64913

AT WORK IN NORTH-CAROLINA TODAY. 48 CASE-REPORTS ON NORTH-CAROLINA NEGROES NOW EMPLOYED OR PREPARING
THEMSELVES FOR EMPLOYMENT...THEIR EDUCATION, JOB QUALIFICATIONS, AND CAREER ASPIRATIONS.   NNORTCGND933

MANAGEMENTS GUIDELINES FOR MEETING THE NEGRO DRIVE FOR JOB EQUALITY. /INDUSTRY/.   NOPINRC63958

THE JOB OUTLOOK FOR NEGRO YOUTH.   NPERRJX64984

NEGROES ARE MOVING UP THE JOB LADDER.   NROSSIX63087

JOB GUIDANCE AND THE DISADVANTAGED.   NSAITCX64308

THE JOB HUNT. JOB SEEKING BEHAVIOR OF UNEMPLOYED WORKERS IN A LOCAL ECONOMY.   NSHEPHL66128

THE JOB HUNT. JOB SEEKING BEHAVIOR OF UNEMPLOYED WORKERS IN A LOCAL ECONOMY.   NSHEPHL66128

A NOTE ON RACIAL DIFFERENCES IN JOB VALUES AND DESIRES.   NSINGSL56142

NEGRO JOB STATUS AND EDUCATION.   NTURNRH53213

TWO STATE REPORT ON JOB DISCRIMINATION. /NEW-YORK NEW-JERSEY/   NUSDLAB58844

JOB RIGHTS FOR NEGROES -- PRESSURE ON EMPLOYERS.   NUSNEWR66270

A STUDY OF SOME ASPECTS OF JOB SATISFACTION AMONG NEGRO WHITE-COLLAR WORKERS.   NWEATMD54296

INTEREST PATTERN FAKING BY FEMALE JOB APPLICANTS. /ASPIRATIONS/   WBECKJA63633

ON THE JOB, WOMEN ACT MUCH LIKE MEN. /OCCUPATIONS/   WBUSIWX63667

A STUDY OF JOB MOTIVATIONS, ACTIVITIES, AND SATISFACTIONS OF PRESENT AND PROSPECTIVE WOMEN COLLEGE
FACULTY MEMBERS. /OCCUPATIONS/   WCOOKWX60252

ADDRESS TO CONFERENCE ON EDUCATION AND JOB OPPORTUNITIES FOR WOMEN RETURNING TO THE LABOR-MARKET.   WDOUTAX62741

STUDY OF JOB OPPORTUNITIES FOR WOMEN COLLEGE GRADUATES. /OCCUPATIONS/   WINTEAP58861

IN QUEST OF WIDER HORIZONS. THE WOMAN AFTER FORTY THINKS ABOUT A JOB. /ASPIRATIONS/   WJEWIVA62882

RESEARCH AND YOUR JOB. /TECHNOLOGICAL-CHANGE/   WKEYSMD64900

PART-TIME JOB OPPORTUNITIES FOR WOMEN.   WMEREJL60970

HELP WANTED -- FEMALE. A STUDY OF DEMAND AND SUPPLY IN A LOCAL JOB MARKET FOR WOMEN. /MANPOWER/   WSMITGM64121

JOB OPPORTUNITIES FOR WOMEN COLLEGE GRADUATES.   WSWERSX64145

SPEECH ABOUT JOB OPPORTUNITIES FOR GIRLS BEFORE THE MARYLAND STATE PERSONNEL AND GUIDANCE ASSOCIATION.   WTERLRX64148

JOB HORIZONS FOR COLLEGE WOMEN IN THE 1960-S.   WUSDLAB64202

WORLD OF WORK CONFERENCE ON CAREER AND JOB OPPORTUNITIES, WASHINGTON, DC, JULY 1962.   WUSDLAB64242

THE OFFICIAL WORD ON JOB RIGHTS FOR WOMEN.   WUSNEWR65246

JOB-APPLICANTS
   4. CURRENT PROBLEMS IN TEST PERFORMANCE OF JOB-APPLICANTS.   GDUGARD66651

JOB-CHOICE
   HOW DOES RELIGION AFFECT JOB-CHOICE.   JHARVBS65731

JOB-CORPS
   LOW-INCOME YOUTH. UNEMPLOYMENT, VOCATIONAL TRAINING, AND THE JOB-CORPS.   GPURCFX66208

JOB-DEVELOPMENT
   JOB-DEVELOPMENT FOR YOUTH.   GBENNGX66877

   PROBLEMS AND TRENDS IN JOB-DEVELOPMENT AND EMPLOYMENT PROGRAMS.   NPURYMT63028

JOB-EQUALITY
   PUTTING NEGROES ON A JOB-EQUALITY BASIS.   NWOODCA45339

JOB-HOLDERS
   MULTIPLE JOB-HOLDERS IN DECEMBER, 1959.   GBANCGX60418

JOB-LESS
   BEHIND LOS-ANGELES. JOB-LESS NEGROES AND THE BOOM. /UNEMPLOYMENT CALIFORNIA/   NMOYNDP65860

JOB-MARKET
   REALITIES OF THE JOB-MARKET FOR THE HIGH SCHOOL DROPOUT.   GBIENHX64111

   THE NEGRO WORKER IN THE CHICAGO JOB-MARKET. /ILLINOIS/   NBAROHX66055

JOB-MOBILITY
   ATTITUDE TOWARD JOB-MOBILITY AMONG HOUSEHOLD HEADS IN LOW-INCOME AREAS OF THE RURAL SOUTH.   NDUNKJX64300

JOB-OPPORTUNITIES
   EDUCATIONAL ACHIEVEMENT AND JOB-OPPORTUNITIES. A VICIOUS CIRCLE.   NBLALHM58084

   A STUDY OF JOB-OPPORTUNITIES IN THE STATE OF FLORIDA FOR NEGRO COLLEGE GRADUATES.   NDECKPM60261

JOB-RELATED
   JOB-RELATED EXPENSES OF THE WORKING-MOTHERS.   WADDILK63862

JOB-SEARCH
   RACIAL DIFFERENCES IN MIGRATION AND JOB-SEARCH. A CASE-STUDY.   NLURIMX66712

JOBHOLDERS
   MULTIPLE JOBHOLDERS IN MAY, 1963.   GBOGAFA64460

JOBLESS
   THE NEW LOST GENERATION. JOBLESS YOUTH.   GHARRMX64759

JOBLESSNESS
   AUTOMATION AND JOBLESSNESS. IS RETRAINING THE ANSWER.   GGLAZWX62866

JOBS
   ADDRESS TO COMMUNITY RELATIONS SERVICE STAFF TRAINING SESSION, JANUARY 12, 1967, ON JOBS NOW. /NEGRO
   PUERTO-RICAN YOUTH/   CCOLEBX67918

   SENIORITY AND POSTWAR JOBS. RUBBER INDUSTRY. /NEGRO WOMEN/   CLABORR44028

   NEGRO WOMEN AND THEIR JOBS.   CUSDLAB54262

   THE EROSION OF JOBS AND SKILLS.   GAFLCIO63864

   HOW MANY JOBS. WHAT KIND OF JOBS.   GALLECX65870

   HOW MANY JOBS. WHAT KIND OF JOBS.   GALLECX65870

   JOBS, WAGES AND CHANGING TECHNOLOGY.   GARONRL65747

   TEXAS PROVIDES JOBS FOR MINORITY-GROUPS.   GCARRHX66558

   JOBS FOR THE HARD-TO-EMPLOY IN PRIVATE ENTERPRISE.   GCASSFH66744

   FINAL REPORT ON JOBS II PROJECT. /CHICAGO ILLINOIS/   GCHICBC65319

   AUTOMATION. THE IMPACT ON JOBS AND PEOPLE.   GCOONRB64871

   SCHOOLING, DISCRIMINATION, AND JOBS.   GHENNJF63278

   AUTOMATION, JOBS, AND MANPOWER.   GKILLCC63755

   EFFECTS OF TECHNOLOGICAL-CHANGE ON THE NATURE OF JOBS.   GLEVILA64623

   JOBS, MEN AND MACHINES. PROBLEMS OF AUTOMATION.   GMARKCX64949

   JOBS, 1960-1970. THE CHANGING PATTERN. /EMPLOYMENT-TRENDS/   GNEWYSE60108

   THE MOVEMENT OF LABOR BETWEEN FARM AND NONFARM JOBS.   GPERKBX66150

   JOBS WITHOUT CREED OR COLOR.   GRAUSWX45583

   RACE, JOBS, AND POLITICS. THE STORY OF FEPC.   GRUCHLX53266

   JOBS TARGET -- EMPLOYMENT.   GUSCHACND383

   PEOPLE, SKILLS, AND JOBS.   GUSDLAB63491

   ADOLESCENTS NEED JOBS.   ITHOMHX61629

   STUDY SHOWS FEW JEWS HAVE TOP JOBS IN AUTO INDUSTRY.   JNATIJM63748

   JEWISH LAW STUDENT AND NEW-YORK JOBS. /EMPLOYMENT DISCRIMINATION/   JRIGHXX64757

   THE JEWISH LAW STUDENT AND NEW-YORK JOBS -- DISCRIMINATORY EFFECTS IN LAW FIRM HIRING PRACTICES.
   /OCCUPATIONS/   JYALELJ64774

   JEWISH LAW STUDENT AND NEW-YORK JOBS.   JYOUNJX65775

   MORE ROOM AT THE TOP. COMPANY EXPERIENCE IN EMPLOYING NEGROES IN PROFESSIONAL AND MANAGEMENT JOBS.
   /INDUSTRY/   NBIRDCX63080

JOBS   (CONTINUATION)
    THE STATUS OF JOBS AND OCCUPATIONS AS EVALUATED BY AN URBAN NEGRO SAMPLE.   NBROWMC55126

    JOBS FOR NEGROES. ONE COMPANY-S ANSWER. /CASE-STUDY INDUSTRY/   NBUSIMX64142

    BRINGING BETTER JOBS TO NEGROES. /EMPLOYMENT-AGENCY/   NBUSIWX62146

    THE NEGRO DRIVE FOR JOBS.   NBUSIWX63154

    JOBS FOR NEGROES -- THE GAINS, THE PROBLEMS, AND THE NEW HIRING LAW. /TITLE-VII/   NBUSIWX65151

    JOBS AND THE COLOR LINE.   NCHILRR57205

    DUAL PARTS OF DESEGREGATION. LEGISLATION TO EDUCATE AND TRAIN NEGROES FOR BETTER JOBS.   NDUSCJX63311

    NEW HOPE FOR RURAL DIXIE. FIRMS IN CAROLINAS CREATE JOBS FOR NEGROES.   NEBONXX64317

    NEW JOBS FOR NEGROES.   NEDELHX66320

    NEGROES AND JOBS.   NGOLDNX66428

    REGIONS, RACE AND JOBS.   NHENDVW67517

    NEGRO JOBS AND EDUCATION.   NKUEBJX63315

    JOBS AND COLOR. NEGRO EMPLOYMENT IN TENNESSEE STATE GOVERNMENT.   NLONGHH62706

    JOBS AND THE LAW. /LOUISVILLE KENTUCKY/   NLOUIHR65717

    JOBS FOR NEGROES. HOW MUCH PROGRESS IN SIGHT.   NNEWSXX63912

    WILL NEGROES GET JOBS NOW.   NNORTHR45948

    HIRING NEGROES FOR BETTER JOBS. EXPERIENCE OF LEADING COMPANIES. /INDUSTRY/   NOPINRC64957

    JOBS FOR THE NEGRO. THE UNFINISHED REVOLUTION.   NRANDAP64034

    HOW NEGRO WORKERS FEEL ABOUT THEIR JOBS.   NROSEAW51292

    THE STRUGGLE FOR JOBS AND FOR NEGRO RIGHTS IN THE TRADE UNIONS.   NSIMOHX50139

    JOBS FOR NEGROES. SOME NORTH-SOUTH PLANT STUDIES. /CASE-STUDY/   NSTEEEH53174

    NEGROES GO NORTH, WEST. JOBS TAKE THEM FAR AFIELD FROM THE SOUTH.   NUSNEWR51272

    NEGROES. BIG ADVANCES IN JOBS, WEALTH, STATUS.   NUSNEWR58271

    FOR NEGROES. MORE AND BETTER JOBS IN GOVERNMENT.   NUSNEWR62268

    JOBS FOR NEGROES -- IS THERE A REAL SHORTAGE.   NUSNEWR63269

    OPPORTUNITIES AND REQUIREMENTS FOR INITIAL EMPLOYMENT OF SCHOOL LEAVERS. WITH EMPHASIS ON OFFICE AND
    RETAIL JOBS. /EMPLOYMENT-SELECTION/   WCOOKFS66705

    A SURVEY OF WOMEN-S APTITUDES FOR ARMY JOBS. /MILITARY/   WFUCHEF63772

    JOBS AND TRAINING FOR WOMEN TECHNICIANS. /TRAINING/   WMEYEMB61975

    FIRST JOBS OF COLLEGE WOMEN -- REPORT ON WOMEN GRADUATES, CLASS OF 1957.   WUSDLAB59194

    GREAT STRIDES MADE IN JOBS FOR WOMEN IN FEDERAL SERVICE.   WUSDLAB62041

    FUTURE JOBS FOR HIGH SCHOOL GIRLS.   WUSDLAB65196

JOBSEEKERS
    SHOWING THE WAY IN PREPARING NEGRO JOBSEEKERS.   NWESTZJ66317

JOBSITE
    RACIAL DISCRIMINATION ON THE JOBSITE. COMPETING THEORIES AND COMPETING FORUMS.   NMEYEBI65210

JOHNSON
    CONGRESS AND THE JOHNSON POVERTY PROGRAM.   GCONGDX66356

JOURNALISTS
    WOMEN JOURNALISTS AND TODAY-S WORLD. /OCCUPATIONS/   WKEYSMD65021

JOURNEY
    THE NEGRO-S JOURNEY TO THE CITY -- PART I.   NNEWMDK65908

    THE NEGRO-S JOURNEY TO THE CITY -- PART II.   NNEWMDK65909

JUNIOR
    A STUDY OF THE ACCULTURATION AND SOCIAL ASPIRATIONS OF SIXTY JUNIOR HIGH SCHOOL STUDENTS FROM THE MEXICAN
    ETHNIC GROUP.   MJONEBM62421

    TECHNICAL EDUCATION IN THE JUNIOR COLLEGE.   WHARRNC64825

JURISDICTION
    OPINION CONCERNING THE SCOPE AND AUTHORITY OF THE JURISDICTION THAT MAY BE GRANTED TO CITY OR COUNTY
    HUMAN-RELATIONS-COMMISSIONS IN THE FIELDS OF EMPLOYMENT AND HOUSING. /CALIFORNIA/   GCALAGO63512

    SUMMARY FACT SHEETS FOR STATE PUBLIC AGENCIES WITH JURISDICTION OVER DISCRIMINATION IN EMPLOYMENT. GUSCCMC65416

    SOCIAL AND ECONOMIC SURVEY OF POTAWATOMIE JURISDICTION.   IUSDINT57660

JUSTICE
    THE ETHICS OF COMPENSATORY JUSTICE.PREFERENTIAL-TREATMENT/   GLICHRX64900

    THE NEGRO REVOLUTION. A QUEST FOR JUSTICE.   NHATCJF66648

    EQUAL JUSTICE IN AN UNEQUAL WORLD. EQUALITY FOR THE NEGRO -- THE PROBLEM OF SPECIAL TREATMENT.   NKAPLJX66645

    SUMMARY JUSTICE -- THE NEGRO GI IN KOREA. /MILITARY/   NMARSTX51755

JUVENILE
    EMPLOYABILITY AND THE JUVENILE ARREST RECORD.   GSPAREV66839

    COLOR, CLASS, PERSONALITY, AND JUVENILE DELINQUENCY.   NCLARKB59210

JUVENILE-DELINQUENCY
   FACTORS ASSOCIATED WITH SCHOOL DROPOUTS AND **JUVENILE-DELINQUENCY** AMONG LOWER-CLASS CHILDREN.   GPALMFX63671

   THE RELATIONSHIP OF THE SOCIAL-STRUCTURE OF AN INDIAN COMMUNITY TO ADULT AND **JUVENILE-DELINQUENCY**.
   /POVERTY ECONOMIC-STATUS/   IMINNMS63218

   THE RELATIONSHIP OF **JUVENILE-DELINQUENCY**, RACE, AND ECONOMIC STATUS.   NBLUEJT48097

JUVENILES
   SOCIO-ECONOMIC CLASS AND AREA AS CORRELATES OF ILLEGAL BEHAVIOR AMONG **JUVENILES**.   NCLARJP62209

   GOAL-ORIENTATIONS AND ILLEGAL BEHAVIOR AMONG **JUVENILES**.   NCLARJP63208

KANSAS
   COMMISSION ENFORCEMENT OF STATE LAWS AGAINST DISCRIMINATION. A COMPARATIVE ANALYSIS OF THE **KANSAS** ACT.   GOYSORB65657

   A REVIEW OF THE ECONOMIC AND CULTURAL PROBLEMS OF WICHITA, **KANSAS**.   NBANNWM65051

   SALARIED WOMEN IN UPPER LEVEL POSITIONS IN **KANSAS** BUSINESS FIRMS.   WSTOCFT59143

KANSAS-CITY
   INCOME, EDUCATION AND UNEMPLOYMENT IN NEIGHBORHOODS. **KANSAS-CITY**, MISSOURI. /DEMOGRAPHY/   CUSDLAB63464

   AREAS OF COMMISSION CONCERN. /**KANSAS-CITY** MISSOURI/   GKANCIC62840

   RACIAL INTEGRATION IN EMPLOYMENT -- FINDINGS IN TWO **KANSAS-CITY** HOSPITALS.   NGIBSHX54402

   THE NEGRO WORKER OF **KANSAS-CITY**. A STUDY OF TRADE UNION AND ORGANIZED LABOR RELATIONS.   NKANCIU40634

   UNIVERSITY OF **KANSAS-CITY** PROJECT FOR CONTINUING EDUCATION OF WOMEN.   WBERRJX63640

KENNEDY
   THE CIVIL-RIGHTS PROGRAMS OF THE **KENNEDY** ADMINISTRATION.   NSULLDF64190

KENTUCKY
   EXPLANATION AND DIGEST OF THE 1966 **KENTUCKY** CIVIL-RIGHTS-ACT COVERING EMPLOYMENT AND PUBLIC
   ACCOMODATIONS. ENACTED JANUARY 27 1966, EFFECTIVE JULY 1 1966.   GKENTCHND844

   NEGRO EMPLOYMENT IN **KENTUCKY** STATE AGENCIES.   NKENTCH66643

   BRICKS WITHOUT STRAW. STUDIES OF COMMUNITY UNEMPLOYMENT PROBLEMS, THE NEGROES DILEMMA. /LOUISVILLE
   KENTUCKY/   NLOUIHR64715

   JOBS AND THE LAW. /LOUISVILLE **KENTUCKY**/   NLOUIHR65717

   PATTERNS OF DISCRIMINATION STUDY -- LOUISVILLE HUMAN-RELATIONS-COMMISSION. /**KENTUCKY**/   NLOUIHR66582

   FACTS FOR ACTION. /LOUISVILLE **KENTUCKY**/   NLOUIHR66716

   LOUISVILLE. SPECIAL REPORT. /CASE-STUDY **KENTUCKY**/   NMUSEBX64868

   A SURVEY OF THE ECONOMIC AND CULTURAL CONDITIONS OF THE NEGRO POPULATION OF LOUISVILLE, **KENTUCKY** AND A
   REVIEW OF THE PROGRAM AND ACTIVITIES OF THE LOUISVILLE URBAN-LEAGUE. JANUARY-FEBRUARY, 1948.   NNATLUL48903

   LOUISVILLE. /**KENTUCKY**/   NSOUTRC64162

   IMPROVED CONDITIONS FOR NEGROES IN LOUISVILLE. /**KENTUCKY**/   NUSDLAB45820

KERN
   FARM MECHANIZATION AND LABOR STABILIZATION. PART II IN A SERIES ON TECHNOLOGICAL-CHANGE AND FARM LABOR
   USE. **KERN** COUNTY, CALIFORNIA, 1961. /NEGRO MEXICAN-AMERICAN/   CMETZWH65389

KERN-COUNTY
   THE FARM WORKER IN A CHANGING AGRICULTURE. PART I IN A SERIES ON TECHNOLOGICAL-CHANGE AND FARM LABOR USE,
   KERN-COUNTY, CALIFORNIA, 1961.   GMETZWH64387

KEY
   EDUCATION OF THE MINORITY POOR -- THE **KEY** TO THE WAR-ON-POVERTY.   GCLARKB66915

   KEY QUESTIONS ON THE POVERTY PROBLEM.   GKEYSLH64943

   UNDERSTANDING THE HUMAN FACTOR. THE **KEY** TO SUPERVISORY SUCCESS.   GPRESCP59201

   SOCIAL DEVELOPMENT. **KEY** TO THE GREAT SOCIETY. /SOCIO-ECONOMIC WELFARE/   GUSDHEW66639

   PUERTO-RICANS, **KEY** SOURCE OF LABOR.   PNEWYDC56817

   WOMANPOWER -- **KEY** TO MANAGEMENT MANPOWER SHORTAGE.   WLLOYBJ62633

   TRAINING. **KEY** TO EMPLOYMENT.   WPETEEX62057

KINSHIP
   KINSHIP AS A FACTOR AFFECTING CANTONESE ECONOMIC ADAPTATION IN THE UNITED STATES.   OBARNML66698

KITCHEN
   FROM **KITCHEN** TO CAREER. /WORK-FAMILY-CONFLICT/   WLEWIAB65930

KLAMATH
   KLAMATH INDIANS IN TWO NON-INDIAN COMMUNITIES. KLAMATH-FALLS AND EUGENE-SPRINGFIELD. /OREGON/   ILIVIMG59582

   LIVELIHOOD AND TRIBAL GOVERNMENT ON THE **KLAMATH** INDIAN RESERVATION.   ISTERTX61624

   MODERN **KLAMATH**. DEMOGRAPHY AND ECONOMY.   ISTERTX65625

   KLAMATH INDIAN TRIBE.   IUSSENA56673

   REVIEW APPRAISAL. **KLAMATH** INDIAN ASSETS.   IUSSENA59674

KLAMATH-FALLS
   KLAMATH INDIANS IN TWO NON-INDIAN COMMUNITIES. **KLAMATH-FALLS** AND EUGENE-SPRINGFIELD. /OREGON/   ILIVIMG59582

KLINEBERG
   NEGRO INTELLIGENCE AND SELECTIVE MIGRATION. A PHILADELPHIA TEST OF THE **KLINEBERG** HYPOTHESIS.
   /PENNSYLVANIA/   NLEEXES51673

KNOWLEDGE
   IN SEARCH OF A FUTURE. A STUDY OF CAREER-SEEKING EXPERIENCES OF SELECTED NEGRO HIGH SCHOOL GRADUATES IN
   WASHINGTON-DC WHICH WAS AN EFFORT TO PROVIDE **KNOWLEDGE** HELPFUL IN SOLVING ONE OF THE MOST CRITICAL

KNOWLEDGE   (CONTINUATION)
PROBLEMS FACING URBAN AMERICA TODAY.   NGRIEES63454

   THE RIGHT TO KNOWLEDGE. /COLLEGE EDUCATION/   NHEALHX64306

   KNOWLEDGE AND INTERESTS CONCERNING SIXTEEN OCCUPATIONS AMONG ELEMENTARY AND SECONDARY SCHOOL STUDENTS.
   /ASPIRATIONS/   WMELSRC63968

KOREA
   REPORT ON KOREA. /MILITARY/   NMARSTX51754

   SUMMARY JUSTICE -- THE NEGRO GI IN KOREA. /MILITARY/   NMARSTX51755

LABOR
   ANNUAL FARM LABOR REPORT. 1965, CALIFORNIA DEPARTMENT OF EMPLOYMENT, FARM LABOR SERVICE. /NEGRO
   MEXICAN-AMERICAN WOMEN/   CCALDEM66906

   ANNUAL FARM LABOR REPORT, 1965, CALIFORNIA DEPARTMENT OF EMPLOYMENT, FARM LABOR SERVICE. /NEGRO
   MEXICAN-AMERICAN WOMEN/   CCALDEM66906

   REPORT ON OAKLAND SCHOOLS. AN INVESTIGATION UNDER SECTION 1421 OF THE CALIFORNIA LABOR CODE OF THE
   OAKLAND UNIFIED SCHOOL DISTRICT 1962-1963. /NEGRO ORIENTAL MEXICAN-AMERICAN/   CCALDIR63710

   LABOR UNIONISM IN AMERICAN AGRICULTURE. /NEGRO MEXICAN-AMERICAN ORIENTAL/   CJAMISM45005

   FARM MECHANIZATION AND LABOR STABILIZATION. PART II IN A SERIES ON TECHNOLOGICAL-CHANGE AND FARM LABOR
   USE, KERN COUNTY, CALIFORNIA, 1961. /NEGRO MEXICAN-AMERICAN/   CMETZWH65389

   FARM MECHANIZATION AND LABOR STABILIZATION. PART II IN A SERIES ON TECHNOLOGICAL-CHANGE AND FARM LABOR
   USE, KERN COUNTY, CALIFORNIA, 1961. /NEGRO MEXICAN-AMERICAN/   CMETZWH65389

   THE MIGRANT LABOR PROBLEM -- ITS STATE AND INTERSTATE ASPECTS. /NEGRO MEXICAN-AMERICAN/   CPALEHA63098

   LABOR LOOKS AT AUTOMATION.   GAFLCICND863

   ORGANIZED LABOR AND RACIAL MINORITIES. /UNION/   GBAILLH51575

   PROJECTIONS TO 1975. THE GROWTH AND STRUCTURE OF THE LABOR FORCE.   GBAKESS65702

   LABOR UNIONS IN ACTION. A STUDY OF THE MAINSPRINGS OF UNIONISM.   GBARBJX48421

   DIMENSIONS OF THE FARM LABOR PROBLEM.   GBISHCE67915

   FARM LABOR IN THE UNITED STATES.   GBISHCE67916

   ORGANIZED LABOR AND THE INTEGRATION OF ETHNIC GROUPS. /UNION/   GBLOCHD58455

   ORGANIZED LABOR AND MINORITY GROUPS. /UNION/   GBLUEJT47457

   THE SUBSTANCE OF AMERICAN FAIR-EMPLOYMENT-PRACTICES LEGISLATION. II. EMPLOYMENT-AGENCIES, LABOR
   ORGANIZATIONS, AND OTHERS.   GBONFAE67136

   MIGRANT LABOR IN WISCONSIN.   GBRANEX63796

   MANPOWER IMPLICATIONS OF TECHNOLOGICAL-CHANGE. RESEARCH FINDINGS OF THE US DEPARTMENT OF LABOR.   GBRANSX63876

   DISCRIMINATORY ASPECTS OF THE LABOR MARKET OF THE 60-S.   GBUCKLF

   GUIDE TO LAWFUL AND UNLAWFUL PRE-EMPLOYMENT INQUIRIES BY EMPLOYERS, EMPLOYMENT-AGENCIES, AND LABOR
   ORGANIZATIONS UNDER THE CALIFORNIA FAIR-EMPLOYMENT-PRACTICE ACT, LABOR CODE, SECTIONS 1410-1432.   GCALDIR60527

   GUIDE TO LAWFUL AND UNLAWFUL PRE-EMPLOYMENT INQUIRIES BY EMPLOYERS, EMPLOYMENT-AGENCIES, AND LABOR
   ORGANIZATIONS UNDER THE CALIFORNIA FAIR-EMPLOYMENT-PRACTICE ACT, LABOR CODE, SECTIONS 1410-1432.   GCALDIR60527

   EMPLOYMENT PRACTICES, CITY OF PASADENA, AN INVESTIGATION UNDER SECTION 1421 OF THE CALIFORNIA LABOR CODE
   1963-1965.   GCALFEPND531

   LABOR AND CIVIL-RIGHTS. /CALIFORNIA UNION/   GCALLFX59544

   LABOR AND CIVIL-RIGHTS 1964. /CALIFORNIA UNION/   GCALLFX64545

   THE ITINERANT FARM LABOR PROJECT REPORT. /MIGRANT-WORKERS CALIFORNIA/   GCALVRS60553

   THE COMMUNITY LOOKS AT MIGRANT LABOR. /MIGRANT-WORKERS/   GCCNSLC59926

   SEMINAR ON MANPOWER POLICY AND PROGRAM. LABOR LOOKS AT AUTOMATION AND CIVIL-RIGHTS.   GCONWJT65496

   REPORTS OF THE MEETINGS OF THE COMMITTEE OF OFFICIALS ON MIGRATORY FARM LABOR OF THE ATLANTIC SEABOARD
   STATES. /MIGRANT-WORKERS/   GCOUNSG58932

   MIGRATORY-LABOR IN THE WEST. BACKGROUND INFORMATION FOR THE WESTERN INTERSTATE CONFERENCE ON MIGRATORY
   LABOR. /MIGRANT-WORKERS/   GCOUNSG60931

   SUGAR BEET LABOR IN NORTHERN COLORADO. /MIGRANT-WORKERS/   GDAVIIF58939

   REPORT AND RECOMMENDATIONS OF DELAWARE COMMITTEE ON MIGRATORY LABOR. /MIGRANT-WORKERS/   GDELACM58945

   EFFECT OF MECHANIZATION ON EMPLOYMENT OF MIGRATORY LABOR IN AGRICULTURE AND FOOD PROCESSING.
   /MIGRANT-WORKERS/   GDELASE59946

   DISCRIMINATION BY LABOR UNIONS IN THE EXERCISE OF STATUTORY BARGAINING POWERS.   GDCDDEM45646

   LABOR AND THE CIVIL-RIGHTS REVOLUTION. /UNION/   GFLEIHX60685

   PUSH-BUTTON LABOR. /TECHNOLOGICAL-CHANGE UNEMPLOYMENT/   GFORTXX54047

   LABOR LOOKS AT THE CRISES IN CIVIL-RIGHTS. /UNION/   GGOLDHX58975

   LABOR LAW -- UNION MEMBERSHIP DENIED ON THE BASIS OF RACIAL DISCRIMINATION. /WISCONSIN LEGISLATION/ GKAUFET58014

   LABOR AND THE EMANCIPATION PROCLAMATION. /UNION/   GKRONJL65861

   POPULATION CHANGE AND THE SUPPLY OF LABOR.   GLEBESX60276

   THE ADAPTATION OF LABOR RESOURCES TO CHANGING NEEDS. /MOBILITY/   GLESTRA66532

   UNIONS BEFORE THE BAR. HISTORICAL TRIALS SHOWING THE EVOLUTION OF LABOR RIGHTS IN THE US.   GLIEBEX50901

   THE POSITION OF MINORITIES IN THE AMERICAN LABOR MOVEMENT. /UNION/   GMARSRX66946

PROGRESS IN MEETING PROBLEMS OF MIGRATORY LABOR IN MARYLAND.   GMARYGC60955

THE FARM WORKER IN A CHANGING AGRICULTURE. PART I IN A SERIES ON TECHNOLOGICAL-CHANGE AND FARM LABOR USE,
KERN-COUNTY, CALIFORNIA, 1961.   GMETZWH64387

TEENAGE LABOR PROBLEMS AND THE NEIGHBORHOOD-YOUTH-CORPS.   GMCONJD66726

INTER-GROUP RELATIONS WITHIN LABOR AND INDUSTRY.   GNATLCL49042

PROCEEDINGS OF THE NATIONAL-SHARECROPPERS-FUND CONFERENCE ON MIGRATORY LABOR AND LOW-INCOME FARMERS.
NOVEMBER 13 1957.   GNATLSF57299

NEW-YORK STATE-COMMISSION-AGAINST-DISCRIMINATION, STATEMENT BEFORE THE US SENATE SUBCOMMITTEE ON LABOR
AND LABOR-MANAGEMENT RELATIONS.   GNEWYSA52102

MIGRANT FARM LABOR IN NEW-YORK.   GNEWYSE58109

MIGRANT FARM LABOR IN NEW-YORK STATE.   GNEWYSJ63112

A HELPING HAND. SEASONAL FARM LABOR IN NEW-YORK STATE. /MIGRANT-WORKERS/   GNEWYSX63087

MIGRATORY LABOR IN OHIO. A REPORT BY THE GOVERNOR-S COMMITTEE, AUGUST 1962.   GOHICGC62095

GUIDE TO EMPLOYERS, EMPLOYMENT-AGENCIES AND LABOR UNIONS DEFINING PROPER AND IMPROPER PRE-EMPLOYMENT
INQUIRIES. /PENNSYLVANIA/   GPENNHRND164

THE MOVEMENT OF LABOR BETWEEN FARM AND NONFARM JOBS.   GPERKBX66150

HUMAN RESOURCES IN THE URBAN ECONOMY. PART II -- THE LABOR FORCE PERFORMANCE OF MINORITY-GROUPS.   GPERLMX63169

CIVIL-RIGHTS AND LIBERTIES AND LABOR UNIONS.   GRAUHJL57217

THE MIGRANT LABOR PROBLEM IN WISCONSIN.   GRAUSEX62218

NATIONAL EMPLOYMENT, SKILLS, AND EARNINGS OF FARM LABOR.   GSCHUTW67964

ORGANIZED LABOR AND THE MINORITY WORKER NEED EACH OTHER. /UNION/   GSHISBX59305

LABOR AND FAIR-EMPLOYMENT PRACTICE. /UNION/   GSLAIDX67840

A MIGRANT LABOR CRISIS IN IMMOKALEE. /FLORIDA/   GSOWOWT59328

MINORITY-GROUP INTEGRATION BY LABOR AND MANAGEMENT. A STUDY OF THE EMPLOYMENT PRACTICES OF THE LARGER
EMPLOYERS, AND THE MEMBERSHIP PRACTICES OF THE LARGER LABOR UNIONS WITH RESPECT TO RACE, RELIGION, AND
NATIONAL ORIGIN, CONNECTICUT, 1951.   GSTETHG53598

MINORITY-GROUP INTEGRATION BY LABOR AND MANAGEMENT. A STUDY OF THE EMPLOYMENT PRACTICES OF THE LARGER
EMPLOYERS, AND THE MEMBERSHIP PRACTICES OF THE LARGER LABOR UNIONS WITH RESPECT TO RACE, RELIGION, AND
NATIONAL ORIGIN, CONNECTICUT, 1951.   GSTETHG53598

LABOR UNIONS AND FAIR-EMPLOYMENT-PRACTICES LEGISLATION.   GTIMBEX54357

SOCIAL RESPONSIBILITIES OF ORGANIZED LABOR. /UNION/   GTITCJA57358

FARM LABOR ADJUSTMENTS TO CHANGING TECHNOLOGY.   GTOLLGS67974

MIGRATORY FARM LABOR CONFERENCE, PROCEEDINGS.   GUSDLAB57359

MAJOR AGRICULTURAL MIGRANT LABOR DEMAND AREAS.   GUSDLAB61509

HOUSING FOR MIGRANT AGRICULTURAL WORKERS. LABOR CAMP STANDARDS.   GUSDLAB62508

CONSOLIDATED INVENTORY OF DEPARTMENT OF LABOR RESEARCH ON LABOR-FORCE EMPLOYMENT AND UNEMPLOYMENT.   GUSDLAB64441

CONSOLIDATED INVENTORY OF DEPARTMENT OF LABOR RESEARCH ON AUTOMATION AND TECHNOLOGICAL-CHANGE.   GUSDLAB64619

FARM LABOR DEVELOPMENTS -- EMPLOYMENT AND WAGE SUPPLEMENT.   GUSDLAB66446

LABOR WEEK. RULES ON HIRING, PROMOTING -- QUESTIONS ANSWERED.   GUSNEWR66518

MIGRATORY LABOR.   GUSSENA59469

MIGRATORY LABOR BILLS.   GUSSENA63305

PROGRESS IN MEETING PROBLEMS OF MIGRATORY LABOR IN MARYLAND.   GUVMADA62529

PROBLEMS OF MIGRANT LABOR.   GWALLFX61221

MEMBERSHIP DISCRIMINATION IN LABOR UNIONS.   GWASHLR64541

FEDERAL REMEDIES FOR RACIAL DISCRIMINATION BY LABOR UNIONS.   GWEISLX62597

MIGRATORY LABOR IN DELAWARE.   GWELFCD56548

THE CONSTITUTION AND THE LABOR UNION.   GWELLHX61549

LABOR AND CIVIL-RIGHTS IN CHICAGO. /ILLINOIS UNION/   GWESTJX66551

LABOR AND THE PUBLIC INTEREST. /UNION/   GWIRTWW64572

LABOR LOOKS AT EQUAL RIGHTS IN EMPLOYMENT. /UNION/   GWOLLJA64579

SAN-CARLOS APACHE WAGE LABOR.   IADAMWX57522

REPORT ON INDIAN FARM LABOR ACTIVITY.   IUSDLAB66668

LEGACY OF THE JEWISH LABOR MOVEMENT.   JTYLEGX65766

CALIFORNIA-S FARM LABOR PROBLEMS. /MIGRANT-WORKERS/   MCALSSE63380

MIGRATORY LABOR IN COLORADO.   MCOLOLC60382

MIGRATORY LABOR IN COLORADO. REPORT TO THE COLORADO GENERAL ASSEMBLY.   MCOLOLC62383

MIGRATORY LABOR IN THE WEST.   MCOUNSH60386

MERCHANTS OF LABOR. THE MEXICAN BRACERO STORY.   MGALAEX66397

A HISTORY OF THE INTERRELATIONSHIPS BETWEEN IMPORTED MEXICAN LABOR, DOMESTIC MIGRANTS, AND THE TEXAS AGRICULTURAL ECONOMY.   MGRAVRP60405

MEXICAN-AMERICAN LABOR PROBLEMS IN TEXAS.   MJONELB65318

SURVEY ON TRANSIENT MEXICAN LABOR REQUIREMENTS.   MLOSACAND430

TERMINATION OF THE BRACERO PROGRAM. SOME EFFECTS ON FARM LABOR AND MIGRANT HOUSING NEEDS.   MMCELRC65385

THE MEXICAN FARM LABOR SUPPLY PROGRAM -- ITS FRIENDS AND FOES.   MPFEIOG63456

AN ANALYSIS OF THE MEXICAN-AMERICAN MIGRANT LABOR FORCE IN THE STOCKBRIDGE AREA. /MICHIGAN/   MRODRFX66464

THE EFFECTS OF IMPORTED MEXICAN FARM LABOR IN A CALIFORNIA COUNTY.   MROONJF61465

A SELECTIVE BIBLIOGRAPHY OF CALIFORNIA LABOR HISTORY.   MSLOBMX64495

FAMILY ORGANIZATION IN FIVE TYPES OF MIGRATORY WAGE LABOR.   MSOLIML61496

MEXICAN FARM LABOR CONSULTANTS REPORT.   .   MUSDLAB59508

FARM LABOR.   MUSHOUR58509

MEXICAN FARM LABOR PROGRAM.   MUSHOUR63984

THE SOUTHERN LABOR STORY. /UNION/   NAFLCIO58006

LABOR OPPOSES PREJUDICE. /UNION/   NAMERFX55012

OAKLAND LABOR BACKS UP YOUTH. /TRAINING/   NAWNEMX66875

NEGRO LABOR IN THE AUTO INDUSTRY.   NBAILLH43045

ORGANIZED LABOR AND THE NEGRO WORKER. /UNION/   NBAINMX63046

MISSISSIPPI. BATTLEFRONT FOR LABOR. /UNION/   NBARTBX65057

REFLECTIONS ON THE NEGRO AND LABOR. /UNION/   NBELLDX63073

NEGROES AND ORGANIZED LABOR. /UNION/   NBLOCHD62091

LABOR AND LABORING CLASSES.   NBLOOGF50095

ORGANIZED LABOR AND MINORITY-GROUPS POLICY AND PRACTICES. /UNION/   NBLUEJT47256

LABOR AND THE SOUTHERN NEGRO.   NBRADCX57107

NEGRO AMERICAN LABOR COUNCIL IS ACTIVE IN NEW-YORK STATE.   NBROOTR61119

DISCRIMINATORY ASPECTS OF THE LABOR MARKET OF THE 60-S.   NBUCKLF61130

SOUTH-S TENSION SEIZES LABOR. /UNION/   NBUSIWX56882

AMERICAN LABOR ATTACKS ITS OWN SEGREGATION PROBLEM. /UNION/   NCHASWX58194

LABOR UNIONS AND THE NEGRO.   NCOMMXX59228

WAR ECONOMICS AND NEGRO LABOR.   NDAVIFG42260

NEGROES AND THE LABOR MOVEMENT. RECORD OF THE LEFT WING UNIONS.   NDOYLWX62287

LABOR IN AMERICA. A HISTORY.   NDULLFR49301

THE CONSTITUTIONAL RIGHT TO MEMBERSHIP IN A LABOR UNION -- FIFTH AND FOURTEENTH AMENDMENTS.   NELLIGH59330

LABOR IN AMERICA.   NFAULHU57345

IS LABOR COLOR BLIND. /UNION/   NFLEIHX59359

HISTORY OF THE LABOR MOVEMENT IN THE UNITED STATES. /UNION/   NFONEPS47370

INTER-INDUSTRY LABOR MOBILITY AMONG MEN, 1957-60.   NGALLLE66392

SOUTHERN LABOR FIGHTS BACK. /UNION/   NGOOGGX48434

LABOR LAW AND THE NEGRO.   NGOULWB64889

SITUATIONAL PRESSURES AND FUNCTIONAL ROLE OF THE ETHNIC LABOR LEADERS. /UNION/   NGREESX53453

ORGANIZED LABOR AND THE NEGRO WORKER. /UNION/   NGROBGX60460

RACIAL DISCRIMINATION IN AMERICAN LABOR UNIONS.   NGUHAME65464

THE USE OF NEGRO LABOR IN SOUTHERN INDUSTRY. /OCCUPATIONAL-PATTERNS/   NHALLDE53477

THE OPPORTUNITIES AND DIFFICULTIES OF ORGANIZING NEGRO LABOR IN THE PRESENT EMERGENCY. /UNION/   NHALLWX42259

RECENT DEVELOPMENTS IN RACE-RELATIONS AND ORGANIZED LABOR.   NHENDVW66213

NAACP LABOR MANUAL. A GUIDE TO ACTION.   NHILLHX58531

LABOR AND SEGREGATION. /UNION/   NHILLHX59529

LABOR UNIONS AND THE NEGRO.   NHILLHX59530

RACISM WITHIN ORGANIZED LABOR. A REPORT OF THE FIVE YEARS OF THE AFL-CIO, 1955-1960. /UNION/   NHILLHX60542

HAS ORGANIZED LABOR FAILED THE NEGRO WORKER. /UNION/   NHILLHX62526

THE ILGWU TODAY -- THE DECAY OF A LABOR UNION.   NHILLHX62528

ORGANIZED LABOR AND THE NEGRO WAGE-EARNER. /UNION/   NHILLHX62535

US DEPARTMENT OF LABOR. PUBLIC HEARING, TESTIMONY. /MIGRANT-WORKERS/   NHILLHX63548

THE RACIAL PRACTICES OF ORGANIZED LABOR -- IN THE AGE OF GOMPERS AND AFTER. /UNION/   NHILLHX65541

THE STATUS OF NEGRO LABOR.   NJOHNCS49613

LABOR (CONTINUATION)
THE NEGRO WORKER OF KANSAS-CITY. A STUDY OF TRADE UNION AND ORGANIZED LABOR RELATIONS.   NKANCIU40634

THE MERITOCRACY OF LABOR.   NKEMPMX65293

LABOR UNION AND RACE-RELATIONS. A STUDY OF UNION TACTICS.   NKORNWA50660

LABOR AND TECHNOLOGY ON SELECTED COTTON PLANTATIONS IN THE DELTA AREA OF MISSISSIPPI, 1953-1957.   NLERANL59404

NEGRO FARM LABOR IN THE DELTA AREA OF MISSISSIPPI. SUPPLY AND UTILIZATION.   NLERANL61416

NEGROES AND THE LABOR MOVEMENT -- AN EXCHANGE.   NLIPSSM62043

THE AMERICAN LABOR MOVEMENT.   NLITWLX62698

LABOR IN THE SOUTH. /UNION/   NMARSRX61740

THE NEGRO AND ORGANIZED LABOR. /UNION/   NMARSRX63741

THE NEGRO AND ORGANIZED LABOR. /UNION/   NMARSRX65742

THE POSITION OF MINORITIES IN THE AMERICAN LABOR MOVEMENT. /UNION/   NMARSRX66943

A SOCIOLOGICAL ANALYSIS OF A BI-RACIAL LOCAL LABOR UNION.   NMERCJJ56768

RAILWAY LABOR ACT -- DENIAL OF UNION MEMBERSHIP TO NEGROES.   NMINNLR58800

NEGROES AND THE LABOR MOVEMENT. /UNION/   NNEWXPX62910

NEGRO LABOR AND ITS PROBLEMS.   NNORGPH40930

ORGANIZED LABOR AND THE NEGRO. /UNION/   NNORTHR44944

NATIONAL NEGRO LABOR COUNCIL, THIRD ANNUAL CONVENTION. /UNION/   NPERRPX54987

ORGANIZED LABOR AND THE NEGRO YOUTH. /UNION/   NPOLLSX66723

THE NAACP VERSUS LABOR. /UNION/   NRICHJC62054

LABOR DRIVES TO CLOSE THE SOUTH-S OPEN-SHOP. /UNION/   NRONYVX65072

THE NEGRO IN THE AMERICAN LABOR MOVEMENT. /UNION/   NROSESJ62079

NEGRO LABOR IN THE SOUTHERN CRYSTAL BALL. /EMPLOYMENT/   NRUTHKX49100

THE CIVIL-RIGHTS-ACT OF 1964. RACIAL DISCRIMINATION BY LABOR.UNIONS.   NSAINJL66138

ORGANIZED LABOR IN AMERICAN HISTORY. /UNION/   NTAFTPX64158

WAR LABOR BOARD DECISION ON WAGES OF NEGROES.   NUSDLAB43848

LABOR SUPPLY IN THE SOUTH.   NUSDLAB46824

A LABOR UNIT FOR NEGRO RIGHTS.   NUSDLAB52148

LABOR MONTH IN REVIEW. NEGRO UNEMPLOYMENT.   NUSDLAB63823

LABOR USA. /UNION/   NVELILX59216

PROBLEMS OF MIGRANT LABOR.   NWALLFX61221

NEGRO LABOR. A NATIONAL PROBLEM.   NWEAVRC46304

NEGRO LABOR SINCE 1929.   NWEAVRC50305

LABOR TACKLES THE RACE QUESTION. /UNION/   NWINNFX43554

CIVIL-RIGHTS -- DISCRIMINATION IN LABOR UNIONS.   NYOUNWM64349

SPANISH SPEAKING WORKERS AND THE LABOR MOVEMENT.   PASSPCT56779

LABOR MANAGEMENT ON THE FARM.   PGARDSC58807

LABOR UNIONS AND PUERTO-RICAN MEMBERS IN NEW-YORK CITY.   PGRAYLX63027

NEW-YORK-S LABOR SCANDAL. THE PUERTO-RICAN WORKERS.   PLEVIMX57823

ANNUAL FARM LABOR REPORT. /NEW-JERSEY/   PNEWJSE63831

PUERTO-RICANS, KEY SOURCE OF LABOR.   PNEWYDC56817

CHARACTERISTICS OF POPULATION AND LABOR IN NEW-YORK STATE, 1956 AND 1957. PUERTO-RICANS IN NEW-YORK CITY. PNEWYSE60839

REPORTS OF PUERTO-RICO DEPARTMENT OF LABOR, MIGRATION DIVISION ON PLACEMENT.   PPUERRCND791

LABOR SUPPLY. FAMILY INCOME, AND CONSUMPTION.   WMINCJX60985

LABOR-FORCE PARTICIPATION OF MARRIED WOMEN. A STUDY OF LABOR SUPPLY.   WMINCJX62984

REPORT OF THE COMMITTEE ON PROTECTIVE LABOR LEGISLATION, 1963.   WPRESCO63069

WISCONSIN FAIR-EMPLOYMENT-PRACTICES DIVISION INQUIRY INTO THE CONFLICTS BETWEEN STATE PROTECTIVE LABOR
LEGISLATION AND STATE AND FEDERAL LAWS PROHIBITING DISCRIMINATION BASED ON SEX. /EMPLOYMENT-CONDITIONS/   WUAWXWD65165

SUMMARY OF STATE LABOR LAWS FOR WOMEN.   WUSDLABND219

WHAT ABOUT WOMEN-S ABSENTEEISM AND LABOR TURNOVER.   WUSDLAB65225

LABOR-FORCE
THE NON-WHITE FEMALE IN THE LABOR-FORCE. /WOMEN NEGRO/   CTURNRH51214

NEGRO WOMEN IN THE POPULATION AND IN THE LABOR-FORCE.   CUSDLAB66263

POPULATION AND LABOR-FORCE CHARACTERISTICS OF FIVE SOUTHEASTERN PENNSYLVANIA COUNTIES.   GANDEBXND391

THE AMERICAN LABOR-FORCE. ITS GROWTH AND CHANGING COMPOSITION. /DEMOGRAPHY/   GBANCGX58417

LABOR-FORCE PARTICIPATION AND UNEMPLOYMENT.   GBOWEWG65469

POTENTIAL SUPPLY AND REPLACEMENT OF RURAL MALES OF **LABOR-FORCE** AGE, 1960-70.   GBOWLGK66430

THE CURRENT SITUATION OF THE HIRED FARM **LABOR-FORCE**.   GBOWLGK67920

INTERIM REVISED PROJECTIONS OF US **LABOR-FORCE**, 1965-1975.   GCOOPSX62602

THE OUTLOOK FOR THE **LABOR-FORCE** AT MID-DECADE. /EMPLOYMENT-TRENDS/   GCOOPSX64743

LABOR-FORCE PROJECTIONS BY COLOR, 1970-1980.   GCOOPSX66604

LABOR-FORCE PARTICIPATION OF YOUNG PERSONS AGED 14-24.   GFEARRXND929

CONFERENCE ON UNSKILLED WORKERS IN THE **LABOR-FORCE**. PROBLEMS AND PROSPECTS.   GGITLAL66134

PROJECTIONS OF THE **LABOR-FORCE** OF THE US.   GGOLDHX63787

LABOR-FORCE STATUS OF YOUTH, 1964.   GHAMEHR65756

OCCUPATIONAL MOBILITY FROM THE FARM **LABOR-FORCE**.   GHATHDE67936

CHANGES IN THE **LABOR-FORCE** PARTICIPATION OF THE OLDER WORKER.   GHAUSPM54764

THE STATUS OF THE NONWHITE **LABOR-FORCE** IN ILLINOIS AND THE NATION.   GILLICH57793

THE POOR IN THE WORK FORCE. /**LABOR-FORCE**/   GLEVISA66038

THE **LABOR-FORCE** UNDER CHANGING INCOME AND EMPLOYMENT.   GLONGCX58047

LABOR-FORCE AND EMPLOYMENT, 1960-62.   GMEREJL63067

PROJECTED CHANGES IN THE OCCUPATIONAL STRUCTURE OF THE **LABOR-FORCE**. IMPLICATIONS FOR PUBLIC WELFARE.   GSIFFHX64105

LABOR-FORCE DEVELOPMENTS FOR WHITE AND NONWHITE WORKERS,954-1964.   GUSDLAB64110

CONSOLIDATED INVENTORY OF DEPARTMENT OF LABOR RESEARCH ON **LABOR-FORCE** EMPLOYMENT AND UNEMPLOYMENT.   GUSDLAB64441

THE SECONDARY **LABOR-FORCE** AND THE MEASUREMENT OF UNEMPLOYMENT.   GWILCRC57562

THE ECONOMIC BASIS OF INDIAN LIFE. /INCOME **LABOR-FORCE**/   IKELLWH57076

THE NEGRO IN THE **LABOR-FORCE** OF THE UNITED-STATES.   NBAILLH53044

THE SOURCES OF ECONOMIC GROWTH IN THE UNITED-STATES AND THE ALTERNATIVE BEFORE US. /**LABOR-FORCE**
ECONOMY/   NDENIEF62262

CORRELATIONS BETWEEN INCOME AND **LABOR-FORCE** PARTICIPATION BY RACE.   NDORNSM56283

RECENT MIGRATION TO CHICAGO. /**LABOR-FORCE** ILLINOIS/   NFREERX50967

PLANTATION ORGANIZATION AND THE RESIDENT **LABOR-FORCE**, DELTA AREA, MISSISSIPPI.   NLERANL60403

LABOR-FORCE AND DEMOGRAPHIC FACTORS AFFECTING THE CHANGING RELATIVE STATUS OF THE AMERICAN NEGRO.
1940-1950.   NPHILWM57997

THE NEGRO IN THE **LABOR-FORCE**.   NPURYMT63026

NEGROES IN THE CALIFORNIA AGRICULTURAL **LABOR-FORCE**.   NRECOCW59042

THE EXPECTED-CASES METHOD APPLIED TO THE NON-WHITE MALE **LABOR-FORCE**.   NTURNRH49211

THE NON-WHITE MALE IN THE **LABOR-FORCE**.   NTURNRH49215

THE RELATIVE POSITION OF THE NEGRO MALE IN THE **LABOR-FORCE** OF LARGE AMERICAN CITIES.   NTURNRH51217

POVERTY AREAS OF OUR MAJOR CITIES. THE EMPLOYMENT SITUATION OF NEGRO AND WHITE WORKERS IN METROPOLITAN
AREAS COMPARED IN A SPECIAL **LABOR-FORCE** REPORT.   NWETZJR66114

EDUCATIONAL-ATTAINMENT AND **LABOR-FORCE** PARTICIPATION.   WBOWEWGND652

THE **LABOR-FORCE** PARTICIPATION OF MARRIED WOMEN.   WCAINGG64671

MARRIED WOMEN IN THE **LABOR-FORCE** -- AN ECONOMIC ANALYSIS.   WCAINGG66672

THE FEMALE **LABOR-FORCE** IN METROPOLITAN AREAS. AN INTERNATIONAL COMPARISON.   WCOLLAX62697

AGE OF COMPLETION OF CHILDBEARING AND ITS RELATION TO THE PARTICIPATION OF WOMEN IN THE **LABOR-FORCE**.
UNITED STATES 1910-1955.   WDAYXLH57725

ENTERING THE **LABOR-FORCE**.   WGOLDBX64794

FEMALE **LABOR-FORCE** PARTICIPATION AND ECONOMIC DEVELOPMENT.   WHABESX58811

WOMEN IN THE **LABOR-FORCE**.   WINTELR58869

PROJECTIONS OF POPULATION AND **LABOR-FORCE**.   WINTELR61868

SOME FACTORS WHICH DETERMINE THE DISTRIBUTION OF THE FEMALE WORK-FORCE. /**LABOR-FORCE**/   WJOUROI62883

FEMALE **LABOR-FORCE** MOBILITY AND ITS SIMULATION.   WKORBJX63435

WOMEN AT WORK. /**LABOR-FORCE**/   WKRUGDH64918

FACTORS DETERMINING THE **LABOR-FORCE** PARTICIPATION OF MARRIED WOMEN.   WMAHOTA61951

WOMEN IN THE **LABOR-FORCE**.   WMARCMR60080

LABOR-FORCE PARTICIPATION OF MARRIED WOMEN. A STUDY OF LABOR SUPPLY.   WMINCJX62984

MOTHERS IN THE **LABOR-FORCE**.   WMOUNHS64003

LABOR-FORCE PARTICIPATION OF SUBURBAN MOTHERS.   WMYERGC64011

THE FEMALE **LABOR-FORCE** IN THE UNITED STATES. FACTORS GOVERNING ITS GROWTH AND CHANGING COMPOSITION.   WOPPEVK66096

THE INTERACTION OF DEMAND AND SUPPLY AND ITS EFFECT ON THE FEMALE **LABOR-FORCE** IN THE UNITED STATES.   WOPPEVK66289

THE CHANGING WOMAN WORKER. A STUDY OF THE FEMALE **LABOR-FORCE** IN NEW-JERSEY AND IN THE NATION FROM 1940 TO

LABOR-FORCE   (CONTINUATION)
1958.   WSMITGM60120

THE FEMALE **LABOR-FORCE**. A CASE STUDY IN THE INTERPRETATION OF HISTORICAL STATISTICS.   WSMUTRW60124

LABOR-FORCE SENSITIVITY TO EMPLOYMENT BY AGE, SEX.   WTELLAX65714

LABOR-FORCE PARTICIPATION RATES AND PERCENT DISTRIBUTION OF MOTHERS WITH HUSBAND PRESENT.   WUSDLAB64204

WOMEN IN THE AMERICAN **LABOR-FORCE**. EMPLOYMENT AND UNEMPLOYMENT.   WWILCRX60268

LABOR-MANAGEMENT
REPORT OF INDUSTRY AND **LABOR-MANAGEMENT** CLINICS. IMPLEMENTATION OF EMPLOYMENT IN MERIT PROGRAMS IN NON
FEPC STATES BY DIRECT APPROACH TO TOP MANAGEMENT.   GFISKUR51684

NEW-YORK STATE-COMMISSION-AGAINST-DISCRIMINATION, STATEMENT BEFORE THE US SENATE SUBCOMMITTEE ON LABOR
AND **LABOR-MANAGEMENT** RELATIONS.   GNEWYSA52102

LABOR-MANAGEMENT IRREGULARITIES.   GUSHOUR61345

LABOR-MARKET
A POSITIVE **LABOR-MARKET** POLICY.   GBAKKEW63598

EMPLOYMENT COUNSELING AS AN INTEGRAL PART OF AN ACTIVE **LABOR-MARKET** POLICY.   GEHRLRA65791

TODAY-S REALITIES IN THE FARM **LABOR-MARKET**.   GGOODRC65726

LABOR-MARKET STRATEGIES IN THE WAR-ON-POVERTY. /UNEMPLOYMENT/   GHARBFH65660

CENTRAL ROLE OF INTERGROUP AGENCIES IN THE **LABOR-MARKET**. CHANGING RESEARCH AND PERSONNEL REQUIREMENTS.   GHOPEJX61780

A METHODOLOGICAL APPROACH TO IDENTIFICATION AND CLASSIFICATION OF CERTAIN TYPES OF INACTIVE WORK-SEEKERS.
/UNEMPLOYMENT **LABOR-MARKET**/   GLIEBEE65569

THE STRUCTURE OF THE FARM **LABOR-MARKET** AND MIGRATION PATTERNS.   GMIREWX57499

THE MEASUREMENT AND INTERPRETATION OF JOB VACANCIES. A CONFERENCE REPORT OF THE NATIONAL BUREAU OF
ECONOMIC RESEARCH. /**LABOR-MARKET**/   GNATLBE66611

SUMMARY OF PROCEEDINGS. WORKSHOP ON THE IMPACT OF A TIGHTENING **LABOR-MARKET** ON THE EMPLOYABILITY AND
EMPLOYMENT OF DISADVANTAGED YOUTH.   GNEWYUC66116

EMPLOYMENT POLICY AND THE **LABOR-MARKET**.   GROSSAM65720

UNEMPLOYMENT AND **LABOR-MARKET** POLICY.   GSHULGX66142

FARM **LABOR-MARKET** IN TRANSITION.   GUSDLAB62991

DOMESTIC AND IMPORTED WORKERS IN THE HARVEST **LABOR-MARKET**. SANTA-CLARA COUNTY, CALIFORNIA, 1954.   MFULLVX56396

THE SOCIAL-STRUCTURE OF THE MICHIGAN **LABOR-MARKET**.   NFERMLA65352

THE EMPLOYMENT SITUATION OF WHITE AND NEGRO YOUTH IN THE CITY OF BALTIMORE. INITIAL EXPERIENCES IN THE
LABOR-MARKET. /MARYLAND/   NJOHNHU63735

NEGROES IN A CHANGING **LABOR-MARKET**. /UNEMPLOYMENT/   NKILLCC67653

UNION RACIAL PRACTICES AND THE **LABOR-MARKET**.   NMARSRX62749

STATUS OF NEGROES IN CRAFT UNIONS...PITTSBURGH **LABOR-MARKET**. /PENNSYLVANIA/   NPITTMC65002

THE BACKGROUND OF THE 1947 COLLEGE STUDENT. /**LABOR-MARKET**/   NQUARBX47257

PLACING PUERTO-RICAN WORKERS IN THE NEW-YORK CITY **LABOR-MARKET**.   PMONTHX60830

PUERTO-RICANS IN THE NEW-YORK STATE **LABOR-MARKET**.   PNEWYSE57840

A COMPARISON OF THE OCCUPATIONS OF THE FIRST AND SECOND GENERATION PUERTO-RICANS IN THE MAINLAND
LABOR-MARKET. AND HOW THE WORK OF THE NEW-YORK STATE DEPARTMENT OF LABOR EFFECTS PUERTO-RICANS.   PRAUSC X61846

ADDRESS TO CONFERENCE ON EDUCATION AND JOB OPPORTUNITIES FOR WOMEN RETURNING TO THE **LABOR-MARKET**.   WDOUTAX62741

OLDER WOMEN IN THE **LABOR-MARKET**.   WHUNTEH62271

THE MIDDLE AGED WOMAN AND THE **LABOR-MARKET**.   WJEWIVA62881

WOMEN IN THE **LABOR-MARKET**.   WMUELEL66004

TESTIMONY. PUBLIC HEARING, WOMEN IN PUBLIC AND PRIVATE EMPLOYMENT, CALIFORNIA. /**LABOR-MARKET**/   WSTEPRX66138

WOMEN AND GIRLS IN THE **LABOR-MARKET** TODAY AND TOMORROW.   WWELLJA63263

LABOR-MARKETS
INFORMATION NETWORKS IN **LABOR-MARKETS**.   GREESAX65119

LABOR-MOBILITY
LABOR-MOBILITY IN THE SOUTHERN STATES.   NASHBBX61032

LABOR-MOVEMENT
THE PLACE OF THE NEGRO IN THE AMERICAN **LABOR-MOVEMENT**. /UNION/   NGREESX61452

LABOR-NEGRO
LABOR-NEGRO DIVISION WIDENS. /UNION/   NBUSIWX60152

LABOR-RELATIONS
ECONOMICS OF **LABOR-RELATIONS**. /EQUAL-OPPORTUNITY/   GBLOOGF65885

LABOR-RELATIONS   GFRAEOK60697

CIVIL-RIGHTS PROBLEMS IN PERSONNEL AND **LABOR-RELATIONS**.   GKAMMTX65832

PREJUDICE AND SCIENTIFIC METHOD IN **LABOR-RELATIONS**. /UNION/   GMARRAX52941

STATE LEGISLATION IN **LABOR-RELATIONS** AND DISCRIMINATION IN EMPLOYMENT, 1945.   GSPITRS45332

HOW TO HANDLE RACE **LABOR-RELATIONS**. /UNION/   GSTYLPL50339

CIVIL-RIGHTS PROBLEMS IN PERSONNEL AND **LABOR-RELATIONS**.   NKAMOTCND633

LABOR-S

LABOR-S TASK FORCES. /UNION/   GSLAIDX64318

LABOR-S ROLE. DEMOCRACY ON THE JOB. /UNION/   GSLAIDX66317

LABOR-S RACE PROBLEM. /UNION/   MFORTXX59374

LABOR-S CIVIL-RIGHTS STAND REAFFIRMED AT ATLANTIC-CITY.   NAMERFX58013

LABOR-S GRASS ROOTS. A STUDY OF THE LOCAL UNION.   NBARBJX61052

LABOR-S UNTOLD STORY. /UNION/   NBOYERO55105

THE NEGRO-S PLACE AT LABOR-S TABLE. /UNION/   NBROOTX62122

THE SOUTH TODAY AND LABOR-S TASKS.   NMANNCP53737

LABOR-SUPPLY

THE NEGRO IN THE TEXAS LABOR-SUPPLY.   NHILLFG46524

LABORATORIES

EMPLOYMENT OF WOMEN CHEMISTS IN INDUSTRIAL LABORATORIES. /OCCUPATIONS/   WPARRJB65050

LABORER

WHEN THE MIGRANT LABORER SETTLES DOWN -- A REPORT OF THE FINDINGS OF A PROJECT ON VALUE ASSIMILATION OF IMMIGRANT LABORERS.   MPETECL64454

LABORERS

MEASURING THE ADJUSTMENT OF IMMIGRANT LABORERS. /MEXICAN-AMERICAN NEGRO/   CSHANLW63487

THE ECONOMIC ABSORPTION OF IN-MIGRANT LABORERS IN A NORTHERN INDUSTRIAL COMMUNITY. /MEXICAN-AMERICAN NEGRO/   CSHANLW64486

SOME PROBLEMS IN THE ACCULTURATION OF MEXICAN LABORERS TO A FACTORY.   MALBEPM64356

WHEN THE MIGRANT LABORER SETTLES DOWN -- A REPORT OF THE FINDINGS OF A PROJECT ON VALUE ASSIMILATION OF IMMIGRANT LABORERS.   MPETECL64454

AGRICULTURAL SEASONAL LABORERS OF COLORADO AND CALIFORNIA. /MIGRANT-WORKERS/   NKARRCHND636

LABORFFECTS

A COMPARISON OF THE OCCUPATIONS OF THE FIRST AND SECOND GENERATION PUERTO-RICANS IN THE MAINLAND LABOR-MARKET, AND HOW THE WORK OF THE NEW-YORK STATE DEPARTMENT OF LABORFFECTS PUERTO-RICANS.   PRAUSCX61846

LABORING

LABOR AND LABORING CLASSES.   NBLOOGF50095

LABOUR-FORCE

LABOUR-FORCE ADJUSTMENT OF WORKERS AFFECTED BY TECHNOLOGICAL-CHANGE.   GGOODRC64622

LAKE-ARROWHEAD

LAKE-ARROWHEAD CONFERENCE ON EQUAL-EMPLOYMENT-OPPORTUNITY.   GLOSAFEND916

LAND

DISCRIMINATION -- THE LAW OF THE LAND VERSUS THE LAW OF THE LAND.   GAPRUVJ63402

DISCRIMINATION -- THE LAW OF THE LAND VERSUS THE LAW OF THE LAND.   GAPRUVJ63402

WHITE AND NONWHITE OWNERS OF RURAL LAND IN THE SOUTHEAST.   GBOXLRF65418

THE INVISIBLE LAND. /POVERTY/   GHARRMX66212

MANPOWER TRAINING IN NAVAJO LAND.   IHARTVS63573

UNITED STATES INDIAN POPULATION AND LAND, 1960-1961.   IUSDINT61663

UN-MET NEED IN A LAND OF ABUNDANCE.   NEPSTLA63337

LAND TENURE IN THE SOUTHERN REGION. PROCEEDINGS OF PROFESSIONAL AGRICULTURAL WORKERS TENTH ANNUAL CONFERENCE.   NTUSKIX51218

LANGUAGE

SOME CULTURAL AND ANTHROPOLOGICAL ASPECTS OF ENGLISH AS A SECOND LANGUAGE.   MRUBEAJ66468

CHANGES IN PUBLIC AND PRIVATE LANGUAGE AMONG SPANISH-SPEAKING MIGRANTS TO AN INDUSTRIAL CITY.   MSCHETJ65481

SUGGESTED LANGUAGE FOR A STATE ACT TO ABOLISH DISCRIMINATORY WAGE RATES BASED ON SEX.   WUSDLAB64218

LANSING

COMPARISON OF MEXICANS, NEGROES AND WHITES WITH RESPECT TO OCCUPATIONAL HISTORY, RURAL-URBAN RESIDENCE HISTORY AND ACCULTURIZATION WITHIN THE INSTITUTIONAL STRUCTURE OF LANSING, MICHIGAN.   CGOLDVX60494

A STUDY OF EMPLOYMENT AND TRAINING PATTERNS IN THE LANSING AREA. /MICHIGAN/   NMICFEP58778

LAREDO

THE SOCIAL ASPIRATIONS OF A SELECTED GROUP OF SPANISH NAME PEOPLE IN LAREDO, TEXAS.   MGUERIX59409

LATIN

THE LATIN AMERICAN IS FINDING HIS PLACE.   MDUFFLC66390

LATIN-AMERICAN

PROBLEMS OF THE LATIN-AMERICAN WORKER IN TEXAS.   MGONZHB63404

A CASE-STUDY OF LATIN-AMERICAN UNIONIZATION IN AUSTIN, TEXAS.   MPARISF64452

LATIN-AMERICANS

SOME CHARACTERISTICS OF SPANISH-NAME TEXANS AND FOREIGN LATIN-AMERICANS IN TEXAS HIGHER EDUCATION.   MRENNRR57462

LAUNDRY

NEGRO WOMEN IN THE CLOTHING, CIGAR AND LAUNDRY INDUSTRIES OF PHILADELPHIA, 1960.   CPORTRP43103

LAW

WHAT THE SUPERVISOR SHOULD KNOW ABOUT THE EQUAL-EMPLOYMENT-OPPORTUNITY LAW.   GAHEREX65804

DISCRIMINATION -- THE LAW OF THE LAND VERSUS THE LAW OF THE LAND.   GAPRUVJ63402

DISCRIMINATION -- THE LAW OF THE LAND VERSUS THE LAW OF THE LAND.   GAPRUVJ63402

COMPENSATING EMPLOYEES UNDER THE NEW CIVIL-RIGHTS LAW.   GBENGEJ65436

RACIAL EQUALITY AND THE LAW.   GBERGMX54442

THE NEW CIVIL-RIGHTS LAW AND YOUR BUSINESS.   GBERGNJ64438

A SPECIAL REPORT -- THE EQUAL-EMPLOYMENT-OPPORTUNITY LAW, TITLE-VII OF THE CIVIL-RIGHTS-ACT OF 1964. GBURENAND495

THE OPERATION OF THE NEW-JERSEY LAW AGAINST DISCRIMINATION.   GBUSTJL49507

EQUAL-RIGHTS UNDER THE LAW. PROVIDING FOR EQUAL TREATMENT FOR ALL CITIZENS REGARDLESS OF RACE, RELIGION,
COLOR, NATIONAL ORIGIN OR ANCESTRY. /CALIFORNIA/   GCALAGO60511

CIVIL-RIGHTS-ACT OF 1964, WITH EXPLANATION -- PUBLIC LAW 88-352 -- AS APPROVED BY THE PRESIDENT ON JULY
2, 1964.   GCOMMCH64588

SHOULD CONGRESS PASS A LAW PROHIBITING EMPLOYMENT DISCRIMINATION.   GCONGOX45596

THE ROLE OF LAW IN EQUAL-EMPLOYMENT-OPPORTUNITY.   GCOOKFC66600

DISCRIMINATION AND THE LAW.   GCOUNVX65609

EQUAL-OPPORTUNITIES BY LAW. A CASE-STUDY.   GDUNNDD63654

CIVIL-RIGHTS AND THE LIMITS OF LAW.   GFREUPA64700

RACE-RELATIONS AND AMERICAN LAW.   GGREEJX59981

FAIR-EMPLOYMENT-PRACTICES AND THE LAW.   GHARTPX58763

DEVELOPMENT AND ADMINISTRATION OF THE NEW-YORK STATE LAW AGAINST DISCRIMINATION.   GHIGBJX67143

LABOR LAW -- UNION MEMBERSHIP DENIED ON THE BASIS OF RACIAL DISCRIMINATION. /WISCONSIN LEGISLATION/ GKAUFET58014

RACIAL DISCRIMINATION IN EMPLOYMENT AND THE FEDERAL LAW.   GKOVAIX58026

NJ ANTI-DISCRIMINATION LAW. FIRST ANNUAL REPORT. /NEW-JERSEY/   GLABOLR46871

NY ANTI-DISCRIMINATION LAW. 1946 ANNUAL REPORT. /NEW-YORK/   GLABOLR46872

ENFORCEMENT OF NEW-YORK LAW AGAINST DISCRIMINATION.   GLABORR51879

AN ANALYSIS OF THE EFFECTIVENESS OF THE NEW-YORK STATE LAW AGAINST DISCRIMINATION.   GMARPAW53940

ENFORCEMENT OF THE FEDERAL EQUAL-OPPORTUNITY LAW.   GMARSBX64943

THE LAW AND RACE-RELATIONS.   GMASLWX46147

LAW AND EQUAL-OPPORTUNITY. ANTI-DISCRIMINATION LAW IN MASSACHUSETTS.   GMAYHLH63970

LAW AND EQUAL-OPPORTUNITY. ANTI-DISCRIMINATION LAW IN MASSACHUSETTS.   GMAYHLH63970

PATTERNS OF CONCILIATION UNDER THE NEW-YORK STATE LAW AGAINST DISCRIMINATION.   GNEWXYL51100

RULINGS ON PRE-EMPLOYMENT INQUIRIES RELATING TO RACE, CREED, COLOR OR NATIONAL ORIGIN UNDER THE NEW-YORK
STATE LAW AGAINST DISCRIMINATION.   GNEWYSBND106

STATEMENT TO THE COMMITTEE ON LEGISLATION IN SUPPORT OF AN EFFECTIVE FEDERAL FEP LAW AND OTHER VITAL
CIVIL-RIGHTS LEGISLATION.   GOLIVWX60134

HOW THE NEW CIVIL-RIGHTS LAW AFFECTS YOUR EMPLOYMENT PRACTICES.   GPRENHI64104

THE 1964 CIVIL-RIGHTS LAW. A HARD LOOK.   GRACHCXN0212

OPERATING UNDER THE CIVIL-RIGHTS LAW.   GRESEIA64222

THE NEW FEDERAL FAIR-EMPLOYMENT-PRACTICES ACT -- COMPARISON WITH STATE LAW AND AN ANALYSIS OF RELEVANT
STATE EXPERIENCES. /MISSOURI/   GROBEPC64239

THE LAW AND RACIAL DISCRIMINATION IN EMPLOYMENT.   GROSESJ65255

CASES ARE PEOPLE. AN INTERPRETATION OF THE PENNSYLVANIA FAIR-EMPLOYMENT-PRACTICE LAW.   GSHIREM58304

FAIR-EMPLOYMENT-PRACTICE IN NEW-YORK. LAW, EDUCATION GO HAND IN HAND.   GSULLJD50340

ADMINISTRATIVE LAW -- HUMAN-RELATIONS COMMISSIONS, PENNSYLVANIA LAW AND DISCRIMINATORY EMPLOYMENT
PRACTICE.   GTEMPLQ63349

ADMINISTRATIVE LAW -- HUMAN-RELATIONS COMMISSIONS, PENNSYLVANIA LAW AND DISCRIMINATORY EMPLOYMENT
PRACTICE.   GTEMPLQ63349

EQUAL UNDER LAW.   GTENBJX65148

LAW OF DISCRIMINATION IN THE EMPLOYMENT OF NONWHITES.   GTURNRH52366

EQUAL-EMPLOYMENT-OPPORTUNITY UNDER FEDERAL LAW.   GUSCOMC66396

FIRST YEAR UNDER NEW-YORK LAW AGAINST DISCRIMINATION.   GUSDLAB47074

LAW AND THE AMERICAN-INDIAN.   IUSCOMC65636

JEWISH LAW GRADUATE. /EMPLOYMENT DISCRIMINATION/   JADLBXX64689

JEWISH LAW STUDENT AND NEW-YORK JOBS. /EMPLOYMENT DISCRIMINATION/   JRIGHXX64757

THE JEWISH LAW STUDENT AND NEW-YORK JOBS -- DISCRIMINATORY EFFECTS IN LAW FIRM HIRING PRACTICES.
/OCCUPATIONS/   JYALELJ64774

THE JEWISH LAW STUDENT AND NEW-YORK JOBS -- DISCRIMINATORY EFFECTS IN LAW FIRM HIRING PRACTICES.
/OCCUPATIONS/   JYALELJ64774

JEWISH LAW STUDENT AND NEW-YORK JOBS.   JYOUNJX65775

RACIAL EQUALITY AND THE LAW. THE ROLE OF LAW IN THE REDUCTION OF DISCRIMINATION IN THE UNITED-STATES. NBERGMX54076

RACIAL EQUALITY AND THE LAW. THE ROLE OF LAW IN THE REDUCTION OF DISCRIMINATION IN THE UNITED-STATES. NBERGMX54076

JOBS FOR NEGROES -- THE GAINS, THE PROBLEMS, AND THE NEW HIRING LAW. /TITLE-VII/   NBUSIWX65151

NEGROES AND THE LAW. /OCCUPATIONS/   NCARLEL64182

LAW   (CONTINUATION)
  THE EVOLUTION OF AMERICAN LAW VIS-A-VIS THE AMERICAN NEGRO.   NGARDHX63395

  LABOR LAW AND THE NEGRO.   NGOULWB64889

  THE NEGRO REVOLUTION AND THE LAW OF COLLECTIVE BARGAINING.   NGOULWB65437

  STATE LAWS AND THE NEGRO. SOCIAL CHANGE AND THE IMPACT OF LAW.   NHILLHX65545

  THE ROLE OF LAW IN SECURING EQUAL-EMPLOYMENT-OPPORTUNITY. LEGAL POWERS AND SOCIAL CHANGE.   NHILLHX66544

  LEGAL EDUCATION. DESEGREGATION IN LAW SCHOOLS.   NLEFLRA57676

  JOBS AND THE LAW. /LOUISVILLE KENTUCKY/   NLOUIHR65717

  RACIAL DISCRIMINATION AND THE FEDERAL LAW. A PROBLEM IN NULLIFICATION.   NLUSKLX63713

  USES OF LAW IN THE STRUGGLE FOR EQUALITY.   NMASLWX55756

  CIVIL-RIGHTS. THE LAW AND THE UNIONS.   NRASKAH64038

  THE LAW AND RACIAL DISCRIMINATION IN EMPLOYMENT.   NROSESJ67078

  SIX MONTHS OPERATION OF NEW-YORK LAW AGAINST DISCRIMINATION.   NUSDLAB46843

  SURVEY OF NEGRO ATTITUDES TOWARD LAW.   NZEITLX65359

  JANE CROW AND THE LAW. SEX DISCRIMINATION AND TITLE-VII.   WMURRPX65010

LAW-SOCIOLOGY
  ANTI-DISCRIMINATION LAWS IN ACTION IN NEW-JERSEY. A LAW-SOCIOLOGY STUDY.   GBLUMAW65459

LAWFUL
  GUIDE TO LAWFUL AND UNLAWFUL PRE-EMPLOYMENT INQUIRIES BY EMPLOYERS, EMPLOYMENT-AGENCIES, AND LABOR
  ORGANIZATIONS UNDER THE CALIFORNIA FAIR-EMPLOYMENT-PRACTICE ACT, LABOR CODE, SECTIONS 1410-1432.   GCALDIR60527

LAWFULNESS
  THE LAWFULNESS OF THE SEGREGATION DECISIONS.   GBLACCX60452

LAWS
  YOUR RIGHTS UNDER FAIR-EMPLOYMENT-PRACTICE LAWS.   GAMERJC60382

  REPORT ON TWENTY STATE ANTI-DISCRIMINATION AGENCIES AND THE LAWS THEY ADMINISTER.   GAMERJD61387

  ANTI-DISCRIMINATION LAWS IN ACTION IN NEW-JERSEY. A LAW-SOCIOLOGY STUDY.   GBLUMAW65459

  EMPLOYMENT DISCRIMINATION. STATE FEPC LAWS AND THE IMPACT OF OF TITLE-VII OF THE CIVIL-RIGHTS-ACT OF
  1964.   GBRYEGL65896

  STATE FAIR-EMPLOMENT LAWS AND THEIR ADMINISTRATION. TEXTS, FEDERAL-STATE COOPERATION, PROHIBITED ACTS. GBURENA64497

  STATE LAWS DEALING WITH NON-DISCRIMINATION IN EMPLOYMENT.   GBUTCGT63508

  DISCRIMINATION AND FAIR-EMPLOYMENT-PRACTICES LAWS.   GCALDWF65699

  COMMISSION ENFORCEMENT OF STATE LAWS AGAINST DISCRIMINATION. A COMPARATIVE ANALYSIS OF THE KANSAS ACT. GDYSCRB65657

  FAIR-EMPLOYMENT-PRACTICES ACT. STATE LAWS GRANTING EQUAL RIGHTS, PRIVILEGES, ETC.   GELWAEX58662

  EDUCATIONAL ASPECTS OF FAIR-EMPLOYMENT-PRACTICES-COMMISION LAWS.   GFLEMJG50687

  SOME GENERAL OBSERVATIONS ON THE ADMINISTRATION OF STATE FAIR-EMPLOYMENT-PRACTICE LAWS.   GGIRARA64721

  COMPARATIVE ANALYSIS OF STATE FAIR-EMPLOYMENT-PRACTICES LAWS.   GHARTPX62762

  STATE FAIR-EMPLOYMENT-PRACTICE LAWS. REPORT PERSUANT TO PROPOSAL 400.   GILLILC57802

  A REVIEW OF STATE FEPC LAWS.   GKOVAIX58860

  SURVEY OF STATE ANTI-DISCRIMINATORY LAWS.   GLABOLR44877

  OPERATION UNDER STATE FEPC LAWS.   GLABOLR45873

  EMPLOYMENT DISCRIMINATION. STATE FAIR-EMPLOYMENT-PRACTICES LAWS AND THE IMPACT OF TITLE-VII OF THE
  CIVIL-RIGHTS-ACT OF 1964.   GLAWXRD65885

  STATE LAWS AGAINST DISCRIMINATION.   GLESKTX61895

  COMPILATION OF LAWS AGAINST DISCRIMINATION. EMPLOYMENT, EDUCATIONAL INSTITUTIONS, PLACES OF PUBLIC
  ACCOMODATION. PUBLIC HOUSING, PUBLICLY ASSISTED HOUSING, PRIVATE HOUSING. /MASSACHUSETTS/   GMASSCAN0963

  STATES LAWS ON RACE AND COLOR.   GMURRPX50034

  EVERYBODY-S BUSINESS. A SUMMARY OF NEW-YORK STATE ANTI-DISCRIMINATION LAWS AND HOW TO USE THEM.   GNATLFC46048

  YOUR RIGHTS... UNDER STATE AND LOCAL FAIR-EMPLOYMENT-PRACTICES LAWS.   GNATLLS55051

  COMPILATION OF LAWS AGAINST DISCRIMINATION, A REFERENCE MANUAL.   GNEWYSA48078

  SUMMARY OF RULES, REGULATIONS, AND LAWS THAT AFFECT SEASONAL FARM WORKERS AND THEIR EMPLOYERS IN NEW-YORK
  STATE. /MIGRANT-WORKERS/   GNEWYSJN0113

  LAWS AGAINST DISCRIMINATION. EMPLOYMENT, PUBLIC ACCOMODATIONS, HOUSING. /OHIO/   GOHIOCR65125

  LAWS ADMINISTERED BY THE PENNSYLVANIA HUMAN-RELATIONS-COMMISSION.   GPENNHRND165

  ENFORCEMENT OF LAWS AGAINST DISCRIMINATION IN EMPLOYMENT.   GRABKSX64211

  EQUAL PROTECTION OF THE LAWS IN NORTH-CAROLINA.   GUSCOMC62397

  BRIEF SUMMARY OF STATE LAWS AGAINST DISCRIMINATION IN PRIVATE EMPLOYMENT. FAIR-EMPLOYMENT-PRACTICE ACTS. GUSDLAB63439

  COVERAGE OF AGRICULTURAL WORKERS UNDER STATE AND FEDERAL LAWS. /MIGRANT-WORKERS/   GUSDLAB64507

  STATE LAWS AGAINST DISCRIMINATION IN EDUCATION.   JHARTPX58730

  YOUR RIGHTS UNDER FAIR-EMPLOYMENT-PRACTICE LAWS. /UNION LEGISLATION/   NAFLCIO60004

  EFFECT OF SCHOOL ASSIGNMENT LAWS ON FEDERAL ADJUDICATION OF INTEGRATION CONTROVERSIES.   NCOLULR57224

LAWS   (CONTINUATION)
RIGHT-TO-WORK **LAWS** AND THE NEGRO WORKER.   NHILLHX58996

STATE **LAWS** AND THE NEGRO. SOCIAL CHANGE AND THE IMPACT OF LAW.   NHILLHX65545

HAVE FAIR-EMPLOYMENT-PRACTICES-COMMISSION **LAWS** INCREASED OPPORTUNITIES FOR NEGROES.   NLETTHA50683

FAIR-EMPLOYMENT-PRACTICE **LAWS** -- EXPERIENCE, EFFECTS, PROSPECTS.   NNORGPH67929

EQUAL PROTECTION OF THE **LAWS** IN PUBLIC HIGHER EDUCATION.   NUSCOMC60302

STATEMENT ON STATE **LAWS**. /EMPLOYMENT-CONDITIONS/   WDAVICX65720

WISCONSIN FAIR-EMPLOYMENT-PRACTICES DIVISION INQUIRY INTO THE CONFLICTS BETWEEN STATE PROTECTIVE LABOR
LEGISLATION AND STATE AND FEDERAL **LAWS** PROHIBITING DISCRIMINATION BASED ON SEX. /EMPLOYMENT-CONDITIONS/   WUAWXWD65165

STATEMENT ON WEIGHT LIFTING, HOURS, SENIORITY **LAWS** AND WOMEN. /EMPLOYMENT-CONDITIONS/   WUAWXWD66164

SUMMARY OF STATE LABOR **LAWS** FOR WOMEN.   WUSDLABND219

LAWS ON SEX DISCRIMINATION IN EMPLOYMENT.   WUSDLAB66K05

FRINGE BENEFIT PROVISIONS FROM STATE MINIMUM WAGE **LAWS** AND ORDERS, SEPTEMBER 1, 1966.
/EMPLOYMENT-CONDITIONS/   WUSDLAB66195

WHY STATE EQUAL-PAY **LAWS**.   WUSDLAB66230

LAWYER
THE NEGRO **LAWYER** IN VIRGINIA. A SURVEY. /OCCUPATIONS/   NFRIEMX65387

THE NEGRO **LAWYER** AND HIS CLIENTS. /OCCUPATIONS/   NHALEWH52476

LAWYERS
THE CAREER PATTERNS OF NEGRO **LAWYERS** IN LOUISIANA. /OCCUPATIONS/   NGUILBM60465

LAYOFFS
UNWANTED WORKERS. PERMANENT **LAYOFFS** AND LONG-TERM UNEMPLOYMENT. /NEGRO WOMEN/   CWILCKC63322

LEADER-S
THE AMERICAN DREAM...EQUAL OPPORTUNITY. A REPORT ON THE COMMUNITY **LEADER-S** CONFERENCE SPONSORED BY
PRESIDENT-S COMMITTEE ON EQUAL-EMPLOYMENT-OPPORTUNITY, MAY 19, 1962.   GPRESCD62105

LEADERS
REGIONAL COMMUNITY **LEADERS** CONFERENCE ON EQUAL-EMPLOYMENT-OPPORTUNITY, PROCEEDINGS.   GPRESCD64113

REPORT BY MEXICAN-AMERICAN **LEADERS**. EDUCATION, EMPLOYMENT, ETC.   MCALDIR64379

EDUCATION OF NEGRO **LEADERS**. INFLUENCES AFFECTING GRADUATE AND PROFESSIONAL STUDIES.   NCALIAX49174

SCHOOL-DESEGREGATION AND NEW INDUSTRY. THE SOUTHERN COMMUNITY **LEADERS** VIEWPOINT.   NCROMRX63243

SITUATIONAL PRESSURES AND FUNCTIONAL ROLE OF THE ETHNIC LABOR **LEADERS**. /UNION/   NGREESX53453

LEADERSHIP
TRADE UNION **LEADERSHIP** COUNCIL --EXPERIMENT IN COMMUNITY ACTION. /DETROIT MICHIGAN/   GBATTRX63426

PREJUDICE -- A THREAT TO THE **LEADERSHIP** ROLE.   GEVANRI62669

NEGRO **LEADERSHIP** IN RURAL GEORGIA COMMUNITIES. OCCUPATIONAL AND SOCIAL ASPECTS.   NEDWAVA42328

A CHALLENGE TO NEGRO **LEADERSHIP**.   NJOHNJG60618

TRADE UNION **LEADERSHIP** COUNCIL. EXPERIMENT IN COMMUNITY ACTION.   NNEWXUT63088

THE NEGRO **LEADERSHIP** CLASS.   NTHOMDC63713

PUERTO-RICAN **LEADERSHIP** IN NEW-YORK.   PGOTSJW66808

WANTED. MORE WOMEN IN EDUCATIONAL **LEADERSHIP**. /OCCUPATIONS/   WNATLCO65016

LEADING
HIRING NEGROES FOR BETTER JOBS. EXPERIENCE OF **LEADING** COMPANIES. /INDUSTRY/   NOPINRC64957

LEAGUE-OF-WOMEN-VOTE
ADDRESS BEFORE **LEAGUE-OF-WOMEN-VOTE**RS, JANUARY 7, 1965. /WORK-WOMAN-ROLE/   WFOWLGH65766

LEARN
WHAT MIGRANT FARM CHILDREN **LEARN**.   GCOLERX66133

LEARNER
THE CONTINUING **LEARNER**. /EDUCATION/   WSOLODX64128

LEARNING
NO FRONTIER TO **LEARNING**. THE MEXICAN STUDENT IN THE UNITED STATES.   MBEALRL57364

THE SPAN OF A WOMEN-S LIFE AND **LEARNING**. /WORK-WOMEN-ROLE/   WAMERCE60606

LEAVERS
OPPORTUNITIES AND REQUIREMENTS FOR INITIAL EMPLOYMENT OF SCHOOL **LEAVERS**. WITH EMPHASIS ON OFFICE AND
RETAIL JOBS. /EMPLOYMENT-SELECTION/   WCOOKFS66705

LEFT
NEGROES AND THE LABOR MOVEMENT. RECORD OF THE **LEFT** WING UNIONS.   NDOYLWX62287

LEFT SECTARIANISM IN THE FIGHT FOR NEGRO RIGHTS AND AGAINST WHITE CHAUVINISM.   NFOSTWZ53375

LEGACY
LEGACY OF THE JEWISH LABOR MOVEMENT.   JTYLEGX65766

LEGAL
EQUALITY BY STATUTES -- **LEGAL** CONTROLS OVER GROUP DISCRIMINATION.   GBERGMX52440

LEGAL DISADVANTAGES OF MIGRATORY WORKERS.   GGIVERA65695

LEGAL RULINGS INTERPRETING THE PROVISIONS OF THE PENNSYLVANIA FAIR-EMPLOYMENT-PRACTICE ACT. GPENNFE58153

LEGAL SANCTIONS AGAINST JOB DISCRIMINATION.   GSIMOCK46311

LEGAL RESTRAINTS ON RACIAL DISCRIMINATION IN EMPLOYMENT.   GSOVEMI66326

LEGAL (CONTINUATION)
DIGEST OF **LEGAL** INTERPRETATIONS ISSUED OR ADOPTED BY THE COMMISSION OCTOBER 9, 1965 THROUGH DECEMBER 31, 1965.   GUSEEOC66509

ADDRESS AT THE CONVOCATION OF THE NAACP **LEGAL** DEFENSE AND EDUCATIONAL FUND. /LEGISLATION/   GWIRTWW66570

THE ROLE OF LAW IN SECURING EQUAL-EMPLOYMENT-OPPORTUNITY. **LEGAL** POWERS AND SOCIAL CHANGE.   NHILLHX66544

LEGAL EDUCATION. DESEGREGATION IN LAW SCHOOLS.   NLEFLRA57676

THE **LEGAL** STATUS OF THE NEGRO.   NMANGCS40735

WOMEN IN **LEGAL** WORK. /OCCUPATIONS/   WGRIFVE58804

REALITIES. EDUCATIONAL, ECONOMIC, **LEGAL** AND PERSONAL NEEDS OF CAREER WOMEN.   WPARKRX66049

LEGAL-STATUS
THE **LEGAL-STATUS** OF THE NEGRO IN THE UNITED STATES.   NMOTLCB66859

LEGALITY
LEGALITY AND VALIDITY OF PERSONNEL TESTS. /LEGISLATION TITLE-VII/   GVINCNX66113

LEGISLATION
NLRB-FEPC. /**LEGISLATION**/   GALBEJM63367

ANTIDISCRIMINATION **LEGISLATION** AS AN INFRINGEMENT OF FREEDOM OF CHOICE.   GAVINAX60409

FREEDOM OF CHOICE IN PERSONAL SERVICE OCCUPATIONS. 13TH AMENDMENT LIMITATIONS ON ANTIDISCRIMINATION
LEGISLATION.   GAVINAX64410

THE RIGHT TO EQUAL TREATMENT. ADMINISTRATIVE ENFORCEMENT OF ANTIDISCRIMINATION **LEGISLATION**.   GBAMBMA61416

FAIR-EMPLOYMENT-PRACTICES **LEGISLATION** OF EIGHT STATES AND TWO CITIES.   GBERGMX51441

PROCESSING EMPLOYMENT DISCRIMINATION CASES. /**LEGISLATION**/   GBLUMAW67117

THE ROLE OF **LEGISLATION** IN ELIMINATING RACIAL DISCRIMINATION.   GBONFAE65462

THE SUBSTANCE OF AMERICAN FAIR-EMPLOYMENT-PRACTICES **LEGISLATION**. II. EMPLOYMENT-AGENCIES, LABOR
ORGANIZATIONS, AND OTHERS.   GBONFAE67136

THE SUBSTANCE OF AMERICAN FAIR-EMPLOYMENT-PRACTICES **LEGISLATION**. I. EMPLOYERS.   GBONFAE67137

FAIR-EMPLOYMENT **LEGISLATION** IN NEW-YORK STATE. ITS HISTORY, DEVELOPMENT, AND SUGGESTED USE ELSEWHERE.   GBRADPX46247

RACE-RELATIONS AND ANTI-DISCRIMINATORY **LEGISLATION**.   GBURMJH51500

THE NLRB AND RACIAL DISCRIMINATION. /**LEGISLATION**/   GCARTRX65560

OUTLOOK REGARDING STATE FEPC **LEGISLATION**.   GCOBBCW46578

TITLE-VII. RELATIONSHIP AND EFFECT ON THE NATIONAL-LABOR- RELATIONS-BOARD. /**LEGISLATION**/   GFUCHRS66702

ANTI-DISCRIMINATION **LEGISLATION** IN THE AMERICAN STATES.   GGRAVWB48734

FEPC **LEGISLATION** IN THE UNITED STATES, FEDERAL, STATE, MUNICIPAL.   GGRAVWB51735

LEGISLATION AGAINST RACIAL OR RELIGIOUS DISCRIMINATION IN EMPLOYMENT, NEW-YORK.   GIVESLM52819

LABOR LAW -- UNION MEMBERSHIP DENIED ON THE BASIS OF RACIAL DISCRIMINATION. /WISCONSIN **LEGISLATION**/   GKAUFET58014

MANAGEMENT-S CONCERN WITH RECENT CIVIL-RIGHTS **LEGISLATION** AFFECTING MANAGEMENT-S OBLIGATIONS TO HIS
EMPLOYEES AND APPLICANTS FOR EMPLOYMENT, MAINLY IN THE STATE OF NEW-YORK.   GKOPPRW65858

THE EFFECT OF STATE FAIR-EMPLOYMENT **LEGISLATION** ON THE ECONOMIC POSITION OF NONWHITE MALES.   GLANDWM66883

LEGISLATION OUTLAWING RACIAL DISCRIMINATION IN EMPLOYMENT.   GLAWYGR45886

THE POLITICS OF ANTIDISCRIMINATION **LEGISLATION**.   GLOCKDX65146

TITLE-VII. RELATIONSHIP AND EFFECT ON EXECUTIVE ORDER 11246. /**LEGISLATION**/   GMANNRD66937

FEP **LEGISLATION** AND ENFORCEMENT IN THE US.   GMEANJE66971

FAIR-EMPLOYMENT-PRACTICES **LEGISLATION**.   GMEINRG57066

MINNESOTA STATE ACT AGAINST DISCRIMINATION, AS APPROVED BY THE MINNESOTA LEGISLATURE, APRIL 1961.
/**LEGISLATION**/   GMINNSCND010

FAIR-EMPLOYMENT-PRACTICES **LEGISLATION**. A SUMMARY OF ITS HISTORY AND DEVELOPMENT WITH STATEMENTS ON BOTH
SIDES.   GMITCJA52016

AN ANALYSIS OF STATE FEPC **LEGISLATION**.   GMORGCA57031

SELECTED ANNOTATED REFERENCES ON FAIR-EMPLOYMENT-PRACTICES **LEGISLATION**.   GNELSRJ52055

REPORT WITH RECOMMENDATIONS ON THE SUBJECT OF FEDERAL FAIR-EMPLOYMENT-PRACTICES **LEGISLATION**.   GNEWYCB53069

FEDERAL **LEGISLATION** FOR A COMPREHENSIVE PROGRAM ON YOUTH EMPLOYMENT.   GNIXORA66847

STATEMENT TO THE COMMITTEE ON LEGISLATION IN SUPPORT OF AN EFFECTIVE FEDERAL FEP LAW AND OTHER VITAL
CIVIL-RIGHTS **LEGISLATION**.   GOLIVWX60134

STATEMENT TO THE COMMITTEE ON **LEGISLATION** IN SUPPORT OF AN EFFECTIVE FEDERAL FEP LAW AND OTHER VITAL
CIVIL-RIGHTS LEGISLATION.   GOLIVWX60134

TITLE-VII. REPORTING AND RECORD KEEPING. /**LEGISLATION**/   GPEARHG66149

DISCRIMINATION IN UNION MEMBERSHIP. DENIAL OF DUE PROCESS UNDER FEDERAL COLLECTIVE BARGAINING
LEGISLATION.   GPRESSB58126

TITLE-VII. RELATIONSHIP AND EFFECT ON STATE ACTION. /**LEGISLATION**/   GPURDJW66209

TITLE-VII. LIMITATIONS AND QUALIFICATIONS. /**LEGISLATION**/   GRACHCX66214

TITLE-VII. COVERAGE AND COMMENTS. /**LEGISLATION**/   GSCHMCT66287

FREEDOM TO WORK. /FEPC **LEGISLATION**/   GSMITSX55320

LEGISLATION   (CONTINUATION)
STATE LEGISLATION IN LABOR-RELATIONS AND DISCRIMINATION IN EMPLOYMENT, 1945.   GSPITRS45332

LABOR UNIONS AND FAIR-EMPLOYMENT-PRACTICES LEGISLATION.   GTIMBEX54357

HIRING AND PROMOTION SYSTEMS UNDER FAIR-EMPLOYMENT-PRACTICES LEGISLATION.   GUSOLAB67116

THE DYNAMICS OF STATE CAMPAIGNS FOR FAIR-EMPLOYMENT-PRACTICES LEGISLATION.   GUVCHCE50211

LEGALITY AND VALIDITY OF PERSONNEL TESTS. /LEGISLATION TITLE-VII/   GVINCNX66113

TITLE-VII. COMPLAINT PROCEDURES AND REMEDIES. /LEGISLATION/   GWALKRW66538

ADDRESS AT THE CONVOCATION OF THE NAACP LEGAL DEFENSE AND EDUCATIONAL FUND. /LEGISLATION/   GWIRTWW66570

YOUR RIGHTS UNDER FAIR-EMPLOYMENT-PRACTICE LAWS. /UNION LEGISLATION/   NAFLCIO60004

RACIAL DISCRIMINATION BY A UNION AGAINST EMPLOYEES IT DOES NOT REPRESENT. /LEGISLATION/   NCOLULR52226

RACIAL DISCRIMINATION AND THE DUTY OF FAIR REPRESENTATION. /LEGISLATION/   NCOLULR65225

DUAL PARTS OF DESEGREGATION. LEGISLATION TO EDUCATE AND TRAIN NEGROES FOR BETTER JOBS.   NDUSCJX63311

STATE FAIR-EMPLOYMENT-PRACTICE LEGISLATION UNCONSTITUTIONALLY BURDENS INTERSTATE COMMERCE WHEN APPLIED TO
INTERSTATE AIRLINE.   NHARVLR62499

UNITED STATES HAS STANDING UNDER INTERSTATE COMMERCE ACT AND COMMERCE CLAUSE TO ENJOIN SEGREGATIVE
PRACTICES OF CITY. /LEGISLATION/   NHARVLR64500

THE NATIONAL-LABOR-RELATIONS ACT-AND RACIAL DISCRIMINATION. /LEGISLATION/   NMOLIRL66807

AMENDMENTS TO THE TAFT-HARTLEY. A REJECTION OF RACIAL DISCRIMINATION. /LEGISLATION/   NOSHAJB54964

FAIR-EMPLOYMENT-PRACTICES LEGISLATION.   NPARKRX48974

THE NEGRO AND TITLE-VII. /LEGISLATION/   NPERSPF65562

STATEMENT TO THE NEW-YORK STATE ADVISORY COMMITTEE TO THE US COMMISSION ON CIVIL-RIGHTS, MAY 23, 1966.
/EMPLOYMENT LEGISLATION/   NPOLIEX66004

THE NATIONAL-LABOR-RELATIONS-ACT AND RACIAL DISCRIMINATION. /LEGISLATION/   NSOVEMI62168

RACE DISCRIMINATION AND THE NLRA ACT. THE BRAVE NEW WORLD OF MIRANDA. /LEGISLATION/   NSOVEMI63169

LEGISLATION AGAINST DISCRIMINATION IN EMPLOYMENT.   NUSOLAB45825

ANTI-DISCRIMINATION LEGISLATION IN 1947.   NUSOLAB47810

ANTI-DISCRIMINATION LEGISLATION.   NUSOLAB48149

REPORT OF THE COMMITTEE ON PROTECTIVE LABOR LEGISLATION, 1963.   WPRESCO63069

WISCONSIN FAIR-EMPLOYMENT-PRACTICES DIVISION INQUIRY INTO THE CONFLICTS BETWEEN STATE PROTECTIVE LABOR
LEGISLATION AND STATE AND FEDERAL LAWS PROHIBITING DISCRIMINATION BASED ON SEX. /EMPLOYMENT-CONDITIONS/ WUAWXWD65165

SEX AND THE CIVIL-RIGHTS-ACT. /LEGISLATION/   WUHLXGX66200

DIGEST OF STATE LEGISLATION OF SPECIAL INTEREST TO WOMEN WORKERS.   WUSOLABND191

LEGISLATIVE
THE CIVIL-RIGHTS-ACT OF 1964. WHAT IT MEANS -- TO EMPLOYERS, BUSINESSMEN, UNIONS, EMPLOYEES,
MINORITY-GROUPS. TEXT, ANALYSIS, LEGISLATIVE HISTORY.   GBUREON64492

REPORT OF NEW-YORK STATE JOINT LEGISLATIVE COMMITTEE ON MIGRANT-LABOR.   GNEWYSLND115

TITLE-VII. LEGISLATIVE HISTORY.   GVAASFJ66534

THE PROPOSED LEGISLATIVE DEATH KNELL OF PRIVATE DISCRIMINATORY EMPLOYMENT PRACTICES.   GWILSAX45566

A STUDY OF STATE AND LOCAL LEGISLATIVE AND ADMINISTRATIVE ACTS DESIGNED TO MEET PROBLEMS OF HUMAN-RIGHTS. GWISCLR52573

THE CIVIL-RIGHTS FIGHT. A LOOK AT THE LEGISLATIVE RECORD.   NAFLCIO60005

LEGISLATURE
REPORT TO THE GOVERNOR AND THE LEGISLATURE OF THE COMMISSION ON MANPOWER, AUTOMATION AND TECHNOLOGY,
1964. /CALIFORNIA/   GCALCMA65515

MINNESOTA STATE ACT AGAINST DISCRIMINATION, AS APPROVED BY THE MINNESOTA LEGISLATURE, APRIL 1961.
/LEGISLATION/   GMINNSCND010

STATEMENT BEFORE CALIFORNIA LEGISLATURE ASSEMBLY, INTERIM SUBCOMMITTEE ON ECONOMIC OPPORTUNITY ON BEHALF
OF CHINATOWN-NORTH BEACH DISTRICT COUNCIL.   OWONGLJ64771

LENGTH
ILLINOIS JOB SEEKERS SURVEY. EDUCATION, SKILLS, LENGTH OF UNEMPLOYMENT, AND PERSONAL CHARACTERISTICS.   GILLIDI62004

LESSON
PRINCETON-S LESSON. SCHOOL INTEGRATION IS NOT ENOUGH. /NEW-JERSEY/   GSTREPX64337

LESSONS
LESSONS FROM THE PATTERNS OF UNEMPLOYMENT IN THE LAST FIVE YEARS.   GBANCGX66752

PROVING GROUND FOR FAIR-EMPLOYMENT. SOME LESSONS FROM NEW-YORK STATE-S EXPERIENCE.   GNORTHR47123

THE INEFFECTIVE SOLDIER. LESSONS FOR MANAGEMENT AND THE NATION.   NGINZEX59406

SOME LESSONS FROM WATTS. /LOS-ANGELES CALIFORNIA/   NRUSTBX66098

LEVEL
EDUCATION, SKILL LEVEL, AND EARNINGS OF THE HIRED FARM WORKING FORCE OF 1961.   GCOWHJD63420

PROVING DISCRIMINATION AT THE COMMISSION LEVEL.   GLAMBWH66857

RESOURCE CHARACTERISTICS AND UTILIZATION AND LEVEL OF LIVING ITEMS, RURAL HOUSEHOLDS, NORTH AND WEST
FLORIDA, 1956.   GREUSLA60391

LEVEL OF OCCUPATIONAL ASPIRATIONS AMONG MONTANA INDIANS IN GRADE AND HIGH SCHOOL.   IDOUGGV60550

THE UNEMPLOYMENT RATE AND GRADE LEVEL RELATIONSHIP IN CHICAGO AS REVEALED IN THE 1960 CENSUS. /ILLINOIS/ NHARGAJ65990

LEVEL   (CONTINUATION)
THE EFFECT OF THE GHETTO ON THE DISTRIBUTION AND **LEVEL** OF NONWHITE EMPLOYMENT IN URBAN AREAS.   NKAINJF64631

THE RELATION OF RACIAL SEGREGATION IN EARLY SCHOOLING TO THE **LEVEL** OF ASPIRATION AND ACADEMIC ACHIEVEMENT
OF NEGRO STUDENTS IN A NORTHERN HIGH SCHOOL.   NSAINJN62137

A COMPARATIVE STUDY OF TOP **LEVEL** MALE AND FEMALE EXECUTIVES IN HARRIS-COUNTY. /TEXAS OCCUPATIONS/   WDOLLPA65738

WOMEN GRADUATES OF COOPERATIVE WORK-STUDY PROGRAMS ON THE COLLEGE **LEVEL**. /SKILLS/   WMOSBWB57999

TOP **LEVEL** TRAINING OF WOMEN IN THE UNITED STATES, 1900-60.   WPARRJB62283

MARRIED WOMEN AND THE **LEVEL** OF UNEMPLOYMENT.   WSTEIRL61226

SALARIED WOMEN IN UPPER **LEVEL** POSITIONS IN KANSAS BUSINESS FIRMS.   WSTOCFT59143

THE MOTIVATION FOR WOMEN TO WORK IN HIGH **LEVEL** PROFESSIONAL POSITIONS.   WWALTDE62314

LEVELS
URBAN AND RURAL **LEVELS** OF LIVING. 1960. /ECONOMIC-STATUS/   GCOWHJD65425

LEVELS OF LIVING AMONG WHITES AND NON-WHITES IN THE U.S.   GCOWHJD65614

THE RISING **LEVELS** OF EDUCATION AMONG YOUNG WORKERS.   GCOWHJD65933

SOME EDUCATIONAL IMPLICATIONS OF THE INFLUENCE OF REJECTION ON ASPIRATION **LEVELS** OF MINORITY-GROUP
CHILDREN.   GGOFFRM54366

THE MUTUAL SAVINGS BANKS OF NEW-YORK-CITY. A FOLLOW-UP REPORT ON THE EXCLUSION OF JEWS AT TOP-MANAGEMENT
AND POLICY-MAKING **LEVELS**.   JAMERJC66695

LEVELS OF LIVING OF SPANISH-AMERICAN RURAL AND URBAN FAMILIES IN TWO SOUTH TEXAS COUNTIES.   MCLEMHM63381

OCCUPATIONAL AND EDUCATIONAL **LEVELS** OF ASPIRATION OF MEXICAN-AMERICAN YOUTH.   MDEHOAX61388

LEVELS OF ASPIRATION OF MEXICAN-AMERICANS IN EL-PASO SCHOOLS. /TEXAS/   MNALLFX59447

NEW-MEXICO COUNTY INDUSTRIAL COMPOSITION AND **LEVELS** OF LIVING.   MSANOAD63479

WORKING AT IMPROVING THE MOTIVATIONAL AND ACHIEVEMENT **LEVELS** OF THE DEPRIVED.   NHARREC63367

ASPIRATION **LEVELS** OF NEGRO DELINQUENT, DEPENDENT, AND PUBLIC SCHOOL BOYS.   NMITCLE57804

LIBERAL
LIBERAL ARTS WOMEN GRADUATES. CLASS OF 1958. /WORK-WOMEN-ROLE/   WLICHMW59933

LIBERALISM
LIBERALISM AND THE NEGRO. /ASPIRATIONS/   NCOMMXX64467

THE NEW CHALLENGE TO **LIBERALISM**.   NTYLEGX63539

LIBERALS
NEGRO MILITANTS, JEWISH **LIBERALS**, AND THE UNIONS.   NBROOTR61121

LIBERTIES
CIVIL-RIGHTS AND **LIBERTIES** AND LABOR UNIONS.   GRAUHJL57217

LIBERTY
LIBERTY IN THE BIG CORPORATION.   GWESTAF61557

LIBRARIANS
CHARACTERISTICS OF NEGRO COLLEGE CHIEF **LIBRARIANS**. /OCCUPATIONS/   NPOLLFM64005

LIBRARIES
SPECIAL WOMEN-S COLLECTIONS IN US **LIBRARIES**.   WBELLMS59636

LIBRARY
LIBRARY RESOURCES AND SERVICES IN WHITE AND NEGRO COLLEGES. /EDUCATION/   NSAMOTX65128

LIFE
LIFE INSURANCE. THE PATIENT IMPROVES. /DISCRIMINATION/   GANTIDL59399

LIFE INSURANCE COMPANIES. /DISCRIMINATION/   GANTIDL62398

ASSIMILATION IN AMERICAN **LIFE**. THE ROLE OF RACE, RELIGION, AND NATIONAL ORIGINS.   GGORDMM64729

RACE AND NATIONALITY IN AMERICAN **LIFE**.   GHANDOX57758

UNEMPLOYMENT AS A WAY OF **LIFE**.   GJACOPX66527

INDIANS AND OTHER AMERICANS, TWO WAYS OF **LIFE** MEET.   IFEYXHE59558

THE ECONOMIC BASIS OF INDIAN **LIFE**. /INCOME LABOR-FORCE/   IKELLWH57076

LIFE ON THE BLACKFEET INDIAN RESERVATION TODAY.   IMUSEPI57593

ECONOMIC STRUCTURE AND THE **LIFE** OF THE JEWS.   JKUZNSX60738

GLIMPSES OF JEWISH **LIFE** IN SAN-FRANCISCO. /CALIFORNIA/   JZARCMM64776

PERCEIVED **LIFE** CHANCES IN THE OPPORTUNITY STRUCTURE. A STUDY OF A TRI-ETHNIC HIGH SCHOOL.   MGUERCX62410

NEGRO FAMILY **LIFE** IN AMERICA.   NBILLAX65499

BLACK METROPOLIS. A STUDY OF NEGRO **LIFE** IN A NORTHERN CITY.   NDRAKSC45291

THE NEGRO-S NEW ECONOMIC **LIFE**.   NHUGHEJ56583

VOCATIONAL ORIENTATION TOWARD A REWARDING **LIFE**.   NJONEAM65622

CULTURE, CLASS AND FAMILY **LIFE** AMONG LOW-INCOME NEGROES.   NLEWIHX67691

FOUNDATIONS OF RACISM IN AMERICAN **LIFE**.   NODELJH64953

HOUGH, CLEVELAND, OHIO -- A STUDY OF SOCIAL **LIFE** AND CHANGE.   NSUSSMB59192

READJUSTMENTS OF VETERANS TO CIVILIAN **LIFE**.   NUSDLAB46839

NEGRO FAMILIES IN RURAL WISCONSIN, A STUDY OF THEIR COMMUNITY **LIFE**.   NWISCGC59331

LIFE   (CONTINUATION)
   CHINESE IN AMERICAN LIFE. SOME ASPECTS OF THEIR HISTORY, STATUS, PROBLEMS AND CONTRIBUTIONS.   OKUNGSW62737

   LIFE AMONG THE GARMENT WORKERS.   PBRAEPX58782

   THE SPAN OF A WOMEN-S LIFE AND LEARNING. /WORK-WOMEN-ROLE/   WAMERCE60606

   LIFE GOALS AND VOCATIONAL CHOICE. /WORK-WOMAN-ROLE/   WASTIAW64620

   THE POST-PARENTAL PHASE IN THE LIFE CYCLE OF 50 COLLEGE EDUCATED WOMEN. /WORK-FAMILY-CONFLICT/   WDAVIIX60717

   EDUCATION AND A WOMAN-S LIFE. /WORK-WOMAN-ROLE/   WDENNLE63729

   TABLES OF WORKING LIFE FOR WOMEN, 1950.   WGARFSH57180

   LIFE STYLES OF EDUCATED WOMEN. /WORK-FAMILY-CONFLICT/   WGINZEX66785

   LIFE INSURANCE SELLING AS A CAREER FOR WOMEN. /OCCUPATIONS/   WLEITSF61926

   ATTITUDES TOWARD CAREER AND MARRIAGE AND THE DEVELOPMENT OF LIFE STYLES IN YOUNG WOMEN.
   /WORK-FAMILY-CONFLICT/   WMATTEX64962

   EDUCATION AND A WOMAN-S LIFE.   WMONSKJ63987

   WOMEN-S CHANGING ROLES THROUGH THE LIFE CYCLE.   WNEUGBL59025

   ROLE OF WOMEN IN AMERICAN ECONOMIC LIFE.   WNORRLW56036

   A NEW LIFE PATTERN FOR THE COLLEGE-EDUCATED WOMAN. /WORK-FAMILY-CONFLICT/   WSTEIER65133

   A STUDY OF THE LIFE PLANNING OF 550 FRESHMEN WOMEN AT PURDUE UNIVERSITY. /WORK-FAMILY-CONFLICT/   WZISSCX64285

LIFE-STYLE
   A DEMONSTRATION PROJECT DESIGNED TO TEST THE LIFE-STYLE AND THE GROWTH POTENTIAL OF URBAN DROPOUTS FROM
   DISADVANTAGED HOMES.   GCLEAMP66130

   SPANISH-AMERICANS OF THE SOUTHWEST. LIFE-STYLE PATTERNS AND THEIR IMPLICATIONS.   MHAYDRG66114

LIFETIME
   LIFETIME AND RECENT MIGRATION. /DEMOGRAPHY/   CUSBURC63172

   LIFETIME INCOME AND ECONOMIC GROWTH.   NMILLHP65782

LIFTING
   STATEMENT ON WEIGHT LIFTING, HOURS, SENIORITY LAWS AND WOMEN. /EMPLOYMENT-CONDITIONS/   WUAWXWD66164

LIMIT
   THE UPPER LIMIT OF ABILITY AMONG AMERICAN NEGROES.   NJENKMD48607

LIMITATIONS
   FREEDOM OF CHOICE IN PERSONAL SERVICE OCCUPATIONS. 13TH AMENDMENT LIMITATIONS ON ANTIDISCRIMINATION
   LEGISLATION.   GAVINAX64410

   STATISTICS ON APPRENTICESHIP AND THEIR LIMITATIONS.   GGROOPX64745

   TITLE-VII. LIMITATIONS AND QUALIFICATIONS. /LEGISLATION/   GRACHCX66214

   THE CALIFORNIA FAIR-EMPLOYMENT-PRACTICES-COMMISSION. ITS HISTORY, ACCOMPLISHMENTS, AND LIMITATIONS.   GTOBRMC63361

   THE NEGRO WORKER-S CULTURAL AND OCCUPATIONAL LIMITATIONS.   NMCPICM61729

LIMITED
   THE LIMITED POTENTIAL FOR NEGRO-WHITE JOB EQUALITY.   NCHALWE65188

LIMITS
   CIVIL-RIGHTS AND THE LIMITS OF LAW.   GFREUPA64700

   THE ROLE AND LIMITS OF NATIONAL MANPOWER POLICIES.   GWEBEAR66760

LINK
   CRAFT UNIONS. A LINK IN THE CIRCLE OF NEGRO DISCRIMINATION.   NBLOCHC57088

LIST
   SELECTED LIST OF REFERENCES ON MINORITY-GROUP EMPLOYMENT IN THE PUBLIC SERVICE.   GSIMPDX64312

   A SELECTED LIST OF REFERENCES RELATING TO DISCRIMINATION AND SEGREGATION IN EDUCATION, 1949 TO JUNE 1955.   NTUSKIX55220

LITERACY
   LITERACY, AND THE NEGRO AND WORLD-WAR-II.   NAPTHHX46028

LITERATURE
   A SURVEY OF CURRENT LITERATURE ON AUTOMATION AND OTHER TECHNOLOGICAL-CHANGES. A SELECTED ANNOTATED
   BIBLIOGRAPHY.   GUSDLAB64825

   THE PROBLEM OF CULTURAL BIAS IN SELECTION. I. BACKGROUND AND LITERATURE. /TESTING/   NCAMPJT65179

LITIGATION
   THE INDIVIDUAL RIGHT TO ELIMINATE EMPLOYMENT DISCRIMINATION BY LITIGATION.   GBLUMAW66566

LITTLE-ROCK
   TWO PLANTS -- LITTLE-ROCK. /CASE-STUDY INDUSTRY ARKANSAS/   NECKAEW55319

LIVE
   SENIOR CITIZENS AND HOW THEY LIVE. AN ANALYSIS OF 1960 CENSUS DATA. PART II. THE AGING NONWHITE AND HIS
   HOUSING. /ECONOMIC-STATUS/   GUSHHFX63321

   PLACING INDIANS WHO LIVE ON RESERVATIONS. A COOPERATIVE PROGRAM.   IUSDLAB59667

LIVES
   DIGEST OF CASE STUDIES ON CONTINUITIES AND DISCONTINUITIES IN THE EMPLOYMENT-EDUCATION-FAMILY PATTERNS OF
   WOMEN-S LIVES.   WDELAPJ60224

   CHANGING PATTERNS IN WOMEN-S LIVES IN 1960. /WORK-WOMAN-ROLE/   WHAWKAL60834

   CHANGING REALITIES IN WOMEN-S LIVES. /WORK-WOMAN-ROLE/   WKEYSMD65893

   FACING THE FACTS ABOUT WOMEN-S LIVES TODAY. /WORK-WOMAN-ROLE/   WKEYSMD65895

   SOURCES OF SATISFACTION IN THE LIVES OF WORKING WOMEN.   WLAURMW61923

LIVES   (CONTINUATION)
   WORK IN THE LIVES OF MARRIED WOMEN.   WNATLMC57021

   ONE WOMAN. TWO LIVES. /WORK-FAMILY-CONFLICT/   WTIMEXX61155

   CHANGING CULTURAL CONCEPTS IN WOMEN-S LIVES. /WORK-WOMAN-ROLE/   WUSEERH64255

LIVING
   URBAN AND RURAL LEVELS OF LIVING. 1960. /ECONOMIC-STATUS/   GCOWHJD65425

   LEVELS OF LIVING AMONG WHITES AND NON-WHITES IN THE U.S.   GCOWHJD65614

   RESOURCE CHARACTERISTICS AND UTILIZATION AND LEVEL OF LIVING ITEMS, RURAL HOUSEHOLDS, NORTH AND WEST
   FLORIDA, 1956.   GREUSLA60391

   POPULATION CHARACTERISTICS, LIVING CONDITIONS AND INCOME OF INDIAN FAMILIES, NORTHERN-CHEYENNE
   RESERVATION, JULY, 1961.   IUSDINT63656

   POPULATION CHARACTERISTICS, LIVING CONDITIONS, AND INCOME OF INDIAN FAMILIES, FORT-PECK RESERVATION,
   1951-1961.   IUSDINT63657

   POPULATION CHARACTERISTICS, LIVING CONDITIONS AND INCOMES OF INDIAN FAMILIES, FORT-BELKNAP RESERVATION.   IUSDINT63658

   POPULATION CHARACTERISTICS, LIVING CONDITIONS AND INCOMES OF INDIAN FAMILIES, ROCKY-BAY-S RESERVATION.   IUSDINT63659

   LEVELS OF LIVING OF SPANISH-AMERICAN RURAL AND URBAN FAMILIES IN TWO SOUTH TEXAS COUNTIES.   MCLEMHM63381

   NEW-MEXICO COUNTY INDUSTRIAL COMPOSITION AND LEVELS OF LIVING.   MSANDAC63479

   RECENT SOUTHERN INDUSTRIALIZATION AND ITS IMPLICATIONS FOR NEGROES LIVING IN THE SOUTH.
   /EMPLOYMENT-TRENDS/   NCHICCA53204

   A HISTORICAL REVIEW OF THE IMPACT OF SOCIAL AND ECONOMIC STRUCTURE ON NEGRO CULTURE AND HOW IT INFLUENCES
   FAMILY LIVING.   NJACKJX64596

   A WOMAN-S GUIDE TO EARNING A GOOD LIVING.   WWINTEX61270

LOAN
   PATTERNS OF DISCRIMINATION IN THE FINANCIAL INSTITUTIONS OF THE DISTRICT-OF-COLUMBIA. THE BANKING,
   SAVINGS AND LOAN, AND INSURANCE INDUSTRIES.   GDISTCC66642

LOANS
   APPROACHES TO INCOME IMPROVEMENT. EXPERIENCES OF FAMILIES RECEIVING PRODUCTION LOANS UNDER THE FARMERS
   HOME ADMINISTRATION.   GHENOWE59422

LOCAL
   FEPC. AN ADMINISTRATIVE STUDY OF SELECTED STATE AND LOCAL PROGRAMS.   GALFOAL54869

   STATE AND LOCAL CONTRACTS AND SUBCONTRACTS.   GCONWJE64599

   LOCAL REGULATION OF DISCRIMINATORY EMPLOYMENT PRACTICES.   GELSOAX47661

   CALIFORNIA LOCAL GOVERNMENT AND INTEGRATION.   GFORDJA63695

   LOCAL CONTRACTS AND SUB-CONTRACTS. THE ROLES OF CITY GOVERNMENT AND PRIVATE CITIZENS GROUPS.   GJONEMX64829

   MISSOURI LOCAL GOVERNMENT ACTION IN THE AREA OF HUMAN-RIGHTS.   GMISSCH63022

   WHAT TITLE-VII MEANS FOR THE LOCAL OFFICE. /SES/   GMITCHR66018

   DIGEST OF FINDINGS FROM A WORKING CONFERENCE OF LOCAL COUNCILS. /FEPC/   GNATLCS45045

   YOUR RIGHTS... UNDER STATE AND LOCAL FAIR-EMPLOYMENT-PRACTICES LAWS.   GNATLLS55051

   HANDBOOK FOR LOCAL UNION FAIR PRACTICES COMMITTEES. REVISED EDITION.   GUAWXFPND369

   HOW ACCURATE ARE ESTIMATES OF STATE AND LOCAL UNEMPLOYMENT.   GULLMJX63975

   A STUDY OF STATE AND LOCAL LEGISLATIVE AND ADMINISTRATIVE ACTS DESIGNED TO MEET PROBLEMS OF HUMAN-RIGHTS. GWISCLR52573

   FEDERAL INDIAN POLICY AS IT AFFECTS LOCAL INDIAN AFFAIRS.   IMCKIFX64086

   DEALING WITH INTER-RACIAL TENSIONS ON LOCAL UNION GRASS ROOTS BASIS.   NANDEEC50894

   LABOR-S GRASS ROOTS. A STUDY OF THE LOCAL UNION.   NBARBJX61052

   A SOCIOLOGICAL ANALYSIS OF A BI-RACIAL LOCAL LABOR UNION.   NMERCJJ56768

   OPINION BY HONORABLE BENJAMIN LENCHER. CITY OF PITTSBURGH VS PLUMBERS LOCAL UNION NO 27. /PENNSYLVANIA/   NPITTLJ65001

   THE JOB HUNT. JOB SEEKING BEHAVIOR OF UNEMPLOYED WORKERS IN A LOCAL ECONOMY.   NSHEPHL66128

   PUERTO-RICAN INTEGRATION IN A GARMENT UNION LOCAL.   PHELFRB57815

   HELP WANTED — FEMALE. A STUDY OF DEMAND AND SUPPLY IN A LOCAL JOB MARKET FOR WOMEN. /MANPOWER/   WSMITGM64121

LOCALS
   NLRB DECERTIFIES RACIALLY SEGREGATED UNION LOCALS.   NCHECOX64890

   UNION LOCALS AND THE UNDER-UTILIZATION OF NEGRO WORKERS.   NJONEBA66884

   AN ANALYSIS OF THE IMPLEMENTATION OF THE UAW-CIO-S FAIR PRACTICES AND ANTI-DISCRIMINATION POLICIES IN
   SELECTED CHICAGO LOCALS. /UNION/   NJONEJE51883

LOCATION
   NEGRO FARM OPERATORS. NUMBER, LOCATION AND RECENT TRENDS.   NBEALCL58064

LOCKHEED
   CARRYING OUT A PLAN FOR JOB INTEGRATION AND DOING IT -- IN THE HEART OF GEORGIA -- WITHOUT A SINGLE
   UNPLEASANT INCIDENT. THAT-S THE EXPERIENCE OF LOCKHEED AIRCRAFT CORPORATION AT ITS MARIETTA PLANT.
   /INDUSTRY/   NBUSIWX63148

   REPORT AND SUMMARY OF THE AIR FORCE ON ACTIONS TAKEN BY LOCKHEED AIRCRAFT CORPORATION AT THE AIR FORCE
   PLANT NO 6 IN MARIETTA, GEORGIA. /INDUSTRY/   NPRESCO61013

LOCKHEED-AIRCRAFT-CO
   PLAN FOR EQUAL-JOB-OPPORTUNITY AT LOCKHEED-AIRCRAFT-CORP. /INDUSTRY CASE-STUDY/   NUSDLAB61838

LONG-RANGE
   LONG-RANGE CAUSES AND CONSEQUENCES OF THE EMPLOYMENT OF MARRIED WOMEN.   WBLOORC65884

LONG-TERM
  UNWANTED WORKERS. PERMANENT LAYOFFS AND **LONG-TERM** UNEMPLOYMENT. /NEGRO WOMEN/   CWILCRC63322

  LONG-TERM MANPOWER PROJECTIONS.   GGORDRA64525

  LONG-TERM MANPOWER PROJECTIONS. PROCEEDINGS OF A CONFERENCE CONDUCTED BY THE RESEARCH PROGRAM ON
  UNEMPLOYMENT AND THE AMERICAN ECONOMY.   GGORDRA65613

  LONG-TERM UNEMPLOYMENT IN THE 1960-S.   GHOLLSS65124

  LONG-TERM UNEMPLOYMENT IN THE UNITED STATES.   GMEREJL61995

  PUBLIC WORK AND THE **LONG-TERM** UNEMPLOYED.   GROSSMS66844

  HELPING THE **LONG-TERM** UNEMPLOYED. /INCOME-MAINTENANCE TRAINING/   GUSDLAB62221

  FAMILY CHARACTERISTICS OF THE **LONG-TERM** UNEMPLOYED.   GUSDLAB63762

LONGEVITY
  LONGEVITY AND HEALTH-STATUS OF THE NEGRO AMERICAN.   NGOLDMS63431

LONGSHORE
  A STUDY OF THE **LONGSHORE** INDUSTRY IN NEW-ORLEANS WITH EMPHASIS ON NEGRO LONGSHOREMEN. /LOUISIANA/   NORTICF56962

LONGSHOREMEN
  A STUDY OF THE LONGSHORE INDUSTRY IN NEW-ORLEANS WITH EMPHASIS ON NEGRO **LONGSHOREMEN**. /LOUISIANA/   NORTICF56962

LOS-ANGELES
  NEGROES AND MEXICAN-AMERICANS IN SOUTH AND EAST **LOS-ANGELES**. AN ANALYSIS OF A SPECIAL US CENSUS SURVEY OF
  NOVEMBER 1965. /CALIFORNIA/   CCALDIR66168

  THE URBAN REALITY. A COMPARATIVE STUDY OF THE SOCIO-ECONOMIC SITUATION OF MEXICAN-AMERICANS, NEGROES AND
  ANGLO-CAUCASIANS IN **LOS-ANGELES** COUNTY. /CALIFORNIA/   CLOSACH65708

  INCOME, EDUCATION AND UNEMPLOYMENT IN NEIGHBORHOODS. **LOS-ANGELES**, CALIFORNIA. /DEMOGRAPHY/   CUSDLAB63565

  HARD-CORE UNEMPLOYMENT AND POVERTY IN **LOS-ANGELES**. /CALIFORNIA NEGRO MEXICAN-AMERICAN/   CUVCAIIND524

  REPORT. EVALUATION STUDY OF YOUTH TRAINING AND EMPLOYMENT PROJECT, EAST **LOS-ANGELES**. /NEGRO
  MEXICAN-AMERICAN CALIFORNIA/   CWEINJL64310

  JOB BIAS IN L A. /**LOS-ANGELES** CALIFORNIA/   GANTIOL57397

  SOME PROBLEMS IN MINORITY-GROUP EDUCATION IN THE **LOS-ANGELES** PUBLIC SCHOOLS. /CALIFORNIA/   GBULLPX63489

  LOS-ANGELES CITY SCHOOLS. AN INVESTIGATION OF EMPLOYMENT PRACTICES. /CALIFORNIA/   GCALFEP64536

  A SUMMARY REPORT OF PRACTICES AND PROGRAMS DESIGNED TO REDUCE THE NUMBER OF DROPOUTS IN THE HIGH SCHOOLS
  OF **LOS-ANGELES** COUNTY. /CALIFORNIA/   GDELMDT66147

  SURVEY OF MINORITY-GROUP EMPLOYMENT AND PATIENT CARE IN PRIVATE HOSPITAL FACILITIES IN **LOS-ANGELES**
  COUNTY. /CALIFORNIA/   GLOSACCND914

  TESTIMONY OF HUMAN RELATIONS. /**LOS-ANGELES** CALIFORNIA/   GLOSACCND915

  REPORTS ON THE PATTERN OF EMPLOYMENT OF MINORITY-GROUP PERSONS IN DEPARTMENT OF COUNTY
  GOVERNMENT.**LOS-ANGELES** CALIFORNIA/   GLOSACC62913

  PROPOSED POLICY REGARDING STATISTICS ON EMPLOYMENT. /**LOS-ANGELES** CALIFORNIA/   GLOSACC64912

  REPORT OF FINDINGS AND RECOMMENDATIONS RESULTING FROM AN ANALYSIS OF THE EMPLOYMENT PRACTICES IN THE
  VARIOUS DEPARTMENTS OF THE CITY OF **LOS-ANGELES**. /CALIFORNIA/   GLOSAOC63917

  US COMMISSION-ON-CIVIL-RIGHTS, HEARINGS. **LOS-ANGELES** AND SAN-FRANCISCO, CALIFORNIA. JANUARY 25-26, 1960,
  JANUARY 27-28, 1960.   GUSCOMC60400

  SUB-EMPLOYMENT IN THE SLUMS OF **LOS-ANGELES**. /CALIFORNIA/   GUSDLAB66514

  LAKE ARROWHEAD CONFERENCE ON EQUAL-EMPLOYMENT-OPPORTUNITY, OCTOBER 22-24, 1963 -- RECORD OF PROCEEDINGS.
  LOS-ANGELES, CALIFORNIA.   GUSFEDE63513

  A CENSUS OF INDIANS IN **LOS-ANGELES**. /CALIFORNIA/   IPRICJA67606

  THE MIGRATION AND ADAPTATION OF AMERICAN INDIANS TO **LOS-ANGELES**. /CALIFORNIA/   IPRICJA67608

  AMERICAN-INDIANS IN **LOS-ANGELES**. A STUDY OF ADAPTATION TO A CITY. /CALIFORNIA/   IUVCALA66675

  A REPORT ON THE JEWISH POPULATION OF **LOS-ANGELES**. /CALIFORNIA/   JMASAGX59746

  BACKGROUND AND AMBITION OF MALE MEXICAN-AMERICAN HIGH SCHOOL SENIORS IN **LOS-ANGELES**. /CALIFORNIA/   MHELLCS63414

  SOME NOTES ON THE MEXICAN POPULATION OF **LOS-ANGELES** COUNTY. /CALIFORNIA/   MLOSACDND431

  MEXICAN-AMERICAN FAMILIES. **LOS-ANGELES** COUNTY. /CALIFORNIA/   MMCNAPH57435

  MEXICAN-AMERICANS IN THE **LOS-ANGELES** REGION. /CALIFORNIA/   MORTIMX62449

  REPORT FROM **LOS-ANGELES**. /CALIFORNIA/   NBUGGJA66131

  FIGHTING POVERTY. THE VIEW FROM WATTS. /**LOS-ANGELES** CALIFORNIA/   NBULLPX66135

  SOME PRACTICAL STUDIES IN PUBLIC TRANSPORTATION. /EMPLOYMENT-CONDITIONS WATTS **LOS-ANGELES** CALIFORNIA/   NCARLJX65593

  THE NEGRO IN **LOS-ANGELES** COUNTY. /CALIFORNIA/   NLOSACC63709

  PROPOSALS FOR THE IMPROVEMENT OF HUMAN RELATIONS IN THE **LOS-ANGELES** METROPOLITAN AREA. /EMPLOYMENT
  CALIFORNIA/   NLOSACC65365

  BEHIND **LOS-ANGELES**. JOB-LESS NEGROES AND THE BOOM. /UNEMPLOYMENT CALIFORNIA/   NMOYNDP65860

  WATTS ONE YEAR LATER. /TRAINING CALIFORNIA **LOS-ANGELES**/   NPAGEDX66970

  SOME LESSONS FROM WATTS. /**LOS-ANGELES** CALIFORNIA/   NRUSTBX66098

  THE WATTS MANIFESTO AND THE MCCONE REPORT. /**LOS-ANGELES** CALIFORNIA/   NRUSTBX66099

  THE MAYOR AND THE FIRE CHIEF. THE FIGHT OVER INTEGRATING THE **LOS-ANGELES** FIRE DEPARTMENT. /CALIFORNIA
  CASE-STUDY/   NSHERFP59130

LOS-ANGELES   (CONTINUATION)
PROGRESS IN WATTS -- THE LOS-ANGELES ASTD COMMUNITY AFFAIRS PROGRAM. /CALIFORNIA/   NTRAIAD66580

PREJUDICE IS NOT THE WHOLE STORY. EXAMINATION OF THREE CASES OF NEGRO UPGRADING IN TRACTION COMPANIES IN
PHILADELPHIA, LOS-ANGELES AND CHICAGO. /PENNSYLVANIA CALIFORNIA ILLINOIS/   NWECKJE45308

LOSS
UNUSED MANPOWER. THE NATION-S LOSS.   GUSDLAB66504

LOST
THE NEW LOST GENERATION. JOBLESS YOUTH.   GHARRMX64759

LOUISIANA
THE EMPLOYMENT OF NEGRO WOMEN AS DOMESTIC-SERVANTS IN NEW-ORLEANS. /LOUISIANA/   CGILMHX44403

INCOME, EDUCATION AND UNEMPLOYMENT IN NEIGHBORHOODS. NEW-ORLEANS, LOUISIANA. /DEMOGRAPHY/   CUSDLAB63469

RURAL INDUSTRIALIZATION IN A LOUISIANA COMMUNITY. /ECONOMIC-STATUS OCCUPATIONS/   GBERTAL59393

STUDY OF OCCUPATIONAL CHARACTERISTICS OF NON-WHITES IN THE EAST BATON-ROUGE AREA. /LOUISIANA/   GHARRWRND760

THE EFFECTS OF INDUSTRIALIZATION ON RURAL LOUISIANA. A STUDY OF PLANT EMPLOYEES.   GPRICPH58395

US COMMISSION-ON-CIVIL-RIGHTS. HEARINGS. NEW-ORLEANS, LOUISIANA. SEPTEMBER 27-28, 1960, MAY 5-6, 1961. GUSCOMC61403

SUB-EMPLOYMENT IN THE SLUMS OF NEW-ORLEANS. /LOUISIANA/   GUSDLAB66512

THE FRENCH AND THE NON-FRENCH IN LOUISIANA. A STUDY OF THE RELEVANCE OF ETHNIC FACTORS IN RURAL
DEVELOPMENT. /ECONOMIC-STATUS/   NBERTAL65394

INCOME AND RELATED CHARACTERISTICS OF RURAL HOUSEHOLDS IN THE CENTRAL LOUISIANA MIXED FARMING AREA.   NBOLTBX60398

RESOURCE USE AND ADJUSTMENT. RURAL FAMILIES IN THE CENTRAL LOUISIANA MIXED FARMING AREA.   NBOLTBX61396

FARM INCOME PREDICTIONS FOR SMALL FARMS IN THE CENTRAL LOUISIANA MIXED FARMING AREA.   NBOLTBX62399

SEGREGATION DEAL. NEW-ORLEANS REGION FEPC PERMITS COMPROMISE. /LOUISIANA/   NBUSIWX45161

EFFECTS OF UNEMPLOYMENT ON WHITE AND NEGRO PRISON-ADMISSIONS IN LOUISIANA.   NDOBBDA58277

THE CAREER PATTERNS OF NEGRO LAWYERS IN LOUISIANA. /OCCUPATIONS/   NGUILBM60465

COLLEGE, COLOR, AND EMPLOYMENT. RACIAL DIFFERENTIALS IN POSTGRADUATE EMPLOYMENT AMONG 1964 GRADUATES OF
LOUISIANA COLLEGES.   NHUSOCF66328

THE SCHOOL DROPOUT IN LOUISIANA 1963-1964.   NLOUISD64714

A STUDY OF THE LONGSHORE INDUSTRY IN NEW-ORLEANS WITH EMPHASIS ON NEGRO LONGSHOREMEN. /LOUISIANA/   NORTICF56962

NEGRO EMPLOYMENT IN THREE COMPANIES IN THE NEW-ORLEANS AREA. /CASE-STUDY LOUISIANA/   NUSDLAB55828

THREE COMPANIES -- NEW-ORLEANS AREA. /CASE-STUDY LOUISIANA/   NWISSHW55332

LOUISVILLE
BRICKS WITHOUT STRAW. STUDIES OF COMMUNITY UNEMPLOYMENT PROBLEMS. THE NEGROES DILEMMA. /LOUISVILLE
KENTUCKY/   NLGUIHR64715

JOBS AND THE LAW. /LOUISVILLE KENTUCKY/   NLOUIHR65717

PATTERNS OF DISCRIMINATION STUDY -- LOUISVILLE HUMAN-RELATIONS-COMMISSION. /KENTUCKY/   NLGUIHR66582

FACTS FOR ACTION. /LOUISVILLE KENTUCKY/   NLOUIHR66716

LOUISVILLE. SPECIAL REPORT. /CASE-STUDY KENTUCKY/   NMUSEBX64868

A SURVEY OF THE ECONOMIC AND CULTURAL CONDITIONS OF THE NEGRO POPULATION OF LOUISVILLE, KENTUCKY AND A
REVIEW OF THE PROGRAM AND ACTIVITIES OF THE LOUISVILLE URBAN-LEAGUE. JANUARY-FEBRUARY, 1948.   NNATLUL48903

A SURVEY OF THE ECONOMIC AND CULTURAL CONDITIONS OF THE NEGRO POPULATION OF LOUISVILLE, KENTUCKY AND A
REVIEW OF THE PROGRAM AND ACTIVITIES OF THE LOUISVILLE URBAN-LEAGUE. JANUARY-FEBRUARY, 1948.   NNATLUL48903

LOUISVILLE. /KENTUCKY/   NSOUTRC64162

IMPROVED CONDITIONS FOR NEGROES IN LOUISVILLE. /KENTUCKY/   NUSDLAB45820

LOW
THE EFFECT OF LOW EDUCATIONAL-ATTAINMENT ON INCOMES. A COMPARATIVE STUDY OF SELECTED ETHNIC GROUPS.
/NEGRO MEXICAN-AMERICAN/   CFOGEWX66367

DISCRIMINATION AND LOW INCOMES.   GANTOAX59401

SOME DETERMINANTS OF LOW FAMILY INCOME.   GCREADX61621

HOUSING DEFICIENCIES OF AGRICULTURAL WORKERS AND OTHER LOW INCOME GROUPS.   MMCMIOX62434

THE EFFECT OF LOW EDUCATIONAL ATTAINMENT ON INCOMES. A COMPARATIVE STUDY OF SELECTED ETHNIC GROUPS.   OFOGEWX66721

LOW-INCOME
IMPLICATIONS OF THE STUDIES. /DISCRIMINATION LOW-INCOME NEGRO PUERTO-RICAN POLICY-RECOMMENDATIONS/ CABRACX59001

THE POOR PAY MORE. CONSUMER PRACTICES OF LOW-INCOME FAMILIES.   GCAPLDX63310

LOW-INCOME FAMILIES AND MEASURES OF INCOME INEQUALITY.   GGOLDSF62725

HOME INTERVIEW STUDY OF LOW-INCOME HOUSEHOLDS IN DETROIT, MICHIGAN.   GGREEAI65472

POVERTY IN TEXAS. THE DISTRIBUTION OF LOW-INCOME FAMILIES.   GKUVLWP65867

THE LOW-INCOME PROBLEM IN AGRICULTURE.   GMOOREJ64030

PROCEEDINGS OF THE NATIONAL-SHARECROPPERS-FUND CONFERENCE ON MIGRATORY LABOR AND LOW-INCOME FARMERS.
NOVEMBER 13 1957.   GNATLSF57299

LOW-INCOME YOUTH. UNEMPLOYMENT, VOCATIONAL TRAINING, AND THE JOB-CORPS.   GPURCFX66208

FAMILY INCOME AND RELATED CHARACTERISTICS AMONG LOW-INCOME COUNTIES AND STATES.   GRODOAL64241

FARM AND NON-FARM EMPLOYMENT OPPORTUNITIES FOR LOW-INCOME FARM FAMILIES.   GRUTTVW59270

LOW-INCOME   (CONTINUATION)
    LOW-INCOME FAMILIES AND UNRELATED INDIVIDUALS IN THE UNITED STATES. 1964. /DEMOGRAPHY/   GUSBURC65151

    CONSUMER EXPENDITURES AND INCOME WITH EMPHASIS ON LOW-INCOME FAMILIES.   GUSDLAB64833

    COOPERATIVE EXTENSION SERVICE WORK WITH LOW-INCOME FAMILIES.   IUSDAGR63638

    POVERTY AMONG SPANISH-AMERICANS IN TEXAS. LOW-INCOME FAMILIES IN A MINORITY-GROUP.   MUPHAWK66511

    ATTITUDE TOWARD JOB-MOBILITY AMONG HOUSEHOLD HEADS IN LOW-INCOME AREAS OF THE RURAL SOUTH.   NDUNKJX64300

    CHILD REARING AMONG LOW-INCOME FAMILIES. /ECONOMIC-STATUS/   NLEWIHX61040

    CULTURE, CLASS AND FAMILY LIFE AMONG LOW-INCOME NEGROES.   NLEWIHX67691

    THE ECONOMIC AND SOCIAL ADJUSTMENT OF LOW-INCOME FEMALE-HEADED FAMILIES.   WBERNSE65458

    WOMEN-S EARNINGS IN LOW-INCOME FAMILIES.   WUSDLAB66236

    THE EVOLVING LOW-INCOME PROBLEM IN AGRICULTURE. /ECONOMIC-STATUS/   WWELCFJ60227

LOW-INCOMES
    RAISING LOW-INCOMES THROUGH IMPROVED EDUCATION.   GCOMIED65591

    DISCRIMINATION AND LOW-INCOMES.   NSLAIDX61021

LOW-SKILL
    BREAKING THE BARRIERS OF OCCUPATIONAL ISOLATION. A REPORT ON UPGRADING LOW-SKILL, LOW-WAGE WORKERS.   CPROJAX66237
    /NEGRO   PUERTO-RICAN/

LOW-WAGE
    BREAKING THE BARRIERS OF OCCUPATIONAL ISOLATION. A REPORT ON UPGRADING LOW-SKILL, LOW-WAGE WORKERS.   CPROJAX66237
    /NEGRO   PUERTO-RICAN/

LOWER
    TEXAS GROWERS AND WORKERS ON THE FARM, LOWER RIO-GRANDE VALLEY.   GTEXAEC59352

    SOME ASPECTS OF VOCATIONAL ASPIRATIONS AND VALUE ORIENTATION AMONG NEGRO BOYS IN THE LOWER SOCIO-ECONOMIC   NSCHMWX63139
    CLASSES.

    THE LOWER STATUS PUERTO-RICAN FAMILY.   PBRAMJX62783

    SCHOOL AND COMMUNITY COURSE. THE LOWER STATUS PUERTO-RICAN FAMILY.   PBRAMJX63784

    A MEMORANDUM ON THE MOTIVATIONS OF MIDDLE AGED WOMEN IN THE LOWER EDUCATIONAL BRACKETS TO RETURN TO WORK.   WJEWIVA61880
    /ASPIRATIONS/

    A PILOT STUDY OF THE MOTIVATIONS AND PROBLEMS OF MIDDLE AGED HOMEMAKERS IN LOWER SOCIO-ECONOMIC GROUPS IN   WJEWIVA62883
    SEEKING EMPLOYMENT. /ASPIRATIONS/

LOWER-BLUE-COLLAR
    CHARACTERISTICS OF THE LOWER-BLUE-COLLAR CLASS.SOCIO-ECONOMIC/   NCCHEAK63219

LOWER-CLASS
    LOWER-CLASS DELINQUENCY AND WORK PROGRAMS.   GMARTJM66854

    FACTORS ASSOCIATED WITH SCHOOL DROPOUTS AND JUVENILE-DELINQUENCY AMONG LOWER-CLASS CHILDREN.   GPALMFX63671

    OCCUPATIONAL ASPIRATIONS OF LOWER-CLASS NEGRO AND WHITE YOUTH.   NANTOAX59027

    LOWER-CLASS NEGRO MOTHERS ASPIRATIONS FOR THEIR CHILDREN.   NBELLRR65074

    A COMPARISON OF THE SOCIAL CHARACTERISTICS AND EDUCATIONAL ASPIRATIONS OF NORTHERN, LOWER-CLASS, NEGRO   NCAGLLT66904
    PARENTS WHO ACCEPTED AND DECLINED AN OPPORTUNITY FOR INTEGRATED EDUCATION FOR THEIR CHILDREN.

    SOME WORK-RELATED CULTURAL DEPRIVATIONS OF LOWER-CLASS NEGRO YOUTHS.   NHIMEJS64554

    CRUCIBLE OF IDENTITY. THE NEGRO LOWER-CLASS FAMILY.   NRAINLX66032

LOWER-CLASSES
    THE AMERICAN LOWER-CLASSES. A TYPOLOGICAL APPROACH.   GMILLSM64727

LOWER-EAST-SIDE
    POVERTY ON THE LOWER-EAST-SIDE. SELECTED ASPECTS OF THE MOBILIZATION-FOR-YOUTH EXPERIENCE.   GBARRSX64130

LUISENO
    THE LUISENO INDIANS IN 1965.   IPRICJA65607

MACHINE
    PATTERNS OF DISCRIMINATION IN THE GLASS AND MACHINE TOOL INDUSTRIES IN OHIO.   GOHIOCR66126

    PATTERNS OF DISCRIMINATION IN THE MACHINE TOOL INDUSTRY IN OHIO.   GOHIOCR66128

    THE NAVAJO IN THE MACHINE AGE. HUMAN RESOURCES ARE IMPORTANT TOO.   INAPIAX58594

MACHINES
    JOBS, MEN AND MACHINES. PROBLEMS OF AUTOMATION.   GMARKCX64949

    FARMERS, WORKERS, AND MACHINES. TECHNOLOGICAL AND SOCIAL-CHANGE IN FARM INDUSTRIES OF ARIZONA.   MPADFHX65450

MACON
    FACTORS AFFECTING THE PRESENT FARMING PROGRAMS OF ONE HUNDRED NEGRO FARMS IN THE PATRONAGE AREA OF THE   NBRONCA51337
    MACON COUNTY TRAINING SCHOOL, IN ALABAMA, WITH EMPHASIS FOR IMPROVEMENT.

    VOCATIONAL CHOICES OF NEGRO HIGH SCHOOL STUDENTS IN MACON COUNTY, ALABAMA, AND THEIR RELATIONSHIP TO   NCHAPEJ49351
    BASIC OCCUPATIONAL ACTIVITES OF THE SCHOOL COMMUNITIES. /ASPIRATIONS/

    THE EVALUATION OF PRACTICES CARRIED ON BY TWO HUNDRED NEGRO FARMERS IN THE PRODUCTION OF COTTON IN MACON   NGOLDSM48350
    COUNTY, ALABAMA.

    A STUDY OF FARM MANAGEMENT PRACTICES ON 100 NEGRO FARMS IN MACON COUNTY, ALABAMA, 1949.   NSHAWBJ50339

    THE INFLUENCE OF TUSKEGEE-INSTITUTE ON THE HEALTH, EDUCATIONAL, ECONOMIC, AND POLITICAL ASPECTS OF THE   NSHIEAR51342
    NEGRO POPULATION OF MACON COUNTY, ALABAMA.

MAINLAND
    A COMPARISON OF THE OCCUPATIONS OF THE FIRST AND SECOND GENERATION PUERTO-RICANS IN THE MAINLAND   PRAUSCX61846
    LABOR-MARKET, AND HOW THE WORK OF THE NEW-YORK STATE DEPARTMENT OF LABORFFECTS PUERTO-RICANS.

MAINSTREAM
    THE INDIAN TESTS THE MAINSTREAM.   IMCNIDX66585

    INTO THE MAINSTREAM. /RACE-RELATIONS SOUTH ECONOMIC-STATUS/   NJOHNCS47007

MAJOR
    AN EXPERIMENT TO TEST THREE MAJOR ISSUES OF WORK PROGRAM METHODOLOGY WITHIN MOBILIZATION-FOR-YOUTH-S
    INTEGRATED SERVICES TO OUT-OF-SCHOOL UNEMPLOYED YOUTH. /NEGRO PUERTO-RICAN/   CMOBIFY66024

    THE SCHOOL DROPOUT PROBLEM IN MAJOR CITIES OF NEW-YORK STATE. ROCHESTER -- PART I. /NEGRO PUERTO-RICAN/ CNEWYSD62090

    ANTIDISCRIMINATION PROVISIONS IN MAJOR CONTRACTS, 1961.   GLUDELE62923

    MAJOR AGRICULTURAL MIGRANT LABOR DEMAND AREAS.   GUSDLAB61509

    TECHNOLOGICAL TRENDS IN 36 MAJOR AMERICAN INDUSTRIES.   GUSDLAB64802

    TECHNOLOGICAL TRENDS IN MAJOR AMERICAN INDUSTRIES. /EMPLOYMENT/   GUSDLAB66637

    A COMPARISON OF MAJOR UNITED STATES RELIGIOUS GROUPS. /ECONOMIC-STATUS/   JLAZRBX61033

    THE DETERMINATION OF CERTAIN MAJOR FACTORS AFFECTING THE NEGRO VETERAN IN THE ON-THE-JOB TRAINING PROGRAM
    IN VOCATIONAL AGRICULTURE IN THE STATE OF ALABAMA AS A BASIS FOR PLANNING A MORE EFFECTIVE PROGRAM.   NBATTEF49338

    SUMMARY OF MAJOR POINTS, TALK ON EMPLOYMENT, MCCONE-COMMISSION SERIES.   NBULLPX66898

    THE EMPLOYMENT OF NEGROES IN THE US BY MAJOR OCCUPATION AND INDUSTRY.   NHOPEJX53567

    NEGRO COLLEGES. LONG IGNORED. SOUTHERN SCHOOLS NOW COURTED BY MAJOR UNIVERSITIES AND FOUNDATIONS.   NLANGEX64304

    MAJOR POLITICAL ISSUES WHICH DIRECTLY CONCERN NEGROES.   NMILLJE48250

    POVERTY AREAS OF OUR MAJOR CITIES. THE EMPLOYMENT SITUATION OF NEGRO AND WHITE WORKERS IN METROPOLITAN
    AREAS COMPARED IN A SPECIAL LABOR-FORCE REPORT.   NWETZJR66114

MAJORS
    WHAT BRINGS AND HOLDS WOMAN SCIENCE MAJORS. /OCCUPATIONS/   WDEMEAL63728

    SOME INTELLECTUAL ATTRIBUTES AND EDUCATIONAL INTERESTS OF UNIVERSITY WOMEN IN VARIOUS MAJORS.
    /ASPIRATIONS/   WGENTLX60790

MALADJUSTED
    WORKING MOTHERS AND MALADJUSTED CHILDREN.   WHANDHX57818

MALE
    UNIONISM, MIGRATION, AND THE MALE NONWHITE-WHITE UNEMPLOYMENT DIFFERENTIAL.   GRAPPLA66216

    PROBLEMS OF NAVAJO MALE GRADUATES OF INTERMOUNTAIN SCHOOL DURING THEIR FIRST YEAR OF EMPLOYMENT.   IBAKEJE59533

    ANALYSIS OF MALE NAVAHO STUDENTS PERCEPTIONS OF OCCUPATIONAL OPPORTUNITIES AND THEIR ATTITUDES TOWARD
    DEVELOPMENT OF SKILLS AND TRAITS NECESSARY FOR OCCUPATIONAL COMPETENCE.   IDESPCW65548

    BACKGROUND AND AMBITION OF MALE MEXICAN-AMERICAN HIGH SCHOOL SENIORS IN LOS-ANGELES. /CALIFORNIA/   MHELLCS63414

    SEX, STATUS AND THE UNDEREMPLOYMENT OF THE NEGRO MALE.   NCLARKB67212

    THE EDUCATIONAL AND OCCUPATIONAL ASPIRATIONS AND PLANS OF NEGRO AND WHITE MALE ELEMENTARY SCHOOL
    STUDENTS.   NHOLLRG59562

    ACHIEVEMENT OF MALE HIGH SCHOOL DROPOUTS AND GRADUATES IN ALABAMA VOCATIONAL SCHOOLS.   NMILLGJ65791

    THE EXPECTED-CASES METHOD APPLIED TO THE NON-WHITE MALE LABOR-FORCE.   NTURNRH49211

    THE NON-WHITE MALE IN THE LABOR-FORCE.   NTURNRH49215

    THE RELATIVE POSITION OF THE NEGRO MALE IN THE LABOR-FORCE OF LARGE AMERICAN CITIES.   NTURNRH51217

    OCCUPATIONAL ASPIRATIONS OF NEGRO MALE HIGH SCHOOL STUDENTS.   NUZELOX61278

    NEGRO MALE IDENTIFICATION PROBLEMS.   NWOROIX62341

    A COMPARATIVE STUDY OF TOP LEVEL MALE AND FEMALE EXECUTIVES IN HARRIS-COUNTY. /TEXAS OCCUPATIONS/   WDOLLPA65738

MALE-FEMALE
    A COMPARISON OF THE MALE-FEMALE ROLES IN ENGINEERING. /OCCUPATION/   WROBISS63083

MALES
    RURAL-FARM MALES ENTERING AND LEAVING WORKING AGES, 1940-50 AND 1950-60. REPLACEMENT RATIOS AND RATES.
    /OCCUPATIONS/   GBOWLGK56433

    POTENTIAL SUPPLY AND REPLACEMENT OF RURAL MALES OF LABOR-FORCE AGE, 1960-70.   GBOWLGK66430

    A NOTE ON OCCUPATIONAL MOBILITY FOR WHITE AND NONWHITE MALES, 1950 TO 1965.   GJAFFAJ66820

    THE EFFECT OF STATE FAIR-EMPLOYMENT LEGISLATION ON THE ECONOMIC POSITION OF NONWHITE MALES.   GLANDWM66883

    THE ASSOCIATION OF INCOME AND EDUCATION FOR MALES, BY REGION, RACE, AND AGE.   GLASSRL65998

    VALUE ORIENTATIONS OF YOUNG MEXICAN-AMERICAN MALES AS REFLECTED IN THEIR WORK PATTERNS AND EMPLOYMENT
    PREFERENCES.   MWADDJO62513

    RECENT MIGRATION OF YOUNG MALES INTO HOUSTON, TEXAS.   MWAGODW57515

    AND ANGELS WALK WHERE ONLY MALES TREAD. THE EMERGENCE OF WOMANPOWER. /MANPOWER/   WMATHJP66959

MAN
    MAN, WORK AND SOCIETY. A READER IN THE SOCIOLOGY OF OCCUPATIONS.   GNOSOSX62336

    MOST NOTORIOUS VICTORY. MAN IN AN AGE OF AUTOMATION.   GSELIBB66841

    EDUCATION AND TRAINING. THE BRIDGE BETWEEN MAN AND HIS WORK.   GUSDHEW65156

    THE INDIAN AND THE WHITE MAN.   IWASHWE64682

    TEXAS-S THIRD MAN. THE TEXAS MEXICAN.   MPAREAX63451

    LAST MAN IN. RACIAL ACCESS TO UNIONS.   NGREESX59451

    RICH MAN, POOR MAN. /INCOME/   NMILLHP64784

MAN   (CONTINUATION)
    RICH MAN, POOR MAN. /INCOME/   NMILLHP64784

    MAN IN METROPOLIS. /RESIDENTIAL-SEGREGATION GHETTO/   NSCHILB65106

MAN-S
    THE BLACK MAN-S BURDEN. /DISCRIMINATION ECONOMIC-STATUS/   NREDDJS43546

MANAGEMENT
    MANAGEMENT GUIDE. EQUAL-EMPLOYMENT-OPPORTUNITY.   GASSOIC63407

    COUNSELOR-S VIEWS ON CHANGING MANAGEMENT POLICIES.   GCOXXTX63618

    PLANT INSPECTION SURVEY BY MANAGEMENT -- MINORITY-GROUP INTEGRATION. /COLORADO/   GDENNGHND632

    RACIAL STATISTICS AS A MANAGEMENT TOOL.   GDOARLE66645

    REPORT OF INDUSTRY AND LABOR-MANAGEMENT CLINICS. IMPLEMENTATION OF EMPLOYMENT IN MERIT PROGRAMS IN NON
    FEPC STATES BY DIRECT APPROACH TO TOP MANAGEMENT.   GFISKUR51684

    MANAGEMENT AND MINORITY GROUPS. A STUDY OF ATTITUDES AND PRACTICES IN HIRING AND UPGRADING. GMARKPI57085

    INTERRACIAL HUMAN RELATIONS IN MANAGEMENT, A COMPILED REPORT PRESENTED ORALLY...JANUARY 17 1951.   GMCKEIX51926

    MANAGEMENT AND MERIT EMPLOYMENT.   GNEWYSAND084

    MINORITY-GROUP INTEGRATION BY LABOR AND MANAGEMENT. A STUDY OF THE EMPLOYMENT PRACTICES OF THE LARGER
    EMPLOYERS, AND THE MEMBERSHIP PRACTICES OF THE LARGER LABOR UNIONS WITH RESPECT TO RACE, RELIGION, AND
    NATIONAL ORIGIN, CONNECTICUT, 1951.   GSTETHG53598

    INDIAN RELOCATION. PROBLEMS OF DEPENDENCY AND MANAGEMENT IN THE CITY.   IABLCJX65085

    LARGE CORPORATIONS ACCUSED OF DISCRIMINATION AGAINST JEWS IN MANAGEMENT, EXECUTIVE CAPACITIES BY
    AMERICAN-JEWISH-COMMITTEE.   JWORLOX64773

    THE MANAGEMENT OF RACIAL INTEGRATION IN BUSINESS, A SPECIAL REPORT TO MANAGEMENT.   NALEXRD64868

    THE MANAGEMENT OF RACIAL INTEGRATION IN BUSINESS, A SPECIAL REPORT TO MANAGEMENT.   NALEXRD64868

    MORE ROOM AT THE TOP. COMPANY EXPERIENCE IN EMPLOYING NEGROES IN PROFESSIONAL AND MANAGEMENT JOBS.
     /INDUSTRY/   NBIRDCX63080

    HOW MANAGEMENT CAN INTEGRATE NEGROES IN WAR INDUSTRIES.   NDAVIJA42255

    RACIAL STATISTICS AS A MANAGEMENT TOOL.   NDOARLE66276

    THE MANAGEMENT OF RACIAL INTEGRATION IN BUSINESS.   NDORIGF64282

    THE NEGRO AND EQUAL-EMPLOYMENT-OPPORTUNITIES. A REVIEW OF MANAGEMENT EXPERIENCES IN TWENTY COMPANIES. NFERMLA66790

    THE INEFFECTIVE SOLDIER. LESSONS FOR MANAGEMENT AND THE NATION.   NGINZEX59406

    A MANAGEMENT PERSPECTIVE TOWARD NEGRO ECONOMIC PRESSURES.   NHOFFHX65558

    WHAT THE GOVERNMENT REQUIRES OF MANAGEMENT AND UNIONS.   NHORTRX64291

    MANAGEMENT, RACIAL DISCRIMINATION AND APPRENTICE TRAINING   NKOVAIX64663

    MANAGEMENT COMPLIANCE WITH PRESIDENTIAL DIRECTIVES.   NLAWRRG64296

    MANAGEMENT POLICIES AND BI-RACIAL INTEGRATION IN INDUSTRY.   NMOHRFT54806

    COMMENTS ON MANAGEMENT PROBLEMS.   NNATLIC43921

    MANAGEMENT VERSUS JIM-CROW. /INDUSTRY/   NPURCTV62023

    MANAGEMENT SOCIAL RESPONSIBILITY AND RACIAL EMPLOYMENT IN THE MEAT-PACKING INDUSTRY.   NPURCTV67123

    MANAGEMENT AND MINORITY-GROUPS. A STUDY OF ATTITUDES AND PRACTICES IN HIRING AND UPGRADING. NROSEBX59080

    A STUDY OF FARM MANAGEMENT PRACTICES ON 100 NEGRO FARMS IN MACON COUNTY, ALABAMA, 1949.   NSHAWBJ50339

    HOW MANAGEMENT VIEWS ITS RACE-RELATIONS RESPONSIBILITIES.   NSTRAGX67181

    LABOR MANAGEMENT ON THE FARM.   PGARDSC58807

    WOMANPOWER -- KEY TO MANAGEMENT MANPOWER SHORTAGE.   WLLOYBJ62633

    A STUDY OF WOMEN IN OFFICE MANAGEMENT POSITIONS WITH IMPLICATIONS FOR BUSINESS EDUCATION. /OCCUPATIONS/   WRUSHEM57096

    TODAY-S BUSINESS WOMAN. HER CHARACTERISTICS, HER NEED FOR FURTHER EDUCATION, HER FUTURE IN MANAGEMENT.
    /OCCUPATIONS/   WTHOMMH63152

    MANAGEMENT PROBLEMS OF HOMEMAKERS EMPLOYED OUTSIDE THE HOME. /WORK-FAMILY-CONFLICT/   WUSDHEW61174

MANAGEMENT-S
    MANAGEMENT-S CONCERN WITH RECENT CIVIL-RIGHTS LEGISLATION AFFECTING MANAGEMENT-S OBLIGATIONS TO HIS
    EMPLOYEES AND APPLICANTS FOR EMPLOYMENT, MAINLY IN THE STATE OF NEW-YORK.   GKOPPRW65858

    MANAGEMENT-S CONCERN WITH RECENT CIVIL-RIGHTS LEGISLATION AFFECTING MANAGEMENT-S OBLIGATIONS TO HIS
    EMPLOYEES AND APPLICANTS FOR EMPLOYMENT, MAINLY IN THE STATE OF NEW-YORK.   GKOPPRW65858

MANAGEMENTS
    MANAGEMENTS GUIDELINES FOR MEETING THE NEGRO DRIVE FOR JOB EQUALITY. /INDUSTRY/.   NOPINRC63958

MANAGER-S
    THE FEDERAL MANAGER-S ROLE IN DEMOCRACY-S UNFINISHED BUSINESS.   GCLINRX61577

MANAGERIAL
    SELECTING AND TRAINING NEGROES FOR MANAGERIAL POSITIONS.   NEDUCTS64322

MANAGERS
    ON-THE-JOB EXPERIENCES OF NEGRO MANAGERS.   NBLANJW64917

    PROGRESS IN PLANS-FOR-PROGRESS FOR NEGRO MANAGERS.   NLOCKHC65701

    WOMEN AS EXECUTIVES AND MANAGERS. /OCCUPATIONS/   WMAHRAH65953

MANAGING
    MANAGING YOUR MANPOWER. NEGRO EMPLOYMENT PROBLEM.   NBROOTR63118

MANAGING   (CONTINUATION)
  MANAGING WOMEN EMPLOYEES IN SMALL BUSINESS.   WUSSMBA62248

MANDATORY
  NON-DISCRIMINATION CLAUSE IN GOVERNMENT CONTRACTS IS MANDATORY.   NUSDLAB43833

MANHATTAN
  INCOME, EDUCATION AND UNEMPLOYMENT IN NEIGHBORHOODS. NEW-YORK-CITY -- MANHATTAN.   /DEMOGRAPHY/   CUSDLAB63473

MANIFESTO
  THE WATTS MANIFESTO AND THE MCCONE REPORT.   /LOS-ANGELES CALIFORNIA/   NRUSTBX66099

MANPOWER
  AN EXPERIMENT IN MANPOWER DEVELOPMENT.   /TRAINING MISSISSIPPI NEGRO WOMEN/   CSELFHO66325

  ACTION FOR EMPLOYMENT. A DEMONSTRATION NEIGHBORHOOD MANPOWER PROJECT.   GALLCTO66361

  MANPOWER DEVELOPMENT PROGRAMS FOR FARM PEOPLE.   GALLECC67910

  MANPOWER RETRAINING IN THE SOUTH-S RURAL POPULATION -- AN OPPORTUNITY FOR DEVELOPMENT.   GBACHFT63413

  AN INTEGRATED POSITIVE MANPOWER POLICY.   GBAKKEW65753

  AUTOMATION, PRODUCTIVITY AND MANPOWER PROBLEMS.   GBOKXDX64736

  MANPOWER DEVELOPMENT. CHARGES AND CHALLENGES. /TECHNOLOGICAL-CHANGE TRAINING/   GBOLIAC65528

  MANPOWER IMPLICATIONS OF TECHNOLOGICAL-CHANGE. RESEARCH FINDINGS OF THE US DEPARTMENT OF LABOR.   GBRANSX63876

  REPORT TO THE GOVERNOR AND THE LEGISLATURE OF THE COMMISSION ON MANPOWER, AUTOMATION AND TECHNOLOGY,
  1964. /CALIFORNIA/   GCALCMA65515

  MANPOWER RESOURCES OF THE SAN-FRANCISCO OAKLAND BAY AREA 1960-1970.   /CALIFORNIA/   GCALDEM63520

  MANPOWER DEVELOPMENT TRAINING. TOTAL NUMBER OF NEW ENROLLEES DURING THE MONTH BY RACE AND OCCUPATION
  STATEWIDE AND BY ADMINISTRATIVE AREA, SEPTEMBER, 1966, OCTOBER, 1966. /CALIFORNIA/   GCALDEM66518

  MANPOWER PROGRAM IMPLICATIONS OF SKILL IMBALANCES. /TRAINING/   GCASSFH66565

  ECONOMIC MANPOWER AND SOCIAL-WELFARE.   GCLAGEX65794

  1964 MANPOWER SURVEY. /CHICAGO ILLINOIS/   GCOMIEF64592

  PUBLIC WELFARE, AUTOMATION, AND EXPERIMENTAL MANPOWER PROGRAMS.   GCONFAP63545

  SEMINAR ON MANPOWER POLICY AND PROGRAM. LABOR LOOKS AT AUTOMATION AND CIVIL-RIGHTS.   GCCNWJT65496

  SEMINAR ON MANPOWER POLICY AND PROGRAM -- AUTOMATION, SKILL, AND MANPOWER PREDICTIONS.   GCROSER66148

  SEMINAR ON MANPOWER POLICY AND PROGRAM -- AUTOMATION, SKILL, AND MANPOWER PREDICTIONS.   GCROSER66148

  MANPOWER POLICIES FOR A DEMOCRATIC SOCIETY.   GDAVIHX65629

  FARM MANPOWER POLICY.   GFULLVX67931

  PROJECTIONS OF MANPOWER REQUIREMENTS AND SUPPLY.   GGOLDHX66933

  US MANPOWER AND EMPLOYMENT POLICY. A REVIEW ESSAY.   GGORDMS65728

  LONG-TERM MANPOWER PROJECTIONS.   GGORDRA64525

  LONG-TERM MANPOWER PROJECTIONS. PROCEEDINGS OF A CONFERENCE CONDUCTED BY THE RESEARCH PROGRAM ON
  UNEMPLOYMENT AND THE AMERICAN ECONOMY.   GGORDRA65613

  MANPOWER IN THE UNITED STATES. PROBLEMS AND POLICIES.   GHABEWX54750

  EDUCATION, MANPOWER AND ECONOMIC-GROWTH.   GHARBFH64741

  REFLECTIONS ON THE MANPOWER REVOLUTION.   GHECKAX64937

  REALIZING THE MANPOWER POTENTIALITIES OF MINORITY-GROUP YOUTH.   GHOLLJH58778

  THE COMMUNITY ACTION AGENCY-S ROLE IN COMPREHENSIVE MANPOWER PROGRAMS -- PLANNING AND PROBLEMS.   GKANERD66863

  MANPOWER POLICY, POVERTY AND THE STATE OF THE ECONOMY.   GKERSJA66733

  AUTOMATION, JOBS, AND MANPOWER.   GKILLCC63755

  THE MANPOWER REVOLUTION -- A CALL FOR DEBATE.   GKIRSGC64860

  MANPOWER PROBLEMS AND THE BUSINESS COMMUNITY.   GKRUGDHND865

  UNEMPLOYMENT INSURANCE AND MANPOWER POLICY. /INCOME-MAINTENANCE/   GKRUGDH65628

  EMPLOYMENT PROBLEMS OF YOUTH AND MANPOWER PROGRAMS.   GKRUGDH66864

  COUNSELOR-S GUIDE TO OCCUPATIONAL AND OTHER MANPOWER INFORMATION. AN ANNOTATED BIBLIOGRAPHY.   GLAFADP65782

  MANPOWER PLANNING IN A FREE SOCIETY.   GLESTRA66155

  FEDERAL MANPOWER POLICIES AND PROGRAMS TO COMBAT UNEMPLOYMENT.   GLEVISA64897

  WORK RELIEF. SOCIAL WELFARE STYLE.   /MANPOWER UNEMPLOYMENT/   GLEVISA66531

  AN ACTIVE EMPLOYER MANPOWER POLICY.   GLIVEER66567

  THE ROLE OF JOB CREATION PROGRAMS.   /MANPOWER/   GMANGGL65728

  THE MANPOWER REVOLUTION. ITS POLICY CONSEQUENCES. EXCERPTS FROM SENATE HEARINGS BEFORE THE CLARK
  SUBCOMMITTEE.   GMANGGL66217

  THE ROLE OF THE EMPLOYER IN MANPOWER POLICY.   /INDUSTRY/   GMYERCA66527

  MANPOWER AND EDUCATION.   GNATLEA56047

  A POLICY FOR SKILLED MANPOWER.   GNATLMC54876

  GOVERNMENT AND MANPOWER.   /POLICY-RECOMMENDATIONS/   GNATLMC64956

MANPOWER   (CONTINUATION)
MANPOWER UNLIMITED. /INDUSTRY INTEGRATION/   GNEWYSA57086

MANPOWER POLICY AND PROGRAMMES IN THE UNITED STATES.   GORGAEC64776

TRENDS AND PERSPECTIVES IN MANPOWER POLICY.   GREHNGX65654

COORDINATION AMONG FEDERAL MANPOWER PROGRAMS.   GROBSRT66721

THE HIGH COST OF DISCRIMINATION. THE WASTE IN MANPOWER, MORALE, AND PRODUCTIVITY COSTS AMERICAN INDUSTRY
30 BILLION DOLLARS A YEAR.   GROPEEX63244

AUTOMATION, MANPOWER, AND EDUCATION.   GROSEJM66008

THE NEXT 20 YEARS IN MANPOWER.   GROSSAM66083

THE MANPOWER PROBLEMS OF AUTOMATION.   GSALNEX65769

A BENEFIT-COST ANALYSIS OF MANPOWER RETRAINING.   GSOMEGJ64157

MANPOWER NEEDS BY INDUSTRY TO 1975.   GSTAMHX65768

CURRENT MANPOWER PROBLEMS. AN INTRODUCTORY SURVEY.   GSTURAF64837

MANPOWER PROJECTIONS. SOME CONCEPTUAL PROBLEMS AND RESEARCH NEEDS. /EMPLOYMENT-TRENDS/   GSWERSX66535

COORDINATION OF MANPOWER PROGRAMS.   GTAYLHC66967

THE ROLE OF MANPOWER POLICY IN ACHIEVING AGGREGATE GOALS. /EMPLOYMENT INCOME/   GTHURLC66640

MANPOWER DEVELOPMENT AND TRAINING.   GUSDHEW65763

MANPOWER. THE CHALLENGE OF THE 1960-S.   GUSDLAB60488

MANPOWER REPORT OF THE PRESIDENT.   GUSDLAB62700

MEETING THE MANPOWER PROBLEMS OF. I. AREA REDEVELOPMENT, II. AUTOMATION.   GUSDLAB62708

MANPOWER RESEARCH PROGRAMS.   GUSDLAB62981

BRIDGE TO EMPLOYMENT. DEMONSTRATION MANPOWER PROGRAMS.   GUSDLAB63442

UTILIZING OUR MANPOWER RESOURCES. SPECIAL APPLICANT GROUPS.   GUSDLAB63665

MANPOWER REPORT OF THE PRESIDENT AND A REPORT ON MANPOWER REQUIREMENTS, RESOURCES, UTILIZATION, AND
TRAINING.   GUSDLAB63830

MANPOWER REPORT OF THE PRESIDENT AND A REPORT ON MANPOWER REQUIREMENTS, RESOURCES, UTILIZATION, AND
TRAINING.   GUSDLAB63830

MANPOWER REPORT OF THE PRESIDENT AND A REPORT ON MANPOWER REQUIREMENTS, RESOURCES, UTILIZATION, AND
TRAINING.   GUSDLAB64829

MANPOWER REPORT OF THE PRESIDENT AND A REPORT ON MANPOWER REQUIREMENTS, RESOURCES, UTILIZATION, AND
TRAINING.   GUSDLAB64829

SEMINAR ON MANPOWER POLICY AND PROGRAM MEASUREMENT OF TECHNOLOGICAL-CHANGE.   GUSDLAB64980

SEMINAR ON MANPOWER POLICY AND PROGRAM. CYBERNATION AND SOCIAL CHANGE.   GUSDLAB64982

OCCUPATIONAL DEVELOPMENTS. SHORTAGES OF SKILLED TECHNICAL MANPOWER HIGHEST IN RECENT YEARS.   GUSDLAB65561

MANPOWER IMPLICATIONS OF AUTOMATION.   GUSDLAB65608

MANPOWER. RESEARCH AND TRAINING.   GUSDLAB65710

SELECTED MANPOWER INDICATORS FOR STATES.   GUSDLAB65826

MANPOWER REPORT OF THE PRESIDENT AND A REPORT ON MANPOWER REQUIREMENTS, RESOURCES, UTILIZATION, AND
TRAINING.   GUSDLAB65828

MANPOWER REPORT OF THE PRESIDENT AND A REPORT ON MANPOWER REQUIREMENTS, RESOURCES, UTILIZATION, AND
TRAINING.   GUSDLAB65828

AMERICA-S INDUSTRIAL AND OCCUPATIONAL MANPOWER REQUIREMENTS, 1964-75.   GUSDLAB66437

REPORT ON MANPOWER RESEARCH AND TRAINING UNDER THE MDTA.   GUSDLAB66493

UNUSED MANPOWER. THE NATION-S LOSS.   GUSDLAB66504

YOUNG WORKERS. A REPRINT FROM THE 1966 MANPOWER REPORT.   GUSDLAB66505

EMPLOYMENT SERVICE TASK FORCE REPORT. /MANPOWER SES/   GUSDLAB66559

MANPOWER TASKS FOR 1966.   GUSDLAB66663

MANPOWER REPORT OF THE PRESIDENT AND A REPORT ON MANPOWER REQUIREMENTS, RESOURCES, UTILIZATION, AND
TRAINING.   GUSDLAB66827

MANPOWER REPORT OF THE PRESIDENT AND A REPORT ON MANPOWER REQUIREMENTS, RESOURCES, UTILIZATION, AND
TRAINING.   GUSDLAB66827

DISCRIMINATION AND FULL UTILIZATION OF MANPOWER RESOURCES, 1952.   GUSSENA52347

NATION-S MANPOWER REVOLUTION.   GUSSENA63331

HEARINGS RELATING TO THE TRAINING AND UTILIZATION OF THE MANPOWER RESOURCES OF THE NATION.   GUSSENA63618

MANPOWER RETRAINING.   GUSSENA63822

TOWARDS FULL EMPLOYMENT. PROPOSALS FOR A COMPREHENSIVE EMPLOYMENT AND MANPOWER POLICY IN THE UNITED
STATES.   GUSSENA64332

SELECTED READINGS IN EMPLOYMENT AND MANPOWER.   GUSSENA64334

THE ROLE AND LIMITS OF NATIONAL MANPOWER POLICIES.   GWEBEAR66760

MANPOWER PROGRAMS. THEIR CONTRIBUTION TO THE ACHIEVEMENT OF EQUAL-OPPORTUNITY MANPOWER ADMINISTRATION.   GWHITHC65558

MANPOWER   (CONTINUATION)
    MANPOWER PROGRAMS. THEIR CONTRIBUTION TO THE ACHIEVEMENT OF EQUAL-OPPORTUNITY MANPOWER ADMINISTRATION.   GWHITHC65558

    MANPOWER TRAINING. SOME COST DIMENSIONS.   GYOUNSX67144

    MANPOWER AND TRAINING. TRENDS, OUTLOOK AND PROGRAMS.   GZEISJS63704

    MANPOWER SERVICES TO ARIZONA INDIANS. /SES/   IARIZSE66912

    MANPOWER SERVICES ON THE NAVAJO RESERVATION.   IGRAFMF66565

    MANPOWER TRAINING IN NAVAJO LAND.   IHARTVS63573

    SOCIAL AND CULTURAL CONSIDERATIONS IN THE DEVELOPMENT OF MANPOWER PROGRAMS FOR INDIANS.   IKELLWH67579

    NATIONAL CONFERENCE ON MANPOWER PROGRAMS FOR INDIANS. SUMMATION.   IKRUGDH67811

    MANPOWER TRAINING AND THE NEGRO WORKER.   NBRAZWF66110

    MANAGING YOUR MANPOWER. NEGRO EMPLOYMENT PROBLEM.   NBROOTR63118

    SEGREGATION AND MANPOWER WASTE.   NGINZEX60413

    PSYCHOLOGY AND MANPOWER POLICY.   NGINZEX66412

    REALIZING THE MANPOWER POTENTIALITIES OF MINORITY-GROUP YOUTH.   NHOLLJH58561

    EXPERIMENTAL AND DEMONSTRATION MANPOWER PROJECT FOR THE RECRUITMENT, TRAINING, PLACEMENT AND FOLLOW-UP OF
    RURAL UNEMPLOYED WORKERS IN TEN NORTH FLORIDA CITIES. FINAL REPORT. /PARTICIPANTS/   NJACKTA66597

    THE NEGRO AS AN AMERICAN. /MANPOWER/   NJOHNXX63336

    WASTED MANPOWER -- BERKELEY CHALLENGE AND OPPORTUNITY. WORKSHOP COSPONSORED WITH THE BERKELEY UNIFIED
    SCHOOL-DISTRICT MARCH 15-16, 1963. /CALIFORNIA/   NKENNVD63642

    EMPLOYMENT OF NEGRO MANPOWER IN CALVERT COUNTY, MARYLAND.   NLERANL60401

    MANPOWER SERVICES FOR EQUAL-EMPLOYMENT-OPPORTUNITY.   NLEVILX64685

    INTELLIGENCE IN THE UNITED STATES. A SURVEY -- WITH CONCLUSIONS FOR MANPOWER UTILIZATION IN EDUCATION AND
    EMPLOYMENT.   NMINEJB57796

    COMMISSION ON MANPOWER UTILIZATION REPORTS.   NNATLAI55872

    MOBILIZING MANPOWER.   NPATEJE43977

    BLUEPRINT FOR TALENT. SEARCHING AMERICA-S HIDDEN MANPOWER.   NPLAURL57003

    WASTE OF MANPOWER -- RACE AND EMPLOYMENT IN A SOUTHERN STATE.   NROBEGX62064

    UTILIZATION OF NEGRO MANPOWER.   NUSDDEF59239

    IMPACT OF OFFICE AUTOMATION IN THE INTERNAL REVENUE SERVICE. A STUDY OF THE MANPOWER IMPLICATIONS DURING
    THE FIRST STAGES OF THE CHANGEOVER. /ECONOMIC-STATUS/   NUSDLAB63198

    EDUCATION AND MANPOWER.   WDAVIHX60941

    FINAL REPORT. EXPERIMENTAL AND DEMONSTRATION MANPOWER PROJECT FOR THE RECRUITMENT, TRAINING, PLACEMENT
    AND FOLLOW-UP OF RURAL UNEMPLOYED WORKERS IN TEN NORTH FLORIDA COUNTIES.   WFLORMP66326

    IMPLICATIONS FROM RECENT RESEARCH ON COLLEGE STUDENTS. /MANPOWER/   WHEISPX59838

    STUDENTS TODAY -- MEN AND WOMEN OF TOMORROW. /MANPOWER/   WHEISPX61841

    WOMANPOWER -- KEY TO MANAGEMENT MANPOWER SHORTAGE.   WLLOYBJ62633

    AND ANGELS WALK WHERE ONLY MALES TREAD. THE EMERGENCE OF WOMANPOWER. /MANPOWER/   WMATHJP66959

    MANPOWER IMPLICATIONS OF AUTOMATION.   WORGAEC64045

    HELP WANTED -- FEMALE. A STUDY OF DEMAND AND SUPPLY IN A LOCAL JOB MARKET FOR WOMEN. /MANPOWER/   WSMITGM64121

    HEALTH MANPOWER SOURCE BOOK. SECTION 2. NURSING PERSONNEL.   WUSDHEW66177

    THE NURSING SHORTAGE AND THE NURSE TRAINING ACT OF 1964. /MANPOWER/   WYETTDX66246

MANPOWER-DEVELOPMENT
    THE TRAINING OF MIGRANT FARM WORKERS. A FOLLOW-UP STUDY OF TWO EXPERIMENTAL AND DEMONSTRATION PROGRAMS
    UNDER THE MANPOWER-DEVELOPMENT-AND-TRAINING-ACT. /MEXICAN-AMERICAN AMERICAN-INDIAN/   CUNIVOD66054

    TRAINING DISADVANTAGED GROUPS UNDER THE MANPOWER-DEVELOPMENT-TRAINING-ACT.   GHELPCW63501

    RETRAINING UNDER THE MANPOWER-DEVELOPMENT-ACT. A COST-BENEFIT ANALYSIS.   GPAGEDA64775

    ANNUAL REPORT OF THE SECRETARY OF HEALTH, EDUCATION, AND WELFARE TO THE CONGRESS ON TRAINING ACTIVITIES
    UNDER THE MANPOWER-DEVELOPMENT-AND-TRAINING-ACT, 1965.   GUSDHEW66978

    CHARACTERISTICS OF 6000 WHITE AND NONWHITE PERSONS ENROLLED IN MANPOWER-DEVELOPMENT-AND-TRAINING-ACT
    TRAINING.   GUSDLAB63197

    FACTORS IN WORKERS DECISIONS TO FOREGO RETRAINING UNDER THE MANPOWER-DEVELOPMENT-AND-RETRAINING-ACT.   NBRAZWF64318

    OCCUPATIONAL TRAINING OF WOMEN UNDER THE MANPOWER-DEVELOPMENT-AND-TRAINING-ACT.   WUSDLAB64179

MANUAL
    SELF APPRAISAL FOR MERIT PROMOTION. A RESEARCH MANUAL.   GBOWMGW63467

    MANUAL OF INTERGROUP RELATIONS.   GDEANJP55630

    FEPC REFERENCE MANUAL.   GNATLCJ48040

    COMPILATION OF LAWS AGAINST DISCRIMINATION. A REFERENCE MANUAL.   GNEWYSA48078

    FIELD MANUAL ON EQUAL-EMPLOYMENT-OPPORTUNITY UNDER GOVERNMENT CONTRACTS.   GPRESCD65107

    NAACP LABOR MANUAL. A GUIDE TO ACTION.   NHILLHX58531

MANUFACTURING
    ANALYSIS OF THE TECHNIQUES OF RACIAL INTEGRATION IN THREE MANUFACTURING FIRMS. /INDUSTRY/   NCAMPFX54178

MANUFACTURING   (CONTINUATION)
    WOMEN EMPLOYEES IN **MANUFACTURING** BY INDUSTRY, JANUARY, 1959.   WEMPLAE59752

MAP
    DISTRIBUTION OF SPANISH-NAME PEOPLE IN THE SOUTHWEST. TABLES AND **MAP**.   MHOLLSX56417

MARCH-ON-WASHINGTON-
    WHEN NEGROES MARCH. THE **MARCH-ON-WASHINGTON**-MOVEMENT IN THE ORGANIZATIONAL POLITICS FOR FEPC.   NGARFHX59396

MARGINAL
    MARGINAL EMPLOYABILITY.   GFURFPH62705

    THE **MARGINAL** SEX. /WORK-WOMAN-ROLE/   WFREEMX62771

MARGINALITY
    EDUCATION AND **MARGINALITY**. A STUDY OF THE NEGRO COLLEGE GRADUATE.   NCUTHMV49936

MARIETTA
    CARRYING OUT A PLAN FOR JOB INTEGRATION AND DOING IT -- IN THE HEART OF GEORGIA -- WITHOUT A SINGLE
    UNPLEASANT INCIDENT. THAT-S THE EXPERIENCE OF LOCKHEED AIRCRAFT CORPORATION AT ITS **MARIETTA** PLANT.
    /INDUSTRY/   NBUSIWX63148

    REPORT AND SUMMARY OF THE AIR FORCE ON ACTIONS TAKEN BY LOCKHEED AIRCRAFT CORPORATION AT THE AIR FORCE
    PLANT NO 6 IN **MARIETTA**. GEORGIA. /INDUSTRY/   NPRESCD61013

MARITAL
    MARITAL AND FAMILY CHARACTERISTICS OF WORKERS, MARCH 1963.   GPERRVC64168

    MARITAL AND FAMILY CHARACTERISTICS OF WORKERS, MARCH 1960.   GSCHIJX61284

    MARITAL AND FAMILY CHARACTERISTICS OF WORKERS, MARCH 1961.   GSCHIJX62285

    MARITAL AND FAMILY CHARACTERISTICS OF WORKERS, MARCH 1962.   GSCHIJX63286

    MARITAL AND FAMILY CHARACTERISTICS OF WORKERS, MARCH 1964.   GUSDLAB64201

    MARITAL DISAGREEMENT IN WORKING WIFE MARRIAGES AS A FUNCTION OF HUSBAND-S ATTITUDE TOWARDS WIFE-S
    EMPLOYMENT. /WORK-FAMILY-CONFLICT/   WGIANAX57779

MARITAL-STATUS
    EMPLOYMENT AND PERSONAL CHARACTERISTICS. EMPLOYMENT BY AGE, RACE, NATIVITY, EDUCATION, **MARITAL-STATUS**,
    HOUSEHOLD RELATIONSHIPS, ETC. /DEMOGRAPHY/   CUSBURC53372

    NONWHITE POPULATION BY RACE. NEGROES, INDIANS, JAPANESE, CHINESE, FILIPINOS. BY AGE, SEX, **MARITAL-STATUS**,
    EDUCATION, EMPLOYMENT-STATUS, OCCUPATIONAL-STATUS, INCOME, ETC. /DEMOGRAPHY/   CUSBURC53378

    NONWHITE POPULATION BY RACE. NEGROES, INDIANS, JAPANESE,CHINESE, FILIPINOS. BY AGE, SEX,
    MARITAL-STATUS,EDUCATION, EMPLOYMENT-STATUS, OCCUPATIONAL-STATUS, INCOME, ETC. /DEMOGRAPHY/   CUSBURC63176

    DISCRIMINATION IN EMPLOYMENT OR OCCUPATION ON THE BASIS OF **MARITAL-STATUS**.   WINTELR62865

    AGE AND **MARITAL-STATUS** AND THEIR RELATIONSHIP TO SUCCESS IN PRACTICAL NURSING. /OCCUPATIONS/   WMEADLX63967

MARKET
    DISCRIMINATORY ASPECTS OF THE LABOR **MARKET** OF THE 60-S.   GBUCKLF

    MINORITIES IN THE **MARKET** PLACE.   GDEMSHX65869

    NEGRO **MARKET**. GROWING, CHANGING, CHALLENGING.   NBLACLE63493

    ECONOMIC TRENDS IN THE NEGRO **MARKET**. /ECONOMIC-STATUS/   NBRIMAF64891

    DISCRIMINATORY ASPECTS OF THE LABOR **MARKET** OF THE 60-S.   NBUCKLF61130

    ETHNOMICS -- NEGRO MUST BE FULL PARTICIPANT IN **MARKET** PLACE.   NBUNKHC65122

    THE **MARKET** FOR NEGRO EDUCATORS IN COLLEGES AND UNIVERSITIES OUTSIDE THE SOUTH.   NROSEHM61076

    THE ACADEMIC **MARKET** PLACE. /OCCUPATIONS/   WCAPLTX58679

    WOMEN-S CHANGING ROLE IN THE US EMPLOYMENT **MARKET**.   WMUNTEE56007

    HELP WANTED -- FEMALE. A STUDY OF DEMAND AND SUPPLY IN A LOCAL JOB **MARKET** FOR WOMEN. /MANPOWER/   WSMITGM64121

MARKETPLACE
    THE NEGRO-S FORCE IN **MARKETPLACE**. /EMPLOYMENT/   NBUSIWX62156

MARKETS
    FREE MEN AND FREE **MARKETS**. /TECHNOLOGICAL-CHANGE GUARANTEED-INCOME/   GTHEORX63682

MARKOV
    FUTURE OCCUPATIONAL DIFFERENCES BETWEEN THE RACES. A **MARKOV** APPROACH.   NLEWISX66693

MARRIAGE
    EMPLOYMENT, EDUCATION AND **MARRIAGE** OF YOUNG NEGRO ADULTS.   NCOXXOC41934

    ROLE EXPECTATIONS OF YOUNG WOMEN REGARDING **MARRIAGE** AND A CAREER. /ASPIRATIONS WORK-FAMILY-CONFLICT/   WEMPELT58751

    MARRIAGE AND CAREERS FOR GIRLS. /WORK-FAMILY-CONFLICT/   WGARFSH57774

    MARRIAGE AND CAREER CONFLICTS IN GIRLS AND YOUNG WOMEN. /WORK-FAMILY-CONFLICT/   WMATTEX60961

    ATTITUDES TOWARD CAREER AND **MARRIAGE** AND THE DEVELOPMENT OF LIFE STYLES IN YOUNG WOMEN.
    /WORK-FAMILY-CONFLICT/   WMATTEX64962

    WORK AND **MARRIAGE**. /WORK-FAMILY-CONFLICT/   WMEYEAE58974

    CAREERS FOR WOMEN AFTER **MARRIAGE** AND CHILDREN. /WORK-FAMILY-CONFLICT/   WONEIBP65043

    MARRIAGE, FAMILY, AND SOCIETY. A READER. /WORK-FAMILY-CONFLICT/   WRODMHX65084

MARRIAGES
    MARITAL DISAGREEMENT IN WORKING WIFE **MARRIAGES** AS A FUNCTION OF HUSBAND-S ATTITUDE TOWARDS WIFE-S
    EMPLOYMENT. /WORK-FAMILY-CONFLICT/   WGIANAX57779

MARRIED
    UNEMPLOYMENT OF **MARRIED** WOMEN.   WALTMSX63757

    THE PROSPECT FOR ADVANCEMENT IN BUSINESS OF THE **MARRIED** WOMAN COLLEGE GRADUATE. /OCCUPATIONS/   WBECKEL64632

MARRIED   (CONTINUATION)
LONG-RANGE CAUSES AND CONSEQUENCES OF THE EMPLOYMENT OF MARRIED WOMEN.   WBLOORC65884

THE RELATIONSHIP OF PARENTAL IDENTIFICATION TO SEX ROLE ACCEPTANCE IN MARRIED, SINGLE, CAREER AND
NON-CAREER WOMEN. /WORK-WOMEN-ROLE/   WBREYCH64654

THE LABOR-FORCE PARTICIPATION OF MARRIED WOMEN.   WCAINGG64671

MARRIED WOMEN IN THE LABOR-FORCE -- AN ECONOMIC ANALYSIS.   WCAINGG66672

STATUS IMPLICATIONS OF THE EMPLOYMENT OF MARRIED WOMEN IN THE UNITED STATES.   WDAYXLH61726

MARRIED WOMEN AT UTAH STATE UNIVERSITY, SPRING QUARTER, 1960. /TRAINING/   WFREDCX61769

ATTITUDES OF WOMEN REGARDING GAINFUL EMPLOYMENT OF MARRIED WOMEN. /ASPIRATIONS/   WGLENHM59789

A FUNCTIONAL APPROACH TO THE GAINFUL EMPLOYMENT OF MARRIED WOMEN.   WHACKHM61812

ATTITUDES OF COLLEGE STUDENTS TOWARD EMPLOYMENT AMONG MARRIED WOMEN. /WORK-FAMILY-CONFLICT/   WHEWEVH64482

FACTORS DETERMINING THE LABOR-FORCE PARTICIPATION OF MARRIED WOMEN.   WMAHOTA61951

LABOR-FORCE PARTICIPATION OF MARRIED WOMEN. A STUDY OF LABOR SUPPLY.   WMINCJX62984

ROLES OF THE MARRIED WOMAN IN SCIENCE. /OCCUPATIONS/   WMOTZAB61002

WORK IN THE LIVES OF MARRIED WOMEN.   WNATLMC57021

CORRELATES OF PRESENT AND FUTURE WORK STATUS OF MARRIED WOMEN.   WSOBOMB60125

THE VOCATIONAL ROLES OF OLDER MARRIED WOMEN. /WORK-WOMAN-ROLE/   WSTEIAX61136

MARRIED WOMEN AND THE LEVEL OF UNEMPLOYMENT.   WSTEIRL61226

THE MARRIED FEMALE SCHOOL TEACHER. A CONTINUED STUDY. /WORK-FAMILY-CONFLICT/   WSTEPCM60139

AN ANALYSIS OF FACTORS INFLUENCING MARRIED WOMEN-S ACTUAL OR PLANNED WORK PARTICIPATION.   WWELLMW61261

MARSHALL
THE ROLE OF CIVIL-RIGHTS ORGANIZATIONS. A MARSHALL PLAN APPROACH.   NTUCKSX66209

MARTYRS
NEGRO TEACHERS. MARTYRS TO INTEGRATION. /OCCUPATIONS/   NCOXXOC53935

MARYLAND
INCOME, EDUCATION AND UNEMPLOYMENT IN NEIGHBORHOODS. BALTIMORE, MARYLAND. /DEMOGRAPHY/   CUSDLAB63452

COMMUNITY VALUES IN EDUCATION AND OCCUPATIONAL SELECTION. A STUDY OF YOUTH IN EMMITSBURG, MARYLAND.   GLEONRC64894

PROGRESS IN MEETING PROBLEMS OF MIGRATORY LABOR IN MARYLAND.   GMARYGC60955

THE HOUSING PROBLEM OF THE MIGRANT-WORKER IN MARYLAND.   GMARYSD59956

MARYLAND TB -- VD HEALTH PROGRAM AMONG AGRICULTURAL MIGRANTS.   GMARYSD65958

MIGRANT CREWS IN EASTERN MARYLAND.   GSHOSAL65306

REPORTS ON APPRENTICESHIP, NINE STATE ADVISORY COMMITTEES. /CALIFORNIA   FLORIDA   MARYLAND CONNECTICUT
WASHINGTON-DC NEW-JERSEY NEW-YORK TENNESSEE WISCONSIN/   GUSCOMC64407

REPORT ON MARYLAND. EMPLOYMENT.   GUSCOMC64411

PROGRESS IN MEETING PROBLEMS OF MIGRATORY LABOR IN MARYLAND.   GUVMADA62529

TOWARD EQUALITY, BALTIMORE-S PROGRESS-REPORT, A CHRONICLE OF PROGRESS SINCE WORLD-WAR-II TOWARD THE
ACHIEVEMENT OF EQUAL-RIGHTS AND OPPORTUNITIES FOR NEGROES IN MARYLAND 1946-1958.   NBALTUL58048

TOWARD EQUALITY, BALTIMORE-S PROGRESS-REPORT, 1962 SUPPLEMENT. /MARYLAND/   NBALTUL62049

WAR INDUSTRY EMPLOYMENT FOR NEGROES IN MARYLAND.   NBRYSWO43129

SOME TENDENCIES IN DEMOGRAPHIC TRENDS IN MARYLAND, 1950-1956.   NJACKEG57070

THE EMPLOYMENT SITUATION OF WHITE AND NEGRO YOUTH IN THE CITY OF BALTIMORE. INITIAL EXPERIENCES IN THE
LABOR-MARKET. /MARYLAND/   NJOHNHU63735

EMPLOYMENT OF NEGRO MANPOWER IN CALVERT COUNTY, MARYLAND.   NLERANL60401

THE EMPLOYMENT SITUATION OF WHITE AND NEGRO YOUTH IN THE CITY OF BALTIMORE. /MARYLAND/   NLEVEBX63684

INCOME, EMPLOYMENT STATUS AND CHANGE IN CALVERT COUNTY, MARYLAND.   NROHRWC58400

OCCUPATIONAL DISTRIBUTION OF EMPLOYED COLORED WORKERS OF MARYLAND.   NUSDLAB40834

CONCERN FOR AGRICULTURAL MIGRANTS IN MARYLAND.   PUVMAXX64856

SPEECH ABOUT JOB OPPORTUNITIES FOR GIRLS BEFORE THE MARYLAND STATE PERSONNEL AND GUIDANCE ASSOCIATION.   WTERLRX64148

MASSACHUSETTS
INCOME, EDUCATION AND UNEMPLOYMENT IN NEIGHBORHOODS. BOSTON, MASSACHUSETTS. /DEMOGRAPHY/   CUSDLAB63454

NOW. MASSACHUSETTS PLAN FOR EQUAL-EMPLOYMENT-OPPORTUNITY.   GGCULJX63732

COMPILATION OF LAWS AGAINST DISCRIMINATION. EMPLOYMENT, EDUCATIONAL INSTITUTIONS, PLACES OF PUBLIC
ACCOMODATION, PUBLIC HOUSING, PUBLICLY ASSISTED HOUSING, PRIVATE HOUSING. /MASSACHUSETTS/   GMASSCAND963

LAW AND EQUAL-OPPORTUNITY. ANTI-DISCRIMINATION LAW IN MASSACHUSETTS.   GMAYHLH63970

FAIR-EMPLOYMENT IN MASSACHUSETTS. PART I.   GMCKEES52927

FAIR-EMPLOYMENT IN MASSACHUSETTS, PART II.   GMCKEES52928

MASSACHUSETTS FAIR-EMPLOYMENT-PRACTICE ACT OF 1946.   GUSDLAB46075

SUB-EMPLOYMENT IN THE SLUMS OF BOSTON. /MASSACHUSETTS/   GUSDLAB66518

THE NEGRO IN BOSTON. /MASSACHUSETTS/   NEDWARM61327

FINAL REPORT. EQUAL-EMPLOYMENT-OPPORTUNITY IN THE TRANSPORTATION INDUSTRY. /MASSACHUSETTS/   NMASSCA66964

MASSACHUSETTS (CONTINUATION)
REPORT OF THE COMMISSION ON THE EMPLOYMENT PROBLEMS OF NEGROES TO GOVERNOR SALTONSTALL. /MASSACHUSETTS/   NMASSCE42757

THE VOICE OF THE GHETTO. A REPORT ON TWO BOSTON NEIGHBORHOOD MEETINGS. /MASSACHUSETTS/   NUSCOMC67149

SHORTAGE OR SURPLUS. AN ASSESSMENT OF BOSTON WOMANPOWER IN INDUSTRY, GOVERNMENT, AND RESEARCH. JUNE 7-8,
1963. /MASSACHUSETTS/   WUSDLAB66217

THE NEXT STEP -- A GUIDE TO PART-TIME OPPORTUNITIES IN GREATER BOSTON FOR THE EDUCATED WOMAN.
/MASSACHUSETTS/   WWHITMS64266

MATCHED
INTELLIGENCE AND EDUCATIONAL ACHIEVEMENT OF A MATCHED SAMPLE OF WHITE AND NEGRO STUDENTS.   NMCQURX60730

MATERIAL
A COMPILATION OF STATISTICAL DATA, CHARTS AND OTHER RESOURCE MATERIAL FOR CONFERENCE PARTICIPANTS.
/APPRENTICESHIP CALIFORNIA YOUTH/   GCALCNA60516

SCHOOL, MINORITIES AND EQUAL-RIGHTS, SELECTED MATERIAL. /CALIFORNIA/   GCALSLIND549

NEGRO RESPONSES TO VERBAL AND NON-VERBAL TEST MATERIAL.   NBEANKL47914

MATERIALS
THE EDUCATION OF THE SPANISH-SPEAKING IN THE SOUTHWEST -- AN ANALYSIS OF THE 1960 CENSUS MATERIALS.   MSAMOJX63469

MATERIALS RELATING TO THE EDUCATION OF SPANISH-SPEAKING PEOPLE IN THE UNITED STATES, AN ANNOTATED
BIBLIOGRAPHY.   MSANCGI59478

MATERIALS COLLECTION ON WOMEN.   WSMITCLND118

MATERNAL
MATERNAL EMPLOYMENT. SITUATIONAL AND ATTITUDINAL VARIABLES. /WORK-FAMILY-CONFLICT/   WBRIEDX61655

RELATIONS AMONG MATERNAL EMPLOYMENT INDICES AND DEVELOPMENTAL CHARACTERISTICS OF CHILDREN.
/WORK-FAMILY-CONFLICT/   WBURCLG61665

WHAT ASPECTS OF CHILD BEHAVIOR SHOULD BE STUDIED IN RELATION TO MATERNAL EMPLOYMENT.   WHARTRE61829

MATERNITY
MATERNITY BENEFIT PROVISIONS FOR EMPLOYED WOMEN. /EMPLOYMENT-CONDITIONS/   WUSDLAB60206

MATHEMATICIANS
WOMEN MATHEMATICIANS IN INDUSTRY. /OCCUPATIONS/   WSENDVL64111

MATHEMATICS
REPORT OF THE EXPLORATORY STATISTICAL SURVEY OF THE EDUCATIONAL-ATTAINMENT, NUMBER, AND AVAILABILITY OF
THE MEMBERSHIP OF THE AMERICAN ASSOCIATION OF UNIVERSITY WOMEN FOR TEACHING IN THE FIELDS OF SCIENCE AND
MATHEMATICS. /OCCUPATIONS/   WDOLAEF57735

RUTGERS -- THE STATE UNIVERSITY, FORD FOUNDATION PROGRAM FOR THE RETRAINING IN MATHEMATICS OF COLLEGE
GRADUATE WOMEN. /TRAINING/   WMARTHM63957

MATHEMATICS RETRAINING PROGRAM. NOTES AND COMMENTS, APRIL 1964, 1965, 1966. /TRAINING/   WRUTGMR64097

REPORT -- 1965-66 -- RETRAINING PROGRAM IN MATHEMATICS AND SCIENCE FOR COLLEGE GRADUATE WOMEN.   WRUTGMR66098

MATRIARCHY
THE NEGRO MATRIARCHY. /WOMEN ECONOMIC-STATUS/   NBATTMX65313

MATRIX
THE MATRIX. /POVERTY UNEMPLOYMENT/   GMYRDGX64955

MATURE
RESOURCES FOR THE EMPLOYMENT OF MATURE WOMEN AND/OR THEIR CONTINUING EDUCATION. A SELECTED BIBLIOGRAPHY
AND AIDS.   WBERNML66746

RECRUITMENT OF THE MATURE WOMAN.   WCULPPX61382

COUNSELING THE MATURE WOMAN.   WDOLAEF66733

COUNSELING OF GIRLS AND MATURE WOMEN.   WHEDGJN64994

REPORT ON UNDERGRADUATE COUNSELING AND CONTINUING EDUCATION AND GUIDANCE FOR MATURE WOMAN.   WNICOHG64032

MATURE WOMEN IN DOCTORAL PROGRAMS. /OCCUPATIONS/   WRANDKS65073

IMPLICATIONS OF TWO PILOT PROJECTS IN TRAINING MATURE WOMEN AS COUNSELORS.   WRIOCMJ65082

MAYOR
INTERIM REPORT TO THE MAYOR ON ITS INQUIRY INTO CHARGES OF RACIAL BIAS IN THE CITY BUILDING AND
CONSTRUCTION INDUSTRY. /NEW-YORK NEGRO PUERTO-RICAN/   CNEWYCO64917

THE MAYOR AND THE FIRE CHIEF. THE FIGHT OVER INTEGRATING THE LOS-ANGELES FIRE DEPARTMENT. /CALIFORNIA
CASE-STUDY/   NSHERFP59130

MCCONE
THE WATTS MANIFESTO AND THE MCCONE REPORT. /LOS-ANGELES CALIFORNIA/   NRUSTBX66099

MCCONE-COMMISSION
SUMMARY OF MAJOR POINTS, TALK ON EMPLOYMENT, MCCONE-COMMISSION SERIES.   NBULLPX66898

MCCONE-REPORT
EMPLOYMENT AND TRAINING, THE MCCONE-REPORT -- SIX MONTHS LATER.   NBULLPXND134

MDTA
RACIAL CHARACTERISTICS, MDTA TRAINEES, SAN-FRANCISCO. /CALIFORNIA NEGRO MEXICAN-AMERICAN/   CELTOEX63332

MDTA MOVES TO THE FRONT.   GDALYVR66625

MDTA INSTITUTIONAL TRAINING OF NONWHITES.   GMARSJX66944

GRADUATES OF THE NORFOLK PROJECT ONE YEAR LATER. /MDTA TRAINING/   GQUINPA65771

TRAINING OF PUBLIC ASSISTANCE RECIPIENTS UNDER THE MDTA.   GROSORG66258

REPORT ON MANPOWER RESEARCH AND TRAINING UNDER THE MDTA.   GUSDLAB66493

MDTA COMES TO THE OWYHEE RESERVATION.   IFISHCR66559

MDTA   (CONTINUATION)
MDTA PROJECT UPLIFT. /TRAINING/   NFILIJE66354

TESTIMONY, PUBLIC HEARING, WOMEN IN PUBLIC AND PRIVATE EMPLOYMENT, CALIFORNIA. /MDTA EEO/   WINGRLX66859

MEANS
CULTURAL AND RELATED RESTRAINTS AND MEANS OF OVERCOMING THEM. /MEXICAN-AMERICAN NEGRO INTEGRATION/   CSHANLW65485

THE CIVIL-RIGHTS-ACT OF 1964. WHAT IT MEANS -- TO EMPLOYERS, BUSINESSMEN, UNIONS, EMPLOYEES,
MINORITY-GROUPS. TEXT, ANALYSIS, LEGISLATIVE HISTORY.   GBUREON64492

ENDS AND MEANS IN THE WAR-ON-POVERTY.   GLAMPRJ66881

WHAT TITLE-VII MEANS FOR THE LOCAL OFFICE. /SES/   GMITCHR66018

AMBITIONS OF MEXICAN-AMERICAN YOUTH -- GOALS AND MEANS OF MOBILITY OF HIGH SCHOOL SENIORS.   MHELLCS64413

WHAT THE ECONOMIC-OPPORTUNITY-ACT MEANS TO THE NEGRO.   NWOLFDP65337

WHAT THE EQUAL-PAY PRINCIPLE MEANS TO WOMEN.   WUSDLAB64227

MEASUREMENT
THE MEANING AND MEASUREMENT OF PARTIAL AND DISGUISED UNEMPLOYMENT.   GDUCOLJ57955

UNEMPLOYMENT. ITS SCOPE, MEASUREMENT, AND EFFECT ON POVERTY.   GFERGRH65012

SOME SUGGESTED APPROACHES FOR TEST DEVELOPMENT AND MEASUREMENT.   GKRUGRE66863

THE MEASUREMENT AND INTERPRETATION OF JOB VACANCIES. A CONFERENCE REPORT OF THE NATIONAL BUREAU OF
ECONOMIC RESEARCH. /LABOR-MARKET/   GNATLBE66611

SEMINAR ON MANPOWER POLICY AND PROGRAM MEASUREMENT OF TECHNOLOGICAL-CHANGE.   GUSDLAB64980

THE SECONDARY LABOR-FORCE AND THE MEASUREMENT OF UNEMPLOYMENT.   GWILCRC57562

THE MEASUREMENT OF ASSIMILATION. THE SPOKANE INDIANS. /WASHINGTON/   IROYXPX66613

MEASURES
LOW-INCOME FAMILIES AND MEASURES OF INCOME INEQUALITY.   GGOLDSF62725

MEASURING
MEASURING THE ADJUSTMENT OF IMMIGRANT LABORERS. /MEXICAN-AMERICAN NEGRO/   CSHANLW63487

MEAT-PACKING
MANAGEMENT SOCIAL RESPONSIBILITY AND RACIAL EMPLOYMENT IN THE MEAT-PACKING INDUSTRY.   NPURCTV67123

MECHANICAL
THE MECHANICAL COTTON-PICKER, NEGRO MIGRATION, AND THE INTEGRATION MOVEMENT.   NDILLHCND274

MECHANICS
VOCATIONAL GRADUATES IN AUTO MECHANICS. A FOLLOW-UP STUDY OF NEGRO AND WHITE YOUTH. /OCCUPATIONS/   NLEVEBX66036

MECHANIZATION
FARM MECHANIZATION AND LABOR STABILIZATION. PART II IN A SERIES ON TECHNOLOGICAL-CHANGE AND FARM LABOR
USE. KERN COUNTY, CALIFORNIA, 1961. /NEGRO MEXICAN-AMERICAN/   CMETZWH65389

EFFECT OF MECHANIZATION ON EMPLOYMENT OF MIGRATORY LABOR IN AGRICULTURE AND FOOD PROCESSING.
/MIGRANT-WORKERS/   GDELASE59946

MECHANIZATION AND THE TEXAS MIGRANT.   MTEXACC64499

THE RELATIONSHIP BETWEEN MECHANIZATION OF COTTON PRODUCTION AND ATTENDANCE AND ENROLLMENT IN THE RURAL
SCHOOLS OF COAHOMA COUNTY, MISSISSIPPI.   NMCLABF51349

MEDICAL
MEDICAL SERVICE JOB OPPORTUNITIES 1964-66, SAN-FRANCISCO BAY AREA. /CALIFORNIA/   GCALDEM64521

MEDICAL SCHOOL QUOTAS. /EDUCATION DISCRIMINATION/   JBRAVHX58707

A PRELIMINARY REPORT ON MEDICAL STAFF APPOINTMENTS HELD BY NEGRO PHYSICIANS AT PREDOMINANTLY WHITE
HOSPITALS. /CHICAGO ILLINOIS/   NCHICCO60201

THE SEARCH FOR NEGRO MEDICAL STUDENTS. /EDUCATION/   NFALLAG63343

MEDICAL SOCIETY OF THE DISTRICT OF COLUMBIA TO ADMIT NEGRO PHYSICIANS. /OCCUPATIONS/   NJOURNM52628

OPTIMAL UTILIZATION OF MEDICAL WOMANPOWER. /OCCUPATIONS/   WBAUMLX66630

SURVEY OF WOMEN PHYSICIANS GRADUATING FROM MEDICAL SCHOOL, 1925-1940. /OCCUPATIONS/   WDYKMRA57745

REPORT ON THE SURVEY OF FEMALE PHYSICIANS GRADUATING FROM MEDICAL SCHOOL BETWEEN 1925 AND 1940.
/OCCUPATIONS/   WHANNFX58819

SUPPLY OF MEDICAL WOMEN IN THE UNITED STATES. /OCCUPATIONS/   WWRIGKW66277

ADMISSION OF WOMEN TO MEDICAL SCHOOL.   WWULSJH66278

MEDICINE
ETHNIC GROUPS AND THE PRACTICE OF MEDICINE. /OCCUPATIONS/   GLIEBSX58042

PROGRESS AND PORTENTS FOR THE NEGRO IN MEDICINE. /OCCUPATIONS/   NCOBBWM48217

NEGROES IN MEDICINE. /OCCUPATIONS/   NNATLMF52877

NEW OPPORTUNITIES FOR NEGROES IN MEDICINE. /OCCUPATIONS/   NNATLMF62878

A REPORT ON COMMUNITY FACTORS IN NASHVILLE RELATED TO THE NEGRO IN MEDICINE. /TENNESSEE/   NVALIPX56281

MEDICINE AS A CAREER FOR WOMEN. /OCCUPATIONS/   WAMERMW65607

DISCUSSION. WOMEN IN MEDICINE. /OCCUPATIONS/   WGRIFAM65803

BARRIERS TO THE CAREER CHOICE OF ENGINEERING, MEDICINE, OR SCIENCE AMONG AMERICAN WOMEN. /OCCUPATIONS/   WROSSAS65091

MEETING
MEETING TODAYS CHALLENGE FOR EMPLOYMENT. /AMERICAN-INDIAN NEGRO MEXICAN-AMERICAN/   CARIZSE65403

PROGRESS IN MEETING PROBLEMS OF MIGRATORY LABOR IN MARYLAND.   GMARYGC60955

MEETING (CONTINUATION)
MEETING THE MANPOWER PROBLEMS OF. I. AREA REDEVELOPMENT, II. AUTOMATION.   GUSDLAB62708

PROGRESS IN **MEETING** PROBLEMS OF MIGRATORY LABOR IN MARYLAND.   GUVMADA62529

REPORT OF INDIAN RECRUITMENT AND TRAINING **MEETING** AT ALBUQUERQUE, NEW-MEXICO, ON DECEMBER 6, 1966.   IUSDLAB66321

MINUTES OF INDIAN EMPLOYMENT **MEETING** HELD NOVEMBER 29-30, 1966 IN BISMARK, NORTH-DAKOTA.   IUSDLAB66322

MEETING THE PSYCHOLOGICAL CRISES OF NEGRO YOUTH THROUGH A COORDINATED GUIDANCE SERVICE.   NBRAZWF58111

MANAGEMENTS GUIDELINES FOR **MEETING** THE NEGRO DRIVE FOR JOB EQUALITY. /INDUSTRY/.   NOPINRC63958

MEETING THE NEEDS OF THE PUERTO-RICAN MIGRANT.   PMONTHK59829

MEETINGS
REPORTS OF THE **MEETINGS** OF THE COMMITTEE OF OFFICIALS ON MIGRATORY FARM LABOR OF THE ATLANTIC SEABOARD
STATES. /MIGRANT-WORKERS/   GCOUNSG58932

THE VOICE OF THE GHETTO. A REPORT ON TWO BOSTON NEIGHBORHOOD **MEETINGS**. /MASSACHUSETTS/   NUSCCMC67149

MEMBERS
PERSONS BY FAMILY CHARACTERISTICS. FAMILY **MEMBERS** BY SOCIAL, ECONOMIC AND HOUSING CHARACTERISTICS OF
FAMILIES. /DEMOGRAPHY/   CUSBURC63180

THE RIGHTS AND RESPONSIBILITY OF UNION **MEMBERS**. /ANTIDISCRIMINATION/   GGOLDAX58974

HERE-S HOW MERIT EMPLOYMENT PROGRAMS WORK. A REPORT ON PROGRESS AND PROBLEMS IN THE EMPLOYMENT OF
MINORITY-GROUP **MEMBERS**.   GILLISC56803

THE INFLUENCE OF DISCRIMINATION ON MINORITY-GROUP **MEMBERS** IN ITS RELATION TO ATTEMPTS TO COMBAT
DISCRIMINATION.   GSAENGX48273

THE INFLUENCE OF A BORDER CITY UNION ON THE RACE ATTITUDES OF ITS **MEMBERS**.   NROSEAW53293

LABOR UNIONS AND PUERTO-RICAN **MEMBERS** IN NEW-YORK CITY.   PGRAYLX63027

A STUDY OF JOB MOTIVATIONS, ACTIVITIES, AND SATISFACTIONS OF PRESENT AND PROSPECTIVE WOMEN COLLEGE
FACULTY **MEMBERS**. /OCCUPATIONS/   WCOOKWX60252

MEMBERSHIP
STATEMENT ON SURVEYS AND STATISTICS AS TO RACIAL AND ETHNIC COMPOSITION OF WORK-FORCE OR UNION
MEMBERSHIP. /CALIFORNIA/   GCALFEP63539

LABOR LAW -- UNION **MEMBERSHIP** DENIED ON THE BASIS OF RACIAL DISCRIMINATION. /WISCONSIN LEGISLATION/   GKAUFET58014

DISCRIMINATION IN UNION **MEMBERSHIP**. DENIAL OF DUE PROCESS UNDER FEDERAL COLLECTIVE BARGAINING
LEGISLATION.   GPRESSB58126

MINORITY-GROUP INTEGRATION BY LABOR AND MANAGEMENT. A STUDY OF THE EMPLOYMENT PRACTICES OF THE LARGER
EMPLOYERS, AND THE **MEMBERSHIP** PRACTICES OF THE LARGER LABOR UNIONS WITH RESPECT TO RACE, RELIGION, AND
NATIONAL ORIGIN. CONNECTICUT, 1951.   GSTETHG53598

MEMBERSHIP DISCRIMINATION IN LABOR UNIONS.   GWASHLR64541

CONSEQUENCES OF DISCRIMINATORY UNION **MEMBERSHIP** POLICY.   GWESTRL53019

TRADE UNION COMPLIANCE WITH PRESIDENTIAL DIRECTIVES, **MEMBERSHIP** ACCEPTANCE, SENIORITY, ETC.   NCOOPJX64294

THE CONSTITUTIONAL RIGHT TO **MEMBERSHIP** IN A LABOR UNION -- FIFTH AND FOURTEENTH AMENDMENTS.   NELLIGH59330

MEMBERSHIP POLICIES OF INTERNATIONAL UNIONS AS THEY AFFECT NEGRO WORKERS.   NGRANLB41442

THE PROBLEMS OF RACIAL DISCRIMINATION IN UNION **MEMBERSHIP**.   NJENKHX47605

RECENT TRENDS OF **MEMBERSHIP** OF INTERNATIONAL UNIONS AS THEY AFFECT NEGRO WORKERS.   NJOHNRA44620

RAILWAY LABOR ACT -- DENIAL OF UNION **MEMBERSHIP** TO NEGROES.   NMINNLR58800

RACIAL DISCRIMINATION IN UNION **MEMBERSHIP**.   NPROMHJ59127

REPORT OF THE EXPLORATORY STATISTICAL SURVEY OF THE EDUCATIONAL-ATTAINMENT, NUMBER, AND AVAILABILITY OF
THE **MEMBERSHIP** OF THE AMERICAN ASSOCIATION OF UNIVERSITY WOMEN FOR TEACHING IN THE FIELDS OF SCIENCE AND
MATHEMATICS. /OCCUPATIONS/   WOOLAEF57735

MEMORANDUM
MEMORANDUM OF UNDERSTANDING BETWEEN CALIFORNIA STATE FAIR- EMPLOYMENT-PRACTICE-COMMISSION AND
BANK-OF-AMERICA NATIONAL TRUST AND SAVINGS ASSOCIATION.   GCALFEPND537

MEMORANDUM ON IDENTITY AND NEGRO YOUTH.   NERIKEX64338

A **MEMORANDUM** ON THE MOTIVATIONS OF MIDDLE AGED WOMEN IN THE LOWER EDUCATIONAL BRACKETS TO RETURN TO WORK.
/ASPIRATIONS/   WJEWIVA61880

MEMPHIS
INCOME, EDUCATION AND UNEMPLOYMENT IN NEIGHBORHOODS. **MEMPHIS**, TENNESSEE. /DEMOGRAPHY/   CUSDLAB63466

US COMMISSION-ON-CIVIL-RIGHTS, HEARINGS. **MEMPHIS**, TENNESSEE. JUNE 25-26, 1962.   GUSCCMC62401

MEMPHIS. SPECIAL REPORT. /CASE-STUDY/   NMUSEBX64869

MEN
OCCUPATIONS BY EARNINGS AND EDUCATION. STATISTICS FOR **MEN** 18-64 YEARS OLD, BY COLOR, IN SELECTED
OCCUPATIONS. /DEMOGRAPHY/   CUSBURC63178

MORTALITY BY OCCUPATION AND INDUSTRY AMONG **MEN** 20 TO 64 YEARS OF AGE. UNITED STATES, 1950. /DEMOGRAPHY/   GGURALX62748

MEN WITHOUT WORK. THE ECONOMICS OF UNEMPLOYMENT.   GLEBESX65891

JOBS, **MEN** AND MACHINES. PROBLEMS OF AUTOMATION.   GMARKCX64949

AN EXPERIMENT IN RETRAINING UNEMPLOYED **MEN** FOR PRACTICAL NURSING CAREERS.   GPEIMSC66139

OUT-OF-SCHOOL YOUTH -- TWO YEARS LATER. A 1965 RE-SURVEY OF YOUNG **MEN**.   GPERRVC66774

ONE-THIRD OF A NATION. A REPORT ON YOUNG **MEN** FOUND UNQUALIFIED FOR MILITARY SERVICE.   GPRESTM64316

ALL MANNER OF **MEN**. /FEPC/   GROSSMX48260

MEN   (CONTINUATION)
    MERIT AND MEN.   GSCHRJX46289

    FREE MEN AND FREE MARKETS.   /TECHNOLOGICAL-CHANGE GUARANTEED-INCOME/   GTHEORX63682

    AN ECONOMICAL AND HISTORICAL ANALYSIS OF THE CAUSES OF VARIATION AMONG NORTHERN STANDARD METROPOLITAN
    AREAS IN PRODUCTIVITY OF NEGRO MEN IN 1949.   NBATCAB61060

    DECLINE IN THE RELATIVE INCOME OF NEGRO MEN.   NBATCAB64058

    RELATIVE INCOME OF NEGRO MEN. SOME RECENT DATA.   NFEINRX66349

    INTER-INDUSTRY LABOR MOBILITY AMONG MEN. 1957-60.   NGALLLE66392

    EMPLOYMENT PATTERNS OF NEGRO MEN AND WOMEN.   NGINZEX66416

    WE CALL ALL MEN BROTHERS. /UNION/   NMEANGX57763

    RACE RELATIONS. QUESTIONS AND ANSWERS FOR PERSONNEL MEN.   NSHOSAX64132

    OCCUPATIONS FOR MEN AND WOMEN AFTER 45.   WANGEJL63615

    ON THE JOB. WOMEN ACT MUCH LIKE MEN. /OCCUPATIONS/   WBUSIWX63667

    THE STATUS OF WOMEN IN THE PROFESSIONS RELATIVE TO THE STATUS OF MEN. /OCCUPATIONS/   WCAVARS57684

    STUDENTS TODAY -- MEN AND WOMEN OF TOMORROW. /MANPOWER/   WHEISPX61841

    PAY DIFFERENCES BETWEEN MEN AND WOMEN. /DISCRIMINATION/   WSANBHX64100

MENOMINEE
    THE MENOMINEE TERMINATION CRISIS. BARRIERS IN THE WAY OF A RAPID CULTURAL TRANSITION.   IAMESDW59525

    MENOMINEE WOMEN AND CULTURE CHANGE.   ISPINLS62622

MENTAL
    A STUDY OF THE MENTAL HEALTH PROBLEMS OF MEXICAN-AMERICAN RESIDENTS. /TEXAS/   MTEXASD61500

    THE JAPANESE SOCIAL STRUCTURE AND THE SOURCE OF MENTAL STRAINS OF JAPANESE IMMIGRANTS IN THE US.   OIGAXMX57732

    NONTRADITIONALLY TRAINED WOMEN AS MENTAL HEALTH COUNSELORS/PSYCHOTHERAPISTS.   WMAGOTM66779

MENTALITIES
    THE MENTALITIES OF NEGRO AND WHITE WORKERS. AN EXPERIMENTAL SCHOOL-S INTERPRETATION OF NEGRO TRADE
    UNIONISM.   NVALIPX49280

MERCED-COUNTY
    THE SETTLEMENT OF MERCED-COUNTY, CALIFORNIA.   OGRAHJC57728

MERCHANDISE
    A STUDY OF EMPLOYMENT PATTERNS IN THE GENERAL MERCHANDISE GROUP RETAIL STORES IN NEW-YORK-CITY.   GWATKDO66588

MERCHANTS
    MERCHANTS OF LABOR. THE MEXICAN BRACERO STORY.   MGALAEX66397

MERIT
    QUESTIONS AND ANSWERS ABOUT EMPLOYMENT ON MERIT.   GAMERFC50379

    EMPLOYMENT BY MERIT ALONE.   GBOWMGW61466

    SELF APPRAISAL FOR MERIT PROMOTION. A RESEARCH MANUAL.   GBOWMGW63467

    MERIT EMPLOYMENT. NON-DISCRIMINATION IN INDUSTRY.   GBULLPX60897

    MINORITY-GROUPS AND MERIT SYSTEM PRACTICE.   GCALPPA65547

    MERIT EMPLOYMENT IN CHICAGO. /ILLINOIS/   GCHICMC56566

    REPORT OF INDUSTRY AND LABOR-MANAGEMENT CLINICS. IMPLEMENTATION OF EMPLOYMENT IN MERIT PROGRAMS IN NON
    FEPC STATES BY DIRECT APPROACH TO TOP MANAGEMENT.   GFISKUR51684

    GUIDE TO MERIT EMPLOYMENT. A RESTATEMENT OF INDUSTRY PRINCIPLES AND PRACTICES.   GFOODECND694

    A STUDY OF MERIT EMPLOYMENT IN 100 ILLINOIS FIRMS.   GILLICH56794

    HERE-S HOW MERIT EMPLOYMENT PROGRAMS WORK. A REPORT ON PROGRESS AND PROBLEMS IN THE EMPLOYMENT OF
    MINORITY-GROUP MEMBERS.   GILLISC56803

    WE BELIEVE IN EMPLOYMENT ON MERIT, BUT...   GLELAWC63893

    MERIT EMPLOYMENT IN MICHIGAN. A PICTORIAL REPORT.   GMICFEP63981

    MANAGEMENT AND MERIT EMPLOYMENT.   GNEWYSANDO84

    MERIT EMPLOYMENT -- UNFINISHED BUSINESS.   GPURYMJ62210

    EQUAL-OPPORTUNITY UNDER THE MERIT SYSTEM.   GROSEHS66253

    MERIT AND MEN.   GSCHRJX46289

    JOB QUOTAS AND THE MERIT SYSTEM.   NCHASET63195

    EMPLOYMENT ON MERIT. THE CONTINUING CHALLENGE TO BUSINESS. NEGRO-S ECONOMIC LOT.   NMORRJJ57854

MERIT-EMPLOYMENT
    A POSITIVE PROGRAM FOR MERIT-EMPLOYMENT.   GDOUGMX60650

MERITOCRACY
    THE MERITOCRACY OF LABOR.   NKEMPMX65293

MERRILL-TRUST-FUND
    MERRILL-TRUST-FUND TO IMPROVE THE EMPLOYMENT OPPORTUNITIES OF THE MIGRANT FARM WORKERS OF MEXICAN ORIGIN.   MBISHCS62365

MESQUAKIE
    BICULTURATION OF MESQUAKIE TEENAGE BOYS.   IPOLGSX60605

METHOD
    THEORY, METHOD AND FINDINGS IN THE STUDY OF ACCULTURATION. A REVIEW. /MEXICAN-AMERICAN NEGRO/   CPETECX65989

METHOD   (CONTINUATION)
   PREJUDICE AND SCIENTIFIC METHOD IN LABOR-RELATIONS. /UNION/   GMARRAX52941

   THE EXPECTED-CASES METHOD APPLIED TO THE NCN-WHITE MALE LABOR-FORCE.   NTURNRH49211

METHODIST
   INTEGRATION IN PROFESSIONAL EDUCATION. THE STORY OF PERKINS, SOUTHERN METHODIST UNIVERSITY. /VOCATIONS/   NCUNNMX56579

METHODOLOGICAL
   A METHODOLOGICAL APPROACH TO IDENTIFICATION AND CLASSIFICATION OF CERTAIN TYPES OF INACTIVE WORK-SEEKERS.
   /UNEMPLOYMENT LABOR-MARKET/   GLIEBEE65569

METHODOLOGY
   AN EXPERIMENT TO TEST THREE MAJOR ISSUES OF WORK PROGRAM METHODOLOGY WITHIN MOBILIZATION-FOR-YOUTH-S
   INTEGRATED SERVICES TO OUT-OF-SCHOOL UNEMPLOYED YOUTH. /NEGRO PUERTO-RICAN/   CMOBIFY66024

METHODS
   METHODS OF ADJUSTING TO AUTOMATION AND TECHNOLOGICAL-CHANGE. /INDUSTRY/   GBOKXDX64737

   PROGRESS WITHOUT FEDERAL COMPULSION. ARGUING THE CASE FOR COMPROMISE METHODS.   GNORTHR52122

   MOBILITY. METHODS OF JOB SEARCH, ATTITUDES, AND MOTIVATION OF DISPLACED WORKERS.   GSHEPHL64621

   MOVING AHEAD. AIMS AND METHODS. /CIVIL-RIGHTS ANTIDISCRIMINATION/   GWOFFHX62577

   CASE-STUDIES IN URBAN-LEAGUE METHODS.   NCOLUUL59227

METROPOLIS
   THE NEWCOMERS. NEGROES AND PUERTO-RICANS IN A CHANGING METROPOLIS   CHANDOX59481

   BLACK METROPOLIS. A STUDY OF NEGRO LIFE IN A NORTHERN CITY.   NDRAKSC45291

   MAN IN METROPOLIS. /RESIDENTIAL-SEGREGATION GHETTO/   NSCHILB65106

   THE DEEPENING CRISIS IN METROPOLIS.   NSILBCE65136

METROPOLITAN
   MOBILITY FOR METROPOLITAN AREAS.   CUSBURC63173

   THE NEXT STEPS TOWARD EQUALITY OF OPPORTUNITY IN THE SYRACUSE METROPOLITAN AREA. REPORT OF THE SYRACUSE
   CONFERENCE ON HUMAN RIGHTS AND HOUSING, JULY 2-3 1962. /NEW-YORK/   GNEWYSB62103

   RACIAL CHANGES IN METROPOLITAN AREAS, 1950-1960. /DEMOGRAPHY/   GSCHNLF63288

   POPULATION OF THE UNITED STATES BY METROPOLITAN AND NONMETROPOLITAN RESIDENCE. /DEMOGRAPHY/   GUSBURC66159

   MEXICAN-AMERICAN AND TOTAL EMPLOYMENT IN SELECTED STATES AND STANDARD METROPOLITAN STATISTICAL AREAS.   MUSCISC63504

   MIGRATION AND OPPORTUNITY. A STUDY OF STANDARD METROPOLITAN AREAS IN THE UNITED-STATES.   NBALATR63047

   AN ECONOMICAL AND HISTORICAL ANALYSIS OF THE CAUSES OF VARIATION AMONG NORTHERN STANDARD METROPOLITAN
   AREAS IN PRODUCTIVITY OF NEGRO MEN IN 1949.   NBATCAB61060

   NEGRO EMPLOYMENT IN THE BIRMINGHAM METROPOLITAN AREA. /ALABAMA CASE-STUDY/   NHAWLLT55502

   PROPOSALS FOR THE IMPROVEMENT OF HUMAN RELATIONS IN THE LOS-ANGELES METROPOLITAN AREA. /EMPLOYMENT
   CALIFORNIA/   NLOSACC65365

   RACIAL CHANGES IN METROPOLITAN AREAS, 1950-1960. /DEMOGRAPHY MIGRATION/   NSCHNLF65109

   THE CHANGING COLOR COMPOSITION OF METROPOLITAN AREAS. /DEMOGRAPHY/   NSHARHX62125

   EMPLOYMENT IN METROPOLITAN WASHINGTON. /WASHINGTON-DC/   NUSDLAB63260

   POVERTY AREAS OF OUR MAJOR CITIES. THE EMPLOYMENT SITUATION OF NEGRO AND WHITE WORKERS IN METROPOLITAN
   AREAS COMPARED IN A SPECIAL LABOR-FORCE REPORT.   NWETZJR66114

   THE FEMALE LABOR-FORCE IN METROPOLITAN AREAS. AN INTERNATIONAL COMPARISON.   WCOLLAX62697

   A SURVEY OF THE SOCIAL AND OCCUPATIONAL CHARACTERISTICS OF A METROPOLITAN NURSE. COMPLEMENT.
   /OCCUPATIONAL-DISTRIBUTION/   WDEUTIX56730

   A SURVEY OF THE SOCIAL AND OCCUPATIONAL CHARACTERISTICS OF A METROPOLITAN NURSE COMPLEMENT.   WDEUTIX57369

MEXICAN
   PREJUDICE TOWARD MEXICAN AND NEGRO AMERICANS. A COMPARISON.   CPINKAX63458

   THE INTEGRATION OF AMERICANS OF MEXICAN, PUERTO-RICAN, AND ORIENTAL DESCENT.   CYINGJM56519

   SOME PROBLEMS IN THE ACCULTURATION OF MEXICAN LABORERS TO A FACTORY.   MALBEPM64356

   NO FRONTIER TO LEARNING. THE MEXICAN STUDENT IN THE UNITED STATES.   MBEALRL57364

   MERRILL-TRUST-FUND TO IMPROVE THE EMPLOYMENT OPPORTUNITIES OF THE MIGRANT FARM WORKERS OF MEXICAN ORIGIN.   MBISHCS62365

   MERCHANTS OF LABOR. THE MEXICAN BRACERO STORY.   MGALAEX66397

   MEXICAN GREEN CARDERS. PRELIMINARY REPORT.   MGALLLX62399

   THE MEXICAN IN THE NORTHERN URBAN AREA. A COMPARISON OF TWO GENERATIONS.   MGOLDNX59403

   A HISTORY OF THE INTERRELATIONSHIPS BETWEEN IMPORTED MEXICAN LABOR, DOMESTIC MIGRANTS, AND THE TEXAS
   AGRICULTURAL ECONOMY.   MGRAVRP60405

   MEXICAN IMMIGRATION TO THE UNITED STATES. THE RECORD AND ITS IMPLICATIONS.   MGREBLX66406

   MEXICAN CULTURAL PATTERNS.   MIMMASM57420

   A STUDY OF THE ACCULTURATION AND SOCIAL ASPIRATIONS OF SIXTY JUNIOR HIGH SCHOOL STUDENTS FROM THE MEXICAN
   ETHNIC GROUP.   MJONEBM62421

   SURVEY ON TRANSIENT MEXICAN LABOR REQUIREMENTS.   MLOSACAND430

   SOME NOTES ON THE MEXICAN POPULATION OF LOS-ANGELES COUNTY. /CALIFORNIA/   MLOSACOND431

   TEXAS-S THIRD MAN. THE TEXAS MEXICAN.   MPAREAX63451

   THE MEXICAN FARM LABOR SUPPLY PROGRAM -- ITS FRIENDS AND FOES.   MPFEIDG63456

MEXICAN   (CONTINUATION)
    THE EFFECTS OF IMPORTED MEXICAN FARM LABOR IN A CALIFORNIA COUNTY.   MROONJF61465

    THE AMERICAN OF MEXICAN DESCENT.   MSANCGI61477

    THE MEXICAN IMMIGRANT WORKER IN SOUTHWESTERN AGRICULTURE.   MTHOMAN56501

    INFORMATION CONCERNING ENTRY OF MEXICAN AGRICULTURAL WORKERS INTO THE UNITED STATES.   MUSDLAB59335

    MEXICAN FARM LABOR CONSULTANTS REPORT.   MUSDLAB59508

    MEXICAN FARM LABOR PROGRAM.   MUSHOUR63984

    THREE BASIC THEMES IN MEXICAN AND PUERTO-RICAN FAMILIES.   PTRENRD58800

MEXICAN-AMERICAN
    MEETING TODAYS CHALLENGE FOR EMPLOYMENT. /AMERICAN-INDIAN NEGRO MEXICAN-AMERICAN/   CARIZSE65403

    TESTIMONY. PUBLIC HEARING. WOMEN IN PUBLIC AND PRIVATE EMPLOYMENT, CALIFORNIA. /MEXICAN-AMERICAN/   CARYWSX66621

    THE ECONOMY AND THE MINORITY POOR. /NEGRO AMERICAN-INDIAN MEXICAN-AMERICAN PUERTO-RICAN/   CBATCAB66879

    REPORT TO GOVERNOR EDMUND G BROWN. SECOND ETHNIC SURVEY OF EMPLOYMENT AND PROMOTION IN STATE GOVERNMENT.
    /CALIFORNIA NEGRO MEXICAN-AMERICAN/   CBECKWL65070

    HUMAN-RESOURCE PROBLEMS OF THE COMING DECADE. /EMPLOYMENT NEGRO MEXICAN-AMERICAN/   CBULLPX66136

    SPANISH-SPEAKING CHILDREN. /MEXICAN-AMERICAN PUERTO-RICAN EDUCATION/   CBURMJH60287

    THE PUSH OF AN ELBOW. CIVIL-RIGHTS AND OUR SPANISH-SPEAKING MINORITY. /MEXICAN-AMERICAN PUERTO-RICAN/ CBURMJH60371

    CHARACTERISTICS OF RETRAINING APPLICANTS. /CALIFORNIA NEGRO MEXICAN-AMERICAN WOMEN/   CCALDEM66166

    ANNUAL FARM LABOR REPORT, 1965. CALIFORNIA DEPARTMENT OF EMPLOYMENT, FARM LABOR SERVICE. /NEGRO
    MEXICAN-AMERICAN WOMEN/   CCALDEM66906

    RACIAL DISTRIBUTION OF SELECTED UNEMPLOYMENT INSURANCE AND EMPLOYMENT SERVICE DATA. JULY-DECEMBER 1966.
    /NEGRO MEXICAN-AMERICAN/   CCALDEM67907

    REPORT ON OAKLAND SCHOOLS. AN INVESTIGATION UNDER SECTION 1421 OF THE CALIFORNIA LABOR CODE OF THE
    OAKLAND UNIFIED SCHOOL DISTRICT 1962-1963. /NEGRO ORIENTAL MEXICAN-AMERICAN/   CCALDIR63710

    TRAINING AID. CULTURAL DIFFERENCES, TRAINING IN NONDISCRIMINATION, READING ASSIGNMENTS. /EMPLOYMENT
    MEXICAN-AMERICAN NEGRO/   CCALDSW65447

    RACIAL CHARACTERISTICS. MDTA TRAINEES, SAN-FRANCISCO. /CALIFORNIA NEGRO MEXICAN-AMERICAN/   CELTOEX63332

    THE EFFECT OF LOW EDUCATIONAL-ATTAINMENT ON INCOMES. A COMPARATIVE STUDY OF SELECTED ETHNIC GROUPS.
    /NEGRO MEXICAN-AMERICAN/   CFOGEWX66367

    APACHE, NAVAHO, AND SPANIARD. /MEXICAN-AMERICAN AMERICAN-INDIAN/   CFORBJX60561

    ECONOMIC, SOCIAL, AND DEMOGRAPHIC CHARACTERISTICS OF SPANISH-AMERICAN WAGE WORKERS ON US FARMS.
    /PUERTO-RICAN MEXICAN-AMERICAN/   CFRIERE63805

    THE NATION-S CHILDREN. VOL I. THE FAMILY AND SOCIAL-CHANGE. VOL II. DEVELOPMENT AND EDUCATION. VOL III.
    PROBLEMS AND PROSPECTS. /NEGRO PUERTO-RICAN MEXICAN-AMERICAN WOMEN/   CGINZEX60720

    FAMILY STRUCTURE AND SCHOOL PERFORMANCE. A COMPARATIVE STUDY OF STUDENTS FROM THREE ETHNIC BACKGROUNDS IN
    AN INTEGRATED SCHOOL. /MEXICAN-AMERICAN AMERICAN-INDIAN/   CGRIFJX65407

    UNDER-ACHIEVEMENT AMONG MINORITY-GROUP STUDENTS. AN ANALYSIS AND A PROPOSAL. /YOUTH NEGRO
    MEXICAN-AMERICAN PUERTO-RICAN/   CHOBACW63555

    THE FORGOTTEN PEOPLE. /MIGRANT-WORKERS MEXICAN-AMERICAN PUERTO-RICAN NEGRO/   CJACOPX59600

    LABOR UNIONISM IN AMERICAN AGRICULTURE. /NEGRO MEXICAN-AMERICAN ORIENTAL/   CJAMISM45005

    AT THE PREVAILING RATE. /MEXICAN-AMERICAN NEGRO UNION/   CLEBETX57371

    FARM MECHANIZATION AND LABOR STABILIZATION. PART II IN A SERIES ON TECHNOLOGICAL-CHANGE AND FARM LABOR
    USE. KERN COUNTY, CALIFORNIA, 1961. /NEGRO MEXICAN-AMERICAN/   CMETZWH65389

    POVERTY IN THE SOUTHWEST. A COMPARATIVE STUDY OF MEXICAN-AMERICAN, NONWHITE AND ANGLO FAMILIES. /NEGRO/ CMITTFG66777

    THE MIGRANT LABOR PROBLEM -- ITS STATE AND INTERSTATE ASPECTS. /NEGRO MEXICAN-AMERICAN/   CPALEHA63098

    THE IMMIGRANT. VALUE ORIENTATIONS AND VOCATIONAL ASPIRATIONS. /NEGRO MEXICAN-AMERICAN/   CPETECL64988

    THEORY, METHOD AND FINDINGS IN THE STUDY OF ACCULTURATION. A REVIEW. /MEXICAN-AMERICAN NEGRO/   CPETECX65989

    NEW PROBLEM OF LARGE SCALE UNEMPLOYABILITY. /NEGRO MEXICAN-AMERICAN AMERICAN-INDIAN/   CROSEAM64553

    THE SPANISH-SPEAKING PEOPLE IN THE UNITED STATES. /PUERTO-RICAN MEXICAN-AMERICAN/   CRUBIEBND848

    SPANISH-SPEAKING PEOPLE IN THE UNITED STATES. A PILOT REPORT. /MEXICAN-AMERICAN PUERTO-RICAN/   CSAMOJX63474

    OCCUPATIONAL AND RESIDENTIAL ADJUSTMENT OF RURAL MIGRANTS. /NEGRO MEXICAN-AMERICAN/   CSHANLW61119

    THE URBAN ADJUSTMENT OF IMMIGRANTS. THE RELATIONSHIP OF EDUCATION TO OCCUPATIONAL AND TOTAL FAMILY
    INCOME. /NEGRO MEXICAN-AMERICAN/   CSHANLW63122

    THE ASSIMILATION AND ACCULTURATION OF MIGRANTS TO URBAN AREAS. /MEXICAN-AMERICAN NEGRO/   CSHANLW63484

    MEASURING THE ADJUSTMENT OF IMMIGRANT LABORERS. /MEXICAN-AMERICAN NEGRO/   CSHANLW63487

    THE ECONOMIC ABSORPTION AND CULTURAL INTEGRATION OF IMMIGRANT MEXICAN-AMERICAN AND NEGRO WORKERS.   CSHANLW64124

    THE ECONOMIC ABSORPTION OF IN-MIGRANT LABORERS IN A NORTHERN INDUSTRIAL COMMUNITY. /MEXICAN-AMERICAN
    NEGRO/   CSHANLW64486

    URBAN ADJUSTMENT AND ITS RELATIONSHIP TO THE SOCIAL ANTECEDENTS OF IMMIGRANT WORKERS. /NEGRO
    MEXICAN-AMERICAN/   CSHANLW65121

    CULTURAL AND RELATED RESTRAINTS AND MEANS OF OVERCOMING THEM. /MEXICAN-AMERICAN NEGRO INTEGRATION/   CSHANLW65485

    FINAL REPORT. EXPERIMENTAL AND DEMONSTRATION ON-JOB-TRAINING PROJECT. /MIGRANT-WORKERS MEXICAN-AMERICAN
    NEGRO ARIZONA/   CSKILTO66324

MEXICAN-AMERICAN   (CONTINUATION)
THE TRAINING OF MIGRANT FARM WORKERS. A FOLLOW-UP STUDY OF TWO EXPERIMENTAL AND DEMONSTRATION PROGRAMS
UNDER THE MANPOWER-DEVELOPMENT-AND-TRAINING-ACT. /MEXICAN-AMERICAN AMERICAN-INDIAN/   CUNIVOD66054

OAK GLEN -- A TRAINING CAMP FOR UNEMPLOYED YOUTH. /NEGRO MEXICAN-AMERICAN/   CUSDLAB66323

HARD-CORE UNEMPLOYMENT AND POVERTY IN LOS-ANGELES. /CALIFORNIA NEGRO MEXICAN-AMERICAN/   CUVCAIIND524

ECONOMIC ABSORPTION AND CULTURAL INTEGRATION OF THE URBAN NEWCOMER. /NEGRO MEXICAN-AMERICAN/   CUVIOIP65277

REPORT. EVALUATION STUDY OF YOUTH TRAINING AND EMPLOYMENT PROJECT, EAST LOS-ANGELES. /NEGRO
MEXICAN-AMERICAN CALIFORNIA/   CWEINJL64310

FRUSTRATION ON THE FARM. /MEXICAN-AMERICAN ORIENTAL UNION/   GCORTJC57372

OBSTACLES TO ASSIMILATION OF THE MEXICAN-AMERICAN IN THE UNITED STATES.   MBEALRL60362

EMPLOYMENT PROBLEMS OF THE MEXICAN-AMERICAN.   MBULLPX64369

A STUDY OF AMERICAN AND MEXICAN-AMERICAN CULTURE VALUES AND THEIR SIGNIFICANCE IN EDUCATION.   MCABRYA63373

REPORT BY MEXICAN-AMERICAN LEADERS. EDUCATION, EMPLOYMENT, ETC.   MCALDIR64379

OCCUPATIONAL AND EDUCATIONAL LEVELS OF ASPIRATION OF MEXICAN-AMERICAN YOUTH.   MDEHOAX61388

SOME NON-INTELLECTUAL CORRELATES OF ACADEMIC ACHIEVEMENT AMONG MEXICAN-AMERICAN SECONDARY SCHOOL
STUDENTS.   MGILLLJ62401

BACKGROUND AND AMBITION OF MALE MEXICAN-AMERICAN HIGH SCHOOL SENIORS IN LOS-ANGELES. /CALIFORNIA/   MHELLCS63414

AMBITIONS OF MEXICAN-AMERICAN YOUTH -- GOALS AND MEANS OF MOBILITY OF HIGH SCHOOL SENIORS.   MHELLCS64413

MEXICAN-AMERICAN YOUTH. FORGOTTEN YOUTH AT THE CROSSROADS.   MHELLCS66416

MEXICAN-AMERICAN LABOR PROBLEMS IN TEXAS.   MJONELB65318

THE MEXICAN-AMERICAN WORKERS OF SAN-ANTONIO. /TEXAS/   MLANDRG66427

PROSPECTUS OF THE MEXICAN-AMERICAN STUDY PROJECT.   MMARSRX64437

MEXICAN-AMERICAN FAMILIES. LOS-ANGELES COUNTY. /CALIFORNIA/   MMCNAPH57435

SOME DIFFERENCES IN FACTORS RELATED TO EDUCATIONAL ACHIEVEMENT OF TWO MEXICAN-AMERICAN GROUPS. MMONTPX60443

CLASS CONSCIOUSNESS AND SOCIAL MOBILITY IN A MEXICAN-AMERICAN COMMUNITY.   MPENAFX63453

A SURVEY OF THE PROBLEMS INVOLVED IN THE AMERICANIZATION OF THE MEXICAN-AMERICAN.   MREYEIX57463

AN ANALYSIS OF THE MEXICAN-AMERICAN MIGRANT LABOR FORCE IN THE STOCKBRIDGE AREA. /MICHIGAN/   MRCDRFX66464

SOCIAL MOBILITY AND IMPUTATIONS OF WITCHCRAFT IN A MEXICAN-AMERICAN NEIGHBORHOOD OF TEXAS.   MRUBEAJ66467

A STUDY OF THE MENTAL HEALTH PROBLEMS OF MEXICAN-AMERICAN RESIDENTS. /TEXAS/   MTEXASD61500

MEXICAN-AMERICAN AND TOTAL EMPLOYMENT IN SELECTED STATES AND STANDARD METROPOLITAN STATISTICAL AREAS.   MUSCISC63504

MEXICAN-AMERICAN STUDY PROJECT, ADVANCE REPORT 3, BIBLIOGRAPHY.   MUVCALM66510

VALUE ORIENTATIONS OF YOUNG MEXICAN-AMERICAN MALES AS REFLECTED IN THEIR WORK PATTERNS AND EMPLOYMENT
PREFERENCES.   MWADDJO62513

EMPLOYMENT PROBLEMS OF THE MEXICAN-AMERICAN.   MWOODMJ64518

MEXICAN-AMERICANS
NEGROES AND MEXICAN-AMERICANS IN SOUTH AND EAST LOS-ANGELES. AN ANALYSIS OF A SPECIAL US CENSUS SURVEY OF
NOVEMBER 1965. /CALIFORNIA/   CCALDIR66168

NEGROES AND MEXICAN-AMERICANS IN THE CALIFORNIA STATE GOVERNMENT, A COOPERATIVE PROJECT.   CCALOGB65171

THE URBAN REALITY. A COMPARATIVE STUDY OF THE SOCIO-ECONOMIC SITUATION OF MEXICAN-AMERICANS, NEGROES AND
ANGLO-CAUCASIANS IN LOS-ANGELES COUNTY. /CALIFORNIA/   CLOSACH65708

THE PREDICTION AND EXPLANATION OF ECONOMIC ABSORPTION AMONG MEXICAN-AMERICANS, NEGROES, AND ANGLOS IN A
NORTHERN INDUSTRIAL COMMUNITY.   CSHANLW63120

THE PREDICTION OF ECONOMIC ABSORPTION AND CULTURAL INTEGRATION AMONG MEXICAN-AMERICANS, NEGROES, AND
ANGLOS IN A NORTHERN INDUSTRIAL COMMUNITY.   CSHANLW66123

MEXICAN-AMERICANS AND CIVIL-RIGHTS.   MALMAAS64357

THE CIVIL-RIGHTS SITUATION OF MEXICAN-AMERICANS AND SPANISH-AMERICANS.   MBURMJH61370

REACTION TO MEXICAN-AMERICANS, A BACKGROUND PAPER.   MCABRYA65372

EDUCATION AND INCOME OF MEXICAN-AMERICANS IN THE SOUTHWEST.   MFOGEWX65393

MEXICAN-AMERICANS, A BACKGROUND PAPER.   MGUZMRX65411

MEXICAN-AMERICANS ON THE MOVE.   MGUZMRX66412

CLASS AS AN EXPLANATION OF ETHNIC DIFFERENCES IN MOBILITY ASPIRATIONS -- THE CASE OF MEXICAN-AMERICANS.   MHELLCS65415

STUDY OF SOCIO-CULTURAL FACTORS THAT INHIBIT OR ENCOURAGE DELINQUENCY AMONG MEXICAN-AMERICANS. MLOSARW58432

THE MEXICAN-AMERICANS OF SOUTH TEXAS.   MMADSWX64436

STATEMENT ON EMPLOYMENT PROBLEMS OF MEXICAN-AMERICANS IN CALIFORNIA.   MMORADX63445

LEVELS OF ASPIRATION OF MEXICAN-AMERICANS IN EL-PASO SCHOOLS. /TEXAS/   MNALLFX59447

MEXICAN-AMERICANS IN THE LOS-ANGELES REGION. /CALIFORNIA/   MORTIMX62449

ACROSS THE TRACKS. MEXICAN-AMERICANS IN A TEXAS CITY.   MRUBEAJ66466

MEXICAN-AMERICANS IN URBAN PUBLIC HIGH SCHOOLS. AN EXPLORATION OF THE DROP-OUT PROGRAM.   MSHELPM59488

THE MUTUAL IMAGES AND EXPECTATIONS OF ANGLO-AMERIANS AND MEXICAN-AMERICANS.   MSIMMOG61490

MEXICAN-AMERICANS. SELECTED REFERENCES.   MUSDLAB67011

MEXICAN-AMERICANS   (CONTINUATION)
    EMPLOYMENT PROBLEMS OF MEXICAN-AMERICANS.   MWOODMJ65446

MEXICANS
    SPANISH-SPEAKING AMERICANS. MEXICANS AND PUERTO-RICANS IN THE UNITED STATES.   CBLAIBX59366

    COMPARISON OF MEXICANS, NEGROES AND WHITES WITH RESPECT TO OCCUPATIONAL HISTORY, RURAL-URBAN RESIDENCE
    HISTORY AND ACCULTURIZATION WITHIN THE INSTITUTIONAL STRUCTURE OF LANSING, MICHIGAN.   CGOLDVX60494

MEXICO
    HANDBOOK OF AMERICAN-INDIANS NORTH OF MEXICO.   ISMITIB59619

MIAMI
    NEGRO EMPLOYMENT IN MIAMI. /FLORIDA/   NFLORC062366

MICHIGAN
    COMPARISON OF MEXICANS, NEGROES AND WHITES WITH RESPECT TO OCCUPATIONAL HISTORY, RURAL-URBAN RESIDENCE
    HISTORY AND ACCULTURIZATION WITHIN THE INSTITUTIONAL STRUCTURE OF LANSING, MICHIGAN.   CGOLDVX60494

    INCOME, EDUCATION AND UNEMPLOYMENT IN NEIGHBORHOODS. DETROIT, MICHIGAN. /DEMOGRAPHY/   CUSDLAB63461

    TRADE UNION LEADERSHIP COUNCIL --EXPERIMENT IN COMMUNITY ACTION. /DETROIT MICHIGAN/   GBATTRX63426

    A SUMMARY ANALYSIS OF FIVE YEARS OF CLAIMS EXPERIENCE BY THE MICHIGAN
    FAIR-EMPLOYMENT-PRACTICES-COMMISSION, FEBRUARY, 1961.   GCOUSFR61612

    A SUMMARY ANALYSIS OF SIX YEARS OF CLAIMS EXPERIENCE BY THE MICHIGAN FAIR-EMPLOYMENT
    PRACTICES-COMMISSION, FEBRUARY 1962.   GCOUSFR62613

    EMPLOYMENT IN CIVIL-SERVICE OF MINORITY-GROUPS. /DETROIT MICHIGAN/   GDETRCC63638

    EMPLOYMENT AND INCOME BY AGE, SEX, COLOR AND RESIDENCE. /DETROIT MICHIGAN/   GDETRCC63948

    REPORT ON AND ANALYSIS OF SECOND CENSUS OF CITY EMPLOYEES TO DETERMINE BASES FOR FUTURE PERSONNEL
    DEVELOPMENTS. /DETROIT MICHIGAN/   GDETRCC66639

    A STUDY OF FAIR-EMPLOYMENT-PRACTICES OF THE CITY GOVERNMENT. /GRAND-RAPIDS MICHIGAN/   GGRANRH66733

    HOME INTERVIEW STUDY OF LOW-INCOME HOUSEHOLDS IN DETROIT, MICHIGAN.   GGREEAI65472

    STUDY OF SERVICES TO DEAL WITH POVERTY IN DETROIT, MICHIGAN.   GGREEAI65480

    A STUDY OF UNEMPLOYMENT, TRAINING AND PLACEMENT PATTERNS IN THE MUSKEGON AREA. /MICHIGAN/   GMICFEA57979

    FOUR YEARS ON THE JOB IN MICHIGAN. /FEPC/   GMICFEP60980

    SPECIAL REPORT, AN INVESTIGATION OF THE PERSONNEL POLICIES AND PRACTICES OF THE MICHIGAN STATE HIGHWAY
    DEPARTMENT, MARCH 1961.   GMICFEP61983

    MERIT EMPLOYMENT IN MICHIGAN. A PICTORIAL REPORT.   GMICFEP63981

    US COMMISSION-ON-CIVIL-RIGHTS. HEARINGS. DETROIT, MICHIGAN. DEC 14-15 1960.   GUSCCMC61399

    REPORT ON EMPLOYMENT PROBLEMS OF NONWHITE YOUTH IN MICHIGAN.   GUSCOMC66408

    DETROIT-S INSURED UNEMPLOYED AND EMPLOYABLE WELFARE RECIPIENTS. /MICHIGAN/   GWICKED63561

    AN ANALYSIS OF THE MEXICAN-AMERICAN MIGRANT LABOR FORCE IN THE STOCKBRIDGE AREA. /MICHIGAN/   MRODRFX66464

    DETROIT FEELS BRUNT OF NEGRO PRESSURE. /MICHIGAN/   NBUSIWX63149

    STUDY OF DETROIT POLICE DEPARTMENT PERSONNEL PRACTICES. /MICHIGAN OCCUPATIONS/   NDETRCC63267

    THE SOCIAL-STRUCTURE OF THE MICHIGAN LABOR-MARKET.   NFERMLA65352

    CONFLICT RESPONSE. DETROIT NEGROES FACE UNEMPLOYMENT. /MICHIGAN/   NLEGGJC59678

    SURVEY OF ALBION, MICHIGAN.   NMICCRC64772

    NILES COMMUNITY SELF SURVEY. /MICHIGAN/   NMICCRC65771

    EMPLOYMENT DISTRIBUTION STUDY OF THE CONSTRUCTION INDUSTRY IN MICHIGAN.   NMICCRC66606

    A STUDY OF NON-WHITE EMPLOYMENT IN THE STATE SERVICE. /MICHIGAN/   NMICCSC64775

    A FOLLOW-UP STUDY OF NON-WHITE EMPLOYMENT IN THE STATE SERVICE. /MICHIGAN/   NMICCSC65774

    A STUDY OF EMPLOYMENT AND TRAINING PATTERNS IN THE LANSING AREA. /MICHIGAN/   NMICFEP58778

    EQUAL-EMPLOYMENT-OPPORTUNITY IN THE SUBURBAN SHOPPING CENTER. FACT OR FICTION. /MICHIGAN/   NMICFEP63777

    EMPLOYMENT PROBLEMS OF NEGROES IN MICHIGAN.   NUSDLAB41816

    HARD-CORE UNEMPLOYMENT IN DETROIT. CAUSES AND REMEDIES. /MICHIGAN/   NWACHHMND289

    CONFERENCE ON WOMEN IN THE UPPER PENINSULA ECONOMY. REPORT. /MICHIGAN/   WMICDLA64976

    WOMEN WORKERS IN MICHIGAN, 1960.   WUSDLAB64240

MICHIGAN-S
    A REPORT ON THE CHARACTERISTICS OF MICHIGAN-S NON-WHITE POPULATION.   NMICCRC65773

MID-CENTURY
    THE AMERICAN NEGRO AT MID-CENTURY.   NPOPURB58008

MID-CONTINENT
    MIGRATORY FARM WORKERS IN THE MID-CONTINENT STREAMS.   GUSDAGR60425

MID-SIXTIES
    POVERTY IN THE UNITED STATES IN THE MID-SIXTIES.   GCHILCX64922

MIDCENTURY
    EDUCATED WOMEN -- A MIDCENTURY EVALUATION. /WORK-WOMAN-ROLE/   WDOLAEF56734

    THE AMERICAN WOMAN AT MIDCENTURY. /WORK-WOMAN-ROLE/   WYOUNLM61279

MIDCONTINENT
    MIGRATORY FARMWORKERS IN THE MIDCONTINENT STREAM.   GMETZWH60440

MIDDLE

THE NEGRO MIDDLE CLASS IS RIGHT IN THE MIDDLE. /ECONOMIC-STATUS/   NCORDDX66030

THE NEGRO MIDDLE CLASS IS RIGHT IN THE MIDDLE. /ECONOMIC-STATUS/   NCORDDX66030

POTENTIALITIES OF WOMEN IN THE MIDDLE YEARS. /WORK-FAMILY-CONFLICT/   WGROSIH56806

A MEMORANDUM ON THE MOTIVATIONS OF MIDDLE AGED WOMEN IN THE LOWER EDUCATIONAL BRACKETS TO RETURN TO WORK. /ASPIRATIONS/   WJEWIVA61880

THE MIDDLE AGED WOMAN AND THE LABOR-MARKET.   WJEWIVA62881

A PILOT STUDY OF THE MOTIVATIONS AND PROBLEMS OF MIDDLE AGED HOMEMAKERS IN LOWER SOCIO-ECONOMIC GROUPS IN SEEKING EMPLOYMENT. /ASPIRATIONS/   WJEWIVA62883

MIDDLE-CLASS

DESEGREGATION AND THE ECONOMIC FUTURE OF THE NEGRO MIDDLE-CLASS.   NBRIMAF65890

BLACK BOURGEOISIE. THE RISE OF A MIDDLE-CLASS IN THE UNITED STATES.   NFRAZEF57371

THE NEGRO MIDDLE-CLASS AND DESEGREGATION.   NFRAZEF57381

THE NEGRO-S MIDDLE-CLASS DREAM.   NLINCCE64695

MIDDLESEX-COUNTY

REPORT ON A SURVEY OF EMPLOYMENT POLICIES AND PRACTICES INVOLVING MINORITY-GROUPS IN MIDDLESEX-COUNTY, NEW-JERSEY.   GNEWJDE52061

MIDST

IN THE MIDST OF PLENTY. THE POOR IN AMERICA. /ECONOMIC-STATUS/   NBAGDBH64877

MIDWEST

THE QUEST FOR IDENTITY AND STATUS. FACETS OF THE DESEGREGATION PROCESS IN THE UPPER MIDWEST. /ECONOMIC-STATUS/   NTILLJA61161

MIGRANT

THE MIGRANT LABOR PROBLEM -- ITS STATE AND INTERSTATE ASPECTS. /NEGRO MEXICAN-AMERICAN/   CPALEHA63098

THE TRAINING OF MIGRANT FARM WORKERS. A FOLLOW-UP STUDY OF TWO EXPERIMENTAL AND DEMONSTRATION PROGRAMS UNDER THE MANPOWER-DEVELOPMENT-AND-TRAINING-ACT. /MEXICAN-AMERICAN AMERICAN-INDIAN/   CUNIVOD66054

MIGRANT LABOR IN WISCONSIN.   GBRANEX63796

WHAT MIGRANT FARM CHILDREN LEARN.   GCOLERX66133

THE COMMUNITY LOOKS AT MIGRANT LABOR. /MIGRANT-WORKERS/   GCONSLO59926

MIGRANT PROJECT 1959. /MIGRANT-WORKERS/   GFLORBH59690

THE MIGRANT PROJECT. /MIGRANT-WORKERS/   GFLORHN60689

SELECTED STATE PROGRAMS IN MIGRANT EDUCATION.   GHANEGE64004

MIGRANT FARM LABOR IN NEW-YORK.   GNEWYSE58109

EMPLOYMENT AND EARNINGS OF MIGRANT FARM WORKERS IN NEW-YORK STATE.   GNEWYSE60110

MIGRANT FARM LABOR IN NEW-YORK STATE.   GNEWYSJ63112

THE MIGRANT LABOR PROBLEM IN WISCONSIN.   GRAUSEX62218

MIGRANT CREWS IN EASTERN MARYLAND.   GSHOSAL65306

THE HARVESTERS. THE STORY OF THE MIGRANT PEOPLE.   GSHOTLR61684

A MIGRANT LABOR CRISIS IN IMMOKALEE. /FLORIDA/   GSOWDWT59328

THE WORLD OF THE MIGRANT CHILD.   GSUTTEX57344

SELECTED STATE PROGRAMS IN MIGRANT EDUCATION.   GUSDHEW63505

PROGRAMS OF NATIONAL ORGANIZATIONS FOR MIGRANT FARM WORKERS AND THEIR FAMILIES.   GUSDLAB61202

MAJOR AGRICULTURAL MIGRANT LABOR DEMAND AREAS.   GUSDLAB61509

HOUSING FOR MIGRANT AGRICULTURAL WORKERS. LABOR CAMP STANDARDS.   GUSDLAB62508

PROBLEMS OF MIGRANT LABOR.   GWALLFX61221

THE HARVEST OF DESPAIR. THE MIGRANT FARM WORKER.   GWRIGDX65604

PERCEIVED OPPORTUNITIES, EXPECTATIONS, AND THE DECISION TO REMAIN ON RELOCATION. THE CASE OF THE NAVAHO INDIAN MIGRANT TO DENVER, COLORADO.   IGRAVTD65567

VALUES, EXPECTATIONS AND RELOCATION. THE NAVAHO MIGRANT TO DENVER. /COLORADO/   IGRAVTD66146

MERRILL-TRUST-FUND TO IMPROVE THE EMPLOYMENT OPPORTUNITIES OF THE MIGRANT FARM WORKERS OF MEXICAN ORIGIN.   MBISHCS62365

EDUCATING MIGRANT CHILDREN IN COLORADO.   MCOLOSD61384

TERMINATION OF THE BRACERO PROGRAM. SOME EFFECTS ON FARM LABOR AND MIGRANT HOUSING NEEDS.   MMCELRC65385

WHEN THE MIGRANT LABORER SETTLES DOWN -- A REPORT OF THE FINDINGS OF A PROJECT ON VALUE ASSIMILATION OF IMMIGRANT LABORERS.   MPETECL64454

AN ANALYSIS OF THE MEXICAN-AMERICAN MIGRANT LABOR FORCE IN THE STOCKBRIDGE AREA. /MICHIGAN/   MRCDRFX66464

URBANIZATION OF THE MIGRANT. PROCESSES AND OUTCOMES. A RESEARCH PROPOSAL.   MSIMMOG64491

MECHANIZATION AND THE TEXAS MIGRANT.   MTEXACC64499

PROCEEDINGS OF THE CONFERENCE ON EDUCATION FOR ADULT MIGRANT WORKERS. /TEXAS/   MTEXACM62498

THE MIGRANT PROBLEM AND PRESSURE GROUP POLITICS.   MTOMARD61502

SOCIAL AND ATTITUDINAL CHARACTERISTICS OF SPANISH-SPEAKING MIGRANT AND EX-MIGRANT WORKERS IN THE SOUTHWEST.   MULIBHX66503

PROBLEMS OF MIGRANT LABOR.   NWALLFX61221

MIGRANT   (CONTINUATION)
   MEETING THE NEEDS OF THE PUERTO-RICAN MIGRANT.   PMONTHK59829

   PATTERNS OF SOCIAL ACCOMODATION OF THE MIGRANT PUERTO-RICAN IN THE AMERICAN SOCIAL STRUCTURE.   PSEDAEX58850

MIGRANT-LABOR
   BUREAU OF MIGRANT-LABOR REPORT. /NEW-JERSEY NEGRO PUERTO-RICAN/   CNEWJDL61907

   HEALTH PROBLEMS OF MIGRANT-LABOR.   GMIREMX59013

   REPORT OF NEW-YORK STATE JOINT LEGISLATIVE COMMITTEE ON MIGRANT-LABOR.   GNEWYSLND115

   CONCLUSIONS AND RECOMMENDATIONS, FIRST CONFERENCE ON MIGRANT-LABOR.   GTEXACO59351

MIGRANT-LABOR--THE
   MIGRANT-LABOR--THE NATIONAL RESPONSIBILITY.   GMITCJP59954

MIGRANT-WORKER
   THE HEALTH OF THE MIGRANT-WORKER. /EMPLOYMENT-CONDITIONS/   GLINDJR66603

   THE HOUSING PROBLEM OF THE MIGRANT-WORKER IN MARYLAND.   GMARYSD59956

   THE MIGRANT-WORKER.   MSCHOWE66687

MIGRANT-WORKERS
   THE FORGOTTEN PEOPLE. /MIGRANT-WORKERS MEXICAN-AMERICAN PUERTO-RICAN NEGRO/   CJACOPX59600

   FINAL REPORT. EXPERIMENTAL AND DEMONSTRATION ON-JOB-TRAINING PROJECT. /MIGRANT-WORKERS MEXICAN-AMERICAN
   NEGRO ARIZONA/   CSKILTO66324

   STILL THE HARVEST OF SHAME. /MIGRANT-WORKERS/   GBENNFX64500

   THE ITINERANT FARM LABOR PROJECT REPORT. /MIGRANT-WORKERS CALIFORNIA/   GCALVRS60553

   A SOCIAL PROFILE OF AGRICULTURAL MIGRATORY PEOPLE IN COLORADO. /MIGRANT-WORKERS/   GCOLOSD59919

   THE COMMUNITY LOOKS AT MIGRANT LABOR. /MIGRANT-WORKERS/   GCCNSLC59926

   REPORTS OF THE MEETINGS OF THE COMMITTEE OF OFFICIALS ON MIGRATORY FARM LABOR OF THE ATLANTIC SEABOARD
   STATES. /MIGRANT-WORKERS/   GCOUNSG58932

   MIGRATORY-LABOR IN THE WEST. BACKGROUND INFORMATION FOR THE WESTERN INTERSTATE CONFERENCE ON MIGRATORY
   LABOR. /MIGRANT-WORKERS/   GCOUNSG60931

   SUGAR BEET LABOR IN NORTHERN COLORADO. /MIGRANT-WORKERS/   GDAVIIF58939

   REPORT AND RECOMMENDATIONS OF DELAWARE COMMITTEE ON MIGRATORY LABOR. /MIGRANT-WORKERS/   GDELACM58945

   EFFECT OF MECHANIZATION ON EMPLOYMENT OF MIGRATORY LABOR IN AGRICULTURE AND FOOD PROCESSING.
   /MIGRANT-WORKERS/   GDELASE59946

   MIGRANT PROJECT 1959. /MIGRANT-WORKERS/   GFLORBH59690

   THE MIGRANT PROJECT. /MIGRANT-WORKERS/   GFLORHN60689

   MIGRANT-WORKERS PLIGHT.   GFORTXX59045

   THEY FOLLOW THE SUN. /MIGRANT-WORKERS/   GKOOSEL57691

   SOME REGIONAL DIFFERENCES IN WAGES OF AGRICULTURAL WORKERS. /MIGRANT-WORKERS/   GMAITST60436

   THE CALIFORNIA FARM WORKER. STILL IN DUBIOUS BATTLE. /MIGRANT-WORKERS UNION/   GMEISDX60461

   CHARACTERISTICS OF FARM WORKERS AS RELATED TO STABILIZATION OF THE WORK FORCE. /MIGRANT-WORKERS/ GMETZWH62504

   SUMMARY OF RULES, REGULATIONS, AND LAWS THAT AFFECT SEASONAL FARM WORKERS AND THEIR EMPLOYERS IN NEW-YORK
   STATE. /MIGRANT-WORKERS/   GNEWYSJND113

   A HELPING HAND. SEASONAL FARM LABOR IN NEW-YORK STATE. /MIGRANT-WORKERS/   GNEWYSX63087

   GRAPE WORKERS WIN NEW GAINS. /MIGRANT-WORKERS UNION CALIFORNIA/   GROSSLX66557

   THE EDUCATIONAL STATUS OF A MINORITY. /MIGRANT-WORKERS/   GSAMOJX63501

   THE IMMOKALEE STORY. /MIGRANT-WORKERS FLORIDA/   GSCWDWT58327

   AGRICULTURAL WORKERS AND WORKMEN-S COMPENSATION. /MIGRANT-WORKERS/   GUSDLAB64506

   COVERAGE OF AGRICULTURAL WORKERS UNDER STATE AND FEDERAL LAWS. /MIGRANT-WORKERS/   GUSDLAB64507

   VOLUNTARY FARM EMPLOYMENT SERVICE. /MIGRANT-WORKERS/   GUSSENA64306

   COMMON GROUND. /NEW-JERSEY MIGRANT-WORKERS/   GWILLLB59565

   CALIFORNIA-S FARM LABOR PROBLEMS. /MIGRANT-WORKERS/   MCALSSE63380

   STRANGERS IN OUR FIELDS. /MIGRANT-WORKERS/   MGALAEX56400

   COMPREHENSIVE REPORT OF THE OFFICE OF THE BISHOP-S COMMITTEE FOR MIGRANT-WORKERS.   MNATLCBND082

   HOW UNIONS ARE SIGNING THEM UP. /MIGRANT-WORKERS CALIFORNIA/   MWINGWX66536

   US DEPARTMENT OF LABOR, PUBLIC HEARING, TESTIMONY. /MIGRANT-WORKERS/   NHILLHX63548

   AGRICULTURAL SEASONAL LABORERS OF COLORADO AND CALIFORNIA. /MIGRANT-WORKERS/   NKARRCHND636

   TESTIMONY, PUBLIC HEARING, WOMEN IN PUBLIC AND PRIVATE EDUCATION, CALIFORNIA. /FEP
   EMPLOYMENT-CONDITIONS DISCRIMINATION MIGRANT-WORKERS/   WBLOCHX66649

   STATEMENT, PUBLIC HEARING, WOMEN IN PUBLIC AND PRIVATE EMPLOYMENT, CALIFORNIA. /EMPLOYMENT-CONDITIONS
   MIGRANT-WORKERS/   WKAUFDX66886

   TESTIMONY, PUBLIC HEARING, WOMEN IN PUBLIC AND PRIVATE EMPLOYMENT, CALIFORNIA. /FEP MIGRANT-WORKERS
   EMPLOYMENT-CONDITIONS/   WLLOYMX66940

   STATEMENT, PUBLIC HEARING, WOMEN IN PUBLIC AND PRIVATE EMPLOYMENT, CALIFORNIA. /FEP
   EMPLOYMENT-CONDITIONS MIGRANT-WORKERS/   WMILLJJ66979

   TESTIMONY, PUBLIC HEARING, WOMEN IN PUBLIC AND PRIVATE EMPLOYMENT, CALIFORNIA. /FEP

MIGRANT-WORKERS   (CONTINUATION)
   EMPLOYMENT-CONDITIONS   MIGRANT-WORKERS/   WPEEVMX66052

   TESTIMONY, PUBLIC HEARING, WOMEN IN PUBLIC AND PRIVATE EMPLOYMENT, CALIFORNIA.   /FEP
   EMPLOYMENT-CONDITIONS DISCRIMINATION   MIGRANT-WORKERS/   WSPENNX66129

   TESTIMONY, PUBLIC HEARING, WOMEN IN PUBLIC AND PRIVATE EMPLOYMENT, CALIFORNIA.   /EMPLOYMENT-CONDITIONS
   MIGRANT-WORKERS/   WWEBEJX66258

   TESTIMONY, PUBLIC HEARING, WOMEN IN PUBLIC AND PRIVATE EMPLOYMENT, CALIFORNIA.   /FEP
   EMPLOYMENT-CONDITIONS MIGRANT-WORKERS/   WWOMEIX66273

MIGRANTS
   OCCUPATIONAL AND RESIDENTIAL ADJUSTMENT OF RURAL MIGRANTS. /NEGRO   MEXICAN-AMERICAN/   CSHANLW61119

   THE ASSIMILATION AND ACCULTURATION OF MIGRANTS TO URBAN AREAS.   /MEXICAN-AMERICAN   NEGRO/   CSHANLW63484

   HEALTH OF MIGRANTS. /CALIFORNIA/   GCALDIR60522

   MIGRANTS. /ECONOMIC-STATUS/   GKURTAX60866

   MARYLAND TB -- VD HEALTH PROGRAM AMONG AGRICULTURAL MIGRANTS.   GMARYSD65958

   CONDITIONS FOR MIGRANTS -- A NATIONAL DISGRACE.   GSCHWLX66556

   HEALTH WORK AMONG MIGRANTS IN 1958 BY THE NEW-JERSEY STATE DEPARTMENT OF HEALTH.   GSHEPAC59301

   THE ECONOMIC ABSORPTION OF NAVAHO INDIAN MIGRANTS IN DENVER, COLORADO.   IWEPPRS65684

   A HISTORY OF THE INTERRELATIONSHIPS BETWEEN IMPORTED MEXICAN LABOR, DOMESTIC MIGRANTS, AND THE TEXAS
   AGRICULTURAL ECONOMY.   MGRAVRP60405

   TEXAS MIGRANTS PROGRAM. /TRAINING   EDUCATION/   MMACNBL67335

   CHANGES IN PUBLIC AND PRIVATE LANGUAGE AMONG SPANISH-SPEAKING MIGRANTS TO AN INDUSTRIAL CITY.   MSCHETJ65481

   NONWHITE MIGRANTS TO AND FROM SELECTED CITIES.   NPRICDO48019

   DISTANCE OF MIGRATION AND SOCIO-ECONOMIC STATUS OF MIGRANTS.   NROSEAM58291

   MIGRANTS POSE PROBLEMS FOR NEW-JERSEY FARMERS WHO NEED THEM.   PCUNNJT57793

   MIGRANTS AND CULTURE CHANGE.   PPAULIX55843

   AN ANALYSIS OF UNEMPLOYED PUERTO-RICAN MIGRANTS IN NEW-YORK CITY.   PREMEGN58847

   CONCERN FOR AGRICULTURAL MIGRANTS IN MARYLAND.   PUVMAXX64856

   TESTIMONY PRESENTED AT PUBLIC HEARING, MARCH 31 -- APRIL 1, 1966. /FEP EMPLOYMENT-CONDITIONS
   DISCRIMINATION MIGRANTS/   WCALACW62675

   TESTIMONY PRESENTED AT PUBLIC HEARING, APRIL 28, 1966. SAN-FRANCISCO, CALIFORNIA. /FEP
   EMPLOYMENT-CONDITIONS DISCRIMINATION MIGRANTS/   WCALACW62676

   TESTIMONY PRESENTED AT PUBLIC HEARING, FEBRUARY 24-25, 1966. /FEP EMPLOYMENT-CONDITIONS   DISCRIMINATION
   MIGRANTS/   WCALACW66674

   REPORT OF THE CALIFORNIA ADVISORY COMMISSION ON THE STATUS OF WOMEN. /FEP EMPLOYMENT-CONDITIONS
   DISCRIMINATION MIGRANTS/   WCALACW67673

   TESTIMONY, PUBLIC HEARING, WOMEN IN PUBLIC AND PRIVATE EMPLOYMENT, CALIFORNIA. /FEP
   EMPLOYMENT-CONDITIONS DISCRIMINATION MIGRANTS/   WCLIFFG66692

MIGRATION
   LIFETIME AND RECENT MIGRATION. /DEMOGRAPHY/   CUSBURC63172

   MIGRATION PATTERNS OF THE RURAL-FARM POPULATION. THIRTEEN ECONOMIC REGIONS OF THE UNITED STATES,
   1940-1950.   GBOWLGK57415

   MIGRATION OF POPULATION IN THE SOUTH. SITUATION AND PROSPECTS.   GBOWLGK58397

   NET MIGRATION OF THE POPULATION, 1950-60, BY AGE, SEX, AND COLOR. VOL II, ANALYTICAL GROUPINGS OF
   COUNTIES. /INCOME/   GBOWLGK65434

   THE COMPOSITION OF NET MIGRATION AMONG COUNTIES IN THE UNITED STATES, 1950-60.   GBOWLGK66414

   CONTINUITY AND CHANGE IN SOUTHERN MIGRATION. /DEMOGRAPHY/   GHAMICH65757

   THE STRUCTURE OF THE FARM LABOR-MARKET AND MIGRATION PATTERNS.   GMIREWX57499

   UNIONISM, MIGRATION, AND THE MALE NONWHITE-WHITE UNEMPLOYMENT DIFFERENTIAL.   GRAPPLA66216

   MIGRATION OF THE TEXAS FARM POPULATION.   GSKRARL57315

   SOME NEW EVIDENCE ON EDUCATIONAL SELECTIVITY IN MIGRATION FROM THE SOUTH.   GSUVAEM65345

   THE MIGRATION AND ADAPTATION OF AMERICAN INDIANS TO LOS-ANGELES. /CALIFORNIA/   IPRICJA67608

   MIGRATION TO SOUTHWEST TEXAS. PEOPLES AND WORDS.   MNORMAX56448

   RECENT MIGRATION OF YOUNG MALES INTO HOUSTON, TEXAS.   MWAGODW57515

   MIGRATION AND OPPORTUNITY. A STUDY OF STANDARD METROPOLITAN AREAS IN THE UNITED-STATES.   NBALATR63047

   THE MECHANICAL COTTON-PICKER, NEGRO MIGRATION, AND THE INTEGRATION MOVEMENT.   NDILLHCND274

   EDUCATIONAL PATTERNS IN SOUTHERN MIGRATION.   NFEINRX65348

   RECENT MIGRATION TO CHICAGO. /LABOR-FORCE   ILLINOIS/   NFREERX50967

   THE NEGRO MIGRATION. /ECONOMIC-STATUS/   NGRIEGXND982

   EDUCATIONAL SELECTIVITY OF NET MIGRATION FROM THE SOUTH.   NHAMICH59986

   THE NEGRO LEAVES THE SOUTH. /DEMOGRAPHY MIGRATION/   NHAMICH64479

   NEGRO INTERNAL MIGRATION IN THE UNITED STATES. 1870-1960.   NJORGJM62624

   NEGRO INTELLIGENCE AND SELECTIVE MIGRATION. A PHILADELPHIA TEST OF THE KLINEBERG HYPOTHESIS.

MIGRATION   (CONTINUATION)
   /PENNSYLVANIA/   NLEEXES51673

   RACIAL DIFFERENCES IN MIGRATION AND JOB-SEARCH. A CASE-STUDY.   NLURIMX66712

   NEGRO MIGRATION IN THE UNITED STATES.   NPURDLX54024

   SPECIAL PROBLEMS OF NEGRO MIGRATION DURING THE WAR.   NREIDID47362

   DISTANCE OF MIGRATION AND SOCIO-ECONOMIC STATUS OF MIGRANTS.   NROSEAM58291

   MIGRATION PATTERNS OF NEGROES FROM A RURAL NORTHEASTERN MISSISSIPPI COMMUNITY. /DEMOGRAPHY/   NRUBIMX60094

   RACIAL CHANGES IN METROPOLITAN AREAS, 1950-1960. /DEMOGRAPHY MIGRATION/   NSCHNLF65109

   MIGRATION AND ADJUSTMENT EXPERIENCES OF RURAL WORKERS IN INDIANAPOLIS. /INDIANA/   NSMITED53143

   MIGRATION, MOBILITY, AND THE ASSIMILATION OF THE NEGRO.   NTAEUIB58363

   THE CHANGING CHARACTER OF NEGRO MIGRATION. /DEMOGRAPHY/   NTAEUKE65194

   SOCIAL AND ECONOMIC IMPLICATIONS OF MIGRATION FOR THE NEGRO IN THE PRESENT SOCIAL ORDER.   NVALIPX42261

   NEW ASPECTS OF PUERTO-RICAN MIGRATION.   PCARLRC59785

   MIGRATION TRENDS.   PDECOPP59794

   THE IMPACT OF PUERTO-RICAN MIGRATION ON GOVERNMENTAL SERVICES IN NEW-YORK CITY.   PDWORMB57797

   SOME ECONOMIC ASPECTS OF PUERTO-RICAN MIGRATION TO THE UNITED STATES.   PFLEIBM61804

   THE IMPACT OF PUERTO-RICAN MIGRATION TO THE UNITED STATES. /EMPLOYMENT/   PFLEIBM63437

   SOME ECONOMIC ASPECTS OF PUERTO-RICAN MIGRATION TO THE UNITED STATES.   PFLEIBM63803

   IMPLICATIONS OF PUERTO-RICAN MIGRATION TO THE CONTINENT OUTSIDE NEW-YORK CITY.   PGERNAC56808

   SOME ECONOMIC CONSEQUENCES OF THE PUERTO-RICAN MIGRATION INTO PERTH-AMBOY, 1949-1954. /NEW-JERSEY/ PGOLUFX55812

   NOTES ON MIGRATION AND WORKERS ATTITUDES TOWARD IT.   PGREGPX61857

   PUERTO-RICANS IN PHILADELPHIA. MIGRATION AND ACCOMODATION. /PENNSYLVANIA/   PKOSSJD65822

   REPORTS OF PUERTO-RICO DEPARTMENT OF LABOR, MIGRATION DIVISION ON PLACEMENT.   PPUERRDND791

   THE MIGRATION DIVISION -- POLICY, FUNCTIONS, OBJECTIVES.   PPUERRD57789

MIGRATORY
   A SOCIAL PROFILE OF AGRICULTURAL MIGRATORY PEOPLE IN COLORADO. /MIGRANT-WORKERS/   GCOLOSD59919

   REPORTS OF THE MEETINGS OF THE COMMITTEE OF OFFICIALS ON MIGRATORY FARM LABOR OF THE ATLANTIC SEABOARD
   STATES. /MIGRANT-WORKERS/   GCOUNSG58932

   MIGRATORY-LABOR IN THE WEST. BACKGROUND INFORMATION FOR THE WESTERN INTERSTATE CONFERENCE ON MIGRATORY
   LABOR. /MIGRANT-WORKERS/   GCOUNSG60931

   REPORT AND RECOMMENDATIONS OF DELAWARE COMMITTEE ON MIGRATORY LABOR. /MIGRANT-WORKERS/   GDELACM58945

   EFFECT OF MECHANIZATION ON EMPLOYMENT OF MIGRATORY LABOR IN AGRICULTURE AND FOOD PROCESSING.
   /MIGRANT-WORKERS/   GDELASE59946

   LEGAL DISADVANTAGES OF MIGRATORY WORKERS.   GGIVERA65695

   MIGRATORY FARM WORKERS IN THE ATLANTIC COAST STREAM. I. CHANGES IN NEW-YORK, 1953 AND 1957.   GLARSOF60406

   THE MIGRATORY WORKER IN THE FARM ECONOMY.   GLEVILA61357

   PROGRESS IN MEETING PROBLEMS OF MIGRATORY LABOR IN MARYLAND.   GMARYGC60955

   MIGRATORY FARM WORKERS IN THE ATLANTIC COAST STREAM.   GMETZWH55426

   MIGRATORY FARMWORKERS IN THE MIDCONTINENT STREAM.   GMETZWH60440

   MIGRATORY FARM WORKERS IN THE ATLANTIC COAST STREAM. WESTERN NEW-YORK, JUNE 1953.   GMOTHJR54405

   AN EXPERIMENT IN VOCATIONAL EDUCATION FOR CHILDREN OF MIGRATORY FARM WORKERS, JULY-AUGUST 1956.   GNATLCRND046

   PROCEEDINGS OF THE NATIONAL-SHARECROPPERS-FUND CONFERENCE ON MIGRATORY LABOR AND LOW-INCOME FARMERS.
   NOVEMBER 13 1957.   GNATLSF57299

   MIGRATORY LABOR IN OHIO, A REPORT BY THE GOVERNOR-S COMMITTEE, AUGUST 1962.   GOHIOGC62095

   MIGRATORY WORKERS IN NEW-YORK, CHANGES, 1953, 1957, AND 1958.   GSHAREF59428

   MIGRATORY FARM WORKERS IN THE ATLANTIC COAST STREAM. II. EDUCATION OF NEW-YORK WORKERS AND THEIR
   CHILDREN, 1953 AND 1957.   GSHAREF60427

   INCOMES OF MIGRATORY AGRICULTURAL WORKERS.   GTEXAAE60350

   MIGRATORY FARM WORKERS IN THE MID-CONTINENT STREAMS.   GUSDAGR60425

   SELECTED REFERENCES ON MIGRATORY WORKERS AND THEIR FAMILIES. PROBLEMS AND PROGRAMS.   GUSDLAB56204

   MIGRATORY FARM LABOR CONFERENCE, PROCEEDINGS.   GUSDLAB57359

   SELECTED REFERENCES ON DOMESTIC MIGRATORY AGRICULTURAL WORKERS, THEIR FAMILIES, PROBLEMS, AND PROGRAMS,
   1955-1960.   GUSDLAB61495

   MIGRATORY LABOR.   GUSSENA59469

   MIGRATORY LABOR BILLS.   GUSSENA63305

   PROGRESS IN MEETING PROBLEMS OF MIGRATORY LABOR IN MARYLAND.   GUVMADA62529

   MIGRATORY LABOR IN DELAWARE.   GWELFCD56548

   MIGRATORY WORKERS IN NEW-YORK STATE, 1959 AND COMPARISONS WITH 1953, 1957, AND 1958.   GWHYTDR60407

   MIGRATORY LABOR IN COLORADO.   MCOLOLC60382

MIGRATORY   (CONTINUATION)
  MIGRATORY LABOR IN COLORADO. REPORT TO THE COLORADO GENERAL ASSEMBLY.   MCOLOLC62383

  MIGRATORY LABOR IN THE WEST.   MCOUNSH60386

  A PLANNED COMMUNITY FOR MIGRATORY FARM WORKERS.   MFEERAB62392

  MIGRATORY AGRICULTURAL WORKERS IN THE UNITED STATES.   MJORGJM60422

  INCOMES OF MIGRATORY AGRICULTURAL WORKERS.   MMETZWH60439

  FAMILY ORGANIZATION IN FIVE TYPES OF MIGRATORY WAGE LABOR.   MSOLIML61496

  NO HARVEST FOR THE REAPER. THE STORY OF THE MIGRATORY AGRICULTURAL WORKER IN THE UNITED STATES.   NHILLHX59534

  THE FIRST 10 YEARS...THE PUERTO-RICAN MIGRATORY PROBLEM.   PCASTCX58786

MIGRATORY-LABOR
  MIGRATORY-LABOR IN THE WEST. BACKGROUND INFORMATION FOR THE WESTERN INTERSTATE CONFERENCE ON MIGRATORY
  LABOR. /MIGRANT-WORKERS/   GCOUNSG60931

MILITANTS
  NEGRO MILITANTS, JEWISH LIBERALS, AND THE UNIONS.   NBROOTR61121

MILITARY
  ONE-THIRD OF A NATION. A REPORT ON YOUNG MEN FOUND UNQUALIFIED FOR MILITARY SERVICE.   GPRESTM64316

  CIVILIAN PERSONNEL -- NONDISCRIMINATION IN EMPLOYMENT. /MILITARY/   GUSDAIR62189

  SUPERVISOR DEVELOPMENT PROGRAM, BASIC COURSE. NONDISCRIMINATION POLICY. /MILITARY/   GUSDARM56192

  A TIME FOR ACTION. PROCEEDINGS OF THE NATIONAL CONFERENCE ON EQUAL-EMPLOYMENT-OPPORTUNITY, 1962.
  /MILITARY/   GUSDARM62193

  A BIBLIOGRAPHY OF CIVIL-RIGHTS AND CIVIL-LIBERTIES. /EMPLOYMENT   UNION   MILITARY/   NBROOAD62117

  THE NEGRO IN THE US ARMY. /MILITARY/   NDWYERJ53312

  INTEGRATION IN THE ARMED SERVICES. /MILITARY/   NEVANJC56340

  THE 1960 AUDIT OF NEGRO VETERANS AND SERVICEMAN. /MILITARY/   NFELDJA61350

  THE NEGRO IN THE ARMY TODAY. /MILITARY/   NHASTWH42466

  REPORT ON KOREA. /MILITARY/   NMARSTX51754

  SUMMARY JUSTICE -- THE NEGRO GI IN KOREA. /MILITARY/   NMARSTX51755

  RACIAL INTEGRATION IN THE ARMED FORCES. /MILITARY/   NMOSKCC66855

  THE NEGRO IN THE NAVY. /MILITARY/   NMUELWR45865

  THE NEGRO AND THE NATIONAL GUARD. /MILITARY/   NNEWTIG62915

  BREAKTHROUGH ON THE COLOR FRONT. /MILITARY/   NNICHLX54920

  FREEDOM TO SERVE. /MILITARY/   NPRESCE50015

  THE NEGRO POLICY OF THE AMERICAN ARMY SINCE WORLD-WAR-II. /MILITARY/   NREDDLD53044

  THE IMPACT OF MILITARY SERVICE UPON THE RACIAL ATTITUDES OF NEGRO SERVICEMEN IN WORLD-WAR II.   NROBEHW53065

  INTEGRATION IN THE ARMED SERVICES. A PROGRESS REPORT. /MILITARY/   NUSDDEF55195

  INTEGRATION AND THE NEGRO OFFICER IN THE ARMED FORCES OF THE UNITED STATES OF AMERICA. /MILITARY/   NUSDDEF62240

  SEGREGATION IN THE ARMED FORCES. /MILITARY/   NUSDLAB44151

  THE NEGRO IN THE ARMED FORCES. /MILITARY/   NWEILFD47309

  WHAT THE NEGRO THINKS OF THE ARMY. /MILITARY/   NWHITWX42465

  A SURVEY OF WOMEN-S APTITUDES FOR ARMY JOBS. /MILITARY/   WFUCHEF63772

MILWAUKEE
  INCOME, EDUCATION AND UNEMPLOYMENT IN NEIGHBORHOODS. MILWAUKEE, WISCONSIN. /DEMOGRAPHY/   CUSDLAB63467

  MILWAUKEE. A FAIR DEAL. /WISCONSIN EEO/   GWINTEL66569

  THE NEGRO IN MILWAUKEE. PROGRESS AND PORTENT, 1863-1963. /WISCONSIN/   NMILWCC63792

  EMPLOYMENT AS IT RELATES TO NEGROES IN THE MILWAUKEE INDUSTRIAL AREA. /WISCONSIN/   NMILWUL48793

MINIMUM
  EMPLOYMENT EFFECTS OF STATE MINIMUM WAGES FOR WOMEN.   WPETEJX59059

  FRINGE BENEFIT PROVISIONS FROM STATE MINIMUM WAGE LAWS AND ORDERS, SEPTEMBER 1, 1966.
  /EMPLOYMENT-CONDITIONS/   WUSDLAB66195

MINNEAPOLIS
  INCOME, EDUCATION AND UNEMPLOYMENT IN NEIGHBORHOODS. MINNEAPOLIS -- ST-PAUL, MINNESOTA. /DEMOGRAPHY/   CUSDLAB63468

  SURVEY AND ANALYSIS OF NON-WHITE EMPLOYMENT BY THE CITY OF MINNEAPOLIS. /MINNESOTA/   GMINLMH65002

  MUNICIPAL FEPC IN MINNEAPOLIS. /MINNESOTA/   GSURVXX47341

  REPORT OF TWIN-CITIES EQUAL-OPPORTUNITY REVIEW. /MINNEAPOLIS ST-PAUL MINNESOTA/   GUSCISC64131

  THE MINNESOTA INDIAN IN MINNEAPOLIS.   IMINLCW56545

MINNESOTA
  INCOME, EDUCATION AND UNEMPLOYMENT IN NEIGHBORHOODS. MINNEAPOLIS -- ST-PAUL, MINNESOTA. /DEMOGRAPHY/   CUSDLAB63468

  SURVEY AND ANALYSIS OF NON-WHITE EMPLOYMENT BY THE CITY OF MINNEAPOLIS. /MINNESOTA/   GMINLMH65002

  MINNESOTA STATE ACT AGAINST DISCRIMINATION, AS APPROVED BY THE MINNESOTA LEGISLATURE, APRIL 1961.
  /LEGISLATION/   GMINNSCND010

  MINNESOTA STATE ACT AGAINST DISCRIMINATION, AS APPROVED BY THE MINNESOTA LEGISLATURE, APRIL 1961.

MINNESOTA   (CONTINUATION)
    /LEGISLATION/   GMINNSCNDO10

    MUNICIPAL FEPC IN MINNEAPOLIS. /MINNESOTA/   GSURVXX47341

    REPORT OF TWIN-CITIES EQUAL-OPPORTUNITY REVIEW. /MINNEAPOLIS ST-PAUL MINNESOTA/   GUSCISC64131

    THE MINNESOTA INDIAN IN MINNEAPOLIS.   IMINLCW56545

    THE NEGRO WORKER IN MINNESOTA. A REPORT.   NMINNGI45798

    THE NEGRO WORKER-S PROGRESS IN MINNESOTA. A REPORT.   NMINNGI49799

    THE NEGRO POPULATION IN DULUTH MINNESOTA, 1950. /DEMOGRAPHY/   NTURBGX52210

    REPORT OF ARROWHEAD REGIONAL CONFERENCE ON THE STATUS OF WOMEN IN NORTHERN MINNESOTA. WARRORC66216

    UNIVERSITY OF MINNESOTA -- THE MINNESOTA PLAN. /EDUCATION/   WSCHLVX63103

    UNIVERSITY OF MINNESOTA -- THE MINNESOTA PLAN. /EDUCATION/   WSCHLVX63103

    MINNESOTA PLAN FOR WOMEN-S CONTINUING EDUCATION. A PROGRESS REPORT.   WSENDVL61298

MINORITIES
    ECONOMIC GROWTH AND EMPLOYMENT OPPORTUNITIES FOR MINORITIES. /NEGRO WOMEN/   CHIESOL64775

    EMPLOYING MINORITIES SUCCESSFULLY.   GAMERFC48378

    ORGANIZED LABOR AND RACIAL MINORITIES. /UNION/   GBAILLH51575

    AMERICAN MINORITIES. A TEXTBOOK OF READINGS IN INTERGROUP RELATIONS.   GBARRML57424

    ONE AMERICA. THE HISTORY, CONTRIBUTIONS, AND PRESENT PROBLEMS OF OUR RACIAL AND NATIONAL MINORITIES. GBROWFJ45477

    SCHOOL. MINORITIES AND EQUAL-RIGHTS, SELECTED MATERIAL. /CALIFORNIA/   GCALSLIND549

    MINORITIES AND THE AMERICAN PROMISE. THE CONFLICT OF PRINCIPLE AND PRACTICE.   GCOLESG54580

    MINORITIES IN THE MARKET PLACE.   GDEMSHX65869

    FURNISHING EQUAL-OPPORTUNITY FOR MINORITIES IN CIVIL-SERVICE.   GGREGGX62070

    CURRENT INTERNATIONAL UNION POLICIES AFFECTING MINORITIES AND THEIR IMPLEMENTATION.   GHOPEJX49781

    EMPLOYMENT PROBLEMS OF RACIAL MINORITIES.   GHOPEJX61002

    PART IV. EMPLOYMENT PROBLEMS OF RACIAL MINORITIES.   GINDURR61813

    MINORITIES IN AMERICAN SOCIETY.   GMARDCF62938

    ETHNIC AND ECONOMIC MINORITIES. UNION-S FUTURE OR UNRECRUITABLE.   GMARSRX63945

    THE POSITION OF MINORITIES IN THE AMERICAN LABOR MOVEMENT. /UNION/   GMARSRX66946

    INDUSTRY-S EXPERIMENT TOWARDS INTEGRATION OF MINORITIES INTO INDUSTRY.   GRUBIAX46265

    THESE OUR PEOPLE. MINORITIES IN AMERICAN CULTURE.   GSCHERA49281

    POWER AS A PRIMARY CONCEPT IN THE STUDY OF MINORITIES.   GSCHERA56058

    RACIAL AND CULTURAL MINORITIES.   GSIMPGE65314

    THE ECONOMIC SITUATION OF NATIONAL MINORITIES IN THE UNITED STATES OF AMERICA.   GTHOMJA47354

    RECRUITING MINORITIES FOR PUBLIC EMPLOYMENT. EXPERIENCE REPORT 105.   GUSCCNM66420

    MINORITIES IN DEFENSE.   GUSOFPM42519

    JOB OPPORTUNITIES FOR MINORITIES IN THE SEATTLE AREA. /WASHINGTON/   GUVWAIL48532

    INTEGRATION OF MINORITIES.   MLANDRX60426

    THE POSITION OF MINORITIES IN THE AMERICAN LABOR MOVEMENT. /UNION/   NMARSRX66943

    AN INDUSTRIAL EXPERIMENT TOWARDS INTEGRATION OF MINORITIES INTO INDUSTRY.   NRUBIAX46093

MINORITY
    THE ECONOMY AND THE MINORITY POOR. /NEGRO AMERICAN-INDIAN MEXICAN-AMERICAN PUERTO-RICAN/ CBATCAB66879

    THE PUSH OF AN ELBOW. CIVIL-RIGHTS AND OUR SPANISH-SPEAKING MINORITY. /MEXICAN-AMERICAN PUERTO-RICAN/ CBURMJH60371

    RECENT TRENDS IN THE STUDY OF MINORITY AND RACE-RELATIONS. /NEGRO PUERTO-RICAN ORIENTAL/ CGORDMM63977

    MINORITY PEOPLES IN A NATION AT WAR.   GANNAOA42549

    BENEFIT POLICIES IN RELATION TO RECRUITMENT OF OLDER WORKERS, HANDICAPPED, AND MINORITY GROUPS. GBARRGJ51425

    INEQUALITY OF OPPORTUNITY IN HIGHER EDUCATION. A STUDY OF MINORITY GROUP AND RELATED BARRIERS TO COLLEGE
    ADMISSION.   GBERKDS48446

    ORGANIZED LABOR AND MINORITY GROUPS. /UNION/   GBLUEJT47457

    THE MINORITY CHILD AND THE SCHOOLS.   GBULLPX62488

    SAN-MATEO AREA MINORITY JOB SURVEY. /CALIFORNIA/   GCALFEP65542

    FAIR-EMPLOYMENT-PRACTICES EQUAL GOOD EMPLOYMENT PRACTICES. GUIDELINES FOR TESTING AND SELECTING MINORITY
    JOB APPLICANTS. /CALIFORNIA/   GCALFEP66540

    EDUCATION OF THE MINORITY POOR -- THE KEY TO THE WAR-ON-POVERTY.   GCLARKB66915

    MINORITY PROGRAM CALLS FOR COMMUNITY ACTION.   GCRAICE65619

    MINORITY IN THE ENTERPRISE.   GFOLEAS52692

    CURRENT MINORITY POLICIES AND THEIR IMPLEMENTATION IN INTERNATIONAL UNIONS.   GHOPEJX51782

    MINORITY UTILIZATION PRACTICES -- RATIONAL OR SENTIMENTAL.   GHOPEJX51783

MINORITY   (CONTINUATION)
      PROTECTING RIGHTS OF MINORITY EMPLOYEES.   GKINGRL60854

      MINORITY RIGHTS AND THE PUBLIC INTEREST.   GLUSKLX42924

      MANAGEMENT AND MINORITY GROUPS. A STUDY OF ATTITUDES AND PRACTICES IN HIRING AND UPGRADING.   GMARKPI57085

      SURVEY OF OHIO COLLEGE AND UNIVERSITY PLACEMENT OFFICES WITH REGARD TO JOB PLACEMENT OF MINORITY
      STUDENTS.   GOHIOCR62132

      MINORITY RIGHTS AND THE UNION SHOP.   GREADFT64220

      MINORITY PROBLEMS.   GRCSEAM65249

      THE EDUCATIONAL STATUS OF A MINORITY. /MIGRANT-WORKERS/   GSAMOJX63501

      THE PRACTICES OF CRAFT UNIONS IN WASHINGTON-DC WITH RESPECT TO MINORITY GROUPS IN CIVIL-RIGHTS IN THE
      NATION-S CAPITOL.   GSEGABD59294

      ORGANIZED LABOR AND THE MINORITY WORKER NEED EACH OTHER. /UNION/   GSHISBX59305

      FROM SCHOOL TO JOB. GUIDANCE FOR MINORITY YOUTH.   GTANNAX63156

      STUDY OF MINORITY GROUP EMPLOYMENT IN THE FEDERAL GOVERNMENT, 1966.   GUSCISC66767

      MINORITY WORKER HIRING AND REFERRAL IN SAN-FRANCISCO. /CALIFORNIA/   GUSDLAB58076

      AMERICAN MINORITY RELATIONS. THE SOCIOLOGY OF RACE AND ETHNIC GROUPS.   GVANDJW63535

      THE MINORITY NEWCOMER IN OPEN AND CLOSED GROUPS.   GZILLRC59595

      AMERICAN-INDIANS. NEGLECTED MINORITY. /ECONOMIC-STATUS/   IDENNLB66547

      A CULTURAL MINORITY IMPROVES ITSELF.   MATKIJA61361

      EDUCATIONAL STATUS OF A MINORITY.   MSAMOJX63470

      VOCATIONAL GUIDANCE FOR MINORITY YOUTH.   NBABOIX59038

      MINORITY PROGRAM CALLS FOR COMMUNITY ACTION.   NCRAICE65240

      AN INSIGHT INTO STRUCTURAL UNEMPLOYMENT -- THE EXPERIENCE OF A MINORITY GROUP IN A PROSPEROUS COMMUNITY.   NGERSWJ65634

      ECONOMICS FOR THE MINORITY. /POVERTY/   NHARRMX65488

      NEGRO MINORITY. /ECONOMIC-STATUS/   NJOHNCS42550

      TRADE UNIONS AND MINORITY PROBLEMS.   NJOUROS53891

      GUIDANCE AND MINORITY YOUTH.   NLONGHH62705

      STUDY OF ECONOMIC AND CULTURAL ACTIVITIES IN THE WARREN AREA AS THEY RELATE TO MINORITY PEOPLE. /OHIO/   NWARRUL64986

      MINORITY REPORT. /EEO/   WDAVICX63718

MINORITY-GROUP
      UNDER-ACHIEVEMENT AMONG MINORITY-GROUP STUDENTS. AN ANALYSIS AND A PROPOSAL. /YOUTH NEGRO
      MEXICAN-AMERICAN PUERTO-RICAN/   CHOBACW63555

      JOB ADJUSTMENT PROBLEMS OF DELINQUENT MINORITY-GROUP YOUTH.   GAMOSWE64874

      THE MINORITY-GROUP WORKER IN CAMDEN COUNTY. /NEW-JERSEY/   GBOGITX54057

      COUNSELING MINORITY-GROUP YOUTH. DEVELOPING THE EXPERIENCE OF EQUALITY THROUGH EDUCATION.   GBRIGWA62473

      SOME PROBLEMS IN MINORITY-GROUP EDUCATION IN THE LOS-ANGELES PUBLIC SCHOOLS. /CALIFORNIA/   GBULLPX63489

      HOW TO RECRUIT MINORITY-GROUP COLLEGE GRADUATES. ITS PROBLEMS, ITS TECHNIQUES, ITS SOURCES, ITS
      OPPORTUNITIES.   GCALVRX63555

      PLANT INSPECTION SURVEY BY MANAGEMENT -- MINORITY-GROUP INTEGRATION. /COLORADO/   GDENNGHND632

      SOME CONSIDERATIONS AS TO THE CONTRIBUTIONS OF SOCIAL, PERSONALITY, AND RACIAL FACTORS TO SCHOOL
      RETARDATION IN MINORITY-GROUP CHILDREN.   GDEUTMP56641

      MINORITY-GROUP AND CLASS STATUS AS RELATED TO SOCIAL AND PERSONALITY FACTORS IN SCHOLASTIC ACHIEVEMENT.   GDEUTMP60640

      SOME EDUCATIONAL IMPLICATIONS OF THE INFLUENCE OF REJECTION ON ASPIRATION LEVELS OF MINORITY-GROUP
      CHILDREN.   GGOFFRM54366

      EXPANDED UTILIZATION OF MINORITY-GROUP WORKERS.   GGRAYCJ51736

      REALIZING THE MANPOWER POTENTIALITIES OF MINORITY-GROUP YOUTH.   GHOLLJH58778

      HERE-S HOW MERIT EMPLOYMENT PROGRAMS WORK. A REPORT ON PROGRESS AND PROBLEMS IN THE EMPLOYMENT OF
      MINORITY-GROUP MEMBERS.   GILLISC56803

      TESTING MINORITY-GROUP APPLICANTS.   GKETCWA66942

      TESTING MINORITY-GROUP APPLICANTS FOR EMPLOYMENT.   GLOCKHC65907

      SURVEY OF MINORITY-GROUP EMPLOYMENT AND PATIENT CARE IN PRIVATE HOSPITAL FACILITIES IN LOS-ANGELES
      COUNTY. /CALIFORNIA/   GLOSACCND914

      MINORITY-GROUP WORKERS IN INDUSTRY.   GMEYESM56058

      PROBLEMS, RESEARCH, AND RECOMMENDATIONS IN THE EMPLOYMENT TESTING OF MINORITY-GROUP APPLICANTS.   GNEWCMR66163

      REPORT OF A PRELIMINARY STUDY OF EMPLOYMENT PRACTICES INVOLVING MINORITY-GROUP WORKERS, ESSEX-COUNTY,
      NEW-JERSEY.   GNEWJDE46059

      1964 MINORITY-GROUP STUDY.   GPRESCD64111

      STUDY OF MINORITY-GROUP EMPLOYMENT IN THE FEDERAL GOVERNMENT.   GPRESCD64116

      HELPING TO OVERCOME MINORITY-GROUP PROBLEMS.   GRUDDEN63267

      THE INFLUENCE OF DISCRIMINATION ON MINORITY-GROUP MEMBERS IN ITS RELATION TO ATTEMPTS TO COMBAT

MINORITY-GROUP   (CONTINUATION)
DISCRIMINATION.   GSAENGX48273

SELECTED LIST OF REFERENCES ON **MINORITY-GROUP** EMPLOYMENT IN THE PUBLIC SERVICE.   GSIMPDX64312

PROBLEMS AND APPROACHES IN INTEGRATING **MINORITY-GROUP** WORK FORCES.   GSPERBJ53330

MINORITY-GROUP INTEGRATION BY LABOR AND MANAGEMENT. A STUDY OF THE EMPLOYMENT PRACTICES OF THE LARGER
EMPLOYERS. AND THE MEMBERSHIP PRACTICES OF THE LARGER LABOR UNIONS WITH RESPECT TO RACE, RELIGION, AND
NATIONAL ORIGIN. CONNECTICUT, 1951.   GSTETHG53598

STUDY OF **MINORITY-GROUP** EMPLOYMENT IN THE FEDERAL GOVERNMENT.   GUSDLAB63500

TESTING OF **MINORITY-GROUP** APPLICANTS FOR EMPLOYMENT.   GWALLPX66539

A **MINORITY-GROUP** IN AMERICAN SOCIETY.   GYINGJM66589

CITY EMPLOYMENT SURVEY. PERCENTAGE OF **MINORITY-GROUP** EMPLOYEES BY DEPARTMENT. /YONKERS NEW-YORK/ GYONKCC66592

POVERTY AMONG SPANISH-AMERICANS IN TEXAS. LOW-INCOME FAMILIES IN A **MINORITY-GROUP**.   MUPHAWK66511

MINORITY-GROUP INTEGRATION IN HOSPITALS.   NBABOIX61037

MINORITY-GROUP ATTITUDES OF NEGROES AND IMPLICATIONS FOR GUIDANCE.   NENGLWH57333

REALIZING THE MANPOWER POTENTIALITIES OF **MINORITY-GROUP** YOUTH.   NHOLLJH58561

NEGRO REACTIONS TO **MINORITY-GROUP** STATUS.   NJOHNRA57619

MINORITY-GROUP STUDY. JUNE 1963. NEGRO AND TOTAL EMPLOYMENT IN SELECTED AGENCIES.   NPRESCD63010

STUDY OF **MINORITY-GROUP** EMPLOYMENT IN THE FEDERAL-GOVERNMENT, 1963.   NUSCISC63228

STUDY OF **MINORITY-GROUP** EMPLOYMENT IN THE FEDERAL GOVERNMENT, 1965.   NUSCISC65229

MINORITY-GROUPS
MINORITY-GROUPS IN NEVADA. /NEGRO AMERICAN-INDIAN/   CRUSCER66807

SIGNIFICANT TRENDS IN THE NEW-YORK STATE ECONOMY, WITH SPECIAL REFERENCE TO **MINORITY-GROUPS**.
/PUERTO-RICAN NEGRO/   CRUSSVR59482

STRENGTHENING THE INTEGRATION OF **MINORITY-GROUPS**. THE PROBLEM IS TACKLED AS A UNION PROBLEM.   GALGCME52107

APTITUDE TESTING, TRAINING, AND EMPLOYEE DEVELOPMENT, WITH A SECTION ON THE EMPLOYMENT OF
MINORITY-GROUPS.   GAMERMA49389

THE CIVIL-RIGHTS-ACT OF 1964. WHAT IT MEANS -- TO EMPLOYERS, BUSINESSMEN, UNIONS, EMPLOYEES,
MINORITY-GROUPS. TEXT, ANALYSIS, LEGISLATIVE HISTORY.   GBUREON64492

THE CALIFORNIA PLAN FOR EQUAL-OPPORTUNITY IN APPRENTICESHIP FOR **MINORITY-GROUPS**.   GCALDIR63523

MINORITY-GROUPS AND MERIT SYSTEM PRACTICE.   GCALPPA65547

TEXAS PROVIDES JOBS FOR **MINORITY-GROUPS**.   GCARRHX66558

MINORITY-GROUPS CONFERENCE ON EQUAL-EMPLOYMENT-OPPORTUNITIES.   GCHURRX55572

EMPLOYMENT IN CIVIL-SERVICE OF **MINORITY-GROUPS**. /DETROIT MICHIGAN/   GDETRCC63638

VOCATIONAL TRAINING TO IMPROVE JOB OPPORTUNITIES FOR **MINORITY-GROUPS**. COMMENT.   GFINEMX64681

UNDERSTANDING **MINORITY-GROUPS**.   GGITTJB56973

DEVELOPMENT OF TRAINING INCENTIVES FOR THE YOUTH OF **MINORITY-GROUPS**. /ECONOMIC-STATUS/   GGRANLB57979

MINORITY-GROUPS. EMPLOYMENT PROBLEMS, REFERENCES.   GHESLMR63773

THE CITY GOVERNMENT AND **MINORITY-GROUPS**.   GINTECM63816

MINORITY-GROUPS AND ECONOMIC-STATUS IN NEW-YORK STATE.   GLANGGE59884

GUIDANCE, TRAINING AND APPRENTICESHIP FACTORS AFFECTING **MINORITY-GROUPS**.   GNATLAM60037

MINORITY-GROUPS. SEGREGATION AND INTEGRATION.   GNATLCN55044

REPORT ON A SURVEY OF EMPLOYMENT POLICIES AND HIRING PRACTICES INVOLVING **MINORITY-GROUPS** IN HUDSON-COUNTY,
NEW-JERSEY.   GNEWJDE51060

REPORT ON A SURVEY OF EMPLOYMENT POLICIES AND PRACTICES INVOLVING **MINORITY-GROUPS** IN MIDDLESEX-COUNTY,
NEW-JERSEY.   GNEWJDE52061

REPORT ON EMPLOYMENT AND IMAGE OF **MINORITY-GROUPS** ON TELEVISION.   GNEWYSB63105

HUMAN RESOURCES IN THE URBAN ECONOMY. PART II -- THE LABOR FORCE PERFORMANCE OF **MINORITY-GROUPS**. GPERLMX63169

EMPLOYMENT PROGRAM FOR **MINORITY-GROUPS**.   GTHAMME50353

SERVICE TO **MINORITY-GROUPS**. 1958.   GUSDLAB58497

VOCATIONAL-TRAINING TO IMPROVE JOB OPPORTUNITIES FOR **MINORITY-GROUPS**.   GWALSJP64540

CALIFORNIA-S **MINORITY-GROUPS** PROGRAM.   GWOODMJ64581

MINORITY-GROUPS AND THEIR EDUCATION IN HAY-COUNTY, TEXAS.   MMEADBS59438

ORGANIZED LABOR AND **MINORITY-GROUPS** POLICY AND PRACTICES. /UNION/   NBLUEJT47256

TRAINING FOR **MINORITY-GROUPS**. PROBLEMS OF RACIAL IMBALANCE AND SEGREGATION.   NFUSFDR66014

WHAT SHOULD THE BUSINESS RESPONSE BE TO THE NEGRO REVOLUTION. A PUBLIC RELATIONS PROGRAM FOR DEALING WITH
MINORITY-GROUPS.   NLANGJF65671

MINORITY-GROUPS AND INTERGROUP RELATIONS IN THE SAN-FRANCISCO BAY AREA. /CALIFORNIA/   NRECOCW63043

MANAGEMENT AND **MINORITY-GROUPS**. A STUDY OF ATTITUDES AND PRACTICES IN HIRING AND UPGRADING.   NROSEBX59080

MINORITY-GROUPS IN CALIFORNIA.   NUSDLAB66826

MINUTES
MINUTES OF INDIAN EMPLOYMENT MEETING HELD NOVEMBER 29-30, 1966 IN BISMARK, NORTH-DAKOTA.   IUSDLAB66322

MIRANDA
RACE DISCRIMINATION AND THE NLRA ACT. THE BRAVE NEW WORLD OF MIRANDA. /LEGISLATION/   NSOVEMI63169

MISSISSIPPI
AN EXPERIMENT IN MANPOWER DEVELOPMENT. /TRAINING MISSISSIPPI NEGRO WOMEN/   CSELFHO66325

MISSISSIPPI. BATTLEFRONT FOR LABOR. /UNION/   NBARTBX65057

THE PRICE OF DEFIANCE. /MISSISSIPPI RACE/   NBUSIWX62159

THE GENERAL CONDITIONS OF MISSISSIPPI NEGROES.   NCOUNFO63929

THE CHANGING ECONOMIC STATUS OF THE MISSISSIPPI NEGRO.   NEATHBJ64314

THE THORNTONS OF MISSISSIPPI. PEONAGE ON THE PLANTATION. /POVERTY/   NGOODPX66433

LABOR AND TECHNOLOGY ON SELECTED COTTON PLANTATIONS IN THE DELTA AREA OF MISSISSIPPI, 1953-1957.   NLERANL59404

PLANTATION ORGANIZATION AND THE RESIDENT LABOR-FORCE, DELTA AREA, MISSISSIPPI.   NLERANL60403

NEGRO FARM LABOR IN THE DELTA AREA OF MISSISSIPPI. SUPPLY AND UTILIZATION.   NLERANL61416

THE RELATIONSHIP BETWEEN MECHANIZATION OF COTTON PRODUCTION AND ATTENDANCE AND ENROLLMENT IN THE RURAL
SCHOOLS OF COAHOMA COUNTY, MISSISSIPPI.   NMCLABF51349

MIGRATION PATTERNS OF NEGROES FROM A RURAL NORTHEASTERN MISSISSIPPI COMMUNITY. /DEMOGRAPHY/   NRUBIMX60094

A CRITICAL APPRAISAL OF PROFESSION TRAINING OF NEGRO TEACHERS IN OKTIBBEHA COUNTY MISSISSIPPI.   NWILLMM50234

MISSISSIPPI WORKERS. WHERE THEY COME FROM AND HOW THEY PERFORM. A STUDY OF WORKING FORCES IN SELECTED
MISSISSIPPI INDUSTRIAL PLANTS.   NWOFFBM55333

MISSISSIPPI WORKERS. WHERE THEY COME FROM AND HOW THEY PERFORM. A STUDY OF WORKING FORCES IN SELECTED
MISSISSIPPI INDUSTRIAL PLANTS.   NWOFFBM55333

THE RURAL WORKING HOMEMAKER. ALCORN-COUNTY, MISSISSIPPI. /WORK-FAMILY-CONFLICT/   WBRYAES61660

MISSOURI
INCOME, EDUCATION AND UNEMPLOYMENT IN NEIGHBORHOODS. KANSAS-CITY, MISSOURI. /DEMOGRAPHY/   CUSDLAB63464

INCOME, EDUCATION AND UNEMPLOYMENT IN NEIGHBORHOODS. ST-LOUIS, MISSOURI. /DEMOGRAPHY/   CUSDLAB63481

FINAL REPORT. THE YOUTH TRAINING PROJECT, SEPTEMBER 1, 1963--JANUARY 31, 1965. /ST-LOUIS MISSOURI
TESTING/   GJEWIEV65568

AREAS OF COMMISSION CONCERN. /KANSAS-CITY MISSOURI/   GKANCIC62840

TECHNICAL REPORT NUMBER 1. EMPLOYMENT PRACTICES IN THE HOTEL, MOTEL AND RESTAURANT INDUSTRY OF MISSOURI.   GMILLRX66020

TECHNICAL REPORT NUMBER 2. EMPLOYMENT PRACTICES OF SELECTED MISSOURI PUBLIC UTILITIES. NATURAL GAS AND
ELECTRIC.   GMILLRX66021

MISSOURI LOCAL GOVERNMENT ACTION IN THE AREA OF HUMAN-RIGHTS.   GMISSCH63022

THE NEW FEDERAL FAIR-EMPLOYMENT-PRACTICES ACT -- COMPARISON WITH STATE LAW AND AN ANALYSIS OF RELEVANT
STATE EXPERIENCES. /MISSOURI/   GROBEPC64239

THEY DID IT IN ST-LOUIS. /INDUSTRY INTEGRATION MISSOURI/   GROSSMX47262

A REPORT TO THE US COMMISSION ON CIVIL-RIGHTS. /MISSOURI/   GUSCOMC63406

SUB-EMPLOYMENT IN THE SLUMS OF ST-LOUIS. /MISSOURI/   GUSDLAB66517

NEGROES IN MISSOURI.   NCAMPRR60180

STUDY OF HUMAN-RIGHTS IN MISSOURI.   NMISSCH60802

EQUAL-EMPLOYMENT-OPPORTUNITIES IN MISSOURI STATE AGENCIES. A SURVEY OF NEGRO EMPLOYMENT, SPRING-SUMMER
1963.   NMISSCH64801

THE NEGRO IN THE ST-LOUIS ECONOMY. /MISSOURI/   NSOBEIX54178

REPORT ON THE MISSOURI COMMISSION ON THE STATUS OF WOMEN. /WORK-WOMEN-ROLE/   WCOLUMX64700

MISSOURI-BASIN
INDIANS OF THE MISSOURI-BASIN -- CULTURAL FACTORS IN THEIR SOCIAL AND ECONOMIC ADJUSTMENT.   IREIFBX58610

MIT
WOMEN AND THE SCIENTIFIC PROFESSIONS. THE MIT SYMPOSIUM ON AMERICAN WOMEN IN SCIENCE AND ENGINEERING.
/OCCUPATIONS/   WMATTJA65963

MIXED
INTERPERSONAL RELATIONS IN ETHNICALLY MIXED SMALL WORK GROUPS.   GSCOTWW59291

INCOME AND RELATED CHARACTERISTICS OF RURAL HOUSEHOLDS IN THE CENTRAL LOUISIANA MIXED FARMING AREA.   NBOLTBX60398

RESOURCE USE AND ADJUSTMENT. RURAL FAMILIES IN THE CENTRAL LOUISIANA MIXED FARMING AREA.   NBOLTBX61396

FARM INCOME PREDICTIONS FOR SMALL FARMS IN THE CENTRAL LOUISIANA MIXED FARMING AREA.   NBOLTBX62399

NEXT IT-S A MIXED POLICE FORCE. INTEGRATIONISTS LATEST GOAL IN NATION-S CAPITAL. /WASHINGTON-DC/   NUSNEWR57274

MMPI
NEGRO-WHITE DIFFERENCES ON THE MMPI. /TESTING/   NHOKAJE60559

MOBILITY
MOBILITY FOR METROPOLITAN AREAS.   CUSBURC63173

MOBILITY FOR STATES AND STATE ECONOMIC AREAS. /DEMOGRAPHY/   CUSBURC63174

EDUCATION AND OCCUPATIONAL MOBILITY. A REGRESSION ANALYSIS.   GDUNCOD63652

VERTICAL MOBILITY AND PREJUDICE.   GGREEJX53738

OCCUPATIONAL MOBILITY FROM THE FARM LABOR-FORCE.   GHATHDE67936

A NOTE ON OCCUPATIONAL MOBILITY FOR WHITE AND NONWHITE MALES, 1950 TO 1965.   GJAFFAJ66820

THE ADAPTATION OF LABOR RESOURCES TO CHANGING NEEDS. /MOBILITY/   GLESTRA66532

MOBILITY   (CONTINUATION)
GEOGRAPHIC MOBILITY AND EMPLOYMENT STATUS, MARCH 1962-MARCH 1963.   GSABESX64271

MOBILITY, METHODS OF JOB SEARCH, ATTITUDES, AND MOTIVATION OF DISPLACED WORKERS.   GSHEPHL64621

POPULATION MOBILITY WITHIN THE UNITED STATES.   GSHRYHS64309

MOBILITY AND WORKER ADAPTATION TO ECONOMIC CHANGE IN THE US.   GTRAVHX63836

MOBILITY OF THE POPULATION OF THE UNITED STATES, JANUARY 1, 1950 TO FEBRUARY 1, 1965. /DEMOGRAPHY/   GUSBURC65161

MOBILITY OF THE POPOFATION FO THE UNITED STATES, MARCH 1964 TO MARCH 1965. /DEMOGRAPHY/   GUSBURC66158

RELOCATION RIDDLES. /MOBILITY EDUCATION/   ITAYLFX65560

JEWISH AND ITALIAN IMMIGRATION AND SUBSEQUENT STATUS MOBILITY.   JSTROFL58764

AMBITIONS OF MEXICAN-AMERICAN YOUTH -- GOALS AND MEANS OF MOBILITY OF HIGH SCHOOL SENIORS.   MHELLCS64413

CLASS AS AN EXPLANATION OF ETHNIC DIFFERENCES IN MOBILITY ASPIRATIONS -- THE CASE OF MEXICAN-AMERICANS.   MHELLCS65415

CLASS CONSCIOUSNESS AND SOCIAL MOBILITY IN A MEXICAN-AMERICAN COMMUNITY.   MPENAFX63453

SOCIAL MOBILITY AND IMPUTATIONS OF WITCHCRAFT IN A MEXICAN-AMERICAN NEIGHBORHOOD OF TEXAS.   MRUBEAJ66467

INTER-INDUSTRY LABOR MOBILITY AMONG MEN, 1957-60.   NGALLLE66392

INTRA-PLANT MOBILITY OF NEGRO AND WHITE WORKERS.   NGARBAP65394

RECENT TRENDS IN THE OCCUPATIONAL MOBILITY OF NEGROES, 1930-1960.   NHARENX65484

SOME COMPARISONS AMONG NEGRO-WHITE COLLEGE STUDENTS. SOCIAL AMBITION AND ESTIMATED SOCIAL MOBILITY.   NHARREE66786

OCCUPATIONAL MOBILITY AND ATTITUDES TOWARD NEGROES.   NHODGRWND355

ATTITUDES TOWARD SOCIAL MOBILITY AS REVEALED BY SAMPLES OF NEGRO AND WHITE BOYS.   NMONTJB58809

NEGRO-WHITE DIFFERENCES IN GEOGRAPHIC MOBILITY.   NMUELEX66864

STATUS POSITION, MOBILITY, AND ETHNIC IDENTIFICATION OF THE NEGRO.   NPARKSX64973

RACIAL AND FAMILY EXPERIENCE CORRELATES OF MOBILITY ASPIRATION.   NSMITHP62144

MIGRATION, MOBILITY, AND THE ASSIMILATION OF THE NEGRO.   NTAEUIB58363

NEGRO-WHITE DIFFERENTIALS IN GEOGRAPHIC MOBILITY, 1964, 1965. /DEMOGRAPHY/   NUSDCOM64194

FEMALE LABOR-FORCE MOBILITY AND ITS SIMULATION.   WKORBJX63435

WHY WOMEN START AND STOP WORKING. A STUDY IN MOBILITY.   WROSECX65088

MOBILIZATION
THE EFFECT OF THE WAR ECONOMY ON THE SOUTH. HOW MOBILIZATION WILL AFFECT POSITION OF THE NEGRO.   NJACKJX51595

MOBILIZATION-FOR-YOU
AN EXPERIMENT TO TEST THREE MAJOR ISSUES OF WORK PROGRAM METHODOLOGY WITHIN MOBILIZATION-FOR-YOUTH-S
INTEGRATED SERVICES TO OUT-OF-SCHOOL UNEMPLOYED YOUTH. /NEGRO PUERTO-RICAN/   CMOBIFY66024

POVERTY ON THE LOWER-EAST-SIDE. SELECTED ASPECTS OF THE MOBILIZATION-FOR-YOUTH EXPERIENCE.   GBARRSX64130

MASTER ANNOTATED BIBLIOGRAPHY OF PAPERS OF MOBILIZATION-FOR-YOUTH. PUBLISHED, UNPUBLISHED AND PRESENTED
AT CONFERENCES.   GMOBIFY65025

MOBILIZING
MOBILIZING MANPOWER.   NPATEJE43977

MODEL
A MODEL STATE FAIR-EMPLOYMENT-PRACTICE BILL.   GNAACNL45036

MODERN
THE QUEST FOR THE DREAM. THE DEVELOPMENT OF CIVIL-RIGHTS AND HUMAN-RELATIONS IN MODERN AMERICA.   GROCHJP63057

THE INDIANS IN MODERN AMERICA.   IBAIRDA56532

MODERN KLAMATH. DEMOGRAPHY AND ECONOMY.   ISTERTX65625

MODERN AMERICAN CAREER WOMEN. /OCCUPATIONS/   WCLYMEX59693

WOMEN IN THE MODERN WORLD. /WORK-WOMAN-ROLE/   WFIRKEX63764

THE MODERN MOTHER-S DILEMMA. /WORK-FAMILY-CONFLICT/   WGRUESM57984

HIGH SCHOOL FRESHMAN AND SENIORS VIEW THE ROLE OF WOMEN IN MODERN SOCIETY. /WORK-FAMILY-CONFLICT/   WKERNKK65892

THE IDENTITY OF MODERN WOMAN. /WORK-WOMAN-ROLE/   WKRECHS65381

WOMEN AND MODERN SCIENCE. /OCCUPATIONS/   WLEWIND57932

MODIFICATION
IDENTIFICATION AND MODIFICATION OF THE SOCIAL-PSYCHOLOGICAL CORRELATES OF ECONOMIC DEPENDENCY. PROJECT
FINAL REPORT.   GKIMMPR66137

MOHAWKS
MOHAWKS. ROUND TRIP TO THE HIGH STEEL.   IBLUMRX65539

MONEY
MONEY BENEFITS OF EDUCATION BY SEX AND RACE IN NEW-YORK STATE, 1956.   GGREEWX61741

MONTANA
LEVEL OF OCCUPATIONAL ASPIRATIONS AMONG MONTANA INDIANS IN GRADE AND HIGH SCHOOL.   IDOUGGV60550

MONTGOMERY
OCCUPATIONAL ESTABLISHMENT OF FORMER STUDENTS OF VOCATIONAL AGRICULTURE IN MONTGOMERY TRAINING SCHOOL
AREA. /ALABAMA/   NSCOTCOND346

MORALE
THE HIGH COST OF DISCRIMINATION. THE WASTE IN MANPOWER, MORALE, AND PRODUCTIVITY COSTS AMERICAN INDUSTRY
30 BILLION DOLLARS A YEAR.   GROPEEX63244

MORRIS
SUMMARY OF A SURVEY OF SOCIAL AND ECONOMIC CONDITIONS IN MORRIS COUNTY NEW-JERSEY AS THEY AFFECT THE NEGRO.   NKERNJH57645

MORTALITY
MORTALITY BY OCCUPATION AND INDUSTRY AMONG MEN 20 TO 64 YEARS OF AGE. UNITED STATES, 1950. /DEMOGRAPHY/   GGURALX62748

MOTEL
TECHNICAL REPORT NUMBER 1. EMPLOYMENT PRACTICES IN THE HOTEL, MOTEL AND RESTAURANT INDUSTRY OF MISSOURI.   GMILLRX66020

MOTHER
SO YOU WANT TO BE A WORKING MOTHER.   WBENJLX66456

THE CASE FOR THE WORKING MOTHER.   WCOTTDW65708

ON BEING SOMETHING OTHER THAN MOTHER AND BEING MOTHER TOO. /WORK-FAMILY-CONFLICT/   WGOLDMR63793

ON BEING SOMETHING OTHER THAN MOTHER AND BEING MOTHER TOO. /WORK-FAMILY-CONFLICT/   WGOLDMR63793

THE EMPLOYED MOTHER IN AMERICA.   WNYEXFI63040

THE MOTHER WHO WORKS OUTSIDE THE HOUSE.   WWEINVX61259

MOTHER-S
RELATION OF MOTHER-S EMPLOYMENT TO INTELLECTUAL PERFORMANCE OF NEGRO COLLEGE STUDENTS.   NEPPSEG64336

THE MODERN MOTHER-S DILEMMA. /WORK-FAMILY-CONFLICT/   WGRUESM57984

MOTHERHOOD
THE CASE AGAINST FULL-TIME MOTHERHOOD. /EMPLOYMENT/   WROSSAS65092

MOTHERS
CLASS DIFFERENCES IN THE SOCIALIZATION PRACTICES OF NEGRO MOTHERS.   CKAMICKND632

THE CHILD-REARING ATTITUDES OF DISADVANTAGED NEGRO MOTHERS AND SOME EDUCATIONAL IMPLICATIONS.   CRADINX65031

NEGRO ADC MOTHERS LOOK FOR WORK. /WOMEN/   CWILLJJ58324

LOWER-CLASS NEGRO MOTHERS ASPIRATIONS FOR THEIR CHILDREN.   NBELLRR65074

A STUDY TO DETERMINE THE EMPLOYMENT POTENTIAL OF MOTHERS RECEIVING AID-TO-DEPENDENT-CHILDREN ASSISTANCE.   WBROODJ64656

AN EXPLORATORY STUDY OF EMPLOYERS ATTITUDES TOWARD WORKING MOTHERS.   WCONYJE61704

EMPLOYERS ATTITUDES TOWARD WORKING MOTHERS.   WCONYJE63703

WORKING MOTHERS AND MALADJUSTED CHILDREN.   WHANDHX57818

CHILDREN OF WORKING MOTHERS, 1960.   WHERZEX64123

THE NATION-S WORKING MOTHERS AND THE NEED FOR DAY CARE. ADDRESS. /EMPLOYMENT-CONDITIONS/   WKEYSMD65897

WORKING MOTHERS AND THEIR ARRANGEMENTS FOR CARE OF THEIR CHILDREN. /EMPLOYMENT-CONDITIONS/   WLAJEHC59922

CHILDREN AND WORKING MOTHERS.   WMACCEE58949

PROFESSIONAL AND NON-PROFESSIONAL WOMEN AS MOTHERS.   WMERIFH55971

MOTHERS AT WORK.   WMETRLI63973

MOTHERS IN THE LABOR-FORCE.   WMOUNHS64003

LABOR-FORCE PARTICIPATION OF SUBURBAN MOTHERS.   WMYERGC64011

WHY COLLEGE-TRAINED MOTHERS WORK.   WROSSJE65770

CHILD CARE ARRANGEMENTS OF FULLTIME WORKING MOTHERS. /EMPLOYMENT-CONDITIONS/   WUSDHEW59171

CHILD CARE ARRANGEMENTS OF THE NATION-S WORKING MOTHERS. A PRELIMINARY REPORT.   WUSDHEW65172

CRITERIA FOR ASSESSING FEASIBILITY OF MOTHERS EMPLOYMENT AND ADEQUACY OF CHILD CARE PLANS.   WUSDHEW66173

LABOR-FORCE PARTICIPATION RATES AND PERCENT DISTRIBUTION OF MOTHERS WITH HUSBAND PRESENT.   WUSDLAB64204

WHO ARE THE WORKING MOTHERS.   WUSDLAB66805

PART-TIME WORKING MOTHERS -- A CASE-STUDY.   WWORTNB60245

MOTIVATING
MOTIVATING NEGRO YOUTH IN RHODE-ISLAND.   NMINIBC65797

MOTIVATION
MOBILITY, METHODS OF JOB SEARCH, ATTITUDES, AND MOTIVATION OF DISPLACED WORKERS.   GSHEPHL64621

ANOMIE AND ACHIEVEMENT MOTIVATION. A STUDY OF PERSONALITY DEVELOPMENT WITHIN CULTURAL DISORGANIZATION.   IKERCAC59018

THE MOTIVATION OF THE UNDERPRIVILEGED WORKER.   NDAVIAX46254

MOTIVATION AND PERFORMANCE OF NEGRO STUDENTS.   NEPPSEG66335

COMMUNITY FACTORS AFFECTING MOTIVATION AND ACHIEVEMENT IN A DECADE OF DECISION. /EDUCATION/   NGRANLB62441

MOTIVATION AND ASPIRATION IN THE NEGRO COLLEGE.   NGURIPX66352

ACHIEVEMENT MOTIVATION CHARACTERISTICS OF NEGRO COLLEGE FRESHMEN.   NHARREC59492

WORK MOTIVATION OF COLLEGE ALUMNAE. FIVE-YEAR FOLLOWUP.   WEYDELD67223

A COMMENTARY ON THE MOTIVATION AND EDUCATION OF COLLEGE WOMEN. /ASPIRATIONS/   WHEISPX62837

THE MOTIVATION OF COLLEGE WOMEN TODAY. A CLOSER LOOK. /ASPIRATIONS/   WHEISPX62839

THE MOTIVATION OF COLLEGE WOMEN TODAY. THE CULTURAL SETTING. /ASPIRATIONS/   WHEISPX63840

THE MOTIVATION FOR WOMEN TO WORK IN HIGH LEVEL PROFESSIONAL POSITIONS.   WWALTDE62314

MOTIVATIONAL
MOTIVATIONAL PROBLEMS IN TRAINING.   GWISPLG65141

MOTIVATIONAL   (CONTINUATION)
WORKING AT IMPROVING THE **MOTIVATIONAL** AND ACHIEVEMENT LEVELS OF THE DEPRIVED.   NHARREC63367

SOCIAL ROLE EXPECTATION. **MOTIVATIONAL** VARIABLE IN GIRLS. /ASPIRATIONS/   WHANSDE64821

MOTIVATIONS
A STUDY OF JOB **MOTIVATIONS**, ACTIVITIES, AND SATISFACTIONS OF PRESENT AND PROSPECTIVE WOMEN COLLEGE
FACULTY MEMBERS. /OCCUPATIONS/   WCOOKWX60252

A MEMORANDUM ON THE **MOTIVATIONS** OF MIDDLE AGED WOMEN IN THE LOWER EDUCATIONAL BRACKETS TO RETURN TO WORK.
/ASPIRATIONS/   WJEWIVA61880

A PILOT STUDY OF THE **MOTIVATIONS** AND PROBLEMS OF MIDDLE AGED HOMEMAKERS IN LOWER SOCIO-ECONOMIC GROUPS IN
SEEKING EMPLOYMENT. /ASPIRATIONS/   WJEWIVA62883

MOTIVE
THE ACHIEVEMENT **MOTIVE** IN WOMEN. A STUDY OF THE IMPLICATIONS FOR CAREER DEVELOPMENT.   WBARURX66453

MOTOROLA
PRESS SWALLOWS **MOTOROLA** HOAX. /TESTING/   GWESTOL65552

HIRING TESTS WAIT FOR THE SCORE. MYART VS **MOTOROLA**.   NBUSIWX65150

THE **MOTOROLA** CASE. /TESTING/   NFRENRL65385

MOVEMENT
FAIR-EMPLOYMENT-PRACTICE-COMMISSION **MOVEMENT** IN PERSPECTIVE.   GKESSLC56846

THE PRESENT STATUS OF THE CULTURE FAIR TESTING **MOVEMENT**.   GLAMBNM64880

THE POSITION OF MINORITIES IN THE AMERICAN LABOR **MOVEMENT**. /UNION/   GMARSRX66946

THE **MOVEMENT** OF LABOR BETWEEN FARM AND NONFARM JOBS.   GPERKBX66150

LEGACY OF THE JEWISH LABOR **MOVEMENT**.   JTYLEGX65766

THE MECHANICAL COTTON-PICKER. NEGRO MIGRATION, AND THE INTEGRATION **MOVEMENT**.   NDILLHCND274

NEGROES AND THE LABOR **MOVEMENT**. RECORD OF THE LEFT WING UNIONS.   NDOYLWX62287

HISTORY OF THE LABOR **MOVEMENT** IN THE UNITED STATES. /UNION/   NFONEPS47370

NEGROES AND THE LABOR **MOVEMENT** -- AN EXCHANGE.   NLIPSSM62043

THE AMERICAN LABOR **MOVEMENT**.   NLITWLX62698

THE POSITION OF MINORITIES IN THE AMERICAN LABOR **MOVEMENT**. /UNION/   NMARSRX66943

THE CIVIL-RIGHTS **MOVEMENT** AND EMPLOYMENT.   NMCKERB64722

PROBLEMS AND PROSPECTS OF THE NEGRO **MOVEMENT**. /EMPLOYMENT/   NMURPRJ66866

NEGROES AND THE LABOR **MOVEMENT**. /UNION/   NNEWXPX62910

THE NEGRO IN THE AMERICAN LABOR **MOVEMENT**. /UNION/   NROSESJ62079

SOCIAL-CLASS FACTORS UNDERLYING THE CIVIL-RIGHTS **MOVEMENT**.   NSCOTJW66112

THE POLITICS OF PREJUDICE. THE ANTI-JAPANESE **MOVEMENT** IN CALIFORNIA AND THE STRUGGLE FOR JAPANESE
EXCLUSION.   ODANIRX61716

SPANISH SPEAKING WORKERS AND THE LABOR **MOVEMENT**.   PASSPCT56779

THE GREAT BACK-TO-WORK **MOVEMENT**. /WORK-FAMILY-CONFLICT/   WBELLDX56635

MOVEMENTS
THE SOCIAL POLITICS OF FEPC. A STUDY IN REFORM PRESSURE **MOVEMENTS**.   GKESSLC48847

MOYNIHAN
SAVAGE DISCOVERY. THE **MOYNIHAN** REPORT.   GRYANWX65489

MOYNIHAN-REPORT
THE NEGRO FAMILY AND THE **MOYNIHAN-REPORT**.   NCARPLX66184

MULTIPLE
MULTIPLE JOB-HOLDERS IN DECEMBER, 1959.   GBANCGX60418

MULTIPLE JOBHOLDERS IN MAY, 1963.   GBOGAFA64460

MULTIRACIAL
EMPLOYMENT POLICY PROBLEMS IN A **MULTIRACIAL** SOCIETY.   GSIMPGE62313

MUNICIPAL
RACE AND SOCIO-ECONOMIC STATUS IN **MUNICIPAL** PERSONNEL SELECTION.   GBIANJC67590

THE PRESENT STATUS AND PROGRAMS OF FEPC. FEDERAL, STATE, AND **MUNICIPAL**.   GBRAZBR51472

FEPC LEGISLATION IN THE UNITED STATES. FEDERAL, STATE, **MUNICIPAL**.   GGRAVWB51735

MUNICIPAL FAIR-EMPLOYMENT-PRACTICES IN NEBRASKA.   GNEBRLR62086

GOVERNMENTAL FAIR-EMPLOYMENT AGENCIES. AN APPRAISAL OF FEDERAL, STATE, AND **MUNICIPAL** EFFORTS TO END JOB
DISCRIMINATION.   GNORGPH62120

MUNICIPAL FAIR-EMPLOYMENT ORDINANCES AS A VALID EXERCISE OF THE POLICE POWER.   GNORTDL64093

MUNICIPAL HUMAN-RELATIONS COMMISSION. A SURVEY OF PROGRAMS IN SELECTED CITIES OF THE UNITED STATES.   GRICHCM63236

MUNICIPAL FEPC IN MINNEAPOLIS. /MINNESOTA/   GSURVXX47341

MUNICIPAL-EMPLOYEES
ETHNIC SURVEY OF **MUNICIPAL-EMPLOYEES**. A REPORT ON THE NUMBER AND DISTRIBUTION OF NEGROES AND
PUERTO-RICANS AND OTHER EMPLOYEES BY THE CITY OF NEW-YORK.   CNEWYCC64916

MUSKEGON
A STUDY OF UNEMPLOYMENT, TRAINING AND PLACEMENT PATTERNS IN THE **MUSKEGON** AREA. /MICHIGAN/   GMICFEA57979

MUTUAL
THE **MUTUAL** SAVINGS BANKS OF NEW-YORK-CITY. /DISCRIMINATION/   JAMERJC65694

MUTUAL   (CONTINUATION)
THE **MUTUAL** SAVINGS BANKS OF NEW-YORK-CITY. A FOLLOW-UP REPORT ON THE EXCLUSION OF JEWS AT TOP-MANAGEMENT
AND POLICY-MAKING LEVELS.   JAMERJC66695

THE **MUTUAL** IMAGES AND EXPECTATIONS OF ANGLO-AMERICANS AND MEXICAN-AMERICANS.   MSIMMOG61490

MYART
HIRING TESTS WAIT FOR THE SCORE. **MYART** VS MOTOROLA.   NBUSIWX65150

MYRDALIAN
THE **MYRDALIAN** HYPOTHESES. RANK ORDER OF DISCRIMINATION.   GEDMUER44495

MYTHS
EXPLODING THE **MYTHS**. EXPANDING EMPLOYMENT OPPORTUNITIES FOR CAREER WOMEN.   WUVCAEC66249

NAACP
ADDRESS AT THE CONVOCATION OF THE **NAACP** LEGAL DEFENSE AND EDUCATIONAL FUND. /LEGISLATION/   GWIRTWW66570

NAACP AND THE AFL-CIO. AN OVERVIEW. /UNION/   NGROSJA62461

NAACP VIEWS CONDITIONS.   NGUSCKI63469

NAACP LABOR MANUAL. A GUIDE TO ACTION.   NHILLHX58531

THE **NAACP** VERSUS LABOR. /UNION/   NRICHJC62054

NARRAGANSETT
THE DETRIBALIZATION OF THE **NARRAGANSETT** INDIANS. A CASE STUDY.   IBOISEX56886

NARRAGANSETT SURVIVAL. A STUDY OF GROUP PERSISTENCE THROUGH ADAPTED TRAITS.   IBOISEX59887

NASHVILLE
EMPLOYMENT OPPORTUNITY FOR **NASHVILLE** NEGROES. /TENNESSEE/   NCOMUCE60230

EMPLOYMENT OPPORTUNITIES FOR **NASHVILLE** NEGROES. /TENNESSEE/   NHENDVW60516

A REPORT ON COMMUNITY FACTORS IN **NASHVILLE** RELATED TO THE NEGRO IN MEDICINE. /TENNESSEE/   NVALIPX56281

NATION
MINORITY PEOPLES IN A **NATION** AT WAR.   GANNAOA42549

POVERTY AND DEPRIVATION IN THE UNITED STATES. THE PLIGHT OF TWO-FIFTHS OF A **NATION**.   GCONFOE62873

THE STATUS OF THE NONWHITE LABOR-FORCE IN ILLINOIS AND THE **NATION**.   GILLICH57793

IMPROVING THE WORK SKILLS OF THE **NATION**.   GNATLMC55052

ONE-THIRD OF A **NATION**. A REPORT ON YOUNG MEN FOUND UNQUALIFIED FOR MILITARY SERVICE.   GPRESTM64316

HEARINGS RELATING TO THE TRAINING AND UTILIZATION OF THE MANPOWER RESOURCES OF THE **NATION**.   GUSSENA63618

A COMPARISON OF TUITION-AND-FEE CHARGES IN NEGRO INSTITUTIONS WITH CHARGES IN INSTITUTIONS OF THE
SOUTHEAST AND OF THE **NATION**. 1962-1963. /EDUCATION/   NOAMILX64127

HUMAN-RESOURCES. THE WEALTH OF A **NATION**. /YOUTH/   NGINZEX58405

THE INEFFECTIVE SOLDIER. LESSONS FOR MANAGEMENT AND THE **NATION**.   NGINZEX59406

THE ECONOMIC-STATUS OF NEGROES. IN THE **NATION** AND IN THE SOUTH.   NHENDVW63515

THE SOCIAL REVOLUTION. CHALLENGE TO THE **NATION**. /CIVIL-RIGHTS/   NYOUNWM63600

THE CHANGING WOMAN WORKER. A STUDY OF THE FEMALE LABOR-FORCE IN NEW-JERSEY AND IN THE **NATION** FROM 1940 TO
1958.   WSMITGM60120

NATION-S
THE **NATION-S** CHILDREN. VOL I. THE FAMILY AND SOCIAL-CHANGE. VOL II. DEVELOPMENT AND EDUCATION. VOL III.
PROBLEMS AND PROSPECTS. /NEGRO PUERTO-RICAN MEXICAN-AMERICAN WOMEN/   CGINZEX60720

FAIR-EMPLOYMENT IN THE **NATION-S** CAPITAL. A STUDY OF PROGRESS AND DILEMMA. /WASHINGTON-DC/   GSAWYDA62279

THE PRACTICES OF CRAFT UNIONS IN WASHINGTON-DC WITH RESPECT TO MINORITY GROUPS IN CIVIL-RIGHTS IN THE
NATION-S CAPITOL.   GSEGABD59294

UNUSED MANPOWER. THE **NATION-S** LOSS.   GUSDLAB66504

YOUTH. THE **NATION-S** RICHEST RESOURCE. THEIR EDUCATION AND EMPLOYMENT NEEDS.   GUSINCC53514

NATION-S MANPOWER REVOLUTION.   GUSSENA63331

RACIAL DISCRIMINATION IN THE **NATION-S** APPRENTICESHIP TRAINING PROGRAM.   NHILLHX62539

NEXT IT-S A MIXED POLICE FORCE. INTEGRATIONISTS LATEST GOAL IN **NATION-S** CAPITAL. /WASHINGTON-DC/   NUSNEWR57274

ALL THESE PEOPLE. THE **NATION-S** HUMAN RESOURCES IN THE SOUTH.   NVANCRB45282

THE **NATION-S** WORKING MOTHERS AND THE NEED FOR DAY CARE. ADDRESS. /EMPLOYMENT-CONDITIONS/   WKEYSMD65897

CHILD CARE ARRANGEMENTS OF THE **NATION-S** WORKING MOTHERS. A PRELIMINARY REPORT.   WUSDHEW65172

CHANGING PROFILE OF THE **NATION-S** WORK-FORCE.   WWIRTWW63271

NATIONAL
AUTOMATION AND ECONOMIC PROGRESS. A SUMMARY OF THE REPORT OF THE **NATIONAL** COMMISSION ON TECHNOLOGY,
AUTOMATION, AND ECONOMIC PROGRESS.   GBOWEHR66748

ONE AMERICA. THE HISTORY, CONTRIBUTIONS, AND PRESENT PROBLEMS OF OUR RACIAL AND **NATIONAL** MINORITIES.   GBROWFJ45477

EQUAL-RIGHTS UNDER THE LAW. PROVIDING FOR EQUAL TREATMENT FOR ALL CITIZENS REGARDLESS OF RACE, RELIGION,
COLOR, **NATIONAL** ORIGIN OR ANCESTRY. /CALIFORNIA/   GCALAGO60511

MEMORANDUM OF UNDERSTANDING BETWEEN CALIFORNIA STATE FAIR- EMPLOYMENT-PRACTICE-COMMISSION AND
BANK-OF-AMERICA **NATIONAL** TRUST AND SAVINGS ASSOCIATION.   GCALFEPND537

A **NATIONAL** PROGRAM FOR THE IMPROVEMENT OF WELFARE SERVICES AND THE REDUCTION OF WELFARE DEPENDENCY.   GCOHENE65664

ASSIMILATION IN AMERICAN LIFE. THE ROLE OF RACE, RELIGION, AND **NATIONAL** ORIGINS.   GGORDMM64729

CIVIL-RIGHTS -- A **NATIONAL** CHALLENGE.   GHANNJA61988

NATIONAL   (CONTINUATION)
DISCRIMINATION AND **NATIONAL** WELFARE.   GMACIRM49025

NATIONAL POLITICS OF FAIR-EMPLOYMENT.   GMCKEEX52950

MIGRANT-LABOR--THE **NATIONAL** RESPONSIBILITY.   GMITCJP59954

THE MEASUREMENT AND INTERPRETATION OF JOB VACANCIES. A CONFERENCE REPORT OF THE **NATIONAL** BUREAU OF
ECONOMIC RESEARCH. /LABOR-MARKET/   GNATLBE66611

RULINGS ON PRE-EMPLOYMENT INQUIRIES RELATING TO RACE, CREED, COLOR OR **NATIONAL** ORIGIN UNDER THE NEW-YORK
STATE LAW AGAINST DISCRIMINATION.   GNEWYSBND106

NATIONAL EMPLOYMENT, SKILLS, AND EARNINGS OF FARM LABOR.   GSCHUTW67964

CONDITIONS FOR MIGRANTS -- A **NATIONAL** DISGRACE.   GSCHWLX66556

MINORITY-GROUP INTEGRATION BY LABOR AND MANAGEMENT. A STUDY OF THE EMPLOYMENT PRACTICES OF THE LARGER
EMPLOYERS, AND THE MEMBERSHIP PRACTICES OF THE LARGER LABOR UNIONS WITH RESPECT TO RACE, RELIGION, AND
NATIONAL ORIGIN, CONNECTICUT, 1951.   GSTETHG53598

THE ECONOMIC SITUATION OF **NATIONAL** MINORITIES IN THE UNITED STATES OF AMERICA.   GTHOMJA47354

THE **NATIONAL** CONFERENCE AND THE REPORTS OF THE STATE ADVISORY COMMITTEES TO THE U.S. COMMISSION ON
CIVIL-RIGHTS, 1959.   GUSCCMC60405

A TIME FOR ACTION. PROCEEDINGS OF THE **NATIONAL** CONFERENCE ON EQUAL-EMPLOYMENT-OPPORTUNITY, 1962.
 /MILITARY/   GUSDARM62193

PROGRAMS OF **NATIONAL** ORGANIZATIONS FOR MIGRANT FARM WORKERS AND THEIR FAMILIES.   GUSOLAB61202

THE ROLE AND LIMITS OF **NATIONAL** MANPOWER POLICIES.   GWEBEAR66760

NATIONAL CONFERENCE ON MANPOWER PROGRAMS FOR INDIANS. SUMMATION.   IKRUGDH67811

THE NEGRO IN THE **NATIONAL** ECONOMY.   NBRIMAF66115

THE **NATIONAL** TECHNICAL ASSOCIATION. /OCCUPATIONS/   NEVANJC43258

PROBLEMS AND OPPORTUNITIES CONFRONTING NEGROES IN THE FIELD OF BUSINESS, REPORT ON THE **NATIONAL**
CONFERENCE ON SMALL BUSINESS. /OCCUPATIONS/   NFITZNH63358

DISCRIMINATION AND **NATIONAL** WELFARE. A SERIES OF ADDRESSES AND DISCUSSIONS.   NMACIRM49731

THE NEGRO FAMILY. THE CASE FOR **NATIONAL** ACTION.   NMCYNDP65862

A **NATIONAL** SKILLS-BANK, WHAT IT IS, HOW IT OPERATES.   NNATLULND893

THE NEGRO AND THE **NATIONAL** GUARD. /MILITARY/   NNEWTIG62915

NATIONAL NEGRO LABOR COUNCIL, THIRD ANNUAL CONVENTION. /UNION/   NPERRPX54987

NEGRO WORKERS AND THE **NATIONAL** DEFENSE PROGRAM.   NUSOLAB41253

NEGRO LABOR. A **NATIONAL** PROBLEM.   NWEAVRC46304

COMPLAINTS ALLEGING DISCRIMINATION BECAUSE OF PUERTO-RICAN **NATIONAL** ORIGIN, JULY 1, 1945-SEPTEMBER 1,
1958.   PNEWYSA58836

PROGRESS AND PROSPECTS. THE REPORT OF THE SECOND **NATIONAL** CONFERENCE OF GOVERNORS COMMISSIONS ON THE
STATUS OF WOMEN. /EMPLOYMENT-CONDITIONS/   WGOVECS65798

A **NATIONAL** INQUIRY OF PRIVATE HOUSEHOLD-EMPLOYEES AND EMPLOYERS.   WNATLCH66014

PROFESSIONAL WOMANPOWER AS A **NATIONAL** RESOURCE.   WPARRJB61051

NATIONAL-LABOR-
TITLE-VII. RELATIONSHIP AND EFFECT ON THE **NATIONAL-LABOR-** RELATIONS-BOARD. /LEGISLATION/   GFUCHRS66702

NATIONAL-LABOR-RELAT
THE **NATIONAL-LABOR-RELATIONS** ACT-AND RACIAL DISCRIMINATION. /LEGISLATION/   NMOLIRL66807

THE RACIAL ISSUE AS AN ANTI UNION TOOL AND THE **NATIONAL-LABOR-RELATIONS-**BOARD.   NSACHRX63888

THE **NATIONAL-LABOR-RELATIONS-**ACT AND RACIAL DISCRIMINATION. /LEGISLATION/   NSOVEMI62168

NATIONAL-SHARECROPPE
PROCEEDINGS OF THE **NATIONAL-SHARECROPPERS-**FUND CONFERENCE ON MIGRATORY LABOR AND LOW-INCOME FARMERS.
NOVEMBER 13 1957.   GNATLSF57299

NATIONALITY
RACE, **NATIONALITY**, AND RELIGION -- THEIR RELATIONSHIP TO APPOINTMENT POLICIES AND CASEWORK.   GHAGEDJ57752

RACE AND **NATIONALITY** IN AMERICAN LIFE.   GHANDOX57758

NATIONWIDE
AUTOMATION. **NATIONWIDE** STUDIES IN THE US.   GGREELX64614

NATIVITY
EMPLOYMENT AND PERSONAL CHARACTERISTICS. EMPLOYMENT BY AGE, RACE, **NATIVITY**, EDUCATION, MARITAL-STATUS,
HOUSEHOLD RELATIONSHIPS, ETC. /DEMOGRAPHY/   CUSBURC53372

NATIVITY AND PARENTAGE. /DEMOGRAPHY/   CUSBURC63175

NATURALIZATION
NATURALIZATION AND ASSIMILATION PRONENESS OF CALIFORNIA IMMIGRANT POPULATIONS.   MKRASWX63425

NAVAHO
APACHE, **NAVAHO**, AND SPANIARD. /MEXICAN-AMERICAN AMERICAN-INDIAN/   CFORBJX60561

ANALYSIS OF MALE **NAVAHO** STUDENTS PERCEPTIONS OF OCCUPATIONAL OPPORTUNITIES AND THEIR ATTITUDES TOWARD
DEVELOPMENT OF SKILLS AND TRAITS NECESSARY FOR OCCUPATIONAL COMPETENCE.   IDESPCW65548

A STUDY OF **NAVAHO** URBAN RELOCATION IN DENVER COLORADO.   IGRAVTD64566

PERCEIVED OPPORTUNITIES, EXPECTATIONS, AND THE DECISION TO REMAIN ON RELOCATION. THE CASE OF THE **NAVAHO**
INDIAN MIGRANT TO DENVER, COLORADO.   IGRAVTD65567

VALUES, EXPECTATIONS AND RELOCATION. THE **NAVAHO** MIGRANT TO DENVER. /COLORADO/   IGRAVTD66146

NAVAHO   (CONTINUATION)
    THE ROLE OF WOMEN IN A CHANGING NAVAHO SOCIETY.   IHAMALS57985

    FRUITLAND, NEW-MEXICO. A NAVAHO COMMUNITY IN TRANSITION.   ISASATT60615

    CHANGE AND RESISTANCE IN AN ISOLATED NAVAHO COMMUNITY.   ISHEPMX64618

    NAVAHO.   IVOGTEZ61679

    THE ECONOMIC ABSORPTION OF NAVAHO INDIAN MIGRANTS IN DENVER, COLORADO.   IWEPPRS65684

    ECONOMIC FACTORS IN NAVAHO URBAN RELOCATION.   IWEPPRS65685

NAVAJO
    PROBLEMS OF NAVAJO MALE GRADUATES OF INTERMOUNTAIN SCHOOL DURING THEIR FIRST YEAR OF EMPLOYMENT.   IBAKEJE59533

    DOORWAY TOWARD THE LIGHT. THE STORY OF THE SPECIAL NAVAJO EDUCATION PROGRAM.   ICGOMLM62646

    MANPOWER SERVICES ON THE NAVAJO RESERVATION.   IGRAFMF66565

    MANPOWER TRAINING IN NAVAJO LAND.   IHARTVS63573

    THE NAVAJO IN THE MACHINE AGE. HUMAN RESOURCES ARE IMPORTANT TOO.   INAPIAX58594

    THE ECONOMIC DEVELOPMENT AND URBANIZATION OF THE NAVAJO INDIAN RESERVATION.   ISELLCL62616

    YOU ASKED ABOUT THE NAVAJO. EDUCATION, HEALTH, AND ECONOMIC PROBLEMS OF THE NAVAJO.   IUSDINT57664

    YOU ASKED ABOUT THE NAVAJO. EDUCATION, HEALTH, AND ECONOMIC PROBLEMS OF THE NAVAJO.   IUSDINT57664

NAVAJOES
    TRAINING NAVAJOES FOR THE FUTURE.   ILINDVX64581

NAVAJOS
    THE NAVAJOS.   INAVATP64598

    THE NAVAJOS.   IUNDERM56635

NAVY
    EQUAL-EMPLOYMENT-OPPORTUNITY GUIDE FOR DEPARTMENT OF THE NAVY CONTRACTORS.   GUSDDEF64433

    THE NEGRO IN THE NAVY. /MILITARY/   NMUELWR45865

NEBRASKA
    MUNICIPAL FAIR-EMPLOYMENT-PRACTICES IN NEBRASKA.   GNEBRLR62086

NECESSARY
    ANALYSIS OF MALE NAVAHO STUDENTS PERCEPTIONS OF OCCUPATIONAL OPPORTUNITIES AND THEIR ATTITUDES TOWARD
    DEVELOPMENT OF SKILLS AND TRAITS NECESSARY FOR OCCUPATIONAL COMPETENCE.   IDESPCW65548

    IS DISCRIMINATION AGAINST TALENTED WOMEN NECESSARY.   WWARNCF61220

NECESSITIES
    POLITICAL NECESSITIES OF ABUNDANCE. /GUARANTEED-INCOME/   GTHEORX64610

    THE POLITICAL NECESSITIES OF ABUNDANCE. /GUARANTEED-INCOME/   GTHEORX64968

NEED
    ESTIMATED NEED FOR SKILLED-WORKERS, 1965-75. /EMPLOYMENT/   GSALTAF66534

    ORGANIZED LABOR AND THE MINORITY WORKER NEED EACH OTHER. /UNION/   GSHISBX59305

    APPRENTICESHIP. AN EVALUATION OF THE NEED.   GSTRAGX65715

    ADOLESCENTS NEED JOBS.   ITHOMHX61629

    JEWS NEED NOT APPLY. /DISCRIMINATION EMPLOYMENT/   JWEISAX58770

    UN-MET NEED IN A LAND OF ABUNDANCE.   NEPSTLA63337

    TRAINING FOR TOMORROW-S SCIENTISTS AND TECHNICIANS. A COMMUNITY APPROACH TO A COMMUNITY NEED.   NFINLOE60356

    YOU NEED TO SEE IT TO BELIEVE IT. REPORT OF THE 1963 SUMMER STUDY-SKILLS PROGRAMS. /COLLEGE EDUCATION/   NMARTWD63303

    SOME CORRELATES OF HIGH NEED FOR ACHIEVEMENT AMONG URBAN NORTHERN NEGROES.   NNUTTRL46951

    MIGRANTS POSE PROBLEMS FOR NEW-JERSEY FARMERS WHO NEED THEM.   PCUNNJT57793

    WHAT NURSES NEED IS A CHANCE TO GROW. /OCCUPATIONAL-STATUS/   WGINSEX62786

    THE NATION-S WORKING MOTHERS AND THE NEED FOR DAY CARE. ADDRESS. /EMPLOYMENT-CONDITIONS/   WKEYSMD65897

    TODAY-S BUSINESS WOMAN. HER CHARACTERISTICS, HER NEED FOR FURTHER EDUCATION, HER FUTURE IN MANAGEMENT.
    /OCCUPATIONS/   WTHOMMH63152

NEEDED
    ISSUES AND PROBLEMS IN INTEGRATING NEEDED SUPPORTIVE SERVICES IN NEIGHBORHOOD-YOUTH-CORPS PROJECTS.   GBATTMX66131

    SECURING SKILLS NEEDED FOR SUCCESS. COMMUNITY JOB TRAINING FOR NEGROES.   NBLUMAA66099

    ARE NEGRO SCHOOLS OF NURSING NEEDED TODAY.   WCARNME64910

    NEEDED. UNIQUE PATTERNS FOR EDUCATING WOMEN. /WORK-WOMEN-ROLE/   WIRISLD62874

    WOMANPOWER NEEDED.   WKEYSMD66901

NEEDLE
    THE OLD-TIMERS AND THE NEWCOMERS. ETHNIC-GROUP RELATIONS IN A NEEDLE TRADE UNION.   NHERBWX53519

NEEDS
    THE ADAPTATION OF LABOR RESOURCES TO CHANGING NEEDS. /MOBILITY/   GLESTRA66532

    MANPOWER NEEDS BY INDUSTRY TO 1975.   GSTAMHX65768

    MANPOWER PROJECTIONS. SOME CONCEPTUAL PROBLEMS AND RESEARCH NEEDS. /EMPLOYMENT-TRENDS/   GSWERSX66535

    YOUNG WORKERS. THEIR SPECIAL TRAINING NEEDS.   GUSDLAB63506

    YOUTH. THE NATION-S RICHEST RESOURCE. THEIR EDUCATION AND EMPLOYMENT NEEDS.   GUSINCC53514

NEEDS   (CONTINUATION)
   A POLICY TO MEET INDIAN NEEDS TODAY.   IERNSRC59556

   NEEDS AND RESOURCES OF THE JICARILLA APACHE INDIAN TRIBE.   ISTANRI58623

   BASIC NEEDS OF INDIAN PEOPLE.   IUSDINT57643

   BASIC NEEDS OF SPANISH-AMERICAN FARM FAMILIES IN NEW-MEXICO.   MGRISGXND408

   TERMINATION OF THE BRACERO PROGRAM. SOME EFFECTS ON FARM LABOR AND MIGRANT HOUSING NEEDS.   MMCELRC65385

   NEGRO EDUCATION IN AMERICA. ITS ADEQUACY, PROBLEMS AND NEEDS.   NCLIFVA62215

   PROBLEMS AND NEEDS OF NEGRO CHILDREN AND YOUTH RESULTING FROM FAMILY DISORGANIZATION.   NFRAZEF50382

   PROBLEMS AND NEEDS OF NEGRO ADOLESCENT WORKERS.   NGRANLB40980

   INTELLECTUALLY SUPERIOR NEGRO YOUTH. THEIR PROBLEMS AND NEEDS. /EDUCATION/   NJENKMD50606

   WHO NEEDS THE NEGRO. /OCCUPATIONAL-STATUS TECHNOLOGICAL-CHANGE/   NWILLSM64232

   MEETING THE NEEDS OF THE PUERTO-RICAN MIGRANT.   PMONTHK59829

   CONTINUING EDUCATION OF WOMEN. NEEDS, ASPIRATIONS, AND PLANS.   WBERRJX63641

   INVESTIGATION OF DIFFERENCES IN OCCUPATIONAL PREFERENCES, STEREOTYPIC THINKING, AND PSYCHOLOGICAL NEEDS
   AMONG UNDERGRADUATE WOMEN STUDENTS IN SELECTED CURRICULAR AREAS. /ASPIRATIONS/   WKITTRE60313

   WHEN WILL THE EDUCATIONAL NEEDS OF WOMEN BE MET. SOME QUESTIONS FOR THE COUNSELOR.   WNEUMRR63026

   REALITIES. EDUCATIONAL, ECONOMIC, LEGAL AND PERSONAL NEEDS OF CAREER WOMEN.   WPARKRX66049

   NEEDS AND OPPORTUNITIES IN OUR SOCIETY FOR THE EDUCATED WOMAN.   WPETEEX63054

   FULL PARTNERSHIP FOR WOMEN -- WHAT STILL NEEDS TO BE DONE.   WVITAIX63218

NEGLECTED
   AMERICAN-INDIANS. NEGLECTED MINORITY. /ECONOMIC-STATUS/   IDENNLB66547

   NEGLECTED TALENTS. BACKGROUND AND PROSPECTS OF NEGRO COLLEGE GRADUATES.   NNATLOR66880

NEGRO
   IMPLICATIONS OF THE STUDIES. /DISCRIMINATION LOW-INCOME NEGRO PUERTO-RICAN POLICY-RECOMMENDATIONS/   CABRACX59001

   MEETING TODAYS CHALLENGE FOR EMPLOYMENT. /AMERICAN-INDIAN NEGRO MEXICAN-AMERICAN/   CARIZSE65403

   THE ECONOMY AND THE MINORITY POOR. /NEGRO AMERICAN-INDIAN MEXICAN-AMERICAN PUERTO-RICAN/   CBATCAB66879

   REPORT TO GOVERNOR EDMUND G BROWN. SECOND ETHNIC SURVEY OF EMPLOYMENT AND PROMOTION IN STATE GOVERNMENT.
   /CALIFORNIA NEGRO MEXICAN-AMERICAN/   CBECKWL65070

   HUMAN-RESOURCE PROBLEMS OF THE COMING DECADE. /EMPLOYMENT NEGRO MEXICAN-AMERICAN/   CBULLPX66136

   CHARACTERISTICS OF RETRAINING APPLICANTS. /CALIFORNIA NEGRO MEXICAN-AMERICAN WOMEN/   CCALDEM66166

   ANNUAL FARM LABOR REPORT, 1965, CALIFORNIA DEPARTMENT OF EMPLOYMENT, FARM LABOR SERVICE. /NEGRO
   MEXICAN-AMERICAN WOMEN/   CCALDEM66906

   RACIAL DISTRIBUTION OF SELECTED UNEMPLOYMENT INSURANCE AND EMPLOYMENT SERVICE DATA. JULY-DECEMBER 1966.
   /NEGRO MEXICAN-AMERICAN/   CCALDEM67907

   REPORT ON OAKLAND SCHOOLS. AN INVESTIGATION UNDER SECTION 1421 OF THE CALIFORNIA LABOR CODE OF THE
   OAKLAND UNIFIED SCHOOL DISTRICT 1962-1963. /NEGRO ORIENTAL MEXICAN-AMERICAN/   CCALDIR63710

   TRAINING AID. CULTURAL DIFFERENCES, TRAINING IN NONDISCRIMINATION, READING ASSIGNMENTS. /EMPLOYMENT
   MEXICAN-AMERICAN NEGRO/   CCALDSW65447

   INTEGRATION IN PROFESSIONAL NURSING. /OCCUPATIONS NEGRO WOMEN/   CCARNME62183

   THE DISCRIMINATION CASE. /NEGRO PUERTO-RICAN SES/   CCOHEHX65917

   ADDRESS TO COMMUNITY RELATIONS SERVICE STAFF TRAINING SESSION, JANUARY 12, 1967, ON JOBS NOW. /NEGRO
   PUERTO-RICAN YOUTH/   CCOLEBX67918

   WOMEN AT WORK. /NEGRO/   CDECTMX61376

   THE EVALUATION OF WORK BY FEMALES, 1940-1950. /WOMEN NEGRO/   CDORNSM56284

   THE VALUES OF NEGRO WOMEN COLLEGE STUDENTS.   CEAGLOW45313

   RACIAL CHARACTERISTICS, MDTA TRAINEES, SAN-FRANCISCO. /CALIFORNIA NEGRO MEXICAN-AMERICAN/   CELTOEX63332

   THE EFFECT OF LOW EDUCATIONAL-ATTAINMENT ON INCOMES. A COMPARATIVE STUDY OF SELECTED ETHNIC GROUPS.
   /NEGRO MEXICAN-AMERICAN/   CFOGEWX66367

   OPPORTUNITIES IN NURSING FOR DISADVANTAGED YOUTH. /WOMEN NEGRO OCCUPATIONS/   CFRAKFX66375

   THE EMPLOYMENT OF NEGRO WOMEN AS DOMESTIC-SERVANTS IN NEW-ORLEANS. /LOUISIANA/   CGILMHX44403

   THE NATION-S CHILDREN. VOL I. THE FAMILY AND SOCIAL-CHANGE. VOL II. DEVELOPMENT AND EDUCATION. VOL III.
   PROBLEMS AND PROSPECTS. /NEGRO PUERTO-RICAN MEXICAN-AMERICAN WOMEN/   CGINZEX60720

   FACTORS AFFECTING EDUCATIONAL-ATTAINMENT IN DEPRESSED URBAN AREAS. /NEGRO PUERTO-RICAN/   CGOLDML63426

   NEGRO NURSES IN HOSPITALS. /WOMEN NEGRO/   CGOLDXX60374

   NEGRO NURSES IN HOSPITALS. /WOMEN NEGRO/   CGOLDXX60374

   RECENT TRENDS IN THE STUDY OF MINORITY AND RACE-RELATIONS. /NEGRO PUERTO-RICAN ORIENTAL/   CGORDMM63977

   A NOTE ON THE VALUES OF SOUTHERN COLLEGE WOMEN, WHITE AND NEGRO.   CGRAYSW47445

   ECONOMIC GROWTH AND EMPLOYMENT OPPORTUNITIES FOR MINORITIES. /NEGRO WOMEN/   CHIESOL64775

   UNDER-ACHIEVEMENT AMONG MINORITY-GROUP STUDENTS. AN ANALYSIS AND A PROPOSAL. /YOUTH NEGRO
   MEXICAN-AMERICAN PUERTO-RICAN/   CHOBACW63555

   WOMEN WHO WORK. /NEGRO/   CHUTCGX52589

DEVELOPING NEW-YORK CITY-S HUMAN RESOURCES. VOL 1. /NEGRO PUERTO-RICAN/   CINSTOP66034

THE FORGOTTEN PEOPLE. /MIGRANT-WORKERS MEXICAN-AMERICAN PUERTO-RICAN NEGRO/   CJACOPX59600

LABOR UNIONISM IN AMERICAN AGRICULTURE. /NEGRO MEXICAN-AMERICAN ORIENTAL/   CJAMISM45005

CLASS DIFFERENCES IN THE SOCIALIZATION PRACTICES OF NEGRO MOTHERS.   CKAMICKND632

REGISTRIES AND INTERGROUP RELATIONS. /NEGRO WOMEN DISCRIMINATION/   CKASUMX59013

THE NEGRO WOMAN AT WORK. ADDRESS TO CONFERENCE ON THE NEGRO WOMAN IN THE USA.   CKEYSMD65646

THE NEGRO WOMAN AT WORK. ADDRESS TO CONFERENCE ON THE NEGRO WOMAN IN THE USA.   CKEYSMD65646

SENIORITY AND POSTWAR JOBS. RUBBER INDUSTRY. /NEGRO WOMEN/   CLABORR44028

AT THE PREVAILING RATE. /MEXICAN-AMERICAN NEGRO UNION/   CLEBETX57371

CULTURAL DIFFERENCES IN AMERICAN ETHNIC GROUPS. BIBLIOGRAPHY. /AMERICAN-INDIAN NEGRO SPANISH-AMERICAN/   CLIBRCX64899

CHANGING PATTERNS OF PREJUDICE. /NEGRO PUERTO-RICAN ORIENTAL AMERICAN-INDIAN/   CMARRAJ62055

FARM MECHANIZATION AND LABOR STABILIZATION. PART II IN A SERIES ON TECHNOLOGICAL-CHANGE AND FARM LABOR
USE. KERN COUNTY, CALIFORNIA, 1961. /NEGRO MEXICAN-AMERICAN/   CMETZWH65389

POVERTY IN THE SOUTHWEST. A COMPARATIVE STUDY OF MEXICAN-AMERICAN, NONWHITE AND ANGLO FAMILIES. /NEGRO/   CMITTFG66777

AN EXPERIMENT TO TEST THREE MAJOR ISSUES OF WORK PROGRAM METHODOLOGY WITHIN MOBILIZATION-FOR-YOUTH-S
INTEGRATED SERVICES TO OUT-OF-SCHOOL UNEMPLOYED YOUTH. /NEGRO PUERTO-RICAN/   CMOBIFY66024

BUREAU OF MIGRANT-LABOR REPORT. /NEW-JERSEY NEGRO PUERTO-RICAN/   CNEWJDL61907

INTERIM REPORT TO THE MAYOR ON ITS INQUIRY INTO CHARGES OF RACIAL BIAS IN THE CITY BUILDING AND
CONSTRUCTION INDUSTRY. /NEW-YORK NEGRO PUERTO-RICAN/   CNEWYCO64917

THE SCHOOL DROPOUT PROBLEM IN MAJOR CITIES OF NEW-YORK STATE. ROCHESTER -- PART I. /NEGRO PUERTO-RICAN/   CNEWYSD62090

THE NEGRO COLLEGE WOMAN.   CNOBLJL54924

THE NEGRO WOMAN COLLEGE GRADUATE.   CNOBLJL55925

THE AMERICAN NEGRO WOMAN.   CNOBLJL66923

FACTS ON ADC IN NORTH-CAROLINA. /NEGRO AMERICAN-INDIAN/   CNORTCS59934

THE MIGRANT LABOR PROBLEM -- ITS STATE AND INTERSTATE ASPECTS. /NEGRO MEXICAN-AMERICAN/   CPALEHA63098

THE IMMIGRANT. VALUE ORIENTATIONS AND VOCATIONAL ASPIRATIONS. /NEGRO MEXICAN-AMERICAN/   CPETECL64988

THEORY, METHOD AND FINDINGS IN THE STUDY OF ACCULTURATION. A REVIEW. /MEXICAN-AMERICAN NEGRO/   CPETECX65989

PREJUDICE TOWARD MEXICAN AND NEGRO AMERICANS. A COMPARISON.   CPINKAX63458

NEGRO WOMEN IN THE CLOTHING, CIGAR AND LAUNDRY INDUSTRIES OF PHILADELPHIA, 1960.   CPORTRP43103

BREAKING THE BARRIERS OF OCCUPATIONAL ISOLATION. A REPORT ON UPGRADING LOW-SKILL, LOW-WAGE WORKERS.
/NEGRO PUERTO-RICAN/   CPROJAX66237

THE CHILD-REARING ATTITUDES OF DISADVANTAGED NEGRO MOTHERS AND SOME EDUCATIONAL IMPLICATIONS.   CRADINX65031

NEW PROBLEM OF LARGE SCALE UNEMPLOYABILITY. /NEGRO MEXICAN-AMERICAN AMERICAN-INDIAN/   CROSEAM64553

MINORITY-GROUPS IN NEVADA. /NEGRO AMERICAN-INDIAN/   CRUSCER66807

SIGNIFICANT TRENDS IN THE NEW-YORK STATE ECONOMY, WITH SPECIAL REFERENCE TO MINORITY-GROUPS.
/PUERTO-RICAN NEGRO/   CRUSSVR59482

SECRETARIAL TRAINING WITH SPEECH IMPROVEMENT. AN EXPERIMENTAL AND DEMONSTRATION PROJECT. /NEGRO WOMEN/   CSAINMD66320

SOCIO-ECONOMIC DIFFERENTIALS AMONG NONWHITE RACES. /NEGRO ORIENTAL AMERICAN-INDIAN/   CSCHMCF65107

AN EXPERIMENT IN MANPOWER DEVELOPMENT. /TRAINING MISSISSIPPI NEGRO WOMEN/   CSELFHO66325

THE ENDURING SLUMS. /NEGRO PUERTO-RICAN/   CSELIDX57034

OCCUPATIONAL AND RESIDENTIAL ADJUSTMENT OF RURAL MIGRANTS. /NEGRO MEXICAN-AMERICAN/   CSHANLW61119

THE URBAN ADJUSTMENT OF IMMIGRANTS. THE RELATIONSHIP OF EDUCATION TO OCCUPATIONAL AND TOTAL FAMILY
INCOME. /NEGRO MEXICAN-AMERICAN/   CSHANLW63122

THE ASSIMILATION AND ACCULTURATION OF MIGRANTS TO URBAN AREAS. /MEXICAN-AMERICAN NEGRO/   CSHANLW63484

MEASURING THE ADJUSTMENT OF IMMIGRANT LABORERS. /MEXICAN-AMERICAN NEGRO/   CSHANLW63487

THE ECONOMIC ABSORPTION AND CULTURAL INTEGRATION OF IMMIGRANT MEXICAN-AMERICAN AND NEGRO WORKERS.   CSHANLW64124

THE ECONOMIC ABSORPTION OF IN-MIGRANT LABORERS IN A NORTHERN INDUSTRIAL COMMUNITY. /MEXICAN-AMERICAN
NEGRO/   CSHANLW64486

URBAN ADJUSTMENT AND ITS RELATIONSHIP TO THE SOCIAL ANTECEDENTS OF IMMIGRANT WORKERS. /NEGRO
MEXICAN-AMERICAN/   CSHANLW65121

CULTURAL AND RELATED RESTRAINTS AND MEANS OF OVERCOMING THEM. /MEXICAN-AMERICAN NEGRO INTEGRATION/   CSHANLW65485

FINAL REPORT. EXPERIMENTAL AND DEMONSTRATION ON-JOB-TRAINING PROJECT. /MIGRANT-WORKERS MEXICAN-AMERICAN
NEGRO ARIZONA/   CSKILTO66324

SEX DIFFERENCES IN OCCUPATIONAL CHOICE PATTERNS AMONG ADOLESCENTS. /ASPIRATIONS WOMEN NEGRO/   CSPREJX62999

NO TIME FOR PREJUDICE. /WOMEN NEGRO OCCUPATIONS/   CSTAUMK61132

THE NON-WHITE FEMALE IN THE LABOR-FORCE. /WOMEN NEGRO/   CTURNRH51214

NEGRO POPULATION. MARCH 1964. /WOMEN DEMOGRAPHY/   CUSBURC64376

NEGRO POPULATION. MARCH 1965. /WOMEN DEMOGRAPHY/   CUSBURC65377

SELECTED BIBLIOGRAPHY FOR DISADVANTAGED YOUTH. /NEGRO PUERTO-RICAN/   CUSDHEWND855

NEGRO   (CONTINUATION)
    OPPORTUNITIES FOR NEGRO WOMEN AS DIETICIANS. /OCCUPATIONS/   CUSDLAB43837

    NEGRO WOMEN AND THEIR JOBS.   CUSDLAB54262

    THE CHANGING STATUS OF NEGRO WOMEN WORKERS.   CUSDLAB64072

    NEGRO WOMEN WORKERS IN 1960.   CUSDLAB64264

    CURRENT DATA ON NONWHITE WOMEN WORKERS. /NEGRO/   CUSDLAB65261

    NEGRO WOMEN IN THE POPULATION AND IN THE LABOR-FORCE.   CUSDLAB66263

    OAK GLEN -- A TRAINING CAMP FOR UNEMPLOYED YOUTH. /NEGRO MEXICAN-AMERICAN/   CUSDLAB66323

    POVERTY IN THE UNITED STATES, HEARINGS. /AMERICAN-INDIAN NEGRO PUERTO-RICAN EMPLOYMENT/   CUSHOUR64346

    HARD-CORE UNEMPLOYMENT AND POVERTY IN LOS-ANGELES. /CALIFORNIA NEGRO MEXICAN-AMERICAN/   CUVCAIIND524

    ECONOMIC ABSORPTION AND CULTURAL INTEGRATION OF THE URBAN NEWCOMER. /NEGRO MEXICAN-AMERICAN/   CUVICIP65277

    REPORT. EVALUATION STUDY OF YOUTH TRAINING AND EMPLOYMENT PROJECT, EAST LOS-ANGELES. /NEGRO
      MEXICAN-AMERICAN CALIFORNIA/   CWEINJL64310

    UNWANTED WORKERS. PERMANENT LAYOFFS AND LONG-TERM UNEMPLOYMENT. /NEGRO WOMEN/   CWILCRC63322

    NEGRO ADC MOTHERS LOOK FOR WORK. /WOMEN/   CWILLJJ58324

    SOCIAL-STRATIFICATION AND ACADEMIC ACHIEVEMENT. /NEGRO ORIENTAL/   CWILSAB63325

    FINAL REPORT OF THE YMCA YOUTH AND WORK PROJECT 1962-1966. /NEGRO PUERTO-RICAN TRAINING/   CYMCAYA66329

    THE NEGRO GIRL AND POVERTY. /WOMEN/   CYOUNMB65636

    ECONOMIC-TRENDS IN EXTENSION WORK WITH NEGRO FARMERS IN ALABAMA, 1936-1948.   GGAINRL48341

    POVERTY AND THE NEGRO.   GSHEPHL65965

    SOCIAL FACTORS IN OCCUPATIONAL AND EDUCATIONAL ASPIRATIONS OF NEGRO AND WHITE STUDENTS.   NADDIDP61002

    THE NEW NEGRO   NAHMAMH61007

    NEGRO PLATFORM WORKERS. /INDUSTRY CASE-STUDY/   NAMERCR45011

    GROWING UP NEGRO.   NAMERCX63009

    NEGRO EMPLOYMENT-TRENDS IN THE SOUTH.   NAMERFX53015

    THE NEGRO WORKER. /INDUSTRY/   NAMERMA42017

    AUDIT OF NEGRO VETERANS AND SERVICEMEN, 1960. /PUBLIC-EMPLOYMENT/   NAMERVC60019

    A STUDY OF THE OCCUPATIONAL AWARENESS OF A SELECTED GROUP OF NINTH GRADE NEGRO STUDENTS.   NAMOSWE60020

    NEGRO YOUTH AND EMPLOYMENT OPPORTUNITIES. /UNEMPLOYMENT EDUCATION/   NAMOSWE63021

    INTELLIGENCE OF THE AMERICAN NEGRO.   NANTIDL63911

    NEGRO AND WHITE YOUTH IN ELMIRA. /NEW-YORK/   NANTOAX59026

    OCCUPATIONAL ASPIRATIONS OF LOWER-CLASS NEGRO AND WHITE YOUTH.   NANTOAX59027

    AMERICAN NEGRO AND IMMIGRANT EXPERIENCES. SIMILARITIES AND DIFFERENCES.   NAPPEJJ66805

    LITERACY, AND THE NEGRO AND WORLD-WAR-II.   NAPTHHX46028

    THE NEW NEGRO CASUALTIES. /OCCUPATIONS TEACHERS/   NARISJM65029

    THE NEGRO STEELWORKERS OF PITTSBURGH AND THE UNIONS. /PENNSYLVANIA/   NAUGUTX47035

    EGO DEVELOPMENT AMONG SEGREGATED NEGRO CHILDREN. /ASPIRATIONS/   NAUSUDP65036

    THE DILEMMA OF THE NEGRO PROFESSIONAL.   NBACKKX64039

    NEGRO EMPLOYMENT IN FEDERAL-GOVERNMENT.   NBAERMF61042

    THE NEGRO AUTOMOBILE-WORKERS. /OCCUPATIONS/   NBAILLH43043

    NEGRO LABOR IN THE AUTO INDUSTRY.   NBAILLH43045

    THE NEGRO IN THE LABOR-FORCE OF THE UNITED-STATES.   NBAILLH53044

    ORGANIZED LABOR AND THE NEGRO WORKER. /UNION/   NBAINMX63046

    NEGRO HIRING -- SOME CASE-STUDIES. /INDUSTRY/   NBAMBJJ49050

    THE NEGRO VANGUARD. /CIVIL-RIGHTS/   NBARDRX59878

    NEGRO UNEMPLOYMENT. A CASE-STUDY.   NBAROHX63054

    THE NEGRO WORKER IN THE CHICAGO JOB-MARKET. /ILLINOIS/   NBAROHX66055

    AN ECONOMICAL AND HISTORICAL ANALYSIS OF THE CAUSES OF VARIATION AMONG NORTHERN STANDARD METROPOLITAN
    AREAS IN PRODUCTIVITY OF NEGRO MEN IN 1949.   NBATCAB61060

    DECLINE IN THE RELATIVE INCOME OF NEGRO MEN.   NBATCAB64058

    ECONOMIC FORCES SERVING THE ENDS OF THE NEGRO PROTEST. /UNEMPLOYMENT/   NBATCAB65059

    POVERTY. THE SPECIAL CASE OF THE NEGRO.   NBATCAB65061

    NEGRO ADDICT OCCUPATIONAL HISTORY.   NBATEWM66880

    THE DETERMINATION OF CERTAIN MAJOR FACTORS AFFECTING THE NEGRO VETERAN IN THE ON-THE-JOB TRAINING PROGRAM
    IN VOCATIONAL AGRICULTURE IN THE STATE OF ALABAMA AS A BASIS FOR PLANNING A MORE EFFECTIVE PROGRAM.   NBATTEF49338

    THE NEGRO MATRIARCHY. /WOMEN ECONOMIC-STATUS/   NBATTMX65313

    THE EMPLOYABILITY OF THE CHAMPAIGN-URBANA, ILLINOIS, NEGRO.   NBEAKJR64062

NEGRO FARM OPERATORS. NUMBER, LOCATION AND RECENT TRENDS.	NBEALCL58064
THE NEGRO IN AMERICAN AGRICULTURE.	NBEALCL66063
NEGRO RESPONSES TO VERBAL AND NON-VERBAL TEST MATERIAL.	NBEANKL47914
THE AGING NEGRO. SOME IMPLICATIONS FOR SOCIAL-WELFARE SERVICES.	NBEATWM60066
PLACEMENT AND CAREER COUNSELING AT PREDOMINANTLY NEGRO COLLEGES.	NBEAUAG66067
EMPLOYMENT AND INCOME OF NEGRO WORKERS. 1940-1952.	NBEDEMS53071
REFLECTIONS ON THE NEGRO AND LABOR. /UNION/	NBELLDX63073
LOWER-CLASS NEGRO MOTHERS ASPIRATIONS FOR THEIR CHILDREN.	NBELLRR65074
CHILDREN AND INCOME IN NEGRO FAMILIES.	NBERNEH46077
NEGRO FAMILY LIFE IN AMERICA.	NBILLAX65499
A STUDY OF THE NEGRO COMMUNITY IN CHAMPAIGN-URBANA, ILLINOIS.	NBINDAM61079
PRE-COLLEGE PREPARATION OF NEGRO STUDENTS.	NBINDAM66139
NEGRO MARKET. GROWING, CHANGING, CHALLENGING.	NBLACLE63493
ECONOMIC DISCRIMINATION AND NEGRO INCREASES.	NBLALHM56083
ON-THE-JOB EXPERIENCES OF NEGRO MANAGERS.	NBLANJW64917
CRAFT UNIONS. A LINK IN THE CIRCLE OF NEGRO DISCRIMINATION.	NBLOCHD57088
CRAFT UNIONS AND THE NEGRO IN HISTORICAL PERSPECTIVE.	NBLOCHD58087
THE EMPLOYMENT OF THE NEW-YORK NEGRO IN RETROSPECT.	NBLOCHD59090
DISCRIMINATION AGAINST THE NEGRO IN EMPLOYMENT IN NEW-YORK, 1920-1963.	NBLOCHD65089
THE ORIGIN AND DEVELOPMENT OF THE NEGRO VISITING TEACHER IN ALABAMA. /OCCUPATIONS/	NBOATRF49345
THE AMERICAN REVOLUTION. PAGES FROM A NEGRO WORKER-S NOTEBOOK.	NBOGGJX63101
THE NEGRO SCHOLAR AND PROFESSIONAL IN AMERICA.	NBONDHM66103
LABOR AND THE SOUTHERN NEGRO.	NBRADCX57107
MEETING THE PSYCHOLOGICAL CRISES OF NEGRO YOUTH THROUGH A COORDINATED GUIDANCE SERVICE.	NBRAZWF58111
CURRICULUM CHOICE IN THE NEGRO COLLEGE.	NBRAZWF60109
OCCUPATIONAL CHOICE IN THE NEGRO COLLEGE.	NBRAZWF60112
CORRELATES OF SOUTHERN NEGRO PERSONALITY.	NBRAZWF64496
MANPOWER TRAINING AND THE NEGRO WORKER.	NBRAZWF66110
NEGRO PROGRESS. WHAT THE FACTS SHOW.	NBREIGX52113
ECONOMIC TRENDS IN THE NEGRO MARKET. /ECONOMIC-STATUS/	NBRIMAF64891
DESEGREGATION AND THE ECONOMIC FUTURE OF THE NEGRO MIDDLE-CLASS.	NBRIMAF65890
THE NEGRO IN THE NATIONAL ECONOMY.	NBRIMAF66115
THE NEGRO REVOLUTION IN AMERICA.	NBRINWX64116
FACTORS AFFECTING THE PRESENT FARMING PROGRAMS OF ONE HUNDRED NEGRO FARMS IN THE PATRONAGE AREA OF THE MACON COUNTY TRAINING SCHOOL, IN ALABAMA, WITH EMPHASIS FOR IMPROVEMENT.	NBRONCA51337
NEGRO AMERICAN LABOR COUNCIL IS ACTIVE IN NEW-YORK STATE.	NBROOTR61119
NEGRO MILITANTS, JEWISH LIBERALS, AND THE UNIONS.	NBROOTR61121
MANAGING YOUR MANPOWER. NEGRO EMPLOYMENT PROBLEM.	NBROOTR63118
GRADUATE AND PROFESSIONAL EDUCATION IN NEGRO INSTITUTIONS. /ECONOMIC-STATUS/	NBROWAX58893
THE NEGRO GRADUATE, 1950-1960. /COLLEGE EDUCATION/	NBROWAX60125
NEGRO UNEMPLOYMENT. A CASE-STUDY.	NBROWHX63894
THE STATUS OF JOBS AND OCCUPATIONS AS EVALUATED BY AN URBAN NEGRO SAMPLE.	NBROWMC55126
A COMPARISON OF THE VOCATIONAL ASPIRATIONS OF PAIRED SIXTH-GRADE WHITE AND NEGRO CHILDREN WHO ATTEND SEGREGATED SCHOOLS.	NBROWRG65895
THE NEGRO BIDS FOR UNION POWER.	NBRUNDX60128
A COMPARISON OF THE ACADEMIC ACHIEVEMENTS OF WHITE AND NEGRO HIGH SCHOOL GRADUATES. /EDUCATION/	NBULLHA50132
ETHNOMICS -- NEGRO MUST BE FULL PARTICIPANT IN MARKET PLACE.	NBUNKHC65122
THE NEGRO AND TITLE-VII.	NBURENA65137
THE VOICES OF NEGRO PROTEST IN AMERICA.	NBURNHX63902
NEGRO PRESSURE ON UNIONS.	NBUSIWX60155
NEGRO UNIONISTS ORGANIZE FOR ACTION.	NBUSIWX60157
AFL-CIO COUNCIL GETS NEGRO DEMAND FOR MORE ACTION ON BIAS IN UNIONS.	NBUSIWX61144
DETROIT FEELS BRUNT OF NEGRO PRESSURE. /MICHIGAN/	NBUSIWX63149
THE NEGRO DRIVE FOR JOBS.	NBUSIWX63154
AIDING NEGRO BUSINESSMEN. SMALL BUSINESS OPPORTUNITIES CORPORATION, PHILADELPHIA. /PENNSYLVANIA/	NBUSIWX64143

INDUSTRY RUSHES FOR NEGRO GRADS.   NBUSIWX64297

A COMPARISON OF THE SOCIAL CHARACTERISTICS AND EDUCATIONAL ASPIRATIONS OF NORTHERN, LOWER-CLASS, NEGRO
PARENTS WHO ACCEPTED AND DECLINED AN OPPORTUNITY FOR INTEGRATED EDUCATION FOR THEIR CHILDREN.   NCAGLLT66904

NEGRO CALIFORNIANS. POPULATION, EMPLOYMENT, INCOME, EDUCATION.   NCALDIR63167

DISTRIBUTION OF NEGRO PUPULATION IN THE UNITED STATES. /DEMOGRAPHY/   NCALEWC56069

EDUCATION OF NEGRO LEADERS. INFLUENCES AFFECTING GRADUATE AND PROFESSIONAL STUDIES.   NCALIAX49174

THE ULTIMATE CONQUEST OF NEGRO ECONOMIC INEQUALITY.   NCALLEX64175

THE NEGRO IN SYRACUSE. /NEW-YORK/   NCAMPAKND177

JOB HOLDING AMONG NEGRO YOUTH.   NCAPLNX66013

THE NEGRO FAMILY AND THE MOYNIHAN-REPORT.   NCARPLX66184

INTEGRATING THE NEGRO TEACHER OUT OF A JOB. /OCCUPATIONS/   NCARTBX65999

THE PSYCHOLOGY OF THE NEGRO UNDER DISCRIMINATION.   NCAYTHR51187

RESEARCH ON NEGRO JOB SUCCESS.   NCHALWE62189

A MORE PRODUCTIVE ROLE FOR THE NEGRO IN THE SOUTH-S ECONOMY.   NCHALWE64912

THE COUNSELOR AND THE NEGRO STUDENT.   NCHAPAA66192

DOMESTIC-SERVICE AND THE NEGRO.   NCHAPDX64193

VOCATIONAL CHOICES OF NEGRO HIGH SCHOOL STUDENTS IN MACON COUNTY, ALABAMA, AND THEIR RELATIONSHIP TO
BASIC OCCUPATIONAL ACTIVITES OF THE SCHOOL COMMUNITIES. /ASPIRATIONS/   NCHAPEJ49351

THE NEGRO AND EMPLOYMENT-OPPORTUNITIES IN THE SOUTH. CHATTANOOGA REGION. /TENNESSEE/   NCHATCC62197

SOME RECENT UNITED STATES SUPREME COURT DECISIONS AFFECTING THE RIGHTS OF NEGRO WORKERS.   NCHICCA47914

A PRELIMINARY REPORT ON MEDICAL STAFF APPOINTMENTS HELD BY NEGRO PHYSICIANS AT PREDOMINANTLY WHITE
HOSPITALS. /CHICAGO ILLINOIS/   NCHICCO60201

GRADUATE EDUCATION. PUBLIC SERVICE. AND THE NEGRO.   NCIKIWI66207

THE NEGRO STUDENT AT INTEGRATED COLLEGES.   NCLARKB63214

THE NEGRO COLLEGE STUDENT. SOME FACTS AND SOME CONCERNS.   NCLARKB64307

SEX, STATUS AND THE UNDEREMPLOYMENT OF THE NEGRO MALE.   NCLARKB67212

TEST BIAS. VALIDITY OF THE SCHOLASTIC APTITUDE TEST FOR NEGRO AND WHITE STUDENTS IN INTEGRATED COLLEGES. NCLEATA66923

THE NEGRO IN CLEVELAND, 1950-1963. /OHIO/   NCLEVUL64916

NEGRO EDUCATION IN AMERICA. ITS ADEQUACY, PROBLEMS AND NEEDS.   NCLIFVA62215

EDUCATING THE AMERICAN NEGRO.   NCLIFVA66227

PROGRESS AND PORTENTS FOR THE NEGRO IN MEDICINE. /OCCUPATIONS/   NCOBBWM48217

NOT TO THE SWIFT. PROGRESS AND PROSPECTS OF THE NEGRO IN SCIENCE AND THE PROFESSIONS. /OCCUPATIONS/ NCOBBWM58216

THE NEGRO AND EDUCATION.   NCOHEEE63220

LABOR UNIONS AND THE NEGRO.   NCOMMXX59228

LIBERALISM AND THE NEGRO. /ASPIRATIONS/   NCOMMXX64467

A COMPARATIVE STUDY OF THE OCCUPATIONAL INTERESTS OF NEGRO AND WHITE ADOLESCENT BOYS.   NCONNSM65471

THE ROLE OF THE NEGRO IN THE ORGANIZATION OF THE CIO. /UNION/   NCOOPJE56235

THE NEGRO MIDDLE CLASS IS RIGHT IN THE MIDDLE. /ECONOMIC-STATUS/   NCCRODX66030

EMPLOYMENT. EDUCATION AND MARRIAGE OF YOUNG NEGRO ADULTS.   NCOXXOC41934

NEGRO TEACHERS. MARTYRS TO INTEGRATION. /OCCUPATIONS/   NCOXXOC53935

REASONS FOR BELATED EDUCATION. A STUDY OF THE PLIGHT OF THE OLDER NEGRO TEACHERS. /OCCUPATIONS/   NCUNNGE58244

EDUCATION AND MARGINALITY. A STUDY OF THE NEGRO COLLEGE GRADUATE.   NCUTHMV49936

NEGRO SUBORDINATION AND WHITE GAINS. /INCOME OCCUPATIONAL-STATUS/   NCUTRPX65245

THE NEGRO AMERICAN. /EMPLOYMENT INCOME ECONOMIC-STATUS/   NDAEDXX65246

A COMPARISON OF TUITION-AND-FEE CHARGES IN NEGRO INSTITUTIONS WITH CHARGES IN INSTITUTIONS OF THE
SOUTHEAST AND OF THE NATION. 1962-1963. /EDUCATION/   NDAMILX64127

THE RELATIVE PROGRESS OF THE AMERICAN NEGRO SINCE 1950.   NDANIWG63250

THE MEANING OF NEGRO STRATEGY.   NDANZDX64468

WAR ECONOMICS AND NEGRO LABOR.   NDAVIFG42260

NEGRO EMPLOYMENT IN THE FEDERAL GOVERNMENT.   NDAVIJA45259

POSTWAR EMPLOYMENT AND THE NEGRO WORKER.   NDAVIJA46258

NEGRO EMPLOYMENT, A PROGRESS REPORT.   NDAVIJA52256

TVA AND NEGRO EMPLOYMENT. /TENNESSEE/   NDAVIJH55253

THE AMERICAN NEGRO REFERENCE BOOK.   NDAVIJP66260

TRADE UNIONS PRACTICES AND THE NEGRO WORKER -- THE ESTABLISHMENT AND IMPLEMENTATION OF AFL-CIO
ANTI-DISCRIMINATION POLICY.   NDAVINF60312

A STUDY OF JOB-OPPORTUNITIES IN THE STATE OF FLORIDA FOR NEGRO COLLEGE GRADUATES.   NDECKPM60261

NEGRO EMPLOYMENT IN SOUTHERN INDUSTRY.   NDEWEDX52270

FOUR STUDIES OF NEGRO EMPLOYMENT IN THE UPPER SOUTH.   NDEWEDX55269

OCCUPATIONAL SHIFTS IN NEGRO EMPLOYMENT.   NDIAMDE65273

THE MECHANICAL COTTON-PICKER, NEGRO MIGRATION, AND THE INTEGRATION MOVEMENT.   NDILLHCND274

EFFECTS OF UNEMPLOYMENT ON WHITE AND NEGRO PRISON-ADMISSIONS IN LOUISIANA.   NDOBBDA58277

NEGRO EMPLOYMENT OPPORTUNITIES DURING AND AFTER THE WAR.   NDODDAE45949

DESEGREGATION AND THE EMPLOYMENT OF NEGRO TEACHERS. /OCCUPATIONS/   NDODDHH55950

THE PROGRESS OF THE NEGRO IN HIGHER EDUCATION, 1950-1960.   NDODDHH63278

THE NEGRO FAMILY-S SEARCH FOR ECONOMIC SECURITY.   NDOUGJH64285

THE URBAN NEGRO FAMILY.   NDOUGJH66286

BLACK METROPOLIS. A STUDY OF NEGRO LIFE IN A NORTHERN CITY.   NDRAKSC45291

RECENT TRENDS IN RESEARCH ON THE NEGRO IN THE UNITED STATES.   NDRAKSC57290

THE AMERICAN DREAM AND THE NEGRO.   NDRAKSC63288

THE SOCIAL AND ECONOMIC STATUS OF THE NEGRO IN THE UNITED STATES.   NDRAKSC65289

NEGRO SCHOLARS IN SCIENTIFIC RESEARCH.   NDREWCR50294

THE NEGRO IN DENTAL EDUCATION.   NDUMMCO59302

CERTAIN ASPECTS OF THE ECONOMIC DEVELOPMENT OF THE AMERICAN NEGRO 1864-1960.   NDUMOAL45303

THE NEGRO POPULATION OF CHICAGO. A STUDY OF RESIDENTIAL SUCCESSION. /ILLINOIS OCCUPATIONAL-PATTERNS/   NDUNCOD57306

NEGRO EMPLOYMENT PROBLEM.   NDUNSRA63310

THE NEGRO IN THE US ARMY. /MILITARY/   NDWYERJ53312

THE NEGRO TEACHER AND DESEGREGATION.   NDWYERJ57956

THE CHANGING ECONOMIC STATUS OF THE MISSISSIPPI NEGRO.   NEATHBJ64314

THE NEGRO PROFESSIONAL CLASS. /OCCUPATIONAL-PATTERNS/   NEDWAGF59324

CHANGES IN OCCUPATIONS AS THEY AFFECT THE NEGRO.   NEDWAGF64323

OCCUPATIONAL-MOBILITY OF NEGRO PROFESSIONAL WORKERS.   NEDWAGF64326

THE NEGRO IN BOSTON. /MASSACHUSETTS/   NEDWARM61327

NEGRO LEADERSHIP IN RURAL GEORGIA COMMUNITIES. OCCUPATIONAL AND SOCIAL ASPECTS.   NEDWAVA42328

RELATION OF MOTHER-S EMPLOYMENT TO INTELLECTUAL PERFORMANCE OF NEGRO COLLEGE STUDENTS.   NEPPSEG64336

FAMILY AND ACHIEVEMENT. A PROPOSAL TO STUDY THE EFFECT OF FAMILY SOCIALIZATION ON ACHIEVEMENT AND
PERFORMANCE AMONG URBAN NEGRO AMERICANS.   NEPPSEG65334

MOTIVATION AND PERFORMANCE OF NEGRO STUDENTS.   NEPPSEG66335

ON SPECIAL-TRAINING-UNIT PERFORMANCE AS AN INDEX OF NEGRO ABILITY.   NERICRW46339

MEMORANDUM ON IDENTITY AND NEGRO YOUTH.   NERIKEX64338

CIVIL-RIGHTS, 1960-63. THE NEGRO CAMPAIGN TO WIN EQUAL RIGHTS AND OPPORTUNITIES IN THE UNITED STATES.   NFACTOF64341

THE NEGRO INTEGRATED.   NFALCNS45342

THE SEARCH FOR NEGRO MEDICAL STUDENTS. /EDUCATION/   NFALLAG63343

AN ECONOMIC AND SOCIAL PROFILE OF THE NEGRO AMERICAN.   NFEINRX65347

RELATIVE INCOME OF NEGRO MEN. SOME RECENT DATA.   NFEINRX66349

THE 1960 AUDIT OF NEGRO VETERANS AND SERVICEMAN. /MILITARY/   NFELDJA61350

THE STRUGGLE OF NEGRO TEACHERS IN FLORIDA FOR EQUAL SALARIES. /OCCUPATIONS/   NFERGML49961

THE NEGRO AND EQUAL-EMPLOYMENT-OPPORTUNITIES. A REVIEW OF MANAGEMENT EXPERIENCES IN TWENTY COMPANIES.   NFERMLA66790

YOUNG NEGRO TALENT. SURVEY OF THE EXPERIENCES AND EXPECTATIONS OF NEGRO AMERICANS WHO GRADUATED FROM
COLLEGE IN 1961.   NFICHJH64867

YOUNG NEGRO TALENT. SURVEY OF THE EXPERIENCES AND EXPECTATIONS OF NEGRO AMERICANS WHO GRADUATED FROM
COLLEGE IN 1961.   NFICHJH64867

CAREER PREPARATION AND EXPECTATIONS OF NEGRO COLLEGE STUDENTS.   NFICHJH66789

NEGRO EMPLOYMENT IN MIAMI. /FLORIDA/   NFLORCO62366

THE NEGRO BUSINESSMAN. IN SEARCH OF A TRADITION. /OCCUPATIONS/   NFOLEEP66369

GRANTS AND PROJECTS RELATED TO THE DEVELOPMENT OF THE AMERICAN NEGRO. ALL FISCAL YEARS THROUGH JUNE 10,
1966.   NFORDFX66133

NEGRO BUSINESSMEN OF NEW-ORLEANS.   NFORTXX49054

LEFT SECTARIANISM IN THE FIGHT FOR NEGRO RIGHTS AND AGAINST WHITE CHAUVINISM.   NFOSTWZ53375

ETHNIC FAMILY PATTERNS. THE NEGRO FAMILY IN THE UNITED STATES.   NFRAZEF48379

PROBLEMS AND NEEDS OF NEGRO CHILDREN AND YOUTH RESULTING FROM FAMILY DISORGANIZATION.   NFRAZEF50382

THE INTEGRATION OF THE NEGRO INTO AMERICAN SOCIETY.   NFRAZEF51578

THE NEGRO MIDDLE-CLASS AND DESEGREGATION.   NFRAZEF57381

THE **NEGRO** IN THE UNITED STATES.   NFRAZEF57966

THE **NEGRO** FAMILY IN CHICAGO. /ILLINOIS/   NFRAZEF64380

THE **NEGRO** LAWYER IN VIRGINIA. A SURVEY. /OCCUPATIONS/   NFRIEMX65387

A **NEGRO** BUSINESS-MAN SPEAKS HIS MIND.   NFULLSB63390

THE **NEGRO** AND POVERTY.   NGALLLE67393

INTRA-PLANT MOBILITY OF **NEGRO** AND WHITE WORKERS.   NGARBAP65394

THE EVOLUTION OF AMERICAN LAW VIS-A-VIS THE AMERICAN **NEGRO**.   NGARDHX63395

ECONOMIC ADVANCES OF THE AMERICAN **NEGRO**.   NGERSGX65082

SOCIAL-STRUCTURE AND THE **NEGRO** REVOLT. AN EXAMINATION OF SOME HYPOTHESES. /SOCIO-ECONOMIC/   NGESCJA64400

THE **NEGRO** POTENTIAL. /EMPLOYMENT INCOME EDUCATION/   NGINZEX56409

EXPANDING **NEGRO** OPPORTUNITIES. /OCCUPATIONAL-STATUS/   NGINZEX60404

THE **NEGRO** AND HIS WORK.   NGINZEX61407

THE **NEGRO** CHALLENGE TO THE BUSINESS COMMUNITY. /INDUSTRY/   NGINZEX64408

THE TROUBLESOME PRESENCE. AMERICAN DEMOCRACY AND THE **NEGRO**.   NGINZEX64414

EMPLOYMENT PATTERNS OF **NEGRO** MEN AND WOMEN.   NGINZEX66416

POVERTY AND THE **NEGRO**.   NGINZEX66971

THE GUIDANCE OF **NEGRO** YOUTH.   NGINZEX67417

ASPIRATIONS OF **NEGRO** AND WHITE STUDENTS.   NGISTNP63419

THE RELATIVE SIZE OF THE **NEGRO** POPULATION AND NEGRO OCCUPATIONAL-STATUS.   NGLENND64424

THE RELATIVE SIZE OF THE NEGRO POPULATION AND **NEGRO** OCCUPATIONAL-STATUS.   NGLENND64424

REPLY TO CUTRIGHT ON **NEGRO** SUBORDINATION. /OCCUPATIONAL-STATUS/   NGLENND65425

THE ROLE OF WHITE RESISTANCE AND FACILITATION IN THE **NEGRO** STRUGGLE FOR EQUALITY.   NGLENND65676

EDUCATIONAL IMPERATIVE. THE **NEGRO** IN THE CHANGING SOUTH.   NGOLDFH63429

LONGEVITY AND HEALTH-STATUS OF THE **NEGRO** AMERICAN.   NGOLDMS63431

THE EVALUATION OF PRACTICES CARRIED ON BY TWO HUNDRED **NEGRO** FARMERS IN THE PRODUCTION OF COTTON IN MACON
COUNTY, ALABAMA.   NGOLDSM48350

NOTE ON **NEGRO** ALIENATION.   NGORDDX65976

LABOR LAW AND THE **NEGRO**.   NGOULWB64889

THE **NEGRO** REVOLUTION AND THE LAW OF COLLECTIVE BARGAINING.   NGOULWB65437

THE **NEGRO** SALARIED WORKER. /EMPLOYMENT-SELECTION/   NGOURJC65438

PROBLEMS AND NEEDS OF **NEGRO** ADOLESCENT WORKERS.   NGRANLB40980

MEMBERSHIP POLICIES OF INTERNATIONAL UNIONS AS THEY AFFECT **NEGRO** WORKERS.   NGRANLB41442

THE **NEGRO** AND ECONOMIC OPPORTUNITY.   NGRANLB41443

BARRIERS TO **NEGRO** WAR EMPLOYMENT.   NGRANLB42440

THE **NEGRO** RECORD IN EQUAL-OPPORTUNITIES.   NGRANLB58596

THE VOCATIONAL PREFERENCE OF **NEGRO** CHILDREN.   NGRAYSW44446

NEGRO DIALECT. THE LAST BARRIER TO INTEGRATION.   NGREEGC63447

THE PLACE OF THE **NEGRO** IN THE AMERICAN LABOR-MOVEMENT. /UNION/   NGREESX61452

IN SEARCH OF A FUTURE. A STUDY OF CAREER-SEEKING EXPERIENCES OF SELECTED **NEGRO** HIGH SCHOOL GRADUATES IN
WASHINGTON-DC WHICH WAS AN EFFORT TO PROVIDE KNOWLEDGE HELPFUL IN SOLVING ONE OF THE MOST CRITICAL
PROBLEMS FACING URBAN AMERICA TODAY.   NGRIEES63454

THE **NEGRO** MIGRATION. /ECONOMIC-STATUS/   NGRIEGXND982

ORGANIZED LABOR AND THE **NEGRO** WORKER. /UNION/   NGROBGX60460

SOME PERSONALITY CHARACTERISTICS OF SOUTHERN **NEGRO** STUDENTS.   NGROSMM57462

THE CAREER PATTERNS OF **NEGRO** LAWYERS IN LOUISIANA. /OCCUPATIONS/   NGUILBM60465

MOTIVATION AND ASPIRATION IN THE **NEGRO** COLLEGE.   NGURIPX66352

SOCIAL-CLASS CONSTRAINTS ON THE OCCUPATIONAL ASPIRATIONS OF STUDENTS ATTENDING SOME PREDOMINANTLY **NEGRO**
COLLEGES.   NGURIPX66467

SOME CHARACTERISTICS OF STUDENTS FROM POVERTY BACKGROUNDS ATTENDING PREDOMINANTLY **NEGRO** COLLEGES IN THE
CEEP SOUTH.   NGURIPX66468

NEGRO YEARBOOK.   NGUZMJP47470

HIRING **NEGRO** WORKERS. /INDUSTRY/   NHABBSX64473

CHIEF EXECUTIVES VIEW **NEGRO** EMPLOYMENT. /INDUSTRY/   NHABBSX65471

THE **NEGRO** AS AN EMPLOYEE. /INDUSTRY/   NHABBSX65474

COMPANY EXPERIENCE WITH **NEGRO** EMPLOYMENT. /INDUSTRY/   NHABBSX66472

THE **NEGRO** LAWYER AND HIS CLIENTS. /OCCUPATIONS/   NHALEWH52476

THE USE OF **NEGRO** LABOR IN SOUTHERN INDUSTRY. /OCCUPATIONAL-PATTERNS/   NHALLDE53477

NEGRO   (CONTINUATION)

THE OPPORTUNITIES AND DIFFICULTIES OF ORGANIZING **NEGRO** LABOR IN THE PRESENT EMERGENCY. /UNION/   NHALLWX42259

THE **NEGRO** LEAVES THE SOUTH. /DEMOGRAPHY MIGRATION/   NHAMICH64479

ATTITUDES OF WHITE DEPARTMENT STORE EMPLOYEES TOWARD **NEGRO** CO-WORKERS. /CASE-STUDY/   NHARDJX52482

CHANGING OCCUPATIONAL-STATUS OF **NEGRO** EDUCATION.   NHARENX62483

HIGHER EDUCATION FOR THE **NEGRO**.   NHARLBW65486

ACHIEVEMENT MOTIVATION CHARACTERISTICS OF **NEGRO** COLLEGE FRESHMEN.   NHARREC59492

THE STATUS OF THE **NEGRO** CPA IN THE UNITED STATES. /OCCUPATIONS/   NHARRLJ62494

A STUDY OF THE EFFECTS OF EFFORTS TO IMPROVE EMPLOYMENT-OPPORTUNITIES OF NEGROES ON THE UTILIZATION OF **NEGRO** WORKERS.   NHARTJW64496

PICKETING BY NEGROES TO OBTAIN EMPLOYMENT IN PROPORTION TO **NEGRO** CUSTOMERS HELD UNLAWFUL.   NHARVLR49498

THE **NEGRO** IN THE ARMY TODAY. /MILITARY/   NHASTWH42466

THE **NEGRO** REVOLUTION. A QUEST FOR JUSTICE.   NHATCJF66648

DEMOGRAPHIC FACTORS IN THE INTEGRATION OF THE **NEGRO**.   NHAUSPM65501

DEMOGRAPHIC AND SOCIAL FACTORS IN THE POVERTY OF THE **NEGRO**.   NHAUSPM66992

NEGRO EMPLOYMENT IN THE BIRMINGHAM METROPOLITAN AREA. /ALABAMA CASE-STUDY/   NHAWLLT55502

THE **NEGRO** FEDERAL-GOVERNMENT WORKER.   NHAYELJ42504

THE ECONOMIC IMBALANCE. AN INQUIRY INTO THE ECONOMIC-STATUS OF NEGROES IN THE UNITED STATES, 1935-1960, WITH IMPLICATIONS FOR **NEGRO** EDUCATION.   NHENDVW60512

ECONOMIC OPPORTUNITY AND **NEGRO** EDUCATION.   NHENDVW62513

SOME PERSONAL AND SOCIOLOGICAL VARIABLES ASSOCIATED WITH OCCUPATIONAL-CHOICES OF **NEGRO** YOUTH.   NHERSPF65520

IS THERE A BREAKDOWN OF THE **NEGRO** FAMILY.   NHERZEX66521

THE **NEGRO** IN THE TEXAS LABOR-SUPPLY.   NHILLFG46524

THE **NEGRO** WORKER IN INDUSTRY.   NHILLHX57533

RIGHT-TO-WORK LAWS AND THE **NEGRO** WORKER.   NHILLHX58996

LABOR UNIONS AND THE **NEGRO**.   NHILLHX59530

APPRENTICES, SKILLED CRAFTSMEN AND THE **NEGRO**. AN ANALYSIS.   NHILLHX60525

THE **NEGRO** WAGE-EARNER AND APPRENTICESHIP TRAINING PROGRAMS. A CRITICAL ANALYSIS WITH RECOMMENDATIONS.   NHILLHX60532

HAS ORGANIZED LABOR FAILED THE **NEGRO** WORKER. /UNION/   NHILLHX62526

ORGANIZED LABOR AND THE **NEGRO** WAGE-EARNER. /UNION/   NHILLHX62535

UNIONS AND THE **NEGRO** COMMUNITY.   NHILLHX64997

STATE LAWS AND THE **NEGRO**. SOCIAL CHANGE AND THE IMPACT OF LAW.   NHILLHX65545

SOCIAL-CLASSES. A FRAME OF REFERENCE FOR THE STUDY OF **NEGRO** SOCIETY.   NHILLMC43551

SOME WORK-RELATED CULTURAL DEPRIVATIONS OF LOWER-CLASS **NEGRO** YOUTHS.   NHIMEJS64554

NEGRO TEEN-AGE CULTURE.   NHIMEJX61071

THE ASSESSMENT OF ADJUSTMENT OF AGED **NEGRO** WOMEN IN A SOUTHERN CITY.   NHIMEJX62072

A MANAGEMENT PERSPECTIVE TOWARD **NEGRO** ECONOMIC PRESSURES.   NHOFFHX65558

PREPARATION OF THE **NEGRO** COLLEGE GRADUATE FOR BUSINESS. /EMPLOYMENT-SELECTION/   NHOLLJH65560

THE **NEGRO** AND HIGHER EDUCATION.   NHOLLJX65305

THE EDUCATIONAL AND OCCUPATIONAL ASPIRATIONS AND PLANS OF **NEGRO** AND WHITE MALE ELEMENTARY SCHOOL STUDENTS.   NHOLLRG59562

URBAN-LEAGUE UPGRADES **NEGRO** WORKERS.   NHOLMAX66563

NEGRO EMPLOYMENT IN THREE SOUTHERN PLANTS OF INTERNATIONAL HARVESTER COMPANY. /CASE-STUDY/   NHOPEJX55572

THE **NEGRO** IN THE FEDERAL-GOVERNMENT.   NHOPEJX63576

THE **NEGRO** IN OUR ECONOMY.   NHUGHWH48587

THE EFFECT OF A CHANGING AGRICULTURAL PATTERN ON **NEGRO** FARMERS OF SOUTH-CAROLINA.   NHURSRL56253

THE AFL-CIO AND THE **NEGRO**. /UNION/   NHUTCJXND590

JACKSONVILLE LOOKS AT ITS **NEGRO** COMMUNITY. /FLORIDA/   NJACKCC46598

THE EFFECT OF THE WAR ECONOMY ON THE SOUTH. HOW MOBILIZATION WILL AFFECT POSITION OF THE **NEGRO**.   NJACKJX51595

A HISTORICAL REVIEW OF THE IMPACT OF SOCIAL AND ECONOMIC STRUCTURE ON **NEGRO** CULTURE AND HOW IT INFLUENCES FAMILY LIVING.   NJACKJX64596

THE **NEGRO** WORKER ASSERTS HIS RIGHTS. /UNION/   NJACOPA63601

DIFFERENTIAL CHARACTERISTICS OF SUPERIOR AND UNSELECTED **NEGRO** COLLEGE STUDENTS.   NJENKMD48608

INTELLECTUALLY SUPERIOR **NEGRO** YOUTH. THEIR PROBLEMS AND NEEDS. /EDUCATION/   NJENKMD50606

GROWING UP IN THE BLACK BELT. **NEGRO** YOUTH IN THE RURAL SOUTH.   NJOHNCS41611

THE **NEGRO**.   NJOHNCS42544

NEGRO MINORITY. /ECONOMIC-STATUS/   NJOHNCS42550

PATTERNS OF NEGRO SEGREGATION.   NJOHNCS43008

THE NEGRO WAR WORKER IN SAN-FRANCISCO. /CALIFORNIA/   NJOHNCS44612

THE STATUS OF NEGRO LABOR.   NJOHNCS49613

THE SOCIO-ECONOMIC BACKGROUND OF NEGRO HEALTH STATUS.   NJOHNCS49616

THE EMPLOYMENT SITUATION OF WHITE AND NEGRO YOUTH IN THE CITY OF BALTIMORE. INITIAL EXPERIENCES IN THE
LABOR-MARKET. /MARYLAND/   NJOHNHU63735

A CHALLENGE TO NEGRO LEADERSHIP.   NJOHNJG60618

RECENT TRENDS OF MEMBERSHIP OF INTERNATIONAL UNIONS AS THEY AFFECT NEGRO WORKERS.   NJCHNRA44620

NEGRO REACTIONS TO MINORITY-GROUP STATUS.   NJOHNRA57619

TAPPING THE NEGRO POTENTIAL. /INDUSTRY EMPLOYMENT-SELECTION PROMOTION/   NJOHNTX65621

THE NEGRO AS AN AMERICAN. /MANPOWER/   NJOHNXX63336

UNION LOCALS AND THE UNDER-UTILIZATION OF NEGRO WORKERS.   NJONEBA66884

EFFORTS OF NEGRO TEACHERS IN THE SOUTHERN STATES TO OBTAIN EQUALIZATION OF SALARIES.   NJONEER48343

THE AMERICAN NEGRO AND THE CURRENT SCENE.   NJONEJAND738

THE CHANGING STATUS OF THE NEGRO IN SOUTHERN AGRICULTURE.   NJONELW50623

NEGRO YOUTH IN THE SOUTH. /EDUCATION EMPLOYMENT/   NJONELW60010

NEGRO INTERNAL MIGRATION IN THE UNITED STATES. 1870-1960.   NJORGJM62624

RELATIVE PROGRESS OF THE AMERICAN NEGRO SINCE 1950.   NJOURNE63626

STUDIES IN THE HIGHER EDUCATION OF NEGRO AMERICANS.   NJOURNE66627

MEDICAL SOCIETY OF THE DISTRICT OF COLUMBIA TO ADMIT NEGRO PHYSICIANS. /OCCUPATIONS/   NJOURNM52628

THE NEGRO WORKER OF KANSAS-CITY. A STUDY OF TRADE UNION AND ORGANIZED LABOR RELATIONS.   NKANCIU40634

EQUAL JUSTICE IN AN UNEQUAL WORLD. EQUALITY FOR THE NEGRO -- THE PROBLEM OF SPECIAL TREATMENT.   NKAPLJX66645

EFFECTS OF ANXIETY, THREAT, AND RACIAL ENVIRONMENT ON TASK PERFORMANCE OF NEGRO COLLEGE STUDENTS.   NKATZIX63640

THE SOCIO-ECONOMIC ADJUSTMENT OF THE NEGRO IN SEATTLE BETWEEN 1940 AND 1950. /WASHINGTON/   NKENNTH54273

NEGRO EMPLOYMENT IN KENTUCKY STATE AGENCIES.   NKENTCH66643

NEGRO VISIBILITY.   NKEPHWM54543

EMPLOYMENT PROBLEMS OF THE OLDER NEGRO WORKER.   NKERNJH50644

SUMMARY OF A SURVEY OF SOCIAL AND ECONOMIC CONDITIONS IN MORRIS COUNTY NEW-JERSEY AS THEY AFFECT THE
NEGRO.   NKERNJH57645

NEGRO ENGINEERS AND STUDENTS REPORT ON THEIR PROFESSION. /OCCUPATIONS/   NKIEHRX58647

CHANGING PATTERNS OF NEGRO EMPLOYMENT. /OCCUPATIONAL-PATTERNS/   NKIFEAX64649

THE NEGRO IN AMERICAN BUSINESS. THE CONFLICT BETWEEN SEPARATISM AND INTEGRATION.   NKINZRH50654

SOCIAL-STATUS AND ASPIRATIONS IN PHILADELPHIA-S NEGRO POPULATION. /PENNSYLVANIA/   NKLEIRJ62655

CHARACTERISTICS OF THE AMERICAN NEGRO.   NKLINOX44656

A STUDY OF PROFESSIONAL PREPARATION OF NEGRO TEACHERS OF EXCEPTIONAL CHILDREN IN NORTH-CAROLINA COUNTY
AND CITY PUBLIC SCHOOLS.   NKNIGOB65023

THE NEGRO UNION OFFICIAL. A STUDY OF SPONSORSHIP AND CONTROL.   NKORNWA52661

THE NEGRO IN FEDERAL EMPLOYMENT. THE QUEST FOR EQUAL-OPPORTUNITY.   NKRISSX67143

NEGRO JOBS AND EDUCATION.   NKUEBJX63315

THE NEGRO AND APPRENTICESHIPS.   NKURSHX65669

NEGRO COLLEGES. LONG IGNORED, SOUTHERN SCHOOLS NOW COURTED BY MAJOR UNIVERSITIES AND FOUNDATIONS.   NLANGEX64304

WHAT SHOULD THE BUSINESS RESPONSE BE TO THE NEGRO REVOLUTION. A PUBLIC RELATIONS PROGRAM FOR DEALING WITH
MINORITY-GROUPS.   NLANGJF65671

VOCATIONAL ASPIRATIONS OF NEGRO YOUTH IN CALIFORNIA.   NLAWRPF50368

NEGRO INTELLIGENCE AND SELECTIVE MIGRATION. A PHILADELPHIA TEST OF THE KLINEBERG HYPOTHESIS.
/PENNSYLVANIA/   NLEEXES51673

NEGRO AND WHITE IN A CONNECTICUT TOWN.   NLEEXFF61674

EMPLOYMENT OF NEGRO MANPOWER IN CALVERT COUNTY, MARYLAND.   NLERANL60401

NEGRO FARM LABOR IN THE DELTA AREA OF MISSISSIPPI. SUPPLY AND UTILIZATION.   NLERANL61416

THE EMPLOYMENT SITUATION OF WHITE AND NEGRO YOUTH IN THE CITY OF BALTIMORE. /MARYLAND/   NLEVEBX63684

VOCATIONAL GRADUATES IN AUTO MECHANICS. A FOLLOW-UP STUDY OF NEGRO AND WHITE YOUTH. /OCCUPATIONS/   NLEVEBX66036

DESEGREGATION, INTEGRATION, AND THE NEGRO COMMUNITY.   NLEWIHX56073

THE CHANGING NEGRO FAMILY.   NLEWIHX60690

AN ECONOMIC ANALYSIS OF SPECIFIED INCORPORATED AND UNINCORPORATED FARMERS COOPERATIVE ASSOCIATIONS
OPERATED BY NEGRO FARMERS IN ALABAMA.   NLIGHMB53340

THE ABSENT FATHER HAUNTS THE NEGRO FAMILY.   NLINCCE65694

A PILOT STUDY OF PERSONALITY FACTORS RELATED TO OCCUPATIONAL ASPIRATIONS OF NEGRO COLLEGE STUDENTS.   NLITTLW66697

TEACHER SUPPLY AND DEMAND IN THE NEGRO COLLEGE.   NLLOYRG54045

PROGRESS IN PLANS-FOR-PROGRESS FOR NEGRO MANAGERS.   NLOCKHC65701

THE PROGRESS OF THE NEGRO AFTER A CENTURY OF EMANCIPATION.   NLOGARW63046

JOBS AND COLOR. NEGRO EMPLOYMENT IN TENNESSEE STATE GOVERNMENT.   NLONGHH62706

THE NEGRO IN LOS-ANGELES COUNTY. /CALIFORNIA/   NLOSACC63709

NEGRO AND WHITE CHILDREN-S PLANS FOR THEIR FUTURES. /ASPIRATIONS/   NLOTTAJ63487

HOW INTEGRATION IS WORKING OUT IN INDUSTRY. THE NEGRO WORKER.   NMANARX56734

THE LEGAL STATUS OF THE NEGRO.   NMANGCS40735

THE NEGRO AND ORGANIZED LABOR. /UNION/   NMARSRX63741

UNIONS AND THE NEGRO COMMUNITY.   NMARSRX64061

THE NEGRO WORKER AND THE TRADE UNIONS. A FOOT IN THE DOOR.   NMARSRX65058

THE NEGRO AND ORGANIZED LABOR. /UNION/   NMARSRX65742

NEGRO PARTICIPATION IN APPRENTICESHIP PROGRAMS.   NMARSRX66327

THE NEGRO WORKER.   NMARSRX67057

NEGRO PARTICIPATION IN APPRENTICESHIP PROGRAMS.   NMARSRX67118

NEGRO STATUS IN THE BOILERMAKERS UNION.   NMARSTX44753

SUMMARY JUSTICE -- THE NEGRO GI IN KOREA. /MILITARY/   NMARSTX51755

THE CIO AND THE NEGRO IN THE SOUTH. /UNION/   NMASOJR45323

THE RURAL NEGRO POPULATION OF THE SOUTH IN TRANSITION.   NMAYOSC63762

NEGRO VERSUS WHITE INTELLIGENCE. A CONTINUING CONTROVERSY.   NMCCOWM58062

POSTWAR STATUS OF NEGRO WORKERS IN SAN-FRANCISCO AREA. /CALIFORNIA/   NMCENDX50721

THE PREDOMINANTLY NEGRO COLLEGES AND UNIVERSITIES IN TRANSITION.   NMCGREJ65720

THE ROLE OF THE NEGRO IN THE HEALING PROFESSIONS IN CONTEMPORARY AMERICA. /OCCUPATIONS/ NMCPHEL55728

THE NEGRO WORKER-S CULTURAL AND OCCUPATIONAL LIMITATIONS.   NMCPICM61729

FACTORS AFFECTING FARM PLACEMENT OF NEGRO VOCATIONAL AGRICULTURE STUDENTS IN ALABAMA.   NMCQUFT45348

INTELLIGENCE AND EDUCATIONAL ACHIEVEMENT OF A MATCHED SAMPLE OF WHITE AND NEGRO STUDENTS. NMCQURX60730

CIVIL-RIGHTS STRATEGIES FOR NEGRO EMPLOYMENT.   NMEIEAX67764

THE FACTS ON NEGRO PHYSICIANS. /OCCUPATIONS/   NMENZRX49766

DISCRIMINATION IN THE HIRING AND ASSIGNMENT OF NEGRO TEACHERS IN PUBLIC SCHOOL SYSTEMS. NMICLRX66068

THE NEGRO AMERICAN. A BIBLIOGRAPHY.   NMILLEW66129

PROGRESS AND PROSPECTS FOR THE NEGRO WORKER.   NMILLHP65783

THE NEGRO IN MILWAUKEE. PROGRESS AND PORTENT, 1863-1963. /WISCONSIN/   NMILWCC63792

MOTIVATING NEGRO YOUTH IN RHODE-ISLAND.   NMINIBC65797

THE NEGRO WORKER IN MINNESOTA. A REPORT.   NMINNGI45798

THE NEGRO WORKER-S PROGRESS IN MINNESOTA. A REPORT.   NMINNGI49799

EQUAL-EMPLOYMENT-OPPORTUNITIES IN MISSOURI STATE AGENCIES. A SURVEY OF NEGRO EMPLOYMENT, SPRING-SUMMER
1963.   NMISSCH64801

ASPIRATION LEVELS OF NEGRO DELINQUENT, DEPENDENT, AND PUBLIC SCHOOL BOYS.   NMITCLE57804

ATTITUDES TOWARD SOCIAL MOBILITY AS REVEALED BY SAMPLES OF NEGRO AND WHITE BOYS.   NMONTJB58809

THE NEGRO AND THE UNION.   NMORGSX59851

THE NEGRO GHETTO. PROBLEMS AND ALTERNATIVES.   NMORRRL65852

THE UTILIZATION OF NEGRO TEACHERS IN THE COLLEGES OF NEW-YORK STATE.   NMOSSJA60857

A STUDY OF THE POTENTIAL SUPPLY OF NEGRO TEACHERS FOR THE COLLEGES OF NEW-YORK STATE.   NMOSSJA61858

THE NEGRO AND EMPLOYMENT OPPORTUNITIES IN THE SOUTH.   NMOSSJA62856

THE LEGAL-STATUS OF THE NEGRO IN THE UNITED STATES.   NMOTLCB66859

EMPLOYMENT, INCOME, AND THE ORDEAL OF THE NEGRO FAMILY.   NMOYNDP65861

THE NEGRO FAMILY. THE CASE FOR NATIONAL ACTION.   NMOYNDP65862

THE NEGRO IN THE NAVY. /MILITARY/   NMUELWR45865

PROBLEMS AND PROSPECTS OF THE NEGRO MOVEMENT. /EMPLOYMENT/   NMURPRJ66866

THE STATUS OF THE NEGRO PHYSICIAN IN NEW-YORK STATE. /OCCUPATIONS/   NMURRPM55867

SOCIAL TRENDS IN AMERICA AND STRATEGIC APPROACHES TO THE NEGRO PROBLEM.   NMYRDGX48871

SOUTHERN NEGRO. 1952.   NNATIXX52873

RECRUITING NEGRO COLLEGE GRADUATES.   NNATLIC64231

GOALS IN NEGRO EMPLOYMENT. /INDUSTRY/   NNATLIC65874

NEGRO WORKERS AFTER THE WAR.   NNATLNC45879

NEGLECTED TALENTS. BACKGROUND AND PROSPECTS OF NEGRO COLLEGE GRADUATES.   NNATLOR66880

SELECTED STUDIES OF NEGRO EMPLOYMENT IN THE SOUTH.   NNATLPA55881

INTER-RACIAL PLANNING FOR COMMUNITY ORGANIZATION... EMPLOYMENT PROBLEMS OF THE NEGRO.   NNATLUL44900

NEGRO WORKERS IN THE BUILDING TRADES IN SELECTED CITIES. NORFOLK, VIRGINIA. /INDUSTRY/   NNATLUL46894

NEGRO WORKERS IN THE BUILDING TRADES IN CERTAIN CITIES.   NNATLUL47904

A SURVEY OF THE ECONOMIC AND CULTURAL CONDITIONS OF THE NEGRO POPULATION OF LOUISVILLE, KENTUCKY AND A
REVIEW OF THE PROGRAM AND ACTIVITIES OF THE LOUISVILLE URBAN-LEAGUE. JANUARY-FEBRUARY, 1948.   NNATLUL48903

APPRENTICESHIP AND TRAINING OPPORTUNITIES FOR NEGRO YOUTHS IN SELECTED URBAN-LEAGUE CITIES.   NNATLUL61885

ECONOMIC AND SOCIAL STATUS OF THE NEGRO IN THE UNITED STATES.   NNATLUL62083

AUTOMATION AND THE RETRAINING OF NEGRO WORKERS.   NNATLUL62886

DOUBLE JEOPARDY -- THE OLDER NEGRO IN AMERICA TODAY.   NNATLUL64887

THE PLACE OF THE NEGRO FARMER IN THE CHANGING ECONOMY OF THE COTTON SOUTH.   NNEALEE50905

ECONOMIC-STATUS OF THE NEGRO.   NNEWMDKND957

CORPORATE HIRING POLICIES AND THE NEGRO. /INDUSTRY/   NNEWSXX64911

THE NEGRO AND THE NATIONAL GUARD. /MILITARY/   NNEWTIG62915

THE URBAN-LEAGUE AND THE VOCATIONAL GUIDANCE AND ADJUSTMENT OF NEGRO YOUTH.   NNICHLE52922

NEGRO LABOR AND ITS PROBLEMS.   NNORGPH40930

EMPLOYING THE NEGRO IN AMERICAN INDUSTRY   NNORGPH59932

THE NEGRO AND UNIONISM IN THE BIRMINGHAM, ALABAMA IRON AND STEEL INDUSTRY.   NNORTHR43941

THE NEGRO IN THE RAILWAY UNIONS.   NNORTHR44943

ORGANIZED LABOR AND THE NEGRO. /UNION/   NNORTHR44944

UNIONS AND NEGRO EMPLOYMENT.   NNORTHR46947

LAST HIRED. FIRST FIRED. THOUGH NEGRO WORKERS HAVE MADE IMPRESSIVE GAINS THEY MIGHT BE FIRST TO FEEL THE
BITE OF RECESSION.   NNORTHR49940

THE NEGRO AND EMPLOYMENT OPPORTUNITY. PROBLEMS AND PRACTICES.   NNORTHR65949

MANAGEMENTS GUIDELINES FOR MEETING THE NEGRO DRIVE FOR JOB EQUALITY. /INDUSTRY/.   NOPINRC63958

ECONOMIC AND SOCIAL STATUS OF THE NEGRO IN THE UNITED STATES.   NORSHMX61961

THE AGED NEGRO AND HIS INCOME.   NORSHMX64960

A STUDY OF THE LONGSHORE INDUSTRY IN NEW-ORLEANS WITH EMPHASIS ON NEGRO LONGSHOREMEN. /LOUISIANA/   NORTICF56962

NEGRO EMPLOYMENT IN THE TEXTILE INDUSTRIES OF NORTH AND SOUTH-CAROLINA. /NORTH-CAROLINA/   NOSBUDD66963

BLACK ODYSSEY. THE STORY OF THE NEGRO IN AMERICA.   NOTTLRX45966

THE NEGRO IN SCHOOL ADMINISTRATION.   NOVERXX61967

EMPLOYMENT SECURITY AND THE NEGRO.   NOXLELA40969

STATUS POSITION, MOBILITY, AND ETHNIC IDENTIFICATION OF THE NEGRO.   NPARKSX64973

THE NEGRO AMERICAN.   NPARSTX66976

THE INDUSTRIAL INTEGRATION OF THE NEGRO.   NPATITH63978

NEGRO YOUTH -- EDUCATION, EMPLOYMENT, AND CIVIL-RIGHTS.   NPEARAX64980

TRENDS IN THE ECONOMIC-STATUS OF THE NEGRO PEOPLE. /OCCUPATIONAL-PATTERNS/   NPERLVX52983

THE NEGRO IN SOUTHERN AGRICULTURE.   NPERLVX53982

THE JOB OUTLOOK FOR NEGRO YOUTH.   NPERRJX64984

NATIONAL NEGRO LABOR COUNCIL. THIRD ANNUAL CONVENTION. /UNION/   NPERRPX54987

THE NEGRO AND TITLE-VII. /LEGISLATION/   NPERSPF65562

FATHER-ABSENCE AND NEGRO ADULT PERSONALITY. A RESEARCH NOTE.   NPETTTFND990

NEGRO AMERICAN INTELLIGENCE. A NEW LOOK AT AN OLD CONTROVERSY.   NPETTTF63063

NEGRO AMERICAN PERSONALITY.   NPETTTF64991

A PROFILE OF THE NEGRO AMERICAN.   NPETTTF64992

THE NEW NEGRO. EMERGING AMERICAN.   NPFAUHW63993

COUNSELING NEGRO STUDENTS. AN EDUCATIONAL DILEMMA.   NPHILWB59996

LABOR-FORCE AND DEMOGRAPHIC FACTORS AFFECTING THE CHANGING RELATIVE STATUS OF THE AMERICAN NEGRO.
1940-1950.   NPHILWM57997

NEGRO BUSINESS AND BUSINESS EDUCATION. THEIR PRESENT AND PROSPECTIVE DEVELOPMENT.   NPIERJA47998

A REGIONAL STUDY OF THE NEGRO.   NPIERWG41999

THE NEGRO REVOLUTION AND EMPLOYMENT.   NPOLIEX64219

CHARACTERISTICS OF NEGRO COLLEGE CHIEF LIBRARIANS. /OCCUPATIONS/   NPOLLFM64005

ORGANIZED LABOR AND THE NEGRO YOUTH. /UNION/   NPOLLSX66723

THE AMERICAN NEGRO AT MID-CENTURY.   NPOPURB58008

RETREATISM AND OCCUPATIONAL ASPIRATIONS AMONG WHITE AND **NEGRO** HIGH SCHOOL SENIORS.   NPOWEEC61009

NEGRO AND TOTAL EMPLOYMENT BY GRADE AND SALARY GROUPS, JUNE 1961 AND JUNE 1962.   NPRESCD62011

NEGRO EMPLOYMENT IN THE FEDERAL GOVERNMENT BY CIVIL SERVICE REGION, STATE AND PAY CATEGORIES, JUNE 1962.   NPRESCD62012

MINORITY-GROUP STUDY. JUNE 1963. **NEGRO** AND TOTAL EMPLOYMENT IN SELECTED AGENCIES.   NPRESCD63010

CHARACTERISTICS OF **NEGRO** EMPLOYMENT IN FEDERAL AGENCIES IN ATLANTA, GEORGIA.   NPRESCP60016

CHANGING CHARACTERISTICS OF THE **NEGRO** POPULATION.   NPRICDO65018

THE YOUNG **NEGRO** IN AMERICA 1960-1980.   NPROCSD66021

THE HOPES OF **NEGRO** WORKERS FOR THEIR CHILDREN.   NPURCTV64022

NEGRO MIGRATION IN THE UNITED STATES.   NPURDLX54024

THE **NEGRO** IN THE LABOR-FORCE.   NPURYMT63026

THE **NEGRO** IN THE INDUSTRIAL DEVELOPMENT OF THE SOUTH.   NRABOSH53029

CRUCIBLE OF IDENTITY. THE **NEGRO** LOWER-CLASS FAMILY.   NRAINLX66032

THE **NEGRO** CONGRESS.   NRANDAP40576

JOBS FOR THE **NEGRO**. THE UNFINISHED REVOLUTION.   NRANDAP64034

THE **NEGRO** ISSUE IN CALIFORNIA.   NRECOCW48041

THE **NEGRO** POLICY OF THE AMERICAN ARMY SINCE WORLD-WAR-II. /MILITARY/   NREDDLD53044

ACCOMODATION BETWEEN **NEGRO** AND WHITE EMPLOYEES IN A WEST COAST AIRCRAFT INDUSTRY, 1942-1944.
/CASE-STUDY/   NREEDBA47045

A CRITICAL SUMMARY. THE **NEGRO** ON THE HOME FRONT IN WORLD-WARS I AND II.   NREIDID43048

SPECIAL PROBLEMS OF **NEGRO** MIGRATION DURING THE WAR.   NREIDID47362

THE AMERICAN **NEGRO**.   NREIDID56047

THE **NEGRO** TOBACCO WORKER AND HIS UNION IN DURHAM, NORTH-CAROLINA.   NRICEJD41053

WIDER HORIZONS FOR **NEGRO** WORKERS.   NRICHCX64058

OCCUPATIONAL ATTITUDES OF **NEGRO** WORKERS.   NRICHEX43056

GRADUATE EDUCATION OF **NEGRO** PSYCHOLOGISTS.   NRICHTW56057

THE NEW ANTI-POVERTY IDEOLOGY AND THE **NEGRO**.   NRIESFX65060

IN DEFENSE OF THE **NEGRO** FAMILY.   NRIESFX66059

ANNUAL FAMILY AND OCCUPATIONAL EARNINGS OF RESIDENTS OF TWO **NEGRO** HOUSING PROJECTS IN ATLANTA 1937-1944.
/GEORGIA/   NRITTAL45062

NEGRO EDUCATION -- FOR WHAT.   NROBEGX61063

THE IMPACT OF MILITARY SERVICE UPON THE RACIAL ATTITUDES OF **NEGRO** SERVICEMEN IN WORLD-WAR II.   NROBEHW53065

NEGRO AMERICAN COLLEGE YOUTH-S OUTLOOK ON THE FUTURE.   NROBESO57067

THE RELATIONSHIP BETWEEN TEST INTELLIGENCE OF THIRD GRADE **NEGRO** CHILDREN AND THE OCCUPATIONS OF THEIR
PARENTS.   NROBIML47070

THE **NEGRO** IN AMERICA.   NROSEAM48319

THE **NEGRO** IN POST-WAR AMERICA.   NROSEAM50294

NEW AND EMERGING **NEGRO** PROBLEMS.   NROSEAM60295

SOCIAL CHANGE AND THE **NEGRO** PROBLEM.   NROSEAM64296

THE **NEGRO** PROTEST.   NROSEAM65074

THE AMERICAN **NEGRO** PROBLEM IN THE CONTEXT OF SOCIAL CHANGE.   NROSEAM65289

HOW **NEGRO** WORKERS FEEL ABOUT THEIR JOBS.   NROSEAW51292

THE MARKET FOR **NEGRO** EDUCATORS IN COLLEGES AND UNIVERSITIES OUTSIDE THE SOUTH.   NROSEHM61076

THE **NEGRO** IN INDUSTRY.   NROSERX53077

THE **NEGRO** IN THE AMERICAN LABOR MOVEMENT.   /UNION/   NROSESJ62079

THE **NEGRO** IN THE AMERICAN ECONOMY.   NROSSAM67082

WILL THE **NEGRO** SUCCEED.   NROSSAM67085

A REVIEW OF RESEARCH ON THE **NEGRO** AND EMPLOYMENT IN THE SOUTH.   NROWARL65703

NEGRO EMPLOYMENT IN BIRMINGHAM. THREE CASES. /ALABAMA/   NROWARL67091

THE **NEGRO** POLICEMAN IN THE SOUTH. /OCCUPATIONS/   NRUDWEM60095

NEGRO POLICE EMPLOYMENT IN THE URBAN SOUTH.   NRUDWEM61134

NEGRO LABOR IN THE SOUTHERN CRYSTAL BALL. /EMPLOYMENT/   NRUTHKX49100

CUSTOMER REACTIONS TO THE INTEGRATION OF **NEGRO** SALES PERSONNEL.   NSAENGX50101

THE RELATION OF RACIAL SEGREGATION IN EARLY SCHOOLING TO THE LEVEL OF ASPIRATION AND ACADEMIC ACHIEVEMENT
OF **NEGRO** STUDENTS IN A NORTHERN HIGH SCHOOL.   NSAINJN62137

THE EFFECT OF SEGREGATION ON THE ASPIRATIONS OF **NEGRO** YOUTH.   NSAINJN66136

LIBRARY RESOURCES AND SERVICES IN WHITE AND **NEGRO** COLLEGES. /EDUCATION/   NSAMOTX65128

THE NORTH AMERICAN NEGRO. /DISCRIMINATION/   NSANCLA42537

NEGRO UNEMPLOYMENT -- WHAT CITY BUSINESSMEN ARE DOING ABOUT IT.   NSCHMJC64108

SOME ASPECTS OF VOCATIONAL ASPIRATIONS AND VALUE ORIENTATION AMONG NEGRO BOYS IN THE LOWER SOCIO-ECONOMIC CLASSES.   NSCHMWX63139

THE CULTURE OF UNEMPLOYMENT. SOME NOTES ON NEGRO CHILDREN.   NSCHWMX64110

NEGRO CAREER EXPECTATIONS.   NSEXTPX63117

NEGRO EMPLOYMENT.   NSHAFHB59118

A STUDY OF FARM MANAGEMENT PRACTICES ON 100 NEGRO FARMS IN MACON COUNTY, ALABAMA, 1949.   NSHAWBJ50339

POVERTY AND THE NEGRO.   NSHEPHL65127

THE INFLUENCE OF TUSKEGEE-INSTITUTE ON THE HEALTH, EDUCATIONAL, ECONOMIC, AND POLITICAL ASPECTS OF THE NEGRO POPULATION OF MACON COUNTY, ALABAMA.   NSHIEAR51342

THE TESTING OF NEGRO INTELLIGENCE.   NSHUEAX66145

EMPLOYMENT EXPERIENCES OF NEGRO PHILADELPHIANS. A DESCRIPTIVE STUDY OF THE EMPLOYMENT EXPERIENCES, PERCEPTIONS, AND ASPIRATIONS OF SELECTED PHILADELPHIA WHITES AND NON-WHITES.   NSIEGAI59718

ON THE COST OF BEING A NEGRO. /INCOME EDUCATION/   NSIEGPM65146

THE CITY AND THE NEGRO.   NSILBCE62134

THE BUSINESSMAN AND THE NEGRO. /INDUSTRY/   NSILBCE63133

THE ECONOMICS OF THE NEGRO PROBLEM.   NSILBCE64137

THE STRUGGLE FOR JOBS AND FOR NEGRO RIGHTS IN THE TRADE UNIONS.   NSIMOHX50139

SOCIAL CHARACTERISTICS OF HIGH SCHOOL SENIORS IN URBAN NEGRO HIGH SCHOOLS IN TWO STATES.   NSMITBF56147

THE DISAPPEARING NEGRO FARMER OF FLORIDA, 1920-1950.   NSMITCU56364

ON BEING A NEGRO IN 1960. /OCCUPATIONAL-STATUS/   NSMITCU60275

THE CHANGING NUMBER AND DISTRIBUTION OF THE AGED NEGRO POPULATION OF THE UNITED STATES. /DEMOGRAPHY/   NSMITLT58145

THE NEGRO COMMUNITY AND THE DEVELOPMENT OF NEGRO POTENTIAL.   NSMUTRW57146

THE NEGRO COMMUNITY AND THE DEVELOPMENT OF NEGRO POTENTIAL.   NSMUTRW57146

THE GENERAL CONDITION OF THE ALABAMA NEGRO.   NSNCCXX65187

THE NEGRO IN THE ST-LOUIS ECONOMY. /MISSOURI/   NSOBEIX54178

PERSONAL AND ON-THE-JOB CHARACTERISTICS RELATED TO NEGRO PERCEPTIONS OF DISCRIMINATION.   NSOLDHX56152

OCCUPATIONAL PRESTIGE IN A NEGRO COMMUNITY.   NSOLZRX61153

RIOTS, GHETTOS AND THE NEGRO REVOLT.   NSOSKWX67154

ECONOMIC VALUE OF THE NEGRO TO THE SOUTH. PAST, PRESENT, AND POTENTIAL.   NSOUTRC45158

HOUSTON -- THE NEGRO AND EMPLOYMENT OPPORTUNITIES IN THE SOUTH, THE FIRST OF A SERIES OF EMPLOYMENT STUDIES IN SOUTHERN CITIES. /TEXAS/   NSOUTRC61161

THE NEGRO AND EMPLOYMENT OPPORTUNITIES IN THE SOUTH.   NSOUTRC62151

ATLANTA -- THE NEGRO AND EMPLOYMENT OPPORTUNITIES IN THE SOUTH, THE THIRD OF A SERIES OF EMPLOYMENT STUDIES IN SOUTHERN CITIES. /GEORGIA/   NSOUTRC62155

CHATTANOOGA -- THE NEGRO AND EMPLOYMENT OPPORTUNITIES IN THE SOUTH, THE SECOND OF A SERIES OF EMPLOYMENT STUDIES IN SOUTHERN CITIES. /TENNESSEE/   NSOUTRC62156

A STUDY OF NEGRO FARMERS IN SOUTH-CAROLINA.   NSOUTRC62165

RACIAL WORK AND NEGRO WASTE IN SOUTHERN EMPLOYMENT.   NSCUTRC62300

ACCULTURATION AND NEGRO BLUE-COLLAR WORKERS.   NSTAMRX64171

SOUTHERN CITIES EMPLOYING NEGRO POLICEMEN -- INCLUDING NORTH-CAROLINA CITIES OVER 15,000 POPULATION.   NSTEEDL46173

THE POVERTY-DEPENDENCY SYNDROME OF THE ADC FEMALE-BASED NEGRO FAMILY.   NSTROFL64074

MIGRATION, MOBILITY, AND THE ASSIMILATION OF THE NEGRO.   NTAEUIB58363

IS THE NEGRO AN IMMIGRANT GROUP.   NTAEUKE63195

THE NEGRO AS AN IMMIGRANT GROUP. RECENT TRENDS IN RACIAL AND ETHNIC SEGREGATION IN CHICAGO. /ILLINOIS/   NTAEUKE64196

THE CHANGING CHARACTER OF NEGRO MIGRATION. /DEMOGRAPHY/   NTAEUKE65194

THE NEGRO POPULATION IN THE UNITED STATES. /DEMOGRAPHY/   NTAEUKE65198

CAREER PATTERNS OF TEACHERS IN NEGRO COLLEGES.   NTHOMDC58204

THE NEGRO LEADERSHIP CLASS.   NTHOMDC63713

NEGRO WORKER LIFTS HIS SIGHTS. /ASPIRATIONS/   NTHOMJA462C2

ON IMPROVING THE ECONOMIC STATUS OF THE NEGRO.   NTOBIJX65206

FULL EMPLOYMENT AND THE NEGRO WORKER.   NTOWNWS45162

THE ROLE OF THE COUNSELOR IN THE GUIDANCE OF NEGRO STUDENTS.   NTRUEDL60208

THE NEGRO POPULATION IN DULUTH MINNESOTA, 1950. /DEMOGRAPHY/   NTURBGX52210

OCCUPATIONAL CHOICES OF NEGRO HIGH SCHOOL SENIORS IN TEXAS.   NTURNBA57165

THE RELATIVE POSITION OF THE NEGRO MALE IN THE LABOR-FORCE OF LARGE AMERICAN CITIES.   NTURNRH51217

NEGRO JOB STATUS AND EDUCATION.   NTURNRH53213

THE NEW NEGRO. /UNION/   NTYLEGX67221

UTILIZATION OF NEGRO MANPOWER.   NUSDDEF59239

INTEGRATION AND THE NEGRO OFFICER IN THE ARMED FORCES OF THE UNITED STATES OF AMERICA. /MILITARY/   NUSDDEF62240

THE NEGRO IN THE WEST. SOME FACTS RELATING TO SOCIAL AND ECONOMIC CONDITIONS. NO 1. THE NEGRO WORKER.   NUSDLABND256

THE NEGRO IN THE WEST. SOME FACTS RELATING TO SOCIAL AND ECONOMIC CONDITIONS. NO 1. THE NEGRO WORKER.   NUSDLABND256

NEGRO WORKERS AND THE NATIONAL DEFENSE PROGRAM.   NUSDLAB41253

EQUAL-PAY FOR WHITE AND NEGRO TEACHERS. /OCCUPATIONS/   NUSDLAB41817

NEGRO PARTICIPATION IN DEFENSE WORK.   NUSDLAB41829

NEGRO EMPLOYMENT IN AIRPLANE PLANTS. /INDUSTRY/   NUSDLAB43827

OCCUPATIONAL STATUS OF NEGRO RAILROAD WORKERS.   NUSDLAB43836

VOCATIONAL EDUCATION FOR NEGRO YOUTH IN TEXAS.   NUSDLAB49847

A LABOR UNIT FOR NEGRO RIGHTS.   NUSDLAB52148

NEGRO EMPLOYMENT IN THREE COMPANIES IN THE NEW-ORLEANS AREA. /CASE-STUDY LOUISIANA/   NUSDLAB55828

THE NEGRO WAGE-EARNER AND APPRENTICESHIP TRAINING PROGRAMS.   NUSDLAB60249

LABOR MONTH IN REVIEW. NEGRO UNEMPLOYMENT.   NUSDLAB63823

NEGRO EMPLOYMENT IN 1965.   NUSDLAB65247

BIBLIOGRAPHY ON THE ECONOMIC-STATUS OF THE NEGRO.   NUSDLAB65254

FACULTY EDUCATION AND INCOME IN NEGRO AND WHITE COLLEGES.   NUSDLAB65819

THE UNITED STATES EMPLOYMENT SERVICE AND THE NEGRO WORK APPLICANT.   NUSWAMC44276

OCCUPATIONAL ASPIRATIONS OF NEGRO MALE HIGH SCHOOL STUDENTS.   NUZELOX61278

SOCIAL AND ECONOMIC IMPLICATIONS OF MIGRATION FOR THE NEGRO IN THE PRESENT SOCIAL ORDER.   NVALIPX42261

THE MENTALITIES OF NEGRO AND WHITE WORKERS. AN EXPERIMENTAL SCHOOL-S INTERPRETATION OF NEGRO TRADE
UNIONISM.   NVALIPX49280

THE MENTALITIES OF NEGRO AND WHITE WORKERS. AN EXPERIMENTAL SCHOOL-S INTERPRETATION OF NEGRO TRADE
UNIONISM.   NVALIPX49280

A REPORT ON COMMUNITY FACTORS IN NASHVILLE RELATED TO THE NEGRO IN MEDICINE. /TENNESSEE/   NVALIPX56281

DEMOGRAPHIC CHARACTERISTICS OF THE NEGRO POPULATION IN THE UNITED STATES.   NVALIPX63279

THE NEGRO AND DISCRIMINATION IN EMPLOYMENT.   NWACHDD65288

THE SITUATION OF THE NEGRO IN THE U.S.   NWAGECW57290

CHANGE IN THE STATUS OF THE NEGRO IN AMERICAN SOCIETY.   NWALKHJ57291

NORTH-CAROLINA AND THE NEGRO.   NWAYNCM64295

A STUDY OF SOME ASPECTS OF JOB SATISFACTION AMONG NEGRO WHITE-COLLAR WORKERS.   NWEATMD54296

THE ROLE OF THE NEGRO COLLEGE.   NWEAVEK44297

DEFENSE INDUSTRIES AND THE NEGRO.   NWEAVRC42552

THE EMPLOYMENT OF THE NEGRO IN WAR INDUSTRIES.   NWEAVRC43225

THE NEGRO COMES OF AGE IN INDUSTRY.   NWEAVRC43301

RECENT EVENTS IN NEGRO UNION RELATIONSHIPS.   NWEAVRC44306

NEGRO EMPLOYMENT IN THE AIRCRAFT INDUSTRY.   NWEAVRC45302

NEGRO LABOR. A NATIONAL PROBLEM.   NWEAVRC46304

THE NEGRO GHETTO.   NWEAVRC48303

NEGRO LABOR SINCE 1929.   NWEAVRC50305

THE CHANGING STRUCTURE OF THE AMERICAN CITY AND THE NEGRO.   NWEAVRC64299

PREJUDICE IS NOT THE WHOLE STORY. EXAMINATION OF THREE CASES OF NEGRO UPGRADING IN TRACTION COMPANIES IN
PHILADELPHIA. LOS-ANGELES AND CHICAGO. /PENNSYLVANIA CALIFORNIA ILLINOIS/   NWECKJE45308

THE NEGRO IN THE ARMED FORCES. /MILITARY/   NWEILFD47309

THE NEGRO IN THE US. A RESEARCH GUIDE.   NWELSEK65304

NEGRO EMPLOYMENT PRACTICES IN THE CHATTANOOGA AREA. /TENNESSEE/   NWESSWH55314

A SURVEY OF EMPLOYMENT OPPORTUNITIES AS THEY RELATE TO THE NEGRO IN NEW-ROCHELLE, NEW-YORK, 1955.   NWESTCU55316

SUMMARY OF RESEARCH DURING 1964 RELATED TO THE NEGRO AND NEGRO EDUCATION.   NWESTEX66315

SUMMARY OF RESEARCH DURING 1964 RELATED TO THE NEGRO AND NEGRO EDUCATION.   NWESTEX66315

SHOWING THE WAY IN PREPARING NEGRO JOBSEEKERS.   NWESTZJ66317

POVERTY AREAS OF OUR MAJOR CITIES. THE EMPLOYMENT SITUATION OF NEGRO AND WHITE WORKERS IN METROPOLITAN
AREAS COMPARED IN A SPECIAL LABOR-FORCE REPORT.   NWETZJR66114

THE PLACEMENT OF NEGRO COLLEGE GRADUATES IN BUSINESS ORGANIZATIONS.   NWHITEW64321

COMPARATIVE STUDY OF SOCIO-ECONOMIC AND SOCIAL-PSYCHOLOGICAL DETERMINANTS OF EDUCATIONAL AND OCCUPATIONAL

NEGRO   (CONTINUATION)
ASPIRATIONS OF NEGRO AND WHITE COLLEGE SENIORS.   NWHITRM59319

THE NEGRO ENTREPRENEUR.   NWHITWL66320

WHAT THE NEGRO THINKS OF THE ARMY. /MILITARY/   NWHITWX42465

THE VOCATIONAL GUIDANCE AND EDUCATION OF NEGROES. THE NEGRO AND THE BATTLE OF PRODUCTION.   NWILKDA42233

PLACING THE NEGRO WORKER.   NWILKWH41323

A CRITICAL APPRAISAL OF PROFESSION TRAINING OF NEGRO TEACHERS IN OKTIBBEHA COUNTY MISSISSIPPI.   NWILLMM50234

WHO NEEDS THE NEGRO. /OCCUPATIONAL-STATUS TECHNOLOGICAL-CHANGE/   NWILLSM64232

AUTOMATION AND THE NEGRO. WILL WE SURVIVE.   NWILSCE65326

WHITE EMPLOYERS AND NEGRO WORKERS.   NWILSLX43327

NEGRO FAMILIES IN RURAL WISCONSIN. A STUDY OF THEIR COMMUNITY LIFE.   NWISCGC59331

EDUCATION-S CHALLENGE TO AMERICAN NEGRO YOUTH.   NWOLFDP62336

WHAT THE ECONOMIC-OPPORTUNITY-ACT MEANS TO THE NEGRO.   NWOLFDP65337

POSTWAR TRENDS IN NEGRO EMPLOYMENT.   NWOLFSL47334

NEGRO MALE IDENTIFICATION PROBLEMS.   NWOROIX62341

AFTER HIGH SCHOOL WHAT...HIGHLIGHTS OF A STUDY OF CAREER PLANS OF NEGRO AND WHITE RURAL YOUTH IN THREE
FLORIDA COUNTIES. /ASPIRATIONS/   NYOUMEG65390

NEGRO ENTREPRENEURSHIP IN SOUTHERN ECONOMIC DEVELOPMENT.   NYOUNHB64346

SOME SOCIOLOGICAL ASPECTS OF VOCATIONAL GUIDANCE OF NEGRO CHILDREN.   NYOUNMN44348

THE NEGRO REVOLT.   NYOUNWM63352

THE INTERMINGLED REVOLUTIONS -- THE NEGRO AND AUTOMATION.   NYOUNWM64299

SURVEY OF NEGRO ATTITUDES TOWARD LAW.   NZEITLX65359

ARE NEGRO SCHOOLS OF NURSING NEEDED TODAY.   WCARNME64910

EXPERIENCES OF NEGRO HIGH SCHOOL GIRLS WITH DOMESTIC PLACEMENT AGENCIES. /HOUSEHOLD-WORKERS/   WRUSSRD62135

NEGRO-AMERICAN
TRANSFORMATION OF THE NEGRO-AMERICAN. /EDUCATION EMPLOYMENT INCOME/   NBROOLX65123

A FIVE-CITY SURVEY OF NEGRO-AMERICAN EMPLOYEES OF THE FEDERAL GOVERNMENT.   NPRESCP57017

NEGRO-AMERICANS
TRENDS IN THE EMPLOYMENT OF NEGRO-AMERICANS IN UPPER-LEVEL WHITE-COLLAR POSITIONS OF THE FEDERAL
GOVERNMENT.   GPRESCP60200

NEGRO-LABOR
DEVELOPMENTS IN THE NEGRO-LABOR ALLIANCE. /UNION/   NSTROEK56185

NEGRO-OWNED
THE CENSUS OF NEGRO-OWNED BUSINESSES. /PHILADELPHIA PENNSYLVANIA OCCUPATIONS/   NDREXIT64295

NEGRO-S
IS EQUALITY UNFAIR. NEGRO-S PLEA FOR PREFERENTIAL-TREATMENT.   NAMERXX63008

THE NEGRO-S PLACE AT LABOR-S TABLE. /UNION/   NBROOTX62122

THE NEGRO-S FORCE IN MARKETPLACE. /EMPLOYMENT/   NBUSIWX62156

THE NEGRO-S CHANGING PLACE IN SOUTHERN AGRICULTURE.   NCHRIDE58206

NEGRO-S REAL PROBLEM. /DISCRIMINATION/   NGISSIX65418

THE NEGRO-S FUTURE THROUGH FAIR-EMPLOYMENT-PRACTICES.   NHODGEN62557

THE NEGRO-S NEW ECONOMIC LIFE.   NHUGHEJ56583

THE NEGRO-S MIDDLE-CLASS DREAM.   NLINCCE64695

EMPLOYMENT ON MERIT. THE CONTINUING CHALLENGE TO BUSINESS. NEGRO-S ECONOMIC LOT.   NMORRJJ57854

THE NEGRO-S JOURNEY TO THE CITY -- PART I.   NNEWMDK65908

THE NEGRO-S JOURNEY TO THE CITY -- PART II.   NNEWMDK65909

NEGRO-S SEARCH FOR A BETTER JOB.   NNEWSXX64913

THE NEGRO-S ADVENTURE IN GENERAL BUSINESS.   NOAKXVV49952

THE NEGRO-S OCCUPATIONAL PROGRESS.   NRUSSJL66096

THE NEGRO-S SHARE.   NSTERRX43179

WITH THE NEGRO-S HELP.   NWEAVRC42307

THE NEGRO-S PARTICIPATION IN AMERICAN BUSINESS.   NYOUNHB63347

NEGRO-UNION
THE ROOTS OF THE NEGRO-UNION ALLIANCE. /UNION/   NMARSRX66746

NEGRO-WHITE
THE NEGRO-WHITE PROBLEM. WHAT CAN THE UNIONS DO ABOUT IT.   NCATHDX57186

THE LIMITED POTENTIAL FOR NEGRO-WHITE JOB EQUALITY.   NCHALWE65188

SOCIAL INFLUENCES IN NEGRO-WHITE INTELLIGENCE DIFFERENCES.   NDEUTMX64268

THE ANATOMY OF THE NEGRO-WHITE INCOME DIFFERENTIAL.   NGALLLE65391

SOME COMPARISONS AMONG NEGRO-WHITE COLLEGE STUDENTS. SOCIAL AMBITION AND ESTIMATED SOCIAL MOBILITY.   NHARREE66786

NEGROES   (CONTINUATION)
NEGROES IN AMERICAN SOCIETY.   NDAVIMR49252

NEGROES AND THE SERVICE INDUSTRIES. /OCCUPATIONS/   NDIAMOE64272

WHY SHOULD NEGROES WORK. /ASPIRATIONS/   NDIZAJE66015

NEGROES AND THE LABOR MOVEMENT. RECORD OF THE LEFT WING UNIONS.   NOOYLWX62287

COMPARATIVE PSYCHOLOGICAL STUDIES OF NEGROES AND WHITES IN THE UNITED STATES.   NDREGRM60292

RECENT RESEARCH IN PSYCHOLOGICAL COMPARISONS OF NEGROES AND WHITES IN THE UNITED STATES.   NDREGRM65293

DUAL PARTS OF DESEGREGATION, LEGISLATION TO EDUCATE AND TRAIN NEGROES FOR BETTER JOBS.   NDUSCJX63311

ETHNIC AND CLASS PREFERENCES AMONG COLLEGE NEGROES.   NEBOIAX60315

NEW HOPE FOR RURAL DIXIE. FIRMS IN CAROLINAS CREATE JOBS FOR NEGROES.   NEBONXX64317

NEW JOBS FOR NEGROES.   NEDELHX66320

SELECTING AND TRAINING NEGROES FOR MANAGERIAL POSITIONS.   NEDUCTS64322

NEGROES. VOCATIONAL GUIDANCE AND COUNSELING IN THE SOUTHERN FIELD.   NEDWAGL47325

THE HIGHER EDUCATION OF NEGROES IN THE UNITED STATES.   NEELLWC55329

MINORITY-GROUP ATTITUDES OF NEGROES AND IMPLICATIONS FOR GUIDANCE.   NENGLWH57333

THE NEGROES WHO DO NOT WANT TO END SEGREGATION. /EMPLOYMENT/   NFAGGHL55255

THE TECHNIQUE OF INTRODUCING NEGROES INTO THE PLANT. /INDUSTRY/   NFELDHX42351

PROBLEMS AND OPPORTUNITIES CONFRONTING NEGROES IN THE FIELD OF BUSINESS, REPORT ON THE NATIONAL
CONFERENCE ON SMALL BUSINESS. /OCCUPATIONS/   NFITZNH63358

FORTUNE PRESS ANALYSIS, NEGROES. /EMPLOYMENT/   NFORTUN45052

THE NEGROES WAR.   NFORTXX42541

THE CULTURAL-BACKGROUND OF SOUTHERN NEGROES.   NFRAZEF57378

WHEN NEGROES MARCH. THE MARCH-ON-WASHINGTON-MOVEMENT IN THE ORGANIZATIONAL POLITICS FOR FEPC.   NGARFHX59396

AT WORK IN INDUSTRY TODAY. 50 CASE-REPORTS ON NEGROES AT WORK.   NGENEEX64398

OCCUPATIONAL DIFFERENTIATION OF NEGROES AND WHITES IN THE UNITED STATES.   NGIBBJP65401

THE NEGROES.   NGLAZNX63420

CHANGES IN THE AMERICAN OCCUPATIONAL-STRUCTURE AND OCCUPATIONAL GAINS OF NEGROES DURING THE 1940-S.   NGLENND62422

OCCUPATIONAL BENEFITS TO WHITES FROM THE SUBORDINATION OF NEGROES. /DISCRIMINATION/   NGLENND63423

NEGROES AND JOBS.   NGOLDNX66428

THE WAR-TIME EMPLOYMENT OF NEGROES IN THE FEDERAL-GOVERNMENT.   NGOLICL45432

NEGROES AND WAR PRODUCTION.   NGRANLB42444

NEGROES IN FIVE NEW-YORK CITIES. A STUDY OF PROBLEMS, ACHIEVEMENTS AND TRENDS. /RACE-RELATIONS/   NGRIEES58455

EFFECTS OF ON-THE-JOB EXPERIENCE WITH NEGROES UPON RACIAL ATTITUDES OF WHITE WORKERS IN UNION SHOPS. NGUNDRH50466

RECENT TRENDS IN THE OCCUPATIONAL MOBILITY OF NEGROES, 1930-1960.   NHARENX65484

EFFECTS OF AUTOMATION ON THE POSITION OF NEGROES IN A SOUTHERN INDUSTRIAL PLANT.   NHARTJW64495

A STUDY OF THE EFFECTS OF EFFORTS TO IMPROVE EMPLOYMENT-OPPORTUNITIES OF NEGROES ON THE UTILIZATION OF
NEGRO WORKERS.   NHARTJW64496

PICKETING BY NEGROES TO OBTAIN EMPLOYMENT IN PROPORTION TO NEGRO CUSTOMERS HELD UNLAWFUL.   NHARVLR49498

A CENTURY OF CHANGE. NEGROES IN THE US ECONOMY, 1860-1960. /OCCUPATIONAL-PATTERNS/   NHAYEMX62506

PREFERENTIAL-TREATMENT FOR NEGROES.   NHECHFM64509

NEGROES IN THE GOVERNMENT EMPLOYMENT.   NHENDEW43510

THE ECONOMIC IMBALANCE. AN INQUIRY INTO THE ECONOMIC-STATUS OF NEGROES IN THE UNITED STATES, 1935-1960,
WITH IMPLICATIONS FOR NEGRO EDUCATION.   NHENDVW60512

EMPLOYMENT OPPORTUNITIES FOR NASHVILLE NEGROES. /TENNESSEE/   NHENDVW60516

THE ECONOMIC-STATUS OF NEGROES. IN THE NATION AND IN THE SOUTH.   NHENDVW63515

THE PATTERN OF JOB DISCRIMINATION AGAINST NEGROES.   NHILLHX65536

OCCUPATIONAL MOBILITY AND ATTITUDES TOWARD NEGROES.   NHODGRWND355

INDUSTRIAL INTEGRATION OF NEGROES. THE UPGRADING PROCESS.   NHOPEJX52571

THE EMPLOYMENT OF NEGROES IN THE US BY MAJOR OCCUPATION AND INDUSTRY.   NHOPEJX53567

THE PROBLEM OF UNEMPLOYMENT AS IT RELATES TO NEGROES.   NHOPEJX60573

THE POST-WAR INDUSTRIAL OUTLOOK FOR NEGROES.   NHOWAUG44579

NO MORE COUSIN TOMS. THE CLASH BETWEEN THE UNIONS AND THE NEGROES.   NJACOPX63602

THE UPPER LIMIT OF ABILITY AMONG AMERICAN NEGROES.   NJENKMD48607

REVIEW OF EVIDENCE RELATING TO EFFECTS OF DESEGREGATION ON THE INTELLECTUAL PERFORMANCE OF NEGROES.   NKATZIX64637

A STUDY OF THE EMPLOYMENT OPPORTUNITIES FOR NEGROES IN BREWERIES OF THE UNITED STATES. /INDUSTRY/   NKERNJH51897

OPPORTUNITIES FOR NEGROES IN ENGINEERING. /OCCUPATIONS/   NKIEHRX58648

OPPORTUNITIES FOR NEGROES IN ENGINEERING -- A SECOND REPORT. /OCCUPATIONS/   NKIEHRX64333

NEGROES IN A CHANGING LABOR-MARKET. /UNEMPLOYMENT/   NKILLCC67653

OFFICIAL ADVICE ON EMPLOYING NEGROES.   NLABORR42030

THE EMPLOYMENT OF NEGROES IN PUBLIC WELFARE IN ELEVEN SOUTHERN STATES, 1936-1949. /OCCUPATIONS/   NLARKJR52672

CONFLICT RESPONSE. DETROIT NEGROES FACE UNEMPLOYMENT. /MICHIGAN/   NLEGGJC59678

ECONOMIC DEPRIVATION AND EXTREMISM. A STUDY OF UNEMPLOYED NEGROES.   NLEGGJC61680

ECONOMIC CRISIS AND EXPECTATIONS OF VIOLENCE. A STUDY OF UNEMPLOYED NEGROES .   NLEGGJC64679

HAVE FAIR-EMPLOYMENT-PRACTICES-COMMISSION LAWS INCREASED OPPORTUNITIES FOR NEGROES.   NLETTHA50683

SOME CORRELATES OF ANOMIE AMONG RURAL NEGROES.   NLEWICE66688

PROGRESS IN INTERRACIAL RELATIONSHIPS. INEQUALITIES FOR NEGROES.   NLEWIES43689

HIGHER EDUCATION FOR NEGROES. A TOUGH SITUATION.   NLEWIHX49692

CULTURE, CLASS AND FAMILY LIFE AMONG LOW-INCOME NEGROES.   NLEWIHX67691

NEGROES AND THE LABOR MOVEMENT -- AN EXCHANGE.   NLIPSSM62043

EDUCATIONAL CHANGES AFFECTING AMERICAN NEGROES.   NLOGARW64704

BRICKS WITHOUT STRAW. STUDIES OF COMMUNITY UNEMPLOYMENT PROBLEMS, THE NEGROES DILEMMA. /LOUISVILLE
KENTUCKY/   NLOUIHR64715

FAMILY PATTERNS, ACHIEVEMENTS, AND ASPIRATIONS OF URBAN NEGROES.   NLYSTMH61718

THE IMPORTANCE OF CONTACT IN DETERMINING ATTITUDES TOWARD NEGROES.   NMACKBK48488

SOME ATTITUDES TOWARD EMPLOYING NEGROES AS TEACHERS IN A NORTHERN UNIVERSITY.   NMARCFL48054

FACILITATIVE AND INHIBITIVE FACTORS IN TRAINING PROGRAM RECRUITMENT AMONG RURAL NEGROES.   NMARSCP65738

SOME FACTORS INFLUENCING THE UPGRADING OF NEGROES IN THE SOUTHERN PETROLEUM REFINING INDUSTRY.
/CASE-STUDY/   NMARSRX63748

REPORT OF THE COMMISSION ON THE EMPLOYMENT PROBLEMS OF NEGROES TO GOVERNOR SALTONSTALL. /MASSACHUSETTS/   NMASSCE42757

FROM PLANTATION TO GHETTO. AN INTERPRETIVE HISTORY OF AMERICAN NEGROES.   NMEIEAX66765

RECENT TRENDS IN THE ECONOMIC-STATUS OF NEGROES.   NMILLHP63785

MAJOR POLITICAL ISSUES WHICH DIRECTLY CONCERN NEGROES.   NMILLJE48250

EMPLOYMENT AS IT RELATES TO NEGROES IN THE MILWAUKEE INDUSTRIAL AREA. /WISCONSIN/   NMILWUL48793

RAILWAY LABOR ACT -- DENIAL OF UNION MEMBERSHIP TO NEGROES.   NMINNLR58800

REPRESENTATION OF NEGROES AND WHITES AS EMPLOYEES IN THE FEDERAL PRISON SYSTEM.   NMORGGD62849

AMERICAN NEGROES -- A WASTED RESOURCE. /INDUSTRY/   NMORRJJ57853

BEHIND LOS-ANGELES. JOB-LESS NEGROES AND THE BOOM. /UNEMPLOYMENT CALIFORNIA/   NMOYNDP65860

NEGROES IN MEDICINE. /OCCUPATIONS/   NNATLMF52877

NEW OPPORTUNITIES FOR NEGROES IN MEDICINE. /OCCUPATIONS/   NNATLMF62878

INTEGRATION OF NEGROES IN DEPARTMENT STORES.   NNATLUL46891

NEGROES AND THE BUILDING TRADES UNION.   NNATLUL57902

JOBS FOR NEGROES. HOW MUCH PROGRESS IN SIGHT.   NNEWSXX63912

NEGROES AND THE LABOR MOVEMENT. /UNION/   NNEWXPX62910

THE EMPLOYMENT OF NEGROES AS DRIVER SALESMEN IN THE BAKING INDUSTRY.   NNEWYSA60919

AT WORK IN NORTH-CAROLINA TODAY. 48 CASE-REPORTS ON NORTH-CAROLINA NEGROES NOW EMPLOYED OR PREPARING
THEMSELVES FOR EMPLOYMENT...THEIR EDUCATION, JOB QUALIFICATIONS, AND CAREER ASPIRATIONS.   NNORTCGND933

NEGROES IN A WAR INDUSTRY. THE CASE OF SHIPBUILDING.   NNCRTHR43942

WILL NEGROES GET JOBS NOW.   NNCRTHR45948

THE INTELLIGENCE OF AMERICAN NEGROES.   NNORTRD56935

SOME CORRELATES OF HIGH NEED FOR ACHIEVEMENT AMONG URBAN NORTHERN NEGROES.   NNUTTRL46951

AN HISTORICAL SURVEY AND ANALYSIS OF THE PROGRESS OF NEGROES IN PUBLIC-SERVICE 1932-1952.   NOLIVLW56955

THE CONTROVERSY OVER EQUAL-RIGHTS FOR NEGROES.   NOPINRC56956

HIRING NEGROES FOR BETTER JOBS. EXPERIENCE OF LEADING COMPANIES. /INDUSTRY/   NOPINRC64957

NEWARK. NEGROES MOVE TOWARD POWER. /NEW-JERSEY/   NOSHEJX65965

THE INTRODUCTION OF NEGROES INTO WHITE DEPARTMENTS. /CASE-STUDY INDUSTRY/   NPALMER55972

STATUS OF NEGROES IN CRAFT UNIONS...PITTSBURGH LABOR-MARKET. /PENNSYLVANIA/   NPITTMC65002

CHANGING EMPLOYMENT PATTERNS OF NEGROES, 1920-1950.   NPRESHB62125

COMPANY EXPERIENCE WITH THE EMPLOYMENT OF NEGROES. /INDUSTRY/   NPRINUI54020

COMBATING DISCRIMINATION IN THE EMPLOYMENT OF NEGROES IN WAR INDUSTRIES AND GOVERNMENT AGENCIES. NRAMSLA43128

DISCRIMINATION AND THE OCCUPATIONAL PROGRESS OF NEGROES.   NRAYAEX61040

NEGROES IN THE CALIFORNIA AGRICULTURAL LABOR-FORCE.   NRECOCW59042

NEGROES IN THE UNITED STATES. THEIR EMPLOYMENT AND ECONOMIC STATUS.   NRINGHH53061

NEGROES ARE MOVING UP THE JOB LADDER.   NROSSIX63087

NEGROES   (CONTINUATION)
ARE NEGROES READY FOR EQUALITY.   NROWACT60090

MIGRATION PATTERNS OF NEGROES FROM A RURAL NORTHEASTERN MISSISSIPPI COMMUNITY. /DEMOGRAPHY/   NRUBIMX60094

NEGROES IN THE WORK GROUP. HOW 33 BUSINESS AND INDUSTRIAL FIRMS OFFERED EQUAL-EMPLOYMENT-OPPORTUNITIES TO
ALL.   NSEIDJX50114

NEGROES IN THE NORTH.   NSHAFHB65799

CIVIL-RIGHTS. EMPLOYMENT. AND THE SOCIAL STATUS OF AMERICAN NEGROES.   NSHEPHL66129

JOBS FOR NEGROES. SOME NORTH-SOUTH PLANT STUDIES. /CASE-STUDY/   NSTEEEH53174

TRAINING OF NEGROES IN THE SKILLED-TRADES.   NSTEEHG54176

MORE SALARIED POSITIONS ARE OPENED TO NEGROES BY BUSINESS AND INDUSTRY HERE. /NEW-YORK/   NSTETOX63154

A BRIEF SURVEY OF HIGHER EDUCATION FOR NEGROES.   NSTOKMS64180

SO THE NEGROES WANT WORK. /UNION/   NSTREGX41462

NOTES ON THE CONDITIONS OF NEGROES. /EDUCATION DISCRIMINATION/   NSTREGX45463

INTERESTS OF NEGROES AND WHITES.   NSTROEK52186

NEGROES IN CITIES. /DEMOGRAPHY SEGREGATION/   NTAEUKE65197

DISCRIMINATION AGAINST NEGROES.   NTHOMPX43203

EMPLOYMENT GAINS AND THE DETERMINANTS OF THE OCCUPATIONAL DISTRIBUTION OF NEGROES.   NTHURLC67971

EMPLOYMENT PROBLEMS OF NEGROES IN MICHIGAN.   NUSDLAB41816

NEW TRAINING PLAN FOR NEGROES.   NUSDLAB41832

BI-RACIAL COOPERATION IN PLACEMENT OF NEGROES.   NUSDLAB42811

EMPLOYMENT OF NEGROES BY FEDERAL-GOVERNMENT.   NUSDLAB43818

TRAINING NEGROES FOR WAR WORK.   NUSDLAB43845

WAR LABOR BOARD DECISION ON WAGES OF NEGROES.   NUSDLAB43848

OCCUPATIONAL DISTRIBUTION OF NEGROES IN 1940.   NUSDLAB44835

IMPROVED CONDITIONS FOR NEGROES IN LOUISVILLE. /KENTUCKY/   NUSDLAB45820

NEGROES IN NEW-YORK CITY. OCCUPATIONAL DISTRIBUTION.   NUSDLAB49831

NEGROES IN APPRENTICESHIPS. NEW-YORK STATE.   NUSDLAB60830

CONFERENCE ON PROBLEMS IN EMPLOYMENT CONFRONTING NEGROES IN NEW-JERSEY, OCTOBER 18 1962.   NUSDLAB62242

THE ECONOMIC SITUATION OF NEGROES IN THE UNITED STATES.   NUSDLAB62243

EMPLOYMENT OF NEGROES BY GOVERNMENT-CONTRACTORS.   NUSDLAB64814

EMPLOYMENT OF NEGROES IN THE FEDERAL-GOVERNMENT, JUNE 1964.   NUSDLAB65815

THE EMPLOYMENT OF NEGROES. SOME DEMOGRAPHIC CONSIDERATIONS.   NUSDLAB66245

THE NEGROES IN THE UNITED STATES. THEIR ECONOMIC AND SOCIAL SITUATION.   NUSDLAB66257

NEGROES GO NORTH, WEST. JOBS TAKE THEM FAR AFIELD FROM THE SOUTH.   NUSNEWR51272

UNION BAN ON NEGROES UPHELD.   NUSNEWR57209

NEGROES. BIG ADVANCES IN JOBS, WEALTH, STATUS.   NUSNEWR58271

FOR NEGROES. MORE AND BETTER JOBS IN GOVERNMENT.   NUSNEWR62268

FORCED HIRING OF NEGROES.   NUSNEWR63207

JOBS FOR NEGROES -- IS THERE A REAL SHORTAGE.   NUSNEWR63269

UNIONS FEEL GROWING PRESSURE TO TAKE MORE NEGROES.   NUSNEWR64292

JOB RIGHTS FOR NEGROES -- PRESSURE ON EMPLOYERS.   NUSNEWR66270

NEW PUSH FOR HIRING OF NEGROES.   NUSNEWR66273

EMPLOYMENT AND THE ECONOMIC STATUS OF NEGROES IN THE UNITED STATES.   NUSSENA52333

EMPLOYMENT AND ECONOMIC STATUS OF NEGROES IN THE US.   NUSSENA54275

NEGROES IN SCIENCE. /OCCUPATIONS/   NVIORJX65284

SPECIAL REPORT. A SURVEY OF NEGROES EMPLOYED BY THE STATE OF WEST-VIRGINIA.   NVIRGHR64318

NEGROES ON THE SALES FORCE. THE QUIET INTEGRATION.   NVOGLAJ64286

THE POST-WAR OUTLOOK FOR NEGROES IN SMALL BUSINESS, THE ENGINEERING AND THE TECHNICAL VOCATIONS.   NWALKJO46580

EMPLOYMENT OF NEGROES IN UNITED STATES WAR INDUSTRIES.   NWEAVRC44300

SIGNIFICANT ACHIEVEMENTS OF NEGROES IN EDUCATION 1907-1947. /OCCUPATIONS/   NWHITMJ48249

THE OPPORTUNITIES FOR BUSINESS OWNERSHIP AMONG NEGROES.   NWHITWL66231

THE VOCATIONAL GUIDANCE AND EDUCATION OF NEGROES. THE NEGRO AND THE BATTLE OF PRODUCTION.   NWILKDA42233

WAR AND POSTWAR TRENDS IN EMPLOYMENT OF NEGROES.   NWOLFSL45335

PUTTING NEGROES ON A JOB-EQUALITY BASIS.   NWOODCA45339

THE ADJUSTMENT OF NEGROES IN A NORTHERN INDUSTRIAL COMMUNITY.   NZIMMBG62360

NEIGHBOR
TEXAS GOOD NEIGHBOR.   MSOUTSS62497

NEIGHBORHOOD
ACTION FOR EMPLOYMENT. A DEMONSTRATION NEIGHBORHOOD MANPOWER PROJECT.   GALLCTO66361

SOCIAL MOBILITY AND IMPUTATIONS OF WITCHCRAFT IN A MEXICAN-AMERICAN NEIGHBORHOOD OF TEXAS.   MRUBEAJ66467

THE ROLE OF ORGANIZATIONAL STRUCTURES. UNION VERSUS NEIGHBORHOOD IN A TENSION SITUATION.   NREITOC53050

THE VOICE OF THE GHETTO. A REPORT ON TWO BOSTON NEIGHBORHOOD MEETINGS. /MASSACHUSETTS/   NUSCOMC67149

NEIGHBORHOOD-YOUTH-C
ISSUES AND PROBLEMS IN INTEGRATING NEEDED SUPPORTIVE SERVICES IN NEIGHBORHOOD-YOUTH-CORPS PROJECTS.   GBATTMX66131

TEENAGE LABOR PROBLEMS AND THE NEIGHBORHOOD-YOUTH-CORPS.   GMOONJD66726

NEIGHBORHOODS
INCOME, EDUCATION AND UNEMPLOYMENT IN NEIGHBORHOODS. ATLANTA, GEORGIA. /DEMOGRAPHY/   CUSDLAB63451

INCOME, EDUCATION AND UNEMPLOYMENT IN NEIGHBORHOODS. BALTIMORE, MARYLAND. /DEMOGRAPHY/   CUSDLAB63452

INCOME, EDUCATION AND UNEMPLOYMENT IN NEIGHBORHOODS. BIRMINGHAM, ALABAMA. /DEMOGRAPHY/   CUSDLAB63453

INCOME, EDUCATION AND UNEMPLOYMENT IN NEIGHBORHOODS. BOSTON, MASSACHUSETTS. /DEMOGRAPHY/   CUSDLAB63454

INCOME, EDUCATION AND UNEMPLOYMENT IN NEIGHBORHOODS. BUFFALO, NEW-YORK. /DEMOGRAPHY/   CUSDLAB63455

INCOME, EDUCATION AND UNEMPLOYMENT IN NEIGHBORHOODS. CHICAGO, ILLINOIS. /DEMOGRAPHY/   CUSDLAB63456

INCOME, EDUCATION AND UNEMPLOYMENT IN NEIGHBORHOODS. CINCINNATI, OHIO. /DEMOGRAPHY/   CUSDLAB63457

INCOME, EDUCATION AND UNEMPLOYMENT IN NEIGHBORHOODS. CLEVELAND, OHIO. /CEMOGRAPHY/   CUSDLAB63458

INCOME, EDUCATION AND UNEMPLOYMENT IN NEIGHBORHOODS. DALLAS, TEXAS. /DEMOGRAPHY/   CUSDLAB63459

INCOME, EDUCATION AND UNEMPLOYMENT IN NEIGHBORHOODS. DENVER, COLORADO. /DEMOGRAPHY/   CUSDLAB63460

INCOME, EDUCATION AND UNEMPLOYMENT IN NEIGHBORHOODS. DETROIT, MICHIGAN. /DEMOGRAPHY/   CUSDLAB63461

INCOME, EDUCATION AND UNEMPLOYMENT IN NEIGHBORHOODS. HOUSTON, TEXAS. /DEMOGRAPHY/   CUSDLAB63462

INCOME, EDUCATION AND UNEMPLOYMENT IN NEIGHBORHOODS. INDIANAPOLIS, INDIANA. /DEMOGRAPHY/   CUSDLAB63463

INCOME, EDUCATION AND UNEMPLOYMENT IN NEIGHBORHOODS. KANSAS-CITY, MISSOURI. /DEMOGRAPHY/   CUSDLAB63464

INCOME, EDUCATION AND UNEMPLOYMENT IN NEIGHBORHOODS. MEMPHIS, TENNESSEE. /DEMOGRAPHY/   CUSDLAB63466

INCOME, EDUCATION AND UNEMPLOYMENT IN NEIGHBORHOODS. MILWAUKEE, WISCONSIN. /DEMOGRAPHY/   CUSDLAB63467

INCOME, EDUCATION AND UNEMPLOYMENT IN NEIGHBORHOODS. MINNEAPOLIS -- ST-PAUL, MINNESOTA. /DEMOGRAPHY/   CUSDLAB63468

INCOME, EDUCATION AND UNEMPLOYMENT IN NEIGHBORHOODS. NEW-ORLEANS, LOUISIANA. /DEMOGRAPHY/   CUSDLAB63469

INCOME, EDUCATION AND UNEMPLOYMENT IN NEIGHBORHOODS. NEWARK, NEW-JERSEY. /DEMOGRAPHY/   CUSDLAB63470

INCOME, EDUCATION AND UNEMPLOYMENT IN NEIGHBORHOODS. NEW-YORK-CITY -- BROOKLYN. /DEMOGRAPHY/   CUSDLAB63471

INCOME, EDUCATION AND UNEMPLOYMENT IN NEIGHBORHOODS. NEW-YORK-CITY -- THE BRONX. /DEMOGRAPHY/   CUSDLAB63472

INCOME, EDUCATION AND UNEMPLOYMENT IN NEIGHBORHOODS. NEW-YORK-CITY -- MANHATTAN. /DEMOGRAPHY/   CUSDLAB63473

INCOME, EDUCATION AND UNEMPLOYMENT IN NEIGHBORHOODS. NEW-YORK-CITY -- QUEENS. /DEMOGRAPHY/   CUSDLAB63474

INCOME, EDUCATION AND UNEMPLOYMENT IN NEIGHBORHOODS. NEW-YORK-CITY -- STATEN-ISLAND. /DEMOGRAPHY/   CUSDLAB63475

INCOME, EDUCATION AND UNEMPLOYMENT IN NEIGHBORHOODS. OAKLAND, CALIFORNIA. /DEMOGRAPHY/   CUSDLAB63476

INCOME, EDUCATION AND UNEMPLOYMENT IN NEIGHBORHOODS. OKLAHOMA-CITY, OKLAHOMA. /DEMOGRAPHY/   CUSDLAB63477

INCOME, EDUCATION AND UNEMPLOYMENT IN NEIGHBORHOODS. PHILADELPHIA, PENNSYLVANIA. /DEMOGRAPHY/   CUSDLAB63478

INCOME, EDUCATION AND UNEMPLOYMENT IN NEIGHBORHOODS. PITTSBURGH, PENNSYLVANIA. /DEMOGRAPHY/   CUSDLAB63479

INCOME, EDUCATION AND UNEMPLOYMENT IN NEIGHBORHOODS. PHOENIX, ARIZONA. /DEMOGRAPHY/   CUSDLAB63480

INCOME, EDUCATION AND UNEMPLOYMENT IN NEIGHBORHOODS. ST-LOUIS, MISSOURI. /DEMOGRAPHY/   CUSDLAB63481

INCOME, EDUCATION AND UNEMPLOYMENT IN NEIGHBORHOODS. SAN-ANTONIO, TEXAS. /DEMOGRAPHY/   CUSDLAB63482

INCOME, EDUCATION AND UNEMPLOYMENT IN NEIGHBORHOODS. SAN-DIEGO, CALIFORNIA. /DEMOGRAPHY/   CUSDLAB63483

INCOME, EDUCATION AND UNEMPLOYMENT IN NEIGHBORHOODS. SAN-FRANCISCO, CALIFORNIA. /DEMOGRAPHY/   CUSDLAB63484

INCOME, EDUCATION AND UNEMPLOYMENT IN NEIGHBORHOODS. SEATTLE, WASHINGTON. /DEMOGRAPHY/   CUSDLAB63485

INCOME, EDUCATION AND UNEMPLOYMENT IN NEIGHBORHOODS. TAMPA, ST-PETERSBURG FLORIDA. /DEMOGRAPHY/   CUSDLAB63486

INCOME, EDUCATION AND UNEMPLOYMENT IN NEIGHBORHOODS. WASHINGTON-DC. /DEMOGRAPHY/   CUSDLAB63487

INCOME, EDUCATION AND UNEMPLOYMENT IN NEIGHBORHOODS. LOS-ANGELES, CALIFORNIA. /DEMOGRAPHY/   CUSDLAB63565

THE SOCIO-ECONOMIC AND PHYSICAL CHARACTERISTICS OF THE VARIOUS NEIGHBORHOODS IN PUEBLO. /COLORADO/   GPUEBRP65459

NEIGHBORS
STRANGERS THEN NEIGHBORS. FROM PILGRIMS TO PUERTO-RICANS.   PSENICX61308

THE PUERTO-RICANS, STRANGERS -- THEN NEIGHBORS.   PSENICX65307

NET
NET MIGRATION OF THE POPULATION, 1950-60, BY AGE, SEX, AND COLOR. VOL II, ANALYTICAL GROUPINGS OF
COUNTIES. /INCOME/   GBOWLGK65434

THE COMPOSITION OF NET MIGRATION AMONG COUNTIES IN THE UNITED STATES, 1950-60.   GBOWLGK66414

EDUCATIONAL SELECTIVITY OF NET MIGRATION FROM THE SOUTH.   NHAMICH59986

NETWORKS
INFORMATION NETWORKS IN LABOR-MARKETS.   GREESAX65119

NEVADA
MINORITY-GROUPS IN NEVADA. /NEGRO AMERICAN-INDIAN/   CRUSCER66807

NEW-ENGLAND
   PART I. THE NEW-ENGLAND EXPERIENCE RETRAINING THE UNEMPLOYED.   GFEDERB62930

NEW-HAVEN
   A CLIMATE OF CHANGE. THE NEW-HAVEN STORY. /CONNECTICUT/   NFARRGR65344

   WORKERS WANTED. A STUDY OF EMPLOYERS HIRING POLICIES, PREFERENCES, AND PRACTICES IN NEW-HAVEN AND
   CHARLOTTE. /CONNECTICUT NORTH-CAROLINA/   NNOLAEW49928

NEW-HAVEN-S
   A SURVEY OF NEW-HAVEN-S NEWCOMERS. THE PUERTO-RICANS. /CONNECTICUT/   PDONCDX59796

NEW-JERSEY
   BUREAU OF MIGRANT-LABOR REPORT. /NEW-JERSEY NEGRO PUERTO-RICAN/   CNEWJDL61907

   INCOME, EDUCATION AND UNEMPLOYMENT IN NEIGHBORHOODS. NEWARK, NEW-JERSEY. /DEMOGRAPHY/   CUSDLAB63470

   REPORTS ON THE WORK OF THE FEPC IN NEW-JERSEY AND NEW-YORK.   GAMERCR46372

   ANTI-DISCRIMINATION LAWS IN ACTION IN NEW-JERSEY. A LAW-SOCIOLOGY STUDY.   GBLUMAW65459

   THE MINORITY-GROUP WORKER IN CAMDEN COUNTY. /NEW-JERSEY/   GBOGITX54057

   THE OPERATION OF THE NEW-JERSEY LAW AGAINST DISCRIMINATION.   GBUSTJL49507

   NJ ANTI-DISCRIMINATION LAW. FIRST ANNUAL REPORT. /NEW-JERSEY/   GLABOLR46871

   REPORT ON SECOND ANNUAL SPRING CONFERENCE ON CIVIL-RIGHTS OF NEW-JERSEY COMMISSION-ON-CIVIL-RIGHTS, APRIL
   23, 1966.   GNEWJCC66056

   REPORT OF A PRELIMINARY STUDY OF EMPLOYMENT PRACTICES INVOLVING MINORITY-GROUP WORKERS, ESSEX-COUNTY,
   NEW-JERSEY.   GNEWJDE46059

   REPORT ON A SURVEY OF EMPLOYMENT POLICIES AND HIRING PRACTICES INVOLVING MINORITY-GROUPS IN HUDON-COUNTY,
   NEW-JERSEY.   GNEWJDE51060

   REPORT ON A SURVEY OF EMPLOYMENT POLICIES AND PRACTICES INVOLVING MINORITY-GROUPS IN MIDDLESEX-COUNTY,
   NEW-JERSEY.   GNEWJDE52061

   RAILROAD, EMPLOYMENT IN THE NEW-YORK AND NEW-JERSEY.   GNEWYSA58101

   HEALTH WORK AMONG MIGRANTS IN 1958 BY THE NEW-JERSEY STATE DEPARTMENT OF HEALTH.   GSHEPAC59301

   PRINCETON-S LESSON. SCHOOL INTEGRATION IS NOT ENOUGH. /NEW-JERSEY/   GSTREPX64337

   US COMMISSION-ON-CIVIL-RIGHTS, HEARINGS. NEWARK, NEW-JERSEY. SEPTEMBER 11-12, 1962.   GUSCOMC62402

   HOUSING, EMPLOYMENT OPPORTUNITIES AND APPRENTICESHIP TRAINING, REPORT. /NEW-JERSEY/   GUSCOMC63404

   REPORTS ON APPRENTICESHIP, NINE STATE ADVISORY COMMITTEES. /CALIFORNIA FLORIDA MARYLAND CONNECTICUT
   WASHINGTON-DC NEW-JERSEY NEW-YORK TENNESSEE WISCONSIN/   GUSCOMC64407

   EXPANDING EMPLOYMENT OPPORTUNITIES IN NEWARK. EXPERIENCE REPORT 101. /NEW-JERSEY/   GUSCONM65418

   COMMON GROUND. /NEW-JERSEY MIGRANT-WORKERS/   GWILLLB59565

   SUMMARY OF A SURVEY OF SOCIAL AND ECONOMIC CONDITIONS IN MORRIS COUNTY NEW-JERSEY AS THEY AFFECT THE
   NEGRO.   NKERNJH57645

   SURVEY OF EQUAL-EMPLOYMENT-OPPORTUNITIES IN NEW-JERSEY INVESTOR-OWNED PUBLIC UTILITIES.   NLEVIMJ66607

   NEWARK. NEGROES MOVE TOWARD POWER. /NEW-JERSEY/   NOSHEJX65965

   TWO STATE REPORT ON JOB DISCRIMINATION. /NEW-YORK NEW-JERSEY/   NUSDLAB58844

   CONFERENCE ON PROBLEMS IN EMPLOYMENT CONFRONTING NEGROES IN NEW-JERSEY, OCTOBER 18 1962.   NUSDLAB62242

   PUERTO-RICAN FARM WORKERS IN NEW-JERSEY.   PAINERO59777

   MIGRANTS POSE PROBLEMS FOR NEW-JERSEY FARMERS WHO NEED THEM.   PCUNNJT57793

   THE PUERTO-RICAN WORKER IN PERTH-AMBOY, NEW-JERSEY.   PGOLUFT56811

   SOME ECONOMIC CONSEQUENCES OF THE PUERTO-RICAN MIGRATION INTO PERTH-AMBOY, 1949-1954. /NEW-JERSEY/   PGOLUFX55812

   ANNUAL FARM LABOR REPORT. /NEW-JERSEY/   PNEWJSE63831

   THE CHANGING WOMAN WORKER. A STUDY OF THE FEMALE LABOR-FORCE IN NEW-JERSEY AND IN THE NATION FROM 1940 TO
   1958.   WSMITGM60120

NEW-MEXICO
   INDIANS WORK AT THEIR OWN SKI RESORT. /NEW-MEXICO/   ILINDVX66580

   INDIAN RELOCATION AND THE NEW-MEXICO SEC.   ISANDJN62615

   FRUITLAND, NEW-MEXICO. A NAVAHO COMMUNITY IN TRANSITION.   ISASATT60615

   REPORT OF INDIAN RECRUITMENT AND TRAINING MEETING AT ALBUQUERQUE, NEW-MEXICO, ON DECEMBER 6, 1966.   IUSDLAB66321

   BASIC NEEDS OF SPANISH-AMERICAN FARM FAMILIES IN NEW-MEXICO.   MGRISGXND408

   THE SPANISH-AMERICANS IN NEW-MEXICO.   MKNOWCS61424

   PATRON-PEON PATTERN AMONG THE SPANISH-AMERICANS OF NEW-MEXICO.   MKNOWCS66423

   ANALYSIS OF POPULATION CHANGES IN NEW-MEXICO COUNTIES.   MPIERGK61457

   NEW-MEXICO COUNTY INDUSTRIAL COMPOSITION AND LEVELS OF LIVING.   MSANDAD63479

   RURAL PEOPLE AND THEIR RESOURCES, NORTH-CENTRAL NEW-MEXICO.   MTAYLMM60402

NEW-ORLEANS
   THE EMPLOYMENT OF NEGRO WOMEN AS DOMESTIC-SERVANTS IN NEW-ORLEANS. /LOUISIANA/   CGILMHX44403

   INCOME, EDUCATION AND UNEMPLOYMENT IN NEIGHBORHOODS. NEW-ORLEANS, LOUISIANA. /DEMOGRAPHY/   CUSDLAB63469

   US COMMISSION-ON-CIVIL-RIGHTS, HEARINGS. NEW-ORLEANS, LOUISIANA. SEPTEMBER 27-28, 1960, MAY 5-6, 1961. GUSCOMC61403

   SUB-EMPLOYMENT IN THE SLUMS OF NEW-ORLEANS. /LOUISIANA/   GUSDLAB66512

NEW-ORLEANS   (CONTINUATION)
SEGREGATION DEAL. NEW-ORLEANS REGION FEPC PERMITS COMPROMISE. /LOUISIANA/   NBUSIWX45161

NEGRO BUSINESSMEN OF NEW-ORLEANS.   NFORTXX49054

A STUDY OF THE LONGSHORE INDUSTRY IN NEW-ORLEANS WITH EMPHASIS ON NEGRO LONGSHOREMEN. /LOUISIANA/ NORTICF56962

NEGRO EMPLOYMENT IN THREE COMPANIES IN THE NEW-ORLEANS AREA. /CASE-STUDY LOUISIANA/   NUSDLAB55828

THREE COMPANIES -- NEW-ORLEANS AREA. /CASE-STUDY LOUISIANA/   NWISSHW55332

NEW-ROCHELLE
A SURVEY OF EMPLOYMENT OPPORTUNITIES AS THEY RELATE TO THE NEGRO IN NEW-ROCHELLE, NEW-YORK, 1955.   NWESTCU55316

NEW-YORK
DEVELOPING NEW-YORK CITY-S HUMAN RESOURCES. VOL 1. /NEGRO PUERTO-RICAN/   CINSTOP66034

ETHNIC SURVEY OF MUNICIPAL-EMPLOYEES. A REPORT ON THE NUMBER AND DISTRIBUTION OF NEGROES AND
PUERTO-RICANS AND OTHER EMPLOYEES BY THE CITY OF NEW-YORK.   CNEWYC064916

INTERIM REPORT TO THE MAYOR CN ITS INQUIRY INTO CHARGES OF RACIAL BIAS IN THE CITY BUILDING AND
CONSTRUCTION INDUSTRY. /NEW-YORK NEGRO PUERTO-RICAN/   CNEWYC064917

THE SCHOOL DROPOUT PROBLEM IN MAJOR CITIES OF NEW-YORK STATE. ROCHESTER -- PART I. /NEGRO PUERTO-RICAN/   CNEWYSD62090

SIGNIFICANT TRENDS IN THE NEW-YORK STATE ECONOMY, WITH SPECIAL REFERENCE TO MINORITY-GROUPS.
/PUERTO-RICAN NEGRO/   CRUSSVR59482

INCOME, EDUCATION AND UNEMPLOYMENT IN NEIGHBORHOODS. BUFFALO, NEW-YORK. /DEMOGRAPHY/   CUSDLAB63455

REPORTS CN THE WORK OF THE FEPC IN NEW-JERSEY AND NEW-YORK.   GAMERCR46372

FAIR-EMPLOYMENT LEGISLATION IN NEW-YORK STATE. ITS HISTORY, DEVELOPMENT, AND SUGGESTED USE ELSEWHERE. GBRADPX46247

POVERTY IN NEW-YORK CITY. FACTS FOR PLANNING COMMUNITY ACTION.   GCOMCCN64210

FEPC. NEW-YORK VERSION.   GFORTXX50696

MONEY BENEFITS OF EDUCATION BY SEX AND RACE IN NEW-YORK STATE, 1956.   GGREEWX61741

NEW-YORK STATE-COMMISSION-AGAINST-DISCRIMINATION.   GHIGBJX55995

DEVELOPMENT AND ADMINISTRATION OF THE NEW-YORK STATE LAW AGAINST DISCRIMINATION.   GHIGBJX67143

NEW-YORK STATE-S PROGRAM AGAINST DISCRIMINATION IN EMPLOYMENT. THE WORK OF THE NEW-YORKEW-YORK
STATE-COMMISSION-AGAINST-DISCRIMINATION.   GINDUBX57812

LEGISLATION AGAINST RACIAL OR RELIGIOUS DISCRIMINATION IN EMPLOYMENT, NEW-YORK.   GIVESLM52819

MANAGEMENT-S CONCERN WITH RECENT CIVIL-RIGHTS LEGISLATION AFFECTING MANAGEMENT-S OBLIGATIONS TO HIS
EMPLOYEES AND APPLICANTS FOR EMPLOYMENT, MAINLY IN THE STATE OF NEW-YORK.   GKOPPRW65858

NY ANTI-DISCRIMINATION LAW. 1946 ANNUAL REPORT. /NEW-YORK/   GLABOLR46872

ENFORCEMENT OF NEW-YORK LAW AGAINST DISCRIMINATION.   GLABORR51879

MINORITY-GROUPS AND ECONOMIC-STATUS IN NEW-YORK STATE.   GLANGGE59884

MIGRATORY FARM WORKERS IN THE ATLANTIC COAST STREAM. I. CHANGES IN NEW-YORK, 1953 AND 1957.   GLARSOF60406

AN ANALYSIS OF THE EFFECTIVENESS OF THE NEW-YORK STATE LAW AGAINST DISCRIMINATION.   GMARPAW53940

MIGRATORY FARM WORKERS IN THE ATLANTIC COAST STREAM. WESTERN NEW-YORK, JUNE 1953.   GMOTHJR54405

EVERYBODY-S BUSINESS. A SUMMARY OF NEW-YORK STATE ANTI-DISCRIMINATION LAWS AND HOW TO USE THEM.   GNATLFC46048

PATTERNS OF CONCILIATION UNDER THE NEW-YORK STATE LAW AGAINST DISCRIMINATION.   GNEWXYL51100

THE NEW-YORK STATE COMMISSION AGAINST DISCRIMINATION. A NEW TECHNIQUE FOR AN OLD PROBLEM.   GNEWYSA47107

NEW-YORK STATE-COMMISSION-AGAINST-DISCRIMINATION, STATEMENT BEFORE THE US SENATE SUBCOMMITTEE ON LABOR
AND LABOR-MANAGEMENT RELATIONS.   GNEWYSA52102

COMMUNICATIONS EMPLOYEES AND GOOD SERVICE. /NEW-YORK/   GNEWYSA54077

THE BANKING INDUSTRY. VERIFIED COMPLAINTS AND INFORMAL INVESTIGATIONS. /NEW-YORK/   GNEWYSA58076

EMPLOYMENT IN DEPARTMENT STORES. /NEW-YORK/   GNEWYSA58079

EMPLOYMENT IN THE HOTEL INDUSTRY. /NEW-YORK/   GNEWYSA58081

THE INSURANCE INDUSTRY -- VERIFIED COMPLAINTS AND INFORMAL INVESTIGATIONS HANDLED BY THE NEW-YORK STATE
COMMISSION AGAINST DISCRIMINATION, JULY 1 1945-SEPTEMBER 15, 1958.   GNEWYSA58082

RAILROAD. EMPLOYMENT IN THE NEW-YORK AND NEW-JERSEY.   GNEWYSA58101

INVESTIGATION OF CHARGES OF DISCRIMINATORY PRACTICES IN THE NEW-YORK STATE-EMPLOYMENT-SERVICE.   GNEWYSA59083

RULINGS ON PRE-EMPLOYMENT INQUIRIES RELATING TO RACE, CREED, COLOR OR NATIONAL ORIGIN UNDER THE NEW-YORK
STATE LAW AGAINST DISCRIMINATION.   GNEWYSBND106

THE NEXT STEPS TOWARD EQUALITY OF OPPORTUNITY IN THE SYRACUSE METROPOLITAN AREA. REPORT OF THE SYRACUSE
CONFERENCE ON HUMAN RIGHTS AND HOUSING, JULY 2-3 1962. /NEW-YORK/   GNEWYSB62103

REPORT OF INQUIRY CONCERNING CHARGES OF DISCRIMINATING PRACTICES IN THE NEW-YORK STATE THRUWAY AUTHORITY. GNEWYSB64104

MIGRANT FARM LABOR IN NEW-YORK.   GNEWYSE58109

EMPLOYMENT AND EARNINGS OF MIGRANT FARM WORKERS IN NEW-YORK STATE.   GNEWYSE60110

SUMMARY OF RULES, REGULATIONS, AND LAWS THAT AFFECT SEASONAL FARM WORKERS AND THEIR EMPLOYERS IN NEW-YORK
STATE. /MIGRANT-WORKERS/   GNEWYSJND113

MIGRANT FARM LABOR IN NEW-YORK STATE.   GNEWYSJ63112

REPORT OF NEW-YORK STATE JOINT LEGISLATIVE COMMITTEE ON MIGRANT-LABOR.   GNEWYSLND115

A HELPING HAND. SEASONAL FARM LABOR IN NEW-YORK STATE. /MIGRANT-WORKERS/   GNEWYSX63087

PROVING GROUND FOR FAIR-EMPLOYMENT. SOME LESSONS FROM NEW-YORK STATE-S EXPERIENCE.   GNORTHR47123

COMBATING DISCRIMINATION IN EMPLOYMENT IN NEW-YORK STATE.   GRACKFX49215

MIGRATORY WORKERS IN NEW-YORK. CHANGES, 1953, 1957, AND 1958.   GSHAREF59428

MIGRATORY FARM WORKERS IN THE ATLANTIC COAST STREAM. II. EDUCATION OF NEW-YORK WORKERS AND THEIR
CHILDREN. 1953 AND 1957.   GSHAREF60427

A SURVEY OF DISCRIMINATION IN THE BUILDING TRADES INDUSTRY, NEW-YORK CITY.   GSHAUDF63300

PUBLIC ASSISTANCE RECIPIENTS IN NEW-YORK STATE, JANUARY-FEBRUARY 1957.   GSNYDEM58114

FAIR-EMPLOYMENT-PRACTICE IN NEW-YORK. LAW, EDUCATION GO HAND IN HAND.   GSULLJD50340

REPORTS ON APPRENTICESHIP. NINE STATE ADVISORY COMMITTEES. /CALIFORNIA FLORIDA MARYLAND CONNECTICUT
WASHINGTON-DC NEW-JERSEY NEW-YORK TENNESSEE WISCONSIN/   GUSCOMC64407

FIRST YEAR UNDER NEW-YORK LAW AGAINST DISCRIMINATION.   GUSDLAB47074

SUB-EMPLOYMENT IN THE SLUMS OF NEW-YORK.   GUSDLAB66511

YOUTH IN NEW-YORK CITY. OUT OF SCHOOL AND OUT OF WORK.   GVOGAAS62074

MIGRATORY WORKERS IN NEW-YORK STATE, 1959 AND COMPARISONS WITH 1953, 1957, AND 1958.   GWHYTDR60407

APPRENTICESHIP TRAINING IN NEW-YORK. OPENINGS IN 1963.   GWORKDL63582

CITY EMPLOYMENT SURVEY. PERCENTAGE OF MINORITY-GROUP EMPLOYEES BY DEPARTMENT. /YONKERS NEW-YORK/   GYONKCC66592

THE INDIAN TODAY IN NEW-YORK STATE.   INEWYSF56601

THE INDIAN TODAY IN NEW-YORK STATE.   INEWYSI64602

THE SPIRIT OF THE GHETTO. STUDIES OF THE JEWISH QUARTER OF NEW-YORK.   JHAPGHX65989

JEWS IN AND OUT OF NEW-YORK CITY. /ECONOMIC-STATUS/   JLAZRBX61034

JEWISH LAW STUDENT AND NEW-YORK JOBS. /EMPLOYMENT DISCRIMINATION/   JRIGHXX64757

THE JEWISH LAW STUDENT AND NEW-YORK JOBS -- DISCRIMINATORY EFFECTS IN LAW FIRM HIRING PRACTICES.
/OCCUPATIONS/   JYALELJ64774

JEWISH LAW STUDENT AND NEW-YORK JOBS.   JYOUNJX65775

NEGRO AND WHITE YOUTH IN ELMIRA. /NEW-YORK/   NANTCAX59026

PROGRESS TOWARD INTEGRATION. FOUR CASE-STUDIES. /EMPLOYMENT FEPC NEW-YORK/   NBACKSX59040

THE EMPLOYMENT OF THE NEW-YORK NEGRO IN RETROSPECT.   NBLOCHD59090

DISCRIMINATION AGAINST THE NEGRO IN EMPLOYMENT IN NEW-YORK, 1920-1963.   NBLOCHD65089

NEGRO AMERICAN LABOR COUNCIL IS ACTIVE IN NEW-YORK STATE.   NBROOTR61119

OPERATION ACHIEVEMENT. /NEW-YORK EMPLOYMENT/   NCALVIJ63176

THE NEGRO IN SYRACUSE. /NEW-YORK/   NCAMPAKND177

OUTREACH IN ROCHESTER. /NEW-YORK/   NCROFES66242

FROM 1790 TO 1960. NEGROES IN NEW-YORK.   NCROMFX61121

RACE, OCCUPATION, AND SOCIAL-CLASS IN NEW-YORK.   NFRUMRM58388

RACE-RELATIONS IN ROCHESTER. A PROFILE FOR 1957. /NEW-YORK/   NGRIEES57457

RACE-RELATIONS IN THE ALBANY TROY AREA. A PROFILE FOR 1957. /NEW-YORK/   NGRIEES57503

NEGROES IN FIVE NEW-YORK CITIES. A STUDY OF PROBLEMS, ACHIEVEMENTS AND TRENDS. /RACE-RELATIONS/   NGRIEES58455

RACE-RELATIONS IN BROOME-COUNTY, A PROFILE FOR 1958. /NEW-YORK/   NGRIEES58456

RACE-RELATIONS IN SYRACUSE. A PROFILE. /NEW-YORK/   NGRIEES58458

YOUTH IN THE GHETTO. A STUDY OF THE CONSEQUENCES OF POWERLESSNESS AND A BLUEPRINT FOR CHANGE. /NEW-YORK/ NHARLYO64485

NEW-YORK CITY COMMISSION ON HUMAN RIGHTS, CONSTRUCTION TRADES HEARING, TESTIMONY. /INDUSTRY/   NHILLHX66546

THE UTILIZATION OF NEGRO TEACHERS IN THE COLLEGES OF NEW-YORK STATE.   NMOSSJA60857

A STUDY OF THE POTENTIAL SUPPLY OF NEGRO TEACHERS FOR THE COLLEGES OF NEW-YORK STATE.   NMOSSJA61858

THE STATUS OF THE NEGRO PHYSICIAN IN NEW-YORK STATE. /OCCUPATIONS/   NMURRPM55867

STATEMENT TO THE NEW-YORK STATE ADVISORY COMMITTEE TO THE US COMMISSION ON CIVIL-RIGHTS, MAY 23, 1966.
/EMPLOYMENT LEGISLATION/   NPOLIEX66004

A SURVEY OF DISCRIMINATION IN THE BUILDING TRADES INDUSTRY. NEW-YORK CITY.   NSHAUDX63126

MORE SALARIED POSITIONS ARE OPENED TO NEGROES BY BUSINESS AND INDUSTRY HERE. /NEW-YORK/   NSTETDX63154

ECONOMIC STRUCTURE OF THE HARLEM COMMUNITY. /NEW-YORK/   NSTEVHR64177

SIX MONTHS OPERATION OF NEW-YORK LAW AGAINST DISCRIMINATION.   NUSDLAB46843

NEGROES IN NEW-YORK CITY. OCCUPATIONAL DISTRIBUTION.   NUSDLAB49831

TWO STATE REPORT ON JOB DISCRIMINATION. /NEW-YORK NEW-JERSEY/   NUSDLAB58844

NEGROES IN APPRENTICESHIPS, NEW-YORK STATE.   NUSDLAB60830

A SURVEY OF EMPLOYMENT OPPORTUNITIES AS THEY RELATE TO THE NEGRO IN NEW-ROCHELLE, NEW-YORK, 1955.   NWESTCU55316

CHINESE PEOPLE AND CHINA-TOWN IN NEW-YORK CITY.   OWUXXCT58772

80 PUERTO-RICAN FAMILIES IN NEW-YORK CITY.   PBERLBB58780

EAST-HARLEM BLOCK COMMUNITY DEVELOPMENT PROGRAM. /NEW-YORK/   PBORDDXND781

A PUERTO-RICAN IN NEW-YORK.   PDIAZEX61795

THE IMPACT OF PUERTO-RICAN MIGRATION ON GOVERNMENTAL SERVICES IN NEW-YORK CITY.   PDWORMB57797

THE PUERTO-RICANS IN NEW-YORK.   PEAGLMX59303

IMPLICATIONS OF PUERTO-RICAN MIGRATION TO THE CONTINENT OUTSIDE NEW-YORK CITY.   PGERNAC56808

PUERTO-RICAN LEADERSHIP IN NEW-YORK.   PGOTSJW66808

LABOR UNIONS AND PUERTO-RICAN MEMBERS IN NEW-YORK CITY.   PGRAYLX63027

THE PUERTO-RICAN WORKERS IN NEW-YORK.   PGRAYLX63813

PUERTO-RICAN INTEGRATION IN THE SKIRT INDUSTRY IN NEW-YORK CITY.   PHELFBH59481

PUERTO-RICANS IN NEW-YORK.   PILLIIX56818

SUPPLEMENTARY REPORT ON PUERTO-RICANS IN BUFFALO. /NEW-YORK/   PIMSETP62820

LA VIDA. A PUERTO-RICAN FAMILY IN THE CULTURE OF POVERTY -- SAN-JUAN AND NEW-YORK.   PLEWIOX66825

PLACING PUERTO-RICAN WORKERS IN THE NEW-YORK CITY LABOR-MARKET.   PMONTHX60830

POPULATIONS OF NEW-YORK STATE. REPORT NO 2. THE PUERTO-RICAN POPULATION OF THE NEW-YORK-CITY AREA.   PNEWYC062838

SOME CHARACTERISTICS OF PUBLIC ASSISTANCE CASES IN NEW-YORK CITY, AUGUST, 1959.   PNEWYDW60835

PUERTO-RICAN EMPLOYMENT IN NEW-YORK CITY HOTELS. /OCCUPATIONS/   PNEWYSA58837

PUERTO-RICANS IN THE NEW-YORK STATE LABOR-MARKET.   PNEWYSE57840

CHARACTERISTICS OF POPULATION AND LABOR IN NEW-YORK STATE, 1956 AND 1957. PUERTO-RICANS IN NEW-YORK CITY.   PNEWYSE60839

CHARACTERISTICS OF POPULATION AND LABOR IN NEW-YORK STATE, 1956 AND 1957. PUERTO-RICANS IN NEW-YORK CITY.   PNEWYSE60839

A COMPARISON OF THE OCCUPATIONS OF THE FIRST AND SECOND GENERATION PUERTO-RICANS IN THE MAINLAND
LABOR-MARKET, AND HOW THE WORK OF THE NEW-YORK STATE DEPARTMENT OF LABORFFECTS PUERTO-RICANS.   PRAUSCX61846

AN ANALYSIS OF UNEMPLOYED PUERTO-RICAN MIGRANTS IN NEW-YORK CITY.   PREMEGN58847

CHANGES IN SELECTED PERSONALITY CHARACTERISTICS AND PERSISTENCE IN THE CAREER CHOICES OF WOMEN ASSOCIATED
WITH A FOUR YEAR COLLEGE EDUCATION AT ONE OF THE COLLEGES OF THE CITY UNIVERSITY OF NEW-YORK.
/ASPIRATIONS/   WLEINMX64925

NEW-YORK WOMEN. A REPORT AND RECOMMENDATIONS FROM THE NEW-YORK GOVERNOR-S COMMITTEE ON THE EDUCATION AND
EMPLOYMENT OF WOMEN.   WNEWYGW64799

NEW-YORK WOMEN. A REPORT AND RECOMMENDATIONS FROM THE NEW-YORK GOVERNOR-S COMMITTEE ON THE EDUCATION AND
EMPLOYMENT OF WOMEN.   WNEWYGW64799

SECOND CAREER. /WORK-FAMILY-CONFLICT NEW-YORK/   WSCHWJX60108

NEW-YORK-CITY

INCOME, EDUCATION AND UNEMPLOYMENT IN NEIGHBORHOODS. NEW-YORK-CITY -- BROOKLYN. /DEMOGRAPHY/   CUSDLAB63471

INCOME, EDUCATION AND UNEMPLOYMENT IN NEIGHBORHOODS. NEW-YORK-CITY -- THE BRONX. /DEMOGRAPHY/   CUSDLAB63472

INCOME, EDUCATION AND UNEMPLOYMENT IN NEIGHBORHOODS. NEW-YORK-CITY -- MANHATTAN. /DEMOGRAPHY/   CUSDLAB63473

INCOME, EDUCATION AND UNEMPLOYMENT IN NEIGHBORHOODS. NEW-YORK-CITY -- QUEENS. /DEMOGRAPHY/   CUSDLAB63474

INCOME, EDUCATION AND UNEMPLOYMENT IN NEIGHBORHOODS. NEW-YORK-CITY -- STATEN-ISLAND. /DEMOGRAPHY/   CUSDLAB63475

REPORT OF THE DIAGNOSTIC SURVEY OF TENANT HOUSEHOLDS IN THE WEST SIDE URBAN-RENEWAL AREA OF
NEW-YORK-CITY.   GGREEAI65474

YOUTH AND WORK IN NEW-YORK-CITY.   GKOHLMC62855

A STUDY OF EMPLOYMENT PATTERNS IN THE GENERAL MERCHANDISE GROUP RETAIL STORES IN NEW-YORK-CITY.   GWATKDO66588

THE MUTUAL SAVINGS BANKS OF NEW-YORK-CITY. /DISCRIMINATION/   JAMERJC65694

THE MUTUAL SAVINGS BANKS OF NEW-YORK-CITY. A FOLLOW-UP REPORT ON THE EXCLUSION OF JEWS AT TOP-MANAGEMENT
AND POLICY-MAKING LEVELS.   JAMERJC66695

THE ADJUSTMENT OF PUERTO-RICANS IN NEW-YORK-CITY.   PFITZJP59801

POPULATIONS OF NEW-YORK STATE. REPORT NO 2. THE PUERTO-RICAN POPULATION OF THE NEW-YORK-CITY AREA.   PNEWYC062838

NEW-YORK-S

NEW-YORK-S NONDISCRIMINATION EMPLOYMENT POLICY.   NHARRCV65491

DISCRIMINATION IN THE HIRING HALL. A CASE-STUDY OF PRESSURES TO PROMOTE INTEGRATION IN NEW-YORK-S BREWERY
INDUSTRY.   NLANGGE59670

NEW-YORK-S PUERTO-RICANS.   PGLAZNX58211

NEW-YORK-S LABOR SCANDAL. THE PUERTO-RICAN WORKERS.   PLEVIMX57823

NEW-YORKEW-YORK

NEW-YORK STATE-S PROGRAM AGAINST DISCRIMINATION IN EMPLOYMENT. THE WORK OF THE NEW-YORKEW-YORK
STATE-COMMISSION-AGAINST-DISCRIMINATION.   GINDUBX57812

NEWARK

INCOME, EDUCATION AND UNEMPLOYMENT IN NEIGHBORHOODS. NEWARK, NEW-JERSEY. /DEMOGRAPHY/   CUSDLAB63470

US COMMISSION-ON-CIVIL-RIGHTS, HEARINGS. NEWARK, NEW-JERSEY. SEPTEMBER 11-12, 1962.   GUSCOMC62402

EXPANDING EMPLOYMENT OPPORTUNITIES IN NEWARK. EXPERIENCE REPORT 101. /NEW-JERSEY/   GUSCONM65418

NEWARK. NEGROES MOVE TOWARD POWER. /NEW-JERSEY/   NOSHEJX65965

NEWCOMER

ECONOMIC ABSORPTION AND CULTURAL INTEGRATION OF THE URBAN NEWCOMER. /NEGRO MEXICAN-AMERICAN/   CUVIOIP65277

NEWCOMER   (CONTINUATION)
   THE MINORITY NEWCOMER IN OPEN AND CLOSED GROUPS.   GZILLRC59595

   THE PUERTO-RICAN NEWCOMER.   PPUERRD60790

NEWCOMERS
   THE NEWCOMERS. NEGROES AND PUERTO-RICANS IN A CHANGING METROPOLIS   CHANDOX59481

   THE OLD-TIMERS AND THE NEWCOMERS. ETHNIC-GROUP RELATIONS IN A NEEDLE TRADE UNION.   NHERBWX53519

   A SURVEY OF NEW-HAVEN-S NEWCOMERS. THE PUERTO-RICANS. /CONNECTICUT/   PDONCDX59796

NEWS
   HUMAN-RELATIONS NEWS OF CHICAGO. /ILLINOIS/   GCHICHR59565

   THE REAL NEWS ABOUT AUTOMATION.   NSILBCE65035

NEWSPAPERS
   CAREERS FOR NEGROES ON NEWSPAPERS. /OCCUPATIONS/   NAMERNG66018

NILES
   NILES COMMUNITY SELF SURVEY. /MICHIGAN/   NMICCRC65771

NJ
   NJ ANTI-DISCRIMINATION LAW. FIRST ANNUAL REPORT. /NEW-JERSEY/   GLABOLR46871

NLRA
   RACE DISCRIMINATION AND THE NLRA ACT. THE BRAVE NEW WORLD OF MIRANDA. /LEGISLATION/   NSOVEMI63169

NLRB
   THE NLRB AND RACIAL DISCRIMINATION. /LEGISLATION/   GCARTRX65560

   UNION RACIAL DISCRIMINATION -- RECENT DEVELOPMENTS BEFORE THE NLRB AND THEIR IMPLICATIONS UNDER TITLE-VII
   OF THE CIVIL-RIGHTS-ACT OF 1964.   GGEORLJ65714

   NLRB -- FEPC.   GJEFFAX63822

   RACIAL AND RELIGIOUS DISCRIMINATION IN EMPLOYMENT AND THE ROLE OF THE NLRB.   GMALOWH61935

   DISCRIMINATION AND THE NLRB. THE SCOPE OF THE BOARD POWER UNDER SECTIONS 8A3 AND 8B2.   GUVCHLR64212

   NLRB CRACKS DOWN ON UNION BIAS.   NBUSIWX64887

   NLRB DECERTIFIES RACIALLY SEGREGATED UNION LOCALS.   NCHECDX64890

   RACIAL DISCRIMINATION AND THE NLRB. THE HUGHES TOOL CASE, PART ONE.   NVIRGLR64017

   RACIAL DISCRIMINATION AND THE NLRB. THE HUGHES TOOL CASE, PART TWO.   NVIRGLR64018

NLRB-FEPC
   NLRB-FEPC. /LEGISLATION/   GALBEJM63367

NON-CAREER
   THE RELATIONSHIP OF PARENTAL IDENTIFICATION TO SEX ROLE ACCEPTANCE IN MARRIED, SINGLE, CAREER AND
   NON-CAREER WOMEN. /WORK-WOMEN-ROLE/   WBREYCH64654

   PERCEPTIONS OF ROLE CONFLICTS AND SELF CONFLICTS AMONG CAREER AND NON-CAREER COLLEGE EDUCATED WOMEN.
   /WORK-FAMILY-CONFLICT/   WMORGDD62996

NON-DISCRIMINATION
   MERIT EMPLOYMENT. NON-DISCRIMINATION IN INDUSTRY.   GBULLPX60897

   STATE LAWS DEALING WITH NON-DISCRIMINATION IN EMPLOYMENT.   GBUTCGT63508

   THE POLICY OF NON-DISCRIMINATION IN EMPLOYMENT IN THE FEDERAL GOVERNMENT.   GPRESCP55198

   SOME QUESTIONS AND ANSWERS ON THE NON-DISCRIMINATION POLICY OF THE FEDERAL GOVERNMENT.   GPRESCP55199

   NON-DISCRIMINATION CLAUSE IN GOVERNMENT CONTRACTS IS MANDATORY.   NUSDLAB43833

   INTERNATIONAL-HARVESTER-S NON-DISCRIMINATION POLICY. /CASE-STUDY/   NUSDLAB54822

NON-ENGLISH
   PLACEMENT OF NON-ENGLISH SPEAKING APPLICANTS.   GWATSMMND544

NON-FARM
   CHARACTERISTICS OF THE U.S. POPULATION BY FARM AND NON-FARM ORIGIN.   GBEALCL64423

   FARM AND NON-FARM EMPLOYMENT OPPORTUNITIES FOR LOW-INCOME FARM FAMILIES.   GRUTTVW59270

NON-FRENCH
   THE FRENCH AND THE NON-FRENCH IN LOUISIANA. A STUDY OF THE RELEVANCE OF ETHNIC FACTORS IN RURAL
   DEVELOPMENT. /ECONOMIC-STATUS/   NBERTAL65394

NON-INDIAN
   KLAMATH INDIANS IN TWO NON-INDIAN COMMUNITIES. KLAMATH-FALLS AND EUGENE-SPRINGFIELD. /OREGON/   ILIVIMG59582

NON-INTELLECTUAL
   SOME NON-INTELLECTUAL CORRELATES OF ACADEMIC ACHIEVEMENT AMONG MEXICAN-AMERICAN SECONDARY SCHOOL
   STUDENTS.   MGILLLJ62401

NON-PRACTITIONERS
   PRACTITIONERS AND NON-PRACTITIONERS IN A GROUP OF WOMEN PHYSICIANS. /ASPIRATIONS/   WGLICRX65791

NON-PROFESSIONAL
   PROFESSIONAL AND NON-PROFESSIONAL WOMEN AS MOTHERS.   WMERIFH55971

NON-SEGREGATION
   NON-SEGREGATION. OR QUALITY IN SCHOOLS OF THE DEEP SOUTH. /ECONOMIC-STATUS/   NBRITNX54892

NON-VERBAL
   NEGRO RESPONSES TO VERBAL AND NON-VERBAL TEST MATERIAL.   NBEANKL47914

NON-WHITE
   THE NON-WHITE FEMALE IN THE LABOR-FORCE. /WOMEN NEGRO/   CTURNRH51214

   EMPLOYMENT OF WHITE AND NON-WHITE PERSONS. 1955. /DEMOGRAPHY/   CUSBURC56373

   ECONOMIC-STATUS OF NON-WHITE WORKERS, 1955-1962. /OCCUPATIONAL-DISTRIBUTION/   GKESSMA63848

NON-WHITE   (CONTINUATION)
SURVEY AND ANALYSIS OF NON-WHITE EMPLOYMENT BY THE CITY OF MINNEAPOLIS.   /MINNESOTA/   GMINLMH65002

SECOND SURVEY OF NON-WHITE EMPLOYEES IN STATE GOVERNMENT IN PENNSYLVANIA.   GPENNHR65167

THE SAN-FRANCISCO NON-WHITE POPULATION 1950-1960. /CALIFORNIA/   GROSETXND250

SURVEY OF NON-WHITE EMPLOYEES IN STATE GOVERNMENT. /PENNSYLVANIA/   GSTRUJW63338

A REPORT ON THE CHARACTERISTICS OF MICHIGAN-S NON-WHITE POPULATION.   NMICCRC65773

A STUDY OF NON-WHITE EMPLOYMENT IN THE STATE SERVICE. /MICHIGAN/   NMICCSC64775

A FOLLOW-UP STUDY OF NON-WHITE EMPLOYMENT IN THE STATE SERVICE.   /MICHIGAN/   NMICCSC65774

THE NON-WHITE IN PROVIDENCE.   /RHODE-ISLAND/   NRHODIUND052

THE EXPECTED-CASES METHOD APPLIED TO THE NON-WHITE MALE LABOR-FORCE.   NTURNRH49211

THE NON-WHITE MALE IN THE LABOR-FORCE.   NTURNRH49215

NON-WHITES
LEVELS OF LIVING AMONG WHITES AND NON-WHITES IN THE U.S.   GCOWHJD65614

STUDY OF OCCUPATIONAL CHARACTERISTICS OF NON-WHITES IN THE EAST BATON-ROUGE AREA. /LOUISIANA/   GHARRWRND760

REPORT OF 1961 - 1962 SURVEY OF PHILADELPHIA BANKS AND ATTACHED COMPOSITE TABULATION OF NON-WHITES.
/PENNSYLVANIA/   GPHILCH62180

A CAREER BREAK FOR NON-WHITES.   NBUSIWX60147

SOME CHANGES IN THE RELATIVE STATUS OF AMERICAN NON-WHITES, 1940 TO 1960. /INCOME   OCCUPATIONAL-STATUS
ECUCATION/   NGLENND63421

EMPLOYMENT EXPERIENCES OF NEGRO PHILADELPHIANS. A DESCRIPTIVE STUDY OF THE EMPLOYMENT EXPERIENCES,
PERCEPTIONS, AND ASPIRATIONS OF SELECTED PHILADELPHIA WHITES AND NON-WHITES.   NSIEGAI59718

NONDISCRIMINATION
TRAINING AID. CULTURAL DIFFERENCES, TRAINING IN NONDISCRIMINATION, READING ASSIGNMENTS. /EMPLOYMENT
MEXICAN-AMERICAN NEGRO/   CCALDSW65447

NONDISCRIMINATION IN THE FEDERAL-SERVICES.   GDAVIJA46628

NONDISCRIMINATION IN FEDERALLY-ASSISTED PROGRAMS OF THE DEPARTMENT-OF-THE-TREASURY,
DEPARTMENT-OF-DEFENSE, ATOMIC-ENERGY-COMMISSION, CIVIL-AERONAUTICS-BOARD, FEDERAL-AVIATION-AGENCY,
VETERANS-ADMINISTRATION.   GFEDERX64673

NONDISCRIMINATION IN EMPLOYMENT. EXECUTIVE-ORDER 10925.   GGINSGJ61718

THE NONDISCRIMINATION CLAUSE IN GOVERNMENT CONTRACTS.   GPASLRS57148

REPORT OF THE SPECIAL COMMITTEE CN NONDISCRIMINATION OF THE BOARD OF PUBLIC EDUCATION, PHILADELPHIA.
/PENNSYLVANIA/   GPHILBE64172

COMPLIANCE GUIDE, RECOMMENDATIONS FOR OBTAINING COMPLIANCE WITH THE NONDISCRIMINATION PROVISIONS IN
GOVERNMENT CONTRACTS.   GPRESCH58119

ENFORCEMENT OF NONDISCRIMINATION REQUIREMENTS FOR GOVERNMENT CONTRACT WORK.   GSPECWH63329

CIVILIAN PERSONNEL -- NONDISCRIMINATION IN EMPLOYMENT. /MILITARY/   GUSDAIR62189

SUPERVISOR DEVELOPMENT PROGRAM, BASIC COURSE, NONDISCRIMINATION POLICY. /MILITARY/   GUSDARM56192

THE FEDERAL NONDISCRIMINATION POLICY IN THE VETERANS-ADMINISTRATION.   GUSVETA59521

NONDISCRIMINATION IN THE FEDERAL SERVICES.   NDAVIJA46257

NEW-YORK-S NONDISCRIMINATION EMPLOYMENT POLICY.   NHARRCV65491

WORKING RULES FOR ASSURING NONDISCRIMINATION IN HOSPITAL ADMINISTRATION.   NYALELJ64600

NONFARM
EDUCATIONAL STATUS, COLLEGE PLANS, AND OCCUPATIONAL-STATUS OF FARM AND NONFARM YOUTHS. OCTOBER 1959.   GCOWHJD61427

SCHOOL DROPOUT RATES AMONG FARM AND NONFARM YOUTH 1950 AND 1960.   GCOWHJD63421

CHARACTERISTICS OF SCHOOL DROPOUTS AND HIGH SCHOOL GRADUATES, FARM AND NONFARM, 1960.   GCOWHJD64419

THE MOVEMENT OF LABOR BETWEEN FARM AND NONFARM JOBS.   GPERKBX66150

NONFEDERAL
SURVEY OF SALARIES AND EMPLOYMENT-CONDITIONS IN NONFEDERAL PSYCHIATRIC HOSPITALS.   WAMERNA65611

NONMETROPOLITAN
POPULATION OF THE UNITED STATES BY METROPOLITAN AND NONMETROPOLITAN RESIDENCE. /DEMOGRAPHY/   GUSBURC66159

NONTRADITIONALLY
NONTRADITIONALLY TRAINED WOMEN AS MENTAL HEALTH COUNSELORS/PSYCHOTHERAPISTS.   WMAGOTM66779

NONWHITE
POVERTY IN THE SOUTHWEST. A COMPARATIVE STUDY OF MEXICAN-AMERICAN, NONWHITE AND ANGLO FAMILIES. /NEGRO/   CMITTFG66777

SOCIO-ECONOMIC DIFFERENTIALS AMONG NONWHITE RACES. /NEGRO ORIENTAL AMERICAN-INDIAN/   CSCHMCF65107

NONWHITE POPULATION BY RACE. NEGROES, INDIANS, JAPANESE, CHINESE, FILIPINOS. BY AGE, SEX, MARITAL-STATUS,
EDUCATION, EMPLOYMENT-STATUS, OCCUPATIONAL-STATUS, INCOME, ETC. /DEMOGRAPHY/   CUSBURC53378

NONWHITE POPULATION BY RACE. NEGROES, INDIANS, JAPANESE,CHINESE, FILIPINOS. BY AGE, SEX,
MARITAL-STATUS,EDUCATION, EMPLOYMENT-STATUS, OCCUPATIONAL-STATUS, INCOME, ETC. /DEMOGRAPHY/   CUSBURC63176

CURRENT DATA ON NONWHITE WOMEN WORKERS. /NEGRO/   CUSDLAB65261

WHITE AND NONWHITE OWNERS OF RURAL LAND IN THE SOUTHEAST.   GBOXLRF65418

NONWHITE EMPLOYMENT IN THE UNITED STATES.   GBUCKLF63479

SOCIOECONOMIC DIFFERENCES BETWEEN WHITE AND NONWHITE FARM POPULATIONS IN THE SOUTH.   GCOWHJD64616

DISCRIMINATION AND THE WHITE -- NONWHITE UNEMPLOYMENT DIFFERENTIALS.   GGILMHJ63716

NONWHITE   (CONTINUATION)
NONWHITE OCCUPATIONAL STATUS, BY REGION, AS RELATED TO PERCENT OF NONWHITE.   GGUEREW63746

NONWHITE OCCUPATIONAL STATUS, BY REGION, AS RELATED TO PERCENT OF NONWHITE.   GGUEREW63746

THE STATUS OF THE NONWHITE LABOR-FORCE IN ILLINOIS AND THE NATION.   GILLICH57793

NONWHITE POPULATION IN ILLINOIS, 1950-1960.   GILLICH61791

A NOTE ON OCCUPATIONAL MOBILITY FOR WHITE AND NONWHITE MALES, 1950 TO 1965.   GJAFFAJ66820

THE EFFECT OF STATE FAIR-EMPLOYMENT LEGISLATION ON THE ECONOMIC POSITION OF NONWHITE MALES.   GLANDWM66883

CHANGING PATTERNS IN EMPLOYMENT OF NONWHITE WORKERS.   GRUSSJL66269

REPORT ON EMPLOYMENT PROBLEMS OF NONWHITE YOUTH IN MICHIGAN.   GUSCOMC66408

NONWHITE FARM OPERATORS IN THE UNITED STATES.   GUSDLAB41077

CHARACTERISTICS OF 6000 WHITE AND NONWHITE PERSONS ENROLLED IN MANPOWER-DEVELOPMENT-AND-TRAINING-ACT
TRAINING.   GUSDLAB63197

LABOR-FORCE DEVELOPMENTS FOR WHITE AND NONWHITE WORKERS,954-1964.   GUSDLAB64110

SENIOR CITIZENS AND HOW THEY LIVE. AN ANALYSIS OF 1960 CENSUS DATA. PART II. THE AGING NONWHITE AND HIS
HOUSING. /ECONOMIC-STATUS/   GUSHHFX63321

PERCENT NONWHITE AND DISCRIMINATION IN THE SOUTH.   NBLALHM57085

CHANGES IN NONWHITE EMPLOYMENT 1960-1966.   NCAMPJT66010

THE EFFECT OF THE GHETTO ON THE DISTRIBUTION AND LEVEL OF NONWHITE EMPLOYMENT IN URBAN AREAS.   NKAINJF64631

ECONOMIC STATUS OF NONWHITE WORKERS, 1955-62.   NKESSMA63019

NONWHITE MIGRANTS TO AND FROM SELECTED CITIES.   NPRICDO48019

SOCIAL SECURITY PROGRAM STATISTICS RELATING TO NONWHITE FAMILIES AND CHILDREN.   NUSDHEW58241

NONWHITE-WHITE
UNIONISM, MIGRATION, AND THE MALE NONWHITE-WHITE UNEMPLOYMENT DIFFERENTIAL.   GRAPPLA66216

NONWHITES
RELATIVE SOCIOECONOMIC STATUS OF SOUTHERN WHITES AND NONWHITES, 1950 AND 1960.   GCOWHJD64615

THE ATTRACTIVENESS OF THE SOUTH TO WHITES AND NONWHITES. AN ECOLOGICAL STUDY.   GHEERDM63769

WARTIME EMPLOYMENT PATTERNS OF NONWHITES AND FEMALE WORKERS IN SOUTHERN INDUSTRY.   GHOPEJX46485

A REPORT ON EMPLOYMENT OF NONWHITES IN CHICAGO. /ILLINOIS/   GILLICH55792

MDTA INSTITUTIONAL TRAINING OF NONWHITES.   GMARSJX66944

LAW OF DISCRIMINATION IN THE EMPLOYMENT OF NONWHITES.   GTURNRH52366

THE EDUCATIONAL OUTLOOK FOR NONWHITES IN FLORIDA.   NABRAAA66141

FOCI OF DISCRIMINATION IN THE EMPLOYMENT OF NONWHITES.   NTURNRH52212

NORFOLK
GRADUATES OF THE NORFOLK PROJECT ONE YEAR LATER. /MDTA TRAINING/   GQUINPA65771

WHAT MASSIVE RESISTANCE COSTS NORFOLK AND ITS BUSINESSMEN. /VIRGINIA/   NBUSIWX58165

NEGRO WORKERS IN THE BUILDING TRADES IN SELECTED CITIES. NORFOLK, VIRGINIA. /INDUSTRY/   NNATLUL46894

NORTH
RESOURCE CHARACTERISTICS AND UTILIZATION AND LEVEL OF LIVING ITEMS, RURAL HOUSEHOLDS, NORTH AND WEST
FLORIDA, 1956.   GREUSLA60391

INCOME, RESOURCES, AND ADJUSTMENT POTENTIALS AMONG RURAL FAMILIES IN NORTH AND WEST FLORIDA.   GREUSLA62388

COMPARATIVE STUDIES OF NORTH AMERICAN-INDIANS.   IDRIVHE57954

HANDBOOK OF AMERICAN-INDIANS NORTH OF MEXICO.   ISMITIB59619

A CHRONICLE OF RACE-RELATIONS -- THE UNITED STATES, NORTH AND SOUTH.   NDUBOWE41298

EXPERIMENTAL AND DEMONSTRATION MANPOWER PROJECT FOR THE RECRUITMENT, TRAINING, PLACEMENT AND FOLLOW-UP OF
RURAL UNEMPLOYED WORKERS IN TEN NORTH FLORIDA CITIES. FINAL REPORT. /PARTICIPANTS/   NJACKTA66597

INTEGRATION NORTH AND SOUTH.   NLOTHDX56710

NEGRO EMPLOYMENT IN THE TEXTILE INDUSTRIES OF NORTH AND SOUTH-CAROLINA. /NORTH-CAROLINA/   NOSBUDD66963

THE NORTH AMERICAN NEGRO. /DISCRIMINATION/   NSANCLA42537

NEGROES IN THE NORTH.   NSHAFHB65799

NEGROES GO NORTH, WEST. JOBS TAKE THEM FAR AFIELD FROM THE SOUTH.   NUSNEWR51272

ATTITUDES TOWARD WOMEN COLLEGE TEACHERS IN INSTITUTIONS OF HIGHER EDUCATION ACCREDITED BY THE NORTH
CENTRAL ASSOCIATION.   WBERWHD62475

FINAL REPORT. EXPERIMENTAL AND DEMONSTRATION MANPOWER PROJECT FOR THE RECRUITMENT, TRAINING, PLACEMENT
AND FOLLOW-UP OF RURAL UNEMPLOYED WORKERS IN TEN NORTH FLORIDA COUNTIES.   WFLORMP66326

NORTH-CAROLINA
FACTS ON ADC IN NORTH-CAROLINA. /NEGRO AMERICAN-INDIAN/   CNORTCS59934

SURVEY OF EMPLOYMENT IN STATE GOVERNMENT. /NORTH-CAROLINA/   GNORTCG64121

EQUAL PROTECTION OF THE LAWS IN NORTH-CAROLINA.   GUSCOMC62397

HEALTH PRACTICES AND EDUCATIONAL ASPIRATIONS AS INDICATORS OF ACCULTURATION AND SOCIAL-CLASS AMONG THE
EASTERN CHEROKEE. /NORTH-CAROLINA/   IKUPFHJ62216

A STUDY OF PROFESSIONAL PREPARATION OF NEGRO TEACHERS OF EXCEPTIONAL CHILDREN IN NORTH-CAROLINA COUNTY

NORTH-CAROLINA   (CONTINUATION)
AND CITY PUBLIC SCHOOLS.   NKNIGOB65023

WORKERS WANTED. A STUDY OF EMPLOYERS HIRING POLICIES, PREFERENCES, AND PRACTICES IN NEW-HAVEN AND
CHARLOTTE. /CONNECTICUT NORTH-CAROLINA/   NNOLAEW49928

AT WORK IN NORTH-CAROLINA TODAY. 48 CASE-REPORTS ON NORTH-CAROLINA NEGROES NOW EMPLOYED OR PREPARING
THEMSELVES FOR EMPLOYMENT...THEIR EDUCATION, JOB QUALIFICATIONS, AND CAREER ASPIRATIONS.   NNCRTCGND933

AT WORK IN NORTH-CAROLINA TODAY. 48 CASE-REPORTS ON NORTH-CAROLINA NEGROES NOW EMPLOYED OR PREPARING
THEMSELVES FOR EMPLOYMENT...THEIR EDUCATION, JOB QUALIFICATIONS, AND CAREER ASPIRATIONS.   NNORTCGND933

EMPLOYMENT IN STATE GOVERNMENT. /NORTH-CAROLINA/   NNORTCG66092

NEGRO EMPLOYMENT IN THE TEXTILE INDUSTRIES OF NORTH AND SOUTH-CAROLINA. /NORTH-CAROLINA/   NOSBUDD66963

THE NEGRO TOBACCO WORKER AND HIS UNION IN DURHAM, NORTH-CAROLINA.   NRICEJD41053

SOUTHERN CITIES EMPLOYING NEGRO POLICEMEN -- INCLUDING NORTH-CAROLINA CITIES OVER 15,000 POPULATION.   NSTEEDL46173

CHARLOTTE. /NORTH-CAROLINA/   NWATTPX64294

NORTH-CAROLINA AND THE NEGRO.   NWAYNCM64295

NORTH-CENTRAL
RURAL PEOPLE AND THEIR RESOURCES, NORTH-CENTRAL NEW-MEXICO.   MTAYLMM60402

NORTH-DAKOTA
MINUTES OF INDIAN EMPLOYMENT MEETING HELD NOVEMBER 29-30, 1966 IN BISMARK, NORTH-DAKOTA.   IUSDLAB66322

NORTH-SOUTH
JOBS FOR NEGROES. SOME NORTH-SOUTH PLANT STUDIES. /CASE-STUDY/   NSTEEEH53174

NORTHEAST
INCOMES OF RURAL FAMILIES IN NORTHEAST TEXAS.   GSOUTJH59325

NORTHEASTERN
MIGRATION PATTERNS OF NEGROES FROM A RURAL NORTHEASTERN MISSISSIPPI COMMUNITY. /DEMOGRAPHY/   NRUBIMX60094

NORTHERN
THE PREDICTION AND EXPLANATION OF ECONOMIC ABSORPTION AMONG MEXICAN-AMERICANS, NEGROES, AND ANGLOS IN A
NORTHERN INDUSTRIAL COMMUNITY.   CSHANLW63120

THE ECONOMIC ABSORPTION OF IN-MIGRANT LABORERS IN A NORTHERN INDUSTRIAL COMMUNITY. /MEXICAN-AMERICAN
NEGRO/   CSHANLW64486

THE PREDICTION OF ECONOMIC ABSORPTION AND CULTURAL INTEGRATION AMONG MEXICAN-AMERICANS, NEGROES, AND
ANGLOS IN A NORTHERN INDUSTRIAL COMMUNITY.   CSHANLW66123

SUGAR BEET LABOR IN NORTHERN COLORADO. /MIGRANT-WORKERS/   GDAVIIF58939

THE MEXICAN IN THE NORTHERN URBAN AREA. A COMPARISON OF TWO GENERATIONS.   MGOLDNX59403

AN ECONOMICAL AND HISTORICAL ANALYSIS OF THE CAUSES OF VARIATION AMONG NORTHERN STANDARD METROPOLITAN
AREAS IN PRODUCTIVITY OF NEGRO MEN IN 1949.   NBATCAB61060

A COMPARISON OF THE SOCIAL CHARACTERISTICS AND EDUCATIONAL ASPIRATIONS OF NORTHERN, LOWER-CLASS, NEGRO
PARENTS WHO ACCEPTED AND DECLINED AN OPPORTUNITY FOR INTEGRATED EDUCATION FOR THEIR CHILDREN.   NCAGLLT66904

BLACK METROPOLIS. A STUDY OF NEGRO LIFE IN A NORTHERN CITY.   NDRAKSC45291

THE EFFECTS OF SOUTHERN WHITE WORKERS ON RACE-RELATIONS IN NORTHERN PLANTS.   NKILLLM52650

SOME ATTITUDES TOWARD EMPLOYING NEGROES AS TEACHERS IN A NORTHERN UNIVERSITY.   NMARCFL48054

SOME CORRELATES OF HIGH NEED FOR ACHIEVEMENT AMONG URBAN NORTHERN NEGROES.   NNUTTRL46951

THE RELATION OF RACIAL SEGREGATION IN EARLY SCHOOLING TO THE LEVEL OF ASPIRATION AND ACADEMIC ACHIEVEMENT
OF NEGRO STUDENTS IN A NORTHERN HIGH SCHOOL.   NSAINJN62137

CIVIL-RIGHTS AND THE NORTHERN GHETTO.   NSTUDOT64188

THE ADJUSTMENT OF NEGROES IN A NORTHERN INDUSTRIAL COMMUNITY.   NZIMMBG62360

REPORT OF ARROWHEAD REGIONAL CONFERENCE ON THE STATUS OF WOMEN IN NORTHERN MINNESOTA.   WARRORC66216

NORTHERN-CHEYENNE
POPULATION CHARACTERISTICS, LIVING CONDITIONS AND INCOME OF INDIAN FAMILIES, NORTHERN-CHEYENNE
RESERVATION, JULY, 1961.   IUSDINT63656

NORTHWEST
INDIANS OF THE NORTHWEST COAST.   IDCUCPX63549

NOTE
A NOTE ON THE VALUES OF SOUTHERN COLLEGE WOMEN, WHITE AND NEGRO.   CGRAYSW47445

A NOTE ON OCCUPATIONAL MOBILITY FOR WHITE AND NONWHITE MALES, 1950 TO 1965.   GJAFFAJ66820

NOTE ON NEGRO ALIENATION.   NGORDOX65976

FATHER-ABSENCE AND NEGRO ADULT PERSONALITY. A RESEARCH NOTE.   NPETTTFND990

A NOTE ON RACIAL DIFFERENCES IN JOB VALUES AND DESIRES.   NSINGSL56142

NOTES
SOME NOTES ON THE MEXICAN POPULATION OF LOS-ANGELES COUNTY. /CALIFORNIA/   MLOSACOND431

THE CULTURE OF UNEMPLOYMENT. SOME NOTES ON NEGRO CHILDREN.   NSCHWMX64110

NOTES ON THE CONDITIONS OF NEGROES. /EDUCATION DISCRIMINATION/   NSTREGX45463

NOTES ON MIGRATION AND WORKERS ATTITUDES TOWARD IT.   PGREGPX61857

THE EDUCATION OF WOMEN -- INFORMATION AND RESEARCH NOTES.   WAMERCEND605

NOTES ON THE ROLE OF CHOICE IN THE PSYCHOLOGY OF PROFESSIONAL WOMEN. /OCCUPATIONS/   WBAILLX64623

NOTES ON WOMEN IN INDUSTRY -- PRESENTED AT AMERICAN PSYCHOLOGICAL SYMPOSIUM, SEPT 1963. /DISCRIMINATION/   WGILMBV63970

NOTES (CONTINUATION)
MATHEMATICS RETRAINING PROGRAM. **NOTES** AND COMMENTS, APRIL 1964, 1965, 1966. /TRAINING/   WRUTGMR64097

NOTICE
DISCRIMINATION. A **NOTICE** TO INDUSTRY.   NFORTXX55051

NSA-S
NSA-S PROFESSIONAL STATUS SURVEY, 1964. /ECONOMIC-STATUS/   WNATLSA65023

NULLIFICATION
RACIAL DISCRIMINATION AND THE FEDERAL LAW. A PROBLEM IN **NULLIFICATION**.   NLUSKLX63713

NUMBER
ETHNIC SURVEY OF MUNICIPAL-EMPLOYEES. A REPORT ON THE **NUMBER** AND DISTRIBUTION OF NEGROES AND
PUERTO-RICANS AND OTHER EMPLOYEES BY THE CITY OF NEW-YORK.   CNEWYCC64916

MANPOWER DEVELOPMENT TRAINING. TOTAL **NUMBER** OF NEW ENROLLEES DURING THE MONTH BY RACE AND OCCUPATION
STATEWIDE AND BY ADMINISTRATIVE AREA, SEPTEMBER, 1966, OCTOBER, 1966. /CALIFORNIA/   GCALDEM66518

A SUMMARY REPORT OF PRACTICES AND PROGRAMS DESIGNED TO REDUCE THE **NUMBER** OF DROPOUTS IN THE HIGH SCHOOLS
OF LOS-ANGELES COUNTY. /CALIFORNIA/   GDELMDT66147

CHANGES IN THE **NUMBER** AND COMPOSITION OF THE POOR. /DEMOGRAPHY/   GMILLHP65656

TECHNICAL REPORT **NUMBER** 1. EMPLOYMENT PRACTICES IN THE HOTEL, MOTEL AND RESTAURANT INDUSTRY OF MISSOURI.   GMILLRX66020

TECHNICAL REPORT **NUMBER** 2. EMPLOYMENT PRACTICES OF SELECTED MISSOURI PUBLIC UTILITIES. NATURAL GAS AND
ELECTRIC.   GMILLRX66021

NEGRO FARM OPERATORS. **NUMBER**, LOCATION AND RECENT TRENDS.   NBEALCL58064

THE CHANGING **NUMBER** AND DISTRIBUTION OF THE AGED NEGRO POPULATION OF THE UNITED STATES. /DEMOGRAPHY/   NSMITLT58145

REPORT OF THE EXPLORATORY STATISTICAL SURVEY OF THE EDUCATIONAL-ATTAINMENT, **NUMBER**, AND AVAILABILITY OF
THE MEMBERSHIP OF THE AMERICAN ASSOCIATION OF UNIVERSITY WOMEN FOR TEACHING IN THE FIELDS OF SCIENCE AND
MATHEMATICS. /OCCUPATIONS/   WDOLAEF57735

NURSE
INITIATION INTO A WOMAN-S PROFESSION. IDENTITY PROBLEMS IN THE STATUS TRANSITION OF CO-ED TO STUDENT
NURSE.   WDAVIFX66723

A SURVEY OF THE SOCIAL AND OCCUPATIONAL CHARACTERISTICS OF A METROPOLITAN **NURSE**. COMPLEMENT.
/OCCUPATIONAL-DISTRIBUTION/   WDEUTIX56730

A SURVEY OF THE SOCIAL AND OCCUPATIONAL CHARACTERISTICS OF A METROPOLITAN **NURSE** COMPLEMENT.   WDEUTIX57369

UPDATING TRAINING FOR THE RETURNING **NURSE**, SOCIAL WORKER AND TEACHER.   WNATLCP61018

THE NURSING SHORTAGE AND THE **NURSE** TRAINING ACT OF 1964. /MANPOWER/   WYETTDX66246

NURSES
NEGRO **NURSES** IN HOSPITALS. /WOMEN NEGRO/   CGOLDXX60374

THE BLS STUDY OF **NURSES** SALARIES AND EMPLOYMENT CONDITIONS.   WAMERJN57378

SURVEY OF EMPLOYMENT-CONDITIONS OF **NURSES** EMPLOYED BY PHYSICIANS AND/OR DENTISTS, JULY 1964.   WAMERNA65610

INACTIVE **NURSES**. AN UNTAPPED RECRUITMENT SOURCE.   WBARKAE65628

THE OCCUPATIONAL-STATUS OF **NURSES**.   WDEVEGX62731

WHAT **NURSES** NEED IS A CHANCE TO GROW. /OCCUPATIONAL-STATUS/   WGINSEX62786

TWENTY THOUSAND **NURSES** TELL THEIR STORY. /SOCIO-ECONOMIC/   WHUGHEC58851

EMPLOYMENT AND CONDITIONS OF WORK OF **NURSES**.   WINTELO60862

PROFESSIONAL STANDARDS AND ECONOMIC-STATUS OF **NURSES** IN THE UNITED STATES.   WKRUGOH60917

THE SHORTAGE OF **NURSES** AND CONDITIONS OF WORK IN NURSING. /OCCUPATIONS/   WKRUSMX58920

NURSES AND OTHER HOSPITAL PERSONNEL -- THEIR EARNINGS AND EMPLOYMENT-CONDITIONS.   WUSDLAB61211

NURSING
INTEGRATION IN PROFESSIONAL **NURSING**. /OCCUPATIONS NEGRO WOMEN/   CCARNME62183

OPPORTUNITIES IN **NURSING** FOR DISADVANTAGED YOUTH. /WOMEN NEGRO OCCUPATIONS/   CFRAKFX66375

AN EXPERIMENT IN RETRAINING UNEMPLOYED MEN FOR PRACTICAL **NURSING** CAREERS.   GPEIMSC66139

FACTS ABOUT **NURSING**.   WAMERNA66608

SURVEY OF SALARIES AND PERSONNEL PRACTICES FOR TEACHERS AND ADMINISTRATORS IN **NURSING** EDUCATIONAL
PROGRAMS, DECEMBER 1965.   WAMERNA66612

ARE NEGRO SCHOOLS OF **NURSING** NEEDED TODAY.   WCARNME64910

ROLE CONCEPTION AND CAREER ASPIRATION. A STUDY OF IDENTITY IN **NURSING**.   WCORWRG61707

NURSING PROFESSION. FIVE SOCIOLOGICAL SURVEYS.   WDAVIFX66722

SOCIAL FACTORS WHICH AFFECT CAREER CHOICE IN PSYCHIATRIC **NURSING**.   WDOUGAM61740

DROP-OUTS FROM SCHOOLS OF **NURSING**. THE EFFECT OF SELF- AND ROLE PERCEPTION.   WKIBRAK58902

THE SHORTAGE OF NURSES AND CONDITIONS OF WORK IN **NURSING**. /OCCUPATIONS/   WKRUSMX58920

AGE AND MARITAL-STATUS AND THEIR RELATIONSHIP TO SUCCESS IN PRACTICAL **NURSING**. /OCCUPATIONS/   WMEADLX63967

HEALTH MANPOWER SOURCE BOOK. SECTION 2. **NURSING** PERSONNEL.   WUSDHEW66177

THE **NURSING** SHORTAGE AND THE NURSE TRAINING ACT OF 1964. /MANPOWER/   WYETTDX66246

NURSING-S
NURSING-S ECONOMIC PLIGHT. /ECONOMIC-STATUS/   WMOSEEX65000

NURSING-STUDENTS
CAREER DECISIONS AND PROFESSIONAL EXPECTATIONS OF **NURSING-STUDENTS**. /ASPIRATIONS/   WFOXXDJ61767

NY ANTI-DISCRIMINATION LAW. 1946 ANNUAL REPORT.   /NEW-YORK/   GLABOLR46872

OAK
OAK GLEN -- A TRAINING CAMP FOR UNEMPLOYED YOUTH.   /NEGRO MEXICAN-AMERICAN/   CUSDLAB66323

OAKLAND
REPORT ON OAKLAND SCHOOLS. AN INVESTIGATION UNDER SECTION 1421 OF THE CALIFORNIA LABOR CODE OF THE
OAKLAND UNIFIED SCHOOL DISTRICT 1962-1963.   /NEGRO ORIENTAL MEXICAN-AMERICAN/   CCALDIR63710

REPORT ON OAKLAND SCHOOLS. AN INVESTIGATION UNDER SECTION 1421 OF THE CALIFORNIA LABOR CODE OF THE
OAKLAND UNIFIED SCHOOL DISTRICT 1962-1963.   /NEGRO ORIENTAL MEXICAN-AMERICAN/   CCALDIR63710

INCOME, EDUCATION AND UNEMPLOYMENT IN NEIGHBORHOODS. OAKLAND, CALIFORNIA.   /DEMOGRAPHY/   CUSDLAB63476

MANPOWER RESOURCES OF THE SAN-FRANCISCO OAKLAND BAY AREA 1960-1970.   /CALIFORNIA/   GCALDEM63520

SUB-EMPLOYMENT IN THE SLUMS OF OAKLAND.   /CALIFORNIA/   GUSDLAB66521

OAKLAND LABOR BACKS UP YOUTH.   /TRAINING/   NAWNEMX66875

INTERIM REPORT ON OAKLAND SCHOOLS.   /CALIFORNIA/   NCALFEP66169

THE ECONOMIC-STATUS OF NEGROES IN THE SAN-FRANCISCO OAKLAND BAY AREA. A REPORT BASED ON THE 1960 CENSUS
OF POPULATION. /CALIFORNIA/   NCALFES63172

OBJECTIVE
OBJECTIVE ACCESS IN THE OPPORTUNITY STRUCTURE. THE ASSESSMENT OF THREE ETHNIC GROUPS WITH RESPECT TO
QUANTIFIED SOCIAL STRUCTURAL VARIABLES.   MRENDGX63461

OBJECTIVES
THE MIGRATION DIVISION -- POLICY, FUNCTIONS, OBJECTIVES.   PPUERRD57789

OBLIGATIONS
TEXTS OF RULES AND REGULATIONS OF PRESIDENT-S COMMITTEE ON EQUAL-EMPLOYMENT-OPPORTUNITY RELATING TO
OBLIGATIONS OF GOVERNMENT CONTRACTORS AND SUBCONTRACTORS, EFFECTIVE JULY 22, 1961. A BNA SPECIAL REPORT.   GBURENA61498

MANAGEMENT-S CONCERN WITH RECENT CIVIL-RIGHTS LEGISLATION AFFECTING MANAGEMENT-S OBLIGATIONS TO HIS
EMPLOYEES AND APPLICANTS FOR EMPLOYMENT, MAINLY IN THE STATE OF NEW-YORK.   GKOPPRW65858

OBSERVATIONS
SOME GENERAL OBSERVATIONS ON THE ADMINISTRATION OF STATE FAIR-EMPLOYMENT-PRACTICE LAWS.   GGIRARA64721

OBSTACLES
OBSTACLES TO DESEGREGATION IN AMERICA-S URBAN AREAS.   GGRIEGX64743

OBSTACLES TO ASSIMILATION OF THE MEXICAN-AMERICAN IN THE UNITED STATES.   MBEALRL60362

PERSONAL AND ENVIRONMENTAL OBSTACLES TO PRODUCTION ADJUSTMENTS ON SOUTH-CAROLINA PIEDMONT AREA FARMS.   NTAYLCC58411

OCCUPATION
OCCUPATIONAL CHARACTERISTICS, DATA ON AGE, RACE, EDUCATION, WORK EXPERIENCE, INCOME, ETC. FOR WORKERS IN
EACH OCCUPATION.   CUSBURC63177

OCCUPATION BY INDUSTRY.   /DEMOGRAPHY/   CUSBURC63179

MANPOWER DEVELOPMENT TRAINING. TOTAL NUMBER OF NEW ENROLLEES DURING THE MONTH BY RACE AND OCCUPATION
STATEWIDE AND BY ADMINISTRATIVE AREA, SEPTEMBER, 1966, OCTOBER, 1966. /CALIFORNIA/   GCALDEM66518

MORTALITY BY OCCUPATION AND INDUSTRY AMONG MEN 20 TO 64 YEARS OF AGE. UNITED STATES, 1950. /DEMOGRAPHY/   GGURALX62748

DISCRIMINATION IN THE FIELD OF EMPLOYMENT AND OCCUPATION.   GINTELC58817

RACE, OCCUPATION, AND SOCIAL-CLASS IN NEW-YORK.   NFRUMRM58388

THE EMPLOYMENT OF NEGROES IN THE US BY MAJOR OCCUPATION AND INDUSTRY.   NHOPEJX53567

WHITE-COLLAR WOMEN. THE SECRETARIAL-STENOGRAPHIC OCCUPATION.   WBRYACD57659

DISCRIMINATION IN EMPLOYMENT OR OCCUPATION ON THE BASIS OF MARITAL-STATUS.   WINTELR62865

A COMPARISON OF THE MALE-FEMALE ROLES IN ENGINEERING. /OCCUPATION/   WROBISS63083

OCCUPATION-PATTERNS
OCCUPATION-PATTERNS OF SPANISH-AMERICANS IN SELECTED AREAS OF TEXAS.   MSKRARL62494

OCCUPATIONAL
COMPARISON OF MEXICANS, NEGROES AND WHITES WITH RESPECT TO OCCUPATIONAL HISTORY, RURAL-URBAN RESIDENCE
HISTORY AND ACCULTURIZATION WITHIN THE INSTITUTIONAL STRUCTURE OF LANSING, MICHIGAN.   CGOLDVX60494

BREAKING THE BARRIERS OF OCCUPATIONAL ISOLATION. A REPORT ON UPGRADING LOW-SKILL, LOW-WAGE WORKERS.
/NEGRO PUERTO-RICAN/   CPROJAX66237

OCCUPATIONAL AND RESIDENTIAL ADJUSTMENT OF RURAL MIGRANTS. /NEGRO MEXICAN-AMERICAN/   CSHANLW61119

THE URBAN ADJUSTMENT OF IMMIGRANTS. THE RELATIONSHIP OF EDUCATION TO OCCUPATIONAL AND TOTAL FAMILY
INCOME. /NEGRO MEXICAN-AMERICAN/   CSHANLW63122

SEX DIFFERENCES IN OCCUPATIONAL CHOICE PATTERNS AMONG ADOLESCENTS. /ASPIRATIONS WOMEN NEGRO/   CSPREJX62999

OCCUPATIONAL CHARACTERISTICS, DATA ON AGE, RACE, EDUCATION, WORK EXPERIENCE, INCOME, ETC. FOR WORKERS IN
EACH OCCUPATION.   CUSBURC63177

FORMAL OCCUPATIONAL TRAINING OF ADULT WORKERS, ITS EXTENT, NATURE, AND USE.   GBEDEMX64448

OCCUPATIONAL DISCRIMINATION. SOME THEORETICAL PROPOSITIONS.   GBLALHM62454

EFFECTS OF TECHNOLOGICAL-CHANGE ON OCCUPATIONAL EMPLOYMENT PATTERNS IN THE UNITED STATES.   GCLAGEX64625

THE SCHOOL COUNSELOR AT WORK ON OCCUPATIONAL DISCRIMINATION.   GDIXALX46643

EDUCATION AND OCCUPATIONAL MOBILITY. A REGRESSION ANALYSIS.   GDUNCOD63652

ATTITUDE TOWARD OCCUPATIONAL CHANGE AS AN INDICATOR OF PROSPECTS FOR ADJUSTMENT.   GDUNKJE64653

CHANGING EMPHASIS IN OCCUPATIONAL TEST DEVELOPMENT.   GDVORBJ65650

THE VALIDITY OF OCCUPATIONAL APTITUDE TESTS.   GGHISEE66788

OCCUPATIONAL   (CONTINUATION)
THE POSITION OF RACIAL GROUPS IN OCCUPATIONAL STRUCTURES.   GGLICCE47722

OCCUPATIONAL EMPLOYMENT STATISTICS. SOURCES AND DATA.   GGREEHX66627

NONWHITE OCCUPATIONAL STATUS. BY REGION. AS RELATED TO PERCENT OF NONWHITE.   GGUEREW63746

STUDY CF OCCUPATIONAL CHARACTERISTICS OF NON-WHITES IN THE EAST BATON-ROUGE AREA. /LOUISIANA/   GHARRWRND76G

OCCUPATIONAL MOBILITY FROM THE FARM LABOR-FORCE.   GHATHDE67936

A NOTE ON OCCUPATIONAL MOBILITY FOR WHITE AND NONWHITE MALES. 1950 TO 1965.   GJAFFAJ66820

COUNSELOR-S GUIDE TO OCCUPATIONAL AND OTHER MANPOWER INFORMATION. AN ANNOTATED BIBLIOGRAPHY.   GLAFADP65782

COMMUNITY VALUES IN EDUCATION AND OCCUPATIONAL SELECTION. A STUDY OF YOUTH IN EMMITSBURG, MARYLAND.   GLEONRC64894

SOCIAL-STATUS AND EDUCATIONAL AND OCCUPATIONAL ASPIRATION.   GSEWEWH57297

PROJECTED CHANGES IN THE OCCUPATIONAL STRUCTURE OF THE LABOR-FORCE. IMPLICATIONS FOR PUBLIC WELFARE.   GSIFFHX64105

OCCUPATIONAL DEVELOPMENTS. SHORTAGES OF SKILLED TECHNICAL MANPOWER HIGHEST IN RECENT YEARS.   GUSDLAB65561

AMERICA-S INDUSTRIAL AND OCCUPATIONAL MANPOWER REQUIREMENTS, 1964-75.   GUSDLAB66437

ANALYSIS OF MALE NAVAHO STUDENTS PERCEPTIONS OF OCCUPATIONAL OPPORTUNITIES AND THEIR ATTITUDES TOWARD
DEVELOPMENT OF SKILLS AND TRAITS NECESSARY FCR OCCUPATIONAL COMPETENCE.   IDESPCW65548

ANALYSIS OF MALE NAVAHO STUDENTS PERCEPTIONS OF OCCUPATIONAL OPPORTUNITIES AND THEIR ATTITUDES TOWARD
DEVELOPMENT OF SKILLS AND TRAITS NECESSARY FOR OCCUPATIONAL COMPETENCE.   IDESPCW65548

LEVEL OF OCCUPATIONAL ASPIRATICNS AMONG MONTANA INDIANS IN GRADE AND HIGH SCHOOL.   IDOUGGV60550

OCCUPATIONAL AND EDUCATIONAL LEVELS OF ASPIRATION OF MEXICAN-AMERICAN YOUTH.   MDEHGAX61388

OCCUPATIONAL CHANGE AMONG SPANISH-AMERICANS IN ATASCOSA-COUNTY AND SAN-ANTONIO, TEXAS.   MSKRARL66492

SOCIAL FACTORS IN OCCUPATIONAL AND EDUCATIONAL ASPIRATIONS OF NEGRO AND WHITE STUDENTS.   NADDIDP61002

A STUDY OF THE OCCUPATIONAL AWARENESS OF A SELECTED GROUP OF NINTH GRADE NEGRO STUDENTS.   NAMOSWE60020

OCCUPATIONAL ASPIRATIONS OF LOWER-CLASS NEGRC AND WHITE YOUTH.   NANTOAX59027

NEGRC ADDICT OCCUPATIONAL HISTCRY.   NBATEWM66880

DISCRIMINATION AND THE OCCUPATIONAL PROGRESS OF NEGRCES. A COMMENT.   NBECKGS62068

OCCUPATIONAL CHOICE IN THE NEGRO COLLEGE.   NBRAZWF60112

VOCATICNAL CHOICES UF NEGRO HIGH SCHOOL STUDENTS IN MACON COUNTY, ALABAMA, AND THEIR RELATIONSHIP TO
BASIC OCCUPATIONAL ACTIVITES OF THE SCHOOL COMMUNITIES. /ASPIRATIONS/   NCHAPEJ49351

A COMPARATIVE STUDY OF THE OCCUPATIONAL INTERESTS OF NEGRO AND WHITE ADOLESCENT BOYS.   NCONNSM65471

OCCUPATIONAL SHIFTS IN NEGRO EMPLOYMENT.   NDIAMDE65273

NEGRO LEADERSHIP IN RURAL GEORGIA COMMUNITIES. OCCUPATIONAL AND SOCIAL ASPECTS.   NEDWAVA42328

I G PERFORMANCE. EDUCATIONAL AND OCCUPATIONAL ASPIRATIONS OF YOUTH IN A SOUTHERN CITY -- A RACIAL
COMPARISON.   NGEISPX62397

OCCUPATIONAL DIFFERENTIATION OF NEGROES AND WHITES IN THE UNITED STATES.   NGIBBJP65401

OCCUPATIONAL CHOICE. AN APPRCACH TO A GENERAL THEORY.   NGINZEX51410

CHANGES IN THE AMERICAN OCCUPATIONAL-STRUCTURE AND OCCUPATIONAL GAINS OF NEGROES DURING THE 1940-S.   NGLENND62422

OCCUPATIONAL BENEFITS TO WHITES FROM THE SUBORDINATICN OF NEGROES. /DISCRIMINATION/   NGLENND63423

OCCUPATIONAL CHOICE AND THE TEACHING CAREER.   NGUBAEG59463

SOCIAL-CLASS CONSTRAINTS ON THE OCCUPATIONAL ASPIRATIONS OF STUDENTS ATTENDING SOME PREDOMINANTLY NEGRO
COLLEGES.   NGURIPX66467

RECENT TRENDS IN THE OCCUPATIONAL MOBILITY OF NEGROES. 1930-1960.   NHARENX65484

A STUDY CF OCCUPATIONAL ATTITUDES.   NHARREC53493

OCCUPATIONAL MOBILITY AND ATTITUDES TOWARD NEGROES.   NHCDGRWND355

OCCUPATIONAL ASSIMILATION AS A CCMPETITIVE PRUCESS.   NHODGRW65556

THE EDUCATIONAL AND OCCUPATIONAL ASPIRATIONS AND PLANS OF NEGRO AND WHITE MALE ELEMENTARY SCHOOL
STUDENTS.   NHOLLRG59562

THE OCCUPATIONAL SITUATION UF CENTRAL HARLEM YOUTH.   NHOUSLX65577

FUTURE OCCUPATIONAL DIFFERENCES BETWEEN THE RACES. A MARKOV APPROACH.   NLEWISX66693

A PILOT STUDY OF PERSONALITY FACTORS RELATED TO OCCUPATIONAL ASPIRATIONS OF NEGRO COLLEGE STUDENTS.   NLITTLW66697

THE NEGRO WORKER-S CULTURAL AND OCCUPATIONAL LIMITATIONS.   NMCPICM61729

RETREATISM AND OCCUPATIONAL ASPIRATICNS AMONG WHITE AND NEGRO HIGH SCHOOL SENIORS.   NPOWEEC61009

DISCRIMINATION AND THE OCCUPATIONAL PROGRESS OF NEGRCES.   NRAYAEX61040

OCCUPATIONAL ATTITUDES OF NEGRO WORKERS.   NRICHEX43056

ANNUAL FAMILY AND OCCUPATIONAL EARNINGS OF RESIDENTS OF TWO NEGRO HOUSING PROJECTS IN ATLANTA 1937-1944.
/GECRGIA/   NRITTAL45062

THE NEGRO-S OCCUPATIONAL PROGRESS.   NRUSSJL66096

OCCUPATIONAL ESTABLISHMENT OF FORMER STUDENTS OF VOCATIONAL AGRICULTURE IN MONTGCMERY TRAINING SCHOOL
AREA. /ALABAMA/   NSCOTCDND346

THE CHANGING OCCUPATIONAL STRUCTURE OF THE SOUTH.   NSIMPRL65140

OCCUPATIONAL   (CONTINUATION)
OCCUPATIONAL PRESTIGE IN A NEGRO COMMUNITY.   NSOLZRX61153

EMPLOYMENT GAINS AND THE DETERMINANTS OF THE **OCCUPATIONAL** DISTRIBUTION OF NEGROES.   NTHURLC67971

OCCUPATIONAL CHOICES OF NEGRO HIGH SCHOOL SENIORS IN TEXAS.   NTURNBA57165

OCCUPATIONAL PATTERNS OF INEQUALITY.   NTURNRH54216

OCCUPATIONAL DISTRIBUTION CF EMPLOYED COLORED WORKERS OF MARYLAND.   NUSDLAB40834

OCCUPATIONAL STATUS OF NEGRO RAILROAD WORKERS.   NUSDLAB43836

OCCUPATIONAL DISTRIBUTION OF NEGROES IN 1940.   NUSDLAB44835

NEGROES IN NEW-YORK CITY. **OCCUPATIONAL** DISTRIBUTION.   NUSDLAB49831

ENHANCING THE **OCCUPATIONAL** OUTLOOK AND VOCATIONAL ASPIRATIONS OF SOUTHERN SECONDARY YOUTH. A CONFERENCE
OF SECONDARY SCHOOL PRINCIPALS AND COUNSELORS.   NUSDLAB65334

OCCUPATIONAL ASPIRATIONS OF NEGRO MALE HIGH SCHOOL STUDENTS.   NUZELOX61278

ETHNIC STATUS AND **OCCUPATIONAL** DILEMMAS.   NVOLLHM66287

COMPARATIVE STUDY OF SOCIO-ECONOMIC AND SOCIAL-PSYCHOLOGICAL DETERMINANTS OF EDUCATIONAL AND **OCCUPATIONAL**
ASPIRATIONS OF NEGRO AND WHITE COLLEGE SENIORS.   NWHITRM59319

OCCUPATIONAL PLANS AND ASPIRATIONS. PUERTO-RICAN AND AMERICAN HIGH SCHOOL SENIORS COMPARED.   PSILVRM63100

A SURVEY OF THE SOCIAL AND **OCCUPATIONAL** CHARACTERISTICS OF A METROPOLITAN NURSE. COMPLEMENT.
/OCCUPATIONAL-DISTRIBUTION/   WDEUTIX56730

A SURVEY OF THE SOCIAL AND **OCCUPATIONAL** CHARACTERISTICS OF A METROPOLITAN NURSE COMPLEMENT.   WDEUTIX57369

OCCUPATIONAL TRAINING OF WOMEN IN THE UNITED STATES.   WINTELR64866

INVESTIGATION OF DIFFERENCES IN **OCCUPATIONAL** PREFERENCES, STEREOTYPIC THINKING, AND PSYCHOLOGICAL NEEDS
AMONG UNDERGRADUATE WOMEN STUDENTS IN SELECTED CURRICULAR AREAS. /ASPIRATIONS/   WKITTRE60313

OCCUPATIONAL VALUES AND OCCUPATIONAL SELECTION.   WRAVIMJ57077

OCCUPATIONAL VALUES AND **OCCUPATIONAL** SELECTION.   WRAVIMJ57077

OCCUPATIONAL CHOICE AMONG CAREER ORIENTED COLLEGE WOMEN. /ASPIRATIONS/   WSIMPRL61115

OCCUPATIONAL PLANNING BY YOUNG WOMEN, A STUDY OF OCCUPATIONAL EXPERIENCES, ASPIRATIONS, ATTITUDES, AND
PLANS CF COLLEGE AND HIGH SCHOOL GIRLS.   WSLOCWL56116

OCCUPATIONAL PLANNING BY YOUNG WOMEN, A STUDY OF **OCCUPATIONAL** EXPERIENCES, ASPIRATIONS, ATTITUDES, AND
PLANS CF COLLEGE AND HIGH SCHOOL GIRLS.   WSLOCWL56116

WOMEN IN INDUSTRY -- PATTERNS OF WOMEN-S WORK AND **OCCUPATIONAL** HEALTH AND SAFETY. /OCCUPATIONS/   WSPIRES60301

OCCUPATIONAL TRAINING OF WOMEN UNDER THE MANPOWER-DEVELOPMENT-AND-TRAINING-ACT.   WUSDLAB64179

VOCATIONAL INTERESTS AND **OCCUPATIONAL** ADJUSTMENT OF COLLEGE WOMEN.   WWARRPA59222

OCCUPATIONAL PLANNING FOR WOMEN.   WZAPOMW61282

OCCUPATIONAL-CHOICES
SOME PERSONAL AND SOCIOLOGICAL VARIABLES ASSOCIATED WITH **OCCUPATIONAL-CHOICES** OF NEGRO YOUTH.   NHERSPF65520

OCCUPATIONAL-DISTRIB
ECONOMIC-STATUS OF NON-WHITE WORKERS, 1955-1962. /OCCUPATIONAL-DISTRIBUTION/   GKESSMA63848

A SURVEY OF THE SOCIAL AND OCCUPATIONAL CHARACTERISTICS OF A METROPOLITAN NURSE. COMPLEMENT.
/OCCUPATIONAL-DISTRIBUTION/   WDEUTIX56730

OCCUPATIONAL-MOBILIT
OCCUPATIONAL-MOBILITY OF NEGRO PROFESSIONAL WORKERS.   NEDWAGF64326

OCCUPATIONAL-PATTERN
CHILDREN OF THE GILDED GHETTO. CONFLICT RESOLUTION OF THREE GENERATIONS OF AMERICAN JEWS.
/OCCUPATIONAL-PATTERNS/   JKRAMJR61736

OCCUPATIONAL-PATTERNS OF RURAL AND URBAN SPANISH-AMERICANS IN TWO SOUTH TEXAS COUNTIES.   MCOTHML66385

THE NEGRO POPULATION OF CHICAGO. A STUDY OF RESIDENTIAL SUCCESSION. /ILLINOIS OCCUPATIONAL-PATTERNS/   NDUNCOD57306

THE NEGRO PROFESSIONAL CLASS. /OCCUPATIONAL-PATTERNS/   NEDWAGF59324

THE USE OF NEGRO LABOR IN SOUTHERN INDUSTRY. /OCCUPATIONAL-PATTERNS/   NHALLDE53477

A CENTURY OF CHANGE. NEGROES IN THE US ECONOMY, 1860-1960. /OCCUPATIONAL-PATTERNS/   NHAYEMX62506

CHANGING PATTERNS OF NEGRO EMPLOYMENT. /OCCUPATIONAL-PATTERNS/   NKIFEAX64649

TRENDS IN THE ECONOMIC-STATUS OF THE NEGRO PEOPLE. /OCCUPATIONAL-PATTERNS/   NPERLVX52983

OCCUPATIONAL-STATUS
NONWHITE POPULATION BY RACE. NEGROES, INDIANS, JAPANESE, CHINESE, FILIPINOS. BY AGE, SEX, MARITAL-STATUS,
EDUCATION, EMPLOYMENT-STATUS, OCCUPATIONAL-STATUS, INCOME, ETC. /DEMOGRAPHY/   CUSBURC53378

NONWHITE POPULATION BY RACE. NEGROES, INDIANS, JAPANESE,CHINESE, FILIPINOS. BY AGE, SEX,
MARITAL-STATUS,EDUCATION, EMPLOYMENT-STATUS, OCCUPATIONAL-STATUS, INCOME, ETC. /DEMOGRAPHY/   CUSBURC63176

EDUCATIONAL STATUS, COLLEGE PLANS, AND OCCUPATIONAL-STATUS OF FARM AND NONFARM YOUTHS. OCTOBER 1959.   GCOWHJD61427

NEGRO SUBORDINATION AND WHITE GAINS. /INCOME OCCUPATIONAL-STATUS/   NCUTRPX65245

TUSKEGEE LOOKS AT ITS VETERANS. /OCCUPATIONAL-STATUS/   NDERBIA46251

DISCRIMINATION 1963. /OCCUPATIONAL-STATUS/   NFINLOX63355

EXPANDING NEGRO OPPORTUNITIES. /OCCUPATIONAL-STATUS/   NGINZEX60404

SOME CHANGES IN THE RELATIVE STATUS OF AMERICAN NON-WHITES, 1940 TO 1960. /INCOME OCCUPATIONAL-STATUS
EDUCATION/   NGLENND63421

OCCUPATIONAL-STATUS (CONTINUATION)
THE RELATIVE SIZE OF THE NEGRO POPULATION AND NEGRO **OCCUPATIONAL-STATUS**.   NGLENND64424

REPLY TO CUTRIGHT ON NEGRO SUBORDINATION. /**OCCUPATIONAL-STATUS**/   NGLENND65425

CHANGING **OCCUPATIONAL-STATUS** OF NEGRO EDUCATION.   NHARENX62483

ON BEING A NEGRO IN 1960. /**OCCUPATIONAL-STATUS**/   NSMITCU60275

WHO NEEDS THE NEGRO. /**OCCUPATIONAL-STATUS** TECHNOLOGICAL-CHANGE/   NWILLSM64232

THE **OCCUPATIONAL-STATUS** OF NURSES.   WOEVEGX62731

WHAT NURSES NEED IS A CHANCE TO GROW. /**OCCUPATIONAL-STATUS**/   WGINSEX62786

OCCUPATIONAL-STRATIF
RESIDENTIAL DISTRIBUTION AND **OCCUPATIONAL-STRATIFICATION**.   NDUNCOD55307

OCCUPATIONAL-STRUCTU
CHANGES IN THE AMERICAN **OCCUPATIONAL-STRUCTURE** AND OCCUPATIONAL GAINS OF NEGROES DURING THE 1940-S.   NGLENND62422

OCCUPATIONS
INTEGRATION IN PROFESSIONAL NURSING. /**OCCUPATIONS** NEGRO WOMEN/   CCARNME62183

OPPORTUNITIES IN NURSING FOR DISADVANTAGED YOUTH. /WOMEN NEGRO **OCCUPATIONS**/   CFRAKFX66375

NO TIME FOR PREJUDICE. /WOMEN NEGRO **OCCUPATIONS**/   CSTAUMK61132

OCCUPATIONS BY EARNINGS AND EDUCATION. STATISTICS FOR MEN 18-64 YEARS OLD, BY COLOR, IN SELECTED
OCCUPATIONS. /DEMOGRAPHY/   CUSBURC63178

OCCUPATIONS BY EARNINGS AND EDUCATION. STATISTICS FOR MEN 18-64 YEARS OLD, BY COLOR, IN SELECTED
OCCUPATIONS. /DEMOGRAPHY/   CUSBURC63178

OPPORTUNITIES FOR NEGRO WOMEN AS DIETICIANS. /**OCCUPATIONS**/   CUSDLAB43837

FREEDOM OF CHOICE IN PERSONAL SERVICE **OCCUPATIONS**. 13TH AMENDMENT LIMITATIONS ON ANTIDISCRIMINATION
LEGISLATION.   GAVINAX64410

IMPLICATIONS OF THE RECENT CENSUSES FOR PROFESSIONAL AGRICULTURAL WORKERS. /**OCCUPATIONS**/   GBEALCL61412

RURAL INDUSTRIALIZATION IN A LOUISIANA COMMUNITY. /ECONOMIC-STATUS **OCCUPATIONS**/   GBERTAL59393

RURAL-FARM MALES ENTERING AND LEAVING WORKING AGES, 1940-50 AND 1950-60. REPLACEMENT RATIOS AND RATES.
/**OCCUPATIONS**/   GBOWLGK56433

THE EMPLOYED POOR. THEIR CHARACTERISTICS AND **OCCUPATIONS**.   GCUMMLD65623

ETHNIC GROUPS AND THE PRACTICE OF MEDICINE. /**OCCUPATIONS**/   GLIEBSX58042

RURAL INDUSTRIALIZATION. A SUMMARY OF FIVE STUDIES. /UNEMPLOYMENT **OCCUPATIONS**/   GMAITST61383

MAN, WORK AND SOCIETY. A READER IN THE SOCIOLOGY OF **OCCUPATIONS**.   GNOSOSX62336

THE EFFECTS OF AUTOMATION ON **OCCUPATIONS** AND WORKERS IN PENNSYLVANIA.   GPENNSE65641

ADAPTATION OF PAPAGO WORKERS TO OFF-RESERVATION **OCCUPATIONS**.   IWADDJX66680

WHO SHALL BE OUR DOCTORS. /**OCCUPATIONS** DISCRIMINATION/   JBLOCLX57706

THE JEWISH LAW STUDENT AND NEW-YORK JOBS -- DISCRIMINATORY EFFECTS IN LAW FIRM HIRING PRACTICES.
/**OCCUPATIONS**/   JYALELJ64774

CAREERS FOR NEGROES ON NEWSPAPERS. /**OCCUPATIONS**/   NAMERNG66018

THE CHARACTERISTICS OF THE SUPPLY OF NEGROES FOR PROFESSIONAL **OCCUPATIONS**.   NANDERW65024

CHANGING PATTERNS IN AGRICULTURAL PRODUCTIONS, WEST-VIRGINIA, 1920-1950. /**OCCUPATIONS**/   NANGLRA54254

THE NEW NEGRO CASUALTIES. /**OCCUPATIONS** TEACHERS/   NARISJM65029

THE NEGRO AUTOMOBILE-WORKERS. /**OCCUPATIONS**/   NBAILLH43043

THE ORIGIN AND DEVELOPMENT OF THE NEGRO VISITING TEACHER IN ALABAMA. /**OCCUPATIONS**/   NBOATRF49345

THE STATUS OF JOBS AND **OCCUPATIONS** AS EVALUATED BY AN URBAN NEGRO SAMPLE.   NBROWMC55126

NEGROES AND THE LAW. /**OCCUPATIONS**/   NCARLEL64182

INTEGRATING THE NEGRO TEACHER OUT OF A JOB. /**OCCUPATIONS**/   NCARTBX65999

PROGRESS AND PORTENTS FOR THE NEGRO IN MEDICINE. /**OCCUPATIONS**/   NCOBBWM48217

NOT TO THE SWIFT. PROGRESS AND PROSPECTS OF THE NEGRO IN SCIENCE AND THE PROFESSIONS. /**OCCUPATIONS**/   NCOBBWM58216

DISPLACED TEACHERS. /**OCCUPATIONS**/   NCOMMXX65229

NEGRO TEACHERS. MARTYRS TO INTEGRATION. /**OCCUPATIONS**/   NCOXXOC53935

REASONS FOR BELATED EDUCATION. A STUDY OF THE PLIGHT OF THE OLDER NEGRO TEACHERS. /**OCCUPATIONS**/   NCUNNGE58244

NEGROES AS TEACHING ASSISTANTS IN SOME PUBLICLY SUPPORTED UNIVERSITIES. /**OCCUPATIONS**/   NDANIWG62248

STUDY OF DETROIT POLICE DEPARTMENT PERSONNEL PRACTICES. /MICHIGAN **OCCUPATIONS**/   NDETRCC63267

NEGROES AND THE SERVICE INDUSTRIES. /**OCCUPATIONS**/   NDIAMDE64272

DESEGREGATION AND THE EMPLOYMENT OF NEGRO TEACHERS. /**OCCUPATIONS**/   NDODDHH55950

THE CENSUS OF NEGRO-OWNED BUSINESSES. /PHILADELPHIA PENNSYLVANIA **OCCUPATIONS**/   NDREXIT64295

CHANGES IN **OCCUPATIONS** AS THEY AFFECT THE NEGRO.   NEDWAGF64323

THE NATIONAL TECHNICAL ASSOCIATION. /**OCCUPATIONS**/   NEVANJC43258

THE STRUGGLE OF NEGRO TEACHERS IN FLORIDA FOR EQUAL SALARIES. /**OCCUPATIONS**/   NFERGML49961

PROBLEMS AND OPPORTUNITIES CONFRONTING NEGROES IN THE FIELD OF BUSINESS. REPORT ON THE NATIONAL

OCCUPATIONS   (CONTINUATION)

CONFERENCE ON SMALL BUSINESS. /OCCUPATIONS/	NFITZNH63358
THE NEGRO BUSINESSMAN. IN SEARCH OF A TRADITION. /OCCUPATIONS/	NFOLEEP66369
THE NEGRO LAWYER IN VIRGINIA. A SURVEY. /OCCUPATIONS/	NFRIEMX65387
THE CAREER PATTERNS OF NEGRO LAWYERS IN LOUISIANA. /OCCUPATIONS/	NGUILBM60465
THE NEGRO LAWYER AND HIS CLIENTS. /OCCUPATIONS/	NHALEWH52476
THE STATUS OF THE NEGRO CPA IN THE UNITED STATES. /OCCUPATIONS/	NHARRLJ62494
MEDICAL SOCIETY OF THE DISTRICT OF COLUMBIA TO ADMIT NEGRO PHYSICIANS. /OCCUPATIONS/	NJOURNM52628
NEGRO ENGINEERS AND STUDENTS REPORT ON THEIR PROFESSION. /OCCUPATIONS/	NKIEHRX58647
OPPORTUNITIES FOR NEGROES IN ENGINEERING. /OCCUPATIONS/	NKIEHRX58648
OPPORTUNITIES FOR NEGROES IN ENGINEERING -- A SECOND REPORT. /OCCUPATIONS/	NKIEHRX64333
THE EMPLOYMENT OF NEGROES IN PUBLIC WELFARE IN ELEVEN SOUTHERN STATES, 1936-1949. /OCCUPATIONS/	NLARKJR52672
VOCATIONAL GRADUATES IN AUTO MECHANICS. A FOLLOW-UP STUDY OF NEGRO AND WHITE YOUTH. /OCCUPATIONS/	NLEVEBX66036
THE ROLE OF THE NEGRO IN THE HEALING PROFESSIONS IN CONTEMPORARY AMERICA. /OCCUPATIONS/	NMCPHEL55728
THE FACTS ON NEGRO PHYSICIANS. /OCCUPATIONS/	NMENZRX49766
THE STATUS OF THE NEGRO PHYSICIAN IN NEW-YORK STATE. /OCCUPATIONS/	NMURRPM55867
NEGROES IN MEDICINE. /OCCUPATIONS/	NNATLMF52877
NEW OPPORTUNITIES FOR NEGROES IN MEDICINE. /OCCUPATIONS/	NNATLMF62878
THE USE OF COLORED PERSONS IN SKILLED OCCUPATIONS.	NOCONWB41094
CHARACTERISTICS OF NEGRO COLLEGE CHIEF LIBRARIANS. /OCCUPATIONS/	NPOLLFM64005
THE AMERICAN FARMER. /OCCUPATIONS/	NPOPURB63007
I AM A CONTROVERSIAL DENTIST. /OCCUPATIONS/	NREEDET62046
THE RELATIONSHIP BETWEEN TEST INTELLIGENCE OF THIRD GRADE NEGRO CHILDREN AND THE OCCUPATIONS OF THEIR PARENTS.	NROBIML47070
THE NEGRO POLICEMAN IN THE SOUTH. /OCCUPATIONS/	NRUDWEM60095
EQUAL-PAY FOR WHITE AND NEGRO TEACHERS. /OCCUPATIONS/	NUSDLAB41817
NEGROES IN SCIENCE. /OCCUPATIONS/	NVIORJX65284
SIGNIFICANT ACHIEVEMENTS OF NEGROES IN EDUCATION 1907-1947. /OCCUPATIONS/	NWHITMJ48249
RESOURCE UNITS IN THE TEACHING OF OCCUPATIONS -- AN EXPERIMENT IN GUIDANCE OF PUERTO-RICAN TEENAGERS.	PNEWYCC56834
PUERTO-RICAN EMPLOYMENT IN NEW-YORK CITY HOTELS. /OCCUPATIONS/	PNEWYSA58837
A COMPARISON OF THE OCCUPATIONS OF THE FIRST AND SECOND GENERATION PUERTO-RICANS IN THE MAINLAND LABOR-MARKET, AND HOW THE WORK OF THE NEW-YORK STATE DEPARTMENT OF LABOR EFFECTS PUERTO-RICANS.	PRAUSCX61846
WOMEN IN THE PROFESSIONAL WORLD. /OCCUPATIONS/	WALPEEJ62604
MEDICINE AS A CAREER FOR WOMEN. /OCCUPATIONS/	WAMERMW65607
ENGINEERING TALENT IN SHORT SUPPLY. /OCCUPATIONS/	WAMONRX62613
OCCUPATIONS FOR MEN AND WOMEN AFTER 45.	WANGEJL63615
NOTES ON THE ROLE OF CHOICE IN THE PSYCHOLOGY OF PROFESSIONAL WOMEN. /OCCUPATIONS/	WBAILLX64623
CAREERS FOR WOMEN IN SCIENCE. /OCCUPATIONS/	WBARBMS58627
OPTIMAL UTILIZATION OF MEDICAL WOMANPOWER. /OCCUPATIONS/	WBAUMLX66630
THE PROSPECT FOR ADVANCEMENT IN BUSINESS OF THE MARRIED WOMAN COLLEGE GRADUATE. /OCCUPATIONS/	WBECKEL64632
ACADEMIC WOMEN. /OCCUPATIONS/	WBERNJX64638
THE PRESENT SITUATION IN THE ACADEMIC WORLD OF WOMEN TRAINED IN ENGINEERING. /OCCUPATIONS/	WBERNJX65639
THE COMMITMENT REQUIRED OF A WOMAN ENTERING A SCIENTIFIC PROFESSION. /OCCUPATIONS/	WBETTBX65645
THE PRESENT SITUATION OF WOMAN SCIENTISTS AND ENGINEERS IN INDUSTRY AND GOVERNMENT. /OCCUPATIONS/	WBOLTRH65650
ARE WOMEN EXECUTIVES PEOPLE. /OCCUPATIONS/	WBOWMGW65653
PANEL DISCUSSION. THE COMMITTMENT REQUIRED OF A WOMAN ENTERING A SCIENTIFIC PROFESSION. /OCCUPATIONS/	WBUNTMI65663
PETTICOATS RUSTLE ON EXECUTIVE LADDER. /OCCUPATIONS/	WBUSIWX62668
ON THE JOB, WOMEN ACT MUCH LIKE MEN. /OCCUPATIONS/	WBUSIWX63667
WOMEN AS GOVERNMENT EMPLOYEES. /OCCUPATIONS/	WBUSIWX63669
THE ACADEMIC MARKET PLACE. /OCCUPATIONS/	WCAPLTX58679
THE STATUS OF WOMEN IN THE PROFESSIONS RELATIVE TO THE STATUS OF MEN. /OCCUPATIONS/	WCAVARS57684
A SOURCE FOR COLLEGE FACULTIES. /OCCUPATIONS/	WCLAYFL62691
MODERN AMERICAN CAREER WOMEN. /OCCUPATIONS/	WCLYMEX59693
ENCOURAGING SCIENTIFIC TALENT. /OCCUPATIONS/	WCOLECG56694
SEX-ROLE AND PROFESSIONALISM. A STUDY OF HIGH SCHOOL TEACHERS. /OCCUPATIONS/	WCOLCJX63698

A STUDY OF JOB MOTIVATIONS, ACTIVITIES, AND SATISFACTIONS OF PRESENT AND PROSPECTIVE WOMEN COLLEGE

OCCUPATIONS   (CONTINUATION)
FACULTY MEMBERS. /OCCUPATIONS/   WCOOKWX60252

WOMAN AS POTENTIAL SCIENTISTS. /OCCUPATIONS/   WCROSKP63710

THE WOMAN EXECUTIVE. /OCCUPATIONS/   WCUSSMX58712

CAREERS AS CONCERNS OF BLUE-COLLAR GIRLS. /OCCUPATIONS/   WDAVIEX64721

WHAT BRINGS AND HOLDS WOMAN SCIENCE MAJORS. /OCCUPATIONS/   WDEMEAL63728

REPORT OF THE EXPLORATORY STATISTICAL SURVEY OF THE EDUCATIONAL-ATTAINMENT, NUMBER, AND AVAILABILITY OF THE MEMBERSHIP OF THE AMERICAN ASSOCIATION OF UNIVERSITY WOMEN FOR TEACHING IN THE FIELDS OF SCIENCE AND MATHEMATICS. /OCCUPATIONS/   WDOLAEF57735

A COMPARATIVE STUDY OF TOP LEVEL MALE AND FEMALE EXECUTIVES IN HARRIS-COUNTY. /TEXAS OCCUPATIONS/   WDOLLPA65738

SURVEY OF WOMEN PHYSICIANS GRADUATING FROM MEDICAL SCHOOL, 1925-1940. /OCCUPATIONS/   WDYKMRA57745

ACADEMIC WOMAN. /OCCUPATIONS/   WECKERE59746

ACADEMIC WOMEN. /OCCUPATIONS/   WELLMMX65749

THE STATUS OF WOMEN IN PROFESSIONAL SOCIOLOGY. /OCCUPATIONS/   WFAVASF60757

WOMEN PHYSICIANS IN THE TWENTY-FIRST CENTURY. /OCCUPATIONS/   WFAYXMX66758

FACTORS ASSOCIATED WITH GRADUATE SCHOOL ATTENDANCE AND ROLE DEFINITION OF THE WOMAN DOCTORAL CANDIDATES AT THE PENNSYLVANIA STATE UNIVERSITY. /OCCUPATIONS/   WFIELJC61763

WOMEN IN INDUSTRY. /OCCUPATIONS/   WGILBLM62782

CLOSING THE GAP. /OCCUPATIONS/   WGILBLM65781

WOMEN IN BANKING. /OCCUPATIONS/   WGILDGN59783

WOMEN IN EXECUTIVE POSTS. /OCCUPATIONS/   WGIVEJN60787

DISCUSSION. WOMEN IN MEDICINE. /OCCUPATIONS/   WGRIFAM65803

WOMEN IN LEGAL WORK. /OCCUPATIONS/   WGRIFVE58804

CAREERS FOR WOMEN IN RETAILING. /OCCUPATIONS/   WGROSSB59807

WOMEN AS BOSSES. /OCCUPATIONS/   WHAMMKX56817

REPORT ON THE SURVEY OF FEMALE PHYSICIANS GRADUATING FROM MEDICAL SCHOOL BETWEEN 1925 AND 1940. /OCCUPATIONS/   WHANNFX58819

PANEL DISCUSSION. THE CASE FOR AND AGAINST THE EMPLOYMENT OF WOMEN. /OCCUPATIONS/   WHARRTW65824

LADY AND ONE-THIRD SCHOLAR. /OCCUPATIONS/   WHEALAK63835

GIFTED WOMEN IN THE TRADE UNIONS. /OCCUPATIONS/   WHILLBX62845

STUDY OF JOB OPPORTUNITIES FOR WOMEN COLLEGE GRADUATES. /OCCUPATIONS/   WINTEAP58861

WOMEN PROFESSORS AT BROWN. /OCCUPATIONS/   WKEENBC62887

WOMEN JOURNALISTS AND TODAY-S WORLD. /OCCUPATIONS/   WKEYSMD65021

ENHANCING THE ROLE OF WOMEN IN SCIENCE, ENGINEERING, AND THE SOCIAL SCIENCES. /OCCUPATIONS/   WKILLJR65903

CAREER OPPORTUNITIES FOR WOMEN IN BUSINESS. /OCCUPATIONS/   WKINGAG63904

THAT GIRL IN THE OFFICE. /OCCUPATIONS/   WKNIGRX61910

THE FEMALE PHYSICIAN IN PUBLIC HEALTH. CONFLICT AND RECONCILIATION OF THE SEX AND PROFESSIONAL ROLES. /OCCUPATIONS/   WKOSAJX64915

THE SHORTAGE OF NURSES AND CONDITIONS OF WORK IN NURSING. /OCCUPATIONS/   WKRUSMX58920

WHY NOBODY WANTS WOMEN IN SCIENCE. /OCCUPATIONS/   WKUNDRB65919

LIFE INSURANCE SELLING AS A CAREER FOR WOMEN. /OCCUPATIONS/   WLEITSF61926

WOMEN AND MODERN SCIENCE. /OCCUPATIONS/   WLEWIND57932

WOMEN AS EXECUTIVES AND MANAGERS. /OCCUPATIONS/   WMAHRAH65953

WOMEN ARE TRAINING FOR BUSINESS. /OCCUPATIONS/   WMARSEM62956

WOMEN IN EDUCATION. /OCCUPATIONS/   WMASOVC62958

WOMEN AND THE SCIENTIFIC PROFESSIONS. THE MIT SYMPOSIUM ON AMERICAN WOMEN IN SCIENCE AND ENGINEERING. /OCCUPATIONS/   WMATTJA65963

EXECUTIVE CAREERS FOR WOMEN. /OCCUPATIONS/   WMAULFX61065

TESTIMONY. PUBLIC HEARING, WOMEN IN PUBLIC AND PRIVATE EMPLOYMENT, CALIFORNIA. /OCCUPATIONS EMPLOYMENT-CONDITIONS/   WMCLALX66947

AGE AND MARITAL-STATUS AND THEIR RELATIONSHIP TO SUCCESS IN PRACTICAL NURSING. /OCCUPATIONS/   WMEADLX63967

KNOWLEDGE AND INTERESTS CONCERNING SIXTEEN OCCUPATIONS AMONG ELEMENTARY AND SECONDARY SCHOOL STUDENTS. /ASPIRATIONS/   WMELSRC63968

WOMEN IN UNIVERSITY TEACHING. /OCCUPATIONS/   WMILLMM61981

EMERGING OPPORTUNITIES FOR QUALIFIED WOMEN. /OCCUPATIONS/   WMILLRX66982

ROLES OF THE MARRIED WOMAN IN SCIENCE. /OCCUPATIONS/   WMOTZAB61002

CAREERS FOR WOMEN IN BIOLOGICAL SCIENCES. /OCCUPATIONS/   WMURPMC60009

WANTED. MORE WOMEN IN EDUCATIONAL LEADERSHIP. /OCCUPATIONS/   WNATLCO65016

WOMEN IN SCIENTIFIC CAREERS. /OCCUPATIONS/   WNATLSF61022

OCCUPATIONS   (CONTINUATION)
  EMPLOYMENT OF WOMEN CHEMISTS IN INDUSTRIAL LABORATORIES. /OCCUPATIONS/   WPARRJB65050

  SHOULD WOMEN BE TRAINED IN THE SCIENCES.   /OCCUPATIONS/   WPINEMX58061

  WHO CHOOSES SOCIAL WORK, WHEN AND WHY.   /OCCUPATIONS/   WPINSAM63062

  WOMEN ON COLLEGE AND UNIVERSITY FACULTIES. A HISTORICAL SURVEY AND A STUDY OF THEIR PRESENT ACADEMIC
  STATUS. /OCCUPATIONS/   WPOLLLA65063

  MATURE WOMEN IN DOCTORAL PROGRAMS.   /OCCUPATIONS/   WRANDKS65073

  THE UNTAPPED RESOURCE...   /OCCUPATIONS/   WRASKBL59074

  NEW SOURCES OF COLLEGE TEACHERS.   /OCCUPATIONS/   WRILESB61287

  CLIMBING A CAREER PYRAMID -- IN SKIRTS.   /OCCUPATIONS/   WROEXAV64086

  PSYCHOLOGY OF OCCUPATIONS.   WROEXAX56085

  WOMEN IN SCIENCE.   /OCCUPATIONS/   WROEXAX66455

  BARRIERS TO THE CAREER CHOICE OF ENGINEERING, MEDICINE, OR SCIENCE AMONG AMERICAN WOMEN. /OCCUPATIONS/   WROSSAS65091

  WOMEN IN SCIENCE. WHY SO FEW. /OCCUPATIONS/   WROSSAS65094

  A STUDY OF WOMEN IN OFFICE MANAGEMENT POSITIONS WITH IMPLICATIONS FOR BUSINESS EDUCATION. /OCCUPATIONS/   WRUSHEM57096

  PART-TIME ASSIGNMENT OF WOMEN IN TEACHING. /OCCUPATIONS/   WSAMPJX65099

  WOMEN MATHEMATICIANS IN INDUSTRY. /OCCUPATIONS/   WSENDVL64111

  WOMEN EXECUTIVES. FACT AND FANCY. /OCCUPATIONS/   WSLOTCT58117

  WOMEN IN PROFESSIONAL ENGINEERING. /OCCUPATIONS/   WSOCIOW62127

  WOMEN IN INDUSTRY -- PATTERNS OF WOMEN-S WORK AND OCCUPATIONAL HEALTH AND SAFETY. /OCCUPATIONS/   WSPIRES60301

  WOMEN IN TECHNOLOGY. /OCCUPATIONS/   WSTEIER62153

  TODAY-S BUSINESS WOMAN. HER CHARACTERISTICS, HER NEED FOR FURTHER EDUCATION, HER FUTURE IN MANAGEMENT.
  /OCCUPATIONS/   WTHOMMH63152

  THE ROLE OF WOMEN IN PROFESSIONAL ENGINEERING. /OCCUPATIONS/   WTORPWG62157

  WOMEN IN COLLEGE AND UNIVERSITY TEACHING. /OCCUPATIONS/   WTOTAJV65159

  OCCUPATIONS AND SALARIES OF WOMEN IN THE FEDERAL SERVICE.   WUSCISC62168

  EMPLOYMENT AND CHARACTERISTICS OF WOMEN ENGINEERS. /OCCUPATIONS/   WUSDLAB56989

  OCCUPATIONS AND SALARIES OF WOMEN FEDERAL EMPLOYEES.   WUSDLAB57992

  CLERICAL OCCUPATIONS FOR WOMEN -- TODAY AND TOMORROW. /OCCUPATIONS/   WUSDLAB64188

  CLERICAL OCCUPATIONS FOR WOMEN -- TODAY AND TOMORROW. /OCCUPATIONS/   WUSDLAB64188

  WOMEN EXECUTIVES IN THE FEDERAL-GOVERNMENT. /OCCUPATIONS/   WWARNWL62993

  STATISTICS ON WOMEN PROFESSIONAL ENGINEERS. /OCCUPATIONS/   WWEBBJR66226

  THE WOMEN PHYSICIANS DILEMMA. /OCCUPATIONS/   WWILLJJ66269

  SUPPLY OF MEDICAL WOMEN IN THE UNITED STATES. /OCCUPATIONS/   WWRIGKW66277

OFF-RESERVATION
  ADAPTATION OF PAPAGO WORKERS TO OFF-RESERVATION OCCUPATIONS.   IWADDJX66680

OFFENDER
  WORK PROGRAMS AND THE YOUTHFUL OFFENDER.   GCOLEEX66131

OFFICE
  WEAPONS AGAINST DISCRIMINATION IN PUBLIC OFFICE.   GAVINAX62411

  I STATEMENT BEFORE THE HOUSE POST OFFICE AND CIVIL SERVICE SUBCOMMITTEE ON POSTAL OPERATIONS, II
  DISCRIMINATION, PLANNED AND ACCIDENTAL. /TESTING/   GENNEWH67928

  WHAT TITLE-VII MEANS FOR THE LOCAL OFFICE. /SES/   GMITCHR66018

  EQUAL-EMPLOYMENT-OPPORTUNITY IN THE US POST OFFICE DEPARTMENT, A SUPPLEMENTAL REPORT TO THE POSTMASTER
  GENERAL.   GUSPODA63516

  RELOCATEES FROM GALLUP AREA TO THE DENVER FIELD EMPLOYMENT ASSISTANCE OFFICE. /COLORADO/   IGRAVTDND438

  COMPREHENSIVE REPORT OF THE OFFICE OF THE BISHOP-S COMMITTEE FOR MIGRANT-WORKERS.   MNATLCBND082

  IMPACT OF OFFICE AUTOMATION IN THE INTERNAL REVENUE SERVICE. A STUDY OF THE MANPOWER IMPLICATIONS DURING
  THE FIRST STAGES OF THE CHANGEOVER. /ECONOMIC-STATUS/   NUSDLAB63198

  OPPORTUNITIES AND REQUIREMENTS FOR INITIAL EMPLOYMENT OF SCHOOL LEAVERS. WITH EMPHASIS ON OFFICE AND
  RETAIL JOBS. /EMPLOYMENT-SELECTION/   WCOOKFS66705

  WHEN THE COMPUTER TAKES OVER THE OFFICE. /TECHNOLOGICAL-CHANGE/   WHOOSIR60000

  AUTOMATION IN THE OFFICE. /TECHNOLOGICAL-CHANGE/   WHOOSIR61848

  THAT GIRL IN THE OFFICE. /OCCUPATIONS/   WKNIGRX61910

  OFFICE WORK AND AUTOMATION. /TECHNOLOGICAL-CHANGE/   WLEVIHS56929

  AUTOMATION AND EMPLOYMENT OPPORTUNITIES FOR OFFICE WORKERS. THE EFFECT OF ELECTRONIC COMPUTERS ON
  EMPLOYMENT OF CLERICAL WORKERS, WITH A SPECIAL REPORT ON PROGRAMMERS.   WPASCWX58178

  A STUDY OF WOMEN IN OFFICE MANAGEMENT POSITIONS WITH IMPLICATIONS FOR BUSINESS EDUCATION. /OCCUPATIONS/   WRUSHEM57096

  OFFICE AUTOMATION AND WHITE-COLLAR EMPLOYMENT.   WSMITGM59122

OFFICER
  INTEGRATION AND THE NEGRO OFFICER IN THE ARMED FORCES OF THE UNITED STATES OF AMERICA. /MILITARY/   NUSDDEF62240

OFFICES
SURVEY OF OHIO COLLEGE AND UNIVERSITY PLACEMENT **OFFICES** WITH REGARD TO JOB PLACEMENT OF MINORITY
STUDENTS.   GOHIOCR62132

OFFICIAL
SOLVING AN AMERICAN DILEMMA. THE ROLE OF THE FEPC **OFFICIAL**. A COMPARATIVE STUDY OF STATE CIVIL-RIGHTS
COMMISSIONS.   GLLOYKM64317

THE NEGRO UNION **OFFICIAL**. A STUDY OF SPONSORSHIP AND CONTROL.   NKORNWA52661

OFFICIAL ADVICE ON EMPLOYING NEGROES.   NLABORR42030

THE **OFFICIAL** WORD ON JOB RIGHTS FOR WOMEN.   WUSNEWR65246

OFFICIALS
REPORTS OF THE MEETINGS OF THE COMMITTEE OF **OFFICIALS** ON MIGRATORY FARM LABOR OF THE ATLANTIC SEABOARD
STATES. /MIGRANT-WORKERS/   GCOUNSG58932

A GUIDE TO GOVERNMENT **OFFICIALS**. /CIVIL-RIGHTS/   GOREGBLND135

OHIO
CURRENT POPULATION REPORTS -- SPECIAL CENSUS OF CLEVELAND, **OHIO**. /DEMOGRAPHY/   CUSBURC65379

INCOME, EDUCATION AND UNEMPLOYMENT IN NEIGHBORHOODS. CINCINNATI, **OHIO**. /DEMOGRAPHY/   CUSDLAB63457

INCOME, EDUCATION AND UNEMPLOYMENT IN NEIGHBORHOODS. CLEVELAND, **OHIO**. /DEMOGRAPHY/   CUSDLAB63458

SURVEY OF **OHIO** COLLEGE AND UNIVERSITY PLACEMENT OFFICES WITH REGARD TO JOB PLACEMENT OF MINORITY
STUDENTS.   GOHIOCR62132

RACIAL DISCRIMINATION IN THE CINCINNATI BUILDING TRADES. A COMPREHENSIVE REPORT AND RECOMMENDATIONS.
/**OHIO**/   GOHIOCR64129

LAWS AGAINST DISCRIMINATION. EMPLOYMENT, PUBLIC ACCOMODATIONS, HOUSING. /**OHIO**/   GOHIOCR65125

PATTERNS OF DISCRIMINATION IN THE GLASS AND MACHINE TOOL INDUSTRIES IN **OHIO**.   GOHIOCR66126

PATTERNS OF DISCRIMINATION IN THE GLASS INDUSTRY IN **OHIO**.   GOHIOCR66127

PATTERNS OF DISCRIMINATION IN THE MACHINE TOOL INDUSTRY IN **OHIO**.   GOHIOCR66128

MIGRATORY LABOR IN **OHIO**. A REPORT BY THE GOVERNOR-S COMMITTEE, AUGUST 1962.   GOHIOGC62095

SUB-EMPLOYMENT IN THE SLUMS OF CLEVELAND. /**OHIO**/   GUSDLAB66516

THE NEGRO IN CLEVELAND, 1950-1963. /**OHIO**/   NCLEVUL64916

MONTHLY SUMMARY OF EVENTS AND TRENDS IN RACE-RELATIONS. /CINCINNATI **OHIO** CASE-STUDY UNION/ NFISKUX44357

RACIAL DISCRIMINATION IN EMPLOYMENT IN THE CINCINNATI AREA. /**OHIO**/   NKUHNAX62668

RACIAL DISCRIMINATION IN THE CINCINNATI BUILDING TRADES. REPORT AND RECOMMENDATIONS. /**OHIO**/ NOHIOCR66605

HOUGH, CLEVELAND, **OHIO** -- A STUDY OF SOCIAL LIFE AND CHANGE.   NSUSSMB59192

STUDY OF ECONOMIC AND CULTURAL ACTIVITIES IN THE WARREN AREA AS THEY RELATE TO MINORITY PEOPLE. /**OHIO**/ NWARRUL64986

OKLAHOMA
INCOME, EDUCATION AND UNEMPLOYMENT IN NEIGHBORHOODS. OKLAHOMA-CITY, **OKLAHOMA**. /DEMOGRAPHY/ CUSDLAB63477

OKLAHOMA GEARS FOR THE CIVIL-RIGHTS-ACT.   GJELTMM66823

EMPLOYMENT SURVEY. /TULSA **OKLAHOMA**/   GTULSCR66364

OKLAHOMA-CITY
INCOME, EDUCATION AND UNEMPLOYMENT IN NEIGHBORHOODS. **OKLAHOMA-CITY**, OKLAHOMA. /DEMOGRAPHY/ CUSDLAB63477

OKTIBBEHA
A CRITICAL APPRAISAL OF PROFESSION TRAINING OF NEGRO TEACHERS IN **OKTIBBEHA** COUNTY MISSISSIPPI. NWILLMM50234

OLD-TIMERS
THE **OLD-TIMERS** AND THE NEWCOMERS. ETHNIC-GROUP RELATIONS IN A NEEDLE TRADE UNION.   NHERBWX53519

OLDER
BENEFIT POLICIES IN RELATION TO RECRUITMENT OF **OLDER** WORKERS, HANDICAPPED, AND MINORITY GROUPS. GBARRGJ51425

CHANGES IN THE LABOR-FORCE PARTICIPATION OF THE **OLDER** WORKER.   GHAUSPM54764

THE SOCIAL AND POLITICAL REACTIONS OF **OLDER** NEGROES TO UNEMPLOYMENT.   NAIKEMX66865

REASONS FOR BELATED EDUCATION. A STUDY OF THE PLIGHT OF THE **OLDER** NEGRO TEACHERS. /OCCUPATIONS/ NCUNNGE58244

EMPLOYMENT PROBLEMS OF THE **OLDER** NEGRO WORKER.   NKERNJH50644

DOUBLE JEOPARDY -- THE **OLDER** NEGRO IN AMERICA TODAY.   NNATLUL64887

OLDER WOMEN IN THE LABOR-MARKET.   WHUNTEH62271

VOCATIONAL TRAINING OF THE **OLDER** WOMAN.   WKINGCR66906

THE VOCATIONAL ROLES OF **OLDER** MARRIED WOMEN. /WORK-WOMAN-ROLE/   WSTEIAX61136

ON-JOB-TRAINING
FINAL REPORT. EXPERIMENTAL AND DEMONSTRATION **ON-JOB-TRAINING** PROJECT. /MIGRANT-WORKERS MEXICAN-AMERICAN
NEGRO ARIZONA/   CSKILTO66324

ON-THE-JOB
THE DETERMINATION OF CERTAIN MAJOR FACTORS AFFECTING THE NEGRO VETERAN IN THE **ON-THE-JOB** TRAINING PROGRAM
IN VOCATIONAL AGRICULTURE IN THE STATE OF ALABAMA AS A BASIS FOR PLANNING A MORE EFFECTIVE PROGRAM. NBATTEF49338

ON-THE-JOB EXPERIENCES OF NEGRO MANAGERS.   NBLANJW64917

EFFECTS OF **ON-THE-JOB** EXPERIENCE WITH NEGROES UPON RACIAL ATTITUDES OF WHITE WORKERS IN UNION SHOPS. NGUNDRH50466

PERSONAL AND **ON-THE-JOB** CHARACTERISTICS RELATED TO NEGRO PERCEPTIONS OF DISCRIMINATION.   NSOLOHX56152

OPEN-SHOP
LABOR DRIVES TO CLOSE THE SOUTH-S **OPEN-SHOP**. /UNION/   NRONYVX65072

OPENING
 OPENING THE DOOR TO EMPLOYMENT. /EEO/   NGEORCH64399

OPENINGS
 APPRENTICESHIP TRAINING IN NEW-YORK. OPENINGS IN 1963.   GWORKDL63582

OPERATION
 THE OPERATION OF THE NEW-JERSEY LAW AGAINST DISCRIMINATION.   GBUSTJL49507

 OPERATION UNDER STATE FEPC LAWS.   GLABOLR45873

 OPERATION BOOTSTRAP FOR THE AMERICAN-INDIAN.   IUSHOUR59669

 OPERATION ACHIEVEMENT. /NEW-YORK EMPLOYMENT/   NCALVIJ63176

 SIX MONTHS OPERATION OF NEW-YORK LAW AGAINST DISCRIMINATION.   NUSDLAB46843

OPERATIONS
 I STATEMENT BEFORE THE HOUSE POST OFFICE AND CIVIL SERVICE SUBCOMMITTEE ON POSTAL OPERATIONS, II
 DISCRIMINATION. PLANNED AND ACCIDENTAL. /TESTING/   GENNEWH67928

 REPORT ON THE STRUCTURE AND OPERATIONS OF THE PRESIDENT-S COMMITTEE ON EQUAL-EMPLOYMENT-OPPORTUNITY.   GKHEETW62852

 FEPC. REPORT ON OPERATIONS.   GLABOLR45870

OPERATOR
 UNITED STATES CENSUS OF AGRICULTURE. COLOR, RACE, AND TENURE OF FARM OPERATOR. GENERAL REPORT, VOLUME II.
 /DEMOGRAPHY/   CUSBURC59382

OPERATORS
 NONWHITE FARM OPERATORS IN THE UNITED STATES.   GUSDLAB41077

 NEGRO FARM OPERATORS. NUMBER, LOCATION AND RECENT TRENDS.   NBEALCL58064

 COLOR, RACE AND TENURE OF FARM OPERATORS.   NUSBURC62225

OPINION
 OPINION CONCERNING THE SCOPE AND AUTHORITY OF THE JURISDICTION THAT MAY BE GRANTED TO CITY OR COUNTY
 HUMAN-RELATIONS-COMMISSIONS IN THE FIELDS OF EMPLOYMENT AND HOUSING. /CALIFORNIA/   GCALAGC63512

 OPINION BY HONORABLE BENJAMIN LENCHER. CITY OF PITTSBURGH VS PLUMBERS LOCAL UNION NO 27. /PENNSYLVANIA/ NPITTLJ65001

OPINIONS
 SOME ATTITUDES AND OPINIONS OF EMPLOYED WOMEN.   WRAMSGV63132

OPPORTUNITIES
 OPPORTUNITIES IN NURSING FOR DISADVANTAGED YOUTH. /WOMEN NEGRO OCCUPATIONS/   CFRAKFX66375

 ECONOMIC GROWTH AND EMPLOYMENT OPPORTUNITIES FOR MINORITIES. /NEGRO WOMEN/   CHIESDL64775

 OPPORTUNITIES FOR NEGRO WOMEN AS DIETICIANS. /OCCUPATIONS/   CUSDLAB43837

 EMPLOYMENT OPPORTUNITIES FOR HIGH SCHOOL DROPOUTS, A STUDY OF EMPLOYERS PRACTICES, NEEDS AND ATTITUDES IN
 THE DISTRICT OF COLUMBIA. /WASHINGTON-DC/   GBURESS57499

 MEDICAL SERVICE JOB OPPORTUNITIES 1964-66, SAN-FRANCISCO BAY AREA. /CALIFORNIA/   GCALDEM64521

 HOTEL AND RESTAURANT JOB OPPORTUNITIES, SAN-FRANCISCO BAY AREA, 1964-1966. /CALIFORNIA/   GCALDEM65517

 HOW TO RECRUIT MINORITY-GROUP COLLEGE GRADUATES, ITS PROBLEMS, ITS TECHNIQUES, ITS SOURCES, ITS
 OPPORTUNITIES.   GCALVRX63555

 VOCATIONAL TRAINING TO IMPROVE JOB OPPORTUNITIES FOR MINORITY-GROUPS. COMMENT.   GFINEMX64681

 JOB OPPORTUNITIES FROM FEPC ACTION.   GHOWDEX65785

 SPECIAL REPORT ON EMPLOYMENT OPPORTUNITIES IN ILLINOIS.   GILLIIR48801

 PSYCHOLOGICAL TESTING FOR EFFECTIVE EMPLOYMENT PRACTICES AND EQUAL JOB OPPORTUNITIES.   GKETCWA65849

 JOB OPPORTUNITIES AND POVERTY.   GMEANGC65674

 FARM AND NON-FARM EMPLOYMENT OPPORTUNITIES FOR LOW-INCOME FARM FAMILIES.   GRUTTVW59270

 HOUSING, EMPLOYMENT OPPORTUNITIES AND APPRENTICESHIP TRAINING, REPORT. /NEW-JERSEY/   GUSCOMC63404

 EXPANDING EMPLOYMENT OPPORTUNITIES IN NEWARK. EXPERIENCE REPORT 101. /NEW-JERSEY/   GUSCONM65418

 JOB OPPORTUNITIES FOR MINORITIES IN THE SEATTLE AREA. /WASHINGTON/   GUVWAIL48532

 VOCATIONAL-TRAINING TO IMPROVE JOB OPPORTUNITIES FOR MINORITY-GROUPS.   GWALSJP64540

 BROADENING WORK OPPORTUNITIES FOR INDIAN YOUTH.   IARCHMS61526

 ANALYSIS OF MALE NAVAHO STUDENTS PERCEPTIONS OF OCCUPATIONAL OPPORTUNITIES AND THEIR ATTITUDES TOWARD
 DEVELOPMENT OF SKILLS AND TRAITS NECESSARY FOR OCCUPATIONAL COMPETENCE.   IDESPCW65548

 PAPAGO INDIANS, EVALUATION OF OPPORTUNITIES FOR PERMANENT RELOCATION.   IFITZKXND440

 PERCEIVED OPPORTUNITIES, EXPECTATIONS, AND THE DECISION TO REMAIN ON RELOCATION. THE CASE OF THE NAVAHO
 INDIAN MIGRANT TO DENVER, COLORADO.   IGRAVTD65567

 AMERICAN-INDIANS SEEK NEW OPPORTUNITIES.   IUSDINTND665

 PLANNING CONSTRUCTIVE ECONOMIC OPPORTUNITIES FOR THE JEWISH AGED.   JBARSIX59700

 MERRILL-TRUST-FUND TO IMPROVE THE EMPLOYMENT OPPORTUNITIES OF THE MIGRANT FARM WORKERS OF MEXICAN ORIGIN. MBISHCS62365

 PROCEEDINGS OF EMPLOYMENT OPPORTUNITIES EDUCATIONAL CONFERENCE.   MCOUNMA62930

 FAIR-EMPLOYMENT AND YOUTH. ISI SE PUEDE -- IT CAN BE DONE. RE. YOUTH AND OPPORTUNITIES.   MWEBBEB66516

 NEGRO YOUTH AND EMPLOYMENT OPPORTUNITIES. /UNEMPLOYMENT EDUCATION/   NAMOSWE63021

 TOWARD EQUALITY. BALTIMORE-S PROGRESS-REPORT, A CHRONICLE OF PROGRESS SINCE WORLD-WAR-II TOWARD THE
 ACHIEVEMENT OF EQUAL-RIGHTS AND OPPORTUNITIES FOR NEGROES IN MARYLAND 1946-1958.   NBALTUL58048

 AIDING NEGRO BUSINESSMEN. SMALL BUSINESS OPPORTUNITIES CORPORATION, PHILADELPHIA. /PENNSYLVANIA/   NBUSINX64143

OPPORTUNITIES   (CONTINUATION)
   NEW OPPORTUNITIES FOR NEGROES...IN EDUCATION...IN CAREERS.   NCHANTX63190

   NEGRO EMPLOYMENT OPPORTUNITIES DURING AND AFTER THE WAR.   NDODDAE45949

   CIVIL-RIGHTS. 1960-63. THE NEGRO CAMPAIGN TO WIN EQUAL RIGHTS AND OPPORTUNITIES IN THE UNITED STATES.   NFACTOF64341

   PROBLEMS AND OPPORTUNITIES CONFRONTING NEGROES IN THE FIELD OF BUSINESS, REPORT ON THE NATIONAL
   CONFERENCE ON SMALL BUSINESS. /OCCUPATIONS/   NFITZNH63358

   EXPANDING NEGRO OPPORTUNITIES. /OCCUPATIONAL-STATUS/   NGINZEX60404

   THE OPPORTUNITIES AND DIFFICULTIES OF ORGANIZING NEGRO LABOR IN THE PRESENT EMERGENCY. /UNION/   NHALLWX42259

   EMPLOYMENT OPPORTUNITIES FOR NASHVILLE NEGROES. /TENNESSEE/   NHENDVW60516

   A STUDY OF THE EMPLOYMENT OPPORTUNITIES FOR NEGROES IN BREWERIES OF THE UNITED STATES. /INDUSTRY/   NKERNJH51897

   OPPORTUNITIES FOR NEGROES IN ENGINEERING. /OCCUPATIONS/   NKIEHRX58648

   OPPORTUNITIES FOR NEGROES IN ENGINEERING -- A SECOND REPORT. /OCCUPATIONS/   NKIEHRX64333

   HAVE FAIR-EMPLOYMENT-PRACTICES-COMMISSION LAWS INCREASED OPPORTUNITIES FOR NEGROES.   NLETTHA50683

   A PROPOSAL FOR THE PREVENTION AND CONTROL OF DELINQUENCY BY EXPANDING OPPORTUNITIES.   NMOBIFY62263

   THE NEGRO AND EMPLOYMENT OPPORTUNITIES IN THE SOUTH.   NMOSSJA62856

   NEW OPPORTUNITIES FOR NEGROES IN MEDICINE. /OCCUPATIONS/   NNATLMF62878

   APPRENTICESHIP AND TRAINING OPPORTUNITIES FOR NEGRO YOUTHS IN SELECTED URBAN-LEAGUE CITIES.   NNATLUL61885

   HOUSTON -- THE NEGRO AND EMPLOYMENT OPPORTUNITIES IN THE SOUTH, THE FIRST OF A SERIES OF EMPLOYMENT
   STUDIES IN SOUTHERN CITIES. /TEXAS/   NSOUTRC61161

   THE NEGRO AND EMPLOYMENT OPPORTUNITIES IN THE SOUTH.   NSOUTRC62151

   ATLANTA -- THE NEGRO AND EMPLOYMENT OPPORTUNITIES IN THE SOUTH, THE THIRD OF A SERIES OF EMPLOYMENT
   STUDIES IN SOUTHERN CITIES. /GEORGIA/   NSOUTRC62155

   CHATTANOOGA -- THE NEGRO AND EMPLOYMENT OPPORTUNITIES IN THE SOUTH, THE SECOND OF A SERIES OF EMPLOYMENT
   STUDIES IN SOUTHERN CITIES. /TENNESSEE/   NSOUTRC62156

   A SURVEY OF EMPLOYMENT OPPORTUNITIES AS THEY RELATE TO THE NEGRO IN NEW-ROCHELLE, NEW-YORK, 1955.   NWESTCU55316

   THE OPPORTUNITIES FOR BUSINESS OWNERSHIP AMONG NEGROES.   NWHITWL66231

   THE URBAN-LEAGUE EXPANDS OPPORTUNITIES.   NYOUNWM66355

   OPPORTUNITIES AND REQUIREMENTS FOR INITIAL EMPLOYMENT OF SCHOOL LEAVERS. WITH EMPHASIS ON OFFICE AND
   RETAIL JOBS. /EMPLOYMENT-SELECTION/   WCOOKFS66705

   ADDRESS TO CONFERENCE ON EDUCATION AND JOB OPPORTUNITIES FOR WOMEN RETURNING TO THE LABOR-MARKET.   WDOUTAX62741

   STUDY OF JOB OPPORTUNITIES FOR WOMEN COLLEGE GRADUATES. /OCCUPATIONS/   WINTEAP58861

   NEW OPPORTUNITIES AND NEW RESPONSIBILITIES FOR WOMEN. /WORK-WOMAN-ROLE/   WKEYSMD64899

   CAREER OPPORTUNITIES FOR WOMEN IN BUSINESS.   /OCCUPATIONS/   WKINGAG63904

   PART-TIME JOB OPPORTUNITIES FOR WOMEN.   WMEREJL60970

   EMERGING OPPORTUNITIES FOR QUALIFIED WOMEN. /OCCUPATIONS/   WMILLRX66982

   TEACHING. OPPORTUNITIES FOR WOMEN COLLEGE GRADUATES.   WNATLEA64019

   AUTOMATION AND EMPLOYMENT OPPORTUNITIES FOR OFFICE WORKERS. THE EFFECT OF ELECTRONIC COMPUTERS ON
   EMPLOYMENT OF CLERICAL WORKERS, WITH A SPECIAL REPORT ON PROGRAMMERS.   WPASCWX58178

   NEEDS AND OPPORTUNITIES IN OUR SOCIETY FOR THE EDUCATED WOMAN.   WPETEEX63054

   JOB OPPORTUNITIES FOR WOMEN COLLEGE GRADUATES.   WSWERSX64145

   SPEECH ABOUT JOB OPPORTUNITIES FOR GIRLS BEFORE THE MARYLAND STATE PERSONNEL AND GUIDANCE ASSOCIATION.   WTERLRX64148

   TRAINING OPPORTUNITIES FOR WOMEN AND GIRLS.   WUSDLAB60221

   WORLD OF WORK CONFERENCE ON CAREER AND JOB OPPORTUNITIES. WASHINGTON, DC, JULY 1962.   WUSDLAB64242

   PROFESSIONAL OPPORTUNITIES FOR WOMEN, PROCEEDINGS.   WUVCAEB66250

   EXPLODING THE MYTHS. EXPANDING EMPLOYMENT OPPORTUNITIES FOR CAREER WOMEN.   WUVCAEC66249

   OPPORTUNITIES FOR WOMEN THROUGH EDUCATION.   WUVMICC65251

   THE NEXT STEP -- A GUIDE TO PART-TIME OPPORTUNITIES IN GREATER BOSTON FOR THE EDUCATED WOMAN.
    /MASSACHUSETTS/   WWHITMS64266

   THE COLLEGE GIRL LOOKS AHEAD TO HER CAREER OPPORTUNITIES.   WZAPOMW56280

OPPORTUNITIES-INDUST
   OPPORTUNITIES-INDUSTRIALIZATION-CENTER. CRAFTSMEN WITH CONFIDENCE. /TRAINING/   GSULLLH66220

OPPORTUNITY
   EQUAL JOB OPPORTUNITY IS GOOD BUSINESS.   GAMERJC54381

   MANPOWER RETRAINING IN THE SOUTH-S RURAL POPULATION -- AN OPPORTUNITY FOR DEVELOPMENT.   GBACHFT63413

   INEQUALITY OF OPPORTUNITY IN HIGHER EDUCATION. A STUDY OF MINORITY GROUP AND RELATED BARRIERS TO COLLEGE
   ADMISSION.   GBERKDS48446

   APPROACHING EQUALITY OF OPPORTUNITY IN HIGHER EDUCATION.   GBROWFJ55476

   PROMOTING EQUAL JOB OPPORTUNITY, A GUIDE FOR EMPLOYERS. /CALIFORNIA/   GCALFEP63538

   CIVIL-RIGHTS. EMPLOYMENT OPPORTUNITY, AND ECONOMIC GROWTH.   GFEILJG65677

   IMPROVING INDUSTRIAL RACE-RELATIONS -- PART I. EQUAL JOB OPPORTUNITY -- SLOGAN OR REALITY.   GFLEMHC63363

OPPORTUNITY   (CONTINUATION)
EQUALITY OF EDUCATIONAL **OPPORTUNITY**.   GLIEBMX59902

PROCEEDINGS OF CONFERENCE ON EDUCATION FOR **OPPORTUNITY**, OPPORTUNITY FOR EDUCATION.   GMICFEP61982

PROCEEDINGS OF CONFERENCE ON EDUCATION FOR OPPORTUNITY, **OPPORTUNITY** FOR EDUCATION.   GMICFEP61982

PROFILE IN BLACK AND WHITE. DISCRIMINATION AND INEQUALITY OF **OPPORTUNITY**.   GNATLULND085

THE NEXT STEPS TOWARD EQUALITY OF **OPPORTUNITY** IN THE SYRACUSE METROPOLITAN AREA. REPORT OF THE SYRACUSE
CONFERENCE ON HUMAN RIGHTS AND HOUSING, JULY 2-3 1962. /NEW-YORK/   GNEWYSB62103

POVERTY, AFFLUENCE AND **OPPORTUNITY**.   GORNAOA64140

THE INDUSTRIAL PSYCHOLOGIST. SELECTION AND EQUAL-EMPLOYMENT **OPPORTUNITY**.   GPARRJA66147

THE AMERICAN DREAM...EQUAL **OPPORTUNITY**, A REPORT ON THE COMMUNITY LEADER-S CONFERENCE SPONSORED BY
PRESIDENT-S COMMITTEE ON EQUAL-EMPLOYMENT-OPPORTUNITY, MAY 19, 1962.   GPRESCD62105

EQUAL ECONOMIC **OPPORTUNITY**. A REPORT.   GPRESCG53117

EQUAL JOB **OPPORTUNITY** AS SET FORTH IN EXECUTIVE ORDERS 10479 AND 10557.   GPRESCH56191

FOURTH ANNUAL REPORT ON EQUAL JOB **OPPORTUNITY**. 1956-1957, PRESIDENT-S COMMITTEE ON GOVERNMENT CONTRACTS.   GPRESCH57122

EQUALITY OF JOB **OPPORTUNITY** AND CIVIL-RIGHTS.   GREUTWP60223

CONFERENCE ON EQUAL JOB **OPPORTUNITY**.   GUSDLAB56027

A GUIDE TO INDUSTRIAL-RELATIONS IN THE UNITED STATES. EQUAL JOB **OPPORTUNITY** UNDER COLLECTIVE-BARGAINING.   GUSDLAB58449

FEDERAL EQUALITY OF **OPPORTUNITY** IN EMPLOYMENT ACT.   GUSSENA52350

BETTER ECONOMIC **OPPORTUNITY** FOR INDIANS.   IBECKJX66536

INDIAN INDUSTRIAL DEVELOPMENT PROGRAM. A NEW INDUSTRIAL **OPPORTUNITY**.   IUSDINT64653

EQUALITY OF **OPPORTUNITY**.   JKLINOX58735

PERCEIVED LIFE CHANCES IN THE **OPPORTUNITY** STRUCTURE. A STUDY OF A TRI-ETHNIC HIGH SCHOOL.   MGUERCX62410

OBJECTIVE ACCESS IN THE **OPPORTUNITY** STRUCTURE. THE ASSESSMENT OF THREE ETHNIC GROUPS WITH RESPECT TO
QUANTIFIED SOCIAL STRUCTURAL VARIABLES.   MRENDGX63461

MIGRATION AND **OPPORTUNITY**. A STUDY OF STANDARD METROPOLITAN AREAS IN THE UNITED-STATES.   NBALATR63047

A COMPARISON OF THE SOCIAL CHARACTERISTICS AND EDUCATIONAL ASPIRATIONS OF NORTHERN, LOWER-CLASS, NEGRO
PARENTS WHO ACCEPTED AND DECLINED AN **OPPORTUNITY** FOR INTEGRATED EDUCATION FOR THEIR CHILDREN.   NCAGLLT66904

THEY MAKE **OPPORTUNITY** KNOCK. /INDUSTRY URBAN-LEAGUE/   NCHEMWX63200

EQUALITY OF EDUCATIONAL **OPPORTUNITY**.   NCOLEJS66223

EMPLOYMENT **OPPORTUNITY** FOR NASHVILLE NEGROES. /TENNESSEE/   NCOMUCE60230

PROMOTION SYSTEMS AND EQUAL-EMPLOYMENT **OPPORTUNITY**.   NDOERPB66280

EQUAL EDUCATIONAL **OPPORTUNITY**. ANOTHER ASPECT.   NGIOVPC64279

THE NEGRO AND ECONOMIC **OPPORTUNITY**.   NGRANLB41443

ECONOMIC **OPPORTUNITY** AND NEGRO EDUCATION.   NHENDVW62513

EQUALITY OF **OPPORTUNITY**. A UNION APPROACH TO FAIR EMPLOYMENT.   NHOPEJX56570

EQUALITY OF EMPLOYMENT **OPPORTUNITY**. A PROCESS ANALYSIS OF UNION INITIATIVE.   NHOPEJX60569

WASTED MANPOWER -- BERKELEY CHALLENGE AND **OPPORTUNITY**. WORKSHOP COSPONSORED WITH THE BERKELEY UNIFIED
SCHOOL-DISTRICT MARCH 15-16, 1963. /CALIFORNIA/   NKENNVD63642

CONFERENCE ON EQUAL JOB **OPPORTUNITY**.   NMCKIGB56725

PROGRAM AIDS FOR VOCATIONAL **OPPORTUNITY** PROGRAM.   NNATLUL49895

EQUAL **OPPORTUNITY** AND EQUAL PAY.   NNORTHR64937

THE NEGRO AND EMPLOYMENT **OPPORTUNITY**. PROBLEMS AND PRACTICES.   NNORTHR65949

THE AMERICAN DREAM...EQUAL **OPPORTUNITY**.   NPRESCD62014

THE SOUTH -- AMERICA-S **OPPORTUNITY** NO 1.   NSOUTRC45164

STATEMENT BEFORE CALIFORNIA LEGISLATURE ASSEMBLY, INTERIM SUBCOMMITTEE ON ECONOMIC OPPORTUNITY ON BEHALF
OF CHINATOWN-NORTH BEACH DISTRICT COUNCIL.   OWONGLJ64771

OPPORTUNTIES
COORDINATED PLANNING FOR ECONOMIC **OPPORTUNTIES** FOR JEWISH AGED.   JRABIDX59751

ORDER
EQUAL-EMPLOYMENT-OPPORTUNITY AND EXECUTIVE **ORDER** 10925.   GBIRNOX62451

THE MYRDALIAN HYPOTHESES. RANK **ORDER** OF DISCRIMINATION.   GEDMUER44495

TITLE-VII. RELATIONSHIP AND EFFECT ON EXECUTIVE **ORDER** 11246. /LEGISLATION/   GMANNRD66937

TECHNOLOGICAL-CHANGE AND THE SOCIAL **ORDER**. /SOUTH/   NNOLAEW65927

SOCIAL AND ECONOMIC IMPLICATIONS OF MIGRATION FOR THE NEGRO IN THE PRESENT SOCIAL **ORDER**.   NVALIPX42261

ORDERS
EQUAL JOB OPPORTUNITY AS SET FORTH IN EXECUTIVE **ORDERS** 10479 AND 10557.   GPRESCH56191

FRINGE BENEFIT PROVISIONS FROM STATE MINIMUM WAGE LAWS AND **ORDERS**, SEPTEMBER 1, 1966.
/EMPLOYMENT-CONDITIONS/   WUSDLAB66195

ORDINANCES
ANALYSIS OF CITY **ORDINANCES** AGAINST RACIAL AND RELIGIOUS DISCRIMINATION IN EMPLOYMENT.   GAMERJCND380

MUNICIPAL FAIR-EMPLOYMENT **ORDINANCES** AS A VALID EXERCISE OF THE POLICE POWER.   GNORTDL64093

ORDINANCES   (CONTINUATION)
     CIVIL-RIGHTS ORDINANCES.   GRHYNCS63234

 OREGON
     KLAMATH INDIANS IN TWO NON-INDIAN COMMUNITIES. KLAMATH-FALLS AND EUGENE-SPRINGFIELD.   /OREGON/   ILIVIMG59582

     THE SELF-SUPPORTING WOMAN IN OREGON.   WKNILNO60034

ORGANIZATION
     STATE ORGANIZATION FOR FAIR-EMPLOYMENT-PRACTICES.   GDUFFJX44522

     REGICNAL ORGANIZATION, BUREAU-OF-INDIAN-AFFAIRS.   ITAYLTW57627

     FAMILY ORGANIZATION IN FIVE TYPES OF MIGRATORY WAGE LABOR.   MSOLIML61496

     THE ROLE OF THE NEGRO IN THE ORGANIZATION OF THE CIO. /UNION/   NCOOPJE56235

     PLANTATION ORGANIZATION AND THE RESIDENT LABOR-FORCE, DELTA AREA, MISSISSIPPI.   NLERANL60403

     INTER-RACIAL PLANNING FOR COMMUNITY ORGANIZATION... EMPLOYMENT PROBLEMS OF THE NEGRO.   NNATLUL44900

ORGANIZATIONAL
     WHEN NEGROES MARCH. THE MARCH-ON-WASHINGTON-MOVEMENT IN THE ORGANIZATIONAL POLITICS FOR FEPC.   NGARFHX59396

     THE ROLE OF ORGANIZATIONAL STRUCTURES. UNION VERSUS NEIGHBORHOOD IN A TENSION SITUATION.   NREITDC53050

ORGANIZATIONS
     THE SUBSTANCE OF AMERICAN FAIR-EMPLOYMENT-PRACTICES LEGISLATION. II. EMPLOYMENT-AGENCIES, LABOR
     ORGANIZATIONS, AND OTHERS.   GBONFAE67136

     GUIDE TO LAWFUL AND UNLAWFUL PRE-EMPLOYMENT INQUIRIES BY EMPLOYERS, EMPLOYMENT-AGENCIES, AND LABOR
     ORGANIZATIONS UNDER THE CALIFORNIA FAIR-EMPLOYMENT-PRACTICE ACT, LABOR CODE, SECTIONS 1410-1432.   GCALDIR60527

     PROGRAMS OF NATIONAL ORGANIZATIONS FOR MIGRANT FARM WORKERS AND THEIR FAMILIES.   GUSDLAB61202

     THE ROLE OF CIVIL-RIGHTS ORGANIZATIONS. A MARSHALL PLAN APPROACH.   NTUCKSX66209

     THE PLACEMENT OF NEGRO COLLEGE GRADUATES IN BUSINESS ORGANIZATIONS.   NWHITEW64321

ORGANIZE
     NEGRO UNIONISTS ORGANIZE FOR ACTION.   NBUSIWX60157

ORGANIZED
     ORGANIZED LABOR AND RACIAL MINORITIES. /UNION/   GBAILLH51575

     ORGANIZED LABOR AND THE INTEGRATION OF ETHNIC GROUPS. /UNION/   GBLOCHD58455

     ORGANIZED LABOR AND MINORITY GROUPS. /UNION/   GBLUEJT47457

     ORGANIZED LABOR AND THE MINORITY WORKER NEED EACH OTHER. /UNION/   GSHISBX59305

     SOCIAL RESPONSIBILITIES OF ORGANIZED LABOR. /UNION/   GTITCJA57358

     ORGANIZED LABOR AND THE NEGRO WORKER. /UNION/   NBAINMX63046

     NEGROES AND ORGANIZED LABOR. /UNION/   NBLOCHD62091

     ORGANIZED LABOR AND MINORITY-GROUPS POLICY AND PRACTICES. /UNION/   NBLUEJT47256

     ORGANIZED LABOR AND THE NEGRO WORKER. /UNION/   NGROBGX60460

     RECENT DEVELOPMENTS IN RACE-RELATIONS AND ORGANIZED LABOR.   NHENDVW66213

     RACISM WITHIN ORGANIZED LABOR. A REPORT OF THE FIVE YEARS OF THE AFL-CIO, 1955-1960. /UNION/   NHILLHX60542

     HAS ORGANIZED LABOR FAILED THE NEGRO WORKER. /UNION/   NHILLHX62526

     ORGANIZED LABOR AND THE NEGRO WAGE-EARNER. /UNION/   NHILLHX62535

     THE RACIAL PRACTICES OF ORGANIZED LABOR -- IN THE AGE OF GOMPERS AND AFTER. /UNION/   NHILLHX65541

     THE NEGRO WORKER OF KANSAS-CITY. A STUDY OF TRADE UNION AND ORGANIZED LABOR RELATIONS.   NKANCIU40634

     THE NEGRO AND ORGANIZED LABOR. /UNION/   NMARSRX63741

     THE NEGRO AND ORGANIZED LABOR. /UNION/   NMARSRX65742

     ORGANIZED LABOR AND THE NEGRO. /UNION/   NNORTHR44944

     ORGANIZED LABOR AND THE NEGRO YOUTH. /UNION/   NPOLLSX66723

     ORGANIZED LABOR IN AMERICAN HISTORY. /UNION/   NTAFTPX64158

ORGANIZING
     ORGANIZING THE UNEMPLOYED. THE CHICAGO PROJECT. /ILLINOIS/   GFLACRX64964

     THE OPPORTUNITIES AND DIFFICULTIES OF ORGANIZING NEGRO LABOR IN THE PRESENT EMERGENCY. /UNION/   NHALLWX42259

ORIENTAL
     REPORT ON OAKLAND SCHOOLS. AN INVESTIGATION UNDER SECTION 1421 OF THE CALIFORNIA LABOR CODE OF THE
     OAKLAND UNIFIED SCHOOL DISTRICT 1962-1963. /NEGRO ORIENTAL MEXICAN-AMERICAN/   CCALDIR63710

     RECENT TRENDS IN THE STUDY OF MINORITY AND RACE-RELATIONS. /NEGRO PUERTO-RICAN ORIENTAL/   CGORDMM63977

     LABOR UNIONISM IN AMERICAN AGRICULTURE. /NEGRO MEXICAN-AMERICAN ORIENTAL/   CJAMISM45005

     CHANGING PATTERNS OF PREJUDICE. /NEGRO PUERTO-RICAN ORIENTAL AMERICAN-INDIAN/   CMARRAJ62055

     SOCIO-ECONOMIC DIFFERENTIALS AMONG NONWHITE RACES. /NEGRO ORIENTAL AMERICAN-INDIAN/   CSCHMCF65107

     SOCIAL-STRATIFICATION AND ACADEMIC ACHIEVEMENT. /NEGRO ORIENTAL/   CWILSAB63325

     THE INTEGRATION OF AMERICANS OF MEXICAN, PUERTO-RICAN, AND ORIENTAL DESCENT.   CYINGJM56519

     FRUSTRATION ON THE FARM. /MEXICAN-AMERICAN ORIENTAL UNION/   GCORTJC57372

     WESTERNERS FROM THE EAST. ORIENTAL IMMIGRANTS REAPPRAISED.   ODANIRX66084

     OUR ORIENTAL AMERICANS.   ORITTXX65758

ORIENTATION
    VALUE ORIENTATION, ROLE CONFLICT, AND ALIENATION FROM WORK. A CROSS-CULTURAL STUDY.   MZURCLA65520

    VOCATIONAL ORIENTATION TOWARD A REWARDING LIFE.   NJONEAM65622

    SOME ASPECTS OF VOCATIONAL ASPIRATIONS AND VALUE ORIENTATION AMONG NEGRO BOYS IN THE LOWER SOCIO-ECONOMIC
    CLASSES.   NSCHMWX63139

    ASSIMILATION OF CHINESE IN AMERICA. CHANGES IN ORIENTATION AND SOCIAL PERCEPTIONS.   OFONGSL65722

    FAMILIAL CORRELATES OF ORIENTATION TOWARD FUTURE EMPLOYMENT AMONG COLLEGE WOMEN. /ASPIRATIONS/   WSIEGAX63572

ORIENTATIONS
    THE IMMIGRANT. VALUE ORIENTATIONS AND VOCATIONAL ASPIRATIONS. /NEGRO MEXICAN-AMERICAN/   CPETECL64988

    VALUE ORIENTATIONS OF YOUNG MEXICAN-AMERICAN MALES AS REFLECTED IN THEIR WORK PATTERNS AND EMPLOYMENT
    PREFERENCES.   MWAJDJO62513

ORIENTED
    OCCUPATIONAL CHOICE AMONG CAREER ORIENTED COLLEGE WOMEN. /ASPIRATIONS/   WSIMPRL61115

    INTEREST AND VALUES OF CAREER AND HOME MAKING ORIENTED WOMEN.   WWAGMMX66761

ORIGIN
    CHARACTERISTICS OF THE U.S. POPULATION BY FARM AND NON-FARM ORIGIN.   GBEALCL64423

    EQUAL-RIGHTS UNDER THE LAW. PROVIDING FOR EQUAL TREATMENT FOR ALL CITIZENS REGARDLESS OF RACE, RELIGION,
    COLOR, NATIONAL ORIGIN OR ANCESTRY. /CALIFORNIA/   GCALAGO60511

    RULINGS ON PRE-EMPLOYMENT INQUIRIES RELATING TO RACE, CREED, COLOR OR NATIONAL ORIGIN UNDER THE NEW-YORK
    STATE LAW AGAINST DISCRIMINATION.   GNEWYSBND106

    MINORITY-GROUP INTEGRATION BY LABOR AND MANAGEMENT. A STUDY OF THE EMPLOYMENT PRACTICES OF THE LARGER
    EMPLOYERS, AND THE MEMBERSHIP PRACTICES OF THE LARGER LABOR UNIONS WITH RESPECT TO RACE, RELIGION, AND
    NATIONAL ORIGIN, CONNECTICUT, 1951.   GSTETHG53598

    MERRILL-TRUST-FUND TO IMPROVE THE EMPLOYMENT OPPORTUNITIES OF THE MIGRANT FARM WORKERS OF MEXICAN ORIGIN.   MBISHCS62365

    THE ORIGIN AND DEVELOPMENT OF THE NEGRO VISITING TEACHER IN ALABAMA. /OCCUPATIONS/   NBOATRF49345

    COMPLAINTS ALLEGING DISCRIMINATION BECAUSE OF PUERTO-RICAN NATIONAL ORIGIN, JULY 1, 1945-SEPTEMBER 1,
    1958.   PNEWYSA58836

ORIGINS
    ASSIMILATION IN AMERICAN LIFE. THE ROLE OF RACE, RELIGION, AND NATIONAL ORIGINS.   GGORDMM64729

    SOCIAL ORIGINS AND CAREER PREPARATION AMONG FILIPINOS IN AMERICAN UNIVERSITIES.   OBELTAG61703

OURAY
    AN EVALUATION OF THE 10-YEAR DEVELOPMENT PROGRAM OF THE UTE TRIBE OF THE UINTAH AND OURAY RESERVATION,
    UTAH.   IUSDINT58648

OUT-OF-SCHOOL
    AN EXPERIMENT TO TEST THREE MAJOR ISSUES OF WORK PROGRAM METHODOLOGY WITHIN MOBILIZATION-FOR-YOUTH-S
    INTEGRATED SERVICES TO OUT-OF-SCHOOL UNEMPLOYED YOUTH. /NEGRO PUERTO-RICAN/   CMOBIFY66024

    SOCIAL DYNAMITE. THE REPORT OF THE CONFERENCE ON UNEMPLOYED, OUT-OF-SCHOOL YOUTH IN URBAN AREAS, MAY
    24-26, 1961.   GNATLCC61039

    OUT-OF-SCHOOL YOUTH -- TWO YEARS LATER. A 1965 RE-SURVEY OF YOUNG MEN.   GPERRVC66774

    EVALUATION AND SKILL TRAINING OF OUT-OF-SCHOOL, HARD-CORE UNEMPLOYED YOUTH FOR TRAINING AND PLACEMENT.   GSMITAE65140

OUTLAWING
    LEGISLATION OUTLAWING RACIAL DISCRIMINATION IN EMPLOYMENT.   GLAWYGR45886

OUTLAWS
    UAW OUTLAWS DISCRIMINATION. /UNION/   GUAWXIU56370

OUTLOOK
    OUTLOOK REGARDING STATE FEPC LEGISLATION.   GCO3BCW46578

    THE OUTLOOK FOR THE LABOR-FORCE AT MID-DECADE. /EMPLOYMENT-TRENDS/   GCOOPSX64743

    THE OUTLOOK OF WORKING CLASS YOUTH. /DROP-OUT ASPIRATION/   GMILLSM62570

    THE OUTLOOK FOR TECHNOLOGICAL-CHANGE AND EMPLOYMENT.   GNATLCO66897

    THE OUTLOOK FOR A NEW FEPC. THE 80TH CONGRESS AND JOB DISCRIMINATION.   GROSSMX47261

    MANPOWER AND TRAINING. TRENDS, OUTLOOK AND PROGRAMS.   GZEISJS63704

    THE EDUCATIONAL OUTLOOK FOR NONWHITES IN FLORIDA.   NABRAAA66141

    JOB OUTLOOK FOR YOUTH.   NEBONXX63316

    THE POST-WAR INDUSTRIAL OUTLOOK FOR NEGROES.   NHOWAUG44579

    RACE DISCRIMINATION IN TRADE UNIONS. RECORD AND OUTLOOK.   NNORTHR46945

    THE JOB OUTLOOK FOR NEGRO YOUTH.   NPERRJX64984

    NEGRO AMERICAN COLLEGE YOUTH-S OUTLOOK ON THE FUTURE.   NROBESO57067

    ENHANCING THE OCCUPATIONAL OUTLOOK AND VOCATIONAL ASPIRATIONS OF SOUTHERN SECONDARY YOUTH. A CONFERENCE
    OF SECONDARY SCHOOL PRINCIPALS AND COUNSELORS.   NUSDLAB65334

    THE POST-WAR OUTLOOK FOR NEGROES IN SMALL BUSINESS, THE ENGINEERING AND THE TECHNICAL VOCATIONS.   NWALKJO46580

    THE ROLE OUTLOOK OF EDUCATED WOMEN. /ASPIRATIONS/   WANGRSS64484

    OUTLOOK FOR WOMEN.   WPETEEX65055

OUTREACH
    OUTREACH IN ROCHESTER. /NEW-YORK/   NCROFES66242

    OUTREACH -- THE AFFIRMATIVE APPROACH. /EMPLOYMENT SES/   NFRANWH66698

OVERVIEW
    ECONOMIC EXPANSION AND PERSISTING UNEMPLOYMENT. AN OVERVIEW.   GREESAX66722

OVERVIEW   (CONTINUATION)
    NAACP AND THE AFL-CIO. AN **OVERVIEW**. /UNION/   NGROSJA62461

OWNERS
    WHITE AND NONWHITE **OWNERS** OF RURAL LAND IN THE SOUTHEAST.   GBOXLRF65418

OWNERSHIP
    THE OPPORTUNITIES FOR BUSINESS **OWNERSHIP** AMONG NEGROES.   NWHITWL66231

OWYHEE
    MDTA COMES TO THE **OWYHEE** RESERVATION.   IFISHCR66559

PACKINGHOUSE
    THE SELF-SURVEY OF THE **PACKINGHOUSE** UNION. A TECHNIQUE FOR EFFECTING CHANGE. /CASE-STUDY/   NHOPEJX53574

PACT
    ANTI-DISCRIMINATION **PACT** SIGNED IN PHILADELPHIA. /PENNSYLVANIA/   GPUBLWX63207

PAIRED
    A COMPARISON OF THE VOCATIONAL ASPIRATIONS OF **PAIRED** SIXTH-GRADE WHITE AND NEGRO CHILDREN WHO ATTEND
    SEGREGATED SCHOOLS.   NBROWRG65895

PALOUSE
    THE PHYSICAL GEOGRAPHY OF THE **PALOUSE** REGION, WASHINGTON AND IDAHO, AND ITS RELATION TO THE AGRICULTURAL
    ECCNCMY.   OSHROCR58762

PANEL
    PANEL DISCUSSION. THE COMMITTMENT REQUIRED OF A WOMAN ENTERING A SCIENTIFIC PROFESSION. /OCCUPATIONS/   WBUNTMI65663

    PANEL DISCUSSION. THE CASE FOR AND AGAINST THE EMPLOYMENT OF WOMEN. /OCCUPATIONS/   WHARRTW65824

PAPAGO
    PAPAGO RESERVATION REPORT.   IARIZCI62527

    PAPAGO INDIANS. EVALUATION OF OPPORTUNITIES FOR PERMANENT RELOCATION.   IFITZKXND440

    ADAPTATION OF **PAPAGO** WORKERS TO OFF-RESERVATION OCCUPATIONS.   IWADDJX66680

PAPER
    REACTION TO MEXICAN-AMERICANS, A BACKGROUND **PAPER**.   MCABRYA65372

    MEXICAN-AMERICANS. A BACKGROUND **PAPER**.   MGUZMRX65411

    POSITION **PAPER** ON EMPLOYMENT INTEGRATION.   NKELLKP64641

PAPERS
    MASTER ANNOTATED BIBLIOGRAPHY OF **PAPERS** OF MOBILIZATION-FOR-YOUTH. PUBLISHED, UNPUBLISHED AND PRESENTED
    AT CONFERENCES.   GMOBIFY65025

PARADOX
    THE ECONOMICS OF POVERTY. AN AMERICAN **PARADOX**.   GWEISBA65666

PARENTAGE
    NATIVITY AND **PARENTAGE**. /DEMOGRAPHY/   CUSBURC63175

    PUERTO-RICANS IN THE UNITED STATES. SOCIAL AND ECONOMIC DATA FOR PERSONS OF PUERTO-RICAN BIRTH AND
    PARENTAGE. /DEMOGRAPHY/   PUSBURC63182

PARENTAL
    THE RELATIONSHIP OF **PARENTAL** IDENTIFICATION TO SEX ROLE ACCEPTANCE IN MARRIED, SINGLE, CAREER AND
    NON-CAREER WOMEN. /WORK-WOMEN-ROLE/   WBREYCH64654

PARENTS
    A COMPARISON OF THE SOCIAL CHARACTERISTICS AND EDUCATIONAL ASPIRATIONS OF NORTHERN, LOWER-CLASS, NEGRO
    PARENTS WHO ACCEPTED AND DECLINED AN OPPORTUNITY FOR INTEGRATED EDUCATION FOR THEIR CHILDREN.   NCAGLLT66904

    THE RELATIONSHIP BETWEEN TEST INTELLIGENCE OF THIRD GRADE NEGRO CHILDREN AND THE OCCUPATIONS OF THEIR
    PARENTS.   NROBIML47070

PARLEY
    PARLEY ON CIVIL-RIGHTS.   GAMERFX57873

PARLIAMENTARY
    FEPC -- A CASE HISTORY IN **PARLIAMENTARY** MANEUVER.   GMASLWX46959

PAROLE
    EMPLOYMENT-TRENDS AMONG CALIFORNIA YOUTH AUTHORITY WARDS ON **PAROLE**. 1948-62.   MCALDYA63378

PART-TIME
    UNEMPLOYMENT AMONG FULL-TIME AND **PART-TIME** WORKERS.   GSTEIRL64336

    WOMEN **PART-TIME** WORKERS IN THE U.S.   WHEWEAX62843

    PART-TIME CARE. THE DAY-CARE PROBLEM. /EMPLOYMENT-CONDITIONS/   WHOSLEM64540

    PART-TIME EMPLOYMENT FOR WOMEN WITH FAMILY RESPONSIBILITIES. /WORK-FAMILY-CONFLICT/   WINTELR57867

    PARTICIPATION IN **PART-TIME** WORK BY WOMEN COLLEGE STUDENTS.   WISAALE57875

    PART-TIME JOB OPPORTUNITIES FOR WOMEN.   WMEREJL60970

    PART-TIME ASSIGNMENT OF WOMEN IN TEACHING. /OCCUPATIONS/   WSAMPJX65099

    PART-TIME EMPLOYMENT.   WSCHWJX64107

    PART-TIME PROGRAM FOR PROFESSIONALLY TRAINED WOMEN. /TRAINING/   WTACKAL66147

    PART-TIME EMPLOYMENT FOR WOMEN.   WUSDLAB60213

    THE NEXT STEP -- A GUIDE TO **PART-TIME** OPPORTUNITIES IN GREATER BOSTON FOR THE EDUCATED WOMAN.
    /MASSACHUSETTS/   WWHITMS64266

    PART-TIME WORKING MOTHERS -- A CASE-STUDY.   WWORTNB60245

PARTIAL
    PARTIAL INVENTORY OF ON-GOING RESEARCH IN EQUAL-EMPLOYMENT-OPPORTUNITIES.   GANDEBR67589

    THE MEANING AND MEASUREMENT OF **PARTIAL** AND DISGUISED UNEMPLOYMENT.   GDUCOLJ57955

PARTICIPANT
ETHNOMICS -- NEGRO MUST BE FULL **PARTICIPANT** IN MARKET PLACE.   NBUNKHC65122

PARTICIPANTS
A COMPILATION OF STATISTICAL DATA, CHARTS AND OTHER RESOURCE MATERIAL FOR CONFERENCE **PARTICIPANTS**.
/APPRENTICESHIP CALIFORNIA YOUTH/   GCALCNA60516

EXPERIMENTAL AND DEMONSTRATION MANPOWER PROJECT FOR THE RECRUITMENT, TRAINING, PLACEMENT AND FOLLOW-UP OF
RURAL UNEMPLOYED WORKERS IN TEN NORTH FLORIDA CITIES. FINAL REPORT. /PARTICIPANTS/   NJACKTA66597

PARTICIPATION
LABOR-FORCE **PARTICIPATION** AND UNEMPLOYMENT.   GBOWEWG65469

PARTICIPATION OF THE POOR. A REEXAMINATION.   GCAHNEX66905

LABOR-FORCE **PARTICIPATION** OF YOUNG PERSONS AGED 14-24.   GFEARRXND929

CHANGES IN THE LABOR-FORCE **PARTICIPATION** OF THE OLDER WORKER.   GHAUSPM54764

CORRELATIONS BETWEEN INCOME AND LABOR-FORCE **PARTICIPATION** BY RACE.   NDORNSM56283

NEGRO **PARTICIPATION** IN APPRENTICESHIP PROGRAMS.   NMARSRX66327

NEGRO **PARTICIPATION** IN APPRENTICESHIP PROGRAMS.   NMARSRX67118

NEGRO **PARTICIPATION** IN DEFENSE WORK.   NUSDLAB41829

THE NEGRO-S **PARTICIPATION** IN AMERICAN BUSINESS.   NYOUNHB63347

EDUCATIONAL-ATTAINMENT AND LABOR-FORCE **PARTICIPATION**.   WBOWEWGND652

THE LABOR-FORCE **PARTICIPATION** OF MARRIED WOMEN.   WCAINGG64671

AGE OF COMPLETION OF CHILDBEARING AND ITS RELATION TO THE **PARTICIPATION** OF WOMEN IN THE LABOR-FORCE.
UNITED STATES 1910-1955.   WDAYXLH57725

FEMALE LABOR-FORCE **PARTICIPATION** AND ECONOMIC DEVELOPMENT.   WHABESX58811

PARTICIPATION IN PART-TIME WORK BY WOMEN COLLEGE STUDENTS.   WISAALE57875

TRENDS IN THE **PARTICIPATION** OF WOMEN IN THE WORKING-FORCE.   WJAFFAH56878

TRENDS IN WOMEN-S WORK **PARTICIPATION**.   WLESECE58928

A CONFERENCE TO ENLIST THE **PARTICIPATION** OF 50 INSTITUTIONS OF HIGHER EDUCATION IN SPECIFIC R AND D
PROGRAMS TO PREPARE WOMEN FOR PRODUCTIVE EMPLOYMENT.   WLLOYBJ64937

FACTORS DETERMINING THE LABOR-FORCE **PARTICIPATION** OF MARRIED WOMEN.   WMAHOTA61951

LABOR-FORCE **PARTICIPATION** OF MARRIED WOMEN. A STUDY OF LABOR SUPPLY.   WMINCJX62984

LABOR-FORCE **PARTICIPATION** OF SUBURBAN MOTHERS.   WMYERGC64011

LABOR-FORCE **PARTICIPATION** RATES AND PERCENT DISTRIBUTION OF MOTHERS WITH HUSBAND PRESENT.   WUSDLAB64204

AN ANALYSIS OF FACTORS INFLUENCING MARRIED WOMEN-S ACTUAL OR PLANNED WORK **PARTICIPATION**.   WWELLMW61261

PARTNERSHIP
FULL **PARTNERSHIP** FOR WOMEN -- WHAT STILL NEEDS TO BE DONE.   WVITAIX63218

PARTNERSHIP TEACHING PROGRAM. PROGRESS REPORT -- JAN-OCT 1965. SECTION I. /TRAINING/   WWOMEEA65275

PASADENA
EMPLOYMENT PRACTICES, CITY OF **PASADENA**, AN INVESTIGATION UNDER SECTION 1421 OF THE CALIFORNIA LABOR CODE
1963-1965.   GCALFEPND531

PAST
INDIANS OF CALIFORNIA, **PAST** AND PRESENT.   IQUINFX60609

ECONOMIC VALUE OF THE NEGRO TO THE SOUTH. **PAST**, PRESENT, AND POTENTIAL.   NSOUTRC45158

SEGREGATION. A COLOR PATTERN FROM THE **PAST** -- OUR STRUGGLE TO WIPE IT OUT.   NSURVGX47191

PATIENT
LIFE INSURANCE. THE **PATIENT** IMPROVES. /DISCRIMINATION/   GANTIOL59399

SURVEY OF MINORITY-GROUP EMPLOYMENT AND **PATIENT** CARE IN PRIVATE HOSPITAL FACILITIES IN LOS-ANGELES
COUNTY. /CALIFORNIA/   GLOSACCND914

PATRON-PEON
PATRON-PEON PATTERN AMONG THE SPANISH-AMERICANS OF NEW-MEXICO.   MKNOWCS66423

PATRONAGE
FACTORS AFFECTING THE PRESENT FARMING PROGRAMS OF ONE HUNDRED NEGRO FARMS IN THE **PATRONAGE** AREA OF THE
MACON COUNTY TRAINING SCHOOL, IN ALABAMA, WITH EMPHASIS FOR IMPROVEMENT.   NBRONCA51337

PATTERN
REPORTS ON THE **PATTERN** OF EMPLOYMENT OF MINORTY-GROUP PERSONS IN DEPARTMENT OF COUNTY
GOVERNMENT.LOS-ANGELES CALIFORNIA/   GLOSACC62913

JOBS, 1960-1970. THE CHANGING **PATTERN**. /EMPLOYMENT-TRENDS/   GNEWYSE60108

PATTERN FOR PROGRESS, SEVENTH REPORT, FINAL REPORT TO PRESIDENT EISENHOWER FROM THE COMMITTEE ON
GOVERNMENT CONTRACTS.   GPRESCH60123

THE **PATTERN** OF DEPENDENT POVERTY IN CALIFORNIA.   GRAABEX64120

RACIAL AND ETHNIC EMPLOYMENT **PATTERN** SURVEY OF THE CITY AND COUNTY OF SAN-FRANCISCO GOVERNMENT.
DEPARTMENTAL ANALYSIS. /CALIFORNIA/   GSANFHR65264

THE CHANGING **PATTERN** IN EMPLOYMENT. /EQUAL-EMPLOYMENT-OPPORTUNITY/   GWALLLM63520

A DECISIVE **PATTERN** IN AMERICAN JEWISH HISTORY.   JRIVIEX58325

PATRON-PEON **PATTERN** AMONG THE SPANISH-AMERICANS OF NEW-MEXICO.   MKNOWCS66423

THE **PATTERN** OF JOB DISCRIMINATION AGAINST NEGROES.   NHILLHX65536

THE EFFECT OF A CHANGING AGRICULTURAL **PATTERN** ON NEGRO FARMERS OF SOUTH-CAROLINA.   NHURSRL56253

PATTERN   (CONTINUATION)
SEGREGATION. A COLOR **PATTERN** FROM THE PAST -- OUR STRUGGLE TO WIPE IT OUT.   NSURVGX47191

INTEREST **PATTERN** FAKING BY FEMALE JOB APPLICANTS. /ASPIRATIONS/   WBECKJA63633

A NEW LIFE **PATTERN** FOR THE COLLEGE-EDUCATED WOMAN. /WORK-FAMILY-CONFLICT/   WSTEIER65133

PATTERNING
SITUATIONAL **PATTERNING** AND INTERGROUP RELATIONS.   GKOHNML56145

PATTERNS
CHANGING **PATTERNS** OF PREJUDICE. /NEGRO PUERTO-RICAN ORIENTAL AMERICAN-INDIAN/   CMARRAJ62055

SEX DIFFERENCES IN OCCUPATIONAL CHOICE **PATTERNS** AMONG ADOLESCENTS. /ASPIRATIONS WOMEN NEGRO/   CSPREJX62999

LESSONS FROM THE **PATTERNS** OF UNEMPLOYMENT IN THE LAST FIVE YEARS.   GBANCGX66752

MIGRATION **PATTERNS** OF THE RURAL-FARM POPULATION. THIRTEEN ECONOMIC REGIONS OF THE UNITED STATES,
1940-1950.   GBOWLGK57415

EFFECTS OF TECHNOLOGICAL-CHANGE ON OCCUPATIONAL EMPLOYMENT **PATTERNS** IN THE UNITED STATES.   GCLAGEX64625

A STUDY OF **PATTERNS** OF DISCRIMINATION IN EMPLOYMENT FOR THE EQUAL-EMPLOYMENT-OPPORTUNITY-COMMISSION,
WASHINGTON-DC.   GCOUSFR66478

PATTERNS OF DISCRIMINATION IN THE FINANCIAL INSTITUTIONS OF THE DISTRICT-OF-COLUMBIA. THE BANKING,
SAVINGS AND LOAN, AND INSURANCE INDUSTRIES.   GDISTCC66642

WARTIME EMPLOYMENT **PATTERNS** OF NONWHITES AND FEMALE WORKERS IN SOUTHERN INDUSTRY.   GHOPEJX46485

ETHNIC **PATTERNS** IN AMERICAN CITIES.   GLIEBSX63904

A STUDY OF UNEMPLOYMENT, TRAINING AND PLACEMENT **PATTERNS** IN THE MUSKEGON AREA. /MICHIGAN/   GMICFEA57979

THE STRUCTURE OF THE FARM LABOR-MARKET AND MIGRATION **PATTERNS**.   GMIREWX57499

PATTERNS OF CONCILIATION UNDER THE NEW-YORK STATE LAW AGAINST DISCRIMINATION.   GNEWXYL51100

PATTERNS OF DISCRIMINATION IN THE GLASS AND MACHINE TOOL INDUSTRIES IN OHIO.   GOHIOCR66126

PATTERNS OF DISCRIMINATION IN THE GLASS INDUSTRY IN OHIO.   GOHIOCR66127

PATTERNS OF DISCRIMINATION IN THE MACHINE TOOL INDUSTRY IN OHIO.   GOHIOCR66128

CHANGING **PATTERNS** IN EMPLOYMENT OF NONWHITE WORKERS.   GRUSSJL66269

A STUDY OF EMPLOYMENT **PATTERNS** IN THE GENERAL MERCHANDISE GROUP RETAIL STORES IN NEW-YORK-CITY.   GWATKDC66588

FINAL REPORT. **PATTERNS** OF DISCRIMINATION STUDY -- WISCONSIN.   GWISCIC66587

PATTERNS OF EXCLUSION FROM THE EXECUTIVE-SUITE. COMMERCIAL BANKING.   JAMERJC66696

BARRIERS. **PATTERNS** OF DISCRIMINATION AGAINST JEWS.   JBELTNC58702

THE JEWS. SOCIAL **PATTERNS** OF AN AMERICAN GROUP.   JSKLAMX58149

AN ANALYSIS OF CURRENT **PATTERNS** IN HUMAN RESOURCE DEVELOPMENT IN SAN-ANTONIO, TEXAS.   MDAVIHW66387

SPANISH-AMERICANS OF THE SOUTHWEST. LIFE-STYLE **PATTERNS** AND THEIR IMPLICATIONS.   MHAYDRG66114

MEXICAN CULTURAL **PATTERNS**.   MIMMASM57420

VALUE ORIENTATIONS OF YOUNG MEXICAN-AMERICAN MALES AS REFLECTED IN THEIR WORK **PATTERNS** AND EMPLOYMENT
PREFERENCES.   MWADOJO62513

CHANGING **PATTERNS** IN AGRICULTURAL PRODUCTIONS, WEST-VIRGINIA, 1920-1950. /OCCUPATIONS/   NANGLRA54254

EDUCATIONAL **PATTERNS** IN SOUTHERN MIGRATION.   NFEINRX65348

ETHNIC FAMILY **PATTERNS**. THE NEGRO FAMILY IN THE UNITED STATES.   NFRAZEF48379

EMPLOYMENT **PATTERNS** OF NEGRO MEN AND WOMEN.   NGINZEX66416

THE CAREER **PATTERNS** OF NEGRO LAWYERS IN LOUISIANA. /OCCUPATIONS/   NGUILBM60465

PATTERNS OF EMPLOYMENT DISCRIMINATION.   NHILLHX62537

RACIAL INEQUALITY IN EMPLOYMENT. THE **PATTERNS** OF DISCRIMINATION.   NHILLHX65540

TRENDS IN **PATTERNS** OF RACE-RELATIONS IN THE SOUTH SINCE MAY 17 1954.   NHOPEJX56575

PATTERNS OF NEGRO SEGREGATION.   NJOHNCS43008

CHANGING **PATTERNS** OF NEGRO EMPLOYMENT. /OCCUPATIONAL-PATTERNS/   NKIFEAX64649

PATTERNS OF DISCRIMINATION STUDY -- LOUISVILLE HUMAN-RELATIONS-COMMISSION. /KENTUCKY/   NLCUIHR66582

FAMILY **PATTERNS**, ACHIEVEMENTS, AND ASPIRATIONS OF URBAN NEGROES.   NLYSTMH61718

A STUDY OF EMPLOYMENT AND TRAINING **PATTERNS** IN THE LANSING AREA. /MICHIGAN/   NMICFEP58778

CHANGING EMPLOYMENT **PATTERNS** OF NEGROES, 1920-1950.   NPRESHB62125

MIGRATION **PATTERNS** OF NEGROES FROM A RURAL NORTHEASTERN MISSISSIPPI COMMUNITY. /DEMOGRAPHY/   NRUBIMX60094

CAREER **PATTERNS** OF TEACHERS IN NEGRO COLLEGES.   NTHOMDC58204

OCCUPATIONAL **PATTERNS** OF INEQUALITY.   NTURNRH54216

PATTERNS OF SOCIAL ACCOMODATION OF THE MIGRANT PUERTO-RICAN IN THE AMERICAN SOCIAL STRUCTURE.   PSEDAEX58850

DIGEST OF CASE STUDIES ON CONTINUITIES AND DISCONTINUITIES IN THE EMPLOYMENT-EDUCATION-FAMILY **PATTERNS** OF
WOMEN-S LIVES.   WDELAPJ60224

THE CHANGING **PATTERNS** OF WOMEN-S WORK. SOME PSYCHOLOGICAL CORRELATES.   WGINZEX58784

COLLEGE WOMEN-S IDENTIFICATIONS WITH THEIR FATHERS IN RELATION TO VOCATIONAL INTEREST **PATTERNS**.
/ASPIRATIONS/   WHALLWJ63815

PATTERNS (CONTINUATION)
PATTERNS IN WOMANPOWER. A PILOT STUDY.   WHANSEB62820

SOME IMPLICATIONS ON CURRENT CHANGES IN SEX ROLE **PATTERNS**. /WORK-WOMAN-ROLE/   WHARTRE60828

CHANGING **PATTERNS** IN WOMEN-S LIVES IN 1960. /WORK-WOMAN-ROLE/   WHAWKAL60834

NEEDED. UNIQUE **PATTERNS** FOR EDUCATING WOMEN. /WORK-WOMEN-ROLE/   WIRISLD62874

PSYCHOLOGICAL AND SOCIOLOGICAL FACTORS IN PREDICTION OF CAREER **PATTERNS** OF WOMEN. /ASPIRATIONS/   WMULVMC61080

PSYCHOLOGICAL AND SOCIOLOGICAL FACTORS IN PREDICTION OF CAREER **PATTERNS** FOR WOMEN. /ASPIRATIONS/   WMULVMC63006

SOME IMPLICATIONS OF THE EMPLOYMENT **PATTERNS** OF WOMEN UNDER SOCIAL-SECURITY.   WPOLIEJ59454

WOMEN IN INDUSTRY -- **PATTERNS** OF WOMEN-S WORK AND OCCUPATIONAL HEALTH AND SAFETY. /OCCUPATIONS/   WSPIRES60301

NEW **PATTERNS** OF EMPLOYMENT.   WUVMICC66685

PAY
THE POOR **PAY** MORE. CONSUMER PRACTICES OF LOW-INCOME FAMILIES.   GCAPLDX63310

EQUAL OPPORTUNITY AND EQUAL **PAY**.   NNORTHR64937

THE PRICE WE **PAY** FOR DISCRIMINATION. /SOUTH ECONOMY/   NPATTBX64979

NEGRO EMPLOYMENT IN THE FEDERAL GOVERNMENT BY CIVIL SERVICE REGION, STATE AND **PAY** CATEGORIES, JUNE 1962.   NPRESCD62012

EQUAL **PAY** FOR WOMEN. /DISCRIMINATION/   WCOMMXX63701

PAY DIFFERENCES BETWEEN MEN AND WOMEN. /DISCRIMINATION/   WSANBHX64100

PAYS
THE PRICE BUSINESS **PAYS**. /INDUSTRY DISCRIMINATION/   GROPEEX49245

PEACE
BROKEN **PEACE** PIPES. A 400 YEAR HISTORY OF THE AMERICAN-INDIAN.   IPEITIM64604

PENINSULA
CONFERENCE ON WOMEN IN THE UPPER **PENINSULA** ECONOMY. REPORT. /MICHIGAN/   WMICDLA64976

PENNSYLVANIA
INCOME, EDUCATION AND UNEMPLOYMENT IN NEIGHBORHOODS. PHILADELPHIA, **PENNSYLVANIA**. /DEMOGRAPHY/   CUSDLAB63478

INCOME, EDUCATION AND UNEMPLOYMENT IN NEIGHBORHOODS. PITTSBURGH, **PENNSYLVANIA**. /DEMOGRAPHY/   CUSDLAB63479

POPULATION AND LABOR-FORCE CHARACTERISTICS OF FIVE SOUTHEASTERN **PENNSYLVANIA** COUNTIES.   GANDEBXND391

SPECIAL ASSIMILATION PROBLEMS OF UNDERPRIVILEGED IMMIGRANTS TO PHILADELPHIA. /PENNSYLVANIA/   GPENNEL62502

LEGAL RULINGS INTERPRETING THE PROVISIONS OF THE **PENNSYLVANIA** FAIR-EMPLOYMENT-PRACTICE ACT.   GPENNFE58153

EMPLOYMENT PRACTICES IN **PENNSYLVANIA**.   GPENNGC53159

GUIDE TO EMPLOYERS, EMPLOYMENT-AGENCIES AND LABOR UNIONS DEFINING PROPER AND IMPROPER PRE-EMPLOYMENT
INQUIRIES. /PENNSYLVANIA/   GPENNHRND164

LAWS ADMINISTERED BY THE **PENNSYLVANIA** HUMAN-RELATIONS-COMMISSION.   GPENNHRND165

EMPLOYMENT PRACTICES OF THE PHILADELPHIA SCHOOL DISTRICT. /PENNSYLVANIA/   GPENNHR62162

FAIR EMPLOYMENT SURVEY OF THE WESTCHESTER AREA. /PENNSYLVANIA/   GPENNHR65163

SECOND SURVEY OF NON-WHITE EMPLOYEES IN STATE GOVERNMENT IN **PENNSYLVANIA**.   GPENNHR65167

THE EFFECTS OF AUTOMATION ON OCCUPATIONS AND WORKERS IN **PENNSYLVANIA**.   GPENNSE65641

REPORT OF THE SPECIAL COMMITTEE ON NONDISCRIMINATION OF THE BOARD OF PUBLIC EDUCATION, PHILADELPHIA.
/PENNSYLVANIA/   GPHILBE64172

SUMMARY OF TESTIMONY -- HOTEL RESTAURANT HEARINGS, APPENDIX A. /PHILADELPHIA PENNSYLVANIA/   GPHILCH60181

FINDINGS OF FACT, CONCLUSIONS AND ACTION OF THE COMMISSION ON HUMAN-RELATIONS IN RE. INVESTIGATIVE PUBLIC
HEARINGS INTO ALLEGED DISCRIMINATORY PRACTICE BY THE HOTEL AND RESTAURANT INDUSTRY IN PHILADELPHIA.
/PENNSYLVANIA/   GPHILCH61176

REPORT OF PROGRESS IN THE INTEGRATION OF HOTEL AND RESTAURANT EMPLOYMENT, APRIL 1961 TO MARCH 1962.
/PHILADELPHIA PENNSYLVANIA/   GPHILCH62178

REPORT OF 1961 - 1962 SURVEY OF PHILADELPHIA BANKS AND ATTACHED COMPOSITE TABULATION OF NON-WHITES.
/PENNSYLVANIA/   GPHILCH62180

A SPECIAL REPORT. CITY CONTRACT COMPLIANCE. PROGRESS IN 1963. /PHILADELPHIA PENNSYLVANIA/   GPHILCH64179

ANTI-DISCRIMINATION PACT SIGNED IN PHILADELPHIA. /PENNSYLVANIA/   GPUBLWX63207

CASES ARE PEOPLE. AN INTERPRETATION OF THE **PENNSYLVANIA** FAIR-EMPLOYMENT-PRACTICE LAW.   GSHIREM58304

SURVEY OF NON-WHITE EMPLOYEES IN STATE GOVERNMENT. /PENNSYLVANIA/   GSTRUJW63338

ADMINISTRATIVE LAW -- HUMAN-RELATIONS COMMISSIONS, **PENNSYLVANIA** LAW AND DISCRIMINATORY EMPLOYMENT
PRACTICE.   GTEMPLQ63349

SUB-EMPLOYMENT IN THE SLUMS OF PHILADELPHIA. /PENNSYLVANIA/   GUSDLAB66522

THE NEGRO STEELWORKERS OF PITTSBURGH AND THE UNIONS. /PENNSYLVANIA/   NAUGUTX47035

CASE-STUDY OF A RIOT THE PHILADELPHIA STORY. /PENNSYLVANIA/   NBERSLE66078

AIDING NEGRO BUSINESSMEN. SMALL BUSINESS OPPORTUNITIES CORPORATION, PHILADELPHIA. /PENNSYLVANIA/   NBUSIWX64143

THE CENSUS OF NEGRO-OWNED BUSINESSES. /PHILADELPHIA PENNSYLVANIA OCCUPATIONS/   NDREXIT64295

SOCIAL-STATUS AND ASPIRATIONS IN PHILADELPHIA-S NEGRO POPULATION. /PENNSYLVANIA/   NKLEIRJ62655

SELF-HELP IN PHILADELPHIA. /TRAINING PENNSYLVANIA/   NLEESHX64675

NEGRO INTELLIGENCE AND SELECTIVE MIGRATION. A PHILADELPHIA TEST OF THE KLINEBERG HYPOTHESIS.

PENNSYLVANIA   (CONTINUATION)
    /PENNSYLVANIA/   NLEEXES51673

    REPORT OF THE 1961-1962 SURVEY OF PHILADELPHIA BANKS. /PENNSYLVANIA/   NPHILCH62995

    OPINION BY HONORABLE BENJAMIN LENCHER. CITY OF PITTSBURGH VS PLUMBERS LOCAL UNION NO 27. /PENNSYLVANIA/ NPITTLJ65001

    STATUS OF NEGROES IN CRAFT UNIONS...PITTSBURGH LABOR-MARKET. /PENNSYLVANIA/   NPITTMC65002

    DESEGREGATION. A COMMUNITY DESIGN. /PHILADELPHIA PENNSYLVANIA/   NSCHEGX61104

    PREJUDICE IS NOT THE WHOLE STORY. EXAMINATION OF THREE CASES OF NEGRO UPGRADING IN TRACTION COMPANIES IN
    PHILADELPHIA. LOS-ANGELES AND CHICAGO. /PENNSYLVANIA CALIFORNIA ILLINOIS/   NWECKJE45308

    PUERTO-RICANS IN PHILADELPHIA. MIGRATION AND ACCOMODATION. /PENNSYLVANIA/   PKOSSJD65822

    PUERTO-RICANS IN PHILADELPHIA. /PENNSYLVANIA/   PMETARX59826

    PHILADELPHIA-S PUERTO-RICAN POPULATION. WITH 1960 CENSUS DATA. /PENNSYLVANIA/   PPITTCH64844

    FACTORS ASSOCIATED WITH GRADUATE SCHOOL ATTENDANCE AND ROLE DEFINITION OF THE WOMAN DOCTORAL CANDIDATES
    AT THE PENNSYLVANIA STATE UNIVERSITY. /OCCUPATIONS/   WFIELJC61763

PEONAGE
    THE THORNTONS OF MISSISSIPPI. PEONAGE ON THE PLANTATION. /POVERTY/   NGOODPX66433

PERCEIVED
    PERCEIVED OPPORTUNITIES. EXPECTATIONS. AND THE DECISION TO REMAIN ON RELOCATION. THE CASE OF THE NAVAHO
    INDIAN MIGRANT TO DENVER. COLORADO.   IGRAVTD65567

    PERCEIVED LIFE CHANCES IN THE OPPORTUNITY STRUCTURE. A STUDY OF A TRI-ETHNIC HIGH SCHOOL.   MGUERCX62410

PERCENT
    NONWHITE OCCUPATIONAL STATUS. BY REGION. AS RELATED TO PERCENT OF NONWHITE.   GGUEREW63746

    PERCENT NONWHITE AND DISCRIMINATION IN THE SOUTH.   NBLALHM57085

    LABOR-FORCE PARTICIPATION RATES AND PERCENT DISTRIBUTION OF MOTHERS WITH HUSBAND PRESENT.   WUSDLAB64204

PERCENTAGE
    CITY EMPLOYMENT SURVEY. PERCENTAGE OF MINORITY-GROUP EMPLOYEES BY DEPARTMENT. /YONKERS NEW-YORK/   GYONKCC66592

PERCEPTION
    DROP-OUTS FROM SCHOOLS OF NURSING. THE EFFECT OF SELF- AND ROLE PERCEPTION.   WKIBRAK58902

PERCEPTIONS
    ANALYSIS OF MALE NAVAHO STUDENTS PERCEPTIONS OF OCCUPATIONAL OPPORTUNITIES AND THEIR ATTITUDES TOWARD
    DEVELOPMENT OF SKILLS AND TRAITS NECESSARY FOR OCCUPATIONAL COMPETENCE.   IDESPCW65548

    EMPLOYMENT EXPERIENCES OF NEGRO PHILADELPHIANS. A DESCRIPTIVE STUDY OF THE EMPLOYMENT EXPERIENCES.
    PERCEPTIONS. AND ASPIRATIONS OF SELECTED PHILADELPHIA WHITES AND NON-WHITES.   NSIEGAI59718

    PERSONAL AND ON-THE-JOB CHARACTERISTICS RELATED TO NEGRO PERCEPTIONS OF DISCRIMINATION.   NSOLDHX56152

    ASSIMILATION OF CHINESE IN AMERICA. CHANGES IN ORIENTATION AND SOCIAL PERCEPTIONS.   OFONGSL65722

    PERCEPTIONS OF ROLE CONFLICTS AND SELF CONFLICTS AMONG CAREER AND NON-CAREER COLLEGE EDUCATED WOMEN.
    /WORK-FAMILY-CONFLICT/   WMORGOD62996

    HIGH SCHOOL GUIDANCE COUNSELOR-S PERCEPTIONS OF SELECTED CAREERS FOR WOMEN COLLEGE GRADUATES.   WSWOPMR63146

PERFORM
    MISSISSIPPI WORKERS. WHERE THEY COME FROM AND HOW THEY PERFORM. A STUDY OF WORKING FORCES IN SELECTED
    MISSISSIPPI INDUSTRIAL PLANTS.   NWOFFBM55333

PERFORMANCE
    FAMILY STRUCTURE AND SCHOOL PERFORMANCE. A COMPARATIVE STUDY OF STUDENTS FROM THREE ETHNIC BACKGROUNDS IN
    AN INTEGRATED SCHOOL. /MEXICAN-AMERICAN AMERICAN-INDIAN/   CGRIFJX65407

    4. CURRENT PROBLEMS IN TEST PERFORMANCE OF JOB-APPLICANTS.   GDUGARD66651

    3 CURRENT PROBLEMS IN TEST PERFORMANCE OF JOB APPLICANTS.   GLOPEFM66909

    HUMAN RESOURCES IN THE URBAN ECONOMY. PART II -- THE LABOR FORCE PERFORMANCE OF MINORITY-GROUPS.   GPERLMX63169

    TEST PERFORMANCE IN RELATION TO ETHNIC GROUP AND SOCIAL CLASS.   GROBESO63683

    RELATION OF MOTHER-S EMPLOYMENT TO INTELLECTUAL PERFORMANCE OF NEGRO COLLEGE STUDENTS.   NEPPSEG64336

    FAMILY AND ACHIEVEMENT. A PROPOSAL TO STUDY THE EFFECT OF FAMILY SOCIALIZATION ON ACHIEVEMENT AND
    PERFORMANCE AMONG URBAN NEGRO AMERICANS.   NEPPSEG65334

    MOTIVATION AND PERFORMANCE OF NEGRO STUDENTS.   NEPPSEG66335

    ON SPECIAL-TRAINING-UNIT PERFORMANCE AS AN INDEX OF NEGRO ABILITY.   NERICRW46339

    I Q PERFORMANCE. EDUCATIONAL AND OCCUPATIONAL ASPIRATIONS OF YOUTH IN A SOUTHERN CITY -- A RACIAL
    COMPARISON.   NGEISPX62397

    THE MEANINGFULNESS OF NEGRO-WHITE DIFFERENCES IN INTELLIGENCE TEST PERFORMANCE.   NHICKRA66740

    EFFECTS OF ANXIETY. THREAT. AND RACIAL ENVIRONMENT ON TASK PERFORMANCE OF NEGRO COLLEGE STUDENTS.   NKATZIX63640

    REVIEW OF EVIDENCE RELATING TO EFFECTS OF DESEGREGATION ON THE INTELLECTUAL PERFORMANCE OF NEGROES.   NKATZIX64637

    NEGRO-WHITE DIFFERENCES IN INTELLIGENCE TEST PERFORMANCE.   NKLINOX63657

    THE PROBLEM OF CULTURAL BIAS IN SELECTION. II. ETHNIC BACKGROUND AND TEST PERFORMANCE.   NROBESO65068

    THE EFFECT OF SPECIAL INSTRUCTION UPON TEST PERFORMANCE OF HIGH SCHOOL STUDENTS IN TENNESSEE.   NROBESO66961

    RELATIONSHIP BETWEEN THE EDUCATIONAL GOALS AND THE ACADEMIC PERFORMANCE OF WOMEN. A CONFIRMATION.   WWEITHX59260

PERFORMING-ARTS
    EMPLOYMENT-PRACTICES IN THE PERFORMING-ARTS.   GUSHOUR63337

PERKINS
    INTEGRATION IN PROFESSIONAL EDUCATION. THE STORY OF PERKINS. SOUTHERN METHODIST UNIVERSITY. /VOCATIONS/ NCUNNMX56579

PERPETUATION
PUBLIC WELFARE. POVERTY -- PREVENTION OR **PERPETUATION**. A STUDY OF THE STATE DEPARTMENT OF PUBLIC
ASSISTANCE OF THE STATE OF WASHINGTON.   GGREEAI64479

PERSISTENCE
NARRAGANSETT SURVIVAL. A STUDY OF GROUP **PERSISTENCE** THROUGH ADAPTED TRAITS.   IBOISEX59887

CHANGES IN SELECTED PERSONALITY CHARACTERISTICS AND **PERSISTENCE** IN THE CAREER CHOICES OF WOMEN ASSOCIATED
WITH A FOUR YEAR COLLEGE EDUCATION AT ONE OF THE COLLEGES OF THE CITY UNIVERSITY OF NEW-YORK.
/ASPIRATIONS/   WLEINMX64925

PERSISTENT
THE EVIDENCE OF **PERSISTENT** UNEMPLOYMENT.   GINDURR59814

HIGH SCHOOL GRADUATES AND DROPOUTS -- A NEW LOOK AT A **PERSISTENT** PROBLEM.   NLIVIAH58044

PERSISTING
ECONOMIC EXPANSION AND **PERSISTING** UNEMPLOYMENT. AN OVERVIEW.   GREESAX66722

PERSONAL
EMPLOYMENT AND **PERSONAL** CHARACTERISTICS. EMPLOYMENT BY AGE, RACE, NATIVITY, EDUCATION, MARITAL-STATUS,
HOUSEHOLD RELATIONSHIPS, ETC. /DEMOGRAPHY/   CUSBURC53372

FREEDOM OF CHOICE IN **PERSONAL** SERVICE OCCUPATIONS. 13TH AMENDMENT LIMITATIONS ON ANTIDISCRIMINATION
LEGISLATION.   GAVINAX64410

ILLINOIS JOB SEEKERS SURVEY. EDUCATION, SKILLS, LENGTH OF UNEMPLOYMENT, AND **PERSONAL** CHARACTERISTICS.   GILLIDI62004

SOME **PERSONAL** AND SOCIOLOGICAL VARIABLES ASSOCIATED WITH OCCUPATIONAL-CHOICES OF NEGRO YOUTH.   NHERSPF65520

TO WIN THESE RIGHTS. A **PERSONAL** STORY OF THE CIO IN THE SOUTH. /UNION/   NMASOJR52324

PERSONAL AND ON-THE-JOB CHARACTERISTICS RELATED TO NEGRO PERCEPTIONS OF DISCRIMINATION.   NSOLDHX56152

PERSONAL AND ENVIRONMENTAL OBSTACLES TO PRODUCTION ADJUSTMENTS ON SOUTH-CAROLINA PIEDMONT AREA FARMS.   NTAYLCC58411

PERSONAL SATISFACTIONS. /WORK-WOMAN-ROLE/   WNYEXFI63038

REALITIES. EDUCATIONAL, ECONOMIC, LEGAL AND **PERSONAL** NEEDS OF CAREER WOMEN.   WPARKRX66049

PERSONALITY
SOME CONSIDERATIONS AS TO THE CONTRIBUTIONS OF SOCIAL, **PERSONALITY**, AND RACIAL FACTORS TO SCHOOL
RETARDATION IN MINORITY-GROUP CHILDREN.   GDEUTMP56641

MINORITY-GROUP AND CLASS STATUS AS RELATED TO SOCIAL AND **PERSONALITY** FACTORS IN SCHOLASTIC ACHIEVEMENT.   GDEUTMP60640

THE FALLACIES OF **PERSONALITY** TESTING.   GWHYTWH54560

ACCULTURATION, SELF-IDENTIFICATION, AND **PERSONALITY** ADJUSTMENT.   ICHANNA65543

ANOMIE AND ACHIEVEMENT MOTIVATION. A STUDY OF **PERSONALITY** DEVELOPMENT WITHIN CULTURAL DISORGANIZATION.   IKERCAC59018

CORRELATES OF SOUTHERN NEGRO **PERSONALITY**.   NBRAZWF64496

COLOR, CLASS, **PERSONALITY**, AND JUVENILE DELINQUENCY.   NCLARKB59210

SOME **PERSONALITY** CHARACTERISTICS OF SOUTHERN NEGRO STUDENTS.   NGROSMM57462

A PILOT STUDY OF **PERSONALITY** FACTORS RELATED TO OCCUPATIONAL ASPIRATIONS OF NEGRO COLLEGE STUDENTS.   NLITTLW66697

FATHER-ABSENCE AND NEGRO ADULT **PERSONALITY**. A RESEARCH NOTE.   NPETTTFND990

NEGRO AMERICAN **PERSONALITY**.   NPETTTF64991

ACHIEVEMENT, CULTURE AND **PERSONALITY**. THE CASE OF THE JAPANESE-AMERICANS.   OCAUDWX61711

THE DEVELOPMENT OF BEHAVIOR AND **PERSONALITY**. /WORK-WOMEN-ROLE/   WANDEJE60614

AN INVERTED FACTOR ANALYSIS OF **PERSONALITY** DIFFERENCES BETWEEN CAREER AND HOMEMAKING-ORIENTED WOMEN.
/ASPIRATIONS/   WAVILDL64316

INTEREST AND **PERSONALITY** CORRELATES OF CAREER-MOTIVATED AND HOMEMAKING-MOTIVATED COLLEGE WOMEN.
/ASPIRATIONS/   WHOYTDP58850

CHANGES IN SELECTED **PERSONALITY** CHARACTERISTICS AND PERSISTENCE IN THE CAREER CHOICES OF WOMEN ASSOCIATED
WITH A FOUR YEAR COLLEGE EDUCATION AT ONE OF THE COLLEGES OF THE CITY UNIVERSITY OF NEW-YORK.
/ASPIRATIONS/   WLEINMX64925

PERSONNEL
RACE AND SOCIO-ECONOMIC STATUS IN MUNICIPAL **PERSONNEL** SELECTION.   GBIANJC67590

EQUAL-OPPORTUNITIES PLAN STRESSED IN STATE **PERSONNEL** BOARD DOCUMENT. /CALIFORNIA/   GCALSEM64548

ETHNIC CENSUS OF EXAMINATION COMPETITORS, JAN-JUNE 1965, CALIFORNIA STATE **PERSONNEL** BOARD.   GCALSPB65551

REPORT ON AND ANALYSIS OF SECOND CENSUS OF CITY EMPLOYEES TO DETERMINE BASES FOR FUTURE **PERSONNEL**
DEVELOPMENTS. /DETROIT MICHIGAN/   GDETRCC66639

PERSONNEL TESTING.   GGUIORM65693

CENTRAL ROLE OF INTERGROUP AGENCIES IN THE LABOR-MARKET. CHANGING RESEARCH AND **PERSONNEL** REQUIREMENTS.   GHOPEJX61780

CIVIL-RIGHTS PROBLEMS IN **PERSONNEL** AND LABOR-RELATIONS.   GKAMMTX65832

PERSONNEL TESTING, JANUARY 1960.   GMERCMA60976

SPECIAL REPORT. AN INVESTIGATION OF THE **PERSONNEL** POLICIES AND PRACTICES OF THE MICHIGAN STATE HIGHWAY
DEPARTMENT, MARCH 1961.   GMICFEP61983

PERSONNEL SELECTION TESTS AND FAIR-EMPLOYMENT-PRACTICES.   GSEASHX51293

CIVILIAN **PERSONNEL** -- NONDISCRIMINATION IN EMPLOYMENT. /MILITARY/   GUSDAIR62189

PLACEMENT OF PROFESSIONAL **PERSONNEL**.   GUSOLAB52492

LEGALITY AND VALIDITY OF **PERSONNEL** TESTS. /LEGISLATION TITLE-VII/   GVINCNX66113

EMPLOYMENT OF JEWISH **PERSONNEL** IN THE AUTOMOBILE INDUSTRY. /DISCRIMINATION/   JRIGHXX63756

PERSONNEL   (CONTINUATION)
THE PERSONNEL JOB IN A CHANGING WORLD. /INDUSTRY/   NBLUOJW64093

STUDY OF DETROIT POLICE DEPARTMENT PERSONNEL PRACTICES. /MICHIGAN OCCUPATIONS/   NDETRCC63267

PERSONNEL PRACTICES AND WARTIME CHANGES. /EMPLOYMENT/   NHAASFJ46548

CIVIL-RIGHTS PROBLEMS IN PERSONNEL AND LABOR-RELATIONS.   NKAMOTCND633

UPDATING GUIDANCE AND PERSONNEL PRACTICES.   NROUSRJ62089

CUSTOMER REACTIONS TO THE INTEGRATION OF NEGRO SALES PERSONNEL.   NSAENGX50101

RACE RELATIONS. QUESTIONS AND ANSWERS FOR PERSONNEL MEN.   NSHOSAX64132

SURVEY OF SALARIES AND PERSONNEL PRACTICES FOR TEACHERS AND ADMINISTRATORS IN NURSING EDUCATIONAL
PROGRAMS, DECEMBER 1965.   WAMERNA66612

SPEECH ABOUT JOB OPPORTUNITIES FOR GIRLS BEFORE THE MARYLAND STATE PERSONNEL AND GUIDANCE ASSOCIATION.   WTERLRX64148

HEALTH MANPOWER SOURCE BOOK. SECTION 2. NURSING PERSONNEL.   WUSDHEW66177

NURSES AND OTHER HOSPITAL PERSONNEL -- THEIR EARNINGS AND EMPLOYMENT-CONDITIONS.   WUSDLAB61211

PERSONS
EMPLOYMENT OF WHITE AND NON-WHITE PERSONS. 1955. /DEMOGRAPHY/   CUSBURC56373

PERSONS BY FAMILY CHARACTERISTICS. FAMILY MEMBERS BY SOCIAL, ECONOMIC AND HOUSING CHARACTERISTICS OF
FAMILIES. /DEMOGRAPHY/   CUSBURC63180

PERSONS OF SPANISH-SURNAME. SOCIAL AND ECONOMIC DATA FOR WHITE PERSONS OF SPANISH SURNAME IN 5
SOUTHWESTERN STATES. /DEMOGRAPHY/   CUSBURC63181

PERSONS OF SPANISH-SURNAME. SOCIAL AND ECONOMIC DATA FOR WHITE PERSONS OF SPANISH SURNAME IN 5
SOUTHWESTERN STATES. /DEMOGRAPHY/   CUSBURC63181

TRENDS IN THE INCOME OF FAMILIES AND PERSONS IN THE UNITED STATES. 1947-1960. /DEMOGRAPHY/   CUSBURC63381

INCOME IN 1964 OF FAMILIES AND PERSONS IN THE UNITED STATES. /DEMOGRAPHY/   CUSBURC65375

LABOR-FORCE PARTICIPATION OF YOUNG PERSONS AGED 14-24.   GFEARRXND929

REPORTS ON THE PATTERN OF EMPLOYMENT OF MINORTY-GROUP PERSONS IN DEPARTMENT OF COUNTY
GOVERNMENT.LOS-ANGELES CALIFORNIA/   GLOSACC62913

CHARACTERISTICS OF 6000 WHITE AND NONWHITE PERSONS ENROLLED IN MANPOWER-DEVELOPMENT-AND-TRAINING-ACT
TRAINING.   GUSDLAB63197

THE USE OF COLORED PERSONS IN SKILLED OCCUPATIONS.   NOCONWB41094

PUERTO-RICANS IN THE UNITED STATES. SOCIAL AND ECONOMIC DATA FOR PERSONS OF PUERTO-RICAN BIRTH AND
PARENTAGE. /DEMOGRAPHY/   PUSBURC63182

PERSPECTIVE
YOUTH EMPLOYMENT PROGRAMS IN PERSPECTIVE.   GBENJJG65006

US WELFARE POLICIES IN PERSPECTIVE.   GGORDMS63742

FAIR-EMPLOYMENT-PRACTICE-COMMISSION MOVEMENT IN PERSPECTIVE.   GKESSLC56846

TRAINING IN THE PERSPECTIVE OF TECHNOLOGICAL-CHANGE.   GSTRIHE66669

CRAFT UNIONS AND THE NEGRO IN HISTORICAL PERSPECTIVE.   NBLOCHD58087

A MANAGEMENT PERSPECTIVE TOWARD NEGRO ECONOMIC PRESSURES.   NHOFFHX65558

PERSPECTIVES
THE WAR-ON-POVERTY. PERSPECTIVES AND PROSPECTS.   GMILLSM65953

TRENDS AND PERSPECTIVES IN MANPOWER POLICY.   GREHNGX65654

NEW PERSPECTIVES ON POVERTY.   GSHOSAB65685

THE AMERICAN INDIAN. PERSPECTIVES FOR STUDY OF SOCIAL CHANGE.   IEGGAFR66552

PERSPECTIVES IN AMERICAN INDIAN CULTURE CHANGE.   ISPICEH61621

SOCIOLOGICAL PERSPECTIVES IN UNEMPLOYMENT RESEARCH.   NFERMLA64353

POLITICAL PERSPECTIVES.   NMOYNDP65863

COUNSELING GIRLS TOWARD NEW PERSPECTIVES.   WMIDDAR65190

PERSUADER
INVISIBLE PERSUADER ON PROMOTIONS.   JUVMIIT65768

PERTH-AMBOY
THE PUERTO-RICAN WORKER IN PERTH-AMBOY. NEW-JERSEY.   PGOLUFT56811

SOME ECONOMIC CONSEQUENCES OF THE PUERTO-RICAN MIGRATION INTO PERTH-AMBOY, 1949-1954. /NEW-JERSEY/   PGOLUFX55812

PETROLEUM
SOME FACTORS INFLUENCING THE UPGRADING OF NEGROES IN THE SOUTHERN PETROLEUM REFINING INDUSTRY.
/CASE-STUDY/   NMARSRX63748

PHD
GRADUATE EDUCATION FOR WOMEN. THE RADCLIFFE PHD.   WRADCCX56072

PHENOMENON
AMERICAN INDIANS. WHITE AND BLACK. THE PHENOMENON OF TRANSCULTURATION.   IHALLAI63571

PHILADELPHIA
NEGRO WOMEN IN THE CLOTHING, CIGAR AND LAUNDRY INDUSTRIES OF PHILADELPHIA, 1960.   CPORTRP43103

INCOME, EDUCATION AND UNEMPLOYMENT IN NEIGHBORHOODS. PHILADELPHIA, PENNSYLVANIA. /DEMOGRAPHY/   CUSDLAB63478

SPECIAL ASSIMILATION PROBLEMS OF UNDERPRIVILEGED IMMIGRANTS TO PHILADELPHIA. /PENNSYLVANIA/   GPENNEL62502

EMPLOYMENT PRACTICES OF THE PHILADELPHIA SCHOOL DISTRICT. /PENNSYLVANIA/   GPENNHR62162

PHILADELPHIA   (CONTINUATION)
REPORT OF THE SPECIAL COMMITTEE ON NONDISCRIMINATION OF THE BOARD OF PUBLIC EDUCATION. PHILADELPHIA.
/PENNSYLVANIA/   GPHILBE64172

SUMMARY OF TESTIMONY -- HOTEL RESTAURANT HEARINGS, APPENDIX A. /PHILADELPHIA PENNSYLVANIA/   GPHILCH60181

FINDINGS OF FACT, CONCLUSIONS AND ACTION OF THE COMMISSION ON HUMAN-RELATIONS IN RE. INVESTIGATIVE PUBLIC
HEARINGS INTO ALLEGED DISCRIMINATORY PRACTICE BY THE HOTEL AND RESTAURANT INDUSTRY IN PHILADELPHIA.
/PENNSYLVANIA/   GPHILCH61176

REPORT OF PROGRESS IN THE INTEGRATION OF HOTEL AND RESTAURANT EMPLOYMENT, APRIL 1961 TO MARCH 1962.
/PHILADELPHIA PENNSYLVANIA/   GPHILCH62178

REPORT OF 1961 - 1962 SURVEY OF PHILADELPHIA BANKS AND ATTACHED COMPOSITE TABULATION OF NON-WHITES.
/PENNSYLVANIA/   GPHILCH62180

A SPECIAL REPORT, CITY CONTRACT COMPLIANCE. PROGRESS IN 1963. /PHILADELPHIA PENNSYLVANIA/   GPHILCH64179

ANTI-DISCRIMINATION PACT SIGNED IN PHILADELPHIA. /PENNSYLVANIA/   GPUBLWX63207

SUB-EMPLOYMENT IN THE SLUMS OF PHILADELPHIA. /PENNSYLVANIA/   GUSDLAB66522

CASE-STUDY OF A RIOT THE PHILADELPHIA STORY. /PENNSYLVANIA/   NBERSLE66078

AIDING NEGRO BUSINESSMEN. SMALL BUSINESS OPPORTUNITIES CORPORATION, PHILADELPHIA. /PENNSYLVANIA/   NBUSIWX64143

THE CENSUS OF NEGRO-OWNED BUSINESSES. /PHILADELPHIA PENNSYLVANIA OCCUPATIONS/   NDREXIT64295

SELF-HELP IN PHILADELPHIA. /TRAINING PENNSYLVANIA/   NLEESHX64675

NEGRO INTELLIGENCE AND SELECTIVE MIGRATION. A PHILADELPHIA TEST OF THE KLINEBERG HYPOTHESIS.
/PENNSYLVANIA/   NLEEXES51673

REPORT OF THE 1961-1962 SURVEY OF PHILADELPHIA BANKS. /PENNSYLVANIA/   NPHILCH62995

DESEGREGATION. A COMMUNITY DESIGN. /PHILADELPHIA PENNSYLVANIA/   NSCHEGX61104

EMPLOYMENT EXPERIENCES OF NEGRO PHILADELPHIANS. A DESCRIPTIVE STUDY OF THE EMPLOYMENT EXPERIENCES,
PERCEPTIONS, AND ASPIRATIONS OF SELECTED PHILADELPHIA WHITES AND NON-WHITES.   NSIEGAI59718

PREJUDICE IS NOT THE WHOLE STORY. EXAMINATION OF THREE CASES OF NEGRO UPGRADING IN TRACTION COMPANIES IN
PHILADELPHIA. LOS-ANGELES AND CHICAGO. /PENNSYLVANIA CALIFORNIA ILLINOIS/   NWECKJE45308

PUERTO-RICANS IN PHILADELPHIA. MIGRATION AND ACCOMODATION. /PENNSYLVANIA/   PKOSSJD65822

PUERTO-RICANS IN PHILADELPHIA. /PENNSYLVANIA/   PMETARX59826

PHILADELPHIA-S
SOCIAL-STATUS AND ASPIRATIONS IN PHILADELPHIA-S NEGRO POPULATION. /PENNSYLVANIA/   NKLEIRJ62655

PHILADELPHIA-S PUERTO-RICAN POPULATION, WITH 1960 CENSUS DATA. /PENNSYLVANIA/   PPITTCH64844

PHILADELPHIANS
EMPLOYMENT EXPERIENCES OF NEGRO PHILADELPHIANS. A DESCRIPTIVE STUDY OF THE EMPLOYMENT EXPERIENCES,
PERCEPTIONS, AND ASPIRATIONS OF SELECTED PHILADELPHIA WHITES AND NON-WHITES.   NSIEGAI59718

PHOENIX
INCOME, EDUCATION AND UNEMPLOYMENT IN NEIGHBORHOODS. PHOENIX, ARIZONA. /DEMOGRAPHY/   CUSDLAB63480

SUB-EMPLOYMENT IN THE SLUMS OF PHOENIX. /ARIZONA/   GUSDLAB66513

PHYSICIAN
THE STATUS OF THE NEGRO PHYSICIAN IN NEW-YORK STATE. /OCCUPATIONS/   NMURRPM55867

THE FEMALE PHYSICIAN IN PUBLIC HEALTH. CONFLICT AND RECONCILIATION OF THE SEX AND PROFESSIONAL ROLES.
/OCCUPATIONS/   WKOSAJX64915

PHYSICIANS
A PRELIMINARY REPORT ON MEDICAL STAFF APPOINTMENTS HELD BY NEGRO PHYSICIANS AT PREDOMINANTLY WHITE
HOSPITALS. /CHICAGO ILLINOIS/   NCHICCO60201

MEDICAL SOCIETY OF THE DISTRICT OF COLUMBIA TO ADMIT NEGRO PHYSICIANS. /OCCUPATIONS/   NJOURNM52628

THE FACTS ON NEGRO PHYSICIANS. /OCCUPATIONS/   NMENZRX49766

SURVEY OF EMPLOYMENT-CONDITIONS OF NURSES EMPLOYED BY PHYSICIANS AND/OR DENTISTS, JULY 1964.   WAMERNA65610

SURVEY OF WOMEN PHYSICIANS GRADUATING FROM MEDICAL SCHOOL, 1925-1940. /OCCUPATIONS/   WDYKMRA57745

WOMEN PHYSICIANS IN THE TWENTY-FIRST CENTURY. /OCCUPATIONS/   WFAYXMX66758

PRACTITIONERS AND NON-PRACTITIONERS IN A GROUP OF WOMEN PHYSICIANS. /ASPIRATIONS/   WGLICRX65791

REPORT ON THE SURVEY OF FEMALE PHYSICIANS GRADUATING FROM MEDICAL SCHOOL BETWEEN 1925 AND 1940.
/OCCUPATIONS/   WHANNFX58819

THE WOMEN PHYSICIANS DILEMMA. /OCCUPATIONS/   WWILLJJ66269

PICKETING
PICKETING BY NEGROES TO OBTAIN EMPLOYMENT IN PROPORTION TO NEGRO CUSTOMERS HELD UNLAWFUL.   NHARVLR49498

PIEDMONT
CHARACTERISTICS, RESOURCES, AND INCOMES OF RURAL HOUSEHOLDS, PIEDMONT AREA, SOUTH-CAROLINA.   GBURCTA62408

PERSONAL AND ENVIRONMENTAL OBSTACLES TO PRODUCTION ADJUSTMENTS ON SOUTH-CAROLINA PIEDMONT AREA FARMS.   NTAYLCC58411

PILOT
SPANISH-SPEAKING PEOPLE IN THE UNITED STATES. A PILOT REPORT. /MEXICAN-AMERICAN PUERTO-RICAN/   CSAMGJX63474

A PILOT STUDY OF THE EMPLOYMENT EXPERIENCES OF HIGH SCHOOL GRADUATES.   GPHILCH65177

A PILOT STUDY OF AN INTEGRATED WORK FORCE.   NCOUSFR58611

A PILOT STUDY OF PERSONALITY FACTORS RELATED TO OCCUPATIONAL ASPIRATIONS OF NEGRO COLLEGE STUDENTS.   NLITTLW66697

PATTERNS IN WOMANPOWER. A PILOT STUDY.   WHANSEB62820

A PILOT STUDY OF THE MOTIVATIONS AND PROBLEMS OF MIDDLE AGED HOMEMAKERS IN LOWER SOCIO-ECONOMIC GROUPS IN

PILOT (CONTINUATION)
SEEKING EMPLOYMENT. /ASPIRATIONS/   WJEWIVA62883

PILOT PROJECTS FOR CONTINUING EDUCATION FOR WOMEN.   WMERRMH63972

IMPLICATIONS OF TWO PILOT PROJECTS IN TRAINING MATURE WOMEN AS COUNSELORS.   WRIOCMJ65082

PITTSBURGH
INCOME, EDUCATION AND UNEMPLOYMENT IN NEIGHBORHOODS. PITTSBURGH, PENNSYLVANIA. /DEMOGRAPHY/   CUSDLAB63479

THE NEGRO STEELWORKERS OF PITTSBURGH AND THE UNIONS. /PENNSYLVANIA/   NAUGUTX47035

OPINION BY HONORABLE BENJAMIN LENCHER. CITY OF PITTSBURGH VS PLUMBERS LOCAL UNION NO 27. /PENNSYLVANIA/   NPITTLJ65001

STATUS OF NEGROES IN CRAFT UNIONS...PITTSBURGH LABOR-MARKET. /PENNSYLVANIA/   NPITTMC65002

PLACE
MINORITIES IN THE MARKET PLACE.   GDEMSHX65869

THE LATIN AMERICAN IS FINDING HIS PLACE.   MDUFFLC66390

THE NEGRO-S PLACE AT LABOR-S TABLE. /UNION/   NBROOTX62122

ETHNOMICS -- NEGRO MUST BE FULL PARTICIPANT IN MARKET PLACE.   NBUNKHC65122

THE NEGRO-S CHANGING PLACE IN SOUTHERN AGRICULTURE.   NCHRIDE58206

THE PLACE OF THE NEGRO IN THE AMERICAN LABOR-MOVEMENT. /UNION/   NGREESX61452

THE PLACE OF THE NEGRO FARMER IN THE CHANGING ECONOMY OF THE COTTON SOUTH.   NNEALEE50905

SERVICING THE HARD TO PLACE.   PYANGRX61859

LET-S PUT WOMEN IN THEIR PLACE. /INDUSTRY/   WALBEGS61602

THE ACADEMIC MARKET PLACE. /OCCUPATIONS/   WCAPLTX58679

REVOLUTION WITHOUT IDEOLOGY. THE CHANGING PLACE OF WOMEN IN AMERICA. /WORK-WOMEN-ROLE/   WDEGLCN64727

A WOMAN-S PLACE. /WORK-WOMAN-ROLE/   WGRUMOX61379

PLACEMENT
A STUDY OF UNEMPLOYMENT, TRAINING AND PLACEMENT PATTERNS IN THE MUSKEGON AREA. /MICHIGAN/   GMICFEA57979

SURVEY OF OHIO COLLEGE AND UNIVERSITY PLACEMENT OFFICES WITH REGARD TO JOB PLACEMENT OF MINORITY
STUDENTS.   GOHIOCR62132

SURVEY OF OHIO COLLEGE AND UNIVERSITY PLACEMENT OFFICES WITH REGARD TO JOB PLACEMENT OF MINORITY
STUDENTS.   GOHIOCR62132

EVALUATION AND SKILL TRAINING OF OUT-OF-SCHOOL, HARD-CORE UNEMPLOYED YOUTH FOR TRAINING AND PLACEMENT.   GSMITAE65140

PLACEMENT OF PROFESSIONAL PERSONNEL.   GUSDLAB52492

PLACEMENT OF NON-ENGLISH SPEAKING APPLICANTS.   GWATSMMND544

PLACEMENT EXPERIENCES OF APPLICANTS TO A PRIVATE EMPLOYMENT-AGENCY.   NANTIOL55901

PLACEMENT AND CAREER COUNSELING AT PREDOMINANTLY NEGRO COLLEGES.   NBEAUAG66067

EXPERIMENTAL AND DEMONSTRATION MANPOWER PROJECT FOR THE RECRUITMENT, TRAINING, PLACEMENT AND FOLLOW-UP OF
RURAL UNEMPLOYED WORKERS IN TEN NORTH FLORIDA CITIES. FINAL REPORT. /PARTICIPANTS/   NJACKTA66597

PLACEMENT SERVICE OF THE AMERICAN FRIENDS SERVICE COMMITTEE. A TECHNIQUE IN RACE-RELATIONS.   NLOESFS46703

FACTORS AFFECTING FARM PLACEMENT OF NEGRO VOCATIONAL AGRICULTURE STUDENTS IN ALABAMA.   NMCQUFT45348

BI-RACIAL COOPERATION IN PLACEMENT OF NEGROES.   NUSDLAB42811

THE PLACEMENT OF NEGRO COLLEGE GRADUATES IN BUSINESS ORGANIZATIONS.   NWHITEW64321

REPORTS OF PUERTO-RICO DEPARTMENT OF LABOR, MIGRATION DIVISION ON PLACEMENT.   PPUERRDND791

FINAL REPORT. EXPERIMENTAL AND DEMONSTRATION MANPOWER PROJECT FOR THE RECRUITMENT, TRAINING, PLACEMENT
AND FOLLOW-UP OF RURAL UNEMPLOYED WORKERS IN TEN NORTH FLORIDA COUNTIES.   WFLORMP66326

EXPERIENCES OF NEGRO HIGH SCHOOL GIRLS WITH DOMESTIC PLACEMENT AGENCIES. /HOUSEHOLD-WORKERS/   WRUSSRD62135

PLACEMENTS
INCREASED INDUSTRIAL PLACEMENTS OF WORKERS.   NUSDLAB41821

PLACES
COMPILATION OF LAWS AGAINST DISCRIMINATION, EMPLOYMENT, EDUCATIONAL INSTITUTIONS, PLACES OF PUBLIC
ACCOMODATION, PUBLIC HOUSING, PUBLICLY ASSISTED HOUSING, PRIVATE HOUSING. /MASSACHUSETTS/   GMASSCAND963

PLACING
PLACING INDIANS WHO LIVE ON RESERVATIONS. A COOPERATIVE PROGRAM.   IUSDLAB59667

PLACING THE NEGRO WORKER.   NWILKWH41323

PLACING PUERTO-RICAN WORKERS IN THE NEW-YORK CITY LABOR-MARKET.   PMONTHX60830

PLAINS
SELECTED REFERENCES ON THE PLAINS INDIANS.   IEWERJC60816

PLAN
SAN FRANCISCO-S PLAN FOR DEMOCRATIC RACIAL-RELATIONS. /CALIFORNIA/   GBAYXAC43427

THE CALIFORNIA PLAN FOR EQUAL-OPPORTUNITY IN APPRENTICESHIP FOR MINORITY-GROUPS.   GCALDIR63523

EQUAL-OPPORTUNITIES PLAN STRESSED IN STATE PERSONNEL BOARD DOCUMENT. /CALIFORNIA/   GCALSEM64548

NOW. MASSACHUSETTS PLAN FOR EQUAL-EMPLOYMENT-OPPORTUNITY.   GGOULJX63732

US PLAN TO BREAK CYCLE OF BIAS AND POVERTY.   GRICHEX66235

GUARANTEED-INCOME PLAN.   GSHAFHB66801

FAMILY PLAN AND REHABILITATION PROGRAMS, STANDING-ROCK RESERVATION.   IUSDINT64649

PLAN (CONTINUATION)
CARRYING OUT A **PLAN** FOR JOB INTEGRATION AND DOING IT -- IN THE HEART OF GEORGIA -- WITHOUT A SINGLE
UNPLEASANT INCIDENT. THAT-S THE EXPERIENCE OF LOCKHEED AIRCRAFT CORPORATION AT ITS MARIETTA PLANT.
/INDUSTRY/   NBUSIWX63148

THE ROLE OF CIVIL-RIGHTS ORGANIZATIONS. A MARSHALL **PLAN** APPROACH.   NTUCKSX66209

NEW TRAINING **PLAN** FOR NEGROES.   NUSDLAB41832

PLAN FOR EQUAL-JOB-OPPORTUNITY AT LOCKHEED-AIRCRAFT-CORP. /INDUSTRY CASE-STUDY/   NUSDLAB61838

UNIVERSITY OF MINNESOTA -- THE MINNESOTA **PLAN**. /EDUCATION/   WSCHLVX63103

MINNESOTA **PLAN** FOR WOMEN-S CONTINUING EDUCATION. A PROGRESS REPORT.   WSENDVL61298

PLAN-FOR-PROGRESS
WESTERN-ELECTRIC AND ITS **PLAN-FOR-PROGRESS**. A THREE YEAR REPORT. /INDUSTRY/   GWESTEC64553

PLANNED
I STATEMENT BEFORE THE HOUSE POST OFFICE AND CIVIL SERVICE SUBCOMMITTEE ON POSTAL OPERATIONS, II
DISCRIMINATION. **PLANNED** AND ACCIDENTAL. /TESTING/   GENNEWH67928

A **PLANNED** COMMUNITY FOR MIGRATORY FARM WORKERS.   MFEERAB62392

AN ANALYSIS OF FACTORS INFLUENCING MARRIED WOMEN-S ACTUAL OR **PLANNED** WORK PARTICIPATION.   WWELLMW61261

PLANNING
POVERTY IN NEW-YORK CITY. FACTS FOR **PLANNING** COMMUNITY ACTION.   GCOMCCN64210

THE COMMUNITY ACTION AGENCY-S ROLE IN COMPREHENSIVE MANPOWER PROGRAMS -- **PLANNING** AND PROBLEMS.   GKANERD66863

MANPOWER **PLANNING** IN A FREE SOCIETY.   GLESTRA66155

PLANNING CONSTRUCTIVE ECONOMIC OPPORTUNITIES FOR THE JEWISH AGED.   JBARSIX59700

COORDINATED **PLANNING** FOR ECONOMIC OPPORTUNTIES FOR JEWISH AGED.   JRABIOX59751

THE DETERMINATION OF CERTAIN MAJOR FACTORS AFFECTING THE NEGRO VETERAN IN THE ON-THE-JOB TRAINING PROGRAM
IN VOCATIONAL AGRICULTURE IN THE STATE OF ALABAMA AS A BASIS FOR **PLANNING** A MORE EFFECTIVE PROGRAM.   NBATTEF49338

PLANNING THE END OF THE AMERICAN GHETTO. A PROGRAM OF ECONOMIC DEVELOPMENT FOR EQUAL-RIGHTS.   NHILLHX66538

INTER-RACIAL **PLANNING** FOR COMMUNITY ORGANIZATION... EMPLOYMENT PROBLEMS OF THE NEGRO.   NNATLUL44900

OCCUPATIONAL **PLANNING** BY YOUNG WOMEN, A STUDY OF OCCUPATIONAL EXPERIENCES, ASPIRATIONS, ATTITUDES, AND
PLANS OF COLLEGE AND HIGH SCHOOL GIRLS.   WSLOCWL56116

OCCUPATIONAL **PLANNING** FOR WOMEN.   WZAPOMW61282

A STUDY OF THE LIFE **PLANNING** OF 550 FRESHMEN WOMEN AT PURDUE UNIVERSITY. /WORK-FAMILY-CONFLICT/   WZISSCX64285

PLANS
EDUCATIONAL STATUS, COLLEGE **PLANS**, AND OCCUPATIONAL-STATUS OF FARM AND NONFARM YOUTHS. OCTOBER 1959.   GCOWHJD61427

BACKGROUND FACTORS RELATING TO COLLEGE **PLANS** AND COLLEGE ENROLLMENT AMONG PUBLIC HIGH SCHOOL STUDENTS.
/ASPIRATIONS/   GEDUCTS57959

PLANS-FOR-PROGRESS. A FIRST YEAR REPORT BY THE **PLANS** FOR PROGRESS ADVISORY COUNCIL.   GPRESCD64112

THE EDUCATIONAL AND OCCUPATIONAL ASPIRATIONS AND **PLANS** OF NEGRO AND WHITE MALE ELEMENTARY SCHOOL
STUDENTS.   NHOLLRG59562

NEGRO AND WHITE CHILDREN-S **PLANS** FOR THEIR FUTURES. /ASPIRATIONS/   NLOTTAJ63487

AFTER HIGH SCHOOL WHAT...HIGHLIGHTS OF A STUDY OF CAREER **PLANS** OF NEGRO AND WHITE RURAL YOUTH IN THREE
FLORIDA COUNTIES. /ASPIRATIONS/   NYOUMEG65390

OCCUPATIONAL **PLANS** AND ASPIRATIONS. PUERTO-RICAN AND AMERICAN HIGH SCHOOL SENIORS COMPARED.   PSILVRM63100

CONTINUING EDUCATION OF WOMEN. NEEDS, ASPIRATIONS, AND **PLANS**.   WBERRJX63641

POST-HIGH SCHOOL **PLANS** FOR SENIOR GIRLS IN RELATION TO SCHOLASTIC APTITUDE. /ASPIRATIONS/   WMILLRX61983

OCCUPATIONAL PLANNING BY YOUNG WOMEN, A STUDY OF OCCUPATIONAL EXPERIENCES, ASPIRATIONS, ATTITUDES, AND
PLANS OF COLLEGE AND HIGH SCHOOL GIRLS.   WSLOCWL56116

BACKGROUND FACTORS AND COLLEGE GOING **PLANS** AMONG HIGH APTITUDE PUBLIC HIGH SCHOOL SENIORS. /ASPIRATIONS/   WSTICGX56141

CRITERIA FOR ASSESSING FEASIBILITY OF MOTHERS EMPLOYMENT AND ADEQUACY OF CHILD CARE **PLANS**.   WUSDHEW66173

THE RELATIONSHIP OF SELECTED VARIABLES TO CAREER-MARRIAGE **PLANS** OF UNIVERSITY FRESHMAN WOMEN.
/WORK-FAMILY-CONFLICT/   WZISSCX62284

PLANS-FOR-PROGRESS
REMARKS AT THE **PLANS-FOR-PROGRESS** CONFERENCE.   GHUMPHH65788

PLANS-FOR-PROGRESS. A FIRST YEAR REPORT BY THE PLANS FOR PROGRESS ADVISORY COUNCIL.   GPRESCD64112

PLANS-FOR-PROGRESS.   GTROURX62163

PROGRESS IN **PLANS-FOR-PROGRESS** FOR NEGRO MANAGERS.   NLOCKHC65701

PLANS-FOR-PROGRESS.   NMATTEG66759

PLANS-FOR-PROGRESS. ATLANTA SURVEY. /GEORGIA/   NSOUTRC63163

PLANT
PLANT INSPECTION SURVEY BY MANAGEMENT -- MINORITY-GROUP INTEGRATION. /COLORADO/   GDENNGHND632

THE EFFECTS OF INDUSTRIALIZATION ON RURAL LOUISIANA. A STUDY OF **PLANT** EMPLOYEES.   GPRICPH58395

EMPLOYMENT INTEGRATION AND RACIAL WAGE DIFFERENCE IN A SOUTHERN **PLANT**.   GWEINRX59988

CARRYING OUT A PLAN FOR JOB INTEGRATION AND DOING IT -- IN THE HEART OF GEORGIA -- WITHOUT A SINGLE
UNPLEASANT INCIDENT. THAT-S THE EXPERIENCE OF LOCKHEED AIRCRAFT CORPORATION AT ITS MARIETTA **PLANT**.
/INDUSTRY/   NBUSIWX63148

THE TECHNIQUE OF INTRODUCING NEGROES INTO THE **PLANT**. /INDUSTRY/   NFELDHX42351

PLANT (CONTINUATION)
EFFECTS OF AUTOMATION ON THE POSITION OF NEGROES IN A SOUTHERN INDUSTRIAL **PLANT**.   NHARTJW64495

SOLVING RACIAL PROBLEMS IN YOUR **PLANT**. /INDUSTRY/   NMODEIX45805

REPORT AND SUMMARY OF THE AIR FORCE ON ACTIONS TAKEN BY LOCKHEED AIRCRAFT CORPORATION AT THE AIR FORCE
PLANT NO 6 IN MARIETTA, GEORGIA. /INDUSTRY/   NPRESCD61013

THE INTERVENTION OF THE UNION IN THE **PLANT**.   NSEXTBX53116

JOBS FOR NEGROES. SOME NORTH-SOUTH **PLANT** STUDIES. /CASE-STUDY/   NSTEEEH53174

EMPLOYMENT INTEGRATION AND WAGE DIFFERENCES IN A SOUTHERN **PLANT**.   NWEINRX59311

PLANTATION
THE THORNTONS OF MISSISSIPPI. PEONAGE ON THE **PLANTATION**. /POVERTY/   NGOODPX66433

PLANTATION ORGANIZATION AND THE RESIDENT LABOR-FORCE, DELTA AREA, MISSISSIPPI.   NLERANL60403

FROM **PLANTATION** TO GHETTO. AN INTERPRETIVE HISTORY OF AMERICAN NEGROES.   NMEIEAX66765

SOCIAL AND CULTURAL CHANGE IN THE **PLANTATION** AREA.   NRUBIMX54297

PLANTATIONS
LABOR AND TECHNOLOGY ON SELECTED COTTON **PLANTATIONS** IN THE DELTA AREA OF MISSISSIPPI, 1953-1957.   NLERANL59404

PLANTS
TWO **PLANTS** -- LITTLE-ROCK. /CASE-STUDY INDUSTRY ARKANSAS/   NECKAEW55319

NEGRO EMPLOYMENT IN THREE SOUTHERN **PLANTS** OF INTERNATIONAL HARVESTER COMPANY. /CASE-STUDY/   NHOPEJX55572

THE EFFECTS OF SOUTHERN WHITE WORKERS ON RACE-RELATIONS IN NORTHERN **PLANTS**.   NKILLLM52650

NEGRO EMPLOYMENT IN AIRPLANE **PLANTS**. /INDUSTRY/   NUSDLAB43827

MISSISSIPPI WORKERS. WHERE THEY COME FROM AND HOW THEY PERFORM. A STUDY OF WORKING FORCES IN SELECTED
MISSISSIPPI INDUSTRIAL **PLANTS**.   NWOFFBM55333

PLATFORM
NEGRO **PLATFORM** WORKERS. /INDUSTRY CASE-STUDY/   NAMERCR45011

PLIGHT
POVERTY AND DEPRIVATION IN THE UNITED STATES. THE **PLIGHT** OF TWO-FIFTHS OF A NATION.   GCONFOE62873

MIGRANT-WORKERS **PLIGHT**.   GFORTXX59045

WHERE THE REAL POVERTY IS. **PLIGHT** OF AMERICAN-INDIANS.   IUSNEWR66671

REASONS FOR BELATED EDUCATION. A STUDY OF THE **PLIGHT** OF THE OLDER NEGRO TEACHERS. /OCCUPATIONS/   NCUVNGE58244

NURSING-S ECONOMIC **PLIGHT**. /ECONOMIC-STATUS/   WMOSEEX65000

PLUMBERS
OPINION BY HONORABLE BENJAMIN LENCHER. CITY OF PITTSBURGH VS **PLUMBERS** LOCAL UNION NO 27. /PENNSYLVANIA/   NPITTLJ65001

PLUMBING
JOINT STAND REJECTS RACIAL QUOTAS FOR **PLUMBING** APPRENTICES.   GAIRCHR63867

PLURALISM
ASSIMILATION OR **PLURALISM**.   OKITADX65734

POCAHONTAS
RACE RELATIONSHIP IN THE **POCAHONTAS** COAL FIELD.   NMINARD52794

POLEMIC
ON THEORIES OF AUTOMATION. A **POLEMIC** AGAINST DANIEL BELL AND OTHERS. /UNEMPLOYMENT/   GSELIBB66609

POLICE
EVALUATING JOB APPLICANTS WITH **POLICE** RECORDS. /CALIFORNIA/   GCALFEP66532

MUNICIPAL FAIR-EMPLOYMENT ORDINANCES AS A VALID EXERCISE OF THE **POLICE** POWER.   GNORTDL64093

STUDY OF DETROIT **POLICE** DEPARTMENT PERSONNEL PRACTICES. /MICHIGAN OCCUPATIONS/   NDETRCC63267

NEGRO **POLICE** EMPLOYMENT IN THE URBAN SOUTH.   NRUDWEM61134

NEXT IT-S A MIXED **POLICE** FORCE. INTEGRATIONISTS LATEST GOAL IN NATION-S CAPITAL. /WASHINGTON-DC/   NUSNEWR57274

POLICEMAN
THE NEGRO **POLICEMAN** IN THE SOUTH. /OCCUPATIONS/   NRUDWEM60095

POLICEMEN
SOUTHERN CITIES EMPLOYING NEGRO **POLICEMEN** -- INCLUDING NORTH-CAROLINA CITIES OVER 15,000 POPULATION. NSTEEDL46173

POLICIES
POLICIES FOR THE PROMOTION OF ECONOMIC GROWTH.   GACKLGX66680

BENEFIT **POLICIES** IN RELATION TO RECRUITMENT OF OLDER WORKERS, HANDICAPPED, AND MINORITY GROUPS.   GBARRGJ51425

POLICIES AND PRACTICES OF DISCRIMINATION COMMISSIONS. /FEPC/   GCARTEA56559

COUNSELOR-S VIEWS ON CHANGING MANAGEMENT **POLICIES**.   GCOXXTX63618

MANPOWER **POLICIES** FOR A DEMOCRATIC SOCIETY.   GDAVIHX65629

POLICIES AFFECTING INCOME-DISTRIBUTION. /EMPLOYMENT INCOME-MAINTENANCE/   GFERNFL65662

US WELFARE **POLICIES** IN PERSPECTIVE.   GGORDMS63742

MANPOWER IN THE UNITED STATES. PROBLEMS AND **POLICIES**.   GHABEWX54750

RACE, NATIONALITY, AND RELIGION -- THEIR RELATIONSHIP TO APPOINTMENT **POLICIES** AND CASEWORK.   GHAGEDJ57752

GOVERNMENT REGULATION OF UNION **POLICIES**.   GHICKRX66774

CURRENT INTERNATIONAL UNION **POLICIES** AFFECTING MINORITIES AND THEIR IMPLEMENTATION.   GHOPEJX49781

CURRENT MINORITY **POLICIES** AND THEIR IMPLEMENTATION IN INTERNATIONAL UNIONS.   GHOPEJX51782

POLICIES   (CONTINUATION)
FEDERAL MANPOWER **POLICIES** AND PROGRAMS TO COMBAT UNEMPLOYMENT.   GLEVISA64897

SPECIAL REPORT. AN INVESTIGATION OF THE PERSONNEL **POLICIES** AND PRACTICES OF THE MICHIGAN STATE HIGHWAY
DEPARTMENT, MARCH 1961.   GMICFEP61983

REPORT ON A SURVEY OF EMPLOYMENT **POLICIES** AND HIRING PRACTICES INVOLVING MINORITY-GROUPS IN HUDON-COUNTY,
NEW-JERSEY.   GNEWJDE51060

REPORT ON A SURVEY OF EMPLOYMENT **POLICIES** AND PRACTICES INVOLVING MINORITY-GROUPS IN MIDDLESEX-COUNTY,
NEW-JERSEY.   GNEWJDE52061

THE ROLE AND LIMITS OF NATIONAL MANPOWER **POLICIES**.   GWEBEAR66760

MEMBERSHIP **POLICIES** OF INTERNATIONAL UNIONS AS THEY AFFECT NEGRO WORKERS.   NGRANLB41442

AN ANALYSIS OF THE IMPLEMENTATION OF THE UAW-CIO-S FAIR PRACTICES AND ANTI-DISCRIMINATION **POLICIES** IN
SELECTED CHICAGO LOCALS.   /UNION/   NJONEJE51883

EQUAL-EMPLOYMENT-OPPORTUNITY. COMPANY **POLICIES** AND EXPERIENCE.   NMILLGW64070

MANAGEMENT **POLICIES** AND BI-RACIAL INTEGRATION IN INDUSTRY.   NMOHRFT54806

CORPORATE HIRING **POLICIES** AND THE NEGRO. /INDUSTRY/   NNEWSXX64911

WORKERS WANTED. A STUDY OF EMPLOYERS HIRING **POLICIES**, PREFERENCES, AND PRACTICES IN NEW-HAVEN AND
CHARLOTTE. /CONNECTICUT NORTH-CAROLINA/   NNOLAEW49928

IN THE UNIONS. RACIAL **POLICIES**.   NNORTHR47939

INDUSTRY-S RACIAL EMPLOYMENT **POLICIES**.   NNORTHR67938

POLICY
A POSITIVE LABOR-MARKET **POLICY**.   GBAKKEW63598

AN INTEGRATED POSITIVE MANPOWER **POLICY**.   GBAKKEW65753

THE ELIMINATION OF POVERTY. A PRIMARY GOAL OF PUBLIC **POLICY**.   GCOHEWJ64925

SEMINAR ON MANPOWER **POLICY** AND PROGRAM. LABOR LOOKS AT AUTOMATION AND CIVIL-RIGHTS.   GCONWJT65496

SEMINAR ON MANPOWER **POLICY** AND PROGRAM -- AUTOMATION, SKILL, AND MANPOWER PREDICTIONS.   GCROSER66148

EMPLOYMENT COUNSELING AS AN INTEGRAL PART OF AN ACTIVE LABOR-MARKET **POLICY**.   GEHRLRA65791

FARM MANPOWER **POLICY**.   GFULLVX67931

SOME PROPOSALS FOR GOVERNMENT **POLICY** IN AN AUTOMATING SOCIETY.   GGANSHJ65696

US MANPOWER AND EMPLOYMENT **POLICY**. A REVIEW ESSAY.   GGORDMS65728

CRITICAL ISSUES IN EMPLOYMENT **POLICY**, A REPORT. /UNEMPLOYMENT/   GHARBFH66476

MANPOWER **POLICY**. POVERTY AND THE STATE OF THE ECONOMY.   GKERSJA66733

UNEMPLOYMENT INSURANCE AND MANPOWER **POLICY**. /INCOME-MAINTENANCE/   GKRUGOH65628

AN ACTIVE EMPLOYER MANPOWER **POLICY**.   GLIVEER66567

IMPACT OF COMPANY **POLICY** UPON DISCRIMINATION.   GLONDJX54908

URBAN POVERTY AND PUBLIC **POLICY**.   GLONGNE64856

PUBLIC **POLICY**, PRIVATE ENTERPRISE AND THE REDUCTION OF POVERTY.   GLONGNE65121

PROPOSED **POLICY** REGARDING STATISTICS ON EMPLOYMENT. /LOS-ANGELES CALIFORNIA/   GLOSACC64912

THE MANPOWER REVOLUTION. ITS **POLICY** CONSEQUENCES. EXCERPTS FROM SENATE HEARINGS BEFORE THE CLARK
SUBCOMMITTEE.   GMANGGL66217

THE ROLE OF EMPLOYMENT **POLICY**. /ANTI-POVERTY/   GMINSHX65655

THE ROLE OF THE EMPLOYER IN MANPOWER **POLICY**. /INDUSTRY/   GMYERCA66527

IMPLEMENTATION OF THE FEDERAL FAIR-EMPLOYMENT **POLICY**.   GNATLAI49038

A **POLICY** FOR SKILLED MANPOWER.   GNATLMC54876

PUBLIC **POLICY** AND UNEMPLOYMENT.   GOATEJF64542

MANPOWER **POLICY** AND PROGRAMMES IN THE UNITED STATES.   GORGAEC64776

THE **POLICY** OF NON-DISCRIMINATION IN EMPLOYMENT IN THE FEDERAL GOVERNMENT.   GPRESCP55198

SOME QUESTIONS AND ANSWERS ON THE NON-DISCRIMINATION **POLICY** OF THE FEDERAL GOVERNMENT.   GPRESCP55199

FIRST ANNUAL REPORT, PRESIDENT-S COMMITTEE ON GOVERNMENT EMPLOYMENT **POLICY**, APRIL 30 1956.   GPRESCP56193

SECOND ANNUAL REPORT, PRESIDENT-S COMMITTEE ON GOVERNMENT EMPLOYMENT **POLICY**, 1957.   GPRESCP57194

THIRD ANNUAL REPORT, PRESIDENT-S COMMITTEE ON GOVERNMENT EMPLOYMENT **POLICY**, 1958.   GPRESCP58195

FOURTH ANNUAL REPORT, PRESIDENT-S COMMITTEE ON GOVERNMENT EMPLOYMENT **POLICY**.   GPRESCP59196

TRENDS AND PERSPECTIVES IN MANPOWER **POLICY**.   GREHNGX65654

EMPLOYMENT **POLICY** AND THE LABOR-MARKET.   GROSSAM65720

UNEMPLOYMENT AND LABOR-MARKET **POLICY**.   GSHULGX66142

EMPLOYMENT **POLICY** PROBLEMS IN A MULTIRACIAL SOCIETY.   GSIMPGE62313

A **POLICY** FOR FULL EMPLOYMENT.   GSOLORX62323

THE ROLE OF MANPOWER **POLICY** IN ACHIEVING AGGREGATE GOALS. /EMPLOYMENT INCOME/   GTHURLC66640

THE ROLE OF REDISTRIBUTION IN SOCIAL **POLICY**.   GTITMRM65359

SUPERVISOR DEVELOPMENT PROGRAM, BASIC COURSE, NONDISCRIMINATION **POLICY**. /MILITARY/   GUSDARM56192

POLICY   (CONTINUATION)
SEMINAR ON MANPOWER POLICY AND PROGRAM MEASUREMENT OF TECHNOLOGICAL-CHANGE.   GUSDLAB64980

SEMINAR ON MANPOWER POLICY AND PROGRAM. CYBERNATION AND SOCIAL CHANGE.   GUSDLAB64982

TOWARDS FULL EMPLOYMENT. PROPOSALS FOR A COMPREHENSIVE EMPLOYMENT AND MANPOWER POLICY IN THE UNITED
STATES.   GUSSENA64332

THE FEDERAL NONDISCRIMINATION POLICY IN THE VETERANS-ADMINISTRATION.   GUSVETA59521

CONSEQUENCES OF DISCRIMINATORY UNION MEMBERSHIP POLICY.   GWESTRL53019

CIVIL-RIGHTS POLICY IN THE FEDERAL SYSTEM. PROPOSALS FOR A BETTER USE OF ADMINISTRATIVE PROCESS.   GWITHJX65575

US GOVERNMENT POLICY TOWARD AMERICAN INDIANS. A FEW BASIC FACTS.   IELLIMB57554

A POLICY TO MEET INDIAN NEEDS TODAY.   IERNSRC59556

FEDERAL INDIAN POLICY AS IT AFFECTS LOCAL INDIAN AFFAIRS.   IMCKIFX64086

INDIAN AFFAIRS. A STUDY OF THE CHANGES IN POLICY OF THE UNITED STATES TOWARD INDIANS.   ITYLESL64634

ORGANIZED LABOR AND MINORITY-GROUPS POLICY AND PRACTICES. /UNION/   NBLUEJT47256

TRADE UNIONS PRACTICES AND THE NEGRO WORKER -- THE ESTABLISHMENT AND IMPLEMENTATION OF AFL-CIO
ANTI-DISCRIMINATION POLICY.   NDAVINF60312

PSYCHOLOGY AND MANPOWER POLICY.   NGINZEX66412

NEW-YORK-S NONDISCRIMINATION EMPLOYMENT POLICY.   NHARRCV65491

INTER-AGENCY POLICY ON RACIAL BIAS.   NLABORR43029

UNION STRUCTURE AND PUBLIC POLICY. THE CONTROL OF UNION RACIAL PRACTICES.   NMARSRX63752

THE NEGRO POLICY OF THE AMERICAN ARMY SINCE WORLD-WAR-II. /MILITARY/   NREDDLD53044

PUBLIC POLICY AND DISCRIMINATION IN APPRENTICESHIP.   NSTRAGX65182

INTERNATIONAL-HARVESTER-S NON-DISCRIMINATION POLICY. /CASE-STUDY/   NUSDLAB54822

THE MIGRATION DIVISION -- POLICY, FUNCTIONS, OBJECTIVES.   PPUERRD57789

POLICY RESOLUTION ADOPTED BY AFL-CIO 6TH CONSTITUTIONAL CONVENTION, SAN FRANCISCO, DEC 1965. /EEO/ WAFLCIO65617

VOCATIONAL EDUCATION AND FEDERAL POLICY.   WLEVISA63039

POLICY-MAKING
THE MUTUAL SAVINGS BANKS OF NEW-YORK-CITY. A FOLLOW-UP REPORT ON THE EXCLUSION OF JEWS AT TOP-MANAGEMENT
AND POLICY-MAKING LEVELS.   JAMERJC66695

POLICY-RECOMMENDATIO
IMPLICATIONS OF THE STUDIES. /DISCRIMINATION LOW-INCOME NEGRO PUERTO-RICAN POLICY-RECOMMENDATIONS/ CABRACX59001

GOVERNMENT AND MANPOWER. /POLICY-RECOMMENDATIONS/   GNATLMC64956

THE CIRCLE OF FUTILITY. /COMPENSATORY-EDUCATION POLICY-RECOMMENDATIONS/   NSCHRPX64125

TO FULFILL THESE RIGHTS. /POLICY-RECOMMENDATIONS/   NUSDLAB66248

POLITICAL
DROPOUTS. A POLITICAL PROBLEM. /EMPLOYMENT/   GMILLSM62354

THE STRATEGY AND POLITICAL ECONOMY OF THE WAR-AGAINST-POVERTY.   GORNAOA64958

POLITICAL NECESSITIES OF ABUNDANCE. /GUARANTEED-INCOME/   GTHEORX64610

THE POLITICAL NECESSITIES OF ABUNDANCE. /GUARANTEED-INCOME/   GTHEORX64968

ECONOMIC. POLITICAL AND PSYCHOLOGICAL ASPECTS OF EMPLOYMENT.   GUPHOWH64528

JICARILLA APACHE POLITICAL AND ECONOMIC STRUCTURES.   IWILSHC64235

THE SOCIAL AND POLITICAL REACTIONS OF OLDER NEGROES TO UNEMPLOYMENT.   NAIKEMX66865

SOUTHERN RACIAL ATTITUDES. CONFLICT, AWARENESS AND POLITICAL CHANGE.   NMATTDR62758

MAJOR POLITICAL ISSUES WHICH DIRECTLY CONCERN NEGROES.   NMILLJE48250

POLITICAL PERSPECTIVES.   NMOYNDP65863

THE INFLUENCE OF TUSKEGEE-INSTITUTE ON THE HEALTH, EDUCATIONAL, ECONOMIC, AND POLITICAL ASPECTS OF THE
NEGRO POPULATION OF MACON COUNTY, ALABAMA.   NSHIEAR51342

REPORT OF THE COMMITTEE ON CIVIL AND POLITICAL RIGHTS.   WPRESCO63065

POLITICS
POVERTY AND POLITICS.   GHARRMX64935

THE SOCIAL POLITICS OF FEPC. A STUDY IN REFORM PRESSURE MOVEMENTS.   GKESSLC48847

THE POLITICS OF ANTIDISCRIMINATION LEGISLATION.   GLOCKDX65146

NATIONAL POLITICS OF FAIR-EMPLOYMENT.   GMCKEEX52950

RACE, JOBS, AND POLITICS. THE STORY OF FEPC.   GRUCHLX53266

THE MIGRANT PROBLEM AND PRESSURE GROUP POLITICS.   MTOMARD61502

WHEN NEGROES MARCH. THE MARCH-ON-WASHINGTON-MOVEMENT IN THE ORGANIZATIONAL POLITICS FOR FEPC.   NGARFHX59396

POVERTY, RACE AND POLITICS.   NMILLSM65790

THE POLITICS OF PREJUDICE. THE ANTI-JAPANESE MOVEMENT IN CALIFORNIA AND THE STRUGGLE FOR JAPANESE
EXCLUSION.   ODANIRX61716

POOR
THE ECONOMY AND THE MINORITY POOR. /NEGRO AMERICAN-INDIAN MEXICAN-AMERICAN PUERTO-RICAN/   CBATCAB66879

POOR   (CONTINUATION)
    AMERICA-S POOR. REALITY AND CHANGE. /RETRAINING SKILLS UNEMPLOYMENT/   GAMERFX66674

    PARTICIPATION OF THE POOR. A REEXAMINATION.   GCAHNEX66905

    THE POOR PAY MORE. CONSUMER PRACTICES OF LOW-INCOME FAMILIES.   GCAPLDX63310

    EDUCATION OF THE MINORITY POOR -- THE KEY TO THE WAR-ON-POVERTY.   GCLARKB66915

    THE WEIGHT OF THE POOR -- A STRATEGY TO END POVERTY. /GUARANTEED-INCOME/   GCLOWRX66525

    THE EMPLOYED POOR. THEIR CHARACTERISTICS AND OCCUPATIONS.   GCUMMLD65623

    WHO ARE THE AMERICAN POOR.   GFALTEK64031

    JOB AND CAREER DEVELOPMENT FOR THE POOR...THE HUMAN SERVICES. INCLUDES BIBLIOGRAPHY.   GGOLDGS66360

    A PUBLIC EMPLOYMENT PROGRAM FOR THE UNEMPLOYED POOR.   GGREEAI65473

    PROGRAMS IN AID OF THE POOR.   GLEVISA65601

    THE POOR IN THE WORK FORCE. /LABOR-FORCE/   GLEVISA66038

    PROGRAMS IN AID OF THE POOR. /ANTI-POVERTY/   GLEVISA66729

    THE NOW VISIBLE POOR.   GMACDDX64947

    THE AMERICAN POOR.   GMILLHP63987

    CHANGES IN THE NUMBER AND COMPOSITION OF THE POOR. /DEMOGRAPHY/   GMILLHP65656

    CHILDREN OF THE POOR.   GORSHMX63141

    COUNTING THE POOR. ANOTHER LOOK AT THE POVERTY PROFILE.   GORSHMX65142

    WHO-S WHO AMONG THE POOR.   GORSHMX65144

    MORE ABOUT THE POOR IN 1964.   GORSHMX66280

    THE POOR IN CITY AND SUBURB. 1964.   GORSHMX66282

    RECOUNTING THE POOR -- A FIVE-YEAR REVIEW.   GORSHMX66642

    NEW CAREERS FOR THE POOR.   GPEARAX65099

    INVESTING IN POOR PEOPLE. AN ECONOMIST-S VIEW.   GSCHUTW65842

    THE YOUNG WHO ARE POOR.   GSHEPHL65966

    THE DISADVANTAGED POOR. EDUCATION AND EMPLOYMENT.   GUSCHAC66187

    THE EMPLOYABILITY OF CHIPPEWA INDIANS AND POOR WHITES.   ILIEBLX66041

    IN THE MIDST OF PLENTY. THE POOR IN AMERICA. /ECONOMIC-STATUS/   NBAGDBH64877

    THE POOR OF HARLEM. SOCIAL FUNCTIONING OF THE UNDERCLASS.   NGORDJX65435

    SOME ASSUMPTIONS ABOUT THE POOR.   NHERZEX63522

    RICH MAN. POOR MAN. /INCOME/   NMILLHP64784

    COOPERATIVES. CREDIT UNIONS, AND POOR PEOPLE.   NSOUTRC66524

    THE EMPLOYED POOR. A CASE-STUDY. /WASHINGTON-DC/   NWILLCV65989

POPULATION
    NONWHITE POPULATION BY RACE. NEGROES, INDIANS, JAPANESE, CHINESE, FILIPINOS. BY AGE, SEX, MARITAL-STATUS,
    EDUCATION, EMPLOYMENT-STATUS, OCCUPATIONAL-STATUS, INCOME, ETC. /DEMOGRAPHY/   CUSBURC53378

    INCOME OF THE ELDERLY POPULATION. /DEMOGRAPHY/   CUSBURC63171

    NONWHITE POPULATION BY RACE. NEGROES, INDIANS, JAPANESE,CHINESE, FILIPINOS. BY AGE, SEX,
    MARITAL-STATUS,EDUCATION, EMPLOYMENT-STATUS, OCCUPATIONAL-STATUS, INCOME, ETC. /DEMOGRAPHY/   CUSBURC63176

    NEGRO POPULATION. MARCH 1964. /WOMEN DEMOGRAPHY/   CUSBURC64376

    NEGRO POPULATION. MARCH 1965. /WOMEN DEMOGRAPHY/   CUSBURC65377

    CURRENT POPULATION REPORTS -- SPECIAL CENSUS OF CLEVELAND, OHIO. /DEMOGRAPHY/ CUSBURC65379

    NEGRO WOMEN IN THE POPULATION AND IN THE LABOR-FORCE.   CUSDLAB66263

    POPULATION AND LABOR-FORCE CHARACTERISTICS OF FIVE SOUTHEASTERN PENNSYLVANIA COUNTIES.   GANDEBXND391

    MANPOWER RETRAINING IN THE SOUTH-S RURAL POPULATION -- AN OPPORTUNITY FOR DEVELOPMENT.   GBACHFT63413

    RECENT POPULATION TRENDS IN THE UNITED STATES WITH EMPHASIS ON RURAL AREAS. /EDUCATION/   GBEALCL63426

    CHARACTERISTICS OF THE U.S. POPULATION BY FARM AND NON-FARM ORIGIN.   GBEALCL64423

    WORK EXPERIENCE OF THE POPULATION IN 1965.   GBOGAFA66138

    THE POPULATION OF THE UNITED STATES.   GBOGUDJ59461

    MIGRATION PATTERNS OF THE RURAL-FARM POPULATION. THIRTEEN ECONOMIC REGIONS OF THE UNITED STATES,
    1940-1950.   GBOWLGK57415

    MIGRATION OF POPULATION IN THE SOUTH. SITUATION AND PROSPECTS.   GBOWLGK58397

    CHARACTERISTICS OF THE POPULATION OF HIRED FARMWORKER HOUSEHOLDS. /ECONOMIC-STATUS/   GBOWLGK65424

    NET MIGRATION OF THE POPULATION, 1950-60, BY AGE, SEX, AND COLOR. VOL II, ANALYTICAL GROUPINGS OF
    COUNTIES. /INCOME/   GBOWLGK65434

    WORK EXPERIENCE OF THE POPULATION IN 1959.   GCOOPSX60603

    NONWHITE POPULATION IN ILLINOIS. 1950-1960.   GILLICH61791

    POPULATION CHANGE AND POVERTY REDUCTION, 1947-1975.   GLAMPRJ66882

POPULATION   (CONTINUATION)
POPULATION CHANGE AND THE SUPPLY OF LABOR.   GLEBESX60276

WORK EXPERIENCE OF THE POPULATION IN 1960.   GROSECX60257

THE SAN-FRANCISCO NON-WHITE POPULATION 1950-1960. /CALIFORNIA/   GROSETXND250

WORK EXPERIENCE OF THE POPULATION IN 1962.   GSABESX64272

POPULATION MOBILITY WITHIN THE UNITED STATES.   GSHRYHS64309

MIGRATION OF THE TEXAS FARM POPULATION.   GSKRARL57315

MOBILITY OF THE POPULATION OF THE UNITED STATES, JANUARY 1, 1950 TO FEBRUARY 1, 1965. /DEMOGRAPHY/   GUSBURC65161

POPULATION OF THE UNITED STATES BY METROPOLITAN AND NONMETROPOLITAN RESIDENCE. /DEMOGRAPHY/   GUSBURC66159

CHARACTERISTICS OF THE POPULATION OF HIRED FARMWORKER HOUSEHOLDS.   GUSDAGR65422

AMERICAN INDIANS IN CALIFORNIA. POPULATION, EDUCATION, EMPLOYMENT, INCOME.   ICALDIR65541

POPULATION AND INCOME CENSUS. WIND-RIVER RESERVATION, WYOMING.   IUSDINT60655

UNITED STATES INDIAN POPULATION AND LAND, 1960-1961.   IUSDINT61663

POPULATION CHARACTERISTICS, LIVING CONDITIONS AND INCOME OF INDIAN FAMILIES, NORTHERN-CHEYENNE
RESERVATION, JULY, 1961.   IUSDINT63656

POPULATION CHARACTERISTICS, LIVING CONDITIONS, AND INCOME OF INDIAN FAMILIES, FORT-PECK RESERVATION,
1951-1961.   IUSDINT63657

POPULATION CHARACTERISTICS, LIVING CONDITIONS AND INCOMES OF INDIAN FAMILIES, FORT-BELKNAP RESERVATION.   IUSDINT63658

POPULATION CHARACTERISTICS, LIVING CONDITIONS AND INCOMES OF INDIAN FAMILIES, ROCKY-BAY-S RESERVATION.   IUSDINT63659

JEWISH POPULATION IN THE UNITED STATES, 1960. /DEMOGRAPHY/   JCHENAX61712

JEWISH POPULATION IN THE UNITED STATES, 1961. /DEMOGRAPHY/   JCHENAX62713

A REPORT ON THE JEWISH POPULATION OF LOS-ANGELES. /CALIFORNIA/   JMASAGX59746

THE SPANISH-SURNAME POPULATION OF TEXAS.   MBROWHL64286

A STATISTICAL PROFILE OF THE SPANISH-SURNAME POPULATION OF TEXAS.   MBROWHL64368

CALIFORNIANS OF SPANISH SURNAME. POPULATION, EMPLOYMENT, INCOME, EDUCATION.   MCALDIR64377

SOME NOTES ON THE MEXICAN POPULATION OF LOS-ANGELES COUNTY. /CALIFORNIA/   MLOSACDND431

ANALYSIS OF POPULATION CHANGES IN NEW-MEXICO COUNTIES.   MPIERGK61457

THE CONCENTRATION OF SPANISH-SURNAME POPULATION IN THE FIVE SOUTHWESTERN STATES.   MUSCOMC62505

POPULATION DISTRIBUTION AND COMPOSITION IN THE NEW SOUTH.   NBOGUDJ54102

NEGRO CALIFORNIANS, POPULATION, EMPLOYMENT, INCOME, EDUCATION.   NCALDIR63167

DISTRIBUTION OF NEGRO POPULATION IN THE UNITED STATES. /DEMOGRAPHY/   NCALEWC56069

THE ECONOMIC-STATUS OF NEGROES IN THE SAN-FRANCISCO OAKLAND BAY AREA. A REPORT BASED ON THE 1960 CENSUS
OF POPULATION. /CALIFORNIA/   NCALFES63172

THE NEGRO POPULATION OF CHICAGO. A STUDY OF RESIDENTIAL SUCCESSION. /ILLINOIS OCCUPATIONAL-PATTERNS/   NDUNCOD57306

THE RELATIVE SIZE OF THE NEGRO POPULATION AND NEGRO OCCUPATIONAL-STATUS.   NGLENND64424

SOCIAL-STATUS AND ASPIRATIONS IN PHILADELPHIA-S NEGRO POPULATION. /PENNSYLVANIA/   NKLEIRJ62655

THE RURAL NEGRO POPULATION OF THE SOUTH IN TRANSITION.   NMAYOSC63762

A REPORT ON THE CHARACTERISTICS OF MICHIGAN-S NON-WHITE POPULATION.   NMICCRC65773

A SURVEY OF THE ECONOMIC AND CULTURAL CONDITIONS OF THE NEGRO POPULATION OF LOUISVILLE, KENTUCKY AND A
REVIEW OF THE PROGRAM AND ACTIVITIES OF THE LOUISVILLE URBAN-LEAGUE. JANUARY-FEBRUARY, 1948.   NNATLUL48903

CHANGING CHARACTERISTICS OF THE NEGRO POPULATION.   NPRICDO65018

THE INFLUENCE OF TUSKEGEE-INSTITUTE ON THE HEALTH, EDUCATIONAL, ECONOMIC, AND POLITICAL ASPECTS OF THE
NEGRO POPULATION OF MACON COUNTY, ALABAMA.   NSHIEAR51342

THE CHANGING NUMBER AND DISTRIBUTION OF THE AGED NEGRO POPULATION OF THE UNITED STATES. /DEMOGRAPHY/   NSMITLT58145

SOUTHERN CITIES EMPLOYING NEGRO POLICEMEN -- INCLUDING NORTH-CAROLINA CITIES OVER 15,000 POPULATION.   NSTEEDL46173

THE NEGRO POPULATION IN THE UNITED STATES. /DEMOGRAPHY/   NTAEUKE65198

THE NEGRO POPULATION IN DULUTH MINNESOTA, 1950. /DEMOGRAPHY/   NTURBGX52210

DEMOGRAPHIC CHARACTERISTICS OF THE NEGRO POPULATION IN THE UNITED STATES.   NVALIPX63279

CHINESE IMMIGRATION AND POPULATION CHANGES SINCE 1940.   OLEEXRX57740

POPULATIONS OF NEW-YORK STATE. REPORT NO 2. THE PUERTO-RICAN POPULATION OF THE NEW-YORK-CITY AREA.   PNEWYCO62838

CHARACTERISTICS OF POPULATION AND LABOR IN NEW-YORK STATE, 1956 AND 1957. PUERTO-RICANS IN NEW-YORK CITY.   PNEWYSE60839

PHILADELPHIA-S PUERTO-RICAN POPULATION, WITH 1960 CENSUS DATA. /PENNSYLVANIA/   PPITTCH64844

IMPLICATIONS OF POPULATION REDISTRIBUTION.   PSENICX57851

CENSUS OF POPULATION. 1960. PUERTO-RICANS IN THE UNITED STATES.   PUSBURC63854

WORLD-S WORKING POPULATION. SOME DEMOGRAPHIC ASPECTS.   WINTELR56871

PROJECTIONS OF POPULATION AND LABOR-FORCE.   WINTELR61868

POPULATIONS
SOCIOECONOMIC DIFFERENCES BETWEEN WHITE AND NONWHITE FARM POPULATIONS IN THE SOUTH.   GCOWHJD64616

POPULATIONS   (CONTINUATION)
NATURALIZATION AND ASSIMILATION PRONENESS OF CALIFORNIA IMMIGRANT **POPULATIONS**.   MKRASWX63425

POPULATIONS OF NEW-YORK STATE. REPORT NO 2. THE PUERTO-RICAN POPULATION OF THE NEW-YORK-CITY AREA.   PNEWYCO62838

PORTENT
THE NEGRO IN MILWAUKEE, PROGRESS AND **PORTENT**, 1863-1963. /WISCONSIN/   NMILWCC63792

PORTENTS
PROGRESS AND **PORTENTS** FOR THE NEGRO IN MEDICINE. /OCCUPATIONS/   NCOBBWM48217

PROSPECTS FOR EQUAL-EMPLOYMENT. CONFLICTING **PORTENTS**.   NMARSRX65744

PORTERS
THE BROTHERHOOD OF SLEEPING CAR **PORTERS**. /UNION/   NBRAZBR46108

POSITION
THE **POSITION** OF RACIAL GROUPS IN OCCUPATIONAL STRUCTURES.   GGLICCE47722

THE EFFECT OF STATE FAIR-EMPLOYMENT LEGISLATION ON THE ECONOMIC **POSITION** OF NONWHITE MALES.   GLANDWM66883

THE **POSITION** OF MINORITIES IN THE AMERICAN LABOR MOVEMENT. /UNION/   GMARSRX66946

EFFECTS OF AUTOMATION ON THE **POSITION** OF NEGROES IN A SOUTHERN INDUSTRIAL PLANT.   NHARTJW64495

THE EFFECT OF THE WAR ECONOMY ON THE SOUTH. HOW MOBILIZATION WILL AFFECT **POSITION** OF THE NEGRO.   NJACKJX51595

POSITION PAPER ON EMPLOYMENT INTEGRATION.   NKELLKP64641

THE **POSITION** OF MINORITIES IN THE AMERICAN LABOR MOVEMENT. /UNION/   NMARSRX66943

STATUS **POSITION**, MOBILITY, AND ETHNIC IDENTIFICATION OF THE NEGRO.   NPARKSX64973

THE RELATIVE **POSITION** OF THE NEGRO MALE IN THE LABOR-FORCE OF LARGE AMERICAN CITIES.   NTURNRH51217

THE WORKING WIFE AND HER FAMILY-S ECONOMIC **POSITION**.   WCARRMS62681

THE IMPACT OF CULTURAL CHANGE ON WOMEN-S **POSITION**. /BLUE-COLLAR ASPIRATIONS/   WKONOGX66913

POSITION CHOICES AND CAREERS. ELEMENTS OF A THEORY. /ASPIRATIONS/   WTIEDDV58154

POSITIONS
TRENDS IN THE EMPLOYMENT OF NEGRO-AMERICANS IN UPPER-LEVEL WHITE-COLLAR **POSITIONS** OF THE FEDERAL GOVERNMENT.   GPRESCP60200

SELECTING AND TRAINING NEGROES FOR MANAGERIAL **POSITIONS**.   NEDUCTS64322

MORE SALARIED **POSITIONS** ARE OPENED TO NEGROES BY BUSINESS AND INDUSTRY HERE. /NEW-YORK/   NSTETDX63154

A STUDY OF WOMEN IN OFFICE MANAGEMENT **POSITIONS** WITH IMPLICATIONS FOR BUSINESS EDUCATION. /OCCUPATIONS/   WRUSHEM57096

SALARIED WOMEN IN UPPER LEVEL **POSITIONS** IN KANSAS BUSINESS FIRMS.   WSTOCFT59143

THE MOTIVATION FOR WOMEN TO WORK IN HIGH LEVEL PROFESSIONAL **POSITIONS**.   WWALTDE62314

POSITIVE
A **POSITIVE** LABOR-MARKET POLICY.   GBAKKEW63598

AN INTEGRATED **POSITIVE** MANPOWER POLICY.   GBAKKEW65753

POSITIVE ACTION ON UNEMPLOYMENT.   GCASSFH63562

A **POSITIVE** PROGRAM FOR MERIT-EMPLOYMENT.   GDOUGMX60650

POST
I STATEMENT BEFORE THE HOUSE **POST** OFFICE AND CIVIL SERVICE SUBCOMMITTEE ON POSTAL OPERATIONS, II DISCRIMINATION. PLANNED AND ACCIDENTAL. /TESTING/   GENNEWH67928

EQUAL-EMPLOYMENT-OPPORTUNITY IN THE US **POST** OFFICE DEPARTMENT, A SUPPLEMENTAL REPORT TO THE POSTMASTER GENERAL.   GUSPODA63516

POST GRADUATION ROLE PREFERENCE OF SENIOR WOMEN IN COLLEGE. /ASPIRATION/   WCHRIHX56690

POST-HIGH
POST-HIGH SCHOOL PLANS FOR SENIOR GIRLS IN RELATION TO SCHOLASTIC APTITUDE. /ASPIRATIONS/   WMILLRX61983

POST-PARENTAL
THE **POST-PARENTAL** PHASE IN THE LIFE CYCLE OF 50 COLLEGE EDUCATED WOMEN. /WORK-FAMILY-CONFLICT/   WDAVIIX60717

POST-WAR
THE **POST-WAR** INDUSTRIAL OUTLOOK FOR NEGROES.   NHOWAUG44579

THE NEGRO IN **POST-WAR** AMERICA.   NROSEAM50294

THE **POST-WAR** OUTLOOK FOR NEGROES IN SMALL BUSINESS, THE ENGINEERING AND THE TECHNICAL VOCATIONS.   NWALKJO46580

POSTAL
I STATEMENT BEFORE THE HOUSE POST OFFICE AND CIVIL SERVICE SUBCOMMITTEE ON **POSTAL** OPERATIONS, II DISCRIMINATION. PLANNED AND ACCIDENTAL. /TESTING/   GENNEWH67928

POSTGRADUATE
COLLEGE, COLOR, AND EMPLOYMENT. RACIAL DIFFERENTIALS IN **POSTGRADUATE** EMPLOYMENT AMONG 1964 GRADUATES OF LOUISIANA COLLEGES.   NHUSOCF66328

POSTMASTER
EQUAL-EMPLOYMENT-OPPORTUNITY IN THE US POST OFFICE DEPARTMENT, A SUPPLEMENTAL REPORT TO THE **POSTMASTER** GENERAL.   GUSPODA63516

POSTS
WOMEN IN EXECUTIVE **POSTS**. /OCCUPATIONS/   WGIVEJN60787

POSTWAR
SENIORITY AND **POSTWAR** JOBS. RUBBER INDUSTRY. /NEGRO WOMEN/   CLABORR44028

POSTWAR EMPLOYMENT DISCRIMINATION.   GWEISAJ47547

POSTWAR EMPLOYMENT AND THE NEGRO WORKER.   NDAVIJA46258

POSTWAR STATUS OF NEGRO WORKERS IN SAN-FRANCISCO AREA. /CALIFORNIA/   NMCENDX50721

POSTWAR (CONTINUATION)
WAR AND **POSTWAR** TRENDS IN EMPLOYMENT OF NEGROES.   NWOLFSL45335

POSTWAR TRENDS IN NEGRO EMPLOYMENT.   NWOLFSL47334

POTAWATOMIE
SOCIAL AND ECONOMIC SURVEY OF **POTAWATOMIE** JURISDICTION.   IUSDINT57660

POTENTIAL
POTENTIAL SUPPLY AND REPLACEMENT OF RURAL MALES OF LABOR-FORCE AGE, 1960-70.   GBOWLGK66430

A DEMONSTRATION PROJECT DESIGNED TO TEST THE LIFE-STYLE AND THE GROWTH **POTENTIAL** OF URBAN DROPOUTS FROM
DISADVANTAGED HOMES.   GCLEAMP66130

POTENTIAL ECONOMIC GAINS FROM ELIMINATING DISCRIMINATION.   GCOUNEA66204

THE LIMITED **POTENTIAL** FOR NEGRO-WHITE JOB EQUALITY.   NCHALWE65188

THE NEGRO **POTENTIAL**. /EMPLOYMENT INCOME EDUCATION/   NGINZEX56409

TAPPING THE NEGRO **POTENTIAL**. /INDUSTRY EMPLOYMENT-SELECTION PROMOTION/   NJOHNTX65621

A STUDY OF THE **POTENTIAL** SUPPLY OF NEGRO TEACHERS FOR THE COLLEGES OF NEW-YORK STATE.   NMOSSJA61858

THE NEGRO COMMUNITY AND THE DEVELOPMENT OF NEGRO **POTENTIAL**.   NSMUTRW57146

ECONOMIC VALUE OF THE NEGRO TO THE SOUTH. PAST, PRESENT, AND **POTENTIAL**.   NSOUTRC45158

RELEASING HUMAN **POTENTIAL**.   PEASTHP61798

A STUDY TO DETERMINE THE EMPLOYMENT **POTENTIAL** OF MOTHERS RECEIVING AID-TO-DEPENDENT-CHILDREN ASSISTANCE. WBROODJ64656

WOMAN AS **POTENTIAL** SCIENTISTS. /OCCUPATIONS/   WCROSKP63710

THE **POTENTIAL** OF WOMEN. /WORK-WOMAN-ROLE/   WFARBSM63756

POTENTIALITIES
REALIZING THE MANPOWER **POTENTIALITIES** OF MINORITY-GROUP YOUTH.   GHOLLJH58778

REALIZING THE MANPOWER **POTENTIALITIES** OF MINORITY-GROUP YOUTH.   NHOLLJH58561

POTENTIALITIES OF WOMEN IN THE MIDDLE YEARS. /WORK-FAMILY-CONFLICT/   WGROSIH56806

POTENTIALS
INCOME, RESOURCES, AND ADJUSTMENT **POTENTIALS** AMONG RURAL FAMILIES IN NORTH AND WEST FLORIDA.   GREUSLA62388

POVERTY
POVERTY IN THE SOUTHWEST. A COMPARATIVE STUDY OF MEXICAN-AMERICAN, NONWHITE AND ANGLO FAMILIES. /NEGRO/ CMITTFG66777

POVERTY IN THE UNITED STATES. HEARINGS. /AMERICAN-INDIAN NEGRO PUERTO-RICAN EMPLOYMENT/   CUSHOUR64346

HARD-CORE UNEMPLOYMENT AND **POVERTY** IN LOS-ANGELES. /CALIFORNIA NEGRO MEXICAN-AMERICAN/   CUVCAIIND524

THE NEGRO GIRL AND **POVERTY**. /WOMEN/   CYOUNMB65636

TRICKLING DOWN. THE RELATIONSHIP BETWEEN ECONOMIC GROWTH AND THE EXTENT OF **POVERTY** AMONG AMERICAN
FAMILIES.   GANDEWH64392

THE INVISIBLE AMERICANS. /**POVERTY** UNEMPLOYMENT/   GBAGDBH63754

POVERTY ON THE LOWER-EAST-SIDE. SELECTED ASPECTS OF THE MOBILIZATION-FOR-YOUTH EXPERIENCE.   GBARRSX64130

THE ECONOMICS OF **POVERTY**.   GBATCAB66751

POVERTY IN RURAL AREAS OF THE UNITED STATES.   GBIRDAR64450

RURAL **POVERTY**.   GBURCLE65490

POVERTY IN THE UNITED STATES IN THE MID-SIXTIES.   GCHILCX64922

THE WEIGHT OF THE POOR -- A STRATEGY TO END **POVERTY**. /GUARANTEED-INCOME/   GCLOWRX66525

THE ELIMINATION OF **POVERTY**. A PRIMARY GOAL OF PUBLIC POLICY.   GCOHEWJ64925

POVERTY IN NEW-YORK CITY. FACTS FOR PLANNING COMMUNITY ACTION.   GCOMCCN64210

POVERTY AND DEPRIVATION IN THE UNITED STATES. THE PLIGHT OF TWO-FIFTHS OF A NATION.   GCONFOE62873

CONGRESS AND THE JOHNSON **POVERTY** PROGRAM.   GCONGDX66356

SOME DEMOGRAPHIC ASPECTS OF **POVERTY** IN THE UNITED STATES.   GDAVIKX65663

POVERTY IN PLENTY.   GDUNNGH64927

UNEMPLOYMENT. ITS SCOPE, MEASUREMENT, AND EFFECT ON **POVERTY**.   GFERGRH65012

POVERTY AMID AFFLUENCE.   GFISHLX66682

POVERTY AND INCOME-MAINTENANCE FOR THE UNEMPLOYED.   GGORDMS65661

PUBLIC WELFARE. **POVERTY** -- PREVENTION OR PERPETUATION. A STUDY OF THE STATE DEPARTMENT OF PUBLIC
ASSISTANCE OF THE STATE OF WASHINGTON.   GGREEAI64479

STUDY OF SERVICES TO DEAL WITH **POVERTY** IN DETROIT, MICHIGAN.   GGREEAI65480

THE OTHER AMERICA. /**POVERTY**/   GHARRMX63099

POVERTY AND POLITICS.   GHARRMX64935

A SOCIAL REFORMER-S VIEW OF **POVERTY**.   GHARRMX65659

THE WORLD OF **POVERTY**.   GHARRMX66136

THE INVISIBLE LAND. /**POVERTY**/   GHARRMX66212

ADOLESCENCE. CULTURAL DEPRIVATION, **POVERTY**, AND THE DROPOUT.   GHUNTDE66939

UNEMPLOYMENT AND **POVERTY**.   GJOHNHG65826

POVERTY   (CONTINUATION)
  MANPCWER POLICY, **POVERTY** AND THE STATE OF THE ECONOMY.   GKERSJA66733

  POVERTY, AGGREGATE DEMAND, AND ECONOMIC STRUCTURE.   GKERSJA66941

  PROGRESS OR **POVERTY**. THE US AT THE CROSSROADS.   GKEYSLH64862

  KEY QUESTIONS ON THE **POVERTY** PROBLEM.   GKEYSLH64943

  WEALTH AND POWER IN AMERICA. /ECONOMY **POVERTY**/   GKOLKGX62690

  POVERTY IN TEXAS. THE DISTRIBUTION OF LOW-INCOME FAMILIES.   GKUVLWP65867

  INCOME-DISTRIBUTION AND **POVERTY**.   GLAMPRJ65658

  POPULATION CHANGE AND POVERTY REDUCTION, 1947-1975.   GLAMPRJ66882

  URBAN **POVERTY** AND PUBLIC POLICY.   GLONGNE64856

  PUBLIC POLICY, PRIVATE ENTERPRISE AND THE REDUCTION CF **POVERTY**.   GLONGNE65121

  JOB OPPORTUNITIES AND POVERTY.   GMEANGC65674

  THE FACE OF **POVERTY** IN THE UNITED STATES.   GMILLHP64853

  THE DIMENSIONS OF **POVERTY**.   GMILLHP65952

  POVERTY AMERICAN STYLE.   GMILLHP66989

  THE WAR ON **POVERTY**.   GMYRDGX64851

  THE MATRIX. /**POVERTY** UNEMPLOYMENT/   GMYRDGX64955

  FACTS CN THE MANY FACES OF **POVERTY**.   GNATLUL65084

  PUVERTY, AFFLUENCE AND OPPORTUNITY.   GORNAOA64140

  POVERTY AMID AFFLUENCE.   GORNAOA66320

  POVERTY IN THE CITIES.   GORNAOA67138

  COUNTING THE POOR. ANOTHER LOOK AT THE **POVERTY** PROFILE.   GORSHMX65142

  CONSUMPTION, WORK, AND **POVERTY**.   GORSHMX65959

  THE PATTERN OF DEPENDENT **POVERTY** IN CALIFORNIA.   GRAABEX64120

  US PLAN TO BREAK CYCLE OF BIAS AND **POVERTY**.   GRICHEX66235

  POVERTY AS A PUBLIC ISSUE.   GSELIBB65686

  POVERTY AND THE NEGRO.   GSHEPHL65965

  NEW PERSPECTIVES ON **POVERTY**.   GSHOSAB65685

  THE CAUSES OF **POVERTY**.   GTHURLC67972

  THE CONCEPT OF **POVERTY**. /ECCNOMIC-OPPORTUNITY/   GUSCHAC65186

  THE ECONOMICS OF **POVERTY**. AN AMERICAN PARADOX.   GWEISBA65666

  POVERTY IN AFFLUENCE.   GWILLRE65665

  POVERTY AND THE CRITERIA FOR PUBLIC EXPENDITURES.   GWOLOHX65990

  AMERICAN INDIAN CAPITAL CONFERENCE ON **POVERTY**. MAY 9-12, 1964. FINDINGS.   IAMERIN64087

  THE RELATIONSHIP OF THE SOCIAL-STRUCTURE OF AN INDIAN COMMUNITY TO ADULT AND JUVENILE-DELINQUENCY.
  /**POVERTY** ECONOMIC-STATUS/   IMINNMS63218

  THE WAR AGAINST **POVERTY** -- THE AMERICAN-INDIAN.   INASHPX64597

  WHERE THE REAL **POVERTY** IS. PLIGHT OF AMERICAN-INDIANS.   IUSNEWR66671

  INCIAN **POVERTY** AND INDIAN HEALTH.   IWAGNCJ64681

  POVERTY, COMMUNITY AND POWER. /ECONOMIC-STATUS/   IWARRCX65668

  THEIR HERITAGE -- **POVERTY**.   MARAGMX66358

  THE BURDEN OF **POVERTY**.   MMITTFG66442

  POVERTY AMONG SPANISH-AMERICANS IN TEXAS. LOW-INCOME FAMILIES IN A MINORITY-GROUP.   MUPHAWK66511

  DIFFERENTIALS IN THE INCIDENCE OF **POVERTY** IN TEXAS. /ECONOMIC-STATUS/   MUPHAWK66533

  POVERTY. THE SPECIAL CASE OF THE NEGRO.   NBATCAB65061

  POVERTY IN THE GHETTO.   NBULLPX65138

  FIGHTING **POVERTY**. THE VIEW FROM WATTS. /LOS-ANGELES CALIFORNIA/   NBULLPX66135

  RACE AND **POVERTY**.   NDENTJH64263

  SOUTHERN **POVERTY** AND THE RACIAL DIVISION-OF-LABOR.   NDEWEOX62271

  GOALS IN THE WAR ON **POVERTY**. /ECONOMIC-STATUS/   NECKSOX66957

  THE DEEP SOUTH LOOKS UP. /**POVERTY** EMPLOYMENT/   NFORTXX43050

  THE NEGRO AND **POVERTY**.   NGALLLE67393

  POVERTY AND THE NEGRO.   NGINZEX66971

  THE THCRNTONS OF MISSISSIPPI. PECNAGE ON THE PLANTATION. /**POVERTY**/   NGOODPX66433

  SOME CHARACTERISTICS OF STUDENTS FROM **POVERTY** BACKGRCUNDS ATTENDING PREDCMINANTLY NEGRO COLLEGES IN THE
  DEEP SCUTH.   NGURIPX66468

POVERTY   (CONTINUATION)
    ECONOMICS FOR THE MINORITY. /POVERTY/   NHARRMX65488

    DEMOGRAPHIC AND SOCIAL FACTORS IN THE POVERTY OF THE NEGRO.   NHAUSPM66992

    BEYOND POVERTY OF INCOME.   NHENDGX67214

    THE WASTED AMERICANS. /POVERTY/   NMAYXEX64760

    POVERTY, RACE AND POLITICS.   NMILLSM65790

    PROGRESS AGAINST POVERTY.   NNATLSFND882

    EMPLOYMENT, RACE AND POVERTY.   NROSSAM67086

    RACE AND POVERTY.   NSCHALX64102

    REFLECTIONS ON POVERTY WITHIN AGRICULTURE.   NSCHUTW50144

    POVERTY AND THE NEGRO.   NSHEPHL65127

    POVERTY. /SOUTH ANTI-POVERTY/   NULMXAX66712

    POVERTY AREAS OF OUR MAJOR CITIES. THE EMPLOYMENT SITUATION OF NEGRO AND WHITE WORKERS IN METROPOLITAN
    AREAS COMPARED IN A SPECIAL LABOR-FORCE REPORT.   NWETZJR66114

    POVERTY IN THE UNITED STATES.   NWOLFDP64338

    POVERTY IN THE GARDEN SPOT, VOLS I AND II.   PELIZCX66031

    THE CULTURE OF POVERTY.   PLEWIOX66824

    LA VIDA. A PUERTO-RICAN FAMILY IN THE CULTURE OF POVERTY -- SAN-JUAN AND NEW-YORK.   PLEWIOX66825

    SPANISH HARLEM, AN ANATOMY OF POVERTY.   PSEXTPC65853

    WOMEN IN POVERTY.   WUSDLAB64237

    WOMEN IN POVERTY.   WWASHBB65667

POVERTY-DEPENDENCY
    THE POVERTY-DEPENDENCY SYNDROME OF THE ADC FEMALE-BASED NEGRO FAMILY.   NSTROFL64074

POWER
    POWER AS A DIMENSION OF EDUCATION.   GDODSDW62647

    THE FEDERAL INTEREST IN EMPLOYMENT DISCRIMINATION. HEREIN THE CONSTITUTIONAL SCOPE OF EXECUTIVE POWER TO
    WITHOLD APPROPRIATE FUNDS.   GFERGCC64679

    WEALTH AND POWER IN AMERICA. /ECONOMY POVERTY/   GKOLKGX62690

    MUNICIPAL FAIR-EMPLOYMENT ORDINANCES AS A VALID EXERCISE OF THE POLICE POWER.   GNORTDL64093

    THE CIVIL-RIGHTS-ACT OF 1964 -- SOURCE AND SCOPE OF CONGRESSIONAL POWER.   GNORTUL65672

    POWER AS A PRIMARY CONCEPT IN THE STUDY OF MINORITIES.   GSCHERA56058

    DISCRIMINATION AND THE NLRB. THE SCOPE OF THE BOARD POWER UNDER SECTIONS 8A3 AND 8B2.   GUVCHLR64212

    POVERTY, COMMUNITY AND POWER. /ECONOMIC-STATUS/   IWARRCX65668

    THE NEGRO BIDS FOR UNION POWER.   NBRUNDX60128

    DARK GHETTO. DILEMMAS OF SOCIAL POWER.   NCLARKB65211

    NEWARK. NEGROES MOVE TOWARD POWER. /NEW-JERSEY/   NOSHEJX65965

POWERLESSNESS
    YOUTH IN THE GHETTO. A STUDY OF THE CONSEQUENCES OF POWERLESSNESS AND A BLUEPRINT FOR CHANGE. /NEW-YORK/   NHARLYO64485

POWERS
    DISCRIMINATION BY LABOR UNIONS IN THE EXERCISE OF STATUTORY BARGAINING POWERS.   GDODDEM45646

    THE ROLE OF LAW IN SECURING EQUAL-EMPLOYMENT-OPPORTUNITY. LEGAL POWERS AND SOCIAL CHANGE. NHILLHX66544

PRACTICE
    THE PRACTICE OF UNIONISM.   GBARBJX56422

    GOVENOR-S CODE OF FAIR PRACTICE /CALIFORNIA/   GCALOGB63546

    MINORITY-GROUPS AND MERIT SYSTEM PRACTICE.   GCALPPA65547

    FAIR PRACTICE IN EMPLOYMENT.   GCHALFK48563

    MINORITIES AND THE AMERICAN PROMISE. THE CONFLICT OF PRINCIPLE AND PRACTICE.   GCOLESG54580

    EMPLOYMENT PRACTICE GUIDE.   GCOMMCH65589

    FAIR PRACTICE IN EMPLOYMENT.   GHUDDFP46786

    ETHNIC GROUPS AND THE PRACTICE OF MEDICINE. /OCCUPATIONS/   GLIEBSX58042

    THE PRACTICE OF RACIAL DEMOCRACY.   GNATLIC65593

    FINDINGS OF FACT, CONCLUSIONS AND ACTION OF THE COMMISSION ON HUMAN-RELATIONS IN RE. INVESTIGATIVE PUBLIC
    HEARINGS INTO ALLEGED DISCRIMINATORY PRACTICE BY THE HOTEL AND RESTAURANT INDUSTRY IN PHILADELPHIA.
    /PENNSYLVANIA/   GPHILCH61176

    RHODE-ISLAND COMMISSION-AGAINST-DISCRIMINATION. RULES OF PRACTICE AND PROCEDURE.   GRHODICND232

    LABOR AND FAIR-EMPLOYMENT PRACTICE. /UNION/   GSLAIDX67840

    ADMINISTRATIVE LAW -- HUMAN-RELATIONS COMMISSIONS, PENNSYLVANIA LAW AND DISCRIMINATORY EMPLOYMENT
    PRACTICE.   GTEMPLQ63349

    THE PRACTICE OF RACIAL DEMOCRACY.   NYOUNWM65000

PRACTICES
    CLASS DIFFERENCES IN THE SOCIALIZATION PRACTICES OF NEGRO MOTHERS.   CKAMICKND632

EMPLOYMENT OPPORTUNITIES FOR HIGH SCHOOL DROPOUTS. A STUDY OF EMPLOYERS PRACTICES, NEEDS AND ATTITUDES IN THE DISTRICT OF COLUMBIA. /WASHINGTON-DC/   GBURESS57499

EMPLOYMENT PRACTICES, CITY OF PASADENA, AN INVESTIGATION UNDER SECTION 1421 OF THE CALIFORNIA LABOR CODE 1963-1965.   GCALFEPND531

BANK OF AMERICA EMPLOYMENT PRACTICES. FIRST REPORT BY CALIFORNIA FEPC.   GCALFEP64530

LOS-ANGELES CITY SCHOOLS. AN INVESTIGATION OF EMPLOYMENT PRACTICES. /CALIFORNIA/   GCALFEP64536

FAIR-EMPLOYMENT-PRACTICES EQUAL GOOD EMPLOYMENT PRACTICES. GUIDELINES FOR TESTING AND SELECTING MINORITY JOB APPLICANTS. /CALIFORNIA/   GCALFEP66540

THE POOR PAY MORE. CONSUMER PRACTICES OF LOW-INCOME FAMILIES.   GCAPLDX63310

POLICIES AND PRACTICES OF DISCRIMINATION COMMISSIONS. /FEPC/   GCARTEA56559

A SUMMARY REPORT OF PRACTICES AND PROGRAMS DESIGNED TO REDUCE THE NUMBER OF DROPOUTS IN THE HIGH SCHOOLS OF LOS-ANGELES COUNTY. /CALIFORNIA/   GDELMDT66147

LOCAL REGULATION OF DISCRIMINATORY EMPLOYMENT PRACTICES.   GELSOAX47661

GUIDE TO MERIT EMPLOYMENT. A RESTATEMENT OF INDUSTRY PRINCIPLES AND PRACTICES.   GFOODECND694

EMPLOYMENT PRACTICES, FAIR AND UNFAIR.   GFORDJA65450

MINORITY UTILIZATION PRACTICES -- RATIONAL OR SENTIMENTAL.   GHOPEJX51783

DISCRIMINATION WITHOUT PREJUDICE. A STUDY OF PROMOTION PRACTICES IN INDUSTRY.   GKAHNRL64733

UNFAIR EMPLOYMENT PRACTICES AS VIEWED BY PRIVATE EMPLOYMENT COUNSELORS.   GKEENVX52015

PSYCHOLOGICAL TESTING FOR EFFECTIVE EMPLOYMENT PRACTICES AND EQUAL JOB OPPORTUNITIES.   GKETCWA65849

DISCRIMINATION IN EMPLOYMENT. FEDERAL AND STATE PRACTICES IN ANTI-DISCRIMINATION.   GLEITRD49892

REPORT OF FINDINGS AND RECOMMENDATIONS RESULTING FROM AN ANALYSIS OF THE EMPLOYMENT PRACTICES IN THE VARIOUS DEPARTMENTS OF THE CITY OF LOS-ANGELES. /CALIFORNIA/   GLOSAOC63917

MANAGEMENT AND MINORITY GROUPS. A STUDY OF ATTITUDES AND PRACTICES IN HIRING AND UPGRADING.   GMARKPI57085

THE RACIAL PRACTICES OF THE ILGWU -- A REPLY.   GMARSRX64059

SPECIAL REPORT. AN INVESTIGATION OF THE PERSONNEL POLICIES AND PRACTICES OF THE MICHIGAN STATE HIGHWAY DEPARTMENT, MARCH 1961.   GMICFEP61983

TECHNICAL REPORT NUMBER 1. EMPLOYMENT PRACTICES IN THE HOTEL, MOTEL AND RESTAURANT INDUSTRY OF MISSOURI.   GMILLRX66020

TECHNICAL REPORT NUMBER 2. EMPLOYMENT PRACTICES OF SELECTED MISSOURI PUBLIC UTILITIES. NATURAL GAS AND ELECTRIC.   GMILLRX66021

REPORT OF A PRELIMINARY STUDY OF EMPLOYMENT PRACTICES INVOLVING MINORITY-GROUP WORKERS, ESSEX-COUNTY, NEW-JERSEY.   GNEWJDE46059

REPORT ON A SURVEY OF EMPLOYMENT POLICIES AND HIRING PRACTICES INVOLVING MINORITY-GROUPS IN HUDON-COUNTY, NEW-JERSEY.   GNEWJDE51060

REPORT ON A SURVEY OF EMPLOYMENT POLICIES AND PRACTICES INVOLVING MINORITY-GROUPS IN MIDDLESEX-COUNTY, NEW-JERSEY.   GNEWJDE52061

INVESTIGATION OF CHARGES OF DISCRIMINATORY PRACTICES IN THE NEW-YORK STATE-EMPLOYMENT-SERVICE.   GNEWYSA59083

REPORT OF INQUIRY CONCERNING CHARGES OF DISCRIMINATING PRACTICES IN THE NEW-YORK STATE THRUWAY AUTHORITY.   GNEWYSB64104

EMPLOYMENT PRACTICES IN PENNSYLVANIA.   GPENNGC53159

EMPLOYMENT PRACTICES OF THE PHILADELPHIA SCHOOL DISTRICT. /PENNSYLVANIA/   GPENNHR62162

FAIR-EMPLOYMENT IS GOOD BUSINESS. EXAMPLES OF FAIR PRACTICES FOR TITLE-VII OF THE CIVIL-RIGHTS-ACT OF 1964.   GPOTOII65188

HOW THE NEW CIVIL-RIGHTS LAW AFFECTS YOUR EMPLOYMENT PRACTICES.   GPRENHI64104

THE PRACTICES OF CRAFT UNIONS IN WASHINGTON-DC WITH RESPECT TO MINORITY GROUPS IN CIVIL-RIGHTS IN THE NATION-S CAPITOL.   GSEGABD59294

MINORITY-GROUP INTEGRATION BY LABOR AND MANAGEMENT. A STUDY OF THE EMPLOYMENT PRACTICES OF THE LARGER EMPLOYERS, AND THE MEMBERSHIP PRACTICES OF THE LARGER LABOR UNIONS WITH RESPECT TO RACE, RELIGION, AND NATIONAL ORIGIN, CONNECTICUT, 1951.   GSTETHG53598

MINORITY-GROUP INTEGRATION BY LABOR AND MANAGEMENT. A STUDY OF THE EMPLOYMENT PRACTICES OF THE LARGER EMPLOYERS, AND THE MEMBERSHIP PRACTICES OF THE LARGER LABOR UNIONS WITH RESPECT TO RACE, RELIGION, AND NATIONAL ORIGIN. CONNECTICUT, 1951.   GSTETHG53598

HANDBOOK FOR LOCAL UNION FAIR PRACTICES COMMITTEES. REVISED EDITION.   GUAWXFPND369

THE PROPOSED LEGISLATIVE DEATH KNELL OF PRIVATE DISCRIMINATORY EMPLOYMENT PRACTICES.   GWILSAX45566

EMPLOYMENT PRACTICES, CITY OF SAN-DIEGO, 1963-1964. /CALIFORNIA/   GZOOKDX64596

HEALTH PRACTICES AND EDUCATIONAL ASPIRATIONS AS INDICATORS OF ACCULTURATION AND SOCIAL-CLASS AMONG THE EASTERN CHEROKEE. /NORTH-CAROLINA/   IKUPFHJ62216

THE JEWISH LAW STUDENT AND NEW-YORK JOBS -- DISCRIMINATORY EFFECTS IN LAW FIRM HIRING PRACTICES. /OCCUPATIONS/   JYALELJ64774

ORGANIZED LABOR AND MINORITY-GROUPS POLICY AND PRACTICES. /UNION/   NBLUEJT47256

TRADE UNIONS PRACTICES AND THE NEGRO WORKER -- THE ESTABLISHMENT AND IMPLEMENTATION OF AFL-CIO ANTI-DISCRIMINATION POLICY.   NDAVINF60312

STUDY OF DETROIT POLICE DEPARTMENT PERSONNEL PRACTICES. /MICHIGAN OCCUPATIONS/   NDETRCC63267

THE EVALUATION OF PRACTICES CARRIED ON BY TWO HUNDRED NEGRO FARMERS IN THE PRODUCTION OF COTTON IN MACON COUNTY, ALABAMA.   NGOLDSM48350

PERSONNEL PRACTICES AND WARTIME CHANGES. /EMPLOYMENT/   NHAASFJ46548

PRACTICES   (CONTINUATION)
UNITED STATES HAS STANDING UNDER INTERSTATE COMMERCE ACT AND COMMERCE CLAUSE TO ENJOIN SEGREGATIVE
PRACTICES OF CITY. /LEGISLATION/   NHARVLR64500

THE RACIAL **PRACTICES** OF ORGANIZED LABOR -- IN THE AGE OF GOMPERS AND AFTER. /UNION/   NHILLHX65541

AN ANALYSIS OF THE IMPLEMENTATION OF THE UAW-CIO-S FAIR **PRACTICES** AND ANTI-DISCRIMINATION POLICIES IN
SELECTED CHICAGO LOCALS. /UNION/   NJONEJE51883

SOME FACTORS INFLUENCING UNION RACIAL **PRACTICES**.   NMARSRX62747

UNION RACIAL **PRACTICES** AND THE LABOR-MARKET.   NMARSRX62749

UNION RACIAL **PRACTICES**.   NMARSRX63750

UNION STRUCTURE AND PUBLIC POLICY. THE CONTROL OF UNION RACIAL **PRACTICES**.   NMARSRX63752

REPORT OF THE COMMITTEE ON UNFAIR EMPLOYMENT **PRACTICES**.   NNEBRLC51906

WORKERS WANTED. A STUDY OF EMPLOYERS HIRING POLICIES, PREFERENCES, AND **PRACTICES** IN NEW-HAVEN AND
CHARLOTTE. /CONNECTICUT NORTH-CAROLINA/   NNOLAEW49928

THE NEGRO AND EMPLOYMENT OPPORTUNITY. PROBLEMS AND **PRACTICES**.   NNGRTHR65949

MANAGEMENT AND MINORITY-GROUPS. A STUDY OF ATTITUDES AND **PRACTICES** IN HIRING AND UPGRADING.   NROSEBX59080

UPDATING GUIDANCE AND PERSONNEL **PRACTICES**.   NROUSRJ62089

THE DROPOUT AND THE DELINQUENT. PROMISING **PRACTICES** GLEANED FROM A YEAR OF STUDY.   NSCHRDX63141

A STUDY OF FARM MANAGEMENT **PRACTICES** ON 100 NEGRO FARMS IN MACON COUNTY, ALABAMA, 1949.   NSHAWBJ50339

ECONOMIC AND SOCIAL CONSEQUENCES OF RACIAL DISCRIMINATORY **PRACTICES**.   NUNITNX63224

CHANGING EMPLOYMENT **PRACTICES** IN THE CONSTRUCTION INDUSTRY. EXPERIENCE REPORT 102.   NUSCONM65233

NEGRO EMPLOYMENT **PRACTICES** IN THE CHATTANOOGA AREA. /TENNESSEE/   NWESSWH55314

SURVEY OF SALARIES AND PERSONNEL **PRACTICES** FOR TEACHERS AND ADMINISTRATORS IN NURSING EDUCATIONAL
PROGRAMS, DECEMBER 1965.   WAMERNA66612

PRACTITIONERS
PRACTITIONERS AND NON-PRACTITIONERS IN A GROUP OF WOMEN PHYSICIANS. /ASPIRATIONS/   WGLICRX65791

PRE-COLLEGE
PRE-COLLEGE PREPARATION OF NEGRO STUDENTS.   NBINDAM66139

PRE-EMPLOYMENT
GUIDE TO LAWFUL AND UNLAWFUL **PRE-EMPLOYMENT** INQUIRIES BY EMPLOYERS, EMPLOYMENT-AGENCIES, AND LABOR
ORGANIZATIONS UNDER THE CALIFORNIA FAIR-EMPLOYMENT-PRACTICE ACT, LABOR CODE, SECTIONS 1410-1432.   GCALDIR60527

FAIR-EMPLOYMENT-PRACTICE ACT...FEPC RULES AND REGULATIONS... GUIDE TO **PRE-EMPLOYMENT** INQUIRIES.
/CALIFORNIA/   GCALFEP61533

FAIR-EMPLOYMENT-PRACTICE-COMMISSION GUIDE TO UNLAWFUL **PRE-EMPLOYMENT** INQUIRIES.   GCURRRO060889

RULINGS ON **PRE-EMPLOYMENT** INQUIRIES RELATING TO RACE, CREED, COLOR OR NATIONAL ORIGIN UNDER THE NEW-YORK
STATE LAW AGAINST DISCRIMINATION.   GNEWYSBND106

GUIDE TO EMPLOYERS, EMPLOYMENT-AGENCIES AND LABOR UNIONS DEFINING PROPER AND IMPROPER **PRE-EMPLOYMENT**
INQUIRIES. /PENNSYLVANIA/   GPENNHRND164

PRE-WHITE-HOUSE
TO FULFILL THESE RIGHTS. SUMMARY REPORT OF **PRE-WHITE-HOUSE** CONFERENCES.   WYWCAXX66079

PREDICTING
CULTURAL EXPOSURE AND RACE AS VARIABLES IN **PREDICTING** TRAINING AND JOB SUCCESS. /TESTING/   NLOCKHCND700

PREDICTION
THE **PREDICTION** AND EXPLANATION OF ECONOMIC ABSORPTION AMONG MEXICAN-AMERICANS, NEGROES, AND ANGLOS IN A
NORTHERN INDUSTRIAL COMMUNITY.   CSHANLW63120

THE **PREDICTION** OF ECONOMIC ABSORPTION AND CULTURAL INTEGRATION AMONG MEXICAN-AMERICANS, NEGROES, AND
ANGLOS IN A NORTHERN INDUSTRIAL COMMUNITY.   CSHANLW66123

PSYCHOLOGICAL AND SOCIOLOGICAL FACTORS IN **PREDICTION** OF CAREER PATTERNS OF WOMEN. /ASPIRATIONS/   WMULVMC61080

PSYCHOLOGICAL AND SOCIOLOGICAL FACTORS IN **PREDICTION** OF CAREER PATTERNS FOR WOMEN. /ASPIRATIONS/   WMULVMC63006

PREDICTIONS
SEMINAR ON MANPOWER POLICY AND PROGRAM -- AUTOMATION, SKILL, AND MANPOWER **PREDICTIONS**.   GCROSER66148

FARM INCOME **PREDICTIONS** FOR SMALL FARMS IN THE CENTRAL LOUISIANA MIXED FARMING AREA.   NBOLTBX62399

PREDICTOR
ROLE CONCEPTION AS A **PREDICTOR** OF ADULT FEMALE ROLES. /WORK-WOMAN-ROLE/   WANGRSS66619

PREDICTORS
WORK VALUES AND BACKGROUND FACTORS AS **PREDICTORS** OF WOMEN-S DESIRE TO WORK. /ASPIRATIONS/   WEYDELC62754

PREFERENCE
THE VOCATIONAL **PREFERENCE** OF NEGRO CHILDREN.   NGRAYSW44446

POST GRADUATION ROLE **PREFERENCE** OF SENIOR WOMEN IN COLLEGE. /ASPIRATION/   WCHRIHX56690

SOME CORRELATES OF HOMEMAKING VS CAREER **PREFERENCE** AMONG COLLEGE HOME ECONOMICS STUDENTS.
/WORK-FAMILY-CONFLICT/   WVETTLX64257

PREFERENCES
VALUE ORIENTATIONS OF YOUNG MEXICAN-AMERICAN MALES AS REFLECTED IN THEIR WORK PATTERNS AND EMPLOYMENT
PREFERENCES.   MWADDJO62513

ETHNIC AND CLASS **PREFERENCES** AMONG COLLEGE NEGROES.   NEBOIAX60315

WORKERS WANTED. A STUDY OF EMPLOYERS HIRING POLICIES, **PREFERENCES**, AND PRACTICES IN NEW-HAVEN AND
CHARLOTTE. /CONNECTICUT NORTH-CAROLINA/   NNOLAEW49928

INVESTIGATION OF DIFFERENCES IN OCCUPATIONAL **PREFERENCES**, STEREOTYPIC THINKING, AND PSYCHOLOGICAL NEEDS

PREFERENCES   (CONTINUATION)
    AMONG UNDERGRADUATE WOMEN STUDENTS IN SELECTED CURRICULAR AREAS. /ASPIRATIONS/   WKITTRE60313

PREFERENTIAL-HIRING
    PREFERENTIAL-HIRING FOR NEGROES. A DEBATE.   NAMERCX63010

PREFERENTIAL-TREATME
    THE ETHICS OF COMPENSATORY JUSTICE.PREFERENTIAL-TREATMENT/   GLICHRX64900

    IS EQUALITY UNFAIR. NEGRO-S PLEA FOR PREFERENTIAL-TREATMENT.   NAMERXX63008

    PREFERENTIAL-TREATMENT FOR NEGROES.   NHECHFM64509

    INDUSTRY ON TRIAL. /PREFERENTIAL-TREATMENT/   NKAPPLX63635

PREJUDICE
    CHANGING PATTERNS OF PREJUDICE. /NEGRO PUERTO-RICAN ORIENTAL   AMERICAN-INDIAN/   CMARRAJ62055

    PREJUDICE TOWARD MEXICAN AND NEGRO AMERICANS. A COMPARISON.   CPINKAX63458

    NO TIME FOR PREJUDICE. /WOMEN NEGRO OCCUPATIONS/   CSTAUMK61132

    THE NATURE OF PREJUDICE.   GALLPGX58871

    CONTROLLING GROUP PREJUDICE.   GANNAOA46547

    PREJUDICE AND DECISION-MAKING. /EMPLOYMENT DISCRIMINATION/   GDAILCA66926

    PREJUDICE -- A THREAT TO THE LEADERSHIP ROLE.   GEVANRI62669

    PUNISHMENT WITHOUT CRIME. WHAT YOU CAN DO ABOUT PREJUDICE. /DISCRIMINATION/   GFINESA49962

    VERTICAL MOBILITY AND PREJUDICE.   GGREEJX53738

    DISCRIMINATION WITHOUT PREJUDICE. A STUDY OF PROMOTION PRACTICES IN INDUSTRY.   GKAHNRL64733

    PREJUDICE AND SCIENTIFIC METHOD IN LABOR-RELATIONS. /UNION/   GMARRAX52941

    PREJUDICE AND ECONOMIC DOGMA.   GROUCJX55263

    HOW WELL DOES TV FIGHT PREJUDICE.   GTUCKJN56363

    LABOR OPPOSES PREJUDICE. /UNION/   NAMERFX55012

    DISCRIMINATION WITHOUT PREJUDICE. /INDUSTRY/   NBLOORO55094

    THE UAW FIGHTS RACE PREJUDICE. /UNION/   NHOWEIX49581

    PREJUDICE. SUPERSTITION. AND ECONOMICS.   NHOWERW56582

    RACE PREJUDICE AND DISCRIMINATION. READINGS IN INTERGROUP RELATIONS IN THE US.   NROSEAM51075

    PREJUDICE COSTS TOO MUCH.   NSHISBX56538

    SOCIAL-MOBILITY AND PREJUDICE.   NSILBFB59138

    PREJUDICE IS NOT THE WHOLE STORY. EXAMINATION OF THREE CASES OF NEGRO UPGRADING IN TRACTION COMPANIES IN
    PHILADELPHIA, LOS-ANGELES AND CHICAGO. /PENNSYLVANIA CALIFORNIA ILLINOIS/   NWECKJE45308

    WHAT PRICE PREJUDICE -- ON THE ECONOMICS OF DISCRIMINATION.   NYOUNWM63356

    THE POLITICS OF PREJUDICE. THE ANTI-JAPANESE MOVEMENT IN CALIFORNIA AND THE STRUGGLE FOR JAPANESE
    EXCLUSION.   ODANIRX61716

    WOMAN AT WORK -- A STUDY IN PREJUDICE. /DISCRIMINATION/   WMARMJX66954

PRELIMINARY
    GOVERNMENT CONTRACTS AND SOCIAL CONTROL. A PRELIMINARY INQUIRY.   GMILLAS55985

    REPORT OF A PRELIMINARY STUDY OF EMPLOYMENT PRACTICES INVOLVING MINORITY-GROUP WORKERS, ESSEX-COUNTY,
    NEW-JERSEY.   GNEWJDE46059

    DIVISION OF AUTHORITY UNDER TITLE-VII OF THE CIVIL-RIGHTS-ACT OF 1964. A PRELIMINARY STUDY IN
    FEDERAL-STATE INTERAGENCY RELATIONS.   GROSESJ66254

    DIMENSIONS IN DISCRIMINATION. A PRELIMINARY SURVEY OF SAN-DIEGO-S COMMUNITY PROBLEMS OF DISCRIMINATION
    PART II. /CALIFORNIA/   GSANDLW65274

    UTE INDIAN SURVEY -- PRELIMINARY REPORT. SOCIAL AND ECONOMIC CHARACTERISTICS.   IBRIGYUND442

    PRELIMINARY REPORT ON SURVEY OF ACTIVE APPRENTICE'S. /CALIFORNIA/   MCALDIR62376

    MEXICAN GREEN CARDERS. PRELIMINARY REPORT.   MGALLLX62399

    A PRELIMINARY REPORT ON MEDICAL STAFF APPOINTMENTS HELD BY NEGRO PHYSICIANS AT PREDOMINANTLY WHITE
    HOSPITALS. /CHICAGO ILLINOIS/   NCHICCO60201

    CHILD CARE ARRANGEMENTS OF THE NATION-S WORKING MOTHERS. A PRELIMINARY REPORT.   WUSDHEW65172

PREPARATION
    AN ASSESSMENT OF THE SUITABILITY OF THE FACETED STRUCTURE OF THE WRU EDUCATION THESAURUS AS A FRAMEWORK
    FOR PREPARATION OF A THESAURUS OF EQUAL-EMPLOYMENT-OPPORTUNITY TERMS.   GBARHGC66162

    THE ROLE OF THE SECONDARY SCHOOLS IN THE PREPARATION OF YOUTH FOR EMPLOYMENT.   GKAUFJJ67940

    THE ROLE OF THE SECONDARY SCHOOLS IN THE PREPARATION OF YOUTH FOR EMPLOYMENT. SUMMARY, CONCLUSIONS. AND
    RECOMMENDATIONS.   GKAUFJJ67963

    PRE-COLLEGE PREPARATION OF NEGRO STUDENTS.   NBINDAM66139

    CAREER PREPARATION AND EXPECTATIONS OF NEGRO COLLEGE STUDENTS.   NFICHJH66789

    PREPARATION OF THE NEGRO COLLEGE GRADUATE FOR BUSINESS. /EMPLOYMENT-SELECTION/   NHOLLJH65560

    A STUDY OF PROFESSIONAL PREPARATION OF NEGRO TEACHERS OF EXCEPTIONAL CHILDREN IN NORTH-CAROLINA COUNTY
    AND CITY PUBLIC SCHOOLS.   NKNIGOB65023

    THE PREPARATION OF DISADVANTAGED YOUTH FOR EMPLOYMENT AND CIVIC RESPONSIBILITIES.   NPERRJX64985

PREPARATION   (CONTINUATION)
SOCIAL ORIGINS AND CAREER **PREPARATION** AMONG FILIPINOS IN AMERICAN UNIVERSITIES.   OBELTAG61703

PREPARE
A CONFERENCE TO ENLIST THE PARTICIPATION OF 50 INSTITUTIONS OF HIGHER EDUCATION IN SPECIFIC R AND D
PROGRAMS TO **PREPARE** WOMEN FOR PRODUCTIVE EMPLOYMENT.   WLLOYBJ64937

PREPARING
AT WORK IN NORTH-CAROLINA TODAY. 48 CASE-REPORTS ON NORTH-CAROLINA NEGROES NOW EMPLOYED OR **PREPARING**
THEMSELVES FOR EMPLOYMENT...THEIR EDUCATION, JOB QUALIFICATIONS, AND CAREER ASPIRATIONS.   NNORTCGND933

SHOWING THE WAY IN **PREPARING** NEGRO JOBSEEKERS.   NWESTZJ66317

PRESCRIPTION
THE PUERTO-RICAN WORKER CONFRONTS THE COMPLEX URBAN SOCIETY -- A **PRESCRIPTION** FOR CHANGE.   PCAROLA67874

PRESIDENT
CIVIL-RIGHTS-ACT OF 1964, WITH EXPLANATION -- PUBLIC LAW 88-352 -- AS APPROVED BY THE **PRESIDENT** ON JULY
2, 1964.   GCOMMCH64588

ECONOMIC REPORTS OF THE **PRESIDENT**.   GCOUNEAND239

HOW THE **PRESIDENT** IS WINNING THE WAR ON DISCRIMINATION.   GFACTMA56670

REPORT TO THE **PRESIDENT**, NOVEMBER 26, 1963 BY THE PRESIDENT-S COMMITTEE ON EQUAL-EMPLOYMENT-OPPORTUNITY.   GPRESCO64114

FIVE YEARS OF PROGRESS, 1953-1958. A REPORT TO **PRESIDENT** EISENHOWER BY THE PRESIDENT-S COMMITTEE ON
GOVERNMENT CONTRACTS.   GPRESCH58121

PATTERN FOR PROGRESS, SEVENTH REPORT, FINAL REPORT TO **PRESIDENT** EISENHOWER FROM THE COMMITTEE ON
GOVERNMENT CONTRACTS.   GPRESCH60123

MANPOWER REPORT OF THE **PRESIDENT**.   GUSDLAB62700

MANPOWER REPORT OF THE **PRESIDENT** AND A REPORT ON MANPOWER REQUIREMENTS, RESOURCES, UTILIZATION, AND
TRAINING.   GUSDLAB63830

MANPOWER REPORT OF THE **PRESIDENT** AND A REPORT ON MANPOWER REQUIREMENTS, RESOURCES, UTILIZATION, AND
TRAINING.   GUSDLAB64829

MANPOWER REPORT OF THE **PRESIDENT** AND A REPORT ON MANPOWER REQUIREMENTS, RESOURCES, UTILIZATION, AND
TRAINING.   GUSDLAB65828

MANPOWER REPORT OF THE **PRESIDENT** AND A REPORT ON MANPOWER REQUIREMENTS, RESOURCES, UTILIZATION, AND
TRAINING.   GUSDLAB66827

PRESIDENT-S
TEXTS OF RULES AND REGULATIONS OF **PRESIDENT-S** COMMITTEE ON EQUAL-EMPLOYMENT-OPPORTUNITY RELATING TO
OBLIGATIONS OF GOVERNMENT CONTRACTORS AND SUBCONTRACTORS, EFFECTIVE JULY 22, 1961. A BNA SPECIAL REPORT.   GBURENA61498

RULES AND REGULATIONS OF THE **PRESIDENT-S** COMMITTEE ON EQUAL-EMPLOYMENT-OPPORTUNITY AS AMENDED.   GBURENA63496

THE FIRST NINE MONTHS. REPORT OF THE **PRESIDENT-S** COMMITTEE ON EQUAL-EMPLOYMENT-OPPORTUNITY.   GFEDEBJ62672

THE JOB AHEAD FOR THE **PRESIDENT-S** COMMITTEE ON EQUAL-EMPLOYMENT-OPPORTUNITY.   GHOLLJR61999

REPORT ON THE STRUCTURE AND OPERATIONS OF THE **PRESIDENT-S** COMMITTEE ON EQUAL-EMPLOYMENT-OPPORTUNITY.   GKHEETW62852

THE AMERICAN DREAM...EQUAL OPPORTUNITY, A REPORT ON THE COMMUNITY LEADER-S CONFERENCE SPONSORED BY
PRESIDENT-S COMMITTEE ON EQUAL-EMPLOYMENT-OPPORTUNITY, MAY 19, 1962.   GPRESCO62105

THE FIRST NINE MONTHS -- SPECIAL YEAR-END REPORT, APRIL 7, 1961-JANUARY 15, 1962, **PRESIDENT-S** COMMITTEE
ON EQUAL-EMPLOYMENT-OPPORTUNITY.   GPRESCO62108

REPORT TO THE PRESIDENT, NOVEMBER 26, 1963 BY THE **PRESIDENT-S** COMMITTEE ON EQUAL-EMPLOYMENT-OPPORTUNITY.   GPRESCO64114

FIRST REPORT, **PRESIDENT-S** COMMITTEE ON GOVERNMENT CONTRACTS.   GPRESCH54120

SECOND ANNUAL REPORT, THE **PRESIDENT-S** COMMITTEE ON GOVERNMENT CONTRACTS.   GPRESCH55124

FOURTH ANNUAL REPORT ON EQUAL JOB OPPORTUNITY, 1956-1957, **PRESIDENT-S** COMMITTEE ON GOVERNMENT CONTRACTS.   GPRESCH57122

FIVE YEARS OF PROGRESS, 1953-1958, A REPORT TO PRESIDENT EISENHOWER BY THE **PRESIDENT-S** COMMITTEE ON
GOVERNMENT CONTRACTS.   GPRESCH58121

FIRST ANNUAL REPORT, **PRESIDENT-S** COMMITTEE ON GOVERNMENT EMPLOYMENT POLICY, APRIL 30 1956.   GPRESCP56193

SECOND ANNUAL REPORT, **PRESIDENT-S** COMMITTEE ON GOVERNMENT EMPLOYMENT POLICY, 1957.   GPRESCP57194

THIRD ANNUAL REPORT, **PRESIDENT-S** COMMITTEE ON GOVERNMENT EMPLOYMENT POLICY, 1958.   GPRESCP58195

FOURTH ANNUAL REPORT, **PRESIDENT-S** COMMITTEE ON GOVERNMENT EMPLOYMENT POLICY.   GPRESCP59196

PRESIDENT-S COMMITTEE ON EQUAL-EMPLOYMENT-OPPORTUNITY.   GTAYLHX62348

REPORT OF **PRESIDENT-S** COMMISSION ON STATUS OF WOMEN.   WPRESCO63993

PRESIDENT-S-COMMITTE
REPORT BY **PRESIDENT-S-COMMITTEE-ON-EQUAL-OPPORTUNITY**.   NUSDLAB62840

PRESIDENTIAL
TRADE UNION COMPLIANCE WITH **PRESIDENTIAL** DIRECTIVES, MEMBERSHIP ACCEPTANCE, SENIORITY, ETC.   NCOOPJX64294

MANAGEMENT COMPLIANCE WITH **PRESIDENTIAL** DIRECTIVES.   NLAWRRG64296

PRESIDENTS
SECRETARY-S CONFERENCE WITH COLLEGE **PRESIDENTS** AND EXECUTIVES. /EDUCATION EMPLOYMENT/   NUSDLAB63301

PRESS
PRESS SWALLOWS MOTOROLA HOAX. /TESTING/   GWESTOL65552

FORTUNE **PRESS** ANALYSIS, NEGROES. /EMPLOYMENT/   NFORTUN45052

PRESSURE
THE SOCIAL POLITICS OF FEPC. A STUDY IN REFORM **PRESSURE** MOVEMENTS.   GKESSLC48847

THE MIGRANT PROBLEM AND **PRESSURE** GROUP POLITICS.   MTOMARD61502

NEGRO **PRESSURE** ON UNIONS.   NBUSIWX60155

PRESSURE   (CONTINUATION)
   MORE RACE PRESSURE ON BUSINESS.   NBUSIWX62153

   DETROIT FEELS BRUNT OF NEGRO PRESSURE. /MICHIGAN/   NBUSIWX63149

   UNIONS FEEL GROWING PRESSURE TO TAKE MORE NEGROES.   NUSNEWR64292

   JOB RIGHTS FOR NEGROES -- PRESSURE ON EMPLOYERS.   NUSNEWR66270

PRESSURES
   SITUATIONAL PRESSURES AND FUNCTIONAL ROLE OF THE ETHNIC LABOR LEADERS. /UNION/   NGREESX53453

   A MANAGEMENT PERSPECTIVE TOWARD NEGRO ECONOMIC PRESSURES.   NHOFFHX65558

   DISCRIMINATION IN THE HIRING HALL. A CASE-STUDY OF PRESSURES TO PROMOTE INTEGRATION IN NEW-YORK-S BREWERY
   INDUSTRY.   NLANGGE59670

PRESTIGE
   OCCUPATIONAL PRESTIGE IN A NEGRO COMMUNITY.   NSOLZRX61153

PREVENTION
   PUBLIC WELFARE. POVERTY -- PREVENTION OR PERPETUATION. A STUDY OF THE STATE DEPARTMENT OF PUBLIC
   ASSISTANCE OF THE STATE OF WASHINGTON.   GGREEAI64479

   A PROPOSAL FOR THE PREVENTION AND CONTROL OF DELINQUENCY BY EXPANDING OPPORTUNITIES.   NMOBIFY62263

PRICE
   THE PRICE BUSINESS PAYS. /INDUSTRY DISCRIMINATION/   GROPEEX49245

   THE PRICE OF DEFIANCE. /MISSISSIPPI RACE/   NBUSIWX62159

   THE PRICE WE PAY FOR DISCRIMINATION. /SOUTH ECONOMY/   NPATTBX64979

   WHAT PRICE PREJUDICE -- ON THE ECONOMICS OF DISCRIMINATION.   NYOUNWM63356

PRINCETON-MANPOWER-S
   UNEMPLOYMENT IN A PROSPEROUS ECONOMY. A REPORT OF THE PRINCETON-MANPOWER-SYMPOSIUM.   GBOWEWG65749

PRINCETON-S
   PRINCETON-S LESSON. SCHOOL INTEGRATION IS NOT ENOUGH. /NEW-JERSEY/   GSTREPX64337

PRINCIPAL
   A STUDY OF ELEMENTARY SCHOOL TEACHER-S ATTITUDES TOWARD THE WOMAN PRINCIPAL AND TOWARD ELEMENTARY
   PRINCIPALSHIP AS A CAREER. /DISCRIMINATION/   WBARTAK58629

PRINCIPALS
   ENHANCING THE OCCUPATIONAL OUTLOOK AND VOCATIONAL ASPIRATIONS OF SOUTHERN SECONDARY YOUTH. A CONFERENCE
   OF SECONDARY SCHOOL PRINCIPALS AND COUNSELORS.   NUSDLAB65334

PRINCIPLE
   MINORITIES AND THE AMERICAN PROMISE. THE CONFLICT OF PRINCIPLE AND PRACTICE.   GCOLESG54580

   WHAT THE EQUAL-PAY PRINCIPLE MEANS TO WOMEN.   WUSDLAB64227

PRINCIPLES
   GUIDE TO MERIT EMPLOYMENT. A RESTATEMENT OF INDUSTRY PRINCIPLES AND PRACTICES.   GFOODECND694

   PRINCIPLES ESTABLISHED BY THE FEPC.   GLABOLR45874

PRISON
   REPRESENTATION OF NEGROES AND WHITES AS EMPLOYEES IN THE FEDERAL PRISON SYSTEM.   NMORGGD62849

PRISON-ADMISSIONS
   EFFECTS OF UNEMPLOYMENT ON WHITE AND NEGRO PRISON-ADMISSIONS IN LOUISIANA.   NDOBBDA58277

PRIVACY
   THE CONGRESSIONAL HEARINGS AND ISSUES IN PSYCHOLOGICAL TESTING. INVASIONS OF PRIVACY AND TEST BIAS.   GGORDJEND934

PRIVATE
   TESTIMONY. PUBLIC HEARING. WOMEN IN PUBLIC AND PRIVATE EMPLOYMENT, CALIFORNIA. /MEXICAN-AMERICAN/   CARYWSX66621

   JOBS FOR THE HARD-TO-EMPLOY IN PRIVATE ENTERPRISE.   GCASSFH66744

   LOCAL CONTRACTS AND SUB-CONTRACTS. THE ROLES OF CITY GOVERNMENT AND PRIVATE CITIZENS GROUPS.   GJONEMX64829

   UNFAIR EMPLOYMENT PRACTICES AS VIEWED BY PRIVATE EMPLOYMENT COUNSELORS.   GKEENVX52015

   PUBLIC POLICY, PRIVATE ENTERPRISE AND THE REDUCTION OF POVERTY.   GLONGNE65121

   SURVEY OF MINORITY-GROUP EMPLOYMENT AND PATIENT CARE IN PRIVATE HOSPITAL FACILITIES IN LOS-ANGELES
   COUNTY. /CALIFORNIA/   GLOSACCND914

   COMPILATION OF LAWS AGAINST DISCRIMINATION. EMPLOYMENT, EDUCATIONAL INSTITUTIONS, PLACES OF PUBLIC
   ACCOMODATION. PUBLIC HOUSING, PUBLICLY ASSISTED HOUSING, PRIVATE HOUSING. /MASSACHUSETTS/   GMASSCAND963

   SEMINARS ON PRIVATE ADJUSTMENTS TO AUTOMATION AND TECHNOLOGICAL-CHANGE.   GPRESCL64772

   BRIEF SUMMARY OF STATE LAWS AGAINST DISCRIMINATION IN PRIVATE EMPLOYMENT. FAIR-EMPLOYMENT-PRACTICE ACTS.   GUSDLAB63439

   THE PROPOSED LEGISLATIVE DEATH KNELL OF PRIVATE DISCRIMINATORY EMPLOYMENT PRACTICES.   GWILSAX45566

   CHANGES IN PUBLIC AND PRIVATE LANGUAGE AMONG SPANISH-SPEAKING MIGRANTS TO AN INDUSTRIAL CITY.   MSCHETJ65481

   PLACEMENT EXPERIENCES OF APPLICANTS TO A PRIVATE EMPLOYMENT-AGENCY.   NANTIDL55901

   RACIAL DISCRIMINATION AND PRIVATE EDUCATION.   NMILLAS57069

   PRIVATE BUSINESS AND EDUCATION IN THE SOUTH.   NMILLHH60780

   TESTIMONY. PUBLIC HEARING. WOMEN IN PUBLIC AND PRIVATE EMPLOYMENT, CALIFORNIA. /DISCRIMINATION EEOC/   WBALEHX66625

   TESTIMONY. PUBLIC HEARING. WOMEN IN PUBLIC AND PRIVATE EMPLOYMENT, CALIFORNIA. /EMPLOYMENT-CONDITIONS/   WBECHCX66631

   STATEMENT. PUBLIC HEARING. WOMEN IN PUBLIC AND PRIVATE EMPLOYMENT, CALIFORNIA. /FEP
   EMPLOYMENT-CONDITIONS DISCRIMINATION/   WBELAJX66634

   STATEMENT. PUBLIC HEARING. WOMEN IN PUBLIC AND PRIVATE EMPLOYMENT, CALIFORNIA. /FEP
   EMPLOYMENT-CONDITIONS DISCRIMINATION/   WBENNSJ66637

PRIVATE   (CONTINUATION)
TESTIMONY, PUBLIC HEARING, WOMEN IN PUBLIC AND **PRIVATE** EDUCATION, CALIFORNIA. /FEP
EMPLOYMENT-CONDITIONS DISCRIMINATION MIGRANT-WORKERS/   WBLOCHX66649

TESTIMONY, PUBLIC HEARING, WOMAN IN PUBLIC AND **PRIVATE** EMPLOYMENT, CALIFORNIA. /DISCRIMINATION/   WBROWAX66657

TESTIMONY, PUBLIC HEARING, WOMEN IN PUBLIC AND **PRIVATE** EMPLOYMENT, CALIFORNIA. /EMPLOYMENT-CONDITIONS/   WCHANHD66687

TESTIMONY, PUBLIC HEARING, WOMEN IN PUBLIC AND **PRIVATE** EMPLOYMENT, CALIFORNIA. /FEP
EMPLOYMENT-CONDITIONS DISCRIMINATION MIGRANTS/   WCLIFFG66692

TESTIMONY, PUBLIC HEARING, WOMEN IN PUBLIC AND **PRIVATE** EMPLOYMENT, CALIFORNIA. /DISCRIMINATION/   WCOLLNX66696

TESTIMONY, PUBLIC HEARING, WOMEN IN PUBLIC AND **PRIVATE** EMPLOYMENT, CALIFORNIA. /EMPLOYMENT-CONDITIONS/   WCOMPBX66702

TESTIMONY, PUBLIC HEARING, WOMEN IN PUBLIC AND **PRIVATE** EMPLOYMENT, CALIFORNIA. /TRAINING/   WCUMMGX66711

TESTIMONY, PUBLIC HEARING, WOMEN IN PUBLIC AND **PRIVATE** EMPLOYMENT, CALIFORNIA. /EMPLOYMENT-CONDITIONS/   WDIBRJX66732

TESTIMONY, PUBLIC HEARING, WOMAN IN PUBLIC AND **PRIVATE** EMPLOYMENT, CALIFORNIA. /DISCRIMINATION/   WDORAMX66739

TESTIMONY, PUBLIC HEARING, WOMEN IN PUBLIC AND **PRIVATE** EMPLOYMENT, CALIFORNIA. /EMPLOYMENT-CONDITIONS/   WEVANSX66753

TESTIMONY, PUBLIC HEARING, WOMEN IN PUBLIC AND **PRIVATE** EMPLOYMENT, CALIFORNIA. /EMPLOYMENT-CONDITIONS/   WFEINBX66760

TESTIMONY, PUBLIC HEARING, WOMEN IN PUBLIC AND **PRIVATE** EMPLOYMENT, CALIFORNIA. /DISCRIMINATION/   WFOOTJX66765

TESTIMONY, PUBLIC HEARING, WOMEN IN PUBLIC AND **PRIVATE** EMPLOYMENT, CALIFORNIA. /EMPLOYMENT-CONDITIONS/   WGABELX66773

TESTIMONY, PUBLIC HEARING, WOMEN IN PUBLIC AND **PRIVATE** EMPLOYMENT, CALIFORNIA. /DISCRIMINATION/   WGEIGPX66776

TESTIMONY, PUBLIC HEARING, WOMEN IN PUBLIC AND **PRIVATE** EMPLOYMENT, CALIFORNIA. /DEMOGRAPHY/   WGERSMX66777

TESTIMONY, PUBLIC HEARING, WOMEN IN PUBLIC AND **PRIVATE** EMPLOYMENT, CALIFORNIA. /EMPLOYMENT-CONDITIONS/   WGILBRX66780

TESTIMONY, PUBLIC HEARING, WOMEN IN PUBLIC AND **PRIVATE** EMPLOYMENT, CALIFORNIA. /EMPLOYMENT-CONDITIONS/   WGLENEM66788

TESTIMONY, PUBLIC HEARING, WOMEN IN PUBLIC AND **PRIVATE** EMPLOYMENT, CALIFORNIA. /DISCRIMINATION
WORK-FAMILY-CONFLICT/   WGUPTRC66808

TESTIMONY, PUBLIC HEARING, WOMEN IN PUBLIC AND **PRIVATE** EMPLOYMENT, CALIFORNIA. /EMPLOYMENT-CONDITIONS/   WGUPTRC66809

TESTIMONY, PUBLIC HEARING, WOMEN IN PUBLIC AND **PRIVATE** EMPLOYMENT, CALIFORNIA. /EMPLOYMENT-CONDITIONS/   WHEALWX66836

TESTIMONY, PUBLIC HEARING, WOMEN IN PUBLIC AND **PRIVATE** EMPLOYMENT, CALIFORNIA. /DISCRIMINATION/   WHILLHX66844

TESTIMONY, PUBLIC HEARING, WOMEN IN PUBLIC AND **PRIVATE** EMPLOYMENT, CALIFORNIA. /MOTA EEO/   WINGRLX66859

STATEMENT, PUBLIC HEARING, WOMEN IN PUBLIC AND **PRIVATE** EMPLOYMENT, CALIFORNIA. /EMPLOYMENT-CONDITIONS
MIGRANT-WORKERS/   WKAUFOX66886

TESTIMONY, PUBLIC HEARING, WOMEN IN PUBLIC AND **PRIVATE** EMPLOYMENT, CALIFORNIA. /EMPLOYMENT-CONDITIONS/   WKELLET66888

STATEMENT, PUBLIC HEARING, WOMEN IN PUBLIC AND **PRIVATE** EMPLOYMENT, CALIFORNIA. /EMPLOYMENT-CONDITIONS/   WKENNVX66890

STATEMENT, PUBLIC HEARING, WOMEN IN PUBLIC AND **PRIVATE** EMPLOYMENT, CALIFORNIA. /EMPLOYMENT-CONDITIONS/   WKNIGTF66911

TESTIMONY, PUBLIC HEARING, WOMEN IN PUBLIC AND **PRIVATE** EMPLOYMENT, CALIFORNIA. /FEP MIGRANT-WORKERS
EMPLOYMENT-CONDITIONS/   WLLOYMX66940

TESTIMONY, PUBLIC HEARING, WOMEN IN PUBLIC AND **PRIVATE** EMPLOYMENT, CALIFORNIA. /FEP   EMPLOYMENT
CONDITIONS/   WLOWEDX66943

TESTIMONY, PUBLIC HEARING, WOMEN IN PUBLIC AND **PRIVATE** EMPLOYMENT, CALIFORNIA. /EMPLOYMENT-CONDITIONS/   WMACKJW66950

TESTIMONY, PUBLIC HEARING, WOMEN IN PUBLIC AND **PRIVATE** EMPLOYMENT, CALIFORNIA. /OCCUPATIONS
EMPLOYMENT-CONDITIONS/   WMCLALX66947

TESTIMONY, PUBLIC HEARING, WOMEN IN PUBLIC AND **PRIVATE** EMPLOYMENT, CALIFORNIA. /BLUE-COLLAR
EMPLOYMENT-CONDITIONS/   WMENGVX66969

STATEMENT, PUBLIC HEARING, WOMEN IN PUBLIC AND **PRIVATE** EMPLOYMENT, CALIFORNIA. /FEP
EMPLOYMENT-CONDITIONS MIGRANT-WORKERS/   WMILLJJ66979

TESTIMONY, PUBLIC HEARING, WOMEN IN PUBLIC AND **PRIVATE** EMPLOYMENT, CALIFORNIA. /EMPLOYMENT-CONDITIONS/   WMILLKL66980

TESTIMONY, PUBLIC HEARING, WOMEN IN PUBLIC AND **PRIVATE** EMPLOYMENT, CALIFORNIA. /EMPLOYMENT-CONDITIONS/   WMORAMX66995

TESTIMONY, PUBLIC HEARING, WOMEN IN PUBLIC AND **PRIVATE** EMPLOYMENT, CALIFORNIA.   WMOTHWA66001

TESTIMONY, PUBLIC HEARING, WOMEN IN PUBLIC AND **PRIVATE** EMPLOYMENT, CALIFORNIA. /EMPLOYMENT-CONDITIONS/   WMYRIRX66013

A NATIONAL INQUIRY OF **PRIVATE** HOUSEHOLD-EMPLOYEES AND EMPLOYERS.   WNATLCH66014

TESTIMONY, PUBLIC HEARING, WOMEN IN PUBLIC AND **PRIVATE** EMPLOYMENT, CALIFORNIA. /EMPLOYMENT-CONDITIONS/   WPALMGX66047

TESTIMONY, PUBLIC HEARING, WOMEN IN PUBLIC AND **PRIVATE** EMPLOYMENT, CALIFORNIA. /FEP
EMPLOYMENT-CONDITIONS MIGRANT-WORKERS/   WPEEVMX66052

REPORT OF THE COMMITTEE ON **PRIVATE** EMPLOYMENT, 1963.   WPRESCO63068

TESTIMONY, PUBLIC HEARING, WOMEN IN PUBLIC AND **PRIVATE** EMPLOYMENT, CALIFORNIA. /EMPLOYMENT-CONDITIONS/   WRILEEX66081

TESTIMONY, PUBLIC HEARING, WOMEN IN PUBLIC AND **PRIVATE** EMPLOYMENT, CALIFORNIA. /FEP
EMPLOYMENT-CONDITIONS/   WSCHRPX66104

TESTIMONY, PUBLIC HEARING, WOMEN IN PUBLIC AND **PRIVATE** EMPLOYMENT, CALIFORNIA. /EMPLOYMENT-CONDITIONS/   WSHEAHX66112

TESTIMONY, PUBLIC HEARING, WOMEN IN PUBLIC AND **PRIVATE** EMPLOYMENT, CALIFORNIA. /FEP
EMPLOYMENT-CONDITIONS DISCRIMINATION/   WSMITWH66123

TESTIMONY, PUBLIC HEARING, WOMEN IN PUBLIC AND **PRIVATE** EMPLOYMENT, CALIFORNIA. /FEP
EMPLOYMENT-CONDITIONS DISCRIMINATION MIGRANT-WORKERS/   WSPENNX66129

TESTIMONY, PUBLIC HEARING, WOMEN IN PUBLIC AND **PRIVATE** EMPLOYMENT, CALIFORNIA. /LABOR-MARKET/   WSTEPRX66138

TESTIMONY, PUBLIC HEARING, WOMEN IN PUBLIC AND **PRIVATE** EMPLOYMENT, CALIFORNIA. /FEPC/   WSTERAX66140

TESTIMONY, PUBLIC HEARING, WOMEN IN PUBLIC AND **PRIVATE** EMPLOYMENT, CALIFORNIA. /EMPLOYMENT-CONDITIONS/   WTHOMOX66151

PRIVATE   (CONTINUATION)
TESTIMONY, PUBLIC HEARING, WOMEN IN PUBLIC AND **PRIVATE** EMPLOYMENT, CALIFORNIA. /EMPLOYMENT-CONDITIONS
DISCRIMINATION/   WTHOMGX66149

TO IMPROVE THE STATUS OF **PRIVATE** HOUSEHOLD WORK. /HOUSEHOLD-WORKERS/   WUSDLAB65220

WOMEN **PRIVATE** HOUSEHOLD-WORKERS FACT SHEET.   WUSDLAB66238

STATEMENT, PUBLIC HEARING, WOMEN IN PUBLIC AND **PRIVATE** EMPLOYMENT, CALIFORNIA. /FEP
EMPLOYMENT-CONDITIONS DISCRIMINATION/   WVAILLX66256

TESTIMONY, PUBLIC HEARING, WOMEN IN PUBLIC AND **PRIVATE** EMPLOYMENT, CALIFORNIA. /EMPLOYMENT-CONDITIONS
MIGRANT-WORKERS/   WWEBEJX66258

TESTIMONY, PUBLIC HEARING, WOMEN IN PUBLIC AND **PRIVATE** EMPLOYMENT, CALIFORNIA. /FEP
EMPLOYMENT-CONDITIONS MIGRANT-WORKERS/   WWCMEIX66273

TESTIMONY, PUBLIC HEARING, WOMEN IN PUBLIC AND **PRIVATE** EMPLOYMENT, CALIFORNIA. /EMPLOYMENT-CONDITIONS/   WWOODWX66276

PRIVATE-HOUSEHOLD
PRIVATE-HOUSEHOLD EMPLOYMENT -- SUMMARY OF FIRST AND SECOND CONSULTATIONS. /HOUSEHOLD-WORKERS/   WUSDLAB64212

PRIVILEGES
FAIR-EMPLOYMENT-PRACTICES ACT, STATE LAWS GRANTING EQUAL RIGHTS, **PRIVILEGES**, ETC.   GELWAEX58662

PROCEDURE
RHODE-ISLAND COMMISSION-AGAINST-DISCRIMINATION, RULES OF PRACTICE AND **PROCEDURE**.   GRHODICND232

PROCEDURES
HIRING **PROCEDURES** AND SELECTION STANDARDS IN THE SAN-FRANCISCO BAY AREA. /CALIFORNIA/   GMALMTF55934

GUIDELINES ON EMPLOYMENT TESTING **PROCEDURES**.   GUSEEOC66510

TITLE-VII. COMPLAINT **PROCEDURES** AND REMEDIES. /LEGISLATION/   GWALKRW66538

PROCEEDINGS
LONG-TERM MANPOWER PROJECTIONS. **PROCEEDINGS** OF A CONFERENCE CONDUCTED BY THE RESEARCH PROGRAM ON
UNEMPLOYMENT AND THE AMERICAN ECONOMY.   GGORDRA65613

PROCEEDINGS OF CONFERENCE ON EDUCATION FOR OPPORTUNITY, OPPORTUNITY FOR EDUCATION.   GMICFEP61982

PROCEEDINGS OF THE NATIONAL-SHARECROPPERS-FUND CONFERENCE ON MIGRATORY LABOR AND LOW-INCOME FARMERS.
NOVEMBER 13 1957.   GNATLSF57299

SUMMARY OF **PROCEEDINGS**. WORKSHOP ON THE IMPACT OF A TIGHTENING LABOR-MARKET ON THE EMPLOYABILITY AND
EMPLOYMENT OF DISADVANTAGED YOUTH.   GNEWYUC66116

COMMISSIONS FOR HUMAN RIGHTS, 15TH ANNUAL CONFERENCE, **PROCEEDINGS**.   GPENNHR63166

REGIONAL COMMUNITY LEADERS CONFERENCE ON EQUAL-EMPLOYMENT-OPPORTUNITY, **PROCEEDINGS**.   GPRESCO64113

A TIME FOR ACTION, **PROCEEDINGS** OF THE NATIONAL CONFERENCE ON EQUAL-EMPLOYMENT-OPPORTUNITY, 1962.
/MILITARY/   GUSDARM62193

MIGRATORY FARM LABOR CONFERENCE, **PROCEEDINGS**.   GUSDLAB57359

LAKE ARROWHEAD CONFERENCE ON EQUAL-EMPLOYMENT-OPPORTUNITY, OCTOBER 22-24, 1963 -- RECORD OF **PROCEEDINGS**.
LOS-ANGELES, CALIFORNIA.   GUSFEDE63513

PROCEEDINGS OF THE CONFERENCE ON INDIAN TRIBES AND TREATIES.   IUVMNCC56676

PROCEEDINGS OF THE 50TH ANNIVERSARY OBSERVANCE OF THE AMERICAN JEWISH COMMITTEE. APRIL 10-14, 1957. THE
PURSUIT OF EQUALITY AT HOME AND ABROAD. /ECONOMIC-OPPORTUNITY/   JAMERJC58692

TRANSCRIPT OF **PROCEEDINGS** OF THE INTERIM SUBCOMMITTEE ON SPECIAL EMPLOYMENT PROBLEMS. /CALIFORNIA/   MCALAIC64374

PROCEEDINGS OF EMPLOYMENT OPPORTUNITIES EDUCATIONAL CONFERENCE.   MCOUNMA62930

PROCEEDINGS OF THE CONFERENCE ON EDUCATION FOR ADULT MIGRANT WORKERS. /TEXAS/   MTEXACM62498

LAND TENURE IN THE SOUTHERN REGION. **PROCEEDINGS** OF PROFESSIONAL AGRICULTURAL WORKERS TENTH ANNUAL
CONFERENCE.   NTUSKIX51218

FIRST CATALYST ON CAMPUS CONFERENCE, **PROCEEDINGS**. /WORK-WOMEN-ROLE/   WCATAXX64683

PROFESSIONAL OPPORTUNITIES FOR WOMEN, **PROCEEDINGS**.   WUVCAEB66250

3RD ANNUAL WOMEN-S CONFERENCE, **PROCEEDINGS**.   WUVUTXX66254

PROCESS
DISCRIMINATION IN UNION MEMBERSHIP. DENIAL OF DUE **PROCESS** UNDER FEDERAL COLLECTIVE BARGAINING
LEGISLATION.   GPRESSB58126

CIVIL-RIGHTS POLICY IN THE FEDERAL SYSTEM. PROPOSALS FOR A BETTER USE OF ADMINISTRATIVE **PROCESS**.   GWITHJX65575

THE DISPLACED PERSON AND THE SOCIAL AGENCY. A STUDY OF THE CASEWORK **PROCESS** AND ITS RELATION TO IMMIGRANT
ADJUSTMENT.   JCRYSDX58714

GATEKEEPERS IN THE **PROCESS** OF ASSIMILATION.   MKURTNR66270

CPI -- CHEMICAL **PROCESS** INDUSTRIES -- TAKES LEAD IN ANTI-BIAS DRIVE. /INDUSTRY/   NCHEMWX61199

OCCUPATIONAL ASSIMILATION AS A COMPETITIVE **PROCESS**.   NHODGRW65556

INDUSTRIAL INTEGRATION OF NEGROES. THE UPGRADING **PROCESS**.   NHOPEJX52571

EQUALITY OF EMPLOYMENT OPPORTUNITY. A **PROCESS** ANALYSIS OF UNION INITIATIVE.   NHOPEJX60569

THE QUEST FOR IDENTITY AND STATUS. FACETS OF THE DESEGREGATION **PROCESS** IN THE UPPER MIDWEST.
/ECONOMIC-STATUS/   NTILLJA61161

PROCESSES
URBANIZATION OF THE MIGRANT. **PROCESSES** AND OUTCOMES. A RESEARCH PROPOSAL.   MSIMMOG64491

PROCESSING
PROCESSING EMPLOYMENT DISCRIMINATION CASES. /LEGISLATION/   GBLUMAW67117

EFFECT OF MECHANIZATION ON EMPLOYMENT OF MIGRATORY LABOR IN AGRICULTURE AND FOOD **PROCESSING**.

PROCESSING   (CONTINUATION)
    /MIGRANT-WORKERS/   GDELASE59946

PROCLAMATION
    LABOR AND THE EMANCIPATION PROCLAMATION. /UNION/   GKRONJL65861

PROCUREMENT
    FEDERAL PROCUREMENT AND EQUAL-OPPORTUNITY EMPLOYMENT.   GPOWETX64190

PRODUCTION
    APPROACHES TO INCOME IMPROVEMENT. EXPERIENCES OF FAMILIES RECEIVING PRODUCTION LOANS UNDER THE FARMERS
    HOME ADMINISTRATION.   GHENDWE59422

    THE EVALUATION OF PRACTICES CARRIED ON BY TWO HUNDRED NEGRO FARMERS IN THE PRODUCTION OF COTTON IN MACON
    COUNTY, ALABAMA.   NGOLDSM48350

    NEGROES AND WAR PRODUCTION.   NGRANLB42444

    THE RELATIONSHIP BETWEEN MECHANIZATION OF COTTON PRODUCTION AND ATTENDANCE AND ENROLLMENT IN THE RURAL
    SCHOOLS OF COAHOMA COUNTY, MISSISSIPPI.   NMCLABF51349

    PERSONAL AND ENVIRONMENTAL OBSTACLES TO PRODUCTION ADJUSTMENTS ON SOUTH-CAROLINA PIEDMONT AREA FARMS.   NTAYLCC58411

    THE VOCATIONAL GUIDANCE AND EDUCATION OF NEGROES. THE NEGRO AND THE BATTLE OF PRODUCTION.   NWILKDA42233

PRODUCTIONS
    CHANGING PATTERNS IN AGRICULTURAL PRODUCTIONS, WEST-VIRGINIA, 1920-1950. /OCCUPATIONS/   NANGLRA54254

PRODUCTIVE
    THE RELATIONSHIP BETWEEN UNEARNED INCOME AND INDIVIDUAL PRODUCTIVE EFFORT ON THE JICARILLA APACHE INDIAN
    RESERVATION.   IWILSHC61687

    A MORE PRODUCTIVE ROLE FOR THE NEGRO IN THE SOUTH-S ECONOMY.   NCHALWE64912

    A CONFERENCE TO ENLIST THE PARTICIPATION OF 50 INSTITUTIONS OF HIGHER EDUCATION IN SPECIFIC R AND D
    PROGRAMS TO PREPARE WOMEN FOR PRODUCTIVE EMPLOYMENT.   WLLOYBJ64937

PRODUCTIVITY
    AUTOMATION, PRODUCTIVITY AND MANPOWER PROBLEMS.   GBOKXDX64736

    TECHNOLOGICAL-CHANGE, PRODUCTIVITY, AND EMPLOYMENT IN THE UNITED STATES.   GGREELX64739

    THE HIGH COST OF DISCRIMINATION. THE WASTE IN MANPOWER, MORALE, AND PRODUCTIVITY COSTS AMERICAN INDUSTRY
    30 BILLION DOLLARS A YEAR.   GROPEEX63244

    AN ECONOMICAL AND HISTORICAL ANALYSIS OF THE CAUSES OF VARIATION AMONG NORTHERN STANDARD METROPOLITAN
    AREAS IN PRODUCTIVITY OF NEGRO MEN IN 1949.   NBATCAB61060

    BEHAVIOR AND PRODUCTIVITY IN BI-RACIAL WORK GROUPS.   NKATZIX58638

PROFESSION
    NEGRO ENGINEERS AND STUDENTS REPORT ON THEIR PROFESSION. /OCCUPATIONS/   NKIEHRX58647

    A CRITICAL APPRAISAL OF PROFESSION TRAINING OF NEGRO TEACHERS IN OKTIBBEHA COUNTY MISSISSIPPI. NWILLMM50234

    THE COMMITMENT REQUIRED OF A WOMAN ENTERING A SCIENTIFIC PROFESSION. /OCCUPATIONS/   WBETTBX65645

    PANEL DISCUSSION. THE COMMITTMENT REQUIRED OF A WOMAN ENTERING A SCIENTIFIC PROFESSION. /OCCUPATIONS/   WBUNTMI65663

    NURSING PROFESSION. FIVE SOCIOLOGICAL SURVEYS.   WDAVIFX66722

    INITIATION INTO A WOMAN-S PROFESSION. IDENTITY PROBLEMS IN THE STATUS TRANSITION OF CO-ED TO STUDENT
    NURSE.   WDAVIFX66723

PROFESSIONAL
    INTEGRATION IN PROFESSIONAL NURSING. /OCCUPATIONS NEGRO WOMEN/   CCARNME62183

    CHARACTERISTICS OF PROFESSIONAL WORKERS. /DEMOGRAPHY/   CUSBURC63167

    IMPLICATIONS OF THE RECENT CENSUSES FOR PROFESSIONAL AGRICULTURAL WORKERS. /OCCUPATIONS/   GBEALCL61412

    PLACEMENT OF PROFESSIONAL PERSONNEL.   GUSDLAB52492

    THE CHARACTERISTICS OF THE SUPPLY OF NEGROES FOR PROFESSIONAL OCCUPATIONS.   NANDERW65024

    THE DILEMMA OF THE NEGRO PROFESSIONAL.   NBACKKX64039

    MORE ROOM AT THE TOP. COMPANY EXPERIENCE IN EMPLOYING NEGROES IN PROFESSIONAL AND MANAGEMENT JOBS.
    /INDUSTRY/   NBIRDCX63080

    THE NEGRO SCHOLAR AND PROFESSIONAL IN AMERICA.   NBONDHM66103

    GRADUATE AND PROFESSIONAL EDUCATION IN NEGRO INSTITUTIONS. /ECONOMIC-STATUS/   NBROWAX58893

    EDUCATION OF NEGRO LEADERS. INFLUENCES AFFECTING GRADUATE AND PROFESSIONAL STUDIES.   NCALIAX49174

    INTEGRATION IN PROFESSIONAL EDUCATION. THE STORY OF PERKINS, SOUTHERN METHODIST UNIVERSITY. /VOCATIONS/   NCUNNMX56579

    THE NEGRO PROFESSIONAL CLASS. /OCCUPATIONAL-PATTERNS/   NEDWAGF59324

    OCCUPATIONAL-MOBILITY OF NEGRO PROFESSIONAL WORKERS.   NEDWAGF64326

    A STUDY OF PROFESSIONAL PREPARATION OF NEGRO TEACHERS OF EXCEPTIONAL CHILDREN IN NORTH-CAROLINA COUNTY
    AND CITY PUBLIC SCHOOLS.   NKNIGOB65023

    LAND TENURE IN THE SOUTHERN REGION. PROCEEDINGS OF PROFESSIONAL AGRICULTURAL WORKERS TENTH ANNUAL
    CONFERENCE.   NTUSKIX51218

    WOMEN IN THE PROFESSIONAL WORLD. /OCCUPATIONS/   WALPEEJ62604

    NOTES ON THE ROLE OF CHOICE IN THE PSYCHOLOGY OF PROFESSIONAL WOMEN. /OCCUPATIONS/   WBAILLX64623

    THE STATUS OF WOMEN IN PROFESSIONAL SOCIOLOGY. /OCCUPATIONS/   WFAVASF60757

    CAREER DECISIONS AND PROFESSIONAL EXPECTATIONS OF NURSING-STUDENTS. /ASPIRATIONS/   WFOXXDJ61767

    THE FEMALE PHYSICIAN IN PUBLIC HEALTH. CONFLICT AND RECONCILIATION OF THE SEX AND PROFESSIONAL ROLES.
    /OCCUPATIONS/   WKOSAJX64915

PROFESSIONAL   (CONTINUATION)
    PROFESSIONAL STANDARDS AND ECONOMIC-STATUS OF NURSES IN THE UNITED STATES.   WKRUGDH60917

    PROFESSIONAL AND NON-PROFESSIONAL WOMEN AS MOTHERS.   WMERIFH55971

    NSA-S PROFESSIONAL STATUS SURVEY, 1964. /ECONOMIC-STATUS/   WNATLSA65023

    PROFESSIONAL WOMANPOWER AS A NATIONAL RESOURCE.   WPARRJB61051

    WOMEN IN PROFESSIONAL ENGINEERING. /OCCUPATIONS/   WSOCIOW62127

    THE ROLE OF WOMEN IN PROFESSIONAL ENGINEERING. /OCCUPATIONS/   WTORPWG62157

    PROFESSIONAL OPPORTUNITIES FOR WOMEN, PROCEEDINGS.   WUVCAEB66250

    THE MOTIVATION FOR WOMEN TO WORK IN HIGH LEVEL PROFESSIONAL POSITIONS.   WWALTDE62314

    STATISTICS ON WOMEN PROFESSIONAL ENGINEERS. /OCCUPATIONS/   WWEBBJR66226

PROFESSIONALISM
    SEX-ROLE AND PROFESSIONALISM. A STUDY OF HIGH SCHOOL TEACHERS. /OCCUPATIONS/   WCOLOJX63698

PROFESSIONALLY
    PART-TIME PROGRAM FOR PROFESSIONALLY TRAINED WOMEN. /TRAINING/   WTACKAL66147

PROFESSIONS
    PARNASSUS RESTRICTED. JOB DISCRIMINATION IN THE PROFESSIONS.   GGOLDMH46724

    VOCATIONS AND PROFESSIONS.   GLUTZPX40925

    NOT TO THE SWIFT. PROGRESS AND PROSPECTS OF THE NEGRO IN SCIENCE AND THE PROFESSIONS. /OCCUPATIONS/   NCOBBWM58216

    THE ROLE OF THE NEGRO IN THE HEALING PROFESSIONS IN CONTEMPORARY AMERICA. /OCCUPATIONS/   NMCPHEL55728

    THE STATUS OF WOMEN IN THE PROFESSIONS RELATIVE TO THE STATUS OF MEN. /OCCUPATIONS/   WCAVARS57684

    WOMEN AND THE SCIENTIFIC PROFESSIONS. THE MIT SYMPOSIUM ON AMERICAN WOMEN IN SCIENCE AND ENGINEERING.
    /OCCUPATIONS/   WMATTJA65963

PROFESSORS
    WOMEN PROFESSORS AT BROWN. /OCCUPATIONS/   WKEENBC62887

PROFILE
    A SOCIAL PROFILE OF AGRICULTURAL MIGRATORY PEOPLE IN COLORADO. /MIGRANT-WORKERS/   GCOLOSD59919

    PROFILE IN BLACK AND WHITE. DISCRIMINATION AND INEQUALITY OF OPPORTUNITY.   GNATLULND0085

    COUNTING THE POOR. ANOTHER LOOK AT THE POVERTY PROFILE.   GORSHMX65142

    A STATISTICAL PROFILE OF THE SPANISH-SURNAME POPULATION OF TEXAS.   MBROWHL64368

    AN ECONOMIC AND SOCIAL PROFILE OF THE NEGRO AMERICAN.   NFEINRX65347

    RACE-RELATIONS IN ROCHESTER, A PROFILE FOR 1957. /NEW-YORK/   NGRIEES57457

    RACE-RELATIONS IN THE ALBANY TROY AREA. A PROFILE FOR 1957. /NEW-YORK/   NGRIEES57503

    RACE-RELATIONS IN BROOME-COUNTY, A PROFILE FOR 1958. /NEW-YORK/   NGRIEES58456

    RACE-RELATIONS IN SYRACUSE. A PROFILE. /NEW-YORK/   NGRIEES58458

    A PROFILE OF THE NEGRO AMERICAN.   NPETTTF64992

    HUMAN-RELATIONS IN ANN-ARBOR, A COMMUNITY PROFILE.   NPIKEJX67101

    CHANGING PROFILE OF THE NATION-S WORK-FORCE.   WWIRTWW63271

PROFILES
    PUERTO-RICAN PROFILES.   PNEWYCC64832

    INTEREST PROFILES OF UNIVERSITY WOMEN. /ASPIRATIONS/   WMITCED57986

PROGRAM
    AN EXPERIMENT TO TEST THREE MAJOR ISSUES OF WORK PROGRAM METHODOLOGY WITHIN MOBILIZATION-FOR-YOUTH-S
    INTEGRATED SERVICES TO OUT-OF-SCHOOL UNEMPLOYED YOUTH. /NEGRO PUERTO-RICAN/   CMOBIFY66024

    REPORT OF THE CALIFORNIA STATE ADVISORY COMMITTEE TO THE UNITED STATES COMMISSION ON CIVIL-RIGHTS ON
    CALIFORNIA-S PROGRAM FOR EQUAL-OPPORTUNITY IN APPRENTICESHIP.   GBECKWL62432

    EQUAL-OPPORTUNITY IN APPRENTICESHIP AND TRAINING -- THE CALIFORNIA PROGRAM.   GCALDIR65524

    MANPOWER PROGRAM IMPLICATIONS OF SKILL IMBALANCES. /TRAINING/   GCASSFH66565

    A NATIONAL PROGRAM FOR THE IMPROVEMENT OF WELFARE SERVICES AND THE REDUCTION OF WELFARE DEPENDENCY.   GCOHENE65664

    CONGRESS AND THE JOHNSON POVERTY PROGRAM.   GCONGDX66356

    SEMINAR ON MANPOWER POLICY AND PROGRAM. LABOR LOOKS AT AUTOMATION AND CIVIL-RIGHTS.   GCONWJT65496

    MINORITY PROGRAM CALLS FOR COMMUNITY ACTION.   GCRAICE65619

    SEMINAR ON MANPOWER POLICY AND PROGRAM -- AUTOMATION, SKILL, AND MANPOWER PREDICTIONS.   GCROSER66148

    A POSITIVE PROGRAM FOR MERIT-EMPLOYMENT.   GDOUGMX60650

    THE FEDERAL ANTI-POVERTY PROGRAM AND SOME IMPLICATIONS OF SUBPROFESSIONAL TRAINING.   GGORDJE65135

    LONG-TERM MANPOWER PROJECTIONS. PROCEEDINGS OF A CONFERENCE CONDUCTED BY THE RESEARCH PROGRAM ON
    UNEMPLOYMENT AND THE AMERICAN ECONOMY.   GGORDRA65613

    A PUBLIC EMPLOYMENT PROGRAM FOR THE UNEMPLOYED POOR.   GGREEAI65473

    NEW-YORK STATE-S PROGRAM AGAINST DISCRIMINATION IN EMPLOYMENT. THE WORK OF THE NEW-YORK
    STATE-COMMISSION-AGAINST-DISCRIMINATION.   GINDUBX57812

    DEVELOPING FAIR-EMPLOYMENT PROGRAMS. A PROGRAM FOR THE SMALLER COMPANY.   GJENSJJ66785

    IMPLICATIONS OF THE ANTI-POVERTY PROGRAM FOR EDUCATION AND EMPLOYMENT.   GLEVILA65781

MARYLAND TB -- VD HEALTH **PROGRAM** AMONG AGRICULTURAL MIGRANTS.   GMARYSD65958

A HUMAN-RELATIONS **PROGRAM** FOR SAN-FRANCISCO. /CALIFORNIA/   GMITCJP64277

FEDERAL LEGISLATION FOR A COMPREHENSIVE **PROGRAM** ON YOUTH EMPLOYMENT.   GNIXORA66847

STATE EXECUTIVE AUTHORITY TO PROMOTE CIVIL-RIGHTS. AN ACTION **PROGRAM** FOR THE 1960-S.   GSILAJX63310

EMPLOYMENT **PROGRAM** FOR MINORITY-GROUPS.   GTHAMME50353

EQUAL-EMPLOYMENT-OPPORTUNITY TRAINING, A **PROGRAM** FOR AFFIRMATIVE-ACTION.   GUSCISC63384

SUPERVISOR DEVELOPMENT **PROGRAM**, BASIC COURSE, NONDISCRIMINATION POLICY. /MILITARY/   GUSDARM56192

FAMILY CHARACTERISTICS OF THE LONG TERM UNEMPLOYED. A REPORT ON A STUDY OF CLAIMANTS UNDER THE TEMPORARY
EXTENDED UNEMPLOYMENT COMPENSATION **PROGRAM**, 1961-2.   GUSDLAB61445

SEMINAR ON MANPOWER POLICY AND **PROGRAM** MEASUREMENT OF TECHNOLOGICAL-CHANGE.   GUSDLAB64980

SEMINAR ON MANPOWER POLICY AND **PROGRAM**. CYBERNATION AND SOCIAL CHANGE.   GUSDLAB64982

EXAMINATION OF THE WAR-ON-POVERTY **PROGRAM**.   GUSHOUR65824

CALIFORNIA-S MINORITY-GROUPS **PROGRAM**.   GWOODMJ64581

THE WOL APPRENTICESHIP TRAINING **PROGRAM**. REPORT OF A YEAR-S EXPERIMENT.   GWORKDL65584

A LOOK AT THE FEPC-S AFFIRMATIVE-ACTION **PROGRAM**.   GYABRSX65588

DOORWAY TOWARD THE LIGHT. THE STORY OF THE SPECIAL NAVAJO EDUCATION **PROGRAM**.   ICOOMLM62646

A **PROGRAM** FOR INDIAN CITIZENS. A SUMMARY REPORT.   IFUNDFT61562

THE AMERICAN INDIAN RELOCATION **PROGRAM**.   IMADILX56587

DOCUMENTARY HISTORY OF THE FOX PROJECT, 1948-1959. A **PROGRAM** IN ACTION ANTHROPOLOGY.   INETTRM60599

AN EVALUATION OF THE 10-YEAR DEVELOPMENT **PROGRAM** OF THE UTE TRIBE OF THE UINTAH AND OURAY RESERVATION,
UTAH.   IUSDINT58648

EMPLOYMENT ASSISTANCE **PROGRAM**.   IUSDINT64647

INDIAN INDUSTRIAL DEVELOPMENT **PROGRAM**. A NEW INDUSTRIAL OPPORTUNITY.   IUSDINT64653

A FOLLOWUP STUDY OF 1963 RECIPIENTS OF THE SERVICES OF THE EMPLOYMENT ASSISTANCE **PROGRAM**,
BUREAU-OF-INDIAN-AFFAIRS.   IUSDINT66650

PLACING INDIANS WHO LIVE ON RESERVATIONS. A COOPERATIVE **PROGRAM**.   IUSDLAB59667

TEXAS MIGRANTS **PROGRAM**. /TRAINING EDUCATION/   MMACNBL67335

TERMINATION OF THE BRACERO **PROGRAM**. SOME EFFECTS ON FARM LABOR AND MIGRANT HOUSING NEEDS.   MMCELRC65385

THE MEXICAN FARM LABOR SUPPLY **PROGRAM** -- ITS FRIENDS AND FOES.   MPFEIDG63456

TEXAS AND THE BRACERO **PROGRAM**.   MSCRUOM63482

MEXICAN-AMERICANS IN URBAN PUBLIC HIGH SCHOOLS. AN EXPLORATION OF THE DROP-OUT **PROGRAM**.   MSHELPM59488

MEXICAN FARM LABOR **PROGRAM**.   MUSHOUR63984

THE DETERMINATION OF CERTAIN MAJOR FACTORS AFFECTING THE NEGRO VETERAN IN THE ON-THE-JOB TRAINING **PROGRAM**
IN VOCATIONAL AGRICULTURE IN THE STATE OF ALABAMA AS A BASIS FOR PLANNING A MORE EFFECTIVE PROGRAM.   NBATTEF49338

THE DETERMINATION OF CERTAIN MAJOR FACTORS AFFECTING THE NEGRO VETERAN IN THE ON-THE-JOB TRAINING PROGRAM
IN VOCATIONAL AGRICULTURE IN THE STATE OF ALABAMA AS A BASIS FOR PLANNING A MORE EFFECTIVE **PROGRAM**.   NBATTEF49338

MINORITY **PROGRAM** CALLS FOR COMMUNITY ACTION.   NCRAICE65240

RACIAL DISCRIMINATION IN THE NATION-S APPRENTICESHIP TRAINING **PROGRAM**.   NHILLHX62539

PLANNING THE END OF THE AMERICAN GHETTO. A **PROGRAM** OF ECONOMIC DEVELOPMENT FOR EQUAL-RIGHTS.   NHILLHX66538

WHAT SHOULD THE BUSINESS RESPONSE BE TO THE NEGRO REVOLUTION. A PUBLIC RELATIONS **PROGRAM** FOR DEALING WITH
MINORITY-GROUPS.   NLANGJF65671

A UNIQUE REGIONAL **PROGRAM** OF PSYCHOLOGICAL RESEARCH AND TRAINING IN THE SOUTH.   NLANGMC56032

FACILITATIVE AND INHIBITIVE FACTORS IN TRAINING **PROGRAM** RECRUITMENT AMONG RURAL NEGROES.   NMARSCP65738

SHARECROPPERS IN THE 60-S. A REPORT AND A **PROGRAM**.   NNATLSF61883

A SURVEY OF THE ECONOMIC AND CULTURAL CONDITIONS OF THE NEGRO POPULATION OF LOUISVILLE, KENTUCKY AND A
REVIEW OF THE **PROGRAM** AND ACTIVITIES OF THE LOUISVILLE URBAN-LEAGUE. JANUARY-FEBRUARY, 1948.   NNATLUL48903

PROGRAM AIDS FOR VOCATIONAL OPPORTUNITY PROGRAM.   NNATLUL49895

PROGRAM AIDS FOR VOCATIONAL OPPORTUNITY **PROGRAM**.   NNATLUL49895

UNEMPLOYMENT AND THE AMERICAN ECONOMY. RESEARCH **PROGRAM** ON UNEMPLOYMENT.   NROSSAM63259

AN ANALYSIS OF SELECTIVE FACTORS INFLUENCING FARM INCOME IN HALE COUNTY, AS A BASIS FOR ESTABLISHING A
MORE EFFECTIVE VOCATIONAL AGRICULTURAL **PROGRAM**. /ALABAMA/   NSALTDR52347

PROGRESS IN WATTS -- THE LOS-ANGELES ASTD COMMUNITY AFFAIRS **PROGRAM**. /CALIFORNIA/   NTRAIAD66580

SOCIAL SECURITY **PROGRAM** STATISTICS RELATING TO NONWHITE FAMILIES AND CHILDREN.   NUSDHEW58241

NEGRO WORKERS AND THE NATIONAL DEFENSE **PROGRAM**.   NUSDLAB41253

UNION **PROGRAM** FOR ELIMINATING DISCRIMINATION.   NUSDLAB63846

HEARING BEFORE THE AD HOC SUBCOMMITTEE ON THE WAR-ON-POVERTY **PROGRAM**.   NYOUNWM64350

EAST-HARLEM BLOCK COMMUNITY DEVELOPMENT **PROGRAM**. /NEW-YORK/   PBORODXND781

RUTGERS -- THE STATE UNIVERSITY. FORD FOUNDATION **PROGRAM** FOR THE RETRAINING IN MATHEMATICS OF COLLEGE

PROGRAM   (CONTINUATION)
GRADUATE WOMEN. /TRAINING/   WMARTHM63957

  MATHEMATICS RETRAINING PROGRAM. NOTES AND COMMENTS, APRIL 1964, 1965, 1966. /TRAINING/   WRUTGMR64097

  REPORT -- 1965-66 -- RETRAINING PROGRAM IN MATHEMATICS AND SCIENCE FOR COLLEGE GRADUATE WOMEN.   WRUTGMR66098

  PART-TIME PROGRAM FOR PROFESSIONALLY TRAINED WOMEN. /TRAINING/   WTACKAL66147

  PARTNERSHIP TEACHING PROGRAM. PROGRESS REPORT -- JAN-OCT 1965. SECTION I. /TRAINING/   WWOMEEA65275

PROGRAMMERS
  AUTOMATION AND EMPLOYMENT OPPORTUNITIES FOR OFFICE WORKERS. THE EFFECT OF ELECTRONIC COMPUTERS ON
  EMPLOYMENT OF CLERICAL WORKERS. WITH A SPECIAL REPORT ON PROGRAMMERS.   WPASCWX58178

PROGRAMMES
  MANPOWER POLICY AND PROGRAMMES IN THE UNITED STATES.   GORGAEC64776

PROGRAMS
  THE TRAINING OF MIGRANT FARM WORKERS. A FOLLOW-UP STUDY OF TWO EXPERIMENTAL AND DEMONSTRATION PROGRAMS
  UNDER THE MANPOWER-DEVELOPMENT-AND-TRAINING-ACT.   /MEXICAN-AMERICAN AMERICAN-INDIAN/   CUNIVOD66054

  FEPC. AN ADMINISTRATIVE STUDY OF SELECTED STATE AND LOCAL PROGRAMS.   GALFOAL54869

  THE ROLE OF GOVERNMENT-SPONSORED TRAINING AND RETRAINING PROGRAMS.   GALLECC65758

  MANPOWER DEVELOPMENT PROGRAMS FOR FARM PEOPLE.   GALLECC67910

  PROGRAMS TO AID THE UNEMPLOYED IN THE 1960-S.   GBECKJX65430

  YOUTH EMPLOYMENT PROGRAMS IN PERSPECTIVE.   GBENJJG65006

  THE PRESENT STATUS AND PROGRAMS OF FEPC. FEDERAL, STATE, AND MUNICIPAL.   GBRAZBR51472

  ACTION PROGRAMS FOR FEPC ADVISORY COMMITTEES. /CALIFORNIA/   GCALFEP66528

  WORK PROGRAMS AND THE YOUTHFUL OFFENDER.   GCOLEEX66131

  PUBLIC WELFARE, AUTOMATION, AND EXPERIMENTAL MANPOWER PROGRAMS.   GCONFAP63545

  A SUMMARY REPORT OF PRACTICES AND PROGRAMS DESIGNED TO REDUCE THE NUMBER OF DROPOUTS IN THE HIGH SCHOOLS
  OF LOS-ANGELES COUNTY. /CALIFORNIA/   GDELMDT66147

  NONDISCRIMINATION IN FEDERALLY-ASSISTED PROGRAMS OF THE DEPARTMENT-OF-THE-TREASURY,
  DEPARTMENT-OF-DEFENSE, ATOMIC-ENERGY-COMMISSION, CIVIL-AERONAUTICS-BOARD, FEDERAL-AVIATION-AGENCY,
  VETERANS-ADMINISTRATION.   GFEDERX64673

  REPORT OF INDUSTRY AND LABOR-MANAGEMENT CLINICS. IMPLEMENTATION OF EMPLOYMENT IN MERIT PROGRAMS IN NON
  FEPC STATES BY DIRECT APPROACH TO TOP MANAGEMENT.   GFISKUR51684

  SELECTED STATE PROGRAMS IN MIGRANT EDUCATION.   GHANEGE64004

  HERE-S HOW MERIT EMPLOYMENT PROGRAMS WORK. A REPORT ON PROGRESS AND PROBLEMS IN THE EMPLOYMENT OF
  MINORITY-GROUP MEMBERS.   GILLISC56803

  DEVELOPING FAIR-EMPLOYMENT PROGRAMS. A PROGRAM FOR THE SMALLER COMPANY.   GJENSJJ66785

  THE COMMUNITY ACTION AGENCY-S ROLE IN COMPREHENSIVE MANPOWER PROGRAMS -- PLANNING AND PROBLEMS.   GKANERD66863

  EMPLOYMENT PROBLEMS OF YOUTH AND MANPOWER PROGRAMS.   GKRUGDH66864

  FEDERAL MANPOWER POLICIES AND PROGRAMS TO COMBAT UNEMPLOYMENT.   GLEVISA64897

  PROGRAMS IN AID OF THE POOR.   GLEVISA65601

  PROGRAMS IN AID OF THE POOR. /ANTI-POVERTY/   GLEVISA66729

  DEVELOPING FAIR-EMPLOYMENT PROGRAMS. GUIDELINES FOR SELECTION.   GLOCKHC66780

  THE ROLE OF JOB CREATION PROGRAMS. /MANPOWER/   GMANGGL65728

  LOWER-CLASS DELINQUENCY AND WORK PROGRAMS.   GMARTJM66854

  APPRENTICE PROGRAMS.   GPRESCD64106

  MUNICIPAL HUMAN-RELATIONS COMMISSION. A SURVEY OF PROGRAMS IN SELECTED CITIES OF THE UNITED STATES.   GRICHCM63236

  COORDINATION AMONG FEDERAL MANPOWER PROGRAMS.   GROBSRT66721

  COORDINATION OF MANPOWER PROGRAMS.   GTAYLHC66967

  BIBLIOGRAPHY ON VOLUNTARY FAIR-EMPLOYMENT PROGRAMS.   GUSCOMC65392

  PROGRAMS FOR HIGH SCHOOL DROPOUTS. EXPERIENCE REPORT 101.   GUSCONF64976

  SELECTED STATE PROGRAMS IN MIGRANT EDUCATION.   GUSDHEW63505

  SELECTED REFERENCES ON MIGRATORY WORKERS AND THEIR FAMILIES. PROBLEMS AND PROGRAMS.   GUSDLAB56204

  PROGRAMS OF NATIONAL ORGANIZATIONS FOR MIGRANT FARM WORKERS AND THEIR FAMILIES.   GUSDLAB61202

  SELECTED REFERENCES ON DOMESTIC MIGRATORY AGRICULTURAL WORKERS, THEIR FAMILIES, PROBLEMS, AND PROGRAMS,
  1955-1960.   GUSDLAB61495

  MANPOWER RESEARCH PROGRAMS.   GUSDLAB62981

  BRIDGE TO EMPLOYMENT. DEMONSTRATION MANPOWER PROGRAMS.   GUSDLAB63442

  EQUAL-OPPORTUNITY IN APPRENTICESHIP PROGRAMS.   GUSHOUR61343

  IMPLICATIONS OF GOVERNMENT-SPONSORED TRAINING PROGRAMS. /TECHNOLOGICAL-CHANGE/   GWALSJP64620

  MANPOWER PROGRAMS. THEIR CONTRIBUTION TO THE ACHIEVEMENT OF EQUAL-OPPORTUNITY MANPOWER ADMINISTRATION.   GWHITHC65558

  MANPOWER AND TRAINING. TRENDS, OUTLOOK AND PROGRAMS.   GZEISJS63704

  SOCIAL AND CULTURAL CONSIDERATIONS IN THE DEVELOPMENT OF MANPOWER PROGRAMS FOR INDIANS. IKELLWH67579

  NATIONAL CONFERENCE ON MANPOWER PROGRAMS FOR INDIANS. SUMMATION.   IKRUGDH67811

FAMILY PLAN AND REHABILITATION **PROGRAMS**, STANDING-ROCK RESERVATION.   IUSDINT64649

VOCATIONAL TRAINING **PROGRAMS** FOR AMERICAN-INDIANS.   IUSDLAB64009

WORKING WITH STUDENTS INSIDE AND OUTSIDE THE CLASSROOM IN ADULT BASIC EDUCATION **PROGRAMS**.   NBRAZWF64285

FACTORS AFFECTING THE PRESENT FARMING **PROGRAMS** OF ONE HUNDRED NEGRO FARMS IN THE PATRONAGE AREA OF THE
MACON COUNTY TRAINING SCHOOL, IN ALABAMA, WITH EMPHASIS FOR IMPROVEMENT.   NBRONCA51337

THE NEGRO WAGE-EARNER AND APPRENTICESHIP TRAINING **PROGRAMS**. A CRITICAL ANALYSIS WITH RECOMMENDATIONS.   NHILLHX60532

APPRENTICESHIP TRAINING **PROGRAMS** AND RACIAL DISCRIMINATION.   NKOVAIX65024

NEGRO PARTICIPATION IN APPRENTICESHIP **PROGRAMS**.   NMARSRX66327

NEGRO PARTICIPATION IN APPRENTICESHIP **PROGRAMS**.   NMARSRX67118

YOU NEED TO SEE IT TO BELIEVE IT. REPORT OF THE 1963 SUMMER STUDY-SKILLS **PROGRAMS**. /COLLEGE EDUCATION/   NMARTWD63303

PROBLEMS AND TRENDS IN JOB-DEVELOPMENT AND EMPLOYMENT **PROGRAMS**.   NPURYMT63028

THE CIVIL-RIGHTS **PROGRAMS** OF THE KENNEDY ADMINISTRATION.   NSULLDF64190

EQUAL-OPPORTUNITY IN FARM **PROGRAMS** -- AN APPRAISAL OF SERVICES RENDERED BY AGENCIES OF THE UNITED STATES
DEPARTMENT OF AGRICULTURE.   NUSCOMC65232

THE NEGRO WAGE-EARNER AND APPRENTICESHIP TRAINING **PROGRAMS**.   NUSDLAB60249

SURVEY OF SALARIES AND PERSONNEL PRACTICES FOR TEACHERS AND ADMINISTRATORS IN NURSING EDUCATIONAL
PROGRAMS, DECEMBER 1965.   WAMERNA66612

RESEARCH REPORT. SURVEY OF CONTINUING EDUCATION **PROGRAMS**.   WFIELBX64762

A CONFERENCE TO ENLIST THE PARTICIPATION OF 50 INSTITUTIONS OF HIGHER EDUCATION IN SPECIFIC R AND D
PROGRAMS TO PREPARE WOMEN FOR PRODUCTIVE EMPLOYMENT.   WLLOYBJ64937

A SURVEY OF SPECIAL EDUCATIONAL **PROGRAMS** FOR ADULT WOMEN IN UNIVERSITY EXTENSION DIVISIONS AND EVENING
COLLEGES AS OF SPRING 1965.   WLORIRK66942

WOMEN GRADUATES OF COOPERATIVE WORK-STUDY **PROGRAMS** ON THE COLLEGE LEVEL. /SKILLS/   WMOSBWB57999

MATURE WOMEN IN DOCTORAL **PROGRAMS**. /OCCUPATIONS/   WRANDKS65073

UNIVERSITY **PROGRAMS** OF CONTINUING EDUCATION FOR THE ADULT WOMAN.   WTINKAH64156

TRADE AND INDUSTRIAL EDUCATION FOR GIRLS AND WOMEN. A DIRECTORY OF TRAINING **PROGRAMS**.   WUSDHEW60175

WHY CONTINUING EDUCATION **PROGRAMS** FOR WOMEN.   WUSDLAB63229

PROGRESS
1963 REPORT OF **PROGRESS** IN HUMAN-RIGHTS.   GALASSC63366

AUTOMATION AND ECONOMIC **PROGRESS**. A SUMMARY OF THE REPORT OF THE NATIONAL COMMISSION ON TECHNOLOGY,
AUTOMATION, AND ECONOMIC PROGRESS.   GBOWEHR66748

AUTOMATION AND ECONOMIC PROGRESS. A SUMMARY OF THE REPORT OF THE NATIONAL COMMISSION ON TECHNOLOGY,
AUTOMATION, AND ECONOMIC **PROGRESS**.   GBOWEHR66748

PROGRESS IN CIVIL-RIGHTS TO 1964. /EEO/   GFLEIHX65106

HERE-S HOW MERIT EMPLOYMENT PROGRAMS WORK. A REPORT ON **PROGRESS** AND PROBLEMS IN THE EMPLOYMENT OF
MINORITY-GROUP MEMBERS.   GILLISC56803

PROGRESS OR POVERTY. THE US AT THE CROSSROADS.   GKEYSLH64862

PROGRESS IN MEETING PROBLEMS OF MIGRATORY LABOR IN MARYLAND.   GMARYGC60955

THE PEOPLE TAKE THE LEAD. A RECORD OF **PROGRESS** IN CIVIL-RIGHTS, 1948-1957.   GNATLLS57049

THE PEOPLE TAKE THE LEAD. A RECORD OF **PROGRESS** IN CIVIL-RIGHTS, 1954-1963.   GNATLLS63050

PROGRESS WITHOUT FEDERAL COMPULSION. ARGUING THE CASE FOR COMPROMISE METHODS.   GNORTHR52122

REPORT OF **PROGRESS** IN THE INTEGRATION OF HOTEL AND RESTAURANT EMPLOYMENT, APRIL 1961 TO MARCH 1962.
/PHILADELPHIA PENNSYLVANIA/   GPHILCH62178

A SPECIAL REPORT. CITY CONTRACT COMPLIANCE. **PROGRESS** IN 1963. /PHILADELPHIA PENNSYLVANIA/   GPHILCH64179

PLANS-FOR-PROGRESS. A FIRST YEAR REPORT BY THE PLANS FOR **PROGRESS** ADVISORY COUNCIL.   GPRESCD64112

FIVE YEARS OF **PROGRESS**, 1953-1958. A REPORT TO PRESIDENT EISENHOWER BY THE PRESIDENT-S COMMITTEE ON
GOVERNMENT CONTRACTS.   GPRESCH58121

PATTERN FOR **PROGRESS**. SEVENTH REPORT. FINAL REPORT TO PRESIDENT EISENHOWER FROM THE COMMITTEE ON
GOVERNMENT CONTRACTS.   GPRESCH60123

PROGRESS IN FAIR-EMPLOYMENT-PRACTICES.   GRIGHXX59238

FEPC IN THE STATES. A **PROGRESS** REPORT.   GRORTJX58246

FAIR-EMPLOYMENT IN THE NATION-S CAPITAL. A STUDY OF **PROGRESS** AND DILEMMA. /WASHINGTON-DC/   GSAWYDA62279

FAIR-EMPLOYMENT IN THE FEDERAL SERVICE. A **PROGRESS** REPORT ON CONSTRUCTIVE STEPS.   GUSCISC52386

PROGRESS TOWARD FAIR-EMPLOYMENT-PRACTICES.   GUSDLAB45078

PROGRESS IN MEETING PROBLEMS OF MIGRATORY LABOR IN MARYLAND.   GUVMADA62529

PROGRESS IN EMPLOYMENT ASSISTANCE.   IDAVIRC62546

CONSTRAINTS ON ECONOMIC **PROGRESS** ON THE ROSEBUD SIOUX INDIAN RESERVATION.   IEICHCK60553

INDIAN AFFAIRS 1964. A **PROGRESS** REPORT FROM THE COMMISSIONER OF INDIAN AFFAIRS.   IUSDINT64652

THE NEGROES **PROGRESS** TOWARD EMPLOYMENT EQUALITY.   NAUGUTX58034

PROGRESS TOWARD INTEGRATION. FOUR CASE-STUDIES. /EMPLOYMENT FEPC NEW-YORK/   NBACKSX59040

PROGRESS   (CONTINUATION)
   TOWARD EQUALITY, BALTIMORE-S PROGRESS-REPORT, A CHRONICLE OF **PROGRESS** SINCE WORLD-WAR-II TOWARD THE
   ACHIEVEMENT OF EQUAL-RIGHTS AND OPPORTUNITIES FOR NEGROES IN MARYLAND 1946-1958.   NBALTUL58048

   DISCRIMINATION AND THE OCCUPATIONAL **PROGRESS** OF NEGROES. A COMMENT.   NBECKGS62068

   NEGRO **PROGRESS**. WHAT THE FACTS SHOW.   NBREIGX52113

   ECONOMIC **PROGRESS** IN BLACK AND WHITE.   NBRIMAF66114

   PROGRESS AND PORTENTS FOR THE NEGRO IN MEDICINE. /OCCUPATIONS/   NCOBBWM48217

   NOT TO THE SWIFT. **PROGRESS** AND PROSPECTS OF THE NEGRO IN SCIENCE AND THE PROFESSIONS. /OCCUPATIONS/   NCOBBWM58216

   THE RELATIVE **PROGRESS** OF THE AMERICAN NEGRO SINCE 1950.   NDANIWG63250

   NEGRO EMPLOYMENT. A **PROGRESS** REPORT.   NDAVIJA52256

   THE **PROGRESS** OF THE NEGRO IN HIGHER EDUCATION, 1950-1960.   NDODDHH63278

   RELATIVE **PROGRESS** OF THE AMERICAN NEGRO SINCE 1950.   NJOURNE63626

   PROGRESS IN INTERRACIAL RELATIONSHIPS. INEQUALITIES FOR NEGROES.   NLEWIES43689

   PROGRESS IN PLANS-FOR-PROGRESS FOR NEGRO MANAGERS.   NLOCKHC65701

   THE **PROGRESS** OF THE NEGRO AFTER A CENTURY OF EMANCIPATION.   NLOGARW63046

   PROGRESS IN RACE-RELATIONS.   NMCNIRX51727

   PROGRESS AND PROSPECTS FOR THE NEGRO WORKER.   NMILLHP65783

   THE NEGRO IN MILWAUKEE, **PROGRESS** AND PORTENT, 1863-1963. /WISCONSIN/   NMILWCC63792

   THE NEGRO WORKER-S **PROGRESS** IN MINNESOTA. A REPORT.   NMINNGI49799

   PROGRESS AGAINST POVERTY.   NNATLSFND882

   JOBS FOR NEGROES. HOW MUCH **PROGRESS** IN SIGHT.   NNEWSXX63912

   SOUTHERN TRADITION AND REGIONAL **PROGRESS**.   NNICHWH60322

   AN HISTORICAL SURVEY AND ANALYSIS OF THE **PROGRESS** OF NEGROES IN PUBLIC-SERVICE 1932-1952.   NOLIVLW56955

   DISCRIMINATION AND THE OCCUPATIONAL **PROGRESS** OF NEGROES.   NRAYAEX61040

   THE NEGRO-S OCCUPATIONAL **PROGRESS**.   NRUSSJL66096

   PROGRESS IN WATTS -- THE LOS-ANGELES ASTD COMMUNITY AFFAIRS PROGRAM. /CALIFORNIA/   NTRAIAD66580

   INTEGRATION IN THE ARMED SERVICES. A **PROGRESS** REPORT. /MILITARY/   NUSDDEF55195

   SOUTHERN RACE **PROGRESS**. THE WAVERING COLOR LINE.   NWOOFTJ57340

   PROGRESS OF THE COMMISSION ON THE STATUS OF WOMAN. /WORK-WOMAN-ROLE/   WELLIKX63748

   PROGRESS AND PROSPECTS. THE REPORT OF THE SECOND NATIONAL CONFERENCE OF GOVERNORS COMMISSIONS ON THE
   STATUS OF WOMEN. /EMPLOYMENT-CONDITIONS/   WGOVECS65798

   PROGRESS AND PROSPECTS. /EMPLOYMENT-CONDITIONS/   WGOVECS66215

   WOMAN-S CENTURY OF **PROGRESS**. IS IT TO END IN REGRESSION. /WORK-WOMAN-ROLE/   WMCKARC58946

   SOCIAL WORK DEGREE **PROGRESS** REPORT. /TRAINING/   WNYUYUG66031

   MINNESOTA PLAN FOR WOMEN-S CONTINUING EDUCATION. A **PROGRESS** REPORT.   WSENDVL61298

   REPORT ON **PROGRESS** IN 1965 ON THE STATUS OF WOMEN. /EDUCATION EMPLOYMENT-CONDITIONS/   WUSINCS65860

   PARTNERSHIP TEACHING PROGRAM. **PROGRESS** REPORT -- JAN-OCT 1965. SECTION I. /TRAINING/   WWOMEEA65275

PROGRESS-REPORT
   TOWARD EQUALITY, BALTIMORE-S **PROGRESS-REPORT**, A CHRONICLE OF PROGRESS SINCE WORLD-WAR-II TOWARD THE
   ACHIEVEMENT OF EQUAL-RIGHTS AND OPPORTUNITIES FOR NEGROES IN MARYLAND 1946-1958.   NBALTUL58048

   TOWARD EQUALITY, BALTIMORE-S **PROGRESS-REPORT**, 1962 SUPPLEMENT. /MARYLAND/   NBALTUL62049

PROHIBIT
   BRIEF SUBMITTED IN SUPPORT OF SENATE BILL NO 984, A BILL TO **PROHIBIT** DISCRIMINATION IN EMPLOYMENT....   GTUTTCH47368

PROHIBITED
   STATE FAIR-EMPLOYMENT LAWS AND THEIR ADMINISTRATION. TEXTS, FEDERAL-STATE COOPERATION, **PROHIBITED** ACTS.   GBURENA64497

PROHIBITING
   SHOULD CONGRESS PASS A LAW **PROHIBITING** EMPLOYMENT DISCRIMINATION.   GCONGDX45596

   WISCONSIN FAIR-EMPLOYMENT-PRACTICES DIVISION INQUIRY INTO THE CONFLICTS BETWEEN STATE PROTECTIVE LABOR
   LEGISLATION AND STATE AND FEDERAL LAWS **PROHIBITING** DISCRIMINATION BASED ON SEX. /EMPLOYMENT-CONDITIONS/   WUAWXWD65165

PROJECT
   NEGROES AND MEXICAN-AMERICANS IN THE CALIFORNIA STATE GOVERNMENT, A COOPERATIVE **PROJECT**.   CCALOGB65171

   SECRETARIAL TRAINING WITH SPEECH IMPROVEMENT. AN EXPERIMENTAL AND DEMONSTRATION **PROJECT**. /NEGRO WOMEN/   CSAINMD66320

   FINAL REPORT. EXPERIMENTAL AND DEMONSTRATION ON-JOB-TRAINING **PROJECT**. /MIGRANT-WORKERS MEXICAN-AMERICAN
   NEGRO ARIZONA/   CSKILTO66324

   REPORT. EVALUATION STUDY OF YOUTH TRAINING AND EMPLOYMENT **PROJECT**, EAST LOS-ANGELES. /NEGRO
   MEXICAN-AMERICAN CALIFORNIA/   CWEINJL64310

   FINAL REPORT OF THE YMCA YOUTH AND WORK **PROJECT** 1962-1966. /NEGRO PUERTO-RICAN TRAINING/   CYMCAYA66329

   ACTION FOR EMPLOYMENT. A DEMONSTRATION NEIGHBORHOOD MANPOWER **PROJECT**.   GALLCTO66361

   AMBITIOUS EDUCATION IMPROVEMENT **PROJECT** UNDER WAY IN SOUTH.   GAMERCE64370

   THE ITINERANT FARM LABOR **PROJECT** REPORT. /MIGRANT-WORKERS CALIFORNIA/   GCALVRS60553

   FINAL REPORT ON JOBS II **PROJECT**. /CHICAGO ILLINOIS/   GCHICBC65319

PROJECT (CONTINUATION)
A DEMONSTRATION **PROJECT** DESIGNED TO TEST THE LIFE-STYLE AND THE GROWTH POTENTIAL OF URBAN DROPOUTS FROM DISADVANTAGED HOMES.   GCLEAMP66130

ORGANIZING THE UNEMPLOYED. THE CHICAGO **PROJECT**. /ILLINOIS/   GFLACRX64964

MIGRANT **PROJECT** 1959. /MIGRANT-WORKERS/   GFLORBH59690

THE MIGRANT **PROJECT**. /MIGRANT-WORKERS/   GFLORHN60689

ADULT AND YOUTH EMPLOYMENT **PROJECT**, AUGUST-SEPTEMBER 1965.   GHEALDV65646

ADULT AND YOUTH EMPLOYMENT **PROJECT**, APRIL-MAY 1965.   GHEALDV65647

FINAL REPORT. THE YOUTH TRAINING **PROJECT**, SEPTEMBER 1, 1963--JANUARY 31, 1965. /ST-LOUIS MISSOURI TESTING/   GJEWIEV65568

IDENTIFICATION AND MODIFICATION OF THE SOCIAL-PSYCHOLOGICAL CORRELATES OF ECONOMIC DEPENDENCY. **PROJECT** FINAL REPORT.   GKIMMPR66137

GRADUATES OF THE NORFOLK **PROJECT** ONE YEAR LATER. /MDTA TRAINING/   GQUINPA65771

DOCUMENTARY HISTORY OF THE FOX **PROJECT**, 1948-1959. A PROGRAM IN ACTION ANTHROPOLOGY.   INETTRM60599

THE FOX **PROJECT**. /ECONOMY/   ITAXXSX58157

PROSPECTUS OF THE MEXICAN-AMERICAN STUDY **PROJECT**.   MMARSRX64437

SAN-ANTONIO **PROJECT**. /TEXAS/   MNATLCA63081

WHEN THE MIGRANT LABORER SETTLES DOWN -- A REPORT OF THE FINDINGS OF A **PROJECT** ON VALUE ASSIMILATION OF IMMIGRANT LABORERS.   MPETECL64454

MEXICAN-AMERICAN STUDY **PROJECT**. ADVANCE REPORT 3, BIBLIOGRAPHY.   MUVCALM66510

SAN-ANTONIO **PROJECT**. /TEXAS/   MWAGNJA63514

TWO YEAR REPORT ON THE YOUTH GUIDANCE **PROJECT**, 1958-1959. /CHICAGO ILLINOIS/   NCHICULND203

MDTA **PROJECT** UPLIFT. /TRAINING/   NFILIJE66354

THE IMPLICATIONS OF **PROJECT** CLEAR. /DESEGREGATION/   NFORMPB55372

EXPERIMENTAL AND DEMONSTRATION MANPOWER **PROJECT** FOR THE RECRUITMENT, TRAINING, PLACEMENT AND FOLLOW-UP OF RURAL UNEMPLOYED WORKERS IN TEN NORTH FLORIDA CITIES. FINAL REPORT. /PARTICIPANTS/   NJACKTA66597

EXPERIMENTAL FEATURES OF THE TUSKEGEE-INSTITUTE RETRAINING **PROJECT**.   NTUSKIX65765

DEMONSTRATIONAL FEATURES OF THE TUSKEGEE-INSTITUTE. RETRAINING **PROJECT**.   NTUSKIX65766

UNIVERSITY OF KANSAS-CITY **PROJECT** FOR CONTINUING EDUCATION OF WOMEN.   WBERRJX63640

FINAL REPORT. EXPERIMENTAL AND DEMONSTRATION MANPOWER **PROJECT** FOR THE RECRUITMENT, TRAINING, PLACEMENT AND FOLLOW-UP OF RURAL UNEMPLOYED WORKERS IN TEN NORTH FLORIDA COUNTIES.   WFLORMP66326

PROJECTED
PROJECTED CHANGES IN THE OCCUPATIONAL STRUCTURE OF THE LABOR-FORCE. IMPLICATIONS FOR PUBLIC WELFARE.   GSIFFHX64105

PROJECTIONS
PROJECTIONS TO 1975. THE GROWTH AND STRUCTURE OF THE LABOR FORCE.   GBAKESS65702

INTERIM REVISED **PROJECTIONS** OF US LABOR-FORCE, 1965-1975.   GCOOPSX62602

LABOR-FORCE **PROJECTIONS** BY COLOR, 1970-1980.   GCOOPSX66604

PROJECTIONS OF THE LABOR-FORCE OF THE US.   GGOLDHX63787

PROJECTIONS OF MANPOWER REQUIREMENTS AND SUPPLY.   GGOLDHX66933

LONG-TERM MANPOWER **PROJECTIONS**.   GGORDRA64525

LONG-TERM MANPOWER **PROJECTIONS**. PROCEEDINGS OF A CONFERENCE CONDUCTED BY THE RESEARCH PROGRAM ON UNEMPLOYMENT AND THE AMERICAN ECONOMY.   GGORDRA65613

MANPOWER **PROJECTIONS**. SOME CONCEPTUAL PROBLEMS AND RESEARCH NEEDS. /EMPLOYMENT-TRENDS/   GSWERSX66535

PROJECTIONS OF SCHOOL AND COLLEGE ENROLLMENT IN THE UNITED STATES TO 1985. /DEMOGRAPHY/   GUSBURC66160

PROJECTIONS OF POPULATION AND LABOR-FORCE.   WINTELR61868

PROJECTS
ISSUES AND PROBLEMS IN INTEGRATING NEEDED SUPPORTIVE SERVICES IN NEIGHBORHOOD-YOUTH-CORPS **PROJECTS**.   GBATTMX66131

GRANTS AND **PROJECTS** RELATED TO THE DEVELOPMENT OF THE AMERICAN NEGRO. ALL FISCAL YEARS THROUGH JUNE 10, 1966.   NFORDFX66133

TWO **PROJECTS** FOR DROPOUT YOUTH.   NJEWIEA64609

ANNUAL FAMILY AND OCCUPATIONAL EARNINGS OF RESIDENTS OF TWO NEGRO HOUSING **PROJECTS** IN ATLANTA 1937-1944. /GEORGIA/   NRITTAL45062

PILOT **PROJECTS** FOR CONTINUING EDUCATION FOR WOMEN.   WMERRMH63972

IMPLICATIONS OF TWO PILOT **PROJECTS** IN TRAINING MATURE WOMEN AS COUNSELORS.   WRIOCMJ65082

PROMOTABILITY
WHAT HELPS OR HARMS **PROMOTABILITY**.   GBOWMGW64468

PROMOTE
STATE EXECUTIVE AUTHORITY TO **PROMOTE** CIVIL-RIGHTS. AN ACTION PROGRAM FOR THE 1960-S.   GSILAJX63310

DISCRIMINATION IN THE HIRING HALL. A CASE-STUDY OF PRESSURES TO **PROMOTE** INTEGRATION IN NEW-YORK-S BREWERY INDUSTRY.   NLANGGE59670

PROMOTING
PROMOTING EQUAL JOB OPPORTUNITY, A GUIDE FOR EMPLOYERS. /CALIFORNIA/   GCALFEP63538

THE ROLE OF GOVERNMENT IN **PROMOTING** FULL EMPLOYMENT.   GROSSAM66084

PROMOTING (CONTINUATION)
LABOR WEEK. RULES ON HIRING, **PROMOTING** -- QUESTIONS ANSWERED.   GUSNEWR66518

PROMOTING EQUAL-EMPLOYMENT THROUGH THE PUBLIC EMPLOYMENT SERVICE.   NLEVILX62686

PROMOTION
REPORT TO GOVERNOR EDMUND G BROWN. SECOND ETHNIC SURVEY OF EMPLOYMENT AND **PROMOTION** IN STATE GOVERNMENT.
/CALIFORNIA NEGRO MEXICAN-AMERICAN/   CBECKWL65070

POLICIES FOR THE **PROMOTION** OF ECONOMIC GROWTH.   GACKLGX66680

SECOND ETHNIC SURVEY OF EMPLOYMENT AND **PROMOTION** IN STATE GOVERNMENT. /CALIFORNIA/   GBECKWL65433

SELF APPRAISAL FOR MERIT **PROMOTION**. A RESEARCH MANUAL.   GBOWMGW63467

DISCRIMINATORY **PROMOTION** SYSTEMS.   GDOERPB67115

DISCRIMINATION WITHOUT PREJUDICE. A STUDY OF **PROMOTION** PRACTICES IN INDUSTRY.   GKAHNRL64733

HIRING AND **PROMOTION** SYSTEMS UNDER FAIR-EMPLOYMENT-PRACTICES LEGISLATION.   GUSDLAB67116

PROMOTION SYSTEMS AND EQUAL-EMPLOYMENT OPPORTUNITY.   NDOERPB66280

TAPPING THE NEGRO POTENTIAL. /INDUSTRY EMPLOYMENT-SELECTION **PROMOTION**/   NJOHNTX65621

PROMOTIONS
INVISIBLE PERSUADER ON **PROMOTIONS**.   JUVMIIT65768

PROMOTIONS SYSTEMS AND EQUAL-EMPLOYMENT-OPPORTUNITY.   NDOERPB66279

PROPOSAL
UNDER-ACHIEVEMENT AMONG MINORITY-GROUP STUDENTS. AN ANALYSIS AND A **PROPOSAL**. /YOUTH NEGRO
MEXICAN-AMERICAN PUERTO-RICAN/   CHOBACW63555

STATE FAIR-EMPLOYMENT-PRACTICE LAWS. REPORT PERSUANT TO **PROPOSAL** 400.   GILLILC57802

URBANIZATION OF THE MIGRANT. PROCESSES AND OUTCOMES. A RESEARCH **PROPOSAL**.   MSIMMOG64491

FAMILY AND ACHIEVEMENT. A **PROPOSAL** TO STUDY THE EFFECT OF FAMILY SOCIALIZATION ON ACHIEVEMENT AND
PERFORMANCE AMONG URBAN NEGRO AMERICANS.   NEPPSEG65334

A **PROPOSAL** FOR THE PREVENTION AND CONTROL OF DELINQUENCY BY EXPANDING OPPORTUNITIES.   NMOBIFY62263

EQUALITY BETWEEN THE SEXES. AN IMMODEST **PROPOSAL**. /WORK-WOMEN-ROLE/   WROSSAS64132

PROPOSALS
STATE CIVIL-RIGHTS STATUTES. SOME **PROPOSALS**.   GBONFAE64463

SOME **PROPOSALS** FOR GOVERNMENT POLICY IN AN AUTOMATING SOCIETY.   GGANSHJ65696

TOWARDS FULL EMPLOYMENT. **PROPOSALS** FOR A COMPREHENSIVE EMPLOYMENT AND MANPOWER POLICY IN THE UNITED
STATES.   GUSSENA64332

CIVIL-RIGHTS POLICY IN THE FEDERAL SYSTEM. **PROPOSALS** FOR A BETTER USE OF ADMINISTRATIVE PROCESS. GWITHJX65575

PROPOSALS FOR THE IMPROVEMENT OF HUMAN RELATIONS IN THE LOS-ANGELES METROPOLITAN AREA. /EMPLOYMENT
CALIFORNIA/   NLOSACC65365

RACIAL DISCRIMINATION IN EMPLOYMENT. **PROPOSALS** FOR CORRECTIVE ACTION.   NPOLLDX63006

PROPOSITIONS
OCCUPATIONAL DISCRIMINATION. SOME THEORETICAL **PROPOSITIONS**.   GBLALHM62454

DESEGREGATION. SOME **PROPOSITIONS** AND RESEARCH SUGGESTIONS.   NSUCHEA58189

CAREER DEVELOPMENT OF WOMEN. SOME **PROPOSITIONS**.   WTIEDDV59153

PROSPECT
THE **PROSPECT** FOR ADVANCEMENT IN BUSINESS OF THE MARRIED WOMAN COLLEGE GRADUATE. /OCCUPATIONS/   WBECKEL64632

PROSPECTIVE
NEGRO BUSINESS AND BUSINESS EDUCATION. THEIR PRESENT AND **PROSPECTIVE** DEVELOPMENT.   NPIERJA47998

A STUDY OF JOB MOTIVATIONS, ACTIVITIES, AND SATISFACTIONS OF PRESENT AND **PROSPECTIVE** WOMEN COLLEGE
FACULTY MEMBERS. /OCCUPATIONS/   WCOOKWX60252

PROSPECTS
THE NATION-S CHILDREN. VOL I. THE FAMILY AND SOCIAL-CHANGE. VOL II. DEVELOPMENT AND EDUCATION. VOL III.
PROBLEMS AND **PROSPECTS**. /NEGRO PUERTO-RICAN MEXICAN-AMERICAN WOMEN/   CGINZEX60720

MIGRATION OF POPULATION IN THE SOUTH. SITUATION AND **PROSPECTS**.   GBOWLGK58397

ATTITUDE TOWARD OCCUPATIONAL CHANGE AS AN INDICATOR OF **PROSPECTS** FOR ADJUSTMENT.   GDUNKJE64653

CONFERENCE ON UNSKILLED WORKERS IN THE LABOR-FORCE. PROBLEMS AND **PROSPECTS**.   GGITLAL66134

PROSPECTS FOR EDUCATION AND EMPLOYMENT.   GLEAGWVND890

EQUAL-EMPLOYMENT-OPPORTUNITIES. PROBLEMS AND **PROSPECTS**.   GMARSRX65056

URBAN DIFFERENTIATION. PROBLEMS AND **PROSPECTS**.   GMCELDX65051

COMMENTS ON EQUAL-EMPLOYMENT-OPPORTUNITIES. PROBLEMS AND **PROSPECTS**.   GMCKER865930

THE WAR-ON-POVERTY. PERSPECTIVES AND **PROSPECTS**.   GMILLSM65953

JEWISH ECONOMIC **PROSPECTS** IN 1965.   JPUCKWX65750

NOT TO THE SWIFT. PROGRESS AND **PROSPECTS** OF THE NEGRO IN SCIENCE AND THE PROFESSIONS. /OCCUPATIONS/ NCOBBWM58216

PROSPECTS FOR EQUAL-EMPLOYMENT. CONFLICTING PORTENTS.   NMARSRX65744

PROGRESS AND **PROSPECTS** FOR THE NEGRO WORKER.   NMILLHP65783

PROBLEMS AND **PROSPECTS** OF THE NEGRO MOVEMENT. /EMPLOYMENT/   NMURPRJ66866

NEGLECTED TALENTS. BACKGROUND AND **PROSPECTS** OF NEGRO COLLEGE GRADUATES.   NNATLOR66880

FAIR-EMPLOYMENT-PRACTICE LAWS -- EXPERIENCE, EFFECTS, **PROSPECTS**.   NNORGPH67929

PROSPECTS   (CONTINUATION)
PROGRESS AND PROSPECTS. THE REPORT OF THE SECOND NATIONAL CONFERENCE OF GOVERNORS COMMISSIONS ON THE
STATUS CF WOMEN. /EMPLOYMENT-CONDITIONS/   WGOVECS65798

   PROGRESS AND PROSPECTS. /EMPLOYMENT-CONDITIONS/   WGOVECS66215

   PRCBLEMS AND PROSPECTS OF WORKING WOMEN.   WWESTRC62214

PROSPECTUS
   PROSPECTUS OF THE MEXICAN-AMERICAN STUDY PROJECT.   MMARSRX64437

PROSPERITY
   PROSPERITY THROUGH EQUALITY.   NMILLLX63788

PROSPEROUS
   UNEMPLOYMENT IN A PROSPEROUS ECONOMY. A REPORT OF THE PRINCETON-MANPOWER-SYMPOSIUM.   GBOWEWG65749

   AN INSIGHT INTO STRUCTURAL UNEMPLOYMENT -- THE EXPERIENCE OF A MINORITY GROUP IN A PROSPEROUS COMMUNITY.   NGERSWJ65634

PROTECTING
   PROTECTING RIGHTS OF MINORITY EMPLOYEES.   GKINGRL60854

PROTECTION
   EQUAL PROTECTION OF THE LAWS IN NORTH-CAROLINA.   GUSCOMC62397

   EQUAL PROTECTION OF THE LAWS IN PUBLIC HIGHER EDUCATION.   NUSCOMC60302

PROTECTIVE
   REPORT OF THE COMMITTEE ON PROTECTIVE LABOR LEGISLATION, 1963.   WPRESCO63069

   WISCONSIN FAIR-EMPLOYMENT-PRACTICES DIVISION INQUIRY INTO THE CONFLICTS BETWEEN STATE PROTECTIVE LABOR
   LEGISLATION AND STATE AND FEDERAL LAWS PROHIBITING DISCRIMINATION BASED CN SEX. /EMPLOYMENT-CONDITIONS/   WUAWXWD65165

PROTEST
   ECCNCMIC FCRCES SERVING THE ENDS OF THE NEGRC PROTEST. /UNEMPLOYMENT/   NBATCAB65059

   THE VOICES OF NEGRO PROTEST IN AMERICA.   NBURNHX63902

   THE ECONOMICS OF PROTEST.   NHARRMX67489

   THE NEGRC PROTEST.   NRCSEAM65074

PROVIDENCE
   THE NON-WHITE IN PROVIDENCE. /RHODE-ISLAND/   NRHODIUND052

PROVISIONS
   THE CONTROVERSY OVER THE EQUAL-EMPLOYMENT-OPPORTUNITY PROVISIONS OF THE CIVIL-RIGHTS BILL. PRO AND CON.   GCONGOX64594

   ANTIDISCRIMINATICN PROVISIONS IN MAJCR CONTRACTS, 1961.   GLUDELE62923

   LEGAL RULINGS INTERPRETING THE PROVISIONS OF THE PENNSYLVANIA FAIR-EMPLOYMENT-PRACTICE ACT.   GPENNFE58153

   COMPLIANCE GUIDE. RECOMMENDATIONS FOR OBTAINING COMPLIANCE WITH THE NONDISCRIMINATION PROVISIONS IN
   GOVERNMENT CONTRACTS.   GPRESCH58119

   MATFRNITY BENEFIT PROVISIONS FOR EMPLOYED WOMEN. /EMPLOYMENT-CONDITIONS/   WUSDLAB60206

   WOMEN ANC THE EQUAL-EMPLOYMENT PROVISIONS OF THE CIVIL-RIGHTS-ACT.   WUSDLAB65234

   FRINGE BENEFIT PROVISIONS FRCM STATE MINIMUM WAGE LAWS AND ORDERS, SEPTEMBER 1, 1966.
   /EMPLOYMENT-CONDITIONS/   WUSDLAB66195

PSYCHIATRIC
   SURVEY OF SALARIES AND EMPLOYMENT-CONDITIONS IN NONFEDERAL PSYCHIATRIC HOSPITALS.   WAMERNA65611

   SOCIAL FACTORS WHICH AFFECT CAREER CHOICE IN PSYCHIATRIC NURSING.   WDOUGAM61740

PSYCHOLOGICAL
   THE USE OF PSYCHOLOGICAL TESTS IN INDUSTRY.   GALBRLE63368

   THE IMPLICATIONS OF THE CIVIL-RIGHTS-ACT OF 1964 FOR PSYCHOLOGICAL ASSESSMENT IN INDUSTRY. /TESTING/   GASHXPX66405

   PSYCHOLOGICAL TESTING. SOME PROBLEMS AND SOLUTIONS. /INDUSTRY/   GFRENWL66101

   THE CONGRESSIONAL HEARINGS AND ISSUES IN PSYCHOLOGICAL TESTING. INVASIONS OF PRIVACY AND TEST BIAS.   GGORDJEND934

   PSYCHOLOGICAL TESTING FOR EFFECTIVE EMPLOYMENT PRACTICES AND EQUAL JOB OPPORTUNITIES.   GKETCWA65849

   PSYCHOLOGICAL TESTS AND FAIR EMPLOYMENT. A STUDY OF EMPLOYMENT TESTING IN THE SAN-FRANCISCO BAY AREA.
   /CALIFCRNIA/   GRUSHJT66268

   PSYCHOLOGICAL TESTING IN INDUSTRY. A CRITICAL EVALUATION.   GSTANES64635

   ECCNCMIC, POLITICAL AND PSYCHOLOGICAL ASPECTS OF EMPLOYMENT.   GUPHOWH64528

   FAIR-EMPLOYMENT-PRACTICES-COMMISSION EXPERIENCES WITH PSYCHOLOGICAL TESTING.   NASHXPX65031

   MEETING THE PSYCHOLOGICAL CRISES OF NEGRO YOUTH THROUGH A COORDINATED GUIDANCE SERVICE.   NBRAZWF58111

   WHAT ARE THE PSYCHOLOGICAL EFFECTS OF SEGREGATION UNDER CONDITIONS OF EQUAL FACILITIES.   NCHEIIX49198

   DESEGREGATION. A PSYCHOLOGICAL ANALYSIS.   NCOOKSW57234

   COMPARATIVE PSYCHOLOGICAL STUDIES OF NEGROES AND WHITES IN THE UNITED STATES.   NDREGRM60292

   RECENT RESEARCH IN PSYCHOLOGICAL COMPARISONS OF NEGROES AND WHITES IN THE UNITED STATES.   NDREGRM65293

   A UNIQUE REGIONAL PROGRAM OF PSYCHOLOGICAL RESEARCH AND TRAINING IN THE SOUTH.   NLANGMC56032

   NOTES CN WCMEN IN INDUSTRY -- PRESENTED AT AMERICAN PSYCHOLOGICAL SYMPOSIUM, SEPT 1963. /DISCRIMINATION/ WGILMBV63970

   THE CHANGING PATTERNS OF WOMEN-S WORK. SOME PSYCHOLOGICAL CORRELATES.   WGINZEX58784

   PSYCHOLOGICAL PROBLEMS OF WOMEN IN DIFFERENT SOCIAL ROLES. /WORK-WOMAN-ROLE/   WJAHOMX55879

   INVESTIGATION OF DIFFERENCES IN OCCUPATIONAL PREFERENCES, STEREOTYPIC THINKING, AND PSYCHOLOGICAL NEEDS
   AMCNG UNDERGRADUATE WOMEN STUDENTS IN SELECTED CURRICULAR AREAS. /ASPIRATIONS/   WKITTRE60313

   PSYCHOLOGICAL AND SOCIOLOGICAL FACTORS IN PREDICTION OF CAREER PATTERNS OF WOMEN. /ASPIRATIONS/   WMULVMC61080

PSYCHOLOGICAL   (CONTINUATION)
  PSYCHOLOGICAL AND SOCIOLOGICAL FACTORS IN PREDICTION OF CAREER PATTERNS FOR WOMEN. /ASPIRATIONS/   WMULVMC63006

PSYCHOLOGIST
  THE INDUSTRIAL PSYCHOLOGIST. SELECTION AND EQUAL-EMPLOYMENT OPPORTUNITY.   GPARRJA66147

  WHAT THE INDUSTRIAL PSYCHOLOGIST MUST KNOW ABOUT TODAY-S AND TOMORROW-S WOMAN.   WPERLEX63100

PSYCHOLOGISTS
  GRADUATE EDUCATION OF NEGRO PSYCHOLOGISTS.   NRICHTW56057

PSYCHOLOGY
  THE PSYCHOLOGY OF THE NEGRO UNDER DISCRIMINATION.   NCAYTHR51187

  PSYCHOLOGY AND MANPOWER POLICY.   NGINZEX66412

  NOTES ON THE ROLE OF CHOICE IN THE PSYCHOLOGY OF PROFESSIONAL WOMEN. /OCCUPATIONS/   WBAILLX64623

  PSYCHOLOGY OF OCCUPATIONS.   WROEXAX56085

PSYCHOTHERAPISTS
  NONTRADITIONALLY TRAINED WOMEN AS MENTAL HEALTH COUNSELORS/PSYCHOTHERAPISTS.   WMAGOTM66779

PUBLIC
  TESTIMONY. PUBLIC HEARING, WOMEN IN PUBLIC AND PRIVATE EMPLOYMENT, CALIFORNIA. /MEXICAN-AMERICAN/   CARYWSX66621

  TESTIMONY. PUBLIC HEARING, WOMEN IN PUBLIC AND PRIVATE EMPLOYMENT, CALIFORNIA. /MEXICAN-AMERICAN/   CARYWSX66621

  AUTOMATION AND PUBLIC WELFARE.   GAMERPW64798

  WEAPONS AGAINST DISCRIMINATION IN PUBLIC OFFICE.   GAVINAX62411

  SOME PROBLEMS IN MINORITY-GROUP EDUCATION IN THE LOS-ANGELES PUBLIC SCHOOLS. /CALIFORNIA/   GBULLPX63489

  THE ELIMINATION OF POVERTY. A PRIMARY GOAL OF PUBLIC POLICY.   GCOHEWJ64925

  CIVIL-RIGHTS-ACT OF 1964, WITH EXPLANATION -- PUBLIC LAW 88-352 -- AS APPROVED BY THE PRESIDENT ON JULY
  2, 1964.   GCO4MCH64588

  PUBLIC WELFARE, AUTOMATION, AND EXPERIMENTAL MANPOWER PROGRAMS.   GCONFAP63545

  BACKGROUND FACTORS RELATING TO COLLEGE PLANS AND COLLEGE ENROLLMENT AMONG PUBLIC HIGH SCHOOL STUDENTS.
  /ASPIRATIONS/   GEDUCTS57959

  FAIR-EMPLOYMENT-PRACTICES IN THE PUBLIC SERVICE.   GFRIELL62701

  PUBLIC WELFARE. POVERTY -- PREVENTION OR PERPETUATION. A STUDY OF THE STATE DEPARTMENT OF PUBLIC
  ASSISTANCE OF THE STATE OF WASHINGTON.   GGREEAI64479

  PUBLIC WELFARE. POVERTY -- PREVENTION OR PERPETUATION. A STUDY OF THE STATE DEPARTMENT OF PUBLIC
  ASSISTANCE OF THE STATE OF WASHINGTON.   GGREEAI64479

  A PUBLIC EMPLOYMENT PROGRAM FOR THE UNEMPLOYED POOR.   GGREEAI65473

  AGGRESSIVE RECRUITMENT AND THE PUBLIC SERVICE.   GGREGGX61071

  EXPLANATION AND DIGEST OF THE 1966 KENTUCKY CIVIL-RIGHTS-ACT COVERING EMPLOYMENT AND PUBLIC
  ACCOMODATIONS, ENACTED JANUARY 27 1966, EFFECTIVE JULY 1 1966.   GKENTCHND844

  URBAN POVERTY AND PUBLIC POLICY.   GLONGNE64856

  PUBLIC POLICY, PRIVATE ENTERPRISE AND THE REDUCTION OF POVERTY.   GLONGNE65121

  MINORITY RIGHTS AND THE PUBLIC INTEREST.   GLUSKLX42924

  COMPILATION OF LAWS AGAINST DISCRIMINATION, EMPLOYMENT, EDUCATIONAL INSTITUTIONS, PLACES OF PUBLIC
  ACCOMODATION. PUBLIC HOUSING, PUBLICLY ASSISTED HOUSING, PRIVATE HOUSING. /MASSACHUSETTS/   GMASSCAND963

  COMPILATION OF LAWS AGAINST DISCRIMINATION, EMPLOYMENT, EDUCATIONAL INSTITUTIONS, PLACES OF PUBLIC
  ACCOMODATION. PUBLIC HOUSING, PUBLICLY ASSISTED HOUSING, PRIVATE HOUSING. /MASSACHUSETTS/   GMASSCAND963

  TECHNICAL REPORT NUMBER 2. EMPLOYMENT PRACTICES OF SELECTED MISSOURI PUBLIC UTILITIES. NATURAL GAS AND
  ELECTRIC.   GMILLRX66021

  PUBLIC POLICY AND UNEMPLOYMENT.   GOATEJF64542

  LAWS AGAINST DISCRIMINATION. EMPLOYMENT, PUBLIC ACCOMODATIONS, HOUSING. /OHIO/   GOHIOCR65125

  REPORT OF THE SPECIAL COMMITTEE ON NONDISCRIMINATION OF THE BOARD OF PUBLIC EDUCATION, PHILADELPHIA.
  /PENNSYLVANIA/   GPHILBE64172

  FINDINGS OF FACT, CONCLUSIONS AND ACTION OF THE COMMISSION ON HUMAN-RELATIONS IN RE. INVESTIGATIVE PUBLIC
  HEARINGS INTO ALLEGED DISCRIMINATORY PRACTICE BY THE HOTEL AND RESTAURANT INDUSTRY IN PHILADELPHIA.
  /PENNSYLVANIA/   GPHILCH61176

  TRAINING OF PUBLIC ASSISTANCE RECIPIENTS UNDER THE MDTA.   GROSORG66258

  PUBLIC WORK AND THE LONG-TERM UNEMPLOYED.   GROSSMS66844

  POVERTY AS A PUBLIC ISSUE.   GSELIBB65686

  EDUCATION AND INCOME. INEQUALITIES IN OUR PUBLIC SCHOOLS.   GSEXTPX61298

  PROJECTED CHANGES IN THE OCCUPATIONAL STRUCTURE OF THE LABOR-FORCE. IMPLICATIONS FOR PUBLIC WELFARE.   GSIFFHX64105

  SELECTED LIST OF REFERENCES ON MINORITY-GROUP EMPLOYMENT IN THE PUBLIC SERVICE.   GSIMPDX64312

  PUBLIC ASSISTANCE RECIPIENTS IN NEW-YORK STATE, JANUARY-FEBRUARY 1957.   GSNYDEM58114

  SUMMARY FACT SHEETS FOR STATE PUBLIC AGENCIES WITH JURISDICTION OVER DISCRIMINATION IN EMPLOYMENT.   GUSCCMC65416

  RECENT TRENDS IN PUBLIC EMPLOYMENT.   GUSCONMND419

  RECRUITING MINORITIES FOR PUBLIC EMPLOYMENT. EXPERIENCE REPORT 105.   GUSCONM66420

  LABOR AND THE PUBLIC INTEREST. /UNION/   GWIRTWW64572

  POVERTY AND THE CRITERIA FOR PUBLIC EXPENDITURES.   GWOLOHX65990

  INSURANCE. BANKING. PUBLIC UTILITIES. /DISCRIMINATION EMPLOYMENT/   JSIMOBX58763

  CHANGES IN PUBLIC AND PRIVATE LANGUAGE AMONG SPANISH-SPEAKING MIGRANTS TO AN INDUSTRIAL CITY.   MSCHETJ65481

  MEXICAN-AMERICANS IN URBAN PUBLIC HIGH SCHOOLS. AN EXPLORATION OF THE DROP-OUT PROGRAM.   MSHELPM59488

  RACIAL DESEGREGATION IN THE PUBLIC SERVICE, WITH PARTICULAR REFERENCE TO THE US GOVERNMENT.   NBROWVJ54127

  SOME PRACTICAL STUDIES IN PUBLIC TRANSPORTATION. /EMPLOYMENT-CONDITIONS WATTS LOS-ANGELES CALIFORNIA/ NCARLJX65593

  GRADUATE EDUCATION. PUBLIC SERVICE, AND THE NEGRO.   NCIKIWI66207

  SOCIAL AND ECONOMIC IMPLICATIONS OF INTEGRATING IN THE PUBLIC SCHOOLS.   NCLARKB65213

  US DEPARTMENT OF LABOR, PUBLIC HEARING, TESTIMONY. /MIGRANT-WORKERS/   NHILLHX63548

  A STUDY OF PROFESSIONAL PREPARATION OF NEGRO TEACHERS OF EXCEPTIONAL CHILDREN IN NORTH-CAROLINA COUNTY
  AND CITY PUBLIC SCHOOLS.   NKNIGOB65023

  WHAT SHOULD THE BUSINESS RESPONSE BE TO THE NEGRO REVOLUTION. A PUBLIC RELATIONS PROGRAM FOR DEALING WITH
  MINORITY-GROUPS.   NLANGJF65671

  THE EMPLOYMENT OF NEGROES IN PUBLIC WELFARE IN ELEVEN SOUTHERN STATES, 1936-1949. /OCCUPATIONS/   NLARKJR52672

  PROMOTING EQUAL-EMPLOYMENT THROUGH THE PUBLIC EMPLOYMENT SERVICE.   NLEVILX62686

  SURVEY OF EQUAL-EMPLOYMENT-OPPORTUNITIES IN NEW-JERSEY INVESTOR-OWNED PUBLIC UTILITIES.   NLEVIMJ66607

  UNION STRUCTURE AND PUBLIC POLICY. THE CONTROL OF UNION RACIAL PRACTICES.   NMARSRX63752

  DISCRIMINATION IN THE HIRING AND ASSIGNMENT OF NEGRO TEACHERS IN PUBLIC SCHOOL SYSTEMS.   NMICLRX66068

  ASPIRATION LEVELS OF NEGRO DELINQUENT, DEPENDENT, AND PUBLIC SCHOOL BOYS.   NMITCLE57804

  PUBLIC POLICY AND DISCRIMINATION IN APPRENTICESHIP.   NSTRAGX65182

  EQUAL PROTECTION OF THE LAWS IN PUBLIC HIGHER EDUCATION.   NUSCOMC60302

  PUBLIC EMPLOYMENT IN SAVANNAH, GEORGIA. EXPERIENCE REPORT 104.   NUSCONM66235

  SOME CHARACTERISTICS OF PUBLIC ASSISTANCE CASES IN NEW-YORK CITY, AUGUST, 1959.   PNEWYDW60835

  TESTIMONY. PUBLIC HEARING. WOMEN IN PUBLIC AND PRIVATE EMPLOYMENT, CALIFORNIA. /DISCRIMINATION EEOC/ WBALEHX66625

  TESTIMONY. PUBLIC HEARING. WOMEN IN PUBLIC AND PRIVATE EMPLOYMENT, CALIFORNIA. /DISCRIMINATION EEOC/ WBALEHX66625

  TESTIMONY. PUBLIC HEARING. WOMEN IN PUBLIC AND PRIVATE EMPLOYMENT, CALIFORNIA. /EMPLOYMENT-CONDITIONS/ WBECHCX66631

  TESTIMONY. PUBLIC HEARING. WOMEN IN PUBLIC AND PRIVATE EMPLOYMENT, CALIFORNIA. /EMPLOYMENT-CONDITIONS/ WBECHCX66631

  STATEMENT. PUBLIC HEARING. WOMEN IN PUBLIC AND PRIVATE EMPLOYMENT, CALIFORNIA. /FEP
  EMPLOYMENT-CONDITIONS DISCRIMINATION/   WBELAJX66634

  STATEMENT. PUBLIC HEARING. WOMEN IN PUBLIC AND PRIVATE EMPLOYMENT, CALIFORNIA. /FEP
  EMPLOYMENT-CONDITIONS DISCRIMINATION/   WBELAJX66634

  STATEMENT. PUBLIC HEARING. WOMEN IN PUBLIC AND PRIVATE EMPLOYMENT, CALIFORNIA. /FEP
  EMPLOYMENT-CONDITIONS DISCRIMINATION/   WBENNSJ66637

  STATEMENT. PUBLIC HEARING. WOMEN IN PUBLIC AND PRIVATE EMPLOYMENT, CALIFORNIA. /FEP
  EMPLOYMENT-CONDITIONS DISCRIMINATION/   WBENNSJ66637

  TESTIMONY. PUBLIC HEARING. WOMEN IN PUBLIC AND PRIVATE EDUCATION, CALIFORNIA. /FEP
  EMPLOYMENT-CONDITIONS DISCRIMINATION MIGRANT-WORKERS/   WBLOCHX66649

  TESTIMONY. PUBLIC HEARING. WOMEN IN PUBLIC AND PRIVATE EDUCATION, CALIFORNIA. /FEP
  EMPLOYMENT-CONDITIONS DISCRIMINATION MIGRANT-WORKERS/   WBLOCHX66649

  TESTIMONY. PUBLIC HEARING. WOMAN IN PUBLIC AND PRIVATE EMPLOYMENT, CALIFORNIA. /DISCRIMINATION/   WBROWAX66657

  TESTIMONY. PUBLIC HEARING. WOMAN IN PUBLIC AND PRIVATE EMPLOYMENT, CALIFORNIA. /DISCRIMINATION/   WBROWAX66657

  TESTIMONY PRESENTED AT PUBLIC HEARING, MARCH 31 -- APRIL 1, 1966. /FEP EMPLOYMENT-CONDITIONS
  DISCRIMINATION MIGRANTS/   WCALACW62675

  TESTIMONY PRESENTED AT PUBLIC HEARING, APRIL 28, 1966. SAN-FRANCISCO, CALIFORNIA. /FEP
  EMPLOYMENT-CONDITIONS DISCRIMINATION MIGRANTS/   WCALACW62676

  TESTIMONY PRESENTED AT PUBLIC HEARING, FEBRUARY 24-25, 1966. /FEP EMPLOYMENT-CONDITIONS DISCRIMINATION
  MIGRANTS/   WCALACW66674

  TESTIMONY PRESENTED AT PUBLIC HEARING, APRIL 29, 1966. SAN-FRANCISCO, CALIFORNIA. /FEP
  EMPLOYMENT-CONDITIONS CHILDREN/   WCALACW66677

  TESTIMONY. PUBLIC HEARING. WOMEN IN PUBLIC AND PRIVATE EMPLOYMENT, CALIFORNIA. /EMPLOYMENT-CONDITIONS/ WCHANHO66687

  TESTIMONY. PUBLIC HEARING. WOMEN IN PUBLIC AND PRIVATE EMPLOYMENT, CALIFORNIA. /EMPLOYMENT-CONDITIONS/ WCHANHO66687

  TESTIMONY. PUBLIC HEARING. WOMEN IN PUBLIC AND PRIVATE EMPLOYMENT, CALIFORNIA. /FEP
  EMPLOYMENT-CONDITIONS DISCRIMINATION MIGRANTS/   WCLIFFG66692

  TESTIMONY. PUBLIC HEARING. WOMEN IN PUBLIC AND PRIVATE EMPLOYMENT, CALIFORNIA. /FEP
  EMPLOYMENT-CONDITIONS DISCRIMINATION MIGRANTS/   WCLIFFG66692

  TESTIMONY. PUBLIC HEARING. WOMEN IN PUBLIC AND PRIVATE EMPLOYMENT, CALIFORNIA. /DISCRIMINATION/   WCOLLNX66696

  TESTIMONY. PUBLIC HEARING. WOMEN IN PUBLIC AND PRIVATE EMPLOYMENT, CALIFORNIA. /DISCRIMINATION/   WCOLLNX66696

  TESTIMONY. PUBLIC HEARING. WOMEN IN PUBLIC AND PRIVATE EMPLOYMENT, CALIFORNIA. /EMPLOYMENT-CONDITIONS/ WCOMPBX66702

  TESTIMONY. PUBLIC HEARING. WOMEN IN PUBLIC AND PRIVATE EMPLOYMENT, CALIFORNIA. /EMPLOYMENT-CONDITIONS/ WCOMPBX66702

  TESTIMONY. PUBLIC HEARING. WOMEN IN PUBLIC AND PRIVATE EMPLOYMENT, CALIFORNIA. /TRAINING/   WCUMMGX66711

  TESTIMONY. PUBLIC HEARING. WOMEN IN PUBLIC AND PRIVATE EMPLOYMENT, CALIFORNIA. /TRAINING/   WCUMMGX66711

  TESTIMONY. PUBLIC HEARING. WOMEN IN PUBLIC AND PRIVATE EMPLOYMENT, CALIFORNIA. /EMPLOYMENT-CONDITIONS/ WDIBRJX66732

TESTIMCNY, **PUBLIC** HEARING, WCMEN IN PUBLIC AND PRIVATE EMPLOYMENT, CALIFORNIA. /EMPLOYMENT-CONDITIONS/   WDIBRJX66732

TESTIMCNY, **PUBLIC** HEARING, WCMAN IN PUBLIC AND PRIVATE EMPLOYMENT, CALIFORNIA. /DISCRIMINATION/   WDORAMX66739

TESTIMONY, PUBLIC HEARING, WCMAN IN **PUBLIC** AND PRIVATE EMPLOYMENT, CALIFORNIA. /DISCRIMINATION/   WDORAMX66739

TESTIMCNY, **PUBLIC** HEARING, WCMEN IN PUBLIC AND PRIVATE EMPLOYMENT, CALIFCRNIA. /EMPLOYMENT-CONDITIONS/   WEVANSX66753

TESTIMCNY, PUBLIC HEARING, WCMEN IN **PUBLIC** AND PRIVATE EMPLOYMENT, CALIFORNIA. /EMPLOYMENT-CONDITIONS/   WEVANSX66753

TESTIMCNY, **PUBLIC** HEARING, WOMEN IN PUBLIC AND PRIVATE EMPLOYMENT, CALIFORNIA. /EMPLOYMENT-CONDITIONS/   WFEINBX66760

TESTIMCNY, PUBLIC HEARING, WCMEN IN **PUBLIC** AND PRIVATE EMPLOYMENT, CALIFORNIA. /EMPLOYMENT-CONDITIONS/   WFEINBX66760

TESTIMCNY, PUBLIC HEARING, WCMEN IN PUBLIC AND PRIVATE EMPLOYMENT, CALIFORNIA. /DISCRIMINATION/   WFOOTJX66765

TESTIMCNY, PUBLIC HEARING, WCMEN IN PUBLIC AND PRIVATE EMPLOYMENT, CALIFORNIA. /DISCRIMINATION/   WFOOTJX66765

TESTIMCNY, **PUBLIC** HEARING, WCMEN IN PUBLIC AND PRIVATE EMPLOYMENT, CALIFCRNIA. /EMPLOYMENT-CONDITIONS/   WGABELX66773

TESTIMCNY, PUBLIC HEARING, WCMEN IN PUBLIC AND PRIVATE EMPLOYMENT, CALIFORNIA. /EMPLOYMENT-CONDITIONS/   WGABELX66773

TESTIMCNY, **PUBLIC** HEARING, WCMEN IN PUBLIC AND PRIVATE EMPLOYMENT, CALIFCRNIA. /DISCRIMINATION/   WGEIGPX66776

TESTIMCNY, PUBLIC HEARING, WCMEN IN **PUBLIC** AND PRIVATE EMPLOYMENT, CALIFORNIA. /DISCRIMINATION/   WGEIGPX66776

TESTIMONY, PUBLIC HEARING, WCMEN IN PUBLIC AND PRIVATE EMPLOYMENT, CALIFORNIA. /DEMOGRAPHY/   WGERSMX66777

TESTIMCNY, PUBLIC HEARING, WCMEN IN PUBLIC AND PRIVATE EMPLOYMENT, CALIFORNIA. /DEMOGRAPHY/   WGERSMX66777

TESTIMCNY, PUBLIC HEARING, WCMEN IN PUBLIC AND PRIVATE EMPLOYMENT, CALIFORNIA. /EMPLOYMENT-CONDITIONS/   WGILBRX66780

TESTIMCNY, PUBLIC HEARING, WCMEN IN **PUBLIC** AND PRIVATE EMPLOYMENT, CALIFORNIA. /EMPLOYMENT-CONDITIONS/   WGILBRX66780

TESTIMCNY, PUBLIC HEARING, WCMEN IN PUBLIC AND PRIVATE EMPLOYMENT, CALIFORNIA. /EMPLOYMENT-CONDITIONS/   WGLENEM66788

TESTIMCNY, PUBLIC HEARING, WCMEN IN PUBLIC AND PRIVATE EMPLOYMENT, CALIFORNIA. /EMPLOYMENT-CONDITIONS/   WGLENEM66788

TESTIMCNY, **PUBLIC** HEARING, WCMEN IN PUBLIC AND PRIVATE EMPLOYMENT, CALIFORNIA. /DISCRIMINATION
WORK-FAMILY-CONFLICT/   WGUPTRC66808

TESTIMCNY, PUBLIC HEARING, WCMEN IN **PUBLIC** AND PRIVATE EMPLOYMENT, CALIFORNIA. /DISCRIMINATION
WORK-FAMILY-CONFLICT/   WGUPTRC66808

TESTIMCNY, **PUBLIC** HEARING, WCMEN IN PUBLIC AND PRIVATE EMPLOYMENT, CALIFORNIA. /EMPLOYMENT-CONDITIONS/   WGUPTRC66809

TESTIMCNY, PUBLIC HEARING, WOMEN IN **PUBLIC** AND PRIVATE EMPLOYMENT, CALIFORNIA. /EMPLOYMENT-CONDITIONS/   WGUPTRC66809

TESTIMCNY, **PUBLIC** HEARING, WCMEN IN PUBLIC AND PRIVATE EMPLOYMENT, CALIFORNIA. /EMPLOYMENT-CONDITIONS/   WHEALWX66836

TESTIMCNY, PUBLIC HEARING, WOMEN IN PUBLIC AND PRIVATE EMPLOYMENT, CALIFORNIA. /EMPLOYMENT-CONDITIONS/   WHEALWX66836

TESTIMCNY, PUBLIC HEARING, WCMEN IN **PUBLIC** AND PRIVATE EMPLOYMENT, CALIFORNIA. /DISCRIMINATION/   WHILLHX66844

TESTIMCNY, **PUBLIC** HEARING, WCMEN IN PUBLIC AND PRIVATE EMPLOYMENT, CALIFORNIA. /DISCRIMINATION/   WHILLHX66844

TESTIMCNY, PUBLIC HEARING, WCMEN IN PUBLIC AND PRIVATE EMPLOYMENT, CALIFORNIA. /MDTA EEO/   WINGRLX66859

TESTIMCNY, PUBLIC HEARING, WCMEN IN **PUBLIC** AND PRIVATE EMPLOYMENT, CALIFCRNIA. /MDTA EEO/   WINGRLX66859

STATEMENT, **PUBLIC** HEARING, WCMEN IN PUBLIC AND PRIVATE EMPLOYMENT, CALIFORNIA. /EMPLOYMENT-CONDITIONS
MIGRANT-WORKERS/   WKAUFDX66886

STATEMENT, PUBLIC HEARING, WCMEN IN **PUBLIC** AND PRIVATE EMPLOYMENT, CALIFORNIA. /EMPLOYMENT-CONDITIONS
MIGRANT-WORKERS/   WKAUFDX66886

TESTIMCNY, PUBLIC HEARING, WOMEN IN PUBLIC AND PRIVATE EMPLOYMENT, CALIFORNIA. /EMPLOYMENT-CONDITIONS/   WKELLET66888

TESTIMCNY, PUBLIC HEARING, WCMEN IN **PUBLIC** AND PRIVATE EMPLOYMENT, CALIFORNIA. /EMPLOYMENT-CONDITIONS/   WKELLET66888

STATEMENT, **PUBLIC** HEARING, WCMEN IN PUBLIC AND PRIVATE EMPLOYMENT, CALIFORNIA. /EMPLOYMENT-CONDITIONS/   WKENNVX66890

STATEMENT, PUBLIC HEARING, WCMEN IN PUBLIC AND PRIVATE EMPLOYMENT, CALIFORNIA. /EMPLOYMENT-CONDITIONS/   WKENNVX66890

STATEMENT, **PUBLIC** HEARING, WCMEN IN PUBLIC AND PRIVATE EMPLOYMENT, CALIFCRNIA. /EMPLOYMENT-CONDITIONS/   WKNIGTF66911

STATEMENT, PUBLIC HEARING, WCMEN IN **PUBLIC** AND PRIVATE EMPLOYMENT, CALIFORNIA. /EMPLOYMENT-CONDITIONS/   WKNIGTF66911

THE FEMALE PHYSICIAN IN **PUBLIC** HEALTH. CONFLICT AND RECONCILIATION OF THE SEX AND PROFESSIONAL ROLES.
/OCCUPATIONS/   WKOSAJX64915

TESTIMCNY, **PUBLIC** HEARING, WCMEN IN PUBLIC AND PRIVATE EMPLOYMENT, CALIFORNIA. /FEP MIGRANT-WORKERS
EMPLCYMENT-CONDITIONS/   WLLOYMX66940

TESTIMCNY, PUBLIC HEARING, WCMEN IN **PUBLIC** AND PRIVATE EMPLOYMENT, CALIFORNIA. /FEP MIGRANT-WORKERS
EMPLCYMENT-CONDITIONS/   WLLOYMX66940

TESTIMCNY, **PUBLIC** HEARING, WOMEN IN PUBLIC AND PRIVATE EMPLOYMENT, CALIFORNIA. /FEP EMPLOYMENT
CCNDITIONS/   WLOWEDX66943

TESTIMCNY, PUBLIC HEARING, WCMEN IN **PUBLIC** AND PRIVATE EMPLOYMENT, CALIFORNIA. /FEP EMPLOYMENT
CCNDITIONS/   WLOWEDX66943

TESTIMCNY, **PUBLIC** HEARING, WCMEN IN PUBLIC AND PRIVATE EMPLOYMENT, CALIFORNIA. /EMPLOYMENT-CONDITIONS/   WMACKJW66950

TESTIMCNY, PUBLIC HEARING, WCMEN IN **PUBLIC** AND PRIVATE EMPLOYMENT, CALIFORNIA. /EMPLOYMENT-CONDITIONS/   WMACKJW66950

TESTIMCNY, **PUBLIC** HEARING, WCMEN IN PUBLIC AND PRIVATE EMPLOYMENT, CALIFORNIA. /OCCUPATIONS
EMPLOYMENT-CONDITIONS/   WMCLALX66947

TESTIMCNY, PUBLIC HEARING, WCMEN IN **PUBLIC** AND PRIVATE EMPLOYMENT, CALIFORNIA. /OCCUPATIONS
EMPLCYMENT-CONDITIONS/   WMCLALX66947

TESTIMCNY, **PUBLIC** HEARING, WCMEN IN PUBLIC AND PRIVATE EMPLOYMENT, CALIFORNIA. /BLUE-COLLAR
EMPLOYMENT-CONDITIONS/   WMENGVX66969

TESTIMCNY, PUBLIC HEARING, WCMEN IN **PUBLIC** AND PRIVATE EMPLOYMENT, CALIFORNIA. /BLUE-COLLAR

PUBLIC   (CONTINUATION)
EMPLOYMENT-CONDITIONS/   WMENGVX66969

    STATEMENT, **PUBLIC** HEARING, WOMEN IN PUBLIC AND PRIVATE EMPLOYMENT, CALIFORNIA. /FEP
    EMPLOYMENT-CONDITIONS MIGRANT-WORKERS/   WMILLJJ66979

    STATEMENT, PUBLIC HEARING, WOMEN IN **PUBLIC** AND PRIVATE EMPLOYMENT, CALIFORNIA. /FEP
    EMPLOYMENT-CONDITIONS MIGRANT-WORKERS/   WMILLJJ66979

    TESTIMONY, **PUBLIC** HEARING, WOMEN IN PUBLIC AND PRIVATE EMPLOYMENT, CALIFORNIA. /EMPLOYMENT-CONDITIONS/   WMILLKL66980

    TESTIMONY, PUBLIC HEARING, WOMEN IN **PUBLIC** AND PRIVATE EMPLOYMENT, CALIFORNIA. /EMPLOYMENT-CONDITIONS/   WMILLKL66980

    TESTIMONY, **PUBLIC** HEARING, WOMEN IN PUBLIC AND PRIVATE EMPLOYMENT, CALIFORNIA. /EMPLOYMENT-CONDITIONS/   WMORAMX66995

    TESTIMONY, PUBLIC HEARING, WOMEN IN **PUBLIC** AND PRIVATE EMPLOYMENT, CALIFORNIA. /EMPLOYMENT-CONDITIONS/   WMORAMX66995

    TESTIMONY, **PUBLIC** HEARING, WOMEN IN PUBLIC AND PRIVATE EMPLOYMENT, CALIFORNIA.   WMOTHWA66001

    TESTIMONY, **PUBLIC** HEARING, WOMEN IN PUBLIC AND PRIVATE EMPLOYMENT, CALIFORNIA.   WMOTHWA66001

    TESTIMONY, **PUBLIC** HEARING, WOMEN IN PUBLIC AND PRIVATE EMPLOYMENT, CALIFORNIA. /EMPLOYMENT-CONDITIONS/   WMYRIRX66013

    TESTIMONY, PUBLIC HEARING, WOMEN IN **PUBLIC** AND PRIVATE EMPLOYMENT, CALIFORNIA. /EMPLOYMENT-CONDITIONS/   WMYRIRX66013

    TESTIMONY, PUBLIC HEARING, WOMEN IN **PUBLIC** AND PRIVATE EMPLOYMENT, CALIFORNIA. /EMPLOYMENT-CONDITIONS/   WPALMGX66047

    TESTIMONY, PUBLIC HEARING, WOMEN IN **PUBLIC** AND PRIVATE EMPLOYMENT, CALIFORNIA. /EMPLOYMENT-CONDITIONS/   WPALMGX66047

    TESTIMONY, **PUBLIC** HEARING, WOMEN IN PUBLIC AND PRIVATE EMPLOYMENT, CALIFORNIA. /FEP
    EMPLOYMENT-CONDITIONS MIGRANT-WORKERS/   WPEEVMX66052

    TESTIMONY, PUBLIC HEARING, WOMEN IN **PUBLIC** AND PRIVATE EMPLOYMENT, CALIFORNIA. /FEP
    EMPLOYMENT-CONDITIONS MIGRANT-WORKERS/   WPEEVMX66052

    TESTIMONY, **PUBLIC** HEARING, WOMEN IN PUBLIC AND PRIVATE EMPLOYMENT, CALIFORNIA. /EMPLOYMENT-CONDITIONS/   WRILEEX66081

    TESTIMONY, PUBLIC HEARING, WOMEN IN **PUBLIC** AND PRIVATE EMPLOYMENT, CALIFORNIA. /EMPLOYMENT-CONDITIONS/   WRILEEX66081

    TESTIMONY, **PUBLIC** HEARING, WOMEN IN PUBLIC AND PRIVATE EMPLOYMENT, CALIFORNIA. /FEP
    EMPLOYMENT-CONDITIONS/   WSCHRPX66104

    TESTIMONY, PUBLIC HEARING, WOMEN IN **PUBLIC** AND PRIVATE EMPLOYMENT, CALIFORNIA. /FEP
    EMPLOYMENT-CONDITIONS/   WSCHRPX66104

    TESTIMONY, PUBLIC HEARING, WOMEN IN **PUBLIC** AND PRIVATE EMPLOYMENT, CALIFORNIA. /EMPLOYMENT-CONDITIONS/   WSHEAHX66112

    TESTIMONY, PUBLIC HEARING, WOMEN IN **PUBLIC** AND PRIVATE EMPLOYMENT, CALIFORNIA. /EMPLOYMENT-CONDITIONS/   WSHEAHX66112

    TESTIMONY, **PUBLIC** HEARING, WOMEN IN PUBLIC AND PRIVATE EMPLOYMENT, CALIFORNIA. /FEP
    EMPLOYMENT-CONDITIONS DISCRIMINATION/   WSMITWH66123

    TESTIMONY, PUBLIC HEARING, WOMEN IN **PUBLIC** AND PRIVATE EMPLOYMENT, CALIFORNIA. /FEP
    EMPLOYMENT-CONDITIONS DISCRIMINATION/   WSMITWH66123

    TESTIMONY, **PUBLIC** HEARING, WOMEN IN PUBLIC AND PRIVATE EMPLOYMENT, CALIFORNIA. /FEP
    EMPLOYMENT-CONDITIONS DISCRIMINATION MIGRANT-WORKERS/   WSPENNX66129

    TESTIMONY, PUBLIC HEARING, WOMEN IN **PUBLIC** AND PRIVATE EMPLOYMENT, CALIFORNIA. /FEP
    EMPLOYMENT-CONDITIONS DISCRIMINATION MIGRANT-WORKERS/   WSPENNX66129

    TESTIMONY, **PUBLIC** HEARING, WOMEN IN PUBLIC AND PRIVATE EMPLOYMENT, CALIFORNIA. /LABOR-MARKET/   WSTEPRX66138

    TESTIMONY, PUBLIC HEARING, WOMEN IN **PUBLIC** AND PRIVATE EMPLOYMENT, CALIFORNIA. /LABOR-MARKET/   WSTEPRX66138

    TESTIMONY, **PUBLIC** HEARING, WOMEN IN PUBLIC AND PRIVATE EMPLOYMENT, CALIFORNIA. /FEPC/   WSTERAX66140

    TESTIMONY, PUBLIC HEARING, WOMEN IN **PUBLIC** AND PRIVATE EMPLOYMENT, CALIFORNIA. /FEPC/   WSTERAX66140

    BACKGROUND FACTORS AND COLLEGE GOING PLANS AMONG HIGH APTITUDE **PUBLIC** HIGH SCHOOL SENIORS. /ASPIRATIONS/   WSTICGX56141

    TESTIMONY, **PUBLIC** HEARING, WOMEN IN PUBLIC AND PRIVATE EMPLOYMENT, CALIFORNIA. /EMPLOYMENT-CONDITIONS/   WTHOMDX66151

    TESTIMONY, PUBLIC HEARING, WOMEN IN **PUBLIC** AND PRIVATE EMPLOYMENT, CALIFORNIA. /EMPLOYMENT-CONDITIONS/   WTHOMDX66151

    TESTIMONY, **PUBLIC** HEARING, WOMEN IN PUBLIC AND PRIVATE EMPLOYMENT, CALIFORNIA. /EMPLOYMENT-CONDITIONS
    DISCRIMINATION/   WTHOMGX66149

    TESTIMONY, PUBLIC HEARING, WOMEN IN **PUBLIC** AND PRIVATE EMPLOYMENT, CALIFORNIA. /EMPLOYMENT-CONDITIONS
    DISCRIMINATION/   WTHOMGX66149

    STATEMENT, **PUBLIC** HEARING, WOMEN IN PUBLIC AND PRIVATE EMPLOYMENT, CALIFORNIA. /FEP
    EMPLOYMENT-CONDITIONS DISCRIMINATION/   WVAILLX66256

    STATEMENT, PUBLIC HEARING, WOMEN IN **PUBLIC** AND PRIVATE EMPLOYMENT, CALIFORNIA. /FEP
    EMPLOYMENT-CONDITIONS DISCRIMINATION/   WVAILLX66256

    TESTIMONY, **PUBLIC** HEARING, WOMEN IN PUBLIC AND PRIVATE EMPLOYMENT, CALIFORNIA. /EMPLOYMENT-CONDITIONS
    MIGRANT-WORKERS/   WWEBEJX66258

    TESTIMONY, PUBLIC HEARING, WOMEN IN **PUBLIC** AND PRIVATE EMPLOYMENT, CALIFORNIA. /EMPLOYMENT-CONDITIONS
    MIGRANT-WORKERS/   WWEBEJX66258

    TESTIMONY, **PUBLIC** HEARING, WOMEN IN PUBLIC AND PRIVATE EMPLOYMENT, CALIFORNIA. /FEP
    EMPLOYMENT-CONDITIONS MIGRANT-WORKERS/   WWOMEIX66273

    TESTIMONY, PUBLIC HEARING, WOMEN IN **PUBLIC** AND PRIVATE EMPLOYMENT, CALIFORNIA. /FEP
    EMPLOYMENT-CONDITIONS MIGRANT-WORKERS/   WWOMEIX66273

    TESTIMONY, **PUBLIC** HEARING, WOMEN IN PUBLIC AND PRIVATE EMPLOYMENT, CALIFORNIA. /EMPLOYMENT-CONDITIONS/   WWOODWX66276

    TESTIMONY, PUBLIC HEARING, WOMEN IN **PUBLIC** AND PRIVATE EMPLOYMENT, CALIFORNIA. /EMPLOYMENT-CONDITIONS/   WWOODWX66276

PUBLIC-EMPLOYMENT
AUDIT OF NEGRO VETERANS AND SERVICEMEN, 1960. /PUBLIC-EMPLOYMENT/   NAMERVC60019

    TRENDS IN **PUBLIC-EMPLOYMENT**.   NKRUGDH61667

PUBLIC-SERVICE
AN HISTORICAL SURVEY AND ANALYSIS OF THE PROGRESS OF NEGROES IN **PUBLIC-SERVICE** 1932-1952.   NOLIVLW56955

PUEBLO
THE SOCIO-ECONOMIC AND PHYSICAL CHARACTERISTICS OF THE VARIOUS NEIGHBORHOODS IN **PUEBLO**. /COLORADO/   GPUEBRP65459

PUERTO-RICAN
IMPLICATIONS OF THE STUDIES. /DISCRIMINATION LOW-INCOME NEGRO **PUERTO-RICAN** POLICY-RECOMMENDATIONS/   CABRACX59001

THE ECONOMY AND THE MINORITY POOR. /NEGRO AMERICAN-INDIAN MEXICAN-AMERICAN **PUERTO-RICAN**/   CBATCAB66879

SPANISH-SPEAKING CHILDREN. /MEXICAN-AMERICAN **PUERTO-RICAN** EDUCATION/   CBURMJH60287

THE PUSH OF AN ELBOW. CIVIL-RIGHTS AND OUR SPANISH-SPEAKING MINORITY. /MEXICAN-AMERICAN **PUERTO-RICAN**/   CBURMJH60371

THE DISCRIMINATION CASE. /NEGRO **PUERTO-RICAN** SES/   CCOHEHX65917

ADDRESS TO COMMUNITY RELATIONS SERVICE STAFF TRAINING SESSION, JANUARY 12, 1967, ON JOBS NOW. /NEGRO **PUERTO-RICAN** YOUTH/   CCOLEBX67918

ECONOMIC, SOCIAL, AND DEMOGRAPHIC CHARACTERISTICS OF SPANISH-AMERICAN WAGE WORKERS ON US FARMS. /**PUERTO-RICAN** MEXICAN-AMERICAN/   CFRIERE63805

THE NATION-S CHILDREN. VOL I. THE FAMILY AND SOCIAL-CHANGE. VOL II. DEVELOPMENT AND EDUCATION. VOL III. PROBLEMS AND PROSPECTS. /NEGRO **PUERTO-RICAN** MEXICAN-AMERICAN WOMEN/   CGINZEX60720

FACTORS AFFECTING EDUCATIONAL-ATTAINMENT IN DEPRESSED URBAN AREAS. /NEGRO **PUERTO-RICAN**/   CGOLDML63426

RECENT TRENDS IN THE STUDY OF MINORITY AND RACE-RELATIONS. /NEGRO **PUERTO-RICAN** ORIENTAL/   CGORDMM63977

UNDER-ACHIEVEMENT AMONG MINORITY-GROUP STUDENTS. AN ANALYSIS AND A PROPOSAL. /YOUTH NEGRO MEXICAN-AMERICAN **PUERTO-RICAN**/   CHOBACW63555

DEVELOPING NEW-YORK CITY-S HUMAN RESOURCES. VOL 1. /NEGRO **PUERTO-RICAN**/   CINSTOP66034

THE FORGOTTEN PEOPLE. /MIGRANT-WORKERS MEXICAN-AMERICAN **PUERTO-RICAN** NEGRO/   CJACOPX59600

CHANGING PATTERNS OF PREJUDICE. /NEGRO **PUERTO-RICAN** ORIENTAL AMERICAN-INDIAN/   CMARRAJ62055

AN EXPERIMENT TO TEST THREE MAJOR ISSUES OF WORK PROGRAM METHODOLOGY WITHIN MOBILIZATION-FOR-YOUTH-S INTEGRATED SERVICES TO OUT-OF-SCHOOL UNEMPLOYED YOUTH. /NEGRO **PUERTO-RICAN**/   CMOBIFY66024

BUREAU OF MIGRANT-LABOR REPORT. /NEW-JERSEY NEGRO **PUERTO-RICAN**/   CNEWJOL61907

INTERIM REPORT TO THE MAYOR ON ITS INQUIRY INTO CHARGES OF RACIAL BIAS IN THE CITY BUILDING AND CONSTRUCTION INDUSTRY. /NEW-YORK NEGRO **PUERTO-RICAN**/   CNEWYCO64917

THE SCHOOL DROPOUT PROBLEM IN MAJOR CITIES OF NEW-YORK STATE. ROCHESTER -- PART I. /NEGRO **PUERTO-RICAN**/   CNEWYSD62090

BREAKING THE BARRIERS OF OCCUPATIONAL ISOLATION. A REPORT ON UPGRADING LOW-SKILL, LOW-WAGE WORKERS. /NEGRO **PUERTO-RICAN**/   CPROJAX66237

THE SPANISH-SPEAKING PEOPLE IN THE UNITED STATES. /**PUERTO-RICAN** MEXICAN-AMERICAN/   CRUBIEBND848

SIGNIFICANT TRENDS IN THE NEW-YORK STATE ECONOMY, WITH SPECIAL REFERENCE TO MINORITY-GROUPS. /**PUERTO-RICAN** NEGRO/   CRUSSVR59482

SPANISH-SPEAKING PEOPLE IN THE UNITED STATES. A PILOT REPORT. /MEXICAN-AMERICAN **PUERTO-RICAN**/   CSAMOJX63474

THE ENDURING SLUMS. /NEGRO **PUERTO-RICAN**/   CSELIOX57034

SELECTED BIBLIOGRAPHY FOR DISADVANTAGED YOUTH. /NEGRO **PUERTO-RICAN**/   CUSDHEWND855

POVERTY IN THE UNITED STATES, HEARINGS. /AMERICAN-INDIAN NEGRO **PUERTO-RICAN** EMPLOYMENT/   CUSHOUR64346

THE INTEGRATION OF AMERICANS OF MEXICAN, **PUERTO-RICAN**, AND ORIENTAL DESCENT.   CYINGJM56519

FINAL REPORT OF THE YMCA YOUTH AND WORK PROJECT 1962-1966. /NEGRO **PUERTO-RICAN** TRAINING/   CYMCAYA66329

PUERTO-RICAN FARM WORKERS IN NEW-JERSEY.   PAINERO59777

80 **PUERTO-RICAN** FAMILIES IN NEW-YORK CITY.   PBERLBB58780

THE **PUERTO-RICAN** COMMUNITY IN AMERICA. RAPID ACCULTURATION.   PBOWALX62889

THE LOWER STATUS **PUERTO-RICAN** FAMILY.   PBRAMJX62783

SCHOOL AND COMMUNITY COURSE. THE LOWER STATUS **PUERTO-RICAN** FAMILY.   PBRAMJX63784

THE **PUERTO-RICAN** WORKER CONFRONTS THE COMPLEX URBAN SOCIETY -- A PRESCRIPTION FOR CHANGE.   PCARDLA67874

NEW ASPECTS OF **PUERTO-RICAN** MIGRATION.   PCARLRC59785

THE FIRST 10 YEARS...THE **PUERTO-RICAN** MIGRATORY PROBLEM.   PCASTCX58786

A **PUERTO-RICAN** IN NEW-YORK.   PDIAZEX61795

THE IMPACT OF **PUERTO-RICAN** MIGRATION ON GOVERNMENTAL SERVICES IN NEW-YORK CITY.   PDWORMB57797

SOME ECONOMIC ASPECTS OF **PUERTO-RICAN** MIGRATION TO THE UNITED STATES.   PFLEIBM61804

THE IMPACT OF **PUERTO-RICAN** MIGRATION TO THE UNITED STATES. /EMPLOYMENT/   PFLEIBM63437

SOME ECONOMIC ASPECTS OF **PUERTO-RICAN** MIGRATION TO THE UNITED STATES.   PFLEIBM63803

IMPLICATIONS OF **PUERTO-RICAN** MIGRATION TO THE CONTINENT OUTSIDE NEW-YORK CITY.   PGERNAC56808

THE **PUERTO-RICAN** WORKER IN PERTH-AMBOY, NEW-JERSEY.   PGOLUFT56811

SOME ECONOMIC CONSEQUENCES OF THE **PUERTO-RICAN** MIGRATION INTO PERTH-AMBOY, 1949-1954. /NEW-JERSEY/   PGOLUFX55812

PUERTO-RICAN LEADERSHIP IN NEW-YORK.   PGOTSJW66808

LABOR UNIONS AND **PUERTO-RICAN** MEMBERS IN NEW-YORK CITY.   PGRAYLX63027

THE **PUERTO-RICAN** WORKERS IN NEW-YORK.   PGRAYLX63813

PUERTO-RICAN INTEGRATION IN THE SKIRT INDUSTRY IN NEW-YORK CITY.   PHELFBH59481

PUERTO-RICAN INTEGRATION IN A GARMENT UNION LOCAL.   PHELFRB57815

THE **PUERTO-RICAN** SECTION. A STUDY IN SOCIAL TRANSITION.   PHERNJX59816

PUERTO-RICAN   (CONTINUATION)
  NEW-YORK-S LABOR SCANDAL. THE PUERTO-RICAN WORKERS.   PLEVIMX57823

  LA VIDA. A PUERTO-RICAN FAMILY IN THE CULTURE OF POVERTY -- SAN-JUAN AND NEW-YORK.   PLEWIOX66825

  BIBLIOGRAPHY ON THE PUERTO-RICAN. HIS CULTURE AND SOCIETY.   PMOBIFYND024

  CULTURAL VALUES AND THE PUERTO-RICAN.   PMONSJX57828

  MEETING THE NEEDS OF THE PUERTO-RICAN MIGRANT.   PMONTHK59829

  PLACING PUERTO-RICAN WORKERS IN THE NEW-YORK CITY LABOR-MARKET.   PMONTHX60830

  RESOURCE UNITS IN THE TEACHING OF OCCUPATIONS -- AN EXPERIMENT IN GUIDANCE OF PUERTO-RICAN TEENAGERS.   PNEWYCC56834

  THE PUERTO-RICAN STUDY, 1953-1957.   PNEWYCC58833

  PUERTO-RICAN PROFILES.   PNEWYCC64832

  POPULATIONS OF NEW-YORK STATE. REPORT NO 2. THE PUERTO-RICAN POPULATION OF THE NEW-YORK-CITY AREA.   PNEWYCO62838

  COMPLAINTS ALLEGING DISCRIMINATION BECAUSE OF PUERTO-RICAN NATIONAL ORIGIN, JULY 1, 1945-SEPTEMBER 1,
  1958.   PNEWYSA58836

  PUERTO-RICAN EMPLOYMENT IN NEW-YORK CITY HOTELS. /OCCUPATIONS/   PNEWYSA58837

  PUERTO-RICAN CULTURE.   PORTIRX62841

  PHILADELPHIA-S PUERTO-RICAN POPULATION, WITH 1960 CENSUS DATA. /PENNSYLVANIA/   PPITTCH64844

  THE PUERTO-RICAN NEWCOMER.   PPUERRD60790

  AN ANALYSIS OF UNEMPLOYED PUERTO-RICAN MIGRANTS IN NEW-YORK CITY.   PREMEGN58847

  PATTERNS OF SOCIAL ACCOMODATION OF THE MIGRANT PUERTO-RICAN IN THE AMERICAN SOCIAL STRUCTURE.   PSEDAEX58850

  OCCUPATIONAL PLANS AND ASPIRATIONS. PUERTO-RICAN AND AMERICAN HIGH SCHOOL SENIORS COMPARED.   PSILVRM63100

  THREE BASIC THEMES IN MEXICAN AND PUERTO-RICAN FAMILIES.   PTRENRD58800

  PUERTO-RICANS IN THE UNITED STATES. SOCIAL AND ECONOMIC DATA FOR PERSONS OF PUERTO-RICAN BIRTH AND
  PARENTAGE. /DEMOGRAPHY/   PUSBURC63182

PUERTO-RICANS
  SPANISH-SPEAKING AMERICANS. MEXICANS AND PUERTO-RICANS IN THE UNITED STATES.   CBLAIBX59366

  THE NEWCOMERS. NEGROES AND PUERTO-RICANS IN A CHANGING METROPOLIS   CHANDOX59481

  ETHNIC SURVEY OF MUNICIPAL-EMPLOYEES. A REPORT ON THE NUMBER AND DISTRIBUTION OF NEGROES AND
  PUERTO-RICANS AND OTHER EMPLOYEES BY THE CITY OF NEW-YORK.   CNEWYCO64916

  A SURVEY OF NEW-HAVEN-S NEWCOMERS. THE PUERTO-RICANS. /CONNECTICUT/   PDONCOX59796

  THE PUERTO-RICANS IN NEW-YORK.   PEAGLMX59303

  THE PUERTO-RICANS.   PELMARM66677

  THE INTEGRATION OF PUERTO-RICANS.   PFITZJP55802

  THE ADJUSTMENT OF PUERTO-RICANS IN NEW-YORK-CITY.   PFITZJP59801

  DISCRIMINATION AGAINST PUERTO-RICANS.   PGARCAX58806

  NEW-YORK-S PUERTO-RICANS.   PGLAZNX58211

  THE PUERTO-RICANS.   PGLAZNX63809

  PUERTO-RICANS IN NEW-YORK.   PILLIIX56818

  SUPPLEMENTARY REPORT ON PUERTO-RICANS IN BUFFALO. /NEW-YORK/   PIMSETP62820

  PUERTO-RICANS IN PHILADELPHIA. MIGRATION AND ACCOMODATION. /PENNSYLVANIA/   PKOSSJD65822

  PUERTO-RICANS IN PHILADELPHIA. /PENNSYLVANIA/   PMETARX59826

  PUERTO-RICANS, KEY SOURCE OF LABOR.   PNEWYDC56817

  PUERTO-RICANS IN THE NEW-YORK STATE LABOR-MARKET.   PNEWYSE57840

  CHARACTERISTICS OF POPULATION AND LABOR IN NEW-YORK STATE, 1956 AND 1957. PUERTO-RICANS IN NEW-YORK CITY. PNEWYSE60839

  HELPING PUERTO-RICANS HELP THEMSELVES.   PPUERRD58787

  THE PUERTO-RICANS.   PRANDCX58845

  A COMPARISON OF THE OCCUPATIONS OF THE FIRST AND SECOND GENERATION PUERTO-RICANS IN THE MAINLAND
  LABOR-MARKET. AND HOW THE WORK OF THE NEW-YORK STATE DEPARTMENT OF LABORFFECTS PUERTO-RICANS.   PRAUSCX61846

  A COMPARISON OF THE OCCUPATIONS OF THE FIRST AND SECOND GENERATION PUERTO-RICANS IN THE MAINLAND
  LABOR-MARKET. AND HOW THE WORK OF THE NEW-YORK STATE DEPARTMENT OF LABORFFECTS PUERTO-RICANS.   PRAUSCX61846

  THE PUERTO-RICANS IN THE UNITED STATES.   PSENICX56852

  STRANGERS THEN NEIGHBORS. FROM PILGRIMS TO PUERTO-RICANS.   PSENICX61308

  THE PUERTO-RICANS, STRANGERS -- THEN NEIGHBORS.   PSENICX65307

  PUERTO-RICANS IN THE UNITED STATES. SOCIAL AND ECONOMIC DATA FOR PERSONS OF PUERTO-RICAN BIRTH AND
  PARENTAGE. /DEMOGRAPHY/   PUSBURC63182

  CENSUS OF POPULATION. 1960. PUERTO-RICANS IN THE UNITED STATES.   PUSBURC63854

PUERTO-RICO
  UP FROM PUERTO-RICO.   PPADIEX58842

  HOW TO HIRE AGRICULTURAL WORKERS FROM PUERTO-RICO.   PPUERRDND788

  REPORTS OF PUERTO-RICO DEPARTMENT OF LABOR. MIGRATION DIVISION ON PLACEMENT.   PPUERRDND791

PURDUE
A STUDY OF THE LIFE PLANNING OF 550 FRESHMEN WOMEN AT **PURDUE** UNIVERSITY. /WORK-FAMILY-CONFLICT/   WZISSCX64285

PUSH-BUTTON
PUSH-BUTTON LABOR. /TECHNOLOGICAL-CHANGE UNEMPLOYMENT/   GFORTXX54047

QED
QED. /WORK-WOMEN-ROLE/   WDOLAEF64736

QUALIFICATIONS
TITLE-VII. LIMITATIONS AND **QUALIFICATIONS**. /LEGISLATION/   GRACHCX66214

AT WORK IN NORTH-CAROLINA TODAY. 48 CASE-REPORTS ON NORTH-CAROLINA NEGROES NOW EMPLOYED OR PREPARING
THEMSELVES FOR EMPLOYMENT...THEIR EDUCATION, JOB **QUALIFICATIONS**, AND CAREER ASPIRATIONS.   NNORTCGND933

QUALIFIED
EMERGING OPPORTUNITIES FOR **QUALIFIED** WOMEN. /OCCUPATIONS/   WMILLRX66982

QUALITY
NON-SEGREGATION, OR **QUALITY** IN SCHOOLS OF THE DEEP SOUTH. /ECONOMIC-STATUS/   NBRITNX54892

QUANTIFIED
OBJECTIVE ACCESS IN THE OPPORTUNITY STRUCTURE. THE ASSESSMENT OF THREE ETHNIC GROUPS WITH RESPECT TO
QUANTIFIED SOCIAL STRUCTURAL VARIABLES.   MRENDGX63461

QUANTITATIVE
UNEMPLOYMENT IN THE UNITED STATES. **QUANTITATIVE** DIMENSIONS.   GBOWEWG65464

A **QUANTITATIVE** ANALYSIS OF WHITE-NONWHITE INCOME DIFFERENTIALS IN THE US IN 1939.   GZEMAMX55594

HIDDEN UNEMPLOYMENT 1953-62. A **QUANTITATIVE** ANALYSIS BY AGE AND SEX.   NDERNTX66264

QUEENS
INCOME, EDUCATION AND UNEMPLOYMENT IN NEIGHBORHOODS. NEW-YORK-CITY -- **QUEENS**. /DEMOGRAPHY/   CUSDLAB63474

QUERIES
QUERIES CONCERNING INDUSTRY AND SOCIETY GROWING OUT OF STUDY OF ETHNIC RELATIONS IN INDUSTRY.   GHUGHEC59787

QUESTIONING
QUESTIONING APPLICANTS FOR EMPLOYMENT, A GUIDE FOR APPLICATION FORMS AND INTERVIEWS UNDER THE HAWAII
FAIR-EMPLOYMENT-PRACTICES ACT.   GHAWADL64767

QUESTIONNAIRE
SELF-ANALYSIS **QUESTIONNAIRE**. /EEO INDUSTRY/   GPRESCD63115

A **QUESTIONNAIRE** PORTRAIT OF THE FRESHMAN COED. AFTER COLLEGE WHAT. /ASPIRATIONS/   WLLOYBJ66938

QUESTIONS
QUESTIONS AND ANSWERS ABOUT EMPLOYMENT ON MERIT.   GAMERFC50379

KEY **QUESTIONS** ON THE POVERTY PROBLEM.   GKEYSLH64943

SOME **QUESTIONS** AND ANSWERS ON THE CIVIL-RIGHTS BILL.   GLEADCCND888

QUESTIONS AND ANSWERS ABOUT PERMANENT FAIR-EMPLOYMENT-PRACTICES COMMISSIONS.   GNORTMT45124

42 **QUESTIONS** AND ANSWERS ABOUT FAIR-EMPLOYMENT-PRACTICES.   GOREGBLND138

SOME **QUESTIONS** AND ANSWERS ON THE NON-DISCRIMINATION POLICY OF THE FEDERAL GOVERNMENT.   GPRESCP55199

LABOR WEEK. RULES ON HIRING, PROMOTING -- **QUESTIONS** ANSWERED.   GUSNEWR66518

QUESTIONS REGARDING AMERICAN-INDIAN CRIMINALITY.   ISTEWOX64302

ANSWERS TO **QUESTIONS** ABOUT AMERICAN-INDIANS.   IUSDINT65642

RACE RELATIONS. **QUESTIONS** AND ANSWERS FOR PERSONNEL MEN.   NSHOSAX64132

WHEN WILL THE EDUCATIONAL NEEDS OF WOMEN BE MET. SOME **QUESTIONS** FOR THE COUNSELOR.   WNEUMRR63026

QUOTAS
JOINT STAND REJECTS RACIAL **QUOTAS** FOR PLUMBING APPRENTICES.   GAIRCHR63867

MEDICAL SCHOOL **QUOTAS**. /EDUCATION DISCRIMINATION/   JBRAVHX58707

JOB **QUOTAS** AND THE MERIT SYSTEM.   NCHASET63195

QUOTAS FOR NEGROES.   NCHASET64196

RACE
EMPLOYMENT AND PERSONAL CHARACTERISTICS. EMPLOYMENT BY AGE, **RACE**, NATIVITY, EDUCATION, MARITAL-STATUS,
HOUSEHOLD RELATIONSHIPS, ETC. /DEMOGRAPHY/   CUSBURC53372

NONWHITE POPULATION BY **RACE**. NEGROES, INDIANS, JAPANESE, CHINESE, FILIPINOS. BY AGE, SEX, MARITAL-STATUS,
EDUCATION, EMPLOYMENT-STATUS, OCCUPATIONAL-STATUS, INCOME, ETC. /DEMOGRAPHY/   CUSBURC53378

UNITED STATES CENSUS OF AGRICULTURE. COLOR, **RACE**, AND TENURE OF FARM OPERATOR. GENERAL REPORT, VOLUME II.
/DEMOGRAPHY/   CUSBURC59382

NONWHITE POPULATION BY **RACE**. NEGROES, INDIANS, JAPANESE,CHINESE, FILIPINOS. BY AGE, SEX,
MARITAL-STATUS,EDUCATION, EMPLOYMENT-STATUS, OCCUPATIONAL-STATUS, INCOME, ETC. /DEMOGRAPHY/   CUSBURC63176

OCCUPATIONAL CHARACTERISTICS, DATA ON AGE, **RACE**, EDUCATION, WORK EXPERIENCE, INCOME, ETC. FOR WORKERS IN
EACH OCCUPATION.   CUSBURC63177

RACE, EMPLOYMENT TESTS, AND EQUAL-OPPORTUNITY.   GASHXPX65406

RACE AND ETHNIC RELATIONS.   GBERRBX65449

RACE AND SOCIO-ECONOMIC STATUS IN MUNICIPAL PERSONNEL SELECTION.   GBIANJC67590

EQUAL-RIGHTS UNDER THE LAW. PROVIDING FOR EQUAL TREATMENT FOR ALL CITIZENS REGARDLESS OF **RACE**, RELIGION,
COLOR, NATIONAL ORIGIN OR ANCESTRY. /CALIFORNIA/   GCALAGO60511

MANPOWER DEVELOPMENT TRAINING. TOTAL NUMBER OF NEW ENROLLEES DURING THE MONTH BY **RACE** AND OCCUPATION
STATEWIDE AND BY ADMINISTRATIVE AREA, SEPTEMBER, 1966, OCTOBER, 1966. /CALIFORNIA/   GCALDEM66518

ELIMINATION OF **RACE** DISCRIMINATION IN THE APPLICATION BLANK.   GDARTCX47626

RACE (CONTINUATION)

ASSIMILATION IN AMERICAN LIFE. THE ROLE OF **RACE**, RELIGION, AND NATIONAL ORIGINS.   GGORDMM64729

MONEY BENEFITS OF EDUCATION BY SEX AND **RACE** IN NEW-YORK STATE, 1956.   GGREEWX61741

RACE, NATIONALITY, AND RELIGION -- THEIR RELATIONSHIP TO APPOINTMENT POLICIES AND CASEWORK.   GHAGEDJ57752

RACE AND NATIONALITY IN AMERICAN LIFE.   GHANDOX57758

ETHNIC AND **RACE** BARRIERS.   GKAHLJA57831

URBANISM, **RACE**, AND ANOMIA.   GKILLLX62853

THE ASSOCIATION OF INCOME AND EDUCATION FOR MALES, BY REGION, **RACE**, AND AGE.   GLASSRL65998

STATES LAWS ON **RACE** AND COLOR.   GMURRPX50034

RULINGS ON PRE-EMPLOYMENT INQUIRIES RELATING TO **RACE**, CREED, COLOR OR NATIONAL ORIGIN UNDER THE NEW-YORK
STATE LAW AGAINST DISCRIMINATION.   GNEWYSBND106

RACE, ETHNICITY, AND THE ACHIEVEMENT SYNDROME.   GROSEBC59252

RACE, JOBS, AND POLITICS. THE STORY OF FEPC.   GRUCHLX53266

MINORITY-GROUP INTEGRATION BY LABOR AND MANAGEMENT. A STUDY OF THE EMPLOYMENT PRACTICES OF THE LARGER
EMPLOYERS, AND THE MEMBERSHIP PRACTICES OF THE LARGER LABOR UNIONS WITH RESPECT TO **RACE**, RELIGION, AND
NATIONAL ORIGIN, CONNECTICUT, 1951.   GSTETHG53598

HOW TO HANDLE **RACE** LABOR-RELATIONS. /UNION/   GSTYLPL50339

RACE, INDIVIDUAL AND COLLECTIVE BEHAVIOR.   GTHOMET58356

RACE TROUBLES HURT UNIONS TOO.   GUSNEWR56517

AMERICAN MINORITY RELATIONS. THE SOCIOLOGY OF **RACE** AND ETHNIC GROUPS.   GVANDJW63535

LABOR-S **RACE** PROBLEM. /UNION/   MFORTXX59374

RACE AND SOCIAL-CLASS AS SEPARATE FACTORS RELATED TO SOCIAL ENVIRONMENT. /ASPIRATIONS/   NBLOORX63096

THE RELATIONSHIP OF JUVENILE-DELINQUENCY, **RACE**, AND ECONOMIC STATUS.   NBLUEJT48097

RACE ISSUE AND UNIONS IN THE SOUTH.   NBUSIWX56160

RACE PROBLEMS BUILD UP FOR UNIONS.   NBUSIWX58880

SOUTH-S **RACE** DISPUTES INVOLVE BUSINESSMAN.   NBUSIWX60162

MORE **RACE** PRESSURE ON BUSINESS.   NBUSIWX62153

THE PRICE OF DEFIANCE. /MISSISSIPPI **RACE**/   NBUSIWX62159

RACE HATE. NEWEST UNION-BUSTING WEAPON IN THE SOUTH.   NCAREJB58181

RACE, APTITUDE AND VOCATIONAL INTERESTS.   NCHANNN65191

RACE AND POVERTY.   NDENTJH64263

CORRELATIONS BETWEEN INCOME AND LABOR-FORCE PARTICIPATION BY **RACE**.   NDORNSM56283

INDUSTRY AND **RACE** IN THE SOUTHERN US.   NEDMOMS65321

RACE, OCCUPATION, AND SOCIAL-CLASS IN NEW-YORK.   NFRUMRM58388

EMPLOYMENT SECURITY, SENIORITY AND **RACE**. THE ROLE OF TITLE-VII OF THE CIVIL-RIGHTS-ACT OF 1964.   NGOULWB67864

REGIONS, **RACE** AND JOBS.   NHENDVW67517

THE UAW FIGHTS **RACE** PREJUDICE. /UNION/   NHOWEIX49581

UNION HELD GUILTY OF **RACE** DISCRIMINATION.   NLABORR45027

CULTURAL EXPOSURE AND **RACE** AS VARIABLES IN PREDICTING TRAINING AND JOB SUCCESS. /TESTING/   NLOCKHCND700

RACE AND THE SCHOOLS.   NMEYEAE58769

POVERTY, **RACE** AND POLITICS.   NMILLSM65790

RACE RELATIONSHIP IN THE POCAHONTAS COAL FIELD.   NMINARD52794

THE DESIGNATION OF **RACE** OR COLOR ON FORMS.   NMINDAX66795

RACE, ECONOMIC ATTITUDES, AND BEHAVIOR.   NMORGJX62850

EDUCATION AND **RACE**.   NNATLUL66888

RACE DISCRIMINATION IN UNIONS.   NNORTHR45946

RACE DISCRIMINATION IN TRADE UNIONS. RECORD AND OUTLOOK.   NNORTHR46945

WASTE OF MANPOWER -- **RACE** AND EMPLOYMENT IN A SOUTHERN STATE.   NROBEGX62064

RACE PREJUDICE AND DISCRIMINATION. READINGS IN INTERGROUP RELATIONS IN THE US.   NROSEAM51075

THE INFLUENCE OF A BORDER CITY UNION ON THE **RACE** ATTITUDES OF ITS MEMBERS.   NROSEAW53293

EMPLOYMENT, **RACE** AND POVERTY.   NROSSAM67086

RACE AND POVERTY.   NSCHALX64102

RACE RELATIONS. QUESTIONS AND ANSWERS FOR PERSONNEL MEN.   NSHOSAX64132

RACE DISCRIMINATION AND THE NLRA ACT. THE BRAVE NEW WORLD OF MIRANDA. /LEGISLATION/   NSOVEMI63169

SOCIALIZATION, **RACE** AND THE AMERICAN HIGH SCHOOL. /EDUCATION/   NTENHWP65201

EDITORIAL COMMENT. FEPC HEARINGS REDUCE **RACE** PROBLEM TO LOWEST TERMS -- EQUAL-ECONOMIC-OPPORTUNITY.   NTHOMCH43160

RACE AND INTELLIGENCE. AN EVALUATION.   NTUMIMM63065

RACE   (CONTINUATION)
    COLOR. RACE AND TENURE OF FARM OPERATORS.   NUSBURC62225

    IMPACT OF THE RACE ISSUE ON UNIONS IN THE SOUTH.   NUSNEWR56208

    LABOR TACKLES THE RACE QUESTION. /UNION/   NWINNFX43554

    SOUTHERN RACE PROGRESS. THE WAVERING COLOR LINE.   NWOOFTJ57340

    EMPLOYEE CHOICE AND SOME PROBLEMS OF RACE AND REMEDIES IN REPRESENTATION CAMPAIGNS.   NYALELJ63599

    A LOOK AT THE OTHER WOMAN. /RACE DISCRIMINATION/   WWALDSX65017

RACE-RELATIONS
    RECENT TRENDS IN THE STUDY OF MINORITY AND RACE-RELATIONS. /NEGRO PUERTO-RICAN ORIENTAL/   CGORDMM63977

    SOCIAL STRUCTURE AND RACE-RELATIONS.   GBONIES66135

    RACE-RELATIONS AND ANTI-DISCRIMINATORY LEGISLATION.   GBURMJH51500

    IMPROVING INDUSTRIAL RACE-RELATIONS -- PART I. EQUAL JOB OPPORTUNITY -- SLOGAN OR REALITY.   GFLEMHC63363

    RACE-RELATIONS AND AMERICAN LAW.   GGREEJX59981

    HOW RACE-RELATIONS AFFECT YOUR BUSINESS.   GKHEETW63850

    RACE-RELATIONS FRONTIERS IN HAWAII.   GLINDAW61744

    THE LAW AND RACE-RELATIONS.   GMASLWX46147

    RACE-RELATIONS. PROBLEMS AND THEORY.   GMASUJX63064

    TESTIMONY TO THE SUBCOMMITTEE ON RACE-RELATIONS AND URBAN PROBLEMS. /SES CALIFORNIA/   GREDMWX64221

    THE CHANGING ECONOMIC BACKGROUND OF AMERICAN RACE-RELATIONS.   GROSEAW50288

    IMPROVING INDUSTRIAL RACE-RELATIONS -- PART 2. HUMAN PROBLEMS IN IMPROVING INDUSTRIAL RACE-RELATIONS.   GSHOSAB63307

    IMPROVING INDUSTRIAL RACE-RELATIONS -- PART 2. HUMAN PROBLEMS IN IMPROVING INDUSTRIAL RACE-RELATIONS.   GSHOSAB63307

    RACE-RELATIONS IN AN INDUSTRIAL SOCIETY. /EMPLOYMENT GRIEVANCE-PROCEDURES/   NBACOEF63041

    INDUSTRIALIZATION AND RACE-RELATIONS.   NBLUMHX65100

    RACE-RELATIONS AND SOCIAL-CHANGE.   NBURGME65140

    A CHRONICLE OF RACE-RELATIONS -- THE UNITED STATES, NORTH AND SOUTH.   NDUBOWE41298

    A CHRONICLE OF RACE-RELATIONS. FEPC.   NDUBOWE43297

    RACE-RELATIONS IN THE UNITED-STATES 1916-1947.   NDUBOWE48299

    MONTHLY SUMMARY OF EVENTS AND TRENDS IN RACE-RELATIONS. /CINCINNATI OHIO CASE-STUDY UNION/   NFISKUX44357

    AREAS OF RESEARCH IN RACE-RELATIONS.   NFRAZEF58376

    TESTIMONY BEFORE STATE SENATE FACT FINDING SUBCOMMITTEE ON RACE-RELATIONS AND URBAN PROBLEMS, FINAL
    HEARING. JANUARY 20 1965. /CALIFORNIA FEPC/   NGRAHCX65439

    RACE-RELATIONS IN ROCHESTER, A PROFILE FOR 1957. /NEW-YORK/   NGRIEES57457

    RACE-RELATIONS IN THE ALBANY TROY AREA. A PROFILE FOR 1957. /NEW-YORK/   NGRIEES57503

    NEGROES IN FIVE NEW-YORK CITIES. A STUDY OF PROBLEMS, ACHIEVEMENTS AND TRENDS. /RACE-RELATIONS/   NGRIEES58455

    RACE-RELATIONS IN BROOME-COUNTY, A PROFILE FOR 1958. /NEW-YORK/   NGRIEES58456

    RACE-RELATIONS IN SYRACUSE. A PROFILE. /NEW-YORK/   NGRIEES58458

    ECONOMIC DIMENSIONS IN RACE-RELATIONS.   NHENDVW61511

    RECENT DEVELOPMENTS IN RACE-RELATIONS AND ORGANIZED LABOR.   NHENDVW66213

    TRENDS IN PATTERNS OF RACE-RELATIONS IN THE SOUTH SINCE MAY 17 1954.   NHOPEJX56575

    RACE-RELATIONS IN INDUSTRIAL RELATIONS.   NHUGHEC46586

    RACE-RELATIONS AND THE SOCIOLOGICAL IMAGINATION.   NHUGHEC63585

    INDUSTRIALIZATION AND RACE-RELATIONS.   NHUNTGX65588

    PRESENT STATUS OF RACE-RELATIONS IN THE SOUTH.   NJOHNCS44615

    INTO THE MAINSTREAM. /RACE-RELATIONS SOUTH ECONOMIC-STATUS/   NJOHNCS47007

    THE EFFECTS OF SOUTHERN WHITE WORKERS ON RACE-RELATIONS IN NORTHERN PLANTS.   NKILLLM52650

    LABOR UNION AND RACE-RELATIONS. A STUDY OF UNION TACTICS.   NKORNWA50660

    PLACEMENT SERVICE OF THE AMERICAN FRIENDS SERVICE COMMITTEE. A TECHNIQUE IN RACE-RELATIONS.   NLOESFS46703

    INDUSTRIALIZATION AND RACE-RELATIONS IN THE SOUTHERN US.   NMARSRX65739

    PROGRESS IN RACE-RELATIONS.   NMCNIRX51727

    HOW MANAGEMENT VIEWS ITS RACE-RELATIONS RESPONSIBILITIES.   NSTRAGX67181

    RACE-RELATIONS IN THE SOUTH, 1963.   NTUSKIX64219

    THE IMPACT OF RACE-RELATIONS ON INDUSTRIAL RELATIONS IN THE SOUTH.   NWHEEJH64230

    STATEMENT BEFORE CALIFORNIA SENATE SUB-COMMITTEE ON RACE-RELATIONS AND URBAN PROBLEMS.   OLOWXHW64745

RACES
    SOCIO-ECONOMIC DIFFERENTIALS AMONG NONWHITE RACES. /NEGRO ORIENTAL AMERICAN-INDIAN/   CSCHMCF65107

    FUTURE OCCUPATIONAL DIFFERENCES BETWEEN THE RACES. A MARKOV APPROACH.   NLEWISX66693

RACIAL
    RACIAL DISTRIBUTION OF SELECTED UNEMPLOYMENT INSURANCE AND EMPLOYMENT SERVICE DATA. JULY-DECEMBER 1966.

CCALDEM67907

RACIAL CHARACTERISTICS, MDTA TRAINEES. SAN-FRANCISCO. /CALIFORNIA NEGRO MEXICAN-AMERICAN/   CELTOEX63332

INTERIM REPORT TO THE MAYOR CN ITS INQUIRY INTO CHARGES OF RACIAL BIAS IN THE CITY BUILDING AND
CONSTRUCTION INDUSTRY. /NEW-YORK NEGRO PUERTO-RICAN/   CNEWYCO64917

JOINT STAND REJECTS RACIAL QUOTAS FOR PLUMBING APPRENTICES.   GAIRCHR63867

ANALYSIS OF CITY ORDINANCES AGAINST RACIAL AND RELIGIOUS DISCRIMINATION IN EMPLOYMENT.   GAMERJCND380

RACIAL DESEGREGATION AND INTEGRATION.   GANNADA56578

ORGANIZED LABOR AND RACIAL MINORITIES. /UNION/   GBAILLH51575

RACIAL EQUALITY AND THE LAW.   GBERGMX54442

RECENT RESEARCH ON RACIAL RELATIONS IN THE USA.   GBLUMHX58458

THE ROLE OF LEGISLATION IN ELIMINATING RACIAL DISCRIMINATION.   GBONFAE65462

ONE AMERICA. THE HISTORY, CONTRIBUTIONS, AND PRESENT PROBLEMS OF OUR RACIAL AND NATIONAL MINORITIES.   GBROWFJ45477

STATEMENT CN SURVEYS AND STATISTICS AS TO RACIAL AND ETHNIC COMPOSITION OF WORK-FORCE OR UNION
MEMBERSHIP. /CALIFORNIA/   GCALFEP63539

THE NLRB AND RACIAL DISCRIMINATION. /LEGISLATION/   GCARTRX65560

ECONOMIC COSTS OF RACIAL DISCRIMINATION IN EMPLOYMENT.   GCOUNEA62205

SOME CONSIDERATIONS AS TO THE CONTRIBUTIONS OF SOCIAL, PERSONALITY, AND RACIAL FACTORS TO SCHOOL
RETARDATION IN MINORITY-GROUP CHILDREN.   GDEUTMP56641

RACIAL STATISTICS AS A MANAGEMENT TOOL.   GDOARLE66645

UNION RACIAL DISCRIMINATION -- RECENT DEVELOPMENTS BEFORE THE NLRB AND THEIR IMPLICATIONS UNDER TITLE-VII
OF THE CIVIL-RIGHTS-ACT OF 1964.   GGEORLJ65714

RACIAL INTEGRATION IN EMPLOYMENT.   GGIBSHX54969

THE POSITION OF RACIAL GROUPS IN OCCUPATIONAL STRUCTURES.   GGLICCE47722

THE FAIR REPRESENTATION DOCTRINE. AN EFFECTIVE WEAPON AGAINST UNION RACIAL DISCRIMINATION.   GHERRNM64772

DEMOGRAPHIC CHANGE AND RACIAL GHETTOS. THE CRISIS OF AMERICAN CITIES.   GHILLHX66691

EMPLOYMENT PROBLEMS OF RACIAL MINORITIES.   GHOPEJX61002

PART IV. EMPLOYMENT PROBLEMS OF RACIAL MINORITIES.   GINDURR61813

LEGISLATION AGAINST RACIAL OR RELIGIOUS DISCRIMINATION IN EMPLOYMENT, NEW-YORK.   GIVESLM52819

RACIAL DISCRIMINATION IN UNIONS.   GKAHNSD65011

LABOR LAW -- UNION MEMBERSHIP DENIED ON THE BASIS OF RACIAL DISCRIMINATION. /WISCONSIN LEGISLATION/   GKAUFET58014

RACIAL DISCRIMINATION IN EMPLOYMENT AND THE FEDERAL LAW.   GKOVAIX58026

LEGISLATION OUTLAWING RACIAL DISCRIMINATION IN EMPLOYMENT.   GLAWYGR45886

RACIAL AND RELIGIOUS DISCRIMINATION IN EMPLOYMENT AND THE ROLE OF THE NLRB.   GMALOWH61935

THE RACIAL PRACTICES OF THE ILGWU -- A REPLY.   GMARSRX64059

THE PRACTICE OF RACIAL DEMOCRACY.   GNATLIC65593

RACIAL DISCRIMINATION IN THE CINCINNATI BUILDING TRADES. A COMPREHENSIVE REPORT AND RECOMMENDATIONS.
/OHIO/   GOHICCR64129

THEY AND WE. RACIAL AND ETHNIC RELATIONS IN THE UNITED STATES.   GROSEPI64251

THE LAW AND RACIAL DISCRIMINATION IN EMPLOYMENT.   GROSESJ65255

RACIAL AND ETHNIC EMPLOYMENT PATTERN SURVEY OF THE CITY AND COUNTY OF SAN-FRANCISCO GOVERNMENT.
DEPARTMENTAL ANALYSIS. /CALIFORNIA/   GSANFHR65264

RACIAL CHANGES IN METROPOLITAN AREAS. 1950-1960. /DEMOGRAPHY/   GSCHNLF63288

RACIAL AND ETHNIC RELATIONS. SELECTED READINGS.   GSEGABE66154

RACIAL AND CULTURAL MINORITIES.   GSIMPGE65314

LEGAL RESTRAINTS ON RACIAL DISCRIMINATION IN EMPLOYMENT.   GSOVEMI66326

EMPLOYMENT INTEGRATION AND RACIAL WAGE DIFFERENCE IN A SOUTHERN PLANT.   GWEINRX59988

FEDERAL REMEDIES FOR RACIAL DISCRIMINATION BY LABOR UNIONS.   GWEISLX62597

THE MANAGEMENT OF RACIAL INTEGRATION IN BUSINESS, A SPECIAL REPORT TO MANAGEMENT.   NALEXRD64868

RACIAL EQUALITY AND THE LAW. THE ROLE OF LAW IN THE REDUCTION OF DISCRIMINATION IN THE UNITED-STATES.   NBERGMX54076

RACIAL DISCRIMINATION IN THE FEDERAL SERVICE. A STUDY IN THE SOCIOLOGY OF ADMINISTRATION.   NBRADWC53106

RACIAL DESEGREGATION IN THE PUBLIC SERVICE, WITH PARTICULAR REFERENCE TO THE US GOVERNMENT.   NBROWVJ54127

RACIAL ATTITUDES AND THE EMPLOYMENT OF NEGROES.   NBULLHA51133

ANALYSIS OF THE TECHNIQUES OF RACIAL INTEGRATION IN THREE MANUFACTURING FIRMS. /INDUSTRY/   NCAMPFX54178

RACIAL DISCRIMINATION BY A UNION AGAINST EMPLOYEES IT DOES NOT REPRESENT. /LEGISLATION/   NCCLULR52226

RACIAL DISCRIMINATION AND THE DUTY OF FAIR REPRESENTATION. /LEGISLATION/   NCOLULR65225

SOUTHERN POVERTY AND THE RACIAL DIVISION-OF-LABOR.   NDEWEDX62271

RACIAL STATISTICS AS A MANAGEMENT TOOL.   NDOARLE66276

THE MANAGEMENT OF **RACIAL** INTEGRATION IN BUSINESS.   NDORIGF64282

HISTORY OF **RACIAL** SEGREGATION IN THE UNITED STATES.   NFRANJH56060

THE **RACIAL** ISSUE.   NFRAZEF47384

TRAINING FOR MINORITY-GROUPS. PROBLEMS OF **RACIAL** IMBALANCE AND SEGREGATION.   NFUSFDR66014

I Q PERFORMANCE. EDUCATIONAL AND OCCUPATIONAL ASPIRATIONS OF YOUTH IN A SOUTHERN CITY -- A **RACIAL**
COMPARISON.   NGEISPX62397

RACIAL INTEGRATION IN EMPLOYMENT -- FINDINGS IN TWO KANSAS-CITY HOSPITALS.   NGIBSHX54402

LAST MAN IN. **RACIAL** ACCESS TO UNIONS.   NGREESX59451

RACIAL DISCRIMINATION IN AMERICAN LABOR UNIONS.   NGUHAME65464

EFFECTS OF ON-THE-JOB EXPERIENCE WITH NEGROES UPON **RACIAL** ATTITUDES OF WHITE WORKERS IN UNION SHOPS. NGUNDRH50466

RACIAL DISCRIMINATION BY UNIONS.   NHALLGD57987

RACIAL CONTRASTS IN INCOME.   NHARPRM60487

RECENT EFFECTS OF **RACIAL** CONFLICT ON SOUTHERN INDUSTRIAL DEVELOPMENT.   NHILLHX59543

RACIAL DISCRIMINATION IN THE NATION-S APPRENTICESHIP TRAINING PROGRAM.   NHILLHX62539

RACIAL INEQUALITY IN EMPLOYMENT. THE PATTERNS OF DISCRIMINATION.   NHILLHX65540

THE **RACIAL** PRACTICES OF ORGANIZED LABOR -- IN THE AGE OF GOMPERS AND AFTER. /UNION/   NHILLHX65541

EFFORTS TO ELIMINATE **RACIAL** DISCRIMINATION IN INDUSTRY -- WITH PARTICULAR REFERENCE TO THE SOUTH.   NHOPEJX54566

THE KNITTING OF **RACIAL** GROUPS IN INDUSTRY.   NHUGHEC46584

COLLEGE, COLOR, AND EMPLOYMENT. **RACIAL** DIFFERENTIALS IN POSTGRADUATE EMPLOYMENT AMONG 1964 GRADUATES OF
LOUISIANA COLLEGES.   NHUSOCF66328

RACIAL DIFFERENCES AND THE FUTURE. /INTELLIGENCE EQUAL-OPPORTUNITY/   NINGLDJ64067

THE PROBLEMS OF **RACIAL** DISCRIMINATION IN UNION MEMBERSHIP.   NJENKHX47605

TO STEM THIS TIDE. A SURVEY OF **RACIAL** TENSION AREAS IN THE U.S.   NJOHNCS43617

EFFECTS OF ANXIETY, THREAT, AND **RACIAL** ENVIRONMENT ON TASK PERFORMANCE OF NEGRO COLLEGE STUDENTS.   NKATZIX63640

CIVIL-RIGHTS -- **RACIAL** DISCRIMINATION IN TEACHER HIRING AND ASSIGNMENT FORBIDDEN.   NKELLPL66734

RACIAL CRISIS IN AMERICA.   NKILLLM64652

MANAGEMENT. **RACIAL** DISCRIMINATION AND APPRENTICE TRAINING   NKOVAIX64663

APPRENTICESHIP TRAINING PROGRAMS AND **RACIAL** DISCRIMINATION.   NKOVAIX65024

RACIAL DISCRIMINATION IN EMPLOYMENT IN THE CINCINNATI AREA. /OHIO/   NKUHNAX62668

INTER-AGENCY POLICY ON **RACIAL** BIAS.   NLABORR43029

RACIAL DIFFERENCES IN MIGRATION AND JOB-SEARCH. A CASE-STUDY.   NLURIMX66712

RACIAL DISCRIMINATION AND THE FEDERAL LAW. A PROBLEM IN NULLIFICATION.   NLUSKLX63713

SOME FACTORS INFLUENCING UNION **RACIAL** PRACTICES.   NMARSRX62747

UNION **RACIAL** PRACTICES AND THE LABOR-MARKET.   NMARSRX62749

UNION **RACIAL** PROBLEMS IN THE SOUTH.   NMARSRX62751

RACIAL FACTORS INFLUENCING ENTRY TO THE SKILLED TRADES. /UNION/   NMARSRX63745

UNION **RACIAL** PRACTICES.   NMARSRX63750

UNION STRUCTURE AND PUBLIC POLICY. THE CONTROL OF UNION **RACIAL** PRACTICES.   NMARSRX63752

SOUTHERN **RACIAL** ATTITUDES. CONFLICT, AWARENESS AND POLITICAL CHANGE.   NMATTOR62758

RACIAL DISCRIMINATION ON THE JOBSITE. COMPETING THEORIES AND COMPETING FORUMS.   NMEYEBI65210

RACIAL DISCRIMINATION AND PRIVATE EDUCATION.   NMILLAS57069

SOLVING **RACIAL** PROBLEMS IN YOUR PLANT. /INDUSTRY/   NMODEIX45805

THE NATIONAL-LABOR-RELATIONS ACT-AND **RACIAL** DISCRIMINATION. /LEGISLATION/   NMOLIRL66807

RACIAL INTEGRATION IN THE ARMED FORCES. /MILITARY/   NMOSKCC66855

RACIAL ASPECTS OF RECONVERSION.   NNATLUL45896

RACIAL DISCRIMINATION IN EMPLOYMENT. BIBLIOGRAPHY.   NNORGPH62931

IN THE UNIONS. **RACIAL** POLICIES.   NNORTHR47939

INDUSTRY-S **RACIAL** EMPLOYMENT POLICIES.   NNORTHR67938

RACIAL DISCRIMINATION IN THE CINCINNATI BUILDING TRADES. REPORT AND RECOMMENDATIONS. /OHIO/   NOHIOCR66605

AMENDMENTS TO THE TAFT-HARTLEY. A REJECTION OF **RACIAL** DISCRIMINATION. /LEGISLATION/   NOSHAJB54964

THE IMPACT OF SOCIO-ECONOMIC CHANGE ON **RACIAL** GROUPS IN A RURAL SETTING.   NPELLRJ62981

RACIAL DIFFERENCES IN INTELLIGENCE.   NPLOTLX59064

RACIAL DISCRIMINATION IN EMPLOYMENT. PROPOSALS FOR CORRECTIVE ACTION.   NPOLLDX63006

RACIAL DISCRIMINATION IN UNION MEMBERSHIP.   NPROMHJ59127

MANAGEMENT SOCIAL RESPONSIBILITY AND **RACIAL** EMPLOYMENT IN THE MEAT-PACKING INDUSTRY.   NPURCTV67123

RACIAL   (CONTINUATION)
THE IMPACT OF MILITARY SERVICE UPON THE **RACIAL** ATTITUDES OF NEGRO SERVICEMEN IN WORLD-WAR II.   NROBEHW53065

AMERICAN ENTERPRISE AND THE **RACIAL** CRISIS.   NROBIJX63069

THE LAW AND **RACIAL** DISCRIMINATION IN EMPLOYMENT.   NROSESJ67078

THE **RACIAL** ISSUE AS AN ANTI UNION TOOL AND THE NATIONAL-LABOR-RELATIONS-BOARD.   NSACHRX63888

THE CIVIL-RIGHTS-ACT OF 1964. **RACIAL** DISCRIMINATION BY LABOR UNIONS.   NSAINJL66138

THE RELATION OF **RACIAL** SEGREGATION IN EARLY SCHOOLING TO THE LEVEL OF ASPIRATION AND ACADEMIC ACHIEVEMENT   NSAINJN62137
OF NEGRO STUDENTS IN A NORTHERN HIGH SCHOOL.

RACIAL CHANGES IN METROPOLITAN AREAS. 1950-1960. /DEMOGRAPHY MIGRATION/   NSCHNLF65109

A NOTE ON **RACIAL** DIFFERENCES IN JOB VALUES AND DESIRES.   NSINGSL56142

RACIAL AND FAMILY EXPERIENCE CORRELATES OF MOBILITY ASPIRATION.   NSMITHP62144

RACIAL WORK AND NEGRO WASTE IN SOUTHERN EMPLOYMENT.   NSOUTRC62300

THE NATIONAL-LABOR-RELATIONS-ACT AND **RACIAL** DISCRIMINATION. /LEGISLATION/   NSOVEMI62168

THE NEGRO AS AN IMMIGRANT GROUP. RECENT TRENDS IN **RACIAL** AND ETHNIC SEGREGATION IN CHICAGO. /ILLINOIS/   NTAEUKE64196

RACIAL DISCRIMINATION IN UNIONS.   NTEMPLQ65200

ECONOMIC AND SOCIAL CONSEQUENCES OF **RACIAL** DISCRIMINATORY PRACTICES.   NUNITNX63224

RACIAL DISCRIMINATION AND THE NLRB. THE HUGHES TOOL CASE, PART ONE.   NVIRGLR64017

RACIAL DISCRIMINATION AND THE NLRB. THE HUGHES TOOL CASE, PART TWO.   NVIRGLR64018

THE PRACTICE OF **RACIAL** DEMOCRACY.   NYCUNWM65000

RACIAL-RELATIONS
SAN FRANCISCO-S PLAN FOR DEMOCRATIC **RACIAL-RELATIONS**. /CALIFORNIA/   GBAYXAC43427

RACIALLY
NLRB DECERTIFIES **RACIALLY** SEGREGATED UNION LOCALS.   NCHECDX64890

RACISM
THE ECONOMICS OF **RACISM**.   NHARRMX61490

RACISM WITHIN ORGANIZED LABOR. A REPORT OF THE FIVE YEARS OF THE AFL-CIO, 1955-1960. /UNION/   NHILLHX60542

FOUNDATIONS OF **RACISM** IN AMERICAN LIFE.   NODELJH64953

RACISM STYMIES UNIONS IN THE SOUTH.   NSEGABD57113

RADCLIFFE
GRADUATE EDUCATION FOR WOMEN. THE **RADCLIFFE** PHD.   WRADCCX56072

RADCLIFFE INSTITUTE FOR INDEPENDENT STUDY. /TRAINING/   WSMITCX63119

RAILROAD
RAILROAD. EMPLOYMENT IN THE NEW-YORK AND NEW-JERSEY.   GNEWYSA58101

OCCUPATIONAL STATUS OF NEGRO **RAILROAD** WORKERS.   NUSDLAB43836

RAILROADS
RAILROADS BEFORE THE FEPC.   GLAWYGR45887

RAILWAY
RAILWAY LABOR ACT -- DENIAL OF UNION MEMBERSHIP TO NEGROES.   NMINNLR58800

THE NEGRO IN THE **RAILWAY** UNIONS.   NNORTHR44943

RAISING
RAISING LOW-INCOMES THROUGH IMPROVED EDUCATION.   GCOMIED65591

SPANISH-AMERICANS **RAISING** EDUCATIONAL SIGHTS.   MSKRARL65493

RAISING THE STATUS OF HOUSEHOLD EMPLOYMENT. /HOUSEHOLD-WORKERS/   WMORRMM66998

RANK
THE MYRDALIAN HYPOTHESES. **RANK** ORDER OF DISCRIMINATION.   GEDMUER44495

RATE
AT THE PREVAILING **RATE**. /MEXICAN-AMERICAN NEGRO UNION/   CLEBETX57371

DROPOUTS AND THE **RATE** OF UNEMPLOYMENT. /YOUTH/   NDUNCBX65304

THE UNEMPLOYMENT **RATE** AND GRADE LEVEL RELATIONSHIP IN CHICAGO AS REVEALED IN THE 1960 CENSUS. /ILLINOIS/   NHARGAJ65990

DISCRIMINATION IN **RATE** OF COMPENSATION BETWEEN COLORED AND WHITE TEACHERS HELD UNCONSTITUTIONAL.   NHARVLR40497

RATES
WAGE **RATES** AND UNEMPLOYMENT.   GBACKJX64876

RURAL-FARM MALES ENTERING AND LEAVING WORKING AGES, 1940-50 AND 1950-60. REPLACEMENT RATIOS AND **RATES**.   GBOWLGK56433
/OCCUPATIONS/

SCHOOL DROPOUT **RATES** AMONG FARM AND NONFARM YOUTH 1950 AND 1960.   GCOWHJD63421

LABOR-FORCE PARTICIPATION **RATES** AND PERCENT DISTRIBUTION OF MOTHERS WITH HUSBAND PRESENT.   WUSDLAB64204

SUGGESTED LANGUAGE FOR A STATE ACT TO ABOLISH DISCRIMINATORY WAGE **RATES** BASED ON SEX.   WUSDLAB64218

RATIOS
RURAL-FARM MALES ENTERING AND LEAVING WORKING AGES, 1940-50 AND 1950-60. REPLACEMENT **RATIOS** AND RATES.   GBOWLGK56433
/OCCUPATIONS/

RE-EVALUATION
EXCLUSIONS AND ADAPTATIONS. A **RE-EVALUATION** OF THE CULTURE-OF-POVERTY THEME.   NCOHERXND221

RE-EXAMINED
INCREASING STRUCTURAL UNEMPLOYMENT **RE-EXAMINED**.   GSTOIVX66001

RE-SURVEY
OUT-OF-SCHOOL YOUTH -- TWO YEARS LATER. A 1965 RE-SURVEY OF YOUNG MEN.   GPERRVC66774

REACTION
REACTION TO MEXICAN-AMERICANS, A BACKGROUND PAPER.   MCABRYA65372

REACTIONS
THE SOCIAL AND POLITICAL REACTIONS OF OLDER NEGROES TO UNEMPLOYMENT.   NAIKEMX66865

NEGRO REACTIONS TO MINORITY-GROUP STATUS.   NJOHNRA57619

CUSTOMER REACTIONS TO THE INTEGRATION OF NEGRO SALES PERSONNEL.   NSAENGX50101

READER
MAN, WORK AND SOCIETY. A READER IN THE SOCIOLOGY OF OCCUPATIONS.   GNOSOSX62336

MARRIAGE, FAMILY, AND SOCIETY. A READER. /WORK-FAMILY-CONFLICT/   WRODMHX65084

READINGS
AMERICAN MINORITIES. A TEXTBOOK OF READINGS IN INTERGROUP RELATIONS.   GBARRML57424

RACIAL AND ETHNIC RELATIONS. SELECTED READINGS.   GSEGABE66154

SELECTED READINGS IN EMPLOYMENT AND MANPOWER.   GUSSENA64334

RACE PREJUDICE AND DISCRIMINATION. READINGS IN INTERGROUP RELATIONS IN THE US.   NROSEAM51075

READJUSTMENTS
READJUSTMENTS OF VETERANS TO CIVILIAN LIFE.   NUSDLAB46839

REALITIES
REALITIES OF THE JOB-MARKET FOR THE HIGH SCHOOL DROPOUT.   GBIENHX64111

TODAY-S REALITIES IN THE FARM LABOR-MARKET.   GGOODRC65726

CHANGING REALITIES IN WOMEN-S LIVES. /WORK-WOMAN-ROLE/   WKEYSMD65893

REALITIES. EDUCATIONAL, ECONOMIC, LEGAL AND PERSONAL NEEDS OF CAREER WOMEN.   WPARKRX66049

REALITY
THE URBAN REALITY. A COMPARATIVE STUDY OF THE SOCIO-ECONOMIC SITUATION OF MEXICAN-AMERICANS, NEGROES AND
ANGLO-CAUCASIANS IN LOS-ANGELES COUNTY. /CALIFORNIA/   CLOSACH65708

AMERICA-S POOR. REALITY AND CHANGE. /RETRAINING SKILLS UNEMPLOYMENT/   GAMERFX66674

IMPROVING INDUSTRIAL RACE-RELATIONS -- PART I. EQUAL JOB OPPORTUNITY -- SLOGAN OR REALITY. GFLEMHC63363

THE REALITY OF EQUAL-OPPORTUNITY IN FEDERAL EMPLOYMENT.   GMACYJW66933

GIVING REALITY TO THE PROMISE OF EQUALITY.   GROBIJB64240

REALIZING
REALIZING THE MANPOWER POTENTIALITIES OF MINORITY-GROUP YOUTH.   GHOLLJH58778

REALIZING THE MANPOWER POTENTIALITIES OF MINORITY-GROUP YOUTH.   NHOLLJH58561

REAPER
NO HARVEST FOR THE REAPER. THE STORY OF THE MIGRATORY AGRICULTURAL WORKER IN THE UNITED STATES. NHILLHX59534

REAPPRAISAL
HIGHER EDUCATION FOR WOMEN. TIME FOR REAPPRAISAL.   WDOLAEF63952

REAPPRAISED
WESTERNERS FROM THE EAST. ORIENTAL IMMIGRANTS REAPPRAISED.   ODANIRX66084

REARING
CHILD REARING AMONG LOW-INCOME FAMILIES. /ECONOMIC-STATUS/   NLEWIHX61040

REASONS
A STUDY OF THE REASONS FOR FAILURE ON THE JOB OF SOME GRADUATES OF INTERMOUNTAIN SCHOOL.   IFISHLX60560

REASONS FOR BELATED EDUCATION. A STUDY OF THE PLIGHT OF THE OLDER NEGRO TEACHERS. /OCCUPATIONS/ NCUNNGE58244

REBUILDING
REBUILDING CITIES. THE EFFECTS OF DISPLACEMENT AND RELOCATION ON SMALL BUSINESS.   NZIMMBG64247

RECESSION
LAST HIRED. FIRST FIRED. THOUGH NEGRO WORKERS HAVE MADE IMPRESSIVE GAINS THEY MIGHT BE FIRST TO FEEL THE
BITE OF RECESSION.   NNORTHR49940

RECIPIENTS
TRAINING OF PUBLIC ASSISTANCE RECIPIENTS UNDER THE MDTA.   GROSORG66258

PUBLIC ASSISTANCE RECIPIENTS IN NEW-YORK STATE, JANUARY-FEBRUARY 1957.   GSNYDEM58114

DETROIT-S INSURED UNEMPLOYED AND EMPLOYABLE WELFARE RECIPIENTS. /MICHIGAN/   GWICKED63561

INSURED UNEMPLOYED AND EMPLOYABLE WELFARE RECIPIENTS.   GWICKEX63637

A FOLLOWUP STUDY OF 1963 RECIPIENTS OF THE SERVICES OF THE EMPLOYMENT ASSISTANCE PROGRAM,
BUREAU-OF-INDIAN-AFFAIRS.   IUSDINT66650

RECOMMENDATIONS
REPORT AND RECOMMENDATIONS OF DELAWARE COMMITTEE ON MIGRATORY LABOR. /MIGRANT-WORKERS/   GDELACM58945

THE ROLE OF THE SECONDARY SCHOOLS IN THE PREPARATION OF YOUTH FOR EMPLOYMENT. SUMMARY, CONCLUSIONS, AND
RECOMMENDATIONS.   GKAUFJJ67963

REPORT OF FINDINGS AND RECOMMENDATIONS RESULTING FROM AN ANALYSIS OF THE EMPLOYMENT PRACTICES IN THE
VARIOUS DEPARTMENTS OF THE CITY OF LOS-ANGELES. /CALIFORNIA/   GLOSAOC63917

PROBLEMS, RESEARCH, AND RECOMMENDATIONS IN THE EMPLOYMENT TESTING OF MINORITY-GROUP APPLICANTS. GNEWCMR66163

REPORT WITH RECOMMENDATIONS ON THE SUBJECT OF FEDERAL FAIR-EMPLOYMENT-PRACTICES LEGISLATION. GNEWYCB53069

RACIAL DISCRIMINATION IN THE CINCINNATI BUILDING TRADES. A COMPREHENSIVE REPORT AND RECOMMENDATIONS.
/OHIO/   GOHIOCR64129

COMPLIANCE GUIDE. RECOMMENDATIONS FOR OBTAINING COMPLIANCE WITH THE NONDISCRIMINATION PROVISIONS IN

RECOMMENDATIONS   (CONTINUATION)
GOVERNMENT CONTRACTS.   GPRESCH58119

CONCLUSIONS AND **RECOMMENDATIONS**, FIRST CONFERENCE ON MIGRANT-LABOR.   GTEXACO59351

THE NEGRO WAGE-EARNER AND APPRENTICESHIP TRAINING PROGRAMS. A CRITICAL ANALYSIS WITH **RECOMMENDATIONS**.   NHILLHX60532

TWENTY YEARS OF STATE FAIR-EMPLOYMENT-PRACTICE COMMISSIONS. A CRITICAL ANALYSIS WITH **RECOMMENDATIONS**.   NHILLHX64550

RACIAL DISCRIMINATION IN THE CINCINNATI BUILDING TRADES. REPORT AND **RECOMMENDATIONS**. /OHIO/   NOHIOCR66605

NEW-YORK WOMEN. A REPORT AND **RECOMMENDATIONS** FROM THE NEW-YORK GOVERNOR-S COMMITTEE ON THE EDUCATION AND
EMPLOYMENT OF WOMEN.   WNEWYGW64799

RECONCILIATION
THE FEMALE PHYSICIAN IN PUBLIC HEALTH. CONFLICT AND **RECONCILIATION** OF THE SEX AND PROFESSIONAL ROLES.
/OCCUPATIONS/   WKOSAJX64915

RECONVERSION
RACIAL ASPECTS OF **RECONVERSION**.   NNATLUL45896

RECORD
THE PEOPLE TAKE THE LEAD. A **RECORD** OF PROGRESS IN CIVIL-RIGHTS, 1948-1957.   GNATLLS57049

THE PEOPLE TAKE THE LEAD. A **RECORD** OF PROGRESS IN CIVIL-RIGHTS, 1954-1963.   GNATLLS63050

TITLE-VII. REPORTING AND **RECORD** KEEPING. /LEGISLATION/   GPEARHG66149

EMPLOYABILITY AND THE JUVENILE ARREST **RECORD**.   GSPAREV66839

TOLERANCE IN INDUSTRY. THE **RECORD**.   GTURNHC50365

LAKE ARROWHEAD CONFERENCE ON EQUAL-EMPLOYMENT-OPPORTUNITY, OCTOBER 22-24, 1963 -- **RECORD** OF PROCEEDINGS.
LOS-ANGELES, CALIFORNIA.   GUSFEDE63513

MEXICAN IMMIGRATION TO THE UNITED STATES. THE **RECORD** AND ITS IMPLICATIONS.   MGREBLX66406

THE CIVIL-RIGHTS FIGHT. A LOOK AT THE LEGISLATIVE **RECORD**.   NAFLCIO60005

NEGROES AND THE LABOR MOVEMENT. **RECORD** OF THE LEFT WING UNIONS.   NDOYLWX62287

THE NEGRO **RECORD** IN EQUAL-OPPORTUNITIES.   NGRANLB58596

RACE DISCRIMINATION IN TRADE UNIONS. **RECORD** AND OUTLOOK.   NNORTHR46945

DESEGREGATION IN AMERICAN SOCIETY. THE **RECORD** OF A GENERATION OF CHANGE.   NYINGJM63345

RECORDS
EVALUATING JOB APPLICANTS WITH POLICE **RECORDS**. /CALIFORNIA/   GCALFEP66532

RECRUIT
HOW TO **RECRUIT** MINORITY-GROUP COLLEGE GRADUATES, ITS PROBLEMS, ITS TECHNIQUES, ITS SOURCES, ITS
OPPORTUNITIES.   GCALVRX63555

RECRUITING
RECRUITING MINORITIES FOR PUBLIC EMPLOYMENT. EXPERIENCE REPORT 105.   GUSCONM66420

RECRUITING NEGRO COLLEGE GRADUATES.   NNATLIC64231

EFFECTIVE COLLEGE **RECRUITING**. /TECHNOLOGICAL-CHANGE/   WODIOGS61042

RECRUITMENT
BENEFIT POLICIES IN RELATION TO **RECRUITMENT** OF OLDER WORKERS, HANDICAPPED, AND MINORITY GROUPS.   GBARRGJ51425

AGGRESSIVE **RECRUITMENT** AND THE PUBLIC SERVICE.   GGREGGX61071

REPORT OF INDIAN **RECRUITMENT** AND TRAINING MEETING AT ALBUQUERQUE, NEW-MEXICO, ON DECEMBER 6, 1966.   IUSDLAB66321

EXPERIMENTAL AND DEMONSTRATION MANPOWER PROJECT FOR THE **RECRUITMENT**, TRAINING, PLACEMENT AND FOLLOW-UP OF
RURAL UNEMPLOYED WORKERS IN TEN NORTH FLORIDA CITIES. FINAL REPORT. /PARTICIPANTS/   NJACKTA66597

FACILITATIVE AND INHIBITIVE FACTORS IN TRAINING PROGRAM **RECRUITMENT** AMONG RURAL NEGROES.   NMARSCP65738

REVOLUTION IN EVOLUTION. /COLLEGE **RECRUITMENT**/   NSCOTFG66111

INACTIVE NURSES. AN UNTAPPED **RECRUITMENT** SOURCE.   WBARKAE65628

RECRUITMENT OF THE MATURE WOMAN.   WCULPPX61382

FINAL REPORT. EXPERIMENTAL AND DEMONSTRATION MANPOWER PROJECT FOR THE **RECRUITMENT**, TRAINING, PLACEMENT
AND FOLLOW-UP OF RURAL UNEMPLOYED WORKERS IN TEN NORTH FLORIDA COUNTIES.   WFLORMP66326

REDEVELOPMENT
MEETING THE MANPOWER PROBLEMS OF. I. AREA **REDEVELOPMENT**, II. AUTOMATION.   GUSDLAB62708

REDISTRIBUTION
THE ROLE OF **REDISTRIBUTION** IN SOCIAL POLICY.   GTITMRM65359

IMPLICATIONS OF POPULATION **REDISTRIBUTION**.   PSENICX57851

REDRESS
URBAN JOB DISCRIMINATION. ABUSES AND **REDRESS**.   GRICOLX66237

REDUCE
A SUMMARY REPORT OF PRACTICES AND PROGRAMS DESIGNED TO **REDUCE** THE NUMBER OF DROPOUTS IN THE HIGH SCHOOLS
OF LOS-ANGELES COUNTY. /CALIFORNIA/   GDELMDT66147

EDITORIAL COMMENT. FEPC HEARINGS **REDUCE** RACE PROBLEM TO LOWEST TERMS -- EQUAL-ECONOMIC-OPPORTUNITY.   NTHOMCH43160

REDUCTION
A NATIONAL PROGRAM FOR THE IMPROVEMENT OF WELFARE SERVICES AND THE **REDUCTION** OF WELFARE DEPENDENCY.   GCOHENE65664

POPULATION CHANGE AND POVERTY **REDUCTION**, 1947-1975.   GLAMPRJ66882

PUBLIC POLICY, PRIVATE ENTERPRISE AND THE **REDUCTION** OF POVERTY.   GLONGNE65121

THE **REDUCTION** OF INTERGROUP TENSIONS.   GWILLRM47564

RACIAL EQUALITY AND THE LAW. THE ROLE OF LAW IN THE **REDUCTION** OF DISCRIMINATION IN THE UNITED-STATES.   NBERGMX54076

REEXAMINATION
PARTICIPATION OF THE POOR. A REEXAMINATION.   GCAHNEX66905

REFERENCE
SIGNIFICANT TRENDS IN THE NEW-YORK STATE ECONOMY, WITH SPECIAL REFERENCE TO MINORITY-GROUPS.
/PUERTO-RICAN NEGRO/   CRUSSVR59482

HUMAN CAPITAL. A THEORETICAL AND EMPIRICAL ANALYSIS WITH SPECIAL REFERENCE TO EDUCATION.   GBECKGS64700

FEPC REFERENCE MANUAL.   GNATLCJ48040

COMPILATION OF LAWS AGAINST DISCRIMINATION. A REFERENCE MANUAL.   GNEWYSA48078

INCOME-DISTRIBUTION AS A FACTOR IN REGIONAL GROWTH, WITH SPECIAL REFERENCE TO THE SOUTHEAST UNITED
STATES. /DISCRIMINATION/   GPHILEW65773

REFERENCE ENCYCLOPEDIA ON THE AMERICAN-INDIAN.   IKLEIBA67899

HIGHER EDUCATION OF SOUTHWESTERN INDIANS WITH REFERENCE TO SUCCESS AND FAILURE.   IMCGRGD62584

EMPLOYMENT ASSISTANCE REFERENCE BIBLIOGRAPHY.   IUSDINTN0452

RACIAL DESEGREGATION IN THE PUBLIC SERVICE, WITH PARTICULAR REFERENCE TO THE US GOVERNMENT. NBROWVJ54127

THE AMERICAN NEGRO REFERENCE BOOK.   NDAVIJP66260

SOCIAL-CLASSES. A FRAME OF REFERENCE FOR THE STUDY OF NEGRO SOCIETY.   NHILLMC43551

EFFORTS TO ELIMINATE RACIAL DISCRIMINATION IN INDUSTRY -- WITH PARTICULAR REFERENCE TO THE SOUTH. NHOPEJX54566

WOMEN AND HIGHER EDUCATION WITH SPECIAL REFERENCE TO THE UNIVERSITY OF WISCONSIN.   WFREDEB62768

REFERENCES
MINORITY-GROUPS. EMPLOYMENT PROBLEMS, REFERENCES.   GHESLMR63773

CIVIL-RIGHTS AND EMPLOYMENT, SELECTED REFERENCES.   GMICSUSND984

SELECTED ANNOTATED REFERENCES ON FAIR-EMPLOYMENT-PRACTICES LEGISLATION.   GNELSRJ52055

SELECTED LIST OF REFERENCES ON MINORITY-GROUP EMPLOYMENT IN THE PUBLIC SERVICE.   GSIMPDX64312

DROPOUTS -- SELECTED REFERENCES.   GUSDHEW64764

SELECTED REFERENCES ON MIGRATORY WORKERS AND THEIR FAMILIES. PROBLEMS AND PROGRAMS.   GUSDLAB56204

SELECTED REFERENCES ON DOMESTIC MIGRATORY AGRICULTURAL WORKERS, THEIR FAMILIES, PROBLEMS, AND PROGRAMS,
1955-1960.   GUSDLAB61495

SELECTED REFERENCES ON THE PLAINS INDIANS.   IEWERJC60816

MEXICAN-AMERICANS. SELECTED REFERENCES.   MUSDLAB67011

A SELECTED LIST OF REFERENCES RELATING TO DISCRIMINATION AND SEGREGATION IN EDUCATION, 1949 TO JUNE 1955. NTUSKIX55220

REFERRAL
MINORITY WORKER HIRING AND REFERRAL IN SAN-FRANCISCO. /CALIFORNIA/   GUSDLAB58076

REFINING
SOME FACTORS INFLUENCING THE UPGRADING OF NEGROES IN THE SOUTHERN PETROLEUM REFINING INDUSTRY.
/CASE-STUDY/   NMARSRX63748

REFORM
THE SOCIAL POLITICS OF FEPC. A STUDY IN REFORM PRESSURE MOVEMENTS.   GKESSLC48847

REFORMER-S
A SOCIAL REFORMER-S VIEW OF POVERTY.   GHARRMX65659

REGION
THE EMERGING RURAL SOUTH. A REGION UNDER CONFRONTATION BY MASS SOCIETY.   GBERTAL66140

NONWHITE OCCUPATIONAL STATUS, BY REGION, AS RELATED TO PERCENT OF NONWHITE.   GGUEREW63746

THE ASSOCIATION OF INCOME AND EDUCATION FOR MALES, BY REGION, RACE, AND AGE.   GLASSRL65998

MEXICAN-AMERICANS IN THE LOS-ANGELES REGION. /CALIFORNIA/   MORTIMX62449

SEGREGATION DEAL. NEW-ORLEANS REGION FEPC PERMITS COMPROMISE. /LOUISIANA/   NBUSIWX45161

THE NEGRO AND EMPLOYMENT-OPPORTUNITIES IN THE SOUTH. CHATTANOOGA REGION. /TENNESSEE/   NCHATCC62197

NEGRO EMPLOYMENT IN THE FEDERAL GOVERNMENT BY CIVIL SERVICE REGION, STATE AND PAY CATEGORIES, JUNE 1962. NPRESCD62012

LAND TENURE IN THE SOUTHERN REGION. PROCEEDINGS OF PROFESSIONAL AGRICULTURAL WORKERS TENTH ANNUAL
CONFERENCE.   NTUSKIX51218

THE PHYSICAL GEOGRAPHY OF THE PALOUSE REGION, WASHINGTON AND IDAHO, AND ITS RELATION TO THE AGRICULTURAL
ECONOMY.   OSHROCR58762

REGIONAL
SOME GENERAL ASPECTS OF RECENT REGIONAL DEVELOPMENT. /SOUTH/   GHENDJM64142

SOME REGIONAL DIFFERENCES IN WAGES OF AGRICULTURAL WORKERS. /MIGRANT-WORKERS/   GMAITST60436

INCOME-DISTRIBUTION AS A FACTOR IN REGIONAL GROWTH, WITH SPECIAL REFERENCE TO THE SOUTHEAST UNITED
STATES. /DISCRIMINATION/   GPHILEW65773

REGIONAL COMMUNITY LEADERS CONFERENCE ON EQUAL-EMPLOYMENT-OPPORTUNITY, PROCEEDINGS.   GPRESCD64113

REGIONAL ORGANIZATION. BUREAU-OF-INDIAN-AFFAIRS.   ITAYLTW57627

REGIONAL CONFERENCES ON IMPLEMENTING THE CIVIL-RIGHTS-ACT.   NFREYMX66386

A UNIQUE REGIONAL PROGRAM OF PSYCHOLOGICAL RESEARCH AND TRAINING IN THE SOUTH.   NLANGMC56032

SOUTHERN TRADITION AND REGIONAL PROGRESS.   NNICHWH60322

A REGIONAL STUDY OF THE NEGRO.   NPIERWG41999

REPORT OF ARROWHEAD REGIONAL CONFERENCE ON THE STATUS OF WOMEN IN NORTHERN MINNESOTA.   WARRORC66216

REGIONS

MIGRATION PATTERNS OF THE RURAL-FARM POPULATION. THIRTEEN ECONOMIC **REGIONS** OF THE UNITED STATES, 1940-1950. .... GBCWLGK57415

REGIONS, RACE AND JOBS. NHENDVW67517

REGISTRIES

REGISTRIES AND INTERGROUP RELATIONS. /NEGRO WOMEN DISCRIMINATION/ CKASUMX59013

REGRESSION

EDUCATION AND OCCUPATIONAL MOBILITY. A **REGRESSION** ANALYSIS. GDUNCOD63652

WOMAN-S CENTURY OF PROGRESS. IS IT TO END IN **REGRESSION**. /WORK-WOMAN-ROLE/ WMCKARC58946

REGULATION

LOCAL **REGULATION** OF DISCRIMINATORY EMPLOYMENT PRACTICES. GELSOAX47661

FAIR-EMPLOYMENT-PRACTICES ACT AND **REGULATION** 30. /HAWAII/ GHAWADL64766

GOVERNMENT **REGULATION** OF UNION POLICIES. GHICKRX66774

REGULATIONS

TEXTS OF RULES AND **REGULATIONS** OF PRESIDENT-S COMMITTEE ON EQUAL-EMPLOYMENT-OPPORTUNITY RELATING TO OBLIGATIONS OF GOVERNMENT CONTRACTORS AND SUBCONTRACTORS, EFFECTIVE JULY 22, 1961. A BNA SPECIAL REPORT. GBURENA61498

RULES AND **REGULATIONS** OF THE PRESIDENT-S COMMITTEE ON EQUAL-EMPLOYMENT-OPPORTUNITY AS AMENDED. GBURENA63496

FAIR-EMPLOYMENT-PRACTICE ACT...FEPC RULES AND **REGULATIONS**... GUIDE TO PRE-EMPLOYMENT INQUIRIES. /CALIFORNIA/ GCALFEP61533

SUMMARY OF RULES, **REGULATIONS**, AND LAWS THAT AFFECT SEASONAL FARM WORKERS AND THEIR EMPLOYERS IN NEW-YORK STATE. /MIGRANT-WORKERS/ GNEWYSJND113

GOVERNMENT CONTRACT EMPLOYMENT. RULES AND **REGULATIONS**... EFFECTIVE JULY 22, 1961, AS AMENDED SEPTEMBER 7, 1963. .... GPRESCD63110

REHABILITATION

UNTAPPED GOOD. THE **REHABILITATION** OF SCHOOL DROPOUTS. GCHANNM66803

CIVIL-RIGHTS AND THE **REHABILITATION** OF AFDC CLIENTS. GSETSLX64296

FAMILY PLAN AND **REHABILITATION** PROGRAMS, STANDING-ROCK RESERVATION. IUSDINT64649

EDUCABILITY AND **REHABILITATION**. THE FUTURE OF THE WELFARE CLASS. NHESSRD64523

NO LONGER SUPERFLUOUS -- THE EDUCATIONAL **REHABILITATION** OF THE HARD-CORE UNEMPLOYED. NPALLNJ65332

REJECTION

SOME EDUCATIONAL IMPLICATIONS OF THE INFLUENCE OF **REJECTION** ON ASPIRATION LEVELS OF MINORITY-GROUP CHILDREN. GGOFFRM54366

AMENDMENTS TO THE TAFT-HARTLEY. A **REJECTION** OF RACIAL DISCRIMINATION. /LEGISLATION/ NOSHAJB54964

REJECTS

JOINT STAND **REJECTS** RACIAL QUOTAS FOR PLUMBING APPRENTICES. GAIRCHR63867

RELATED

CULTURAL AND **RELATED** RESTRAINTS AND MEANS OF OVERCOMING THEM. /MEXICAN-AMERICAN NEGRO INTEGRATION/ ... CSHANLW65485

INEQUALITY OF OPPORTUNITY IN HIGHER EDUCATION. A STUDY OF MINORITY GROUP AND **RELATED** BARRIERS TO COLLEGE ADMISSION. GBERKDS48446

MINORITY-GROUP AND CLASS STATUS AS **RELATED** TO SOCIAL AND PERSONALITY FACTORS IN SCHOLASTIC ACHIEVEMENT. ... GDEUTMP60640

NONWHITE OCCUPATIONAL STATUS, BY REGION, AS **RELATED** TO PERCENT OF NONWHITE. GGUEREW63746

CHARACTERISTICS OF FARM WORKERS AS **RELATED** TO STABILIZATION OF THE WORK FORCE. /MIGRANT-WORKERS/ ... GMETZWH62504

FAMILY INCOME AND **RELATED** CHARACTERISTICS AMONG LOW-INCOME COUNTIES AND STATES. GRODOAL64241

SOME DIFFERENCES IN FACTORS **RELATED** TO EDUCATIONAL ACHIEVEMENT OF TWO MEXICAN-AMERICAN GROUPS. ... MMONTPX60443

RACE AND SOCIAL-CLASS AS SEPARATE FACTORS **RELATED** TO SOCIAL ENVIRONMENT. /ASPIRATIONS/ ... NBLOORX63096

INCOME AND **RELATED** CHARACTERISTICS OF RURAL HOUSEHOLDS IN THE CENTRAL LOUISIANA MIXED FARMING AREA. ... NBOLTBX60398

GRANTS AND PROJECTS **RELATED** TO THE DEVELOPMENT OF THE AMERICAN NEGRO. ALL FISCAL YEARS THROUGH JUNE 10, 1966. .... NFORDFX66133

PROBLEMS FOR ADULT EDUCATION **RELATED** TO ACQUIRING CAPABILITIES FOR WORK. NGOLDFH63430

A PILOT STUDY OF PERSONALITY FACTORS **RELATED** TO OCCUPATIONAL ASPIRATIONS OF NEGRO COLLEGE STUDENTS. ... NLITTLW66697

PERSONAL AND ON-THE-JOB CHARACTERISTICS **RELATED** TO NEGRO PERCEPTIONS OF DISCRIMINATION. ... NSOLDHX56152

AN EMPIRICAL STUDY OF HIGH SCHOOL DROPOUTS IN REGARD TO TEN POSSIBLY **RELATED** FACTORS. ... NTHOMRJ54159

A REPORT ON COMMUNITY FACTORS IN NASHVILLE **RELATED** TO THE NEGRO IN MEDICINE. /TENNESSEE/ ... NVALIPX56281

SUMMARY OF RESEARCH DURING 1964 **RELATED** TO THE NEGRO AND NEGRO EDUCATION. NWESTEX66315

RELATION

EMPLOYMENT-STATUS AND WORK CHARACTERISTICS. STATISTICS ON THE **RELATION** BETWEEN EMPLOYMENT AND SOCIAL AND ECONOMIC CHARACTERISTICS. /DEMOGRAPHY/ CUSBURC63170

BENEFIT POLICIES IN **RELATION** TO RECRUITMENT OF OLDER WORKERS, HANDICAPPED, AND MINORITY GROUPS. ... GBARRGJ51425

TEST PERFORMANCE IN **RELATION** TO ETHNIC GROUP AND SOCIAL CLASS. GROBESO63683

THE INFLUENCE OF DISCRIMINATION ON MINORITY-GROUP MEMBERS IN ITS **RELATION** TO ATTEMPTS TO COMBAT DISCRIMINATION. GSAENGX48273

THE DISPLACED PERSON AND THE SOCIAL AGENCY. A STUDY OF THE CASEWORK PROCESS AND ITS **RELATION** TO IMMIGRANT ADJUSTMENT. JCRYSDX58714

RELATION OF MOTHER-S EMPLOYMENT TO INTELLECTUAL PERFORMANCE OF NEGRO COLLEGE STUDENTS. ... NEPPSEG64336

THE **RELATION** OF RACIAL SEGREGATION IN EARLY SCHOOLING TO THE LEVEL OF ASPIRATION AND ACADEMIC ACHIEVEMENT

RELATION (CONTINUATION)
OF NEGRO STUDENTS IN A NORTHERN HIGH SCHOOL.

NSAINJN62137

THE PHYSICAL GEOGRAPHY OF THE PALOUSE REGION, WASHINGTON AND IDAHO, AND ITS **RELATION** TO THE AGRICULTURAL
ECONOMY.

OSHROCR58762

AGE OF COMPLETION OF CHILDBEARING AND ITS **RELATION** TO THE PARTICIPATION OF WOMEN IN THE LABOR-FORCE.
UNITED STATES 1910-1955.

WDAYXLH57725

COLLEGE WOMEN-S IDENTIFICATIONS WITH THEIR FATHERS IN **RELATION** TO VOCATIONAL INTEREST PATTERNS.
/ASPIRATIONS/

WHALLWJ63815

WHAT ASPECTS OF CHILD BEHAVIOR SHOULD BE STUDIED IN **RELATION** TO MATERNAL EMPLOYMENT.

WHARTRE61829

POST-HIGH SCHOOL PLANS FOR SENIOR GIRLS IN **RELATION** TO SCHOLASTIC APTITUDE. /ASPIRATIONS/

WMILLRX61983

RELATIONS
ADDRESS TO COMMUNITY **RELATIONS** SERVICE STAFF TRAINING SESSION, JANUARY 12, 1967, ON JOBS NOW. /NEGRO
PUERTO-RICAN YOUTH/

CCOLEBX67918

REGISTRIES AND INTERGROUP **RELATIONS**. /NEGRO WOMEN DISCRIMINATION/

CKASUMX59013

AMERICAN MINORITIES, A TEXTBOOK OF READINGS IN INTERGROUP **RELATIONS**.

GBARRML57424

RACE AND ETHNIC **RELATIONS**.

GBERRBX65449

RECENT RESEARCH ON RACIAL **RELATIONS** IN THE USA.

GBLUMHX58458

MANUAL OF INTERGROUP **RELATIONS**.

GDEANJP55630

INTERGROUP **RELATIONS** IN THE FEDERAL-SERVICE .

GDOUGJH61649

INTERGROUP **RELATIONS** WITHIN BUSINESS AND INDUSTRY.

GGENECC49713

QUERIES CONCERNING INDUSTRY AND SOCIETY GROWING OUT OF STUDY OF ETHNIC **RELATIONS** IN INDUSTRY.

GHUGHEC59787

SITUATIONAL PATTERNING AND INTERGROUP **RELATIONS**.

GKOHNML56145

TESTIMONY OF HUMAN **RELATIONS**. /LOS-ANGELES CALIFORNIA/

GLOSACCND915

ETHNIC **RELATIONS** IN THE UNITED STATES.

GMCDOEC53050

INTERRACIAL HUMAN **RELATIONS** IN MANAGEMENT, A COMPILED REPORT PRESENTED ORALLY...JANUARY 17 1951.

GMCKEIX51926

INTER-GROUP **RELATIONS** WITHIN LABOR AND INDUSTRY.

GNATLCL49042

NEW-YORK STATE-COMMISSION-AGAINST-DISCRIMINATION, STATEMENT BEFORE THE US SENATE SUBCOMMITTEE ON LABOR
AND LABOR-MANAGEMENT **RELATIONS**.

GNEWYSA52102

THEY AND WE, RACIAL AND ETHNIC **RELATIONS** IN THE UNITED STATES.

GROSEPI64251

DIVISION OF AUTHORITY UNDER TITLE-VII OF THE CIVIL-RIGHTS-ACT OF 1964. A PRELIMINARY STUDY IN
FEDERAL-STATE INTERAGENCY **RELATIONS**.

GROSESJ66254

INTERPERSONAL **RELATIONS** IN ETHNICALLY MIXED SMALL WORK GROUPS.

GSCOTWW59291

RACIAL AND ETHNIC **RELATIONS**. SELECTED READINGS.

GSEGABE66154

AMERICAN MINORITY **RELATIONS**, THE SOCIOLOGY OF RACE AND ETHNIC GROUPS.

GVANDJW63535

HUMAN RESOURCES, **RELATIONS** AND PROBLEMS ON THE FORT-HALL INDIAN RESERVATION.

IHARMHC61572

THE OLD-TIMERS AND THE NEWCOMERS. ETHNIC-GROUP **RELATIONS** IN A NEEDLE TRADE UNION.

NHERBWX53519

THE NATURAL HISTORY OF SOCIAL CONFLICT AND WHITE-NEGRO **RELATIONS**.

NHIMEJS49553

CHANGING STRUCTURES OF WHITE-NEGRO **RELATIONS** IN THE SOUTH.

NHIMEJS51552

WHAT ARE SOME INDUSTRIAL **RELATIONS** APPROACHES TO INTEGRATION.

NHOMAHL63564

RACE-RELATIONS IN INDUSTRIAL **RELATIONS**.

NHUGHEC46586

THE NEGRO WORKER OF KANSAS-CITY. A STUDY OF TRADE UNION AND ORGANIZED LABOR **RELATIONS**.

NKANCIU40634

WHAT SHOULD THE BUSINESS RESPONSE BE TO THE NEGRO REVOLUTION. A PUBLIC **RELATIONS** PROGRAM FOR DEALING WITH
MINORITY-GROUPS.

NLANGJF65671

PROPOSALS FOR THE IMPROVEMENT OF HUMAN **RELATIONS** IN THE LOS-ANGELES METROPOLITAN AREA. /EMPLOYMENT
CALIFORNIA/

NLCSACC65365

MINORITY-GROUPS AND INTERGROUP **RELATIONS** IN THE SAN-FRANCISCO BAY AREA. /CALIFORNIA/

NRECOCW63043

RACE PREJUDICE AND DISCRIMINATION. READINGS IN INTERGROUP **RELATIONS** IN THE US.

NROSEAM51075

RACE **RELATIONS**. QUESTIONS AND ANSWERS FOR PERSONNEL MEN.

NSHOSAX64132

THE IMPACT OF RACE-RELATIONS ON INDUSTRIAL **RELATIONS** IN THE SOUTH.

NWHEEJH64230

RELATIONS AMONG MATERNAL EMPLOYMENT INDICES AND DEVELOPMENTAL CHARACTERISTICS OF CHILDREN.
/WORK-FAMILY-CONFLICT/

WBURCLG61665

RELATIONSHIP
THE URBAN ADJUSTMENT OF IMMIGRANTS. THE **RELATIONSHIP** OF EDUCATION TO OCCUPATIONAL AND TOTAL FAMILY
INCOME. /NEGRO MEXICAN-AMERICAN/

CSHANLW63122

URBAN ADJUSTMENT AND ITS **RELATIONSHIP** TO THE SOCIAL ANTECEDENTS OF IMMIGRANT WORKERS. /NEGRO
MEXICAN-AMERICAN/

CSHANLW65121

TRICKLING DOWN. THE **RELATIONSHIP** BETWEEN ECONOMIC GROWTH AND THE EXTENT OF POVERTY AMONG AMERICAN
FAMILIES.

GANDEWH64392

TITLE-VII. **RELATIONSHIP** AND EFFECT ON THE NATIONAL-LABOR- RELATIONS-BOARD. /LEGISLATION/

GFUCHRS66702

RACE, NATIONALITY, AND RELIGION -- THEIR **RELATIONSHIP** TO APPOINTMENT POLICIES AND CASEWORK.

GHAGEDJ57752

TITLE-VII. **RELATIONSHIP** AND EFFECT ON EXECUTIVE ORDER 11246. /LEGISLATION/

GMANNRD66937

TITLE-VII. **RELATIONSHIP** AND EFFECT ON STATE ACTION. /LEGISLATION/

GPURDJW66209

RELATIONSHIP   (CONTINUATION)
THE **RELATIONSHIP** OF THE SOCIAL-STRUCTURE OF AN INDIAN COMMUNITY TO ADULT AND JUVENILE-DELINQUENCY.
/POVERTY ECONOMIC-STATUS/   IMINNMS63218

THE **RELATIONSHIP** BETWEEN UNEARNED INCOME AND INDIVIDUAL PRODUCTIVE EFFORT ON THE JICARILLA APACHE INDIAN
RESERVATION.   IWILSHC61687

THE **RELATIONSHIP** OF JUVENILE-DELINQUENCY, RACE, AND ECONOMIC STATUS.   NBLUEJT48097

VOCATIONAL CHOICES OF NEGRO HIGH SCHOOL STUDENTS IN MACON COUNTY, ALABAMA, AND THEIR **RELATIONSHIP** TO
BASIC OCCUPATIONAL ACTIVITES OF THE SCHOOL COMMUNITIES. /ASPIRATIONS/   NCHAPEJ49351

THE UNEMPLOYMENT RATE AND GRADE LEVEL **RELATIONSHIP** IN CHICAGO AS REVEALED IN THE 1960 CENSUS. /ILLINOIS/ NHARGAJ65990

THE **RELATIONSHIP** BETWEEN MECHANIZATION OF COTTON PRODUCTION AND ATTENDANCE AND ENROLLMENT IN THE RURAL
SCHOOLS OF COAHOMA COUNTY, MISSISSIPPI.   NMCLABF51349

RACE **RELATIONSHIP** IN THE POCAHONTAS COAL FIELD.   NMINARD52794

THE **RELATIONSHIP** BETWEEN TEST INTELLIGENCE OF THIRD GRADE NEGRO CHILDREN AND THE OCCUPATIONS OF THEIR
PARENTS.   NROBIML47070

THE **RELATIONSHIP** OF PARENTAL IDENTIFICATION TO SEX ROLE ACCEPTANCE IN MARRIED, SINGLE, CAREER AND
NON-CAREER WOMEN. /WORK-WOMEN-ROLE/   WBREYCH64654

AGE AND MARITAL-STATUS AND THEIR **RELATIONSHIP** TO SUCCESS IN PRACTICAL NURSING. /OCCUPATIONS/   WMEADLX63967

RELATIONSHIP BETWEEN THE EDUCATIONAL GOALS AND THE ACADEMIC PERFORMANCE OF WOMEN. A CONFIRMATION.   WWEITHX59260

THE **RELATIONSHIP** OF SELECTED VARIABLES TO CAREER-MARRIAGE PLANS OF UNIVERSITY FRESHMAN WOMEN.
/WORK-FAMILY-CONFLICT/   WZISSCX62284

RELATIONSHIPS
EMPLOYMENT AND PERSONAL CHARACTERISTICS. EMPLOYMENT BY AGE, RACE, NATIVITY, EDUCATION, MARITAL-STATUS,
HOUSEHOLD **RELATIONSHIPS**, ETC. /DEMOGRAPHY/   CUSBURC53372

PROGRESS IN INTERRACIAL **RELATIONSHIPS**. INEQUALITIES FOR NEGROES.   NLEWIES43689

RECENT EVENTS IN NEGRO UNION **RELATIONSHIPS**.   NWEAVRC44306

RELIABLE
ARE JOB TESTS **RELIABLE**.   GFUERJS65703

RELIEF
WORK **RELIEF**. SOCIAL WELFARE STYLE. /MANPOWER UNEMPLOYMENT/   GLEVISA66531

RELIGION
EQUAL-RIGHTS UNDER THE LAW. PROVIDING FOR EQUAL TREATMENT FOR ALL CITIZENS REGARDLESS OF RACE, **RELIGION**,
COLOR, NATIONAL ORIGIN OR ANCESTRY. /CALIFORNIA/   GCALAGO60511

ASSIMILATION IN AMERICAN LIFE. THE ROLE OF RACE, **RELIGION**, AND NATIONAL ORIGINS.   GGORDMY64729

RACE, NATIONALITY, AND **RELIGION** -- THEIR RELATIONSHIP TO APPOINTMENT POLICIES AND CASEWORK.   GHAGEDJ57752

MINORITY-GROUP INTEGRATION BY LABOR AND MANAGEMENT. A STUDY OF THE EMPLOYMENT PRACTICES OF THE LARGER
EMPLOYERS, AND THE MEMBERSHIP PRACTICES OF THE LARGER LABOR UNIONS WITH RESPECT TO RACE, **RELIGION**, AND
NATIONAL ORIGIN, CONNECTICUT, 1951.   GSTETHG53598

HOW DOES **RELIGION** AFFECT JOB-CHOICE.   JHARVBS65731

RELIGIOUS
ANALYSIS OF CITY ORDINANCES AGAINST RACIAL AND **RELIGIOUS** DISCRIMINATION IN EMPLOYMENT.   GAMERJCND380

LEGISLATION AGAINST RACIAL OR **RELIGIOUS** DISCRIMINATION IN EMPLOYMENT, NEW-YORK.   GIVESLM52819

RACIAL AND **RELIGIOUS** DISCRIMINATION IN EMPLOYMENT AND THE ROLE OF THE NLRB.   GMALOWH61935

A COMPARISON OF MAJOR UNITED STATES **RELIGIOUS** GROUPS. /ECONOMIC-STATUS/   JLAZRBX61033

RELOCATED
RELOCATED AMERICAN INDIANS IN THE SAN-FRANCISCO BAY AREA. SOCIAL INTERACTION AND INDIAN IDENTITY.
/CALIFORNIA/   IALBCJX64523

RELOCATEES
RELOCATEES FROM GALLUP AREA TO THE DENVER FIELD EMPLOYMENT ASSISTANCE OFFICE. /COLORADO/   IGRAVTDND438

SAN-FRANCISCO **RELOCATEES**. /CALIFORNIA/   ITAXXSXND441

RELOCATION
INDIAN **RELOCATION**. PROBLEMS OF DEPENDENCY AND MANAGEMENT IN THE CITY.   IABLOJX65085

PAPAGO INDIANS. EVALUATION OF OPPORTUNITIES FOR PERMANENT **RELOCATION**.   IFITZKXND440

A STUDY OF NAVAHO URBAN **RELOCATION** IN DENVER COLORADO.   IGRAVTD64566

PERCEIVED OPPORTUNITIES, EXPECTATIONS, AND THE DECISION TO REMAIN ON **RELOCATION**. THE CASE OF THE NAVAHO
INDIAN MIGRANT TO DENVER, COLORADO.   IGRAVTC65567

VALUES, EXPECTATIONS AND **RELOCATION**. THE NAVAHO MIGRANT TO DENVER. /COLORADO/   IGRAVTD66146

THE AMERICAN INDIAN **RELOCATION** PROGRAM.   IMADILX56587

RELOCATION OF THE DISPLACED WORKER.   IMETZWX63081

INDIAN **RELOCATION** AND THE NEW-MEXICO SEC.   ISANDJN62615

RELOCATION RIDDLES. /MOBILITY EDUCATION/   ITAYLFX65560

THE BUREAU OF INDIAN AFFAIRS VOLUNTARY **RELOCATION** SERVICES.   IUSDINT60644

ECONOMIC FACTORS IN NAVAHO URBAN **RELOCATION**.   IWEPPRS65685

REBUILDING CITIES. THE EFFECTS OF DISPLACEMENT AND **RELOCATION** ON SMALL BUSINESS.   NZIMMBG64247

RELUCTANT
THE **RELUCTANT** SOUTH. /INTEGRATION/   NFICHJH59464

REMARKS
REMARKS AT THE PLANS-FOR-PROGRESS CONFERENCE.   GHUMPHH65788

REMARKS   (CONTINUATION)
    REMARKS ON EQUAL-EMPLOYMENT-OPPORTUNITIES.   GMCKERB65931

    THE INDIANS AND THE GREAT SOCIETY. REMARKS.   IMONDWX66591

REMEDIES
    TITLE-VII. COMPLAINT PROCEDURES AND REMEDIES. /LEGISLATION/   GWALKRW66538

    FEDERAL REMEDIES FOR RACIAL DISCRIMINATION BY LABOR UNIONS.   GWEISLX62597

    HARD-CORE UNEMPLOYMENT IN DETROIT. CAUSES AND REMEDIES. /MICHIGAN/   NWACHHMND289

    EMPLOYEE CHOICE AND SOME PROBLEMS OF RACE AND REMEDIES IN REPRESENTATION CAMPAIGNS.   NYALELJ63599

REPLACEMENT
    RURAL-FARM MALES ENTERING AND LEAVING WORKING AGES, 1940-50 AND 1950-60. REPLACEMENT RATIOS AND RATES.
    /OCCUPATIONS/   GBOWLGK56433

    POTENTIAL SUPPLY AND REPLACEMENT OF RURAL MALES OF LABOR-FORCE AGE, 1960-70.   GBOWLGK66430

REPORT
    REPORT TO GOVERNOR EDMUND G BROWN. SECOND ETHNIC SURVEY OF EMPLOYMENT AND PROMOTION IN STATE GOVERNMENT.
    /CALIFORNIA NEGRO MEXICAN-AMERICAN/   CBECKWL65070

    ANNUAL FARM LABOR REPORT, 1965, CALIFORNIA DEPARTMENT OF EMPLOYMENT, FARM LABOR SERVICE. /NEGRO
    MEXICAN-AMERICAN WOMEN/   CCALDEM66906

    REPORT ON OAKLAND SCHOOLS. AN INVESTIGATION UNDER SECTION 1421 OF THE CALIFORNIA LABOR CODE OF THE
    OAKLAND UNIFIED SCHOOL DISTRICT 1962-1963. /NEGRO ORIENTAL MEXICAN-AMERICAN/   CCALDIR63710

    BUREAU OF MIGRANT-LABOR REPORT. /NEW-JERSEY NEGRO PUERTO-RICAN/   CNEWJOL61907

    ETHNIC SURVEY OF MUNICIPAL-EMPLOYEES, A REPORT ON THE NUMBER AND DISTRIBUTION OF NEGROES AND
    PUERTO-RICANS AND OTHER EMPLOYEES BY THE CITY OF NEW-YORK.   CNEWYCC64916

    INTERIM REPORT TO THE MAYOR ON ITS INQUIRY INTO CHARGES OF RACIAL BIAS IN THE CITY BUILDING AND
    CONSTRUCTION INDUSTRY. /NEW-YORK NEGRO PUERTO-RICAN/   CNEWYCO64917

    BREAKING THE BARRIERS OF OCCUPATIONAL ISOLATION. A REPORT ON UPGRADING LOW-SKILL, LOW-WAGE WORKERS.
    /NEGRO PUERTO-RICAN/   CPROJAX66237

    SPANISH-SPEAKING PEOPLE IN THE UNITED STATES. A PILOT REPORT. /MEXICAN-AMERICAN PUERTO-RICAN/   CSAMOJX63474

    FINAL REPORT. EXPERIMENTAL AND DEMONSTRATION ON-JOB-TRAINING PROJECT. /MIGRANT-WORKERS MEXICAN-AMERICAN
    NEGRO ARIZONA/   CSKILTO66324

    UNITED STATES CENSUS OF AGRICULTURE. COLOR, RACE, AND TENURE OF FARM OPERATOR. GENERAL REPORT, VOLUME II.
    /DEMOGRAPHY/   CUSBURC59382

    REPORT. EVALUATION STUDY OF YOUTH TRAINING AND EMPLOYMENT PROJECT, EAST LOS-ANGELES. /NEGRO
    MEXICAN-AMERICAN CALIFORNIA/   CWEINJL64310

    FINAL REPORT OF THE YMCA YOUTH AND WORK PROJECT 1962-1966. /NEGRO PUERTO-RICAN TRAINING/   CYMCAYA66329

    1963 REPORT OF PROGRESS IN HUMAN-RIGHTS.   GALASSC63366

    REPORT ON TWENTY STATE ANTI-DISCRIMINATION AGENCIES AND THE LAWS THEY ADMINISTER.   GAMERJD61387

    REPORT OF THE CALIFORNIA STATE ADVISORY COMMITTEE TO THE UNITED STATES COMMISSION ON CIVIL-RIGHTS ON
    CALIFORNIA-S PROGRAM FOR EQUAL-OPPORTUNITY IN APPRENTICESHIP.   GBECKWL62432

    AUTOMATION AND ECONOMIC PROGRESS. A SUMMARY OF THE REPORT OF THE NATIONAL COMMISSION ON TECHNOLOGY,
    AUTOMATION, AND ECONOMIC PROGRESS.   GBOWEHR66748

    UNEMPLOYMENT IN A PROSPEROUS ECONOMY. A REPORT OF THE PRINCETON-MANPOWER-SYMPOSIUM.   GBOWEWG65749

    A SPECIAL REPORT -- THE EQUAL-EMPLOYMENT-OPPORTUNITY LAW, TITLE-VII OF THE CIVIL-RIGHTS-ACT OF 1964. GBURENAN0495

    TEXTS OF RULES AND REGULATIONS OF PRESIDENT-S COMMITTEE ON EQUAL-EMPLOYMENT-OPPORTUNITY RELATING TO
    OBLIGATIONS OF GOVERNMENT CONTRACTORS AND SUBCONTRACTORS, EFFECTIVE JULY 22, 1961. A BNA SPECIAL REPORT. GBURENA61498

    REPORT TO THE GOVERNOR AND THE LEGISLATURE OF THE COMMISSION ON MANPOWER, AUTOMATION AND TECHNOLOGY,
    1964. /CALIFORNIA/   GCALCMA65515

    BANK OF AMERICA EMPLOYMENT PRACTICES. FIRST REPORT BY CALIFORNIA FEPC.   GCALFEP64530

    AFFIRMATIVE-ACTIONS IN EMPLOYMENT. A SPECIAL FEPC REPORT. /CALIFORNIA/   GCALFEP65529

    THE ITINERANT FARM LABOR PROJECT REPORT. /MIGRANT-WORKERS CALIFORNIA/   GCALVRS60553

    FINAL REPORT ON JOBS II PROJECT. /CHICAGO ILLINOIS/   GCHICBC65319

    REPORT AND RECOMMENDATIONS OF DELAWARE COMMITTEE ON MIGRATORY LABOR. /MIGRANT-WORKERS/   GDELACM58945

    A SUMMARY REPORT OF PRACTICES AND PROGRAMS DESIGNED TO REDUCE THE NUMBER OF DROPOUTS IN THE HIGH SCHOOLS
    OF LOS-ANGELES COUNTY. /CALIFORNIA/   GDELMDT66147

    REPORT ON AND ANALYSIS OF SECOND CENSUS OF CITY EMPLOYEES TO DETERMINE BASES FOR FUTURE PERSONNEL
    DEVELOPMENTS. /DETROIT MICHIGAN/   GDETRCC66639

    THE FIRST NINE MONTHS. REPORT OF THE PRESIDENT-S COMMITTEE ON EQUAL-EMPLOYMENT-OPPORTUNITY.   GFEDEBJ62672

    REPORT OF INDUSTRY AND LABOR-MANAGEMENT CLINICS. IMPLEMENTATION OF EMPLOYMENT IN MERIT PROGRAMS IN NON
    FEPC STATES BY DIRECT APPROACH TO TOP MANAGEMENT.   GFISKUR51684

    REPORT OF THE DIAGNOSTIC SURVEY OF TENANT HOUSEHOLDS IN THE WEST SIDE URBAN-RENEWAL AREA OF
    NEW-YORK-CITY.   GGREEAI65474

    CRITICAL ISSUES IN EMPLOYMENT POLICY, A REPORT. /UNEMPLOYMENT/   GHARBFH66476

    A REPORT ON EMPLOYMENT OF NONWHITES IN CHICAGO. /ILLINOIS/   GILLICH55792

    SPECIAL REPORT ON EMPLOYMENT OPPORTUNITIES IN ILLINOIS.   GILLIIR48801

    STATE FAIR-EMPLOYMENT-PRACTICE LAWS. REPORT PERSUANT TO PROPOSAL 400.   GILLILC57802

    HERE-S HOW MERIT EMPLOYMENT PROGRAMS WORK. A REPORT ON PROGRESS AND PROBLEMS IN THE EMPLOYMENT OF
    MINORITY-GROUP MEMBERS.   GILLISC56803

REPORT OF THE SURVEY OF EMPLOYEES OF THE STATE OF INDIANA, SEPTEMBER 1961.   GINDICR61806

FINAL REPORT. THE YOUTH TRAINING PROJECT, SEPTEMBER 1, 1963--JANUARY 31, 1965. /ST-LOUIS MISSOURI
TESTING/   GJEWIEV65568

REPORT ON THE STRUCTURE AND OPERATIONS OF THE PRESIDENT-S COMMITTEE ON EQUAL-EMPLOYMENT-OPPORTUNITY.   GKHEETW62852

IDENTIFICATION AND MODIFICATION OF THE SOCIAL-PSYCHOLOGICAL CORRELATES OF ECONOMIC DEPENDENCY. PROJECT
FINAL REPORT.   GKIMMPR66137

FEPC. REPORT ON OPERATIONS.   GLABOLR45870

NJ ANTI-DISCRIMINATION LAW. FIRST ANNUAL REPORT. /NEW-JERSEY/   GLABOLR46871

NY ANTI-DISCRIMINATION LAW. 1946 ANNUAL REPORT. /NEW-YORK/   GLABOLR46872

REPORT OF FINDINGS AND RECOMMENDATIONS RESULTING FROM AN ANALYSIS OF THE EMPLOYMENT PRACTICES IN THE
VARIOUS DEPARTMENTS OF THE CITY OF LOS-ANGELES. /CALIFORNIA/   GLOSAOC63917

INTERRACIAL HUMAN RELATIONS IN MANAGEMENT, A COMPILED REPORT PRESENTED ORALLY...JANUARY 17 1951.   GMCKEIX51926

SPECIAL REPORT. AN INVESTIGATION OF THE PERSONNEL POLICIES AND PRACTICES OF THE MICHIGAN STATE HIGHWAY
DEPARTMENT, MARCH 1961.   GMICFEP61983

MERIT EMPLOYMENT IN MICHIGAN. A PICTORIAL REPORT.   GMICFEP63981

TECHNICAL REPORT NUMBER 1. EMPLOYMENT PRACTICES IN THE HOTEL, MOTEL AND RESTAURANT INDUSTRY OF MISSOURI.   GMILLRX66020

TECHNICAL REPORT NUMBER 2. EMPLOYMENT PRACTICES OF SELECTED MISSOURI PUBLIC UTILITIES. NATURAL GAS AND
ELECTRIC.   GMILLRX66021

THE MEASUREMENT AND INTERPRETATION OF JOB VACANCIES. A CONFERENCE REPORT OF THE NATIONAL BUREAU OF
ECONOMIC RESEARCH. /LABOR-MARKET/   GNATLBE66611

SOCIAL DYNAMITE. THE REPORT OF THE CONFERENCE ON UNEMPLOYED, OUT-OF-SCHOOL YOUTH IN URBAN AREAS, MAY
24-26, 1961.   GNATLCC61039

REPORT ON SECOND ANNUAL SPRING CONFERENCE ON CIVIL-RIGHTS OF NEW-JERSEY COMMISSION-ON-CIVIL-RIGHTS, APRIL
23, 1966.   GNEWJCC66056

REPORT OF A PRELIMINARY STUDY OF EMPLOYMENT PRACTICES INVOLVING MINORITY-GROUP WORKERS, ESSEX-COUNTY,
NEW-JERSEY.   GNEWJDE46059

REPORT ON A SURVEY OF EMPLOYMENT POLICIES AND HIRING PRACTICES INVOLVING MINORITY-GROUPS IN HUDON-COUNTY,
NEW-JERSEY.   GNEWJDE51060

REPORT ON A SURVEY OF EMPLOYMENT POLICIES AND PRACTICES INVOLVING MINORITY-GROUPS IN MIDDLESEX-COUNTY,
NEW-JERSEY.   GNEWJDE52061

REPORT WITH RECOMMENDATIONS ON THE SUBJECT OF FEDERAL FAIR-EMPLOYMENT-PRACTICES LEGISLATION.   GNEWYCB53069

THE NEXT STEPS TOWARD EQUALITY OF OPPORTUNITY IN THE SYRACUSE METROPOLITAN AREA. REPORT OF THE SYRACUSE
CONFERENCE ON HUMAN RIGHTS AND HOUSING, JULY 2-3 1962. /NEW-YORK/   GNEWYSB62103

REPORT ON EMPLOYMENT AND IMAGE OF MINORITY-GROUPS ON TELEVISION.   GNEWYSB63105

REPORT OF INQUIRY CONCERNING CHARGES OF DISCRIMINATING PRACTICES IN THE NEW-YORK STATE THRUWAY AUTHORITY.   GNEWYSB64104

REPORT OF NEW-YORK STATE JOINT LEGISLATIVE COMMITTEE ON MIGRANT-LABOR.   GNEWYSLND115

RACIAL DISCRIMINATION IN THE CINCINNATI BUILDING TRADES. A COMPREHENSIVE REPORT AND RECOMMENDATIONS.
/OHIO/   GOHIOCR64129

MIGRATORY LABOR IN OHIO. A REPORT BY THE GOVERNOR-S COMMITTEE, AUGUST 1962.   GOHIOGC62095

REPORT OF THE SPECIAL COMMITTEE ON NONDISCRIMINATION OF THE BOARD OF PUBLIC EDUCATION, PHILADELPHIA.
/PENNSYLVANIA/   GPHILBE64172

REPORT OF PROGRESS IN THE INTEGRATION OF HOTEL AND RESTAURANT EMPLOYMENT, APRIL 1961 TO MARCH 1962.
/PHILADELPHIA PENNSYLVANIA/   GPHILCH62178

REPORT OF 1961 - 1962 SURVEY OF PHILADELPHIA BANKS AND ATTACHED COMPOSITE TABULATION OF NON-WHITES.
/PENNSYLVANIA/   GPHILCH62180

A SPECIAL REPORT, CITY CONTRACT COMPLIANCE. PROGRESS IN 1963. /PHILADELPHIA PENNSYLVANIA/   GPHILCH64179

THE AMERICAN DREAM...EQUAL OPPORTUNITY, A REPORT ON THE COMMUNITY LEADER-S CONFERENCE SPONSORED BY
PRESIDENT-S COMMITTEE ON EQUAL-EMPLOYMENT-OPPORTUNITY, MAY 19, 1962.   GPRESCD62105

THE FIRST NINE MONTHS — SPECIAL YEAR-END REPORT, APRIL 7, 1961-JANUARY 15, 1962, PRESIDENT-S COMMITTEE
ON EQUAL-EMPLOYMENT-OPPORTUNITY.   GPRESCD62108

PLANS-FOR-PROGRESS, A FIRST YEAR REPORT BY THE PLANS FOR PROGRESS ADVISORY COUNCIL.   GPRESCD64112

REPORT TO THE PRESIDENT, NOVEMBER 26, 1963 BY THE PRESIDENT-S COMMITTEE ON EQUAL-EMPLOYMENT-OPPORTUNITY.   GPRESCD64114

EQUAL ECONOMIC OPPORTUNITY. A REPORT.   GPRESCG53117

FIRST REPORT. PRESIDENT-S COMMITTEE ON GOVERNMENT CONTRACTS.   GPRESCH54120

SECOND ANNUAL REPORT, THE PRESIDENT-S COMMITTEE ON GOVERNMENT CONTRACTS.   GPRESCH55124

FOURTH ANNUAL REPORT ON EQUAL JOB OPPORTUNITY, 1956-1957, PRESIDENT-S COMMITTEE ON GOVERNMENT CONTRACTS.   GPRESCH57122

FIVE YEARS OF PROGRESS, 1953-1958, A REPORT TO PRESIDENT EISENHOWER BY THE PRESIDENT-S COMMITTEE ON
GOVERNMENT CONTRACTS.   GPRESCH58121

PATTERN FOR PROGRESS. SEVENTH REPORT, FINAL REPORT TO PRESIDENT EISENHOWER FROM THE COMMITTEE ON
GOVERNMENT CONTRACTS.   GPRESCH60123

PATTERN FOR PROGRESS. SEVENTH REPORT, FINAL REPORT TO PRESIDENT EISENHOWER FROM THE COMMITTEE ON
GOVERNMENT CONTRACTS.   GPRESCH60123

FIRST ANNUAL REPORT. PRESIDENT-S COMMITTEE ON GOVERNMENT EMPLOYMENT POLICY, APRIL 30 1956.   GPRESCP56193

SECOND ANNUAL REPORT, PRESIDENT-S COMMITTEE ON GOVERNMENT EMPLOYMENT POLICY, 1957.   GPRESCP57194

THIRD ANNUAL REPORT, PRESIDENT-S COMMITTEE ON GOVERNMENT EMPLOYMENT POLICY, 1958.   GPRESCP58195

REPORT   (CONTINUATION)
    FOURTH ANNUAL REPORT, PRESIDENT-S COMMITTEE ON GOVERNMENT EMPLOYMENT POLICY.   GPRESCP59196

    ONE-THIRD OF A NATION. A REPORT ON YOUNG MEN FOUND UNQUALIFIED FOR MILITARY SERVICE.   GPRESTM64316

    FEPC IN THE STATES. A PROGRESS REPORT.   GRORTJX58246

    SAVAGE DISCOVERY. THE MOYNIHAN REPORT.   GRYANWX65489

    FINAL REPORT OF SAN-FRANCISCO CALIFORNIA COMMISSION ON EQUAL-EMPLOYMENT-OPPORTUNITY.   GSANFCE60275

    FAIR-EMPLOYMENT IN THE FEDERAL SERVICE. A PROGRESS REPORT ON CONSTRUCTIVE STEPS.   GUSCISC52386

    REPORT OF TWIN-CITIES EQUAL-OPPORTUNITY REVIEW. /MINNEAPOLIS ST-PAUL MINNESOTA/   GUSCISC64131

    EMPLOYMENT, 1961 US COMMISSION-ON-CIVIL-RIGHTS REPORT, VOLUME 3.   GUSCOMC61395

    THE 50 STATES REPORT.   GUSCOMC61415

    HOUSING, EMPLOYMENT OPPORTUNITIES AND APPRENTICESHIP TRAINING, REPORT. /NEW-JERSEY/   GUSCOMC63404

    A REPORT TO THE US COMMISSION ON CIVIL-RIGHTS. /MISSOURI/   GUSCOMC63406

    REPORT ON FLORIDA OF THE US COMMISSION ON CIVIL-RIGHTS.   GUSCOMC63409

    REPORT ON WASHINGTON-DC. EMPLOYMENT.   GUSCOMC63412

    REPORT ON MARYLAND. EMPLOYMENT.   GUSCOMC64411

    REPORT ON EMPLOYMENT PROBLEMS OF NONWHITE YOUTH IN MICHIGAN.   GUSCOMC66408

    FINAL REPORT. US COMMISSION ON FAIR-EMPLOYMENT-PRACTICES, JUNE 28, 1946.   GUSCOMF47417

    PROGRAMS FOR HIGH SCHOOL DROPOUTS. EXPERIENCE REPORT 101.   GUSCONF64976

    EXPANDING EMPLOYMENT OPPORTUNITIES IN NEWARK. EXPERIENCE REPORT 101. /NEW-JERSEY/   GUSCONM65418

    RECRUITING MINORITIES FOR PUBLIC EMPLOYMENT. EXPERIENCE REPORT 105.   GUSCONM66420

    THE HIRED FARM WORKING FORCE OF 1964. A STATISTICAL REPORT.   GUSDAGR65424

    HEALTH, EDUCATION, AND WELFARE ASPECTS OF THE ECONOMIC REPORT OF THE PRESENT AND ANNUAL REPORT OF THE
    COUNCIL OF ECONOMIC ADVISORS.   GUSDHEW66711

    HEALTH, EDUCATION, AND WELFARE ASPECTS OF THE ECONOMIC REPORT OF THE PRESENT AND ANNUAL REPORT OF THE
    COUNCIL OF ECONOMIC ADVISORS.   GUSDHEW66711

    ANNUAL REPORT OF THE SECRETARY OF HEALTH, EDUCATION, AND WELFARE TO THE CONGRESS ON TRAINING ACTIVITIES
    UNDER THE MANPOWER-DEVELOPMENT-AND-TRAINING-ACT, 1965.   GUSDHEW66978

    SCHOOL AND EARLY EMPLOYMENT EXPERIENCE OF YOUTH. A REPORT ON SEVEN COMMUNITIES, 1952-57.   GUSDLAB60494

    FAMILY CHARACTERISTICS OF THE LONG TERM UNEMPLOYED. A REPORT ON A STUDY OF CLAIMANTS UNDER THE TEMPORARY
    EXTENDED UNEMPLOYMENT COMPENSATION PROGRAM, 1961-2.   GUSDLAB61445

    MANPOWER REPORT OF THE PRESIDENT.   GUSDLAB62700

    MANPOWER REPORT OF THE PRESIDENT AND A REPORT ON MANPOWER REQUIREMENTS, RESOURCES, UTILIZATION, AND
    TRAINING.   GUSDLAB63830

    MANPOWER REPORT OF THE PRESIDENT AND A REPORT ON MANPOWER REQUIREMENTS, RESOURCES, UTILIZATION, AND
    TRAINING.   GUSDLAB63830

    MANPOWER REPORT OF THE PRESIDENT AND A REPORT ON MANPOWER REQUIREMENTS, RESOURCES, UTILIZATION, AND
    TRAINING.   GUSDLAB64829

    MANPOWER REPORT OF THE PRESIDENT AND A REPORT ON MANPOWER REQUIREMENTS, RESOURCES, UTILIZATION, AND
    TRAINING.   GUSDLAB64829

    MANPOWER REPORT OF THE PRESIDENT AND A REPORT ON MANPOWER REQUIREMENTS, RESOURCES, UTILIZATION, AND
    TRAINING.   GUSDLAB65828

    MANPOWER REPORT OF THE PRESIDENT AND A REPORT ON MANPOWER REQUIREMENTS, RESOURCES, UTILIZATION, AND
    TRAINING.   GUSDLAB65828

    REPORT ON MANPOWER RESEARCH AND TRAINING UNDER THE MDTA.   GUSDLAB66493

    YOUNG WORKERS. A REPRINT FROM THE 1966 MANPOWER REPORT.   GUSDLAB66505

    EMPLOYMENT SERVICE TASK FORCE REPORT. /MANPOWER SES/   GUSDLAB66559

    MANPOWER REPORT OF THE PRESIDENT AND A REPORT ON MANPOWER REQUIREMENTS, RESOURCES, UTILIZATION, AND
    TRAINING.   GUSDLAB66827

    MANPOWER REPORT OF THE PRESIDENT AND A REPORT ON MANPOWER REQUIREMENTS, RESOURCES, UTILIZATION, AND
    TRAINING.   GUSDLAB66827

    FIRST REPORT. US FAIR-EMPLOYMENT-PRACTICE-COMMITTEE.   GUSFEPC45512

    FINAL REPORT. US FAIR-EMPLOYMENT-PRACTICE-COMMITTEE.   GUSFEPC47511

    EQUAL-EMPLOYMENT-OPPORTUNITY ACT OF 1962. REPORT TO ACCOMPANY HR 10144.   GUSHOUR62340

    EQUAL-EMPLOYMENT-OPPORTUNITY ACT OF 1963, REPORT TO ACCOMPANY HR 405.   GUSHOUR63341

    EQUAL-EMPLOYMENT-OPPORTUNITY IN THE US POST OFFICE DEPARTMENT. A SUPPLEMENTAL REPORT TO THE POSTMASTER
    GENERAL.   GUSPODA6351(

    WESTERN-ELECTRIC AND ITS PLAN-FOR-PROGRESS, A THREE YEAR REPORT. /INDUSTRY/   GWESTEC64553

    FINAL REPORT. PATTERNS OF DISCRIMINATION STUDY -- WISCONSIN.   GWISCIC66587

    THE WDL APPRENTICESHIP TRAINING PROGRAM. REPORT OF A YEAR-S EXPERIMENT.   GWORKDL65584

    PAPAGO RESERVATION REPORT.   IARIZCI62527

    ARIZONA RESERVATIONS ECONOMICS. SURVEY REPORT.   IARIZCI63528

    BAILEYS REPORT ON SEMINOLES.   IBAILAL57531

REPORT   (CONTINUATION)
REPORT. SUMMER 1960.   IBAILAL60530

UTE INDIAN SURVEY -- PRELIMINARY REPORT, SOCIAL AND ECONOMIC CHARACTERISTICS.   IBRIGYUND442

A PROGRAM FOR INDIAN CITIZENS. A SUMMARY REPORT.   IFUNDFT61562

REPORT TO THE SECRETARY OF THE INTERIOR BY THE TASK FORCE ON INDIAN AFFAIRS.   IUSDINT61641

INDIAN AFFAIRS 1964. A PROGRESS REPORT FROM THE COMMISSIONER OF INDIAN AFFAIRS.   IUSDINT64652

REPORT OF INDIAN RECRUITMENT AND TRAINING MEETING AT ALBUQUERQUE, NEW-MEXICO, ON DECEMBER 6, 1966.   IUSDLAB66321

REPORT ON INDIAN FARM LABOR ACTIVITY.   IUSDLAB66668

THE MUTUAL SAVINGS BANKS OF NEW-YORK-CITY. A FOLLOW-UP REPORT ON THE EXCLUSION OF JEWS AT TOP-MANAGEMENT
AND POLICY-MAKING LEVELS.   JAMERJC66695

A REPORT ON THE JEWISH POPULATION OF LOS-ANGELES. /CALIFORNIA/   JMASAGX59746

PRELIMINARY REPORT ON SURVEY OF ACTIVE APPRENTICES. /CALIFORNIA/   MCALDIR62376

REPORT BY MEXICAN-AMERICAN LEADERS. EDUCATION, EMPLOYMENT, ETC.   MCALDIR64379

MIGRATORY LABOR IN COLORADO. REPORT TO THE COLORADO GENERAL ASSEMBLY.   MCOLOLC62383

MEXICAN GREEN CARDERS. PRELIMINARY REPORT.   MGALLLX62399

COMPREHENSIVE REPORT OF THE OFFICE OF THE BISHOP-S COMMITTEE FOR MIGRANT-WORKERS.   MNATLCBND082

WHEN THE MIGRANT LABORER SETTLES DOWN -- A REPORT OF THE FINDINGS OF A PROJECT ON VALUE ASSIMILATION OF
IMMIGRANT LABORERS.   MPETECL64454

MEXICAN FARM LABOR CONSULTANTS REPORT.   MUSDLAB59508

MEXICAN-AMERICAN STUDY PROJECT. ADVANCE REPORT 3, BIBLIOGRAPHY.   MUVCALM66510

SUMMARY REPORT OF THE STUDY OF DROP-OUTS IN THE THREE SENIOR HIGH SCHOOLS, COMPTON UNION HIGH SCHOOL
DISTRICT. /CALIFORNIA/   MWHITNX60517

THE MANAGEMENT OF RACIAL INTEGRATION IN BUSINESS, A SPECIAL REPORT TO MANAGEMENT.   NALEXRD64868

REPORT FROM LOS-ANGELES. /CALIFORNIA/   NBUGGJA66131

FINAL REPORT. EMPLOYMENT AND TRAINING, REPORT FOR GOVERNOR-S COMMISSION.   NBULLPX65483

FINAL REPORT. EMPLOYMENT AND TRAINING, REPORT FOR GOVERNOR-S COMMISSION.   NBULLPX65483

INTERIM REPORT ON OAKLAND SCHOOLS. /CALIFORNIA/   NCALFEP66169

THE ECONOMIC-STATUS OF NEGROES IN THE SAN-FRANCISCO OAKLAND BAY AREA. A REPORT BASED ON THE 1960 CENSUS
OF POPULATION. /CALIFORNIA/   NCALFES63172

ETHNIC CENSUS OF EXAMINATION COMPETITORS. REPORT OF EXAMINATIONS GIVEN JULY THROUGH DECEMBER, 1965,
SUMMARY. /TESTING CALIFORNIA/   NCALFPB66173

A PRELIMINARY REPORT ON MEDICAL STAFF APPOINTMENTS HELD BY NEGRO PHYSICIANS AT PREDOMINANTLY WHITE
HOSPITALS. /CHICAGO ILLINOIS/   NCHICCO60201

TWO YEAR REPORT ON THE YOUTH GUIDANCE PROJECT, 1958-1959. /CHICAGO   ILLINOIS/   NCHICULND203

ABC REPORT 1964. /COLLEGE   EDUCATION/   NDARTCX64309

NEGRO EMPLOYMENT. A PROGRESS REPORT.   NDAVIJA52256

PROBLEMS AND OPPORTUNITIES CONFRONTING NEGROES IN THE FIELD OF BUSINESS, REPORT ON THE NATIONAL
CONFERENCE ON SMALL BUSINESS. /OCCUPATIONS/   NFITZNH63358

RACISM WITHIN ORGANIZED LABOR. A REPORT OF THE FIVE YEARS OF THE AFL-CIO, 1955-1960. /UNION/   NHILLHX60542

EXPERIMENTAL AND DEMONSTRATION MANPOWER PROJECT FOR THE RECRUITMENT, TRAINING, PLACEMENT AND FOLLOW-UP OF
RURAL UNEMPLOYED WORKERS IN TEN NORTH FLORIDA CITIES. FINAL REPORT. /PARTICIPANTS/   NJACKTA66597

NEGRO ENGINEERS AND STUDENTS REPORT ON THEIR PROFESSION. /OCCUPATIONS/   NKIEHRX58647

OPPORTUNITIES FOR NEGROES IN ENGINEERING -- A SECOND REPORT. /OCCUPATIONS/   NKIEHRX64333

REPORT ON KOREA. /MILITARY/   NMARSTX51754

YOU NEED TO SEE IT TO BELIEVE IT. REPORT OF THE 1963 SUMMER STUDY-SKILLS PROGRAMS. /COLLEGE   EDUCATION/   NMARTWD63303

FINAL REPORT. EQUAL-EMPLOYMENT-OPPORTUNITY IN THE TRANSPORTATION INDUSTRY. /MASSACHUSETTS/   NMASSCA66964

REPORT OF THE COMMISSION ON THE EMPLOYMENT PROBLEMS OF NEGROES TO GOVERNOR SALTONSTALL. /MASSACHUSETTS/   NMASSCE42757

A REPORT ON THE CHARACTERISTICS OF MICHIGAN-S NON-WHITE POPULATION.   NMICCRC65773

THE NEGRO WORKER IN MINNESOTA. A REPORT.   NMINNGI45798

THE NEGRO WORKER-S PROGRESS IN MINNESOTA. A REPORT.   NMINNGI49799

LOUISVILLE. SPECIAL REPORT. /CASE-STUDY KENTUCKY/   NMUSEBX64868

MEMPHIS. SPECIAL REPORT. /CASE-STUDY/   NMUSEBX64869

SHARECROPPERS IN THE 60-S. A REPORT AND A PROGRAM.   NNATLSF61883

REPORT OF THE COMMITTEE ON UNFAIR EMPLOYMENT PRACTICES.   NNEBRLC51906

RACIAL DISCRIMINATION IN THE CINCINNATI BUILDING TRADES. REPORT AND RECOMMENDATIONS. /OHIO/   NOHIOCR66605

REPORT OF THE 1961-1962 SURVEY OF PHILADELPHIA BANKS. /PENNSYLVANIA/   NPHILCH62995

REPORT AND SUMMARY OF THE AIR FORCE ON ACTIONS TAKEN BY LOCKHEED AIRCRAFT CORPORATION AT THE AIR FORCE
PLANT NO 6 IN MARIETTA, GEORGIA. /INDUSTRY/   NPRESCD61013

GOVERNOR-S CIVIL-RIGHTS TASK FORCE. REPORT. /RHODE-ISLAND/   NRHODIC64051

THE WATTS MANIFESTO AND THE MCCONE REPORT. /LOS-ANGELES CALIFORNIA/   NRUSTBX66099

1961 COMMISSION ON CIVIL-RIGHTS **REPORT** BOOK 3. EMPLOYMENT.   NUSCOMC61231

THE VOICE OF THE GHETTO. A **REPORT** ON TWO BOSTON NEIGHBORHOOD MEETINGS.   /MASSACHUSETTS/   NUSCOMC67149

CHANGING EMPLOYMENT PRACTICES IN THE CONSTRUCTION INDUSTRY. EXPERIENCE **REPORT** 102.   NUSCONM65233

CITY CONTRACTORS AND FAIR-EMPLOYMENT. EXPERIENCE **REPORT** 103.   NUSCONM66234

PUBLIC EMPLOYMENT IN SAVANNAH, GEORGIA. EXPERIENCE **REPORT** 104.   NUSCONM66235

INTEGRATION IN THE ARMED SERVICES. A PROGRESS **REPORT**. /MILITARY/   NUSDDEF55195

THEY ARE AMERICA. A **REPORT** TO THE AMERICAN PEOPLE.   NUSDLAB57250

TWO STATE **REPORT** ON JOB DISCRIMINATION. /NEW-YORK NEW-JERSEY/   NUSDLAB58844

REPORT BY PRESIDENT-S-COMMITTEE-ON-EQUAL-OPPORTUNITY.   NUSDLAB62840

SUMMARY **REPORT**. EQUAL-EMPLOYMENT-OPPORTUNITY CONFERENCE.   NUSNAAS63267

A **REPORT** ON COMMUNITY FACTORS IN NASHVILLE RELATED TO THE NEGRO IN MEDICINE.   /TENNESSEE/   NVALIPX56281

SPECIAL **REPORT**. A SURVEY OF NEGROES EMPLOYED BY THE STATE OF WEST-VIRGINIA.   NVIRGHR64318

TO FULFILL THESE RIGHTS. **REPORT** ON THE WHITE-HOUSE-CONFERENCE.   /EEO/   NWATTPX66545

POVERTY AREAS OF OUR MAJOR CITIES. THE EMPLOYMENT SITUATION OF NEGRO AND WHITE WORKERS IN METROPOLITAN
AREAS COMPARED IN A SPECIAL LABOR-FORCE **REPORT**.   NWETZJR66114

REPORT FROM A SPANISH HARLEM FORTRESS.   PHAMMRX64153

SIX MONTHS **REPORT**.   PHAUGJX60814

SUPPLEMENTARY **REPORT** ON PUERTO-RICANS IN BUFFALO. /NEW-YORK/   PIMSETP62820

ANNUAL FARM LABOR **REPORT**. /NEW-JERSEY/   PNEWJSE63831

POPULATIONS OF NEW-YORK STATE. **REPORT** NO 2. THE PUERTO-RICAN POPULATION OF THE NEW-YORK-CITY AREA.   PNEWYCO62838

PROBLEMS OF WORKING WOMEN. SUMMARY **REPORT** OF A CONFERENCE.   WAFLCIO61618

REPORT OF ARROWHEAD REGIONAL CONFERENCE ON THE STATUS OF WOMEN IN NORTHERN MINNESOTA.   WARRORC66216

REPORT OF THE CALIFORNIA ADVISORY COMMISSION ON THE STATUS OF WOMEN. /FEP EMPLOYMENT-CONDITIONS
DISCRIMINATION MIGRANTS/   WCALACW67673

REPORT ON THE FIRST CONFERENCE ON THE STATUS OF WOMEN. /WORK-WOMEN-ROLE/   WCOLUMX64699

REPORT ON THE MISSOURI COMMISSION ON THE STATUS OF WOMEN. /WORK-WOMEN-ROLE/   WCOLUMX64700

MINORITY **REPORT**. /EEO/   WDAVICX63718

REPORT OF THE EXPLORATORY STATISTICAL SURVEY OF THE EDUCATIONAL-ATTAINMENT, NUMBER, AND AVAILABILITY OF
THE MEMBERSHIP OF THE AMERICAN ASSOCIATION OF UNIVERSITY WOMEN FOR TEACHING IN THE FIELDS OF SCIENCE AND
MATHEMATICS. /OCCUPATIONS/   WDOLAEF57735

RESEARCH **REPORT**. SURVEY OF CONTINUING EDUCATION PROGRAMS.   WFIELBX64762

FINAL **REPORT**. EXPERIMENTAL AND DEMONSTRATION MANPOWER PROJECT FOR THE RECRUITMENT, TRAINING, PLACEMENT
AND FOLLOW-UP OF RURAL UNEMPLOYED WORKERS IN TEN NORTH FLORIDA COUNTIES.   WFLORMP66326

PROGRESS AND PROSPECTS. THE **REPORT** OF THE SECOND NATIONAL CONFERENCE OF GOVERNORS COMMISSIONS ON THE
STATUS OF WOMEN. /EMPLOYMENT-CONDITIONS/   WGOVECS65798

REPORT ON THE SURVEY OF FEMALE PHYSICIANS GRADUATING FROM MEDICAL SCHOOL BETWEEN 1925 AND 1940.
/OCCUPATIONS/   WHANNFX58819

FIRST **REPORT**. IOWA GOVERNOR-S COMMISSION ON THE STATUS OF WOMEN. /EMPLOYMENT-CONDITIONS/   WIOWAGC64796

CONFERENCE ON WOMEN IN THE UPPER PENINSULA ECONOMY. **REPORT**. /MICHIGAN/   WMICOLA64976

NEW-YORK WOMEN. A **REPORT** AND RECOMMENDATIONS FROM THE NEW-YORK GOVERNOR-S COMMITTEE ON THE EDUCATION AND
EMPLOYMENT OF WOMEN.   WNEWYGW64799

REPORT ON UNDERGRADUATE COUNSELING AND CONTINUING EDUCATION AND GUIDANCE FOR MATURE WOMAN.   WNICOHG64032

SOCIAL WORK DEGREE PROGRESS **REPORT**. /TRAINING/   WNYUYUG66031

AUTOMATION AND EMPLOYMENT OPPORTUNITIES FOR OFFICE WORKERS. THE EFFECT OF ELECTRONIC COMPUTERS ON
EMPLOYMENT OF CLERICAL WORKERS, WITH A SPECIAL **REPORT** ON PROGRAMMERS.   WPASCWX58178

REPORT OF THE COMMITTEE ON CIVIL AND POLITICAL RIGHTS.   WPRESCO63065

REPORT OF THE COMMITTEE ON EDUCATION. /EQUAL-OPPORTUNITY COUNSELING/   WPRESCO63066

REPORT OF THE COMMITTEE ON FEDERAL EMPLOYMENT.   WPRESCO63067

REPORT OF THE COMMITTEE ON PRIVATE EMPLOYMENT, 1963.   WPRESCO63068

REPORT OF THE COMMITTEE ON PROTECTIVE LABOR LEGISLATION, 1963.   WPRESCO63069

REPORT OF THE COMMITTEE ON SOCIAL INSURANCE AND TAXES, 1963.   WPRESCO63070

REPORT OF PRESIDENT-S COMMISSION ON STATUS OF WOMEN.   WPRESCO63993

REPORT -- 1965-66 -- RETRAINING PROGRAM IN MATHEMATICS AND SCIENCE FOR COLLEGE GRADUATE WOMEN.   WRUTGMR66098

MINNESOTA PLAN FOR WOMEN-S CONTINUING EDUCATION. A PROGRESS **REPORT**.   WSENDVL61298

FIVE THOUSAND WOMEN COLLEGE GRADUATES **REPORT**.   WSHOSRX56113

REPORT OF CONFERENCE ON EMPLOYMENT PROBLEMS OF WORKING WOMEN.   WSTATUI63131

CHILD CARE ARRANGEMENTS OF THE NATION-S WORKING MOTHERS. A PRELIMINARY **REPORT**.   WUSDHEW65172

FIRST JOBS OF COLLEGE WOMEN -- **REPORT** ON WOMEN GRADUATES, CLASS OF 1957.   WUSDLAB59194

WOMAN-S DESTINY -- CHOICE OR CHANCE. **REPORT** OF CONFERENCE AT THE UNIVERSITY OF WASHINGTON, NOVEMBER

REPORT   (CONTINUATION)
  21-22. 1963.   WUSDLAB65233

  REPORT ON PROGRESS IN 1965 ON THE STATUS OF WOMEN. /EDUCATION EMPLOYMENT-CONDITIONS/   WUSINCS65860

  WISCONSIN WOMEN. REPORT OF THE WISCONSIN GOVERNOR-S COMMISSION ON THE STATUS OF WOMEN.   WWISXGC65272

  PARTNERSHIP TEACHING PROGRAM. PROGRESS REPORT -- JAN-OCT 1965. SECTION I. /TRAINING/   WWOMEEA65275

  TO FULFILL THESE RIGHTS. SUMMARY REPORT OF PRE-WHITE-HOUSE CONFERENCES.   WYWCAXX66079

REPORTING
  TITLE-VII. REPORTING AND RECORD KEEPING. /LEGISLATION/   GPEARHG66149

REPORTS
  CURRENT POPULATION REPORTS -- SPECIAL CENSUS OF CLEVELAND, OHIO. /DEMOGRAPHY/   CUSBURC65379

  REPORTS ON THE WORK OF THE FEPC IN NEW-JERSEY AND NEW-YORK.   GAMERCR46372

  ECONOMIC REPORTS OF THE PRESIDENT.   GCOUNEAND239

  REPORTS OF THE MEETINGS OF THE COMMITTEE OF OFFICIALS ON MIGRATORY FARM LABOR OF THE ATLANTIC SEABOARD
  STATES. /MIGRANT-WORKERS/   GCOUNSG58932

  REPORTS ON THE PATTERN OF EMPLOYMENT OF MINORTY-GROUP PERSONS IN DEPARTMENT OF COUNTY
  GOVERNMENT.LOS-ANGELES CALIFORNIA/   GLOSACC62913

  THE NATIONAL CONFERENCE AND THE REPORTS OF THE STATE ADVISORY COMMITTEES TO THE U.S. COMMISSION ON
  CIVIL-RIGHTS. 1959.   GUSCOMC60405

  REPORTS ON APPRENTICESHIP, NINE STATE ADVISORY COMMITTEES. /CALIFORNIA FLORIDA MARYLAND CONNECTICUT
  WASHINGTON-DC NEW-JERSEY NEW-YORK TENNESSEE WISCONSIN/   GUSCCMC64407

  ANNUAL REPORTS OF US DEPARTMENT OF THE INTERIOR.   IUSDINTND666

  ADL REPORTS ON SOCIAL, EMPLOYMENT, EDUCATIONAL AND HOUSING DISCRIMINATION.   JANTIDL57690

  COMMISSION ON MANPOWER UTILIZATION REPORTS.   NNATLAI55872

  REPORTS OF PUERTO-RICO DEPARTMENT OF LABOR, MIGRATION DIVISION ON PLACEMENT.   PPUERRDND791

REPRESENTATION
  THE DUTY OF FAIR REPRESENTATION.   GCOXXAX57617

  THE FAIR REPRESENTATION DOCTRINE. AN EFFECTIVE WEAPON AGAINST UNION RACIAL DISCRIMINATION. GHERRNM64772

  UNION-S DUTY OF FAIR REPRESENTATION AND THE CIVIL-RIGHTS-ACT OF 1964.   GSHERHL65302

  UNION DEMOCRACY AND FAIR REPRESENTATION. FEDERAL RESPONSIBILITY IN A FEDERAL SYSTEM.   GWELLHX58550

  RACIAL DISCRIMINATION AND THE DUTY OF FAIR REPRESENTATION. /LEGISLATION/   NCOLULR65225

  REPRESENTATION OF NEGROES AND WHITES AS EMPLOYEES IN THE FEDERAL PRISON SYSTEM.   NMORGGD62849

  EMPLOYEE CHOICE AND SOME PROBLEMS OF RACE AND REMEDIES IN REPRESENTATION CAMPAIGNS.   NYALELJ63599

REPRINT
  YOUNG WORKERS. A REPRINT FROM THE 1966 MANPOWER REPORT.   GUSDLAB66505

REQUIREMENTS
  INTERINDUSTRY EMPLOYMENT REQUIREMENTS.   GALTEJX65369

  PROJECTIONS OF MANPOWER REQUIREMENTS AND SUPPLY.   GGOLDHX66933

  CENTRAL ROLE OF INTERGROUP AGENCIES IN THE LABOR-MARKET. CHANGING RESEARCH AND PERSONNEL REQUIREMENTS. GHOPEJX61780

  TESTS AND THE REQUIREMENTS OF THE JOB.   GMETZJH65119

  ENFORCEMENT OF NONDISCRIMINATION REQUIREMENTS FOR GOVERNMENT CONTRACT WORK.   GSPECWH63329

  MANPOWER REPORT OF THE PRESIDENT AND A REPORT ON MANPOWER REQUIREMENTS, RESOURCES, UTILIZATION, AND
  TRAINING.   GUSDLAB63830

  MANPOWER REPORT OF THE PRESIDENT AND A REPORT ON MANPOWER REQUIREMENTS, RESOURCES, UTILIZATION, AND
  TRAINING.   GUSDLAB64829

  MANPOWER REPORT OF THE PRESIDENT AND A REPORT ON MANPOWER REQUIREMENTS, RESOURCES, UTILIZATION, AND
  TRAINING.   GUSDLAB65828

  AMERICA-S INDUSTRIAL AND OCCUPATIONAL MANPOWER REQUIREMENTS, 1964-75.   GUSDLAB66437

  MANPOWER REPORT OF THE PRESIDENT AND A REPORT ON MANPOWER REQUIREMENTS, RESOURCES, UTILIZATION, AND
  TRAINING.   GUSDLAB66827

  SURVEY ON TRANSIENT MEXICAN LABOR REQUIREMENTS.   MLOSACAND430

  OPPORTUNITIES AND REQUIREMENTS FOR INITIAL EMPLOYMENT OF SCHOOL LEAVERS. WITH EMPHASIS ON OFFICE AND
  RETAIL JOBS. /EMPLOYMENT-SELECTION/   WCCOKFS66705

RESEARCH
  PARTIAL INVENTORY OF ON-GOING RESEARCH IN EQUAL-EMPLOYMENT-OPPORTUNITIES.   GANDEBR67589

  RECENT RESEARCH ON RACIAL RELATIONS IN THE USA.   GBLUMHX58458

  SELF APPRAISAL FOR MERIT PROMOTION. A RESEARCH MANUAL.   GBOWMGW63467

  MANPOWER IMPLICATIONS OF TECHNOLOGICAL-CHANGE. RESEARCH FINDINGS OF THE US DEPARTMENT OF LABOR. GBRANSX63876

  NEW DIRECTIONS IN US EMPLOYMENT-SERVICE APTITUDE TEST RESEARCH.   GDVORBJ65656

  LONG-TERM MANPOWER PROJECTIONS. PROCEEDINGS OF A CONFERENCE CONDUCTED BY THE RESEARCH PROGRAM ON
  UNEMPLOYMENT AND THE AMERICAN ECONOMY.   GGORDRA65613

  CENTRAL ROLE OF INTERGROUP AGENCIES IN THE LABOR-MARKET. CHANGING RESEARCH AND PERSONNEL REQUIREMENTS. GHOPEJX61780

  ECONOMIC GROWTH. EQUAL-OPPORTUNITY, RESEARCH, JOINT EFFORT. EMPLOYMENT.   GILLIGC63798

  THE MEASUREMENT AND INTERPRETATION OF JOB VACANCIES. A CONFERENCE REPORT OF THE NATIONAL BUREAU OF

RESEARCH   (CONTINUATION)
ECCNOMIC RESEARCH. /LABOR-MARKET/   GNATLBE66611

PROBLEMS, RESEARCH, AND RECOMMENDATIONS IN THE EMPLOYMENT TESTING OF MINORITY-GROUP APPLICANTS.   GNEWCMR66163

RESEARCH BULLETIN ON INTERGRCUP-RELATIONS. /EEO/   GSMITCX62319

MANPOWER PROJECTIONS. SOME CONCEPTUAL PROBLEMS AND RESEARCH NEEDS. /EMPLOYMENT-TRENDS/   GSWERSX66535

SEGREGATION AND DESEGREGATION. A DIGEST OF RECENT RESEARCH.   GTUMIMM57164

MANPCWER RESEARCH PROGRAMS.   GUSDLAB62981

CONSOLIDATED INVENTORY OF DEPARTMENT OF LABOR RESEARCH ON LABOR-FORCE EMPLOYMENT AND UNEMPLOYMENT.   GUSDLAB64441

CONSOLIDATED INVENTORY OF DEPARTMENT OF LABOR RESEARCH ON AUTOMATION AND TECHNOLOGICAL-CHANGE.   GUSDLAB64619

UNEMPLOYMENT AND RETRAINING. AN ANNOTATED BIBLIOGRAPHY OF RESEARCH.   GUSDLAB65503

MANPCWER, RESEARCH AND TRAINING.   GUSDLAB65710

REPORT ON MANPOWER RESEARCH AND TRAINING UNDER THE MCTA.   GUSDLAB66493

URBANIZATION OF THE MIGRANT. PROCESSES AND OUTCOMES. A RESEARCH PROPOSAL.   MSIMMOG64491

RESEARCH ON NEGRO JOB SUCCESS.   NCHALWE62189

RECENT TRENDS IN RESEARCH ON THE NEGRO IN THE UNITED STATES.   NDRAKSC57290

RECENT RESEARCH IN PSYCHOLOGICAL COMPARISONS OF NEGROES AND WHITES IN THE UNITED STATES.   NDREGRM65293

NEGRO SCHOLARS IN SCIENTIFIC RESEARCH.   NDREWCR50294

SOCIOLOGICAL PERSPECTIVES IN UNEMPLOYMENT RESEARCH.   NFERMLA64353

AREAS OF RESEARCH IN RACE-RELATIONS.   NFRAZEF58376

A UNIQUE REGIONAL PROGRAM OF PSYCHOLOGICAL RESEARCH AND TRAINING IN THE SOUTH.   NLANGMC56032

FATHER-ABSENCE AND NEGRO ADULT PERSONALITY. A RESEARCH NOTE.   NPETTTFND990

UNEMPLOYMENT AND THE AMERICAN ECONOMY. RESEARCH PROGRAM ON UNEMPLOYMENT.   NROSSAM63259

A REVIEW OF RESEARCH ON THE NEGRO AND EMPLOYMENT IN THE SOUTH.   NROWARL65703

DESEGREGATION. SOME PROPOSITIONS AND RESEARCH SUGGESTIONS.   NSUCHEA58189

THE NEGRO IN THE US. A RESEARCH GUIDE.   NWELSEK65304

SUMMARY OF RESEARCH DURING 1964 RELATED TO THE NEGRO AND NEGRO EDUCATION.   NWESTEX66315

THE EDUCATION OF WOMEN -- INFORMATION AND RESEARCH NCTES.   WAMERCEND605

RESEARCH REPORT. SURVEY OF CONTINUING EDUCATION PROGRAMS.   WFIELBX64762

IMPLICATIONS FROM RECENT RESEARCH ON COLLEGE STUDENTS. /MANPOWER/   WHEISPX59838

RESEARCH AND YOUR JOB. /TECHNOLOGICAL-CHANGE/   WKEYSMD64900

SUMMARY OF CURRENT RESEARCH CN WOMEN-S ROLES.   WNOBLJL59035

SHORTAGE OR SURPLUS. AN ASSESSMENT OF BOSTON WOMANPOWER IN INDUSTRY, GOVERNMENT, AND RESEARCH. JUNE 7-8,
1963. /MASSACHUSETTS/   WUSDLAB66217

RESERVATION
PAPAGO RESERVATION REPORT.   IARIZCI62527

INDIANS IN RURAL AND RESERVATION AREAS. /CALIFORNIA/   ICALACI66542

CONSTRAINTS ON ECONOMIC PROGRESS ON THE ROSEBUD SIOUX INDIAN RESERVATION.   IEICHCK60553

MCTA CCMES TO THE OWYHEE RESERVATION.   IFISHCR66559

MANPOWER SERVICES ON THE NAVAJO RESERVATION.   IGRAFMF66565

HUMAN RESOURCES, RELATIONS AND PROBLEMS ON THE FORT-HALL INDIAN RESERVATION.   IHARMHC61572

LIFE ON THE BLACKFEET INDIAN RESERVATION TODAY.   IMUSEPI57593

ECCNOMY AND CONDITIONS OF THE FORT-HALL INDIAN RESERVATION.   INYBRNX64603

THE ECONOMIC DEVELOPMENT AND URBANIZATION OF THE NAVAJO INDIAN RESERVATION.   ISELLCL62616

THE SIOUX CN THE RESERVATION.   ISHAWLC60617

LIVELIHOOD AND TRIBAL GOVERNMENT ON THE KLAMATH INDIAN RESERVATION.   ISTERTX61624

AN EVALUATION OF THE 10-YEAR DEVELOPMENT PROGRAM OF THE UTE TRIBE OF THE UINTAH AND OURAY RESERVATION,
UTAH.   IUSDINT58648

POPULATION AND INCOME CENSUS. WIND-RIVER RESERVATION, WYOMING.   IUSDINT60655

POPULATION CHARACTERISTICS, LIVING CONDITIONS AND INCOME OF INDIAN FAMILIES, NORTHERN-CHEYENNE
RESERVATION, JULY, 1961.   IUSDINT63656

POPULATION CHARACTERISTICS, LIVING CONDITIONS, AND INCOME OF INDIAN FAMILIES, FORT-PECK RESERVATION,
1951-1961.   IUSDINT63657

POPULATION CHARACTERISTICS, LIVING CONDITIONS AND INCOMES OF INDIAN FAMILIES, FORT-BELKNAP RESERVATION.   IUSDINT63658

POPULATION CHARACTERISTICS, LIVING CONDITIONS AND INCOMES CF INDIAN FAMILIES, ROCKY-BAY-S RESERVATION.   IUSDINT63659

FAMILY PLAN AND REHABILITATICN PROGRAMS, STANDING-ROCK RESERVATION.   IUSDINT64649

THE RELATIONSHIP BETWEEN UNEARNED INCOME AND INDIVIDUAL PRODUCTIVE EFFORT ON THE JICARILLA APACHE INDIAN
RESERVATION.   IWILSHC61687

RESERVATIONS
ARIZONA RESERVATIONS ECONOMICS. SURVEY REPORT.   IARIZCI63528

RESERVATIONS   (CONTINUATION)
AMERICA-S CONCENTRATION CAMPS, THE FACTS ABOUT OUR INDIAN **RESERVATIONS** TODAY.   IEMBRCB56555

INDIANS ON FEDERAL **RESERVATIONS** IN THE US.   IUSDHEW58196

PLACING INDIANS WHO LIVE ON **RESERVATIONS**. A COOPERATIVE PROGRAM.   IUSDLAB59667

RESIDENCE
COMPARISON OF MEXICANS, NEGROES AND WHITES WITH RESPECT TO OCCUPATIONAL HISTORY, RURAL-URBAN **RESIDENCE**
HISTORY AND ACCULTURIZATION WITHIN THE INSTITUTIONAL STRUCTURE OF LANSING, MICHIGAN.   CGOLDVX60494

EMPLOYMENT AND INCOME BY AGE, SEX, COLOR AND **RESIDENCE**. /DETROIT MICHIGAN/   GDETRCC63948

POPULATION OF THE UNITED STATES BY METROPOLITAN AND NONMETROPOLITAN **RESIDENCE**. /DEMOGRAPHY/   GUSBURC66159

RESIDENT
PLANTATION ORGANIZATION AND THE **RESIDENT** LABOR-FORCE, DELTA AREA, MISSISSIPPI.   NLERANL60403

RESIDENTIAL
OCCUPATIONAL AND **RESIDENTIAL** ADJUSTMENT OF RURAL MIGRANTS. /NEGRO MEXICAN-AMERICAN/   CSHANLW61119

RESIDENTIAL SEGREGATION OF SOCIAL-CLASSES AND ASPIRATIONS OF HIGH SCHOOL BOYS.   GWILSAB59568

THE EFFECT OF **RESIDENTIAL** SEGREGATION UPON EDUCATIONAL ACHIEVEMENT AND ASPIRATIONS.   GWILSAB60567

RESIDENTIAL SEGREGATION IN THE URBAN SOUTHWEST.   MMOORJW66444

RESIDENTIAL DISTRIBUTION AND OCCUPATIONAL-STRATIFICATION.   NDUNCOD55307

THE NEGRO POPULATION OF CHICAGO. A STUDY OF **RESIDENTIAL** SUCCESSION. /ILLINOIS OCCUPATIONAL-PATTERNS/   NDUNCOD57306

RESIDENTIAL SEGREGATION AND SOCIAL DIFFERENTIATION.   NDUNCOD59305

RESIDENTIAL-SEGREGAT
EQUALITY AND BEYOND. /RESIDENTIAL-SEGREGATION/   NGRIEGX66459

MAN IN METROPOLIS. /RESIDENTIAL-SEGREGATION GHETTO/   NSCHILB65106

RESIDENTS
A STUDY OF THE MENTAL HEALTH PROBLEMS OF MEXICAN-AMERICAN **RESIDENTS**. /TEXAS/   MTEXASD61500

ANNUAL FAMILY AND OCCUPATIONAL EARNINGS OF **RESIDENTS** OF TWO NEGRO HOUSING PROJECTS IN ATLANTA 1937-1944.
/GEORGIA/   NRITTAL45062

RESISTANCE
CHANGE AND **RESISTANCE** IN AN ISOLATED NAVAHO COMMUNITY.   ISHEPMX64618

WHAT MASSIVE **RESISTANCE** COSTS NORFOLK AND ITS BUSINESSMEN. /VIRGINIA/   NBUSIWX58165

THE ROLE OF WHITE **RESISTANCE** AND FACILITATION IN THE NEGRO STRUGGLE FOR EQUALITY.   NGLENND65676

UNION **RESISTANCE**. SOUTHERN STYLE.   NGCULHM48436

COMMUNITY **RESISTANCE** TO AND ACCEPTANCE OF DESEGREGATION.   NKILLLM65651

RESOLUTION
CIVIL-RIGHTS **RESOLUTION**.   GAMERFX59872

CHILDREN OF THE GILDED GHETTO. CONFLICT **RESOLUTION** OF THREE GENERATIONS OF AMERICAN JEWS.
/OCCUPATIONAL-PATTERNS/   JKRAMJR61736

POLICY **RESOLUTION** ADOPTED BY AFL-CIO 6TH CONSTITUTIONAL CONVENTION, SAN FRANCISCO, DEC 1965. /EEO/   WAFLCIO65617

RESOURCE
A COMPILATION OF STATISTICAL DATA, CHARTS AND OTHER **RESOURCE** MATERIAL FOR CONFERENCE PARTICIPANTS.
/APPRENTICESHIP CALIFORNIA YOUTH/   GCALCNA60516

HUMAN CAPITAL AS A SOUTHERN **RESOURCE**.   GCOLBMR63994

RESOURCE CHARACTERISTICS AND UTILIZATION AND LEVEL OF LIVING ITEMS, RURAL HOUSEHOLDS, NORTH AND WEST
FLORIDA, 1956.   GREUSLA60391

YOUTH, THE NATION-S RICHEST **RESOURCE**. THEIR EDUCATION AND EMPLOYMENT NEEDS.   GUSINCC53514

AN ANALYSIS OF CURRENT PATTERNS IN HUMAN **RESOURCE** DEVELOPMENT IN SAN-ANTONIO, TEXAS.   MDAVIHW66387

RESOURCE USE AND ADJUSTMENT. RURAL FAMILIES IN THE CENTRAL LOUISIANA MIXED FARMING AREA.   NBOLTBX61396

AMERICAN NEGROES -- A WASTED **RESOURCE**. /INDUSTRY/   NMORRJJ57853

INDUSTRY-S MOST UNDERDEVELOPED **RESOURCE**.   NNATLUL64890

RESOURCE UNITS IN THE TEACHING OF OCCUPATIONS -- AN EXPERIMENT IN GUIDANCE OF PUERTO-RICAN TEENAGERS.   PNEWYCC56834

PROFESSIONAL WOMANPOWER AS A NATIONAL **RESOURCE**.   WPARRJB61051

THE UNTAPPED **RESOURCE**... /OCCUPATIONS/   WRASKBL59074

RESOURCES
DEVELOPING NEW-YORK CITY-S HUMAN **RESOURCES**. VOL 1. /NEGRO PUERTO-RICAN/   CINSTOP66034

CHARACTERISTICS, **RESOURCES**, AND INCOMES OF RURAL HOUSEHOLDS, PIEDMONT AREA, SOUTH-CAROLINA.   GBURCTA62408

MANPOWER **RESOURCES** OF THE SAN-FRANCISCO OAKLAND BAY AREA 1960-1970. /CALIFORNIA/   GCALDEM63520

THE ADAPTATION OF LABOR **RESOURCES** TO CHANGING NEEDS. /MOBILITY/   GLESTRA66532

RESOURCES AND INCOMES OF RURAL FAMILIES IN THE COASTAL PLAIN AREAS OF GEORGIA.   GMCARWC59392

HUMAN **RESOURCES** IN THE URBAN ECONOMY. PART II -- THE LABOR FORCE PERFORMANCE OF MINORITY-GROUPS.   GPERLMX63169

INCOME, **RESOURCES**, AND ADJUSTMENT POTENTIALS AMONG RURAL FAMILIES IN NORTH AND WEST FLORIDA.   GREUSLA62388

UTILIZING OUR MANPOWER **RESOURCES**. SPECIAL APPLICANT GROUPS.   GUSDLAB63665

MANPOWER REPORT OF THE PRESIDENT AND A REPORT ON MANPOWER REQUIREMENTS, **RESOURCES**, UTILIZATION, AND
TRAINING.   GUSDLAB63830

MANPOWER REPORT OF THE PRESIDENT AND A REPORT ON MANPOWER REQUIREMENTS, **RESOURCES**, UTILIZATION, AND

RESOURCES   (CONTINUATION)
    TRAINING.   GUSDLAB64829

    MANPOWER REPORT OF THE PRESIDENT AND A REPORT ON MANPOWER REQUIREMENTS, **RESOURCES**, UTILIZATION, AND
    TRAINING.   GUSDLAB65828

    MANPOWER REPORT OF THE PRESIDENT AND A REPORT ON MANPOWER REQUIREMENTS, **RESOURCES**, UTILIZATION, AND
    TRAINING.   GUSDLAB66827

    DISCRIMINATION AND FULL UTILIZATION OF MANPOWER **RESOURCES**, 1952.   GUSSENA52347

    HEARINGS RELATING TO THE TRAINING AND UTILIZATION OF THE MANPOWER **RESOURCES** OF THE NATION.   GUSSENA63618

    HUMAN **RESOURCES** SURVEY OF THE COLVILLE CONFEDERATE TRIBES.   IBLOOJA59538

    HUMAN **RESOURCES**, RELATIONS AND PROBLEMS ON THE FORT-HALL INDIAN RESERVATION.   IHARMHC61572

    THE NAVAJO IN THE MACHINE AGE. HUMAN **RESOURCES** ARE IMPORTANT TOO.   INAPIAX58594

    NEEDS AND **RESOURCES** OF THE JICARILLA APACHE INDIAN TRIBE.   ISTANRI58623

    RURAL PEOPLE AND THEIR **RESOURCES**, NORTH-CENTRAL NEW-MEXICO.   MTAYLMM60402

    OF HUMAN **RESOURCES** AND THE SOUTH.   NROSSJX50088

    LIBRARY **RESOURCES** AND SERVICES IN WHITE AND NEGRO COLLEGES. /EDUCATION/   NSAMGTX65128

    ALL THESE PEOPLE. THE NATION-S HUMAN **RESOURCES** IN THE SOUTH.   NVANCRB45282

    RESOURCES FOR THE EMPLOYMENT OF MATURE WOMEN AND/OR THEIR CONTINUING EDUCATION. A SELECTED BIBLIOGRAPHY
    AND AIDS.   WBERNML66746

RESPONSE
    WHAT SHOULD THE BUSINESS **RESPONSE** BE TO THE NEGRO REVOLUTION. A PUBLIC RELATIONS PROGRAM FOR DEALING WITH
    MINORITY-GROUPS.   NLANGJF65671

    CONFLICT **RESPONSE**. DETROIT NEGROES FACE UNEMPLOYMENT. /MICHIGAN/   NLEGGJC59678

RESPONSES
    NEGRO **RESPONSES** TO VERBAL AND NON-VERBAL TEST MATERIAL.   NBEANKL47914

RESPONSIBILITIES
    FUNCTIONS AND **RESPONSIBILITIES** OF FEPC. /CALIFORNIA/   GCALDIR63526

    SOCIAL **RESPONSIBILITIES** OF ORGANIZED LABOR. /UNION/   GTITCJA57358

    FEDERAL AGENCIES WITH PRIMARY CIVIL-RIGHTS **RESPONSIBILITIES**.   GUSDLAB65447

    THE PREPARATION OF DISADVANTAGED YOUTH FOR EMPLOYMENT AND CIVIC **RESPONSIBILITIES**.   NPERRJX64985

    HOW MANAGEMENT VIEWS ITS RACE-RELATIONS **RESPONSIBILITIES**.   NSTRAGX67181

    PART-TIME EMPLOYMENT FOR WOMEN WITH FAMILY **RESPONSIBILITIES**. /WORK-FAMILY-CONFLICT/   WINTELR57867

    NEW OPPORTUNITIES AND NEW **RESPONSIBILITIES** FOR WOMEN. /WORK-WOMAN-ROLE/   WKEYSMD64899

RESPONSIBILITY
    EQUAL-EMPLOYMENT-OPPORTUNITY -- AN EMPLOYMENT-SERVICE **RESPONSIBILITY**.   GFANTAX64671

    THE RIGHTS AND **RESPONSIBILITY** OF UNION MEMBERS. /ANTIDISCRIMINATION/   GGOLDAX58974

    MIGRANT-LABOR--THE NATIONAL **RESPONSIBILITY**.   GMITCJP59954

    UNION DEMOCRACY AND FAIR REPRESENTATION. FEDERAL **RESPONSIBILITY** IN A FEDERAL SYSTEM.   GWELLHX58550

    MANAGEMENT SOCIAL **RESPONSIBILITY** AND RACIAL EMPLOYMENT IN THE MEAT-PACKING INDUSTRY.   NPURCTV67123

RESTAURANT
    HOTEL AND **RESTAURANT** JOB OPPORTUNITIES, SAN-FRANCISCO BAY AREA, 1964-1966. /CALIFORNIA/   GCALDEM65517

    TECHNICAL REPORT NUMBER 1. EMPLOYMENT PRACTICES IN THE HOTEL, MOTEL AND **RESTAURANT** INDUSTRY OF MISSOURI. GMILLRX66020

    SUMMARY OF TESTIMONY -- HOTEL **RESTAURANT** HEARINGS, APPENDIX A. /PHILADELPHIA PENNSYLVANIA/   GPHILCH60181

    FINDINGS OF FACT, CONCLUSIONS AND ACTION OF THE COMMISSION ON HUMAN-RELATIONS IN RE. INVESTIGATIVE PUBLIC
    HEARINGS INTO ALLEGED DISCRIMINATORY PRACTICE BY THE HOTEL AND **RESTAURANT** INDUSTRY IN PHILADELPHIA.
    /PENNSYLVANIA/   GPHILCH61176

    REPORT OF PROGRESS IN THE INTEGRATION OF HOTEL AND **RESTAURANT** EMPLOYMENT, APRIL 1961 TO MARCH 1962.
    /PHILADELPHIA PENNSYLVANIA/   GPHILCH62178

RESTRAINTS
    CULTURAL AND RELATED **RESTRAINTS** AND MEANS OF OVERCOMING THEM. /MEXICAN-AMERICAN NEGRO INTEGRATION/   CSHANLW65485

    LEGAL **RESTRAINTS** ON RACIAL DISCRIMINATION IN EMPLOYMENT.   GSOVEMI66326

RESURVEY
    COLLEGE WOMEN SEVEN YEARS AFTER GRADUATION -- **RESURVEY** OF WOMEN GRADUATES CLASS OF 1957.   WUSDLAB66185

RETAIL
    A STUDY OF EMPLOYMENT PATTERNS IN THE GENERAL MERCHANDISE GROUP **RETAIL** STORES IN NEW-YORK-CITY. GWATKDO66588

    OPPORTUNITIES AND REQUIREMENTS FOR INITIAL EMPLOYMENT OF SCHOOL LEAVERS. WITH EMPHASIS ON OFFICE AND
    RETAIL JOBS. /EMPLOYMENT-SELECTION/   WCOOKFS66705

    THE **RETAIL** CLERKS. /TECHNOLOGICAL-CHANGE/   WHARRMX62823

RETAILING
    CAREERS FOR WOMEN IN **RETAILING**. /OCCUPATIONS/   WGROSSB59807

RETARDATION
    SOME CONSIDERATIONS AS TO THE CONTRIBUTIONS OF SOCIAL, PERSONALITY, AND RACIAL FACTORS TO SCHOOL
    RETARDATION IN MINORITY-GROUP CHILDREN.   GDEUTMP56641

RETENTION
    RETENTION AND WITHDRAWAL OF COLLEGE STUDENTS. /DROP-OUT/   WIFFERE57854

RETIREMENT
    THE DRIFT TO EARLY **RETIREMENT**. /TECHNOLOGICAL-CHANGE/   GFALTEK65032

RETRAINING

CHARACTERISTICS OF **RETRAINING** APPLICANTS. /CALIFORNIA NEGRO MEXICAN-AMERICAN WOMEN/   CCALDEM66166

THE ROLE OF GOVERNMENT-SPONSORED TRAINING AND **RETRAINING** PROGRAMS.   GALLECC65758

AMERICA-S POOR. REALITY AND CHANGE. /**RETRAINING** SKILLS UNEMPLOYMENT/   GAMERFX66674

MANPOWER **RETRAINING** IN THE SOUTH-S RURAL POPULATION -- AN OPPORTUNITY FOR DEVELOPMENT.   GBACHFT63413

A BENEFIT-COST ANALYSIS OF THE ECONOMIC EFFECTIVENESS OF **RETRAINING** THE UNEMPLOYED.   GBORUME64142

THE COST OF **RETRAINING** THE HARD-CORE UNEMPLOYED.   GBORUME65745

THE ECONOMIC EFFECTIVENESS OF **RETRAINING** THE UNEMPLOYED.   GBORUME66919

PART I. THE NEW-ENGLAND EXPERIENCE **RETRAINING** THE UNEMPLOYED.   GFEDERB62930

AUTOMATION AND JOBLESSNESS. IS **RETRAINING** THE ANSWER.   GGLAZWX62866

RETRAINING UNDER THE MANPOWER-DEVELOPMENT-ACT. A COST-BENEFIT ANALYSIS.   GPAGEDA64775

AN EXPERIMENT IN **RETRAINING** UNEMPLOYED MEN FOR PRACTICAL NURSING CAREERS.   GPEIMSC66139

RETRAINING, AN EVALUATION OF GAINS AND COSTS.   GSOMEGG65717

A BENEFIT-COST ANALYSIS OF MANPOWER **RETRAINING**.   GSOMEGJ64157

UNEMPLOYMENT AND **RETRAINING**. AN ANNOTATED BIBLIOGRAPHY OF RESEARCH.   GUSDLAB65503

MANPOWER **RETRAINING**.   GUSSENA63822

FACTORS IN WORKERS DECISIONS TO FOREGO **RETRAINING** UNDER THE MANPOWER-DEVELOPMENT-AND-RETRAINING-ACT.   NBRAZWF64318

AUTOMATION AND THE **RETRAINING** OF NEGRO WORKERS.   NNATLUL62886

EXPERIMENTAL FEATURES OF THE TUSKEGEE-INSTITUTE **RETRAINING** PROJECT.   NTUSKIX65765

DEMONSTRATIONAL FEATURES OF THE TUSKEGEE-INSTITUTE. **RETRAINING** PROJECT.   NTUSKIX65766

RUTGERS -- THE STATE UNIVERSITY. FORD FOUNDATION PROGRAM FOR THE **RETRAINING** IN MATHEMATICS OF COLLEGE GRADUATE WOMEN. /TRAINING/   WMARTHM63957

MATHEMATICS **RETRAINING** PROGRAM. NOTES AND COMMENTS, APRIL 1964, 1965, 1966. /TRAINING/   WRUTGMR64097

REPORT -- 1965-66 -- **RETRAINING** PROGRAM IN MATHEMATICS AND SCIENCE FOR COLLEGE GRADUATE WOMEN.   WRUTGMR66098

RETREATISM

RETREATISM AND OCCUPATIONAL ASPIRATIONS AMONG WHITE AND NEGRO HIGH SCHOOL SENIORS.   NPOWEEC61009

RETURNING

ADDRESS TO CONFERENCE ON EDUCATION AND JOB OPPORTUNITIES FOR WOMEN **RETURNING** TO THE LABOR-MARKET.   WDOUTAX62741

UPDATING TRAINING FOR THE **RETURNING** NURSE, SOCIAL WORKER AND TEACHER.   WNATLCP61018

REVEALED

SOUTHERN ECONOMIC DEVELOPMENT AS **REVEALED** BY THE CHANGING STRUCTURE OF EMPLOYMENT.   NDUNNES62309

THE UNEMPLOYMENT RATE AND GRADE LEVEL RELATIONSHIP IN CHICAGO AS **REVEALED** IN THE 1960 CENSUS. /ILLINOIS/   NHARGAJ65990

ATTITUDES TOWARD SOCIAL MOBILITY AS **REVEALED** BY SAMPLES OF NEGRO AND WHITE BOYS.   NMONTJB58809

REVENUE

IMPACT OF OFFICE AUTOMATION IN THE INTERNAL **REVENUE** SERVICE. A STUDY OF THE MANPOWER IMPLICATIONS DURING THE FIRST STAGES OF THE CHANGEOVER. /ECONOMIC-STATUS/   NUSDLAB63198

REVIEW

THEORY, METHOD AND FINDINGS IN THE STUDY OF ACCULTURATION. A **REVIEW**. /MEXICAN-AMERICAN NEGRO/   CPETECX65989

REVIEW AND ANALYSIS OF CITY CERTIFICATIONS AND APPOINTMENTS. /BERKELEY CALIFORNIA/   GBERKCM64444

EMPLOYMENT **REVIEW**. /DES-MOINES IOWA/   GDESMCH65635

US MANPOWER AND EMPLOYMENT POLICY. A **REVIEW** ESSAY.   GGORDMS65728

A **REVIEW** OF STATE FEPC LAWS.   GKOVAIX58860

RECOUNTING THE POOR -- A FIVE-YEAR **REVIEW**.   GORSHMX66642

REPORT OF TWIN-CITIES EQUAL-OPPORTUNITY **REVIEW**. /MINNEAPOLIS ST-PAUL MINNESOTA/   GUSCISC64131

REVIEW APPRAISAL. KLAMATH INDIAN ASSETS.   IUSSENA59674

A **REVIEW** OF THE ECONOMIC AND CULTURAL PROBLEMS OF WICHITA, KANSAS.   NBANNWM65051

THE NEGRO AND EQUAL-EMPLOYMENT-OPPORTUNITIES. A **REVIEW** OF MANAGEMENT EXPERIENCES IN TWENTY COMPANIES.   NFERMLA66790

A HISTORICAL **REVIEW** OF THE IMPACT OF SOCIAL AND ECONOMIC STRUCTURE ON NEGRO CULTURE AND HOW IT INFLUENCES FAMILY LIVING.   NJACKJX64596

REVIEW OF EVIDENCE RELATING TO EFFECTS OF DESEGREGATION ON THE INTELLECTUAL PERFORMANCE OF NEGROES.   NKATZIX64637

A SURVEY OF THE ECONOMIC AND CULTURAL CONDITIONS OF THE NEGRO POPULATION OF LOUISVILLE, KENTUCKY AND A **REVIEW** OF THE PROGRAM AND ACTIVITIES OF THE LOUISVILLE URBAN-LEAGUE. JANUARY-FEBRUARY, 1948.   NNATLUL48903

TOWARD FAIR EMPLOYMENT. A **REVIEW**.   NROSERX65130

A **REVIEW** OF RESEARCH ON THE NEGRO AND EMPLOYMENT IN THE SOUTH.   NROWARL65703

LABOR MONTH IN **REVIEW**. NEGRO UNEMPLOYMENT.   NUSDLAB63823

FANTASY, FACT AND THE FUTURE...A **REVIEW** OF THE STATUS OF WOMEN AND POSSIBLE IMPLICATIONS FOR WOMEN-S EDUCATION AND ROLE IN THE NEXT DECADE.   WFITZLE63963

REVIEWS

GUIDE FOR INVESTIGATIONS AND COMPLIANCE **REVIEWS** IN EQUAL-EMPLOYMENT-OPPORTUNITY.   GPRESCD62109

REVOLT

REVOLT IN THE SOUTH. /UNION DISCRIMINATION/   NFORTXX56881

REVOLT (CONTINUATION)

SOCIAL-STRUCTURE AND THE NEGRO **REVOLT**. AN EXAMINATION OF SOME HYPOTHESES. /SOCIO-ECONOMIC/   NGESCJA64400

RIOTS, GHETTOS AND THE NEGRO **REVOLT**.   NSOSKWX67154

THE NEGRO **REVOLT**.   NYOUNWM63352

REVOLUTION

LABOR AND THE CIVIL-RIGHTS **REVOLUTION**. /UNION/   GFLEIHX60685

REFLECTIONS ON THE MANPOWER **REVOLUTION**.   GHECKAX64937

THE MANPOWER **REVOLUTION** -- A CALL FOR DEBATE.   GKIRSGC64860

THE MANPOWER **REVOLUTION**. ITS POLICY CONSEQUENCES. EXCERPTS FROM SENATE HEARINGS BEFORE THE CLARK SUBCOMMITTEE.   GMANGGL66217

THE GUARANTEED-INCOME. NEXT STEP IN ECONOMIC **REVOLUTION**.   GTHEORX66626

NATION-S MANPOWER **REVOLUTION**.   GUSSENA63331

TALES OF THE DELANO **REVOLUTION**.   MVALDLX66512

THE AMERICAN **REVOLUTION**. PAGES FROM A NEGRO WORKER-S NOTEBOOK.   NBOGGJX63101

THE NEGRO **REVOLUTION** IN AMERICA.   NBRINWX64116

THE NEGRO **REVOLUTION** AND THE LAW OF COLLECTIVE BARGAINING.   NGOULWB65437

THE NEGRO **REVOLUTION**. A QUEST FOR JUSTICE.   NHATCJF66648

WHAT SHOULD THE BUSINESS RESPONSE BE TO THE NEGRO **REVOLUTION**. A PUBLIC RELATIONS PROGRAM FOR DEALING WITH MINORITY-GROUPS.   NLANGJF65671

THE CIVIL-RIGHTS **REVOLUTION** AND THE BUSINESSMAN.   NMCKERB64723

THE NEGRO **REVOLUTION** AND EMPLOYMENT.   NPOLIEX64219

THE UNFINISHED **REVOLUTION**. /TRAINING/   NRANDAP62036

TODAY-S CIVIL-RIGHTS **REVOLUTION**.   NRANDAP63035

JOBS FOR THE NEGRO. THE UNFINISHED **REVOLUTION**.   NRANDAP64034

REVOLUTION IN EVOLUTION. /COLLEGE RECRUITMENT/   NSCOTFG66111

THE NEW **REVOLUTION** IN THE COTTON ECONOMY.   NSTREJH57184

THE SOCIAL **REVOLUTION**. CHALLENGE TO THE NATION. /CIVIL-RIGHTS/   NYOUNWM63600

REVOLUTION WITHOUT IDEOLOGY. THE CHANGING PLACE OF WOMEN IN AMERICA. /WORK-WOMEN-ROLE/   WDEGLCN64727

REVOLUTIONS

THE INTERMINGLED **REVOLUTIONS** -- THE NEGRO AND AUTOMATION.   NYOUNWM64299

RHODE-ISLAND

RHODE-ISLAND COMMISSION-AGAINST-DISCRIMINATION, RULES OF PRACTICE AND PROCEDURE.   GRHODICND232

MOTIVATING NEGRO YOUTH IN **RHODE-ISLAND**.   NMINIBC65797

GOVERNOR-S CIVIL-RIGHTS TASK FORCE. REPORT. /**RHODE-ISLAND**/   NRHODIC64051

THE NON-WHITE IN PROVIDENCE. /**RHODE-ISLAND**/   NRHODIUND052

RIGHT

THE **RIGHT** TO EQUAL TREATMENT. ADMINISTRATIVE ENFORCEMENT OF ANTIDISCRIMINATION LEGISLATION.   GBAMBMA61416

THE INDIVIDUAL **RIGHT** TO ELIMINATE EMPLOYMENT DISCRIMINATION BY LITIGATION.   GBLUMAW66566

THE **RIGHT** TO JOIN A UNION.   GSU4MCW47342

THE **RIGHT** TO EQUAL-OPPORTUNITY.   MGLICLB66694

THE NEGRO MIDDLE CLASS IS **RIGHT** IN THE MIDDLE. /ECONOMIC-STATUS/   NCORDDX66030

THE CONSTITUTIONAL **RIGHT** TO MEMBERSHIP IN A LABOR UNION -- FIFTH AND FOURTEENTH AMENDMENTS.   NELLIGH59330

THE **RIGHT** TO KNOWLEDGE. /COLLEGE EDUCATION/   NHEALHX64306

RIGHT-TO-WORK

RIGHT-TO-WORK LAWS AND THE NEGRO WORKER.   NHILLHX58996

RIGHT-TO-WORK-LAWS

RIGHT-TO-WORK-LAWS AND CIVIL-RIGHTS. /UNION/   GHERLAK64771

RIGHTS

VIGOROUS **RIGHTS** EFFORTS PLEDGED BY CONVENTION.   GAMERFX59577

EQUAL **RIGHTS** FOR ALL.   GAMERFX66376

YOUR **RIGHTS** UNDER FAIR-EMPLOYMENT-PRACTICE LAWS.   GAMERJC60382

FAIR-EMPLOYMENT-PRACTICES ACT. STATE LAWS GRANTING EQUAL **RIGHTS**, PRIVILEGES, ETC.   GELWAEX58662

THE **RIGHTS** AND RESPONSIBILITY OF UNION MEMBERS. /ANTIDISCRIMINATION/   GGOLDAX58974

SOME BASIC CONSTITUTIONAL **RIGHTS** OF ECONOMIC SIGNIFICANCE.   GHALERX51754

PROTECTING **RIGHTS** OF MINORITY EMPLOYEES.   GKINGRL60854

UNIONS BEFORE THE BAR. HISTORICAL TRIALS SHOWING THE EVOLUTION OF LABOR **RIGHTS** IN THE US.   GLIEBEX50901

MINORITY **RIGHTS** AND THE PUBLIC INTEREST.   GLUSKLX42924

EQUAL **RIGHTS** -- HERE AND NOW.   GMEANGX63972

YOUR **RIGHTS**... UNDER STATE AND LOCAL FAIR-EMPLOYMENT-PRACTICES LAWS.   GNATLLS55051

THE NEXT STEPS TOWARD EQUALITY OF OPPORTUNITY IN THE SYRACUSE METROPOLITAN AREA. REPORT OF THE SYRACUSE

RIGHTS   (CONTINUATION)
CONFERENCE ON HUMAN **RIGHTS** AND HOUSING, JULY 2-3 1962. /NEW-YORK/   GNEWYSB62103

COMMISSIONS FOR HUMAN **RIGHTS**, 15TH ANNUAL CONFERENCE, PROCEEDINGS.   GPENNHR63166

TO SECURE THESE **RIGHTS**.   GPRESCC47192

MINORITY **RIGHTS** AND THE UNION SHOP.   GREADFT64220

LABOR LOOKS AT EQUAL **RIGHTS** IN EMPLOYMENT. /UNION/   GWOLLJA64579

EQUAL **RIGHTS** FOR THE SATURDAY SABBATH OBSERVER. /EMPLOYMENT DISCRIMINATION/   JHARTPX63729

YOUR **RIGHTS** UNDER FAIR-EMPLOYMENT-PRACTICE LAWS. /UNION LEGISLATION/   NAFLCIO60004

A CIVIL **RIGHTS** INVENTORY OF SAN FRANCISCO. PART I. /UNION/   NBABOIX58893

SOME RECENT UNITED STATES SUPREME COURT DECISIONS AFFECTING THE **RIGHTS** OF NEGRO WORKERS.   NCHICCA47914

CIVIL-RIGHTS. 1960-63. THE NEGRO CAMPAIGN TO WIN EQUAL **RIGHTS** AND OPPORTUNITIES IN THE UNITED STATES. NFACTOF64341

LEFT SECTARIANISM IN THE FIGHT FOR NEGRO **RIGHTS** AND AGAINST WHITE CHAUVINISM.   NFOSTWZ53375

NEW-YORK CITY COMMISSION ON HUMAN **RIGHTS**, CONSTRUCTION TRADES HEARING, TESTIMONY. /INDUSTRY/   NHILLHX66546

THE NEGRO WORKER ASSERTS HIS **RIGHTS**. /UNION/   NJACOPA63601

TO WIN THESE **RIGHTS**. A PERSONAL STORY OF THE CIO IN THE SOUTH. /UNION/   NMASOJR52324

UNION **RIGHTS** AND UNION DUTIES.   NSEIDJI43115

THE STRUGGLE FOR JOBS AND FOR NEGRO **RIGHTS** IN THE TRADE UNIONS.   NSIMOHX50139

A LABOR UNIT FOR NEGRO **RIGHTS**.   NUSDLAB52148

TO FULFILL THESE **RIGHTS**. /POLICY-RECOMMENDATIONS/   NUSDLAB66248

JOB **RIGHTS** FOR NEGROES -- PRESSURE ON EMPLOYERS.   NUSNEWR66270

TO FULFILL THESE **RIGHTS**. REPORT ON THE WHITE-HOUSE-CONFERENCE. /EEO/   NWATTPX66545

REPORT OF THE COMMITTEE ON CIVIL AND POLITICAL **RIGHTS**.   WPRESCO63065

THE OFFICIAL WORD ON JOB **RIGHTS** FOR WOMEN.   WUSNEWR65246

TO FULFILL THESE **RIGHTS**. SUMMARY REPORT OF PRE-WHITE-HOUSE CONFERENCES.   WYWCAXX66079

RIO-GRANDE
TEXAS GROWERS AND WORKERS ON THE FARM, LOWER **RIO-GRANDE** VALLEY.   GTEXAEC59352

RIOT
CASE-STUDY OF A **RIOT** THE PHILADELPHIA STORY. /PENNSYLVANIA/   NBERSLE66078

THE HARLEM **RIOT**. A STUDY IN MASS FRUSTRATION.   NOLANHX43954

RIOTS
RIOTS, GHETTOS AND THE NEGRO REVOLT.   NSOSKWX67154

ROCHESTER
THE SCHOOL DROPOUT PROBLEM IN MAJOR CITIES OF NEW-YORK STATE. **ROCHESTER** -- PART I. /NEGRO PUERTO-RICAN/ CNEWYSD62090

OUTREACH IN **ROCHESTER**. /NEW-YORK/   NCROFES66242

RACE-RELATIONS IN **ROCHESTER**, A PROFILE FOR 1957. /NEW-YORK/   NGRIEES57457

ROCKY-BAY-S
POPULATION CHARACTERISTICS, LIVING CONDITIONS AND INCOMES OF INDIAN FAMILIES, **ROCKY-BAY-S** RESERVATION. IUSDINT63659

ROCKY-MOUNTAIN
FAMILY COMPOSITION AND CHARACTERISTICS OF AN ECONOMICALLY DEPRIVED CROSS-CULTURAL **ROCKY-MOUNTAIN** AREA. MANDRWH66359

ROLE
THE **ROLE** OF GOVERNMENT-SPONSORED TRAINING AND RETRAINING PROGRAMS.   GALLECC65758

THE **ROLE** OF LEGISLATION IN ELIMINATING RACIAL DISCRIMINATION.   GBONFAE65462

THE FEDERAL MANAGER-S **ROLE** IN DEMOCRACY-S UNFINISHED BUSINESS.   GCLINRX61577

THE **ROLE** OF WAGES IN A GREAT SOCIETY.   GCONFOE66872

THE **ROLE** OF LAW IN EQUAL-EMPLOYMENT-OPPORTUNITY.   GCOOKFC66600

PREJUDICE -- A THREAT TO THE LEADERSHIP **ROLE**.   GEVANRI62669

THE **ROLE** OF GOVERNMENT. /TECHNOLOGICAL-CHANGE/   GGOLDAX62865

ASSIMILATION IN AMERICAN LIFE. THE **ROLE** OF RACE, RELIGION, AND NATIONAL ORIGINS.   GGORDMM64729

THE **ROLE** OF THE UNITED STATES EMPLOYMENT-SERVICE IN A CHANGING ECONOMY.   GHABEWX64649

CENTRAL **ROLE** OF INTERGROUP AGENCIES IN THE LABOR-MARKET. CHANGING RESEARCH AND PERSONNEL REQUIREMENTS. GHOPEJX61780

THE COMMUNITY ACTION AGENCY-S **ROLE** IN COMPREHENSIVE MANPOWER PROGRAMS -- PLANNING AND PROBLEMS.   GKANERD66863

THE **ROLE** OF THE SECONDARY SCHOOLS IN THE PREPARATION OF YOUTH FOR EMPLOYMENT.   GKAUFJJ67940

THE **ROLE** OF THE SECONDARY SCHOOLS IN THE PREPARATION OF YOUTH FOR EMPLOYMENT. SUMMARY, CONCLUSIONS, AND
RECOMMENDATIONS.   GKAUFJJ67963

THE NEW **ROLE** OF THE EMPLOYMENT SERVICE IN SERVING THE DISADVANTAGED. /SES/   GLEVILA66599

SOLVING AN AMERICAN DILEMMA. THE **ROLE** OF THE FEPC OFFICIAL, A COMPARATIVE STUDY OF STATE CIVIL-RIGHTS
COMMISSIONS.   GLLOYKM64317

RACIAL AND RELIGIOUS DISCRIMINATION IN EMPLOYMENT AND THE **ROLE** OF THE NLRB.   GMALOWH61935

THE **ROLE** OF JOB CREATION PROGRAMS. /MANPOWER/   GMANGGL65728

THE **ROLE** OF EMPLOYMENT POLICY. /ANTI-POVERTY/   GMINSHX65655

ROLE   (CONTINUATION)
    INCREASING EMPLOYABILITY OF YOUTH. THE **ROLE** OF WORK TRAINING.   GMOEDMX66852

    THE **ROLE** OF THE EMPLOYER IN MANPOWER POLICY. /INDUSTRY/   GMYERCA66527

    THE **ROLE** OF AGRICULTURAL TECHNOLOGY IN SOUTHERN SOCIAL CHANGE.   GRAPEAX46037

    THE **ROLE** OF GOVERNMENT IN PROMOTING FULL EMPLOYMENT.   GROSSAM66084

    LABOR-S **ROLE**. DEMOCRACY ON THE JOB. /UNION/   GSLAIDX66317

    THE **ROLE** OF MANPOWER POLICY IN ACHIEVING AGGREGATE GOALS. /EMPLOYMENT INCOME/   GTHURLC66640

    THE **ROLE** OF REDISTRIBUTION IN SOCIAL POLICY.   GTITMRM65359

    FEDERAL **ROLE** IN URBAN AFFAIRS.   GUSSENA66351

    THE **ROLE** AND LIMITS OF NATIONAL MANPOWER POLICIES.   GWEBEAR66760

    THE **ROLE** OF WOMEN IN A CHANGING NAVAHO SOCIETY.   IHAMALS57985

    THE CHANGING **ROLE** OF THE INDIAN IN ARIZONA.   IKELLWH58577

    THE **ROLE** OF THE BUREAU-OF-INDIAN-AFFAIRS SINCE 1933.   IZIMMWX57248

    VALUE ORIENTATION. **ROLE** CONFLICT. AND ALIENATION FROM WORK. A CROSS-CULTURAL STUDY.   MZURCLA65520

    RACIAL EQUALITY AND THE LAW. THE **ROLE** OF LAW IN THE REDUCTION OF DISCRIMINATION IN THE UNITED-STATES.   N9ERGMX54076

    A MORE PRODUCTIVE **ROLE** FOR THE NEGRO IN THE SOUTH-S ECONOMY.   NCHALWE64912

    THE **ROLE** OF THE NEGRO IN THE ORGANIZATION OF THE CIO. /UNION/   NCOOPJE56235

    THE **ROLE** OF WHITE RESISTANCE AND FACILITATION IN THE NEGRO STRUGGLE FOR EQUALITY.   NGLENND65676

    EMPLOYMENT SECURITY. SENIORITY AND RACE. THE **ROLE** OF TITLE-VII OF THE CIVIL-RIGHTS-ACT OF 1964.   NGOULWB67864

    SITUATIONAL PRESSURES AND FUNCTIONAL **ROLE** OF THE ETHNIC LABOR LEADERS. /UNION/   NGREESX53453

    THE **ROLE** OF LAW IN SECURING EQUAL-EMPLOYMENT-OPPORTUNITY. LEGAL POWERS AND SOCIAL CHANGE.   NHILLHX66544

    STATEMENT AND TESTIMONY ON FEDERAL **ROLE** IN URBAN AFFAIRS. /EMPLOYMENT GHETTO/   NKENNRF66017

    THE **ROLE** OF THE NEGRO IN THE HEALING PROFESSIONS IN CONTEMPORARY AMERICA. /OCCUPATIONS/   NMCPHEL55728

    THE **ROLE** OF ORGANIZATIONAL STRUCTURES. UNION VERSUS NEIGHBORHOOD IN A TENSION SITUATION.   NREITDC53050

    THE **ROLE** OF THE COUNSELOR IN THE GUIDANCE OF NEGRO STUDENTS.   NTRUEDL60208

    THE **ROLE** OF CIVIL-RIGHTS ORGANIZATIONS. A MARSHALL PLAN APPROACH.   NTUCKSX66209

    THE **ROLE** OF THE NEGRO COLLEGE.   NWEAVEK44297

    THE **ROLE** OUTLOOK OF EDUCATED WOMEN. /ASPIRATIONS/   WANGRSS64484

    ROLE CONCEPTION AS A PREDICTOR OF ADULT FEMALE ROLES. /WORK-WOMAN-ROLE/   WANGRSS66619

    NOTES ON THE **ROLE** OF CHOICE IN THE PSYCHOLOGY OF PROFESSIONAL WOMEN. /OCCUPATIONS/   WBAILLX64623

    THE RELATIONSHIP OF PARENTAL IDENTIFICATION TO SEX **ROLE** ACCEPTANCE IN MARRIED, SINGLE, CAREER AND
    NON-CAREER WOMEN. /WORK-WOMEN-ROLE/   WBREYCH64654

    POST GRADUATION **ROLE** PREFERENCE OF SENIOR WOMEN IN COLLEGE. /ASPIRATION/   WCHRIHX56690

    ROLE CONCEPTION AND CAREER ASPIRATION. A STUDY OF IDENTITY IN NURSING.   WCORWRG61707

    ROLE EXPECTATIONS OF YOUNG WOMEN REGARDING MARRIAGE AND A CAREER. /ASPIRATIONS WORK-FAMILY-CONFLICT/   WEMPELT58751

    FACTORS ASSOCIATED WITH GRADUATE SCHOOL ATTENDANCE AND **ROLE** DEFINITION OF THE WOMAN DOCTORAL CANDIDATES
    AT THE PENNSYLVANIA STATE UNIVERSITY. /OCCUPATIONS/   WFIELJC61763

    FANTASY, FACT AND THE FUTURE...A REVIEW OF THE STATUS OF WOMEN AND POSSIBLE IMPLICATIONS FOR WOMEN-S
    EDUCATION AND **ROLE** IN THE NEXT DECADE.   WFITZLE63963

    THE **ROLE** OF THE EDUCATED WOMAN. AN EMPIRICAL STUDY OF THE ATTITUDES OF A GROUP OF COLLEGE WOMEN.
    /WORK-WOMAN-ROLE/   WFREEMB65770

    COUNSELING IMPLICATIONS OF WOMAN-S CHANGING **ROLE**.   WGASSGZ59775

    SOCIAL **ROLE** EXPECTATION. MOTIVATIONAL VARIABLE IN GIRLS. /ASPIRATIONS/   WHANSDE64821

    SOME IMPLICATIONS ON CURRENT CHANGES IN SEX **ROLE** PATTERNS. /WORK-WOMAN-ROLE/   WHARTRE60828

    THE **ROLE** OF THE EDUCATED WOMAN. /WORK-WOMAN-ROLE/   WJONECX64009

    HIGH SCHOOL FRESHMAN AND SENIORS VIEW THE **ROLE** OF WOMEN IN MODERN SOCIETY. /WORK-FAMILY-CONFLICT/   WKERNKK65892

    DROP-OUTS FROM SCHOOLS OF NURSING. THE EFFECT OF SELF- AND **ROLE** PERCEPTION.   WKIBRAK58902

    ENHANCING THE **ROLE** OF WOMEN IN SCIENCE, ENGINEERING, AND THE SOCIAL SCIENCES. /OCCUPATIONS/   WKILLJR65903

    THE AMERICAN WOMAN-S **ROLE**. /WORK-WOMAN-ROLE/   WKIUCFX62909

    ECONOMIC **ROLE** OF WOMEN 45-65. /WORK-WOMAN-ROLE/   WKYRKHX56921

    PERCEPTIONS OF **ROLE** CONFLICTS AND SELF CONFLICTS AMONG CAREER AND NON-CAREER COLLEGE EDUCATED WOMEN.
    /WORK-FAMILY-CONFLICT/   WMORGDD62996

    WOMEN-S CHANGING **ROLE** IN THE US EMPLOYMENT MARKET.   WMUNTEE56007

    ROLE OF WOMEN IN AMERICAN ECONOMIC LIFE.   WNORRLW56036

    THE CHANGING **ROLE** OF COLLEGE WOMEN. A BIBLIOGRAPHY. /WORK-WOMAN-ROLE/   WSCHWJX62106

    CONCEPT OF THE FEMININE **ROLE**. /WORK-WOMAN-ROLE/   WSTEIAX63135

    ROLE OF WOMEN. /WORK-WOMAN-ROLE/   WTHOMJL56380

    THE **ROLE** OF WOMEN IN PROFESSIONAL ENGINEERING. /OCCUPATIONS/   WTORPWG62157

ROLE   (CONTINUATION)
THE CHANGING **ROLE** OF WOMEN IN OUR CHANGING SOCIETY.   WUSOLAB62253

HOW WOMEN-S **ROLE** IN US IS CHANGING.   WUSNEWR66245

ROLES
LOCAL CONTRACTS AND SUB-CONTRACTS. THE **ROLES** OF CITY GOVERNMENT AND PRIVATE CITIZENS GROUPS. GJONEMX64829

ROLE CONCEPTION AS A PREDICTOR OF ADULT FEMALE **ROLES**. /WORK-WOMAN-ROLE/   WANGRSS66619

WOMAN-S **ROLES**. HOW GIRLS SEE THEM. /WORK-WOMAN-ROLE/   WHARTRE62830

PSYCHOLOGICAL PROBLEMS OF WOMEN IN DIFFERENT SOCIAL **ROLES**. /WORK-WOMAN-ROLE/   WJAHOMX55879

THE FEMALE PHYSICIAN IN PUBLIC HEALTH. CONFLICT AND RECONCILIATION OF THE SEX AND PROFESSIONAL **ROLES**.
/OCCUPATIONS/   WKOSAJX64915

ROLES OF THE MARRIED WOMAN IN SCIENCE. /OCCUPATIONS/   WMOTZAB61002

WOMEN-S TWO **ROLES**. /WORK-FAMILY-CONFLICT/   WMYRDAX56012

WOMEN-S CHANGING **ROLES** THROUGH THE LIFE CYCLE.   WNEUGBL59025

SUMMARY OF CURRENT RESEARCH ON WOMEN-S **ROLES**.   WNOBLJL59035

A COMPARISON OF THE MALE-FEMALE **ROLES** IN ENGINEERING. /OCCUPATION/   WROBISS63083

SOME CHANGING **ROLES** OF WOMEN IN SUBURBIA. A SOCIAL ANTHROPOLOGICAL CASE STUDY. /WORK-FAMILY-CONFLICT/ WSCOFNE60109

THE VOCATIONAL **ROLES** OF OLDER MARRIED WOMEN. /WORK-WOMAN-ROLE/   WSTEIAX61136

ROOTS
THE HISTORICAL **ROOTS** OF FAIR-EMPLOYMENT.   GFLEMJG46688

SOME SOCIOLOGICAL **ROOTS** OF VOCATIONAL CHOICES.   GYOUNME46593

DEALING WITH INTER-RACIAL TENSIONS ON LOCAL UNION GRASS **ROOTS** BASIS.   NANDEEC50894

LABOR-S GRASS **ROOTS**. A STUDY OF THE LOCAL UNION.   NBARBJX61052

THE **ROOTS** OF THE NEGRO-UNION ALLIANCE. /UNION/   NMARSRX66746

THE **ROOTS** OF AMBIVALENCE IN AMERICAN WOMEN. /WORK-FAMILY-CONFLICT/   WROSSASND133

ROSEBUD
CONSTRAINTS ON ECONOMIC PROGRESS ON THE **ROSEBUD** SIOUX INDIAN RESERVATION.   IEICHCK60553

RUBBER
SENIORITY AND POSTWAR JOBS. **RUBBER** INDUSTRY. /NEGRO WOMEN/   CLABORR44028

SENIORITY IN THE AKRON **RUBBER** INDUSTRY.   NUSOLAB44841

RULES
TEXTS OF **RULES** AND REGULATIONS OF PRESIDENT-S COMMITTEE ON EQUAL-EMPLOYMENT-OPPORTUNITY RELATING TO
OBLIGATIONS OF GOVERNMENT CONTRACTORS AND SUBCONTRACTORS, EFFECTIVE JULY 22, 1961. A BNA SPECIAL REPORT.   GBURENA61498

RULES AND REGULATIONS OF THE PRESIDENT-S COMMITTEE ON EQUAL-EMPLOYMENT-OPPORTUNITY AS AMENDED. GBURENA63496

FAIR-EMPLOYMENT-PRACTICE ACT...FEPC **RULES** AND REGULATIONS... GUIDE TO PRE-EMPLOYMENT INQUIRIES.
/CALIFORNIA/   GCALFEP61533

SUMMARY OF **RULES**, REGULATIONS, AND LAWS THAT AFFECT SEASONAL FARM WORKERS AND THEIR EMPLOYERS IN NEW-YORK
STATE. /MIGRANT-WORKERS/   GNEWYSJND113

RULES ON EMPLOYMENT INQUIRIES.   GOREGBLND139

GOVERNMENT CONTRACT EMPLOYMENT. **RULES** AND REGULATIONS... EFFECTIVE JULY 22, 1961, AS AMENDED SEPTEMBER 7,
1963.   GPRESCD63110

RHODE-ISLAND COMMISSION-AGAINST-DISCRIMINATION. **RULES** OF PRACTICE AND PROCEDURE.   GRHODICND232

LABOR WEEK. **RULES** ON HIRING, PROMOTING -- QUESTIONS ANSWERED.   GUSNEWR66518

WORKING **RULES** FOR ASSURING NONDISCRIMINATION IN HOSPITAL ADMINISTRATION.   NYALELJ64600

ANTI-NEPOTISM **RULES** IN AMERICAN COLLEGES AND UNIVERSITIES -- THEIR EFFECT ON THE FACULTY EMPLOYMENT OF
WOMEN.   WDOLAEF60951

RULINGS
RULINGS ON PRE-EMPLOYMENT INQUIRIES RELATING TO RACE, CREED, COLOR OR NATIONAL ORIGIN UNDER THE NEW-YORK
STATE LAW AGAINST DISCRIMINATION.   GNEWYSBND106

LEGAL **RULINGS** INTERPRETING THE PROVISIONS OF THE PENNSYLVANIA FAIR-EMPLOYMENT-PRACTICE ACT. GPENNFE58153

RURAL
OCCUPATIONAL AND RESIDENTIAL ADJUSTMENT OF **RURAL** MIGRANTS. /NEGRO MEXICAN-AMERICAN/   CSHANLW61119

INCOMES OF **RURAL** FAMILIES IN THE BLACKLAND PRAIRIES.   GADKIWG63410

MANPOWER RETRAINING IN THE SOUTH-S **RURAL** POPULATION -- AN OPPORTUNITY FOR DEVELOPMENT.   GBACHFT63413

RECENT POPULATION TRENDS IN THE UNITED STATES WITH EMPHASIS ON **RURAL** AREAS. /EDUCATION/   GBEALCL63426

RURAL INDUSTRIALIZATION IN A LOUISIANA COMMUNITY. /ECONOMIC-STATUS OCCUPATIONS/   GBERTAL59393

THE EMERGING **RURAL** SOUTH. A REGION UNDER CONFRONTATION BY MASS SOCIETY.   GBERTAL66140

POVERTY IN **RURAL** AREAS OF THE UNITED STATES.   GBIRDAR64450

POTENTIAL SUPPLY AND REPLACEMENT OF **RURAL** MALES OF LABOR-FORCE AGE, 1960-70.   GBOWLGK66430

WHITE AND NONWHITE OWNERS OF **RURAL** LAND IN THE SOUTHEAST.   GBOXLRF65418

RURAL POVERTY.   GBURCLE65490

CHARACTERISTICS, RESOURCES, AND INCOMES OF **RURAL** HOUSEHOLDS, PIEDMONT AREA, SOUTH-CAROLINA. GBURCTA62408

URBAN AND **RURAL** LEVELS OF LIVING. 1960. /ECONOMIC-STATUS/   GCOWHJC65425

RURAL (CONTINUATION)

RURAL INDUSTRIALIZATION. A SUMMARY OF FIVE STUDIES. /UNEMPLOYMENT OCCUPATIONS/   GMAITST61383

RESOURCES AND INCOMES OF **RURAL** FAMILIES IN THE COASTAL PLAIN AREAS OF GEORGIA.   GMCARWC59392

THE EFFECTS OF INDUSTRIALIZATION ON **RURAL** LOUISIANA. A STUDY OF PLANT EMPLOYEES.   GPRICPH58395

RESOURCE CHARACTERISTICS AND UTILIZATION AND LEVEL OF LIVING ITEMS, **RURAL** HOUSEHOLDS, NORTH AND WEST FLORIDA, 1956.   GREUSLA60391

INCOME, RESOURCES, AND ADJUSTMENT POTENTIALS AMONG **RURAL** FAMILIES IN NORTH AND WEST FLORIDA.   GREUSLA62388

INCOMES OF **RURAL** FAMILIES IN NORTHEAST TEXAS.   GSOUTJF59325

RURAL PEOPLE IN THE AMERICAN ECONOMY.   GUSDAGR66507

INDIANS IN **RURAL** AND RESERVATION AREAS. /CALIFORNIA/   ICALACI66542

LEVELS OF LIVING OF SPANISH-AMERICAN **RURAL** AND URBAN FAMILIES IN TWO SOUTH TEXAS COUNTIES.   MCLEMHM63381

OCCUPATIONAL-PATTERNS OF **RURAL** AND URBAN SPANISH-AMERICANS IN TWO SOUTH TEXAS COUNTIES.   MCOTHML66385

INCOMES OF **RURAL** AND URBAN SPANISH-AMERICANS IN TWO SOUTH TEXAS COUNTIES.   MDICKBE65389

RURAL PEOPLE AND THEIR RESOURCES, NORTH-CENTRAL NEW-MEXICO.   MTAYLMM60402

SOME DEMOGRAPHIC CHARACTERISTICS OF **RURAL** YOUTH.   NBEEGJA63072

THE FRENCH AND THE NON-FRENCH IN LOUISIANA. A STUDY OF THE RELEVANCE OF ETHNIC FACTORS IN **RURAL** DEVELOPMENT. /ECONOMIC-STATUS/   NBERTAL65394

INCOME AND RELATED CHARACTERISTICS OF **RURAL** HOUSEHOLDS IN THE CENTRAL LOUISIANA MIXED FARMING AREA.   NBOLTBX60398

RESOURCE USE AND ADJUSTMENT. **RURAL** FAMILIES IN THE CENTRAL LOUISIANA MIXED FARMING AREA.   NBOLTBX61396

ATTITUDE TOWARD JOB-MOBILITY AMONG HOUSEHOLD HEADS IN LOW-INCOME AREAS OF THE **RURAL** SOUTH.   NDUNKJX64300

NEW HOPE FOR **RURAL** DIXIE. FIRMS IN CAROLINAS CREATE JOBS FOR NEGROES.   NEBONXX64317

NEGRO LEADERSHIP IN **RURAL** GEORGIA COMMUNITIES. OCCUPATIONAL AND SOCIAL ASPECTS.   NEDWAVA42328

EXPERIMENTAL AND DEMONSTRATION MANPOWER PROJECT FOR THE RECRUITMENT, TRAINING, PLACEMENT AND FOLLOW-UP OF **RURAL** UNEMPLOYED WORKERS IN TEN NORTH FLORIDA CITIES. FINAL REPORT. /PARTICIPANTS/   NJACKTA66597

GROWING UP IN THE BLACK BELT. NEGRO YOUTH IN THE **RURAL** SOUTH.   NJOHNCS41611

SOME CORRELATES OF ANOMIE AMONG **RURAL** NEGROES.   NLEWICE66688

FACILITATIVE AND INHIBITIVE FACTORS IN TRAINING PROGRAM RECRUITMENT AMONG **RURAL** NEGROES.   NMARSCP65738

THE **RURAL** NEGRO POPULATION OF THE SOUTH IN TRANSITION.   NMAYOSC63762

THE RELATIONSHIP BETWEEN MECHANIZATION OF COTTON PRODUCTION AND ATTENDANCE AND ENROLLMENT IN THE **RURAL** SCHOOLS OF COAHOMA COUNTY, MISSISSIPPI.   NMCLABF51349

THE IMPACT OF SOCIO-ECONOMIC CHANGE ON RACIAL GROUPS IN A **RURAL** SETTING.   NPELLRJ62981

MIGRATION PATTERNS OF NEGROES FROM A **RURAL** NORTHEASTERN MISSISSIPPI COMMUNITY. /DEMOGRAPHY/   NRUBIMX60094

MIGRATION AND ADJUSTMENT EXPERIENCES OF **RURAL** WORKERS IN INDIANAPOLIS. /INDIANA/   NSMITED53143

NEGRO FAMILIES IN **RURAL** WISCONSIN. A STUDY OF THEIR COMMUNITY LIFE.   NWISCGC59331

AFTER HIGH SCHOOL WHAT...HIGHLIGHTS OF A STUDY OF CAREER PLANS OF NEGRO AND WHITE **RURAL** YOUTH IN THREE FLORIDA COUNTIES. /ASPIRATIONS/   NYOUMEG65390

THE **RURAL** WORKING HOMEMAKER. ALCORN-COUNTY, MISSISSIPPI. /WORK-FAMILY-CONFLICT/   WBRYAES61660

FINAL REPORT. EXPERIMENTAL AND DEMONSTRATION MANPOWER PROJECT FOR THE RECRUITMENT, TRAINING, PLACEMENT AND FOLLOW-UP OF **RURAL** UNEMPLOYED WORKERS IN TEN NORTH FLORIDA COUNTIES.   WFLORMP66326

ACCESS OF GIRLS AND WOMEN TO EDUCATION IN **RURAL** AREAS. A COMPARATIVE STUDY.   WUNESCO64166

RURAL-FARM

RURAL-FARM MALES ENTERING AND LEAVING WORKING AGES, 1940-50 AND 1950-60. REPLACEMENT RATIOS AND RATES. /OCCUPATIONS/   GBOWLGK56433

MIGRATION PATTERNS OF THE **RURAL-FARM** POPULATION. THIRTEEN ECONOMIC REGIONS OF THE UNITED STATES, 1940-1950.   GBOWLGK57415

RURAL-URBAN

COMPARISON OF MEXICANS, NEGROES AND WHITES WITH RESPECT TO OCCUPATIONAL HISTORY, **RURAL-URBAN** RESIDENCE HISTORY AND ACCULTURATION WITHIN THE INSTITUTIONAL STRUCTURE OF LANSING, MICHIGAN.   CGCLDVX60494

RURAL-URBAN DIFFERENCES IN ASPIRATIONS.   GMIDDRX59573

RUTGERS

RUTGERS -- THE STATE UNIVERSITY. FORD FOUNDATION PROGRAM FOR THE RETRAINING IN MATHEMATICS OF COLLEGE GRADUATE WOMEN. /TRAINING/   WMARTHM63957

SABBATH

EQUAL RIGHTS FOR THE SATURDAY **SABBATH** OBSERVER. /EMPLOYMENT DISCRIMINATION/   JHARTPX63729

SAFETY

WOMEN IN INDUSTRY -- PATTERNS OF WOMEN-S WORK AND OCCUPATIONAL HEALTH AND **SAFETY**. /OCCUPATIONS/   WSPIRES60301

SALARIED

THE NEGRO **SALARIED** WORKER. /EMPLOYMENT-SELECTION/   NGOURJC65438

MORE **SALARIED** POSITIONS ARE OPENED TO NEGROES BY BUSINESS AND INDUSTRY HERE. /NEW-YORK/   NSTETDX63154

SALARIED WOMEN IN UPPER LEVEL POSITIONS IN KANSAS BUSINESS FIRMS.   WSTOCFT59143

SALARIES

STUDY OF THE SHORTAGE AND **SALARIES** OF SCIENTISTS AND ENGINEERS.   GUSSENA54353

THE STRUGGLE OF NEGRO TEACHERS IN FLORIDA FOR EQUAL **SALARIES**. /OCCUPATIONS/   NFERGML49961

EFFORTS OF NEGRO TEACHERS IN THE SOUTHERN STATES TO OBTAIN EQUALIZATION OF **SALARIES**.   NJONEER48343

SALARIES   (CONTINUATION)
THE BLS STUDY OF NURSES **SALARIES** AND EMPLOYMENT CONDITIONS.   WAMERJN57378

SURVEY OF **SALARIES** AND EMPLOYMENT-CONDITIONS IN NONFEDERAL PSYCHIATRIC HOSPITALS.   WAMERNA65611

SURVEY OF **SALARIES** AND PERSONNEL PRACTICES FOR TEACHERS AND ADMINISTRATORS IN NURSING EDUCATIONAL
PROGRAMS, DECEMBER 1965.   WAMERNA66612

OCCUPATIONS AND **SALARIES** OF WOMEN IN THE FEDERAL SERVICE.   WUSCISC62168

OCCUPATIONS AND **SALARIES** OF WOMEN FEDERAL EMPLOYEES.   WUSDLAB57992

SALARY
NEGRO AND TOTAL EMPLOYMENT BY GRADE AND **SALARY** GROUPS, JUNE 1961 AND JUNE 1962.   NPRESCD62011

SALES
CUSTOMER REACTIONS TO THE INTEGRATION OF NEGRO **SALES** PERSONNEL.   NSAENGX50101

NEGROES ON THE **SALES** FORCE. THE QUIET INTEGRATION.   NVOGLAJ64286

SALESMEN
THE EMPLOYMENT OF NEGROES AS DRIVER **SALESMEN** IN THE BAKING INDUSTRY.   NNEWYSA60919

SALTONSTALL
REPORT OF THE COMMISSION ON THE EMPLOYMENT PROBLEMS OF NEGROES TO GOVERNOR **SALTONSTALL**. /MASSACHUSETTS/   NMASSCE42757

SAMPLE
THE STATUS OF JOBS AND OCCUPATIONS AS EVALUATED BY AN URBAN NEGRO **SAMPLE**.   NBROWMC55126

INTELLIGENCE AND EDUCATIONAL ACHIEVEMENT OF A MATCHED **SAMPLE** OF WHITE AND NEGRO STUDENTS. NMCQURX60730

SAMPLES
ATTITUDES TOWARD SOCIAL MOBILITY AS REVEALED BY **SAMPLES** OF NEGRO AND WHITE BOYS.   NMONTJB58809

SAN-ANTONIO
INCOME, EDUCATION AND UNEMPLOYMENT IN NEIGHBORHOODS. **SAN-ANTONIO**, TEXAS. /DEMOGRAPHY/   CUSDLAB63482

SUB-EMPLOYMENT IN THE SLUMS OF **SAN-ANTONIO**. /TEXAS/   GUSDLAB66515

AN ANALYSIS OF CURRENT PATTERNS IN HUMAN RESOURCE DEVELOPMENT IN **SAN-ANTONIO**, TEXAS.   MDAVIHW66387

THE MEXICAN-AMERICAN WORKERS OF **SAN-ANTONIO**. /TEXAS/   MLANDRG66427

SAN-ANTONIO PROJECT. /TEXAS/   MNATLCA63081

ECONOMIC BASE STUDY OF **SAN-ANTONIO** AND TWENTY-SEVEN COUNTY AREAS. /TEXAS/   MSANACP64476

OCCUPATIONAL CHANGE AMONG SPANISH-AMERICANS IN ATASCOSA-COUNTY AND **SAN-ANTONIO**, TEXAS.   MSKRARL66492

SAN-ANTONIO PROJECT. /TEXAS/   MWAGNJA63514

SAN-CARLOS
SAN-CARLOS APACHE WAGE LABOR.   IADAMWX57522

DEVELOPMENT OF THE **SAN-CARLOS** APACHE CATTLE INDUSTRY. /CALIFORNIA/   IGETTHT58563

THE **SAN-CARLOS** INDIAN CATTLE INDUSTRY. /CALIFORNIA/   IGETTHT63564

SAN-DIEGO
INCOME, EDUCATION AND UNEMPLOYMENT IN NEIGHBORHOODS. **SAN-DIEGO**, CALIFORNIA. /DEMOGRAPHY/   CUSDLAB63483

EMPLOYMENT PRACTICES, CITY OF **SAN-DIEGO**, 1963-1964. /CALIFORNIA/   GZOOKDX64596

SAN-DIEGO-S
DIMENSIONS IN DISCRIMINATION, A PRELIMINARY SURVEY OF **SAN-DIEGO-S** COMMUNITY PROBLEMS OF DISCRIMINATION
PART II. /CALIFORNIA/   GSANDLW65274

SAN-FRANCISCO
RACIAL CHARACTERISTICS, MDTA TRAINEES, **SAN-FRANCISCO**. /CALIFORNIA NEGRO MEXICAN-AMERICAN/ CELTCEX63332

INCOME, EDUCATION AND UNEMPLOYMENT IN NEIGHBORHOODS. **SAN-FRANCISCO**, CALIFORNIA. /DEMOGRAPHY/   CUSDLAB63484

A CIVIL-RIGHTS INVENTORY OF **SAN-FRANCISCO**. PART I. EMPLOYMENT. /CALIFORNIA/   GBABOIX58606

MANPOWER RESOURCES OF THE **SAN-FRANCISCO** OAKLAND BAY AREA 1960-1970. /CALIFORNIA/   GCALDEM63520

MEDICAL SERVICE JOB OPPORTUNITIES 1964-66, **SAN-FRANCISCO** BAY AREA. /CALIFORNIA/   GCALDEM64521

HOTEL AND RESTAURANT JOB OPPORTUNITIES, **SAN-FRANCISCO** BAY AREA, 1964-1966. /CALIFORNIA/   GCALDEM65517

BAY AREA CONFERENCE ON FULL-EMPLOYMENT. /**SAN-FRANCISCO** CALIFORNIA/   GHIRSFI64776

HIRING PROCEDURES AND SELECTION STANDARDS IN THE **SAN-FRANCISCO** BAY AREA. /CALIFORNIA/   GMALMTF55934

A HUMAN-RELATIONS PROGRAM FOR **SAN-FRANCISCO**. /CALIFORNIA/   GMITCJP64277

THE **SAN-FRANCISCO** NON-WHITE POPULATION 1950-1960. /CALIFORNIA/   GROSETXND250

PSYCHOLOGICAL TESTS AND FAIR EMPLOYMENT. A STUDY OF EMPLOYMENT TESTING IN THE **SAN-FRANCISCO** BAY AREA.
/CALIFORNIA/   GRUSHJT66268

FINAL REPORT OF **SAN-FRANCISCO** CALIFORNIA COMMISSION ON EQUAL-EMPLOYMENT-OPPORTUNITY.   GSANFCE60275

RACIAL AND ETHNIC EMPLOYMENT PATTERN SURVEY OF THE CITY AND COUNTY OF **SAN-FRANCISCO** GOVERNMENT.
DEPARTMENTAL ANALYSIS. /CALIFORNIA/   GSANFHR65264

US COMMISSION-ON-CIVIL-RIGHTS, HEARINGS. LOS-ANGELES AND **SAN-FRANCISCO**, CALIFORNIA. JANUARY 25-26, 1960,
JANUARY 27-28, 1960.   GUSCCMC60400

MINORITY WORKER HIRING AND REFERRAL IN **SAN-FRANCISCO**. /CALIFORNIA/   GUSDLAB58076

SUB-EMPLOYMENT IN THE SLUMS OF **SAN-FRANCISCO**. /CALIFORNIA/   GUSDLAB66519

RELOCATED AMERICAN INDIANS IN THE **SAN-FRANCISCO** BAY AREA. SOCIAL INTERACTION AND INDIAN IDENTITY.
/CALIFORNIA/   IALBOJX64523

SAN-FRANCISCO RELOCATEES. /CALIFORNIA/   ITAXXSXND441

GLIMPSES OF JEWISH LIFE IN **SAN-FRANCISCO**. /CALIFORNIA/   JZARCMM64776

SAN-FRANCISCO   (CONTINUATION)
THE ECONOMIC-STATUS OF NEGROES IN THE **SAN-FRANCISCO** OAKLAND BAY AREA. A REPORT BASED ON THE 1960 CENSUS
OF POPULATION. /CALIFORNIA/   NCALFES63172

SOCIAL-DEPENDENCY IN THE **SAN-FRANCISCO** BAY AREA. TODAY AND TOMORROW. /CALIFORNIA/   NGREEMX63449

THE NEGRO WAR WORKER IN **SAN-FRANCISCO**. /CALIFORNIA/   NJOHNCS44612

POSTWAR STATUS OF NEGRO WORKERS IN **SAN-FRANCISCO** AREA. /CALIFORNIA/   NMCENDX50721

MINORITY-GROUPS AND INTERGROUP RELATIONS IN THE **SAN-FRANCISCO** BAY AREA. /CALIFORNIA/   NRECOCW63043

TESTIMONY PRESENTED AT PUBLIC HEARING, APRIL 28, 1966. **SAN-FRANCISCO**, CALIFORNIA. /FEP
EMPLOYMENT-CONDITIONS DISCRIMINATION MIGRANTS/   WCALACW62676

TESTIMONY PRESENTED AT PUBLIC HEARING, APRIL 29, 1966. **SAN-FRANCISCO**, CALIFORNIA. /FEP
EMPLOYMENT-CONDITIONS CHILDREN/   WCALACW66677

SAN-JUAN
LA VIDA. A PUERTO-RICAN FAMILY IN THE CULTURE OF POVERTY -- **SAN-JUAN** AND NEW-YORK.   PLEWIOX66825

SAN-MATEO
SAN-MATEO AREA MINORITY JOB SURVEY. /CALIFORNIA/   GCALFEP65542

SANCTIONS
LEGAL **SANCTIONS** AGAINST JOB DISCRIMINATION.   GSIMOCK46311

SANTA-CLARA
DOMESTIC AND IMPORTED WORKERS IN THE HARVEST LABOR-MARKET. **SANTA-CLARA** COUNTY, CALIFORNIA, 1954.   MFULLVX56396

SATISFACTION
A STUDY OF SOME ASPECTS OF JOB **SATISFACTION** AMONG NEGRO WHITE-COLLAR WORKERS.   NWEATMD54296

SOURCES OF **SATISFACTION** IN THE LIVES OF WORKING WOMEN.   WLAURMW61923

SATISFACTIONS
A STUDY OF JOB MOTIVATIONS, ACTIVITIES, AND **SATISFACTIONS** OF PRESENT AND PROSPECTIVE WOMEN COLLEGE
FACULTY MEMBERS. /OCCUPATIONS/   WCOOKWX60252

PERSONAL **SATISFACTIONS**. /WORK-WOMAN-ROLE/   WNYEXFI63038

SAVANNAH
PUBLIC EMPLOYMENT IN **SAVANNAH**, GEORGIA. EXPERIENCE REPORT 104.   NUSCONM66235

SAVINGS
MEMORANDUM OF UNDERSTANDING BETWEEN CALIFORNIA STATE FAIR- EMPLOYMENT-PRACTICE-COMMISSION AND
BANK-OF-AMERICA NATIONAL TRUST AND **SAVINGS** ASSOCIATION.   GCALFEPND537

PATTERNS OF DISCRIMINATION IN THE FINANCIAL INSTITUTIONS OF THE DISTRICT-OF-COLUMBIA. THE BANKING,
SAVINGS AND LOAN, AND INSURANCE INDUSTRIES.   GDISTCC66642

THE MUTUAL **SAVINGS** BANKS OF NEW-YORK-CITY. /DISCRIMINATION/   JAMERJC65694

THE MUTUAL **SAVINGS** BANKS OF NEW-YORK-CITY. A FOLLOW-UP REPORT ON THE EXCLUSION OF JEWS AT TOP-MANAGEMENT
AND POLICY-MAKING LEVELS.   JAMERJC66695

SCHOLAR
THE NEGRO **SCHOLAR** AND PROFESSIONAL IN AMERICA.   NBONDHM66103

LADY AND ONE-THIRD **SCHOLAR**. /OCCUPATIONS/   WHEALAK63835

SCHOLARS
NEGRO **SCHOLARS** IN SCIENTIFIC RESEARCH.   NDREWCR50294

SCHOLASTIC
MINORITY-GROUP AND CLASS STATUS AS RELATED TO SOCIAL AND PERSONALITY FACTORS IN **SCHOLASTIC** ACHIEVEMENT.   GDEUTMP60640

TEST BIAS. VALIDITY OF THE **SCHOLASTIC** APTITUDE TEST FOR NEGRO AND WHITE STUDENTS IN INTEGRATED COLLEGES.   NCLEATA66923

POST-HIGH SCHOOL PLANS FOR SENIOR GIRLS IN RELATION TO **SCHOLASTIC** APTITUDE. /ASPIRATIONS/   WMILLRX61983

SCHOOL
REPORT ON OAKLAND SCHOOLS. AN INVESTIGATION UNDER SECTION 1421 OF THE CALIFORNIA LABOR CODE OF THE
OAKLAND UNIFIED **SCHOOL** DISTRICT 1962-1963. /NEGRO ORIENTAL MEXICAN-AMERICAN/   CCALDIR63710

FAMILY STRUCTURE AND **SCHOOL** PERFORMANCE. A COMPARATIVE STUDY OF STUDENTS FROM THREE ETHNIC BACKGROUNDS IN
AN INTEGRATED SCHOOL. /MEXICAN-AMERICAN AMERICAN-INDIAN/   CGRIFJX65407

FAMILY STRUCTURE AND **SCHOOL** PERFORMANCE. A COMPARATIVE STUDY OF STUDENTS FROM THREE ETHNIC BACKGROUNDS IN
AN INTEGRATED **SCHOOL**. /MEXICAN-AMERICAN AMERICAN-INDIAN/   CGRIFJX65407

THE **SCHOOL** DROPOUT PROBLEM IN MAJOR CITIES OF NEW-YORK STATE. ROCHESTER -- PART I. /NEGRO PUERTO-RICAN/   CNEWYSD62090

SCHOOL ENROLLMENT. /DEMOGRAPHY/   CUSBURC63183

REALITIES OF THE JOB-MARKET FOR THE HIGH **SCHOOL** DROPOUT.   GBIENHX64111

EMPLOYMENT OF HIGH **SCHOOL** GRADUATES AND DROPOUTS IN 1964.   GBOGAFA65750

EMPLOYMENT OF **SCHOOL** AGE YOUTH, OCTOBER 1965.   GBOGAFA66918

EMPLOYMENT OPPORTUNITIES FOR HIGH **SCHOOL** DROPOUTS, A STUDY OF EMPLOYERS PRACTICES, NEEDS AND ATTITUDES IN
THE DISTRICT OF COLUMBIA. /WASHINGTON-DC/   GBURESS57499

SCHOOL. MINORITIES AND EQUAL-RIGHTS, SELECTED MATERIAL. /CALIFORNIA/   GCALSLIND549

UNTAPPED GOOD. THE REHABILITATION OF **SCHOOL** DROPOUTS.   GCHANNM66803

EMPLOYMENT OF JUNE 1959 HIGH **SCHOOL** GRADUATES, OCTOBER 1959.   GCOOPSX60601

SCHOOL DROPOUT RATES AMONG FARM AND NONFARM YOUTH 1950 AND 1960.   GCOWHJD63421

CHARACTERISTICS OF **SCHOOL** DROPOUTS AND HIGH SCHOOL GRADUATES, FARM AND NONFARM, 1960.   GCOWHJD64419

CHARACTERISTICS OF SCHOOL DROPOUTS AND HIGH **SCHOOL** GRADUATES, FARM AND NONFARM, 1960.   GCOWHJD64419

SOME CONSIDERATIONS AS TO THE CONTRIBUTIONS OF SOCIAL, PERSONALITY, AND RACIAL FACTORS TO **SCHOOL**
RETARDATION IN MINORITY-GROUP CHILDREN.   GDEUTMP56641

THE SCHOOL COUNSELOR AT WORK ON OCCUPATIONAL DISCRIMINATION.   GDIXALX46643

BACKGROUND FACTORS RELATING TO COLLEGE PLANS AND COLLEGE ENROLLMENT AMONG PUBLIC HIGH SCHOOL STUDENTS.
/ASPIRATIONS/   GEDUCTS57959

SCHOOL DROPOUTS. A COMMENTARY AND ANNOTATED BIBLIOGRAPHY.   GMILLSM64071

SCHOOL FAILURES AND DROPOUTS.   GNEISEG63054

FACTORS ASSOCIATED WITH SCHOOL DROPOUTS AND JUVENILE-DELINQUENCY AMONG LOWER-CLASS CHILDREN.   GPALMFX63671

EMPLOYMENT PRACTICES OF THE PHILADELPHIA SCHOOL DISTRICT. /PENNSYLVANIA/   GPENNHR62162

A PILOT STUDY OF THE EMPLOYMENT EXPERIENCES OF HIGH SCHOOL GRADUATES.   GPHILCH65177

EMPLOYMENT OF HIGH SCHOOL GRADUATES AND DROPOUTS IN 1962.   GSCHIJX63282

PRINCETON-S LESSON. SCHOOL INTEGRATION IS NOT ENOUGH. /NEW-JERSEY/   GSTREPX64337

APPROACHES TO THE SCHOOL DROPOUT PROBLEM.   GSULLNV65653

FROM SCHOOL TO JOB. GUIDANCE FOR MINORITY YOUTH.   GTANNAX63156

PROJECTIONS OF SCHOOL AND COLLEGE ENROLLMENT IN THE UNITED STATES TO 1985. /DEMOGRAPHY/   GUSBURC66160

PROGRAMS FOR HIGH SCHOOL DROPOUTS. EXPERIENCE REPORT 101.   GUSCONF64976

SCHOOL AND EARLY EMPLOYMENT EXPERIENCE OF YOUTH. A REPORT ON SEVEN COMMUNITIES, 1952-57.   GUSDLAB60494

EMPLOYMENT OF HIGH SCHOOL GRADUATES AND DROPOUTS IN 1965.   GUSDLAB66073

YOUTH IN NEW-YORK CITY. OUT OF SCHOOL AND OUT OF WORK.   GVOGAAS62074

RESIDENTIAL SEGREGATION OF SOCIAL-CLASSES AND ASPIRATIONS OF HIGH SCHOOL BOYS.   GWILSAB59568

PROBLEMS OF NAVAJO MALE GRADUATES OF INTERMOUNTAIN SCHOOL DURING THEIR FIRST YEAR OF EMPLOYMENT. IBAKEJE59533

LEVEL OF OCCUPATIONAL ASPIRATIONS AMONG MONTANA INDIANS IN GRADE AND HIGH SCHOOL.   IDOUGGV60550

A STUDY OF THE REASONS FOR FAILURE ON THE JOB OF SOME GRADUATES OF INTERMOUNTAIN SCHOOL.   IFISHLX60560

MEDICAL SCHOOL QUOTAS. /EDUCATION DISCRIMINATION/   JBRAVHX58707

SOME NON-INTELLECTUAL CORRELATES OF ACADEMIC ACHIEVEMENT AMONG MEXICAN-AMERICAN SECONDARY SCHOOL
STUDENTS.   MGILLLJ62401

PERCEIVED LIFE CHANCES IN THE OPPORTUNITY STRUCTURE. A STUDY OF A TRI-ETHNIC HIGH SCHOOL.   MGUERCX62410

BACKGROUND AND AMBITION OF MALE MEXICAN-AMERICAN HIGH SCHOOL SENIORS IN LOS-ANGELES. /CALIFORNIA/ MHELLCS63414

AMBITIONS OF MEXICAN-AMERICAN YOUTH -- GOALS AND MEANS OF MOBILITY OF HIGH SCHOOL SENIORS.   MHELLCS64413

A STUDY OF THE ACCULTURATION AND SOCIAL ASPIRATIONS OF SIXTY JUNIOR HIGH SCHOOL STUDENTS FROM THE MEXICAN
ETHNIC GROUP.   MJONEBM62421

DIFFERENCES IN DROPOUT AND OTHER SCHOOL BEHAVIOR BETWEEN TWO GROUPS OF TENTH GRADE BOYS IN AN URBAN HIGH
SCHOOL.   MMUNORF57446

DIFFERENCES IN DROPOUT AND OTHER SCHOOL BEHAVIOR BETWEEN TWO GROUPS OF TENTH GRADE BOYS IN AN URBAN HIGH
SCHOOL.   MMUNORF57446

SUMMARY REPORT OF THE STUDY OF DROP-OUTS IN THE THREE SENIOR HIGH SCHOOLS, COMPTON UNION HIGH SCHOOL
DISTRICT. /CALIFORNIA/   MWHITNX60517

SCHOOL ATTENDANCE AND ATTAINMENT. FUNCTION AND DYSFUNCTION OF SCHOOL AND FAMILY SOCIAL SYSTEMS.
/EMPLOYMENT DROP-OUT/   NBERTAL62882

SCHOOL ATTENDANCE AND ATTAINMENT. FUNCTION AND DYSFUNCTION OF SCHOOL AND FAMILY SOCIAL SYSTEMS.
/EMPLOYMENT DROP-OUT/   NBERTAL62882

FACTORS AFFECTING THE PRESENT FARMING PROGRAMS OF ONE HUNDRED NEGRO FARMS IN THE PATRONAGE AREA OF THE
MACON COUNTY TRAINING SCHOOL, IN ALABAMA, WITH EMPHASIS FOR IMPROVEMENT.   NBRONCA51337

A COMPARISON OF THE ACADEMIC ACHIEVEMENTS OF WHITE AND NEGRO HIGH SCHOOL GRADUATES. /EDUCATION/ NBULLHA50132

VOCATIONAL CHOICES OF NEGRO HIGH SCHOOL STUDENTS IN MACON COUNTY, ALABAMA, AND THEIR RELATIONSHIP TO
BASIC OCCUPATIONAL ACTIVITES OF THE SCHOOL COMMUNITIES. /ASPIRATIONS/   NCHAPEJ49351

VOCATIONAL CHOICES OF NEGRO HIGH SCHOOL STUDENTS IN MACON COUNTY, ALABAMA, AND THEIR RELATIONSHIP TO
BASIC OCCUPATIONAL ACTIVITES OF THE SCHOOL COMMUNITIES. /ASPIRATIONS/   NCHAPEJ49351

EFFECT OF SCHOOL ASSIGNMENT LAWS ON FEDERAL ADJUDICATION OF INTEGRATION CONTROVERSIES.   NCOLULR57224

SOME FACTORS WHICH DISTINGUISH DROP-OUTS FROM HIGH SCHOOL GRADUATES.   NGRAGWL49978

IN SEARCH OF A FUTURE. A STUDY OF CAREER-SEEKING EXPERIENCES OF SELECTED NEGRO HIGH SCHOOL GRADUATES IN
WASHINGTON-DC WHICH WAS AN EFFORT TO PROVIDE KNOWLEDGE HELPFUL IN SOLVING ONE OF THE MOST CRITICAL
PROBLEMS FACING URBAN AMERICA TODAY.   NGRIEES63454

THE EDUCATIONAL AND OCCUPATIONAL ASPIRATIONS AND PLANS OF NEGRO AND WHITE MALE ELEMENTARY SCHOOL
STUDENTS.   NHOLLRG59562

HIGH SCHOOL GRADUATES AND DROPOUTS -- A NEW LOOK AT A PERSISTENT PROBLEM.   NLIVIAH58044

THE SCHOOL DROPOUT IN LOUISIANA 1963-1964.   NLOUISD64714

DISCRIMINATION IN THE HIRING AND ASSIGNMENT OF NEGRO TEACHERS IN PUBLIC SCHOOL SYSTEMS.   NMICLRX66068

ACHIEVEMENT OF MALE HIGH SCHOOL DROPOUTS AND GRADUATES IN ALABAMA VOCATIONAL SCHOOLS.   NMILLGJ65791

ASPIRATION LEVELS OF NEGRO DELINQUENT, DEPENDENT, AND PUBLIC SCHOOL BOYS.   NMITCLE57804

FACTORS INVOLVED IN STUDENT ELIMINATION FROM HIGH SCHOOL.   NMOORPL54079

THE NEGRO IN SCHOOL ADMINISTRATION.   NOVERXX61967

RETREATISM AND OCCUPATIONAL ASPIRATIONS AMONG WHITE AND NEGRO HIGH SCHOOL SENIORS.   NPOWEEC61009

SCHOOL   (CONTINUATION)
THE EFFECT OF SPECIAL INSTRUCTION UPON TEST PERFORMANCE OF HIGH SCHOOL STUDENTS IN TENNESSEE.   NROBESO66961

THE RELATION OF RACIAL SEGREGATION IN EARLY SCHOOLING TO THE LEVEL OF ASPIRATION AND ACADEMIC ACHIEVEMENT
OF NEGRO STUDENTS IN A NORTHERN HIGH SCHOOL.   NSAINJN62137

OCCUPATIONAL ESTABLISHMENT OF FORMER STUDENTS OF VOCATIONAL AGRICULTURE IN MONTGOMERY TRAINING SCHOOL
AREA. /ALABAMA/   NSCOTCDND346

SOCIAL CHARACTERISTICS OF HIGH SCHOOL SENIORS IN URBAN NEGRO HIGH SCHOOLS IN TWO STATES.   NSMITBF56147

SCHOOL DESEGREGATION IN 1966. THE SLOW UNDOING.   NSOUTRC66150

SOCIALIZATION, RACE AND THE AMERICAN HIGH SCHOOL. /EDUCATION/   NTENHWP65201

AN EMPIRICAL STUDY OF HIGH SCHOOL DROPOUTS IN REGARD TO TEN POSSIBLY RELATED FACTORS.   NTHOMRJ54159

OCCUPATIONAL CHOICES OF NEGRO HIGH SCHOOL SENIORS IN TEXAS.   NTURNBA57165

ENHANCING THE OCCUPATIONAL OUTLOOK AND VOCATIONAL ASPIRATIONS OF SOUTHERN SECONDARY YOUTH. A CONFERENCE
OF SECONDARY SCHOOL PRINCIPALS AND COUNSELORS.   NUSOLAB65334

OCCUPATIONAL ASPIRATIONS OF NEGRO MALE HIGH SCHOOL STUDENTS.   NUZELOX61278

AFTER HIGH SCHOOL WHAT...HIGHLIGHTS OF A STUDY OF CAREER PLANS OF NEGRO AND WHITE RURAL YOUTH IN THREE
FLORIDA COUNTIES. /ASPIRATIONS/   NYOUMEG65390

SCHOOL AND COMMUNITY COURSE. THE LOWER STATUS PUERTO-RICAN FAMILY.   PBRAMJX63784

OCCUPATIONAL PLANS AND ASPIRATIONS. PUERTO-RICAN AND AMERICAN HIGH SCHOOL SENIORS COMPARED.   PSILVRM63100

A STUDY OF ELEMENTARY SCHOOL TEACHER-S ATTITUDES TOWARD THE WOMAN PRINCIPAL AND TOWARD ELEMENTARY
PRINCIPALSHIP AS A CAREER. /DISCRIMINATION/   WBARTAK58629

BACK TO SCHOOL. /WORK-FAMILY-CONFLICT/   WCARNCO62680

SEX-ROLE AND PROFESSIONALISM. A STUDY OF HIGH SCHOOL TEACHERS. /OCCUPATIONS/   WCOLOJX63698

OPPORTUNITIES AND REQUIREMENTS FOR INITIAL EMPLOYMENT OF SCHOOL LEAVERS. WITH EMPHASIS ON OFFICE AND
RETAIL JOBS. /EMPLOYMENT-SELECTION/   WCOOKFS667C5

SURVEY OF WOMEN PHYSICIANS GRADUATING FROM MEDICAL SCHOOL, 1925-1940. /OCCUPATIONS/   WDYKMRA57745

FACTORS ASSOCIATED WITH GRADUATE SCHOOL ATTENDANCE AND ROLE DEFINITION OF THE WOMAN DOCTORAL CANDIDATES
AT THE PENNSYLVANIA STATE UNIVERSITY. /OCCUPATIONS/   WFIELJC61763

WHO GOES TO GRADUATE SCHOOL. /EDUCATION/   WGROPGL59805

REPORT ON THE SURVEY OF FEMALE PHYSICIANS GRADUATING FROM MEDICAL SCHOOL BETWEEN 1925 AND 1940.
/OCCUPATIONS/   WHANNFX58819

HIGH SCHOOL FRESHMAN AND SENIORS VIEW THE ROLE OF WOMEN IN MODERN SOCIETY. /WORK-FAMILY-CONFLICT/   WKERNKK65892

KNOWLEDGE AND INTERESTS CONCERNING SIXTEEN OCCUPATIONS AMONG ELEMENTARY AND SECONDARY SCHOOL STUDENTS.
/ASPIRATIONS/   WMELSRC63968

POST-HIGH SCHOOL PLANS FOR SENIOR GIRLS IN RELATION TO SCHOLASTIC APTITUDE. /ASPIRATIONS/   WMILLRX61983

EXPERIENCES OF NEGRO HIGH SCHOOL GIRLS WITH DOMESTIC PLACEMENT AGENCIES. /HOUSEHOLD-WORKERS/   WRUSSRD62135

SCHOOL DROPOUTS. THE FEMALE SPECIES.   WSCHRDX62105

OCCUPATIONAL PLANNING BY YOUNG WOMEN, A STUDY OF OCCUPATIONAL EXPERIENCES, ASPIRATIONS, ATTITUDES, AND
PLANS OF COLLEGE AND HIGH SCHOOL GIRLS.   WSLOCWL56116

THE MARRIED FEMALE SCHOOL TEACHER. A CONTINUED STUDY. /WORK-FAMILY-CONFLICT/   WSTEPCM60139

BACKGROUND FACTORS AND COLLEGE GOING PLANS AMONG HIGH APTITUDE PUBLIC HIGH SCHOOL SENIORS. /ASPIRATIONS/   WSTICGX56141

HIGH SCHOOL GUIDANCE COUNSELOR-S PERCEPTIONS OF SELECTED CAREERS FOR WOMEN COLLEGE GRADUATES.   WSWOPMR63146

FUTURE JOBS FOR HIGH SCHOOL GIRLS.   WUSOLAB65196

ADMISSION OF WOMEN TO MEDICAL SCHOOL.   WWULSJH66278

SCHOOL-DESEGREGATION
SCHOOL-DESEGREGATION AND NEW INDUSTRY. THE SOUTHERN COMMUNITY LEADERS VIEWPOINT.   NCROMRX63243

SCHOOL-DISTRICT
WASTED MANPOWER -- BERKELEY CHALLENGE AND OPPORTUNITY. WORKSHOP COSPONSORED WITH THE BERKELEY UNIFIED
SCHOOL-DISTRICT MARCH 15-16, 1963. /CALIFORNIA/   NKEVNVD63642

SCHOOL-S
THE MENTALITIES OF NEGRO AND WHITE WORKERS. AN EXPERIMENTAL SCHOOL-S INTERPRETATION OF NEGRO TRADE
UNIONISM.   NVALIPX49280

SCHOOLING
SCHOOLING, DISCRIMINATION, AND JOBS.   GHEVNJF63278

THE RELATION OF RACIAL SEGREGATION IN EARLY SCHOOLING TO THE LEVEL OF ASPIRATION AND ACADEMIC ACHIEVEMENT
OF NEGRO STUDENTS IN A NORTHERN HIGH SCHOOL.   NSAINJN62137

SCHOOLS
REPORT ON OAKLAND SCHOOLS. AN INVESTIGATION UNDER SECTION 1421 OF THE CALIFORNIA LABOR CODE OF THE
OAKLAND UNIFIED SCHOOL DISTRICT 1962-1963. /NEGRO ORIENTAL MEXICAN-AMERICAN/   CCALDIR63710

THE MINORITY CHILD AND THE SCHOOLS.   GBULLPX62488

SOME PROBLEMS IN MINORITY-GROUP EDUCATION IN THE LOS-ANGELES PUBLIC SCHOOLS. /CALIFORNIA/   GBULLPX63489

LOS-ANGELES CITY SCHOOLS. AN INVESTIGATION OF EMPLOYMENT PRACTICES. /CALIFORNIA/   GCALFEP64536

A SUMMARY REPORT OF PRACTICES AND PROGRAMS DESIGNED TO REDUCE THE NUMBER OF DROPOUTS IN THE HIGH SCHOOLS
OF LOS-ANGELES COUNTY. /CALIFORNIA/   GDELMDT66147

THE ROLE OF THE SECONDARY SCHOOLS IN THE PREPARATION OF YOUTH FOR EMPLOYMENT.   GKAUFJJ67940

THE ROLE OF THE SECONDARY SCHOOLS IN THE PREPARATION OF YOUTH FOR EMPLOYMENT. SUMMARY, CONCLUSIONS. AND

SCHOOLS   (CONTINUATION)
RECOMMENDATIONS.   GKAUFJJ67963

EDUCATION AND INCOME. INEQUALITIES IN OUR PUBLIC SCHOOLS.   GSEXTPX61298

LEVELS OF ASPIRATION OF MEXICAN-AMERICANS IN EL-PASO SCHOOLS. /TEXAS/   MNALLFX59447

MEXICAN-AMERICANS IN URBAN PUBLIC HIGH SCHOOLS. AN EXPLORATION OF THE DROP-OUT PROGRAM.   MSHELPM59488

SUMMARY REPORT OF THE STUDY OF DROP-OUTS IN THE THREE SENIOR HIGH SCHOOLS, COMPTON UNION HIGH SCHOOL
DISTRICT. /CALIFORNIA/   MWHITNX60517

NON-SEGREGATION, OR QUALITY IN SCHOOLS OF THE DEEP SOUTH. /ECONOMIC-STATUS/   NBRITNX54892

A COMPARISON OF THE VOCATIONAL ASPIRATIONS OF PAIRED SIXTH-GRADE WHITE AND NEGRO CHILDREN WHO ATTEND
SEGREGATED SCHOOLS.   NBROWRG65895

INTERIM REPORT ON OAKLAND SCHOOLS. /CALIFORNIA/   NCALFEP66169

SOCIAL AND ECONOMIC IMPLICATIONS OF INTEGRATING IN THE PUBLIC SCHOOLS.   NCLARKB65213

HOW GOOD ARE OUR SCHOOLS.   NCONNCX66232

A STUDY OF PROFESSIONAL PREPARATION OF NEGRO TEACHERS OF EXCEPTIONAL CHILDREN IN NORTH-CAROLINA COUNTY
AND CITY PUBLIC SCHOOLS.   NKNIGOB65023

NEGRO COLLEGES. LONG IGNORED, SOUTHERN SCHOOLS NOW COURTED BY MAJOR UNIVERSITIES AND FOUNDATIONS.   NLANGEX64304

LEGAL EDUCATION. DESEGREGATION IN LAW SCHOOLS.   NLEFLRA57676

THE SCHOOLS.   NMAYEMX62761

THE RELATIONSHIP BETWEEN MECHANIZATION OF COTTON PRODUCTION AND ATTENDANCE AND ENROLLMENT IN THE RURAL
SCHOOLS OF COAHOMA COUNTY, MISSISSIPPI.   NMCLABF51349

RACE AND THE SCHOOLS.   NMEYEAE58769

ACHIEVEMENT OF MALE HIGH SCHOOL DROPOUTS AND GRADUATES IN ALABAMA VOCATIONAL SCHOOLS.   NMILLGJ65791

SOCIAL CHARACTERISTICS OF HIGH SCHOOL SENIORS IN URBAN NEGRO HIGH SCHOOLS IN TWO STATES.   NSMITBF56147

ARE NEGRO SCHOOLS OF NURSING NEEDED TODAY.   WCARNME64910

DROP-OUTS FROM SCHOOLS OF NURSING. THE EFFECT OF SELF- AND ROLE PERCEPTION.   WKIBRAK58902

SCIENCE
NOT TO THE SWIFT. PROGRESS AND PROSPECTS OF THE NEGRO IN SCIENCE AND THE PROFESSIONS. /OCCUPATIONS/ NCOBBWM58216

NEGROES IN SCIENCE. /OCCUPATIONS/   NVIORJX65284

CAREERS FOR WOMEN IN SCIENCE. /OCCUPATIONS/   WBARBMS58627

WHAT BRINGS AND HOLDS WOMAN SCIENCE MAJORS. /OCCUPATIONS/   WDEMEAL63728

REPORT OF THE EXPLORATORY STATISTICAL SURVEY OF THE EDUCATIONAL-ATTAINMENT, NUMBER, AND AVAILABILITY OF
THE MEMBERSHIP OF THE AMERICAN ASSOCIATION OF UNIVERSITY WOMEN FOR TEACHING IN THE FIELDS OF SCIENCE AND
MATHEMATICS. /OCCUPATIONS/   WDOLAEF57735

ENHANCING THE ROLE OF WOMEN IN SCIENCE, ENGINEERING, AND THE SOCIAL SCIENCES. /OCCUPATIONS/   WKILLJR65903

WHY NOBODY WANTS WOMEN IN SCIENCE. /OCCUPATIONS/   WKUNDRB65919

WOMEN AND MODERN SCIENCE. /OCCUPATIONS/   WLEWIND57932

WOMEN AND THE SCIENTIFIC PROFESSIONS. THE MIT SYMPOSIUM ON AMERICAN WOMEN IN SCIENCE AND ENGINEERING.
/OCCUPATIONS/   WMATTJA65963

ROLES OF THE MARRIED WOMAN IN SCIENCE. /OCCUPATIONS/   WMOTZAB61002

WOMEN IN SCIENCE. /OCCUPATIONS/   WROEXAX66455

BARRIERS TO THE CAREER CHOICE OF ENGINEERING, MEDICINE, OR SCIENCE AMONG AMERICAN WOMEN. /OCCUPATIONS/ WROSSAS65091

WOMEN IN SCIENCE. WHY SO FEW. /OCCUPATIONS/   WROSSAS65094

REPORT -- 1965-66 -- RETRAINING PROGRAM IN MATHEMATICS AND SCIENCE FOR COLLEGE GRADUATE WOMEN.   WRUTGMR66098

SCIENCES
ENHANCING THE ROLE OF WOMEN IN SCIENCE, ENGINEERING, AND THE SOCIAL SCIENCES. /OCCUPATIONS/   WKILLJR65903

CAREERS FOR WOMEN IN BIOLOGICAL SCIENCES. /OCCUPATIONS/   WMURPMC60009

SHOULD WOMEN BE TRAINED IN THE SCIENCES. /OCCUPATIONS/   WPINEMX58061

SCIENTIFIC
PREJUDICE AND SCIENTIFIC METHOD IN LABOR-RELATIONS. /UNION/   GMARRAX52941

NEGRO SCHOLARS IN SCIENTIFIC RESEARCH.   NDREWCR50294

THE COMMITMENT REQUIRED OF A WOMAN ENTERING A SCIENTIFIC PROFESSION. /OCCUPATIONS/   WBETTBX65645

PANEL DISCUSSION. THE COMMITTMENT REQUIRED OF A WOMAN ENTERING A SCIENTIFIC PROFESSION. /OCCUPATIONS/ WBUNTMI65663

ENCOURAGING SCIENTIFIC TALENT. /OCCUPATIONS/   WCOLECG56694

WOMEN AND THE SCIENTIFIC PROFESSIONS. THE MIT SYMPOSIUM ON AMERICAN WOMEN IN SCIENCE AND ENGINEERING.
/OCCUPATIONS/   WMATTJA65963

WOMEN IN SCIENTIFIC CAREERS. /OCCUPATIONS/   WNATLSF61022

SCIENTISTS
STUDY OF THE SHORTAGE AND SALARIES OF SCIENTISTS AND ENGINEERS.   GUSSENA54353

TRAINING FOR TOMORROW-S SCIENTISTS AND TECHNICIANS. A COMMUNITY APPROACH TO A COMMUNITY NEED.   NFINLOE60356

THE PRESENT SITUATION OF WOMAN SCIENTISTS AND ENGINEERS IN INDUSTRY AND GOVERNMENT. /OCCUPATIONS/   WBOLTRH65650

WOMAN AS POTENTIAL SCIENTISTS. /OCCUPATIONS/   WCROSKP63710

SEABOARD
REPORTS OF THE MEETINGS OF THE COMMITTEE OF OFFICIALS ON MIGRATORY FARM LABOR OF THE ATLANTIC **SEABOARD** STATES. /MIGRANT-WORKERS/ GCOUNSG58932

SEARCH
MOBILITY. METHODS OF JOB **SEARCH**, ATTITUDES, AND MOTIVATION OF DISPLACED WORKERS. GSHEPHL64621

THE NEGRO FAMILY-S **SEARCH** FOR ECONOMIC SECURITY. NDOUGJH64285

THE **SEARCH** FOR NEGRO MEDICAL STUDENTS. /EDUCATION/ NFALLAG63343

THE NEGRO BUSINESSMAN. IN **SEARCH** OF A TRADITION. /OCCUPATIONS/ NFOLEEP66369

IN **SEARCH** OF A FUTURE. A STUDY OF CAREER-SEEKING EXPERIENCES OF SELECTED NEGRO HIGH SCHOOL GRADUATES IN WASHINGTON-DC WHICH WAS AN EFFORT TO PROVIDE KNOWLEDGE HELPFUL IN SOLVING ONE OF THE MOST CRITICAL PROBLEMS FACING URBAN AMERICA TODAY. NGRIEES63454

NEGRO-S **SEARCH** FOR A BETTER JOB. NNEWSXX64913

TALENT **SEARCH** FOR WOMANPOWER. WHARREX65826

SEARCHING
BLUEPRINT FOR TALENT. **SEARCHING** AMERICA-S HIDDEN MANPOWER. NPLAURL57003

SEASONAL
SUMMARY OF RULES, REGULATIONS, AND LAWS THAT AFFECT **SEASONAL** FARM WORKERS AND THEIR EMPLOYERS IN NEW-YORK STATE. /MIGRANT-WORKERS/ GNEWYSJND113

A HELPING HAND. **SEASONAL** FARM LABOR IN NEW-YORK STATE. /MIGRANT-WORKERS/ GNEWYSX63087

AGRICULTURAL **SEASONAL** LABORERS OF COLORADO AND CALIFORNIA. /MIGRANT-WORKERS/ NKARRCHND636

SEATTLE
INCOME, EDUCATION AND UNEMPLOYMENT IN NEIGHBORHOODS. **SEATTLE**, WASHINGTON. /DEMOGRAPHY/ CUSDLAB63485

JOB OPPORTUNITIES FOR MINORITIES IN THE **SEATTLE** AREA. /WASHINGTON/ GUVWAIL48532

THE SOCIO-ECONOMIC ADJUSTMENT OF THE NEGRO IN **SEATTLE** BETWEEN 1940 AND 1950. /WASHINGTON/ NKENNTH54273

SEC
INDIAN RELOCATION AND THE NEW-MEXICO **SEC**. ISANDJN62615

SECONDARY
THE ROLE OF THE **SECONDARY** SCHOOLS IN THE PREPARATION OF YOUTH FOR EMPLOYMENT. GKAUFJJ67940

THE ROLE OF THE **SECONDARY** SCHOOLS IN THE PREPARATION OF YOUTH FOR EMPLOYMENT. SUMMARY, CONCLUSIONS, AND RECOMMENDATIONS. GKAUFJJ67963

THE **SECONDARY** LABOR-FORCE AND THE MEASUREMENT OF UNEMPLOYMENT. GWILCRC57562

SOME NON-INTELLECTUAL CORRELATES OF ACADEMIC ACHIEVEMENT AMONG MEXICAN-AMERICAN **SECONDARY** SCHOOL STUDENTS. MGILLLJ62401

ENHANCING THE OCCUPATIONAL OUTLOOK AND VOCATIONAL ASPIRATIONS OF SOUTHERN **SECONDARY** YOUTH. A CONFERENCE OF SECONDARY SCHOOL PRINCIPALS AND COUNSELORS. NUSDLAB65334

ENHANCING THE OCCUPATIONAL OUTLOOK AND VOCATIONAL ASPIRATIONS OF SOUTHERN SECONDARY YOUTH. A CONFERENCE OF **SECONDARY** SCHOOL PRINCIPALS AND COUNSELORS. NUSDLAB65334

KNOWLEDGE AND INTERESTS CONCERNING SIXTEEN OCCUPATIONS AMONG ELEMENTARY AND **SECONDARY** SCHOOL STUDENTS. /ASPIRATIONS/ WMELSRC63968

SECRETARIAL
SECRETARIAL TRAINING WITH SPEECH IMPROVEMENT. AN EXPERIMENTAL AND DEMONSTRATION PROJECT. /NEGRO WOMEN/ ... CSAINMD66320

SECRETARIAL-STENOGRA
WHITE-COLLAR WOMEN. THE **SECRETARIAL-STENOGRAPHIC** OCCUPATION. WBRYACD57659

SECRETARY
ANNUAL REPORT OF THE **SECRETARY** OF HEALTH, EDUCATION, AND WELFARE TO THE CONGRESS ON TRAINING ACTIVITIES UNDER THE MANPOWER-DEVELOPMENT-AND-TRAINING-ACT, 1965. .... GUSDHEW66978

REPORT TO THE **SECRETARY** OF THE INTERIOR BY THE TASK FORCE ON INDIAN AFFAIRS. IUSDINT61641

SECRETARY-S
SECRETARY-S CONFERENCE WITH COLLEGE PRESIDENTS AND EXECUTIVES. /EDUCATION EMPLOYMENT/ NUSDLAB63301

SECTARIANISM
LEFT **SECTARIANISM** IN THE FIGHT FOR NEGRO RIGHTS AND AGAINST WHITE CHAUVINISM. NFOSTWZ53375

SECURITY
SECURITY. CIVIL-LIBERTIES AND UNIONS. GFLEIHX57686

CYBERNATION AND JOB **SECURITY**. /UNEMPLOYMENT/ GMANGGL66529

VOCATIONAL-TECHNICAL EDUCATION AND ECONOMIC **SECURITY**. GSWANJC66155

SOCIAL **SECURITY** AND THE AMERICAN-INDIAN. IUSDHEW60639

THE NEGRO FAMILY-S SEARCH FOR ECONOMIC **SECURITY**. NDOUGJH64285

EMPLOYMENT **SECURITY**, SENIORITY AND RACE. THE ROLE OF TITLE-VII OF THE CIVIL-RIGHTS-ACT OF 1964. ... NGOULWB67864

EMPLOYMENT **SECURITY** AND THE NEGRO. NOXLELA40969

SOCIAL **SECURITY** PROGRAM STATISTICS RELATING TO NONWHITE FAMILIES AND CHILDREN. NUSDHEW58241

SEGREGATED
EDUCATION OF THE DEPRIVED AND **SEGREGATED**. GBANKSC65419

EGO DEVELOPMENT AMONG **SEGREGATED** NEGRO CHILDREN. /ASPIRATIONS/ NAUSUDP65036

A COMPARISON OF THE VOCATIONAL ASPIRATIONS OF PAIRED SIXTH-GRADE WHITE AND NEGRO CHILDREN WHO ATTEND **SEGREGATED** SCHOOLS. NBROWRG65895

NLRB DECERTIFIES RACIALLY **SEGREGATED** UNION LOCALS. NCHECDX64890

ATLANTA-S **SEGREGATED** APPROACH TO INTEGRATED EMPLOYMENT. /GEORGIA/ NTHOMHX62205

SEGREGATION
THE LAWFULNESS OF THE **SEGREGATION** DECISIONS.   GBLACCX60452

MINORITY-GROUPS. **SEGREGATION** AND INTEGRATION.   GNATLCN55044

SEGREGATION AND DESEGREGATION. A DIGEST OF RECENT RESEARCH.   GTUMIMM57164

HOW DEPARTMENT X ELIMINATED **SEGREGATION**.   GUSCISC49388

RESIDENTIAL **SEGREGATION** OF SOCIAL-CLASSES AND ASPIRATIONS OF HIGH SCHOOL BOYS.   GWILSAB59568

THE EFFECT OF RESIDENTIAL **SEGREGATION** UPON EDUCATIONAL ACHIEVEMENT AND ASPIRATIONS.   GWILSAB60567

CAN **SEGREGATION** SURVIVE IN AN INDUSTRIAL SOCIETY.   GYINGJM58590

RESIDENTIAL **SEGREGATION** IN THE URBAN SOUTHWEST.   MMOORJW66444

SEGREGATION DEAL. NEW-ORLEANS REGION FEPC PERMITS COMPROMISE. /LOUISIANA/   NBUSIWX45161

AMERICAN LABOR ATTACKS ITS OWN **SEGREGATION** PROBLEM. /UNION/   NCHASWX58194

WHAT ARE THE PSYCHOLOGICAL EFFECTS OF **SEGREGATION** UNDER CONDITIONS OF EQUAL FACILITIES.   NCHEIIX49198

THE ECONOMICS OF **SEGREGATION**.   NDILLWP58275

RESIDENTIAL **SEGREGATION** AND SOCIAL DIFFERENTIATION.   NDUNCOD59305

THE NEGROES WHO DO NOT WANT TO END **SEGREGATION**. /EMPLOYMENT/   NFAGGHL55255

HISTORY OF RACIAL **SEGREGATION** IN THE UNITED STATES.   NFRANJH56060

TRAINING FOR MINORITY-GROUPS. PROBLEMS OF RACIAL IMBALANCE AND **SEGREGATION**.   NFUSFDR66014

SEGREGATION AND MANPOWER WASTE.   NGINZEX60413

LABOR AND **SEGREGATION**. /UNION/   NHILLHX59529

PATTERNS OF NEGRO **SEGREGATION**.   NJOHNCS43008

THE RELATION OF RACIAL **SEGREGATION** IN EARLY SCHOOLING TO THE LEVEL OF ASPIRATION AND ACADEMIC ACHIEVEMENT
OF NEGRO STUDENTS IN A NORTHERN HIGH SCHOOL.   NSAINJN62137

THE EFFECT OF **SEGREGATION** ON THE ASPIRATIONS OF NEGRO YOUTH.   NSAINJN66136

SEGREGATION. A COLOR PATTERN FROM THE PAST -- OUR STRUGGLE TO WIPE IT OUT.   NSURVGX47191

THE NEGRO AS AN IMMIGRANT GROUP. RECENT TRENDS IN RACIAL AND ETHNIC **SEGREGATION** IN CHICAGO. /ILLINOIS/ NTAEUKE64196

NEGROES IN CITIES. /DEMOGRAPHY **SEGREGATION**/   NTAEUKE65197

A SELECTED LIST OF REFERENCES RELATING TO DISCRIMINATION AND **SEGREGATION** IN EDUCATION, 1949 TO JUNE 1955. NTUSKIX55220

SEGREGATION IN THE ARMED FORCES. /MILITARY/   NUSOLAB44151

UNIONS AND **SEGREGATION**.   NYOUNJE56357

SEGREGATIVE
UNITED STATES HAS STANDING UNDER INTERSTATE COMMERCE ACT AND COMMERCE CLAUSE TO ENJOIN **SEGREGATIVE**
PRACTICES OF CITY. /LEGISLATION/   NHARVLR64500

SELECTING
FAIR-EMPLOYMENT-PRACTICES EQUAL GOOD EMPLOYMENT PRACTICES. GUIDELINES FOR TESTING AND **SELECTING** MINORITY
JOB APPLICANTS. /CALIFORNIA/   GCALFEP66540

SELECTING AND TRAINING NEGROES FOR MANAGERIAL POSITIONS.   NEDUCTS64322

SELECTION
RACE AND SOCIO-ECONOMIC STATUS IN MUNICIPAL PERSONNEL **SELECTION**.   GBIANJC67590

COMMUNITY VALUES IN EDUCATION AND OCCUPATIONAL **SELECTION**. A STUDY OF YOUTH IN EMMITSBURG, MARYLAND. GLEONRC64894

DEVELOPING FAIR-EMPLOYMENT PROGRAMS. GUIDELINES FOR **SELECTION**.   GLOCKHC66780

HIRING PROCEDURES AND **SELECTION** STANDARDS IN THE SAN-FRANCISCO BAY AREA. /CALIFORNIA/   GMALMTF55934

RECENT TRENDS IN THE TEST **SELECTION** OF APPRENTICES.   GMOTLAW53033

THE INDUSTRIAL PSYCHOLOGIST. **SELECTION** AND EQUAL-EMPLOYMENT OPPORTUNITY.   GPARRJA66147

PERSONNEL **SELECTION** TESTS AND FAIR-EMPLOYMENT-PRACTICES.   GSEASHX51293

FACTORS AFFECTING EMPLOYEE **SELECTION** IN TWO CULTURES. /DISCRIMINATION/   GTRIAHC63083

THE ETHNICS OF EXECUTIVE **SELECTION**.   JWARDLB65769

DIFFERENTIAL **SELECTION** AMONG APPLICANTS FROM DIFFERENT SOCIO-ECONOMIC AND ETHNIC BACKGROUNDS.   NBARRRS65056

THE PROBLEM OF CULTURAL BIAS IN **SELECTION**. I. BACKGROUND AND LITERATURE. /TESTING/   NCAMPJT65179

THE PROBLEMS OF CULTURAL BIAS IN **SELECTION**. POSSIBLE SOLUTION TO THE PROBLEM OF CULTURAL BIAS IN TESTS. NKRUGRE64731

THE PROBLEM OF CULTURAL BIAS IN **SELECTION**. II. ETHNIC BACKGROUND AND TEST PERFORMANCE.   NROBESO65068

OCCUPATIONAL VALUES AND OCCUPATIONAL **SELECTION**.   WRAVIMJ57077

SELECTIVE
A **SELECTIVE** BIBLIOGRAPHY ON DISCRIMINATION IN HOUSING AND EMPLOYMENT.   GNEWYLF60075

A **SELECTIVE** BIBLIOGRAPHY OF CALIFORNIA LABOR HISTORY.   MSLOBMX64495

NEGRO INTELLIGENCE AND **SELECTIVE** MIGRATION. A PHILADELPHIA TEST OF THE KLINEBERG HYPOTHESIS.
/PENNSYLVANIA/   NLEEXES51673

AN ANALYSIS OF **SELECTIVE** FACTORS INFLUENCING FARM INCOME IN HALE COUNTY, AS A BASIS FOR ESTABLISHING A
MORE EFFECTIVE VOCATIONAL AGRICULTURAL PROGRAM. /ALABAMA/   NSALTDR52347

SELECTIVITY
SOME NEW EVIDENCE ON EDUCATIONAL **SELECTIVITY** IN MIGRATION FROM THE SOUTH.   GSUVAEM65345

SELECTIVITY (CONTINUATION)
EDUCATIONAL **SELECTIVITY** OF NET MIGRATION FROM THE SOUTH.   NHAMICH59986

SELF-ANALYSIS
SELF-ANALYSIS QUESTIONNAIRE. /EEO INDUSTRY/   GPRESCD63115

SELF-HELP
SELF-HELP IN PHILADELPHIA. /TRAINING PENNSYLVANIA/   NLEESHX64675

SELF-IDENTIFICATION
ACCULTURATION. **SELF-IDENTIFICATION**, AND PERSONALITY ADJUSTMENT.   ICHANNA65543

SELF-IMPOSED
THE PROBLEM OF **SELF-IMPOSED** INEQUALITIES.   GWATTWW66223

SELF-SUPPORTING
THE **SELF-SUPPORTING** WOMAN IN OREGON.   WKNILNO60034

SELF-SURVEY
THE **SELF-SURVEY** OF THE PACKINGHOUSE UNION. A TECHNIQUE FOR EFFECTING CHANGE. /CASE-STUDY/   NHOPEJX53574

SELLING
LIFE INSURANCE **SELLING** AS A CAREER FOR WOMEN. /OCCUPATIONS/   WLEITSF61926

SEMINAR
SEMINAR CN MANPOWER POLICY AND PROGRAM. LABOR LOOKS AT AUTOMATION AND CIVIL-RIGHTS.   GCONWJT65496

SEMINAR CN MANPOWER POLICY AND PROGRAM -- AUTOMATION, SKILL, AND MANPOWER PREDICTIONS.   GCROSER66148

SEMINAR ON MANPOWER POLICY AND PROGRAM MEASUREMENT OF TECHNOLOGICAL-CHANGE.   GUSDLAB64980

SEMINAR CN MANPOWER POLICY AND PROGRAM. CYBERNATION AND SOCIAL CHANGE.   GUSDLAB64982

SEMINARS
SEMINARS ON PRIVATE ADJUSTMENTS TO AUTOMATION AND TECHNOLOGICAL-CHANGE.   GPRESCL64772

SEMINOLE
THE PRESENT STATUS OF THE FLORIDA **SEMINOLE** INDIANS.   IPEITIM59284

SEMINOLES
BAILEYS REPORT ON **SEMINOLES**.   IBAILAL57531

SENATE
THE MANPOWER REVOLUTION. ITS POLICY CONSEQUENCES. EXCERPTS FROM **SENATE** HEARINGS BEFORE THE CLARK
SUBCOMMITTEE.   GMANGGL66217

NEW-YORK STATE-COMMISSION-AGAINST-DISCRIMINATION. STATEMENT BEFORE THE US **SENATE** SUBCOMMITTEE ON LABOR
AND LABOR-MANAGEMENT RELATIONS.   GNEWYSA52102

BRIEF SUBMITTED IN SUPPORT OF **SENATE** BILL NO 984, A BILL TO PROHIBIT DISCRIMINATION IN EMPLOYMENT.... GTUTTCH47368

TESTIMONY BEFORE STATE **SENATE** FACT FINDING SUBCOMMITTEE ON RACE-RELATIONS AND URBAN PROBLEMS. FINAL
HEARING, JANUARY 20 1965. /CALIFORNIA FEPC/   NGRAHCX65439

STATEMENT BEFORE CALIFORNIA **SENATE** SUB-COMMITTEE ON RACE-RELATIONS AND URBAN PROBLEMS.   OLOWXHW64745

SENIOR
SENIOR CITIZENS AND HOW THEY LIVE. AN ANALYSIS OF 1960 CENSUS DATA. PART II. THE AGING NONWHITE AND HIS
HOUSING. /ECONOMIC-STATUS/   GUSHHFX63321

SUMMARY REPORT OF THE STUDY CF DROP-OUTS IN THE THREE **SENIOR** HIGH SCHOOLS, COMPTON UNION HIGH SCHOOL
DISTRICT. /CALIFORNIA/   MWHITNX60517

POST GRADUATION ROLE PREFERENCE OF **SENIOR** WOMEN IN COLLEGE. /ASPIRATION/   WCHRIHX56690

POST-HIGH SCHOOL PLANS FOR **SENIOR** GIRLS IN RELATION TO SCHOLASTIC APTITUDE. /ASPIRATIONS/   WMILLRX61983

SENIORITY
SENIORITY AND POSTWAR JOBS. RUBBER INDUSTRY. /NEGRO WOMEN/   CLABORR44028

TRADE UNION COMPLIANCE WITH PRESIDENTIAL DIRECTIVES, MEMBERSHIP ACCEPTANCE, **SENIORITY**, ETC.   NCOOPJX64294

EMPLOYMENT SECURITY, **SENIORITY** AND RACE. THE ROLE OF TITLE-VII OF THE CIVIL-RIGHTS-ACT OF 1964. NGOULWB67864

SENIORITY IN THE AKRON RUBBER INDUSTRY.   NUSDLAB44841

SENIORITY IN THE AUTOMOBILE INDUSTRY.   NUSDLAB44842

STATEMENT CN **SENIORITY**. /UNION/   WDAVICX65719

STATEMENT ON WEIGHT LIFTING, HOURS, **SENIORITY** LAWS AND WOMEN. /EMPLOYMENT-CONDITIONS/   WUAWXWD66164

SENIORS
BACKGROUND AND AMBITION OF MALE MEXICAN-AMERICAN HIGH SCHOOL **SENIORS** IN LOS-ANGELES. /CALIFORNIA/ MHELLCS63414

AMBITIONS OF MEXICAN-AMERICAN YOUTH -- GOALS AND MEANS OF MOBILITY OF HIGH SCHOOL **SENIORS**.   MHELLCS64413

RETREATISM AND OCCUPATIONAL ASPIRATIONS AMONG WHITE AND NEGRO HIGH SCHOOL **SENIORS**.   NPOWEEC61009

SOCIAL CHARACTERISTICS OF HIGH SCHOOL **SENIORS** IN URBAN NEGRO HIGH SCHOOLS IN TWO STATES.   NSMITBF56147

OCCUPATIONAL CHOICES OF NEGRO HIGH SCHOOL **SENIORS** IN TEXAS.   NTURNBA57165

COMPARATIVE STUDY OF SOCIO-ECONOMIC AND SOCIAL-PSYCHOLOGICAL DETERMINANTS OF EDUCATIONAL AND OCCUPATIONAL
ASPIRATIONS OF NEGRO AND WHITE COLLEGE **SENIORS**.   NWHITRM59319

OCCUPATIONAL PLANS AND ASPIRATIONS. PUERTO-RICAN AND AMERICAN HIGH SCHOOL **SENIORS** COMPARED.   PSILVRM63100

HIGH SCHOOL FRESHMAN AND **SENIORS** VIEW THE ROLE OF WOMEN IN MODERN SOCIETY. /WORK-FAMILY-CONFLICT/ WKERNKK65892

BACKGROUND FACTORS AND COLLEGE GOING PLANS AMONG HIGH APTITUDE PUBLIC HIGH SCHOOL **SENIORS**. /ASPIRATIONS/ WSTICGX56141

SEPARATISM
THE NEGRO IN AMERICAN BUSINESS. THE CONFLICT BETWEEN **SEPARATISM** AND INTEGRATION.   NKINZRH50654

SERIES
FARM MECHANIZATION AND LABOR STABILIZATION. PART II IN A **SERIES** ON TECHNOLOGICAL-CHANGE AND FARM LABOR
USE, KERN COUNTY, CALIFORNIA, 1961. /NEGRO MEXICAN-AMERICAN/   CMETZWH65389

SERIES   (CONTINUATION)
THE FARM WORKER IN A CHANGING AGRICULTURE. PART I IN A SERIES ON TECHNOLOGICAL-CHANGE AND FARM LABOR USE,
KERN-COUNTY, CALIFORNIA, 1961.   GMETZWH64387

SUMMARY OF MAJOR POINTS, TALK ON EMPLOYMENT, MCCONE-COMMISSION SERIES.   NBULLPX66898

DISCRIMINATION AND NATIONAL WELFARE. A SERIES OF ADDRESSES AND DISCUSSIONS.   NMACIRM49731

HOUSTON -- THE NEGRO AND EMPLOYMENT OPPORTUNITIES IN THE SOUTH, THE FIRST OF A SERIES OF EMPLOYMENT
STUDIES IN SOUTHERN CITIES. /TEXAS/   NSOUTRC61161

ATLANTA -- THE NEGRO AND EMPLOYMENT OPPORTUNITIES IN THE SOUTH, THE THIRD OF A SERIES OF EMPLOYMENT
STUDIES IN SOUTHERN CITIES. /GEORGIA/   NSOUTRC62155

CHATTANOOGA -- THE NEGRO AND EMPLOYMENT OPPORTUNITIES IN THE SOUTH, THE SECOND OF A SERIES OF EMPLOYMENT
STUDIES IN SOUTHERN CITIES. /TENNESSEE/   NSOUTRC62156

SERVANT
THE VANISHING SERVANT AND THE CONTEMPORARY STATUS-SYSTEM OF THE AMERICAN SOUTH.   NANDEAX53022

SERVICE
ANNUAL FARM LABOR REPORT, 1965, CALIFORNIA DEPARTMENT OF EMPLOYMENT, FARM LABOR SERVICE. /NEGRO
MEXICAN-AMERICAN WOMEN/   CCALDEM66906

RACIAL DISTRIBUTION OF SELECTED UNEMPLOYMENT INSURANCE AND EMPLOYMENT SERVICE DATA. JULY-DECEMBER 1966.
/NEGRO MEXICAN-AMERICAN/   CCALDEM67907

ADDRESS TO COMMUNITY RELATIONS SERVICE STAFF TRAINING SESSION, JANUARY 12, 1967, ON JOBS NOW. /NEGRO
PUERTO-RICAN YOUTH/   CCOLEBX67918

FREEDOM OF CHOICE IN PERSONAL SERVICE OCCUPATIONS. 13TH AMENDMENT LIMITATIONS ON ANTIDISCRIMINATION
LEGISLATION.   GAVINAX64410

EFFECTS ON ECONOMIC GROWTH OF THE EMPLOYMENT SHIFT TO SERVICE INDUSTRIES.   GBRADME64797

MEDICAL SERVICE JOB OPPORTUNITIES 1964-66, SAN-FRANCISCO BAY AREA. /CALIFORNIA/   GCALDEM64521

EQUAL-EMPLOYMENT-OPPORTUNITY. A CHALLENGE TO THE EMPLOYMENT SERVICE.   GCASSFH66561

I STATEMENT BEFORE THE HOUSE POST OFFICE AND CIVIL SERVICE SUBCOMMITTEE ON POSTAL OPERATIONS, II
DISCRIMINATION. PLANNED AND ACCIDENTAL. /TESTING/   GENNEWH67928

FAIR-EMPLOYMENT-PRACTICES IN THE PUBLIC SERVICE.   GFRIELL62701

AGGRESSIVE RECRUITMENT AND THE PUBLIC SERVICE.   GGREGGX61071

THE NEW ROLE OF THE EMPLOYMENT SERVICE IN SERVING THE DISADVANTAGED. /SES/   GLEVILA66599

COMMUNICATIONS EMPLOYEES AND GOOD SERVICE. /NEW-YORK/   GNEWYSA54077

ONE-THIRD OF A NATION. A REPORT ON YOUNG MEN FOUND UNQUALIFIED FOR MILITARY SERVICE.   GPRESTM64316

SELECTED LIST OF REFERENCES ON MINORITY-GROUP EMPLOYMENT IN THE PUBLIC SERVICE.   GSIMPDX64312

FAIR-EMPLOYMENT IN THE FEDERAL SERVICE.   GUSCISC51385

FAIR-EMPLOYMENT IN THE FEDERAL SERVICE, A PROGRESS REPORT ON CONSTRUCTIVE STEPS.   GUSCISC52386

SERVICE TO MINORITY-GROUPS. 1958.   GUSDLAB58497

EMPLOYMENT SERVICE TASK FORCE REPORT. /MANPOWER SES/   GUSDLAB66559

VOLUNTARY FARM EMPLOYMENT SERVICE. /MIGRANT-WORKERS/   GUSSENA64306

COOPERATIVE EXTENSION SERVICE WORK WITH LOW-INCOME FAMILIES.   IUSDAGR63638

RACIAL DISCRIMINATION IN THE FEDERAL SERVICE. A STUDY IN THE SOCIOLOGY OF ADMINISTRATION. NBRADWC53106

MEETING THE PSYCHOLOGICAL CRISES OF NEGRO YOUTH THROUGH A COORDINATED GUIDANCE SERVICE. NBRAZWF58111

RACIAL DESEGREGATION IN THE PUBLIC SERVICE, WITH PARTICULAR REFERENCE TO THE US GOVERNMENT. NBROWVJ54127

GRADUATE EDUCATION, PUBLIC SERVICE, AND THE NEGRO.   NCIKIWI66207

NEGROES AND THE SERVICE INDUSTRIES. /OCCUPATIONS/   NDIAMDE64272

PROMOTING EQUAL-EMPLOYMENT THROUGH THE PUBLIC EMPLOYMENT SERVICE.   NLEVILX62686

PLACEMENT SERVICE OF THE AMERICAN FRIENDS SERVICE COMMITTEE. A TECHNIQUE IN RACE-RELATIONS. NLOESFS46703

PLACEMENT SERVICE OF THE AMERICAN FRIENDS SERVICE COMMITTEE. A TECHNIQUE IN RACE-RELATIONS. NLOESFS46703

A STUDY OF NON-WHITE EMPLOYMENT IN THE STATE SERVICE. /MICHIGAN/   NMICCSC64775

A FOLLOW-UP STUDY OF NON-WHITE EMPLOYMENT IN THE STATE SERVICE. /MICHIGAN/   NMICCSC65774

NEGRO EMPLOYMENT IN THE FEDERAL GOVERNMENT BY CIVIL SERVICE REGION, STATE AND PAY CATEGORIES, JUNE 1962. NPRESCD62012

THE IMPACT OF MILITARY SERVICE UPON THE RACIAL ATTITUDES OF NEGRO SERVICEMEN IN WORLD-WAR II. NROBEHW53065

IMPACT OF OFFICE AUTOMATION IN THE INTERNAL REVENUE SERVICE. A STUDY OF THE MANPOWER IMPLICATIONS DURING
THE FIRST STAGES OF THE CHANGEOVER. /ECONOMIC-STATUS/   NUSDLAB63198

THE UNITED STATES EMPLOYMENT SERVICE AND THE NEGRO WORK APPLICANT.   NUSWAMC44276

OCCUPATIONS AND SALARIES OF WOMEN IN THE FEDERAL SERVICE.   WUSCISC62168

GREAT STRIDES MADE IN JOBS FOR WOMEN IN FEDERAL SERVICE.   WUSDLAB62041

WOMEN IN FEDERAL SERVICE, 1939-59.   WWIRTWH62181

SERVICEMAN
THE 1960 AUDIT OF NEGRO VETERANS AND SERVICEMAN. /MILITARY/   NFELDJA61350

SERVICEMEN
AUDIT OF NEGRO VETERANS AND SERVICEMEN, 1960. /PUBLIC-EMPLOYMENT/   NAMERVC60019

THE IMPACT OF MILITARY SERVICE UPON THE RACIAL ATTITUDES OF NEGRO SERVICEMEN IN WORLD-WAR II. NROBEHW53065

SERVICES

AN EXPERIMENT TO TEST THREE MAJOR ISSUES OF WORK PROGRAM METHODOLOGY WITHIN MOBILIZATION-FOR-YOUTH-S INTEGRATED **SERVICES** TO OUT-OF-SCHOOL UNEMPLOYED YOUTH. /NEGRO PUERTO-RICAN/   CMOBIFY66024

ISSUES AND PROBLEMS IN INTEGRATING NEEDED SUPPORTIVE **SERVICES** IN NEIGHBORHOOD-YOUTH-CORPS PROJECTS.   GBATTMX66131

A NATIONAL PROGRAM FOR THE IMPROVEMENT OF WELFARE **SERVICES** AND THE REDUCTION OF WELFARE DEPENDENCY.   GCOHENE65664

JOB AND CAREER DEVELOPMENT FOR THE POOR...THE HUMAN **SERVICES**. INCLUDES BIBLIOGRAPHY.   GGOLDGS66360

STUDY OF **SERVICES** TO DEAL WITH POVERTY IN DETROIT, MICHIGAN.   GGREEAI65480

MANPOWER **SERVICES** TO ARIZONA INDIANS. /SES/   IARIZSE66912

MANPOWER **SERVICES** ON THE NAVAJO RESERVATION.   IGRAFMF66565

COUNSELLING **SERVICES**.   ITHOMBXND439

THE BUREAU OF INDIAN AFFAIRS VOLUNTARY RELOCATION **SERVICES**.   IUSDINT60644

A FOLLOWUP STUDY OF 1963 RECIPIENTS OF THE **SERVICES** OF THE EMPLOYMENT ASSISTANCE PROGRAM, BUREAU-OF-INDIAN-AFFAIRS.   IUSDINT66650

THE AGING NEGRO. SOME IMPLICATIONS FOR SOCIAL-WELFARE **SERVICES**.   NBEATWM60066

NEGROES AND GOVERNMENTAL **SERVICES**. AN APPRAISAL.   NBOYDWM46252

NONDISCRIMINATION IN THE FEDERAL **SERVICES**.   NDAVIJA46257

INTEGRATION IN THE ARMED **SERVICES**. /MILITARY/   NEVANJC56340

MANPOWER **SERVICES** FOR EQUAL-EMPLOYMENT-OPPORTUNITY.   NLEVILX64685

LIBRARY RESOURCES AND **SERVICES** IN WHITE AND NEGRO COLLEGES. /EDUCATION/   NSAMOTX65128

EQUAL-OPPORTUNITY IN FARM PROGRAMS -- AN APPRAISAL OF **SERVICES** RENDERED BY AGENCIES OF THE UNITED STATES DEPARTMENT OF AGRICULTURE.   NUSCOMC65232

INTEGRATION IN THE ARMED **SERVICES**. A PROGRESS REPORT. /MILITARY/   NUSDDEF55195

THE IMPACT OF PUERTO-RICAN MIGRATION ON GOVERNMENTAL **SERVICES** IN NEW-YORK CITY.   PDWORMB57797

DAY CARE **SERVICES**. FORM AND SUBSTANCE. /EMPLOYMENT-CONDITIONS/   WHOFFGL61846

WOMEN WORKERS. WORKING HOURS AND **SERVICES**.   WKLEIVX65908

SERVICING

SERVICING THE HARD TO PLACE.   PYANGRX61859

SES

THE DISCRIMINATION CASE. /NEGRO PUERTO-RICAN SES/   CCOHEHX65917

THE NEW ROLE OF THE EMPLOYMENT SERVICE IN SERVING THE DISADVANTAGED. /SES/   GLEVILA66599

WHAT TITLE-VII MEANS FOR THE LOCAL OFFICE. /SES/   GMITCHR66018

TESTIMONY TO THE SUBCOMMITTEE ON RACE-RELATIONS AND URBAN PROBLEMS. /SES CALIFORNIA/   GREDMWX64221

EMPLOYMENT SERVICE TASK FORCE REPORT. /MANPOWER SES/   GUSDLAB66559

MANPOWER SERVICES TO ARIZONA INDIANS. /SES/   IARIZSE66912

OUTREACH -- THE AFFIRMATIVE APPROACH. /EMPLOYMENT SES/   NFRANWH66698

SEX

SEX DIFFERENCES IN OCCUPATIONAL CHOICE PATTERNS AMONG ADOLESCENTS. /ASPIRATIONS WOMEN NEGRO/   CSPREJX62999

NONWHITE POPULATION BY RACE. NEGROES, INDIANS, JAPANESE, CHINESE, FILIPINOS. BY AGE, SEX, MARITAL-STATUS, EDUCATION, EMPLOYMENT-STATUS, OCCUPATIONAL-STATUS, INCOME, ETC. /DEMOGRAPHY/   CUSBURC53378

NONWHITE POPULATION BY RACE. NEGROES, INDIANS, JAPANESE, CHINESE, FILIPINOS. BY AGE, SEX, MARITAL-STATUS, EDUCATION, EMPLOYMENT-STATUS, OCCUPATIONAL-STATUS, INCOME, ETC. /DEMOGRAPHY/   CUSBURC63176

NET MIGRATION OF THE POPULATION, 1950-60, BY AGE, SEX, AND COLOR. VOL II, ANALYTICAL GROUPINGS OF COUNTIES. /INCOME/   GBOWLGK65434

EMPLOYMENT AND INCOME BY AGE, SEX, COLOR AND RESIDENCE. /DETROIT MICHIGAN/   GDETRCC63948

MONEY BENEFITS OF EDUCATION BY SEX AND RACE IN NEW-YORK STATE, 1956.   GGREEWX61741

SEX, STATUS AND THE UNDEREMPLOYMENT OF THE NEGRO MALE.   NCLARKB67212

HIDDEN UNEMPLOYMENT 1953-62. A QUANTITATIVE ANALYSIS BY AGE AND SEX.   NDERNTX66264

THE RELATIONSHIP OF PARENTAL IDENTIFICATION TO SEX ROLE ACCEPTANCE IN MARRIED, SINGLE, CAREER AND NON-CAREER WOMEN. /WORK-WOMEN-ROLE/   WBREYCH64654

SEX AS A FACTOR IN THE DETERMINATION OF EDUCATIONAL CHOICE. /ASPIRATIONS/   WDOLEAA64737

THE MARGINAL SEX. /WORK-WOMAN-ROLE/   WFREEMX62771

SOME IMPLICATIONS ON CURRENT CHANGES IN SEX ROLE PATTERNS. /WORK-WOMAN-ROLE/   WHARTRE60828

CLASSIFICATION ON THE BASIS OF SEX AND THE 1964 CIVIL-RIGHTS-ACT.   WIOWALR65102

THE FEMALE PHYSICIAN IN PUBLIC HEALTH. CONFLICT AND RECONCILIATION OF THE SEX AND PROFESSIONAL ROLES. /OCCUPATIONS/   WKOSAJX64915

JANE CROW AND THE LAW. SEX DISCRIMINATION AND TITLE-VII.   WMURRPX65010

SEX AND EQUAL-OPPORTUNITY IN HIGHER EDUCATION.   WPUNKHH61071

LABOR-FORCE SENSITIVITY TO EMPLOYMENT BY AGE, SEX.   WTELLAX65714

WISCONSIN FAIR-EMPLOYMENT-PRACTICES DIVISION INQUIRY INTO THE CONFLICTS BETWEEN STATE PROTECTIVE LABOR LEGISLATION AND STATE AND FEDERAL LAWS PROHIBITING DISCRIMINATION BASED ON SEX. /EMPLOYMENT-CONDITIONS/   WUAWXWD65165

SEX AND THE CIVIL-RIGHTS-ACT. /LEGISLATION/   WUHLXGX66200

SEX   (CONTINUATION)
    SUGGESTED LANGUAGE FOR A STATE ACT TO ABOLISH DISCRIMINATORY WAGE RATES BASED ON SEX.   WUSDLAB64218

    LAWS ON SEX DISCRIMINATION IN EMPLOYMENT.   WUSDLAB66K05

SEX-ROLE
    SEX-ROLE AND PROFESSIONALISM. A STUDY OF HIGH SCHOOL TEACHERS.   /OCCUPATIONS/   WCOLOJX63698

SEXES
    EQUALITY BETWEEN THE SEXES. AN IMMODEST PROPOSAL. /WORK-WOMEN-ROLE/   WROSSAS64132

SHARECROPPERS
    SHARECROPPERS IN THE 60-S. A REPORT AND A PROGRAM.   NNATLSF61883

SHIFT
    EFFECTS ON ECONOMIC GROWTH OF THE EMPLOYMENT SHIFT TO SERVICE INDUSTRIES.   GBRADME64797

SHIFTS
    OCCUPATIONAL SHIFTS IN NEGRO EMPLOYMENT.   NDIAMDE65273

SHIPBUILDING
    NEGROES IN A WAR INDUSTRY. THE CASE OF SHIPBUILDING.   NNORTHR43942

SHOP
    MINORITY RIGHTS AND THE UNION SHOP.   GREADFT64220

SHOPPING
    EQUAL-EMPLOYMENT-OPPORTUNITY IN THE SUBURBAN SHOPPING CENTER. FACT OR FICTION. /MICHIGAN/   NMICFEP63777

SHOPS
    EFFECTS OF ON-THE-JOB EXPERIENCE WITH NEGROES UPON RACIAL ATTITUDES OF WHITE WORKERS IN UNION SHOPS.   NGUNDRH50466

SHORTAGE
    STUDY OF THE SHORTAGE AND SALARIES OF SCIENTISTS AND ENGINEERS.   GUSSENA54353

    JOBS FOR NEGROES -- IS THERE A REAL SHORTAGE.   NUSNEWR63269

    THE SHORTAGE OF NURSES AND CONDITIONS OF WORK IN NURSING. /OCCUPATIONS/   WKRUSMX58920

    WOMANPOWER -- KEY TO MANAGEMENT MANPOWER SHORTAGE.   WLLOYBJ62633

    SHORTAGE OR SURPLUS. AN ASSESSMENT OF BOSTON WOMANPOWER IN INDUSTRY, GOVERNMENT, AND RESEARCH. JUNE 7-8,
    1963. /MASSACHUSETTS/   WUSDLAB66217

    THE NURSING SHORTAGE AND THE NURSE TRAINING ACT OF 1964. /MANPOWER/   WYETTDX66246

SHORTAGES
    OCCUPATIONAL DEVELOPMENTS. SHORTAGES OF SKILLED TECHNICAL MANPOWER HIGHEST IN RECENT YEARS.   GUSDLAB65561

SIMULATION
    FEMALE LABOR-FORCE MOBILITY AND ITS SIMULATION.   WKORBJX63435

SINGLE
    CARRYING OUT A PLAN FOR JOB INTEGRATION AND DOING IT -- IN THE HEART OF GEORGIA -- WITHOUT A SINGLE
    UNPLEASANT INCIDENT. THAT-S THE EXPERIENCE OF LOCKHEED AIRCRAFT CORPORATION AT ITS MARIETTA PLANT.
    /INDUSTRY/   NBUSIWX63148

    THE RELATIONSHIP OF PARENTAL IDENTIFICATION TO SEX ROLE ACCEPTANCE IN MARRIED, SINGLE, CAREER AND
    NON-CAREER WOMEN. /WORK-WOMEN-ROLE/   WBREYCH64654

SIOUX
    CONSTRAINTS ON ECONOMIC PROGRESS ON THE ROSEBUD SIOUX INDIAN RESERVATION.   IEICHCK60553

    THE SIOUX ON THE RESERVATION.   ISHAWLC60617

    CULTURAL AND ECONOMIC-STATUS OF THE SIOUX PEOPLE.   IUSDINT64645

SITUATION
    THE URBAN REALITY. A COMPARATIVE STUDY OF THE SOCIO-ECONOMIC SITUATION OF MEXICAN-AMERICANS, NEGROES AND
    ANGLO-CAUCASIANS IN LOS-ANGELES COUNTY. /CALIFORNIA/   CLOSACH65708

    MIGRATION OF POPULATION IN THE SOUTH. SITUATION AND PROSPECTS.   GBOWLGK58397

    THE CURRENT SITUATION OF THE HIRED FARM LABOR-FORCE.   GBOWLGK67920

    THE ECONOMIC SITUATION OF NATIONAL MINORITIES IN THE UNITED STATES OF AMERICA.   GTHOMJA47354

    THE CIVIL-RIGHTS SITUATION OF MEXICAN-AMERICANS AND SPANISH-AMERICANS.   MBURMJH61370

    THE OCCUPATIONAL SITUATION OF CENTRAL HARLEM YOUTH.   NHOUSLX65577

    THE EMPLOYMENT SITUATION OF WHITE AND NEGRO YOUTH IN THE CITY OF BALTIMORE. INITIAL EXPERIENCES IN THE
    LABOR-MARKET. /MARYLAND/   NJOHNHU63735

    THE EMPLOYMENT SITUATION OF WHITE AND NEGRO YOUTH IN THE CITY OF BALTIMORE. /MARYLAND/   NLEVEBX63684

    HIGHER EDUCATION FOR NEGROES. A TOUGH SITUATION.   NLEWIHX49692

    THE ROLE OF ORGANIZATIONAL STRUCTURES. UNION VERSUS NEIGHBORHOOD IN A TENSION SITUATION.   NREITDC53050

    THE ECONOMIC SITUATION OF NEGROES IN THE UNITED STATES.   NUSDLAB62243

    THE EMPLOYMENT SITUATION.   NUSDLAB66206

    THE NEGROES IN THE UNITED STATES. THEIR ECONOMIC AND SOCIAL SITUATION.   NUSDLAB66257

    THE SITUATION OF THE NEGRO IN THE U.S.   NWAGECW57290

    POVERTY AREAS OF OUR MAJOR CITIES. THE EMPLOYMENT SITUATION OF NEGRO AND WHITE WORKERS IN METROPOLITAN
    AREAS COMPARED IN A SPECIAL LABOR-FORCE REPORT.   NWETZJR66114

    THE PRESENT SITUATION IN THE ACADEMIC WORLD OF WOMEN TRAINED IN ENGINEERING. /OCCUPATIONS/   WBERNJX65639

    THE PRESENT SITUATION OF WOMAN SCIENTISTS AND ENGINEERS IN INDUSTRY AND GOVERNMENT. /OCCUPATIONS/   WBCLTRH65650

SITUATIONAL
    SITUATIONAL PATTERNING AND INTERGROUP RELATIONS.   GKOHNML56145

    SITUATIONAL PRESSURES AND FUNCTIONAL ROLE OF THE ETHNIC LABOR LEADERS. /UNION/   NGREESX53453

SITUATIONAL   (CONTINUATION)
    MATERNAL EMPLOYMENT. SITUATIONAL AND ATTITUDINAL VARIABLES. /WORK-FAMILY-CONFLICT/   WBRIEDX61655

SIZE
    THE RELATIVE SIZE OF THE NEGRO POPULATION AND NEGRO OCCUPATIONAL-STATUS.   NGLENND64424

SKILL
    MANPOWER PROGRAM IMPLICATIONS OF SKILL IMBALANCES. /TRAINING/   GCASSFH66565

    EDUCATION, SKILL LEVEL, AND EARNINGS OF THE HIRED FARM WORKING FORCE OF 1961.   GCOWHJD63420

    SEMINAR ON MANPOWER POLICY AND PROGRAM -- AUTOMATION, SKILL, AND MANPOWER PREDICTIONS.   GCROSER66148

    EVALUATION AND SKILL TRAINING OF OUT-OF-SCHOOL, HARD-CORE UNEMPLOYED YOUTH FOR TRAINING AND PLACEMENT.   GSMITAE65140

SKILLED
    A POLICY FOR SKILLED MANPOWER.   GNATLMC54876

    THE SKILLED WORK FORCE OF THE UNITED STATES.   GUSDLAB55498

    OCCUPATIONAL DEVELOPMENTS. SHORTAGES OF SKILLED TECHNICAL MANPOWER HIGHEST IN RECENT YEARS.   GUSDLAB65561

    APPRENTICES, SKILLED CRAFTSMEN AND THE NEGRO. AN ANALYSIS.   NHILLHX60525

    RACIAL FACTORS INFLUENCING ENTRY TO THE SKILLED TRADES. /UNION/   NMARSRX63745

    THE USE OF COLORED PERSONS IN SKILLED OCCUPATIONS.   NOCONWB41094

SKILLED-TRADES
    TRAINING OF NEGROES IN THE SKILLED-TRADES.   NSTEEHG54176

SKILLED-WORKERS
    ESTIMATED NEED FOR SKILLED-WORKERS, 1965-75. /EMPLOYMENT/   GSALTAF66534

SKILLS
    THE EROSION OF JOBS AND SKILLS.   GAFLCIO63864

    AMERICA-S POOR. REALITY AND CHANGE. /RETRAINING SKILLS UNEMPLOYMENT/   GAMERFX66674

    AN ANALYSIS OF THE EXPERIENCED HIRED FARM WORKING FORCE, 1948-1957. /SKILLS/   GCOWHJD60423

    ILLINOIS JOB SEEKERS SURVEY. EDUCATION, SKILLS, LENGTH OF UNEMPLOYMENT, AND PERSONAL CHARACTERISTICS.   GILLIDI62004

    IMPROVING THE WORK SKILLS OF THE NATION.   GNATLMC55052

    NATIONAL EMPLOYMENT, SKILLS, AND EARNINGS OF FARM LABOR.   GSCHUTW67964

    PEOPLE, SKILLS, AND JOBS.   GUSDLAB63491

    ANALYSIS OF MALE NAVAHO STUDENTS PERCEPTIONS OF OCCUPATIONAL OPPORTUNITIES AND THEIR ATTITUDES TOWARD
    DEVELOPMENT OF SKILLS AND TRAITS NECESSARY FOR OCCUPATIONAL COMPETENCE.   IDESPCW65548

    SECURING SKILLS NEEDED FOR SUCCESS. COMMUNITY JOB TRAINING FOR NEGROES.   NBLUMAA66099

    ARMING THE UNEMPLOYED WITH SKILLS. /TRAINING/   NCOONRB66927

    WOMEN GRADUATES OF COOPERATIVE WORK-STUDY PROGRAMS ON THE COLLEGE LEVEL. /SKILLS/   WMOSBWB57999

SKILLS-BANK
    A NATIONAL SKILLS-BANK. WHAT IT IS, HOW IT OPERATES.   NNATLULND893

SKIRT
    PUERTO-RICAN INTEGRATION IN THE SKIRT INDUSTRY IN NEW-YORK CITY.   PHELFBH59481

SLOGAN
    IMPROVING INDUSTRIAL RACE-RELATIONS -- PART I. EQUAL JOB OPPORTUNITY -- SLOGAN OR REALITY.   GFLEMHC63363

SLUM
    THE CULTURE OF THE SLUM.   GDAVIAX63132

SLUMS
    THE ENDURING SLUMS. /NEGRO PUERTO-RICAN/   CSELIDX57034

    SLUMS AND SOCIAL INSECURITY.   GSCHOAL65122

    SUB-EMPLOYMENT IN THE SLUMS OF NEW-YORK.   GUSDLAB66511

    SUB-EMPLOYMENT IN THE SLUMS OF NEW-ORLEANS. /LOUISIANA/   GUSDLAB66512

    SUB-EMPLOYMENT IN THE SLUMS OF PHOENIX. /ARIZONA/   GUSDLAB66513

    SUB-EMPLOYMENT IN THE SLUMS OF LOS-ANGELES. /CALIFORNIA/   GUSDLAB66514

    SUB-EMPLOYMENT IN THE SLUMS OF SAN-ANTONIO. /TEXAS/   GUSDLAB66515

    SUB-EMPLOYMENT IN THE SLUMS OF CLEVELAND. /OHIO/   GUSDLAB66516

    SUB-EMPLOYMENT IN THE SLUMS OF ST-LOUIS. /MISSOURI/   GUSDLAB66517

    SUB-EMPLOYMENT IN THE SLUMS OF BOSTON. /MASSACHUSETTS/   GUSDLAB66518

    SUB-EMPLOYMENT IN THE SLUMS OF SAN-FRANCISCO. /CALIFORNIA/   GUSDLAB66519

    A SHARPER LOOK AT UNEMPLOYMENT IN US CITIES, AND SLUMS.   GUSDLAB66520

    SUB-EMPLOYMENT IN THE SLUMS OF OAKLAND. /CALIFORNIA/   GUSDLAB66521

    SUB-EMPLOYMENT IN THE SLUMS OF PHILADELPHIA. /PENNSYLVANIA/   GUSDLAB66522

    SLUMS AND SUBURBS. /TRAINING/   NCONAJB61920

SMALL
    INTERPERSONAL RELATIONS IN ETHNICALLY MIXED SMALL WORK GROUPS.   GSCOTWW59291

    FARM INCOME PREDICTIONS FOR SMALL FARMS IN THE CENTRAL LOUISIANA MIXED FARMING AREA.   NBOLTBX62399

    AIDING NEGRO BUSINESSMEN. SMALL BUSINESS OPPORTUNITIES CORPORATION, PHILADELPHIA. /PENNSYLVANIA/   NBUSIWX64143

    PROBLEMS AND OPPORTUNITIES CONFRONTING NEGROES IN THE FIELD OF BUSINESS, REPORT ON THE NATIONAL

SMALL   (CONTINUATION)
    CONFERENCE ON **SMALL** BUSINESS. /OCCUPATIONS/   NFITZNH63358

    THE POST-WAR OUTLOOK FOR NEGROES IN **SMALL** BUSINESS, THE ENGINEERING AND THE TECHNICAL VOCATIONS.   NWALKJO46580

    REBUILDING CITIES. THE EFFECTS OF DISPLACEMENT AND RELOCATION ON **SMALL** BUSINESS.   NZIMMBG64247

    MANAGING WOMEN EMPLOYEES IN **SMALL** BUSINESS.   WUSSMBA62248

SOCIAL
    ECONOMIC, **SOCIAL**, AND DEMOGRAPHIC CHARACTERISTICS OF SPANISH-AMERICAN WAGE WORKERS ON US FARMS.
      /PUERTO-RICAN MEXICAN-AMERICAN/   CFRIERE63805

    URBAN ADJUSTMENT AND ITS RELATIONSHIP TO THE **SOCIAL** ANTECEDENTS OF IMMIGRANT WORKERS.   /NEGRO
    MEXICAN-AMERICAN/   CSHANLW65121

    GENERAL **SOCIAL** AND ECONOMIC CHARACTERISTICS. SUMMARY, US CENSUS OF 1960. /DEMOGRAPHY/   CUSBURC62374

    EMPLOYMENT-STATUS AND WORK CHARACTERISTICS. STATISTICS ON THE RELATION BETWEEN EMPLOYMENT AND **SOCIAL** AND
    ECONOMIC CHARACTERISTICS. /DEMOGRAPHY/   CUSBURC63170

    PERSONS BY FAMILY CHARACTERISTICS. FAMILY MEMBERS BY **SOCIAL**, ECONOMIC AND HOUSING CHARACTERISTICS OF
    FAMILIES. /DEMOGRAPHY/   CUSBURC63180

    PERSONS OF SPANISH-SURNAME. **SOCIAL** AND ECONOMIC DATA FOR WHITE PERSONS OF SPANISH SURNAME IN 5
    SOUTHWESTERN STATES. /DEMOGRAPHY/   CUSBURC63181

    THE **SOCIAL** MEANING OF DISCRIMINATION.   GANTOAX60400

    SOCIAL STRUCTURE AND RACE-RELATIONS.   GBONIES66135

    ECONOMIC AND **SOCIAL** DEPRIVATIONS. ITS EFFECTS ON CHILDREN AND FAMILIES IN THE UNITED STATES -- A SELECTED
    BIBLIOGRAPHY.   GCHILCX64571

    A **SOCIAL** PROFILE OF AGRICULTURAL MIGRATORY PEOPLE IN COLORADO. /MIGRANT-WORKERS/   GCOLOSO59919

    SOCIAL INTEGRATION, ATTITUDES AND UNION ACTIVITY.   GDEANLR54944

    SOME CONSIDERATIONS AS TO THE CONTRIBUTIONS OF **SOCIAL**, PERSONALITY, AND RACIAL FACTORS TO SCHOOL
    RETARDATION IN MINORITY-GROUP CHILDREN.   GDEUTMP56641

    MINORITY-GROUP AND CLASS STATUS AS RELATED TO **SOCIAL** AND PERSONALITY FACTORS IN SCHOLASTIC ACHIEVEMENT. GDEUTMP60640

    TECHNOLOGY AND **SOCIAL** CHANGE.   GGINZEX64972

    A **SOCIAL** REFORMER-S VIEW OF POVERTY.   GHARRMX65659

    THE **SOCIAL** POLITICS OF FEPC. A STUDY IN REFORM PRESSURE MOVEMENTS.   GKESSLC48847

    WORK RELIEF. **SOCIAL** WELFARE STYLE. /MANPOWER UNEMPLOYMENT/   GLEVISA66531

    CYBERNATION AND **SOCIAL** CHANGE. /TECHNOLOGICAL-CHANGE/   GMICADN64673

    GOVERNMENT CONTRACTS AND **SOCIAL** CONTROL. A PRELIMINARY INQUIRY.   GMILLAS55985

    SOCIAL DYNAMITE. THE REPORT OF THE CONFERENCE ON UNEMPLOYED, OUT-OF-SCHOOL YOUTH IN URBAN AREAS, MAY
    24-26, 1961.   GNATLCC61039

    THE ROLE OF AGRICULTURAL TECHNOLOGY IN SOUTHERN **SOCIAL** CHANGE.   GRAPEAX46037

    TEST PERFORMANCE IN RELATION TO ETHNIC GROUP AND **SOCIAL** CLASS.   GROBESO63683

    SLUMS AND **SOCIAL** INSECURITY.   GSCHOAL65122

    SOCIAL RESPONSIBILITIES OF ORGANIZED LABOR. /UNION/   GTITCJA57358

    THE ROLE OF REDISTRIBUTION IN **SOCIAL** POLICY.   GTITMRM65359

    SOCIAL DEVELOPMENT. KEY TO THE GREAT SOCIETY. /SOCIO-ECONOMIC WELFARE/   GUSDHEW66639

    SEMINAR ON MANPOWER POLICY AND PROGRAM. CYBERNATION AND **SOCIAL** CHANGE.   GUSDLAB64982

    RELOCATED AMERICAN INDIANS IN THE SAN-FRANCISCO BAY AREA. **SOCIAL** INTERACTION AND INDIAN IDENTITY.
    /CALIFORNIA/   IALBOJX64523

    UTE INDIAN SURVEY -- PRELIMINARY REPORT, **SOCIAL** AND ECONOMIC CHARACTERISTICS.   IBRIGYUND442

    THE AMERICAN INDIAN, PERSPECTIVES FOR STUDY OF **SOCIAL** CHANGE.   IEGGAFR66552

    SOCIAL SURVEY OF AMERICAN-INDIAN URBAN INTEGRATION.   IHIRAJXND444

    SOCIAL AND CULTURAL CONSIDERATIONS IN THE DEVELOPMENT OF MANPOWER PROGRAMS FOR INDIANS.   IKELLWH67579

    INDIANS OF THE MISSOURI-BASIN -- CULTURAL FACTORS IN THEIR **SOCIAL** AND ECONOMIC ADJUSTMENT.   IREIFBX58610

    SOCIAL SECURITY AND THE AMERICAN-INDIAN.   IUSDHEW60639

    SOCIAL AND ECONOMIC SURVEY OF POTAWATOMIE JURISDICTION.   IUSDINT57660

    ADL REPORTS ON **SOCIAL**, EMPLOYMENT, EDUCATIONAL AND HOUSING DISCRIMINATION.   JANTIDL57690

    THE DISPLACED PERSON AND THE **SOCIAL** AGENCY. A STUDY OF THE CASEWORK PROCESS AND ITS RELATION TO IMMIGRANT
    ADJUSTMENT.   JCRYSDX58714

    SOCIAL CHARACTERISTICS OF AMERICAN JEWS.   JGLAZNX60726

    ON THE **SOCIAL** SCENE. /EQUAL-OPPORTUNITY/   JLEEXAM58739

    DEMOGRAPHIC AND **SOCIAL** ASPECTS.   JSHERBC64759

    THE JEWS. **SOCIAL** PATTERNS OF AN AMERICAN GROUP.   JSKLAMX58149

    ECONOMIC, **SOCIAL** AND DEMOGRAPHIC CHARACTERISTICS OF SPANISH-AMERICAN WAGE WORKERS ON US FARMS.   MFRIERE63394

    THE **SOCIAL** ASPIRATIONS OF A SELECTED GROUP OF SPANISH NAME PEOPLE IN LAREDO, TEXAS.   MGUERIX59409

    A STUDY OF THE ACCULTURATION AND **SOCIAL** ASPIRATIONS OF SIXTY JUNIOR HIGH SCHOOL STUDENTS FROM THE MEXICAN
    ETHNIC GROUP.   MJONEBM62421

CLASS CONSCIOUSNESS AND **SOCIAL** MOBILITY IN A MEXICAN-AMERICAN COMMUNITY.   MPENAFX63453

OBJECTIVE ACCESS IN THE OPPORTUNITY STRUCTURE. THE ASSESSMENT OF THREE ETHNIC GROUPS WITH RESPECT TO
QUANTIFIED **SOCIAL** STRUCTURAL VARIABLES.   MRENDGX63461

SOCIAL MOBILITY AND IMPUTATIONS OF WITCHCRAFT IN A MEXICAN-AMERICAN NEIGHBORHOOD OF TEXAS.   MRUBEAJ66467

SOCIAL AND ATTITUDINAL CHARACTERISTICS OF SPANISH-SPEAKING MIGRANT AND EX-MIGRANT WORKERS IN THE
SOUTHWEST.   MULIBHX66503

SOCIAL FACTORS IN OCCUPATIONAL AND EDUCATIONAL ASPIRATIONS OF NEGRO AND WHITE STUDENTS.   NADDIDP61002

THE **SOCIAL** AND POLITICAL REACTIONS OF OLDER NEGROES TO UNEMPLOYMENT.   NAIKEMX66865

SCHOOL ATTENDANCE AND ATTAINMENT. FUNCTION AND DYSFUNCTION OF SCHOOL AND FAMILY **SOCIAL** SYSTEMS.
/EMPLOYMENT DROP-OUT/   NBERTAL62982

RACE AND SOCIAL-CLASS AS SEPARATE FACTORS RELATED TO **SOCIAL** ENVIRONMENT. /ASPIRATIONS/   NBLOORX63096

A COMPARISON OF THE **SOCIAL** CHARACTERISTICS AND EDUCATIONAL ASPIRATIONS OF NORTHERN, LOWER-CLASS, NEGRO
PARENTS WHO ACCEPTED AND DECLINED AN OPPORTUNITY FOR INTEGRATED EDUCATION FOR THEIR CHILDREN.   NCAGLLT66904

CARK GHETTO. DILEMMAS OF **SOCIAL** POWER.   NCLARKB65211

SOCIAL AND ECONOMIC IMPLICATIONS OF INTEGRATING IN THE PUBLIC SCHOOLS.   NCLARKB65213

SOCIAL INFLUENCES IN NEGRO-WHITE INTELLIGENCE DIFFERENCES.   NDEUTMX64268

THE **SOCIAL** AND ECONOMIC STATUS OF THE NEGRO IN THE UNITED STATES.   NDRAKSC65289

RESIDENTIAL SEGREGATION AND **SOCIAL** DIFFERENTIATION.   NDUNCOD59305

NEGRO LEADERSHIP IN RURAL GEORGIA COMMUNITIES. OCCUPATIONAL AND **SOCIAL** ASPECTS.   NEDWAVA42328

AN ECONOMIC AND **SOCIAL** PROFILE OF THE NEGRO AMERICAN.   NFEINRX65347

DESEGREGATION OF **SOCIAL** AGENCIES IN THE SOUTH.   NGOLDJX65427

THE POOR OF HARLEM. **SOCIAL** FUNCTIONING OF THE UNDERCLASS.   NGORDJX65435

DO CORPORATIONS HAVE A **SOCIAL** DUTY. /INDUSTRY/   NHACKAX63475

SOME COMPARISONS AMONG NEGRO-WHITE COLLEGE STUDENTS. **SOCIAL** AMBITION AND ESTIMATED SOCIAL MOBILITY. NHARREE66786

SOME COMPARISONS AMONG NEGRO-WHITE COLLEGE STUDENTS. SOCIAL AMBITION AND ESTIMATED **SOCIAL** MOBILITY. NHARREE66786

DEMOGRAPHIC AND **SOCIAL** FACTORS IN THE POVERTY OF THE NEGRO.   NHAUSPM66992

A SOCIOLOGICAL INTERPRETATION OF **SOCIAL** CHANGE IN THE SOUTH.   NHEBERX46508

CHANGES IN THE **SOCIAL** STRATIFICATION OF THE SOUTH.   NHEBERX56507

STATE LAWS AND THE NEGRO. **SOCIAL** CHANGE AND THE IMPACT OF LAW.   NHILLHX65545

THE ROLE OF LAW IN SECURING EQUAL-EMPLOYMENT-OPPORTUNITY. LEGAL POWERS AND **SOCIAL** CHANGE.   NHILLHX66544

THE NATURAL HISTORY OF **SOCIAL** CONFLICT AND WHITE-NEGRO RELATIONS.   NHIMEJS49553

A HISTORICAL REVIEW OF THE IMPACT OF **SOCIAL** AND ECONOMIC STRUCTURE ON NEGRO CULTURE AND HOW IT INFLUENCES
FAMILY LIVING.   NJACKJX64596

SUMMARY OF A SURVEY OF **SOCIAL** AND ECONOMIC CONDITIONS IN MORRIS COUNTY NEW-JERSEY AS THEY AFFECT THE
NEGRO.   NKERNJH57645

ATTITUDES TOWARD **SOCIAL** MOBILITY AS REVEALED BY SAMPLES OF NEGRO AND WHITE BOYS.   NMONTJB58809

SOCIAL TRENDS IN AMERICA AND STRATEGIC APPROACHES TO THE NEGRO PROBLEM.   NMYRDGX48871

ECONOMIC AND **SOCIAL** STATUS OF THE NEGRO IN THE UNITED STATES.   NNATLUL62083

TECHNOLOGICAL-CHANGE AND THE **SOCIAL** ORDER. /SOUTH/   NNOLAEW65927

ECONOMIC AND **SOCIAL** STATUS OF THE NEGRO IN THE UNITED STATES.   NORSHMX61961

MANAGEMENT **SOCIAL** RESPONSIBILITY AND RACIAL EMPLOYMENT IN THE MEAT-PACKING INDUSTRY.   NPURCTV67123

SOCIAL CHANGE AND THE NEGRO PROBLEM.   NROSEAM64296

THE AMERICAN NEGRO PROBLEM IN THE CONTEXT OF **SOCIAL** CHANGE.   NROSEAM65289

SOCIAL AND CULTURAL CHANGE IN THE PLANTATION AREA.   NRUBIMX54297

CIVIL-RIGHTS, EMPLOYMENT, AND THE **SOCIAL** STATUS OF AMERICAN NEGROES.   NSHEPHL66129

DESEGREGATION AND INTEGRATION IN **SOCIAL** WORK.   NSIMOSM56262

SOCIAL CHARACTERISTICS OF HIGH SCHOOL SENIORS IN URBAN NEGRO HIGH SCHOOLS IN TWO STATES.   NSMITBF56147

HOUGH. CLEVELAND. OHIO -- A STUDY OF **SOCIAL** LIFE AND CHANGE.   NSUSSMB59192

ECONOMIC AND **SOCIAL** CONSEQUENCES OF RACIAL DISCRIMINATORY PRACTICES.   NUNITNX63224

SOCIAL SECURITY PROGRAM STATISTICS RELATING TO NONWHITE FAMILIES AND CHILDREN.   NUSDHEW58241

THE NEGRO IN THE WEST. SOME FACTS RELATING TO **SOCIAL** AND ECONOMIC CONDITIONS. NO 1. THE NEGRO WORKER. NUSDLABND256

THE NEGROES IN THE UNITED STATES. THEIR ECONOMIC AND **SOCIAL** SITUATION.   NUSDLAB66257

SOCIAL AND ECONOMIC IMPLICATIONS OF MIGRATION FOR THE NEGRO IN THE PRESENT SOCIAL ORDER.   NVALIPX42261

SOCIAL AND ECONOMIC IMPLICATIONS OF MIGRATION FOR THE NEGRO IN THE PRESENT **SOCIAL** ORDER.   NVALIPX42261

SOCIAL CLASS AND COLOR CASTE IN AMERICA.   NWARNWL62292

THE **SOCIAL** REVOLUTION. CHALLENGE TO THE NATION. /CIVIL-RIGHTS/   NYOUNWM63600

SOCIAL ORIGINS AND CAREER PREPARATION AMONG FILIPINOS IN AMERICAN UNIVERSITIES.   OBELTAG61703

SOCIAL   (CONTINUATION)
ASSIMILATION OF CHINESE IN AMERICA. CHANGES IN ORIENTATION AND **SOCIAL** PERCEPTIONS.   OFONGSL65722

THE JAPANESE **SOCIAL** STRUCTURE AND THE SOURCE OF MENTAL STRAINS OF JAPANESE IMMIGRANTS IN THE US.   OIGAXMX57732

THE PUERTO-RICAN SECTION. A STUDY IN **SOCIAL** TRANSITION.   PHERNJX59816

PATTERNS OF **SOCIAL** ACCOMODATION OF THE MIGRANT PUERTO-RICAN IN THE AMERICAN SOCIAL STRUCTURE.   PSEDAEX58850

PATTERNS OF SOCIAL ACCOMODATION OF THE MIGRANT PUERTO-RICAN IN THE AMERICAN **SOCIAL** STRUCTURE.   PSEDAEX58850

PUERTO-RICANS IN THE UNITED STATES. **SOCIAL** AND ECONOMIC DATA FOR PERSONS OF PUERTO-RICAN BIRTH AND
PARENTAGE. /DEMOGRAPHY/   PUSBURC63182

THE ECONOMIC AND **SOCIAL** ADJUSTMENT OF LOW-INCOME FEMALE-HEADED FAMILIES.   WBERNSE65458

A SURVEY OF THE **SOCIAL** AND OCCUPATIONAL CHARACTERISTICS OF A METROPOLITAN NURSE. COMPLEMENT.
/OCCUPATIONAL-DISTRIBUTION/   WDEUTIX56730

A SURVEY OF THE **SOCIAL** AND OCCUPATIONAL CHARACTERISTICS OF A METROPOLITAN NURSE COMPLEMENT.   WDEUTIX57369

SOCIAL FACTORS WHICH AFFECT CAREER CHOICE IN PSYCHIATRIC NURSING.   WDOUGAM61740

THE EFFECT OF THE **SOCIAL** CONTEXT IN THE VOCATIONAL COUNSELING OF COLLEGE WOMEN.   WGURIMG63810

SOCIAL ROLE EXPECTATION. MOTIVATIONAL VARIABLE IN GIRLS. /ASPIRATIONS/   WHANSDE64821

PSYCHOLOGICAL PROBLEMS OF WOMEN IN DIFFERENT **SOCIAL** ROLES. /WORK-WOMAN-ROLE/   WJAHOMX55879

ENHANCING THE ROLE OF WOMEN IN SCIENCE, ENGINEERING, AND THE **SOCIAL** SCIENCES. /OCCUPATIONS/   WKILLJR65903

UPDATING TRAINING FOR THE RETURNING NURSE. **SOCIAL** WORKER AND TEACHER.   WNATLCP61018

SOCIAL WORK DEGREE PROGRESS REPORT. /TRAINING/   WNYUYUG66031

WHO CHOOSES **SOCIAL** WORK, WHEN AND WHY. /OCCUPATIONS/   WPINSAM63062

REPORT OF THE COMMITTEE ON **SOCIAL** INSURANCE AND TAXES, 1963.   WPRESCO63070

SOME CHANGING ROLES OF WOMEN IN SUBURBIA. A **SOCIAL** ANTHROPOLOGICAL CASE STUDY. /WORK-FAMILY-CONFLICT/   WSCOFNE60109

SOCIAL-CHANGE
THE NATION-S CHILDREN. VOL I. THE FAMILY AND **SOCIAL-CHANGE**. VOL II. DEVELOPMENT AND EDUCATION. VOL III.
PROBLEMS AND PROSPECTS. /NEGRO PUERTO-RICAN MEXICAN-AMERICAN WOMEN/   CGINZEX60720

FARMERS, WORKERS, AND MACHINES. TECHNOLOGICAL AND **SOCIAL-CHANGE** IN FARM INDUSTRIES OF ARIZONA.   MPADFHX65450

RACE-RELATIONS AND **SOCIAL-CHANGE**.   NBURGME65140

IMPACT ON THE INDIVIDUAL. /**SOCIAL-CHANGE**   SOUTH/   NWRIGSJ63344

SOCIAL-CLASS
HEALTH PRACTICES AND EDUCATIONAL ASPIRATIONS AS INDICATORS OF ACCULTURATION AND **SOCIAL-CLASS** AMONG THE
EASTERN CHEROKEE. /NORTH-CAROLINA/   IKUPFHJ62216

RACE AND **SOCIAL-CLASS** AS SEPARATE FACTORS RELATED TO SOCIAL ENVIRONMENT. /ASPIRATIONS/   NBLOORX63096

RACE, OCCUPATION, AND **SOCIAL-CLASS** IN NEW-YORK.   NFRUMRM58388

SOCIAL-CLASS CONSTRAINTS ON THE OCCUPATIONAL ASPIRATIONS OF STUDENTS ATTENDING SOME PREDOMINANTLY NEGRO
COLLEGES.   NGURIPX66467

SOCIAL-CLASS FACTORS UNDERLYING THE CIVIL-RIGHTS MOVEMENT.   NSCOTJW66112

SOCIAL-CLASSES
RESIDENTIAL SEGREGATION OF **SOCIAL-CLASSES** AND ASPIRATIONS OF HIGH SCHOOL BOYS.   GWILSAB59568

SOCIAL-CLASSES. A FRAME OF REFERENCE FOR THE STUDY OF NEGRO SOCIETY.   NHILLMC43551

SOCIAL-DEPENDENCY
SOCIAL-DEPENDENCY IN THE SAN-FRANCISCO BAY AREA. TODAY AND TOMORROW. /CALIFORNIA/   NGREEMX63449

SOCIAL-MOBILITY
SOCIAL-MOBILITY IN INDUSTRIAL SOCIETY.   NLIPSSM59696

SOCIAL-MOBILITY AND PREJUDICE.   NSILBFB59138

SOCIAL-PSYCHOLOGICAL
IDENTIFICATION AND MODIFICATION OF THE **SOCIAL-PSYCHOLOGICAL** CORRELATES OF ECONOMIC DEPENDENCY. PROJECT
FINAL REPORT.   GKIMMPR66137

COMPARATIVE STUDY OF SOCIO-ECONOMIC AND **SOCIAL-PSYCHOLOGICAL** DETERMINANTS OF EDUCATIONAL AND OCCUPATIONAL
ASPIRATIONS OF NEGRO AND WHITE COLLEGE SENIORS.   NWHITRM59319

SOCIAL-ROLES
CHANGING **SOCIAL-ROLES** IN THE NEW SOUTH.   NHIMEJS62998

SOCIAL-SECURITY
SOME IMPLICATIONS OF THE EMPLOYMENT PATTERNS OF WOMEN UNDER **SOCIAL-SECURITY**.   WPOLIEJ59454

SOCIAL-STATUS
SOCIAL-STATUS AND EDUCATIONAL AND OCCUPATIONAL ASPIRATION.   GSEWEWH57297

SOCIAL-STATUS AND ASPIRATIONS IN PHILADELPHIA-S NEGRO POPULATION. /PENNSYLVANIA/   NKLEIRJ62655

SOCIAL-STRATIFICATIO
SOCIAL-STRATIFICATION AND ACADEMIC ACHIEVEMENT. /NEGRO ORIENTAL/   CWILSAB63325

SOCIAL-STRUCTURE
THE RELATIONSHIP OF THE **SOCIAL-STRUCTURE** OF AN INDIAN COMMUNITY TO ADULT AND JUVENILE-DELINQUENCY.
/POVERTY ECONOMIC-STATUS/   IMINNMS63218

THE **SOCIAL-STRUCTURE** OF THE MICHIGAN LABOR-MARKET.   NFERMLA65352

SOCIAL-STRUCTURE AND THE NEGRO REVOLT. AN EXAMINATION OF SOME HYPOTHESES. /SOCIO-ECONOMIC/   NGESCJA64400

SOCIAL-WELFARE
ECONOMIC MANPOWER AND **SOCIAL-WELFARE**.   GCLAGEX65794

SOCIAL-WELFARE   (CONTINUATION)
     THE AGING NEGRO. SOME IMPLICATIONS FOR **SOCIAL-WELFARE** SERVICES.   NBEATWM60066

SOCIALIZATION
     CLASS DIFFERENCES IN THE **SOCIALIZATION** PRACTICES OF NEGRO MOTHERS.   CKAMICKND632

     FAMILY AND ACHIEVEMENT. A PROPOSAL TO STUDY THE EFFECT OF FAMILY **SOCIALIZATION** ON ACHIEVEMENT AND
     PERFORMANCE AMONG URBAN NEGRO AMERICANS.   NEPPSEG65334

     SOCIALIZATION. RACE AND THE AMERICAN HIGH SCHOOL. /EDUCATION/   NTENHWP65201

SOCIETY
     THE EMERGING RURAL SOUTH. A REGION UNDER CONFRONTATION BY MASS **SOCIETY**.   GBERTAL66140

     THE ROLE OF WAGES IN A GREAT **SOCIETY**.   GCONFOE66872

     MANPOWER POLICIES FOR A DEMOCRATIC **SOCIETY**.   GDAVIHX65629

     SOME PROPOSALS FOR GOVERNMENT POLICY IN AN AUTOMATING **SOCIETY**.   GGANSHJ65696

     QUERIES CONCERNING INDUSTRY AND **SOCIETY** GROWING OUT OF STUDY OF ETHNIC RELATIONS IN INDUSTRY.   GHUGHEC59787

     MANPOWER PLANNING IN A FREE **SOCIETY**.   GLESTRA66155

     MINORITIES IN AMERICAN **SOCIETY**.   GMARDCF62938

     MAN. WORK AND **SOCIETY**. A READER IN THE SOCIOLOGY OF OCCUPATIONS.   GNOSOSX62336

     FOUNDATION FOR THE GREAT **SOCIETY**. /EEO/   GROOSFD66242

     EMPLOYMENT POLICY PROBLEMS IN A MULTIRACIAL **SOCIETY**.   GSIMPGE62313

     SOCIAL DEVELOPMENT. KEY TO THE GREAT **SOCIETY**. /SOCIO-ECONOMIC WELFARE/   GUSDHEW66639

     CAN SEGREGATION SURVIVE IN AN INDUSTRIAL **SOCIETY**.   GYINGJM58590

     A MINORITY-GROUP IN AMERICAN **SOCIETY**.   GYINGJM66589

     THE ROLE OF WOMEN IN A CHANGING NAVAHO **SOCIETY**.   IHAMALS57985

     THE INDIANS AND THE GREAT **SOCIETY**. REMARKS.   IMONDWX66591

     A JEW WITHIN AMERICAN **SOCIETY** -- A STUDY IN ETHNIC INDIVIDUALITY.   JSHERCB61311

     THE SPANISH-SPEAKING PEOPLE IN AMERICAN **SOCIETY**.   MSAMOJX64472

     RACE-RELATIONS IN AN INDUSTRIAL **SOCIETY**. /EMPLOYMENT GRIEVANCE-PROCEDURES/   NBACOEF63041

     NEGROES IN AMERICAN **SOCIETY**.   NDAVIMR49252

     THE INTEGRATION OF THE NEGRO INTO AMERICAN **SOCIETY**.   NFRAZEF51578

     SOCIAL-CLASSES. A FRAME OF REFERENCE FOR THE STUDY OF NEGRO **SOCIETY**.   NHILLMC43551

     MEDICAL **SOCIETY** OF THE DISTRICT OF COLUMBIA TO ADMIT NEGRO PHYSICIANS. /OCCUPATIONS/   NJOURNM52628

     SOCIAL-MOBILITY IN INDUSTRIAL **SOCIETY**.   NLIPSSM59696

     CHANGE IN THE STATUS OF THE NEGRO IN AMERICAN **SOCIETY**.   NWALKHJ57291

     DESEGREGATION IN AMERICAN **SOCIETY**. THE RECORD OF A GENERATION OF CHANGE.   NYINGJM63345

     THE PUERTO-RICAN WORKER CONFRONTS THE COMPLEX URBAN **SOCIETY** -- A PRESCRIPTION FOR CHANGE.   PCAROLA67874

     BIBLIOGRAPHY ON THE PUERTO-RICAN. HIS CULTURE AND **SOCIETY**.   PMOBIFYND024

     HIGH SCHOOL FRESHMAN AND SENIORS VIEW THE ROLE OF WOMEN IN MODERN **SOCIETY**. /WORK-FAMILY-CONFLICT/ WKERNKK65892

     NEEDS AND OPPORTUNITIES IN OUR **SOCIETY** FOR THE EDUCATED WOMAN.   WPETEEX63054

     MARRIAGE. FAMILY. AND **SOCIETY**. A READER. /WORK-FAMILY-CONFLICT/   WRODMHX65084

     THE CHANGING ROLE OF WOMEN IN OUR CHANGING **SOCIETY**.   WUSDLAB62253

     THE EDUCATION OF WOMEN AND GIRLS IN A CHANGING **SOCIETY**. A SELECTED BIBLIOGRAPHY WITH ANNOTATIONS. WWIGNTX65267

SOCIO-CULTURAL
     STUDY OF **SOCIO-CULTURAL** FACTORS THAT INHIBIT OR ENCOURAGE DELINQUENCY AMONG MEXICAN-AMERICANS.   MLOSARW58432

     THE **SOCIO-CULTURAL** SETTING.   WNYEXFI63039

SOCIO-ECONOMIC
     THE URBAN REALITY. A COMPARATIVE STUDY OF THE **SOCIO-ECONOMIC** SITUATION OF MEXICAN-AMERICANS, NEGROES AND
     ANGLO-CAUCASIANS IN LOS-ANGELES COUNTY. /CALIFORNIA/   CLOSACH65708

     SOCIO-ECONOMIC DIFFERENTIALS AMONG NONWHITE RACES. /NEGRO ORIENTAL AMERICAN-INDIAN/   CSCHMCF65107

     RACE AND **SOCIO-ECONOMIC** STATUS IN MUNICIPAL PERSONNEL SELECTION.   GBIANJC67590

     THE **SOCIO-ECONOMIC** AND PHYSICAL CHARACTERISTICS OF THE VARIOUS NEIGHBORHOODS IN PUEBLO. /COLORADO/ GPUEBRP65459

     SOCIAL DEVELOPMENT. KEY TO THE GREAT SOCIETY. /**SOCIO-ECONOMIC** WELFARE/   GUSDHEW66639

     SPANISH-SPEAKING AND ENGLISH SPEAKING CHILDREN IN SOUTHWEST TEXAS. A COMPARATIVE STUDY OF INTELLIGENCE,
     SOCIO-ECONOMIC STATUS. AND ACHIEVEMENT.   MRATLYX60460

     DIFFERENTIAL SELECTION AMONG APPLICANTS FROM DIFFERENT **SOCIO-ECONOMIC** AND ETHNIC BACKGROUNDS.   NBARRRS65056

     SOCIO-ECONOMIC CLASS AND AREA AS CORRELATES OF ILLEGAL BEHAVIOR AMONG JUVENILES.   NCLARJP62209

     CHARACTERISTICS OF THE LOWER-BLUE-COLLAR CLASS.**SOCIO-ECONOMIC**/   NCOHEAK63219

     SOCIAL-STRUCTURE AND THE NEGRO REVOLT. AN EXAMINATION OF SOME HYPOTHESES. /**SOCIO-ECONOMIC**/   NGESCJA64400

     THE **SOCIO-ECONOMIC** BACKGROUND OF NEGRO HEALTH STATUS.   NJOHNCS49616

     THE **SOCIO-ECONOMIC** ADJUSTMENT OF THE NEGRO IN SEATTLE BETWEEN 1940 AND 1950. /WASHINGTON/   NKENNTH54273

     THE IMPACT OF **SOCIO-ECONOMIC** CHANGE ON RACIAL GROUPS IN A RURAL SETTING.   NPELLRJ62981

SOCIO-ECONOMIC   (CONTINUATION)
DISTANCE OF MIGRATION AND **SOCIO-ECONOMIC** STATUS OF MIGRANTS.   NROSEAM58291

SOME ASPECTS OF VOCATIONAL ASPIRATIONS AND VALUE ORIENTATION AMONG NEGRO BOYS IN THE LOWER **SOCIO-ECONOMIC**
CLASSES.   NSCHPWX63139

COMPARATIVE STUDY OF **SOCIO-ECONOMIC** AND SOCIAL-PSYCHOLOGICAL DETERMINANTS OF EDUCATIONAL AND OCCUPATIONAL
ASPIRATIONS OF NEGRO AND WHITE COLLEGE SENIORS.   NWHITRM59319

TWENTY THOUSAND NURSES TELL THEIR STORY. /**SOCIO-ECONOMIC**/   WHUGHEC58851

A PILOT STUDY OF THE MOTIVATIONS AND PROBLEMS OF MIDDLE AGED HOMEMAKERS IN LOWER **SOCIO-ECONOMIC** GROUPS IN
SEEKING EMPLOYMENT. /ASPIRATIONS/   WJEWIVA62883

SOCIOECONOMIC
RELATIVE **SOCIOECONOMIC** STATUS OF SOUTHERN WHITES AND NONWHITES, 1950 AND 1960.   GCOWHJD64615

SOCIOECONOMIC DIFFERENCES BETWEEN WHITE AND NONWHITE FARM POPULATIONS IN THE SOUTH.   GCOWHJD64616

SOCIOLOGICAL
SOME **SOCIOLOGICAL** ROOTS OF VOCATIONAL CHOICES.   GYOUNME46593

ON DESEGREGATION AND MATTERS **SOCIOLOGICAL**. /ECONOMIC-STATUS/   NCAMPEQ61909

SOCIOLOGICAL PERSPECTIVES IN UNEMPLOYMENT RESEARCH.   NFERMLA64353

A **SOCIOLOGICAL** INTERPRETATION OF SOCIAL CHANGE IN THE SOUTH.   NHEBERX46508

SOME PERSONAL AND **SOCIOLOGICAL** VARIABLES ASSOCIATED WITH OCCUPATIONAL-CHOICES OF NEGRO YOUTH.   NHERSPF65520

RACE-RELATIONS AND THE **SOCIOLOGICAL** IMAGINATION.   NHUGHEC63585

A **SOCIOLOGICAL** ANALYSIS OF A BI-RACIAL LOCAL LABOR UNION.   NMERCJJ56768

SOME **SOCIOLOGICAL** ASPECTS OF VOCATIONAL GUIDANCE OF NEGRO CHILDREN.   NYOUNMN44348

NURSING PROFESSION. FIVE **SOCIOLOGICAL** SURVEYS.   WDAVIFX66722

PSYCHOLOGICAL AND **SOCIOLOGICAL** FACTORS IN PREDICTION OF CAREER PATTERNS OF WOMEN. /ASPIRATIONS/   WMULVMC61080

PSYCHOLOGICAL AND **SOCIOLOGICAL** FACTORS IN PREDICTION OF CAREER PATTERNS FOR WOMEN. /ASPIRATIONS/   WMULVMC63006

SOCIOLOGY
MAN, WORK AND SOCIETY. A READER IN THE **SOCIOLOGY** OF OCCUPATIONS.   GNOSOSX62336

AMERICAN MINORITY RELATIONS. THE **SOCIOLOGY** OF RACE AND ETHNIC GROUPS.   GVANDJW63535

RACIAL DISCRIMINATION IN THE FEDERAL SERVICE. A STUDY IN THE **SOCIOLOGY** OF ADMINISTRATION.   NBRADWC53106

SOCIOLOGY OF EMANCIPATION.   NCOLLHX65491

THE STATUS OF WOMEN IN PROFESSIONAL **SOCIOLOGY**. /OCCUPATIONS/   WFAVASF60757

SOLDIER
THE INEFFECTIVE **SOLDIER**. LESSONS FOR MANAGEMENT AND THE NATION.   NGINZEX59406

SOLUTION
RECOGNITION OF DISCRIMINATION -- A **SOLUTION**.   GBLOCHD58456

THE PROBLEMS OF CULTURAL BIAS IN SELECTION. POSSIBLE **SOLUTION** TO THE PROBLEM OF CULTURAL BIAS IN TESTS.   NKRUGRE64731

SOLUTIONS
PSYCHOLOGICAL TESTING. SOME PROBLEMS AND **SOLUTIONS**. /INDUSTRY/   GFRENWL66101

POSSIBLE **SOLUTIONS** TO THE PROBLEM OF CULTURAL BIAS IN TESTS.   GKRUGRE64946

SOLVING
SOLVING AN AMERICAN DILEMMA. THE ROLE OF THE FEPC OFFICIAL, A COMPARATIVE STUDY OF STATE CIVIL-RIGHTS
COMMISSIONS.   GLLOYKM64317

IN SEARCH OF A FUTURE. A STUDY OF CAREER-SEEKING EXPERIENCES OF SELECTED NEGRO HIGH SCHOOL GRADUATES IN
WASHINGTON-DC WHICH WAS AN EFFORT TO PROVIDE KNOWLEDGE HELPFUL IN **SOLVING** ONE OF THE MOST CRITICAL
PROBLEMS FACING URBAN AMERICA TODAY.   NGRIEES63454

SOLVING RACIAL PROBLEMS IN YOUR PLANT. /INDUSTRY/   NMODEIX45805

SOURCE
THE CIVIL-RIGHTS-ACT OF 1964 -- **SOURCE** AND SCOPE OF CONGRESSIONAL POWER.   GNORTUL65672

THE JAPANESE SOCIAL STRUCTURE AND THE **SOURCE** OF MENTAL STRAINS OF JAPANESE IMMIGRANTS IN THE US.   OIGAXMX57732

PUERTO-RICANS. KEY **SOURCE** OF LABOR.   PNEWYDC56817

INACTIVE NURSES. AN UNTAPPED RECRUITMENT **SOURCE**.   WBARKAE65628

A **SOURCE** FOR COLLEGE FACULTIES. /OCCUPATIONS/   WCLAYFL62691

HEALTH MANPOWER **SOURCE** BOOK. SECTION 2. NURSING PERSONNEL.   WUSDHEW66177

SOURCES
SOURCES AND STRUCTURE OF FAMILY INCOME. /DEMOGRAPHY/   CUSBURC63184

HOW TO RECRUIT MINORITY-GROUP COLLEGE GRADUATES. ITS PROBLEMS, ITS TECHNIQUES, ITS **SOURCES**, ITS
OPPORTUNITIES.   GCALVRX63555

OCCUPATIONAL EMPLOYMENT STATISTICS, **SOURCES** AND DATA.   GGREEHX66627

THE **SOURCES** OF ECONOMIC GROWTH IN THE UNITED-STATES AND THE ALTERNATIVE BEFORE US. /LABOR-FORCE
ECONOMY/   NDENIEF62262

SOURCES OF SATISFACTION IN THE LIVES OF WORKING WOMEN.   WLAURMW61923

NEW **SOURCES** OF COLLEGE TEACHERS. /OCCUPATIONS/   WRILESB61287

SOUTH
NEGROES AND MEXICAN-AMERICANS IN **SOUTH** AND EAST LOS-ANGELES. AN ANALYSIS OF A SPECIAL US CENSUS SURVEY OF
NOVEMBER 1965. /CALIFORNIA/   CCALDIR66168

AMBITIONS EDUCATION IMPROVEMENT PROJECT UNDER WAY IN **SOUTH**.   GAMERCE64370

THE EMERGING RURAL SOUTH. A REGION UNDER CONFRONTATION BY MASS SOCIETY.   GBERTAL66140

MIGRATION OF POPULATION IN THE SOUTH. SITUATION AND PROSPECTS.   GBOWLGK58397

SOCIOECONOMIC DIFFERENCES BETWEEN WHITE AND NONWHITE FARM POPULATIONS IN THE SOUTH.   GCOWHJD64616

THE ATTRACTIVENESS OF THE SOUTH TO WHITES AND NONWHITES. AN ECOLOGICAL STUDY.   GHEERDM63769

SOME GENERAL ASPECTS OF RECENT REGIONAL DEVELOPMENT. /SOUTH/   GHENDJM64142

THE DEEP SOUTH IN TRANSFORMATION.   GHIGHRB65056

THE AMERICAN SOUTH IN THE 1960-S.   GLEISAX64730

ECONOMICS IN THE SOUTH.   GMITCBX57017

SOME NEW EVIDENCE ON EDUCATIONAL SELECTIVITY IN MIGRATION FROM THE SOUTH.   GSUVAEM65345

LEVELS OF LIVING OF SPANISH-AMERICAN RURAL AND URBAN FAMILIES IN TWO SOUTH TEXAS COUNTIES.   MCLEMHM63381

OCCUPATIONAL-PATTERNS OF RURAL AND URBAN SPANISH-AMERICANS IN TWO SOUTH TEXAS COUNTIES.   MCOTHML66385

INCOMES OF RURAL AND URBAN SPANISH-AMERICANS IN TWO SOUTH TEXAS COUNTIES.   MDICKBE65389

THE MEXICAN-AMERICANS OF SOUTH TEXAS.   MMADSWX64436

NEGRO EMPLOYMENT-TRENDS IN THE SOUTH.   NAMERFX53015

THE VANISHING SERVANT AND THE CONTEMPORARY STATUS-SYSTEM OF THE AMERICAN SOUTH.   NANDEAX53022

THE OTHER SIDE OF JORDAN. NEGROES OUTSIDE THE SOUTH.   NASHMHS60033

PERCENT NONWHITE AND DISCRIMINATION IN THE SOUTH.   NBLALHM57085

URBANIZATION AND DISCRIMINATION IN THE SOUTH.   NBLALHM59086

THE FUTURE OF THE COLOR LINE. /SOUTH/   NBLUMHX65327

POPULATION DISTRIBUTION AND COMPOSITION IN THE NEW SOUTH.   NBOGUDJ54102

NON-SEGREGATION. OR QUALITY IN SCHOOLS OF THE DEEP SOUTH. /ECONOMIC-STATUS/   NBRITNX54892

RACE ISSUE AND UNIONS IN THE SOUTH.   NBUSIWX56160

NEW BUSINESS WAYS IN THE SOUTH.   NBUSIWX61158

RACE HATE. NEWEST UNION-BUSTING WEAPON IN THE SOUTH.   NCAREJB58181

THE NEGRO AND EMPLOYMENT-OPPORTUNITIES IN THE SOUTH. CHATTANOOGA REGION. /TENNESSEE/   NCHATCC62197

RECENT SOUTHERN INDUSTRIALIZATION AND ITS IMPLICATIONS FOR NEGROES LIVING IN THE SOUTH.
/EMPLOYMENT-TRENDS/   NCHICCA53204

THE EMERGING SOUTH.   NCLARTD61055

FOUR STUDIES OF NEGRO EMPLOYMENT IN THE UPPER SOUTH.   NDEWEDX55269

A CHRONICLE OF RACE-RELATIONS -- THE UNITED STATES, NORTH AND SOUTH.   NDUBOWE41298

ATTITUDE TOWARD JOB-MOBILITY AMONG HOUSEHOLD HEADS IN LOW-INCOME AREAS OF THE RURAL SOUTH.   NDUNKJX64300

THE RELUCTANT SOUTH. /INTEGRATION/   NFICHJH59464

THE DEEP SOUTH LOOKS UP. /POVERTY EMPLOYMENT/   NFORTXX43050

REVOLT IN THE SOUTH. /UNION DISCRIMINATION/   NFORTXX56881

EDUCATIONAL IMPERATIVE. THE NEGRO IN THE CHANGING SOUTH.   NGOLDFH63429

DESEGREGATION OF SOCIAL AGENCIES IN THE SOUTH.   NGOLDJX65427

SOME CHARACTERISTICS OF STUDENTS FROM POVERTY BACKGROUNDS ATTENDING PREDOMINANTLY NEGRO COLLEGES IN THE
DEEP SOUTH.   NGURIPX66468

EDUCATIONAL SELECTIVITY OF NET MIGRATION FROM THE SOUTH.   NHAMICH59986

THE NEGRO LEAVES THE SOUTH. /DEMOGRAPHY MIGRATION/   NHAMICH64479

A SOCIOLOGICAL INTERPRETATION OF SOCIAL CHANGE IN THE SOUTH.   NHEBERX46508

CHANGES IN THE SOCIAL STRATIFICATION OF THE SOUTH.   NHEBERX56507

ECONOMIC DIMENSIONS. /SOUTH INCOME TECHNOLOGY/   NHENDVW63514

THE ECONOMIC-STATUS OF NEGROES. IN THE NATION AND IN THE SOUTH.   NHENDVW63515

CHANGING STRUCTURES OF WHITE-NEGRO RELATIONS IN THE SOUTH.   NHIMEJS51552

CHANGING SOCIAL-ROLES IN THE NEW SOUTH.   NHIMEJS62998

EFFORTS TO ELIMINATE RACIAL DISCRIMINATION IN INDUSTRY -- WITH PARTICULAR REFERENCE TO THE SOUTH.   NHOPEJX54566

TRENDS IN PATTERNS OF RACE-RELATIONS IN THE SOUTH SINCE MAY 17 1954.   NHOPEJX56575

THE EFFECT OF THE WAR ECONOMY ON THE SOUTH. HOW MOBILIZATION WILL AFFECT POSITION OF THE NEGRO.   NJACKJX51595

GROWING UP IN THE BLACK BELT. NEGRO YOUTH IN THE RURAL SOUTH.   NJOHNCS41611

PRESENT STATUS OF RACE-RELATIONS IN THE SOUTH.   NJOHNCS44615

INTO THE MAINSTREAM. /RACE-RELATIONS SOUTH ECONOMIC-STATUS/   NJOHNCS47007

NEXT STEPS IN EDUCATION IN THE SOUTH.   NJOHNCS54614

NEGRO YOUTH IN THE SOUTH. /EDUCATION EMPLOYMENT/   NJONELW60010

A UNIQUE REGIONAL PROGRAM OF PSYCHOLOGICAL RESEARCH AND TRAINING IN THE SOUTH.   NLANGMC56032

SOUTH   (CONTINUATION)
      INTEGRATION NORTH AND SOUTH.   NLOTHDX56710

      THE SOUTH TODAY AND LABOR-S TASKS.   NMANNCP53737

      SOME FACTORS INFLUENCING THE GROWTH OF UNIONS IN THE SOUTH.   NMARSRX60060

      LABOR IN THE SOUTH. /UNION/   NMARSRX61740

      UNION RACIAL PROBLEMS IN THE SOUTH.   NMARSRX62751

      THE CIO AND THE NEGRO IN THE SOUTH. /UNION/   NMASOJR45323

      TO WIN THESE RIGHTS. A PERSONAL STORY OF THE CIO IN THE SOUTH.   /UNION/   NMASOJR52324

      THE RURAL NEGRO POPULATION OF THE SOUTH IN TRANSITION.   NMAYOSC63762

      THE SOUTH IN CONTINUITY AND CHANGE.   NMCKIJC65726

      PRIVATE BUSINESS AND EDUCATION IN THE SOUTH.   NMILLHH60780

      THE NEGRO AND EMPLOYMENT OPPORTUNITIES IN THE SOUTH.   NMOSSJA62856

      SELECTED STUDIES OF NEGRO EMPLOYMENT IN THE SOUTH.   NNATLPA55881

      THE PLACE OF THE NEGRO FARMER IN THE CHANGING ECONOMY OF THE COTTON SOUTH.   NNEALEE50905

      INDUSTRY COMES OF AGE IN THE SOUTH.   NNOLAEW53926

      TECHNOLOGICAL-CHANGE AND THE SOCIAL ORDER. /SOUTH/   NNOLAEW65927

      DEMOGRAPHIC ASPECTS OF CONTEMPORARY CHANGE. /SOUTH/   NPARRCH63975

      THE PRICE WE PAY FOR DISCRIMINATION. /SOUTH ECONOMY/   NPATTBX64979

      THE NEGRO IN THE INDUSTRIAL DEVELOPMENT OF THE SOUTH.   NRABOSH53029

      URBANIZATION IN THE SOUTH.   NREISLX65049

      THE MARKET FOR NEGRO EDUCATORS IN COLLEGES AND UNIVERSITIES OUTSIDE THE SOUTH.   NROSEHM61076

      OF HUMAN RESOURCES AND THE SOUTH.   NROSSJX50088

      A REVIEW OF RESEARCH ON THE NEGRO AND EMPLOYMENT IN THE SOUTH.   NROWARL65703

      THE NEGRO POLICEMAN IN THE SOUTH. /OCCUPATIONS/   NRUDWEM60095

      NEGRO POLICE EMPLOYMENT IN THE URBAN SOUTH.   NRUDWEM61134

      RACISM STYMIES UNIONS IN THE SOUTH.   NSEGABD57113

      THE CHANGING OCCUPATIONAL STRUCTURE OF THE SOUTH.   NSIMPRL65140

      CHANGES IN THE CONTEMPORARY SOUTH.   NSINDAX64141

      ECONOMIC VALUE OF THE NEGRO TO THE SOUTH. PAST, PRESENT, AND POTENTIAL.   NSOUTRC45158

      THE SOUTH -- AMERICA-S OPPORTUNITY NO 1.   NSOUTRC45164

      HOUSTON -- THE NEGRO AND EMPLOYMENT OPPORTUNITIES IN THE SOUTH, THE FIRST OF A SERIES OF EMPLOYMENT
      STUDIES IN SOUTHERN CITIES. /TEXAS/   NSOUTRC61161

      THE NEGRO AND EMPLOYMENT OPPORTUNITIES IN THE SOUTH.   NSOUTRC62151

      ATLANTA -- THE NEGRO AND EMPLOYMENT OPPORTUNITIES IN THE SOUTH, THE THIRD OF A SERIES OF EMPLOYMENT
      STUDIES IN SOUTHERN CITIES. /GEORGIA/   NSOUTRC62155

      CHATTANOOGA -- THE NEGRO AND EMPLOYMENT OPPORTUNITIES IN THE SOUTH, THE SECOND OF A SERIES OF EMPLOYMENT
      STUDIES IN SOUTHERN CITIES. /TENNESSEE/   NSOUTRC62156

      DEMOGRAPHIC AND ECONOMIC CHANGE IN THE SOUTH, 1940-1960.   NSPENJJ63716

      RACE-RELATIONS IN THE SOUTH, 1963.   NTUSKIX64219

      POVERTY. /SOUTH ANTI-POVERTY/   NULMXAX66712

      LABOR SUPPLY IN THE SOUTH.   NUSDLAB46824

      NEGROES GO NORTH, WEST. JOBS TAKE THEM FAR AFIELD FROM THE SOUTH.   NUSNEWR51272

      IMPACT OF THE RACE ISSUE ON UNIONS IN THE SOUTH.   NUSNEWR56208

      ALL THESE PEOPLE. THE NATION-S HUMAN RESOURCES IN THE SOUTH.   NVANCRB45282

      THE URBAN SOUTH.   NVANCRB54283

      THE IMPACT OF RACE-RELATIONS ON INDUSTRIAL RELATIONS IN THE SOUTH.   NWHEEJH64230

      IMPACT ON THE INDIVIDUAL. /SOCIAL-CHANGE SOUTH/   NWRIGSJ63344

SOUTH-CAROLINA
      CHARACTERISTICS, RESOURCES, AND INCOMES OF RURAL HOUSEHOLDS, PIEDMONT AREA, SOUTH-CAROLINA.   GBURCTA62408

      THE EFFECT OF A CHANGING AGRICULTURAL PATTERN ON NEGRO FARMERS OF SOUTH-CAROLINA.   NHURSRL56253

      NEGRO EMPLOYMENT IN THE TEXTILE INDUSTRIES OF NORTH AND SOUTH-CAROLINA. /NORTH-CAROLINA/   NOSBUDD66963

      A STUDY OF NEGRO FARMERS IN SOUTH-CAROLINA.   NSOUTRC62165

      PERSONAL AND ENVIRONMENTAL OBSTACLES TO PRODUCTION ADJUSTMENTS ON SOUTH-CAROLINA PIEDMONT AREA FARMS.   NTAYLCC58411

SOUTH-S
      MANPOWER RETRAINING IN THE SOUTH-S RURAL POPULATION -- AN OPPORTUNITY FOR DEVELOPMENT.   GBACHFT63413

      SOUTH-S TENSION SEIZES LABOR. /UNION/   NBUSIWX56882

      SOUTH-S RACE DISPUTES INVOLVE BUSINESSMAN.   NBUSIWX60162

      A MORE PRODUCTIVE ROLE FOR THE NEGRO IN THE SOUTH-S ECONOMY.   NCHALWE64912

SOUTH-S   (CONTINUATION)
LABOR DRIVES TO CLOSE THE **SOUTH-S** OPEN-SHOP.   /UNION/   NRONYVX65072

SOUTHEAST
WHITE AND NONWHITE OWNERS OF RURAL LAND IN THE **SOUTHEAST**.   GBOXLRF65418

INCOME-DISTRIBUTION AS A FACTOR IN REGIONAL GROWTH, WITH SPECIAL REFERENCE TO THE **SOUTHEAST** UNITED
STATES. /DISCRIMINATION/   GPHILEW65773

A COMPARISON OF TUITION-AND-FEE CHARGES IN NEGRO INSTITUTIONS WITH CHARGES IN INSTITUTIONS OF THE
SOUTHEAST AND OF THE NATION. 1962-1963.   /EDUCATION/   NDAMILX64127

SOUTHEASTERN
POPULATION AND LABOR-FORCE CHARACTERISTICS OF FIVE **SOUTHEASTERN** PENNSYLVANIA COUNTIES.   GANDEBXND391

SOUTHERN
A NOTE ON THE VALUES OF **SOUTHERN** COLLEGE WOMEN, WHITE AND NEGRO.   CGRAYSW47445

HUMAN CAPITAL AS A **SOUTHERN** RESOURCE.   GCOLBMR63994

HUMAN CAPITAL IN **SOUTHERN** DEVELOPMENT 1939-1963.   GCOLBMR65793

RELATIVE SOCIOECONOMIC STATUS OF **SOUTHERN** WHITES AND NONWHITES, 1950 AND 1960.   GCOWHJD64615

ESSAYS IN **SOUTHERN** ECONOMIC DEVELOPMENT.   GGREEMX64450

CONTINUITY AND CHANGE IN **SOUTHERN** MIGRATION.   /DEMOGRAPHY/   GHAMICH65757

WARTIME EMPLOYMENT PATTERNS OF NONWHITES AND FEMALE WORKERS IN **SOUTHERN** INDUSTRY.   GHOPEJX46485

THE ROLE OF AGRICULTURAL TECHNOLOGY IN **SOUTHERN** SOCIAL CHANGE.   GRAPEAX46037

EMPLOYMENT INTEGRATION AND RACIAL WAGE DIFFERENCE IN A **SOUTHERN** PLANT.   GWEINRX59988

THE **SOUTHERN** LABOR STORY.   /UNION/   NAFLCIO58006

STAFF TRAINING WITH A **SOUTHERN** ACCENT.   NAMERFX65016

LABOR-MOBILITY IN THE **SOUTHERN** STATES.   NASHBBX61032

LABOR AND THE **SOUTHERN** NEGRO.   NBRADCX57107

CORRELATES OF **SOUTHERN** NEGRO PERSONALITY.   NBRAZWF64496

RECENT **SOUTHERN** INDUSTRIALIZATION AND ITS IMPLICATIONS FOR NEGROES LIVING IN THE SOUTH.
/EMPLOYMENT-TRENDS/   NCHICCA53204

THE NEGRO-S CHANGING PLACE IN **SOUTHERN** AGRICULTURE.   NCHRIDE58206

SCHOOL-DESEGREGATION AND NEW INDUSTRY. THE **SOUTHERN** COMMUNITY LEADERS VIEWPOINT.   NCROMRX63243

INTEGRATION IN PROFESSIONAL EDUCATION. THE STORY OF PERKINS, **SOUTHERN** METHODIST UNIVERSITY. /VOCATIONS/ NCUNNMX56579

NEGRO EMPLOYMENT IN **SOUTHERN** INDUSTRY.   NDEWEDX52270

SOUTHERN POVERTY AND THE RACIAL DIVISION-OF-LABOR.   NDEWEDX62271

CASTE AND CLASS IN A **SOUTHERN** TOWN.   NDOLLJX49281

RECENT **SOUTHERN** ECONOMIC DEVELOPMENT.   NDUNNES62308

SOUTHERN ECONOMIC DEVELOPMENT AS REVEALED BY THE CHANGING STRUCTURE OF EMPLOYMENT.   NDUNNES62309

INDUSTRY AND RACE IN THE **SOUTHERN** US.   NEDMOMS65321

NEGROES. VOCATIONAL GUIDANCE AND COUNSELING IN THE **SOUTHERN** FIELD.   NEDWAGL47325

EDUCATIONAL PATTERNS IN **SOUTHERN** MIGRATION.   NFEINRX65348

THE CULTURAL-BACKGROUND OF **SOUTHERN** NEGROES.   NFRAZEF57378

I Q PERFORMANCE, EDUCATIONAL AND OCCUPATIONAL ASPIRATIONS OF YOUTH IN A **SOUTHERN** CITY -- A RACIAL
COMPARISON.   NGEISPX62397

SOUTHERN LABOR FIGHTS BACK.   /UNION/   NGOOGGX48434

UNION RESISTANCE, **SOUTHERN** STYLE.   NGOULHM48436

SOME PERSONALITY CHARACTERISTICS OF **SOUTHERN** NEGRO STUDENTS.   NGROSMM57462

THE USE OF NEGRO LABOR IN **SOUTHERN** INDUSTRY. /OCCUPATIONAL-PATTERNS/   NHALLOE53477

EFFECTS OF AUTOMATION ON THE POSITION OF NEGROES IN A **SOUTHERN** INDUSTRIAL PLANT.   NHARTJW64495

RECENT EFFECTS OF RACIAL CONFLICT ON **SOUTHERN** INDUSTRIAL DEVELOPMENT.   NHILLHX59543

THE ASSESSMENT OF ADJUSTMENT OF AGED NEGRO WOMEN IN A **SOUTHERN** CITY.   NHIMEJX62072

NEGRO EMPLOYMENT IN THREE **SOUTHERN** PLANTS OF INTERNATIONAL HARVESTER COMPANY. /CASE-STUDY/   NHOPEJX55572

EFFORTS OF NEGRO TEACHERS IN THE **SOUTHERN** STATES TO OBTAIN EQUALIZATION OF SALARIES.   NJONEER48343

THE CHANGING STATUS OF THE NEGRO IN **SOUTHERN** AGRICULTURE.   NJONELW50623

THE EFFECTS OF **SOUTHERN** WHITE WORKERS ON RACE-RELATIONS IN NORTHERN PLANTS.   NKILLLM52650

NEGRO COLLEGES. LONG IGNORED, **SOUTHERN** SCHOOLS NOW COURTED BY MAJOR UNIVERSITIES AND FOUNDATIONS.   NLANGEX64304

THE EMPLOYMENT OF NEGROES IN PUBLIC WELFARE IN ELEVEN **SOUTHERN** STATES, 1936-1949. /OCCUPATIONS/   NLARKJR52672

SOME FACTORS INFLUENCING THE UPGRADING OF NEGROES IN THE **SOUTHERN** PETROLEUM REFINING INDUSTRY.
/CASE-STUDY/   NMARSRX63748

INDUSTRIALIZATION AND RACE-RELATIONS IN THE **SOUTHERN** US.   NMARSRX65739

SOUTHERN RACIAL ATTITUDES. CONFLICT, AWARENESS AND POLITICAL CHANGE.   NMATTDR62758

SOUTHERN NEGRO. 1952.   NNATIXX52873

SOUTHERN   (CONTINUATION)
SOUTHERN TRADITION AND REGIONAL PROGRESS.   NNICHWH60322

THE NEGRO IN SOUTHERN AGRICULTURE.   NPERLVX53982

WASTE OF MANPOWER -- RACE AND EMPLOYMENT IN A SOUTHERN STATE.   NROBEGX62064

NEGRO LABOR IN THE SOUTHERN CRYSTAL BALL. /EMPLOYMENT/   NRUTHKX49100

HOUSTON -- THE NEGRO AND EMPLOYMENT OPPORTUNITIES IN THE SOUTH, THE FIRST OF A SERIES OF EMPLOYMENT
STUDIES IN SOUTHERN CITIES. /TEXAS/   NSOUTRC61161

ATLANTA -- THE NEGRO AND EMPLOYMENT OPPORTUNITIES IN THE SOUTH, THE THIRD OF A SERIES OF EMPLOYMENT
STUDIES IN SOUTHERN CITIES. /GEORGIA/   NSOUTRC62155

CHATTANOOGA -- THE NEGRO AND EMPLOYMENT OPPORTUNITIES IN THE SOUTH, THE SECOND OF A SERIES OF EMPLOYMENT
STUDIES IN SOUTHERN CITIES. /TENNESSEE/   NSOUTRC62156

RACIAL WORK AND NEGRO WASTE IN SOUTHERN EMPLOYMENT.   NSOUTRC62300

SOUTHERN CITIES EMPLOYING NEGRO POLICEMEN -- INCLUDING NORTH-CAROLINA CITIES OVER 15,000 POPULATION.   NSTEEDL46173

SOUTHERN UNIONS AND THE INTEGRATION ISSUE.   NTREWHL56207

LAND TENURE IN THE SOUTHERN REGION. PROCEEDINGS OF PROFESSIONAL AGRICULTURAL WORKERS TENTH ANNUAL
CONFERENCE.   NTUSKIX51218

ENHANCING THE OCCUPATIONAL OUTLOOK AND VOCATIONAL ASPIRATIONS OF SOUTHERN SECONDARY YOUTH. A CONFERENCE
OF SECONDARY SCHOOL PRINCIPALS AND COUNSELORS.   NUSDLA865334

EMPLOYMENT INTEGRATION AND WAGE DIFFERENCES IN A SOUTHERN PLANT.   NWEINRX59311

THE BURDEN OF SOUTHERN HISTORY.   NWOODCV60061

SOUTHERN RACE PROGRESS. THE WAVERING COLOR LINE.   NWOOFTJ57340

NEGRO ENTREPRENEURSHIP IN SOUTHERN ECONOMIC DEVELOPMENT.   NYOUNHB64346

THE CHANGING STATUS OF THE SOUTHERN WOMAN. /WORK-WOMAN-ROLE/   WJOHNGG65884

SOUTHWEST
POVERTY IN THE SOUTHWEST. A COMPARATIVE STUDY OF MEXICAN-AMERICAN, NONWHITE AND ANGLO FAMILIES. /NEGRO/   CMITTFG66777

INDIANS OF THE SOUTHWEST.   IATKIMJ63529

SPANISH-AMERICANS OF THE SOUTHWEST.   MCLAPRF66112

EDUCATION AND INCOME OF MEXICAN-AMERICANS IN THE SOUTHWEST.   MFOGEWX65393

SPANISH-AMERICANS OF THE SOUTHWEST. LIFE-STYLE PATTERNS AND THEIR IMPLICATIONS.   MHAYDRG66114

DISTRIBUTION OF SPANISH-NAME PEOPLE IN THE SOUTHWEST. TABLES AND MAP.   MHOLLSX56417

THE SOUTHWEST. OLD AND NEW.   MHOLLWE61418

RESIDENTIAL SEGREGATION IN THE URBAN SOUTHWEST.   MMOORJW66444

MIGRATION TO SOUTHWEST TEXAS. PEOPLES AND WORDS.   MNORMAX56448

SPANISH-SPEAKING AND ENGLISH SPEAKING CHILDREN IN SOUTHWEST TEXAS. A COMPARATIVE STUDY OF INTELLIGENCE,
SOCIO-ECONOMIC STATUS, AND ACHIEVEMENT.   MRATLYX60460

THE EDUCATION OF THE SPANISH-SPEAKING IN THE SOUTHWEST -- AN ANALYSIS OF THE 1960 CENSUS MATERIALS.   MSAMOJX63469

THE SPANISH-SPEAKING PEOPLE OF THE SOUTHWEST.   MSAUNLX58480

SOCIAL AND ATTITUDINAL CHARACTERISTICS OF SPANISH-SPEAKING MIGRANT AND EX-MIGRANT WORKERS IN THE
SOUTHWEST.   MULIBHX66503

SOUTHWESTERN
PERSONS OF SPANISH-SURNAME. SOCIAL AND ECONOMIC DATA FOR WHITE PERSONS OF SPANISH SURNAME IN 5
SOUTHWESTERN STATES. /DEMOGRAPHY/   CUSBURC63181

HIGHER EDUCATION OF SOUTHWESTERN INDIANS WITH REFERENCE TO SUCCESS AND FAILURE.   IMCGRGD62584

THE MEXICAN IMMIGRANT WORKER IN SOUTHWESTERN AGRICULTURE.   MTHOMAN56501

THE CONCENTRATION OF SPANISH-SURNAME POPULATION IN THE FIVE SOUTHWESTERN STATES.   MUSCCMC62505

SPANIARD
APACHE. NAVAHO. AND SPANIARD. /MEXICAN-AMERICAN AMERICAN-INDIAN/   CFORBJX60561

SPANISH
PERSONS OF SPANISH-SURNAME. SOCIAL AND ECONOMIC DATA FOR WHITE PERSONS OF SPANISH SURNAME IN 5
SOUTHWESTERN STATES. /DEMOGRAPHY/   CUSBURC63181

CALIFORNIANS OF SPANISH SURNAME. POPULATION, EMPLOYMENT, INCOME, EDUCATION.   MCALDIR64377

THE SOCIAL ASPIRATIONS OF A SELECTED GROUP OF SPANISH NAME PEOPLE IN LAREDO, TEXAS.   MGUERIX59409

CONTRASTS BETWEEN SPANISH FOLK AND ANGLO URBAN CULTURAL VALUES. /EDUCATION ASPIRATIONS/   MVALDBX64449

SPANISH SPEAKING WORKERS AND THE LABOR MOVEMENT.   PASSPCT56779

REPORT FROM A SPANISH HARLEM FORTRESS.   PHAMMRX64153

SPANISH HARLEM. AN ANATOMY OF POVERTY.   PSEXTPC65853

ISLAND IN THE CITY. THE WORLD OF SPANISH HARLEM.   PWAKEDX59858

SPANISH-AMERICAN
ECONOMIC. SOCIAL. AND DEMOGRAPHIC CHARACTERISTICS OF SPANISH-AMERICAN WAGE WORKERS ON US FARMS.
/PUERTO-RICAN MEXICAN-AMERICAN/   CFRIERE63805

CULTURAL DIFFERENCES IN AMERICAN ETHNIC GROUPS. BIBLIOGRAPHY. /AMERICAN-INDIAN NEGRO SPANISH-AMERICAN/   CLIBRCX64899

LEVELS OF LIVING OF SPANISH-AMERICAN RURAL AND URBAN FAMILIES IN TWO SOUTH TEXAS COUNTIES.   MCLEMHM63381

ECONOMIC. SOCIAL AND DEMOGRAPHIC CHARACTERISTICS OF SPANISH-AMERICAN WAGE WORKERS ON US FARMS.   MFRIERE63394

SPANISH-AMERICAN   (CONTINUATION)
  BASIC NEEDS OF SPANISH-AMERICAN FARM FAMILIES IN NEW-MEXICO.   MGRISGXND408

SPANISH-AMERICANS
  THE CIVIL-RIGHTS SITUATION OF MEXICAN-AMERICANS AND SPANISH-AMERICANS.   MBURMJH61370

  SPANISH-AMERICANS OF THE SOUTHWEST.   MCLAPRF66112

  OCCUPATIONAL-PATTERNS OF RURAL AND URBAN SPANISH-AMERICANS IN TWO SOUTH TEXAS COUNTIES.   MCOTHML66385

  INCOMES OF RURAL AND URBAN SPANISH-AMERICANS IN TWO SOUTH TEXAS COUNTIES.   MDICKBE65389

  SPANISH-AMERICANS OF THE SOUTHWEST. LIFE-STYLE PATTERNS AND THEIR IMPLICATIONS.   MHAYDRG66114

  SPANISH-AMERICANS.   MHOYEHC64419

  THE SPANISH-AMERICANS IN NEW-MEXICO.   MKNOWCS61424

  PATRON-PEON PATTERN AMONG THE SPANISH-AMERICANS OF NEW-MEXICO.   MKNOWCS66423

  OCCUPATION-PATTERNS OF SPANISH-AMERICANS IN SELECTED AREAS OF TEXAS.   MSKRARL62494

  SPANISH-AMERICANS RAISING EDUCATIONAL SIGHTS.   MSKRARL65493

  OCCUPATIONAL CHANGE AMONG SPANISH-AMERICANS IN ATASCOSA-COUNTY AND SAN-ANTONIO, TEXAS.   MSKRARL66492

  POVERTY AMONG SPANISH-AMERICANS IN TEXAS. LOW-INCOME FAMILIES IN A MINORITY-GROUP.   MUPHAWK66511

SPANISH-NAME
  DISTRIBUTION OF SPANISH-NAME PEOPLE IN THE SOUTHWEST. TABLES AND MAP.   MHOLLSX56417

  SOME CHARACTERISTICS OF SPANISH-NAME TEXANS AND FOREIGN LATIN-AMERICANS IN TEXAS HIGHER EDUCATION.   MRENNRR57462

SPANISH-SPEAKING
  SPANISH-SPEAKING AMERICANS. MEXICANS AND PUERTO-RICANS IN THE UNITED STATES.   CBLAIBX59366

  SPANISH-SPEAKING CHILDREN. /MEXICAN-AMERICAN PUERTO-RICAN EDUCATION/   CBURMJH60287

  THE PUSH OF AN ELBOW. CIVIL-RIGHTS AND OUR SPANISH-SPEAKING MINORITY. /MEXICAN-AMERICAN PUERTO-RICAN/   CBURMJH60371

  THE SPANISH-SPEAKING PEOPLE IN THE UNITED STATES. /PUERTO-RICAN MEXICAN-AMERICAN/   CRUBIEBND848

  SPANISH-SPEAKING PEOPLE IN THE UNITED STATES. A PILOT REPORT. /MEXICAN-AMERICAN PUERTO-RICAN/   CSAMOJX63474

  SPANISH-SPEAKING AND ENGLISH SPEAKING CHILDREN IN SOUTHWEST TEXAS. A COMPARATIVE STUDY OF INTELLIGENCE,
  SOCIO-ECONOMIC STATUS, AND ACHIEVEMENT.   MRATLYX60460

  THE SPANISH-SPEAKING PEOPLE IN THE UNITED STATES.   MSAMOJX62473

  THE EDUCATION OF THE SPANISH-SPEAKING IN THE SOUTHWEST -- AN ANALYSIS OF THE 1960 CENSUS MATERIALS.   MSAMCJX63469

  THE GENERAL STATUS OF THE SPANISH-SPEAKING PEOPLE IN THE UNITED STATES.   MSAMOJX63471

  THE SPANISH-SPEAKING PEOPLE IN AMERICAN SOCIETY.   MSAMOJX64472

  SPANISH-SPEAKING PEOPLES.   MSAMOJX64475

  MATERIALS RELATING TO THE EDUCATION OF SPANISH-SPEAKING PEOPLE IN THE UNITED STATES. AN ANNOTATED
  BIBLIOGRAPHY.   MSANCGI59478

  THE SPANISH-SPEAKING PEOPLE OF THE SOUTHWEST.   MSAUNLX58480

  CHANGES IN PUBLIC AND PRIVATE LANGUAGE AMONG SPANISH-SPEAKING MIGRANTS TO AN INDUSTRIAL CITY.   MSCHETJ65481

  SOCIAL AND ATTITUDINAL CHARACTERISTICS OF SPANISH-SPEAKING MIGRANT AND EX-MIGRANT WORKERS IN THE
  SOUTHWEST.   MULIBHX66503

SPANISH-SURNAME
  PERSONS OF SPANISH-SURNAME. SOCIAL AND ECONOMIC DATA FOR WHITE PERSONS OF SPANISH SURNAME IN 5
  SOUTHWESTERN STATES. /DEMOGRAPHY/   CUSBURC63181

  THE SPANISH-SURNAME POPULATION OF TEXAS.   MBROWHL64286

  A STATISTICAL PROFILE OF THE SPANISH-SURNAME POPULATION OF TEXAS.   MBROWHL64368

  THE CONCENTRATION OF SPANISH-SURNAME POPULATION IN THE FIVE SOUTHWESTERN STATES.   MUSCOMC62505

SPEAKING
  PLACEMENT OF NON-ENGLISH SPEAKING APPLICANTS.   GWATSMMND544

  SPANISH-SPEAKING AND ENGLISH SPEAKING CHILDREN IN SOUTHWEST TEXAS. A COMPARATIVE STUDY OF INTELLIGENCE,
  SOCIO-ECONOMIC STATUS, AND ACHIEVEMENT.   MRATLYX60460

  STRICTLY SPEAKING. /EMPLOYMENT/   NLONGMX62048

  SPANISH SPEAKING WORKERS AND THE LABOR MOVEMENT.   PASSPCT56779

  SPEAKING FOR THE WORKING CLASS WIFE. /BLUE-COLLAR/   WSEXTPC62299

SPECIAL
  NEGROES AND MEXICAN-AMERICANS IN SOUTH AND EAST LOS-ANGELES. AN ANALYSIS OF A SPECIAL US CENSUS SURVEY OF
  NOVEMBER 1965. /CALIFORNIA/   CCALDIR66168

  SIGNIFICANT TRENDS IN THE NEW-YORK STATE ECONOMY, WITH SPECIAL REFERENCE TO MINORITY-GROUPS.
  /PUERTO-RICAN NEGRO/   CRUSSVR59482

  CURRENT POPULATION REPORTS -- SPECIAL CENSUS OF CLEVELAND, OHIO. /DEMOGRAPHY/   CUSBURC65379

  HUMAN CAPITAL. A THEORETICAL AND EMPIRICAL ANALYSIS WITH SPECIAL REFERENCE TO EDUCATION.   GBECKGS64700

  A SPECIAL REPORT -- THE EQUAL-EMPLOYMENT-OPPORTUNITY LAW, TITLE-VII OF THE CIVIL-RIGHTS-ACT OF 1964.   GBURENAND495

  TEXTS OF RULES AND REGULATIONS OF PRESIDENT-S COMMITTEE ON EQUAL-EMPLOYMENT-OPPORTUNITY RELATING TO
  OBLIGATIONS OF GOVERNMENT CONTRACTORS AND SUBCONTRACTORS, EFFECTIVE JULY 22, 1961. A BNA SPECIAL REPORT.   GBURENA61498

  AFFIRMATIVE-ACTIONS IN EMPLOYMENT. A SPECIAL FEPC REPORT. /CALIFORNIA/   GCALFEP65529

  SPECIAL REPORT ON EMPLOYMENT OPPORTUNITIES IN ILLINOIS.   GILLIIR48801

SPECIAL   (CONTINUATION)
SPECIAL REPORT. AN INVESTIGATION OF THE PERSONNEL POLICIES AND PRACTICES OF THE MICHIGAN STATE HIGHWAY
DEPARTMENT. MARCH 1961.   GMICFEP61983

SPECIAL ASSIMILATION PROBLEMS OF UNDERPRIVILEGED IMMIGRANTS TO PHILADELPHIA. /PENNSYLVANIA/   GPENNEL62502

REPORT OF THE SPECIAL COMMITTEE CN NCNDISCRIMINATION OF THE BOARD OF PUBLIC EDUCATION, PHILADELPHIA.
/PENNSYLVANIA/   GPHILBE64172

A SPECIAL REPORT. CITY CONTRACT COMPLIANCE. PROGRESS IN 1963. /PHILADELPHIA PENNSYLVANIA/   GPHILCH64179

INCOME-DISTRIBUTION AS A FACTOR IN REGIONAL GROWTH, WITH SPECIAL REFERENCE TO THE SOUTHEAST UNITED
STATES. /DISCRIMINATION/   GPHILEW65773

THE FIRST NINE MONTHS -- SPECIAL YEAR-END REPORT, APRIL 7, 1961-JANUARY 15, 1962, PRESIDENT-S COMMITTEE
CN EQUAL-EMPLOYMENT-OPPORTUNITY.   GPRESCD62108

YOUNG WORKERS. THEIR SPECIAL TRAINING NEEDS.   GUSDLAB63506

UTILIZING OUR MANPOWER RESOURCES. SPECIAL APPLICANT GROUPS.   GUSDLAB63665

DOORWAY TOWARD THE LIGHT. THE STORY OF THE SPECIAL NAVAJO EDUCATION PROGRAM.   ICOOMLM62646

TRANSCRIPT OF PROCEEDINGS OF THE INTERIM SUBCOMMITTEE ON SPECIAL EMPLOYMENT PROBLEMS. /CALIFORNIA/   MCALAIC64374

THE MANAGEMENT OF RACIAL INTEGRATION IN BUSINESS, A SPECIAL REPORT TO MANAGEMENT.   NALEXRD64868

POVERTY. THE SPECIAL CASE OF THE NEGRO.   NBATCAB65061

EQUAL JUSTICE IN AN UNEQUAL WORLD. EQUALITY FOR THE NEGRO -- THE PROBLEM OF SPECIAL TREATMENT.   NKAPLJX66645

LOUISVILLE. SPECIAL REPORT. /CASE-STUDY KENTUCKY/   NMUSEBX64868

MEMPHIS. SPECIAL REPORT. /CASE-STUDY/   NMUSEBX64869

SPECIAL PROBLEMS OF NEGRO MIGRATION DURING THE WAR.   NREIDID47362

THE EFFECT OF SPECIAL INSTRUCTION UPON TEST PERFORMANCE OF HIGH SCHOOL STUDENTS IN TENNESSEE.   NROBESO66961

SPECIAL ISSUE ON EQUAL-EMPLOYMENT.   NUSGESA63266

SPECIAL REPORT. A SURVEY OF NEGROES EMPLOYED BY THE STATE OF WEST-VIRGINIA.   NVIRGHR64318

POVERTY AREAS OF OUR MAJOR CITIES. THE EMPLOYMENT SITUATION OF NEGRO AND WHITE WORKERS IN METROPOLITAN
AREAS COMPARED IN A SPECIAL LABOR-FORCE REPORT.   NWETZJR66114

SPECIAL WOMEN-S COLLECTIONS IN US LIBRARIES.   WBELLMS59636

WOMEN AND HIGHER EDUCATION WITH SPECIAL REFERENCE TO THE UNIVERSITY OF WISCONSIN.   WFREDEB62768

SPECIAL SUPPLEMENT ON THE AMERICAN FEMALE. /WORK-WOMAN-ROLE/   WHARPXX62822

A SURVEY OF SPECIAL EDUCATIONAL PROGRAMS FOR ADULT WOMEN IN UNIVERSITY EXTENSION DIVISIONS AND EVENING
COLLEGES AS CF SPRING 1965.   WLORIRK66942

AUTOMATION AND EMPLOYMENT OPPORTUNITIES FOR OFFICE WORKERS. THE EFFECT OF ELECTRONIC COMPUTERS ON
EMPLOYMENT OF CLERICAL WORKERS, WITH A SPECIAL REPORT ON PROGRAMMERS.   WPASCWX58178

DIGEST OF STATE LEGISLATION OF SPECIAL INTEREST TO WOMEN WORKERS.   WUSDLABND191

SPECIAL-TRAINING-UNI
ON SPECIAL-TRAINING-UNIT PERFORMANCE AS AN INDEX OF NEGRO ABILITY.   NERICRW46339

SPECIFICATIONS
EMPLOYER SPECIFICATIONS FOR DEFENSE WORKERS.   NUSDLAB41244

SPEECH
SECRETARIAL TRAINING WITH SPEECH IMPROVEMENT. AN EXPERIMENTAL AND DEMONSTRATION PROJECT. /NEGRO WOMEN/   CSAINMD66320

SPEECH ABOUT JOB OPPORTUNITIES FOR GIRLS BEFORE THE MARYLAND STATE PERSONNEL AND GUIDANCE ASSOCIATION.   WTERLRX64148

SPOKANE
ASSIMILATION OF THE SPOKANE INDIANS. /WASHINGTON/   IROYXPX61612

THE MEASUREMENT CF ASSIMILATION. THE SPOKANE INDIANS. /WASHINGTON/   IROYXPX66613

ASSIMILATION OF THE SPOKANE INDIANS. /WASHINGTON/   ISTONCX62626

SPONSORSHIP
THE NEGRO UNION OFFICIAL. A STUDY OF SPONSORSHIP AND CONTROL.   NKORNWA52661

ST-LOUIS
INCOME. EDUCATION AND UNEMPLOYMENT IN NEIGHBORHOODS. ST-LOUIS, MISSOURI. /DEMOGRAPHY/   CUSDLAB63481

FINAL REPORT. THE YOUTH TRAINING PROJECT, SEPTEMBER 1, 1963--JANUARY 31, 1965. /ST-LOUIS MISSOURI
TESTING/   GJEWIEV65568

THEY DID IT IN ST-LOUIS. /INDUSTRY INTEGRATION MISSOURI/   GROSSMX47262

SUB-EMPLOYMENT IN THE SLUMS OF ST-LOUIS. /MISSOURI/   GUSDLAB66517

THE NEGRO IN THE ST-LOUIS ECONOMY. /MISSOURI/   NSOBEIX54178

ST-PAUL
INCOME. EDUCATION AND UNEMPLOYMENT IN NEIGHBORHOODS. MINNEAPOLIS -- ST-PAUL, MINNESOTA. /DEMOGRAPHY/   CUSDLAB63468

REPORT OF TWIN-CITIES EQUAL-OPPORTUNITY REVIEW. /MINNEAPOLIS ST-PAUL MINNESOTA/   GUSCISC64131

ST-PETERSBURG
INCOME. EDUCATION AND UNEMPLOYMENT IN NEIGHBORHOODS. TAMPA, ST-PETERSBURG FLORIDA. /DEMOGRAPHY/   CUSDLAB63486

STABILITY
THE QUESTS FOR ECONOMIC STABILITY AND EQUAL-EMPLOYMENT-OPPORTUNITY.   GBRIMAF66475

STABILIZATION
FARM MECHANIZATION AND LABOR STABILIZATION. PART II IN A SERIES ON TECHNOLOGICAL-CHANGE AND FARM LABOR
USE, KERN COUNTY, CALIFORNIA, 1961. /NEGRO MEXICAN-AMERICAN/   CMETZWH65389

CHARACTERISTICS OF FARM WORKERS AS RELATED TO STABILIZATION OF THE WORK FORCE. /MIGRANT-WORKERS/   GMETZWH62504

STAFF

ADDRESS TO COMMUNITY RELATIONS SERVICE **STAFF** TRAINING SESSION, JANUARY 12, 1967, ON JOBS NOW.   /NEGRO PUERTO-RICAN YOUTH/ — CCOLEBX67918

STAFF TRAINING WITH A SOUTHERN ACCENT. — NAMERFX65016

A PRELIMINARY REPORT ON MEDICAL **STAFF** APPOINTMENTS HELD BY NEGRO PHYSICIANS AT PREDOMINANTLY WHITE HOSPITALS. /CHICAGO ILLINOIS/ — NCHICC060201

STANDARD

MEXICAN-AMERICAN AND TOTAL EMPLOYMENT IN SELECTED STATES AND **STANDARD** METROPOLITAN STATISTICAL AREAS. — MUSCISC63504

MIGRATION AND OPPORTUNITY. A STUDY OF **STANDARD** METROPOLITAN AREAS IN THE UNITED-STATES. — NBALATR63047

AN ECONOMICAL AND HISTORICAL ANALYSIS OF THE CAUSES OF VARIATION AMONG NORTHERN **STANDARD** METROPOLITAN AREAS IN PRODUCTIVITY OF NEGRO MEN IN 1949. — NBATCAB61060

STANDARDS

CONTRACTOR GROUP HITS REVISED EQUAL EMPLOYMENT **STANDARDS**. — GAIRCHR63866

HIRING PROCEDURES AND SELECTION **STANDARDS** IN THE SAN-FRANCISCO BAY AREA. /CALIFORNIA/ — GMALMTF55934

EQUAL-EMPLOYMENT-OPPORTUNITY. SHOULD HIRING **STANDARDS** BE RELAXED. — GMAYFHX64968

HOUSING FOR MIGRANT AGRICULTURAL WORKERS. LABOR CAMP **STANDARDS**. — GUSDLAB62508

PROFESSIONAL **STANDARDS** AND ECONOMIC-STATUS OF NURSES IN THE UNITED STATES. — WKRUGDH60917

STANDING-ROCK

FAMILY PLAN AND REHABILITATION PROGRAMS, **STANDING-ROCK** RESERVATION. — IUSDINT64649

STATE

REPORT TO GOVERNOR EDMUND G BROWN. SECOND ETHNIC SURVEY OF EMPLOYMENT AND PROMOTION IN **STATE** GOVERNMENT. /CALIFORNIA NEGRO MEXICAN-AMERICAN/ — CBECKWL65070

NEGROES AND MEXICAN-AMERICANS IN THE CALIFORNIA **STATE** GOVERNMENT, A COOPERATIVE PROJECT. — CCALOGB65171

THE SCHOOL DROPOUT PROBLEM IN MAJOR CITIES OF NEW-YORK **STATE**. ROCHESTER -- PART I. /NEGRO PUERTO-RICAN/ — CNEWYSD62090

THE MIGRANT LABOR PROBLEM -- ITS **STATE** AND INTERSTATE ASPECTS. /NEGRO MEXICAN-AMERICAN/ — CPALEHA63098

SIGNIFICANT TRENDS IN THE NEW-YORK **STATE** ECONOMY, WITH SPECIAL REFERENCE TO MINORITY-GROUPS. /PUERTO-RICAN NEGRO/ — CRUSSVR59482

MOBILITY FOR STATES AND **STATE** ECONOMIC AREAS. /DEMOGRAPHY/ — CUSBURC63174

STATE OF BIRTH. /DEMOGRAPHY/ — CUSBURC63185

FEPC. AN ADMINISTRATIVE STUDY OF SELECTED **STATE** AND LOCAL PROGRAMS. — GALFOAL54869

STATE FAIR-EMPLOYMENT-PRACTICES-COMMISSIONS -- A SELECTED BIBLIOGRAPHY. — GAMERCR46373

STATE FAIR-EMPLOYMENT-PRACTICES-COMMISSION -- WHAT THE PEOPLE SAY. — GAMERCR47374

EVALUATION OF **STATE** FAIR-EMPLOYMENT-PRACTICES-COMMISSIONS. EXPERIENCES AND FORECASTS. — GAMERCR49371

REPORT ON TWENTY **STATE** ANTI-DISCRIMINATION AGENCIES AND THE LAWS THEY ADMINISTER. — GAMERJD61387

REPORT OF THE CALIFORNIA **STATE** ADVISORY COMMITTEE TO THE UNITED STATES COMMISSION ON CIVIL-RIGHTS ON CALIFORNIA-S PROGRAM FOR EQUAL-OPPORTUNITY IN APPRENTICESHIP. — GBECKWL62432

SECOND ETHNIC SURVEY OF EMPLOYMENT AND PROMOTION IN **STATE** GOVERNMENT. /CALIFORNIA/ — GBECKWL65433

STATE CIVIL-RIGHTS STATUTES. SOME PROPOSALS. — GBONFAE64463

FAIR-EMPLOYMENT LEGISLATION IN NEW-YORK **STATE**. ITS HISTORY, DEVELOPMENT, AND SUGGESTED USE ELSEWHERE. — GBRADPX46247

THE PRESENT STATUS AND PROGRAMS OF FEPC. FEDERAL, **STATE**, AND MUNICIPAL. — GBRAZBR51472

EMPLOYMENT DISCRIMINATION. **STATE** FEPC LAWS AND THE IMPACT OF OF TITLE-VII OF THE CIVIL-RIGHTS-ACT OF 1964. — GBRYEGL65896

STATE FAIR-EMPLOMENT LAWS AND THEIR ADMINISTRATION. TEXTS, FEDERAL-STATE COOPERATION, PROHIBITED ACTS. — GBURENA64497

STATE LAWS DEALING WITH NON-DISCRIMINATION IN EMPLOYMENT. — GBUTCGT63508

MEMORANDUM OF UNDERSTANDING BETWEEN CALIFORNIA **STATE** FAIR- EMPLOYMENT-PRACTICE-COMMISSION AND BANK-OF-AMERICA NATIONAL TRUST AND SAVINGS ASSOCIATION. — GCALFEPND537

EQUAL-OPPORTUNITIES PLAN STRESSED IN **STATE** PERSONNEL BOARD DOCUMENT. /CALIFORNIA/ — GCALSEM64548

ETHNIC CENSUS OF EXAMINATION COMPETITORS, JAN-JUNE 1965, CALIFORNIA **STATE** PERSONNEL BOARD. — GCALSPB65551

OUTLOOK REGARDING **STATE** FEPC LEGISLATION. — GCOBBCW46578

STATE AND LOCAL CONTRACTS AND SUBCONTRACTS. — GCONWJE64599

STATE ORGANIZATION FOR FAIR-EMPLOYMENT-PRACTICES. — GDUFFJX44522

COMMISSION ENFORCEMENT OF **STATE** LAWS AGAINST DISCRIMINATION. A COMPARATIVE ANALYSIS OF THE KANSAS ACT. — GDYSORB65657

FAIR-EMPLOYMENT-PRACTICES ACT. **STATE** LAWS GRANTING EQUAL RIGHTS, PRIVILEGES, ETC. — GELWAEX58662

SOME GENERAL OBSERVATIONS ON THE ADMINISTRATION OF **STATE** FAIR-EMPLOYMENT-PRACTICE LAWS. — GGIRARA64721

FEPC LEGISLATION IN THE UNITED STATES, FEDERAL, **STATE**, MUNICIPAL. — GGRAVWB51735

PUBLIC WELFARE. POVERTY -- PREVENTION OR PERPETUATION. A STUDY OF THE **STATE** DEPARTMENT OF PUBLIC ASSISTANCE OF THE STATE OF WASHINGTON. — GGREEAI64479

PUBLIC WELFARE. POVERTY -- PREVENTION OR PERPETUATION. A STUDY OF THE STATE DEPARTMENT OF PUBLIC ASSISTANCE OF THE **STATE** OF WASHINGTON. — GGREEAI64479

MONEY BENEFITS OF EDUCATION BY SEX AND RACE IN NEW-YORK **STATE**, 1956. — GGREEWX61741

SELECTED **STATE** PROGRAMS IN MIGRANT EDUCATION. — GHANEGE64004

COMPARATIVE ANALYSIS OF **STATE** FAIR-EMPLOYMENT-PRACTICES LAWS. — GHARTPX62762

DEVELOPMENT AND ADMINISTRATION OF THE NEW-YORK **STATE** LAW AGAINST DISCRIMINATION.   GHIGBJX67143

STATE FAIR-EMPLOYMENT-PRACTICE LAWS. REPORT PERSUANT TO PROPOSAL 400.   GILLILC57802

REPORT OF THE SURVEY OF EMPLOYEES OF THE **STATE** OF INDIANA, SEPTEMBER 1961.   GINDICR61806

MANPOWER POLICY, POVERTY AND THE **STATE** OF THE ECONOMY.   GKERSJA66733

MANAGEMENT-S CONCERN WITH RECENT CIVIL-RIGHTS LEGISLATION AFFECTING MANAGEMENT-S OBLIGATIONS TO HIS
EMPLOYEES AND APPLICANTS FOR EMPLOYMENT, MAINLY IN THE **STATE** OF NEW-YORK.   GKOPPRW65858

A REVIEW OF **STATE** FEPC LAWS.   GKOVAIX58860

COMMON CARRIERS AND THE **STATE** FEPC.   GKOVAIX63025

SURVEY OF **STATE** ANTI-DISCRIMINATORY LAWS.   GLABOLR44877

OPERATION UNDER **STATE** FEPC LAWS.   GLABOLR45873

THE EFFECT OF **STATE** FAIR-EMPLOYMENT LEGISLATION ON THE ECONOMIC POSITION OF NONWHITE MALES.   GLANDWM66883

MINORITY-GROUPS AND ECONOMIC-STATUS IN NEW-YORK **STATE**.   GLANGGE59884

EMPLOYMENT DISCRIMINATION. **STATE** FAIR-EMPLOYMENT-PRACTICES LAWS AND THE IMPACT OF TITLE-VII OF THE
CIVIL-RIGHTS-ACT OF 1964.   GLAWXRD65885

DISCRIMINATION IN EMPLOYMENT. FEDERAL AND **STATE** PRACTICES IN ANTI-DISCRIMINATION.   GLEITRD49892

STATE LAWS AGAINST DISCRIMINATION.   GLESKTX61895

SOLVING AN AMERICAN DILEMMA. THE ROLE OF THE FEPC OFFICIAL. A COMPARATIVE STUDY OF **STATE** CIVIL-RIGHTS
COMMISSIONS.   GLLOYKM64317

AN ANALYSIS OF THE EFFECTIVENESS OF THE NEW-YORK **STATE** LAW AGAINST DISCRIMINATION.   GMARPAW53940

FAIR-EMPLOYMENT **STATE** BY STATE.   GMASLWX45960

FAIR-EMPLOYMENT STATE BY **STATE**.   GMASLWX45960

ETHNIC SURVEY OF EMPLOYMENT IN **STATE** GOVERNMENT. /CALIFORNIA/   GMESPFA63977

SPECIAL REPORT. AN INVESTIGATION OF THE PERSONNEL POLICIES AND PRACTICES OF THE MICHIGAN **STATE** HIGHWAY
DEPARTMENT, MARCH 1961.   GMICFEP61983

MINNESOTA **STATE** ACT AGAINST DISCRIMINATION, AS APPROVED BY THE MINNESOTA LEGISLATURE, APRIL 1961.
/LEGISLATION/   GMINNSCND010

AN ANALYSIS OF **STATE** FEPC LEGISLATION.   GMORGCA57031

A MODEL **STATE** FAIR-EMPLOYMENT-PRACTICE BILL.   GNAACNL45036

EVERYBODY-S BUSINESS. A SUMMARY OF NEW-YORK **STATE** ANTI-DISCRIMINATION LAWS AND HOW TO USE THEM.   GNATLFC46048

YOUR RIGHTS... UNDER **STATE** AND LOCAL FAIR-EMPLOYMENT-PRACTICES LAWS.   GNATLLS55051

PATTERNS OF CONCILIATION UNDER THE NEW-YORK **STATE** LAW AGAINST DISCRIMINATION.   GNEWXYL51100

THE NEW-YORK **STATE** COMMISSION AGAINST DISCRIMINATION. A NEW TECHNIQUE FOR AN OLD PROBLEM.   GNEWYSA47107

THE INSURANCE INDUSTRY -- VERIFIED COMPLAINTS AND INFORMAL INVESTIGATIONS HANDLED BY THE NEW-YORK **STATE**
COMMISSION AGAINST DISCRIMINATION, JULY 1 1945-SEPTEMBER 15, 1958.   GNEWYSA58082

RULINGS ON PRE-EMPLOYMENT INQUIRIES RELATING TO RACE, CREED, COLOR OR NATIONAL ORIGIN UNDER THE NEW-YORK
STATE LAW AGAINST DISCRIMINATION.   GNEWYSBND106

REPORT OF INQUIRY CONCERNING CHARGES OF DISCRIMINATING PRACTICES IN THE NEW-YORK **STATE** THRUWAY AUTHORITY.   GNEWYSB64104

EMPLOYMENT AND EARNINGS OF MIGRANT FARM WORKERS IN NEW-YORK **STATE**.   GNEWYSE60110

SUMMARY OF RULES, REGULATIONS, AND LAWS THAT AFFECT SEASONAL FARM WORKERS AND THEIR EMPLOYERS IN NEW-YORK
STATE. /MIGRANT-WORKERS/   GNEWYSJND113

MIGRANT FARM LABOR IN NEW-YORK **STATE**.   GNEWYSJ63112

REPORT OF NEW-YORK **STATE** JOINT LEGISLATIVE COMMITTEE ON MIGRANT-LABOR.   GNEWYSLND115

A HELPING HAND. SEASONAL FARM LABOR IN NEW-YORK **STATE**. /MIGRANT-WORKERS/   GNEWYSX63087

GOVERNMENTAL FAIR-EMPLOYMENT AGENCIES. AN APPRAISAL OF FEDERAL, **STATE**, AND MUNICIPAL EFFORTS TO END JOB
DISCRIMINATION.   GNORGPH62120

SURVEY OF EMPLOYMENT IN **STATE** GOVERNMENT. /NORTH-CAROLINA/   GNORTCG64121

SECOND SURVEY OF NON-WHITE EMPLOYEES IN **STATE** GOVERNMENT IN PENNSYLVANIA.   GPENNHR65167

TITLE-VII. RELATIONSHIP AND EFFECT ON **STATE** ACTION. /LEGISLATION/   GPURDJW66209

COMBATING DISCRIMINATION IN EMPLOYMENT IN NEW-YORK **STATE**.   GRACKFX49215

THE NEW FEDERAL FAIR-EMPLOYMENT-PRACTICES ACT -- COMPARISON WITH **STATE** LAW AND AN ANALYSIS OF RELEVANT
STATE EXPERIENCES. /MISSOURI/   GROBEPC64239

THE NEW FEDERAL FAIR-EMPLOYMENT-PRACTICES ACT -- COMPARISON WITH STATE LAW AND AN ANALYSIS OF RELEVANT
STATE EXPERIENCES. /MISSOURI/   GROBEPC64239

SUPPLEMENTARY ACTIVITIES FOR **STATE** GOVERNMENTS SEEKING TO ELIMINATE DISCRIMINATION.   GROUTFB64264

HEALTH WORK AMONG MIGRANTS IN 1958 BY THE NEW-JERSEY **STATE** DEPARTMENT OF HEALTH.   GSHEPAC59301

STATE EXECUTIVE AUTHORITY TO PROMOTE CIVIL-RIGHTS. AN ACTION PROGRAM FOR THE 1960-S.   GSILAJX63310

PUBLIC ASSISTANCE RECIPIENTS IN NEW-YORK **STATE**, JANUARY-FEBRUARY 1957.   GSNYDEM58114

STATE LEGISLATION IN LABOR-RELATIONS AND DISCRIMINATION IN EMPLOYMENT, 1945.   GSPITRS45332

THE CALIFORNIA FEPC. STEPCHILD OF THE **STATE** AGENCIES.   GSTANLR65333

SURVEY OF NON-WHITE EMPLOYEES IN **STATE** GOVERNMENT. /PENNSYLVANIA/   GSTRUJW63338

STATE   (CONTINUATION)
   HOW ACCURATE ARE ESTIMATES OF STATE AND LOCAL UNEMPLOYMENT.   GULLMJX63975

   THE NATIONAL CONFERENCE AND THE REPORTS OF THE STATE ADVISORY COMMITTEES TO THE U.S. COMMISSION ON
   CIVIL-RIGHTS. 1959.   GUSCCMC60405

   REPORTS ON APPRENTICESHIP. NINE STATE ADVISORY COMMITTEES. /CALIFORNIA   FLORIDA   MARYLAND   CONNECTICUT
   WASHINGTON-DC NEW-JERSEY NEW-YORK TENNESSEE WISCONSIN/   GUSCOMC64407

   SUMMARY FACT SHEETS FOR STATE PUBLIC AGENCIES WITH JURISDICTION OVER DISCRIMINATION IN EMPLOYMENT. GUSCOMC65416

   SELECTED BIBLIOGRAPHY ON STATE FAIR-EMPLOYMENT-PRACTICE COMMISSIONS.   GUSCOMC66414

   SELECTED STATE PROGRAMS IN MIGRANT EDUCATION.   GUSDHEW63505

   BRIEF SUMMARY OF STATE LAWS AGAINST DISCRIMINATION IN PRIVATE EMPLOYMENT. FAIR-EMPLOYMENT-PRACTICE ACTS. GUSDLAB63439

   COVERAGE OF AGRICULTURAL WORKERS UNDER STATE AND FEDERAL LAWS. /MIGRANT-WORKERS/   GUSDLAB64507

   THE DYNAMICS OF STATE CAMPAIGNS FOR FAIR-EMPLOYMENT-PRACTICES LEGISLATION.   GUVCHCE50211

   MIGRATORY WORKERS IN NEW-YORK STATE, 1959 AND COMPARISONS WITH 1953, 1957, AND 1958.   GWHYTDR60407

   A STUDY OF STATE AND LOCAL LEGISLATIVE AND ADMINISTRATIVE ACTS DESIGNED TO MEET PROBLEMS OF HUMAN-RIGHTS. GWISCLR52573

   THE INDIAN TODAY IN NEW-YORK STATE.   INEWYSF56601

   THE INDIAN TODAY IN NEW-YORK STATE.   INEWYSI64602

   STATE LAWS AGAINST DISCRIMINATION IN EDUCATION.   JHARTPX58730

   THE DETERMINATION OF CERTAIN MAJOR FACTORS AFFECTING THE NEGRO VETERAN IN THE ON-THE-JOB TRAINING PROGRAM
   IN VOCATIONAL AGRICULTURE IN THE STATE OF ALABAMA AS A BASIS FOR PLANNING A MORE EFFECTIVE PROGRAM. NBATTEF49338

   NEGRO AMERICAN LABOR COUNCIL IS ACTIVE IN NEW-YORK STATE.   NBROOTR61119

   A STUDY OF JOB-OPPORTUNITIES IN THE STATE OF FLORIDA FOR NEGRO COLLEGE GRADUATES.   NDECKPM60261

   TESTIMONY BEFORE STATE SENATE FACT FINDING SUBCOMMITTEE ON RACE-RELATIONS AND URBAN PROBLEMS, FINAL
   HEARING. JANUARY 20 1965. /CALIFORNIA FEPC/   NGRAHCX65439

   STATE FAIR-EMPLOYMENT-PRACTICE LEGISLATION UNCONSTITUTIONALLY BURDENS INTERSTATE COMMERCE WHEN APPLIED TO
   INTERSTATE AIRLINE.   NHARVLR62499

   TWENTY YEARS OF STATE FAIR-EMPLOYMENT-PRACTICE COMMISSIONS. A CRITICAL ANALYSIS WITH RECOMMENDATIONS. NHILLHX64550

   STATE LAWS AND THE NEGRO. SOCIAL CHANGE AND THE IMPACT OF LAW.   NHILLHX65545

   NEGRO EMPLOYMENT IN KENTUCKY STATE AGENCIES.   NKENTCH66643

   JOBS AND COLOR. NEGRO EMPLOYMENT IN TENNESSEE STATE GOVERNMENT.   NLONGHH62706

   A STUDY OF NON-WHITE EMPLOYMENT IN THE STATE SERVICE. /MICHIGAN/   NMICCSC64775

   A FOLLOW-UP STUDY OF NON-WHITE EMPLOYMENT IN THE STATE SERVICE. /MICHIGAN/   NMICCSC65774

   EQUAL-EMPLOYMENT-OPPORTUNITIES IN MISSOURI STATE AGENCIES. A SURVEY OF NEGRO EMPLOYMENT, SPRING-SUMMER
   1963.   NMISSCH64801

   THE UTILIZATION OF NEGRO TEACHERS IN THE COLLEGES OF NEW-YORK STATE.   NMOSSJA60857

   A STUDY OF THE POTENTIAL SUPPLY OF NEGRO TEACHERS FOR THE COLLEGES OF NEW-YORK STATE.   NMOSSJA61858

   THE STATUS OF THE NEGRO PHYSICIAN IN NEW-YORK STATE. /OCCUPATIONS/   NMURRPM55867

   EMPLOYMENT IN STATE GOVERNMENT. /NORTH-CAROLINA/   NNORTCG66092

   STATEMENT TO THE NEW-YORK STATE ADVISORY COMMITTEE TO THE US COMMISSION ON CIVIL-RIGHTS, MAY 23, 1966.
   /EMPLOYMENT LEGISLATION/   NPOLIEX66004

   NEGRO EMPLOYMENT IN THE FEDERAL GOVERNMENT BY CIVIL SERVICE REGION, STATE AND PAY CATEGORIES, JUNE 1962. NPRESCD62012

   WASTE OF MANPOWER -- RACE AND EMPLOYMENT IN A SOUTHERN STATE.   NROBEGX62064

   OUR WELFARE STATE AND THE WELFARE OF FARM PEOPLE.   NSCHUTW64143

   THE EXPERIENCE OF STATE FAIR-EMPLOYMENT COMMISSIONS. A COMPARATIVE STUDY.   NSUTIAX65343

   TWO STATE REPORT ON JOB DISCRIMINATION. /NEW-YORK NEW-JERSEY/   NUSDLAB58844

   NEGROES IN APPRENTICESHIPS. NEW-YORK STATE.   NUSDLAB60830

   SPECIAL REPORT. A SURVEY OF NEGROES EMPLOYED BY THE STATE OF WEST-VIRGINIA.   NVIRGHR64318

   POPULATIONS OF NEW-YORK STATE. REPORT NO 2. THE PUERTO-RICAN POPULATION OF THE NEW-YORK-CITY AREA. PNEWYCO62838

   PUERTO-RICANS IN THE NEW-YORK STATE LABOR-MARKET.   PNEWYSE57840

   CHARACTERISTICS OF POPULATION AND LABOR IN NEW-YORK STATE, 1956 AND 1957. PUERTO-RICANS IN NEW-YORK CITY. PNEWYSE60839

   A COMPARISON OF THE OCCUPATIONS OF THE FIRST AND SECOND GENERATION PUERTO-RICANS IN THE MAINLAND
   LABOR-MARKET. AND HOW THE WORK OF THE NEW-YORK STATE DEPARTMENT OF LABORFFECTS PUERTO-RICANS.   PRAUSCX61846

   STATEMENT ON STATE LAWS. /EMPLOYMENT-CONDITIONS/   WDAVICX65720

   FACTORS ASSOCIATED WITH GRADUATE SCHOOL ATTENDANCE AND ROLE DEFINITION OF THE WOMAN DOCTORAL CANDIDATES
   AT THE PENNSYLVANIA STATE UNIVERSITY. /OCCUPATIONS/   WFIELJC61763

   MARRIED WOMEN AT UTAH STATE UNIVERSITY, SPRING QUARTER, 1960. /TRAINING/   WFREDCX61769

   RUTGERS -- THE STATE UNIVERSITY. FORD FOUNDATION PROGRAM FOR THE RETRAINING IN MATHEMATICS OF COLLEGE
   GRADUATE WOMEN. /TRAINING/   WMARTHM63957

   EMPLOYMENT EFFECTS OF STATE MINIMUM WAGES FOR WOMEN.   WPETEJX59059

   SPEECH ABOUT JOB OPPORTUNITIES FOR GIRLS BEFORE THE MARYLAND STATE PERSONNEL AND GUIDANCE ASSOCIATION. WTERLRX64148

   WISCONSIN FAIR-EMPLOYMENT-PRACTICES DIVISION INQUIRY INTO THE CONFLICTS BETWEEN STATE PROTECTIVE LABOR

STATE   (CONTINUATION)
  LEGISLATION AND **STATE** AND FEDERAL LAWS PROHIBITING DISCRIMINATION BASED ON SEX. /EMPLOYMENT-CONDITIONS/   WUAWXWD65165

  WISCONSIN FAIR-EMPLOYMENT-PRACTICES DIVISION INQUIRY INTO THE CONFLICTS BETWEEN **STATE** PROTECTIVE LABOR
  LEGISLATION AND STATE AND FEDERAL LAWS PROHIBITING DISCRIMINATION BASED ON SEX. /EMPLOYMENT-CONDITIONS/   WUAWXWC65165

  DIGEST OF **STATE** LEGISLATION OF SPECIAL INTEREST TO WOMEN WORKERS.   WUSDLABND191

  SUMMARY OF **STATE** LABOR LAWS FOR WOMEN.   WUSDLABND219

  SUGGESTED LANGUAGE FOR A **STATE** ACT TO ABOLISH DISCRIMINATORY WAGE RATES BASED ON SEX.   WUSDLAB64218

  FRINGE BENEFIT PROVISIONS FROM **STATE** MINIMUM WAGE LAWS AND ORDERS, SEPTEMBER 1, 1966.
  /EMPLOYMENT-CONDITIONS/   WUSDLAB66195

  WHY **STATE** EQUAL-PAY LAWS.   WUSDLAB66230

STATE-COMMISSION-AGA
  NEW-YORK **STATE-COMMISSION-AGAINST-DISCRIMINATION**.   GHIGBJX55995

  NEW-YORK STATE-S PROGRAM AGAINST DISCRIMINATION IN EMPLOYMENT. THE WORK OF THE NEW-YORKEW-YORK
  STATE-COMMISSION-AGAINST-DISCRIMINATION.   GINDUBX57812

  NEW-YORK **STATE-COMMISSION-AGAINST-DISCRIMINATION**, STATEMENT BEFORE THE US SENATE SUBCOMMITTEE ON LABOR
  AND LABOR-MANAGEMENT RELATIONS.   GNEWYSA52102

STATE-EMPLOYMENT-SER
  INVESTIGATION OF CHARGES OF DISCRIMINATORY PRACTICES IN THE NEW-YORK **STATE-EMPLOYMENT-SERVICE**.   GNEWYSA59083

  THE **STATE-EMPLOYMENT-SER**VICE AND THE ATTITUDE OF UNEMPLOYABLE DROPOUTS.   NHARRIE66991

STATE-PERSONNEL-BOAR
  ETHNIC CENSUS OF EXAMINATION COMPETITORS, JULY-DEC 1965, CALIFORNIA **STATE-PERSONNEL-BOARD**.   GCALSPB65552

STATE-S
  NEW-YORK **STATE-S** PROGRAM AGAINST DISCRIMINATION IN EMPLOYMENT. THE WORK OF THE NEW-YORKEW-YORK
  STATE-COMMISSION-AGAINST-DISCRIMINATION.   GINDUBX57812

  PROVING GROUND FOR FAIR-EMPLOYMENT. SOME LESSONS FROM NEW-YORK **STATE-S** EXPERIENCE.   GNORTHR47123

STATEMENT
  STATEMENT ON SURVEYS AND STATISTICS AS TO RACIAL AND ETHNIC COMPOSITION OF WORK-FORCE OR UNION
  MEMBERSHIP. /CALIFORNIA/   GCALFEP63539

  I **STATEMENT** BEFORE THE HOUSE POST OFFICE AND CIVIL SERVICE SUBCOMMITTEE ON POSTAL OPERATIONS, II
  DISCRIMINATION. PLANNED AND ACCIDENTAL. /TESTING/   GENNEWH67928

  STATEMENT ON BEHALF OF AMERICAN JEWISH CONGRESS ON DISCRIMINATION IN EMPLOYMENT.   GMASLWX61961

  NEW-YORK STATE-COMMISSION-AGAINST-DISCRIMINATION, **STATEMENT** BEFORE THE US SENATE SUBCOMMITTEE ON LABOR
  AND LABOR-MANAGEMENT RELATIONS.   GNEWYSA52102

  STATEMENT TO THE COMMITTEE ON LEGISLATION IN SUPPORT OF AN EFFECTIVE FEDERAL FEP LAW AND OTHER VITAL
  CIVIL-RIGHTS LEGISLATION.   GOLIVWX60134

  STATEMENT ON EMPLOYMENT PROBLEMS OF MEXICAN-AMERICANS IN CALIFORNIA.   MMORADX63445

  STATEMENT AND TESTIMONY ON FEDERAL ROLE IN URBAN AFFAIRS. /EMPLOYMENT GHETTO/   NKENNRF66017

  STATEMENT TO THE NEW-YORK STATE ADVISORY COMMITTEE TO THE US COMMISSION ON CIVIL-RIGHTS, MAY 23, 1966.
  /EMPLOYMENT LEGISLATION/   NPOLIEX66004

  STATEMENT BEFORE CALIFORNIA SENATE SUB-COMMITTEE ON RACE-RELATIONS AND URBAN PROBLEMS.   OLOWXHW64745

  STATEMENT BEFORE CALIFORNIA LEGISLATURE ASSEMBLY, INTERIM SUBCOMMITTEE ON ECONOMIC OPPORTUNITY ON BEHALF
  OF CHINATOWN-NORTH BEACH DISTRICT COUNCIL.   OWONGLJ64771

  STATEMENT, PUBLIC HEARING, WOMEN IN PUBLIC AND PRIVATE EMPLOYMENT, CALIFORNIA. /FEP
  EMPLOYMENT-CONDITIONS DISCRIMINATION/   WBELAJX66634

  STATEMENT, PUBLIC HEARING, WOMEN IN PUBLIC AND PRIVATE EMPLOYMENT, CALIFORNIA. /FEP
  EMPLOYMENT-CONDITIONS DISCRIMINATION/   WBENNSJ66637

  STATEMENT ON SENIORITY. /UNION/   WDAVICX65719

  STATEMENT ON STATE LAWS. /EMPLOYMENT-CONDITIONS/   WDAVICX65720

  STATEMENT, PUBLIC HEARING, WOMEN IN PUBLIC AND PRIVATE EMPLOYMENT, CALIFORNIA. /EMPLOYMENT-CONDITIONS
  MIGRANT-WORKERS/   WKAUFDX66886

  STATEMENT, PUBLIC HEARING, WOMEN IN PUBLIC AND PRIVATE EMPLOYMENT, CALIFORNIA. /EMPLOYMENT-CONDITIONS/   WKENNVX66890

  STATEMENT, PUBLIC HEARING, WOMEN IN PUBLIC AND PRIVATE EMPLOYMENT, CALIFORNIA. /EMPLOYMENT-CONDITIONS/   WKNIGTF66911

  STATEMENT, PUBLIC HEARING, WOMEN IN PUBLIC AND PRIVATE EMPLOYMENT, CALIFORNIA. /FEP
  EMPLOYMENT-CONDITIONS MIGRANT-WORKERS/   WMILLJJ66979

  STATEMENT ON WEIGHT LIFTING, HOURS, SENIORITY LAWS AND WOMEN. /EMPLOYMENT-CONDITIONS/   WUAWXWD66164

  STATEMENT, PUBLIC HEARING, WOMEN IN PUBLIC AND PRIVATE EMPLOYMENT, CALIFORNIA. /FEP
  EMPLOYMENT-CONDITIONS DISCRIMINATION/   WVAILLX66256

STATEMENTS
  FAIR-EMPLOYMENT-PRACTICES LEGISLATION, A SUMMARY OF ITS HISTORY AND DEVELOPMENT WITH **STATEMENTS** ON BOTH
  SIDES.   GMITCJA52016

  STATEMENTS RELATING TO THE IMPACT OF TECHNOLOGICAL-CHANGE. /INDUSTRY/   GNATLCT66848

STATEN-ISLAND
  INCOME, EDUCATION AND UNEMPLOYMENT IN NEIGHBORHOODS. NEW-YORK-CITY -- **STATEN-ISLAND**. /DEMOGRAPHY/   CUSDLAB63475

STATES
  SPANISH-SPEAKING AMERICANS. MEXICANS AND PUERTO-RICANS IN THE UNITED **STATES**.   CBLAIBX59366

  THE SPANISH-SPEAKING PEOPLE IN THE UNITED **STATES**. /PUERTO-RICAN MEXICAN-AMERICAN/   CRUBIEBND848

  SPANISH-SPEAKING PEOPLE IN THE UNITED **STATES**. A PILOT REPORT. /MEXICAN-AMERICAN PUERTO-RICAN/   CSAMOJX63474

  UNITED **STATES** CENSUS OF AGRICULTURE. COLOR, RACE, AND TENURE OF FARM OPERATOR. GENERAL REPORT, VOLUME II.

/DEMOGRAPHY/   CUSBURC59382

MOBILITY FOR STATES AND STATE ECONOMIC AREAS. /DEMOGRAPHY/   CUSBURC63174

PERSONS OF SPANISH-SURNAME. SOCIAL AND ECONOMIC DATA FOR WHITE PERSONS OF SPANISH SURNAME IN 5
SOUTHWESTERN STATES. /DEMOGRAPHY/   CUSBURC63181

TRENDS IN THE INCOME OF FAMILIES AND PERSONS IN THE UNITED STATES. 1947-1960. /DEMOGRAPHY/   CUSBURC63381

STATISTICAL ABSTRACT OF THE UNITED STATES. 1964. /DEMOGRAPHY/   CUSBURC64380

INCOME IN 1964 OF FAMILIES AND PERSONS IN THE UNITED STATES. /DEMOGRAPHY/   CUSBURC65375

POVERTY IN THE UNITED STATES, HEARINGS. /AMERICAN-INDIAN NEGRO PUERTO-RICAN EMPLOYMENT/   CUSHOUR64346

CIVIL-RIGHTS IN THE UNITED STATES, 1953.   GAMERJC53388

WHERE THE STATES STAND ON CIVIL-RIGHTS.   GBARNRX62423

RECENT POPULATION TRENDS IN THE UNITED STATES WITH EMPHASIS ON RURAL AREAS. /EDUCATION/   GBEALCL63426

REPORT OF THE CALIFORNIA STATE ADVISORY COMMITTEE TO THE UNITED STATES COMMISSION ON CIVIL-RIGHTS ON
CALIFORNIA-S PROGRAM FOR EQUAL-OPPORTUNITY IN APPRENTICESHIP.   GBECKWL62432

A SPECULATIVE VIEW OF THE UNITED STATES IN 1985 AND BEYOND. /TECHNOLOGICAL-CHANGE/   GBELLDX62612

FAIR-EMPLOYMENT-PRACTICES LEGISLATION OF EIGHT STATES AND TWO CITIES.   GBERGMX51441

POVERTY IN RURAL AREAS OF THE UNITED STATES.   GBIRDAR64450

FARM LABOR IN THE UNITED STATES.   GBISHCE67916

THE POPULATION OF THE UNITED STATES.   GBOGUDJ59461

UNEMPLOYMENT IN THE UNITED STATES. QUANTITATIVE DIMENSIONS.   GBOWEWG65464

MIGRATION PATTERNS OF THE RURAL-FARM POPULATION. THIRTEEN ECONOMIC REGIONS OF THE UNITED STATES,
1940-1950.   GBOWLGK57415

THE COMPOSITION OF NET MIGRATION AMONG COUNTIES IN THE UNITED STATES, 1950-60.   GBOWLGK66414

NONWHITE EMPLOYMENT IN THE UNITED STATES.   GBUCKLF63479

ECONOMIC AND SOCIAL DEPRIVATIONS. ITS EFFECTS ON CHILDREN AND FAMILIES IN THE UNITED STATES -- A SELECTED
BIBLIOGRAPHY.   GCHILCX64571

POVERTY IN THE UNITED STATES IN THE MID-SIXTIES.   GCHILCX64922

EFFECTS OF TECHNOLOGICAL-CHANGE ON OCCUPATIONAL EMPLOYMENT PATTERNS IN THE UNITED STATES.   GCLAGEX64625

POVERTY AND DEPRIVATION IN THE UNITED STATES. THE PLIGHT OF TWO-FIFTHS OF A NATION.   GCONFOE62873

REPORTS OF THE MEETINGS OF THE COMMITTEE OF OFFICIALS ON MIGRATORY FARM LABOR OF THE ATLANTIC SEABOARD
STATES. /MIGRANT-WORKERS/   GCOUNSG58932

SOME DEMOGRAPHIC ASPECTS OF POVERTY IN THE UNITED STATES.   GDAVIKX65663

REPORT OF INDUSTRY AND LABOR-MANAGEMENT CLINICS. IMPLEMENTATION OF EMPLOYMENT IN MERIT PROGRAMS IN NON
FEPC STATES BY DIRECT APPROACH TO TOP MANAGEMENT.   GFISKUR51684

FEPC -- HOW IT WORKS IN SEVEN STATES.   GFURNJC52706

ANTI-DISCRIMINATION LEGISLATION IN THE AMERICAN STATES.   GGRAVWB48734

FEPC LEGISLATION IN THE UNITED STATES, FEDERAL, STATE, MUNICIPAL.   GGRAVWB51735

TECHNOLOGICAL-CHANGE, PRODUCTIVITY, AND EMPLOYMENT IN THE UNITED STATES.   GGREELX64739

STATES AS FAIR-EMPLOYERS.   GGROVHE61744

MORTALITY BY OCCUPATION AND INDUSTRY AMONG MEN 20 TO 64 YEARS OF AGE. UNITED STATES, 1950. /DEMOGRAPHY/   GGURALX62748

MANPOWER IN THE UNITED STATES. PROBLEMS AND POLICIES.   GHABEWX54750

THE ROLE OF THE UNITED STATES EMPLOYMENT-SERVICE IN A CHANGING ECONOMY.   GHABEWX64649

STRUCTURAL UNEMPLOYMENT IN THE UNITED STATES.   GKILLCC66800

THE TENURE STATUS OF FARMWORKERS IN THE UNITED STATES.   GMAIEFH60417

ETHNIC RELATIONS IN THE UNITED STATES.   GMCDOEC53050

LONG-TERM UNEMPLOYMENT IN THE UNITED STATES.   GMEREJL61995

THE FACE OF POVERTY IN THE UNITED STATES.   GMILLHP64853

INCOME-DISTRIBUTION IN THE UNITED STATES. /DEMOGRAPHY/   GMILLHP66778

INCOME AND WELFARE IN THE UNITED STATES.   GMORGJN62032

STATES LAWS ON RACE AND COLOR.   GMURRPX50034

WHITE UNEMPLOYMENT IN THE UNITED STATES, 1947-1958, AN ANALYSIS OF TRENDS.   GNEWYSA58089

MANPOWER POLICY AND PROGRAMMES IN THE UNITED STATES.   GORGAEC64776

INCOME-DISTRIBUTION AS A FACTOR IN REGIONAL GROWTH, WITH SPECIAL REFERENCE TO THE SOUTHEAST UNITED
STATES. /DISCRIMINATION/   GPHILEW65773

MUNICIPAL HUMAN-RELATIONS COMMISSION, A SURVEY OF PROGRAMS IN SELECTED CITIES OF THE UNITED STATES.   GRICHCM63236

FAMILY INCOME AND RELATED CHARACTERISTICS AMONG LOW-INCOME COUNTIES AND STATES.   GRODOAL64241

FEPC IN THE STATES. A PROGRESS REPORT.   GRORTJX58246

THEY AND WE, RACIAL AND ETHNIC RELATIONS IN THE UNITED STATES.   GROSEPI64251

POPULATION MOBILITY WITHIN THE UNITED STATES.   GSHRYHS64309

THE ECONOMIC SITUATION OF NATIONAL MINORITIES IN THE UNITED STATES OF AMERICA.   GTHOMJA47354

LOW-INCOME FAMILIES AND UNRELATED INDIVIDUALS IN THE UNITED STATES. 1964. /DEMOGRAPHY/   GUSBURC65151

MOBILITY OF THE POPULATION OF THE UNITED STATES, JANUARY 1, 1950 TO FEBRUARY 1, 1965. /DEMOGRAPHY/   GUSBURC65161

MOBILITY OF THE POPOFATION FO THE UNITED STATES, MARCH 1964 TO MARCH 1965. /DEMOGRAPHY/   GUSBURC66158

POPULATION OF THE UNITED STATES BY METROPOLITAN AND NONMETROPOLITAN RESIDENCE. /DEMOGRAPHY/   GUSBURC66159

PROJECTIONS OF SCHOOL AND COLLEGE ENROLLMENT IN THE UNITED STATES TO 1985. /DEMOGRAPHY/   GUSBURC66160

THE 50 STATES REPORT.   GUSCOMC61415

NONWHITE FARM OPERATORS IN THE UNITED STATES.   GUSDLAB41077

THE SKILLED WORK FORCE OF THE UNITED STATES.   GUSDLAB55498

A GUIDE TO INDUSTRIAL-RELATICNS IN THE UNITED STATES. EQUAL JOB OPPORTUNITY UNDER COLLECTIVE-BARGAINING.   GUSDLAB58449

SELECTED MANPOWER INDICATORS FOR STATES.   GUSDLAB65826

EMPLOYMENT AND EARNINGS STATISTICS FOR THE UNITED STATES, 1909-1966.   GUSDLAB66832

TOWARDS FULL EMPLOYMENT. PROPOSALS FOR A COMPREHENSIVE EMPLOYMENT AND MANPOWER POLICY IN THE UNITED
STATES.   GUSSENA64332

EMPLOYMENT AND UNEMPLOYMENT IN THE UNITED STATES.   GWOFLSX64759

THE UNITED STATES INDIAN.   ICOLLJX56544

THE PRESENT DAY DISTRIBUTION OF UNITED STATES INDIANS.   ITAXXSX56628

INDIAN AFFAIRS. A STUDY OF THE CHANGES IN POLICY OF THE UNITED STATES TOWARD INDIANS.   ITYLESL64634

UNITED STATES INDIAN POPULATION AND LAND, 1960-1961.   IUSDINT61663

JEWISH POPULATION IN THE UNITED STATES, 1960. /DEMOGRAPHY/   JCHENAX61712

JEWISH POPULATION IN THE UNITED STATES, 1961. /DEMOGRAPHY/   JCHENAX62713

A COMPARISON OF MAJOR UNITED STATES RELIGIOUS GROUPS. /ECONOMIC-STATUS/   JLAZRBX61033

NO FRONTIER TO LEARNING. THE MEXICAN STUDENT IN THE UNITED STATES.   MBEALRL57364

OBSTACLES TO ASSIMILATION OF THE MEXICAN-AMERICAN IN THE UNITED STATES.   MBEALRL60362

MEXICAN IMMIGRATION TO THE UNITED STATES. THE RECORD AND ITS IMPLICATIONS.   MGREBLX66406

MIGRATORY AGRICULTURAL WORKERS IN THE UNITED STATES.   MJORGJM60422

THE SPANISH-SPEAKING PEOPLE IN THE UNITED STATES.   MSAMOJX62473

THE GENERAL STATUS OF THE SPANISH-SPEAKING PEOPLE IN THE UNITED STATES.   MSAMOJX63471

MATERIALS RELATING TO THE EDUCATION OF SPANISH-SPEAKING PEOPLE IN THE UNITED STATES, AN ANNOTATED
BIBLIOGRAPHY.   MSANCGI59478

MEXICAN-AMERICAN AND TOTAL EMPLOYMENT IN SELECTED STATES AND STANDARD METROPOLITAN STATISTICAL AREAS.   MUSCISC63504

THE CONCENTRATION OF SPANISH-SURNAME POPULATION IN THE FIVE SOUTHWESTERN STATES.   MUSCOMC62505

INFORMATION CONCERNING ENTRY OF MEXICAN AGRICULTURAL WORKERS INTO THE UNITED STATES.   MUSDLAB59335

LABOR-MOBILITY IN THE SOUTHERN STATES.   NASHBBX61032

DISTRIBUTION OF NEGRO POPULATION IN THE UNITED STATES. /DEMOGRAPHY/   NCALEWC56069

SOME RECENT UNITED STATES SUPREME COURT DECISIONS AFFECTING THE RIGHTS OF NEGRO WORKERS.   NCHICCA47914

RECENT TRENDS IN RESEARCH ON THE NEGRO IN THE UNITED STATES.   NDRAKSC57290

THE SOCIAL AND ECONOMIC STATUS OF THE NEGRO IN THE UNITED STATES.   NDRAKSC65289

COMPARATIVE PSYCHOLOGICAL STUDIES OF NEGROES AND WHITES IN THE UNITED STATES.   NDREGRM60292

RECENT RESEARCH IN PSYCHOLOGICAL COMPARISONS OF NEGROES AND WHITES IN THE UNITED STATES.   NDREGRM65293

A CHRONICLE OF RACE-RELATIONS -- THE UNITED STATES, NORTH AND SOUTH.   NDUBOWE41298

THE HIGHER EDUCATION OF NEGROES IN THE UNITED STATES.   NEELLWC55329

CIVIL-RIGHTS, 1960-63. THE NEGRO CAMPAIGN TO WIN EQUAL RIGHTS AND OPPORTUNITIES IN THE UNITED STATES.   NFACTOF64341

HISTORY OF THE LABOR MOVEMENT IN THE UNITED STATES. /UNION/   NFONEPS47370

HISTORY OF RACIAL SEGREGATION IN THE UNITED STATES.   NFRANJH56060

ETHNIC FAMILY PATTERNS. THE NEGRO FAMILY IN THE UNITED STATES.   NFRAZEF48379

BLACK BOURGEOISIE. THE RISE OF A MIDDLE-CLASS IN THE UNITED STATES.   NFRAZEF57371

THE NEGRO IN THE UNITED STATES.   NFRAZEF57966

OCCUPATIONAL DIFFERENTIATION OF NEGROES AND WHITES IN THE UNITED STATES.   NGIBBJP65401

THE STATUS OF THE NEGRO CPA IN THE UNITED STATES. /OCCUPATIONS/   NHARRLJ62494

UNITED STATES HAS STANDING UNDER INTERSTATE COMMERCE ACT AND COMMERCE CLAUSE TO ENJOIN SEGREGATIVE
PRACTICES OF CITY. /LEGISLATION/   NHARVLR64500

THE ECONOMIC IMBALANCE. AN INQUIRY INTO THE ECONOMIC-STATUS OF NEGROES IN THE UNITED STATES, 1935-1960,
WITH IMPLICATIONS FOR NEGRO EDUCATION.   NHENDVW60512

NO HARVEST FOR THE REAPER. THE STORY OF THE MIGRATORY AGRICULTURAL WORKER IN THE UNITED STATES.   NHILLHX59534

EFFORTS OF NEGRO TEACHERS IN THE SOUTHERN STATES TO OBTAIN EQUALIZATION OF SALARIES.   NJONEER48343

STATES   (CONTINUATION)
NEGRO INTERNAL MIGRATION IN THE UNITED **STATES**. 1870-1960.   NJORGJM62624

A STUDY OF THE EMPLOYMENT OPPORTUNITIES FOR NEGROES IN BREWERIES OF THE UNITED **STATES**. /INDUSTRY/   NKERNJH51897

THE EMPLOYMENT OF NEGROES IN PUBLIC WELFARE IN ELEVEN SOUTHERN **STATES**, 1936-1949. /OCCUPATIONS/   NLARKJR52672

INTELLIGENCE IN THE UNITED **STATES**. A SURVEY -- WITH CONCLUSIONS FOR MANPOWER UTILIZATION IN EDUCATION AND
EMPLOYMENT.   NMINEJB57796

THE LEGAL-STATUS OF THE NEGRO IN THE UNITED **STATES**.   NMOTLCB66859

ECONOMIC AND SOCIAL STATUS OF THE NEGRO IN THE UNITED **STATES**.   NNATLUL62083

ECONOMIC AND SOCIAL STATUS OF THE NEGRO IN THE UNITED **STATES**.   NORSHMX61961

NEGRO MIGRATION IN THE UNITED **STATES**.   NPURDLX54024

NEGROES IN THE UNITED **STATES**. THEIR EMPLOYMENT AND ECONOMIC STATUS.   NRINGHH53061

SOCIAL CHARACTERISTICS OF HIGH SCHOOL SENIORS IN URBAN NEGRO HIGH SCHOOLS IN TWO **STATES**.   NSMITBF56147

THE CHANGING NUMBER AND DISTRIBUTION OF THE AGED NEGRO POPULATION OF THE UNITED STATES. /DEMOGRAPHY/   NSMITLT58145

THE NEGRO POPULATION IN THE UNITED **STATES**. /DEMOGRAPHY/   NTAEUKE65198

EQUAL-OPPORTUNITY IN FARM PROGRAMS -- AN APPRAISAL OF SERVICES RENDERED BY AGENCIES OF THE UNITED STATES
DEPARTMENT OF AGRICULTURE.   NUSCOMC65232

INTEGRATION AND THE NEGRO OFFICER IN THE ARMED FORCES OF THE UNITED **STATES** OF AMERICA. /MILITARY/   NUSDDEF62240

THE ECONOMIC SITUATION OF NEGROES IN THE UNITED **STATES**.   NUSDLAB62243

THE NEGROES IN THE UNITED **STATES**. THEIR ECONOMIC AND SOCIAL SITUATION.   NUSDLAB66257

EMPLOYMENT AND THE ECONOMIC STATUS OF NEGROES IN THE UNITED **STATES**.   NUSSENA52333

THE UNITED **STATES** EMPLOYMENT SERVICE AND THE NEGRO WORK APPLICANT.   NUSWAMC44276

DEMOGRAPHIC CHARACTERISTICS OF THE NEGRO POPULATION IN THE UNITED **STATES**.   NVALIPX63279

EMPLOYMENT OF NEGROES IN UNITED **STATES** WAR INDUSTRIES.   NWEAVRC44300

POVERTY IN THE UNITED **STATES**.   NWOLFDP64338

KINSHIP AS A FACTOR AFFECTING CANTONESE ECONOMIC ADAPTATION IN THE UNITED **STATES**.   OBARNML66698

THE FUI-CH-IAO IN THE UNITED **STATES** OF AMERICA.   OLEEXRH58742

THE CHINESE IN THE UNITED **STATES** OF AMERICA.   OLEEXRH60741

SOME ECONOMIC ASPECTS OF PUERTO-RICAN MIGRATION TO THE UNITED **STATES**.   PFLEIBM61804

THE IMPACT OF PUERTO-RICAN MIGRATION TO THE UNITED **STATES**. /EMPLOYMENT/   PFLEIBM63437

SOME ECONOMIC ASPECTS OF PUERTO-RICAN MIGRATION TO THE UNITED **STATES**.   PFLEIBM63803

THE PUERTO-RICANS IN THE UNITED **STATES**.   PSENICX56852

PUERTO-RICANS IN THE UNITED **STATES**. SOCIAL AND ECONOMIC DATA FOR PERSONS OF PUERTO-RICAN BIRTH AND
PARENTAGE. /DEMOGRAPHY/   PUSBURC63182

CENSUS OF POPULATION. 1960. PUERTO-RICANS IN THE UNITED **STATES**.   PUSBURC63854

AGE OF COMPLETION OF CHILDBEARING AND ITS RELATION TO THE PARTICIPATION OF WOMEN IN THE LABOR-FORCE.
UNITED **STATES** 1910-1955.   WDAYXLH57725

STATUS IMPLICATIONS OF THE EMPLOYMENT OF MARRIED WOMEN IN THE UNITED **STATES**.   WDAYXLH61726

OCCUPATIONAL TRAINING OF WOMEN IN THE UNITED **STATES**.   WINTELR64866

PROFESSIONAL STANDARDS AND ECONOMIC-STATUS OF NURSES IN THE UNITED **STATES**.   WKRUGDH60917

THE FEMALE LABOR-FORCE IN THE UNITED **STATES**. FACTORS GOVERNING ITS GROWTH AND CHANGING COMPOSITION.   WOPPEVK66096

THE INTERACTION OF DEMAND AND SUPPLY AND ITS EFFECT ON THE FEMALE LABOR-FORCE IN THE UNITED **STATES**.   WOPPEVK66289

TOP LEVEL TRAINING OF WOMEN IN THE UNITED **STATES**. 1900-60.   WPARRJB62283

STATUS OF WOMEN IN THE UNITED **STATES**.   WPETEEX64056

BACKGROUND FACTS ON WOMEN WORKERS IN THE UNITED **STATES**.   WUSDLAB66638

SUPPLY OF MEDICAL WOMEN IN THE UNITED **STATES**. /OCCUPATIONS/   WWRIGKW66277

WOMEN TODAY. TRENDS AND ISSUES IN THE UNITED **STATES**. /WORK-WOMAN-ROLE/   WYWCAXX63078

STATEWIDE
MANPOWER DEVELOPMENT TRAINING. TOTAL NUMBER OF NEW ENROLLEES DURING THE MONTH BY RACE AND OCCUPATION
STATEWIDE AND BY ADMINISTRATIVE AREA, SEPTEMBER, 1966, OCTOBER, 1966. /CALIFORNIA/   GCALDEM66518

STATISTICAL
STATISTICAL ABSTRACT OF THE UNITED STATES. 1964. /DEMOGRAPHY/   CUSBURC64380

A COMPILATION OF **STATISTICAL** DATA, CHARTS AND OTHER RESOURCE MATERIAL FOR CONFERENCE PARTICIPANTS.
/APPRENTICESHIP CALIFORNIA YOUTH/   GCALCNA60516

THE HIRED FARM WORKING FORCE OF 1964. A **STATISTICAL** REPORT.   GUSDAGR65424

A **STATISTICAL** PROFILE OF THE SPANISH-SURNAME POPULATION OF TEXAS.   MBROWHL64368

MEXICAN-AMERICAN AND TOTAL EMPLOYMENT IN SELECTED STATES AND STANDARD METROPOLITAN **STATISTICAL** AREAS.   MUSCISC63504

REPORT OF THE EXPLORATORY **STATISTICAL** SURVEY OF THE EDUCATIONAL-ATTAINMENT, NUMBER, AND AVAILABILITY OF
THE MEMBERSHIP OF THE AMERICAN ASSOCIATION OF UNIVERSITY WOMEN FOR TEACHING IN THE FIELDS OF SCIENCE AND
MATHEMATICS. /OCCUPATIONS/   WOOLAEF57735

STATISTICS
EMPLOYMENT-STATUS AND WORK CHARACTERISTICS. **STATISTICS** ON THE RELATION BETWEEN EMPLOYMENT AND SOCIAL AND

STATISTICS   (CONTINUATION)
  ECONOMIC CHARACTERISTICS. /DEMOGRAPHY/   CUSBURC63170

    OCCUPATIONS BY EARNINGS AND EDUCATION. STATISTICS FOR MEN 18-64 YEARS OLD, BY COLOR, IN SELECTED
    OCCUPATIONS. /DEMOGRAPHY/   CUSBURC63178

    STATEMENT ON SURVEYS AND STATISTICS AS TO RACIAL AND ETHNIC COMPOSITION OF WORK-FORCE OR UNION
    MEMBERSHIP. /CALIFORNIA/   GCALFEP63539

    RACIAL STATISTICS AS A MANAGEMENT TOOL.   GDOARLE66645

    OCCUPATIONAL EMPLOYMENT STATISTICS, SOURCES AND DATA.   GGREEHX66627

    STATISTICS ON APPRENTICESHIP AND THEIR LIMITATIONS.   GGROOPX64745

    PROPOSED POLICY REGARDING STATISTICS ON EMPLOYMENT. /LOS-ANGELES CALIFORNIA/   GLOSACC64912

    TESTIMONY BEFORE SUBCOMMITTEE ON ECONOMIC STATISTICS, MAY 17, 1965.   GUSCONG65421

    FAMILY INCOME STATISTICS.   GUSDLAB49029

    EMPLOYMENT AND EARNINGS STATISTICS FOR THE UNITED STATES, 1909-1966.   GUSDLAB66832

    STATISTICS CONCERNING INDIAN EDUCATION, FISCAL YEAR 1956.   IUSDINT56661

    RACIAL STATISTICS AS A MANAGEMENT TOOL.   NDOARLE66276

    SOCIAL SECURITY PROGRAM STATISTICS RELATING TO NONWHITE FAMILIES AND CHILDREN.   NUSDHEW58241

    THE FEMALE LABOR-FORCE. A CASE STUDY IN THE INTERPRETATION OF HISTORICAL STATISTICS.   WSMUTRW60124

    STATISTICS ON WOMEN PROFESSIONAL ENGINEERS. /OCCUPATIONS/   WWEBBJR66226

STATUS
  THE CHANGING STATUS OF NEGRO WOMEN WORKERS.   CUSDLAB64072

  RACE AND SOCIO-ECONOMIC STATUS IN MUNICIPAL PERSONNEL SELECTION.   GBIANJC67590

  THE PRESENT STATUS AND PROGRAMS OF FEPC. FEDERAL, STATE, AND MUNICIPAL.   GBRAZBR51472

  EDUCATIONAL STATUS, COLLEGE PLANS, AND OCCUPATIONAL-STATUS OF FARM AND NONFARM YOUTHS. OCTOBER 1959.   GCOWHJD61427

  RELATIVE SOCIOECONOMIC STATUS OF SOUTHERN WHITES AND NONWHITES, 1950 AND 1960.   GCOWHJD64615

  MINORITY-GROUP AND CLASS STATUS AS RELATED TO SOCIAL AND PERSONALITY FACTORS IN SCHOLASTIC ACHIEVEMENT.   GDEUTMP60640

  NONWHITE OCCUPATIONAL STATUS, BY REGION, AS RELATED TO PERCENT OF NONWHITE.   GGUEREW63746

  LABOR-FORCE STATUS OF YOUTH, 1964.   GHAMEHR65756

  THE STATUS OF THE NONWHITE LABOR-FORCE IN ILLINOIS AND THE NATION.   GILLICH57793

  THE PRESENT STATUS OF THE CULTURE FAIR TESTING MOVEMENT.   GLAMBNM64880

  THE TENURE STATUS OF FARMWORKERS IN THE UNITED STATES.   GMAIEFH60417

  GEOGRAPHIC MOBILITY AND EMPLOYMENT STATUS, MARCH 1962-MARCH 1963.   GSABESX64271

  THE EDUCATIONAL STATUS OF A MINORITY. /MIGRANT-WORKERS/   GSAMOJX63501

  SOME PROBLEMS INVOLVED IN THE CHANGING STATUS OF THE AMERICAN INDIAN.   IBARNML56534

  THE PRESENT STATUS OF THE FLORIDA SEMINOLE INDIANS.   IPEITIM59284

  JEWISH AND ITALIAN IMMIGRATION AND SUBSEQUENT STATUS MOBILITY.   JSTROFL58764

  SPANISH-SPEAKING AND ENGLISH SPEAKING CHILDREN IN SOUTHWEST TEXAS. A COMPARATIVE STUDY OF INTELLIGENCE,
  SOCIO-ECONOMIC STATUS, AND ACHIEVEMENT.   MRATLYX60460

  EDUCATIONAL STATUS OF A MINORITY.   MSAMOJX63470

  THE GENERAL STATUS OF THE SPANISH-SPEAKING PEOPLE IN THE UNITED STATES.   MSAMOJX63471

  THE RELATIONSHIP OF JUVENILE-DELINQUENCY, RACE, AND ECONOMIC STATUS.   NBLUEJT48097

  THE STATUS OF JOBS AND OCCUPATIONS AS EVALUATED BY AN URBAN NEGRO SAMPLE.   NBROWMC55126

  SEX, STATUS AND THE UNDEREMPLOYMENT OF THE NEGRO MALE.   NCLARKB67212

  THE SOCIAL AND ECONOMIC STATUS OF THE NEGRO IN THE UNITED STATES.   NDRAKSC65289

  THE CHANGING ECONOMIC STATUS OF THE MISSISSIPPI NEGRO.   NEATHBJ64314

  SOME CHANGES IN THE RELATIVE STATUS OF AMERICAN NON-WHITES, 1940 TO 1960. /INCOME OCCUPATIONAL-STATUS
  EDUCATION/   NGLENND63421

  THE STATUS OF THE NEGRO CPA IN THE UNITED STATES. /OCCUPATIONS/   NHARRLJ62494

  PRESENT STATUS OF RACE-RELATIONS IN THE SOUTH.   NJOHNCS44615

  THE STATUS OF NEGRO LABOR.   NJOHNCS49613

  THE SOCIO-ECONOMIC BACKGROUND OF NEGRO HEALTH STATUS.   NJOHNCS49616

  NEGRO REACTIONS TO MINORITY-GROUP STATUS.   NJOHNRA57619

  THE CHANGING STATUS OF THE NEGRO IN SOUTHERN AGRICULTURE.   NJONELW50623

  ECONOMIC STATUS OF NONWHITE WORKERS, 1955-62.   NKESSMA63019

  THE LEGAL STATUS OF THE NEGRO.   NMANGCS40735

  NEGRO STATUS IN THE BOILERMAKERS UNION.   NMARSTX44753

  POSTWAR STATUS OF NEGRO WORKERS IN SAN-FRANCISCO AREA. /CALIFORNIA/   NMCENDX50721

  THE STATUS OF THE NEGRO PHYSICIAN IN NEW-YORK STATE. /OCCUPATIONS/   NMURRPM55867

  ECONOMIC AND SOCIAL STATUS OF THE NEGRO IN THE UNITED STATES.   NNATLUL62083

STATUS   (CONTINUATION)
ECCNOMIC AND SOCIAL STATUS OF THE NEGRO IN THE UNITED STATES.   NORSHMX61961

STATUS POSITION, MOBILITY, AND ETHNIC IDENTIFICATION OF THE NEGRO.   NPARKSX64973

LABOR-FORCE AND DEMOGRAPHIC FACTORS AFFECTING THE CHANGING RELATIVE STATUS OF THE AMERICAN NEGRO.
1940-1950.   NPHILWM57997

STATUS OF NEGROES IN CRAFT UNIONS...PITTSBURGH LABOR-MARKET. /PENNSYLVANIA/   NPITTMC65002

NEGROES IN THE UNITED STATES. THEIR EMPLOYMENT AND ECONOMIC STATUS.   NRINGHH53061

INCOME, EMPLOYMENT STATUS AND CHANGE IN CALVERT COUNTY, MARYLAND.   NROHRWC58400

DISTANCE OF MIGRATION AND SOCIO-ECONOMIC STATUS OF MIGRANTS.   NROSEAM58291

CIVIL-RIGHTS, EMPLOYMENT, AND THE SOCIAL STATUS OF AMERICAN NEGROES.   NSHEPHL66129

THE QUEST FOR IDENTITY AND STATUS. FACETS OF THE DESEGREGATION PROCESS IN THE UPPER MIDWEST.
/ECONOMIC-STATUS/   NTILLJA61161

ON IMPROVING THE ECONOMIC STATUS OF THE NEGRO.   NTOBIJX65206

NEGRO JOB STATUS AND EDUCATION.   NTURNRH53213

OCCUPATIONAL STATUS OF NEGRO RAILROAD WORKERS.   NUSDLAB43836

NEGROES. BIG ADVANCES IN JOBS, WEALTH, STATUS.   NUSNEWR58271

EMPLOYMENT AND THE ECONOMIC STATUS OF NEGROES IN THE UNITED STATES.   NUSSENA52333

EMPLOYMENT AND ECONOMIC STATUS OF NEGROES IN THE US.   NUSSENA54275

ETHNIC STATUS AND OCCUPATIONAL DILEMMAS.   NVOLLHM66287

CHANGE IN THE STATUS OF THE NEGRO IN AMERICAN SOCIETY.   NWALKHJ57291

SOME CANTONESE-AMERICAN PROBLEMS OF STATUS ADJUSTMENT.   OBARNML58699

CHINESE IN AMERICAN LIFE. SOME ASPECTS OF THEIR HISTORY, STATUS, PROBLEMS AND CONTRIBUTIONS.   OKUNGSW62737

THE LOWER STATUS PUERTO-RICAN FAMILY.   PBRAMJX62783

SCHOOL AND COMMUNITY COURSE. THE LOWER STATUS PUERTO-RICAN FAMILY.   PBRAMJX63784

REPORT OF ARROWHEAD REGIONAL CONFERENCE ON THE STATUS OF WOMEN IN NORTHERN MINNESOTA.   WARRORC66216

REPORT OF THE CALIFORNIA ADVISORY COMMISSION ON THE STATUS OF WOMEN. /FEP EMPLOYMENT-CONDITIONS
DISCRIMINATION MIGRANTS/   WCALACW67673

THE STATUS OF WOMEN IN THE PROFESSIONS RELATIVE TO THE STATUS OF MEN. /OCCUPATIONS/   WCAVARS57684

THE STATUS OF WOMEN IN THE PROFESSIONS RELATIVE TO THE STATUS OF MEN. /OCCUPATIONS/   WCAVARS57684

THE CHANGING STATUS OF WOMEN.   WCHICRC62689

REPORT ON THE FIRST CONFERENCE ON THE STATUS OF WOMEN. /WORK-WOMEN-ROLE/   WCOLUMX64699

REPORT ON THE MISSOURI COMMISSION ON THE STATUS OF WOMEN. /WORK-WOMEN-ROLE/   WCOLUMX64700

INITIATION INTO A WOMAN-S PROFESSION. IDENTITY PROBLEMS IN THE STATUS TRANSITION OF CO-ED TO STUDENT
NURSE.   WDAVIFX66723

STATUS IMPLICATIONS OF THE EMPLOYMENT OF MARRIED WOMEN IN THE UNITED STATES.   WDAYXLH61726

PROGRESS OF THE COMMISSION ON THE STATUS OF WOMAN. /WORK-WOMAN-ROLE/   WELLIKX63748

THE STATUS OF WOMEN IN PROFESSIONAL SOCIOLOGY. /OCCUPATIONS/   WFAVASF60757

FANTASY, FACT AND THE FUTURE...A REVIEW OF THE STATUS OF WOMEN AND POSSIBLE IMPLICATIONS FOR WOMEN-S
EDUCATION AND ROLE IN THE NEXT DECADE.   WFITZLE63963

PROGRESS AND PROSPECTS. THE REPORT OF THE SECOND NATIONAL CONFERENCE OF GOVERNORS COMMISSIONS ON THE
STATUS OF WOMEN. /EMPLOYMENT-CONDITIONS/   WGOVECS65798

THE STATUS OF WOMEN. /DISCRIMINATION/   WHERZNK60377

FIRST REPORT, IOWA GOVERNOR-S COMMISSION ON THE STATUS OF WOMEN. /EMPLOYMENT-CONDITIONS/   WIOWAGC64796

THE CHANGING STATUS OF THE SOUTHERN WOMAN. /WORK-WOMAN-ROLE/   WJOHNGG65884

WOMEN-S STATUS -- WOMEN TODAY AND THEIR EDUCATION.   WLLOYEX56941

RAISING THE STATUS OF HOUSEHOLD EMPLOYMENT. /HOUSEHOLD-WORKERS/   WMORRMM66998

NSA-S PROFESSIONAL STATUS SURVEY, 1964. /ECCNOMIC-STATUS/   WNATLSA65023

STATUS OF WOMEN IN THE UNITED STATES.   WPETEEX64056

WOMEN ON COLLEGE AND UNIVERSITY FACULTIES. A HISTORICAL SURVEY AND A STUDY OF THEIR PRESENT ACADEMIC
STATUS. /OCCUPATIONS/   WPOLLLA65063

REPORT OF PRESIDENT-S COMMISSION ON STATUS OF WOMEN.   WPRESCO63993

CORRELATES OF PRESENT AND FUTURE WORK STATUS OF MARRIED WOMEN.   WSOBCMB60125

UNIONS AND THE CHANGING STATUS OF WOMEN WORKERS.   WUSDLABND224

GOVERNORS COMMISSIONS ON THE STATUS OF WOMEN.   WUSDLAB64199

TO IMPROVE THE STATUS OF PRIVATE HOUSEHOLD WORK. /HOUSEHOLD-WORKERS/   WUSDLAB65220

WISCONSIN GOVERNOR-S CONFERENCE ON THE CHANGING STATUS OF WOMEN, JAN 31-FEB 1 1964.   WUSDLAB65232

REPORT ON PROGRESS IN 1965 ON THE STATUS OF WOMEN. /EDUCATION EMPLOYMENT-CONDITIONS/   WUSINCS65860

WISCONSIN WOMEN. REPORT OF THE WISCONSIN GOVERNOR-S COMMISSION ON THE STATUS OF WOMEN.   WWISXGC65272

STATUS-SYSTEM
THE VANISHING SERVANT AND THE CONTEMPORARY STATUS-SYSTEM OF THE AMERICAN SOUTH.   NANDEAX53022

STATUTES
    EQUALITY BY **STATUTES** -- LEGAL CONTROLS OVER GROUP DISCRIMINATION.   GBERGMX52440

    STATE CIVIL-RIGHTS **STATUTES**. SOME PROPOSALS.   GBONFAE64463

STATUTORY
    DISCRIMINATION BY LABOR UNIONS IN THE EXERCISE OF **STATUTORY** BARGAINING POWERS.   GOODDEM45646

STEEL
    MOHAWKS. ROUND TRIP TO THE HIGH **STEEL**.   IBLUMRX65539

    THE NEGRO AND UNIONISM IN THE BIRMINGHAM, ALABAMA IRON AND **STEEL** INDUSTRY.   NNORTHR43941

STEELWORKERS
    THE NEGRO **STEELWORKERS** OF PITTSBURGH AND THE UNIONS. /PENNSYLVANIA/   NAUGUTX47035

STEREOTYPIC
    INVESTIGATION OF DIFFERENCES IN OCCUPATIONAL PREFERENCES, **STEREOTYPIC** THINKING, AND PSYCHOLOGICAL NEEDS
    AMONG UNDERGRADUATE WOMEN STUDENTS IN SELECTED CURRICULAR AREAS. /ASPIRATIONS/   WKITTRE60313

STOCKBRIDGE
    AN ANALYSIS OF THE MEXICAN-AMERICAN MIGRANT LABOR FORCE IN THE **STOCKBRIDGE** AREA. /MICHIGAN/   MRODRFX66464

STORE
    ATTITUDES OF WHITE DEPARTMENT **STORE** EMPLOYEES TOWARD NEGRO CO-WORKERS. /CASE-STUDY/   NHARDJX52482

STORES
    EMPLOYMENT IN DEPARTMENT **STORES**. /NEW-YORK/   GNEWYSA58079

    A STUDY OF EMPLOYMENT PATTERNS IN THE GENERAL MERCHANDISE GROUP RETAIL **STORES** IN NEW-YORK-CITY.   GWATKDO66588

    INTEGRATION OF NEGROES IN DEPARTMENT **STORES**.   NNATLUL46891

STORY
    RACE, JOBS, AND POLITICS. THE STORY OF FEPC.   GRUCHLX53266

    THE HARVESTERS. THE **STORY** OF THE MIGRANT PEOPLE.   GSHOTLR61684

    THE IMMOKALEE **STORY**. /MIGRANT-WORKERS FLORIDA/   GSOWDWT58327

    DOORWAY TOWARD THE LIGHT. THE **STORY** OF THE SPECIAL NAVAJO EDUCATION PROGRAM.   ICOOMLM62646

    MERCHANTS OF LABOR. THE MEXICAN BRACERO **STORY**.   MGALAEX66397

    THE BRACERO **STORY**.   MSOTOAX59370

    THE SOUTHERN LABOR **STORY**. /UNION/   NAFLCIO58006

    CASE-STUDY OF A RIOT THE PHILADELPHIA **STORY**. /PENNSYLVANIA/   NBERSLE66078

    LABOR-S UNTOLD **STORY**. /UNION/   NBOYERO55105

    INTEGRATION IN PROFESSIONAL EDUCATION. THE **STORY** OF PERKINS, SOUTHERN METHODIST UNIVERSITY. /VOCATIONS/   NCUNNMX56579

    A CLIMATE OF CHANGE. THE NEW-HAVEN **STORY**. /CONNECTICUT/   NFARRGR65344

    NO HARVEST FOR THE REAPER. THE **STORY** OF THE MIGRATORY AGRICULTURAL WORKER IN THE UNITED STATES.   NHILLHX59534

    TO WIN THESE RIGHTS. A PERSONAL **STORY** OF THE CIO IN THE SOUTH. /UNION/   NMASOJR52324

    THE URBAN-LEAGUE **STORY** 1910-1960.   NNATLUL60899

    BLACK ODYSSEY. THE **STORY** OF THE NEGRO IN AMERICA.   NOTTLRX45966

    PREJUDICE IS NOT THE WHOLE **STORY**. EXAMINATION OF THREE CASES OF NEGRO UPGRADING IN TRACTION COMPANIES IN
    PHILADELPHIA, LOS-ANGELES AND CHICAGO. /PENNSYLVANIA CALIFORNIA ILLINOIS/   NWECKJE45308

    THE **STORY** OF EAST-HARLEM-YOUTH-EMPLOYMENT-SERVICE, INC.   PEASTHY64799

    TWENTY THOUSAND NURSES TELL THEIR **STORY**. /SOCIO-ECONOMIC/   WHUGHEC58851

STRAINS
    THE JAPANESE SOCIAL STRUCTURE AND THE SOURCE OF MENTAL **STRAINS** OF JAPANESE IMMIGRANTS IN THE US.   OIGAXMX57732

STRANGERS
    THE FIRST LOOK AT **STRANGERS**.   IBUNKRX59899

    STRANGERS IN OUR FIELDS. /MIGRANT-WORKERS/   MGALAEX56400

    STRANGERS THEN NEIGHBORS. FROM PILGRIMS TO PUERTO-RICANS.   PSENICX61308

    THE PUERTO-RICANS, **STRANGERS** -- THEN NEIGHBORS.   PSENICX65307

STRATEGIC
    SOCIAL TRENDS IN AMERICA AND **STRATEGIC** APPROACHES TO THE NEGRO PROBLEM.   NMYRDGX48871

STRATEGIES
    LABOR-MARKET **STRATEGIES** IN THE WAR-ON-POVERTY. /UNEMPLOYMENT/   GHARBFH65660

    STRATEGIES IN THE WAR-ON-POVERTY.   GMACHFX65657

    CIVIL-RIGHTS **STRATEGIES** FOR NEGRO EMPLOYMENT.   NMEIEAX67764

STRATEGY
    THE WEIGHT OF THE POOR -- A **STRATEGY** TO END POVERTY. /GUARANTEED-INCOME/   GCLOWRX66525

    THE **STRATEGY** AND POLITICAL ECONOMY OF THE WAR-AGAINST-POVERTY.   GORNAOA64958

    THE MEANING OF NEGRO **STRATEGY**.   NDANZDX64468

    THE CONGRESS-OF-RACIAL-EQUALITY AND ITS **STRATEGY**.   NRICHMX65055

    THE URBAN-LEAGUE AND ITS **STRATEGY**.   NYOUNWM65354

STRATIFICATION
    ETHNIC **STRATIFICATION**. A COMPARATIVE APPROACH.   GSHIBTX65303

    CHANGES IN THE SOCIAL **STRATIFICATION** OF THE SOUTH.   NHEBERX56507

STREAM
MIGRATORY FARM WORKERS IN THE ATLANTIC COAST STREAM. I. CHANGES IN NEW-YORK, 1953 AND 1957.   GLARSOF60406

MIGRATORY FARM WORKERS IN THE ATLANTIC COAST STREAM.   GMETZWH55426

MIGRATORY FARMWORKERS IN THE MIDCONTINENT STREAM.   GMETZWH60440

MIGRATORY FARM WORKERS IN THE ATLANTIC COAST STREAM. WESTERN NEW-YORK, JUNE 1953.   GMOTHJR54405

MIGRATORY FARM WORKERS IN THE ATLANTIC COAST STREAM, II. EDUCATION OF NEW-YORK WORKERS AND THEIR
CHILDREN. 1953 AND 1957.   GSHAREF60427

STREAMS
MIGRATORY FARM WORKERS IN THE MID-CONTINENT STREAMS.   GUSDAGR60425

STRIKE
HUELGA. THE FIRST 100 DAYS OF THE GREAT DELANO STRIKE. /UNION/   MNELSEX66028

STRUCTURAL
STRUCTURAL UNEMPLOYMENT AND AGGREGATE DEMAND.   GGILPEG66632

HAS STRUCTURAL UNEMPLOYMENT WORSENED.   GGORDRA64731

STRUCTURAL UNEMPLOYMENT IN THE UNITED STATES.   GKILLCC66800

INCREASING STRUCTURAL UNEMPLOYMENT RE-EXAMINED.   GSTOIVX66001

OBJECTIVE ACCESS IN THE OPPORTUNITY STRUCTURE. THE ASSESSMENT OF THREE ETHNIC GROUPS WITH RESPECT TO
QUANTIFIED SOCIAL STRUCTURAL VARIABLES.   MRENDGX63461

AN INSIGHT INTO STRUCTURAL UNEMPLOYMENT -- THE EXPERIENCE OF A MINORITY GROUP IN A PROSPEROUS COMMUNITY.   NGERSWJ65634

STRUCTURE
COMPARISON OF MEXICANS. NEGROES AND WHITES WITH RESPECT TO OCCUPATIONAL HISTORY, RURAL-URBAN RESIDENCE
HISTORY AND ACCULTURIZATION WITHIN THE INSTITUTIONAL STRUCTURE OF LANSING, MICHIGAN.   CGOLDVX60494

FAMILY STRUCTURE AND SCHOOL PERFORMANCE. A COMPARATIVE STUDY OF STUDENTS FROM THREE ETHNIC BACKGROUNDS IN
AN INTEGRATED SCHOOL. /MEXICAN-AMERICAN AMERICAN-INDIAN/   CGRIFJX65407

SOURCES AND STRUCTURE OF FAMILY INCOME. /DEMOGRAPHY/   CUSBURC63184

PROJECTIONS TO 1975. THE GROWTH AND STRUCTURE OF THE LABOR FORCE.   GBAKESS65702

WHITE COLLAR EMPLOYMENT. TRENDS AND STRUCTURE.   GBANYCA61420

AN ASSESSMENT OF THE SUITABILITY OF THE FACETED STRUCTURE OF THE WRU EDUCATION THESAURUS AS A FRAMEWORK
FOR PREPARATION OF A THESAURUS OF EQUAL-EMPLOYMENT-OPPORTUNITY TERMS.   GBARHGC66162

SOCIAL STRUCTURE AND RACE-RELATIONS.   GBONIES66135

POVERTY. AGGREGATE DEMAND, AND ECONOMIC STRUCTURE.   GKERSJA66941

REPORT ON THE STRUCTURE AND OPERATIONS OF THE PRESIDENT-S COMMITTEE ON EQUAL-EMPLOYMENT-OPPORTUNITY.   GKHEETW62852

THE STRUCTURE OF THE FARM LABOR-MARKET AND MIGRATION PATTERNS.   GMIREWX57499

THE STRUCTURE OF UNEMPLOYMENT AND AUTOMATION.   GNAVIPX57007

PROJECTED CHANGES IN THE OCCUPATIONAL STRUCTURE OF THE LABOR-FORCE. IMPLICATIONS FOR PUBLIC WELFARE.   GSIFFHX64105

THE CHANGING STRUCTURE OF UNEMPLOYMENT. AN ECONOMETRIC STUDY.   GTHURLC65970

ECONOMIC STRUCTURE AND THE LIFE OF THE JEWS.   JKUZNSX60738

PERCEIVED LIFE CHANCES IN THE OPPORTUNITY STRUCTURE. A STUDY OF A TRI-ETHNIC HIGH SCHOOL.   MGUERCX62410

OBJECTIVE ACCESS IN THE OPPORTUNITY STRUCTURE. THE ASSESSMENT OF THREE ETHNIC GROUPS WITH RESPECT TO
QUANTIFIED SOCIAL STRUCTURAL VARIABLES.   MRENDGX63461

SOUTHERN ECONOMIC DEVELOPMENT AS REVEALED BY THE CHANGING STRUCTURE OF EMPLOYMENT.   NDUNNES62309

FACTORY FOLKWAYS. A STUDY OF INSTITUTIONAL STRUCTURE AND CHANGE.   NELLSJS52331

A HISTORICAL REVIEW OF THE IMPACT OF SOCIAL AND ECONOMIC STRUCTURE ON NEGRO CULTURE AND HOW IT INFLUENCES
FAMILY LIVING.   NJACKJX64596

UNION STRUCTURE AND PUBLIC POLICY. THE CONTROL OF UNION RACIAL PRACTICES.   NMARSRX63752

THE CHANGING OCCUPATIONAL STRUCTURE OF THE SOUTH.   NSIMPRL65140

ECONOMIC STRUCTURE OF THE HARLEM COMMUNITY. /NEW-YORK/   NSTEVHR64177

THE CHANGING STRUCTURE OF THE AMERICAN CITY AND THE NEGRO.   NWEAVRC64299

THE JAPANESE SOCIAL STRUCTURE AND THE SOURCE OF MENTAL STRAINS OF JAPANESE IMMIGRANTS IN THE US.   OIGAXMX57732

PATTERNS OF SOCIAL ACCOMODATION OF THE MIGRANT PUERTO-RICAN IN THE AMERICAN SOCIAL STRUCTURE.   PSEDAEX58850

STRUCTURES
THE POSITION OF RACIAL GROUPS IN OCCUPATIONAL STRUCTURES.   GGLICCE47722

JICARILLA APACHE POLITICAL AND ECONOMIC STRUCTURES.   IWILSHC64235

CHANGING STRUCTURES OF WHITE-NEGRO RELATIONS IN THE SOUTH.   NHIMEJS51552

THE ROLE OF ORGANIZATIONAL STRUCTURES. UNION VERSUS NEIGHBORHOOD IN A TENSION SITUATION.   NREITDC53050

STRUGGLE
INTRODUCTION. THE STRUGGLE FOR EQUALITY AND ITS IMPACT ON INDUSTRIAL-RELATIONS.   GSTEIBX64335

STRUGGLE FOR EQUALITY. SYMPOSIUM.   JMCLABX64747

THE STRUGGLE OF NEGRO TEACHERS IN FLORIDA FOR EQUAL SALARIES. /OCCUPATIONS/   NFERGML49961

THE ROLE OF WHITE RESISTANCE AND FACILITATION IN THE NEGRO STRUGGLE FOR EQUALITY.   NGLENND65676

USES OF LAW IN THE STRUGGLE FOR EQUALITY.   NMASLWX55756

BEYOND TODAY-S STRUGGLE.   NNATLUL65884

STUDENTS   (CONTINUATION)
FACTORS AFFECTING FARM PLACEMENT OF NEGRO VOCATIONAL AGRICULTURE STUDENTS IN ALABAMA.   NMCQUFT45348

INTELLIGENCE AND EDUCATIONAL ACHIEVEMENT OF A MATCHED SAMPLE OF WHITE AND NEGRO STUDENTS.   NMCQURX60730

COUNSELING NEGRO STUDENTS. AN EDUCATIONAL DILEMMA.   NPHILWB59996

THE EFFECT OF SPECIAL INSTRUCTION UPON TEST PERFORMANCE OF HIGH SCHOOL STUDENTS IN TENNESSEE.   NROBESO66961

THE RELATION OF RACIAL SEGREGATION IN EARLY SCHOOLING TO THE LEVEL OF ASPIRATION AND ACADEMIC ACHIEVEMENT
OF NEGRO STUDENTS IN A NORTHERN HIGH SCHOOL.   NSAINJN62137

OCCUPATIONAL ESTABLISHMENT OF FORMER STUDENTS OF VOCATIONAL AGRICULTURE IN MONTGOMERY TRAINING SCHOOL
AREA. /ALABAMA/   NSCOTCCN0346

THE ROLE OF THE COUNSELOR IN THE GUIDANCE OF NEGRO STUDENTS.   NTRUEDL60208

OCCUPATIONAL ASPIRATIONS OF NEGRO MALE HIGH SCHOOL STUDENTS.   NUZELOX61278

IMPLICATIONS FROM RECENT RESEARCH ON COLLEGE STUDENTS. /MANPOWER/   WHEISPX59838

STUDENTS TODAY -- MEN AND WOMEN OF TOMORROW. /MANPOWER/   WHEISPX61841

ATTITUDES OF COLLEGE STUDENTS TOWARD EMPLOYMENT AMONG MARRIED WOMEN. /WORK-FAMILY-CONFLICT/   WHEWEVH64482

RETENTION AND WITHDRAWAL OF COLLEGE STUDENTS. /DROP-OUT/   WIFFERE57854

PARTICIPATION IN PART-TIME WORK BY WOMEN COLLEGE STUDENTS.   WISAALE57875

INVESTIGATION OF DIFFERENCES IN OCCUPATIONAL PREFERENCES, STEREOTYPIC THINKING, AND PSYCHOLOGICAL NEEDS
AMONG UNDERGRADUATE WOMEN STUDENTS IN SELECTED CURRICULAR AREAS. /ASPIRATIONS/   WKITTRE60313

KNOWLEDGE AND INTERESTS CONCERNING SIXTEEN OCCUPATIONS AMONG ELEMENTARY AND SECONDARY SCHOOL STUDENTS.
/ASPIRATIONS/   WMELSRC63968

THE EMPLOYMENT OF STUDENTS, OCTOBER 1961.   WROSECX62087

CHARACTERISTICS OF WOMEN-S COLLEGE STUDENTS.   WROWEFB64095

SOME CORRELATES OF HOMEMAKING VS CAREER PREFERENCE AMONG COLLEGE HOME ECONOMICS STUDENTS.
/WORK-FAMILY-CONFLICT/   WVETTLX64257

STUDIES
IMPLICATIONS OF THE STUDIES. /DISCRIMINATION LOW-INCOME NEGRO PUERTO-RICAN POLICY-RECOMMENDATIONS/   CABRACX59001

AUTOMATION. NATIONWIDE STUDIES IN THE US.   GGREELX64614

RURAL INDUSTRIALIZATION. A SUMMARY OF FIVE STUDIES. /UNEMPLOYMENT OCCUPATIONS/   GMAITST61383

STUDIES IN UNEMPLOYMENT.   GUSSENA60352

COMPARATIVE STUDIES OF NORTH AMERICAN-INDIANS.   IDRIVHE57954

THE SPIRIT OF THE GHETTO. STUDIES OF THE JEWISH QUARTER OF NEW-YORK.   JHAPGHX65989

EDUCATION OF NEGRO LEADERS. INFLUENCES AFFECTING GRADUATE AND PROFESSIONAL STUDIES.   NCALIAX49174

SOME PRACTICAL STUDIES IN PUBLIC TRANSPORTATION. /EMPLOYMENT-CONDITIONS WATTS LOS-ANGELES CALIFORNIA/ NCARLJX65593

FOUR STUDIES OF NEGRO EMPLOYMENT IN THE UPPER SOUTH.   NDEWEDX55269

COMPARATIVE PSYCHOLOGICAL STUDIES OF NEGROES AND WHITES IN THE UNITED STATES.   NDREGRM60292

STUDIES IN THE HIGHER EDUCATION OF NEGRO AMERICANS.   NJOURNE66627

BRICKS WITHOUT STRAW. STUDIES OF COMMUNITY UNEMPLOYMENT PROBLEMS, THE NEGROES DILEMMA. /LOUISVILLE
KENTUCKY/   NLCUIHR64715

SELECTED STUDIES OF NEGRO EMPLOYMENT IN THE SOUTH.   NNATLPA55881

HOUSTON -- THE NEGRO AND EMPLOYMENT OPPORTUNITIES IN THE SOUTH, THE FIRST OF A SERIES OF EMPLOYMENT
STUDIES IN SOUTHERN CITIES. /TEXAS/   NSOUTRC61161

ATLANTA -- THE NEGRO AND EMPLOYMENT OPPORTUNITIES IN THE SOUTH, THE THIRD OF A SERIES OF EMPLOYMENT
STUDIES IN SOUTHERN CITIES. /GEORGIA/   NSOUTRC62155

CHATTANOOGA -- THE NEGRO AND EMPLOYMENT OPPORTUNITIES IN THE SOUTH, THE SECOND OF A SERIES OF EMPLOYMENT
STUDIES IN SOUTHERN CITIES. /TENNESSEE/   NSOUTRC62156

JOBS FOR NEGROES. SOME NORTH-SOUTH PLANT STUDIES. /CASE-STUDY/   NSTEEEH53174

DIGEST OF CASE STUDIES ON CONTINUITIES AND DISCONTINUITIES IN THE EMPLOYMENT-EDUCATION-FAMILY PATTERNS OF
WOMEN-S LIVES.   WDELAPJ60224

STUDY
THE EFFECT OF LOW EDUCATIONAL-ATTAINMENT ON INCOMES. A COMPARATIVE STUDY OF SELECTED ETHNIC GROUPS.
/NEGRO MEXICAN-AMERICAN/   CFOGEWX66367

RECENT TRENDS IN THE STUDY OF MINORITY AND RACE-RELATIONS. /NEGRO PUERTO-RICAN ORIENTAL/   CGORDMM63977

FAMILY STRUCTURE AND SCHOOL PERFORMANCE. A COMPARATIVE STUDY OF STUDENTS FROM THREE ETHNIC BACKGROUNDS IN
AN INTEGRATED SCHOOL. /MEXICAN-AMERICAN AMERICAN-INDIAN/   CGRIFJX65407

THE URBAN REALITY. A COMPARATIVE STUDY OF THE SOCIO-ECONOMIC SITUATION OF MEXICAN-AMERICANS, NEGROES AND
ANGLO-CAUCASIANS IN LOS-ANGELES COUNTY. /CALIFORNIA/   CLOSACF65708

POVERTY IN THE SOUTHWEST. A COMPARATIVE STUDY OF MEXICAN-AMERICAN, NONWHITE AND ANGLO FAMILIES. /NEGRO/ CMITTFG66777

THEORY, METHOD AND FINDINGS IN THE STUDY OF ACCULTURATION. A REVIEW. /MEXICAN-AMERICAN NEGRO/   CPETECX65989

THE TRAINING OF MIGRANT FARM WORKERS. A FOLLOW-UP STUDY OF TWO EXPERIMENTAL AND DEMONSTRATION PROGRAMS
UNDER THE MANPOWER-DEVELOPMENT-AND-TRAINING-ACT. /MEXICAN-AMERICAN AMERICAN-INDIAN/   CUNIVOC66054

REPORT. EVALUATION STUDY OF YOUTH TRAINING AND EMPLOYMENT PROJECT, EAST LOS-ANGELES. /NEGRO
MEXICAN-AMERICAN CALIFORNIA/   CWEINJL64310

FEPC. AN ADMINISTRATIVE STUDY OF SELECTED STATE AND LOCAL PROGRAMS.   GALFOAL54869

LABOR UNIONS IN ACTION. A STUDY OF THE MAINSPRINGS OF UNIONISM.   GBARBJX48421

INEQUALITY OF OPPORTUNITY IN HIGHER EDUCATION. A **STUDY** OF MINORITY GROUP AND RELATED BARRIERS TO COLLEGE ADMISSION.   GBERKDS48446

ANTI-DISCRIMINATION LAWS IN ACTION IN NEW-JERSEY. A LAW-SOCIOLOGY **STUDY**.   GBLUMAW65459

EMPLOYMENT OPPORTUNITIES FOR HIGH SCHOOL DROPOUTS, A **STUDY** OF EMPLOYERS PRACTICES, WEEDS AND ATTITUDES IN THE DISTRICT OF COLUMBIA. /WASHINGTON-DC/   GBURESS57499

A **STUDY** OF PATTERNS OF DISCRIMINATION IN EMPLOYMENT FOR THE EQUAL-EMPLOYMENT-OPPORTUNITY-COMMISSION, WASHINGTON-DC.   GCCUSFR66478

A **STUDY** OF FAIR-EMPLOYMENT-PRACTICES OF THE CITY GOVERNMENT. /GRAND-RAPIDS MICHIGAN/   GGRANRH66733

PUBLIC WELFARE. POVERTY -- PREVENTION OR PERPETUATION. A **STUDY** OF THE STATE DEPARTMENT OF PUBLIC ASSISTANCE OF THE STATE CF WASHINGTON.   GGREEAI64479

HOME INTERVIEW **STUDY** OF LOW-INCOME HOUSEHOLDS IN DETROIT, MICHIGAN.   GGREEAI65472

STUDY OF SERVICES TO DEAL WITH POVERTY IN DETROIT, MICHIGAN.   GGREEAI65480

STUDY OF OCCUPATIONAL CHARACTERISTICS OF NON-WHITES IN THE EAST BATON-ROUGE AREA. /LOUISIANA/   GHARRWRND760

THE ATTRACTIVENESS OF THE SOUTH TO WHITES AND NONWHITES. AN ECOLOGICAL **STUDY**.   GHEERDM63769

QUERIES CONCERNING INDUSTRY AND SOCIETY GROWING OUT CF **STUDY** OF ETHNIC RELATIONS IN INDUSTRY.   GHUGHEC59787

A **STUDY** OF MERIT EMPLOYMENT IN 100 ILLINOIS FIRMS.   GILLICH56794

DISCRIMINATION WITHOUT PREJUDICE. A **STUDY** OF PROMOTION PRACTICES IN INDUSTRY.   GKAHNRL64733

THE SOCIAL POLITICS OF FEPC. A **STUDY** IN REFORM PRESSURE MOVEMENTS.   GKESSLC48847

COMMUNITY VALUES IN EDUCATION AND OCCUPATIONAL SELECTION. A **STUDY** OF YOUTH IN EMMITSBURG, MARYLAND.   GLEONRC64894

SOLVING AN AMERICAN DILEMMA. THE ROLE OF THE FEPC OFFICIAL, A COMPARATIVE **STUDY** OF STATE CIVIL-RIGHTS COMMISSIONS.   GLLOYKM64317

MANAGEMENT AND MINORITY GROUPS. A **STUDY** OF ATTITUDES AND PRACTICES IN HIRING AND UPGRADING.   GMARKPI57085

A **STUDY** OF UNEMPLOYMENT, TRAINING AND PLACEMENT PATTERNS IN THE MUSKEGON AREA. /MICHIGAN/   GMICFEA57979

REPORT OF A PRELIMINARY **STUDY** OF EMPLOYMENT PRACTICES INVOLVING MINORITY-GROUP WORKERS, ESSEX-COUNTY, NEW-JERSEY.   GNEWJDE46059

A PILOT **STUDY** OF THE EMPLOYMENT EXPERIENCES CF HIGH SCHOOL GRADUATES.   GPHILCH65177

1964 MINORITY-GROUP **STUDY**.   GPRESCD64111

STUDY OF MINORITY-GROUP EMPLOYMENT IN THE FEDERAL GOVERNMENT.   GPRESCD64116

THE EFFECTS OF INDUSTRIALIZATION ON RURAL LOUISIANA. A **STUDY** OF PLANT EMPLOYEES.   GPRICPH58395

DIVISION OF AUTHORITY UNDER TITLE-VII OF THE CIVIL-RIGHTS-ACT OF 1964. A PRELIMINARY **STUDY** IN FEDERAL-STATE INTERAGENCY RELATIONS.   GROSESJ66254

PSYCHOLOGICAL TESTS AND FAIR EMPLOYMENT. A **STUDY** OF EMPLOYMENT TESTING IN THE SAN-FRANCISCO BAY AREA. /CALIFORNIA/   GRUSHJT66268

FAIR-EMPLOYMENT IN THE NATION-S CAPITAL. A **STUDY** OF PROGRESS AND DILEMMA. /WASHINGTON-DC/   GSAWYDA62279

POWER AS A PRIMARY CONCEPT IN THE **STUDY** OF MINORITIES.   GSCHERA56058

MINORITY-GROUP INTEGRATION BY LABOR AND MANAGEMENT. A **STUDY** OF THE EMPLOYMENT PRACTICES OF THE LARGER EMPLOYERS. AND THE MEMBERSHIP PRACTICES OF THE LARGER LABOR UNIONS WITH RESPECT TO RACE, RELIGION, AND NATIONAL ORIGIN. CONNECTICUT. 1951.   GSTETHG53598

THE CHANGING STRUCTURE OF UNEMPLOYMENT. AN ECONOMETRIC **STUDY**.   GTHURLC65970

STUDY OF MINORITY GROUP EMPLOYMENT IN THE FEDERAL GOVERNMENT, 1966.   GUSCISC66767

FAMILY CHARACTERISTICS OF THE LONG TERM UNEMPLOYED. A REPORT ON A **STUDY** OF CLAIMANTS UNDER THE TEMPORARY EXTENDED UNEMPLOYMENT COMPENSATION PROGRAM, 1961-2.   GUSDLAB61445

STUDY OF MINORITY-GROUP EMPLOYMENT IN THE FEDERAL GOVERNMENT.   GUSDLAB63500

STUDY OF THE SHORTAGE AND SALARIES OF SCIENTISTS AND ENGINEERS.   GUSSENA54353

A **STUDY** OF EMPLOYMENT PATTERNS IN THE GENERAL MERCHANDISE GROUP RETAIL STORES IN NEW-YORK-CITY.   GWATKDO66588

FINAL REPORT. PATTERNS OF DISCRIMINATION **STUDY** -- WISCONSIN.   GWISCIC66587

A **STUDY** OF STATE AND LOCAL LEGISLATIVE AND ADMINISTRATIVE ACTS DESIGNED TO MEET PROBLEMS OF HUMAN-RIGHTS.   GWISCLR52573

THE DETRIBALIZATION OF THE NARRAGANSETT INDIANS. A CASE **STUDY**.   IBOISEX56886

NARRAGANSETT SURVIVAL. A **STUDY** OF GROUP PERSISTENCE THROUGH ADAPTED TRAITS.   IBOISEX59887

THE AMERICAN INDIAN. PERSPECTIVES FOR **STUDY** OF SOCIAL CHANGE.   IEGGAFR66552

A **STUDY** OF THE REASONS FOR FAILURE ON THE JOB OF SOME GRADUATES OF INTERMOUNTAIN SCHOOL.   IFISHLX60560

A **STUDY** OF NAVAHO URBAN RELOCATION IN DENVER COLORADO.   IGRAVTD64566

ANOMIE AND ACHIEVEMENT MOTIVATION. A **STUDY** OF PERSONALITY DEVELOPMENT WITHIN CULTURAL DISORGANIZATION.   IKERCAC59018

INDIAN AFFAIRS. A **STUDY** OF THE CHANGES IN POLICY OF THE UNITED STATES TOWARD INDIANS.   ITYLESL64634

A FOLLOWUP **STUDY** OF 1963 RECIPIENTS OF THE SERVICES OF THE EMPLOYMENT ASSISTANCE PROGRAM, BUREAU-OF-INDIAN-AFFAIRS.   IUSDINT66650

AMERICAN-INDIANS IN LOS-ANGELES. A **STUDY** OF ADAPTATION TO A CITY. /CALIFORNIA/   IUVCALA66675

THE DISPLACED PERSON AND THE SOCIAL AGENCY. A **STUDY** CF THE CASEWORK PROCESS AND ITS RELATION TO IMMIGRANT ADJUSTMENT.   JCRYSDX58714

STUDY SHOWS FEW JEWS HAVE TOP JOBS IN AUTO INDUSTRY.   JNATIJM63748

A JEW WITHIN AMERICAN SOCIETY -- A **STUDY** IN ETHNIC INDIVIDUALITY.   JSHERCB61311

STUDY   (CONTINUATION)

A STUDY OF AMERICAN AND MEXICAN-AMERICAN CULTURE VALUES AND THEIR SIGNIFICANCE IN EDUCATION.   MCABRYA63373

PERCEIVED LIFE CHANCES IN THE OPPORTUNITY STRUCTURE. A STUDY OF A TRI-ETHNIC HIGH SCHOOL.   MGUERCX62410

A STUDY OF THE ACCULTURATION AND SOCIAL ASPIRATIONS OF SIXTY JUNIOR HIGH SCHOOL STUDENTS FROM THE MEXICAN
ETHNIC GROUP.   MJONEBM62421

STUDY OF SOCIO-CULTURAL FACTORS THAT INHIBIT OR ENCOURAGE DELINQUENCY AMONG MEXICAN-AMERICANS.   MLOSARW58432

PROSPECTUS OF THE MEXICAN-AMERICAN STUDY PROJECT.   MMARSRX64437

SPANISH-SPEAKING AND ENGLISH SPEAKING CHILDREN IN SOUTHWEST TEXAS. A COMPARATIVE STUDY OF INTELLIGENCE,
SOCIC-ECCNCMIC STATUS, AND ACHIEVEMENT.   MRATLYX60460

ECCNCMIC BASE STUDY OF SAN-ANTONIO AND TWENTY-SEVEN COUNTY AREAS. /TEXAS/   MSANACP64476

A STUDY OF THE MENTAL HEALTH PROBLEMS OF MEXICAN-AMERICAN RESIDENTS. /TEXAS/   MTEXASD61500

MEXICAN-AMERICAN STUDY PROJECT, ADVANCE REPORT 3, BIBLIOGRAPHY.   MUVCALM66510

SUMMARY REPORT OF THE STUDY OF DROP-OUTS IN THE THREE SENIOR HIGH SCHOOLS, COMPTON UNION HIGH SCHOOL
CISTRICT. /CALIFORNIA/   MWHITNX60517

VALUE ORIENTATION, ROLE CONFLICT, AND ALIENATION FROM WORK. A CROSS-CULTURAL STUDY.   MZURCLA65520

A STUDY OF THE OCCUPATIONAL AWARENESS OF A SELECTED GROUP OF NINTH GRADE NEGRO STUDENTS.   NAMOSWE60020

MIGRATION AND OPPORTUNITY. A STUDY OF STANDARD METROPOLITAN AREAS IN THE UNITED-STATES.   NBALATR63047

LABOR-S GRASS ROOTS. A STUDY OF THE LOCAL UNION.   NBARBJX61052

THE FRENCH AND THE NON-FRENCH IN LOUISIANA. A STUDY OF THE RELEVANCE OF ETHNIC FACTORS IN RURAL
DEVELOPMENT. /ECONOMIC-STATUS/   NBERTAL65394

A STUDY OF THE NEGRO COMMUNITY IN CHAMPAIGN-URBANA, ILLINOIS.   NBINDAM61079

RACIAL DISCRIMINATION IN THE FEDERAL SERVICE. A STUDY IN THE SOCIOLOGY OF ADMINISTRATION.   NBRADWC53106

A COMPARATIVE STUDY OF THE OCCUPATIONAL INTERESTS OF NEGRO AND WHITE ADOLESCENT BOYS.   NCONNSM65471

A PILOT STUDY OF AN INTEGRATED WORK FORCE.   NCOUSFR58611

REASCNS FOR BELATED EDUCATION. A STUDY OF THE PLIGHT OF THE OLDER NEGRO TEACHERS. /OCCUPATIONS/   NCUNNGE58244

EDUCATION AND MARGINALITY. A STUDY OF THE NEGRO COLLEGE GRADUATE.   NCUTHMV49936

A STUDY OF JOB-OPPORTUNITIES IN THE STATE OF FLORIDA FOR NEGRO COLLEGE GRADUATES.   NDECKPM60261

STUDY OF DETROIT POLICE DEPARTMENT PERSONNEL PRACTICES. /MICHIGAN OCCUPATIONS/   NDETRCC63267

BLACK METROPOLIS. A STUDY OF NEGRO LIFE IN A NORTHERN CITY.   NDRAKSC45291

THE NEGRO POPULATION OF CHICAGO. A STUDY OF RESIDENTIAL SUCCESSION. /ILLINOIS OCCUPATIONAL-PATTERNS/   NDUNCOD57306

FACTORY FOLKWAYS. A STUDY OF INSTITUTIONAL STRUCTURE AND CHANGE.   NELLSJS52331

FAMILY AND ACHIEVEMENT. A PROPOSAL TO STUDY THE EFFECT OF FAMILY SOCIALIZATION ON ACHIEVEMENT AND
PERFORMANCE AMONG URBAN NEGRO AMERICANS.   NEPPSEG65334

NEGROES IN FIVE NEW-YORK CITIES. A STUDY OF PROBLEMS, ACHIEVEMENTS AND TRENDS. /RACE-RELATIONS/   NGRIEES58455

IN SEARCH OF A FUTURE. A STUDY OF CAREER-SEEKING EXPERIENCES OF SELECTED NEGRO HIGH SCHOOL GRADUATES IN
WASHINGTON-DC WHICH WAS AN EFFORT TO PROVIDE KNOWLEDGE HELPFUL IN SOLVING ONE OF THE MOST CRITICAL
PROBLEMS FACING URBAN AMERICA TODAY.   NGRIEES63454

YOUTH IN THE GHETTO. A STUDY OF THE CONSEQUENCES OF POWERLESSNESS AND A BLUEPRINT FOR CHANGE. /NEW-YORK/   NHARLYO64485

A STUDY OF OCCUPATIONAL ATTITUDES.   NHARREC53493

A STUDY OF THE EFFECTS OF EFFORTS TO IMPROVE EMPLOYMENT-OPPORTUNITIES OF NEGROES ON THE UTILIZATION OF
NEGRO WORKERS.   NHARTJW64496

SOCIAL-CLASSES. A FRAME OF REFERENCE FOR THE STUDY OF NEGRO SOCIETY.   NHILLMC43551

THE NEGRO WORKER OF KANSAS-CITY. A STUDY OF TRADE UNION AND ORGANIZED LABOR RELATIONS.   NKANCIU40634

A STUDY OF THE EMPLOYMENT OPPORTUNITIES FOR NEGROES IN BREWERIES OF THE UNITED STATES. /INDUSTRY/   NKERNJH51897

A STUDY OF PROFESSIONAL PREPARATION OF NEGRO TEACHERS OF EXCEPTIONAL CHILDREN IN NORTH-CAROLINA COUNTY
AND CITY PUBLIC SCHOOLS.   NKNIGOB65023

LABOR UNION AND RACE-RELATIONS. A STUDY OF UNION TACTICS.   NKORNWA50660

THE NEGRO UNION OFFICIAL. A STUDY OF SPONSORSHIP AND CONTROL.   NKORNWA52661

ECCNCMIC DEPRIVATION AND EXTREMISM. A STUDY OF UNEMPLOYED NEGROES.   NLEGGJC61680

ECONOMIC CRISIS AND EXPECTATIONS OF VIOLENCE. A STUDY OF UNEMPLOYED NEGROES .   NLEGGJC64679

VOCATICNAL GRADUATES IN AUTO MECHANICS. A FOLLOW-UP STUDY OF NEGRO AND WHITE YOUTH. /OCCUPATIONS/   NLEVEBX66036

A PILOT STUDY OF PERSONALITY FACTORS RELATED TO OCCUPATIONAL ASPIRATIONS OF NEGRO COLLEGE STUDENTS.   NLITTLW66697

PATTERNS OF DISCRIMINATION STUDY -- LOUISVILLE HUMAN-RELATIONS-COMMISSION. /KENTUCKY/   NLOUIHR66582

HOSPITAL EMPLOYMENT STUDY.   NMCGODJ66583

EMPLOYMENT DISTRIBUTION STUDY OF THE CONSTRUCTION INDUSTRY IN MICHIGAN.   NMICCRC66606

A STUDY OF NON-WHITE EMPLOYMENT IN THE STATE SERVICE. /MICHIGAN/   NMICCSC64775

A FOLLOW-UP STUDY OF NON-WHITE EMPLOYMENT IN THE STATE SERVICE. /MICHIGAN/   NMICCSC65774

A STUDY OF EMPLOYMENT AND TRAINING PATTERNS IN THE LANSING AREA. /MICHIGAN/   NMICFEP58778

STUDY OF HUMAN-RIGHTS IN MISSOURI.   NMISSCH60802

A STUDY OF THE POTENTIAL SUPPLY OF NEGRO TEACHERS FOR THE COLLEGES OF NEW-YORK STATE.   NMOSSJA61858

WORKERS WANTED. A **STUDY** OF EMPLOYERS HIRING POLICIES, PREFERENCES, AND PRACTICES IN NEW-HAVEN AND CHARLOTTE. /CONNECTICUT NORTH-CAROLINA/   NNOLAEW49928

THE HARLEM RIOT. A **STUDY** IN MASS FRUSTRATION.   NOLANHX43954

A **STUDY** OF THE LONGSHORE INDUSTRY IN NEW-ORLEANS WITH EMPHASIS ON NEGRO LONGSHOREMEN. /LOUISIANA/   NORTICF56962

A REGIONAL **STUDY** OF THE NEGRO.   NPIERWG41999

MINORITY-GROUP **STUDY**. JUNE 1963. NEGRO AND TOTAL EMPLOYMENT IN SELECTED AGENCIES.   NPRESCD63010

MANAGEMENT AND MINORITY-GROUPS. A **STUDY** OF ATTITUDES AND PRACTICES IN HIRING AND UPGRADING. NROSEBX59080

THE DROPOUT AND THE DELINQUENT. PROMISING PRACTICES GLEANED FROM A YEAR OF **STUDY**.   NSCHRDX63141

A **STUDY** OF FARM MANAGEMENT PRACTICES ON 100 NEGRO FARMS IN MACON COUNTY, ALABAMA, 1949.   NSHAWBJ50339

EMPLOYMENT EXPERIENCES OF NEGRO PHILADELPHIANS. A DESCRIPTIVE **STUDY** OF THE EMPLOYMENT EXPERIENCES, PERCEPTIONS, AND ASPIRATIONS OF SELECTED PHILADELPHIA WHITES AND NON-WHITES.   NSIEGAI59718

A **STUDY** OF NEGRO FARMERS IN SOUTH-CAROLINA.   NSOUTRC62165

HOUGH, CLEVELAND, OHIO -- A **STUDY** OF SOCIAL LIFE AND CHANGE.   NSUSSMB59192

THE EXPERIENCE OF STATE FAIR-EMPLOYMENT COMMISSIONS. A COMPARATIVE **STUDY**.   NSUTIAX65343

AN EMPIRICAL **STUDY** OF HIGH SCHOOL DROPOUTS IN REGARD TO TEN POSSIBLY RELATED FACTORS.   NTHOMRJ54159

STUDY OF MINORITY-GROUP EMPLOYMENT IN THE FEDERAL-GOVERNMENT, 1963.   NUSCISC63228

STUDY OF MINORITY-GROUP EMPLOYMENT IN THE FEDERAL GOVERNMENT, 1965.   NUSCISC65229

IMPACT OF OFFICE AUTOMATION IN THE INTERNAL REVENUE SERVICE. A **STUDY** OF THE MANPOWER IMPLICATIONS DURING THE FIRST STAGES OF THE CHANGEOVER. /ECONOMIC-STATUS/   NUSDLAB63198

STUDY OF ECONOMIC AND CULTURAL ACTIVITIES IN THE WARREN AREA AS THEY RELATE TO MINORITY PEOPLE. /OHIO/   NWARRUL64986

A **STUDY** OF SOME ASPECTS OF JOB SATISFACTION AMONG NEGRO WHITE-COLLAR WORKERS.   NWEATMD54296

COMPARATIVE **STUDY** OF SOCIO-ECONOMIC AND SOCIAL-PSYCHOLOGICAL DETERMINANTS OF EDUCATIONAL AND OCCUPATIONAL ASPIRATIONS OF NEGRO AND WHITE COLLEGE SENIORS.   NWHITRM59319

NEGRO FAMILIES IN RURAL WISCONSIN, A **STUDY** OF THEIR COMMUNITY LIFE.   NWISCGC59331

MISSISSIPPI WORKERS. WHERE THEY COME FROM AND HOW THEY PERFORM. A **STUDY** OF WORKING FORCES IN SELECTED MISSISSIPPI INDUSTRIAL PLANTS.   NWOFFBM55333

AFTER HIGH SCHOOL WHAT...HIGHLIGHTS OF A **STUDY** OF CAREER PLANS OF NEGRO AND WHITE RURAL YOUTH IN THREE FLORIDA COUNTIES. /ASPIRATIONS/   NYOUMEG65390

CONTRASTIVE ACCULTURATION OF CALIFORNIA JAPANESE. COMPARATIVE APPROACH TO THE **STUDY** OF IMMIGRANTS.   OBEFUHX65701

CALIFORNIA-S FRUIT AND VEGETABLE CANNING INDUSTRY. AN ECONOMIC **STUDY**.   OBENJMP61704

THE EFFECT OF LOW EDUCATIONAL ATTAINMENT ON INCOMES. A COMPARATIVE **STUDY** OF SELECTED ETHNIC GROUPS.   OFOGEWX66721

THE PUERTO-RICAN SECTION. A **STUDY** IN SOCIAL TRANSITION.   PHERNJX59816

THE PUERTO-RICAN **STUDY**. 1953-1957.   PNEWYCC58833

THE BLS **STUDY** OF NURSES SALARIES AND EMPLOYMENT CONDITIONS.   WAMERJN57378

A **STUDY** OF ELEMENTARY SCHOOL TEACHER-S ATTITUDES TOWARD THE WOMAN PRINCIPAL AND TOWARD ELEMENTARY PRINCIPALSHIP AS A CAREER. /DISCRIMINATION/   WBARTAK58629

THE ACHIEVEMENT MOTIVE IN WOMEN. A **STUDY** OF THE IMPLICATIONS FOR CAREER DEVELOPMENT.   WBARURX66453

A **STUDY** TO DETERMINE THE EMPLOYMENT POTENTIAL OF MOTHERS RECEIVING AID-TO-DEPENDENT-CHILDREN ASSISTANCE.   WBROODJ64656

SEX-ROLE AND PROFESSIONALISM. A **STUDY** OF HIGH SCHOOL TEACHERS. /OCCUPATIONS/   WCOLOJX63698

AN EXPLORATORY **STUDY** OF EMPLOYERS ATTITUDES TOWARD WORKING MOTHERS.   WCONYJE61704

A **STUDY** OF JOB MOTIVATIONS, ACTIVITIES, AND SATISFACTIONS OF PRESENT AND PROSPECTIVE WOMEN COLLEGE FACULTY MEMBERS. /OCCUPATIONS/   WCOOKWX60252

ROLE CONCEPTION AND CAREER ASPIRATION. A **STUDY** OF IDENTITY IN NURSING.   WCORWRG61707

A COMPARATIVE **STUDY** OF TOP LEVEL MALE AND FEMALE EXECUTIVES IN HARRIS-COUNTY. /TEXAS OCCUPATIONS/   WDOLLPA65738

STUDY OF ADOLESCENT GIRLS. /ASPIRATIONS/   WDOUVEX57742

THE ROLE OF THE EDUCATED WOMAN. AN EMPIRICAL **STUDY** OF THE ATTITUDES OF A GROUP OF COLLEGE WOMEN. /WORK-WOMAN-ROLE/   WFREEMB65770

PATTERNS IN WOMANPOWER. A PILOT **STUDY**.   WHANSEB62820

STUDY OF JOB OPPORTUNITIES FOR WOMEN COLLEGE GRADUATES. /OCCUPATIONS/   WINTEAP58861

A PILOT **STUDY** OF THE MOTIVATIONS AND PROBLEMS OF MIDDLE AGED HOMEMAKERS IN LOWER SOCIO-ECONOMIC GROUPS IN SEEKING EMPLOYMENT. /ASPIRATIONS/   WJEWIVA62883

WOMAN AT WORK -- A **STUDY** IN PREJUDICE. /DISCRIMINATION/   WMARMJX66954

LABOR-FORCE PARTICIPATION OF MARRIED WOMEN. A **STUDY** OF LABOR SUPPLY.   WMINCJX62984

WOMEN ON COLLEGE AND UNIVERSITY FACULTIES. A HISTORICAL SURVEY AND A **STUDY** OF THEIR PRESENT ACADEMIC STATUS. /OCCUPATIONS/   WPOLLLA65063

WHY WOMEN START AND STOP WORKING. A **STUDY** IN MOBILITY.   WROSECX65088

WORKING WIVES. AN ECONOMETRIC **STUDY**.   WROSERX58089

A **STUDY** OF WOMEN IN OFFICE MANAGEMENT POSITIONS WITH IMPLICATIONS FOR BUSINESS EDUCATION. /OCCUPATIONS/   WRUSHEM57096

SOME CHANGING ROLES OF WOMEN IN SUBURBIA. A SOCIAL ANTHROPOLOGICAL CASE **STUDY**. /WORK-FAMILY-CONFLICT/   WSCOFNE60109

OCCUPATIONAL PLANNING BY YOUNG WOMEN. A **STUDY** OF OCCUPATIONAL EXPERIENCES, ASPIRATIONS, ATTITUDES, AND

STUDY   (CONTINUATION)
PLANS OF COLLEGE AND HIGH SCHOOL GIRLS.   WSLOCWL56116

RADCLIFFE INSTITUTE FOR INDEPENDENT STUDY. /TRAINING/   WSMITCX63119

THE CHANGING WOMAN WORKER. A STUDY OF THE FEMALE LABOR-FORCE IN NEW-JERSEY AND IN THE NATION FROM 1940 TO
1958.   WSMITGM60120

HELP WANTED -- FEMALE. A STUDY OF DEMAND AND SUPPLY IN A LOCAL JOB MARKET FOR WOMEN. /MANPOWER/   WSMITGM64121

THE FEMALE LABOR-FORCE. A CASE STUDY IN THE INTERPRETATION OF HISTORICAL STATISTICS.   WSMUTRW60124

THE MARRIED FEMALE SCHOOL TEACHER. A CONTINUED STUDY. /WORK-FAMILY-CONFLICT/   WSTEPCM60139

ACCESS OF GIRLS AND WOMEN TO EDUCATION IN RURAL AREAS. A COMPARATIVE STUDY.   WUNESCO64166

GOVERNMENT CAREERS FOR WOMEN -- A STUDY.   WUSDLAB57198

FIFTEEN YEARS AFTER COLLEGE -- A STUDY OF ALUMNAE OF THE CLASS OF 1945.   WUSDLAB62193

A STUDY OF THE LIFE PLANNING OF 550 FRESHMEN WOMEN AT PURDUE UNIVERSITY. /WORK-FAMILY-CONFLICT/   WZISSCX64285

STUDY-SKILLS
YOU NEED TO SEE IT TO BELIEVE IT. REPORT OF THE 1963 SUMMER STUDY-SKILLS PROGRAMS. /COLLEGE EDUCATION/   NMARTWD63303

STYLE
WORK RELIEF. SOCIAL WELFARE STYLE. /MANPOWER UNEMPLOYMENT/   GLEVISA66531

POVERTY AMERICAN STYLE.   GMILLHP66989

UNION RESISTANCE. SOUTHERN STYLE.   NGOULHM48436

STYLES
LIFE STYLES OF EDUCATED WOMEN. /WORK-FAMILY-CONFLICT/   WGINZEX66785

ATTITUDES TOWARD CAREER AND MARRIAGE AND THE DEVELOPMENT OF LIFE STYLES IN YOUNG WOMEN.
/WORK-FAMILY-CONFLICT/   WMATTEX64962

SUB-COMMITTEE
STATEMENT BEFORE CALIFORNIA SENATE SUB-COMMITTEE ON RACE-RELATIONS AND URBAN PROBLEMS.   OLOWXHW64745

SUB-CONTRACTS
LOCAL CONTRACTS AND SUB-CONTRACTS. THE ROLES OF CITY GOVERNMENT AND PRIVATE CITIZENS GROUPS. GJONEMX64829

SUB-EMPLOYMENT
SUB-EMPLOYMENT IN THE SLUMS OF NEW-YORK.   GUSDLAB66511

SUB-EMPLOYMENT IN THE SLUMS OF NEW-ORLEANS. /LOUISIANA/   GUSDLAB66512

SUB-EMPLOYMENT IN THE SLUMS OF PHOENIX. /ARIZONA/   GUSDLAB66513

SUB-EMPLOYMENT IN THE SLUMS OF LOS-ANGELES. /CALIFORNIA/   GUSDLAB66514

SUB-EMPLOYMENT IN THE SLUMS OF SAN-ANTONIO. /TEXAS/   GUSDLAB66515

SUB-EMPLOYMENT IN THE SLUMS OF CLEVELAND. /OHIO/   GUSDLAB66516

SUB-EMPLOYMENT IN THE SLUMS OF ST-LOUIS. /MISSOURI/   GUSDLAB66517

SUB-EMPLOYMENT IN THE SLUMS OF BOSTON. /MASSACHUSETTS/   GUSDLAB66518

SUB-EMPLOYMENT IN THE SLUMS OF SAN-FRANCISCO. /CALIFORNIA/   GUSDLAB66519

SUB-EMPLOYMENT IN THE SLUMS OF OAKLAND. /CALIFORNIA/   GUSDLAB66521

SUB-EMPLOYMENT IN THE SLUMS OF PHILADELPHIA. /PENNSYLVANIA/   GUSDLAB66522

SUBCOMMITTEE
HEARING OF THE SUBCOMMITTEE ON ECONOMIC DEVELOPMENT, EDITED TRANSCRIPT, JANUARY 28 AND 29, 1964.
/CALIFORNIA FEP/   GCALAIW64510

I STATEMENT BEFORE THE HOUSE POST OFFICE AND CIVIL SERVICE SUBCOMMITTEE ON POSTAL OPERATIONS, II
DISCRIMINATION. PLANNED AND ACCIDENTAL. /TESTING/   GENNEWH67928

THE MANPOWER REVOLUTION. ITS POLICY CONSEQUENCES. EXCERPTS FROM SENATE HEARINGS BEFORE THE CLARK
SUBCOMMITTEE.   GMANGGL66217

NEW-YORK STATE-COMMISSION-AGAINST-DISCRIMINATION, STATEMENT BEFORE THE US SENATE SUBCOMMITTEE ON LABOR
AND LABOR-MANAGEMENT RELATIONS.   GNEWYSA52102

TESTIMONY TO THE SUBCOMMITTEE ON RACE-RELATIONS AND URBAN PROBLEMS. /SES CALIFORNIA/   GREDMWX64221

TESTIMONY BEFORE SUBCOMMITTEE ON ECONOMIC STATISTICS, MAY 17, 1965.   GUSCONG65421

TRANSCRIPT OF PROCEEDINGS OF THE INTERIM SUBCOMMITTEE ON SPECIAL EMPLOYMENT PROBLEMS. /CALIFORNIA/   MCALAIC64374

TESTIMONY BEFORE STATE SENATE FACT FINDING SUBCOMMITTEE ON RACE-RELATIONS AND URBAN PROBLEMS, FINAL
HEARING. JANUARY 20 1965. /CALIFORNIA FEPC/   NGRAHCX65439

HEARING BEFORE THE AD HOC SUBCOMMITTEE ON THE WAR-ON-POVERTY PROGRAM.   NYOUNWM64350

STATEMENT BEFORE CALIFORNIA LEGISLATURE ASSEMBLY, INTERIM SUBCOMMITTEE ON ECONOMIC OPPORTUNITY ON BEHALF
OF CHINATOWN-NORTH BEACH DISTRICT COUNCIL.   OWONGLJ64771

SUBCONTRACTORS
TEXTS OF RULES AND REGULATIONS OF PRESIDENT-S COMMITTEE ON EQUAL-EMPLOYMENT-OPPORTUNITY RELATING TO
OBLIGATIONS OF GOVERNMENT CONTRACTORS AND SUBCONTRACTORS, EFFECTIVE JULY 22, 1961. A BNA SPECIAL REPORT.   GBURENA61498

SUBCONTRACTS
STATE AND LOCAL CONTRACTS AND SUBCONTRACTS.   GCONWJE64599

SUBORDINATION
NEGRO SUBORDINATION AND WHITE GAINS. /INCOME OCCUPATIONAL-STATUS/   NCUTRPX65245

OCCUPATIONAL BENEFITS TO WHITES FROM THE SUBORDINATION OF NEGROES. /DISCRIMINATION/   NGLENND63423

REPLY TO CUTRIGHT ON NEGRO SUBORDINATION. /OCCUPATIONAL-STATUS/   NGLENND65425

SUBPROFESSIONAL
THE FEDERAL ANTI-POVERTY PROGRAM AND SOME IMPLICATIONS OF SUBPROFESSIONAL TRAINING.   GGORDJE65135

SUBURB
THE POOR IN CITY AND SUBURB, 1964.   GORSHMX66282

SUBURBAN
EQUAL-EMPLOYMENT-OPPORTUNITY IN THE SUBURBAN SHOPPING CENTER. FACT OR FICTION. /MICHIGAN/   NMICFEP63777

LABOR-FORCE PARTICIPATION OF SUBURBAN MOTHERS.   WMYERGC64011

SUBURBIA
SOME CHANGING ROLES OF WOMEN IN SUBURBIA. A SOCIAL ANTHROPOLOGICAL CASE STUDY. /WORK-FAMILY-CONFLICT/   WSCOFNE60109

SUBURBS
SLUMS AND SUBURBS. /TRAINING/   NCONAJB61920

SUCCESS
UNDERSTANDING THE HUMAN FACTOR. THE KEY TO SUPERVISORY SUCCESS.   GPRESCP59201

HIGHER EDUCATION OF SOUTHWESTERN INDIANS WITH REFERENCE TO SUCCESS AND FAILURE.   IMCGRGD62584

SECURING SKILLS NEEDED FOR SUCCESS. COMMUNITY JOB TRAINING FOR NEGROES.   NBLUMAA66099

RESEARCH ON NEGRO JOB SUCCESS.   NCHALWE62189

CULTURAL EXPOSURE AND RACE AS VARIABLES IN PREDICTING TRAINING AND JOB SUCCESS. /TESTING/   NLOCKHCND700

AGE AND MARITAL-STATUS AND THEIR RELATIONSHIP TO SUCCESS IN PRACTICAL NURSING. /OCCUPATIONS/   WMEADLX63967

SUCCESSION
THE NEGRO POPULATION OF CHICAGO. A STUDY OF RESIDENTIAL SUCCESSION. /ILLINOIS OCCUPATIONAL-PATTERNS/   NDUNCOD57306

SUGAR
SUGAR BEET LABOR IN NORTHERN COLORADO. /MIGRANT-WORKERS/   GDAVIIF58939

SUIT
EARNINGS IN THE WOMEN-S AND MISSES COAT AND SUIT INDUSTRY.   WUSDLAB57988

SUITABILITY
AN ASSESSMENT OF THE SUITABILITY OF THE FACETED STRUCTURE OF THE WRU EDUCATION THESAURUS AS A FRAMEWORK
FOR PREPARATION OF A THESAURUS OF EQUAL-EMPLOYMENT-OPPORTUNITY TERMS.   GBARHGC66162

SUMMARY
GENERAL SOCIAL AND ECONOMIC CHARACTERISTICS. SUMMARY. US CENSUS OF 1960. /DEMOGRAPHY/   CUSBURC62374

FEDERAL CIVIL-RIGHTS-ACT OF 1960. SUMMARY AND ANALYSIS.   GAMERJD60385

THE CIVIL-RIGHTS AND CIVIL-LIBERTIES DECISIONS OF THE US SUPREME COURT FOR THE 1962-63 TERM. A SUMMARY
AND ANALYSIS.   GAMERJD63384

AUTOMATION AND ECONOMIC PROGRESS. A SUMMARY OF THE REPORT OF THE NATIONAL COMMISSION ON TECHNOLOGY,
AUTOMATION, AND ECONOMIC PROGRESS.   GBOWEHR66748

APPRENTICESHIP AND TESTS. FEP SUMMARY OF LATEST DEVELOPMENTS.   GBUREON65491

A SUMMARY ANALYSIS OF FIVE YEARS OF CLAIMS EXPERIENCE BY THE MICHIGAN
FAIR-EMPLOYMENT-PRACTICES-COMMISSION, FEBRUARY, 1961.   GCOUSFR61612

A SUMMARY ANALYSIS OF SIX YEARS OF CLAIMS EXPERIENCE BY THE MICHIGAN FAIR-EMPLOYMENT
PRACTICES-COMMISSION, FEBRUARY 1962.   GCOUSFR62613

A SUMMARY REPORT OF PRACTICES AND PROGRAMS DESIGNED TO REDUCE THE NUMBER OF DROPOUTS IN THE HIGH SCHOOLS
OF LOS-ANGELES COUNTY. /CALIFORNIA/   GDELMDT66147

THE ROLE OF THE SECONDARY SCHOOLS IN THE PREPARATION OF YOUTH FOR EMPLOYMENT. SUMMARY, CONCLUSIONS. AND
RECOMMENDATIONS.   GKAUFJJ67963

RURAL INDUSTRIALIZATION. A SUMMARY OF FIVE STUDIES. /UNEMPLOYMENT OCCUPATIONS/   GMAITST61383

FAIR-EMPLOYMENT-PRACTICES LEGISLATION. A SUMMARY OF ITS HISTORY AND DEVELOPMENT WITH STATEMENTS ON BOTH
SIDES.   GMITCJA52016

EVERYBODY-S BUSINESS. A SUMMARY OF NEW-YORK STATE ANTI-DISCRIMINATION LAWS AND HOW TO USE THEM.   GNATLFC46048

SUMMARY OF RULES, REGULATIONS, AND LAWS THAT AFFECT SEASONAL FARM WORKERS AND THEIR EMPLOYERS IN NEW-YORK
STATE. /MIGRANT-WORKERS/   GNEWYSJND113

SUMMARY OF PROCEEDINGS. WORKSHOP ON THE IMPACT OF A TIGHTENING LABOR-MARKET ON THE EMPLOYABILITY AND
EMPLOYMENT OF DISADVANTAGED YOUTH.   GNEWYUC66116

SUMMARY OF TESTIMONY -- HOTEL RESTAURANT HEARINGS, APPENDIX A. /PHILADELPHIA PENNSYLVANIA/   GPHILCH60181

SUMMARY FACT SHEETS FOR STATE PUBLIC AGENCIES WITH JURISDICTION OVER DISCRIMINATION IN EMPLOYMENT. GUSCOMC65416

BRIEF SUMMARY OF STATE LAWS AGAINST DISCRIMINATION IN PRIVATE EMPLOYMENT. FAIR-EMPLOYMENT-PRACTICE ACTS.   GUSDLAB63439

A PROGRAM FOR INDIAN CITIZENS. A SUMMARY REPORT.   IFUNDFT61562

SUMMARY REPORT OF THE STUDY OF DROP-OUTS IN THE THREE SENIOR HIGH SCHOOLS, COMPTON UNION HIGH SCHOOL
DISTRICT. /CALIFORNIA/   MWHITNX60517

SUMMARY OF MAJOR POINTS, TALK ON EMPLOYMENT, MCCONE-COMMISSION SERIES.   NBULLPX66898

ETHNIC CENSUS OF EXAMINATION COMPETITORS. REPORT OF EXAMINATIONS GIVEN JULY THROUGH DECEMBER, 1965,
SUMMARY. /TESTING CALIFORNIA/   NCALFPB66173

MONTHLY SUMMARY OF EVENTS AND TRENDS IN RACE-RELATIONS. /CINCINNATI OHIO CASE-STUDY UNION/   NFISKUX44357

SUMMARY OF A SURVEY OF SOCIAL AND ECONOMIC CONDITIONS IN MORRIS COUNTY NEW-JERSEY AS THEY AFFECT THE
NEGRO.   NKERNJH57645

SUMMARY JUSTICE -- THE NEGRO GI IN KOREA. /MILITARY/   NMARSTX51755

REPORT AND SUMMARY OF THE AIR FORCE ON ACTIONS TAKEN BY LOCKHEED AIRCRAFT CORPORATION AT THE AIR FORCE
PLANT NO 6 IN MARIETTA. GEORGIA. /INDUSTRY/   NPRESCD61013

A CRITICAL SUMMARY. THE NEGRO ON THE HOME FRONT IN WORLD-WARS I AND II.   NREIDID43048

SUMMARY REPORT. EQUAL-EMPLOYMENT-OPPORTUNITY CONFERENCE.   NUSNAAS63267

SUMMARY OF RESEARCH DURING 1964 RELATED TO THE NEGRO AND NEGRO EDUCATION.   NWESTEX66315

SUMMARY   (CONTINUATION)
    A SUMMARY IN FACTS AND FIGURES.   PPUERRDN0792

    PROBLEMS OF WORKING WOMEN. SUMMARY REPORT OF A CONFERENCE.   WAFLCIO61618

    SUMMARY OF CURRENT RESEARCH ON WOMEN-S ROLES.   WNOBLJL59035

    SUMMARY OF STATE LABOR LAWS FOR WOMEN.   WUSDLABND219

    PRIVATE-HOUSEHOLD EMPLOYMENT -- SUMMARY OF FIRST AND SECOND CONSULTATIONS. /HOUSEHOLD-WORKERS/   WUSDLAB64212

    TO FULFILL THESE RIGHTS. SUMMARY REPORT OF PRE-WHITE-HOUSE CONFERENCES.   WYWCAXX66079

SUMMATION
    NATIONAL CONFERENCE ON MANPOWER PROGRAMS FOR INDIANS. SUMMATION.   IKRUGDH67811

SUPERSTITION
    PREJUDICE. SUPERSTITION. AND ECONOMICS.   NHOWERW56582

SUPERVISING
    SOME GUIDES FOR SUPERVISING WOMEN WORKERS.   WGRANLJ63800

SUPERVISION
    TERMINATION OF FEDERAL SUPERVISION. DISINTEGRATION AND THE AMERICAN-INDIANS.   ILAFAOX57075

SUPERVISOR
    WHAT THE SUPERVISOR SHOULD KNOW ABOUT THE EQUAL-EMPLOYMENT-OPPORTUNITY LAW.   GAHEREX65804

    SUPERVISOR DEVELOPMENT PROGRAM, BASIC COURSE, NONDISCRIMINATION POLICY. /MILITARY/   GUSDARM56192

SUPERVISORY
    UNDERSTANDING THE HUMAN FACTOR. THE KEY TO SUPERVISORY SUCCESS.   GPRESCP59201

SUPPLEMENT
    FARM LABOR DEVELOPMENTS -- EMPLOYMENT AND WAGE SUPPLEMENT.   GUSDLAB66446

    TOWARD EQUALITY, BALTIMORE-S PROGRESS-REPORT. 1962 SUPPLEMENT. /MARYLAND/   NBALTUL62049

    SPECIAL SUPPLEMENT ON THE AMERICAN FEMALE. /WORK-WOMAN-ROLE/   WHARPXX62822

SUPPLEMENTAL
    EQUAL-EMPLOYMENT-OPPORTUNITY IN THE US POST OFFICE DEPARTMENT. A SUPPLEMENTAL REPORT TO THE POSTMASTER
    GENERAL.   GUSPODA63516

SUPPLEMENTARY
    THE HIRED FARM WORKING FORCE OF 1963 WITH SUPPLEMENTARY DATA FOR 1962. /ECONOMIC-STATUS/   GBOWLGK65432

    SUPPLEMENTARY ACTIVITIES FOR STATE GOVERNMENTS SEEKING TO ELIMINATE DISCRIMINATION.   GROUTFB64264

    SUPPLEMENTARY REPORT ON PUERTO-RICANS IN BUFFALO. /NEW-YORK/   PIMSETP62820

SUPPLY
    POTENTIAL SUPPLY AND REPLACEMENT OF RURAL MALES OF LABOR-FORCE AGE, 1960-70.   GBOWLGK66430

    EQUAL-EMPLOYMENT-OPPORTUNITY IN THE DEFENSE SUPPLY AGENCY.   GDEFESA64631

    PROJECTIONS OF MANPOWER REQUIREMENTS AND SUPPLY.   GGOLDHX66933

    POPULATION CHANGE AND THE SUPPLY OF LABOR.   GLEBESX60276

    THE MEXICAN FARM LABOR SUPPLY PROGRAM -- ITS FRIENDS AND FOES.   MPFEIDG63456

    THE CHARACTERISTICS OF THE SUPPLY OF NEGROES FOR PROFESSIONAL OCCUPATIONS.   NANDERW65024

    NEGRO FARM LABOR IN THE DELTA AREA OF MISSISSIPPI. SUPPLY AND UTILIZATION.   NLERANL61416

    TEACHER SUPPLY AND DEMAND IN THE NEGRO COLLEGE.   NLLOYRG54045

    A STUDY OF THE POTENTIAL SUPPLY OF NEGRO TEACHERS FOR THE COLLEGES OF NEW-YORK STATE.   NMOSSJA61858

    LABOR SUPPLY IN THE SOUTH.   NUSDLAB46824

    ENGINEERING TALENT IN SHORT SUPPLY. /OCCUPATIONS/   WAMONRX62613

    LABOR SUPPLY. FAMILY INCOME, AND CONSUMPTION.   WMINCJX60985

    LABOR-FORCE PARTICIPATION OF MARRIED WOMEN. A STUDY OF LABOR SUPPLY.   WMINCJX62984

    THE INTERACTION OF DEMAND AND SUPPLY AND ITS EFFECT ON THE FEMALE LABOR-FORCE IN THE UNITED STATES.   WOPPEVK66289

    HELP WANTED -- FEMALE. A STUDY OF DEMAND AND SUPPLY IN A LOCAL JOB MARKET FOR WOMEN. /MANPOWER/   WSMITGM64121

    SUPPLY OF MEDICAL WOMEN IN THE UNITED STATES. /OCCUPATIONS/   WWRIGKW66277

SUPPORT
    STATEMENT TO THE COMMITTEE ON LEGISLATION IN SUPPORT OF AN EFFECTIVE FEDERAL FEP LAW AND OTHER VITAL
    CIVIL-RIGHTS LEGISLATION.   GOLIVWX60134

    BRIEF SUBMITTED IN SUPPORT OF SENATE BILL NO 984, A BILL TO PROHIBIT DISCRIMINATION IN EMPLOYMENT....   GTUTTCH47368

    EXECUTIVE SUPPORT OF CIVIL-RIGHTS.   NSOUTRC62159

SUPPORTIVE
    ISSUES AND PROBLEMS IN INTEGRATING NEEDED SUPPORTIVE SERVICES IN NEIGHBORHOOD-YOUTH-CORPS PROJECTS.   GBATTMX66131

SUPREME-COURT
    THE SUPREME-COURT AND GROUP DISCRIMINATION SINCE 1937.   GBERGMX49443

SURNAME
    PERSONS OF SPANISH-SURNAME. SOCIAL AND ECONOMIC DATA FOR WHITE PERSONS OF SPANISH SURNAME IN 5
    SOUTHWESTERN STATES. /DEMOGRAPHY/   CUSBURC63181

    CALIFORNIANS OF SPANISH SURNAME. POPULATION, EMPLOYMENT, INCOME, EDUCATION.   MCALDIR64377

SURPLUS
    SHORTAGE OR SURPLUS. AN ASSESSMENT OF BOSTON WOMANPOWER IN INDUSTRY, GOVERNMENT, AND RESEARCH. JUNE 7-8,
    1963. /MASSACHUSETTS/   WUSDLAB66217

SURVEY
    REPORT TO GOVERNOR EDMUND G BROWN. SECOND ETHNIC SURVEY OF EMPLOYMENT AND PROMOTION IN STATE GOVERNMENT.

CBECKWL65070

NEGROES AND MEXICAN-AMERICANS IN SOUTH AND EAST LOS-ANGELES. AN ANALYSIS OF A SPECIAL US CENSUS **SURVEY** OF
NOVEMBER 1965. /CALIFORNIA/   CCALDIR66168

ETHNIC **SURVEY** OF MUNICIPAL-EMPLOYEES. A REPORT ON THE NUMBER AND DISTRIBUTION OF NEGROES AND
PUERTO-RICANS AND OTHER EMPLOYEES BY THE CITY OF NEW-YORK.   CNEWYCO64916

A FIVE-STATE **SURVEY** OF DISCRIMINATION BY COMMERCIAL EMPLOYMENT AGENCIES.   GAMERJD63386

SECOND ETHNIC **SURVEY** OF EMPLOYMENT AND PROMOTION IN STATE GOVERNMENT. /CALIFORNIA/   GBECKWL65433

COMMUNITY **SURVEY**. LONG BEACH, CALIFORNIA.   GCALFEPND541

SAN-MATEO AREA MINORITY JOB **SURVEY**. /CALIFORNIA/   GCALFEP65542

1964 MANPOWER **SURVEY**. /CHICAGO ILLINOIS/   GCOMIEF64592

PLANT INSPECTION **SURVEY** BY MANAGEMENT -- MINORITY-GROUP INTEGRATION. /COLORADO/   GDENNGHND632

REPORT OF THE DIAGNOSTIC **SURVEY** OF TENANT HOUSEHOLDS IN THE WEST SIDE URBAN-RENEWAL AREA OF
NEW-YORK-CITY.   GGREEAI65474

ILLINOIS JOB SEEKERS **SURVEY**. EDUCATION, SKILLS, LENGTH OF UNEMPLOYMENT, AND PERSONAL CHARACTERISTICS.   GILLIDI62004

ILLINOIS JOB SEEKER-S **SURVEY**.   GILLIGC62795

REPORT OF THE **SURVEY** OF EMPLOYEES OF THE STATE OF INDIANA, SEPTEMBER 1961.   GINDICR61806

SURVEY OF STATE ANTI-DISCRIMINATORY LAWS.   GLABOLR44877

SURVEY OF MINORITY-GROUP EMPLOYMENT AND PATIENT CARE IN PRIVATE HOSPITAL FACILITIES IN LOS-ANGELES
COUNTY. /CALIFORNIA/   GLOSACCND914

ETHNIC **SURVEY** OF EMPLOYMENT IN STATE GOVERNMENT. /CALIFORNIA/   GMESPFA63977

SURVEY AND ANALYSIS OF NON-WHITE EMPLOYMENT BY THE CITY OF MINNEAPOLIS. /MINNESOTA/   GMINLMH65002

REPORT ON A **SURVEY** OF EMPLOYMENT POLICIES AND HIRING PRACTICES INVOLVING MINORITY-GROUPS IN HUDON-COUNTY,
NEW-JERSEY.   GNEWJDE51060

REPORT ON A **SURVEY** OF EMPLOYMENT POLICIES AND PRACTICES INVOLVING MINORITY-GROUPS IN MIDDLESEX-COUNTY,
NEW-JERSEY.   GNEWJDE52061

SURVEY OF EMPLOYMENT IN STATE GOVERNMENT. /NORTH-CAROLINA/   GNCRTCG64121

SURVEY OF OHIO COLLEGE AND UNIVERSITY PLACEMENT OFFICES WITH REGARD TO JOB PLACEMENT OF MINORITY
STUDENTS.   GOHIOCR62132

FAIR EMPLOYMENT **SURVEY** OF THE WESTCHESTER AREA. /PENNSYLVANIA/   GPENNHR65163

SECOND **SURVEY** OF NON-WHITE EMPLOYEES IN STATE GOVERNMENT IN PENNSYLVANIA.   GPENNHR65167

REPORT OF 1961 - 1962 **SURVEY** OF PHILADELPHIA BANKS AND ATTACHED COMPOSITE TABULATION OF NON-WHITES.
/PENNSYLVANIA/   GPHILCH62180

MUNICIPAL HUMAN-RELATIONS COMMISSION. A **SURVEY** OF PROGRAMS IN SELECTED CITIES OF THE UNITED STATES.   GRICHCM63236

DIMENSIONS IN DISCRIMINATION. A PRELIMINARY **SURVEY** OF SAN-DIEGO-S COMMUNITY PROBLEMS OF DISCRIMINATION
PART II. /CALIFORNIA/   GSANDLW65274

RACIAL AND ETHNIC EMPLOYMENT PATTERN **SURVEY** OF THE CITY AND COUNTY OF SAN-FRANCISCO GOVERNMENT.
DEPARTMENTAL ANALYSIS. /CALIFORNIA/   GSANFHR65264

A **SURVEY** OF DISCRIMINATION IN THE BUILDING TRADES INDUSTRY, NEW-YORK CITY.   GSHAUDF63300

SURVEY OF NON-WHITE EMPLOYEES IN STATE GOVERNMENT. /PENNSYLVANIA/   GSTRUJW63338

CURRENT MANPOWER PROBLEMS. AN INTRODUCTORY **SURVEY**.   GSTURAF64837

EMPLOYMENT **SURVEY**. /TULSA OKLAHOMA/   GTULSCR66364

A **SURVEY** OF CURRENT LITERATURE ON AUTOMATION AND OTHER TECHNOLOGICAL-CHANGES. A SELECTED ANNOTATED
BIBLIOGRAPHY.   GUSDLAB64825

ETHNIC **SURVEY** OF APPRENTICES. /CALIFORNIA/   GWEBBEB65546

CITY EMPLOYMENT **SURVEY**. PERCENTAGE OF MINORITY-GROUP EMPLOYEES BY DEPARTMENT. /YONKERS NEW-YORK/   GYONKCC66592

ARIZONA RESERVATIONS ECONOMICS. **SURVEY** REPORT.   IARIZCI63528

HUMAN RESOURCES **SURVEY** OF THE COLVILLE CONFEDERATE TRIBES.   IBLOOJA59538

UTE INDIAN **SURVEY** -- PRELIMINARY REPORT, SOCIAL AND ECONOMIC CHARACTERISTICS.   IBRIGYUND442

SOCIAL **SURVEY** OF AMERICAN-INDIAN URBAN INTEGRATION.   IHIRAJXND444

SOCIAL AND ECONOMIC **SURVEY** OF POTAWATOMIE JURISDICTION.   IUSDINT57660

INDIAN UNEMPLOYMENT **SURVEY**, JULY 1963.   IUSHOUR63670

PRELIMINARY REPORT ON **SURVEY** OF ACTIVE APPRENTICES. /CALIFORNIA/   MCALDIR62376

SURVEY ON TRANSIENT MEXICAN LABOR REQUIREMENTS.   MLOSACAND430

A **SURVEY** OF THE PROBLEMS INVOLVED IN THE AMERICANIZATION OF THE MEXICAN-AMERICAN.   MREYEIX57463

EMPLOYMENT AND EMPLOYABILITY AMONG CALIFORNIA YOUTH AUTHORITY WARDS. A **SURVEY**.   MSECKJP62483

EMPLOYMENT **SURVEY** OF DES-MOINES FIRMS. /IOWA/   NDESMCH65265

YOUNG NEGRO TALENT. **SURVEY** OF THE EXPERIENCES AND EXPECTATIONS OF NEGRO AMERICANS WHO GRADUATED FROM
COLLEGE IN 1961.   NFICHJH64867

THE NEGRO LAWYER IN VIRGINIA. A **SURVEY**. /OCCUPATIONS/   NFRIEMX65387

TO STEM THIS TIDE. A **SURVEY** OF RACIAL TENSION AREAS IN THE U.S.   NJOHNCS43617

SURVEY·   (CONTINUATION)
   SUMMARY OF A **SURVEY** OF SOCIAL AND ECONOMIC CONDITIONS IN MORRIS COUNTY NEW-JERSEY AS THEY AFFECT THE
   NEGRO.   NKERNJH57645

   SURVEY OF EQUAL-EMPLOYMENT-OPPORTUNITIES IN NEW-JERSEY INVESTOR-OWNED PUBLIC UTILITIES.   NLEVIMJ66607

   SURVEY OF ALBION, MICHIGAN.   NMICCRC64772

   NILES COMMUNITY SELF **SURVEY.** /MICHIGAN/   NMICCRC65771

   INTELLIGENCE IN THE UNITED STATES. A **SURVEY** -- WITH CONCLUSIONS FOR MANPOWER UTILIZATION IN EDUCATION AND
   EMPLOYMENT.   NMINEJB57796

   EQUAL-EMPLOYMENT-OPPORTUNITIES IN MISSOURI STATE AGENCIES. A **SURVEY** OF NEGRO EMPLOYMENT, SPRING-SUMMER
   1963.   NMISSCH64801

   A **SURVEY** OF THE ECONOMIC AND CULTURAL CONDITIONS OF THE NEGRO POPULATION OF LOUISVILLE, KENTUCKY AND A
   REVIEW OF THE PROGRAM AND ACTIVITIES OF THE LOUISVILLE URBAN-LEAGUE. JANUARY-FEBRUARY, 1948.   NNATLUL48903

   SURVEY OF UNEMPLOYMENT IN SELECTED URBAN-LEAGUE CITIES.   NNATLUL61898

   AN HISTORICAL **SURVEY** AND ANALYSIS OF THE PROGRESS OF NEGROES IN PUBLIC-SERVICE 1932-1952.   NOLIVLW56955

   REPORT OF THE 1961-1962 **SURVEY** OF PHILADELPHIA BANKS. /PENNSYLVANIA/   NPHILCH62995

   A FIVE-CITY **SURVEY** OF NEGRO-AMERICAN EMPLOYEES OF THE FEDERAL GOVERNMENT.   NPRESCP57017

   A **SURVEY** OF DISCRIMINATION IN THE BUILDING TRADES INDUSTRY. NEW-YORK CITY.   NSHAUDX63126

   PLANS-FOR-PROGRESS. ATLANTA **SURVEY.** /GEORGIA/   NSOUTRC63163

   A BRIEF **SURVEY** OF HIGHER EDUCATION FOR NEGROES.   NSTOKMS64180

   SPECIAL REPORT. A **SURVEY** OF NEGROES EMPLOYED BY THE STATE OF WEST-VIRGINIA.   NVIRGHR64318

   1966 EMPLOYMENT **SURVEY** IN THE TEXTILE INDUSTRY OF THE CAROLINAS.   NWALLPA66591

   A **SURVEY** OF EMPLOYMENT OPPORTUNITIES AS THEY RELATE TO THE NEGRO IN NEW-ROCHELLE, NEW-YORK, 1955.   NWESTCU55316

   SURVEY OF NEGRO ATTITUDES TOWARD LAW.   NZEITLX65359

   A **SURVEY** OF NEW-HAVEN-S NEWCOMERS. THE PUERTO-RICANS. /CONNECTICUT/   PDONCDX59796

   SURVEY OF EMPLOYMENT-CONDITIONS OF NURSES EMPLOYED BY PHYSICIANS AND/OR DENTISTS, JULY 1964.   WAMERNA65610

   SURVEY OF SALARIES AND EMPLOYMENT-CONDITIONS IN NONFEDERAL PSYCHIATRIC HOSPITALS.   WAMERNA65611

   SURVEY OF SALARIES AND PERSONNEL PRACTICES FOR TEACHERS AND ADMINISTRATORS IN NURSING EDUCATIONAL
   PROGRAMS, DECEMBER 1965.   WAMERNA66612

   A **SURVEY** OF THE SOCIAL AND OCCUPATIONAL CHARACTERISTICS OF A METROPOLITAN NURSE. COMPLEMENT.
   /OCCUPATIONAL-DISTRIBUTION/   WDEUTIX56730

   A **SURVEY** OF THE SOCIAL AND OCCUPATIONAL CHARACTERISTICS OF A METROPOLITAN NURSE COMPLEMENT.   WDEUTIX57369

   REPORT OF THE EXPLORATORY STATISTICAL **SURVEY** OF THE EDUCATIONAL-ATTAINMENT, NUMBER, AND AVAILABILITY OF
   THE MEMBERSHIP OF THE AMERICAN ASSOCIATION OF UNIVERSITY WOMEN FOR TEACHING IN THE FIELDS OF SCIENCE AND
   MATHEMATICS. /OCCUPATIONS/   WDOLAEF57735

   SURVEY OF WOMEN PHYSICIANS GRADUATING FROM MEDICAL SCHOOL, 1925-1940. /OCCUPATIONS/   WDYKMRA57745

   RESEARCH REPORT. **SURVEY** OF CONTINUING EDUCATION PROGRAMS.   WFIELBX64762

   A **SURVEY** OF WOMEN-S APTITUDES FOR ARMY JOBS. /MILITARY/   WFUCHEF63772

   REPORT ON THE **SURVEY** OF FEMALE PHYSICIANS GRADUATING FROM MEDICAL SCHOOL BETWEEN 1925 AND 1940.
   /OCCUPATIONS/   WHANNFX58819

   A **SURVEY** OF SPECIAL EDUCATIONAL PROGRAMS FOR ADULT WOMEN IN UNIVERSITY EXTENSION DIVISIONS AND EVENING
   COLLEGES AS OF SPRING 1965.   WLORIRK66942

   NSA-S PROFESSIONAL STATUS **SURVEY**, 1964. /ECONOMIC-STATUS/   WNATLSA65023

   WOMEN ON COLLEGE AND UNIVERSITY FACULTIES. A HISTORICAL **SURVEY** AND A STUDY OF THEIR PRESENT ACADEMIC
   STATUS. /OCCUPATIONS/   WPOLLLA65063

SURVEYS
   STATEMENT ON **SURVEYS** AND STATISTICS AS TO RACIAL AND ETHNIC COMPOSITION OF WORK-FORCE OR UNION
   MEMBERSHIP. /CALIFORNIA/   GCALFEP63539

   NURSING PROFESSION. FIVE SOCIOLOGICAL **SURVEYS**.   WDAVIFX66722

SURVIVAL
   NARRAGANSETT **SURVIVAL.** A STUDY OF GROUP PERSISTENCE THROUGH ADAPTED TRAITS.   IBOISEX59887

   THE INDIAN TRIBES OF THE US. ETHNIC AND CULTURAL **SURVIVAL**.   IMCNIDX61586

SURVIVE
   CAN SEGREGATION **SURVIVE** IN AN INDUSTRIAL SOCIETY.   GYINGJM58590

   AUTOMATION AND THE NEGRO. WILL WE **SURVIVE**.   NWILSCE65326

SURVIVORS
   WOMEN HOUSEHOLD WORKERS COVERED BY OLD AGE, **SURVIVORS**, AND DISABILITY INSURANCE.   WPOLIEJ65285

SYMPOSIUM
   SYMPOSIUM ON CHEROKEE AND INDIAN CULTURE.   IFENTWN61620

   STRUGGLE FOR EQUALITY. **SYMPOSIUM**.   JMCLABX64747

   NOTES ON WOMEN IN INDUSTRY -- PRESENTED AT AMERICAN PSYCHOLOGICAL **SYMPOSIUM**, SEPT 1963. /DISCRIMINATION/ WGILMBV63970

   WOMEN AND THE SCIENTIFIC PROFESSIONS. THE MIT **SYMPOSIUM** ON AMERICAN WOMEN IN SCIENCE AND ENGINEERING.
   /OCCUPATIONS/   WMATTJA65963

SYNDROME
   RACE, ETHNICITY, AND THE ACHIEVEMENT **SYNDROME**.   GROSEBC59252

   THE POVERTY-DEPENDENCY **SYNDROME** OF THE ADC FEMALE-BASED NEGRO FAMILY.   NSTROFL64074

SYRACUSE
THE NEXT STEPS TOWARD EQUALITY OF OPPORTUNITY IN THE **SYRACUSE** METROPOLITAN AREA. REPORT OF THE SYRACUSE
CONFERENCE ON HUMAN RIGHTS AND HOUSING, JULY 2-3 1962. /NEW-YORK/   GNEWYSB62103

THE NEXT STEPS TOWARD EQUALITY OF OPPORTUNITY IN THE **SYRACUSE** METROPOLITAN AREA. REPORT OF THE SYRACUSE
CONFERENCE ON HUMAN RIGHTS AND HOUSING, JULY 2-3 1962. /NEW-YORK/   GNEWYSB62103

THE NEGRO IN **SYRACUSE**. /NEW-YORK/   NCAMPAKND177

RACE-RELATIONS IN **SYRACUSE**. A PROFILE. /NEW-YORK/   NGRIEES58458

SYSTEM
MINORITY-GROUPS AND MERIT **SYSTEM** PRACTICE.   GCALPPA65547

EQUAL-OPPORTUNITY UNDER THE MERIT **SYSTEM**.   GROSEHS66253

UNION DEMOCRACY AND FAIR REPRESENTATION. FEDERAL RESPONSIBILITY IN A FEDERAL **SYSTEM**.   GWELLHX58550

CIVIL-RIGHTS POLICY IN THE FEDERAL **SYSTEM**. PROPOSALS FOR A BETTER USE OF ADMINISTRATIVE PROCESS.   GWITHJX65575

JOB QUOTAS AND THE MERIT **SYSTEM**.   NCHASET63195

REPRESENTATION OF NEGROES AND WHITES AS EMPLOYEES IN THE FEDERAL PRISON **SYSTEM**.   NMORGGD62849

SYSTEMS
DISCRIMINATORY PROMOTION **SYSTEMS**.   GDOERPB67115

HIRING AND PROMOTION **SYSTEMS** UNDER FAIR-EMPLOYMENT-PRACTICES LEGISLATION.   GUSDLAB67116

SCHOOL ATTENDANCE AND ATTAINMENT. FUNCTION AND DYSFUNCTION OF SCHOOL AND FAMILY SOCIAL **SYSTEMS**.
/EMPLOYMENT DROP-OUT/   NBERTAL62882

PROMOTIONS **SYSTEMS** AND EQUAL-EMPLOYMENT-OPPORTUNITY.   NDOERPB66279

PROMOTION **SYSTEMS** AND EQUAL-EMPLOYMENT OPPORTUNITY.   NDOERPB66280

DISCRIMINATION IN THE HIRING AND ASSIGNMENT OF NEGRO TEACHERS IN PUBLIC SCHOOL **SYSTEMS**.   NMICLRX66068

TABLES
DISTRIBUTION OF SPANISH-NAME PEOPLE IN THE SOUTHWEST. **TABLES** AND MAP.   MHOLLSX56417

TABLES OF WORKING LIFE FOR WOMEN, 1950.   WGARFSH57180

TABULATION
REPORT OF 1961 - 1962 SURVEY OF PHILADELPHIA BANKS AND ATTACHED COMPOSITE **TABULATION** OF NON-WHITES.
/PENNSYLVANIA/   GPHILCH62180

TACTICS
LABOR UNION AND RACE-RELATIONS. A STUDY OF UNION **TACTICS**.   NKORNWA50660

TAFT-HARTLEY
AMENDMENTS TO THE **TAFT-HARTLEY**. A REJECTION OF RACIAL DISCRIMINATION. /LEGISLATION/   NOSHAJB54964

TAILORING
TAILORING THE TECHNIQUES TO ELIMINATE AND PREVENT EMPLOYMENT DISCRIMINATION.   GSPITHX64331

TALENT
WASTED **TALENT**. /EDUCATION/   NBONDHM60888

YOUNG NEGRO **TALENT**. SURVEY OF THE EXPERIENCES AND EXPECTATIONS OF NEGRO AMERICANS WHO GRADUATED FROM
COLLEGE IN 1961.   NFICHJH64867

BLUEPRINT FOR **TALENT**. SEARCHING AMERICA-S HIDDEN MANPOWER.   NPLAURL57003

ENGINEERING **TALENT** IN SHORT SUPPLY. /OCCUPATIONS/   WAMONRX62613

OUR GREATEST WASTE OF **TALENT** IS WOMEN. /WORK-WOMEN-ROLE/   WBUNTMI61662

ENCOURAGING SCIENTIFIC **TALENT**. /OCCUPATIONS/   WCOLECG56694

TALENT SEARCH FOR WOMANPOWER.   WHARREX65826

GUIDING CREATIVE **TALENT**. /WORK-WOMAN-ROLE/   WTORREP62158

TALENTED
IS DISCRIMINATION AGAINST **TALENTED** WOMEN NECESSARY.   WWARNCF61220

TALENTS
NEGLECTED **TALENTS**. BACKGROUND AND PROSPECTS OF NEGRO COLLEGE GRADUATES.   NNATLOR66880

TAMPA
INCOME. EDUCATION AND UNEMPLOYMENT IN NEIGHBORHOODS. **TAMPA**, ST-PETERSBURG FLORIDA. /DEMOGRAPHY/   CUSDLAB63486

TARGET
BUSINESS -- NEXT **TARGET** FOR INTEGRATION. /INDUSTRY/   GPERRJX63170

JOBS **TARGET** -- EMPLOYMENT.   GUSCHACND383

TASK
LABOR-S **TASK** FORCES. /UNION/   GSLAIDX64318

TASK FORCE FOR EQUAL-OPPORTUNITY IN BUSINESS.   GUSDCOM65432

EMPLOYMENT SERVICE **TASK** FORCE REPORT. /MANPOWER SES/   GUSDLAB66559

REPORT TO THE SECRETARY OF THE INTERIOR BY THE **TASK** FORCE ON INDIAN AFFAIRS.   IUSDINT61641

EFFECTS OF ANXIETY, THREAT, AND RACIAL ENVIRONMENT ON **TASK** PERFORMANCE OF NEGRO COLLEGE STUDENTS.   NKATZIX63640

GOVERNOR-S CIVIL-RIGHTS **TASK** FORCE. REPORT. /RHODE-ISLAND/   NRHODIC64051

TASKS
MANPOWER **TASKS** FOR 1966.   GUSDLAB66663

THE SOUTH TODAY AND LABOR-S **TASKS**.   NMANNCP53737

TASTES
WELFARE CRITERIA AND CHANGING **TASTES**.   GWECKRS62987

TAXES
REPORT OF THE COMMITTEE ON SOCIAL INSURANCE AND **TAXES**, 1963.   WPRESCO63070

TB
MARYLAND **TB** -- VD HEALTH PROGRAM AMONG AGRICULTURAL MIGRANTS.   GMARYSD65958

TEACHER
THE ORIGIN AND DEVELOPMENT OF THE NEGRO VISITING **TEACHER** IN ALABAMA. /OCCUPATIONS/   NBOATRF49345

CHANGES AND CHALLENGES IN THE 60-S. /INTEGRATION TECHNOLOGICAL-CHANGE **TEACHER**/   NBRAGEW63312

INTEGRATING THE NEGRO **TEACHER** OUT OF A JOB. /OCCUPATIONS/   NCARTBX65999

THE NEGRO **TEACHER** AND DESEGREGATION.   NDWYERJ57956

THE NEXT STEP. **TEACHER** INTEGRATION.   NJANSPA66603

CIVIL-RIGHTS -- RACIAL DISCRIMINATION IN **TEACHER** HIRING AND ASSIGNMENT FORBIDDEN.   NKELLPL66734

TEACHER SUPPLY AND DEMAND IN THE NEGRO COLLEGE.   NLLOYRG54045

THE **TEACHER** COMES INTO HER OWN. /WORK-FAMILY-CONFLICT/   WMCINMC61945

UPDATING TRAINING FOR THE RETURNING NURSE, SOCIAL WORKER AND **TEACHER**.   WNATLCP61018

THE MARRIED FEMALE SCHOOL **TEACHER**. A CONTINUED STUDY. /WORK-FAMILY-CONFLICT/   WSTEPCM60139

TEACHER-S
A STUDY OF ELEMENTARY SCHOOL **TEACHER-S** ATTITUDES TOWARD THE WOMAN PRINCIPAL AND TOWARD ELEMENTARY
PRINCIPALSHIP AS A CAREER. /DISCRIMINATION/   WBARTAK58629

TEACHERS
CHARACTERISTICS OF **TEACHERS**. /DEMOGRAPHY/   CUSBURC63168

THE NEW NEGRO CASUALTIES. /OCCUPATIONS **TEACHERS**/   NARISJM65029

DISPLACED **TEACHERS**. /OCCUPATIONS/   NCOMMXX65229

NEGRO **TEACHERS**. MARTYRS TO INTEGRATION. /OCCUPATIONS/   NCOXXOC53935

REASONS FOR BELATED EDUCATION. A STUDY OF THE PLIGHT OF THE OLDER NEGRO **TEACHERS**. /OCCUPATIONS/ NCUNNGE58244

DESEGREGATION AND THE EMPLOYMENT OF NEGRO **TEACHERS**. /OCCUPATIONS/   NDODDHH55950

THE STRUGGLE OF NEGRO **TEACHERS** IN FLORIDA FOR EQUAL SALARIES. /OCCUPATIONS/   NFERGML49961

DISCRIMINATION IN RATE OF COMPENSATION BETWEEN COLORED AND WHITE **TEACHERS** HELD UNCONSTITUTIONAL. NHARVLR40497

EFFORTS OF NEGRO **TEACHERS** IN THE SOUTHERN STATES TO OBTAIN EQUALIZATION OF SALARIES.   NJONEER48343

A STUDY OF PROFESSIONAL PREPARATION OF NEGRO **TEACHERS** OF EXCEPTIONAL CHILDREN IN NORTH-CAROLINA COUNTY
AND CITY PUBLIC SCHOOLS.   NKNIGOB65023

SOME ATTITUDES TOWARD EMPLOYING NEGROES AS **TEACHERS** IN A NORTHERN UNIVERSITY.   NMARCFL48054

DISCRIMINATION IN THE HIRING AND ASSIGNMENT OF NEGRO **TEACHERS** IN PUBLIC SCHOOL SYSTEMS.   NMICLRX66068

THE UTILIZATION OF NEGRO **TEACHERS** IN THE COLLEGES OF NEW-YORK STATE.   NMOSSJA60857

A STUDY OF THE POTENTIAL SUPPLY OF NEGRO **TEACHERS** FOR THE COLLEGES OF NEW-YORK STATE.   NMOSSJA61858

TEACHERS OF CULTURALLY DISADVANTAGED AMERICAN YOUTH.   NROUSRX63310

CAREER PATTERNS OF **TEACHERS** IN NEGRO COLLEGES.   NTHOMDC58204

EQUAL-PAY FOR WHITE AND NEGRO **TEACHERS**. /OCCUPATIONS/   NUSDLAB41817

A CRITICAL APPRAISAL OF PROFESSION TRAINING OF NEGRO **TEACHERS** IN OKTIBBEHA COUNTY MISSISSIPPI.   NWILLMM50234

SURVEY OF SALARIES AND PERSONNEL PRACTICES FOR **TEACHERS** AND ADMINISTRATORS IN NURSING EDUCATIONAL
PROGRAMS, DECEMBER 1965.   WAMERNA66612

ATTITUDES TOWARD WOMEN COLLEGE **TEACHERS** IN INSTITUTIONS OF HIGHER EDUCATION ACCREDITED BY THE NORTH
CENTRAL ASSOCIATION.   WBERWHD62475

SEX-ROLE AND PROFESSIONALISM. A STUDY OF HIGH SCHOOL **TEACHERS**. /OCCUPATIONS/   WCOLOJX63698

NEW SOURCES OF COLLEGE **TEACHERS**. /OCCUPATIONS/   WRILESB61287

TEACHING
NEGROES AS **TEACHING** ASSISTANTS IN SOME PUBLICLY SUPPORTED UNIVERSITIES. /OCCUPATIONS/   NDANIWG62248

OCCUPATIONAL CHOICE AND THE **TEACHING** CAREER.   NGUBAEG59463

RESOURCE UNITS IN THE **TEACHING** OF OCCUPATIONS -- AN EXPERIMENT IN GUIDANCE OF PUERTO-RICAN TEENAGERS. PNEWYCC56834

REPORT OF THE EXPLORATORY STATISTICAL SURVEY OF THE EDUCATIONAL-ATTAINMENT, NUMBER, AND AVAILABILITY OF
THE MEMBERSHIP OF THE AMERICAN ASSOCIATION OF UNIVERSITY WOMEN FOR **TEACHING** IN THE FIELDS OF SCIENCE AND
MATHEMATICS. /OCCUPATIONS/   WDOLAEF57735

WOMEN IN UNIVERSITY **TEACHING**. /OCCUPATIONS/   WMILLMM61981

TEACHING. OPPORTUNITIES FOR WOMEN COLLEGE GRADUATES.   WNATLEA64019

PART-TIME ASSIGNMENT OF WOMEN IN **TEACHING**. /OCCUPATIONS/   WSAMPJX65099

WOMEN IN COLLEGE AND UNIVERSITY **TEACHING**. /OCCUPATIONS/   WTOTAJV65159

PARTNERSHIP **TEACHING** PROGRAM. PROGRESS REPORT -- JAN-OCT 1965. SECTION I. /TRAINING/   WWOMEEA65275

TECHNICAL
TECHNICAL REPORT NUMBER 1. EMPLOYMENT PRACTICES IN THE HOTEL, MOTEL AND RESTAURANT INDUSTRY OF MISSOURI. GMILLRX66020

TECHNICAL REPORT NUMBER 2. EMPLOYMENT PRACTICES OF SELECTED MISSOURI PUBLIC UTILITIES. NATURAL GAS AND
ELECTRIC.   GMILLRX66021

OCCUPATIONAL DEVELOPMENTS. SHORTAGES OF SKILLED **TECHNICAL** MANPOWER HIGHEST IN RECENT YEARS.   GUSDLAB65561

THE NATIONAL **TECHNICAL** ASSOCIATION. /OCCUPATIONS/   NEVANJC43258

TECHNICAL   (CONTINUATION)
THE POST-WAR OUTLOOK FOR NEGROES IN SMALL BUSINESS, THE ENGINEERING AND THE TECHNICAL VOCATIONS.   NWALKJ046580

TECHNICAL EDUCATION IN THE JUNIOR COLLEGE.   WHARRNC64825

TECHNICIANS
TRAINING FOR TOMORROW-S SCIENTISTS AND TECHNICIANS. A COMMUNITY APPROACH TO A COMMUNITY NEED.   NFINLOE60356

JOBS AND TRAINING FOR WOMEN TECHNICIANS. /TRAINING/   WMEYEMB61975

TECHNIQUE
THE NEW-YORK STATE COMMISSION AGAINST DISCRIMINATION. A NEW TECHNIQUE FOR AN OLD PROBLEM.   GNEWYSA47107

THE TECHNIQUE OF INTRODUCING NEGROES INTO THE PLANT. /INDUSTRY/   NFELDHX42351

THE SELF-SURVEY OF THE PACKINGHOUSE UNION. A TECHNIQUE FOR EFFECTING CHANGE. /CASE-STUDY/   NHOPEJX53574

PLACEMENT SERVICE OF THE AMERICAN FRIENDS SERVICE COMMITTEE. A TECHNIQUE IN RACE-RELATIONS.   NLOESFS46703

TECHNIQUES
HOW TO RECRUIT MINORITY-GROUP COLLEGE GRADUATES, ITS PROBLEMS, ITS TECHNIQUES, ITS SOURCES, ITS
OPPORTUNITIES.   GCALVRX63555

TAILORING THE TECHNIQUES TO ELIMINATE AND PREVENT EMPLOYMENT DISCRIMINATION.   GSPITHX64331

ANALYSIS OF THE TECHNIQUES OF RACIAL INTEGRATION IN THREE MANUFACTURING FIRMS. /INDUSTRY/   NCAMPFX54178

EQUAL-EMPLOYMENT-OPPORTUNITY. CHANGING PROBLEMS, CHANGING TECHNIQUES.   NHOPEJX63568

TECHNOLOGICAL
IMPLICATIONS OF AUTOMATION AND OTHER TECHNOLOGICAL DEVELOPMENTS, A SELECTED BIBLIOGRAPHY.   GUSDLAB63450

TECHNOLOGICAL TRENDS IN 36 MAJOR AMERICAN INDUSTRIES.   GUSDLAB64802

TECHNOLOGICAL TRENDS IN MAJOR AMERICAN INDUSTRIES. /EMPLOYMENT/   GUSDLAB66637

FARMERS, WORKERS, AND MACHINES. TECHNOLOGICAL AND SOCIAL-CHANGE IN FARM INDUSTRIES OF ARIZONA.   MPADFHX65450

TECHNOLOGICAL-CHANGE
FARM MECHANIZATION AND LABOR STABILIZATION. PART II IN A SERIES ON TECHNOLOGICAL-CHANGE AND FARM LABOR
USE, KERN COUNTY, CALIFORNIA, 1961. /NEGRO MEXICAN-AMERICAN/   CMETZWH65389

A SPECULATIVE VIEW OF THE UNITED STATES IN 1985 AND BEYOND. /TECHNOLOGICAL-CHANGE/   GBELLDX62612

METHODS OF ADJUSTING TO AUTOMATION AND TECHNOLOGICAL-CHANGE. /INDUSTRY/   GBOKXDX64737

MANPOWER DEVELOPMENT. CHARGES AND CHALLENGES. /TECHNOLOGICAL-CHANGE TRAINING/   GBOLIAC65528

MANPOWER IMPLICATIONS OF TECHNOLOGICAL-CHANGE. RESEARCH FINDINGS OF THE US DEPARTMENT OF LABOR.   GBRANSX63876

THE GREAT EMPLOYMENT CONTROVERSY. /TECHNOLOGICAL-CHANGE/   GBUCKWX62875

EFFECTS OF TECHNOLOGICAL-CHANGE ON OCCUPATIONAL EMPLOYMENT PATTERNS IN THE UNITED STATES.   GCLAGEX64625

AUTOMATION AND TECHNOLOGICAL-CHANGE.   GDUNLJT62698

THE DRIFT TO EARLY RETIREMENT. /TECHNOLOGICAL-CHANGE/   GFALTEK65032

PUSH-BUTTON LABOR. /TECHNOLOGICAL-CHANGE UNEMPLOYMENT/   GFORTXX54047

THE ROLE OF GOVERNMENT. /TECHNOLOGICAL-CHANGE/   GGOLDAX62865

LABOUR-FORCE ADJUSTMENT OF WORKERS AFFECTED BY TECHNOLOGICAL-CHANGE.   GGOODRC64622

TWENTY YEARS OF ECONOMIC AND INDUSTRIAL CHANGE. /TECHNOLOGICAL-CHANGE EMPLOYMENT/   GGORDRA65675

TECHNOLOGICAL-CHANGE, PRODUCTIVITY, AND EMPLOYMENT IN THE UNITED STATES.   GGREELX64739

THE IMPACT OF TECHNOLOGICAL-CHANGE.   GHABEWX63615

THE ACCIDENTAL CENTURY. /TECHNOLOGICAL-CHANGE/   GHARRMX65597

EFFECTS OF TECHNOLOGICAL-CHANGE ON THE NATURE OF JOBS.   GLEVILA64623

THE FARM WORKER IN A CHANGING AGRICULTURE. PART I IN A SERIES ON TECHNOLOGICAL-CHANGE AND FARM LABOR USE,
KERN-COUNTY, CALIFORNIA, 1961.   GMETZWH64387

CYBERNATION. THE SILENT CONQUEST. /TECHNOLOGICAL-CHANGE/   GMICADN62978

CYBERNATION AND SOCIAL CHANGE. /TECHNOLOGICAL-CHANGE/   GMICADN64673

THE OUTLOOK FOR TECHNOLOGICAL-CHANGE AND EMPLOYMENT.   GNATLCO66897

EDUCATIONAL IMPLICATIONS OF TECHNOLOGICAL-CHANGE.   GNATLCO66898

STATEMENTS RELATING TO THE IMPACT OF TECHNOLOGICAL-CHANGE. /INDUSTRY/   GNATLCT66848

THE EMPLOYMENT IMPACT OF TECHNOLOGICAL-CHANGE.   GNATLCT66849

ADJUSTING TO CHANGE. /TECHNOLOGICAL-CHANGE/   GNATLCT66850

SEMINARS ON PRIVATE ADJUSTMENTS TO AUTOMATION AND TECHNOLOGICAL-CHANGE.   GPRESCL64772

TECHNOLOGICAL-CHANGE AND VOCATIONAL COUNSELING.   GSAMLJX64843

TRAINING IN THE PERSPECTIVE OF TECHNOLOGICAL-CHANGE.   GSTRIHE66669

FREE MEN AND FREE MARKETS. /TECHNOLOGICAL-CHANGE GUARANTEED-INCOME/   GTHECRX63682

CONSOLIDATED INVENTORY OF DEPARTMENT OF LABOR RESEARCH ON AUTOMATION AND TECHNOLOGICAL-CHANGE.   GUSDLAB64619

A SURVEY OF CURRENT LITERATURE ON AUTOMATION AND OTHER TECHNOLOGICAL-CHANGES. A SELECTED ANNOTATED
BIBLIOGRAPHY.   GUSDLAB64825

SEMINAR ON MANPOWER POLICY AND PROGRAM MEASUREMENT OF TECHNOLOGICAL-CHANGE.   GUSDLAB64980

IMPLICATIONS OF GOVERNMENT-SPONSORED TRAINING PROGRAMS. /TECHNOLOGICAL-CHANGE/   GWALSJP64620

THE PACE OF TECHNOLOGICAL-CHANGE AND THE FACTORS AFFECTING IT.   GWOLFSL64624

TECHNOLOGICAL-CHANGE (CONTINUATION)
CHANGES AND CHALLENGES IN THE 60-S. /INTEGRATION TECHNOLOGICAL-CHANGE TEACHER/   NBRAGEW63312

RECENT COLLECTIVE-BARGAINING AND TECHNOLOGICAL-CHANGE.   NDAVILM64942

TECHNOLOGICAL-CHANGE AND THE SOCIAL ORDER. /SOUTH/   NNOLAEW65927

NO TIME FOR TRAGIC IRONIES. /EMPLOYMENT TECHNOLOGICAL-CHANGE/   NPURYMT63027

WHO NEEDS THE NEGRO. /OCCUPATIONAL-STATUS TECHNOLOGICAL-CHANGE/   NWILLSM64232

THE RETAIL CLERKS. /TECHNOLOGICAL-CHANGE/   WHARRMX62823

WHEN THE COMPUTER TAKES OVER THE OFFICE. /TECHNOLOGICAL-CHANGE/   WHOOSIR60000

AUTOMATION IN THE OFFICE. /TECHNOLOGICAL-CHANGE/   WHOOSIR61848

RESEARCH AND YOUR JOB. /TECHNOLOGICAL-CHANGE/   WKEYSMD64900

AUTOMATION AND EMPLOYMENT. /TECHNOLOGICAL-CHANGE/   WKREPJX64916

OFFICE WORK AND AUTOMATION. /TECHNOLOGICAL-CHANGE/   WLEVIHS56929

PROBLEM AREAS IN TRAINING FOR AUTOMATED WORK. /TECHNOLOGICAL-CHANGE/   WLIPSOX64936

EFFECTIVE COLLEGE RECRUITING. /TECHNOLOGICAL-CHANGE/   WODIOGS61042

TECHNOLOGY
JOBS, WAGES AND CHANGING TECHNOLOGY.   GARONRL65747

6. TEST TECHNOLOGY AND EQUAL-EMPLOYMENT-OPPORTUNITY.   GBAYRAG66428

AUTOMATION AND ECONOMIC PROGRESS. A SUMMARY OF THE REPORT OF THE NATIONAL COMMISSION ON TECHNOLOGY,
AUTOMATION, AND ECONOMIC PROGRESS.   GBOWEHR66748

REPORT TO THE GOVERNOR AND THE LEGISLATURE OF THE COMMISSION ON MANPOWER, AUTOMATION AND TECHNOLOGY,
1964. /CALIFORNIA/   GCALCMA65515

TECHNOLOGY AND SOCIAL CHANGE.   GGINZEX64972

TECHNOLOGY AND THE AMERICAN ECONOMY.   GNATLCT66602

THE ROLE OF AGRICULTURAL TECHNOLOGY IN SOUTHERN SOCIAL CHANGE.   GRAPEAX46037

FARM LABOR ADJUSTMENTS TO CHANGING TECHNOLOGY.   GTOLLGS67974

ECONOMIC DIMENSIONS. /SOUTH INCOME TECHNOLOGY/   NHENDVW63514

LABOR AND TECHNOLOGY ON SELECTED COTTON PLANTATIONS IN THE DELTA AREA OF MISSISSIPPI, 1953-1957. NLERANL59404

TECHNOLOGY AND WOMEN-S WORK.   WBAKEEF64624

WOMEN IN TECHNOLOGY. /OCCUPATIONS/   WSTEIER62153

WOMEN TELEPHONE WORKERS AND CHANGING TECHNOLOGY.   WUSDLAB63239

TEEN-AGE
NEGRO TEEN-AGE CULTURE.   NHIMEJX61071

TEENAGE
TEENAGE LABOR PROBLEMS AND THE NEIGHBORHOOD-YOUTH-CORPS.   GMOONJD66726

BICULTURATION OF MESQUAKIE TEENAGE BOYS.   IPOLGSX60605

TEENAGERS
EMPLOYMENT OF TEENAGERS. JUNE 1966.   NROSSAM66081

RESOURCE UNITS IN THE TEACHING OF OCCUPATIONS -- AN EXPERIMENT IN GUIDANCE OF PUERTO-RICAN TEENAGERS. PNEWYCC56834

TELEPHONE
WOMEN TELEPHONE WORKERS AND CHANGING TECHNOLOGY.   WUSDLAB63239

TELEVISION
REPORT ON EMPLOYMENT AND IMAGE OF MINORITY-GROUPS ON TELEVISION.   GNEWYSB63105

TEMPORARY
FAMILY CHARACTERISTICS OF THE LONG TERM UNEMPLOYED. A REPORT ON A STUDY OF CLAIMANTS UNDER THE TEMPORARY
EXTENDED UNEMPLOYMENT COMPENSATION PROGRAM, 1961-2.   GUSDLAB61445

TENANT
REPORT OF THE DIAGNOSTIC SURVEY OF TENANT HOUSEHOLDS IN THE WEST SIDE URBAN-RENEWAL AREA OF
NEW-YORK-CITY.   GGREEAI65474

TENNESSEE
INCOME, EDUCATION AND UNEMPLOYMENT IN NEIGHBORHOODS. MEMPHIS, TENNESSEE. /DEMOGRAPHY/   CUSDLAB63466

US COMMISSION-ON-CIVIL-RIGHTS, HEARINGS. MEMPHIS, TENNESSEE. JUNE 25-26, 1962.   GUSCOMC62401

REPORTS ON APPRENTICESHIP, NINE STATE ADVISORY COMMITTEES. /CALIFORNIA FLORIDA MARYLAND CONNECTICUT
WASHINGTON-DC NEW-JERSEY NEW-YORK TENNESSEE WISCONSIN/   GUSCOMC64407

THE NEGRO AND EMPLOYMENT-OPPORTUNITIES IN THE SOUTH. CHATTANOOGA REGION. /TENNESSEE/   NCHATCC62197

EMPLOYMENT OPPORTUNITY FOR NASHVILLE NEGROES. /TENNESSEE/   NCOMUCE60230

TVA AND NEGRO EMPLOYMENT. /TENNESSEE/   NDAVIJH55253

EMPLOYMENT OPPORTUNITIES FOR NASHVILLE NEGROES. /TENNESSEE/   NHENDVW60516

JOBS AND COLOR. NEGRO EMPLOYMENT IN TENNESSEE STATE GOVERNMENT.   NLONGHH62706

THE EFFECT OF SPECIAL INSTRUCTION UPON TEST PERFORMANCE OF HIGH SCHOOL STUDENTS IN TENNESSEE.   NROBESO66961

CHATTANOOGA -- THE NEGRO AND EMPLOYMENT OPPORTUNITIES IN THE SOUTH, THE SECOND OF A SERIES OF EMPLOYMENT
STUDIES IN SOUTHERN CITIES. /TENNESSEE/   NSOUTRC62156

A REPORT ON COMMUNITY FACTORS IN NASHVILLE RELATED TO THE NEGRO IN MEDICINE. /TENNESSEE/   NVALIPX56281

NEGRO EMPLOYMENT PRACTICES IN THE CHATTANOOGA AREA. /TENNESSEE/   NWESSWH55314

TENSION

SOUTH-S **TENSION** SEIZES LABOR.   /UNION/
NBUSIWX56882

TO STEM THIS TIDE, A SURVEY CF RACIAL **TENSION** AREAS IN THE U.S.
NJOHNCS43617

THE ROLE OF ORGANIZATIONAL STRUCTURES. UNION VERSUS NEIGHBORHOOD IN A **TENSION** SITUATION.
NREITDC53050

TENSIONS

THE REDUCTION UF INTERGROUP **TENSIONS**.
GWILLRM47564

CEALING WITH INTER-RACIAL **TENSIONS** ON LOCAL UNION GRASS ROOTS BASIS.
NANDEEC50894

TENURE

UNITED STATES CENSUS OF AGRICULTURE. COLOR, RACE, AND **TENURE** OF FARM OPERATOR. GENERAL REPORT, VOLUME II. /CEMOGRAPHY/
CUSBURC59382

JOB **TENURE** OF AMERICAN WORKERS.
GHAMEHR63755

THE **TENURE** STATUS OF FARMWORKERS IN THE UNITED STATES.
GMAIEFH60417

LAND **TENURE** IN THE SOUTHERN REGION. PROCEEDINGS OF PROFESSIONAL AGRICULTURAL WORKERS TENTH ANNUAL CONFERENCE.
NTUSKIX51218

COLOR, RACE AND **TENURE** JF FARM OPERATORS.
NUSBURC62225

TERM

THE CIVIL-RIGHTS AND CIVIL-LIBERTIES DECISIONS OF THE US SUPREME COURT FCR THE 1962-63 **TERM**. A SUMMARY ANC ANALYSIS.
GAMERJD63384

FAMILY CHARACTERISTICS UF THE LONG **TERM** UNEMPLOYED. A REPORT ON A STUDY OF CLAIMANTS UNDER THE TEMPORARY EXTENDED UNEMPLOYMENT CUMPENSATICN PROGRAM, 1961-2.
GUSDLAB61445

TERMINATION

THE MENOMINEE **TERMINATION** CRISIS. BARRIERS IN THE WAY OF A RAPID CULTURAL TRANSITION.
IAMESDW59525

TERMINATION OF FEDERAL SUPERVISION. DISINTEGRATION AND THE AMERICAN-INDIANS.
ILAFAOX57075

TERMINATION OF THE BRACERO PROGRAM. SOME EFFECTS ON FARM LABOR AND MIGRANT HOUSING NEEDS.
MMCELRC65385

TEST

AN EXPERIMENT TO **TEST** THREE MAJOR ISSUES OF WORK PROGRAM METHODOLOGY WITHIN MOBILIZATICN-FOR-YOUTH-S INTEGRATED SERVICES TO JUT-OF-SCHOOL UNEMPLOYED YOUTH. /NEGRO   PUERTO-RICAN/
CMOBIFY66024

6. **TEST** TECHNOLOGY AND EQUAL-EMPLOYMENT-OPPORTUNITY.
GBAYRAG66428

A CEMCNSTRATION PROJECT CESIGNED TO **TEST** THE LIFE-STYLE AND THE GROWTH POTENTIAL OF URBAN DROPOUTS FROM CISACVANTAGED HOMES.
GCLEAMP66130

4. CURRENT PROBLEMS IN **TEST** PERFORMANCE OF JCB-APPLICANTS.
GDUGARD66651

CHANGING EMPHASIS IN OCCUPATIONAL **TEST** DEVELCPMENT.
GDVCRBJ65650

NEW DIRECTIONS IN US EMPLOYMENT-SERVICE APTITUDE **TEST** RESEARCH.
GOVORBJ65656

THE CONGRESSIONAL HEARINGS AND ISSUES IN PSYCHOLOGICAL TESTING. INVASIONS OF PRIVACY AND **TEST** BIAS.
GGORDJEND934

SOME SUGGESTED APPROACHES FOR **TEST** DEVELOPMENT AND MEASUREMENT.
GKRUGRE66863

3 CURRENT PROBLEMS IN **TEST** PERFORMANCE OF JOB APPLICANTS.
GLOPEFM66909

RECENT TRENDS IN THE **TEST** SELECTION OF APPRENTICES.
GMOTLAW53033

TEST PERFORMANCE IN RELATICN TO ETHNIC GROUP AND SOCIAL CLASS.
GROBESO63683

NEGRO RESPONSES TO VERBAL ANC NON-VERBAL **TEST** MATERIAL.
NBEANKL47914

TEST BIAS. VALIDITY OF THE SCHOLASTIC APTITUDE TEST FOR NEGRO AND WHITE STUDENTS IN INTEGRATED COLLEGES.
NCLEATA66923

TEST BIAS. VALIDITY OF THE SCHOLASTIC APTITUDE **TEST** FOR NEGRO AND WHITE STUDENTS IN INTEGRATED COLLEGES.
NCLEATA66923

THE MEANINGFULNESS OF NEGRO-WHITE DIFFERENCES IN INTELLIGENCE **TEST** PERFORMANCE.
NHICKRA66740

NEGRC-WHITE DIFFERENCES IN INTELLIGENCE **TEST** PERFORMANCE.
NKLINOX63657

NEGRO INTELLIGENCE AND SELECTIVE MIGRATION. A PHILADELPHIA **TEST** OF THE KLINEBERG HYPOTHESIS. /PENNSYLVANIA/
NLEEXES51673

THE PROBLEM OF CULTURAL BIAS IN SELECTION. II. ETHNIC BACKGROUND AND **TEST** PERFORMANCE.
NROBESC65068

THE EFFECT OF SPECIAL INSTRUCTION UPCN **TEST** PERFORMANCE OF HIGH SCHOOL STUDENTS IN TENNESSEE.
NROBESO66961

THE RELATIONSHIP BETWEEN **TEST** INTELLIGENCE OF THIRD GRADE NEGRO CHILDREN AND THE OCCUPATIONS OF THEIR PARENTS.
NROBIML47070

TESTIMONY

TESTIMONY. PUBLIC HEARING. WCMEN IN PUBLIC AND PRIVATE EMPLOYMENT, CALIFORNIA. /MEXICAN-AMERICAN/
CARYWSX66621

TESTIMONY OF HUMAN RELATIONS. /LOS-ANGELES CALIFORNIA/
GLOSACCND915

SUMMARY OF **TESTIMONY** -- HOTEL RESTAURANT HEARINGS, APPENDIX A. /PHILADELPHIA PENNSYLVANIA/
GPHILCH60181

TESTIMONY TO THE SUBCOMMITTEE ON RACE-RELATICNS AND URBAN PROBLEMS. /SES CALIFORNIA/
GREDMWX64221

TESTIMONY BEFORE SUBCOMMITTEE ON ECONOMIC STATISTICS, MAY 17, 1965.
GUSCONG65421

TESTIMONY BEFORE STATE SENATE FACT FINDING SUBCOMMITTEE ON RACE-RELATIONS AND URBAN PROBLEMS, FINAL HEARING, JANUARY 20 1965. /CALIFORNIA FEPC/
NGRAHCX65439

EQUAL-EMPLOYMENT-OPPORTJNITY, HEARING, **TESTIMONY**.
NHILLHX62547

LS DEPARTMENT OF LABOR, PUBLIC HEARING, **TESTIMONY**. /MIGRANT-WORKERS/
NHILLHX63548

NEW-YORK CITY COMMISSION ON HUMAN RIGHTS, CONSTRUCTION TRADES HEARING, **TESTIMONY**. /INDUSTRY/
NHILLHX66546

STATEMENT AND **TESTIMONY** ON FEDERAL ROLE IN URBAN AFFAIRS. /EMPLOYMENT GHETTO/
NKENNRF66017

TESTIMONY. PUBLIC HEARING. WCMEN IN PUBLIC AND PRIVATE EMPLOYMENT, CALIFORNIA. /DISCRIMINATION EEOC/
WBALEHX66625

TESTIMONY. PUBLIC HEARING. WCMEN IN PUBLIC AND PRIVATE EMPLOYMENT, CALIFORNIA. /EMPLOYMENT-CONDITIONS/
WBECHCX66631

TESTIMONY   (CONTINUATION)
    TESTIMONY, PUBLIC HEARING, WOMEN IN PUBLIC AND PRIVATE EDUCATION, CALIFORNIA. /FEP
    EMPLOYMENT-CONDITIONS DISCRIMINATION MIGRANT-WORKERS/   WBLOCHX66649

    TESTIMONY, PUBLIC HEARING, WOMAN IN PUBLIC AND PRIVATE EMPLOYMENT, CALIFORNIA. /DISCRIMINATION/   WBROWAX66657

    TESTIMONY PRESENTED AT PUBLIC HEARING, MARCH 31 -- APRIL 1, 1966. /FEP EMPLOYMENT-CONDITIONS
    DISCRIMINATION MIGRANTS/   WCALACW62675

    TESTIMONY PRESENTED AT PUBLIC HEARING, APRIL 28, 1966. SAN-FRANCISCO, CALIFORNIA. /FEP
    EMPLOYMENT-CONDITIONS DISCRIMINATION MIGRANTS/   WCALACW62676

    TESTIMONY PRESENTED AT PUBLIC HEARING, FEBRUARY 24-25, 1966. /FEP EMPLOYMENT-CONDITIONS DISCRIMINATION
    MIGRANTS/   WCALACW66674

    TESTIMONY PRESENTED AT PUBLIC HEARING, APRIL 29, 1966. SAN-FRANCISCO, CALIFORNIA. /FEP
    EMPLOYMENT-CONDITIONS CHILDREN/   WCALACW66677

    TESTIMONY, PUBLIC HEARING, WOMEN IN PUBLIC AND PRIVATE EMPLOYMENT, CALIFORNIA. /EMPLOYMENT-CONDITIONS/   WCHANHD66687

    TESTIMONY, PUBLIC HEARING, WOMEN IN PUBLIC AND PRIVATE EMPLOYMENT, CALIFORNIA. /FEP
    EMPLOYMENT-CONDITIONS DISCRIMINATION MIGRANTS/   WCLIFFG66692

    TESTIMONY, PUBLIC HEARING, WOMEN IN PUBLIC AND PRIVATE EMPLOYMENT, CALIFORNIA. /DISCRIMINATION/   WCOLLNX66696

    TESTIMONY, PUBLIC HEARING, WOMEN IN PUBLIC AND PRIVATE EMPLOYMENT, CALIFORNIA. /EMPLOYMENT-CONDITIONS/   WCOMPBX66702

    TESTIMONY, PUBLIC HEARING, WOMEN IN PUBLIC AND PRIVATE EMPLOYMENT, CALIFORNIA. /TRAINING/   WCUMMGX66711

    TESTIMONY, PUBLIC HEARING, WOMEN IN PUBLIC AND PRIVATE EMPLOYMENT, CALIFORNIA. /EMPLOYMENT-CONDITIONS/   WDIBRJX66732

    TESTIMONY, PUBLIC HEARING, WOMAN IN PUBLIC AND PRIVATE EMPLOYMENT, CALIFORNIA. /DISCRIMINATION/   WDORAMX66739

    TESTIMONY, PUBLIC HEARING, WOMEN IN PUBLIC AND PRIVATE EMPLOYMENT, CALIFORNIA. /EMPLOYMENT-CONDITIONS/   WEVANSX66753

    TESTIMONY, PUBLIC HEARING, WOMEN IN PUBLIC AND PRIVATE EMPLOYMENT, CALIFORNIA. /EMPLOYMENT-CONDITIONS/   WFEINBX66760

    TESTIMONY, PUBLIC HEARING, WOMEN IN PUBLIC AND PRIVATE EMPLOYMENT, CALIFORNIA. /DISCRIMINATION/   WFOOTJX66765

    TESTIMONY, PUBLIC HEARING, WOMEN IN PUBLIC AND PRIVATE EMPLOYMENT, CALIFORNIA. /EMPLOYMENT-CONDITIONS/   WGABELX66773

    TESTIMONY, PUBLIC HEARING, WOMEN IN PUBLIC AND PRIVATE EMPLOYMENT, CALIFORNIA. /DISCRIMINATION/   WGEIGPX66776

    TESTIMONY, PUBLIC HEARING, WOMEN IN PUBLIC AND PRIVATE EMPLOYMENT, CALIFORNIA. /DEMOGRAPHY/   WGERSMX66777

    TESTIMONY, PUBLIC HEARING, WOMEN IN PUBLIC AND PRIVATE EMPLOYMENT, CALIFORNIA. /EMPLOYMENT-CONDITIONS/   WGILBRX66780

    TESTIMONY, PUBLIC HEARING, WOMEN IN PUBLIC AND PRIVATE EMPLOYMENT, CALIFORNIA. /EMPLOYMENT-CONDITIONS/   WGLENEM66788

    TESTIMONY, PUBLIC HEARING, WOMEN IN PUBLIC AND PRIVATE EMPLOYMENT, CALIFORNIA. /DISCRIMINATION
    WORK-FAMILY-CONFLICT/   WGUPTRC66808

    TESTIMONY, PUBLIC HEARING, WOMEN IN PUBLIC AND PRIVATE EMPLOYMENT, CALIFORNIA. /EMPLOYMENT-CONDITIONS/   WGUPTRC66809

    TESTIMONY, PUBLIC HEARING, WOMEN IN PUBLIC AND PRIVATE EMPLOYMENT, CALIFORNIA. /EMPLOYMENT-CONDITIONS/   WHEALWX66836

    TESTIMONY, PUBLIC HEARING, WOMEN IN PUBLIC AND PRIVATE EMPLOYMENT, CALIFORNIA. /DISCRIMINATION/   WHILLHX66844

    TESTIMONY, PUBLIC HEARING, WOMEN IN PUBLIC AND PRIVATE EMPLOYMENT, CALIFORNIA. /MOTA EEO/   WINGRLX66859

    TESTIMONY, PUBLIC HEARING, WOMEN IN PUBLIC AND PRIVATE EMPLOYMENT, CALIFORNIA. /EMPLOYMENT-CONDITIONS/   WKELLET66888

    TESTIMONY, PUBLIC HEARING, WOMEN IN PUBLIC AND PRIVATE EMPLOYMENT, CALIFORNIA. /FEP MIGRANT-WORKERS
    EMPLOYMENT-CONDITIONS/   WLLOYMX66940

    TESTIMONY, PUBLIC HEARING, WOMEN IN PUBLIC AND PRIVATE EMPLOYMENT, CALIFORNIA. /FEP EMPLOYMENT
    CONDITIONS/   WLOWEDX66943

    TESTIMONY, PUBLIC HEARING, WOMEN IN PUBLIC AND PRIVATE EMPLOYMENT, CALIFORNIA. /EMPLOYMENT-CONDITIONS/   WMACKJW66950

    TESTIMONY, PUBLIC HEARING, WOMEN IN PUBLIC AND PRIVATE EMPLOYMENT, CALIFORNIA. /OCCUPATIONS
    EMPLOYMENT-CONDITIONS/   WMCLALX66947

    TESTIMONY, PUBLIC HEARING, WOMEN IN PUBLIC AND PRIVATE EMPLOYMENT, CALIFORNIA. /BLUE-COLLAR
    EMPLOYMENT-CONDITIONS/   WMENGVX66969

    TESTIMONY, PUBLIC HEARING, WOMEN IN PUBLIC AND PRIVATE EMPLOYMENT, CALIFORNIA. /EMPLOYMENT-CONDITIONS/   WMILLKL66980

    TESTIMONY, PUBLIC HEARING, WOMEN IN PUBLIC AND PRIVATE EMPLOYMENT, CALIFORNIA. /EMPLOYMENT-CONDITIONS/   WMORAMX66995

    TESTIMONY, PUBLIC HEARING, WOMEN IN PUBLIC AND PRIVATE EMPLOYMENT, CALIFORNIA.   WMOTHWA66001

    TESTIMONY, PUBLIC HEARING, WOMEN IN PUBLIC AND PRIVATE EMPLOYMENT, CALIFORNIA. /EMPLOYMENT-CONDITIONS/   WMYRIRX66013

    TESTIMONY, PUBLIC HEARING, WOMEN IN PUBLIC AND PRIVATE EMPLOYMENT, CALIFORNIA. /EMPLOYMENT-CONDITIONS/   WPALMGX66047

    TESTIMONY, PUBLIC HEARING, WOMEN IN PUBLIC AND PRIVATE EMPLOYMENT, CALIFORNIA. /FEP
    EMPLOYMENT-CONDITIONS MIGRANT-WORKERS/   WPEEVMX66052

    TESTIMONY, PUBLIC HEARING, WOMEN IN PUBLIC AND PRIVATE EMPLOYMENT, CALIFORNIA. /EMPLOYMENT-CONDITIONS/   WRILEEX66081

    TESTIMONY, PUBLIC HEARING, WOMEN IN PUBLIC AND PRIVATE EMPLOYMENT, CALIFORNIA. /FEP
    EMPLOYMENT-CONDITIONS/   WSCHRPX66104

    TESTIMONY, PUBLIC HEARING, WOMEN IN PUBLIC AND PRIVATE EMPLOYMENT, CALIFORNIA. /EMPLOYMENT-CONDITIONS/   WSHEAHX66112

    TESTIMONY, PUBLIC HEARING, WOMEN IN PUBLIC AND PRIVATE EMPLOYMENT, CALIFORNIA. /FEP
    EMPLOYMENT-CONDITIONS DISCRIMINATION/   WSMITWH66123

    TESTIMONY, PUBLIC HEARING, WOMEN IN PUBLIC AND PRIVATE EMPLOYMENT, CALIFORNIA. /FEP
    EMPLOYMENT-CONDITIONS DISCRIMINATION MIGRANT-WORKERS/   WSPENNX66129

    TESTIMONY, PUBLIC HEARING, WOMEN IN PUBLIC AND PRIVATE EMPLOYMENT, CALIFORNIA. /LABOR-MARKET/   WSTEPRX66138

    TESTIMONY, PUBLIC HEARING, WOMEN IN PUBLIC AND PRIVATE EMPLOYMENT, CALIFORNIA. /FEPC/   WSTERAX66140

    TESTIMONY, PUBLIC HEARING, WOMEN IN PUBLIC AND PRIVATE EMPLOYMENT, CALIFORNIA. /EMPLOYMENT-CONDITIONS/   WTHOMDX66151

    TESTIMONY, PUBLIC HEARING, WOMEN IN PUBLIC AND PRIVATE EMPLOYMENT, CALIFORNIA. /EMPLOYMENT-CONDITIONS

TESTIMONY   (CONTINUATION)
    DISCRIMINATION/   WTHOMGX66149

    TESTIMONY, PUBLIC HEARING, WOMEN IN PUBLIC AND PRIVATE EMPLOYMENT, CALIFORNIA.   /EMPLOYMENT-CONDITIONS
    MIGRANT-WORKERS/   WWEBEJX66258

    TESTIMONY, PUBLIC HEARING, WOMEN IN PUBLIC AND PRIVATE EMPLOYMENT, CALIFORNIA.   /FEP
    EMPLOYMENT-CONDITIONS MIGRANT-WORKERS/   WWOMEIX66273

    TESTIMONY, PUBLIC HEARING, WOMEN IN PUBLIC AND PRIVATE EMPLOYMENT, CALIFORNIA.   /EMPLOYMENT-CONDITIONS/   WWOODWX66276

TESTING
    APTITUDE TESTING, TRAINING, AND EMPLOYEE DEVELOPMENT, WITH A SECTION ON THE EMPLOYMENT OF
    MINORITY-GROUPS.   GAMERMA49389

    TESTING THE UNTESTABLES.   GARNSSX64404

    THE IMPLICATIONS OF THE CIVIL-RIGHTS-ACT OF 1964 FOR PSYCHOLOGICAL ASSESSMENT IN INDUSTRY. /TESTING/ GASHXPX66405

    FAIR-EMPLOYMENT-PRACTICES EQUAL GOOD EMPLOYMENT PRACTICES. GUIDELINES FOR TESTING AND SELECTING MINORITY
    JOB APPLICANTS. /CALIFORNIA/   GCALFEP66540

    TESTING OF CULTURALLY DIFFERENT GROUPS.   GCAMPJX64093

    AN INVESTIGATION OF ITEM BIAS. /TESTING/   GCLEATA66924

    TESTING THE DISADVANTAGED.   GCULHMM65651

    I STATEMENT BEFORE THE HOUSE POST OFFICE AND CIVIL SERVICE SUBCOMMITTEE ON POSTAL OPERATIONS, II
    DISCRIMINATION. PLANNED AND ACCIDENTAL. /TESTING/   GENNEWH67928

    TESTING AND TITLE-VII. /   GFLINCX65120

    PSYCHOLOGICAL TESTING. SOME PROBLEMS AND SOLUTIONS. /INDUSTRY/   GFRENWL66101

    THE CONGRESSIONAL HEARINGS AND ISSUES IN PSYCHOLOGICAL TESTING. INVASIONS OF PRIVACY AND TEST BIAS. GGORDJEND934

    CIVIL-SERVICE TESTING AND JOB DISCRIMINATION.   GGORDJE66281

    PERSONNEL TESTING.   GGUIORM65693

    TRENDS IN EMPLOYEE TESTING.   GHABBSX65112

    FINAL REPORT. THE YOUTH TRAINING PROJECT, SEPTEMBER 1, 1963--JANUARY 31, 1965. /ST-LOUIS MISSOURI
    TESTING/   GJEWIEV65568

    PSYCHOLOGICAL TESTING FOR EFFECTIVE EMPLOYMENT PRACTICES AND EQUAL JOB OPPORTUNITIES.   GKETCWA65849

    TESTING MINORITY-GROUP APPLICANTS.   GKETCWA66942

    THE PRESENT STATUS OF THE CULTURE FAIR TESTING MOVEMENT.   GLAMBNM64880

    TESTING MINORITY-GROUP APPLICANTS FOR EMPLOYMENT.   GLOCKHC65907

    THE INDUSTRIAL SETTING. PROBLEMS AND EXPERIENCES. /TESTING/   GLOPEFM65910

    PERSONNEL TESTING, JANUARY 1960.   GMERCMA60976

    PROBLEMS, RESEARCH, AND RECOMMENDATIONS IN THE EMPLOYMENT TESTING OF MINORITY-GROUP APPLICANTS.   GNEWCMR66163

    PSYCHOLOGICAL TESTS AND FAIR EMPLOYMENT. A STUDY OF EMPLOYMENT TESTING IN THE SAN-FRANCISCO BAY AREA.
    /CALIFORNIA/   GRUSHJT66268

    PSYCHOLOGICAL TESTING IN INDUSTRY. A CRITICAL EVALUATION.   GSTANES64635

    GUIDELINES ON EMPLOYMENT TESTING PROCEDURES.   GUSEEOC66510

    TESTING OF MINORITY-GROUP APPLICANTS FOR EMPLOYMENT.   GWALLPX66539

    PRESS SWALLOWS MOTOROLA HOAX. /TESTING/   GWESTOL65552

    THE FALLACIES OF PERSONALITY TESTING.   GWHYTWH54560

    FAIR-EMPLOYMENT-PRACTICES-COMMISSION EXPERIENCES WITH PSYCHOLOGICAL TESTING.   NASHXPX65031

    CAT ON A HOT TIN ROOF. /TESTING/   NBONDHM58497

    ETHNIC CENSUS OF EXAMINATION COMPETITORS. REPORT OF EXAMINATIONS GIVEN JULY THROUGH DECEMBER, 1965,
    SUMMARY. /TESTING CALIFORNIA/   NCALFPB66173

    THE PROBLEM OF CULTURAL BIAS IN SELECTION. I. BACKGROUND AND LITERATURE. /TESTING/   NCAMPJT65179

    THE MOTOROLA CASE. /TESTING/   NFRENRL65385

    NEGRO-WHITE DIFFERENCES ON THE MMPI. /TESTING/   NHOKAJE60559

    CULTURAL EXPOSURE AND RACE AS VARIABLES IN PREDICTING TRAINING AND JOB SUCCESS. /TESTING/   NLOCKHCND700

    THE TESTING OF NEGRO INTELLIGENCE.   NSHUEAX66145

TESTS
    THE USE OF PSYCHOLOGICAL TESTS IN INDUSTRY.   GALBRLE63368

    RACE, EMPLOYMENT TESTS, AND EQUAL-OPPORTUNITY.   GASHXPX65406

    APPRENTICESHIP AND TESTS. FEP SUMMARY OF LATEST DEVELOPMENTS.   GBUREON65491

    ARE JOB TESTS RELIABLE.   GFUERJS65703

    THE VALIDITY OF OCCUPATIONAL APTITUDE TESTS.   GGHISEE66788

    EMPLOYMENT TESTS AND DISCRIMINATORY HIRING.   GGUIORM66747

    POSSIBLE SOLUTIONS TO THE PROBLEM OF CULTURAL BIAS IN TESTS.   GKRUGRE64946

    TESTS AND THE REQUIREMENTS OF THE JOB.   GMETZJH65119

    PSYCHOLOGICAL TESTS AND FAIR EMPLOYMENT. A STUDY OF EMPLOYMENT TESTING IN THE SAN-FRANCISCO BAY AREA.

TESTS   (CONTINUATION)
/CALIFORNIA/   GRUSHJT66268

PERSONNEL SELECTION TESTS AND FAIR-EMPLOYMENT-PRACTICES.   GSEASHX51293

LEGALITY AND VALIDITY OF PERSONNEL TESTS. /LEGISLATION TITLE-VII/   GVINCNX66113

THE INDIAN TESTS THE MAINSTREAM.   IMCNIDX66585

HIRING TESTS WAIT FOR THE SCORE. MYART VS MOTOROLA.   NBUSIWX65150

THE PROBLEMS OF CULTURAL BIAS IN SELECTION, POSSIBLE SOLUTION TO THE PROBLEM OF CULTURAL BIAS IN TESTS.   NKRUGRE64731

TEXANS
SOME CHARACTERISTICS OF SPANISH-NAME TEXANS AND FOREIGN LATIN-AMERICANS IN TEXAS HIGHER EDUCATION.   MRENNRR57462

TEXAS
INCOME, EDUCATION AND UNEMPLOYMENT IN NEIGHBORHOODS. DALLAS, TEXAS. /DEMOGRAPHY/   CUSDLAB63459

INCOME, EDUCATION AND UNEMPLOYMENT IN NEIGHBORHOODS. HOUSTON, TEXAS. /DEMOGRAPHY/   CUSDLAB63462

INCOME, EDUCATION AND UNEMPLOYMENT IN NEIGHBORHOODS. SAN-ANTONIO, TEXAS. /DEMOGRAPHY/   CUSDLAB63482

TEXAS PROVIDES JOBS FOR MINORITY-GROUPS.   GCARRHX66558

AN EQUAL-OPPORTUNITIES COMMITTEE AT WORK IN TEXAS.   GDESHEA66633

POVERTY IN TEXAS. THE DISTRIBUTION OF LOW-INCOME FAMILIES.   GKUVLWP65867

MIGRATION OF THE TEXAS FARM POPULATION.   GSKRARL57315

INCOMES OF RURAL FAMILIES IN NORTHEAST TEXAS.   GSOUTJH59325

TEXAS GROWERS AND WORKERS ON THE FARM, LOWER RIO-GRANDE VALLEY.   GTEXAEC59352

SUB-EMPLOYMENT IN THE SLUMS OF SAN-ANTONIO. /TEXAS/   GUSDLAB66515

THE SPANISH-SURNAME POPULATION OF TEXAS.   MBROWHL64286

A STATISTICAL PROFILE OF THE SPANISH-SURNAME POPULATION OF TEXAS.   MBROWHL64368

LEVELS OF LIVING OF SPANISH-AMERICAN RURAL AND URBAN FAMILIES IN TWO SOUTH TEXAS COUNTIES.   MCLEMHM63381

OCCUPATIONAL-PATTERNS OF RURAL AND URBAN SPANISH-AMERICANS IN TWO SOUTH TEXAS COUNTIES.   MCOTHML66385

AN ANALYSIS OF CURRENT PATTERNS IN HUMAN RESOURCE DEVELOPMENT IN SAN-ANTONIO, TEXAS.   MDAVIHW66387

INCOMES OF RURAL AND URBAN SPANISH-AMERICANS IN TWO SOUTH TEXAS COUNTIES.   MDICKBE65389

PROBLEMS OF THE LATIN-AMERICAN WORKER IN TEXAS.   MGONZHB63404

A HISTORY OF THE INTERRELATIONSHIPS BETWEEN IMPORTED MEXICAN LABOR, DOMESTIC MIGRANTS, AND THE TEXAS
AGRICULTURAL ECONOMY.   MGRAVRP60405

THE SOCIAL ASPIRATIONS OF A SELECTED GROUP OF SPANISH NAME PEOPLE IN LAREDO, TEXAS.   MGUERIX59409

MEXICAN-AMERICAN LABOR PROBLEMS IN TEXAS.   MJONELB65318

THE MEXICAN-AMERICAN WORKERS OF SAN-ANTONIO. /TEXAS/   MLANDRG66427

THE OTHER TEXAS.   MLOOKXX63429

TEXAS MIGRANTS PROGRAM. /TRAINING EDUCATION/   MMACNBL67335

THE MEXICAN-AMERICANS OF SOUTH TEXAS.   MMADSWX64436

MINORITY-GROUPS AND THEIR EDUCATION IN HAY-COUNTY, TEXAS.   MMEADBS59438

LEVELS OF ASPIRATION OF MEXICAN-AMERICANS IN EL-PASO SCHOOLS. /TEXAS/   MNALLFX59447

SAN-ANTONIO PROJECT. /TEXAS/   MNATLCA63081

MIGRATION TO SOUTHWEST TEXAS. PEOPLES AND WORDS.   MNORMAX56448

TEXAS-S THIRD MAN. THE TEXAS MEXICAN.   MPAREAX63451

A CASE-STUDY OF LATIN-AMERICAN UNIONIZATION IN AUSTIN, TEXAS.   MPARISF64452

SPANISH-SPEAKING AND ENGLISH SPEAKING CHILDREN IN SOUTHWEST TEXAS. A COMPARATIVE STUDY OF INTELLIGENCE,
SOCIO-ECONOMIC STATUS, AND ACHIEVEMENT.   MRATLYX60460

SOME CHARACTERISTICS OF SPANISH-NAME TEXANS AND FOREIGN LATIN-AMERICANS IN TEXAS HIGHER EDUCATION.   MRENNRR57462

ACROSS THE TRACKS. MEXICAN-AMERICANS IN A TEXAS CITY.   MRUBEAJ66466

SOCIAL MOBILITY AND IMPUTATIONS OF WITCHCRAFT IN A MEXICAN-AMERICAN NEIGHBORHOOD OF TEXAS.   MRUBEAJ66467

ECONOMIC BASE STUDY OF SAN-ANTONIO AND TWENTY-SEVEN COUNTY AREAS. /TEXAS/   MSANACP64476

TEXAS AND THE BRACERO PROGRAM.   MSCRUOM63482

OCCUPATION-PATTERNS OF SPANISH-AMERICANS IN SELECTED AREAS OF TEXAS.   MSKRARL62494

OCCUPATIONAL CHANGE AMONG SPANISH-AMERICANS IN ATASCOSA-COUNTY AND SAN-ANTONIO, TEXAS.   MSKRARL66492

TEXAS GOOD NEIGHBOR.   MSOUTSS62497

MECHANIZATION AND THE TEXAS MIGRANT.   MTEXACC64499

PROCEEDINGS OF THE CONFERENCE ON EDUCATION FOR ADULT MIGRANT WORKERS. /TEXAS/   MTEXACM62498

A STUDY OF THE MENTAL HEALTH PROBLEMS OF MEXICAN-AMERICAN RESIDENTS. /TEXAS/   MTEXASD61500

POVERTY AMONG SPANISH-AMERICANS IN TEXAS. LOW-INCOME FAMILIES IN A MINORITY-GROUP.   MUPHAWK66511

DIFFERENTIALS IN THE INCIDENCE OF POVERTY IN TEXAS. /ECONOMIC-STATUS/   MUPHAWK66533

SAN-ANTONIO PROJECT. /TEXAS/   MWAGNJA63514

TEXAS   (CONTINUATION)
    RECENT MIGRATION OF YOUNG MALES INTO HOUSTON, TEXAS.   MWAGODW57515

    THE NEGRO IN THE TEXAS LABOR-SUPPLY.   NHILLFG46524

    HOUSTON -- THE NEGRO AND EMPLOYMENT OPPORTUNITIES IN THE SOUTH, THE FIRST OF A SERIES OF EMPLOYMENT
    STUDIES IN SOUTHERN CITIES. /TEXAS/   NSOUTRC61161

    OCCUPATIONAL CHOICES OF NEGRO HIGH SCHOOL SENIORS IN TEXAS.   NTURNBA57165

    VOCATIONAL EDUCATION FOR NEGRO YOUTH IN TEXAS.   NUSDLAB49847

    A COMPARATIVE STUDY OF TOP LEVEL MALE AND FEMALE EXECUTIVES IN HARRIS-COUNTY. /TEXAS OCCUPATIONS/   WDOLLPA65738

TEXAS-S
    TEXAS-S THIRD MAN. THE TEXAS MEXICAN.   MPAREAX63451

TEXT
    THE CIVIL-RIGHTS-ACT OF 1964. WHAT IT MEANS -- TO EMPLOYERS, BUSINESSMEN, UNIONS, EMPLOYEES,
    MINORITY-GROUPS. TEXT, ANALYSIS, LEGISLATIVE HISTORY.   GBUREON64492

TEXTBOOK
    AMERICAN MINORITIES. A TEXTBOOK OF READINGS IN INTERGROUP RELATIONS.   GBARRML57424

TEXTILE
    NEGRO EMPLOYMENT IN THE TEXTILE INDUSTRIES OF NORTH AND SOUTH-CAROLINA. /NORTH-CAROLINA/   NOSBUDD66963

    1966 EMPLOYMENT SURVEY IN THE TEXTILE INDUSTRY OF THE CAROLINAS.   NWALLPA66591

TEXTS
    TEXTS OF RULES AND REGULATIONS OF PRESIDENT-S COMMITTEE ON EQUAL-EMPLOYMENT-OPPORTUNITY RELATING TO
    OBLIGATIONS OF GOVERNMENT CONTRACTORS AND SUBCONTRACTORS, EFFECTIVE JULY 22, 1961. A BNA SPECIAL REPORT.   GBURENA61498

    STATE FAIR-EMPLOMENT LAWS AND THEIR ADMINISTRATION. TEXTS, FEDERAL-STATE COOPERATION, PROHIBITED ACTS.   GBURENA64497

THEME
    EXCLUSIONS AND ADAPTATIONS. A RE-EVALUATION OF THE CULTURE-OF-POVERTY THEME.   NCOHERXND221

THEMES
    THREE BASIC THEMES IN MEXICAN AND PUERTO-RICAN FAMILIES.   PTRENRD58800

THEORETICAL
    HUMAN CAPITAL. A THEORETICAL AND EMPIRICAL ANALYSIS WITH SPECIAL REFERENCE TO EDUCATION.   GBECKGS64700

    OCCUPATIONAL DISCRIMINATION. SOME THEORETICAL PROPOSITIONS.   GBLALHM62454

THEORIES
    ON THEORIES OF AUTOMATION. A POLEMIC AGAINST DANIEL BELL AND OTHERS. /UNEMPLOYMENT/   GSELIBB66609

    RACIAL DISCRIMINATION ON THE JOBSITE. COMPETING THEORIES AND COMPETING FORUMS.   NMEYEBI65210

THEORY
    THEORY, METHOD AND FINDINGS IN THE STUDY OF ACCULTURATION. A REVIEW. /MEXICAN-AMERICAN NEGRO/   CPETECX65989

    RACE-RELATIONS. PROBLEMS AND THEORY.   GMASUJX63064

    AN ALTERNATIVE THEORY OF ECONOMIC DISCRIMINATION.   GTHURLC67969

    OCCUPATIONAL CHOICE. AN APPROACH TO A GENERAL THEORY.   NGINZEX51410

    POSITION CHOICES AND CAREERS. ELEMENTS OF A THEORY. /ASPIRATIONS/   WTIEDDV58154

THREAT
    PREJUDICE -- A THREAT TO THE LEADERSHIP ROLE.   GEVANRI62669

    EFFECTS OF ANXIETY, THREAT, AND RACIAL ENVIRONMENT ON TASK PERFORMANCE OF NEGRO COLLEGE STUDENTS. NKATZIX63640

THRUWAY
    REPORT OF INQUIRY CONCERNING CHARGES OF DISCRIMINATING PRACTICES IN THE NEW-YORK STATE THRUWAY AUTHORITY.   GNEWYSB64104

TIME
    NO TIME FOR PREJUDICE. /WOMEN NEGRO OCCUPATIONS/   CSTAUMK61132

    EQUALITY IN OUR TIME. WHAT WE SAID, AND WHAT WE DID NOT SAY.   GLOWESH63921

    A TIME FOR ACTION. PROCEEDINGS OF THE NATIONAL CONFERENCE ON EQUAL-EMPLOYMENT-OPPORTUNITY, 1962.
    /MILITARY/   GUSDARM62193

    A STITCH IN TIME CAN SERVE ALL.   GWOLLMX54580

    NO TIME FOR TRAGIC IRONIES. /EMPLOYMENT TECHNOLOGICAL-CHANGE/   NPURYMT63027

    HIGHER EDUCATION FOR WOMEN. TIME FOR REAPPRAISAL.   WDOLAEF63952

    TIME, WORK, AND WELFARE.   WMORGJX65997

TITLE-VII
    COVERAGE UNDER TITLE-VII OF THE CIVIL-RIGHTS-ACT.   GBENEMC66435

    DISCRIMINATION, UNIONS, AND TITLE-VII.   GBLAKGR64453

    EMPLOYMENT DISCRIMINATION. STATE FEPC LAWS AND THE IMPACT OF OF TITLE-VII OF THE CIVIL-RIGHTS-ACT OF
    1964.   GBRYEGL65896

    A SPECIAL REPORT -- THE EQUAL-EMPLOYMENT-OPPORTUNITY LAW, TITLE-VII OF THE CIVIL-RIGHTS-ACT OF 1964.   GBURENAND495

    TESTING AND TITLE-VII.   GFLINCX65120

    TITLE-VII. RELATIONSHIP AND EFFECT ON THE NATIONAL-LABOR- RELATIONS-BOARD. /LEGISLATION/   GFUCHRS66702

    UNION RACIAL DISCRIMINATION -- RECENT DEVELOPMENTS BEFORE THE NLRB AND THEIR IMPLICATIONS UNDER TITLE-VII
    OF THE CIVIL-RIGHTS-ACT OF 1964.   GGEORLJ65714

    A TALE OF 22 CITIES. TITLE-VII OF THE CIVIL-RIGHTS-ACT OF 1964.   GKOTHCA65732

    EMPLOYMENT DISCRIMINATION. STATE FAIR-EMPLOYMENT-PRACTICES LAWS AND THE IMPACT OF TITLE-VII OF THE
    CIVIL-RIGHTS-ACT OF 1964.   GLAWXRD65885

    TITLE-VII. RELATIONSHIP AND EFFECT ON EXECUTIVE ORDER 11246. /LEGISLATION/   GMANNRD66937

TITLE-VII   (CONTINUATION)
    WHAT TITLE-VII MEANS FOR THE LOCAL OFFICE. /SES/   GMITCHR66018

    TITLE-VII. REPORTING AND RECORD KEEPING. /LEGISLATION/   GPEARHG66149

    FAIR-EMPLOYMENT IS GOOD BUSINESS. EXAMPLES OF FAIR PRACTICES FOR TITLE-VII OF THE CIVIL-RIGHTS-ACT OF
    1964.   GPOTOII65188

    TITLE-VII. RELATIONSHIP AND EFFECT ON STATE ACTION. /LEGISLATION/   GPURDJW66209

    TITLE-VII. LIMITATIONS AND QUALIFICATIONS. /LEGISLATION/   GRACHCX66214

    DIVISION OF AUTHORITY UNDER TITLE-VII OF THE CIVIL-RIGHTS-ACT OF 1964. A PRELIMINARY STUDY IN
    FEDERAL-STATE INTERAGENCY RELATIONS.   GROSESJ66254

    TITLE-VII. COVERAGE AND COMMENTS. /LEGISLATION/   GSCHMCT66287

    TITLE-VII. LEGISLATIVE HISTORY.   GVAASFJ66534

    LEGALITY AND VALIDITY OF PERSONNEL TESTS. /LEGISLATION TITLE-VII/   GVINCNX66113

    THE CORPORATION AND TITLE-VII.   GVIOTVH66113

    TITLE-VII. COMPLAINT PROCEDURES AND REMEDIES. /LEGISLATION/   GWALKRW66538

    THE NEGRO AND TITLE-VII.   NBURENA65137

    JOBS FOR NEGROES -- THE GAINS, THE PROBLEMS, AND THE NEW HIRING LAW. /TITLE-VII/   NBUSIWX65151

    EMPLOYMENT SECURITY, SENIORITY AND RACE. THE ROLE OF TITLE-VII OF THE CIVIL-RIGHTS-ACT OF 1964.   NGOULWB67864

    TITLE-VII. EQUAL-EMPLOYMENT SECTION. CIVIL-RIGHTS-ACT OF 1964. THE WAR-AGAINST-POVERTY.   NHILLHX65549

    THE NEGRO AND TITLE-VII. /LEGISLATION/   NPERSPF65562

    JANE CROW AND THE LAW. SEX DISCRIMINATION AND TITLE-VII.   WMURRPX65010

TOBACCO
    THE NEGRO TOBACCO WORKER AND HIS UNION IN DURHAM, NORTH-CAROLINA.   NRICEJD41053

TOKENISM
    THE CASE AGAINST TOKENISM.   NKINGML62144

TOLERANCE
    TOLERANCE IN INDUSTRY. THE RECORD.   GTURNHC50365

TOOL
    RACIAL STATISTICS AS A MANAGEMENT TOOL.   GDOARLE66645

    PATTERNS OF DISCRIMINATION IN THE GLASS AND MACHINE TOOL INDUSTRIES IN OHIO.   GOHIOCR66126

    PATTERNS OF DISCRIMINATION IN THE MACHINE TOOL INDUSTRY IN OHIO.   GOHIOCR66128

    RACIAL STATISTICS AS A MANAGEMENT TOOL.   NDOARLE66276

    THE RACIAL ISSUE AS AN ANTI UNION TOOL AND THE NATIONAL-LABOR-RELATIONS-BOARD.   NSACHRX63888

    RACIAL DISCRIMINATION AND THE NLRB. THE HUGHES TOOL CASE, PART ONE.   NVIRGLR64017

    RACIAL DISCRIMINATION AND THE NLRB. THE HUGHES TOOL CASE, PART TWO.   NVIRGLR64018

TOOLS
    FAIR-EMPLOYMENT WORKS -- TOOLS FOR HUMAN-RELATIONS.   GTHOMJA51355

TOP-MANAGEMENT
    THE MUTUAL SAVINGS BANKS OF NEW-YORK-CITY. A FOLLOW-UP REPORT ON THE EXCLUSION OF JEWS AT TOP-MANAGEMENT
    AND POLICY-MAKING LEVELS.   JAMERJC66695

TOTAL
    THE URBAN ADJUSTMENT OF IMMIGRANTS. THE RELATIONSHIP OF EDUCATION TO OCCUPATIONAL AND TOTAL FAMILY
    INCOME. /NEGRO MEXICAN-AMERICAN/   CSHANLW63122

    MANPOWER DEVELOPMENT TRAINING. TOTAL NUMBER OF NEW ENROLLEES DURING THE MONTH BY RACE AND OCCUPATION
    STATEWIDE AND BY ADMINISTRATIVE AREA, SEPTEMBER, 1966, OCTOBER, 1966. /CALIFORNIA/   GCALDEM66518

    MEXICAN-AMERICAN AND TOTAL EMPLOYMENT IN SELECTED STATES AND STANDARD METROPOLITAN STATISTICAL AREAS. MUSCISC63504

    NEGRO AND TOTAL EMPLOYMENT BY GRADE AND SALARY GROUPS, JUNE 1961 AND JUNE 1962.   NPRESCD62011

    MINORITY-GROUP STUDY, JUNE 1963. NEGRO AND TOTAL EMPLOYMENT IN SELECTED AGENCIES.   NPRESCD63010

TOWN
    CASTE AND CLASS IN A SOUTHERN TOWN.   NDOLLJX49281

    NEGRO AND WHITE IN A CONNECTICUT TOWN.   NLEEXFF61674

TRADE
    TRADE UNION LEADERSHIP COUNCIL --EXPERIMENT IN COMMUNITY ACTION. /DETROIT MICHIGAN/   GBATTRX63426

    TRADE UNION COMPLIANCE WITH PRESIDENTIAL DIRECTIVES, MEMBERSHIP ACCEPTANCE, SENIORITY, ETC.   NCOOPJX64294

    TRADE UNIONS PRACTICES AND THE NEGRO WORKER -- THE ESTABLISHMENT AND IMPLEMENTATION OF AFL-CIO
    ANTI-DISCRIMINATION POLICY.   NDAVINF60312

    THE OLD-TIMERS AND THE NEWCOMERS. ETHNIC-GROUP RELATIONS IN A NEEDLE TRADE UNION.   NHERBWX53519

    TRADE UNIONS AND MINORITY PROBLEMS.   NJOUROS53891

    THE NEGRO WORKER OF KANSAS-CITY. A STUDY OF TRADE UNION AND ORGANIZED LABOR RELATIONS.   NKANCIU40634

    THE NEGRO WORKER AND THE TRADE UNIONS. A FOOT IN THE DOOR.   NMARSRX65058

    TRADE UNION LEADERSHIP COUNCIL. EXPERIMENT IN COMMUNITY ACTION.   NNEWXUT63088

    RACE DISCRIMINATION IN TRADE UNIONS. RECORD AND OUTLOOK.   NNORTHR46945

    DISCRIMINATION AND THE TRADE UNIONS.   NNORTHR49936

    THE STRUGGLE FOR JOBS AND FOR NEGRO RIGHTS IN THE TRADE UNIONS.   NSIMOHX50139

TRADE (CONTINUATION)
THE MENTALITIES OF NEGRO AND WHITE WORKERS. AN EXPERIMENTAL SCHOOL-S INTERPRETATION OF NEGRO **TRADE** UNIONISM.   NVALIPX49280

GIFTED WOMEN IN THE **TRADE** UNIONS. /OCCUPATIONS/   WHILLBX62845

TRADE AND INDUSTRIAL EDUCATION FOR GIRLS AND WOMEN. A DIRECTORY OF TRAINING PROGRAMS.   WUSDHEW60175

TRADES
RACIAL DISCRIMINATION IN THE CINCINNATI BUILDING **TRADES**. A COMPREHENSIVE REPORT AND RECOMMENDATIONS. /OHIO/   GOHIOCR64129

A SURVEY OF DISCRIMINATION IN THE BUILDING **TRADES** INDUSTRY, NEW-YORK CITY.   GSHAUDF63300

NEW-YORK CITY COMMISSION ON HUMAN RIGHTS, CONSTRUCTION **TRADES** HEARING, TESTIMONY. /INDUSTRY/   NHILLHX66546

RACIAL FACTORS INFLUENCING ENTRY TO THE SKILLED **TRADES**. /UNION/   NMARSRX63745

NEGRO WORKERS IN THE BUILDING **TRADES** IN SELECTED CITIES. NORFOLK, VIRGINIA. /INDUSTRY/   NNATLUL46894

NEGRO WORKERS IN THE BUILDING **TRADES** IN CERTAIN CITIES.   NNATLUL47904

NEGROES AND THE BUILDING **TRADES** UNION.   NNATLUL57902

RACIAL DISCRIMINATION IN THE CINCINNATI BUILDING **TRADES**. REPORT AND RECOMMENDATIONS. /OHIO/   NOHIOCR66605

A SURVEY OF DISCRIMINATION IN THE BUILDING **TRADES** INDUSTRY. NEW-YORK CITY.   NSHAUDX63126

TRADITION
THE NEGRO BUSINESSMAN. IN SEARCH OF A **TRADITION**. /OCCUPATIONS/   NFOLEEP66369

THE OPTIMISTIC **TRADITION** AND AMERICAN YOUTH.   NGINZEX61411

SOUTHERN **TRADITION** AND REGIONAL PROGRESS.   NNICHWH60322

TRAIN
DUAL PARTS OF DESEGREGATION. LEGISLATION TO EDUCATE AND **TRAIN** NEGROES FOR BETTER JOBS.   NDUSCJX63311

TRAINED
THE PRESENT SITUATION IN THE ACADEMIC WORLD OF WOMEN **TRAINED** IN ENGINEERING. /OCCUPATIONS/   WBERNJX65639

NONTRADITIONALLY **TRAINED** WOMEN AS MENTAL HEALTH COUNSELORS/PSYCHOTHERAPISTS.   WMAGOTM66779

SHOULD WOMEN BE **TRAINED** IN THE SCIENCES. /OCCUPATIONS/   WPINEMX58061

PART-TIME PROGRAM FOR PROFESSIONALLY **TRAINED** WOMEN. /TRAINING/   WTACKAL66147

EVERYBODY-S TALKING ABOUT **TRAINED** WORKERS FOR THE FUTURE.   WUSDLAB63243

TRAINEES
RACIAL CHARACTERISTICS, MDTA **TRAINEES**, SAN-FRANCISCO. /CALIFORNIA NEGRO MEXICAN-AMERICAN/   CELTOEX63332

TRAINING
TRAINING AID. CULTURAL DIFFERENCES, TRAINING IN NONDISCRIMINATION, READING ASSIGNMENTS. /EMPLOYMENT MEXICAN-AMERICAN NEGRO/   CCALDSW65447

TRAINING AID. CULTURAL DIFFERENCES, **TRAINING** IN NONDISCRIMINATION, READING ASSIGNMENTS. /EMPLOYMENT MEXICAN-AMERICAN NEGRO/   CCALDSW65447

ADDRESS TO COMMUNITY RELATIONS SERVICE STAFF **TRAINING** SESSION, JANUARY 12, 1967, ON JOBS NOW. /NEGRO PUERTO-RICAN YOUTH/   CCOLEBX67918

SECRETARIAL **TRAINING** WITH SPEECH IMPROVEMENT. AN EXPERIMENTAL AND DEMONSTRATION PROJECT. /NEGRO WOMEN/   CSAINMD66320

AN EXPERIMENT IN MANPOWER DEVELOPMENT. /**TRAINING** MISSISSIPPI NEGRO WOMEN/   CSELFHC66325

THE **TRAINING** OF MIGRANT FARM WORKERS. A FOLLOW-UP STUDY OF TWO EXPERIMENTAL AND DEMONSTRATION PROGRAMS UNDER THE MANPOWER-DEVELOPMENT-AND-TRAINING-ACT. /MEXICAN-AMERICAN AMERICAN-INDIAN/   CUNIVOD66054

OAK GLEN -- A **TRAINING** CAMP FOR UNEMPLOYED YOUTH. /NEGRO MEXICAN-AMERICAN/   CUSDLAB66323

REPORT. EVALUATION STUDY OF YOUTH **TRAINING** AND EMPLOYMENT PROJECT, EAST LOS-ANGELES. /NEGRO MEXICAN-AMERICAN CALIFORNIA/   CWEINJL64310

FINAL REPORT OF THE YMCA YOUTH AND WORK PROJECT 1962-1966. /NEGRO PUERTO-RICAN **TRAINING**/   CYMCAYA66329

THE ROLE OF GOVERNMENT-SPONSORED **TRAINING** AND RETRAINING PROGRAMS.   GALLECC65758

APTITUDE TESTING, **TRAINING**, AND EMPLOYEE DEVELOPMENT, WITH A SECTION ON THE EMPLOYMENT OF MINORITY-GROUPS.   GAMERMA49389

FORMAL OCCUPATIONAL **TRAINING** OF ADULT WORKERS, ITS EXTENT, NATURE, AND USE.   GBEDEMX64448

MANPOWER DEVELOPMENT. CHARGES AND CHALLENGES. /TECHNOLOGICAL-CHANGE **TRAINING**/   GBOLIAC65528

TRAINING THE HARD-CORE UNEMPLOYED.   GBROOLB64795

MANPOWER DEVELOPMENT **TRAINING**. TOTAL NUMBER OF NEW ENROLLEES DURING THE MONTH BY RACE AND OCCUPATION STATEWIDE AND BY ADMINISTRATIVE AREA, SEPTEMBER, 1966, OCTOBER, 1966. /CALIFORNIA/   GCALDEM66518

EQUAL-OPPORTUNITY IN APPRENTICESHIP AND **TRAINING** -- THE CALIFORNIA PROGRAM.   GCALDIR65524

MANPOWER PROGRAM IMPLICATIONS OF SKILL IMBALANCES. /**TRAINING**/   GCASSFH66565

VOCATIONAL **TRAINING** TO IMPROVE JOB OPPORTUNITIES FOR MINORITY-GROUPS. COMMENT.   GFINEMX64681

VOCATIONAL **TRAINING**   GFREEMX60699

TRAINING AND DEVELOPMENT.   GFUGAGR64704

THE FEDERAL ANTI-POVERTY PROGRAM AND SOME IMPLICATIONS OF SUBPROFESSIONAL **TRAINING**.   GGORDJE65135

DEVELOPMENT OF **TRAINING** INCENTIVES FOR THE YOUTH OF MINORITY-GROUPS. /ECONOMIC-STATUS/   GGRANLB57979

TRAINING DISADVANTAGED GROUPS UNDER THE MANPOWER-DEVELOPMENT-TRAINING-ACT.   GHELPCW63501

WAR-ON-POVERTY. /EMPLOYMENT **TRAINING**/   GHUMPHH64739

FINAL REPORT. THE YOUTH **TRAINING** PROJECT, SEPTEMBER 1, 1963--JANUARY 31, 1965. /ST-LOUIS MISSOURI

  GJEWIEV65568

MDTA INSTITUTIONAL TRAINING OF NONWHITES.   GMARSJX66944

A STUDY OF UNEMPLOYMENT, TRAINING AND PLACEMENT PATTERNS IN THE MUSKEGON AREA. /MICHIGAN/   GMICFEA57979

INCREASING EMPLOYABILITY OF YOUTH. THE ROLE OF WORK TRAINING.   GMOEDMX66852

GUIDANCE, TRAINING AND APPRENTICESHIP FACTORS AFFECTING MINORITY-GROUPS.   GNATLAM60037

LOW-INCOME YOUTH, UNEMPLOYMENT, VOCATIONAL TRAINING, AND THE JOB-CORPS.   GPURCFX66208

GRADUATES OF THE NORFOLK PROJECT ONE YEAR LATER. /MDTA TRAINING/   GQUINPA65771

TRAINING OF PUBLIC ASSISTANCE RECIPIENTS UNDER THE MDTA.   GROSORG66258

EVALUATION AND SKILL TRAINING OF OUT-OF-SCHOOL, HARD-CORE UNEMPLOYED YOUTH FOR TRAINING AND PLACEMENT.   GSMITAE65140

EVALUATION AND SKILL TRAINING OF OUT-OF-SCHOOL, HARD-CORE UNEMPLOYED YOUTH FOR TRAINING AND PLACEMENT.   GSMITAE65140

TRAINING IN THE PERSPECTIVE OF TECHNOLOGICAL-CHANGE.   GSTRIHE66669

OPPORTUNITIES-INDUSTRIALIZATION-CENTER. CRAFTSMEN WITH CONFIDENCE. /TRAINING/   GSULLLH66220

EQUAL-EMPLOYMENT-OPPORTUNITY TRAINING, A PROGRAM FOR AFFIRMATIVE-ACTION.   GUSCISC63384

HOUSING, EMPLOYMENT OPPORTUNITIES AND APPRENTICESHIP TRAINING, REPORT. /NEW-JERSEY/   GUSCOMC63404

EDUCATION AND TRAINING, THE BRIDGE BETWEEN MAN AND HIS WORK.   GUSDHEW65156

MANPOWER DEVELOPMENT AND TRAINING.   GUSDHEW65763

THE YOUTH WE HAVEN-T SERVED. /EDUCATION TRAINING/   GUSDHEW66002

ANNUAL REPORT OF THE SECRETARY OF HEALTH, EDUCATION, AND WELFARE TO THE CONGRESS ON TRAINING ACTIVITIES
UNDER THE MANPOWER-DEVELOPMENT-AND-TRAINING-ACT, 1965.   GUSDHEW66978

HELPING THE LONG-TERM UNEMPLOYED. /INCOME-MAINTENANCE TRAINING/   GUSDLAB62221

CHARACTERISTICS OF 6000 WHITE AND NONWHITE PERSONS ENROLLED IN MANPOWER-DEVELOPMENT-AND-TRAINING-ACT
TRAINING.   GUSDLAB63197

YOUNG WORKERS. THEIR SPECIAL TRAINING NEEDS.   GUSDLAB63506

MANPOWER REPORT OF THE PRESIDENT AND A REPORT ON MANPOWER REQUIREMENTS, RESOURCES, UTILIZATION, AND
TRAINING.   GUSDLAB63830

MANPOWER REPORT OF THE PRESIDENT AND A REPORT ON MANPOWER REQUIREMENTS, RESOURCES, UTILIZATION, AND
TRAINING.   GUSDLAB64829

MANPOWER. RESEARCH AND TRAINING.   GUSDLAB65710

MANPOWER REPORT OF THE PRESIDENT AND A REPORT ON MANPOWER REQUIREMENTS, RESOURCES, UTILIZATION, AND
TRAINING.   GUSDLAB65828

REPORT ON MANPOWER RESEARCH AND TRAINING UNDER THE MDTA.   GUSDLAB66493

MANPOWER REPORT OF THE PRESIDENT AND A REPORT ON MANPOWER REQUIREMENTS, RESOURCES, UTILIZATION, AND
TRAINING.   GUSDLAB66827

HEARINGS RELATING TO THE TRAINING AND UTILIZATION OF THE MANPOWER RESOURCES OF THE NATION.   GUSSENA63618

IMPLICATIONS OF GOVERNMENT-SPONSORED TRAINING PROGRAMS. /TECHNOLOGICAL-CHANGE/   GWALSJP64620

MOTIVATIONAL PROBLEMS IN TRAINING.   GWISPLG65141

APPRENTICESHIP TRAINING IN NEW-YORK. OPENINGS IN 1963.   GWORKDL63582

THE WOL APPRENTICESHIP TRAINING PROGRAM. REPORT OF A YEAR-S EXPERIMENT.   GWORKDL65584

MANPOWER TRAINING. SOME COST DIMENSIONS.   GYOUNSX67144

MANPOWER AND TRAINING. TRENDS, OUTLOOK AND PROGRAMS.   GZEISJS63704

MANPOWER TRAINING IN NAVAJO LAND.   IHARTVS63573

TRAINING NAVAJOES FOR THE FUTURE.   ILINDVX64581

VOCATIONAL TRAINING PROGRAMS FOR AMERICAN-INDIANS.   IUSDLAB64009

REPORT OF INDIAN RECRUITMENT AND TRAINING MEETING AT ALBUQUERQUE, NEW-MEXICO, ON DECEMBER 6, 1966.   IUSDLAB66321

TEXAS MIGRANTS PROGRAM. /TRAINING EDUCATION/   MMACNBL67335

STAFF TRAINING WITH A SOUTHERN ACCENT.   NAMERFX65016

OAKLAND LABOR BACKS UP YOUTH. /TRAINING/   NAWNEMX66875

THE DETERMINATION OF CERTAIN MAJOR FACTORS AFFECTING THE NEGRO VETERAN IN THE ON-THE-JOB TRAINING PROGRAM
IN VOCATIONAL AGRICULTURE IN THE STATE OF ALABAMA AS A BASIS FOR PLANNING A MORE EFFECTIVE PROGRAM.   NBATTEF49338

SECURING SKILLS NEEDED FOR SUCCESS. COMMUNITY JOB TRAINING FOR NEGROES.   NBLUMAA66099

JOB TRAINING THROUGH ADULT-EDUCATION.   NBLUMAA67098

MANPOWER TRAINING AND THE NEGRO WORKER.   NBRAZWF66110

FACTORS AFFECTING THE PRESENT FARMING PROGRAMS OF ONE HUNDRED NEGRO FARMS IN THE PATRONAGE AREA OF THE
MACON COUNTY TRAINING SCHOOL, IN ALABAMA, WITH EMPHASIS FOR IMPROVEMENT.   NBRONCA51337

EMPLOYMENT AND TRAINING. THE MCCONE-REPORT -- SIX MONTHS LATER.   NBULLPXND134

FINAL REPORT. EMPLOYMENT AND TRAINING. REPORT FOR GOVERNOR-S COMMISSION.   NBULLPX65483

SLUMS AND SUBURBS. /TRAINING/   NCONAJB61920

ARMING THE UNEMPLOYED WITH SKILLS. /TRAINING/   NCOONRB66927

SELECTING AND **TRAINING** NEGROES FOR MANAGERIAL POSITIONS.   NEDUCTS64322

MDTA PROJECT UPLIFT. /**TRAINING**/   NFILIJE66354

TRAINING FOR TOMORROW-S SCIENTISTS AND TECHNICIANS. A COMMUNITY APPROACH TO A COMMUNITY NEED.   NFINLOE60356

TRAINING FOR MINORITY-GROUPS. PROBLEMS OF RACIAL IMBALANCE AND SEGREGATION.   NFUSFDR66014

THE NEGRO WAGE-EARNER AND APPRENTICESHIP **TRAINING** PROGRAMS. A CRITICAL ANALYSIS WITH RECOMMENDATIONS.   NHILLHX60532

RACIAL DISCRIMINATION IN THE NATION-S APPRENTICESHIP **TRAINING** PROGRAM.   NHILLHX62539

EXPERIMENTAL AND DEMONSTRATION MANPOWER PROJECT FOR THE RECRUITMENT, **TRAINING**, PLACEMENT AND FOLLOW-UP OF
RURAL UNEMPLOYED WORKERS IN TEN NORTH FLORIDA CITIES. FINAL REPORT. /PARTICIPANTS/   NJACKTA66597

MANAGEMENT, RACIAL DISCRIMINATION AND APPRENTICE **TRAINING**   NKOVAIX64663

APPRENTICESHIP **TRAINING** PROGRAMS AND RACIAL DISCRIMINATION.   NKOVAIX65024

A UNIQUE REGIONAL PROGRAM OF PSYCHOLOGICAL RESEARCH AND **TRAINING** IN THE SOUTH.   NLANGMC56032

SELF-HELP IN PHILADELPHIA. /**TRAINING** PENNSYLVANIA/   NLEESHX64675

CULTURAL EXPOSURE AND RACE AS VARIABLES IN PREDICTING **TRAINING** AND JOB SUCCESS. /TESTING/   NLOCKHCND700

FACILITATIVE AND INHIBITIVE FACTORS IN **TRAINING** PROGRAM RECRUITMENT AMONG RURAL NEGROES.   NMARSCP65738

A STUDY OF EMPLOYMENT AND **TRAINING** PATTERNS IN THE LANSING AREA. /MICHIGAN/   NMICFEP58778

HELP FOR THE HARD-CORE UNEMPLOYED. /**TRAINING**/   NMILLJN66787

APPRENTICESHIP AND **TRAINING** OPPORTUNITIES FOR NEGRO YOUTHS IN SELECTED URBAN-LEAGUE CITIES.   NNATLUL61885

WATTS ONE YEAR LATER. /**TRAINING** CALIFORNIA LOS-ANGELES/   NPAGEDX66970

THE UNFINISHED REVOLUTION. /**TRAINING**/   NRANDAP62036

OCCUPATIONAL ESTABLISHMENT OF FORMER STUDENTS OF VOCATIONAL AGRICULTURE IN MONTGOMERY **TRAINING** SCHOOL
AREA. /ALABAMA/   NSCOTCDND346

TRAINING OF NEGROES IN THE SKILLED-TRADES.   NSTEEHG54176

NEW **TRAINING** PLAN FOR NEGROES.   NUSDLAB41832

TRAINING NEGROES FOR WAR WORK.   NUSDLAB43845

THE NEGRO WAGE-EARNER AND APPRENTICESHIP **TRAINING** PROGRAMS.   NUSDLAB60249

A CRITICAL APPRAISAL OF PROFESSION **TRAINING** OF NEGRO TEACHERS IN OKTIBBEHA COUNTY MISSISSIPPI.   NWILLMM50234

CONTINUING EDUCATION -- FOCUS ON COUNSELING AND **TRAINING**.   WAAUWFX65616

TESTIMONY, PUBLIC HEARING, WOMEN IN PUBLIC AND PRIVATE EMPLOYMENT, CALIFORNIA. /**TRAINING**/   WCU4MGX66711

FINAL REPORT. EXPERIMENTAL AND DEMONSTRATION MANPOWER PROJECT FOR THE RECRUITMENT, **TRAINING**, PLACEMENT
AND FOLLOW-UP OF RURAL UNEMPLOYED WORKERS IN TEN NORTH FLORIDA COUNTIES.   WFLORMP66326

MARRIED WOMEN AT UTAH STATE UNIVERSITY, SPRING QUARTER, 1960. /**TRAINING**/   WFREDCX61769

THE COMPARATIVE ACADEMIC ACHIEVEMENT OF YOUNG AND OLD. /**TRAINING**/   WHALFIT62813

VOCATIONAL GUIDANCE AND **TRAINING** OF GIRLS AND WOMEN. /COUNSELING/   WINTELO64863

OCCUPATIONAL **TRAINING** OF WOMEN IN THE UNITED STATES.   WINTELR64866

VOCATIONAL **TRAINING** OF THE OLDER WOMAN.   WKINGCR66906

PROBLEM AREAS IN **TRAINING** FOR AUTOMATED WORK. /TECHNOLOGICAL-CHANGE/   WLIPSOX64936

WOMEN ARE **TRAINING** FOR BUSINESS. /OCCUPATIONS/   WMARSEM62956

RUTGERS -- THE STATE UNIVERSITY. FORD FOUNDATION PROGRAM FOR THE RETRAINING IN MATHEMATICS OF COLLEGE
GRADUATE WOMEN. /**TRAINING**/   WMARTHM63957

JOBS AND **TRAINING** FOR WOMEN TECHNICIANS. /**TRAINING**/   WMEYEMB61975

JOBS AND TRAINING FOR WOMEN TECHNICIANS. /**TRAINING**/   WMEYEMB61975

UPDATING **TRAINING** FOR THE RETURNING NURSE, SOCIAL WORKER AND TEACHER.   WNATLCP61018

SOCIAL WORK DEGREE PROGRESS REPORT. /**TRAINING**/   WNYUYUG66031

TOP LEVEL **TRAINING** OF WOMEN IN THE UNITED STATES, 1900-60.   WPARRJB62283

TRAINING. KEY TO EMPLOYMENT.   WPETEEX62057

IMPLICATIONS OF TWO PILOT PROJECTS IN **TRAINING** MATURE WOMEN AS COUNSELORS.   WRIOCMJ65082

MATHEMATICS RETRAINING PROGRAM. NOTES AND COMMENTS, APRIL 1964, 1965, 1966. /**TRAINING**/   WRUTGMR64097

RADCLIFFE INSTITUTE FOR INDEPENDENT STUDY. /**TRAINING**/   WSMITCX63119

PART-TIME PROGRAM FOR PROFESSIONALLY TRAINED WOMEN. /**TRAINING**/   WTACKAL66147

TRADE AND INDUSTRIAL EDUCATION FOR GIRLS AND WOMEN. A DIRECTORY OF **TRAINING** PROGRAMS.   WUSDHEW60175

TRAINING OPPORTUNITIES FOR WOMEN AND GIRLS.   WUSDLAB60221

OCCUPATIONAL **TRAINING** OF WOMEN UNDER THE MANPOWER-DEVELOPMENT-AND-TRAINING-ACT.   WUSDLAB64179

TRAINING WOMEN AND GIRLS FOR WORK.   WWELLJA60262

PARTNERSHIP TEACHING PROGRAM. PROGRESS REPORT -- JAN-OCT 1965. SECTION I. /**TRAINING**/   WWOMEEA65275

THE NURSING SHORTAGE AND THE NURSE **TRAINING** ACT OF 1964. /MANPOWER/   WYETTDX66246

TRAINS
ARAPAHOE INDIAN **TRAINS** FOR SPACE AGE.   IUSDLAB66960

TRAITS

NARRAGANSETT SURVIVAL. A STUDY OF GROUP PERSISTENCE THROUGH ADAPTED TRAITS.   IBOISEX59887

ANALYSIS OF MALE NAVAHO STUDENTS PERCEPTIONS OF OCCUPATIONAL OPPORTUNITIES AND THEIR ATTITUDES TOWARD
DEVELOPMENT OF SKILLS AND TRAITS NECESSARY FOR OCCUPATIONAL COMPETENCE.   IDESPCW65548

TRANSCRIPT

HEARING OF THE SUBCOMMITTEE ON ECONOMIC DEVELOPMENT. EDITED TRANSCRIPT, JANUARY 28 AND 29, 1964.
/CALIFORNIA FEP/   GCALAIW64510

TRANSCRIPT OF PROCEEDINGS OF THE INTERIM SUBCOMMITTEE ON SPECIAL EMPLOYMENT PROBLEMS. /CALIFORNIA/ MCALAIC64374

TRANSCULTURATION

AMERICAN INDIANS, WHITE AND BLACK. THE PHENOMENON OF TRANSCULTURATION.   IHALLAI63571

TRANSFORMATION

THE DEEP SOUTH IN TRANSFORMATION.   GHIGHRB65056

TRANSFORMATION OF THE NEGRO-AMERICAN. /EDUCATION EMPLOYMENT INCOME/   NBROOLX65123

TRANSIENT

SURVEY ON TRANSIENT MEXICAN LABOR REQUIREMENTS.   MLOSACAND430

TRANSITION

FARM LABOR-MARKET IN TRANSITION.   GUSDLAB62991

THE MENOMINEE TERMINATION CRISIS. BARRIERS IN THE WAY OF A RAPID CULTURAL TRANSITION.   IAMESDW59525

FRUITLAND, NEW-MEXICO. A NAVAHO COMMUNITY IN TRANSITION.   ISASATT60615

HARLEM. A COMMUNITY IN TRANSITION.   NCLARJH64309

THE RURAL NEGRO POPULATION OF THE SOUTH IN TRANSITION.   NMAYOSC63762

THE PREDOMINANTLY NEGRO COLLEGES AND UNIVERSITIES IN TRANSITION.   NMCGREJ65720

THE PUERTO-RICAN SECTION. A STUDY IN SOCIAL TRANSITION.   PHERNJX59816

INITIATION INTO A WOMAN-S PROFESSION. IDENTITY PROBLEMS IN THE STATUS TRANSITION OF CO-ED TO STUDENT
NURSE.   WDAVIFX66723

TRANSPORTATION

CIVIL-RIGHTS IN AIR TRANSPORTATION AND GOVERNMENT INITIATIVE.   GDIXORX63644

SOME PRACTICAL STUDIES IN PUBLIC TRANSPORTATION. /EMPLOYMENT-CONDITIONS WATTS LOS-ANGELES CALIFORNIA/ NCARLJX65593

FINAL REPORT. EQUAL-EMPLOYMENT-OPPORTUNITY IN THE TRANSPORTATION INDUSTRY. /MASSACHUSETTS/   NMASSCA66964

TREATMENT

THE RIGHT TO EQUAL TREATMENT. ADMINISTRATIVE ENFORCEMENT OF ANTIDISCRIMINATION LEGISLATION.   GBAMBMA61416

EQUAL-RIGHTS UNDER THE LAW. PROVIDING FOR EQUAL TREATMENT FOR ALL CITIZENS REGARDLESS OF RACE, RELIGION,
COLOR, NATIONAL ORIGIN OR ANCESTRY. /CALIFORNIA/   GCALAGO60511

EQUAL JUSTICE IN AN UNEQUAL WORLD. EQUALITY FOR THE NEGRO -- THE PROBLEM OF SPECIAL TREATMENT.   NKAPLJX66645

TREND

THE TREND SINCE 1944 ON THE COLOR LINE IN INDUSTRY.   NOPINRC51959

TRENDS

RECENT TRENDS IN THE STUDY OF MINORITY AND RACE-RELATIONS. /NEGRO PUERTO-RICAN ORIENTAL/   CGORDMM63977

SIGNIFICANT TRENDS IN THE NEW-YORK STATE ECONOMY, WITH SPECIAL REFERENCE TO MINORITY-GROUPS.
/PUERTO-RICAN NEGRO/   CRUSSVR59482

TRENDS IN THE INCOME OF FAMILIES AND PERSONS IN THE UNITED STATES. 1947-1960. /DEMOGRAPHY/   CUSBURC63381

WHITE COLLAR EMPLOYMENT. TRENDS AND STRUCTURE.   GBANYCA61420

RECENT POPULATION TRENDS IN THE UNITED STATES WITH EMPHASIS ON RURAL AREAS. /EDUCATION/   GBEALCL63426

TRENDS IN EMPLOYEE TESTING.   GHABBSX65112

RECENT TRENDS IN THE TEST SELECTION OF APPRENTICES.   GMOTLAW53033

WHITE UNEMPLOYMENT IN THE UNITED STATES, 1947-1958, AN ANALYSIS OF TRENDS.   GNEWYSA58089

TRENDS IN THE EMPLOYMENT OF NEGRO-AMERICANS IN UPPER-LEVEL WHITE-COLLAR POSITIONS OF THE FEDERAL
GOVERNMENT.   GPRESCP60200

TRENDS AND PERSPECTIVES IN MANPOWER POLICY.   GREHNGX65654

RECENT TRENDS IN PUBLIC EMPLOYMENT.   GUSCONMND419

TECHNOLOGICAL TRENDS IN 36 MAJOR AMERICAN INDUSTRIES.   GUSDLAB64802

TECHNOLOGICAL TRENDS IN MAJOR AMERICAN INDUSTRIES. /EMPLOYMENT/   GUSDLAB66637

MANPOWER AND TRAINING. TRENDS, OUTLOOK AND PROGRAMS.   GZEISJS63704

NEGRO FARM OPERATORS. NUMBER, LOCATION AND RECENT TRENDS.   NBEALCL58064

ECONOMIC TRENDS IN THE NEGRO MARKET. /ECONOMIC-STATUS/   NBRIMAF64891

RECENT TRENDS IN RESEARCH ON THE NEGRO IN THE UNITED STATES.   NDRAKSC57290

MONTHLY SUMMARY OF EVENTS AND TRENDS IN RACE-RELATIONS. /CINCINNATI OHIO CASE-STUDY UNION/   NFISKUX44357

NEGROES IN FIVE NEW-YORK CITIES. A STUDY OF PROBLEMS, ACHIEVEMENTS AND TRENDS. /RACE-RELATIONS/   NGRIEES58455

RECENT TRENDS IN THE OCCUPATIONAL MOBILITY OF NEGROES, 1930-1960.   NHARENX65484

TRENDS IN PATTERNS OF RACE-RELATIONS IN THE SOUTH SINCE MAY 17 1954.   NHOPEJX56575

SOME TENDENCIES IN DEMOGRAPHIC TRENDS IN MARYLAND, 1950-1956.   NJACKEG57070

RECENT TRENDS OF MEMBERSHIP OF INTERNATIONAL UNIONS AS THEY AFFECT NEGRO WORKERS.   NJOHNRA44620

TRENDS IN PUBLIC-EMPLOYMENT.   NKRUGDH61667

TRENDS (CONTINUATION)
RECENT **TRENDS** IN THE ECONOMIC-STATUS OF NEGROES.   NMILLHP63785

SOCIAL **TRENDS** IN AMERICA AND STRATEGIC APPROACHES TO THE NEGRO PROBLEM.   NMYRDGX48871

TRENDS IN THE ECONOMIC-STATUS OF THE NEGRO PEOPLE. /OCCUPATIONAL-PATTERNS/   NPERLVX52983

PROBLEMS AND **TRENDS** IN JOB-DEVELOPMENT AND EMPLOYMENT PROGRAMS.   NPURYMT63028

THE NEGRO AS AN IMMIGRANT GROUP. RECENT **TRENDS** IN RACIAL AND ETHNIC SEGREGATION IN CHICAGO. /ILLINOIS/   NTAEUKE64196

WAR AND POSTWAR **TRENDS** IN EMPLOYMENT OF NEGROES.   NWOLFSL45335

POSTWAR **TRENDS** IN NEGRO EMPLOYMENT.   NWOLFSL47334

MIGRATION **TRENDS**.   PDECOPP59794

TRENDS IN THE PARTICIPATION CF WOMEN IN THE WORKING-FORCE.   WJAFFAH56878

TRENDS IN WOMEN-S EMPLOYMENT.   WKEYSMD65644

TRENDS IN WOMEN-S WORK PARTICIPATION.   WLESECE58928

WOMEN-S EDUCATION. FACTS, FINDINGS, AND APPARENT **TRENDS**.   WNEWCMX64028

TRENDS IN EDUCATIONAL-ATTAINMENT OF WOMEN.   WUSDLAB65222

TRENDS IN EDUCATIONAL-ATTAINMENT OF WOMEN.   WUSDLAB67806

WOMEN TODAY. **TRENDS** AND ISSUES IN THE UNITED STATES. /WORK-WOMAN-ROLE/   WYWCAXX63078

WOMEN-S WORK. FACTS, FINDINGS, AND APPARENT **TRENDS**.   WZAPCMW64283

TRI-ETHNIC
ACCULTURATION. ACCESS AND ALCOHOL IN A **TRI-ETHNIC** COMMUNITY.   MGRAVTD67214

PERCEIVED LIFE CHANCES IN THE OPPORTUNITY STRUCTURE. A STUDY OF A **TRI-ETHNIC** HIGH SCHOOL.   MGUERCX62410

TRIAL
INDUSTRY ON **TRIAL**. /PREFERENTIAL-TREATMENT/   NKAPPLX63635

TRIALS
UNIONS BEFORE THE BAR. HISTORICAL **TRIALS** SHOWING THE EVOLUTION OF LABOR RIGHTS IN THE US.   GLIEBEX50901

TRIBAL
LIVELIHOOD AND **TRIBAL** GOVERNMENT ON THE KLAMATH INDIAN RESERVATION.   ISTERTX61624

TRIBE
NEEDS AND RESOURCES OF THE JICARILLA APACHE INDIAN **TRIBE**.   ISTANRI58623

AN EVALUATION OF THE 10-YEAR DEVELOPMENT PROGRAM OF THE UTE **TRIBE** OF THE UINTAH AND OURAY RESERVATION, UTAH.   IUSDINT58648

KLAMATH INDIAN **TRIBE**.   IUSSENA56673

TRIBES
HUMAN RESOURCES SURVEY OF THE COLVILLE CONFEDERATE **TRIBES**.   IBLOOJA59538

THE INDIAN **TRIBES** OF THE US. ETHNIC AND CULTURAL SURVIVAL.   IMCNIDX61586

PROCEEDINGS OF THE CONFERENCE ON INDIAN **TRIBES** AND TREATIES.   IUVMNCC56676

TROY
RACE-RELATIONS IN THE ALBANY **TROY** AREA. A PROFILE FOR 1957. /NEW-YORK/   NGRIEES57503

TRUST
MEMORANDUM OF UNDERSTANDING BETWEEN CALIFORNIA STATE FAIR- EMPLOYMENT-PRACTICE-COMMISSION AND
BANK-OF-AMERICA NATIONAL **TRUST** AND SAVINGS ASSOCIATION.   GCALFEPND537

TRUTH
THE **TRUTH** ABOUT THE ILGWU. /UNION/   NTYLEGX62222

TUITION-AND-FEE
A COMPARISON OF **TUITION-AND-FEE** CHARGES IN NEGRO INSTITUTIONS WITH CHARGES IN INSTITUTIONS OF THE
SOUTHEAST AND OF THE NATION. 1962-1963. /EDUCATION/   NDAMILX64127

TULSA
EMPLOYMENT SURVEY. /TULSA OKLAHOMA/   GTULSCR66364

TURNOVER
WHAT ABOUT WOMEN-S ABSENTEEISM AND LABOR **TURNOVER**.   WUSDLAB65225

TUSKEGEE
TUSKEGEE LOOKS AT ITS VETERANS. /OCCUPATIONAL-STATUS/   NDERBIA46251

TUSKEGEE-INSTITUTE
THE INFLUENCE OF **TUSKEGEE-INSTITUTE** ON THE HEALTH, EDUCATIONAL, ECONOMIC, AND POLITICAL ASPECTS OF THE
NEGRO POPULATION OF MACON COUNTY, ALABAMA.   NSHIEAR51342

EXPERIMENTAL FEATURES OF THE **TUSKEGEE-INSTITUTE** RETRAINING PROJECT.   NTUSKIX65765

DEMONSTRATIONAL FEATURES OF THE **TUSKEGEE-INSTITUTE**. RETRAINING PROJECT.   NTUSKIX65766

TV
HOW WELL DOES **TV** FIGHT PREJUDICE.   GTUCKJN56363

TVA
TVA AND NEGRO EMPLOYMENT. /TENNESSEE/   NDAVIJH55253

TWIN-CITIES
REPORT OF **TWIN-CITIES** EQUAL-OPPORTUNITY REVIEW. /MINNEAPOLIS ST-PAUL MINNESOTA/   GUSCISC64131

TYPE
DISCRIMINATION IN HOUSING AND EMPLOYMENT. WHAT **TYPE** OF PROBLEM IS IT.   GPEDDWX64150

TYPES
A METHODOLOGICAL APPROACH TO IDENTIFICATION AND CLASSIFICATION OF CERTAIN **TYPES** OF INACTIVE WORK-SEEKERS.
/UNEMPLOYMENT LABOR-MARKET/   GLIEBEE65569

TYPES   (CONTINUATION)
  FAMILY ORGANIZATION IN FIVE **TYPES** OF MIGRATORY WAGE LABOR.   MSOLIML61496

TYPOLOGICAL
  THE AMERICAN LOWER-CLASSES. A **TYPOLOGICAL** APPROACH.   GMILLSM64727

UAW
  UAW OUTLAWS DISCRIMINATION. /UNION/   GUAWXIU56370

  THE UAW FIGHTS RACE PREJUDICE. /UNION/   NHOWEIX49581

  WOMEN IN THE UAW.   /EEO/   WUAWXCC66163

UAW-CIO-S
  AN ANALYSIS OF THE IMPLEMENTATION OF THE **UAW-CIO-S** FAIR PRACTICES AND ANTI-DISCRIMINATION POLICIES IN
  SELECTED CHICAGO LOCALS. /UNION/   NJONEJE51883

UINTAH
  AN EVALUATION OF THE 10-YEAR DEVELOPMENT PROGRAM OF THE UTE TRIBE OF THE **UINTAH** AND OURAY RESERVATION,
  UTAH.   IUSDINT58648

UNCONSTITUTIONAL
  DISCRIMINATION IN RATE OF COMPENSATION BETWEEN COLORED AND WHITE TEACHERS HELD **UNCONSTITUTIONAL**. NHARVLR40497

UNCONSTITUTIONALLY
  STATE FAIR-EMPLOYMENT-PRACTICE LEGISLATION **UNCONSTITUTIONALLY** BURDENS INTERSTATE COMMERCE WHEN APPLIED TO
  INTERSTATE AIRLINE.   NHARVLR62499

UNDER-ACHIEVEMENT
  UNDER-ACHIEVEMENT AMONG MINORITY-GROUP STUDENTS. AN ANALYSIS AND A PROPOSAL. /YOUTH NEGRO
  MEXICAN-AMERICAN PUERTO-RICAN/   CHOBACW63555

UNDER-UTILIZATION
  UNION LOCALS AND THE **UNDER-UTILIZATION** OF NEGRO WORKERS.   NJONEBA66884

UNDERCLASS
  THE POOR OF HARLEM. SOCIAL FUNCTIONING OF THE **UNDERCLASS**.   NGORDJX65435

UNDERDEVELOPED
  INDUSTRY-S MOST **UNDERDEVELOPED** RESOURCE.   NNATLUL64890

UNDEREMPLOYMENT
  SEX. STATUS AND THE **UNDEREMPLOYMENT** OF THE NEGRO MALE.   NCLARKB67212

UNDERGRADUATE
  INVESTIGATION OF DIFFERENCES IN OCCUPATIONAL PREFERENCES, STEREOTYPIC THINKING, AND PSYCHOLOGICAL NEEDS
  AMONG **UNDERGRADUATE** WOMEN STUDENTS IN SELECTED CURRICULAR AREAS. /ASPIRATIONS/   WKITTRE60313

  REPORT ON **UNDERGRADUATE** COUNSELING AND CONTINUING EDUCATION AND GUIDANCE FOR MATURE WOMAN.   WNICOHG64032

UNDERPRIVILEGED
  SPECIAL ASSIMILATION PROBLEMS OF **UNDERPRIVILEGED** IMMIGRANTS TO PHILADELPHIA. /PENNSYLVANIA/   GPENNEL62502

  THE MOTIVATION OF THE **UNDERPRIVILEGED** WORKER.   NDAVIAX46254

UNDERUTILIZATION
  UNDERUTILIZATION OF WOMEN WORKERS.   WUSDLAB66223

UNEARNED
  THE RELATIONSHIP BETWEEN **UNEARNED** INCOME AND INDIVIDUAL PRODUCTIVE EFFORT ON THE JICARILLA APACHE INDIAN
  RESERVATION.   IWILSHC61687

UNEDUCATED
  THE **UNEDUCATED**.   NGINZEX53415

UNEMPLOYABILITY
  NEW PROBLEM OF LARGE SCALE **UNEMPLOYABILITY**. /NEGRO MEXICAN-AMERICAN AMERICAN-INDIAN/   CROSEAM64553

UNEMPLOYABLE
  THE STATE-EMPLOYMENT-SERVICE AND THE ATTITUDE OF **UNEMPLOYABLE** DROPOUTS.   NHARRIE66991

UNEMPLOYABLES
  UNEMPLOYMENT AND **UNEMPLOYABLES**.   GFOXXWM65697

  THE **UNEMPLOYABLES**.   NNEWSXX66914

UNEMPLOYED
  AN EXPERIMENT TO TEST THREE MAJOR ISSUES OF WORK PROGRAM METHODOLOGY WITHIN MOBILIZATION-FOR-YOUTH-S
  INTEGRATED SERVICES TO OUT-OF-SCHOOL **UNEMPLOYED** YOUTH. /NEGRO PUERTO-RICAN/   CMOBIFY66024

  OAK GLEN -- A TRAINING CAMP FOR **UNEMPLOYED** YOUTH. /NEGRO MEXICAN-AMERICAN/   CUSDLAB66323

  IN AID OF THE **UNEMPLOYED**.   GBECKJX64878

  PROGRAMS TO AID THE **UNEMPLOYED** IN THE 1960-S.   GBECKJX65430

  A BENEFIT-COST ANALYSIS OF THE ECONOMIC EFFECTIVENESS OF RETRAINING THE **UNEMPLOYED**.   GBORUME64142

  THE COST OF RETRAINING THE HARD-CORE **UNEMPLOYED**.   GBORUME65745

  THE ECONOMIC EFFECTIVENESS OF RETRAINING THE **UNEMPLOYED**.   GBORUME66919

  TRAINING THE HARD-CORE **UNEMPLOYED**.   GBROOLB64795

  PART I. THE NEW-ENGLAND EXPERIENCE RETRAINING THE **UNEMPLOYED**.   GFEDERB62930

  ORGANIZING THE **UNEMPLOYED**. THE CHICAGO PROJECT. /ILLINOIS/   GFLACRX64964

  POVERTY AND INCOME-MAINTENANCE FOR THE **UNEMPLOYED**.   GGORDMS65661

  A PUBLIC EMPLOYMENT PROGRAM FOR THE **UNEMPLOYED** POOR.   GGREEAI65473

  SOME ISSUES IN KNOWING THE **UNEMPLOYED**.   GGURSOR64749

  A PORTRAIT OF THE **UNEMPLOYED**.   GKALICB66012

  SOCIAL DYNAMITE. THE REPORT OF THE CONFERENCE ON **UNEMPLOYED**, OUT-OF-SCHOOL YOUTH IN URBAN AREAS, MAY
  24-26, 1961.   GNATLCC61039

UNEMPLOYED   (CONTINUATION)
AN EXPERIMENT IN RETRAINING UNEMPLOYED MEN FOR PRACTICAL NURSING CAREERS.   GPEIMSC66139

PUBLIC WORK AND THE LONG-TERM UNEMPLOYED.   GROSSMS66844

WHO ARE THE UNEMPLOYED.   GSEIDBX54295

EVALUATION AND SKILL TRAINING OF OUT-OF-SCHOOL, HARD-CORE UNEMPLOYED YOUTH FOR TRAINING AND PLACEMENT.   GSMITAE65140

WORK HISTORY, ATTITUDES, AND INCOME OF THE UNEMPLOYED.   GSTEIRL63838

FAMILY CHARACTERISTICS OF THE LONG TERM UNEMPLOYED. A REPORT ON A STUDY OF CLAIMANTS UNDER THE TEMPORARY
EXTENDED UNEMPLOYMENT COMPENSATION PROGRAM, 1961-2.   GUSDLAB61445

HELPING THE LONG-TERM UNEMPLOYED. /INCOME-MAINTENANCE TRAINING/   GUSDLAB62221

FAMILY CHARACTERISTICS OF THE LONG-TERM UNEMPLOYED.   GUSDLAB63762

THE UNEMPLOYED. WHY THEY STARTED LOOKING FOR WORK.   GUSDLAB65979

DETROIT-S INSURED UNEMPLOYED AND EMPLOYABLE WELFARE RECIPIENTS. /MICHIGAN/   GWICKED63561

INSURED UNEMPLOYED AND EMPLOYABLE WELFARE RECIPIENTS.   GWICKEX63637

COUNTING THE EMPLOYED AND THE UNEMPLOYED.   GWOLFSL63578

THE INVISIBLE UNEMPLOYED.   NBELLDX58029

ARMING THE UNEMPLOYED WITH SKILLS. /TRAINING/   NCOONRB66927

EXPERIMENTAL AND DEMONSTRATION MANPOWER PROJECT FOR THE RECRUITMENT, TRAINING, PLACEMENT AND FOLLOW-UP OF
RURAL UNEMPLOYED WORKERS IN TEN NORTH FLORIDA CITIES. FINAL REPORT. /PARTICIPANTS/   NJACKTA66597

ECONOMIC DEPRIVATION AND EXTREMISM. A STUDY OF UNEMPLOYED NEGROES.   NLEGGJC61680

ECONOMIC CRISIS AND EXPECTATIONS OF VIOLENCE. A STUDY OF UNEMPLOYED NEGROES .   NLEGGJC64679

HELP FOR THE HARD-CORE UNEMPLOYED. /TRAINING/   NMILLJN66787

NO LONGER SUPERFLUOUS -- THE EDUCATIONAL REHABILITATION OF THE HARD-CORE UNEMPLOYED.   NPALLNJ65332

THE JOB HUNT. JOB SEEKING BEHAVIOR OF UNEMPLOYED WORKERS IN A LOCAL ECONOMY.   NSHEPHL66128

AN ANALYSIS OF UNEMPLOYED PUERTO-RICAN MIGRANTS IN NEW-YORK CITY.   PREMEGN58847

FINAL REPORT. EXPERIMENTAL AND DEMONSTRATION MANPOWER PROJECT FOR THE RECRUITMENT, TRAINING, PLACEMENT
AND FOLLOW-UP OF RURAL UNEMPLOYED WORKERS IN TEN NORTH FLORIDA COUNTIES.   WFLORMP66326

UNEMPLOYMENT
RACIAL DISTRIBUTION OF SELECTED UNEMPLOYMENT INSURANCE AND EMPLOYMENT SERVICE DATA. JULY-DECEMBER 1966.
/NEGRO MEXICAN-AMERICAN/   CCALDEM67907

INCOME, EDUCATION AND UNEMPLOYMENT IN NEIGHBORHOODS. ATLANTA, GEORGIA. /DEMOGRAPHY/   CUSDLAB63451

INCOME, EDUCATION AND UNEMPLOYMENT IN NEIGHBORHOODS. BALTIMORE, MARYLAND. /DEMOGRAPHY/   CUSDLAB63452

INCOME, EDUCATION AND UNEMPLOYMENT IN NEIGHBORHOODS. BIRMINGHAM, ALABAMA. /DEMOGRAPHY/   CUSDLAB63453

INCOME, EDUCATION AND UNEMPLOYMENT IN NEIGHBORHOODS. BOSTON, MASSACHUSETTS. /DEMOGRAPHY/   CUSDLAB63454

INCOME, EDUCATION AND UNEMPLOYMENT IN NEIGHBORHOODS. BUFFALO, NEW-YORK. /DEMOGRAPHY/   CUSDLAB63455

INCOME, EDUCATION AND UNEMPLOYMENT IN NEIGHBORHOODS. CHICAGO, ILLINOIS. /DEMOGRAPHY/   CUSDLAB63456

INCOME, EDUCATION AND UNEMPLOYMENT IN NEIGHBORHOODS. CINCINNATI, OHIO. /DEMOGRAPHY/   CUSDLAB63457

INCOME, EDUCATION AND UNEMPLOYMENT IN NEIGHBORHOODS. CLEVELAND, OHIO. /DEMOGRAPHY/   CUSDLAB63458

INCOME, EDUCATION AND UNEMPLOYMENT IN NEIGHBORHOODS. DALLAS, TEXAS. /DEMOGRAPHY/   CUSDLAB63459

INCOME, EDUCATION AND UNEMPLOYMENT IN NEIGHBORHOODS. DENVER, COLORADO. /DEMOGRAPHY/   CUSDLAB63460

INCOME, EDUCATION AND UNEMPLOYMENT IN NEIGHBORHOODS. DETROIT, MICHIGAN. /DEMOGRAPHY/   CUSDLAB63461

INCOME, EDUCATION AND UNEMPLOYMENT IN NEIGHBORHOODS. HOUSTON, TEXAS. /DEMOGRAPHY/   CUSDLAB63462

INCOME, EDUCATION AND UNEMPLOYMENT IN NEIGHBORHOODS. INDIANAPOLIS, INDIANA. /DEMOGRAPHY/   CUSDLAB63463

INCOME, EDUCATION AND UNEMPLOYMENT IN NEIGHBORHOODS. KANSAS-CITY, MISSOURI. /DEMOGRAPHY/   CUSDLAB63464

INCOME, EDUCATION AND UNEMPLOYMENT IN NEIGHBORHOODS. MEMPHIS, TENNESSEE. /DEMOGRAPHY/   CUSDLAB63466

INCOME, EDUCATION AND UNEMPLOYMENT IN NEIGHBORHOODS. MILWAUKEE, WISCONSIN. /DEMOGRAPHY/   CUSDLAB63467

INCOME, EDUCATION AND UNEMPLOYMENT IN NEIGHBORHOODS. MINNEAPOLIS -- ST-PAUL, MINNESOTA. /DEMOGRAPHY/   CUSDLAB63468

INCOME, EDUCATION AND UNEMPLOYMENT IN NEIGHBORHOODS. NEW-ORLEANS, LOUISIANA. /DEMOGRAPHY/   CUSDLAB63469

INCOME, EDUCATION AND UNEMPLOYMENT IN NEIGHBORHOODS. NEWARK, NEW-JERSEY. /DEMOGRAPHY/   CUSDLAB63470

INCOME, EDUCATION AND UNEMPLOYMENT IN NEIGHBORHOODS. NEW-YORK-CITY -- BROOKLYN. /DEMOGRAPHY/   CUSDLAB63471

INCOME, EDUCATION AND UNEMPLOYMENT IN NEIGHBORHOODS. NEW-YORK-CITY -- THE BRONX. /DEMOGRAPHY/   CUSDLAB63472

INCOME, EDUCATION AND UNEMPLOYMENT IN NEIGHBORHOODS. NEW-YORK-CITY -- MANHATTAN. /DEMOGRAPHY/   CUSDLAB63473

INCOME, EDUCATION AND UNEMPLOYMENT IN NEIGHBORHOODS. NEW-YORK-CITY -- QUEENS. /DEMOGRAPHY/   CUSDLAB63474

INCOME, EDUCATION AND UNEMPLOYMENT IN NEIGHBORHOODS. NEW-YORK-CITY -- STATEN-ISLAND. /DEMOGRAPHY/   CUSDLAB63475

INCOME, EDUCATION AND UNEMPLOYMENT IN NEIGHBORHOODS. OAKLAND, CALIFORNIA. /DEMOGRAPHY/   CUSDLAB63476

INCOME, EDUCATION AND UNEMPLOYMENT IN NEIGHBORHOODS. OKLAHOMA-CITY, OKLAHOMA. /DEMOGRAPHY/   CUSDLAB63477

INCOME, EDUCATION AND UNEMPLOYMENT IN NEIGHBORHOODS. PHILADELPHIA, PENNSYLVANIA. /DEMOGRAPHY/   CUSDLAB63478

INCOME, EDUCATION AND UNEMPLOYMENT IN NEIGHBORHOODS. PITTSBURGH, PENNSYLVANIA. /DEMOGRAPHY/   CUSDLAB63479

INCOME, EDUCATION AND UNEMPLOYMENT IN NEIGHBORHOODS. PHOENIX, ARIZONA. /DEMOGRAPHY/   CUSDLAB63480

UNEMPLOYMENT   (CONTINUATION)
    INCOME, EDUCATION AND UNEMPLOYMENT IN NEIGHBORHOODS. ST-LOUIS, MISSOURI. /DEMOGRAPHY/   CUSDLAB63481

    INCOME, EDUCATION AND UNEMPLOYMENT IN NEIGHBORHOODS. SAN-ANTONIO, TEXAS. /DEMOGRAPHY/   CUSDLAB63482

    INCOME, EDUCATION AND UNEMPLOYMENT IN NEIGHBORHOODS. SAN-DIEGO, CALIFORNIA. /DEMOGRAPHY/   CUSDLAB63483

    INCOME, EDUCATION AND UNEMPLOYMENT IN NEIGHBORHOODS. SAN-FRANCISCO, CALIFORNIA. /DEMOGRAPHY/   CUSDLAB63484

    INCOME, EDUCATION AND UNEMPLOYMENT IN NEIGHBORHOODS. SEATTLE, WASHINGTON. /DEMOGRAPHY/   CUSDLAB63485

    INCOME, EDUCATION AND UNEMPLOYMENT IN NEIGHBORHOODS. TAMPA, ST-PETERSBURG FLORIDA. /DEMOGRAPHY/   CUSDLAB63486

    INCOME, EDUCATION AND UNEMPLOYMENT IN NEIGHBORHOODS. WASHINGTON-DC. /DEMOGRAPHY/   CUSDLAB63487

    INCOME, EDUCATION AND UNEMPLOYMENT IN NEIGHBORHOODS. LOS-ANGELES, CALIFORNIA. /DEMOGRAPHY/   CUSDLAB63565

    HARD-CORE UNEMPLOYMENT AND POVERTY IN LOS-ANGELES. /CALIFORNIA NEGRO MEXICAN-AMERICAN/   CUVCAIIND524

    UNWANTED WORKERS. PERMANENT LAYOFFS AND LONG-TERM UNEMPLOYMENT. /NEGRO WOMEN/   CWILCRC63322

    THE SPECTER OF MASS YOUTH UNEMPLOYMENT.   GAMERFX65377

    AMERICA-S POOR. REALITY AND CHANGE. /RETRAINING SKILLS UNEMPLOYMENT/   GAMERFX66674

    WAGE RATES AND UNEMPLOYMENT.   GBACKJX64876

    THE INVISIBLE AMERICANS. /POVERTY UNEMPLOYMENT/   GBAGDBH63754

    LESSONS FROM THE PATTERNS OF UNEMPLOYMENT IN THE LAST FIVE YEARS.   GBANCGX66752

    UNEMPLOYMENT IN THE UNITED STATES. QUANTITATIVE DIMENSIONS.   GBOWEWG65464

    LABOR-FORCE PARTICIPATION AND UNEMPLOYMENT.   GBOWEWG65469

    UNEMPLOYMENT IN A PROSPEROUS ECONOMY. A REPORT OF THE PRINCETON-MANPOWER-SYMPOSIUM.   GBOWEWG65749

    POSITIVE ACTION ON UNEMPLOYMENT.   GCASSFH63562

    THE MEANING AND MEASUREMENT OF PARTIAL AND DISGUISED UNEMPLOYMENT.   GDUCOLJ57955

    UNEMPLOYMENT. ITS SCOPE, MEASUREMENT, AND EFFECT ON POVERTY.   GFERGRH65012

    WHERE UNEMPLOYMENT HITS THE HARDEST.   GFOLSMB64109

    PUSH-BUTTON LABOR. /TECHNOLOGICAL-CHANGE UNEMPLOYMENT/   GFORTXX54047

    UNEMPLOYMENT AND UNEMPLOYABLES.   GFOXXWM65697

    THE WHITE-NON-WHITE UNEMPLOYMENT DIFFERENTIAL.   GGILMHJ63436

    DISCRIMINATION AND THE WHITE -- NONWHITE UNEMPLOYMENT DIFFERENTIALS.   GGILMHJ63716

    ECONOMIC DISCRIMINATION AND UNEMPLOYMENT.   GGILMHJ65717

    STRUCTURAL UNEMPLOYMENT AND AGGREGATE DEMAND.   GGILPEG66632

    A CONFERENCE ON UNEMPLOYMENT.   GGORDMS63727

    UNEMPLOYMENT AND AMERICAN ECONOMY.   GGORDRA64526

    HAS STRUCTURAL UNEMPLOYMENT WORSENED.   GGORDRA64731

    LONG-TERM MANPOWER PROJECTIONS. PROCEEDINGS OF A CONFERENCE CONDUCTED BY THE RESEARCH PROGRAM ON
    UNEMPLOYMENT AND THE AMERICAN ECONOMY.   GGORDRA65613

    LABOR-MARKET STRATEGIES IN THE WAR-ON-POVERTY. /UNEMPLOYMENT/   GHARBFH65660

    CRITICAL ISSUES IN EMPLOYMENT POLICY, A REPORT. /UNEMPLOYMENT/   GHARBFH66476

    INTRODUCTION TO ECONOMICS OF GROWTH, UNEMPLOYMENT, AND INFLATION.   GHERMHX64938

    LONG-TERM UNEMPLOYMENT IN THE 1960-S.   GHOLLSS65124

    ILLINOIS JOB SEEKERS SURVEY. EDUCATION, SKILLS, LENGTH OF UNEMPLOYMENT, AND PERSONAL CHARACTERISTICS.   GILLIDI62004

    THE EVIDENCE OF PERSISTENT UNEMPLOYMENT.   GINDURR59814

    UNEMPLOYMENT AS A WAY OF LIFE.   GJACOPX66527

    UNEMPLOYMENT AND POVERTY.   GJOHNHG65826

    STRUCTURAL UNEMPLOYMENT IN THE UNITED STATES.   GKILLCC66800

    UNEMPLOYMENT INSURANCE AND MANPOWER POLICY. /INCOME-MAINTENANCE/   GKRUGDH65628

    MEN WITHOUT WORK, THE ECONOMICS OF UNEMPLOYMENT.   GLEBESX65891

    FEDERAL MANPOWER POLICIES AND PROGRAMS TO COMBAT UNEMPLOYMENT.   GLEVISA64897

    WORK RELIEF. SOCIAL WELFARE STYLE. /MANPOWER UNEMPLOYMENT/   GLEVISA66531

    A METHODOLOGICAL APPROACH TO IDENTIFICATION AND CLASSIFICATION OF CERTAIN TYPES OF INACTIVE WORK-SEEKERS.
    /UNEMPLOYMENT LABOR-MARKET/   GLIEBEE65569

    RURAL INDUSTRIALIZATION. A SUMMARY OF FIVE STUDIES. /UNEMPLOYMENT OCCUPATIONS/   GMAITST61383

    CYBERNATION AND JOB SECURITY. /UNEMPLOYMENT/   GMANGGL66529

    LONG-TERM UNEMPLOYMENT IN THE UNITED STATES.   GMEREJL61995

    A STUDY OF UNEMPLOYMENT, TRAINING AND PLACEMENT PATTERNS IN THE MUSKEGON AREA. /MICHIGAN/   GMICFEA57979

    CHALLENGE TO AFFLUENCE. /UNEMPLOYMENT/   GMYRDGX63035

    THE MATRIX. /POVERTY UNEMPLOYMENT/   GMYRDGX64955

    THE STRUCTURE OF UNEMPLOYMENT AND AUTOMATION.   GNAVIPX57007

UNEMPLOYMENT   (CONTINUATION)
   WHITE UNEMPLOYMENT IN THE UNITED STATES, 1947-1958, AN ANALYSIS OF TRENDS.   GNEWYSA58089

   PUBLIC POLICY AND UNEMPLOYMENT.   GOATEJF64542

   THE BATTLE AGAINST UNEMPLOYMENT.   GOKUNAX65133

   LOW-INCOME YOUTH, UNEMPLOYMENT, VOCATIONAL TRAINING, AND THE JOB-CORPS.   GPURCFX66208

   UNIONISM, MIGRATION, AND THE MALE NONWHITE-WHITE UNEMPLOYMENT DIFFERENTIAL.   GRAPPLA66216

   ECONOMIC EXPANSION AND PERSISTING UNEMPLOYMENT. AN OVERVIEW.   GREESAX66722

   ON THEORIES OF AUTOMATION. A POLEMIC AGAINST DANIEL BELL AND OTHERS. /UNEMPLOYMENT/   GSELIBB66609

   UNEMPLOYMENT AND LABOR-MARKET POLICY.   GSHULGX66142

   UNEMPLOYMENT AMONG FULL-TIME AND PART-TIME WORKERS.   GSTEIRL64336

   INCREASING STRUCTURAL UNEMPLOYMENT RE-EXAMINED.   GSTOIVX66001

   THE CHANGING STRUCTURE OF UNEMPLOYMENT. AN ECONOMETRIC STUDY.   GTHURLC65970

   HOW ACCURATE ARE ESTIMATES OF STATE AND LOCAL UNEMPLOYMENT.   GULLMJX63975

   EMPLOYMENT AND UNEMPLOYMENT.   GUSCONG62977

   FAMILY CHARACTERISTICS OF THE LONG TERM UNEMPLOYED. A REPORT ON A STUDY OF CLAIMANTS UNDER THE TEMPORARY
   EXTENDED UNEMPLOYMENT COMPENSATION PROGRAM, 1961-2.   GUSDLAB61445

   CONSOLIDATED INVENTORY OF DEPARTMENT OF LABOR RESEARCH ON LABOR-FORCE EMPLOYMENT AND UNEMPLOYMENT.   GUSDLAB64441

   UNEMPLOYMENT AND RETRAINING. AN ANNOTATED BIBLIOGRAPHY OF RESEARCH.   GUSDLAB65503

   A SHARPER LOOK AT UNEMPLOYMENT IN US CITIES, AND SLUMS.   GUSDLAB66520

   STUDIES IN UNEMPLOYMENT.   GUSSENA60352

   AUTOMATION AND UNEMPLOYMENT.   GWARDRX62821

   THE SECONDARY LABOR-FORCE AND THE MEASUREMENT OF UNEMPLOYMENT.   GWILCRC57562

   EMPLOYMENT AND UNEMPLOYMENT IN THE UNITED STATES.   GWOFLSX64759

   INDIAN UNEMPLOYMENT SURVEY, JULY 1963.   IUSHOUR63670

   THE SOCIAL AND POLITICAL REACTIONS OF OLDER NEGROES TO UNEMPLOYMENT.   NAIKEMX66865

   NEGRO YOUTH AND EMPLOYMENT OPPORTUNITIES. /UNEMPLOYMENT EDUCATION/   NAMOSWE63021

   NEGRO UNEMPLOYMENT. A CASE-STUDY.   NBAROHX63054

   ECONOMIC FORCES SERVING THE ENDS OF THE NEGRO PROTEST. /UNEMPLOYMENT/   NBATCAB65059

   THE SQUARE AND I. /UNEMPLOYMENT YOUTH/   NBEANLX63065

   NEGRO UNEMPLOYMENT. A CASE-STUDY.   NBROWHX63894

   HIDDEN UNEMPLOYMENT 1953-62. A QUANTITATIVE ANALYSIS BY AGE AND SEX.   NDERNTX66264

   EFFECTS OF UNEMPLOYMENT ON WHITE AND NEGRO PRISON-ADMISSIONS IN LOUISIANA.   NDOBBDA58277

   DROPOUTS AND THE RATE OF UNEMPLOYMENT. /YOUTH/   NDUNCBX65304

   SOCIOLOGICAL PERSPECTIVES IN UNEMPLOYMENT RESEARCH.   NFERMLA64353

   AN INSIGHT INTO STRUCTURAL UNEMPLOYMENT -- THE EXPERIENCE OF A MINORITY GROUP IN A PROSPEROUS COMMUNITY. NGERSWJ65634

   THE UNEMPLOYMENT RATE AND GRADE LEVEL RELATIONSHIP IN CHICAGO AS REVEALED IN THE 1960 CENSUS. /ILLINOIS/ NHARGAJ65990

   THE PROBLEM OF UNEMPLOYMENT AS IT RELATES TO NEGROES.   NHOPEJX60573

   NEGROES IN A CHANGING LABOR-MARKET. /UNEMPLOYMENT/   NKILLCC67653

   CONFLICT RESPONSE, DETROIT NEGROES FACE UNEMPLOYMENT. /MICHIGAN/   NLEGGJC59678

   BRICKS WITHOUT STRAW. STUDIES OF COMMUNITY UNEMPLOYMENT PROBLEMS, THE NEGROES DILEMMA. /LOUISVILLE
   KENTUCKY/   NLOUIHR64715

   BEHIND LOS-ANGELES. JOB-LESS NEGROES AND THE BOOM. /UNEMPLOYMENT CALIFORNIA/   NMOYNDP65860

   SURVEY OF UNEMPLOYMENT IN SELECTED URBAN-LEAGUE CITIES.   NNATLUL61898

   UNEMPLOYMENT AND THE AMERICAN ECONOMY. RESEARCH PROGRAM ON UNEMPLOYMENT.   NROSSAM63259

   UNEMPLOYMENT AND THE AMERICAN ECONOMY. RESEARCH PROGRAM ON UNEMPLOYMENT.   NROSSAM63259

   NEGRO UNEMPLOYMENT -- WHAT CITY BUSINESSMEN ARE DOING ABOUT IT.   NSCHMJC64108

   THE CULTURE OF UNEMPLOYMENT. SOME NOTES ON NEGRO CHILDREN.   NSCHWMX64110

   LABOR MONTH IN REVIEW. NEGRO UNEMPLOYMENT.   NUSDLAB63823

   HARD-CORE UNEMPLOYMENT IN DETROIT. CAUSES AND REMEDIES. /MICHIGAN/   NWACHHMND289

   UNEMPLOYMENT OF MARRIED WOMEN.   WALTMSX63757

   MARRIED WOMEN AND THE LEVEL OF UNEMPLOYMENT.   WSTEIRL61226

   WOMEN IN THE AMERICAN LABOR-FORCE. EMPLOYMENT AND UNEMPLOYMENT.   WWILCRX60268

UNEQUAL
   EQUAL JUSTICE IN AN UNEQUAL WORLD. EQUALITY FOR THE NEGRO -- THE PROBLEM OF SPECIAL TREATMENT.   NKAPLJX66645

UNFAIR
   EMPLOYMENT PRACTICES. FAIR AND UNFAIR.   GFORDJA65450

   UNFAIR EMPLOYMENT PRACTICES AS VIEWED BY PRIVATE EMPLOYMENT COUNSELORS.   GKEENVX52015

UNFAIR (CONTINUATION)

IS EQUALITY UNFAIR. NEGRO-S PLEA FOR PREFERENTIAL-TREATMENT.   NAMERXX63008

REPORT OF THE COMMITTEE ON UNFAIR EMPLOYMENT PRACTICES.   NNEBRLC51906

UNINCORPORATED

AN ECONOMIC ANALYSIS OF SPECIFIED INCORPORATED AND UNINCORPORATED FARMERS COOPERATIVE ASSOCIATIONS
OPERATED BY NEGRO FARMERS IN ALABAMA.   NLIGHMB53340

UNION

AT THE PREVAILING RATE. /MEXICAN-AMERICAN NEGRO UNION/   CLEBETX57371

STRENGTHENING THE INTEGRATION OF MINORITY-GROUPS. THE PROBLEM IS TACKLED AS A UNION PROBLEM.   GALGOME52107

ORGANIZED LABOR AND RACIAL MINORITIES. /UNION/   GBAILLH51575

TRADE UNION LEADERSHIP COUNCIL --EXPERIMENT IN COMMUNITY ACTION. /DETROIT MICHIGAN/ GBATTRX63426

ORGANIZED LABOR AND THE INTEGRATION OF ETHNIC GROUPS. /UNION/   GBLOCHD58455

ORGANIZED LABOR AND MINORITY GROUPS. /UNION/   GBLUEJT47457

STATEMENT ON SURVEYS AND STATISTICS AS TO RACIAL AND ETHNIC COMPOSITION OF WORK-FORCE OR UNION
MEMBERSHIP. /CALIFORNIA/   GCALFEP63539

LABOR AND CIVIL-RIGHTS. /CALIFORNIA UNION/   GCALLFX59544

LABOR AND CIVIL-RIGHTS 1964. /CALIFORNIA UNION/   GCALLFX64545

FRUSTRATION ON THE FARM. /MEXICAN-AMERICAN ORIENTAL UNION/   GCORTJC57372

SOCIAL INTEGRATION, ATTITUDES AND UNION ACTIVITY.   GDEANLR54944

LABOR AND THE CIVIL-RIGHTS REVOLUTION. /UNION/   GFLEIHX60685

UNION RACIAL DISCRIMINATION -- RECENT DEVELOPMENTS BEFORE THE NLRB AND THEIR IMPLICATIONS UNDER TITLE-VII
OF THE CIVIL-RIGHTS-ACT OF 1964.   GGEORLJ65714

THE RIGHTS AND RESPONSIBILITY OF UNION MEMBERS. /ANTIDISCRIMINATION/   GGOLDAX58974

LABOR LOOKS AT THE CRISES IN CIVIL-RIGHTS. /UNION/   GGOLDHX58975

RIGHT-TO-WORK-LAWS AND CIVIL-RIGHTS. /UNION/   GHERLAK64771

THE FAIR REPRESENTATION DOCTRINE. AN EFFECTIVE WEAPON AGAINST UNION RACIAL DISCRIMINATION.   GHERRNM64772

GOVERNMENT REGULATION OF UNION POLICIES.   GHICKRX66774

CURRENT INTERNATIONAL UNION POLICIES AFFECTING MINORITIES AND THEIR IMPLEMENTATION.   GHOPEJX49781

THE AFL FIGHTS BIGOTRY. /UNION/   GJEWILCND824

LABOR LAW -- UNION MEMBERSHIP DENIED ON THE BASIS OF RACIAL DISCRIMINATION. /WISCONSIN LEGISLATION/   GKAUFET58014

LABOR AND THE EMANCIPATION PROCLAMATION. /UNION/   GKRONJL65861

PREJUDICE AND SCIENTIFIC METHOD IN LABOR-RELATIONS. /UNION/   GMARRAX52941

THE POSITION OF MINORITIES IN THE AMERICAN LABOR MOVEMENT. /UNION/   GMARSRX66946

THE CALIFORNIA FARM WORKER. STILL IN DUBIOUS BATTLE. /MIGRANT-WORKERS UNION/   GMEISDX60461

DISCRIMINATION IN UNION MEMBERSHIP. DENIAL OF DUE PROCESS UNDER FEDERAL COLLECTIVE BARGAINING
LEGISLATION.   GPRESSB58126

MINORITY RIGHTS AND THE UNION SHOP.   GREADFT64220

GRAPE WORKERS WIN NEW GAINS. /MIGRANT-WORKERS UNION CALIFORNIA/   GROSSLX66557

ORGANIZED LABOR AND THE MINORITY WORKER NEED EACH OTHER. /UNION/   GSHISBX59305

LABOR-S TASK FORCES. /UNION/   GSLAIDX64318

LABOR-S ROLE. DEMOCRACY ON THE JOB. /UNION/   GSLAIDX66317

LABOR AND FAIR-EMPLOYMENT PRACTICE. /UNION/   GSLAIDX67840

HOW TO HANDLE RACE LABOR-RELATIONS. /UNION/   GSTYLPL50339

THE RIGHT TO JOIN A UNION.   GSUMMCW47342

SOCIAL RESPONSIBILITIES OF ORGANIZED LABOR. /UNION/   GTITCJA57358

HANDBOOK FOR LOCAL UNION FAIR PRACTICES COMMITTEES. REVISED EDITION.   GUAWXFPND369

UAW OUTLAWS DISCRIMINATION. /UNION/   GUAWXIU56370

UNION DEMOCRACY AND FAIR REPRESENTATION. FEDERAL RESPONSIBILITY IN A FEDERAL SYSTEM. GWELLHX58550

THE CONSTITUTION AND THE LABOR UNION.   GWELLHX61549

LABOR AND CIVIL-RIGHTS IN CHICAGO. /ILLINOIS UNION/   GWESTJX66551

CONSEQUENCES OF DISCRIMINATORY UNION MEMBERSHIP POLICY.   GWESTRL53019

LABOR AND THE PUBLIC INTEREST. /UNION/   GWIRTWW64572

LABOR LOOKS AT EQUAL RIGHTS IN EMPLOYMENT. /UNION/   GWOLLJA64579

THE INCIDENCE OF ANTIDISCRIMINATION CLAUSES IN UNION CONTRACTS.   GWORTMS65681

LABOR-S RACE PROBLEM. /UNION/   MFORTXX59374

HUELGA. THE FIRST 100 DAYS OF THE GREAT DELANO STRIKE. /UNION/   MNELSEX66028

SUMMARY REPORT OF THE STUDY OF DROP-OUTS IN THE THREE SENIOR HIGH SCHOOLS, COMPTON UNION HIGH SCHOOL
DISTRICT. /CALIFORNIA/   MWHITNX60517

THE SOUTHERN LABOR STORY. /UNION/   NAFLCIO58006

YOUR RIGHTS UNDER FAIR-EMPLOYMENT-PRACTICE LAWS.   /UNION LEGISLATION/   NAFLCIO60004

LABOR OPPOSES PREJUDICE.   /UNION/   NAMERFX55012

CEALING WITH INTER-RACIAL TEASIONS ON LOCAL UNION GRASS ROOTS BASIS.   NANOEEC50894

A CIVIL RIGHTS INVENTORY OF SAN FRANCISCO. PART I.   /UNION/   NBABOIX58893

ORGANIZED LABOR AND THE NEGRC WORKER.   /UNION/   NBAINMX63046

LABOR-S GRASS ROOTS. A STUDY OF THE LOCAL UNION.   NBARBJX61052

MISSISSIPPI. BATTLEFRONT FOR LABOR.   /UNION/   NBARTBX65057

REFLECTIONS ON THE NEGRO AND LABOR.   /UNION/   NBELLDX63073

THE ANTI-LABOR FRONT.   /UNION/   NBERNVH43555

NEGROES AND ORGANIZED LABOR.   /UNION/   NBLOCHD62091

CRGANIZED LABOR AND MINORITY-GROUPS POLICY AND PRACTICES. /UNION/   NBLUEJT47256

LABOR-S UNTOLD STORY.   /UNION/   NBOYERO55105

THE BROTHERHOOD OF SLEEPING CAR PORTERS.   /UNION/   NBRAZBR46108

A BIBLIOGRAPHY OF CIVIL-RIGHTS AND CIVIL-LIBERTIES. /EMPLOYMENT UNION   MILITARY/   NBROOAD62117

THE NEGRO-S PLACE AT LABOR-S TABLE.   /UNION/   NBROOTX62122

NEW SQUEEZE ON CCNSTRUCTION.   /UNION/   NBROOTX66631

THE NEGRC BIDS FOR UNION POWER.   NBRUNDX60128

UNION FIGHTS DISCRIMINATION.   NBUSIWX51164

UNION BIAS.   NBUSIWX54879

SOUTH-S TENSION SEIZES LABOR.   /UNION/   NBUSIWX56882

LABOR-NEGRO DIVISION WIDENS.   /UNION/   NBUSIWX60152

NLRB CRACKS DOWN ON UNION BIAS.   NBUSIWX64887

AMERICAN LABOR ATTACKS ITS OWN SEGREGATION PROBLEM.   /UNION/   NCHASWX58194

NLRB DECERTIFIES RACIALLY SEGREGATED UNION LOCALS.   NCHECDX64890

RACIAL DISCRIMINATION BY A UNION AGAINST EMPLOYEES IT DOES NOT REPRESENT. /LEGISLATION/   NCOLULR52226

THE ROLE OF THE NEGRO IN THE ORGANIZATION OF THE CIO.   /UNION/   NCOOPJE56235

TRADE UNION COMPLIANCE WITH PRESIDENTIAL DIRECTIVES, MEMBERSHIP ACCEPTANCE, SENIORITY, ETC.   NCOOPJX64294

THE CONSTITUTIONAL RIGHT TO MEMBERSHIP IN A LABOR UNION -- FIFTH AND FOURTEENTH AMENDMENTS.   NELLIGH59330

MONTHLY SUMMARY OF EVENTS ANC TRENDS IN RACE-RELATIONS. /CINCINNATI OHIO CASE-STUDY UNION/   NFISKUX44357

WE OPEN THE GATES.   /UNION/   NFLEIHX58361

IS LABOR COLOR BLIND.   /UNION/   NFLEIHX59359

HISTORY OF THE LABOR MOVEMENT IN THE UNITED STATES.   /UNION/   NFONEPS47370

REVOLT IN THE SOUTH.   /UNION DISCRIMINATION/   NFORTXX56881

SOUTHERN LABOR FIGHTS BACK.   /UNION/   NGOOGGX48434

UNION RESISTANCE. SOUTHERN STYLE.   NGOULHM48436

SITUATIONAL PRESSURES AND FUNCTIONAL ROLE OF THE ETHNIC LABOR LEADERS.   /UNION/   NGREESX53453

THE PLACE OF THE NEGRO IN THE AMERICAN LABOR-MOVEMENT. /UNION/   NGREESX61452

ORGANIZED LABOR AND THE NEGRO WORKER.   /UNION/   NGROBGX60460

NAACP AND THE AFL-CIO. AN OVERVIEW. /UNION/   NGROSJA62461

EFFECTS OF ON-THE-JOB EXPERIENCE WITH NEGROES UPON RACIAL ATTITUDES OF WHITE WORKERS IN UNION SHOPS.   NGUNDRH50466

THE CPPORTUNITIES AND DIFFICULTIES OF ORGANIZING NEGRO LABOR IN THE PRESENT EMERGENCY.   /UNION/   NHALLWX42259

THE CLO-TIMERS AND THE NEWCOMERS. ETHNIC-GROUP RELATIONS IN A NEEDLE TRADE UNION.   NHERBWX53519

LABOR AND SEGREGATION.   /UNION/   NHILLHX59529

RACISM WITHIN ORGANIZED LABOR. A REPORT OF THE FIVE YEARS OF THE AFL-CIO, 1955-1960. /UNION/   NHILLHX60542

HAS ORGANIZED LABOR FAILED THE NEGRO WORKER. /UNION/   NHILLHX62526

THE ILGWU TODAY -- THE DECAY OF A LABOR UNION.   NHILLHX62528

ORGANIZED LABOR AND THE NEGRC WAGE-EARNER.   /UNION/   NHILLHX62535

THE ILGWU -- FACT AND FICTION.   /UNION/   NHILLHX63527

THE RACIAL PRACTICES OF ORGANIZED LABOR -- IN THE AGE OF GOMPERS AND AFTER. /UNION/   NHILLHX65541

THE SELF-SURVEY OF THE PACKINGHOUSE UNION. A TECHNIQUE FOR EFFECTING CHANGE. /CASE-STUDY/   NHOPEJX53574

EQUALITY OF OPPORTUNITY. A UNION APPROACH TO FAIR EMPLOYMENT.   NHOPEJX56570

EQUALITY OF EMPLOYMENT OPPORTUNITY. A PROCESS ANALYSIS OF UNION INITIATIVE.   NHOPEJX60569

THE UAW FIGHTS RACE PREJUDICE.   /UNION/   NHOWEIX49581

THE AFL-CIC AND THE NEGRO.   /UNION/   NHUTCJXND590

THE NEGRO WORKER ASSERTS HIS RIGHTS. /UNION/   NJACOPA63601

THE PROBLEMS OF RACIAL DISCRIMINATION IN UNION MEMBERSHIP.   NJENKHX47605

UNION LOCALS AND THE UNDER-UTILIZATION OF NEGRO WORKERS.   NJONEBA66884

AN ANALYSIS OF THE IMPLEMENTATION OF THE UAW-CIO-S FAIR PRACTICES AND ANTI-DISCRIMINATION POLICIES IN
SELECTED CHICAGO LOCALS. /UNION/   NJONEJE51883

THE NEGRO WORKER OF KANSAS-CITY. A STUDY OF TRADE UNION AND ORGANIZED LABOR RELATIONS.   NKANCIU40634

LABOR UNION AND RACE-RELATIONS. A STUDY OF UNION TACTICS.   NKORNWA50660

LABOR UNION AND RACE-RELATIONS. A STUDY OF UNION TACTICS.   NKORNWA50660

THE NEGRO UNION OFFICIAL. A STUDY OF SPONSORSHIP AND CONTROL.   NKORNWA52661

IDEOLOGY AND INTERESTS. THE DETERMINANTS OF UNION ACTION.   NKORNWA53659

UNION HELD GUILTY OF RACE DISCRIMINATION.   NLABORR45027

LABOR IN THE SOUTH. /UNION/   NMARSRX61740

SOME FACTORS INFLUENCING UNION RACIAL PRACTICES.   NMARSRX62747

UNION RACIAL PRACTICES AND THE LABOR-MARKET.   NMARSRX62749

UNION RACIAL PROBLEMS IN THE SOUTH.   NMARSRX62751

THE NEGRO AND ORGANIZED LABOR. /UNION/   NMARSRX63741

RACIAL FACTORS INFLUENCING ENTRY TO THE SKILLED TRADES. /UNION/   NMARSRX63745

UNION RACIAL PRACTICES.   NMARSRX63750

UNION STRUCTURE AND PUBLIC POLICY. THE CONTROL OF UNION RACIAL PRACTICES.   NMARSRX63752

UNION STRUCTURE AND PUBLIC POLICY. THE CONTROL OF UNION RACIAL PRACTICES.   NMARSRX63752

THE NEGRO AND ORGANIZED LABOR. /UNION/   NMARSRX65742

THE ROOTS OF THE NEGRO-UNION ALLIANCE. /UNION/   NMARSRX66746

THE POSITION OF MINORITIES IN THE AMERICAN LABOR MOVEMENT. /UNION/   NMARSRX66943

NEGRO STATUS IN THE BOILERMAKERS UNION.   NMARSTX44753

THE CIO AND THE NEGRO IN THE SOUTH. /UNION/   NMASOJR45323

TO WIN THESE RIGHTS. A PERSONAL STORY OF THE CIO IN THE SOUTH. /UNION/   NMASOJR52324

WORK AND COLOR. /UNION/   NMASOLR52063

WE CALL ALL MEN BROTHERS. /UNION/   NMEANGX57763

A SOCIOLOGICAL ANALYSIS OF A BI-RACIAL LOCAL LABOR UNION.   NMERCJJ56768

DIXIE IN BLACK AND WHITE. /UNION/   NMEZEAG47492

RAILWAY LABOR ACT -- DENIAL OF UNION MEMBERSHIP TO NEGROES.   NMINNLR58800

THE NEGRO AND THE UNION.   NMORGSX59851

NEGROES AND THE BUILDING TRADES UNION.   NNATLUL57902

NEGROES AND THE LABOR MOVEMENT. /UNION/   NNEWXPX62910

TRADE UNION LEADERSHIP COUNCIL. EXPERIMENT IN COMMUNITY ACTION.   NNEWXUT63088

ORGANIZED LABOR AND THE NEGRO. /UNION/   NNORTHR44944

NATIONAL NEGRO LABOR COUNCIL, THIRD ANNUAL CONVENTION. /UNION/   NPERRPX54987

OPINION BY HONORABLE BENJAMIN LENCHER. CITY OF PITTSBURGH VS PLUMBERS LOCAL UNION NO 27. /PENNSYLVANIA/   NPITTLJ65001

ORGANIZED LABOR AND THE NEGRO YOUTH. /UNION/   NPOLLSX66723

RACIAL DISCRIMINATION IN UNION MEMBERSHIP.   NPROMHJ59127

THE ROLE OF ORGANIZATIONAL STRUCTURES. UNION VERSUS NEIGHBORHOOD IN A TENSION SITUATION.   NREITOC53050

THE NEGRO TOBACCO WORKER AND HIS UNION IN DURHAM, NORTH-CAROLINA.   NRICEJD41053

THE NAACP VERSUS LABOR. /UNION/   NRICHJC62054

LABOR DRIVES TO CLOSE THE SOUTH-S OPEN-SHOP. /UNION/   NRONYVX65072

THE INFLUENCE OF A BORDER CITY UNION ON THE RACE ATTITUDES OF ITS MEMBERS.   NROSEAW53293

THE NEGRO IN THE AMERICAN LABOR MOVEMENT. /UNION/   NROSESJ62079

THE RACIAL ISSUE AS AN ANTI UNION TOOL AND THE NATIONAL-LABOR-RELATIONS-BOARD.   NSACHRX63888

UNION RIGHTS AND UNION DUTIES.   NSEIDJI43115

UNION RIGHTS AND UNION DUTIES.   NSEIDJI43115

THE INTERVENTION OF THE UNION IN THE PLANT.   NSEXTBX53116

SO THE NEGROES WANT WORK. /UNION/   NSTREGX41462

DEVELOPMENTS IN THE NEGRO-LABOR ALLIANCE. /UNION/   NSTROEK56185

ORGANIZED LABOR IN AMERICAN HISTORY. /UNION/   NTAFTPX64158

THE TRUTH ABOUT THE ILGWU. /UNION/   NTYLEGX62222

THE NEW NEGRO. /UNION/   NTYLEGX67221

UNION   (CONTINUATION)
 UNION PROGRAM FOR ELIMINATING DISCRIMINATION.   NUSDLAB63846

 UNION BAN ON NEGROES UPHELD.   NUSNEWR57209

 LABOR USA. /UNION/   NVELILX59216

 RECENT EVENTS IN NEGRO UNION RELATIONSHIPS.   NWEAVRC44306

 LABOR TACKLES THE RACE QUESTION. /UNION/   NWINNFX43554

 PUERTO-RICAN INTEGRATION IN A GARMENT UNION LOCAL.   PHELFRB57815

 STATEMENT ON SENIORITY. /UNION/   WDAVICX65719

UNION-BUSTING
 RACE HATE. NEWEST UNION-BUSTING WEAPON IN THE SOUTH.   NCAREJB58181

UNION-S
 ETHNIC AND ECONOMIC MINORITIES. UNION-S FUTURE OR UNRECRUITABLE.   GMARSRX63945

 UNION-S DUTY OF FAIR REPRESENTATION AND THE CIVIL-RIGHTS-ACT OF 1964.   GSHERHL65302

UNIONISM
 LABOR UNIONISM IN AMERICAN AGRICULTURE. /NEGRO MEXICAN-AMERICAN ORIENTAL/   CJAMISM45005

 LABOR UNIONS IN ACTION. A STUDY OF THE MAINSPRINGS OF UNIONISM.   GBARBJX48421

 THE PRACTICE OF UNIONISM.   GBARBJX56422

 UNIONISM. MIGRATION, AND THE MALE NONWHITE-WHITE UNEMPLOYMENT DIFFERENTIAL.   GRAPPLA66216

 THE NEGRO AND UNIONISM IN THE BIRMINGHAM, ALABAMA IRON AND STEEL INDUSTRY.   NNORTHR43941

 THE MENTALITIES OF NEGRO AND WHITE WORKERS. AN EXPERIMENTAL SCHOOL-S INTERPRETATION OF NEGRO TRADE
 UNIONISM.   NVALIPX49280

UNIONISTS
 NEGRO UNIONISTS ORGANIZE FOR ACTION.   NBUSIWX60157

UNIONIZATION
 A CASE-STUDY OF LATIN-AMERICAN UNIONIZATION IN AUSTIN, TEXAS.   MPARISF64452

UNIONS
 UNIONS URGED TO FOLLOW THROUGH ON PLEDGES TO COMBAT JOB BIAS.   GAFLCIO63365

 LABOR UNIONS IN ACTION. A STUDY OF THE MAINSPRINGS OF UNIONISM.   GBARBJX48421

 DISCRIMINATION, UNIONS, AND TITLE-VII.   GBLAKGR64453

 THE CIVIL-RIGHTS-ACT OF 1964. WHAT IT MEANS -- TO EMPLOYERS, BUSINESSMEN, UNIONS, EMPLOYEES,
 MINORITY-GROUPS. TEXT, ANALYSIS, LEGISLATIVE HISTORY.   GBUREON64492

 HOW WELL CAN UNIONS KEEP PLEDGE ON BIAS.   GBUSIWX62505

 DISCRIMINATION BY LABOR UNIONS IN THE EXERCISE OF STATUTORY BARGAINING POWERS.   GDODDEM45646

 SECURITY. CIVIL-LIBERTIES AND UNIONS.   GFLEIHX57686

 CURRENT MINORITY POLICIES AND THEIR IMPLEMENTATION IN INTERNATIONAL UNIONS.   GHOPEJX51782

 RACIAL DISCRIMINATION IN UNIONS.   GKAHNSD65011

 UNIONS BEFORE THE BAR. HISTORICAL TRIALS SHOWING THE EVOLUTION OF LABOR RIGHTS IN THE US.   GLIEBEX50901

 GUIDE TO EMPLOYERS, EMPLOYMENT-AGENCIES AND LABOR UNIONS DEFINING PROPER AND IMPROPER PRE-EMPLOYMENT
 INQUIRIES. /PENNSYLVANIA/   GPENNHRND164

 CIVIL-RIGHTS AND LIBERTIES AND LABOR UNIONS.   GRAUHJL57217

 THE PRACTICES OF CRAFT UNIONS IN WASHINGTON-DC WITH RESPECT TO MINORITY GROUPS IN CIVIL-RIGHTS IN THE
 NATICN-S CAPITOL.   GSEGABD59294

 MINORITY-GROUP INTEGRATION BY LABOR AND MANAGEMENT. A STUDY OF THE EMPLOYMENT PRACTICES OF THE LARGER
 EMPLOYERS, AND THE MEMBERSHIP PRACTICES OF THE LARGER LABOR UNIONS WITH RESPECT TO RACE, RELIGION, AND
 NATIONAL ORIGIN, CONNECTICUT, 1951.   GSTETHG53598

 LABOR UNIONS AND FAIR-EMPLOYMENT-PRACTICES LEGISLATICN.   GTIMBEX54357

 RACE TROUBLES HURT UNIONS TOO.   GUSNEWR56517

 MEMBERSHIP DISCRIMINATION IN LABOR UNIONS.   GWASHLR64541

 FEDERAL REMEDIES FOR RACIAL DISCRIMINATION BY LABOR UNIONS.   GWEISLX62597

 DISCRIMINATION IN CRAFT UNIONS.   GYABRSM65587

 HOW UNIONS ARE SIGNING THEM UP. /MIGRANT-WORKERS CALIFORNIA/   MWINGWX66536

 THE FATE OF THE UNIONS.   NARONSX64030

 THE NEGRO STEELWCRKERS OF PITTSBURGH AND THE UNIONS. /PENNSYLVANIA/   NAUGUTX47035

 CRAFT UNIONS. A LINK IN THE CIRCLE OF NEGRO DISCRIMINATION.   NBLOCHD57088

 CRAFT UNIONS AND THE NEGRO IN HISTORICAL PERSPECTIVE.   NBLOCHD58087

 NEGRO MILITANTS, JEWISH LIBERALS, AND THE UNIONS.   NBROOTR61121

 RACE ISSUE AND UNIONS IN THE SOUTH.   NBUSIWX56160

 RACE PROBLEMS BUILD UP FOR UNIONS.   NBUSIWX58880

 NEGRO PRESSURE ON UNIONS.   NBUSIWX60155

 AFL-CIO COUNCIL GETS NEGRO DEMAND FOR MORE ACTION ON BIAS IN UNIONS.   NBUSIWX61144

 THE NEGRO-WHITE PROBLEM. WHAT CAN THE UNIONS DO ABOUT IT.   NCATHDX57186

UNIONS   (CONTINUATION)
    LABOR UNIONS AND THE NEGRO.   NCOMMXX59228

    TRADE UNIONS PRACTICES AND THE NEGRO WORKER -- THE ESTABLISHMENT AND IMPLEMENTATION OF AFL-CIO
    ANTI-DISCRIMINATION POLICY.   NDAVINF60312

    NEGROES AND THE LABOR MOVEMENT. RECORD OF THE LEFT WING UNIONS.   NDOYLWX62287

    UNIONS AND DISCRIMINATION.   NFLEIHX59360

    BIAS IN UNIONS.   NFORTXX57373

    MEMBERSHIP POLICIES OF INTERNATIONAL UNIONS AS THEY AFFECT NEGRO WORKERS.   NGRANLB41442

    LAST MAN IN. RACIAL ACCESS TO UNIONS.   NGREESX59451

    RACIAL DISCRIMINATION IN AMERICAN LABOR UNIONS.   NGUHAME65464

    RACIAL DISCRIMINATION BY UNIONS.   NHALLGD57987

    LABOR UNIONS AND THE NEGRO.   NHILLHX59530

    UNIONS AND THE NEGRO COMMUNITY.   NHILLHX64997

    WHAT THE GOVERNMENT REQUIRES OF MANAGEMENT AND UNIONS.   NHORTRX64291

    NO MORE COUSIN TOMS. THE CLASH BETWEEN THE UNIONS AND THE NEGROES.   NJACOPX63602

    RECENT TRENDS OF MEMBERSHIP OF INTERNATIONAL UNIONS AS THEY AFFECT NEGRO WORKERS.   NJOHNRA44620

    TRADE UNIONS AND MINORITY PROBLEMS.   NJOUROS53891

    JIM CROW IN BUILDING UNIONS.   NLIFEMX66493

    SOME FACTORS INFLUENCING THE GROWTH OF UNIONS IN THE SOUTH.   NMARSRX60060

    UNIONS AND THE NEGRO COMMUNITY.   NMARSRX64061

    THE NEGRO WORKER AND THE TRADE UNIONS. A FOOT IN THE DOOR.   NMARSRX65058

    THE NEGRO IN THE RAILWAY UNIONS.   NNORTHR44943

    RACE DISCRIMINATION IN UNIONS.   NNORTHR45946

    RACE DISCRIMINATION IN TRADE UNIONS. RECORD AND OUTLOOK.   NNORTHR46945

    UNIONS AND NEGRO EMPLOYMENT.   NNORTHR46947

    IN THE UNIONS. RACIAL POLICIES.   NNORTHR47939

    DISCRIMINATION AND THE TRADE UNIONS.   NNORTHR49936

    STATUS OF NEGROES IN CRAFT UNIONS...PITTSBURGH LABOR-MARKET. /PENNSYLVANIA/   NPITTMC65002

    CIVIL-RIGHTS. THE LAW AND THE UNIONS.   NRASKAH64038

    THE CIVIL-RIGHTS-ACT OF 1964. RACIAL DISCRIMINATION BY LABOR UNIONS.   NSAINJL66138

    RACISM STYMIES UNIONS IN THE SOUTH.   NSEGABD57113

    THE STRUGGLE FOR JOBS AND FOR NEGRO RIGHTS IN THE TRADE UNIONS.   NSIMOHX50139

    COOPERATIVES, CREDIT UNIONS, AND POOR PEOPLE.   NSOUTRC66524

    RACIAL DISCRIMINATION IN UNIONS.   NTEMPLQ65200

    SOUTHERN UNIONS AND THE INTEGRATION ISSUE.   NTREWHL56207

    IMPACT OF THE RACE ISSUE ON UNIONS IN THE SOUTH.   NUSNEWR56208

    UNIONS FEEL GROWING PRESSURE TO TAKE MORE NEGROES.   NUSNEWR64292

    UNIONS AND SEGREGATION.   NYOUNJE56357

    CIVIL-RIGHTS -- DISCRIMINATION IN LABOR UNIONS.   NYOUNWM64349

    LABOR UNIONS AND PUERTO-RICAN MEMBERS IN NEW-YORK CITY.   PGRAYLX63027

    GIFTED WOMEN IN THE TRADE UNIONS. /OCCUPATIONS/   WHILLBX62845

    UNIONS AND THE CHANGING STATUS OF WOMEN WORKERS.   WUSDLABND224

UNITED
    SPANISH-SPEAKING AMERICANS. MEXICANS AND PUERTO-RICANS IN THE UNITED STATES.   CBLAIBX59366

    THE SPANISH-SPEAKING PEOPLE IN THE UNITED STATES. /PUERTO-RICAN MEXICAN-AMERICAN/   CRUBIEBND848

    SPANISH-SPEAKING PEOPLE IN THE UNITED STATES. A PILOT REPORT. /MEXICAN-AMERICAN PUERTO-RICAN/   CSAMOJX63474

    UNITED STATES CENSUS OF AGRICULTURE. COLOR, RACE, AND TENURE OF FARM OPERATOR. GENERAL REPORT, VOLUME II.
    /DEMOGRAPHY/   CUSBURC59382

    TRENDS IN THE INCOME OF FAMILIES AND PERSONS IN THE UNITED STATES. 1947-1960. /DEMOGRAPHY/   CUSBURC63381

    STATISTICAL ABSTRACT OF THE UNITED STATES. 1964. /DEMOGRAPHY/   CUSBURC64380

    INCOME IN 1964 OF FAMILIES AND PERSONS IN THE UNITED STATES. /DEMOGRAPHY/   CUSBURC65375

    POVERTY IN THE UNITED STATES, HEARINGS. /AMERICAN-INDIAN NEGRO PUERTO-RICAN EMPLOYMENT/   CUSHOUR64346

    CIVIL-RIGHTS IN THE UNITED STATES, 1953.   GAMERJC53388

    RECENT POPULATION TRENDS IN THE UNITED STATES WITH EMPHASIS ON RURAL AREAS. /EDUCATION/   GBEALCL63426

    REPORT OF THE CALIFORNIA STATE ADVISORY COMMITTEE TO THE UNITED STATES COMMISSION ON CIVIL-RIGHTS ON
    CALIFORNIA-S PROGRAM FOR EQUAL-OPPORTUNITY IN APPRENTICESHIP.   GBECKWL62432

    A SPECULATIVE VIEW OF THE UNITED STATES IN 1985 AND BEYOND. /TECHNOLOGICAL-CHANGE/   GBELLDX62612

POVERTY IN RURAL AREAS OF THE UNITED STATES.   GBIRDAR64450

FARM LABOR IN THE UNITED STATES.   GBISHCE67916

THE POPULATION OF THE UNITED STATES.   GBOGUDJ59461

UNEMPLOYMENT IN THE UNITED STATES. QUANTITATIVE DIMENSIONS.   GBOWEWG65464

MIGRATION PATTERNS OF THE RURAL-FARM POPULATION. THIRTEEN ECONOMIC REGIONS OF THE UNITED STATES,
1940-1950.   GBOWLGK57415

THE COMPOSITION OF NET MIGRATION AMONG COUNTIES IN THE UNITED STATES, 1950-60.   GBOWLGK66414

NONWHITE EMPLOYMENT IN THE UNITED STATES.   GBUCKLF63479

ECONOMIC AND SOCIAL DEPRIVATIONS. ITS EFFECTS ON CHILDREN AND FAMILIES IN THE UNITED STATES -- A SELECTED
BIBLIOGRAPHY.   GCHILCX64571

POVERTY IN THE UNITED STATES IN THE MID-SIXTIES.   GCHILCX64922

EFFECTS OF TECHNOLOGICAL-CHANGE ON OCCUPATIONAL EMPLOYMENT PATTERNS IN THE UNITED STATES.   GCLAGEX64625

POVERTY AND DEPRIVATION IN THE UNITED STATES. THE PLIGHT OF TWO-FIFTHS OF A NATION.   GCONFOE62873

SOME DEMOGRAPHIC ASPECTS OF POVERTY IN THE UNITED STATES.   GDAVIKX65663

FEPC LEGISLATION IN THE UNITED STATES, FEDERAL, STATE, MUNICIPAL.   GGRAVWB51735

TECHNOLOGICAL-CHANGE, PRODUCTIVITY, AND EMPLOYMENT IN THE UNITED STATES.   GGREELX64739

MORTALITY BY OCCUPATION AND INDUSTRY AMONG MEN 20 TO 64 YEARS OF AGE. UNITED STATES, 1950.   /DEMOGRAPHY/   GGURALX62748

MANPOWER IN THE UNITED STATES. PROBLEMS AND POLICIES.   GHABEWX54750

THE ROLE OF THE UNITED STATES EMPLOYMENT-SERVICE IN A CHANGING ECONOMY.   GHABEWX64649

STRUCTURAL UNEMPLOYMENT IN THE UNITED STATES.   GKILLCC66800

THE TENURE STATUS OF FARMWORKERS IN THE UNITED STATES.   GMAIEFH60417

ETHNIC RELATIONS IN THE UNITED STATES.   GMCDOEC53050

LONG-TERM UNEMPLOYMENT IN THE UNITED STATES.   GMEREJL61995

THE FACE OF POVERTY IN THE UNITED STATES.   GMILLHP64853

INCOME-DISTRIBUTION IN THE UNITED STATES. /DEMOGRAPHY/   GMILLHP66778

INCOME AND WELFARE IN THE UNITED STATES.   GMORGJN62032

WHITE UNEMPLOYMENT IN THE UNITED STATES, 1947-1958, AN ANALYSIS OF TRENDS.   GNEWYSA58089

MANPOWER POLICY AND PROGRAMMES IN THE UNITED STATES.   GORGAEC64776

INCOME-DISTRIBUTION AS A FACTOR IN REGIONAL GROWTH, WITH SPECIAL REFERENCE TO THE SOUTHEAST UNITED
STATES. /DISCRIMINATION/   GPHILEW65773

MUNICIPAL HUMAN-RELATIONS COMMISSION. A SURVEY OF PROGRAMS IN SELECTED CITIES OF THE UNITED STATES.   GRICHCM63236

THEY AND WE. RACIAL AND ETHNIC RELATIONS IN THE UNITED STATES.   GROSEPI64251

POPULATION MOBILITY WITHIN THE UNITED STATES.   GSHRYHS64309

THE ECONOMIC SITUATION OF NATIONAL MINORITIES IN THE UNITED STATES OF AMERICA.   GTHOMJA47354

LOW-INCOME FAMILIES AND UNRELATED INDIVIDUALS IN THE UNITED STATES. 1964. /DEMOGRAPHY/   GUSBURC65151

MOBILITY OF THE POPULATION OF THE UNITED STATES, JANUARY 1, 1950 TO FEBRUARY 1, 1965. /DEMOGRAPHY/   GUSBURC65161

MOBILITY OF THE POPOFATION FO THE UNITED STATES, MARCH 1964 TO MARCH 1965. /DEMOGRAPHY/   GUSBURC66158

POPULATION OF THE UNITED STATES BY METROPOLITAN AND NONMETROPOLITAN RESIDENCE. /DEMOGRAPHY/   GUSBURC66159

PROJECTIONS OF SCHOOL AND COLLEGE ENROLLMENT IN THE UNITED STATES TO 1985. /DEMOGRAPHY/   GUSBURC66160

NONWHITE FARM OPERATORS IN THE UNITED STATES.   GUSDLAB41077

THE SKILLED WORK FORCE OF THE UNITED STATES.   GUSDLAB55498

A GUIDE TO INDUSTRIAL-RELATIONS IN THE UNITED STATES. EQUAL JOB OPPORTUNITY UNDER COLLECTIVE-BARGAINING.   GUSDLAB58449

EMPLOYMENT AND EARNINGS STATISTICS FOR THE UNITED STATES, 1909-1966.   GUSDLAB66832

TOWARDS FULL EMPLOYMENT. PROPOSALS FOR A COMPREHENSIVE EMPLOYMENT AND MANPOWER POLICY IN THE UNITED
STATES.   GUSSENA64332

EMPLOYMENT AND UNEMPLOYMENT IN THE UNITED STATES.   GWOFLSX64759

THE UNITED STATES INDIAN.   ICOLLJX56544

THE PRESENT DAY DISTRIBUTION OF UNITED STATES INDIANS.   ITAXXSX56628

INDIAN AFFAIRS. A STUDY OF THE CHANGES IN POLICY OF THE UNITED STATES TOWARD INDIANS.   ITYLESL64634

UNITED STATES INDIAN POPULATION AND LAND, 1960-1961.   IUSDINT61663

JEWISH POPULATION IN THE UNITED STATES, 1960. /DEMOGRAPHY/   JCHENAX61712

JEWISH POPULATION IN THE UNITED STATES, 1961. /DEMOGRAPHY/   JCHENAX62713

A COMPARISON OF MAJOR UNITED STATES RELIGIOUS GROUPS. /ECONOMIC-STATUS/   JLAZRBX61033

NO FRONTIER TO LEARNING. THE MEXICAN STUDENT IN THE UNITED STATES.   MBEALRL57364

OBSTACLES TO ASSIMILATION OF THE MEXICAN-AMERICAN IN THE UNITED STATES.   MBEALRL60362

MEXICAN IMMIGRATION TO THE UNITED STATES. THE RECORD AND ITS IMPLICATIONS.   MGREBLX66406

MIGRATORY AGRICULTURAL WORKERS IN THE UNITED STATES.   MJORGJM60422

THE SPANISH-SPEAKING PEOPLE IN THE UNITED STATES.   MSAMOJX62473

THE GENERAL STATUS OF THE SPANISH-SPEAKING PEOPLE IN THE UNITED STATES.   MSAMOJX63471

MATERIALS RELATING TO THE EDUCATION OF SPANISH-SPEAKING PEOPLE IN THE UNITED STATES, AN ANNOTATED
BIBLIOGRAPHY.   MSANCGI59478

INFORMATION CONCERNING ENTRY OF MEXICAN AGRICULTURAL WORKERS INTO THE UNITED STATES.   MUSDLAB59335

DISTRIBUTION OF NEGRO POPULATION IN THE UNITED STATES. /DEMOGRAPHY/   NCALEWC56069

SOME RECENT UNITED STATES SUPREME COURT DECISIONS AFFECTING THE RIGHTS OF NEGRO WORKERS.   NCHICCA47914

RECENT TRENDS IN RESEARCH ON THE NEGRO IN THE UNITED STATES.   NDRAKSC57290

THE SOCIAL AND ECONOMIC STATUS OF THE NEGRO IN THE UNITED STATES.   NDRAKSC65289

COMPARATIVE PSYCHOLOGICAL STUDIES OF NEGROES AND WHITES IN THE UNITED STATES.   NDREGRM60292

RECENT RESEARCH IN PSYCHOLOGICAL COMPARISONS OF NEGROES AND WHITES IN THE UNITED STATES.   NDREGRM65293

A CHRONICLE OF RACE-RELATIONS -- THE UNITED STATES, NORTH AND SOUTH.   NDUBOWE41298

THE HIGHER EDUCATION OF NEGROES IN THE UNITED STATES.   NEELLWC55329

CIVIL-RIGHTS, 1960-63. THE NEGRO CAMPAIGN TO WIN EQUAL RIGHTS AND OPPORTUNITIES IN THE UNITED STATES. NFACTOF64341

HISTORY OF THE LABOR MOVEMENT IN THE UNITED STATES. /UNION/   NFONEPS47370

HISTORY OF RACIAL SEGREGATION IN THE UNITED STATES.   NFRANJH56060

ETHNIC FAMILY PATTERNS. THE NEGRO FAMILY IN THE UNITED STATES.   NFRAZEF48379

BLACK BOURGEOISIE. THE RISE OF A MIDDLE-CLASS IN THE UNITED STATES.   NFRAZEF57371

THE NEGRO IN THE UNITED STATES.   NFRAZEF57966

OCCUPATIONAL DIFFERENTIATION OF NEGROES AND WHITES IN THE UNITED STATES.   NGIBBJP65401

THE STATUS OF THE NEGRO CPA IN THE UNITED STATES. /OCCUPATIONS/   NHARRLJ62494

UNITED STATES HAS STANDING UNDER INTERSTATE COMMERCE ACT AND COMMERCE CLAUSE TO ENJOIN SEGREGATIVE
PRACTICES OF CITY. /LEGISLATION/   NHARVLR64500

THE ECONOMIC IMBALANCE. AN INQUIRY INTO THE ECONOMIC-STATUS OF NEGROES IN THE UNITED STATES, 1935-1960,
WITH IMPLICATIONS FOR NEGRO EDUCATION.   NHENDVW60512

NO HARVEST FOR THE REAPER. THE STORY OF THE MIGRATORY AGRICULTURAL WORKER IN THE UNITED STATES.   NHILLHX59534

NEGRO INTERNAL MIGRATION IN THE UNITED STATES. 1870-1960.   NJORGJM62624

A STUDY OF THE EMPLOYMENT OPPORTUNITIES FOR NEGROES IN BREWERIES OF THE UNITED STATES. /INDUSTRY/   NKERNJH51897

INTELLIGENCE IN THE UNITED STATES, A SURVEY -- WITH CONCLUSIONS FOR MANPOWER UTILIZATION IN EDUCATION AND
EMPLOYMENT.   NMINEJB57796

THE LEGAL-STATUS OF THE NEGRO IN THE UNITED STATES.   NMOTLCB66859

ECONOMIC AND SOCIAL STATUS OF THE NEGRO IN THE UNITED STATES.   NNATLUL62083

ECONOMIC AND SOCIAL STATUS OF THE NEGRO IN THE UNITED STATES.   NORSHMX61961

NEGRO MIGRATION IN THE UNITED STATES.   NPURDLX54024

NEGROES IN THE UNITED STATES. THEIR EMPLOYMENT AND ECONOMIC STATUS.   NRINGHH53061

THE CHANGING NUMBER AND DISTRIBUTION OF THE AGED NEGRO POPULATION OF THE UNITED STATES. /DEMOGRAPHY/ NSMITLT58145

THE NEGRO POPULATION IN THE UNITED STATES. /DEMOGRAPHY/   NTAEUKE65198

EQUAL-OPPORTUNITY IN FARM PROGRAMS -- AN APPRAISAL OF SERVICES RENDERED BY AGENCIES OF THE UNITED STATES
DEPARTMENT OF AGRICULTURE.   NUSCOMC65232

INTEGRATION AND THE NEGRO OFFICER IN THE ARMED FORCES OF THE UNITED STATES OF AMERICA. /MILITARY/   NUSDDEF62240

THE ECONOMIC SITUATION OF NEGROES IN THE UNITED STATES.   NUSDLAB62243

THE NEGROES IN THE UNITED STATES. THEIR ECONOMIC AND SOCIAL SITUATION.   NUSDLAB66257

EMPLOYMENT AND THE ECONOMIC STATUS OF NEGROES IN THE UNITED STATES.   NUSSENA52333

THE UNITED STATES EMPLOYMENT SERVICE AND THE NEGRO WORK APPLICANT.   NUSWAMC44276

DEMOGRAPHIC CHARACTERISTICS OF THE NEGRO POPULATION IN THE UNITED STATES.   NVALIPX63279

EMPLOYMENT OF NEGROES IN UNITED STATES WAR INDUSTRIES.   NWEAVRC44300

POVERTY IN THE UNITED STATES.   NWOLFDP64338

KINSHIP AS A FACTOR AFFECTING CANTONESE ECONOMIC ADAPTATION IN THE UNITED STATES.   OBARNML66698

THE HUI-CH-IAO IN THE UNITED STATES OF AMERICA.   OLEEXRH58742

THE CHINESE IN THE UNITED STATES OF AMERICA.   OLEEXRH60741

SOME ECONOMIC ASPECTS OF PUERTO-RICAN MIGRATION TO THE UNITED STATES.   PFLEIBM61804

THE IMPACT OF PUERTO-RICAN MIGRATION TO THE UNITED STATES. /EMPLOYMENT/   PFLEIBM63437

SOME ECONOMIC ASPECTS OF PUERTO-RICAN MIGRATION TO THE UNITED STATES.   PFLEIBM63803

THE PUERTO-RICANS IN THE UNITED STATES.   PSENICX56852

PUERTO-RICANS IN THE UNITED STATES. SOCIAL AND ECONOMIC DATA FOR PERSONS OF PUERTO-RICAN BIRTH AND
PARENTAGE. /DEMOGRAPHY/   PUSBURC63182

UNITED   (CONTINUATION)
CENSUS OF POPULATION. 1960. PUERTO-RICANS IN THE **UNITED** STATES.   PUSBURC63854

AGE OF COMPLETION OF CHILDBEARING AND ITS RELATION TO THE PARTICIPATION OF WOMEN IN THE LABOR-FORCE.
UNITED STATES 1910-1955.   WDAYXLH57725

STATUS IMPLICATIONS OF THE EMPLOYMENT OF MARRIED WOMEN IN THE **UNITED** STATES.   WDAYXLH61726

OCCUPATIONAL TRAINING OF WOMEN IN THE **UNITED** STATES.   WINTELR64866

PROFESSIONAL STANDARDS AND ECONOMIC-STATUS OF NURSES IN THE **UNITED** STATES.   WKRUGOH60917

THE FEMALE LABOR-FORCE IN THE **UNITED** STATES. FACTORS GOVERNING ITS GROWTH AND CHANGING COMPOSITION.   WOPPEVK66096

THE INTERACTION OF DEMAND AND SUPPLY AND ITS EFFECT ON THE FEMALE LABOR-FORCE IN THE **UNITED** STATES.   WOPPEVK66289

TOP LEVEL TRAINING OF WOMEN IN THE **UNITED** STATES, 1900-60.   WPARRJB62283

STATUS OF WOMEN IN THE **UNITED** STATES.   WPETEEX64056

BACKGROUND FACTS ON WOMEN WORKERS IN THE **UNITED** STATES.   WUSDLAB66638

SUPPLY OF MEDICAL WOMEN IN THE **UNITED** STATES. /OCCUPATIONS/   WWRIGKW66277

WOMEN TODAY. TRENDS AND ISSUES IN THE **UNITED** STATES. /WORK-WOMAN-ROLE/   WYWCAXX63078

UNITED-STATES
THE NEGRO IN THE LABOR-FORCE OF THE **UNITED-STATES**.   NBAILLH53044

MIGRATION AND OPPORTUNITY. A STUDY OF STANDARD METROPOLITAN AREAS IN THE **UNITED-STATES**.   NBALATR63047

RACIAL EQUALITY AND THE LAW. THE ROLE OF LAW IN THE REDUCTION OF DISCRIMINATION IN THE **UNITED-STATES**.   NBERGMX54076

THE SOURCES OF ECONOMIC GROWTH IN THE **UNITED-STATES** AND THE ALTERNATIVE BEFORE US. /LABOR-FORCE
ECONOMY/   NDENIEF62262

RACE-RELATIONS IN THE **UNITED-STATES** 1916-1947.   NDUBOWE48299

UNIVERSITIES
NEGROES AS TEACHING ASSISTANTS IN SOME PUBLICLY SUPPORTED **UNIVERSITIES**. /OCCUPATIONS/   NDANIWG62248

NEGRO COLLEGES. LONG IGNORED, SOUTHERN SCHOOLS NOW COURTED BY MAJOR **UNIVERSITIES** AND FOUNDATIONS.   NLANGEX64304

THE PREDOMINANTLY NEGRO COLLEGES AND **UNIVERSITIES** IN TRANSITION.   NMCGREJ65720

THE MARKET FOR NEGRO EDUCATORS IN COLLEGES AND **UNIVERSITIES** OUTSIDE THE SOUTH.   NROSEHM61076

SOCIAL ORIGINS AND CAREER PREPARATION AMONG FILIPINOS IN AMERICAN **UNIVERSITIES**.   OBELTAG61703

ANTI-NEPOTISM RULES IN AMERICAN COLLEGES AND UNIVERSITIES -- THEIR EFFECT ON THE FACULTY EMPLOYMENT OF
WOMEN.   WDOLAEF60951

UNIVERSITY
SURVEY OF OHIO COLLEGE AND **UNIVERSITY** PLACEMENT OFFICES WITH REGARD TO JOB PLACEMENT OF MINORITY
STUDENTS.   GOHIOCR62132

JEWS IN COLLEGE AND **UNIVERSITY** ADMINISTRATION.   JAMERJC66693

INTEGRATION IN PROFESSIONAL EDUCATION. THE STORY OF PERKINS, SOUTHERN METHODIST **UNIVERSITY**. /VOCATIONS/   NCUNNMX56579

SOME ATTITUDES TOWARD EMPLOYING NEGROES AS TEACHERS IN A NORTHERN **UNIVERSITY**.   NMARCFL48054

UNIVERSITY OF KANSAS-CITY PROJECT FOR CONTINUING EDUCATION OF WOMEN.   WBERRJX63640

REPORT OF THE EXPLORATORY STATISTICAL SURVEY OF THE EDUCATIONAL-ATTAINMENT, NUMBER, AND AVAILABILITY OF
THE MEMBERSHIP OF THE AMERICAN ASSOCIATION OF **UNIVERSITY** WOMEN FOR TEACHING IN THE FIELDS OF SCIENCE AND
MATHEMATICS. /OCCUPATIONS/   WDOLAEF57735

FACTORS ASSOCIATED WITH GRADUATE SCHOOL ATTENDANCE AND ROLE DEFINITION OF THE WOMAN DOCTORAL CANDIDATES
AT THE PENNSYLVANIA STATE **UNIVERSITY**. /OCCUPATIONS/   WFIELJC61763

MARRIED WOMEN AT UTAH STATE **UNIVERSITY**, SPRING QUARTER, 1960. /TRAINING/   WFREDCX61769

WOMEN AND HIGHER EDUCATION WITH SPECIAL REFERENCE TO THE **UNIVERSITY** OF WISCONSIN.   WFREDEB62768

SOME INTELLECTUAL ATTRIBUTES AND EDUCATIONAL INTERESTS OF **UNIVERSITY** WOMEN IN VARIOUS MAJORS.
/ASPIRATIONS/   WGENTLX60790

CHANGES IN SELECTED PERSONALITY CHARACTERISTICS AND PERSISTENCE IN THE CAREER CHOICES OF WOMEN ASSOCIATED
WITH A FOUR YEAR COLLEGE EDUCATION AT ONE OF THE COLLEGES OF THE CITY **UNIVERSITY** OF NEW-YORK.
/ASPIRATIONS/   WLEINMX64925

A SURVEY OF SPECIAL EDUCATIONAL PROGRAMS FOR ADULT WOMEN IN **UNIVERSITY** EXTENSION DIVISIONS AND EVENING
COLLEGES AS OF SPRING 1965.   WLORIRK66942

RUTGERS -- THE STATE **UNIVERSITY**, FORD FOUNDATION PROGRAM FOR THE RETRAINING IN MATHEMATICS OF COLLEGE
GRADUATE WOMEN. /TRAINING/   WMARTHM63957

WOMEN IN **UNIVERSITY** TEACHING. /OCCUPATIONS/   WMILLMM61981

INTEREST PROFILES OF **UNIVERSITY** WOMEN. /ASPIRATIONS/   WMITCED57986

WOMEN ON COLLEGE AND **UNIVERSITY** FACULTIES. A HISTORICAL SURVEY AND A STUDY OF THEIR PRESENT ACADEMIC
STATUS. /OCCUPATIONS/   WPOLLLA65063

UNIVERSITY OF MINNESOTA -- THE MINNESOTA PLAN. /EDUCATION/   WSCHLVX63103

UNIVERSITY PROGRAMS OF CONTINUING EDUCATION FOR THE ADULT WOMAN.   WTINKAH64156

WOMEN IN COLLEGE AND **UNIVERSITY** TEACHING. /OCCUPATIONS/   WTOTAJV65159

WOMAN-S DESTINY -- CHOICE OR CHANCE. REPORT OF CONFERENCE AT THE **UNIVERSITY** OF WASHINGTON, NOVEMBER
21-22. 1963.   WUSDLAB65233

THE RELATIONSHIP OF SELECTED VARIABLES TO CAREER-MARRIAGE PLANS OF **UNIVERSITY** FRESHMAN WOMEN.
/WORK-FAMILY-CONFLICT/   WZISSCX62284

A STUDY OF THE LIFE PLANNING OF 550 FRESHMEN WOMEN AT PURDUE **UNIVERSITY**. /WORK-FAMILY-CONFLICT/   WZISSCX64285

UNLAWFUL
GUIDE TO LAWFUL AND **UNLAWFUL** PRE-EMPLOYMENT INQUIRIES BY EMPLOYERS, EMPLOYMENT-AGENCIES, AND LABOR
ORGANIZATIONS UNDER THE CALIFORNIA FAIR-EMPLOYMENT-PRACTICE ACT, LABOR CODE, SECTIONS 1410-1432.   GCALDIR60527

FAIR-EMPLOYMENT-PRACTICE-COMMISSION GUIDE TO **UNLAWFUL** PRE-EMPLOYMENT INQUIRIES.   GCURRRO60889

PICKETING BY NEGROES TO OBTAIN EMPLOYMENT IN PROPORTION TO NEGRO CUSTOMERS HELD **UNLAWFUL**.   NHARVLR49498

UNPUBLISHED
MASTER ANNOTATED BIBLIOGRAPHY OF PAPERS OF MOBILIZATION-FOR-YOUTH. PUBLISHED, **UNPUBLISHED** AND PRESENTED
AT CONFERENCES.   GMOBIFY65025

UNQUALIFIED
ONE-THIRD OF A NATION. A REPORT ON YOUNG MEN FOUND **UNQUALIFIED** FOR MILITARY SERVICE.   GPRESTM64316

UNRECRUITABLE
ETHNIC AND ECONOMIC MINORITIES. UNION-S FUTURE OR **UNRECRUITABLE**.   GMARSRX63945

UNRELATED
LOW-INCOME FAMILIES AND **UNRELATED** INDIVIDUALS IN THE UNITED STATES. 1964. /DEMOGRAPHY/   GUSBURC65151

UNSELECTED
DIFFERENTIAL CHARACTERISTICS OF SUPERIOR AND **UNSELECTED** NEGRO COLLEGE STUDENTS.   NJENKMD48608

UNSKILLED
CONFERENCE ON **UNSKILLED** WORKERS IN THE LABOR-FORCE. PROBLEMS AND PROSPECTS.   GGITLAL66134

UNTAPPED
UNTAPPED GOOD. THE REHABILITATION OF SCHOOL DROPOUTS.   GCHANNM66803

INACTIVE NURSES. AN **UNTAPPED** RECRUITMENT SOURCE.   WBARKAE65628

THE **UNTAPPED** RESOURCE... /OCCUPATIONS/   WRASKBL59074

UNTESTABLES
TESTING THE **UNTESTABLES**.   GARNSSX64404

UNUSED
UNUSED MANPOWER. THE NATION-S LOSS.   GUSDLAB66504

UNWANTED
UNWANTED WORKERS. PERMANENT LAYOFFS AND LONG-TERM UNEMPLOYMENT. /NEGRO WOMEN/   CWILCRC63322

UPDATING
UPDATING GUIDANCE AND PERSONNEL PRACTICES.   NROUSRJ62089

UPDATING TRAINING FOR THE RETURNING NURSE, SOCIAL WORKER AND TEACHER.   WNATLCP61018

UPGRADES
URBAN-LEAGUE **UPGRADES** NEGRO WORKERS.   NHOLMAX66563

UPGRADING
BREAKING THE BARRIERS OF OCCUPATIONAL ISOLATION. A REPORT ON **UPGRADING** LOW-SKILL, LOW-WAGE WORKERS.
/NEGRO PUERTO-RICAN/   CPROJAX66237

MANAGEMENT AND MINORITY GROUPS. A STUDY OF ATTITUDES AND PRACTICES IN HIRING AND **UPGRADING**.   GMARKPI57085

INDUSTRIAL INTEGRATION OF NEGROES. THE **UPGRADING** PROCESS.   NHOPEJX52571

SOME FACTORS INFLUENCING THE **UPGRADING** OF NEGROES IN THE SOUTHERN PETROLEUM REFINING INDUSTRY.
/CASE-STUDY/   NMARSRX63748

MANAGEMENT AND MINORITY-GROUPS. A STUDY OF ATTITUDES AND PRACTICES IN HIRING AND **UPGRADING**.   NROSEBX59080

PREJUDICE IS NOT THE WHOLE STORY. EXAMINATION OF THREE CASES OF NEGRO **UPGRADING** IN TRACTION COMPANIES IN
PHILADELPHIA, LOS-ANGELES AND CHICAGO. /PENNSYLVANIA CALIFORNIA ILLINOIS/   NWECKJE45308

UPLIFT
MDTA PROJECT **UPLIFT**. /TRAINING/   NFILIJE66354

UPPER
FOUR STUDIES OF NEGRO EMPLOYMENT IN THE **UPPER** SOUTH.   NDEWEDX55269

THE **UPPER** LIMIT OF ABILITY AMONG AMERICAN NEGROES.   NJENKMD48607

THE QUEST FOR IDENTITY AND STATUS. FACETS OF THE DESEGREGATION PROCESS IN THE **UPPER** MIDWEST.
/ECONOMIC-STATUS/   NTILLJA61161

CONFERENCE ON WOMEN IN THE **UPPER** PENINSULA ECONOMY. REPORT. /MICHIGAN/   WMICOLA64976

SALARIED WOMEN IN **UPPER** LEVEL POSITIONS IN KANSAS BUSINESS FIRMS.   WSTOCFT59143

UPPER-LEVEL
TRENDS IN THE EMPLOYMENT OF NEGRO-AMERICANS IN **UPPER-LEVEL** WHITE-COLLAR POSITIONS OF THE FEDERAL
GOVERNMENT.   GPRESCP60200

URBAN
FACTORS AFFECTING EDUCATIONAL-ATTAINMENT IN DEPRESSED **URBAN** AREAS. /NEGRO PUERTO-RICAN/   CGOLDML63426

THE **URBAN** REALITY. A COMPARATIVE STUDY OF THE SOCIO-ECONOMIC SITUATION OF MEXICAN-AMERICANS, NEGROES AND
ANGLO-CAUCASIANS IN LOS-ANGELES COUNTY. /CALIFORNIA/   CLOSACH65708

THE **URBAN** ADJUSTMENT OF IMMIGRANTS. THE RELATIONSHIP OF EDUCATION TO OCCUPATIONAL AND TOTAL FAMILY
INCOME. /NEGRO MEXICAN-AMERICAN/   CSHANLW63122

THE ASSIMILATION AND ACCULTURATION OF MIGRANTS TO **URBAN** AREAS. /MEXICAN-AMERICAN NEGRO/   CSHANLW63484

URBAN ADJUSTMENT AND ITS RELATIONSHIP TO THE SOCIAL ANTECEDENTS OF IMMIGRANT WORKERS. /NEGRO
MEXICAN-AMERICAN/   CSHANLW65121

ECONOMIC ABSORPTION AND CULTURAL INTEGRATION OF THE **URBAN** NEWCOMER. /NEGRO MEXICAN-AMERICAN/   CUVIOIP65277

A DEMONSTRATION PROJECT DESIGNED TO TEST THE LIFE-STYLE AND THE GROWTH POTENTIAL OF **URBAN** DROPOUTS FROM
DISADVANTAGED HOMES.   GCLEAMP66130

URBAN AND RURAL LEVELS OF LIVING. 1960. /ECONOMIC-STATUS/   GCOWHJD65425

OBSTACLES TO DESEGREGATION IN AMERICA-S **URBAN** AREAS.   GGRIEGX64743

URBAN POVERTY AND PUBLIC POLICY.   GLONGNE64856

URBAN DIFFERENTIATION. PROBLEMS AND PROSPECTS.   GMCELDX65051

SOCIAL DYNAMITE. THE REPORT OF THE CONFERENCE ON UNEMPLOYED, OUT-OF-SCHOOL YOUTH IN URBAN AREAS, MAY
24-26, 1961.   GNATLCC61039

DISCRIMINATION IN URBAN EMPLOYMENT.   GPALMEN47145

HUMAN RESOURCES IN THE URBAN ECONOMY. PART II -- THE LABOR FORCE PERFORMANCE OF MINORITY-GROUPS.   GPERLMX63169

TESTIMONY TO THE SUBCOMMITTEE ON RACE-RELATIONS AND URBAN PROBLEMS. /SES CALIFORNIA/   GREDMWX64221

URBAN JOB DISCRIMINATION. ABUSES AND REDRESS.   GRICOLX66237

FEDERAL ROLE IN URBAN AFFAIRS.   GUSSENA66351

DILEMMAS OF URBAN AMERICA.   GWEAVRC66707

A STUDY OF NAVAHO URBAN RELOCATION IN DENVER COLORADO.   IGRAVTD64566

SOCIAL SURVEY OF AMERICAN-INDIAN URBAN INTEGRATION.   IHIRAJXND444

CORRELATES OF ADJUSTMENT AMONG AMERICAN-INDIANS IN AN URBAN ENVIRONMENT.   IMARTHW64588

ECONOMIC FACTORS IN NAVAHO URBAN RELOCATION.   IWEPPRS65685

LEVELS OF LIVING OF SPANISH-AMERICAN RURAL AND URBAN FAMILIES IN TWO SOUTH TEXAS COUNTIES.   MCLEMHM63381

OCCUPATIONAL-PATTERNS OF RURAL AND URBAN SPANISH-AMERICANS IN TWO SOUTH TEXAS COUNTIES.   MCOTHML66385

INCOMES OF RURAL AND URBAN SPANISH-AMERICANS IN TWO SOUTH TEXAS COUNTIES.   MDICKBE65389

THE MEXICAN IN THE NORTHERN URBAN AREA. A COMPARISON OF TWO GENERATIONS.   MGOLDNX59403

RESIDENTIAL SEGREGATION IN THE URBAN SOUTHWEST.   MMOORJW66444

DIFFERENCES IN DROPOUT AND OTHER SCHOOL BEHAVIOR BETWEEN TWO GROUPS OF TENTH GRADE BOYS IN AN URBAN HIGH
SCHOOL.   MMUNORF57446

MEXICAN-AMERICANS IN URBAN PUBLIC HIGH SCHOOLS. AN EXPLORATION OF THE DROP-OUT PROGRAM.   MSHELPM59488

SELF RADIUS AND GOALS OF YOUTH IN DIFFERENT URBAN AREAS.   MSHERCW61489

CONTRASTS BETWEEN SPANISH FOLK AND ANGLO URBAN CULTURAL VALUES. /EDUCATION ASPIRATIONS/   MVALDBX64449

THE STATUS OF JOBS AND OCCUPATIONS AS EVALUATED BY AN URBAN NEGRO SAMPLE.   NBROWMC55126

THE URBAN NEGRO FAMILY.   NDOUGJH66286

FAMILY AND ACHIEVEMENT. A PROPOSAL TO STUDY THE EFFECT OF FAMILY SOCIALIZATION ON ACHIEVEMENT AND
PERFORMANCE AMONG URBAN NEGRO AMERICANS.   NEPPSEG65334

TESTIMONY BEFORE STATE SENATE FACT FINDING SUBCOMMITTEE ON RACE-RELATIONS AND URBAN PROBLEMS, FINAL
HEARING, JANUARY 20 1965. /CALIFORNIA FEPC/   NGRAHCX65439

IN SEARCH OF A FUTURE. A STUDY OF CAREER-SEEKING EXPERIENCES OF SELECTED NEGRO HIGH SCHOOL GRADUATES IN
WASHINGTON-DC WHICH WAS AN EFFORT TO PROVIDE KNOWLEDGE HELPFUL IN SOLVING ONE OF THE MOST CRITICAL
PROBLEMS FACING URBAN AMERICA TODAY.   NGRIEES63454

THE EFFECT OF THE GHETTO ON THE DISTRIBUTION AND LEVEL OF NONWHITE EMPLOYMENT IN URBAN AREAS.   NKAINJF64631

STATEMENT AND TESTIMONY ON FEDERAL ROLE IN URBAN AFFAIRS. /EMPLOYMENT GHETTO/   NKENNRF66017

FAMILY PATTERNS, ACHIEVEMENTS, AND ASPIRATIONS OF URBAN NEGROES.   NLYSTMH61718

URBAN DESEGREGATION.   NNORTLK65950

SOME CORRELATES OF HIGH NEED FOR ACHIEVEMENT AMONG URBAN NORTHERN NEGROES.   NNUTTRL46951

DISCRIMINATION IN URBAN EMPLOYMENT.   NPALMEN47971

NEGRO POLICE EMPLOYMENT IN THE URBAN SOUTH.   NRUDWEM61134

SOCIAL CHARACTERISTICS OF HIGH SCHOOL SENIORS IN URBAN NEGRO HIGH SCHOOLS IN TWO STATES.   NSMITBF56147

THE URBAN SOUTH.   NVANCRB54283

STATEMENT BEFORE CALIFORNIA SENATE SUB-COMMITTEE ON RACE-RELATIONS AND URBAN PROBLEMS.   OLOWXHW64745

THE PUERTO-RICAN WORKER CONFRONTS THE COMPLEX URBAN SOCIETY -- A PRESCRIPTION FOR CHANGE.   PCARDLA67874

URBAN-LEAGUE
THEY MAKE OPPORTUNITY KNOCK. /INDUSTRY URBAN-LEAGUE/   NCHEMWX63200

CASE-STUDIES IN URBAN-LEAGUE METHODS.   NCOLUUL59227

URBAN-LEAGUE UPGRADES NEGRO WORKERS.   NHOLMAX66563

NEW LOOK FOR THE URBAN-LEAGUE.   NMONIAX65808

A SURVEY OF THE ECONOMIC AND CULTURAL CONDITIONS OF THE NEGRO POPULATION OF LOUISVILLE, KENTUCKY AND A
REVIEW OF THE PROGRAM AND ACTIVITIES OF THE LOUISVILLE URBAN-LEAGUE. JANUARY-FEBRUARY, 1948.   NNATLUL48903

THE URBAN-LEAGUE STORY 1910-1960.   NNATLUL60899

APPRENTICESHIP AND TRAINING OPPORTUNITIES FOR NEGRO YOUTHS IN SELECTED URBAN-LEAGUE CITIES.   NNATLUL61885

SURVEY OF UNEMPLOYMENT IN SELECTED URBAN-LEAGUE CITIES.   NNATLUL61898

THE URBAN-LEAGUE AND THE VOCATIONAL GUIDANCE AND ADJUSTMENT OF NEGRO YOUTH.   NNICHLE52922

THE URBAN-LEAGUE AND ITS STRATEGY.   NYOUNWM65354

THE URBAN-LEAGUE EXPANDS OPPORTUNITIES.   NYOUNWM66355

URBAN-RENEWAL
REPORT OF THE DIAGNOSTIC SURVEY OF TENANT HOUSEHOLDS IN THE WEST SIDE URBAN-RENEWAL AREA OF

URBAN-RENEWAL   (CONTINUATION)
    NEW-YORK-CITY.   GGREEAI65474

    URBAN-RENEWAL AND CIVIL-RIGHTS.   NWINTSB64329

URBANISM
    URBANISM, RACE, AND ANOMIA.   GKILLLX62853

URBANIZATION
    THE URBANIZATION OF THE YANKTON INDIANS.   IHURTWR66576

    THE ECONOMIC DEVELOPMENT AND URBANIZATION OF THE NAVAJO INDIAN RESERVATION.   ISELLCL62616

    THE URBANIZATION OF THE DAKOTA INDIANS.   IWHITRX59686

    URBANIZATION OF THE MIGRANT. PROCESSES AND OUTCOMES. A RESEARCH PROPOSAL.   MSIMMOG64491

    URBANIZATION AND DISCRIMINATION IN THE SOUTH.   NBLALHM59086

    URBANIZATION IN THE SOUTH.   NREISLX65049

URGED
    UNIONS URGED TO FOLLOW THROUGH ON PLEDGES TO COMBAT JOB BIAS.   GAFLCIO63365

US
    NEGROES AND MEXICAN-AMERICANS IN SOUTH AND EAST LOS-ANGELES. AN ANALYSIS OF A SPECIAL US CENSUS SURVEY OF
    NOVEMBER 1965.   /CALIFORNIA/   CCALDIR66168

    ECONOMIC, SOCIAL, AND DEMOGRAPHIC CHARACTERISTICS OF SPANISH-AMERICAN WAGE WORKERS ON US FARMS.
    /PUERTO-RICAN MEXICAN-AMERICAN/   CFRIERE63805

    GENERAL SOCIAL AND ECONOMIC CHARACTERISTICS. SUMMARY, US CENSUS OF 1960.   /DEMOGRAPHY/   CUSBURC62374

    THE CIVIL-RIGHTS AND CIVIL-LIBERTIES DECISIONS OF THE US SUPREME COURT FOR THE 1962-63 TERM. A SUMMARY
    AND ANALYSIS.   GAMERJD63384

    MANPOWER IMPLICATIONS OF TECHNOLOGICAL-CHANGE. RESEARCH FINDINGS OF THE US DEPARTMENT OF LABOR.   GBRANSX63876

    INTERIM REVISED PROJECTIONS OF US LABOR-FORCE, 1965-1975.   GCOOPSX62602

    NEW DIRECTIONS IN US EMPLOYMENT-SERVICE APTITUDE TEST RESEARCH.   GDVORBJ65656

    PROJECTIONS OF THE LABOR-FORCE OF THE US.   GGOLDHX63787

    US WELFARE POLICIES IN PERSPECTIVE.   GGORDMS63742

    US MANPOWER AND EMPLOYMENT POLICY. A REVIEW ESSAY.   GGORDMS65728

    AUTOMATION. NATIONWIDE STUDIES IN THE US.   GGREELX64614

    PROGRESS OR POVERTY. THE US AT THE CROSSROADS.   GKEYSLH64862

    UNIONS BEFORE THE BAR. HISTORICAL TRIALS SHOWING THE EVOLUTION OF LABOR RIGHTS IN THE US.   GLIEBEX50901

    GEOGRAPHIC CHANGES IN US EMPLOYMENT FROM 1950 TO 1960.   GMANOSP63855

    FEP LEGISLATION AND ENFORCEMENT IN THE US.   GMEANJE66971

    NEW-YORK STATE-COMMISSION-AGAINST-DISCRIMINATION, STATEMENT BEFORE THE US SENATE SUBCOMMITTEE ON LABOR
    AND LABOR-MANAGEMENT RELATIONS.   GNEWYSA52102

    US PLAN TO BREAK CYCLE OF BIAS AND POVERTY.   GRICHEX66235

    MOBILITY AND WORKER ADAPTATION TO ECONOMIC CHANGE IN THE US.   GTRAVHX63836

    US COMMISSION-ON-CIVIL-RIGHTS, HEARINGS. LOS-ANGELES AND SAN-FRANCISCO, CALIFORNIA. JANUARY 25-26, 1960,
    JANUARY 27-28, 1960.   GUSCOMC60400

    EMPLOYMENT. 1961 US COMMISSION-ON-CIVIL-RIGHTS REPORT, VOLUME 3.   GUSCOMC61395

    US COMMISSION-ON-CIVIL-RIGHTS, HEARINGS. DETROIT, MICHIGAN. DEC 14-15 1960.   GUSCOMC61399

    US COMMISSION-ON-CIVIL-RIGHTS, HEARINGS. NEW-ORLEANS, LOUISIANA. SEPTEMBER 27-28, 1960, MAY 5-6, 1961. GUSCOMC61403

    US COMMISSION-ON-CIVIL-RIGHTS, HEARINGS. MEMPHIS, TENNESSEE. JUNE 25-26, 1962.   GUSCOMC62401

    US COMMISSION-ON-CIVIL-RIGHTS, HEARINGS. NEWARK, NEW-JERSEY. SEPTEMBER 11-12, 1962.   GUSCOMC62402

    A REPORT TO THE US COMMISSION ON CIVIL-RIGHTS.   /MISSOURI/   GUSCOMC63406

    REPORT ON FLORIDA OF THE US COMMISSION ON CIVIL-RIGHTS.   GUSCOMC63409

    FINAL REPORT. US COMMISSION ON FAIR-EMPLOYMENT-PRACTICES, JUNE 28, 1946.   GUSCOMF47417

    A SHARPER LOOK AT UNEMPLOYMENT IN US CITIES, AND SLUMS.   GUSDLAB66520

    FIRST REPORT. US FAIR-EMPLOYMENT-PRACTICE-COMMITTEE.   GUSFEPC45512

    FINAL REPORT. US FAIR-EMPLOYMENT-PRACTICE-COMMITTEE.   GUSFEPC47511

    EQUAL-EMPLOYMENT-OPPORTUNITY IN THE US POST OFFICE DEPARTMENT. A SUPPLEMENTAL REPORT TO THE POSTMASTER
    GENERAL.   GUSPODA63516

    A QUANTITATIVE ANALYSIS OF WHITE-NONWHITE INCOME DIFFERENTIALS IN THE US IN 1939.   GZEMAMX55594

    US GOVERNMENT POLICY TOWARD AMERICAN INDIANS. A FEW BASIC FACTS.   IELLIMB57554

    THE INDIAN TRIBES OF THE US. ETHNIC AND CULTURAL SURVIVAL.   IMCNIDX61586

    INDIANS ON FEDERAL RESERVATIONS IN THE US.   IUSDHEW58196

    ANNUAL REPORTS OF US DEPARTMENT OF THE INTERIOR.   IUSDINTND666

    ECONOMIC, SOCIAL AND DEMOGRAPHIC CHARACTERISTICS OF SPANISH-AMERICAN WAGE WORKERS ON US FARMS.   MFRIERE63394

    RACIAL DESEGREGATION IN THE PUBLIC SERVICE, WITH PARTICULAR REFERENCE TO THE US GOVERNMENT.   NBROWVJ54127

    THE SOURCES OF ECONOMIC GROWTH IN THE UNITED-STATES AND THE ALTERNATIVE BEFORE US.   /LABOR-FORCE

UTILIZING
UTILIZING OUR MANPOWER RESOURCES. SPECIAL APPLICANT GROUPS.   GUSDLAB63665

VACANCIES
THE MEASUREMENT AND INTERPRETATION OF JOB VACANCIES. A CONFERENCE REPORT OF THE NATIONAL BUREAU OF
ECCNCMIC RESEARCH.   /LABOR-MARKET/   GNATLBE66611

VALID
MUNICIPAL FAIR-EMPLOYMENT ORDINANCES AS A VALID EXERCISE OF THE POLICE POWER. GNORTDL64093

VALIDATION
THE VALIDATION OF ACCULTURATION. A CONDITION TO ETHNIC ASSIMILATION.   OBROOLX55708

VALIDITY
THE VALIDITY OF OCCUPATIONAL APTITUDE TESTS.   GGHISEE66788

LEGALITY AND VALIDITY OF PERSONNEL TESTS.   /LEGISLATION TITLE-VII/   GVINCNX66113

TEST BIAS. VALIDITY OF THE SCHOLASTIC APTITUDE TEST FOR NEGRO AND WHITE STUDENTS IN INTEGRATED COLLEGES.   NCLEATA66923

VALUE
THE IMMIGRANT. VALUE ORIENTATIONS AND VOCATIONAL ASPIRATIONS.   /NEGRO MEXICAN-AMERICAN/   CPETECL64988

THE ECCNCMIC VALUE OF EDUCATION.   GSCHUTW63895

WHEN THE MIGRANT LABORER SETTLES DOWN -- A REPORT OF THE FINDINGS OF A PROJECT ON VALUE ASSIMILATION OF
IMMIGRANT LABORERS.   MPETECL64454

VALUE ORIENTATIONS OF YOUNG MEXICAN-AMERICAN MALES AS REFLECTED IN THEIR WORK PATTERNS AND EMPLOYMENT
PREFERENCES.   MWADDJO62513

VALUE ORIENTATION. ROLE CONFLICT, AND ALIENATION FROM WORK. A CROSS-CULTURAL STUDY.   MZURCLA65520

SOME ASPECTS OF VOCATIONAL ASPIRATIONS AND VALUE ORIENTATION AMONG NEGRO BOYS IN THE LOWER SOCIO-ECONOMIC
CLASSES.   NSCHMWX63139

ECCNCMIC VALUE OF THE NEGRO TO THE SCUTH. PAST, PRESENT, AND POTENTIAL.   NSOUTRC45158

VALUE CHANGE IN COLLEGE WOMEN.   /WORK-WOMEN-ROLE/   WBROWDR62658

VALUES
THE VALUES OF NEGRO WOMEN COLLEGE STUDENTS.   CEAGLOW45313

A NOTE ON THE VALUES OF SOUTHERN COLLEGE WOMEN. WHITE AND NEGRO.   CGRAYSW47445

COMMUNITY VALUES IN EDUCATION AND OCCUPATIONAL SELECTION. A STUDY OF YOUTH IN EMMITSBURG, MARYLAND.   GLEONRC64894

VALUES. EXPECTATIONS AND RELOCATION. THE NAVAHO MIGRANT TO DENVER.   /COLORADO/   IGRAVTD66146

A STUDY OF AMERICAN AND MEXICAN-AMERICAN CULTURE VALUES AND THEIR SIGNIFICANCE IN EDUCATION.   MCABRYA63373

IMPLICATIONS OF CULTURAL VALUES IN EDUCATION.   MVALDBX64448

CONTRASTS BETWEEN SPANISH FOLK AND ANGLO URBAN CULTURAL VALUES.   /EDUCATION ASPIRATIONS/   MVALDBX64449

A NOTE ON RACIAL DIFFERENCES IN JOB VALUES AND DESIRES.   NSINGSL56142

CULTURAL VALUES AND THE PUERTO-RICAN.   PMONSJX57828

WORK VALUES AND BACKGROUND FACTORS AS PREDICTORS OF WOMEN-S DESIRE TO WORK.   /ASPIRATIONS/   WEYDELD62754

CHANGING VALUES IN COLLEGE.   /WORK-WOMAN-ROLE/   WJACOPE57877

OCCUPATIONAL VALUES AND OCCUPATIONAL SELECTION.   WRAVIMJ57077

INTEREST AND VALUES OF CAREER AND HOME MAKING ORIENTED WOMEN.   WWAGMMX66761

VARIABLE
SOCIAL ROLE EXPECTATION. MOTIVATIONAL VARIABLE IN GIRLS. /ASPIRATIONS/   WHANSDE64821

VARIABLES
OBJECTIVE ACCESS IN THE OPPORTUNITY STRUCTURE. THE ASSESSMENT OF THREE ETHNIC GROUPS WITH RESPECT TO
QUANTIFIED SOCIAL STRUCTURAL VARIABLES.   MRENDGX63461

SOME PERSONAL AND SOCIOLOGICAL VARIABLES ASSOCIATED WITH OCCUPATIONAL-CHOICES OF NEGRO YOUTH.   NHERSPF65520

CULTURAL EXPOSURE AND RACE AS VARIABLES IN PREDICTING TRAINING AND JOB SUCCESS.   /TESTING/   NLOCKHCND700

MATERNAL EMPLOYMENT. SITUATIONAL AND ATTITUDINAL VARIABLES. /WORK-FAMILY-CONFLICT/   WBRIEDX61655

THE RELATIONSHIP OF SELECTED VARIABLES TO CAREER-MARRIAGE PLANS OF UNIVERSITY FRESHMAN WOMEN.
/WORK-FAMILY-CONFLICT/   WZISSCX62284

VARIATION
AN ECONOMICAL AND HISTORICAL ANALYSIS OF THE CAUSES OF VARIATION AMONG NORTHERN STANDARD METROPOLITAN
AREAS IN PRODUCTIVITY OF NEGRO MEN IN 1949.   NBATCAB61060

VD
MARYLAND TB -- VD HEALTH PROGRAM AMONG AGRICULTURAL MIGRANTS.   GMARYSD65958

VEGETABLE
CALIFORNIA-S FRUIT AND VEGETABLE CANNING INDUSTRY. AN ECONOMIC STUDY.   OBENJMP61704

VERBAL
NEGRO RESPONSES TO VERBAL AND NON-VERBAL TEST MATERIAL.   NBEANKL47914

VERIFIED
THE BANKING INDUSTRY. VERIFIED COMPLAINTS AND INFORMAL INVESTIGATIONS.   /NEW-YORK/   GNEWYSA58076

THE INSURANCE INDUSTRY -- VERIFIED COMPLAINTS AND INFORMAL INVESTIGATIONS HANDLED BY THE NEW-YORK STATE
COMMISSION AGAINST DISCRIMINATION. JULY 1 1945-SEPTEMBER 15, 1958.   GNEWYSA58082

VERTICAL
VERTICAL MOBILITY AND PREJUDICE.   GGREEJX53738

VETERAN
THE DETERMINATION OF CERTAIN MAJOR FACTORS AFFECTING THE NEGRO VETERAN IN THE ON-THE-JOB TRAINING PROGRAM
IN VOCATIONAL AGRICULTURE IN THE STATE OF ALABAMA AS A BASIS FOR PLANNING A MORE EFFECTIVE PROGRAM.   NBATTEF49338

VETERANS
AUDIT OF NEGRO **VETERANS** AND SERVICEMEN, 1960. /PUBLIC-EMPLOYMENT/

NAMERVC60019

TUSKEGEE LOOKS AT ITS **VETERANS**. /OCCUPATIONAL-STATUS/

NDERBIA46251

THE 1960 AUDIT OF NEGRO **VETERANS** AND SERVICEMAN. /MILITARY/

NFELDJA61350

READJUSTMENTS OF **VETERANS** TO CIVILIAN LIFE.

NUSDLAB46839

VETERANS-ADMINISTRAT
NONDISCRIMINATION IN FEDERALLY-ASSISTED PROGRAMS OF THE DEPARTMENT-OF-THE-TREASURY,
DEPARTMENT-OF-DEFENSE. ATOMIC-ENERGY-COMMISSION, CIVIL-AERONAUTICS-BOARD, FEDERAL-AVIATION-AGENCY,
VETERANS-ADMINISTRATION.

GFEDERX64673

THE FEDERAL NONDISCRIMINATION POLICY IN THE **VETERANS-ADMINISTRATION**.

GUSVETA59521

VIEW
A SPECULATIVE **VIEW** OF THE UNITED STATES IN 1985 AND BEYOND. /TECHNOLOGICAL-CHANGE/

GBELLDX62612

A SOCIAL REFORMER-S **VIEW** OF POVERTY.

GHARRMX65659

INVESTING IN POOR PEOPLE. AN ECONOMIST-S **VIEW**.

GSCHUTW65842

FIGHTING POVERTY. THE **VIEW** FROM WATTS. /LOS-ANGELES CALIFORNIA/

NBULLPX66135

CHIEF EXECUTIVES **VIEW** NEGRO EMPLOYMENT. /INDUSTRY/

NHABBSX65471

HIGH SCHOOL FRESHMAN AND SENIORS **VIEW** THE ROLE OF WOMEN IN MODERN SOCIETY. /WORK-FAMILY-CONFLICT/

WKERNKK65892

WOMEN **VIEW** THEIR WORKING WORLD.

WRAMSGV63104

VIEWPOINT
SCHOOL-DESEGREGATION AND NEW INDUSTRY. THE SOUTHERN COMMUNITY LEADERS **VIEWPOINT**.

NCROMRX63243

VIEWS
COUNSELOR-S **VIEWS** ON CHANGING MANAGEMENT POLICIES.

GCOXXTX63618

NAACP **VIEWS** CONDITIONS.

NGUSCKI63469

HOW MANAGEMENT **VIEWS** ITS RACE-RELATIONS RESPONSIBILITIES.

NSTRAGX67181

VIOLENCE
CASTE. ECONOMY, AND **VIOLENCE**.

NDAVIAX45938

ECONOMIC CRISIS AND EXPECTATIONS OF **VIOLENCE**. A STUDY OF UNEMPLOYED NEGROES .

NLEGGJC64679

VIRGINIA
WHAT MASSIVE RESISTANCE COSTS NORFOLK AND ITS BUSINESSMEN. /VIRGINIA/

NBUSIWX58165

THE NEGRO LAWYER IN **VIRGINIA**. A SURVEY. /OCCUPATIONS/

NFRIEMX65387

NEGRO WORKERS IN THE BUILDING TRADES IN SELECTED CITIES. NORFOLK, **VIRGINIA**. /INDUSTRY/

NNATLUL46894

VISIBILITY
NEGRO **VISIBILITY**.

NKEPHWM54543

VISIBLE
THE NOW **VISIBLE** POOR.

GMACDDX64947

VOCATIONAL
THE IMMIGRANT. VALUE ORIENTATIONS AND **VOCATIONAL** ASPIRATIONS. /NEGRO MEXICAN-AMERICAN/

CPETECL64988

VOCATIONAL TRAINING TO IMPROVE JOB OPPORTUNITIES FOR MINORITY-GROUPS. COMMENT.

GFINEMX64681

VOCATIONAL TRAINING

GFREEMX60699

AN EXPERIMENT IN **VOCATIONAL** EDUCATION FOR CHILDREN OF MIGRATORY FARM WORKERS, JULY-AUGUST 1956.

GNATLCRND046

LOW-INCOME YOUTH, UNEMPLOYMENT, **VOCATIONAL** TRAINING, AND THE JOB-CORPS.

GPURCFX66208

TECHNOLOGICAL-CHANGE AND **VOCATIONAL** COUNSELING.

GSAMLJX64843

SOME SOCIOLOGICAL ROOTS OF **VOCATIONAL** CHOICES.

GYOUNME46593

VOCATIONAL TRAINING PROGRAMS FOR AMERICAN-INDIANS.

IUSDLAB64009

VOCATIONAL GUIDANCE FOR MINORITY YOUTH.

NBABOIX59038

THE DETERMINATION OF CERTAIN MAJOR FACTORS AFFECTING THE NEGRO VETERAN IN THE ON-THE-JOB TRAINING PROGRAM
IN **VOCATIONAL** AGRICULTURE IN THE STATE OF ALABAMA AS A BASIS FOR PLANNING A MORE EFFECTIVE PROGRAM.

NBATTEF49338

A COMPARISON OF THE **VOCATIONAL** ASPIRATIONS OF PAIRED SIXTH-GRADE WHITE AND NEGRO CHILDREN WHO ATTEND
SEGREGATED SCHOOLS.

NBROWRG65895

RACE, APTITUDE AND **VOCATIONAL** INTERESTS.

NCHANNN65191

VOCATIONAL CHOICES OF NEGRO HIGH SCHOOL STUDENTS IN MACON COUNTY, ALABAMA, AND THEIR RELATIONSHIP TO
BASIC OCCUPATIONAL ACTIVITES OF THE SCHOOL COMMUNITIES. /ASPIRATIONS/

NCHAPEJ49351

NEGROES. **VOCATIONAL** GUIDANCE AND COUNSELING IN THE SOUTHERN FIELD.

NEDWAGL47325

THE **VOCATIONAL** PREFERENCE OF NEGRO CHILDREN.

NGRAYSW44446

VOCATIONAL ORIENTATION TOWARD A REWARDING LIFE.

NJONEAM65622

VOCATIONAL ASPIRATIONS OF NEGRO YOUTH IN CALIFORNIA.

NLAWRPF50368

VOCATIONAL GRADUATES IN AUTO MECHANICS. A FOLLOW-UP STUDY OF NEGRO AND WHITE YOUTH. /OCCUPATIONS/

NLEVEBX66036

FACTORS AFFECTING FARM PLACEMENT OF NEGRO **VOCATIONAL** AGRICULTURE STUDENTS IN ALABAMA.

NMCQUFT45348

ACHIEVEMENT OF MALE HIGH SCHOOL DROPOUTS AND GRADUATES IN ALABAMA **VOCATIONAL** SCHOOLS.

NMILLGJ65791

PROGRAM AIDS FOR **VOCATIONAL** OPPORTUNITY PROGRAM.

NNATLUL49895

THE URBAN-LEAGUE AND THE **VOCATIONAL** GUIDANCE AND ADJUSTMENT OF NEGRO YOUTH.

NNICHLE52922

AN ANALYSIS OF SELECTIVE FACTORS INFLUENCING FARM INCOME IN HALE COUNTY, AS A BASIS FOR ESTABLISHING A

VOCATIONAL   (CONTINUATION)
    MORE EFFECTIVE VOCATIONAL AGRICULTURAL PROGRAM. /ALABAMA/   NSALTOR52347

    SOME ASPECTS OF VOCATIONAL ASPIRATIONS AND VALUE ORIENTATION AMONG NEGRO BOYS IN THE LOWER SOCIO-ECONOMIC
    CLASSES.   NSCHMWX63139

    OCCUPATIONAL ESTABLISHMENT OF FORMER STUDENTS OF VOCATIONAL AGRICULTURE IN MONTGOMERY TRAINING SCHOOL
    AREA. /ALABAMA/   NSCOTCOND346

    VOCATIONAL GUIDANCE BIBLIOGRAPHY.   NTANNAX40199

    VOCATIONAL EDUCATION FOR NEGRO YOUTH IN TEXAS.   NUSDLAB49847

    ENHANCING THE OCCUPATIONAL OUTLOOK AND VOCATIONAL ASPIRATIONS OF SOUTHERN SECONDARY YOUTH. A CONFERENCE
    OF SECONDARY SCHOOL PRINCIPALS AND COUNSELORS.   NUSDLAB65334

    THE VOCATIONAL GUIDANCE AND EDUCATION OF NEGROES. THE NEGRO AND THE BATTLE OF PRODUCTION.   NWILKOA42233

    SOME SOCIOLOGICAL ASPECTS OF VOCATIONAL GUIDANCE OF NEGRO CHILDREN.   NYOUNMN44348

    LIFE GOALS AND VOCATIONAL CHOICE. /WORK-WOMAN-ROLE/   WASTIAW64620

    THE EFFECT OF THE SOCIAL CONTEXT IN THE VOCATIONAL COUNSELING OF COLLEGE WOMEN.   WGURIMG63810

    COLLEGE WOMEN-S IDENTIFICATIONS WITH THEIR FATHERS IN RELATION TO VOCATIONAL INTEREST PATTERNS.
     /ASPIRATIONS/   WHALLWJ63815

    VOCATIONAL GUIDANCE AND TRAINING OF GIRLS AND WOMEN. /COUNSELING/   WINTELO64863

    VOCATIONAL TRAINING OF THE OLDER WOMAN.   WKINGCR66906

    VOCATIONAL EDUCATION AND FEDERAL POLICY.   WLEVISA63039

    THE VOCATIONAL ROLES OF OLDER MARRIED WOMEN. /WORK-WOMAN-ROLE/   WSTEIAX61136

    VOCATIONAL INTERESTS AND OCCUPATIONAL ADJUSTMENT OF COLLEGE WOMEN.   WWARRPA59222

VOCATIONAL-TECHNICAL
    VOCATIONAL-TECHNICAL EDUCATION AND ECONOMIC SECURITY.   GSWANJC66155

VOCATIONAL-TRAINING
    VOCATIONAL-TRAINING TO IMPROVE JOB OPPORTUNITIES FOR MINORITY-GROUPS.   GWALSJP64540

VOCATIONS
    VOCATIONS AND PROFESSIONS.   GLUTZPX40925

    INTEGRATION IN PROFESSIONAL EDUCATION. THE STORY OF PERKINS, SOUTHERN METHODIST UNIVERSITY. /VOCATIONS/   NCUNNMX56579

    THE POST-WAR OUTLOOK FOR NEGROES IN SMALL BUSINESS, THE ENGINEERING AND THE TECHNICAL VOCATIONS.   NWALKJO46580

VOLUNTARY
    BIBLIOGRAPHY ON VOLUNTARY FAIR-EMPLOYMENT PROGRAMS.   GUSCOMC65392

    VOLUNTARY FARM EMPLOYMENT SERVICE. /MIGRANT-WORKERS/   GUSSENA64306

    THE BUREAU OF INDIAN AFFAIRS VOLUNTARY RELOCATION SERVICES.   IUSDINT60644

WAGE
    ECONOMIC, SOCIAL, AND DEMOGRAPHIC CHARACTERISTICS OF SPANISH-AMERICAN WAGE WORKERS ON US FARMS.
     /PUERTO-RICAN MEXICAN-AMERICAN/   CFRIERE63805

    WAGE RATES AND UNEMPLOYMENT.   GBACKJX64876

    FARM LABOR DEVELOPMENTS -- EMPLOYMENT AND WAGE SUPPLEMENT.   GUSDLAB66446

    EMPLOYMENT INTEGRATION AND RACIAL WAGE DIFFERENCE IN A SOUTHERN PLANT.   GWEINRX59988

    SAN-CARLOS APACHE WAGE LABOR.   IADAMWX57522

    ECONOMIC, SOCIAL AND DEMOGRAPHIC CHARACTERISTICS OF SPANISH-AMERICAN WAGE WORKERS ON US FARMS.   MFRIERE63394

    FAMILY ORGANIZATION IN FIVE TYPES OF MIGRATORY WAGE LABOR.   MSOLIML61496

    EMPLOYMENT INTEGRATION AND WAGE DIFFERENCES IN A SOUTHERN PLANT.   NWEINRX59311

    SUGGESTED LANGUAGE FOR A STATE ACT TO ABOLISH DISCRIMINATORY WAGE RATES BASED ON SEX.   WUSDLAB64218

    FRINGE BENEFIT PROVISIONS FROM STATE MINIMUM WAGE LAWS AND ORDERS, SEPTEMBER 1, 1966.
     /EMPLOYMENT-CONDITIONS/   WUSDLAB66195

WAGE-EARNER
    THE NEGRO WAGE-EARNER AND APPRENTICESHIP TRAINING PROGRAMS. A CRITICAL ANALYSIS WITH RECOMMENDATIONS.   NHILLHX60532

    ORGANIZED LABOR AND THE NEGRO WAGE-EARNER. /UNION/   NHILLHX62535

    THE NEGRO WAGE-EARNER AND APPRENTICESHIP TRAINING PROGRAMS.   NUSDLAB60249

WAGES
    JOBS, WAGES AND CHANGING TECHNOLOGY.   GARONRL65747

    THE ROLE OF WAGES IN A GREAT SOCIETY.   GCONFOE66872

    SOME REGIONAL DIFFERENCES IN WAGES OF AGRICULTURAL WORKERS. /MIGRANT-WORKERS/   GMAITST60436

    WAR LABOR BOARD DECISION ON WAGES OF NEGROES.   NUSDLAB43848

    EMPLOYMENT AND WAGES IN THE US.   NWOYTWS53343

    WOMEN-S WAGES.   WINTELR60870

    EMPLOYMENT EFFECTS OF STATE MINIMUM WAGES FOR WOMEN.   WPETEJX59059

WAR
    MINORITY PEOPLES IN A NATION AT WAR.   GANNAOA42549

    HOW THE PRESIDENT IS WINNING THE WAR ON DISCRIMINATION.   GFACTMA56670

    THE WAR ON POVERTY.   GMYRDGX64851

WAR   (CONTINUATION)
    INDUSTRY EMPLOYMENT GROWTH SINCE WORLD WAR II.   GUSOLAB63831

    THE WAR AGAINST POVERTY -- THE AMERICAN-INDIAN.   INASHPX64597

    WAR INDUSTRY EMPLOYMENT FOR NEGROES IN MARYLAND.   NBRYSWO43129

    WAR ECONOMICS AND NEGRO LABOR.   NDAVIFG42260

    HOW MANAGEMENT CAN INTEGRATE NEGROES IN WAR INDUSTRIES.   NDAVIJA42255

    NEGRO EMPLOYMENT OPPORTUNITIES DURING AND AFTER THE WAR.   NOODDAE45949

    GOALS IN THE WAR ON POVERTY. /ECONOMIC-STATUS/   NECKSOX66957

    THE NEGROES WAR.   NFORTXX42541

    BARRIERS TO NEGRO WAR EMPLOYMENT.   NGRANLB42440

    NEGROES AND WAR PRODUCTION.   NGRANLB42444

    THE EFFECT OF THE WAR ECONOMY ON THE SOUTH. HOW MOBILIZATION WILL AFFECT POSITION OF THE NEGRO.   NJACKJX51595

    THE NEGRO WAR WORKER IN SAN-FRANCISCO. /CALIFORNIA/   NJCHNCS44612

    NEGRO WORKERS AFTER THE WAR.   NNATLNC45879

    NEGROES IN A WAR INDUSTRY. THE CASE OF SHIPBUILDING.   NNORTHR43942

    COMBATING DISCRIMINATION IN THE EMPLOYMENT OF NEGROES IN WAR INDUSTRIES AND GOVERNMENT AGENCIES. NRAMSLA43128

    SPECIAL PROBLEMS OF NEGRO MIGRATION DURING THE WAR.   NREIDID47362

    TRAINING NEGROES FOR WAR WORK.   NUSOLAB43845

    WAR LABOR BOARD DECISION ON WAGES OF NEGROES.   NUSOLAB43848

    THE EMPLOYMENT OF THE NEGRO IN WAR INDUSTRIES.   NWEAVRC43225

    EMPLOYMENT OF NEGROES IN UNITED STATES WAR INDUSTRIES.   NWEAVRC44300

    WAR AND POSTWAR TRENDS IN EMPLOYMENT OF NEGROES.   NWOLFSL45335

WAR-AGAINST-POVERTY
    THE STRATEGY AND POLITICAL ECONOMY OF THE WAR-AGAINST-POVERTY.   GORNAOA64958

    TITLE-VII. EQUAL-EMPLOYMENT SECTION. CIVIL-RIGHTS-ACT OF 1964. THE WAR-AGAINST-POVERTY.   NHILLHX65549

WAR-ON-POVERTY
    EDUCATION OF THE MINORITY POOR -- THE KEY TO THE WAR-ON-POVERTY.   GCLARKB66915

    THE FOUNDATIONS OF THE WAR-ON-POVERTY.   GGALLLE65932

    LABOR-MARKET STRATEGIES IN THE WAR-ON-POVERTY. /UNEMPLOYMENT/   GHARBFH65660

    WAR-ON-POVERTY. /EMPLOYMENT TRAINING/   GHUMPHH64739

    ENDS AND MEANS IN THE WAR-ON-POVERTY.   GLAMPRJ66881

    STRATEGIES IN THE WAR-ON-POVERTY.   GMACHFX65657

    THE WAR-ON-POVERTY. PERSPECTIVES AND PROSPECTS.   GMILLSM65953

    THE MIXED-UP WAR-ON-POVERTY.   GSILBCE65038

    EXAMINATION OF THE WAR-ON-POVERTY PROGRAM.   GUSHOUR65824

    THE WAR-ON-POVERTY.   GUSSENA64355

    THE INDIAN BUREAU AND THE WAR-ON-POVERTY.   INASHPX64134

    HEARING BEFORE THE AD HOC SUBCOMMITTEE ON THE WAR-ON-POVERTY PROGRAM.   NYOUNWM64350

WAR-TIME
    THE WAR-TIME EMPLOYMENT OF NEGROES IN THE FEDERAL-GOVERNMENT.   NGOLICL45432

WARDS
    EMPLOYMENT-TRENDS AMONG CALIFORNIA YOUTH AUTHORITY WARDS ON PAROLE. 1948-62.   MCALDYA63378

    EMPLOYMENT AND EMPLOYABILITY AMONG CALIFORNIA YOUTH AUTHORITY WARDS. A SURVEY.   MSECKJP62483

WARREN
    STUDY OF ECONOMIC AND CULTURAL ACTIVITIES IN THE WARREN AREA AS THEY RELATE TO MINORITY PEOPLE. /OHIO/   NWARRUL64986

WARTIME
    WARTIME EMPLOYMENT PATTERNS OF NONWHITES AND FEMALE WORKERS IN SOUTHERN INDUSTRY.   GHOPEJX46485

    PERSONNEL PRACTICES AND WARTIME CHANGES. /EMPLOYMENT/   NHAASFJ46548

WASHINGTON
    INCOME, EDUCATION AND UNEMPLOYMENT IN NEIGHBORHOODS. SEATTLE, WASHINGTON. /DEMOGRAPHY/   CUSOLAB63485

    PUBLIC WELFARE. POVERTY -- PREVENTION OR PERPETUATION. A STUDY OF THE STATE DEPARTMENT OF PUBLIC
    ASSISTANCE OF THE STATE OF WASHINGTON.   GGREEAI64479

    JOB OPPORTUNITIES FOR MINORITIES IN THE SEATTLE AREA. /WASHINGTON/   GUVWAIL48532

    ASSIMILATION OF THE SPOKANE INDIANS. /WASHINGTON/   IROYXPX61612

    THE MEASUREMENT OF ASSIMILATION. THE SPOKANE INDIANS. /WASHINGTON/   IROYXPX66613

    ASSIMILATION OF THE SPOKANE INDIANS. /WASHINGTON/   ISTONCX62626

    THE SOCIO-ECONOMIC ADJUSTMENT OF THE NEGRO IN SEATTLE BETWEEN 1940 AND 1950. /WASHINGTON/   NKENNTH54273

    EMPLOYMENT IN METROPOLITAN WASHINGTON. /WASHINGTON-DC/   NUSOLAB63260

    THE PHYSICAL GEOGRAPHY OF THE PALOUSE REGION, WASHINGTON AND IDAHO, AND ITS RELATION TO THE AGRICULTURAL

  ECONOMY.   OSHROCR58762

  WORLD OF WORK CONFERENCE ON CAREER AND JOB OPPORTUNITIES, WASHINGTON, DC, JULY 1962.   WUSDLAB64242

  WOMAN-S DESTINY -- CHOICE OR CHANCE. REPORT OF CONFERENCE AT THE UNIVERSITY OF WASHINGTON, NOVEMBER   WUSDLAB65233
  21-22, 1963.

WASHINGTON-DC
  INCOME, EDUCATION AND UNEMPLOYMENT IN NEIGHBORHOODS. WASHINGTON-DC. /DEMOGRAPHY/   CUSDLAB63487

  EMPLOYMENT OPPORTUNITIES FOR HIGH SCHOOL DROPOUTS. A STUDY OF EMPLOYERS PRACTICES, NEEDS AND ATTITUDES IN
  THE DISTRICT OF COLUMBIA. /WASHINGTON-DC/   GBURESS57499

  A STUDY OF PATTERNS OF DISCRIMINATION IN EMPLOYMENT FOR THE EQUAL-EMPLOYMENT-OPPORTUNITY-COMMISSION,
  WASHINGTON-DC.   GCOUSFR66478

  FAIR-EMPLOYMENT IN THE NATION-S CAPITAL. A STUDY OF PROGRESS AND DILEMMA. /WASHINGTON-DC/   GSAWYDA62279

  THE PRACTICES OF CRAFT UNIONS IN WASHINGTON-DC WITH RESPECT TO MINORITY GROUPS IN CIVIL-RIGHTS IN THE
  NATION-S CAPITOL.   GSEGABD59294

  REPORT ON WASHINGTON-DC. EMPLOYMENT.   GUSCOMC63412

  REPORTS ON APPRENTICESHIP, NINE STATE ADVISORY COMMITTEES. /CALIFORNIA FLORIDA MARYLAND CONNECTICUT
  WASHINGTON-DC NEW-JERSEY NEW-YORK TENNESSEE WISCONSIN/   GUSCOMC64407

  IN SEARCH OF A FUTURE. A STUDY OF CAREER-SEEKING EXPERIENCES OF SELECTED NEGRO HIGH SCHOOL GRADUATES IN
  WASHINGTON-DC WHICH WAS AN EFFORT TO PROVIDE KNOWLEDGE HELPFUL IN SOLVING ONE OF THE MOST CRITICAL
  PROBLEMS FACING URBAN AMERICA TODAY.   NGRIEES63454

  EMPLOYMENT IN METROPOLITAN WASHINGTON. /WASHINGTON-DC/   NUSDLAB63260

  NEXT IT-S A MIXED POLICE FORCE. INTEGRATIONISTS LATEST GOAL IN NATION-S CAPITAL. /WASHINGTON-DC/   NUSNEWR57274

  THE EMPLOYED POOR. A CASE-STUDY. /WASHINGTON-DC/   NWILLCV65989

WASTE
  THE HIGH COST OF DISCRIMINATION. THE WASTE IN MANPOWER, MORALE, AND PRODUCTIVITY COSTS AMERICAN INDUSTRY
  30 BILLION DOLLARS A YEAR.   GROPEEX63244

  DISCRIMINATION...AN ECONOMIC WASTE.   GWACHWWND536

  SEGREGATION AND MANPOWER WASTE.   NGINZEX60413

  WASTE OF MANPOWER -- RACE AND EMPLOYMENT IN A SOUTHERN STATE.   NROBEGX62064

  RACIAL WORK AND NEGRO WASTE IN SOUTHERN EMPLOYMENT.   NSOUTRC62300

  OUR GREATEST WASTE OF TALENT IS WOMEN. /WORK-WOMEN-ROLE/   WBUNTMI61662

  A HUGE WASTE. EDUCATED WOMANPOWER.   WBUNTMI61900

  WOMANPOWER -- WANTON WASTE OR WISHFUL THINKING.   WWESTEM62265

WASTED
  WASTED TALENT. /EDUCATION/   NBONDHM60888

  WASTED MANPOWER -- BERKELEY CHALLENGE AND OPPORTUNITY. WORKSHOP COSPONSORED WITH THE BERKELEY UNIFIED
  SCHOOL-DISTRICT MARCH 15-16, 1963. /CALIFORNIA/   NKENNVD63642

  THE WASTED AMERICANS. /POVERTY/   NMAYXEX64760

  AMERICAN NEGROES -- A WASTED RESOURCE. /INDUSTRY/   NMORRJJ57853

  IS COLLEGE EDUCATION WASTED ON WOMEN.   WSANFNX57102

WATTS
  FIGHTING POVERTY. THE VIEW FROM WATTS. /LOS-ANGELES CALIFORNIA/   NBULLPX66135

  SOME PRACTICAL STUDIES IN PUBLIC TRANSPORTATION. /EMPLOYMENT-CONDITIONS WATTS LOS-ANGELES CALIFORNIA/   NCARLJX65593

  WATTS ONE YEAR LATER. /TRAINING CALIFORNIA LOS-ANGELES/   NPAGEDX66970

  SOME LESSONS FROM WATTS. /LOS-ANGELES CALIFORNIA/   NRUSTBX66098

  THE WATTS MANIFESTO AND THE MCCONE REPORT. /LOS-ANGELES CALIFORNIA/   NRUSTBX66099

  PROGRESS IN WATTS -- THE LOS-ANGELES ASTD COMMUNITY AFFAIRS PROGRAM. /CALIFORNIA/   NTRAIAD66580

WDL
  THE WDL APPRENTICESHIP TRAINING PROGRAM. REPORT OF A YEAR-S EXPERIMENT.   GWORKDL65584

WEALTH
  WEALTH AND POWER IN AMERICA. /ECONOMY POVERTY/   GKOLKGX62690

  HUMAN-RESOURCES, THE WEALTH OF A NATION. /YOUTH/   NGINZEX58405

  NEGROES. BIG ADVANCES IN JOBS, WEALTH, STATUS.   NUSNEWR58271

WEAPON
  THE FAIR REPRESENTATION DOCTRINE. AN EFFECTIVE WEAPON AGAINST UNION RACIAL DISCRIMINATION.   GHERRNM64772

  RACE HATE. NEWEST UNION-BUSTING WEAPON IN THE SOUTH.   NCAREJB58181

WEAPONS
  WEAPONS AGAINST DISCRIMINATION IN PUBLIC OFFICE.   GAVINAX62411

WEIGHT
  THE WEIGHT OF THE POOR -- A STRATEGY TO END POVERTY. /GUARANTEED-INCOME/   GCLOWRX66525

  STATEMENT ON WEIGHT LIFTING, HOURS, SENIORITY LAWS AND WOMEN. /EMPLOYMENT-CONDITIONS/   WUAWXWD66164

WELFARE
  AUTOMATION AND PUBLIC WELFARE.   GAMERPW64798

  A NATIONAL PROGRAM FOR THE IMPROVEMENT OF WELFARE SERVICES AND THE REDUCTION OF WELFARE DEPENDENCY.   GCOHENE65664

  A NATIONAL PROGRAM FOR THE IMPROVEMENT OF WELFARE SERVICES AND THE REDUCTION OF WELFARE DEPENDENCY.   GCOHENE65664

WELFARE (CONTINUATION)

PUBLIC WELFARE, AUTOMATION, AND EXPERIMENTAL MANPOWER PROGRAMS.   GCCNFAP63545

US WELFARE POLICIES IN PERSPECTIVE.   GGORDMS63742

PUBLIC WELFARE. POVERTY -- PREVENTION OR PERPETUATION. A STUDY OF THE STATE DEPARTMENT OF PUBLIC
ASSISTANCE OF THE STATE OF WASHINGTON.   GGREEAI64479

WORK RELIEF. SOCIAL WELFARE STYLE. /MANPOWER UNEMPLOYMENT/   GLEVISA66531

DISCRIMINATION AND NATIJNAL WELFARE.   GMACIRM49025

INCOME AND WELFARE IN THE UNITED STATES.   GMORGJN62032

PROJECTED CHANGES IN THE OCCUPATIONAL STRUCTURE OF THE LABOR-FORCE. IMPLICATIONS FOR PUBLIC WELFARE.   GSIFFHX64105

WHITE-NONWHITE DIFFERENTIALS IN HEALTH, EDUCATION, AND WELFARE.   GUSDHEW65435

SOCIAL DEVELOPMENT. KEY TO THE GREAT SOCIETY. /SOCIO-ECONOMIC WELFARE/   GUSDHEW66639

HEALTH, EDUCATION, AND WELFARE ASPECTS OF THE ECONOMIC REPORT OF THE PRESENT AND ANNUAL REPORT OF THE
COUNCIL OF ECONOMIC ADVISORS.   GUSDHEW66711

ANNUAL REPORT OF THE SECRETARY OF HEALTH, EDUCATION, AND WELFARE TO THE CONGRESS ON TRAINING ACTIVITIES
UNCER THE MANPOWER-DEVELOPMENT-AND-TRAINING-ACT, 1965.   GUSDHEW66978

WELFARE CRITERIA AND CHANGING TASTES.   GWECKRS62987

DETRCIT-S INSURED UNEMPLOYED AND EMPLOYABLE WELFARE RECIPIENTS. /MICHIGAN/   GWICKEC63561

INSURED UNEMPLOYED AND EMPLOYABLE WELFARE RECIPIENTS.   GWICKEX63637

EDUCABILITY AND REHABILITATICN. THE FUTURE OF THE WELFARE CLASS.   NHESSRD64523

THE EMPLOYMENT OF NEGROES IN PUBLIC WELFARE IN ELEVEN SOUTHERN STATES, 1936-1949. /OCCUPATIONS/   NLARKJR52672

DISCRIMINATION AND NATIJNAL WELFARE. A SERIES OF ADDRESSES AND DISCUSSIONS.   NMACIRM49731

OUR WELFARE STATE AND THE WELFARE OF FARM PEOPLE.   NSCHUTW64143

OUR WELFARE STATE AND THE WELFARE OF FARM PEOPLE.   NSCHUTW64143

TIME, WORK, AND WELFARE.   WMORGJX65997

WEST

MIGRATORY-LABOR IN THE WEST. BACKGROUND INFORMATION FOR THE WESTERN INTERSTATE CONFERENCE ON MIGRATORY
LABOR. /MIGRANT-WORKERS/   GCOUNSG60931

REPORT OF THE DIAGNOSTIC SURVEY OF TENANT HOUSEHOLDS IN THE WEST SIDE URBAN-RENEWAL AREA OF
NEW-YORK-CITY.   GGREEAI65474

RESOURCE CHARACTERISTICS AND UTILIZATION AND LEVEL OF LIVING ITEMS, RURAL HOUSEHOLDS, NORTH AND WEST
FLORIDA, 1956.   GREUSLA60391

INCOME, RESOURCES, AND ADJUSTMENT POTENTIALS AMONG RURAL FAMILIES IN NORTH AND WEST FLORIDA.   GREUSLA62388

MIGRATCRY LABOR IN THE WEST.   MCOUNSH60386

ACCOMOCATION BETWEEN NEGRO AND WHITE EMPLOYEES IN A WEST COAST AIRCRAFT INDUSTRY, 1942-1944.
/CASE-STUDY/   NREEDBA47045

THE NEGRO IN THE WEST. SOME FACTS RELATING TC SOCIAL AND ECONOMIC CONDITIONS. NO 1. THE NEGRO WORKER.   NUSOLABND256

NEGROES GO NORTH, WEST. JOBS TAKE THEM FAR AFIELD FROM THE SOUTH.   NUSNEWR51272

WEST-VIRGINIA

CHANGING PATTERNS IN AGRICULTURAL PRODUCTIONS, WEST-VIRGINIA, 1920-1950. /OCCUPATIONS/   NANGLRA54254

SPECIAL REPORT. A SURVEY OF NEGROES EMPLOYED BY THE STATE OF WEST-VIRGINIA.   NVIRGHR64318

WESTCHESTER

FAIR EMPLOYMENT SURVEY JF THE WESTCHESTER AREA. /PENNSYLVANIA/   GPENNHR65163

WESTERN

MIGRATCRY-LABOR IN THE WEST. BACKGROUND INFORMATION FOR THE WESTERN INTERSTATE CONFERENCE ON MIGRATORY
LABOR. /MIGRANT-WORKERS/   GCOUNSG6C931

MIGRATORY FARM WORKERS IN THE ATLANTIC COAST STREAM. WESTERN NEW-YORK, JUNE 1953.   GMCTHJR54405

WESTERN-ELECTRIC

WESTERN-ELECTRIC AND ITS PLAN-FOR-PROGRESS. A THREE YEAR REPORT. /INDUSTRY/   GWESTEC64553

WESTERNERS

WESTERNERS FROM THE EAST. ORIENTAL IMMIGRANTS REAPPRAISED.   ODANIRX66084

WHITE

A NOTE ON THE VALUES OF SOUTHERN COLLEGE WOMEN, WHITE AND NEGRO.   CGRAYSW47445

EMPLOYMENT OF WHITE AND NON-WHITE PERSONS. 1955. /DEMOGRAPHY/   CUSBURC56373

PERSONS OF SPANISH-SURNAME. SOCIAL AND ECONOMIC DATA FOR WHITE PERSONS OF SPANISH SURNAME IN 5
SOUTHWESTERN STATES. /DEMOGRAPHY/   CUSBURC63181

WHITE COLLAR EMPLOYMENT. TRENDS AND STRUCTURE.   GBANYCA6142C

WHITE AND NONWHITE OWNERS OF RURAL LAND IN THE SOUTHEAST.   GBOXLRF65418

SOCIOECONOMIC DIFFERENCES BETWEEN WHITE AND NONWHITE FARM POPULATIONS IN THE SOUTH.   GCOWHJD64616

DISCRIMINATION AND THE WHITE -- NONWHITE UNEMPLOYMENT DIFFERENTIALS.   GGILMHJ63716

A NOTE ON OCCUPATIONAL MOBILITY FOR WHITE AND NONWHITE MALES, 1950 TO 1965.   GJAFFAJ66820

PROFILE IN BLACK AND WHITE. CISCRIMINATION AND INEQUALITY OF OPPORTUNITY.   GNATLULND085

WHITE UNEMPLOYMENT IN THE UNITED STATES. 1947-1958, AN ANALYSIS OF TRENDS.   GNEWYSA58089

CHARACTERISTICS OF 6000 WHITE AND NONWHITE PERSONS ENROLLED IN MANPOWER-DEVELOPMENT-AND-TRAINING-ACT

WHITE   (CONTINUATION)

TRAINING.   GUSDLAB63197

LABOR-FORCE DEVELOPMENTS FOR WHITE AND NONWHITE WORKERS,954-1964.   GUSDLAB64110

AMERICAN INDIANS, WHITE AND BLACK. THE PHENOMENON OF TRANSCULTURATION.   IHALLAI63571

THE INDIAN AND THE WHITE MAN.   IWASHWE64682

AMERICAN-INDIANS AND WHITE PEOPLE.   IWAXXRH61224

SOCIAL FACTORS IN OCCUPATIONAL AND EDUCATIONAL ASPIRATIONS OF NEGRO AND WHITE STUDENTS.   NADDIDP61002

NEGRO AND WHITE YOUTH IN ELMIRA. /NEW-YORK/   NANTOAX59026

OCCUPATIONAL ASPIRATIONS OF LOWER-CLASS NEGRO AND WHITE YOUTH.   NANTOAX59027

CONFRONTATION. BLACK AND WHITE. /CIVIL-RIGHTS/   NBENNLX65881

ECONOMIC PROGRESS IN BLACK AND WHITE.   NBRIMAF66114

A COMPARISON OF THE VOCATIONAL ASPIRATIONS OF PAIRED SIXTH-GRADE WHITE AND NEGRO CHILDREN WHO ATTEND
SEGREGATED SCHOOLS.   NBROWRG65895

A COMPARISON OF THE ACADEMIC ACHIEVEMENTS OF WHITE AND NEGRO HIGH SCHOOL GRADUATES. /EDUCATION/   NBULLHA50132

A PRELIMINARY REPORT ON MEDICAL STAFF APPOINTMENTS HELD BY NEGRO PHYSICIANS AT PREDOMINANTLY WHITE
HOSPITALS. /CHICAGO ILLINOIS/   NCHICCO60201

TEST BIAS. VALIDITY OF THE SCHOLASTIC APTITUDE TEST FOR NEGRO AND WHITE STUDENTS IN INTEGRATED COLLEGES. NCLEATA66923

A COMPARATIVE STUDY OF THE OCCUPATIONAL INTERESTS OF NEGRO AND WHITE ADOLESCENT BOYS.   NCONNSM65471

NEGRO SUBORDINATION AND WHITE GAINS. /INCOME OCCUPATIONAL-STATUS/   NCUTRPX65245

EFFECTS OF UNEMPLOYMENT ON WHITE AND NEGRO PRISON-ADMISSIONS IN LOUISIANA.   NDOBBDA58277

LEFT SECTARIANISM IN THE FIGHT FOR NEGRO RIGHTS AND AGAINST WHITE CHAUVINISM.   NFOSTWZ53375

INTRA-PLANT MOBILITY OF NEGRO AND WHITE WORKERS.   NGARBAP65394

ASPIRATIONS OF NEGRO AND WHITE STUDENTS.   NGISTNP63419

THE ROLE OF WHITE RESISTANCE AND FACILITATION IN THE NEGRO STRUGGLE FOR EQUALITY.   NGLENND65676

EFFECTS OF ON-THE-JOB EXPERIENCE WITH NEGROES UPON RACIAL ATTITUDES OF WHITE WORKERS IN UNION SHOPS. NGUNDRH50466

ATTITUDES OF WHITE DEPARTMENT STORE EMPLOYEES TOWARD NEGRO CO-WORKERS. /CASE-STUDY/   NHARDJX52482

DISCRIMINATION IN RATE OF COMPENSATION BETWEEN COLORED AND WHITE TEACHERS HELD UNCONSTITUTIONAL.   NHARVLR40497

THE EDUCATIONAL AND OCCUPATIONAL ASPIRATIONS AND PLANS OF NEGRO AND WHITE MALE ELEMENTARY SCHOOL
STUDENTS.   NHOLLRG59562

THE EMPLOYMENT SITUATION OF WHITE AND NEGRO YOUTH IN THE CITY OF BALTIMORE. INITIAL EXPERIENCES IN THE
LABOR-MARKET. /MARYLAND/   NJOHNHU63735

EFFECTS OF WHITE AUTHORITARIANISM IN BI-RACIAL WORK GROUPS.   NKATZIX60639

THE EFFECTS OF SOUTHERN WHITE WORKERS ON RACE-RELATIONS IN NORTHERN PLANTS.   NKILLLM52650

NEGRO AND WHITE IN A CONNECTICUT TOWN.   NLEEXFF61674

THE EMPLOYMENT SITUATION OF WHITE AND NEGRO YOUTH IN THE CITY OF BALTIMORE. /MARYLAND/   NLEVEBX63684

VOCATIONAL GRADUATES IN AUTO MECHANICS. A FOLLOW-UP STUDY OF NEGRO AND WHITE YOUTH. /OCCUPATIONS/   NLEVEBX66036

NEGRO AND WHITE CHILDREN-S PLANS FOR THEIR FUTURES. /ASPIRATIONS/   NLOTTAJ63487

NEGRO VERSUS WHITE INTELLIGENCE. A CONTINUING CONTROVERSY.   NMCCOWM58062

INTELLIGENCE AND EDUCATIONAL ACHIEVEMENT OF A MATCHED SAMPLE OF WHITE AND NEGRO STUDENTS.   NMCQURX60730

DIXIE IN BLACK AND WHITE. /UNION/   NMEZEAG47492

ATTITUDES TOWARD SOCIAL MOBILITY AS REVEALED BY SAMPLES OF NEGRO AND WHITE BOYS.   NMONTJB58809

THE INTRODUCTION OF NEGROES INTO WHITE DEPARTMENTS. /CASE-STUDY INDUSTRY/   NPALMER55972

RETREATISM AND OCCUPATIONAL ASPIRATIONS AMONG WHITE AND NEGRO HIGH SCHOOL SENIORS.   NPOWEEC61009

BLACK FAMILIES AND THE WHITE HOUSE.   NRAINLX66033

ACCOMODATION BETWEEN NEGRO AND WHITE EMPLOYEES IN A WEST COAST AIRCRAFT INDUSTRY, 1942-1944.
/CASE-STUDY/   NREEDBA47045

LIBRARY RESOURCES AND SERVICES IN WHITE AND NEGRO COLLEGES. /EDUCATION/   NSAMOTX65128

CRISIS IN BLACK AND WHITE.   NSILBCE65135

EQUAL-PAY FOR WHITE AND NEGRO TEACHERS. /OCCUPATIONS/   NUSDLAB41817

FACULTY EDUCATION AND INCOME IN NEGRO AND WHITE COLLEGES.   NUSDLAB65819

THE MENTALITIES OF NEGRO AND WHITE WORKERS. AN EXPERIMENTAL SCHOOL-S INTERPRETATION OF NEGRO TRADE
UNIONISM.   NVALIPX49280

POVERTY AREAS OF OUR MAJOR CITIES. THE EMPLOYMENT SITUATION OF NEGRO AND WHITE WORKERS IN METROPOLITAN
AREAS COMPARED IN A SPECIAL LABOR-FORCE REPORT.   NWETZJR66114

COMPARATIVE STUDY OF SOCIO-ECONOMIC AND SOCIAL-PSYCHOLOGICAL DETERMINANTS OF EDUCATIONAL AND OCCUPATIONAL
ASPIRATIONS OF NEGRO AND WHITE COLLEGE SENIORS.   NWHITRM59319

WHITE EMPLOYERS AND NEGRO WORKERS.   NWILSLX43327

AFTER HIGH SCHOOL WHAT...HIGHLIGHTS OF A STUDY OF CAREER PLANS OF NEGRO AND WHITE RURAL YOUTH IN THREE
FLORIDA COUNTIES. /ASPIRATIONS/   NYOUMEG65390

WHITE-COLLAR
TRENDS IN THE EMPLOYMENT OF NEGRO-AMERICANS IN UPPER-LEVEL WHITE-COLLAR POSITIONS OF THE FEDERAL

WHITE-COLLAR   (CONTINUATION)
  GOVERNMENT.   GPRESCP60200

  A STUDY OF SOME ASPECTS OF JOB SATISFACTION AMONG NEGRO WHITE-COLLAR WORKERS.   NWEATMD54296

  WHITE-COLLAR WOMEN. THE SECRETARIAL-STENOGRAPHIC OCCUPATION.   WBRYACD57659

  OFFICE AUTOMATION AND WHITE-COLLAR EMPLOYMENT.   WSMITGM59122

  AUTOMATION AND THE WHITE-COLLAR WORKER.   WSTIEJX57142

WHITE-HOUSE-CONFEREN
  TO FULFILL THESE RIGHTS. REPORT ON THE WHITE-HOUSE-CONFERENCE. /EEO/   NWATTPX66545

WHITE-NEGRO
  THE NATURAL HISTORY OF SOCIAL CONFLICT AND WHITE-NEGRO RELATIONS.   NHIMEJS49553

  CHANGING STRUCTURES OF WHITE-NEGRO RELATIONS IN THE SOUTH.   NHIMEJS51552

WHITE-NON-WHITE
  THE WHITE-NON-WHITE UNEMPLOYMENT DIFFERENTIAL.   GGILMHJ63436

WHITE-NONWHITE
  HIGHLIGHTS OF WHITE-NONWHITE DIFFERENTIALS.   GHUYCEE65790

  WHITE-NONWHITE DIFFERENTIALS IN HEALTH, EDUCATION, AND WELFARE.   GUSDHEW65435

  A QUANTITATIVE ANALYSIS OF WHITE-NONWHITE INCOME DIFFERENTIALS IN THE US IN 1939.   GZEMAMX55594

WHITES
  COMPARISON OF MEXICANS, NEGROES AND WHITES WITH RESPECT TO OCCUPATIONAL HISTORY, RURAL-URBAN RESIDENCE
  HISTORY AND ACCULTURIZATION WITHIN THE INSTITUTIONAL STRUCTURE OF LANSING, MICHIGAN.   CGOLDVX60494

  RELATIVE SOCIOECONOMIC STATUS OF SOUTHERN WHITES AND NONWHITES, 1950 AND 1960.   GCOWHJD64615

  LEVELS OF LIVING AMONG WHITES AND NON-WHITES IN THE U.S.   GCOWHJC65614

  THE ATTRACTIVENESS OF THE SOUTH TO WHITES AND NONWHITES. AN ECOLOGICAL STUDY.   GHEERDM63769

  THE EMPLOYABILITY OF CHIPPEWA INDIANS AND POOR WHITES.   ILIEBLX66041

  COMPARATIVE PSYCHOLOGICAL STUDIES OF NEGROES AND WHITES IN THE UNITED STATES.   NDREGRM60292

  RECENT RESEARCH IN PSYCHOLOGICAL COMPARISONS OF NEGROES AND WHITES IN THE UNITED STATES.   NDREGRM65293

  OCCUPATIONAL DIFFERENTIATION OF NEGROES AND WHITES IN THE UNITED STATES.   NGIBBJP65401

  OCCUPATIONAL BENEFITS TO WHITES FROM THE SUBORDINATION OF NEGROES. /DISCRIMINATION/   NGLENND63423

  REPRESENTATION OF NEGROES AND WHITES AS EMPLOYEES IN THE FEDERAL PRISON SYSTEM.   NMORGGD62849

  EMPLOYMENT EXPERIENCES OF NEGRO PHILADELPHIANS. A DESCRIPTIVE STUDY OF THE EMPLOYMENT EXPERIENCES,
  PERCEPTIONS, AND ASPIRATIONS OF SELECTED PHILADELPHIA WHITES AND NON-WHITES.   NSIEGAI59718

  INTERESTS OF NEGROES AND WHITES.   NSTROEK52186

WICHITA
  A REVIEW OF THE ECONOMIC AND CULTURAL PROBLEMS OF WICHITA, KANSAS.   NBANNWM65051

WIFE
  THE WORKING WIFE AND HER FAMILY-S ECONOMIC POSITION.   WCARRMS62681

  MARITAL DISAGREEMENT IN WORKING WIFE MARRIAGES AS A FUNCTION OF HUSBAND-S ATTITUDE TOWARDS WIFE-S
  EMPLOYMENT. /WORK-FAMILY-CONFLICT/   WGIANAX57779

  THE HOMEMAKER AND THE WORKING WIFE. /WORK-FAMILY-CONFLICT/   WKOMAMX62912

  SPEAKING FOR THE WORKING CLASS WIFE. /BLUE-COLLAR/   WSEXTPC62299

WIFE-S
  MARITAL DISAGREEMENT IN WORKING WIFE MARRIAGES AS A FUNCTION OF HUSBAND-S ATTITUDE TOWARDS WIFE-S
  EMPLOYMENT. /WORK-FAMILY-CONFLICT/   WGIANAX57779

WIND-RIVER
  POPULATION AND INCOME CENSUS. WIND-RIVER RESERVATION, WYOMING.   IUSDINT60655

WISCONSIN
  INCOME, EDUCATION AND UNEMPLOYMENT IN NEIGHBORHOODS. MILWAUKEE, WISCONSIN. /DEMOGRAPHY/   CUSDLAB63467

  MIGRANT LABOR IN WISCONSIN.   GBRANEX63796

  LABOR LAW -- UNION MEMBERSHIP DENIED ON THE BASIS OF RACIAL DISCRIMINATION. /WISCONSIN LEGISLATION/   GKAUFET58014

  THE MIGRANT LABOR PROBLEM IN WISCONSIN.   GRAUSEX62218

  REPORTS ON APPRENTICESHIP, NINE STATE ADVISORY COMMITTEES. /CALIFORNIA FLORIDA MARYLAND CONNECTICUT
  WASHINGTON-DC NEW-JERSEY NEW-YORK TENNESSEE WISCONSIN/   GUSCOMC64407

  MILWAUKEE. A FAIR DEAL. /WISCONSIN EEO/   GWINTEL66569

  FINAL REPORT, PATTERNS OF DISCRIMINATION STUDY -- WISCONSIN.   GWISCIC66587

  THE NEGRO IN MILWAUKEE, PROGRESS AND PORTENT, 1863-1963. /WISCONSIN/   NMILWCC63792

  EMPLOYMENT AS IT RELATES TO NEGROES IN THE MILWAUKEE INDUSTRIAL AREA. /WISCONSIN/   NMILWUL48793

  NEGRO FAMILIES IN RURAL WISCONSIN. A STUDY OF THEIR COMMUNITY LIFE.   NWISCGC59331

  WOMEN AND HIGHER EDUCATION WITH SPECIAL REFERENCE TO THE UNIVERSITY OF WISCONSIN.   WFREDEB62768

  WISCONSIN FAIR-EMPLOYMENT-PRACTICES DIVISION INQUIRY INTO THE CONFLICTS BETWEEN STATE PROTECTIVE LABOR
  LEGISLATION AND STATE AND FEDERAL LAWS PROHIBITING DISCRIMINATION BASED ON SEX. /EMPLOYMENT-CONDITIONS/   WUAWXWD65165

  WISCONSIN GOVERNOR-S CONFERENCE ON THE CHANGING STATUS OF WOMEN, JAN 31-FEB 1 1964.   WUSDLAB65232

  WISCONSIN WOMEN. REPORT OF THE WISCONSIN GOVERNOR-S COMMISSION ON THE STATUS OF WOMEN.   WWISXGC65272

  WISCONSIN WOMEN. REPORT OF THE WISCONSIN GOVERNOR-S COMMISSION ON THE STATUS OF WOMEN.   WWISXGC65272

WITCHCRAFT
   SOCIAL MOBILITY AND IMPUTATICNS OF WITCHCRAFT IN A MEXICAN-AMERICAN NEIGHBORHOOD OF TEXAS.   MRUBEAJ66467

WITHDRAWAL
   RETENTION AND WITHDRAWAL OF COLLEGE STUDENTS. /DROP-OUT/   WIFFERE57854

WIVES
   WORKING WIVES.   WLINDFX63108

   FRESHMEN INTERVIEW WORKING WIVES.   WMAYXEE59964

   WORKING WIVES. AN ECONOMETRIC STUDY.   WROSERX58089

   FAMILY CHARACTERISTICS OF WORKING WIVES.   WUSBURC59169

WOMAN
   THE NEGRO WOMAN AT WORK. ADDRESS TO CONFERENCE ON THE NEGRO WOMAN IN THE USA.   CKEYSMD65646

   THE NEGRO WOMAN AT WORK. ADDRESS TO CONFERENCE ON THE NEGRO WOMAN IN THE USA.   CKEYSMD65646

   THE NEGRO COLLEGE WOMAN.   CNOBLJL54924

   THE NEGRO WOMAN COLLEGE GRADUATE.   CNOBLJL55925

   THE AMERICAN NEGRO WOMAN.   CNOBLJL66923

   CHANGE AND CHOICE FOR THE COLLEGE WOMAN. /WORK-WOMAN-ROLE/   WAAUWJX62601

   A STUDY OF ELEMENTARY SCHOCL TEACHER-S ATTITUDES TOWARD THE WOMAN PRINCIPAL AND TOWARD ELEMENTARY
   PRINCIPALSHIP AS A CAREER. /DISCRIMINATION/   WBARTAK58629

   THE PROSPECT FOR ADVANCEMENT IN BUSINESS OF THE MARRIED WOMAN COLLEGE GRADUATE. /OCCUPATIONS/   WBECKEL64632

   THE COMMITMENT REQUIRED OF A WOMAN ENTERING A SCIENTIFIC PROFESSION. /OCCUPATIONS/   WBETTBX65645

   THE PRESENT SITUATION OF WOMAN SCIENTISTS ANC ENGINEERS IN INDUSTRY AND GOVERNMENT. /OCCUPATIONS/   WBOLTRH65650

   TESTIMONY, PUBLIC HEARING, WOMAN IN PUBLIC AND PRIVATE EMPLOYMENT, CALIFORNIA. /DISCRIMINATION/   WBROWAX66657

   PANEL DISCUSSION. THE COMMITTMENT REQUIRED OF A WOMAN ENTERING A SCIENTIFIC PROFESSION. /OCCUPATIONS/   WBUNTMI65663

   WOMAN WORKERS IN CALIFORNIA, 1949-SEPTEMBER 1966.   WCALDIR67269

   WOMAN AS POTENTIAL SCIENTISTS. /OCCUPATIONS/   WCROSKP63710

   RECRUITMENT OF THE MATURE WOMAN.   WCULPPX61382

   THE WOMAN EXECUTIVE. /OCCUPATIONS/   WCUSSMX58712

   THE WOMAN IN AMERICA. /WORK-WOMEN-ROLE/   WDAEOXX64714

   WHAT BRINGS AND HOLDS WOMAN SCIENCE MAJORS. /OCCUPATIONS/   WDEMEAL63728

   COUNSELING THE MATURE WOMAN.   WDOLAEF66733

   TESTIMONY, PUBLIC HEARING, WOMAN IN PUBLIC AND PRIVATE EMPLOYMENT, CALIFORNIA. /DISCRIMINATION/   WDORAMX66739

   WHAT EVERY ABLE WOMAN SHOULD KNOW. /WORK-PATTERN ASPIRATIONS/   WDREWEM61743

   ACADEMIC WOMAN. /OCCUPATIONS/   WECKERE59746

   PROGRESS OF THE COMMISSION ON THE STATUS OF WOMAN. /WORK-WOMAN-ROLE/   WELLIKX63748

   FACTORS ASSOCIATED WITH GRADUATE SCHOOL ATTENDANCE AND ROLE DEFINITION OF THE WOMAN DOCTORAL CANDIDATES
   AT THE PENNSYLVANIA STATE UNIVERSITY. /OCCUPATIONS/   WFIELJC61763

   THE ROLE OF THE EDUCATED WOMAN. AN EMPIRICAL STUDY OF THE ATTITUDES OF A GROUP OF COLLEGE WOMEN.
   /WORK-WOMAN-ROLE/   WFREEMB65770

   A PLEA FOR THE UNCOMMON WOMAN. /WOMAN-WORK-ROLE/   WGETTRG57778

   THE WORKING WOMAN. BARRIERS IN EMPLOYMENT. /DISCRIMINATION/   WHARREX64827

   THE MIDDLE AGED WOMAN AND THE LABOR-MARKET.   WJEWIVA62881

   IN QUEST OF WIDER HORIZONS. THE WOMAN AFTER FORTY THINKS ABOUT A JOB. /ASPIRATIONS/   WJEWIVA62882

   THE CHANGING STATUS OF THE SOUTHERN WOMAN. /WORK-WOMAN-ROLE/   WJOHNGG65884

   THE ROLE OF THE EDUCATED WOMAN. /WORK-WOMAN-ROLE/   WJONECX64009

   VOCATIONAL TRAINING OF THE OLDER WOMAN.   WKINGCR66906

   THE SELF-SUPPORTING WOMAN IN OREGON.   WKNILNG60034

   THE IDENTITY OF MODERN WOMAN. /WORK-WOMAN-ROLE/   WKRECHS65381

   THE WOMAN IN AMERICA. /WORK-WOMEN-ROLE/   WLIFTRJ65935

   WOMAN AT WORK -- A STUDY IN PREJUDICE. /DISCRIMINATION/   WMARMJX66954

   ROLES OF THE MARRIED WOMAN IN SCIENCE. /OCCUPATIONS/   WMOTZAB61002

   REPORT ON UNDERGRADUATE COUNSELING AND CONTINUING EDUCATION AND GUIDANCE FOR MATURE WOMAN.   WNICOHG64032

   WHAT THE INDUSTRIAL PSYCHOLOGIST MUST KNOW ABOUT TODAY-S AND TOMORROW-S WOMAN.   WPERLEX63100

   NEEDS AND OPPORTUNITIES IN OUR SOCIETY FOR THE EDUCATED WOMAN.   WPETEEX63054

   A GOOD WOMAN IS HARD TO FIND. /WORK-FAMILY-CONFLICT/   WROSSAS64093

   THE CHANGING WOMAN WORKER. A STUDY OF THE FEMALE LABOR-FORCE IN NEW-JERSEY AND IN THE NATION FROM 1940 TO
   1958.   WSMITGW60120

   A NEW LIFE PATTERN FOR THE COLLEGE-EDUCATED WOMAN. /WORK-FAMILY-CONFLICT/   WSTEIER65133

   TODAY-S BUSINESS WOMAN. HER CHARACTERISTICS, HER NEED FOR FURTHER EDUCATION, HER FUTURE IN MANAGEMENT.
   /OCCUPATIONS/   WTHOMMH63152

WOMAN   (CONTINUATION)
    ONE WOMAN. TWO LIVES. /WORK-FAMILY-CONFLICT/   WTIMEXX61155

    UNIVERSITY PROGRAMS OF CONTINUING EDUCATION FOR THE ADULT WOMAN.   WTINKAH64156

    A LOOK AT THE OTHER WOMAN. /RACE DISCRIMINATION/   WWALDSX65017

    THE NEXT STEP -- A GUIDE TO PART-TIME OPPORTUNITIES IN GREATER BOSTON FOR THE EDUCATED WOMAN.
    /MASSACHUSETTS/   WWHITMS64266

    THE AMERICAN WOMAN AT MIDCENTURY. /WORK-WOMAN-ROLE/   WYOUNLM61279

WOMAN-S
    INITIATION INTO A WOMAN-S PROFESSION. IDENTITY PROBLEMS IN THE STATUS TRANSITION OF CO-ED TO STUDENT
    NURSE.   WDAVIFX66723

    EDUCATION AND A WOMAN-S LIFE. /WORK-WOMAN-ROLE/   WDENNLE63729

    COUNSELING IMPLICATIONS OF WOMAN-S CHANGING ROLE.   WGASSGZ59775

    A WOMAN-S PLACE. /WORK-WOMAN-ROLE/   WGRUMDX61379

    WOMAN-S ROLES. HOW GIRLS SEE THEM. /WORK-WOMAN-ROLE/   WHARTRE62830

    A WOMAN-S WORLD. /WORK-WOMAN-ROLE/   WINDUBX63857

    THE AMERICAN WOMAN-S ROLE. /WORK-WOMAN-ROLE/   WKIUCFX62909

    WOMAN-S CENTURY OF PROGRESS. IS IT TO END IN REGRESSION. /WORK-WOMAN-ROLE/   WMCKARC58946

    EDUCATION AND A WOMAN-S LIFE.   WMONSKJ63987

    WOMAN-S DESTINY -- CHOICE OR CHANCE. REPORT OF CONFERENCE AT THE UNIVERSITY OF WASHINGTON, NOVEMBER
    21-22. 1963.   WUSDLAB65233

    A WOMAN-S GUIDE TO EARNING A GOOD LIVING.   WWINTEX61270

WOMAN-WORK-ROLE
    A PLEA FOR THE UNCOMMON WOMAN. /WOMAN-WORK-ROLE/   WGETTRG57778

    THE AMERICAN COLLEGE. /WOMAN-WORK-ROLE/   WSANFNX62101

WOMANHOOD
    COUNSELING TODAY-S GIRLS FOR TOMORROW-S WOMANHOOD.   WWESTEM65210

WOMANPOWER
    OPTIMAL UTILIZATION OF MEDICAL WOMANPOWER. /OCCUPATIONS/   WBAUMLX66630

    A HUGE WASTE. EDUCATED WOMANPOWER.   WBUNTMI61900

    CALIFORNIA WOMANPOWER.   WCALDIR66267

    PATTERNS IN WOMANPOWER. A PILOT STUDY.   WHANSEB62820

    TALENT SEARCH FOR WOMANPOWER.   WHARREX65826

    WOMANPOWER NEEDED.   WKEYSMD66901

    WOMANPOWER -- KEY TO MANAGEMENT MANPOWER SHORTAGE.   WLLOYBJ62633

    AND ANGELS WALK WHERE ONLY MALES TREAD. THE EMERGENCE OF WOMANPOWER. /MANPOWER/   WMATHJP66959

    WOMANPOWER.   WNATLMC57020

    PROFESSIONAL WOMANPOWER AS A NATIONAL RESOURCE.   WPARRJB61051

    CURIOUS QUEST FOR WOMANPOWER.   WREEVNX63078

    WHAT ABOUT WOMANPOWER IN THE SPACE AGE.   WSTEIER62134

    SHORTAGE OR SURPLUS. AN ASSESSMENT OF BOSTON WOMANPOWER IN INDUSTRY, GOVERNMENT, AND RESEARCH. JUNE 7-8,
    1963. /MASSACHUSETTS/   WUSDLAB66217

    WOMANPOWER -- WANTON WASTE OR WISHFUL THINKING.   WWESTEM62265

WOMEN
    TESTIMONY. PUBLIC HEARING. WOMEN IN PUBLIC AND PRIVATE EMPLOYMENT. CALIFORNIA. /MEXICAN-AMERICAN/   CARYWSX66621

    CHARACTERISTICS OF RETRAINING APPLICANTS. /CALIFORNIA NEGRO MEXICAN-AMERICAN WOMEN/   CCALDEM66166

    ANNUAL FARM LABOR REPORT. 1965. CALIFORNIA DEPARTMENT OF EMPLOYMENT. FARM LABOR SERVICE. /NEGRO
    MEXICAN-AMERICAN WOMEN/   CCALDEM66906

    INTEGRATION IN PROFESSIONAL NURSING. /OCCUPATIONS NEGRO WOMEN/   CCARNME62183

    WOMEN AT WORK. /NEGRO/   CDECTMX61376

    THE EVALUATION OF WORK BY FEMALES. 1940-1950. /WOMEN NEGRO/   CDORNSM56284

    THE VALUES OF NEGRO WOMEN COLLEGE STUDENTS.   CEAGLOW45313

    OPPORTUNITIES IN NURSING FOR DISADVANTAGED YOUTH. /WOMEN NEGRO OCCUPATIONS/   CFRAKFX66375

    THE EMPLOYMENT OF NEGRO WOMEN AS DOMESTIC-SERVANTS IN NEW-ORLEANS. /LOUISIANA/   CGILMHX44403

    THE NATION-S CHILDREN. VOL I. THE FAMILY AND SOCIAL-CHANGE. VOL II. DEVELOPMENT AND EDUCATION. VOL III.
    PROBLEMS AND PROSPECTS. /NEGRO PUERTO-RICAN MEXICAN-AMERICAN WOMEN/   CGINZEX60720

    NEGRO NURSES IN HOSPITALS. /WOMEN NEGRO/   CGOLDXX60374

    A NOTE ON THE VALUES OF SOUTHERN COLLEGE WOMEN, WHITE AND NEGRO.   CGRAYSW47445

    ECONOMIC GROWTH AND EMPLOYMENT OPPORTUNITIES FOR MINORITIES. /NEGRO WOMEN/   CHIESDL64775

    WOMEN WHO WORK. /NEGRO/   CHUTCGX52589

    REGISTRIES AND INTERGROUP RELATIONS. /NEGRO WOMEN DISCRIMINATION/   CKASUMX59013

    SENIORITY AND POSTWAR JOBS. RUBBER INDUSTRY. /NEGRO WOMEN/   CLABORR44028

NEGRO WOMEN IN THE CLOTHING, CIGAR AND LAUNDRY INDUSTRIES OF PHILADELPHIA, 1960.   CPORTRP43103

SECRETARIAL TRAINING WITH SPEECH IMPROVEMENT. AN EXPERIMENTAL AND DEMONSTRATION PROJECT. /NEGRO WOMEN/   CSAINMD66320

AN EXPERIMENT IN MANPOWER DEVELOPMENT. /TRAINING MISSISSIPPI NEGRO WOMEN/   CSELFHO66325

SEX DIFFERENCES IN OCCUPATIONAL CHOICE PATTERNS AMONG ADOLESCENTS. /ASPIRATIONS WOMEN NEGRO/   CSPREJX62999

NO TIME FOR PREJUDICE. /WOMEN NEGRO OCCUPATIONS/   CSTAUMK61132

THE NON-WHITE FEMALE IN THE LABOR-FORCE. /WOMEN NEGRO/   CTURNRH51214

NEGRO POPULATION. MARCH 1964. /WOMEN DEMOGRAPHY/   CUSBURC64376

NEGRO POPULATION. MARCH 1965. /WOMEN DEMOGRAPHY/   CUSBURC65377

OPPORTUNITIES FOR NEGRO WOMEN AS DIETICIANS. /OCCUPATIONS/   CUSDLAB43837

NEGRO WOMEN AND THEIR JOBS.   CUSDLAB54262

THE CHANGING STATUS OF NEGRO WOMEN WORKERS.   CUSDLAB64072

NEGRO WOMEN WORKERS IN 1960.   CUSDLAB64264

CURRENT DATA ON NONWHITE WOMEN WORKERS. /NEGRO/   CUSDLAB65261

NEGRO WOMEN IN THE POPULATION AND IN THE LABOR-FORCE.   CUSDLAB66263

UNWANTED WORKERS. PERMANENT LAYOFFS AND LONG-TERM UNEMPLOYMENT. /NEGRO WOMEN/   CWILCRC63322

NEGRO ADC MOTHERS LOOK FOR WORK. /WOMEN/   CWILLJJ58324

THE NEGRO GIRL AND POVERTY. /WOMEN/   CYOUNMB65636

THE ROLE OF WOMEN IN A CHANGING NAVAHO SOCIETY.   IHAMALS57985

MENOMINEE WOMEN AND CULTURE CHANGE.   ISPINLS62622

THE NEGRO MATRIARCHY. /WOMEN ECONOMIC-STATUS/   NBATTMX65313

EMPLOYMENT PATTERNS OF NEGRO MEN AND WOMEN.   NGINZEX66416

THE ASSESSMENT OF ADJUSTMENT OF AGED NEGRO WOMEN IN A SOUTHERN CITY.   NHIMEJX62072

PROBLEMS OF WORKING WOMEN. SUMMARY REPORT OF A CONFERENCE.   WAFLCIO61618

LET-S PUT WOMEN IN THEIR PLACE. /INDUSTRY/   WALBEGS61602

WOMEN IN THE PROFESSIONAL WORLD. /OCCUPATIONS/   WALPEEJ62604

UNEMPLOYMENT OF MARRIED WOMEN.   WALTMSX63757

THE EDUCATION OF WOMEN -- INFORMATION AND RESEARCH NOTES.   WAMERCEND605

MEDICINE AS A CAREER FOR WOMEN. /OCCUPATIONS/   WAMERMW65607

OCCUPATIONS FOR MEN AND WOMEN AFTER 45.   WANGEJL63615

THE ROLE OUTLOOK OF EDUCATED WOMEN. /ASPIRATIONS/   WANGRSS64484

REPORT OF ARROWHEAD REGIONAL CONFERENCE ON THE STATUS OF WOMEN IN NORTHERN MINNESOTA.   WARRORC66216

AN INVERTED FACTOR ANALYSIS OF PERSONALITY DIFFERENCES BETWEEN CAREER AND HOMEMAKING-ORIENTED WOMEN.
/ASPIRATIONS/   WAVILDL64316

NOTES ON THE ROLE OF CHOICE IN THE PSYCHOLOGY OF PROFESSIONAL WOMEN. /OCCUPATIONS/   WBAILLX64623

TESTIMONY, PUBLIC HEARING. WOMEN IN PUBLIC AND PRIVATE EMPLOYMENT, CALIFORNIA. /DISCRIMINATION EEOC/   WBALEHX66625

CAREERS FOR WOMEN IN SCIENCE. /OCCUPATIONS/   WBARBMS58627

THE ACHIEVEMENT MOTIVE IN WOMEN. A STUDY OF THE IMPLICATIONS FOR CAREER DEVELOPMENT.   WBARURX66453

TESTIMONY, PUBLIC HEARING. WOMEN IN PUBLIC AND PRIVATE EMPLOYMENT, CALIFORNIA. /EMPLOYMENT-CONDITIONS/   WBECHCX66631

STATEMENT, PUBLIC HEARING. WOMEN IN PUBLIC AND PRIVATE EMPLOYMENT, CALIFORNIA. /FEP
EMPLOYMENT-CONDITIONS DISCRIMINATION/   WBELAJX66634

STATEMENT, PUBLIC HEARING. WOMEN IN PUBLIC AND PRIVATE EMPLOYMENT, CALIFORNIA. /FEP
EMPLOYMENT-CONDITIONS DISCRIMINATION/   WBENNSJ66637

ACADEMIC WOMEN. /OCCUPATIONS/   WBERNJX64638

THE PRESENT SITUATION IN THE ACADEMIC WORLD OF WOMEN TRAINED IN ENGINEERING. /OCCUPATIONS/   WBERNJX65639

RESOURCES FOR THE EMPLOYMENT OF MATURE WOMEN AND/OR THEIR CONTINUING EDUCATION. A SELECTED BIBLIOGRAPHY
AND AIDS.   WBERNML66746

UNIVERSITY OF KANSAS-CITY PROJECT FOR CONTINUING EDUCATION OF WOMEN.   WBERRJX63640

CONTINUING EDUCATION OF WOMEN. NEEDS, ASPIRATIONS, AND PLANS.   WBERRJX63641

COUNSELING GIRLS AND WOMEN. AWARENESS. ANALYSIS. ACTION.   WBERRJX66642

ATTITUDES TOWARD WOMEN COLLEGE TEACHERS IN INSTITUTIONS OF HIGHER EDUCATION ACCREDITED BY THE NORTH
CENTRAL ASSOCIATION.   WBERWHD62475

WOMEN. EMANCIPATION IS STILL TO COME. /WORK-FAMILY-CONFLICT/   WBETTBX64646

THE COLLEGE AND THE CONTINUING EDUCATION OF WOMEN.   WBLACGW63648

TESTIMONY, PUBLIC HEARING. WOMEN IN PUBLIC AND PRIVATE EDUCATION, CALIFORNIA. /FEP
EMPLOYMENT-CONDITIONS DISCRIMINATION MIGRANT-WORKERS/   WBLOCHX66649

LONG-RANGE CAUSES AND CONSEQUENCES OF THE EMPLOYMENT OF MARRIED WOMEN.   WBLOORO65884

ASCENT OF WOMEN. /WORK-WOMEN-ROLE/   WBORGEM63651

ARE WOMEN EXECUTIVES PEOPLE. /OCCUPATIONS/   WBOWMGW65653

THE RELATIONSHIP OF PARENTAL IDENTIFICATION TO SEX ROLE ACCEPTANCE IN MARRIED, SINGLE, CAREER AND
NON-CAREER WOMEN. /WORK-WOMEN-ROLE/   WBREYCH64654

VALUE CHANGE IN COLLEGE WOMEN. /WORK-WOMEN-ROLE/   WBROWDR62658

WHITE-COLLAR WOMEN. THE SECRETARIAL-STENOGRAPHIC OCCUPATION.   WBRYACD57659

OUR GREATEST WASTE OF TALENT IS WOMEN. /WORK-WOMEN-ROLE/   WBUNTMI61662

CONTINUING EDUCATION FOR WOMEN.   WBUNTMI61664

ON THE JOB, WOMEN ACT MUCH LIKE MEN. /OCCUPATIONS/   WBUSIWX63667

WOMEN AS GOVERNMENT EMPLOYEES. /OCCUPATIONS/   WBUSIWX63669

THE LABOR-FORCE PARTICIPATION OF MARRIED WOMEN.   WCAINGG64671

MARRIED WOMEN IN THE LABOR-FORCE -- AN ECONOMIC ANALYSIS.   WCAINGG66672

REPORT OF THE CALIFORNIA ADVISORY COMMISSION ON THE STATUS OF WOMEN. /FEP EMPLOYMENT-CONDITIONS
 DISCRIMINATION MIGRANTS/   WCALACW67673

EARNINGS AND HOURS OF WOMEN AGRICULTURAL WORKERS.   WCALDIR64268

WOMEN WORKERS IN CALIFORNIA. JANUARY 1949-AUGUST 1964.   WCALIDL64678

AMERICAN WOMEN. THE CHANGING IMAGE. /WORK-WOMEN-ROLE/   WCASSBB62682

THE STATUS OF WOMEN IN THE PROFESSIONS RELATIVE TO THE STATUS OF MEN. /OCCUPATIONS/   WCAVARS57684

TESTIMONY, PUBLIC HEARING, WOMEN IN PUBLIC AND PRIVATE EMPLOYMENT, CALIFORNIA. /EMPLOYMENT-CONDITIONS/   WCHANHD66687

THE CHANGING STATUS OF WOMEN.   WCHICRC62689

POST GRADUATION ROLE PREFERENCE OF SENIOR WOMEN IN COLLEGE. /ASPIRATION/   WCHRIHX56690

TESTIMONY, PUBLIC HEARING, WOMEN IN PUBLIC AND PRIVATE EMPLOYMENT, CALIFORNIA. /FEP
 EMPLOYMENT-CONDITIONS DISCRIMINATION MIGRANTS/   WCLIFFG66692

MODERN AMERICAN CAREER WOMEN. /OCCUPATIONS/   WCLYMEX59693

TESTIMONY, PUBLIC HEARING, WOMEN IN PUBLIC AND PRIVATE EMPLOYMENT, CALIFORNIA. /DISCRIMINATION/   WCOLLNX66696

REPORT ON THE FIRST CONFERENCE ON THE STATUS OF WOMEN. /WORK-WOMEN-ROLE/   WCOLUMX64699

REPORT ON THE MISSOURI COMMISSION ON THE STATUS OF WOMEN. /WORK-WOMEN-ROLE/   WCOLUMX64700

EQUAL PAY FOR WOMEN. /DISCRIMINATION/   WCOMMXX63701

TESTIMONY, PUBLIC HEARING, WOMEN IN PUBLIC AND PRIVATE EMPLOYMENT, CALIFORNIA. /EMPLOYMENT-CONDITIONS/   WCOMPBX66702

A STUDY OF JOB MOTIVATIONS, ACTIVITIES, AND SATISFACTIONS OF PRESENT AND PROSPECTIVE WOMEN COLLEGE
FACULTY MEMBERS. /OCCUPATIONS/   WCOOKWX60252

ON EDUCATING WOMEN HIGHLY. /WORK-WOMEN-ROLE/   WCORMML67706

FOCUS ON THE FUTURE FOR WOMEN. /WORK-WOMEN-ROLE/   WCRONDH56709

TESTIMONY, PUBLIC HEARING, WOMEN IN PUBLIC AND PRIVATE EMPLOYMENT, CALIFORNIA. /TRAINING/   WCUMMGX66711

WHAT ABOUT WOMEN. /WORK-WOMEN-ROLE/   WCUTLJH61713

WORK, WOMEN, AND CHILDREN. /WORK-FAMILY-CONFLICT/   WDAVIHX60715

THE POST-PARENTAL PHASE IN THE LIFE CYCLE OF 50 COLLEGE EDUCATED WOMEN. /WORK-FAMILY-CONFLICT/   WDAVIIX60717

EDUCATION OF WOMEN -- SIGNS FOR THE FUTURE.   WDAVIOD57044

THE EDUCATION OF WOMEN -- SIGNS FOR THE FUTURE.   WDAVIOD59937

AGE OF COMPLETION OF CHILDBEARING AND ITS RELATION TO THE PARTICIPATION OF WOMEN IN THE LABOR-FORCE.
UNITED STATES 1910-1955.   WDAYXLH57725

STATUS IMPLICATIONS OF THE EMPLOYMENT OF MARRIED WOMEN IN THE UNITED STATES.   WDAYXLH61726

REVOLUTION WITHOUT IDEOLOGY. THE CHANGING PLACE OF WOMEN IN AMERICA. /WORK-WOMEN-ROLE/   WDEGLCN64727

TESTIMONY, PUBLIC HEARING, WOMEN IN PUBLIC AND PRIVATE EMPLOYMENT, CALIFORNIA. /EMPLOYMENT-CONDITIONS/   WDIBRJX66732

EDUCATED WOMEN -- A MIDCENTURY EVALUATION. /WORK-WOMAN-ROLE/   WDOLAEF56734

REPORT OF THE EXPLORATORY STATISTICAL SURVEY OF THE EDUCATIONAL-ATTAINMENT, NUMBER, AND AVAILABILITY OF
THE MEMBERSHIP OF THE AMERICAN ASSOCIATION OF UNIVERSITY WOMEN FOR TEACHING IN THE FIELDS OF SCIENCE AND
MATHEMATICS. /OCCUPATIONS/   WDOLAEF57735

ANTI-NEPOTISM RULES IN AMERICAN COLLEGES AND UNIVERSITIES -- THEIR EFFECT ON THE FACULTY EMPLOYMENT OF
WOMEN.   WDOLAEF60951

HIGHER EDUCATION FOR WOMEN. TIME FOR REAPPRAISAL.   WDOLAEF63952

ADDRESS TO CONFERENCE ON EDUCATION AND JOB OPPORTUNITIES FOR WOMEN RETURNING TO THE LABOR-MARKET.   WDOUTAX62741

SURVEY OF WOMEN PHYSICIANS GRADUATING FROM MEDICAL SCHOOL, 1925-1940. /OCCUPATIONS/   WDYKMRA57745

WHAT-S THE USE OF EDUCATING WOMEN. /WORK-WOMAN-ROLE/   WEDDYED63747

ACADEMIC WOMEN. /OCCUPATIONS/   WELLMMX65749

ROLE EXPECTATIONS OF YOUNG WOMEN REGARDING MARRIAGE AND A CAREER. /ASPIRATIONS WORK-FAMILY-CONFLICT/   WEMPELT58751

WOMEN EMPLOYEES IN MANUFACTURING BY INDUSTRY, JANUARY, 1959.   WEMPLAE59752

TESTIMONY, PUBLIC HEARING, WOMEN IN PUBLIC AND PRIVATE EMPLOYMENT, CALIFORNIA. /EMPLOYMENT-CONDITIONS/   WEVANSX66753

THE POTENTIAL OF WOMEN. /WORK-WOMAN-ROLE/   WFARBSM63756

THE CHALLENGE TO WOMEN. /WORK-WOMAN-ROLE/   WFARBSM66755

THE STATUS OF WOMEN IN PROFESSIONAL SOCIOLOGY. /OCCUPATIONS/   WFAVASF60757

WOMEN PHYSICIANS IN THE TWENTY-FIRST CENTURY. /OCCUPATIONS/   WFAYXMX66758

TESTIMONY, PUBLIC HEARING, WOMEN IN PUBLIC AND PRIVATE EMPLOYMENT, CALIFORNIA. /EMPLOYMENT-CONDITIONS/   WFEINBX66760

WOMEN IN THE MODERN WORLD. /WORK-WOMAN-ROLE/   WFIRKEX63764

FANTASY, FACT AND THE FUTURE...A REVIEW OF THE STATUS OF WOMEN AND POSSIBLE IMPLICATIONS FOR WOMEN-S
EDUCATION AND ROLE IN THE NEXT DECADE.   WFITZLE63963

EMPLOYMENT PROBLEMS OF WORKING WOMEN.   WFLAGJJ63130

TESTIMONY, PUBLIC HEARING, WOMEN IN PUBLIC AND PRIVATE EMPLOYMENT, CALIFORNIA. /DISCRIMINATION/   WFOOTJX66765

MARRIED WOMEN AT UTAH STATE UNIVERSITY, SPRING QUARTER, 1960. /TRAINING/   WFREDCX61769

WOMEN AND HIGHER EDUCATION WITH SPECIAL REFERENCE TO THE UNIVERSITY OF WISCONSIN.   WFREDEB62768

THE ROLE OF THE EDUCATED WOMAN. AN EMPIRICAL STUDY OF THE ATTITUDES OF A GROUP OF COLLEGE WOMEN.
/WORK-WOMAN-ROLE/   WFREEMB65770

TESTIMONY, PUBLIC HEARING, WOMEN IN PUBLIC AND PRIVATE EMPLOYMENT, CALIFORNIA. /EMPLOYMENT-CONDITIONS/   WGABELX66773

TABLES OF WORKING LIFE FOR WOMEN, 1950.   WGARFSH57180

TESTIMONY, PUBLIC HEARING, WOMEN IN PUBLIC AND PRIVATE EMPLOYMENT, CALIFORNIA. /DISCRIMINATION/   WGEIGPX66776

SOME INTELLECTUAL ATTRIBUTES AND EDUCATIONAL INTERESTS OF UNIVERSITY WOMEN IN VARIOUS MAJORS.
/ASPIRATIONS/   WGENTLX60790

TESTIMONY, PUBLIC HEARING, WOMEN IN PUBLIC AND PRIVATE EMPLOYMENT, CALIFORNIA. /DEMOGRAPHY/   WGERSMX66777

WOMEN IN INDUSTRY. /OCCUPATIONS/   WGILBLM62782

TESTIMONY, PUBLIC HEARING, WOMEN IN PUBLIC AND PRIVATE EMPLOYMENT, CALIFORNIA. /EMPLOYMENT-CONDITIONS/   WGILBRX66780

WOMEN IN BANKING. /OCCUPATIONS/   WGILDGN59783

NOTES ON WOMEN IN INDUSTRY -- PRESENTED AT AMERICAN PSYCHOLOGICAL SYMPOSIUM, SEPT 1963. /DISCRIMINATION/   WGILMBV63970

LIFE STYLES OF EDUCATED WOMEN. /WORK-FAMILY-CONFLICT/   WGINZEX66785

WOMEN IN EXECUTIVE POSTS. /OCCUPATIONS/   WGIVEJN60787

TESTIMONY, PUBLIC HEARING, WOMEN IN PUBLIC AND PRIVATE EMPLOYMENT, CALIFORNIA. /EMPLOYMENT-CONDITIONS/   WGLENEM66788

ATTITUDES OF WOMEN REGARDING GAINFUL EMPLOYMENT OF MARRIED WOMEN. /ASPIRATIONS/   WGLENHM59789

ATTITUDES OF WOMEN REGARDING GAINFUL EMPLOYMENT OF MARRIED WOMEN. /ASPIRATIONS/   WGLENHM59789

PRACTITIONERS AND NON-PRACTITIONERS IN A GROUP OF WOMEN PHYSICIANS. /ASPIRATIONS/   WGLICRX65791

A TURNING TO TAKE NEXT -- ALTERNATIVE GOALS IN THE EDUCATION OF WOMEN. /WORK-WOMAN-ROLE/   WGOLDFH65792

PROGRESS AND PROSPECTS. THE REPORT OF THE SECOND NATIONAL CONFERENCE OF GOVERNORS COMMISSIONS ON THE
STATUS OF WOMEN. /EMPLOYMENT-CONDITIONS/   WGOVECS65798

SOME GUIDES FOR SUPERVISING WOMEN WORKERS.   WGRANLJ63800

DISCUSSION. WOMEN IN MEDICINE. /OCCUPATIONS/   WGRIFAM65803

WOMEN IN LEGAL WORK. /OCCUPATIONS/   WGRIFVE58804

POTENTIALITIES OF WOMEN IN THE MIDDLE YEARS. /WORK-FAMILY-CONFLICT/   WGROSIH56806

CAREERS FOR WOMEN IN RETAILING. /OCCUPATIONS/   WGROSSB59807

TESTIMONY, PUBLIC HEARING, WOMEN IN PUBLIC AND PRIVATE EMPLOYMENT, CALIFORNIA. /DISCRIMINATION
WORK-FAMILY-CONFLICT/   WGUPTRC66808

TESTIMONY, PUBLIC HEARING, WOMEN IN PUBLIC AND PRIVATE EMPLOYMENT, CALIFORNIA. /EMPLOYMENT-CONDITIONS/   WGUPTRC66809

THE EFFECT OF THE SOCIAL CONTEXT IN THE VOCATIONAL COUNSELING OF COLLEGE WOMEN.   WGURIMG63810

A FUNCTIONAL APPROACH TO THE GAINFUL EMPLOYMENT OF MARRIED WOMEN.   WHACKHM61812

THE COMPARATIVE ACADEMIC ACHIEVEMENT OF WOMEN FORTY YEARS OF AGE AND OVER AND WOMEN EIGHTEEN TO TWENTY
FIVE.   WHALFIT61814

THE COMPARATIVE ACADEMIC ACHIEVEMENT OF WOMEN FORTY YEARS OF AGE AND OVER AND WOMEN EIGHTEEN TO TWENTY
FIVE.   WHALFIT61814

WOMEN AS BOSSES. /OCCUPATIONS/   WHAMMKX56817

PANEL DISCUSSION. THE CASE FOR AND AGAINST THE EMPLOYMENT OF WOMEN. /OCCUPATIONS/   WHARRTW65824

TESTIMONY, PUBLIC HEARING, WOMEN IN PUBLIC AND PRIVATE EMPLOYMENT, CALIFORNIA. /EMPLOYMENT-CONDITIONS/   WHEALWX66836

COUNSELING OF GIRLS AND MATURE WOMEN.   WHEDGJN64994

STUDENTS TODAY -- MEN AND WOMEN OF TOMORROW. /MANPOWER/   WHEISPX61841

A COMMENTARY ON THE MOTIVATION AND EDUCATION OF COLLEGE WOMEN. /ASPIRATIONS/   WHEISPX62837

THE MOTIVATION OF COLLEGE WOMEN TODAY. A CLOSER LOOK. /ASPIRATIONS/   WHEISPX62839

THE MOTIVATION OF COLLEGE WOMEN TODAY. THE CULTURAL SETTING. /ASPIRATIONS/   WHEISPX63840

THE STATUS OF WOMEN. /DISCRIMINATION/   WHERZNK60377

WOMEN PART-TIME WORKERS IN THE U.S.   WHEWEAX62843

ATTITUDES OF COLLEGE STUDENTS TOWARD EMPLOYMENT AMONG MARRIED WOMEN. /WORK-FAMILY-CONFLICT/   WHEWEVH64482

GIFTED WOMEN IN THE TRADE UNIONS. /OCCUPATIONS/   WHILLBX62845

TESTIMCNY, PUBLIC HEARING, WOMEN IN PUBLIC AND PRIVATE EMPLOYMENT, CALIFORNIA. /DISCRIMINATION/   WHILLHX66844

INTEREST AND PERSONALITY CORRELATES OF CAREER-MOTIVATED AND HOMEMAKING-MOTIVATED COLLEGE WOMEN.
/ASPIRATIONS/   WHOYTDP58850

CLDER WOMEN IN THE LABOR-MARKET.   WHUNTEH62271

WOMEN WORKERS IN ILLINOIS.   WILLIBE64330

WOMEN IN THE WORK-FORCE.   WINDUBX65858

TESTIMCNY, PUBLIC HEARING, WOMEN IN PUBLIC AND PRIVATE EMPLOYMENT, CALIFORNIA. /MDTA EEO/   WINGRLX66859

WORKING WOMEN...WHO ARE THEY.   WINSTOL60873

STUDY OF JOB OPPORTUNITIES FOR WOMEN COLLEGE GRADUATES. /OCCUPATIONS/   WINTEAP58861

VOCATIONAL GUIDANCE AND TRAINING OF GIRLS AND WOMEN. /COUNSELING/   WINTELO64863

PART-TIME EMPLOYMENT FOR WOMEN WITH FAMILY RESPONSIBILITIES. /WORK-FAMILY-CONFLICT/   WINTELR57867

CHILD CARE FACILITIES FOR WOMEN WORKERS. /EMPLOYMENT-CONDITIONS/   WINTELR58864

WOMEN IN THE LABCR-FORCE.   WINTELR58869

OCCUPATIONAL TRAINING OF WOMEN IN THE UNITED STATES.   WINTELR64866

FIRST REPORT. IOWA GOVERNOR-S COMMISSION ON THE STATUS OF WOMEN. /EMPLOYMENT-CONDITIONS/   WIOWAGC64796

CONFERENCE ON EMPLOYMENT PROBLEMS OF WORKING WOMEN.   WIOWAGC64797

NEEDED. UNIQUE PATTERNS FOR EDUCATING WOMEN. /WORK-WOMEN-ROLE/   WIRISLD62874

PARTICIPATION IN PART-TIME WCRK BY WOMEN COLLEGE STUCENTS.   WISAALE57875

ABSENTEEISM AMONG WOMEN WORKERS IN INDUSTRY.   WISAMVX62876

TRENDS IN THE PARTICIPATION CF WOMEN IN THE WORKING-FORCE.   WJAFFAH56878

PSYCHOLOGICAL PRCBLEMS OF WOMEN IN DIFFERENT SOCIAL ROLES. /WORK-WOMAN-ROLE/   WJAHOMX55879

A MEMORANDUM ON THE MOTIVATICNS OF MIDDLE AGED WOMEN IN THE LOWER EDUCATIONAL BRACKETS TO RETURN TO WORK.
/ASPIRATIONS/   WJEWIVA61880

STATEMENT, PUBLIC HEARING, WOMEN IN PUBLIC AND PRIVATE EMPLOYMENT, CALIFORNIA. /EMPLOYMENT-CONDITIONS
MIGRANT-WORKERS/   WKAUFDX66886

WOMEN PROFESSORS AT BROWN. /OCCUPATIONS/   WKEENBC62887

TESTIMCNY, PUBLIC HEARING, WOMEN IN PUBLIC AND PRIVATE EMPLOYMENT, CALIFCRNIA. /EMPLOYMENT-CONDITIONS/   WKELLET66888

AMERICAN WOMEN WHO WORK.   WKENDBX65225

AN AMERICAN ANACHRONISM, THE IMAGE OF WOMEN AND WORK. /WORK-WOMAN-ROLE/   WKENNKX64891

STATEMENT, PUBLIC HEARING, WOMEN IN PUBLIC AND PRIVATE EMPLOYMENT, CALIFORNIA. /EMPLOYMENT-CONDITIONS/   WKENNVX66890

HIGH SCHOOL FRESHMAN AND SENIORS VIEW THE ROLE OF WOMEN IN MODERN SOCIETY. /WORK-FAMILY-CONFLICT/   WKERNKK65892

NEW HORIZONS FOR WOMEN. /WORK-WOMAN-ROLE/   WKEYSMD64898

NEW CPPORTUNITIES AND NEW RESPCNSIBILITIES FOR WOMEN. /WORK-WOMAN-ROLE/   WKEYSMD64899

WOMEN JOURNALISTS AND TODAY-S WORLD. /OCCUPATIONS/   WKEYSMD65021

ENHANCING THE ROLE OF WOMEN IN SCIENCE, ENGINEERING, AND THE SOCIAL SCIENCES. /OCCUPATIONS/   WKILLJR65903

CAREER OPPORTUNITIES FOR WOMEN IN BUSINESS. /OCCUPATIONS/   WKINGAG63904

INVESTIGATION OF DIFFERENCES IN OCCUPATIONAL PREFERENCES, STEREOTYPIC THINKING, AND PSYCHOLOGICAL NEEDS
AMONG UNDERGRADUATE WOMEN STUDENTS IN SELECTED CURRICULAR AREAS. /ASPIRATIONS/   WKITTRE60313

WOMEN WORKERS. WORKING HOURS AND SERVICES.   WKLEIVX65908

STATEMENT, PUBLIC HEARING, WOMEN IN PUBLIC AND PRIVATE EMPLOYMENT, CALIFORNIA. /EMPLOYMENT-CONDITIONS/   WKNIGTF66911

WOMEN AT WORK. /LABOR-FORCE/   WKRUGDH64918

WOMEN AT WORK.   WKRUGDH64997

WHY NOBODY WANTS WOMEN IN SCIENCE. /OCCUPATIONS/   WKUNDRB65919

ECONOMIC ROLE OF WOMEN 45-65. /WORK-WOMAN-RCLE/   WKYRKHX56921

SOURCES OF SATISFACTION IN THE LIVES OF WORKING WOMEN.   WLAURMW61923

CHANGES IN SELECTED PERSONALITY CHARACTERISTICS AND PERSISTENCE IN THE CAREER CHOICES OF WOMEN ASSOCIATED
WITH A FOUR YEAR COLLEGE EDUCATION AT ONE OF THE COLLEGES OF THE CITY UNIVERSITY OF NEW-YORK.
/ASPIRATIONS/   WLEINMX64925

LIFE INSURANCE SELLING AS A CAREER FOR WOMEN. /OCCUPATIONS/   WLEITSF61926

TODAY-S WOMEN COLLEGE GRADUATES. /WORK-WOMEN-ROLE/   WLEOPAK59927

WOMEN AND MODERN SCIENCE. /OCCUPATIONS/   WLEWIND57932

LIBERAL ARTS WOMEN GRADUATES, CLASS OF 1958. /WORK-WOMEN-ROLE/   WLICHMW59933

A CONFERENCE TO ENLIST THE PARTICIPATION OF 50 INSTITUTIONS OF HIGHER EDUCATION IN SPECIFIC R AND D
PROGRAMS TO PREPARE WOMEN FOR PRODUCTIVE EMPLOYMENT.   WLLOYBJ64937

WOMEN-S STATUS -- WOMEN TODAY AND THEIR EDUCATION.   WLLOYEX56941

TESTIMONY, PUBLIC HEARING, WOMEN IN PUBLIC AND PRIVATE EMPLOYMENT, CALIFORNIA. /FEP MIGRANT-WORKERS
EMPLOYMENT-CONDITIONS/   WLLOYMX66940

A SURVEY OF SPECIAL EDUCATIONAL PROGRAMS FOR ADULT WOMEN IN UNIVERSITY EXTENSION DIVISIONS AND EVENING

WOMEN   (CONTINUATION)
   COLLEGES AS OF SPRING 1965.   WLORIRK66942

      TESTIMCNY, PUBLIC HEARING, WOMEN IN PUBLIC AND PRIVATE EMPLOYMENT, CALIFORNIA. /FEP EMPLOYMENT
      CONDITIONS/   WLOWEDX66943

      TESTIMCNY, PUBLIC HEARING, WOMEN IN PUBLIC AND PRIVATE EMPLOYMENT, CALIFORNIA. /EMPLOYMENT-CONDITIONS/   WMACKJW66950

      NONTRADITIONALLY TRAINED WOMEN AS MENTAL HEALTH COUNSELORS/PSYCHOTHERAPISTS.   WMAGOTM66779

      FACTORS DETERMINING THE LABOR-FORCE PARTICIPATION OF MARRIED WOMEN.   WMAHOTA61951

      WOMEN AS EXECUTIVES AND MANAGERS. /OCCUPATIONS/   WMAHRAH65953

      WOMEN IN THE LABOR-FORCE.   WMARCMR60080

      WOMEN AND WORK.   WMARRAF61955

      WOMEN ARE TRAINING FOR BUSINESS. /OCCUPATIONS/   WMARSEM62956

      RUTGERS -- THE STATE UNIVERSITY, FORD FOUNDATION PROGRAM FOR THE RETRAINING IN MATHEMATICS OF COLLEGE
      GRADUATE WOMEN. /TRAINING/   WMARTHM63957

      WOMEN IN EDUCATION. /OCCUPATICNS/   WMASOVC62958

      MARRIAGE AND CAREER CONFLICTS IN GIRLS AND YOUNG WOMEN. /WORK-FAMILY-CONFLICT/   WMATTEX60961

      ATTITUDES TOWARD CAREER AND MARRIAGE AND THE DEVELOPMENT OF LIFE STYLES IN YOUNG WOMEN.
      /WORK-FAMILY-CONFLICT/   WMATTEX64962

      WOMEN AND THE SCIENTIFIC PROFESSIONS. THE MIT SYMPOSIUM ON AMERICAN WOMEN IN SCIENCE AND ENGINEERING.
      /OCCUPATIONS/   WMATTJA65963

      WOMEN AND THE SCIENTIFIC PROFESSIONS. THE MIT SYMPOSIUM ON AMERICAN WOMEN IN SCIENCE AND ENGINEERING.
      /OCCUPATIONS/   WMATTJA65963

      EXECUTIVE CAREERS FOR WOMEN. /OCCUPATIONS/   WMAULFX61065

      TESTIMCNY, PUBLIC HEARING, WOMEN IN PUBLIC AND PRIVATE EMPLOYMENT, CALIFCRNIA. /OCCUPATIONS
      EMPLCYMENT-CONDITIONS/   WMCLALX66947

      AMERICAN WOMEN /WORK-WJMEN-ROLE/   WMEADMX65966

      TESTIMCNY, PUBLIC HEARING, WOMEN IN PUBLIC AND PRIVATE EMPLOYMENT, CALIFORNIA. /BLUE-COLLAR
      EMPLOYMENT-CONDITIONS/   WMENGVX66969

      PART-TIME JOB OPPORTUNITIES FOR WOMEN.   WMEREJL60970

      PROFESSIONAL AND NON-PROFESSIONAL WOMEN AS MOTHERS.   WMERIFH55971

      PILOT PROJECTS FOR CONTINUING EDUCATION FOR WOMEN.   WMERRMH63972

      JOBS AND TRAINING FOR WOMEN TECHNICIANS. /TRAINING/   WMEYEMB61975

      CONFERENCE ON WOMEN IN THE UPPER PENINSULA ECONOMY. REPORT. /MICHIGAN/   WMICDLA64976

      STATEMENT, PUBLIC HEARING, WOMEN IN PUBLIC AND PRIVATE EMPLOYMENT, CALIFORNIA. /FEP
      EMPLOYMENT-CONDITIONS MIGRANT-WORKERS/   WMILLJJ66979

      TESTIMONY, PUBLIC HEARING, WOMEN IN PUBLIC AND PRIVATE EMPLOYMENT, CALIFORNIA. /EMPLOYMENT-CONDITIONS/   WMILLKL66980

      WOMEN IN UNIVERSITY TEACHING. /OCCUPATIONS/   WMILLMM61981

      EMERGING OPPORTUNITIES FOR QUALIFIED WOMEN. /OCCUPATIONS/   WMILLRX66982

      LABOR-FORCE PARTICIPATIJN OF MARRIED WOMEN. A STUDY OF LABOR SUPPLY.   WMINCJX62984

      INTEREST PROFILES OF UNIVERSITY WOMEN. /ASPIRATIONS/   WMITCED57986

      TESTIMCNY, PUBLIC HEARING, WOMEN IN PUBLIC AND PRIVATE EMPLOYMENT, CALIFORNIA. /EMPLOYMENT-CONDITIONS/   WMORAMX66995

      PERCEPTIONS OF ROLE CONFLICTS AND SELF CONFLICTS AMONG CAREER AND NON-CAREER COLLEGE EDUCATED WOMEN.
      /WORK-FAMILY-CONFLICT/   WMORGDD62996

      WOMEN GRADUATES OF COOPERATIVE WORK-STUDY PROGRAMS ON THE COLLEGE LEVEL. /SKILLS/   WMOSBWB57999

      TESTIMCNY, PUBLIC HEARING, WOMEN IN PUBLIC AND PRIVATE EMPLOYMENT, CALIFORNIA.   WMOTHWA66001

      WOMEN IN THE LABOR-MARKET.   WMUELEL66004

      NEW HORIZONS FOR COLLEGE WOMEN. /WORK-WOMEN-ROLE/   WMULLLC60005

      PSYCHOLOGICAL AND SOCIOLOGICAL FACTORS IN PREDICTICN OF CAREER PATTERNS OF WOMEN. /ASPIRATIONS/   WMULVMC61080

      PSYCHOLOGICAL AND SOCIOLOGICAL FACTORS IN PREDICTION OF CAREER PATTERNS FOR WOMEN. /ASPIRATIONS/   WMULVMC63006

      CAREERS FOR WOMEN IN BIOLOGICAL SCIENCES. /OCCUPATIONS/   WMURPMC60009

      TESTIMONY, PUBLIC HEARING, WOMEN IN PUBLIC AND PRIVATE EMPLOYMENT, CALIFORNIA. /EMPLOYMENT-CONDITIONS/   WMYRIRX66013

      WANTED. MORE WOMEN IN EDUCATIONAL LEADERSHIP. /OCCUPATIONS/   WNATLCO65016

      TEACHING. OPPORTUNITIES FOR WOMEN COLLEGE GRADUATES.   WNATLEA64019

      WORK IN THE LIVES OF MARRIED WOMEN.   WNATLMC57021

      WOMEN IN SCIENTIFIC CAREERS. /OCCUPATIONS/   WNATLSF61022

      WHEN WILL THE EDUCATIONAL NEEDS OF WOMEN BE MET. SOME QUESTIONS FOR THE COUNSELOR.   WNEUMRR63026

      A CENTURY OF HIGHER EDUCATION FOR AMERICAN WOMEN.   WNEWCMX59027

      WHAT EDUCATED WOMEN WANT. /ASPIRATIONS/   WNEWSXX66029

      NEW-YORK WOMEN. A REPORT AND RECOMMENDATIONS FROM THE NEW-YORK GOVERNOR-S COMMITTEE ON THE EDUCATION AND
      EMPLOYMENT OF WOMEN.   WNEWYGW64799

      NEW-YORK WOMEN. A REPORT AND RECOMMENDATIONS FROM THE NEW-YORK GOVERNOR-S COMMITTEE ON THE EDUCATION AND

451

WOMEN   (CONTINUATION)
  EMPLOYMENT OF WOMEN.   WNEWYGW64799

  ROLE OF WOMEN IN AMERICAN ECONOMIC LIFE.   WNORRLW56036

  CAREERS FOR WOMEN AFTER MARRIAGE AND CHILDREN. /WORK-FAMILY-CONFLICT/   WONEIBP65043

  TESTIMONY. PUBLIC HEARING, WOMEN IN PUBLIC AND PRIVATE EMPLOYMENT, CALIFORNIA. /EMPLOYMENT-CONDITIONS/   WPALMGX66047

  REALITIES. EDUCATIONAL, ECONOMIC, LEGAL AND PERSONAL NEEDS OF CAREER WOMEN.   WPARKRX66049

  TOP LEVEL TRAINING OF WOMEN IN THE UNITED STATES, 1900-60.   WPARRJB62283

  EMPLOYMENT OF WOMEN CHEMISTS IN INDUSTRIAL LABORATORIES. /OCCUPATIONS/   WPARRJB65050

  TESTIMONY. PUBLIC HEARING, WOMEN IN PUBLIC AND PRIVATE EMPLOYMENT, CALIFORNIA. /FEP
  EMPLOYMENT-CONDITIONS MIGRANT-WORKERS/   WPEEVMX66052

  STATUS OF WOMEN IN THE UNITED STATES.   WPETEEX64056

  WORKING WOMEN.   WPETEEX64058

  OUTLOOK FOR WOMEN.   WPETEEX65055

  EMPLOYMENT EFFECTS OF STATE MINIMUM WAGES FOR WOMEN.   WPETEJX59059

  SHOULD WOMEN BE TRAINED IN THE SCIENCES. /OCCUPATIONS/   WPINEMX58061

  SOME IMPLICATIONS OF THE EMPLOYMENT PATTERNS OF WOMEN UNDER SOCIAL-SECURITY.   WPOLIEJ59454

  WOMEN HOUSEHOLD WORKERS COVERED BY OLD AGE, SURVIVORS, AND DISABILITY INSURANCE.   WPOLIEJ65285

  WOMEN ON COLLEGE AND UNIVERSITY FACULTIES. A HISTORICAL SURVEY AND A STUDY OF THEIR PRESENT ACADEMIC
  STATUS. /OCCUPATIONS/   WPOLLLA65063

  AMERICAN WOMEN. /WORK-WOMAN-ROLE/   WPRESCO63064

  REPORT OF PRESIDENT-S COMMISSION ON STATUS OF WOMEN.   WPRESCO63993

  WOMEN AT WORK. 1. THE FACTS AND WHY WOMEN WORK. 2. THE SIGNIFICANCE.   WQUINFX62992

  WOMEN AT WORK. 1. THE FACTS AND WHY WOMEN WORK. 2. THE SIGNIFICANCE.   WQUINFX62992

  GRADUATE EDUCATION FOR WOMEN. THE RADCLIFFE PHD.   WRADCCX56072

  WOMEN VIEW THEIR WORKING WORLD.   WRAMSGV63104

  SOME ATTITUDES AND OPINIONS OF EMPLOYED WOMEN.   WRAMSGV63132

  MATURE WOMEN IN DOCTORAL PROGRAMS. /OCCUPATIONS/   WRANDKS65073

  UNFINISHED BUSINESS. CONTINUING EDUCATION FOR WOMEN.   WRAUSEX61076

  SECOND CHANCE. NEW EDUCATION FOR WOMEN.   WRAUSEX62075

  SOME CONTINUITIES AND DISCONTINUITIES IN THE EDUCATION OF WOMEN. /WORK-FAMILY-CONFLICT/   WRIESDX56079

  WOMEN. THEIR ORBITS AND THEIR EDUCATION. /WORK-FAMILY-CONFLICT/   WRIESDX58080

  TESTIMONY. PUBLIC HEARING, WOMEN IN PUBLIC AND PRIVATE EMPLOYMENT, CALIFORNIA. /EMPLOYMENT-CONDITIONS/   WRILEEX66081

  IMPLICATIONS OF TWO PILOT PROJECTS IN TRAINING MATURE WOMEN AS COUNSELORS.   WRIOCMJ65082

  WOMEN IN SCIENCE. /OCCUPATIONS/   WROEXAX66455

  WHY WOMEN START AND STOP WORKING. A STUDY IN MOBILITY.   WROSECX65088

  THE ROOTS OF AMBIVALENCE IN AMERICAN WOMEN. /WORK-FAMILY-CONFLICT/   WROSSASND133

  BARRIERS TO THE CAREER CHOICE OF ENGINEERING, MEDICINE, OR SCIENCE AMONG AMERICAN WOMEN. /OCCUPATIONS/   WROSSAS65091

  WOMEN IN SCIENCE. WHY SO FEW. /OCCUPATIONS/   WROSSAS65094

  AMBIVALENCE IN AMERICAN WOMEN. /WORK-FAMILY-CONFLICT/   WROSSAS66090

  A STUDY OF WOMEN IN OFFICE MANAGEMENT POSITIONS WITH IMPLICATIONS FOR BUSINESS EDUCATION. /OCCUPATIONS/   WRUSHEM57096

  REPORT -- 1965-66 -- RETRAINING PROGRAM IN MATHEMATICS AND SCIENCE FOR COLLEGE GRADUATE WOMEN.   WRUTGMR66098

  PART-TIME ASSIGNMENT OF WOMEN IN TEACHING. /OCCUPATIONS/   WSAMPJX65099

  PAY DIFFERENCES BETWEEN MEN AND WOMEN. /DISCRIMINATION/   WSANBHX64100

  IS COLLEGE EDUCATION WASTED ON WOMEN.   WSANFNX57102

  A NEW WORLD FOR WORKING WOMEN.   WSCHNWF63140

  TESTIMONY. PUBLIC HEARING, WOMEN IN PUBLIC AND PRIVATE EMPLOYMENT, CALIFORNIA. /FEP
  EMPLOYMENT-CONDITIONS/   WSCHRPX66104

  THE CHANGING ROLE OF COLLEGE WOMEN. A BIBLIOGRAPHY. /WORK-WOMAN-ROLE/   WSCHWJX62106

  SOME CHANGING ROLES OF WOMEN IN SUBURBIA. A SOCIAL ANTHROPOLOGICAL CASE STUDY. /WORK-FAMILY-CONFLICT/   WSCOFNE60109

  EDUCATING TOMORROW-S WOMEN.   WSENDVL64110

  WOMEN MATHEMATICIANS IN INDUSTRY. /OCCUPATIONS/   WSENDVL64111

  TESTIMONY. PUBLIC HEARING, WOMEN IN PUBLIC AND PRIVATE EMPLOYMENT, CALIFORNIA. /EMPLOYMENT-CONDITIONS/   WSHEAHX66112

  FIVE THOUSAND WOMEN COLLEGE GRADUATES REPORT.   WSHOSRX56113

  FAMILIAL CORRELATES OF ORIENTATION TOWARD FUTURE EMPLOYMENT AMONG COLLEGE WOMEN. /ASPIRATIONS/   WSIEGAX63572

  OCCUPATIONAL CHOICE AMONG CAREER ORIENTED COLLEGE WOMEN. /ASPIRATIONS/   WSIMPRL61115

  OCCUPATIONAL PLANNING BY YOUNG WOMEN, A STUDY OF OCCUPATIONAL EXPERIENCES, ASPIRATIONS, ATTITUDES, AND
  PLANS OF COLLEGE AND HIGH SCHOOL GIRLS.   WSLOCWL56116

WOMEN EXECUTIVES. FACT AND FANCY. /OCCUPATIONS/   WSLOTCT58117

MATERIALS COLLECTION ON WOMEN.   WSMITCLND118

HELP WANTED -- FEMALE. A STUDY OF DEMAND AND SUPPLY IN A LOCAL JOB MARKET FOR WOMEN. /MANPOWER/   WSMITGM64121

TESTIMONY, PUBLIC HEARING. WOMEN IN PUBLIC AND PRIVATE EMPLOYMENT, CALIFORNIA. /FEP
EMPLOYMENT-CONDITIONS DISCRIMINATION/   WSMITWH66123

WOMEN AND WORK IN AMERICA.   WSMUTRW59148

CORRELATES OF PRESENT AND FUTURE WORK STATUS OF MARRIED WOMEN.   WSOBOMB60125

WOMEN IN PROFESSIONAL ENGINEERING. /OCCUPATIONS/   WSOCIOW62127

TESTIMONY, PUBLIC HEARING. WOMEN IN PUBLIC AND PRIVATE EMPLOYMENT, CALIFORNIA. /FEP
EMPLOYMENT-CONDITIONS DISCRIMINATION MIGRANT-WORKERS/   WSPENNX66129

WOMEN IN INDUSTRY -- PATTERNS OF WOMEN-S WORK AND OCCUPATIONAL HEALTH AND SAFETY. /OCCUPATIONS/   WSPIRES60301

REPORT OF CONFERENCE ON EMPLOYMENT PROBLEMS OF WORKING WOMEN.   WSTATUI63131

THE VOCATIONAL ROLES OF OLDER MARRIED WOMEN. /WORK-WOMAN-ROLE/   WSTEIAX61136

WOMEN IN TECHNOLOGY. /OCCUPATIONS/   WSTEIER62153

MARRIED WOMEN AND THE LEVEL OF UNEMPLOYMENT.   WSTEIRL61226

TESTIMONY, PUBLIC HEARING. WOMEN IN PUBLIC AND PRIVATE EMPLOYMENT, CALIFORNIA. /LABOR-MARKET/   WSTEPRX66138

TESTIMONY, PUBLIC HEARING. WOMEN IN PUBLIC AND PRIVATE EMPLOYMENT, CALIFORNIA. /FEPC/   WSTERAX66140

SALARIED WOMEN IN UPPER LEVEL POSITIONS IN KANSAS BUSINESS FIRMS.   WSTOCFT59143

ARE WOMEN WORKERS UNPREDICTABLE.   WSUJAWW58144

JOB OPPORTUNITIES FOR WOMEN COLLEGE GRADUATES.   WSWERSX64145

ROOM AT THE TOP FOR COLLEGE WOMEN.   WSWERSX64767

HIGH SCHOOL GUIDANCE COUNSELOR-S PERCEPTIONS OF SELECTED CAREERS FOR WOMEN COLLEGE GRADUATES.   WSWOPMR63146

PART-TIME PROGRAM FOR PROFESSIONALLY TRAINED WOMEN. /TRAINING/   WTACKAL66147

TESTIMONY, PUBLIC HEARING. WOMEN IN PUBLIC AND PRIVATE EMPLOYMENT, CALIFORNIA. /EMPLOYMENT-CONDITIONS/   WTHOMDX66151

TESTIMONY, PUBLIC HEARING. WOMEN IN PUBLIC AND PRIVATE EMPLOYMENT, CALIFORNIA. /EMPLOYMENT-CONDITIONS
DISCRIMINATION/   WTHOMGX66149

ROLE OF WOMEN. /WORK-WOMAN-ROLE/   WTHOMJL56380

CAREER DEVELOPMENT OF WOMEN. SOME PROPOSITIONS.   WTIEDDV59153

THE ROLE OF WOMEN IN PROFESSIONAL ENGINEERING. /OCCUPATIONS/   WTORPWG62157

WOMEN IN COLLEGE AND UNIVERSITY TEACHING. /OCCUPATIONS/   WTOTAJV65159

WOMEN AND WORK.   WTURNMB64160

WOMEN IN THE UAW. /EEJ/   WUAWXCC66163

STATEMENT ON WEIGHT LIFTING, HOURS, SENIORITY LAWS AND WOMEN. /EMPLOYMENT-CONDITIONS/   WUAWXWD66164

ACCESS OF GIRLS AND WOMEN TO EDUCATION IN RURAL AREAS. A COMPARATIVE STUDY.   WUNESCO64166

FEDERAL CAREERS FOR WOMEN.   WUSCISC61167

OCCUPATIONS AND SALARIES OF WOMEN IN THE FEDERAL SERVICE.   WUSCISC62168

FEDERAL EMPLOYMENT OF WOMEN.   WUSCISC66483

TRADE AND INDUSTRIAL EDUCATION FOR GIRLS AND WOMEN. A DIRECTORY OF TRAINING PROGRAMS.   WUSDHEW60175

THE HEALTH OF WOMEN WHO WORK.   WUSDHEW65170

DIGEST OF STATE LEGISLATION OF SPECIAL INTEREST TO WOMEN WORKERS.   WUSDLABND191

SUMMARY OF STATE LABOR LAWS FOR WOMEN.   WUSDLABND219

UNIONS AND THE CHANGING STATUS OF WOMEN WORKERS.   WUSDLABND224

EMPLOYMENT AND CHARACTERISTICS OF WOMEN ENGINEERS. /OCCUPATIONS/   WUSDLAB56989

EMPLOYMENT OF JUNE 1955 WOMEN COLLEGE GRADUATES.   WUSDLAB56990

GOVERNMENT CAREERS FOR WOMEN -- A STUDY.   WUSDLAB57198

OCCUPATIONS AND SALARIES OF WOMEN FEDERAL EMPLOYEES.   WUSDLAB57992

FIRST JOBS OF COLLEGE WOMEN -- REPORT ON WOMEN GRADUATES, CLASS OF 1957.   WUSDLAB59194

FIRST JOBS OF COLLEGE WOMEN -- REPORT ON WOMEN GRADUATES, CLASS OF 1957.   WUSDLAB59194

TRAINING OPPORTUNITIES FOR WOMEN AND GIRLS.   WUSDLAB60221

MATERNITY BENEFIT PROVISIONS FOR EMPLOYED WOMEN. /EMPLOYMENT-CONDITIONS/   WUSDLAB60206

PART-TIME EMPLOYMENT FOR WOMEN.   WUSDLAB60213

GREAT STRIDES MADE IN JOBS FOR WOMEN IN FEDERAL SERVICE.   WUSDLAB62041

EMPLOYMENT PROBLEMS OF WOMEN.   WUSDLAB62189

WOMEN WORKERS IN 1960. GEOGRAPHICAL DIFFERENCES.   WUSDLAB62241

THE CHANGING ROLE OF WOMEN IN OUR CHANGING SOCIETY.   WUSDLAB62253

WHAT-S NEW ABOUT WOMEN WORKERS.   WUSDLAB63226

WOMEN   (CONTINUATION)
WHY CONTINUING EDUCATION PROGRAMS FOR WOMEN.   WUSDLAB63229

WOMEN TELEPHONE WORKERS AND CHANGING TECHNOLOGY.   WUSDLAB63239

OCCUPATIONAL TRAINING OF WOMEN UNDER THE MANPOWER-DEVELOPMENT-AND-TRAINING-ACT.   WUSDLAB64179

CLERICAL OCCUPATIONS FOR WOMEN -- TODAY AND TOMORROW. /OCCUPATIONS/   WUSDLAB64188

GOVERNORS COMMISSIONS ON THE STATUS OF WOMEN.   WUSDLAB64199

JOB HORIZONS FOR COLLEGE WOMEN IN THE 1960-S.   WUSDLAB64202

WHAT THE EQUAL-PAY PRINCIPLE MEANS TO WOMEN.   WUSDLAB64227

WOMEN IN POVERTY.   WUSDLAB64237

WOMEN WORKERS IN MICHIGAN, 1960.   WUSDLAB64240

TRENDS IN EDUCATIONAL-ATTAINMENT OF WOMEN.   WUSDLAB65222

WISCONSIN GOVERNOR-S CONFERENCE ON THE CHANGING STATUS OF WOMEN, JAN 31-FEB 1 1964.   WUSDLAB65232

WOMEN AND THE EQUAL-EMPLOYMENT PROVISIONS OF THE CIVIL-RIGHTS-ACT.   WUSDLAB65234

COLLEGE WOMEN SEVEN YEARS AFTER GRADUATION -- RESURVEY OF WOMEN GRADUATES CLASS OF 1957.   WUSDLAB66185

COLLEGE WOMEN SEVEN YEARS AFTER GRADUATION -- RESURVEY OF WOMEN GRADUATES CLASS OF 1957.   WUSDLAB66185

1965 HANDBOOK ON WOMEN WORKERS.   WUSDLAB66200

BIBLIOGRAPHY ON AMERICAN WOMEN WORKERS.   WUSDLAB66201

UNDERUTILIZATION OF WOMEN WORKERS.   WUSDLAB66223

WHY WOMEN WORK.   WUSDLAB66231

WOMEN PRIVATE HOUSEHOLD-WORKERS FACT SHEET.   WUSDLAB66238

BACKGROUND FACTS ON WOMEN WORKERS IN THE UNITED STATES.   WUSDLAB66638

TRENDS IN EDUCATIONAL-ATTAINMENT OF WOMEN.   WUSDLAB67806

REPORT ON PROGRESS IN 1965 ON THE STATUS OF WOMEN. /EDUCATION EMPLOYMENT-CONDITIONS/   WUSINCS65860

EQUAL-PAY FOR WOMEN. ITS EFFECT.   WUSNEWR64244

THE OFFICIAL WORD ON JOB RIGHTS FOR WOMEN.   WUSNEWR65246

MANAGING WOMEN EMPLOYEES IN SMALL BUSINESS.   WUSSMBA62248

PROFESSIONAL OPPORTUNITIES FOR WOMEN, PROCEEDINGS.   WUVCAEB66250

EXPLODING THE MYTHS. EXPANDING EMPLOYMENT OPPORTUNITIES FOR CAREER WOMEN.   WUVCAEC66249

CONTINUING EDUCATION FOR WOMEN.   WUVCHCF61686

OPPORTUNITIES FOR WOMEN THROUGH EDUCATION.   WUVMICC65251

STATEMENT. PUBLIC HEARING. WOMEN IN PUBLIC AND PRIVATE EMPLOYMENT, CALIFORNIA. /FEP   WVAILLX66256
  EMPLOYMENT-CONDITIONS DISCRIMINATION/

FULL PARTNERSHIP FOR WOMEN -- WHAT STILL NEEDS TO BE DONE.   WVITAIX63218

INTEREST AND VALUES OF CAREER AND HOME MAKING ORIENTED WOMEN.   WWAGMMX66761

THE MOTIVATION FOR WOMEN TO WORK IN HIGH LEVEL PROFESSIONAL POSITIONS.   WWALTDE62314

IS DISCRIMINATION AGAINST TALENTED WOMEN NECESSARY.   WWARNCF61220

WOMEN EXECUTIVES IN THE FEDERAL-GOVERNMENT. /OCCUPATIONS/   WWARNWL62993

VOCATIONAL INTERESTS AND OCCUPATIONAL ADJUSTMENT OF COLLEGE WOMEN.   WWARRPA59222

WOMEN IN POVERTY.   WWASHBB65667

STATISTICS ON WOMEN PROFESSIONAL ENGINEERS. /OCCUPATIONS/   WWEBBJR66226

TESTIMONY. PUBLIC HEARING. WOMEN IN PUBLIC AND PRIVATE EMPLOYMENT, CALIFORNIA. /EMPLOYMENT-CONDITIONS
MIGRANT-WORKERS/   WWEBEJX66258

RELATIONSHIP BETWEEN THE EDUCATIONAL GOALS AND THE ACADEMIC PERFORMANCE OF WOMEN. A CONFIRMATION.   WWEITHX59260

TRAINING WOMEN AND GIRLS FOR WORK.   WWELLJA60262

WOMEN AND GIRLS IN THE LABOR-MARKET TODAY AND TOMORROW.   WWELLJA63263

PROBLEMS AND PROSPECTS OF WORKING WOMEN.   WWESTRC62214

THE EDUCATION OF WOMEN AND GIRLS IN A CHANGING SOCIETY. A SELECTED BIBLIOGRAPHY WITH ANNOTATIONS.   WWIGNTX65267

WOMEN IN THE AMERICAN LABOR-FORCE. EMPLOYMENT AND UNEMPLOYMENT.   WWILCRX60268

THE WOMEN PHYSICIANS DILEMMA. /OCCUPATIONS/   WWILLJJ66269

WOMEN IN FEDERAL SERVICE, 1939-59.   WWIRTWW62181

WISCONSIN WOMEN. REPORT OF THE WISCONSIN GOVERNOR-S COMMISSION ON THE STATUS OF WOMEN.   WWISXGC65272

WISCONSIN WOMEN. REPORT OF THE WISCONSIN GOVERNOR-S COMMISSION ON THE STATUS OF WOMEN.   WWISXGC65272

TESTIMONY. PUBLIC HEARING. WOMEN IN PUBLIC AND PRIVATE EMPLOYMENT, CALIFORNIA. /FEP   WWOMEIX66273
  EMPLOYMENT-CONDITIONS MIGRANT-WORKERS/

TESTIMONY. PUBLIC HEARING. WOMEN IN PUBLIC AND PRIVATE EMPLOYMENT, CALIFORNIA. /EMPLOYMENT-CONDITIONS/   WWOODWX66276

SUPPLY OF MEDICAL WOMEN IN THE UNITED STATES. /OCCUPATIONS/   WWRIGKW66277

ADMISSION OF WOMEN TO MEDICAL SCHOOL.   WWULSJH66278

WOMEN   (CONTINUATION)
  WOMEN TODAY. TRENDS AND ISSUES IN THE UNITED STATES. /WORK-WOMAN-ROLE/   WYWCAXX63078

  COLLEGE WOMEN AND EMPLOYMENT.   WZAPOMW59281

  OCCUPATIONAL PLANNING FOR WOMEN.   WZAPOMW61282

  THE RELATIONSHIP OF SELECTED VARIABLES TO CAREER-MARRIAGE PLANS OF UNIVERSITY FRESHMAN WOMEN.
  /WORK-FAMILY-CONFLICT/   WZISSCX62284

  A STUDY OF THE LIFE PLANNING OF 550 FRESHMEN WOMEN AT PURDUE UNIVERSITY. /WORK-FAMILY-CONFLICT/   WZISSCX64285

WOMEN-S
  WOMEN-S EDUCATION.   WAAUWEFN0274

  THE SPAN OF A WOMEN-S LIFE AND LEARNING. /WORK-WOMEN-ROLE/   WAMERCE60606

  TECHNOLOGY AND WOMEN-S WORK.   WBAKEEF64624

  THE INTERRUPTION AND RESUMPTION OF WOMEN-S CAREERS.   WBARURX66457

  SPECIAL WOMEN-S COLLECTIONS IN US LIBRARIES.   WBELLMS59636

  COMMUNITY WOMEN-S GROUPS TAKE ACTION. /HOUSEHOLD-WORKERS/   WBUFFDX66661

  FACTORS INFLUENCING WOMEN-S DECISIONS ABOUT HIGHER EDUCATION. /ASPIRATIONS/   WDAVIOD59716

  DIGEST OF CASE STUDIES ON CONTINUITIES AND DISCONTINUITIES IN THE EMPLOYMENT-EDUCATION-FAMILY PATTERNS OF
  WOMEN-S LIVES.   WDELAPJ60224

  WORK VALUES AND BACKGROUND FACTORS AS PREDICTORS OF WOMEN-S DESIRE TO WORK. /ASPIRATIONS/   WEYDELD62754

  FANTASY, FACT AND THE FUTURE...A REVIEW OF THE STATUS OF WOMEN AND POSSIBLE IMPLICATIONS FOR WOMEN-S
  EDUCATION AND ROLE IN THE NEXT DECADE.   WFITZLE63963

  A SURVEY OF WOMEN-S APTITUDES FOR ARMY JOBS. /MILITARY/   WFUCHEF63772

  THE CHANGING PATTERNS OF WOMEN-S WORK. SOME PSYCHOLOGICAL CORRELATES.   WGINZEX58784

  COLLEGE WOMEN-S IDENTIFICATIONS WITH THEIR FATHERS IN RELATION TO VOCATIONAL INTEREST PATTERNS.
  /ASPIRATIONS/   WHALLWJ63815

  CHANGING PATTERNS IN WOMEN-S LIVES IN 1960. /WORK-WOMAN-ROLE/   WHAWKAL60834

  WOMEN-S WAGES.   WINTELR60870

  TRENDS IN WOMEN-S EMPLOYMENT.   WKEYSMD65644

  CHANGING REALITIES IN WOMEN-S LIVES. /WORK-WOMAN-ROLE/   WKEYSMD65893

  FACING THE FACTS ABOUT WOMEN-S LIVES TODAY. /WORK-WOMAN-ROLE/   WKEYSMD65895

  THE IMPACT OF CULTURAL CHANGE ON WOMEN-S POSITION. /BLUE-COLLAR ASPIRATIONS/   WKONOGX66913

  TRENDS IN WOMEN-S WORK PARTICIPATION.   WLESECE58928

  WOMEN-S STATUS -- WOMEN TODAY AND THEIR EDUCATION.   WLLOYEX56941

  WOMEN-S CHANGING ROLE IN THE US EMPLOYMENT MARKET.   WMUNTEE56007

  WOMEN-S TWO ROLES. /WORK-FAMILY-CONFLICT/   WMYRDAX56012

  WOMEN-S CHANGING ROLES THROUGH THE LIFE CYCLE.   WNEUGBL59025

  WOMEN-S EDUCATION. FACTS, FINDINGS, AND APPARENT TRENDS.   WNEWCMX64028

  SUMMARY OF CURRENT RESEARCH ON WOMEN-S ROLES.   WNOBLJL59035

  CHARACTERISTICS OF WOMEN-S COLLEGE STUDENTS.   WROWEFB64095

  MINNESOTA PLAN FOR WOMEN-S CONTINUING EDUCATION. A PROGRESS REPORT.   WSENDVL61298

  WOMEN IN INDUSTRY -- PATTERNS OF WOMEN-S WORK AND OCCUPATIONAL HEALTH AND SAFETY. /OCCUPATIONS/   WSPIRES60301

  WOMEN-S ATTITUDES TOWARD CAREERS.   WSTEIAX59137

  SOME ASPECTS OF WOMEN-S AMBITIONS.   WTURNRH64162

  EARNINGS IN THE WOMEN-S AND MISSES COAT AND SUIT INDUSTRY.   WUSDLAB57988

  WHAT ABOUT WOMEN-S ABSENTEEISM AND LABOR TURNOVER.   WUSDLAB65225

  WOMEN-S EARNINGS IN LOW-INCOME FAMILIES.   WUSDLAB66236

  THE FUROR OVER WOMEN-S EDUCATION.   WUSEERH63215

  CHANGING CULTURAL CONCEPTS IN WOMEN-S LIVES. /WORK-WOMAN-ROLE/   WUSEERH64255

  HOW WOMEN-S ROLE IN US IS CHANGING.   WUSNEWR66245

  3RD ANNUAL WOMEN-S CONFERENCE, PROCEEDINGS.   WUVUTXX66254

  AN ANALYSIS OF FACTORS INFLUENCING MARRIED WOMEN-S ACTUAL OR PLANNED WORK PARTICIPATION.   WWELLMW61261

  WOMEN-S WORK. FACTS, FINDINGS, AND APPARENT TRENDS.   WZAPOMW64283

WORK
  WOMEN AT WORK. /NEGRO/   CDECTMX61376

  THE EVALUATION OF WORK BY FEMALES, 1940-1950. /WOMEN NEGRO/   CDORNSM56284

  WOMEN WHO WORK. /NEGRO/   CHUTCGX52589

  THE NEGRO WOMAN AT WORK. ADDRESS TO CONFERENCE ON THE NEGRO WOMAN IN THE USA.   CKEYSMD65646

  AN EXPERIMENT TO TEST THREE MAJOR ISSUES OF WORK PROGRAM METHODOLOGY WITHIN MOBILIZATION-FOR-YOUTH-S
  INTEGRATED SERVICES TO OUT-OF-SCHOOL UNEMPLOYED YOUTH. /NEGRO PUERTO-RICAN/   CMOBIFY66024

  EMPLOYMENT-STATUS AND WORK CHARACTERISTICS. STATISTICS ON THE RELATION BETWEEN EMPLOYMENT AND SOCIAL AND

ECONOMIC CHARACTERISTICS. /DEMOGRAPHY/   CUSBURC63170

OCCUPATIONAL CHARACTERISTICS, DATA ON AGE, RACE, EDUCATION, WORK EXPERIENCE, INCOME, ETC. FOR WORKERS IN
EACH OCCUPATION.   CUSBURC63177

NEGRO ADC MOTHERS LOOK FOR WORK. /WOMEN/   CWILLJJ58324

FINAL REPORT OF THE YMCA YOUTH AND WORK PROJECT 1962-1966. /NEGRO   PUERTO-RICAN TRAINING/ CYMCAYA66329

REPORTS ON THE WORK OF THE FEPC IN NEW-JERSEY AND NEW-YORK.   GAMERCR46372

THE COMING CRISIS. YOUTH WITHOUT WORK.   GAMERFX63375

WORK EXPERIENCE OF THE POPULATION IN 1965.   GBOGAFA66138

WORK PROGRAMS AND THE YOUTHFUL OFFENDER.   GCOLEEX66131

WORK EXPERIENCE OF THE POPULATION IN 1959.   GCOOPSX60603

AN EQUAL-OPPORTUNITIES COMMITTEE AT WORK IN TEXAS.   GDESHEA66633

THE SCHOOL COUNSELOR AT WORK ON OCCUPATIONAL DISCRIMINATION.   GDIXALX46643

ECONOMIC-TRENDS IN EXTENSION WORK WITH NEGRO FARMERS IN ALABAMA, 1936-1948.   GGAINRL48341

EDUCATIONAL-ATTAINMENT OF THE WORK FORCE.   GHAMMHR66145

INCOME WITHOUT WORK. /GUARANTEED-INCOME/   GHAZLHX66523

HERE-S HOW MERIT EMPLOYMENT PROGRAMS WORK. A REPORT ON PROGRESS AND PROBLEMS IN THE EMPLOYMENT OF
MINORITY-GROUP MEMBERS.   GILLISC56803

NEW-YORK STATE-S PROGRAM AGAINST DISCRIMINATION IN EMPLOYMENT. THE WORK OF THE NEW-YORKEW-YORK
STATE-COMMISSION-AGAINST-DISCRIMINATION.   GINDUBX57812

YOUTH AND WORK IN NEW-YORK-CITY.   GKOHLMC62855

MEN WITHOUT WORK. THE ECONOMICS OF UNEMPLOYMENT.   GLEBESX65891

THE POOR IN THE WORK FORCE. /LABOR-FORCE/   GLEVISA66038

WORK RELIEF. SOCIAL WELFARE STYLE. /MANPOWER UNEMPLOYMENT/   GLEVISA66531

LOWER-CLASS DELINQUENCY AND WORK PROGRAMS.   GMARTJM66854

CHARACTERISTICS OF FARM WORKERS AS RELATED TO STABILIZATION OF THE WORK FORCE. /MIGRANT-WORKERS/ GMETZWH62504

INCREASING EMPLOYABILITY OF YOUTH. THE ROLE OF WORK TRAINING.   GMOEDMX66852

IMPROVING THE WORK SKILLS OF THE NATION.   GNATLMC55052

MAN. WORK AND SOCIETY. A READER IN THE SOCIOLOGY OF OCCUPATIONS.   GNOSOSX62336

CONSUMPTION. WORK, AND POVERTY.   GORSHMX65959

WORK EXPERIENCE OF THE POPULATION IN 1960.   GROSECX60257

PUBLIC WORK AND THE LONG-TERM UNEMPLOYED.   GROSSMS66844

WORK EXPERIENCE OF THE POPULATION IN 1962.   GSABESX64272

INTERPERSONAL RELATIONS IN ETHNICALLY MIXED SMALL WORK GROUPS.   GSCOTWW59291

THE BALANCED ETHNIC WORK GROUP.   GSCOTWW61290

HEALTH WORK AMONG MIGRANTS IN 1958 BY THE NEW-JERSEY STATE DEPARTMENT OF HEALTH.   GSHEPAC59301

FREEDOM TO WORK. /FEPC LEGISLATION/   GSMITSX55320

ENFORCEMENT OF NONDISCRIMINATION REQUIREMENTS FOR GOVERNMENT CONTRACT WORK.   GSPECWH63329

PROBLEMS AND APPROACHES IN INTEGRATING MINORITY-GROUP WORK FORCES.   GSPERBJ53330

WORK HISTORY. ATTITUDES. AND INCOME OF THE UNEMPLOYED.   GSTEIRL63838

EDUCATION FOR A CHANGING WORLD OF WORK. /YOUTH/   GUSDHEW63834

EDUCATION AND TRAINING. THE BRIDGE BETWEEN MAN AND HIS WORK.   GUSDHEW65156

THE SKILLED WORK FORCE OF THE UNITED STATES.   GUSDLAB55498

THE UNEMPLOYED. WHY THEY STARTED LOOKING FOR WORK.   GUSDLAB65979

YOUTH IN NEW-YORK CITY. OUT OF SCHOOL AND OUT OF WORK.   GVOGAAS62074

BROADENING WORK OPPORTUNITIES FOR INDIAN YOUTH.   IARCHMS61526

INDIANS WORK AT THEIR OWN SKI RESORT. /NEW-MEXICO/   ILINDVX66580

COOPERATIVE EXTENSION SERVICE WORK WITH LOW-INCOME FAMILIES.   IUSDAGR63638

ADL AT WORK. THE CRUMBLING WALLS. /EMPLOYMENT DISCRIMINATION/   JADLBXX63688

VALUE ORIENTATIONS OF YOUNG MEXICAN-AMERICAN MALES AS REFLECTED IN THEIR WORK PATTERNS AND EMPLOYMENT
PREFERENCES.   MWADDJO62513

VALUE ORIENTATION, ROLE CONFLICT, AND ALIENATION FROM WORK. A CROSS-CULTURAL STUDY.   MZURCLA65520

MAKING APPRENTICESHIP WORK.   NAMERFX66014

NEGROES AT WORK.   NBROOTR61120

A PILOT STUDY OF AN INTEGRATED WORK FORCE.   NCOUSFR58611

WHY SHOULD NEGROES WORK. /ASPIRATIONS/   NDIZAJE66015

AT WORK IN INDUSTRY TODAY. 50 CASE-REPORTS ON NEGROES AT WORK.   NGENEEX64398

AT WORK IN INDUSTRY TODAY. 50 CASE-REPORTS ON NEGROES AT WORK.   NGENEEX64398

THE NEGRO AND HIS WORK.   NGINZEX61407

PROBLEMS FOR ADULT EDUCATION RELATED TO ACQUIRING CAPABILITIES FOR WORK.   NGOLDFH63430

INTEGRATING THE WORK FORCE.   NINDURP66593

BEHAVIOR AND PRODUCTIVITY IN BI-RACIAL WORK GROUPS.   NKATZIX58638

EFFECTS OF WHITE AUTHORITARIANISM IN BI-RACIAL WORK GROUPS.   NKATZIX60639

WORK AND COLOR. /UNION/   NMASOLR52063

AT WORK IN NORTH-CAROLINA TODAY. 48 CASE-REPORTS ON NORTH-CAROLINA NEGROES NOW EMPLOYED OR PREPARING
THEMSELVES FOR EMPLOYMENT...THEIR EDUCATION, JOB QUALIFICATIONS, AND CAREER ASPIRATIONS.   NNORTCGND933

WHY THEY DON-T WANT TO WORK. /ASPIRATIONS/   NSCHWMX64022

NEGROES IN THE WORK GROUP. HOW 33 BUSINESS AND INDUSTRIAL FIRMS OFFERED EQUAL-EMPLOYMENT-OPPORTUNITIES TO
ALL.   NSEIDJX50114

DESEGREGATION AND INTEGRATION IN SOCIAL WORK.   NSIMOSM56262

RACIAL WORK AND NEGRO WASTE IN SOUTHERN EMPLOYMENT.   NSOUTRC62300

SO THE NEGROES WANT WORK. /UNION/   NSTREGX41462

NEGRO PARTICIPATION IN DEFENSE WORK.   NUSDLAB41829

TRAINING NEGROES FOR WAR WORK.   NUSDLAB43845

THE UNITED STATES EMPLOYMENT SERVICE AND THE NEGRO WORK APPLICANT.   NUSWAMC44276

A COMPARISON OF THE OCCUPATIONS OF THE FIRST AND SECOND GENERATION PUERTO-RICANS IN THE MAINLAND
LABOR-MARKET. AND HOW THE WORK OF THE NEW-YORK STATE DEPARTMENT OF LABORFFECTS PUERTO-RICANS.   PRAUSCX61846

TECHNOLOGY AND WOMEN-S WORK.   WBAKEEF64624

WORK, WOMEN, AND CHILDREN. /WORK-FAMILY-CONFLICT/   WDAVIHX60715

WORK VALUES AND BACKGROUND FACTORS AS PREDICTORS OF WOMEN-S DESIRE TO WORK. /ASPIRATIONS/   WEYDELD62754

WORK VALUES AND BACKGROUND FACTORS AS PREDICTORS OF WOMEN-S DESIRE TO WORK. /ASPIRATIONS/   WEYDELD62754

WORK MOTIVATION OF COLLEGE ALUMNAE. FIVE-YEAR FOLLOWUP.   WEYDELD67223

THE CHANGING PATTERNS OF WOMEN-S WORK. SOME PSYCHOLOGICAL CORRELATES.   WGINZEX58784

WOMEN IN LEGAL WORK. /OCCUPATIONS/   WGRIFVE58804

THE DECISION TO WORK. /ASPIRATIONS/   WHOFFLW63847

EMPLOYMENT AND CONDITIONS OF WORK OF NURSES.   WINTELO60862

PARTICIPATION IN PART-TIME WORK BY WOMEN COLLEGE STUDENTS.   WISAALE57875

A MEMORANDUM ON THE MOTIVATIONS OF MIDDLE AGED WOMEN IN THE LOWER EDUCATIONAL BRACKETS TO RETURN TO WORK.
/ASPIRATIONS/   WJEWIVA61880

AMERICAN WOMEN WHO WORK.   WKENDBX65225

AN AMERICAN ANACHRONISM, THE IMAGE OF WOMEN AND WORK. /WORK-WOMAN-ROLE/   WKENNKX64891

WOMEN AT WORK. /LABOR-FORCE/   WKRUGDH64918

WOMEN AT WORK.   WKRUGDH64997

THE SHORTAGE OF NURSES AND CONDITIONS OF WORK IN NURSING. /OCCUPATIONS/   WKRUSMX58920

TRENDS IN WOMEN-S WORK PARTICIPATION.   WLESECE58928

OFFICE WORK AND AUTOMATION. /TECHNOLOGICAL-CHANGE/   WLEVIHS56929

PROBLEM AREAS IN TRAINING FOR AUTOMATED WORK. /TECHNOLOGICAL-CHANGE/   WLIPSOX64936

WOMAN AT WORK -- A STUDY IN PREJUDICE. /DISCRIMINATION/   WMARMJX66954

WOMEN AND WORK.   WMARRAF61955

MOTHERS AT WORK.   WMETRLI63973

WORK AND MARRIAGE. /WORK-FAMILY-CONFLICT/   WMEYEAE58974

TIME, WORK, AND WELFARE.   WMORGJX65997

WORK IN THE LIVES OF MARRIED WOMEN.   WNATLMC57021

SOCIAL WORK DEGREE PROGRESS REPORT. /TRAINING/   WNYUYUG66031

WHO CHOOSES SOCIAL WORK, WHEN AND WHY. /OCCUPATIONS/   WPINSAM63062

WOMEN AT WORK. 1. THE FACTS AND WHY WOMEN WORK. 2. THE SIGNIFICANCE.   WQUINFX62992

WOMEN AT WORK. 1. THE FACTS AND WHY WOMEN WORK. 2. THE SIGNIFICANCE.   WQUINFX62992

WHY COLLEGE-TRAINED MOTHERS WORK.   WROSSJE65770

WOMEN AND WORK IN AMERICA.   WSMUTRW59148

CORRELATES OF PRESENT AND FUTURE WORK STATUS OF MARRIED WOMEN.   WSOBOMB60125

COMMITMENT TO WORK. /ASPIRATIONS/   WSOBOMG63126

WOMEN IN INDUSTRY -- PATTERNS OF WOMEN-S WORK AND OCCUPATIONAL HEALTH AND SAFETY. /OCCUPATIONS/   WSPIRES60301

WOMEN AND WORK.   WTURNMB64160

WORK   (CONTINUATION)
    THE HEALTH OF WOMEN WHO WORK.   WUSDHEW65170

    WORLD CF WORK CONFERENCE ON CAREER AND JOB OPPORTUNITIES, WASHINGTON, DC, JULY 1962.   WUSDLAB64242

    TO IMPROVE THE STATUS OF PRIVATE HOUSEHOLD WORK. /HOUSEHOLD-WORKERS/   WUSDLAB65220

    WHY WOMEN WORK.   WUSDLAB66231

    EQUAL-PAY FOR EQUAL WORK.   WUSHOUR62020

    THE MOTIVATION FOR WOMEN TO WORK IN HIGH LEVEL PROFESSIONAL POSITIONS.   WWALTDE62314

    TRAINING WOMEN AND GIRLS FOR WORK.   WWELLJA60262

    AN ANALYSIS OF FACTORS INFLUENCING MARRIED WOMEN-S ACTUAL OR PLANNED WORK PARTICIPATION.   WWELLMW61261

    WOMEN-S WORK. FACTS, FINDINGS, AND APPARENT TRENDS.   WZAPCMW64283

WORK-FAMILY-CONFLICT
    THE GREAT BACK-TO-WORK MOVEMENT. /WORK-FAMILY-CONFLICT/   WBELLDX56635

    WOMEN. EMANCIPATION IS STILL TC COME. /WORK-FAMILY-CONFLICT/   WBETTBX64646

    MATERNAL EMPLOYMENT. SITUATICNAL AND ATTITUDINAL VARIABLES. /WORK-FAMILY-CONFLICT/   WBRIEDX61655

    THE RURAL WORKING HOMEMAKER. ALCORN-COUNTY, MISSISSIPPI. /WORK-FAMILY-CONFLICT/   WBRYAES61660

    RELATIONS AMONG MATERNAL EMPLOYMENT INDICES AND DEVELOPMENTAL CHARACTERISTICS OF CHILDREN.
    /WORK-FAMILY-CONFLICT/   WBURCLG61665

    BACK FROM THE HOME TO BUSINESS. /WORK-FAMILY-CONFLICT/   WBUSIWX61666

    BACK TC SCHOOL. /WORK-FAMILY-CONFLICT/   WCARNCO62680

    WORK, WOMEN, AND CHILDREN. /WORK-FAMILY-CONFLICT/   WDAVIHX60715

    THE POST-PARENTAL PHASE IN THE LIFE CYCLE OF 50 COLLEGE EDUCATED WOMEN. /WORK-FAMILY-CONFLICT/   WDAVIIX60717

    ROLE EXPECTATIONS OF YOUNG WOMEN REGARDING MARRIAGE AND A CAREER. /ASPIRATIONS WORK-FAMILY-CONFLICT/ WEMPELT58751

    MARRIAGE AND CAREERS FOR GIRLS. /WORK-FAMILY-CONFLICT/   WGARFSH57774

    MARITAL DISAGREEMENT IN WORKING WIFE MARRIAGES AS A FUNCTION OF HUSBAND-S ATTITUDE TOWARDS WIFE-S
    EMPLOYMENT. /WORK-FAMILY-CONFLICT/   WGIANAX57779

    LIFE STYLES OF EDUCATED WOMEN. /WORK-FAMILY-CONFLICT/   WGINZEX66785

    ON BEING SOMETHING OTHER THAN MOTHER AND BEING MOTHER TOO. /WORK-FAMILY-CONFLICT/   WGOLDMR63793

    TRAPPED HOUSEWIFE. /WORK-FAMILY-CONFLICT/   WGRAYHX62801

    POTENTIALITIES OF WOMEN IN THE MIDDLE YEARS. /WORK-FAMILY-CONFLICT/   WGROSIH56806

    THE MODERN MOTHER-S DILEMMA. /WORK-FAMILY-CONFLICT/   WGRUESM57984

    TESTIMONY. PUBLIC HEARING, WOMEN IN PUBLIC AND PRIVATE EMPLOYMENT, CALIFORNIA. /DISCRIMINATION
    WORK-FAMILY-CONFLICT/   WGUPTRC66808

    ATTITUDES OF COLLEGE STUDENTS TOWARD EMPLOYMENT AMONG MARRIED WOMEN. /WORK-FAMILY-CONFLICT/   WHEWEVH64482

    PART-TIME EMPLOYMENT FOR WOMEN WITH FAMILY RESPONSIBILITIES. /WORK-FAMILY-CONFLICT/   WINTELR57867

    HIGH SCHOOL FRESHMAN AND SENIORS VIEW THE ROLE OF WOMEN IN MODERN SOCIETY. /WORK-FAMILY-CONFLICT/   WKERNKK65892

    THE HOMEMAKER AND THE WORKING WIFE. /WORK-FAMILY-CONFLICT/   WKOMAMX62912

    FROM KITCHEN TO CAREER. /WORK-FAMILY-CONFLICT/   WLEWIAB65930

    MARRIAGE AND CAREER CONFLICTS IN GIRLS AND YOUNG WOMEN. /WORK-FAMILY-CONFLICT/   WMATTEX60961

    ATTITUDES TOWARD CAREER AND MARRIAGE AND THE DEVELOPMENT OF LIFE STYLES IN YOUNG WOMEN.
    /WORK-FAMILY-CONFLICT/   WMATTEX64962

    THE TEACHER COMES INTO HER OWN. /WORK-FAMILY-CONFLICT/   WMCINMC61945

    WORK AND MARRIAGE. /WORK-FAMILY-CONFLICT/   WMEYEAE58974

    PERCEPTIONS OF ROLE CONFLICTS AND SELF CONFLICTS AMONG CAREER AND NON-CAREER COLLEGE EDUCATED WOMEN.
    /WORK-FAMILY-CONFLICT/   WMORGDD62996

    WOMEN-S TWO ROLES. /WORK-FAMILY-CONFLICT/   WMYRDAX56012

    CAREERS AFTER FORTY. /WORK-FAMILY-CONFLICT/   WNIEMJX58033

    CAREERS FOR WOMEN AFTER MARRIAGE AND CHILDREN. /WORK-FAMILY-CONFLICT/   WONEIBP65043

    SOME CONTINUITIES AND DISCONTINUITIES IN THE EDUCATION OF WOMEN. /WORK-FAMILY-CONFLICT/   WRIESDX56079

    WOMEN. THEIR ORBITS AND THEIR EDUCATION. /WORK-FAMILY-CONFLICT/   WRIESDX58080

    MARRIAGE, FAMILY, AND SOCIETY. A READER. /WORK-FAMILY-CONFLICT/   WROOMHX65084

    THE ROOTS OF AMBIVALENCE IN AMERICAN WOMEN. /WORK-FAMILY-CONFLICT/   WROSSASND133

    A GOOD WOMAN IS HARD TO FIND. /WORK-FAMILY-CONFLICT/   WROSSAS64093

    AMBIVALENCE IN AMERICAN WOMEN. /WORK-FAMILY-CONFLICT/   WROSSAS66090

    SECOND CAREER. /WORK-FAMILY-CONFLICT NEW-YORK/   WSCHWJX60108

    SOME CHANGING ROLES OF WOMEN IN SUBURBIA. A SOCIAL ANTHROPOLOGICAL CASE STUDY. /WORK-FAMILY-CONFLICT/ WSCOFNE60109

    A NEW LIFE PATTERN FOR THE COLLEGE-EDUCATED WOMAN. /WORK-FAMILY-CONFLICT/   WSTEIER65133

    THE MARRIED FEMALE SCHOOL TEACHER. A CONTINUED STUDY. /WORK-FAMILY-CONFLICT/   WSTEPCM60139

    CNE WOMAN, TWO LIVES. /WORK-FAMILY-CONFLICT/   WTIMEXX61155

WORK-FAMILY-CONFLICT (CONTINUATION)
MANAGEMENT PROBLEMS OF HOMEMAKERS EMPLOYED OUTSIDE THE HOME. /WORK-FAMILY-CONFLICT/   WUSDHEW61174

SOME CORRELATES OF HOMEMAKING VS CAREER PREFERENCE AMONG COLLEGE HOME ECONOMICS STUDENTS.
/WORK-FAMILY-CONFLICT/   WVETTLX64257

THE RELATIONSHIP OF SELECTED VARIABLES TO CAREER-MARRIAGE PLANS OF UNIVERSITY FRESHMAN WOMEN.
/WORK-FAMILY-CONFLICT/   WZISSCX62284

A STUDY OF THE LIFE PLANNING OF 550 FRESHMEN WOMEN AT PURDUE UNIVERSITY.   /WORK-FAMILY-CONFLICT/   WZISSCX64285

WORK-FORCE
STATEMENT ON SURVEYS AND STATISTICS AS TO RACIAL AND ETHNIC COMPOSITION OF WORK-FORCE OR UNION
MEMBERSHIP. /CALIFORNIA/   GCALFEP63539

CHANGING COMPOSITION OF THE AMERICAN WORK-FORCE.   GCOOPSX59928

THE INTEGRATED WORK-FORCE. WHERE ARE WE NOW.   GMULFRH66116

INTEGRATION IN THE WORK-FORCE. WHY AND HOW.   NNATLUL55901

WOMEN IN THE WORK-FORCE.   WINDUBX65858

SOME FACTORS WHICH DETERMINE THE DISTRIBUTION OF THE FEMALE WORK-FORCE.   /LABOR-FORCE/   WJOUROI62883

CHANGING PROFILE OF THE NATION-S WORK-FORCE.   WWIRTWW63271

WORK-PATTERN
WHAT EVERY ABLE WOMAN SHOULD KNOW. /WORK-PATTERN ASPIRATIONS/   WDREWEM61743

WORK-RELATED
SOME WORK-RELATED CULTURAL DEPRIVATIONS OF LOWER-CLASS NEGRO YOUTHS.   NHIMEJS64554

WORK-SEEKERS
A METHODOLOGICAL APPROACH TO IDENTIFICATION AND CLASSIFICATION OF CERTAIN TYPES OF INACTIVE WORK-SEEKERS.
/UNEMPLOYMENT LABOR-MARKET/   GLIEBEE65569

WORK-STUDY
WOMEN GRADUATES CF COOPERATIVE WORK-STUDY PRCGRAMS ON THE COLLEGE LEVEL.   /SKILLS/   WMOSBWB57999

WORK-WOMAN-ROLE
CHANGE AND CHOICE FOR THE COLLEGE WOMAN. /WORK-WOMAN-ROLE/   WAAUWJX62601

ROLE CONCEPTION AS A PREDICTOR OF ADULT FEMALE ROLES. /WORK-WOMAN-ROLE/   WANGRSS66619

LIFE GOALS AND VOCATIONAL CHOICE. /WORK-WOMAN-ROLE/   WASTIAW64620

THE FACTS, THE HOPES, AND THE POSSIBILITIES. /WORK-WOMAN-ROLE/   WBANNMC63626

GROWING UP FEMALE. /WORK-WOMAN-ROLE/   WBETTBX62883

EDUCATION AND A WOMAN-S LIFE. /WORK-WOMAN-ROLE/   WDENNLE63729

EDUCATED WOMEN -- A MIDCENTURY EVALUATION. /WORK-WOMAN-ROLE/   WDOLAEF56734

WHAT-S THE USE OF EDUCATING WOMEN. /WORK-WOMAN-ROLE/   WEDDYED63747

PROGRESS OF THE COMMISSION ON THE STATUS OF WOMAN. /WORK-WOMAN-ROLE/   WELLIKX63748

THE POTENTIAL OF WOMEN. /WORK-WOMAN-ROLE/   WFARBSM63756

THE CHALLENGE TO WOMEN. /WORK-WOMAN-ROLE/   WFARBSM66755

WOMEN IN THE MODERN WORLD. /WORK-WOMAN-ROLE/   WFIRKEX63764

ADDRESS BEFORE LEAGUE-OF-WOMEN-VOTERS, JANUARY 7, 1965. /WORK-WOMAN-ROLE/   WFOWLGH65766

THE ROLE OF THE EDUCATED WOMAN. AN EMPIRICAL STUDY OF THE ATTITUDES OF A GROUP OF COLLEGE WOMEN.
/WORK-WOMAN-ROLE/   WFREEMB65770

THE MARGINAL SEX. /WORK-WOMAN-ROLE/   WFREEMX62771

A TURNING TO TAKE NEXT -- ALTERNATIVE GOALS IN THE EDUCATION OF WOMEN. /WORK-WOMAN-ROLE/   WGOLDFH65792

A WOMAN-S PLACE. /WORK-WOMAN-ROLE/   WGRUMDX61379

SPECIAL SUPPLEMENT ON THE AMERICAN FEMALE. /WORK-WOMAN-ROLE/   WHARPXX62822

SOME IMPLICATIONS ON CURRENT CHANGES IN SEX ROLE PATTERNS. /WORK-WOMAN-ROLE/   WHARTRE60828

WOMAN-S ROLES. HOW GIRLS SEE THEM. /WORK-WOMAN-ROLE/   WHARTRE62830

CHANGING PATTERNS IN WOMEN-S LIVES IN 1960. /WORK-WOMAN-ROLE/   WHAWKAL60834

A WOMAN-S WORLD. /WORK-WOMAN-ROLE/   WINDUBX63857

CHANGING VALUES IN COLLEGE. /WORK-WOMAN-ROLE/   WJACOPE57877

PSYCHOLOGICAL PROBLEMS OF WOMEN IN DIFFERENT SOCIAL ROLES. /WORK-WOMAN-ROLE/   WJAHOMX55879

THE CHANGING STATUS OF THE SOUTHERN WOMAN. /WORK-WOMAN-ROLE/   WJOHNGG65884

THE ROLE OF THE EDUCATED WOMAN. /WORK-WOMAN-ROLE/   WJONECX64009

AN AMERICAN ANACHRONISM. THE IMAGE OF WOMEN AND WORK. /WORK-WOMAN-ROLE/   WKENNKX64891

NEW HORIZONS FOR WOMEN. /WORK-WOMAN-ROLE/   WKEYSMD64898

NEW OPPORTUNITIES AND NEW RESPONSIBILITIES FOR WOMEN. /WORK-WOMAN-ROLE/   WKEYSMD64899

CHANGING REALITIES IN WOMEN-S LIVES. /WORK-WOMAN-ROLE/   WKEYSMD65893

FACING THE FACTS ABOUT WOMEN-S LIVES TODAY. /WORK-WOMAN-ROLE/   WKEYSMD65895

NOT TOO LITTLE OR TOO LATE. /WORK-WOMAN-ROLE/   WKINGAG56905

THE AMERICAN WOMAN-S ROLE. /WORK-WOMAN-ROLE/   WKIUCFX62909

THE IDENTITY OF MODERN WOMAN. /WORK-WOMAN-ROLE/   WKRECHS65381

WORK-WOMAN-ROLE   (CONTINUATION)
    ECONOMIC ROLE OF WOMEN 45-65. /WORK-WOMAN-ROLE/   WKYRKHX56921

    WOMAN-S CENTURY OF PROGRESS. IS IT TO END IN REGRESSION. /WORK-WOMAN-ROLE/   WMCKARC58946

    PERSONAL SATISFACTIONS. /WORK-WOMAN-ROLE/   WNYEXFI63038

    AMERICAN WOMEN. /WORK-WOMAN-ROLE/   WPRESCO63064

    THE CHANGING ROLE OF COLLEGE WOMEN. A BIBLIOGRAPHY. /WORK-WOMAN-ROLE/   WSCHWJX62106

    THE VOCATIONAL ROLES OF OLDER MARRIED WOMEN. /WORK-WOMAN-ROLE/   WSTEIAX61136

    CONCEPT OF THE FEMININE ROLE. /WORK-WOMAN-ROLE/   WSTEIAX63135

    ROLE OF WOMEN. /WORK-WOMAN-ROLE/   WTHOMJL56380

    GUIDING CREATIVE TALENT. /WORK-WOMAN-ROLE/   WTORREP62158

    CHANGING CULTURAL CONCEPTS IN WOMEN-S LIVES. /WORK-WOMAN-ROLE/   WUSEERH64255

    THE AMERICAN WOMAN AT MIDCENTURY. /WORK-WOMAN-ROLE/   WYOUNLM61279

    WOMEN TODAY. TRENDS AND ISSUES IN THE UNITED STATES. /WORK-WOMAN-ROLE/   WYWCAXX63078

WORK-WOMEN-ROLE
    THE SPAN OF A WOMEN-S LIFE AND LEARNING. /WORK-WOMEN-ROLE/   WAMERCE60606

    THE DEVELOPMENT OF BEHAVIOR AND PERSONALITY. /WORK-WOMEN-ROLE/   WANDEJE60614

    ASCENT OF WOMEN. /WORK-WOMEN-ROLE/   WBORGEM63651

    THE RELATIONSHIP OF PARENTAL IDENTIFICATION TO SEX ROLE ACCEPTANCE IN MARRIED, SINGLE, CAREER AND
    NON-CAREER WOMEN. /WORK-WOMEN-ROLE/   WBREYCH64654

    VALUE CHANGE IN COLLEGE WOMEN. /WORK-WOMEN-ROLE/   WBROWDR62658

    OUR GREATEST WASTE OF TALENT IS WOMEN. /WORK-WOMEN-ROLE/   WBUNTMI61662

    AMERICAN WOMEN. THE CHANGING IMAGE. /WORK-WOMEN-ROLE/   WCASSBB62682

    FIRST CATALYST ON CAMPUS CONFERENCE, PROCEEDINGS. /WORK-WOMEN-ROLE/   WCATAXX64683

    REPORT ON THE FIRST CONFERENCE ON THE STATUS OF WOMEN. /WORK-WOMEN-ROLE/   WCOLUMX64699

    REPORT ON THE MISSOURI COMMISSION ON THE STATUS OF WOMEN. /WORK-WOMEN-ROLE/   WCOLUMX64700

    ON EDUCATING WOMEN HIGHLY. /WORK-WOMEN-ROLE/   WCORMML67706

    FOCUS ON THE FUTURE FOR WOMEN. /WORK-WOMEN-ROLE/   WCRONDH56709

    WHAT ABOUT WOMEN. /WORK-WOMEN-ROLE/   WCUTLJH61713

    THE WOMAN IN AMERICA. /WORK-WOMEN-ROLE/   WDAEDXX64714

    REVOLUTION WITHOUT IDEOLOGY. THE CHANGING PLACE OF WOMEN IN AMERICA. /WORK-WOMEN-ROLE/   WDEGLCN64727

    QED. /WORK-WOMEN-ROLE/   WDOLAEF64736

    NEEDED. UNIQUE PATTERNS FOR EDUCATING WOMEN. /WORK-WOMEN-ROLE/   WIRISLD62874

    TODAY-S WOMEN COLLEGE GRADUATES. /WORK-WOMEN-ROLE/   WLEOPAK59927

    LIBERAL ARTS WOMEN GRADUATES. CLASS OF 1958. /WORK-WOMEN-ROLE/   WLICHMW59933

    THE WOMAN IN AMERICA. /WORK-WOMEN-ROLE/   WLIFTRJ65935

    AMERICAN WOMEN /WORK-WOMEN-ROLE/   WMEADMX65966

    NEW HORIZONS FOR COLLEGE WOMEN. /WORK-WOMEN-ROLE/   WMULLLC60005

    EQUALITY BETWEEN THE SEXES. AN IMMODEST PROPOSAL. /WORK-WOMEN-ROLE/   WROSSAS64132

WORKER
    THE MINORITY-GROUP WORKER IN CAMDEN COUNTY. /NEW-JERSEY/   GBOGITX54057

    CHANGES IN THE LABOR-FORCE PARTICIPATION OF THE OLDER WORKER.   GHAUSPM54764

    THE MIGRATORY WORKER IN THE FARM ECONOMY.   GLEVILA61357

    THE CALIFORNIA FARM WORKER. STILL IN DUBIOUS BATTLE. /MIGRANT-WORKERS UNION/   GMEISDX60461

    THE FARM WORKER IN A CHANGING AGRICULTURE. PART I IN A SERIES ON TECHNOLOGICAL-CHANGE AND FARM LABOR USE,
    KERN-COUNTY, CALIFORNIA. 1961.   GMETZWH64387

    ORGANIZED LABOR AND THE MINORITY WORKER NEED EACH OTHER. /UNION/   GSHISBX59305

    MOBILITY AND WORKER ADAPTATION TO ECONOMIC CHANGE IN THE US.   GTRAVHX63836

    MINORITY WORKER HIRING AND REFERRAL IN SAN-FRANCISCO. /CALIFORNIA/   GUSDLAB58076

    THE HARVEST OF DESPAIR. THE MIGRANT FARM WORKER.   GWRIGDX65604

    RELOCATION OF THE DISPLACED WORKER.   IMETZWX63081

    PROBLEMS OF THE LATIN-AMERICAN WORKER IN TEXAS.   MGONZHB63404

    THE MEXICAN IMMIGRANT WORKER IN SOUTHWESTERN AGRICULTURE.   MTHOMAN56501

    THE NEGRO WORKER. /INDUSTRY/   NAMERMA42017

    ORGANIZED LABOR AND THE NEGRO WORKER. /UNION/   NBAINMX63046

    THE NEGRO WORKER IN THE CHICAGO JOB-MARKET. /ILLINOIS/   NBAROHX66055

    MANPOWER TRAINING AND THE NEGRO WORKER.   NBRAZWF66110

    THE MOTIVATION OF THE UNDERPRIVILEGED WORKER.   NDAVIAX46254

  POSTWAR EMPLOYMENT AND THE NEGRO WORKER.   NDAVIJA46258

  TRADE UNIONS PRACTICES AND THE NEGRO WORKER -- THE ESTABLISHMENT AND IMPLEMENTATION OF AFL-CIO
  ANTI-DISCRIMINATION POLICY.   NDAVINF60312

  THE NEGRO SALARIED WORKER. /EMPLOYMENT-SELECTION/   NGOURJC65438

  ORGANIZED LABOR AND THE NEGRC WORKER. /UNION/   NGROBGX60460

  THE NEGRO FEDERAL-GOVERNMENT WORKER.   NHAYELJ42504

  THE NEGRO WORKER IN INDUSTRY.   NHILLHX57533

  RIGHT-TO-WORK LAWS AND THE NEGRO WORKER.   NHILLHX58996

  NO HARVEST FOR THE REAPER. THE STORY OF THE MIGRATORY AGRICULTURAL WORKER IN THE UNITED STATES.   NHILLHX59534

  HAS ORGANIZED LABOR FAILED THE NEGRO WORKER. /UNION/   NHILLHX62526

  THE NEGRO WORKER ASSERTS HIS RIGHTS. /UNION/   NJACOPA63601

  THE NEGRO WAR WORKER IN SAN-FRANCISCO. /CALIFORNIA/   NJOHNCS44612

  THE NEGRO WORKER OF KANSAS-CITY. A STUDY OF TRADE UNION AND ORGANIZED LABOR RELATIONS.   NKANCIU40634

  EMPLOYMENT PROBLEMS OF THE OLDER NEGRO WORKER.   NKERNJH50644

  HOW INTEGRATION IS WORKING OUT IN INDUSTRY. THE NEGRO WORKER.   NMANARX56734

  THE NEGRO WORKER AND THE TRADE UNIONS. A FOOT IN THE DOOR.   NMARSRX65058

  THE NEGRO WORKER.   NMARSRX67057

  PROGRESS AND PROSPECTS FOR THE NEGRO WORKER.   NMILLHP65783

  THE NEGRO WORKER IN MINNESOTA. A REPORT.   NMINNGI45798

  THE NEGRO TOBACCO WORKER AND HIS UNION IN DURHAM, NORTH-CAROLINA.   NRICEJD41053

  NEGRO WORKER LIFTS HIS SIGHTS. /ASPIRATIONS/   NTHOMJA46202

  FULL EMPLOYMENT AND THE NEGRO WORKER.   NTOWNWS45162

  THE NEGRO IN THE WEST, SOME FACTS RELATING TO SOCIAL AND ECONOMIC CONDITIONS. NO 1. THE NEGRO WORKER. NUSDLABND256

  PLACING THE NEGRO WORKER.   NWILKWH41323

  THE PUERTO-RICAN WORKER CONFRONTS THE COMPLEX URBAN SOCIETY -- A PRESCRIPTION FOR CHANGE.   PCARDLA67874

  THE PUERTO-RICAN WORKER IN PERTH-AMBOY, NEW-JERSEY.   PGOLUFT56811

  UPDATING TRAINING FOR THE RETURNING NURSE, SOCIAL WORKER AND TEACHER.   WNATLCP61018

  THE CHANGING WOMAN WORKER. A STUDY OF THE FEMALE LABOR-FORCE IN NEW-JERSEY AND IN THE NATION FROM 1940 TO
  1958.   WSMITGM60120

  AUTOMATION AND THE WHITE-COLLAR WORKER.   WSTIEJX57142

WORKER-S
  THE AMERICAN REVOLUTION. PAGES FROM A NEGRO WORKER-S NOTEBOOK.   NBOGGJX63101

  THE NEGRO WORKER-S CULTURAL AND OCCUPATIONAL LIMITATIONS.   NMCPICM61729

  THE NEGRO WORKER-S PROGRESS IN MINNESOTA. A REPORT.   NMINNGI49799

WORKERS
  ECONOMIC, SOCIAL, AND DEMOGRAPHIC CHARACTERISTICS OF SPANISH-AMERICAN WAGE WORKERS ON US FARMS.
  /PUERTO-RICAN MEXICAN-AMERICAN/   CFRIERE63805

  BREAKING THE BARRIERS OF OCCUPATIONAL ISOLATION. A REPORT ON UPGRADING LOW-SKILL, LOW-WAGE WORKERS.
  /NEGRO PUERTO-RICAN/   CPROJAX66237

  THE ECONOMIC ABSORPTION AND CULTURAL INTEGRATION OF IMMIGRANT MEXICAN-AMERICAN AND NEGRO WORKERS.   CSHANLW64124

  URBAN ADJUSTMENT AND ITS RELATIONSHIP TO THE SOCIAL ANTECEDENTS OF IMMIGRANT WORKERS. /NEGRO
  MEXICAN-AMERICAN/   CSHANLW65121

  THE TRAINING OF MIGRANT FARM WORKERS. A FOLLOW-UP STUDY OF TWO EXPERIMENTAL AND DEMONSTRATION PROGRAMS
  UNDER THE MANPOWER-DEVELOPMENT-AND-TRAINING-ACT. /MEXICAN-AMERICAN AMERICAN-INDIAN/   CUNIVOC66054

  CHARACTERISTICS OF PROFESSIONAL WORKERS. /DEMOGRAPHY/   CUSBURC63167

  OCCUPATIONAL CHARACTERISTICS. DATA ON AGE, RACE, EDUCATION, WORK EXPERIENCE, INCOME, ETC. FOR WORKERS IN
  EACH OCCUPATION.   CUSBURC63177

  THE CHANGING STATUS OF NEGRO WOMEN WORKERS.   CUSDLAB64072

  NEGRO WOMEN WORKERS IN 1960.   CUSDLAB64264

  CURRENT DATA ON NONWHITE WOMEN WORKERS. /NEGRO/   CUSDLAB65261

  UNWANTED WORKERS. PERMANENT LAYOFFS AND LONG-TERM UNEMPLOYMENT. /NEGRO WOMEN/   CWILCRC63322

  BENEFIT POLICIES IN RELATION TO RECRUITMENT OF OLDER WORKERS, HANDICAPPED, AND MINORITY GROUPS.   GBARRGJ51425

  IMPLICATIONS OF THE RECENT CENSUSES FOR PROFESSIONAL AGRICULTURAL WORKERS. /OCCUPATIONS/   GBEALCL61412

  FORMAL OCCUPATIONAL TRAINING OF ADULT WORKERS, ITS EXTENT, NATURE, AND USE.   GBEDEMX64448

  THE RISING LEVELS OF EDUCATION AMONG YOUNG WORKERS.   GCOWHJD65933

  CONFERENCE ON UNSKILLED WORKERS IN THE LABOR-FORCE. PROBLEMS AND PROSPECTS.   GGITLAL66134

  LEGAL DISADVANTAGES OF MIGRATORY WORKERS.   GGIVERA65695

  LABOUR-FORCE ADJUSTMENT OF WORKERS AFFECTED BY TECHNOLOGICAL-CHANGE.   GGOODRC64622

  EXPANDED UTILIZATION OF MINORITY-GROUP WORKERS.   GGRAYCJ51736

WORKERS   (CONTINUATION)
        JOB TENURE OF AMERICAN WORKERS.   GHAMEHR63755

WARTIME EMPLOYMENT PATTERNS OF NONWHITES AND FEMALE WORKERS IN SOUTHERN INDUSTRY.   GHOPEJX46485

EDUCATIONAL-ATTAINMENT OF WORKERS, MARCH, 1962.   GJOHNDF63828

EDUCATIONAL ATTAINMENT OF WORKERS, MARCH 1964.   GJOHNDF65784

ECONOMIC-STATUS OF NON-WHITE WORKERS, 1955-1962. /OCCUPATIONAL-DISTRIBUTION/   GKESSMA63848

MIGRATORY FARM WORKERS IN THE ATLANTIC COAST STREAM. I. CHANGES IN NEW-YORK, 1953 AND 1957.   GLARSOF60406

SOME REGIONAL DIFFERENCES IN WAGES OF AGRICULTURAL WORKERS. /MIGRANT-WORKERS/   GMAITST60436

MIGRATORY FARM WORKERS IN THE ATLANTIC COAST STREAM.   GMETZWH55426

CHARACTERISTICS OF FARM WORKERS AS RELATED TO STABILIZATION OF THE WORK FORCE. /MIGRANT-WORKERS/   GMETZWH62504

MINORITY-GROUP WORKERS IN INDUSTRY.   GMEYESM56058

MIGRATORY FARM WORKERS IN THE ATLANTIC COAST STREAM. WESTERN NEW-YORK, JUNE 1953.   GMOTHJR54405

AN EXPERIMENT IN VOCATIONAL EDUCATION FOR CHILDREN OF MIGRATORY FARM WORKERS, JULY-AUGUST 1956.   GNATLCRND046

REPORT OF A PRELIMINARY STUDY OF EMPLOYMENT PRACTICES INVOLVING MINORITY-GROUP WORKERS, ESSEX-COUNTY,
NEW-JERSEY.   GNEWJDE46059

EMPLOYMENT AND EARNINGS OF MIGRANT FARM WORKERS IN NEW-YORK STATE.   GNEWYSE60110

SUMMARY OF RULES, REGULATIONS, AND LAWS THAT AFFECT SEASONAL FARM WORKERS AND THEIR EMPLOYERS IN NEW-YORK
STATE. /MIGRANT-WORKERS/   GNEWYSJND113

THE EFFECTS OF AUTOMATION ON OCCUPATIONS AND WORKERS IN PENNSYLVANIA.   GPENNSE65641

MARITAL AND FAMILY CHARACTERISTICS OF WORKERS, MARCH 1963.   GPERRVC64168

GRAPE WORKERS WIN NEW GAINS. /MIGRANT-WORKERS UNION CALIFORNIA/   GROSSLX66557

CHANGING PATTERNS IN EMPLOYMENT OF NONWHITE WORKERS.   GRUSSJL66269

FAMILY CHARACTERISTICS OF WORKERS. 1959.   GSCHIJX60283

MARITAL AND FAMILY CHARACTERISTICS OF WORKERS, MARCH 1960.   GSCHIJX61284

MARITAL AND FAMILY CHARACTERISTICS OF WORKERS, MARCH 1961.   GSCHIJX62285

MARITAL AND FAMILY CHARACTERISTICS OF WORKERS, MARCH 1962.   GSCHIJX63286

MIGRATORY WORKERS IN NEW-YORK, CHANGES, 1953, 1957, AND 1958.   GSHAREF59428

MIGRATORY FARM WORKERS IN THE ATLANTIC COAST STREAM, II. EDUCATION OF NEW-YORK WORKERS AND THEIR
CHILDREN, 1953 AND 1957.   GSHAREF60427

MIGRATORY FARM WORKERS IN THE ATLANTIC COAST STREAM, II. EDUCATION OF NEW-YORK WORKERS AND THEIR
CHILDREN, 1953 AND 1957.   GSHAREF60427

MOBILITY, METHODS OF JOB SEARCH, ATTITUDES, AND MOTIVATION OF DISPLACED WORKERS.   GSHEPHL64621

UNEMPLOYMENT AMONG FULL-TIME AND PART-TIME WORKERS.   GSTEIRL64336

INCOMES OF MIGRATORY AGRICULTURAL WORKERS.   GTEXAAE60350

TEXAS GROWERS AND WORKERS ON THE FARM, LOWER RIO-GRANDE VALLEY.   GTEXAEC59352

MIGRATORY FARM WORKERS IN THE MID-CONTINENT STREAMS.   GUSDAGR60425

SELECTED REFERENCES ON MIGRATORY WORKERS AND THEIR FAMILIES. PROBLEMS AND PROGRAMS.   GUSDLAB56204

PROGRAMS OF NATIONAL ORGANIZATIONS FOR MIGRANT FARM WORKERS AND THEIR FAMILIES.   GUSDLAB61202

SELECTED REFERENCES ON DOMESTIC MIGRATORY AGRICULTURAL WORKERS, THEIR FAMILIES, PROBLEMS, AND PROGRAMS,
1955-1960.   GUSDLAB61495

HOUSING FOR MIGRANT AGRICULTURAL WORKERS. LABOR CAMP STANDARDS.   GUSDLAB62508

YOUNG WORKERS. THEIR SPECIAL TRAINING NEEDS.   GUSDLAB63506

LABOR-FORCE DEVELOPMENTS FOR WHITE AND NONWHITE WORKERS,954-1964.   GUSDLAB64110

MARITAL AND FAMILY CHARACTERISTICS OF WORKERS, MARCH 1964.   GUSDLAB64201

AGRICULTURAL WORKERS AND WORKMEN-S COMPENSATION. /MIGRANT-WORKERS/   GUSDLAB64506

COVERAGE OF AGRICULTURAL WORKERS UNDER STATE AND FEDERAL LAWS. /MIGRANT-WORKERS/   GUSDLAB64507

YOUNG WORKERS. A REPRINT FROM THE 1966 MANPOWER REPORT.   GUSDLAB66505

MIGRATORY WORKERS IN NEW-YORK STATE, 1959 AND COMPARISONS WITH 1953, 1957, AND 1958.   GWHYTDR60407

ADAPTATION OF PAPAGO WORKERS TO OFF-RESERVATION OCCUPATIONS.   IWADDJX66680

MERRILL-TRUST-FUND TO IMPROVE THE EMPLOYMENT OPPORTUNITIES OF THE MIGRANT FARM WORKERS OF MEXICAN ORIGIN.   MBISHCS62365

A PLANNED COMMUNITY FOR MIGRATORY FARM WORKERS.   MFEERAB62392

ECONOMIC, SOCIAL AND DEMOGRAPHIC CHARACTERISTICS OF SPANISH-AMERICAN WAGE WORKERS ON US FARMS.   MFRIERE63394

DOMESTIC AND IMPORTED WORKERS IN THE HARVEST LABOR-MARKET, SANTA-CLARA COUNTY, CALIFORNIA, 1954.   MFULLVX56396

MIGRATORY AGRICULTURAL WORKERS IN THE UNITED STATES.   MJORGJM60422

THE MEXICAN-AMERICAN WORKERS OF SAN-ANTONIO. /TEXAS/   MLANDRG66427

HOUSING DEFICIENCIES OF AGRICULTURAL WORKERS AND OTHER LOW INCOME GROUPS.   MMCMIOX62434

INCOMES OF MIGRATORY AGRICULTURAL WORKERS.   MMETZWH60439

FARMERS, WORKERS, AND MACHINES. TECHNOLOGICAL AND SOCIAL-CHANGE IN FARM INDUSTRIES OF ARIZONA.   MPADFHX65450

WORKERS   (CONTINUATION)
    PROCEEDINGS OF THE CONFERENCE ON EDUCATION FOR ADULT MIGRANT WORKERS. /TEXAS/   MTEXACM62498

    SOCIAL AND ATTITUDINAL CHARACTERISTICS OF SPANISH-SPEAKING MIGRANT AND EX-MIGRANT WORKERS IN THE
    SOUTHWEST.   MULIBHX66503

    INFORMATION CONCERNING ENTRY OF MEXICAN AGRICULTURAL WORKERS INTO THE UNITED STATES.   MUSDLAB59335

    NEGRO PLATFORM WORKERS. /INDUSTRY CASE-STUDY/   NAMERCR45011

    EMPLOYMENT AND INCOME OF NEGRO WORKERS. 1940-1952.   NBEDEMS53071

    FACTORS IN WORKERS DECISIONS TO FOREGO RETRAINING UNDER THE MANPOWER-DEVELOPMENT-AND-RETRAINING-ACT.   NBRAZWF64318

    SOME RECENT UNITED STATES SUPREME COURT DECISIONS AFFECTING THE RIGHTS OF NEGRO WORKERS.   NCHICCA47914

    OCCUPATIONAL-MOBILITY OF NEGRO PROFESSIONAL WORKERS.   NEDWAGF64326

    INTRA-PLANT MOBILITY OF NEGRO AND WHITE WORKERS.   NGARBAP65394

    PROBLEMS AND NEEDS OF NEGRO ADOLESCENT WORKERS.   NGRANLB40980

    MEMBERSHIP POLICIES OF INTERNATIONAL UNIONS AS THEY AFFECT NEGRO WORKERS.   NGRANLB41442

    EFFECTS OF ON-THE-JOB EXPERIENCE WITH NEGROES UPON RACIAL ATTITUDES OF WHITE WORKERS IN UNION SHOPS.   NGUNDRH50466

    HIRING NEGRO WORKERS. /INDUSTRY/   NHABBSX64473

    A STUDY OF THE EFFECTS OF EFFORTS TO IMPROVE EMPLOYMENT-OPPORTUNITIES OF NEGROES ON THE UTILIZATION OF
    NEGRO WORKERS.   NHARTJW64496

    URBAN-LEAGUE UPGRADES NEGRO WORKERS.   NHOLMAX66563

    EXPERIMENTAL AND DEMONSTRATION MANPOWER PROJECT FOR THE RECRUITMENT, TRAINING, PLACEMENT AND FOLLOW-UP OF
    RURAL UNEMPLOYED WORKERS IN TEN NORTH FLORIDA CITIES. FINAL REPORT. /PARTICIPANTS/   NJACKTA66597

    RECENT TRENDS OF MEMBERSHIP OF INTERNATIONAL UNIONS AS THEY AFFECT NEGRO WORKERS.   NJOHNRA44620

    UNION LOCALS AND THE UNDER-UTILIZATION OF NEGRO WORKERS.   NJONEBA66884

    ECONOMIC STATUS OF NONWHITE WORKERS, 1955-62.   NKESSMA63019

    THE EFFECTS OF SOUTHERN WHITE WORKERS ON RACE-RELATIONS IN NORTHERN PLANTS.   NKILLLM52650

    ATTITUDES TOWARD ETHNIC FARM WORKERS IN COACHELLA-VALLEY. /CALIFORNIA/   NMCDOEC55719

    POSTWAR STATUS OF NEGRO WORKERS IN SAN-FRANCISCO AREA. /CALIFORNIA/   NMCENDX50721

    NEGRO WORKERS AFTER THE WAR.   NNATLNC45879

    NEGRO WORKERS IN THE BUILDING TRADES IN SELECTED CITIES. NORFOLK, VIRGINIA. /INDUSTRY/   NNATLUL46894

    NEGRO WORKERS IN THE BUILDING TRADES IN CERTAIN CITIES.   NNATLUL47904

    AUTOMATION AND THE RETRAINING OF NEGRO WORKERS.   NNATLUL62886

    WORKERS WANTED. A STUDY OF EMPLOYERS HIRING POLICIES, PREFERENCES, AND PRACTICES IN NEW-HAVEN AND
    CHARLOTTE. /CONNECTICUT NORTH-CAROLINA/   NNOLAEW49928

    LAST HIRED. FIRST FIRED. THOUGH NEGRO WORKERS HAVE MADE IMPRESSIVE GAINS THEY MIGHT BE FIRST TO FEEL THE
    BITE OF RECESSION.   NNORTHR49940

    THE HOPES OF NEGRO WORKERS FOR THEIR CHILDREN.   NPURCTV64022

    WIDER HORIZONS FOR NEGRO WORKERS.   NRICHCX64058

    OCCUPATIONAL ATTITUDES OF NEGRO WORKERS.   NRICHEX43056

    HOW NEGRO WORKERS FEEL ABOUT THEIR JOBS.   NROSEAW51292

    THE JOB HUNT. JOB SEEKING BEHAVIOR OF UNEMPLOYED WORKERS IN A LOCAL ECONOMY.   NSHEPHL66128

    MIGRATION AND ADJUSTMENT EXPERIENCES OF RURAL WORKERS IN INDIANAPOLIS. /INDIANA/   NSMITED53143

    ACCULTURATION AND NEGRO BLUE-COLLAR WORKERS.   NSTAMRX64171

    LAND TENURE IN THE SOUTHERN REGION. PROCEEDINGS OF PROFESSIONAL AGRICULTURAL WORKERS TENTH ANNUAL
    CONFERENCE.   NTUSKIX51218

    OCCUPATIONAL DISTRIBUTION OF EMPLOYED COLORED WORKERS OF MARYLAND.   NUSDLAB40834

    EMPLOYER SPECIFICATIONS FOR DEFENSE WORKERS.   NUSDLAB41244

    NEGRO WORKERS AND THE NATIONAL DEFENSE PROGRAM.   NUSDLAB41253

    INCREASED INDUSTRIAL PLACEMENTS OF WORKERS.   NUSDLAB41821

    OCCUPATIONAL STATUS OF NEGRO RAILROAD WORKERS.   NUSDLAB43836

    THE MENTALITIES OF NEGRO AND WHITE WORKERS. AN EXPERIMENTAL SCHOOL-S INTERPRETATION OF NEGRO TRADE
    UNIONISM.   NVALIPX49280

    A STUDY OF SOME ASPECTS OF JOB SATISFACTION AMONG NEGRO WHITE-COLLAR WORKERS.   NWEATMD54296

    POVERTY AREAS OF OUR MAJOR CITIES. THE EMPLOYMENT SITUATION OF NEGRO AND WHITE WORKERS IN METROPOLITAN
    AREAS COMPARED IN A SPECIAL LABOR-FORCE REPORT.   NWETZJR66114

    WHITE EMPLOYERS AND NEGRO WORKERS.   NWILSLX43327

    MISSISSIPPI WORKERS. WHERE THEY COME FROM AND HOW THEY PERFORM. A STUDY OF WORKING FORCES IN SELECTED
    MISSISSIPPI INDUSTRIAL PLANTS.   NWOFFBM55333

    PUERTO-RICAN FARM WORKERS IN NEW-JERSEY.   PAINERO59777

    SPANISH SPEAKING WORKERS AND THE LABOR MOVEMENT.   PASSPCT56779

    LIFE AMONG THE GARMENT WORKERS.   PBRAEPX58782

    THE PUERTO-RICAN WORKERS IN NEW-YORK.   PGRAYLX63813

NOTES CN MIGRATION AND WORKERS ATTITUDES TOWARD IT.   PGREGPX61857

NEW-YORK-S LABOR SCANDAL. THE PUERTO-RICAN WORKERS.   PLEVIMX57823

PLACING PUERTO-RICAN WORKERS IN THE NEW-YORK CITY LABOR-MARKET.   PMONTHX60830

HOW TO HIRE AGRICULTURAL WORKERS FROM PUERTO-RICO.   PPUERRDND788

EARNINGS AND HOURS OF WOMEN AGRICULTURAL WORKERS.   WCALDIR64268

WOMAN WORKERS IN CALIFORNIA, 1949-SEPTEMBER 1966.   WCALDIR67269

WOMEN WORKERS IN CALIFORNIA. JANUARY 1949-AUGUST 1964.   WCALIDL64678

FINAL REPORT. EXPERIMENTAL AND DEMONSTRATION MANPOWER PROJECT FOR THE RECRUITMENT, TRAINING, PLACEMENT
AND FOLLOW-UP OF RURAL UNEMPLOYED WORKERS IN TEN NORTH FLORIDA COUNTIES.   WFLORMP66326

SOME GUIDES FOR SUPERVISING WOMEN WORKERS.   WGRANLJ63800

WOMEN PART-TIME WORKERS IN THE U.S.   WHEWEAX62843

WOMEN WORKERS IN ILLINOIS.   WILLIBE64330

CHILD CARE FACILITIES FOR WOMEN WORKERS. /EMPLOYMENT-CONDITIONS/   WINTELR58864

ABSENTEEISM AMONG WOMEN WORKERS IN INDUSTRY.   WISAMVX62876

WOMEN WORKERS. WORKING HOURS AND SERVICES.   WKLEIVX65908

AUTOMATICN AND EMPLOYMENT OPPORTUNITIES FOR OFFICE WORKERS. THE EFFECT OF ELECTRONIC COMPUTERS ON
EMPLOYMENT OF CLERICAL WORKERS, WITH A SPECIAL REPORT ON PROGRAMMERS.   WPASCWX58178

AUTOMATION AND EMPLOYMENT OPPORTUNITIES FOR OFFICE WORKERS. THE EFFECT OF ELECTRONIC COMPUTERS ON
EMPLOYMENT OF CLERICAL WORKERS, WITH A SPECIAL REPORT ON PROGRAMMERS.   WPASCWX58178

WOMEN HOUSEHOLD WORKERS COVERED BY OLD AGE, SURVIVORS, AND DISABILITY INSURANCE.   WPOLIEJ65285

ARE WOMEN WORKERS UNPREDICTABLE.   WSUJAWW58144

DIGEST OF STATE LEGISLATION OF SPECIAL INTEREST TO WOMEN WORKERS.   WUSDLABND191

UNIONS AND THE CHANGING STATUS OF WOMEN WORKERS.   WUSDLABND224

WOMEN WORKERS IN 1960. GEOGRAPHICAL DIFFERENCES.   WUSDLAB62241

WHAT-S NEW ABOUT WOMEN WORKERS.   WUSDLAB63226

WOMEN TELEPHONE WORKERS AND CHANGING TECHNOLOGY.   WUSDLAB63239

EVERYBODY-S TALKING ABOUT TRAINED WORKERS FOR THE FUTURE.   WUSDLAB63243

WOMEN WORKERS IN MICHIGAN, 1960.   WUSDLAB64240

1965 HANDBOOK ON WOMEN WORKERS.   WUSDLAB66200

BIBLIOGRAPHY ON AMERICAN WOMEN WORKERS.   WUSDLAB66201

UNDERUTILIZATION OF WOMEN WORKERS.   WUSDLAB66223

BACKGROUND FACTS ON WOMEN WORKERS IN THE UNITED STATES.   WUSDLAB66638

WORKING

RURAL-FARM MALES ENTERING AND LEAVING WORKING AGES, 1940-50 AND 1950-60. REPLACEMENT RATIOS AND RATES.
/OCCUPATIONS/   GBOWLGK56433

THE HIRED FARM WORKING FORCE OF 1963 WITH SUPPLEMENTARY DATA FOR 1962. /ECONOMIC-STATUS/   GBOWLGK65432

THE HIRED FARM WORKING FORCE OF 1958. /ECONOMIC-STATUS/   GCOWHJD59430

AN ANALYSIS OF THE EXPERIENCED HIRED FARM WORKING FORCE, 1948-1957. /SKILLS/   GCOWHJD60423

EDUCATION, SKILL LEVEL, AND EARNINGS OF THE HIRED FARM WORKING FORCE OF 1961.   GCOWHJD63420

THE HIRED FARM WORKING FORCE OF 1960. /ECONOMIC-STATUS/   GFRIERE62431

THE HIRED FARM WORKING FORCE OF 1956. /ECONOMIC-STATUS/   GMAITST58428

THE HIRED FARM WORKING FORCE OF 1957. /ECONOMIC-STATUS/   GMAITST59429

THE HIRED FARM WORKING FORCE OF 1958.   GMAITST61384

HOW INTEGRATION IS WORKING OUT IN INDUSTRY.   GMANARX56936

THE OUTLOOK OF WORKING CLASS YOUTH. /DROP-OUT ASPIRATION/   GMILLSM62570

DIGEST OF FINDINGS FROM A WORKING CONFERENCE OF LOCAL COUNCILS. /FEPC/   GNATLCS45045

THE HIRED FARM WORKING FORCE OF 1964. A STATISTICAL REPORT.   GUSDAGR65424

WORKING WITH STUDENTS INSIDE AND OUTSIDE THE CLASSROOM IN ADULT BASIC EDUCATION PROGRAMS.   NBRAZWF64285

WORKING AT IMPROVING THE MOTIVATIONAL AND ACHIEVEMENT LEVELS OF THE DEPRIVED.   NHARREC63367

HOW INTEGRATION IS WORKING OUT IN INDUSTRY. THE NEGRO WORKER.   NMANARX56734

MISSISSIPPI WORKERS. WHERE THEY COME FROM AND HOW THEY PERFORM. A STUDY OF WORKING FORCES IN SELECTED
MISSISSIPPI INDUSTRIAL PLANTS.   NWOFFBM55333

WORKING RULES FOR ASSURING NCNDISCRIMINATION IN HOSPITAL ADMINISTRATION.   NYALELJ64600

PROBLEMS OF WORKING WOMEN. SUMMARY REPORT OF A CONFERENCE.   WAFLCIO61618

SO YOU WANT TO BE A WORKING MOTHER.   WBENJLX66456

THE RURAL WORKING HOMEMAKER. ALCORN-COUNTY, MISSISSIPPI. /WORK-FAMILY-CONFLICT/   WBRYAES61660

THE WORKING WIFE AND HER FAMILY-S ECONOMIC POSITION.   WCARRMS62681

WORKING   (CONTINUATION)
AN EXPLORATORY STUDY OF EMPLOYERS ATTITUDES TOWARD WORKING MOTHERS.   WCONYJE61704

EMPLOYERS ATTITUDES TOWARD WORKING MOTHERS.   WCONYJE63703

THE CASE FOR THE WORKING MOTHER.   WCOTTDW65708

EMPLOYMENT PROBLEMS OF WORKING WOMEN.   WFLAGJJ63130

TABLES OF WORKING LIFE FOR WOMEN, 1950.   WGARFSH57180

MARITAL DISAGREEMENT IN WORKING WIFE MARRIAGES AS A FUNCTION OF HUSBAND-S ATTITUDE TOWARDS WIFE-S
EMPLOYMENT. /WORK-FAMILY-CONFLICT/   WGIANAX57779

WORKING MOTHERS AND MALADJUSTED CHILDREN.   WHANDHX57818

THE WORKING WOMAN. BARRIERS IN EMPLOYMENT. /DISCRIMINATION/   WHARREX64827

CHILDREN OF WORKING MOTHERS, 1960.   WHERZEX64123

WORKING WOMEN...WHO ARE THEY.   WINSTOL60873

WORLD-S WORKING POPULATION. SOME DEMOGRAPHIC ASPECTS.   WINTELR56871

CONFERENCE ON EMPLOYMENT PROBLEMS OF WORKING WOMEN.   WIOWAGC64797

THE NATION-S WORKING MOTHERS AND THE NEED FOR DAY CARE. ADDRESS. /EMPLOYMENT-CONDITIONS/   WKEYSMD65897

WOMEN WORKERS. WORKING HOURS AND SERVICES.   WKLEIVX65908

THE HOMEMAKER AND THE WORKING WIFE. /WORK-FAMILY-CONFLICT/   WKOMAMX62912

WORKING MOTHERS AND THEIR ARRANGEMENTS FOR CARE OF THEIR CHILDREN. /EMPLOYMENT-CONDITIONS/   WLAJEHC59922

SOURCES OF SATISFACTION IN THE LIVES OF WORKING WOMEN.   WLAURMW61923

WORKING WIVES.   WLINDFX63108

CHILDREN AND WORKING MOTHERS.   WMACCEE58949

FRESHMEN INTERVIEW WORKING WIVES.   WMAYXEE59964

WORKING WOMEN.   WPETEEX64058

WOMEN VIEW THEIR WORKING WORLD.   WRAMSGV63104

WHY WOMEN START AND STOP WORKING. A STUDY IN MOBILITY.   WROSECX65088

WORKING WIVES. AN ECONOMETRIC STUDY.   WROSERX58089

A NEW WORLD FOR WORKING WOMEN.   WSCHNWF63140

SPEAKING FOR THE WORKING CLASS WIFE. /BLUE-COLLAR/   WSEXTPC62299

REPORT OF CONFERENCE ON EMPLOYMENT PROBLEMS OF WORKING WOMEN.   WSTATUI63131

FAMILY CHARACTERISTICS OF WORKING WIVES.   WUSBURC59169

CHILD CARE ARRANGEMENTS OF FULLTIME WORKING MOTHERS. /EMPLOYMENT-CONDITICNS/   WUSDHEW59171

CHILD CARE ARRANGEMENTS OF THE NATION-S WORKING MOTHERS. A PRELIMINARY REPORT.   WUSDHEW65172

WHO ARE THE WORKING MOTHERS.   WUSDLAB66B05

PROBLEMS AND PROSPECTS OF WORKING WOMEN.   WWESTRC62214

PART-TIME WORKING MOTHERS -- A CASE-STUDY.   WWORTNB60245

WORKING-CLASS
ECONOMIC INSECURITY AND WORKING-CLASS CONSCIOUSNESS.   NLEGGJC64677

WORKING-FORCE
TRENDS IN THE PARTICIPATION OF WOMEN IN THE WORKING-FORCE.   WJAFFAH56878

WORKING-MOTHERS
JOB-RELATED EXPENSES OF THE WORKING-MOTHERS.   WADDILK63862

WORKING-WIFE
THE WORKING-WIFE HOUSEHOLD. PARTS 1 AND 2.   WLINDFX66117

WORKMEN-S
AGRICULTURAL WORKERS AND WORKMEN-S COMPENSATION. /MIGRANT-WORKERS/   GUSDLAB64506

WORKSHOP
SUMMARY OF PROCEEDINGS. WORKSHOP ON THE IMPACT OF A TIGHTENING LABOR-MARKET ON THE EMPLOYABILITY AND
EMPLOYMENT OF DISADVANTAGED YOUTH.   GNEWYUC66116

WASTED MANPOWER -- BERKELEY CHALLENGE AND OPPORTUNITY. WORKSHOP COSPONSORED WITH THE BERKELEY UNIFIED
SCHOOL-DISTRICT MARCH 15-16, 1963. /CALIFORNIA/   NKENNVD63642

WORLD
THE WORLD OF POVERTY.   GHARRMX66136

THE WORLD OF THE MIGRANT CHILD.   GSUTTEX57344

EDUCATION FOR A CHANGING WORLD OF WORK. /YOUTH/   GUSDHEW63834

INDUSTRY EMPLOYMENT GROWTH SINCE WORLD WAR II.   GUSDLAB63831

THE PERSONNEL JOB IN A CHANGING WORLD. /INDUSTRY/   NBLOOJW64093

EQUAL JUSTICE IN AN UNEQUAL WORLD. EQUALITY FOR THE NEGRO -- THE PROBLEM OF SPECIAL TREATMENT.   NKAPLJX66645

RACE DISCRIMINATION AND THE NLRA ACT. THE BRAVE NEW WORLD OF MIRANDA. /LEGISLATION/   NSOVEMI63169

ISLAND IN THE CITY. THE WORLD OF SPANISH HARLEM.   PWAKEDX59858

WOMEN IN THE PROFESSIONAL WORLD. /OCCUPATIONS/   WALPEEJ62604

WORLD   (CONTINUATION)
    THE PRESENT SITUATION IN THE ACADEMIC WORLD OF WOMEN TRAINED IN ENGINEERING. /OCCUPATIONS/   WBERNJX65639

    WOMEN IN THE MODERN WORLD. /WORK-WOMAN-ROLE/   WFIRKEX63764

    A WOMAN-S WORLD. /WORK-WOMAN-ROLE/   WINDUBX63857

    WOMEN JOURNALISTS AND TODAY-S WORLD. /OCCUPATIONS/   WKEYSMD65021

    WOMEN VIEW THEIR WORKING WORLD.   WRAMSGV63104

    A NEW WORLD FOR WORKING WOMEN.   WSCHNWF63140

    WORLD OF WORK CONFERENCE ON CAREER AND JOB OPPORTUNITIES, WASHINGTON, DC, JULY 1962.   WUSDLAB64242

WORLD-S
    WORLD-S WORKING POPULATION. SOME DEMOGRAPHIC ASPECTS.   WINTELR56871

WORLD-WAR
    THE IMPACT OF MILITARY SERVICE UPON THE RACIAL ATTITUDES OF NEGRO SERVICEMEN IN WORLD-WAR II.   NROBEHW53065

WORLD-WAR-II
    LITERACY, AND THE NEGRO AND WORLD-WAR-II.   NAPTHHX46028

    TOWARD EQUALITY, BALTIMORE-S PROGRESS-REPORT, A CHRONICLE OF PROGRESS SINCE WORLD-WAR-II TOWARD THE
    ACHIEVEMENT OF EQUAL-RIGHTS AND OPPORTUNITIES FOR NEGROES IN MARYLAND 1946-1958.   NBALTUL58048

    THE NEGRO POLICY OF THE AMERICAN ARMY SINCE WORLD-WAR-II. /MILITARY/   NREDDLD53044

WORLD-WARS
    A CRITICAL SUMMARY. THE NEGRO ON THE HOME FRONT IN WORLD-WARS I AND II.   NREIDID43048

WYOMING
    POPULATION AND INCOME CENSUS. WIND-RIVER RESERVATION, WYOMING.   IUSDINT60655

YANKTON
    THE URBANIZATION OF THE YANKTON INDIANS.   IHURTWR66576

YEARBOOK
    AMERICAN JEWISH YEARBOOK.   JFINEMXND720

    NEGRO YEARBOOK.   NGUZMJP47470

YMCA
    FINAL REPORT OF THE YMCA YOUTH AND WORK PROJECT 1962-1966. /NEGRO PUERTO-RICAN TRAINING/   CYMCAYA66329

YONKERS
    CITY EMPLOYMENT SURVEY. PERCENTAGE OF MINORITY-GROUP EMPLOYEES BY DEPARTMENT. /YONKERS NEW-YORK/   GYONKCC66592

YOUNG
    THE RISING LEVELS OF EDUCATION AMONG YOUNG WORKERS.   GCOWHJD65933

    LABOR-FORCE PARTICIPATION OF YOUNG PERSONS AGED 14-24.   GFEARRXND929

    OUT-OF-SCHOOL YOUTH -- TWO YEARS LATER. A 1965 RE-SURVEY OF YOUNG MEN.   GPERRVC66774

    ONE-THIRD OF A NATION. A REPORT ON YOUNG MEN FOUND UNQUALIFIED FOR MILITARY SERVICE.   GPRESTM64316

    THE YOUNG WHO ARE POOR.   GSHEPHL65966

    YOUNG WORKERS. THEIR SPECIAL TRAINING NEEDS.   GUSDLAB63506

    YOUNG WORKERS. A REPRINT FROM THE 1966 MANPOWER REPORT.   GUSDLAB66505

    VALUE ORIENTATIONS OF YOUNG MEXICAN-AMERICAN MALES AS REFLECTED IN THEIR WORK PATTERNS AND EMPLOYMENT
    PREFERENCES.   MWADDJO62513

    RECENT MIGRATION OF YOUNG MALES INTO HOUSTON, TEXAS.   MWAGODW57515

    EMPLOYMENT, EDUCATION AND MARRIAGE OF YOUNG NEGRO ADULTS.   NCOXXOC41934

    YOUNG NEGRO TALENT. SURVEY OF THE EXPERIENCES AND EXPECTATIONS OF NEGRO AMERICANS WHO GRADUATED FROM
    COLLEGE IN 1961.   NFICHJH64867

    THE YOUNG NEGRO IN AMERICA 1960-1980.   NPROCSD66021

    ROLE EXPECTATIONS OF YOUNG WOMEN REGARDING MARRIAGE AND A CAREER. /ASPIRATIONS WORK-FAMILY-CONFLICT/   WEMPELT58751

    THE COMPARATIVE ACADEMIC ACHIEVEMENT OF YOUNG AND OLD. /TRAINING/   WHALFIT62813

    MARRIAGE AND CAREER CONFLICTS IN GIRLS AND YOUNG WOMEN. /WORK-FAMILY-CONFLICT/   WMATTEX60961

    ATTITUDES TOWARD CAREER AND MARRIAGE AND THE DEVELOPMENT OF LIFE STYLES IN YOUNG WOMEN.
    /WORK-FAMILY-CONFLICT/   WMATTEX64962

    OCCUPATIONAL PLANNING BY YOUNG WOMEN, A STUDY OF OCCUPATIONAL EXPERIENCES, ASPIRATIONS, ATTITUDES, AND
    PLANS OF COLLEGE AND HIGH SCHOOL GIRLS.   WSLOCWL56116

YOUTH
    ADDRESS TO COMMUNITY RELATIONS SERVICE STAFF TRAINING SESSION, JANUARY 12, 1967, ON JOBS NOW. /NEGRO
    PUERTO-RICAN YOUTH/   CCOLEBX67918

    OPPORTUNITIES IN NURSING FOR DISADVANTAGED YOUTH. /WOMEN NEGRO OCCUPATIONS/   CFRAKFX66375

    UNDER-ACHIEVEMENT AMONG MINORITY-GROUP STUDENTS. AN ANALYSIS AND A PROPOSAL. /YOUTH NEGRO
    MEXICAN-AMERICAN PUERTO-RICAN/   CHOBACW63555

    AN EXPERIMENT TO TEST THREE MAJOR ISSUES OF WORK PROGRAM METHODOLOGY WITHIN MOBILIZATION-FOR-YOUTH-S
    INTEGRATED SERVICES TO OUT-OF-SCHOOL UNEMPLOYED YOUTH. /NEGRO PUERTO-RICAN/   CMOBIFY66024

    SELECTED BIBLIOGRAPHY FOR DISADVANTAGED YOUTH. /NEGRO PUERTO-RICAN/   CUSDHEWND855

    OAK GLEN -- A TRAINING CAMP FOR UNEMPLOYED YOUTH. /NEGRO MEXICAN-AMERICAN/   CUSDLAB66323

    REPORT. EVALUATION STUDY OF YOUTH TRAINING AND EMPLOYMENT PROJECT, EAST LOS-ANGELES. /NEGRO
    MEXICAN-AMERICAN CALIFORNIA/   CWEINJL64310

    FINAL REPORT OF THE YMCA YOUTH AND WORK PROJECT 1962-1966. /NEGRO PUERTO-RICAN TRAINING/   CYMCAYA66329

YOUTH   (CONTINUATION)
THE COMING CRISIS. YOUTH WITHOUT WORK.   GAMERFX63375

THE SPECTER OF MASS YOUTH UNEMPLOYMENT.   GAMERFX65377

JOB ADJUSTMENT PROBLEMS OF DELINQUENT MINORITY-GROUP YOUTH.   GAMOSWE64874

YOUTH EMPLOYMENT PROGRAMS IN PERSPECTIVE.   GBENJJG65006

JOB-DEVELOPMENT FOR YOUTH.   GBENNGX66877

EMPLOYMENT OF SCHOOL AGE YOUTH, OCTOBER 1965.   GBOGAFA66918

COUNSELING MINORITY-GROUP YOUTH. DEVELOPING THE EXPERIENCE OF EQUALITY THROUGH EDUCATION.   GBRIGWA62473

A COMPILATION OF STATISTICAL DATA, CHARTS AND OTHER RESOURCE MATERIAL FOR CONFERENCE PARTICIPANTS.
/APPRENTICESHIP CALIFORNIA YOUTH/   GCALCNA60516

SCHOOL DROPOUT RATES AMONG FARM AND NONFARM YOUTH 1950 AND 1960.   GCOWHJD63421

BASIC ISSUES AFFECTING YOUTH EMPLOYMENT.   GFREEMK64005

DEVELOPMENT OF TRAINING INCENTIVES FOR THE YOUTH OF MINORITY-GROUPS. /ECONOMIC-STATUS/   GGRANLB57979

LABOR-FORCE STATUS OF YOUTH, 1964.   GHAMEHR65756

THE NEW LOST GENERATION. JOBLESS YOUTH.   GHARRMX64759

ADULT AND YOUTH EMPLOYMENT PROJECT, AUGUST-SEPTEMBER 1965.   GHEALDV65646

ADULT AND YOUTH EMPLOYMENT PROJECT, APRIL-MAY 1965.   GHEALDV65647

REALIZING THE MANPOWER POTENTIALITIES OF MINORITY-GROUP YOUTH.   GHOLLJH58778

FINAL REPORT. THE YOUTH TRAINING PROJECT, SEPTEMBER 1, 1963--JANUARY 31, 1965. /ST-LOUIS MISSOURI
TESTING/   GJEWIEV65568

THE ROLE OF THE SECONDARY SCHOOLS IN THE PREPARATION OF YOUTH FOR EMPLOYMENT.   GKAUFJJ67940

THE ROLE OF THE SECONDARY SCHOOLS IN THE PREPARATION OF YOUTH FOR EMPLOYMENT. SUMMARY, CONCLUSIONS. AND
RECOMMENDATIONS.   GKAUFJJ67963

YOUTH AND WORK IN NEW-YORK-CITY.   GKOHLMC62855

EMPLOYMENT PROBLEMS OF YOUTH AND MANPOWER PROGRAMS.   GKRUGDH66864

COMMUNITY VALUES IN EDUCATION AND OCCUPATIONAL SELECTION. A STUDY OF YOUTH IN EMMITSBURG, MARYLAND.   GLEONRC64894

YOUTH EMPLOYMENT ACT.   GLEVISA63898

THE OUTLOOK OF WORKING CLASS YOUTH. /DROP-OUT ASPIRATION/   GMILLSM62570

INCREASING EMPLOYABILITY OF YOUTH. THE ROLE OF WORK TRAINING.   GMOEDMX66852

ECONOMIC FACTORS INFLUENCING EDUCATIONAL-ATTAINMENTS AND ASPIRATIONS OF FARM YOUTH.   GMOOREJ64386

SOCIAL DYNAMITE. THE REPORT OF THE CONFERENCE ON UNEMPLOYED, OUT-OF-SCHOOL YOUTH IN URBAN AREAS, MAY
24-26, 1961.   GNATLCC61039

SUMMARY OF PROCEEDINGS. WORKSHOP ON THE IMPACT OF A TIGHTENING LABOR-MARKET ON THE EMPLOYABILITY AND
EMPLOYMENT OF DISADVANTAGED YOUTH.   GNEWYUC66116

FEDERAL LEGISLATION FOR A COMPREHENSIVE PROGRAM ON YOUTH EMPLOYMENT.   GNIXORA66847

OUT-OF-SCHOOL YOUTH -- TWO YEARS LATER. A 1965 RE-SURVEY OF YOUNG MEN.   GPERRVC66774

LOW-INCOME YOUTH, UNEMPLOYMENT, VOCATIONAL TRAINING, AND THE JOB-CORPS.   GPURCFX66208

EVALUATION AND SKILL TRAINING OF OUT-OF-SCHOOL, HARD-CORE UNEMPLOYED YOUTH FOR TRAINING AND PLACEMENT.   GSMITAE65140

FROM SCHOOL TO JOB. GUIDANCE FOR MINORITY YOUTH.   GTANNAX63156

REPORT ON EMPLOYMENT PROBLEMS OF NONWHITE YOUTH IN MICHIGAN.   GUSCOMC66408

EDUCATION FOR A CHANGING WORLD OF WORK. /YOUTH/   GUSDHEW63834

THE YOUTH WE HAVEN-T SERVED. /EDUCATION TRAINING/   GUSDHEW66002

SCHOOL AND EARLY EMPLOYMENT EXPERIENCE OF YOUTH. A REPORT ON SEVEN COMMUNITIES, 1952-57.   GUSDLAB60494

YOUTH. THE NATION-S RICHEST RESOURCE. THEIR EDUCATION AND EMPLOYMENT NEEDS.   GUSINCC53514

PROBLEMS OF YOUTH. A FACT BOOK. /EMPLOYMENT/   GUSLIBC64823

YOUTH IN NEW-YORK CITY. OUT OF SCHOOL AND OUT OF WORK.   GVOGAAS62074

CHILDREN AND YOUTH IN THE 1960-S.   GWHITHC60559

BROADENING WORK OPPORTUNITIES FOR INDIAN YOUTH.   IARCHMS61526

WARRIOR DROPOUTS. /YOUTH/   IWAXXRH67812

EMPLOYMENT-TRENDS AMONG CALIFORNIA YOUTH AUTHORITY WARDS ON PAROLE. 1948-62.   MCALDYA63378

OCCUPATIONAL AND EDUCATIONAL LEVELS OF ASPIRATION OF MEXICAN-AMERICAN YOUTH.   MDEHOAX61388

AMBITIONS OF MEXICAN-AMERICAN YOUTH -- GOALS AND MEANS OF MOBILITY OF HIGH SCHOOL SENIORS.   MHELLCS64413

MEXICAN-AMERICAN YOUTH. FORGOTTEN YOUTH AT THE CROSSROADS.   MHELLCS66416

MEXICAN-AMERICAN YOUTH. FORGOTTEN YOUTH AT THE CROSSROADS.   MHELLCS66416

CAREERS FOR YOUTH.   MMEXIEC63441

EMPLOYMENT AND EMPLOYABILITY AMONG CALIFORNIA YOUTH AUTHORITY WARDS. A SURVEY.   MSECKJP62483

SELF RADIUS AND GOALS OF YOUTH IN DIFFERENT URBAN AREAS.   MSHERCW61489

FAIR-EMPLOYMENT AND YOUTH. ISI SE PUEDE -- IT CAN BE DONE. RE. YOUTH AND OPPORTUNITIES.   MWEBBEB66516

YOUTH   (CONTINUATION)
    FAIR-EMPLOYMENT AND YOUTH. ISI SE PUEDE -- IT CAN BE DONE. RE. YOUTH AND OPPORTUNITIES.   MWEBBEB66516

    NEGRO YOUTH AND EMPLOYMENT OPPORTUNITIES. /UNEMPLOYMENT EDUCATION/   NAMOSWE63021

    DISADVANTAGED YOUTH -- RECOGNIZING THE PROBLEM.   NAMOSWE64331

    NEGRO AND WHITE YOUTH IN ELMIRA. /NEW-YORK/   NANTOAX59026

    OCCUPATIONAL ASPIRATIONS OF LOWER-CLASS NEGRO AND WHITE YOUTH.   NANTOAX59027

    OAKLAND LABOR BACKS UP YOUTH. /TRAINING/   NAWNEMX66875

    VOCATIONAL GUIDANCE FOR MINORITY YOUTH.   NBABOIX59038

    THE SQUARE AND I. /UNEMPLOYMENT YOUTH/   NBEANLX63065

    SOME DEMOGRAPHIC CHARACTERISTICS OF RURAL YOUTH.   NBEEGJA63072

    MEETING THE PSYCHOLOGICAL CRISES OF NEGRO YOUTH THROUGH A COORDINATED GUIDANCE SERVICE.   NBRAZWF58111

    JOB HOLDING AMONG NEGRO YOUTH.   NCAPLNX66013

    TWO YEAR REPORT ON THE YOUTH GUIDANCE PROJECT, 1958-1959. /CHICAGO   ILLINOIS/   NCHICULN0203

    DROPOUTS AND THE RATE OF UNEMPLOYMENT. /YOUTH/   NDUNCBX65304

    JOB OUTLOOK FOR YOUTH.   NEBONXX63316

    MEMORANDUM ON IDENTITY AND NEGRO YOUTH.   NERIKEX64338

    PROBLEMS AND NEEDS OF NEGRO CHILDREN AND YOUTH RESULTING FROM FAMILY DISORGANIZATION.   NFRAZEF50382

    I Q PERFORMANCE, EDUCATIONAL AND OCCUPATIONAL ASPIRATIONS OF YOUTH IN A SOUTHERN CITY -- A RACIAL
    COMPARISON.   NGEISPX62397

    HUMAN-RESOURCES. THE WEALTH OF A NATION. /YOUTH/   NGINZEX58405

    THE OPTIMISTIC TRADITION AND AMERICAN YOUTH.   NGINZEX61411

    THE GUIDANCE OF NEGRO YOUTH.   NGINZEX67417

    YOUTH IN THE GHETTO. A STUDY OF THE CONSEQUENCES OF POWERLESSNESS AND A BLUEPRINT FOR CHANGE. /NEW-YORK/   NHARLYO64485

    SOME PERSONAL AND SOCIOLOGICAL VARIABLES ASSOCIATED WITH OCCUPATIONAL-CHOICES OF NEGRO YOUTH.   NHERSPF65520

    REALIZING THE MANPOWER POTENTIALITIES OF MINORITY-GROUP YOUTH.   NHOLLJH58561

    THE OCCUPATIONAL SITUATION OF CENTRAL HARLEM YOUTH.   NHOUSLX65577

    INTELLECTUALLY SUPERIOR NEGRO YOUTH. THEIR PROBLEMS AND NEEDS. /EDUCATION/   NJENKMD50606

    TWO PROJECTS FOR DROPOUT YOUTH.   NJEWIEA64609

    GROWING UP IN THE BLACK BELT. NEGRO YOUTH IN THE RURAL SOUTH.   NJOHNCS41611

    THE EMPLOYMENT SITUATION OF WHITE AND NEGRO YOUTH IN THE CITY OF BALTIMORE. INITIAL EXPERIENCES IN THE
    LABOR-MARKET. /MARYLAND/   NJOHNHU63735

    NEGRO YOUTH IN THE SOUTH. /EDUCATION EMPLOYMENT/   NJONELW60010

    VOCATIONAL ASPIRATIONS OF NEGRO YOUTH IN CALIFORNIA.   NLAWRPF50368

    THE EMPLOYMENT SITUATION OF WHITE AND NEGRO YOUTH IN THE CITY OF BALTIMORE. /MARYLAND/   NLEVEBX63684

    VOCATIONAL GRADUATES IN AUTO MECHANICS. A FOLLOW-UP STUDY OF NEGRO AND WHITE YOUTH. /OCCUPATIONS/   NLEVEBX66036

    GUIDANCE AND MINORITY YOUTH.   NLONGHH62705

    THE NEXT GENERATION. /YOUTH/   NMICHDX65770

    MOTIVATING NEGRO YOUTH IN RHODE-ISLAND.   NMINIBC65797

    THE URBAN-LEAGUE AND THE VOCATIONAL GUIDANCE AND ADJUSTMENT OF NEGRO YOUTH.   NNICHLE52922

    NEGRO YOUTH -- EDUCATION, EMPLOYMENT, AND CIVIL-RIGHTS.   NPEARAX64980

    THE JOB OUTLOOK FOR NEGRO YOUTH.   NPERRJX64984

    THE PREPARATION OF DISADVANTAGED YOUTH FOR EMPLOYMENT AND CIVIC RESPONSIBILITIES.   NPERRJX64985

    ORGANIZED LABOR AND THE NEGRO YOUTH. /UNION/   NPOLLSX66723

    TEACHERS OF CULTURALLY DISADVANTAGED AMERICAN YOUTH.   NROUSRX63310

    THE EFFECT OF SEGREGATION ON THE ASPIRATIONS OF NEGRO YOUTH.   NSAINJN66136

    VOCATIONAL EDUCATION FOR NEGRO YOUTH IN TEXAS.   NUSDLAB49847

    ENHANCING THE OCCUPATIONAL OUTLOOK AND VOCATIONAL ASPIRATIONS OF SOUTHERN SECONDARY YOUTH. A CONFERENCE
    OF SECONDARY SCHOOL PRINCIPALS AND COUNSELORS.   NUSDLAB65334

    EDUCATION-S CHALLENGE TO AMERICAN NEGRO YOUTH.   NWOLFDP62336

    AFTER HIGH SCHOOL WHAT...HIGHLIGHTS OF A STUDY OF CAREER PLANS OF NEGRO AND WHITE RURAL YOUTH IN THREE
    FLORIDA COUNTIES. /ASPIRATIONS/   NYOUMEG65390

    WHY JUAN CAN-T READ. /YOUTH EDUCATION/   PARNORX62778

YOUTH-S
    NEGRO AMERICAN COLLEGE YOUTH-S OUTLOOK ON THE FUTURE.   NROBESO57067

YOUTHFUL
    WORK PROGRAMS AND THE YOUTHFUL OFFENDER.   GCOLEEX66131

YOUTHS
    EDUCATIONAL STATUS, COLLEGE PLANS, AND OCCUPATIONAL-STATUS OF FARM AND NONFARM YOUTHS. OCTOBER 1959.   GCOWHJD61427

    SOME WORK-RELATED CULTURAL DEPRIVATIONS OF LOWER-CLASS NEGRO YOUTHS.   NHIMEJS64554

Bibliography

C

CABRACX59001   ABRAMS C   *NY STATE COMM AGAINST DISCR
IMPLICATIONS OF THE STUDIES. /DISCRIMINATION LOW-INCOME
NEGRO PUERTO-RICAN POLICY-RECOMMENDATIONS/
DISCRIMINATION AND LOW INCOMES. ED BY AARON ANTONOVSKY AND
LEWIS L LORWIN. NEW SCHOOL FOR SOCIAL RESEARCH. NEW YORK.
1959. PP 15-46.

CARIZSE65403   ARIZONA SES
MEETING TODAYS CHALLENGE FOR EMPLOYMENT. /AMERICAN-INDIAN
NEGRO MEXICAN-AMERICAN/
ARIZONA STATE EMPLOYMENT SERVICE. EMPLOYMENT SECURITY
COMMISSION. TUCSON, ARIZONA. JAN 1965. 12 PP.

CARYWSX66621   ARYWITZ S   *CAL STATE LABOR COMMISSIONER
TESTIMONY, PUBLIC HEARING, WOMEN IN PUBLIC AND PRIVATE
EMPLOYMENT, CALIFORNIA. /MEXICAN-AMERICAN/
CALIFORNIA ADVISORY COMMISSION ON THE STATUS OF WOMEN.
STUDY COMMITTEE NO 1, ON PUBLIC AND PRIVATE EMPLOYMENT.
HEARINGS. SACRAMENTO, CALIFORNIA. FEB 24-25 1966. VOL 1,
PP 30-38.

CBATCAB66879   BATCHELDER AB   *US CHAMBER OF COMMERCE
THE ECONOMY AND THE MINORITY POOR.
/NEGRO AMERICAN-INDIAN MEXICAN-AMERICAN PUERTO-RICAN/
THE DISADVANTAGED POOR. EDUCATION AND EMPLOYMENT. US CHAMBER
OF COMMERCE. TASK FORCE ON ECONOMIC GROWTH AND OPPORTUNITY.
WASHINGTON, DC. 1966. PP 123-152.

CBECKWL65070   BECKER WL
REPORT TO GOVERNOR EDMUND G BROWN. SECOND ETHNIC SURVEY OF
EMPLOYMENT AND PROMOTION IN STATE GOVERNMENT.
/CALIFORNIA NEGRO MEXICAN-AMERICAN/
CALIFORNIA, GOVERNOR-S OFFICE. SACRAMENTO, CALIFORNIA. 1965.

CBLAIBX59366   BLAIR B   LIVELY AO
TRIMBLE GW   *NATIONAL COUNCIL OF CHURCHES
SPANISH-SPEAKING AMERICANS. MEXICANS AND PUERTO-RICANS IN
THE UNITED STATES.
BUREAU OF RESEARCH AND SURVEY, HOME MISSION RESEARCH UNIT.
A STUDY CONDUCTED FOR THE NATIONAL COUNCIL OF CHURCHES OF
CHRIST IN THE UNITED STATES OF AMERICA, HOME MISSIONS
DIVISION. NEW YORK. 1959.

CBULLPX66136   BULLOCK P
HUMAN-RESOURCE PROBLEMS OF THE COMING DECADE. /EMPLOYMENT
NEGRO MEXICAN-AMERICAN/
UNIVERSITY OF CALIFORNIA, INSTITUTE OF INDUSTRIAL RELATIONS.
UNPUBLISHED PAPER. LOS ANGELES, CALIFORNIA. NOV 1966. 17 PP.

CBURMJH60287   BURMA JH
SPANISH-SPEAKING CHILDREN. /MEXICAN-AMERICAN PUERTO-RICAN
EDUCATION/
THE NATION-S CHILDREN. ED BY ELI GINZBERG. COLUMBIA
UNIVERSITY PRESS. NEW YORK. 1960. PP 78-102.

CBURMJH60371   BURMA JH   JORGENSON J
THE PUSH OF AN ELBOW. CIVIL-RIGHTS AND OUR SPANISH-SPEAKING
MINORITY. /MEXICAN-AMERICAN PUERTO-RICAN/
FRONTIER, JULY 1960. PP 10-12.

CCALDEM66166   CALIFORNIA DEPT OF EMPLOYMENT
CHARACTERISTICS OF RETRAINING APPLICANTS. /CALIFORNIA
NEGRO MEXICAN-AMERICAN WOMEN/
CALIFORNIA DEPARTMENT OF EMPLOYMENT. REPORT 513, NO 61.
SACRAMENTO, CALIFORNIA. OCT 21 1966. 4 PP.

CCALDEM66906   CALIFORNIA DEPT OF EMPLOYMENT
ANNUAL FARM LABOR REPORT, 1965, CALIFORNIA DEPARTMENT OF
EMPLOYMENT, FARM LABOR SERVICE. /NEGRO MEXICAN-AMERICAN
WOMEN/
CALIFORNIA DEPARTMENT OF EMPLOYMENT, FARM LABOR SERVICE.
RIVERSIDE, CALIFORNIA. SEPT 1966. 68 PP.

CCALDEM67907   CALIFORNIA DEPT OF EMPLOYMENT
RACIAL DISTRIBUTION OF SELECTED UNEMPLOYMENT INSURANCE AND
EMPLOYMENT SERVICE DATA. JULY-DECEMBER 1966. /NEGRO
MEXICAN-AMERICAN/
CALIFORNIA DEPARTMENT OF EMPLOYMENT, REPORT 130, NO 17
SUPPLEMENT. MAR 8 1967. 8 PP.

CCALDIR63710   CAL DEPT OF INDUSTRIAL RELS
REPORT ON OAKLAND SCHOOLS. AN INVESTIGATION UNDER SECTION
1421 OF THE CALIFORNIA LABOR CODE OF THE OAKLAND UNIFIED
SCHOOL DISTRICT 1962-1963. /NEGRO ORIENTAL
MEXICAN-AMERICAN/
CALIFORNIA DEPARTMENT OF INDUSTRIAL RELATIONS, FAIR
EMPLOYMENT PRACTICE COMMISSION. SACRAMENTO, CALIFORNIA.
32 PP.

CCALDIR66168   CAL DEPT OF INDUSTRIAL RELS
NEGROES AND MEXICAN-AMERICANS IN SOUTH AND EAST LOS-ANGELES.
AN ANALYSIS OF A SPECIAL US CENSUS SURVEY OF NOVEMBER
1965. /CALIFORNIA/
CALIFORNIA DEPARTMENT OF INDUSTRIAL RELATIONS, DIVISION OF
FAIR EMPLOYMENT PRACTICES. SAN FRANCISCO, CALIFORNIA. JULY
1966. 39 PP.

CCALDSW65447   CAL DEPT OF SOCIAL WELFARE
TRAINING AID. CULTURAL DIFFERENCES, TRAINING IN
NONDISCRIMINATION, READING ASSIGNMENTS. /EMPLOYMENT
MEXICAN-AMERICAN NEGRO/
CALIFORNIA DEPARTMENT OF SOCIAL WELFARE. SAN FRANCISCO,
CALIFORNIA. SEPT 1965. 184 PP.

CCALUGB65171   CAL OFFICE OF THE GOVERNOR   CAL NEWSPAPER PUBLISHERS
CAL STATE PERSONNEL BOARD
NEGROES AND MEXICAN-AMERICANS IN THE CALIFORNIA STATE
GOVERNMENT, A COOPERATIVE PROJECT.
CALIFORNIA OFFICE OF THE GOVERNOR EDMUND G BROWN, SELECTED
CALIFORNIA NEWSPAPER PUBLISHERS, AND THE STATE PERSONNEL
BOARD. SACRAMENTO, CALIFORNIA. 1965. 100 PLUS PP.

CCARNME62183   CARNEGIE ME   OSBORNE EM
INTEGRATION IN PROFESSIONAL NURSING. /OCCUPATIONS NEGRO
WOMEN/
THE CRISIS, JAN 1962.

CCOHEHX65917   COHEN H
THE DISCRIMINATION CASE. /NEGRO PUERTO-RICAN SES/
THE DEMONICS OF BUREAUCRACY. THE IOWA STATE UNIVERSITY

PRESS. AMES, IOWA. 1965. PP 167-218.

CCOLEBX67918   COLE B
ADDRESS TO COMMUNITY RELATIONS SERVICE STAFF TRAINING
SESSION, JANUARY 12, 1967, ON JOBS NOW. /NEGRO
PUERTO-RICAN YOUTH/
JOBS NOW. COMMUNITY RELATIONS SERVICE STAFF TRAINING
SESSION. CHICAGO, ILLINOIS. JAN 1967. 26 PP.

CDECTMX61376   DECTER M
WOMEN AT WORK. /NEGRO/
COMMENTARY, VOL 31, MAR 1961. PP 243-250.

CDORNSM56284   DORNBUSCH SM   KERR DM
THE EVALUATION OF WORK BY FEMALES, 1940-1950. /WOMEN
NEGRO/
AMERICAN JOURNAL OF SOCIOLOGY, VOL 61, NO 4, JAN 1956.
PP 340-344.

CEAGLOW45313   EAGLESON OW   BELL ES
THE VALUES OF NEGRO WOMEN COLLEGE STUDENTS.
JOURNAL OF SOCIAL PSYCHOLOGY, VOL 22, 1945. PP 149-154.

CELTOEX63332   ELTON E   *CAL DEPARTMENT OF EMPLOYMENT
RACIAL CHARACTERISTICS, MDTA TRAINEES, SAN-FRANCISCO.
/CALIFORNIA NEGRO MEXICAN-AMERICAN/
CALIFORNIA DEPARTMENT OF EMPLOYMENT. SACRAMENTO, CALIFORNIA.
MAY 14 1963. 12 PP.

CFOGEWX66367   FOGEL W
THE EFFECT OF LOW EDUCATIONAL-ATTAINMENT ON INCOMES. A
COMPARATIVE STUDY OF SELECTED ETHNIC GROUPS. /NEGRO
MEXICAN-AMERICAN/
JOURNAL OF HUMAN RESOURCES, VOL 1, FALL 1966. PP 22-40.

CFORBJX60561   FORBES J
APACHE, NAVAHO, AND SPANIARD. /MEXICAN-AMERICAN
AMERICAN-INDIAN/
UNIVERSITY OF OKLAHOMA PRESS. NORMAN, OKLAHOMA. 1960.

CFRAKFX66375   FRAKELTON F
OPPORTUNITIES IN NURSING FOR DISADVANTAGED YOUTH.
/WOMEN NEGRO OCCUPATIONS/
NURSING OUTLOOK, VOL 14, AP 1966. PP 26 PLUS.

CFRIERE63805   FRIEND RE   BAUM S
ECONOMIC, SOCIAL, AND DEMOGRAPHIC CHARACTERISTICS OF
SPANISH-AMERICAN WAGE WORKERS ON US FARMS. /PUERTO-RICAN
MEXICAN-AMERICAN/
US DEPARTMENT OF AGRICULTURE, ECONOMIC RESEARCH SERVICE,
ECONOMIC AND STATISTICAL ANALYSIS DIVISION, AGRICULTURAL
ECONOMIC REPORT NO 27. WASHINGTON, DC. 1963. 21 PP.

CGILMHX44403   GILMORE H   WILSON L
THE EMPLOYMENT OF NEGRO WOMEN AS DOMESTIC-SERVANTS IN
NEW-ORLEANS. /LOUISIANA/
SOCIAL FORCES, VOL 22, NO 3, MAR 1944. PP 318-323.

CGINZEX60720   GINZBERG E ED
THE NATION-S CHILDREN. VOL I. THE FAMILY AND SOCIAL-CHANGE.
VOL II. DEVELOPMENT AND EDUCATION. VOL III. PROBLEMS AND
PROSPECTS. /NEGRO PUERTO-RICAN MEXICAN-AMERICAN WOMEN/
COLUMBIA UNIVERSITY PRESS. NEW YORK. 1960.

CGOLDML63426   GOLDBERG ML
FACTORS AFFECTING EDUCATIONAL-ATTAINMENT IN DEPRESSED URBAN
AREAS. /NEGRO PUERTO-RICAN/
EDUCATION IN DEPRESSED AREAS. ED BY A HARRY PASSOW. COLUMBIA
UNIVERSITY, TEACHERS COLLEGE. NEW YORK. 1963. PP 68-97.

CGOLDVX60494   GOLDKIND V
COMPARISON OF MEXICANS, NEGROES AND WHITES WITH RESPECT TO
OCCUPATIONAL HISTORY, RURAL-URBAN RESIDENCE HISTORY AND
ACCULTURIZATION WITHIN THE INSTITUTIONAL STRUCTURE OF
LANSING, MICHIGAN.
MICHIGAN STATE UNIVERSITY. PHD DISSERTATION. EAST LANSING,
MICHIGAN. 1960.

CGOLDXX60374   GOLDSTEIN
NEGRO NURSES IN HOSPITALS. /WOMEN NEGRO/
AMERICAN JOURNAL OF NURSING, VOL 60. FEB 1960. PP 215 PLUS.

CGORDMM63977   GORDON MM
RECENT TRENDS IN THE STUDY OF MINORITY AND RACE-RELATIONS.
/NEGRO PUERTO-RICAN ORIENTAL/
ANNALS OF AMERICAN ACADEMY OF POLITICAL AND SOCIAL SCIENCE,
VOL 350, NOV 1963. PP 148-156.

CGRAYSW47445   GRAY SW
A NOTE ON THE VALUES OF SOUTHERN COLLEGE WOMEN, WHITE AND
NEGRO.
JOURNAL OF SOCIAL PSYCHOLOGY, VOL 25, 1947. PP 239-241.

CGRIFJX65407   GRIFFEN J
FAMILY STRUCTURE AND SCHOOL PERFORMANCE. A COMPARATIVE
STUDY OF STUDENTS FROM THREE ETHNIC BACKGROUNDS IN AN
INTEGRATED SCHOOL. /MEXICAN-AMERICAN AMERICAN-INDIAN/
UNIVERSITY OF PENNSYLVANIA. PHD DISSERTATION. PHILADELPHIA,
PENNSYLVANIA. 1965.

CHANDOX59481   HANDLIN O
THE NEWCOMERS. NEGROES AND PUERTO-RICANS IN A CHANGING
METROPOLIS
HARVARD UNIVERSITY PRESS. CAMBRIDGE, MASSACHUSETTS. 1959.

CHIESDL64775   HIESTAND DL
ECONOMIC GROWTH AND EMPLOYMENT OPPORTUNITIES FOR MINORITIES.
/NEGRO WOMEN/
COLUMBIA UNIVERSITY PRESS. NEW YORK. 1964. 127 PP.

CHOBACW63555   HOBART CW
UNDER-ACHIEVEMENT AMONG MINORITY-GROUP STUDENTS. AN ANALYSIS
AND A PROPOSAL. /YOUTH NEGRO MEXICAN-AMERICAN
PUERTO-RICAN/
PHYLON, VOL 24, NO 2, SUMMER 1963. PP 184-196.

CHUTCGX52589   HUTCHINS G
WOMEN WHO WORK. /NEGRO/
INTERNATIONAL PUBLICATIONS. NEW YORK. 1952. 96 PP.

CINSTOP66034   INST OF PUBLIC ADMINISTRATION
DEVELOPING NEW-YORK CITY-S HUMAN RESOURCES. VOL 1.
/NEGRO   PUERTO-RICAN/
INSTITUTE OF PUBLIC ADMINISTRATION. NEW YORK. JUNE 1966.
PP 1-48.

CJACOPX59600   JACOBS P
THE FORGOTTEN PEOPLE. /MIGRANT-WORKERS MEXICAN-AMERICAN
PUERTO-RICAN NEGRO/
THE REPORTER, JAN 22 1959. PP 13-20.

CJAMISM45005   JAMIESON SM
LABOR UNIONISM IN AMERICAN AGRICULTURE. /NEGRO
MEXICAN-AMERICAN ORIENTAL/
US DEPARTMENT OF LABOR, BUREAU OF LABOR STATISTICS. GPO.
WASHINGTON, DC. 1945. 457 PP.

CKAMICKND632   KAMII CK   RADIN NL
CLASS DIFFERENCES IN THE SOCIALIZATION PRACTICES OF NEGRO
MOTHERS.
UNIVERSITY OF MICHIGAN. MIMEOGRAPHED. ANN ARBOR, MICHIGAN.
ND. 27 PP.

CKASUMX59013   KASUN M
REGISTRIES AND INTERGROUP RELATIONS. /NEGRO WOMEN
DISCRIMINATION/
AMERICAN JOURNAL OF NURSING, VOL 59, FEB 1959. PP 234-235.

CKEYSMD65646   KEYSERLING MD   *US DEPARTMENT OF LABOR
THE NEGRO WOMAN AT WORK. ADDRESS TO CONFERENCE ON THE NEGRO
WOMAN IN THE USA.
US DEPARTMENT OF LABOR, WOMAN-S BUREAU. GPO. WASHINGTON, DC.
1965. 12 PP.

CLABJRR44028   LABOR RELS REFERENCE MANUAL
SENIORITY AND POSTWAR JOBS. RUBBER INDUSTRY. /NEGRO WOMEN/
LABOR RELATIONS REFERENCE MANUAL, VOL 14, MARCH 1 1944.
PP 2505-2507.

CLEBETX57371   LE BERTHON T
AT THE PREVAILING RATE. /MEXICAN-AMERICAN NEGRO   UNION/
COMMONWEAL, VOL 67, NO 5, NOV 1 1957. PP 122-125.

CLIBRCX64899   THE LIBRARY COUNSELOR
CULTURAL DIFFERENCES IN AMERICAN ETHNIC GROUPS.
BIBLIOGRAPHY. /AMERICAN-INDIAN NEGRO SPANISH-AMERICAN/
THE LIBRARY COUNSELOR, VOL 19, JULY 1964. PP 1-27.

CLOSACH65708   LOS ANGELES COMM HUM RELS
THE URBAN REALITY. A COMPARATIVE STUDY OF THE SOCIO-ECONOMIC
SITUATION OF MEXICAN-AMERICANS, NEGROES AND
ANGLO-CAUCASIANS IN LOS-ANGELES COUNTY. /CALIFORNIA/
LOS ANGELES COMMISSION ON HUMAN RELATIONS. LOS ANGELES,
CALIFORNIA. JUNE 1965. 54 PP.

CMARRAJ62055   MARROW AJ
CHANGING PATTERNS OF PREJUDICE. /NEGRO PUERTO-RICAN
ORIENTAL AMERICAN-INDIAN/
CHILTON PRESS. PHILADELPHIA, PENNSYLVANIA. 1962. 271 PP.

CMETZWH65389   METZLER WH
FARM MECHANIZATION AND LABOR STABILIZATION. PART II IN A
SERIES ON TECHNOLOGICAL-CHANGE AND FARM LABOR USE,
KERN COUNTY, CALIFORNIA, 1961. /NEGRO MEXICAN-AMERICAN/
UNIVERSITY OF CALIFORNIA. BERKELEY, CALIFORNIA. JAN 1965.
58 PP.

CMITTFG66777   MITTELBACH FG   MARSHALL GF
POVERTY IN THE SOUTHWEST. A COMPARATIVE STUDY OF
MEXICAN-AMERICAN, NONWHITE AND ANGLO FAMILIES. /NEGRO/
AMERICAN STATISTICAL ASSOCIATION, PROCEEDINGS. 1966.
PP 477-484.

CMOBIFY66024   MOBILIZATION FOR YOUTH
AN EXPERIMENT TO TEST THREE MAJOR ISSUES OF WORK PROGRAM
METHODOLOGY WITHIN MOBILIZATION-FOR-YOUTH-S INTEGRATED
SERVICES TO OUT-OF-SCHOOL UNEMPLOYED YOUTH.
/NEGRO PUERTO-RICAN/
MOBILIZATION FOR YOUTH, INC., DIVISION OF EMPLOYMENT
OPPORTUNITIES. EIGHT MONTH REPORT TO THE OFFICE OF MANPOWER
POLICY, EVALUATION AND RESEARCH. DEC 16 1965-AUG 15 1966.
NEW YORK. 1966.

CNEWJDL61907   NJ DEPT LABOR AND INDUSTRY
BUREAU OF MIGRANT-LABOR REPORT. /NEW-JERSEY NEGRO
PUERTO-RICAN/
NEW JERSEY DEPARTMENT OF LABOR AND INDUSTRY. TRENTON,
NEW JERSEY. 1961. 6 PP.

CNEWYCO64916   NYC COMM ON HUMAN RIGHTS
ETHNIC SURVEY OF MUNICIPAL-EMPLOYEES. A REPORT ON THE NUMBER
AND DISTRIBUTION OF NEGROES AND PUERTO-RICANS AND OTHER
EMPLOYEES BY THE CITY OF NEW-YORK.
NEW YORK CITY COMMISSION ON HUMAN RIGHTS. NEW YORK.
MAR 19 1964. 2 VOLS.

CNEWYCO64917   NYC COMM ON HUMAN RIGHTS
INTERIM REPORT TO THE MAYOR ON ITS INQUIRY INTO CHARGES OF
RACIAL BIAS IN THE CITY BUILDING AND CONSTRUCTION
INDUSTRY. /NEW-YORK NEGRO PUERTO-RICAN/
NEW YORK CITY, COMMISSION ON HUMAN RIGHTS. NEW YORK. 1964.

CNEWYSD62090   NY STATE DIVISION FOR YOUTH
THE SCHOOL DROPOUT PROBLEM IN MAJOR CITIES OF NEW-YORK
STATE. ROCHESTER -- PART I. /NEGRO PUERTO-RICAN/
NEW YORK STATE DIVISION FOR YOUTH. ALBANY, NEW YORK.
MAY 1962.

CNOBLJL54924   NOBLE JL
THE NEGRO COLLEGE WOMAN.
COLUMBIA UNIVERSITY, TEACHERS COLLEGE. NEW YORK. 1954.

CNOBLJL55925   NOBLE JL
THE NEGRO WOMAN COLLEGE GRADUATE.
COLUMBIA UNIVERSITY PRESS. NEW YORK. 1955.

CNOBLJL66923   NOBLE JL
THE AMERICAN NEGRO WOMAN.
THE AMERICAN NEGRO REFERENCE BOOK. ED BY JOHN P DAVIS.
PRENTICE-HALL. ENGLEWOOD CLIFFS, NEW JERSEY. 1966.

CNORTCS59934   N CAROLINA S BRD PUB WELFARE
FACTS ON ADC IN NORTH-CAROLINA. /NEGRO AMERICAN-INDIAN/
NORTH CAROLINA STATE BOARD OF PUBLIC WELFARE. RALEIGH,
NORTH CAROLINA. 1959. 34 PP.

CPALEHA63098   PALEY HA
THE MIGRANT LABOR PROBLEM -- ITS STATE AND INTERSTATE
ASPECTS. /NEGRO MEXICAN-AMERICAN/
JOURNAL OF NEGRO EDUCATION, VOL 32, NO 1, WINTER 1963.

PP 35-42.

CPETECL64988   PETERSON CL   KRASS BM
SHANNON LW
THE IMMIGRANT. VALUE ORIENTATIONS AND VOCATIONAL
ASPIRATIONS. /NEGRO MEXICAN-AMERICAN/
MIDWEST SOCIOLOGICAL SOCIETY MEETINGS, PAPER. KANSAS CITY,
KANSAS. 1964.

CPETECX65989   PETERSON CL   SCHEFF TJ
THEORY, METHOD AND FINDINGS IN THE STUDY OF ACCULTURATION. A
REVIEW. /MEXICAN-AMERICAN NEGRO/
INTERNATIONAL REVIEW OF COMMUNITY DEVELOPMENT, NOS 13-14,
1965. PP 155-176.

CPINKAX63458   PINKNEY A
PREJUDICE TOWARD MEXICAN AND NEGRO AMERICANS. A COMPARISON.
PHYLON, 4TH QUARTER, WINTER 1963. PP 353-359.

CPORTRP43103   PORTER RP
NEGRO WOMEN IN THE CLOTHING, CIGAR AND LAUNDRY INDUSTRIES OF
PHILADELPHIA, 1960.
JOURNAL OF NEGRO EDUCATION, VOL 12, NO 1, WINTER 1943.
PP 21-23.

CPROJAX66237   PROJECT ADVANCE   CORNELL UNIVERSITY
PUERTO RICAN FORUM   NEW YORK URBAN LEAGUE
BREAKING THE BARRIERS OF OCCUPATIONAL ISOLATION. A REPORT ON
UPGRADING LOW-SKILL, LOW-WAGE WORKERS.
/NEGRO PUERTO-RICAN/
CORNELL UNIVERSITY, PUERTO RICAN FORUM, NEW YORK URBAN
LEAGUE. NEW YORK. SKILL ADVANCEMENT INC. 1966.

CRADINX65031   RADIN N   KAMII CK
THE CHILD-REARING ATTITUDES OF DISADVANTAGED NEGRO MOTHERS
AND SOME EDUCATIONAL IMPLICATIONS.
JOURNAL OF NEGRO EDUCATION, VOL 34, SPRING 1965. PP 138-146.

CROSEAM64553   ROSE AM
NEW PROBLEM OF LARGE SCALE UNEMPLOYABILITY.
/NEGRO MEXICAN-AMERICAN AMERICAN-INDIAN/
AMERICAN JOURNAL OF ECONOMICS AND SOCIOLOGY, VOL 23, NO 4,
OCT 1964. PP 337-350.

CRUBIEBND848   RUBIN EB   *US COMM ON CIVIL RIGHTS
THE SPANISH-SPEAKING PEOPLE IN THE UNITED STATES.
/PUERTO-RICAN MEXICAN-AMERICAN/
US COMMISSION ON CIVIL RIGHTS. GPO. WASHINGTON, DC. 10 PP.

CRUSCER66807   RUSCO ER
MINORITY-GROUPS IN NEVADA. /NEGRO AMERICAN-INDIAN/
UNIVERSITY OF NEVADA, BUREAU OF GOVERNMENTAL RESEARCH. RENO,
NEVADA. 1966. 52 PP.

CRUSSVR59482   RUSSELL VR
SIGNIFICANT TRENDS IN THE NEW-YORK STATE ECONOMY, WITH
SPECIAL REFERENCE TO MINORITY-GROUPS. /PUERTO-RICAN
NEGRO/
DISCRIMINATION AND LOW INCOMES, ED BY AARON ANTONOVSKY AND
LEWIS L LORWIN. NEW SCHOOL FOR SOCIAL RESEARCH. NEW YORK.
1959. PP 71-99.

CSAINMD66320   ST MARY-S DOMINICAN COLLEGE   *US DEPARTMENT OF LABOR
SECRETARIAL TRAINING WITH SPEECH IMPROVEMENT. AN
EXPERIMENTAL AND DEMONSTRATION PROJECT. /NEGRO WOMEN/
ST MARY-S DOMINICAN COLLEGE. US DEPARTMENT OF LABOR, OFFICE
OF MANPOWER POLICY, EVALUATION AND RESEARCH. NEW ORLEANS,
LOUISIANA. AUG 31 1966. 150 PP.

CSAMOJX63474   SAMORA J   *US COMM ON CIVIL RIGHTS
SPANISH-SPEAKING PEOPLE IN THE UNITED STATES. A PILOT
REPORT. /MEXICAN-AMERICAN PUERTO-RICAN/
US COMMISSION ON CIVIL RIGHTS. UNPUBLISHED MANUSCRIPT.
WASHINGTON, DC. 1963.

CSCHMCF65107   SCHMID CF   NOBBE CE
SOCIO-ECONOMIC DIFFERENTIALS AMONG NONWHITE RACES. /NEGRO
ORIENTAL AMERICAN-INDIAN/
AMERICAN SOCIOLOGICAL REVIEW, VOL 30, DEC 1965. PP 909-922.

CSELFHO66325   SELF HELP OPPORTUNITY CENTER   *US DEPARTMENT OF LABOR
*JACKSON STATE COLLEGE
AN EXPERIMENT IN MANPOWER DEVELOPMENT. /TRAINING
MISSISSIPPI WOMEN/
JACKSON STATE COLLEGE. US DEPARTMENT OF LABOR, OFFICE OF
MANPOWER EVALUATION, POLICY AND RESEARCH. JACKSON,
MISSISSIPPI. NOV 1966. 105 PP.

CSELIDX57034   SELIGMAN D
THE ENDURING SLUMS. /NEGRO PUERTO-RICAN/
FORTUNE, DEC 1957. PP 144-148 FF.

CSHANLW61119   SHANNON LW
OCCUPATIONAL AND RESIDENTIAL ADJUSTMENT OF RURAL MIGRANTS.
/NEGRO MEXICAN-AMERICAN/
LABOR MOBILITY AND POPULATION IN AGRICULTURE. IOWA STATE
UNIVERSITY PRESS. AMES, IOWA. 1961. PP 122-149.

CSHANLW63120   SHANNON LW
THE PREDICTION AND EXPLANATION OF ECONOMIC ABSORPTION AMONG
MEXICAN-AMERICANS, NEGROES, AND ANGLOS IN A NORTHERN
INDUSTRIAL COMMUNITY.
PACIFIC SOCIOLOGICAL ASSOCIATION, PAPER. PORTLAND, OREGON.
1963.

CSHANLW63122   SHANNON LW   KRASS E
THE URBAN ADJUSTMENT OF IMMIGRANTS. THE RELATIONSHIP OF
EDUCATION TO OCCUPATIONAL AND TOTAL FAMILY INCOME.
/NEGRO MEXICAN-AMERICAN/
PACIFIC SOCIOLOGICAL REVIEW, VOL 6, NO 1, SPRING 1963.
PP 37-42.

CSHANLW63484   SHANNON LW   *UNIV OF WIS URBAN PROGRAM
THE ASSIMILATION AND ACCULTURATION OF MIGRANTS TO URBAN
AREAS. /MEXICAN-AMERICAN NEGRO/
THE UNIVERSITY OF WISCONSIN URBAN PROGRAM. MADISON,
WISCONSIN. 1963. 27 PP.

CSHANLW63487   SHANNON LW   LETTAU K
MEASURING THE ADJUSTMENT OF IMMIGRANT LABORERS.
/MEXICAN-AMERICAN NEGRO/
SOUTHWESTERN SOCIAL SCIENCE QUARTERLY, SEPT 1963.
PP 139-148.

CSHANLW64124   SHANNON LW   AND KRASS EM
THE ECONOMIC ABSORPTION AND CULTURAL INTEGRATION OF
IMMIGRANT MEXICAN-AMERICAN AND NEGRO WORKERS.
STATE UNIVERSITY OF IOWA, DEPARTMENT OF SOCIOLOGY AND
ANTHROPOLOGY. IOWA CITY, IOWA. 1964. 413 PP.

CSHANLW64486 SHANNON LW KRASS EM
THE ECONOMIC ABSORPTION OF IN-MIGRANT LABORERS IN A NORTHERN INDUSTRIAL COMMUNITY. /MEXICAN-AMERICAN NEGRO/
AMERICAN JOURNAL OF ECONOMICS AND SOCIOLOGY, VOL 23, JAN 1964. PP 65-84.

CSHANLW65121 SHANNON LW
URBAN ADJUSTMENT AND ITS RELATIONSHIP TO THE SOCIAL ANTECEDENTS OF IMMIGRANT WORKERS. /NEGRO MEXICAN-AMERICAN/
INTERNATIONAL REVIEW OF COMMUNITY DEVELOPMENT, NO 13-14, 1965. PP 177-188.

CSHANLW65485 SHANNON LW
CULTURAL AND RELATED RESTRAINTS AND MEANS OF OVERCOMING THEM. /MEXICAN-AMERICAN NEGRO INTEGRATION/
THE ECONOMIC DEVELOPMENT OF AGRICULTURE. IOWA STATE UNIVERSITY PRESS. AMES, IOWA. 1965. PP 66-80, CHAPTER 4.

CSHANLW66123 SHANNON LW MORGAN P
THE PREDICTION OF ECONOMIC ABSORPTION AND CULTURAL INTEGRATION AMONG MEXICAN-AMERICANS, NEGROES, AND ANGLOS IN A NORTHERN INDUSTRIAL COMMUNITY.
HUMAN ORGANIZATION, VOL 25, NO 2, SUMMER 1966. PP 154-162.

CSKILTO66324 SKILL TRAINING OPPOR PROJECT *ARIZONA COUNCIL OF CHURCHES *US DEPARTMENT OF LABOR
FINAL REPORT. EXPERIMENTAL AND DEMONSTRATION ON-JOB-TRAINING PROJECT. /MIGRANT-WORKERS MEXICAN-AMERICAN NEGRO ARIZONA/
ARIZONA COUNCIL OF CHURCHES. MIGRANT OPPORTUNITY PROGRAM. PHOENIX, ARIZONA. AP 12 1966. 64 PP.

CSPREJX62999 SPREY J
SEX DIFFERENCES IN OCCUPATIONAL CHOICE PATTERNS AMONG ADOLESCENTS. /ASPIRATIONS WOMEN NEGRO/
SOCIAL PROBLEMS, VOL 10, SUMMER 1962. PP 11-22.

CSTAUMK61132 STAUPERS MK
NO TIME FOR PREJUDICE. /WOMEN NEGRO OCCUPATIONS/
MACMILLAN. NEW YORK. 1961. 206 PP.

CTURNRH51214 TURNER RH
THE NON-WHITE FEMALE IN THE LABOR-FORCE. /WOMEN NEGRO/
AMERICAN JOURNAL OF SOCIOLOGY, VOL 56, NO 5, 1951. PP 438-447.

CUNIVOD66054 UNIVERSITY OF DENVER
THE TRAINING OF MIGRANT FARM WORKERS. A FOLLOW-UP STUDY OF TWO EXPERIMENTAL AND DEMONSTRATION PROGRAMS UNDER THE MANPOWER-DEVELOPMENT-AND-TRAINING-ACT. /MEXICAN-AMERICAN AMERICAN-INDIAN/
UNIVERSITY OF DENVER, GRADUATE SCHOOL OF SOCIAL WORK. DENVER, COLORADO. 1966. 187 PP.

CUSBURC53372 US BUREAU OF THE CENSUS
EMPLOYMENT AND PERSONAL CHARACTERISTICS. EMPLOYMENT BY AGE, RACE, NATIVITY, EDUCATION, MARITAL-STATUS, HOUSEHOLD RELATIONSHIPS, ETC. /DEMOGRAPHY/
US DEPARTMENT OF COMMERCE, BUREAU OF THE CENSUS. GPO. WASHINGTON, DC. 1953. 145 PP.

CUSBURC53378 US BUREAU OF THE CENSUS
NONWHITE POPULATION BY RACE. NEGROES, INDIANS, JAPANESE, CHINESE, FILIPINOS. BY AGE, SEX, MARITAL-STATUS, EDUCATION, EMPLOYMENT-STATUS, OCCUPATIONAL-STATUS, INCOME, ETC. /DEMOGRAPHY/
US DEPARTMENT OF COMMERCE, BUREAU OF THE CENSUS. GPO. WASHINGTON, DC. 1953. 88 PP.

CUSBURC56373 US BUREAU OF THE CENSUS
EMPLOYMENT OF WHITE AND NON-WHITE PERSONS. 1955. /DEMOGRAPHY/
US DEPARTMENT OF COMMERCE, BUREAU OF THE CENSUS, CURRENT POPULATION REPORTS, SERIES P-50, NO 66. GPO. WASHINGTON, DC. MAR 1956.

CUSBURC59382 US BUREAU OF THE CENSUS
UNITED STATES CENSUS OF AGRICULTURE. COLOR, RACE, AND TENURE OF FARM OPERATOR. GENERAL REPORT, VOLUME II. /DEMOGRAPHY/
US DEPARTMENT OF COMMERCE, BUREAU OF THE CENSUS. GPO. WASHINGTON, DC. 1959. PP 1032-1033.

CUSBURC62374 US BUREAU OF THE CENSUS
GENERAL SOCIAL AND ECONOMIC CHARACTERISTICS. SUMMARY, US CENSUS OF 1960. /DEMOGRAPHY/
US DEPARTMENT OF COMMERCE, BUREAU OF THE CENSUS, FINAL REPORT PC-1-1C. GPO. WASHINGTON, DC. 1962. 344 PP.

CUSBURC63167 US BUREAU OF THE CENSUS
CHARACTERISTICS OF PROFESSIONAL WORKERS. /DEMOGRAPHY/
US DEPARTMENT OF COMMERCE, BUREAU OF THE CENSUS, FINAL REPORT PC-2-7E. GPO. WASHINGTON, DC. 1963. 145 PP.

CUSBURC63168 US BUREAU OF THE CENSUS
CHARACTERISTICS OF TEACHERS. /DEMOGRAPHY/
US DEPARTMENT OF COMMERCE, BUREAU OF THE CENSUS, FINAL REPORT PC-2-7D. GPO. WASHINGTON, DC. 1963. 58 PP.

CUSBURC63169 US BUREAU OF THE CENSUS
EDUCATIONAL-ATTAINMENT. /DEMOGRAPHY/
US DEPARTMENT OF COMMERCE, BUREAU OF THE CENSUS, FINAL REPORT.PC-2-5B. GPO. WASHINGTON, D.C. 1963. 188 PP.

CUSBURC63170 US BUREAU OF THE CENSUS
EMPLOYMENT-STATUS AND WORK CHARACTERISTICS. STATISTICS ON THE RELATION BETWEEN EMPLOYMENT AND SOCIAL AND ECONOMIC CHARACTERISTICS. /DEMOGRAPHY/
US DEPARTMENT OF COMMERCE, BUREAU OF THE CENSUS, FINAL REPORT PC-2-6A. GPO. WASHINGTON, DC. 1963. 226 PP.

CUSBURC63171 US BUREAU OF THE CENSUS
INCOME OF THE ELDERLY POPULATION. /DEMOGRAPHY/
US DEPARTMENT OF COMMERCE, BUREAU OF THE CENSUS, FINAL REPORT PC-2-8B. GPO. WASHINGTON, DC. 1963. 207 PP.

CUSBURC63172 US BUREAU OF THE CENSUS
LIFETIME AND RECENT MIGRATION. /DEMOGRAPHY/
US DEPARTMENT OF COMMERCE, BUREAU OF THE CENSUS, FINAL REPORT PC-2-2D. GPO. WASHINGTON, DC. 1963. 493 PP.

CUSBURC63173 US BUREAU OF THE CENSUS
MOBILITY FOR METROPOLITAN AREAS.
US DEPARTMENT OF COMMERCE, BUREAU OF THE CENSUS, FINAL REPORT PC-2-2C. GPO. WASHINGTON, DC. 1963. 348 PP.

CUSBURC63174 US BUREAU OF THE CENSUS
MOBILITY FOR STATES AND STATE ECONOMIC AREAS. /DEMOGRAPHY/
US DEPARTMENT OF COMMERCE, BUREAU OF THE CENSUS, FINAL REPORT PC-2-2B. GPO. WASHINGTON, DC. 1963. 468 PP.

CUSBURC63175 US BUREAU OF THE CENSUS
NATIVITY AND PARENTAGE. /DEMOGRAPHY/
US DEPARTMENT OF COMMERCE, BUREAU OF THE CENSUS, FINAL REPORT PC-2-1A. GPO. WASHINGTON, DC. 1963. 153 PP.

CUSBURC63176 US BUREAU OF THE CENSUS
NONWHITE POPULATION BY RACE. NEGROES, INDIANS, JAPANESE, CHINESE, FILIPINOS. BY AGE, SEX, MARITAL-STATUS, EDUCATION, EMPLOYMENT-STATUS, OCCUPATIONAL-STATUS, INCOME, ETC. /DEMOGRAPHY/
US DEPARTMENT OF COMMERCE, BUREAU OF THE CENSUS, FINAL REPORT PC-2-1C. GPO. WASHINGTON, DC. 1963. 255 PP.

CUSBURC63177 US BUREAU OF THE CENSUS
OCCUPATIONAL CHARACTERISTICS, DATA ON AGE, RACE, EDUCATION, WORK EXPERIENCE, INCOME, ETC. FOR WORKERS IN EACH OCCUPATION.
US DEPARTMENT OF COMMERCE, BUREAU OF THE CENSUS, FINAL REPORT PC-2-7A. GPO. WASHINGTON, DC. 1963. 530 PP.

CUSBURC63178 US BUREAU OF THE CENSUS
OCCUPATIONS BY EARNINGS AND EDUCATION. STATISTICS FOR MEN 18-64 YEARS OLD, BY COLOR, IN SELECTED OCCUPATIONS. /DEMOGRAPHY/
US DEPARTMENT OF COMMERCE, BUREAU OF THE CENSUS, FINAL REPORT PC-2-7B. GPO. WASHINGTON, DC. 1963. 304 PP.

CUSBURC63179 US BUREAU OF THE CENSUS
OCCUPATION BY INDUSTRY. /DEMOGRAPHY/
US DEPARTMENT OF COMMERCE, BUREAU OF THE CENSUS, FINAL REPORT PC-2-7C. GPO. WASHINGTON, DC. 1963. 146 PP.

CUSBURC63180 US BUREAU OF THE CENSUS
PERSONS BY FAMILY CHARACTERISTICS. FAMILY MEMBERS BY SOCIAL, ECONOMIC AND HOUSING CHARACTERISTICS OF FAMILIES. /DEMOGRAPHY/
US DEPARTMENT OF COMMERCE, BUREAU OF THE CENSUS, FINAL REPORT PC-2-4B. GPO. WASHINGTON, DC. 205 PP.

CUSBURC63181 US BUREAU OF THE CENSUS
PERSONS OF SPANISH-SURNAME. SOCIAL AND ECONOMIC DATA FOR WHITE PERSONS OF SPANISH SURNAME IN 5 SOUTHWESTERN STATES. /DEMOGRAPHY/
US DEPARTMENT OF COMMERCE, BUREAU OF THE CENSUS, FINAL REPORT PC-2-1B. GPO. WASHINGTON, DC. 1963. 202 PP.

CUSBURC63183 US BUREAU OF THE CENSUS
SCHOOL ENROLLMENT. /DEMOGRAPHY/
US DEPARTMENT OF COMMERCE, BUREAU OF THE CENSUS, FINAL REPORT PC-2-5A. GPO. WASHINGTON, DC. 1963. 132 PP.

CUSBURC63184 US BUREAU OF THE CENSUS
SOURCES AND STRUCTURE OF FAMILY INCOME. /DEMOGRAPHY/
US DEPARTMENT OF COMMERCE, BUREAU OF THE CENSUS, FINAL REPORT PC-2-4C. GPO. WASHINGTON, DC. 1963. 235 PP.

CUSBURC63185 US BUREAU OF THE CENSUS
STATE OF BIRTH. /DEMOGRAPHY/
US DEPARTMENT OF COMMERCE, BUREAU OF THE CENSUS, FINAL REPORT PC-2-2A. GPO. WASHINGTON, DC. 1963. 176 PP.

CUSBURC63381 US BUREAU OF THE CENSUS
TRENDS IN THE INCOME OF FAMILIES AND PERSONS IN THE UNITED STATES. 1947-1960. /DEMOGRAPHY/
US DEPARTMENT OF COMMERCE, BUREAU OF THE CENSUS, TECHNICAL PAPER NO 8, PREPARED BY HERMAN P MILLER. GPO. WASHINGTON, DC. 1963. 349 PP.

CUSBURC64376 US BUREAU OF THE CENSUS
NEGRO POPULATION. MARCH 1964. /WOMEN DEMOGRAPHY/
US DEPARTMENT OF COMMERCE, BUREAU OF THE CENSUS, CURRENT POPULATION REPORTS, SERIES P-20, NO 142. GPO. WASHINGTON, DC. 1964.

CUSBURC64380 US BUREAU OF THE CENSUS
STATISTICAL ABSTRACT OF THE UNITED STATES. 1964. /DEMOGRAPHY/
US DEPARTMENT OF COMMERCE, BUREAU OF THE CENSUS. GPO. WASHINGTON, DC. 1964.

CUSBURC65375 US BUREAU OF THE CENSUS
INCOME IN 1964 OF FAMILIES AND PERSONS IN THE UNITED STATES. /DEMOGRAPHY/
US DEPARTMENT OF COMMERCE, BUREAU OF THE CENSUS, CURRENT POPULATION REPORTS, CONSUMER INCOME, SERIES P-60, NO 47. GPO. WASHINGTON, DC. SEPT 24 1965.

CUSBURC65377 US BUREAU OF THE CENSUS
NEGRO POPULATION. MARCH 1965. /WOMEN DEMOGRAPHY/
US DEPARTMENT OF COMMERCE, BUREAU OF THE CENSUS, CURRENT POPULATION REPORTS, SERIES P-20, NO 145. GPO. WASHINGTON, DC. 1965.

CUSBURC65379 US BUREAU OF THE CENSUS
CURRENT POPULATION REPORTS -- SPECIAL CENSUS OF CLEVELAND, OHIO. /DEMOGRAPHY/
US DEPARTMENT OF COMMERCE, BUREAU OF THE CENSUS. GPO. WASHINGTON, DC. 1965.

CUSDHEWND855 US DEPT OF HEALTH ED WELFARE
SELECTED BIBLIOGRAPHY FOR DISADVANTAGED YOUTH. /NEGRO PUERTO-RICAN/
US DEPARTMENT OF HEALTH, EDUCATION AND WELFARE, OFFICE OF EDUCATION. GPO. WASHINGTON, DC. 11 PP.

CUSDLAB43837 US DEPARTMENT OF LABOR
OPPORTUNITIES FOR NEGRO WOMEN AS DIETICIANS. /OCCUPATIONS/
US DEPARTMENT OF LABOR, MONTHLY LABOR REVIEW, VOL 57, NO 1, JULU 1943. PP 104-105.

CUSDLAB54262 US DEPARTMENT OF LABOR
NEGRO WOMEN AND THEIR JOBS.
US DEPARTMENT OF LABOR, WOMEN-S BUREAU. LEAFLET NO 19. GPO. WASHINGTON, DC. 1954. 10 PP.

CUSDLAB63451 US DEPARTMENT OF LABOR
INCOME, EDUCATION AND UNEMPLOYMENT IN NEIGHBORHOODS. ATLANTA, GEORGIA. /DEMOGRAPHY/
US DEPARTMENT OF LABOR, BUREAU OF LABOR STATISTICS. GPO. WASHINGTON, DC. JAN 1963. 30PP.

CUSDLAB63452 US DEPARTMENT OF LABOR
INCOME, EDUCATION AND UNEMPLOYMENT IN NEIGHBORHOODS. BALTIMORE, MARYLAND. /DEMOGRAPHY/
US DEPARTMENT OF LABOR, BUREAU OF LABOR STATISTICS. GPO. WASHINGTON, DC. JAN 1963. 32PP.

CUSDLAB63453 US DEPARTMENT OF LABOR
INCOME, EDUCATION AND UNEMPLOYMENT IN NEIGHBORHOODS.

BIRMINGHAM, ALABAMA. /DEMOGRAPHY/
US DEPARTMENT OF LABOR, BUREAU OF LABOR STATISTICS. GPO.
WASHINGTON, DC. JAN 1963. 22 PP.

CUSDLAB63454　US DEPARTMENT OF LABOR
INCOME, EDUCATION AND UNEMPLOYMENT IN NEIGHBORHOODS.
BOSTON, MASSACHUSETTS. /DEMOGRAPHY/
US DEPARTMENT OF LABOR, BUREAU OF LABOR STATISTICS. GPO.
WASHINGTON, DC. JAN 1963. 28 PP.

CUSDLAB63455　US DEPARTMENT OF LABOR
INCOME, EDUCATION AND UNEMPLOYMENT IN NEIGHBORHOODS.
BUFFALO, NEW-YORK. /DEMOGRAPHY/
US DEPARTMENT OF LABOR, BUREAU OF LABOR STATISTICS. GPO.
WASHINGTON, DC. JAN 1963. 32 PP.

CUSDLAB63456　US DEPARTMENT OF LABOR
INCOME, EDUCATION AND UNEMPLOYMENT IN NEIGHBORHOODS.
CHICAGO, ILLINOIS. /DEMOGRAPHY/
US DEPARTMENT OF LABOR, BUREAU OF LABOR STATISTICS. GPO.
WASHINGTON, DC. JAN 1963. 97 PP.

CUSDLAB63457　US DEPARTMENT OF LABOR
INCOME, EDUCATION AND UNEMPLOYMENT IN NEIGHBORHOODS.
CINCINNATI, OHIO. /DEMOGRAPHY/
US DEPARTMENT OF LABOR, BUREAU OF LABOR STATISTICS. GPO.
WASHINGTON, DC. JAN 1963. 28 PP.

CUSDLAB63458　US DEPARTMENT OF LABOR
INCOME, EDUCATION AND UNEMPLOYMENT IN NEIGHBORHOODS.
CLEVELAND, OHIO. /DEMOGRAPHY/
US DEPARTMENT OF LABOR, BUREAU OF LABOR STATISTICS. GPO.
WASHINGTON, DC. JAN 1963. 30 PP.

CUSDLAB63459　US DEPARTMENT OF LABOR
INCOME, EDUCATION AND UNEMPLOYMENT IN NEIGHBORHOODS.
DALLAS, TEXAS. /DEMOGRAPHY/
US DEPARTMENT OF LABOR, BUREAU OF LABOR STATISTICS. GPO.
WASHINGTON, DC. JAN 1963. 20 PP.

CUSDLAB63460　US DEPARTMENT OF LABOR
INCOME, EDUCATION AND UNEMPLOYMENT IN NEIGHBORHOODS.
DENVER, COLORADO. /DEMOGRAPHY/
US DEPARTMENT OF LABOR, BUREAU OF LABOR STATISTICS. GPO.
WASHINGTON, DC. JAN 1963. 24 PP.

CUSDLAB63461　US DEPARTMENT OF LABOR
INCOME, EDUCATION AND UNEMPLOYMENT IN NEIGHBORHOODS.
DETROIT, MICHIGAN. /DEMOGRAPHY/
US DEPARTMENT OF LABOR, BUREAU OF LABOR STATISTICS. GPO.
WASHINGTON, DC. JAN 1963. 58 PP.

CUSDLAB63462　US DEPARTMENT OF LABOR
INCOME, EDUCATION AND UNEMPLOYMENT IN NEIGHBORHOODS.
HOUSTON, TEXAS. /DEMOGRAPHY/
US DEPARTMENT OF LABOR, BUREAU OF LABOR STATISTICS. GPO.
WASHINGTON, DC. JAN 1963. 29 PP.

CUSDLAB63463　US DEPARTMENT OF LABOR
INCOME, EDUCATION AND UNEMPLOYMENT IN NEIGHBORHOODS.
INDIANAPOLIS, INDIANA. /DEMOGRAPHY/
US DEPARTMENT OF LABOR, BUREAU OF LABOR STATISTICS. GPO.
WASHINGTON, DC. JAN 1963. 30 PP.

CUSDLAB63464　US DEPARTMENT OF LABOR
INCOME, EDUCATION AND UNEMPLOYMENT IN NEIGHBORHOODS.
KANSAS-CITY, MISSOURI. /DEMOGRAPHY/
US DEPARTMENT OF LABOR, BUREAU OF LABOR STATISTICS. GPO.
WASHINGTON, DC. JAN 1963. 28 PP.

CUSDLAB63466　US DEPARTMENT OF LABOR
INCOME, EDUCATION AND UNEMPLOYMENT IN NEIGHBORHOODS.
MEMPHIS, TENNESSEE. /DEMOGRAPHY/
US DEPARTMENT OF LABOR, BUREAU OF LABOR STATISTICS. GPO.
WASHINGTON, DC. JAN 1963. 22 PP.

CUSDLAB63467　US DEPARTMENT OF LABOR
INCOME, EDUCATION AND UNEMPLOYMENT IN NEIGHBORHOODS.
MILWAUKEE, WISCONSIN. /DEMOGRAPHY/
US DEPARTMENT OF LABOR, BUREAU OF LABOR STATISTICS. GPO.
WASHINGTON, DC. JAN 1963. 28 PP.

CUSDLAB63468　US DEPARTMENT OF LABOR
INCOME, EDUCATION AND UNEMPLOYMENT IN NEIGHBORHOODS.
MINNEAPOLIS -- ST-PAUL, MINNESOTA. /DEMOGRAPHY/
US DEPARTMENT OF LABOR, BUREAU OF LABOR STATISTICS. GPO.
WASHINGTON, DC. JAN 1963. 32 PP.

CUSDLAB63469　US DEPARTMENT OF LABOR
INCOME, EDUCATION AND UNEMPLOYMENT IN NEIGHBORHOODS.
NEW-ORLEANS, LOUISIANA. /DEMOGRAPHY/
US DEPARTMENT OF LABOR, BUREAU OF LABOR STATISTICS. GPO.
WASHINGTON, DC. JAN 1963. 30 PP.

CUSDLAB63470　US DEPARTMENT OF LABOR
INCOME, EDUCATION AND UNEMPLOYMENT IN NEIGHBORHOODS.
NEWARK, NEW-JERSEY. /DEMOGRAPHY/
US DEPARTMENT OF LABOR, BUREAU OF LABOR STATISTICS. GPO.
WASHINGTON, DC. JAN 1963. 31 PP.

CUSDLAB63471　US DEPARTMENT OF LABOR
INCOME, EDUCATION AND UNEMPLOYMENT IN NEIGHBORHOODS.
NEW-YORK-CITY -- BROOKLYN. /DEMOGRAPHY/
US DEPARTMENT OF LABOR, BUREAU OF LABOR STATISTICS. GPO.
WASHINGTON, DC. JAN 1963. 84 PP.

CUSDLAB63472　US DEPARTMENT OF LABOR
INCOME, EDUCATION AND UNEMPLOYMENT IN NEIGHBORHOODS.
NEW-YORK-CITY -- THE BRONX. /DEMOGRAPHY/
US DEPARTMENT OF LABOR, BUREAU OF LABOR STATISTICS. GPO.
WASHINGTON, DC. JAN 1963. 47 PP.

CUSDLAB63473　US DEPARTMENT OF LABOR
INCOME, EDUCATION AND UNEMPLOYMENT IN NEIGHBORHOODS.
NEW-YORK-CITY -- MANHATTAN. /DEMOGRAPHY/
US DEPARTMENT OF LABOR, BUREAU OF LABOR STATISTICS. GPO.
WASHINGTON, DC. JAN 1963. 44 PP.

CUSDLAB63474　US DEPARTMENT OF LABOR
INCOME, EDUCATION AND UNEMPLOYMENT IN NEIGHBORHOODS.
NEW-YORK-CITY -- QUEENS. /DEMOGRAPHY/
US DEPARTMENT OF LABOR, BUREAU OF LABOR STATISTICS. GPO.
WASHINGTON, DC. JAN 1963. 71 PP.

CUSDLAB63475　US DEPARTMENT OF LABOR
INCOME, EDUCATION AND UNEMPLOYMENT IN NEIGHBORHOODS.
NEW-YORK-CITY -- STATEN-ISLAND. /DEMOGRAPHY/
US DEPARTMENT OF LABOR, BUREAU OF LABOR STATISTICS. GPO.
WASHINGTON, DC. JAN 1963. 19 PP.

CUSDLAB63476　US DEPARTMENT OF LABOR
INCOME, EDUCATION AND UNEMPLOYMENT IN NEIGHBORHOODS.
OAKLAND, CALIFORNIA. /DEMOGRAPHY/
US DEPARTMENT OF LABOR, BUREAU OF LABOR STATISTICS. GPO.
WASHINGTON, DC. JAN 1963. 23 PP.

CUSDLAB63477　US DEPARTMENT OF LABOR
INCOME, EDUCATION AND UNEMPLOYMENT IN NEIGHBORHOODS.
OKLAHOMA-CITY, OKLAHOMA. /DEMOGRAPHY/
US DEPARTMENT OF LABOR, BUREAU OF LABOR STATISTICS. GPO.
WASHINGTON, DC. JAN 1963. 19 PP.

CUSDLAB63478　US DEPARTMENT OF LABOR
INCOME, EDUCATION AND UNEMPLOYMENT IN NEIGHBORHOODS.
PHILADELPHIA, PENNSYLVANIA. /DEMOGRAPHY/
US DEPARTMENT OF LABOR, BUREAU OF LABOR STATISTICS. GPO.
WASHINGTON, DC. JAN 1963. 52 PP.

CUSDLAB63479　US DEPARTMENT OF LABOR
INCOME, EDUCATION AND UNEMPLOYMENT IN NEIGHBORHOODS.
PITTSBURGH, PENNSYLVANIA. /DEMOGRAPHY/
US DEPARTMENT OF LABOR, BUREAU OF LABOR STATISTICS. GPO.
WASHINGTON, DC. JAN 1963. 30 PP.

CUSDLAB63480　US DEPARTMENT OF LABOR
INCOME, EDUCATION AND UNEMPLOYMENT IN NEIGHBORHOODS.
PHOENIX, ARIZONA. /DEMOGRAPHY/
US DEPARTMENT OF LABOR, BUREAU OF LABOR STATISTICS. GPO.
WASHINGTON, DC. JAN 1963. 20 PP.

CUSDLAB63481　US DEPARTMENT OF LABOR
INCOME, EDUCATION AND UNEMPLOYMENT IN NEIGHBORHOODS.
ST-LOUIS, MISSOURI. /DEMOGRAPHY/
US DEPARTMENT OF LABOR, BUREAU OF LABOR STATISTICS. GPO.
WASHINGTON, DC. JAN 1963. 30 PP.

CUSDLAB63482　US DEPARTMENT OF LABOR
INCOME, EDUCATION AND UNEMPLOYMENT IN NEIGHBORHOODS.
SAN-ANTONIO, TEXAS. /DEMOGRAPHY/
US DEPARTMENT OF LABOR, BUREAU OF LABOR STATISTICS. GPO.
WASHINGTON, DC. JAN 1963. 26 PP.

CUSDLAB63483　US DEPARTMENT OF LABOR
INCOME, EDUCATION AND UNEMPLOYMENT IN NEIGHBORHOODS.
SAN-DIEGO, CALIFORNIA. /DEMOGRAPHY/
US DEPARTMENT OF LABOR, BUREAU OF LABOR STATISTICS. GPO.
WASHINGTON, DC. JAN 1963. 28 PP.

CUSDLAB63484　US DEPARTMENT OF LABOR
INCOME, EDUCATION AND UNEMPLOYMENT IN NEIGHBORHOODS.
SAN-FRANCISCO, CALIFORNIA. /DEMOGRAPHY/
US DEPARTMENT OF LABOR, BUREAU OF LABOR STATISTICS. GPO
WASHINGTON, DC. JAN 1963. 34 PP.

CUSDLAB63485　US DEPARTMENT OF LABOR
INCOME, EDUCATION AND UNEMPLOYMENT IN NEIGHBORHOODS.
SEATTLE, WASHINGTON. /DEMOGRAPHY/
US DEPARTMENT OF LABOR, BUREAU OF LABOR STATISTICS. GPO.
WASHINGTON, DC. JAN 1963. 27 PP.

CUSDLAB63486　US DEPARTMENT OF LABOR
INCOME, EDUCATION AND UNEMPLOYMENT IN NEIGHBORHOODS.
TAMPA, ST-PETERSBURG FLORIDA. /DEMOGRAPHY/
US DEPARTMENT OF LABOR, BUREAU OF LABOR STATISTICS. GPO.
WASHINGTON, DC. JAN 1963. 24 PP.

CUSDLAB63487　US DEPARTMENT OF LABOR
INCOME, EDUCATION AND UNEMPLOYMENT IN NEIGHBORHOODS.
WASHINGTON-DC. /DEMOGRAPHY/
US DEPARTMENT OF LABOR, BUREAU OF LABOR STATISTICS. GPO.
WASHINGTON, DC. JAN 1963. 34 PP.

CUSDLAB63565　US DEPARTMENT OF LABOR
INCOME, EDUCATION AND UNEMPLOYMENT IN NEIGHBORHOODS.
LOS-ANGELES, CALIFORNIA. /DEMOGRAPHY/
US DEPARTMENT OF LABOR, BUREAU OF LABOR STATISTICS. GPO.
WASHINGTON, DC. JAN 1963. 81 PP.

CUSDLAB64072　US DEPARTMENT OF LABOR
THE CHANGING STATUS OF NEGRO WOMEN WORKERS.
US DEPARTMENT OF LABOR, MONTHLY LABOR REVIEW, VOL 87, NO 6,
JUNE 1964. PP 671-673.

CUSDLAB64264　US DEPARTMENT OF LABOR
NEGRO WOMEN WORKERS IN 1960.
US DEPARTMENT OF LABOR, WOMEN-S BUREAU. BULLETIN 287. GPO.
WASHINGTON, DC. 1964. 55 PP.

CUSDLAB65261　US DEPARTMENT OF LABOR
CURRENT DATA ON NONWHITE WOMEN WORKERS. /NEGRO/
US DEPARTMENT OF LABOR, WOMEN-S BUREAU. GPO. WASHINGTON, DC.
JUNE 1965. 12 PP.

CUSDLAB66263　US DEPARTMENT OF LABOR
NEGRO WOMEN IN THE POPULATION AND IN THE LABOR-FORCE.
US DEPARTMENT OF LABOR, WOMEN-S BUREAU. GPO. WASHINGTON, DC.
JUNE 1966. 34 PP.

CUSDLAB66323　US DEPARTMENT OF LABOR
OAK GLEN -- A TRAINING CAMP FOR UNEMPLOYED YOUTH. /NEGRO
MEXICAN-AMERICAN/
US DEPARTMENT OF LABOR, OFFICE OF MANPOWER POLICY,
EVALUATION AND RESEARCH. MANPOWER/AUTOMATION RESEARCH
MONOGRAPH NO 5. WASHINGTON, DC. MAY 1966. 69 PP.

CUSHOUR64346　US HOUSE OF REPRESENTATIVES
POVERTY IN THE UNITED STATES, HEARINGS. /AMERICAN-INDIAN
NEGRO PUERTO-RICAN EMPLOYMENT/
US HOUSE OF REPRESENTATIVES, COMMITTEE ON EDUCATION AND
LABOR. 88TH CONGRESS, 2ND SESSION. HEARINGS. GPO.
WASHINGTON, DC. 1964. 304 PP.

CUVCAIIN0524　UCLA INSTITUTE OF IND RELS　　*US DEPARTMENT OF COMMERCE
HARD-CORE UNEMPLOYMENT AND POVERTY IN LOS-ANGELES.
/CALIFORNIA NEGRO MEXICAN-AMERICAN/
US DEPARTMENT OF COMMERCE, AREA REDEVELOPMENT
ADMINISTRATION. GPO. WASHINGTON, DC. 579 PP.

CUVIOIP65277　U OF IOWA INST OF PUB AFFAIRS
ECONOMIC ABSORPTION AND CULTURAL INTEGRATION OF THE URBAN
NEWCOMER. /NEGRO MEXICAN-AMERICAN/
EMERGING PROBLEMS IN HOUSING AND URBAN DEVELOPMENT.
UNIVERSITY OF IOWA, INSTITUTE OF PUBLIC AFFAIRS. IOWA CITY,
IOWA. 1965. PP 24-46.

CWEINJL64310　WEINBERG JL　　*US DEPARTMENT OF LABOR
REPORT, EVALUATION STUDY OF YOUTH TRAINING AND EMPLOYMENT
PROJECT, EAST LOS-ANGELES. /NEGRO MEXICAN-AMERICAN
CALIFORNIA/
US DEPARTMENT OF LABOR, OFFICE OF MANPOWER, AUTOMATION AND

TRAINING, DIVISION CF SPECIAL PROGRAMS. GPO. WASHINGTON, DC.
AUG 14 1964. 52 PP.

CWILCRC63322   WILCOCK RC   FRANKE WH
UNWANTED WORKERS. PERMANENT LAYOFFS AND LONG-TERM
   UNEMPLOYMENT.   /NEGRO WOMEN/
THE FREE PRESS-OF GLENCOE. NEW YORK. 1963. 340.

CWILLJJ58324   WILLIAMS JJ
NEGRO ADC MOTHERS LOOK FOR WORK. /WOMEN/
UNIVERSITY OF MICHIGAN PRESS. ANN ARBOR, MICHIGAN. 1958.
105 PP.

CWILSAB63325   WILSON AB
SOCIAL-STRATIFICATION AND ACADEMIC ACHIEVEMENT. /NEGRO
   ORIENTAL/
EDUCATION IN DEPRESSED AREAS. ED BY A HARRY PASSOW. COLUMBIA
UNIVERSITY, TEACHERS COLLEGE. NEW YORK. 1963. PP 217-234.

CYINGJM56519   YINGER JM   SIMPSON GE
THE INTEGRATION OF AMERICANS OF MEXICAN, PUERTO-RICAN, AND
   ORIENTAL CESCENT.
THE ANNALS OF THE AMERICAN ACADEMY OF POLITICAL AND SOCIAL
SCIENCE. VOL 304, MAR 1956. PP 124-131.

CYMCAYA66329   YMCA YOUTH AND WORK PROJECT   *YMCA VOCATL SERVICE CENTER
FINAL REPORT OF THE YMCA YOUTH AND WORK PROJECT 1962-1966.
   /NEGRO PUERTO-RICAN TRAINING/
YMCA VOCATIONAL SERVICE CENTER. BASIC SYSTEMS INCORPORATED.
BROOKLYN, NEW YORK. AP 29 1966. 92 PP.

CYOUNMB65636   YOUNG MB
THE NEGRO GIRL AND POVERTY. /WOMEN/
THE AMERICAN CHILD, VOL 47, NO 3, MAY 1965. PP 11-13.

GABRACX56861 ABRAMS C
CIVIL-RIGHTS IN 1956.
COMMENTARY, AUG 1956. PP 101-109.

GABRACX58361 ABRAMS C   *ANTI-DEFAMATION LEAGUE
LAST HIRED -- FIRST FIRED. /DISCRIMINATION/
ANTI-DEFAMATION LEAGUE OF B-NAI B-RITH, ADL BULLETIN,
MAY 1958.

GACKLGX66680 ACKLEY G   *US DEPARTMENT OF LABOR
POLICIES FOR THE PROMOTION OF ECONOMIC GROWTH.
US DEPARTMENT OF LABOR, MANPOWER ADMINISTRATION, SEMINAR ON
MANPOWER POLICY AND PROGRAM. JAN 1966. 33 PP.

GADKIWG63410 ADKINS WG
INCOMES OF RURAL FAMILIES IN THE BLACKLAND PRAIRIES.
TEXAS A AND M UNIVERSITY. COLLEGE STATION, TEXAS. MAY 1963.
20 PP.

GAFLCIOND863 AFL-CIO
LABOR LOOKS AT AUTOMATION.
AFL-CIO, PUBLICATION NO 21. WASHINGTON, DC. 36 PP. ND.

GAFLCIO63365 AFL-CIO NEWS
UNIONS URGED TO FOLLOW THROUGH ON PLEDGES TO COMBAT JOB
  BIAS.
AFL-CIO NEWS, JUNE 13 1963.

GAFLCIO63864 AFL-CIO DEPT OF RESEARCH
THE EROSION OF JOBS AND SKILLS.
AMERICAN FEDERATIONIST, OCT 1963. 7 PP.

GAHEREX65804 AHERN E
WHAT THE SUPERVISOR SHOULD KNOW ABOUT THE
  EQUAL-EMPLOYMENT-OPPORTUNITY LAW.
SUPERVISORY MANAGEMENT, VOL 10, NO 9, SEPT 1965. PP 11-16.

GAIRCHR63866 AIR COND HEATING REFRIG NEWS
CONTRACTOR GROUP HITS REVISED EQUAL EMPLOYMENT STANDARDS.
AIR CONDITIONING, HEATING, AND REFRIGERATION NEWS,
AUG 5 1963.

GAIRCHR63867 AIR COND HEATING REFRIG NEWS
JOINT STAND REJECTS RACIAL QUOTAS FOR PLUMBING APPRENTICES.
AIR CONDITIONING, HEATING, AND REFRIGERATION NEWS,
AUG 26 1963.

GALASSC63366 ALASKA STATE COMM HUM RIGHTS
1963 REPORT OF PROGRESS IN HUMAN-RIGHTS.
ALASKA STATE COMMISSION FOR HUMAN RIGHTS. ANCHORAGE, ALASKA.
1963. 20 PP.

GALBEJM63367 ALBERT JM
NLRB-FEPC. /LEGISLATION/
VANDERBILT LAW REVIEW, VOL 16, JUNE 1963. PP 547-593.

GALBRLE63368 ALBRIGHT LE   GLENNON JR
SMITH WJ
THE USE OF PSYCHOLOGICAL TESTS IN INDUSTRY.
HOWARD ALLEN, INC. CLEVELAND, OHIO. 1963. 192 PP.

GALFOAL54869 ALFORD AL
FEPC. AN ADMINISTRATIVE STUDY OF SELECTED STATE AND LOCAL
  PROGRAMS.
PRINCETON UNIVERSITY. PHD THESIS. PRINCETON, NEW JERSEY.
1954.

GALGJME52107 ALGOR ME
STRENGTHENING THE INTEGRATION OF MINORITY-GROUPS. THE
  PROBLEM IS TACKLED AS A UNION PROBLEM.
JOURNAL OF EDUCATIONAL SOCIOLOGY, VOL 25, FEB 1952.
PP 337-342.

GALLCTO66361 ALLEGHENY CC IMPROVE NBRHOOD
ACTION FOR EMPLOYMENT. A DEMONSTRATION NEIGHBORHOOD
  MANPOWER PROJECT.
ALLEGHENY COUNCIL TO IMPROVE OUR NEIGHBORHOOD. PITTSBURGH,
PENNSYLVANIA. 1966. 63 PP.

GALLECC65758 ALLER CC
THE ROLE OF GOVERNMENT-SPONSORED TRAINING AND RETRAINING
  PROGRAMS.
UNEMPLOYMENT IN A PROSPEROUS ECONOMY. A REPORT OF THE
PRINCETON MANPOWER SYMPOSIUM. ED BY W G BOWEN AND F H
HARBISON. PRINCETON UNIVERSITY. PRINCETON, NEW JERSEY. 1965.
PP 126-141.

GALLECC67910 ALLER CC
MANPOWER DEVELOPMENT PROGRAMS FOR FARM PEOPLE.
FARM LABOR IN THE UNITED STATES. ED BY C E BISHOP. COLUMBIA
UNIVERSITY PRESS. NEW YORK. 1967. PP 115-136.

GALLECX65870 ALLER C
HOW MANY JOBS. WHAT KIND OF JOBS.
AFL-CIO INDUSTRIAL UNION DEPARTMENT, IUD AGENDA, VOL 1,
NO 8, SEPT 1965. PP 9-11.

GALLPGX58871 ALLPORT G
THE NATURE OF PREJUDICE.
DOUBLEDAY-ANCHOR. NEW YORK. 1958.

GALTEJX65369 ALTERMAN J   *US DEPARTMENT OF LABOR
INTERINDUSTRY EMPLOYMENT REQUIREMENTS.
US DEPARTMENT OF LABOR, MONTHLY LABOR REVIEW, JULY 1965.

GAMERCE64370 AMERICAN CC ON EDUCATION
AMBITIOUS EDUCATION IMPROVEMENT PROJECT UNDER WAY IN SOUTH.
EXPANDING OPPORTUNITIES, VOL 1, NO 2, SEPT 1964. 8 PP.

GAMERCR46372 AM COUNCIL ON RACE RELATIONS
REPORTS ON THE WORK OF THE FEPC IN NEW-JERSEY AND NEW-YORK.
AMERICAN COUNCIL ON RACE RELATIONS. SAN FRANCISCO,
CALIFORNIA. 1946.

GAMERCR46373 AM COUNCIL ON RACE RELATIONS
STATE FAIR-EMPLOYMENT-PRACTICES-COMMISSIONS -- A SELECTED
  BIBLIOGRAPHY.
AMERICAN COUNCIL ON RACE RELATIONS. CHICAGO, ILLINOIS. 1946.

GAMERCR47374 AM COUNCIL ON RACE RELATIONS

STATE FAIR-EMPLOYMENT-PRACTICES-COMMISSION -- WHAT THE
  PEOPLE SAY.
AMERICAN COUNCIL ON RACE RELATIONS. CHICAGO, ILLINOIS. 1947.
13 PP.

GAMERCR49371 AM COUNCIL ON RACE RELATIONS
EVALUATION OF STATE FAIR-EMPLOYMENT-PRACTICES-COMMISSIONS.
  EXPERIENCES AND FORECASTS.
AMERICAN COUNCIL ON RACE RELATIONS. CHICAGO, ILLINOIS.
MAR 1949.

GAMERCX66756 AMERICAN CHILD
THE GUARANTEED-INCOME.
AMERICAN CHILD, VOL 48, SUMMER 1966. ENTIRE ISSUE.

GAMERFC48378 AM FRIENDS SERVICE COMMITTEE
EMPLOYING MINORITIES SUCCESSFULLY.
AMERICAN FRIENDS SERVICE COMMITTEE, INC. UNPUBLISHED PAPER.
PHILADELPHIA, PENNSYLVANIA. 1948.

GAMERFC50379 AM FRIENDS SERVICE COMMITTEE
QUESTIONS AND ANSWERS ABOUT EMPLOYMENT ON MERIT.
AMERICAN FRIENDS SERVICE COMMITTEE. PHILADELPHIA,
PENNSYLVANIA. 1950. 20 PP.

GAMERFX57873 AMERICAN FEDERATIONIST
PARLEY ON CIVIL-RIGHTS.
AMERICAN FEDERATIONIST, VOL 64, NO 7, JULY 1957. PP 23FF.

GAMERFX59577 AMERICAN FEDERATIONIST
VIGOROUS RIGHTS EFFORTS PLEDGED BY CONVENTION.
AMERICAN FEDERATIONIST, VOL 66, NO 9, OCT 1959. PP 20-21.

GAMERFX59872 AMERICAN FEDERATIONIST
CIVIL-RIGHTS RESOLUTION.
AMERICAN FEDERATIONIST, VOL 66, NO 9, OCT 1959. PP 21-23.

GAMERFX63375 AMERICAN FEDERATIONIST
THE COMING CRISIS. YOUTH WITHOUT WORK.
THE AMERICAN FEDERATIONIST, VOL 70, NO 4, AP 1963. PP 8-15.

GAMERFX65377 AMERICAN FEDERATIONIST
THE SPECTER OF MASS YOUTH UNEMPLOYMENT.
THE AMERICAN FEDERATIONIST, VOL 72, NO 5, MAY 1965. PP 8-15.

GAMERFX66376 AMERICAN FEDERATIONIST
EQUAL RIGHTS FOR ALL.
THE AMERICAN FEDERATIONIST, VOL 71, NO 3, MAR 1966. PP 1-4.

GAMERFX66674 AMERICAN FEDERATIONIST
AMERICA-S POOR. REALITY AND CHANGE. /RETRAINING SKILLS
  UNEMPLOYMENT/
THE AMERICAN FEDERATIONIST, VOL 73, NO 4, AP 1966.
25 PP. ENTIRE ISSUE.

GAMERJCND380 AMERICAN JEWISH COMMITTEE
ANALYSIS OF CITY ORDINANCES AGAINST RACIAL AND RELIGIOUS
  DISCRIMINATION IN EMPLOYMENT.
AMERICAN JEWISH COMMITTEE. NEW YORK. ND.

GAMERJC53388 AMERICAN JEWISH CONGRESS   NAACP
CIVIL-RIGHTS IN THE UNITED STATES, 1953.
AMERICAN JEWISH CONGRESS AND NATIONAL ASSOCIATION FOR THE
ADVANCEMENT OF COLORED PEOPLE. NEW YORK. 1954. 189 PP.

GAMERJC54381 AMERICAN JEWISH COMMITTEE
EQUAL JOB OPPORTUNITY IS GOOD BUSINESS.
AMERICAN JEWISH COMMITTEE. NEW YORK. 1954.

GAMERJC60382 AMERICAN JEWISH COMMITTEE
YOUR RIGHTS UNDER FAIR-EMPLOYMENT-PRACTICE LAWS.
AMERICAN JEWISH COMMITTEE. NEW YORK. 1960.

GAMERJC64383 AMERICAN JEWISH COMMITTEE
INTEGRATION IN BUSINESS AND INDUSTRY. A SELECTED, ANNOTATED
  BIBLIOGRAPHY.
AMERICAN JEWISH COMMITTEE, INSTITUTE OF HUMAN RELATIONS.
NEW YORK. FEB 3 1964. 4 PP.

GAMERJD60385 AMERICAN JEWISH CONGRESS
FEDERAL CIVIL-RIGHTS-ACT OF 1960, SUMMARY AND ANALYSIS.
AMERICAN JEWISH CONGRESS, COMMISSION ON LAW AND SOCIAL
ACTION. NEW YORK. 1960. 14 PP.

GAMERJD61387 AMERICAN JEWISH CONGRESS
REPORT ON TWENTY STATE ANTI-DISCRIMINATION AGENCIES AND THE
  LAWS THEY ADMINISTER.
AMERICAN JEWISH CONGRESS, COMMISSION ON LAW AND SOCIAL
ACTION. NEW YORK. MIMEOGRAPHED. DEC 1961. 27 PP.

GAMERJD63384 AMERICAN JEWISH CONGRESS
THE CIVIL-RIGHTS AND CIVIL-LIBERTIES DECISIONS OF THE US
  SUPREME COURT FOR THE 1962-63 TERM. A SUMMARY AND
  ANALYSIS.
AMERICAN JEWISH CONGRESS, COMMISSION ON LAW AND SOCIAL
ACTION. NEW YORK. 1963. 88 PP.

GAMERJD63386 AMERICAN JEWISH CONGRESS
A FIVE-STATE SURVEY OF DISCRIMINATION BY COMMERCIAL
  EMPLOYMENT AGENCIES.
NATION-S MANPOWER REVOLUTION. US SENATE, COMMITTEE ON LABOR,
EDUCATION AND WELFARE, SUBCOMMITTEE ON EMPLOYMENT AND
MANPOWER. 88TH CONGRESS, 1ST SESSION. GPO. WASHINGTON, DC.
JUNE 1963. PP 771-773.

GAMERMA49389 AMERICAN MANAGEMENT ASSN
APTITUDE TESTING, TRAINING, AND EMPLOYEE DEVELOPMENT, WITH
  A SECTION ON THE EMPLOYMENT OF MINORITY-GROUPS.
AMERICAN MANAGEMENT ASSOCIATION. NEW YORK. 1949. 23 PP.

GAMERPW64798 AMERICAN PUBLIC WELFARE ASSN
AUTOMATION AND PUBLIC WELFARE.
AMERICAN FOUNDATION ON AUTOMATION AND EMPLOYMENT, INC.
PROCEEDINGS. CHICAGO, ILLINOIS. JUNE 1964. 69 PP.

GAMOSWE64874 AMOS WE
JOB ADJUSTMENT PROBLEMS OF DELINQUENT MINORITY-GROUP YOUTH.
VOCATIONAL GUIDANCE QUARTERLY, VOL 13, WINTER 1964-65.
PP 87-90.

GANDEBR67589 ANDERSON BR *EEOC
PARTIAL INVENTORY OF ON-GOING RESEARCH IN
EQUAL-EMPLOYMENT-OPPORTUNITIES.
EQUAL EMPLOYMENT OPPORTUNITY COMMISSION, OFFICE OF RESEARCH
AND REPORTS. WASHINGTON, DC. FEB 1 1967. 175 PP.

GANDEBXND391 ANDERSON B *OPPORS INDIZATION CENTER
POPULATION AND LABOR-FORCE CHARACTERISTICS OF FIVE
SOUTHEASTERN PENNSYLVANIA COUNTIES.
OPPORTUNITIES INDUSTRIALIZATION CENTER, RECORDS MANAGEMENT
AND EVALVATION DEPARTMENT. ND.

GANDEWH64392 ANDERSON WHL
TRICKLING DOWN. THE RELATIONSHIP BETWEEN ECONOMIC GROWTH AND
THE EXTENT OF POVERTY AMONG AMERICAN FAMILIES.
QUARTERLY JOURNAL OF ECONOMICS, NOV 1964, PP 511-524.

GANNAOA42549 ANNALS OF AAPSS
MINORITY PEOPLES IN A NATION AT WAR.
ANNALS OF THE AMERICAN ACADEMY OF POLITICAL AND SOCIAL
SCIENCE, VOL 223, SEPT 1942. ENTIRE ISSUE.

GANNAOA46547 ANNALS OF AAPSS
CONTROLLING GROUP PREJUDICE.
ANNALS OF THE AMERICAN ACADEMY OF POLITICAL AND SOCIAL
SCIENCE, VOL 244, MAR 1946. ENTIRE ISSUE.

GANNAOA56578 ANNALS OF AAPSS
RACIAL DESEGREGATION AND INTEGRATION.
ANNALS OF THE AMERICAN ACADEMY OF POLITICAL AND SOCIAL
SCIENCE, VOL 304, 1956. ENTIRE ISSUE.

GANTIDL57397 ANTI-DEFAMATION LEAGUE
JOB BIAS IN L A. /LOS-ANGELES CALIFORNIA/
ANTI-DEFAMATION LEAGUE OF B-NAI B-RITH, ADL BULLETIN,
SEPT 1957.

GANTIDL59399 ANTI-DEFAMATION LEAGUE
LIFE INSURANCE. THE PATIENT IMPROVES. /DISCRIMINATION/
ANTI-DEFAMATION LEAGUE OF B-NAI B-RITH, ADL BULLETIN,
JUNE 1959.

GANTIDL61393 ANTI-DEFAMATION LEAGUE
BANK BARRIERS /DISCRIMINATION/
ANTI-DEFAMATION LEAGUE OF B-NAI B-RITH, ADL BULLETIN,
NOV 1961.

GANTIDL62398 ANTI-DEFAMATION LEAGUE
LIFE INSURANCE COMPANIES. /DISCRIMINATION/
ANTI-DEFAMATION LEAGUE OF B-NAI B-RITH, ADL BULLETIN,
OCT 1962.

GANTIDL63396 ANTI-DEFAMATION LEAGUE
INDUSTRY AND HUMAN-RIGHTS.
ANTI-DEFAMATION LEAGUE OF B-NAI B-RITH, ADL BULLETIN,
JUNE 1963.

GANTOAX59401 ANTONOVSKY A ED LORWIN LL ED
*NY STATE COMM AGAINST DISCR
DISCRIMINATION AND LOW INCOMES.
NEW SCHOOL FOR SOCIAL RESEARCH. NEW YORK. 1959. 381 PP.

GANTJAX60400 ANTONOVSKY A *NY STATE COMM AGAINST DISCR
THE SOCIAL MEANING OF DISCRIMINATION.
DISCRIMINATION AND LOW INCOMES. ED BY AARON ANTONOVSKY AND
LOUIS L LORWIN. NEW SCHOOL FOR SOCIAL RESEARCH. NEW YORK.
1959. ALSO PHYLON, VOL 21, NO 1, 1ST QUARTER 1960. PP 81-95.

GAPRUVJ63402 APRUZZESE VJ
DISCRIMINATION -- THE LAW OF THE LAND VERSUS THE LAW OF THE
LAND.
LABOR LAW JOURNAL, VOL 14, JULY 1963. PP 597-600.

GARNSSX64404 ARNSTEIN S *US DEPARTMENT OF LABOR
TESTING THE UNTESTABLES.
US DEPARTMENT OF LABOR, OCCUPATIONAL OUTLOOK QUARTERLY, SEPT
1964. PP 21-24.

GARGNRL65747 ARONSON RL
JOBS, WAGES AND CHANGING TECHNOLOGY.
CORNELL UNIVERSITY, STATE SCHOOL OF INDUSTRIAL AND LABOR
RELATIONS, BULLETIN 55. ITHACA, NEW YORK. 1965. 74 PP.

GASHXPX65406 ASH P
RACE, EMPLOYMENT TESTS, AND EQUAL-OPPORTUNITY.
NATIONAL ASSOCIATION OF INTERGROUP RELATIONS OFFICERS
CONVENTION, PAPER. CHICAGO, ILLINOIS. OCT 21 1965. ALSO
INDUSTRIAL MANAGEMENT, VOL 8, NO 3, MAR 1966. PP 8-12.

GASHXPX66405 ASH P
THE IMPLICATIONS OF THE CIVIL-RIGHTS-ACT OF 1964 FOR
PSYCHOLOGICAL ASSESSMENT IN INDUSTRY. /TESTING/
AMERICAN PSYCHOLOGICAL CONVENTION, 72ND ANNUAL CONVENTION.
SYMPOSIUM, LEGAL ISSUES WHICH CONFRONT THE PSYCHOLOGIST AND
COMMUNITY, PAPER. CHICAGO, ILLINOIS. SEPT 5 1965. ALSO
AMERICAN PSYCHOLOGIST, VOL 21, NO 8, AUG 1966. PP 797-803.

GASSOIC63407 ASSOC INDUSTRIES OF CLEVELAND
MANAGEMENT GUIDE. EQUAL-EMPLOYMENT-OPPORTUNITY.
ASSOCIATED INDUSTRIES OF CLEVELAND. CLEVELAND, OHIO. 1963.
20 PP.

GATKIJA61408 ATKINS JA *COLORADO STATE DEPT OF ED
HUMAN-RELATIONS IN COLORADO. 1858-1959.
COLORADO STATE DEPARTMENT OF EDUCATION. DENVER, COLORADO.
1961. 196 PP.

GAVINAX60409 AVINS A
ANTIDISCRIMINATION LEGISLATION AS AN INFRINGEMENT OF FREEDOM
OF CHOICE.
NEW YORK LAW FORUM, VOL 6, NO 1, 1960. PP 13-37.

GAVINAX62411 AVINS A
WEAPONS AGAINST DISCRIMINATION IN PUBLIC OFFICE.
SYRACUSE LAW REVIEW, VOL 14, FALL 1962. PP 24-41.

GAVINAX64410 AVINS A
FREEDOM OF CHOICE IN PERSONAL SERVICE OCCUPATIONS. 13TH
AMENDMENT LIMITATIONS ON ANTIDISCRIMINATION LEGISLATION.
CORNELL LAW QUARTERLY, VOL 49, 1964. PP 228-256.

GBABOJIX58606 BABOW I HOWDEN E
*CC CIVIC UNITY SAN FRANCISCO
A CIVIL-RIGHTS INVENTORY OF SAN-FRANCISCO. PART I,
EMPLOYMENT. /CALIFORNIA/
COUNCIL FOR CIVIC UNITY OF SAN FRANCISCO. SAN FRANCISCO,
CALIFORNIA. 1958. 352 PP.

GBACHFT63413 BACHMURA FT
MANPOWER RETRAINING IN THE SOUTH-S RURAL POPULATION -- AN

OPPORTUNITY FOR DEVELOPMENT.
ASSOCIATION OF SOUTHERN AGRICULTURAL WORKERS, PROCEEDINGS.
MEMPHIS, TENNESSEE. 1963.

GBACKJX64876 BACKMAN J *NATL INDUSTRIAL CONF BOARD
WAGE RATES AND UNEMPLOYMENT.
NATIONAL INDUSTRIAL CONFERENCE BOARD, PUBLIC AFFAIRS
CONFERENCE REPORT NO 1, VOLUNTARY AND INVOLUNTARY
UNEMPLOYMENT, ED MARTIN R GAINSBRUGH. NEW YORK. 1964.

GBAGDBH63754 BAGDIKIAN BH
THE INVISIBLE AMERICANS. /POVERTY UNEMPLOYMENT/
SATURDAY EVENING POST, NO 45, DEC 21 1963. PP 28-38.

GBAILLH51575 BAILER LH
ORGANIZED LABOR AND RACIAL MINORITIES. /UNION/
ANNALS OF THE AMERICAN ACADEMY OF POLITICAL AND SOCIAL
SCIENCE, VOL 274, MAR 1951. PP 101-107.

GBAILSK66913 BAILEY SK
COORDINATING THE GREAT-SOCIETY.
REPORTER, MAR 24,1966. PP 1-6

GBAKESS65702 BAKER SS *NATL INDUSTRIAL CONF BOARD
PROJECTIONS TO 1975. THE GROWTH AND STRUCTURE OF THE LABOR
FORCE.
NATIONAL INDUSTRIAL CONFERENCE BOARD, CONFERENCE BOARD
RECORD, VOL 2, OCT 1966. PP 45-54.

GBAKKEW63598 BAKKE EW
A POSITIVE LABOR-MARKET POLICY.
CHARLES E MERRILL BOOKS, INC. COLUMBUS, OHIO. 1963.

GBAKKEW65753 BAKKE EW
AN INTEGRATED POSITIVE MANPOWER POLICY.
EMPLOYMENT POLICY AND THE LABOR MARKET. ED BY A M ROSS.
UNIVERSITY OF CALIFORNIA PRESS. BERKELEY, CALIFORNIA. 1965.
PP 358-378.

GBAMBMA61416 BAMBERGER MA LEWIN N
THE RIGHT TO EQUAL TREATMENT. ADMINISTRATIVE ENFORCEMENT OF
ANTIDISCRIMINATION LEGISLATION.
HARVARD LAW REVIEW, JAN 1961. PP 526-589.

GBANCGX58417 BANCROFT G
THE AMERICAN LABOR-FORCE. ITS GROWTH AND CHANGING
COMPOSITION. /DEMOGRAPHY/
JOHN WILEY AND SONS. NEW YORK. 1958.

GBANCGX60418 BANCROFT G *US DEPARTMENT OF LABOR
MULTIPLE JOB-HOLDERS IN DECEMBER, 1959.
US DEPARTMENT OF LABOR, MONTHLY LABOR REVIEW, VOL 83, NO 10,
OCT 1960.

GBANCGX66752 BANCROFT G
LESSONS FROM THE PATTERNS OF UNEMPLOYMENT IN THE LAST FIVE
YEARS.
PROSPERITY AND UNEMPLOYMENT. ED BY R A GORDON AND M S
GORDON. JOHN WILEY AND SONS, INC. 1966. PP 191-226.

GBANKSC65419 BANK ST COLLEGE OF EDUCATION
EDUCATION OF THE DEPRIVED AND SEGREGATED.
BANK STREET COLLEGE OF EDUCATION. DEDHAM, MASSACHUSETTS.
1965. 59 PP.

GBANYCA61420 BANY CA *US DEPARTMENT OF LABOR
WHITE COLLAR EMPLOYMENT. TRENDS AND STRUCTURE.
US DEPARTMENT OF LABOR, MONTHLY LABOR REVIEW, VOL 84, NO 3,
FEB 1961. 26 PP.

GBARBJX48421 BARBASH J
LABOR UNIONS IN ACTION, A STUDY OF THE MAINSPRINGS OF
UNIONISM.
HARPERS. NEW YORK. 1948.

GBARBJX56422 BARBASH J
THE PRACTICE OF UNIONISM.
HARPERS. NEW YORK. 1956. 465 PP.

GBARDBX66533 BARD B
WHY DROPOUT CAMPAIGNS FAIL.
SATURDAY REVIEW, VOL 49, NO 38, SEPT 17 1966. PP 78 PLUS.

GBARHGC66162 BARHYDT GC
AN ASSESSMENT OF THE SUITABILITY OF THE FACETED STRUCTURE OF
THE WRU EDUCATION THESAURUS AS A FRAMEWORK FOR PREPARATION
OF A THESAURUS OF EQUAL-EMPLOYMENT-OPPORTUNITY TERMS.
THE UNIVERSITY OF MICHIGAN-WAYNE STATE UNIVERSITY, INSTITUTE
OF LABOR AND INDUSTRIAL RELATIONS. ANN ARBOR, MICHIGAN.
1966. 20 PP.

GBARNRX62423 BARNETT R GARAI J
WHERE THE STATES STAND ON CIVIL-RIGHTS.
STERLING PUBLISHING CO. NEW YORK. 1962. 160 PP.

GBARRGJ51425 BARRY GJ *US DEPARTMENT OF LABOR
BENEFIT POLICIES IN RELATION TO RECRUITMENT OF OLDER
WORKERS, HANDICAPPED, AND MINORITY GROUPS.
US DEPARTMENT OF LABOR, EMPLOYMENT SECURITY REVIEW, VOL 18,
NO 12, DEC 1951. PP 19-20.

GBARRML57424 BARRON ML
AMERICAN MINORITIES, A TEXTBOOK OF READINGS IN INTERGROUP
RELATIONS.
ALFRED A KNOPF. NEW YORK. 1957. 518 PP.

GBARRSX64130 BARR S *MOBILIZATION FOR YOUTH INC
POVERTY ON THE LOWER-EAST-SIDE. SELECTED ASPECTS OF THE
MOBILIZATION-FOR-YOUTH EXPERIENCE.
MOBILIZATION FOR YOUTH, INC, TRAINING INSTITUTE PROGRAM ON
URBAN COMMUNITY DEVELOPMENT, APR 27 - MAY 1 1964, PAPER.
NEW YORK. 1964.

GBATCAB66751 BATCHELDER AB
THE ECONOMICS OF POVERTY.
JOHN WILEY AND SONS. NEW YORK. 1966. 214 PP.

GBATTMX66131 BATTLE M *NYU CENT STUDY UNEMP YOUTH
ISSUES AND PROBLEMS IN INTEGRATING NEEDED SUPPORTIVE
SERVICES IN NEIGHBORHOOD-YOUTH-CORPS PROJECTS.
NEW YORK UNIVERSITY, GRADUATE SCHOOL OF SOCIAL WORK, CENTER
FOR THE STUDY OF UNEMPLOYED YOUTH. NEW YORK. FEB 1966. 8 PP.

GBATTRX63426 BATTLE R SHEFFIELD H
TRADE UNION LEADERSHIP COUNCIL --EXPERIMENT IN COMMUNITY
ACTION. /DETROIT MICHIGAN/
NEW UNIVERSITY THOUGHT, VOL 3, SEPT-OCT 1963. PP 34-41.

GBAYRAG66428 BAYROFF AG
6. TEST TECHNOLOGY AND EQUAL-EMPLOYMENT-OPPORTUNITY.

PERSONNEL PSYCHOLOGY, VOL 19, SPRING 1966. PP PP 35.

GBAYXAC43427 BAY AREA CC AGAINST DISCR
SAN FRANCISCO-S PLAN FOR DEMOCRATIC RACIAL-RELATIONS.
/CALIFORNIA/
BAY AREA COUNCIL AGAINST DISCRIMINATION. SAN FRANCISCO,
CALIFORNIA. 1943. 12 PP.

GBEALCL61412 BEALE CL
IMPLICATIONS OF THE RECENT CENSUSES FOR PROFESSIONAL
AGRICULTURAL WORKERS. /OCCUPATIONS/
ASSOCIATION OF PROFESSIONAL AGRICULTURAL WORKERS,
PROCEEDINGS. TUSKEGEE, ALABAMA. DEC 1961.

GBEALCL63426 BEALE CL   BOGUE DJ
*US DEPARTMENT OF AGRICULTURE
RECENT POPULATION TRENDS IN THE UNITED STATES WITH EMPHASIS
ON RURAL AREAS. /EDUCATION/
US DEPARTMENT OF AGRICULTURE. GPO. WASHINGTON, DC. JAN 1963.
48 PP.

GBEALCL64423 BEALE CL   HUDSON JC
BANKS VJ   *US DEPARTMENT OF AGRICULTURE
CHARACTERISTICS OF THE U.S. POPULATION BY FARM AND
NON-FARM ORIGIN.
US DEPARTMENT OF AGRICULTURE, ECONOMIC RESEARCH SERVICE.
GPO. WASHINGTON, DC. 1964. 23 PP.

GBECKGS57429 BECKER GS
THE ECONOMICS OF DISCRIMINATION.
UNIVERSITY OF CHICAGO PRESS. CHICAGO, ILLINOIS. 1957.
137 PP.

GBECKGS64700 BECKER GS   *NATL BUREAU OF EC RESEARCH
HUMAN CAPITAL. A THEORETICAL AND EMPIRICAL ANALYSIS WITH
SPECIAL REFERENCE TO EDUCATION.
NATIONAL BUREAU OF ECONOMIC RESEARCH. COLUMBIA UNIVERSITY
PRESS. NEW YORK. 1964. 187 PP.

GBECKJX64878 BECKER J
IN AID OF THE UNEMPLOYED.
JOHNS HOPKINS PRESS. BALTIMORE, MARYLAND. 1964. 300 PP.

GBECKJX65430 BECKER J   HABER W
LEVITAN S   *UPJOHN INST EMPLOY RESEARCH
PROGRAMS TO AID THE UNEMPLOYED IN THE 1960-S.
THE W.E. UPJOHN INSTITUTE FOR EMPLOYMENT RESEARCH.
KALAMAZOO, MICHIGAN. JAN 1965.

GBECKWL62431 BECKER WL
AFTER FEPC -- WHAT.
JOURNAL OF INTERGROUP RELATIONS, VOL 3, NO 4, AUG 1962.
PP 337-343.

GBECKWL62432 BECKER WL   *CAL ADVSY COMT TO US CR COMM
REPORT OF THE CALIFORNIA STATE ADVISORY COMMITTEE TO THE
UNITED STATES COMMISSION ON CIVIL-RIGHTS ON CALIFORNIA-S
PROGRAM FOR EQUAL-OPPORTUNITY IN APPRENTICESHIP.
US COMMISSION ON CIVIL RIGHTS, CALIFORNIA STATE ADVISORY
COMMITTEE. 1962. 15 PP.

GBECKWL65433 BECKER WL   *CAL OFFICE OF THE GOVERNOR
SECOND ETHNIC SURVEY OF EMPLOYMENT AND PROMOTION IN STATE
GOVERNMENT. /CALIFORNIA/
CALIFORNIA GOVERNOR-S OFFICE. SACRAMENTO, CALIFORNIA.
JULY 1965. 6 PP.

GBEDEMX64448 BEDELL M   BOWLBY R
*US DEPARTMENT OF LABOR
FORMAL OCCUPATIONAL TRAINING OF ADULT WORKERS, ITS EXTENT,
NATURE, AND USE.
US DEPARTMENT OF LABOR, OFFICE OF MANPOWER, AUTOMATION, AND
TRAINING, MANPOWER-AUTOMATION RESEARCH MONOGRAPH NO 2. GPO.
WASHINGTON, DC. DEC 1964. 48 PP.

GBELLDX62612 BELL D
A SPECULATIVE VIEW OF THE UNITED STATES IN 1985 AND BEYOND.
/TECHNOLOGICAL-CHANGE/
BOSTON, MASSACHUSETTS. JUNE 1962. MULTILITHED. 48 PP.

GBENEDX65434 BENETAR D   KNIGHT R
SCHLER N   FOWLER G
IMPLICATIONS FOR BUSINESS OF THE CIVIL-RIGHTS-ACT OF 1964.
RECORD OF THE BAR ASSOCIATION OF THE CITY OF NEW YORK,
VOL 20, 1965. PP 128-147.

GBENEMC66435 BENEWITZ MC
COVERAGE UNDER TITLE-VII OF THE CIVIL-RIGHTS-ACT.
LABOR LAW JOURNAL, MAY 1966. PP 285-291.

GBENGEJ65436 BENGE EJ   *BUREAU OF BUSINESS PRACTICE
COMPENSATING EMPLOYEES UNDER THE NEW CIVIL-RIGHTS LAW.
BUREAU OF BUSINESS PRACTICE. WATERFORD, CONNECTICUT. 1965.

GBENJJG65006 BENJAMIN JG   LESH S
FREEDMAN MK   *US DEPT OF HEALTH ED WELFARE
YOUTH EMPLOYMENT PROGRAMS IN PERSPECTIVE.
US DEPARTMENT OF HEALTH, EDUCATION, AND WELFARE, WELFARE
ADMINISTRATION, OFFICE OF JUVENILE DELINQUENCY AND YOUTH
DEVELOPMENT. GPO. WASHINGTON, DC. 1965. 121 PP.

GBENNFX64500 BENNETT F
STILL THE HARVEST OF SHAME. /MIGRANT-WORKERS/
COMMONWEAL, VOL 80, NO 3, AP 10 1964. PP 83-86.

GBENNGX66877 BENNETT G   *NYU CENTER STUDY UNEMP YOUTH
JOB-DEVELOPMENT FOR YOUTH.
NEW YORK UNIVERSITY, GRADUATE SCHOOL OF SOCIAL WORK, CENTER
FOR THE STUDY OF UNEMPLOYED YOUTH. NEW YORK. FEB 1966.
11 PP.

GBERGMX49443 BERGER M
THE SUPREME-COURT AND GROUP DISCRIMINATION SINCE 1937.
COLUMBIA LAW REVIEW, VOL 49, NO 2, FEB 1949. PP 201-230.

GBERGMX51441 BERGER M
FAIR-EMPLOYMENT-PRACTICES LEGISLATION OF EIGHT STATES AND
TWO CITIES.
ANNALS OF THE AMERICAN ACADEMY OF POLITICAL AND SOCIAL
SCIENCE. MAY 1951. PP 34-40.

GBERGMX52440 BERGER M
EQUALITY BY STATUTES -- LEGAL CONTROLS OVER GROUP
DISCRIMINATION.
COLUMBIA UNIVERSITY PRESS. NEW YORK. 1952. 238 PP.

GBERGMX54442 BERGER M   *UNESCO
RACIAL EQUALITY AND THE LAW.
UNITED NATIONS EDUCATIONAL, SCIENTIFIC AND CULTURAL
ORGANIZATION. PARIS, FRANCE. 1954.

GBERGNJ64438 BERGEN NJ CHAMBER OF COMMERCE
THE NEW CIVIL-RIGHTS LAW AND YOUR BUSINESS.
PRENTICE-HALL. ENGLEWOOD CLIFFS, NEW JERSEY. 1964. 39 PP.

GBERGRK64437 BERG RK
EQUAL-EMPLOYMENT-OPPORTUNITY UNDER CIVIL-RIGHTS-ACT OF 1964.
BROOKLYN LAW REVIEW, VOL 31, DEC 1964. PP 62-97.

GBERKCM64444 BERKELEY CITY MANAGER
REVIEW AND ANALYSIS OF CITY CERTIFICATIONS AND APPOINTMENTS.
/BERKELEY CALIFORNIA/
BERKELEY CITY MANAGER. BERKELEY, CALIFORNIA. FEB 7 1964.
19 PP.

GBERKDS48446 BERKOWITZ DS
INEQUALITY OF OPPORTUNITY IN HIGHER EDUCATION. A STUDY OF
MINORITY GROUP AND RELATED BARRIERS TO COLLEGE ADMISSION.
WILLIAMS PRESS. ALBANY, NEW YORK. 1948. 203 PP.

GBERLAA66222 BERLE AA
ECONOMIC EQUALITY AND GOVERNMENT ACTION.
ALL MEN ARE CREATED EQUAL. ED BY W W WATTENBERG. WAYNE STATE
UNIVERSITY PRESS. DETROIT, MICHIGAN. 1966. PP 63-82.

GBERNBI62447 BERNHARD BI   *ANTI-DEFAMATION LEAGUE
THE CONSCIENCE OF THE GOVERNMENT. /ANTIDISCRIMINATION/
THE ADMINISTRATION AND CIVIL RIGHTS. ANTI-DEFAMATION LEAGUE
OF B-NAI B-RITH, ADL BULLETIN, MAR 1962. PP 7-8.

GBERNYX64448 BERNSTEIN Y   *PHILADELPHIA COMM HUMAN RELS
FAIR-EMPLOYMENT-PRACTICE ACTS AND THE COURTS.
PHILADELPHIA COMMISSION ON HUMAN RELATIONS. MIMEOGRAPHED.
PHILADELPHIA, PENNSYLVANIA. DEC 1964. 10 PP.

GBERRBX65449 BERRY B
RACE AND ETHNIC RELATIONS.
HOUGHTON MIFFLIN CO. BOSTON, MASSACHUSETTS. 3RD ED. 1965.
435 PP.

GBERTAL59393 BERTRAND AL   OSBORNE HW
RURAL INDUSTRIALIZATION IN A LOUISIANA COMMUNITY.
/ECONOMIC-STATUS OCCUPATIONS/
LOUISIANA STATE UNIVERSITY. BATON ROUGE, LOUISIANA. JUNE
1959. 40 PP.

GBERTAL66140 BERTRAND AL
THE EMERGING RURAL SOUTH. A REGION UNDER CONFRONTATION BY
MASS SOCIETY.
RURAL SOCIOLOGY, VOL 31, NO 4, DEC 1966. PP 449-457.

GBIANJC67590 BIANCHINI JC   DANIELSON WF
HEATH RW   HILLIARD CA
RACE AND SOCIO-ECONOMIC STATUS IN MUNICIPAL PERSONNEL
SELECTION.
CITY OF BERKELEY, DIVISION OF PERSONNEL. BERKELEY,
CALIFORNIA. JAN 1967. 15 PP.

GBIENHX64111 BIENSTALK H   *NATIONAL EDUCATION ASSN
REALITIES OF THE JOB-MARKET FOR THE HIGH SCHOOL DROPOUT.
GUIDANCE AND THE SCHOOL DROPOUT. ED BY D. SCHREIBER.
NATIONAL EDUCATION ASSOCIATION. WASHINGTON, DC. 1964.
PP 84-108.

GBIRDAR64450 BIRD AR   *US DEPARTMENT OF AGRICULTURE
POVERTY IN RURAL AREAS OF THE UNITED STATES.
US DEPARTMENT OF AGRICULTURE, RESOURCE DEVELOPMENT ECONOMICS
DIVISION, AGRICULTURAL ECONOMIC REPORT NO 63. GPO.
WASHINGTON, DC. 1964.

GBIRNOX62451 BIRNBAUM O
EQUAL-EMPLOYMENT-OPPORTUNITY AND EXECUTIVE ORDER 10925.
KANSAS LAW REVIEW, VOL 2, OCT 1962. PP 17-34.

GBISHCE67915 BISHOP CE
DIMENSIONS OF THE FARM LABOR PROBLEM.
FARM LABOR IN THE UNITED STATES. ED BY C E BISHOP. COLUMBIA
UNIVERSITY PRESS. NEW YORK. 1967. PP 1-18.

GBISHCE67916 BISHOP CE ED
FARM LABOR IN THE UNITED STATES.
COLUMBIA UNIVERSITY PRESS. NEW YORK. 1967. 143 PP.

GBLACCX60452 BLACK C
THE LAWFULNESS OF THE SEGREGATION DECISIONS.
YALE LAW JOURNAL, VOL 69, NO 3, JAN 1960. PP 421-436.

GBLAKGR64453 BLAKEY GR
DISCRIMINATION, UNIONS, AND TITLE-VII.
AMERICA, VOL 3, NO 9, AUG 29 1964. PP 210-212.

GBLALHM62454 BLALOCK HM
OCCUPATIONAL DISCRIMINATION. SOME THEORETICAL PROPOSITIONS.
SOCIAL PROBLEMS, VOL 9, WINTER 1962. PP 240-247.

GBLOCHD58455 BLOCH HD
ORGANIZED LABOR AND THE INTEGRATION OF ETHNIC GROUPS.
/UNION/
JOURNAL OF HUMAN RELATIONS, SUMMER 1958.

GBLOCHD58456 BLOCH HD
RECOGNITION OF DISCRIMINATION -- A SOLUTION.
JOURNAL OF SOCIAL PSYCHOLOGY, VOL 48, NOV 1958. PP 291-295.

GBLOOGF65885 BLOOM GF   NORTHRUP HR
ECONOMICS OF LABOR-RELATIONS. /EQUAL-OPPORTUNITY/
R D IRWIN. HOMEWOOD, ILLINOIS. 1965. CHAPTER 25, PP 851-870.

GBLUEJT47457 BLUE JT
ORGANIZED LABOR AND MINORITY GROUPS. /UNION/
QUARTERLY REVIEW OF HIGHER EDUCATION AMONG NEGROES, VOL 15,
JULY 1947. PP 170-177.

GBLUMAW65459 BLUMROSEN AW
ANTI-DISCRIMINATION LAWS IN ACTION IN NEW-JERSEY. A
LAW-SOCIOLOGY STUDY.
RUTGERS LAW REVIEW, VOL 19, NO 2, WINTER 1965. PP 189-287.

GBLUMAW66566 BLUMROSEN AW
THE INDIVIDUAL RIGHT TO ELIMINATE EMPLOYMENT DISCRIMINATION
BY LITIGATION.
INDUSTRIAL RELATIONS RESEARCH ASSOCIATION, PROCEEDINGS, 19TH
ANNUAL WINTER MEETING. SAN FRANCISCO, CALIFORNIA.
DEC 28-29 1966. PP 88-98.

GBLUMAW67117 BLUMROSEN AW   *US DEPARTMENT OF LABOR
PROCESSING EMPLOYMENT DISCRIMINATION CASES. /LEGISLATION/
US DEPARTMENT OF LABOR, MONTHLY LABOR REVIEW, VOL 90,
MAR 1967. PP 25-26.

GBLUMHX58458 BLUMER H
RECENT RESEARCH ON RACIAL RELATIONS IN THE USA.
INTERNATIONAL SOCIAL SCIENCE BULLETIN, VOL 10, NO 3, 1958.
PP 403-447.

GBOGAFA64460 BOGAN FA   HAMEL HR
*US DEPARTMENT OF LABOR
MULTIPLE JOBHOLDERS IN MAY, 1963.
US DEPARTMENT OF LABOR, MONTHLY LABOR REVIEW, VOL 87, NO 3,
REPORT NO 39, MAR 1964. 18 PP.

GBOGAFA65750 BOGAN FA   *US DEPARTMENT OF LABOR
EMPLOYMENT OF HIGH SCHOOL GRADUATES AND DROPOUTS IN 1964.
US DEPARTMENT OF LABOR, MONTHLY LABOR REVIEW, VOL 88, NO 6,
JUNE 1965. PP 637-644.

GBOGAFA66138 BOGAN FA   SWANSTROM TE
*US DEPARTMENT OF LABOR
WORK EXPERIENCE OF THE POPULATION IN 1965.
US DEPARTMENT OF LABOR, SPECIAL LABOR FORCE REPORT NO 76.
DEC 1966. PP 1369-1377 PLUS.

GBOGAFA66918 BOGAN FA   *US DEPARTMENT OF LABOR
EMPLOYMENT OF SCHOOL AGE YOUTH, OCTOBER 1965.
US DEPARTMENT OF LABOR, MONTHLY LABOR REVIEW, VOL 89, JULY
1966. PP 739-743.

GBOGITX54057 BOGIA T   *NEW JERSEY DEPT OF EDUCATION
THE MINORITY-GROUP WORKER IN CAMDEN COUNTY. /NEW-JERSEY/
NEW JERSEY DEPARTMENT OF EDUCATION, DIVISION AGAINST
DISCRIMINATION. NEWARK, NEW JERSEY. NOV 1954.

GBOGUDJ59461 BOGUE DJ
THE POPULATION OF THE UNITED STATES.
GLENCOE FREE PRESS. NEW YORK. 1959.

GBOKXDX64736 BOK D   *US DEPARTMENT OF LABOR
AUTOMATION, PRODUCTIVITY AND MANPOWER PROBLEMS.
US DEPARTMENT OF LABOR, PRESIDENT-S COMMITTEE ON
LABOR-MANAGEMENT POLICY, DISCUSSION PAPER. 1964. 20 PP.

GBOKXDX64737 BOK D   KOSSORIS MD
*US DEPARTMENT OF LABOR
METHODS OF ADJUSTING TO AUTOMATION AND TECHNOLOGICAL-CHANGE.
/INDUSTRY/
US DEPARTMENT OF LABOR, PRESIDENT-S COMMITTEE ON
LABOR-MANAGEMENT POLICY. WASHINGTON, DC. 1964. 33 PP.

GBOLIAC65528 BOLINO AC
MANPOWER DEVELOPMENT. CHARGES AND CHALLENGES.
/TECHNOLOGICAL-CHANGE TRAINING/
MICHIGAN BUSINESS REVIEW, VOL 17, NO 4, JULY 1965. PP 31-37.

GBONFAE64463 BONFIELD AE
STATE CIVIL-RIGHTS STATUTES. SOME PROPOSALS.
IOWA LAW REVIEW, VOL 49, 1964. P 1067.

GBONFAE65462 BONFIELD AE
THE ROLE OF LEGISLATION IN ELIMINATING RACIAL
DISCRIMINATION.
RACE, VOL 7, OCT 1965. PP 107-122.

GBONFAE67136 BONFIELD AE
THE SUBSTANCE OF AMERICAN FAIR-EMPLOYMENT-PRACTICES
LEGISLATION. II. EMPLOYMENT-AGENCIES, LABOR ORGANIZATIONS,
AND OTHERS.
NORTHWESTERN UNIVERSITY LAW REVIEW, VOL 62, NO 1, MAR-AP
1967. PP 19-44)

GBONFAE67137 BONFIELD AE
THE SUBSTANCE OF AMERICAN FAIR-EMPLOYMENT-PRACTICES
LEGISLATION. I. EMPLOYERS.
NORTHWESTERN UNIVERSITY LAW REVIEW, VOL 61, NO 6, JAN-FEB
1967. PP 907-975.

GBONIES66135 BONILLA ES
SOCIAL STRUCTURE AND RACE-RELATIONS.
KNOWING THE DISADVANTAGED. ED BY STATEN W WEBSTER. CHANDLER
PUBLISHING CO. SAN FRANCISCO, CALIFORNIA. 1966. PP 104-117.

GBORUME64142 BORUS ME
A BENEFIT-COST ANALYSIS OF THE ECONOMIC EFFECTIVENESS OF
RETRAINING THE UNEMPLOYED.
YALE UNIVERSITY, YALE ECONOMIC ESSAYS, VOL 4, NO 2, FALL
1964.

GBORUME65745 BORUS ME
THE COST OF RETRAINING THE HARD-CORE UNEMPLOYED.
LABOR LAW JOURNAL, SEPT 1965. PP 574-583. ALSO MICHIGAN
STATE UNIVERSITY, SCHOOL OF LABOR AND INDUSTRIAL RELATIONS,
REPRINT SERIES NO 76.

GBORUME66919 BORUS ME
THE ECONOMIC EFFECTIVENESS OF RETRAINING THE UNEMPLOYED.
FEDERAL RESERVE BANK OF BOSTON, RESEARCH REPORT NO 35.
BOSTON, MASSACHUSETTS. JULY 1966. 219 PP.

GBOWEHR66748 BOWEN HR   MANGUM GL
AUTOMATION AND ECONOMIC PROGRESS. A SUMMARY OF THE REPORT OF
THE NATIONAL COMMISSION ON TECHNOLOGY, AUTOMATION, AND
ECONOMIC PROGRESS.
PRENTICE-HALL, INC. SPECTRUM BOOKS. ENGLEWOOD CLIFFS,
NEW JERSEY. 1966. 170 PP.

GBOWEWG65464 BOWEN WG   *PRINCETON UNIVERSITY
UNEMPLOYMENT IN THE UNITED STATES. QUANTITATIVE DIMENSIONS.
UNEMPLOYMENT IN A PROSPEROUS ECONOMY. REPORT OF THE
PRINCETON MANPOWER SYMPOSIUM. ED BY WILLIAM G BOWEN AND
FREDERICK H HARBISON. PRINCETON UNIVERSITY. PRINCETON,
NEW JERSEY. MAY 13-14, 1965. PP 15-40.

GBOWEWG65469 BOWEN WG   FINEGAN TA
LABOR-FORCE PARTICIPATION AND UNEMPLOYMENT.
EMPLOYMENT POLICY AND THE LABOR MARKET. ED BY ARTHUR M ROSS.
UNIVERSITY OF CALIFORNIA PRESS. BERKELEY, CALIFORNIA. 1965.

GBOWEWG65749 BOWEN WG   HARBISON FH
UNEMPLOYMENT IN A PROSPEROUS ECONOMY. A REPORT OF THE
PRINCETON-MANPOWER-SYMPOSIUM.
PRINCETON UNIVERSITY, INDUSTRIAL RELATIONS SECTION, REPORT
SERIES NO 108. PRINCETON, NEW JERSEY. 1965. 173 PP.

GBOWLGK56433 BOWLES GK   TAEUBER C
*US BUREAU OF THE CENSUS   *US DEPARTMENT OF AGRICULTURE
RURAL-FARM MALES ENTERING AND LEAVING WORKING AGES, 1940-50
AND 1950-60. REPLACEMENT RATIOS AND RATES. /OCCUPATIONS/
US BUREAU OF THE CENSUS. US DEPARTMENT OF AGRICULTURE. GPO.
WASHINGTON, DC. AUG 1956. 65 PP.

GBOWLGK57415 BOWLES GK

GBOWLGK58397 BOWLES GK
MIGRATION OF POPULATION IN THE SOUTH. SITUATION AND
PROSPECTS.
ASSOCIATION OF SOUTHERN AGRICULTURAL WORKERS, PROCEEDINGS.
LITTLE ROCK, ARKANSAS. 1958.

GBOWLGK65424 BOWLES GK   BEALE CL
*US DEPARTMENT OF AGRICULTURE
CHARACTERISTICS OF THE POPULATION OF HIRED FARMWORKER
HOUSEHOLDS. /ECONOMIC-STATUS/
US DEPARTMENT OF AGRICULTURE. GPO. WASHINGTON, DC. AUG 1965.
21 PP.

GBOWLGK65432 BOWLES GK   SELLERS WE
*US DEPARTMENT OF AGRICULTURE
THE HIRED FARM WORKING FORCE OF 1963 WITH SUPPLEMENTARY DATA
FOR 1962. /ECONOMIC-STATUS/
US DEPARTMENT OF AGRICULTURE. GPO. WASHINGTON, DC. MAY 1965.
63 PP.

GBOWLGK65434 BOWLES GK   TRAVER JD
*US DEPARTMENT OF AGRICULTURE
NET MIGRATION OF THE POPULATION, 1950-60, BY AGE, SEX, AND
COLOR. VOL II, ANALYTICAL GROUPINGS OF COUNTIES. /INCOME/
US DEPARTMENT OF AGRICULTURE, ECONOMIC RESEARCH SERVICE.
GPO. WASHINGTON, DC. NOV 1965. 189 PP.

GBOWLGK66414 BOWLES GK   TARVER JD
THE COMPOSITION OF NET MIGRATION AMONG COUNTIES IN THE
UNITED STATES, 1950-60.
AGRICULTURAL ECONOMICS RESEARCH, JAN 1966. PP 13-19.

GBOWLGK66430 BOWLES GK   BEALE CL
BRADSHAW BS   *US DEPARTMENT OF AGRICULTURE
POTENTIAL SUPPLY AND REPLACEMENT OF RURAL MALES OF
LABOR-FORCE AGE, 1960-70.
US DEPARTMENT OF AGRICULTURE, ECONOMIC RESEARCH SERVICE,
STATISTICAL BULLETIN NO 378. GPO. WASHINGTON, DC. OCT 1966.
145 PP.

GBOWLGK67920 BOWLES GK
THE CURRENT SITUATION OF THE HIRED FARM LABOR-FORCE.
FARM LABOR IN THE UNITED STATES. ED BY C E BISHOP. COLUMBIA
UNIVERSITY PRESS. NEW YORK. 1967. PP 19-40.

GBOWMGW61466 BOWMAN GW
EMPLOYMENT BY MERIT ALONE.
OFFICE EXECUTIVE, VOL 36, MAY 1961. PP 14-15, 37.

GBOWMGW63467 BOWMAN GW   *NATL CONF CHRISTIANS-JEWS
SELF APPRAISAL FOR MERIT PROMOTION, A RESEARCH MANUAL.
NATIONAL CONFERENCE OF CHRISTIANS AND JEWS. NEW YORK. 1963.
39 PP.

GBOWMGW64468 BOWMAN GW
WHAT HELPS OR HARMS PROMOTABILITY.
HARVARD BUSINESS REVIEW, VOL 42, JAN-FEB 1964. PP 6-8.

GBOXLRF65418 BOXLEY RF   *US DEPARTMENT OF AGRICULTURE
WHITE AND NONWHITE OWNERS OF RURAL LAND IN THE SOUTHEAST.
US DEPARTMENT OF AGRICULTURE, ECONOMIC RESEARCH SERVICE.
GPO. WASHINGTON, DC. JUNE 1965. 23 PP.

GBRADDS65679 BRADY DS   *US DEPT OF HEALTH ED WELFARE
AGE AND INCOME-DISTRIBUTION. /DEMOGRAPHY/
US DEPARTMENT OF HEALTH, EDUCATION, AND WELFARE, SOCIAL
SECURITY ADMINISTRATION, DIVISION OF RESEARCH AND
STATISTICS, RESEARCH REPORT NO 8. GPO. WASHINGTON, DC. 1965.
62 PP.

GBRADME64797 BRADLEY ME
EFFECTS ON ECONOMIC GROWTH OF THE EMPLOYMENT SHIFT TO
SERVICE INDUSTRIES.
INDUSTRIAL LABOR RELATIONS RESEARCH, VOL 9, NO 3, 1964.
PP 3-6.

GBRADPX46247 BRADLEY P ED   *YMCA
FAIR-EMPLOYMENT LEGISLATION IN NEW-YORK STATE. ITS HISTORY,
DEVELOPMENT, AND SUGGESTED USE ELSEWHERE.
YMCA. ASSOCIATION PRESS. NEW YORK. 1946. 48 PP.

GBRANEX63796 BRANDEIS E
MIGRANT LABOR IN WISCONSIN.
LABOR MANAGEMENT AND SOCIAL POLICY. ESSAYS IN THE JOHN R
COMMONS TRADITION. UNIVERSITY OF WISCONSIN PRESS. MADISON,
WISCONSIN. 1963. PP 197-300.

GBRANSX63876 BRANDWEIN S
MANPOWER IMPLICATIONS OF TECHNOLOGICAL-CHANGE. RESEARCH
FINDINGS OF THE US DEPARTMENT OF LABOR.
LABOR LAW JOURNAL, VOL 14, AUG 1963. PP 655-661.

GBRAVHX59471 BRAVERMAN H   *ANTI-DEFAMATION LEAGUE
BUCK STOPS HERE. /DISCRIMINATION/
ANTI-DEFAMATION LEAGUE OF B-NAI B-RITH, ADL BULLETIN, JUNE
1959.

GBRAZBR51472 BRAZAEL BR
THE PRESENT STATUS AND PROGRAMS OF FEPC. FEDERAL, STATE, AND
MUNICIPAL.
JOURNAL OF NEGRO EDUCATION, VOL 20, SUMMER 1951. PP 378-397.

GBRIGWA62473 BRIGGS WA   HUMMEL DL
COUNSELING MINORITY-GROUP YOUTH. DEVELOPING THE EXPERIENCE
OF EQUALITY THROUGH EDUCATION.
F.J. HEER PRINTING COMPANY. COLUMBUS, OHIO. 1962. 139 PP.

GBRIMAF66475 BRIMMER AF   *NATIONAL URBAN LEAGUE
THE QUESTS FOR ECONOMIC STABILITY AND
EQUAL-EMPLOYMENT-OPPORTUNITY.
NATIONAL URBAN LEAGUE EQUAL OPPORTUNITY DAY DINNER, REMARKS.
NEW YORK. NOV 18 1966. 22 PP.

GBRONYX57921 BRONZEN Y
THE ECONOMICS OF AUTOMATION.
AMERICAN ECONOMIC REVIEW, MAY 1957. PP 239-344.

GBRODLB64795 BROOKS LB   *US DEPT OF HEALTH ED WELFARE
TRAINING THE HARD-CORE UNEMPLOYED.
US DEPARTMENT OF HEALTH, EDUCATION, AND WELFARE. GPO.
WASHINGTON, DC. 1964. 99 PP.

GBROWFJ45477 BROWN FJ ED   ROUCEK J ED
ONE AMERICA. THE HISTORY, CONTRIBUTIONS, AND PRESENT
PROBLEMS OF OUR RACIAL AND NATIONAL MINORITIES.
PRENTICE-HALL. NEW YORK. REVISED ED. 1945. 717 PP.

MIGRATION PATTERNS OF THE RURAL-FARM POPULATION. THIRTEEN
ECONOMIC REGIONS OF THE UNITED STATES, 1940-1950.
RURAL SOCIOLOGY, MAR 1957. PP 1-11.

GBROWFJ55476 BROWN FJ   *AMERICAN CC ON EDUCATION
APPROACHING EQUALITY OF OPPORTUNITY IN HIGHER EDUCATION.
AMERICAN COUNCIL OF EDUCATION, COMMITTEE ON EQUALITY OF
OPPORTUNITY IN HIGHER EDUCATION, NATIONAL CONFERENCE REPORT.
WASHINGTON, DC. 1955. 132 PP.

GBRYEGL65896 BRYENTON GL
EMPLOYMENT DISCRIMINATION. STATE FEPC LAWS AND THE IMPACT OF
OF TITLE-VII OF THE CIVIL-RIGHTS-ACT OF 1964.
WESTERN RESERVE LAW REVIEW, VOL 16, MAY 1965. PP 608-659.

GBUCKLF   BUCKLEY LF
DISCRIMINATORY ASPECTS OF THE LABOR MARKET OF THE 60-S.
REVIEW OF SOCIAL ECCNOMY, VOL 19, MAR 1961. PP25-42.

GBUCKLF63479 BUCKLEY LF
NONWHITE EMPLOYMENT IN THE UNITED STATES.
INTERRACIAL REVIEW, VOL 36, FEB 1963. PP 32-33.

GBUCKWX62875 BUCKINGHAM W
THE GREAT EMPLOYMENT CONTROVERSY. /TECHNOLOGICAL-CHANGE/
ANNALS OF THE AMERICAN ACADEMY OF POLITICAL AND SOCIAL
SCIENCE, VOL 340, MAR 1962. PP 46-52.

GBUFFLR64484 BUFFALO LAW REVIEW
CONFERENCE ISSUE -- TOWARD EQUAL-OPPORTUNITY IN EMPLOYMENT.
BUFFALO LAW REVIEW, VOL 14, NO 1, FALL 1964.

GBULLPX60897 BULLOCK P   *UCLA INSTITUTE OF IND RELS
MERIT EMPLOYMENT. NON-DISCRIMINATION IN INDUSTRY.
UNIVERSITY OF CALIFORNIA, INSTITUTE OF INDUSTRIAL RELATIONS.
LOS ANGELES, CALIFORNIA. 1960. 101 PP.

GBULLPX61523 BULLOCK P   *UCLA INSTITUTE OF IND RELS
COMBATING DISCRIMINATION IN EMPLOYMENT.
UNIVERSITY OF CALIFORNIA, INSTITUTE OF INDUSTRIAL RELATIONS,
REPRINT NO 104. LOS ANGELES, CALIFORNIA. 1961. 14 PP. ALSO
CALIFORNIA MANAGEMENT REVIEW, VOL 3, SUMMER 1961. PP 18-32.

GBULLPX62488 BULLOCK P   SINGLETON R
*UCLA INSTITUTE OF IND RELS
THE MINORITY CHILD AND THE SCHOOLS.
UNIVERSITY OF CALIFORNIA, INSTITUTE OF INDUSTRIAL RELATIONS.
LOS ANGELES, CALIFORNIA. 1962.

GBULLPX63489 BULLOCK P   SINGLETON R
*UCLA INSTITUTE OF IND RELS
SOME PROBLEMS IN MINORITY-GROUP EDUCATION IN THE LOS-ANGELES
PUBLIC SCHOOLS. /CALIFORNIA/
UNIVERSITY OF CALIFORNIA, INSTITUTE OF INDUSTRIAL RELATIONS.
LOS ANGELES, CALIFORNIA. 1963.

GBULLPX66486 BULLOCK P   *UCLA INSTITUTE OF IND RELS
EQUAL-OPPORTUNITY IN EMPLOYMENT.
UNIVERSITY OF CALIFORNIA, INSTITUTE OF INDUSTRIAL RELATIONS.
LOS ANGELES, CALIFORNIA. 1966. 114 PP.

GBURCLE65490 BURCHINAL LG   SIFF H
RURAL POVERTY.
POVERTY IN AMERICA. ED BY LOUIS A FERMAN, JOYCE L KORNBLUH,
AND ALAN HABER. UNIVERSITY OF MICHIGAN PRESS. ANN ARBOR,
MICHIGAN. 1965. PP 100-111.

GBURCTA62408 BURCH TA   LANHAM WJ
BUTLER CP
CHARACTERISTICS, RESOURCES, AND INCOMES OF RURAL HOUSEHOLDS,
PIEDMONT AREA, SOUTH-CAROLINA.
CLEMSON AGRICULTURAL COLLEGE. CLEMSON, SOUTH CAROLINA.
OCT 1962. 16 PP.

GBURENAN0495 BUREAU OF NATIONAL AFFAIRS
A SPECIAL REPORT -- THE EQUAL-EMPLOYMENT-OPPORTUNITY LAW,
TITLE-VII OF THE CIVIL-RIGHTS-ACT OF 1964.
BUREAU OF NATIONAL AFFAIRS, INC. WASHINGTON, DC. ND.

GBURENA61498 BUREAU OF NATIONAL AFFAIRS
TEXTS OF RULES AND REGULATIONS OF PRESIDENT-S COMMITTEE ON
EQUAL-EMPLOYMENT-OPPORTUNITY RELATING TO OBLIGATIONS OF
GOVERNMENT CONTRACTORS AND SUBCONTRACTORS, EFFECTIVE JULY
22, 1961. A BNA SPECIAL REPORT.
BUREAU OF NATIONAL AFFAIRS, INC. WASHINGTON, DC. JULY 21
1961. 11 PP.

GBURENA63496 BUREAU OF NATIONAL AFFAIRS
RULES AND REGULATIONS OF THE PRESIDENT-S COMMITTEE ON
EQUAL-EMPLOYMENT-OPPORTUNITY AS AMENDED.
BUREAU OF NATIONAL AFFAIRS, INC. A SPECIAL REPORT.
WASHINGTON, DC. SEPT 6 1963.

GBURENA64497 BUREAU OF NATIONAL AFFAIRS
STATE FAIR-EMPLOMENT LAWS AND THEIR ADMINISTRATION. TEXTS,
FEDERAL-STATE COOPERATION, PROHIBITED ACTS.
BUREAU OF NATIONAL AFFAIRS, INC. WASHINGTON, DC. 1964.
285 PP.

GBURENA65494 BUREAU OF NATIONAL AFFAIRS
FAIR-EMPLOYMENT-PRACTICES.
BUREAU OF NATIONAL AFFAIRS, INC, LABOR POLICY AND PRACTICES,
VOL 6, WASHINGTON, DC. 1965.

GBUREON64492 BUREAU OF NATIONAL AFFAIRS
THE CIVIL-RIGHTS-ACT OF 1964. WHAT IT MEANS -- TO EMPLOYERS,
BUSINESSMEN, UNIONS, EMPLOYEES, MINORITY-GROUPS. TEXT,
ANALYSIS, LEGISLATIVE HISTORY.
BUREAU OF NATIONAL AFFAIRS, INC. WASHINGTON, DC. 1964.
424 PP.

GBUREON65491 BUREAU OF NATIONAL AFFAIRS
APPRENTICESHIP AND TESTS, FEP SUMMARY OF LATEST
DEVELOPMENTS.
BUREAU OF NATIONAL AFFAIRS, INC. WASHINGTON, DC.
APRIL 29 1965.

GBUREON66493 BUREAU OF NATIONAL AFFAIRS
EQUAL-EMPLOYMENT-ACT OF 1966.
BUREAU OF NATIONAL AFFAIRS, INC, FAIR EMPLOYMENT PRACTICES,
NO 31, AP 8 1966. 8 PP.

GBURESS57499 BUREAU SOC SCIENCE RESEARCH
EMPLOYMENT OPPORTUNITIES FOR HIGH SCHOOL DROPOUTS, A STUDY
OF EMPLOYERS PRACTICES, NEEDS AND ATTITUDES IN THE
DISTRICT OF COLUMBIA. /WASHINGTON-DC/
BUREAU OF SOCIAL SCIENCE RESEARCH, INC. PREPARED FOR THE US
EMPLOYMENT SERVICE FOR THE DISTRICT OF COLUMBIA. WASHINGTON,
DC. 1957. 118 PP.

GBURMJH51500 BURMA JH
RACE-RELATIONS AND ANTI-DISCRIMINATORY LEGISLATION.
AMERICAN JOURNAL OF SOCIOLOGY, VOL 56, MAY 1951. PP 416-423.

GBUSIWX61502 BUSINESS WEEK
EQUAL-JOB-RIGHTS.
BUSINESS WEEK, MAR 11 1961. P 120.

GBUSIWX62505 BUSINESS WEEK
HOW WELL CAN UNIONS KEEP PLEDGE ON BIAS.
BUSINESS WEEK, NOV 24 1962. PP 54-56.

GBUSIWX65502 BUSINESS WEEK
BUSINESS WIDENS ITS HIRING RANGE.
BUSINESS WEEK, DEC 4 1965. PP 125-126.

GBUSTJL49507 BUSTARD JL
THE OPERATION OF THE NEW-JERSEY LAW AGAINST DISCRIMINATION.
JOURNAL OF NEGRO EDUCATION, VOL 18, SPRING 1949. PP 123-133.

GBUTCGT63508 BUTCHER GT   *US LIBRARY OF CONGRESS LRS
STATE LAWS DEALING WITH NON-DISCRIMINATION IN EMPLOYMENT.
US LIBRARY OF CONGRESS, LEGISLATIVE REFERENCE SERVICE. GPO.
WASHINGTON, DC. JULY 24 1963. 54 PP.

GCAHNEX66905 CAHN E   *US OFFICE OF EC OPPORTUNITY
PARTICIPATION OF THE POOR. A REEXAMINATION.
THE SOCIETY FOR THE STUDY OF SOCIAL PROBLEMS, 16TH ANNUAL
MEETING, PAPER. MIAMI BEACH, FLORIDA. AUG 27 1966.

GCALAGO60511 CAL ATTORNEY GENERALS OFFICE
EQUAL-RIGHTS UNDER THE LAW. PROVIDING FOR EQUAL TREATMENT
FOR ALL CITIZENS REGARDLESS OF RACE, RELIGION, COLOR,
NATIONAL ORIGIN OR ANCESTRY. /CALIFORNIA/
CALIFORNIA ATTORNEY GENERAL-S OFFICE. SACRAMENTO,
CALIFORNIA. 1960. 14 PP.

GCALAGO63512 CAL ATTORNEY GENERALS OFFICE
OPINION CONCERNING THE SCOPE AND AUTHORITY OF THE
JURISDICTION THAT MAY BE GRANTED TO CITY OR COUNTY
HUMAN-RELATIONS-COMMISSIONS IN THE FIELDS OF EMPLOYMENT
AND HOUSING. /CALIFORNIA/
CALIFORNIA ATTORNEY GENERAL-S OFFICE, OPINION NO 63/156.
SACRAMENTO, CALIFORNIA. OCT 14 1963. 5 PP.

GCALAIW64510 CAL ASSEMBLY INTERIM COMT WM
HEARING OF THE SUBCOMMITTEE ON ECONOMIC DEVELOPMENT, EDITED
TRANSCRIPT, JANUARY 28 AND 29, 1964. /CALIFORNIA/
CALIFORNIA ASSEMBLY COMMITTEE, INTERIM COMMITTEE ON WAYS AND
MEANS. SACRAMENTO, CALIFORNIA. 1964. 98 PP.

GCALBOE64513 CALIFORNIA BOARD OF EDUCATION
TOWARD EQUAL-EMPLOYMENT-OPPORTUNITY. /CALIFORNIA/
CALIFORNIA BOARD OF EDUCATION, COMMISSION ON EQUAL
OPPORTUNITIES IN EDUCATION. SACRAMENTO, CALIFORNIA. 1964.
19 PP.

GCALCMA65515 CAL COMM MANPOWER AUTOM TECH
REPORT TO THE GOVERNOR AND THE LEGISLATURE OF THE COMMISSION
ON MANPOWER, AUTOMATION AND TECHNOLOGY, 1964.
/CALIFORNIA/
CALIFORNIA COMMISSION ON MANPOWER, AUTOMATION AND
TECHNOLOGY. SAN FRANCISCO, CALIFORNIA. 1965. 39 PP.

GCALCNA60516 CAL CONF ON APPRENTICESHIP
A COMPILATION OF STATISTICAL DATA, CHARTS AND OTHER RESOURCE
MATERIAL FOR CONFERENCE PARTICIPANTS. /APPRENTICESHIP
CALIFORNIA YOUTH/
CALIFORNIA INTERDEPARTMENTAL COMMITTEE CN YOUTH EMPLOYMENT.
SAN FRANCISCO, CALIFORNIA. 1960. 11 PP.

GCALDEM63520 CALIFORNIA DEPT OF EMPLOYMENT
MANPOWER RESOURCES OF THE SAN-FRANCISCO OAKLAND BAY AREA
1960-1970. /CALIFORNIA/
CALIFORNIA DEPARTMENT OF EMPLOYMENT, RESEARCH AND STATISTICS
SECTION. STUDIES OF THE SAN FRANCISCO-OAKLAND BAY AREA LABOR
MARKET NUMBER 1. SAN FRANCISCO, CALIFORNIA. MAY 1963. 64 PP.

GCALDEM64521 CALIFORNIA DEPT OF EMPLOYMENT
MEDICAL SERVICE JOB OPPORTUNITIES 1964-66, SAN-FRANCISCO
BAY AREA. /CALIFORNIA/
CALIFORNIA DEPARTMENT OF EMPLOYMENT, RESEARCH AND STATISTICS
SECTION. STUDIES OF THE SAN FRANCISCO BAY AREA NUMBER 2.
SAN FRANCISCO, CALIFORNIA. JULY 1964. 82 PP.

GCALDEM65517 CALIFORNIA DEPT OF EMPLOYMENT
HOTEL AND RESTAURANT JOB OPPORTUNITIES, SAN-FRANCISCO BAY
AREA, 1964-1966. /CALIFORNIA/
CALIFORNIA DEPARTMENT OF EMPLOYMENT, COASTAL AREA, RESEARCH
AND STATISTICS SECTION. STUDIES OF THE SAN FRANCISCO BAY
AREA LABOR MARKET, NUMBER 3. SAN FRANCISCO, CALIFORNIA.
MAR 1965. 49 PP.

GCALDEM66518 CALIFORNIA DEPT OF EMPLOYMENT
MANPOWER DEVELOPMENT TRAINING. TOTAL NUMBER OF NEW ENROLLEES
DURING THE MONTH BY RACE AND OCCUPATION STATEWIDE AND BY
ADMINISTRATIVE AREA, SEPTEMBER, 1966, OCTOBER, 1966.
/CALIFORNIA/
CALIFORNIA DEPARTMENT OF LABOR, REPORT 513L, NO 23.
SACRAMENTO, CALIFORNIA. OCT, NOV 1966. 6 PP.

GCALDIR60522 CAL DEPT OF INDUSTRIAL RELS
HEALTH OF MIGRANTS. /CALIFORNIA/
CALIFORNIA-S HEALTH, VOL 17, NO 2, AP 15, 1960. 3 PP.

GCALDIR60527 CAL DEPT OF INDUSTRIAL RELS
GUIDE TO LAWFUL AND UNLAWFUL PRE-EMPLOYMENT INQUIRIES BY
EMPLOYERS, EMPLOYMENT-AGENCIES, AND LABOR ORGANIZATIONS
UNDER THE CALIFORNIA FAIR-EMPLOYMENT-PRACTICE ACT, LABOR
CODE, SECTIONS 1410-1432.
CALIFORNIA DEPARTMENT OF INDUSTRIAL RELATIONS, DIVISION OF
FAIR EMPLOYMENT PRACTICES. SAN FRANCISCO, CALIFORNIA. 1960.
5 PP.

GCALDIR63523 CAL DEPT OF INDUSTRIAL RELS
THE CALIFORNIA PLAN FOR EQUAL-OPPORTUNITY IN APPRENTICESHIP
FOR MINORITY-GROUPS.
CALIFORNIA DEPARTMENT OF INDUSTRIAL RELATIONS, DIVISION OF
APPRENTICESHIP STANDARDS. SAN FRANCISCO, CALIFORNIA.
FEB 1963. 21 PP.

GCALDIR63526 CAL DEPT OF INDUSTRIAL RELS
FUNCTIONS AND RESPONSIBILITIES OF FEPC. /CALIFORNIA/
CALIFORNIA DEPARTMENT OF INDUSTRIAL RELATIONS, DIVISION OF
FAIR EMPLOYMENT PRACTICES, INFORMATIONAL MEMO NO 12. SAN
FRANCISCO, CALIFORNIA. SEPT 13 1963. 8 PP.

GCALDIR65524 CAL DEPT OF INDUSTRIAL RELS
EQUAL-OPPORTUNITY IN APPRENTICESHIP AND TRAINING -- THE
CALIFORNIA PROGRAM.
CALIFORNIA DEPARTMENT OF INDUSTRIAL RELATIONS, DIVISION OF
APPRENTICESHIP STANDARDS. SAN FRANCISCO, CALIFORNIA.
MIMEOGRAPHED. JUNE 1965. 10 PP.

GCALDWF65699   CALDWELL   WF
DISCRIMINATION AND FAIR-EMPLOYMENT-PRACTICES LAWS.
LABOR LAW JOURNAL, VOL 16, JULY 1965. PP 394-403.

GCALFEPND531   CALIFORNIA FEPC
EMPLOYMENT PRACTICES, CITY OF PASADENA, AN INVESTIGATION
   UNDER SECTION 1421 OF THE CALIFORNIA LABOR CODE 1963-1965.
CALIFORNIA FAIR EMPLOYMENT PRACTICE COMMISSION. CALIFORNIA
DEPARTMENT OF INDUSTRIAL RELATIONS. SAN FRANCISCO,
CALIFORNIA. ND. 11 PP.

GCALFEPND537   CALIFORNIA FEPC
MEMORANDUM OF UNDERSTANDING BETWEEN CALIFORNIA STATE FAIR-
   EMPLOYMENT-PRACTICE-COMMISSION AND BANK-OF-AMERICA
   NATIONAL TRUST AND SAVINGS ASSOCIATION.
CALIFORNIA FAIR EMPLOYMENT PRACTICE COMMISSION.
SAN FRANCISCO, CALIFORNIA. ND. 6 PP.

GCALFEPND541   CALIFORNIA FEPC
COMMUNITY SURVEY. LONG BEACH, CALIFORNIA.
CALIFORNIA FAIR EMPLOYMENT PRACTICES COMMISSION, WOMEN-S
ADVISORY COUNCIL. SAN FRANCISCO, CALIFORNIA. ND. 22 PP.

GCALFEP61533   CALIFORNIA FEPC
FAIR-EMPLOYMENT-PRACTICE ACT...FEPC RULES AND REGULATIONS...
   GUIDE TO PRE-EMPLOYMENT INQUIRIES. /CALIFORNIA/
CALIFORNIA FAIR EMPLOYMENT PRACTICE COMMISSION.
SAN FRANCISCO, CALIFORNIA. MAY 1961. 27 PP.

GCALFEP63538   CALIFORNIA FEPC
PROMOTING EQUAL JOB OPPORTUNITY, A GUIDE FOR EMPLOYERS.
   /CALIFORNIA/
CALIFORNIA FAIR EMPLOYMENT PRACTICE COMMISSION.
SAN FRANCISCO, CALIFORNIA. DEC 1963. 9 PP.

GCALFEP63539   CALIFORNIA FEPC
STATEMENT ON SURVEYS AND STATISTICS AS TO RACIAL AND ETHNIC
   COMPOSITION OF WORK-FORCE OR UNION MEMBERSHIP.
   /CALIFORNIA/
CALIFORNIA FAIR EMPLOYMENT PRACTICE COMMISSION. SACRAMENTO,
CALIFORNIA. NOV 1963. 4 PP.

GCALFEP64530   CALIFORNIA FEPC
BANK OF AMERICA EMPLOYMENT PRACTICES. FIRST REPORT BY
   CALIFORNIA FEPC.
CALIFORNIA FAIR EMPLOYMENT PRACTICE COMMISSION. SAN
FRANCISCO, CALIFORNIA. SEPT 1964. 20 PP.

GCALFEP64536   CALIFORNIA FEPC
LOS-ANGELES CITY SCHOOLS. AN INVESTIGATION OF EMPLOYMENT
   PRACTICES. /CALIFORNIA/
CALIFORNIA FAIR EMPLOYMENT PRACTICES COMMISSION.
SAN FRANCISCO, CALIFORNIA. OCT 1964. 5 PP. PLUS.

GCALFEP65529   CALIFORNIA FEPC
AFFIRMATIVE-ACTIONS IN EMPLOYMENT. A SPECIAL FEPC REPORT.
   /CALIFORNIA/
CALIFORNIA FAIR EMPLOYMENT PRACTICE COMMISSION. SAN
FRANCISCO, CALIFORNIA. 1965. 7 PP.

GCALFEP65542   CALIFORNIA FEPC
SAN-MATEO AREA MINORITY JOB SURVEY. /CALIFORNIA/
CALIFORNIA FAIR EMPLOYMENT PRACTICE COMMISSION.
SAN FRANCISCO, CALIFORNIA. JUNE 1965. 7 PP.

GCALFEP66528   CALIFORNIA FEPC
ACTION PROGRAMS FOR FEPC ADVISORY COMMITTEES. /CALIFORNIA/
CALIFORNIA, FAIR EMPLOYMENT PRACTICES COMMISION. SAN
FRANCISCO, CALIFORNIA. 1966. 7 PP.

GCALFEP66532   CALIFORNIA FEPC
EVALUATING JOB APPLICANTS WITH POLICE RECORDS. /CALIFORNIA/
CALIFORNIA FAIR EMPLOYMENT PRACTICE COMMISSION.
SAN FRANCISCO, CALIFORNIA. JULY 1966. 4 PP.

GCALFEP66540   CALIFORNIA FEPC
FAIR-EMPLOYMENT-PRACTICES EQUAL GOOD EMPLOYMENT PRACTICES.
   GUIDELINES FOR TESTING AND SELECTING MINORITY JOB
   APPLICANTS. /CALIFORNIA/
CALIFORNIA FAIR EMPLOYMENT PRACTICE COMMISSION, TECHNICAL
ADVISORY COMMITTEE ON TESTING. SACRAMENTO, CALIFORNIA.
MAY 1966.

GCALLFX59544   CALIFORNIA LABOR FEDERATION
LABOR AND CIVIL-RIGHTS. /CALIFORNIA UNION/
CALIFORNIA LABOR FEDERATION, AFL-CIO. SAN FRANCISCO,
CALIFORNIA. 1959.

GCALLFX64545   CALIFORNIA LABOR FEDERATION
LABOR AND CIVIL-RIGHTS 1964. /CALIFORNIA UNION/
CALIFORNIA LABOR FEDERATION, AFL-CIO. SAN FRANCISCO,
CALIFORNIA. AUG 1964. 10 PP.

GCALOGB63546   CAL OFFICE OF THE GOVENOR
GOVENOR-S CODE OF FAIR PRACTICE /CALIFORNIA/
CALIFORNIA OFFICE OF THE GOVENOR. SACRAMENTO, CALIFORNIA.
JULY 24 1963.

GCALPPA65547   CAL PUBLIC PERSONNEL ASSN
MINORITY-GROUPS AND MERIT SYSTEM PRACTICE.
CALIFORNIA PUBLIC PERSONNEL ASSOCIATION, REPORT NO 653.
CHICAGO, ILLINOIS. 1965.

GCALSEM64548   CALIFORNIA STATE EMPLOYEE
EQUAL-OPPORTUNITIES PLAN STRESSED IN STATE PERSONNEL BOARD
   DOCUMENT. /CALIFORNIA/
CALIFORNIA STATE EMPLOYEE, VOL 36, JAN 16 1964. P 4.

GCALSLIND549   CALIFORNIA STATE LIBRARY   *CALIFORNIA DEPT OF EDUCATION
SCHOOL, MINORITIES AND EQUAL-RIGHTS, SELECTED MATERIAL.
   /CALIFORNIA/
CALIFORNIA STATE DEPARTMENT OF OF EDUCATION, BUREAU OF
INTERGROUP RELATIONS. SACRAMENTO, CALIFORNIA. ND. 13 PP.

GCALSPB65551   CAL STATE PERSONNEL BOARD
ETHNIC CENSUS OF EXAMINATION COMPETITORS, JAN-JUNE 1965.
   CALIFORNIA STATE PERSONNEL BOARD.
CALIFORNIA STATE PERSONNEL BOARD. SACRAMENTO, CALIFORNIA.
JUNE 1965.

GCALSPB65552   CAL STATE PERSONNEL BOARD
ETHNIC CENSUS OF EXAMINATION COMPETITORS, JULY-DEC 1965,
   CALIFORNIA STATE-PERSONNEL-BOARD.
CALIFORNIA STATE PERSONNEL BOARD. SACRAMENTO, CALIFORNIA.
JUNE 1965.

GCALVRS60553   CAL VOCATIONAL REHAB SERVICE
THE ITINERANT FARM LABOR PROJECT REPORT. /MIGRANT-WORKERS
   CALIFORNIA/
CALIFORNIA VOCATIONAL REHABILITATION SERVICE. SACRAMENTO,
CALIFORNIA. JAN 4 1960. 10 PP.

GCALVRX63555   CALVERT   R
HOW TO RECRUIT MINORITY-GROUP COLLEGE GRADUATES, ITS
   PROBLEMS, ITS TECHNIQUES, ITS SOURCES, ITS OPPORTUNITIES.
THE PERSONNEL JOURNAL, INC. SWARTHMORE, PENNSYLVANIA. 1963.
41 PP.

GCAMPJX64093   CAMPBELL   J   *EDUCATIONAL TESTING SERVICE
TESTING OF CULTURALLY DIFFERENT GROUPS.
EDUCATIONAL TESTING SERVICE, RESEARCH BULLETIN RB-64-34.
PRINCETON, NEW JERSEY. 1964. 22 PP.

GCAPLDX63310   CAPLOVITZ   D
THE POOR PAY MORE. CONSUMER PRACTICES OF LOW-INCOME
   FAMILIES.
FREE PRESS OF GLENCOE. NEW YORK. 1963. 220 PP.

GCARRHX66558   CARR   H   *US DEPARTMENT OF LABOR
TEXAS PROVIDES JOBS FOR MINORITY-GROUPS.
US DEPARTMENT OF LABOR, EMPLOYMENT SERVICE REVIEW,
VOL 3, NO 4, AP 1966. PP 32-33.

GCARTEA56559   CARTER   EA
POLICIES AND PRACTICES OF DISCRIMINATION COMMISSIONS.
   /FEPC/
ANNALS OF THE AMERICAN ACADEMY OF POLITICAL AND SOCIAL
SCIENCE, VOL 304, MAR 1956. PP 62-77.

GCARTRX65560   CARTER   R
THE NLRB AND RACIAL DISCRIMINATION. /LEGISLATION/
LAW IN TRANSITION QUARTERLY, VOL 2, NO 2, SPRING 1965.
PP 87-96.

GCASSFH63562   CASSELL   FH
POSITIVE ACTION ON UNEMPLOYMENT.
INTEGRATED EDUCATION, VOL 1, JUNE 1963. P 36.

GCASSFH66561   CASSELL   FH   *US DEPARTMENT OF LABOR
EQUAL-EMPLOYMENT-OPPORTUNITY. A CHALLENGE TO THE EMPLOYMENT
   SERVICE.
US DEPARTMENT OF LABOR, EMPLOYMENT SERVICE REVIEW, VOL 3,
NO 8, AUG 1966. PP 1-3, 17.

GCASSFH66565   CASSELL   FH
MANPOWER PROGRAM IMPLICATIONS OF SKILL IMBALANCES.
   /TRAINING/
INDUSTRIAL RELATIONS RESEARCH ASSOCIATION, PROCEEDINGS,
19TH ANNUAL WINTER MEETING. SAN FRANCISCO, CALIFORNIA.
DEC 28-29 1966. PP 230-239.

GCASSFH66744   CASSELL   FH
JOBS FOR THE HARD-TO-EMPLOY IN PRIVATE ENTERPRISE.
CRITICAL ISSUES IN EMPLOYMENT POLICY. ED BY F H HARBISON AND
J D MOONEY. PRINCETON UNIVERSITY, INDUSTRIAL RELATIONS
SECTION. PRINCETON, NEW JERSEY. 1966. PP 77-94.

GCHALFK48563   CHALMERS   FK   HEIGHT   DI
FAIR PRACTICE IN EMPLOYMENT.
WOMEN-S PRESS. NEW YORK. 1948.

GCHANNM66803   CHANSKY   NM
UNTAPPED GOOD. THE REHABILITATION OF SCHOOL DROPOUTS.
CHARLES C THOMAS, PUBLISHERS. SPRINGFIELD, ILLINOIS. 1966.
267 PP.

GCHICBC65319   CHICAGO BOYS CLUBS   CHICAGO YOUTH CENTERS
YMCA OF METROPOLITAN CHICAGO   *US DEPARTMENT OF LABOR
FINAL REPORT ON JOBS II PROJECT. /CHICAGO ILLINOIS/
CHICAGO BOYS CLUBS, CHICAGO YOUTH CENTERS, AND YMCA OF
METROPOLITAN CHICAGO. US DEPARTMENT OF LABOR, OFFICE OF
MANPOWER, AUTOMATION AND TRAINING. GPO. WASHINGTON, DC.
AUG 27 1965. 262 PP.

GCHICHR59565   CHICAGO COMM ON HUMAN RELS
HUMAN-RELATIONS NEWS OF CHICAGO. /ILLINOIS/
CHICAGO COMMISSION ON HUMAN RELATIONS, HUMAN RELATIONS NEWS
OF CHICAGO, VOL 1, NO 1, AP 1959.

GCHICHR62568   CHICAGO COMM ON HUMAN RELS
YOUR CIVIL-RIGHTS. /CHICAGO ILLINOIS/
CHICAGO COMMISSION ON HUMAN RELATIONS. CHICAGO, ILLINOIS.
OCT 15 1962. 46 PP.

GCHICMC56566   CHI MAYORS COMT COM WELFARE
MERIT EMPLOYMENT IN CHICAGO. /ILLINOIS/
CHICAGO MAYOR-S COMMITTEE ON COMMUNITY WELFARE, SUBCOMMITTEE
ON EMPLOYMENT AND COMMUNITY SERVICES. CHICAGO, ILLINOIS.
FEB 1956. 26 PP.

GCHILCX64571   CHILMAN   C
ECONOMIC AND SOCIAL DEPRIVATIONS. ITS EFFECTS ON CHILDREN
   AND FAMILIES IN THE UNITED STATES -- A SELECTED
   BIBLIOGRAPHY.
JOURNAL OF MARRIAGE AND THE FAMILY, VOL 26, NO 4, NOV 1964.
PP 495-498.

GCHILCX64922   CHILMAN   C   SUSSMAN   MB
POVERTY IN THE UNITED STATES IN THE MIO-SIXTIES.
JOURNAL OF MARRIAGE AND THE FAMILY, VOL 26, NOV 1964.
PP 391-398.

GCHURRX55572   CHURCH   R   *US DEPARTMENT OF LABOR
MINORITY-GROUPS CONFERENCE ON
   EQUAL-EMPLOYMENT-OPPORTUNITIES.
US DEPARTMENT OF LABOR, MONTHLY LABOR REVIEW, VOL 78,
SEPT 1955. PP 1017-1019.

GCLAGEX64625   CLAGUE   E
EFFECTS OF TECHNOLOGICAL-CHANGE ON OCCUPATIONAL EMPLOYMENT
   PATTERNS IN THE UNITED STATES.
ORGANIZATION FOR ECONOMIC COOPERATION AND DEVELOPMENT,
NORTH AMERICAN JOINT CONFERENCE. THE REQUIREMENTS OF
AUTOMATED JOBS AND THEIR POLICY IMPLICATIONS.
WASHINGTON, DC. DEC 8-10 1964. PP 103-118.

GCLAGEX65794   CLAGUE   E   *US DEPARTMENT OF LABOR
ECONOMIC MANPOWER AND SOCIAL-WELFARE.
UNIVERSITY OF CHICAGO SYMPOSIUM, ADDRESS. US DEPARTMENT OF
LABOR. GPO. WASHINGTON, DC. 1965. 14 PP.

GCLARKB60574   CLARK   KB
DISADVANTAGED STUDENTS AND DISCRIMINATION.
SEARCH FOR TALENT, NO 7, 1960. PP 12-19.

GCLARKB66915   CLARK   KB   *US CHAMBER OF COMMERCE
EDUCATION OF THE MINORITY POOR -- THE KEY TO THE
   WAR-ON-POVERTY.
THE DISADVANTAGED POOR. EDUCATION AND EMPLOYMENT. US CHAMBER

OF COMMERCE, TASK FORCE ON ECONOMIC GROWTH AND OPPORTUNITY.
WASHINGTON, DC. 1966. PP 173-188.

GCLEAMP66130   CLEAVES MP
A DEMONSTRATION PROJECT DESIGNED TO TEST THE LIFE-STYLE AND
    THE GROWTH POTENTIAL OF URBAN DROPOUTS FROM DISADVANTAGED
    HOMES.
WESTERN MARYLAND COLLEGE. MASTERS THESIS. WESTMINSTER,
MARYLAND. 1966.

GCLEATA66924   CLEARY TA   HILTON TL
*EDUCATIONAL TESTING SERVICE
AN INVESTIGATION OF ITEM BIAS. /TESTING/
EDUCATIONAL TESTING SERVICE, RESEARCH BULLETIN RB-66-17.
PRINCETON, NEW JERSEY. AP 1966. 20 PP.

GCLINRX61577   CLINCHY R
THE FEDERAL MANAGER-S ROLE IN DEMOCRACY-S UNFINISHED
    BUSINESS.
CIVIL SERVICE JOURNAL, VOL 2, OCT-DEC 1961. PP 5-7.

GCLOWRX66525   CLOWARD R   PIVEN FF
THE WEIGHT OF THE POOR -- A STRATEGY TO END POVERTY.
    /GUARANTEED-INCOME/
THE NATION, VOL 202, NO 18, MAY 2, 1966. 7 PP.

GCOBBCW46578   COBB CW
OUTLOOK REGARDING STATE FEPC LEGISLATION.
JOURNAL OF NEGRO HISTORY, VOL 31, JULY 1946. PP 247-253.

GCOHEFS46579   COHEN FS
THE PEOPLE VS. DISCRIMINATION. THE FEPC FIGHT INITIATES A
    NEW EPOCH.
COMMENTARY, MAR 1946. PP 17-22.

GCOHENE65664   COHEN NE
A NATIONAL PROGRAM FOR THE IMPROVEMENT OF WELFARE SERVICES
    AND THE REDUCTION OF WELFARE DEPENDENCY.
POVERTY IN AMERICA. ED BY M S GORDON. CHANDLER PUBLISHING
CO. SAN FRANCISCO, CALIFORNIA. 1965. PP 278-298.

GCOHEWJ64925   COHEN WJ
THE ELIMINATION OF POVERTY. A PRIMARY GOAL OF PUBLIC POLICY.
POVERTY IN PLENTY. ED BY G H DUNNE. P J KENEDY AND SONS.
NEW YORK. 1964. PP 24-47.

GCOLBMR63994   COLBERG MR
HUMAN CAPITAL AS A SOUTHERN RESOURCE.
SOUTHERN ECONOMIC JOURNAL, VOL 29, JAN 1963. PP 157-166.

GCOLBMR65793   COLBERG MR
HUMAN CAPITAL IN SOUTHERN DEVELOPMENT 1939-1963.
UNIVERSITY OF NORTH CAROLINA PRESS. CHAPEL HILL,
NORTH CAROLINA. 1965. 135 PP.

GCOLEEX66131   COLE E   *NYU CEN STUDY UNEMP YOUTH
WORK PROGRAMS AND THE YOUTHFUL OFFENDER.
NEW YORK UNIVERSITY, GRADUATE SCHOOL OF SOCIAL WORK, CENTER
FOR THE STUDY OF UNEMPLOYED YOUTH. NEW YORK. JUNE 1966.

GCOLERX66133   COLES R
WHAT MIGRANT FARM CHILDREN LEARN.
KNOWING THE DISADVANTAGED. ED BY STATEN W WEBSTER. CHANDLER
PUBLISHING CO. SAN FRANCISCO, CALIFORNIA. 1966. PP 236-243.

GCOLESG54580   COLE SG   COLE MW
MINORITIES AND THE AMERICAN PROMISE. THE CONFLICT OF
    PRINCIPLE AND PRACTICE.
HARPERS. NEW YORK. 1954. 319 PP.

GCOLOSD59919   COLORADO STATE DEPT OF ED
A SOCIAL PROFILE OF AGRICULTURAL MIGRATORY PEOPLE IN
    COLORADO. /MIGRANT-WORKERS/
COLORADO STATE DEPARTMENT OF EDUCATION, RESOURCE REPORT E-1.
DENVER, COLORADO. 1959. 27 PP.

GCOMCCN64210   COMM CC GTR NEW YORK
POVERTY IN NEW-YORK CITY. FACTS FOR PLANNING COMMUNITY
    ACTION.
COMMUNITY COUNCIL OF GREATER NEW YORK, RESEARCH DEPARTMENT.
NEW YORK. NOV 1964. 34 PP.

GCOMIED65591   COMT FOR ECONOMIC DEVELOPMENT
RAISING LOW-INCOMES THROUGH IMPROVED EDUCATION.
COMMITTEE FOR ECONOMIC DEVELOPMENT, RESEARCH AND POLICY
COMMITTEE, STATEMENT. SEPT 1965. 51 PP.

GCOMIEF64592   COMMITTEE FOR FULL EMPLOYMENT   *CHI ASSN COMMMRCE INDUSTRY
1964 MANPOWER SURVEY. /CHICAGO ILLINOIS/
CHICAGO ASSOCIATION OF COMMERCE AND INDUSTRY. CHICAGO,
ILLINOIS. 1964. 44 PP.

GCOMMCH64588   COMMERCE CLEARING HOUSE
CIVIL-RIGHTS-ACT OF 1964, WITH EXPLANATION -- PUBLIC
    LAW 88-352 -- AS APPROVED BY THE PRESIDENT ON
    JULY 2, 1964.
COMMERCE CLEARING HOUSE, INC. CHICAGO, ILLINOIS. 1964.
108 PP.

GCOMMCH64590   COMMERCE CLEARING HOUSE
FAIR-EMPLOYMENT-PRACTICES UNDER THE CIVIL-RIGHTS-ACT OF
    1964.
COMMERCE CLEARING HOUSE, INC. CHICAGO, ILLINOIS. 1964.
24 PP.

GCOMMCH65589   COMMERCE CLEARING HOUSE
EMPLOYMENT PRACTICE GUIDE.
COMMERCE CLEARING HOUSE, INC. CHICAGO, ILLINOIS. 1965.

GCONFAP63545   CONF AUTOMATION PUB WELFARE
PUBLIC WELFARE, AUTOMATION, AND EXPERIMENTAL MANPOWER
    PROGRAMS.
AMERICAN FOUNDATION ON AUTOMATION AND EMPLOYMENT. NEW YORK.
OCT 1963. 19 PP.

GCONFOE62873   CONFERENCE ON EC PROGRESS
POVERTY AND DEPRIVATION IN THE UNITED STATES. THE PLIGHT OF
    TWO-FIFTHS OF A NATION.
CONFERENCE ON ECONOMIC PROGRESS. WASHINGTON, DC. AP 1962.
97 PP.

GCONFOE66872   CONFERENCE ON EC PROGRESS
THE ROLE OF WAGES IN A GREAT SOCIETY.
CONFERENCE ON ECONOMIC PROGRESS. WASHINGTON, DC. 1966.
124 PP.

GCONGDX45596   CONGRESSIONAL DIGEST
SHOULD CONGRESS PASS A LAW PROHIBITING EMPLOYMENT
    DISCRIMINATION.
CONGRESSIONAL DIGEST, VOL 24, NO 6-7, JUNE-JULY 1945.

PP 163-192.

GCONGDX50597   CONGRESSIONAL DIGEST
STORM CENTER OF THE FIGHT -- FEPC.
CONGRESSIONAL DIGEST, VOL 29, NO 2, FEB 1950. P 43.

GCONGDX64594   CONGRESSIONAL DIGEST
THE CONTROVERSY OVER THE EQUAL-EMPLOYMENT-OPPORTUNITY
    PROVISIONS OF THE CIVIL-RIGHTS BILL. PRO AND CON.
CONGRESSIONAL DIGEST, VOL 43, MAR 1964. PP 64796.

GCONGDX66356   CONGRESSIONAL DIGEST
CONGRESS AND THE JOHNSON POVERTY PROGRAM.
CONGRESSIONAL DIGEST, VOL 45, MAR 1966. PP 67-96.

GCONSLO59926   CONSUMERS LEAGUE OF NEW YORK
THE COMMUNITY LOOKS AT MIGRANT LABOR. /MIGRANT-WORKERS/
CONSUMERS LEAGUE OF NEW YORK. NEW YORK. 1959. 15 PP.

GCONWJE64599   CONWAY JE
STATE AND LOCAL CONTRACTS AND SUBCONTRACTS.
BUFFALO LAW REVIEW, VOL 14, 1964. PP 130-139.

GCONWJT65496   CONWAY JT   *US DEPARTMENT OF LABOR
SEMINAR ON MANPOWER POLICY AND PROGRAM. LABOR LOOKS AT
    AUTOMATION AND CIVIL-RIGHTS.
US DEPARTMENT OF LABOR, OFFICE OF MANPOWER, AUTOMATION,
AND TRAINING. GPO. WASHINGTON, DC. FEB 1965. 26 PP.

GCOOKFC66600   COOKSEY FC
THE ROLE OF LAW IN EQUAL-EMPLOYMENT-OPPORTUNITY.
BOSTON COLLEGE INDUSTRIAL AND COMMERCIAL LAW REVIEW, VOL 7,
NO 3, SPRING 1966. PP 417-430.

GCOONRB64871   COONEY RB
AUTOMATION. THE IMPACT ON JOBS AND PEOPLE.
AMERICAN FEDERATIONIST, VOL 71, MAY 1964. PP 3-8.

GCOOPSX59928   COOPER S   *US DEPARTMENT OF LABOR
CHANGING COMPOSITION OF THE AMERICAN WORK-FORCE.
US DEPARTMENT OF LABOR, BUREAU OF LABOR STATISTICS,
OCCUPATIONAL OUTLOOK QUARTERLY, VOL 3, NO 2, MAY 1959.
PP 20-23.

GCOOPSX60601   COOPER S   *US DEPARTMENT OF LABOR
EMPLOYMENT OF JUNE 1959 HIGH SCHOOL GRADUATES, OCTOBER 1959.
US DEPARTMENT OF LABOR, MONTHLY LABOR REVIEW, VOL 83, NO 5,
MAY 1960. 7 PP.

GCOOPSX60603   COOPER S   *US DEPARTMENT OF LABOR
WORK EXPERIENCE OF THE POPULATION IN 1959.
US DEPARTMENT OF LABOR, MONTHLY LABOR REVIEW, VOL 83, NO 12,
DEC 1960. 35 PP.

GCOOPSX62602   COOPER S   *US DEPARTMENT OF LABOR
INTERIM REVISED PROJECTIONS OF US LABOR-FORCE, 1965-1975.
US DEPARTMENT OF LABOR, MONTHLY LABOR REVIEW, OCT 1962.
PP 1089-1099.

GCOOPSX64743   COOPER S   JOHNSTON DF
THE OUTLOOK FOR THE LABOR-FORCE AT MID-DECADE.
    /EMPLOYMENT-TRENDS/
AMERICAN STATISTICAL ASSOCIATION, BUSINESS AND ECONOMICS
SECTION, PROCEEDINGS. 1964. PP 367-383.

GCOOPSX66604   COOPER S   JOHNSTON DF
*US DEPARTMENT OF LABOR
LABOR-FORCE PROJECTIONS BY COLOR, 1970-1980.
US DEPARTMENT OF LABOR, MONTHLY LABOR REVIEW, SEPT 1966.
PP 965-982. ALSO US DEPARTMENT OF LABOR, BUREAU OF LABOR
STATISTICS. SPECIAL LABOR FORCE REPORT NO 73.

GCORTJC57372   CORT JC
FRUSTRATION ON THE FARM.
    /MEXICAN-AMERICAN ORIENTAL UNION/
COMMONWEAL, VOL 66, NO 16, JULY 19 1957. PP 394-396.

GCOUNEAND239   COUNCIL OF ECONOMIC ADVISORS
ECONOMIC REPORTS OF THE PRESIDENT.
COUNCIL OF ECONOMIC ADVISORS. GPO. WASHINGTON, DC.
PUBLISHED ANNUALLY.

GCOUNEA62205   COUNCIL OF ECONOMIC ADVISORS
ECONOMIC COSTS OF RACIAL DISCRIMINATION IN EMPLOYMENT.
COUNCIL OF ECONOMIC ADVISERS. GPO. WASHINGTON, DC.
SEPT 24 1962. 9 PP.

GCOUNEA66204   COUNCIL OF ECONOMIC ADVISORS
POTENTIAL ECONOMIC GAINS FROM ELIMINATING DISCRIMINATION.
COUNCIL OF ECONOMIC ADVISERS. GPO. WASHINGTON, DC. 1966.

GCOUNSG58932   COUNCIL OF STATE GOVERNMENTS
REPORTS OF THE MEETINGS OF THE COMMITTEE OF OFFICIALS ON
    MIGRATORY FARM LABOR OF THE ATLANTIC SEABOARD STATES.
    /MIGRANT-WORKERS/
COUNCIL OF STATE GOVERNMENTS. WASHINGTON, DC. 1958. 31 PP.

GCOUNSG60931   COUNCIL OF STATE GOVERNMENTS
MIGRATORY-LABOR IN THE WEST. BACKGROUND INFORMATION FOR THE
    WESTERN INTERSTATE CONFERENCE ON MIGRATORY LABOR.
    /MIGRANT-WORKERS/
COUNCIL OF STATE GOVERNMENTS. SAN FRANCISCO, CALIFORNIA.
AP 1960. 14 PP.

GCOUNVX64608   COUNTRYMAN V
THE CONSTITUTION AND JOB DISCRIMINATION.
WASHINGTON LAW REVIEW, VOL 39, 1964. PP 74-95.

GCOUNVX65609   COUNTRYMAN V ED
DISCRIMINATION AND THE LAW.
UNIVERSITY OF CHICAGO PRESS. CHICAGO, ILLINOIS. 1965.
170 PP.

GCOUNVX65610   COUNTRYMAN V   WILLIAMS JS
MING WM
DISCRIMINATION IN EMPLOYMENT.
DISCRIMINATION AND THE LAW. ED BY VERN COUNTRYMAN.
UNIVERSITY OF CHICAGO PRESS. CHICAGO, ILLINOIS. 1965.
PP 21-50.

GCOUSFR61612   COUSENS FR
A SUMMARY ANALYSIS OF FIVE YEARS OF CLAIMS EXPERIENCE BY TH
    MICHIGAN FAIR-EMPLOYMENT-PRACTICES-COMMISSION,
    FEBRUARY, 1961.
MICHIGAN FAIR EMPLOYMENT PRACTICES COMMISSION. DETROIT,
MICHIGAN. 1961. 9 PP.

GCOUSFR62613   COUSENS FR
A SUMMARY ANALYSIS OF SIX YEARS OF CLAIMS EXPERIENCE BY THE
    MICHIGAN FAIR-EMPLOYMENT PRACTICES-COMMISSION, FEBRUARY

1962.
MICHIGAN FAIR EMPLOYMENT PRACTICES COMMISSION. DETROIT,
MICHIGAN. 1962. 5 PP.

GCOUSFR66478   COUSENS FR   MILLER   JA
*U OF MICH-WAYNE STATE U ILIR
A STUDY OF PATTERNS OF DISCRIMINATION IN EMPLOYMENT FOR THE
EQUAL-EMPLOYMENT-OPPORTUNITY-COMMISSION, WASHINGTON-DC.
UNIVERSITY OF MICHIGAN-WAYNE STATE UNIVERSITY, INSTITUTE OF
LABOR AND INDUSTRIAL RELATIONS. ANN ARBOR-DETROIT, MICHIGAN.
SEPT 1966. 300 PP.

GCOWHJD59430   COWHIG JD   MAITLAND ST
*US DEPARTMENT OF AGRICULTURE
THE HIRED FARM WORKING FORCE OF 1958. /ECONOMIC-STATUS/
US DEPARTMENT OF AGRICULTURE. GPO. WASHINGTON, DC. DEC 1959.
29 PP.

GCOWHJD60423   COWHIG JD   MAITLAND ST
*US DEPARTMENT OF AGRICULTURE
AN ANALYSIS OF THE EXPERIENCED HIRED FARM WORKING FORCE,
   1948-1957. /SKILLS/
US DEPARTMENT OF AGRICULTURE. GPO. WASHINGTON, DC. AP 1960.
19 PP.

GCOWHJD61427   COWHIG JD   NAM CB
*US BUREAU OF THE CENSUS   *US DEPARTMENT OF AGRICULTURE
EDUCATIONAL STATUS, COLLEGE PLANS, AND OCCUPATIONAL-STATUS
   OF FARM AND NONFARM YOUTHS. OCTOBER 1959.
US BUREAU OF THE CENSUS. US DEPARTMENT OF AGRICULTURE. GPO.
WASHINGTON, DC. AUG 1961. 33 PP.

GCOWHJD63420   COWHIG JD   *US DEPARTMENT OF AGRICULTURE
EDUCATION, SKILL LEVEL, AND EARNINGS OF THE HIRED FARM
   WORKING FORCE OF 1961.
US DEPARTMENT OF AGRICULTURE. GPO. WASHINGTON, DC. MAR 1963.
21 PP.

GCOWHJD63421   COWHIG JD   *US DEPARTMENT OF AGRICULTURE
SCHOOL DROPOUT RATES AMONG FARM AND NONFARM YOUTH 1950 AND
   1960.
US DEPARTMENT OF AGRICULTURE. GPO. WASHINGTON, DC.
SEPT 1963. 30 PP.

GCOWHJD64419   COWHIG JD   *US DEPARTMENT OF AGRICULTURE
CHARACTERISTICS OF SCHOOL DROPOUTS AND HIGH SCHOOL
   GRADUATES, FARM AND NONFARM, 1960.
US DEPARTMENT OF AGRICULTURE, AGRICULTURAL ECONOMIC REPORT.
GPO. WASHINGTON, DC. DEC 1964. 32 PP.

GCOWHJD64615   COWHIG JD   BEALE CL
RELATIVE SOCIOECONOMIC STATUS OF SOUTHERN WHITES AND
   NONWHITES, 1950 AND 1960.
SOUTHWESTERN SOCIAL SCIENCE QUARTERLY, SEPT 1964.
PP 113-124.

GCOWHJD64616   COWHIG JD   BEALE CL
SOCIOECONOMIC DIFFERENCES BETWEEN WHITE AND NONWHITE FARM
   POPULATIONS IN THE SOUTH.
SOCIAL FORCES, VOL 42, NO 3, MAR 1964. PP 354-362.

GCOWHJD65425   COWHIG JD   *US DEPARTMENT OF AGRICULTURE
URBAN AND RURAL LEVELS OF LIVING. 1960. /ECONOMIC-STATUS/
US DEPARTMENT OF AGRICULTURE. GPO. WASHINGTON, DC.
JULY 1965. 18 PP.

GCOWHJD65614   COWHIG JD   BEALE C
*US DEPT OF HEALTH ED WELFARE
LEVELS OF LIVING AMONG WHITES AND NON-WHITES IN THE U.S.
US DEPARTMENT OF HEALTH, EDUCATION, AND WELFARE, INDICATORS,
OCT 1965.

GCOWHJD65933   COWHIG JD   BEALE CL
*US DEPARTMENT OF LABOR
THE RISING LEVELS OF EDUCATION AMONG YOUNG WORKERS.
US DEPARTMENT OF LABOR, MONTHLY LABOR REVIEW, VOL 88, NO 6,
JUNE 1965. PP 625-629.

GCOXXAX57617   COX A
THE DUTY OF FAIR REPRESENTATION.
VILLANOVA LAW REVIEW, VOL 2, JAN 1957. PP 151-177.

GCOXXTX63618   COX T
COUNSELOR-S VIEWS ON CHANGING MANAGEMENT POLICIES.
PUBLIC RELATIONS JOURNAL, VOL 19, NOV 1963.

GCRAICE65619   CRAIG CE   *US DEPARTMENT OF LABOR
MINORITY PROGRAM CALLS FOR COMMUNITY ACTION.
US DEPARTMENT OF LABOR, EMPLOYMENT SERVICE REVIEW, VOL 2,
NO 8, AUG 1965. PP 10-12.

GCRAICE66620   CRAIG CE   RICHARDS WW
*US DEPARTMENT OF LABOR
ARIZONA-S EXPERIENCE UNDER THE CIVIL-RIGHTS-ACT.
US DEPARTMENT OF LABOR, EMPLOYMENT SERVICE REVIEW, VOL 3,
NO 8, AUG 1966. PP 11-13.

GCREADX61621   CREAMER D
SOME DETERMINANTS OF LOW FAMILY INCOME.
ECONOMIC DEVELOPMENT AND CULTURE CHANGE, AP 1961. P 437 FF.

GCROSER66148   CROSSMAN ER   *US DEPARTMENT OF LABOR
SEMINAR ON MANPOWER POLICY AND PROGRAM -- AUTOMATION, SKILL,
   AND MANPOWER PREDICTIONS.
US DEPARTMENT OF LABOR, MANPOWER ADMINISTRATION, OFFICE OF
MANPOWER, POLICY, EVALUATION AND RESEARCH. GPO. WASHINGTON,
DC. SEPT 1966. 37 PP.

GCULHMM65651   CULHANE MM   *US DEPARTMENT OF LABOR
TESTING THE DISADVANTAGED.
US DEPARTMENT OF LABOR, EMPLOYMENT SERVICE REVIEW, VOL 2,
NO 5, MAY 1965. PP 8-9.

GCUMMLD65623   CUMMINGS LD   *US DEPARTMENT OF LABOR
THE EMPLOYED POOR. THEIR CHARACTERISTICS AND OCCUPATIONS.
US DEPARTMENT OF LABOR, MONTHLY LABOR REVIEW, JULY 1965.
PP 828-841.

GCURRRO60889   CURRAN RO   *LEAGUE OF CALIFORNIA CITIES
FAIR-EMPLOYMENT-PRACTICE-COMMISSION GUIDE TO UNLAWFUL
   PRE-EMPLOYMENT INQUIRIES.
LEAGUE OF CALIFORNIA CITIES, CITY ATTORNEYS DEPARTMENT,
ANNUAL CONFERENCE. OCT 25 1960. BERKELEY, CALIFORNIA. 1960.
5 PP.

GDAILCA66926   DAILEY CA
PREJUDICE AND DECISION-MAKING. /EMPLOYMENT DISCRIMINATION/
PERSONNEL ADMINISTRATION, VOL 29, SEPT-OCT 1966. PP 6-13.

GDALYVR66625   DALY VR   *US DEPARTMENT OF LABOR

MDTA MOVES TO THE FRONT.
US DEPARTMENT OF LABOR, EMPLOYMENT SERVICE REVIEW, VOL 3,
NO 10, OCT 1966. PP 28-29.

GDARTCX47626   DARTNELL CORPORATION
ELIMINATION OF RACE DISCRIMINATION IN THE APPLICATION BLANK.
DARTNELL CORPORATION. CHICAGO, ILLINOIS. 1947. 7 PP.

GDAVIAX63132   DAVIS A   *MOBILIZATION FOR YOUTH INC
THE CULTURE OF THE SLUM.
MOBILIZATION FOR YOUTH, INC. NEW YORK. JAN 1963.

GDAVIHX65629   DAVID H
MANPOWER POLICIES FOR A DEMOCRATIC SOCIETY.
COLUMBIA UNIVERSITY PRESS. NEW YORK. 1965. 121 PP.

GDAVIIF58939   DAVIS IF   METZLER WH
SUGAR BEET LABOR IN NORTHERN COLORADO. /MIGRANT-WORKERS/
COLORADO STATE UNIVERSITY, EXPERIMENT STATION. FORT COLLINS,
COLORADO. 1958. 102 PP.

GDAVIJA46628   DAVIS JA
NONDISCRIMINATION IN THE FEDERAL-SERVICES.
ANNALS OF THE AMERICAN ACADEMY OF POLITICAL AND SOCIAL
SCIENCE, NO 244, MAR 1946. PP 65-74.

GDAVIKX65663   DAVIS K
SOME DEMOGRAPHIC ASPECTS OF POVERTY IN THE UNITED STATES.
POVERTY IN AMERICA. ED BY M S GORDON. CHANDLER PUBLISHING
CO. SAN FRANCISCO, CALIFORNIA. 1965. PP 299-319.

GDAVIMX64870   DAVID M
INCOMES AND DEPENDENCY IN THE COMING DECADES.
AMERICAN JOURNAL OF ECONOMICS AND SOCIOLOGY, VOL 23,
JULY 1964. PP 249-267.

GDAVIWG65629   DAVIS WG
A COMMON GOAL -- EQUAL-EMPLOYMENT-OPPORTUNITY.
THE AMERICAN FEDERATIONIST, VOL 72, NO 6, JUNE 1965. PP 1-4.

GDEANJP55630   DEAN JP
MANUAL OF INTERGROUP RELATIONS.
UNIVERSITY OF CHICAGO PRESS. CHICAGO, ILLINOIS. 1955.
194 PP.

GDEANLR54944   DEAN LR
SOCIAL INTEGRATION, ATTITUDES AND UNION ACTIVITY.
INDUSTRIAL AND LABOR RELATIONS REVIEW, OCT 1954.

GDEFESA64631   DEFENSE SUPPLY AGENCY
EQUAL-EMPLOYMENT-OPPORTUNITY IN THE DEFENSE SUPPLY AGENCY.
DEFENSE SUPPLY AGENCY. ALEXANDRIA, VIRGINIA. JUNE 1964.
15 PP.

GDELACM58545   DELAWARE COMT MIGRATORY LABOR
REPORT AND RECOMMENDATIONS OF DELAWARE COMMITTEE ON
   MIGRATORY LABOR. /MIGRANT-WORKERS/
DELAWARE LABOR COMMISSION, COMMITTEE ON MIGRATORY LABOR.
WILMINGTON, DELAWARE. 1958. 11 PP.

GDELASE59546   DELAWARE SES
EFFECT OF MECHANIZATION ON EMPLOYMENT OF MIGRATORY LABOR IN
   AGRICULTURE AND FOOD PROCESSING. /MIGRANT-WORKERS/
DELAWARE STATE EMPLOYMENT SERVICE. WILMINGTON, DELAWARE.
1959.

GDELMDT66147   DELMET DT
A SUMMARY REPORT OF PRACTICES AND PROGRAMS DESIGNED TO
   REDUCE THE NUMBER OF DROPOUTS IN THE HIGH SCHOOLS OF
   LOS-ANGELES COUNTY. /CALIFORNIA/
THE DISADVANTAGED AND POTENTIAL DROPOUT. COMPENSATORY
PROGRAMS. ED BY JOHN C GOWAN AND GEORGE D DEMOS. CHARLES C
THOMAS, PUBLISHER. SPRINGFIELD, ILLINOIS. 1966. PP 462-480.

GDEMSHX65869   DEMSETZ H
MINORITIES IN THE MARKET PLACE.
NORTH CAROLINA LAW REVIEW, VOL 43, NO 2, FEB 1965.
PP 271-297.

GDENNGHN0632   DENNY GH   *COLORADO ANTI-DISCR COMM
PLANT INSPECTION SURVEY BY MANAGEMENT -- MINORITY-GROUP
   INTEGRATION. /COLORADO/
COLORADO ANTIDISCRIMINATION COMMISSION. DENVER, COLORADO.
NO. 12 PP.

GDERNTX64947   DERNBERG T
ECONOMICS AND THE CIVIL-RIGHTS CRISIS.
THE ACTIVIST, VOL 4, NO 3, SPRING 1964. PP 141-145.

GDESHEA66633   DE SHAZO EA
AN EQUAL-OPPORTUNITIES COMMITTEE AT WORK IN TEXAS.
SOCIAL SCIENCE, VOL 41, NO 2, AP 1966. PP 99-106.

GDESMCH65635   DES MOINES COMM ON HUM RIGHTS
EMPLOYMENT REVIEW. /DES-MOINES IOWA/
COMMISSION ON HUMAN RIGHTS. DES MOINES, IOWA. FEB 8 1965.
5 PP PLUS.

GDETRCC63638   DETROIT COMM COMMUNITY RELS
EMPLOYMENT IN CIVIL-SERVICE OF MINORITY-GROUPS. /DETROIT
   MICHIGAN/
DETROIT COMMISSION ON COMMUNITY RELATIONS. DETROIT,
MICHIGAN. 1963. . PP.

GDETRCC63948   DETROIT COMM COMMUNITY RELS
EMPLOYMENT AND INCOME BY AGE, SEX, COLOR AND RESIDENCE.
   /DETROIT MICHIGAN/
DETROIT COMMISSION ON COMMUNITY RELATIONS. DETROIT,
MICHIGAN. MAY 1963. 20 PP.

GDETRCC66639   DETROIT COMM COMMUNITY RELS
REPORT ON AND ANALYSIS OF SECOND CENSUS OF CITY EMPLOYEES TO
   DETERMINE BASES FOR FUTURE PERSONNEL DEVELOPMENTS.
   /DETROIT MICHIGAN/
DETROIT COMMISSION ON COMMUNITY RELATIONS. DETROIT,
MICHIGAN. MAR 24 1966. 14 PP.

GDEUTMP56641   DEUTSCH MP
SOME CONSIDERATIONS AS TO THE CONTRIBUTIONS OF SOCIAL,
   PERSONALITY, AND RACIAL FACTORS TO SCHOOL RETARDATION IN
   MINORITY-GROUP CHILDREN.
AMERICAN PSYCHOLOGICAL ASSOCIATION, CONVENTION, PAPER.
CHICAGO, ILLINOIS. SEPT 1956.

GDEUTMP60640   DEUTSCH MP   *CORNELL SOCT APPLIED ANTHRO
MINORITY-GROUP AND CLASS STATUS AS RELATED TO SOCIAL AND
   PERSONALITY FACTORS IN SCHOLASTIC ACHIEVEMENT.
CORNELL UNIVERSITY, SOCIETY FOR APPLIED ANTHROPOLOGY,
MONOGRAPH NO 2. ITHACA, NEW YORK. 1960. 32 PP.

GDISTCC66642 DC COMMRS COUNCIL ON HUM RELS
PATTERNS OF DISCRIMINATION IN THE FINANCIAL INSTITUTIONS OF
THE DISTRICT-OF-COLUMBIA. THE BANKING, SAVINGS AND LOAN,
AND INSURANCE INDUSTRIES.
DISTRICT OF COLUMBIA COMMISSIONERS COUNCIL ON HUMAN
RELATIONS. WASHINGTON, DC. JUNE 1966. 105 PLUS PP.

GDIXALX46643 DIX L
THE SCHOOL COUNSELOR AT WORK ON OCCUPATIONAL DISCRIMINATION.
OCCUPATIONS, VOL 24, FEB 1946. PP 261-265.

GDIXORX63644 DIXON R
CIVIL-RIGHTS IN AIR TRANSPORTATION AND GOVERNMENT
INITIATIVE.
VIRGINIA LAW REVIEW, VOL 49, NO 2, MAR 1963- PP 205-231.

GDOARLE66645 DOAR LE   *US DEPARTMENT OF LABOR
RACIAL STATISTICS AS A MANAGEMENT TOOL.
US DEPARTMENT OF LABOR, EMPLOYMENT SERVICE REVIEW, VOL 3,
NO 10, OCT 1966. PP 18-II.

GDODDEM45646 DODD EM
DISCRIMINATION BY LABOR UNIONS IN THE EXERCISE OF STATUTORY
BARGAINING POWERS.
HARVARD LAW REVIEW, VOL 58, FEB 1945. PP 448-455.

GDODSDW62647 DODSON DW
POWER AS A DIMENSION OF EDUCATION.
THE JOURNAL OF EDUCATIONAL SOCIOLOGY, VOL 35, NO 5, 1962.
13 PP.

GDOERPB67115 DOERINGER PB   *US DEPARTMENT OF LABOR
DISCRIMINATORY PROMOTION SYSTEMS.
US DEPARTMENT OF LABOR, MONTHLY LABOR REVIEW, VOL 90,
MAR 1967. PP 27-28.

GDONACX64648 DONAHUE C
EQUAL-EMPLOYMENT-OPPORTUNITY.
FEDERAL BAR JOURNAL, VOL 24, WINTER 1964. PP 76-86.

GDOUGJH61649 DOUGLASS JH
INTERGROUP RELATIONS IN THE FEDERAL-SERVICE .
JOURNAL OF INTERGROUP RELATIONS, VOL 2, WINTER 1960-1961.
PP 37-48.

GDOUGMX60650 DOUGLAS M
A POSITIVE PROGRAM FOR MERIT-EMPLOYMENT.
SECOND ANNUAL KANSAS CONFERENCE ON CIVIL RIGHTS, SPEECH.
KANSAS STATE UNIVERSITY. TOPEKA KANSAS. MAY 7 1960. ALSO
KANSAS ANTI-DISCRIMINATION COMMISSION, REPRINT. TOPEKA,
KANSAS. 1960. 6 PP.

GDUCOLJ57955 DUCOFF LJ   HAGOOD MJ
*NATL BUREAU OF EC RESEARCH
THE MEANING AND MEASUREMENT OF PARTIAL AND DISGUISED
UNEMPLOYMENT.
THE MEASUREMENT AND BEHAVIOR OF UNEMPLOYMENT. NATIONAL
BUREAU OF ECONOMIC RESEARCH. NEW YORK. 1957.

GDUFFJX44522 DUFFY J   *U OF CAL BUREAU PUBLIC ADM
STATE ORGANIZATION FOR FAIR-EMPLOYMENT-PRACTICES.
UNIVERSITY OF CALIFORNIA, BUREAU OF PUBLIC ADMINISTRATION.
BERKELY, CALIFORNIA. 1944.

GDUGARD66651 DUGAN RD
4. CURRENT PROBLEMS IN TEST PERFORMANCE OF JOB-APPLICANTS.
PERSONNEL PSYCHOLOGY, VOL 19, SPRING 1966. PP 18-24.

GDUNCOD63652 DUNCAN OD   HODGE RW
EDUCATION AND OCCUPATIONAL MOBILITY. A REGRESSION ANALYSIS.
AMERICAN JOURNAL OF SOCIOLOGY, VOL 68, NO 6, 1963.
PP 629-644.

GDUNKJE64653 DUNKELBERGER JE
ATTITUDE TOWARD OCCUPATIONAL CHANGE AS AN INDICATOR OF
PROSPECTS FOR ADJUSTMENT.
ASSOCIATION OF SOUTHERN AGRICULTURAL WORKERS CONFERENCE,
AGRICULTURAL ECONOMICS AND RURAL SOCIOLOGY SECTION, PAPER.
ATLANTA, GEORGIA. FEB 4 1964. 16 PP.

GDUNLJT62698 DUNLOP JT ED
AUTOMATION AND TECHNOLOGICAL-CHANGE.
PRENTICE-HALL, INC. ENGLEWOOD CLIFFS, NEW JERSEY. 1962.
184 PP.

GDUNNAA62655 DUNNIGAN AA
EQUAL-EMPLOYMENT-OPPORTUNITIES TODAY.
THE AMERICAN TEACHERS ASSOCIATION BULLETIN, VOL 35, MR.
1962. PP 21-22.

GDUNNDD63654 DUNN DD
EQUAL-OPPORTUNITIES BY LAW. A CASE-STUDY.
UNIVERSITY OF WISCONSIN. MASTERS THESIS. MADISON, WISCONSIN.
1963.

GDUNNGH64927 DUNNE GH
POVERTY IN PLENTY.
P J KENEDY AND SONS. NEW YORK. 1964. 142 PP.

GDVORBJ65650 DVORAK BJ   *US DEPARTMENT OF LABOR
CHANGING EMPHASIS IN OCCUPATIONAL TEST DEVELOPMENT.
US DEPARTMENT OF LABOR, EMPLOYMENT SERVICE REVIEW, VOL 2,
NO 8, AUG 1965. PP 45-47.

GDVORBJ65656 DVORAK BJ   DROEGE RC
SEILER J
NEW DIRECTIONS IN US EMPLOYMENT-SERVICE APTITUDE TEST
RESEARCH.
THE PERSONNEL AND GUIDANCE JOURNAL, VOL 44, OCT 1965. PP
136-141.

GDYSORB65657 DYSON RB   DYSON ED
COMMISSION ENFORCEMENT OF STATE LAWS AGAINST DISCRIMINATION.
A COMPARATIVE ANALYSIS OF THE KANSAS ACT.
KANSAS LAW REVIEW, VOL 14, NO 1, OCT 1965. PP 29-58.

GEDELHX63658 EDELSBERG H   BRODY DA
*ANTI-DEFAMATION LEAGUE
CIVIL-RIGHTS IN THE 88TH CONGRESS, FIRST SESSION, 1963.
ANTI-DEFAMATION LEAGUE OF B-NAI B-RITH. NEW YORK. DEC 1963.
14 PP.

GEDMUER44495 EDMUNDS ER
THE MYRDALIAN HYPOTHESES. RANK ORDER OF DISCRIMINATION.
PHYLON, VOL 15, NO 3, 3RD QUARTER 1944. PP 297-303.

GEDUCTS57959 EDUCATIONAL TESTING SERVICE
BACKGROUND FACTORS RELATING TO COLLEGE PLANS AND COLLEGE
ENROLLMENT AMONG PUBLIC HIGH SCHOOL STUDENTS.
/ASPIRATIONS/

EDUCATIONAL TESTING SERVICE. PRINCETON, NEW JERSEY. 1957.

GEHRLRA65791 EHRLE RA
EMPLOYMENT COUNSELING AS AN INTEGRAL PART OF AN ACTIVE
LABOR-MARKET POLICY.
VOCATIONAL GUIDANCE QUARTERLY, VOL 13, NO 4, 1965.
PP 270-275.

GELSOAX47661 ELSON A   SCHANFIELD L
LOCAL REGULATION OF DISCRIMINATORY EMPLOYMENT PRACTICES.
YALE LAW JOURNAL, VOL 56, NO 3, FEB 1947. PP 431-457.

GELWAEX58662 ELWARD E   *US LIBRARY OF CONGRESS
FAIR-EMPLOYMENT-PRACTICES ACT, STATE LAWS GRANTING EQUAL
RIGHTS, PRIVILEGES, ETC.
COUNCIL OF STATE GOVERNMENTS. CHICAGO, ILLINOIS. 1958.
88 PP.

GENNEWH67928 ENNEIS WH   *EEOC
I STATEMENT BEFORE THE HOUSE POST OFFICE AND CIVIL SERVICE
SUBCOMMITTEE ON POSTAL OPERATIONS, II DISCRIMINATION.
PLANNED AND ACCIDENTAL. /TESTING/
EQUAL EMPLOYMENT OPPORTUNITY COMMISSION, OFFICE OF RESEARCH
AND REPORTS, RESEARCH REPORT 1967-16, AP 1967. 29 PP.

GEVANRI62669 EVANS RI
PREJUDICE -- A THREAT TO THE LEADERSHIP ROLE.
PERSONNEL ADMINISTRATION, VOL 25, JAN-FEB 1962. PP 17-23.

GFACTMA56670 FACTORY MNGMT AND MAINTENANCE
HOW THE PRESIDENT IS WINNING THE WAR ON DISCRIMINATION.
FACTORY MANAGEMENT AND MAINTENANCE, JAN 1956. PP 104-105.

GFALTEK64031 FALTERMAYER EK
WHO ARE THE AMERICAN POOR.
FORTUNE, MAR 1964. PP 118-119, 218-229.

GFALTEK65032 FALTERMAYER EK
THE DRIFT TO EARLY RETIREMENT. /TECHNOLOGICAL-CHANGE/
FORTUNE, MAY 1965. PP 112-115 FF.

GFANTAX64671 FANTACI A   *US DEPARTMENT OF LABOR
EQUAL-EMPLOYMENT-OPPORTUNITY -- AN EMPLOYMENT-SERVICE
RESPONSIBILITY.
US DEPARTMENT OF LABOR, EMPLOYMENT SERVICE REVIEW, VOL 1,
NO 3, MAR 1964. PP 31-33.

GFEARRXND929 FEARN R
LABOR-FORCE PARTICIPATION OF YOUNG PERSONS AGED 14-24.
UNIVERSITY OF CHICAGO. PHD DISSERTATION. CHICAGO, ILLINOIS.
ND.

GFEDEBJ62672 FEDERAL BAR JOURNAL
THE FIRST NINE MONTHS. REPORT OF THE PRESIDENT-S COMMITTEE
ON EQUAL-EMPLOYMENT-OPPORTUNITY.
FEDERAL BAR JOURNAL, VOL 22, SUMMER 1962. PP 255-257.

GFEDERB62930 FEDERAL RESERVE BANK BOSTON
PART I. THE NEW-ENGLAND EXPERIENCE RETRAINING THE
UNEMPLOYED.
NEW ENGLAND BUSINESS REVIEW, AUG 1962. PP 1-4.

GFEDERX64673 FEDERAL REGISTER
NONDISCRIMINATION IN FEDERALLY-ASSISTED PROGRAMS OF THE
DEPARTMENT-OF-THE-TREASURY, DEPARTMENT-OF-DEFENSE,
ATOMIC-ENERGY-COMMISSION, CIVIL-AERONAUTICS-BOARD,
FEDERAL-AVIATION-AGENCY, VETERANS-ADMINISTRATION.
FEDERAL REGISTER, VOL 29, NO 254, DEC 31 1964.
PP 19275-19304.

GFEILJG62675 FEILD JG   *ANTI-DEFAMATION LEAGUE
EQUAL-EMPLOYMENT-OPPORTUNITY. /DISCRIMINATION/
THE ADMINISTRATION AND CIVIL RIGHTS. ANTI-DEFAMATION LEAGUE
OF B-NAI B-RITH, ADL BULLETIN, MAR 1962. PP 14-16.

GFEILJG64676 FEILD JG
FEPC -- HINDSIGHT AND FORESIGHT.
BUFFALO LAW REVIEW, VOL 14, NO 1, FALL 1964. PP 16-21.

GFEILJG65677 FEILD JG   MISTER M
CIVIL-RIGHTS, EMPLOYMENT OPPORTUNITY, AND ECONOMIC GROWTH.
UNIVERSITY OF DETROIT LAW JOURNAL, FALL 1965.

GFERGCC64679 FERGUSON CC
THE FEDERAL INTEREST IN EMPLOYMENT DISCRIMINATION. HEREIN
THE CONSTITUTIONAL SCOPE OF EXECUTIVE POWER TO WITHOLD
APPROPRIATE FUNDS.
BUFFALO LAW REVIEW, VOL 14, 1964. PP 1-15.

GFERGRH65012 FERGUSON RH
UNEMPLOYMENT. ITS SCOPE, MEASUREMENT, AND EFFECT ON POVERTY.
CORNELL UNIVERSITY, NEW YORK STATE SCHOOL OF INDUSTRIAL AND
LABOR RELATIONS. ITHACA, NEW YORK. 1965. 76 PP.

GFERMIX60680 FERMAN I
DISCRIMINATION IN EMPLOYMENT.
NEW YORK LAW FORUM, VOL 6, 1960. PP 59-68.

GFERNFL65662 FERNBACH FL
POLICIES AFFECTING INCOME-DISTRIBUTION. /EMPLOYMENT
INCOME-MAINTENANCE/
POVERTY IN AMERICA. ED BY M S GORDON. CHANDLER PUBLISHING
CO. SAN FRANCISCO, CALIFORNIA. 1965. PP 115-127.

GFINEMX64681 FINE M   CULBERSON GW
VOCATIONAL TRAINING TO IMPROVE JOB OPPORTUNITIES FOR
MINORITY-GROUPS. COMMENT.
BUFFALO LAW REVIEW, VOL 14, 1964. PP 170 FF.

GFINESA49962 FINEBERG SA
PUNISHMENT WITHOUT CRIME. WHAT YOU CAN DO ABOUT PREJUDICE.
/DISCRIMINATION/
DOUBLEDAY AND CO. NEW YORK. 1949. 337 PP.

GFISHLX66682 FISHMAN L ED
POVERTY AMID AFFLUENCE.
YALE UNIVERSITY PRESS. NEW HAVEN, CONNECTICUT. 1966.

GFISKUR51684 FISK UNIV RACE RELS INSTITUTE
REPORT OF INDUSTRY AND LABOR-MANAGEMENT CLINICS.
IMPLEMENTATION OF EMPLOYMENT IN MERIT PROGRAMS IN NON FEPC
STATES BY DIRECT APPROACH TO TOP MANAGEMENT.
FISK UNIVERSITY, RACE RELATIONS INSTITUTE. NASHVILLE,
TENNESSEE. 1951. 6 PP.

GFLACRX64964 FLACKS R
ORGANIZING THE UNEMPLOYED. THE CHICAGO PROJECT. /ILLINOIS/
CHICAGO, ILLINOIS. UNPUBLISHED. AP 7 1964. 10 PP.

GFLEIHX57686 FLEISCHMAN H   *AFL-CIO

SECURITY, CIVIL-LIBERTIES AND UNIONS.
AFL-CIO, PUBLICATION NO 31, WASHINGTON, DC. 1957. 52 PP.

GFLEIHX60685 FLEISCHMAN H
LABOR AND THE CIVIL-RIGHTS REVOLUTION. /UNION/
THE NEW LEADER, AP 18 1960. ALSO NEW YORK CITY, NATIONAL
LABOR SERVICE, INSTITUTE OF HUMAN RELATIONS. 5 PP. ALSO
AMERICAN JEWISH COMMITTEE, INSTITUTE OF HUMAN RELATIONS.
NEW YORK.

GFLEIHX65106 FLEISCHMAN H
PROGRESS IN CIVIL-RIGHTS TO 1964. /EEO/
LEGAL ASPECTS OF THE CIVIL RIGHTS MOVEMENT. ED BY D KING AND
C QUICK. WAYNE STATE UNIVERSITY PRESS. DETROIT, MICHIGAN.
1965. PP 269-301.

GFLEMHC63363 FLEMING HC
IMPROVING INDUSTRIAL RACE-RELATIONS -- PART I. EQUAL JOB
   OPPORTUNITY -- SLOGAN OR REALITY.
PERSONNEL ADMINISTRATION, VOL 26, MAR-AP 1963. PP 25-28.

GFLE4JG46688 FLEMING JG
THE HISTORICAL ROOTS OF FAIR-EMPLOYMENT.
PHYLON, VOL 7, NO 1, 1946. PP 21-31.

GFLE4JG50687 FLEMING JG
EDUCATIONAL ASPECTS OF FAIR-EMPLOYMENT-PRACTICES-COMMISION
   LAWS.
JOURNAL OF NEGRO EDUCATION, VOL 19, NO1, WINTER 1950.
PP 7-15.

GFLINCX65120 FLINCHER C
TESTING AND TITLE-VII.
ATLANTA ECONOMIC REVIEW, JUNE 1965. PP 15-19.

GFLO4BH59690 FLORIDA STATE BOARD HEALTH
MIGRANT PROJECT 1959. /MIGRANT-WORKERS/
JACKSONVILLE, FLORIDA. JULY, 1959. 55 PP.

GFLO4HN60689 FLORIDA HEALTH NOTES
THE MIGRANT PROJECT. /MIGRANT-WORKERS/
FLORIDA HEALTH NOTES, JAN 1960. 22 PP.

GFOLEAS52692 FOLEY AS
MINORITY IN THE ENTERPRISE.
SOCIAL ORDER, VOL 2, MAY 1952. PP 221-226.

GFOLSFM54693 FOLSOM FM
EQUAL-OPPORTUNITY IN EMPLOYMENT.
US SENATE COMMITTEE ON LABOR AND PUBLIC WELFARE,
SUBCOMMITTEE ON CIVIL RIGHTS, STATEMENT. GPO.
WASHINGTON, DC. FEB 23 1954.

GFOLSMB64109 FOLSOM MB
WHERE UNEMPLOYMENT HITS THE HARDEST.
SATURDAY REVIEW, JAN 11 1964. PP 21-26.

GFOOJECND694 FOOD EMPLOYERS COUNCIL INC
GUIDE TO MERIT EMPLOYMENT, A RESTATEMENT OF INDUSTRY
   PRINCIPLES AND PRACTICES.
FOOD EMPLOYERS COUNCIL, INC. LOS ANGELES, CALIFORNIA. ND.
7 PP.

GFORDJA63695 FORD JA
CALIFORNIA LOCAL GOVERNMENT AND INTEGRATION.
PERSONNEL MANAGEMENT, VOL 3, NO 4, JULY-AUG 1963.

GFORDJA65450 FORD JA   *CALIFORNIA FEPC
EMPLOYMENT PRACTICES, FAIR AND UNFAIR.
TRAINING AID. CULTURAL DIFFERENCES. TRAINING IN
NONDISCRIMINATION, READING ASSIGNMENTS. CALIFORNIA STATE
DEPARTMENT OF SOCIAL WELFARE. SAN FRANCISCO, CALIFORNIA.
SEPT 1965. PP 177-180.

GFORTXX40459 FORTUNE
THE DISPOSSESSED.
FORTUNE, VOL 20, FEB 1940. PP 94-95, 118-126.

GFORTXX50696 FORTUNE
FEPC. NEW-YORK VERSION.
FORTUNE, SEPT 1950. PP 50 FF.

GFORTXX54047 FORTUNE
PUSH-BUTTON LABOR. /TECHNOLOGICAL-CHANGE UNEMPLOYMENT/
FORTUNE, AUG 1954. PP 50-52.

GFORTXX59045 FORTUNE
MIGRANT-WORKERS PLIGHT.
FORTUNE, NOV 1959. PP 274-276.

GFOXXWM65697 FOX WM
UNEMPLOYMENT AND UNEMPLOYABLES.
BUSINESS HORIZONS. VOL 8, SUMMER 1965. PP 59-72.

GFRAEOK60697 FRAENKEL OK   *ACLU
LABOR-RELATIONS
THE SUPREME COURT AND CIVIL LIBERTIES. HOW THE COURT HAS
PROTECTED THE BILL OF RIGHTS. OCEANA PUBLICATIONS, INC. NEW
YORK. 1960. PP 121-136.

GFREEMK64005 FREEDMAN MK
BASIC ISSUES AFFECTING YOUTH EMPLOYMENT.
NATIONAL COMMITTEE ON EMPLOYMENT OF YOUTH. NEW YORK.
FEB 1964, 148 PP.

GFREEMX60699 FREEDMAN M
VOCATIONAL TRAINING
AMERICAN CHILD, VOL 47, NO 4, NOV 1960. PP 9-12.

GFRENWL66101 FRENCH WL
PSYCHOLOGICAL TESTING. SOME PROBLEMS AND SOLUTIONS.
   /INDUSTRY/
PERSONNEL ADMINISTRATION, VOL 2, NO 2, 1966. PP 19-24.

GFREUPA64700 FREUND PA
CIVIL-RIGHTS AND THE LIMITS OF LAW.
BUFFALO LAW REVIEW, VOL 14, 1964. PP 199 FF.

GFRIELL62701 FRIEDLAND LL
FAIR-EMPLOYMENT-PRACTICES IN THE PUBLIC SERVICE.
PUBLIC PERSONNEL REVIEW, VOL 23, AP 1962. PP 109-113.

GFRIERE62431 FRIEND RE   STANSBERRY RR
*US DEPARTMENT OF AGRICULTURE
THE HIRED FARM WORKING FORCE OF 1960. /ECONOMIC-STATUS/
US DEPARTMENT OF AGRICULTURE. GPO. WASHINGTON, DC.
JULY 1962. 55 PP.

GFUCHRS66702 FUCHS RS   ELLIS DB.
TITLE-VII. RELATIONSHIP AND EFFECT ON THE NATIONAL-LABOR-

RELATIONS-BOARD. /LEGISLATION/
BOSTON COLLEGE INDUSTRIAL AND COMMERCIAL LAW REVIEW, VOL 7,
NO 3, SPRING 1966. PP 575-600.

GFUERJS65703 FUERST JS
ARE JOB TESTS RELIABLE.
FOCUS MIDWEST, VOL 4, NO-S 1-2, JAN-FEB 1965. PP 14-15.

GFUGAGR64704 FUGAL GR
TRAINING AND DEVELOPMENT.
SYMPOSIUM. EQUAL EMPLOYMENT OPPORTUNITY. COMPANY POLICIES
AND EXPERIENCES. MANAGEMENT REVIEW, VOL 53, AP 1964.

GFULLVX67931 FULLER V
FARM MANPOWER POLICY.
FARM LABOR IN THE UNITED STATES. ED BY C E BISHOP. COLUMBIA
UNIVERSITY. NEW YORK. 1967. PP 97-114.

GFURFPH62705 FURFEY PH   HARTE TJ
WALSH ME
MARGINAL EMPLOYABILITY.
CATHOLIC UNIVERSITY OF AMERICA PRESS. WASHINGTON, DC. 1962.
92 PP.

GFURNJC52706 FURNAS JC
FEPC -- HOW IT WORKS IN SEVEN STATES.
LOOK, OCT 21 1952.

GGAINRL48341 GAINES RL
ECONOMIC-TRENDS IN EXTENSION WORK WITH NEGRO FARMERS IN
   ALABAMA, 1936-1948.
TUSKEGEE INSTITUTE. THESIS. TUSKEGEE, ALABAMA. 1948. 123 PP.

GGALLLE65932 GALLAWAY LE
THE FOUNDATIONS OF THE WAR-ON-POVERTY.
AMERICAN ECONOMIC REVIEW, MARCH 1965. PP 122FF.

GGANSHJ65696 GANS HJ
SOME PROPOSALS FOR GOVERNMENT POLICY IN AN AUTOMATING
   SOCIETY.
THE CORRESPONDENT, NO 30, JAN-FEB 1964. PP 74-82. ALSO IN
NEW PERSPECTIVES ON POVERTY, EDS ARTHUR B SHOSTAK AND
WILLIAM GOMBERG. PRENTICE-HALL, INC. ENGLEWOOD CLIFFS,
NEW JERSEY. 1965. PP 142-157.

GGARDBB55707 GARDNER BB   MOORE DG
HUMAN-RELATIONS IN INDUSTRY.
RICHARD D IRWIN. HOMEWOOD, ILLINOIS. 3RD EDITION. 1955.
427 PP.

GGENECC49713 GENERAL CABLE CORPORATION
INTERGROUP RELATIONS WITHIN BUSINESS AND INDUSTRY.
CONFERENCE OF BUSINESS, INDUSTRIAL, LABOR, AND SOCIAL
SCIENCE LEADERS AND EXPERTS, PROCEEDINGS. GENERAL CABLE
CORPORATION. NEW YORK. DEC 17 1948, JAN 24 1949. 19 PP.

GGEORLJ65714 GEORGETOWN LAW JOURNAL
UNION RACIAL DISCRIMINATION -- RECENT DEVELOPMENTS BEFORE
   THE NLRB AND THEIR IMPLICATIONS UNDER TITLE-VII OF THE
   CIVIL-RIGHTS-ACT OF 1964.
GEORGETOWN LAW JOURNAL, VOL 53, NO 4, SUMMER 1965.
PP 1103-1115.

GGHISEE66788 GHISELLI EE
THE VALIDITY OF OCCUPATIONAL APTITUDE TESTS.
JOHN WILEY AND SONS, INC. NEW YORK. 1966. 155 PP.

GGIBSHX54969 GIBSON H
RACIAL INTEGRATION IN EMPLOYMENT.
PUBLICATION NO 8, JUNE 1954. AVAILABLE AT US EQUAL
EMPLOYMENT OPPORTUNITY COMMISSION, OFFICE OF RESEARCH.
WASHINGTON, DC.

GGILMHJ63436 GILMAN HJ
THE WHITE-NON-WHITE UNEMPLOYMENT DIFFERENTIAL.
HUMAN RESOURCES IN THE URBAN ECONOMY. ED BY MARK PERLMAN.
JOHNS HOPKINS PRESS. BALTIMORE, MARYLAND. 1963. PP 75-113.

GGILMHJ63716 GILMAN HJ
DISCRIMINATION AND THE WHITE -- NONWHITE UNEMPLOYMENT
   DIFFERENTIALS.
UNIVERSITY OF CHICAGO. PHD DISSERTATION. CHICAGO, ILLINOIS.
1963.

GGILMHJ65717 GILMAN HJ
ECONOMIC DISCRIMINATION AND UNEMPLOYMENT.
AMERICAN ECONOMIC REVIEW, VOL 55, NO 5, PART I, DEC 1965.

GGILPEG66632 GILPATRICK EG
STRUCTURAL UNEMPLOYMENT AND AGGREGATE DEMAND.
JOHNS HOPKINS PRESS. BALTIMORE, MARYLAND. 1966. 235 PP.

GGINSGJ61718 GINSBURG GJ
NONDISCRIMINATION IN EMPLOYMENT. EXECUTIVE-ORDER 10925.
MILITARY LAW REVIEW, OCT 1961. PP 141-150.

GGINZEX64972 GINZBERG E
TECHNOLOGY AND SOCIAL CHANGE.
COLUMBIA UNIVERSITY PRESS. NEW YORK. 1964.

GGIRARA64721 GIRARD RA   JAFFE LL
SOME GENERAL OBSERVATIONS ON THE ADMINISTRATION OF STATE
   FAIR-EMPLOYMENT-PRACTICE LAWS.
BUFFALO LAW REVIEW, VOL 14, 1964. PP 114-120.

GGITLAL66134 GITLOW AL ED
CONFERENCE ON UNSKILLED WORKERS IN THE LABOR-FORCE. PROBLEMS
   AND PROSPECTS.
NEW YORK UNIVERSITY, SCHOOL OF BUSINESS AND THE PRESIDENT-S
COMMITTEE ON EMPLOYMENT OF THE HANDICAPPED. NEW YORK.
SEPT 29, 1966.

GGITTJB56973 GITTLER JB
UNDERSTANDING MINORITY-GROUPS.
JOHN WILEY AND SONS. NEW YORK. 1956.

GGIVERA65695 GIVENS RA
LEGAL DISADVANTAGES OF MIGRATORY WORKERS.
LABOR LAW JOURNAL, VOL 16, SEPT 1965. PP 584-596.

GGLAZWX62866 GLAZIER W
AUTOMATION AND JOBLESSNESS. IS RETRAINING THE ANSWER.
ATLANTIC MONTHLY, VOL 210, AUG 1962. PP 43-47.

GGLICCE47722 GLICK CE
THE POSITION OF RACIAL GROUPS IN OCCUPATIONAL STRUCTURES.
SOCIAL FORCES, VOL 26, NO 2, DEC 1947. PP 206-211.

GGOFFRM54366 GOFF RM
SOME EDUCATIONAL IMPLICATIONS OF THE INFLUENCE OF REJECTION

ON ASPIRATION LEVELS OF MINORITY-GROUP CHILDREN.
JOURNAL OF EXPERIMENTAL EDUCATION, VOL 23, 1954. PP 179-183.

GGOLDAX58974 GOLDBERG A
THE RIGHTS AND RESPONSIBILITY OF UNION MEMBERS.
/ANTIDISCRIMINATION/
AMERICAN FEDERATIONIST, VOL 65, NO 2, FEB 1958. PP 15-19.

GGOLDAX62865 GOLDBERG A
THE ROLE OF GOVERNMENT. /TECHNOLOGICAL-CHANGE/
ANNALS OF THE AMERICAN ACADEMY OF POLITICAL AND SOCIAL
SCIENCE, VOL 340, MAR 1962. PP 110-116.

GGOLDGS66360 GOLDBERG GS
JOB AND CAREER DEVELOPMENT FOR THE POOR...THE HUMAN
SERVICES. INCLUDES BIBLIOGRAPHY.
YESHIVA UNIVERSITY INFORMATION RETRIEVAL CENTER ON THE
DISADVANTAGED, IRCD BULLETIN. VOL 2, NO 4, SEPT 1966. 11 PP.

GGOLDHX58975 GOLDEN H   *JEWISH LABOR COMMISSION
LABOR LOOKS AT THE CRISES IN CIVIL-RIGHTS. /UNION/
JEWISH LABOR COMMISSION. NEW YORK. 1958.

GGOLDHX63787 GOLDSTEIN H   *US DEPARTMENT OF LABOR
PROJECTIONS OF THE LABOR-FORCE OF THE US.
US DEPARTMENT OF LABOR, BUREAU OF LABOR STATISTICS. GPO.
WASHINGTON, DC. 1963. 45 PP.

GGOLDHX66933 GOLDSTEIN H
PROJECTIONS OF MANPOWER REQUIREMENTS AND SUPPLY.
INDUSTRIAL RELATIONS, VOL 5, MAY 1966. PP 17-27.

GGOLDMH46724 GOLDBERG MH
PARNASSUS RESTRICTED. JOB DISCRIMINATION IN THE PROFESSIONS.
SCHOOL AND SOCIETY, VOL 64, JULY 6 1946. PP 4-5.

GGOLDSF62725 GOLDSMITH SF
LOW-INCOME FAMILIES AND MEASURES OF INCOME INEQUALITY.
REVIEW OF SOCIAL ECONOMY, VOL 20, MAR 1962. PP 1-25.

GGOODRC64622 GOODWIN RC
LABOUR-FORCE ADJUSTMENT OF WORKERS AFFECTED BY
TECHNOLOGICAL-CHANGE.
ORGANIZATION FOR ECONOMIC COOPERATION AND DEVELOPMENT,
NORTH AMERICAN JOINT CONFERENCE. THE REQUIREMENTS OF
AUTOMATED JOBS. WASHINGTON, DC. DEC 8-10 1964. PP 277-292.

GGOODRC65726 GOODWIN RC
TODAY-S REALITIES IN THE FARM LABOR-MARKET.
NATIONAL FARM LABOR CONFERENCE, SPEECH. WASHINGTON, DC. ALSO
US DEPARTMENT OF LABOR, NEWS, 1964-1965.

GGORDJEN0934 GORDON JE
THE CONGRESSIONAL HEARINGS AND ISSUES IN PSYCHOLOGICAL
TESTING. INVASIONS OF PRIVACY AND TEST BIAS.
THE UNIVERSITY OF MICHIGAN. ANN ARBOR, MICHIGAN. NO. 27PP.

GGORDJE65135 GORDON JE
THE FEDERAL ANTI-POVERTY PROGRAM AND SOME IMPLICATIONS OF
SUBPROFESSIONAL TRAINING.
AMERICAN PSYCHOLOGIST, VOL 20, NO 5, MAY 1965.

GGORDJE66281 GORDON JE
CIVIL-SERVICE TESTING AND JOB DISCRIMINATION.
UNIVERSITY OF MICHIGAN, SCHOOL OF SOCIAL WORK. ANN ARBOR,
MICHIGAN. MIMEOGRAPHED PAPER. JUNE 17 1966.

GGORDMM64729 GORDON MM
ASSIMILATION IN AMERICAN LIFE. THE ROLE OF RACE, RELIGION,
AND NATIONAL ORIGINS.
OXFORD UNIVERSITY PRESS. NEW YORK. 1964. 286 PP.

GGORDMS63727 GORDON MS
A CONFERENCE ON UNEMPLOYMENT.
INDUSTRIAL RELATIONS, VOL 2, NO 3, MAY 1963. PP 1-6.

GGORDMS63742 GORDON MS
US WELFARE POLICIES IN PERSPECTIVE.
INDUSTRIAL RELATIONS, VOL 2, FEB 1963. PP 33-61.

GGORDMS65661 GORDON MS
POVERTY AND INCOME-MAINTENANCE FOR THE UNEMPLOYED.
POVERTY IN AMERICA. ED BY M S GORDON. CHANDLER PUBLISHING
CO. SAN FRANCISCO, CALIFORNIA. 1965. PP 253-264.

GGORDMS65728 GORDON MS   *UCLA INSTITUTE OF IND RELS
US MANPOWER AND EMPLOYMENT POLICY. A REVIEW ESSAY.
UNIVERSITY OF CALIFORNIA, INSTITUTE OF INDUSTRIAL RELATIONS,
REPRINT NO 249. LOS ANGELES, CALIFORNIA. 1965.

GGORDRA64525 GORDON RA   *U OF CAL BERKELY INST OF IR
LONG-TERM MANPOWER PROJECTIONS.
UNIVERSITY OF CALIFORNIA, INSTITUTE OF INDUSTRIAL RELATIONS.
BERKELY, CALIFORNIA. 1964.

GGORDRA64526 GORDON RA   ROSS A
*U OF CAL BERKELEY INST OF IR
UNEMPLOYMENT AND AMERICAN ECONOMY.
UNIVERSITY OF CALIFORNIA, INSTITUTE OF INDUSTRIAL RELATIONS.
BERKELEY, CALIFORNIA. 1964.

GGORDRA64731 GORDON RA
HAS STRUCTURAL UNEMPLOYMENT WORSENED.
INDUSTRIAL RELATIONS, VOL 3, NO 3, MAY 1964. PP 53 FF.

GGORDRA65613 GORDON RA   *U OF CAL BERKELEY INST OF IR
LONG-TERM MANPOWER PROJECTIONS. PROCEEDINGS OF A CONFERENCE
CONDUCTED BY THE RESEARCH PROGRAM ON UNEMPLOYMENT AND THE
AMERICAN ECONOMY.
UNIVERSITY OF CALIFORNIA, INSTITUTE OF INDUSTRIAL RELATIONS.
BERKELEY, CALIFORNIA. 1965. 64 PP.

GGORDRA65675 GORDON RA   *US DEPARTMENT OF LABOR
TWENTY YEARS OF ECONOMIC AND INDUSTRIAL CHANGE.
/TECHNOLOGICAL-CHANGE EMPLOYMENT/
US DEPARTMENT OF LABOR, MANPOWER ADMINISTRATION, SEMINAR ON
MANPOWER POLICY AND PROGRAM. AP 1965. 46 PP.

GGOULJX63732 GOULD J
NOW, MASSACHUSETTS PLAN FOR EQUAL-EMPLOYMENT-OPPORTUNITY.
INDUSTRY, VOL 29, DEC 1963. PP 10-11, 34.

GGRANLB57979 GRANGER LB   *PRES-S COMT GOVT CONTRACTS
DEVELOPMENT OF TRAINING INCENTIVES FOR THE YOUTH OF
MINORITY-GROUPS. /ECONOMIC-STATUS/
PRESIDENT-S COMMITTEE ON GOVERNMENT CONTRACTS. WASHINGTON,
DC. 1957.

GGRANRH66733 GRAND RAPIDS HUMAN RELS COMM
A STUDY OF FAIR-EMPLOYMENT-PRACTICES OF THE CITY GOVERNMENT.

/GRAND-RAPIDS MICHIGAN/
GRAND RAPIDS HUMAN RELATIONS COMMISSION. GRAND RAPIDS,
MICHIGAN. AUG 1966. 17 PP.

GGRAVWB48734 GRAVES WB   *US LIBRARY OF CONGRESS
ANTI-DISCRIMINATION LEGISLATION IN THE AMERICAN STATES.
US LIBRARY OF CONGRESS, LEGISLATIVE REFERENCE SERVICE,
PUBLIC AFFAIRS BULLETIN NO 65. GPO. WASHINGTON, DC. 1948.
92 PP.

GGRAVWB51735 GRAVES WB   *US LIBRARY OF CONGRESS
FEPC LEGISLATION IN THE UNITED STATES, FEDERAL, STATE,
MUNICIPAL.
US LIBRARY OF CONGRESS, LEGISLATIVE REFERENCE SERVICE,
PUBLIC AFFAIRS BULLETIN NO 3. GPO. WASHINGTON, DC. 1951.
239 PP.

GGRAYCJ51736 GRAY CJ   BEATTY D
*US DEPARTMENT OF LABOR
EXPANDED UTILIZATION OF MINORITY-GROUP WORKERS.
US DEPARTMENT OF LABOR, EMPLOYMENT SECURITY REVIEW, VOL 18,
NO 4, AP 1951. PP 34-36.

GGREEAI64479 GREENLEIGH ASSOCIATES INC
PUBLIC WELFARE. POVERTY -- PREVENTION OR PERPETUATION. A
STUDY OF THE STATE DEPARTMENT OF PUBLIC ASSISTANCE OF THE
STATE OF WASHINGTON.
GREENLEIGH ASSOCIATES, INC. NEW YORK. 1964. 277 PP.

GGREEAI65472 GREENLEIGH ASSOCIATES INC
HOME INTERVIEW STUDY OF LOW-INCOME HOUSEHOLDS IN DETROIT,
MICHIGAN.
GREENLEIGH ASSOCIATES, INC. NEW YORK. 1965. 104 PP.

GGREEAI65473 GREENLEIGH ASSOCIATES INC
A PUBLIC EMPLOYMENT PROGRAM FOR THE UNEMPLOYED POOR.
GREENLEIGH ASSOCIATES, INC. NEW YORK. NOV 1965. 85 PP.

GGREEAI65474 GREENLEIGH ASSOCIATES INC
REPORT OF THE DIAGNOSTIC SURVEY OF TENANT HOUSEHOLDS IN THE
WEST SIDE URBAN-RENEWAL AREA OF NEW-YORK-CITY.
GREENLEIGH ASSOCIATES, INC. NEW YORK. 1965.

GGREEAI65480 GREENLEIGH ASSOCIATES INC
STUDY OF SERVICES TO DEAL WITH POVERTY IN DETROIT, MICHIGAN.
GREENLEIGH ASSOCIATES, INC. NEW YORK. 1965. 136 PP.

GGREEHX66627 GREENSPAN H   KILGALLON JJ
*US DEPARTMENT OF LABOR
OCCUPATIONAL EMPLOYMENT STATISTICS, SOURCES AND DATA.
US DEPARTMENT OF LABOR, REPORT NO 305. GPO. WASHINGTON, DC.
JUNE 1966. 87 PP.

GGREEJX53738 GREENBLUM J   PEARLIN LI
VERTICAL MOBILITY AND PREJUDICE.
CLASS, STATUS, AND POWER. ED BY REINHARD BENDIX AND
S.M. LIPSET. THE FREE PRESS. GLENCOE, ILLINOIS. 1953.
PP 480-491.

GGREEJX59981 GREENBERG J
RACE-RELATIONS AND AMERICAN LAW.
COLUMBIA UNIVERSITY PRESS. NEW YORK. 1959. 480 PP.

GGREELX64614 GREENBERG L   WEINBERG E
*US DEPARTMENT OF LABOR
AUTOMATION. NATIONWIDE STUDIES IN THE US.
US DEPARTMENT OF LABOR, BUREAU OF LABOR STATISTICS. GPO.
WASHINGTON, DC. 1964. 29 PP.

GGREELX64739 GREENBERG L   *OECD
TECHNOLOGICAL-CHANGE, PRODUCTIVITY, AND EMPLOYMENT IN THE
UNITED STATES.
ORGANIZATION FOR ECONOMIC COOPERATION AND DEVELOPMENT,
CONFERENCE ON MANPOWER IMPLICATIONS OF AUTOMATION, PAPER.
WASHINGTON, DC. DEC 8-10 1964.

GGREEMX64450 GREENHUT M   WHITMAN WT
ESSAYS IN SOUTHERN ECONOMIC DEVELOPMENT.
UNIVERSITY OF NORTH CAROLINA PRESS. CHAPEL HILL, NORTH
CAROLINA. 1964.

GGREEWX61741 GREENWALD W   WINTRAUB RE
MONEY BENEFITS OF EDUCATION BY SEX AND RACE IN NEW-YORK
STATE, 1950.
JOURNAL OF EDUCATIONAL SOCIOLOGY, VOL 34, MAR 1961.
PP 312-319.

GGREGGX61071 GREGORY G   *NYC CIVIL SERVICE COMM
AGGRESSIVE RECRUITMENT AND THE PUBLIC SERVICE.
PUBLIC PERSONNEL ASSOCIATION. 1961 ANNUAL CONFERENCE,
ADDRESS. NEW YORK CITY CIVIL SERVICE COMMISSION. NEW YORK.
1961. 3 PP.

GGREGGX62070 GREGORY G   *NYC CIVIL SERVICE COMM
FURNISHING EQUAL-OPPORTUNITY FOR MINORITIES IN
CIVIL-SERVICE.
PUBLIC PERSONNEL ADMINISTRATION, 1962 ANNUAL CONFERENCE,
ADDRESS. NEW YORK CITY CIVIL SERVICE COMMISSION. NEW YORK.
1962. 8 PP.

GGRIEGX64743 GRIER G   GRIER E
OBSTACLES TO DESEGREGATION IN AMERICA-S URBAN AREAS.
RACE. VOL 6, NO 1, JULY 1964. 15 PP.

GGROJPX64745 GROOM P   *US DEPARTMENT OF LABOR
STATISTICS ON APPRENTICESHIP AND THEIR LIMITATIONS.
US DEPARTMENT OF LABOR, MONTHLY LABOR REVIEW, VOL 87, 1964.
P 391.

GGROVHE61744 GROVES HE
STATES AS FAIR-EMPLOYERS.
HOWARD LAW JOURNAL, VOL 7, WINTER 1961. PP 1-16.

GGUEREW63746 GUERNSEY EW
NONWHITE OCCUPATIONAL STATUS, BY REGION, AS RELATED TO
PERCENT OF NONWHITE.
FLORIDA STATE UNIVERSITY. MASTER-S THESIS. TALLAHASSEE,
FLORIDA. 1963.

GGUIORM65693 GUION RM
PERSONNEL TESTING.
MCGRAW-HILL. NEW YORK. 1965. 585 PP.

GGUIORM66747 GUION RM
EMPLOYMENT TESTS AND DISCRIMINATORY HIRING.
INDUSTRIAL RELATIONS, VOL 5, FEB 1966. PP 20-37. ALSO
US DEPARTMENT OF LABOR, EMPLOYMENT SERVICE REVIEW, VOL 3,
NO 8. AUG 1966. PP 71-76.

GGURALX62748 GURALNICK L   *US DEPT OF HEALTH ED WELFARE

MORTALITY BY OCCUPATION AND INDUSTRY AMONG MEN 20 TO 64
YEARS OF AGE, UNITED STATES, 1950. /DEMOGRAPHY/
US DEPARTMENT OF HEALTH, EDUCATION AND WELFARE, NATIONAL
OFFICE OF US PUBLIC HEALTH, VITAL STATISTICS, SPECIAL
REPORT, VOL 52, NO 2, 1962.

GGURSOR64749 GURSSLIN OR   ROACH JL
SOME ISSUES IN KNOWING THE UNEMPLOYED.
SOCIAL PROBLEMS, VOL 12, NO 1, 1964. PP 86-98.

GHABSSX65112 HABBE S   *NATL INDUSTRIAL CONF BOARD
TRENDS IN EMPLOYEE TESTING.
NATIONAL INDUSTRIAL CONFERENCE BOARD, CONFERENCE BOARD
RECORD, VOL 2, DEC 1965. PP 46-47.

GHABEWX54750 HABER W   *INDUSTRIAL RELS RESEARCH ASS
MANPOWER IN THE UNITED STATES. PROBLEMS AND POLICIES.
INDUSTRIAL RELATIONS RESEARCH ASSOCIATION, PUBLICATION 11.
NEW YORK. 1954. 225 PP.

GHABEWX63615 HABER W   FERMAN LA
HUDSON JR   *UPJOHN INST EMPLOY RESEARCH
THE IMPACT OF TECHNOLOGICAL-CHANGE.
THE W E UPJOHN INSTITUTE FOR EMPLOYMENT RESEARCH. KALAMAZOO,
MICHIGAN. 1963. 62 PP.

GHABEWX64649 HABER W   KRUGER DH
THE ROLE OF THE UNITED STATES EMPLOYMENT-SERVICE IN A
CHANGING ECONOMY.
THE W E UPJOHN INSTITUTE FOR EMPLOYMENT RESEARCH. KALAMAZOO,
MICHIGAN. 1964. 122 PP.

GHAGAJJ63751 HAGAN JJ   JAMES JH
GUIDELINES FOR INITIATING FAIR-EMPLOYMENT-PRACTICES.
PERSONNEL JOURNAL, VOL 40, MAY-JUNE 1963. PP 53-59.

GHAGEDJ57752 HAGER DJ
RACE, NATIONALITY, AND RELIGION -- THEIR RELATIONSHIP TO
APPOINTMENT POLICIES AND CASEWORK.
NATIONAL PROBATION AND PAROLE ASSOCIATION JOURNAL, VOL 3,
NO 2, AP 1957.

GHALERX51754 HALE R
SOME BASIC CONSTITUTIONAL RIGHTS OF ECONOMIC SIGNIFICANCE.
COLUMBIA LAW REVIEW, VOL 51, NO 3, MAR 1951. PP 271-326.

GHAMEHR63755 HAMEL HR   *US DEPARTMENT OF LABOR
JOB TENURE OF AMERICAN WORKERS.
US DEPARTMENT OF LABOR, MONTHLY LABOR REVIEW, VOL 86, NO 10,
REPORT NO 36, OCT 1963. 8 PP.

GHAMEHR65756 HAMEL HR   *US DEPARTMENT OF LABOR
LABOR-FORCE STATUS OF YOUTH, 1964.
US DEPARTMENT OF LABOR, MONTHLY LABOR REVIEW, SPECIAL LABOR
FORCE REPORT NO 56, AUG 1965. PP 932-937.

GHAMICH65757 HAMILTON CH
CONTINUITY AND CHANGE IN SOUTHERN MIGRATION. /DEMOGRAPHY/
THE SOUTH IN CONTINUITY AND CHANGE. ED BY JOHN C MCKINNEY
AND EDGAR T THOMPSON. DUKE UNIVERSITY PRESS. DURHAM, NORTH
CAROLINA. 1965. PP 53-78.

GHAMMHR66145 HAMMEL HR   *US DEPARTMENT OF LABOR
EDUCATIONAL-ATTAINMENT OF THE WORK FORCE.
US DEPARTMENT OF LABOR, OCCUPATIONAL OUTLOOK QUARTERLY, VOL
10, NO 3, SEPT 1966. PP 24-25.

GHANDOX57758 HANDLIN O
RACE AND NATIONALITY IN AMERICAN LIFE.
LITTLE BROWN AND COMPANY. BOSTON, MASSACHUSETTS. 1957.

GHANEGE64004 HANEY GE   *US DEPT OF HEALTH ED WELFARE
SELECTED STATE PROGRAMS IN MIGRANT EDUCATION.
US DEPARTMENT OF HEALTH, EDUCATION, AND WELFARE, OFFICE OF
EDUCATION. GPO. WASHINGTON, DC. 1964. 74 PP.

GHANNJA61988 HANNAH JA
CIVIL-RIGHTS -- A NATIONAL CHALLENGE.
SOUTH DAKOTA LAW REVIEW, VOL 6, SPRING 1961. PP 1-30.

GHARBFH64741 HARBISON FH   MYERS CA
EDUCATION, MANPOWER AND ECONOMIC-GROWTH.
MCGRAW-HILL BOOK CO. NEW YORK. 1964. 223 PP.

GHARBFH65660 HARBISON FH
LABOR-MARKET STRATEGIES IN THE WAR-ON-POVERTY.
/UNEMPLOYMENT/
POVERTY IN AMERICA. ED BY M S GORDON. CHANDLER PUBLISHING
CO. SAN FRANCISCO, CALIFORNIA. 1965.

GHARBFH66476 HARBISON FH ED   MOONEY JD ED
CRITICAL ISSUES IN EMPLOYMENT POLICY, A REPORT.
/UNEMPLOYMENT/
PRINCETON UNIVERSITY, 2ND MANPOWER SYMPOSIUM, 1966.
PRINCETON UNIVERSITY PRESS. PRINCETON, NEW JERSEY. 1966.
162 PP.

GHARRMX63099 HARRINGTON M
THE OTHER AMERICA. /POVERTY/
MACMILLAN. NEW YORK. 1963. 186 PP.

GHARRMX64759 HARRINGTON M
THE NEW LOST GENERATION. JOBLESS YOUTH.
THE NEW YORK TIMES MAGAZINE. MAY 24 1964.

GHARRMX64935 HARRINGTON M
POVERTY AND POLITICS.
POVERTY IN PLENTY. ED BY G H DUNNE. P J KENEDY AND SONS.
1964. PP 48-60.

GHARRMX65597 HARRINGTON M
THE ACCIDENTAL CENTURY. /TECHNOLOGICAL-CHANGE/
THE MACMILLAN CO. NEW YORK. 1965. 322 PP.

GHARRMX65659 HARRINGTON M
A SOCIAL REFORMER-S VIEW OF POVERTY.
POVERTY IN AMERICA. ED BY M S GORDON. CHANDLER PUBLISHING
CO. SAN FRANCISCO, CALIFORNIA. 1965. PP 27-37.

GHARRMX66136 HARRINGTON M
THE WORLD OF POVERTY.
THE AMERICAN FEDERATIONIST, VOL 73, AP 1966. PP 2-5.

GHARRMX66212 HARRINGTON M
THE INVISIBLE LAND. /POVERTY/
KNOWING THE DISADVANTAGED. ED BY STATEN W WEBSTER. CHANDLER
PUBLISHING CO. SAN FRANCISCO, CALIFORNIA. 1966. PP 6-19.

GHARRWRN0760 HARRISON WR
STUDY OF OCCUPATIONAL CHARACTERISTICS OF NON-WHITES IN THE

EAST BATON-ROUGE AREA. /LOUISIANA/
SOUTHERN UNIVERSITY THOUGHT, VOL 40, NO 3. RESEARCH ISSUE.

GHARTPX58763 HARTMAN P   *ANTI-DEFAMATION LEAGUE
FAIR-EMPLOYMENT-PRACTICES AND THE LAW.
BARRIERS. PATTERNS OF DISCRIMINATION AGAINST JEWS. ED BY
N C BELTH. ANTI-DEFAMATION LEAGUE OF B-NAI B-RITH. NEW YORK.
1958. PP 58-60.

GHARTPX62762 HARTMAN P   *ANTI-DEFAMATION LEAGUE
COMPARATIVE ANALYSIS OF STATE FAIR-EMPLOYMENT-PRACTICES
LAWS.
ANTI-DEFAMATION LEAGUE OF B-NAI B-RITH. NEW YORK. 1962.

GHATHDE67936 HATHAWAY DE
OCCUPATIONAL MOBILITY FROM THE FARM LABOR-FORCE.
FARM LABOR IN THE UNITED STATES. ED BY C E BISHOP. COLUMBIA
UNIVERSITY PRESS. NEW YORK. 1967. PP 71-96.

GHAUSPM54764 HAUSER PM
CHANGES IN THE LABOR-FORCE PARTICIPATION OF THE OLDER
WORKER.
AMERICAN JOURNAL OF SOCIOLOGY, VOL 59, NO 4, JAN 1954.
PP 312-323.

GHAWADL64766 HAWAII DEPT LABOR IND RELS
FAIR-EMPLOYMENT-PRACTICES ACT AND REGULATION 30. /HAWAII/
HAWAII DEPARTMENT OF LABOR AND INDUSTRIAL RELATIONS,
ENFORCEMENT DIVISION. HONOLULU, HAWAII. JUNE 1964. 12 PP.

GHAWADL64767 HAWAII DEPT LABOR IND RELS
QUESTIONING APPLICANTS FOR EMPLOYMENT, A GUIDE FOR
APPLICATION FORMS AND INTERVIEWS UNDER THE HAWAII
FAIR-EMPLOYMENT-PRACTICES ACT.
HAWAII DEPARTMENT OF LABOR AND INDUSTRIAL RELATIONS,
ENFORCEMENT DIVISION. HONOLULU, HAWAII. DEC 1964. 7 PP.

GHAZLHX66523 HAZLITT H
INCOME WITHOUT WORK. /GUARANTEED-INCOME/
THE FREEMAN, VOL 54, NO 9, SEPT 1966. PP 20-36.

GHEALDV65646 HEALAS DV
ADULT AND YOUTH EMPLOYMENT PROJECT, AUGUST-SEPTEMBER 1965.
MAYOR-S YOUTH EMPLOYMENT PROJECT. DETROIT, MICHIGAN. 1965.
53 PP.

GHEALDV65647 HEALAS DV
ADULT AND YOUTH EMPLOYMENT PROJECT, APRIL-MAY 1965.
MAYOR-S YOUTH EMPLOYMENT PROJECT. DETROIT, MICHIGAN. 1965.
26 PP.

GHECKAX64937 HECKSCHER A
REFLECTIONS ON THE MANPOWER REVOLUTION.
AMERICAN SCHOLAR, VOL 33, AUTUMN 1964. PP 568-578.

GHEERDM63769 HEER DM
THE ATTRACTIVENESS OF THE SOUTH TO WHITES AND NONWHITES. AN
ECOLOGICAL STUDY.
AMERICAN SOCIOLOGICAL REVIEW, VOL 28, NO 1, FEB 1963.
PP 101-107.

GHELPCW63501 HELPER CW   *US DEPARTMENT OF LABOR
TRAINING DISADVANTAGED GROUPS UNDER THE
MANPOWER-DEVELOPMENT-TRAINING-ACT.
US DEPARTMENT OF LABOR, OFFICE OF MANPOWER, AUTOMATION, AND
TRAINING, MANPOWER EVALUATION REPORT NO 1. GPO. WASHINGTON,
DC. NOV 1963. 24 PP.

GHENDJM64142 HENDERSON JM
SOME GENERAL ASPECTS OF RECENT REGIONAL DEVELOPMENT.
/SOUTH/
ESSAYS IN SOUTHERN ECONOMIC DEVELOPMENT. ED BY M.L. GREENHUT
AND W. T. WHITMAN. UNIVERSITY OF NORTH CAROLINA PRESS.
CHAPEL HILL, NORTH CAROLINA. 1964. CHAPTER 5.

GHENDWE59422 HENDRIX WE   *US DEPARTMENT OF AGRICULTURE
APPROACHES TO INCOME IMPROVEMENT. EXPERIENCES OF FAMILIES
RECEIVING PRODUCTION LOANS UNDER THE FARMERS HOME
ADMINISTRATION.
US DEPARTMENT OF AGRICULTURE. GPO. WASHINGTON, DC. AUG 1959.
44 PP.

GHENNJF63278 HENNING JF
SCHOOLING, DISCRIMINATION, AND JOBS.
INTEGRATED EDUCATION, VOL 1, NO 6, DEC 1963-JAN 1964.
PP 43-45. ALSO US SENATE, COMMITTEE ON LABOR AND PUBLIC
WELFARE, SUBCOMMITTEE ON EMPLOYMENT AND MANPOWER. NATION-S
MANPOWER REVOLUTION, HEARINGS, PART II. GPO. WASHINGTON, DC.
1963. PP 403-404.

GHENNJF63770 HENNING JF
EXPANDING APPRENTICESHIP FOR ALL AMERICANS.
THE AMERICAN FEDERATIONIST, VOL 70, JULY 1963. PP 1-5.

GHERLAK64771 HERLING AK
RIGHT-TO-WORK-LAWS AND CIVIL-RIGHTS. /UNION/
WALKING TOGETHER. RELIGION AND LABOR COUNCIL OF AMERICA.
AP 16 1964. 2 PP.

GHERMHX64538 HERMAN H
INTRODUCTION TO ECONOMICS OF GROWTH, UNEMPLOYMENT, AND
INFLATION.
APPLETON-CENTURY-CROFT. NEW YORK. 1964.

GHERRNM64772 HERRING NM
THE FAIR REPRESENTATION DOCTRINE. AN EFFECTIVE WEAPON
AGAINST UNION RACIAL DISCRIMINATION.
MARYLAND LAW REVIEW, VOL 24, JAN 3 1964. P 144.

GHESLMR63773 HESLET MR   *US LIBRARY OF CONGRESS
MINORITY-GROUPS. EMPLOYMENT PROBLEMS, REFERENCES.
US LIBRARY OF CONGRESS, LEGISLATIVE REFERENCE SERVICE. GPO.
WASHINGTON, DC. OCT 16 1963. 7 PP.

GHICKRX66774 HICKEY R
GOVERNMENT REGULATION OF UNION POLICIES.
BOSTON COLLEGE INDUSTRIAL AND COMMERCIAL LAW REVIEW, VOL 7,
1966. PP 191-237.

GHIGBJX55995 HIGBE J
NEW-YORK STATE-COMMISSION-AGAINST-DISCRIMINATION.
SYRACUSE UNIVERSITY. PHD DISSERTATION. SYRACUSE, NEW YORK.
1955.

GHIGBJX67143 HIGBEE J
DEVELOPMENT AND ADMINISTRATION OF THE NEW-YORK STATE LAW
AGAINST DISCRIMINATION.
UNIVERSITY OF ALABAMA PRESS. UNIVERSITY, ALABAMA. 1967.

GHIGHRB65056 HIGHSAW RB ED

THE DEEP SOUTH IN TRANSFORMATION.
UNIVERSITY OF ALABAMA PRESS. MONTGOMERY, ALABAMA. 1965.

GHILL HX66691   HILL H
DEMOGRAPHIC CHANGE AND RACIAL GHETTOS. THE CRISIS OF
    AMERICAN CITIES.
JOURNAL OF URBAN LAW, VOL 44, WINTER 1966. PP 231-285.

GHIRSFI64776   HIRSCH FI
BAY AREA CONFERENCE ON FULL-EMPLOYMENT. /SAN-FRANCISCO
    CALIFORNIA/
LABOR TODAY, VOL 3, NO 3, JUNE-JULY 1964. PP 19-22 PLUS.

GHOLL JH58778   HOLLAND JH
REALIZING THE MANPOWER POTENTIALITIES OF MINORITY-GROUP
    YOUTH.
NATIONAL URBAN LEAGUE, ANNUAL CONFERENCE, ADDRESS. OMAHA,
NEBRASKA. 1958.

GHOLL JR61999   HOLLEMAN JR
THE JOB AHEAD FOR THE PRESIDENT-S COMMITTEE ON
    EQUAL-EMPLOYMENT-OPPORTUNITY.
INDUSTRIAL RELATIONS RESEARCH ASSOCIATION, PROCEEDINGS.
SPRING 1961. PP 618-621.

GHOLL SS65124   HOLLAND SS   *US DEPARTMENT OF LABOR
LONG-TERM UNEMPLOYMENT IN THE 1960-S.
US DEPARTMENT OF LABOR, MONTHLY LABOR REVIEW, SPECIAL LABOR
FORCE REPORT NO 58, VOL 88, SEPT 1965.

GHOPE JX46485   HOPE J
WARTIME EMPLOYMENT PATTERNS OF NONWHITES AND FEMALE WORKERS
    IN SOUTHERN INDUSTRY.
THE QUARTERLY REVIEW OF HIGHER EDUCATION AMONG NEGROES,
VOL 14, NO 3, JULY 1946. PP 146-153.

GHOPE JX49781   HOPE J
CURRENT INTERNATIONAL UNION POLICIES AFFECTING MINORITIES
    AND THEIR IMPLEMENTATION.
FISK UNIVERSITY. NASHVILLE, TENNESSEE. UNPUBLISHED
MANUSCRIPT. 1949.

GHOPE JX51782   HOPE J
CURRENT MINORITY POLICIES AND THEIR IMPLEMENTATION IN
    INTERNATIONAL UNIONS.
AMERICAN JOURNAL OF ECONOMICS AND SOCIOLOGY, VOL 10,
JULY 1951.

GHOPE JX51783   HOPE J
MINORITY UTILIZATION PRACTICES -- RATIONAL OR SENTIMENTAL.
SOCIAL RESEARCH, VOL 18, JULY 1951. PP 152-170.

GHOPE JX61002   HOPE J   TONER J
VIA E
EMPLOYMENT PROBLEMS OF RACIAL MINORITIES.
INDUSTRIAL RELATIONS RESEARCH ASSOCIATION, ANNALS. 1961.
PP 139-150.

GHOPE JX61780   HOPE J
CENTRAL ROLE OF INTERGROUP AGENCIES IN THE LABOR-MARKET.
    CHANGING RESEARCH AND PERSONNEL REQUIREMENTS.
JOURNAL OF INTERGROUP RELATIONS, VOL 2, NO 2, SPRING 1961.
PP 132-144.

GHOWD EX65785   HOWDEN E
JOB OPPORTUNITIES FROM FEPC ACTION.
HUMAN RELATIONS NEWS AND REPORT, VOL 1, NO 5, 1965. 2 PP.

GHUDD FP46786   HUDDLE FP
FAIR PRACTICE IN EMPLOYMENT.
EDITORIAL RESEARCH REPORTS, VOL 1, NO 3, JAN 18 1946. 51 PP.

GHUGH EC59787   HUGHES EC
QUERIES CONCERNING INDUSTRY AND SOCIETY GROWING OUT OF
    STUDY OF ETHNIC RELATIONS IN INDUSTRY.
AMERICAN SOCIOLOGICAL REVIEW, VOL 14, NO 2, AP 1959.
PP 211-220.

GHUMP HH64739   HUMPHREY HH
WAR-ON-POVERTY. /EMPLOYMENT TRAINING/
MCGRAW-HILL BOOK CO. NEW YORK. 1964. 206 PP.

GHUMP HH65788   HUMPHREY HH
REMARKS AT THE PLANS-FOR-PROGRESS CONFERENCE.
PRESIDENT-S COMMITTEE ON EQUAL EMPLOYMENT OPPORTUNITY,
REMARKS. JAN 26 1965. 17 PP.

GHUNT DE66939   HUNT DE
ADOLESCENCE. CULTURAL DEPRIVATION, POVERTY, AND THE DROPOUT.
REVIEW OF EDUCATIONAL RESEARCH, VOL 36, OCT 1966.
PP 463-473.

GHUNT HX63789   HUNTON H
IMPLEMENTING AFFIRMATIVE ACTION WITH AIR-FORCE CONTRACTORS.
INTERRACIAL REVIEW, VOL 36, FEB 1963. PP 36-38.

GHUYC EE65790   HUYCH EE   *US DEPT OF HEALTH ED WELFARE
HIGHLIGHTS OF WHITE-NONWHITE DIFFERENTIALS.
US DEPARTMENT OF HEALTH, EDUCATION AND WELFARE. HEALTH,
EDUCATION AND WELFARE INDICATORS, FEB-OCT 1965. PP 3-5.

GILLI CH55792   ILLINOIS COMM ON HUMAN RELS
A REPORT ON EMPLOYMENT OF NONWHITES IN CHICAGO. /ILLINOIS/
ILLINOIS COMMISSION ON HUMAN RELATIONS. CHICAGO, ILLINOIS.
NOV 4 1955. 8 PP.

GILLI CH56794   ILLINOIS COMM ON HUMAN RELS
A STUDY OF MERIT EMPLOYMENT IN 100 ILLINOIS FIRMS.
ILLINOIS COMMISSION ON HUMAN RELATIONS. CHICAGO, ILLINOIS.
MAY 1956.

GILLI CH57793   ILLINOIS COMM ON HUMAN RELS
THE STATUS OF THE NONWHITE LABOR-FORCE IN ILLINOIS AND THE
    NATION.
ILLINOIS COMMISSION ON HUMAN RELATIONS. CHICAGO, ILLINOIS.
AUG 1957. 9 PP.

GILLI CH61791   ILLINOIS COMM ON HUMAN RELS
NONWHITE POPULATION IN ILLINOIS, 1950-1960.
CHICAGO COMMISSION ON HUMAN RIGHTS. CHICAGO, ILLINOIS.
NOV 1961. 7 PLUS PP.

GILLI DI62004   ILLINOIS DEPARTMENT OF LABOR   ILL GOVR-S COMT ON UNEMPLOY
ILLINOIS JOB SEEKERS SURVEY. EDUCATION, SKILLS, LENGTH OF
    UNEMPLOYMENT, AND PERSONAL CHARACTERISTICS.
ILLINOIS DEPARTMENT OF LABOR, RESEARCH AND STATISTICS
SECTION. SPRINGFIELD, ILLINOIS. 1962.

GILLI FEND795   ILLINOIS FEPC
FAIR-EMPLOYMENT-PRACTICE ACT OF ILLINOIS.

ILLINOIS FAIR EMPLOYMENT PRACTICE COMMISSION. CHICAGO,
ILLINOIS. NO. 13 PP.

GILLI GC62799   ILLINOIS GOVRS COMT UNEMPLOY
ILLINOIS JOB SEEKER-S SURVEY.
ILLINOIS GOVERNOR-S COMMITTEE ON UNEMPLOYMENT. CHICAGO,
ILLINOIS. 1962. TWO VOLS.

GILLI GC63798   ILLINOIS GOVRS COMT UNEMPLOY
ECONOMIC GROWTH, EQUAL-OPPORTUNITY, RESEARCH, JOINT EFFORT.
    EMPLOYMENT.
ILLINOIS INFORMATION SERVICE. SPRINGFIELD, ILLINOIS. 1963.
217 PP.

GILLI IR48801   ILLINOIS INTERRACIAL COMM
SPECIAL REPORT ON EMPLOYMENT OPPORTUNITIES IN ILLINOIS.
ILLINOIS INTERRACIAL COMMISSION. SPRINGFIELD, ILLINOIS.
1948. 114 PP.

GILLI LC57802   ILLINOIS LEGISLATIVE COUNCIL
STATE FAIR-EMPLOYMENT-PRACTICE LAWS. REPORT PERSUANT TO
    PROPOSAL 400.
ILLINOIS LEGISLATIVE COUNCIL, RESEARCH DEPARTMENT, BULLETIN
NO 3-123. SPRINGFIELD, ILLINOIS. DEC 1957. 27 PP.

GILLI SC56803   ILL STATE CHAMBER OF COMMERCE
HERE-S HOW MERIT EMPLOYMENT PROGRAMS WORK. A REPORT ON
    PROGRESS AND PROBLEMS IN THE EMPLOYMENT OF MINORITY-GROUP
    MEMBERS.
ILLINOIS STATE CHAMBER OF COMMERCE. CHICAGO, ILLINOIS.
1956. 19 PP.

GINDI CRND804   INDIANA CIVIL RIGHTS COMM
CIVIL-RIGHTS IN INDIANA.
INDIANA CIVIL RIGHTS COMMISSION. INDIANAPOLIS, INDIANIA. ND.
15 PP.

GINDI CR61806   INDIANA CIVIL RIGHTS COMM
REPORT OF THE SURVEY OF EMPLOYEES OF THE STATE OF INDIANA,
    SEPTEMBER 1961.
INDIANA CIVIL RIGHTS COMMISSION. INDIANAPOLIS, INDIANA.
1961. 3 PP.

GINDJ BX51811   INDUSTRIAL BULLETIN
DEMOCRACY ON THE JOB.
INDUSTRIAL BULLETIN, OCT 1951. PP 24-27, 31.

GINDJ BX57812   INDUSTRIAL BULLETIN
NEW-YORK STATE-S PROGRAM AGAINST DISCRIMINATION IN
    EMPLOYMENT. THE WORK OF THE NEW-YORK
NEW-YORK STATE-COMMISSION-AGAINST-DISCRIMINATION.
INDUSTRIAL BULLETIN, VOL 36, MAR 1957. PP 12-16.

GINDJ RR59814   INDUSTRIAL RELS RESEARCH ASSN
THE EVIDENCE OF PERSISTENT UNEMPLOYMENT.
INDUSTRIAL RELATIONS RESEARCH ASSOCIATION PROCEEDINGS,
VOL 12, DEC 1959. PP 22-53.

GINDJ RR61813   INDUSTRIAL RELS RESEARCH ASSN
PART IV. EMPLOYMENT PROBLEMS OF RACIAL MINORITIES.
INDUSTRIAL RELATIONS RESEARCH ASSOCIATION PROCEEDINGS,
VOL 14, DEC 1961.

GINTE CM63816   INTERNATL CITY MANAGERS ASSN
THE CITY GOVERNMENT AND MINORITY-GROUPS.
INTERNATIONAL CITY MANAGERS ASSOCIATION, MANAGEMENT
INFORMATION SERVICE, REPORT NO 229. CHICAGO, ILLINOIS.
FEB 1963. 27 PP.

GINTE LC58817   INTERNATIONAL LABOUR CONF
DISCRIMINATION IN THE FIELD OF EMPLOYMENT AND OCCUPATION.
INTERNATIONAL LABOUR CONFERENCE, 42ND SESSION, REPORT IV.
GENEVA, SWITZERLAND. 1958.

GIVES LM52819   IVES LM
LEGISLATION AGAINST RACIAL OR RELIGIOUS DISCRIMINATION IN
    EMPLOYMENT, NEW-YORK.
INDUSTRIAL BULLETIN, OCT 1952. PP 3-5.

GJACJ PX66527   JACOBS P   *U OF CAL BERKELEY INST OF IR
UNEMPLOYMENT AS A WAY OF LIFE.
UNIVERSITY OF CALIFORNIA, INSTITUTE OF INDUSTRIAL RELATIONS,
REPRINT NO 276. BERKELEY, CALIFORNIA. 1966. 18 PP.

GJAFF AJ66820   JAFFE AJ   GORDON JB
A NOTE ON OCCUPATIONAL MOBILITY FOR WHITE AND NONWHITE
    MALES, 1950 TO 1965.
THE NEW YORK STATISTICIAN, VOL 18, NO 4, DEC 1966. PP 1-4.

GJEFF AX63822   JEFFREY A
NLRB -- FEPC.
VANDERBILT LAW REVIEW, VOL 16, 1963. PP 547-593.

GJELT MM66823   JELTZ MM   *US DEPARTMENT OF LABOR
OKLAHOMA GEARS FOR THE CIVIL-RIGHTS-ACT.
US DEPARTMENT OF LABOR, EMPLOYMENT SERVICE REVIEW, VOL 3,
NO 8, AUG 1966. PP 9-10.

GJENS JJ66785   JENSEN JJ
DEVELOPING FAIR-EMPLOYMENT PROGRAMS. A PROGRAM FOR THE
    SMALLER COMPANY.
PERSONNEL JOURNAL, VOL 43, NO 4, JULY-AUG 1966. PP 57-62.

GJEWI EV65568   JEWISH EMPLOY VOCAT SERVICE
FINAL REPORT. THE YOUTH TRAINING PROJECT,
    SEPTEMBER 1, 1963--JANUARY 31, 1965. /ST-LOUIS MISSOURI
    TESTING/
JEWISH EMPLOYMENT AND VOCATIONAL SERVICE. ST LOUIS,
MISSOURI. 1965. 76 PP.

GJEWI LCND824   JEWISH LABOR COMMITTEE
THE AFL FIGHTS BIGOTRY. /UNION/
JEWISH LABOR COMMITTEE. NEW YORK. ND. 40 PP.

GJOHN DF63828   JOHNSTON DF   *US DEPARTMENT OF LABOR
EDUCATIONAL-ATTAINMENT OF WORKERS, MARCH, 1962.
US DEPARTMENT OF LABOR, MONTHLY LABOR REVIEW, VOL 86, NO 7,
REPORT NO 33, JULY 1963. 8 PP.

GJOHN DF65784   JOHNSTON DF   *US DEPARTMENT OF LABOR
EDUCATIONAL ATTAINMENT OF WORKERS, MARCH 1964.
US DEPARTMENT OF LABOR, MONTHLY LABOR REVIEW, VOL 88, NO 5,
MAY 1965. 29 PP.

GJOHN GW50825   JOHNSON GW
THE FOES OF THE FEPC.
THE REPORTER, AUG 15 1950. PP 32-34.

GJOHN HG65826   JOHNSON HG
UNEMPLOYMENT AND POVERTY.

WEST VIRGINIA UNIVERSITY CONFERENCE, POVERTY AMIDST
AFFLUENCE. PAPER. MORGANTOWN, WEST VIRGINIA. MAY 1965.
PROCEEDINGS PUBLISHED BY YALE UNIVERSITY PRESS. NEW HAVEN,
CONNECTICUT. 1966.

GJOHNMW65827   JOHNSON MW
ISSUES AND ANSWERS. /EEO/
EQUAL EMPLOYMENT OPPORTUNITY CONFERENCE. SPEECH. MARCH 31
1965. OAKLAND, CALIFORNIA. ALAMEDA COUNTY HUMAN RELATIONS
COMMISSION. MIMEOGRAPHED. MARCH 1965. 7 PP.

GJONEMX64829   JONES M
LOCAL CONTRACTS AND SUB-CONTRACTS. THE ROLES OF CITY
GOVERNMENT AND PRIVATE CITIZENS GROUPS.
BUFFALO LAW REVIEW, VOL 14, 1964. PP 140-147.

GKAHLJA57831   KAHL JA
ETHNIC AND RACE BARRIERS.
THE AMERICAN CLASS STRUCTURE. NEW YORK. RINEHART. 1957.
CHAPTER 8.

GKAHNRL64733   KAHN RL   GURIN G
QUINN RP   BAAR E
KRAUT AI   *UM ISR SURVEY RESEARCH CENT
DISCRIMINATION WITHOUT PREJUDICE. A STUDY OF PROMOTION
PRACTICES IN INDUSTRY.
UNIVERTY OF MICHIGAN, INSTITUTE FOR SOCIAL RESEARCH, SURVEY
RESEARCH CENTER. ANN ARBOR, MICHIGAN. NOV 1964. 45 PP.

GKAHNSD65011   KAHN SD
RACIAL DISCRIMINATION IN UNIONS.
TEMPLE LAW QUARTERLY, VOL 38, 1965. PP 311-341.

GKALICB66012   KALISH CB   *US DEPARTMENT OF LABOR
A PORTRAIT OF THE UNEMPLOYED.
US DEPARTMENT OF LABOR, MONTHLY LABOR REVIEW, JAN 1966.
PP 7-14.

GKAMMTX65832   KAMMHOLZ T
CIVIL-RIGHTS PROBLEMS IN PERSONNEL AND LABOR-RELATIONS.
ILLINOIS BUSINESS JOURNAL, VOL 353, 1965. PP 464-479.

GKANCIC62840   KANSAS CITY COMM ON HUM RELS
AREAS OF COMMISSION CONCERN. /KANSAS-CITY MISSOURI/
KANSAS CITY COMMISSION ON HUMAN RELATIONS, KANSAS CITY,
MISSOURI. AP 15 1962. 12 PP.

GKANERD66863   KANE RD   *NYU CENT STUDY UNEMP YOUTH
THE COMMUNITY ACTION AGENCY-S ROLE IN COMPREHENSIVE MANPOWER
PROGRAMS -- PLANNING AND PROBLEMS.
NEW YORK UNIVERSITY, GRADUATE SCHOOL OF SOCIAL WORK, CENTER
FOR THE STUDY OF UNEMPLOYED YOUTH. NEW YORK. FEB 1966.
27 PP.

GKARTWX67215   KART W
EQUAL-EMPLOYMENT.
TRAINING IN BUSINESS AND INDUSTRY, VOL 4, NO 2, FEB 1967.
PP 48-53.

GKAUFET58014   KAUFMANN ET
LABOR LAW -- UNION MEMBERSHIP DENIED ON THE BASIS OF RACIAL
DISCRIMINATION. /WISCONSIN LEGISLATION/
WISCONSIN LAW REVIEW, VOL 1958, MAR 1958, PP 294-311.

GKAUFJJ67940   KAUFMAN JJ   SCHAEFER CJ
LEWIS MV   STEVENS DW
HOUSE EW
THE ROLE OF THE SECONDARY SCHOOLS IN THE PREPARATION OF
YOUTH FOR EMPLOYMENT.
PENNSYLVANIA STATE UNIVERSITY, INSTITUTE FOR RESEARCH ON
HUMAN RESOURCES. UNIVERSITY PARK, PENNSYLVANIA. FEB 1967.
435 PP.

GKAUFJJ67963   KAUFMAN JJ   SCHAEFER CJ
LEWIS MV   STEVENS DW
HOUSE EW
THE ROLE OF THE SECONDARY SCHOOLS IN THE PREPARATION OF
YOUTH FOR EMPLOYMENT. SUMMARY, CONCLUSIONS. AND
RECOMMENDATIONS.
PENNSYLVANIA STATE UNIVERSITY, INSTITUTE FOR RESEARCH ON
HUMAN RESOURCES. UNIVERSITY PARK, PENNSYLVANIA. FEB 1967.
20 PP.

GKAUFSF64841   KAUFER SF   LESKES T
*AMERICAN JEWISH COMMITTEE.
THE PEOPLE TAKE THE LEAD.
AMERICAN JEWISH COMMITTEE, INSTITUTE OF HUMAN RELATIONS.
NEW YORK. JAN 1964. 52 PP.

GKEENVX52015   KEENAN V   KERR WA
UNFAIR EMPLOYMENT PRACTICES AS VIEWED BY PRIVATE EMPLOYMENT
COUNSELORS.
JOURNAL OF APPLIED PSYCHOLOGY, VOL 36, NO 6, DEC 1952.
PP 361-364.

GKENNJF63842   KENNEDY JF   *US CONFERENCE OF MAYORS
CITY PROBLEMS OF 1963. /ANTIDISCRIMINATION/
US CONFERENCE OF MAYORS, ADDRESS. WASHINGTON, DC. PP 2-9.

GKENTCHND844   KENTUCKY COMM ON HUMAN RIGHTS
EXPLANATION AND DIGEST OF THE 1966 KENTUCKY CIVIL-RIGHTS-ACT
COVERING EMPLOYMENT AND PUBLIC ACCOMODATIONS, ENACTED
JANUARY 27 1966, EFFECTIVE JULY 1 1966.
KENTUCKY COMMISSION ON HUMAN RIGHTS, FRANKFORT, KENTUCKY.
NO. 9 PP.

GKERSJA66733   KERSHAW JA
MANPOWER POLICY, POVERTY AND THE STATE OF THE ECONOMY.
CRITICAL ISSUES IN EMPLOYMENT POLICY. ED BY F H HARBISON AND
J D MOONEY. PRINCETON UNIVERSITY, INDUSTRIAL RELATIONS
SECTION. PRINCETON, NEW JERSEY. 1966. PP 39-52.

GKERSJA66941   KERSHAW JA   LEVINE RA
POVERTY, AGGREGATE DEMAND, AND ECONOMIC STRUCTURE.
JOURNAL OF HUMAN RESOURCES, VOL 1, SUMMER 1966. PP 67-70.

GKESSLC48847   KESSELMAN LC
THE SOCIAL POLITICS OF FEPC. A STUDY IN REFORM PRESSURE
MOVEMENTS.
UNIVERSITY OF NORTH CAROLINA PRESS. CHAPEL HILL, NORTH
CAROLINA. 1948. 253 PP.

GKESSLC56846   KESSELMAN LC
FAIR-EMPLOYMENT-PRACTICE-COMMISSION MOVEMENT IN PERSPECTIVE.
JOURNAL OF NEGRO HISTORY, VOL 31, JAN 1956. PP 30-46.

GKESSMA63848   KESSLER MA   *US DEPARTMENT OF LABOR
ECONOMIC-STATUS OF NON-WHITE WORKERS, 1955-1962.
/OCCUPATIONAL-DISTRIBUTION/
US DEPARTMENT OF LABOR, SPECIAL LABOR FORCE REPORT NO 33.

MONTHLY LABOR REVIEW, VOL 86, NO 7, 1963. PP 780-793.

GKETCWA65849   KETCHAM WA
PSYCHOLOGICAL TESTING FOR EFFECTIVE EMPLOYMENT PRACTICES AND
EQUAL JOB OPPORTUNITIES.
CONFERENCE ON SELECTIVE EMPLOYMENT PRACTICES AND EQUAL JOB
OPPORTUNITIES, PAPER. SPONSORED BY PSYCHODYNAMICS RESEARCH
AND ASSOCIATES, INC. DEARBORN, MICHIGAN. MAY 28 1965.

GKETCWA66942   KETCHAM WA
TESTING MINORITY-GROUP APPLICANTS.
UNIVERSITY OF MICHIGAN, BUREAU OF INDUSTRIAL RELATIONS.
PERSONNEL TECHNIQUES SEMINAR, PAPER. ANN ARBOR,
MICHIGAN. JAN 26, 1966. 5 PP.

GKEYSLH64862   KEYSERLING LH
PROGRESS OR POVERTY. THE US AT THE CROSSROADS.
CONFERENCE ON ECONOMIC PROGRESS. WASHINGTON, DC. DEC 1964.
150 PP.

GKEYSLH64943   KEYSERLING LH
KEY QUESTIONS ON THE POVERTY PROBLEM.
POVERTY IN PLENTY. ED BY G H DUNNE. P J KENEDY AND SONS.
NEW YORK. 1964. PP 91-117.

GKHEETW62852   KHEEL TW
REPORT ON THE STRUCTURE AND OPERATIONS OF THE PRESIDENT-S
COMMITTEE ON EQUAL-EMPLOYMENT-OPPORTUNITY.
PRENTICE-HALL. ENGLEWOOD CLIFFS, NEW JERSEY. 1962.

GKHEETW63850   KHEEL TW
HOW RACE-RELATIONS AFFECT YOUR BUSINESS.
PRENTICE-HALL. ENGLEWOOD CLIFFS, NEW JERSEY. 1963. 36 PP.

GKHEETW64851   KHEEL TW
GUIDE TO FAIR-EMPLOYMENT-PRACTICES.
PRENTICE-HALL. ENGLEWOOD CLIFFS, NEW JERSEY. 1964.

GKILLCC62861   KILLINGSWORTH CC ED
AUTOMATION.
ANNALS OF THE AMERICAN ACADEMY OF POLITICAL AND SOCIAL
SCIENCE, VOL 340, MAR 1962. ENTIRE ISSUE.

GKILLCC63755   KILLINGSWORTH CC
AUTOMATION, JOBS, AND MANPOWER.
NATION-S MANPOWER REVOLUTION. US SENATE, COMMITTEE ON LABOR
AND PUBLIC WELFARE, HEARINGS, PART 5, GPO. WASHINGTON, DC.
1963. PP 1461-1483.

GKILLCC66800   KILLINGSWORTH CC
STRUCTURAL UNEMPLOYMENT IN THE UNITED STATES.
EMPLOYMENT PROBLEMS OF AUTOMATION AND ADVANCED TECHNOLOGY.
AN INTERNATIONAL PERSPECTIVE. ED BY J STIEBER. MACMILLAN AND
CO. LONDON. 1966. PP 128-156.

GKILLLX62853   KILLIAN L   GRIGG C
URBANISM, RACE, AND ANOMIA.
AMERICAN JOURNAL OF SOCIOLOGY, VOL 67, 1962. PP 661-665.

GKIMMPR66137   KIMMEL PR
IDENTIFICATION AND MODIFICATION OF THE SOCIAL-PSYCHOLOGICAL
CORRELATES OF ECONOMIC DEPENDENCY. PROJECT FINAL REPORT.
US DEPARTMENT OF HEALTH, EDUCATION, AND WELFARE, WELFARE
ADMINISTRATION. WASHINGTON, DC. MAR 1966.

GKINGRL60854   KING RL
PROTECTING RIGHTS OF MINORITY EMPLOYEES.
LABOR LAW JOURNAL, VOL 11, FEB 1960. PP 143-154.

GKIRSGC64860   KIRSTEIN GC
THE MANPOWER REVOLUTION -- A CALL FOR DEBATE.
THE NATION, VOL 198, FEB 10 1964. PP 140-144.

GKOHLMC62855   KOHLER MC
YOUTH AND WORK IN NEW-YORK-CITY.
TACONIC FOUNDATION. NEW YORK. MAR 1962.

GKOHNML56145   KOHN ML   WILLIAMS RM
SITUATIONAL PATTERNING AND INTERGROUP RELATIONS.
AMERICAN SOCIOLOGICAL REVIEW, VOL 21, 1956. PP 164-174.

GKOLKGX62690   KOLKO G
WEALTH AND POWER IN AMERICA. /ECONOMY POVERTY/
FREDERICK A PRAEGER, INC. NEW YORK. 1962. 178 PP.

GKONVMR47856   KONVITZ MR
THE CONSTITUTION AND CIVIL-RIGHTS.
COLUMBIA UNIVERSITY PRESS. NEW YORK. 1947. 245 PP.

GKONVMR61477   KONVITZ MR
A CENTURY-OF CIVIL-RIGHTS.
WITH A STUDY OF STATE LAW AGAINST DISCRIMINATION BY THEODORE
LESKES. COLUMBIA UNIVERSITY PRESS. NEW YORK CITY. 1961.
293 PP.

GKOOSEL57691   KOOS EL   *FLORIDA STATE BOARD HEALTH
THEY FOLLOW THE SUN. /MIGRANT-WORKERS/
FLORIDA STATE BOARD OF HEALTH. JACKSONVILLE, FLORIDA. 1957.
55 PP.

GKOPPRW65858   KOPP RW
MANAGEMENT-S CONCERN WITH RECENT CIVIL-RIGHTS LEGISLATION
AFFECTING MANAGEMENT-S OBLIGATIONS TO HIS EMPLOYEES AND
APPLICANTS FOR EMPLOYMENT, MAINLY IN THE STATE OF
NEW-YORK.
LABOR LAW JOURNAL, VOL 16, NO 2, FEB 1965. PP 67-86.

GKOTHCA65732   KOTHE CA ED   *NATL ASSN MANUFACTURERS
A TALE OF 22 CITIES. TITLE-VII OF THE CIVIL-RIGHTS-ACT OF
1964.
NATIONAL ASSOCIATION OF MANUFACTURERS. NEW YORK. 1965.
168 PP.

GKOVAIX58026   KOVARSKY I
RACIAL DISCRIMINATION IN EMPLOYMENT AND THE FEDERAL LAW.
OREGON LAW REVIEW, VOL 38, DEC 1958. PP 54-85.

GKOVAIX58860   KOVARSKY I
A REVIEW OF STATE FEPC LAWS.
LABOR LAW JOURNAL, VOL 9, JULY 1958. PP 478-494.

GKOVAIX63025   KOVARSKY I
COMMON CARRIERS AND THE STATE FEPC.
SAINT LOUIS UNIVERSITY LAW JOURNAL, VOL 8, WINTER 1963.
PP 175-189.

GKRONJL65861   KRONER JL
LABOR AND THE EMANCIPATION PROCLAMATION. /UNION/
LEGAL ASPECTS OF THE CIVIL RIGHTS MOVEMENT. ED BY DONALD
KING AND CHARLES QUICK. WAYNE STATE UNIVERSITY PRESS.

DETROIT, MICHIGAN. 1965. PP 79-86.

GKRUEAO63862 KRUEGER AO
THE ECONOMICS OF DISCRIMINATION.
JOURNAL OF POLITICAL ECONOMY, OCT 1963. PP 481-486.

GKRUGDHND865 KRUGER DH
MANPOWER PROBLEMS AND THE BUSINESS COMMUNITY.
MICHIGAN STATE UNIVERSITY, SCHOOL OF LABOR AND INDUSTRIAL
RELATIONS. MANUSCRIPT. LANSING, MICHIGAN. ND. 14 PP.

GKRUGDH65628 KRUGER DH   *US DEPARTMENT OF LABOR
UNEMPLOYMENT INSURANCE AND MANPOWER POLICY.
/INCOME-MAINTENANCE/
US DEPARTMENT OF LABOR, UNEMPLOYMENT INSURANCE REVIEW,
AUG 1965. PP 21-25.

GKRUGDH66864 KRUGER DH
EMPLOYMENT PROBLEMS OF YOUTH AND MANPOWER PROGRAMS.
MIDWEST REGIONAL CONFERENCE ON YOUTH EMPLOYMENT, NATIONAL
COMMITTEE ON EMPLOYMENT OF YOUTH, ADDRESS. DETROIT,
MICHIGAN. OCT 20 1966. 11 PP.

GKRUGRE64946 KRUG RE   *EDUCATICNAL TESTING SERVICE
POSSIBLE SOLUTIONS TO THE PROBLEM OF CULTURAL BIAS IN TESTS.
SELECTING AND TRAINING NEGROES FOR MANAGERIAL POSITIONS.
PROCEEDINGS OF THE EXECUTIVE STUDY CONFERENCE, EDUCATIONAL
TESTING SERVICE. PRINCETON, NEW JERSEY. NOV 10-11, 1964.
PP 77-85.

GKRUGRE66863 KRUG RE
SOME SUGGESTED APPROACHES FOR TEST DEVELOPMENT AND
MEASUREMENT.
PERSONNEL PSYCHOLOGY, VOL 19, SPRING 1966. PP 24-35.

GKURTAX60866 KURTH A
MIGRANTS. /ECONOMIC-STATUS/
CHILDREN AND YOUTH IN THE 1960-S. 1960 WHITE HOUSE
CONFERENCE ON CHILDREN AND YOUTH, SURVEY PAPERS. GOLDEN
ANNIVERSARY WHITE HOUSE CONFERENCE ON CHILDREN AND YOUTH,
INC. WASHINGTON, DC. 1960. PP 205-218.

GKUVLWP65867 KUVLESKY WP   WRIGHT DE
POVERTY IN TEXAS. THE DISTRIBUTION OF LOW-INCOME FAMILIES.
TEXAS A AND M UNIVERSITY, TEXAS AGRICULTURAL EXPERIMENT
STATION, DEPARTMENTAL INFORMATION REPORT NO 64-5. COLLEGE
STATION, TEXAS. OCT 1965.

GLABJLJ65819 LABOR LAW JOURNAL
DISCRIMINATION AND FAIR-EMPLOYMENT-PRACTICES.
LABOR LAW JOURNAL, VOL 16, NO 7, JULY 1965. PP 349 FF.

GLABJLR44877 LABOR LAW REFERENCE MANUAL
SURVEY OF STATE ANTI-DISCRIMINATORY LAWS.
LABOR LAW REFERENCE MANUAL, VOL 15, SEPT 1 1944.
PP 2618-2621.

GLABJLR45870 LABOR LAW REFERENCE MANUAL
FEPC. REPORT ON OPERATIONS.
LABOR LAW REFERENCE MANUAL, VOL 16, MAR 1 1945.
PP 2549-2552.

GLABJLR45873 LABOR LAW REFERENCE MANUAL
OPERATION UNDER STATE FEPC LAWS.
LABOR LAW REFERENCE MANUAL, VOL 16, MAR 1 1945.
PP 2553-2556.

GLABJLR45874 LABOR LAW REFERENCE MANUAL
PRINCIPLES ESTABLISHED BY THE FEPC.
LABOR LAW REFERENCE MANUAL, VOL 16, MAR 1 1945.
PP 2542-2548.

GLABJLR46871 LABOR LAW REFERENCE MANUAL
NJ ANTI-DISCRIMINATION LAW. FIRST ANNUAL REPORT.
/NEW-JERSEY/
LABOR LAW REFERENCE MANUAL, VOL 19, NOV 1 1946. PP 119-120.

GLABJLR46872 LABOR LAW REFERENCE MANUAL
NY ANTI-DISCRIMINATION LAW. 1946 ANNUAL REPORT. /NEW-YORK/
LABOR LAW REFERENCE MANUAL, VOL 19, NOV 1 1946. PP 116-118.

GLABJRR51879 LABOR RELATIONS REPORTER
ENFORCEMENT OF NEW-YORK LAW AGAINST DISCRIMINATION.
LABOR RELATIONS REPORTER, VOL 27, NO 39, MAR 19 1951.
PP 231-239.

GLAFADP65782 LAFAYETTE DP   *US DEPARTMENT OF LABOR
COUNSELOR-S GUIDE TO OCCUPATIONAL AND OTHER MANPOWER
INFORMATION. AN ANNOTATED BIBLIOGRAPHY.
US DEPARTMENT OF LABOR, BUREAU OF LABOR STATISTICS, BULLETIN
NO 1421. GPO. WASHINGTON, DC. 1965. 87 PP.

GLAMBNM64880 LAMBERT NM
THE PRESENT STATUS OF THE CULTURE FAIR TESTING MOVEMENT.
PSYCHOLOGY IN THE SCHOOLS, VOL 1, NO 3, JULY 1964.
PP 318-330.

GLAMBWH66857 LAMB WH
PROVING DISCRIMINATION AT THE COMMISSION LEVEL.
TEMPLE LAW QUARTERLY, VOL 39, NO 3, SPRING 1966. PP 299-338.

GLAMPRJ65658 LAMPMAN RJ
INCOME-DISTRIBUTION AND POVERTY.
POVERTY IN AMERICA. ED BY M S GORDON. CHANDLER PUBLISHING
CO. SAN FRANCISCO, CALIFORNIA. 1965. PP 102-114.

GLAMPRJ66881 LAMPMAN RJ
ENDS AND MEANS IN THE WAR-ON-POVERTY.
WEST VIRGINIA UNIVERSITY CONFERENCE, POVERTY AMIDST
AFFLUENCE, MAY 1965. PAPER. YALE UNIVERSITY PRESS.
NEW HAVEN, CONNECTICUT. 1966.

GLAMPRJ66882 LAMPMAN RJ
POPULATION CHANGE AND POVERTY REDUCTION, 1947-1975.
WEST VIRGINIA UNIVERSITY CONFERENCE, POVERTY AMIDST
AFFLUENCE, MAY 1965. PAPER. YALE UNIVERSITY PRESS.
NEW HAVEN, CONNECTICUT. 1966.

GLANDWM66883 LANDES WM
THE EFFECT OF STATE FAIR-EMPLOYMENT LEGISLATION ON THE
ECONOMIC POSITION OF NONWHITE MALES.
HARVARD UNIVERSITY. PHD DISSERTATION. CAMBRIDGE,
MASSACHUSSETTS. 1966.

GLANGGE59884 LANG GE   *NY STATE COMM AGAINST DISCR
MINORITY-GROUPS AND ECONOMIC-STATUS IN NEW-YORK STATE.
DISCRIMINATION AND LOW INCOMES, ED BY AARON ANTONOVSKY AND
LEWIS L LORWIN. NEW SCHOOL FOR SOCIAL RESEARCH, NEW YORK.
1959.

GLARSOF60406 LARSON OF   SHARP EF
MIGRATORY FARM WORKERS IN THE ATLANTIC COAST STREAM.
I. CHANGES IN NEW-YORK, 1953 AND 1957.
CORNELL UNIVERSITY. ITHACA, NEW YORK. MAY 1960. 62 PP.

GLASSRL65998 LASSITER RL
THE ASSOCIATION OF INCOME AND EDUCATION FOR MALES, BY
REGION, RACE, AND AGE.
SOUTHERN ECONOMIC JOURNAL, VOL 32, JULY 1965. PP 15-22.

GLAWXRD65885 LAW REVIEW DIGEST
EMPLOYMENT DISCRIMINATION. STATE FAIR-EMPLOYMENT-PRACTICES
LAWS AND THE IMPACT OF TITLE-VII OF THE CIVIL-RIGHTS-ACT
OF 1964.
LAW REVIEW DIGEST, VOL 15, 1965. PP 30-53.

GLAWYGR45886 LAWYERS GUILD REVIEW
LEGISLATION OUTLAWING RACIAL DISCRIMINATION IN EMPLOYMENT.
LAWYERS GUILD REVIEW, VOL 5, NO 2, 1945.

GLAWYGR45887 LAWYERS GUILD REVIEW
RAILROADS BEFORE THE FEPC.
LAWYERS GUILD REVIEW, VOL 4, NO 2, 1944. P 32. ALSO YEARBOOK
OF AMERICAN LABOR. 1945. PP 398-440.

GLEADCCND888 LEADERSHIP CONF CIVIL RIGHTS
SOME QUESTIONS AND ANSWERS ON THE CIVIL-RIGHTS BILL.
LEADERSHIP CONFERENCE ON CIVIL RIGHTS, WASHINGTON, DC. ND.
24 PP.

GLEAGWVND890 LEAGUE OF WOMEN VOTERS
PROSPECTS FOR EDUCATION AND EMPLOYMENT.
LEAGUE OF WOMEN VOTERS. WASHINGTON, DC. 24 PP. ND.

GLEBESX60276 LEBERGOTT S   *NATL BUREAU OF EC RESEARCH
POPULATION CHANGE AND THE SUPPLY OF LABOR.
DEMOGRAPHIC AND ECONOMIC CHANGE IN DEVELOPED AREAS. NATIONAL
BUREAU OF ECONOMIC RESEARCH. SPECIAL CONFERENCE SERIES, 11.
PRINCETON UNIVERSITY PRESS. PRINCETON, NEW JERSEY. 1960.

GLEBESX65891 LEBERGOTT S ED
MEN WITHOUT WORK, THE ECONOMICS OF UNEMPLOYMENT.
PRENTICE-HALL. ENGLEWOOD CLIFFS, NEW JERSEY. 1965. 183 PP.

GLEISAX64730 LEISERSON A ED
THE AMERICAN SOUTH IN THE 1960-S.
PRAEGER. NEW YORK. 1964. 242 PP.

GLEITRD49892 LEITER RD
DISCRIMINATION IN EMPLOYMENT. FEDERAL AND STATE PRACTICES IN
ANTI-DISCRIMINATION.
AMERICAN JOURNAL OF ECONOMICS AND SOCIOLOGY, VOL 8, JULY
1949. PP 337-350.

GLELAWC63893 LELAND WC
WE BELIEVE IN EMPLOYMENT ON MERIT, BUT...
MINNESOTA LAW REVIEW, VOL 37, MAR 1963. PP 246-267.

GLEONRC64894 LEONARD RC
COMMUNITY VALUES IN EDUCATION AND OCCUPATIONAL SELECTION. A
STUDY OF YOUTH IN EMMITSBURG, MARYLAND.
CATHOLIC UNIVERSITY. PHD DISSERTATION. WASHINGTON, DC. 1964.

GLESKTX61895 LESKES T
STATE LAWS AGAINST DISCRIMINATION.
A CENTURY OF CIVIL RIGHTS. MILTON R KONVITZ. COLUMBIA
UNIVERSITY PRESS. NEW YORK. 1961.

GLESTRA66155 LESTER RA
MANPOWER PLANNING IN A FREE SOCIETY.
PRINCETON UNIVERSITY PRESS. PRINCETON, NEW JERSEY. 1966.
227 PP.

GLESTRA66532 LESTER RA   *US DEPARTMENT OF LABOR
THE ADAPTATION OF LABOR RESOURCES TO CHANGING NEEDS.
/MOBILITY/
US DEPARTMENT OF LABOR, MONTHLY LABOR REVIEW, VOL 89, NO 3,
MAR 1966. PP 245-249.

GLEVILA61357 LEVINE LA
THE MIGRATORY WORKER IN THE FARM ECONOMY.
INDUSTRIAL RELATIONS RESEARCH ASSOCIATICN, PROCEEDINGS.
CHICAGO, ILLINOIS. 1961. PP 622-630.

GLEVILA64623 LEVINE LA   *OECD
EFFECTS OF TECHNOLOGICAL-CHANGE ON THE NATURE OF JOBS.
ORGANIZATION FOR ECONOMIC COOPERATION AND DEVELOPMENT,
NORTH AMERICAN JOINT CONFERENCE. THE REQUIREMENTS OF
AUTOMATED JOBS. WASHINGTON, DC. DEC 8-10 1964. PP 119-160.

GLEVILA65781 LEVINE LA
IMPLICATIONS OF THE ANTI-POVERTY PROGRAM FOR EDUCATION AND
EMPLOYMENT.
VOCATIONAL GUIDANCE QUARTERLY, VOL 14, NO 1, AUTUMN 1965.
PP 8-15.

GLEVILA66599 LEVINE LA
THE NEW ROLE OF THE EMPLOYMENT SERVICE IN SERVING THE
DISADVANTAGED. /SES/
POVERTY AND HUMAN RESOURCES ABSTRACTS, VOL 1, NO 5,
SEPT-OCT 1966. PP 5-12.

GLEVISA63898 LEVITAN SA   *UPJOHN INST EMPLOY RESEARCH
YOUTH EMPLOYMENT ACT.
THE W E UPJOHN INSTITUTE FOR EMPLOYMENT RESEARCH.
KALAMAZOO, MICHIGAN. 1963.

GLEVISA64896 LEVITAN SA
FEDERAL AID TO DEPRESSED AREAS. AN EVALUATION OF THE
AREA-REDEVELOPMENT-ADMINISTRATION.
JOHN-S HOPKINS PRESS. BALTIMORE, MARYLAND. 1964. 268 PP.

GLEVISA64897 LEVITAN SA   *UPJOHN INST EMPLOY RESEARCH
FEDERAL MANPOWER POLICIES AND PROGRAMS TO COMBAT
UNEMPLOYMENT.
THE W E UPJOHN INSTITUTE FOR EMPLOYMENT RESEARCH.
KALAMAZOO, MICHIGAN. FEB 1964. 41 PP.

GLEVISA65601 LEVITAN SA   *UPJOHN INST EMPLOY RESEARCH
PROGRAMS IN AID OF THE POOR.
W E UPJOHN INSTITUTE FOR EMPLOYMENT RESEARCH, PUBLIC POLICY
INFORMATION BULLETIN. KALAMAZOO, MICHIGAN. 1965. 59 PP.

GLEVISA66038 LEVITAN SA   *US CHAMBER OF COMMERCE
THE POOR IN THE WORK FORCE. /LABOR-FORCE/
THE DISADVANTAGED POOR. EDUCATION AND EMPLOYMENT. US CHAMBER
OF COMMERCE, TASK FORCE ON ECONOMIC GROWTH AND OPPORTUNITY.
WASHINGTON, DC. 1966. PP 297-322.

GLEVISA66531 LEVITAN SA   *UPJOHN INST EMPLOY RESEARCH

WORK RELIEF. SOCIAL WELFARE STYLE. /MANPOWER UNEMPLOYMENT/
THE W E UPJOHN INSTITUTE FOR EMPLOYMENT RESEARCH.
WASHINGTON, DC. JUNE 12, 1966. MIMEOGRAPHED. 18 PP.

GLEVISA66729   LEVITAN SA
PROGRAMS IN AID OF THE POOR. /ANTI-POVERTY/
POVERTY AND HUMAN RESOURCES ABSTRACTS, VOL 1, NO 1,
JAN-FEB 1966. PP 11-25.

GLICHRX64900   LICHTMAN R
THE ETHICS OF COMPENSATORY JUSTICE.
/PREFERENTIAL-TREATMENT/
LAW IN TRANSITION QUARTERLY, VOL 1, 1964. P 76.

GLIEBEE65569   LIEBHAFSKY EE   *U HOUSTON CENT RES BUS ECS
A METHODOLOGICAL APPROACH TO IDENTIFICATION AND
CLASSIFICATION OF CERTAIN TYPES OF INACTIVE WORK-SEEKERS.
/UNEMPLOYMENT LABOR-MARKET/
UNIVERSITY OF HOUSTON, CENTER FOR RESEARCH IN BUSINESS AND
ECONOMICS. HOUSTON, TEXAS. OCT 1965. 130 PP.

GLIEJEX50901   LIEBERMAN E
UNIONS BEFORE THE BAR. HISTORICAL TRIALS SHOWING THE
EVOLUTION OF LABOR RIGHTS IN THE US.
HARPER. NEW YORK. 1950.

GLIEJMX59902   LIEBERMAN M
EQUALITY OF EDUCATIONAL OPPORTUNITY.
HARVARD EDUCATIONAL REVIEW, VOL 29, SUMMER 1959. PP 167-183.

GLIEBSX58042   LIEBERSON S
ETHNIC GROUPS AND THE PRACTICE OF MEDICINE. /OCCUPATIONS/
AMERICAN SOCIOLOGICAL REVIEW, VOL 23, 1958. PP 542-549.

GLIEBSX63904   LIEBERSON S
ETHNIC PATTERNS IN AMERICAN CITIES.
FREE PRESS OF GLENCOE. NEW YORK. 1963. 230 PP.

GLINDAW61744   LIND AW
RACE-RELATIONS FRONTIERS IN HAWAII.
RACE RELATIONS. PROBLEMS AND THEORY. ED BY JITSUICHI
MASUOKA AND PRESTON VALIEN. UNIVERSITY OF NORTH CAROLINA
PRESS. CHAPEL HILL, NORTH CAROLINA. 1961. PP 58-77.

GLINDJR66603   LINDSAY JR   JOHNSTON HL
THE HEALTH OF THE MIGRANT-WORKER. /EMPLOYMENT-CONDITIONS/
JOURNAL OF OCCUPATIONAL HEALTH, VOL 8, NO 1, JAN 1966.
PP 27-30.

GLIVEER66567   LIVERNASH ER
AN ACTIVE EMPLOYER MANPOWER POLICY.
INDUSTRIAL RELATIONS RESEARCH ASSOCIATION, 19TH ANNUAL
WINTER MEETINGS. PROCEEDINGS. SAN FRANCISCO, CALIFORNIA.
DEC 28-29 1966. PP 208-218.

GLLOYKM64317   LLOYD KM
SOLVING AN AMERICAN DILEMMA. THE ROLE OF THE FEPC OFFICIAL.
A COMPARATIVE STUDY OF STATE CIVIL-RIGHTS COMMISSIONS.
STANFORD UNIVERSITY, PHD DISSERTATION. STANFORD, CALIFORNIA.
1964. 317 PP.

GLOCKDX65146   LOCKARD D
THE POLITICS OF ANTIDISCRIMINATION LEGISLATION.
HARVARD JOURNAL ON LEGISLATION, VOL 3, 1965. PP 3-61.

GLOCKHC65907   LOCKWOOD HC
TESTING MINORITY-GROUP APPLICANTS FOR EMPLOYMENT.
PERSONNEL JOURNAL, VOL 44, NO 7, JULY-AUG 1965. PP 356-360.

GLOCKHC66780   LOCKWOOD HC
DEVELOPING FAIR-EMPLOYMENT PROGRAMS. GUIDELINES FOR
SELECTION.
PERSONNEL JOURNAL, VOL 43, NO 4, JULY-AUG 1966. PP 50-57.

GLOCKHC66906   LOCKWOOD HC   *US DEPARTMENT OF LABOR
CRITICAL PROBLEMS IN ACHIEVING EQUAL-EMPLOYMENT-OPPORTUNITY.
PERSONNEL PSYCHOLOGY, VOL 19, SPRING 1966. PP 3-9. ALSO IN
US DEPARTMENT OF LABOR, EMPLOYMENT SERVICE REVIEW, VOL 3,
NO 8, AUG 1966. PP 14-17.

GLONDJX54908   LONDON J   HAMMETT R
IMPACT OF COMPANY POLICY UPON DISCRIMINATION.
SOCIOLOGY AND SOCIOLOGICAL RESEARCH, VOL 39, NOV 1954.
PP 88-91.

GLONGCX58C47   LONG C   *NATL BUREAU OF EC RESEARCH
THE LABOR-FORCE UNDER CHANGING INCOME AND EMPLOYMENT.
NATIONAL BUREAU OF ECONOMIC RESEARCH. NEW YORK. 1958.

GLONGNE64856   LONG NE
URBAN POVERTY AND PUBLIC POLICY.
BUSINESS AND GOVERNMENT REVIEW, VOL 5, JULY-AUG, 1964.
PP 31-38.

GLONGNE65121   LONG NE   *NATL ASSN MANUFACTURERS
PUBLIC POLICY, PRIVATE ENTERPRISE AND THE REDUCTION OF
POVERTY.
NATIONAL ASSOCIATION OF MANUFACTURERS. NEW YORK. 1965.
14 PP.

GLOPEFM65910   LOPEZ FM
THE INDUSTRIAL SETTING. PROBLEMS AND EXPERIENCES. /TESTING/
NEW YORK STATE PSYCHOLOGICAL ASSOCIATION, 1965 CONVENTION,
PAPER. GROSSINGER, NEW YORK. AP 29-MAY 2 1965.

GLOPEFM66909   LOPEZ FM
3 CURRENT PROBLEMS IN TEST PERFORMANCE OF JOB APPLICANTS.
PERSONNEL PSYCHOLOGY, VOL 19, SPRING 1966. PP 10-18.

GLOSACCND914   LA COUNTY CCMM ON HUM RELS
SURVEY OF MINORITY-GROUP EMPLOYMENT AND PATIENT CARE IN
PRIVATE HOSPITAL FACILITIES IN LOS-ANGELES COUNTY.
/CALIFORNIA/
LOS ANGELES COUNTY COMMISSION ON HUMAN RELATIONS.
LOS ANGELES, CALIFORNIA. 8 PP.

GLOSACCND915   LA COUNTY CCMM ON HUM RELS
TESTIMONY ON HUMAN RELATIONS. /LOS-ANGELES CALIFORNIA/
LOS ANGELES COUNTY COMMISSION ON HUMAN RELATIONS.
LOS ANGELES, CALIFORNIA. 12 PP.

GLOSACC62913   LA COUNTY CCMM ON HUM RELS
REPORTS ON THE PATTERN OF EMPLOYMENT OF MINORTY-GROUP
PERSONS IN DEPARTMENT OF COUNTY GOVERNMENT.
/LOS-ANGELES CALIFORNIA/
LOS ANGELES COUNTY COMMISSION ON HUMAN RELATIONS.
LOS ANGELES, CALIFORNIA. JAN 8 1962. 4 PP, AND AP 4 1962.
3 PP.

GLOSACC64912   LA COUNTY CCMM ON HUM RELS

PROPOSED POLICY REGARDING STATISTICS ON EMPLOYMENT.
/LOS-ANGELES CALIFORNIA/
LOS ANGELES COUNTY COMMISSION ON HUMAN RELATIONS.
LOS ANGELES, CALIFORNIA. JUNE 1964. 1 P.

GLOSAFEND916   LA FEDERAL EXECUTIVE BOARD
LAKE-ARROWHEAD CONFERENCE ON EQUAL-EMPLOYMENT-OPPORTUNITY.
LOS ANGELES FEDERAL EXECUTIVE BOARD, LOS ANGELES,
CALIFORNIA. NO. 150 PP.

GLOSAOC63917   LA CITY ADMV OFFICER OFFICE
REPORT OF FINDINGS AND RECOMMENDATIONS RESULTING FROM AN
ANALYSIS OF THE EMPLOYMENT PRACTICES IN THE VARIOUS
DEPARTMENTS OF THE CITY OF LOS-ANGELES. /CALIFORNIA/
LOS ANGELES OFFICE OF THE CITY ADMINISTRATIVE OFFICER.
LOS ANGELES, CALIFORNIA. MAR 8 1963. 6 PP.

GLOWESH63921   LOWELL SH   *NYC COMM ON HUMAN RIGHTS
EQUALITY IN OUR TIME. WHAT WE SAID, AND WHAT WE DID NOT SAY.
ANTI-DEFAMATION LEAGUE TESTIMONIAL BREAKFAST SPEECH. NYC
CITY COMMISSION ON HUMAN RIGHTS, NEW YORK. 1963. 12 PP.

GLUDELE62923   LUDEN LE   *US DEPARTMENT OF LABOR
ANTIDISCRIMINATION PROVISIONS IN MAJOR CONTRACTS, 1961.
US DEPARTMENT OF LABOR, MONTHLY LABOR REVIEW, VOL 85,
JUNE 1962. PP 643-651.

GLUSKLX42924   LUSKY L
MINORITY RIGHTS AND THE PUBLIC INTEREST.
YALE LAW JOURNAL, VOL 52, NO 1, DEC 1942. PP 1-41.

GLUTZPX40925   LUTZ P ED
VOCATIONS AND PROFESSIONS.
ASSOCIATION PRESS. NEW YORK. 1940. 145 PP.

GMACDDX64947   MACDONALD D
THE NOW VISIBLE POOR.
POVERTY IN PLENTY. ED BY G H DUNNE. P J KENEDY AND SONS.
NEW YORK. 1964. PP 61-69.

GMACHFX65657   MACHLUP F
STRATEGIES IN THE WAR-ON-POVERTY.
POVERTY IN AMERICA. ED BY M S GORDON. CHANDLER PUBLISHING
CO. SAN FRANCISCO, CALIFORNIA. 1965. PP 445-465.

GMACIRM49025   MACIVER RM ED
DISCRIMINATION AND NATIONAL WELFARE.
HARPER. NEW YORK. 1949.

GMACYJW66933   MACY JW   *US DEPARTMENT OF LABOR
THE REALITY OF EQUAL-OPPORTUNITY IN FEDERAL EMPLOYMENT.
US DEPARTMENT OF LABOR, EMPLOYMENT SERVICE REVIEW, VOL 3,
NO 8, AUG 1966. PP 40-44.

GMAIEFH60417   MAIER FH   MAITLAND ST
BOWLES GK   *US DEPARTMENT OF AGRICULTURE
THE TENURE STATUS OF FARMWORKERS IN THE UNITED STATES.
US DEPARTMENT OF AGRICULTURE. GPO. WASHINGTON, DC.
JULY 1960. 91 PP.

GMAITST58428   MAITLAND ST   *US DEPARTMENT OF AGRICULTURE
THE HIRED FARM WORKING FORCE OF 1956. /ECONOMIC-STATUS/
US DEPARTMENT OF AGRICULTURE. GPO. WASHINGTON, DC. AP 1958.
50 PP.

GMAITST59429   MAITLAND ST   FISHER CA
*US DEPARTMENT OF AGRICULTURE
THE HIRED FARM WORKING FORCE OF 1957. /ECONOMIC-STATUS/
US DEPARTMENT OF AGRICULTURE. GPO. WASHINGTON, DC.
JUNE 1959. 67 PP.

GMAITST60436   MAITLAND ST   COWHIG JD
*US DEPARTMENT OF AGRICULTURE
SOME REGIONAL DIFFERENCES IN WAGES OF AGRICULTURAL WORKERS.
/MIGRANT-WORKERS/
ASSOCIATION OF SOUTHERN AGRICULTURAL WORKERS, PAPER.
WASHINGTON, DC. FEB 1960.

GMAITST61383   MAITLAND ST   FRIEND RE
*US DEPARTMENT OF AGRICULTURE
RURAL INDUSTRIALIZATION. A SUMMARY OF FIVE STUDIES.
/UNEMPLOYMENT OCCUPATIONS/
US DEPARTMENT OF AGRICULTURE. GPO. WASHINGTON, DC. NOV 1961.
37 PP.

GMAITST61384   MAITLAND ST   STANSBERRY RR
FRIEND RE   *US DEPARTMENT OF AGRICULTURE
THE HIRED FARM WORKING FORCE OF 1958.
US DEPARTMENT OF AGRICULTURE. GPO. WASHINGTON, DC. AP 1961.
53 PP.

GMALMTF55934   MALM TF
HIRING PROCEDURES AND SELECTION STANDARDS IN THE
SAN-FRANCISCO BAY AREA. /CALIFORNIA/
INDUSTRIAL AND LABOR RELATIONS REVIEW, JAN 1955. PP 231-252.

GMALOWH61935   MALONEY WH
RACIAL AND RELIGIOUS DISCRIMINATION IN EMPLOYMENT AND THE
ROLE OF THE NLRB.
MARYLAND LAW REVIEW, VOL 21, SUMMER 1961. PP 219-232.

GMANARX56936   MANAGEMENT REVIEW
HOW INTEGRATION IS WORKING OUT IN INDUSTRY.
MANAGEMENT REVIEW, JULY 1956. PP 547-549.

GMANGGL65728   MANGUM GL
THE ROLE OF JOB CREATION PROGRAMS. /MANPOWER/
UNEMPLOYMENT IN A PROSPEROUS ECONOMY. A REPORT OF THE
PRINCETON-MANPOWER-SYMPOSIUM. ED BY W G BOWEN AND
F H HARBISON. PRINCETON UNIVERSITY. PRINCETON, NEW JERSEY.
1965. PP 107-125.

GMANGGL66217   MANGUM GL ED
THE MANPOWER REVOLUTION. ITS POLICY CONSEQUENCES. EXCERPTS
FROM SENATE HEARINGS BEFORE THE CLARK SUBCOMMITTEE.
DOUBLEDAY AND CO., ANCHOR BOOKS. NEW YORK. 1966. 580 PP.

GMANGGL66526   MANGUM GL
THE COMPUTER AND THE AMERICAN ECONOMY.
DUKE UNIVERSITY, SEMINAR ON THE IMPACT OF THE COMPUTER ON
SOCIETY, PAPER. DURHAM, NORTH CAROLINA. MAY 6-7 1966.
20 PP.

GMANGGL66529   MANGUM GL
CYBERNATION AND JOB SECURITY. /UNEMPLOYMENT/
LABOR LAW JOURNAL, JAN 1966. PP 18-25.

GMANNRD66937   MANNING RD   DOMESICK SR
TITLE-VII. RELATIONSHIP AND EFFECT ON EXECUTIVE ORDER 11246.
/LEGISLATION/

BOSTON COLLEGE INDUSTRIAL AND COMMERCIAL LAW REVIEW, VOL 7,
NO 3, SPRING 1966. PP 561-574.

GMANJSP63855 MANOR SP   *US DEPARTMENT OF LABOR
GEOGRAPHIC CHANGES IN US EMPLOYMENT FROM 1950 TO 1960.
US DEPARTMENT OF LABOR, MONTHLY LABOR REVIEW, VOL 86, NO 1,
JAN 1963. PP 1-10.

GMARDCF62938 MARDEN CF   MEYERS G
MINORITIES IN AMERICAN SOCIETY.
AMERICAN BOOK CO. NEW YORK. 1952. 2ND ED. 1962. 493 PP.

GMARKCX64949 MARKHAM C
JOBS, MEN AND MACHINES. PROBLEMS OF AUTOMATION.
AMERICAN FOUNDATION ON AUTOMATION AND EMPLOYMENT, CONFERENCE
ON SOLUTIONS TO PROBLEMS OF AUTOMATION AND EMPLOYMENT.
F A PRAEGER. NEW YORK. 1964.

GMARKPI57085 MARKET PSYCHOLOGY INC.   *NY STATE COMM AGAINST DISCR
MANAGEMENT AND MINORITY GROUPS, A STUDY OF ATTITUDES AND
   PRACTICES IN HIRING AND UPGRADING.
NEW YORK STATE COMMISSION AGAINST DISCRIMINATION. NEW YORK.
JUNE 1957.

GMARPAW53940 MARPLE AW
AN ANALYSIS OF THE EFFECTIVENESS OF THE NEW-YORK STATE LAW
   AGAINST DISCRIMINATION.
UNIVERSITY OF ILLINOIS, INSTITUTE OF LABOR AND INDUSTRIAL
RELATIONS. MASTER-S THESIS. CHAMPAIGN, ILLINOIS. 1953.

GMARRAX52941 MARROW A
PREJUDICE AND SCIENTIFIC METHOD IN LABOR-RELATIONS. /UNION/
INDUSTRIAL AND LABOR RELATIONS REVIEW. VOL 5, NO 4, JULY
1952. PP 593-598.

GMARSBX62942 MARSHALL B   *ANTI-DEFAMATION LEAGUE
THE ENFORCEMENT OF CIVIL-RIGHTS. /DISCRIMINATION/
ANTI-DEFAMATION LEAGUE OF B-NAI B-RITH, ADL BULLETIN,
MAR 1962. PP 9-13.

GMARSBX64943 MARSHALL B
ENFORCEMENT OF THE FEDERAL EQUAL-OPPORTUNITY LAW.
LABOR RELATIONS REVIEW, VOL 57, 1964. PP 181-182.

GMARSJX66944 MARSHALL J   *US DEPARTMENT OF LABOR
MDTA INSTITUTIONAL TRAINING OF NONWHITES.
US DEPARTMENT OF LABOR, EMPLOYMENT SERVICE REVIEW, VOL 3,
NO 8, AUG 1966. PP 67-69.

GMARSRX63945 MARSHALL R
ETHNIC AND ECONOMIC MINORITIES. UNION-S FUTURE OR
   UNRECRUITABLE.
ANNALS OF THE AMERICAN ACADEMY OF POLITICAL AND SOCIAL
SCIENCE, VOL 350, NOV 1963. PP 63-73.

GMARSRX64059 MARSHALL R
THE RACIAL PRACTICES OF THE ILGWU -- A REPLY.
INDUSTRIAL AND RACIAL RELATIONS REVIEW, VOL 17, NO 4,
JULY 1964. PP 622-626.

GMARSRX65056 MARSHALL R
EQUAL-EMPLOYMENT-OPPORTUNITIES. PROBLEMS AND PROSPECTS.
INDUSTRIAL RELATIONS RESEARCH ASSOCIATION, PROCEEDINGS.
SPRING 1965. PP 453-468. ALSO IN LABOR LAW JOURNAL, VOL 16,
AUG 1965. PP 453-476.

GMARSRX66546 MARSHALL R
THE POSITION OF MINORITIES IN THE AMERICAN LABOR MOVEMENT.
   /UNION/
LABOR IN A CHANGING AMERICA. ED BY WILLIAM HABER. BASIC
BOOKS, INC. NEW YORK. 1966. PP 238-251.

GMARTJM66854 MARTIN JM   *NYU CENT STUDY UNEMP YOUTH
LOWER-CLASS DELINQUENCY AND WORK PROGRAMS.
NEW YORK UNIVERSITY, GRADUATE SCHOOL OF SOCIAL WORK, CENTER
FOR THE STUDY OF UNEMPLOYED YOUTH, NEW YORK. FEB 1966.
26 PP.

GMARTRG46947 MARTIN RG
FEPC RALLY.
NEW REPUBLIC, VOL 114, MAR 18 1946. PP 379-381.

GMARYGC60955 MD GOVRS COMT MIGRATORY LABOR
PROGRESS IN MEETING PROBLEMS OF MIGRATORY LABOR IN MARYLAND.
UNIVERSITY OF MARYLAND, AGRICULTURAL EXTENSION SERVICE.
COLLEGE PARK, MARYLAND. MAR 1960. 17 PP.

GMARYSD59956 MARYLAND STATE DEPT OF HEALTH
THE HOUSING PROBLEM OF THE MIGRANT-WORKER IN MARYLAND.
MARYLAND STATE DEPARTMENT OF HEALTH, BUREAU OF ENVIRONMENTAL
HYGIENE. BALTIMORE, MARYLAND. 1959. 9 PP.

GMARYSD65958 MARYLAND STATE DEPT OF HEALTH
MARYLAND T8 -- VD HEALTH PROGRAM AMONG AGRICULTURAL
   MIGRANTS.
MARYLAND STATE DEPARTMENT OF HEALTH, MONTHLY BULLETIN,
VOL 31, NO 5, MAY 1965. BALTIMORE, MARYLAND.

GMASLWX45960 MASLOW W
FAIR-EMPLOYMENT STATE BY STATE.
NATION, VOL 160, AP 14 1945. PP 410-411.

GMASLWX46147 MASLOW W
THE LAW AND RACE-RELATIONS.
ANNALS OF THE AMERICAN ACADEMY OF POLITICAL AND SOCIAL
SCIENCE, VOL 244, MAR 1946. PP 75-81.

GMASLWX46959 MASLOW W
FEPC -- A CASE HISTORY IN PARLIAMENTARY MANEUVER.
UNIVERSITY OF CHICAGO LAW REVIEW, VOL 13, 1946. P 407.

GMASLWX61961 MASLOW W
STATEMENT ON BEHALF OF AMERICAN JEWISH CONGRESS ON
   DISCRIMINATION IN EMPLOYMENT.
US HOUSE OF REPRESENTATIVES, COMMITTEE ON EDUCATION AND
LABOR. REPRINTED BY AMERICAN JEWISH CONGRESS. NEW YORK.
NOV 3 1961. 11 PP.

GMASSCAND963 MASS COMM AGAINST DISCR
COMPILATION OF LAWS AGAINST DISCRIMINATION, EMPLOYMENT,
   EDUCATIONAL INSTITUTIONS, PLACES OF PUBLIC ACCOMODATION,
   PUBLIC HOUSING, PUBLICLY ASSISTED HOUSING, PRIVATE
   HOUSING. /MASSACHUSETTS/
MASSACHUSETTS COMMISSION AGAINST DISCRIMINATION, BOSTON,
MASSACHUSETTS. NO. 15 PP.

GMASJJX63064 MASUKOA J   VALIEN P
RACE-RELATIONS. PROBLEMS AND THEORY.
UNIVERSITY OF NORTH CAROLINA PRESS. CHAPEL HILL, NORTH
CAROLINA. 1963.

GMATTEG64967 MATTISON EG
THE COMMUNITY APPROACH. /EEO/
SYMPOSIUM. EQUAL EMPLOYMENT OPPORTUNITY, COMPANY POLICIES
AND EXPERIENCES. MANAGEMENT REVIEW, VOL 53, AP 1964.

GMAYFHX64968 MAYFIELD H
EQUAL-EMPLOYMENT-OPPORTUNITY. SHOULD HIRING STANDARDS BE
   RELAXED.
PERSONNEL JOURNAL, VOL 61, SEPT-OCT 1964. PP 8-17. ALSO
AMERICAN MANAGEMENT ASSOCIATION, INC. NEW YORK. 1964. 10 PP.

GMAYFHX64969 MAYFIELD H
WHAT INDUSTRY CAN DO. /EEO/
SYMPOSIUM. EQUAL EMPLOYMENT OPPORTUNITY, COMPANY POLICIES
AND EXPERIENCES. MANAGEMENT REVIEW, VOL 53, AP 1964.

GMAYHLH63970 MAYHEW LH
LAW AND EQUAL-OPPORTUNITY. ANTI-DISCRIMINATION LAW IN
   MASSACHUSETTS.
HARVARD UNIVERSITY. UNPUBLISHED PHD DISSERTATION.
CAMBRIDGE, MASSACHUSETTS. 1963.

GMCARWC59392 MCARTHUR WC   SAUNDERS FB
RESOURCES AND INCOMES OF RURAL FAMILIES IN THE COASTAL PLAIN
   AREAS OF GEORGIA.
UNIVERSITY OF GEORGIA. ATHENS, GEORGIA. AP 1959. 59 PP.

GMCDJEC53050 MCDONAGH EC   RICHARDS E
ETHNIC RELATIONS IN THE UNITED STATES.
APPLETON-CENTURY-CROFTS. NEW YORK. 1953. 408 PP.

GMCELDX65051 MCELRATH D
URBAN DIFFERENTIATION. PROBLEMS AND PROSPECTS.
LAW AND CONTEMPORARY PROBLEMS, VOL 30, NO 1, WINTER 1965.
PP 103-110.

GMCKEES52927 MCKENNY ES
FAIR-EMPLOYMENT IN MASSACHUSETTS, PART I.
PHYLON, VOL 13, NO 1, 1952. PP 48-53.

GMCKEES52928 MCKENNEY ES
FAIR-EMPLOYMENT IN MASSACHUSETTS, PART II.
PHYLON, VOL 13, NO 2, 1952. PP 141-166.

GMCKEEX52950 MCKENNEY E
NATIONAL POLITICS OF FAIR-EMPLOYMENT.
PHYLON, VOL 13, NO 3, 1952. PP 209-214.

GMCKEIX51926 MCKEE I
INTERRACIAL HUMAN RELATIONS IN MANAGEMENT, A COMPILED REPORT
   PRESENTED ORALLY...JANUARY 17 1951.
AMERICAN UNIVERSITY. WASHINGTON, DC. 1951. 16 PP.

GMCKERB65930 MCKERSIE RB
COMMENTS ON EQUAL-EMPLOYMENT-OPPORTUNITIES. PROBLEMS AND
   PROSPECTS.
LABOR LAW REVIEW, AUG 1965.

GMCKERB65931 MCKERSIE RB
REMARKS ON EQUAL-EMPLOYMENT-OPPORTUNITIES.
INDUSTRIAL RELATIONS RESEARCH ASSOCIATION, SPRING MEETINGS,
PROCEEDINGS. 1965. PP 468-473.

GMCNIRK48932 MCNICKLE RK
DISCRIMINATION IN EMPLOYMENT.
EDITORIAL RESEARCH REPORTS, DEC 17 1948. PP 885-902.

GMEANGC65674 MEANS GC
JOB OPPORTUNITIES AND POVERTY.
POVERTY AS A PUBLIC ISSUE. ED BY BEN B SELIGMAN. THE FREE
PRESS. NEW YORK. 1965. PP 321-335.

GMEANGX63972 MEANY G
EQUAL RIGHTS -- HERE AND NOW.
THE AMERICAN FEDERATIONIST, VOL 70, NO 8, AUG 1963. PP 8-14.

GMEANJE66971 MEANS JE
FEP LEGISLATION AND ENFORCEMENT IN THE US.
INTERNATIONAL LABOR REVIEW, VOL 93, MAR 1966. PP 211-247.

GMEINRG57066 MEINERS RG
FAIR-EMPLOYMENT-PRACTICES LEGISLATION.
DICKINSON LAW REVIEW, VOL 62, OCT 1957. PP 31-69.

GMEISDX60461 MEISTER D
THE CALIFORNIA FARM WORKER. STILL IN DUBIOUS BATTLE.
   /MIGRANT-WORKERS UNION/
NATION, VOL 191, SEPT 24 1960. PP 178-180.

GMELLML50973 MELLOR ML
FAIR-EMPLOYMENT-PRACTICES.
CALIFORNIA LAW REVIEW, VOL 38, AUG 1950. PP 515-524.

GMENDWX62974 MENDELSON W
DISCRIMINATION IN EMPLOYMENT.
DISCRIMINATION. PRENTICE-HALL. ENGLEWOOD CLIFFS, NEW JERSEY.
1962. PP 69-114.

GMERCMA59975 MERCHANTS MANUFACTURERS ASSN
CALIFORNIA FAIR-EMPLOYMENT-PRACTICE ACT.
MERCHANTS AND MANUFACTURERS ASSOCIATION, SURVEY ANALYSIS
NUMBER 45. LOS ANGELES, CALIFORNIA. JULY 1959. 12 PP.

GMERCMA60976 MERCHANTS MANUFACTURERS ASSN
PERSONNEL TESTING, JANUARY 1960.
MERCHANTS AND MANUFACTURERS ASSOCIATION. LOS ANGELES,
CALIFORNIA. JAN 1960. 34 PP.

GMEREJL61995 MEREDITH JL   *US DEPARTMENT OF LABOR
LONG-TERM UNEMPLOYMENT IN THE UNITED STATES.
US DEPARTMENT OF LABOR, MONTHLY LABOR REVIEW, VOL 84, JUNE
1961. PP 601-610.

GMEREJL63067 MEREDITH JL   *US DEPARTMENT OF LABOR
LABOR-FORCE AND EMPLOYMENT, 1960-62.
US DEPARTMENT OF LABOR, MONTHLY LABOR REVIEW, VOL 86, NO 5,
MAY 1963. 7 PP.

GMESPFA63977 MESPLE FA
ETHNIC SURVEY OF EMPLOYMENT IN STATE GOVERNMENT.
   /CALIFORNIA/
REPORT TO CALIFORNIA GOVERNOR EG BROWN. SACRAMENTO,
CALIFORNIA. NOV 27 1963. 7 PP.

GMETZJH65119 METZLER JH   KOHRS EV
TESTS AND THE REQUIREMENTS OF THE JOB.
ARBITRATION JOURNAL, VOL 20, NO 2, 1965. PP 101-111.

GMETZWH55426 METZLER WH   *US DEPARTMENT OF AGRICULTURE

MIGRATORY FARM WORKERS IN THE ATLANTIC COAST STREAM.
US DEPARTMENT OF AGRICULTURE, CIRCULAR NO 966. GPO.
WASHINGTON, DC. 1955. 79 PP.

GMETZWH60440   METZLER WH   SARGENT FO
*US DEPARTMENT OF AGRICULTURE
MIGRATORY FARMWORKERS IN THE MIDCONTINENT STREAM.
US DEPARTMENT OF AGRICULTURE, AGRICULTURAL RESEARCH SERVICE,
PRODUCTION RESEARCH REPORT NO 4. GPO. WASHINGTON, DC.
DEC 1960.

GMETZWH62504   METZLER WH   *US DEPARTMENT OF AGRICULTURE
CHARACTERISTICS OF FARM WORKERS AS RELATED TO STABILIZATION
OF THE WORK FORCE. /MIGRANT-WORKERS/
US DEPARTMENT OF AGRICULTURE, ECONOMIC RESEARCH SERVICE,
FARM ECONOMICS DIVISION. GPO. WASHINGTON, DC. MAR 1962.
5 PP.

GMETZWH64387   METZLER WH
THE FARM WORKER IN A CHANGING AGRICULTURE. PART I IN A
SERIES ON TECHNOLOGICAL-CHANGE AND FARM LABOR USE,
KERN-COUNTY, CALIFORNIA, 1961.
UNIVERSITY OF CALIFORNIA. BERKELEY, CALIFORNIA. SEPT 1964.
98 PP.

GMEYESM56058   MEYERS SM   *NEW JERSEY DEPT OF EDUCATION
MINORITY-GROUP WORKERS IN INDUSTRY.
NEW JERSEY DEPARTMENT OF EDUCATION, DIVISION AGAINST
DISCRIMINATION. TRENTON, NEW JERSEY. OCT 1956. 19 PP.

GMICADN62978   MICHAEL DN   *CENTER STUDY DEMO INSTS
CYBERNATION. THE SILENT CONQUEST. /TECHNOLOGICAL-CHANGE/
CENTER FOR THE STUDY OF DEMOCRATIC INSTITUTIONS.
SANTA BARBARA, CALIFORNIA. 1962.

GMICADN64673   MICHAEL DN   *US DEPARTMENT OF LABOR
CYBERNATION AND SOCIAL CHANGE. /TECHNOLOGICAL-CHANGE/
US DEPARTMENT OF LABOR, MANPOWER ADMINISTRATION, SEMINAR ON
MANPOWER POLICY AND PROGRAM. NOV 1964. 34 PP.

GMICFEA57979   MICHIGAN FEP ADVISORY COUNCIL
A STUDY OF UNEMPLOYMENT, TRAINING AND PLACEMENT PATTERNS IN
THE MUSKEGON AREA. /MICHIGAN/
MICHIGAN FAIR EMPLOYMENT PRACTICES ADVISORY COUNCIL. GREATER
MUSKEGON, MICHIGAN. 1957.

GMICFEP60580   MICHIGAN FEPC
FOUR YEARS ON THE JOB IN MICHIGAN. /FEPC/
MICHIGAN FAIR EMPLOYMENT PRACTICES COMMISSION. LANSING,
MICHIGAN. JUNE 23 1960. 22 PP.

GMICFEP61982   MICHIGAN FEPC
PROCEEDINGS OF CONFERENCE ON EDUCATION FOR OPPORTUNITY,
OPPORTUNITY FOR EDUCATION.
MICHIGAN FAIR EMPLOYMENT PRACTICES COMMISSION. DETROIT,
MICHIGAN. FEB 9 1961. 33 PP.

GMICFEP61983   MICHIGAN FEPC
SPECIAL REPORT, AN INVESTIGATION OF THE PERSONNEL POLICIES
AND PRACTICES OF THE MICHIGAN STATE HIGHWAY DEPARTMENT,
MARCH 1961.
MICHIGAN FAIR EMPLOYMENT PRACTICES COMMISSION. LANSING,
MICHIGAN. 1961. 66 PP.

GMICFEP63981   MICHIGAN FEPC
MERIT EMPLOYMENT IN MICHIGAN. A PICTORIAL REPORT.
MICHIGAN FAIR EMPLOYMENT PRACTICES COMMISSION. LANSING,
MICHIGAN. 1963. 32 PP.

GMICSUSND584   MICH STATE U SCHOOL LABOR IR
CIVIL-RIGHTS AND EMPLOYMENT, SELECTED REFERENCES.
MICHIGAN STATE UNIVERSITY, SCHOOL OF LABOR AND INDUSTRIAL
RELATIONS, PERSONNEL MANAGEMENT PROGRAM SERVICE.
EAST LANSING, MICHIGAN. NO. 3 PP.

GMIDURX59573   MIDDLETON R   GRIGG CM
RURAL-URBAN DIFFERENCES IN ASPIRATIONS.
RURAL SOCIOLOGY, VOL 24, DEC 1959. PP 347-354.

GMILLAS55985   MILLER AS
GOVERNMENT CONTRACTS AND SOCIAL CONTROL. A PRELIMINARY
INQUIRY.
VIRGINIA LAW REVIEW, VOL 41, JAN 1955. PP 27-58.

GMILLGW64986   MILLER GW
EFFECTS ON THE ECONOMY. /EEO/
SYMPOSIUM. EQUAL EMPLOYMENT OPPORTUNITY, COMPANY POLICIES
AND EXPERIENCES. MANAGEMENT REVIEW, VOL 53, AP 1964.

GMILLHP55988   MILLER HP   *US BUREAU OF THE CENSUS
*SOCIAL SCI RESEARCH COUNCIL
INCOME OF THE AMERICAN PEOPLE.
WILEY. NEW YORK. 1955. PREPARED FOR THE SOCIAL SCIENCE
RESEARCH COUNCIL IN COOPERATION WITH THE US DEPARTMENT OF
COMMERCE, BUREAU OF THE CENSUS.

GMILLHP63987   MILLER HP
THE AMERICAN POOR.
THE NATION, VOL 196, JAN 26 1963. PP 65-68.

GMILLHP64853   MILLER HP   *US DEPARTMENT OF LABOR
THE FACE OF POVERTY IN THE UNITED STATES.
US DEPARTMENT OF LABOR, EMPLOYMENT SERVICE REVIEW, VOL 1,
JULY 1964. PP 19-23.

GMILLHP65656   MILLER HP
CHANGES IN THE NUMBER AND COMPOSITION OF THE POOR.
/DEMOGRAPHY/
POVERTY IN AMERICA. ED BY M S GORDON. CHANDLER PUBLISHING
CO. SAN FRANCISCO, CALIFORNIA. 1965. PP 81-101.

GMILLHP65952   MILLER HP
THE DIMENSIONS OF POVERTY.
POVERTY AS A PUBLIC ISSUE. ED BY BEN B SELIGMAN. THE FREE
PRESS. NEW YORK. 1965. PP 20-51.

GMILLHP66778   MILLER HP   *US BUREAU OF THE CENSUS
INCOME-DISTRIBUTION IN THE UNITED STATES. /DEMOGRAPHY/
US BUREAU OF THE CENSUS. GPO. WASHINGTON, DC. 1966. 306 PP.

GMILLHP66589   MILLER HP ED
POVERTY AMERICAN STYLE.
WADSWORTH PUBLISHING COMPANY, INC. BELMONT, CALIFORNIA.
1966.

GMILLRX66020   MILLER R   *MISSOURI COMM ON HUM RIGHTS
TECHNICAL REPORT NUMBER 1, EMPLOYMENT PRACTICES IN THE
HOTEL, MOTEL AND RESTAURANT INDUSTRY OF MISSOURI.
MISSOURI COMMISSION ON HUMAN RIGHTS. JEFFERSON CITY,
MISSOURI. 1966. 58 PLUS PP.

GMILLRX66021   MILLER R   *MISSOURI COMM ON HUM RIGHTS
TECHNICAL REPORT NUMBER 2, EMPLOYMENT PRACTICES OF SELECTED
MISSOURI PUBLIC UTILITIES. NATURAL GAS AND ELECTRIC.
MISSOURI COMMISSION ON HUMAN RIGHTS. JEFFERSON CITY,
MISSOURI. 1966. 48 PP.

GMILLSM62354   MILLER SM
DROPOUTS. A POLITICAL PROBLEM. /EMPLOYMENT/
NATIONAL ECUATION ASSOCIATION. SYMPOSIUM ON SCHOOL DROPOUTS.
PAPER. WASHINGTON, DC. DEC 2-4 1962.

GMILLSM62570   MILLER SM
THE OUTLOOK OF WORKING CLASS YOUTH. /DROP-OUT ASPIRATION/
AMERICAN SOCIOLOGICAL ASSOCIATION, ANNUAL MEETINGS. PAPER.
WASHINGTON, DC. MIMEOGRAPHED. AUG 1962. 17 PP.

GMILLSM64071   MILLER SM   SALEEM BL
BRYCE H   *SYRACUSE U YOUTH DEVEL CENT
SCHOOL DROPOUTS. A COMMENTARY AND ANNOTATED BIBLIOGRAPHY.
SYRACUSE UNIVERSITY, YOUTH DEVELOPMENT CENTER. SYRACUSE,
NEW YORK. 1964. 131 PP.

GMILLSM64727   MILLER SM
THE AMERICAN LOWER-CLASSES. A TYPOLOGICAL APPROACH.
SOCIAL RESEARCH, VOL 31, NO 1, SPRING 1964. PP 1-22.

GMILLSM65553   MILLER SM   REIN M
THE WAR-ON-POVERTY. PERSPECTIVES AND PROSPECTS.
POVERTY AS A PUBLIC ISSUE. ED BY BEN B SELIGMAN. THE FREE
PRESS. NEW YORK. 1965 PP 272-320.

GMINLMH65002   MINNEAPOLIS MAYORS HUM RELS
SURVEY AND ANALYSIS OF NON-WHITE EMPLOYMENT BY THE CITY OF
MINNEAPOLIS. /MINNESOTA/
MINNEAPOLIS MAYOR-S COMMISSION ON HUMAN RELATIONS.
MINNEAPOLIS, MINNESOTA. 1965. 12 PLUS PP.

GMINVSCND010   MINN STATE COMM AGAINST DISCR
MINNESOTA STATE ACT AGAINST DISCRIMINATION, AS APPROVED BY
THE MINNESOTA LEGISLATURE, APRIL 1961. /LEGISLATION/
MINNESOTA STATE COMMISSION AGAINST DISCRIMINATION. ST PAUL,
MINNESOTA. ND. 14 PP.

GMINSHX65655   MINSKY H
THE ROLE OF EMPLOYMENT POLICY. /ANTI-POVERTY/
POVERTY IN AMERICA. ED BY M S GORDON. CHANDLER PUBLISHING
CO. SAN FRANCISCO, CALIFORNIA. 1965. PP 175-200.

GMINSJX65012   MINSKY J
FEPC IN ILLINOIS. FOUR STORMY YEARS.
NOTRE DAME LAWYER, VOL 41, 1965. PP 152-181.

GMIREMX59013   MIRES M
HEALTH PROBLEMS OF MIGRANT-LABOR.
DELAWARE STATE MEDICAL JOURNAL, SEPT 1959. PP 281-284.

GMIREWX57499   MIRENGOFF W   *US DEPARTMENT OF LABOR
THE STRUCTURE OF THE FARM LABOR-MARKET AND MIGRATION
PATTERNS.
US DEPARTMENT OF LABOR, BUREAU OF EMPLOYMENT SECURITY.
CONSULTATION ON MIGRATORY FARM LABOR, PROCEEDINGS. GPO.
WASHINGTON, DC. 1957.

GMISSCH63022   MISSOURI COMM ON HUM RIGHTS
MISSOURI LOCAL GOVERNMENT ACTION IN THE AREA OF
HUMAN-RIGHTS.
MISSOURI COMMISSION ON HUMAN RIGHTS. JEFFERSON CITY,
MISSOURI. SEPT 1963. 30 PP.

GMITCBX57017   MITCHELL B
ECONOMICS IN THE SOUTH.
CURRENT HISTORY, VOL 32, 1957. PP 267-272.

GMITCHR66018   MITCHELL HR   *US DEPARTMENT OF LABOR
WHAT TITLE-VII MEANS FOR THE LOCAL OFFICE. /SES/
US DEPARTMENT OF LABOR, EMPLOYMENT SERVICE REVIEW, VOL 3,
NO 8. AUG 1966. PP 7-8, 10.

GMITCJA52016   MITCHAM JA   *US LIBRARY OF CONGRESS LRS
FAIR-EMPLOYMENT-PRACTICES LEGISLATION, A SUMMARY OF ITS
HISTORY AND DEVELOPMENT WITH STATEMENTS ON BOTH SIDES.
US LIBRARY OF CONGRESS, LEGISLATIVE REFERENCE SERVICE. GPO.
WASHINGTON, DC. SEPT 1952. 45 PP.

GMITCJP59954   MITCHELL JP   *US DEPARTMENT OF LABOR
MIGRANT-LABOR--THE NATIONAL RESPONSIBILITY.
US DEPARTMENT OF LABOR. SPEECH TEXT NO 3007. GPO.
WASHINGTON, DC. NOV 22 1959.

GMITCJP64277   MITCHELL JP   *SAN FRANCISCO MAYOR-S OFFICE
A HUMAN-RELATIONS PROGRAM FOR SAN-FRANCISCO. /CALIFORNIA/
SAN FRANCISCO OFFICE OF THE MAYOR. SAN FRANCISCO,
CALIFORNIA. JAN 2 1964. 31 PP.

GMOBIFY65C25   MOBILIZATION FOR YOUTH INC
MASTER ANNOTATED BIBLIOGRAPHY OF PAPERS OF
MOBILIZATION-FOR-YOUTH. PUBLISHED, UNPUBLISHED AND
PRESENTED AT CONFERENCES.
MOBILIZATION FOR YOUTH, INC, TRAINING DEPARTMENT. NEW YORK.
1965. 81 PP.

GMOEDMX66852   MOED M   *NYU CENT STUDY UNEMP YOUTH
INCREASING EMPLOYABILITY OF YOUTH. THE ROLE OF WORK
TRAINING.
NEW YORK UNIVERSITY, GRADUATE SCHOOL OF SOCIAL WORK, CENTER
FOR THE STUDY OF UNEMPLOYED YOUTH. NEW YORK. FEB 1966.
19 PP.

GMOONJD66726   MOONEY JD
TEENAGE LABOR PROBLEMS AND THE NEIGHBORHOOD-YOUTH-CORPS.
CRITICAL ISSUES IN EMPLOYMENT POLICY. ED BY F H HARBISON AND
J D MOONEY. PRINCETON UNIVERSITY, INDUSTRIAL RELATIONS
SECTION. PRINCETON, NEW JERSEY. 1966. PP 95-117.

GMOOREJ64030   MOORE EJ
THE LOW-INCOME PROBLEM IN AGRICULTURE.
42ND ANNUAL AGRICULTURAL OUTLOOK CONFERENCE. SPEECH.
WASHINGTON, DC. NOV 17 1964.

GMOOREJ64386   MOORE EJ   BAUM EL
GLASGOW RB   *US DEPARTMENT OF AGRICULTURE
ECONOMIC FACTORS INFLUENCING EDUCATIONAL-ATTAINMENTS AND
ASPIRATIONS OF FARM YOUTH.
US DEPARTMENT OF AGRICULTURE. GPO. WASHINGTON, DC. AP 1964.
43 PP.

GMORGCA57031   MORGAN CA
AN ANALYSIS OF STATE FEPC LEGISLATION.
LABOR LAW JOURNAL, VOL 8, JULY 1957. PP 469-478.

GMORGJN62032 MORGAN JN   DAVID M
              COHEN W   BRAZER H
              INCOME AND WELFARE IN THE UNITED STATES.
              MCGRAW HILL. NEW YORK. 1962. 531 PP.

GMOTHJR54405 MOTHER JR   THOMAS HE
              LARSON OF
              MIGRATORY FARM WORKERS IN THE ATLANTIC COAST STREAM. WESTERN
              NEW-YORK, JUNE 1953.
              CORNELL UNIVERSITY. ITHACA, NEW YORK. JUNE 1954. 30 PP.

GMOTLAW53033 MOTLEY AW   *US DEPARTMENT OF LABOR
              RECENT TRENDS IN THE TEST SELECTION OF APPRENTICES.
              US DEPARTMENT OF LABOR, MONTHLY LABOR REVIEW, VOL 76, 1953.
              P 1068.

GMULFRH66116 MULFORD RH
              THE INTEGRATED WORK-FORCE. WHERE ARE WE NOW.
              MANAGEMENT REVIEW, NOV 1966. PP 4-13.

GMURRPX50034 MURRAY P ED   *WOMANS DIV CHRISTIAN SERVICE
              STATES LAWS ON RACE AND COLOR.
              WOMAN-S DIVISION OF CHRISTIAN SERVICE. NO PLACE GIVEN. 1950.
              745 PP.

GMYERCA66527 MYERS CA
              THE ROLE OF THE EMPLOYER IN MANPOWER POLICY. /INDUSTRY/
              PAPER, CONFERENCE ON MANPOWER POLICY, BERKELEY UNEMPLOYMENT
              PROJECT, NEW YORK. JUNE 20-22, 1966. 21 PP.

GMYRDGX63035 MYRDAL G
              CHALLENGE TO AFFLUENCE. /UNEMPLOYMENT/
              PANTHEON BOOKS. NEW YORK. 1963.

GMYRDGX64851 MYRDAL G
              THE WAR ON POVERTY.
              NEW REPUBLIC, VOL 150, FEB 8 1964. PP 14-17.

GMYRDGX64555 MYRDAL G
              THE MATRIX. /POVERTY UNEMPLOYMENT/
              POVERTY IN PLENTY. ED BY G H DUNNE. PJ KENNEDY AND SONS.
              NEW YORK. 1964. PP 118-142.

GNAACNL45036 NAACP NATL LEGAL COMMITTEE   *AM COUNCIL ON RACE RELATIONS
              A MODEL STATE FAIR-EMPLOYMENT-PRACTICE BILL.
              AMERICAN COUNCIL ON RACE RELATIONS. CLEARING HOUSE RELEASE
              NO 2. CHICAGO, ILLINOIS. FEB 28 1945. 9 PP.

GNATLAI49038 NAIRO
              IMPLEMENTATION OF THE FEDERAL FAIR-EMPLOYMENT POLICY.
              NATIONAL ASSOCIATION OF INTERGROUP RELATIONS OFFICIALS.
              CHICAGO, ILLINOIS. JULY 13 1949. 15 PP.

GNATLAM60C37 NAIRO COMM ON MANPOWER
              GUIDANCE, TRAINING AND APPRENTICESHIP FACTORS AFFECTING
              MINORITY-GROUPS.
              NAIRO COMMISSION ON MANPOWER UTILIZATION, SPECIAL REPORT,
              JOURNAL OF INTERGROUP RELATIONS, FEB 1960, ENTIRE ISSUE.

GNATLBE66611 NATL BUREAU OF EC RESEARCH
              THE MEASUREMENT AND INTERPRETATION OF JOB VACANCIES. A
              CONFERENCE REPORT OF THE NATIONAL BUREAU OF ECONOMIC
              RESEARCH. /LABOR-MARKET/
              NATIONAL BUREAU OF ECONOMIC RESEARCH. NEW YORK. 1966.
              593 PP.

GNATLCC61039 NATL COMT CHILDREN YOUTH
              SOCIAL DYNAMITE. THE REPORT OF THE CONFERENCE ON UNEMPLOYED,
              OUT-OF-SCHOOL YOUTH IN URBAN AREAS, MAY 24-26, 1961.
              NATIONAL COMMITTEE FOR CHILDREN AND YOUTH. WASHINGTON, DC.
              1961. 265 PP.

GNATLCJ48040 NATL COM RELS ADVISORY CC
              FEPC REFERENCE MANUAL.
              NATIONAL COMMUNITY RELATIONS ADVISORY COUNCIL, COMMISSION ON
              EMPLOYMENT DISCRIMINATION 1948. NEW YORK. 70 PP.

GNATLCL49042 NATL CONF CHRISTIANS AND JEWS
              INTER-GROUP RELATIONS WITHIN LABOR AND INDUSTRY.
              NATIONAL CONFERENCE OF CHRISTIANS AND JEWS. NEW YORK. 1949.
              90 PP.

GNATLCL54041 NATL CONF CHRISTIANS AND JEWS
              A FAIR CHANCE FOR ALL AMERICANS.
              NATIONAL CONFERENCE OF CHRISTIANS AND JEWS. NEW YORK. 1954.
              18 PP.

GNATLCN55044 NATL CONF ON SOCIAL WELFARE
              MINORITY-GROUPS. SEGREGATION AND INTEGRATION.
              COLUMBIA UNIVERSITY PRESS. NEW YORK. 1955.

GNATLCO66897 NATL COMM TECH AUTOM EC PRGR
              THE OUTLOOK FOR TECHNOLOGICAL-CHANGE AND EMPLOYMENT.
              TECHNOLOGY AND THE AMERICAN ECONOMY. NATIONAL COMMISSION ON
              TECHNOLOGY, AUTOMATION AND ECONOMIC PROGRESS. GPO.
              WASHINGTON, DC. FEB 1966. APPENDIX VOLUME I. 371 PP.

GNATLCO66898 NATL COMM TECH AUTOM EC PRGR
              EDUCATIONAL IMPLICATIONS OF TECHNOLOGICAL-CHANGE.
              TECHNOLOGY AND THE AMERICAN ECONOMY. NATIONAL COMMISSION ON
              TECHNOLOGY, AUTOMATION, AND ECONOMIC PROGRESS. GPO.
              WASHINGTON, DC. FEB 1966. APPENDIX VOLUME 4. 150 PP.

GNATLCRND046 NATIONAL CC OF CHURCHES
              AN EXPERIMENT IN VOCATIONAL EDUCATION FOR CHILDREN OF
              MIGRATORY FARM WORKERS, JULY-AUGUST 1956.
              NATIONAL COUNCIL OF CHURCHES, MIGRANT MINISTRY. NEW YORK.
              12 PP. ND.

GNATLCS45045 NATL CC FOR A PERMANENT FEPC
              DIGEST OF FINDINGS FROM A WORKING CONFERENCE OF LOCAL
              COUNCILS. /FEPC/
              NATIONAL COUNCIL FOR A PERMANENT FAIR EMPLOYMENT PRACTICES
              COMMISSION. WASHINGTON, DC. SEPT 1945. 21 PP.

GNATLCT66602 NATL COMM TECH AUTOM EC PRGR
              TECHNOLOGY AND THE AMERICAN ECONOMY.
              NATIONAL COMMISSION ON TECHNOLOGY, AUTOMATION, AND ECONOMIC
              PROGRESS. REPORT. WASHINGTON, DC. 1966.

GNATLCT66848 NATL COMM TECH AUTOM EC PRGR
              STATEMENTS RELATING TO THE IMPACT OF TECHNOLOGICAL-CHANGE.
              /INDUSTRY/
              TECHNOLOGY AND THE AMERICAN ECONOMY. NATIONAL COMMISSION ON
              TECHNOLOGY, AUTOMATION, AND ECONOMIC PROGRESS.
              WASHINGTON, DC. FEB 1966. APPENDIX VOLUME VI. 307 PP.

GNATLCT66849 NATL COMM TECH AUTOM EC PRGR
              THE EMPLOYMENT IMPACT OF TECHNOLOGICAL-CHANGE.

TECHNOLOGY AND THE AMERICAN ECONOMY. NATIONAL COMMISSION ON
TECHNOLOGY, AUTOMATION, AND ECONOMIC PROGRESS.
WASHINGTON, DC. FEB 1966. APPENDIX VOLUME II. 397 PP.

GNATLCT66850 NATL COMM TECH AUTOM EC PRGR
              ADJUSTING TO CHANGE. /TECHNOLOGICAL-CHANGE/
              TECHNOLOGY AND THE AMERICAN ECONOMY. NATIONAL COMMISSION ON
              TECHNOLOGY, AUTOMATION, AND ECONOMIC PROGRESS. GPO.
              WASHINGTON, DC. FEB 1966. APPENDIX VOLUME III. 274 PP.

GNATLEA56047 NATIONAL EDUCATION ASSN
              MANPOWER AND EDUCATION.
              NATIONAL EDUCATION ASSOCIATION, EDUCATIONAL POLICIES
              COMMISSION. WASHINGTON, DC. 1956. 128 PP.

GNATLEA62126 NATIONAL EDUCATION ASSN
              EDUCATION AND THE DISADVANTAGED AMERICAN.
              NATIONAL EDUCATION ASSOCIATION, EDUCATIONAL POLICIES
              COMMISSION. WASHINGTON, DC. 1962. 39 PP.

GNATLFC46048 NATL FEDN CONSTL LIBERTIES
              EVERYBODY-S BUSINESS, A SUMMARY OF NEW-YORK STATE
              ANTI-DISCRIMINATION LAWS AND HOW TO USE THEM.
              NATIONAL FEDERATION FOR CONSTITUTIONAL LIBERTIES. NEW YORK.
              1946.

GNATLIC65593 NATL INDUSTRIAL CONF BOARD
              THE PRACTICE OF RACIAL DEMOCRACY.
              NATIONAL INDUSTRIAL CONFERENCE BOARD, CONFERENCE BOARD
              RECORD, VOL 2, JUNE 1965. PP 14-18.

GNATLLS55051 NATL LABOR SERVICE
              YOUR RIGHTS... UNDER STATE AND LOCAL
              FAIR-EMPLOYMENT-PRACTICES LAWS.
              NATIONAL LABOR SERVICE. NEW YORK. 1955. 32 PP.

GNATLLS57049 NATL LABOR SERVICE
              THE PEOPLE TAKE THE LEAD. A RECORD OF PROGRESS IN
              CIVIL-RIGHTS, 1948-1957.
              NATIONAL LABOR SERVICE. NEW YORK. 1957.

GNATLLS63050 NATL LABOR SERVICE
              THE PEOPLE TAKE THE LEAD. A RECORD OF PROGRESS IN
              CIVIL-RIGHTS, 1948-1963.
              NATIONAL LABOR SERVICE, INSTITUTE OF HUMAN RELATIONS.
              NEW YORK. 1963. PP 18-26.

GNATLMC54876 NATIONAL MANPOWER COUNCIL
              A POLICY FOR SKILLED MANPOWER.
              NATIONAL MANPOWER COUNCIL. COLUMBIA UNIVERSITY PRESS.
              NEW YORK. 1954. 228 PP.

GNATLMC55052 NATL MANPOWER COUNCIL
              IMPROVING THE WORK SKILLS OF THE NATION.
              COLUMBIA UNIVERSITY PRESS. NEW YORK. 1955.

GNATLMC64956 NATL MANPOWER COUNCIL
              GOVERNMENT AND MANPOWER. /POLICY-RECOMMENDATIONS/
              COLUMBIA UNIVERSITY PRESS. NEW YORK. 1964. 470 PP.

GNATLSF57299 NATL SHARECROPPERS FUND
              PROCEEDINGS OF THE NATIONAL-SHARECROPPERS-FUND CONFERENCE ON
              MIGRATORY LABOR AND LOW-INCOME FARMERS. NOVEMBER 13 1957.
              NATIONAL SHARECROPPERS FUND, INC. NEW YORK. 1957.

GNATLULND085 NATIONAL URBAN LEAGUE
              PROFILE IN BLACK AND WHITE. DISCRIMINATION AND INEQUALITY OF
              OPPORTUNITY.
              NATIONAL URBAN LEAGUE, RESEARCH DEPARTMENT. NEW YORK. 5 PP.

GNATLUL65C84 NATIONAL URBAN LEAGUE
              FACTS ON THE MANY FACES OF POVERTY.
              NATIONAL URBAN LEAGUE. NEW YORK. 1965. 15 PP.

GNAVIPX57007 NAVILLE P
              THE STRUCTURE OF UNEMPLOYMENT AND AUTOMATION.
              INTERNATIONAL SOCIAL SCIENCE BULLETIN, VOL 9, FEB 1957.
              PP 16-30.

GNEBRLR62C86 NEBRASKA LAW REVIEW
              MUNICIPAL FAIR-EMPLOYMENT-PRACTICES IN NEBRASKA.
              NEBRASKA LAW REVIEW, VOL 41, JUNE 1962. PP 816-825.

GNEISEG63054 NEISSER EG
              SCHOOL FAILURES AND DROPOUTS.
              PUBLIC AFFAIRS COMMITTEE, INC, PUBLIC AFFAIRS PAMPHLET
              NO 346. NEW YORK. 1963. 28 PP.

GNELSRJ52055 NELSON RJ   *UNIV OF MINN IND RELS CENTER
              SELECTED ANNOTATED REFERENCES ON FAIR-EMPLOYMENT-PRACTICES
              LEGISLATION.
              UNIVERSITY OF MINNESOTA, INDUSTRIAL RELATIONS CENTER.
              MINNEAPOLIS, MINNESOTA. DEC 1952. 6 PP.

GNEWCMR66163 NEWCOMB MR
              PROBLEMS, RESEARCH, AND RECOMMENDATIONS IN THE EMPLOYMENT
              TESTING OF MINORITY-GROUP APPLICANTS.
              THE UNIVERSITY OF MICHIGAN-WAYNE STATE UNIVERSITY, INSTITUTE
              OF LABOR AND INDUSTRIAL RELATIONS. ANN ARBOR, MICHIGAN.
              1966. 62 PP.

GNEWJCC66056 NEW JERSEY COMM CIVIL RIGHTS
              REPORT ON SECOND ANNUAL SPRING CONFERENCE ON CIVIL-RIGHTS OF
              NEW-JERSEY COMMISSION-ON-CIVIL-RIGHTS, APRIL 23, 1966.
              NEW JERSEY COMMISSION ON CIVIL RIGHTS. TRENTON, NEW JERSEY.
              1966. 29 PP.

GNEWJDE46C59 NEW JERSEY DEPT OF EDUCATION
              REPORT OF A PRELIMINARY STUDY OF EMPLOYMENT PRACTICES
              INVOLVING MINORITY-GROUP WORKERS, ESSEX-COUNTY,
              NEW-JERSEY.
              NEW JERSEY DEPARTMENT OF EDUCATION, DIVISION AGAINST
              DISCRIMINATION. TRENTON, NEW JERSEY. NOV 1946. 7 PP.

GNEWJDE51060 NEW JERSEY DEPT OF EDUCATION
              REPORT ON A SURVEY OF EMPLOYMENT POLICIES AND HIRING
              PRACTICES INVOLVING MINORITY-GROUPS IN HUDSON-COUNTY,
              NEW-JERSEY.
              NEW JERSEY DEPARTMENT OF EDUCATION, DIVISION AGAINST
              DISCRIMINATION. TRENTON, NEW JERSEY. JULY 1951. 14 PP.

GNEWJDE52061 NEW JERSEY DEPT OF EDUCATION
              REPORT ON A SURVEY OF EMPLOYMENT POLICIES AND PRACTICES
              INVOLVING MINORITY-GROUPS IN MIDDLESEX-COUNTY, NEW-JERSEY.
              NEW JERSEY DEPARTMENT OF EDUCATION, DIVISION AGAINST
              DISCRIMINATION. TRENTON, NEW JERSEY. JULY 1952. 13 PP.

GNEWXYL51100 NEW YORK LAW JOURNAL
              PATTERNS OF CONCILIATION UNDER THE NEW-YORK STATE LAW
              AGAINST DISCRIMINATION.

NEW YORK LAW JOURNAL, AP 6, 9, 11, 11 AND 12 1951 ISSUES.
ALSO NEW YORK STATE COMMISSION AGAINST DISCRIMINATION,
REPRINT. ND. 16 PP.

GNEWYCA64068 NEW YORK CHAMBER OF COMMERCE
THE CIVIL-RIGHTS-ACT, IMPLICATIONS FOR BUSINESS.
NEW YORK CHAMBER OF COMMERCE. NEW YORK. 1964. 31 PP.

GNEWYCB53069 NEW YORK BAR ASSOCIATION
REPORT WITH RECOMMENDATIONS ON THE SUBJECT OF FEDERAL
FAIR-EMPLOYMENT-PRACTICES LEGISLATION.
NEW YORK CITY ASSOCIATION OF THE BAR, COMMITTEE ON LABOR AND
SOCIAL SECURITY LEGISLATION. NEW YORK. OCT 1953.

GNEWYLF60075 NEW YORK LAW FORUM
A SELECTIVE BIBLIOGRAPHY ON DISCRIMINATION IN HOUSING AND
EMPLOYMENT.
NEW YORK LAW FORUM, VOL 6, NO 1, 1960. PP 114-117.

GNEWYSAND084 NY STATE COMM AGAINST DISCR
MANAGEMENT AND MERIT EMPLOYMENT.
NEW YORK STATE COMMISSION AGAINST DISCRIMINATION. ALBANY,
NEW YORK. ND. PP.

GNEWYSA47107 NY STATE COMM AGAINST DISCR
THE NEW-YORK STATE COMMISSION AGAINST DISCRIMINATION. A NEW
TECHNIQUE FOR AN OLD PROBLEM.
YALE LAW JOURNAL, VOL 56, MAY 1947. PP 837-862.

GNEWYSA48078 NY STATE COMM AGAINST DISCR
COMPILATION OF LAWS AGAINST DISCRIMINATION, A REFERENCE
MANUAL.
NEW YORK STATE COMMISSION AGAINST DISCRIMINATION. NEW YORK.
1948. 172 PP.

GNEWYSA52102 NY STATE COMM AGAINST DISCR
NEW-YORK STATE-COMMISSION-AGAINST-DISCRIMINATION, STATEMENT
BEFORE THE US SENATE SUBCOMMITTEE ON LABOR AND
LABOR-MANAGEMENT RELATIONS.
NEW YORK STATE COMMISSION AGAINST DISCRIMINATION. NEW YORK.
AP 1952. 17 PP.

GNEWYSA54077 NY STATE COMM AGAINST DISCR
COMMUNICATIONS EMPLOYEES AND GOOD SERVICE. /NEW-YORK/
NEW YORK STATE COMMISSION AGAINST DISCRIMINATION. NEW YORK.
1954. 17 PP.

GNEWYSA57C86 NY STATE COMM AGAINST DISCR
MANPOWER UNLIMITED. /INDUSTRY INTEGRATION/
NEW YORK STATE COMMISSION AGAINST DISCRIMINATION. NEW YORK.
APRIL 1957. 24 PP.

GNEWYSA58076 NY STATE COMM AGAINST DISCR
THE BANKING INDUSTRY. VERIFIED COMPLAINTS AND INFORMAL
INVESTIGATIONS. /NEW-YORK/
NEW YORK STATE COMMISSION AGAINST DISCRIMINATION. NEW YORK.
1958.

GNEWYSA58C79 NY STATE COMM AGAINST DISCR
EMPLOYMENT IN DEPARTMENT STORES. /NEW-YORK/
NEW YORK STATE COMMISSION AGAINST DISCRIMINATION. NEW YORK.
1958. 22 PP.

GNEWYSA58081 NY STATE COMM AGAINST DISCR
EMPLOYMENT IN THE HOTEL INDUSTRY. /NEW-YORK/
NEW YORK STATE COMMISSION AGAINST DISCRIMINATION. NEW YORK.
MAR 1958. 52 PP.

GNEWYSA58082 NY STATE COMM AGAINST DISCR
THE INSURANCE INDUSTRY -- VERIFIED COMPLAINTS AND INFORMAL
INVESTIGATIONS HANDLED BY THE NEW-YORK STATE COMMISSION
AGAINST DISCRIMINATION, JULY 1 1945-SEPTEMBER 15, 1958.
NEW YORK STATE COMMISSION AGAINST DISCRIMINATION. NEW YORK.
19 PP.

GNEWYSA58C89 NY STATE COMM AGAINST DISCR
WHITE UNEMPLOYMENT IN THE UNITED STATES, 1947-1958, AN
ANALYSIS OF TRENDS.
NEW YORK STATE COMMISSION AGAINST DISCRIMINATION, DIVISION
OF RESEARCH TREND REPORTS, NO 2. NEW YORK. APRIL 1958.
7 PP.

GNEWYSA58101 NY STATE COMM AGAINST DISCR   NEW JERSEY DEPT OF EDUCATION
RAILROAD, EMPLOYMENT IN THE NEW-YORK AND NEW-JERSEY.
NEW YORK STATE COMMISSION AGAINST DISCRIMINATION AND NEW
JERSEY DEPARTMENT OF EDUCATION, DIVISION AGAINST
DISCRIMINATION. 1958. 35 PP.

GNEWYSA59083 NY STATE COMM AGAINST DISCR
INVESTIGATION OF CHARGES OF DISCRIMINATORY PRACTICES IN THE
NEW-YORK STATE-EMPLOYMENT-SERVICE.
NEW YORK STATE COMMISSION AGAINST DISCRIMINATION. NEW YORK.
MAY 1959.

GNEWYSBND106 NYS COMM FOR HUMAN RIGHTS
RULINGS ON PRE-EMPLOYMENT INQUIRIES RELATING TO RACE, CREED,
COLOR OR NATIONAL ORIGIN UNDER THE NEW-YORK STATE LAW
AGAINST DISCRIMINATION.
NEW YORK STATE COMMISSION FOR HUMAN RIGHTS. NEW YORK. ND.
20 PP.

GNEWYSB62103 NYS COMM FOR HUMAN RIGHTS
THE NEXT STEPS TOWARD EQUALITY OF OPPORTUNITY IN THE
SYRACUSE METROPOLITAN AREA. REPORT OF THE SYRACUSE
CONFERENCE ON HUMAN RIGHTS AND HOUSING, JULY 2-3 1962.
/NEW-YORK/
NEW YORK STATE COMMISSION FOR HUMAN RIGHTS. SYRACUSE,
NEW YORK. 1962. 65 PP.

GNEWYSB63105 NYS COMM FOR HUMAN RIGHTS
REPORT ON EMPLOYMENT AND IMAGE OF MINORITY-GROUPS ON
TELEVISION.
NEW YORK STATE COMMISSION FOR HUMAN RIGHTS. NEW YORK. APRIL
1963. 14 PP.

GNEWYSB64104 NYS COMM FOR HUMAN RIGHTS   CONWAY JE
REPORT OF INQUIRY CONCERNING CHARGES OF DISCRIMINATING
PRACTICES IN THE NEW-YORK STATE THRUWAY AUTHORITY.
NEW YORK STATE COMMISSION FOR HUMAN RIGHTS. NEW YORK. JUNE
1964. 33 PP.

GNEWYSE58109 NY STATE DEPARTMENT OF LABOR
MIGRANT FARM LABOR IN NEW-YORK.
NEW YORK STATE DEPARTMENT OF LABOR, INDUSTRIAL BULLETIN.
ALBANY, NEW YORK. JUNE 1958.

GNEWYSE60108 NY STATE DEPARTMENT OF LABOR
JOBS, 1960-1970. THE CHANGING PATTERN. /EMPLOYMENT-TRENDS/
NEW YORK STATE DEPARTMENT OF LABOR. ALBANY, NEW YORK. 1960.

GNEWYSE60110 NY STATE DEPARTMENT OF LABOR
EMPLOYMENT AND EARNINGS OF MIGRANT FARM WORKERS IN NEW-YORK
STATE.
NEW YORK STATE DEPARTMENT OF LABOR, PUBLICATION NO B-116.
ALBANY, NEW YORK. AUG 1960.

GNEWYSJND113 NYS IDEPTL COMM FARM AND FOOD
SUMMARY OF RULES, REGULATIONS, AND LAWS THAT AFFECT SEASONAL
FARM WORKERS AND THEIR EMPLOYERS IN NEW-YORK STATE.
/MIGRANT-WORKERS/
NEW YORK STATE INTERDEPARTMENTAL COMMITTEE ON FARM AND FOOD
PROCESSING LABOR, DEPARTMENT OF AGRICULTURE AND MARKETS.
ALBANY, NEW YORK. ISSUED ANNUALLY.

GNEWYSJ63112 NYS IDEPTL COMM FARM AND FOOD
MIGRANT FARM LABOR IN NEW-YORK STATE.
NEW YORK STATE INTERDEPARTMENTAL COMMISSION ON FARM AND FOOD
PROCESSING. ALBANY, NEW YORK. 1963. 16 PP.

GNEWYSLND115 NYS JOINT LEGV COMT MIG LAB
REPORT OF NEW-YORK STATE JOINT LEGISLATIVE COMMITTEE ON
MIGRANT-LABOR.
NEW YORK STATE JOINT LEGISLATIVE COMMITTEE ON MIGRANT LABOR.
ALBANY, NEW YORK. ISSUED ANNUALLY.

GNEWYSX63087 NEW YORK STATE
A HELPING HAND, SEASONAL FARM LABOR IN NEW-YORK STATE.
/MIGRANT-WORKERS/
ALBANY, NEW YORK. 1963. 11 PP.

GNEWYUC66116 NYU CENT STUDY UNEMP YOUTH
SUMMARY OF PROCEEDINGS. WORKSHOP ON THE IMPACT OF A
TIGHTENING LABOR-MARKET ON THE EMPLOYABILITY AND
EMPLOYMENT OF DISADVANTAGED YOUTH.
NEW YORK UNIVERSITY, CENTER FOR THE STUDY OF UNEMPLOYED
YOUTH. NEW YORK. AP 20-21 1966.

GNIXORA66847 NIXON RA   *NYU CENT STUDY UNEMP YOUTH
FEDERAL LEGISLATION FOR A COMPREHENSIVE PROGRAM ON YOUTH
EMPLOYMENT.
NEW YORK UNIVERSITY, GRADUATE SCHOOL OF SOCIAL WORK, CENTER
FOR THE STUDY OF UNEMPLOYED YOUTH. NEW YORK. MAY 1966.
23 PP.

GNIXORM56117 NIXON RM   *ANTI-DEFAMATION LEAGUE
FAIR PLAY STARTS WITH THE BOSS.
/EMPLOYMENT DISCRIMINATION/
ANTI-DEFAMATION LEAGUE OF B-NAI B-RITH, ADL BULLETIN,
FEB 1956.

GNORGPH62120 NORGREN PH
GOVERNMENTAL FAIR-EMPLOYMENT AGENCIES. AN APPRAISAL OF
FEDERAL, STATE, AND MUNICIPAL EFFORTS TO END JOB
DISCRIMINATION.
INDUSTRIAL RELATIONS RESEARCH ASSOCIATION, 14TH ANNUAL
MEETING, PROCEEDINGS. MADISON, WISCONSIN. 1962. PP 120-138.

GNORGPH64091 NORGREN PH   HILL SE
TOWARD FAIR-EMPLOYMENT.
COLUMBIA UNIVERSITY PRESS. NEW YORK. 1964.

GNORGPH64119 NORGREN PH
GOVERNMENT CONTRACTS AND FAIR-EMPLOYMENT-PRACTICES.
LAW AND CONTEMPORARY PROBLEMS, VOL 29, NO 1. WINTER 1964.
PP 225-237.

GNORTCG64121 N CAROLINA GOOD NEIGHBOR CC
SURVEY OF EMPLOYMENT IN STATE GOVERNMENT. /NORTH-CAROLINA/
NORTH CAROLINA GOOD NEIGHBOR COUNCIL. RALEIGH,
NORTH CAROLINA. OCT 1964. REVISED ED, AUG 1966. 43 PP.

GNORTDL64093 NOTRE DAME LAWYER
MUNICIPAL FAIR-EMPLOYMENT ORDINANCES AS A VALID EXERCISE OF
THE POLICE POWER.
NOTRE DAME LAWYER, VOL 39, 1964. PP 607-613.

GNORTHR47123 NORTHRUP HR
PROVING GROUND FOR FAIR-EMPLOYMENT. SOME LESSONS FROM
NEW-YORK STATE-S EXPERIENCE.
COMMENTARY, VOL 4, DEC 1947. PP 552-556.

GNORTHR52122 NORTHRUP HR
PROGRESS WITHOUT FEDERAL COMPULSION. ARGUING THE CASE FOR
COMPROMISE METHODS.
COMMENTARY, VOL 14, SEPT 1952. PP 206-211.

GNORTMT45124 NORTON MT
QUESTIONS AND ANSWERS ABOUT PERMANENT
FAIR-EMPLOYMENT-PRACTICES COMMISSIONS.
US HOUSE OF REPRESENTATIVES. SPEECH. GPO. WASHINGTON, DC.
AP 27 1945.

GNORTUL65672 NORTHWESTERN UNIV LAW REVIEW
THE CIVIL-RIGHTS-ACT OF 1964 -- SOURCE AND SCOPE OF
CONGRESSIONAL POWER.
NORTHWESTERN UNIVERSITY LAW REVIEW. VOL 60, NO 4,
SEPT-OCT 1965. PP 574-584.

GNOSOJSX62336 NOSOW S ED   FORM WH ED
MAN, WORK AND SOCIETY. A READER IN THE SOCIOLOGY OF
OCCUPATIONS.
BASIC BOOKS, INC. NEW YORK. 1962. 612 PP.

GOATEJF64542 OATES JF
PUBLIC POLICY AND UNEMPLOYMENT.
VITAL SPEECHES, VOL 30, NO 19, JULY 15 1964. P 594 FF.

GOHIOCR62132 OHIO CIVIL RIGHTS COMMISSION
SURVEY OF OHIO COLLEGE AND UNIVERSITY PLACEMENT OFFICES WITH
REGARD TO JOB PLACEMENT OF MINORITY STUDENTS.
OHIO CIVIL RIGHTS COMMISSION, COLUMBUS, OHIO. 1962.

GOHIOCR64129 OHIO CIVIL RIGHTS COMMISSION
RACIAL DISCRIMINATION IN THE CINCINNATI BUILDING TRADES.
A COMPREHENSIVE REPORT AND RECOMMENDATIONS. /OHIO/
OHIO CIVIL RIGHTS COMMISSION. COLUMBUS, OHIO. FEB 1964.
46 PP.

GOHIOCR65125 OHIO CIVIL RIGHTS COMMISSION
LAWS AGAINST DISCRIMINATION. EMPLOYMENT, PUBLIC
ACCOMODATIONS, HOUSING. /OHIO/
OHIO CIVIL RIGHTS COMMISSION. COLUMBUS, OHIO. 1965. 22 PP.

GOHIOCR66126 OHIO CIVIL RIGHTS COMMISSION
PATTERNS OF DISCRIMINATION IN THE GLASS AND MACHINE TOOL
INDUSTRIES IN OHIO.
OHIO CIVIL RIGHTS COMMISSION. COLUMBUS, OHIO. 1966.
21 PLUS PP.

GOHIOCR66127 OHIO CIVIL RIGHTS COMMISSION

PATTERNS OF DISCRIMINATION IN THE GLASS INDUSTRY IN OHIO.
OHIO CIVIL RIGHTS COMMISSION. COLUMBUS, OHIO. 1966.
14 PLUS PP.

GOHIOCR66128 OHIO CIVIL RIGHTS COMMISSION
PATTERNS OF DISCRIMINATION IN THE MACHINE TOOL INDUSTRY IN
OHIO.
OHIO CIVIL RIGHTS COMMISSION. COLUMBUS, OHIO. 1966.
15 PLUS PP.

GOHIOGC62095 OHIO GOVRS COMM CIVIL RIGHTS
MIGRATORY LABOR IN OHIO, A REPORT BY THE GOVERNOR-S
COMMITTEE, AUGUST 1962.
OHIO GOVERNOR-S COMMITTEE ON MIGRANT LABOR. COLUMBUS, OHIO.
1962. 38 PP.

GOKUNAX65133 OKUN A
THE BATTLE AGAINST UNEMPLOYMENT.
W W NORTON AND COMPANY. NEW YORK. 1965.

GOLIVWX60134 OLIVER W
STATEMENT TO THE COMMITTEE ON LEGISLATION IN SUPPORT OF AN
EFFECTIVE FEDERAL FEP LAW AND OTHER VITAL CIVIL-RIGHTS
LEGISLATION.
NATIONAL CONFERENCE ON CONSTITUTIONAL RIGHTS AND AMERICAN
FREEDOM, PARK SHERATON HOTEL. SPEECH. NEW YORK. OCT 11TH AND
12TH 1960. 2G PP.

GOREGBLND135 OREGON BUREAU OF LABOR
A GUIDE TO GOVERNMENT OFFICIALS. /CIVIL-RIGHTS/
OREGON BUREAU OF LABOR, CIVIL RIGHTS DIVISION. SALEM,
OREGON. 3 PP.

GOREGBLND138 OREGON BUREAU OF LABOR
42 QUESTIONS AND ANSWERS ABOUT FAIR-EMPLOYMENT-PRACTICES.
OREGON BUREAU OF LABOR, CIVIL RIGHTS DIVISION. PORTLAND,
OREGON. ND. 7 PP.

GOREGBLND139 OREGON BUREAU OF LABOR
RULES ON EMPLOYMENT INQUIRIES.
OREGON BUREAU OF LABOR, FAIR EMPLOYMENT PRACTICES DIVISION.
PORTLAND, OREGON. MIMEOGRAPHED. ND. 5 PP.

GORGAEC64776 ORGANISATION EC COOP DEVEL
MANPOWER POLICY AND PROGRAMMES IN THE UNITED STATES.
ORGANISATION FOR ECONOMIC COOPERATION AND DEVELOPMENT,
REVIEWS OF MANPOWER AND SOCIAL POLICIES. PARIS, FRANCE.
FEB 1964. 209 PP.

GORNAOA64140 ORNATI OA   *MOBILIZATION FOR YOUTH
POVERTY, AFFLUENCE AND OPPORTUNITY.
MOBILIZATION FOR YOUTH, INC. TRAINING INSTITUTE PROGRAM ON
URBAN COMMUNITY DEVELOPMENT PROJECTS. SELECTED ASPECTS OF
THE MOBILIZATION FOR YOUTH EXPERIENCE. NEW YORK. AP 27-MAY 1
1964. 10 PP.

GORNAOA64558 ORNATI OA
THE STRATEGY AND POLITICAL ECONOMY OF THE
WAR-AGAINST-POVERTY.
POVERTY IN PLENTY. ED BY G H DUNNE. P J KENEDY AND SONS.
NEW YORK. 1964. PP 81-90.

GORNAOA66320 ORNATI OA
POVERTY AMID AFFLUENCE.
TWENTIETH CENTURY FUND, INC. NEW YORK. 1966. 208 PP.

GORNAOA67138 ORNATI AO
POVERTY IN THE CITIES.
RESOURCES FOR THE FUTURE, CONFERENCE ON URBAN ECONOMICS,
PAPER. WASHINGTON, DC. JAN 26-28, 1967.

GORSHMX63141 ORSHANSKY M   *US DEPT OF HEALTH ED WELFARE
CHILDREN OF THE POOR.
US DEPARTMENT OF HEALTH, EDUCATION AND WELFARE, SOCIAL
SECURITY BULLETIN, JULY 1963. PP 3-13.

GORSHMX65142 ORSHANSKY M   *US DEPT OF HEALTH ED WELFARE
COUNTING THE POOR, ANOTHER LOOK AT THE POVERTY PROFILE.
US DEPARTMENT OF HEALTH, EDUCATION AND WELFARE, SOCIAL
SECURITY BULLETIN, JAN 1965. PP 3-29.

GORSHMX65144 ORSHANSKY M   *US DEPT OF HEALTH ED WELFARE
WHO-S WHO AMONG THE POOR.
US DEPARTMENT OF HEALTH, EDUCATION AND WELFARE, SOCIAL
SECURITY BULLETIN, JULY 1965. PP 3-32.

GORSHMX65959 ORSHANSKY M
CONSUMPTION, WORK, AND POVERTY.
POVERTY AS A PUBLIC ISSUE. ED BY BEN B SELIGMAN. THE FREE
PRESS. NEW YORK. 1965. PP 52-84.

GORSHMX66280 ORSHANSKY M   *US DEPT OF HEALTH ED WELFARE
MORE ABOUT THE POOR IN 1964.
US DEPARTMENT OF HEALTH, EDUCATION AND WELFARE, SOCIAL
SECURITY BULLETIN, MAY 1966. 37 PP.

GORSHMX66282 ORSHANSKY M   *US DEPT OF HEALTH ED WELFARE
THE POOR IN CITY AND SUBURB, 1964.
US DEPARTMENT OF HEALTH, EDUCATION AND WELFARE, SOCIAL
SECURITY BULLETIN, DEC 1966. 16 PP.

GORSHMX66642 ORSHANSKY M   *US DEPT OF HEALTH ED WELFARE
RECOUNTING THE POOR -- A FIVE-YEAR REVIEW.
US DEPARTMENT OF HEALTH, EDUCATION, AND WELFARE, SOCIAL
SECURITY BULLETIN, VOL 29, NO 4, AP 1966. PP 20-37.

GPAGEDA64775 PAGE DA
RETRAINING UNDER THE MANPOWER-DEVELOPMENT-ACT. A
COST-BENEFIT ANALYSIS.
PUBLIC POLICY, VOL 13, 1964. 9 PP.

GPALMEN47145 PALMER EN
DISCRIMINATION IN URBAN EMPLOYMENT.
AMERICAN JOURNAL OF SOCIOLOGY, VOL 52, JAN 1947. PP 357-361.

GPALMFX63671 PALMORE E   *US DEPT HEALTH ED WELFARE
FACTORS ASSOCIATED WITH SCHOOL DROPOUTS AND
JUVENILE-DELINQUENCY AMONG LOWER-CLASS CHILDREN.
US DEPARTMENT OF HEALTH, EDUCATION, AND WELFARE, SOCIAL
SECURITY BULLETIN. VOL 26, NO 10, OCT 1963. PP 4-9.

GPARRJA66147 PARRISH JA
THE INDUSTRIAL PSYCHOLOGIST. SELECTION AND
EQUAL-EMPLOYMENT OPPORTUNITY.
PERSONNEL PSYCHOLOGY, VOL 19, NO 1, SPRING 1966. PP 1-39.

GPASLRS57148 PASLEY RS
THE NONDISCRIMINATION CLAUSE IN GOVERNMENT CONTRACTS.
VIRGINIA LAW REVIEW, VOL 43, NO 6, OCT 1957. PP 837-871.

GPASSHA63724 PASSOW HA ED
EDUCATION IN DEPRESSED AREAS.
TEACHERS COLLEGE PRESS, COLUMBIA UNIVERSITY, NEW YORK. 1963.
359 PP.

GPEARAX65C99 PEARL A   RIESSMAN F
NEW CAREERS FOR THE POOR.
FREE PRESS. NEW YORK. 1965.

GPEARHG66149 PEARSON HG
TITLE-VII. REPORTING AND RECORD KEEPING. /LEGISLATION/
BOSTON COLLEGE INDUSTRIAL AND COMMERCIAL LAW REVIEW, VOL 7,
NO 3, SPRING 1966. PP 549-560.

GPEDOWX64150 PEDDER W
DISCRIMINATION IN HOUSING AND EMPLOYMENT. WHAT TYPE OF
PROBLEM IS IT.
STANFORD UNIVERSITY, DEPARTMENT OF POLITICAL SCIENCE.
PALO-ALTO, CALIFORNIA. JUNE 1964. 62 PP.

GPEIMSC66139 PEIMER SC   GASS GZ
RUTLEDGE AL
AN EXPERIMENT IN RETRAINING UNEMPLOYED MEN FOR PRACTICAL
NURSING CAREERS.
HOSPITALS JOURNAL OF THE AMERICAN HOSPITAL ASSOCIATION,
VOL 40, NO 20, OCT 16 1966.

GPENNEL62502 PENNSYLVANIA ECONOMY LEAGUE
SPECIAL ASSIMILATION PROBLEMS OF UNDERPRIVILEGED IMMIGRANTS
TO PHILADELPHIA. /PENNSYLVANIA/
PENNSYLVANIA ECONOMY LEAGUE AND BUREAU OF MUNICIPAL
RESEARCH. PHILADELPHIA, PENNSYLVANIA. 1962.

GPENNFE58153 PENNSYLVANIA FEPC
LEGAL RULINGS INTERPRETING THE PROVISIONS OF THE
PENNSYLVANIA FAIR-EMPLOYMENT-PRACTICE ACT.
PENNSYLVANIA FAIR EMPLOYMENT PRACTICE COMMISSION, DEPARTMENT
OF LABOR AND INDUSTRY. DEC 1958. 14 PP.

GPENNGC53159 PA GOVRS COMM IND RACE RELS
EMPLOYMENT PRACTICES IN PENNSYLVANIA.
PENNSYLVANIA GOVERNOR-S COMMISSION ON INDUSTRIAL RACE
RELATIONS. HARRISBURG, PENNSYLVANIA. FEB 1953. 58 PP.

GPENNHRND164 PENNSYLVANIA HUMAN RELS COMM
GUIDE TO EMPLOYERS, EMPLOYMENT-AGENCIES AND LABOR UNIONS
DEFINING PROPER AND IMPROPER PRE-EMPLOYMENT INQUIRIES.
/PENNSYLVANIA/
PENNSYLVANIA DEPARTMENT OF LABOR AND INDUSTRY, HUMAN
RELATIONS COMMISSION. HARRISBURG, PENNSYLVANIA. ND. 4 PP.

GPENNHRND165 PENNSYLVANIA HUMAN RELS COMM
LAWS ADMINISTERED BY THE PENNSYLVANIA
HUMAN-RELATIONS-COMMISSION.
PENNSYLVANIA DEPARTMENT OF LABOR AND INDUSTRY, HUMAN
RELATIONS COMMISSION. HARRISBURG, PENNSYLVANIA. ND. 18 PP.

GPENNHR62162 PENNSYLVANIA HUMAN RELS COMM
EMPLOYMENT PRACTICES OF THE PHILADELPHIA SCHOOL DISTRICT.
/PENNSYLVANIA/
PENNSYLVANIA DEPARTMENT OF LABOR AND INDUSTRY, HUMAN
RELATIONS COMMISSION. HARRISBURG, PENNSYLVANIA. AUG 1962.
23 PP.

GPENNHR63166 PENNSYLVANIA HUMAN RELS COMM
COMMISSIONS FOR HUMAN RIGHTS, 15TH ANNUAL CONFERENCE,
PROCEEDINGS.
PENNSYLVANIA DEPARTMENT OF LABOR AND INDUSTRY, HUMAN
RELATIONS COMMISSION. HELD IN PITTSBURGH, MAY 21-24 1963.
HARRISBURG, PENNSYLVANIA. 152 PP.

GPENNHR65163 PENNSYLVANIA HUMAN RELS COMM
FAIR EMPLOYMENT SURVEY OF THE WESTCHESTER AREA.
/PENNSYLVANIA/
PENNSYLVANIA DEPARTMENT OF LABOR AND INDUSTRY, HUMAN
RELATIONS COMMISSION. HARRISBURG, PENNSYLVANIA. 1965. 59 PP.

GPENNHR65167 PENNSYLVANIA HUMAN RELS COMM
SECOND SURVEY OF NON-WHITE EMPLOYEES IN STATE GOVERNMENT IN
PENNSYLVANIA.
PENNSYLVANIA DEPARTMENT OF LABOR AND INDUSTRY, HUMAN
RELATIONS COMMISSION. HARRISBURG, PENNSYLVANIA. 1965. 10 PP.

GPENNSE65641 PA STATE EMPLOYMENT SERVICE
THE EFFECTS OF AUTOMATION ON OCCUPATIONS AND WORKERS IN
PENNSYLVANIA.
PENNSYLVANIA STATE EMPLOYMENT SERVICE, AUTOMATION MANPOWER
SERVICES SECTION, TECHNICAL SERVICES DIVISION. HARRISBURG,
PENNSYLVANIA. MAY 1965. 78 PP.

GPERKBX66150 PERKINS B   HATHAWAY DE
THE MOVEMENT OF LABOR BETWEEN FARM AND NONFARM JOBS.
MICHIGAN STATE UNIVERSITY, AGRICULTURAL EXPERIMENT STATION,
RESEARCH BULLETIN 13. 1966. 48 PP.

GPERLMX63169 PERLMAN M ED
HUMAN RESOURCES IN THE URBAN ECONOMY. PART II -- THE LABOR
FORCE PERFORMANCE OF MINORITY-GROUPS.
JOHNS HOPKINS PRESS. 1963. BALTIMORE, MARYLAND. 265 PP.

GPERRJX63170 PERRY J
BUSINESS -- NEXT TARGET FOR INTEGRATION. /INDUSTRY/
HARVARD BUSINESS REVIEW, VOL 41, NO 2, MAR-AP 1963.
PP 104-115.

GPERRVC64168 PERRELLA VC   *US DEPARTMENT OF LABOR
MARITAL AND FAMILY CHARACTERISTICS OF WORKERS, MARCH 1963.
US DEPARTMENT OF LABOR, MONTHLY LABOR REVIEW, VOL 86, NO 2,
REPORT NO 40, FEB 1964. 35 PP.

GPERRVC66774 PERRELLA VC   WALDMAN E
*US DEPARTMENT OF LABOR
OUT-OF-SCHOOL YOUTH -- TWO YEARS LATER. A 1965 RE-SURVEY OF
YOUNG MEN.
US DEPARTMENT OF LABOR, MONTHLY LABOR REVIEW, VOL 89, NO 8,
AUG 1966. PP 860-866.

GPHILBE64172 PHILADELPHIA BRD OF EDUCATION
REPORT OF THE SPECIAL COMMITTEE ON NONDISCRIMINATION OF THE
BOARD OF PUBLIC EDUCATION, PHILADELPHIA. /PENNSYLVANIA/
PHILADELPHIA BOARD OF EDUCATION, SPECIAL COMMITTEE ON
NONDISCRIMINATION. PHILADELPHIA, PENNSYLVANIA. JULY 1964.
191 PP.

GPHILCH60181 PHILADELPHIA COMM HUMAN RELS
SUMMARY OF TESTIMONY -- HOTEL RESTAURANT HEARINGS, APPENDIX
A. /PHILADELPHIA PENNSYLVANIA/
PHILADELPHIA COMMISSION ON HUMAN RELATIONS, DIVISION ON
PUBLIC LAW AND EMPLOYMENT. PHILADELPHIA, PENNSYLVANIA.
NOV 1960. 22 PP.

GPHILCH61176   PHILADELPHIA COMM HUMAN RELS
FINDINGS OF FACT, CONCLUSIONS AND ACTION OF THE COMMISSION
ON HUMAN-RELATIONS IN RE. INVESTIGATIVE PUBLIC HEARINGS
INTO ALLEGED DISCRIMINATORY PRACTICE BY THE HOTEL AND
RESTAURANT INDUSTRY IN PHILADELPHIA. /PENNSYLVANIA/
PHILADELPHIA COMMISSION ON HUMAN RELATIONS. PHILADELPHIA,
PENNSYLVANIA. AP 11 1961. 11 PP.

GPHILCH62178   PHILADELPHIA COMM HUMAN RELS
REPORT OF PROGRESS IN THE INTEGRATION OF HOTEL AND
RESTAURANT EMPLOYMENT, APRIL 1961 TO MARCH 1962.
/PHILADELPHIA PENNSYLVANIA/
PHILADELPHIA COMMISSION ON HUMAN RELATIONS. PHILADELPHIA,
PENNSYLVANIA. JUNE 1962. 12 PP.

GPHILCH62180   PHILADELPHIA COMM HUMAN RELS
REPORT OF 1961 - 1962 SURVEY OF PHILADELPHIA BANKS AND
ATTACHED COMPOSITE TABULATION OF NON-WHITES.
/PENNSYLVANIA/
PHILADELPHIA COMMISSION ON HUMAN RELATIONS, DIVISION OF
PUBLIC LAW AND EMPLOYMENT. PHILADELPHIA, PENNSYLVANIA.
JUNE 5 1962. 34 PP.

GPHILCH64179   PHILADELPHIA COMM HUMAN RELS
A SPECIAL REPORT, CITY CONTRACT COMPLIANCE. PROGRESS IN
1963. /PHILADELPHIA PENNSYLVANIA/
PHILADELPHIA COMMISSION ON HUMAN RELATIONS. PHILADELPHIA,
PENNSYLVANIA. AP 1964. 10 PP.

GPHILCH65177   PHILADELPHIA COMM HUMAN RELS
A PILOT STUDY OF THE EMPLOYMENT EXPERIENCES OF HIGH SCHOOL
GRADUATES.
PHILADELPHIA COMMISSION ON HUMAN RELATIONS. PHILADELPHIA,
PENNSYLVANIA. JULY 1965. 23 PP.

GPHILEW65773   PHILLIPS EW
INCOME-DISTRIBUTION AS A FACTOR IN REGIONAL GROWTH, WITH
SPECIAL REFERENCE TO THE SOUTHEAST UNITED STATES.
/DISCRIMINATION/
UNIVERSITY OF COLORADO. PHD THESIS. BOULDER, COLORADO. 1965.
94 PP.

GPHILMX62616   PHILIPSON M
AUTOMATION IMPLICATIONS FOR THE FUTURE.
VINTAGE BOOKS. NEW YORK. 1962. 456 PP.

GPIERJH64846   PIERSON JH
INSURING FULL EMPLOYMENT.
VIKING PRESS. NEW YORK. 1964. 305 PP.

GPOLIEX65102   POLISAR E
DISCUSSION ON EQUAL-EMPLOYMENT-OPPORTUNITIES.
INDUSTRIAL RELATIONS RESEARCH ASSOCIATION, PROCEEDINGS.
SPRING 1965. PP 473-476.

GPOTOII65188   POTOMAC INSTITUTE INC.
FAIR-EMPLOYMENT IS GOOD BUSINESS. EXAMPLES OF FAIR PRACTICES
FOR TITLE-VII OF THE CIVIL-RIGHTS-ACT OF 1964.
THE POTOMAC INSTITUTE, INC. WASHINGTON, DC. 1965. 22 PP.

GPOTFGX65189   POTTS G   *US DEPARTMENT OF LABOR
CONFERENCE ON EQUAL-EMPLOYMENT-OPPORTUNITY.
US DEPARTMENT OF LABOR, MONTHLY LABOR REVIEW, VOL 88, NO 11,
NOV 1965. PP 1320-1321.

GPOWETX64190   POWERS T
FEDERAL PROCUREMENT AND EQUAL-OPPORTUNITY EMPLOYMENT.
LAW AND CONTEMPORARY PROBLEMS, VOL 29, NO 2, SPRING 1964.
PP 468-487.

GPRENHI64104   PRENTICE-HALL INC
HOW THE NEW CIVIL-RIGHTS LAW AFFECTS YOUR EMPLOYMENT
PRACTICES.
PRENTICE-HALL. ENGLEWOOD CLIFFS, NEW JERSEY. 1964. 47 PP.

GPRESCC47192   PRES-S COMT CIVIL RIGHTS
TO SECURE THESE RIGHTS.
PRESIDENT-S COMMITTEE ON CIVIL-RIGHTS. REPORT. GPO.
WASHINGTON, DC. 1947.

GPRESCD62105   PRESIDENT-S COMMITTEE ON EEO
THE AMERICAN DREAM...EQUAL OPPORTUNITY, A REPORT ON THE
COMMUNITY LEADER-S CONFERENCE SPONSORED BY PRESIDENT-S
COMMITTEE ON EQUAL-EMPLOYMENT-OPPORTUNITY, MAY 19, 1962.
PRESIDENT-S COMMITTEE ON EQUAL EMPLOYMENT OPPORTUNITY. GPO.
WASHINGTON, DC. 1962. 56 PP.

GPRESCD62108   PRESIDENT-S COMMITTEE ON EEO
THE FIRST NINE MONTHS -- SPECIAL YEAR-END REPORT, APRIL 7,
1961-JANUARY 15, 1962, PRESIDENT-S COMMITTEE ON
EQUAL-EMPLOYMENT-OPPORTUNITY.
PRESIDENT-S COMMITTEE ON EQUAL EMPLOYMENT OPPORTUNITY. GPO
WASHINGTON, DC. 1962. 64 PP.

GPRESCD62109   PRESIDENT-S COMMITTEE ON EEO
GUIDE FOR INVESTIGATIONS AND COMPLIANCE REVIEWS IN
EQUAL-EMPLOYMENT-OPPORTUNITY.
PRESIDENT-S COMMITTEE ON EQUAL EMPLOYMENT OPPORTUNITY. GPO.
WASHINGTON, DC. NOV 1962. 16 PP.

GPRESCD63110   PRESIDENT-S COMMITTEE ON EEO
GOVERNMENT CONTRACT EMPLOYMENT. RULES AND REGULATIONS...
EFFECTIVE JULY 22, 1961, AS AMENDED SEPTEMBER 7, 1963.
PRESIDENT-S COMMITTEE ON EQUAL EMPLOYMENT OPPORTUNITY. GPO.
WASHINGTON, DC. NOV 1962. 16 PP.

GPRESCD63115   PRESIDENT-S COMMITTEE ON EEO
SELF-ANALYSIS QUESTIONNAIRE. /EEO INDUSTRY/
PRESIDENT-S COMMITTEE ON EQUAL EMPLOYMENT OPPORTUNITY. GPO.
WASHINGTON, DC. 1963. 5 PP.

GPRESCD64106   PRESIDENT-S COMT ON EEO
APPRENTICE PROGRAMS.
PRESIDENT-S COMMITTEE ON EQUAL EMPLOYMENT OPPORTUNITY,
DAILY LABOR REPORT, NO 87, MAY 4 1964.

GPRESCD64111   PRESIDENT-S COMMITTEE ON EEO
1964 MINORITY-GROUP STUDY.
PRESIDENT-S COMMITTEE ON EQUAL EMPLOYMENT OPPORTUNITY. GPO.
WASHINGTON, DC. 1964.

GPRESCD64112   PRESIDENT-S COMMITTEE ON EEO
PLANS-FOR-PROGRESS, A FIRST YEAR REPORT BY THE PLANS FOR
PROGRESS ADVISORY COUNCIL.
PRESIDENT-S COMMITTEE ON EQUAL EMPLOYMENT OPPORTUNITY,
PLANS FOR PROGRESS. GPO. WASHINGTON, DC. AUG 1964. 21 PP.

GPRESCD64113   PRESIDENT-S COMMITTEE ON EEO
REGIONAL COMMUNITY LEADERS CONFERENCE ON
EQUAL-EMPLOYMENT-OPPORTUNITY, PROCEEDINGS.
PRESIDENT-S COMMITTEE ON EQUAL EMPLOYMENT OPPORTUNITY.
CHICAGO, ILLINOIS. MAY 22 1964.

GPRESCD64114   PRESIDENT-S COMMITTEE ON EEO
REPORT TO THE PRESIDENT, NOVEMBER 26, 1963 BY THE
PRESIDENT-S COMMITTEE ON EQUAL-EMPLOYMENT-OPPORTUNITY.
PRESIDENT-S COMMITTEE ON EQUAL EMPLOYMENT OPPORTUNITY. GPO.
WASHINGTON, DC. 1964. 150 PP.

GPRESCD64116   PRESIDENT-S COMMITTEE ON EEO
STUDY OF MINORITY-GROUP EMPLOYMENT IN THE FEDERAL
GOVERNMENT.
PRESIDENT-S COMMITTEE ON EQUAL EMPLOYMENT OPPORTUNITY.
WASHINGTON, DC. JUNE 1964. 22 PLUS PP.

GPRESCD65107   PRESIDENT-S COMMITTEE ON EEO
FIELD MANUAL ON EQUAL-EMPLOYMENT-OPPORTUNITY UNDER
GOVERNMENT CONTRACTS.
PRESIDENT-S COMMITTEE ON EQUAL EMPLOYMENT OPPORTUNITY. GPO.
WASHINGTON, DC. AP 1965. 73 PP.

GPRESCG53117   PRES COMT GOVT CONTRACT COMPL
EQUAL ECONOMIC OPPORTUNITY. A REPORT.
PRESIDENT-S COMMITTEE ON GOVERNMENT CONTRACT COMPLIANCE.
GPO. WASHINGTON, DC. JAN 16 1953. 111 PP.

GPRESCH54120   PRES-S COMT GOVT CONTRACTS
FIRST REPORT, PRESIDENT-S COMMITTEE ON GOVERNMENT CONTRACTS.
PRESIDENT-S COMMITTEE ON GOVERNMENT CONTRACTS. GPO.
WASHINGTON, DC. SEPT 1954. 20 PP.

GPRESCH55124   PRES-S COMT GOVT CONTRACTS
SECOND ANNUAL REPORT, THE PRESIDENT-S COMMITTEE ON
GOVERNMENT CONTRACTS.
THE PRESIDENT-S COMMITTEE ON GOVERNMENT CONTRACTS.
WASHINGTON, DC. DEC 1955. 18 PP.

GPRESCH56191   PRES-S COMM GOVT CONTRACTS
EQUAL JOB OPPORTUNITY AS SET FORTH IN EXECUTIVE ORDERS 10479
AND 10557.
PRESIDENT-S COMMISSION ON GOVERNMENT CONTRACTS. WASHINGTON,
DC. MAR 1956. 20 PP.

GPRESCH57122   PRES-S COMT GOVT CONTRACTS
FOURTH ANNUAL REPORT ON EQUAL JOB OPPORTUNITY, 1956-1957,
PRESIDENT-S COMMITTEE ON GOVERNMENT CONTRACTS.
PRESIDENT-S COMMITTEE ON GOVERNMENT CONTRACTS. GPO.
WASHINGTON, DC. 1957. 20 PP.

GPRESCH58119   PRES-S COMT GOVT CONTRACTS
COMPLIANCE GUIDE, RECOMMENDATIONS FOR OBTAINING COMPLIANCE
WITH THE NONDISCRIMINATION PROVISIONS IN GOVERNMENT
CONTRACTS.
PRESIDENT-S COMMITTEE ON GOVERNMENT CONTRACTS. GPO.
WASHINGTON, DC. OCT 1958. 70 PP.

GPRESCH58121   PRES-S COMT GOVT CONTRACTS
FIVE YEARS OF PROGRESS, 1953-1958, A REPORT TO PRESIDENT
EISENHOWER BY THE PRESIDENT-S COMMITTEE ON GOVERNMENT
CONTRACTS.
PRESIDENT-S COMMITTEE ON GOVERNMENT CONTRACTS. GPO.
WASHINGTON, DC. 1958. 38 PP.

GPRESCH60123   PRES-S COMT GOVT CONTRACTS
PATTERN FOR PROGRESS, SEVENTH REPORT, FINAL REPORT TO
PRESIDENT EISENHOWER FROM THE COMMITTEE ON GOVERNMENT
CONTRACTS.
PRESIDENT-S COMMITTEE ON GOVERNMENT CONTRACTS. GPO.
WASHINGTON, DC. 1960. 24 PP.

GPRESCL64772   PRES-S COMT LABOR-MANAGE POL
SEMINARS ON PRIVATE ADJUSTMENTS TO AUTOMATION AND
TECHNOLOGICAL-CHANGE.
PRESIDENT-S ADVISORY COMMITTEE ON LABOR-MANAGEMENT POLICY.
GPO. WASHINGTON, DC. MAY-JUNE 1964. 232 PP.

GPRESCP55197   PRES COMT GOVT EMPLOY POLICY
HUMAN-RELATIONS IN FEDERAL EMPLOYMENT.
PRESIDENT-S COMMITTEE ON GOVERNMENT EMPLOYMENT POLICY. GPO.
WASHINGTON, DC. 1955. 8 PP.

GPRESCP55198   PRES COMT GOVT EMPLOY POLICY
THE POLICY OF NON-DISCRIMINATION IN EMPLOYMENT IN THE
FEDERAL GOVERNMENT.
PRESIDENT-S COMMITTEE ON GOVERNMENT EMPLOYMENT POLICY. GPO.
WASHINGTON, DC. 1955. 8 PP.

GPRESCP55199   PRES COMT GOVT EMPLOY POLICY
SOME QUESTIONS AND ANSWERS ON THE NON-DISCRIMINATION POLICY
OF THE FEDERAL GOVERNMENT.
PRESIDENT-S COMMITTEE ON GOVERNMENT EMPLOYMENT POLICY. GPO.
WASHINGTON, DC. 1955. 6 PP.

GPRESCP56193   PRES COMT GOVT EMPLOY POLICY
FIRST ANNUAL REPORT, PRESIDENT-S COMMITTEE ON GOVERNMENT
EMPLOYMENT POLICY, APRIL 30 1956.
PRESIDENT-S COMMITTEE ON GOVERNMENT EMPLOYMENT POLICY. GPO.
WASHINGTON, DC. 1956.

GPRESCP57194   PRES COMT GOVT EMPLOY POLICY
SECOND ANNUAL REPORT, PRESIDENT-S COMMITTEE ON GOVERNMENT
EMPLOYMENT POLICY, 1957.
PRESIDENT-S COMMITTEE ON GOVERNMENT EMPLOYMENT POLICY. GPO.
WASHINGTON, DC. 1957.

GPRESCP58195   PRES COMT GOVT EMPLOY POLICY
THIRD ANNUAL REPORT, PRESIDENT-S COMMITTEE ON GOVERNMENT
EMPLOYMENT POLICY, 1958.
PRESIDENT-S COMMITTEE ON GOVERNMENT EMPLOYMENT POLICY. GPO.
WASHINGTON, DC. 1958.

GPRESCP59196   PRES COMT GOVT EMPLOY POLICY
FOURTH ANNUAL REPORT, PRESIDENT-S COMMITTEE ON GOVERNMENT
EMPLOYMENT POLICY.
PRESIDENT-S COMMITTEE ON GOVERNMENT EMPLOYMENT POLICY. GPO.
WASHINGTON, DC. 1959. 46 PP.

GPRESCP59201   PRES COMT GOVT EMPLOY POLICY
UNDERSTANDING THE HUMAN FACTOR, THE KEY TO SUPERVISORY
SUCCESS.
PRESIDENT-S COMMITTEE ON GOVERNMENT EMPLOYMENT POLICY. GPO.
WASHINGTON, DC. 1959. 32 PP.

GPRESCP60200   PRES COMT GOVT EMPLOY POLICY
TRENDS IN THE EMPLOYMENT OF NEGRO-AMERICANS IN UPPER-LEVEL
WHITE-COLLAR POSITIONS OF THE FEDERAL GOVERNMENT.
PRESIDENT-S COMMITTEE ON GOVERNMENT EMPLOYMENT POLICY. GPO.
WASHINGTON, DC. 1960. 5 PP.

GPRESSB58126 PRESSLER SB   FUNDLER BL
DISCRIMINATION IN UNION MEMBERSHIP. DENIAL OF DUE PROCESS
UNDER FEDERAL COLLECTIVE BARGAINING LEGISLATION.
RUTGERS LAW REVIEW, VOL 12, SUMMER 1958. PP 543-556.

GPRESTM64316 PRES-S TASK FORCE ON MANPOWER
ONE-THIRD OF A NATION. A REPORT ON YOUNG MEN FOUND
UNQUALIFIED FOR MILITARY SERVICE.
THE PRESIDENT-S TASK FORCE ON MANPOWER CONSERVATION. GPO.
WASHINGTON, DC. JAN 1 1964. 86 PP.

GPRICPH58395 PRICE PH   BERTRAND AL
OSBORNE HW
THE EFFECTS OF INDUSTRIALIZATION ON RURAL LOUISIANA. A STUDY
OF PLANT EMPLOYEES.
LOUISIANA STATE UNIVERSITY. BATON ROUGE, LOUISIANA.
JAN 1958. 65 PP.

GPRICWS65688 PRICE WS
THE AFFIRMATIVE-ACTION CONCEPT OF
EQUAL-EMPLOYMENT-OPPORTUNITY.
LABOR LAW JOURNAL. VOL 16, OCT 1965. PP 603-619.

GPUBLWX63207 PUBLISHERS WEEKLY
ANTI-DISCRIMINATION PACT SIGNED IN PHILADELPHIA.
/PENNSYLVANIA/
PUBLISHERS WEEKLY, VOL 184, OCT 14 1963.

GPUEBRP65459 PUEBLO REGIONAL PLANNING COMM
THE SOCIO-ECONOMIC AND PHYSICAL CHARACTERISTICS OF THE
VARIOUS NEIGHBORHOODS IN PUEBLO. /COLORADO/
PUEBLO REGIONAL PLANNING COMMISSION. PUEBLO, COLORADO.
MAR 1965.

GPURCFX66208 PURCELL F   *NYU CENT STUDY UNEMP YOUTH
LOW-INCOME YOUTH, UNEMPLOYMENT, VOCATIONAL TRAINING, AND THE
JOB-CORPS.
NEW YORK UNIVERSITY, GRADUATE SCHOOL OF SOCIAL WORK, CENTER
FOR THE STUDY OF EMPLOYED YOUTH. NEW YORK. JUNE 1966. 24 PP.

GPURDJW66209 PURDY JW
TITLE-VII. RELATIONSHIP AND EFFECT ON STATE ACTION.
/LEGISLATION/
BOSTON COLLEGE INDUSTRIAL AND COMMERCIAL LAW REVIEW, VOL 7,
NO 3, SPRING 1966. PP 525-534.

GPURYMJ62210 PURYEAR MJ
MERIT EMPLOYMENT -- UNFINISHED BUSINESS.
SOCIAL ACTION, DEC 1962.

GQUINPA65771 QUINLAN PA   *US DEPARTMENT OF LABOR
GRADUATES OF THE NORFOLK PROJECT ONE YEAR LATER.
/MDTA TRAINING/
US DEPARTMENT OF LABOR, MANPOWER EVALUATION REPORT NO 5.
GPO. WASHINGTON, DC. 1965. 25 PP.

GRAABEX64120 RAAB E   FOLK H
*CALIF DEPT OF SOC WELFARE
THE PATTERN OF DEPENDENT POVERTY IN CALIFORNIA.
CALIFORNIA DEPARTMENT OF SOCIAL WELFARE, WELFARE STUDY
COMMISSION. SACRAMENTO, CALIFORNIA. MAR 1963. REVISED
JAN 1964.

GRABKSX58213 RABKIN S   PUNER M
*ANTI-DEFAMATION LEAGUE
FEPC. HOW TO ANSWER ITS CRITICS.
BARRIERS. PATTERNS OF DISCRIMINATION AGAINST JEWS. ED BY
NC BELTH. ANTI-DEFAMATION LEAGUE OF B-NAI B-RITH. NEW YORK.
1958. PP 52-58.

GRABKSX64211 RABKIN S
ENFORCEMENT OF LAWS AGAINST DISCRIMINATION IN EMPLOYMENT.
BUFFALO LAW REVIEW, VOL 14, FALL 1964. PP 100-113.

GRACHCXND212 RACHLIN C   *CONGRESS OF RACIAL EQUALITY
THE 1964 CIVIL-RIGHTS LAW, A HARD LOOK.
CONGRESS OF RACIAL EQUALITY, LEGAL DEPARTMENT. NEW YORK.
MIMEOGRAPHED. ND. 19 PP.

GRACHCX66214 RACHLIN C
TITLE-VII. LIMITATIONS AND QUALIFICATIONS. /LEGISLATION/
BOSTON COLLEGE INDUSTRIAL AND COMMERCIAL LAW REVIEW, VOL 7,
NO 3, SPRING 1966. PP 473-494.

GRACKFX49215 RACKOW F   *CORNELL NYS SCHOOL OF ILR
COMBATING DISCRIMINATION IN EMPLOYMENT IN NEW-YORK STATE.
CORNELL UNIVERSITY, NEW YORK STATE SCHOOL OF INDUSTRIAL AND
LABOR RELATIONS, RESEARCH BULLETIN NO 5. ITHACA, NEW YORK.
NOV 1949. 52 PP.

GRAPEAX46037 RAPER A
THE ROLE OF AGRICULTURAL TECHNOLOGY IN SOUTHERN SOCIAL
CHANGE.
SOCIAL FORCES, VOL 25, NO 1, OCT 1946. PP 21-30.

GRAPPLA66216 RAPPING LA
UNIONISM, MIGRATION, AND THE MALE NONWHITE-WHITE
UNEMPLOYMENT DIFFERENTIAL.
THE SOUTHERN ECONOMIC JOURNAL, VOL 32, NO 3, JAN 1966.
PP 317-329. ALSO CARNEGIE INSTITUTE OF TECHNOLOGY, GRADUATE
SCHOOL OF INDUSTRIAL ADMINISTRATION. REPRINT NO 226. 1966.
14 PP.

GRAUHJL57217 RAUH JL
CIVIL-RIGHTS AND LIBERTIES AND LABOR UNIONS.
LABOR LAW JOURNAL, VOL 8, DEC 1957. PP 874-892.

GRAUSEX62218 RAUSHENBUSH E   *WIS GOVRS COMM OF HUM RIGHTS
THE MIGRANT LABOR PROBLEM IN WISCONSIN.
WISCONSIN. GOVERNOR-S COMMISSION ON HUMAN RIGHTS. MADISON,
WISCONSIN. 1962. 52 PP.

GRAUSWX45583 RAUSHENBUSH W   *WORKERS DEFENSE LEAGUE
JOBS WITHOUT CREED OR COLOR.
WORKERS DEFENSE LEAGUE. NEW YORK. 1945. 32 PP.

GRAVIMJ61219 RAVITZ MJ
THE INTERRELATIONSHIPS OF DISCRIMINATION IN EMPLOYMENT, IN
EDUCATION, AND IN HOUSING.
MICHIGAN FAIR EMPLOYMENT PRACTICES COMMISSION, SECOND ANNUAL
STEWARDSHIP CONFERENCE. ADDRESS. LANSING, MICHIGAN.
MAY 13 1961.

GREADFT64220 READ FT
MINORITY RIGHTS AND THE UNION SHOP.
MINNESOTA LAW REVIEW, VOL 49, DEC 1964. P 227.

GREAGMD64845 REAGAN MD
FOR A GUARANTEED-INCOME.
NEW YORK TIMES MAGAZINE, JUNE 7 1964. PP 20, 120-121.

GREDMWX64221 REDMOND W
TESTIMONY TO THE SUBCOMMITTEE ON RACE-RELATIONS AND URBAN
PROBLEMS. /SES CALIFORNIA/
CALIFORNIA STATE ASSEMBLY. SACRAMENTO, CALIFORNIA.
AP 15 1964. 7 PP.

GREESAX65119 REES A
INFORMATION NETWORKS IN LABOR-MARKETS.
AMERICAN ECONOMICS ASSOCIATION, MEETING, PAPER. CHICAGO,
ILLINOIS. DEC 1965.

GREESAX66722 REES A
ECONOMIC EXPANSION AND PERSISTING UNEMPLOYMENT. AN OVERVIEW.
PROSPERITY AND UNEMPLOYMENT. ED BY R A GORDON AND
M S GORDON. JOHN WILEY AND SONS, INC. NEW YORK. 1966.
PP 327-348.

GREHNGX65654 REHN G
TRENDS AND PERSPECTIVES IN MANPOWER POLICY.
POVERTY IN AMERICA. ED BY M S GORDON. CHANDLER PUBLISHING
CO. SAN FRANCISCO, CALIFORNIA. 1965. PP 203-217.

GRESEIA64222 RESEARCH INSTITUTE OF AMERICA
OPERATING UNDER THE CIVIL-RIGHTS LAW.
RESEARCH INSTITUTE OF AMERICA. NEW YORK. SEPT 29 1964.
24 PP.

GREUSLA60391 REUSS LA   GILBRAITH KM
RESOURCE CHARACTERISTICS AND UTILIZATION AND LEVEL OF LIVING
ITEMS, RURAL HOUSEHOLDS, NORTH AND WEST FLORIDA, 1956.
UNIVERSITY OF FLORIDA. GAINESVILLE, FLORIDA. MAR 1960.
130 PP.

GREUSLA62388 REUSS LA   GILBRAITH KM
INCOME, RESOURCES, AND ADJUSTMENT POTENTIALS AMONG RURAL
FAMILIES IN NORTH AND WEST FLORIDA.
UNIVERSITY OF FLORIDA. GAINESVILLE, FLORIDA. DEC 1962. 54 PP.

GREUTWP60223 REUTHER WP
EQUALITY OF JOB OPPORTUNITY AND CIVIL-RIGHTS.
US COMMISSION ON CIVIL RIGHTS. STATEMENT. MIMEOGRAPHED.
DETROIT, MICHIGAN. DEC 14 1960. 14 PP.

GRHODICND232 RHODE ISLAND COMM AGST DISCR
RHODE-ISLAND COMMISSION-AGAINST-DISCRIMINATION, RULES OF
PRACTICE AND PROCEDURE.
RHODE ISLAND COMMISSION AGAINST DISCRIMINATION. PROVIDENCE,
RHODE ISLAND. ND. 5 PLUS PP.

GRHYNCS63234 RHYNE CS   RHYNE B
*NATL INST MUNICIPAL LAW
CIVIL-RIGHTS ORDINANCES.
NATIONAL INSTITUTE OF MUNICIPAL LAW OFFICERS, REPORT NO 148.
WASHINGTON, DC. 1963.

GRICHCM63236 RICHMOND CITY MANAGER
MUNICIPAL HUMAN-RELATIONS COMMISSION, A SURVEY OF PROGRAMS
IN SELECTED CITIES OF THE UNITED STATES.
RICHMOND CITY MANAGER. RICHMOND, CALIFORNIA. MAY 1963.

GRICHEX66235 RICHEY E
US PLAN TO BREAK CYCLE OF BIAS AND POVERTY.
NEGRO DIGEST, VOL 15, NO 9, JULY 1966. PP 33-37.

GRICOLX66237 RICO L
URBAN JOB DISCRIMINATION. ABUSES AND REDRESS.
QUARTERLY REVIEW OF ECONOMICS AND BUSINESS, VOL 6,
WINTER 1966. PP 7-24.

GRIGHXX59238 RIGHTS
PROGRESS IN FAIR-EMPLOYMENT-PRACTICES.
RIGHTS, VOL 2, NO 6, AP-MAY 1959.

GROBEPC64239 ROBERTSON PC   *MISSOURI COMM ON HUM RIGHTS
THE NEW FEDERAL FAIR-EMPLOYMENT-PRACTICES ACT -- COMPARISON
WITH STATE LAW AND AN ANALYSIS OF RELEVANT STATE
EXPERIENCES. /MISSOURI/
THE NATIONAL ASSOCIATION OF MANUFACTURERS. ST LOUIS,
MISSOURI. OCT 1 AND 2 1964. 16 PP.

GROBESO63683 ROBERTS SO
TEST PERFORMANCE IN RELATION TO ETHNIC GROUP AND SOCIAL
CLASS.
FISK UNIVERSITY. NASHVILLE, TENNESSEE. 1963.

GROBIJB64240 ROBISON JB   *CONGRESS OF RACIAL EQUALITY
GIVING REALITY TO THE PROMISE OF EQUALITY.
CONGRESS OF RACIAL EQUALITY. NEW YORK. MIMEOGRAPHED. 1964.
10 PP ALSO IN LAW IN TRANSITION QUARTERLY, SPRING 1964.
PP 104-117.

GROBSRT66721 ROBSON RT   MANGUM GL
COORDINATION AMONG FEDERAL MANPOWER PROGRAMS.
CRITICAL ISSUES IN EMPLOYMENT POLICY. ED BY F H HARBISON AND
J D MOONEY. PRINCETON UNIVERSITY, INDUSTRIAL RELATIONS
SECTION. PRINCETON, NEW JERSEY. 1966. PP 123-155.

GROCHJP63057 ROCHE JP
THE QUEST FOR THE DREAM. THE DEVELOPMENT OF CIVIL-RIGHTS AND
HUMAN-RELATIONS IN MODERN AMERICA.
MACMILLAN. NEW YORK. 1963.

GRODOJAL64241 RODOMSKI AL   MILLS AU
*US DEPT HEALTH ED WELFARE
FAMILY INCOME AND RELATED CHARACTERISTICS AMONG LOW-INCOME
COUNTIES AND STATES.
US DEPARTMENT OF HEALTH, EDUCATION, AND WELFARE, WELFARE
RESEARCH REPORT NO 1. GPO. WASHINGTON, DC. 1964.

GROOSFD66242 ROOSEVELT FD   *ANTI-DEFAMATION LEAGUE
FOUNDATION FOR THE GREAT SOCIETY. /EEO/
ANTI-DEFAMATION LEAGUE OF B-NAI B-RITH, ADL BULLETIN,
JAN 1966.

GROPEEXND243 ROPER E   *CONN COMM ON CIVIL RIGHTS
EXTRAVAGANT INJUSTICE. DISCRIMINATION IN INDUSTRY.
/CONNECTICUT/
CONNECTICUT COMMISSION ON CIVIL RIGHTS. HARTFORD,
CONNECTICUT. ND. PP.

GROPEEX49245 ROPER E   *JTSAM INST RELIG SOC STUDIES
THE PRICE BUSINESS PAYS. /INDUSTRY DISCRIMINATION/
DISCRIMINATION AND NATIONAL WELFARE. ED BY R M MACIVER.
INSTITUTE FOR RELIGIOUS AND SOCIAL STUDIES. JEWISH
THEOLOGICAL SEMINARY OF AMERICA. HARPER BROS. NEW YORK.
1949. PP 15-24.

GROPEEX63244 ROPER E   *NATL CONF CHRISTIANS JEWS
THE HIGH COST OF DISCRIMINATION. THE WASTE IN MANPOWER,

MORALE, AND PRODUCTIVITY COSTS AMERICAN INDUSTRY 30
BILLION DOLLARS A YEAR.
NATIONAL CONFERENCE OF CHRISTIANS AND JEWS. NEW YORK. 1963.
18 PP.

GRORTJX58246   RORTY   J
FEPC IN THE STATES. A PROGRESS REPORT.
ANTIOCH REVIEW, VOL 18, FALL 1958. PP 317-329.

GROSEAM65249   ROSE   AM ED   ROSE   CB ED
MINORITY PROBLEMS.
HARPER AND ROW. NEW YORK. 1965. 434 PP.

GROSEAW50288   ROSE   AW
THE CHANGING ECONOMIC BACKGROUND OF AMERICAN RACE-RELATIONS.
SOUTHWESTERN SOCIAL SCIENCE QUARTERLY, VOL 31, DEC 1950.
PP 159-173.

GROSEBC59252   ROSEN   BC
RACE, ETHNICITY, AND THE ACHIEVEMENT SYNDROME.
AMERICAN SOCIOLOGICAL REVIEW, VOL 24, NO 1, FEB 1959.
PP 47-60.

GROSECX60257   ROSENFELD   C   *US DEPARTMENT OF LABOR
WORK EXPERIENCE OF THE POPULATION IN 1960.
US DEPARTMENT OF LABOR, MONTHLY LABOR REVIEW, VOL 4, NO 12,
REPORT NO 19, DEC 1960. 34 PP.

GROSEHS66253   ROSEN   HS
EQUAL-OPPORTUNITY UNDER THE MERIT SYSTEM.
PUBLIC PERSONNEL REVIEW, JULY 1966. PP 175-179.

GROSEJM66C08   ROSENBERG   JM
AUTOMATION, MANPOWER, AND EDUCATION.
RANDOM HOUSE. NEW YORK. 1966. 179 PP.

GROSEPI64251   ROSE   PI
THEY AND WE, RACIAL AND ETHNIC RELATIONS IN THE UNITED
STATES.
RANDOM HOUSE. NEW YORK. 1964. 177 PP.

GROSESJ65255   ROSEN   SJ
THE LAW AND RACIAL DISCRIMINATION IN EMPLOYMENT.
CALIFORNIA LAW REVIEW, VOL 53, NO 3, AUG 1965. PP 729-799.

GROSESJ66254   ROSEN   SJ
DIVISION OF AUTHORITY UNDER TITLE-VII OF THE
CIVIL-RIGHTS-ACT OF 1964. A PRELIMINARY STUDY IN
FEDERAL-STATE INTERAGENCY RELATIONS.
GEORGE WASHINGTON LAW REVIEW, VOL 34, JUNE 1966. PP 846-892.

GROSETXND250   ROSE   T   KINCH   J
*SAN FRANCISCO CC CIVIC UNITY
THE SAN-FRANCISCO NON-WHITE POPULATION 1950-1960.
/CALIFORNIA/
SAN FRANCISCO COUNCIL FOR CIVIC UNITY. SAN FRANCISCO.
MIMEOGRAPHED. ND. 15 PP.

GROSJRG66258   ROSOFSKY   RG   GOLDSTEIN   B
*US DEPARTMENT OF LABOR
TRAINING OF PUBLIC ASSISTANCE RECIPIENTS UNDER THE MDTA.
US DEPARTMENT OF LABOR, MANPOWER EVALUATION REPORT, NO 6,
AP 1966. GPO. WASHINGTON, DC. 29 PP.

GROSSAM65720   ROSS   AM ED
EMPLOYMENT POLICY AND THE LABOR-MARKET.
UNIVERSITY OF CALIFORNIA PRESS. BERKELEY, CALIFORNIA. 1965.
406 PP.

GROSSAM66083   ROSS   AM
THE NEXT 20 YEARS IN MANPOWER.
THE W E UPJOHN INSTITUTE FOR EMPLOYMENT RESEARCH, 20TH
ANNIVERSARY MEETING. SPEECH. AUGUSTA, MICHIGAN. OCT 6 1966.
22 PP.

GROSSAM66084   ROSS   AM
THE ROLE OF GOVERNMENT IN PROMOTING FULL EMPLOYMENT.
UNIVERSITY OF ILLINOIS, PHI DELTA KAPPA SYMPOSIUM. SPEECH.
URBANA, ILLINOIS. MAR 27-30 1966. 31 PP.

GROSSLX66557   ROSS   L
GRAPE WORKERS WIN NEW GAINS. /MIGRANT-WORKERS   UNION
CALIFORNIA/
LABOR TODAY, VOL 5, NO 4, AUG-SEPT 1966. PP 23-25.

GROSSMS66844   ROSS   MS
PUBLIC WORK AND THE LONG-TERM UNEMPLOYED.
INDUSTRIAL AND LABOR RELATIONS FORUM, VOL 3, NOV 1966.
PP 217-228.

GROSSMX47261   ROSS   M
THE OUTLOOK FOR A NEW FEPC. THE 80TH CONGRESS AND JOB
DISCRIMINATION.
COMMENTARY, VOL 3, AP 1947. PP 301-308.

GROSSMX47262   ROSS   M
THEY DID IT IN ST-LOUIS. /INDUSTRY   INTEGRATION MISSOURI/
COMMENTARY, JULY 1947. PP 9-15.

GROSSMX48260   ROSS   M
ALL MANNER OF MEN. /FEPC/
REYNAL AND HITCHCOCK. NEW YORK. 1948.

GROUCJX55263   ROUCEK   J
PREJUDICE AND ECONOMIC DOGMA.
SOCIAL STUDIES, VOL 46, NO 3, MAR 1955. PP 83-89.

GROUTFB64264   ROUTH   FB
SUPPLEMENTARY ACTIVITIES FOR STATE GOVERNMENTS SEEKING TO
ELIMINATE DISCRIMINATION.
BUFFALO LAW REVIEW, VOL 14, NO 1, FALL 1964. PP 148-150.

GRUBIAX46265   RUBIN   A   SEGAL   G
INDUSTRY-S EXPERIMENT TOWARDS INTEGRATION OF MINORITIES INTO
INDUSTRY.
ANNALS OF THE AMERICAN ACADEMY OF POLITICAL AND SOCIAL
SCIENCE, MAR 1946. PP 53-64.

GRUCHLX53266   RUCHAMES   L
RACE, JOBS, AND POLITICS. THE STORY OF FEPC.
COLUMBIA UNIVERSITY PRESS. NEW YORK. 1953. 255 PP.

GRUDDEN63267   RUDDOCK   EN   *US DEPARTMENT OF LABOR
HELPING TO OVERCOME MINORITY-GROUP PROBLEMS.
US DEPARTMENT OF LABOR, EMPLOYMENT SECURITY REVIEW, VOL 30,
NOS 11 AND 12, NOV AND DEC 1963. P 8.

GRUSHJT66268   RUSMORE   JT   *CALIFORNIA FEPC
PSYCHOLOGICAL TESTS AND FAIR EMPLOYMENT. A STUDY OF
EMPLOYMENT TESTING IN THE SAN-FRANCISCO BAY AREA.

/CALIFORNIA/
CALIFORNIA FAIR EMPLOYMENT PRACTICE COMMISSION, TECHNICAL
ADVISORY COMMITTEE ON TESTING. SACRAMENTO, CALIFORNIA.
JUNE 28 1966. UNPUBLISHED.

GRUSSJL66269   RUSSELL   JL   *US DEPARTMENT OF LABOR
CHANGING PATTERNS IN EMPLOYMENT OF NONWHITE WORKERS.
US DEPARTMENT OF LABOR, MONTHLY LABOR REVIEW, MAY 1966.
PP 503-509.

GRUTTVW59270   RUTTAN   VW
FARM AND NON-FARM EMPLOYMENT OPPORTUNITIES FOR LOW-INCOME
FARM FAMILIES.
PHYLON, VOL 20, NO 3, 1959. PP 248-255.

GRYANWX65485   RYAN   W
SAVAGE DISCOVERY. THE MOYNIHAN REPORT.
THE NATION, VOL 201, NO 17, NOV 22 1965. PP 380-384.

GSABESX64271   SABEN   S   *US DEPARTMENT OF LABOR
GEOGRAPHIC MOBILITY AND EMPLOYMENT STATUS,
MARCH 1962-MARCH 1963.
US DEPARTMENT OF LABOR, MONTHLY LABOR REVIEW, AUG 1964.
PP 873-881. ALSO US DEPARTMENT OF LABOR, BUREAU OF LABOR
STATISTICS, SPECIAL LABOR FORCE REPORT, NO 44. 20 PP.

GSABESX64272   SABEN   S   *US DEPARTMENT OF LABOR
WORK EXPERIENCE OF THE POPULATION IN 1962.
US DEPARTMENT OF LABOR, MONTHLY LABOR REVIEW, VOL 85, NO 1,
REPORT NO 38, JAN 1964. 35 PP.

GSAENGX48273   SAENGER   G   GORDON   NS
*RESEARCH INTERGROUP RELS
THE INFLUENCE OF DISCRIMINATION ON MINORITY-GROUP MEMBERS IN
ITS RELATION TO ATTEMPTS TO COMBAT DISCRIMINATION.
RESEARCH COMMITTEE ON INTERGROUP RELATIONS. NEW YORK. JUNE
1948. 29 PP.

GSALNEX65769   SALNER   E   *US DEPARTMENT OF LABOR
THE MANPOWER PROBLEMS OF AUTOMATION.
US DEPARTMENT OF LABOR, EMPLOYMENT SERVICE REVIEW, VOL 2,
NO 10, OCT 1965. PP 48-54.

GSALTAF66534   SALT   AF   *US DEPARTMENT OF LABOR
ESTIMATED NEED FOR SKILLED-WORKERS, 1965-75. /EMPLOYMENT/
US DEPARTMENT OF LABOR, MONTHLY LABOR REVIEW, VOL 89, NO 4,
AP 1966. PP 365-371.

GSAMLJX64843   SAMLER   J
TECHNOLOGICAL-CHANGE AND VOCATIONAL COUNSELING.
AUTOMATION. THE THREAT AND THE PROMISE. THE ROLE OF THE
COUNSELOR IN THE MANPOWER REVOLUTION. AMERICAN PERSONNEL AND
GUIDANCE ASSOCIATION. WASHINGTON, DC. 1964. PP 57-66.

GSAMOJX63501   SAMORA   J
THE EDUCATIONAL STATUS OF A MINORITY. /MIGRANT-WORKERS/
OHIO STATE UNIVERSITY, COLLEGE OF EDUCATION, BUREAU OF
EDUCATIONAL RESEARCH AND SERVICE. COLUMBUS, OHIO. JUNE 1963.
7 PP.

GSANDLW65274   SAN DIEGO LEAGUE WOMEN VOTERS
DIMENSIONS IN DISCRIMINATION, A PRELIMINARY SURVEY OF
SAN-DIEGO-S COMMUNITY PROBLEMS OF DISCRIMINATION PART II.
/CALIFORNIA/
SAN DIEGO. LEAGUE OF WOMEN VOTERS. SAN DIEGO, CALIFORNIA.
AP 1965. 35 PP.

GSANFCE60275   SAN FRANCISCO COMM EEO
FINAL REPORT OF SAN-FRANCISCO CALIFORNIA COMMISSION ON
EQUAL-EMPLOYMENT-OPPORTUNITY.
SAN FRANCISCO COMMISSION ON EQUAL EMPLOYMENT OPPORTUNITY.
SAN FRANCISCO, CALIFORNIA. 1960. 30 PP.

GSANFHR65264   SAN FRANCISCO HUM RIGHTS COMM
RACIAL AND ETHNIC EMPLOYMENT PATTERN SURVEY OF THE CITY AND
COUNTY OF SAN-FRANCISCO GOVERNMENT. DEPARTMENTAL ANALYSIS.
/CALIFORNIA/
SAN FRANCISCO HUMAN RIGHTS COMMISSION. SAN FRANCISCO,
CALIFORNIA. OCT 1965. 98 PP.

GSAWYDA62279   SAWYER   DA
FAIR-EMPLOYMENT IN THE NATION-S CAPITAL. A STUDY OF PROGRESS
AND DILEMMA. /WASHINGTON-DC/
JOURNAL OF INTERGROUP RELATIONS, VOL 4, WINTER 1962-1963.
PP 37-54.

GSCHEGX66280   SCHERMER   G   *POTOMAC INSTITUTE INC
EMPLOYERS GUIDE TO EQUAL-EMPLOYMENT-OPPORTUNITY.
THE POTOMAC INSTITUTE, INC. WASHINGTON, DC. MAR 1966. 77 PP.

GSCHERA49281   SCHERMERHORN   RA
THESE OUR PEOPLE. MINORITIES IN AMERICAN CULTURE.
HEATH. BOSTON, MASSACHUSETTS. 1949.

GSCHERA56058   SCHERMERHORN   RA
POWER AS A PRIMARY CONCEPT IN THE STUDY OF MINORITIES.
SOCIAL FORCES, VOL 35, OCT 1956. PP 53-56.

GSCHIJX60283   SCHIFFMAN   J   *US DEPARTMENT OF LABOR
FAMILY CHARACTERISTICS OF WORKERS, 1959.
US DEPARTMENT OF LABOR, MONTHLY LABOR REVIEW, VOL 83, NO 7,
AUG 1960. 27 PP.

GSCHIJX61284   SCHIFFMAN   J   *US DEPARTMENT OF LABOR
MARITAL AND FAMILY CHARACTERISTICS OF WORKERS, MARCH 1960.
US DEPARTMENT OF LABOR, MONTHLY LABOR REVIEW, VOL 84, NO 13,
AP 1961. 33 PP.

GSCHIJX62285   SCHIFFMAN   J   *US DEPARTMENT OF LABOR
MARITAL AND FAMILY CHARACTERISTICS OF WORKERS, MARCH 1961.
US DEPARTMENT OF LABOR, MONTHLY LABOR REVIEW, VOL 85, NO 1,
REPORT NO 20, JAN 1962. 43 PP.

GSCHIJX63282   SCHIFFMAN   J   *US DEPARTMENT OF LABOR
EMPLOYMENT OF HIGH SCHOOL GRADUATES AND DROPOUTS IN 1962.
US DEPARTMENT OF LABOR, MONTHLY LABOR REVIEW, VOL 86,
JULY 1963. PP 772-779.

GSCHIJX63286   SCHIFFMAN   J   *US DEPARTMENT OF LABOR
MARITAL AND FAMILY CHARACTERISTICS OF WORKERS, MARCH 1962.
US DEPARTMENT OF LABOR, MONTHLY LABOR REVIEW, VOL 86, NO 1,
REPORT NO 26, JAN 1963. 13 PP.

GSCHMCT66287   SCHMIDT   CT
TITLE-VII. COVERAGE AND COMMENTS. /LEGISLATION/
BOSTON COLLEGE INDUSTRIAL AND COMMERCIAL LAW REVIEW, VOL 7,
NO 3, SPRING 1966. PP 459-472.

GSCHNLF63288   SCHNORE   LF   SHARP   H
RACIAL CHANGES IN METROPOLITAN AREAS, 1950-1960.

/DEMOGRAPHY/
SOCIAL FORCES, VOL 41, 1963. PP 247-252.

GSCHOAL65122 SCHORR AL   *US DEPT OF HEALTH ED WELFARE
SLUMS AND SOCIAL INSECURITY.
US DEPARTMENT OF HEALTH, EDUCATION, AND WELFARE, SOCIAL
SECURITY ADMINISTRATION, RESEARCH REPORT NO 1. WASHINGTON,
DC. 1965.

GSCHRJX46289 SCHREIBER J
MERIT AND MEN.
MENTAL HYGIENE. VOL 30, OCT 1946. PP 606-616.

GSCHJTW63895 SCHULTZ TW
THE ECONOMIC VALUE CF EDUCATION.
COLUMBIA UNIVERSITY PRESS. NEW YORK. 1963.

GSCHJTW65842 SCHULTZ TW
INVESTING IN POOR PEOPLE. AN ECONOMIST-S VIEW.
AMERICAN ECONOMIC REVIEW, VOL 60, MAY 1965. PP 510-520.

GSCHJTW67964 SCHULTZ TW
NATIONAL EMPLOYMENT, SKILLS, AND EARNINGS OF FARM LABOR.
FARM LABOR IN THE UNITED STATES. ED BY C E BISHOP. COLUMBIA
UNIVERSITY PRESS. NEW YORK. 1967. PP 53-70.

GSCHWLX66556 SCHWARTZ L
CONDITIONS FOR MIGRANTS -- A NATIONAL DISGRACE.
FAMILY SERVICE HIGHLIGHTS, VOL 27, NO 2, FEB 1966. PP 58-62.

GSCOTWW59291 SCOTT WW
INTERPERSONAL RELATIONS IN ETHNICALLY MIXED SMALL WORK
    GROUPS.
UNIVERSITY OF SOUTHERN CALIFORNIA. PHD THESIS. LOS ANGELES,
CALIFORNIA. 1959.

GSCOTWW61290 SCOTT WW
THE BALANCED ETHNIC WORK GROUP.
SOCIOLOGY AND SOCIAL RESEARCH, VOL 45, NO 2, JAN 1961.
PP 196-201.

GSCRESX63292 SCREVEN S
BIG BUSINESS FAILS AMERICA. /INDUSTRY/
AMERICA, VOL 108, JAN 12 1963. PP 44-46.

GSEASHX51293 SEASHORE H
PERSONNEL SELECTION TESTS AND FAIR-EMPLOYMENT-PRACTICES.
AMERICAN PSYCHOLOGIST, VOL 6, NO 4, AP 1951. PP 128-129.

GSEGABD59294 SEGAL BD   *NAIRO
THE PRACTICES OF CRAFT UNIONS IN WASHINGTON-DC WITH RESPECT
    TO MINORITY GROUPS IN CIVIL-RIGHTS IN THE NATION-S
    CAPITOL.
NATIONAL ASSOCIATION OF INTERGROUP RELATIONS OFFICIALS.
WASHINGTON, DC. NOV 1959.

GSEGABE66154 SEGAL BE ED
RACIAL AND ETHNIC RELATIONS. SELECTED READINGS.
THOMAS Y. CROWELL CC. NEW YORK. 1966. 491 PP.

GSEIDBX54295 SEIDMAN B
WHO ARE THE UNEMPLOYED.
THE AMERICAN FEDERATIONIST, VOL 61, NO 12, DEC 1954.
PP 11-14.

GSELIBB65686 SELIGMAN BB
POVERTY AS A PUBLIC ISSUE.
THE FREE PRESS. NEW YORK. 1965. 359 PP.

GSELIBB66609 SELIGMAN BB
ON THEORIES OF AUTOMATION. A POLEMIC AGAINST DANIEL BELL AND
    OTHERS. /UNEMPLOYMENT/
DISSENT, VOL 13, NO 3, MAY-JUNE 1966. PP 243-264.

GSELIBB66841 SELIGMAN BB
MOST NOTORIOUS VICTORY. MAN IN AN AGE OF AUTOMATION.
THE FREE PRESS. NEW YORK. 1966. 441 PP.

GSETSLX64296 SETSLEIS L
CIVIL-RIGHTS AND THE REHABILITATION OF AFDC CLIENTS.
SOCIAL WORK, VOL 3, NO 9, AP 1964. PP 3-9.

GSEWEWH57297 SEWELL WH
SOCIAL-STATUS AND EDUCATIONAL AND OCCUPATIONAL ASPIRATION.
AMERICAN SOCIOLOGICAL REVIEW, FEB 1957.

GSEXTPX61298 SEXTON P
EDUCATION AND INCOME. INEQUALITIES IN OUR PUBLIC SCHOOLS.
VIKING PRESS. NEW YORK. 1961. 298 PP.

GSHAFHB66801 SHAFFER HB
GUARANTEED-INCOME PLAN.
EDITORIAL RESEARCH REPORTS. VOL 1, NO 21, JUNE 8 1966.
PP 401-417.

GSHAREF59428 SHARP EF   LARSON OF
LERAY NL   *US DEPARTMENT OF AGRICULTURE
MIGRATORY WORKERS IN NEW-YORK, CHANGES, 1953, 1957, AND
    1958.
US DEPARTMENT OF AGRICULTURE, AGRICULTURAL RESEARCH SERVICE.
GPO. WASHINGTON, DC. AUG 1959. 17 PP.

GSHAREF60427 SHARP EF   LARSON OF
*US DEPARTMENT OF AGRICULTURE
MIGRATORY FARM WORKERS IN THE ATLANTIC COAST STREAM, II.
    EDUCATION OF NEW-YORK WORKERS AND THEIR CHILDREN, 1953 AND
    1957.
US DEPARTMENT OF AGRICULTURE, AGRICULTURAL RESEARCH SERVICE.
GPO. WASHINGTON, DC. MAY 1960.

GSHAUDF63300 SHAUGHNESSY DF
A SURVEY OF DISCRIMINATION IN THE BUILDING TRADES INDUSTRY,
    NEW-YORK CITY.
NEW YORK ADVISORY COMMITTEE TO THE US COMMISSION ON CIVIL
RIGHTS. NEW YORK. AP 1963.

GSHEPAC59301 SHEPARD AC
HEALTH WOKK AMONG MIGRANTS IN 1958 BY THE NEW-JERSEY STATE
    DEPARTMENT OF HEALTH.
PUBLIC HEALTH NEWS, VOL 40, NO 3, MAR 1959. PP 73-78.

GSHEPHL64621 SHEPPARD HL
MOBILITY, METHODS OF JOB SEARCH, ATTITUDES, AND MOTIVATION
    OF DISPLACED WORKERS.
ORGANIZATION FOR ECONOMIC COOPERATION AND DEVELOPMENT,
NORTH AMERICAN JOINT CONFERENCE. THE REQUIREMENTS OF
AUTOMATED JOBS. WASHINGTON, DC. DEC 8-10 1964. PP 293-318.

GSHEPHL65965 SHEPPARD HL
POVERTY AND THE NEGRO.

POVERTY AS A PUBLIC ISSUE. ED BY BEN B SELIGMAN. THE FREE
PRESS. NEW YORK. 1965. PP 118-138.

GSHEPHL65966 SHEPPARD HL
THE YOUNG WHO ARE PCOR.
POVERTY AS A PUBLIC ISSUE. ED BY BEN B SELIGMAN. THE FREE
PRESS. NEW YORK. 1965. PP 102-117.

GSHERHL65302 SHERMAN HL
UNION-S DUTY OF FAIR REPRESENTATION AND THE CIVIL-RIGHTS-ACT
    OF 1964.
MINNESOTA LAW REVIEW, VOL 49, NO 5, AP 1965.

GSHIBTX65303 SHIBUTANI T   KWAN K
ETHNIC STRATIFICATION, A COMPARATIVE APPROACH.
MACMILLAN. NEW YORK. 1965.

GSHIREM58304 SHIRK EM
CASES ARE PEOPLE. AN INTERPRETATION OF THE PENNSYLVANIA
    FAIR-EMPLOYMENT-PRACTICE LAW.
DICKINSON LAW REVIEW, VOL 62, JUNE 1958. PP 289-305.

GSHISBX59305 SHISHKIN B
ORGANIZED LABOR AND THE MINORITY WORKER NEED EACH OTHER.
    /UNION/
THE AMERICAN FEDERATIONIST, VOL 66, NO 11, DEC 1959.
PP 24-25.

GSHOSAB63307 SHOSTAK AB
IMPROVING INDUSTRIAL RACE-RELATIONS -- PART 2, HUMAN
    PROBLEMS IN IMPROVING INDUSTRIAL RACE-RELATIONS.
PERSONNEL ADMINISTRATION, VOL 26, MAR-AP 1963. PP 28-31.

GSHOSAB65685 SHOSTAK AB ED   GOMBERG W ED
NEW PERSPECTIVES ON POVERTY.
PRENTICE-HALL, INC. ENGLEWOOD CLIFFS, NEW JERSEY. 1965.
184 PP.

GSHOSAL65306 SHOSTACK AL   *US DEPARTMENT OF LABOR
MIGRANT CREWS IN EASTERN MARYLAND.
US DEPARTMENT OF LABOR, EMPOLYMENT SERVICE REVIEW, VOL 2,
NOS 1 AND 2, JAN-FEB 1965. PP 32-37.

GSHOTLR61684 SHOTWELL LR
THE HARVESTERS. THE STORY OF THE MIGRANT PEOPLE.
DOUBLEDAY AND CO, INC. NEW YORK. 1961. 242 PP.

GSHRYHS64305 SHRYOCK HS   *U CHI COM FAMILY STUDY CENT
POPULATION MOBILITY WITHIN THE UNITED STATES.
UNIVERSITY OF CHICAGO, COMMUNITY AND FAMILY STUDY CENTER.
CHICAGO, ILLINOIS. 1964.

GSHULGX66142 SHULTZ G   *US DEPARTMENT OF LABOR
UNEMPLOYMENT AND LABOR-MARKET POLICY.
US DEPARTMENT OF LABOR, MONTHLY LABOR REVIEW, JAN 1966.

GSIFFHX64105 SIFF H   *US DEPT OF HEALTH ED WELFARE
PROJECTED CHANGES IN THE OCCUPATIONAL STRUCTURE OF THE
    LABOR-FORCE. IMPLICATIONS FOR PUBLIC WELFARE.
US DEPARTMENT OF HEALTH, EDUCATION, AND WELFARE, WELFARE
ADMINISTRATION, WELFARE IN REVIEW. MARCH 1964. PP 1-15.

GSILAJX63310 SILARD J   *POTOMAC INSTITUTE INC
STATE EXECUTIVE AUTHORITY TO PROMOTE CIVIL-RIGHTS. AN ACTION
    PROGRAM FOR THE 1960-S.
THE POTOMAC INSTITUTE, INC. WASHINGTON, DC. JAN 1963. 59 PP.

GSILBCE65038 SILBERMAN CE
THE MIXED-UP WAR-ON-POVERTY.
FORTUNE. AUG 1965. PP 156-161, 218-226.

GSIMJCK46311 SIMON CK
LEGAL SANCTIONS AGAINST JOB DISCRIMINATION.
MENTAL HYGIENE, VOL 30, OCT 1946. PP 606-623.

GSIMPDX64312 SIMPSON D   HUDSON B
SELECTED LIST OF REFERENCES ON MINORITY-GROUP EMPLOYMENT IN
    THE PUBLIC SERVICE.
UNIVERSITY OF CALIFORNIA, INSTITUTE OF GOVERNMENTAL STUDIES.
BERKELEY, CALIFORNIA. MIMEOGRAPHED. MAY 1964. 34 PP.

GSIMPGE62313 SIMPSON GE
EMPLOYMENT POLICY PROBLEMS IN A MULTIRACIAL SOCIETY.
JOURNAL OF HUMAN RELATIONS, VOL 11, NO 1, AUTUMN 1962. P 43.

GSIMPGE65314 SIMPSON GE   YINGER JM
RACIAL AND CULTURAL MINORITIES.
HARPER AND ROW. NEW YORK. 3RD ED. 1965. 582 PP.

GSKRARL57315 SKRABANEK RL   BOWLES GK
*TEXAS AGL EXPERIMENT STATION
MIGRATION OF THE TEXAS FARM POPULATION.
TEXAS AGRICULTURAL EXPERIMENT STATION, BULLETIN 847. COLLEGE
STATION, TEXAS. 1957. 8 PP.

GSLAIDX64316 SLAIMAN D
CIVIL-RIGHTS. THE FACTS AND THE CHALLENGE.
THE AMERICAN FEDERATIONIST, VOL 71, NO 9, SEPT 1964.
PP 7-12.

GSLAIDX64318 SLAIMAN D
LABOR-S TASK FORCES. /UNION/
THE AMERICAN FEDERATIONIST, VOL 71, NO 3, MAR 1964. PP 5-7.

GSLAIDX66317 SLAIMAN D
LABOR-S ROLE. DEMOCRACY ON THE JOB. /UNION/
THE AMERICAN FEDERATIONIST, VOL 73, NO 11, NOV 1966.
PP 8-12.

GSLAIDX67840 SLAIMAN D
LABOR AND FAIR-EMPLOYMENT PRACTICE. /UNION/
NORTH DAKOTA LAW REVIEW, VOL 43, NO 2, WINTER 1967.
PP 289-298.

GSMITAE65140 SMITH AE   COLLINS HA
MEINDL JL
EVALUATION AND SKILL TRAINING OF OUT-OF-SCHOOL, HARD-CORE
    UNEMPLOYED YOUTH FOR TRAINING AND PLACEMENT.
ST. LOUIS UNIVERSITY, DEPARTMENT OF EDUCATION, EXPERIMENTAL
AND DEMONSTRATION MANPOWER PROGRAM. ST. LOUIS, MISSOURI.
1964-1965.

GSMITCX62319 SMITH COLLEGE
RESEARCH BULLETIN ON INTERGROUP-RELATIONS. /EEO/
SMITH COLLEGE. NORTH HAMPTON, MASSACHUSETTS. JAN 1962.
30 PP.

GSMITSX55320 SMITH S
FREEDOM TO WORK. /FEPC LEGISLATION/
VANTAGE PRESS. NEW YORK. 1955.

GSNOWCX65683   SNOW C
EQUAL-EMPLOYMENT-OPPORTUNITY.
GEORGIA STATE BAR JOURNAL. VOL 2, AUG 1965, PP 27-35.

GSNYDEM58114   SNYDER EM
PUBLIC ASSISTANCE RECIPIENTS IN NEW-YORK STATE,
   JANUARY-FEBRUARY 1957.
NEW YORK STATE INTERDEPARTMENTAL COMMITTEE ON LOW INCOMES.
NEW YORK. 1958.

GSOLORX62323   SOLOW R
A POLICY FOR FULL EMPLOYMENT.
INDUSTRIAL RELATIONS, VOL 2, OCT 1962. PP 1-14.

GSOMEGG65717   SOMERS GG
RETRAINING, AN EVALUATION OF GAINS AND COSTS.
EMPOYMENT POLICY AND THE LABOR MARKET. ED BY A M ROSS.
UNIVERSITY OF CALIFORNIA PRESS. BERKELEY, CALIFORNIA.
1965. PP 271-298.

GSOMEGJ64157   SOMERS GJ   STROMSDORFER EW
A BENEFIT-COST ANALYSIS OF MANPOWER RETRAINING.
INDUSTRIAL RELATIONS RESEARCH ASSOCIATION, 17TH ANNUAL
MEETING, PROCEEDINGS. MADISON, WISCONSIN. DEC 28-29 1964.
PP 172-185.

GSOUTJH59325   SOUTHERN JH   HENDRIX WE
*TEXAS AGL EXPERIMENT STATION
INCOMES OF RURAL FAMILIES IN NORTHEAST TEXAS.
TEXAS A AND M UNIVERSITY, TEXAS AGRICULTURAL EXPERIMENT
STATION, BULLETIN 940. COLLEGE STATION, TEXAS. 1959.

GSOUTSE50324   SOUTHALL SE
INDUSTRY-S UNFINISHED BUSINESS. /CASE-STUDY/
HARPER AND BROTHERS. NEW YORK. 1950. 173 PP.

GSOVEMI66326   SOVERN MI   *TWENTIETH CENTURY FUND
LEGAL RESTRAINTS ON RACIAL DISCRIMINATION IN EMPLOYMENT.
THE TWENTIETH CENTURY FUND. NEW YORK. 1966. 270 PP.

GSOWOWT58327   SOWDER WT   LAURENCE J
THE IMMOKALEE STORY. /MIGRANT-WORKERS FLORIDA/
FLORIDA HEALTH NOTES, OCT 1958.

GSOWOWT59328   SOWDER WT   LAURENCE J
A MIGRANT LABOR CRISIS IN IMMOKALEE. /FLORIDA/
PUBLIC HEALTH REPORTS, VOL 74, NO 1, JAN 1959. PP 77-80.

GSPAREV66839   SPARER EV   *NYU CENT STUDY UNEMP YOUTH
EMPLOYABILITY AND THE JUVENILE ARREST RECORD.
NEW YORK UNIVERSITY, GRADUATE SCHOOL OF SOCIAL WORK, CENTER
FOR THE STUDY OF UNEMPLOYED YOUTH. NEW YORK. JUNE 1966.
14 PP.

GSPECWH63329   SPECK WH
ENFORCEMENT OF NONDISCRIMINATION REQUIREMENTS FOR GOVERNMENT
   CONTRACT WORK.
COLUMBIA LAW REVIEW, VOL 63, NO 2, FEB 1963. PP 243-265.

GSPERBJ53330   SPEROFF BJ
PROBLEMS AND APPROACHES IN INTEGRATING MINORITY-GROUP WORK
   FORCES.
JOURNAL OF SOCIAL PSYCHOLOGY, VOL 37, 1953. PP 271-273.

GSPITHX64331   SPITZ H
TAILORING THE TECHNIQUES TO ELIMINATE AND PREVENT EMPLOYMENT
   DISCRIMINATION.
BUFFALO LAW REVIEW, VOL 14, FALL 1964. PP 79-99.

GSPITRS45332   SPITZ RS   *US DEPARTMENT OF LABOR
STATE LEGISLATION IN LABOR-RELATIONS AND DISCRIMINATION IN
   EMPLOYMENT, 1945.
US DEPARTMENT OF LABOR, MONTHLY LABOR REVIEW, VOL 61,
NOV 1945. PP 984-991.

GSTAMHX65768   STAMBLER H   *US DEPARTMENT OF LABOR
MANPOWER NEEDS BY INDUSTRY TO 1975.
US DEPARTMENT OF LABOR, MONTHLY LABOR REVIEW, VOL 88, NO 3,
MARCH 1965. PP 279-283.

GSTANES64635   STANTON ES
PSYCHOLOGICAL TESTING IN INDUSTRY. A CRITICAL EVALUATION.
PERSONNEL JOURNAL, VOL 43, NO 1, JAN 1964. PP 27-32.

GSTANLR65333   STANFORD LAW REVIEW
THE CALIFORNIA FEPC. STEPCHILD OF THE STATE AGENCIES.
STANFORD LAW REVIEW, VOL 18, NO 1, NOV 1965. PP 187-212.

GSTEIBX64335   STEIN B
INTRODUCTION. THE STRUGGLE FOR EQUALITY AND ITS IMPACT ON
   INDUSTRIAL-RELATIONS.
NEW YORK UNIVERSITY, SEVENTEENTH ANNUAL CONFERENCE ON
LABOR, PROCEEDINGS. BUREAU OF NATIONAL AFFAIRS, INC.
REPRINT. WASHINGTON, DC. 1964. PP 95-105.

GSTEIRL63838   STEIN RL   *US DEPARTMENT OF LABOR
WORK HISTORY, ATTITUDES, AND INCOME OF THE UNEMPLOYED.
US DEPARTMENT OF LABOR, MONTHLY LABOR REVIEW, VOL 86,
DEC 1963. PP 1405-1413.

GSTEIRL64336   STEIN RL   MEREDITH JL
*US DEPARTMENT OF LABOR
UNEMPLOYMENT AMONG FULL-TIME AND PART-TIME WORKERS.
US DEPARTMENT OF LABOR, MONTHLY LABOR REVIEW, VOL 87, NO 9,
REPORT NO 45, SEPT 1964. 5 PP.

GSTETHG53598   STETLER HG   *CONN COMM ON CIVIL RIGHTS
MINORITY-GROUP INTEGRATION BY LABOR AND MANAGEMENT. A STUDY
   OF THE EMPLOYMENT PRACTICES OF THE LARGER EMPLOYERS, AND
   THE MEMBERSHIP PRACTICES OF THE LARGER LABOR UNIONS WITH
   RESPECT TO RACE, RELIGION, AND NATIONAL ORIGIN,
   CONNECTICUT, 1951.
CONNECTICUT COMMISSION ON CIVIL RIGHTS. HARTFORD,
CONNECTICUT. 1953. 67 PP.

GSTOIVX66001   STOIKOV V
INCREASING STRUCTURAL UNEMPLOYMENT RE-EXAMINED.
INDUSTRIAL AND LABOR RELATIONS REVIEW, VOL 19, NO 3, AP
1966. PP 368-376.

GSTRAGX65715   STRAUSS G
APPRENTICESHIP. AN EVALUATION OF THE NEED.
EMPLOYMENT POLICY AND THE LABOR MARKET. ED BY A M ROSS.
UNIVERSITY OF CALIFORNIA PRESS. BERKELEY, CALIFORNIA. 1965.
PP 299-332.

GSTREPX64337   STREIT P
PRINCETON-S LESSON. SCHOOL INTEGRATION IS NOT ENOUGH.
   /NEW-JERSEY/

THE NEW YORK TIMES MAGAZINE, JUNE 21 1964. P 14 PLUS.

GSTRIHE66669   STRINER HE   *US DEPARTMENT OF LABOR
TRAINING IN THE PERSPECTIVE OF TECHNOLOGICAL-CHANGE.
US DEPARTMENT OF LABOR, MANPOWER ADMINISTRATION, SEMINAR ON
MANPOWER POLICY AND PROGRAM. JAN 1966. 25 PP.

GSTRUJW63338   STRUTT JW   *PENNSYLVANIA HUM RELS COMM
SURVEY OF NON-WHITE EMPLOYEES IN STATE GOVERNMENT.
   /PENNSYLVANIA/
PENNSYLVANIA DEPARTMENT OF LABOR AND INDUSTRY, HUMAN
RELATIONS COMMISSION. HARRISBURG, PENNSYLVANIA. MAR 28 1963.
9 PP.

GSTURAF64837   STURMTHAL AF
CURRENT MANPOWER PROBLEMS. AN INTRODUCTORY SURVEY.
UNIVERSITY OF ILLINOIS, INSTITUTE OF LABOR AND INDUSTRIAL
RELATIONS. CHAMPAIGN, ILLINOIS. 1964. 103 PP.

GSTYLPL50339   STYLES PL
HOW TO HANDLE RACE LABOR-RELATIONS. /UNION/
LABOR LAW JOURNAL, VOL 1, AUG 1950. PP 861-865.

GSULLJD50340   SULLIVAN JD
FAIR-EMPLOYMENT-PRACTICE IN NEW-YORK. LAW, EDUCATION GO HAND
   IN HAND.
AMERICA, MAR 4 1950.

GSULLLH66220   SULLIVAN LH   *US DEPARTMENT OF LABOR
OPPORTUNITIES-INDUSTRIALIZATION-CENTER. CRAFTSMEN WITH
   CONFIDENCE. /TRAINING/
US DEPARTMENT OF LABOR, OCCUPATIONAL OUTLOOK QUARTERLY,
VOL 10, NO 4, DEC 1966. PP 20-22.

GSULLNV65653   SULLIVAN NV
APPROACHES TO THE SCHOOL DROPOUT PROBLEM.
POVERTY IN AMERICA. ED BY M S GORDON. CHANDLER PUBLISHING
CO. SAN FRANCISCO, CALIFORNIA. 1965. PP 161-171.

GSUMMCW47342   SUMMERS CW
THE RIGHT TO JOIN A UNION.
COLUMBIA LAW REVIEW, VOL 47, 1947. PP 33 FF.

GSURVXX47341   SURVEY
MUNICIPAL FEPC IN MINNEAPOLIS. /MINNESOTA/
SURVEY, VOL 83, MAR 1947. P 86.

GSUTTEX57344   SUTTON E
THE WORLD OF THE MIGRANT CHILD.
EDUCATIONAL LEADERSHIP, JAN 1957.

GSUVAEM65345   SUVAL EM   HAMILTON H
SOME NEW EVIDENCE ON EDUCATIONAL SELECTIVITY IN MIGRATION
   FROM THE SOUTH.
SOCIAL FORCES, VOL 43, MAY 1965. PP 536-547.

GSWANJC66155   SWANSON JC   *US CHAMBER OF COMMERCE
VOCATIONAL-TECHNICAL EDUCATION AND ECONOMIC SECURITY.
THE DISADVANTAGED POOR. EDUCATION AND EMPLOYMENT. US CHAMBER
OF COMMERCE, TASK FORCE ON ECONOMIC GROWTH AND OPPORTUNITY.
WASHINGTON, DC. 1966. PP 367-396.

GSWERSX66535   SWERDLOFF S   *US DEPARTMENT OF LABOR
MANPOWER PROJECTIONS. SOME CONCEPTUAL PROBLEMS AND RESEARCH
   NEEDS. /EMPLOYMENT-TRENDS/
US DEPARTMENT OF LABOR, MONTHLY LABOR REVIEW, VOL 89, NO 2,
FEB 1966. PP 138-143.

GTANNAX63156   TANNEYHILL A
FROM SCHOOL TO JOB. GUIDANCE FOR MINORITY YOUTH.
PUBLIC AFFAIRS PAMPHLET NO 200. NEW YORK. 1963. 28 PP.

GTAYLHC66967   TAYLOR HC   *US DEPARTMENT OF LABOR
COORDINATION OF MANPOWER PROGRAMS.
US DEPARTMENT OF LABOR, MONTHLY LABOR REVIEW, VOL 89,
SEPT 1966. PP 959-964.

GTAYLHX62347   TAYLOR H
EQUAL-EMPLOYMENT-OPPORTUNITY.
NEW YORK UNIVERSITY, CONFERENCE ON LABOR, PROCEEDINGS.
NO 15. NEW YORK. 1962. PP 35-45.

GTAYLHX62348   TAYLOR H
PRESIDENT-S COMMITTEE ON EQUAL-EMPLOYMENT-OPPORTUNITY.
SOUTHWESTERN LAW JOURNAL, VOL 16, 1962. PP 101-112.

GTEMPLQ63349   TEMPLE LAW QUARTERLY
ADMINISTRATIVE LAW -- HUMAN-RELATIONS COMMISSIONS,
PENNSYLVANIA LAW AND DISCRIMINATORY EMPLOYMENT PRACTICE.
TEMPLE LAW QUARTERLY, VOL 36, 1963. PP 515-550.

GTENBJX65148   TENBROEK J
EQUAL UNDER LAW.
COLLIER BOOKS. NEW YORK. 1965. REVISED EDITION.

GTEXAAE60350   TEXAS AG EXPERIMENTAL STATION
INCOMES OF MIGRATORY AGRICULTURAL WORKERS.
TEXAS AGRICULTURAL EXPERIMENT STATION, BULLETIN NO 950.
COLLEGE STATION, TEXAS. MAR 1960. 12 PP.

GTEXACO59351   TEXAS CC ON MIGRANT LABOR
CONCLUSIONS AND RECOMMENDATIONS, FIRST CONFERENCE ON
   MIGRANT-LABOR.
TEXAS COUNCIL ON MIGRANT LABOR. AUSTIN, TEXAS. NOV 8 1959.
4 PP.

GTEXAEC59352   TEXAS EMPLOYMENT COMMISSION
TEXAS GROWERS AND WORKERS ON THE FARM, LOWER RIO-GRANDE
   VALLEY.
TEXAS EMPLOYMENT COMMISSION. AUSTIN, TEXAS. 1959.

GTHAMME50353   THAMES ME   *US DEPARTMENT OF LABOR
EMPLOYMENT PROGRAM FOR MINORITY-GROUPS.
US DEPARTMENT OF LABOR, EMPLOYMENT SECURITY REVIEW, VOL 17,
NO 11, NOV 1950. PP 7-10.

GTHEJRX63682   THEOBALD R
FREE MEN AND FREE MARKETS. /TECHNOLOGICAL-CHANGE
   GUARANTEED-INCOME/
LARKSON N POTTER, INC. NEW YORK. 1963. 208 PP.

GTHEJRX64610   THEOBALD R
POLITICAL NECESSITIES OF ABUNDANCE. /GUARANTEED-INCOME/
THE AMERICAN CHILD, VOL 46, NO 2, MAR 1964. PP 20-23.

GTHEJRX64968   THEOBALD R
THE POLITICAL NECESSITIES OF ABUNDANCE. /GUARANTEED-INCOME/
POVERTY IN PLENTY. ED BY G H DUNNE. P J KENNEDY AND SONS.
NEW YORK. 1964. PP 70-80.

GTHEORX66626 THEOBALD R ED
THE GUARANTEED-INCOME. NEXT STEP IN ECONOMIC REVOLUTION.
DOUBLEDAY AND COMPANY. NEW YORK. 1966. 233 PP.

GTHOMET58356 THOMPSON ET   HUGHES EC
RACE. INDIVIDUAL AND COLLECTIVE BEHAVIOR.
FREE PRESS. GLENCOE, ILLINOIS. 1958.

GTHO4JA47354 THOMAS JA
THE ECONOMIC SITUATION OF NATIONAL MINORITIES IN THE UNITED
STATES OF AMERICA.
NATIONAL CONFERENCE OF SOCIAL WORK PROCEEDINGS, VOL 74.
COLUMBIA UNIVERSITY PRESS. NEW YORK. 1947. PP 88-95.

GTHO4JA51355 THOMAS JA
FAIR-EMPLOYMENT WORKS -- TOOLS FOR HUMAN-RELATIONS.
OCEANA PUBLICATIONS. NEW YORK. 1951. 33 PP.

GTHURLC65970 THUROW LC
THE CHANGING STRUCTURE OF UNEMPLOYMENT. AN ECONOMETRIC
STUDY.
REVIEW OF ECONOMICS AND STATISTICS, VOL 47, NO 2, MAY 1965.
PP 137-149.

GTHURLC66640 THUROW LC
THE ROLE OF MANPOWER POLICY IN ACHIEVING AGGREGATE GOALS.
/EMPLOYMENT INCOME/
PAPER, CONFERENCE ON MANPOWER POLICY, BERKELEY UNEMPLOYMENT
PROJECT. NEW YORK. JUNE 1966. 41 PP.

GTHURLC67969 THUROW LC
AN ALTERNATIVE THEORY OF ECONOMIC DISCRIMINATION.
HARVARD UNIVERSITY. CAMBRIDGE, MASSACHUSETTS. MAR 1967.
23 PP. MIMEO.

GTHURLC67972 THUROW LC
THE CAUSES OF POVERTY.
QUARTERLY JOURNAL OF ECONOMICS, VOL 81, FEB 1967. PP 40-57.

GTIMBEX54357 TIMBERS E
LABOR UNIONS AND FAIR-EMPLOYMENT-PRACTICES LEGISLATION.
UNIVERSITY OF MICHIGAN. THESIS. ANN ARBOR, MICHIGAN. ALSO
UNIVERSITY MICROFILMS, PUBLICATION NO 7747. ANN ARBOR,
MICHIGAN. 1954.

GTITCJA57358 TITCH JA
SOCIAL RESPONSIBILITIES OF ORGANIZED LABOR. /UNION/
HARPERS. NEW YORK. 1957.

GTITMRM65359 TITMUSS RM   *US DEPT OF HEALTH ED WELFARE
THE ROLE OF REDISTRIBUTION IN SOCIAL POLICY.
US DEPARTMENT OF HEALTH, EDUCATION, AND WELFARE, SOCIAL
SECURITY BULLETIN, JUNE 1965. PP 14-20.

GTOBIJX66973 TOBIN J
THE CASE FOR AN INCOME-GUARANTEE.
PUBLIC INTEREST, NO 4, SUMMER 1966. PP 31-41.

GTOBRMC63361 TOBRINER MC
THE CALIFORNIA FAIR-EMPLOYMENT-PRACTICES-COMMISSION. ITS
HISTORY, ACCOMPLISHMENTS, AND LIMITATIONS.
STANFORD UNIVERSITY. MA THESIS. STANFORD, CALIFORNIA. 1963.

GTOBRMC65360 TOBRINER MC
CALIFORNIA FEPC.
HASTINGS LAW JOURNAL, VOL 16, 1965. PP 333-349.

GTOLLGS67974 TOLLEY GS   FARMER BM
FARM LABOR ADJUSTMENTS TO CHANGING TECHNOLOGY.
FARM LABOR IN THE UNITED STATES. ED BY C E BISHOP. COLUMBIA
UNIVERSITY PRESS. NEW YORK. 1967. PP 41-52.

GTOWEJX64362 TOWER J
FEPC -- SOME PRACTICAL CONSIDERATIONS.
FEDERAL BAR JOURNAL, VOL 24, WINTER 1964. PP 87-92.

GTRAVHX63836 TRAVIS H   *US DEPARTMENT OF LABOR
MOBILITY AND WORKER ADAPTATION TO ECONOMIC CHANGE IN THE US.
US DEPARTMENT OF LABOR, MANPOWER ADMINISTRATION, MANPOWER
RESEARCH BULLETIN NO 1. GPO. WASHINGTON, DC. 1963. 77 PP.

GTRIAHC63083 TRIANDIS HC
FACTORS AFFECTING EMPLOYEE SELECTION IN TWO CULTURES.
/DISCRIMINATION/
JOURNAL OF APPLIED PSYCHOLOGY, VOL 47, NO 2, AP 1963.
PP 89-96.

GTROURX62163 TROUTMAN R   *PRESIDENT-S COMMITTEE ON EEO
PLANS-FOR-PROGRESS.
PRESIDENT-S COMMITTEE ON EQUAL EMPLOYMENT OPPORTUNITY. GPO.
WASHINGTON, DC. AUG 1962. 11 PP PLUS.

GTUCKJN56363 TUCK JN   *ANTI-DEFAMATION LEAGUE
HOW WELL DOES TV FIGHT PREJUDICE.
ANTI-DEFAMATION LEAGUE OF B-NAI B-RITH, ADL BULLETIN, SEPT
1956.

GTULSCR66364 TULSA COMMUNITY RELS COMM
EMPLOYMENT SURVEY. /TULSA OKLAHOMA/
TULSA COMMUNITY RELATIONS COMMISSION. TULSA, OKLAHOMA. 1966.
10 PP.

GTUMIMM57164 TUMIN MM   *ANTI-DEFAMATION LEAGUE
SEGREGATION AND DESEGREGATION. A DIGEST OF RECENT RESEARCH.
ANTI-DEFAMATION LEAGUE OF B-NAI B-RITH. NEW YORK. 1957.
112 PP.

GTURNHC50365 TURNER HC
TOLERANCE IN INDUSTRY. THE RECORD.
EQUALITY IN AMERICA. ED BY G B DEHUSZAR. WILSON COMPANY.
NEW YORK. 1950.

GTURNRH52366 TURNER RH
LAW OF DISCRIMINATION IN THE EMPLOYMENT OF NONWHITES.
AMERICAN JOURNAL OF SOCIOLOGY, NOV 1952. PP 247-256.

GTUSSJE63367 TUSSMAN J ED
DISCRIMINATION AND LIVELIHOOD.
THE SUPREME COURT ON RACIAL DISCRIMINATION. ED BY JOSEPH
TUSSMAN. OXFORD UNIVERSITY PRESS. NEW YORK. 1963.
PP 225-272.

GTUTTCH47368 TUTTLE CH
BRIEF SUBMITTED IN SUPPORT OF SENATE BILL NO 984, A BILL TO
PROHIBIT DISCRIMINATION IN EMPLOYMENT....
US SENATE, COMMITTEE ON LABOR AND PUBLIC WELFARE. 80TH
CONGRESS, 1ST SESSION. JUNE 10 1947. GPO. WASHINGTON, DC.

GUAWXFPND369 UAW FAIR PRACTICES ANTI-DISCR
HANDBOOK FOR LOCAL UNION FAIR PRACTICES COMMITTEES. REVISED
EDITION.
UAW FAIR PRACTICES AND ANTI-DISCRIMINATION DEPARTMENT.
DETROIT, MICHIGAN. NO. 102 PP.

GUAWXIU56370 UAW INTERNATIONAL UNION
UAW OUTLAWS DISCRIMINATION. /UNION/
UAW INTERNATIONAL UNION. DETROIT, MICHIGAN. 1956. 12 PP.

GULLMJX63575 ULLMAN J
HOW ACCURATE ARE ESTIMATES OF STATE AND LOCAL UNEMPLOYMENT.
INDUSTRIAL AND LABOR RELATIONS REVIEW, VOL 16, AP 1963.

GUNITCC62322 UNITED CHURCH OF CHRIST
THE JOB AHEAD IN FAIR-EMPLOYMENT-PRACTICES.
UNITED CHURCH OF CHRIST, COUNCIL FOR CHRISTIAN SOCIAL
ACTION, SOCIAL ACTION, DEC 1962. ENTIRE ISSUE.

GUPHOWH64528 UPHOFF WH ED   *U OF COLORADO CENT LABOR ED
ECONOMIC, POLITICAL AND PSYCHOLOGICAL ASPECTS OF EMPLOYMENT.
UNIVERSITY OF COLORADO, CENTER FOR LABOR EDUCATION AND
RESEARCH. PROCEEDINGS, SYMPOSIUM ON EMPLOYMENT. DENVER.
COLORADO. MAY 22-23 1964. 56 PP.

GUSBURC65151 US BUREAU OF THE CENSUS
LOW-INCOME FAMILIES AND UNRELATED INDIVIDUALS IN THE UNITED
STATES. 1964. /DEMOGRAPHY/
US DEPARTMENT OF COMMERCE, BUREAU OF THE CENSUS, CURRENT
POPULATION REPORTS, SERIES P-60, NO 45. JUNE 1965.

GUSBURC65152 US BUREAU OF THE CENSUS
EDUCATIONAL-ATTAINMENT. MARCH 1964.
US DEPARTMENT OF COMMERCE, BUREAU OF THE CENSUS, CURRENT
POPULATION REPORTS, SERIES P-20, NO 138. MAY 1965.

GUSBURC65161 US BUREAU OF THE CENSUS
MOBILITY OF THE POPULATION OF THE UNITED STATES, JANUARY 1,
1950 TO FEBRUARY 1, 1965. /DEMOGRAPHY/
US DEPARTMENT OF COMMERCE, BUREAU OF THE CENSUS, POPULATION
ESTIMATES, SERIES P-25. GPO. WASHINGTON, DC. MAR 1965.

GUSBURC66158 US BUREAU OF THE CENSUS
MOBILITY OF THE POPCFATION FO THE UNITED STATES, MARCH 1964
TO MARCH 1965. /DEMOGRAPHY/
US DEPARTMENT OF COMMERCE, BUREAU OF THE CENSUS, POPULATION
CHARACTERISTICS, SERIES P-20, NO 150. GPO. WASHINGTON, DC.
AP 1966.

GUSBURC66159 US BUREAU OF THE CENSUS
POPULATION OF THE UNITED STATES BY METROPOLITAN AND
NONMETROPOLITAN RESIDENCE. /DEMOGRAPHY/
US DEPARTMENT OF COMMERCE, BUREAU OF THE CENSUS, POPULATION
CHARACTERISTICS, SERIES P-20, NO 151. GPO. WASHINGTON, DC.
AP 1966.

GUSBURC66160 US BUREAU OF THE CENSUS
PROJECTIONS OF SCHOOL AND COLLEGE ENROLLMENT IN THE UNITED
STATES TO 1985. /DEMOGRAPHY/
US DEPARTMENT OF COMMERCE, BUREAU OF THE CENSUS, POPULATION
ESTIMATES, SERIES P-25, NO 338. GPO. WASHINGTON, DC.
MAY 1966.

GUSCHACND383 US CHAMBER OF COMMERCE
JOBS TARGET -- EMPLOYMENT.
US CHAMBER OF COMMERCE. WASHINGTON, DC. ND. 95 PP.

GUSCHAC65186 US CHAMBER OF COMMERCE
THE CONCEPT OF POVERTY. /ECONOMIC-OPPORTUNITY/
US CHAMBER OF COMMERCE, TASK FORCE ON ECONOMIC GROWTH AND
OPPORTUNITY, WASHINGTON, DC. 1965. 136 PP.

GUSCHAC66187 US CHAMBER OF COMMERCE
THE DISADVANTAGED POOR. EDUCATION AND EMPLOYMENT.
US CHAMBER OF COMMERCE, TASK FORCE ON ECONOMIC GROWTH AND
OPPORTUNITY. WASHINGTON, DC. 1966.

GUSCISC49388 US CIVIL SERVICE COMMISSION
HOW DEPARTMENT X ELIMINATED SEGREGATION.
US CIVIL SERVICE COMMISSION, FAIR EMPLOYMENT BOARD,
INFORMATION BULLETIN NO 4. GPO. WASHINGTON, DC. NOV 21 1949.
2 PP.

GUSCISC51385 US CIVIL SERVICE COMMISSION
FAIR-EMPLOYMENT IN THE FEDERAL SERVICE.
US CIVIL SERVICE COMMISSION. GPO. WASHINGTON, DC. DEC 1951.
14 PP.

GUSCISC52386 US CIVIL SERVICE COMMISSION
FAIR-EMPLOYMENT IN THE FEDERAL SERVICE, A PROGRESS REPORT ON
CONSTRUCTIVE STEPS.
US CIVIL SERVICE COMMISSION, FAIR EMPLOYMENT BOARD,
INFORMATIONAL BULLETIN NO 6. GPO. WASHINGTON, DC. MAR 31
1952. 22 PP.

GUSCISC61387 US CIVIL SERVICE COMMISSION
GRAPHIC PRESENTATION OF FEDERAL-EMPLOYMENT.
US CIVIL SERVICE COMMISSION. GPO. WASHINGTON, DC. 1961.

GUSCISC63384 US CIVIL SERVICE COMMISSION
EQUAL-EMPLOYMENT-OPPORTUNITY TRAINING, A PROGRAM FOR
AFFIRMATIVE-ACTION.
US CIVIL SERVICE COMMISSION, OFFICE OF CAREER DEVELOPMENT.
GPO. WASHINGTON, DC. 1963. 9 PP.

GUSCISC64131 US CIVIL SERVICE COMMISSION
REPORT OF TWIN-CITIES EQUAL-OPPORTUNITY REVIEW.
/MINNEAPOLIS ST-PAUL MINNESOTA/
US CIVIL SERVICE COMMISSION, ST LOUIS REGION. MINNEAPOLIS
AND ST PAUL, MINNESOTA. MARCH 13 1964.

GUSCISC66767 US CIVIL SERVICE COMMISSION
STUDY OF MINORITY GROUP EMPLOYMENT IN THE FEDERAL
GOVERNMENT. 1966.
US CIVIL SERVICE COMMISSION. GPO. WASHINGTON, DC. 1966.

GUSCOMC60400 US COMMISSION ON CIVIL RIGHTS
US COMMISSION-ON-CIVIL-RIGHTS, HEARINGS. LOS-ANGELES AND
SAN-FRANCISCO, CALIFORNIA. JANUARY 25-26, 1960, JANUARY
27-28, 1960.
US COMMISSION ON CIVIL RIGHTS. GPO. WASHINGTON, DC. 1960.
902 PP.

GUSCOMC60405 US COMMISSION ON CIVIL RIGHTS
THE NATIONAL CONFERENCE AND THE REPORTS OF THE STATE
ADVISORY COMMITTEES TO THE U.S. COMMISSION ON
CIVIL-RIGHTS, 1959.
US COMMISSION ON CIVIL RIGHTS. GPO. WASHINGTON, DC. 1960.
433 PP.

GUSCOMC61395 US COMMISSION ON CIVIL RIGHTS
EMPLOYMENT, 1961 US COMMISSION-ON-CIVIL-RIGHTS REPORT,

VOLUME 3.
US COMMISSION ON CIVIL RIGHTS. GPO. WASHINGTON, DC. 1961.
246 PP.

GUSCOMC61399   US COMMISSION ON CIVIL RIGHTS
US COMMISSION-ON-CIVIL-RIGHTS, HEARINGS. DETROIT, MICHIGAN.
DEC 14-15 1960.
US COMMISSION ON CIVIL RIGHTS. GPO. WASHINGTON, DC. 1961.
511 PP.

GUSCOMC61403   US COMMISSION ON CIVIL RIGHTS
US COMMISSION-ON-CIVIL-RIGHTS, HEARINGS. NEW-ORLEANS,
LOUISIANA. SEPTEMBER 27-28, 1960, MAY 5-6, 1961.
US COMMISSION ON CIVIL RIGHTS. GPO. WASHINGTON, DC. 1961.

GUSCOMC61415   US COMMISSION ON CIVIL RIGHTS
THE 50 STATES REPORT.
US COMMISSION ON CIVIL RIGHTS, STATE ADVISORY COMMITTEES.
GPO. WASHINGTON, DC. 1961. 687 PP.

GUSCOMC62397   US COMMISSION ON CIVIL RIGHTS
EQUAL PROTECTION OF THE LAWS IN NORTH-CAROLINA.
US COMMISSION ON CIVIL RIGHTS, NORTH CAROLINA ADVISORY
COMMITTEE. GPO. WASHINGTON, DC. 1962. 251 PP.

GUSCOMC62401   US COMMISSION ON CIVIL RIGHTS
US COMMISSION-ON-CIVIL-RIGHTS, HEARINGS. MEMPHIS, TENNESSEE.
JUNE 25-26, 1962.
US COMMISSION ON CIVIL RIGHTS. GPO. WASHINGTON, DC. 1962
490 PP.

GUSCOMC62402   US COMMISSION ON CIVIL RIGHTS
US COMMISSION-ON-CIVIL-RIGHTS, HEARINGS. NEWARK, NEW-JERSEY.
SEPTEMBER 11-12, 1962.
US COMMISSION ON CIVIL RIGHTS. GPO. WASHINGTON, DC. 1962.
510 PP.

GUSCOMC63398   US COMMISSION ON CIVIL RIGHTS
FREEDOM TO THE FREE. CENTURY OF EMANCIPATION, 1863-1963.
US COMMISSION ON CIVIL RIGHTS. GPO. WASHINGTON, DC. 1963.
246 PP.

GUSCOMC63404   US COMMISSION ON CIVIL RIGHTS
HOUSING, EMPLOYMENT OPPORTUNITIES AND APPRENTICESHIP
TRAINING. REPORT. /NEW-JERSEY/
US COMMISSION ON CIVIL RIGHTS, NEW JERSEY ADVISORY
COMMITTEE. GPO. WASHINGTON, DC. 1963. 62 PP.

GUSCOMC63406   US COMMISSION ON CIVIL RIGHTS
A REPORT TO THE US COMMISSION ON CIVIL-RIGHTS. /MISSOURI/
US COMMISSION ON CIVIL RIGHTS, MISSOURI ADVISORY COMMITTEE.
GPO. WASHINGTON, DC. JUNE 1963. 48 PP.

GUSCOMC63409   US COMMISSION ON CIVIL RIGHTS
REPORT ON FLORIDA OF THE US COMMISSION ON CIVIL-RIGHTS.
US COMMISSION ON CIVIL RIGHTS, FLORIDA STATE ADVISORY
COMMITTEE. GPO. WASHINGTON, DC. 1963. 51 PP.

GUSCOMC63412   US COMMISSION ON CIVIL RIGHTS
REPORT ON WASHINGTON-DC. EMPLOYMENT.
US COMMISSION ON CIVIL RIGHTS, DISTRICT OF COLUMBIA
ADVISORY COMMITTEE. SPECIAL COMMITTEE ON EQUAL EMPLOYMENT.
GPO. WASHINGTON, DC. JULY 1963. 52 PP.

GUSCOMC64407   US COMMISSION ON CIVIL RIGHTS
REPORTS ON APPRENTICESHIP, NINE STATE ADVISORY COMMITTEES.
/CALIFORNIA FLORIDA MARYLAND CONNECTICUT
WASHINGTON-DC NEW-JERSEY NEW-YORK TENNESSEE WISCONSIN/
US COMMISSION ON CIVIL RIGHTS, ADVISORY COMMITTEES OF
CALIFORNIA, CONNECTICUT, DISTRICT OF COLUMBIA, FLORIDA,
MARYLAND, NEW JERSEY, NEW YORK, TENNESSEE, AND WISCONSIN.
GPO. WASHINGTON, DC. JAN 1964.

GUSCOMC64411   US COMMISSION ON CIVIL RIGHTS
REPORT ON MARYLAND. EMPLOYMENT.
US COMMISSION ON CIVIL RIGHTS, MARYLAND ADVISORY COMMITTEE.
GPO. WASHINGTON, DC. FEB 1964.

GUSCOMC65392   US COMMISSION ON CIVIL RIGHTS
BIBLIOGRAPHY ON VOLUNTARY FAIR-EMPLOYMENT PROGRAMS.
US COMMISSION ON CIVIL RIGHTS, INFORMATION CENTER. GPO.
WASHINGTON, DC. AUG 9 1965.

GUSCOMC65416   US COMMISSION ON CIVIL RIGHTS
SUMMARY FACT SHEETS FOR STATE PUBLIC AGENCIES WITH
JURISDICTION OVER DISCRIMINATION IN EMPLOYMENT.
US COMMISSION ON CIVIL RIGHTS. GPO. WASHINGTON, DC.
AUG 1965. 70 PLUS PP.

GUSCOMC66393   US COMMISSION ON CIVIL RIGHTS
BIBLIOGRAPHY ON EQUAL-EMPLOYMENT-OPPORTUNITY.
US COMMISSION ON CIVIL RIGHTS, TECHNICAL INFORMATION CENTER.
GPO. WASHINGTON, DC. NOV 4 1966. 2 PP.

GUSCOMC66396   US COMMISSION ON CIVIL RIGHTS
EQUAL-EMPLOYMENT-OPPORTUNITY UNDER FEDERAL LAW.
US COMMISSION ON CIVIL RIGHTS, CCR SPECIAL PUBLICATION NO 5.
GPO. WASHINGTON, DC. MAR 1966. 10 PP.

GUSCOMC66408   US COMMISSION ON CIVIL RIGHTS
REPORT ON EMPLOYMENT PROBLEMS OF NONWHITE YOUTH IN MICHIGAN.
US COMMISSION ON CIVIL RIGHTS, MICHIGAN STATE ADVISORY
COMMITTEE. GPO. WASHINGTON, DC. 1966. 43 PP.

GUSCOMC66414   US COMMISSION ON CIVIL RIGHTS
SELECTED BIBLIOGRAPHY ON STATE FAIR-EMPLOYMENT-PRACTICE
COMMISSIONS.
US COMMISSION ON CIVIL RIGHTS, TECHNICAL INFORMATION CENTER.
GPO. WASHINGTON, DC. AUG 19 1966. 2 PP.

GUSCOMF47417   US COMMISSION ON FEP
FINAL REPORT, US COMMISSION ON FAIR-EMPLOYMENT-PRACTICES,
JUNE 28, 1946.
US COMMISSION ON FAIR EMPLOYMENT PRACTICES. GPO. WASHINGTON,
DC. 1947. 128 PP.

GUSCONF64976   US CONFERENCE OF MAYORS
PROGRAMS FOR HIGH SCHOOL DROPOUTS, EXPERIENCE REPORT 101.
US CONFERENCE OF MAYORS, COMMUNITY RELATIONS SERVICE.
WASHINGTON, DC. NOV 30 1964. 6 PP.

GUSCONG62977   US CONGRESS
EMPLOYMENT AND UNEMPLOYMENT.
US CONGRESS, JOINT ECONOMIC COMMITTEE, SUBCOMMITTEE ON
ECONOMIC STATISTICS, 87TH CONGRESS, HEARINGS. GPO.
WASHINGTON, DC. 1962.

GUSCONG65421   US CONGRESS
TESTIMONY BEFORE SUBCOMMITTEE ON ECONOMIC STATISTICS, MAY
17, 1965.

US CONGRESS, JOINT ECONOMIC COMMITTEE, SUBCOMMITTEE ON
ECONOMIC STATISTICS, HEARING. 89TH CONGRESS, 1ST SESSION.
GPO. WASHINGTON, DC. 1965.

GUSCONM00419   US CONFERENCE OF MAYORS
RECENT TRENDS IN PUBLIC EMPLOYMENT.
US CONFERENCE OF MAYORS, COMMUNITY RELATIONS SERVICE. GPO.
WASHINGTON, DC. ND. 7 PP.

GUSCONM65418   US CONFERENCE OF MAYORS
EXPANDING EMPLOYMENT OPPORTUNITIES IN NEWARK. EXPERIENCE
REPORT 101. /NEW-JERSEY/
US CONFERENCE OF MAYORS, COMMUNITY RELATIONS SERVICE. GPO.
WASHINGTON, DC. MAR 15 1965. 6 PP.

GUSCONM66420   US CONFERENCE OF MAYORS
RECRUITING MINORITIES FOR PUBLIC EMPLOYMENT. EXPERIENCE
REPORT 105.
US CONFERENCE OF MAYORS, COMMUNITY RELATIONS SERVICE. GPO.
WASHINGTON, DC. AUG 1966. 5 PP.

GUSDAGR60425   METZLER WH   SARGENT FO
#US DEPARTMENT OF AGRICULTURE
MIGRATORY FARM WORKERS IN THE MID-CONTINENT STREAMS.
US DEPARTMENT OF AGRICULTURE, PRODUCTION RESEARCH REPORT
NO 41. GPO. WASHINGTON, DC. DEC 1960.

GUSDAGR65422   US DEPARTMENT OF AGRICULTURE
CHARACTERISTICS OF THE POPULATION OF HIRED FARMWORKER
HOUSEHOLDS.
US DEPARTMENT OF AGRICULTURE, ECONOMIC RESEARCH SERVICE.
AGRICULTURAL RESEARCH REPORT, NO 84, AUG 1965. 21 PP.

GUSDAGR65424   US DEPARTMENT OF AGRICULTURE
THE HIRED FARM WORKING FORCE OF 1964. A STATISTICAL REPORT.
US DEPARTMENT OF AGRICULTURE, ECONOMIC RESEARCH SERVICE.
AGRICULTURAL ECONOMIC REPORT NO 82. GPO. WASHINGTON, DC.
AUG 1965. 29 PP.

GUSDAGR66507   US DEPARTMENT OF AGRICULTURE
RURAL PEOPLE IN THE AMERICAN ECONOMY.
US DEPARTMENT OF AGRICULTURE, ECONOMIC RESEARCH SERVICE.
AGRICULTURAL ECONOMIC REPORT NO 101. WASHINGTON, DC.
OCT 1966. 123 PP.

GUSDAIR62189   US DEPT OF THE AIR FORCE
CIVILIAN PERSONNEL -- NONDISCRIMINATION IN EMPLOYMENT.
/MILITARY/
US DEPARTMENT OF THE AIR FORCE, AIR FORCE REGULATION 40-703.
GPO. WASHINGTON, DC. SEPT 7 1962. 3 PP.

GUSDARM56192   US DEPARTMENT OF THE ARMY
SUPERVISOR DEVELOPMENT PROGRAM, BASIC COURSE,
NONDISCRIMINATION POLICY. /MILITARY/
US DEPARTMENT OF THE ARMY, CIVILIAN PERSONNEL PAMPHLET
NO 41-8-36. WASHINGTON, DC. 1956. 19 PP.

GUSDARM62193   US DEPARTMENT OF THE ARMY
A TIME FOR ACTION, PROCEEDINGS OF THE NATIONAL CONFERENCE ON
EQUAL-EMPLOYMENT-OPPORTUNITY, 1962. /MILITARY/
US DEPARTMENT OF THE ARMY, WASHINGTON, DC. 1962. 70 PP.

GUSDCOM65432   US DEPARTMENT OF COMMERCE
TASK FORCE FOR EQUAL-OPPORTUNITY IN BUSINESS.
US DEPARTMENT OF COMMERCE. GPO. WASHINGTON, DC. AP 1965.

GUSDCOM66431   US DEPARTMENT OF COMMERCE
FRANCHISE COMPANY DATA FOR EQUAL-OPPORTUNITY IN BUSINESS.
US DEPARTMENT OF COMMERCE. GPO. WASHINGTON, DC. MAR 1966.

GUSDDEF64433   US DEPARTMENT OF DEFENSE
EQUAL-EMPLOYMENT-OPPORTUNITY GUIDE FOR
DEPARTMENT OF THE NAVY CONTRACTORS.
US DEPARTMENT OF DEFENSE, OFFICE OF THE ASSISTANT SECRETARY
OF THE NAVY, INSTALLATIONS AND LOGISTICS. GPO. WASHINGTON,
DC. AUG 1964. 25 PP.

GUSDHEW63434   US DEPT OF HEALTH ED WELFARE
EQUAL-EMPLOYMENT-POLICIES.
US DEPARTMENT OF HEALTH, EDUCATION, AND WELFARE, SOCIAL
SECURITY ADMINISTRATION, DIVISION OF MANAGEMENT, OFFICE OF
EMPLOYEE DEVELOPMENT. GPO. WASHINGTON, DC. 1963. 4 PP.

GUSDHEW63505   US DEPT OF HEALTH ED WELFARE
SELECTED STATE PROGRAMS IN MIGRANT EDUCATION.
US DEPARTMENT OF HEALTH, EDUCATION, AND WELFARE, BULLETIN
NO 35. GPO. WASHINGTON, DC. 1963.

GUSDHEW63834   US DEPT OF HEALTH ED WELFARE
EDUCATION FOR A CHANGING WORLD OF WORK. /YOUTH/
US DEPARTMENT OF HEALTH, EDUCATION, AND WELFARE. GPO.
WASHINGTON, DC. 1963. 296 PP.

GUSDHEW64764   US DEPT OF HEALTH ED WELFARE
DROPOUTS -- SELECTED REFERENCES.
US DEPARTMENT OF HEALTH, EDUCATION, AND WELFARE, OFFICE OF
EDUCATION. GPO. WASHINGTON, DC. 1964. 32 PP.

GUSDHEW65156   US DEPT OF HEALTH ED WELFARE
EDUCATION AND TRAINING, THE BRIDGE BETWEEN MAN AND HIS WORK.
US DEPT OF HEALTH, EDUCATION, AND WELFARE, ANNUAL REPORT OF
THE SECRETARY TO THE CONGRESS ON TRAINING ACTIVITIES UNDER
THE MANPOWER DEVELOPMENT AND TRAINING ACT, APRIL 1 1965.
GPO. WASHINGTON, DC. 1965.

GUSDHEW65435   US DEPT OF HEALTH ED WELFARE
WHITE-NONWHITE DIFFERENTIALS IN HEALTH, EDUCATION, AND
WELFARE.
US DEPARTMENT OF HEALTH, EDUCATION, AND WELFARE. GPO.
WASHINGTON, DC. 1965.

GUSDHEW65763   US DEPT OF HEALTH ED WELFARE
MANPOWER DEVELOPMENT AND TRAINING.
US DEPARTMENT OF HEALTH, EDUCATION, AND WELFARE. INDICATORS.
JUNE 1965. PP 13-27.

GUSDHEW66002   US DEPT OF HEALTH ED WELFARE
THE YOUTH WE HAVEN-T SERVED. /EDUCATION TRAINING/
US DEPARTMENT OF HEALTH, EDUCATION, AND WELFARE. GPO.
WASHINGTON, DC. 1966. 51 PP.

GUSDHEW66639   US DEPT OF HEALTH ED WELFARE
SOCIAL DEVELOPMENT. KEY TO THE GREAT SOCIETY.
/SOCIO-ECONOMIC WELFARE/
US DEPARTMENT OF HEALTH, EDUCATION, AND WELFARE, WELFARE
ADMINISTRATION, DIVISION OF RESEARCH, PUBLICATION NO 15.
GPO. WASHINTON, DC. 1966. 92 PP.

GUSDHEW66711   US DEPT OF HEALTH ED WELFARE
HEALTH, EDUCATION, AND WELFARE ASPECTS OF THE ECONOMIC

REPORT OF THE PRESENT AND ANNUAL REPORT OF THE COUNCIL OF
ECONOMIC ADVISORS.
US DEPARTMENT OF HEALTH, EDUCATION, AND WELFARE, INDICATORS.
GPO. WASHINGTON, DC. MAR 1966. PP 7-16.

GUSDHEW66978 US DEPT OF HEALTH EC WELFARE
ANNUAL REPORT OF THE SECRETARY OF HEALTH, EDUCATION, AND
WELFARE TO THE CONGRESS ON TRAINING ACTIVITIES UNDER THE
MANPOWER-DEVELOPMENT-AND-TRAINING-ACT, 1965.
US DEPARTMENT OF HEALTH, EDUCATION, AND WELFARE. GPO.
WASHINGTON, DC. 1966. 92 PP.

GUSDLABND444 US DEPARTMENT OF LABOR
EMPLOYMENT AND EARNINGS.
US DEPARTMENT OF LABOR, BUREAU OF LABOR STATISTICS. GPO.
WASHINGTON, DC. MONTHLY.

GUSDLAB41077 US DEPARTMENT OF LABOR
NONWHITE FARM OPERATORS IN THE UNITED STATES.
US DEPARTMENT OF LABOR, MONTHLY LABOR REVIEW, VOL 53,
AP 1941. PP 399-401.

GUSDLAB45078 US DEPARTMENT OF LABOR
PROGRESS TOWARD FAIR-EMPLOYMENT-PRACTICES.
US DEPARTMENT OF LABOR, MONTHLY LABOR REVIEW, VOL 60,
MAY 1945. PP 1003-1008.

GUSDLAB46075 US DEPARTMENT OF LABOR
MASSACHUSETTS FAIR-EMPLOYMENT-PRACTICE ACT OF 1946.
US DEPARTMENT OF LABOR, MONTHLY LABOR REVIEW, VOL 63,
JULY 1946. P 20.

GUSDLAB47074 US DEPARTMENT OF LABOR
FIRST YEAR UNDER NEW-YORK LAW AGAINST DISCRIMINATION.
US DEPARTMENT OF LABOR, MONTHLY LABOR REVIEW, VOL 64,
JAN 1947. PP 24-27.

GUSDLAB49028 US DEPARTMENT OF LABOR
FAMILY INCOME AND EXPENDITURES.
US DEPARTMENT OF LABOR, MONTHLY LABOR REVIEW, AP 1949.
PP 389-397.

GUSDLAB49029 US DEPARTMENT OF LABOR
FAMILY INCOME STATISTICS.
US DEPARTMENT OF LABOR, MONTHLY LABOR REVIEW, JULY 1949.
PP 34-36.

GUSDLAB52492 US DEPARTMENT OF LABOR
PLACEMENT OF PROFESSIONAL PERSONNEL.
US DEPARTMENT OF LABOR, BUREAU OF EMPLOYMENT SECURITY.
GPO. WASHINGTON, DC. 1952. 45 PP.

GUSDLAB55498 US DEPARTMENT OF LABOR
THE SKILLED WORK FORCE OF THE UNITED STATES.
US DEPARTMENT OF LABOR. GPO. WASHINGTON, DC. 1955. 30 PP.

GUSDLAB56027 US DEPARTMENT OF LABOR
CONFERENCE ON EQUAL JOB OPPORTUNITY.
US DEPARTMENT OF LABOR, MONTHLY LABOR REVIEW, VOL 79, NO 1,
JAN 1956. PP 31-33.

GUSDLAB56204 US DEPARTMENT OF LABOR
SELECTED REFERENCES ON MIGRATORY WORKERS AND THEIR FAMILIES.
PROBLEMS AND PROGRAMS.
US DEPARTMENT OF LABOR, BUREAU OF LABOR STATISTICS. GPO.
WASHINGTON, DC. 1956. 16 PP.

GUSDLAB57359 US DEPARTMENT OF LABOR
MIGRATORY FARM LABOR CONFERENCE, PROCEEDINGS.
US DEPARTMENT OF LABOR. GPO. WASHINGTON, DC. 1957.

GUSDLAB58076 US DEPARTMENT OF LABOR
MINORITY WORKER HIRING AND REFERRAL IN SAN-FRANCISCO.
/CALIFORNIA/
US DEPARTMENT OF LABOR, MONTHLY LABOR REVIEW, VOL 81, NO 10,
OCT 1958. PP 1131-1136.

GUSDLAB58449 US DEPARTMENT OF LABOR
A GUIDE TO INDUSTRIAL-RELATIONS IN THE UNITED STATES. EQUAL
JOB OPPORTUNITY UNDER COLLECTIVE-BARGAINING.
US DEPARTMENT OF LABOR, BUREAU OF LABOR STATISTICS, BULLETIN
NO 38. GPO. WASHINGTON, DC. 1958. 11 PP.

GUSDLAB58497 US DEPARTMENT OF LABOR
SERVICE TO MINORITY-GROUPS. 1958.
US DEPARTMENT OF LABOR. GPO. WASHINGTON, DC. MAR 1958.

GUSDLAB60488 US DEPARTMENT OF LABOR
MANPOWER. THE CHALLENGE OF THE 1960-S.
US DEPARTMENT OF LABOR. GPO. WASHINGTON, DC. 1960. 24 PP.

GUSDLAB60494 US DEPARTMENT OF LABOR
SCHOOL AND EARLY EMPLOYMENT EXPERIENCE OF YOUTH. A REPORT
ON SEVEN COMMUNITIES, 1952-57.
US DEPARTMENT OF LABOR, BUREAU OF LABOR STATISTICS,
BULLETIN NO 1277. GPO. WASHINGTON, DC. 1960.

GUSDLAB61202 US DEPARTMENT OF LABOR
PROGRAMS OF NATIONAL ORGANIZATIONS FOR MIGRANT FARM WORKERS
AND THEIR FAMILIES.
US DEPARTMENT OF LABOR, BULLETIN 236. WASHINGTON, DC.
DEC 1961. 48 PP.

GUSDLAB61445 US DEPARTMENT OF LABOR
FAMILY CHARACTERISTICS OF THE LONG TERM UNEMPLOYED. A REPORT
ON A STUDY OF CLAIMANTS UNDER THE TEMPORARY EXTENDED
UNEMPLOYMENT COMPENSATION PROGRAM, 1961-2.
US DEPARTMENT OF LABOR, BUREAU OF EMPLOYMENT SECURITY. GPO.
WASHINGTON, DC. MAY 1961. 17 PP.

GUSDLAB61495 US DEPARTMENT OF LABOR
SELECTED REFERENCES ON DOMESTIC MIGRATORY AGRICULTURAL
WORKERS, THEIR FAMILIES, PROBLEMS, AND PROGRAMS,
1955-1960.
US DEPARTMENT OF LABOR, BUREAU OF LABOR STANDARDS,
BULLETIN 225. GPO. WASHINGTON, DC. JAN 1961. 38 PP.

GUSDLAB61509 US DEPARTMENT OF LABOR
MAJOR AGRICULTURAL MIGRANT LABOR DEMAND AREAS.
US DEPARTMENT OF LABOR. GPO. WASHINGTON, DC. 1961. 14 PP.

GUSDLAB62221 US DEPARTMENT OF LABOR
HELPING THE LONG-TERM UNEMPLOYED. /INCOME-MAINTENANCE
TRAINING/
US DEPARTMENT OF LABOR, EMPLOYMENT SECURITY REVIEW, VOL 29,
DEC 1962. ENTIRE ISSUE.

GUSDLAB62508 US DEPARTMENT OF LABOR
HOUSING FOR MIGRANT AGRICULTURAL WORKERS. LABOR CAMP
STANDARDS.

US DEPARTMENT OF LABOR, BUREAU OF LABOR STANDARDS, BULLETIN
235. GPO. WASHINGTON, DC. NOV 1962.

GUSDLAB62700 US DEPARTMENT OF LABOR
MANPOWER REPORT OF THE PRESIDENT.
US DEPARTMENT OF LABOR. GPO. WASHINGTON, DC. MAR 1962.

GUSDLAB62708 US DEPARTMENT OF LABOR
MEETING THE MANPOWER PROBLEMS OF. I. AREA REDEVELOPMENT, II.
AUTOMATION.
EMPLOYMENT SECURITY REVIEW, VOL 29, NO 7, JULY 1962. 44 PP.

GUSDLAB62981 US DEPARTMENT OF LABOR
MANPOWER RESEARCH PROGRAMS.
US DEPARTMENT OF LABOR, REPORT OF THE SECRETARY OF LABOR ON
MANPOWER RESEARCH AND TRAINING. GPO. WASHINGTON, DC. 1962.

GUSDLAB62991 US DEPARTMENT OF LABOR
FARM LABOR-MARKET IN TRANSITION.
US DEPARTMENT OF LABOR, EMPLOYMENT SECURITY REVIEW, VOL 29,
JAN 1962. PP 3-36.

GUSDLAB63197 US DEPARTMENT OF LABOR
CHARACTERISTICS OF 6000 WHITE AND NONWHITE PERSONS ENROLLED
IN MANPOWER-DEVELOPMENT-AND-TRAINING-ACT TRAINING.
US DEPARTMENT OF LABOR, OFFICE OF MANPOWER, AUTOMATION, AND
TRAINING. WASHINGTON, DC. AP 1963. 6 PP.

GUSDLAB63439 US DEPARTMENT OF LABOR
BRIEF SUMMARY OF STATE LAWS AGAINST DISCRIMINATION IN
PRIVATE EMPLOYMENT. FAIR-EMPLOYMENT-PRACTICE ACTS.
US DEPARTMENT OF LABOR, BUREAU OF LABOR STANDARDS, FACT
SHEET NO 6-A. GPO. WASHINGTON, DC. JAN 1962, 1963. 5 PP
EACH.

GUSDLAB63442 US DEPARTMENT OF LABOR
BRIDGE TO EMPLOYMENT. DEMONSTRATION MANPOWER PROGRAMS.
US DEPARTMENT OF LABOR, OFFICE OF MANPOWER, AUTOMATION, AND
TRAINING. GPO. WASHINGTON, DC. 1963. 20 PP.

GUSDLAB63450 US DEPARTMENT OF LABOR
IMPLICATIONS OF AUTOMATION AND OTHER TECHNOLOGICAL
DEVELOPMENTS. A SELECTED BIBLIOGRAPHY.
US DEPARTMENT OF LABOR, BUREAU OF LABOR STATISTICS, BULLETIN
NO 1319-1. GPO. WASHINGTON, DC. DEC 1963. 90 PP.

GUSDLAB63491 US DEPARTMENT OF LABOR
PEOPLE, SKILLS, AND JOBS.
US DEPARTMENT OF LABOR, OFFICE OF MANPOWER, AUTOMATION,
AND TRAINING, HIGHLIGHTS FROM THE MANPOWER REPORT OF THE
PRESIDENT. GPO. WASHINGTON, DC. MAR 1963. 29 PP.

GUSDLAB63500 US DEPARTMENT OF LABOR
STUDY OF MINORITY-GROUP EMPLOYMENT IN THE FEDERAL
GOVERNMENT.
US DEPARTMENT OF LABOR, BUREAU OF LABOR STATISTICS. GPO.
WASHINGTON, DC. JUNE. 1963.

GUSDLAB63506 US DEPARTMENT OF LABOR
YOUNG WORKERS. THEIR SPECIAL TRAINING NEEDS.
US DEPARTMENT OF LABOR, MANPOWER ADMINISTRATION, MANPOWER
RESEARCH BULLETIN NO 3. GPO. WASHINGTON, DC. MAY 1963.
19 PP.

GUSDLAB63665 US DEPARTMENT OF LABOR
UTILIZING OUR MANPOWER RESOURCES. SPECIAL APPLICANT GROUPS.
US DEPARTMENT OF LABOR, EMPLOYMENT SECURITY REVIEW,
JUNE 1963.

GUSDLAB63762 US DEPARTMENT OF LABOR
FAMILY CHARACTERISTICS OF THE LONG-TERM UNEMPLOYED.
US DEPARTMENT OF LABOR, BUREAU OF EMPLOYMENT SECURITY. GPO.
WASHINGTON, DC. DEC 1963. 178 PP.

GUSDLAB63830 US DEPARTMENT OF LABOR
MANPOWER REPORT OF THE PRESIDENT AND A REPORT ON MANPOWER
REQUIREMENTS, RESOURCES, UTILIZATION, AND TRAINING.
US DEPARTMENT OF LABOR. GPO. WASHINGTON, DC. MAR 1963.
204 PP.

GUSDLAB63831 US DEPARTMENT OF LABOR
INDUSTRY EMPLOYMENT GROWTH SINCE WORLD WAR II.
US DEPARTMENT OF LABOR, MANPOWER ADMINISTRATION, MANPOWER
REPORT NO 5. GPO. WASHINGTON, DC. 1963.

GUSDLAB64110 US DEPARTMENT OF LABOR
LABOR-FORCE DEVELOPMENTS FOR WHITE AND NONWHITE WORKERS,
1954-1964.
US DEPARTMENT OF LABOR, BUREAU OF LABOR STATISTICS, MONTHLY
REPORT ON THE LABOR FORCE. NOV 1964. PP 11-18.

GUSDLAB64201 US DEPARTMENT OF LABOR
MARITAL AND FAMILY CHARACTERISTICS OF WORKERS, MARCH 1964.
US DEPARTMENT OF LABOR, BUREAU OF LABOR STATISTICS,
SPECIAL LABOR FORCE REPORT NO 50. GPO. WASHINGTON, DC. 1964.

GUSDLAB64441 US DEPARTMENT OF LABOR
CONSOLIDATED INVENTORY OF DEPARTMENT OF LABOR RESEARCH ON
LABOR-FORCE EMPLOYMENT AND UNEMPLOYMENT.
US DEPARTMENT OF LABOR, OFFICE OF MANPOWER, AUTOMATION, AND
TRAINING. GPO. WASHINGTON, DC. 1964. 71 PP.

GUSDLAB64506 US DEPARTMENT OF LABOR
AGRICULTURAL WORKERS AND WORKMEN-S COMPENSATION.
/MIGRANT-WORKERS/
US DEPARTMENT OF LABOR, BUREAU OF LABOR STANDARDS, BULLETIN
206. GPO. WASHINGTON, DC. 1964.

GUSDLAB64507 US DEPARTMENT OF LABOR
COVERAGE OF AGRICULTURAL WORKERS UNDER STATE AND FEDERAL
LAWS. /MIGRANT-WORKERS/
US DEPARTMENT OF LABOR, BUREAU OF LABOR STANDARDS, BULLETIN
264. GPO. WASHINGTON, DC. 1964.

GUSDLAB64619 US DEPARTMENT OF LABOR
CONSOLIDATED INVENTORY OF DEPARTMENT OF LABOR RESEARCH ON
AUTOMATION AND TECHNOLOGICAL-CHANGE.
US DEPARTMENT OF LABOR, MANPOWER ADMINISTRATION, OFFICE OF
MANPOWER, AUTOMATION AND TRAINING. GPO. WASHINGTON, DC.
1964.

GUSDLAB64802 US DEPARTMENT OF LABOR
TECHNOLOGICAL TRENDS IN 36 MAJOR AMERICAN INDUSTRIES.
US DEPARTMENT OF LABOR, BUREAU OF LABOR STATISTICS, OFFICE
OF PRODUCTIVITY AND TECHNOLOGICAL DEVELOPMENT. GPO.
WASHINGTON, DC. 1964.

GUSDLAB64825 US DEPARTMENT OF LABOR
A SURVEY OF CURRENT LITERATURE ON AUTOMATION AND OTHER
TECHNOLOGICAL-CHANGES. A SELECTED ANNOTATED BIBLIOGRAPHY.

US DEPARTMENT OF LABOR, MANPOWER ADMINISTRATION, OFFICE OF
MANPOWER, AUTOMATION AND TRAINING. GPO. WASHINGTON, DC.
1964. 51 PP.

GUSDLAB64829 US DEPARTMENT OF LABOR
MANPOWER REPORT OF THE PRESIDENT AND A REPORT ON MANPOWER
REQUIREMENTS, RESOURCES, UTILIZATION, AND TRAINING.
US DEPARTMENT OF LABOR. GPO. WASHINGTON, DC. MAR 1964.
279 PP.

GUSDLAB64833 US DEPARTMENT OF LABOR
CONSUMER EXPENDITURES AND INCOME WITH EMPHASIS ON LOW-INCOME
FAMILIES.
US DEPARTMENT OF LABOR, BUREAU OF LABOR STATISTICS, REPORT
NO 238-6. GPO. WASHINGTON, DC. JULY 1964. 8 PP.

GUSDLAB64980 US DEPARTMENT OF LABOR
SEMINAR ON MANPOWER POLICY AND PROGRAM MEASUREMENT OF
TECHNOLOGICAL-CHANGE.
US DEPARTMENT OF LABOR. GPO. WASHINGTON, DC. 1964.

GUSDLAB64982 US DEPARTMENT OF LABOR
SEMINAR ON MANPOWER POLICY AND PROGRAM. CYBERNATION AND
SOCIAL CHANGE.
US DEPARTMENT OF LABOR. GPO. WASHINGTON, DC. 1964.

GUSDLAB65026 US DEPARTMENT OF LABOR
CONFERENCE ON EQUAL-EMPLOYMENT-OPPORTUNITY.
US DEPARTMENT OF LABOR, MONTHLY LABOR REVIEW, NOV 1965.
PP 1320-1321.

GUSDLAB65447 US DEPARTMENT OF LABOR
FEDERAL AGENCIES WITH PRIMARY CIVIL-RIGHTS RESPONSIBILITIES.
US DEPARTMENT OF LABOR, BUREAU OF EMPLOYMENT SECURITY. GPO.
WASHINGTON, DC. 1965. 24 PP.

GUSDLAB65503 US DEPARTMENT OF LABOR
UNEMPLOYMENT AND RETRAINING. AN ANNOTATED BIBLIOGRAPHY OF
RESEARCH.
US DEPARTMENT OF LABOR, OFFICE OF POLICY EVALUATION AND
RESEARCH. GPO. WASHINGTON, DC. NOV 1965.

GUSDLAB65561 US DEPARTMENT OF LABOR
OCCUPATIONAL DEVELOPMENTS. SHORTAGES OF SKILLED TECHNICAL
MANPOWER HIGHEST IN RECENT YEARS.
US DEPARTMENT OF LABOR, EMPLOYMENT SERVICE REVIEW, VOL 2,
NO 12, DEC 1965. PP 53-56.

GUSDLAB65608 US DEPARTMENT LABOR
MANPOWER IMPLICATIONS OF AUTOMATION.
US DEPARTMENT OF LABOR, MANPOWER ADMINISTRATION, OFFICE OF
MANPOWER, AUTOMATION AND TRAINING. WASHINGTON, DC.
SEPT 1965. 86 PP.

GUSDLAB65710 US DEPARTMENT OF LABOR
MANPOWER, RESEARCH AND TRAINING.
US DEPARTMENT OF LABOR, REPORT OF THE SECRETARY OF LABOR.
GPO. WASHINGTON, DC. MAR 1965. 219 PP.

GUSDLAB65826 US DEPARTMENT OF LABOR
SELECTED MANPOWER INDICATORS FOR STATES.
US DEPARTMENT OF LABOR, MANPOWER ADMINISTRATION, RESEARCH
BULLETIN NO 4. GPO. WASHINGTON, DC. 1965. 52 PP.

GUSDLAB65828 US DEPARTMENT OF LABOR
MANPOWER REPORT OF THE PRESIDENT AND A REPORT ON MANPOWER
REQUIREMENTS, RESOURCES, UTILIZATION, AND TRAINING.
US DEPARTMENT OF LABOR. GPO. WASHINGTON, DC. MAR 1965.
276 PP.

GUSDLAB65979 US DEPARTMENT OF LABOR
THE UNEMPLOYED. WHY THEY STARTED LOOKING FOR WORK.
US DEPARTMENT OF LABOR, SPECIAL LABOR FORCE REPORT NO 60.
GPO. WASHINGTON, DC. OCT 1965.

GUSDLAB66073 US DEPARTMENT OF LABOR
EMPLOYMENT OF HIGH SCHOOL GRADUATES AND DROPOUTS IN 1965.
US DEPARTMENT OF LABOR, MONTHLY LABOR REVIEW, VOL 89,
JUNE 1966.

GUSDLAB66437 US DEPARTMENT OF LABOR
AMERICA-S INDUSTRIAL AND OCCUPATIONAL MANPOWER REQUIREMENTS,
1964-75.
TECHNOLOGY AND THE AMERICAN ECONOMY, SUPPLEMENT. NATIONAL
COMMISSION ON TECHNOLOGY, AUTOMATION, AND ECONOMIC PROGRESS.
WASHINGTON, DC. JAN 1966. ALSO US DEPARTMENT OF LABOR,
BUREAU OF LABOR STATISTICS. GPO. WASHINGTON, DC.

GUSDLAB66446 US DEPARTMENT OF LABOR
FARM LABOR DEVELOPMENTS -- EMPLOYMENT AND WAGE SUPPLEMENT.
US DEPARTMENT OF LABOR. GPO. WASHINGTON, DC. FEB AND MAR
1966.

GUSDLAB66493 US DEPARTMENT OF LABOR
REPORT ON MANPOWER RESEARCH AND TRAINING UNDER THE MDTA.
US DEPARTMENT OF LABOR, SECRETARY OF LABOR. GPO.
WASHINGTON, DC. 1966.

GUSDLAB66504 US DEPARTMENT OF LABOR
UNUSED MANPOWER. THE NATION-S LOSS.
US DEPARTMENT OF LABOR, MANPOWER ADMINISTRATION. MANPOWER
RESEARCH BULLETIN NO 10. GPO. WASHINGTON, DC. SEPT 1966.
25 PP.

GUSDLAB66505 US DEPARTMENT OF LABOR
YOUNG WORKERS. A REPRINT FROM THE 1966 MANPOWER REPORT.
US DEPARTMENT OF LABOR, MANPOWER ADMINISTRATION. GPO.
WASHINGTON, DC. 1966. 31 PP.

GUSDLAB66511 US DEPARTMENT OF LABOR
SUB-EMPLOYMENT IN THE SLUMS OF NEW-YORK.
US DEPARTMENT OF LABOR, SURVEY. WASHINGTON, DC. 1966. 12 PP.

GUSDLAB66512 US DEPARTMENT OF LABOR
SUB-EMPLOYMENT IN THE SLUMS OF NEW-ORLEANS. /LOUISIANA/
US DEPARTMENT OF LABOR, SURVEY. WASHINGTON, DC. 1966. 8 PP.

GUSDLAB66513 US DEPARTMENT OF LABOR
SUB-EMPLOYMENT IN THE SLUMS OF PHOENIX. /ARIZONA/
US DEPARTMENT OF LABOR, SURVEY. WASHINGTON, DC. 1966. 8 PP.

GUSDLAB66514 US DEPARTMENT OF LABOR
SUB-EMPLOYMENT IN THE SLUMS OF LOS-ANGELES. /CALIFORNIA/
US DEPARTMENT OF LABOR, SURVEY. WASHINGTON, DC. 1966. 8 PP.

GUSDLAB66515 US DEPARTMENT OF LABOR
SUB-EMPLOYMENT IN THE SLUMS OF SAN-ANTONIO. /TEXAS/
US DEPARTMENT OF LABOR, SURVEY. WASHINGTON, DC. 1966. 8 PP.

GUSDLAB66516 US DEPARTMENT OF LABOR
SUB-EMPLOYMENT IN THE SLUMS OF CLEVELAND. /OHIO/
US DEPARTMENT OF LABOR, SURVEY. WASHINGTON, DC. 1966. 8 PP.

GUSDLAB66517 US DEPARTMENT OF LABOR
SUB-EMPLOYMENT IN THE SLUMS OF ST-LOUIS. /MISSOURI/
US DEPARTMENT OF LABOR, SURVEY. WASHINGTON, DC. 1966. 8 PP.

GUSDLAB66518 US DEPARTMENT OF LABOR
SUB-EMPLOYMENT IN THE SLUMS OF BOSTON. /MASSACHUSETTS/
US DEPARTMENT OF LABOR, SURVEY. WASHINGTON, DC. 1966. 9 PP.

GUSDLAB66519 US DEPARTMENT OF LABOR
SUB-EMPLOYMENT IN THE SLUMS OF SAN-FRANCISCO. /CALIFORNIA/
US DEPARTMENT OF LABOR, SURVEY. WASHINGTON, DC. 1966. 8 PP.

GUSDLAB66520 US DEPARTMENT OF LABOR
A SHARPER LOOK AT UNEMPLOYMENT IN US CITIES, AND SLUMS.
US DEPARTMENT OF LABOR, SUMMARY REPORT SUBMITTED TO THE
PRESIDENT BY THE SECRETARY OF LABOR. WASHINGTON, DC. 1966.
12 PP.

GUSDLAB66521 US DEPARTMENT OF LABOR
SUB-EMPLOYMENT IN THE SLUMS OF OAKLAND. /CALIFORNIA/
US DEPARTMENT OF LABOR, SURVEY. WASHINGTON, DC. 1966. 7 PP.

GUSDLAB66522 US DEPARTMENT OF LABOR
SUB-EMPLOYMENT IN THE SLUMS OF PHILADELPHIA. /PENNSYLVANIA/
US DEPARTMENT OF LABOR, SURVEY. WASHINGTON, DC. 1966. 9 PP.

GUSDLAB66559 US DEPARTMENT OF LABOR
EMPLOYMENT SERVICE TASK FORCE REPORT. /MANPOWER SES/
US DEPARTMENT OF LABOR, EMPLOYMENT SERVICE REVIEW, VOL 3,
NO 3, FEB 1966. 38 PP.

GUSDLAB66637 US DEPARTMENT OF LABOR
TECHNOLOGICAL TRENDS IN MAJOR AMERICAN INDUSTRIES.
/EMPLOYMENT/
US DEPARTMENT OF LABOR, BUREAU OF LABOR STATISTICS,
BULLETIN NO 1474. FEB 1966. 269 PP.

GUSDLAB66663 US DEPARTMENT OF LABOR
MANPOWER TASKS FOR 1966.
US DEPARTMENT OF LABOR, EMPLOYMENT SERVICE REVIEW, VOL 3, NO
4, AP 1966. PP 8-12.

GUSDLAB66827 US DEPARTMENT OF LABOR
MANPOWER REPORT OF THE PRESIDENT AND A REPORT ON MANPOWER
REQUIREMENTS, RESOURCES, UTILIZATION, AND TRAINING.
US DEPARTMENT OF LABOR. GPO. WASHINGTON, DC. MAR 1966.
229 PP.

GUSDLAB66832 US DEPARTMENT OF LABOR
EMPLOYMENT AND EARNINGS STATISTICS FOR THE UNITED STATES,
1909-1966.
US DEPARTMENT OF LABOR, BUREAU OF LABOR STATISTICS, BULLETIN
NO 1312-4. GPO. WASHINGTON, DC. 1966. 788 PP.

GUSDLAB67116 US DEPARTMENT OF LABOR
HIRING AND PROMOTION SYSTEMS UNDER FAIR-EMPLOYMENT-PRACTICES
LEGISLATION.
US DEPARTMENT OF LABOR, MONTHLY LABOR REVIEW, VOL 90,
FEB 1967. PP 53-56.

GUSDSTA61507 US DEPARTMENT OF STATE
CONFERENCE ON EQUAL-EMPLOYMENT-OPPORTUNITY, AUGUST 16, 1961.
US DEPARTMENT OF STATE. GPO. WASHINGTON, DC. 1961. 40 PP.

GUSEEOC66509 US EEO COMMISSION
DIGEST OF LEGAL INTERPRETATIONS ISSUED OR ADOPTED BY THE
COMMISSION OCTOBER 9, 1965 THROUGH DECEMBER 31, 1965.
US EQUAL EMPLOYMENT OPPORTUNITY COMMISSION. GPO. WASHINGTON,
DC. 1966. 29 PP.

GUSEEOC66510 US EEO COMMISSION
GUIDELINES ON EMPLOYMENT TESTING PROCEDURES.
US EQUAL EMPLOYMENT OPPORTUNITY COMMISSION. GPO. WASHINGTON,
DC. AUG 24, 1966.

GUSFEDE63513 US FEDERAL EXECUTIVE BOARD
LAKE ARROWHEAD CONFERENCE ON EQUAL-EMPLOYMENT-OPPORTUNITY,
OCTOBER 22-24, 1963 -- RECORD OF PROCEEDINGS. LOS-ANGELES,
CALIFORNIA.
US FEDERAL EXECUTIVE BOARD. GPO. WASHINGTON, DC. 1963.
139 PP.

GUSFEPC45512 US FEP COMMITTEE
FIRST REPORT. US FAIR-EMPLOYMENT-PRACTICE-COMMITTEE.
US FAIR EMPLOYMENT PRACTICE COMMITTEE. GPO. WASHINGTON, DC.
1945.

GUSFEPC47511 US FEP COMMITTEE
FINAL REPORT. US FAIR-EMPLOYMENT-PRACTICE-COMMITTEE.
UNITED STATES FAIR EMPLOYMENT PRACTICE COMMITTEE. GPO.
WASHINGTON, DC. 1947. 128 PP.

GUSHHFX63321 US HOUSING AND HOME FINANCE
SENIOR CITIZENS AND HOW THEY LIVE. AN ANALYSIS OF 1960
CENSUS DATA. PART II. THE AGING NONWHITE AND HIS HOUSING.
/ECONOMIC-STATUS/
US HOUSING AND HOME FINANCE AGENCY, OFFICE OF THE
ADMINISTRATOR. WASHINGTON, DC. NOV 1963.

GUSHOUR61343 US HOUSE OF REPRESENTATIVES
EQUAL-OPPORTUNITY IN APPRENTICESHIP PROGRAMS.
US HOUSE OF REPRESENTATIVES, COMMITTEE ON EDUCATION AND
LABOR, SPECIAL SUBCOMMITTEE ON LABOR. 87TH CONGRESS, 1ST
SESSION. HEARINGS. AUG 21-23 1961. GPO. WASHINGTON, DC.
1961.

GUSHOUR61345 US HOUSE OF REPRESENTATIVES
LABOR-MANAGEMENT IRREGULARITIES.
US HOUSE OF REPRESENTATIVES, COMMITTEE ON EDUCATION AND
LABOR. 87TH CONGRESS, 1ST SESSION. HEARINGS HELD IN NEW YORK
JUNE 3 AND 24 1961. GPO. WASHINGTON, DC. 1961. 104 PP.

GUSHOUR61985 US HOUSE OF REPRESENTATIVES
IMPACT OF AUTOMATION ON EMPLOYMENT.
US HOUSE OF REPRESENTATIVES, COMMITTEE ON EDUCATION AND
LABOR, HEARINGS. GPO. WASHINGTON, DC. 1961.

GUSHOUR62340 US HOUSE OF REPRESENTATIVES
EQUAL-EMPLOYMENT-OPPORTUNITY ACT OF 1962. REPORT TO
ACCOMPANY HR 10144.
US HOUSE OF REPRESENTATIVES, COMMITTEE ON EDUCATION AND
LABOR. 87TH CONGRESS, 2ND SESSION. HOUSE REPORT NO 1370.
GPO. WASHINGTON, DC. 1962. 22 PP.

GUSHOUR62342 US HOUSE OF REPRESENTATIVES
EQUAL-EMPLOYMENT-OPPORTUNITY. PARTS I AND II.
US HOUSE OF REPRESENTATIVES, COMMITTEE ON EDUCATION AND

LABOR, SPECIAL SUBCCMMITTEE ON LABOR. 87TH CONGRESS, 1ST AND
2ND SESSIONS. HEARINGS. OCT 23 1961-JAN 24 1962. GPO.
WASHINGTON, DC. 1962. 1156 PP.

GUSHJUR62344 US HOUSE OF REPRESENTATIVES
INVESTIGATION OF THE GARMENT INDUSTRY.
US HOUSE OF REPRESENTATIVES, COMMITTEE OF EDUCATION AND
LABOR, AD HOC SUBCOMMITTEE ON INVESTIGATION OF THE GARMENT
INDUSTRY. 87TH CONGRESS, 2ND SESSION. HEARINGS. GPO.
WASHINGTON, DC. 1962. 266 PP.

GUSHJUR63337 US HOUSE OF REPRESENTIVES
EMPLOYMENT-PRACTICES IN THE PERFORMING-ARTS.
US HOUSE OF REPRESENTATIVES, COMMITTEE CN EDUCATION AND
LABOR. 87TH CONGRESS, 2ND SESSION. HEARINGS.
OCT 29-NOV 2 1962. GPO. WASHINGTON, DC. 1963. 160 PP.

GUSHJUR63338 US HOUSE OF REPRESENTATIVES
EQUAL-EMPLOYMENT-OPPORTUNITY.
US HOUSE OF REPRESENTATIVES, COMMITTEE CN EDUCATION AND
LABOR, SPECIAL SUBCOMMITTEE ON LABOR, 88TH CONGRESS, 1ST
SESSION. HEARINGS ON HR 405, THE PROPOSED EQUAL EMPLOYMENT
ACT OF 1963. AP-JUNE 1963. GPO. WASHINGTON, DC. 1963.
557 PP.

GUSHJUR63341 US HOUSE OF REPRESENTATIVES
EQUAL-EMPLOYMENT-OPPOKTUNITY ACT OF 1963, REPORT TO
ACCOMPANY HR 405.
US HOUSE OF REPRESENTATIVES, COMMITTEE CN EDUCATION AND
LABOR. 88TH CONGRESS, 1ST SESSION. HOUSE REPORT NO 570. GPO.
WASHINGTON, DC. 1963. 20 PP.

GUSHJUR65339 US HOUSE OF REPRESENTATIVES
EQUAL-EMPLOYMENT-OPPORTUNITY 1965.
US HOUSE OF REPRESENTATIVES, COMMITTEE CN EDUCATION AND
LABOR. 89TH CONGRESS, 1ST SESSION. HEARINGS. JUNE-JULY 1965.
GPO. WASHINGTON, DC. 1965.

GUSHJUR65824 US HOUSE OF REPRESENTATIVES
EXAMINATION OF THE WAR-ON-POVERTY PROGRAM.
US HOUSE OF REPRESENTATIVES, COMMITTEE CN EDUCATION AND
LABOR, SUBCOMMITTEE ON THE WAR ON POVERTY PROGRAM. 89TH
CONGRESS, 1ST SESSION. HEARINGS. GPO. WASHINGTON, DC.
1965. 854 PP.

GUSINCC53514 US IDEPTL COMT CHILDREN YOUTH
YOUTH, THE NATION-S RICHEST RESOURCE. THEIR EDUCATION AND
EMPLOYMENT NEEDS.
US INTERDEPARTMENTAL COMMITTEE ON CHILDREN AND YOUTH. GPO.
WASHINGTON, DC. 1953. 54 PP.

GUSLIBC64823 US LIBRARY OF CONGRESS
PROBLEMS OF YOUTH. A FACT BOOK. /EMPLOYMENT/
US LIBRARY OF CONGRESS, LEGISLATIVE REFERENCE SERVICE. GPO.
WASHINGTON, DC. 1964. 80 PP.

GUSNEWR56517 US NEWS AND WORLD REPORT
RACE TROUBLES HURT UNIONS TOO.
US NEWS AND WORLD REPORT, AP 6 1956. PP 95-99.

GUSNEWR66518 US NEWS AND WORLD REPORT
LABOR WEEK. RULES ON HIRING, PROMOTING -- QUESTIONS
ANSWERED.
US NEWS AND WORLD REPORT, VOL 60, NO 8, FEB 21 1966.
PP 93-96.

GUSOFPM42519 US OFFICE OF PRODUCTION MNGMT
MINORITIES IN DEFENSE.
US OFFICE OF PRODUCTION MANAGEMENT. GPO. WASHINGTON, DC.
1942. 19 PP.

GUSPODA63516 US PO DEPT ADVISORY BOARD
EQUAL-EMPLOYMENT-OPPORTUNITY IN THE US POST OFFICE
DEPARTMENT, A SUPPLEMENTAL REPORT TO THE POSTMASTER
GENERAL.
US POST OFFICE DEPARTMENT ADVISORY BOARD. GPO. WASHINGTON,
DC. AP 1963. 17 PP.

GUSSENA52347 US SENATE
DISCRIMINATION AND FULL UTILIZATION OF MANPOWER RESOURCES,
1952.
US SENATE, COMMITTEE ON LABOR AND PUBLIC WELFARE,
SUBCOMMITTEE ON LABGR MANAGEMENT RELATIONS. 82ND CONGRESS,
2ND SESSION. HEARINGS ON S 1732 AND S 551. GPO. WASHINGTON,
DC. 1952.

GUSSENA52350 US SENATE
FEDERAL EQUALITY OF OPPORTUNITY IN EMPLOYMENT ACT.
US SENATE, COMMITTEE ON LABOR AND PUBLIC WELFARE. 82ND
CONGRESS, 2ND SESSION. SENATE REPORT NO 2080. GPO.
WASHINGTON, DC. 1952.

GUSSENA54330 US SENATE
ANTIDISCRIMINATION IN EMPLOYMENT.
US SENATE, COMMITTEE ON LABOR AND PUBLIC WELFARE. 83RD
CONGRESS, 2ND SESSION. HEARINGS. GPO. WASHINGTON, DC. 1954.
410 PP.

GUSSENA54353 US SENATE
STUDY OF THE SHORTAGE AND SALARIES OF SCIENTISTS AND
ENGINEERS.
US SENATE, COMMITTEE ON POST OFFICE AND CIVIL SERVICE.
83RD CONGRESS, 2ND SESSION. GPO. WASHINGTON, DC. 1954.
20 PP.

GUSSENA59469 US SENATE
MIGRATORY LABOR.
US SENATE, COMMITTEE ON LABOR AND PUBLIC WELFARE,
SUBCOMMITTEE ON MIGRATORY LABOR. 86TH CONGRESS, 1ST SESSION.
HEARINGS. GPO. WASHINGTON, DC. 1959.

GUSSENA60352 US SENATE
STUDIES IN UNEMPLOYMENT.
US SENATE, SPECIAL COMMITTEE ON UNEMPLOYMENT PROBLEMS. 86TH
CONGRESS, 2ND SESSION. PREPARED FOR THE COMMITTEE PURSUANT
TO S 196. GPO. WASHINGTON, DC. 1960.

GUSSENA63305 US SENATE
MIGRATORY LABOR BILLS.
US SENATE, COMMITTEE ON LABOR AND PUBLIC WELFARE,
SUBCOMMITTEE CN MIGRATORY LABOR. 88TH CONGRESS, 1ST SESSION.
HEARINGS. GPO. WASHINGTON, DC. 1963.

GUSSENA63331 US SENATE
NATION-S MANPOWER REVOLUTION.
US SENATE, COMMITTEE ON LABOR AND PUBLIC WELFARE,
SUBCOMMITTEE ON EMPLOYMENT AND MANPOWER. 88TH CONGRESS, 1ST
SESSION. HEARINGS. GPO. WASHINGTON, DC. 1963

GUSSENA63349 US SENATE

EQUAL-EMPLOYMENT-OPPORTUNITY.
US SENATE, COMMITTEE ON LABOR AND PUBLIC WELFARE,
SUBCOMMITTEE ON EMPLOYMENT AND MANPOWER. 88TH CONGRESS, 1ST
SESSION. HEARINGS ON S 773, S 1210, S 1211, AND S 1937.
BILLS RELATING TO EQUAL EMPLOYMENT OPPORTUNITIES,
JULY 24-31 1963, AUG 2 AND 20 1963. GPO. WASHINGTON, DC.
1963.

GUSSENA63618 US SENATE
HEARINGS RELATING TO THE TRAINING AND UTILIZATION OF THE
MANPOWER RESOURCES OF THE NATION.
US SENATE, COMMITTEE ON LABOR AND PUBLIC WELFARE,
SUBCOMMITTEE ON MANPOWER. GPO.
WASHINGTON, DC. 1963. PART ONE, 347 PP.

GUSSENA63822 US SENATE
MANPOWER RETRAINING.
US SENATE, COMMITTEE ON LABOR AND PUBLIC WELFARE,
SUBCOMMITTEE ON EMPLOYMENT AND MANPOWER, HEARINGS. GPO.
WASHINGTON, DC. JULY 16, 18 1963. 214 PP.

GUSSENA64306 US SENATE
VOLUNTARY FARM EMPLCYMENT SERVICE. /MIGRANT-WORKERS/
US SENATE, COMMITTEE ON LABOR AND PUBLIC WELFARE,
SUBCOMMITTEE ON MIGRATORY LABOR. 88TH CCNGRESS, 2ND SESSION.
HEARINGS. GPO. WASHINGTON, DC. 1964.

GUSSENA64332 US SENATE
TOWARDS FULL EMPLOYMENT. PROPCSALS FOR A COMPREHENSIVE
EMPLOYMENT AND MANPOWER POLICY IN THE UNITED STATES.
US SENATE, COMMITTEE ON LABOR AND PUBLIC WELFARE,
SUBCOMMITTEE ON EMPLOYMENT AND MANPOWER. REPORT. 88TH
CONGRESS, 2ND SESSION. GPO. WASHINGTON, DC. 1964. 148 PP.

GUSSENA64334 US SENATE
SELECTED READINGS IN EMPLOYMENT AND MANPOWER.
US SENATE, CUMMITTEE ON LABOR AND PUBLIC WELFARE,
SUBCOMMITTEE ON EMPLOYMENT AND MANPOWER. 88TH CONGRESS, 2ND
SESSION. GPO. WASHINGTON, DC. 1964. 1376 PP.

GUSSENA64348 US SENATE
ECONOMIC-OPPORTUNITY-ACT OF 1964.
US SENATE, COMMITTEE ON LABOR AND PUBLIC WELFARE. HEARINGS.
GPO. WASHINGTON, DC. 1964.

GUSSENA64355 US SENATE
THE WAR-ON-POVERTY.
US SENATE, COMMITTEE ON LABOR AND PUBLIC WELFARE, SELECT
SUBCOMMITTEE ON POVERTY. 88TH CONGRESS, 2ND SESSION.
HEARINGS. GPO. WASHINGTON, DC. 1964.

GUSSENA66351 US SENATE
FEDERAL ROLE IN URBAN AFFAIRS.
US SENATE, COMMITTEE ON GOVERNMENT OPERATIONS, SUBCOMMITTEE
ON EXECUTIVE REORGANIZATION. 89TH CONGRESS, 2ND SESSION.
HEARINGS. AUG 15-19 1966. GPO. WASHINGTCN, DC. 1966.

GUSVETA59521 US VETERANS ADMINISTRATION
THE FEDERAL NONDISCRIMINATION POLICY IN THE
VETERANS-ADMINISTRATION.
US VETERANS ADMINISTRATION, PAMPHLET 07-1. GPO. WASHINGTON,
DC. JAN 1959. 16 PP.

GUVCHCE50211 U CHI COMT CETR ON RACE RELS   *ANTI-DEFAMATION LEAGUE
*AM COUNCIL ON RACE RELATIONS
THE DYNAMICS OF STATE CAMPAIGNS FOR
FAIR-EMPLOYMENT-PRACTICES LEGISLATION.
ANTI-DEFAMATION LEAGUE OF B-NAI B-RITH. AMERICAN COUNCIL ON
RACE RELATICNS. NEW YORK. 1950. 39 PP.

GUVCHLR64212 UNIV OF CHICAGO LAW REVIEW
DISCRIMINATION AND THE NLRB. THE SCOPE OF THE BOARD POWER
UNDER SECTIONS 8A3 AND 8B2.
UNIVERSITY OF CHICAGO LAW REVIEW, VOL 32, AUTUMN 1964.
PP 124-147.

GUVCHLR64213 UNIV OF CHICAGO LAW REVIEW
ENFORCEMENT OF FAIR-EMPLOYMENT UNDER THE CIVIL-RIGHTS-ACT OF
1964.
PP 430-470.

GUVMADA62529 UNIV OF MARYLAND DEPT OF AG
PROGRESS IN MEETING PROBLEMS OF MIGRATORY LABOR IN MARYLAND.
UNIVERSITY OF MARYLAND, DEPARTMENT OF AGRICULTURE.
COLLEGE PARK, MARYLAND. 1962. 37 PP.

GUVWAIL48532 U OF WASH INST LAB ECONOMICS
JOB OPPORTUNITIES FOR MINORITIES IN THE SEATTLE AREA.
/WASHINGTON/
UNIVERSITY OF WASHINGTON, INSTITUTE OF LABOR ECONOMICS.
SEATTLE, WASHINGTON. 1948. 30 PP.

GVAASFJ66534 VAAS FJ
TITLE-VII. LEGISLATIVE HISTORY.
BOSTON COLLEGE INDUSTRIAL AND COMMERCIAL LAW REVIEW, VOL 7,
NO 3, SPRING 1966. PP 431-458.

GVANOJW63535 VANDERZANDEN JW
AMERICAN MINORITY RELATIONS, THE SOCIOLOGY OF RACE AND
ETHNIC GRCUPS.
RONALD PRESS CO. NEW YORK. 1963. 470 PP.

GVINCNX66113 VINCENT N
LEGALITY AND VALIDITY OF PERSONNEL TESTS. /LEGISLATION
TITLE-VII/
BEST-S INSURANCE NEWS, NOL 66, FEB 1966. P 20 PLUS.

GVIOTVH66113 VIOT VH   *NATL INDUSTRIAL CONF BOARD
THE CORPORATION AND TITLE-VII.
NATIONAL INDUSTRIAL CONFERENCE BOARD, CCNFERENCE BOARD
RECORD, AP 1966. PP 16-17.

GVOGAAS62C74 VOGAL AS   KOVAL M
*NEW YORK CITY YOUTH BOARD
YOUTH IN NEW-YORK CITY. OUT OF SCHOOL AND OUT OF WORK.
NEW YORK CITY YOUTH BOARD, OFFICE OF THE MAYOR. NEW YORK.
NOV 1962.

GWACHWWND536 WACHTEL WW
DISCRIMINATION...AN ECONOMIC WASTE.
NATIONAL URBAN LEAGUE, ANNUAL CONVENTION. ADDRESS. ST PAUL,
MINNESOTA. SEPT 6 1951. PUBLISHED BY CALVERT DISTILLERS
CORPORATION. NEW YORK. NO. 20 PP.

GWALKRW66538 WALKER RW
TITLE-VII. COMPLAINT PROCEDURES AND REMEDIES. /LEGISLATION/
BOSTON COLLEGE INDUSTRIAL AND COMMERCIAL LAW REVIEW, VOL 7,
NO 3, SPRING 1966. PP 495-524.

GWALLFX61221 WALLS F   *WASH STATE LEGISLATIVE CC

PROBLEMS OF MIGRANT LABOR.
WASHINGTON STATE LEGISLATIVE COUNCIL. OLYMPIA, WASHINGTON.
MAY 1961. 20 PP.

GWALLLM63520   WALLACE LM   *US VETERANS ADMINISTRATION
THE CHANGING PATTERN IN EMPLOYMENT.
/EQUAL-EMPLOYMENT-OPPORTUNITY/
US VETERANS ADMINISTRATION, PERSONNEL INFORMATION BULLETIN
NO 169. GPO. WASHINGTON, DC. AP 1963. PP 10-12.

GWALLPX66539   WALLACE P   KISSINGER B
REYNOLDS B   *US EEO COMMISSION
TESTING OF MINORITY-GROUP APPLICANTS FOR EMPLOYMENT.
US EQUAL EMPLOYMENT OPPORTUNITY COMMISSION, OFFICE OF
RESEARCH AND REPORTS. WASHINGTON, DC. MAR 1966. 30 PP.

GWALSJP64540   WALSH JP
VOCATIONAL-TRAINING TO IMPROVE JOB OPPORTUNITIES FOR
MINORITY-GROUPS.
BUFFALO LAW REVIEW, VOL 14, 1964. PP 151-164.

GWALSJP64620   WALSH JP
IMPLICATIONS OF GOVERNMENT-SPONSORED TRAINING PROGRAMS.
/TECHNOLOGICAL-CHANGE/
ORGANIZATION FOR ECONOMIC COOPERATION AND DEVELOPMENT,
NORTH AMERICAN JOINT CONFERENCE. THE REQUIREMENTS OF
AUTOMATED JOBS. WASHINGTON, DC. DEC 8-10 1964. PP 345-356.

GWARDRX62821   WARD R
AUTOMATION AND UNEMPLOYMENT.
NEW UNIVERSITY THOUGHT, VOL 2, WINTER 1962. PP 29-46.

GWASHLR64541   WASHINGTON LAW REVIEW
MEMBERSHIP DISCRIMINATION IN LABOR UNIONS.
WASHINGTON LAW REVIEW, VOL 39, 1964. PP 293-297.

GWATKDO66588   WATKINS DO   MCKINNEY D
*NYC COMM ON HUMAN RIGHTS
A STUDY OF EMPLOYMENT PATTERNS IN THE GENERAL MERCHANDISE
GROUP RETAIL STORES IN NEW-YORK-CITY.
NEW YORK CITY COMMISSION ON HUMAN RIGHTS. NEW YORK.
JUNE 30 1966. 2 VOLS. 148 PP.

GWATSMMND544   WATSON MM   *US DEPARTMENT OF LABOR
PLACEMENT OF NON-ENGLISH SPEAKING APPLICANTS.
US DEPARTMENT OF LABOR, EMPLOYMENT SECURITY REVIEW, VOL 17,
NO 11. P 29.

GWATTWW66223   WATTENBERG WW
THE PROBLEM OF SELF-IMPOSED INEQUALITIES.
ALL MEN ARE CREATED EQUAL. ED BY W W WATTENBERG. WAYNE STATE
UNIVERSITY PRESS. DETROIT, MICHIGAN. 1966. PP 117-136.

GWEAVRC66707   WEAVER RC
DILEMMAS OF URBAN AMERICA.
HARVARD UNIVERSITY PRESS. CAMBRIDGE, MASSACHUSETTS. 1966.
138 PP.

GWEBBEB65546   WEBB EB   *CAL DEPT OF INDUSTRIAL RELS
ETHNIC SURVEY OF APPRENTICES. /CALIFORNIA/
CALIFORNIA DEPARTMENT OF INDUSTRIAL RELATIONS.
SAN FRANCISCO, CALIFORNIA. OCT 29 1965.

GWEBEAR66760   WEBER AR
THE ROLE AND LIMITS OF NATIONAL MANPOWER POLICIES.
INDUSTRIAL RELATIONS RESEARCH ASSOCIATION, PROCEEDINGS.
MADISON, WISCONSIN. 1966. PP 32-50.

GWECKRS62987   WECKSTEIN RS
WELFARE CRITERIA AND CHANGING TASTES.
AMERICAN ECONOMIC REVIEW, VOL 52, MAR 1962. PP 133-153.

GWEINRX59588   WEINTRAUB R
EMPLOYMENT INTEGRATION AND RACIAL WAGE DIFFERENCE IN A
SOUTHERN PLANT.
INDUSTRIAL AND LABOR RELATIONS REVIEW, VOL 12, JAN 1959.
PP 214-226.

GWEISAJ47547   WEISS AJ
POSTWAR EMPLOYMENT DISCRIMINATION.
JEWISH SOCIAL SERVICE QUARTERLY, VOL 23, JUNE 1947.
PP 396-405.

GWEISBA65666   WEISBROD BA ED
THE ECONOMICS OF POVERTY. AN AMERICAN PARADOX.
PRENTICE-HALL, INC. ENGLEWOOD CLIFFS, NEW JERSEY. 1965.
180 PP.

GWEISLX62597   WEISS L
FEDERAL REMEDIES FOR RACIAL DISCRIMINATION BY LABOR UNIONS.
GEORGETOWN LAW JOURNAL, VOL 50, NO 3, SPRING 1962.
PP 457-477.

GWELFCD56548   WELFARE COUNCIL OF DELAWARE
MIGRATORY LABOR IN DELAWARE.
WELFARE COUNCIL OF DELAWARE, INC. WILMINGTON, DELAWARE.
MAR 1956. 5 PP.

GWELLHX58550   WELLINGTON H
UNION DEMOCRACY AND FAIR REPRESENTATION. FEDERAL
RESPONSIBILITY IN A FEDERAL SYSTEM.
YALE LAW JOURNAL, VOL 67, 1958. P 1327.

GWELLHX61549   WELLINGTON H
THE CONSTITUTION AND THE LABOR UNION.
YALE LAW JOURNAL, VOL 70, 1961. PP 345-375.

GWESTAF61557   WESTON AF
LIBERTY IN THE BIG CORPORATION.
COLUMBIA UNIVERSITY. NEW YORK. 1961.

GWESTDL65552   WESTBERG DL
PRESS SWALLOWS MOTOROLA HOAX. /TESTING/
FOCUS, VOL 4, NO 1 AND 2, JAN-FEB 1965. PP 10-13.

GWESTEC64553   WESTERN ELECTRIC CO
WESTERN-ELECTRIC AND ITS PLAN-FOR-PROGRESS, A THREE YEAR
REPORT. /INDUSTRY/
WESTERN ELECTRIC CO. NEW YORK. AUG 1964. 22 PP.

GWESTJX66551   WEST J
LABOR AND CIVIL-RIGHTS IN CHICAGO. /ILLINOIS UNION/
POLITICAL AFFAIRS, VOL 45, NOV 1966. PP 15-27.

GWESTRL53019   WESTERN RESERVE LAW REVIEW
CONSEQUENCES OF DISCRIMINATORY UNION MEMBERSHIP POLICY.
WESTERN RESERVE LAW REVIEW, VOL 4, 1953. PP 370FF.

GWHITHC60559   WHITE HOUSE CONFERENCE
CHILDREN AND YOUTH IN THE 1960-S.

GOLDEN ANNIVERSARY WHITE HOUSE CONFERENCE ON CHILDREN AND
YOUTH INC. GPO. WASHINGTON, DC. 1960. 340 PP.

GWHITHC65558   WHITE HOUSE CONFERENCE
MANPOWER PROGRAMS. THEIR CONTRIBUTION TO THE ACHIEVEMENT OF
EQUAL-OPPORTUNITY MANPOWER ADMINISTRATION.
WHITE HOUSE CONFERENCE. WASHINGTON, DC. NOV 1965.

GWHYTDR60407   WHYTE DR   SHARP EF
LARSON OF   LERAY NL
*US DEPARTMENT OF AGRICULTURE
MIGRATORY WORKERS IN NEW-YORK STATE, 1959 AND COMPARISONS
WITH 1953, 1957, AND 1958.
US DEPARTMENT OF AGRICULTURE. GPO. WASHINGTON, DC. AP 1960.
10 PP.

GWHYTWH54560   WHYTE WH
THE FALLACIES OF PERSONALITY TESTING.
FORTUNE, SEPT 1954. PP 117-208.

GWICKED63561   WICKERSHAM ED   *UPJOHN INST EMPLOY RESEARCH
DETROIT-S INSURED UNEMPLOYED AND EMPLOYABLE WELFARE
RECIPIENTS. /MICHIGAN/
THE W E UPJOHN INSTITUTE FOR EMPLOYMENT RESEARCH. KALAMAZOO,
MICHIGAN. AP 1963. 56 PP.

GWICKEX63637   WICKERSHAM E   *UPJOHN INST EMPLOY RESEARCH
INSURED UNEMPLOYED AND EMPLOYABLE WELFARE RECIPIENTS.
THE W E UPJOHN INSTITUTE FOR EMPLOYMENT RESEARCH. KALAMAZOO,
MICHIGAN. 1963.

GWIGGCH65598   WIGGINS CH
THE ILLINOIS FAIR-EMPLOYMENT-PRACTICES-ACT.
UNIVERSITY OF ILLINOIS LAW FORUM, VOL 1965, SUMMER 1965.
PP 267-296.

GWILCRC57562   WILCOCK RC   *NATL BUREAU OF EC RESEARCH
THE SECONDARY LABOR-FORCE AND THE MEASUREMENT OF
UNEMPLOYMENT.
THE MEASUREMENT AND BEHAVIOR OF UNEMPLOYMENT. NATIONAL
BUREAU OF ECONOMIC RESEARCH. NEW YORK. 1957.

GWILLLB59565   WILLETTE LB   *NATL CONSUMERS COMT RES ED
COMMON GROUND. /NEW-JERSEY MIGRANT-WORKERS/
NATIONAL CONSUMERS COMMITTEE FOR RESEARCH AND EDUCATION,
INC. CLEVELAND, OHIO. 1959. 15 PP.

GWILLRE65665   WILL RE ED   VATTER HG ED
POVERTY IN AFFLUENCE.
HARCOURT, BRACE AND WORLD, INC. NEW YORK. 1965. 274 PP.

GWILLRM47564   WILLIAMS RM
THE REDUCTION OF INTERGROUP TENSIONS.
SOCIAL SCIENCE RESEARCH COUNCIL BULLETIN. 1947. 153 PP.

GWILSAB59568   WILSON AB
RESIDENTIAL SEGREGATION OF SOCIAL-CLASSES AND ASPIRATIONS
OF HIGH SCHOOL BOYS.
AMERICAN SOCIOLOGICAL REVIEW, VOL 24, DEC 1959. PP 845.45.

GWILSAB60567   WILSON AB
THE EFFECT OF RESIDENTIAL SEGREGATION UPON EDUCATIONAL
ACHIEVEMENT AND ASPIRATIONS.
UNIVERSITY OF CALIFORNIA. PHD THESIS. BERKELEY,
CALIFORNIA. 1960. PP 85-99.

GWILSAX45566   WILSON A
THE PROPOSED LEGISLATIVE DEATH KNELL OF PRIVATE
DISCRIMINATORY EMPLOYMENT PRACTICES.
VIRGINIA LAW REVIEW, VOL 31, NO 4, SEPT 1945. PP 798-811.

GWINTEL66569   WINTER EL
MILWAUKEE. A FAIR DEAL. /WISCONSIN EEO/
AMERICAN JEWISH COMMITTEE, INSTITUTE OF HUMAN RELATIONS,
REPRINT FROM SATURDAY REVIEW. NEW YORK. 1966. 4 PP.

GWIRTWW64572   WIRTZ WW
LABOR AND THE PUBLIC INTEREST. /UNION/
HARPER AND ROW. NEW YORK. 1964.

GWIRTWW65571   WIRTZ WW
ADDRESS BEFORE THE CIVIL-RIGHTS CONFERENCE.
CIVIL RIGHTS CONFERENCE. ADDRESS. HILTON HOTEL, WASHINGTON,
DC. NOV 17 1965. 18 PP.

GWIRTWW66570   WIRTZ WW
ADDRESS AT THE CONVOCATION OF THE NAACP LEGAL DEFENSE AND
EDUCATIONAL FUND. /LEGISLATION/
NAACP. NEW YORK. MAY 18 1966. 10 PP.

GWISCIC66587   WISC IND COMM EEO DIV
FINAL REPORT, PATTERNS OF DISCRIMINATION
STUDY -- WISCONSIN.
WISCONSIN INDUSTRIAL COMMISSION, EQUAL EMPLOYMENT
OPPORTUNITY DIVISION. WISCONSIN. JUNE 22 1966. 34 PP.

GWISCLR52573   WIS LEGV REFERENCE LIBRARY
A STUDY OF STATE AND LOCAL LEGISLATIVE AND ADMINISTRATIVE
ACTS DESIGNED TO MEET PROBLEMS OF HUMAN-RIGHTS.
WISCONSIN LEGISLATIVE REFERENCE LIBRARY FOR GOVERNOR-S
COMMISSION ON HUMAN RIGHTS, RESEARCH REPORT NO 105. MADISON,
WISCONSIN. JAN 1952.

GWISPLG65141   WISPE LG   *US DEPARTMENT OF LABOR
MOTIVATIONAL PROBLEMS IN TRAINING.
US DEPARTMENT OF LABOR, OCCUPATIONAL OUTLOOK QUARTERLY,
VOL 9, NO 5, SEPT 1965.

GWITHJX65575   WITHERSPOON J
CIVIL-RIGHTS POLICY IN THE FEDERAL SYSTEM. PROPOSALS FOR A
BETTER USE OF ADMINISTRATIVE PROCESS.
YALE LAW JOURNAL, VOL 74, NO 7, JUNE 1965. PP 1171-1244.

GWITTHW64576   WITTENLORN HW
A COMPANY CASE HISTORY. /INDUSTRY EEO/
SYMPOSIUM. EQUAL EMPLOYMENT OPPORTUNITY. COMPANY POLICIES
AND EXPERIENCES. MANAGEMENT REVIEW, VOL 53, AP 1964.

GWOFFHX62577   WOFFORD H   *ANTI-DEFAMATION LEAGUE
MOVING AHEAD. AIMS AND METHODS. /CIVIL-RIGHTS
ANTIDISCRIMINATION/
ANTI-DEFAMATION LEAGUE OF B-NAI B-RITH, ADL BULLETIN,
MAR 1962. PP 2-6.

GWOFLSX64759   WOLFBEIN S
EMPLOYMENT AND UNEMPLOYMENT IN THE UNITED STATES.
SCIENCE RESEARCH ASSOCIATES, INC. CHICAGO, ILLINOIS. 1964.
339 PP.

GWOLFSL63578   WOLFBEIN SL

COUNTING THE EMPLOYED AND THE UNEMPLOYED.
MICHIGAN BUSINESS REVIEW, VOL 14, MAR 1963. PP 1-7.

GWOLFSL64624   WOLFBEIN SL
THE PACE OF TECHNOLOGICAL-CHANGE AND THE FACTORS AFFECTING
    IT.
ORGANIZATION FOR ECONOMIC COOPERATION AND DEVELOPMENT,
NORTH AMERICAN JOINT CONFERENCE. THE REQUIREMENTS OF
AUTOMATED JOBS. WASHINGTON, DC. DEC 8-10 1964. PP 49-72.

GWOLLJA64579   WOLL JA
LABOR LOOKS AT EQUAL RIGHTS IN EMPLOYMENT. /UNION/
FEDERAL BAR JOURNAL, VOL 24, WINTER 1964. P 98.

GWOLLMX54580   WOLL M
A STITCH IN TIME CAN SERVE ALL.
THE AMERICAN FEDERATIONIST, VOL 61, NO 11, NOV 1954. PP 5-6.

GWOLOHX65990   WOLOZIN H
POVERTY AND THE CRITERIA FOR PUBLIC EXPENDITURES.
POVERTY AS A PUBLIC ISSUE. ED BY BEN B SELIGMAN. THE FREE
PRESS. NEW YORK. 1965. PP 336-356.

GWOODMJ64581   WOODS MJ   *US DEPARTMENT OF LABOR
CALIFORNIA-S MINORITY-GROUPS PROGRAM.
US DEPARTMENT OF LABOR, EMPLOYMENT SERVICE REVIEW, VOL 1,
NO 7, JULY 1964. P 40.

GWORKDL63582   WORKERS DEFENSE LEAGUE
APPRENTICESHIP TRAINING IN NEW-YORK. OPENINGS IN 1963.
WORKERS DEFENSE LEAGUE. NEW YORK. 1963.

GWORKDL65584   WORKERS DEFENSE LEAGUE
THE WDL APPRENTICESHIP TRAINING PROGRAM. REPORT OF A YEAR-S
    EXPERIMENT.
WORKERS DEFENSE LEAGUE. NEW YORK. 1965. 25 PP.

GWORTMS64586   WORTMAN MS   LUTHANS F
HOW MANY CONTRACTS BAR DISCRIMINATION IN EMPLOYMENT.
PERSONNEL, VOL 41, NO 1, JAN 1964. PP 75-90.

GWORTMS65585   WORTMAN MS   LUTHANS F
ANTI-DISCRIMINATION CLAUSES REVISITED.
PERSONNEL, VOL 42, NO 5, SEPT-OCT 1965.

GWORTMS65681   WORTMAN MS   LUTHANS F
THE INCIDENCE OF ANTIDISCRIMINATION CLAUSES IN UNION
    CONTRACTS.
LABOR LAW JOURNAL. VOL 16, SEPT 1965. PP 523-532.

GWRIGDX65604   WRIGHT D
THE HARVEST OF DESPAIR. THE MIGRANT FARM WORKER.
BEACON PRESS. BOSTON, MASSACHUSETTS. 1965. 158 PP.

GYABRSM65587   YABROFF SM
DISCRIMINATION IN CRAFT UNIONS.
UNIVERSITY OF CALIFORNIA, GRADUATE SCHOOL OF BUSINESS
ADMINISTRATION. BERKELEY, CALIFORNIA. MIMEOGRAPHED.
NOV 29 1965. 22 PP.

GYABRSX65588   YABROFF S
A LOOK AT THE FEPC-S AFFIRMATIVE-ACTION PROGRAM.
UNIVERSITY OF CALIFORNIA, GRADUATE SCHOOL OF BUSINESS
ADMINISTRATION. BERKELEY, CALIFORNIA. MAY 1965. 23 TYPED PP.

GYINGJM58590   YINGER JM   SIMPSON GE
CAN SEGREGATION SURVIVE IN AN INDUSTRIAL SOCIETY.
ANTIOCH REVIEW, VOL 18, 1958. PP 15-24.

GYINGJM66589   YINGER JM
A MINORITY-GROUP IN AMERICAN SOCIETY.
MCGRAW-HILL, SOCIAL PROBLEMS SERIES. NEW YORK. 1966. 143 PP.

GYONKCC66592   YONKERS CITY COMM HUM RIGHTS
CITY EMPLOYMENT SURVEY. PERCENTAGE OF MINORITY-GROUP
    EMPLOYEES BY DEPARTMENT. /YONKERS NEW-YORK/
YONKERS CITY COMMISSION ON HUMAN RIGHTS. YONKERS, NEW YORK.
JAN 1966. 1 P.

GYOUNME46593   YOUNG ME
SOME SOCIOLOGICAL ROOTS OF VOCATIONAL CHOICES.
PHYLON, VOL 7, NO 2, 2ND QUARTER 1946. PP 156-160.

GYOUNSX67144   YOUNG S
MANPOWER TRAINING, SOME COST DIMENSIONS.
UNIVERSITY OF MASSACHUSETTS, LABOR RELATIONS AND RESEARCH
CENTER. AMHERST, MASSACHUSETTS. 1967. 48 PP.

GZEISJS63704   ZEISEL JS   *US DEPARTMENT OF LABOR
MANPOWER AND TRAINING. TRENDS, OUTLOOK AND PROGRAMS.
US DEPARTMENT OF LABOR, MANPOWER ADMINISTRATION, OFFICE OF
MANPOWER, AUTOMATION AND TRAINING. GPO. WASHINGTON, DC.
JULY 1963. 25 PP.

GZEMAMX55594   ZEMAN M
A QUANTITATIVE ANALYSIS OF WHITE-NONWHITE INCOME
    DIFFERENTIALS IN THE US IN 1939.
UNIVERSITY OF CHICAGO. PHD DISSERTATION. CHICAGO, ILLINOIS.
1955.

GZILLRC59595   ZILLER RC
THE MINORITY NEWCOMER IN OPEN AND CLOSED GROUPS.
UNIVERSITY OF DELAWARE, FELS GROUP DYNAMICS CENTER. NEWARK,
DELAWARE. 1959. 16 PP.

GZOOKDX64596   ZOOK D   HINE R
*CALIFORNIA FEPC
EMPLOYMENT PRACTICES, CITY OF SAN-DIEGO, 1963-1964.
    /CALIFORNIA/
CALIFORNIA FAIR EMPLOYMENT PRACTICES COMMISSION.
SAN FRANCISCO, CALIFORNIA. 1964. 9 PP.

IABLOJX65085 ABLON J
INDIAN RELOCATION. PROBLEMS OF DEPENDENCY AND MANAGEMENT IN
THE CITY.
PHYLON, VOL 26, WINTER 1965. PP 362-371.

IADAMWX57522 ADAMS W
SAN-CARLOS APACHE WAGE LABOR.
UNIVERSITY OF ARIZONA, DEPARTMENT OF ANTHROPOLOGY. TUCSON,
ARIZONA. UNPUBLISHED MANUSCRIPT. 1957.

IALBOJX64523 ALBON J
RELOCATED AMERICAN INDIANS IN THE SAN-FRANCISCO BAY AREA.
SOCIAL INTERACTION AND INDIAN IDENTITY. /CALIFORNIA/
HUMAN ORGANIZATION, VOL 24, 1964. PP 296-304.

IAMERIC61524 AMERICAN INDIAN CONFERENCE
THE VOICE OF THE AMERICAN-INDIAN. DECLARATION OF INDIAN
PURPOSE.
AMERICAN INDIAN CONFERENCE. UNIVERSITY OF CHICAGO. CHICAGO,
ILLINOIS. JUNE 13-20 1961.

IAMERIN64087 AM INDIAN CAP CONF ON POVERTY *COUNCIL ON INDIAN AFFAIRS
AMERICAN INDIAN CAPITAL CONFERENCE ON POVERTY. MAY 9-12,
1964. FINDINGS.
AMERICAN INDIAN CAPITAL CONFERENCE ON POVERTY. WASHINGTON,
DC. 1966. 22 PP.

IAMESDW59525 AMES DW   FISHER BR
THE MENOMINEE TERMINATION CRISIS. BARRIERS IN THE WAY OF A
RAPID CULTURAL TRANSITION.
HUMAN ORGANIZATION, VOL 18, NO 3, FALL 1959.

IARCHMS61526 ARCHERD MS   *US DEPARTMENT OF LABOR
BROADENING WORK OPPORTUNITIES FOR INDIAN YOUTH.
US DEPARTMENT OF LABOR, EMPLOYMENT SECURITY REVIEW, VOL 28,
NO 3, MAR 1961. PP 23-24.

IARIZCI62527 ARIZONA COMM INDIAN AFFAIRS
PAPAGO RESERVATION REPORT.
ARIZONA COMMISSION OF INDIAN AFFAIRS. PHOENIX, ARIZONA.
1962.

IARIZCI63528 ARIZONA COMM INDIAN AFFAIRS
ARIZONA RESERVATIONS ECONOMICS. SURVEY REPORT.
ARIZONA COMMISSION OF INDIAN AFFAIRS. PHOENIX, ARIZONA.
1963.

IARIZSE66912 ARIZONA STATE EMPLOY SERVICE
MANPOWER SERVICES TO ARIZONA INDIANS. /SES/
ARIZONA STATE EMPLOYMENT SERVICE. PHOENIX, ARIZONA. 1966.
14 PP.

IATKIMJ63529 ATKINSON MJ
INDIANS OF THE SOUTHWEST.
THE NAYLOR CO. SAN ANTONIO, TEXAS. 1963.

IBAILAL57531 BAILEY AL   BAILEY H
BAILEYS REPORT ON SEMINOLES.
INDIAN TRUTH, VOL 34, NO 1, JAN-AP 1957. PP 3-4.

IBAILAL60530 BAILEY AL   BAILEY HS
REPORT, SUMMER 1960.
INDIAN TRUTH, VOL 37, NO 3, NOV 1960. PP 1-4.

IBAIRDA56532 BAIREIS DA
THE INDIANS IN MODERN AMERICA.
WISCONSIN STATE HISTORICAL SOCIETY. MADISON, WISCONSIN.
1956.

IBAKEJE59533 BAKER JE
PROBLEMS OF NAVAJO MALE GRADUATES OF INTERMOUNTAIN SCHOOL
DURING THEIR FIRST YEAR OF EMPLOYMENT.
UTAH STATE UNIVERSITY. UNPUBLISHED MASTER-S THESIS. LOGAN
AND CEDAR CITY, UTAH. 1959.

IBARNML56534 BARNETT ML   BAERREIS DA
SOME PROBLEMS INVOLVED IN THE CHANGING STATUS OF THE
AMERICAN INDIAN.
THE INDIAN IN MODERN AMERICA. ED BY DAVID A BAERREIS.
WISCONSIN STATE HISTORICAL SOCIETY. MADISON, WISCONSIN.
1956. PP 50-70.

IBAUMLX64535 BAUMGARTNER L
HEALTH AND ECONOMIC DEVELOPMENT.
ASSOCIATION ON AMERICAN INDIAN AFFAIRS, INDIAN AFFAIRS,
NO 55, JUNE 1964. P 3 PLUS.

IBECKJX66536 BECKER J   *US DEPARTMENT OF LABOR
BETTER ECONOMIC OPPORTUNITY FOR INDIANS.
US DEPARTMENT OF LABOR, EMPLOYMENT SERVICE REVIEW, VOL 3,
NO 3, MAR 1966. PP 31-33.

IBENNRL66451 BENNETT RL
TOWARD A NEW ERA FOR AMERICAN INDIANS. /EMPLOYMENT/
AMERICAN FEDERATIONIST, VOL 73, DEC 1966. PP 14-17.

IBLOOJA59538 BLOODWORTH JA   *US DEPARTMENT OF INTERIOR
HUMAN RESOURCES SURVEY OF THE COLVILLE CONFEDERATE TRIBES.
US DEPARTMENT OF THE INTERIOR, BUREAU OF INDIAN AFFAIRS,
PORTLAND AREA OFFICE. COLVILLE, OREGON. 1959.

IBLUMRX65539 BLUMENFELD R
MOHAWKS. ROUND TRIP TO THE HIGH STEEL.
TRANS-ACTION, VOL 3, NO 1, NOV-DEC 1965. PP 19-21.

IBOISEX56886 BOISSEVAIN E
THE DETRIBALIZATION OF THE NARRAGANSETT INDIANS. A CASE
STUDY.
ETHNOHISTORY, VOL 3, NO 3, SUMMER 1956. PP 225-245.

IBOISEX59887 BOISSEVAIN E
NARRAGANSETT SURVIVAL. A STUDY OF GROUP PERSISTENCE THROUGH
ADAPTED TRAITS.
ETHNOHISTORY, VOL 6, NO 4, FALL 1959. PP 347-362.

IBOTTRV56540 BOTTOMLY RV
WE MUST ASSIST OUR INDIAN BROTHERS TO HELP THEMSELVES.
NATIONAL CONGRESS OF AMERICAN INDIANS. ADDRESS. ALSO IN THE
PEOPLE-S VOICE, HELENA, MONTANA. AP 6 1956.

IBRIGYUN0442 BRIGHAM YOUNG UNIVERSITY
UTE INDIAN SURVEY -- PRELIMINARY REPORT, SOCIAL AND ECONOMIC
CHARACTERISTICS.
AVAILABLE AT US DEPARTMENT OF THE INTERIOR, BUREAU OF
INDIAN AFFAIRS, BRANCH OF EMPLOYMENT ASSISTANCE.
WASHINGTON, DC. ND.

IBUNKRX59899 BUNKER R
THE FIRST LOOK AT STRANGERS.
RUTGERS UNIVERSITY PRESS. NEW BRUNSWICK, NEW JERSEY. 1959.
151 PP.

ICALACI66542 CAL ADVSY COMM INDIAN AFFAIRS
INDIANS IN RURAL AND RESERVATION AREAS. /CALIFORNIA/
CALIFORNIA STATE ADVISORY COMMISSION ON INDIAN AFFAIRS.
SACRAMENTO, CALIFORNIA. 1966.

ICALDIR65541 CAL DEPT OF INDUSTRIAL RELS
AMERICAN INDIANS IN CALIFORNIA. POPULATION, EDUCATION,
EMPLOYMENT, INCOME.
CALIFORNIA DEPARTMENT OF INDUSTRIAL RELATIONS, DIVISION OF
FAIR EMPLOYMENT PRACTICES. SAN FRANCISCO, CALIFORNIA.
NOV 1965. 41 PP.

ICHANNA65543 CHANCE NA
ACCULTURATION, SELF-IDENTIFICATION, AND PERSONALITY
ADJUSTMENT.
AMERICAN ANTHROPOLOGIST, VOL 67, 1965. PP 372-393.

ICOLLJX56544 COLLIER J   HAAS TH
THE UNITED STATES INDIAN.
UNDERSTANDING MINORITY-GROUPS. ED BY JOSEPH B GITTLER. JOHN
WILEY AND SONS. NEW YORK. 1956. PP 33-57.

ICOOMLM62646 COOMBS LM   *US DEPARTMENT OF INTERIOR
DOORWAY TOWARD THE LIGHT. THE STORY OF THE SPECIAL NAVAJO
EDUCATION PROGRAM.
US DEPARTMENT OF THE INTERIOR, BUREAU OF INDIAN AFFAIRS.
GPO. WASHINGTON, DC. 1962.

IDAVIRC62546 DAVIS RC
PROGRESS IN EMPLOYMENT ASSISTANCE.
INDIAN TRUTH, VOL 39, NO 2, SEPT 1962. PP 2-5.

IDENNLB66547 DENNIS LB
AMERICAN-INDIANS. NEGLECTED MINORITY. /ECONOMIC-STATUS/
EDITORIAL RESEARCH REPORTS, VOL 11, NO 8, AUG 24 1966.
PP 23-40.

IDESPCW65548 DESPAIN CW
ANALYSIS OF MALE NAVAHO STUDENTS PERCEPTIONS OF OCCUPATIONAL
OPPORTUNITIES AND THEIR ATTITUDES TOWARD DEVELOPMENT OF
SKILLS AND TRAITS NECESSARY FOR OCCUPATIONAL COMPETENCE.
WASHINGTON STATE UNIVERSITY. EDD DISSERTATION. PULLMAN,
WASHINGTON. 1965.

IDOUCPX63549 DOUCKER P
INDIANS OF THE NORTHWEST COAST.
AMERICAN MUSEUM SCIENCE BOOKS, NATIONAL MUSEUM PRESS.
GARDEN CITY, NEW YORK. 1963.

IDOUGGV60550 DOUGLAS GV
LEVEL OF OCCUPATIONAL ASPIRATIONS AMONG MONTANA INDIANS IN
GRADE AND HIGH SCHOOL.
PENNSYLVANIA STATE UNIVERSITY. PHD DISSERTATION. UNIVERSITY
PARK, PENNSYLVANIA. 1960.

IDOZIEP57C77 DOZIER EP   SIMPSON GE
YINGER JM
THE INTEGRATION OF AMERICANS OF INDIAN DESCENT.
ANNALS OF THE AMERICAN ACADEMY OF POLITICAL AND SOCIAL
SCIENCE, VOL 311, MAY 1957. PP 158 FF.

IDRIVHE57954 DRIVER HE   MASSEY WC
COMPARATIVE STUDIES OF NORTH AMERICAN-INDIANS.
AMERICAN PHILOSOPHICAL SOCIETY, TRANSACTIONS, VOL 47, NO 2,
1957. PP 163-456.

IEGGAFR66552 EGGAN FR
THE AMERICAN INDIAN, PERSPECTIVES FOR STUDY OF SOCIAL
CHANGE.
ALDINE PUBLISHING COMPANY. CHICAGO, ILLINOIS. 1966. 193 PP.

IEICHCK60553 EICHER CK
CONSTRAINTS ON ECONOMIC PROGRESS ON THE ROSEBUD SIOUX
INDIAN RESERVATION.
HARVARD UNIVERSITY. PHD DISSERTATION. CAMBRIDGE,
MASSACHUSETTS. 1960.

IELLIMB57554 ELLIS MB
US GOVERNMENT POLICY TOWARD AMERICAN INDIANS. A FEW BASIC
FACTS.
FRIENDS COMMITTEE ON NATIONAL LEGISLATION. WASHINGTON, DC.
REVISED ED. 1957. 24 PP.

IEMBRCB56555 EMBRY CB
AMERICA-S CONCENTRATION CAMPS, THE FACTS ABOUT OUR INDIAN
RESERVATIONS TODAY.
D MCKAY COMPANY. NEW YORK. 1956. 242 PP.

IERNSRC59556 ERNST RC
A POLICY TO MEET INDIAN NEEDS TODAY.
INDIAN TRUTH, VOL 36, NO 1, JAN-AP 1959. PP 1-4.

IEWERJC58557 EWERS JC
THE BLACKFEET.
UNIVERSITY OF OKLAHOMA PRESS. NORMAN, OKLAHOMA. 1958.

IEWERJC60816 EWERS JC
SELECTED REFERENCES ON THE PLAINS INDIANS.
SMITHSONIAN INSTITUTE, SMITHSONIAN ANTHROPOLOGICAL
BIBLIOGRAPHY NO 1. WASHINGTON, DC. 1960.

IFENTWN61620 FENTON WN   GULICK J
*SMITHSONIAN INSTITUTION
SYMPOSIUM ON CHEROKEE AND INDIAN CULTURE.
SMITHSONIAN INSTITUTION, BUREAU OF AMERICAN ETHNOLOGY,
BULLETIN 180. GPO. WASHINGTON, DC. 1961. 292 PP.

IFEYXHE59558 FEY HE   MCNICKLE D

INDIANS AND OTHER AMERICANS, TWO WAYS OF LIFE MEET.
HARPER. NEW YORK. 1959. 200 PP.

IFISHCR66555   FISH CR   LINDSAY JM
*US DEPARTMENT OF LABOR
MDTA COMES TO THE OWYHEE RESERVATION.
US DEPARTMENT OF LABOR, EMPLOYMENT SERVICE REVIEW, VOL 3,
NO 8, AUG 1966. PP 38-39.

IFISHLX60560   FISH L
A STUDY OF THE REASONS FOR FAILURE ON THE JOB OF SOME
   GRADUATES OF INTERMOUNTAIN SCHOOL.
UTAH STATE UNIVERSITY. MASTER-S THESIS. LOGAN, UTAH. 1960.

IFITZKXND440   FITZGERALD K
PAPAGO INDIANS, EVALUATION OF OPPORTUNITIES FOR PERMANENT
   RELOCATION.
AVAILABLE AT US DEPARTMENT OF THE INTERIOR, BUREAU OF
INDIAN AFFAIRS, BRANCH OF EMPLOYMENT ASSISTANCE.
WASHINGTON, DC. ND.

IFUNDFT61562   FUND FOR THE REPUBLIC INC
A PROGRAM FOR INDIAN CITIZENS. A SUMMARY REPORT.
FUND FOR THE REPUBLIC, INC, COMMISSION ON THE RIGHTS,
LIBERTIES AND RESPONSIBILITIES OF THE AMERICAN INDIANS.
ALBUQUERQUE, NEW MEXICO. 1961. 45 PP.

IGETTHT58563   GETTY HT
DEVELOPMENT OF THE SAN-CARLOS APACHE CATTLE INDUSTRY.
   /CALIFORNIA/
THE KIVA, VOL 23, NC 3, FEB 1958. PP 1-4.

IGETTHT63564   GETTY HT
THE SAN-CARLOS INDIAN CATTLE INDUSTRY. /CALIFORNIA/
UNIVERSITY OF ARIZONA, ANTHROPOLOGICAL PAPERS. TUCSON,
ARIZONA. 1963.

IGRAFMF66565   GRAF MF   *US DEPARTMENT OF LABOR
MANPOWER SERVICES ON THE NAVAJO RESERVATION.
US DEPARTMENT OF LABOR, EMPLOYMENT SERVICE REVIEW, VOL 3,
NO 8, AUG 1966. PP 59-61.

IGRAVTDND438   GRAVES TD
RELOCATEES FROM GALLUP AREA TO THE DENVER FIELD EMPLOYMENT
   ASSISTANCE OFFICE. /COLORADO/
AVAILABLE AT US DEPARTMENT OF THE INTERIOR, BUREAU OF INDIAN
AFFAIRS, BRANCH OF EMPLOYMENT ASSISTANCE. WASHINGTON, DC.
ND.

IGRAVTD64566   GRAVES TD   ALFRED BM
ARSDALE MV   *COLO NAVAHO URBAN RLOCAT RES
A STUDY OF NAVAHO URBAN RELOCATION IN DENVER COLORADO.
UNIVERSITY OF COLORADO, INSTITUTE OF BEHAVIORAL SCIENCE,
NAVAHO URBAN RELOCATION RESEARCH, RESEARCH REPORT NO 1.
JAN 1964.

IGRAVTD65567   GRAVES TD   ARSDALE MV
*COLO NAVAHO URBAN RLOCAT RES
PERCEIVED OPPORTUNITIES, EXPECTATIONS, AND THE DECISION TO
   REMAIN ON RELOCATION. THE CASE OF THE NAVAHO INDIAN
   MIGRANT TO DENVER, COLORADO.
UNIVERSITY OF COLORADO, INSTITUTE OF BEHAVIORAL SCIENCE,
NAVAHO URBAN RELOCATION RESEARCH, RESEARCH REPORT NO 5.
BOULDER, COLORADO. JUNE 1965. 30 PP.

IGRAVTD66146   GRAVES TD   ARSDALE MV
VALUES, EXPECTATIONS AND RELOCATION. THE NAVAHO MIGRANT TO
   DENVER. /COLORADO/
HUMAN ORGANIZATION, VOL 25, NO 4, WINTER 1966. PP 300-307.

IGULIJX60568   GULICK J   *UNIV OF NORTH CAROLINA IRSS
CHEROKEES AT THE CROSSROADS.
UNIVERSITY OF NORTH CAROLINA, INSTITUTE FOR RESEARCH IN
SOCIAL SCIENCE. CHAPEL HILL, NORTH CAROLINA. 1960. 202 PP.

IHADLJN57569   HADLEY JN
THE DEMOGRAPHY OF THE AMERICAN-INDIAN.
ANNALS OF THE AMERICAN ACADEMY OF POLITICAL AND SOCIAL
SCIENCE, VOL 311, MAY 1957.

IHAGAWT61570   HAGAN WT
AMERICAN INDIANS.
UNIVERSITY OF CHICAGO PRESS. CHICAGO, ILLINOIS. 1961.
190 PP.

IHALLAI63571   HALLOWELL AI
AMERICAN INDIANS, WHITE AND BLACK. THE PHENOMENON OF
   TRANSCULTURATION.
CURRENT ANTHROPOLOGY, VOL 4, 1963. PP 519-531.

IHAMALS57985   HAMAMSKY LS
THE ROLE OF WOMEN IN A CHANGING NAVAHO SOCIETY.
AMERICAN ANTHROPOLOGIST, VOL 59, NO 1, FEB 1957. PP 101-107.

IHARMHC61572   HARMSWORTH HC   NYBROTEN N
HUMAN RESOURCES, RELATIONS AND PROBLEMS ON THE FORT-HALL
   INDIAN RESERVATION.
UNIVERSITY OF IDAHO. MOSCOW, IDAHO. 1961.

IHARTVS63573   HART VS
MANPOWER TRAINING IN NAVAJO LAND.
SCHOOL LIFE, VOL 45, MAR 1963. PP 26-29.

IHAVIRJ57574   HAVIGHURST RJ
EDUCATION AMONG AMERICAN-INDIANS. INDIVIDUAL AND CULTURAL
   ASPECTS.
THE ANNALS OF THE AMERICAN ACADEMY OF POLITICAL AND SOCIAL
SCIENCE, VOL 311, MAY 1957. PP 105-115.

IHETZTX58575   HETZEL T   HETZEL R
VISITS MADE TO 20 INDIAN COMMUNITIES.
INDIAN TRUTH, VOL 35, NO 3, JULY-OCT 1958. PP 3-7.

IHIRAJXND444   HIRABAYASHI J
SOCIAL SURVEY OF AMERICAN-INDIAN URBAN INTEGRATION.
AVAILABLE AT US DEPARTMENT OF THE INTERIOR, BUREAU OF
INDIAN AFFAIRS, BRANCH OF EMPLOYMENT ASSISTANCE.
WASHINGTON, DC. ND.

IHUMAOX61820   HUMAN ORGANIZATION
AMERICAN-INDIANS AND THEIR ECONOMIC DEVELOPMENT.
HUMAN ORGANIZATION, WINTER 1961-1962. ENTIRE ISSUE.

IHUMPHH66003   HUMPHREY HH
A NEW DAY FOR THE AMERICAN INDIAN.
THE OPTIMIST, NOV 1966.

IHURTWR66576   HURT WR
THE URBANIZATION OF THE YANKTON INDIANS.
HUMAN ORGANIZATION, VOL 20, WINTER 1961-1962. PP 226-231.

ALSO IN KNOWING THE DISADVANTAGED. ED BY STATEN W WEBSTER.
CHANDLER PUBLISHING COMPANY. SAN FRANCISCO, CALIFORNIA.
1966. PP 77-88.

IKELLWH57076   KELLY WH
THE ECONOMIC BASIS OF INDIAN LIFE. /INCOME LABOR-FORCE/
ANNALS OF THE AMERICAN ACADEMY OF POLITICAL AND SOCIAL
SCIENCE, VOL 311, MAY 1957. PP 71-79.

IKELLWH58577   KELLY WH
THE CHANGING ROLE OF THE INDIAN IN ARIZONA.
UNIVERSITY OF ARIZONA, ARIZONA EXTENSION SERVICE, CIRCULAR
263. TUCSON, ARIZONA. 1958.

IKELLWH67579   KELLY WH
SOCIAL AND CULTURAL CONSIDERATIONS IN THE DEVELOPMENT OF
   MANPOWER PROGRAMS FOR INDIANS.
NATIONAL CONFERENCE ON MANPOWER PROGRAMS FOR INDIANS. PAPER.
KANSAS CITY, MISSOURI. FEB 16 1967. 9 PP.

IKERCAC59018   KERCKHOFF AC
ANOMIE AND ACHIEVEMENT MOTIVATION. A STUDY OF PERSONALITY
   DEVELOPMENT WITHIN A CULTURAL DISORGANIZATION.
SOCIAL FORCES, VOL 37, MAR 1959. PP 201 FF.

IKLEIBA67899   KLEIN B AND CO
REFERENCE ENCYCLOPEDIA ON THE AMERICAN-INDIAN.
B KLEIN AND CO. NEW YORK. 1967.

IKRUGDH67811   KRUGER DH
NATIONAL CONFERENCE ON MANPOWER PROGRAMS FOR INDIANS.
   SUMMATION.
US EMPLOYMENT SERVICE. KANSAS CITY, MISSOURI. FEB 16 1967.
12 PP.

IKUPFHJ62216   KUPFERER HJ
HEALTH PRACTICES AND EDUCATIONAL ASPIRATIONS AS INDICATORS
   OF ACCULTURATION AND SOCIAL-CLASS AMONG THE EASTERN
   CHEROKEE. /NORTH-CAROLINA/
SOCIAL FORCES, VOL 41, NO 2, DEC 1962. PP 154-163.

ILAFAOX57075   LAFARGE O
TERMINATION OF FEDERAL SUPERVISION. DISINTEGRATION AND THE
   AMERICAN-INDIANS.
ANNALS OF THE AMERICAN ACADEMY OF POLITICAL AND SOCIAL
SCIENCE, VOL 311, MAY 1957. PP 41-46.

ILIEBLX66041   LIEBERMAN L
THE EMPLOYABILITY OF CHIPPEWA INDIANS AND POOR WHITES.
MICHIGAN STATE UNIVERSITY. RESEARCH PROPOSAL. EAST LANSING,
MICHIGAN. DEC 20 1966. 8 PP.

ILINDVX64581   LINDSEY V   *US DEPARTMENT OF LABOR
TRAINING NAVAJOES FOR THE FUTURE.
US DEPARTMENT OF LABOR, EMPLOYMENT SERVICE REVIEW, VOL 1,
NO 8, AUG 1964. PP 25-26.

ILINDVX66580   LINDSEY V   *US DEPARTMENT OF LABOR
INDIANS WORK AT THEIR OWN SKI RESORT. /NEW-MEXICO/
US DEPARTMENT OF LABOR, EMPLOYMENT SERVICE REVIEW, VOL 3,
NO 8, AUG 1966. P 54.

ILIVIMG59582   LIVINGSTON MG
KLAMATH INDIANS IN TWO NON-INDIAN COMMUNITIES. KLAMATH-FALLS
   AND EUGENE-SPRINGFIELD. /OREGON/
UNIVERSITY OF OREGON, DEPARTMENT OF ANTHROPOLOGY. MASTER-S
THESIS. EUGENE, OREGON. 1959.

ILURIMO66583   LURIE MO
THE ENDURING INDIAN.
NATURAL HISTORY, VOL 75, NO 9, 1966. PP 10-22.

IMADILX56587   MADIGAN L   *ASSN ON AM INDIAN AFFAIRS
THE AMERICAN INDIAN RELOCATION PROGRAM.
ASSOCIATION ON AMERICAN INDIAN AFFAIRS. NEW YORK. 1956.
22 PP.

IMARTHW64588   MARTIN HW
CORRELATES OF ADJUSTMENT AMONG AMERICAN-INDIANS IN AN URBAN
   ENVIRONMENT.
HUMAN ORGANIZATION, VOL 23, NO 4, WINTER 1964. PP 290-296.

IMAYHMP62589   MAYHALL MP
TODAY -- ACCULTURATION.
THE KIOWAS. UNIVERSITY OF OKLAHOMA PRESS. NORMAN, OKLAHOMA.
1962. PP 270-278.

IMCGRGD62584   MCGRATH GD
HIGHER EDUCATION OF SOUTHWESTERN INDIANS WITH REFERENCE TO
   SUCCESS AND FAILURE.
ARIZONA STATE UNIVERSITY. TEMPE, ARIZONA. 1962. 275 PP.

IMCKIFX64086   MCKINLEY F
FEDERAL INDIAN POLICY AS IT AFFECTS LOCAL INDIAN AFFAIRS.
INDIAN TRUTH, VOL 41, NOS 1-2, JUNE 1964. PP 1-7.

IMCNIDX61586   MCNICKLE D   *LONDON INST OF RACE RELS
THE INDIAN TRIBES OF THE US. ETHNIC AND CULTURAL SURVIVAL.
OXFORD UNIVERSITY PRESS. LONDON, NEW YORK. 1961. 80 PP.

IMCNIDX66585   MCNICKLE D
THE INDIAN TESTS THE MAINSTREAM.
THE NATION, VOL 203, NO 9, SEPT 26 1966. PP 275-279.

IMETZWX63081   METZLER W
RELOCATION OF THE DISPLACED WORKER.
HUMAN ORGANIZATION, VOL 22, SUMMER 1963. PP 142-145.

IMILLFC64590   MILLER FC   CALUKINS DD
CHIPPEWA ADOLESCENTS. A CHANGING GENERATION.
HUMAN ORGANIZATION, VOL 23, NO 2, SUMMER 1964. PP 150-159.

IMINLCW56545   MINNEAPOLIS COM WELFARE CC
THE MINNESOTA INDIAN IN MINNEAPOLIS.
MINNEAPOLIS COMMUNITY WELFARE COUNCIL. MINNEAPOLIS,
MINNESOTA. AP 1956.

IMINNMS63218   MINNIS MS
THE RELATIONSHIP OF THE SOCIAL-STRUCTURE OF AN INDIAN
   COMMUNITY TO ADULT AND JUVENILE-DELINQUENCY. /POVERTY
   ECONOMIC-STATUS/
SOCIAL FORCES, VOL 41, NO 4, MAY 1963. PP 395-403.

IMONDWX66591   MONDALE W
THE INDIANS AND THE GREAT SOCIETY. REMARKS.
CONGRESSIONAL RECORD, AUG 25 1966. PP 19716-19725.

IMUSEPI57593   MUSEUM OF THE PLAINS INDIANS
LIFE ON THE BLACKFEET INDIAN RESERVATION TODAY.
MUSEUM OF THE PLAINS INDIANS. BROWNING, MONTANA. 1957.

INAPIAX58594   NAPIER A   SASAKI   TT
                THE NAVAJO IN THE MACHINE AGE. HUMAN RESOURCES ARE
                  IMPORTANT TOO.
                NEW MEXICO BUSINESS, VOL 2, NO 7, JULY 1958.

INASHPX62595   NASH P
                INDIAN AFFAIRS TODAY.
                UNIVERSITY OF TORONTO, SCHOOL OF GRADUATE STUDIES. ADDRESS.
                PUBLISHED BY DEPARTMENT OF THE INTERIOR. GPO.
                WASHINGTON, DC. DEC 1962.

INASHPX62596   NASH P
                THE NEW TRAIL FOR AMERICAN INDIANS.
                INDIAN TRUTH, VOL 39, NO 1, MAY 1962. PP 1-5.

INASHPX64134   NASH P   *US DEPARTMENT OF INTERIOR
                THE INDIAN BUREAU AND THE WAR-ON-POVERTY.
                CONFERENCE OF SUPERINTENDENTS OF BUREAUS OF INDIAN AFFAIRS,
                SPEECH. SANTA FE, NEW MEXICO. JUNE 1964. 7 PP.

INASHPX64597   NASH P   *US DEPARTMENT OF INTERIOR
                THE WAR AGAINST POVERTY -- THE AMERICAN-INDIAN.
                US DEPARTMENT OF THE INTERIOR, BUREAU OF INDIAN AFFAIRS.
                GPO. WASHINGTON, DC. 1964.

INAVATP64598   NAVAJO TRIBE PR AND INFO DEPT
                THE NAVAJOS.
                NAVAJO TRIBE, PUBLIC RELATIONS AND INFORMATION DEPARTMENT.
                WINDOW ROCK, ARIZONA. AP 1964. 6 PP.

INETTRM60599   NETTING RM ED   PEATTE LR ED
                DOCUMENTARY HISTORY OF THE FOX PROJECT, 1948-1959. A PROGRAM
                  IN ACTION ANTHROPOLOGY.
                UNIVERSITY OF CHICAGO. CHICAGO, ILLINOIS. 1960. 426 PP.

INEWCWW56600   NEWCOMB WW
                THE CULTURE AND ACCULTURATION OF THE DELAWARE INDIANS.
                UNIVERSITY OF MICHIGAN, MUSEUM OF ANTHROPOLOGY, PAPERS,
                NO 10. ANN ARBOR, MICHIGAN. 1956.

INEWYSF56601   NYS DIRECTOR INDIAN SERVICE
                THE INDIAN TODAY IN NEW-YORK STATE.
                NEW YORK STATE DIRECTOR OF INDIAN SERVICE. ALBANY, NEW YORK.
                1956.

INEWYSI64602   NYS IDEPTL COMT INDIAN AFFAIR
                THE INDIAN TODAY IN NEW-YORK STATE.
                NEW YORK STATE INTERDEPARTMENTAL COMMITTEE ON INDIAN
                AFFAIRS. ALBANY, NEW YORK. JULY 1964. 16 PP.

INYBRNX64603   NYBROTEN N ED   *IDAHO U BUR BUS EC RESEARCH
                ECONOMY AND CONDITIONS OF THE FORT-HALL INDIAN RESERVATION.
                IDAHO UNIVERSITY, BUREAU OF BUSINESS AND ECONOMIC RESEARCH,
                REPORT NO 9. MOSCOW, IDAHO. 1964. 198 PP.

IPEITIM59284   PEITHMANN IM
                THE PRESENT STATUS OF THE FLORIDA SEMINOLE INDIANS.
                SOUTHERN FOLKLORE QUARTERLY, VOL 23, SEPT 1959.

IPEITIM64604   PEITHMANN IM
                BROKEN PEACE PIPES. A 400 YEAR HISTORY OF THE
                  AMERICAN-INDIAN.
                THOMAS. SPRINGFIELD, ILLINOIS. 1964.

IPOLGSX60605   POLGAR S
                BICULTURATION OF MESQUAKIE TEENAGE BOYS.
                AMERICAN ANTHROPOLOGIST, VOL 62, 1960. PP 217-235.

IPRICJA65607   PRICE JA   *UCLA
                THE LUISENO INDIANS IN 1965.
                UNIVERSITY OF SOUTHERN CALIFORNIA, DEPARTMENT OF
                ANTHROPOLGY, ETHNOGRAPHIC FIELD SCHOOL. LOS ANGELES,
                CALIFORNIA. 1965. 97 PP.

IPRICJA67606   PRICE JA
                A CENSUS OF INDIANS IN LOS-ANGELES. /CALIFORNIA/
                INDIANS ILLUSTRATED, VOL 1, NO 1, 1967.

IPRICJA67608   PRICE JA
                THE MIGRATION AND ADAPTATION OF AMERICAN INDIANS TO
                  LOS-ANGELES. /CALIFORNIA/
                UNIVERSITY OF SOUTHERN CALIFORNIA, DEPARTMENT OF
                ANTHROPOLOGY. LOS ANGELES, CALIFORNIA. FEB 1967. 15 PP.

IQUINFX60609   QUINN F   *AM FRIENDS SERVICE COMMITTEE
                INDIANS OF CALIFORNIA, PAST AND PRESENT.
                AMERICAN FRIENDS SERVICE COMMITTEE. SAN FRANCISCO,
                CALIFORNIA. 1960.

IREIFBX58610   REIFEL B   *US DEPARTMENT OF INTERIOR
                INDIANS OF THE MISSOURI-BASIN -- CULTURAL FACTORS IN THEIR
                  SOCIAL AND ECONOMIC ADJUSTMENT.
                US DEPARTMENT OF THE INTERIOR, BUREAU OF INDIAN AFFAIRS.
                GPO. WASHINGTON, DC. 1958.

IROYXEP59611   ROY EP
                INDIANS OF DU LAC.
                LOUISIANA STATE UNIVERSITY. UNPUBLISHED MS THESIS.
                BATON ROUGE, LOUISIANA. 1959.

IROYXPX61612   ROY P   *WASH AGL EXPERIMENT STATION
                ASSIMILATION OF THE SPOKANE INDIANS. /WASHINGTON/
                WASHINGTON STATE UNIVERSITY, AGRICULTURE EXPERIMENT STATION,
                BULLETIN NO 628. PULLMAN, WASHINGTON. 1961.

IROYXPX66613   ROY P
                THE MEASUREMENT OF ASSIMILATION. THE SPOKANE INDIANS.
                  /WASHINGTON/
                AMERICAN JOURNAL OF SOCIOLOGY, VOL 67, MAR 1962. PP 541-551.

ISANDJN62615   SANDOVAL JN   LINCOLN AT
                *US DEPARTMENT OF LABOR
                INDIAN RELOCATION AND THE NEW-MEXICO SEC.
                US DEPARTMENT OF LABOR, EMPLOYMENT SECURITY REVIEW, VOL 29,
                NO 3, MAR 1962. PP 16-19.

ISASATT60615   SASAKI TT
                FRUITLAND, NEW-MEXICO. A NAVAHO COMMUNITY IN TRANSITION.
                CORNELL UNIVERSITY PRESS. ITHACA, NEW YORK. 1960. 217 PP.

ISELLCL62616   SELLERS CL
                THE ECONOMIC DEVELOPMENT AND URBANIZATION OF THE NAVAJO
                  INDIAN RESERVATION.
                GEORGIA INSTITUTE OF TECHNOLOGY. ATLANTA, GEORGIA. 1962.

ISHAWLC60617   SHAW LC   *MIT CENTER INTERNATL STUDIES
                THE SIOUX ON THE RESERVATION.
                MASSACHUSETTS INSTITUTE OF TECHNOLOGY, CENTER FOR
                INTERNATIONAL STUDIES. CAMBRIDGE, MASSACHUSETTS. 1960.

ISHEPMX64618   SHEPARDSON M   HAMMOND B
                CHANGE AND RESISTANCE IN AN ISOLATED NAVAHO COMMUNITY.
                AMERICAN ANTHROPOLOGIST, VOL 66, NO 5, OCT 1964.
                PP 1029-1050.

ISMITIB59619   SMITHSONIAN INSTN BUR AM ETHN
                HANDBOOK OF AMERICAN-INDIANS NORTH OF MEXICO.
                SMITHSONIAN INSTITUTION, BUREAU OF AMERICAN ETHNOLOGY,
                BULLETIN NO 30. PAGEANT BOOKS. 1959.

ISPICEH61621   SPICER EH ED
                PERSPECTIVES IN AMERICAN INDIAN CULTURE CHANGE.
                UNIVERSITY OF CHICAGO PRESS. CHICAGO, ILLINOIS. 1961.

ISPINLS62622   SPINDLER LS   *AM ANTHROPOLOGICAL ASSN
                MENOMINEE WOMEN AND CULTURE CHANGE.
                AMERICAN ANTHROPOLOGICAL ASSOCIATION, MEMOIR 91. MENASHA,
                WISCONSIN. 1962. 113 PP.

ISTANRI58623   STANFORD RESEARCH INSTITUTE
                NEEDS AND RESOURCES OF THE JICARILLA APACHE INDIAN TRIBE.
                STANFORD RESEARCH INSTITUTE. MENLO PARK, CALIFORNIA. 1958.
                5 VOLS.

ISTEISX64373   STEINER S
                THE AMERICAN INDIAN. GHETTOS IN THE DESERT.
                THE NATION, VOL 198, JUNE 22 1964. PP 624-627.

ISTERTX61624   STERN T
                LIVELIHOOD AND TRIBAL GOVERNMENT ON THE KLAMATH INDIAN
                  RESERVATION.
                HUMAN ORGANIZATION, VOL 20, WINTER 1961-1962. PP 172-180.

ISTERTX65625   STERN T
                MODERN KLAMATH. DEMOGRAPHY AND ECONOMY.
                THE KLAMATH TRIBE. A PEOPLE AND THEIR RESERVATION.
                UNIVERSITY OF WASHINGTON PRESS. SEATTLE, WASHINGTON. 1965.
                PP 185-195.

ISTEWOX64302   STEWART O
                QUESTIONS REGARDING AMERICAN-INDIAN CRIMINALITY.
                HUMAN ORGANIZATION, VOL 23, NO 1, 1964.

ISTONCX62626   STONE C   ROY P
                ASSIMILATION OF THE SPOKANE INDIANS. /WASHINGTON/
                WASHINGTON STATE UNIVERSITY, DEPARTMENT OF RURAL SOCIOLOGY.
                PULLMAN, WASHINGTON. 1962.

ITAXXSXND441   TAX S   ABLON J
                SAN-FRANCISCO RELOCATEES. /CALIFORNIA/
                AVAILABLE AT THE US DEPARTMENT OF THE INTERIOR, BUREAU OF
                INDIAN AFFAIRS, BRANCH OF EMPLOYMENT ASSISTANCE.
                WASHINGTON, DC. ND.

ITAXXSX56628   TAX S   THOMAS R
                STANLEY S
                THE PRESENT DAY DISTRIBUTION OF UNITED STATES INDIANS.
                AMERICAN ANTHROPOLOGICAL ASSOCIATION, 55TH ANNUAL MEETING.
                PAPER. 1956.

ITAXXSX58157   TAX S
                THE FOX PROJECT. /ECONOMY/
                HUMAN ORGANIZATION, VOL 17, 1958. PP 17-19.

ITAYLFX65560   TAYLOR F
                RELOCATION RIDDLES. /MOBILITY EDUCATION/
                WALL STREET JOURNAL, MAY 21 1965. 2 PP.

ITAYLTW57627   TAYLOR TW
                REGIONAL ORGANIZATION, BUREAU-OF-INDIAN-AFFAIRS.
                HARVARD UNIVERSITY. UNPUBLISHED PHD DISSERTATION. CAMBRIDGE,
                MASSACHUSETTS. 1957.

ITHOMBXND439   THOMPSON B
                COUNSELLING SERVICES.
                AVAILABLE AT US DEPARTMENT OF THE INTERIOR, BUREAU OF INDIAN
                AFFAIRS, BRANCH OF EMPLOYMENT ASSISTANCE. WASHINGTON, DC.
                ND.

ITHOMHX57630   THOMPSON H
                EDUCATION AMONG AMERICAN-INDIANS. INSTITUTIONAL ASPECTS.
                ANNALS OF THE AMERICAN ACADEMY OF POLITICAL AND SOCIAL
                SCIENCE, VOL 311, MAY 1957. PP 95-104.

ITHOMHX61629   THOMPSON H
                ADOLESCENTS NEED JOBS.
                INDIAN EDUCATION, VOL 24, NO 356, MAR 15 1961. PP 1-2.

ITHOMHX61631   THOMPSON H
                EDUCATION FOR THE COMING DECADES.
                INDIAN EDUCATION, VOL 24, NO 352, JAN 15 1961. PP 1-3.

ITHOMLX65632   THOMPSON L   JOSEPH A
                THE HOPI WAY.
                RUSSELL AND RUSSELL. NEW YORK. 1965. 150 PP.

ITYLESL64634   TYLER SL   *BYU INST AM INDIAN STUDIES
                INDIAN AFFAIRS, A STUDY OF THE CHANGES IN POLICY OF THE
                  UNITED STATES TOWARD INDIANS.
                BRIGHAM YOUNG UNIVERSITY, INSTITUTE OF AMERICAN INDIAN
                STUDIES. PROVO, UTAH. 1964. 199 PP.

IUNDERM56635   UNDERHILL RM
                THE NAVAJOS.
                UNIVERSITY OF OKLAHOMA PRESS. NORMAN, OKLAHOMA. 1956.
                299 PP.

IUSCOMC65636   US COMMISSION ON CIVIL RIGHTS
                LAW AND THE AMERICAN-INDIAN.
                MINORITY PROBLEMS. ED BY ARNOLD AND CAROLINE ROSE.
                HARPER AND ROW. NEW YORK. 1965. PP 182-185.

IUSCONG60637   US CONGRESS
                HEARING.
                US CONGRESS, JOINT COMMITTEE ON NAVAJO-HOPI INDIAN
                ADMINISTRATION. JAN 29 1960. 86TH CONGRESS, 2ND SESSION.
                GPO. WASHINGTON, DC. 1960. 38 PP.

IUSDAGR63638   US DEPARTMENT OF AGRICULTURE
                COOPERATIVE EXTENSION SERVICE WORK WITH LOW-INCOME FAMILIES.
                US DEPARTMENT OF AGRICULTURE, FEDERAL EXTENSION SERVICE.
                GPO. WASHINGTON, DC. OCT 1963. 24 PP.

IUSDHEW58196   US DEPT OF HEALTH ED WELFARE
                INDIANS ON FEDERAL RESERVATIONS IN THE US.
                US DEPARTMENT OF HEALTH, EDUCATION AND WELFARE, PUBLIC
                HEALTH SERVICE, DIVISION OF INDIAN HEALTH, PROGRAM ANALYSIS
                AND SPECIAL STUDIES BRANCH. GPO. WASHINGTON, DC. SERIES,
                1958 AND FOLLOWING YEARS.

IUSDHEW60639 US DEPT OF HEALTH EC WELFARE
SOCIAL SECURITY AND THE AMERICAN-INDIAN.
US DEPARTMENT OF HEALTH, EDUCATION AND WELFARE, SOCIAL
SECURITY ADMINISTRATION, BUREAU OF OLD-AGE AND SURVIVORS
INSURANCE. GPO. WASHINGTON, DC. 1960.

IUSDHEW66813 US DEPT OF HEALTH ED WELFARE
INDIAN HEALTH HIGHLIGHTS. /DEMOGRAPHY/
US DEPARTMENT OF HEALTH, EDUCATION, AND WELFARE, PUBLIC
HEALTH SERVICE. GPO. WASHINGTON, DC. JUNE 1966.

IUSDINTND452 US DEPARTMENT OF THE INTERIOR
EMPLOYMENT ASSISTANCE REFERENCE BIBLIOGRAPHY.
AVAILABLE AT US DEPARTMENT OF THE INTERIOR, BUREAU OF INDIAN
AFFAIRS, BRANCH OF EMPLOYMENT ASSISTANCE. WASHINGTON, DC.
ND.

IUSDINTND665 US DEPARTMENT OF INTERIOR
AMERICAN-INDIANS SEEK NEW OPPORTUNITIES.
US DEPARTMENT OF THE INTERIOR, BUREAU OF INDIAN AFFAIRS,
BRANCH OF RELOCATION. DENVER, COLORADO. ND. 3 PP.

IUSDINTND666 US DEPARTMENT OF INTERIOR
ANNUAL REPORTS OF US DEPARTMENT OF THE INTERIOR.
US DEPARTMENT OF INTERIOR, SECRETARY OF THE INTERIOR. GPO.
WASHINGTON, DC.

IUSDINT56661 US DEPARTMENT OF INTERIOR
STATISTICS CONCERNING INDIAN EDUCATION, FISCAL YEAR 1956.
US DEPARTMENT OF THE INTERIOR, BUREAU OF INDIAN AFFAIRS.
GPO. WASHINGTON, DC. 1956.

IUSDINT57643 US DEPARTMENT OF INTERIOR
BASIC NEEDS OF INDIAN PEOPLE.
US DEPARTMENT OF THE INTERIOR, BUREAU OF INDIAN AFFAIRS,
SPECIAL REPORT. WASHINGTON, DC. JUNE 1957.

IUSDINT57660 US DEPARTMENT OF INTERIOR
SOCIAL AND ECONOMIC SURVEY OF POTAWATOMIE JURISDICTION.
US DEPARTMENT OF THE INTERIOR, BUREAU OF INDIAN AFFAIRS.
GPO. WASHINGTON, DC. 1957.

IUSDINT57664 US DEPARTMENT OF INTERIOR
YOU ASKED ABOUT THE NAVAJO. EDUCATION, HEALTH, AND ECONOMIC
PROBLEMS OF THE NAVAJO.
US DEPARTMENT OF THE INTERIOR, BUREAU OF INDIAN AFFAIRS.
HASKELL INSTITUTE. LAWRENCE, KANSAS. 1957. 47 PP.

IUSDINT58648 US DEPARTMENT OF INTERIOR
AN EVALUATION OF THE 10-YEAR DEVELOPMENT PROGRAM OF THE UTE
TRIBE OF THE UINTAH AND OURAY RESERVATION, UTAH.
US DEPARTMENT OF THE INTERIOR, BUREAU OF INDIAN AFFAIRS.
GPO. WASHINGTON, DC. 1958.

IUSDINT59662 US DEPARTMENT OF INTERIOR
TODAY-S DROP-OUT -- TOMORROW-S PROBLEMS.
US DEPARTMENT OF THE INTERIOR, BUREAU OF INDIAN AFFAIRS.
GPO. WASHINGTON, DC. 1959.

IUSDINT60644 US DEPARTMENT OF INTERIOR
THE BUREAU OF INDIAN AFFAIRS VOLUNTARY RELOCATION SERVICES.
US DEPARTMENT OF THE INTERIOR, BUREAU OF INDIAN AFFAIRS.
GPO. WASHINGTON, DC. CIRCA 1960.

IUSDINT60655 US DEPARTMENT OF INTERIOR
POPULATION AND INCOME CENSUS. WIND-RIVER RESERVATION,
WYOMING.
US DEPARTMENT OF THE INTERIOR, BUREAU OF INDIAN AFFAIRS.
BILLINGS, MONTANA. 1960.

IUSDINT61641 US DEPARTMENT OF INTERIOR
REPORT TO THE SECRETARY OF THE INTERIOR BY THE TASK FORCE
ON INDIAN AFFAIRS.
US DEPARTMENT OF THE INTERIOR. WASHINGTON, DC. JULY 10 1961.

IUSDINT61663 US DEPARTMENT OF INTERIOR
UNITED STATES INDIAN POPULATION AND LAND, 1960-1961.
US DEPARTMENT OF THE INTERIOR, BUREAU OF INDIAN AFFAIRS.
GPO. WASHINGTON, DC. OCT 1961.

IUSDINT63656 US DEPARTMENT OF INTERIOR
POPULATION CHARACTERISTICS, LIVING CONDITIONS AND INCOME OF
INDIAN FAMILIES, NORTHERN-CHEYENNE RESERVATION, JULY,
1961.
US DEPARTMENT OF THE INTERIOR, BUREAU OF INDIAN AFFAIRS.
BILLINGS, MONTANA. 1963.

IUSDINT63657 US DEPARTMENT OF INTERIOR
POPULATION CHARACTERISTICS, LIVING CONDITIONS, AND INCOME OF
INDIAN FAMILIES, FORT-PECK RESERVATION, 1951-1961.
US DEPARTMENT OF THE INTERIOR, BUREAU OF INDIAN AFFAIRS.
BILLINGS, MONTANA. 1963.

IUSDINT63658 US DEPARTMENT OF INTERIOR
POPULATION CHARACTERISTICS, LIVING CONDITIONS AND INCOMES OF
INDIAN FAMILIES, FORT-BELKNAP RESERVATION.
US DEPARTMENT OF THE INTERIOR, BUREAU OF INDIAN AFFAIRS.
BILLINGS, MONTANA. 1963.

IUSDINT63659 US DEPARTMENT OF INTERIOR
POPULATION CHARACTERISTICS, LIVING CONDITIONS AND INCOMES OF
INDIAN FAMILIES, ROCKY-BAY-S RESERVATION.
US DEPARTMENT OF THE INTERIOR, BUREAU OF INDIAN AFFAIRS.
BILLINGS, MONTANA. 1963.

IUSDINT64645 US DEPARTMENT OF INTERIOR
CULTURAL AND ECONOMIC-STATUS OF THE SIOUX PEOPLE.
US DEPARTMENT OF THE INTERIOR, BUREAU OF INDIAN AFFAIRS.
STANDING ROCK RESERVATION. BILLINGS, MONTANA. 1964.

IUSDINT64647 US DEPARTMENT OF INTERIOR
EMPLOYMENT ASSISTANCE PROGRAM.
US DEPARTMENT OF THE INTERIOR, BUREAU OF INDIAN AFFAIRS.
GPO. WASHINGTON, DC. OCT 1964. 4 PP.

IUSDINT64649 US DEPARTMENT OF INTERIOR
FAMILY PLAN AND REHABILITATION PROGRAMS, STANDING-ROCK
RESERVATION.
US DEPARTMENT OF INTERIOR, BUREAU OF INDIAN AFFAIRS.
BILLINGS, MONTANA. 1964.

IUSDINT64651 US DEPARTMENT OF INTERIOR
HOPI INDIAN AGENCY.
US DEPARTMENT OF THE INTERIOR, BUREAU OF INDIAN AFFAIRS.
KEAMS CANYON, ARIZONA. 1964.

IUSDINT64652 US DEPARTMENT OF COMMISSIONER
INDIAN AFFAIRS 1964, A PROGRESS REPORT FROM THE COMMISSIONER
OF INDIAN AFFAIRS.

US DEPARTMENT OF THE INTERIOR, BUREAU OF INDIAN AFFAIRS.
GPO. WASHINGTON, DC. 1964.

IUSDINT64653 US DEPARTMENT OF INTERIOR
INDIAN INDUSTRIAL DEVELOPMENT PROGRAM. A NEW INDUSTRIAL
OPPORTUNITY.
US DEPARTMENT OF THE INTERIOR, BUREAU OF INDIAN AFFAIRS.
GPO. WASHINGTON, DC. 1964.

IUSDINT65640 US DEPARTMENT OF INTERIOR
AMERICAN-INDIANS AND THE FEDERAL GOVERNMENT.
US DEPARTMENT OF THE INTERIOR, BUREAU OF INDIAN AFFAIRS.
GPO. WASHINGTON, DC. 1965. 26 PP.

IUSDINT65642 US DEPARTMENT OF INTERIOR
ANSWERS TO QUESTIONS ABOUT AMERICAN-INDIANS.
US DEPARTMENT OF THE INTERIOR, BUREAU OF INDIAN AFFAIRS.
GPO. WASHINGTON, DC. 1965. 36 PP.

IUSDINT66650 US DEPARTMENT OF INTERIOR
A FOLLOWUP STUDY OF 1963 RECIPIENTS OF THE SERVICES OF THE
EMPLOYMENT ASSISTANCE PROGRAM, BUREAU-OF-INDIAN-AFFAIRS.
US DEPARTMENT OF THE INTERIOR, BUREAU OF INDIAN AFFAIRS.
GPO. WASHINGTON, DC. OCT 1966. 53 PP.

IUSDINT66654 US DEPARTMENT OF INTERIOR
INDIANS. /DEMOGRAPHY/
US DEPARTMENT OF THE INTERIOR, BUREAU OF INDIAN AFFAIRS.
GPO. WASHINGTON, DC. JAN 1966. 9 PP.

IUSDLAB59667 US DEPARTMENT OF LABOR
PLACING INDIANS WHO LIVE ON RESERVATIONS. A COOPERATIVE
PROGRAM.
US DEPARTMENT OF LABOR, EMPLOYMENT SECURITY REVIEW, VOL 26,
NO 1, JAN 1959. PP 27-29.

IUSDLAB64009 US DEPARTMENT OF LABOR
VOCATIONAL TRAINING PROGRAMS FOR AMERICAN-INDIANS.
US DEPARTMENT OF LABOR, TRAINING FACTS, REPORT NO 15.
DEC 1964.

IUSDLAB66321 US DEPARTMENT OF LABOR
REPORT OF INDIAN RECRUITMENT AND TRAINING MEETING AT
ALBUQUERQUE, NEW-MEXICO, ON DECEMBER 6, 1966.
US DEPARTMENT OF LABOR, BUREAU OF EMPLOYMENT SECURITY,
OFFICE OF FARM LABOR SERVICE. WASHINGTON, DC. 15 PP.

IUSDLAB66322 US DEPARTMENT OF LABOR
MINUTES OF INDIAN EMPLOYMENT MEETING HELD NOVEMBER 29-30,
1966 IN BISMARK, NORTH-DAKOTA.
US DEPARTMENT OF LABOR. WASHINGTON, DC. 11 PP.

IUSDLAB66668 US DEPARTMENT OF LABOR
REPORT ON INDIAN FARM LABOR ACTIVITY.
US DEPARTMENT OF LABOR, BUREAU OF EMPLOYMENT SECURITY,
OFFICE OF FARM LABOR SERVICE. GPO. WASHINGTON, DC. 1966.
4 PP.

IUSDLAB66960 US DEPARTMENT OF LABOR
ARAPAHOE INDIAN TRAINS FOR SPACE AGE.
US DEPARTMENT OF LABOR, EMPLOYMENT SERVICE REVIEW, VOL 3,
NO 8, AUG 1966. PP 55 PLUS.

IUSHOUR59669 US HOUSE OF REPRESENTATIVES
OPERATION BOOTSTRAP FOR THE AMERICAN-INDIAN.
US HOUSE OF REPRESENTATIVES, COMMITTEE CN INTERIOR AND
INSULAR AFFAIRS. 86TH CONGRESS, 1ST SESSION. GPO.
WASHINGTON, DC. 1959.

IUSHOUR63670 US HOUSE OF REPRESENTATIVES
INDIAN UNEMPLOYMENT SURVEY, JULY 1963.
US HOUSE OF REPRESENTATIVES, COMMITTEE CN INTERIOR AND
INSULAR AFFAIRS, SUBCOMMITTEE ON INDIAN AFFAIRS. REPORT
NO 3, 88TH CONGRESS, 1ST SESSION. GPO. WASHINGTON, DC. 1963.
813 PP.

IUSNEWR62672 US NEWS AND WORLD REPORT
WHY NO INTEGRATION FOR THE AMERICAN-INDIAN.
US NEWS AND WORLD REPORT, VOL 55, SEPT 2 1962. PP 62-66.

IUSNEWR66671 US NEWS AND WORLD REPORT
WHERE THE REAL POVERTY IS. PLIGHT OF AMERICAN-INDIANS.
US NEWS AND WORLD REPORT, VOL 60, AP 25 1966. PP 104-108.

IUSSENA56673 US SENATE
KLAMATH INDIAN TRIBE.
US SENATE, COMMITTEE ON INTERIOR AND INSULAR AFFAIRS. 84TH
CONGRESS, 2ND SESSION. GPO. WASHINGTON, DC. 1956.

IUSSENA59674 US SENATE
REVIEW APPRAISAL. KLAMATH INDIAN ASSETS.
US SENATE, COMMITTEE ON INTERIOR AND INSULAR AFFAIRS. 86TH
CONGRESS, 1ST SESSION. GPO. WASHINGTON, DC. 1959.

IUVCALA66675 UCLA
AMERICAN-INDIANS IN LOS-ANGELES. A STUDY OF ADAPTATION TO A
CITY. /CALIFORNIA/
UNIVERSITY OF SOUTHERN CALIFORNIA, DEPARTMENT OF
ANTHROPOLOGY, ETHNOGRAPHIC FIELD SCHOOL. LOS ANGELES,
CALIFORNIA. 1966. 110 PP.

IUVMNCC56676 UNIVERSITY OF MINNESOTA CCS
PROCEEDINGS OF THE CONFERENCE ON INDIAN TRIBES AND TREATIES.
UNIVERSITY OF MINNESOTA, CENTER FOR CONTINUATION OF STUDY.
AP 1956.

IVOGEFW61677 VOGET FW ED
AMERICAN-INDIANS AND THEIR ECONOMIC DEVELOPMENT.
HUMAN ORGANIZATION, VOL 20, NO 4, WINTER 1961-1962.
SPECIAL ISSUE.

IVOGTEZ57678 VOGT EZ
THE ACCULTURATION OF AMERICAN-INDIANS.
ANNALS OF THE AMERICAN ACADEMY OF POLITICAL AND SOCIAL
SCIENCE, VOL 311, MAY 1957. PP 137-147.

IVOGTEZ61679 VOGT EZ
NAVAHO.
PERSPECTIVES IN AMERICAN CULTURE CHANGE. ED BY EDWARD
SPICER. UNIVERSITY OF CHICAGO PRESS. CHICAGO, ILLINOIS.
1961.

IWADDJX66680 WADDELL J
ADAPTATION OF PAPAGO WORKERS TO OFF-RESERVATION OCCUPATIONS.
UNIVERSITY OF ARIZONA. PHD DISSERTATION. TEMPE, ARIZONA.
1966.

IWAGNCJ64681 WAGNER CJ   RABEAU ES
*US DEPT OF HEALTH ED WELFARE
INDIAN POVERTY AND INDIAN HEALTH.

US DEPARTMENT OF HEALTH, EDUCATION AND WELFARE. REPRINT FROM
HEALTH, EDUCATION, AND WELFARE INDICATORS. GPO. WASHINGTON,
DC. MAR 1964. 43 PP.

IWARRCX65668   WARRIOR C
POVERTY, COMMUNITY AND POWER. /ECONOMIC-STATUS/
NEW UNIVERSITY THOUGHT. VOL 4, NO 2, SUMMER 1965. PP 5-10.

IWASHWE64682   WASHBURN WE ED
THE INDIAN AND THE WHITE MAN.
NEW YORK UNIVERSITY PRESS. NEW YORK. 1964.

IWAXXML64683   WAX ML   WAX RH
DUMONT RV
FORMAL EDUCATION IN AN AMERICAN-INDIAN COMMUNITY.
EMORY UNIVERSITY. ATLANTA, GEORGA. 1964. 133 PP.

IWAXXRH61224   WAX RH   THOMAS RK
AMERICAN-INDIANS AND WHITE PEOPLE.
PHYLON, 4TH QUARTER, WINTER 1961.

IWAXXRH67812   WAX RH
WARRIOR DROPOUTS. /YOUTH/
TRANSACTION. MAY 1967. PP 40-46.

IWEPPRS65684   WEPPNER RS   *COLO NAVAHO URBAN RLOCAT RES
THE ECONOMIC ABSORPTION OF NAVAHO INDIAN MIGRANTS IN DENVER,
   COLORADO.
UNIVERSITY OF COLORADO, INSTITUTE OF BEHAVIORAL SCIENCE,
NAVAHO URBAN RELOCATION RESEARCH, REPORT NO 8, REVISED.
BOULDER, COLORADO. NOV 1965. 86 PP.

IWEPPRS65685   WEPPNER RS   *COLO NAVAHO URBAN RLOCAT RES
ECONOMIC FACTORS IN NAVAHO URBAN RELOCATION.
AMERICAN ANTHROPOLOGICAL ASSOCIATION. ANNUAL MEETING,
SYMPOSIUM. DENVER, COLORADO. NOV 20 1965. ALSO UNIVERSITY
OF COLORADO, INSTITUTE OF BEHAVIORAL SCIENCE, NAVAHO URBAN
RELOCATION RESEARCH, RESEARCH REPORT NO 17, ND. PP 54-71.

IWHITRX59686   WHITE R
THE URBANIZATION OF THE DAKOTA INDIANS.
ST LOUIS UNIVERSITY. UNPUBLISHED MASTER-S THESIS. ST LOUIS,
MISSOURI. 1959.

IWILSHC61687   WILSON HC   WOLFE L
THE RELATIONSHIP BETWEEN UNEARNED INCOME AND INDIVIDUAL
   PRODUCTIVE EFFORT ON THE JICARILLA APACHE INDIAN
   RESERVATION.
ECONOMIC DEVELOPMENT AND CULTURAL CHANGE, VOL 9, 1961.
PP 589-603.

IWILSHC64235   WILSON HC
JICARILLA APACHE POLITICAL AND ECONOMIC STRUCTURES.
UNIVERSITY OF CALIFORNIA PUBLICATIONS IN AMERICAN
ARCHAEOLOGY AND ETHNOLOGY, VOL 48, NO 4, 1964. UNIVERSITY OF
CALIFORNIA PRESS. BERKELEY AND LOS ANGELES, CALIFORNIA.
PP 297-360.

IZIMMWX57248   ZIMMERMAN W
THE ROLE OF THE BUREAU-OF-INDIAN-AFFAIRS SINCE 1933.
ANNALS OF THE AMERICAN ACADEMY OF POLITICAL AND SOCIAL
SCIENCE, VOL 311, MAY 1957.

JADLBXX63688 ADL BULLETIN
ADL AT WORK. THE CRUMBLING WALLS.
/EMPLOYMENT DISCRIMINATION/
ANTI-DEFAMATION LEAGUE OF B-NAI B-RITH, ADL BULLETIN.
SEPT 1963.

JADLBXX64689 ADL BULLETIN
JEWISH LAW GRADUATE. /EMPLOYMENT DISCRIMINATION/
ANTI-DEFAMATION LEAGUE OF B-NAI B-RITH, ADL BULLETIN.
AP 1964.

JAMERJC58692 AMERICAN JEWISH COMMITTEE.
PROCEEDINGS OF THE 50TH ANNIVERSARY OBSERVANCE OF THE
AMERICAN JEWISH COMMITTEE. APRIL 10-14, 1957. THE PURSUIT
OF EQUALITY AT HOME AND ABROAD. /ECONOMIC-OPPORTUNITY/
AMERICAN JEWISH COMMITTEE. NEW YORK. 1958. 305 PP.

JAMERJC60691 AMERICAN JEWISH COMMITTEE
HARVARD LOOKS AT THE EXECUTIVE-SUITE.
COMMITTEE REPORTER, OCT 1960.

JAMERJC65694 AMERICAN JEWISH COMMITTEE
THE MUTUAL SAVINGS BANKS OF NEW-YORK-CITY. /DISCRIMINATION/
AMERICAN JEWISH COMMITTEE, INSTITUTE OF HUMAN RELATIONS.
NEW YORK. OCT 1965. 7 PP.

JAMERJC66693 AMERICAN JEWISH COMMITTEE
JEWS IN COLLEGE AND UNIVERSITY ADMINISTRATION.
AMERICAN JEWISH COMMITTEE, INSTITUTE OF HUMAN RELATIONS.
NEW YORK. MAY 1966. 9 PP.

JAMERJC66695 AMERICAN JEWISH COMMITTEE
THE MUTUAL SAVINGS BANKS OF NEW-YORK-CITY. A FOLLOW-UP
REPORT ON THE EXCLUSION OF JEWS AT TOP-MANAGEMENT AND
POLICY-MAKING LEVELS.
AMERICAN JEWISH COMMITTE. INSTITUTE OF HUMAN RELATIONS.
NEW YORK. NOV 1966. 5 PP.

JAMERJC66696 AMERICAN JEWISH COMMITTEE
PATTERNS OF EXCLUSION FROM THE EXECUTIVE-SUITE. COMMERCIAL
BANKING.
AMERICAN JEWISH COMMITTEE, INSTITUTE OF HUMAN RELATIONS.
NEW YORK. AUG 1966. 12 PP.

JANTIDL57690 ANTI-DEFAMATION LEAGUE
ADL REPORTS ON SOCIAL, EMPLOYMENT, EDUCATIONAL AND HOUSING
DISCRIMINATION.
RIGHTS, DEC 1956-JAN 1957.

JANTJAX58697 ANTONOVSKY A
SOME ASPECTS OF JEWISH DEMOGRAPHY.
THE JEWS -- SOCIAL PATTERNS OF AN AMERICAN GROUP. ED BY
MARSHALL SKLARE. GLENCOE,.ILLINOIS. 1958. PP 45-93.

JBARSIX59700 BARSHOP I
PLANNING CONSTRUCTIVE ECONOMIC OPPORTUNITIES FOR THE JEWISH
AGED.
JOURNAL OF JEWISH COMMUNAL SERVICE, VOL 36, NO 2,
WINTER 1959. PP 186-191.

JBELTNC58702 BELTH NC ED   *ANTI-DEFAMATION LEAGUE
BARRIERS. PATTERNS OF DISCRIMINATION AGAINST JEWS.
ANTI-DEFAMATION LEAGUE OF B-NAI B-RITH. NEW YORK. 1958.
121 PP.

JBLOJLX57706 BLOOMGARDEN L
WHO SHALL BE OUR DOCTORS. /OCCUPATIONS DISCRIMINATION/
COMMENTARY, VOL 23, NO 1, JAN 1957. PP 506-515.

JBLOJLX60705 BLOOMGARDEN L
OUR CHANGING ELITE COLLEGES. /EDUCATION/
COMMENTARY, VOL 29, NO 2, FEB 1960. PP 150-154.

JBRAVHX58707 BRAVERMAN H
MEDICAL SCHOOL QUOTAS. /EDUCATION DISCRIMINATION/
BARRIERS. PATTERNS OF DISCRIMINATION AGAINST JEWS. ED BY
NC BELTH. ANTI-DEFAMATION LEAGUE OF B-NAI B-RITH. NEW YORK.
1958. PP 74-78.

JCHENAX61712 CHENKIN A
JEWISH POPULATION IN THE UNITED STATES, 1960. /DEMOGRAPHY/
AMERICAN JEWISH YEAR BOOK, VOL 62, 1961. PP 62-63.

JCHENAX62713 CHENKIN A
JEWISH POPULATION IN THE UNITED STATES, 1961. /DEMOGRAPHY/
AMERICAN JEWISH YEAR BOOK, VOL 63, 1962. P 136.

JCRYSDX58714 CRYSTAL D
THE DISPLACED PERSON AND THE SOCIAL AGENCY. A STUDY OF THE
CASEWORK PROCESS AND ITS RELATION TO IMMIGRANT ADJUSTMENT.
UNITED HIAS SERVICE. NEW YORK. 1958. 182 PP.

JDAVIHX58717 DAVID H   *AMERICAN JEWISH COMMITTEE
ON THE ECONOMIC SCENE.
PROCEEDINGS OF THE 50TH ANNIVERSARY OBSERVANCE OF THE
AMERICAN JEWISH COMMITTEE. AP 10-14 1958. THE PURSUIT OF
EQUALITY AT HOME AND ABROAD. AMERICAN JEWISH COMMITTEE.
NEW YORK. 1958. PP 43-48.

JEPSTBRND719 EPSTEIN BR   FORSTER A
SOME OF MY BEST FRIENDS... /EMPLOYMENT DISCRIMINATION/
FARRER, STRAUSS, AND CUDAHY. NEW YORK. PART 4, PP 193-259.

JEPSTBR58718 EPSTEIN BR   FORSTER A
*ANTI-DEFAMATION LEAGUE
BARRIERS IN HIGHER EDUCATION.
BARRIERS. PATTERNS OF DISCRIMINATION AGAINST JEWS. ED BY N C
BELTH. ANTI-DEFAMATION LEAGUE OF B-NAI B-RITH. NEW YORK.
1958. PP 60-73.

JFINEMXND720 FINE M ED   HIMMELFARB M ED
*AMERICAN JEWISH COMMITTEE
AMERICAN JEWISH YEARBOOK.
AMERICAN JEWISH COMMITTEE. JEWISH PUBLICATION SOCIETY OF
AMERICA. NEW YORK. ANNUAL.

JFORSAX63723 FORSTER A
DETROIT-S OLD HABIT. /EMPLOYMENT DISCRIMINATION/
ANTI-DEFAMATION LEAGUE OF B-NAI B-RITH, ADL BULLETIN.
NOV 1963.

JGALLBG58724 GALLAGHER BG   *AMERICAN JEWISH COMMITTEE
ON THE EDUCATIONAL SCENE.
PROCEEDINGS OF THE 50TH ANNIVERSARY OBSERVANCE OF THE
AMERICAN JEWISH COMMITTEE. AP 10-14 1957. THE PURSUIT OF
EQUALITY AT HOME AND ABROAD. AMERICAN JEWISH COMMITTEE.
NEW YORK. 1958. PP 55-66.

JGLAZNX60726 GLAZER N
SOCIAL CHARACTERISTICS OF AMERICAN JEWS.
THE JEWS. ED BY LOUIS FINKELSTEIN. HARPER. NEW YORK. 3RD ED
1960. PP 1694-1735.

JGLAZNX63725 GLAZER N   MOYNIHAN DP
THE JEWS.
BEYOND THE MELTING POT. MIT PRESS. CAMBRIDGE.
MASSACHUSETTES. 1963. PP 137-180.

JGOLDNX62727 GOLDBERG N
DEMOGRAPHIC CHARACTERISTICS OF AMERICAN JEWS.
JEWS IN THE MODERN WORLD. VOL 2, ED BY JACOB FRIED.
NEW YORK. 1962.

JHAPGHX65589 HAPGOOD H
THE SPIRIT OF THE GHETTO. STUDIES OF THE JEWISH QUARTER OF
NEW-YORK.
FUNK AND WAGNALLS. NEW YORK. 1965. 300 PP.

JHARTPX58730 HARTMAN P   *ANTI-DEFAMATION LEAGUE
STATE LAWS AGAINST DISCRIMINATION IN EDUCATION.
BARRIERS. PATTERNS OF DISCRIMINATION AGAINST JEWS. ED BY N C
BELTH. ANTI-DEFAMATION LEAGUE OF B-NAI B-RITH. NEW YORK.
1958. PP 89-92.

JHARTPX63729 HARTMAN P
EQUAL RIGHTS FOR THE SATURDAY SABBATH OBSERVER. /EMPLOYMENT
DISCRIMINATION/
ANTI-DEFAMATION LEAGUE OF B-NAI B-RITH, ADL BULLETIN,
MAR 1963.

JHARVBS65731 HARVARD BUSINESS SCHOOL
HOW DOES RELIGION AFFECT JOB-CHOICE.
BUSINESS WEEK, AP 17 1965. ALSO AMERICAN JEWISH COMMITTEE,
INSTITUTE OF HUMAN RELATIONS, REPRINT. NEW YORK. 1965. 2 PP.

JKLINOX58735 KLINEBERG O
EQUALITY OF OPPORTUNITY.
PROCEEDINGS OF THE 50TH ANNIVERSARY OBSERVANCE OF THE
AMERICAN JEWISH COMMITTEE. AP 10-14 1957. THE PURSUIT OF
EQUALITY AT HOME AND ABROAD. AMERICAN JEWISH COMMITTEE.
NEW YORK. 1958. PP 35-42.

JKRAMJR61736 KRAMER JR   LEVENTMAN
CHILDREN OF THE GILDED GHETTO. CONFLICT RESOLUTION OF THREE
GENERATIONS OF AMERICAN JEWS. /OCCUPATIONAL-PATTERNS/
YALE UNIVERSITY PRESS. NEW HAVEN, CONNECTICUT. 1961.

JKUZNSX60738 KUZNETS S
ECONOMIC STRUCTURE AND THE LIFE OF THE JEWS.
THE JEWS. VOL II. ED BY LOUIS FINKELSTEIN. 3RD ED 1960.

JLAZRBX61C33 LAZREWITZ B
A COMPARISON OF MAJOR UNITED STATES RELIGIOUS GROUPS.
/ECONOMIC-STATUS/
JOURNAL OF THE AMERICAN STATISTICAL ASSOCIATION, SEPT 1961.

JLAZRBX61C34 LAZREWITZ B
JEWS IN AND OUT OF NEW-YORK CITY. /ECONOMIC-STATUS/
JEWISH JOURNAL OF SOCIOLOGY, DEC 1961.

JLEEXAM58739 LEE AM
ON THE SOCIAL SCENE. /EQUAL-OPPORTUNITY/
PROCEEDINGS OF THE 50TH ANNIVERSARY OBSERVANCE OF THE
AMERICAN JEWISH COMMITTEE. AP 10-14 1957. THE PURSUIT OF
EQUALITY AT HOME AND ABROAD. AMERICAN JEWISH COMMITTEE.
NEW YORK. 1958. PP 49-54.

JMARCJR58326 MARCUS JR
ESSAYS IN AMERICAN JEWISH HISTORY.
HEBREW UNION COLLEGE. CINCINNATI, OHIO. 1958.

JMASAGX59746 MASARIK G   *JEWISH FEDERATION
A REPORT ON THE JEWISH POPULATION OF LOS-ANGELES.
/CALIFORNIA/
JEWISH FEDERATION-COUNCIL OF GREATER LOS ANGELES, RESEARCH
SERVICE BUREAU. LOS ANGELES, CALIFORNIA. 1959.

JMCLABX64747 MCLAURIN B
STRUGGLE FOR EQUALITY. SYMPOSIUM.
JEWISH FRONTIER, VOL 31, MAR 1964. PP 15-16.

JNATIJM63748 NATIONAL JEWISH MONTHLY
STUDY SHOWS FEW JEWS HAVE TOP JOBS IN AUTO INDUSTRY.
NATIONAL JEWISH MONTHLY, VOL 78, NOV 1963. P 37.

JPILCJX64749 PILCH J
CIVIL-RIGHTS AND JEWISH INSTITUTIONS.
RELIGIOUS EDUCATION, VOL 59, JAN-FEB 1964. PP 86-89.

JPUCKWX65750 PUCKAT W
JEWISH ECONOMIC PROSPECTS IN 1965.
CONGRESS BI-WEEKLY, VOL 32, FEB 15 1965. PP 12-13.

JRABIDX59751 RABINOWITZ D
COORDINATED PLANNING FOR ECONOMIC OPPORTUNTIES FOR JEWISH
AGED.
JOURNAL OF JEWISH COMMUNCAL SERVICE, VOL 36, NO 2, WINTER
1959. PP 181-185.

JREICNX64752 REICH N
ECONOMIC-STATUS.
THE AMERICAN JEW. A REAPPRIASAL. ED BY OSCAR I JANOWEKY.
JEWISH PUBLICATION SOCIETY OF AMERICA. PHILADELPHIA,
PENNSYLVANIA. 1964. PP 53-74.

JRIGHXX57753 RIGHTS
EMPLOYMENT DISCRIMINATION -- PART I.
RIGHTS, VOL 1, NO 4, DEC 1956-JAN 1957.

JRIGHXX57754 RIGHTS

EMPLOYMENT DISCRIMINATION -- PART II.
RIGHTS, VOL 1, NO 5, FEB-MAR 1957.

JRIGHXX59755   RIGHTS
EMPLOYMENT IN INSURANCE COMPANIES.   /DISCRIMINATION/
RIGHTS, VOL 2, NO 8, NOV-DEC 1959.

JRIGHXX63756   RIGHTS
EMPLOYMENT OF JEWISH PERSONNEL IN THE AUTOMOBILE INDUSTRY.
   /DISCRIMINATION/
RIGHTS, VOL 5, NO 2, OCT 1963.

JRIGHXX64757   RIGHTS
JEWISH LAW STUDENT AND NEW-YORK JOBS.   /EMPLOYMENT
   DISCRIMINATION/
RIGHTS, VOL 5, NO 4, JUNE 1964.

JRIVIEX58325   RIVKIN E
A DECISIVE PATTERN IN AMERICAN JEWISH HISTORY.
ESSAYS IN AMERICAN JEWISH HISTORY. UNDER DIRECTION OF J R
MARCUS. HEBREW UNION COLLEGE. CINCINNATI, OHIO. 1958.
PP 23-61.

JSHERBC64759   SHERMAN CB
DEMOGRAPHIC AND SOCIAL ASPECTS.
THE AMERICAN JEW, A REAPPRAISAL. ED BY OSCAR I JANOWSKY.
JEWISH PUBLICATION SOCIETY OF AMERICA. PHILADELPHIA,
PENNSYLVANIA. 1964. PP 27-52.

JSHERCB61311   SHERMAN CB
A JEW WITHIN AMERICAN SOCIETY -- A STUDY IN ETHNIC
   INDIVIDUALITY.
WAYNE STATE UNIVERSITY PRESS. DETROIT, MICHIGAN. 1961.
260 PP.

JSHOSRJ57761   SHOSTECK RJ   *B-NAI B-RITH VOCAT SERV BUR
THE JEWISH COLLEGE STUDENT.
B-NAI B-RITH VOCATIONAL SERVICE. WASHINGTON, DC. 1957.

JSIMJBX58763   SIMON B   *ANTI-DEFAMATION LEAGUE
INSURANCE, BANKING, PUBLIC UTILITIES.   /DISCRIMINATION
   EMPLOYMENT/
BARRIERS. PATTERNS OF DISCRIMINATION AGAINST JEWS. ED BY N C
BELTH. ANTI-DEFAMATION LEAGUE OF B-NAI B-RITH. NEW YORK.
1958. PP 48-52.

JSKLAMX58149   SKLARE M ED
THE JEWS. SOCIAL PATTERNS OF AN AMERICAN GROUP.
THE FREE PRESS. GLENCOE, ILLINOIS. 1958.

JSTROFL58764   STRODTBECK FL
JEWISH AND ITALIAN IMMIGRATION AND SUBSEQUENT STATUS
   MOBILITY.
TALENT AND SOCIETY. ED BY DAVID C MCCLELLAND. VAN NOSTRAND.
PRINCETON, NEW JERSEY. 1958.

JTYLEGX65766   TYLER G
LEGACY OF THE JEWISH LABOR MOVEMENT.
MIDSTREAM, VOL 11, MAR 1965. PP 54-66.

JUVMIIT65768   UM ISR SURVEY RESEARCH CENT
INVISIBLE PERSUADER ON PROMOTIONS.
AMERICAN JEWISH COMMITTEE, INSTITUTE OF HUMAN RELATIONS.
RERRINT. NEW YORK. 1965. 2 PP.

JWARDLB65769   WARD LB
THE ETHNICS OF EXECUTIVE SELECTION.
HARVARD BUSINESS REVIEW, VOL 43, NO 2, MAR-AP 1965. 11 PP.
ALSO IN AMERICAN JEWISH COMMITTEE, INSTITUTE OF HUMAN
RELATIONS. REPRINT. 1965. 11 PP.

JWEISAX58770   WEISS A   *ANTI-DEFAMATION LEAGUE
JEWS NEED NOT APPLY.   /DISCRIMINATION EMPLOYMENT/
BARRIERS. PATTERNS OF DISCRIMINATION AGAINST JEWS. ED BY N C
BELTH. ANTI-DEFAMATION LEAGUE OF B-NAI B-RITH. NEW YORK.
1958. PP 43-48.

JWELLSX60571   WELLES S
THE JEWISH ELAN.
FORTUNE, FEB 1960.

JWORLOX64773   WORLD OVER
LARGE CORPORATIONS ACCUSED OF DISCRIMINATION AGAINST JEWS IN
   MANAGEMENT, EXECUTIVE CAPACITIES BY
   AMERICAN-JEWISH-COMMITTEE.
WORLD OVER, VOL 25, JAN 31 1964. P 5.

JYALELJ64774   YALE LAW JOURNAL
THE JEWISH LAW STUDENT AND NEW-YORK JOBS -- DISCRIMINATORY
   EFFECTS IN LAW FIRM HIRING PRACTICES.   /OCCUPATIONS/
YALE LAW JOURNAL, VOL 73, MAR 1964. PP 625-660.

JYOUNJX65775   YOUNG J
JEWISH LAW STUDENT AND NEW-YORK JOBS.
JEWISH DIGEST, VOL 10, MAR 1965. PP 59-67.

JZARCMM64776   ZARCHIN MM
GLIMPSES OF JEWISH LIFE IN SAN-FRANCISCO.   /CALIFORNIA/
JUDAH L MAGNES MEMORIAL MUSEUM. OAKLAND, CALIFORNIA. 1964.
2ND REVISED ED 264 PP.

MALBEPM64356 ALBERT PM
SOME PROBLEMS IN THE ACCULTURATION OF MEXICAN LABORERS TO A
FACTORY.
SOUTHWEST ANTHROPOLOGICAL ASSOCIATION, SPRING MEETING.
UNPUBLISHED PAPER. MAR 1964.

MALMAAS64357 ALMANZA AS   *LA COUNTY COMM ON HUM RELS
MEXICAN-AMERICANS AND CIVIL-RIGHTS.
LOS ANGELES COUNTY COMMISSION ON HUMAN RELATIONS.
LOS ANGELES, CALIFORNIA. UNPUBLISHED. 1964.

MANDRWH66359 ANDREWS WH
FAMILY COMPOSITION AND CHARACTERISTICS OF AN ECONOMICALLY
DEPRIVED CROSS-CULTURAL ROCKY-MOUNTAIN AREA.
ROCKY MOUNTAIN SOCIAL SCIENCE JOURNAL. AP 1966. PP 122-139.

MARAGMX66358 ARAGON M
THEIR HERITAGE -- POVERTY.
AFL-CIO, INDUSTRIAL UNION DEPARTMENT, IUD AGENDA, VOL 2,
NO 7, JULY 1966. PP 9-13.

MARIARX66360 ARIAS R
THE BARRIO. /EDUCATION INCOME/
AFL-CIO, INDUSTRIAL UNION DEPARTMENT. IVD AGENDA, VOL 2,
NO 7, JULY 1966. PP 15-20.

MATKIJA61361 ATKINS JA   *COLORADO STATE DEPT OF ED
A CULTURAL MINORITY IMPROVES ITSELF.
HUMAN RELATIONS IN COLORADO. COLORADO STATE DEPARTMENT OF
EDUCATION. DENVER, COLORADO. 1961. PP 91-105.

MBARRDN66701 BARRETT DN
DEMOGRAPHIC CHARACTERISTICS.
LA RAZA. ED BY JULIAN SAMORA. UNIVERSITY OF NOTRE DAME
PRESS. NOTRE DAME, INDIANA. 1966. PP 159-199.

MBEALRL57364 BEALS RL
NO FRONTIER TO LEARNING. THE MEXICAN STUDENT IN THE UNITED
STATES.
UNIVERSITY OF MINNESOTA PRESS. MINNEAPOLIS, MINNESOTA. 1957.

MBEALRL60362 BEALS RL
OBSTACLES TO ASSIMILATION OF THE MEXICAN-AMERICAN IN THE
UNITED STATES.
MEXICAN CHRISTIAN INSTITUTE, LECTURE. SAN ANTONIO, TEXAS.
FEB 18 1960.

MBISHCS62365 BISHOPS COMT SPANISH-SPEAKING
MERRILL-TRUST-FUND TO IMPROVE THE EMPLOYMENT OPPORTUNITIES
OF THE MIGRANT FARM WORKERS OF MEXICAN ORIGIN.
BISHOPS COMMITTEE FOR THE SPANISH-SPEAKING. SAN ANTONIO,
TEXAS. JAN 1962. 28 PP.

MBROWHL64286 BROWNING HL   MCLEMORE SD
THE SPANISH-SURNAME POPULATION OF TEXAS.
INSTITUTE OF PUBLIC AFFAIRS, UNIVERSITY OF TEXAS, PUBLIC
AFFAIRS COMMENT, VOL 10, NO 1, JAN 1964.

MBROWHL64368 BROWNING HL   MCLEMORE SD
*U OF TEXAS BUR BUS RESEARCH
A STATISTICAL PROFILE OF THE SPANISH-SURNAME POPULATION OF
TEXAS.
UNIVERSITY OF TEXAS, BUREAU OF BUSINESS RESEARCH. AUSTIN,
TEXAS. JUNE 1964. 83 PP.

MBULLPX64369 BULLOCK P
EMPLOYMENT PROBLEMS OF THE MEXICAN-AMERICAN.
INDUSTRIAL RELATIONS, VOL 3, NO 3, MAY 1964. PP 37-50.
ALSO UNIVERSITY OF SOUTHERN CALIFORNIA, INSTITUTE OF LABOR
AND INDUSTRIAL RELATIONS, REPRINT NO 138. LOS ANGELES,
CALIFORNIA. 1964. 14 PP.

MBURMJH61370 BURMA JH
THE CIVIL-RIGHTS SITUATION OF MEXICAN-AMERICANS AND
SPANISH-AMERICANS.
RACE RELATIONS, PROBLEMS AND THEORY. ED BY JITSUICHI MASUOKA
AND PRESTON VALIEN. UNIVERSITY OF NORTH CAROLINA PRESS.
CHAPEL HILL, NORTH CAROLINA. 1961. PP 155-167.

MCABRYA63373 CABRERA YA
A STUDY OF AMERICAN AND MEXICAN-AMERICAN CULTURE VALUES AND
THEIR SIGNIFICANCE IN EDUCATION.
UNIVERSITY OF COLORADO. EDD DISSERTATION. BOULDER, COLORADO.
1963.

MCABRYA65372 CABRERA YA
REACTION TO MEXICAN-AMERICANS, A BACKGROUND PAPER.
CENTER FOR THE STUDY OF DEMOCRATIC INSTITUTIONS, CONFERENCE.
PAPER. SANTA BARBARA, CALIFORNIA. OCT 29 1965.

MCALAIC64374 CAL ASSEMBLY INTERIM COMT IR
TRANSCRIPT OF PROCEEDINGS OF THE INTERIM SUBCOMMITTEE ON
SPECIAL EMPLOYMENT PROBLEMS. /CALIFORNIA/
CALIFORNIA ASSEMBLY INTERIM COMMITTEE ON INDUSTRIAL
RELATIONS. HEARINGS IN LOS ANGELES JAN 10 1964 ON SPECIAL
EMPLOYMENT PROBLEMS OF THE MEXICAN-AMERICAN. CALIFORNIA
STATE ASSEMBLY. SACRAMENTO, CALIFORNIA. 1964. 101 PP.

MCALDIR62376 CAL DEPT OF INDUSTRIAL RELS
PRELIMINARY REPORT ON SURVEY OF ACTIVE APPRENTICES.
/CALIFORNIA/
CALIFORNIA DEPARTMENT OF INDUSTRIAL RELATIONS, DIVISION OF
APPRENTICESHIP STANDARDS. SAN FRANCISCO, CALIFORNIA.
AP 25 1962.

MCALDIR64377 CAL DEPT OF INDUSTRIAL RELS
CALIFORNIANS OF SPANISH SURNAME. POPULATION, EMPLOYMENT,
INCOME, EDUCATION.
CALIFORNIA DEPARTMENT OF INDUSTRIAL RELATIONS, DIVISION OF
FAIR EMPLOYMENT PRACTICES. MAY 1964. 54 PP.

MCALDIR64379 CAL DEPT OF INDUSTRIAL RELS
REPORT BY MEXICAN-AMERICAN LEADERS. EDUCATION, EMPLOYMENT,
ETC.
CALIFORNIA DEPARTMENT OF INDUSTRIAL RELATIONS, FAIR
EMPLOYMENT PRACTICES COMMISSION. LOS ANGELES, CALIFORNIA.
NOV 1964.

MCALDYA63378 CAL DEPT OF YOUTH AUTHORITY
EMPLOYMENT-TRENDS AMONG CALIFORNIA YOUTH AUTHORITY WARDS ON
PAROLE. 1948-62.
CALIFORNIA DEPARTMENT OF YOUTH AUTHORITY, YOUTH AND ADULT
CORRECTIONS AGENCY, DIVISION OF RESEARCH, RESEARCH REPORT
NO 34. SACRAMENTO, CALIFORNIA. JAN 16 1963.

MCALSSE63380 CALIFORNIA STATE SENATE
CALIFORNIA-S FARM LABOR PROBLEMS. /MIGRANT-WORKERS/
CALIFORNIA STATE SENATE. SACRAMENTO, CALIFORNIA. JAN 1963.
127 PP.

MCLAPRF66112 CLAPP RF   *US DEPT OF HEALTH ED WELFARE
SPANISH-AMERICANS OF THE SOUTHWEST.
US DEPARTMENT OF HEALTH, EDUCATION, AND WELFARE, WELFARE
ADMINISTRATION, WELFARE IN REVIEW. JAN 1966. PP 1-12.

MCLEMHM63381 CLEMENTS HM
LEVELS OF LIVING OF SPANISH-AMERICAN RURAL AND URBAN
FAMILIES IN TWO SOUTH TEXAS COUNTIES.
TEXAS A AND M UNIVERSITY. MS DISSERTATION. COLLEGE STATION,
TEXAS. MAY 1963.

MCOLOLC60382 COLORADO LEGISLATIVE COUNCIL
MIGRATORY LABOR IN COLORADO.
COLORADO LEGISLATIVE COUNCIL. DENVER, COLORADO. NOV 1960.
28 PP.

MCOLOLC62383 COLORADO LEGISLATIVE COUNCIL
MIGRATORY LABOR IN COLORADO. REPORT TO THE COLORADO GENERAL
ASSEMBLY.
COLORADO LEGISLATIVE COUNCIL, RESEARCH PUBLICATION NO 72.
DENVER, COLORADO. DEC 1962.

MCOLOSD61384 COLORADO STATE DEPT OF ED
EDUCATING MIGRANT CHILDREN IN COLORADO.
COLORADO STATE DEPARTMENT OF EDUCATION. DENVER, COLORADO.
1961. 14 PP.

MCOTHML66385 COTHRAN ML
OCCUPATIONAL-PATTERNS OF RURAL AND URBAN SPANISH-AMERICANS
IN TWO SOUTH TEXAS COUNTIES.
TEXAS A AND M UNIVERSITY. MS ESSAY. COLLEGE STATION, TEXAS.
JAN 1966.

MCOUNMA62930 COUNCIL OF MEXICAN-AM AFFAIRS
PROCEEDINGS OF EMPLOYMENT OPPORTUNITIES EDUCATIONAL
CONFERENCE.
COUNCIL OF MEXICAN-AMERICAN AFFAIRS. MAR 31 1962.

MCOUNSH60386 CC OF STATE GOVTS WEST OFFICE
MIGRATORY LABOR IN THE WEST.
COUNCIL OF STATE GOVERNMENTS, WESTERN OFFICE. SAN FRANCISCO,
CALIFORNIA. MAR 1960.

MDAVIHW66387 DAVIS HW
AN ANALYSIS OF CURRENT PATTERNS IN HUMAN RESOURCE
DEVELOPMENT IN SAN-ANTONIO, TEXAS.
UNIVERSITY OF TEXAS. UNPUBLISHED PHD THESIS. AUSTIN, TEXAS.
1966.

MDEHOJAX61388 DEHOYOS A
OCCUPATIONAL AND EDUCATIONAL LEVELS OF ASPIRATION OF
MEXICAN-AMERICAN YOUTH.
MICHIGAN STATE UNIVERSITY. PHD DISSERTATION. EAST LANSING,
MICHIGAN. 1961.

MDICKBE65389 DICKERSON BE
INCOMES OF RURAL AND URBAN SPANISH-AMERICANS IN TWO SOUTH
TEXAS COUNTIES.
TEXAS A AND M UNIVERSITY. MASTER-S ESSAY. COLLEGE STATION,
TEXAS. MAY 1965.

MDUFFLC66390 DUFFIELD LC   *US DEPARTMENT OF LABOR
THE LATIN AMERICAN IS FINDING HIS PLACE.
US DEPARTMENT OF LABOR, EMPLOYMENT SERVICE REVIEW, VOL 3,
NO 8, AUG 1966. PP 35-37.

MFEERAB62392 FEERY AB   *BISHOPS COMT SPANISHSPEAKING
A PLANNED COMMUNITY FOR MIGRATORY FARM WORKERS.
BISHOPS COMMITTEE FOR THE SPANISH-SPEAKING. SAN ANTONIO,
TEXAS. 1962.

MFOGEWX65393 FOGEL W   *UCLA GRAD SCHOOL OF BUS ADM
EDUCATION AND INCOME OF MEXICAN-AMERICANS IN THE SOUTHWEST.
UNIVERSITY OF CALIFORNIA, LOS ANGELES, GRADUATE SCHOOL OF
BUSINESS ADMINISTRATION, DIVISION OF RESEARCH.
MEXICAN-AMERICAN STUDY PROJECT, ADVANCE REPORT 1.
LOS ANGELES, CALIFORNIA. NOV 1965. 30 PP.

MFORTXX59374 FORTUNE
LABOR-S RACE PROBLEM. /UNION/
FORTUNE, VOL 59, MAR 1959. PP 191-192, 194.

MFRIERE63394 FRIEND RE   BAUM S
*US DEPARTMENT OF AGRICULTURE
ECONOMIC, SOCIAL AND DEMOGRAPHIC CHARACTERISTICS OF
SPANISH-AMERICAN WAGE WORKERS ON US FARMS.
US DEPARTMENT OF AGRICULTURE, ECONOMIC RESEARCH SERVICE,
AGRICULTURAL ECONOMIC REPORT NO 27. GPO. WASHINGTON, DC.
MAR 1963.

MFULLVX56396 FULLER V   MAINER JW
VILES GL   *U CAL GIANININ FOUNDATION
DOMESTIC AND IMPORTED WORKERS IN THE HARVEST LABOR-MARKET,
SANTA-CLARA COUNTY, CALIFORNIA, 1954.
UNIVERSITY OF CALIFORNIA, GIANININ FOUNDATION OF
AGRICULTURAL ECONOMICS, REPORT NO 184. BERKELY, CALIFORNIA.
1956.

MGALAEX56400 GALARZA E
STRANGERS IN OUR FIELDS. /MIGRANT-WORKERS/
JOINT US-MEXICAN TRADE UNION COMMITTEE. WASHINGTON, DC.
1956. 80 PP.

MGALAEX66397 GALARZA E
MERCHANTS OF LABOR. THE MEXICAN BRACERO STORY.
MCNALLY AND LOFTIN, PUBLISHERS. SANTA BARBARA, CALIFORNIA.
1966.

MGALLLX62399 GALLARDO L   *US DEPARTMENT OF LABOR
MEXICAN GREEN CARDERS. PRELIMINARY REPORT.

US DEPARTMENT OF LABOR, BUREAU OF EMPLOYMENT SECURITY.
WASHINGTON, DC. JULY 10 1962.

MGILLLJ62401 GILL LJ   SPILKA B
SOME NON-INTELLECTUAL CORRELATES OF ACADEMIC ACHIEVEMENT
    AMONG MEXICAN-AMERICAN SECONDARY SCHOOL STUDENTS.
JOURNAL OF EDUCATIONAL PSYCHOLOGY, VOL 53, JUNE 1962.
PP 144-149.

MGILMNR62402 GILMORE NR   SILMORE GW
BRACERO IN CALIFORNIA.
PACIFIC HISTORICAL REVIEW, VOL 32, AUG 1962. PP 265-282.

MGLICLB66694 GLICK LB
THE RIGHT TO EQUAL-OPPORTUNITY.
LA RAZA. ED BY JULIAN SAMORA. UNIVERSITY OF NOTRE DAME
PRESS. NOTRE DAME, INDIANA. 1966. PP 95-124.

MGOLDNX59403 GOLDNER N
THE MEXICAN IN THE NORTHERN URBAN AREA. A COMPARISON OF TWO
    GENERATIONS.
UNIVERSITY OF MINNESOTA. MASTER-S ESSAY. MINNEAPOLIS,
MINNESOTA. 1959.

MGONZHB63404 GONZALEZ HB
PROBLEMS OF THE LATIN-AMERICAN WORKER IN TEXAS.
US SENATE, COMMITTEE ON LABOR AND PUBLIC WELFARE,
SUBCOMMITTEE ON EMPLOYMENT AND MANPOWER. TESTIMONY.
SEPT 11 1963. 88TH CONGRESS, 1ST SESSION. GPO.
WASHINGTON, DC. 1963. 13 PP.

MGRAVRP60405 GRAVES RP
A HISTORY OF THE INTERRELATIONSHIPS BETWEEN IMPORTED
    MEXICAN LABOR, DOMESTIC MIGRANTS, AND THE TEXAS
    AGRICULTURAL ECONOMY.
UNIVERSITY OF TEXAS. UNPUBLISHED MA THESIS. AUSTIN, TEXAS.
1960.

MGRAVTD67214 GRAVES TD   *U COLO TRI-ETHNIC RES PROJ
ACCULTURATION, ACCESS AND ALCOHOL IN A TRI-ETHNIC COMMUNITY.
UNIVERSITY OF COLORADO, INSTITUTE OF BEHARIORAL SCIENCE,
TRI-ETHNIC RESEARCH PROJECT, RESEARCH REPORT NO 30. BOULDER,
COLORADO. REVISED OCT 1966. 51 PP. ALSO TO APPEAR IN THE
AMERICAN ANTHROPOLOGIST, JUNE OR AUG 1967.

MGREBLX66406 GREBLER L   *UCLA MEX-AM STUDY PROJ
MEXICAN IMMIGRATION TO THE UNITED STATES. THE RECORD AND
    ITS IMPLICATIONS.
MEXICAN-AMERICAN STUDY PROJECT. UNIVERSITY OF SOUTHERN
CALIFORNIA, GRADUATE SCHOOL OF BUSINESS ADMINISTRATION.
LOS ANGELES, CALIFORNIA. JAN 1966.

MGRISGXND408 GRISHAM G   *US DEPARTMENT OF AGRICULTURE
BASIC NEEDS OF SPANISH-AMERICAN FARM FAMILIES IN NEW-MEXICO.
US DEPARTMENT OF AGRICULTURE, FARM SECURITY ADMINISTRATION.
ALBUQUERQUE, NEW MEXICO. ON FILE. ND.

MGUERCX62410 GUERTIN C
PERCEIVED LIFE CHANCES IN THE OPPORTUNITY STRUCTURE. A STUDY
    OF A TRI-ETHNIC HIGH SCHOOL.
UNIVERSITY OF COLORADO. MASTER-S DISSERTATION. BOULDER,
COLORADO. 1962.

MGUERIX59409 GUERRA I
THE SOCIAL ASPIRATIONS OF A SELECTED GROUP OF SPANISH NAME
    PEOPLE IN LAREDO, TEXAS.
UNIVERSITY OF TEXAS. MASTER-S ESSAY. AUSTIN, TEXAS. 1959.

MGUZMRX65411 GUZMAN R   MOORE J
MEXICAN-AMERICANS, A BACKGROUND PAPER.
CENTER FOR THE STUDY OF DEMOCRATIC INSTITUTIONS, CONFERENCE.
PAPER. SANTA BARBARA, CALIFORNIA. OCT 29 1965.

MGUZMRX66412 GUZMAN R
MEXICAN-AMERICANS ON THE MOVE.
AFL-CIO, INDUSTRIAL UNION DEPARTMENT. IUD AGENDA, VOL 2,
NO 7, JULY 1966. PP 2-8.

MHAYDRG66114 HAYDEN RG   *US DEPT OF HEALTH ED WELFARE
SPANISH-AMERICANS OF THE SOUTHWEST. LIFE-STYLE PATTERNS AND
    THEIR IMPLICATIONS.
US DEPARTMENT OF HEALTH, EDUCATION AND WELFARE, WELFARE
ADMINISTRATION, WELFARE IN REVIEW. AP 1966. PP 14-25.

MHELLCS63414 HELLER CS
BACKGROUND AND AMBITION OF MALE MEXICAN-AMERICAN HIGH SCHOOL
    SENIORS IN LOS-ANGELES. /CALIFORNIA/
AMERICAN SOCIOLOGICAL ASSOCIATION, ANNUAL MEETING. PAPER.
LOS ANGELES, CALIFORNIA. 1963.

MHELLCS64413 HELLER CS
AMBITIONS OF MEXICAN-AMERICAN YOUTH -- GOALS AND MEANS OF
    MOBILITY OF HIGH SCHOOL SENIORS.
COLUMBIA UNIVERSITY. UNPUBLISHED PHD DISSERTATION. NEW YORK.
1964.

MHELLCS65415 HELLER CS
CLASS AS AN EXPLANATION OF ETHNIC DIFFERENCES IN MOBILITY
    ASPIRATIONS -- THE CASE OF MEXICAN-AMERICANS.
EASTERN SOCIOLOGICAL SOCIETY, ANNUAL MEETING. PAPER.
NEW YORK. 1965.

MHELLCS66416 HELLER CS
MEXICAN-AMERICAN YOUTH. FORGOTTEN YOUTH AT THE CROSSROADS.
RANDOM HOUSE. NEW YORK. 1966.

MHOLLSX56417 HOLLAND S
DISTRIBUTION OF SPANISH-NAME PEOPLE IN THE SOUTHWEST. TABLES
    AND MAP.
UNIVERSITY OF TEXAS, DEPARTMENT OF HISTORY AND PHILOSOPHY
OF EDUCATION. UNPUBLISHED REPORT. AUSTIN, TEXAS. 1956.

MHOLLWE61418 HOLLUM WE
THE SOUTHWEST. OLD AND NEW.
ALFRED A KNOPF. NEW YORK. 1961.

MHOYEHC64419 HOYER HC
SPANISH-AMERICANS.
ELEVENTH SCHOOL OF MISSIONS. GRETNA, PENNSYLVANIA. ALSO
SILVER BAY CONFERENCE ON THE WORLD MISSION. SILVER BAY,
NEW YORK. 1964.

MIMMASM57420 IMMACULATE SISTER MARY   *WELFARE CC METROPOLITAN CHI
MEXICAN CULTURAL PATTERNS.
SELECTED PAPERS OF INSTITUTE CN CULTURAL PATTERNS OF
NEWCOMERS. WELFARE COUNCIL OF METROPOLITAN CHICAGO.
CHICAGO, ILLINOIS. OCT 1957. PP 41-58.

MJONEBM62421 JONES BM
A STUDY OF THE ACCULTURATION AND SOCIAL ASPIRATIONS OF SIXTY

JUNIOR HIGH SCHOOL STUDENTS FROM THE MEXICAN ETHNIC GROUP.
UNIVERSITY OF TEXAS. UNPUBLISHED MA THESIS. AUSTIN, TEXAS.
1962.

MJONELB65318 JONES LB
MEXICAN-AMERICAN LABOR PROBLEMS IN TEXAS.
UNIVERSITY OF TEXAS, UNPUBLISHED PHD THESIS. AUSTIN, TEXAS.
1965.

MJORGJM60422 JORGENSON JM   WILLIAMS DE
BURMA JH
MIGRATORY AGRICULTURAL WORKERS IN THE UNITED STATES.
GRINNELL COLLEGE. GRINNELL, IOWA. UNPUBLISHED PAPER. 1960.

MKNOWCS61424 KNOWLTON CS
THE SPANISH-AMERICANS IN NEW-MEXICO.
SOCIOLOGY AND SOCIAL RESEARCH, VOL 45, NO 4, JULY 1961.
PP 448-453.

MKNOWCS66423 KNOWLTON CS
PATRON-PEON PATTERN AMONG THE SPANISH-AMERICANS OF
    NEW-MEXICO.
SOCIAL FORCES, OCT 1962. ALSO IN KNOWING THE DISADVANTAGED.
ED BY STATEN W WEBSTER. CHANDLER PUBLISHING CO.
SAN FRANCISCO, CALIFORNIA. 1966. PP 118-126.

MKRASWX63425 KRASSOWSKI W
NATURALIZATION AND ASSIMILATION PRONENESS OF CALIFORNIA
    IMMIGRANT POPULATIONS.
UNIVERSITY OF SOUTHERN CALIFORNIA. PHD DISSERTATION.
LOS ANGELES, CALIFORNIA. 1963.

MKURTNR66270 KURTZ NR
GATEKEEPERS IN THE PROCESS OF ASSIMILATION.
UNIVERSITY OF COLORADO. PHD DISSERTATION. BOULDER, COLORADO.
1966. AVAILABLE IN MIMEO AT THE UNIVERSITY OF COLORADO,
INSTITUTE OF BEHAVICRAL SCIENCE.

MLANDRG66427 LANDOLT RG
THE MEXICAN-AMERICAN WORKERS OF SAN-ANTONIO. /TEXAS/
UNIVERSITY OF TEXAS. UNPUBLISHED PHD THESIS. AUSTIN, TEXAS.
1966.

MLANDRX60426 LANDES R
INTEGRATION OF MINORITIES.
CLAREMONT GRADUATE SCHOOL. CLAREMONT, CALIFORNIA.
UNPUBLISHED PAPER. 1960.

MLOOKXX63429 LOOK
THE OTHER TEXAS.
LOOK, VOL 27, OCT 8 1963. PP 68-70.

MLOSACAND430 LA CHAMBER COMMERCE AG DEPT
SURVEY ON TRANSIENT MEXICAN LABOR REQUIREMENTS.
LOS ANGELES CHAMBER OF COMMERCE, AGRICULTURAL DEPARTMENT.
LOS ANGELES, CALIFORNIA. ND.

MLOSACDND431 LA COUNTY COORDINATING CCS
SOME NOTES ON THE MEXICAN POPULATION OF LOS-ANGELES COUNTY.
    /CALIFORNIA/
UNIVERSITY OF SOUTHERN CALIFORNIA. CITIZENS COMMITTEE FOR
THE DEFENSE OF MEXICAN-AMERICAN YOUTH, ARCHIVE 107/6.
LOS ANGELES, CALIFORNIA. ND.

MLOSARW58432 LA REGION WELFARE PLANNING CC
STUDY OF SOCIO-CULTURAL FACTORS THAT INHIBIT OR ENCOURAGE
    DELINQUENCY AMONG MEXICAN-AMERICANS.
IT-S NEWS, VOL 10, NO 9, FEB 1958.

MMACNBL67335 MACNABB BL   *OEO
TEXAS MIGRANTS PROGRAM. /TRAINING EDUCATION/
COMMUNITIES IN ACTION, VOL 2, NO 2, MAR 1967. PP 21-25.

MMADSWX64436 MADSDEN W
THE MEXICAN-AMERICANS OF SOUTH TEXAS.
HOLT, RINEHART AND WINSTON. NEW YORK. 1967. 112 PP.

MMARSRX64437 MARSHALL R
PROSPECTUS OF THE MEXICAN-AMERICAN STUDY PROJECT.
UNIVERSITY OF SOUTHERN CALIFORNIA. LOS ANGELES, CALIFORNIA.
JAN 27 1964.

MMCBRJG63433 MCBRIDE JG
VANISHING BRACERO.
THE NAYLOR CO. SAN ANTONIO, TEXAS. 1963.

MMCELRC65385 MCELROY RC   GAVETT EE
*US DEPARTMENT OF AGRICULTURE
TERMINATION OF THE BRACERO PROGRAM. SOME EFFECTS ON FARM
    LABOR AND MIGRANT HOUSING NEEDS.
US DEPARTMENT OF AGRICULTURE. GPO. WASHINGTON, DC.
JUNE 1965. 29 PP.

MMCMIOX62434 MCMILLAN O   *CAL GOVRS ADVSY COMM HOUSING
HOUSING DEFICIENCIES OF AGRICULTURAL WORKERS AND OTHER LOW
    INCOME GROUPS.
CALIFORNIA GOVERNOR-S ADVISORY COMMISSICN ON HOUSING
PROBLEMS, DIVISION OF HOUSING, REPORT. SAN FRANCISCO,
CALIFORNIA. NOV 27 1962.

MMCNAPH57435 MCNAMARA PH
MEXICAN-AMERICAN FAMILIES. LOS-ANGELES COUNTY. /CALIFORNIA/
SAINT LOUIS UNIVERSITY. MASTER-S THESIS. ST LOUIS,
MISSOURI. 1957.

MMEADBS59438 MEADOR BS
MINORITY-GROUPS AND THEIR EDUCATION IN HAY-COUNTY, TEXAS.
UNIVERSITY OF TEXAS. PHD DISSERTATION. AUSTIN, TEXAS. 1959.

MMETZWH60439 METZLER WH   SARGENT FO
*TEXAS AGL EXP STATION
INCOMES OF MIGRATORY AGRICULTURAL WORKERS.
TEXAS A AND M COLLEGE, AGRICULTURAL EXPERIMENT STATION,
BULLETIN 950. COLLEGE STATION, TEXAS. MAR 1960. 5 PP.

MMEXIEC63441 MEXICAN-AMERICANS ED CONF
CAREERS FOR YOUTH.
MEXICAN-AMERICANS EDUCATION CONFERENCE, REPORT. PHOENIX,
ARIZONA. JAN 1963.

MMITTFG66442 MITTLEBACH FG   MARSHALL G
THE BURDEN OF POVERTY.
MEXICAN-AMERICAN STUDY PROJECT, ADVANCE REPORT 5.
UNIVERSITY OF SOUTHERN CALIFORNIA, GRADUATE SCHOOL OF
BUSINESS ADMINISTRATION. LOS ANGELES, CALIFORNIA. JULY 1966.
65 PP.

MMONTPX60443 MONTEZ P
SOME DIFFERENCES IN FACTORS RELATED TO EDUCATIONAL
    ACHIEVEMENT OF TWO MEXICAN-AMERICAN GROUPS.

UNIVERSITY OF SOUTHERN CALIFORNIA. MASTER-S DISSERTATION.
LOS ANGELES, CALIFORNIA. 1960.

MMOORJW66444 MOORE JW   MITTELBACH
*UCLA MEXICAN-AM STUDY PROJ
RESIDENTIAL SEGREGATION IN THE URBAN SOUTHWEST.
MEXICAN-AMERICAN STUDY PROJECT. UNIVERSITY OF SOUTHERN
CALIFORNIA, GRADUATE SCHOOL OF BUSINESS ADMINISTRATION.
LOS ANGELES, CALIFORNIA. JUNE 1966.

MMORADX63445 MORALES D
STATEMENT ON EMPLOYMENT PROBLEMS OF MEXICAN-AMERICANS IN
CALIFORNIA.
US SENATE, COMMITTEE ON LABOR AND PUBLIC WELFARE,
SUBCOMMITTEE ON EMPLOYMENT AND MANPOWER. SEPT 11 1963. 88TH
CONGRESS, 1ST SESSION. GPO. WASHINGTON, DC. 1963. 14 PP.

MMUNORF57446 MUNOZ RF
DIFFERENCES IN DROPCUT AND OTHER SCHOOL BEHAVIOR BETWEEN TWO
GROUPS OF TENTH GRADE BOYS IN AN URBAN HIGH SCHOOL.
UNIVERSITY OF SOUTHERN CALIFORNIA. PHD DISSERTATION.
LOS ANGELES, CALIFORNIA. 1957.

MNALLFX59447 NALL F
LEVELS OF ASPIRATION OF MEXICAN-AMERICANS IN EL-PASO
SCHOOLS. /TEXAS/
MICHIGAN STATE UNIVERSITY. PHD DISSERTATION. EAST LANSING,
MICHIGAN. 1959.

MNATLCA63081 NATL CATH CC SPANISH-SPEAKING
SAN-ANTONIO PROJECT. /TEXAS/
NATIONAL CATHOLIC COUNCIL FOR THE SPANISH-SPEAKING. AP 1963.

MNATLCBND0082 NATIONAL CATHOLIC WELFARE CON
COMPREHENSIVE REPORT OF THE OFFICE OF THE BISHOP-S COMMITTEE
FOR MIGRANT-WORKERS.
NATIONAL CATHOLIC WELFARE CONFERENCE, ACMINISTRATIVE BOARD.
ND.

MNELSEX66028 NELSON E
HUELGA. THE FIRST 100 DAYS OF THE GREAT DELANO STRIKE.
/UNION/
FARM WORKERS PRESS. DELANO, CALIFORNIA. 1966. 122 PP.

MNORMAX56448 NORMAN A
MIGRATION TO SOUTHWEST TEXAS. PEOPLES AND WORDS.
SOUTHWESTERN SOCIAL SCIENCE QUARTERLY, VOL 37, SEPT 1 1956.
PP 149-158.

MORTIMX62449 ORTIZ M   *LA ECA WELFARE PLANNING CC
MEXICAN-AMERICANS IN THE LOS-ANGELES REGION. /CALIFORNIA/
EAST CENTRAL AREA WELFARE PLANNING COUNCIL. LOS ANGELES,
CALIFORNIA. AUG 1962.

MPADFHX65450 PADFIELD H   MARTIN WE
FARMERS, WORKERS, AND MACHINES. TECHNOLOGICAL AND
SOCIAL-CHANGE IN FARM INDUSTRIES OF ARIZONA.
UNIVERSITY CF ARIZONA PRESS. TUCSON, ARIZONA. 1965.

MPAREAX63451 PAREDES A
TEXAS-S THIRD MAN. THE TEXAS MEXICAN.
RACE, VOL 4, MAY 1963. PP 49-58.

MPARISF64452 PARIGI SF
A CASE-STUDY OF LATIN-AMERICAN UNIONIZATION IN AUSTIN,
TEXAS.
UNIVERSITY OF TEXAS. UNPUBLISHED PHD THESIS. AUSTIN, TEXAS.
1964.

MPENAFX63453 PENALOSA F
CLASS CONSCIOUSNESS AND SOCIAL MOBILITY IN A
MEXICAN-AMERICAN COMMUNITY.
UNIVERSITY OF SOUTHERN CALIFORNIA. UNPUBLISHED PHD
DISSERTATION. LOS ANGELES, CALIFORNIA. 1963.

MPETECL64454 PETERSON CL
WHEN THE MIGRANT LABORER SETTLES DOWN -- A REPORT OF THE
FINDINGS OF A PROJECT ON VALUE ASSIMILATION OF IMMIGRANT
LABORERS.
UNIVERSITY OF WISCONSIN. MADISON, WISCONSIN. MIMEOGRAPHED.
1964.

MPFEIDG63456 PFEIFFER DG
THE MEXICAN FARM LABOR SUPPLY PROGRAM -- ITS FRIENDS AND
FOES.
UNIVERSITY OF TEXAS. MASTER-S THESIS. AUSTIN, TEXAS. 1963.

MPIERGK61457 PIERSON GK
ANALYSIS OF POPULATION CHANGES IN NEW-MEXICO COUNTIES.
NEW MEXICO BUSINESS, VOL 14, NOV 1961.

MRATLYX60460 RATLIFF Y
SPANISH-SPEAKING AND ENGLISH SPEAKING CHILDREN IN SOUTHWEST
TEXAS. A COMPARATIVE STUDY OF INTELLIGENCE, SOCIO-ECONOMIC
STATUS, AND ACHIEVEMENT.
UNIVERSITY OF TEXAS. UNPUBLISHED MA THESIS. AUSTIN, TEXAS.
1960.

MRENOGX63461 RENDON G   *U COLO TRI-ETHNIC RES PROJ
OBJECTIVE ACCESS IN THE OPPORTUNITY STRUCTURE. THE
ASSESSMENT OF THREE ETHNIC GROUPS WITH RESPECT TO
QUANTIFIED SOCIAL STRUCTURAL VARIABLES.
UNIVERSITY OF COLORADO, INSTITUTE OF BEHAVIORAL SCIENCE,
TRI-ETHNIC RESEARCH PROJECT, REPORT NO 20. BOULDER,
COLORADO. JUNE 1963.

MRENNRR57462 RENNER RR
SOME CHARACTERISTICS OF SPANISH-NAME TEXANS AND FOREIGN
LATIN-AMERICANS IN TEXAS HIGHER EDUCATION.
UNIVERSITY OF TEXAS. PHD DISSERTATION. AUSTIN, TEXAS. 1957.

MREYEIX57463 REYES I
A SURVEY OF THE PROBLEMS INVOLVED IN THE AMERICANIZATION OF
THE MEXICAN-AMERICAN.
UNIVERSITY OF SOUTHERN CALIFORNIA. MASTER-S THESIS.
LOS ANGELES, CALIFORNIA. 1957.

MRODRFX66464 RODRIQUEZ-CANO F
AN ANALYSIS OF THE MEXICAN-AMERICAN MIGRANT LABOR FORCE IN
THE STOCKBRIDGE AREA. /MICHIGAN/
MICHIGAN STATE UNIVERSITY, DEPARTMENT OF SOCIOLOGY. MA
THESIS. EAST LANSING, MICHIGAN. 1966.

MROONJF61465 ROONEY JF
THE EFFECTS OF IMPORTED MEXICAN FARM LABOR IN A CALIFORNIA
COUNTY.
AMERICAN JOURNAL OF ECONOMICS AND SOCIOLOGY, VOL 20,
OCT 1961. PP 513-521.

MRUBEAJ66466 RUBEL AJ

ACROSS THE TRACKS. MEXICAN-AMERICANS IN A TEXAS CITY.
UNIVERSITY OF TEXAS PRESS. AUSTIN, TEXAS. 1966.

MRUBEAJ66467 RUBEL AJ
SOCIAL MOBILITY AND IMPUTATIONS OF WITCHCRAFT IN A
MEXICAN-AMERICAN NEIGHBORHOOD OF TEXAS.
SOUTHERN ANTHROPOLOGICAL SOCIETY. MEETINGS. PAPER.
NEW ORLEANS, LOUSIANA. AP 1966. 7 PP.

MRUBEAJ66468 RUBEL AJ
SOME CULTURAL AND ANTHROPOLOGICAL ASPECTS OF ENGLISH AS A
SECOND LANGUAGE.
AMERICAN EDUCATIONAL RESEARCH ASSOCIATICN, MEETINGS.
REVISION OF A PAPER. CHICAGO, ILLINOIS. FEB 1966. DR ARTHUR
J RUBEL, UNIVERSITY OF NOTRE DAME, DEPARTMENT OF SOCIOLOGY.
NOTRE DAME, INDIANA.

MSAMOJX62473 SAMORA J   *US COMM ON CIVIL RIGHTS
THE SPANISH-SPEAKING PEOPLE IN THE UNITED STATES.
US COMMISSION ON CIVIL RIGHTS. STAFF PAPER. WASHINGTON, DC.
1962.

MSAMOJX63469 SAMORA J
THE EDUCATION OF THE SPANISH-SPEAKING IN THE SOUTHWEST -- AN
ANALYSIS OF THE 1960 CENSUS MATERIALS.
MEXICAN-AMERICAN WORKSHOP SPONSORED BY CAREERS FOR YOUTH AND
THE MEXICAN-AMERICAN COMMUNITY. PAPER. JAN 8 1963.

MSAMOJX63470 SAMORA J
EDUCATIONAL STATUS OF A MINORITY.
THEORY AND PRACTICE, VOL 2, JUNE 1963. PP 144-150.

MSAMOJX63471 SAMORA J
THE GENERAL STATUS OF THE SPANISH-SPEAKING PEOPLE IN THE
UNITED STATES.
SOUTHWEST CONFERENCE CN SOCIAL AND EDUCATIONAL PROBLEMS OF
RURAL AND URBAN MEXICAN-AMERICAN YOUTH. PAPER. OCCIDENTAL
COLLEGE. LOS ANGELES, CALIFORNIA. AP 6 1963.

MSAMOJX64472 SAMORA J
THE SPANISH-SPEAKING PEOPLE IN AMERICAN SOCIETY.
SERVICES TO MEXICAN-AMERICANS. WORKSHOP. SPONSORED BY THE
COMMUNITY COUNCIL OF CENTRAL SANTA CLARA COUNTY, THE
ROSENBERG FOUNDATION OF SAN FRANCISCO AND NATIONAL
INSTITUTE OF MENTAL HEALTH. SAN JOSE, CALIFORNIA. 1964.

MSAMOJX64475 SAMORA J   *US COMM ON CIVIL RIGHTS
SPANISH-SPEAKING PEOPLES.
US COMMISSICN ON CIVIL RIGHTS. STAFF PAPER. WASHINGTON, DC.
FEB 1964.

MSANACP64476 SAN ANTONIO CITY PLAN DEPT
ECONOMIC BASE STUDY OF SAN-ANTONIO AND TWENTY-SEVEN COUNTY
AREAS. /TEXAS/
SAN ANTONIO CITY PLANNING DEPARTMENT. SAN ANTONIO, TEXAS.
AP 1964.

MSANCGI59478 SANCHEZ GI   PUTNAM H
*U TEXAS INST LAT-AM STUDIES
MATERIALS RELATING TO THE EDUCATION OF SPANISH-SPEAKING
PEOPLE IN THE UNITED STATES, AN ANNOTATED BIBLIOGRAPHY.
UNIVERSITY OF TEXAS, INSTITUTE OF LATIN-AMERICAN STUDIES.
AUSTIN, TEXAS. 1959.

MSANCGI61477 SANCHEZ GI
THE AMERICAN OF MEXICAN DESCENT.
CHICAGO JEWISH FORUM, VOL 20, NO 2, WINTER 1961-1962.
PP 120-125. ALSO COLORADO ANTI-DISCRIMINATION COMMISSION.
DENVER, COLCRADO.

MSANOAD63479 SANDOVAL AD
NEW-MEXICO COUNTY INDUSTRIAL COMPOSITION AND LEVELS OF
LIVING.
NEW MEXICO BUSINESS, VOL 16, MAY 1963.

MSAUNLX58480 SAUNDERS L   *ADAMS S CENT CULTURAL STUDIE
THE SPANISH-SPEAKING PEOPLE OF THE SOUTHWEST.
ADAMS STATE COLLEGE, CENTER FOR CULTURAL STUDIES. ALAMOSA,
COLORADO. MAR 1958. 8 PP.

MSCHETJ65481 SCHEFF TJ
CHANGES IN PUBLIC AND PRIVATE LANGUAGE AMONG
SPANISH-SPEAKING MIGRANTS TO AN INDUSTRIAL CITY.
INTERNATIONAL MIGRATION, VOL 3, 1965. PP 78-86.

MSCHOWE66687 SCHOLES WE
THE MIGRANT-WORKER.
LA RAZA. ED BY JULIAN SAMORA. UNIVERSITY OF NOTRE DAME
PRESS. NOTRE DAME, INDIANA. 1966. PP 63-94.

MSCRUOM63482 SCRUGGS OM
TEXAS AND THE BRACERO PROGRAM.
PACIFIC HISTORICAL REVIEW, VOL 32, AUG 1963. PP 251-264.

MSECKJP62483 SECKEL JP
EMPLOYMENT AND EMPLOYABILITY AMONG CALIFORNIA YOUTH
AUTHORITY WARDS. A SURVEY.
DEPARTMENT OF THE YOUTH AUTHORITY, DIVISION OF RESEARCH,
RESEARCH REPORT NO 30. SACRAMENTO, CALIFORNIA. AUG 21 1962.

MSHELPM59488 SHELDON PM
MEXICAN-AMERICANS IN URBAN PUBLIC HIGH SCHOOLS. AN
EXPLORATION UF THE DROP-OUT PROGRAM.
OCCIDENTAL COLLEGE, LABORATORY OF URBAN CULTURE. ROSENBERG
FOUNDATION. SAN FRANCISCO, CALIFORNIA. 1959.

MSHERCW61489 SHERIF CW
SELF RADIUS AND GOALS OF YOUTH IN DIFFERENT URBAN AREAS.
SOUTHWESTERN SOCIAL SCIENCE QUARTERLY, VOL 42, DEC 1961.
PP 259-267.

MSIMMOG61490 SIMMONS OG
THE MUTUAL IMAGES AND EXPECTATIONS OF ANGLO-AMERIANS AND
MEXICAN-AMERICANS.
DAEDALUS, VCL 90, SPRING 1961. PP 206-299. ALSO IN KNOWING
THE DISADVANTAGED. ED BY STATEN W WEBSTER. CHANDLER
PUBLISHING COMPANY. SAN FRANCISO, CALIFORNA. 1966.
PP 127-140.

MSIMMOG64491 SIMMONS OG   HANSON RC
WANDERER JJ   *COLO INST OF BEHAVIORAL SCI
URBANIZATION OF THE MIGRANT. PROCESSES AND OUTCOMES. A
RESEARCH PROPOSAL.
INSTITUTE OF BEHAVIORAL SCIENCE, BUREAU OF SOCIOLOGICAL
RESEARCH. BOULDER, COLORADO. JAN 14 1964.

MSKRARL62494 SKRABANEK RL   DUCOFF LJ
OCCUPATION-PATTERNS OF SPANISH-AMERICANS IN SELECTED AREAS
OF TEXAS.
RURAL SOCIOLOGICAL SOCIETY. PAPER. WASHINGTON, DC. AUG 1962.

MSKRARL65493 SKRABANEK RL
SPANISH-AMERICANS RAISING EDUCATIONAL SIGHTS.
TEXAS AGRICULTURAL PROGRESS, VOL 2, NO 2, SPRING 1965.

MSKRARL66492 SKRABANEK RL   *TEXAS AGL EXP STATION
OCCUPATIONAL CHANGE AMONG SPANISH-AMERICANS IN
   ATASCOSA-COUNTY AND SAN-ANTONIO, TEXAS.
TEXAS A AND M COLLEGE. AGRICULTURAL EXPERIMENT STATION,
BULLETIN 1061. COLLEGE STATION, TEXAS. DEC 1966. 24 PP.

MSLOBMX64495 SLOBODEK M   *UCLA INSTITUTE OF IND RELS
A SELECTIVE BIBLIOGRAPHY OF CALIFORNIA LABOR HISTORY.
UNIVERSITY OF SOUTHERN CALIFORNIA, INSTITUTE OF INDUSTRIAL
RELATIONS. LOS ANGELES, CALIFORNIA. 1964.

MSOLIML61496 SOLIEN DE GONZALEZ NL
FAMILY ORGANIZATION IN FIVE TYPES OF MIGRATORY WAGE LABOR.
AMERICAN ANTHROPOLOGIST, VOL 63, 1961. PP 1264-1280.

MSOTOAX59370 SOTO A
THE BRACERO STORY.
COMMONWEAL, VOL 71, NO 9, NOV 27 1959. PP 258-260.

MSOUTSS62497 SWESTERN SOCIAL SCI QUARTERLY
TEXAS GOOD NEIGHBOR.
SOUTHWESTERN SOCIAL SCIENCE QUARTERLY, VOL 43, SEPT 1962.
PP 118-125.

MTAYLMM60402 TAYLOR MM
RURAL PEOPLE AND THEIR RESOURCES, NORTH-CENTRAL NEW-MEXICO.
NEW MEXICO STATE COLLEGE. UNIVERSITY PARK, NEW MEXICO.
OCT 1960. 28 PP.

MTEXACC64499 TEXAS CC ON MIGRANT LABOR
MECHANIZATION AND THE TEXAS MIGRANT.
TEXAS COUNCIL ON MIGRANT LABOR. AUSTIN, TEXAS. 1964.

MTEXACM62498 TEXAS COMT ON MIG FARM WRKRS TEXAS GOOD NEIGHBOR COMM
PROCEEDINGS OF THE CONFERENCE ON EDUCATION FOR ADULT MIGRANT
   WORKERS. /TEXAS/
TEXAS LEGISLATURE. AUSTIN, TEXAS. 1962.

MTEXASD61500 TEXAS STATE DEPT OF HEALTH
A STUDY OF THE MENTAL HEALTH PROBLEMS OF MEXICAN-AMERICAN
   RESIDENTS. /TEXAS/
TEXAS STATE DEPARTMENT OF HEALTH, DIVISION OF MENTAL HEALTH.
AUSTIN, TEXAS. 1961.

MTHOMAN56501 THOMPSON AN
THE MEXICAN IMMIGRANT WORKER IN SOUTHWESTERN AGRICULTURE.
AMERICAN JOURNAL OF ECONOMICS AND SOCIOLOGY, VOL 16,
OCT 1956. PP 73-81.

MTOMARD61502 TOMASEK RD
THE MIGRANT PROBLEM AND PRESSURE GROUP POLITICS.
THE JOURNAL OF POLITICS, VOL 23, NO 2, MAY 1961. PP 295-319.

MTURNWX65166 TURNER W
NO DICE FOR BRACEROS.
RAMPARTS, VOL 4, NO 5, SEPT 1965. PP 15-26.

MULIBHX66503 ULIBARRI H
SOCIAL AND ATTITUDINAL CHARACTERISTICS OF SPANISH-SPEAKING
   MIGRANT AND EX-MIGRANT WORKERS IN THE SOUTHWEST.
SOCIOLOGY AND SOCIAL RESEARCH, VOL 50, NO 3, AP 1966.
PP 361-370.

MUPHAWK66511 UPHAM WK   LEVER MF
*TEXAS AGL EXP STATION
POVERTY AMONG SPANISH-AMERICANS IN TEXAS. LOW-INCOME
   FAMILIES IN A MINORITY-GROUP.
TEXAS A AND M UNIVERSITY, AGRICULTURAL EXPERMINENT STATION,
DEPARTMENTAL INFORMATION REPORT NO 66-2. COLLEGE STATION,
TEXAS. SEPT 1966. 55 PP.

MUPHAWK66533 UPHAM WK   LEVER MF
DIFFERENTIALS IN THE INCIDENCE OF POVERTY IN TEXAS.
   /ECONOMIC-STATUS/
TEXAS A AND M UNIVERSITY, TEXAS AGRICULTURAL EXPERIMENT
STATION, REPORT NO 66-9. COLLEGE STATION, TEXAS. DEC 1966.
24 PP.

MUSCISC63504 US CIVIL SERVICE COMMISSION *PRESIDENT-S COMMITTEE ON EEO
MEXICAN-AMERICAN AND TOTAL EMPLOYMENT IN SELECTED STATES AND
   STANDARD METROPOLITAN STATISTICAL AREAS.
STUDY OF MINORITY GROUP EMPLOYMENT IN THE FEDERAL
GOVERNMENT. PREPARED BY THE US CIVIL SERVICE COMMISSION FOR
THE PRESIDENT-S COMMITTEE ON EQUAL EMPLOYMENT OPPORTUNITY.
WASHINGTON, DC. JUNE 1963.

MUSCOMC62505 US COMMISSION ON CIVIL RIGHTS
THE CONCENTRATION OF SPANISH-SURNAME POPULATION IN THE FIVE
   SOUTHWESTERN STATES.
US COMMISSION ON CIVIL RIGHTS. WASHINGTON, DC. 1962.

MUSDLAB59335 US DEPARTMENT OF LABOR
INFORMATION CONCERNING ENTRY OF MEXICAN AGRICULTURAL WORKERS
   INTO THE UNITED STATES.
US DEPARTMENT OF LABOR, BUREAU OF EMPLOYMENT SECURITY, FARM
LABOR SERVICE. GPO. WASHINGTON, DC. 1959. 39 PP.

MUSDLAB59508 US DEPARTMENT OF LABOR
MEXICAN FARM LABOR CONSULTANTS REPORT.
US DEPARTMENT OF LABOR, BUREAU OF EMPLOYMENT SECURITY.
WASHINGTON, DC. OCT 1959. 17 PP.

MUSDLAB67011 US DEPARTMENT OF LABOR
MEXICAN-AMERICANS. SELECTED REFERENCES.
US DEPARTMENT OF LABOR, LIBRARY. WASHINGTON, DC. 1967. 7 PP.

MUSHOUR58509 US HOUSE OF REPRESENTATIVES
FARM LABOR.
US HOUSE OF REPRESENTATIVES, COMMITTEE ON AGRICULTURE,
SUBCOMMITTEE ON EQUIPMENT, SUPPLIES, AND MANPOWER. HEARINGS
OF PROBLEMS IN THE SOUTHWEST AND MEXICAN LABOR.
85TH CONGRESS, 2ND SESSION. GPO. WASHINGTON, DC. 1958.

MUSHOUR63984 US HOUSE OF REPRESENTATIVES
MEXICAN FARM LABOR PROGRAM.
US HOUSE OF REPRESENTATIVES, COMMITTEE ON AGRICULTURE,
SUBCOMMITTEE ON EQUIPMENT, SUPPLIES, AND MANPOWER, 88TH
CONGRESS, 1ST SESSION. HEARINGS. GPO. WASHINGTON, DC. 1963.

MUVCALM66510 UCLA MEXICAN-AM STUDY PROJECT
MEXICAN-AMERICAN STUDY PROJECT, ADVANCE REPORT 3,
   BIBLIOGRAPHY.
UNIVERSITY OF SOUTHERN CALIFORNIA, GRADUATE SCHOOL OF
BUSINESS ADMINISTRATION. LOS ANGELES, CALIFORNIA. FEB 1966.
101 PP.

MVALDBX64448 VALDEZ B
IMPLICATIONS OF CULTURAL VALUES IN EDUCATION.
CALIFORNIA DEPARTMENT OF SOCIAL WELFARE. SAN FRANCISCO,
CALIFORNIA. NOV 1964. 4 PP.

MVALDBX64449 VALDEZ B
CONTRASTS BETWEEN SPANISH FOLK AND ANGLO URBAN CULTURAL
   VALUES. /EDUCATION ASPIRATIONS/
CALIFORNIA DEPARTMENT OF SOCIAL WELFARE. SAN FRANCISCO,
CALIFORNIA. NOV 1964. 6 PP.

MVALDLX66512 VALDEZ L   PRUDENCE SISTER MARY
CHAVEZ C
TALES OF THE DELANO REVOLUTION.
RAMPARTS, VOL 5, NO 2, JULY 1966. PP 37-50.

MWADDJO62513 WADDELL JO
VALUE ORIENTATIONS OF YOUNG MEXICAN-AMERICAN MALES AS
   REFLECTED IN THEIR WORK PATTERNS AND EMPLOYMENT
   PREFERENCES.
UNIVERSITY OF TEXAS. UNPUBLISHED MA THESIS. AUSTIN, TEXAS.
1962.

MWAGNJA63514 WAGNER JA   *SAN ANTONIO BISHOPS COMT
SAN-ANTONIO PROJECT. /TEXAS/
SAN ANTONIO BISHOPS COMMITTEE. SAN ANTONIO, TEXAS. 1963.

MWAGODW57515 WAGONER DW
RECENT MIGRATION OF YOUNG MALES INTO HOUSTON, TEXAS.
UNIVERSITY OF TEXAS. MASTER-S THESIS. AUSTIN, TEXAS. 1957.

MWEBBEB66516 WEBB EB   *CAL DEPT OF INDUSTRIAL RELS
FAIR-EMPLOYMENT AND YOUTH. ISI SE PUEDE -- IT CAN BE DONE.
   RE. YOUTH AND OPPORTUNITIES.
CALIFORNIA DEPARTMENT OF INDUSTRIAL RELATIONS, FAIR
EMPLOYMENT PRACTICES COMMISSION. SACRAMENTO, CALIFORNIA.
1966.

MWHITNX60517 WHITAKER N   BURK CJ
*LA COUNTY SUPT OF SCHOOLS
SUMMARY REPORT OF THE STUDY OF DROP-OUTS IN THE THREE
   SENIOR HIGH SCHOOLS, COMPTON UNION HIGH SCHOOL DISTRICT.
   /CALIFORNIA/
OFFICE OF THE LOS ANGELES COUNTY SUPERINTENDENT OF SCHOOLS.
LOS ANGELES, CALIFORNIA. 1960.

MWINGWX66536 WINGO W
HOW UNIONS ARE SIGNING THEM UP. /MIGRANT-WORKERS
   CALIFORNIA/
NATION-S BUSINESS, VOL 54, NO 9, SEPT 1966. PP 36 PLUS.

MWOODMJ64518 WOODS MJ
EMPLOYMENT PROBLEMS OF THE MEXICAN-AMERICAN.
CALIFORNIA ASSEMBLY, SUBCOMMITTEE ON SPECIAL EMPLOYMENT
PROBLEMS. PRESENTATION BY STATE SUPERVISOR OF THE MINORITY
EMPLOYMENT PROGRAM. WEST LOS ANGELES COLLEGE AUDITORIUM.
LOS ANGELES, CALIFORNIA. JAN 10 1964. 13 PP.

MWOODMJ65446 WOODS MJ   *CAL MINORITY EMPLOYMENT PROG
EMPLOYMENT PROBLEMS OF MEXICAN-AMERICANS.
TRAINING AID. CULTURAL DIFFERENCES, TRAINING IN
NONDISCRIMINATION, READING ASSIGNMENTS. CALIFORNIA STATE
DEPARTMENT OF SOCIAL WELFARE, SAN FRANCISCO, CALIFORNIA.
SEPT 1965. PP 155-160.

MZURCLA65520 ZURCHER LA   MEADOW A
ZURCHER SL
VALUE ORIENTATION, ROLE CONFLICT, AND ALIENATION FROM WORK.
   A CROSS-CULTURAL STUDY.
AMERICAN SOCIOLOGICAL REVIEW, VOL 30, AUG 1965.

NABRAAA66141 ABRAHAM AA   SIMMONS GL
THE EDUCATIONAL OUTLOOK FOR NONWHITES IN FLORIDA.
JOURNAL OF NEGRO EDUCATION, VOL 35, NO 4, FALL 1966.
PP 369-380.

NABRACX57510 ABRAMS C
REMOVING JOB BARRIERS.
THE AMERICAN FEDERATIONIST, VOL 64, NO 8, AUG 1957.
PP 20-21.

NADDIDP61002 ADDISON DP
SOCIAL FACTORS IN OCCUPATIONAL AND EDUCATIONAL ASPIRATIONS
   OF NEGRO AND WHITE STUDENTS.
MISSOURI UNIVERSITY. PHD DISSERTATION. COLUMBIA, MISSOURI.
1961.

NAFLCIO58006 AFL-CIO
THE SOUTHERN LABOR STORY. /UNION/
AFL-CIO INDUSTRIAL UNION DEPARTMENT. PUBLICATION NO 25
WASHINGTON, DC. 1958. 42 PP.

NAFLCIO60004 AFL-CIO
YOUR RIGHTS UNDER FAIR-EMPLOYMENT-PRACTICE LAWS. /UNION
   LEGISLATION/
AFL-CIO. WASHINGTON, DC. JAN 1960. 32 PP.

NAFLCIO60005 AFL-CIO
THE CIVIL-RIGHTS FIGHT. A LOOK AT THE LEGISLATIVE RECORD.
AFL-CIO INDUSTRIAL UNION DEPARTMENT. WASHINGTON, DC. SEPT
1960. 29 PP.

NAHMAMH61007 AHMANN MH ED
THE NEW NEGRO
FIDES PUBLISHERS. NOTRE DAME, INDIANA. 1961. 145 PP.

NAIKEMX66865 AIKEN M   FERMAN LA
THE SOCIAL AND POLITICAL REACTIONS OF OLDER NEGROES TO
   UNEMPLOYMENT.
PHYLON, VOL 27, NO 4, WINTER 1966. PP 333-346.

NALEXRD64868 ALEXANDER RD ED
THE MANAGEMENT OF RACIAL INTEGRATION IN BUSINESS, A SPECIAL
   REPORT TO MANAGEMENT.
MCGRAW-HILL CO. NEW YORK. 1964. 147 PP.

NAMERCR45011 AM COUNCIL ON RACE RELATIONS
NEGRO PLATFORM WORKERS. /INDUSTRY CASE-STUDY/
AMERICAN COUNCIL ON RACE RELATIONS. CHICAGO, ILLINOIS. 1945.
48 PP.

NAMERCX63009 AMERICAN CHILD
GROWING UP NEGRO.
AMERICAN CHILD, JAN 1963. ENTIRE ISSUE.

NAMERCX63010 AMERICAN CHILD
PREFERENTIAL-HIRING FOR NEGROES, A DEBATE.
AMERICAN CHILD, VOL 45, NOV 1963. PP 1-23.

NAMERFX53015 AMERICAN FEDERATIONIST
NEGRO EMPLOYMENT-TRENDS IN THE SOUTH.
THE AMERICAN FEDERATIONIST, VOL 60, NO 12, DEC 1953. P 28.

NAMERFX55012 AMERICAN FEDERATIONIST
LABOR OPPOSES PREJUDICE. /UNION/
THE AMERICAN FEDERATIONIST, VOL 62, NO 4, AP 1955. P 22.

NAMERFX58013 AMERICAN FEDERATIONIST
LABOR-S CIVIL-RIGHTS STAND REAFFIRMED AT ATLANTIC-CITY.
THE AMERICAN FEDERATIONIST, VOL 65, NO 2, FFEB 1958. P 27.

NAMERFX65016 AMERICAN FEDERATIONIST
STAFF TRAINING WITH A SOUTHERN ACCENT.
THE AMERICAN FEDERATIONIST, VOL 72, NO 9, SEPT 1965.
PP 19-22.

NAMERFX66014 AMERICAN FEDERATIONIST
MAKING APPRENTICESHIP WORK.
THE AMERICAN FEDERATIONIST, VOL 73, NO 11, NOV 1966.
PP 13-14.

NAMERMA42017 AMERICAN MANAGEMENT ASSN
THE NEGRO WORKER. /INDUSTRY/
AMERICAN MANAGEMENT ASSOCIATION. SPECIAL RESEARCH REPORT
NO 1. NEW YORK. 1942. 32 PP.

NAMERNG66018 AMERICAN NEWSPAPER GUILD
CAREERS FOR NEGROES ON NEWSPAPERS. /OCCUPATIONS/
AMERICAN NEWSPAPER GUILD. WASHINGTON, DC. REVISED 1966.
26 PP.

NAMERVC60019 AMERICAN VETERANS COMMITTEE
AUDIT OF NEGRO VETERANS AND SERVICEMEN, 1960.
   /PUBLIC-EMPLOYMENT/
AMERICAN VETERANS COMMITTEE. WASHINGTON, DC. 1960. 41 PP.

NAMERXX63008 AMERICA
IS EQUALITY UNFAIR. NEGRO-S PLEA FOR PREFERENTIAL-TREATMENT.
AMERICA, VOL 109, 1963. PP 412-413.

NAMOSWE60020 AMOS WE
A STUDY OF THE OCCUPATIONAL AWARENESS OF A SELECTED GROUP OF
   NINTH GRADE NEGRO STUDENTS.
JOURNAL OF NEGRO EDUCATION, VOL 29, 1960. PP 500-503.

NAMOSWE63021 AMOS WE   PERRY J
NEGRO YOUTH AND EMPLOYMENT OPPORTUNITIES. /UNEMPLOYMENT
   EDUCATION/
JOURNAL OF NEGRO EDUCATION, VOL 32, NO 4, FALL 1963.

NAMOSWE64331 AMOS WE   *US DEPARTMENT OF LABOR
DISADVANTAGED YOUTH -- RECOGNIZING THE PROBLEM.
US DEPARTMENT OF LABOR, EMPLOYMENT SERVICE REVIEW,
SEPT 1964. P 43.

NANDEAX53022 ANDERSON A   BOWMAN M
THE VANISHING SERVANT AND THE CONTEMPORARY STATUS-SYSTEM OF
   THE AMERICAN SOUTH.
AMERICAN JOURNAL OF SOCIOLOGY, VOL 59, NO 3, NOV 1953.
PP 215-230.

NANDEBE65023 ANDERSON BE   *US DEPARTMENT OF LABOR
EMPLOYMENT OF NEGROES IN THE FEDERAL-GOVERNMENT.
US DEPARTMENT OF LABOR, MONTHLY LABOR REVIEW, OCT 1965.
PP 1222-1227.

NANDEEC50894 ANDERSON EC
DEALING WITH INTER-RACIAL TENSIONS ON LOCAL UNION GRASS
   ROOTS BASIS.
LABOR AND NATION, FALL 1950. PP 55-56.

NANDERW65024 ANDERSON RW
THE CHARACTERISTICS OF THE SUPPLY OF NEGROES FOR
   PROFESSIONAL OCCUPATIONS.
UNIVERSITY OF ILLINCIS, INSTITUTE OF LABOR AND INDUSTRIAL
RELATIONS. MASTER-S THESIS. CHAMPAIGN, ILLINOIS. 1965.

NANGLRA54254 ANGLIN RA
CHANGING PATTERNS IN AGRICULTURAL PRODUCTIONS,
   WEST-VIRGINIA, 1920-1950. /OCCUPATIONS/
THE QUARTERLY REVIEW OF HIGHER EDUCATION AMONG NEGROES, VOL
22, NO 2, AP 1954. PP 80-97.

NANTIOL55901 ANTI-DEFAMATION LEAGUE
PLACEMENT EXPERIENCES OF APPLICANTS TO A PRIVATE
   EMPLOYMENT-AGENCY.
ANTI-DEFAMATION LEAGUE OF B-NAI B-RITH, BUREAU OF JEWISH
EMPLOYMENT PROBLEMS. SPECIAL REPORT. SEPT 1955. 10 PP.

NANTIOL63511 ANTI-DEFAMATION LEAGUE
INTELLIGENCE OF THE AMERICAN NEGRO.
ANTI-DEFAMATION LEAGUE OF B-NAI B-RITH, RESEARCH REPORTS,
VOL 3, NOV 1963.

NANTOAX59026 ANTONOVSKY A   LERNER MJ
*NY STATE COMM AGAINST DISCR
NEGRO AND WHITE YOUTH IN ELMIRA. /NEW-YORK/
DISCRIMINATION AND LOW INCOMES. ED BY AARON ANTONOVSKY AND
LEWIS L LORWIN. NEW SCHOOL FOR SOCIAL RESEARCH. NEW YORK.
1959.

NANTOAX59027 ANTONOVSKY A   LERNER MJ
OCCUPATIONAL ASPIRATIONS OF LOWER-CLASS NEGRO AND WHITE
   YOUTH.
SOCIAL PROBLEMS, VOL 7, NO 2, FALL 1959. PP 132-138.

NAPPEJJ66805 APPEL JJ
AMERICAN NEGRO AND IMMIGRANT EXPERIENCES. SIMILARITIES AND
   DIFFERENCES.
AMERICAN QUARTERLY, VOL 18, NC 1, SPRING 1966. PP 96-103.

NAPTHHX46028 APTHEKER H
LITERACY, AND THE NEGRO AND WORLD-WAR-II.
JOURNAL OF NEGRO EDUCATION, VOL 15, 1946. PP 595-602.

NARISJM65029 ARISMAN JM
THE NEW NEGRO CASUALTIES. /OCCUPATIONS TEACHERS/
COMMONWEAL, VOL 83, NO 12, DEC 24, 1965. PP 372-373.

NARONSX64030 ARONOWITZ S
THE FATE OF THE UNIONS.
STUDIES ON THE LEFT, VOL 4, NO 1, WINTER 1964. PP 58-73.

NASHBBX61032 ASHBY B   ASHBY P
LABOR-MOBILITY IN THE SOUTHERN STATES.
INDUSTRIAL AND LABOR RELATIONS REVIEW, VOL 14, NO 3,
AP 1961. PP 432-445.

NASHMHS60033 ASHMORE HS
THE OTHER SIDE OF JORDAN. NEGROES OUTSIDE THE SOUTH.
WW NORTON. NEW JERSEY. 1960.

NASHXPX65031 ASH P
FAIR-EMPLOYMENT-PRACTICES-COMMISSION EXPERIENCES WITH
   PSYCHOLOGICAL TESTING.
AMERICAN PSYCHOLOGIST, VOL 20, NO 9, SEPT 1965. PP 797-798.

NAUGUTX47035 AUGUSTINE T
THE NEGRO STEELWORKERS OF PITTSBURGH AND THE UNIONS.
   /PENNSYLVANIA/
UNIVERSITY OF PITTSBURGH. MASTER-S THESIS. PITTSBURGH,
PENNSYLVANIA. 1947.

NAUGUTX58034 AUGUSTINE T
THE NEGROES PROGRESS TOWARD EMPLOYMENT EQUALITY.
PERSONNEL AND GUIDANCE JOURNAL, VOL 36, NO 9, MAY 1958.
PP 632-634.

NAUSUDP65036 AUSUBEL DP   AUSUBEL P
EGO DEVELOPMENT AMONG SEGREGATED NEGRO CHILDREN.
   /ASPIRATIONS/
EDUCATION IN DEPRESSED AREAS. ED BY A HARRY PASSOW, COLUMBIA
UNIVERSITY TEACHERS COLLEGE PRESS. NEW YORK. 1965.
PP 109-141.

NAWNEMX66875 AWNER M
OAKLAND LABOR BACKS UP YOUTH. /TRAINING/
THE AMERICAN FEDERATIONIST, VOL 73, NO 4, AP 1966. PP 14-16.

NBABOIX58893 BABOW I   HOWDEN E
A CIVIL RIGHTS INVENTORY OF SAN FRANCISCO. PART I. /UNION/
SAN FRANCISCO, COUNCIL FOR CIVIC UNITY. SAN FRANCISCO,
CALIFORNIA. JUNE 1958.

NBABOIX59038 BABOW I
VOCATIONAL GUIDANCE FOR MINORITY YOUTH.
UNIVERSITY OF CALIFORNIA, SCHOOL OF SOCIAL WELFARE.
BERKELEY, CALIFORNIA. 1959.

NBABOIX61037 BABOW I
MINORITY-GROUP INTEGRATION IN HOSPITALS.
UNIVERSITY OF CALIFORNIA, SCHOOL OF SOCIAL WELFARE.
BERKELEY, CALIFORNIA. 1961.

NBACKKX64039 BACK K   SIMPSON IH
THE DILEMMA OF THE NEGRO PROFESSIONAL.
JOURNAL OF SOCIAL ISSUES, VOL 20, NO 2, 1964. PP 60-70.

NBACKSX59040 BACKER S   HARRIS H
*NY STATE COMM AGAINST DISCR
PROGRESS TOWARD INTEGRATION. FOUR CASE-STUDIES. /EMPLOYMENT

FEPC NEW-YORK/
DISCRIMINATION AND LOW INCOMES. ED BY AARON ANTONOVSKY AND
LEWIS L LORWIN. NEW SCHOOL FOR SOCIAL RESEARCH. NEW YORK.
1959. PP 281-304.

NBACOEF63041 BACON EF
RACE-RELATIONS IN AN INDUSTRIAL SOCIETY. /EMPLOYMENT
GRIEVANCE-PROCEDURES/
RACE, VOL 4, NO 2, MAY 1963. PP 32-38.

NBAERMF61042 BAER MF
NEGRO EMPLOYMENT IN FEDERAL-GOVERNMENT.
PERSONNEL AND GUIDANCE JOURNAL, VOL 39, FEB 1961.

NBAGOBH64877 BAGDIKIAN BH
IN THE MIDST OF PLENTY. THE POOR IN AMERICA.
/ECONOMIC-STATUS/
BEACON PRESS. BOSTON, MASSACHUSETTS. 1964. 202 PP.

NBAILLH43043 BAILER LH
THE NEGRO AUTOMOBILE-WORKERS. /OCCUPATIONS/
JOURNAL OF POLITICAL ECONOMY, VOL 51, OCT 1943. PP 415-428.

NBAILLH43045 BAILER LH
NEGRO LABOR IN THE AUTO INDUSTRY.
UNIVERSITY OF MICHIGAN. PHD DISSERTATION. ANN ARBOR,
MICHIGAN. 1943.

NBAILLH53044 BAILER LH
THE NEGRO IN THE LABOR-FORCE OF THE UNITED-STATES.
JOURNAL OF NEGRO EDUCATION, VOL 22, NO 3, SUMMER 1953.
PP 297-306.

NBAINMX63046 BAIN M
ORGANIZED LABOR AND THE NEGRO WORKER. /UNION/
NATIONAL REVIEW, VOL 14, JUNE 4 1963.

NBALATR63047 BALAKRISHNAN TR
MIGRATION AND OPPORTUNITY. A STUDY OF STANDARD METROPOLITAN
AREAS IN THE UNITED-STATES.
UNIVERSITY OF MICHIGAN. UNPUBLISHED PHD DISSERTATION.
ANN ARBOR, MICHIGAN. 1963.

NBALTUL58048 BALTIMORE URBAN LEAGUE
TOWARD EQUALITY, BALTIMORE-S PROGRESS-REPORT, A CHRONICLE OF
PROGRESS SINCE WORLD-WAR-II TOWARD THE ACHIEVEMENT OF
EQUAL-RIGHTS AND OPPORTUNITIES FOR NEGROES IN MARYLAND
1946-1958.
BALTIMORE URBAN LEAGUE, THE SIDNEY HOLLANDER FOUNDATION.
BALTIMORE, MARYLAND. 1958. 92 PP.

NBALTUL62049 BALTIMORE URBAN LEAGUE
TOWARD EQUALITY, BALTIMORE-S PROGRESS-REPORT, 1962
SUPPLEMENT. /MARYLAND/
BALTIMORE URBAN LEAGUE. THE SIDNEY HOLLANDER FOUNDATION.
BALTIMORE, MARYLAND. 1962. 17 PP.

NBAMBJJ49050 BAMBRICK JJ   STIEGLITZ H
*NATL INDUSTRIAL CONF BOARD
NEGRO HIRING -- SOME CASE-STUDIES. /INDUSTRY/
NATIONAL INDUSTRIAL CONFERENCE BOARD, CONFERENCE BOARD
MANAGEMENT RECORD, DEC 1949. PP 520-522, 548-549.

NBANNWM65051 BANNER WM   *WICHITA URBAN LEAGUE
A REVIEW OF THE ECONOMIC AND CULTURAL PROBLEMS OF WICHITA,
KANSAS.
WICHITA URBAN LEAGUE. WICHITA, KANSAS. JAN-FEB 1965. 112 PP.

NBARBJX61052 BARBASH J
LABOR-S GRASS ROOTS. A STUDY OF THE LOCAL UNION.
HARPER. NEW YORK. 1961. 250 PP.

NBARDRX59878 BARDOLPH R
THE NEGRO VANGUARD. /CIVIL-RIGHTS/
HOLT, RINEHART AND WINSTON, INC. NEW YORK. 1959. 388 PP.

NBARKNX62053 BARKO N
DROPOUTS TO NOWHERE.
REPORTER, MAR 29, 1962.

NBAROHX63054 BARON H
NEGRO UNEMPLOYMENT. A CASE-STUDY.
NEW UNIVERSITY THOUGHT, VOL 3, SEPT-OCT 1963. PP 279-282.

NBAROHX66055 BARON H   HYMEN B
*US DEPARTMENT OF LABOR
THE NEGRO WORKER IN THE CHICAGO JOB-MARKET. /ILLINOIS/
US DEPARTMENT OF LABOR, EMPLOYMENT SERVICE REVIEW, VOL 3,
NO 8, AUG 1966. PP 32-34.

NBARRRS65056 BARRETT RS   *EDUCATIONAL TESTING SERVICE
DIFFERENTIAL SELECTION AMONG APPLICANTS FROM DIFFERENT
SOCIO-ECONOMIC AND ETHNIC BACKGROUNDS.
SELECTING AND TRAINING NEGROES FOR MANAGERIAL POSITIONS.
EDUCATIONAL TESTING SERVICE. PRINCETON, NEW JERSEY. 1965.
PP 91-102.

NBARTBX65057 BARTON B
MISSISSIPPI. BATTLEFRONT FOR LABOR. /UNION/
THE AMERICAN FEDERATIONIST, VOL 72, NO 10, OCT 1965.
PP 19-20.

NBATCAB61060 BATCHELDER AB
AN ECONOMICAL AND HISTORICAL ANALYSIS OF THE CAUSES OF
VARIATION AMONG NORTHERN STANDARD METROPOLITAN AREAS IN
PRODUCTIVITY OF NEGRO MEN IN 1949.
HARVARD UNIVERSITY. PHD DISSERTATION. CAMBRIDGE,
MASSACHUSETTS. 1961.

NBATCAB64058 BATCHELDER AB
DECLINE IN THE RELATIVE INCOME OF NEGRO MEN.
QUARTERLY JOURNAL OF ECONOMICS, VOL 78, NOV 1964.
PP 525-548.

NBATCAB65059 BATCHELDER AB
ECONOMIC FORCES SERVING THE ENDS OF THE NEGRO PROTEST.
/UNEMPLOYMENT/
ANNALS OF THE AMERICAN ACADEMY OF POLITICAL AND SOCIAL
SCIENCE, VOL 357, JAN 1965.

NBATCAB65061 BATCHELDER AB
POVERTY. THE SPECIAL CASE OF THE NEGRO.
AMERICAN ECONOMIC REVIEW, VOL 55, NO 2, MAY 1965. PP 530-540
ALSO IN THE ECONOMICS OF POVERTY. AN AMERICAN PARADOX. ED
BY BURTON A WEISROD. PRENTICE-HALL. ENGLEWOOD CLIFFS,
NEW JERSEY. 1965. ALSO IN POVERTY IN AMERICA. ED BY LOUIS A
FERMAN, JOYCE L KORNBLUH, AND ALAN HABER. UNIVERSITY OF
MICHIGAN PRESS. ANN ARBOR, MICHIGAN. 1965. PP 112-118.

NBATEWM66880 BATES WM   *US DEPT OF HEALTH ED WELFARE
NEGRO ADDICT OCCUPATIONAL HISTORY.
THE SOCIETY FOR THE STUDY OF SOCIAL PROBLEMS, 16TH ANNUAL
MEETING. PAPER. MIAMI BEACH, FLORIDA. AUG 27 1966.

NBATTEF49338 BATTLE EF
THE DETERMINATION OF CERTAIN MAJOR FACTORS AFFECTING THE
NEGRO VETERAN IN THE ON-THE-JOB TRAINING PROGRAM IN
VOCATIONAL AGRICULTURE IN THE STATE OF ALABAMA AS A BASIS
FOR PLANNING A MORE EFFECTIVE PROGRAM.
TUSKEGEE INSTITUTE. THESIS. TUSKEGEE, ALABAMA. 1949. 37 PP.

NBATTMX65313 BATTLE M   BARNETT J
THE NEGRO MATRIARCHY. /WOMEN ECONOMIC-STATUS/
AMERICAN CHILD, MAY 1965. PP 8-10.

NBEAKJR64062 BEAK JR
THE EMPLOYABILITY OF THE CHAMPAIGN-URBANA, ILLINOIS, NEGRO.
UNIVERSITY OF ILLINOIS, INSTITUTE OF LABOR AND INDUSTRIAL
RELATIONS. MASTER-S THESIS. CHAMPAIGN, ILLINOIS. 1964.

NBEALCL58064 BEALE CL   *US DEPARTMENT OF AGRICULTURE
NEGRO FARM OPERATORS. NUMBER, LOCATION AND RECENT TRENDS.
US DEPARTMENT OF AGRICULTURE. AGRICULTURAL MARKETING
SERVICE. GPO. WASHINGTON, DC. 1958.

NBEALCL66063 BEALE CL
THE NEGRO IN AMERICAN AGRICULTURE.
THE AMERICAN NEGRO REFERENCE BOOK. ED BY JOHN P DAVIS.
PRENTICE-HALL. ENGLEWOOD CLIFFS, NEW JERSEY. 1966.
PP 161-204.

NBEANKL47914 BEAN KL
NEGRO RESPONSES TO VERBAL AND NON-VERBAL TEST MATERIAL.
JOURNAL OF PSYCHOLOGY. VOL 16, 1947. PP 49-56.

NBEANLX63065 BEANE L
THE SQUARE AND I. /UNEMPLOYMENT YOUTH/
AMERICAN CHILD, VOL 45, NO 1, JAN 1963. PP 14-19.

NBEATWM60066 BEATTIE WM
THE AGING NEGRO. SOME IMPLICATIONS FOR SOCIAL-WELFARE
SERVICES.
PHYLON, VOL 21, NO 2, 2ND QUARTER 1960. PP 131-135.

NBEAUAG66067 BEAUMONT AG   *US DEPARTMENT OF LABOR
PLACEMENT AND CAREER COUNSELING AT PREDOMINANTLY NEGRO
COLLEGES.
US DEPARTMENT OF LABOR, EMPLOYMENT SERVICE REVIEW, VOL 3,
NO 8, AUG 1966. PP 4-6, 28.

NBECKGS62068 BECKER GS
DISCRIMINATION AND THE OCCUPATIONAL PROGRESS OF NEGROES.
A COMMENT.
REVIEW OF ECONOMICS AND STATISTICS, VOL 44, MAY 1962.
PP 214-215.

NBECKWL65069 BECKER WL
FAREWELL TO COLOR BLINDNESS.
PUBLIC PERSONNEL REVIEW, VOL 26, NO 3, JULY 1965.
PP 147-150.

NBEDEMS53071 BEDELL MS   *US DEPARTMENT OF LABOR
EMPLOYMENT AND INCOME OF NEGRO WORKERS. 1940-1952.
US DEPARTMENT OF LABOR, MONTHLY LABOR REVIEW, VOL 76,
JUNE 1953. PP 596-601.

NBEEGJA63072 BEEGLE JA   *NATL COMT FOR CHILDREN YOUTH
SOME DEMOGRAPHIC CHARACTERISTICS OF RURAL YOUTH.
NATIONAL COMMITTEE FOR CHILDREN AND YOUTH. WASHINGTON, DC.
SEPT 1963. 11 PP.

NBELLDX58029 BELL D
THE INVISIBLE UNEMPLOYED.
FORTUNE, JULY 1958. PP 105-110 FF.

NBELLDX63073 BELL D
REFLECTIONS ON THE NEGRO AND LABOR. /UNION/
NEW LEADER, VOL 46, JAN 21 1963. PP 18-20.

NBELLRR65074 BELL RR
LOWER-CLASS NEGRO MOTHERS ASPIRATIONS FOR THEIR CHILDREN.
SOCIAL FORCES, VOL 43, MAY 1965. PP 493-500.

NBENNLX65881 BENNETT L
CONFRONTATION. BLACK AND WHITE. /CIVIL-RIGHTS/
JOHNSON PUBLISHING CO. CHICAGO, ILLINOIS. 1965. 317 PP.

NBENNWS64574 BENNETT WS   GIST NP
CLASS AND FAMILY INFLUENCES ON STUDENT ASPIRATIONS.
SOCIAL FORCES, VOL 43, NO 2, DEC 1964. PP 167-173.

NBERGMX54076 BERGER M   *UNESCO
RACIAL EQUALITY AND THE LAW. THE ROLE OF LAW IN THE
REDUCTION OF DISCRIMINATION IN THE UNITED-STATES.
UNITED NATIONS EDUCATION. SCIENTIFIC AND CULTURAL
ORGANIZATION. MARCH 1954. PARIS, FRANCE. 76 PP.

NBERNEH46077 BERNERT EH   FRAZIER FE
CHILDREN AND INCOME IN NEGRO FAMILIES.
SOCIAL FORCES, VOL 25, NO 2, DEC 1946. PP 178-182.

NBERNVH43555 BERNSTEIN VH
THE ANTI-LABOR FRONT. /UNION/
THE ANTIOCH REVIEW, VOL 3, NO 3, FALL 1943. PP 328-340.

NBERSLE66078 BERSON LE
CASE-STUDY OF A RIOT THE PHILADELPHIA STORY. /PENNSYLVANIA/
INSTITUTE OF HUMAN RELATIONS PRESS. PAMPHLET SERIES NO 7.
1966.

NBERTAL62882 BERTRAND AL
SCHOOL ATTENDANCE AND ATTAINMENT, FUNCTION AND DYSFUNCTION
OF SCHOOL AND FAMILY SOCIAL SYSTEMS.
/EMPLOYMENT DROP-OUT/
SOCIAL FORCES, VOL 40, NO 3, MAR 1962. PP 228-233.

NBERTAL65394 BERTRAND AL   BEALE CL
THE FRENCH AND THE NON-FRENCH IN LOUISIANA. A STUDY OF THE
RELEVANCE OF ETHNIC FACTORS IN RURAL DEVELOPMENT.
/ECONOMIC-STATUS/
LOUISIANA STATE UNIVERSITY. BATON ROUGE, LOUISIANA.
DEC 1965. 43 PP.

NBILLAX65499 BILLINGSLEY A   BILLINGSLEY AT
NEGRO FAMILY LIFE IN AMERICA.
SOCIAL SERVICE REVIEW, VOL 39, SEPT 1965. PP 310-319.

NBINDAM61079 BINDMAN AM
A STUDY OF THE NEGRO COMMUNITY IN CHAMPAIGN-URBANA,
ILLINOIS.

UNIVERSITY OF ILLINOIS. UNPUBLISHED MASTER-S THESIS.
CHAMPAIGN, ILLINOIS. 1961.

NBINDAM66139   BINDMAN   AM
PRE-COLLEGE PREPARATION OF NEGRO STUDENTS.
JOURNAL OF NEGRO EDUCATION, VOL 35, NO 4, FALL 1966.
PP 313-321.

NBIRDCX63080   BIRD   C
MORE ROOM AT THE TOP. COMPANY EXPERIENCE IN EMPLOYING
    NEGROES IN PROFESSIONAL AND MANAGEMENT JOBS. /INDUSTRY/
MANAGEMENT REVIEW, VOL 52, NO 3, MAR 1963. PP 4-16.

NBLACLE63493   BLACK   LE
NEGRO MARKET. GROWING, CHANGING, CHALLENGING.
SALES MANAGEMENT, VOL 91, OCT 4 1963. PP 42-47.

NBLAIGE66C81   BLAIR   GE
EDUCATE THE BLACK ONE TOO.
NEW YORK STATE EDUCATION, MAR 1966. 3 PP.

NBLALHM56C83   BLALOCK   HM
ECONOMIC DISCRIMINATION AND NEGRO INCREASES.
AMERICAN SOCIOLOGICAL REVIEW, VOL 21, NO 5, OCT 1956.
PP 584-588.

NBLALHM57085   BLALOCK   HM
PERCENT NONWHITE AND DISCRIMINATION IN THE SOUTH.
AMERICAN SOCIOLOGICAL REVIEW, VOL 22, DEC 1957. PP 677-682.

NBLALHM58084   BLALOCK   HM
EDUCATIONAL ACHIEVEMENT AND JOB-OPPORTUNITIES. A VICIOUS
    CIRCLE.
JOURNAL OF NEGRO EDUCATION, VOL 27, NO 4, FALL 1958.
PP 253-262.

NBLALHM59086   BLALOCK   HM
URBANIZATION AND DISCRIMINATION IN THE SOUTH.
SOCIAL PROBLEMS, VOL 7, 1959. PP 151 FF.

NBLANJW64917   BLANTON   JW   *EDUCATIONAL TESTING SERVICE
ON-THE-JOB EXPERIENCES OF NEGRO MANAGERS.
SELECTING AND TRAINING NEGROES FOR MANAGERIAL POSITIONS.
PROCEEDINGS OF THE EXECUTIVE STUDY CONFERENCE, EDUCATIONAL
TESTING SERVICE. PRINCETON, NEW JERSEY. NOV 10-11, 1964.
PP 141-154.

NBLOCHD55082   BLOCH   HD
THE CIRCLE OF DISCRIMINATION AGAINST NEGROES.
PHYLON, VOL 16, NO 3, 1955. PP 253-262.

NBLOCHD57088   BLOCH   HD
CRAFT UNIONS. A LINK IN THE CIRCLE OF NEGRO DISCRIMINATION.
PHYLON, VOL 18, NO 4, 1957. PP 361-373.

NBLOCHD58C87   BLOCH   HD
CRAFT UNIONS AND THE NEGRO IN HISTORICAL PERSPECTIVE.
JOURNAL OF NEGRO HISTORY, VOL 43, JAN 1958. PP 10-33.

NBLOCHD59C90   BLOCH   HD
THE EMPLOYMENT OF THE NEW-YORK NEGRO IN RETROSPECT.
PHYLON, VOL 20, NO 4, 1959. PP 327-344.

NBLOCHD62091   BLOCH   HD
NEGROES AND ORGANIZED LABOR. /UNION/
JOURNAL OF HUMAN RELATIONS, VOL 10, SUMMER 1962. PP 357-374.

NBLOCHD65089   BLOCH   HD
DISCRIMINATION AGAINST THE NEGRO IN EMPLOYMENT IN NEW-YORK,
    1920-1963.
THE AMERICAN JOURNAL OF ECONOMICS AND SOCIOLOGY, VOL 24,
OCT 1965. PP 361-382.

NBLOCHD66092   BLOCH   HD
SOME EFFECTS OF DISCRIMINATION IN EMPLOYMENT.
AMERICAN JOURNAL OF ECONOMICS AND SOCIOLOGY, VOL 25, NO 1,
JAN 1966. PP 11-25.

NBLOOGF50095   BLOOM   GF   NORTHRUP   HR
LABOR AND LABORING CLASSES.
BLAKISTON. PHILADELPHIA, PENNSYLVANIA. 1950. 749 PP.

NBLOOJW64093   BLOOD   JW ED   *AMERICAN MANAGEMENT ASSN
THE PERSONNEL JOB IN A CHANGING WORLD. /INDUSTRY/
AMERICAN MANAGEMENT ASSOCIATION. NEW YORK. 1964.

NBLOOJRO55094   BLOOD   RO
DISCRIMINATION WITHOUT PREJUDICE. /INDUSTRY/
SOCIAL PROBLEMS, VOL 3, NO 2, OCT 1955. PP 114-117.

NBLOORX63096   BLOOM   R   WHITEMAN   M
DEUTSCH   M
RACE AND SOCIAL-CLASS AS SEPARATE FACTORS RELATED TO SOCIAL
    ENVIRONMENT. /ASPIRATIONS/
AMERICAN JOURNAL OF SOCIOLOGY, VOL 70, JAN 1965. PP 471-476.
ALSO AMERICAN PSYCHOLOGICAL ASSOCIATION MEETING, PAPER.
PHILADELPHIA, PENNSYLVANIA. SEPT 1963.

NBLUEJT47256   BLUE   JT
ORGANIZED LABOR AND MINORITY-GROUPS POLICY AND PRACTICES.
    /UNION/
THE QUARTERLY REVIEW OF HIGHER EDUCATION AMONG NEGROES, VOL
15, NO 3, JULY 1947. PP 170-177.

NBLUEJT48C97   BLUE   JT
THE RELATIONSHIP OF JUVENILE-DELINQUENCY, RACE, AND ECONOMIC
    STATUS.
JOURNAL OF NEGRO EDUCATION, VOL 17, 1948. PP 469-477.

NBLUMAA66099   BLUM   AA   SCHMIDT   CT
SECURING SKILLS NEEDED FOR SUCCESS. COMMUNITY JOB TRAINING
    FOR NEGROES.
MANAGEMENT OF PERSONNEL QUARTERLY, VOL 5, NO 3, FALL 1966.
PP 30-35.

NBLUMAA67C98   BLUM   AA   SCHMIDT   CT
JOB TRAINING THROUGH ADULT-EDUCATION.
EMPLOYMENT, RACE AND POVERTY. ED BY ARTHUR M ROSS AND
HERBERT HILL. HARCOURT, BRACE, AND WORLD. NEW YORK. 1967.
PP 460-478.

NBLUMHX65100   BLUMER   H
INDUSTRIALIZATION AND RACE-RELATIONS.
INDUSTRIALIZATION AND RACE RELATIONS, -- A SYMPOSIUM. ED BY
GUY HUNTER. OXFORD UNIVERSITY PRESS. NEW YORK. 1965.
PP 220-253.

NBLUMHX65327   BLUMER   H
THE FUTURE OF THE COLOR LINE. /SOUTH/
THE SOUTH IN CONTINUITY AND CHANGE. ED BY JOHN C MCKINNEY

AND EDGAR T THOMPSON. DUKE UNIVERSITY PRESS. DURHAM,
NORTH CAROLINA. 1965. PP 322-336.

NBOATRF49345   BOATWRIGHT   RF
THE ORIGIN AND DEVELOPMENT OF THE NEGRO VISITING TEACHER IN
    ALABAMA. /OCCUPATIONS/
TUSKEGEE INSTITUTE. THESIS. TUSKEGEE, ALABAMA. 1949. 66 PP.

NBOGGJX63101   BOGGS   J
THE AMERICAN REVOLUTION. PAGES FROM A NEGRO WORKER-S
    NOTEBOOK.
MONTHLY REVIEW, VOL 15, JULY AND AUG 1963. PP 13-93.

NBOGUDJ54102   BOGUE   DJ
POPULATION DISTRIBUTION AND COMPOSITION IN THE NEW SOUTH.
THE NEW SOUTH AND HIGHER EDUCATION. ED BY JESSIE P GUZMAN.
TUSKEGEE INSTITUTE. TUSKEGEE, ALABAMA. 1954.

NBOLTBX60398   BOLTON   B
INCOME AND RELATED CHARACTERISTICS OF RURAL HOUSEHOLDS IN
    THE CENTRAL LOUISIANA MIXED FARMING AREA.
LOUISIANA STATE UNIVERSITY. BATON ROUGE, LOUISIANA.
MAR 1960. 91 PP.

NBOLTBX61396   BOLTON   B
RESOURCE USE AND ADJUSTMENT. RURAL FAMILIES IN THE CENTRAL
    LOUISIANA MIXED FARMING AREA.
LOUISIANA STATE UNIVERSITY. BATON ROUGE, LOUISIANA.
JUNE 1961. 75 PP.

NBOLTBX62399   BOLTON   B
FARM INCOME PREDICTIONS FOR SMALL FARMS IN THE CENTRAL
    LOUISIANA MIXED FARMING AREA.
LOUISIANA STATE UNIVERSITY. BATON ROUGE, LOUISIANA.
AP 1962. 33 PP.

NBONDHM58497   BOND   HM
CAT ON A HOT TIN ROOF. /TESTING/
JOURNAL OF NEGRO EDUCATION, VOL 27, FALL 1958. PP 519-523.

NBONDHM60888   BOND   HM
WASTED TALENT. /EDUCATION/
THE NATION-S CHILDREN. VOL 2. ED BY ELI GINZBERG. COLUMBIA
UNIVERSITY PRESS. NEW YORK. 1960. PP 116-137.

NBONDHM66103   BOND   HM
THE NEGRO SCHOLAR AND PROFESSIONAL IN AMERICA.
THE AMERICAN NEGRO REFERENCE BOOK. ED BY JOHN P DAVIS.
PRENTICE-HALL. ENGLEWOOD CLIFFS, NEW JERSEY. 1966.
PP 548-589.

NBOYDWM46252   BOYD   WM
NEGROES AND GOVERNMENTAL SERVICES. AN APPRAISAL.
THE QUARTERLY REVIEW OF HIGHER EDUCATION AMONG NEGROES, VOL
14, NO 2, AP 1946. PP 49-54.

NBOYERO55105   BOYER   RO   MORAIS   HM
LABOR-S UNTOLD STORY. /UNION/
CAMERON ASSOCIATES. NEW YORK. 1955. 402 PP.

NBRADCX57107   BRADEN   C
LABOR AND THE SOUTHERN NEGRO.
AMERICAN SOCIALIST, FEB 1957. PP 8-12.

NBRADWC53106   BRADBURY   WC
RACIAL DISCRIMINATION IN THE FEDERAL SERVICE. A STUDY IN THE
    SOCIOLOGY OF ADMINISTRATION.
UNIVERSITY MICROFILMS. PUBLICATION NO 4557. ANN ARBOR,
MICHIGAN. 1953. ALSO AT COLUMBIA UNIVERSITY. THESIS.
NEW YORK. 1953.

NBRAGEW63312   BRAGG   EW
CHANGES AND CHALLENGES IN THE 60-S. /INTEGRATION
    TECHNOLOGICAL-CHANGE   TEACHER/
JOURNAL OF NEGRO EDUCATION, WINTER 1963. PP 25-33.

NBRAZBR46108   BRAZEAL   BR
THE BROTHERHOOD OF SLEEPING CAR PORTERS. /UNION/
HARPER. NEW YORK. 1946.

NBRAZWF58111   BRAZZIEL   WF
MEETING THE PSYCHOLOGICAL CRISES OF NEGRO YOUTH THROUGH A
    COORDINATED GUIDANCE SERVICE.
JOURNAL OF NEGRO EDUCATION, VOL 27, NO 1, WINTER 1958.
PP 79-83.

NBRAZWF60109   BRAZZIEL   WF
CURRICULUM CHOICE IN THE NEGRO COLLEGE.
JOURNAL OF NEGRO EDUCATION, VOL 29, NO 2, SPRING 1960.
PP 207-209.

NBRAZWF60112   BRAZZIEL   WF
OCCUPATIONAL CHOICE IN THE NEGRO COLLEGE.
PERSONNEL AND GUIDANCE JOURNAL, VOL 39, NO 9, 1960.
PP 739-742.

NBRAZWF64285   BRAZZIEL   WF   *VIRGINIA STATE COLLEGE
WORKING WITH STUDENTS INSIDE AND OUTSIDE THE CLASSROOM IN
    ADULT BASIC EDUCATION PROGRAMS.
VIRGINIA STATE COLLEGE. NORFOLK, VIRGINIA. OCT 1964. 7 PP.

NBRAZWF64318   BRAZZIEL   WF   *VIRGINIA STATE COLLEGE
*US DEPARTMENT OF LABOR
FACTORS IN WORKERS DECISIONS TO FOREGO RETRAINING UNDER THE
    MANPOWER-DEVELOPMENT-AND-RETRAINING-ACT.
VIRGINIA STATE COLLEGE, NORFOLK DIVISION. US DEPARTMENT OF
LABOR, OFFICE OF MANPOWER, AUTOMATION AND TRAINING. NORFOLK,
VIRGINIA. JUNE 1964. 57 PP.

NBRAZWF64496   BRAZZIEL   WF
CORRELATES OF SOUTHERN NEGRO PERSONALITY.
JOURNAL OF SOCIAL ISSUES, VOL 20, NO 2, 1964.

NBRAZWF66110   BRAZZIEL   WF
MANPOWER TRAINING AND THE NEGRO WORKER.
JOURNAL OF NEGRO EDUCATION, WINTER 1966. PP 83-87.

NBREIGX52113   BREITMAN   G
NEGRO PROGRESS. WHAT THE FACTS SHOW.
FOURTH INTERNATIONAL, VOL 13, NOV 1952. PP 173-178.

NBRIMAF64891   BRIMMER   AF   *US DEPARTMENT OF COMMERCE
ECONOMIC TRENDS IN THE NEGRO MARKET. /ECONOMIC-STATUS/
MARKETING INFORMATION GUIDE, US DEPARTMENT OF COMMERCE.
GPO. WASHINGTON, DC. MAY 1964. PP 3-7.

NBRIMAF65890   BRIMMER   AF
DESEGREGATION AND THE ECONOMIC FUTURE OF THE NEGRO
    MIDDLE-CLASS.
BOOKER T WASHINGTON ASSOCIATION, 35TH ANNUAL DINNER.

DETROIT, MICHIGAN. JULY 16 1965.

NBRIMAF66114   BRIMMER AF   *US DEPARTMENT OF COMMERCE
ECONOMIC PROGRESS IN BLACK AND WHITE.
US DEPARTMENT OF COMMERCE, OFFICE OF THE SECRETARY. GPO.
WASHINGTON, DC. 1966. SPEECH BY ASSISTANT SECRETARY OF
COMMERCE FOR ECONOMIC AFFAIRS AT ANNUAL BANQUET OF THE
HOUSTON CITIZENS CHAMBER OF COMMERCE. HOUSTON, TEXAS. JAN
21, 1966.

NBRIMAF66115   BRIMMER AF
THE NEGRO IN THE NATIONAL ECONOMY.
THE AMERICAN NEGRO REFERENCE BOOK. ED BY JOHN P DAVIS.
PRENTICE-HALL. ENGLEWOOD CLIFFS, NEW JERSEY. 1966.
PP 251-336.

NBRINWX64116   BRINK W   HARRIS L
THE NEGRO REVOLUTION IN AMERICA.
SIMON AND SCHUSTER. NEW YORK. 1964.

NBRITNX54892   BRITTIN N
NON-SEGREGATION, OR QUALITY IN SCHOOLS OF THE DEEP SOUTH.
/ECONOMIC-STATUS/
ANTIOCH REVIEW, VOL 14, NO 4, DEC 1954. PP 387-397.

NBRONCA51337   BRONSON CA
FACTORS AFFECTING THE PRESENT FARMING PROGRAMS OF ONE
HUNDRED NEGRO FARMS IN THE PATRONAGE AREA OF THE MACON
COUNTY TRAINING SCHOOL, IN ALABAMA, WITH EMPHASIS FOR
IMPROVEMENT.
TUSKEGEE INSTITUTE. THESIS. TUSKEGEE, ALABAMA. 1951. 88 PP.

NBROOAD62117   BROOKS AD
A BIBLIOGRAPHY OF CIVIL-RIGHTS AND CIVIL-LIBERTIES.
/EMPLOYMENT UNION MILITARY/
CIVIL LIBERTIES EDUCATIONAL FOUNDATION. NEW YORK. 1962.
151 PP.

NBROOLX65123   BROOM L   GLENN ND
TRANSFORMATION OF THE NEGRO-AMERICAN. /EDUCATION
EMPLOYMENT INCOME/
HARPER AND ROW. NEW YORK. 1965. 207 PP.

NBROOLX65124   BROOM L   GLENN ND
WHEN WILL AMERICA-S NEGROES CATCH UP. /EMPLOYMENT/
NEW SOCIETY, MAR 25 1965. PP 6-7.

NBROOTR61119   BROOKS TR
NEGRO AMERICAN LABOR COUNCIL IS ACTIVE IN NEW-YORK STATE.
INDUSTRIAL BULLETIN, VOL 40, AP 1961. PP 2-6.

NBROOTR61120   BROOKS TR
NEGROES AT WORK.
COMMONWEAL, MAR 10 1961.

NBROOTR61121   BROOKS TR
NEGRO MILITANTS, JEWISH LIBERALS, AND THE UNIONS.
COMMENTARY, VOL 32, SEPT 1961. PP 209-216.

NBROOTR63118   BROOKS TR
MANAGING YOUR MANPOWER. NEGRO EMPLOYMENT PROBLEM.
DUN-S REVIEW, VOL 82, AUG 1963. PP 59-62.

NBROOTX62122   BROOKS T
THE NEGRO-S PLACE AT LABOR-S TABLE. /UNION/
THE REPORTER, VOL 27, DEC 6 1962. PP 38-39.

NBROOTX66631   BROOKS T
NEW SQUEEZE ON CONSTRUCTION. /UNION/
THE NEW LEADER, VOL 48, NO 17, AUG 29 1966. PP 6-11.

NBROWAX58893   BROWN A
GRADUATE AND PROFESSIONAL EDUCATION IN NEGRO INSTITUTIONS.
/ECONOMIC-STATUS/
JOURNAL OF NEGRO EDUCATION, VOL 27, SUMMER 1958.

NBROWAX60125   BROWN A
THE NEGRO GRADUATE, 1950-1960. /COLLEGE EDUCATION/
NEGRO EDUCATIONAL REVIEW, VOL 11, NO 2, AP 1960. PP 71-81.

NBROWHX63894   BROWN H
NEGRO UNEMPLOYMENT. A CASE-STUDY.
NEW UNVERSITY THOUGHT, VOL 3, NO 2, SEPT-OCT 1963. PP 41-48.

NBROWMC55126   BROWN MC
THE STATUS OF JOBS AND OCCUPATIONS AS EVALUATED BY AN URBAN
NEGRO SAMPLE.
AMERICAN SOCIOLOGICAL REVIEW, VOL 20, NO 5, OCT 1955.
PP 561-566.

NBROWRG65895   BROWN RG
A COMPARISON OF THE VOCATIONAL ASPIRATIONS OF PAIRED
SIXTH-GRADE WHITE AND NEGRO CHILDREN WHO ATTEND
SEGREGATED SCHOOLS.
JOURNAL OF EDUCATIONAL RESEARCH, VOL 58, NO 9, MAY-JUNE
1965. PP 402-404.

NBROWVJ54127   BROWNE VJ
RACIAL DESEGREGATION IN THE PUBLIC SERVICE, WITH PARTICULAR
REFERENCE TO THE US GOVERNMENT.
JOURNAL OF NEGRO EDUCATION, VOL 23, SUMMER 1954. PP 242-248.

NBRUNDX60128   BRUNER D
THE NEGRO BIDS FOR UNION POWER.
THE NATION, MAR 5 1960.

NBRYSWO43129   BRYSON WO
WAR INDUSTRY EMPLOYMENT FOR NEGROES IN MARYLAND.
PHYLON, VOL 4, NO 3, 3RD QUARTER 1943. PP 264-269.

NBUCKLF61130   BUCKLEY LF
DISCRIMINATORY ASPECTS OF THE LABOR MARKET OF THE 60-S.
REVIEW OF SOCIAL ECONOMY, VOL 19, NO 1, MAR 1961.

NBUGGJA66131   BUGGS JA
REPORT FROM LOS-ANGELES. /CALIFORNIA/
JOURNAL OF INTERGROUP RELATIONS, AUTUMN 1966. PP 27-40.

NBULLHA50132   BULLOCK HA
A COMPARISON OF THE ACADEMIC ACHIEVEMENTS OF WHITE AND NEGRO
HIGH SCHOOL GRADUATES. /EDUCATION/
JOURNAL OF EDUCATIONAL RESEARCH, VOL 44, 1950. PP 179-192.

NBULLHA51133   BULLOCK HA
RACIAL ATTITUDES AND THE EMPLOYMENT OF NEGROES.
AMERICAN JOURNAL OF SOCIOLOGY, VOL 56, NO 5, MAR 1951.
PP 438-447.

NBULLPXND134   BULLOCK P
EMPLOYMENT AND TRAINING, THE MCCONE-REPORT -- SIX MONTHS

LATER.
UNIVERSITY OF CALIFORNIA, INSTITUTE OF INDUSTRIAL RELATIONS.
UNPUBLISHED PAPER. LOS ANGELES, CALIFORNIA. ND. 16 PP.

NBULLPX65138   BULLOCK P
POVERTY IN THE GHETTO.
FRONTIER, OCT 1965. PP 5-7. ALSO UNIVERSITY OF CALIFORNIA,
INSTITUTE OF INDUSTRIAL RELATIONS. REPRINT NO 161.
LOS ANGELES, CALIFORNIA. 1966. 6PP.

NBULLPX65483   BULLOCK P   *UCLA INSTITUTE OF IND RELS
FINAL REPORT. EMPLOYMENT AND TRAINING, REPORT FOR GOVERNOR-S
COMMISSION.
UNIVERSITY OF CALIFORNIA, INSTITUTE OF INDUSTRIAL RELATIONS.
LOS ANGELES, CALIFORNIA. UNPUBLISHED PAPER. NOV 9 1965.

NBULLPX66135   BULLOCK P
FIGHTING POVERTY. THE VIEW FROM WATTS. /LOS-ANGELES
CALIFORNIA/
INDUSTRIAL RELATIONS RESEARCH ASSOCIATION, 19TH ANNUAL
MEETING, PAPER. SAN FRANCISCO, CALIFORNIA. DEC 29 1966.
20 PP.

NBULLPX66898   BULLOCK P
SUMMARY OF MAJOR POINTS, TALK ON EMPLOYMENT,
MCCONE-COMMISSION SERIES.
UNIVERSITY OF CALIFORNIA, INSTITUTE OF INDUSTRIAL RELATIONS.
UNPUBLISHED PAPER. LOS ANGELES, CALIFORNIA. JUNE 5 1966.
3 PP.

NBUNKHC65122   BUNKE HC
ETHNOMICS -- NEGRO MUST BE FULL PARTICIPANT IN MARKET PLACE.
BUSINESS AND SOCIETY, SPRING 1965. PP 3-9.

NBURENA65137   BUREAU OF NATIONAL AFFAIRS
THE NEGRO AND TITLE-VII.
BUREAU OF NATIONAL AFFAIRS, SURVEY NO 77. WASHINGTON, DC.
1965. 17 PP.

NBURGME65140   BURGESS ME
RACE-RELATIONS AND SOCIAL-CHANGE.
THE SOUTH IN CONTINUITY AND CHANGE. ED BY JOHN C MCKINNEY
AND EDGAR T THOMPSON. DUKE UNIVERSITY PRESS. DURHAM, NORTH
CAROLINA. 1965. PP 337-358.

NBURNHX63902   BURNS H
THE VOICES OF NEGRO PROTEST IN AMERICA.
OXFORD UNIVERSITY PRESS. NEW YORK. 1963. 88 PP.

NBUSIMX64142   BUSINESS MANAGEMENT
JOBS FOR NEGROES. ONE COMPANY-S ANSWER. /CASE-STUDY
INDUSTRY/
BUSINESS MANAGEMENT, VOL 25, NO 5, FEB 1964. PP 42-45.

NBUSIWX45161   BUSINESS WEEK
SEGREGATION DEAL. NEW-ORLEANS REGION FEPC PERMITS
COMPROMISE. /LOUISIANA/
BUSINESS WEEK, MAY 19 1945. P 107.

NBUSIWX51164   BUSINESS WEEK
UNION FIGHTS DISCRIMINATION.
BUSINESS WEEK, OCT 6 1951. P 40 PLUS.

NBUSIWX54879   BUSINESS WEEK
UNION BIAS.
BUSINESS WEEK, AP 10 1954. P 168.

NBUSIWX56160   BUSINESS WEEK
RACE ISSUE AND UNIONS IN THE SOUTH.
BUSINESS WEEK, AP 14 1956.

NBUSIWX56882   BUSINESS WEEK
SOUTH-S TENSION SEIZES LABOR. /UNION/
BUSINESS WEEK, AP 14 1956. PP 47-48.

NBUSIWX58165   BUSINESS WEEK
WHAT MASSIVE RESISTANCE COSTS NORFOLK AND ITS BUSINESSMEN.
/VIRGINIA/
BUSINESS WEEK, OCT 4 1958. PP 32-34.

NBUSIWX58880   BUSINESS WEEK
RACE PROBLEMS BUILD UP FOR UNIONS.
BUSINESS WEEK, MAY 17 1958. P 138.

NBUSIWX60147   BUSINESS WEEK
A CAREER BREAK FOR NON-WHITES.
BUSINESS WEEK, JAN 2 1960. P 90.

NBUSIWX60152   BUSINESS WEEK
LABOR-NEGRO DIVISION WIDENS. /UNION/
BUSINESS WEEK, JULY 9 1960.

NBUSIWX60155   BUSINESS WEEK
NEGRO PRESSURE ON UNIONS.
BUSINESS WEEK, AP 30 1960. PP 139-141.

NBUSIWX60157   BUSINESS WEEK
NEGRO UNIONISTS ORGANIZE FOR ACTION.
BUSINESS WEEK, JUNE 4 1960. P 80.

NBUSIWX60162   BUSINESS WEEK
SOUTH-S RACE DISPUTES INVOLVE BUSINESSMAN.
BUSINESS WEEK, DEC 17 1960. PP 32, 34.

NBUSIWX61144   BUSINESS WEEK
AFL-CIO COUNCIL GETS NEGRO DEMAND FOR MORE ACTION ON BIAS IN
UNIONS.
BUSINESS WEEK, MAR 4 1961. P 90.

NBUSIWX61145   BUSINESS WEEK
BILLION-DOLLAR PRIZE SPURS INTEGRATION. /INDUSTRY GEORGIA/
BUSINESS WEEK, JUNE 3, 1961.

NBUSIWX61158   BUSINESS WEEK
NEW BUSINESS WAYS IN THE SOUTH.
BUSINESS WEEK, AUG 5 1961. PP 58-63.

NBUSIWX62146   BUSINESS WEEK
BRINGING BETTER JOBS TO NEGROES. /EMPLOYMENT-AGENCY/
BUSINESS WEEK, NOV 3 1962.

NBUSIWX62153   BUSINESS WEEK
MORE RACE PRESSURE ON BUSINESS.
BUSINESS WEEK, MAY 12 1962. PP 130, 132.

NBUSIWX62156   BUSINESS WEEK
THE NEGRO-S FORCE IN MARKETPLACE. /EMPLOYMENT/
BUSINESS WEEK, MAY 26 1962. PP 76-84.

NBUSIWX62159   BUSINESS WEEK

THE PRICE OF DEFIANCE. /MISSISSIPPI RACE/
BUSINESS WEEK, OCT 6 1962. PP 31-32.

NBUSIWX63148 BUSINESS WEEK
CARRYING OUT A PLAN FOR JOB INTEGRATION AND DOING IT -- IN
THE HEART OF GEORGIA -- WITHOUT A SINGLE UNPLEASANT
INCIDENT. THAT-S THE EXPERIENCE OF LOCKHEED AIRCRAFT
CORPORATION AT ITS MARIETTA PLANT. /INDUSTRY/
BUSINESS WEEK, AP 13 1963. PP 90, 92, 96.

NBUSIWX63149 BUSINESS WEEK
DETROIT FEELS BRUNT OF NEGRO PRESSURE. /MICHIGAN/
BUSINESS WEEK, JUNE 29, 1963.

NBUSIWX63154 BUSINESS WEEK
THE NEGRO DRIVE FOR JOBS.
BUSINESS WEEK, AUG 17 1963. PP 52-54, FF.
PP 52-54, 56-58, 60, 65-70, 72, 74.

NBUSIWX64143 BUSINESS WEEK
AIDING NEGRO BUSINESSMEN. SMALL BUSINESS OPPORTUNITIES
CORPORATION, PHILADELPHIA. /PENNSYLVANIA/
BUSINESS WEEK, AP 18 1964.

NBUSIWX64297 BUSINESS WEEK
INDUSTRY RUSHES FOR NEGRO GRADS.
BUSINESS WEEK, AP 25 1964. PP 78-82.

NBUSIWX64298 BUSINESS WEEK
CHICAGO STARTS MOVING ON EQUAL JOB QUESTION. /ILLINOIS/
BUSINESS WEEK, MAY 30 1964. PP 22-23.

NBUSIWX64887 BUSINESS WEEK
NLRB CRACKS DOWN ON UNION BIAS.
BUSINESS WEEK, JULY 11 1964. P 50.

NBUSIWX65150 BUSINESS WEEK
HIRING TESTS WAIT FOR THE SCORE. MYART VS MOTOROLA.
BUSINESS WEEK, FEB 13 1965. PP 45-46.

NBUSIWX65151 BUSINESS WEEK
JOBS FOR NEGROES -- THE GAINS, THE PROBLEMS, AND THE NEW
HIRING LAW. /TITLE-VII/
BUSINESS WEEK, JUNE 12 1965. PP 82-106.

NCAGLLT66904 CAGLE LT   BAKER J
A COMPARISON OF THE SOCIAL CHARACTERISTICS AND EDUCATIONAL
ASPIRATIONS OF NORTHERN, LOWER-CLASS, NEGRO PARENTS WHO
ACCEPTED AND DECLINED AN OPPORTUNITY FOR INTEGRATED
EDUCATION FOR THEIR CHILDREN.
THE SOCIETY FOR THE STUDY OF SOCIAL PROBLEMS, 16TH ANNUAL
MEETING. PAPER. MIAMI BEACH, FLORIDA. AUG 27 1966.

NCALDIR63167 CAL DEPT OF INDUSTRIAL RELS
NEGRO CALIFORNIANS, POPULATION, EMPLOYMENT, INCOME,
EDUCATION.
CALIFORNIA, DEPARTMENT OF INDUSTRIAL RELATIONS, DIVISION OF
FAIR EMPLOYMENT PRACTICES. SAN FRANCISCO, CALIFORNIA. JUNE
1963. 34 PP.

NCALEWC56069 CALEF WC   NELSON HJ
DISTRIBUTION OF NEGRO POPULATION IN THE UNITED STATES.
/DEMOGRAPHY/
GEOGRAPHICAL REVIEW, VOL 46, JAN 1956. PP 82-97.

NCALFEP66169 CALIFORNIA FEPC
INTERIM REPORT ON OAKLAND SCHOOLS. /CALIFORNIA/
CALIFORNIA, FAIR EMPLOYMENT PRACTICE COMMISSION. STATEMENT
BY C L DELLUMS, CHAIRMAN, TO OAKLAND SCHOOL BOARD, JAN 18
1966. SAN FRANCISCO, CALIFORNIA. JAN 13 1966. 6 PP.

NCALFES63172 CALIFORNIA SES
THE ECONOMIC-STATUS OF NEGROES IN THE SAN-FRANCISCO OAKLAND
BAY AREA. A REPORT BASED ON THE 1960 CENSUS OF POPULATION.
/CALIFORNIA/
CALIFORNIA STATE EMPLOYMENT SERVICE. SACRAMENTO, CALIFORNIA.
MAY 1963. 25 PP.

NCALFPB66173 CAL STATE PERSONNEL BOARD
ETHNIC CENSUS OF EXAMINATION COMPETITORS. REPORT OF
EXAMINATIONS GIVEN JULY THROUGH DECEMBER, 1965, SUMMARY.
/TESTING CALIFORNIA/
CALIFORNIA STATE PERSONNEL BOARD. MAR 1966.

NCALIAX49174 CALIVER A   *US DEPT OF HEALTH ED WELFARE
EDUCATION OF NEGRO LEADERS. INFLUENCES AFFECTING GRADUATE
AND PROFESSIONAL STUDIES.
US DEPARTMENT OF HEALTH, EDUCATION, AND WELFARE, OFFICE OF
EDUCATION, FEDERAL SECURITY AGENCY. GPO. WASHINGTON, DC.
1949. 65 PP.

NCALLEX64175 CALLOWAY E   *NEGRO AM LAB CC ST LOUIS DIV
THE ULTIMATE CONQUEST OF NEGRO ECONOMIC INEQUALITY.
ST LOUIS DIVISION OF NEGRO AMERICAN LABOR COUNCIL. ST LOUIS,
MISSOURI. JAN 15 1964. 24 PP.

NCALVIJ63176 CALVET IJ
OPERATION ACHIEVEMENT. /NEW-YORK EMPLOYMENT/
INTERRACIAL REVIEW, VOL 36, SEPT 1963. PP 170-172.

NCAMPAKND177 CAMPBELL AK
THE NEGRO IN SYRACUSE. /NEW-YORK/
BISHOP FOERY-S CATHOLIC NEIGHBOR TRAINING PROGRAM, SPEECH.
9 PP. ND.

NCAMPEQ61909 CAMPBELL EQ
ON DESEGREGATION AND MATTERS SOCIOLOGICAL.
/ECONOMIC-STATUS/
PHYLON, VOL 22, SUMMER 1961. PP 135-145.

NCAMPFX54178 CAMPBELL F
ANALYSIS OF THE TECHNIQUES OF RACIAL INTEGRATION IN THREE
MANUFACTURING FIRMS. /INDUSTRY/
UNIVERSITY OF ILLINOIS, INSTITUTE OF LABOR AND INDUSTRIAL
RELATIONS. MASTER-S THESIS. CHAMPAIGN, ILLINOIS. 1954.

NCAMPJT65179 CAMPBELL JT   *EDUCATIONAL TESTING SERVICE
THE PROBLEM OF CULTURAL BIAS IN SELECTION. I. BACKGROUND AND
LITERATURE. /TESTING/
SELECTING AND TRAINING NEGROES FOR MANAGERIAL POSITIONS.
EDUCATIONAL TESTING SERVICE. PRINCETON, NEW JERSEY. 1965.
PP 57-64.

NCAMPJT66010 CAMPBELL JT   BELCHER LH
*EDUCATIONAL TESTING SERVICE
CHANGES IN NONWHITE EMPLOYMENT 1960-1966.
EDUCATIONAL TESTING SERVICE. PRINCETON, NEW JERSEY. 1966.
25 PP.

NCAMPRR60180 CAMPBELL RR   ROBERTSON PC

*MISSOURI COMM ON HUM RIGHTS
NEGROES IN MISSOURI.
MISSOURI COMMISSION ON HUMAN RIGHTS. JEFFERSON CITY,
MISSOURI. ND, 1960 CENSUS USED. 32 PP.

NCAPLNX66013 CAPLAN N
JOB HOLDING AMONG NEGRO YOUTH.
UNIVERSITY OF MICHIGAN, INSTITUTE FOR SOCIAL RESEARCH,
CENTER FOR GROUP DYNAMICS. UNPUBLISHED PAPER. ANN ARBOR,
MICHIGAN. 1966. 32 PP.

NCAREJB58181 CAREY JB
RACE HATE. NEWEST UNION-BUSTING WEAPON IN THE SOUTH.
THE PROGRESSIVE, VOL 22, JAN 1958. PP 16-18.

NCARLEL64182 CARL EL   CALLAHAN KR
NEGROES AND THE LAW. /OCCUPATIONS/
JOURNAL OF LEGAL EDUCATION, VOL 17, NO 3, 1964-1965.
PP 250-271.

NCARLJX65593 CARLISLE J   *UCLA INSTITUTE OF IND RELS
SOME PRACTICAL STUDIES IN PUBLIC TRANSPORTATION.
/EMPLOYMENT-CONDITIONS WATTS LOS-ANGELES CALIFORNIA/
UNIVERSITY OF CALIFORNIA, INSTITUTE OF INDUSTRIAL RELATIONS.
UNPUBLISHED PAPER. LOS ANGELES, CALIFORNIA. AP 1965. 18 PP.

NCARPLX66184 CARPER L
THE NEGRO FAMILY AND THE MOYNIHAN-REPORT.
DISSENT, MAR-AP 1966. PP 130-140.

NCARTBX65999 CARTER B
INTEGRATING THE NEGRO TEACHER OUT OF A JOB. /OCCUPATIONS/
THE REPORTER, VOL 33, AUG 12 1965. PP 31-33.

NCASSFH66185 CASSEL FH   *US DEPARTMENT OF LABOR
EQUAL-EMPLOYMENT-OPPORTUNITIES.
US DEPARTMENT OF LABOR, EMPLOYMENT SERVICE REVIEW, VOL 3
NO 8, AUG 1966. PP 1-3.

NCATHDX57186 CATHOLIC DIGEST
THE NEGRO-WHITE PROBLEM. WHAT CAN THE UNIONS DO ABOUT IT.
CATHOLIC DIGEST, MAR 1957.

NCAUDHM62911 CAUDILL HM
NIGHT COMES TO THE CUMBERLANDS. /ECONOMIC-STATUS/
LITTLE, BROWN AND CO. BOSTON, MASSACHUSETTS. 1962. 394 PP.

NCAYTHR51187 CAYTON HR
THE PSYCHOLOGY OF THE NEGRO UNDER DISCRIMINATION.
RACE, PREJUDICE AND DISCRIMINATION. ED BY ARNOLD M ROSE.
KNOPF. NEW YORK. 1951. PP 276-290.

NCHALWE62189 CHALMERS WE   DORSEY NW
RESEARCH ON NEGRO JOB SUCCESS.
JOURNAL OF INTERGROUP RELATIONS, VOL 3, NO 4, AUTUMN 1962.
ALSO UNIVERSITY OF ILLINOIS, INSTITUTE OF LABOR AND
INDUSTRIAL RELATIONS. REPRINT NO 120. JAN 1963. 16 PP.

NCHALWE64912 CHALMERS WE   *U OF ILL INST LABOR IND RELS
A MORE PRODUCTIVE ROLE FOR THE NEGRO IN THE SOUTH-S ECONOMY.
UNIVERSITY OF ILLINOIS, INSTITUTE OF LABOR AND INDUSTRIAL
RELATIONS. UNPUBLISHED PAPER. CHAMPAIGN, ILLINOIS. 1964.
48 PP.

NCHALWE65188 CHALMERS WE   *U OF ILL INST LABOR IND RELS
THE LIMITED POTENTIAL FOR NEGRO-WHITE JOB EQUALITY.
UNIVERSITY OF ILLINOIS, INSTITUTE OF LABOR AND INDUSTRIAL
RELATIONS. UNPUBLISHED PAPER. CHAMPAIGN, ILLINOIS. 1965.
39 PP.

NCHANNN65191 CHANSKY NN
RACE, APTITUDE AND VOCATIONAL INTERESTS.
PERSONNEL AND GUIDANCE JOURNAL, VOL 43, NO 8, AP 1965.
PP 780-784.

NCHANTX63190 CHANGING TIMES
NEW OPPORTUNITIES FOR NEGROES...IN EDUCATION...IN CAREERS.
CHANGING TIMES. NEW YORK. AP 1963. 7 PP. ALSO NATIONAL URBAN
LEAGUE. NEW YORK. REPRINT.

NCHAPAA66192 CHAPIN AA   *US DEPARTMENT OF LABOR
THE COUNSELOR AND THE NEGRO STUDENT.
US DEPARTMENT OF LABOR, BUREAU OF LABOR STATISTICS,
OCCUPATIONAL OUTLOOK QUARTERLY, VOL 10, NO 4, DEC 1966.
PP 5-7.

NCHAPDX64193 CHAPLIN D
DOMESTIC-SERVICE AND THE NEGRO.
BLUE-COLLAR WORLD. STUDIES OF THE AMERICAN WORKER. ED BY
ARTHUR SHOSTAK AND WILLIAM GOMBERG. PRENTICE-HALL.
ENGLEWOOD CLIFFS, NEW JERSEY. 1964. PP 527-536.

NCHAPEJ49351 CHAPMAN EJ
VOCATIONAL CHOICES OF NEGRO HIGH SCHOOL STUDENTS IN MACON
COUNTY, ALABAMA, AND THEIR RELATIONSHIP TO BASIC
OCCUPATIONAL ACTIVITES OF THE SCHOOL COMMUNITIES.
/ASPIRATIONS/
TUSKEGEE INSTITUTE. THESIS. TUSKEGEE, ALABAMA. 1949. 109 PP.

NCHASET63195 CHASE ET
JOB QUOTAS AND THE MERIT SYSTEM.
AMERICAN CHILD, VOL 45, NOV 1963. PP 13-19.

NCHASET64196 CHASE ET
QUOTAS FOR NEGROES.
COMMONWEAL, JAN 17 1964.

NCHASWX58194 CHASON W
AMERICAN LABOR ATTACKS ITS OWN SEGREGATION PROBLEM. /UNION/
THE REPORTER, VOL 18, MAY 1958. PP 27-30.

NCHATCC62197 CHATTANOOGA CC COOP ACTION
THE NEGRO AND EMPLOYMENT-OPPORTUNITIES IN THE SOUTH.
CHATTANOOGA REGION. /TENNESSEE/
CHATTANOOGA COUNCIL FOR COOPERATIVE ACTION. CHATTANOOGA,
TENNESSEE. FEB 1962. 16 PP.

NCHECOX64890 CHECKIS LD
NLRB DECERTIFIES RACIALLY SEGREGATED UNION LOCALS.
NEW YORK UNIVERSITY LAW REVIEW, VOL 39, DEC 1964.

NCHEIIX49198 CHEIN I
WHAT ARE THE PSYCHOLOGICAL EFFECTS OF SEGREGATION UNDER
CONDITIONS OF EQUAL FACILITIES.
INTERNATIONAL JOURNAL OF OPINION AND ATTITUDE RESEARCH,
VOL 3, NO 2, SUMMER 1949. PP 229-234.

NCHEMWX61199 CHEMICAL WEEK
CPI -- CHEMICAL PROCESS INDUSTRIES -- TAKES LEAD IN
ANTI-BIAS DRIVE. /INDUSTRY/

CHEMICAL WEEK, VOL 89, OCT 21 1961. PP 77-78 PLUS.

NCHEMWX63200   CHEMICAL WEEK
THEY MAKE OPPORTUNITY KNOCK. /INDUSTRY URBAN-LEAGUE/
CHEMICAL WEEK. OCT 26 1963. ALSO NATIONAL URBAN LEAGUE.
NEW YORK. 1963. 3 PP.

NCHICCA47914   CHICK CA
SOME RECENT UNITED STATES SUPREME COURT DECISIONS AFFECTING
   THE RIGHTS OF NEGRO WORKERS.
JOURNAL OF NEGRO EDUCATION, VOL 16, NO 2, SPRING 1947.
PP 172-179.

NCHICCA53204   CHICK CA
RECENT SOUTHERN INDUSTRIALIZATION AND ITS IMPLICATIONS FOR
   NEGROES LIVING IN THE SOUTH. /EMPLOYMENT-TRENDS/
JOURNAL OF NEGRO EDUCATION, VOL 23, NO 3, SUMMER 1953.
PP 476-483.

NCHICCO60201   CHICAGO COMM ON HUMAN RELS
A PRELIMINARY REPORT ON MEDICAL STAFF APPOINTMENTS HELD BY
   NEGRO PHYSICIANS AT PREDOMINANTLY WHITE HOSPITALS.
   /CHICAGO ILLINOIS/
CHICAGO COMMISSION ON HUMAN RELATIONS. CHICAGO, ILLINOIS.
MAY 1958, REVISED 1960. 16 PP.

NCHICULND203   CHICAGO URBAN LEAGUE
TWO YEAR REPORT ON THE YOUTH GUIDANCE PROJECT, 1958-1959.
   /CHICAGO   ILLINOIS/
CHICAGO URBAN LEAGUE. CHICAGO, ILLINOIS. ND.

NCHICUL58202   CHICAGO URBAN LEAGUE
INTEGRATION ON HOSPITAL APPOINTMENTS AND IN HOSPITAL CARE.
   /CHICAGO ILLINOIS/
CHICAGO URBAN LEAGUE, RESEARCH DEPARTMENT. CHICAGO,
ILLINOIS. 1958.

NCHILRR57205   CHILDERS RR
JOBS AND THE COLOR LINE.
AMERICAN SOCIALIST, JAN 1957. PP 14-15.

NCHRIDE58206   CHRISTENSEN DE
THE NEGRO-S CHANGING PLACE IN SOUTHERN AGRICULTURE.
THE NEGRO IN AMERICAN SOCIETY. FLORIDA STATE UNIVERSITY
STUDIES, NO 28. GROWER PRESS. TAMPA, FLORIDA. 1958.

NCIKIWI66207   CIKINS WI
GRADUATE EDUCATION, PUBLIC SERVICE, AND THE NEGRO.
PUBLIC ADMINISTRATION REVIEW, VOL 26, NO 3, SEPT 1966.
PP 183-191.

NCLARJH64309   CLARKE JH
HARLEM, A COMMUNITY IN TRANSITION.
CITADEL PRESS. NEW YORK. 1964. 223 PP.

NCLARJP62209   CLARK JP   WENNINGER EP
SOCIO-ECONOMIC CLASS AND AREA AS CORRELATES OF ILLEGAL
   BEHAVIOR AMONG JUVENILES.
AMERICAN SOCIOLOGIAL REVIEW, VOL 27, DEC 1962. PP 826-834.

NCLARJP63208   CLARK JP   WENNINGER EP
GOAL-ORIENTATIONS AND ILLEGAL BEHAVIOR AMONG JUVENILES.
SOCIAL FORCES, VOL 42, OCT 1963. PP 49-59.

NCLARKB59210   CLARK KB
COLOR, CLASS, PERSONALITY, AND JUVENILE DELINQUENCY.
JOURNAL OF NEGRO EDUCATION, VOL 28, 1959. PP 240-251.

NCLARKB63214   CLARK KB   PLOTKIN L
*NATL SSF FOR NEGRO STUDENTS
THE NEGRO STUDENT AT INTEGRATED COLLEGES.
NATIONAL SCHOLARSHIP SERVICE AND FUND FOR NEGRO STUDENTS.
NEW YORK. 1963.

NCLARKB64307   CLARK KB
THE NEGRO COLLEGE STUDENT. SOME FACTS AND SOME CONCERNS.
JOURNAL OF THE ASSOCIATION OF COLLEGE ADMISSIONS COUNSELORS,
WINTER 1964. 4 PP.

NCLARKB65211   CLARK KB
DARK GHETTO. DILEMMAS OF SOCIAL POWER.
HARPER AND ROW. NEW YORK. 1965. 240 PP.

NCLARKB65213   CLARK KB   *US DEPARTMENT OF LABOR
SOCIAL AND ECONOMIC IMPLICATIONS OF INTEGRATING IN THE
   PUBLIC SCHOOLS.
US DEPARTMENT OF LABOR, OFFICE OF MANPOWER, AUTOMATION AND
TRAINING. SEMINARS ON MANPOWER POLICY AND PROGRAM. NOV 1965.
22 PP.

NCLARKB67212   CLARK KB
SEX, STATUS AND THE UNDEREMPLOYMENT OF THE NEGRO MALE.
EMPLOYMENT, RACE AND POVERTY. ED BY ARTHUR M ROSS AND
HERBERT HILL. HARCOURT, BRACE, AND WORLD. NEW YORK. 1967.
PP 138-148.

NCLARTD61055   CLARK TD
THE EMERGING SOUTH.
OXFORD UNIVERSITY PRESS. NEW YORK. 1961.

NCLEATA66923   CLEARY TA   *EDUCATIONAL TESTING SERVICE
TEST BIAS. VALIDITY OF THE SCHOLASTIC APTITUDE TEST FOR
   NEGRO AND WHITE STUDENTS IN INTEGRATED COLLEGES.
EDUCATIONAL TESTING SERVICE, RESEARCH BULLETIN RB-66-31.
PRINCETON, NEW JERSEY. JUNE 1966. 23 PP.

NCLEVUL64916   CLEVELAND URBAN LEAGUE
THE NEGRO IN CLEVELAND, 1950-1963. /OHIO/
CLEVELAND URBAN LEAGUE. CLEVELAND, OHIO. JUNE 1964.

NCLIFVA62215   CLIFT VA ED
NEGRO EDUCATION IN AMERICA. ITS ADEQUACY, PROBLEMS AND
   NEEDS.
16TH YEARBOOK OF THE JOHN DEWEY SOCIETY. HARPER AND BROS.
NEW YORK. 1962. 315 PP.

NCLIFVA66227   CLIFT VA
EDUCATING THE AMERICAN NEGRO.
THE AMERICAN NEGRO REFERENCE BOOK. ED BY JOHN P DAVIS.
PRENTICE-HALL. ENGLEWOOD CLIFFS, NEW JERSEY. 1966.
PP 360-395.

NCOBBWM48217   COBB WM   *NAACP
PROGRESS AND PORTENTS FOR THE NEGRO IN MEDICINE.
   /OCCUPATIONS/
NAACP. NEW YORK. 1948.

NCOBBWM58216   COBB WM
NOT TO THE SWIFT. PROGRESS AND PROSPECTS OF THE NEGRO IN
   SCIENCE AND THE PROFESSIONS. /OCCUPATIONS/

JOURNAL OF NEGRO EDUCATION, VOL 27, NO 2, SPRING 1958.
PP 120-126.

NCOCKHW65218   COCKFIELD HW   *US DEPARTMENT OF LABOR
CLEVELAND-S ANNUAL JOB CENTER FOR COLLEGE GRADUATES.
US DEPARTMENT OF LABOR, EMPLOYMENT SERVICE REVIEW, VOL 2,
NO 8, AUG 1965. PP 27-29.

NCOHEAK63219   COHEN AK   HODGES HM
CHARACTERISTICS OF THE LOWER-BLUE-COLLAR CLASS.
   /SOCIO-ECONOMIC/
SOCIAL PROBLEMS, VOL 10, SPRING 1963. PP 303-334.

NCOHEEE63220   COHEN EE
THE NEGRO AND EDUCATION.
AMERICAN CHILD, VOL 45, NO 1, JAN 1963. P 10.

NCOHERXND221   COHEN R   *U PITT LEARNING R AND D CENT
EXCLUSIONS AND ADAPTATIONS. A RE-EVALUATION OF THE
   CULTURE-OF-POVERTY THEME.
UNIVERSITY OF PITTSBURGH, LEARNING RESEARCH AND DEVELOPMENT
CENTER. PITTSBURGH, PENNSYLVANIA. MIMEOGRAPHED. 20 PP.

NCOLEJS66223   COLEMAN JS   *US DEPT OF HEALTH ED WELFARE
EQUALITY OF EDUCATIONAL OPPORTUNITY.
US DEPARTMENT OF HEALTH, EDUCATION AND WELFARE. GPO.
WASHINGTON, DC. 1966. CORRELATIONS SEPARATELY BOUND.

NCOLLHX65491   COLLINS H
SOCIOLOGY OF EMANCIPATION.
PHYLON, VOL 26, NO 2, 2ND QUARTER 1965. PP 148-161.

NCOLULR52226   COLUMBIA LAW REVIEW
RACIAL DISCRIMINATION BY A UNION AGAINST EMPLOYEES IT DOES
   NOT REPRESENT. /LEGISLATION/
COLUMBIA LAW REVIEW, VOL 52, NO 8, DEC 1952. PP 1058-1060.

NCOLULR57224   COLUMBIA LAW REVIEW
EFFECT OF SCHOOL ASSIGNMENT LAWS ON FEDERAL ADJUDICATION OF
   INTEGRATION CONTROVERSIES.
COLUMBIA LAW REVIEW, VOL 57, NO 4, AP 1957. PP 537-552.

NCOLULR65225   COLUMBIA LAW REVIEW
RACIAL DISCRIMINATION AND THE DUTY OF FAIR REPRESENTATION.
   /LEGISLATION/
COLUMBIA LAW REVIEW, VOL 65, NO 2, FEB 1965. PP 273-287.

NCOLUUL59227   COLUMBUS URBAN LEAGUE
CASE-STUDIES IN URBAN-LEAGUE METHODS.
COLUMBUS URBAN LEAGUE. COLUMBUS, OHIO. 1959. 20 PP.

NCOMMXX59228   COMMENTARY
LABOR UNIONS AND THE NEGRO.
COMMENTARY, VOL 28, DEC 1959. PP. 479-488.

NCOMMXX64467   COMMENTARY
LIBERALISM AND THE NEGRO. /ASPIRATIONS/
COMMENTARY, VOL 37, 1964. PP 25-42.

NCOMMXX65229   COMMONWEAL
DISPLACED TEACHERS. /OCCUPATIONS/
COMMONWEAL, VOL 82, SEPT 3 1965. P 613.

NCOMUCE60230   COMMUNITY CONF ON EMPLOYMENT
EMPLOYMENT OPPORTUNITY FOR NASHVILLE NEGROES. /TENNESSEE/
COMMUNITY CONFERENCE ON EMPLOYMENT. FISK UNIVERSITY.
NASHVILLE, TENNESSEE. AP 22-23 1960.

NCONAJB61920   CONANT JB
SLUMS AND SUBURBS. /TRAINING/
MCGRAW-HILL. NEW YORK. 1961. 147 PP.

NCONNCX66232   CONNOR C   DE NUEFVILLE R
HOW GOOD ARE OUR SCHOOLS.
AMERICAN EDUCATION, OCT 1966.

NCONNSM65471   CONNORS SISTER MAUREEN
A COMPARATIVE STUDY OF THE OCCUPATIONAL INTERESTS OF NEGRO
   AND WHITE ADOLESCENT BOYS.
CATHOLIC UNIVERSITY OF AMERICA. PHD DISSERTATION.
WASHINGTON, DC. 1965. 83 PP.

NCONREX47233   CONRAD E
JIM-CROW AMERICA. /DISCRIMINATION/
DUELL, SLOAN, AND PEARCE. NEW YORK. 1947. 237 PP.

NCOOKSW57234   COOK SW
DESEGREGATION. A PSYCHOLOGICAL ANALYSIS.
AMERICAN PSYCHOLOGIST, VOL 12, NO 1, JAN 1957. PP 1-13.

NCOONRB66927   COONEY RB
ARMING THE UNEMPLOYED WITH SKILLS. /TRAINING/
AMERICAN FEDERATIONIST, VOL 73, NO 4, AP 1966. PP 16-18.

NCOOPJE56235   COOPER JE
THE ROLE OF THE NEGRO IN THE ORGANIZATION OF THE CIO.
   /UNION/
NEW YORK UNIVERSITY. MA THESIS, NEW YORK. 1956 OR 1957.

NCOOPJX64294   COOPER J
TRADE UNION COMPLIANCE WITH PRESIDENTIAL DIRECTIVES,
   MEMBERSHIP ACCEPTANCE, SENIORITY, ETC.
SEVENTEENTH ANNUAL CONFERENCE ON LABOR. NEW YORK UNIVERSITY.
NEW YORK. 1964. PP 131-140.

NCORDDX66030   CORDTZ D
THE NEGRO MIDDLE CLASS IS RIGHT IN THE MIDDLE.
   /ECONOMIC-STATUS/
FORTUNE, NOV 1966. PP 174-180, 224-231.

NCOUNFO63929   CC OF FEDERATED ORGANIZATIONS *CORE
*SNCC
THE GENERAL CONDITIONS OF MISSISSIPPI NEGROES.
COFO PAPER NO 1. JACKSON, MISSISSIPPI. MIMEOGRAPHED. 1963.

NCOUSFR5861   COUSENS FR
A PILOT STUDY OF AN INTEGRATED WORK FORCE.
MICHIGAN FAIR EMPLOYMENT PRACTICES COMMISSION. DETROIT,
MICHIGAN. 1958. 36 PP.

NCOXXOC41934   COX OC
EMPLOYMENT, EDUCATION AND MARRIAGE OF YOUNG NEGRO ADULTS.
JOURNAL OF NEGRO EDUCATION, VOL 10, NO 1, JAN 1941.
PP 39-42.

NCOXXOC53935   COX OC
NEGRO TEACHERS. MARTYRS TO INTEGRATION. /OCCUPATIONS/
THE NATION, VOL 176, AP 25 1963. PP 347-348.

NCRAICE65240   CRAIG CE   *US DEPARTMENT OF LABOR

MINORITY PROGRAM CALLS FOR COMMUNITY ACTION.
US DEPARTMENT OF LABOR, EMPLOYMENT SERVICE REVIEW, VOL 2,
NO 8, AUG 1965. PP 10-12.

NCROFES66242   CROFT ES   WILSON J
*US DEPARTMENT OF LABOR
OUTREACH IN ROCHESTER. /NEW-YORK/
US DEPARTMENT OF LABOR, EMPLOYMENT SERVICE REVIEW, VOL 3,
NO 8, AUG 1966. PP 66, 76-77.

NCROMFX61121   CROMIEN F   *NYC COMM ON HUMAN RIGHTS
FROM 1790 TO 1960. NEGROES IN NEW-YORK.
NEW YORK CITY COMMISSION ON HUMAN RIGHTS, RESEARCH REPORT
NO 4. NEW YORK. 1961.

NCROMRX63243   CROMER R
SCHOOL-DESEGREGATION AND NEW INDUSTRY. THE SOUTHERN
   COMMUNITY LEADERS VIEWPOINT.
SOCIAL FORCES, MAY 1963.

NCUNNGE58244   CUNNINGHAM GE
REASONS FOR BELATED EDUCATION. A STUDY OF THE PLIGHT OF THE
   OLDER NEGRO TEACHERS. /OCCUPATIONS/
JOURNAL OF NEGRO EDUCATION, VOL 27, SPRING 1958. PP 195-200.

NCUNNMX56579   CUNNINGGIM M
INTEGRATION IN PROFESSIONAL EDUCATION. THE STORY OF PERKINS,
   SOUTHERN METHODIST UNIVERSITY. /VOCATIONS/
ANNALS OF THE AMERICAN ACADEMY OF POLITICAL AND SOCIAL
SCIENCE, VOL 304, 1956. PP 109-115.

NCUTHMV49936   CUTHBERT MV
EDUCATION AND MARGINALITY. A STUDY OF THE NEGRO COLLEGE
   GRADUATE.
MCGRAW-HILL. NEW YORK. 1949.

NCUTRPX65245   CUTRIGHT P
NEGRO SUBORDINATION AND WHITE GAINS. /INCOME
   OCCUPATIONAL-STATUS/
AMERICAN SOCIOLOGICAL REVIEW, VOL 30, NO 1, FEB 1965.
PP 110-112.

NDAEDXX65246   DAEDALUS
THE NEGRO AMERICAN. /EMPLOYMENT INCOME ECONOMIC-STATUS/
DAEDALUS, VOL 94, NO 4, FALL 1965. PP 743-1166. ALSO VOL 95,
NO 1, WINTER 1966. PP 1-445.

NDALTMX51247   DALTON M
INFORMAL FACTORS IN CAREER ACHIEVEMENT.
AMERICAN JOURNAL OF SOCIOLOGY, VOL 56, NO 5, MAR 1951.
PP 407-415.

NDAMILX64127   D-AMICO L   REED M
A COMPARISON OF TUITION-AND-FEE CHARGES IN NEGRO
   INSTITUTIONS WITH CHARGES IN INSTITUTIONS OF THE SOUTHEAST
   AND OF THE NATION. 1962-1963. /EDUCATION/
JOURNAL OF NEGRO EDUCATION, VOL 33, SPRING 1964. PP 186-190.

NDANIWG62248   DANIEL WG
NEGROES AS TEACHING ASSISTANTS IN SOME PUBLICLY SUPPORTED
   UNIVERSITIES. /OCCUPATIONS/
JOURNAL OF NEGRO EDUCATION, VOL 31, NO 2, SPRING 1962.
PP 202-204.

NDANIWG63249   DANIEL WG
THE RELATIVE EMPLOYMENT AND INCOME OF AMERICAN NEGROES.
JOURNAL OF NEGRO EDUCATION, VOL 32, NO 4, FALL 1963.
PP 349-357.

NDANIWG63250   DANIEL WG ED
THE RELATIVE PROGRESS OF THE AMERICAN NEGRO SINCE 1950.
HOWARD UNIVERSITY PRESS. WASHINGTON, DC. 1963. ALSO JOURNAL
OF NEGRO EDUCATION, VOL 32, NO 4, FALL 1963. PP 311-516.

NDANZDX64468   DANZIG D
THE MEANING OF NEGRO STRATEGY.
COMMENTARY, VOL 37, 1964. PP 41-46.

NDARTCX64305   DARTMOUTH COLLEGE   *ROCKEFELLER FOUNDATION
ABC REPORT 1964. /COLLEGE EDUCATION/
DARTMOUTH COLLEGE, INDEPENDENT SCHOOLS TALENT SEARCH
PROGRAM. ROCKEFELLER FOUNDATION. HANOVER, NEW HAMPSHIRE.
1964. 109 PP.

NDAVIAX45938   DAVIS A
CASTE, ECONOMY, AND VIOLENCE.
AMERICAN JOURNAL OF SOCIOLOGY, VOL 51, JULY 1945. PP 7-15.

NDAVIAX46254   DAVIS A
THE MOTIVATION OF THE UNDERPRIVILEGED WORKER.
INDUSTRY AND SOCIETY. ED BY WILLIAM WHYTE. MCGRAW-HILL.
NEW YORK. 1946. PP 84-106. ALSO BOBBS-MERRILL REPRINT SERIES
NO 62.

NDAVIFG42260   DAVIS FG
WAR ECONOMICS AND NEGRO LABOR.
THE QUARTERLY REVIEW OF HIGHER EDUCATION AMONG NEGROES,
VOL 10, NO 3, JULY 1942. PP 133-168.

NDAVIJA42255   DAVIS JA   *NYS WAR CC COMM DISCR EMPLOY
HOW MANAGEMENT CAN INTEGRATE NEGROES IN WAR INDUSTRIES.
NEW YORK STATE, WAR COUNCIL, COMMISSION ON DISCRIMINATION IN
EMPLOYMENT. ALBANY, NEW YORK. 1942. 43 PP.

NDAVIJA45259   DAVIS JA   DAVIS G
NEGRO EMPLOYMENT IN THE FEDERAL GOVERNMENT.
PHYLON, VOL 6, NO 4, 4TH QUARTER 1945. PP 337-346.

NDAVIJA46257   DAVIS JA
NONDISCRIMINATION IN THE FEDERAL SERVICES.
ANNALS OF THE AMERICAN ACADEMY OF POLITICAL AND SOCIAL
SCIENCE, VOL 244, MAR 1946. PP 65-74.

NDAVIJA46258   DAVIS JA   *COMMON COUNCIL FOR AM UNITY
POSTWAR EMPLOYMENT AND THE NEGRO WORKER.
COMMON COUNCIL FOR AMERICAN UNITY. NEW YORK. 1946. 13 PP.

NDAVIJA52256   DAVIS JA
NEGRO EMPLOYMENT, A PROGRESS REPORT.
FORTUNE, VOL 46, JULY 1952. PP 102-103, 158, 161-162.

NDAVIJH55253   DAVIES JH
TVA AND NEGRO EMPLOYMENT. /TENNESSEE/
JOURNAL OF NEGRO EDUCATION, VOL 24, NO 1, WINTER 1955.
PP 87-90.

NDAVIJP66260   DAVIS JP
THE AMERICAN NEGRO REFERENCE BOOK.
PRENTICE-HALL. ENGLEWOOD CLIFFS, NEW JERSEY. 1966. 969 PP.

NDAVILM64942   DAVID LM   *US DEPARTMENT OF LABOR
RECENT COLLECTIVE-BARGAINING AND TECHNOLOGICAL-CHANGE.
US DEPARTMENT OF LABOR, BUREAU OF LABOR STATISTICS, REPORT
NO 266. GPO. WASHINGTON, DC. MAR 1964.

NDAVIMR49252   DAVIE MR
NEGROES IN AMERICAN SOCIETY.
MCGRAW-HILL. NEW YORK. 1949.

NDAVINF60312   DAVIS NF
TRADE UNIONS PRACTICES AND THE NEGRO WORKER -- THE
   ESTABLISHMENT AND IMPLEMENTATION OF AFL-CIO
   ANTI-DISCRIMINATION POLICY.
UNIVERSITY OF INDIANA. PHD DISSERTATION. BLOOMINGTON,
INDIANA. 1960. 237 PP.

NDECKPM60261   DECKER PM
A STUDY OF JOB-OPPORTUNITIES IN THE STATE OF FLORIDA FOR
   NEGRO COLLEGE GRADUATES.
JOURNAL OF NEGRO EDUCATION, VOL 29, NO 1, WINTER 1960.
PP 93-95.

NDENIEF62262   DENISON EF   *COMT ON ECONOMIC DEVELOPMENT
THE SOURCES OF ECONOMIC GROWTH IN THE UNITED-STATES AND THE
   ALTERNATIVE BEFORE US. /LABOR-FORCE ECONOMY/
COMMITTEE ON ECONOMIC DEVELOPMENT. WASHINGTON, DC. 1962.

NDENTJH64263   DENTON JH
RACE AND POVERTY.
DIABLO PRESS. BERKELEY, CALIFORNIA. 1964.

NDERBIA46251   DERBIGNY IA
TUSKEGEE LOOKS AT ITS VETERANS. /OCCUPATIONAL-STATUS/
THE QUARTERLY REVIEW OF HIGHER EDUCATION AMONG NEGROES, VOL
14, NO 1, JAN 1946. PP 11-18.

NDERNTX66264   DERNBURG T   STRAND K
HIDDEN UNEMPLOYMENT 1953-62. A QUANTITATIVE ANALYSIS BY AGE
   AND SEX.
AMERICAN ECONOMIC REVIEW, MAR 1966. PP 72-95.

NDESMCH65265   DES MOINES COMM ON HUM RIGHTS
EMPLOYMENT SURVEY OF DES-MOINES FIRMS. /IOWA/
DES MOINES COMMISSION ON HUMAN RIGHTS AND JOB
DISCRIMINATION. DES MOINES, IOWA. SUMMER 1965. 82 PP.

NDETRCC63267   DETROIT COMM COMMUNITY RELS
STUDY OF DETROIT POLICE DEPARTMENT PERSONNEL PRACTICES.
   /MICHIGAN OCCUPATIONS/
DETROIT COMMISSION ON COMMUNITY RELATIONS. DETROIT,
MICHIGAN. MAR 27 1963. 43 PP.

NDEUTMX64268   DEUTSCH M   BROWN B
SOCIAL INFLUENCES IN NEGRO-WHITE INTELLIGENCE DIFFERENCES.
JOURNAL OF SOCIAL ISSUES, VOL 20, NO 2, 1964. PP 24-35.

NDEWEDX52270   DEWEY D
NEGRO EMPLOYMENT IN SOUTHERN INDUSTRY.
JOURNAL OF POLITICAL ECONOMY, VOL 60, NO 4, AUG 1952.
PP 279-293.

NDEWEDX55269   DEWEY D   *NATIONAL PLANNING ASSN
FOUR STUDIES OF NEGRO EMPLOYMENT IN THE UPPER SOUTH.
SELECTED STUDIES OF NEGRO EMPLOYMENT IN THE SOUTH. NATIONAL
PLANNING ASSOCIATION, COMMITTEE OF THE SOUTH. REPORT NO 6-4.
WASHINGTON, DC. 1955. PP 146-212.

NDEWEDX62271   DEWEY D
SOUTHERN POVERTY AND THE RACIAL DIVISION-OF-LABOR.
NEW SOUTH, VOL 17, MAY 1962. PP 3-5, 11-13.

NDIAMDE64272   DIAMOND DE
NEGROES AND THE SERVICE INDUSTRIES. /OCCUPATIONS/
CHALLENGE, VOL 13, DEC 1964. PP 33-35.

NDIAMDE65273   DIAMOND DE
OCCUPATIONAL SHIFTS IN NEGRO EMPLOYMENT.
BUSINESS TOPICS, VOL 12, SUMMER 1965. PP 32-44.

NDILLHCND274   DILLINGHAM HC   SLY DF
THE MECHANICAL COTTON-PICKER, NEGRO MIGRATION, AND THE
   INTEGRATION MOVEMENT.
CENTRAL MICHIGAN UNIVERSITY. UNPUBLISHED MANUSCRIPT. MOUNT
PLEASANT, MICHIGAN. ND 12 PP.

NDILLWP58275   DILLINGHAM WP
THE ECONOMICS OF SEGREGATION.
THE NEGRO IN AMERICAN SOCIETY. FLORIDA STATE UNIVERSITY
STUDIES, NO 28. GROWER PRESS. TAMPA, FLORIDA. 1958.

NDIZAJE66015   DIZARD JE
WHY SHOULD NEGROES WORK. /ASPIRATIONS/
UNIVERSITY OF CALIFORNIA, DEPARTMENT OF SOCIOLOGY.
UNPUBLISHED PAPER. BERKELEY, CALIFORNIA. 1966. 19 PP.

NDOARLE66276   DOAR LE   *US DEPARTMENT OF LABOR
RACIAL STATISTICS AS A MANAGEMENT TOOL.
US DEPARTMENT OF LABOR, EMPLOYMENT SERVICE REVIEW, OCT 1966.
PP 18, 22.

NDOBBDA58277   DOBBINS DA   BASS BM
EFFECTS OF UNEMPLOYMENT ON WHITE AND NEGRO PRISON-ADMISSIONS
   IN LOUISIANA.
JOURNAL OF CRIMINAL LAW, CRIMINOLOGY, AND POLICE SCIENCE,
VOL 48, 1958. PP 522-525.

NDODDAE45949   DODD AE
NEGRO EMPLOYMENT OPPORTUNITIES DURING AND AFTER THE WAR.
OPPORTUNITY, AP-JUNE 1945.

NDODDHH55950   DODDY HH
DESEGREGATION AND THE EMPLOYMENT OF NEGRO TEACHERS.
   /OCCUPATIONS/
JOURNAL OF NEGRO EDUCATION, VOL 24, NO 4, FALL 1955.
PP 405-409.

NDODDHH63278   DODDY HH
THE PROGRESS OF THE NEGRO IN HIGHER EDUCATION, 1950-1960.
JOURNAL OF NEGRO EDUCATION, VOL 32, NO 4, 1963 YEARBOOK.
PP 485-492.

NDOERPB66279   DOERINGER PB
PROMOTIONS SYSTEMS AND EQUAL-EMPLOYMENT-OPPORTUNITY.
HARVARD UNIVERSITY. PHD DISSERTATION. CAMBRIDGE,
MASSACHUSETTS. 1966.

NDOERPB66280   DOERINGER PB
PROMOTION SYSTEMS AND EQUAL-EMPLOYMENT OPPORTUNITY.
INDUSTRIAL RELATIONS RESEARCH ASSOCIATION, ANNUAL MEETING,
PAPER. SAN FRANCISCO, CALIFORNIA. DEC 29 1966. 28 PP.

NDOLLJX49281 DOLLARD J
CASTE AND CLASS IN A SOUTHERN TOWN.
HARPER AND ROW. NEW YORK. 1949.

NDORIGF64282 DORIOT GF
THE MANAGEMENT OF RACIAL INTEGRATION IN BUSINESS.
MCGRAW HILL. NEW YORK. 1964.

NDORMMX64953 DORMAN M
WE SHALL OVERCOME. /CIVIL-RIGHTS/
DIAL PRESS. NEW YORK. 1964. 340 PP.

NDORNSM56283 DORNBUSCH SM
CORRELATIONS BETWEEN INCOME AND LABOR-FORCE PARTICIPATION BY
RACE.
AMERICAN JOURNAL OF SOCIOLOGY, VOL 61, JAN 1956. PP 340-344.

NDOUGJH64285 DOUGLAS JH   *US DEPT OF HEALTH ED WELFARE
THE NEGRO FAMILY-S SEARCH FOR ECONOMIC SECURITY.
US DEPARTMENT OF HEALTH, EDUCATION AND WELFARE. GPO.
WASHINGTON, DC. JULY 1964.

NDOUGJH66286 DOUGLAS JH
THE URBAN NEGRO FAMILY.
THE AMERICAN NEGRO REFERENCE BOOK. ED BY JOHN P DAVIS.
PRENTICE-HALL. ENGLEWOOD CLIFFS, NEW JERSEY. 1966.
PP 337-359.

NDOYLWX62287 DOYLE W   LIPSET SM
HILL H   GOODE B
JOHNPOLL BK   SCHULDER DJ
NEGROES AND THE LABOR MOVEMENT. RECORD OF THE LEFT WING
UNIONS.
NEW POLITICS, VOL 2, FALL 1962. PP 142-151.

NDRAKSC45291 DRAKE SC   CLAYTON HR
BLACK METROPOLIS. A STUDY OF NEGRO LIFE IN A NORTHERN CITY.
HARCOURT, BRACE AND WORLD. NEW YORK. 1945.

NDRAKSC57290 DRAKE SC
RECENT TRENDS IN RESEARCH ON THE NEGRO IN THE UNITED STATES.
INTERNATIONAL SOCIAL SCIENCE BULLETIN, VOL 9, NO 4, 1957.
PP 475-494.

NDRAKSC63288 DRAKE SC
THE AMERICAN DREAM AND THE NEGRO.
CENTENNIAL LECTURES, ROOSEVELT UNIVERSITY. CHICAGO,
ILLINOIS. OCCASIONAL PAPER NO 9. 1963.

NDRAKSC65289 DRAKE SC
THE SOCIAL AND ECONOMIC STATUS OF THE NEGRO IN THE
UNITED STATES.
DAEDALUS, VOL 94, NO 4, FALL 1965. PP 771-814.

NDREGRM60292 DREGER RM   MILLER KS
COMPARATIVE PSYCHOLOGICAL STUDIES OF NEGROES AND WHITES IN
THE UNITED STATES.
PSYCHOLOGICAL BULLETIN, VOL 57, 1960. PP 361-402.

NDREGRM65293 DREGER RM   MILLER KS
RECENT RESEARCH IN PSYCHOLOGICAL COMPARISONS OF NEGROES AND
WHITES IN THE UNITED STATES.
SOUTHEASTERN PSYCHOLOGICAL ASSOCIATION MEETING. PAPER.
ATLANTA, GEORGIA. AP 2 1965.

NDREWCR50294 DREW CR
NEGRO SCHOLARS IN SCIENTIFIC RESEARCH.
JOURNAL OF NEGRO HISTORY, VOL 35, NO 2, AP 1950.

NDREXIT64295 DREXEL INST OF TECHNOLOGY
THE CENSUS OF NEGRO-OWNED BUSINESSES. /PHILADELPHIA
PENNSYLVANIA OCCUPATIONS/
DREXEL INSTITUTE OF TECHNOLOGY. PHILADELPHIA, PENNSYLVANIA.
1964.

NDUBOWE41298 DU BOIS WE
A CHRONICLE OF RACE-RELATIONS -- THE UNITED STATES, NORTH
AND SOUTH.
PHYLON, VOL 2, NO 3, 3RD QUARTER. 1941. P 302.

NDUBOWE43297 DUBOIS WEB
A CHRONICLE OF RACE-RELATIONS, FEPC.
PHYLON, VOL 4, NO 3, 3RD QUARTER 1943. PP 286-287. ALSO IN
VOL 5, NO 1, 1ST QUARTER 1944. PP 83-85.

NDUBOWE48299 DUBOIS WEB
RACE-RELATIONS IN THE UNITED-STATES 1916-1947.
PHYLON, VOL 9, NO 3, 3RD QUARTER 1948. PP 234-246.

NDULLFR49301 DULLES FR
LABOR IN AMERICA, A HISTORY.
TY CROWELL. NEW YORK. 1949.

NDUMMCO59302 DUMMET CO
THE NEGRO IN DENTAL EDUCATION.
PHYLON, WINTER 1959. PP 386-387.

NDUMOAL45303 DUMOND AL
CERTAIN ASPECTS OF THE ECONOMIC DEVELOPMENT OF THE AMERICAN
NEGRO 1864-1960.
CATHOLIC UNIVERSITY OF AMERICA PRESS. WASHINGTON, DC.
187 PP.

NDUNCBX65304 DUNCAN B
DROPOUTS AND THE RATE OF UNEMPLOYMENT. /YOUTH/
JOURNAL OF POLITICAL ECONOMY, AP 1965.

NDUNCOD55307 DUNCAN OD   DUNCAN B
RESIDENTIAL DISTRIBUTION AND OCCUPATIONAL-STRATIFICATION.
AMERICAN JOURNAL OF SOCIOLOGY, VOL 60, NO 5, MAR 1955.
PP 493-503.

NDUNCOD57306 DUNCAN OD   DUNCAN B
*U OF CHI COMMUNITY IVENTORY
THE NEGRO POPULATION OF CHICAGO. A STUDY OF RESIDENTIAL
SUCCESSION. /ILLINOIS OCCUPATIONAL-PATTERNS/
UNIVERSITY OF CHICAGO, CHICAGO COMMUNITY INVENTORY.
UNIVERSITY OF CHICAGO PRESS. CHICAGO, ILLINOIS. 1957.

NDUNCOD59305 DUNCAN OD
RESIDENTIAL SEGREGATION AND SOCIAL DIFFERENTIATION.
INTERNATIONAL POPULATION CONFERENCE, VIENNA, 1959.
INTERNATIONAL UNION FOR THE SCIENTIFIC STUDY OF POPULATION.
VIENNA, AUSTRIA. 1959. PP 571-577.

NDUNKJX64300 DUNKELBERGER J
ATTITUDE TOWARD JOB-MOBILITY AMONG HOUSEHOLD HEADS IN
LOW-INCOME AREAS OF THE RURAL SOUTH.
MISSISSIPPI STATE UNIVERSITY. PHD DISSERTATION. STATE

COLLEGE, MISSISSIPPI. 1964.

NDUNNES62308 DUNN ES
RECENT SOUTHERN ECONOMIC DEVELOPMENT.
UNIVERSITY OF FLORIDA PRESS. GAINESVILLE, FLORIDA. 1962.

NDUNNES62309 DUNN ES
SOUTHERN ECONOMIC DEVELOPMENT AS REVEALED BY THE CHANGING
STRUCTURE OF EMPLOYMENT.
UNIVERSITY OF FLORIDA, MONOGRAPHS IN THE SOCIAL SCIENCES
NO 14. GAINESVILLE, FLORIDA. 1962.

NDUNSRA63310 DUN-S REVIEW AND MOD INDUSTRY
NEGRO EMPLOYMENT PROBLEM.
DUN-S REVIEW AND MODERN INDUSTRY, VOL 82, AUG 1963.
PP 59-60.

NDUSCJX63311 DUSCHA J
DUAL PARTS OF DESEGREGATION, LEGISLATION TO EDUCATE AND
TRAIN NEGROES FOR BETTER JOBS.
THE REPORTER, VOL 29, AUG 15 1963. PP 43-46.

NDWYERJ53312 DWYER RJ
THE NEGRO IN THE US ARMY. /MILITARY/
SOCIOLOGY AND SOCIAL RESEARCH, VOL 38, NOV 1953.
PP 103-112.

NDWYERJ57956 DWYER RJ
THE NEGRO TEACHER AND DESEGREGATION.
SOCIOLOGY AND SOCIAL RESEARCH, VOL 42, NO 1, SEPT-OCT 1957.
PP 26-30.

NEATHBJ64314 EATHERLY BJ
THE CHANGING ECONOMIC STATUS OF THE MISSISSIPPI NEGRO.
SOUTHERN METHODIST UNIVERSITY. PHD DISSERTATION. DALLAS,
TEXAS. 1964.

NEBOIAX60315 EBOINE A   MEENES M
ETHNIC AND CLASS PREFERENCES AMONG COLLEGE NEGROES.
JOURNAL OF NEGRO EDUCATION, VOL 29, NO 2, 1960. PP 128-132.

NEBONXX59318 EBONY
PROFITABLE CAREERS -- WITHOUT COLLEGE.
EBONY, VOL 14, JUNE 1959. PP 23-26.

NEBONXX63316 EBONY
JOB OUTLOOK FOR YOUTH.
EBONY, VOL 18, MAY 1963. PP 25-30.

NEBONXX64317 EBONY
NEW HOPE FOR RURAL DIXIE. FIRMS IN CAROLINAS CREATE JOBS FOR
NEGROES.
EBONY, VOL 19, JUNE 1964. PP 50-57.

NECKAEW55319 ECKARD EW   RATCHFORD BU
*NATIONAL PLANNING ASSN
TWO PLANTS -- LITTLE-ROCK. /CASE-STUDY INDUSTRY ARKANSAS/
NATIONAL PLANNING ASSOCIATION, COMMITTEE OF THE SOUTH.
REPORT NO 6-4. WASHINGTON, DC. 1955. PP 334-356.

NECKSOX66957 ECKSTEIN O
GOALS IN THE WAR ON POVERTY. /ECONOMIC-STATUS/
YALE UNIVERSITY PRESS. NEW HAVEN, CONNECTICUT. 1966.

NEDELHX66320 EDELSBERG H   *US DEPARTMENT OF LABOR.
NEW JOBS FOR NEGROES.
US DEPARTMENT OF LABOR, BUREAU OF LABOR STATISTICS.
OCCUPATIONAL OUTLOOK QUARTERLY, VOL 10, NO 4, DEC 1966.
PP 14-15.

NEDMOMS65321 EDMONDSON MS
INDUSTRY AND RACE IN THE SOUTHERN US.
INDUSTRIALIZATION AND RACE RELATIONS. A SYMPOSIUM. ED BY GUY
HUNTER. OXFORD UNIVERSITY PRESS. NEW YORK. 1965. PP 46-60.

NEDUCTS64322 EDUCATIONAL TESTING SERVICE
SELECTING AND TRAINING NEGROES FOR MANAGERIAL POSITIONS.
EDUCATIONAL TESTING SERVICE. PRINCETON, NEW JERSEY. 1964.

NEDWAGF59324 EDWARDS GF
THE NEGRO PROFESSIONAL CLASS. /OCCUPATIONAL-PATTERNS/
GLENCOE FREE PRESS. GLENCOE, ILLINOIS. 1959. 224 PP.

NEDWAGF64323 EDWARDS GF
CHANGES IN OCCUPATIONS AS THEY AFFECT THE NEGRO.
ASSURING FREEDOM TO THE FREE. A CENTURY OF EMANCIPATION IN
THE USA. ED BY ARNOLD M ROSE. WAYNE STATE UNIVERSITY PRESS.
DETROIT, MICHIGAN. 1964.

NEDWAGF64326 EDWARDS GF
OCCUPATIONAL-MOBILITY OF NEGRO PROFESSIONAL WORKERS.
CONTRIBUTIONS TO URBAN SOCIOLOGY. ED BY EW BURGESS AND
D BOGUE. UNIVERSITY OF CHICAGO PRESS. CHICAGO, ILLINOIS.
1964. PP 443-458.

NEDWAGL47325 EDWARDS GL
NEGROES. VOCATIONAL GUIDANCE AND COUNSELING IN THE SOUTHERN
FIELD.
OPPORTUNITY, VOL 25, AP 1947. PP 67-68.

NEDWARM61327 EDWARDS RM   MORRIS LB
*ACTION FOR BOSTON COM DEVEL
THE NEGRO IN BOSTON. /MASSACHUSETTS/
ACTION FOR BOSTON COMMUNITY DEVELOPMENT. BOSTON,
MASSACHUSETTS. OCT 1961. 141 PP.

NEDWAVA42328 EDWARDS VA
NEGRO LEADERSHIP IN RURAL GEORGIA COMMUNITIES. OCCUPATIONAL
AND SOCIAL ASPECTS.
SOCIAL FORCES, VOL 21, NO 1, OCT 1942. PP 90-93.

NEELLWC55329 EELLS WC
THE HIGHER EDUCATION OF NEGROES IN THE UNITED STATES.
JOURNAL OF NEGRO EDUCATION, VOL 1, 1955. PP 426-434.

NELLIGH59330 ELLIS GH
THE CONSTITUTIONAL RIGHT TO MEMBERSHIP IN A LABOR
UNION -- FIFTH AND FOURTEENTH AMENDMENTS.
JOURNAL OF PUBLIC LAW, VOL 8, FALL 1959. PP 580-595.

NELLSJS52331 ELLSWORTH JS
FACTORY FOLKWAYS. A STUDY OF INSTITUTIONAL STRUCTURE AND
CHANGE.
YALE UNIVERSITY PRESS. NEW HAVEN, CONNECTICUT. 1952.

NENGLWH57333 ENGLISH WH
MINORITY-GROUP ATTITUDES OF NEGROES AND IMPLICATIONS FOR
GUIDANCE.
JOURNAL OF NEGRO EDUCATION, VOL 26, 1957. PP 99-107.

NEPPSEG64336 EPPS EG   KATZ I
ALEXSON L
RELATION OF MOTHER-S EMPLOYMENT TO INTELLECTUAL PERFORMANCE
OF NEGRO COLLEGE STUDENTS.
SOCIAL PROBLEMS, VOL 11, SPRING 1964. PP 414-418.

NEPPSEG65334 EPPS EG   *U OF MICH INST SOC RESEARCH
FAMILY AND ACHIEVEMENT. A PROPOSAL TO STUDY THE EFFECT OF
FAMILY SOCIALIZATION ON ACHIEVEMENT AND PERFORMANCE AMONG
URBAN NEGRO AMERICANS.
UNIVERSITY OF MICHIGAN, INSTITUTE FOR SOCIAL RESEARCH.
ANN ARBOR, MICHIGAN. 1965. 19 PP.

NEPPSEG66335 EPPS EG   *U OF MICH INST SOC RESEARCH
MOTIVATION AND PERFORMANCE OF NEGRO STUDENTS.
UNIVERSITY OF MICHIGAN, INSTITUTE FOR SOCIAL RESEARCH.
ANN ARBOR, MICHIGAN. SEPT 1966. 21 PP.

NEPSTLA63337 EPSTEIN LA   *US DEPT OF HEALTH ED WELFARE
UN-MET NEED IN A LAND OF ABUNDANCE.
US DEPARTMENT OF HEALTH, EDUCATION, AND WELFARE, SOCIAL
SECURITY BULLETIN. GPO. WASHINGTON, DC. MAY 1963. PP 3-11.

NERICRW46339 ERICKSON RW
ON SPECIAL-TRAINING-UNIT PERFORMANCE AS AN INDEX OF NEGRO
ABILITY.
JOURNAL OF ABNORMAL AND SOCIAL PSYCHOLOGY, VOL 41, 1946.
P 481.

NERIKEX64338 ERIKSON E
MEMORANDUM ON IDENTITY AND NEGRO YOUTH.
JOURNAL OF SOCIAL ISSUES, VOL 20, OCT 1964. PP 29-42.

NEVANJC43258 EVANS JC
THE NATIONAL TECHNICAL ASSOCIATION. /OCCUPATIONS/
THE QUARTERLY REVIEW OF HIGHER EDUCATION AMONG NEGROES, VOL
2, NO 4, OCT 1943. PP 14-17.

NEVANJC56340 EVANS JC   LANE DA
INTEGRATION IN THE ARMED SERVICES. /MILITARY/
ANNALS OF THE AMERICAN ACADEMY OF POLITICAL AND SOCIAL
SCIENCE. VOL 304, MAR 1956. PP 78-85.

NFACTOF64341 FACTS ON FILE   NEWSYEAR EDS
CIVIL-RIGHTS, 1960-63. THE NEGRO CAMPAIGN TO WIN EQUAL
RIGHTS AND OPPORTUNITIES IN THE UNITED STATES.
FACTS ON FILE. NEW YORK. 1964. 152 PP.

NFAGGHL55255 FAGGET HL
THE NEGROES WHO DO NOT WANT TO END SEGREGATION.
/EMPLOYMENT/
THE QUARTERLY REVIEW OF HIGHER EDUCATION AMONG NEGROES, VOL
23, NO 3, JULY 1955. PP 120-122.

NFALCNS45342 FALCOME NS   *NYS WAR CC COMM DISCR EMPLOY
THE NEGRO INTEGRATED.
NEW YORK STATE WAR COUNCIL COMMITTEE ON DISCRIMINATION IN
EMPLOYMENT. ALBANY, NEW YORK. 1945. 35 PP.

NFALLAG63343 FALL AG
THE SEARCH FOR NEGRO MEDICAL STUDENTS. /EDUCATION/
INTEGRATED EDUCATION, VOL 1, JUNE 1963. PP 15-19.

NFARRGR65344 FARRELL GR   *RUTGERS U URBAN STUDIES CENT
A CLIMATE OF CHANGE, THE NEW-HAVEN STORY. /CONNECTICUT/
RUTGERS -- THE STATE UNIVERSITY, URBAN STUDIES CENTER.
NEW BRUNSWICK, NEW JERSEY. 1965.

NFAULHU57345 FAULKNER HU   STARR M
LABOR IN AMERICA.
OXFORD BOOK COMPANY. NEW YORK. NEW REVISED EDITION 1957.
330 PP.

NFEILJG63346 FEILD JG
A NEW LOOK AT EMPLOYMENT.
NORTH CAROLINA LAW REVIEW, VOL 42, NO 1, DEC 1963.
PP 154-161.

NFEINRX65347 FEIN R
AN ECONOMIC AND SOCIAL PROFILE OF THE NEGRO AMERICAN.
DAEDALUS, VOL 94, NO 4, FALL 1965. PP 815-846.

NFEINRX65348 FEIN R   *BROOKINGS INSTITUTION
EDUCATIONAL PATTERNS IN SOUTHERN MIGRATION.
BROOKINGS INSTITUTION. WASHINGTON, DC. 1965. PP 106-124.

NFEINRX66349 FEIN R
RELATIVE INCOME OF NEGRO MEN. SOME RECENT DATA.
QUARTERLY JOURNAL OF ECONOMICS, VOL 80, MAY 1966.

NFELDHX42351 FELDMAN H
THE TECHNIQUE OF INTRODUCING NEGROES INTO THE PLANT.
/INDUSTRY/
PERSONNEL JOURNAL, SEPT 1942. PP 461-466.

NFELDJA61350 FELDMAN JA
THE 1960 AUDIT OF NEGRO VETERANS AND SERVICEMAN. /MILITARY/
JOURNAL OF INTERGROUP RELATIONS, VOL 2, WINTER 1960-1961.
PP 79-81.

NFERGML49961 FERGUSON ML
THE STRUGGLE OF NEGRO TEACHERS IN FLORIDA FOR EQUAL
SALARIES. /OCCUPATIONS/
TUSKEGEE INSTITUTE. MA ESSAY. TUSKEGEE, ALABAMA. 1949.
44 PP.

NFERMLA64353 FERMAN LA
SOCIOLOGICAL PERSPECTIVES IN UNEMPLOYMENT RESEARCH.
BLUE-COLLAR WORLD. STUDIES OF THE AMERICAN WORKER. ED BY
ARTHUR SHOSTAK AND WILLIAM GOMBERG. PRENTICE-HALL.
ENGLEWOOD CLIFFS, NEW JERSEY. 1964. PP 504-514. ALSO THE
UNIVERSITY OF MICHIGAN-WAYNE STATE UNIVERSITY, INSTITUTE OF
LABOR AND INDUSTRIAL RELATIONS. REPRINT SERIES NO 29.
ANN ARBOR, MICHIGAN. ND.

NFERMLA65352 FERMAN LA
THE SOCIAL-STRUCTURE OF THE MICHIGAN LABOR-MARKET.
MICHIGAN IN THE 1970-S. ED BY WILLIAM HABER. THE UNIVERSITY
OF MICHIGAN, BUREAU OF INDUSTRIAL RELATIONS. ANN ARBOR,
MICHIGAN. PP 241-292.

NFERMLA66790 FERMAN LA   *U OF MICH-WAYNE STATE U ILIR
THE NEGRO AND EQUAL-EMPLOYMENT-OPPORTUNITIES. A REVIEW OF
MANAGEMENT EXPERIENCES IN TWENTY COMPANIES.
THE UNIVERSITY OF MICHIGAN-WAYNE STATE UNIVERSITY, INSTITUTE
OF LABOR AND INDUSTRIAL RELATIONS. ANN ARBOR, MICHIGAN.
DEC 1966. 189 PP.

NFICHJH59464 FICHTER JH
THE RELUCTANT SOUTH. /INTEGRATION/

COMMONWEAL, VOL 70, NO 7, MAY 15 1959. PP 175-177.

NFICHJH64867 FICHTER JH   *NATL OPINION RESEARCH CENTER
YOUNG NEGRO TALENT. SURVEY OF THE EXPERIENCES AND
EXPECTATIONS OF NEGRO AMERICANS WHO GRADUATED FROM COLLEGE
IN 1961.
UNIVERSITY OF CHICAGO, NATIONAL OPINION RESEARCH CENTER.
CHICAGO, ILLINOIS. NOV 1964. 63 PP.

NFICHJH66789 FICHTER JH
CAREER PREPARATION AND EXPECTATIONS OF NEGRO COLLEGE
STUDENTS.
JOURNAL OF NEGRO EDUCATION, VOL 25, NO 4, FALL 1966,
PP 322-335.

NFILIJE66354 FILIPSKI JE   *US DEPARTMENT OF LABOR
MDTA PROJECT UPLIFT. /TRAINING/
US DEPARTMANT OF LABOR, EMPLOYMENT SERVICE REVIEW, VOL3,
NO 8, AUG 1966. PP 18-20.

NFINLOE60356 FINLEY OE   *NATIONAL URBAN LEAGUE
TRAINING FOR TOMORROW-S SCIENTISTS AND TECHNICIANS. A
COMMUNITY APPROACH TO A COMMUNITY NEED.
NATIONAL URBAN LEAGUE. NEW YORK. 1960.

NFINLOX63355 FINLEY O
DISCRIMINATION 1963. /OCCUPATIONAL-STATUS/
AMERICAN CHILD, VOL 45, NO 1, JAN 1963. PP 1-5.

NFISKUX44357 FISK UNIVERSITY
MONTHLY SUMMARY OF EVENTS AND TRENDS IN RACE-RELATIONS.
/CINCINNATI OHIO CASE-STUDY UNION/
FISK UNIVERSITY. NASHVILLE, TENNESSEE. FEB-MAR 1944.

NFITZNH63358 FITZHUGH NH ED
PROBLEMS AND OPPORTUNITIES CONFRONTING NEGROES IN THE FIELD
OF BUSINESS. REPORT ON THE NATIONAL CONFERENCE ON SMALL
BUSINESS. /OCCUPATIONS/
GPO. WASHINGTON, DC. 1963. 102 PP.

NFLEIHX58361 FLEISCHMAN H   RORTY J
*NATIONAL LABOR SERVICE
WE OPEN THE GATES. /UNION/
NATIONAL LABOR SERVICE. NEW YORK. 1958. 64 PP.

NFLEIHX59359 FLEISCHMAN H
IS LABOR COLOR BLIND. /UNION/
PROGRESSIVE, VOL 23, NOV 1959. PP 24-28

NFLEIHX59360 FLEISCHMAN H
UNIONS AND DISCRIMINATION.
THE RECONSTRUCTIONIST, JAN 23 1959.

NFLEMHC66362 FLEMING HC
THE FEDERAL EXECUTIVE AND CIVIL-RIGHTS. 1961-1965.
DAEDALUS, VOL 94, NO 4, FALL 1965. ALSO THE NEGRO AMERICAN.
ED BY TALCOTT PARSONS AND KENNETH CLARK. HOUGHTON MIFFLIN
CO. BOSTON, MASSACHUSETTS. 1966. PP 371-399.

NFLORCO62366 FLORIDA COUNCIL ON HUMAN RELS
NEGRO EMPLOYMENT IN MIAMI. /FLORIDA/
FLORIDA COUNCIL ON HUMAN RELATIONS. NEW SOUTH, VOL 17,
MAY 1962. PP 6-10.

NFOLEEP66369 FOLEY EP
THE NEGRO BUSINESSMAN. IN SEARCH OF A TRADITION.
/OCCUPATIONS/
DAEDALUS, VOL 95, NO 1, WINTER 1966. PP 107-144.

NFONEPS47370 FONER PS
HISTORY OF THE LABOR MOVEMENT IN THE UNITED STATES. /UNION/
INTERNATIONAL PUBLISHERS. NEW YORK. 1947.

NFORDFX66133 FORD FOUNDATION
GRANTS AND PROJECTS RELATED TO THE DEVELOPMENT OF THE
AMERICAN NEGRO. ALL FISCAL YEARS THROUGH JUNE 10, 1966.
THE FORD FOUNDATION. NEW YORK. 1966.

NFORECX51371 FOREMAN C
THE DECADE OF HOPE. /CIVIL-RIGHTS ECONOMIC/
PHYLON, VOL 12, NO 2, 2ND QUARTER 1951. PP 137-150.

NFORMPB55372 FORMAN PB
THE IMPLICATIONS OF PROJECT CLEAR. /DESEGREGATION/
PHYLON, VOL 16, 4TH QUARTER 1955. PP 263-274.

NFORTUN45052 FORTUNE
FORTUNE PRESS ANALYSIS, NEGROES. /EMPLOYMENT/
FORTUNE, VOL 31, NO 5, MAY 1945. PP 233 FF.

NFORTXX42541 FORTUNE
THE NEGROES WAR.
FORTUNE, JUNE 1942. PP 151-158.

NFORTXX43050 FORTUNE
THE DEEP SOUTH LOOKS UP. /POVERTY EMPLOYMENT/
FORTUNE, VOL 28, NO 1, JULY 1943. PP 95-100 FF.

NFORTXX49054 FORTUNE
NEGRO BUSINESSMEN OF NEW-ORLEANS.
FORTUNE, NOV 1949. PP 112-116 FF.

NFORTXX55051 FORTUNE
DISCRIMINATION, A NOTICE TO INDUSTRY.
FORTUNE, NOV 1955. PP 70-72.

NFORTXX56881 FORTUNE
REVOLT IN THE SOUTH. /UNION DISCRIMINATION/
FORTUNE, VOL 53, MAY 1956. PP 215-216.

NFORTXX57373 FORTUNE
BIAS IN UNIONS.
FORTUNE, VOL 55, JUNE 1957. PP 245-246.

NFOSTWZ53375 FOSTER WZ
LEFT SECTARIANISM IN THE FIGHT FOR NEGRO RIGHTS AND AGAINST
WHITE CHAUVINISM.
POLITICAL AFFAIRS, VOL 32, JUNE 1953. PP 17-31.

NFRANJH56060 FRANKLIN JH
HISTORY OF RACIAL SEGREGATION IN THE UNITED STATES.
ANNALS OF THE AMERICAN ACADEMY OF POLITICAL AND SOCIAL
SCIENCE, VOL 304, MAR 1956. PP 1-9.

NFRANWH66698 FRANKLIN WH   *US DEPARTMENT OF LABOR
OUTREACH -- THE AFFIRMATIVE APPROACH. /EMPLOYMENT SES/
US DEPARTMENT OF LABOR, EMPLOYMENT SERVICE REVIEW, VOL 3, NO
8, AUG 1966. PP 64-65.

NFRAZEF47384 FRAZIER EF

THE RACIAL ISSUE.
UNITY AND DIFFERENCE IN AMERICAN LIFE. ED BY RM MACIVER.
HARPER. NEW YORK. 1947. PP 43-60.

NFRAZ EF48379 FRAZIER EF
ETHNIC FAMILY PATTERNS. THE NEGRO FAMILY IN THE
    UNITED STATES.
AMERICAN JOURNAL OF SOCIOLOGY, VOL 54, MAY 1948. PP 432-438.

NFRAZ EF50382 FRAZIER EF
PROBLEMS AND NEEDS OF NEGRO CHILDREN AND YOUTH RESULTING
    FROM FAMILY DISORGANIZATION.
JOURNAL OF NEGRO EDUCATION, VOL 19, 1950. PP 269-277.

NFRAZ EF51578 FRAZIER EF ED
THE INTEGRATION OF THE NEGRO INTO AMERICAN SOCIETY.
HOWARD UNIVERSITY. GRADUATE SCHOOL, DIVISION OF SOCIAL
SCIENCES. PAPERS CONTRIBUTED TO THE 14TH ANNUAL CONFERENCE,
MAY 3-4 1951. HOWARD UNIVERSITY PRESS. WASHINGTON, DC. 1951.
212 PP.

NFRAZ EF57371 FRAZIER EF
BLACK BOURGEOISIE. THE RISE OF A MIDDLE-CLASS IN THE
    UNITED STATES.
GLENCOE FREE PRESS. GLENCOE, ILLINOIS. 1957.

NFRAZ EF57378 FRAZIER EF   *WELFARE CC METROPOLITAN CHI
THE CULTURAL-BACKGROUND OF SOUTHERN NEGROES.
SELECTED PAPERS OF THE INSTITUTE ON CULTURAL PATTERNS OF
NEWCOMERS. WELFARE COUNCIL OF METROPOLITAN CHICAGO. CHICAGO,
ILLINOIS. OCT 1957. PP 1-14.

NFRAZ EF57381 FRAZIER EF
THE NEGRO MIDDLE-CLASS AND DESEGREGATION.
SOCIAL PROBLEMS, VOL 4, 1957. PP 291-301.

NFRAZ EF57966 FRAZIER EF
THE NEGRO IN THE UNITED STATES.
MACMILLAN COMPANY. NEW YORK. REVISED ED. 1957. 769 PP.

NFRAZ EF58376 FRAZIER EF
AREAS OF RESEARCH IN RACE-RELATIONS.
SOCIOLOGY AND SOCIAL RESEARCH, VOL 42, NO 6, JULY-AUG 1958.
PP 424-429.

NFRAZ EF64380 FRAZIER EF
THE NEGRO FAMILY IN CHICAGO. /ILLINOIS/
CONTRIBUTIONS TO URBAN SOCIOLOGY. ED BY EW BURGESS AND DJ
BOGUE. UNIVERSITY OF CHICAGO PRESS. CHICAGO, ILLINOIS. 1964.

NFREE RX50567 FREEDMAN R
RECENT MIGRATION TO CHICAGO. /LABOR-FORCE ILLINOIS/
UNIVERSITY OF CHICAGO PRESS. CHICAGO, ILLINOIS. 1950.
CHAPTER 6.

NFRENRL65385 FRENCH RL
THE MOTOROLA CASE. /TESTING/
INDUSTRIAL PSYCHOLOGIST, VOL 2, AUG 1965. PP 20-50.

NFREYMX66386 FREYMAN M   *US DEPARTMENT OF LABOR
REGIONAL CONFERENCES ON IMPLEMENTING THE CIVIL-RIGHTS-ACT.
US DEPARTMENT OF LABOR, EMPLOYMENT SERVICE REVIEW. VOL 3,
NO 10, OCT 1966. PP 40-41.

NFRIEMX65387 FRIERSON M
THE NEGRO LAWYER IN VIRGINIA. A SURVEY. /OCCUPATIONS/
VIRGINIA LAW REVIEW, VOL 51, 1965. PP 521-545.

NFRUMRM58388 FRUMKIN RM
RACE, OCCUPATION, AND SOCIAL-CLASS IN NEW-YORK.
JOURNAL OF NEGRO EDUCATION, VOL 27, WINTER 1958. PP 62-65.

NFULL SB63390 FULLER SB
A NEGRO BUSINESS-MAN SPEAKS HIS MIND.
US NEWS AND WORLD REPORT, VOL 55, AUGUST 19 1963. PP 58-61.

NFUSF DR66014 FUSFELD DR
TRAINING FOR MINORITY-GROUPS. PROBLEMS OF RACIAL IMBALANCE
    AND SEGREGATION.
UNIVERSITY OF MICHIGAN, DEPARTMENT OF ECONOMICS. UNPUBLISHED
PAPER. ANN ARBOR, MICHIGAN. 1966. 24 PP.

NGALL LE65391 GALLAWAY LE
THE ANATOMY OF THE NEGRO-WHITE INCOME DIFFERENTIAL.
THE NEGRO AND EMPLOYMENT OPPORTUNITY.
PROBLEMS AND PRACTICES. ED BY H R NORTHRUP AND R L ROWAN.
UNIVERSITY OF MICHIGAN, GRADUATE SCHOOL OF BUSINESS
EDUCATION, BUREAU OF INDUSTRIAL RELATIONS. ANN ARBOR,
MICHIGAN. 1965. PP 45-64.

NGALL LE66392 GALLAWAY LE
INTER-INDUSTRY LABOR MOBILITY AMONG MEN, 1957-60.
SOCIAL SECURITY BULLETIN, VOL 29, NO 9, SEPT 1966. PP 10-22.

NGALL LE67393 GALLAWAY LE
THE NEGRO AND POVERTY.
JOURNAL OF BUSINESS, JAN 1967. ALSO LOWELL E GALLAWAY.
UNIVERSITY OF PENNSYLVANIA, WHARTON SCHOOL OF FINANCE AND
COMMERCE, DEPARTMENT OF INDUSTRY. WORKING PAPER NO 8.
MAR 1966. 20 PP.

NGARBAP65394 GARBIN AP   BALLWEG JA
INTRA-PLANT MOBILITY OF NEGRO AND WHITE WORKERS.
AMERICAN JOURNAL OF SOCIOLOGY, VOL 71, NO 3, NOV 1965.
PP 315-319.

NGARDHX63395 GARDNER H
THE EVOLUTION OF AMERICAN LAW VIS-A-VIS THE AMERICAN NEGRO.
AMERICAN BUSINESS LAW JOURNAL, VOL 1, NO 1, 1963. PP 16-24.

NGARFHX59396 GARFINKEL H
WHEN NEGROES MARCH. THE MARCH-ON-WASHINGTON-MOVEMENT IN THE
    ORGANIZATIONAL POLITICS FOR FEPC.
GLENCOE FREE PRESS. GLENCOE, ILLINOIS. 1959.

NGEISPX62397 GEISEL P
I Q PERFORMANCE, EDUCATIONAL AND OCCUPATIONAL ASPIRATIONS
    OF YOUTH IN A SOUTHERN CITY -- A RACIAL COMPARISON.
VANDERBILT UNIVERSITY. PHD DISSERTATION. NASHVILLE,
TENNESSEE. 1962.

NGENEEX64398 GENERAL ELECTRIC
AT WORK IN INDUSTRY TODAY. 50 CASE-REPORTS ON NEGROES AT
    WORK.
GENERAL ELECTRIC. MANAGEMENT DEVELOPMENT AND EMPLOYEE
RELATIONS SERVICES. EQUAL OPPORTUNITIES PROGRESS PUBLICATION
NO ERC-41. SCHENECTADY, NEW YORK. 1964.

NGEORCH64399 GEORGIA COUNCIL ON HUMAN RELS
OPENING THE DOOR TO EMPLOYMENT. /EEO/

GEORGIA COUNCIL ON HUMAN RELATIONS. ATLANTA, GEORGIA. 1964.
8 PP.

NGERSGX65082 GERSH G
ECONOMIC ADVANCES OF THE AMERICAN NEGRO.
CONTEMPORARY REVIEW, VOL 207, SEPT 1965. PP 134-139.

NGERSWJ65634 GERSHENFELD WJ
AN INSIGHT INTO STRUCTURAL UNEMPLOYMENT -- THE EXPERIENCE OF
    A MINORITY GROUP IN A PROSPEROUS COMMUNITY.
ECONOMIC AND BUSINESS BULLETIN, VOL 18, NO 1, SEPT 1965.
PP 21-28.

NGESC JA64400 GESCHWENDER JA
SOCIAL-STRUCTURE AND THE NEGRO REVOLT. AN EXAMINATION OF
    SOME HYPOTHESES. /SOCIO-ECONOMIC/
SOCIAL FORCES, VOL 43, DEC 1964. PP 248-256.

NGIBBJP65401 GIBBS JP
OCCUPATIONAL DIFFERENTIATION OF NEGROES AND WHITES IN THE
    UNITED STATES.
SOCIAL FORCES, VOL 44, DEC 1965. PP 159-165.

NGIBSHX54402 GIBSON H   *KANSAS CITY COM STUDIES
RACIAL INTEGRATION IN EMPLOYMENT -- FINDINGS IN TWO
    KANSAS-CITY HOSPITALS.
KANSAS CITY. COMMUNITY STUDIES, INC PUBLICATION NO 80.
KANSAS CITY, MISSOURI. JULY 1954. 32 PP.

NGINZ EX51410 GINZBERG E   *COLUMBIA U CONSER OF HR PROJ
OCCUPATIONAL CHOICE. AN APPROACH TO A GENERAL THEORY.
COLUMBIA UNIVERSITY, CONSERVATION OF HUMAN RESOURCES
PROJECT. COLUMBIA UNIVERSITY PRESS. NEW YORK. 1951.

NGINZ EX53415 GINZBERG E   BRAY DW
THE UNEDUCATED.
COLUMBIA UNIVERSITY PRESS. NEW YORK. 1953. 246 PP.

NGINZ EX56409 GINZBERG E
THE NEGRO POTENTIAL. /EMPLOYMENT INCOME EDUCATION/
COLUMBIA UNIVERSITY PRESS. NEW YORK. 1956. 144 PP.

NGINZ EX58405 GINZBERG E
HUMAN-RESOURCES, THE WEALTH OF A NATION. /YOUTH/
SIMON AND SCHUSTER. NEW YORK. 1958.

NGINZ EX59406 GINZBERG E   *COLUMBIA U CONSER OF HR PROJ
THE INEFFECTIVE SOLDIER. LESSONS FOR MANAGEMENT AND THE
    NATION.
COLUMBIA UNIVERSITY, CONSERVATION OF HUMAN RESOURCES
PROJECT. COLUMBIA UNIVERSITY PRESS. NEW YORK. 1959. 3 VOLS.

NGINZ EX60404 GINZBERG E
EXPANDING NEGRO OPPORTUNITIES. /OCCUPATIONAL-STATUS/
READINGS IN UNEMPLOYMENT. US SENATE COMMITTEE ON
UNEMPLOYMENT PROBLEMS, 86TH CONGRESS, 2ND SESSION.
WASHINGTON, DC. GPO. 1960. PP 877-906.

NGINZ EX60413 GINZBERG E
SEGREGATION AND MANPOWER WASTE.
PHYLON, VOL 21, NO 4, 1960. PP 311-316.

NGINZ EX61407 GINZBERG E
THE NEGRO AND HIS WORK.
WASHINGTON CENTER FOR METROPOLITAN STUDIES. ADDRESS.
WASHINGTON, DC. NOV 2 1961.

NGINZ EX61411 GINZBERG E   *COLUMBIA U CONSER OF HR PROJ
THE OPTIMISTIC TRADITION AND AMERICAN YOUTH.
COLUMBIA UNIVERSITY, CONSERVATION OF HUMAN RESOURCES
PROJECT. COLUMBIA UNIVERSITY PRESS. NEW YORK. 1961.

NGINZ EX64408 GINZBERG E
THE NEGRO CHALLENGE TO THE BUSINESS COMMUNITY. /INDUSTRY/
MCGRAW-HILL. NEW YORK. 1964. 111 PP.

NGINZ EX64414 GINZBERG E   EICHNER AS
THE TROUBLESOME PRESENCE. AMERICAN DEMOCRACY AND THE NEGRO.
FREE PRESS. NEW YORK. 1964.

NGINZ EX66412 GINZBERG E
PSYCHOLOGY AND MANPOWER POLICY.
AMERICAN PSYCHOLOGIST, VOL 21, NO 6, JUNE 1966. PP 549-554.

NGINZ EX66416 GINZBERG E   HIESTAND D
EMPLOYMENT PATTERNS OF NEGRO MEN AND WOMEN.
THE AMERICAN NEGRO REFERENCE BOOK. ED BY JOHN P DAVIS.
PRENTICE-HALL. ENGLEWOOD CLIFFS, NEW JERSEY. 1966.
PP 205-250.

NGINZ EX66971 GINZBERG E   *US CHAMBER OF COMMERCE
POVERTY AND THE NEGRO.
THE DISADVANTAGED POOR. EDUCATION AND EMPLOYMENT. US CHAMBER
OF COMMERCE, TASK FORCE OF ECONOMIC GROWTH AND OPPORTUNITY.
WASHINGTON, DC. 1966. PP 207-228.

NGINZ EX67417 GINZBERG E   HIESTAND D
THE GUIDANCE OF NEGRO YOUTH.
EMPLOYMENT, RACE AND POVERTY. ED BY ARTHUR M ROSS AND
HERBERT HILL. HARCOURT, BRACE AND WORLD. NEW YORK. 1967.
PP 435-459.

NGIOVPC64279 GIOVANNINI PC
EQUAL EDUCATIONAL OPPORTUNITY. ANOTHER ASPECT.
PETER C GIOVANNINI. NEW YORK PORT OF AUTHORITY. NEW YORK.
MIMEOGRAPHED PAPER. 1964.

NGISS IX65418 GISSEN I   *ANTI-DEFAMATION LEAGUE
NEGRO-S REAL PROBLEM. /DISCRIMINATION/
ANTI-DEFAMATION LEAGUE OF B-NAI B-RITH, ADL BULLETIN.
OCT 1965.

NGISTNP63419 GIST NP   BENNETT WS
ASPIRATIONS OF NEGRO AND WHITE STUDENTS.
SOCIAL FORCES, VOL 42, OCT 1963. PP 40-48.

NGLAZNX63420 GLAZER N   MOYNIHAN DP
THE NEGROES.
BEYOND THE MELTING POT. BY NATHAN GLAZER AND DANIEL P
MOYNIHAN. MASSACHUSETTS INSTITUTE OF TECHNOLOGY PRESS AND
HARVARD PRESS. CAMBRIDGE, MASSACHUSETTS. 1963. PP 25-85.

NGLENND62422 GLENN ND
CHANGES IN THE AMERICAN OCCUPATIONAL-STRUCTURE AND
    OCCUPATIONAL GAINS OF NEGROES DURING THE 1940-S.
SOCIAL FORCES, VOL 41, DEC 1962. PP 188-195.

NGLENND63421 GLENN ND
SOME CHANGES IN THE RELATIVE STATUS OF AMERICAN NON-WHITES,
    1940 TO 1960. /INCOME OCCUPATIONAL-STATUS EDUCATION/

PHYLON, VOL 24, NO 2, SUMMER 1963.

NGLENND63423 GLENN ND
OCCUPATIONAL BENEFITS TO WHITES FROM THE SUBORDINATION OF
NEGROES. /DISCRIMINATION/
AMERICAN SOCIOLOGICAL REVIEW, VOL 28, NO 2, JUNE 1963.
PP 443-448.

NGLENND64424 GLENN ND
THE RELATIVE SIZE OF THE NEGRO POPULATICN AND NEGRO
OCCUPATIONAL-STATUS.
SOCIAL FORCES, VOL 43, NO 1, OCT 1964. PP 42-49.

NGLENND65425 GLENN ND
REPLY TO CUTRIGHT ON NEGRO SUBORDINATION.
/OCCUPATIONAL-STATUS/
AMERICAN SOCIOLOGICAL REVIEW, VOL 30, NO 3, JUNE 1965.
P 416.

NGLENND65676 GLENN ND
THE ROLE OF WHITE RESISTANCE AND FACILITATION IN THE NEGRO
STRUGGLE FOR EQUALITY.
PHYLON, VOL 26, NO 2, SECOND QUARTER, 1965. PP 105-116.

NGOLDFH63429 GOLDMAN FH ED   *UNIV OF CHICAGO CFSOLEFA
EDUCATIONAL IMPERATIVE. THE NEGRO IN THE CHANGING SOUTH.
UNIVERSITY OF CHICAGO, CENTER FOR THE STUDY OF LIBERAL
EDUCATION FOR ADULTS. CHICAGO, ILLINOIS. 1963. 101 PP.

NGOLDFH63430 GOLDMAN FH   *UNIV OF CHICAGO CFSOLEFA
PROBLEMS FOR ADULT EDUCATION RELATED TO ACQUIRING
CAPABILITIES FOR WORK.
EDUCATIONAL IMPERATIVE. THE NEGRO IN THE CHANGING SOUTH.
ED BY F H GOLDMAN. UNIVERSITY OF CHICAGO, CENTER FOR THE
STUDY OF LIBERAL EDUCATION FOR ADULTS. CHICAGO, ILLINOIS.
1963. PP 81-84.

NGOLDJX65427 GOLDEN J
DESEGREGATION OF SOCIAL AGENCIES IN THE SOUTH.
SOCIAL WORK, VOL 10, NO 1, JAN 1965. PP 58-67.

NGOLDMS63431 GOLDSTEIN MS
LONGEVITY AND HEALTH-STATUS OF THE NEGRO AMERICAN.
JOURNAL OF NEGRO EDUCATION, VOL 32, NO 4, 1963. PP 337-348.

NGOLDNX66428 GOLDFINGER N
NEGROES AND JOBS.
THE AMERICAN FEDERATIONIST, VOL 73. NO 11, NOV 1966.
PP 16-20.

NGOLDSM4835O GOLDSBORO SM
THE EVALUATION OF PRACTICES CARRIED ON BY TWO HUNDRED NEGRO
FARMERS IN THE PRODUCTION OF COTTON IN MACON COUNTY,
ALABAMA.
TUSKEGEE INSTITUTE. THESIS. TUSKEGEE, ALABAMA. 1948. 92 PP.

NGOLICL45432 GOLIGHTLY CL   HEMPHILL IW
*US FEP COMMITTEE
THE WAR-TIME EMPLOYMENT OF NEGROES IN THE
FEDERAL-GOVERNMENT.
US FAIR EMPLOYMENT PRACTICES COMMITTEE, DIVISION OF REVIEW
AND ANALYSIS. GPO. WASHINGTON, DC. JAN 1945. 65 PP.

NGOOOPX66433 GOOD P
THE THORNTONS OF MISSISSIPPI. PEONAGE ON THE PLANTATION.
/POVERTY/
THE ATLANTIC MONTHLY, VOL 218, NO 4, SEPT 1966. PP 95-100.

NGOOGGX48434 GOOGE G
SOUTHERN LABOR FIGHTS BACK. /UNION/
THE AMERICAN FEDERATIONIST, VOL 55, NO 4, AP 1948. PP 8-11.

NGORDDX65976 GORDON D
NOTE ON NEGRO ALIENATION.
AMERICAN JOURNAL OF SOCIOLOGY, VOL 70, JAN 1965. PP 477-478.

NGORDJX65435 GORDON J   *NEW YORK OFFICE OF THE MAYOR
THE POOR OF HARLEM. SOCIAL FUNCTIONING OF THE UNDERCLASS.
NEW YORK, OFFICE OF THE MAYOR. INTERDEPARTMENTAL
NEIGHBORHOOD SERVICE CENTER. NEW YORK. JULY 31 1965. 167 PP.

NGOULHM48436 GOULD HM
UNION RESISTANCE, SOUTHERN STYLE.
LABOR AND NATION, JAN 1948. PP 6-9.

NGOULWB64889 GOULD WB
LABOR LAW AND THE NEGRO.
THE NEW LEADER, OCT 12 1964.

NGOULWB65437 GOULD WB
THE NEGRO REVOLUTION AND THE LAW OF COLLECTIVE BARGAINING.
FORDHAM LAW REVIEW, VOL 34, 1965. PP 207-268.

NGOULWB67864 GOULD WB
EMPLOYMENT SECURITY, SENIORITY AND RACE. THE ROLE OF
TITLE-VII OF THE CIVIL-RIGHTS-ACT OF 1964.
HARVARD LAW JOURNAL, VOL 13, NO 1, WINTER 1967. PP 1-50.

NGOURJC65438 GOURLAY JC   *AMERICAN MANAGEMENT ASSN
THE NEGRO SALARIED WORKER. /EMPLOYMENT-SELECTION/
AMERICAN MANAGEMENT ASSOCIATION. RESEARCH STUDY NO 70.
NEW YORK. 1965.

NGRAGWL49978 GRAGG WL
SOME FACTORS WHICH DISTINGUISH DROP-OUTS FROM HIGH SCHOOL
GRADUATES.
OCCUPATIONS, VOL 27, NO 7, AP 1949. PP 457-459.

NGRAHCX65439 GRAHAM C
TESTIMONY BEFORE STATE SENATE FACT FINDING SUBCOMMITTEE ON
RACE-RELATIONS AND URBAN PROBLEMS, FINAL HEARING,
JANUARY 20 1965. /CALIFORNIA FEPC/
CALIFORNIA FAIR EMPLOYMENT PRACTICE COMMISSION.
SAN FRANCISCO, CALIFORNIA. JAN 1965. 13 PP.

NGRANLB40980 GRANGER LB
PROBLEMS AND NEEDS OF NEGRO ADOLESCENT WORKERS.
JOURNAL OF NEGRO EDUCATION, VOL 9, NO 3, JULY 1940.
PP 321-331.

NGRANLB41442 GRANGER LB   *NATIONAL URBAN LEAGUE
MEMBERSHIP POLICIES OF INTERNATIONAL UNIONS AS THEY AFFECT
NEGRO WORKERS.
NATIONAL URBAN LEAGUE. NEW YORK. 1941.

NGRANLB41443 GRANGER LB
THE NEGRO AND ECONOMIC OPPORTUNITY.
NATIONAL CONFERENCE OF SOCIAL WORK PROCEEDINGS, VOL 68.
COLUMBIA UNIVERSITY PRESS. NEW YORK. 1941. PP 75-87.

NGRANLB42440 GRANGER LB
BARRIERS TO NEGRO WAR EMPLOYMENT.
ANNALS OF THE AMERICAN ACADEMY OF POLITICAL AND SOCIAL
SCIENCE, VOL 223, SEPT 1942.

NGRANLB42444 GRANGER LB
NEGROES AND WAR PRODUCTION.
SURVEY GRAPHIC. VOL 31, 1942.

NGRANLB58596 GRANGER LB
THE NEGRO RECORD IN EQUAL-OPPORTUNITIES.
JOURNAL OF HUMAN RELATIONS, VOL 6, NO 4, SUMMER 1958.
PP 105-115.

NGRANLB62441 GRANGER LB
COMMUNITY FACTORS AFFECTING MOTIVATION AND ACHIEVEMENT IN A
DECADE OF DECISION. /EDUCATION/
LOUISIANA EDUCATION ASSOCIATION JOURNAL, MAY-JUNE 1962.

NGRAYSW44446 GRAY SW
THE VOCATIONAL PREFERENCE OF NEGRO CHILCREN.
JOURNAL OF GENETIC PSYCHOLOGY, VOL 64, 1944. PP 239-247.

NGREEGC63447 GREEN GC
NEGRO DIALECT, THE LAST BARRIER TO INTEGRATION.
JOURNAL OF NEGRO EDUCATION, VOL 32, WINTER 1963. PP 81-83.

NGREEMX48448 GREEN M
FAIR EMPLOYMENT IS GOOD BUSINESS AT G FCX OF HARTFORD.
/CASE-STUDY CONNECTICUT/
OPPORTUNITY, SPRING 1948. PP 58-59, 73-75.

NGREEMX63449 GREENFIELD M
SOCIAL-DEPENDENCY IN THE SAN-FRANCISCO BAY AREA. TODAY
AND TOMORROW. /CALIFORNIA/
UNIVERSITY OF CALIFCRNIA, INSTITUTE OF GOVERNMENTAL STUDIES.
BERKELEY, CALIFORNIA. 1963.

NGREESX53453 GREER S
SITUATIONAL PRESSURES AND FUNCTIONAL ROLE OF THE ETHNIC
LABOR LEADERS. /UNION/
SOCIAL FORCES, VOL 32, 1953. PP 41-45.

NGREESX59451 GREER S
LAST MAN IN. RACIAL ACCESS TO UNIONS.
GLENCOE FREE PRESS. GLENCOE, ILLINOIS. 1959. 189 PP.

NGREESX61452 GREER S
THE PLACE OF THE NEGRO IN THE AMERICAN LABOR-MOVEMENT.
/UNION/
AMERICAN REVIEW, VOL 1, WINTER 1961. PP 98-109.

NGRIEES57457 GRIER ES   GRIER G
*NY STATE COMM AGAINST DISCR
RACE-RELATIONS IN ROCHESTER, A PROFILE FOR 1957. /NEW-YORK/
NEW YORK STATE COMMISSION AGAINST DISCRIMINATION. NEW YORK.
AP 1957. 23 PP.

NGRIEES57503 GRIER ES   GRIER G
*NY STATE COMM AGAINST DISCR
RACE-RELATIONS IN THE ALBANY TROY AREA. A PROFILE FOR 1957.
/NEW-YORK/
NEW YORK STATE COMMISSION AGAINST DISCRIMINATION. NEW YORK.
NOV 1957. 51 PP.

NGRIEES58455 GRIER ES   GRIER G
*NY STATE COMM AGAINST DISCR
NEGROES IN FIVE NEW-YORK CITIES. A STUDY OF PROBLEMS,
ACHIEVEMENTS AND TRENDS. /RACE-RELATIONS/
NEW YORK STATE COMMISSION AGAINST DISCRIMINATION. NEW YORK.
AUG 1958.

NGRIEES58456 GRIER ES   GRIER G
*NY STATE COMM AGAINST DISCR
RACE-RELATICNS IN BROOME-COUNTY, A PROFILE FOR 1958.
/NEW-YORK/
NEW YORK STATE COMMISSION AGAINST DISCRIMINATION. NEW YORK.
JUNE 1958. 26 PLUS PP.

NGRIEES58458 GRIER ES   GRIER G
*NY STATE COMM AGAINST DISCR
RACE-RELATIONS IN SYRACUSE. A PROFILE. /NEW-YORK/
NEW YORK STATE COMMISSION AGAINST DISCRIMINATION. NEW YORK.
REVISED ED FEB 1958. 36 PP.

NGRIEES63454 GRIER ES   *WASH CENT FOR METROP STUDIES
IN SEARCH OF A FUTURE. A STUDY OF CAREER-SEEKING EXPERIENCES
OF SELECTED NEGRO HIGH SCHOOL GRADUATES IN WASHINGTON-DC
WHICH WAS AN EFFORT TO PROVIDE KNOWLEDGE HELPFUL IN
SOLVING ONE OF THE MOST CRITICAL PROBLEMS FACING URBAN
AMERICA TODAY.
WASHINGTON CENTER FOR METROPOLITAN STUDIES. WASHINGTON, DC.
JULY 1963. 24 PP.

NGRIEGXND582 GRIER G   GRIER ES
*WASH CENT FOR METROP STUDIES
THE NEGRO MIGRATION. /ECONOMIC-STATUS/
HOUSING YEARBOOK, 1960 AND 1962. WASHINGTON CENTER FOR
METROPOLITAN STUDIES. WASHINGTON, DC. ND.

NGRIEGX66459 GRIER G   GRIER ES
EQUALITY AND BEYOND. /RESIDENTIAL-SEGREGATION/
QUADRANGLE BOOKS. CHICAGO, ILLINOIS. 1966. 115 PP.

NGRIMAP64983 GRIMES AP
EQUALITY IN AMERICA. /ECONOMIC-STATUS/
OXFORD UNIVERSITY PRESS. NEW YORK. 1964.

NGROBGX60460 GROB G
ORGANIZED LABOR AND THE NEGRO WORKER. /UNION/
LABOR HISTORY, VOL 1, NO 2, SPRING 1960. PP 164-176.

NGROSJA62461 GROSS JA
NAACP AND THE AFL-CIO. AN OVERVIEW. /UNION/
NEGRO HISTORICAL BULLETIN, VOL 26, DEC 1962. PP 111-112.

NGROSMM57462 GROSSACK M
SOME PERSONALITY CHARACTERISTICS OF SOUTHERN NEGRO STUDENTS.
JOURNAL OF SOCIAL PSYCHOLOGY, VOL 46, 1957. PP 125-131.

NGUBAEG59463 GUBA EG   JACKSON PW
BIDWELL CE
OCCUPATIONAL CHOICE AND THE TEACHING CAREER.
EDUCATIONAL RESEARCH BULLETIN, VOL 38, 1959. PP 1-12, 27-28.

NGUHAME65464 GUHA ME
RACIAL DISCRIMINATION IN AMERICAN LABOR UNIONS.
VOCATIONAL GUIDANCE QUARTERLY, VOL 13, NO 4, 1965.
PP 237-243.

NGUILBM60465   GUILLORY BM
THE CAREER PATTERNS OF NEGRO LAWYERS IN LOUISIANA.
/OCCUPATIONS/
LOUISIANA STATE UNIVERSITY. MASTERS THESIS. BATON ROUGE,
LOUISIANA. 1960.

NGUNDRH50466   GUNDLACK RH
EFFECTS OF ON-THE-JOB EXPERIENCE WITH NEGROES UPON RACIAL
ATTITUDES OF WHITE WORKERS IN UNION SHOPS.
PSYCHOLOGICAL REPORTS, VOL 2, 1956. PP 67-77. ALSO IN
AMERICAN PSYCHOLOGIST, VOL 5, NO 7, JULY 1950. P 300.

NGURIPX66352   GURIN P   KATZ D
*US DEPT OF HEALTH ED WELFARE *UM ISR SURVEY RESEARCH CENT
MOTIVATION AND ASPIRATION IN THE NEGRO COLLEGE.
UNIVERSITY OF MICHIGAN, INSTITUTE FOR SOCIAL RESEARCH,
SURVEY RESEARCH CENTER. ANN ARBOR, MICHIGAN. NOV 1966.
346 PP.

NGURIPX66467   GURIN P
SOCIAL-CLASS CONSTRAINTS ON THE OCCUPATIONAL ASPIRATIONS OF
STUDENTS ATTENDING SOME PREDOMINANTLY NEGRO COLLEGES.
JOURNAL OF NEGRO EDUCATION, 1966 YEARBOOK.

NGURIPX66468   GURIN P   EPPS E
SOME CHARACTERISTICS OF STUDENTS FROM POVERTY BACKGROUNDS
ATTENDING PREDOMINANTLY NEGRO COLLEGES IN THE DEEP SOUTH.
SOCIAL FORCES, VOL 45, SEPT 1966, PP 27-40.

NGUSCKI63469   GUSCOTT KI
NAACP VIEWS CONDITIONS.
INDUSTRY, VOL 28, JULY 1963. PP 12-13, 29.

NGUZMJP47470   GUZMAN JP ED
NEGRO YEARBOOK.
TUSKEGEE INSTITUTE. TUSKEGEE, ALABAMA. 1947.

NHAASFJ46548   HAAS FJ   FLEMING GJ
PERSONNEL PRACTICES AND WARTIME CHANGES. /EMPLOYMENT/
ANNALS OF THE AMERICAN ACADEMY OF POLITICAL AND SOCIAL
SCIENCE, VOL 244, MAR 1946. PP 48-56.

NHABBSX64473   HABBE S   *NATL INDUSTRIAL CONF BOARD
HIRING NEGRO WORKERS. /INDUSTRY/
NATIONAL INDUSTRIAL CONFERENCE BOARD, CONFERENCE BOARD
RECORD, JUNE 1964. PP 16-19.

NHABBSX65471   HABBE S   *NATL INDUSTRIAL CONF BOARD
CHIEF EXECUTIVES VIEW NEGRO EMPLOYMENT. /INDUSTRY/
NATIONAL INDUSTRIAL CONFERENCE BOARD, CONFERENCE BOARD
RECORD, VOL 2, NO 5, MAY 1965. PP 30-33.

NHABBSX65474   HABBE S   *NATL INDUSTRIAL CONF BOARD
THE NEGRO AS AN EMPLOYEE. /INDUSTRY/
NATIONAL INDUSTRIAL CONFERENCE BOARD, CONFERENCE BOARD
RECORD, VOL 2, NO 9, SEPT 1965. PP 42-46.

NHABBSX66472   HABBE S   *NATL INDUSTRIAL CONF BOARD
COMPANY EXPERIENCE WITH NEGRO EMPLOYMENT. /INDUSTRY/
NATIONAL INDUSTRIAL CONFERENCE BOARD. STUDIES IN PERSONNEL
POLICY, NO 201. NEW YORK. 1966. 2 VOLS, 332 PP.

NHACKAX63475   HACKER A
DO CORPORATIONS HAVE A SOCIAL DUTY. /INDUSTRY/
THE NEW YORK TIMES MAGAZINE, NOV 17 1963. P 21 PLUS.

NHALEWH52476   HALE WH
THE NEGRO LAWYER AND HIS CLIENTS. /OCCUPATIONS/
PHYLON, VOL 13, NO 1, 1ST QUARTER 1952. PP 57-63.

NHALLDE53477   HALL DE
THE USE OF NEGRO LABOR IN SOUTHERN INDUSTRY.
/OCCUPATIONAL-PATTERNS/
UNIVERSITY OF ILLINOIS. MASTERS THESIS. URBANA,
ILLINOIS. 1953.

NHALLGD57987   HALLER GD
RACIAL DISCRIMINATION BY UNIONS.
LABOR LAW JOURNAL, VOL 8, NO 7, JULY 1957. PP 479-481.

NHALLWX42259   HALL W
THE OPPORTUNITIES AND DIFFICULTIES OF ORGANIZING NEGRO LABOR
IN THE PRESENT EMERGENCY. /UNION/
THE QUARTERLY REVIEW OF HIGHER EDUCATION AMONG NEGROES, VOL
10, NO 2, AP 1942. PP 69-73.

NHAMICH59986   HAMILTON CH
EDUCATIONAL SELECTIVITY OF NET MIGRATION FROM THE SOUTH.
SOCIAL FORCES, OCT 1959.

NHAMICH64479   HAMILTON CH
THE NEGRO LEAVES THE SOUTH. /DEMOGRAPHY MIGRATION/
DEMOGRAPHY, VOL 1, NO 1, 1964. PP 273-295.

NHARDJX52482   HARDING J   HOGREFE R
ATTITUDES OF WHITE DEPARTMENT STORE EMPLOYEES TOWARD NEGRO
CO-WORKERS. /CASE-STUDY/
JOURNAL OF SOCIAL ISSUES, VOL 8, NO 1, JAN 1952. PP 18-28.

NHARENX62483   HARE N
CHANGING OCCUPATIONAL-STATUS OF NEGRO EDUCATION.
UNIVERSITY OF CHICAGO. PHD DISSERTATION. CHICAGO, ILLINOIS.
1962.

NHARENX65484   HARE N
RECENT TRENDS IN THE OCCUPATIONAL MOBILITY OF NEGROES,
1930-1960.
SOCIAL FORCES, VOL 44, DEC 1965. PP 166-173.

NHARGAJ65990   HARGRETT AJ
THE UNEMPLOYMENT RATE AND GRADE LEVEL RELATIONSHIP IN
CHICAGO AS REVEALED IN THE 1960 CENSUS. /ILLINOIS/
JOURNAL OF NEGRO EDUCATION, VOL 34, NO 2, SPRING 1965.
PP 121-129.

NHARLBW65486   HARLESTON BW
HIGHER EDUCATION FOR THE NEGRO.
THE ATLANTIC MONTHLY, VOL 216, NOV 1965. PP 139-144.

NHARLYO64485   HARLEM YOUTH OPPORS UNLTD
YOUTH IN THE GHETTO. A STUDY OF THE CONSEQUENCES OF
POWERLESSNESS AND A BLUEPRINT FOR CHANGE. /NEW-YORK/
HARLEM YOUTH OPPORTUNITIES UNLIMITED, INC. NEW YORK. 1964.
2ND EDITION. 620 PP.

NHARPRM60487   HARPER RM
RACIAL CONTRASTS IN INCOME.
ALABAMA LAWYER, VOL 21, JULY 1960. PP 257-260.

NHARRCV65491   HARRIS CV   *US DEPARTMENT OF LABOR

NEW-YORK-S NONDISCRIMINATION EMPLOYMENT POLICY.
US DEPARTMENT OF LABOR, EMPLOYMENT SERVICE REVIEW, VOL 2,
NO 8, AUG 1965. PP 6-9.

NHARREC53493   HARRISON EC
A STUDY OF OCCUPATIONAL ATTITUDES.
JOURNAL OF NEGRO EDUCATION, VOL 22, 1953. PP 471-475.

NHARREC59492   HARRISON EC
ACHIEVEMENT MOTIVATION CHARACTERISTICS OF NEGRO COLLEGE
FRESHMEN.
PERSONNEL AND GUIDANCE JOURNAL, VOL 38, NO 2, OCT 1959.
PP 146-149.

NHARREC63367   HARRISON EC
WORKING AT IMPROVING THE MOTIVATIONAL AND ACHIEVEMENT LEVELS
OF THE DEPRIVED.
JOURNAL OF NEGRO EDUCATION, VOL 32, SUMMER 1963. PP 301-307.

NHARREE66786   HARRIS EE
SOME COMPARISONS AMONG NEGRO-WHITE COLLEGE STUDENTS. SOCIAL
AMBITION AND ESTIMATED SOCIAL MOBILITY.
JOURNAL OF NEGRO EDUCATION, VOL 35, NO 4, FALL 1966.
PP 351-368.

NHARRIE66991   HARRISON IE
THE STATE-EMPLOYMENT-SERVICE AND THE ATTITUDE OF
UNEMPLOYABLE DROPOUTS.
JOURNAL OF NEGRO EDUCATION, VOL 35, NO 2, SPRING 1966.
PP 134-143.

NHARRLJ62494   HARRISON LJ
THE STATUS OF THE NEGRO CPA IN THE UNITED STATES.
/OCCUPATIONS/
JOURNAL OF NEGRO EDUCATION, VOL 31, FALL 1962. PP 503-506.

NHARRMX61490   HARRINGTON M
THE ECONOMICS OF RACISM.
COMMONWEAL, JULY 7 1961. 6 PP.

NHARRMX65488   HARRINGTON M
ECONOMICS FOR THE MINORITY. /POVERTY/
AGENDA, VOL 1, NO 8, SEPT 1965. PP 18-21.

NHARRMX67489   HARRINGTON M
THE ECONOMICS OF PROTEST.
EMPLOYMENT, RACE AND POVERTY. ED BY ARTHUR M ROSS AND
HERBERT HILL. HARCOURT, BRACE, AND WORLD. NEW YORK. 1967.
PP 234-260.

NHARTJW64495   HART JW
EFFECTS OF AUTOMATION ON THE POSITION OF NEGROES IN A
SOUTHERN INDUSTRIAL PLANT.
JOURNAL OF HUMAN RELATIONS, VOL 12, NO 3, 1964. PP 419-421.

NHARTJW64496   HART JW
A STUDY OF THE EFFECTS OF EFFORTS TO IMPROVE
EMPLOYMENT-OPPORTUNITIES OF NEGROES ON THE UTILIZATION OF
NEGRO WORKERS.
JOURNAL OF HUMAN RELATIONS, VOL 12, NO 3, 1964. PP 421-423.

NHARVLR40497   HARVARD LAW REVIEW
DISCRIMINATION IN RATE OF COMPENSATION BETWEEN COLORED AND
WHITE TEACHERS HELD UNCONSTITUTIONAL.
HARVARD LAW REVIEW, VOL 53, NO 4, FEB 1940. PP 669-671.

NHARVLR49498   HARVARD LAW REVIEW
PICKETING BY NEGROES TO OBTAIN EMPLOYMENT IN PROPORTION TO
NEGRO CUSTOMERS HELD UNLAWFUL.
HARVARD LAW REVIEW, VOL 62, NO 6, AP 1949. PP 1077-1079.

NHARVLR62499   HARVARD LAW REVIEW
STATE FAIR-EMPLOYMENT-PRACTICE LEGISLATION
UNCONSTITUTIONALLY BURDENS INTERSTATE COMMERCE WHEN
APPLIED TO INTERSTATE AIRLINE.
HARVARD LAW REVIEW, VOL 76, NO 2, DEC 1962. PP 404-408.

NHARVLR64500   HARVARD LAW REVIEW
UNITED STATES HAS STANDING UNDER INTERSTATE COMMERCE ACT AND
COMMERCE CLAUSE TO ENJOIN SEGREGATIVE PRACTICES OF CITY.
/LEGISLATION/
HARVARD LAW REVIEW, VOL 77, NO 6, AP 1964. PP 1157-1161.

NHASTWH42466   HASTE WH
THE NEGRO IN THE ARMY TODAY. /MILITARY/
ANNALS OF THE AMERICAN ACADEMY OF SOCIAL AND POLITICAL
SCIENCE, VOL 223, SEPT 1942. PP 55-60.

NHATCJF66648   HATCHETT JF
THE NEGRO REVOLUTION. A QUEST FOR JUSTICE.
JOURNAL OF HUMAN RELATIONS, VOL 14, NO 3, THIRD QUARTER
1966, PP 406-421.

NHAUSPM65501   HAUSER PM
DEMOGRAPHIC FACTORS IN THE INTEGRATION OF THE NEGRO.
DAEDALUS, VOL 94, NO 4, FALL 1965. PP 847-877.

NHAUSPM66992   HAUSER PM   *US CHAMBER OF COMMERCE
DEMOGRAPHIC AND SOCIAL FACTORS IN THE POVERTY OF THE NEGRO.
THE DISADVANTAGED POOR. EDUCATION AND EMPLOYMENT. US CHAMBER
OF COMMERCE, TASK FORCE ON ECONOMIC GROWTH AND OPPORTUNITY.
WASHINGTON, DC. 1966. PP 229-262.

NHAWLLT55502   HAWLEY LT   *NATIONAL PLANNING ASSN
NEGRO EMPLOYMENT IN THE BIRMINGHAM METROPOLITAN AREA.
/ALABAMA CASE-STUDY/
SELECTED STUDIES OF NEGRO EMPLOYMENT IN THE SOUTH. NATIONAL
PLANNING ASSOCIATION, COMMITTEE OF THE SOUTH. REPORT NO 6-4.
WASHINGTON, DC. 1955. PP 213-328.

NHAYELJ42504   HAYES LJW
THE NEGRO FEDERAL-GOVERNMENT WORKER.
HOWARD UNIVERSITY. WASHINGTON, DC. 1942. 156 PP.

NHAYEMX62506   HAYES M   *US DEPARTMENT OF LABOR
A CENTURY OF CHANGE. NEGROES IN THE US ECONOMY, 1860-1960.
/OCCUPATIONAL-PATTERNS/
US DEPARTMENT OF LABOR, MONTHLY LABOR REVIEW, VOL 85, NO 12,
1962. PP 1359-1365.

NHEALHX64306   HEALD H
THE RIGHT TO KNOWLEDGE. /COLLEGE EDUCATION/
SCHOOL AND SOCIETY, DEC 12 1964. PP 367-379.

NHEBERX46508   HEBERLE R
A SOCIOLOGICAL INTERPRETATION OF SOCIAL CHANGE IN THE SOUTH.
SOCIAL FORCES, VOL 25, 1946. PP 9-15.

NHEBERX56507   HEBERLE R
CHANGES IN THE SOCIAL STRATIFICATION OF THE SOUTH.

TRANSACTIONS OF THE THIRD WORLD CONGRESS OF SOCIOLOGY,
VOL 3, 1956. PP 96-105.

NHECHFM64509 HECHINGER FM
PREFERENTIAL-TREATMENT FOR NEGROES.
THE REPORTER, DEC 3 1964. PP 22-24.

NHENDEW43510 HENDERSON EW   *US DEPARTMENT OF LABOR
NEGROES IN THE GOVERNMENT EMPLOYMENT.
US DEPARTMENT OF LABOR, MONTHLY LABOR REVIEW, JULY 1943.

NHENDGX67214 HENDERSON G
BEYOND POVERTY OF INCOME.
JOURNAL OF NEGRO EDUCATION, VOL 36, NO 1, WINTER 1967.
PP 42-50.

NHENDVW60512 HENDERSON VW
THE ECONOMIC IMBALANCE. AN INQUIRY INTO THE ECONOMIC-STATUS
OF NEGROES IN THE UNITED STATES, 1935-1960, WITH
IMPLICATIONS FOR NEGRO EDUCATION.
QUARTERLY REVIEW OF EDUCATION AMONG NEGROES, VOL 28, NO 2,
AP 1960. PP 84-98.

NHENDVW60516 HENDERSON VW   *FISK U SOCIAL SCIENCE INST
EMPLOYMENT OPPORTUNITIES FOR NASHVILLE NEGROES. /TENNESSEE/
FISK UNIVERSITY, SOCIAL SCIENCE INSTITUTE. NASHVILLE,
TENNESSEE. SEPT 1960.

NHENDVW61511 HENDERSON VW
ECONOMIC DIMENSIONS IN RACE-RELATIONS.
RACE RELATIONS. PROBLEMS AND THEORY. ED BY J MASUOKA AND
P VALIEN. UNIVERSITY OF NORTH CAROLINA PRESS. CHAPEL HILL,
NORTH CAROLINA. 1961. PP 252-266.

NHENDVW62513 HENDERSON VW
ECONOMIC OPPORTUNITY AND NEGRO EDUCATION.
THE AMERICAN TEACHERS ASSOCIATION BULLETIN, MAR 1962.

NHENDVW63514 HENDERSON VW   *UNIV OF CHICAGO CFSOLEFA
ECONOMIC DIMENSIONS. /SOUTH INCOME TECHNOLOGY/
EDUCATIONAL IMPERATIVE. THE NEGRO IN THE CHANGING SOUTH. ED
BY FREDA H GOLDMAN. CENTER FOR THE STUDY OF LIBERAL
EDUCATION FOR ADULTS. CHICAGO, ILLINOIS. 1963. PP 27-41.

NHENDVW63515 HENDERSON VW   *SOUTHERN REGIONAL COUNCIL
THE ECONOMIC-STATUS OF NEGROES. IN THE NATION AND IN THE
SOUTH.
SOUTHERN REGIONAL COUNCIL, TOWARD REGIONAL REALISM SERIES,
PAMPHLET NO 3. ATLANTA, GEORGIA. 1963. 23 PP.

NHENDVW66213 HENDERSON VW
RECENT DEVELOPMENTS IN RACE-RELATIONS AND ORGANIZED LABOR.
INTERNATIONAL UNION OF ELECTRICAL, RADIO, AND MACHINE
WORKERS, AFL-CIO. 12TH CONSTITUTIONAL CONVENTION. MIAMI
BEACH, FLORIDA. SEPT 6 1966. 11 PP.

NHENDVW67517 HENDERSON VW
REGIONS, RACE AND JOBS.
EMPLOYMENT, RACE AND POVERTY. ED BY ARTHUR M ROSS AND
HERBERT HILL. HARCOURT, BRACE, AND WORLD. NEW YORK. 1967.
PP 76-106.

NHENTNX64518 HENTOFF N
THE NEW EQUALITY.
VIKING PRESS. NEW YORK. 1964, 1965. 246 PP.

NHENTNX65026 HENTOFF N
BEYOND CIVIL-RIGHTS.
MASSACHUSETTS REVIEW, VOL 6, SPRING 1965. PP 581-587.

NHERBWX53519 HERBERG W
THE OLD-TIMERS AND THE NEWCOMERS. ETHNIC-GROUP RELATIONS IN
A NEEDLE TRADE UNION.
JOURNAL OF SOCIAL ISSUES, VOL 9, NO 1, JAN 1953. PP 12-19.

NHERSPF65520 HERSON PF
SOME PERSONAL AND SOCIOLOGICAL VARIABLES ASSOCIATED WITH
OCCUPATIONAL-CHOICES OF NEGRO YOUTH.
JOURNAL OF NEGRO EDUCATION, VOL 34, NO 2, SPRING 1965.
PP 147-151.

NHERZEX63522 HERZOG E   *US DEPT OF HEALTH ED WELFARE
SOME ASSUMPTIONS ABOUT THE POOR.
US DEPARTMENT OF HEALTH, EDUCATION, AND WELFARE, SOCIAL
SERVICE REVIEW, DEC 1963. PP 389-402.

NHERZEX66521 HERZOG E
IS THERE A BREAKDOWN OF THE NEGRO FAMILY.
SOCIAL WORK, JAN 1966. PP 3-10.

NHESSRD64523 HESS RD
EDUCABILITY AND REHABILITATION. THE FUTURE OF THE WELFARE
CLASS.
JOURNAL OF MARRIAGE AND THE FAMILY, NOV 1964. PP 422-429.

NHICKRA66740 HICKS RA
THE MEANINGFULNESS OF NEGRO-WHITE DIFFERENCES IN
INTELLIGENCE TEST PERFORMANCE.
PSYCHOLOGICAL RECORD, VOL 16, NO 1, JAN 1966. PP 43-46.

NHILLFG46524 HILL FG
THE NEGRO IN THE TEXAS LABOR-SUPPLY.
UNIVERSITY OF TEXAS, DEPARTMENT OF ECONOMICS. MA THESIS.
AUSTIN, TEXAS. 1946.

NHILLHX57533 HILL H
THE NEGRO WORKER IN INDUSTRY.
THE NEW LEADER, VOL 40, MAY 6 1957. PP 3-5.

NHILLHX58531 HILL H   *NAACP
NAACP LABOR MANUAL. A GUIDE TO ACTION.
NAACP. NEW YORK. 1958. 76 PP.

NHILLHX58996 HILL H
RIGHT-TO-WORK LAWS AND THE NEGRO WORKER.
THE CRISIS, VOL 65, NO 6, JULY 1958. PP 327-332.

NHILLHX59529 HILL H
LABOR AND SEGREGATION. /UNION/
THE NEW LEADER, OCT 19 1959.

NHILLHX59530 HILL H
LABOR UNIONS AND THE NEGRO.
COMMENTARY, VOL 28, DEC 1959. PP 479-488.

NHILLHX59534 HILL H   *NAACP
NO HARVEST FOR THE REAPER. THE STORY OF THE MIGRATORY
AGRICULTURAL WORKER IN THE UNITED STATES.
NAACP. NEW YORK. 1959. 48 PP.

NHILLHX59543 HILL H
RECENT EFFECTS OF RACIAL CONFLICT ON SOUTHERN INDUSTRIAL
DEVELOPMENT.
PHYLON, VOL 20, NO 4, WINTER 1959. PP 319-326.

NHILLHX60525 HILL H   *NY STATE COMM AGAINST DISCR
APPRENTICES, SKILLED CRAFTSMEN AND THE NEGRO. AN ANALYSIS.
NEW YORK STATE COMMISSION AGAINST DISCRIMINATION. NEW YORK.
1960. 137 PP.

NHILLHX60532 HILL H   *NAACP
THE NEGRO WAGE-EARNER AND APPRENTICESHIP TRAINING PROGRAMS.
A CRITICAL ANALYSIS WITH RECOMMENDATIONS.
NAACP. NEW YORK. 1960. 60 PP.

NHILLHX60542 HILL H   *NAACP
RACISM WITHIN ORGANIZED LABOR. A REPORT OF THE FIVE YEARS OF
THE AFL-CIO, 1955-1960. /UNION/
NAACP, LABOR DEPARTMENT. NEW YORK. 1960. 13 PP. ALSO
JOURNAL OF NEGRO EDUCATION, VOL 30, NO 2, SPRING 1961.
PP 109-118.

NHILLHX62526 HILL H
HAS ORGANIZED LABOR FAILED THE NEGRO WORKER. /UNION/
NEGRO DIGEST, MAY 1962. PP 4-15.

NHILLHX62528 HILL H
THE ILGWU TODAY -- THE DECAY OF A LABOR UNION.
NEW POLITICS, SUMMER 1962. 12 PP.

NHILLHX62535 HILL H
ORGANIZED LABOR AND THE NEGRO WAGE-EARNER. /UNION/
NEW POLITICS, VOL 1, WINTER 1962. PP 8-19.

NHILLHX62537 HILL H
PATTERNS OF EMPLOYMENT DISCRIMINATION.
CRISIS, VOL 69, MAR 1962. PP 137-147.

NHILLHX62539 HILL H
RACIAL DISCRIMINATION IN THE NATION-S APPRENTICESHIP
TRAINING PROGRAM.
PHYLON, VOL 23, NO 3, FALL 1962. PP 215-224.

NHILLHX62547 HILL H
EQUAL-EMPLOYMENT-OPPORTUNITY, HEARING, TESTIMONY.
US HOUSE OF REPRESENTATIVES, COMMITTEE ON EDUCATION AND
LABOR, SPECIAL SUBCOMMITTEE ON LABOR, HEARINGS, PART II.
87TH CONGRESS, 2ND SESSION. GPO. WASHINGTON, DC. 1962.
PP 718-744.

NHILLHX63527 HILL H
THE ILGWU -- FACT AND FICTION. /UNION/
NEW POLITICS, WINTER 1963. 21 PP.

NHILLHX63548 HILL H
US DEPARTMENT OF LABOR, PUBLIC HEARING, TESTIMONY.
/MIGRANT-WORKERS/
US DEPARTMENT OF LABOR. PUBLIC HEARING. GPO. WASHINGTON, DC.
NOV 5 1963. 7 PP.

NHILLHX64550 HILL H
TWENTY YEARS OF STATE FAIR-EMPLOYMENT-PRACTICE COMMISSIONS.
A CRITICAL ANALYSIS WITH RECOMMENDATIONS.
BUFFALO LAW REVIEW, VOL 14, NO 1, FALL 1964. PP 22-69.

NHILLHX64997 HILL H
UNIONS AND THE NEGRO COMMUNITY.
INDUSTRIAL AND LABOR RELATIONS REVIEW, VOL 17, NO 4,
JULY 1964. PP 619-621.

NHILLHX65536 HILL H
THE PATTERN OF JOB DISCRIMINATION AGAINST NEGROES.
MINORITY PROBLEMS. ED BY ARNOLD M ROSE AND CAROLINE B ROSE.
HARPER AND ROW. NEW YORK. 1965. PP 147-157.

NHILLHX65540 HILL H
RACIAL INEQUALITY IN EMPLOYMENT. THE PATTERNS OF
DISCRIMINATION.
ANNALS OF THE AMERICAN ACADEMY OF POLITICAL AND SOCIAL
SCIENCE, VOL 357, JAN 1965. PP 39-47. ALSO IN PROBLEMS AND
PROSPECTS OF THE NEGRO MOVEMENT. ED BY RAYMOND J MURPHY AND
HOWARD ELINSON. WADSWORTH PUBLISHING COMPANY. BELMONT,
CALIFORNIA. 1966. PP 86-107.

NHILLHX65541 HILL H
THE RACIAL PRACTICES OF ORGANIZED LABOR -- IN THE AGE OF
GOMPERS AND AFTER. /UNION/
EMPLOYMENT, RACE AND POVERTY. ED BY ARTHUR M ROSS AND
HERBERT HILL. HARCOURT, BRACE, AND WORLD. NEW YORK. 1967.
PP 365-402. ALSO IN NEW POLITICS, VOL 4, SPRING 1965.
PP 26-46.

NHILLHX65545 HILL H
STATE LAWS AND THE NEGRO. SOCIAL CHANGE AND THE IMPACT OF
LAW.
AFRICAN FORUM, FALL 1965. PP 92-105.

NHILLHX65549 HILL H   *NAACP
TITLE-VII. EQUAL-EMPLOYMENT SECTION. CIVIL-RIGHTS-ACT OF
1964. THE WAR-AGAINST-POVERTY.
NAACP. NEW YORK. JUNE 1965. 39 PP.

NHILLHX66538 HILL H   *NAACP
PLANNING THE END OF THE AMERICAN GHETTO. A PROGRAM OF
ECONOMIC DEVELOPMENT FOR EQUAL-RIGHTS.
NAACP. NEW YORK. 1966. 23 PP.

NHILLHX66544 HILL H
THE ROLE OF LAW IN SECURING EQUAL-EMPLOYMENT-OPPORTUNITY.
LEGAL POWERS AND SOCIAL CHANGE.
BOSTON COLLEGE INDUSTRIAL AND COMMERCIAL LAW REVIEW, VOL 7,
NO 3, SPRING 1966. PP 625-652.

NHILLHX66546 HILL H
NEW-YORK CITY COMMISSION ON HUMAN RIGHTS, CONSTRUCTION
TRADES HEARING, TESTIMONY. /INDUSTRY/
NEW YORK CITY COMMISSION ON HUMAN RIGHTS. CONSTRUCTION
TRADES HEARING. NEW YORK. SEPT 26 1966.

NHILLMC43551 HILL MC   ACKISS TD
SOCIAL-CLASSES. A FRAME OF REFERENCE FOR THE STUDY OF NEGRO
SOCIETY.
SOCIAL FORCES, VOL 22, 1943. PP 92-98.

NHIMEJS49553 HIMES JS
THE NATURAL HISTORY OF SOCIAL CONFLICT AND WHITE-NEGRO
RELATIONS.
PHYLON, VOL 10, NO 1, 1ST QUARTER 1949. PP 50-57.

NHIMEJS51552 HIMES JS

CHANGING STRUCTURES OF WHITE-NEGRO RELATIONS IN THE SOUTH.
PHYLON, VOL 12, NO 3, 3RD QUARTER 1951. PP 227-38.

NHIMEJS62598 HIMES JS
CHANGING SOCIAL-ROLES IN THE NEW SOUTH.
AMERICAN RACE-RELATIONS TODAY. ED BY EARL RAAB. DOUBLEDAY.
GARDEN CITY, NEW YORK. 1962.

NHIMEJS64554 HIMES JS
SOME WORK-RELATED CULTURAL DEPRIVATIONS OF LOWER-CLASS NEGRO
YOUTHS.
JOURNAL OF MARRIAGE AND THE FAMILY, VOL 26, NOV 1964.
PP 447-449. ALSO POVERTY IN AMERICA. ED BY LOUIS A FERMAN,
JOYCE L KORNBLUH AND ALAN HABER. UNIVERSITY OF MICHIGAN
PRESS. ANN ARBOR, MICHIGAN. 1965. PP 384-389.

NHIMEJX61071 HIMES J
NEGRO TEEN-AGE CULTURE.
ANNALS OF THE AMERICAN ACADEMY OF POLITICAL AND SOCIAL
SCIENCE, VOL 338, NOV 1961. PP 91-101.

NHIMEJX62072 HIMES J   HAMELETT ML
THE ASSESSMENT OF ADJUSTMENT OF AGED NEGRO WOMEN IN A
SOUTHERN CITY.
PHYLON, VOL 23, SUMMER 1962. PP 139-147.

NHODGEN62557 HODGES EN
THE NEGRO-S FUTURE THROUGH FAIR-EMPLOYMENT-PRACTICES.
NEGRO HISTORY BULLETIN, VOL 26, OCT 1962. PP 16-18.

NHODGRWND355 HODGE RW   FREIMAN DJ
OCCUPATIONAL MOBILITY AND ATTITUDES TOWARD NEGROES.
UNIVERSITY OF CHICAGO, WORKING PAPER. CHICAGO, ILLINOIS. ND.
30 PP.

NHODGRW65556 HODGE RW   HODGE P
OCCUPATIONAL ASSIMILATION AS A COMPETITIVE PROCESS.
AMERICAN JOURNAL OF SOCIOLOGY, VOL 71, NO 3, NOV 1965.
PP 249-264.

NHOFFHX65558 HOFFMAN H
A MANAGEMENT PERSPECTIVE TOWARD NEGRO ECONOMIC PRESSURES.
PUBLIC RELATIONS QUARTERLY, WINTER 1965. PP 19-24.

NHOKAJE60555 HOKANSON JE   CALDEN G
NEGRO-WHITE DIFFERENCES ON THE MMPI. /TESTING/
JOURNAL OF CLINICAL PSYCHOLOGY, VOL 16, 1960. PP 32-33.

NHOLLJH58561 HOLLAND JH   *NATIONAL URBAN LEAGUE
REALIZING THE MANPOWER POTENTIALITIES OF MINORITY-GROUP
YOUTH.
NATIONAL URBAN LEAGUE. NEW YORK. 1958. 29 PP.

NHOLLJH65560 HOLLAND JH   *EDUCATIONAL TESTING SERVICE
PREPARATION OF THE NEGRO COLLEGE GRADUATE FOR BUSINESS.
/EMPLOYMENT-SELECTION/
SELECTING AND TRAINING NEGROES FOR MANAGERIAL POSITIONS.
EDUCATIONAL TESTING SERVICE. PRINCETON, NEW JERSEY. 1965.
PP 23-34.

NHOLLJX65305 HOLLAND J
THE NEGRO AND HIGHER EDUCATION.
NATIONAL EDUCATION ASSOCIATION, NEA JOURNAL, MAR 1965. 3 PP.

NHOLLRG59562 HOLLOWAY RG   BERREMAN JV
THE EDUCATIONAL AND OCCUPATIONAL ASPIRATIONS AND PLANS OF
NEGRO AND WHITE MALE ELEMENTARY SCHOOL STUDENTS.
PACIFIC SOCIOLOGICAL REVIEW, VOL 2, 1959. PP 59-60.

NHOLMAX66563 HOLMES A   *US DEPARTMENT OF LABOR
URBAN-LEAGUE UPGRADES NEGRO WORKERS.
US DEPARTMENT OF LABOR, EMPLOYMENT SERVICE REVIEW, VOL 3,
NO 8, AUG 1966. PP 25-28.

NHOMAHL63564 HOMAN HL   ENION RA
WHAT ARE SOME INDUSTRIAL RELATIONS APPROACHES TO
INTEGRATION.
PERSONNEL ADMINISTRATION, VOL 26, NOV 1963. PP 55-57.

NHOPEJX52571 HOPE J
INDUSTRIAL INTEGRATION OF NEGROES. THE UPGRADING PROCESS.
HUMAN ORGANIZATION, VOL 11, WINTER 1952. PP 5-14.

NHOPEJX53567 HOPE J
THE EMPLOYMENT OF NEGROES IN THE US BY MAJOR OCCUPATION AND
INDUSTRY.
JOURNAL OF NEGRO EDUCATION, VOL 22, NO 3, SUMMER 1953.
PP 307-321.

NHOPEJX53574 HOPE J
THE SELF-SURVEY OF THE PACKINGHOUSE UNION. A TECHNIQUE FOR
EFFECTING CHANGE. /CASE-STUDY/
JOURNAL OF SOCIAL ISSUES, VOL 9, NO 1, JAN 1953. PP 28 36.

NHOPEJX54566 HOPE J
EFFORTS TO ELIMINATE RACIAL DISCRIMINATION IN
INDUSTRY -- WITH PARTICULAR REFERENCE TO THE SOUTH.
JOURNAL OF NEGRO EDUCATION, VOL 2, 1954. PP 262-272.

NHOPEJX55572 HOPE J   *NATIONAL PLANNING ASSN
NEGRO EMPLOYMENT IN THREE SOUTHERN PLANTS OF INTERNATIONAL
HARVESTER COMPANY. /CASE-STUDY/
SELECTED STUDIES OF NEGRO EMPLOYMENT IN THE SOUTH. NATIONAL
PLANNING ASSOCIATION, COMMITTEE OF THE SOUTH. REPORT NO 6-4.
WASHINGTON, DC. 1955. PP 1-143.

NHOPEJX56570 HOPE J
EQUALITY OF OPPORTUNITY, A UNION APPROACH TO FAIR
EMPLOYMENT.
PUBLIC AFFAIRS PRESS. WASHINGTON, DC. 1956. 142 PP.

NHOPEJX56575 HOPE J
TRENDS IN PATTERNS OF RACE-RELATIONS IN THE SOUTH SINCE
MAY 17 1954.
PHYLON, VOL 17, NO 2, 1956. PP 103-108.

NHOPEJX60569 HOPE J
EQUALITY OF EMPLOYMENT OPPORTUNITY. A PROCESS ANALYSIS OF
UNION INITIATIVE.
READINGS IN UNEMPLOYMENT. US SENATE SPECIAL COMMITTEE ON
UNEMPLOYMENT PROBLEMS. GPO. WASHINGTON, DC. 1960. ALSO
PHYLON, VOL 18, NO 2, 2ND QUARTER 1957. PP 140-154.

NHOPEJX60573 HOPE J
THE PROBLEM OF UNEMPLOYMENT AS IT RELATES TO NEGROES.
STUDIES IN UNEMPLOYMENT. UNITED STATES SENATE. SPECIAL
COMMITTEE ON UNEMPLOYMENT PROBLEMS. GPO. WASHINGTON, DC.
1960. PP 173-223.

NHOPEJX63568 HOPE J

EQUAL-EMPLOYMENT-OPPORTUNITY. CHANGING PROBLEMS, CHANGING
TECHNIQUES.
JOURNAL OF INTERGROUP RELATIONS, VOL 4, WINTER 1962-1963.
PP 29-36.

NHOPEJX63576 HOPE J   SHELTON EE
THE NEGRO IN THE FEDERAL-GOVERNMENT.
JOURNAL OF NEGRO EDUCATION, VOL 32, NO 4, FALL 1963.
PP 367-364.

NHORTRX64291 HORTON R
WHAT THE GOVERNMENT REQUIRES OF MANAGEMENT AND UNIONS.
SEVENTEENTH ANNUAL CONFERENCE ON LABOR. NEW YORK UNIVERSITY.
NEW YORK. 1964. PP 107-123.

NHOUSLX65577 HOUSTON L   *HARYOU-ACT
THE OCCUPATIONAL SITUATION OF CENTRAL HARLEM YOUTH.
HARYOU ACT. NEW YORK. 1965.

NHOWAUG44579 HOWARD UNIV GRAD SCH DIV SSC
THE POST-WAR INDUSTRIAL OUTLOOK FOR NEGROES.
HOWARD UNIVERSITY. GRADUATE SCHOOL. DIVISION OF SOCIAL
SCIENCES. PAPERS AND PROCEEDINGS OF THE 8TH ANNUAL
CONFERENCE. CO-SPONSORED BY A PHILIP RANDOLPH FUND. OCTOBER
18-20 1944. HOWARD UNIVERSITY PRESS. WASHINGTON, DC. 1945.
219 PP.

NHOWEIX49581 HOWE I   WIDICK BJ
THE UAW FIGHTS RACE PREJUDICE. /UNION/
COMMENTARY, VOL 8, SEPT 1949. PP 261-268.

NHOWERW56582 HOWE RW
PREJUDICE. SUPERSTITION, AND ECONOMICS.
PHYLON, VOL 17, NO 3, 3RD QUARTER 1956. PP 215-226.

NHUGHEC46584 HUGHES EC
THE KNITTING OF RACIAL GROUPS IN INDUSTRY.
AMERICAN SOCIOLOGICAL REVIEW, VOL 11, NO 5, OCT 1946.
PP 512-519.

NHUGHEC46586 HUGHES EC
RACE-RELATIONS IN INDUSTRIAL RELATIONS.
INDUSTRY AND SOCIETY. ED BY WILLIAM FOOTE WHYTE.
MCGRAW-HILL. NEW YORK. 1946.

NHUGHEC63585 HUGHES EC
RACE-RELATIONS AND THE SOCIOLOGICAL IMAGINATION.
AMERICAN SOCIOLOGICAL REVIEW, VOL 28, DEC 1963. PP 879-890.

NHUGHEJ56583 HUGHES EJ
THE NEGRO-S NEW ECONOMIC LIFE.
FORTUNE, VOL 54, SEPT 1956. PP 126-131 PLUS.

NHUGHWH48587 HUGHES WH   *SOUTHERN REGIONAL COUNCIL
THE NEGRO IN OUR ECONOMY.
SOUTHERN REGIONAL COUNCIL. ATLANTA, GEORGIA. 1948.

NHUNTGX65588 HUNTER G ED
INDUSTRIALIZATION AND RACE-RELATIONS.
OXFORD UNIVERSITY PRESS. NEW YORK. 1965.

NHURSRL56253 HURST RL
THE EFFECT OF A CHANGING AGRICULTURAL PATTERN ON NEGRO
FARMERS OF SOUTH-CAROLINA.
THE QUARTERLY REVIEW OF HIGHER EDUCATION AMONG NEGROES, VOL
24, NO 4, OCT 1956. PP 146-152.

NHUSOCF66328 HUSON CF   SCHILTZ ME
*NATL OPINION RESEARCH CENTER *US DEPARTMENT OF LABOR
COLLEGE, COLOR, AND EMPLOYMENT. RACIAL DIFFERENTIALS IN
POSTGRADUATE EMPLOYMENT AMONG 1964 GRADUATES OF LOUISIANA
COLLEGES.
UNIVERSITY OF CHICAGO, NATIONAL OPINION RESEARCH CENTER.
US DEPARTMENT OF LABOR, OFFICE OF MANPOWER POLICY,
EVALUATION AND RESEARCH. CHICAGO, ILLINOIS. JULY 1966.
139 PP.

NHUTCJXND590 HUTCHINSON J
THE AFL-CIO AND THE NEGRO. /UNION/
EMPLOYMENT, RACE AND POVERTY. ED BY ARTHUR M ROSS AND
HERBERT HILL. HARCOURT, BRACE, AND WORLD. NEW YORK.
PP 403-434.

NHYMAHH56591 HYMAN HH   SHEATSELY PB
ATTITUDES TOWARD DESEGREGATION.
SCIENTIFIC AMERICAN, VOL 195, 1956. PP 35-39.

NINDURP66593 INDUSTRIAL RELATIONS PANEL *RUTGERS INST MNGMT LAB RELS
INTEGRATING THE WORK FORCE.
RUTGERS -- THE STATE UNIVERSITY, INSTITUTE OF MANAGEMENT AND
LABOR RELATIONS. REPORT NO 2. NEW BRUNSWICK, NEW JERSEY.
JAN 1966. 18 PP.

NINGLDJ64067 INGLE DJ
RACIAL DIFFERENCES AND THE FUTURE. /INTELLIGENCE
EQUAL-OPPORTUNITY/
SCIENCE, VOL 146, OCT 16 1964. PP 375-379.

NJACKCC46598 JACKSONVILLE CC SOC AGENCIES
JACKSONVILLE LOOKS AT ITS NEGRO COMMUNITY. /FLORIDA/
JACKSONVILLE COUNCIL OF SOCIAL AGENCIES. JACKSONVILLE,
FLORIDA. 1946. 113 PP.

NJACKEG57070 JACKSON EG
SOME TENDENCIES IN DEMOGRAPHIC TRENDS IN MARYLAND,
1950-1956.
JOURNAL OF NEGRO EDUCATION, VOL 26, FALL 1957. PP 514-519.

NJACKJX51595 JACKSON J
THE EFFECT OF THE WAR ECONOMY ON THE SOUTH. HOW MOBILIZATION
WILL AFFECT POSITION OF THE NEGRO.
POLITICAL AFFAIRS, FEB 1951. PP 106-123.

NJACKJX64596 JACKSON J   *MOBILIZATION FOR YOUTH
A HISTORICAL REVIEW OF THE IMPACT OF SOCIAL AND ECONOMIC
STRUCTURE ON NEGRO CULTURE AND HOW IT INFLUENCES FAMILY
LIVING.
MOBILIZATION FOR YOUTH, INC. NEW YORK. 1964.

NJACKTA66597 JACKSON TA
EXPERIMENTAL AND DEMONSTRATION MANPOWER PROJECT FOR THE
RECRUITMENT, TRAINING, PLACEMENT AND FOLLOW-UP OF RURAL
UNEMPLOYED WORKERS IN TEN NORTH FLORIDA CITIES. FINAL
REPORT. /PARTICIPANTS/
FLORIDA A AND M UNIVERSITY. TALLAHASSEE, FLORIDA. JAN 31
1966. 152 PP.

NJACOPA63601 JACOBS P
THE NEGRO WORKER ASSERTS HIS RIGHTS. /UNION/
THE STATE OF THE UNIONS. ATHENEUM PRESS. NEW YORK. 1963.

PP 174 FF. ALSO THE REPORTER, JULY 23 1959. PP 16-21.

NJACOPX63602 JACOBS P
NO MORE COUSIN TOMS. THE CLASH BETWEEN THE UNIONS AND THE
NEGROES.
DISSENT, VOL 10, WINTER 1963. PP 6-12.

NJACOJPX67599 JACOBS P
BRINGING UP THE REAR.
EMPLOYMENT RACE AND POVERTY. ED BY ARTHUR M ROSS AND
HERBERT HILL. HARCOURT, BRACE, AND WORLD. NEW YORK. 1967.
PP 107-137.

NJANSPA66603 JANSSEN PA
THE NEXT STEP. TEACHER INTEGRATION.
THE REPORTER, NOV 3 1966. PP 32-34.

NJAVIJK60006 JAVITS JK
DISCRIMINATION -- USA. /EEO/
HARCOURT, BRACE, AND WORLD. NEW YORK. 1960. 310 PP.

NJENKHX47605 JENKINS H
THE PROBLEMS OF RACIAL DISCRIMINATION IN UNION MEMBERSHIP.
LAWYERS GUILD REVIEW, VOL 7, JAN 1947. PP 37-39.

NJENKMD48607 JENKINS MD
THE UPPER LIMIT OF ABILITY AMONG AMERICAN NEGROES.
SCIENTIFIC MONTHLY, VOL 66, 1948. PP 399-401.

NJENKMD48608 JENKINS MD   RANDALL CM
DIFFERENTIAL CHARACTERISTICS OF SUPERIOR AND UNSELECTED
NEGRO COLLEGE STUDENTS.
JOURNAL OF SOCIAL PSYCHOLOGY, VOL 27, 1948. PP 187-202.

NJENKMD50606 JENKINS MD
INTELLECTUALLY SUPERIOR NEGRO YOUTH. THEIR PROBLEMS AND
NEEDS. /EDUCATION/
JOURNAL OF NEGRO EDUCATION, VOL 19, 1950. PP 322-332.

NJEWIEA64609 JEWISH EMPLOY AND VOCAT SERV
TWO PROJECTS FOR DROPOUT YOUTH.
JEWISH EMPLOYMENT AND VOCATIONAL SERVICE. PHILADELPHIA,
PENNSYLVANIA. 1964.

NJOHNCS41611 JOHNSON CS   *AMERICAN CC ON EDUCATION
GROWING UP IN THE BLACK BELT. NEGRO YOUTH IN THE RURAL
SOUTH.
AMERICAN COUNCIL ON EDUCATION. WASHINGTON, DC. 1941. 360 PP.

NJOHNCS42544 JOHNSON CS
THE NEGRO.
AMERICAN JOURNAL OF SOCIOLOGY, VOL 47, NO 6, MAY 1942.
PP 854-864.

NJOHNCS42550 JOHNSON CS
NEGRO MINORITY. /ECONOMIC-STATUS/
ANNALS OF THE AMERICAN ACADEMY OF POLITICAL AND SOCIAL
SCIENCE, VOL 223, SEPT 1942. PP 10-16.

NJOHNCS43008 JOHNSON CS
PATTERNS OF NEGRO SEGREGATION.
HARPER AND BROTHERS. NEW YORK. 1943. 332 PP.

NJOHNCS43617 JOHNSON CS
TO STEM THIS TIDE, A SURVEY OF RACIAL TENSION AREAS IN THE
U.S.
THE PILGRIM PRESS. BOSTON, MASSACHUSETTS. 1943. 142 PP.

NJOHNCS44612 JOHNSON CS
THE NEGRO WAR WORKER IN SAN-FRANCISCO. /CALIFORNIA/
THE JULIUS ROSENWALD FUND. SAN FRANCISCO, CALIFORNIA. 1944.

NJOHNCS44615 JOHNSON CS
PRESENT STATUS OF RACE-RELATIONS IN THE SOUTH.
SOCIAL FORCES, VOL 23, NO 1, OCT 1944. PP 343-348.

NJOHNCS47007 JOHNSON CS   ALLEN E
BOND H   MCCULLOCH M
POLK A
INTO THE MAINSTREAM. /RACE-RELATIONS SOUTH
ECONOMIC-STATUS/
UNIVERSITY OF NORTH CAROLINA PRESS. CHAPEL HILL, NORTH
CAROLINA. 1947. 355 PP.

NJOHNCS49613 JOHNSON CS   VALIEN P
THE STATUS OF NEGRO LABOR.
LABOR IN POSTWAR AMERICA, VOL 2, 1949. PP 553-571.

NJOHNCS49616 JOHNSON CS
THE SOCIO-ECONOMIC BACKGROUND OF NEGRO HEALTH STATUS.
JOURNAL OF NEGRO EDUCATION, VOL 18, 1949. PP 429-435.

NJOHNCS54614 JOHNSON CS
NEXT STEPS IN EDUCATION IN THE SOUTH.
PHYLON, VOL 15, NO 1, 1954. PP 7-20.

NJOHNHU63735 JOHNS HOPKINS UNIVERSITY
THE EMPLOYMENT SITUATION OF WHITE AND NEGRO YOUTH IN THE
CITY OF BALTIMORE. INITIAL EXPERIENCES IN THE
LABOR-MARKET. /MARYLAND/
JOHNS HOPKINS UNIVERSITY, DEPARTMENT OF SOCIAL RELATIONS.
BALTIMORE, MARYLAND. AP 1963. 60 PP.

NJOHNJG60618 JOHNSON JG
A CHALLENGE TO NEGRO LEADERSHIP.
NATIONAL URBAN LEAGUE. ADDRESS. NEW YORK. SEPT 7 1960.

NJOHNRA44620 JOHNSON RA   *NATIONAL URBAN LEAGUE
RECENT TRENDS OF MEMBERSHIP OF INTERNATIONAL UNIONS AS THEY
AFFECT NEGRO WORKERS.
NATIONAL URBAN LEAGUE. NEW YORK. 1944.

NJOHNRA57619 JOHNSON RA
NEGRO REACTIONS TO MINORITY-GROUP STATUS.
AMERICAN MINORITIES. ED BY M L BARRON. ALFRED A KNOPF.
NEW YORK. 1957. PP 192-212.

NJOHNTX65621 JOHNSON T
TAPPING THE NEGRO POTENTIAL. /INDUSTRY
EMPLOYMENT-SELECTION PROMOTION/
INSTITUTE OF APPLIED PSYCHOLOGY REVIEW, VOL 5, SPRING 1965.
PP 64-72.

NJOHNXX63336 JOHNSON   WEAVER
LYFORD   COGLEY
*CENTER FOR STUDY DEMO INSTS
THE NEGRO AS AN AMERICAN. /MANPOWER/
CENTER FOR THE STUDY OF DEMOCRATIC INSTITUTIONS.
SANTA BARBARA, CALIFORNIA. 1963. 19 PP.

NJONEAM65622 JONES AM   *HARYOU-ACT
VOCATIONAL ORIENTATION TOWARD A REWARDING LIFE.
HARYOU-ACT, INC. LIBRARY. NEW YORK. 1965.

NJONEBA66884 JONES BA
UNION LOCALS AND THE UNDER-UTILIZATION OF NEGRO WORKERS.
UNIVERSITY OF ILLINOIS, MA THESIS. CHAMPAIGN, ILLINOIS.
1966.

NJONEER48343 JONES ER
EFFORTS OF NEGRO TEACHERS IN THE SOUTHERN STATES TO OBTAIN
EQUALIZATION OF SALARIES.
TUSKEGEE INSTITUTE. THESIS. TUSKEGEE, ALABAMA. 1948. 61 PP.

NJONEJAND738 JONES JA   *MOBILIZATION FOR YOUTH
THE AMERICAN NEGRO AND THE CURRENT SCENE.
MOBILIZATION FOR YOUTH, INC. NEW YORK. 13 PP.

NJONEJE51883 JONES JE
AN ANALYSIS OF THE IMPLEMENTATION OF THE UAW-CIO-S FAIR
PRACTICES AND ANTI-DISCRIMINATION POLICIES IN SELECTED
CHICAGO LOCALS. /UNION/
UNIVERSITY OF ILLINOIS, MA THESIS. CHAMPAIGN, ILLINOIS.
1951.

NJONELW50623 JONES LW ED   *TUSKEGEE INSTITUTE
THE CHANGING STATUS OF THE NEGRO IN SOUTHERN AGRICULTURE.
TUSKEGEE INSTITUTE. RURAL LIFE INFORMATION SERIES.
BULLETIN NO 3. TUSKEGEE, ALABAMA. 1950.

NJONELW60010 JONES LW
NEGRO YOUTH IN THE SOUTH. /EDUCATION EMPLOYMENT/
THE NATION-S CHILDREN. VOL 3. ED BY ELI GINZBERG. COLUMBIA
UNIVERSITY PRESS. NEW YORK. 1960. PP 51-77.

NJORGJM62624 JORGENSON JM
NEGRO INTERNAL MIGRATION IN THE UNITED STATES. 1870-1960.
UNIVERSITY OF NORTH CAROLINA, DEPARTMENT OF SOCIOLOGY AND
ANTHROPOLOGY. MASTER-S THESIS. CHAPEL HILL, NORTH CAROLINA.
1962.

NJOURNE63626 JOURNAL OF NEGRO EDUCATION
RELATIVE PROGRESS OF THE AMERICAN NEGRO SINCE 1950.
JOURNAL OF NEGRO EDUCATION, VOL 63, FALL 1963. ENTIRE ISSUE.

NJOURNE65625 JOURNAL OF NEGRO EDUCATION
EDUCATION AND CIVIL-RIGHTS IN 1965.
JOURNAL OF NEGRO EDUCATION, VOL 34, SUMMER 1965. ENTIRE
ISSUE.

NJOURNE66627 JOURNAL OF NEGRO EDUCATION
STUDIES IN THE HIGHER EDUCATION OF NEGRO AMERICANS.
JOURNAL OF NEGRO EDUCATION, VOL 35, FALL 1966. ENTIRE ISSUE.

NJOURNM52628 JOURNAL OF NEGRO MEDICAL ASSN
MEDICAL SOCIETY OF THE DISTRICT OF COLUMBIA TO ADMIT NEGRO
PHYSICIANS. /OCCUPATIONS/
JOURNAL OF NEGRO MEDICAL ASSOCIATION, VOL 44, SEPT 1952.
PP 389-391.

NJOUROS53891 JOURNAL OF SOCIAL ISSUES.
TRADE UNIONS AND MINORITY PROBLEMS.
JOURNAL OF SOCIAL ISSUES, NO 2, 1953. ENTIRE ISSUE.

NKAHNTX64629 KAHN T   *LEAGUE FOR IND DEMOCRACY
THE ECONOMICS OF EQUALITY.
LEAGUE FOR INDUSTRIAL DEMOCRACY. NEW YORK. 1964. 70 PP. ALSO
EXCERPTED IN POVERTY IN AMERICA. ED BY LOUIS A FERMAN, JOYCE
L KORNBLUH, AND ALAN HABER. UNIVERSITY OF MICHIGAN PRESS.
ANN ARBOR, MICHIGAN. 1965. PP 153-171.

NKAINJF64631 KAIN JF
THE EFFECT OF THE GHETTO ON THE DISTRIBUTION AND LEVEL OF
NONWHITE EMPLOYMENT IN URBAN AREAS.
AMERICAN STATISTICAL ASSOCIATION, ANNUAL MEETING. CHICAGO,
ILLINOIS. DEC 1964.

NKAINJF66630 KAIN JF
THE BIG CITIES BIG PROBLEM. /GHETTO EMPLOYMENT/
CHALLENGE, VOL 15, NO 1, SEPT-OCT 1966. PP 5-8.

NKAMOTCND633 KAMOMHOLZ TC
CIVIL-RIGHTS PROBLEMS IN PERSONNEL AND LABOR-RELATIONS.
NORTHWESTERN UNIVERSITY, SCHOOL OF LAW, 3RD ANNUAL CORPORATE
COUNSEL INSTITUTE, PROCEEDINGS. PP 179-207.

NKANCIU40634 KANSAS CITY URBAN LEAGUE
THE NEGRO WORKER OF KANSAS-CITY. A STUDY OF TRADE UNION AND
ORGANIZED LABOR RELATIONS.
KANSAS CITY URBAN LEAGUE, DEPARTMENT OF INDUSTRIAL
RELATIONS. KANSAS CITY, MISSOURI. 1940. 62 PP.

NKAPLJX66645 KAPLAN J
EQUAL JUSTICE IN AN UNEQUAL WORLD. EQUALITY FOR THE
NEGRO -- THE PROBLEM OF SPECIAL TREATMENT.
NORTHWESTERN UNIVERSITY LAW REVIEW, VOL 61, NO 3,
JULY-AUGUST 1966. PP 363-410.

NKAPPLX63635 KAPP L
INDUSTRY ON TRIAL. /PREFERENTIAL-TREATMENT/
AMERICAN CHILD, VOL 45, NO 4, NOV 1963.

NKARRCHND636 KARRAKER CH   *PA CITIZENS COMT ON MIG LAB
AGRICULTURAL SEASONAL LABORERS OF COLORADO AND CALIFORNIA.
/MIGRANT-WORKERS/
PENNSYLVANIA CITIZENS COMMITTEE ON MIGRANT LABOR.
LEWISBURG, PENNSYLVANIA. NO. 16 PP.

NKATZIX58638 KATZ I   GOLDSTON J
BENJAMIN L
BEHAVIOR AND PRODUCTIVITY IN BI-RACIAL WORK GROUPS.
HUMAN RELATIONS, VOL 11, MAY 1958. PP 123-141.

NKATZIX60639 KATZ I   BENJAMIN L
EFFECTS OF WHITE AUTHORITARIANISM IN BI-RACIAL WORK GROUPS.
JOURNAL OF ABNORMAL AND SOCIAL PSYCHOLOGY, VOL 61, 1960.
PP 448-456.

NKATZIX63640 KATZ I   GREENBAUM C
EFFECTS OF ANXIETY, THREAT, AND RACIAL ENVIRONMENT ON TASK
PERFORMANCE OF NEGRO COLLEGE STUDENTS.
JOURNAL OF ABNORMAL AND SOCIAL PSYCHOLOGY, VOL 66, NO 6,
1963. PP 562-567.

NKATZIX64637 KATZ I
REVIEW OF EVIDENCE RELATING TO EFFECTS OF DESEGREGATION ON
THE INTELLECTUAL PERFORMANCE OF NEGROES.
NEW YORK UNIVERSITY, RESEARCH CENTER FOR HUMAN RELATIONS.
OFFICE OF NAVAL RESEARCH TECHNICAL REPORT NO 8. NEW YORK.
FEB 1964. 50 PP. ALSO AMERICAN PSYCHOLOGIST, JUNE 1964.

ALSO EDUCATION AND THE METROPOLIS. ED BY HARRY L MILLER
AND MARJORIE B SMILEY. HUNTER COLLEGE, CITY UNIVERSITY OF
NEW YORK. NEW YORK. 1964. PP 373-391.

NKELLKP64641 KELLEY KP
POSITION PAPER ON EMPLOYMENT INTEGRATION.
INTERRACIAL REVIEW, VOL 37, AP 1964. PP 82-84.

NKELLPL66734 KELLOGG PL
CIVIL-RIGHTS -- RACIAL DISCRIMINATION IN TEACHER HIRING AND
ASSIGNMENT FORBIDDEN.
NORTH CAROLINA LAW REVIEW, VOL 45, DEC 1966. PP 166-174.

NKEMPMX65293 KEMPTON M
THE MERITOCRACY OF LABOR.
NEW REPUBLIC, FEB 6 1965. PP 14-17.

NKENNJF63016 KENNEDY JF
DISCRIMINATION IN AMERICA TODAY.
AMERICAN JOURNAL OF ECONOMICS AND SOCIOLOGY, VOL 22, NO 2,
AP 1963. P 286.

NKENNRF66017 KENNEDY RD
STATEMENT AND TESTIMONY ON FEDERAL ROLE IN URBAN AFFAIRS.
/EMPLOYMENT GHETTO/
US SENATE. COMMITTEE ON GOVERNMENT OPERATIONS, SUBCOMMITTEE
ON EXECUTIVE REORGANIZATION. HEARINGS. FEDERAL ROLE IN URBAN
AFFAIRS. PART I. AUG 15-16 1966. GPO. WASHINGTON, DC. 1966.
PP 25-59.

NKENNTH54273 KENNEDEY TH   SMITH CU
THE SOCIO-ECONOMIC ADJUSTMENT OF THE NEGRO IN SEATTLE
BETWEEN 1940 AND 1950. /WASHINGTON/
THE QUARTERLY REVIEW OF HIGHER EDUCATION AMONG NEGROES,
VOL 22, NO 4, OCT 1954. PP 154-159.

NKENNVD63642 KENNEDY VD   *CC OF SOC PLANNING BERKELEY
WASTED MANPOWER -- BERKELEY CHALLENGE AND OPPORTUNITY.
WORKSHOP COSPONSORED WITH THE BERKELEY UNIFIED
SCHOOL-DISTRICT MARCH 15-16, 1963. /CALIFORNIA/
COUNCIL OF SOCIAL PLANNING, BERKELEY AREA. REPORT NO 39.
BERKELEY, CALIFORNIA. 1963. 24 PP.

NKENTCH66643 KENTUCKY COMM ON HUMAN RIGHTS
NEGRO EMPLOYMENT IN KENTUCKY STATE AGENCIES.
KENTUCKY COMMISSION ON HUMAN RIGHTS. FRANKFORT, KENTUCKY.
FEB 1966. 18 PP.

NKEPHWM54543 KEPHART WM
NEGRO VISIBILITY.
AMERICAN SOCIOLOGICAL REVIEW, VOL 19, NO 4, AUG 1954.
PP 462-467.

NKERNJH50644 KERNS JH
EMPLOYMENT PROBLEMS OF THE OLDER NEGRO WORKER.
NEW YORK PUBLIC LIBRARY. NEW YORK. TYPEWRITTEN MANUSCRIPT.
1950.

NKERNJH51897 KERNS JH   *NATIONAL URBAN LEAGUE
A STUDY OF THE EMPLOYMENT OPPORTUNITIES FOR NEGROES IN
BREWERIES OF THE UNITED STATES. /INDUSTRY/
NATIONAL URBAN LEAGUE. NEW YORK. 1951. 73 PP.

NKERNJH57645 KERNS JH   *MORRIS COUNTY URBAN LEAGUE
SUMMARY OF A SURVEY OF SOCIAL AND ECONOMIC CONDITIONS IN
MORRIS COUNTY NEW-JERSEY AS THEY AFFECT THE NEGRO.
MORRIS COUNTY URBAN LEAGUE. MORRISTOWN, NEW JERSEY. 1957.
16 PP.

NKESSMA63019 KESSLER MA   *US DEPARTMENT OF LABOR.
ECONOMIC STATUS OF NONWHITE WORKERS, 1955-62.
US DEPARTMENT OF LABOR, MONTHLY LABOR REVIEW, VOL 86, NO 7,
JULY 1963. PP 780-788.

NKIEHRX58647 KIEHL R
NEGRO ENGINEERS AND STUDENTS REPORT ON THEIR PROFESSION.
/OCCUPATIONS/
JOURNAL OF NEGRO EDUCATION, VOL 27, SPRING 1958. PP 189-194.

NKIEHRX58648 KIEHL R
OPPORTUNITIES FOR NEGROES IN ENGINEERING. /OCCUPATIONS/
PERSONNEL AND GUIDANCE JOURNAL, VOL 37, NOV 1958
PP 219-222.

NKIEHRX64333 KIEHL R
OPPORTUNITIES FOR NEGROES IN ENGINEERING -- A SECOND REPORT.
/OCCUPATIONS/
PERSONNEL AND GUIDANCE JOURNAL, JUNE 1964. PP 1019-1020.

NKIFEAX64649 KIFER A
CHANGING PATTERNS OF NEGRO EMPLOYMENT.
/OCCUPATIONAL-PATTERNS/
INDUSTRIAL RELATIONS, VOL 3, NO 3, MAY 1964. PP 23-36.

NKILLCC67653 KILLINGSWORTH CC
NEGROES IN A CHANGING LABOR-MARKET. /UNEMPLOYMENT/
EMPLOYMENT, RACE AND POVERTY. ED BY ARTHUR M ROSS AND
HERBERT HILL. HARCOURT, BRACE, AND WORLD. NEW YORK. 1967.
PP 49-75.

NKILLLM52650 KILLIAN LM
THE EFFECTS OF SOUTHERN WHITE WORKERS ON RACE-RELATIONS IN
NORTHERN PLANTS.
AMERICAN SOCIOLOGICAL REVIEW, VOL 17, NO 3, JUNE 1952.
PP 327-331.

NKILLLM64652 KILLIAN LM   GRIGG CM
RACIAL CRISIS IN AMERICA.
PRENTICE-HALL. ENGLEWOOD CLIFFS, NEW JERSEY. 1964.

NKILLLM65651 KILLIAN LM   GRIGG CM
COMMUNITY RESISTANCE TO AND ACCEPTANCE OF DESEGREGATION.
JOURNAL OF NEGRO EDUCATION, VOL 34, SUMMER 1965.
PP 268-277.

NKINGML62144 KING ML
THE CASE AGAINST TOKENISM.
THE NEW YORK TIMES MAGAZINE, AUG 5 1962. PP 11 FF.

NKINGML64022 KING MC
WHY WE CAN-T WAIT. /CIVIL-RIGHTS EQUAL-OPPORTUNITY/
HARPER AND ROW. NEW YORK. 1964. 169 PP.

NKINZRH50654 KINZER RH   SAGARIN E
THE NEGRO IN AMERICAN BUSINESS. THE CONFLICT BETWEEN
SEPARATISM AND INTEGRATION.
GREENBERG PUBLISHERS. NEW YORK. 1950. 210 PP.

NKLEIRJ62655 KLEINER RJ   TAYLOR H
*PHILADELPHIA COMM HUMAN RELS

SOCIAL-STATUS AND ASPIRATIONS IN PHILADELPHIA-S NEGRO
POPULATION. /PENNSYLVANIA/
PHILADELPHIA COMMISSION ON HUMAN RELATIONS. PHILADELPHIA,
PENNSYLVANIA. 1962. 16 PP.

NKLINOX44656 KLINEBERG O ED
CHARACTERISTICS OF THE AMERICAN NEGRO.
HARPER AND ROW. NEW YORK. 1944.

NKLINOX63657 KLINEBERG O
NEGRO-WHITE DIFFERENCES IN INTELLIGENCE TEST PERFORMANCE.
AMERICAN PSYCHOLOGIST, VOL 18, NO 4, AP 1963. PP 198-202.

NKNIGOB65023 KNIGHT OB
A STUDY OF PROFESSIONAL PREPARATION OF NEGRO TEACHERS OF
EXCEPTIONAL CHILDREN IN NORTH-CAROLINA COUNTY AND CITY
PUBLIC SCHOOLS.
JOURNAL OF EDUCATIONAL RESEARCH, VOL 58, NO 5, JAN 1965.
PP 195-199.

NKORNWA50660 KORNHAUSER WA
LABOR UNION AND RACE-RELATIONS. A STUDY OF UNION TACTICS.
UNIVERSITY OF CHICAGO. MA THESIS. CHICAGO, ILLINOIS. 1950.

NKORNWA52661 KORNHAUSER WA
THE NEGRO UNION OFFICIAL. A STUDY OF SPONSORSHIP AND
CONTROL.
AMERICAN JOURNAL OF SOCIOLOGY, VOL 57, NO 5, MAR 1952.
PP 443-452.

NKORNWA53659 KORNHAUSER WA
IDEOLOGY AND INTERESTS. THE DETERMINANTS OF UNION ACTION.
JOURNAL OF SOCIAL ISSUES, VOL 9, NO 1, JAN 1953. PP 49-60.

NKOVAIX64663 KOVARSKY I
MANAGEMENT, RACIAL DISCRIMINATION AND APPRENTICE TRAINING
ACADEMY OF MANAGEMENT JOURNAL, VOL 7, NO 3, SEPT 1964.
PP 196-203.

NKOVAIX65024 KOVARSKY I
APPRENTICESHIP TRAINING PROGRAMS AND RACIAL DISCRIMINATION.
IOWA LAW REVIEW, VOL 50, NO 3, SPRING 1965. PP 755-776.

NKRISSX67143 KRISLOV S
THE NEGRO IN FEDERAL EMPLOYMENT. THE QUEST FOR
EQUAL-OPPORTUNITY.
UNIVERSITY OF MINNESOTA PRESS. MINNEAPOLIS, MINNESOTA. 1967.
157 PP.

NKRISSX67665 KRISLOV S
GOVERNMENT AND EQUAL-EMPLOYMENT-OPPORTUNITY.
EMPLOYMENT, RACE AND POVERTY, ED BY ARTHUR M ROSS AND
HERBERT HILL. HARCOURT, BRACE, AND WORLD. NEW YORK. 1967.
PP 337-364.

NKRUEAO63666 KRUEGER AO
THE ECONOMICS OF DISCRIMINATION.
JOURNAL OF POLITICAL ECONOMY, VOL 71, OCT 1963. PP 481-486.

NKRUGDH61667 KRUGER DH
TRENDS IN PUBLIC-EMPLOYMENT.
INDUSTRIAL RELATIONS ASSOCIATION, 14TH ANNUAL MEETING,
PROCEEDINGS. 1961. PP 354-366.

NKRUGRE64731 KRUG RE   *EDUCATIONAL TESTING SERVICE
THE PROBLEMS OF CULTURAL BIAS IN SELECTION, POSSIBLE
SOLUTION TO THE PROBLEM OF CULTURAL BIAS IN TESTS.
SELECTING AND TRAINING NEGROES FOR MANAGERIAL POSITIONS.
EDUCATIONAL TESTING SERVICE. PRINCETON, NEW JERSEY.
NOV 1964. PP 77-85.

NKUEBJX63315 KUEBLER J
NEGRO JOBS AND EDUCATION.
EDITORIAL RESEARCH REPORTS, VOL 1, NO 3, JAN 23 1963.
PP 45-64.

NKUHNAX62668 KUHN A
RACIAL DISCRIMINATION IN EMPLOYMENT IN THE CINNCINATI AREA.
/OHIO/
THE STEPHEN H WILDER FOUNDATION. CINNCINATI, OHIO. 1962.

NKURSHX65669 KURSH H
THE NEGRO AND APPRENTICESHIPS.
APPRENTICESHIPS IN AMERICA. WW NORTON AND CO. NEW YORK.
REVISED ED 1965. PP 97-106.

NLABORR42030 LABOR RELS REFERENCE MANUAL
OFFICIAL ADVICE ON EMPLOYING NEGROES.
LABOR RELATIONS REFERENCE MANUAL, VOL 11, SEPT 1 1942.
PP 2572-2573.

NLABORR43029 LABOR RELS REFERENCE MANUAL
INTER-AGENCY POLICY ON RACIAL BIAS.
LABOR RELATIONS REFERENCE MANUAL, VOL 12, MAR 1 1943.
PP 2559-2560.

NLABORR45027 LABOR RELS REFERENCE MANUAL
UNION HELD GUILTY OF RACE DISCRIMINATION.
LABOR RELATIONS REFERENCE MANUAL, VOL 17, SEPT 1 1945.
PP 2621-2622.

NLANGEX64304 LANGER E
NEGRO COLLEGES. LONG IGNORED, SOUTHERN SCHOOLS NOW COURTED
BY MAJOR UNIVERSITIES AND FOUNDATIONS.
SCIENCE, JULY 29 1964. 3 PP.

NLANGGE59670 LANG GE   *NY STATE COMM AGAINST DISCR
DISCRIMINATION IN THE HIRING HALL. A CASE-STUDY OF PRESSURES
TO PROMOTE INTEGRATION IN NEW-YORK-S BREWERY INDUSTRY.
DISCRIMINATION AND LOW INCOMES. ED BY AARON ANTONOVSKY AND
LOUIS LORWIN. NEW SCHOOL FOR SOCIAL RESEARCH. NEW YORK.
1959. PP 195-247.

NLANGJF65671 LANGDON JF
WHAT SHOULD THE BUSINESS RESPONSE BE TO THE NEGRO
REVOLUTION. A PUBLIC RELATIONS PROGRAM FOR DEALING WITH
MINORITY-GROUPS.
PUBLIC RELATIONS JOURNAL, VOL 21, JUNE 1965. PP 12-17.

NLANGMC56032 LANGHORNE MC
A UNIQUE REGIONAL PROGRAM OF PSYCHOLOGICAL RESEARCH AND
TRAINING IN THE SOUTH.
AMERICAN PSYCHOLOGIST, VOL 11, NO 7, JULY 1956. PP 323-326.

NLARKJR52672 LARKINS JR   *N CAROLINA S BRD PUB WELFARE
THE EMPLOYMENT OF NEGROES IN PUBLIC WELFARE IN ELEVEN
SOUTHERN STATES, 1936-1949. /OCCUPATIONS/
NORTH CAROLINA STATE BOARD OF PUBLIC WELFARE. INFORMATION
BULLETIN NO 17. RALEIGH, NORTH CAROLINA. 1952. 155 PP.

NLAWR PF 50368 LAWRENCE PF
VOCATIONAL ASPIRATICNS OF NEGRO YOUTH IN CALIFORNIA.
JOURNAL OF NEGRO EDUCATION, VOL 19, 1950. PP 47-56.

NLAWR RG 64296 LAWRENCE RG
MANAGEMENT COMPLIANCE WITH PRESIDENTIAL DIRECTIVES.
NEW YORK UNIVERSITY, SEVENTEENTH ANNUAL CONFERENCE ON LABOR.
NEW YORK. 1964. PP 125-130.

NLAWS EX 45035 LAWSON E
EPISODE I. ARTHUR BROWN APPLIES FOR A JOB. /DISCRIMINATION/
JOURNAL OF SOCIAL ISSUES, VOL 1, NO 1, FEB 1945. PP 11-17.

NLEES HX 64675 LEES H
SELF-HELP IN PHILADELPHIA. /TRAINING PENNSYLVANIA/
THE REPORTER, VOL 31, DEC 17 1964. PP 15-17.

NLEEX ES 51673 LEE ES
NEGRO INTELLIGENCE AND SELECTIVE MIGRATION. A PHILADELPHIA
TEST OF THE KLINEBERG HYPOTHESIS. /PENNSYLVANIA/
AMERICAN SOCIOLOGICAL REVIEW, VOL 16, AP 1951. PP 227-233.

NLEEX FF 61674 LEE FF
NEGRO AND WHITE IN A CONNECTICUT TOWN.
BOOKMAN ASSOCIATES. NEW YORK. 1961.

NLEFL RA 57676 LEFLAR RA
LEGAL EDUCATION. DESEGREGATION IN LAW SCHOOLS.
AMERICAN BAR ASSOCIATION JOURNAL, VOL 43, 1957. PP 145-146.

NLEGG JC 59678 LEGGETT JC   STREET D
CONFLICT RESPONSE, DETROIT NEGROES FACE UNEMPLOYMENT.
/MICHIGAN/
AMERICAN SOCIOLOGICAL ASSOCIATION, MEETINGS, PAPER. 1959.

NLEGG JC 61680 LEGGETT JC   STREET D
ECONOMIC DEPRIVATION AND EXTREMISM. A STUDY OF UNEMPLOYED
NEGROES.
AMERICAN JOURNAL OF SOCIOLOGY, VOL 67, JULY 1961. PP 53-57.

NLEGG JC 64677 LEGGETT JC
ECONOMIC INSECURITY AND WORKING-CLASS CONSCIOUSNESS.
AMERICAN SOCIOLOGICAL REVIEW, VOL 29, NO 2, AP 1964.
PP 226-234.

NLEGG JC 64679 LEGGETT JC   STREET D
ECONOMIC CRISIS AND EXPECTATIONS OF VIOLENCE. A STUDY OF
UNEMPLOYEC NEGROES.
BLUE-COLLAR WORLD. STUDIES OF THE AMERICAN WORKER. ED BY
ARTHUR SHOSTAK AND WILLIAM GOMBERG. PRENTICE-HALL.
ENGLEWOOD CLIFFS, NEW JERSEY. 1964. PP 498-504.

NLEIT RD 49681 LEITER RD
DISCRIMINATION IN EMPLOYMENT.
AMERICAN JOURNAL OF ECONOMICS AND SOCIOLOGY, VOL 8, NO 4,
JULY 1949. PP 337-349.

NLERA NL 59404 LERAY NL   CROWE GB
LABOR AND TECHNOLOGY ON SELECTED COTTON PLANTATIONS IN THE
DELTA AREA OF MISSISSIPPI, 1953-1957.
MISSISSIPPI STATE COLLEGE. STATE COLLEGE, MISSISSIPPI.
AP 1959. 23 PP.

NLERA NL 60401 LERAY NL   ROHRER HC
EMPLOYMENT OF NEGRO MANPOWER IN CALVERT COUNTY, MARYLAND.
UNIVERSITY CF MARYLAND. COLLEGE PARK, MARYLAND. MAR 1960.
37 PP.

NLERA NL 60403 LERAY NL   WILBER GL
CROWE GB
PLANTATION ORGANIZATION AND THE RESIDENT LABOR-FORCE, DELTA
AREA, MISSISSIPPI.
MISSISSIPPI STATE COLLEGE. STATE COLLEGE, MISSISSIPPI.
OCT 1960. 24 PP.

NLERA NL 61416 LERAY NL
NEGRO FARM LABOR IN THE DELTA AREA OF MISSISSIPPI. SUPPLY
AND UTILIZATION.
ASSOCIATION OF SOUTHERN AGRICULTURAL WORKERS, PROCEEDINGS.
JACKSON, MISSISSIPPI. 1961.

NLETT HA 50683 LETT HA
HAVE FAIR-EMPLOYMENT-PRACTICES-COMMISSION LAWS INCREASED
OPPORTUNITIES FOR NEGROES.
NATIONAL CONFERENCE OF SOCIAL WORK PROCEEDINGS, VOL 77.
COLUMBIA UNIVERSITY PRESS. NEW YORK. 1950. PP 130-141. ALSO
NEW JERSEY DEPARTMENT OF EDUCATION, DIVISION AGAINST
DISCRIMINATION. TRENTON, NEW JERSEY. 1950.

NLEVE BX 63684 LEVENSON B   *JOHNS HOPKINS DEPT SOC RELS
THE EMPLOYMENT SITUATION OF WHITE AND NEGRO YOUTH IN THE
CITY OF BALTIMORE. /MARYLAND/
JOHNS HOPKINS UNIVERSITY, DEPARTMENT OF SOCIAL RELATIONS.
BALTIMORE, MARYLAND. AP 1963. 60 PP.

NLEVE BX 66C36 LEVENSON B   MCDILL MS
VOCATIONAL GRADUATES IN AUTO MECHANICS. A FOLLOW-UP STUDY OF
NEGRO AND WHITE YOUTH. /OCCUPATIONS/
PHYLON, VOL 27, NO 4, WINTER 1966. PP 347-357.

NLEVI LX 62686 LEVINE L   *US EMPLOYMENT SERVICE
PROMOTING EQUAL-EMPLOYMENT THROUGH THE PUBLIC EMPLOYMENT
SERVICE.
NATIONAL URBAN LEAGUE, CONFERENCE, ADDRESS. GRAND RAPIDS,
MICHIGAN. SEPT 1 1962.

NLEVI LX 64685 LEVINE L   *US EMPLOYMENT SERVICE
MANPOWER SERVICES FOR EQUAL-EMPLOYMENT-OPPORTUNITY.
NATIONAL URBAN LEAGUE, CONFERENCE, ADDRESS. LOUISVILLE,
KENTUCKY. AUG 5 1964.

NLEVI MJ 66607 LEVIN MJ   *NJ DEPT LAW PUBLIC SAFETY
SURVEY OF EQUAL-EMPLOYMENT-OPPORTUNITIES IN NEW-JERSEY
INVESTOR-CWNED PUBLIC UTILITIES.
NEW JERSEY DEPARTMENT OF LAW AND PUBLIC SAFETY, DIVISION ON
CIVIL RIGHTS. TRENTON, NEW JERSEY. JULY 1966. 86 PP.

NLEWI CE 66688 LEWIS CE
SOME CORRELATES OF ANOMIE AMONG RURAL NEGROES.
NORTH CAROLINA STATE UNIVERSITY, DEPARTMENT OF RURAL
SOCIOLOGY. THESIS. RALEIGH, NORTH CAROLINA. 1966. 65 PP.

NLEWI ES 43689 LEWIS ES
PROGRESS IN INTERRACIAL RELATIONSHIPS. INEQUALITIES FOR
NEGROES.
NATIONAL CONFERENCE OF SOCIAL WORK PROCEEDINGS, VOL 70.
COLUMBIA UNIVERSITY PRESS. NEW YORK. 1943. PP 277-289.

NLEWI HX 49692 LEWIS H
HIGHER EDUCATION FOR NEGROES. A TOUGH SITUATION.

PHYLON, VOL 10, NO 4, 4TH QUARTER, 1949. PP 356-361.

NLEWI HX 56073 LEWIS H   HILL M
DESEGREGATION, INTEGRATION, AND THE NEGRO COMMUNITY.
ANNALS OF THE AMERICAN ACADEMY OF POLITICAL AND SOCIAL
SCIENCE, VOL 304, MAR 1956. PP 116-123.

NLEWI HX 60690 LEWIS H
THE CHANGING NEGRO FAMILY.
THE NATIONS CHILDREN, VOL 1. ED BY ELI GINZBERG. COLUMBIA
UNIVERSITY PRESS. NEW YORK. 1960.

NLEWI HX 61C40 LEWIS H   *WASH CENT FOR METROP STUDIES
CHILD REARING AMONG LOW-INCOME FAMILIES. /ECONOMIC-STATUS/
WASHINGTON CENTER FOR METROPOLITAN STUDIES. WASHINGTON, DC.
JUNE 1961. 13 PP.

NLEWI HX 67691 LEWIS H
CULTURE, CLASS AND FAMILY LIFE AMONG LOW-INCOME NEGROES.
EMPLOYMENT, RACE AND POVERTY. ED BY ARTHUR M ROSS AND
HERBERT HILL. HARCOURT, BRACE, AND WORLD. NEW YORK. 1967.
PP 149-174.

NLEWI SX 66693 LIEBERSON S   FUGUITT G
FUTURE OCCUPATIONAL DIFFERENCES BETWEEN THE RACES. A MARKOV
APPROACH.
UNIVERSITY OF WISCONSIN. UNPUBLISHED MANUSCRIPT. MADISON,
WISCONSIN. 1966. 23 PP.

NLIFE MX 66493 LIFE MAGAZINE
JIM CROW IN BUILDING UNIONS.
LIFE MAGAZINE. EDITORIAL. FEBRUARY 18 1966.

NLIGH MB 53340 LIGHTFOOTE MB
AN ECONOMIC ANALYSIS OF SPECIFIED INCORPORATED AND
UNINCORPORATED FARMERS COOPERATIVE ASSOCIATIONS OPERATED
BY NEGRO FARMERS IN ALABAMA.
TUSKEGEE UNIVERSITY. THESIS. 1953. 67 PP.

NLINC CE 64695 LINCOLN CE
THE NEGRO-S MIDDLE-CLASS DREAM.
THE NEW YORK TIMES MAGAZINE, OCT 25 1964.

NLINC CE 65694 LINCOLN CE
THE ABSENT FATHER HAUNTS THE NEGRO FAMILY.
THE NEW YORK TIMES MAGAZINE. NOV 28 1965. P 60 PLUS.

NLIPS SM 59696 LIPSET SM   BENDIX R
SOCIAL-MOBILITY IN INDUSTRIAL SOCIETY.
UNIVERSITY OF CALIFORNIA PRESS. BERKELEY, CALIFORNIA. 1959.

NLIPS SM 62043 LIPSET SM   GOMBERG W
KAHN H   HILL H
NEGROES AND THE LABOR MOVEMENT -- AN EXCHANGE.
NEW POLITICS, VOL 1, NO 3, SPRING 1962. PP 135-141.

NLITT LW 66697 LITTIG LW   *US DEPT OF HEALTH ED WELFARE
A PILOT STUDY OF PERSONALITY FACTORS RELATED TO OCCUPATIONAL
ASPIRATIONS OF NEGRO COLLEGE STUDENTS.
US DEPARTMENT OF HEALTH, EDUCATION AND WELFARE, REPORT TO
THE OFFICE OF EDUCATION. GPO. WASHINGTON, DC. 1966.

NLITW LX 62698 LITWAK L
THE AMERICAN LABOR MOVEMENT.
PRENTICE-HALL SPECTRUM. NEW YORK. 1962.

NLIVI AH 58044 LIVINGSTON AH
HIGH SCHOOL GRADUATES AND DROPOUTS -- A NEW LOOK AT A
PERSISTENT PROBLEM.
SCHOOL REVIEW, VOL 66, 1958. PP 195-203.

NLLOY RG 54045 LLOYD RG   WALKER GH
TEACHER SUPPLY AND CEMAND IN THE NEGRO COLLEGE.
JOURNAL OF NEGRO EDUCATION, VOL 23, NO 4, FALL 1954.
PP 421-427.

NLOCK HC NO 700 LOCKWOOD HC
CULTURAL EXPOSURE AND RACE AS VARIABLES IN PREDICTING
TRAINING AND JOB SUCCESS. /TESTING/
LOCKHEED AIRCRAFT CORPORATION. BURBANK, CALIFORNIA.
UNPUBLISHED MANUSCRIPT. 11 PP.

NLOCK HC 65701 LOCKWOOD HC   *EDUCATICNAL TESTING SERVICE
PROGRESS IN PLANS-FOR-PROGRESS FOR NEGRO MANAGERS.
SELECTING AND TRAINING NEGROES FOR MANAGERIAL POSITIONS.
EDUCATIONAL TESTING SERVICE. PRINCETON, NEW JERSEY. 1965.
PP 1-19.

NLOES FS 46703 LOESCHER FS
PLACEMENT SERVICE OF THE AMERICAN FRIENDS SERVICE COMMITTEE.
A TECHNIQUE IN RACE-RELATIONS.
OCCUPATIONS, VOL 25, NOV 1946. PP 90-93.

NLOGA RW 63046 LOGAN RW
THE PROGRESS OF THE NEGRO AFTER A CENTURY OF EMANCIPATION.
JOURNAL OF NEGRO EDUCATION, VOL 32, NO 4, FALL 1963.
PP 320-328.

NLOGA RW 64704 LOGAN RW
EDUCATIONAL CHANGES AFFECTING AMERICAN NEGROES.
ASSURING FREEDOM TO THE FREE. A CENTURY OF EMANCIPATION IN
THE USA. ED BY ARNOLD M ROSE. WAYNE STATE UNIVERSITY PRESS.
DETROIT, MICHIGAN. 1964.

NLONG HH 62705 LONG HH   *PRESIDENT-S COMMITTEE ON EEO
GUIDANCE AND MINORITY YOUTH.
THE AMERICAN DREAM...EQUAL OPPORTUNITY. REPORT ON THE
COMMUNITY LEADERS CONFERENCE. PRESIDENT-S COMMITTEE ON EQUAL
EMPLOYMENT CPPORTUNITY. GPO. WASHINGTON, DC. MAY 19 1962.

NLONG HH 62706 LONG HH   HENDERSON VW
*TENNESSEE CC ON HUMAN RELS
JOBS AND COLOR. NEGRO EMPLOYMENT IN TENNESSEE STATE
GOVERNMENT.
TENNESSEE COUNCIL ON HUMAN RELATIONS. NASHVILLE, TENNESSEE.
1962.

NLONG MX 62C48 LONG M
STRICTLY SPEAKING. /EMPLOYMENT/
NEW SOUTH, VOL 17, NO 5, MAY 1962. PP 2, 13-15.

NLOSA CC 63709 LA COUNTY CCMM ON HUMAN RELS
THE NEGRO IN LOS-ANGELES COUNTY. /CALIFORNIA/
LOS ANGELES COUNTY COMMISSION ON HUMAN RELATIONS. COMMUNITY
INTELLIGENCE BULLETIN NO 2. LOS ANGELES, CALIFORNIA. 1963.

NLOSA CC 65365 LA COUNTY CCMM ON HUMAN RELS
PROPOSALS FOR THE IMPROVEMENT OF HUMAN RELATIONS IN THE
LOS-ANGELES METROPOLITAN AREA. /EMPLOYMENT CALIFORNIA/
LOS ANGELES COUNTY COMMISSION ON HUMAN RELATIONS.

LOS ANGELES, CALIFORNIA. NOV 2 1965. 74 PP.

NLOTHDX56710 LOTH D   FLEMING H
INTEGRATION NORTH AND SOUTH.
FUND FOR THE REPUBLIC. NEW YORK. 1956. 110 PP.

NLOTTAJ63487 LOTT AJ   LOTT BE
NEGRO AND WHITE CHILDREN-S PLANS FOR THEIR FUTURES.
/ASPIRATIONS/
NEGRO AND WHITE YOUTH. HOLT, RINEHART AND WINSTON. NEW YORK.
1963. PP 61-79.

NLOUIHR64715 LOUISVILLE HUMAN RELS COMM
BRICKS WITHOUT STRAW. STUDIES OF COMMUNITY UNEMPLOYMENT
PROBLEMS, THE NEGROES DILEMMA. /LOUISVILLE KENTUCKY/
LOUISVILLE HUMAN RELATIONS COMMISSION. LOUISVILLE, KENTUCKY.
1964. 12 PP.

NLOUIHR65717 LOUISVILLE HUMAN RELS COMM
JOBS AND THE LAW. /LOUISVILLE KENTUCKY/
LOUISVILLE HUMAN RELATIONS COMMISSION. LOUISVILLE, KENTUCKY.
1965. 44 PP.

NLOUIHR66582 LOUISVILLE HUMAN RELS COMM
PATTERNS OF DISCRIMINATION STUDY -- LOUISVILLE
HUMAN-RELATIONS-COMMISSION. /KENTUCKY/
LOUISVILLE HUMAN RELATIONS COMMISSION, LOUISVILLE, KENTUCKY,
JULY 1966. 31 PP.

NLOUIHR66716 LOUISVILLE HUMAN RELS COMM
FACTS FOR ACTION. /LOUISVILLE KENTUCKY/
LOUISVILLE HUMAN RELATIONS COMMISSION. LOUISVILLE, KENTUCKY.
1966. 16 PP.

NLOUISD64714 LOUISIANA STATE DEPT OF ED
THE SCHOOL DROPOUT IN LOUISIANA 1963-1964.
LOUISIANA STATE DEPARTMENT OF EDUCATION. BULLETIN NO 1026.
BATON ROUGE, LOUISIANA. 1964. 32 PP.

NLURIMX66712 LURIE M   RAYACK E
RACIAL DIFFERENCES IN MIGRATION AND JOB-SEARCH. A
CASE-STUDY.
SOUTHERN ECONOMIC JOURNAL, VOL 33, JULY 1966.

NLUSKLX63713 LUSKY L
RACIAL DISCRIMINATION AND THE FEDERAL LAW. A PROBLEM IN
NULLIFICATION.
COLUMBIA LAW REVIEW, VOL 63, NO 7, NOV 1963. PP 1163-1191.

NLYSTMH61718 LYSTAD MH
FAMILY PATTERNS, ACHIEVEMENTS, AND ASPIRATIONS OF URBAN
NEGROES.
SOCIOLOGY AND SOCIAL RESEARCH, VOL 45, NO 3, AP 1961.
PP 281-288.

NMACIRM49731 MACIVER RM ED   *JTSAM INST RELIG SOC STUDIES
DISCRIMINATION AND NATIONAL WELFARE. A SERIES OF ADDRESSES
AND DISCUSSIONS.
JEWISH THEOLOGICAL SEMINARY OF AMERICA, INSTITUTE FOR
RELIGIOUS AND SOCIAL STUDIES. HARPER. NEW YORK. 1949.
135 PP.

NMACKBK48488 MACKENZIE BK
THE IMPORTANCE OF CONTACT IN DETERMINING ATTITUDES TOWARD
NEGROES.
JOURNAL OF ABNORMAL AND SOCIAL PSYCHOLOGY, VOL 43, NO 1,
JAN 1948. PP 417-441.

NMANARX56734 MANAGEMENT REVIEW
HOW INTEGRATION IS WORKING OUT IN INDUSTRY. THE NEGRO
WORKER.
MANAGEMENT REVIEW, VOL 45, JULY 1956. PP 547-549.

NMANGCS40735 MANGUM CS
THE LEGAL STATUS OF THE NEGRO.
UNIVERSITY OF NORTH CAROLINA PRESS. CHAPEL HILL,
NORTH CAROLINA. 1940.

NMANGMX63736 MANGUM M
THE FIGHT FOR EQUAL-OPPORTUNITY.
AMERICAN JOURNAL OF ECONOMICS AND SOCIOLOGY, VOL 22, NO 4,
OCT 1963. PP 550.

NMANNCP53737 MANN CP   BROWN WH
THE SOUTH TODAY AND LABOR-S TASKS.
POLITICAL AFFAIRS, OCT 1953. PP 31-49.

NMARCFL48054 MARCUSE FL
SOME ATTITUDES TOWARD EMPLOYING NEGROES AS TEACHERS IN A
NORTHERN UNIVERSITY.
JOURNAL OF NEGRO EDUCATION, VOL 17, NO 1, WINTER 1948.
PP 18-26.

NMARSCP65738 MARSH CP   BROWN MM
FACILITATIVE AND INHIBITIVE FACTORS IN TRAINING PROGRAM
RECRUITMENT AMONG RURAL NEGROES.
JOURNAL OF SOCIAL ISSUES, VOL 21, JAN 1965. PP 110-125.

NMARSRX60060 MARSHALL R
SOME FACTORS INFLUENCING THE GROWTH OF UNIONS IN THE SOUTH.
INDUSTRIAL RELATIONS RESEARCH ASSOCIATION, ANNALS. 1960.
PP 166 FF.

NMARSRX61740 MARSHALL R
LABOR IN THE SOUTH. /UNION/
ANTIOCH REVIEW, VOL 21, NO 1, SPRING 1961. PP 80-95.

NMARSRX62747 MARSHALL R
SOME FACTORS INFLUENCING UNION RACIAL PRACTICES.
INDUSTRIAL RELATIONS RESEARCH ASSOCIATION PROCEEDINGS, 1962.
PP 104-119.

NMARSRX62749 MARSHALL R   *US DEPARTMENT OF LABOR
UNION RACIAL PRACTICES AND THE LABOR-MARKET.
US DEPARTMENT OF LABOR, MONTHLY LABOR REVIEW, VOL 85, NO 3,
MAR 1962. PP 268-270.

NMARSRX62751 MARSHALL R
UNION RACIAL PROBLEMS IN THE SOUTH.
INDUSTRIAL RELATIONS, MAY 1962. PP 117-128.

NMARSRX63741 MARSHALL R
THE NEGRO AND ORGANIZED LABOR. /UNION/
JOURNAL OF NEGRO EDUCATION, VOL 32, NO 4, FALL 1963.
PP 375-389.

NMARSRX63745 MARSHALL R
RACIAL FACTORS INFLUENCING ENTRY TO THE SKILLED TRADES.
/UNION/
HUMAN RESOURCES IN THE URBAN COMMUNITY. ED BY MARK PERLMAN.

JOHNS HOPKINS PRESS. BALTIMORE, MARYLAND. 1963. 26 PP.

NMARSRX63748 MARSHALL R
SOME FACTORS INFLUENCING THE UPGRADING OF NEGROES IN THE
SOUTHERN PETROLEUM REFINING INDUSTRY. /CASE-STUDY/
SOCIAL FORCES, VOL 42, NO 2, DEC 1963. PP 186-194.

NMARSRX63750 MARSHALL R
UNION RACIAL PRACTICES.
US SENATE, COMMITTEE ON LABOR AND PUBLIC WELFARE,
SUBCOMMITTEE ON EMPLOYMENT AND MANPOWER, STATEMENT. GPO.
WASHINGTON, DC. 1963. 26 PP.

NMARSRX63752 MARSHALL R
UNION STRUCTURE AND PUBLIC POLICY. THE CONTROL OF UNION
RACIAL PRACTICES.
POLITICAL SCIENCE QUARTERLY, VOL 78, NO 3, SEPT 1963.
PP 445-458.

NMARSRX64061 MARSHALL R
UNIONS AND THE NEGRO COMMUNITY.
INDUSTRIAL AND LABOR RELATIONS REVIEW, VOL 17, NO 2,
JAN 1964. PP 179-202.

NMARSRX65058 MARSHALL R
THE NEGRO WORKER AND THE TRADE UNIONS. A FOOT IN THE DOOR.
WILEY. NEW YORK. 1965.

NMARSRX65739 MARSHALL R
INDUSTRIALIZATION AND RACE-RELATIONS IN THE SOUTHERN US.
INDUSTRIALIZATION AND RACE RELATIONS. A SYMPOSIUM. ED BY
GUY HUNTER. OXFORD UNIVERSITY PRESS. NEW YORK. 1965.
PP 61-96.

NMARSRX65742 MARSHALL R
THE NEGRO AND ORGANIZED LABOR. /UNION/
JOHN WILEY AND SONS. NEW YORK. 1965. 375 PP.

NMARSRX65744 MARSHALL R   *US DEPARTMENT OF LABOR
PROSPECTS FOR EQUAL-EMPLOYMENT. CONFLICTING PORTENTS.
US DEPARTMENT OF LABOR, MONTHLY LABOR REVIEW, VOL 88, NO 6,
JUNE 1965. PP 650-653.

NMARSRX66327 MARSHALL R   BRIGGS VM
*US DEPARTMENT OF LABOR   *UNIVERSITY OF TEXAS
NEGRO PARTICIPATION IN APPRENTICESHIP PROGRAMS.
UNIVERSITY OF TEXAS. US DEPARTMENT OF LABOR, OFFICE OF
MANPOWER POLICY, EVALUATION AND RESEARCH. AUSTIN, TEXAS.
DEC 1966. 499 PP.

NMARSRX66746 MARSHALL R
THE ROOTS OF THE NEGRO-UNION ALLIANCE. /UNION/
AMERICAN FEDERATIONIST, VOL 73, NO 11, NOV 1966. PP 3-8.

NMARSRX66943 MARSHALL R
THE POSITION OF MINORITIES IN THE AMERICAN LABOR MOVEMENT.
/UNION/
LABOR IN A CHANGING AMERICA. ED BY WILLIAM HABER. BASIC
BOOKS, INC. NEW YORK. 1966. PP 238-251.

NMARSRX67057 MARSHALL R
THE NEGRO WORKER.
RANDOM HOUSE. NEW YORK. 1967.

NMARSRX67118 MARSHALL R   BRIGGS VM
NEGRO PARTICIPATION IN APPRENTICESHIP PROGRAMS.
JOURNAL OF HUMAN RESOURCES, WINTER 1967. PP 51-69.

NMARSTX44753 MARSHALL T
NEGRO STATUS IN THE BOILERMAKERS UNION.
CRISIS, MAR 1944.

NMARSTX51754 MARSHALL T   *NAACP
REPORT ON KOREA. /MILITARY/
NAACP. NEW YORK. 1951.

NMARSTX51755 MARSHALL T
SUMMARY JUSTICE -- THE NEGRO GI IN KOREA. /MILITARY/
CRISIS, VOL 58, MAY 1951. PP 297-304, 350-355.

NMARTWD63303 MARTINSON WD
YOU NEED TO SEE IT TO BELIEVE IT, REPORT OF THE 1963 SUMMER
STUDY-SKILLS PROGRAMS. /COLLEGE EDUCATION/
UNITED PRESBYTERIAN CHURCH. BOARD OF NATIONAL MISSIONS.
EDUCATIONAL COUNSELING SERVICE. ATLANTA, GEORGIA. 1963.
20 PP.

NMASLWX55756 MASLOW W
USES OF LAW IN THE STRUGGLE FOR EQUALITY.
SOCIAL RESEARCH, VOL 22, FALL 1955. PP 297-324.

NMASOJR45323 MASON JR
THE CIO AND THE NEGRO IN THE SOUTH. /UNION/
JOURNAL OF NEGRO EDUCATION, VOL 14, FALL 1945. PP 552-561.

NMASOJR52324 MASON JR
TO WIN THESE RIGHTS. A PERSONAL STORY OF THE CIO IN THE
SOUTH. /UNION/
HARPER. NEW YORK. 1952. 206 PP.

NMASOLR52063 MASON LR
WORK AND COLOR. /UNION/
THE NATION, VOL 175, SEPT 27 1952. PP 263-265.

NMASSCA66964 MASS COMM AGAINST DISCR
FINAL REPORT. EQUAL-EMPLOYMENT-OPPORTUNITY IN THE
TRANSPORTATION INDUSTRY. /MASSACHUSETTS/
MASSACHUSETTS COMMISSION AGAINST DISCRIMINATION. BOSTON,
MASSACHUSETTS. JUNE 1966. 26 PLUS PP.

NMASSCE42757 MASS COMM EMPLOY PROBS NEGRO
REPORT OF THE COMMISSION ON THE EMPLOYMENT PROBLEMS OF
NEGROES TO GOVERNOR SALTONSTALL. /MASSACHUSETTS/
MASSACHUSETTS COMMISSION ON THE EMPLOYMENT PROBLEMS OF
NEGROES. BOSTON, MASSACHUSETTS. 1942. 38 PP.

NMATTDR62758 MATTHEWS DR   PROTHRO JW
SOUTHERN RACIAL ATTITUDES. CONFLICT, AWARENESS AND POLITICAL
CHANGE.
ANNALS OF THE AMERICAN ACADEMY OF POLITICAL AND SOCIAL
SCIENES, VOL 344, NOV 1962. PP 108-121.

NMATTEG66759 MATTISON EG   *US DEPARTMENT OF LABOR
PLANS-FOR-PROGRESS.
US DEPARTMENT OF LABOR, OCCUPATIONAL OUTLOOK QUARTERLY,
VOL 10, NO 4, DEC 1966. PP 16-18.

NMAYEMX62761 MAYER M
THE SCHOOLS.
HARPER. NEW YORK. 1962.

NMAYOSC63762 MAYO SC   HAMILTON HC
THE RURAL NEGRO POPULATION OF THE SOUTH IN TRANSITION.
PHYLON, VOL 24, NO 2, 2ND QTR 1963. PP 160-171.

NMAYXEX64760 MAY E
THE WASTED AMERICANS. /POVERTY/
HARPER AND ROW. NEW YORK. 1964. 227 PP.

NMCCOWM58062 MCCORD WM   DEMERATH NJ
NEGRO VERSUS WHITE INTELLIGENCE. A CONTINUING CONTROVERSY.
HARVARD EDUCATIONAL REVIEW, VOL 28, SPRING 1958. PP 120-135.

NMCDOEC55719 MCDONAGH EC
ATTITUDES TOWARD ETHNIC FARM WORKERS IN COACHELLA-VALLEY.
   /CALIFORNIA/
SOCIOLOGY AND SOCIAL RESEARCH, VOL 40, NO 1, SEPT-OCT 1955.
PP 10-18.

NMCENOX50721 MCENTIRE D   TARNOPOL JR
*US DEPARTMENT OF LABOR
POSTWAR STATUS OF NEGRO WORKERS IN SAN-FRANCISCO AREA.
   /CALIFORNIA/
US DEPARTMENT OF LABOR, MONTHLY LABOR REVIEW, VOL 70, NO 6,
JUNE 1950. PP 612-617.

NMCGODJ66583 MCGOUGH DJ   *PHILA CCMM HUMAN RELS
HOSPITAL EMPLOYMENT STUDY.
PHILADELPHIA HUMAN RELATIONS COMMISSION, PHILADELPHIA,
PENNSYLVANIA. JUNE 30 1966. 102 PP.

NMCGREJ65720 MCGRATH EJ   *COLUMBIA U INST OF HIGHER ED
THE PREDOMINANTLY NEGRO COLLEGES AND UNIVERSITIES IN
   TRANSITION.
COLUMBIA UNIVERSITY PRESS, TEACHERS COLLEGE, INSTITUTE OF
HIGHER EDUCATION. NEW YORK. 1965.

NMCKERB64722 MCKERSIE RB
THE CIVIL-RIGHTS MOVEMENT AND EMPLOYMENT.
INDUSTRIAL RELATIONS, VOL 3, NO 3, MAY 1964. PP 1-22.

NMCKERB64723 MCKERSIE RB
THE CIVIL-RIGHTS REVOLUTION AND THE BUSINESSMAN.
BUSINESS TOPICS. MICHIGAN STATE UNIVERSITY. LANSING,
MICHIGAN. MAY 1964.

NMCKIGB56725 MCKIBIN GB   *US DEPARTMENT OF LABOR
CONFERENCE ON EQUAL JOB OPPORTUNITY.
US DEPARTMENT OF LABOR, MONTHLY LABOR REVIEW, VOL 79,
JAN 1956. PP 31-33.

NMCKIJC65726 MCKINNEY JC ED   THOMPSON ET ED
THE SOUTH IN CONTINUITY AND CHANGE.
DUKE UNIVERSITY PRESS. DURHAM, NORTH CAROLINA. 1965. 487 PP.

NMCLABF51349 MCLAURIN BF
THE RELATIONSHIP BETWEEN MECHANIZATION OF COTTON PRODUCTION
   AND ATTENDANCE AND ENROLLMENT IN THE RURAL SCHOOLS OF
   COAHOMA COUNTY, MISSISSIPPI.
TUSKEGEE INSTITUTE. THESIS. TUSKEGEE, ALABAMA. 1951. 59 PP.

NMCNIRX51727 MCNICKLE R
PROGRESS IN RACE-RELATIONS.
EDITORIAL RESEARCH REPORTS, VOL 1, NO 15, AP 1951.

NMCPHEL55728 MCPHERSON EL
THE ROLE OF THE NEGRO IN THE HEALING PROFESSIONS IN
   CONTEMPORARY AMERICA. /OCCUPATIONS/
JOURNAL OF THE NATIONAL MEDICAL ASSOCIATION, VOL 47,
SEPT 1955.

NMCPICM61729 MCPIKE CM
THE NEGRO WORKER-S CULTURAL AND OCCUPATIONAL LIMITATIONS.
UNIVERSITY OF ILLINOIS. INSTITUTE OF LABOR AND INDUSTRIAL
RELATIONS. MASTER-S THESIS. CHAMPAIGN, ILLINOIS. 1961.

NMCQUFT45348 MCQUEEN FT
FACTORS AFFECTING FARM PLACEMENT OF NEGRO VOCATIONAL
   AGRICULTURE STUDENTS IN ALABAMA.
TUSKEGEE INSTITUTE. THESIS. TUSKEGEE, ALABAMA. 1945. 51 PP.

NMCQURX60730 MCQUEEN R   CHURN B
INTELLIGENCE AND EDUCATIONAL ACHIEVEMENT OF A MATCHED
   SAMPLE OF WHITE AND NEGRO STUDENTS.
SCHOOL AND SOCIETY, SEPT 24 1960. PP 327-329.

NMEANGX57763 MEANY G   *NAACP
WE CALL ALL MEN BROTHERS. /UNION/
NAACP. ADDRESS. NEW YORK. 1957.

NMEIEAX66765 MEIER A   RUDWICK EM
FROM PLANTATION TO GHETTO. AN INTERPRETIVE HISTORY OF
   AMERICAN NEGROES.
HILL AND WANG. NEW YORK. 1966. 267 PP.

NMEIEAX67764 MEIER A
CIVIL-RIGHTS STRATEGIES FOR NEGRO EMPLOYMENT.
EMPLOYMENT, RACE, AND POVERTY. ED BY ARTHUR M ROSS AND
HERBERT HILL. HARCOURT, BRACE, AND WORLD. NEW YORK. 1967.
PP 175-204.

NMENZRX49766 MENZES R
THE FACTS ON NEGRO PHYSICIANS. /OCCUPATIONS/
MEDICAL ECONOMICS. DEC 1949. PP 66-75.

NMERCJJ56768 MERCIER JJM
A SOCIOLOGICAL ANALYSIS OF A BI-RACIAL LOCAL LABOR UNION.
LOUISIANA STATE UNIVERSITY. MA THESIS. BATON ROUGE,
LOUISIANA. 1956.

NMEYEAE58769 MEYER AE
RACE AND THE SCHOOLS.
THE ATLANTIC MONTHLY, VOL 201, JAN 1958. PP 29-34.

NMEYEBI65210 MEYER BI
RACIAL DISCRIMINATION ON THE JOBSITE. COMPETING THEORIES AND
   COMPETING FORUMS.
UCLA LAW REVIEW, VOL 12, MAY 1965. PP 1186-1206.

NMEZEAG47492 MEZERIK AG
DIXIE IN BLACK AND WHITE. /UNION/
THE NATION. JUNE 21 1947. PP 740-741.

NMICCRC64772 MICHIGAN CIVIL RIGHTS COMM
SURVEY OF ALBION, MICHIGAN.
MICHIGAN CIVIL RIGHTS COMMISSION. DETROIT, MICHIGAN.
MAR 1964. 26 PP.

NMICCRC65771 MICHIGAN CIVIL RIGHTS COMM
NILES COMMUNITY SELF SURVEY. /MICHIGAN/
MICHIGAN CIVIL RIGHTS COMMISSION. DETROIT, MICHIGAN. 1965.
15 PP.

NMICCRC65773 MICH CIVIL RIGHTS COMM
A REPORT ON THE CHARACTERISTICS OF MICHIGAN-S NON-WHITE
   POPULATION.
MICHIGAN CIVIL RIGHTS COMMISSION, RESEARCH DIVISION.
DETROIT, MICHIGAN. 1965. 5 PP.

NMICCRC66606 MICHIGAN CIVIL RIGHTS COMM
EMPLOYMENT DISTRIBUTION STUDY OF THE CONSTRUCTION
   INDUSTRY IN MICHIGAN.
MICHIGAN CIVIL RIGHTS COMMISSION, DETROIT, MICHIGAN.
JULY 1966. 86 PP.

NMICCSC64775 MICH CIVIL SERVICE COMM
A STUDY OF NON-WHITE EMPLOYMENT IN THE STATE SERVICE.
   /MICHIGAN/
MICHIGAN CIVIL SERVICE COMMISSION, RESEARCH DIVISION.
LANSING, MICHIGAN. MAY 1964. 18 PP.

NMICCSC65774 MICH CIVIL SERVICE COMM
A FOLLOW-UP STUDY OF NON-WHITE EMPLOYMENT IN THE STATE
   SERVICE. /MICHIGAN/
MICHIGAN CIVIL SERVICE COMMISSION, RESEARCH DIVISION.
LANSING, MICHIGAN. JUNE 1965. 20 PP.

NMICFEP58778 MICHIGAN FEPC
A STUDY OF EMPLOYMENT AND TRAINING PATTERNS IN THE LANSING
   AREA. /MICHIGAN/
MICHIGAN FAIR EMPLOYMENT PRACTICES COMMISSION. DETROIT,
MICHIGAN. 1958. 27 PP.

NMICFEP63777 MICHIGAN FEPC
EQUAL-EMPLOYMENT-OPPORTUNITY IN THE SUBURBAN SHOPPING
   CENTER. FACT OR FICTION. /MICHIGAN/
MICHIGAN FAIR EMPLOYMENT PRACTICES COMMISSION. DETROIT,
MICHIGAN. 1963. 17 PP.

NMICHDX65770 MICHAEL D
THE NEXT GENERATION. /YOUTH/
RANDOM HOUSE. NEW YORK. 1965.

NMICLRX66068 MICHIGAN LAW REVIEW
DISCRIMINATION IN THE HIRING AND ASSIGNMENT OF NEGRO
   TEACHERS IN PUBLIC SCHOOL SYSTEMS.
MICHIGAN LAW REVIEW, VOL 64, FEB 1966. PP 692-702.

NMIHLLF62779 MIHLON LF
INDUSTRIAL DISCRIMINATION -- THE SKELETON IN EVERYONE-S
   CLOSET.
FACTORY, VOL 70, AP 1962. PP 80-87.

NMILLAS57069 MILLER AS
RACIAL DISCRIMINATION AND PRIVATE EDUCATION.
UNIVERSITY OF NORTH CAROLINA PRESS. CHAPEL HILL,
NORTH CAROLINA. 1957.

NMILLEW66129 MILLER EW ED
THE NEGRO AMERICAN. A BIBLIOGRAPHY.
HARVARD UNIVERSITY PRESS. CAMBRIDGE, MASSACHUSETTS. 1966.
300 PP.

NMILLGJ65791 MILLET GJ
ACHIEVEMENT OF MALE HIGH SCHOOL DROPOUTS AND GRADUATES IN
   ALABAMA VOCATIONAL SCHOOLS.
GEORGE PEABODY COLLEGE FOR TEACHERS. PHD DISSERTATION.
NASHVILLE, TENNESEE. 1965.

NMILLGW64070 MILLER GW
EQUAL-EMPLOYMENT-OPPORTUNITY. COMPANY POLICIES AND
   EXPERIENCE.
MANAGEMENT REVIEW, VOL 53, AP 1964. PP 4-23.

NMILLHH60780 MILLER HH
PRIVATE BUSINESS AND EDUCATION IN THE SOUTH.
HARVARD BUSINESS REVIEW, VOL 38, JULY-AUG 1960. PP 75-80.

NMILLHP62781 MILLER HP
IS THE INCOME GAP CLOSED. NO.
THE NEW YORK TIMES MAGAZINE, NOV 11 1962. P 50 PLUS.

NMILLHP63785 MILLER HP
RECENT TRENDS IN THE ECONOMIC-STATUS OF NEGROES.
US SENATE, COMMITTEE ON LABOR AND PUBLIC WELFARE,
SUBCOMMITTEE ON EMPLOYMENT AND MANPOWER, HEARINGS,
STATEMENT. 88TH CONGRESS, 1ST SESSION. GPO. WASHINGTON, DC.
JULY 31 1963.

NMILLHP64784 MILLER HP
RICH MAN, POOR MAN. /INCOME/
CROWELL. NEW YORK. 1964

NMILLHP65782 MILLER HP
LIFETIME INCOME AND ECONOMIC GROWTH.
AMERICAN ECONOMIC REVIEW, VOL 55, SEPT 1965. PP 834-843.

NMILLHP65783 MILLER HP
PROGRESS AND PROSPECTS FOR THE NEGRO WORKER.
CHALLENGE, FEB 1965. PP 30-34. ALSO PROBLEMS AND
PROSPECTS OF THE NEGRO LABOR MOVEMENT. ED BY RAYMOND J
MURPHY AND HOWARD ELINSON. WADSORTH PUBLISHING COMPANY.
BELMONT, CALIFORNIA. 1966. PP 108-115.

NMILLHP66630 MILLER HP
THE JOB GAP. /EMPLOYMENT/
THE NEW YORK TIMES MAGAZINE, MAY 8 1966. P 30 FF.

NMILLJE48250 MILLER JE
MAJOR POLITICAL ISSUES WHICH DIRECTLY CONCERN NEGROES.
THE QUARTERLY REVIEW OF HIGHER EDUCATION AMONG NEGROES, VOL
16, NO 4, OCT 1948. PP 140-150.

NMILLJN66787 MILLER JN
HELP FOR THE HARD-CORE UNEMPLOYED. /TRAINING/
CHRISTIAN HERALD, VOL 89, NO 2, FEB 1966. PP 30-32.

NMILLLX63788 MILLER L
PROSPERITY THROUGH EQUALITY.
THE NATION, SEPT 21 1963. PP 157-160, 168.

NMILLSM65789 MILLER SM
ECONOMIC INEQUALITY.
AFL-CIO INDUSTRIAL UNION DEPARTMENT, IUD AGENDA, VOL 1,
NO 8, SEPT 1965. PP 5-8.

NMILLSM65790 MILLER SM
POVERTY, RACE AND POLITICS.
THE NEW SOCIOLOGY. ESSAYS IN SOCIAL SCIENCE AND SOCIAL
THEORY IN HONOR OF C WRIGHT MILLS. ED BY LOUIS HORWITZ.

OXFORD UNIVERSITY PRESS. NEW YORK. 1965.

NMILWCC63792 MILWAUKEE CCMM ON CCM RELS
THE NEGRO IN MILWAUKEE, PROGRESS AND PORTENT, 1863-1963.
/WISCONSIN/
MILWAUKEE CCMMISSION ON COMMUNITY RELATIONS. MILWAUKEE,
WISCONSIN. 1963. 8 PP.

NMILWUL48793 MILWAUKEE URBAN LEAGUE.
EMPLOYMENT AS IT RELATES TO NEGROES IN THE MILWAUKEE
INDUSTRIAL AREA. /WISCONSIN/
MILWAUKEE URBAN LEAGUE. MILWAUKEE, WISCCNSIN. 1948. 7 PP.

NMINARD52794 MINARD RD
RACE RELATICNSHIP IN THE POCAHONTAS COAL FIELD.
JOURNAL OF SOCIAL ISSUES, VOL 8, NO 1, JAN 1952. PP 29-44.

NMINDAX66795 MINDLIN A
THE DESIGNATION OF RACE OR COLOR ON FORMS.
PUBLIC ADMINISTRATION REVIEW, VOL 26, NO 2, JUNE 1966.
PP 110-118.

NMINEJB57796 MINER JB
INTELLIGENCE IN THE UNITED STATES, A SURVEY -- WITH
CONCLUSIONS FOR MANPOWER UTILIZATION IN EDUCATION AND
EMPLOYMENT.
SPRINGER PUBLISHING CO. NEW YORK. 1957. 180 PP.

NMINIBC65797 MINIKINS BC   *US DEPARTMENT OF LABOR
MOTIVATING NEGRO YOUTH IN RHODE-ISLAND.
US DEPARTMENT OF LABOR, EMPLOYMENT SERVICE REVIEW, VOL 2,
NO 8, AUG 1965. PP 4-5.

NMINNGI45798 MINN GOVRS INTER-RACIAL COMM
THE NEGRO WORKER IN MINNESOTA. A REPORT.
MINNESOTA GCVERNOR-S INTER-RACIAL COMMISSION. ST PAUL,
MINNESOTA. 1945.

NMINNGI49799 MINN GOVRS INTER-RACIAL CCMM
THE NEGRO WORKER-S PROGRESS IN MINNESOTA. A REPORT.
MINNESOTA GCVERNOR-S INTER-RACIAL COMMISSION. ST PAUL,
MINNESOTA. JUNE 30 1949. 66 PP.

NMINNLR58800 MINNESOTA LAW REVIEW
RAILWAY LABOR ACT -- DENIAL OF UNION MEMBERSHIP TO NEGROES.
MINNESOTA LAW REVIEW, VOL 42, AP 1958. P 942.

NMISSCH60802 MISSOURI COMM ON HUM RIGHTS
STUDY OF HUMAN-RIGHTS IN MISSOURI.
MISSOURI COMMISSION ON HUMAN RIGHTS. JEFFERSON CITY,
MISSOURI. 1960.

NMISSCH64801 MISSOURI COMM ON HUM RIGHTS
EQUAL-EMPLOYMENT-OFPORTUNITIES IN MISSOURI STATE AGENCIES.
A SURVEY OF NEGRO EMPLOYMENT, SPRING-SUMMER 1963.
MISSOURI COMMISSION ON HUMAN RIGHTS. JEFFERSON CITY,
MISSOURI. 1964. 18 PP.

NMITCJP64295 MITCHEL JP
BUSINESS AND CIVIL-RIGHTS.
VITAL SPEECHES OF THE DAY, JULY 1 1964. PP 549-551.

NMITCLE57804 MITCHELL LE
ASPIRATION LEVELS OF NEGRO DELINQUENT, DEPENDENT, AND PUBLIC
SCHOOL BOYS.
JOURNAL OF NEGRO EDUCATION, VOL 26, WINTER 1957. PP 80-85.

NMOBIFY62263 MOBILIZATION FOR YOUTH
A PROPOSAL FOR THE PREVENTION AND CONTROL OF DELINQUENCY BY
EXPANDING OPPORTUNITIES.
MOBILIZATION FOR YOUTH, INC. NEW YORK. 1562. 640 PP.

NMODEIX45805 MODERN INDUSTRY
SOLVING RACIAL PROBLEMS IN YOUR PLANT. /INDUSTRY/
MODERN INDUSTRY, AP 15 1945. P 78.

NMOHRFT54806 MOHR FT
MANAGEMENT POLICIES AND BI-RACIAL INTEGRATION IN INDUSTRY.
UNIVERSITY OF ILLINCIS. INSTITUTE OF LABOR AND INDUSTRIAL
RELATIONS. MASTER-S THESIS. CHAMPAIGN, ILLINOIS. 1954.

NMOLIRL66807 MOLINAR RL
THE NATIONAL-LABOR-RELATIONS ACT-AND RACIAL DISCRIMINATION.
/LEGISLATION/
BOSTON COLLEGE INDUSTRIAL AND COMMERCIAL LAW REVIEW, VOL 7,
NO 3, SPRING 1966. PP 601-616.

NMONIAX65808 MONISON A
NEW LOOK FOR THE URBAN-LEAGUE.
EBONY, DEC 30 1965.

NMONTJB58809 MONTAGUE JB   EPPS EG
ATTITUDES TOWARD SOCIAL MOBILITY AS REVEALED BY SAMPLES OF
NEGRO AND WHITE BOYS.
PACIFIC SOCIOLOGICAL REVIEW, VOL 1, FALL 1958. PP 81-84.

NMOORPL54079 MOORE PL
FACTORS INVOLVED IN STUDENT ELIMINATION FROM HIGH SCHOOL.
JOURNAL OF NEGRO EDUCATION, VOL 23, 1954. PP 117-122.

NMORGGO62849 MORGAN GO
REPRESENTATION OF NEGROES AND WHITES AS EMPLOYEES IN THE
FEDERAL PRISON SYSTEM.
PHYLON, VOL 23, NO 4, 4TH QUARTER 1962. PP 372-378.

NMORGJX62850 MORGAN J   MARTIN D
RACE, ECONOMIC ATTITUDES, AND BEHAVIOR.
AMERICAN STATISTICAL ASSOCIATION, SOCIAL STATISTICS SECTION,
PROCEEDINGS. 1962. 9 PP.

NMORGSX59851 MORGAN S
THE NEGRO AND THE UNION.
AMERICAN LABOR IN MID-PASSAGE. ED BY BERT COCHRAN. MONTHLY
REVIEW PRESS. NEW YORK. 1959. PP 144-149.

NMORRJJ57853 MORROW JJ
AMERICAN NEGROES -- A WASTED RESOURCE. /INDUSTRY/
HARVARD BUSINESS REVIEW, VOL 35, NO 1, JAN-FEB 1957.
PP 65-74.

NMORRJJ57854 MORROW JJ
EMPLOYMENT ON MERIT. THE CONTINUING CHALLENGE TO BUSINESS,
NEGRO-S ECONOMIC LOT.
MANAGEMENT REVIEW, VOL 46, FEB 1957. PP 9-11.

NMORRRL65852 MORRILL RL
THE NEGRO GHETTO. PROBLEMS AND ALTERNATIVES.
THE GEOGRAPHICAL REVIEW, VOL 55, JULY 1965. PP 339-361.

NMOSKCC66855 MOSKOS CC
RACIAL INTEGRATION IN THE ARMED FORCES. /MILITARY/
AMERICAN JOURNAL OF SOCIOLOGY, VOL 72, NO 2, SEPT 1966.
PP 132-148.

NMOSSJA60857 MOSS JA
THE UTILIZATION OF NEGRO TEACHERS IN THE COLLEGES OF
NEW-YORK STATE.
PHYLON, VOL 21, NO 1, 1ST QUARTER 1960. PP 63-70.

NMOSSJA61858 MOSS JA   MERCER H
A STUDY OF THE POTENTIAL SUPPLY OF NEGRO TEACHERS FOR THE
COLLEGES OF NEW-YORK STATE.
UNICN COLLEGE. SCHENECTADY, NEW YORK. MIMEOGRAPHED.
MAY 1961. 22 PP.

NMOSSJA62856 MOSS JA   *SOUTHERN REGIONAL COUNCIL
THE NEGRO AND EM°LOYMENT OPPORTUNITIES IN THE SOUTH.
SOUTHERN REGIONAL COUNCIL. ATLANTA, GEORGIA. 1962.

NMOTLCB66859 MOTLEY CB
THE LEGAL-STATUS OF THE NEGRO IN THE UNITED STATES.
THE AMERICAN NEGRO REFERENCE BOOK. ED BY JOHN P DAVIS.
PRENTICE-HALL. ENGLEWOOD CLIFFS, NEW JERSEY. 1966.
PP 484-521.

NMOYNDP65860 MOYNIHAN DP
BEHIND LOS-ANGELES. JOB-LESS NEGROES AND THE BOOM.
/UNEMPLOYMENT CALIFORNIA/
THE REPORTER, VOL 33, SEPT 9 1965. P 31.

NMOYNDP65861 MOYNIHAN DP
EMPLOYMENT, INCOME, AND THE ORDEAL OF THE NEGRO FAMILY.
OAEDALUS, VOL 94, NO 4, FALL 1965. PP 745-770.

NMOYNDP65862 MOYNIHAN DP   *US DEPARTMENT OF LABOR
THE NEGRO FAMILY. THE CASE FOR NATIONAL ACTION.
US DEPARTMENT OF LABOR, OFFICE OF POLICY PLANNING AND
RESEARCH. GPO. WASHINGTON, DC. 1965. 78 PP.

NMOYNDP65863 MOYNIHAN DP
POLITICAL PERSPECTIVES.
THE NEGRO CHALLENGE TO THE BUSINESS COMMUNITY. ED BY ELI
GINZBURG. MCGRAW HILL. NEW YORK. 1964.

NMUELEX66864 MUELLER E   *UM ISR SURVEY RESEARCH CENT
NEGRO-WHITE DIFFERENCES IN GEOGRAPHIC MOBILITY.
THE GEOGRAPHIC MOBILITY OF LABOR. JOHN B LANSING AND
EVA MUELLER. UNIVERSITY OF MICHIGAN, INSTITUTE FOR SOCIAL
RESEARCH, SURVEY RESEARCH CENTER. ANN ARBOR, MICHIGAN.

NMUELWR45865 MUELLER WR
THE NEGRO IN THE NAVY. /MILITARY/
SOCIAL FORCES, VOL 24, NO 1, OCT 1945. PP 110-115.
1966. CHAPTER 10.

NMURPRJ66866 MURPHY RJ ED
PROBLEMS AND PROSPECTS OF THE NEGRO MOVEMENT. /EMPLOYMENT/
WADSWORTH PUBLISHING CO. BELMONT, CALIFORNIA. 1966.

NMURRPM55867 MURRAY PM
THE STATUS OF THE NEGRO PHYSICIAN IN NEW-YORK STATE.
/OCCUPATIONS/
NEW YORK STATE JOURNAL OF MEDICINE, VOL 55, 1955.
PP 2980-2981.

NMUSEBX64868 MUSE B   *SOUTHERN REGIONAL COUNCIL
LOUISVILLE. SPECIAL REPORT. /CASE-STUDY KENTUCKY/
SOUTHERN REGIONAL COUNCIL. ATLANTA, GEORGIA. MAY 1964.
45 PP.

NMUSEBX64869 MUSE B   *SOUTHERN REGIONAL COUNCIL
MEMPHIS. SPECIAL REPORT. /CASE-STUDY/
SOUTHERN REGIONAL COUNCIL. ATLANTA, GEORGIA. JULY 1964.
49 PP.

NMYRDGX44870 MYRDAL G
AN AMERICAN DILEMMA.
HARPER. NEW YORK. 1944. 2 VOLS.

NMYRDGX48871 MYRDAL G
SOCIAL TRENDS IN AMERICA AND STRATEGIC APPROACHES TO THE
NEGRO PROBLEM.
PHYLON, VOL 9, NO 3, 3RD QUARTER 1948. PP 196-213.

NNATILR58875 NATL LABOR RELATIONS BOARD
HEARINGS --TRI-CITIES AREA OF ALABAMA.
NATIONAL LABOR RELATIONS BOARD. HEARINGS. JAN 7 1958.

NNATIXX52873 NATION
SOUTHERN NEGRO. 1952.
THE NATION, SEPT 27 1952. PP 261-267.

NNATLAI55872 NAIRO
COMMISSION ON MANPOWER UTILIZATION REPORTS.
NAIRO. WASHINGTON, DC. 1955.

NNATLIC43921 NATL INDUSTRIAL CONF BOARD
COMMENTS ON MANAGEMENT PROBLEMS.
NATIONAL INDUSTRIAL CONFERENCE BOARD, CCNFERENCE BOARD
RECORD, VOL 5, NO 2, FEB 1943. PP 60-63.

NNATLIC64231 NATL INDUSTRIAL CONF BOARD
RECRUITING NEGRO COLLEGE GRADUATES.
NATIONAL INCUSTRIAL CONFERENCE BOARD, CCNFERENCE BOARD
RECORD, AUG 1964.

NNATLIC65874 NATL INDUSTRIAL CONF BOARD
GOALS IN NEGRO EMPLOYMENT. /INDUSTRY/
NATIONAL INDUSTRIAL CONFERENCE BOARD, CCNFERENCE BOARD
RECORD, VOL 2, NO 12, DEC 1965.

NNATLMF52877 NATIONAL MEDICAL FELLOWSHIPS
NEGROES IN MEDICINE. /OCCUPATIONS/
NATIONAL MEDICAL FELLOWSHIPS, INC. CHICAGO, ILLINOIS. 1952.
44 PP.

NNATLMF62878 NATIONAL MEDICAL FELLOWSHIPS
NEW OPPORTUNITIES FOR NEGROES IN MEDICINE. /OCCUPATIONS/
NATIONAL MEDICAL FELLOWSHIPS, INC. CHICAGO, ILLINOIS. 1962.
34 PP.

NNATLNC45879 NATIONAL NEGRO CONGRESS
NEGRO WORKERS AFTER THE WAR.
NATIONAL NEGRO CONGRESS. NEW YORK. 1945. 23 PP.

NNATLOR66880 NATL OPINION RESEARCH CENTER
NEGLECTED TALENTS. BACKGROUND AND PROSPECTS OF NEGRO COLLEGE
GRADUATES.
NATIONAL OPINION RESEARCH CENTER. REPORT NO 112. UNIVERSITY
OF CHICAGO. CHICAGO, ILLINOIS. FEB 1966.

NNATLPA55881 NATIONAL PLANNING ASSN
SELECTED STUDIES OF NEGRO EMPLOYMENT IN THE SOUTH.
NATIONAL PLANNING ASSOCIATICN. REPORT NO 6-4. WASHINGTON,
DC. FEB 1955. 483 PP.

NNATLSFND882 NATIONAL SHARECROPPERS FUND
PROGRESS AGAINST POVERTY.
NATIONAL SHARECROPPERS FUND. NEW YORK. BRCCHURE.

NNATLSF61883 NATIONAL SHARECROPPERS FUND
SHARECROPPERS IN THE 60-S. A REPORT AND A PROGRAM.
NATIONAL SHARECROPPERS FUND, INC. NEW YORK. 1961. 20 PP.

NNATLULND893 NATIONAL URBAN LEAGUE
A NATIONAL SKILLS-BANK, WHAT IT IS, HOW IT OPERATES.
NATIONAL URBAN LEAGUE. NEW YORK. 12 PP.

NNATLUL44900 NATIONAL URBAN LEAGUE
INTER-RACIAL PLANNING FOR COMMUNITY ORGANIZATION...
EMPLOYMENT PROBLEMS OF THE NEGRO.
NATIONAL URBAN LEAGUE. AMERICAN WAR-COMMUNITY SERVICES.
BULLETIN NO 1. NEW YORK. 1944. 15 PP.

NNATLUL45896 NATIONAL URBAN LEAGUE
RACIAL ASPECTS OF RECONVERSION.
NATIONAL URBAN LEAGUE. NEW YORK. 1945. 29 PP.

NNATLUL46891 NATIONAL URBAN LEAGUE
INTEGRATION OF NEGRCES IN DEPARTMENT STORES.
NATIONAL URBAN LEAGUE. NEW YORK. JULY 1946. 14 PP.

NNATLUL46894 NATIONAL URBAN LEAGUE
NEGRO WORKERS IN THE BUILDING TRADES IN SELECTED CITIES.
NORFOLK, VIRGINIA. /INDUSTRY/
NATIONAL URBAN LEAGUE. NEW YORK. 1946. 12 PP.

NNATLUL47904 NATIONAL URBAN LEAGUE
NEGRO WORKERS IN THE BUILDING TRADES IN CERTAIN CITIES.
NATIONAL URBAN LEAGUE. INDUSTRIAL RELATIONS DEPARTMENT.
NEW YORK. 1947.

NNATLUL48903 NATIONAL URBAN LEAGUE
A SURVEY OF THE ECONOMIC AND CULTURAL CONDITIONS OF THE
NEGRO POPULATION CF LOUISVILLE, KENTUCKY AND A REVIEW OF
THE PROGRAM AND ACTIVITIES OF THE LOUISVILLE URBAN-LEAGUE.
JANUARY-FEBRUARY, 1948.
NATIONAL URBAN LEAGUE. DEPARTMENT OF RESEARCH AND COMMUNITY
PROJECTS. NEW YORK. 1948.

NNATLUL49895 NATIONAL URBAN LEAGUE
PROGRAM AIDS FOR VOCATIONAL OPPORTUNITY PROGRAM.
NATIONAL URBAN LEAGUE. NEW YORK. 1949.

NNATLUL55901 NATIONAL URBAN LEAGUE
INTEGRATION IN THE WORK-FORCE, WHY AND HOW.
NATIONAL URBAN LEAGUE. COMMERCE AND INDUSTRY COUNCIL.
NEW YORK. 1955. 12 PP.

NNATLUL57902 NATIONAL URBAN LEAGUE
NEGRCES AND THE BUILDING TRADES UNION.
NATIONAL URBAN LEAGUE. DEPARTMENT OF INDUSTRIAL RELATIONS.
NEW YORK. JAN 17 1957.

NNATLUL60899 NATIONAL URBAN LEAGUE
THE URBAN-LEAGUE STORY 1910-1960.
NATIONAL URBAN LEAGUE. GOLDEN ANNIVERSARY YEARBOOK.
NEW YORK. 1960. 66 PP.

NNATLUL61885 NATIONAL URBAN LEAGUE
APPRENTICESHIP AND TRAINING OPPORTUNITIES FOR NEGRO YOUTHS
IN SELECTED URBAN-LEAGUE CITIES.
NATIONAL URBAN LEAGUE. NEW YORK. 1961.

NNATLUL61898 NATIONAL URBAN LEAGUE
SURVEY OF UNEMPLOYMENT IN SELECTED URBAN-LEAGUE CITIES.
NATIONAL URBAN LEAGUE. NEW YORK. 1961.

NNATLUL62083 NATIONAL URBAN LEAGUE
ECONOMIC AND SOCIAL STATUS OF THE NEGRO IN THE
UNITED STATES.
NATIONAL URBAN LEAGUE. NEW YORK. 1962. 32 PP.

NNATLUL62886 NATIONAL URBAN LEAGUE
AUTOMATION AND THE RETRAINING OF NEGRO WORKERS.
NATIONAL URBAN LEAGUE. TASK FORCE DOCUMENT. NEW YORK. 1962.
54 PP.

NNATLUL64887 NATIONAL URBAN LEAGUE
DOUBLE JEOPARDY -- THE OLDER NEGRO IN AMERICA TODAY.
NATIONAL URBAN LEAGUE. NEW YORK. 1964. 28 PP.

NNATLUL64890 NATIONAL URBAN LEAGUE
INDUSTRY-S MOST UNDERDEVELOPEC RESOURCE.
NATIONAL URBAN LEAGUE. NEW YORK. 1964.

NNATLUL64892 NATIONAL URBAN LEAGUE
LIFELINE TO EQUAL-OPPORTUNITY.
COMMUNITY ACTION ASSEMBLY HANDBOOK. NATIONAL URBAN LEAGUE.
NEW YORK. 1964. 26 PP.

NNATLUL65884 NATIONAL URBAN LEAGUE
BEYOND TODAY-S STRUGGLE.
NATIONAL URBAN LEAGUE. 1964-1965 ANNUAL REPORT. NEW YORK.
1965.

NNATLUL65889 NATIONAL URBAN LEAGUE
GUIDELINES FOR COMMUNITY-ACTION.
NATIONAL URBAN LEAGUE. NEW YORK. 1965. 55 PP.

NNATLUL66888 NATIONAL URBAN LEAGUE
EDUCATION AND RACE.
NATIONAL URBAN LEAGUE. NEW YORK. 1966. 39 PP.

NNEALEE50905 NEAL EE   JONES LW
THE PLACE OF THE NEGRO FARMER IN THE CHANGING ECONOMY OF THE
COTTON SOUTH.
RURAL SOCIOLOGY, VOL 15, MAR 1950. PP 30-41.

NNEBRLC51906 NEBRASKA LEGISLATIVE COUNCIL
REPORT OF THE COMMITTEE ON UNFAIR EMPLOYMENT PRACTICES.
NEBRASKA LEGISLATIVE COUNCIL. COMMITTEE REPORT NO 31.
LINCOLN, NEBRASKA. SEPT 1951. 43 PP.

NNEWMDKND957 NEWMAN DK   *US DEPARTMENT OF LABOR
ECONOMIC-STATUS OF THE NEGRO.
US DEPARTMENT OF LABOR, BUREAU OF LABOR STATISTICS.
WASHINGTON, DC. NO. 38 PP.

NNEWMDK65508 NEWMAN DK   *US DEPARTMENT OF LABOR
THE NEGRO-S JOURNEY TO THE CITY -- PART I.
US DEPARTMENT OF LABOR, MONTHLY LABOR REVIEW, VOL 88, NO 5,
MAY 1965. PP 502-507.

NNEWMDK65909 NEWMAN DK   *US DEPARTMENT OF LABOR
THE NEGRO-S JOURNEY TO THE CITY -- PART II.
US DEPARTMENT OF LABOR, MONTHLY LABOR REVIEW, VOL 88, NO 6,
JUNE 1965. PP 644-650.

NNEWSXX63912 NEWSWEEK
JOBS FOR NEGROES. HCW MUCH PROGRESS IN SIGHT.
NEWSWEEK, VOL 62, JULY 15 1963. PP 68-70, 72.

NNEWSXX64911 NEWSWEEK
CORPORATE HIRING POLICIES AND THE NEGRO. /INDUSTRY/
FREEDOM NOW. ED BY ALAN F WESTIN. BASIC BOOKS, INC.
NEW YORK. 1964.

NNEWSXX64913 NEWSWEEK
NEGRO-S SEARCH FOR A BETTER JOB.
NEWSWEEK, VOL 63, JUNE 8 1964. PP 79-83.

NNEWSXX66914 NEWSWEEK
THE UNEMPLOYABLES.
NEWSWEEK, NOV 7 1966. PP 84-86.

NNEWTIG62915 NEWTON IG
THE NEGRO AND THE NATIONAL GUARD. /MILITARY/
PHYLON, VOL 23, NO 1, 1962. PP 18-28.

NNEWXPX62910 NEW POLITICS
NEGROES AND THE LABCR MOVEMENT. /UNION/
NEW POLITICS, VOL 1, SEPT 1962. PP 135-141.

NNEWXUT63088 NEW UNIVERSITY THOUGHT
TRADE UNION LEADERSHIP COUNCIL. EXPERIMENT IN COMMUNITY
ACTION.
NEW UNIVERSITY THOUGHT, VOL 3, NO 2, SEPT-OCT 1963.
PP 34-41.

NNEWYSA60919 NY STATE COMM AGAINST DISCR
THE EMPLOYMENT OF NEGROES AS CRIVER SALESMEN IN THE BAKING
INDUSTRY.
NEW YORK STATE COMMISSION AGAINST DISCRIMINATION. NEW YORK.
1960.

NNICHLE52922 NICHOLSON LE
THE URBAN-LEAGUE AND THE VOCATIONAL GUICANCE AND ADJUSTMENT
OF NEGRO YOUTH.
JOURNAL OF NEGRO EDUCATION, VOL 21, FALL 1952. PP 448-458.

NNICHLX54920 NICHOLS L
BREAKTHROUGH ON THE COLOR FRONT. /MILITARY/
RANDOM HOUSE. NEW YORK. 1954. 235 PP.

NNICHWH60322 NICHOLLS WH
SOUTHERN TRADITION AND REGIONAL PROGRESS.
UNIVERSITY CF NORTH CAROLINA PRESS. CHAPEL HILL,
NORTH CAROLINA. 1960. 202 PP.

NNOLAEW49928 NOLAND EW   BAKKE EW
WORKERS WANTED. A STUDY OF EMPLOYERS HIRING POLICIES,
PREFERENCES, AND PRACTICES IN NEW-HAVEN AND CHARLOTTE.
/CONNECTICUT NORTH-CAROLINA/
HARPER. NEW YORK. 1949. 233 PP.

NNOLAEW53926 NOLAND EW
INDUSTRY COMES OF AGE IN THE SOUTH.
SOCIAL FORCES, VOL 32, 1953. PP 28-35.

NNOLAEW65527 NOLAND EW
TECHNOLOGICAL-CHANGE AND THE SOCIAL ORDER. /SOUTH/
THE SOUTH IN CONTINUITY AND CHANGE. ED BY JOHN C MCKINNEY
AND EDGAR T THOMPSON. DUKE UNIVERSITY PRESS. DURHAM,
NORTH CAROLINA. 1965. PP 167-197.

NNORGPH40930 NORGREN PH
NEGRO LABOR AND ITS PROBLEMS.
NEW YORK PUBLIC LIBRARY, SCHÖNBURG COLLECTION. NEW YORK.
TYPEWRITTEN SCRIPT DONE AS A PART OF THE MYRDAL STUDY, THE
NEGRO IN AMERICA, SPONSORED BY THE CARNEGIE CORPORATION,
NEW YORK. 1940. 5 VOLS.

NNORGPH59932 NORGREN PH   WEBSTER AN
BORGESON   PATTEN MB
*INDUSTRIAL RELS COUNSELORS
EMPLOYING THE NEGRO IN AMERICAN INDUSTRY
INDUSTRIAL RELATIONS COUNSELORS, INC. INDUSTRIAL RELATIONS
MONOGRAPH NO 17. NEW YORK. 1959. 171 PP.

NNORGPH62931 NORGREN PH   *PRINCETCN UNIV IND RELS SECT
RACIAL DISCRIMINATION IN EMPLOYMENT. BIBLIOGRAPHY.
PRINCETON UNIVERSITY, INDUSTRIAL RELATICNS SECTION.
PRINCETON UNIVERSITY PRESS. PRINCETON, NEW JERSEY.
SEPT 1962.

NNORGPH67929 NORGREN PH
FAIR-EMPLOYMENT-PRACTICE LAWS -- EXPERIENCE, EFFECTS,
PROSPECTS.
EMPLOYMENT, RACE AND POVERTY. ED BY ARTHUR M ROSS AND
HERBERT HILL. HARCOURT, BRACE, AND WORLD. NEW YORK. 1967.
PP 541-572.

NNORTCGND933 N CAROLINA GOOD NEIGHBOR CC
AT WORK IN NORTH-CAROLINA TODAY. 48 CASE-REPORTS ON
NORTH-CAROLINA NEGROES NOW EMPLOYED OR PREPARING
THEMSELVES FOR EMPLOYMENT...THEIR EDUCATION, JOB
QUALIFICATIONS, AND CAREER ASPIRATIONS.
NORTH CAROLINA GOOD NEIGHBOR COUNCIL. RALEIGH, NORTH
CAROLINA. NC. 53 PP.

NNORTCG66092 N CAROLINA GOOD NEIGHBOR CC
EMPLOYMENT IN STATE GOVERNMENT. /NORTH-CAROLINA/
NORTH CAROLINA GOOD NEIGHBOR COUNCIL. RALEIGH, NORTH
CAROLINA. NOV 1966. 40 PP.

NNORTHR43941 NORTHRUP HR
THE NEGRO AND UNIONISM IN THE BIRMINGHAM, ALABAMA IRON AND
STEEL INDUSTRY.
UNIVERSITY OF NORTH CAROLINA PRESS. CHAPEL HILL, NORTH
CAROLINA. 1943.

NNORTHR43942 NORTHRUP HR
NEGROES IN A WAR INDUSTRY. THE CASE OF SHIPBUILDING.
UNIVERSITY OF CHICAGO JOURNAL OF BUSINESS, JULY 1943.
PP 160-172.

NNORTHR44943 NORTHRUP HR
THE NEGRO IN THE RAILWAY UNIONS.
PHYLON, VOL 5, NO 2, 2ND QUARTER, 1944. PP 159-164.

NNORTHR44944   NORTHRUP HR
ORGANIZED LABOR AND THE NEGRO. /UNION/
HARPER AND BROS. NEW YORK. 1944. 312 PP.

NNORTHR45546   NORTHRUP HR
RACE DISCRIMINATION IN UNIONS.
THE AMERICAN MERCURY, AUG 1945. P 96.

NNORTHR45948   NORTHRUP HR   *NY PUBLIC AFFAIRS COMMITTEE
WILL NEGROES GET JOBS NOW.
NEW YORK PUBLIC AFFAIRS COMMITTEE, INC. PUBLIC AFFAIRS
PAMPHLET NO 110. NEW YORK. 1945. 31 PP.

NNORTHR46945   NORTHRUP HR
RACE DISCRIMINATION IN TRADE UNIONS. RECORD AND OUTLOOK.
COMMENTARY, VOL 2, AUG 1946. PP 124-131.

NNORTHR46947   NORTHRUP HR
UNIONS AND NEGRO EMPLOYMENT.
ANNALS OF THE AMERICAN ACADEMY OF POLITICAL AND SOCIAL
SCIENCES, VOL 224, MAR 1946. PP 42-47.

NNORTHR47939   NORTHRUP HR
IN THE UNIONS. RACIAL POLICIES.
SURVEY GRAPHIC, VOL 36, JAN 1947. PP 54-56 PLUS.

NNORTHR49536   NORTHRUP HR
DISCRIMINATION AND THE TRADE UNIONS.
DISCRIMINATION AND NATIONAL WELFARE. ED BY R M MACIVER.
HARPER AND BROTHERS. NEW YORK. 1949. PP 65-76.

NNORTHR49940   NORTHRUP HR
LAST HIRED. FIRST FIRED. THOUGH NEGRO WORKERS HAVE MADE
    IMPRESSIVE GAINS THEY MIGHT BE FIRST TO FEEL THE BITE OF
    RECESSION.
THE REPORTER, DEC 6 1949. PP 9-11.

NNORTHR64937   NORTHRUP HR
EQUAL OPPORTUNITY AND EQUAL PAY.
MANAGEMENT PERSONNEL QUARTERLY, VOL 3, NO 3, FALL 1964.
PP 17-26.

NNORTHR65549   NORTHRUP HR ED   ROWAN RL ED
THE NEGRO AND EMPLOYMENT OPPORTUNITY. PROBLEMS AND
    PRACTICES.
UNIVERSITY OF MICHIGAN, BUREAU OF INDUSTRIAL RELATIONS.
ANN ARBOR, MICHIGAN. 1965.

NNORTHR67938   NORTHRUP HR
INDUSTRY-S RACIAL EMPLOYMENT POLICIES.
EMPLOYMENT, RACE AND POVERTY. ED BY ARTHUR M ROSS AND
HERBERT HILL. HARCOURT, BRACE, AND WORLD. NEW YORK. 1967.
PP 290-307.

NNORTLK65950   NORTHWOOD LK   BARTH AT
URBAN DESEGREGATION.
UNIVERSITY OF WASHINGTON PRESS. SEATTLE, WASHINGTON. 1965.
131 PP.

NNORTRD56535   NORTH RD   *ANTI-DEFAMATION LEAGUE
THE INTELLIGENCE OF AMERICAN NEGROES.
ANTI-DEFAMATION LEAGUE RESEARCH REPORTS, VOL 3, NO 2,
NOV 1956. 8 PP.

NNUTTRL46951   NUTTALL RL
SOME CORRELATES OF HIGH NEED FOR ACHIEVEMENT AMONG URBAN
    NORTHERN NEGROES.
JOURNAL OF ABNORMAL AND SOCIAL PSYCHOLOGY, VOL 68, NO 6,
1946. PP 593-600.

NOAKXVV49952   OAK VV
THE NEGRO-S ADVENTURE IN GENERAL BUSINESS.
ANTIOCH PRESS. YELLOW SPRINGS, OHIO. 1949.

NOCONWB41094   O-CONNER WB   *NATL INDUSTRIAL CONF BOARD
THE USE OF COLORED PERSONS IN SKILLED OCCUPATIONS.
NATIONAL INDUSTRIAL CONFERENCE BOARD, CONFERENCE BOARD
RECORD, DEC 1941. PP 156-158.

NODELJH64953   O-DELL JH
FOUNDATIONS OF RACISM IN AMERICAN LIFE.
FREEDOMWAYS, VOL 4, FALL 1964. PP 513-535.

NOHIOCR66605   OHIO CIVIL RIGHTS COMMISSION
RACIAL DISCRIMINATION IN THE CINCINNATI BUILDING TRADES.
    REPORT AND RECOMMENDATIONS. /OHIO/
OHIO CIVIL RIGHTS COMMISSION, COLUMBUS, OHIO. FEB 24 1966.
46 PP.

NOLANHX43954   OLANSKY H
THE HARLEM RIOT. A STUDY IN MASS FRUSTRATION.
SOCIAL ANALYSIS, VOL 1, 1943. PP 1-29.

NOLIVLW56955   OLIVER LW
AN HISTORICAL SURVEY AND ANALYSIS OF THE PROGRESS OF NEGROES
    IN PUBLIC-SERVICE 1932-1952.
UNIVERSITY OF INDIANA. DOCTORAL DISSERTATION SERIES,
PUBLICATION NO 17. 972. BLOOMINGTON, INDIANA. 1956. 260 PP.
ALSO UNIVERSITY MICROFILMS. ANN ARBOR, MICHIGAN.

NOPINRC51959   OPINION RESEARCH CORPORATION
THE TREND SINCE 1944 ON THE COLOR LINE IN INDUSTRY.
OPINION RESEARCH CORPORATION. THE PUBLIC OPINION INDEX FOR
INDUSTRY, VOL 9, NO 12, DEC 1951. 20 PP.

NOPINRC56956   OPINION RESEARCH CORPORATION
THE CONTROVERSY OVER EQUAL-RIGHTS FOR NEGROES.
OPINION RESEARCH CORPORATION. PRINCETON, NEW JERSEY.
SEPT 1956. PP 1-5, A-1.

NOPINRC63958   OPINION RESEARCH CORPORATION
MANAGEMENTS GUIDELINES FOR MEETING THE NEGRO DRIVE FOR JOB
    EQUALITY. /INDUSTRY/.
OPINION RESEARCH CORPORATION. THE PUBLIC OPINION INDEX FOR
INDUSTRY, VOL 21, NC 9, SEPT 1963.

NOPINRC64957   OPINION RESEARCH CORPORATION
HIRING NEGROES FOR BETTER JOBS. EXPERIENCE OF LEADING
    COMPANIES. /INDUSTRY/
OPINION RESEARCH CORPORATION. THE PUBLIC OPINION INDEX FOR
INDUSTRY, VOL 22, NO 11, NOV 1964.

NORSHMX61961   ORSHANSKY M   KARTER T
*NATIONAL URBAN LEAGUE
ECONOMIC AND SOCIAL STATUS OF THE NEGRO IN THE
    UNITED STATES.
NATIONAL URBAN LEAGUE. NEW YORK. 1961. 32 PP.

NORSHMX64960   ORSHANSKY M   *US DEPT OF HEALTH ED WELFARE
THE AGED NEGRO AND HIS INCOME.
SOCIAL SECURITY BULLETIN. US DEPARTMENT OF HEALTH,
EDUCATION AND WELFARE, SOCIAL SECURITY ADMINISTRATION. GPO.
WASHINGTON, DC. FEB 1964.

NORTICF56562   ORTIQUE CF
A STUDY OF THE LONGSHORE INDUSTRY IN NEW-ORLEANS WITH
    EMPHASIS ON NEGRO LONGSHOREMEN. /LOUISIANA/
UNIVERSITY OF ILLINOIS, INSTITUTE OF LABOR AND INDUSTRIAL
RELATIONS. MASTER-S THESIS. CHAMPAIGN, ILLINOIS. 1956.

NOSBUGR62460   OSBORNE GR
BOYCOTT IN BIRMINGHAM. /ALABAMA/
THE NATION, VOL 194, MAY 5 1962. PP 397-401.

NOSBUDD66963   OSBURN DD   *US EEO COMMISSION
NEGRO EMPLOYMENT IN THE TEXTILE INDUSTRIES OF NORTH AND
    SOUTH-CAROLINA. /NORTH-CAROLINA/
US EQUAL EMPLOYMENT OPPORTUNITY COMMISSION, OFFICE OF
RESEARCH AND REPORTS. GPO. WASHINGTON, DC. DEC 28 1966.
58 PP.

NOSHAJB54964   O SHAUGHNESSY JB
AMENDMENTS TO THE TAFT-HARTLEY. A REJECTION OF RACIAL
    DISCRIMINATION. /LEGISLATION/
LABOR LAW JOURNAL, VOL 5, MAY 1954. PP 330-336, 368.

NOSHEJX65965   O SHEA
NEWARK. NEGROES MOVE TOWARD POWER. /NEW-JERSEY/
THE ATLANTIC MONTHLY, NOV 1965. PP 90-98.

NOTTLRX45966   OTTLEY R
BLACK ODYSSEY. THE STORY OF THE NEGRO IN AMERICA.
CHARLES SCRIBNER-S SONS. NEW YORK. 1948.

NOVERXX61567   OVERVIEW
THE NEGRO IN SCHOOL ADMINISTRATION.
OVERVIEW, VOL 2, JUNE 1961. PP 35-37.

NOWENJA61968   OWENS JA
INTEGRATION IN INDUSTRY.
CATHOLIC DIGEST, AP 1961. PP 40-43.

NOXLELA40969   OXLEY LA   *US DEPARTMENT OF LABOR
EMPLOYMENT SECURITY AND THE NEGRO.
US DEPARTMENT OF LABOR, EMPLOYMENT SECURITY REVIEW, VOL 7,
NO 7, JULY 1940. PP 12-15.

NPAGEDX66970   PAGE D   *US DEPARTMENT OF LABOR
WATTS ONE YEAR LATER. /TRAINING CALIFORNIA LOS-ANGELES/
US DEPARTMENT OF LABOR, EMPLOYMENT SERVICE REVIEW, VOL 3,
NO 8, AUG 1966. PP 21-22.

NPALLNJ65332   PALLONE NJ   *US DEPARTMENT OF LABOR
NO LONGER SUPERFLUOUS -- THE EDUCATIONAL REHABILITATION OF
    THE HARD-CORE UNEMPLOYED.
US DEPARTMENT OF LABOR. GPO. WASHINGTON, DC. JUNE 1965.
60 PP.

NPALMEN47571   PALMER EN
DISCRIMINATION IN URBAN EMPLOYMENT.
AMERICAN JOURNAL OF SOCIOLOGY, VOL 52, NO 4, JAN 1967.
PP 357-361.

NPALMER55972   PALMORE ER
THE INTRODUCTION OF NEGROES INTO WHITE DEPARTMENTS.
    /CASE-STUDY INDUSTRY/
HUMAN ORGANIZATION, VOL 14, SPRING 1955. PP 27-28.

NPARKRX48974   PARKINSON R
FAIR-EMPLOYMENT-PRACTICES LEGISLATION.
HARVARD BUSINESS REVIEW, VOL 26, NO 1, JAN 1948. PP 115-128.

NPARKSX64573   PARKER S   KLEINER RJ
STATUS POSITION, MOBILITY, AND ETHNIC IDENTIFICATION OF THE
    NEGRO.
JOURNAL OF SOCIAL ISSUES, VOL 20, AP 1964. PP 85-102.

NPARRCH63975   PARRISH CH   *UNIV OF CHICAGO CFSOLEFA
DEMOGRAPHIC ASPECTS OF CONTEMPORARY CHANGE. /SOUTH/
EDUCATIONAL IMPERATIVE. THE NEGRO IN THE CHANGING SOUTH. ED
BY FREDA H GOLDMAN. UNIVERSITY OF CHICAGO. CENTER FOR THE
STUDY OF LIBERAL EDUCATION FOR ADULTS, CHICAGO, ILLINOIS.
1963. PP 17-26.

NPARSTX66976   PARSONS T ED   CLARK KB ED
THE NEGRO AMERICAN.
HOUGHTON MIFFLIN CO. BOSTON, MASSACHUSETTS. 1966.
780 PP.

NPATEJE43977   PATE JE
MOBILIZING MANPOWER.
SOCIAL FORCES, VOL 22, NO 2, DEC 1943. PP 151-162.

NPATTBX64579   PATTERSON B   *SOUTHERN REGIONAL COUNCIL
*ANTI-DEFAMATION LEAGUE.
THE PRICE WE PAY FOR DISCRIMINATION. /SOUTH ECONOMY/
SOUTHERN REGIONAL COUNCIL AND THE ANTI-DEFAMATION LEAGUE.
ATLANTA, GEORGIA. JUNE 1964. 45 PP.

NPATTTH63978   PATTEN TH
THE INDUSTRIAL INTEGRATION OF THE NEGRO.
PHYLON, VOL 24, NO 4, WINTER 1963. PP 334-352.

NPEARAX64980   PEARL A
NEGRO YOUTH -- EDUCATION, EMPLOYMENT, AND CIVIL-RIGHTS.
EQUALITY. A PRINCIPLE AND A DILEMMA. TUFTS UNIVERSITY,
LINCOLN FILENE CENTER FOR CITIZENSHIP AND PUBLIC AFFAIRS.
MEDFORD, MASSACHUSETTS. 1964. 14 PP.

NPELLRJ62981   PELLEGRIN RJ   PARENTON VJ
THE IMPACT OF SOCIO-ECONOMIC CHANGE ON RACIAL GROUPS IN A
    RURAL SETTING.
PHYLON, VOL 23, NO 1, 1ST QUARTER 1962. PP 55-60.

NPERLVX52583   PERLO V
TRENDS IN THE ECONOMIC-STATUS OF THE NEGRO PEOPLE.
    /OCCUPATIONAL-PATTERNS/
SCIENCE AND SOCIETY, VOL 16, NO 2, SPRING 1952. PP 115-150.

NPERLVX53982   PERLO V
THE NEGRO IN SOUTHERN AGRICULTURE.
INTERNATIONAL PUBLISHERS. NEW YORK. 1953. 128 PP.

NPERRJX64984   PERRY J
THE JOB OUTLOOK FOR NEGRO YOUTH.
JOURNAL OF NEGRO EDUCATION, SPRING 1964. PP 111-116.

NPERRJX64985   PERRY J
THE PREPARATION OF DISADVANTAGED YOUTH FOR EMPLOYMENT AND

CIVIC RESPONSIBILITIES.
JOURNAL OF NEGRO EDUCATION, VOL 33, NO 3, SUMMER 1964.

NPERR PX54987 PERRY P
NATIONAL NEGRO LABOR COUNCIL, THIRD ANNUAL CONVENTION.
/UNION/
POLITICAL AFFAIRS, FEB 1954. PP 1-8.

NPERS PF65562 PERSONNEL POLICIES FORUM   *BUREAU OF NATIONAL AFFAIRS
THE NEGRO AND TITLE-VII. /LEGISLATION/
THE BUREAU OF NATIONAL AFFAIRS, INC, SURVEY NO 77.
WASHINGTON, DC. JULY 1965. 17 PP.

NPETT TFN0990 PETTIGREW TF
FATHER-ABSENCE AND NEGRO ADULT PERSONALITY. A RESEARCH NOTE.
HARVARD UNIVERSITY. CAMBRIDGE, MASSACHUSETTS. UNPUBLISHED
PAPER. ND.

NPETT TF63063 PETTIGREW TF
NEGRO AMERICAN INTELLIGENCE. A NEW LOOK AT AN OLD
CONTROVERSY.
JOURNAL OF NEGRO EDUCATION, VOL 32, WINTER 1963. PP 6-25.

NPETT TF64991 PETTIGREW TF   THOMPSON DC
NEGRO AMERICAN PERSONALITY.
JOURNAL OF SOCIAL ISSUES, VOL 20, AP 1964. ENTIRE ISSUE.
145 PP.

NPETT TF64992 PETTIGREW TF
A PROFILE OF THE NEGRO AMERICAN.
VAN NOSTRAND. PRINCETON, NEW JERSEY. 1964.

NPFAUHW63993 PFAUTZ HW
THE NEW NEGRO. EMERGING AMERICAN.
PHYLON, VOL 24, NO 4, 4TH QUARTER 1963. PP 360-368.

NPHILCH62995 PHILADELPHIA COMM HUMAN RELS
REPORT OF THE 1961-1962 SURVEY OF PHILADELPHIA BANKS.
/PENNSYLVANIA/
PHILADELPHIA COMMISSION ON HUMAN RELATIONS. PHILADELPHIA,
PENNSYLVANIA. JUNE 1962.

NPHILWB59596 PHILLIPS WB
COUNSELING NEGRO STUDENTS. AN EDUCATIONAL DILEMMA.
CALIFORNIA JOURNAL OF EDUCATIONAL RESEARCH, VOL 10, 1959.
PP 185-188.

NPHILWM57597 PHILLIPS WM
LABOR-FORCE AND DEMOGRAPHIC FACTORS AFFECTING THE CHANGING
RELATIVE STATUS OF THE AMERICAN NEGRO. 1940-1950.
UNIVERSITY OF CHICAGO. THESIS. CHICAGO, ILLINOIS. 1957.
199 PP.

NPIER JA47598 PIERCE JA
NEGRO BUSINESS AND BUSINESS EDUCATION. THEIR PRESENT AND
PROSPECTIVE DEVELOPMENT.
HARPER. NEW YORK. 1947. 338 PP.

NPIER WG41999 PIERSEL WG
A REGIONAL STUDY OF THE NEGRO.
SOCIAL FORCES, VOL 19, NO 3, MAR 1941. PP 390-401.

NPIKE JX67101 PIKER J   *ANN ARBOR HUMAN RELS COMM
HUMAN-RELATIONS IN ANN-ARBOR, A COMMUNITY PROFILE.
ANN ARBOR HUMAN RELATIONS COMMISSION. ANN ARBOR, MICHIGAN.
MAR 1967. 112 PP.

NPITT LJ65001 PITTSBURGH LEGAL JOURNAL
OPINION BY HONORABLE BENJAMIN LENCHER. CITY OF PITTSBURGH VS
PLUMBERS LOCAL UNION NO 27. /PENNSYLVANIA/
PITTSBURGH LEGAL JOURNAL, VOL 113, NO 7, JULY 1 1965. 17 PP.

NPITTMC65002 PITTS MAYOR-S COMM HUM RELS
STATUS OF NEGROES IN CRAFT UNIONS...PITTSBURGH LABOR-MARKET.
/PENNSYLVANIA/
PITTSBURGH, THE MAYOR-S COMMISSION ON HUMAN RELATIONS.
PITTSBURGH, PENNSYLVANIA. JUNE 4 1965. 16 PP.

NPLAURL57003 PLAUT RL   *NATL SSF FOR NEGRO STUDENTS
BLUEPRINT FOR TALENT. SEARCHING AMERICA-S HIDDEN MANPOWER.
NATIONAL SCHOLARSHIP SERVICE AND FUND FOR NEGRO STUDENTS.
NEW YORK. 1957. 41 PP.

NPLOTLX59064 PLOTKIN L
RACIAL DIFFERENCES IN INTELLIGENCE.
AMERICAN PSYCHOLOGIST, VOL 14, AUG 1959. PP 526-527.

NPOLIEX64219 POLISAR E
THE NEGRO REVOLUTION AND EMPLOYMENT.
REPORT CARD, VOL 12, NO 4, AP-MAY 1964.

NPOLIEX66004 POLISAR E
STATEMENT TO THE NEW-YORK STATE ADVISORY COMMITTEE TO THE US
COMMISSION ON CIVIL-RIGHTS, MAY 23, 1966. /EMPLOYMENT
LEGISLATION/
NEW YORK STATE ADVISORY COMMITTEE TO THE US COMMISSION ON
CIVIL RIGHTS. NEW YORK. 1966. 12 PP.

NPOLLDX63006 POLLIT D
RACIAL DISCRIMINATION IN EMPLOYMENT. PROPOSALS FOR
CORRECTIVE ACTION.
BUFFALO LAW REVIEW, VOL 13, FALL 1963. PP 59-92.

NPOLLFM64005 POLLARD FM
CHARACTERISTICS OF NEGRO COLLEGE CHIEF LIBRARIANS.
/OCCUPATIONS/
COLLEGE AND RESEARCH LIBRARIES, VOL 25, JULY 1964.
PP 281-284.

NPOLLSX66723 POLLOCK S
ORGANIZED LABOR AND THE NEGRO YOUTH. /UNION/
LABOR TODAY, VOL 5, NOV 1966. PP 12-14 PLUS.

NPOPURB58008 POPULATION REFERENCE BUREAU
THE AMERICAN NEGRO AT MID-CENTURY.
POPULATION REFERENCE BUREAU, INC. WASHINGTON, DC. NOV 1958.

NPOPURB63007 POPULATION REFERENCE BUREAU
THE AMERICAN FARMER. /OCCUPATIONS/
POPULATION REFERENCE BUREAU, INC, POPULATION BULLETIN.
WASHINGTON, DC. MAY 1963.

NPOWEEC61009 POWELL EC
RETREATISM AND OCCUPATIONAL ASPIRATIONS AMONG WHITE AND
NEGRO HIGH SCHOOL SENIORS.
UNIVERSITY OF KENTUCKY. PHD DISSERTATION. LEXINGTON,
KENTUCKY. 1961.

NPRESCD61013 PRESIDENT-S COMMITTEE ON EEO
REPORT AND SUMMARY OF THE AIR FORCE ON ACTIONS TAKEN BY

LOCKHEED AIRCRAFT CORPORATION AT THE AIR FORCE PLANT NO 6
IN MARIETTA, GEORGIA. /INDUSTRY/
PRESIDENT-S COMMITTEE ON EQUAL EMPLOYMENT OPPORTUNITY. PRESS
RELEASE EEO-6. GPO. WASHINGTON, DC. MAY 25 1961. 11 PP.

NPRESCD62011 PRESIDENT-S COMMITTEE ON EEO
NEGRO AND TOTAL EMPLOYMENT BY GRADE AND SALARY GROUPS,
JUNE 1961 AND JUNE 1962.
PRESIDENT-S COMMITTEE ON EQUAL EMPLOYMENT OPPORTUNITY. GPO.
WASHINGTON, DC. 1962. 40 PP.

NPRESCD62012 PRESIDENT-S COMMITTEE ON EEO
NEGRO EMPLOYMENT IN THE FEDERAL GOVERNMENT BY CIVIL SERVICE
REGION, STATE AND PAY CATEGORIES, JUNE 1962.
PRESIDENT-S COMMITTEE ON EQUAL EMPLOYMENT OPPORTUNITY. GPO.
WASHINGTON, DC. 1962. 22 PP.

NPRESCD62014 PRESIDENT-S COMMITTEE ON EEO
THE AMERICAN DREAM...EQUAL OPPORTUNITY.
PRESIDENT-S COMMITTEE ON EQUAL EMPLOYMENT OPPORTUNITY.
LEADERS CONFERENCE REPORT. GPO. WASHINGTON, DC. MAY 19 1962.

NPRESCD63010 PRESIDENT-S COMMITTEE ON EEO
MINORITY-GROUP STUDY, JUNE 1963. NEGRO AND TOTAL EMPLOYMENT
IN SELECTED AGENCIES.
PRESIDENT-S COMMITTEE ON EQUAL EMPLOYMENT OPPORTUNITY. GPO.
WASHINGTON, DC. 1963. 40 PP.

NPRESCE50015 PRESL COMT EQTY TRTMT OPPOR
FREEDOM TO SERVE. /MILITARY/
PRESIDENTAL COMMITTEE ON EQUALITY OF TREATMENT AND
OPPORTUNITY IN THE ARMED SERVICES. GPO. WASHINGTON, DC.
1950.

NPRESCP57017 PRES COMT GOVT EMPLOY POLICY
A FIVE-CITY SURVEY OF NEGRO-AMERICAN EMPLOYEES OF THE
FEDERAL GOVERNMENT.
PRESIDENT-S COMMITTEE ON GOVERNMENT EMPLOYMENT POLICY. GPO.
WASHINGTON, DC. 1957. 20 PP.

NPRESCP60016 PRES COMT GOVT EMPLOY POLICY
CHARACTERISTICS OF NEGRO EMPLOYMENT IN FEDERAL AGENCIES IN
ATLANTA, GEORGIA.
PRESIDENT-S COMMITTEE ON GOVERNMENT EMPLOYMENT POLICY. GPO.
WASHINGTON, DC. 1960. 4 PP.

NPRESHB62125 PRESSER HB
CHANGING EMPLOYMENT PATTERNS OF NEGROES, 1920-1950.
UNIVERSITY OF NORTH CAROLINA. MASTER-S THESIS. CHAPEL HILL,
NORTH CAROLINA. 1962.

NPRICDO48019 PRICE DO
NONWHITE MIGRANTS TO AND FROM SELECTED CITIES.
AMERICAN JOURNAL OF SOCIOLOGY, VOL 54, NO 3, NOV 1948.
PP 196-201.

NPRICDO65018 PRICE DO   *UNIV OF NORTH CAROLINA IRSS
CHANGING CHARACTERISTICS OF THE NEGRO POPULATION.
UNIVERSITY OF NORTH CAROLINA, INSTITUTE FOR RESEARCH IN
SOCIAL SCIENCE. CHAPEL HILL, NORTH CAROLINA. 1965.

NPRINUI54020 PRINCETON UNIV IND RELS SECT
COMPANY EXPERIENCE WITH THE EMPLOYMENT OF NEGROES.
/INDUSTRY/
PRINCETON UNIVERSITY, INDUSTRIAL RELATIONS SECTION. SELECTED
REFERENCES NO 60. PRINCETON, NEW JERSEY. 1954. 4 PP.

NPROCSD66021 PROCTOR SD
THE YOUNG NEGRO IN AMERICA 1960-1980.
ASSOCIATION PRESS. NEW YORK. 1966. 160 PP.

NPROGXX62059 PROGRESSIVE.
A CENTURY OF STRUGGLE.
PROGRESSIVE, VOL 26, DEC 1962. 58 PP. ENTIRE ISSUE.

NPROMHJ59127 PROMINSKI HJ
RACIAL DISCRIMINATION IN UNION MEMBERSHIP.
UNIVERSITY OF MIAMI LAW REVIEW, VOL 13, SPRING 1959.
PP 364-369.

NPURCTV62023 PURCELL TV
MANAGEMENT VERSUS JIM-CROW. /INDUSTRY/
MANAGEMENT OF PERSONNEL QUARTERLY, SUMMER 1962. PP 2-7.

NPURCTV64022 PURCELL TV
THE HOPES OF NEGRO WORKERS FOR THEIR CHILDREN.
BLUE-COLLAR WORLD. ED BY AB SHOSTAK AND W GOMBERG.
PRENTICE-HALL. ENGLEWOOD CLIFFS, NEW JERSEY. 1964.
PP 144-154.

NPURCTV67123 PURCELL TV
MANAGEMENT SOCIAL RESPONSIBILITY AND RACIAL EMPLOYMENT IN
THE MEAT-PACKING INDUSTRY.
CAMBRIDGE CENTER FOR SOCIAL STUDIES. CAMBRIDGE,
MASSACHUSETTS. MAY 26 1967. UNPUBLISHED WORKING PAPER. 5 PP.

NPURDLX54024 PURDY L
NEGRO MIGRATION IN THE UNITED STATES.
AMERICAN JOURNAL OF ECONOMICS AND SOCIOLOGY, VOL 13, NO 4,
JULY 1954. PP 357-361.

NPURYMT63026 PURYEAR MT   *NATIONAL URBAN LEAGUE
THE NEGRO IN THE LABOR-FORCE.
NATIONAL URBAN LEAGUE, UNPUBLISHED PAPER DONE FOR TACONIC
FOUNDATION ASSESSMENT PROJECT. NEW YORK. JUNE 15 1963.

NPURYMT63027 PURYEAR MT
NO TIME FOR TRAGIC IRONIES. /EMPLOYMENT
TECHNOLOGICAL-CHANGE/
INTERRACIAL REVIEW, VOL 36, FEB 1963. PP 34-35.

NPURYMT63028 PURYEAR MT   *NATIONAL URBAN LEAGUE
PROBLEMS AND TRENDS IN JOB-DEVELOPMENT AND EMPLOYMENT
PROGRAMS.
PROBLEMS AND TRENDS IN CITIES. NATIONAL URBAN LEAGUE,
CONFERENCE. BACKGROUND PAPERS. JULY 28 -- AUG 1 1963.

NQUARBX47257 QUARLES B
THE BACKGROUND OF THE 1947 COLLEGE STUDENT. /LABOR-MARKET/
THE QUARTERLY REVIEW OF HIGHER EDUCATION AMONG NEGROES,
VOL 15, NO 2, AP 1947. PP 87-90.

NRABOSH53029 RABOCK SH
THE NEGRO IN THE INDUSTRIAL DEVELOPMENT OF THE SOUTH.
PHYLON, VOL 14, 3RD QUARTER 1953. PP 319-325.

NRAINLX66032 RAINWATER L
CRUCIBLE OF IDENTITY. THE NEGRO LOWER-CLASS FAMILY.
DAEDALUS, VOL 95, WINTER 1966. PP 172-216.

NRAINLX66033 RAINWATER L   YANCEY WL
BLACK FAMILIES AND THE WHITE HOUSE.
TRANS-ACTION, VOL 3, NO 5, JULY-AUG 1966. PP 6-11.

NRAMSLA43128 RAMSON LA
COMBATING DISCRIMINATION IN THE EMPLOYMENT OF NEGROES IN
   WAR INDUSTRIES AND GOVERNMENT AGENCIES.
JOURNAL OF NEGRO EDUCATION, VOL 12, NO 3, SUMMER 1943.
PP 405-416.

NRANDAP40576 RANDOLPH AP
THE NEGRO CONGRESS.
THE AMERICAN FEDERATIONIST, VOL 47, NO 1, JULY 1940.
PP 24-25.

NRANDAP62036 RANDOLPH AP
THE UNFINISHED REVOLUTION. /TRAINING/
PROGRESSIVE, VOL 26, DEC 1962. PP 20-25.

NRANDAP63035 RANDOLPH AP   REUTHER WP
*AFL-CIO
TODAY-S CIVIL-RIGHTS REVOLUTION.
AFL-CIO INDUSTRIAL UNION DEPARTMENT. WASHINGTON, DC.
NOV 8 1963. 22 PP.

NRANDAP64034 RANDOLPH AP
JOBS FOR THE NEGRO, THE UNFINISHED REVOLUTION.
FREEDOM NOW. ED BY ALAN F WESTIN. BASIC BOOKS, INC.
NEW YORK. 1964. 346 PP.

NRASKAH64038 RASKIN AH
CIVIL-RIGHTS. THE LAW AND THE UNIONS.
THE REPORTER, VOL 31, SEPT 10 1962. PP 23-28.

NRAYAEX61040 RAYACK E
DISCRIMINATION AND THE OCCUPATIONAL PROGRESS OF NEGROES.
REVIEW OF ECONOMICS AND STATISTICS, VOL 43, MAY 1961.
PP 209-214.

NRECOCW48041 RECORD CW
THE NEGRO ISSUE IN CALIFORNIA.
LABOR AND NATION, VOL 4, NO 3, MAY-JUNE 1948. PP 25-27.

NRECOCW59042 RECORD CW
NEGROES IN THE CALIFORNIA AGRICULTURAL LABOR-FORCE.
SOCIAL PROBLEMS, VOL 6, NO 4, SPRING 1959. PP 354-361.

NRECOCW63043 RECORD CW
MINORITY-GROUPS AND INTERGROUP RELATIONS IN THE
   SAN-FRANCISCO BAY AREA. /CALIFORNIA/
UNIVERSITY OF CALIFORNIA. BERKELEY, CALIFORNIA. 1963. 48 PP.

NREDOJS43546 REDDING JS
THE BLACK MAN-S BURDEN. /DISCRIMINATION ECONOMIC-STATUS/
ANTIOCH REVIEW, VOL 3, NO 4, WINTER 1943. PP 587-595.

NREDOLD53044 REDDICK LD
THE NEGRO POLICY OF THE AMERICAN ARMY SINCE WORLD-WAR-II.
   /MILITARY/
JOURNAL OF NEGRO HISTORY, VOL 38, AP 1953. PP 194-215.

NREEDBA47045 REED BA
ACCOMODATION BETWEEN NEGRO AND WHITE EMPLOYEES IN A WEST
   COAST AIRCRAFT INDUSTRY, 1942-1944. /CASE-STUDY/
SOCIAL FORCES, VOL 26, NO 1, OCT 1947. PP 76-84.

NREEDET62046 REED ET
I AM A CONTROVERSIAL DENTIST. /OCCUPATIONS/
INTERRACIAL REVIEW, VOL 35, AP 1962. PP 100-101.

NREIDID43048 REID IDA
A CRITICAL SUMMARY. THE NEGRO ON THE HOME FRONT IN
   WORLD-WARS I AND II.
JOURNAL OF NEGRO EDUCATION, VOL 12, 1943.

NREIDID47362 REID ID
SPECIAL PROBLEMS OF NEGRO MIGRATION DURING THE WAR.
MILBANK MEMORIAL FUND QUARTERLY, VOL 25, NO 3, JULY 1947.
PP 284-292.

NREIDID56047 REID IDA
THE AMERICAN NEGRO.
UNDERSTANDING MINORITY GROUPS. ED BY J B GITTLER.
JOHN WILEY. NEW YORK. 1956.

NREISLX65049 REISSMAN L
URBANIZATION IN THE SOUTH.
THE SOUTH IN CONTINUITY AND CHANGE. ED BY JOHN C MCKINNEY
AND EDGAR T THOMPSON. DUKE UNIVERSITY PRESS. DURHAM,
NORTH CAROLINA. 1965. PP 79-100.

NREITDC53050 REITZES DC
THE ROLE OF ORGANIZATIONAL STRUCTURES. UNION VERSUS
   NEIGHBORHOOD IN A TENSION SITUATION.
JOURNAL OF SOCIAL ISSUES, VOL 9, NO 1, JAN 1953. PP 37-44.

NRENDFW64274 RENDER FW
A MATTER OF THE MOMENT.
THE QUARTERLY REVIEW OF HIGHER EDUCATION AMONG NEGROES,
VOL 32, NO 4, AP 1964. PP 68-71.

NRHODIC64051 RHODE ISLAND COMM AGST DISCR
GOVERNOR-S CIVIL-RIGHTS TASK FORCE. REPORT. /RHODE-ISLAND/
RHODE ISLAND COMMISSION AGAINST DISCRIMINATION. PROVIDENCE,
RHODE ISLAND. JAN 3 1964. PP 4-13.

NRHODIUND052 RHODE ISLAND URBAN LEAGUE
THE NON-WHITE IN PROVIDENCE. /RHODE-ISLAND/
RHODE ISLAND URBAN LEAGUE. PROVIDENCE, RHODE ISLAND. ND.
9 PP.

NRICEJD41053 RICE JD
THE NEGRO TOBACCO WORKER AND HIS UNION IN DURHAM,
   NORTH-CAROLINA.
UNIVERSITY OF NORTH CAROLINA. MA THESIS. CHAPEL HILL,
NORTH CAROLINA. 1941.

NRICHCX64058 RICHMOND C   *US DEPARTMENT OF LABOR
WIDER HORIZONS FOR NEGRO WORKERS.
US DEPARTMENT OF LABOR, OCCUPATIONAL OUTLOOK QUARTERLY,
VOL 8, NO 4, DEC 1964. 3 PP.

NRICHEX43056 RICHARDS E
OCCUPATIONAL ATTITUDES OF NEGRO WORKERS.
SOCIOLOGY AND SOCIAL RESEARCH, VOL 28, SEPT 1943. PP 20-27.

NRICHJC62054 RICH JC
THE NAACP VERSUS LABOR. /UNION/
NEW LEADER, VOL 45, NOV 26 1962. PP 20-21.

NRICHMX65055 RICH M
THE CONGRESS-OF-RACIAL-EQUALITY AND ITS STRATEGY.
THE ANNALS OF THE AMERICAN ACADEMY OF POLITICAL AND SOCIAL
SCIENCE, VOL 357, JAN 1965.

NRICHTW56057 RICHARDS TW
GRADUATE EDUCATION OF NEGRO PSYCHOLOGISTS.
AMERICAN PSYCHOLOGIST, VOL 11, NO 7, JULY 1956. PP 326-327.

NRIESFX65060 RIESSMAN F
THE NEW ANTI-POVERTY IDEOLOGY AND THE NEGRO.
WHITE HOUSE CONFERENCE ON CIVIL RIGHTS, PAPER. WASHINGTON,
DC. NOV 17-18 1965. 21 PP.

NRIESFX66059 RIESSMAN F
IN DEFENSE OF THE NEGRO FAMILY.
DISSENT, MAR-AP 1966. PP 141-155.

NRINGHH53061 RING HH   *US DEPARTMENT OF LABOR
NEGROES IN THE UNITED STATES. THEIR EMPLOYMENT AND ECONOMIC
   STATUS.
US DEPARTMENT OF LABOR, BUREAU OF LABOR STATISTICS.
BULLETIN NO 1119. GPO. WASHINGTON, DC. 1953. 58 PP.

NRITTAL45062 RITTER AL   *US DEPARTMENT OF LABOR
ANNUAL FAMILY AND OCCUPATIONAL EARNINGS OF RESIDENTS OF TWO
   NEGRO HOUSING PROJECTS IN ATLANTA 1937-1944. /GEORGIA/
US DEPARTMENT OF LABOR, MONTHLY LABOR REVIEW, VOL 61,
DEC 1945. PP 1061-1073.

NROBEGX61063 ROBERTS G
NEGRO EDUCATION -- FOR WHAT.
THE NEW YORK TIMES MAGAZINE, NOV 19 1961. ALSO AMERICAN
JEWISH COMMITTEE, INSTITUTE OF HUMAN RELATIONS. NEW YORK.
REPRINT.

NROBEGX62064 ROBERTS G
WASTE OF MANPOWER -- RACE AND EMPLOYMENT IN A SOUTHERN
   STATE.
SOUTH ATLANTIC QUARTERLY, VOL 61, SPRING 1962. PP 141-150.

NROBEHW53065 ROBERTS HW
THE IMPACT OF MILITARY SERVICE UPON THE RACIAL ATTITUDES OF
   NEGRO SERVICEMEN IN WORLD-WAR II.
SOCIAL PROBLEMS, VOL 1, 1953. PP 65-69.

NROBESO57067 ROBERTS SO
NEGRO AMERICAN COLLEGE YOUTH-S OUTLOOK ON THE FUTURE.
AMERICAN PSYCHOLOGIST, VOL 12, NO 7, JULY 1957. P 368.

NROBESO65068 ROBERTS SO   *EDUCATIONAL TESTING SERVICE
THE PROBLEM OF CULTURAL BIAS IN SELECTION. II. ETHNIC
   BACKGROUND AND TEST PERFORMANCE.
SELECTING AND TRAINING NEGROES FOR MANAGERIAL POSITIONS.
EDUCATIONAL TESTING SERVICE. PRINCETON, NEW JERSEY. 1965.
PP 65-75.

NROBESO66961 ROBERTS SO   OPPENHEIM DB
*EDUCATIONAL TESTING SERVICE
THE EFFECT OF SPECIAL INSTRUCTION UPON TEST PERFORMANCE OF
   HIGH SCHOOL STUDENTS IN TENNESSEE.
EDUCATIONAL TESTING SERVICE, RESEARCH BULLETIN RB-66-36.
PRINCETON, NEW JERSEY. JULY 1966. 24 PP.

NROBIJX63069 ROBINSON J
AMERICAN ENTERPRISE AND THE RACIAL CRISIS.
SALES MANAGEMENT, AUG 16 1963. PP 33-37.

NROBIML47070 ROBISON ML   MEENES M
THE RELATIONSHIP BETWEEN TEST INTELLIGENCE OF THIRD GRADE
   NEGRO CHILDREN AND THE OCCUPATIONS OF THEIR PARENTS.
JOURNAL OF NEGRO EDUCATION, VOL 16, SPRING 1947. PP 136-141.

NROHRWC58400 ROHRER WC   LERAY NL
INCOME, EMPLOYMENT STATUS AND CHANGE IN CALVERT COUNTY,
   MARYLAND.
UNIVERSITY OF MARYLAND. COLLEGE PARK, MARYLAND. AUG 1958.
41 PP.

NRONKHO52129 RONKEN HO   LAWRENCE PR
ADMINISTERING CHANGES. A CASE-STUDY OF HUMAN-RELATIONS IN A
   FACTORY.
HARVARD UNIVERSITY, GRADUATE SCHOOL OF BUSINESS
ADMINISTRATION. BOSTON, MASSACHUSETTS. 1952. 324 PP.

NRONYVX65072 RONY V
LABOR DRIVES TO CLOSE THE SOUTH-S OPEN-SHOP. /UNION/
THE REPORTER, VOL 33, NOV 18 1965. PP 31-34.

NROPEEX52073 ROPER E
DISCRIMINATION IN INDUSTRY.
INDUSTRIAL AND LABOR RELATIONS REVIEW. VOL 5, NO 4,
JULY 1952. PP 584-592.

NROSEAM48319 ROSE AM
THE NEGRO IN AMERICA.
BEACON PRESS. BOSTON, MASSACHUSETTES. 1948.

NROSEAM50294 ROSE AM   *ANTI-DEFAMATION LEAGUE
THE NEGRO IN POST-WAR AMERICA.
ANTI-DEFAMATION LEAGUE OF B-NAI B-RITH. NEW YORK. 1950.
34 PP.

NROSEAM51075 ROSE AM
RACE PREJUDICE AND DISCRIMINATION. READINGS IN INTERGROUP
   RELATIONS IN THE US.
KNOPF. NEW YORK. 1951. 605 PP.

NROSEAM58291 ROSE AM
DISTANCE OF MIGRATION AND SOCIO-ECONOMIC STATUS OF MIGRANTS.
AMERICAN SOCIOLOGICAL REVIEW, VOL 23, AUG 1958. PP 420-423.

NROSEAM60295 ROSE AM
NEW AND EMERGING NEGRO PROBLEMS.
JOURNAL OF INTERGROUP RELATIONS, VOL 1, NO 2, AP 1960.
PP 71-74.

NROSEAM64290 ROSE AM ED
ASSURING FREEDOM TO THE FREE. A CENTURY OF EMANCIPATION IN
   THE USA.
WAYNE STATE UNIVERSITY PRESS. DETROIT, MICHIGAN. 1964.
306 PP.

NROSEAM64296 ROSE AM
SOCIAL CHANGE AND THE NEGRO PROBLEM.
THE NEGRO IN AMERICA. 1964. 24 PP.

NROSEAM65074 ROSE AM ED
THE NEGRO PROTEST.
THE ANNALS OF THE AMERICAN ACADEMY OF POLITICAL AND SOCIAL

SCIENCE. VOL 357, JAN 1965. ENTIRE ISSUE.

NROSEAM65289   ROSE AM
THE AMERICAN NEGRO PROBLEM IN THE CONTEXT OF SOCIAL CHANGE.
ANNALS OF THE AMERICAN ACADEMY OF POLITICAL AND SOCIAL
SCIENCE. VOL 357, JAN 1965

NROSEAW51292   ROSE AW
HOW NEGRO WORKERS FEEL ABOUT THEIR JOBS.
PERSONNEL JOURNAL, VOL 29, JAN 1951. PP 292-296.

NROSEAW53293   ROSE AW
THE INFLUENCE OF A BORDER CITY UNION ON THE RACE ATTITUDES
OF ITS MEMBERS.
JOURNAL OF SOCIAL ISSUES, VOL 9, WINTER 1953. PP 20-24.

NROSEBX59080   ROSENBERG B   CHAPIN P
*NY STATE COMM AGAINST DISCR
MANAGEMENT AND MINORITY-GROUPS. A STUDY OF ATTITUDES AND
PRACTICES IN HIRING AND UPGRADING.
DISCRIMINATION AND LOW INCOMES. ED BY AARON ANTONOVSKY AND
LOUIS LORWIN. NEW SCHOOL FOR SOCIAL RESEARCH. NEW YORK.
1959. PP 147-194.

NROSEHM61C76   ROSE HM
THE MARKET FOR NEGRO EDUCATORS IN COLLEGES AND UNIVERSITIES
OUTSIDE THE SOUTH.
JOURNAL OF NEGRO EDUCATION, VOL 30, FALL 1961. PP 432-435.

NROSERX53077   ROSE R
THE NEGRO IN INDUSTRY.
JOURNAL OF COLLEGE PLACEMENT, MAR 1953.

NROSERX65130   ROSE R
TOWARD FAIR EMPLOYMENT. A REVIEW.
THE JOURNAL OF THE INSTITUTE OF RACE RELATIONS, VOL 6, NO 4,
AP 1965. PP 281-287.

NROSESJ62C79   ROSEN SJ
THE NEGRO IN THE AMERICAN LABOR MOVEMENT. /UNION/
YALE LAW SCHOOL, PUBLIC LAW DIVISION. THESIS. NEW HAVEN,
CONNECTICUT. JUNE 1962.

NROSESJ67078   ROSEN SJ
THE LAW AND RACIAL DISCRIMINATION IN EMPLOYMENT.
EMPLOYMENT, RACE AND POVERTY. ED BY ARTHUR M ROSE AND
HERBERT HILL. HARCOURT, BRACE, AND WORLD. NEW YORK. 1967.
PP 479-540. ALSO CALIFORNIA LAW REVIEW, VOL 53, NO 3,
AUG 1965.

NROSSAM63259   ROSS AM
UNEMPLOYMENT AND THE AMERICAN ECONOMY. RESEARCH PROGRAM ON
UNEMPLOYMENT.
JOHN WILEY AND SONS. NEW YORK. 1963. 216 PP.

NROSSAM66081   ROSS AM   *US DEPARTMENT OF LABOR
EMPLOYMENT OF TEENAGERS, JUNE 1966.
US DEPARTMENT OF LABOR, BUREAU OF LABOR STATISTICS,
WASHINGTON, DC. JULY 11 1966. 3 PP.

NROSSAM67082   ROSS AM
THE NEGRO IN THE AMERICAN ECONOMY.
EMPLOYMENT, RACE AND POVERTY. ED BY ARTHUR M ROSS AND
HERBERT HILL. HARCOURT, BRACE, AND WORLD. NEW YORK. 1967.
PP 3-48.

NROSSAM67C85   ROSS AM
WILL THE NEGRO SUCCEED.
EMPLOYMENT, RACE AND POVERTY. ED BY ARTHUR M ROSS AND
HERBERT HILL. HARCOURT, BRACE, AND WORLD. NEW YORK. 1967.
PP 573 FF.

NROSSAM67C86   ROSS AM ED   HILL H ED
EMPLOYMENT, RACE AND POVERTY.
HARCOURT, BRACE AND WORLD. NEW YORK. 1967.

NROSSIX63087   ROSS I
NEGROES ARE MOVING UP THE JOB LADDER.
READER-S DIGEST, DEC 1963. PP 53-57.

NROSSJX50088   ROSS J
OF HUMAN RESOURCES AND THE SOUTH.
SOUTHWEST REVIEW, VOL 35, AUTUMN 1950. PP 276-288.

NROUSRJ62089   ROUSSEVE RJ
UPDATING GUIDANCE AND PERSONNEL PRACTICES.
JOURNAL OF NEGRO EDUCATION, VOL 31, SPRING 1962. PP 182-183.

NROUSRX63310   ROUSSEVE R
TEACHERS OF CULTURALLY DISADVANTAGED AMERICAN YOUTH.
JOURNAL OF NEGRO EDUCATION, VOL 32, NO 2, SPRING 1963.
PP 114-121.

NROWACT60C90   ROWAN CT
ARE NEGROES READY FOR EQUALITY.
SATURDAY EVENING POST, OCT 22 1960.

NROWARL65703   ROWAN RL
A REVIEW OF RESEARCH ON THE NEGRO AND EMPLOYMENT IN THE
SOUTH.
ECONOMICS AND BUSINESS BULLETIN, VOL 17, NO 3, MAR 1965.
PP 20-31.

NROWARL67C91   ROWAN RL
NEGRO EMPLOYMENT IN BIRMINGHAM. THREE CASES. /ALABAMA/
EMPLOYMENT, RACE AND POVERTY. ED BY ARTHUR M ROSS AND
HERBERT HILL. HARCOURT, BRACE, AND WORLD. NEW YORK. 1967.
PP 308-336.

NRUBIAX46C93   RUBIN A   SEGAL GJ
AN INDUSTRIAL EXPERIMENT TOWARDS INTEGRATION OF MINORITIES
INTO INDUSTRY.
ANNALS OF THE AMERICAN ACADEMY OF POLITICAL AND SOCIAL
SCIENCE, MAR 1946. PP 57-64.

NRUBIMX54297   RUBIN M
SOCIAL AND CULTURAL CHANGE IN THE PLANTATION AREA.
JOURNAL OF SOCIAL ISSUES, VOL 10, NO 1, 1954. PP 28-35.

NRUBIMX60C94   RUBIN M
MIGRATION PATTERNS OF NEGROES FROM A RURAL NORTHEASTERN
MISSISSIPPI COMMUNITY. /DEMOGRAPHY/
SOCIAL FORCES, VOL 39, 1960. PP 59-66.

NRUDWEM60095   RUDWICK EM
THE NEGRO POLICEMAN IN THE SOUTH. /OCCUPATIONS/
JOURNAL OF CRIMINAL LAW, CRIMINOLOGY AND POLICE SCIENCE,
VOL 51, JULY-AUG 1960. ALSO SOUTHERN REGIONAL COUNCIL.
ATLANTA, GEORGIA. 1962. 14 PP.

NRUDWEM61134   RUDWICK EM
NEGRO POLICE EMPLOYMENT IN THE URBAN SOUTH.
JOURNAL OF NEGRO EDUCATION, VOL 30, NO 2, SPRING 1961.
PP 102-108.

NRUSSJL66096   RUSSELL JL   *US DEPARTMENT OF LABOR
THE NEGRO-S OCCUPATIONAL PROGRESS.
US DEPARTMENT OF LABOR, OCCUPATIONAL OUTLOOK QUARTERLY,
VOL 10, NO 4, DEC 1966. PP 8-13.

NRUSTBX66097   RUSTIN B
CIVIL-RIGHTS AT THE CROSSROADS.
THE AMERICAN FEDERATIONIST, VOL 73, NO 11, NOV 1966.
PP 16-20.

NRUSTBX66098   RUSTIN B
SOME LESSONS FROM WATTS. /LOS-ANGELES CALIFORNIA/
JOURNAL OF INTERGROUP RELATIONS, AUTUMN 1966. PP 41-48.

NRUSTBX66C99   RUSTIN B
THE WATTS MANIFESTO AND THE MCCONE REPORT. /LOS-ANGELES
CALIFORNIA/
COMMENTARY, MAR 1966. PP 29-35.

NRUTHKX49100   RUTH K
NEGRO LABOR IN THE SOUTHERN CRYSTAL BALL. /EMPLOYMENT/
PHYLON, VOL 10, NO 3, 3RD QUARTER 1949. PP 233-238.

NSACHRX63888   SACHS R
THE RACIAL ISSUE AS AN ANTI UNION TOOL AND THE
NATIONAL-LABOR-RELATIONS-BOARD.
LABOR LAW JOURNAL, VOL 14, OCT 1963.

NSAENGX50101   SAENGER G   GILBERT E
CUSTOMER REACTIONS TO THE INTEGRATION OF NEGRO SALES
PERSONNEL.
INTERNATIONAL JOURNAL OF OPINION AND ATTITUDE RESEARCH,
VOL 4, NO 1, SPRING 1950. PP 57-76. ALSO AMERICAN
PSYCHOLOGIST, VOL 3, NO 7, JULY 1948.

NSAINJL66138   ST JOHN-S LAW REVIEW
THE CIVIL-RIGHTS-ACT OF 1964. RACIAL DISCRIMINATION BY
LABOR UNIONS.
ST JOHN-S LAW REVIEW, VOL 41, JULY 1966. PP 58-81.

NSAINJN62137   ST JOHN NH
THE RELATION OF RACIAL SEGREGATION IN EARLY SCHOOLING TO THE
LEVEL OF ASPIRATION AND ACADEMIC ACHIEVEMENT OF NEGRO
STUDENTS IN A NORTHERN HIGH SCHOOL.
HARVARD UNIVERSITY. PHD DISSERTATION. CAMBRIDGE,
MASSACHUSETTS. 1962.

NSAINJN66136   ST JOHN NH
THE EFFECT OF SEGREGATION ON THE ASPIRATIONS OF NEGRO YOUTH.
HARVARD EDUCATIONAL REVIEW, VOL 36, SUMMER 1966. PP 284-294.

NSAITCX64308   SAITZKY C
JOB GUIDANCE AND THE DISADVANTAGED.
CLEARINGHOUSE, NOV 1964. PP 156-158.

NSALTDR52347   SALTER DR
AN ANALYSIS OF SELECTIVE FACTORS INFLUENCING FARM INCOME
IN HALE COUNTY, AS A BASIS FOR ESTABLISHING A MORE
EFFECTIVE VOCATIONAL AGRICULTURAL PROGRAM. /ALABAMA/
TUSKEGEE INSTITUTE. THESIS. TUSKEGEE, ALABAMA. 1952. 61 PP.

NSAMOTX65128   SAMORE T   *US DEPT OF HEALTH ED WELFARE
LIBRARY RESOURCES AND SERVICES IN WHITE AND NEGRO COLLEGES.
/EDUCATION/
US DEPARTMENT OF HEALTH, EDUCATION, AND WELFARE, INDICATORS.
WASHINGTON, DC. JULY 1965.

NSANCLA42537   SANCHEZ Y SANCHEZ LA
THE NORTH AMERICAN NEGRO. /DISCRIMINATION/
THE ANTIOCH REVIEW, VOL 2, NO 3, SUMMER 1942. PP 357-370.

NSCALEE57272   SCALES EE
INSTITUTIONAL GUIDANCE FACES THE FUTURE.
THE QUARTERLY REVIEW OF HIGHER EDUCATION AMONG NEGROES,
VOL 25, NO 2, AP 1957. PP 86-93.

NSCHALX64102   SCHALLER L   RAWLINGS CW
RACE AND POVERTY.
REGIONAL CHURCH PLANNING OFFICE. OFFICE OF RELIGION AND
RACE. CLEVELAND, OHIO. 1964.

NSCHEGX61104   SCHERMER G   *PHILADELPHIA COMM HUMAN RELS
DESEGREGATION, A COMMUNITY DESIGN. /PHILADELPHIA
PENNSYLVANIA/
PHILADELPHIA COMMISSION ON HUMAN RELATICNS. PHILADELPHIA,
PENNSYLVANIA. 1961. 7 PP.

NSCHEGX64103   SCHERMER G   *AMERICAN MANAGEMENT ASSN
THE DEMAND FOR EQUAL-RIGHTS.
THE PERSONNEL JOB IN A CHANGING WORLD. ED BY JERUME W BLOOD.
AMERICAN MANAGEMENT ASSOCIATION. NEW YORK. 1964.

NSCHILB65106   SCHIVEK LB
MAN IN METROPOLIS. /RESIDENTIAL-SEGREGATION GHETTO/
DOUBLEDAY. GARDEN CITY, NEW YORK. 1965.

NSCHMJC64108   SCHMIDT JC
NEGRO UNEMPLOYMENT -- WHAT CITY BUSINESSMEN ARE DOING ABOUT
IT.
BALTIMORE SUN FEATURES, SEPT 27 1964. 6 PP.

NSCHMWX63139   SCHMIDT W
SOME ASPECTS OF VOCATIONAL ASPIRATIONS AND VALUE ORIENTATION
AMONG NEGRO BOYS IN THE LOWER SOCIO-ECONOMIC CLASSES.
CATHOLIC UNIVERSITY. MASTER-S THESIS. WASHINGTON, DC. 1963.

NSCHNLF65109   SCHNORE LF
RACIAL CHANGES IN METROPOLITAN AREAS, 1950-1960.
/DEMOGRAPHY MIGRATION/
THE URBAN SCENE. FREE PRESS. NEW YORK. 1965. PP. 281-293.

NSCHRDX63141   SCHREIBER D
THE DROPOUT AND THE DELINQUENT. PROMISING PRACTICES GLEANED
FROM A YEAR OF STUDY.
PHI DELTA KAPPA, VOL 44, NO 5, FEB 1963. PP 215-221.

NSCHRPX64125   SCHRAG P
THE CIRCLE OF FUTILITY. /COMPENSATORY-EDUCATION
POLICY-RECOMMENDATIONS/
COMMONWEALTH, MAR 6, 1964. PP 685-688.

NSCHUTW50144   SCHULTZ TW
REFLECTIONS ON POVERTY WITHIN AGRICULTURE.
JOURNAL OF POLITICAL ECONOMY, FEB 1950. PP 1-15.

NSCHJTW64143 SCHULTZ TW
OUR WELFARE STATE AND THE WELFARE OF FARM PEOPLE.
SOCIAL SERVICE REVIEW, JUNE 1964. PP 123-129.

NSCHWMX64022 SCHWARTZ M
WHY THEY DON-T WANT TO WORK. /ASPIRATICNS/
PERSONNEL ADMINISTRATION, VOL 27, MAR 1964. PP 6-10.

NSCHWMX64110 SCHWARTZ M   HENDERSON G
THE CULTURE OF UNEMPLOYMENT. SOME NOTES ON NEGRO CHILDREN.
BLUE-COLLAR WORLD. ED BY A B SHOSTAK AND W GOMBERG.
PRENTICE-HALL. ENGLEWOOD CLIFFS, NEW JERSEY. 1964.
PP 459-468. ALSO THE UNIVERSITY OF MICHIGAN-WAYNE STATE
UNIVERSITY, INSTITUTE OF LABOR AND INDUSTRIAL RELATIONS.
REPRINT SERIES NO 29. ANN ARBOR, MICHIGAN. ND.

NSCOTCDND346 SCOTT CD
OCCUPATIONAL ESTABLISHMENT OF FORMER STUDENTS OF VOCATIONAL
 AGRICULTURE IN MONTGOMERY TRAINING SCHOOL AREA. /ALABAMA/
TUSKEGEE INSTITUTE. THESIS. TUSKEGEE, ALABAMA. 69 PP.

NSCOTFG66111 SCOTT FG
REVOLUTION IN EVOLUTION. /COLLEGE RECRUITMENT/
PERSONNEL JOURNAL, JAN 1966, PP 43-44.

NSCOTJW66112 SCOTT JW
SOCIAL-CLASS FACTORS UNDERLYING THE CIVIL-RIGHTS MOVEMENT.
PHYLON, VOL 27, NO 2, 2ND QUARTER 1966, PP 132-144.

NSEGABD57113 SEGAL BD
RACISM STYMIES UNIONS IN THE SOUTH.
NEW LEADER, VOL 40, NOV 11 1957. PP 14-15 PLUS.

NSEIDJI43115 SEIDMAN JI
UNION RIGHTS AND UNION DUTIES.
HARCOURT, BRACE, AND CO. NEW YORK. 1943. 238 PP.

NSEIDJX50114 SEIDENBERG J   *CORNELL UNIV NYS SCHOOL OFIR
NEGROES IN THE WORK GROUP. HOW 33 BUSINESS AND INDUSTRIAL
 FIRMS OFFERED EQUAL-EMPLOYMENT-OPPORTUNITIES TO ALL.
CORNELL UNIVERSITY, NEW YORK STATE SCHOOL OF INDUSTRIAL
RELATIONS. RESEARCH BULLETIN NO 6. ITHACA, NEW YORK. 1950.
48 PP. ALSO NATIONAL CONFERENCE OF CHRISTIANS AND JEWS.
NEW YORK. 1954. 15 PP.

NSEXTBX53116 SEXTON B
THE INTERVENTION OF THE UNION IN THE PLANT.
JOURNAL OF SOCIAL ISSUES, VOL 9, NO 1, JAN 1953. PP 7-11.

NSEXTPX63117 SEXTON P
NEGRO CAREER EXPECTATIONS.
MERRILL-PALMER QUARTERLY OF BEHAVIOR AND DEVELOPMENT, VOL 9,
NO 4, 1963. PP 303-316.

NSHAFHB59118 SHAFFER HB
NEGRO EMPLOYMENT.
EDITORIAL RESEARCH REPORTS, VOL 2, AUG 1959. PP 575-589.

NSHAFHB65799 SHAFFER HB
NEGROES IN THE NORTH.
EDITORIAL RESEARCH REPORTS, VCL 11, NO 16, OCT 26 1965.
PP 781-797.

NSHARHX62125 SHARP H   SCHNORE LF
THE CHANGING COLOR COMPOSITION OF METROPOLITAN AREAS.
 /DEMOGRAPHY/
LAND ECONOMICS, MAY 1962. PP 169-185.

NSHAUDX63126 SHAUGHNESSY D
A SURVEY OF DISCRIMINATION IN THE BUILDING TRADES INDUSTRY.
 NEW-YORK CITY.
COLUMBIA UNIVERSITY LIBRARY. NEW YORK. AP 1963.

NSHAWBJ50339 SHAW BJ
A STUDY OF FARM MANAGEMENT PRACTICES ON 100 NEGRO FARMS IN
 MACON COUNTY, ALABAMA, 1949.
TUSKEGEE INSTITUTE. THESIS. TUSKEGEE, ALABAMA. 1950. 65 PP.

NSHEPHL65127 SHEPPARD HL
POVERTY AND THE NEGRO.
POVERTY AS A PUBLIC ISSUE. ED BY B B SELIGMAN. THE FREE
PRESS. NEW YORK. 1965. PP 118-138.

NSHEPHL66128 SHEPPARD HL   BELITSKY AH
*UPJOHN INST EMPLOY RESEARCH
THE JOB HUNT. JOB SEEKING BEHAVIOR OF UNEMPLOYED WORKERS IN
 A LOCAL ECONOMY.
JOHNS HOPKINS PRESS. BALTIMORE, MARYLANC. 1966. 270 PP.

NSHEPHL66129 SHEPPARD HL   STRINER HE
*UPJOHN INST EMPLOY RESEARCH
CIVIL-RIGHTS, EMPLOYMENT, AND THE SOCIAL STATUS OF AMERICAN
 NEGROES.
THE W E UPJOHN INSTITUTE FOR EMPLOYMENT RESEARCH. KALAMAZOO,
MICHIGAN. JUNE 1966. 85 PP.

NSHERFP59130 SHERWOOD FP   MARKEY B
*U OF ALA INTER-U CASE PROG
THE MAYOR AND THE FIRE CHIEF. THE FIGHT OVER INTEGRATING THE
 LOS-ANGELES FIRE DEPARTMENT. /CALIFORNIA CASE-STUDY/
UNIVERSITY OF ALABAMA, INTER-UNIVERSITY CASE PROGRAM, CASE
SERIES NO 43. UNIVERSITY OF ALABAMA PRESS. BIRMINGHAM,
ALABAMA. 1959. 24 PP.

NSHIEAR51342 SHIELDS AR
THE INFLUENCE OF TUSKEGEE-INSTITUTE ON THE HEALTH,
 EDUCATIONAL, ECONOMIC, AND POLITICAL ASPECTS OF THE NEGRO
 POPULATION OF MACON COUNTY, ALABAMA.
TUSKEGEE INSTITUTE. THESIS. TUSKEGEE, ALABAMA. 1951. 88 PP.

NSHISBX56538 SHISHKIN B
PREJUDICE COSTS TOO MUCH.
AMERICAN FEDERATIONIST, VOL 63, NO 11, NOV 1956. PP 12-14.

NSHOSAX63131 SHOSTAK A
APPEALS FROM DISCRIMINATION IN FEDERAL EMPLOYMENT. A
 CASE-STUDY.
SOCIAL FORCES, VOL 42, NO 2, CEC 1963. PP 174-178.

NSHOSAX64132 SHOSTAK A
RACE RELATIONS. QUESTIONS AND ANSWERS FOR PERSONNEL MEN.
PERSONNEL ADMINISTRATION, VOL 27, NO 4, JULU-AUG 1964.

NSHUEAX66145 SHUEY A
THE TESTING OF NEGRO INTELLIGENCE.
SOCIAL SCIENCE PRESS. NEW YORK. 1966. 578 PP.

NSIEGAI59718 SIEGEL AI   FEDERMAN P
*APPLIED PSYCHOLOGICAL SERV
EMPLOYMENT EXPERIENCES OF NEGRO PHILADELPHIANS. A

DESCRIPTIVE STUDY OF THE EMPLOYMENT EXPERIENCES,
 PERCEPTIONS, AND ASPIRATIONS OF SELECTED PHILADELPHIA
 WHITES AND NON-WHITES.
APPLIED PSYCHOLOGICAL SERVICES. WAYNE, PENNSYLVANIA. 1959.
43 PP.

NSIEGPM65146 SIEGEL PM
ON THE COST OF BEING A NEGRO. /INCOME EDUCATION/
SOCIOLOGICAL INQUIRY, VOL 35, WINTER 1965. PP 41-57.

NSILBCE62134 SILBERMAN CE
THE CITY AND THE NEGRO.
FORTUNE, MAR 1962. PP 152-153.

NSILBCE63133 SILBERMAN CE
THE BUSINESSMAN AND THE NEGRO. /INDUSTRY/
FORTUNE, VOL 68, NO 3, SEPT 1963. PP 97-99.

NSILBCE64137 SILBERMAN CE
THE ECONOMICS OF THE NEGRO PRCBLEM.
THE NEGRO CHALLENGE TO THE BUSINESS COMMUNITY. ED BY ELI
GINZBURG. MCGRAW HILL. NEW YORK. 1964.

NSILBCE65035 SILBERMAN CE
THE REAL NEWS ABOUT AUTOMATION.
FORTUNE, JAN 1965. PP 124-126, 220-228.

NSILBCE65135 SILBERMAN CE
CRISIS IN BLACK AND WHITE.
RANDOM HOUSE. NEW YORK. 1965.

NSILBCE65136 SILBERMAN CE
THE DEEPENING CRISIS IN METROPOLIS.
JOURNAL OF INTERGROUP RELATIONS, VOL 4, NO 3, SUMMER 1965.
PP 119-131.

NSILBFB59138 SILBERSTEIN FB   SEEMAN M
SOCIAL-MOBILITY AND PREJUDICE.
AMERICAN JOURNAL OF SOCIOLOGY, VOL 65, NO 3, NUV 1959.
PP 258-264.

NSIMUHX50139 SIMON H
THE STRUGGLE FOR JOBS AND FOR NEGRO RIGHTS IN THE TRADE
 UNIONS.
POLITICAL AFFAIRS, FEB 1950. PP 33-48.

NSIMOSM56262 SIMONS SM
DESEGREGATION AND INTEGRATION IN SOCIAL WORK.
JOURNAL OF THE NATIONAL ASSOCIATION OF SOCIAL WORKERS,
VOL 1, NO 4, OCT 1956. PP 20-25.

NSIMPRL65140 SIMPSON RL   NORSWORTHY DR
THE CHANGING OCCUPATIONAL STRUCTURE OF THE SOUTH.
THE SOUTH IN CONTINUITY AND CHANGE. ED BY JOHN C MCKINNEY
AND EDGAR T THOMPSON. DUKE UNIVERSITY PRESS. DURHAM,
NORTH CAROLINA. 1965. PP 198-224.

NSINDAX64141 SINDLER A
CHANGES IN THE CONTEMPORARY SOUTH.
DUKE UNIVERSITY PRESS. DURHAM, NORTH CAROLINA. 1964. 247 PP.

NSINGSL56142 SINGER SL   STEFFLRE B
A NOTE ON RACIAL DIFFERENCES IN JOB VALUES AND DESIRES.
JOURNAL OF SOCIAL PSYCHOLOGY, VOL 43, MAY 1956. PP 333-337.

NSLAIDX61021 SLAIMAN D
DISCRIMINATION AND LOW-INCOMES.
AMERICAN FEDERATIONIST, VOL 68, NO 1, JAN 1961. PP 17-19.

NSMITBF56147 SMITH BF
SOCIAL CHARACTERISTICS OF HIGH SCHOOL SENIORS IN URBAN NEGRO
 HIGH SCHCOLS IN TWO STATES.
JOURNAL OF EDUCATIONAL RESEARCH, VOL 49, NO 7, MAR 1956.
PP 493-503.

NSMITCU56364 SMITH CU
THE DISAPPEARING NEGRO FARMER OF FLORIDA, 1920-1950.
FLORIDA A AND M UNIVERSITY BULLETIN, RESEARCH ISSUE, VOL 9,
NO 3, SEPT 1956. PP 12-18.

NSMITCU60275 SMITH CU
ON BEING A NEGRO IN 1960. /OCCUPATIONAL-STATUS/
THE QUARTERLY REVIEW OF HIGHER EDUCATION AMONG NEGROES,
VOL 28, NO 4, OCT 1960. PP 250-257.

NSMITED53143 SMITH ED
MIGRATION AND ADJUSTMENT EXPERIENCES OF RURAL WORKERS IN
 INDIANAPOLIS. /INDIANA/
UNIVERSITY OF WISCONSIN. PHD THESIS. MADISON, WISCONSIN.
1953.

NSMITHP62144 SMITH HP   ANDERSON M
RACIAL AND FAMILY EXPERIENCE CORRELATES OF MOBILITY
 ASPIRATION.
JOURNAL OF NEGRO EDUCATION, VOL 31, 1962. PP 117-124.

NSMITLT58145 SMITH LT
THE CHANGING NUMBER AND DISTRIBUTION OF THE AGED NEGRO
 POPULATION OF THE UNITED STATES. /DEMOGRAPHY/
PHYLON, VOL 18, NO 4, 4TH QUARTER 1958. PP 339-354.

NSMUTRW57146 SMUTS RW
THE NEGRO COMMUNITY AND THE DEVELOPMENT OF NEGRO POTENTIAL.
JOURNAL OF NEGRO EDUCATION, VOL 26, NO 4, FALL 1957.
PP 456-465.

NSNCCXX65187 SNCC
THE GENERAL CONDITICN OF THE ALABAMA NEGRO.
STUDENT NONVIOLENT COORDINATING COMMITTEE. ATLANTA, GEORGIA.
MAR 1965. 28 PP.

NSOBEIX54178 SOBEL I   *ST LOUIS URBAN LEAGUE
*WASH UNIV DEPT OF IND RELS
THE NEGRO IN THE ST-LOUIS ECONOMY. /MISSOURI/
ST LOUIS URBAN LEAGUE AND WASHINGTON UNIVERSITY, DEPARTMENT
OF INDUSTRIAL RELATIONS. ST LOUIS, MISSOURI. 1954.

NSOLDHX56152 SOLDZ H
PERSONAL AND ON-THE-JOB CHARACTERISTICS RELATED TO NEGRO
 PERCEPTIONS OF DISCRIMINATION.
UNIVERSITY CF ILLINCIS, INSTITUTE OF LABOR AND INDUSTRIAL
RELATIONS. MASTER-S THESIS. CHAMPAIGN, ILLINOIS. 1956.

NSOLZRX61153 SOLZBACHER R
OCCUPATIONAL PRESTIGE IN A NEGRO COMMUNITY.
AMERICAN CATHOLIC SOCIOLOGICAL REVIEW, VOL 22, FALL 1961.
PP 250-257.

NSOSKWX67154 SOSKIN W
RIOTS, GHETTOS AND THE NEGRO REVOLT.

NSOUTCD51166   EMPLOYMENT, RACE AND POVERTY. ED BY ARTHUR M ROSS AND
HERBERT HILL. HARCOURT, BRACE, AND WORLD. NEW YORK. 1967.
PP 205-233.

NSOUTCD51166   SOUTHWIDE CONF DISCR IN HED
DISCRIMINATION IN HIGHER EDUCATION.
SOUTHWIDE CONFERENCE ON DISCRIMINATION IN HIGHER EDUCATION.
SOUTHERN CONFERENCE EDUCATION FUND. NEW ORLEANS, LOUISIANA.
1951. 70 PP.

NSOUTRC45158   SOUTHERN REGIONAL COUNCIL
ECONOMIC VALUE OF THE NEGRO TO THE SOUTH. PAST, PRESENT, AND
POTENTIAL.
SOUTHERN REGIONAL COUNCIL. ATLANTA, GEORGIA. 1945. 12 PP.

NSOUTRC45164   SOUTHERN REGIONAL COUNCIL
THE SOUTH -- AMERICA-S OPPORTUNITY NO 1.
SOUTHERN REGIONAL COUNCIL. ATLANTA, GEORGIA. 1945.

NSOUTRC61160   SOUTHERN REGIONAL COUNCIL
THE FEDERAL EXECUTIVE AND CIVIL-RIGHTS.
SOUTHERN REGIONAL COUNCIL. ATLANTA, GEORGIA. JAN 1961.
48 PP.

NSOUTRC61161   SOUTHERN REGIONAL COUNCIL
HOUSTON -- THE NEGRO AND EMPLOYMENT OPPORTUNITIES IN THE
SOUTH, THE FIRST OF A SERIES OF EMPLOYMENT STUDIES IN
SOUTHERN CITIES. /TEXAS/
SOUTHERN REGIONAL COUNCIL. ATLANTA, GEORGIA. NOV 1961.
22 PP.

NSOUTRC62151   SOUTHERN REGIONAL COUNCIL   ATLANTA COUNCIL ON HUMAN RELS
THE NEGRO AND EMPLOYMENT OPPORTUNITIES IN THE SOUTH.
SOUTHERN REGIONAL COUNCIL, GREATER ATLANTA COUNCIL ON HUMAN
RELATIONS. ATLANTA, GEORGIA. 1962. 21 PP.

NSOUTRC62155   SOUTHERN REGIONAL COUNCIL
ATLANTA -- THE NEGRO AND EMPLOYMENT OPPORTUNITIES IN THE
SOUTH, THE THIRD OF A SERIES OF EMPLOYMENT STUDIES IN
SOUTHERN CITIES. /GEORGIA/
SOUTHERN REGIONAL COUNCIL. ATLANTA, GEORGIA. AP 1962. 21 PP.

NSOUTRC62156   SOUTHERN REGIONAL COUNCIL
CHATTANOOGA -- THE NEGRO AND EMPLOYMENT OPPORTUNITIES IN THE
SOUTH, THE SECOND OF A SERIES OF EMPLOYMENT STUDIES IN
SOUTHERN CITIES. /TENNESSEE/
SOUTHERN REGIONAL COUNCIL. ATLANTA, GEORGIA. FEB 1962.
16 PP.

NSOUTRC62159   SOUTHERN REGIONAL COUNCIL
EXECUTIVE SUPPORT OF CIVIL-RIGHTS.
SOUTHERN REGIONAL COUNCIL. ATLANTA, GEORGIA. MAR 13 1962.
52 PP.

NSOUTRC62165   SOUTHERN REGIONAL COUNCIL
A STUDY OF NEGRO FARMERS IN SOUTH-CAROLINA.
SOUTHERN REGIONAL COUNCIL. ATLANTA, GEORGIA. DEC 1962.
20 PP.

NSOUTRC62300   SOUTHERN REGIONAL COUNCIL.
RACIAL WORK AND NEGRO WASTE IN SOUTHERN EMPLOYMENT.
NEW SOUTH, MAY 1962. 15 PP.

NSOUTRC63157   SOUTHERN REGIONAL COUNCIL
DESEGREGATION IN HIGHER EDUCATION.
SOUTHERN REGIONAL COUNCIL. ATLANTA, GEORGIA. FEB 13 1963.

NSOUTRC63163   SOUTHERN REGIONAL COUNCIL
PLANS-FOR-PROGRESS. ATLANTA SURVEY. /GEORGIA/
SOUTHERN REGIONAL COUNCIL, SPECIAL REPORT. ATLANTA, GEORGIA.
JAN 1963. 15 PP.

NSOUTRC64162   SOUTHERN REGIONAL COUNCIL
LOUISVILLE. /KENTUCKY/
SOUTHERN REGIONAL COUNCIL. ATLANTA, GEORGIA. MAY 1964.
45 PP.

NSOUTRC66150   SOUTHERN REGIONAL COUNCIL
SCHOOL DESEGREGATION IN 1966. THE SLOW UNDOING.
SOUTHERN REGIONAL COUNCIL. ATLANTA, GEORGIA. 1966. 53 PP.

NSOUTRC66524   SOUTHERN REGIONAL COUNCIL
COOPERATIVES, CREDIT UNIONS, AND POOR PEOPLE.
SOUTHERN REGIONAL COUNCIL. ATLANTA, GEORGIA. MAR 1966.
22 PP.

NSOVEMI62168   SOVERN MI
THE NATIONAL-LABOR-RELATIONS-ACT AND RACIAL DISCRIMINATION.
/LEGISLATION/
COLUMBIA LAW REVIEW, VOL 62, AP 1962. PP 563-632.

NSOVEMI63169   SOVERN MI
RACE DISCRIMINATION AND THE NLRA ACT. THE BRAVE NEW WORLD OF
MIRANDA. /LEGISLATION/
NEW YORK UNIVERSITY, CONFERENCE ON LABOR, PROCEEDINGS NO 16.
NEW YORK. 1963. PP 3-18.

NSPENJJ63716   SPENGLER JJ
DEMOGRAPHIC AND ECONOMIC CHANGE IN THE SOUTH, 1940-1960.
CHANGE IN THE CONTEMPORARY SOUTH. ED BY ALLAN P SINDLER.
DUKE UNIVERSITY. DURHAM, NORTH CAROLINA. 1963. 247 PP.

NSTAMRX64171   STAMLER R
ACCULTURATION AND NEGRO BLUE-COLLAR WORKERS.
BLUE-COLLAR WORLD. STUDIES OF THE AMERICAN WORKER. ED BY
ARTHUR SHOSTAK AND WILLIAM GOMBERG. PRENTICE HALL. ENGLEWOOD
CLIFFS, NEW JERSEY. 1964. PP 282-298.

NSTEEDL46173   STEED DL   *N CAROLINA LEAG OF MUNICIP
SOUTHERN CITIES EMPLOYING NEGRO POLICEMEN -- INCLUDING
NORTH-CAROLINA CITIES OVER 15,000 POPULATION.
NORTH CAROLINA LEAGUE OF MUNICIPALITIES. REPORT NO 53.
RALEIGH, NORTH CAROLINA. FEB 1946. 4 PP.

NSTEEEH53174   STEELE EH
JOBS FOR NEGROES. SOME NORTH-SOUTH PLANT STUDIES.
/CASE-STUDY/
SOCIAL FORCES, VOL 32, 1953. PP 152-162

NSTEEHG54176   STEELER HG   *CONN COMM ON CIVIL RIGHTS
TRAINING OF NEGROES IN THE SKILLED-TRADES.
CONNECTICUT COMMISSION ON CIVIL RIGHTS. HARTFORD,
CONNECTICUT. 1954. 62 PP.

NSTEIBX64300   STEIN B
INTRODUCTION. THE STRUGGLE FOR EQUALITY AND ITS IMPACT ON
INDUSTRIAL-RELATIONS.
NEW YORK UNIVERSITY, SEVENTEENTH ANNUAL CONFERENCE ON LABOR.
NEW YORK. 1964. PP 95-105.

NSTERRX43179   STERNER R
THE NEGRO-S SHARE.
HARPER. NEW YORK. 1943.

NSTETDX63154   STETSON D
MORE SALARIED POSITIONS ARE OPENED TO NEGROES BY BUSINESS
AND INDUSTRY HERE. /NEW-YORK/
NEW YORK TIMES, NOV 12 1963. 2 PP. ALSO NEW YORK AMERICAN
JEWISH COMMITTEE, INSTITUTE OF HUMAN RELATIONS. NEW YORK.

NSTEVHR64177   STEVENS HR
ECONOMIC STRUCTURE OF THE HARLEM COMMUNITY. /NEW-YORK/
HARLEM -- A COMMUNITY IN TRANSITION. ED BY JOHN H CLARKE.
THE CITADEL PRESS. NEW YORK. 1964. PP 105-116.

NSTOKMS64180   STOKES MS
A BRIEF SURVEY OF HIGHER EDUCATION FOR NEGROES.
SOCIAL STUDIES, VOL 55, NO 6, NOV 1964. PP 214-221.

NSTRAGX65182   STRAUSS G   INGERMAN S
PUBLIC POLICY AND DISCRIMINATION IN APPRENTICESHIP.
THE HASTINGS LAW JOURNAL. VOL 16, NO 3, FEB 1965. PP 285-
331. ALSO UNIVERSITY OF CALIFORNIA, INSTITUTE OF INDUSTRIAL
RELATIONS. REPRINT NO 260. BERKELEY, CALIFORNIA. 1965.

NSTRAGX67181   STRAUSS G
HOW MANAGEMENT VIEWS ITS RACE-RELATIONS RESPONSIBILITIES.
EMPLOYMENT, RACE AND POVERTY. ED BY ARTHUR M ROSS AND
HERBERT HILL. HARCOURT, BRACE, AND WORLD. NEW YORK. 1967.
PP 261-289.

NSTREGX41462   STREATOR G
SO THE NEGROES WANT WORK. /UNION/
COMMONWEAL, VOL 34, NO 18, AUG 22 1941. PP 414-416.

NSTREGX45463   STREATOR G
NOTES ON THE CONDITIONS OF NEGROES. /EDUCATION
DISCRIMINATION/
COMMONWEAL, VOL 41, NO 18, FEB 16 1945. PP 446-448.

NSTREJH57184   STREET JH
THE NEW REVOLUTION IN THE COTTON ECONOMY.
UNIVERSITY OF NORTH CAROLINA PRESS. CHAPEL HILL, NORTH
CAROLINA. 1957.

NSTROEK52186   STRONG EK
INTERESTS OF NEGROES AND WHITES.
JOURNAL OF SOCIAL PSYCHOLOGY, VOL 35, 1952. PP 139-150.

NSTROEK56185   STRONG EK
DEVELOPMENTS IN THE NEGRO-LABOR ALLIANCE. /UNION/
POLITICAL AFFAIRS, FEB 1956. PP 35-52.

NSTROFL64074   STRODTBECK FL
THE POVERTY-DEPENDENCY SYNDROME OF THE ADC FEMALE-BASED
NEGRO FAMILY.
AMERICAN JOURNAL OF ORTHOPSYCHIATRY, VOL 34, MAR 1964.
PP 216-217.

NSTUDOT64188   STUDIES ON THE LEFT
CIVIL-RIGHTS AND THE NORTHERN GHETTO.
STUDIES ON THE LEFT, VOL 4, NO 3, SUMMER 1964. PP 3-15.

NSUCHEA58189   SUCHMAN EA   *ANTI-DEFAMATION LEAGUE
DESEGREGATION. SOME PROPOSITIONS AND RESEARCH SUGGESTIONS.
ANTI-DEFAMATION LEAGUE. NEW YORK. 1958.

NSULLDF64190   SULLIVAN DF
THE CIVIL-RIGHTS PROGRAMS OF THE KENNEDY ADMINISTRATION.
UNIVERSITY OF OKLAHOMA. DISSERTATION. NORMAN, OKLAHOMA.
1964.

NSURVGX47191   SURVEY GRAPHIC
SEGREGATION. A COLOR PATTERN FROM THE PAST -- OUR STRUGGLE
TO WIPE IT OUT.
SURVEY ASSOCIATES, NEW YORK. 1947. 128 PP.

NSUSSMB59192   SUSSMAN MB   WHITE CR
HOUGH, CLEVELAND, OHIO -- A STUDY OF SOCIAL LIFE AND CHANGE.
WESTERN RESERVE UNIVERSITY PRESS. CLEVELAND, OHIO. 1959.

NSUTIAX65343   SUTIN A
THE EXPERIENCE OF STATE FAIR-EMPLOYMENT COMMISSIONS. A
COMPARATIVE STUDY.
VANDERBILT LAW REVIEW, VOL 18, 1965. PP 965-1046.

NTAEUIB58363   TAEUBER IB
MIGRATION, MOBILITY, AND THE ASSIMILATION OF THE NEGRO.
POPULATION REFERENCE BUREAU, INC, POPULATION BULLETIN,
VOL 14, NO 7, NOV 1958. PP 121-151.

NTAEUKE63195   TAEUBER KE   TAEUBER AF
IS THE NEGRO AN IMMIGRANT GROUP.
INTEGRATED EDUCATION, JUNE 1963. PP 25-28.

NTAEUKE64196   TAEUBER KE   TAEUBER AF
THE NEGRO AS AN IMMIGRANT GROUP. RECENT TRENDS IN RACIAL AND
ETHNIC SEGREGATION IN CHICAGO. /ILLINOIS/
AMERICAN JOURNAL OF SOCIOLOGY, VOL 69, NO 4, JAN 1964.
PP 374-382.

NTAEUKE65194   TAEUBER KE   TAUEBER AF
THE CHANGING CHARACTER OF NEGRO MIGRATION. /DEMOGRAPHY/
AMERICAN JOURNAL OF SOCIOLOGY, VOL 70, JAN 1965. PP 429-441.

NTAEUKE65197   TAEUBER KE   TAEUBER AF
NEGROES IN CITIES. /DEMOGRAPHY SEGREGATION/
ALDINE. CHICAGO, ILLINOIS. 1965.

NTAEUKE65198   TAEUBER KE   TAEUBER AF
THE NEGRO POPULATION IN THE UNITED STATES. /DEMOGRAPHY/
THE AMERICAN NEGRO REFERENCE BOOK. PRENTICE-HALL. ENGLEWOOD
CLIFFS, NEW JERSEY. 1965.

NTAFTPX64158   TAFT P
ORGANIZED LABOR IN AMERICAN HISTORY. /UNION/
HARPER AND BROTHERS. NEW YORK. 1964. CHAPTER 50, PP 664-681.

NTANNAX40199   TANNEYHILL A   *NATIONAL URBAN LEAGUE
VOCATIONAL GUIDANCE BIBLIOGRAPHY.
NATIONAL URBAN LEAGUE. NEW YORK. 9TH ED, 1940.

NTAYLCC58411   TAYLOR CC   BURCH TA
PERSONAL AND ENVIRONMENTAL OBSTACLES TO PRODUCTION
ADJUSTMENTS ON SOUTH-CAROLINA PIEDMONT AREA FARMS.
CLEMSON AGRICULTURAL COLLEGE. CLEMSON, SOUTH CAROLINA.
DEC 1958. 36 PP.

NTEMPLQ65200   TEMPLE LAW QUARTERLY
RACIAL DISCRIMINATION IN UNIONS.

TEMPLE LAW CUARTERLY, VOL 38, SPRING 1965. P 311.

NTENHWP65201   TENHOUTEN WP
SOCIALIZATICN, RACE AND THE AMERICAN HIGH SCHOOL.
    /EDUCATION/
MICHIGAN STATE UNIVERSITY. PHC DISSERTATION. LANSING,
MICHIGAN. 1965.

NTHOMCH43160   THOMPSON CH
EDITORIAL COMMENT. FEPC HEARINGS REDUCE RACE PROBLEM TO
    LOWEST TERMS -- EQUAL-ECONOMIC-OPPORTUNITY.
JOURNAL OF NEGRO EDUCATION, VOL 12, NO 4, FALL 1943.
PP 585-588.

NTHOMDC58204   THOMPSON DC
CAREER PATTERNS OF TEACHERS IN NEGRO COLLEGES.
SOCIAL FORCES, VOL 36, MAR 1958. PP 270-276.

NTHOMDC63713   THOMPSON DC
THE NEGRO LEADERSHIP CLASS.
PRENTICE-HALL. ENGLEWOOD CLIFFS, NEW JERSEY. 1963. 174 PP.

NTHOMHX62205   THOMPSON H
ATLANTA-S SEGREGATEC APPROACH TO INTEGRATED EMPLOYMENT.
    /GEORGIA/
PUBLIC PERSCNNEL REVIEW, VOL 23, AP 1962. PP 117-121.

NTHO4JA46202   THOMAS JA
NEGRO WORKER LIFTS HIS SIGHTS. /ASPIRATIONS/
OPPORTUNITY, VOL 24, AP 1946. PP 54-55.

NTHOMPX43203   THOMAS PX   *NATIONAL URBAN LEAGUE
DISCRIMINATION AGAINST NEGROES.
NATIONAL URBAN LEAGUE. NEW YORK. OCT 1943.

NTHOMRJ54159   THOMAS RJ
AN EMPIRICAL STUDY OF HIGH SCHOOL DROPOUTS IN REGARD TO TEN
    POSSIBLY RELATED FACTORS.
JOURNAL OF EDUCATIONAL SOCIOLCGY, VOL 28, SEPT 1954.
PP 11-18.

NTHURLC67571   THUROW LC
EMPLOYMENT GAINS ANC THE DETERMINANTS OF THE OCCUPATIONAL
    DISTRIBUTION OF NEGROES.
UNIVERSITY OF WISCONSIN, CONFERENCE ON THE EDUCATION AND
    TRAINING OF RACIAL MINORITIES. MADISON, WISCONSIN. MAY 12,
    1967. 23 PP.

NTILLJA61161   TILLMAN JA
THE QUEST FOR IDENTITY AND STATUS. FACETS OF THE
    DESEGREGATION PROCESS IN THE UPPER MIDWEST.
    /ECONOMIC-STATUS/
PHYLON, SUMMER 1961. PP 329-339.

NTOBIJX65206   TOBIN J
ON IMPROVING THE ECCNOMIC STATUS OF THE NEGRO.
DAEDALUS, VOL 94, NO 4, FALL 1965. PP 878-898.

NTOWNWS45162   TOWNSEND WS
FULL EMPLOYMENT AND THE NEGRO WORKER.
JOURNAL OF NEGRO EDUCATION, VOL 14, NO 1, WINTER 1945.
PP 6-10.

NTRAIAD66580   TRAINING AND DEVELOP JOURNAL
PROGRESS IN WATTS -- THE LOS-ANGELES ASTD COMMUNITY AFFAIRS
    PROGRAM. /CALIFORNIA/
TRAINING AND DEVELOPMENT JOURNAL, VOL 20, DEC 1966.
PP 42-44.

NTREWHL56207   TREWHITT HL
SOUTHERN UNIONS AND THE INTEGRATION ISSUE.
THE REPORTER, OCT 4 1956. PP 25-28.

NTRUEDL60208   TRUEBLOOD DL
THE ROLE OF THE COUNSELOR IN THE GUIDANCE OF NEGRO STUDENTS.
HARVARD EDUCATIONAL REVIEW, VOL 30, NO 3, SUMMER 1960.
PP 252-269.

NTUCKSX66209   TUCKER S
THE ROLE OF CIVIL-RIGHTS ORGANIZATIONS. A MARSHALL PLAN
    APPROACH.
BOSTON COLLEGE, INDUSTRIAL AND COMMERCIAL LAW REVIEW, VOL 7,
    NO 3, SPRING 1966. PP 617-624.

NTUMIMM63065   TUMIN MM ED $*NTI-DEFAMATION LEAGUE
RACE AND INTELLIGENCE. AN EVALUATION.
ANTI-DEFAMATION LEAGUE OF B-NAI B-RITH. NEW YORK. 1963.

NTURBGX52210   TURBEVILLE G
THE NEGRO POPULATION IN DULUTH MINNESOTA, 1950.
    /DEMOGRAPHY/
SOCIOLOGY AND SOCIAL RESEARCH, VOL 36, MAR-AP 1952.
PP 231-238.

NTURNBA57165   TURNER BA
OCCUPATIONAL CHOICES OF NEGRO HIGH SCHOOL SENIORS IN TEXAS.
TEXAS SOUTHERN UNIVERSITY. HOUSTON, TEXAS. 1957.

NTURNRH49211   TURNER RH
THE EXPECTED-CASES METHOD APPLIED TO THE NON-WHITE MALE
    LABOR-FORCE.
AMERICAN JOURNAL OF SOCIOLOGY, VOL 55, NO 2, SEPT 1949.
PP 147-156.

NTURNRH49215   TURNER RH
THE NON-WHITE MALE IN THE LABOR-FORCE.
AMERICAN JOURNAL OF SOCIOLOGY, VOL 54, NO 4, JAN 1949.
PP 356-362.

NTURNRH51217   TURNER RH
THE RELATIVE POSITION OF THE NEGRO MALE IN THE LABOR-FORCE
    OF LARGE AMERICAN CITIES.
AMERICAN SOCIOLOGICAL REVIEW, VOL 16, NO 4, AUG 1951.
PP 524-529.

NTURNRH52212   TURNER RH
FOCI OF DISCRIMINATION IN THE EMPLOYMENT OF NONWHITES.
AMERICAN JOURNAL OF SOCIOLOGY, VOL 58, NO 3, NOV 1952.
PP 247-256.

NTURNRH53213   TURNER RH
NEGRO JOB STATUS AND EDUCATION.
SOCIAL FORCES, VOL 32, 1953. PP 45-52.

NTURNRH54216   TURNER RH
OCCUPATIONAL PATTERNS OF INEQUALITY.
AMERICAN JOURNAL OF SOCIOLOGY, VOL 59, NO 5, MAR 1954.
AP 437-447.

NTUSKIX51218   TUSKEGEE INSTITUTE

LAND TENURE IN THE SOUTHERN REGION. PROCEEDINGS OF
    PROFESSIONAL AGRICULTURAL WCRKERS TENTH ANNUAL CONFERENCE.
TUSKEGEE INSTITUTE. TUSKEGEE, ALABAMA. 1951.

NTUSKIX55220   TUSKEGEE INSTITUTE
A SELECTED LIST OF REFERENCES RELATING TO DISCRIMINATION AND
    SEGREGATION IN EDUCATION, 1949 TO JUNE 1955.
TUSKEGEE INSTITUTE, DEPARTMENT OF RECORDS AND RESEARCH,
    RECORDS AND RESEARCH PAMPHLET NO 6. TUSKEGEE, ALABAMA.
    JULY 1955. 9 PP.

NTUSKIX64219   TUSKEGEE INSTITUTE
RACE-RELATIONS IN THE SOUTH, 1963.
TUSKEGEE INSTITUTE. TUSKEGEE, ALABAMA. MAR 12 1964. 42 PP.

NTUSKIX65765   TUSKEGEE INSTITUTE
EXPERIMENTAL FEATURES OF THE TUSKEGEE-INSTITUTE RETRAINING
    PROJECT.
TUSKEGEE INSTITUTE. TUSKEGEE, ALABAMA. VOL 2, OCT 25 1965.
    280 PP.

NTUSKIX65766   TUSKEGEE INSTITUTE
DEMONSTRATIONAL FEATURES OF THE TUSKEGEE-INSTITUTE.
    RETRAINING PROJECT.
TUSKEGEE INSTITUTE, TUSKEGEE, ALABAMA. VOL 1, SEPT 1 1965.
    144 PP.

NTYLEGX62222   TYLER G
THE TRUTH ABOUT THE ILGWU. /UNION/
NEW POLITICS, VOL 2, FALL 1962. PP 6-17.

NTYLEGX63539   TYLER G
THE NEW CHALLENGE TC LIBERALISM.
AMERICAN FEDERATIONIST, VOL 70, NO 11, NOV 1963. PP 1-5.

NTYLEGX67221   TYLER G
THE NEW NEGRO. /UNION/
THE LABOR REVOLUTION. TRADE UNION IN A NEW AMERICA. THE
    VIKING PRESS. NEW YORK. 1967. PP 179-197.

NULMEAX65223   ULMER A
EVERYBODY SEEMED TO LIKE CHARLIE. /DISCRIMINATION/
NEW SOUTH, VOL 20, NO 7,8, JULY, 1965.

NULMXAX66712   ULMER A
POVERTY. /SOUTH ANTI-POVERTY/
NEW SOUTH, VOL 21, NO 1, WINTER 1966. PP 107-115.

NUNITNX63224   UNITED NATIONS
ECONOMIC AND SOCIAL CONSEQUENCES OF RACIAL DISCRIMINATORY
    PRACTICES.
UNITED NATICNS. NEW YORK. 1963.

NUSBURC62225   US BUREAU OF THE CENSUS
COLOR, RACE AND TENURE OF FARM OPERATORS.
US CENSUS OF AGRICULTURE. 1959. US DEPARTMENT OF COMMERCE,
    BUREAU OF THE CENSUS. GPO. WASHINGTON, DC. 1962.

NUSCISC63228   US CIVIL SERVICE COMMISSION
STUDY OF MINORITY-GROUP EMPLOYMENT IN THE
    FEDERAL-GOVERNMENT, 1963.
US CIVIL SERVICE COMMISSION. GPO. WASHINGTON, DC. JUNE 1963.
    20 PP.

NUSCISC65229   US CIVIL SERVICE COMMISSION
STUDY OF MINORITY-GROUP EMPLOYMENT IN THE FEDERAL
    GOVERNMENT, 1965.
US CIVIL SERVICE COMMISSION. GPO. WASHINGTON, DC. 1965.
    193 PP.

NUSCOMC60302   US COMMISSION ON CIVIL RIGHTS
EQUAL PROTECTICN OF THE LAWS IN PUBLIC HIGHER EDUCATION.
US COMMISSION ON CIVIL RIGHTS. GPO. WASHINGTON, DC. 1960.
    326 PP.

NUSCOMC61231   US COMMISSION ON CIVIL RIGHTS
1961 COMMISSION ON CIVIL-RIGHTS REPORT BOOK 3. EMPLOYMENT.
US COMMISSION ON CIVIL RIGHTS. GPO. WASHINGTON, DC. 1961.
    246 PP.

NUSCOMC65232   US COMMISSION ON CIVIL RIGHTS
EQUAL-OPPORTUNITY IN FARM PROGRAMS -- AN APPRAISAL OF
    SERVICES RENDERED BY AGENCIES OF THE UNITED STATES
    DEPARTMENT OF AGRICULTURE.
US COMMISSION ON CIVIL RIGHTS. GPO. WASHINGTON, DC. 1965.
    36 PP.

NUSCOMC67149   US COMMISSION ON CIVIL RIGHTS
THE VOICE OF THE GHETTO. A REPORT ON TWO BOSTON
    NEIGHBORHOOD MEETINGS. /MASSACHUSETTS/
US COMMISSION ON CIVIL RIGHTS, MASSACHUSETTS STATE ADVISORY
    COMMITTEE. WASHINGTON, DC. 1967. 53 PP.

NUSCONM65233   US CONFERENCE OF MAYORS
CHANGING EMPLOYMENT PRACTICES IN THE CONSTRUCTION INDUSTRY.
    EXPERIENCE REPORT 102.
US CONFERENCE OF MAYORS, COMMUNITY RELATIONS SERVICE.
    WASHINGTON, DC. SEPT 1965. 10 PP.

NUSCONM66234   US CONFERENCE OF MAYORS
CITY CONTRACTORS AND FAIR-EMPLOYMENT. EXPERIENCE REPORT 103.
US CONFERENCE OF MAYORS, COMMUNITY RELATIONS SERVICE.
    WASHINGTON, DC. AP 1966. 8 PP.

NUSCONM66235   US CONFERENCE OF MAYORS
PUBLIC EMPLOYMENT IN SAVANNAH, GEORGIA. EXPERIENCE REPORT
    104.
US CONFERENCE OF MAYORS, COMMUNITY RELATIONS SERVICE.
    WASHINGTON, DC. AP 1966. 4 PP.

NUSDCOM64194   US DEPARTMENT OF COMMERCE
NEGRO-WHITE DIFFERENTIALS IN GEOGRAPHIC MOBILITY, 1964,
    1965. /DEMOGRAPHY/
US DEPARTMENT OF COMMERCE, AREA REDEVELOPMENT
    ADMINISTRATION. GPO. WASHINGTON, DC. 1964, 1965.

NUSDOEF55195   US DEPARTMENT OF DEFENSE
INTEGRATION IN THE ARMED SERVICES. A PROGRESS REPORT.
    /MILITARY/
US DEPARTMENT OF DEFENSE, OFFICE OF THE ASSISTANT SECRETARY
    OF DEFENSE FOR MANPOWER AND PERSONNEL. GPO. WASHINGTON, DC.
    1955.

NUSDOEF59239   US DEPARTMENT OF DEFENSE
UTILIZATION OF NEGRC MANPOWER.
US DEPARTMENT OF DEFENSE. GPO. WASHINGTON, DC. 1959.

NUSDOEF62240   US DEPARTMENT OF DEFENSE
INTEGRATION AND THE NEGRO OFFICER IN THE ARMED FORCES OF THE
    UNITED STATES OF AMERICA. /MILITARY/

US DEPARTMENT OF DEFENSE, OFFICE OF THE ASSISTANT SECRETARY. GPO. WASHINGTON, DC. MAR 1962.

NUSDHEW58241 US DEPT OF HEALTH EC WELFARE
SOCIAL SECURITY PROGRAM STATISTICS RELATING TO NONWHITE FAMILIES AND CHILDREN.
US DEPARTMENT OF HEALTH, EDUCATION AND WELFARE, SOCIAL SECURITY ADMINISTRATION. NOTE NO 29. GPO. WASHINGTON, DC. SEPT 8 1958.

NUSDLABND256 US DEPARTMENT OF LABOR
THE NEGRO IN THE WEST, SOME FACTS RELATING TO SOCIAL AND ECONOMIC CONDITIONS. NO 1. THE NEGRO WORKER.
US DEPARTMENT OF LABOR, BUREAU OF LABOR STATISTICS. SAN FRANCISCO, CALIFORNIA. ND. 17 PP.

NUSDLAB40834 US DEPARTMENT OF LABOR
OCCUPATIONAL DISTRIBUTION OF EMPLOYED COLORED WORKERS OF MARYLAND.
US DEPARTMENT OF ALBOR, MONTHLY LABOR REVIEW, VOL 50, NO 2, FEB 1940. PP 350-351.

NUSDLAB41244 US DEPARTMENT OF LABOR
EMPLOYER SPECIFICATIONS FOR DEFENSE WORKERS.
US DEPARTMENT OF LABOR, EMPLOYMENT SECURITY REVIEW, VOL 8, NO 4, AP 1941. PP 17-19.

NUSDLAB41253 US DEPARTMENT OF LABOR
NEGRO WORKERS AND THE NATIONAL DEFENSE PROGRAM.
US DEPARTMENT OF LABOR, BUREAU OF EMPLOYMENT SECURITY. GPO. WASHINGTON, DC. 1941.

NUSDLAB41816 US DEPARTMENT OF LABOR
EMPLOYMENT PROBLEMS OF NEGROES IN MICHIGAN.
US DEPARTMENT OF LABOR, MONTHLY LABOR REVIEW, VOL 52, NO 2, FEB 1941. PP 350-354.

NUSDLAB41817 US DEPARTMENT OF LABOR
EQUAL-PAY FOR WHITE AND NEGRO TEACHERS.
/OCCUPATIONS/
US DEPARTMENT OF LABOR, MONTHLY LABOR REVIEW, VOL 52, NO 2, FEB 1941. P 350.

NUSDLAB41821 US DEPARTMENT OF LABOR
INCREASED INDUSTRIAL PLACEMENTS OF WORKERS.
US DEPARTMENT OF LABOR, MONTHLY LABOR REVIEW, VOL 53, NO 4, OCT 1941. PP 925-926.

NUSDLAB41829 US DEPARTMENT OF LABOR
NEGRO PARTICIPATION IN DEFENSE WORK.
US DEPARTMENT OF LABOR, MONTHLY LABOR REVIEW, JUNE 1941. PP 1388-1390.

NUSDLAB41832 US DEPARTMENT OF LABOR
NEW TRAINING PLAN FOR NEGROES.
US DEPARTMENT OF LABOR, MONTHLY LABOR REVIEW, VOL 53, NO 3, SEPT 1941. PP 620-621.

NUSDLAB42811 US DEPARTMENT OF LABOR
BI-RACIAL COOPERATION IN PLACEMENT OF NEGROES.
US DEPARTMENT OF LABOR, MONTHLY LABOR REVIEW, VOL 55, NO 2, AUG 1942. PP 231-234.

NUSDLAB43818 US DEPARTMENT OF LABOR
EMPLOYMENT OF NEGROES BY FEDERAL-GOVERNMENT.
US DEPARTMENT OF LABOR, MONTHLY LABOR REVIEW, VOL 56, NO 5, MAY 1943. PP 889-891.

NUSDLAB43827 US DEPARTMENT OF LABOR
NEGRO EMPLOYMENT IN AIRPLANE PLANTS. /INDUSTRY/
US DEPARTMENT OF LABOR, MONTHLY LABOR REVIEW, VOL 56, NO 5, MAY 1943. PP 888-889.

NUSDLAB43833 US DEPARTMENT OF LABOR
NON-DISCRIMINATION CLAUSE IN GOVERNMENT CONTRACTS IS MANDATORY.
US DEPARTMENT OF LABOR, MONTHLY LABOR REVIEW, VOL 57, NO 6, DEC 1943. P 1123.

NUSDLAB43836 US DEPARTMENT OF LABOR
OCCUPATIONAL STATUS OF NEGRO RAILROAD WORKERS.
US DEPARTMENT OF LABOR, MONTHLY LABOR REVIEW, VOL 56, NO 3, MAR 1943. PP 484-485.

NUSDLAB43845 US DEPARTMENT OF LABOR
TRAINING NEGROES FOR WAR WORK.
US DEPARTMENT OF LABOR, MONTHLY LABOR REVIEW, VOL 57, NO 5, NOV 1943. PP 952-953.

NUSDLAB43848 US DEPARTMENT OF LABOR
WAR LABOR BOARD DECISION ON WAGES OF NEGROES.
US DEPARTMENT OF LABOR, MONTHLY LABOR REVIEW, VOL 57, NO 1, JULY 1943. PP 31-32.

NUSDLAB44151 US DEPARTMENT OF LABOR
SEGREGATION IN THE ARMED FORCES. /MILITARY/
US DEPARTMENT OF LABOR, SOCIAL SERVICE REVIEW, VOL 18, NO 3, SEPT 1944. PP 369-371.

NUSDLAB44835 US DEPARTMENT OF LABOR
OCCUPATIONAL DISTRIBUTION OF NEGROES IN 1940.
US DEPARTMENT OF LABOR, MONTHLY LABOR REVIEW, VOL 58, NO 4, AP 1944. PP 739.

NUSDLAB44841 US DEPARTMENT OF LABOR
SENIORITY IN THE AKRON RUBBER INDUSTRY.
US DEPARTMENT OF LABOR, MONTHLY LABOR REVIEW, VOL 59, NO 4, OCT 1944. PP 788-796.

NUSDLAB44842 US DEPARTMENT OF LABOR
SENIORITY IN THE AUTOMOBILE INDUSTRY.
US DEPARTMENT OF LABOR, MONTHLY LABOR REVIEW, VOL 59, NO 3, SEPT 1944. PP 463-474.

NUSDLAB45820 US DEPARTMENT OF LABOR
IMPROVED CONDITIONS FOR NEGROES IN LOUISVILLE. /KENTUCKY/
US DEPARTMENT OF LABOR, MONTHLY LABOR REVIEW, VOL 61, NO 4, OCT 1945. PP 727-728.

NUSDLAB45825 US DEPARTMENT OF LABOR
LEGISLATION AGAINST DISCRIMINATION IN EMPLOYMENT.
US DEPARTMENT OF LABOR, MONTHLY LABOR REVIEW, VOL 61, NO 5, NOV 1945. PP 990-991.

NUSDLAB46824 US DEPARTMENT OF LABOR
LABOR SUPPLY IN THE SOUTH.
US DEPARTMENT OF LABOR, MONTHLY LABOR REVIEW, VOL 63, NO 4, OCT 1946 PP 484-494.

NUSDLAB46839 US DEPARTMENT OF LABOR
READJUSTMENTS OF VETERANS TO CIVILIAN LIFE.
US DEPARTMENT OF LABOR, MONTHLY LABOR REVIEW, VOL 63, NO 5, NOV 1946. PP 712-720.

NUSDLAB46843 US DEPARTMENT OF LABOR
SIX MONTHS OPERATION OF NEW-YORK LAW AGAINST DISCRIMINATION.
US DEPARTMENT OF LABOR, MONTHLY LABOR REVIEW, VOL 62, NO 4, AP 1946. PP 593-594.

NUSDLAB47810 US DEPARTMENT OF LABOR
ANTI-DISCRIMINATION LEGISLATION IN 1947.
US DEPARTMENT OF LABOR, MONTHLY LABOR REVIEW, VOL 65, NO 2, AUG 1947. PP 198-199.

NUSDLAB48149 US DEPARTMENT OF LABOR
ANTI-DISCRIMINATION LEGISLATION.
US DEPARTMENT OF LABOR, SOCIAL SERVICE REVIEW, VOL 22, NO 1, MAR 1948. P 87.

NUSDLAB49831 US DEPARTMENT OF LABOR
NEGROES IN NEW-YORK CITY. OCCUPATIONAL DISTRIBUTION.
US DEPARTMENT OF LABOR, MONTHLU LABOR REVIEW, VOL 68, NO 1, JAN 1949. PP 57.

NUSDLAB49847 US DEPARTMENT OF LABOR
VOCATIONAL EDUCATION FOR NEGRO YOUTH IN TEXAS.
US DEPARTMENT OF LABOR, MONTHLY LABOR REVIEW, VOL 68, NO 5, MAY 1949. PP 544-545.

NUSDLAB52148 US DEPARTMENT OF LABOR
A LABOR UNIT FOR NEGRO RIGHTS.
US DEPARTMENT OF LABOR, SOCIAL SERVICE REVIEW, VOL 26, NO 2, MAR 1952. PP 228-229.

NUSDLAB54822 US DEPARTMENT OF LABOR
INTERNATIONAL-HARVESTER-S NON-DISCRIMINATION POLICY.
/CASE-STUDY/
US DEPARTMENT OF LABOR, MONTHLY LABOR REVIEW, VOL 77, NO 1, JAN 1954. PP 16-23.

NUSDLAB55828 US DEPARTMENT OF LABOR
NEGRO EMPLOYMENT IN THREE COMPANIES IN THE NEW-ORLEANS AREA.
/CASE-STUDY LOUISIANA/
US DEPARTMENT OF LABOR, MONTHLY LABOR REVIEW, VOL 78, SEPT 1955. PP 1020-1023.

NUSDLAB57250 US DEPARTMENT OF LABOR
THEY ARE AMERICA, A REPORT TO THE AMERICAN PEOPLE.
US DEPARTMENT OF LABOR. GPO. WASHINGTON, DC. 1957. 83 PP.

NUSDLAB58844 US DEPARTMENT OF LABOR
TWO STATE REPORT ON JOB DISCRIMINATION. /NEW-YORK NEW-JERSEY/
US DEPARTMENT OF LABOR, MONTHLY LABOR REVIEW, VOL 81, NO 10, OCT 1958. PP 1125-1130.

NUSDLAB60249 US DEPARTMENT OF LABOR
THE NEGRO WAGE-EARNER AND APPRENTICESHIP TRAINING PROGRAMS.
US DEPARTMENT OF LABOR. GPO. WASHINGTON, DC. 1960.

NUSDLAB60830 US DEPARTMENT OF LABOR
NEGROES IN APPRENTICESHIPS, NEW-YORK STATE.
US DEPARTMENT OF LABOR, MONTHLY LABOR REVIEW, VOL 83, NO 9, SEPT 1960. PP 952-957.

NUSDLAB61838 US DEPARTMENT OF LABOR
PLAN FOR EQUAL-JOB-OPPORTUNITY AT LOCKHEED-AIRCRAFT-CORP.
/INDUSTRY CASE-STUDY/
US DEPARTMENT OF LABOR, MONTHLY LABOR REVIEW, VOL 84, NO 7, JULY 1961. PP 748-749.

NUSDLAB62242 US DEPARTMENT OF LABOR
CONFERENCE ON PROBLEMS IN EMPLOYMENT CONFRONTING NEGROES IN NEW-JERSEY, OCTOBER 18 1962.
US DEPARTMENT OF LABOR, ADDRESS NO USDL-5443. GPO. WASHINGTON, DC. OCT 19 1962. 11 PP.

NUSDLAB62243 US DEPARTMENT OF LABOR
THE ECONOMIC SITUATION OF NEGROES IN THE UNITED STATES.
US DEPARTMENT OF LABOR. BULLETIN S-3. GPO. WASHINGTON, DC. OCT 1960. REVISED 1962. 41 PP.

NUSDLAB62840 US DEPARTMENT OF LABOR
REPORT BY PRESIDENT-S-COMMITTEE-ON-EQUAL-OPPORTUNITY.
US DEPARTMENT OF LABOR, MONTHLY LABOR REVIEW, VOL 85, NO 6, JUNE 1962. PP 652-654.

NUSDLAB63198 US DEPARTMENT OF LABOR
IMPACT OF OFFICE AUTOMATION IN THE INTERNAL REVENUE SERVICE. A STUDY OF THE MANPOWER IMPLICATIONS DURING THE FIRST STAGES OF THE CHANGEOVER. /ECONOMIC-STATUS/
US DEPARTMENT OF LABOR, BUREAU OF LABOR STATISTICS, BULLETIN NO 1364. GPO. WASHINGTON, DC. JULY 1963.

NUSDLAB63252 US DEPARTMENT OF LABOR
AMERICA IS FOR EVERYBODY.
US DEPARTMENT OF LABOR, BUREAU OF EMPLOYMENT SECURITY. GPO. WASHINGTON, DC. 1963. 19 PP.

NUSDLAB63260 US DEPARTMENT OF LABOR
EMPLOYMENT IN METROPOLITAN WASHINGTON. /WASHINGTON-DC/
US DEPARTMENT OF LABOR, EMPLOYMENT SERVICE FOR THE DISTRICT OF COLUMBIA. GPO. WASHINGTON, DC. JULY 1963. 39 PP.

NUSDLAB63301 US DEPARTMENT OF LABOR
SECRETARY-S CONFERENCE WITH COLLEGE PRESIDENTS AND EXECUTIVES. /EDUCATION EMPLOYMENT/
HOWARD UNIVERSITY. WASHINGTON, DC. JAN 1963. 261 PP.

NUSDLAB63823 US DEPARTMENT OF LABOR
LABOR MONTH IN REVIEW, NEGRO UNEMPLOYMENT.
US DEPARTMENT OF LABOR, MONTHLY LABOR REVIEW, VOL 86, SEPT 1963. PP III-IV.

NUSDLAB63846 US DEPARTMENT OF LABOR
UNION PROGRAM FOR ELIMINATING DISCRIMINATION.
US DEPARTMENT OF LABOR, MONTHLY LABOR REVIEW, VOL 86, NO 1, JAN 1963. PP 58-59.

NUSDLAB64147 US DEPARTMENT OF LABOR
THE CIVIL-RIGHTS-ACT.
US DEPARTMENT OF LABOR, SOCIAL SERVICE REVIEW, VOL 38, NO 3, SEPT 1964. PP 328-329.

NUSDLAB64814 US DEPARTMENT OF LABOR
EMPLOYMENT OF NEGROES BY GOVERNMENT-CONTRACTORS.
US DEPARTMENT OF LABOR, MONTHLY LABOR REVIEW, VOL 87, NO 7, JULY 1964. PP 789-793.

NUSDLAB65247 US DEPARTMENT OF LABOR

NEGRO EMPLOYMENT IN 1965.
US DEPARTMENT OF LABOR. MONTHLY REPORT ON THE LABOR FORCE.
DEC 1965. ALSO CALIFORNIA DEPARTMENT OF INDUSTRIAL
RELATIONS, DIVISION OF FAIR EMPLOYMENT PRACTICES.
INFORMATIONAL MEMO NO 32. SAN FRANCISCO, CALIFORNIA.
FEB 1966. 2 PP.

NUSDLAB65254   US DEPARTMENT OF LABOR
BIBLIOGRAPHY ON THE ECONOMIC-STATUS OF THE NEGRO.
US DEPARTMENT OF LABOR, BUREAU OF LABOR STATISTICS. GPO.
WASHINGTON, DC. NOV 17-18 1965.

NUSDLAB65334   US DEPARTMENT OF LABOR
ENHANCING THE OCCUPATIONAL OUTLOOK AND VOCATIONAL
ASPIRATIONS OF SOUTHERN SECONDARY YOUTH. A CONFERENCE OF
SECONDARY SCHOOL PRINCIPALS AND COUNSELORS.
TUSKEGEE INSTITUTE. TUSKEGEE, ALABAMA. AP 13 1965. 200 PP.

NUSDLAB65813   US DEPARTMENT OF LABOR
CONFERENCE ON EQUAL-EMPLOYMENT-OPPORTUNITY.
US DEPARTMENT OF LABOR, MONTHLY LABOR REVIEW, VOL 88, NO 11,
NOV 1965. PP 1320-1321.

NUSDLAB65815   US DEPARTMENT OF LABOR
EMPLOYMENT OF NEGROES IN THE FEDERAL-GOVERNMENT, JUNE 1964.
US DEPARTMENT OF LABOR, MONTHLY REVIEW, VOL 88, NO 10,
OCT 1965. PP 1222-1227.

NUSDLAB65819   US DEPARTMENT OF LABOR
FACULTY EDUCATION AND INCOME IN NEGRO AND WHITE COLLEGES.
US DEPARTMENT OF LABOR, MONTHLY LABOR REVIEW, VOL 88, NO 5,
MAY 1965. PP 537-540.

NUSDLAB66206   US DEPARTMENT OF LABOR
THE EMPLOYMENT SITUATION.
US SENATE, COMMITTEE ON GOVERNMENT OPERATIONS, SUBCOMMITTEE
ON EXECUTIVE REORGANIZATION. HEARINGS. FEDERAL ROLE IN URBAN
AFFAIRS. PART 2. AUG 17-19 1966. EXHIBIT NO 45. 89TH
CONGRESS, 2ND SESSION. GPO. WASHINGTON, DC. PP 517-528.

NUSDLAB66245   US DEPARTMENT OF LABOR
THE EMPLOYMENT OF NEGROES. SOME DEMOGRAPHIC CONSIDERATIONS.
PROBLEMS AND PROSPECTS OF THE NEGRO MOVEMENT. ED BY RAYMOND
J MURPHY AND HOWARD ELINSON. WADSWORTH PUBLISHING COMPANY.
BELMONT, CALIFORNIA. 1966. PP 116-124.

NUSDLAB66248   US DEPARTMENT OF LABOR
TO FULFILL THESE RIGHTS. /POLICY-RECOMMENDATIONS/
US DEPARTMENT OF LABOR, EMPLOYMENT SERVICE REVIEW, VOL 3,
NO 8, AUG 1966. PP 48-51.

NUSDLAB66257   US DEPARTMENT OF LABOR
THE NEGROES IN THE UNITED STATES. THEIR ECONOMIC AND SOCIAL
SITUATION.
US DEPARTMENT OF LABOR, BUREAU OF LABOR STATISTICS,
BULLETIN 1511. GPO. WASHINGTON, DC. JUNE 1966. 241 PP.

NUSDLAB66826   US DEPARTMENT OF LABOR
MINORITY-GROUPS IN CALIFORNIA.
US DEPARTMENT OF LABOR, MONTHLY LABOR REVIEW, VOL 89, NO 9,
SEPT 1966. PP 978-983.

NUSGESA63266   US GENERAL SERVICES ADM
SPECIAL ISSUE ON EQUAL-EMPLOYMENT.
US GENERAL SERVICES ADMINISTRATION, PERSONNEL DIVISION,
PERSONNEL EXCHANGE, VOL 6, AUG 1963. PP 1-10.

NUSNAAS63267   US NATL AERONAUTICS SPACE ADM
SUMMARY REPORT. EQUAL-EMPLOYMENT-OPPORTUNITY CONFERENCE.
US NATIONAL AERONAUTICS AND SPACE ADMINISTRATION. GPO.
WASHINGTON, DC. JULY 29-31 1963. 25 PP.

NUSNEWR51272   US NEWS AND WORLD REPORT
NEGROES GO NORTH, WEST. JOBS TAKE THEM FAR AFIELD FROM THE
SOUTH.
US NEWS AND WORLD REPORT, NOV 16 1951. PP 50-53.

NUSNEWR56208   US NEWS AND WORLD REPORT
IMPACT OF THE RACE ISSUE ON UNIONS IN THE SOUTH.
US NEWS AND WORLD REPORT, AP 16 1956.

NUSNEWR57209   US NEWS AND WORLD REPORT
UNION BAN ON NEGROES UPHELD.
US NEWS AND WORLD REPORT, OCT 11 1957.

NUSNEWR57274   US NEWS AND WORLD REPORT
NEXT IT-S A MIXED POLICE FORCE. INTEGRATIONISTS LATEST GOAL
IN NATION-S CAPITAL. /WASHINGTON-DC/
US NEWS AND WORLD REPORT, VOL 43, NOV 1 1957. PP 58-60.

NUSNEWR58271   US NEWS AND WORLD REPORT
NEGROES. BIG ADVANCES IN JOBS, WEALTH, STATUS.
US NEWS AND WORLD REPORT, VOL 45, 1958. PP 90-92.

NUSNEWR62268   US NEWS AND WORLD REPORT
FOR NEGROES. MORE AND BETTER JOBS IN GOVERNMENT.
US NEWS AND WORLD REPORT, VOL 52, MAR 5 1962. PP 83-85.

NUSNEWR63207   US NEWS AND WORLD REPORT
FORCED HIRING OF NEGROES.
US NEWS AND WORLD REPORT, JULY 29 1963.

NUSNEWR63269   US NEWS AND WORLD REPORT
JOBS FOR NEGROES -- IS THERE A REAL SHORTAGE.
US NEWS AND WORLD REPORT, VOL 55, AUG 12 1963. PP 28-32.

NUSNEWR64292   US NEWS AND WORLD REPORT
UNIONS FEEL GROWING PRESSURE TO TAKE MORE NEGROES.
US NEWS AND WORLD REPORT, MAY 25 1964. PP 86-89.

NUSNEWR66270   US NEWS AND WORLD REPORT
JOB RIGHTS FOR NEGROES -- PRESSURE ON EMPLOYERS.
US NEWS AND WORLD REPORT, VOL 60, AP 18 1966. PP 84 PLUS.

NUSNEWR66273   US NEWS AND WORLD REPORT
NEW PUSH FOR HIRING OF NEGROES.
US NEWS AND WORLD REPORT, VOL 60, MAR 14 1966. P 110.

NUSSENA52333   US SENATE
EMPLOYMENT AND THE ECONOMIC STATUS OF NEGROES IN THE UNITED
STATES.
US SENATE, COMMITTEE ON LABOR AND PUBLIC WELFARE,
SUBCOMMITTEE ON LABOR AND LABOR-MANAGEMENT RELATIONS, STAFF
REPORT. 82ND CONGRESS, 2ND SESSION. GPO. WASHINGTON, DC.
1952. 20 PP.

NUSSENA54275   US SENATE
EMPLOYMENT AND ECONOMIC STATUS OF NEGROES IN THE US.
US SENATE, COMMITTEE ON LABOR AND PUBLIC WELFARE,
SUBCOMMITTEE ON CIVIL RIGHTS, STAFF REPORT. 83RD CONGRESS,

2ND SESSION. GPO. WASHINGTON, DC. 1954. 20 PP.

NUSWAMC44276   US WAR MANPOWER COMMISSION
THE UNITED STATES EMPLOYMENT SERVICE AND THE NEGRO WORK
APPLICANT.
UNITED STATES WAR MANPOWER COMMISSION, BUREAU OF PLACEMENT.
HANDBOOK. GPO. WASHINGTON, DC. 1944. 56 PP.

NUZELOX61278   UZELL O
OCCUPATIONAL ASPIRATIONS OF NEGRO MALE HIGH SCHOOL STUDENTS.
SOCIOLOGY AND SOCIAL RESEARCH, VOL 45, JAN 1961. PP 202-204.

NVALIPX42261   VALIEN P
SOCIAL AND ECONOMIC IMPLICATIONS OF MIGRATION FOR THE NEGRO
IN THE PRESENT SOCIAL ORDER.
THE QUARTERLY REVIEW OF HIGHER EDUCATION AMONG NEGROES,
VOL 10, NO 2, AP 1942. PP 74-84.

NVALIPX49280   VALIEN P
THE MENTALITIES OF NEGRO AND WHITE WORKERS. AN EXPERIMENTAL
SCHOOL-S INTERPRETATION OF NEGRO TRADE UNIONISM.
SOCIAL FORCES, VOL 27, NO 4, MAY 1949. PP 433-438.

NVALIPX56281   VALIEN P   BOYD I
HOLDEN A
A REPORT ON COMMUNITY FACTORS IN NASHVILLE RELATED TO THE
NEGRO IN MEDICINE. /TENNESSEE/
FISK UNIVERSITY, DEPARTMENT OF SOCIAL SCIENCE. UNPUBLISHED.
NASHVILLE, TENNESSEE. 1956.

NVALIPX63279   VALIEN P
DEMOGRAPHIC CHARACTERISTICS OF THE NEGRO POPULATION IN THE
UNITED STATES.
JOURNAL OF NEGRO EDUCATION, VOL 32, NO 4, FALL 1963.
PP 329-336.

NVANCRB45282   VANCE RB
ALL THESE PEOPLE. THE NATION-S HUMAN RESOURCES IN THE SOUTH.
UNIVERSITY OF NORTH CAROLINA PRESS. CHAPEL HILL, NORTH
CAROLINA. 1945.

NVANCRB54283   VANCE RB ED   DEMERATH NJ ED
THE URBAN SOUTH.
UNIVERSITY OF NORTH CAROLINA PRESS. CHAPEL HILL, NORTH
CAROLINA. 1954.

NVELILX59216   VELIE L
LABOR USA. /UNION/
HARPER AND BROTHERS. NEW YORK. 1959. CHAPTER 14, PP 205-220.

NVIORJX65284   VIORST J
NEGROES IN SCIENCE. /OCCUPATIONS/
SCIENCE NEWS LETTER, VOL 87, AP 3 1965. PP 218-219.

NVIRGHR64318   W VIRGINIA HUMAN RIGHTS COMM
SPECIAL REPORT. A SURVEY OF NEGROES EMPLOYED BY THE STATE
OF WEST-VIRGINIA.
WEST VIRGINIA HUMAN RIGHTS COMMISSION. CHARLESTON, WEST
VIRGINIA. MAY 1964. 15 PP.

NVIRGLR64017   VIRGINIA LAW REVIEW
RACIAL DISCRIMINATION AND THE NLRB. THE HUGHES TOOL CASE,
PART ONE.
VIRGINIA LAW REVIEW, VOL 50, NO 3, 1964. PP 464-534.

NVIRGLR64018   VIRGINIA LAW REVIEW
RACIAL DISCRIMINATION AND THE NLRB. THE HUGHES TOOL CASE,
PART TWO.
VIRGINIA LAW REVIEW, VOL 50, NO 7, 1964. PP 1221-1234.

NVOGLAJ64286   VOGL AJ
NEGROES ON THE SALES FORCE. THE QUIET INTEGRATION.
SALES MANAGEMENT, VOL 93, OCT 16 1964. PP 25-28.

NVOLLHM66287   VOLLMER HM   MILLS DL
ETHNIC STATUS AND OCCUPATIONAL DILEMMAS.
PROFESSIONALIZATION. PRENTICE-HALL. ENGLEWOOD CLIFFS,
NEW JERSEY. 1966. PP 329-340.

NWACHDD65288   WACHTEL DD   *U OF MICH-WAYNE STATE U ILIR
THE NEGRO AND DISCRIMINATION IN EMPLOYMENT.
THE UNIVERSITY OF MICHIGAN-WAYNE STATE UNIVERSITY, INSTITUTE
OF LABOR AND INDUSTRIAL RELATIONS. ANN ARBOR, MICHIGAN.
1965. 112 PP.

NWACHHMND289   WACHTEL HM
HARD-CORE UNEMPLOYMENT IN DETROIT. CAUSES AND REMEDIES.
/MICHIGAN/
INDUSTRIAL RELATIONS RESEARCH ASSOCIATION, 18TH ANNUAL
MEETING, PROCEEDINGS. 9 PP. ALSO THE UNIVERSITY OF MICHIGAN-
WAYNE STATE UNIVERSITY, INSTITUTE OF LABOR AND INDUSTRIAL
RELATIONS. ANN ARBOR, MICHIGAN.

NWAGECW57290   WAGERLY CW
THE SITUATION OF THE NEGRO IN THE U.S.
INTERNATIONAL SOCIAL SCIENCE BULLETIN, VOL 9, NO 4, 1957.
PP 427-428.

NWALKHJ57291   WALKER HJ
CHANGE IN THE STATUS OF THE NEGRO IN AMERICAN SOCIETY.
INTERNATIONAL SOCIAL SCIENCE BULLETIN, VOL 9, NO 4, 1957.
PP 438-474.

NWALKJO46580   WALKER JO
THE POST-WAR OUTLOOK FOR NEGROES IN SMALL BUSINESS, THE
ENGINEERING AND THE TECHNICAL VOCATIONS.
HOWARD UNIVERSITY, GRADUATE SCHOOL, DIVISION OF SOCIAL
SCIENCES, 9TH ANNUAL CONFERENCE, PROCEEDINGS. HOWARD
UNIVERSITY PRESS. WASHINGTON, DC. 1946. 194 PP.

NWALLFX61221   WALLS F   *WASH STATE LEGISLATIVE CC
PROBLEMS OF MIGRANT LABOR.
WASHINGTON STATE LEGISLATIVE COUNCIL. OLYMPIA, WASHINGTON.
MAY 1961. 20 PP.

NWALLPA66591   WALLACE PA   BECKLES MP
*EEOC
1966 EMPLOYMENT SURVEY IN THE TEXTILE INDUSTRY OF THE
CAROLINAS.
EQUAL EMPLOYMENT OPPORTUNITY COMMISSION, OFFICE OF RESEARCH
AND REPORTS. WASHINGTON, DC. DEC 19 1966. 21 PP.

NWARNWL62292   WARNER WL
SOCIAL CLASS AND COLOR CASTE IN AMERICA.
AMERICAN LIFE. DREAM AND REALITY. UNIVERSITY OF CHICAGO
PRESS. CHICAGO, ILLINOIS. REVISED ED. 1962.

NWARKDX64314   WARREN D
WALK IN DIGNITY. /ASPIRATIONS/
VITAL SPEECHES OF THE DAY, JULY 1 1964. PP 572-575.

NWARRUL64986　WARREN URBAN LEAGUE
STUDY OF ECONOMIC AND CULTURAL ACTIVITIES IN THE WARREN AREA
AS THEY RELATE TO MINORITY PEOPLE. /OHIO/
WARREN URBAN LEAGUE. WARREN, OHIO. 1964. 126 PP.

NWATTPX64293　WATTERS P　　　　　　　　*SOUTHERN REGIONAL COUNCIL
BRUNSWICK. /GEORGIA/
SOUTHERN REGIONAL COUNCIL, SPECIAL REPORT. ATLANTA, GEORGIA.
SEPT 1964. 94 PP.

NWATTPX64294　WATTERS P　　　　　　　　*SOUTHERN REGIONAL COUNCIL
CHARLOTTE. /NORTH-CAROLINA/
SOUTHERN REGIONAL COUNCIL, SPECIAL REPORT. ATLANTA, GEORGIA.
MAY 1964. 91 PP.

NWATTPX66545　WATTERS P
TO FULFILL THESE RIGHTS. REPORT ON THE
WHITE-HOUSE-CONFERENCE. /EEO/
NEW SOUTH, SUMMER 1966. PP 26-46.

NWAYNCM64295　WAYNICK CM ED　　　　　　BROOKS JC ED
PITTS EW ED　　　　　　*N CAROLINA MAYORS COPNG COMT
NORTH-CAROLINA AND THE NEGRO.
NORTH CAROLINA MAYORS CO-OPERATING COMMITTEE. RALEIGH, NORTH
CAROLINA. 1964. 309 PP.

NWEATMD54296　WEATHERFORD MD
A STUDY OF SOME ASPECTS OF JOB SATISFACTION AMONG NEGRO
WHITE-COLLAR WORKERS.
AMERICAN UNIVERSITY. MASTERS THESIS. WASHINGTON, DC. 1954.

NWEAVEK44297　WEAVER EK
THE ROLE OF THE NEGRO COLLEGE.
PHYLON, VOL 5, NO 1, 1ST QUARTER 1944. PP 41-50.

NWEAVRC42307　WEAVER RC
WITH THE NEGRO-S HELP.
ATLANTIC MONTHLY, JUNE 1942. PP 696-707.

NWEAVRC42552　WEAVER RC
DEFENSE INDUSTRIES AND THE NEGRO.
ANNALS OF THE AMERICAN ACADEMY OF POLITICAL AND SOCIAL
SCIENCE, VOL 223, SEPT 1942. PP 60-66.

NWEAVRC43225　WEAVER RC
THE EMPLOYMENT OF THE NEGRO IN WAR INDUSTRIES.
JOURNAL OF NEGRO EDUCATION, VOL 12, 1943.

NWEAVRC43301　WEAVER RC
THE NEGRO COMES OF AGE IN INDUSTRY.
ATLANTIC MONTHLY, SEPT 1943. PP 54-59.

NWEAVRC44300　WEAVER RC
EMPLOYMENT OF NEGROES IN UNITED STATES WAR INDUSTRIES.
INTERNATIONAL LABOUR REVIEW, VOL 50, AUG 1944. PP 141-159.

NWEAVRC44306　WEAVER RC
RECENT EVENTS IN NEGRO UNION RELATIONSHIPS.
JOURNAL OF POLITICAL ECONOMY, VOL 52, NO 3, SEPT 1944.
PP 242-243.

NWEAVRC45302　WEAVER RC
NEGRO EMPLOYMENT IN THE AIRCRAFT INDUSTRY.
QUARTERLY JOURNAL OF ECONOMICS, VOL 59, AUG 1945.
PP 597-625.

NWEAVRC46304　WEAVER RC
NEGRO LABOR. A NATIONAL PROBLEM.
HARCOURT, BRACE AND COMPANY. NEW YORK. 1946. 329 PP.

NWEAVRC48303　WEAVER RC
THE NEGRO GHETTO.
HARCOURT, BRACE, AND WORLD. NEW YORK. 1948.

NWEAVRC50305　WEAVER RC
NEGRO LABOR SINCE 1929.
JOURNAL OF NEGRO HISTORY, VOL 35, JAN 1950. PP 20-38.

NWEAVRC63298　WEAVER RC
CHALLENGES TO DEMOCRACY. /ECONOMY/
THE NEGRO AS AN AMERICAN. CENTER FOR THE STUDY OF DEMOCRATIC
INSTITUTIONS. SANTA BARBARA, CALIFORNIA. 1963.

NWEAVRC64299　WEAVER RC
THE CHANGING STRUCTURE OF THE AMERICAN CITY AND THE NEGRO.
ASSURING FREEDOM TO THE FREE. A CENTURY OF EMANCIPATION IN
THE USA. ED BY ARNOLD M ROSE. DETROIT, MICHIGAN. WAYNE STATE
UNIVERSITY PRESS. 1964.

NWECKJE45308　WECKLER JE
PREJUDICE IS NOT THE WHOLE STORY. EXAMINATION OF THREE CASES
OF NEGRO UPGRADING IN TRACTION COMPANIES IN PHILADELPHIA,
LOS-ANGELES AND CHICAGO. /PENNSYLVANIA CALIFORNIA
ILLINOIS/
PUBLIC OPINION QUARTERLY, VOL 9, NO 2, 1945. PP 126-139.

NWEILFD47309　WEIL FDG
THE NEGRO IN THE ARMED FORCES. /MILITARY/
SOCIAL FORCES, VOL 26, NO 1, OCT 1947. PP 94-98.

NWEINRX59311　WEINTRAUB R
EMPLOYMENT INTEGRATION AND WAGE DIFFERENCES IN A SOUTHERN
PLANT.
INDUSTRIAL AND LABOR RELATIONS REVIEW, VOL 12, JAN 1959.
PP 214-226.

NWELSEK65304　WELSCH EK
THE NEGRO IN THE US. A RESEARCH GUIDE.
INDIANA UNIVERSITY PRESS. BLOOMINGTON, INDIANA. 1965.
142 PP.

NWESSWH55314　WESSON WH　　　　　　　*NATIONAL PLANNING ASSN
NEGRO EMPLOYMENT PRACTICES IN THE CHATTANOOGA AREA.
/TENNESSEE/
SELECTED STUDIES OF NEGRO EMPLOYMENT IN THE SOUTH. NATIONAL
PLANNING ASSOCIATION, COMMITTEE OF THE SOUTH. REPORT NO 6-4.
WASHINGTON, DC. 1955. PP 385-483.

NWESTCU55316　WESTCHESTER COUNTY URB LEAG
A SURVEY OF EMPLOYMENT OPPORTUNITIES AS THEY RELATE TO THE
NEGRO IN NEW-ROCHELLE, NEW-YORK. 1955.
WESTCHESTER COUNTY URBAN LEAGUE. WHITE PLAINS, NEW YORK.
JULY-AUG, 1955.

NWESTEX66315　WEST E
SUMMARY OF RESEARCH DURING 1964 RELATED TO THE NEGRO AND
NEGRO EDUCATION.
JOURNAL OF NEGRO EDUCATION, VOL 35, WINTER 1966. PP 62-72.

NWESTZJ66317　WESTON ZJ　　　　　　　*US DEPARTMENT OF LABOR
SHOWING THE WAY IN PREPARING NEGRO JOBSEEKERS.
US DEPARTMENT OF LABOR, EMPLOYMENT SERVICE REVIEW, VOL 3,
NO 8, AUG 1966. PP 45-47.

NWETZJR66114　WETZEL JR　　　　　　　HOLLAND SS
*US DEPARTMENT OF LABOR
POVERTY AREAS OF OUR MAJOR CITIES. THE EMPLOYMENT SITUATION
OF NEGRO AND WHITE WORKERS IN METROPOLITAN AREAS COMPARED
IN A SPECIAL LABOR-FORCE REPORT.
US DEPARTMENT OF LABOR, MONTHLY LABOR REVIEW, VOL 89,
OCT 1966. PP 1105-1110.

NWHEEJH64230　WHEELER JH
THE IMPACT OF RACE-RELATIONS ON INDUSTRIAL RELATIONS IN THE
SOUTH.
INDUSTRIAL RELATIONS RESEARCH ASSOCIATION, PROCEEDINGS.
SPRING 1964. PP 474-481.

NWHITEW64321　WHITLOW EW　　　　　　　*EDUCATIONAL TESTING SERVICE
THE PLACEMENT OF NEGRO COLLEGE GRADUATES IN BUSINESS
ORGANIZATIONS.
SELECTING AND TRAINING NEGROES FOR MANAGERIAL POSITIONS.
EDUCATIONAL TESTING SERVICE. PRINCETON, NEW JERSEY. 1964.
PP 41-50.

NWHITMJ48249　WHITEHEAD MJ
SIGNIFICANT ACHIEVEMENTS OF NEGROES IN EDUCATION 1907-1947.
/OCCUPATIONS/
THE QUARTERLY REVIEW OF HIGHER EDUCATION AMONG NEGROES, VOL
16, NO 1, JAN 1948. PP 1-6.

NWHITRM59319　WHITE RM
COMPARATIVE STUDY OF SOCIO-ECONOMIC AND SOCIAL-PSYCHOLOGICAL
DETERMINANTS OF EDUCATIONAL AND OCCUPATIONAL ASPIRATIONS
OF NEGRO AND WHITE COLLEGE SENIORS.
FLORIDA STATE UNIVERSITY. PHD DISSERTATION. TALLAHASSEE,
FLORIDA. 1959.

NWHITWL66231　WHITE WL　　　　　　　*US CHAMBER OF COMMERCE
THE OPPORTUNITIES FOR BUSINESS OWNERSHIP AMONG NEGROES.
THE DISADVANTAGED POOR. EDUCATION AND EMPLOYMENT. US CHAMBER
OF COMMERCE. TASK FORCE ON ECONOMIC GROWTH AND OPPORTUNITY.
WASHINGTON, DC. 1966. PP 417-434.

NWHITWL66320　WHITE WL　　　　　　　*US DEPARTMENT OF LABOR
THE NEGRO ENTREPRENEUR.
US DEPARTMENT OF LABOR, OCCUPATIONAL OUTLOOK QUARTERLY,
VOL 10, NO 1, FEB 1966. PP 19-22.

NWHITWX42465　WHITE W
WHAT THE NEGRO THINKS OF THE ARMY. /MILITARY/
ANNALS OF THE AMERICAN ACADEMY OF SOCIAL AND POLITICAL
SCIENCE, VOL 223, SEPT 1942. PP 67-72.

NWILKDA42233　WILKERSIN DA
THE VOCATIONAL GUIDANCE AND EDUCATION OF NEGROES. THE NEGRO
AND THE BATTLE OF PRODUCTION.
JOURNAL OF NEGRO EDUCATION, VOL 11, NO 2, AP 1942.
PP 228-239.

NWILKWH41323　WILKINSON WHH　　　　　*US DEPARTMENT OF LABOR
PLACING THE NEGRO WORKER.
US DEPARTMENT OF LABOR, EMPLOYMENT SECURITY REVIEW, VOL 8,
NO 6, JUNE 1941. PP 3-6.

NWILLCV65989　WILLIE CV　　　　　　　RIDDICK WE
THE EMPLOYED POOR. A CASE-STUDY. /WASHINGTON-DC/
POVERTY AS A PUBLIC ISSUE. ED BY BEN B SELIGMAN. THE FREE
PRESS. NEW YORK. 1965. PP 152-176.

NWILLMM50234　WILLIAMS MM
A CRITICAL APPRAISAL OF PROFESSION TRAINING OF NEGRO
TEACHERS IN OKTIBBEHA COUNTY MISSISSIPPI.
TUSKEGEE INSTITUTE. MA ESSAY. TUSKEGEE, ALABAMA. 1950.

NWILLSM64232　WILLHELM SM　　　　　　POWELL EH
WHO NEEDS THE NEGRO. /OCCUPATIONAL-STATUS
TECHNOLOGICAL-CHANGE/
TRANS-ACTION, VOL 1, SEPT-OCT 1964. PP 3-6.

NWILSCE65326　WILSON CE
AUTOMATION AND THE NEGRO. WILL WE SURVIVE.
LIBERATOR, VOL 5, JULY 1965. PP 8-11.

NWILSLX43327　WILSON L　　　　　　　GILMORE H
WHITE EMPLOYERS AND NEGRO WORKERS.
AMERICAN SOCIOLOGICAL REVIEW, VOL 8, NO 6, DEC 1943.
PP 698-705.

NWINNFX43554　WINN F
LABOR TACKLES THE RACE QUESTION. /UNION/
THE ANTIOCH REVIEW, VOL 3, NO 3, FALL 1943. PP 341-360.

NWINTSB64329　WINTERS SB
URBAN-RENEWAL AND CIVIL-RIGHTS.
STUDIES ON THE LEFT, VOL 4, NO 3, SUMMER 1964. PP 16-31.

NWIRTWW63330　WIRTZ WW
TOWARD EQUAL-OPPORTUNITY.
AMERICAN CHILD, VOL 45, NOV 1963. PP 1-4.

NWIRTWX66236　WIRTZ W
ADDRESS. /DISCRIMINATION AFFIRMATIVE-ACTION/
NAACP LEGAL DEFENSE AND EDUCATIONAL FUND, CONVOCATION
ADDRESS. NEW YORK. MAY 18 1966. 10 PP.

NWISCGC59331　WIS GOVRS COMM ON HUM RIGHTS
NEGRO FAMILIES IN RURAL WISCONSIN, A STUDY OF THEIR
COMMUNITY LIFE.
WISCONSIN GOVERNOR-S COMMISSION ON HUMAN RIGHTS. MADISON,
WISCONSIN. 1959. 72 PP.

NWISSHW55332　WISSNER HW　　　　　　*NATIONAL PLANNING ASSN
THREE COMPANIES -- NEW-ORLEANS AREA. /CASE-STUDY
LOUISIANA/
NATIONAL PLANNING ASSOCIATION, COMMITTEE OF THE SOUTH.
REPORT NO 6-4. WASHINGTON, DC. 1955. PP 357-384.

NWOFFBM55333　WOFFORD BM　　　　　　KELLY TA
MISSISSIPPI WORKERS. WHERE THEY COME FROM AND HOW THEY
PERFORM. A STUDY OF WORKING FORCES IN SELECTED MISSISSIPPI
INDUSTRIAL PLANTS.
UNIVERSITY OF ALABAMA PRESS. UNIVERSITY, ALABAMA. 1955.
VOL 1, 148 PP.

NWOLFDP62336　WOLFE DP
EDUCATION-S CHALLENGE TO AMERICAN NEGRO YOUTH.
NEGRO HISTORY BULLETIN, VOL 26, DEC 1962. PP 115-118.

NWOLFDP64338   WOLFE DP ED   BRIMMER AF ED
POVERTY IN THE UNITED STATES.
US HOUSE OF REPRESENTATIVES, COMMITTEE CN EDUCATION AND
LABOR. 86TH CONGRESS, 2ND SESSION. GPO. WASHINGTON, DC.
AP 1964.

NWOLFDP65337   WOLFE DP
WHAT THE ECONOMIC-OPPORTUNITY-ACT MEANS TO THE NEGRO.
JOURNAL OF NEGRO EDUCATION, WINTER 1965.

NWOLFSL45335   WOLFBEIN SL   *US DEPARTMENT OF LABOR
WAR AND POSTWAR TRENDS IN EMPLOYMENT OF NEGROES.
US DEPARTMENT OF LABOR, MONTHLY LABOR REVIEW, VOL 60, NO 1,
JAN 1945. PP 1-6.

NWOLFSL47334   WOLFBEIN SL   *US DEPARTMENT OF LABOR
POSTWAR TRENDS IN NEGRO EMPLOYMENT.
US DEPARTMENT OF LABOR, MONTHLY LABOR REVIEW, VOL 65, NO 6,
DEC 1947. PP 663-665.

NWOODCA45339   WOOD CA
PUTTING NEGROES ON A JOB-EQUALITY BASIS.
FACTORY MANAGEMENT AND MAINTENANCE, OCT 1945. PP 130-1339

NWOODCV60C61   WOODWARD CV
THE BURDEN OF SOUTHERN HISTORY.
LOUISIANA STATE UNIVERSITY PRESS. BATON ROUGE, LOUISIANA.
1960.

NWOOFTJ57340   WOOFTER TJ
SOUTHERN RACE PROGRESS. THE WAVERING COLOR LINE.
PUBLIC AFFAIRS PRESS. NEW YORK. 1957.

NWOROIX62341   WORONOFF I
NEGRO MALE IDENTIFICATION PROBLEMS.
JOURNAL OF EDUCATIONAL SOCIOLOGY, VOL 36, SEPT 1962.
PP 30-32.

NWOYTWS53343   WOYTINSKY WS
EMPLOYMENT AND WAGES IN THE US.
TWENTIETH CENTURY FUND. NEW YORK. 1953. 777 PP.

NWRIGSJ63344   WRIGHT SJ
IMPACT ON THE INDIVIDUAL. /SOCIAL-CHANGE   SOUTH/
EDUCATIONAL IMPERATIVE. THE NEGRO IN THE CHANGING SOUTH. ED
BY FREDA H GOLDMAN. CENTER FOR THE STUDY OF LIBERAL
EDUCATION BY ADULTS. CHICAGO, ILLINOIS. 1963. PP 62-64.

NYALELJ63599   YALE LAW JOURNAL
EMPLOYEE CHOICE AND SOME PROBLEMS OF RACE AND REMEDIES IN
   REPRESENTATION CAMPAIGNS.
YALE LAW JOURNAL, VCL 72, MAY 1963. PP1243-1264.

NYALELJ64600   YALE LAW JOURNAL
WORKING RULES FOR ASSURING NONDISCRIMINATION IN HOSPITAL
   ADMINISTRATION.
YALE LAW JOURNAL, VCL 74, NOV 1964. PP 151-169.

NYINGJM63345   YINGER JM
DESEGREGATION IN AMERICAN SOCIETY. THE RECORD OF A
   GENERATION OF CHANGE.
SOCIOLOGY AND SOCIAL RESEARCH, VOL 47, NO 4, JULY 1963.
PP 428-445.

NYOUMEG65390   YOUMANS EG   GRIGSBY SE
               KING HC
AFTER HIGH SCHOOL WHAT...HIGHLIGHTS OF A STUDY OF CAREER
   PLANS OF NEGRO AND WHITE RURAL YOUTH IN THREE FLORIDA
   COUNTIES. /ASPIRATIONS/
UNIVERSITY OF FLORIDA. GAINESVILLE, FLORIDA. 1965. 19 PP.

NYOUNCE45358   YOUNT CE
ANTI-DISCRIMINATION IN INDUSTRY.
CONFERENCE BOARD MANAGEMENT RECORD, VOL 7, OCT 1945,
PP 286-290.

NYOUNHB63347   YOUNG HB
THE NEGRO-S PARTICIPATION IN AMERICAN BUSINESS.
JOURNAL OF NEGRO EDUCATION, VOL 32, NO 4, 1963 YEARBOOK.
PP 390-401.

NYOUNHB64346   YOUNG HB   HUND JM
NEGRO ENTREPRENEURSHIP IN SOUTHERN ECONCMIC DEVELOPMENT.
ESSAYS IN SOUTHERN ECONOMIC DEVELOPMENT. ED BY MELVIN L
GREENHUT AND W TATE WHITMAN. UNIVERSITY OF NORTH CAROLINA
PRESS. CHAPEL HILL, NORTH CAROLINA. 1964.

NYOUNJE56357   YOUNGDAHL JE
UNIONS AND SEGREGATION.
THE NEW REPUBLIC, JULY 9 1956.

NYOUNMN44348   YOUNG MNE
SOME SOCIOLOGICAL ASPECTS OF VOCATIONAL GUIDANCE OF NEGRO
   CHILDREN.
UNIVERSITY OF PENNSYLVANIA. PHD THESIS. PHILADELPHIA,
PENNSYLVANIA. 1944. 95 PP.

NYOUNWM63352   YOUNG WM
THE NEGRO REVOLT.
AMERICAN CHILD, VOL 45, NO 4, NOV 1963.

NYOUNWM63356   YOUNG WM
WHAT PRICE PREJUDICE -- ON THE ECONOMICS OF DISCRIMINATION.
FREEDOMWAYS, SUMMER 1963.

NYOUNWM63600   YOUNG WM   *NATIONAL URBAN LEAGUE
THE SOCIAL REVOLUTION. CHALLENGE TO THE NATION.
   /CIVIL-RIGHTS/
NATIONAL URBAN LEAGUE. NEW YORK. 1963. 13 PP.

NYOUNWM64299   YOUNG WM
THE INTERMINGLED REVOLUTIONS -- THE NEGRO AND AUTOMATION.
VITAL SPEECHES OF THE DAY, SEPT 1 1964. PP 692-694.

NYOUNWM64349   YOUNG WM
CIVIL-RIGHTS -- DISCRIMINATION IN LABOR UNIONS.
VITAL SPEECHES OF THE DAY, VOL 30, NO 17, JUNE 15 1964.
PP 535-537.

NYOUNWM64350   YOUNG WM
HEARING BEFORE THE AD HOC SUBCOMMITTEE CN THE WAR-ON-POVERTY
   PROGRAM.
US HOUSE OF REPRESENTATIVES, COMMITTEE CN EDUCATION ON
EDUCATION AND LABOR, AD HOC SUBCOMMITTEE ON THE WAR ON
POVERTY PROGRAM. 88TH CONGRESS, 2ND SESSION. GPO.
WASHINGTON, DC. AP 14 1964. 27 PP.

NYOUNWM64351   YOUNG WM
INTEGRATION IN INDUSTRY.
FACTORY MAGAZINE, DEC 1964. PP 49-54.

NYOUNWM64353   YOUNG WM
TO BE EQUAL.
MCGRAW-HILL. NEW YORK. 1964. 254 PP.

NYOUNWM65000   YOUNG WM   *NATL INDUSTRIAL CONF BOARD
THE PRACTICE OF RACIAL DEMOCRACY.
CONFERENCE BOARD RECORD, VOL 2, JUNE 1965. PP 14-18.

NYOUNWM65354   YOUNG WM
THE URBAN-LEAGUE AND ITS STRATEGY.
ANNALS OF THE AMERICAN ACADEMY OF POLITICAL AND SOCIAL
SCIENCE, VOL 357, JAN 1965.

NYOUNWM66355   YOUNG WM
THE URBAN-LEAGUE EXPANDS OPPORTUNITIES.
THE AMERICAN FEDERATIONIST, VOL 73, NO 11, NOV 1966.
PP 14-16.

NZEITLX65359   ZEITZ L
SURVEY OF NEGRO ATTITUDES TOWARD LAW.
RUTGERS LAW REVIEW, VOL 19, NO 2, WINTER 1965, PP 288-316.

NZIMMBG62360   ZIMMER BG
THE ADJUSTMENT OF NEGROES IN A NORTHERN INDUSTRIAL
   COMMUNITY.
SOCIAL PROBLEMS, VOL 9, SPRING 1962. PP 378-386.

NZIMMBG64247   ZIMMER BG
REBUILDING CITIES. THE EFFECTS OF DISPLACEMENT AND
   RELOCATION ON SMALL BUSINESS.
QUADRANGLE BOOKS. CHICAGO, ILLINOIS. 1964. 384 PP.

O

OBARNML58699 BARNETT ML
SOME CANTONESE-AMERICAN PROBLEMS OF STATUS ADJUSTMENT.
PHYLON, VOL 28, JAN 1958. PP 420-427.

OBARNML66698 BARNETT ML
KINSHIP AS A FACTOR AFFECTING CANTONESE ECONOMIC ADAPTATION
IN THE UNITED STATES.
KNOWING THE DISADVANTAGED. ED BY STATEN W WEBSTER. CHANDLER
PUBLISHING CO. SAN FRANCISCO, CALIFORNIA. 1966. PP 192-207.

OBEFUHX65701 BEFU H
CONTRASTIVE ACCULTURATION OF CALIFORNIA JAPANESE.
COMPARATIVE APPROACH TO THE STUDY OF IMMIGRANTS.
HUMAN ORGANIZATION, VOL 24, FALL 1965. PP 209-216.

OBELTAG61703 BELTRAM AG
SOCIAL ORIGINS AND CAREER PREPARATION AMONG FILIPINOS IN
AMERICAN UNIVERSITIES.
UNIVERSITY OF CHICAGO. PHD DISSERTATION, CHICAGO, ILLINOIS.
1961.

OBENJMP61704 BENJAMIN MP
CALIFORNIA-S FRUIT AND VEGETABLE CANNING INDUSTRY. AN
ECONOMIC STUDY.
UNIVERSITY OF CALIFORNIA. PHD DISSERTATION. LOS ANGELES,
CALIFORNIA. 1961.

OBROOLX55708 BROOM L   KITSUSE JI
THE VALIDATION OF ACCULTURATION. A CONDITION TO ETHNIC
ASSIMILATION.
AMERICAN ANTHROPOLOGIST, VOL 57, NO 1, FEB 1955. PP 44-48.

OCALDIR65709 CAL DEPT OF INDUSTRIAL RELS
CALIFORNIANS OF JAPANESE, CHINESE, FILIPINO ANCESTRY.
CALIFORNIA DEPARTMENT OF INDUSTRIAL RELATIONS, DIVISION OF
FAIR EMPLOYMENT PRACTICES. SACRAMENTO, CALIFORNIA.
JUNE 1965. 52 PP.

OCAUDWX61711 CAUDILL W   DE VOS G
ACHIEVEMENT, CULTURE AND PERSONALITY. THE CASE OF THE
JAPANESE-AMERICANS.
AMERICAN ANTHROPOLOGIST, VOL 58, PP 1102-1126. ALSO IN
SOCIAL STRUCTURE AND PERSONALITY. A CASE-BOOK. ED BY YEHUDI
COHEN. HOLT, RINEHART AND WINSTON. NEW YORK. 1961.
PP 391-405.

ODANIRX61716 DANIELS R
THE POLITICS OF PREJUDICE. THE ANTI-JAPANESE MOVEMENT IN
CALIFORNIA AND THE STRUGGLE FOR JAPANESE EXCLUSION.
UNIVERSITY OF SOUTHERN CALIFORNIA. UNPUBLISHED PHD
DISSERTATION. LOS ANGELES, CALIFORNIA. 1961.

ODANIRX66C84 DANIELS R
WESTERNERS FROM THE EAST. ORIENTAL IMMIGRANTS REAPPRAISED.
PACIFIC HISTORICAL REVIEW, VOL 35, NOV 1966. PP 373-383.

OFOGEWX66721 FOGEL W
THE EFFECT OF LOW EDUCATIONAL ATTAINMENT ON INCOMES. A
COMPARATIVE STUDY OF SELECTED ETHNIC GROUPS.
JOURNAL OF HUMAN RESOURCES, VOL 1, FALL 1966. PP 22-40.

OFONGSL65722 FONG SLM
ASSIMILATION OF CHINESE IN AMERICA. CHANGES IN ORIENTATION
AND SOCIAL PERCEPTIONS.
AMERICAN JOURNAL OF SOCIOLOGY, VOL 71, NOV 1965. PP 265-273.

OGRAHJC57728 GRAHAM JC
THE SETTLEMENT OF MERCED-COUNTY, CALIFORNIA.
UNIVERSITY OF SOUTHERN CALIFORNIA. UNPUBLISHED PHD
DISSERTATION. LOS ANGELES, CALIFORNIA. 1957.

OIGAXMX57732 IGA M
THE JAPANESE SOCIAL STRUCTURE AND THE SOURCE OF MENTAL
STRAINS OF JAPANESE IMMIGRANTS IN THE US.
SOCIAL FORCES, VOL 35, NO 3, MAR 1957. PP 271-278.

OKITADX65734 KITAGAWA D
ASSIMILATION OR PLURALISM.
MINORITY PROBLEMS. ED BY ARNOLD AND CAROLINE ROSE. NEW YORK.
HARPER AND ROW. 1965. PP 285-287.

OKUNGSW62737 KUNG SW
CHINESE IN AMERICAN LIFE. SOME ASPECTS OF THEIR HISTORY,
STATUS, PROBLEMS AND CONTRIBUTIONS.
UNIVERSITY OF WASHINGTON PRESS. SEATTLE, WASHINGTON. 1962.
352 PP.

OLEEXRH58742 LEE RH
THE HUI-CH-IAO IN THE UNITED STATES OF AMERICA.
INSTITUTE OF PACIFIC RELATIONS, COLLOQUIUM ON OVERSEAS
CHINESE. NEW YORK. 1958. PP 35-40.

OLEEXRH60741 LEE RH
THE CHINESE IN THE UNITED STATES OF AMERICA.
HONG KONG UNIVERSITY PRESS. HONG KONG, CHINA. 1960. 465 PP.

OLEEXRX57740 LEE R
CHINESE IMMIGRATION AND POPULATION CHANGES SINCE 1940.
SOCIOLOGY AND SOCIAL RESEARCH, VOL 41, NO 3, JAN-FEB 1957.
PP 195-202.

OLOWXHW64745 LOW HW   *CHINESE-AM CITIZENS ALLIANCE
STATEMENT BEFORE CALIFORNIA SENATE SUB-COMMITTEE ON
RACE-RELATIONS AND URBAN PROBLEMS.
CALIFORNIA SENATE, SUB-COMMITTEE ON RACE RELATIONS AND URBAN
PROBLEMS. SAN FRANCISCO, CALIFORNIA. OCT 14 1964.

ORITTXX65758 RITTER ED
OUR ORIENTAL AMERICANS.
MCGRAW-HILL. ST LOUIS, MISSOURI. 1965. 104 PP.

OSHROCR58762 SHROEDER CR
THE PHYSICAL GEOGRAPHY OF THE PALOUSE REGION, WASHINGTON AND
IDAHO, AND ITS RELATION TO THE AGRICULTURAL ECONOMY.
UNIVERSITY OF SOUTHERN CALIFORNIA. UNPUBLISHED PHD
DISSERTATION. LOS ANGELES, CALIFORNIA. 1958.

OTHOMDS56765 THOMAS DS
THE JAPANESE AMERICAN.
UNDERSTANDING MINORITY GROUPS. ED BY JOSEPH B GITTLER. JOHN
WILEY AND SONS. NEW YORK. 1956. PP 33-57.

OWONGLJ64771 WONG LJ   *CHINATOWN-NBEACH DISTRICT CC
STATEMENT BEFORE CALIFORNIA LEGISLATURE ASSEMBLY, INTERIM
SUBCOMMITTEE ON ECONOMIC OPPORTUNITY ON BEHALF OF
CHINATOWN-NORTH BEACH DISTRICT COUNCIL.
CALIFORNIA ASSEMBLY INTERIM SUBCOMMITTEE ON ECONOMIC
OPPORTUNITY. SAN FRANCISCO, CALIFORNIA. DEC 8 1964.

OWUXXCT58772 WU CT
CHINESE PEOPLE AND CHINA-TOWN IN NEW-YORK CITY.
CLARK UNIVERSITY. PHD DISSERTATION. ATLANTA, GEORGIA. 1958.

P

PAINERO59777   AINES RO   *NJ AGL EXPERIMENT STATION
PUERTO-RICAN FARM WORKERS IN NEW-JERSEY.
RUTGERS -- THE STATE UNIVERSITY, DEPARTMENT OF AGRICULTURAL
ECONOMICS, NEW JERSEY AGRICULTURAL EXPERIMENT STATION.
NEW BRUNSWICK, NEW JERSEY. GEB 1959. 5 PP.

PARNORX62778   ARNOLD R
WHY JUAN CAN-T READ. /YOUTH EDUCATION/
COMMONWEAL, VOL 76, NO 5, AP 27 1962. PP 10-12.

PASSPCT56779   ASSN CATHOLIC TRADE UNIONISTS
SPANISH SPEAKING WORKERS AND THE LABOR MOVEMENT.
ASSOCIATION OF CATHOLIC TRADE UNIONISTS. NEW YORK.
MIMEOGRAPHED. 1956.

PBERLBB58780   BERLE BB
80 PUERTO-RICAN FAMILIES IN NEW-YORK CITY.
COLUMBIA UNIVERSITY PRESS. NEW YORK. 1958. 331 PP.

PBORDDXND781   BORDEN D   *EAST HARLEM PROJECT
EAST-HARLEM BLOCK COMMUNITY DEVELOPMENT PROGRAM. /NEW-YORK/
EAST HARLEM PROJECT. NEW YORK. 1ST ED. ND.

PBOWALX62889   BOWMAN L
THE PUERTO-RICAN COMMUNITY IN AMERICA. RAPID ACCULTURATION.
THE HUMANIST, JAN-FEB 1962.

PBRAEPX58782   BRAESTRUP P
LIFE AMONG THE GARMENT WORKERS.
NEW YORK HERALD TRIBUNE, SERIES OF 10 ARTICLES, SEPT 29-OCT
10 1958.

PBRAMJX62783   BRAM J   *MOBILIZATION FOR YOUTH
THE LOWER STATUS PUERTO-RICAN FAMILY.
MOBILIZATION FOR YOUTH, INC. NEW YORK. 1962.

PBRAMJX63784   BRAM J   *MOBILIZATION FOR YOUTH
SCHOOL AND COMMUNITY COURSE. THE LOWER STATUS PUERTO-RICAN
FAMILY.
MOBILIZATION FOR YOUTH, INC. NEW YORK. REVISED ED
MAR 1963. 10 PP.

PCARDLA67874   CARDONA LA
THE PUERTO-RICAN WORKER CONFRONTS THE COMPLEX URBAN
SOCIETY -- A PRESCRIPTION FOR CHANGE.
MAYOR-S COMMUNITY CONFERENCE, ADDRESS. NEW YORK.
AP 15 1967. 36 PP.

PCARLRC59785   CARLTON RC
NEW ASPECTS OF PUERTO-RICAN MIGRATION.
AMERICAN STATISTICAL ASSOCIATION, ANNUAL MEETING, PAPER.
1959.

PCASTCX58786   CASTANO C   *US DEPARTMENT OF LABOR
THE FIRST 10 YEARS...THE PUERTO-RICAN MIGRATORY PROBLEM.
US DEPARTMENT OF LABOR, EMPLOYMENT SECURITY REVIEW, VOL 25,
NO 3, MAR 1958. PP 31-33.

PCUNNJT57793   CUNNINGHAM JT
MIGRANTS POSE PROBLEMS FOR NEW-JERSEY FARMERS WHO NEED THEM.
NEWARK NEWS MAGAZINE, SEPT 1 1957.

PDECOPP59794   DE COLON PP   *PUERTO RICO DEPT OF LABOR
MIGRATION TRENDS.
HUNTER COLLEGE, ADDRESS. MAY 9 1959.
COMMONWEALTH OF PUERTO RICO, DEPARTMENT OF LABOR, MIGRATION
DIVISION. NEW YORK. 1959.

PDIAZEX61795   DIAZ E
A PUERTO-RICAN IN NEW-YORK.
DISSENT, VOL 8, NO 3, SUMMER 1961. PP 383-385.

PDONCDX59796   DONCHIAN D   *NEW HAVEN HUM RELS COUNCIL
A SURVEY OF NEW-HAVEN-S NEWCOMERS. THE PUERTO-RICANS.
/CONNECTICUT/
HUMAN RELATIONS COUNCIL OF GREATER NEW HAVEN. NEW HAVEN,
CONNECTICUT. 1959.

PDWORMB57797   DWORKIS MB
THE IMPACT OF PUERTO-RICAN MIGRATION ON GOVERNMENTAL
SERVICES IN NEW-YORK CITY.
NEW YORK UNIVERSITY PRESS. NEW YORK. 1957.

PEAGLMX59303   EAGLE M
THE PUERTO-RICANS IN NEW-YORK.
STUDIES IN HOUSING AND MINORITY GROUPS. ED BY NATHAN GLAZER
AND DAVIS MCINTIRE. UNIVERSITY OF CALIFORNIA PRESS.
BERKELEY, CALIFORNIA. 1959. PP 144-177.

PEASTHP61798   EAST HARLEM PROJECT   NYC COMM ON HUMAN RIGHTS
RELEASING HUMAN POTENTIAL.
EAST HARLEM PROJECT. NEW YORK CITY COMMISSION ON HUMAN
RIGHTS. NEW YORK. 1961.

PEASTHY64799   E HARLEM YOUTH EMPLOY SERVICE
THE STORY OF EAST-HARLEM-YOUTH-EMPLOYMENT-SERVICE, INC.
EAST HARLEM YOUTH EMPLOYMENT SERVICE, INC. NEW YORK. OCT
1964. 6 PP.

PELIZCX66C31   ELIZABETHTOWN COLLEGE   EPPLEY MA
YANCEY JMY   *LANCASTER COUNTY CAP COMT
POVERTY IN THE GARDEN SPOT, VOLS I AND II.
LANCASTER COUNTY PENNSYLVANIA COMMUNITY ACTION PROGRAM
COMMITTEE. ELIZABETHTOWN, PENNSYLVANIA. JAN 1966. 264 PP.

PELMARM66677   ELMAN RM
THE PUERTO-RICANS.
COMMONWEAL, VOL 83, NO 13, JAN 7 1966. PP 405-408.

PFITZJP55802   FITZPATRICK JP
THE INTEGRATION OF PUERTO-RICANS.
FORDHAM UNIVERSITY. THOUGHT, VOL 30, NO 118, FALL 1955.
PP 402-420.

PFITZJP59801   FITZPATRICK JP
THE ADJUSTMENT OF PUERTO-RICANS IN NEW-YORK-CITY.
THE JOURNAL OF INTERGROUP RELATIONS, VOL 1, WINTER
1959-1960. PP 43-51. ALSO IN AMERICAN RACE RELATIONS TODAY.
ED BY EARL RAAB. DOUBLEDAY AND CO. NEW YORK. 1962. P 176,
FF. ALSO IN MINORITY PROBLEMS. ED BY ARNOLD M ROSE AND

CAROLINE B ROSE. HARPER AND ROW. NEW YORK. 1965. PP 42-49.

PFLEIBM61804   FLEISCHER BM
SOME ECONOMIC ASPECTS OF PUERTO-RICAN MIGRATION TO THE
UNITED STATES.
STANFORD UNIVERSITY. PHD DISSERTATION. PALO ALTO,
CALIFORNIA. 1961.

PFLEIBM63437   FLEISCHER BM
THE IMPACT OF PUERTO-RICAN MIGRATION TO THE UNITED STATES.
/EMPLOYMENT/
HUMAN RESOURCES IN THE URBAN ECONOMY. ED BY MARK PERLMAN.
JOHNS HOPKINS PRESS. BALTIMORE, MARYLAND. 1963. PP 179-194.

PFLEIBM63803   FLEISCHER BM
SOME ECONOMIC ASPECTS OF PUERTO-RICAN MIGRATION TO THE
UNITED STATES.
REVIEW OF ECONOMIC STATISTICS, VOL 45, AUG 1963. PP 245-253.

PGARCAX58806   GARCIA A   *ILL GOURS ADVSY COMM ON CIVR
DISCRIMINATION AGAINST PUERTO-RICANS.
REPORT OF THE GOVERNOR-S ADVISORY COMMISSION ON CIVIL
RIGHTS. ILLINOIS GOVERNOR-S ADVISORY COMMISSION ON CIVIL
RIGHTS. SPRINGFIELD, ILLINOIS. DEC 1958. PP 79-80.

PGARDSC58807   GARDEN STATE COOPERATIVE ASSN
LABOR MANAGEMENT ON THE FARM.
THE GARDEN STATE COOPERATIVE ASSN, INC. TRENTON, NEW JERSEY.
1958. 60 PP.

PGERNAC56808   GERNES AC
IMPLICATIONS OF PUERTO-RICAN MIGRATION TO THE CONTINENT
OUTSIDE NEW-YORK CITY.
UNIVERSITY OF PUERTO RICO, 9TH ANNUAL CONVENTION ON SOCIAL
ORIENTATION, ADDRESS. DEC 10 1955. REPRINTED BY COMMONWEALTH
OF PUERTO RICO, DEPARTMENT OF LABOR, MIGRATION DIVISION.
NEW YORK. 1956. 15 PP.

PGLAZNX58211   GLAZER N
NEW-YORK-S PUERTO-RICANS.
COMMENTARY, VOL 26, 1958. PP 469-478.

PGLAZNX63809   GLAZER N
THE PUERTO-RICANS.
COMMENTARY, JULY 1963. PP 1-9.

PGOLUFT56811   GOLUB FT   *RUTGERS INST MNGMT LAB RELS
THE PUERTO-RICAN WORKER IN PERTH-AMBOY, NEW-JERSEY.
RUTGERS -- THE STATE UNIVERSITY, INSTITUTE OF MANAGEMENT AND
LABOR RELATIONS, OCCASIONAL STUDIES NO 2. NEW BRUNSWICK,
NEW JERSEY. 1956.

PGOLUFX55812   GOLUB F
SOME ECONOMIC CONSEQUENCES OF THE PUERTO-RICAN MIGRATION
INTO PERTH-AMBOY, 1949-1954. /NEW-JERSEY/
RUTGERS --THE STATE UNIVERSITY, INSTITUTE OF MANAGEMENT AND
LABOR RELATIONS. NEW BRUNSWICK, NEW JERSEY. 1955.

PGOTSJW66808   GOTSCH JW
PUERTO-RICAN LEADERSHIP IN NEW-YORK.
NEW YORK UNIVERSITY, MA ESSAY. NEW YORK. JUNE 1966. 77 PP.

PGRAYLX63027   GRAY L
LABOR UNIONS AND PUERTO-RICAN MEMBERS IN NEW-YORK CITY.
CORNELL UNIVERSITY, NEW YORK STATE SCHOOL OF INDUSTRIAL AND
LABOR RELATIONS. ITHACA, NEW YORK. 1963. REPRINT NO 147.

PGRAYLX63813   GRAY L   *OECD
THE PUERTO-RICAN WORKERS IN NEW-YORK.
ORGANIZATION FOR ECONOMIC COOPERATION AND DEVELOPMENT.
PARIS, FRANCE. 1963.

PGREGPX61857   GREGORY P   *UPR MANPOWER RESOURCES PROJ
NOTES ON MIGRATION AND WORKERS ATTITUDES TOWARD IT.
UNIVERSITY OF PUERTO RICO, SOCIAL SCIENCE RESEARCH CENTER,
MANPOWER RESOURCES PROJECT, PRELIMINARY RELEASE.
RIO PIEDRAS, PUERTO RICO. MIMEOGRAPHED. 1961. 10 PP.

PHAMMRX64153   HAMMER RX
REPORT FROM A SPANISH HARLEM FORTRESS.
THE NEW YORK TIMES MAGAZINE, JAN 5 1964. PP 22,32,34,37,39.

PHAUGJX60814   HAUGHTON J   *E HARLEM YOUTH EMPLOY SERV
SIX MONTHS REPORT.
EAST HARLEM YOUTH EMPLOYMENT SERVICE, INC. NEW YORK.
AP 1960. 18 PP.

PHELFBH59481   HELFGOTT BH   *NY STATE COMM AGAINST DISCR
PUERTO-RICAN INTEGRATION IN THE SKIRT INDUSTRY IN
NEW-YORK CITY.
DISCRIMINATION AND LOW INCOMES. ED BY AARON ANTONOVSKY AND
LEWIS L LORWIN. NEW SCHOOL FOR SOCIAL RESEARCH. NEW YORK.
1959. PP 71-99. ALSO NEW YORK STATE COMMISSION AGAINST
DISCRIMINATION. NEW YORK. 1959. 34 PP.

PHELFRB57815   HELFGOTT RB
PUERTO-RICAN INTEGRATION IN A GARMENT UNION LOCAL.
INDUSTRIAL RELATIONS RESEARCH ASSOCIATION, ANNALS. 1957.
P 269 FF.

PHERNJX59816   HERNANDEZ-ALVAREZ J
THE PUERTO-RICAN SECTION. A STUDY IN SOCIAL TRANSITION.
FORDHAM UNIVERSITY, DEPARTMENT OF SOCIOLOGY. UNPUBLISHED
MASTER-S THESIS. NEW YORK. 1959.

PILLIIX56818   ILLICH I
PUERTO-RICANS IN NEW-YORK.
COMMONWEAL, VOL 64, NO 12, JUNE 22 1956. PP 294-297.

PIMSETP62820   IMSE TP
SUPPLEMENTARY REPORT ON PUERTO-RICANS IN BUFFALO.
/NEW-YORK/
CANISIUS COLLEGE. BUFFALO, NEW YORK. JULY 1961, AP 1962.
18 PP, 3 PP.

PKOSSJD65822   KOSS JD
PUERTO-RICANS IN PHILADELPHIA. MIGRATION AND ACCOMODATION.
/PENNSYLVANIA/
UNIVERSITY OF PENNSYLVANIA. PHD DISSERTATION. PHILADELPHIA,
PENNSYLVANIA. 1965.

PLEVIMX57823 LEVITAS M
NEW-YORK-S LABOR SCANDAL. THE PUERTO-RICAN WORKERS.
NEW YORK POST, SERIES OF SIX ARTICLES, JULY 15-19 AND 21
1957.

PLEWIOX66824 LEWIS O
THE CULTURE OF POVERTY.
SCIENTIFIC AMERICAN, OCT 1966. PP 19-25.

PLEWIOX66825 LEWIS O
LA VIDA. A PUERTO-RICAN FAMILY IN THE CULTURE OF
POVERTY -- SAN-JUAN AND NEW-YORK.
RANDOM HOUSE. NEW YORK. 1966. 669 PP.

PMETARX59826 METAUTEN R   *PHILADELPHIA COMM HUMAN RELS
PUERTO-RICANS IN PHILADELPHIA. /PENNSYLVANIA/
PHILADELPHIA COMMISSION ON HUMAN RELATIONS. PHILADELPHIA,
PENNSYLVANIA. 1959.

PMOBIFYNOC024 MOBILIZATION FOR YOUTH
BIBLIOGRAPHY ON THE PUERTO-RICAN. HIS CULTURE AND SOCIETY.
MOBILIZATION FOR YOUTH, INC. NEW YORK. VOL 1, NO 7. ND.

PMONSJX57828 MONSERRAT J   *WELFARE CC METROPOLITAN CHI
CULTURAL VALUES AND THE PUERTO-RICAN.
WELFARE COUNCIL OF METROPOLITAN CHICAGO, SELECTED PAPERS OF
OF INSTITUTE ON CULTURAL PATTERNS ON NEWCOMERS. CHICAGO,
ILLINOIS. OCT 1957. PP 59-70.

PMONTHK59829 MONTROSS HK   *US DEPARTMENT OF LABOR
MEETING THE NEEDS OF THE PUERTO-RICAN MIGRANT.
US DEPARTMENT OF LABOR, EMPLOYMENT SECURITY REVIEW, VOL 26,
NO 1, JAN 1959. PP 31-33.

PMONTHX60830 MONTROSS H   *US DEPARTMENT OF LABOR
PLACING PUERTO-RICAN WORKERS IN THE NEW-YORK CITY
LABOR-MARKET.
US DEPARTMENT OF LABOR, BUREAU OF EMPLOYMENT SECURITY,
MINORITY GROUPS CONFERENCE, ADDRESS. WASHINGTON, DC.
JULY 1960.

PNEWJSE63831 NEW JERSEY SES
ANNUAL FARM LABOR REPORT. /NEW-JERSEY/
NEW JERSEY STATE EMPLOYMENT SERVICE. TRENTON, NEW JERSEY.
1963. 27 PP.

PNEWYCC56834 NEW YORK CITY BOARD OF ED
RESOURCE UNITS IN THE TEACHING OF OCCUPATIONS -- AN
EXPERIMENT IN GUIDANCE OF PUERTO-RICAN TEENAGERS.
NEW YORK CITY BOARD OF EDUCATION, PUERTO RICAN STUDY.
NEW YORK. 1956.

PNEWYCC58833 NEW YORK CITY BOARD OF ED
THE PUERTO-RICAN STUDY, 1953-1957.
NEW YORK CITY BOARD OF EDUCATION. NEW YORK. 1958.

PNEWYCC64832 NEW YORK CITY BOARD OF ED
PUERTO-RICAN PROFILES.
NEW YORK CITY BOARD OF EDUCATION. NEW YORK. 1964. 96 PP.

PNEWYCO62838 NYS COMM FOR HUMAN RIGHTS
POPULATIONS OF NEW-YORK STATE. REPORT NO 2. THE PUERTO-RICAN
POPULATION OF THE NEW-YORK-CITY AREA.
NEW YORK STATE COMMISSION FOR HUMAN RIGHTS. NEW YORK. 1962.

PNEWYDC56817 NYC DEPT COMMERCE PUB EVENTS
PUERTO-RICANS, KEY SOURCE OF LABOR.
NEW YORK CITY DEPARTMENT OF COMMERCE AND PUBLIC EVENTS,
HIGHLIGHTS, VOL 1, NO 8, OCT 1956. PP 1-3.

PNEWYDW60835 NEW YORK CITY DEPT OF WELFARE
SOME CHARACTERISTICS OF PUBLIC ASSISTANCE CASES IN
NEW-YORK CITY, AUGUST, 1959.
NEW YORK CITY DEPARTMENT OF WELFARE. NEW YORK. 1960.

PNEWYSA58836 NY STATE COMM AGAINST DISCR
COMPLAINTS ALLEGING DISCRIMINATION BECAUSE OF PUERTO-RICAN
NATIONAL ORIGIN, JULY 1, 1945-SEPTEMBER 1, 1958.
NEW YORK STATE COMMISSION AGAINST DISCRIMINATION. NEW YORK.
1958.

PNEWYSA58837 NY STATE COMM AGAINST DISCR
PUERTO-RICAN EMPLOYMENT IN NEW-YORK CITY HOTELS.
/OCCUPATIONS/
NEW YORK STATE COMMISSION AGAINST DISCRIMINATION. NEW YORK.
OCT 1958. 9 PP.

PNEWYSE57840 NY STATE DEPARTMENT OF LABOR
PUERTO-RICANS IN THE NEW-YORK STATE LABOR-MARKET.
NEW YORK STATE INDUSTRIAL BULLETIN, VOL 36, NO 8, AUG 1957.
PP 17-19.

PNEWYSE60839 NY STATE DEPARTMENT OF LABOR
CHARACTERISTICS OF POPULATION AND LABOR IN NEW-YORK STATE,
1956 AND 1957. PUERTO-RICANS IN NEW-YORK CITY.
NEW YORK STATE DEPARTMENT OF LABOR. NEW YORK. 1960.

PORTIRX62841 ORTIZ R   *MOBILIZATION FOR YOUTH
PUERTO-RICAN CULTURE.
MOBILIZATION FOR YOUTH INC. TRAINING AND PERSONNEL.
NEW YORK. SEPT 10 1962. 19 PP.

PPADIEX58842 PADILLA E
UP FROM PUERTO-RICO.
COLUMBIA UNIVERSITY PRESS. NEW YORK. 1958.

PPAULIX55843 PAUL I   *HARTFORD SEMINARY FOUNDATION
MIGRANTS AND CULTURE CHANGE.
HARTFORD SEMINARY FOUNDATION BULLETIN, NO 21. WINTER
1955-1956. PP 24-27.

PPITTCH64844 PHILADELPHIA COMM HUMAN RELS
PHILADELPHIA-S PUERTO-RICAN POPULATION, WITH 1960 CENSUS
DATA. /PENNSYLVANIA/
PHILADELPHIA COMMISSION ON HUMAN RELATIONS. PHILADELPHIA,
PENNSYLVANIA. 1964.

PPUERRDND788 PUERTO RICO DEPT OF LABOR *US DEPARTMENT OF LABOR
HOW TO HIRE AGRICULTURAL WORKERS FROM PUERTO-RICO.
COMMONWEALTH OF PUERTO RICO, DEPARTMENT OF LABOR, MIGRATION
DIVISION. IN COOPERATION WITH US DEPARTMENT OF LABOR, BUREAU
OF EMPLOYMENT SECURITY, US EMPLOYMENT SERVICE, FARM
PLACEMENT SERVICE. WASHINGTON, DC. VARIOUS YEARS. 16 PP.

PPUERRDND791 PUERTO RICO DEPT OF LABOR
REPORTS OF PUERTO-RICO DEPARTMENT OF LABOR, MIGRATION
DIVISION ON PLACEMENT.
COMMONWEALTH OF PUERTO RICO, DEPARTMENT OF LABOR, MIGRATION
DIVISION. NEW YORK. MIMEOGRAPHED. VARIOUS YEARS.

PPUERRDND792 PUERTO RICO DEPT OF LABOR
A SUMMARY IN FACTS AND FIGURES.
COMMONWEALTH OF PUERTO RICO, DEPARTMENT OF LABOR, MIGRATION
DIVISION. NEW YORK. VARIOUS YEARS.

PPUERRD57789 PUERTO RICO DEPT OF LABOR
THE MIGRATION DIVISION -- POLICY, FUNCTIONS, OBJECTIVES.
COMMONWEALTH OF PUERTO RICO, DEPARTMENT OF LABOR, MIGRATION
DIVISION. NEW YORK. 1957. 6 PP.

PPUERRD58787 PUERTO RICO DEPT OF LABOR
HELPING PUERTO-RICANS HELP THEMSELVES.
COMMONWEALTH OF PUERTO RICO, DEPARTMENT OF LABOR, MIGRATION
DIVISION. NEW YORK. 1958.

PPUERRD60790 PUERTO RICO DEPT OF LABOR
THE PUERTO-RICAN NEWCOMER.
COMMONWEALTH OF PUERTO RICO, DEPARTMENT OF LABOR, MIGRATION
DIVISION. NEW YORK. 1960.

PRANDCX58845 RAND C
THE PUERTO-RICANS.
OXFORD UNIVERSITY PRESS. NEW YORK. 1958. 178 PP.

PRAUSCX61846 RAUSHENBUSH C
A COMPARISON OF THE OCCUPATIONS OF THE FIRST AND SECOND
GENERATION PUERTO-RICANS IN THE MAINLAND LABOR-MARKET, AND
HOW THE WORK OF THE NEW-YORK STATE DEPARTMENT OF LABOR
AFFECTS PUERTO-RICANS.
PUERTO RICAN POPULATION OF NEW YORK CITY. ED BY A J JAFFE.
COLUMBIA UNIVERSITY, BUREAU OF APPLIED SOCIAL RESEARCH.
NEW YORK. JAN 1961.

PREMEGN58847 REMERI GN
AN ANALYSIS OF UNEMPLOYED PUERTO-RICAN MIGRANTS IN
NEW-YORK CITY.
MONTCLAIR STATE TEACHERS COLLEGE. MASTER-S THESIS.
UPPER MONTCLAIR, NEW JERSEY. 1958.

PSEDAEX58850 SEDA-BONILLA E
PATTERNS OF SOCIAL ACCOMODATION OF THE MIGRANT PUERTO-RICAN
IN THE AMERICAN SOCIAL STRUCTURE.
REVISTA DE CIENCIAS SOCIALES, VOL 11, NO 2, JUNE 1958.
PP 190-201.

PSENICX56852 SENIOR C
THE PUERTO-RICANS IN THE UNITED STATES.
UNDERSTANDING MINORITY GROUPS. ED BY JOSEPH B GITTLER.
JOHN WILEY. NEW YORK. 1956.

PSENICX57851 SENIOR C
IMPLICATIONS OF POPULATION REDISTRIBUTION.
NATIONAL ASSOCIATION OF INTERGROUP RELATIONS OFFICIALS,
11TH ANNUAL CONVENTION. ADDRESS. WASHINGTON, DC. PUBLISHED
BY NAIRO. 1957.

PSENICX61308 SENIOR C   *ANTI-DEFAMATION LEAGUE
STRANGERS THEN NEIGHBORS. FROM PILGRIMS TO PUERTO-RICANS.
ANTI-DEFAMATION LEAGUE OF B-NAI B-RITH. FREEDOM BOOKS.
NEW YORK. 1961. 88 PP.

PSENICX65307 SENIOR C
THE PUERTO-RICANS, STRANGERS -- THEN NEIGHBORS.
QUADRANGLE BOOKS. 2ND ED 1965. CHICAGO, ILLINOIS. 123 PP.

PSEXTPC65853 SEXTON PC
SPANISH HARLEM, AN ANATOMY OF POVERTY.
HARPER AND ROW. NEW YORK. 1965. 208 PP.

PSILVRM63100 SILVA RM
OCCUPATIONAL PLANS AND ASPIRATIONS. PUERTO-RICAN AND
AMERICAN HIGH SCHOOL SENIORS COMPARED.
PENNSYLVANIA STATE UNIVERSITY. MASTERS THESIS. UNIVERSITY
PARK, PENNSYLVANIA. 1963.

PTRENRD58800 TRENT RD
THREE BASIC THEMES IN MEXICAN AND PUERTO-RICAN FAMILIES.
JOURNAL OF SOCIAL PSYCHOLOGY, VOL 48, NOV 1958. PP 167-181.

PUSBURC63182 US BUREAU OF THE CENSUS
PUERTO-RICANS IN THE UNITED STATES. SOCIAL AND ECONOMIC DATA
FOR PERSONS OF PUERTO-RICAN BIRTH AND PARENTAGE.
/DEMOGRAPHY/
US DEPARTMENT OF COMMERCE, BUREAU OF THE CENSUS, FINAL
REPORT PC-2-1D. GPO. WASHINGTON, DC. 1963. 132 PP.

PUSBURC63854 US BUREAU OF THE CENSUS
CENSUS OF POPULATION. 1960, PUERTO-RICANS IN THE UNITED
STATES.
US DEPARTMENT OF COMMERCE, BUREAU OF THE CENSUS. GPO.
WASHINGTON, DC. 1963.

PUVMAXX64856 UNIVERSITY OF MARYLAND   MD GOVRS COMT MIGRATORY LABOR
CONCERN FOR AGRICULTURAL MIGRANTS IN MARYLAND.
UNIVERSITY OF MARYLAND. STATE OF MARYLAND GOVERNORS
COMMITTEE ON MIGRATORY LABOR. COLLEGE PARK, MARYLAND.
FEB 1964. 21 PP.

PWAKEDX59858 WAKEFIELD D
ISLAND IN THE CITY. THE WORLD OF SPANISH HARLEM.
HOUGHTON MIFFLIN CO. BOSTON, MASSACHUSETTS, 1959. 278 PP.

PYANGRX61859 YANGAS R   *E HARLEM YOUTH EMPLOY SERV
SERVICING THE HARD TO PLACE.
EAST HARLEM YOUTH EMPLOYMENT SERVICE, INC. NEW YORK.
JUNE 1961. 25 PP.

W

WAAUWEFND274   AAUW EDUCATIONAL FOUNDATION
WOMEN-S EDUCATION.
AMERICAN ASSOCIATION OF UNIVERSITY WOMEN, EDUCATIONAL
FOUNDATION. WASHINGTON, DC. PERIODIC PUBLICATION.

WAAUWFX65616   AAUW FOUNDATION
CONTINUING EDUCATION -- FOCUS ON COUNSELING AND TRAINING.
WOMEN-S EDUCATION, MAR 1965.

WAAUWJX62601   AAUW JOURNAL
CHANGE AND CHOICE FOR THE COLLEGE WOMAN. /WORK-WOMAN-ROLE/
JOURNAL OF ASSOCIATION OF AMERICAN UNIVERSITY WOMEN,
MAY 1962, ENTIRE ISSUE.

WADDILK63862   ADDISS LK
JOB-RELATED EXPENSES OF THE WORKING-MOTHERS.
CHILDREN, NOV-DEC 1963.

WAFLCIO61618   AFL-CIO
PROBLEMS OF WORKING WOMEN. SUMMARY REPORT OF A CONFERENCE.
AFL-CIO. INDUSTRIAL UNION DEPARTMENT. PUBLICATION NO 43.
WASHINGTON, DC. 1961.

WAFLCIO65617   AFL-CIO
POLICY RESOLUTION ADOPTED BY AFL-CIO 6TH CONSTITUTIONAL
CONVENTION, SAN FRANCISCO, DEC 1965. /EEO/
AFL-CIO. WASHINGTON, DC. 11 PP.

WALBEGS61602   ALBEE GS
LET-S PUT WOMEN IN THEIR PLACE. /INDUSTRY/
SATURDAY EVENING POST, DEC 16 1961. PP 8-10.

WALBJMH61603   ALBJERG MH
WHY DO BRIGHT GIRLS NOT TAKE STIFF COURSES. /ASPIRATIONS/
EDUCATIONAL FORUM, VOL 25, JAN 1961. PP 141-144.

WALPEEJ62604   ALPENFEIS EJ
WOMEN IN THE PROFESSIONAL WORLD. /OCCUPATIONS/
AMERICAN WOMEN. THE CHANGING IMAGE. ED BY BEVERLY B CASSARA.
BEACON PRESS. BOSTON, MASSACHUSETTS. 1962. PP 73-89.

WALTMSX63757   ALTMAN S
UNEMPLOYMENT OF MARRIED WOMEN.
UNIVERSITY OF CALIFORNIA AT LOS ANGELES. PHD THESIS.
LOS ANGELES, CALIFORNIA. 1963.

WAMERCEND605   AMERICAN CC ON EDUCATION
THE EDUCATION OF WOMEN -- INFORMATION AND RESEARCH NOTES.
AMERICAN COUNCIL ON EDUCATION, THE COMMISSION ON THE
EDUCATION OF WOMEN. WASHINGTON, DC. ND. 12 PP.

WAMERCE60606   AMERICAN CC ON EDUCATION
THE SPAN OF A WOMEN-S LIFE AND LEARNING. /WORK-WOMEN-ROLE/
AMERICAN COUNCIL ON EDUCATION, COMMISSION ON THE EDUCATION
OF WOMEN. WASHINGTON, DC. AP 1960.

WAMERJN57378   AMERICAN JOURNAL OF NURSING
THE BLS STUDY OF NURSES SALARIES AND EMPLOYMENT CONDITIONS.
AMERICAN JOURNAL OF NURSING, VOL 57, JULY 1957. P 889.

WAMERMW65607   AMERICAN MEDICAL WOMEN-S ASSN
MEDICINE AS A CAREER FOR WOMEN. /OCCUPATIONS/
AMERICAN MEDICAL WOMEN-S ASSOCIATION. NEW YORK. 1965. 16 PP.

WAMERNA65610   AMERICAN NURSES ASSOCIATION
SURVEY OF EMPLOYMENT-CONDITIONS OF NURSES EMPLOYED BY
PHYSICIANS AND/OR DENTISTS. JULY 1964.
AMERICAN NURSES ASSOCIATION. NEW YORK. MIMEOGRAPHED. 1965.

WAMERNA65611   AMERICAN NURSES ASSOCIATION
SURVEY OF SALARIES AND EMPLOYMENT-CONDITIONS IN NONFEDERAL
PSYCHIATRIC HOSPITALS.
AMERICAN NURSES ASSOCIATION. NEW YORK. MIMEOGRAPHED.
JUNE 1965.

WAMERNA66608   AMERICAN NURSES ASSOCIATION
FACTS ABOUT NURSING.
AMERICAN NURSES ASSOCIATION, ANNUAL, 1956-1966. NEW YORK.
1956-1966.

WAMERNA66612   AMERICAN NURSES ASSOCIATION
SURVEY OF SALARIES AND PERSONNEL PRACTICES FOR TEACHERS AND
ADMINISTRATORS IN NURSING EDUCATIONAL PROGRAMS, DECEMBER
1965.
AMERICAN NURSES ASSOCIATION. NEW YORK. MIMEOGRAPHED. 1966.

WAMONJRX62613 AMON R
ENGINEERING TALENT IN SHORT SUPPLY. /OCCUPATIONS/
NEW YORK STATE, INDUSTRIAL BULLETIN, JUNE 1962.

WANDEJE60614   ANDERSON JE
THE DEVELOPMENT OF BEHAVIOR AND PERSONALITY.
/WORK-WOMEN-ROLE/
DEVELOPMENT AND EDUCATION, THE NATION-S CHILDREN.
ED BY ELI GINZBERG. COLUMBIA UNIVERSITY PRESS. NEW-YORK.
1960.

WANGEJL63615   ANGEL JL
OCCUPATIONS FOR MEN AND WOMEN AFTER 45.
WORLD TRADE ACADEMY PRESS. NEW YORK. 1963.

WANGRSS64484   ANGRIST SS
THE ROLE OUTLOOK OF EDUCATED WOMEN. /ASPIRATIONS/
MARGARET MORRISON CARNEGIE COLLEGE. PITTSBURGH,
PENNSYLVANIA. DEC 1964. 4 PP

WANGRSS66619   ANGRIST SS
ROLE CONCEPTION AS A PREDICTOR OF ADULT FEMALE ROLES.
/WORK-WOMAN-ROLE/
SOCIOLOGY AND SOCIAL RESEARCH, VOL 50, NO 4, JULY 1966.
PP 448-459

WARRURC66216   ARROWHEAD REGIONAL CONFERENCE *US DEPARTMENT OF LABOR
REPORT OF ARROWHEAD REGIONAL CONFERENCE ON THE STATUS OF
WOMEN IN NORTHERN MINNESOTA.
US DEPARTMENT OF LABOR, WOMEN-S BUREAU. ARROWHEAD REGIONAL
CONFERENCE ON THE STATUS OF WOMEN IN NORTHERN MINNESOTA.
JULY 16 1964. PUBLISHED BY US DEPARTMENT OF LABOR, WOMEN-S
BUREAU. GPO. WASHINGTON, DC. 1966.

WASTIAW64620   ASTIN AW   NICHOLS RC
LIFE GOALS AND VOCATIONAL CHOICE. /WORK-WOMAN-ROLE/
JOURNAL OF APPLIED PSYCHOLOGY, 1964. PP 50-58.

WAVILDL64316   AVILA DL
AN INVERTED FACTOR ANALYSIS OF PERSONALITY DIFFERENCES
BETWEEN CAREER AND HOMEMAKING-ORIENTED WOMEN.
/ASPIRATIONS/
UNIVERSITY OF NEBRASKA TEACHERS COLLEGE, EDD DISSERTATION.
LINCOLN, NEBRASKA. 1964. 111 PP.

WBAILLX64623   BAILYN L
NOTES ON THE ROLE OF CHOICE IN THE PSYCHOLOGY OF
PROFESSIONAL WOMEN. /OCCUPATIONS/
DAECALUS, VOL 93, SPRING 1964. PP 700-710.

WBAKEEF64624   BAKER EF
TECHNOLOGY AND WOMEN-S WORK.
COLUMBIA UNIVERSITY PRESS. NEW YORK. 1964. 460 PP.

WBALEHX66625   BALE H   TAYER D
TESTIMONY, PUBLIC HEARING, WOMEN IN PUBLIC AND PRIVATE
EMPLOYMENT, CALIFORNIA. /DISCRIMINATION EEOC/
CALIFORNIA ADVISORY COMMISSION ON THE STATUS OF WOMEN.
STUDY COMMITTEE NO 1, ON PUBLIC AND PRIVATE EMPLOYMENT.
HEARINGS. SACRAMENTO, CALIFORNIA. AP 29 1966. PP 161-179.

WBANNMC63626   BANNING MC
THE FACTS, THE HOPES, AND THE POSSIBILITIES.
/WORK-WOMAN-ROLE/
EDUCATION AND A WOMAN-S LIFE. ED BY LAWRENCE E DENNIS.
AMERICAN COUNCIL ON EDUCATION. WASHINGTON, DC. 1963.
PP 143-149.

WBARBMS58627   BARBER MS   *US DEPARTMENT OF LABOR
CAREERS FOR WOMEN IN SCIENCE. /OCCUPATIONS/
US DEPARTMENT OF LABOR, BUREAU OF LABOR STATISTICS.
OCCUPATIONAL OUTLOOK QUARTERLY, VOL 2, NO 3, SEPT 1958.
PP 27-31.

WBARKAE65628   BARKER AE   STATON EE
*US DEPT OF HEALTH ED WELFARE
INACTIVE NURSES. AN UNTAPPED RECRUITMENT SOURCE.
US DEPARTMENT OF HEALTH, EDUCATION AND WELFARE, PUBLIC
HEALTH REPORTS, VOL 80, NO 7, JULY 1965.

WBARTAK58629   BARTER AK
A STUDY OF ELEMENTARY SCHOOL TEACHER-S ATTITUDES TOWARD THE
WOMAN PRINCIPAL AND TOWARD ELEMENTARY PRINCIPALSHIP AS A
CAREER. /DISCRIMINATION/
UNIVERSITY MICROFILMS. ANN ARBOR, MICHIGAN. 1958. 226 PP.

WBARURX66453   BARUCH R
THE ACHIEVEMENT MOTIVE IN WOMEN. A STUDY OF THE IMPLICATIONS
FOR CAREER DEVELOPMENT.
HARVARD UNIVERSITY. EDD DISSERTATION. CAMBRIDGE,
MASSACHUSETTS. 1966.

WBARURX66457   BARUCH R   *HARVARD CENT FOR RES CAREERS
THE INTERRUPTION AND RESUMPTION OF WOMEN-S CAREERS.
HARVARD UNIVERSITY, GRADUATE SCHOOL OF EDUCATION, CENTER
FOR RESEARCH IN CAREERS, HARVARD STUDIES IN CAREER
DEVELOPMENT NO 50. CAMBRIDGE, MASSACHUSETTS. SEPT 1966.
14 PP.

WBAUMLX66630   BAUMGARTNER L
OPTIMAL UTILIZATION OF MEDICAL WOMANPOWER. /OCCUPATIONS/
JOURNAL OF AMERICAN MEDICAL WOMEN, VOL 21, NO 10, OCT 1966.
PP 832-837.

WBECHCX66631   BECHTOL C
TESTIMONY, PUBLIC HEARING, WOMEN IN PUBLIC AND PRIVATE
EMPLOYMENT, CALIFORNIA. /EMPLOYMENT-CONDITIONS/
CALIFORNIA ADVISORY COMMISSION ON THE STATUS OF WOMEN,
STUDY COMMITTEE NO 1, ON PUBLIC AND PRIVATE EMPLOYMENT.
HEARINGS. SACRAMENTO, CALIFORNIA. MAR 31-AP 1 1966.
PP 118-125.

WBECKEL64632   BECK EL
THE PROSPECT FOR ADVANCEMENT IN BUSINESS OF THE MARRIED
WOMAN COLLEGE GRADUATE. /OCCUPATIONS/
JOURNAL OF THE NATIONAL ASSOCIATION OF WOMEN DEANS AND
COUNCELORS, VOL 27, NO 3 1964. PP 114-119.

WBECKJA63633   BECKER JA
INTEREST PATTERN FAKING BY FEMALE JOB APPLICANTS.
/ASPIRATIONS/
JOURNAL OF INDUSTRIAL PSYCHOLOGY, 1963. PP 51-54.

WBELAJX66634   BELARDI J   *CWBHMC SERVICE WORKERS UNION
STATEMENT, PUBLIC HEARING, WOMEN IN PUBLIC AND PRIVATE
EMPLOYMENT, CALIFORNIA. /FEP EMPLOYMENT-CONDITIONS
DISCRIMINATION/
CALIFORNIA ADVISORY COMMISSION ON THE STATUS OF WOMEN,
STUDY COMMITTEE NO 1, ON PUBLIC AND PRIVATE EMPLOYMENT.
HEARINGS. SACRAMENTO, CALIFORNIA. AP 29 1966. PP 285-294.

WBELLDX56635   BELL D
THE GREAT BACK-TO-WORK MOVEMENT. /WORK-FAMILY-CONFLICT/
FORTUNE, JULY 1956. PP 90-93, 168, 170, 172.

WBELLMS59636   BELL MS
SPECIAL WOMEN-S COLLECTIONS IN US LIBRARIES.
COLLEGE AND RESEARCH LIBRARIES, MAY 1959.

WBENJLX66456   BENJAMIN L
SO YOU WANT TO BE A WORKING MOTHER.
MCGRAW-HILL BOOK CO. NEW YORK. 1966.

WBENNSJ66637   BENNETT SJ
STATEMENT, PUBLIC HEARING, WOMEN IN PUBLIC AND PRIVATE
EMPLOYMENT, CALIFORNIA. /FEP EMPLOYMENT-CONDITIONS
DISCRIMINATION/
CALIFORNIA ADVISORY COMMISSION ON THE STATUS OF WOMEN,
STUDY COMMITTEE NO 1, ON PUBLIC AND PRIVATE EMPLOYMENT.
HEARINGS. SACRAMENTO, CALIFORNIA. MAR 31-AP 1 1966.
PP 98-100.

WBERNJX63643   BERNARD J   SHILLING CW
TYSON JW
INFORMAL COMMUNICATION AMONG BIOSCIENTISTS.

/EMPLOYMENT-CONDITIONS/
BIOLOGICAL SCIENCES COMMUNICATION PROJECT. WASHINGTON, DC.
1963.

WBERNJX64638   BERNARD J
ACADEMIC WOMEN. /OCCUPATIONS/
PENNSYLVANIA STATE UNIVERSITY PRESS. UNIVERSITY PARK,
PENNSYLVANIA. 1964. 331 PP.

WBERNJX65639   BERNARD J
THE PRESENT SITUATION IN THE ACADEMIC WORLD OF WOMEN
  TRAINED IN ENGINEERING. /OCCUPATIONS/
WOMEN AND THE SCIENTIFIC PROFFESSIONS. ED BY JACQUELINE A
MATTFELD AND CAROL G VAN AKEN. MIT PRESS. CAMBRIDGE,
MASSACHUSETTS. 1965. PP 163-182.

WBERNML66746   BERNHARD MEMORIAL LIBRARY
RESOURCES FOR THE EMPLOYMENT OF MATURE WOMEN AND/OR THEIR
  CONTINUING EDUCATION. A SELECTED BIBLIOGRAPHY AND AIDS.
RICHARD J BERNHARD MEMORIAL LIBRARY. NEW YORK. OCT 1966.
24 PP.

WBERNSE65458   BERNARD SE
THE ECONOMIC AND SOCIAL ADJUSTMENT OF LOW-INCOME
  FEMALE-HEADED FAMILIES.
BRANDEIS UNIVERSITY, THE FLORENCE HELLER GRADUATE SCHOOL FOR
ADVANCED STUDIES IN SOCIAL RESEARCH. WALTHAM, MASSACHUSETTS.
PHD DISSERTATION. 1965.

WBERRJX63640   BERRY J
UNIVERSITY OF KANSAS-CITY PROJECT FOR CONTINUING EDUCATION
  OF WOMEN.
EDUCATION AND A WOMEN-S LIFE. ED BY LAWRENCE E DENNIS.
AMERICAN COUNCIL ON EDUCATION. WASHINGTON, DC. 1963.
PP 96-100.

WBERRJX63641   BERRY J   EPSTEIN S
CONTINUING EDUCATION OF WOMEN. NEEDS, ASPIRATIONS, AND
  PLANS.
UNIVERSITY OF KANSAS CITY. KANSAS CITY, MISSOURI. 1963.
41 PP.

WBERRJX66642   BERRY J   KERN KK
MELENEY EK   VETTER L
*MISSOURI DEPT LABOR IR
COUNSELING GIRLS AND WOMEN. AWARENESS. ANALYSIS. ACTION.
UNIVERSITY OF MISSOURI AT KANSAS CITY. KANSAS CITY,
MISSOURI. MAR 1966. 71 PP.

WBERWHD62475   BERWALD HD
ATTITUDES TOWARD WOMEN COLLEGE TEACHERS IN INSTITUTIONS OF
  HIGHER EDUCATION ACCREDITED BY THE NORTH CENTRAL
  ASSOCIATION.
UNIVERSITY OF MINNESOTA. PHD DISSERTATION. MINNEAPOLIS,
MINNESOTA. 1962. 521 PP. 2 VOLS.

WBETTBX62883   BETTELHEIM B
GROWING UP FEMALE. /WORK-WOMAN-ROLE/
HARPER-S, OCT 1962.

WBETTBX64646   BETTELHIEM B
WOMEN. EMANCIPATION IS STILL TO COME.
  /WORK-FAMILY-CONFLICT/
THE NEW REPUBLIC, NOV 7 1964. PP 48-58.

WBETTBX65645   BETTELHIEM B
THE COMMITMENT REQUIRED OF A WOMAN ENTERING A SCIENTIFIC
  PROFESSION. /OCCUPATIONS/
WOMEN AND THE SCIENTIFIC PROFESSIONS. ED BY JACQUELINE A
MATTFELD AND CAROL G VAN AKEN. MIT PRESS. CAMBRIDGE,
MASSACHUSETTES. 1965. PP 3-19.

WBLACGW63648   BLACKWELL GW
THE COLLEGE AND THE CONTINUING EDUCATION OF WOMEN.
EDUCATIONAL RECORD, VOL 44, NO 1, JAN 1963. PP 33-39. ALSO
IN EDUCATION AND A WOMEN-S LIFE. ED BY LAWRENCE E DENNIS.
AMERICAN COUNCIL ON EDUCATION, WASHINGTON, DC. 1963.
PP 72-91.

WBLOCHX66649   BLOCK H   *AMALGAMATED CLOTHING WORKERS
TESTIMONY, PUBLIC HEARING, WOMEN IN PUBLIC AND PRIVATE
  EDUCATION, CALIFORNIA. /FEP EMPLOYMENT-CONDITIONS
  DISCRIMINATION MIGRANT-WORKERS/
CALIFORNIA ADVISORY COMMISSION ON THE STATUS OF WOMEN,
STUDY COMMITTEE NO 1, ON PUBLIC AND PRIVATE EMPLOYMENT.
HEARINGS. SACRAMENTO, CALIFORNIA. MAR 31-AP 1 1966.
PP 32-42.

WBLOORO65884   BLOOD RO
LONG-RANGE CAUSES AND CONSEQUENCES OF THE EMPLOYMENT OF
  MARRIED WOMEN.
JOURNAL OF MARRIAGE AND THE FAMILY, FEB 1965.

WBOLTRH65650   BOLT RH
THE PRESENT SITUATION OF WOMAN SCIENTISTS AND ENGINEERS IN
  INDUSTRY AND GOVERNMENT. /OCCUPATIONS/
WOMEN AND THE SCIENTIFIC PROFESSIONS. ED BY JACQUELINE A
MATTFELD AND CAROL G VAN AKEN. MIT PRESS. CAMBRIDGE,
MASSACHUSETTS. 1965. PP 139-162.

WBORGEM63651   BORGESE EM
ASCENT OF WOMEN. /WORK-WOMEN-ROLE/
GEORGE BRAZILLER. NEW YORK. 1963.

WBOWEWGND0652   BOWEN WG   FINEGAN TA
*PRINCETON U EC DEPT IR SECT
EDUCATIONAL-ATTAINMENT AND LABOR-FORCE PARTICIPATION.
PRINCETON UNIVERSITY, DEPARTMENT OF ECONOMICS, INDUSTRIAL
RELATIONS SECTION. PRINCETON, NEW JERSEY. 15 PP.

WBOWMGW65653   BOWMAN GW   WORTHY BN
GREYSON SA
ARE WOMEN EXECUTIVES PEOPLE. /OCCUPATIONS/
HARVARD BUSINESS REVIEW, VOL 43, NO 4, JULY-AUG 1965.
PP 14-28 PLUS.

WBREYCH64654   BREYTSPRAAK CH
THE RELATIONSHIP OF PARENTAL IDENTIFICATION TO SEX ROLE
  ACCEPTANCE IN MARRIED, SINGLE, CAREER AND NON-CAREER
  WOMEN. /WORK-WOMEN-ROLE/
COLUMBIA UNIVERSITY, PHD DISSERTATION. NEW YORK. 1964.

WBRIEDX61655   BRIELAND D
MATERNAL EMPLOYMENT. SITUATIONAL AND ATTITUDINAL VARIABLES.
  /WORK-FAMILY-CONFLICT/
RESEARCH ISSUES RELATED TO THE EFFECTS OF MATERNAL
EMPLOYMENT ON CHILDREN. ED BY ALBERTA E SIEGEL.
PENNSYLVANIA STATE UNIVERSITY, SOCIAL SCIENCE RESEARCH
CENTER. UNIVERSITY PARK, PENNSYLVANIA. 1961.

WBROODJ64656   BROOKS DJ   *COOK COUNTY DEPT PUBLIC AID
A STUDY TO DETERMINE THE EMPLOYMENT POTENTIAL OF MOTHERS
  RECEIVING AID-TO-DEPENDENT-CHILDREN ASSISTANCE.
COOK COUNTY DEPARTMENT OF PUBLIC AID, CHICAGO, ILLINOIS.
1964. 175 PP.

WBROWAX66657   BROWN A
TESTIMONY, PUBLIC HEARING, WOMAN IN PUBLIC AND PRIVATE
  EMPLOYMENT, CALIFORNIA. /DISCRIMINATION/
CALIFORNIA ADVISORY COMMISSION ON THE STATUS OF WOMEN,
STUDY COMMITTEE NO 1, ON PUBLIC AND PRIVATE EMPLOYMENT.
HEARINGS. SACRAMENTO, CALIFORNIA. MAR 31-AP 1966.
PP 222-226.

WBROWDR62658   BROWN DR
VALUE CHANGE IN COLLEGE WOMEN. /WORK-WOMEN-ROLE/
JOURNAL OF NATIONAL ASSOCIATION OF WOMEN DEANS AND
COUNCELORS, VOL 25, NO 4, JUNE 1962. PP 148-155.

WBRYACD57659   BRYANT CD
WHITE-COLLAR WOMEN. THE SECRETARIAL-STENOGRAPHIC OCCUPATION.
UNIVERSITY OF MISSISSIPPI, UNPUBLISHED MA THESIS.
UNIVERSITY, MISSISSIPPI. 1957.

WBRYAES61660   BRYANT ES   BAILY WC
*MISS AGL EXPERIMENT STATION
THE RURAL WORKING HOMEMAKER. ALCORN-COUNTY, MISSISSIPPI.
  /WORK-FAMILY-CONFLICT/
MISSISSIPPI STATE UNIVERSITY AGRICULTURAL EXPERIMENT
STATION. STATE COLLEGE, MISSISSIPPI. 1961. 21 PP.

WBUFFDX66661   BUFFMIRE D
COMMUNITY WOMEN-S GROUPS TAKE ACTION. /HOUSEHOLD-WORKERS/
ALEXANDRIA GAZETTE, NOV 19 1966.

WBUNTMI61662   BUNTING MI
OUR GREATEST WASTE OF TALENT IS WOMEN. /WORK-WOMEN-ROLE/
LIFE, VOL 50, JAN 13 1961. PP 63-64.

WBUNTMI61664   BUNTING MI   RAUSHENBUSH E
SENDERS VL
CONTINUING EDUCATION FOR WOMEN.
EDUCATIONAL RECORD, VOL 5, OCT 1961. PP 261-286.

WBUNTMI61900   BUNTING MI
A HUGE WASTE. EDUCATED WOMANPOWER.
NEW YORK TIMES MAGAZINE, MAY 7 1961.

WBUNTMI65663   BUNTING MI
PANEL DISCUSSION. THE COMMITTMENT REQUIRED OF A WOMAN
  ENTERING A SCIENTIFIC PROFESSION. /OCCUPATIONS/
WOMEN AND THE SCIENTIFIC PROFESSIONS, ED BY JACQUELINE A
MATTFELD AND CAROL G VAN AKEN. MIT PRESS. CAMBRIDGE,
MASSACHUSETTES. 1965. PP 20-48.

WBURCLG61665   BURCHINAL LG   ROSSMAN JE
RELATIONS AMONG MATERNAL EMPLOYMENT INDICES AND
  DEVELOPMENTAL CHARACTERISTICS OF CHILDREN.
  /WORK-FAMILY-CONFLICT/
MARRIAGE AND FAMILY LIVING, VOL 23, 1961. PP 334-340.

WBUSIWX61666   BUSINESS WEEK
BACK FROM THE HOME TO BUSINESS. /WORK-FAMILY-CONFLICT/
BUSINESS WEEK, OCT 7 1961.

WBUSIWX62668   BUSINESS WEEK
PETTICOATS RUSTLE ON EXECUTIVE LADDER. /OCCUPATIONS/
BUSINESS WEEK, SEPT 29 1962. PP 50-52.

WBUSIWX63667   BUSINESS WEEK
ON THE JOB, WOMEN ACT MUCH LIKE MEN. /OCCUPATIONS/
BUSINESS WEEK, OCT 12 1963. PP 114-115.

WBUSIWX63665   BUSINESS WEEK
WOMEN AS GOVERNMENT EMPLOYEES. /OCCUPATIONS/
BUSINESS WEEK, OCT 12 1963. PP 114-116.

WCAINGG64671   CAIN GG
THE LABOR-FORCE PARTICIPATION OF MARRIED WOMEN.
UNIVERSITY OF CHICAGO, DEPARTMENT OF ECONOMICS, PHD
DISSERTATION. CHICAGO, ILLINOIS. 1964.

WCAINGG66672   CAIN GG
MARRIED WOMEN IN THE LABOR-FORCE -- AN ECONOMIC ANALYSIS.
UNIVERSITY OF CHICAGO PRESS. CHICAGO, ILLINOIS. 1966.
159 PP.

WCALACW62675   CAL ADVSY COMM STATUS WOMEN
TESTIMONY PRESENTED AT PUBLIC HEARING, MARCH 31 -- APRIL 1,
  1966. /FEP EMPLOYMENT-CONDITIONS DISCRIMINATION
  MIGRANTS/
CALIFORNIA ADVISORY COMMISSION ON THE STATUS OF WOMEN,
STUDY COMMITTEE NO 1, ON PUBLIC AND PRIVATE EMPLOYMENT.
SACRAMENTO, CALIFORNIA. 1966. 232 PP.

WCALACW62676   CAL ADVSY COMM STATUS WOMEN
TESTIMONY PRESENTED AT PUBLIC HEARING, APRIL 28, 1966.
  SAN-FRANCISCO, CALIFORNIA. /FEP EMPLOYMENT-CONDITIONS
  DISCRIMINATION MIGRANTS/
CALIFORNIA ADVISORY COMMISSION ON THE STATUS OF WOMEN.
STUDY COMMITTEE NO 1, ON PUBLIC AND PRIVATE EMPLOYMENT,
HEARING. SACRAMENTO, CALIFORNIA. 1966. VOL 1. 129 PP.

WCALACW66674   CAL ADVSY COMM STATUS WOMEN
TESTIMONY PRESENTED AT PUBLIC HEARING, FEBRUARY 24-25, 1966.
  /FEP EMPLOYMENT-CONDITIONS DISCRIMINATION MIGRANTS/
CALIFORNIA ADVISORY COMMISSION ON THE STATUS OF WOMEN.
STUDY COMMITTEE NO 1, ON PUBLIC AND PRIVATE EMPLOYMENT.
SACRAMENTO, CALIFORNIA. 1966. VOLS 1-2. 125 PP.

WCALACW66677   CAL ADVSY COMM STATUS WOMEN
TESTIMONY PRESENTED AT PUBLIC HEARING, APRIL 29, 1966.
  SAN-FRANCISCO, CALIFORNIA. /FEP EMPLOYMENT-CONDITIONS
  CHILDREN/
CALIFORNIA ADVISORY COMMISSION ON THE STATUS OF WOMEN,
STUDY COMMITTEE NO 1, ON PUBLIC AND PRIVATE EMPLOYMENT.
SACRAMENTO, CALIFORNIA. 1966. VOL 2. PP 130-298.

WCALACW67673   CAL ADVSY COMM STATUS WOMEN
REPORT OF THE CALIFORNIA ADVISORY COMMISSION ON THE STATUS
  OF WOMEN. /FEP EMPLOYMENT-CONDITIONS DISCRIMINATION
  MIGRANTS/
CALIFORNIA ADVISORY COMMISSION ON THE STATUS OF WOMEN.
SACRAMENTO, CALIFORNIA. FEB 1967. 121 PP.

WCALOED60445   CALIFORNIA DEPT OF EDUCATION
CAREER GUIDANCE FOR GIRLS. /COUNSELING/
CALIFORNIA STATE DEPARTMENT OF EDUCATION. SACRAMENTO,
CALIFORNIA. 1960.

WCALDIR64268 CALIF DEPT OF INDUSTRIAL RELS
EARNINGS AND HOURS OF WOMEN AGRICULTURAL WORKERS.
CALIFORNIA DEPARTMENT OF INDUSTRIAL RELATIONS, DIVISION OF
LABOR STATISTICS AND RESEARCH. SAN FRANCISCO, CALIFORNIA.
DEC 1964. 25 PP.

WCALDIR66267 CALIF DEPT OF INDUSTRIAL RELS
CALIFORNIA WOMANPOWER.
CALIFORNIA DEPARTMENT OF INDUSTRIAL RELATIONS, DIVISION
OF LABOR STATISTICS AND RESEARCH. SAN FRANCISCO, CALIFORNIA.
JULY 1966. 19 PP.

WCALDIR67269 CALIF DEPT OF INDUSTRIAL RELS
WOMAN WORKERS IN CALIFORNIA, 1949-SEPTEMBER 1966.
CALIFORNIA DEPARTMENT OF INDUSTRIAL RELATIONS, DIVISION OF
LABOR STATISTICS AND RESEARCH. SAN FRANCISCO, CALIFORNIA.
JAN 1967. 20 PP.

WCALIDL64678 CAL DIV LABOR STATS RESEARCH
WOMEN WORKERS IN CALIFORNIA. JANUARY 1949-AUGUST 1964.
CALIFORNIA DIVISION OF LABOR STATISTICS AND RESEARCH.
SAN FRANCISCO, CALIFORNIA. DEC 1964. 25 PP.

WCAPLTX58679 CAPLOW T   MCGEE RG
THE ACADEMIC MARKET PLACE. /OCCUPATIONS/
BASIC BOOKS, INC. NEW YORK. 1958.

WCARNCO62680 CARNEGIE CORP OF NY QUARTERLY
BACK TO SCHOOL. /WORK-FAMILY-CONFLICT/
CARNEGIE CORPORATION OF NEW YORK QUARTERLY, VOL 10, NO 4,
OCT 1962. PP 1-8.

WCARNME64910 CARNEGIE ME
ARE NEGRO SCHOOLS OF NURSING NEEDED TODAY.
NURSING OUTLOOK, VOL 12, NO 2, FEB 1964.

WCARRMS62681 CARROLL MS   *US DEPARTMENT OF LABOR
THE WORKING WIFE AND HER FAMILY-S ECONOMIC POSITION.
US DEPARTMENT OF LABOR, MONTHLY LABOR REVIEW, VOL 85, 1962.
PP 366-374.

WCASSBB62682 CASSARA BB ED
AMERICAN WOMEN. THE CHANGING IMAGE. /WORK-WOMEN-ROLE/
BEACON PRESS. BOSTON, MASSACHUSETTS. 1962.

WCATAXX64683 CATALYST
FIRST CATALYST ON CAMPUS CONFERENCE. PROCEEDINGS.
/WORK-WOMEN-ROLE/
CARNEGIE INSTITUTE OF TECHNOLOGY. PITTSBURGH, PENNSYLVANIA.
MAY 15-16 1964.

WCAVARS57684 CAVAN RS
THE STATUS OF WOMEN IN THE PROFESSIONS RELATIVE TO THE
STATUS OF MEN. /OCCUPATIONS/
QUARTERLY AMERICAN INTERPROFESSIONAL INSTITUTE,
WINTER 1956-1957.

WCHANHD66687 CHANDLER HD   *LAUNDRY DRY CLEANING UNION.
TESTIMONY, PUBLIC HEARING, WOMEN IN PUBLIC AND PRIVATE
EMPLOYMENT, CALIFORNIA. /EMPLOYMENT-CONDITIONS/
CALIFORNIA ADVISORY COMMISSION ON THE STATUS OF WOMEN.
STUDY COMMITTEE NO 1, ON PUBLIC AND PRIVATE EMPLOYMENT.
HEARINGS. SACRAMENTO, CALIFORNIA. MAR 31-AP 1 1966.
PP 158-161.

WCHICRC62689 CHICAGO REGIONAL CONFERENCE   *US DEPARTMENT OF LABOR
THE CHANGING STATUS OF WOMEN.
CHICAGO REGIONAL CONFERENCE. ROOSEVELT UNIVERSITY, CHICAGO,
ILLINOIS. MAY 18-19 1962. PUBLISHED BY US DEPARTMENT OF
LABOR, WOMEN-S BUREAU. GPO. WASHINGTON, DC. 1964.

WCHRIHX56690 CHRISTENSEN H   SWIHART MM
POST GRADUATION ROLE PREFERENCE OF SENIOR WOMEN IN COLLEGE.
/ASPIRATION/
MARRIAGE AND FAMILY LIVING, VOL 18, 1956. P 52.

WCLAYFL62691 CLAYTON FL
A SOURCE FOR COLLEGE FACULTIES. /OCCUPATIONS/
PEMBROKE ALUMNA, VOL 27, OCT 1962.

WCLIFFG66692 CLIFTON FG   *CAL DIV INDUSTRIAL WELFARE
TESTIMONY, PUBLIC HEARING, WOMEN IN PUBLIC AND PRIVATE
EMPLOYMENT, CALIFORNIA. /FEP EMPLOYMENT-CONDITIONS
DISCRIMINATION MIGRANTS/
CALIFORNIA ADVISORY COMMISSION ON THE STATUS OF WOMEN.
STUDY COMMITTEE NO 1, ON PUBLIC AND PRIVATE EMPLOYMENT.
HEARINGS. SACRAMENTO, CALIFORNIA. MAR 31-AP 1 1966.
PP 103-117, 162-168, PP 1-10, SUPPLEMENT TO THESE DAYS
HEARINGS, SPECIALLY BOUND.

WCLYMEX59693 CLYMER E   ERLICH L
MODERN AMERICAN CAREER WOMEN. /OCCUPATIONS/
DODD. NEW YORK. 1959.

WCOLECG56694 COLE CG   *EDUCATIONAL TESTING SERVICE
ENCOURAGING SCIENTIFIC TALENT. /OCCUPATIONS/
EDUCATIONAL TESTING SERVICE, COLLEGE ENTRANCE EXAMINATION
BOARD. PRINCETON, NEW JERSEY. 1956. 259 PP.

WCOLECX69695 COLEMAN C   SHERTZER B
CHANGES IN CAREER ASPIRATIONS.
VOCATIONAL GUIDANCE QUARTERLY, 1963-1964. PP 113-119.

WCOLLAX62697 COLLVER A   LANGOIS E
THE FEMALE LABOR-FORCE IN METROPOLITAN AREAS. AN
INTERNATIONAL COMPARISON.
ECONOMIC DEVELOPMENT AND CULTURAL CHANGE. VOL 10, 1962.
PP 367-385.

WCOLLNX66696 COLLINS N
TESTIMONY, PUBLIC HEARING, WOMEN IN PUBLIC AND PRIVATE
EMPLOYMENT, CALIFORNIA. /DISCRIMINATION/
CALIFORNIA ADVISORY COMMISSION ON THE STATUS OF WOMEN.
STUDY COMMITTEE NO 1, ON PUBLIC AND PRIVATE EMPLOYMENT.
HEARINGS. SACRAMENTO, CALIFORNIA. MAR 31-AP 1 1966.
PP 213-218.

WCOLOJX63698 COLOMBOTOS J
SEX-ROLE AND PROFESSIONALISM. A STUDY OF HIGH SCHOOL
TEACHERS. /OCCUPATIONS/
THE SCHOOL REVIEW, VOL 71, NO 1, 1963. PP 27-40. ALSO IN
PROFESSIONALIZATION. ED BY HOWARD M VOLLMER AND DONALD L
MILLS. PRENTICE-HALL. ENGLEWOOD CLIFFS, NEW JERSEY. 1966.

WCOLUMX64699 COLUMBIA MISSOURIAN
REPORT ON THE FIRST CONFERENCE ON THE STATUS OF WOMEN.
/WORK-WOMEN-ROLE/
COLUMBIA MISSOURIAN, DEC 3 1964.

WCOLUMX64700 COLUMBIA MISSOURIAN
REPORT ON THE MISSOURI COMMISSION ON THE STATUS OF WOMEN.
/WORK-WOMEN-ROLE/
COLUMBIA MISSOURIAN, NOV 29 1964.AND DEC 6 1964.

WCOMMXX63701 COMMONWEAL
EQUAL PAY FOR WOMEN. /DISCRIMINATION/
COMMONWEAL, VOL 78, NO 11, JUNE 7 1963. PP 293-294.
EDITORIAL.

WCOMPBX66702 COMPTON B   *US DEPARTMENT OF LABOR
TESTIMONY, PUBLIC HEARING, WOMEN IN PUBLIC AND PRIVATE
EMPLOYMENT, CALIFORNIA. /EMPLOYMENT-CONDITIONS/
CALIFORNIA ADVISORY COMMISSION ON THE STATUS OF WOMEN,
STUDY COMMITTEE NO 1, ON PUBLIC AND PRIVATE EMPLOYMENT.
HEARINGS. SACRAMENTO, CALIFORNIA. AP 29 1966. PP 238-243.

WCONYJE61704 CONYERS JE
AN EXPLORATORY STUDY OF EMPLOYERS ATTITUDES TOWARD WORKING
MOTHERS.
SOCIOLOGY AND SOCIAL RESEARCH, VOL 45, NO 2, JAN 1961.
PP 145-156.

WCONYJE63703 CONYERS JE
EMPLOYERS ATTITUDES TOWARD WORKING MOTHERS.
THE EMPLOYED MOTHER IN AMERICA. ED BY F IVAN NYE AND LOIS W
HOFFMAN. RAND MCNALLY. CHICAGO,ILLINOIS. 1963. PP 372-383.

WCOOKFS66705 COOK FS
OPPORTUNITIES AND REQUIREMENTS FOR INITIAL EMPLOYMENT OF
SCHOOL LEAVERS. WITH EMPHASIS ON OFFICE AND RETAIL JOBS.
/EMPLOYMENT-SELECTION/
WAYNE STATE UNIVERSITY. DETROIT, MICHIGAN. 1966.

WCOOKWX60252 COOK W
A STUDY OF JOB MOTIVATIONS, ACTIVITIES, AND SATISFACTIONS OF
PRESENT AND PROSPECTIVE WOMEN COLLEGE FACULTY MEMBERS.
/OCCUPATIONS/
UNIVERSITY OF MINNESOTA, COLLEGE OF EDUCATION. MINNEAPOLIS,
MINNESOTA. 1960. 100 PP.

WCORMML67706 CORMACK ML
ON EDUCATING WOMEN HIGHLY. /WORK-WOMEN-ROLE/
FAMILY RELATIONS CONFERENCE. PAPER. EARLHAM COLLEGE.
RICHMOND, INDIANA. AP 10 1962.

WCORWRG61707 CORWIN RG
ROLE CONCEPTION AND CAREER ASPIRATION. A STUDY OF IDENTITY
IN NURSING.
THE SOCIOLOGICAL QUARTERLY, VOL 2, 1961. PP 69-86.

WCOTTDW65708 COTTON DW
THE CASE FOR THE WORKING MOTHER.
STEIN AND DAY. NEW YORK. 1965. 212 PP.

WCRONDH56709 CRONHEIM DH
FOCUS ON THE FUTURE FOR WOMEN. /WORK-WOMEN-ROLE/
JOURNAL OF NATIONAL ASSOCIATION OF WOMEN DEANS AND
COUNSELORS. VOL 19, JUNE 1956.

WCROSKP63710 CROSS KP
WOMAN AS POTENTIAL SCIENTISTS. /OCCUPATIONS/
FARLEIGH DICKINSON UNIVERSITY AND THE US OFFICE OF EMERGENCY
PLANNING, CONFERENCE. THE EXPANDING NEED FOR WOMEN IN
SCIENCE. PAPER. FARLEIGH DICKINSON UNIVERSITY. RUTHERFORD,
NEW JERSEY. DEC 5 1963.

WCULPPX61382 CULPAN P
RECRUITMENT OF THE MATURE WOMAN.
NURSING TIMES, VOL 57, JULY 21 1961. P 919.

WCUMMGX66711 CUMMING G   *CAL DIV OF VOCATIONAL REHAB
TESTIMONY, PUBLIC HEARING, WOMEN IN PUBLIC AND PRIVATE
EMPLOYMENT, CALIFORNIA. /TRAINING/
CALIFORNIA ADVISORY COMMISSION ON THE STATUS OF WOMEN,
STUDY COMMITTEE NO 1, ON PUBLIC AND PRIVATE EMPLOYMENT.
HEARINGS. SACRAMENTO, CALIFORNIA. FEB 24-25 1966. VOL 1,
PP 22-30.

WCUSSMX58712 CUSSLER M
THE WOMAN EXECUTIVE. /OCCUPATIONS/
HARCOURT, BRACE AND WORLD. NEW YORK. 1958.

WCUTLJH61713 CUTLER JH
WHAT ABOUT WOMEN. /WORK-WOMEN-ROLE/
IVES, WASHBURN, INC. NEW YORK. 1961.

WDAEDXX64714 DAEDALUS
THE WOMAN IN AMERICA. /WORK-WOMEN-ROLE/
DAEDALUS, VOL 93, SPRING 1964. ENTIRE ISSUE.

WDAVICX63718 DAVIS C   *UAW WOMEN-S DEPARTMENT
*PRES-S COMMON STATUS WOMEN
MINORITY REPORT. /EEO/
PRESIDENT-S COMMISSION ON THE STATUS OF WOMEN, SUB-COMMITTEE
ON GOVERNMENT CONTRACTS. GPO. WASHINGTON, DC. 1963. 6 PP.

WDAVICX65719 DAVIS C   *UAW WOMEN-S DEPARTMENT
STATEMENT ON SENIORITY. /UNION/
WHITE HOUSE CONFERENCE ON EQUAL EMPLOYMENT OPPORTUNITY.
WASHINGTON, DC. AUG 19 AND 20 1965. 3 PP.

WDAVICX65720 DAVIS C   *UAW WOMEN-S DEPARTMENT
STATEMENT ON STATE LAWS. /EMPLOYMENT-CONDITIONS/
WHITE HOUSE CONFERENCE ON EQUAL EMPLOYMENT OPPORTUNITY.
WASHINGTON, DC. AUG 19 AND 20 1965. 5 PP.

WDAVIEX64721 DAVIS E
CAREERS AS CONCERNS OF BLUE-COLLAR GIRLS. /OCCUPATIONS/
BLUE-COLLAR WORLD. STUDIES OF THE AMERICAN WORKER. ED BY
ARTHUR SHOSTAK AND WILLIAM GOMBERG. PRENTICE-HALL.
ENGLEWOOD CLIFFS, NEW JERSEY. 1964. PP 154-164.

WDAVIFX66722 DAVIS F
NURSING PROFESSION. FIVE SOCIOLOGICAL SURVEYS.
WILEY. NEW YORK. 1966.

WDAVIFX66723 DAVIS F   OLESEN VL
INITIATION INTO A WOMAN-S PROFESSION. IDENTITY PROBLEMS IN
THE STATUS TRANSITION OF CO-ED TO STUDENT NURSE.
SOCIOMETRY, VOL 26, NO 1, MAR 1963. PP 89-101. ALSO IN
PROFESSIONALIZATION. ED BY HOWARD M VOLLMER AND DONALD L
MILLS. PRENTICE-HALL. ENGLEWOOD CLIFFS, NEW JERSEY. 1966.

WDAVIHX60715 DAVID H
WORK, WOMEN, AND CHILDREN. /WORK-FAMILY-CONFLICT/
THE NATION-S CHILDREN. ED BY ELI GINZBERG. COLUMBIA
UNIVERSITY PRESS. NEW YORK. 1960. VOL 3, PP 180-198.

WDAVIHX60941 DAVID H

EDUCATION AND MANPOWER.
COLUMBIA UNIVERSITY PRESS. NEW YORK. 1960. 326 PP.

WDAVIIX60717 DAVIDOFF I   MARKEWICH ME
THE POST-PARENTAL PHASE IN THE LIFE CYCLE OF 50 COLLEGE
    EDUCATED WOMEN. /WORK-FAMILY-CONFLICT/
COLUMBIA UNIVERSITY, TEACHERS COLLEGE= PHD DISSERTATION.
1960.8

WDAVIJA64724 DAVIS JA
GREAT ASPIRATIONS.
ALDINE PUBLISHING CO. CHICAGO, ILLINOIS. 1964. 319 PP.

WDAVIOD57044 DAVID OD ED   *AMERICAN CC ON EDUCATION
EDUCATION OF WOMEN -- SIGNS FOR THE FUTURE.
AMERICAN COUNCIL ON EDUCATION. WASHINGTON, DC. 1957.

WDAVIOD59716 DAVID OD
FACTORS INFLUENCING WOMEN-S DECISIONS ABOUT HIGHER
    EDUCATION. /ASPIRATIONS/
JOURNAL OF THE NATIONAL ASSOCIATION OF WOMEN DEANS AND
COUNSELORS, VOL 23, NO 1, OCT 1959. PP 35-38.

WDAVIOD59537 DAVID OD ED   *AMERICAN CC ON EDUCATION
THE EDUCATION OF WOMEN -- SIGNS FOR THE FUTURE.
AMERICAN COUNCIL ON EDUCATION. WASHINGTON, DC. 1959.

WDAYXLH57725 DAY LH
AGE OF COMPLETION OF CHILDBEARING AND ITS RELATION TO THE
    PARTICIPATION OF WOMEN IN THE LABOR-FORCE. UNITED STATES
    1910-1955.
COLUMBIA UNIVERSITY. PHD DISSERTATION. NEW YORK. 1957.

WDAYXLH61726 DAY LH
STATUS IMPLICATIONS OF THE EMPLOYMENT OF MARRIED WOMEN IN
    THE UNITED STATES.
AMERICAN JOURNAL OF ECONOMICS AND SOCIOLOGY, VOL 20, 1961.
PP 391-397.

WDEGLCN64727 DEGLER CN
REVOLUTION WITHOUT IDEOLOGY. THE CHANGING PLACE OF WOMEN IN
    AMERICA. /WORK-WOMEN-ROLE/
DAEDALUS, VOL 93, SPRING 1964. PP 653-670.

WDELAPJ60224 DELANO PJ
DIGEST OF CASE STUDIES ON CONTINUITIES AND DISCONTINUITIES
    IN THE EMPLOYMENT-EDUCATION-FAMILY PATTERNS OF WOMEN-S
    LIVES.
COLUMBIA UNIVERSITY, TEACHERS COLLEGE. EDD DISSERTATION.
NEW YORK. 1960.

WDEMEAL63728 DEMEMT AL
WHAT BRINGS AND HOLDS WOMAN SCIENCE MAJORS. /OCCUPATIONS/
COLLEGE AND UNIVERSITY, FALL 1963. PP 44-50.

WDENNLE63729 DENNIS LE
EDUCATION AND A WOMAN-S LIFE. /WORK-WOMAN-ROLE/
AMERICAN COUNCIL ON EDUCATION. WASHINGTON, DC. 1963. 153 PP.

WDEUTIX56730 DEUTSCHER I
A SURVEY OF THE SOCIAL AND OCCUPATIONAL CHARACTERISTICS OF A
    METROPOLITAN NURSE. COMPLEMENT.
    /OCCUPATIONAL-DISTRIBUTION/
COMMUNITY STUDIES, INC. KANSAS CITY, MISSOURI. 1956.

WDEUTIX57369 DEUTSCHER I
A SURVEY OF THE SOCIAL AND OCCUPATIONAL CHARACTERISTICS OF A
    METROPOLITAN NURSE COMPLEMENT.
NURSING WORLD, VOL 131, PARTS 1-4, JULY-DEC 1957.

WDEVEGX62731 DEVEREUX G   WEINER FR
THE OCCUPATIONAL-STATUS OF NURSES.
MAN, WORK AND SOCIETY. ED BY S NOSOW. BASIC BOOKS, INC.
NEW YORK. 1962.

WDIBRJX66732 DIBROG J   *BKBNDRS BINDERY WOMENS UNION
TESTIMONY, PUBLIC HEARING, WOMEN IN PUBLIC AND PRIVATE
    EMPLOYMENT, CALIFORNIA. /EMPLOYMENT-CONDITIONS/
CALIFORNIA ADVISORY COMMISSION ON THE STATUS OF WOMEN,
STUDY COMMITTEE NO 1, ON PUBLIC AND PRIVATE EMPLOYMENT.
HEARINGS. SACRAMENTO, CALIFORNIA. MAR 31-AP 1 1966.
PP 92-95.

WDOLAEF56734 DOLAN EF
EDUCATED WOMEN -- A MIDCENTURY EVALUATION.
    /WORK-WOMAN-ROLE/
EDUCATIONAL FORUM, VOL 20, JAN 1956. PP 219-228.

WDOLAEF57735 DOLAN EF
REPORT OF THE EXPLORATORY STATISTICAL SURVEY OF THE
    EDUCATIONAL-ATTAINMENT, NUMBER, AND AVAILABILITY OF THE
    MEMBERSHIP OF THE AMERICAN ASSOCIATION OF UNIVERSITY
    WOMEN FOR TEACHING IN THE FIELDS OF SCIENCE AND
    MATHEMATICS. /OCCUPATIONS/
AMERICAN ASSOCIATION OF UNIVERSITY WOMEN. WASHINGTON, DC.
NOV 15 1957. 60 PP.

WDOLAEF60951 DOLAN EF   DAVIS MP
ANTI-NEPOTISM RULES IN AMERICAN COLLEGES AND
    UNIVERSITIES -- THEIR EFFECT ON THE FACULTY EMPLOYMENT OF
    WOMEN.
HARVARD EDUCATIONAL RECORD, OCT 1960.

WDOLAEF63952 DOLAN EF
HIGHER EDUCATION FOR WOMEN. TIME FOR REAPPRAISAL.
HIGHER EDUCATION, SEPT 1963.

WDOLAEF64736 DOLAN EF
QED. /WORK-WOMEN-ROLE/
JOURNAL OF ASSOCIATION OF AMERICAN UNIVERSITY WOMEN, VOL 57,
NO 3, MAR 1964. PP 136-138.

WDOLAEF66733 DOLAN EF
COUNSELING THE MATURE WOMAN.
JOURNAL OF ASSOCIATION OF AMERICAN UNIVERSITY WOMEN. VOL 59,
1966. PP 62-66.

WDOLEAA64737 DOLE AA
SEX AS A FACTOR IN THE DETERMINATION OF EDUCATIONAL CHOICE.
    /ASPIRATIONS/
JOURNAL OF GENERAL PSYCHOLOGY, VOL 71, 1964. PP 267-278.

WDOLLPA65738 DOLL PA
A COMPARATIVE STUDY OF TOP LEVEL MALE AND FEMALE EXECUTIVES
    IN HARRIS-COUNTY. /TEXAS OCCUPATIONS/
UNIVERSITY OF HOUSTON. PHD DISSERTATION. HOUSTON, TEXAS.
1965.

WDORAMX66739 DORAIS M   *CAL NEWSPAPERS ASSOCIATION
TESTIMONY, PUBLIC HEARING, WOMAN IN PUBLIC AND PRIVATE

EMPLOYMENT, CALIFORNIA. /DISCRIMINATION/
CALIFORNIA ADVISORY COMMISSION ON THE STATUS OF WOMEN,
STUDY COMMITTEE NO 1, ON PUBLIC AND PRIVATE EMPLOYMENT.
HEARINGS. SACRAMENTO, CALIFORNIA. AP 29 1966. PP 157-160.

WDOUGAM61740 DOUGLAS AM
SOCIAL FACTORS WHICH AFFECT CAREER CHOICE IN PSYCHIATRIC
    NURSING.
CATHOLIC UNIVERSITY OF AMERICA PRESS. WASHINGTON, DC. 1961.

WDOUTAX62741 DOUTY A
ADDRESS TO CONFERENCE ON EDUCATION AND JOB OPPORTUNITIES FOR
    WOMEN RETURNING TO THE LABOR-MARKET.
CONFERENCE ON EDUCATION AND JOB OPPORTUNITIES OF WOMEN
RETURNING TO THE LABOR MARKET. PORTLAND STATE COLLEGE.
PORTLAND, OREGON. OCT 24 1962.

WDOUVEX57742 DOUVAN E   KAYE C
*UM ISR SURVEY RESEARCH CENT
STUDY OF ADOLESCENT GIRLS. /ASPIRATIONS/
UNIVERSITY OF MICHIGAN, INSTITUTE FOR SOCIAL RESEARCH,
SURVEY RESEARCH CENTER. ANN ARBOR, MICHIGAN. 1957.

WDREWEM61743 DREWS EM
WHAT EVERY ABLE WOMAN SHOULD KNOW. /WORK-PATTERN
    ASPIRATIONS/
JOURNAL OF NATIONAL ASSOCIATION OF WOMEN DEANS AND
COUNSELORS, VOL 25, OCT 1961. PP 14-20.

WDYKMRA57745 DYKMAN RA   STALNAKER JM
SURVEY OF WOMEN PHYSICIANS GRADUATING FROM MEDICAL SCHOOL,
    1925-1940. /OCCUPATIONS/
JOURNAL OF MEDICAL EDUCATION, VOL 32, NO 13, PART 2, 1957.
PP 3-38.

WECKERE59746 ECKERT RE   STECKLEIN JE
ACADEMIC WOMAN. /OCCUPATIONS/
LIBERAL EDUCATION, VOL 45, OCT 1959. PP 391-397.

WEDDYED63747 EDDY ED
WHAT-S THE USE OF EDUCATING WOMEN. /WORK-WOMAN-ROLE/
SATURDAY REVIEW, VOL 46, MAY 18 1963. PP 66-68.

WELLIKX63748 ELLICKSON K   *US DEPARTMENT OF LABOR
PROGRESS OF THE COMMISSION ON THE STATUS OF WOMAN.
    /WORK-WOMAN-ROLE/
US DEPARTMENT OF LABOR, MONTHLY LABOR REVIEW, VOL 86, NO 2,
FEB 1963. PP 141-144.

WELLMMX65749 ELLMAN M
ACADEMIC WOMEN. /OCCUPATIONS/
COMMENTARY, VOL 39, MAR 1965. PP 67-70.

WEMPELT58751 EMPEY LT
ROLE EXPECTATIONS OF YOUNG WOMEN REGARDING MARRIAGE AND A
    CAREER. /ASPIRATIONS WORK-FAMILY-CONFLICT/
MARRIAGE AND FAMILY LIVING, VOL 20, NO 2, 1958. PP 152-155.

WEMPLAE59752 EMPLOYMENT AND EARNINGS
WOMEN EMPLOYEES IN MANUFACTURING BY INDUSTRY, JANUARY, 1959.
EMPLOYMENT AND EARNINGS, VOL 5, MAY 1959. PP 28-31.

WEVANSX66753 EVANS S   FOSTER D
*WESTERN ELECTRONIC MNFG ASSN
TESTIMONY, PUBLIC HEARING, WOMEN IN PUBLIC AND PRIVATE
    EMPLOYMENT, CALIFORNIA. /EMPLOYMENT-CONDITIONS/
CALIFORNIA ADVISORY COMMISSION ON THE STATUS OF WOMEN.
STUDY COMMITTEE NO 1, ON PUBLIC AND PRIVATE EMPLOYMENT.
HEARINGS. SACRAMENTO, CALIFORNIA. AP 29 1966. PP 103-156.

WEYDELD62754 EYDE LD   *OHIO STATE U BUR BUS RES
WORK VALUES AND BACKGROUND FACTORS AS PREDICTORS OF WOMEN-S
    DESIRE TO WORK. /ASPIRATIONS/
OHIO STATE UNIVERSITY, COLLEGE OF COMMERCE AND
ADMINISTRATION, BUREAU OF BUSINESS RESEARCH. COLUMBUS, OHIO.
1962. 88 PP.

WEYDELD67223 EYDE LD
WORK MOTIVATION OF COLLEGE ALUMNAE. FIVE-YEAR FOLLOWUP.
EASTERN PSYCHOLOGICAL ASSOCIATION, PAPER. BOSTON,
MASSACHUSETTS. AP 1967. 14 PP.

WFARBSM63756 FARBER SM ED   WILSON R ED
THE POTENTIAL OF WOMEN. /WORK-WOMAN-ROLE/
MCGRAW HILL. NEW YORK. 1963. 328 PP.

WFARBSM66755 FARBER SM ED   WILSON RH ED
THE CHALLENGE TO WOMEN. /WORK-WOMAN-ROLE/
BASIC BOOKS, INC. NEW YORK. 1966. 176 PP.

WFAVASF60757 FAVA SF
THE STATUS OF WOMEN IN PROFESSIONAL SOCIOLOGY.
    /OCCUPATIONS/
AMERICAN SOCIOLOGICAL REVIEW, VOL 25, AP 1960.

WFAYXMX66758 FAY M
WOMEN PHYSICIANS IN THE TWENTY-FIRST CENTURY. /OCCUPATIONS/
JOURNAL OF AMERICAN MEDICAL WOMEN, VOL 21, NO 10, OCT 1966.
PP 842-846.

WFEINBX66760 FEINBERG B   WOLF M
*ILGWU
TESTIMONY, PUBLIC HEARING, WOMEN IN PUBLIC AND PRIVATE
    EMPLOYMENT, CALIFORNIA. /EMPLOYMENT-CONDITIONS/
CALIFORNIA ADVISORY COMMISSION ON THE STATUS OF WOMEN,
STUDY COMMITTEE NO 1, ON PUBLIC AND PRIVATE EMPLOYMENT.
HEARINGS. SACRAMENTO, CALIFORNIA. MAR 31-AP 1 1966.
PP 42-56.

WFIELBX64762 FIELD B   *AMERICAN ALUMNI COUNCIL
RESEARCH REPORT. SURVEY OF CONTINUING EDUCATION PROGRAMS.
ALMA MATER, JOURNAL OF THE AMERICAN ALUMNI COUNCIL, VOL 31,
NO 1, JAN 1964. PP 39-40.

WFIELJC61763 FIELD JC
FACTORS ASSOCIATED WITH GRADUATE SCHOOL ATTENDANCE AND ROLE
    DEFINITION OF THE WOMAN DOCTORAL CANDIDATES AT THE
    PENNSYLVANIA STATE UNIVERSITY. /OCCUPATIONS/
PENNSYLVANIA STATE UNIVERSITY. MASTER-S THESIS. UNIVERSITY
PARK, PENNSYLVANIA. 1961.

WFIRKEX63764 FIRKEL E
WOMEN IN THE MODERN WORLD. /WORK-WOMAN-ROLE/
FIDES PUBLISHERS. NOTRE DAME, INDIANA. 1963.

WFITZLE63963 FITZGERALD LE
FANTASY, FACT AND THE FUTURE...A REVIEW OF THE STATUS OF
    WOMEN AND POSSIBLE IMPLICATIONS FOR WOMEN-S EDUCATION AND
    ROLE IN THE NEXT DECADE.
INTERCOLLEGIATE ASSOCIATION OF WOMAN STUDENTS, CONVENTION.

SPEECH. 1963.

WFLAGJJ63130 FLAGLER JJ ED   BOGNANNO MF ED
CRAIG L ED
EMPLOYMENT PROBLEMS OF WORKING WOMEN.
UNIVERSITY OF IOWA, BUREAU OF LABOR AND MANAGEMENT,
CONFERENCE SERIES NO 8. IOWA CITY, IOWA. 1963. 26 PP.

WFLORMP66326 FLORIDA MANPOWER PROJECT   *US DEPARTMENT OF LABOR
*FLORIDA A AND M UNIVERSITY
FINAL REPORT. EXPERIMENTAL AND DEMONSTRATION MANPOWER
PROJECT FOR THE RECRUITMENT, TRAINING, PLACEMENT AND
FOLLOW-UP OF RURAL UNEMPLOYED WORKERS IN TEN NORTH FLORIDA
COUNTIES.
FLORIDA A AND M UNIVERSITY. US DEPARTMENT OF LABOR, OFFICE
OF MANPOWER, AUTOMATION AND TRAINING. TALLAHASSEE, FLORIDA.
JAN 31 1966. 159 PP.

WFOOTJX66765 FOOTE J   *MACHINIST-S UNION
TESTIMONY, PUBLIC HEARING, WOMEN IN PUBLIC AND PRIVATE
EMPLOYMENT, CALIFORNIA. /DISCRIMINATION/
CALIFORNIA ADVISORY COMMISSION ON THE STATUS OF WOMEN,
STUDY COMMITTEE NO 1, ON PUBLIC AND PRIVATE EMPLOYMENT.
HEARINGS. SACRAMENTO, CALIFORNIA. AP 28 1966. PP 71-79.

WFOWLGH65766 FOWLER GH
ADDRESS BEFORE LEAGUE-OF-WOMEN-VOTERS, JANUARY 7, 1965.
/WORK-WOMAN-ROLE/
INSTITUTE ON THE DEVELOPMENT OF HUMAN RESOURCES. NEW YORK.
1965.

WFOXXDJ61767 FOX DJ   DIAMOND L
JACOBOWSKY N
CAREER DECISIONS AND PROFESSIONAL EXPECTATIONS OF
NURSING-STUDENTS. /ASPIRATIONS/
CORNELL UNIVERSITY PRESS. ITHACA, NEW YORK. 1961.

WFREDCX61769 FREDRICKSON C
MARRIED WOMEN AT UTAH STATE UNIVERSITY, SPRING QUARTER,
1960. /TRAINING/
PROCEEDINGS OF THE UTAH ACADEMY OF SCIENCES, ARTS, AND
LETTERS, VOL 38, 1961. PP 50-56.

WFREDEB62768 FRED EB
WOMEN AND HIGHER EDUCATION WITH SPECIAL REFERENCE TO THE
UNIVERSITY OF WISCONSIN.
THE JOURNAL OF EXPERIMENTAL EDUCATION, VOL 31, DEC 1962.

WFREEMB65770 FREEDMAN MB
THE ROLE OF THE EDUCATED WOMAN. AN EMPIRICAL STUDY OF THE
ATTITUDES OF A GROUP OF COLLEGE WOMEN. /WORK-WOMAN-ROLE/
COLLEGE STUDENT PERSONNEL, VOL 6, 1965. PP 145-155.

WFREEMX62771 FREEMAN M
THE MARGINAL SEX. /WORK-WOMAN-ROLE/
COMMONWEAL, VOL 75, NO 19, FEB 2 1962. PP 483-486.

WFUCHEF63772 FUCHS EF   HAMMER CH
A SURVEY OF WOMEN-S APTITUDES FOR ARMY JOBS. /MILITARY/
PERSONNEL PSYCHOLOGY, 1963. PP 151-155.

WGABELX66773 GABEL L   *WAITRESS CAFETERIA WK UNION
TESTIMONY, PUBLIC HEARING, WOMEN IN PUBLIC AND PRIVATE
EMPLOYMENT, CALIFORNIA. /EMPLOYMENT-CONDITIONS/
CALIFORNIA ADVISORY COMMISSION ON THE STATUS OF WOMEN,
STUDY COMMITTEE NO 1, ON PUBLIC AND PRIVATE EMPLOYMENT,
HEARINGS. SACRAMENTO, CALIFORNIA. MAR 31-AP 1 1966.
PP 80-86.

WGARFSH57180 GARFINKLE SH   *US DEPARTMENT OF LABOR
TABLES OF WORKING LIFE FOR WOMEN, 1950.
US DEPARTMENT OF LABOR, BUREAU OF LABOR STATISTICS. GPO.
WASHINGTON, DC. 1957. 33 PP.

WGARFSH57774 GARFINKLE SH   *US DEPARTMENT OF LABOR
MARRIAGE AND CAREERS FOR GIRLS. /WORK-FAMILY-CONFLICT/
OCCUPATIONAL OUTLOOK QUARTERLY, VOL 1, NO 4, DEC 1957.
PP 11-15.

WGASSGZ59775 GASS GZ
COUNSELING IMPLICATIONS OF WOMAN-S CHANGING ROLE.
PERSONNEL AND GUIDANCE JOURNAL, VOL 37, MAR 1959.
PP 482-487.

WGEIGPX66776 GEIGER P   *CAL STATE EMPLOYEES ASSN
TESTIMONY, PUBLIC HEARING, WOMEN IN PUBLIC AND PRIVATE
EMPLOYMENT, CALIFORNIA. /DISCRIMINATION/
CALIFORNIA ADVISORY COMMISSION ON THE STATUS OF WOMEN,
STUDY COMMITTEE NO 1, ON PUBLIC AND PRIVATE EMPLOYMENT,
HEARINGS. SACRAMENTO, CALIFORNIA. FEB 24-25 1966. VOL 1,
PP 38-54.

WGENTLX60790 GENTRY L
SOME INTELLECTUAL ATTRIBUTES AND EDUCATIONAL INTERESTS OF
UNIVERSITY WOMEN IN VARIOUS MAJORS. /ASPIRATIONS/
UNIVERSITY OF MICHIGAN. ANN ARBOR, MICHIGAN. 1960.
MICROFILM. PHD DISSERTATION.

WGERSMX66777 GERSHENSON M   *CAL DEPT INDUSTRIAL WELFARE
TESTIMONY, PUBLIC HEARING, WOMEN IN PUBLIC AND PRIVATE
EMPLOYMENT, CALIFORNIA. /DEMOGRAPHY/
CALIFORNIA ADVISORY COMMISSION ON THE STATUS OF WOMEN,
STUDY COMMITTEE NO 1, ON PUBLIC AND PRIVATE EMPLOYMENT,
HEARINGS. SACRAMENTO, CALIFORNIA. FEB 24-25, 1966. VOL 1,
PP 6-22. VOL 2, LAST 15 PP.

WGETTRG57778 GETTELL RG
A PLEA FOR THE UNCOMMON WOMAN. /WOMAN-WORK-ROLE/
MOUNT HOLYOKE ALUMNAE QUARTERLY, FALL 1957.

WGIANAX57779 GIANOPULOS A   MITCHELL HE
MARITAL DISAGREEMENT IN WORKING WIFE MARRIAGES AS A FUNCTION
OF HUSBAND-S ATTITUDE TOWARDS WIFE-S EMPLOYMENT.
/WORK-FAMILY-CONFLICT/
MARRIAGE AND FAMILY LIVING, VOL 19, NOV 1957. PP 373-378.

WGILBLM62782 GILBRETH LM
WOMEN IN INDUSTRY. /OCCUPATIONS/
AMERICAN WOMEN. THE CHANGING IMAGE. ED BY BEVERLY BRENNER
CASSARA. BEACON PRESS. BOSTON, MASSACHUSETTS. 1962.
PP 90-98.

WGILBLM65781 GILBRETH LM
CLOSING THE GAP. /OCCUPATIONS/
WOMEN AND THE SCIENTIFIC PROFESSIONS. ED BY JACQUELINE A
MATTFELD AND CAROL G VAN AKEN. MIT PRESS. CAMBRIDGE,
MASSACHUSETTS. 1965. PP 215-231.

WGILBRX66780 GILBERT R   *SCREEN EXTRAS GUILD OF LA
TESTIMONY, PUBLIC HEARING, WOMEN IN PUBLIC AND PRIVATE

EMPLOYMENT, CALIFORNIA. /EMPLOYMENT-CONDITIONS/
CALIFORNIA ADVISORY COMMISSION ON THE STATUS OF WOMEN, STUDY
COMMITTEE NO 1, ON PUBLIC AND PRIVATE EMPLOYMENT, HEARINGS.
SACRAMENTO, CALIFORNIA. AP 29 1966. PP 179-200.

WGILDGN59783 GILDERSLEEVE GN
WOMEN IN BANKING. /OCCUPATIONS/
PUBLIC AFFAIRS PRESS. WASHINGTON, DC. 1959. 115 PP.

WGILMBV63970 GILMER BV
NOTES ON WOMEN IN INDUSTRY -- PRESENTED AT AMERICAN
PSYCHOLOGICAL SYMPOSIUM, SEPT 1963. /DISCRIMINATION/
AMERICAN PSYCHOLOGICAL ASSOCIATION, MEETINGS. SEPT 1963.
7 PP.

WGINSEX62786 GINZBERG E
WHAT NURSES NEED IS A CHANCE TO GROW. /OCCUPATIONAL-STATUS/
THE MODERN HOSPITAL. AP 1962. PP 103-106.

WGINZEX58784 GINZBERG E
THE CHANGING PATTERNS OF WOMEN-S WORK. SOME PSYCHOLOGICAL
CORRELATES.
AMERICAN JOURNAL OF ORTHO-PSYCHIATRY, VOL 28, 1958.
PP 313-321.

WGINZEX66785 GINZBERG E
LIFE STYLES OF EDUCATED WOMEN. /WORK-FAMILY-CONFLICT/
COLUMBIA UNIVERSITY PRESS. NEW YORK. 1966. 216 PP.

WGIVEJN60787 GIVEN JN
WOMEN IN EXECUTIVE POSTS. /OCCUPATIONS/
OFFICE EXECUTIVE, DEC 1960. PP 32-33.

WGLENEM66788 GLENN EM   *HOSPITAL EMPLOYEES UNION
TESTIMONY, PUBLIC HEARING, WOMEN IN PUBLIC AND PRIVATE
EMPLOYMENT, CALIFORNIA. /EMPLOYMENT-CONDITIONS/
CALIFORNIA ADVISORY COMMISSION ON THE STATUS OF WOMEN, STUDY
COMMITTEE NO 1, ON PUBLIC AND PRIVATE EMPLOYMENT, HEARINGS.
SACRAMENTO, CALIFORNIA. MAR 31-AP 1 1966. PP 146-147.

WGLENHM59789 GLENN HM
ATTITUDES OF WOMEN REGARDING GAINFUL EMPLOYMENT OF MARRIED
WOMEN. /ASPIRATIONS/
JOURNAL OF HOME ECONOMICS. NO 51. AP 1959. PP 247-252.

WGLICRX65791 GLICK R
PRACTITIONERS AND NON-PRACTITIONERS IN A GROUP OF WOMEN
PHYSICIANS. /ASPIRATIONS/
WESTERN RESERVE UNIVERSITY. PHD DISSERTATION. CLEVELAND,
OHIO. 1965.

WGOLDBX64794 GOLDSTEIN B   STARK H
ENTERING THE LABOR-FORCE.
HOLT, RINEHART, AND WINSTON, INC. NEW YORK. 1964.

WGOLDFH65792 GOLDMAN FH
A TURNING TO TAKE NEXT -- ALTERNATIVE GOALS IN THE EDUCATION
OF WOMEN. /WORK-WOMAN-ROLE/
CENTER FOR THE STUDY OF LIBERAL EDUCATION FOR ADULTS.
BROOKLINE, MASSACHUSETTS. 1965.

WGOLDMR63793 GOLDMAN MR
ON BEING SOMETHING OTHER THAN MOTHER AND BEING MOTHER TOO.
/WORK-FAMILY-CONFLICT/
SARAH LAWRENCE ALUMNAE MAGAZINE, FALL 1963.

WGOVECS65798 GOVRS COMM STATUS OF WOMEN
PROGRESS AND PROSPECTS. THE REPORT OF THE SECOND NATIONAL
CONFERENCE OF GOVERNORS COMMISSIONS ON THE STATUS OF
WOMEN. /EMPLOYMENT-CONDITIONS/
GOVERNORS COMMISSIONS ON THE STATUS OF WOMEN,
INTERDEPARTMENTAL COMMITTEE ON THE STATUS OF WOMEN. CITIZENS
ADVISORY COUNCIL ON THE STATUS OF WOMEN. WASHINGTON, DC.
JULY 28-30 1965. 80 PP.

WGOVECS66215 GOVRS COMMS STATUS OF WOMEN   *US DEPARTMENT OF LABOR
PROGRESS AND PROSPECTS. /EMPLOYMENT-CONDITIONS/
GOVERNORS COMMISSIONS ON THE STATUS OF WOMEN, SECOND
NATIONAL CONFERENCE. REPORT. WASHINGTON, DC.
JULY 28-30 1965. PUBLISHED BY US DEPARTMENT OF LABOR,
WOMEN-S BUREAU. GPO. WASHINGTON, DC. 1966.

WGRANLJ63800 GRANT LJ
SOME GUIDES FOR SUPERVISING WOMEN WORKERS.
SUPERVISORY MANAGEMENT, VOL 8, NO 1, JAN 1963. PP 9-12.

WGRAYHX62801 GRAY H
TRAPPED HOUSEWIFE. /WORK-FAMILY-CONFLICT/
MARRIAGE AND FAMILY LIVING, VOL 24, MAY 1962. PP 179-182.

WGRIFAM65803 GRIFFIN AM   LEYMASTER GR
ROSE JC   KENRICK MM
PETERSON AS
DISCUSSION. WOMEN IN MEDICINE. /OCCUPATIONS/
PRE-MED, COLUMBIA COLLEGE, VOL 4, NO 3, SPRING 1965.
PP 14-23, 45-49.

WGRIFVE58804 GRIFFIN VE   *US DEPARTMENT OF LABOR
WOMEN IN LEGAL WORK. /OCCUPATIONS/
US DEPARTMENT OF LABOR, BUREAU OF LABOR STATISTICS,
OCCUPATIONAL OUTLOOK QUARTERLY, VOL 2, NO 1, FEB 1958.
PP 15 PLUS.

WGROPGL59805 GROPPER GL   FITZPATRICK R
WHO GOES TO GRADUATE SCHOOL. /EDUCATION/
AMERICAN INSTITUTE FOR RESEARCH. PITTSBURGH, PENNSYLVANIA.
1959.

WGROSIH56806 GROSS IH ED
POTENTIALITIES OF WOMEN IN THE MIDDLE YEARS.
/WORK-FAMILY-CONFLICT/
MICHIGAN STATE UNIVERSITY PRESS. EAST LANSING, MICHIGAN.
1956. 198 PP.

WGROSSB59807 GROSSMAN SB   *US DEPARTMENT OF LABOR
CAREERS FOR WOMEN IN RETAILING. /OCCUPATIONS/
US DEPARTMENT OF LABOR, BUREAU OF LABOR STATISTICS,
OCCUPATIONAL OUTLOOK QUARTERLY, VOL 3, NO 3, SEPT 1959.
PP 15-20.

WGRUESM57984 GRUENBERG SM   KRECH HS
THE MODERN MOTHER-S DILEMMA. /WORK-FAMILY-CONFLICT/
PUBLIC AFFAIRS PAMPHLET NO 247. NEW YORK. 1957.

WGRUMDX61379 GRUMBACH D
A WOMAN-S PLACE. /WORK-WOMAN-ROLE/
COMMONWEAL, VOL 74, NO 5, AP 28 1961. PP 117-223.

WGUPTRC66808 GUPTA RC   *CAL FED BUS PROF WOMEN CLUBS
TESTIMONY, PUBLIC HEARING, WOMEN IN PUBLIC AND PRIVATE

EMPLOYMENT, CALIFORNIA. /DISCRIMINATION
WORK-FAMILY-CONFLICT/
CALIFORNIA ADVISORY COMMISSION ON THE STATUS OF WOMEN, STUDY
COMMITTEE NO 1, ON PUBLIC AND PRIVATE EMPLOYMENT, HEARINGS.
SACRAMENTO, CALIFORNIA. FEB 24-25 1966. VOL 1, PP 61-72.

WGUPTRC66809 GUPTA RC   *CAL FED BUS PROF WOMEN CLUBS
TESTIMONY, PUBLIC HEARING, WOMEN IN PUBLIC AND PRIVATE
EMPLOYMENT, CALIFORNIA. /EMPLOYMENT-CONDITIONS/
CALIFORNIA ADVISORY COMMISSION ON THE STATUS OF WOMEN, STUDY
COMMITTEE NO 1, ON PUBLIC AND PRIVATE EMPLOYMENT, HEARINGS.
SACRAMENTO, CALIFORNIA. AP 28 1966. PP 102-114.

WGURIMG63810 GURIN MG   NACHMANN B
SEGAL SJ
THE EFFECT OF THE SOCIAL CONTEXT IN THE VOCATIONAL
COUNSELING OF COLLEGE WOMEN.
JOURNAL OF COUNSELING PSYCHOLOGY, VOL 10, 1963. PP 28-33.

WHABESX58811 HABER S   *RAND CORPORATION
FEMALE LABOR-FORCE PARTICIPATION AND ECONOMIC DEVELOPMENT.
RAND CORPORATION. P-1504. LOS ANGELES, CALIFORNIA. 1958.

WHACKHM61812 HACKER HM
A FUNCTIONAL APPROACH TO THE GAINFUL EMPLOYMENT OF MARRIED
WOMEN.
COLUMBIA UNIVERSITY. DISSERTATION. NEW YORK. 1961.

WHALFIT61814 HALFTER IT
THE COMPARATIVE ACADEMIC ACHIEVEMENT OF WOMEN FORTY YEARS OF
AGE AND OVER AND WOMEN EIGHTEEN TO TWENTY FIVE.
UNIVERSITY OF CHICAGO. PHD DISSERTATION. CHICAGO, ILLINOIS.
1961.

WHALFIT62813 HALFTER IT
THE COMPARATIVE ACADEMIC ACHIEVEMENT OF YOUNG AND OLD.
/TRAINING/
JOURNAL OF NATIONAL ASSOCIATION OF WOMEN DEANS AND
COUNSELORS, VOL 25, NO 2, 1962. PP 60-67.

WHALLWJ63815 HALL WJ
COLLEGE WOMEN-S IDENTIFICATIONS WITH THEIR FATHERS IN
RELATION TO VOCATIONAL INTEREST PATTERNS. /ASPIRATIONS/
UNIVERSITY OF TEXAS. PHD DISSERTATION. AUSTIN, TEXAS. 1963.

WHAMMKX56817 HAMMILL K
WOMEN AS BOSSES. /OCCUPATIONS/
FORTUNE, JUNE 1956.

WHANDHX57818 HAND H
WORKING MOTHERS AND MALADJUSTED CHILDREN.
JOURNAL OF EDUCATIONAL SOCIOLOGY, VOL 30, JAN 1957.
PP 327-352.

WHANNFX58819 HANNETT F
REPORT ON THE SURVEY OF FEMALE PHYSICIANS GRADUATING FROM
MEDICAL SCHOOL BETWEEN 1925 AND 1940. /OCCUPATIONS/
JOURNAL OF THE AMERICAN MEDICAL WOMEN-S ASSOCIATION, VOL 13,
NO 3, MAR 1958. PP 80-85.

WHANSDE64821 HANSON DE
SOCIAL ROLE EXPECTATION. MOTIVATIONAL VARIABLE IN GIRLS.
/ASPIRATIONS/
JOURNAL OF HOME ECONOMICS, VOL 56, NO 5, MAY 1964.
PP 132-136.

WHANSEB62820 HANSL EB
PATTERNS IN WOMANPOWER. A PILOT STUDY.
JOURNAL OF THE NATIONAL ASSOCIATION OF WOMEN DEANS AND
COUNSELORS, VOL 25, NO 2, JAN 1962. PP 25,81-87.

WHARPXX62822 HARPERS
SPECIAL SUPPLEMENT ON THE AMERICAN FEMALE.
/WORK-WOMAN-ROLE/
HARPERS, VOL 225, OCT 1962. PP 117-180.

WHARREX64827 HARRISON E
THE WORKING WOMAN. BARRIERS IN EMPLOYMENT. /DISCRIMINATION/
PUBLIC ADMINISTRATION REVIEW, VOL 24, NO 2, JUNE 1964.
PP 78-85.

WHARREX65826 HARRISON E
TALENT SEARCH FOR WOMANPOWER.
JOURNAL OF ASSOCIATION OF AMERICAN UNIVERSITY WOMEN, VOL 58,
NO 3, 1965. PP 99-101.

WHARRMX62823 HARRINGTON M
THE RETAIL CLERKS. /TECHNOLOGICAL-CHANGE/
JOHN WILEY AND SONS. NEW YORK. 1962.

WHARRNC64825 HARRIS NC
TECHNICAL EDUCATION IN THE JUNIOR COLLEGE.
AMERICAN ASSOCIATION OF JUNIOR COLLEGES. WASHINGTON, DC.
1964.

WHARRTW65824 HARRINGTON TW
PANEL DISCUSSION. THE CASE FOR AND AGAINST THE EMPLOYMENT OF
WOMEN. /OCCUPATIONS/
WOMEN AND THE SCIENTIFIC PROFESSIONS. ED BY JACQUELINE A
MATTFELD AND CAROL G VAN AKEN. MIT PRESS. CAMBRIDGE,
MASSACHUSETTS. 1965. PP 183-214.

WHARTRE60828 HARTLEY RE   *US PUBLIC HEALTH SERVICE
*NATL INST OF MENTAL HEALTH
SOME IMPLICATIONS ON CURRENT CHANGES IN SEX ROLE PATTERNS.
/WORK-WOMAN-ROLE/
US PUBLIC HEALTH SERVICE. NATIONAL INSTITUTE OF MENTAL
HEALTH. WASHINGTON, DC. 1960.

WHARTRE61829 HARTLEY RE
WHAT ASPECTS OF CHILD BEHAVIOR SHOULD BE STUDIED IN RELATION
TO MATERNAL EMPLOYMENT.
RESEARCH ISSUES RELATED TO THE EFFECTS OF MATERNAL
EMPLOYMENT ON CHILDREN. ED BY ALBERTA E SIEGEL. PENNSYLVANIA
STATE UNIVERSITY. SOCIAL SCIENCE RESEARCH CENTER. UNIVERSITY
PARK, PENNSYLVANIA. 1961.

WHARTRE62830 HARTLEY RE
WOMAN-S ROLES. HOW GIRLS SEE THEM. /WORK-WOMAN-ROLE/
JOURNAL OF ASSOCIATION OF AMERICAN UNIVERSITY WOMEN, VOL 55,
MAY 1962. PP 212-216.

WHAVIRJ65833 HAVIGHURST RJ
COUNSELING ADOLESCENT GIRLS IN THE 1960-S.
VOCATIONAL GUIDANCE QUARTERLY, VOL 13, 1965. PP 153-160.

WHAWKAL60834 HAWKES ALR
CHANGING PATTERNS IN WOMEN-S LIVES IN 1960.
/WORK-WOMAN-ROLE/
TEACHERS COLLEGE RECORD. AP 1960.

WHEALAK63835 HEALY AK
LADY AND ONE-THIRD SCHOLAR. /OCCUPATIONS/
EDUCATIONAL FORUM, VOL 27, MAR 1963. PP 313-318.

WHEALWX66836 HEALY W   TWOMEY T
*HOSP AND INST WORKERS UNIONS *CAL CC BUILD SERV EMPS UNION
TESTIMONY, PUBLIC HEARING, WOMEN IN PUBLIC AND PRIVATE
EMPLOYMENT, CALIFORNIA. /EMPLOYMENT-CONDITIONS/
CALIFORNIA ADVISORY COMMISSION ON THE STATUS OF WOMEN, STUDY
COMMITTEE NO 1, ON PUBLIC AND PRIVATE EMPLOYMENT, HEARINGS.
SACRAMENTO, CALIFORNIA. AP 29 1966. PP 217-238.

WHEDGJN64594 HEDGES JN   *US DEPARTMENT OF LABOR
COUNSELING OF GIRLS AND MATURE WOMEN.
US DEPARTMENT OF LABOR, EMPLOYMENT SERVICE REVIEW, NO 1,
1964. PP 23-24.

WHEISPX59838 HEIST P
IMPLICATIONS FROM RECENT RESEARCH ON COLLEGE STUDENTS.
/MANPOWER/
JOURNAL OF THE NATIONAL ASSOCIATION OF WOMEN DEANS AND
COUNSELORS, VOL 22, NO 3, 1959.

WHEISPX61841 HEIST P
STUDENTS TODAY -- MEN AND WOMEN OF TOMORROW. /MANPOWER/
NATIONAL ASSOCIATION OF WOMEN DEANS AND COUNSELORS,
CONVENTION, PAPER. DENVER, COLORADO. MAR 1961.

WHEISPX62837 HEIST P
A COMMENTARY ON THE MOTIVATION AND EDUCATION OF COLLEGE
WOMEN. /ASPIRATIONS/
JOURNAL OF THE NATIONAL ASSOCIATION OF WOMEN DEANS AND
COUNSELORS, VOL 25, JAN 1962. PP 51-59.

WHEISPX62839 HEIST P
THE MOTIVATION OF COLLEGE WOMEN TODAY. A CLOSER LOOK.
/ASPIRATIONS/
JOURNAL OF THE AMERICAN ASSOCIATION OF UNIVERSITY WOMEN.
VOL 55, OCT 1962.

WHEISPX63840 HEIST P
THE MOTIVATION OF COLLEGE WOMEN TODAY. THE CULTURAL SETTING.
/ASPIRATIONS/
JOURNAL OF THE AMERICAN ASSOCIATION OF UNIVERSITY WOMEN,
JAN 1963. PP 55-57.

WHERZEX64123 HERZOG E   *US DEPT OF HEALTH ED WELFARE
CHILDREN OF WORKING MOTHERS, 1960.
US DEPARTMENT OF HEALTH, EDUCATION, AND WELFARE, WELFARE
ADMINISTRATION, CHILDREN-S BUREAU. WASHINGTON, DC.
REPRINT NO 382. 1964.

WHERZNK60377 HERZFELD NK
THE STATUS OF WOMEN. /DISCRIMINATION/
COMMONWEAL, VOL 71, NO 19, FEB 5 1960.

WHEWEAX62843 HEWES A
WOMEN PART-TIME WORKERS IN THE U.S.
INTERNATIONAL LABOUR REVIEW, VOL 86, NO 5, NOV 1962.
PP 443-451.

WHEWEVH64482 HEWER VH   NEUBECK G
ATTITUDES OF COLLEGE STUDENTS TOWARD EMPLOYMENT AMONG
MARRIED WOMEN. /WORK-FAMILY-CONFLICT/
PERSONNEL AND GUIDANCE JOURNAL, VOL 43, 1964. PP 587-592.

WHILLBX62845 HILLMAN B
GIFTED WOMEN IN THE TRADE UNIONS. /OCCUPATIONS/
AMERICAN WOMEN. THE CHANGING IMAGE. ED BY BEVERLY B CASSARA.
BEACON PRESS. BOSTON, MASSACHUSETTS. 1962. PP 99-115.

WHILLHX66844 HILL H   *ASSN WEST PULP PAPER WORKERS
TESTIMONY, PUBLIC HEARING, WOMEN IN PUBLIC AND PRIVATE
EMPLOYMENT, CALIFORNIA. /DISCRIMINATION/
CALIFORNIA ADVISORY COMMISSION ON THE STATUS OF WOMEN, STUDY
COMMITTEE NO 1, ON PUBLIC AND PRIVATE EMPLOYMENT, HEARINGS.
SACRAMENTO, CALIFORNIA. FEB 24-25 1966. VOL 2, PP 89-98.

WHOFFGL61846 HOFFMAN GL   *US DEPT OF HEALTH ED WELFARE
*US DEPARTMENT OF LABOR
DAY CARE SERVICES. FORM AND SUBSTANCE.
/EMPLOYMENT-CONDITIONS/
NATIONAL CONFERENCE ON DAY CARE FOR CHILDREN, REPORT OF.
NOV 17-18 1960. US DEPARTMENT OF HEALTH, EDUCATION AND
WELFARE, US DEPARTMENT OF LABOR, WOMENS BUREAU, CHILDRENS
BUREAU. GPO. WASHINGTON, DC. 1961. 55 PP.

WHOFFLW63847 HOFFMAN LW
THE DECISION TO WORK. /ASPIRATIONS/
THE EMPLOYED MOTHER IN AMERICA. ED BY F IVAN NYE AND LOIS W
HOFFMAN. RAND MCNALLY. CHICAGO, ILLINOIS. 1963. PP 18-39.

WHOOSIR60000 HOOS IR
WHEN THE COMPUTER TAKES OVER THE OFFICE.
/TECHNOLOGICAL-CHANGE/
HARVARD BUSINESS REVIEW, JULY-AUG 1960.

WHOOSIR61848 HOOS IR
AUTOMATION IN THE OFFICE. /TECHNOLOGICAL-CHANGE/
PUBLIC AFFAIRS PRESS. WASHINGTON, DC. 1961. 138 PP.

WHOSLEM64540 HOSLEY EM
PART-TIME CARE. THE DAY-CARE PROBLEM.
/EMPLOYMENT-CONDITIONS/
ANNALS OF THE AMERICAN ACADEMY OF POLITICAL AND SOCIAL
SCIENCES, VOL 355, SEPT 1964. PP 56-61.

WHOYTDP58850 HOYT DP   KENNEDY CE
INTEREST AND PERSONALITY CORRELATES OF CAREER-MOTIVATED
AND HOMEMAKING-MOTIVATED COLLEGE WOMEN. /ASPIRATIONS/
JOURNAL OF COUNSELING PSYCHOLOGY, VOL 51, 1958. PP 44-49.

WHUGHEC58851 HUGHES EC   HUGHES HM
DEUTSCHER I
TWENTY THOUSAND NURSES TELL THEIR STORY. /SOCIO-ECONOMIC/
LIPPINCOTT. PHILADELPHIA, PENNSYLVANIA. 1958. PP 19-46.

WHUNTEH62271 HUNTINGTON EH   *U CAL BERKELEY INST IND RELS
*HELLER COMT RESEARCH SOC ECS
OLDER WOMEN IN THE LABOR-MARKET.
UNIVERSITY OF CALIFORNIA, BERKELEY, INSTITUTE OF INDUSTRIAL
RELATIONS AND HELLER COMMITTEE FOR RESEARCH IN SOCIAL
ECONOMICS, STUDY. BERKELEY, CALIFORNIA. 1962. 258 PP.
UNPUBLISHED TYPESCRIPT.

WIFFERE57854 IFFERT RE   *US DEPT OF HEALTH ED WELFARE
RETENTION AND WITHDRAWAL OF COLLEGE STUDENTS. /DROP-OUT/
US DEPARTMENT OF HEALTH, EDUCATION AND WELFARE, OFFICE OF
EDUCATION. BULLETIN 1958, NO 1. GPO. WASHINGTON, DC. 1957.

WILLIBE64330 ILLINOIS BUR EMPLOY SECURITY
WOMEN WORKERS IN ILLINOIS.
ILLINOIS BUREAU OF EMPLOYMENT SECURITY. CHICAGO, ILLINOIS.
1964.

WINDUBX63857 INDUSTRIAL BULLETIN
A WOMAN-S WORLD. /WORK-WOMAN-ROLE/
INDUSTRIAL BULLETIN, VOL 42, NO 1, JAN 1963. PP 15-20.

WINDUBX65858 INDUSTRIAL BULLETIN
WOMEN IN THE WORK-FORCE.
INDUSTRIAL BULLETIN, VOL 44, NO 3, MAR 1965. PP 22-24.

WINGRLX66859 INGRAM L   *CAL DEPT OF EMPLOYMENT
TESTIMONY, PUBLIC HEARING, WOMEN IN PUBLIC AND PRIVATE
EMPLOYMENT, CALIFORNIA. /MDTA EEO/
CALIFORNIA ADVISORY COMMISSION ON THE STATUS OF WOMEN, STUDY
COMMITTEE NO 1, ON PUBLIC AND PRIVATE EMPLOYMENT. HEARINGS.
SACRAMENTO, CALIFORNIA. FEB 24-25 1966. VOL 2, PP 73-88.

WINSTOL60873 INSTITUTE OF LIFE INSURANCE
WORKING WOMEN...WHO ARE THEY.
INSTITUTE OF LIFE INSURANCE, WOMEN-S DIVISION. NEW YORK.
WINTER 1960.

WINTEAP58861 INTL ASSN PERSONNEL WOMEN
STUDY OF JOB OPPORTUNITIES FOR WOMEN COLLEGE GRADUATES.
/OCCUPATIONS/
INTERNATIONAL ASSOCIATION OF PERSONNEL WOMEN, RESEARCH
COMMITTEE. ST LOUIS, MISSOURI. NOV 1958. 13 PP.

WINTELO60862 INTERNATIONAL LABOUR OFFICE
EMPLOYMENT AND CONDITIONS OF WORK OF NURSES.
INTERNATIONAL LABOUR OFFICE. GENEVA, SWITZERLAND. 1960.
176 PP.

WINTELO64863 INTERNATL LABOUR ORGANIZATION
VOCATIONAL GUIDANCE AND TRAINING OF GIRLS AND WOMEN.
/COUNSELING/
INTERNATIONAL LABOUR ORGANIZATION. GENEVA, SWITZERLAND.
1964. 160 PP.

WINTELR56871 INTERNATIONAL LABOUR REVIEW
WORLD-S WORKING POPULATION. SOME DEMOGRAPHIC ASPECTS.
INTERNATIONAL LABOUR REVIEW, VOL 73, 1956. PP 152-176.

WINTELR57867 INTERNATIONAL LABOUR REVIEW
PART-TIME EMPLOYMENT FOR WOMEN WITH FAMILY RESPONSIBILITIES.
/WORK-FAMILY-CONFLICT/
INTERNATIONAL LABOUR REVIEW, JUNE 1957.

WINTELR58864 INTERNATIONAL LABOUR REVIEW
CHILD CARE FACILITIES FOR WOMEN WORKERS.
/EMPLOYMENT-CONDITIONS/
INTERNATIONAL LABOUR REVIEW, VOL 78, 1958. PP 91-109.

WINTELR58869 INTERNATIONAL LABOUR REVIEW
WOMEN IN THE LABOR-FORCE.
INTERNATIONAL LABOUR REVIEW, VOL 77, 1958. PP 254-272.

WINTELR60870 INTERNATIONAL LABOUR REVIEW
WOMEN-S WAGES.
INTERNATIONAL LABOUR REVIEW, VOL 81, 1960. PP 95-109.

WINTELR61868 INTERNATIONAL LABOUR REVIEW
PROJECTIONS OF POPULATION AND LABOR-FORCE.
INTERNATIONAL LABOUR REVIEW, VOL 83, 1961. PP 378-389.

WINTELR62865 INTERNATIONAL LABOUR REVIEW
DISCRIMINATION IN EMPLOYMENT OR OCCUPATION ON THE BASIS OF
MARITAL-STATUS.
INTERNATIONAL LABOUR REVIEW, VOL 85, MAR-AP 1962.
PP 368-389.

WINTELR64866 INTERNATIONAL LABOUR REVIEW
OCCUPATIONAL TRAINING OF WOMEN IN THE UNITED STATES.
INTERNATIONAL LABOUR REVIEW, VOL 90, DEC 1964. PP 573-574.

WIOWAGC64796 IOWA GOVRS COMM STATUS WOMEN
FIRST REPORT, IOWA GOVERNOR-S COMMISSION ON THE STATUS OF
WOMEN. /EMPLOYMENT-CONDITIONS/
IOWA GOVERNOR-S COMMISSION ON THE STATUS OF WOMEN.
DES MOINES, IOWA. SEPT 1964. 30 PP.

WIOWAGC64797 IOWA GOVRS COMM STATUS WOMEN
CONFERENCE ON EMPLOYMENT PROBLEMS OF WORKING WOMEN.
IOWA GOVERNOR-S COMMISSION ON THE STATUS OF WOMEN.
UNIVERSITY OF IOWA. IOWA CITY, IOWA. MAY 1964.

WIOWALR65102 IOWA LAW REVIEW
CLASSIFICATION ON THE BASIS OF SEX AND THE 1964
CIVIL-RIGHTS-ACT.
IOWA LAW REVIEW, SPRING 1965. PP 778-798.

WIRISLD62874 IRISH LD
NEEDED. UNIQUE PATTERNS FOR EDUCATING WOMEN.
/WORK-WOMEN-ROLE/
COLLEGE BOARD REVIEW, NO 46, WINTER 1962. PP 27-31.

WISAALE57875 ISAACSON LE   AMOS LC
PARTICIPATION IN PART-TIME WORK BY WOMEN COLLEGE STUDENTS.
PERSONNEL AND GUIDANCE JOURNAL, VOL 35, MAR 1957.
PP 445-448.

WISAMVX62876 ISAMBERT-JAMUTI V
ABSENTEEISM AMONG WOMEN WORKERS IN INDUSTRY.
INTERNATIONAL LABOUR REVIEW, MAR 1962.

WJACOPE57877 JACOB PE
CHANGING VALUES IN COLLEGE. /WORK-WOMAN-ROLE/
HARPER AND BROTHERS. NEW YORK. 1957. 174 PP.

WJAFFAH56878 JAFFE AH   *US DEPARTMENT OF LABOR
TRENDS IN THE PARTICIPATION OF WOMEN IN THE WORKING-FORCE.
US DEPARTMENT OF LABOR, MONTHLY LABOR REVIEW, VOL 79, MAY
1956. PP 559-565.

WJAHOMX55879 JAHODA M   HAVEL J
*AMERICAN CC ON EDUCATION
PSYCHOLOGICAL PROBLEMS OF WOMEN IN DIFFERENT SOCIAL ROLES.
/WORK-WOMAN-ROLE/
AMERICAN COUNCIL ON EDUCATION, EDUCATIONAL RECORD, VOL 36,
NO 4, 1955.

WJEWIVA61880 JEWISH VACATION ASSOCIATION
A MEMORANDUM ON THE MOTIVATIONS OF MIDDLE AGED WOMEN IN THE
LOWER EDUCATIONAL BRACKETS TO RETURN TO WORK.
/ASPIRATIONS/
JEWISH VACATION ASSOCIATION, INC, PROJECT ON MIDDLE AGE.

NEW YORK. JAN 1961.

WJEWIVA62881 JEWISH VACATION ASSOCIATION
THE MIDDLE AGED WOMAN AND THE LABOR-MARKET.
JEWISH VACATION ASSOCIATION, INC, REPORT ON A WORKSHOP
SPONSORED BY THE PROJECT ON MIDDLE AGE. NEW YORK. 1962.

WJEWIVA62882 JEWISH VACATION ASSOCIATION
IN QUEST OF WIDER HORIZONS. THE WOMAN AFTER FORTY THINKS
ABOUT A JOB. /ASPIRATIONS/
JEWISH VACATION ASSOCIATION, INC, PROJECT ON MIDDLE AGE.
NEW YORK. 1962.

WJEWIVA62883 JEWISH VACATION ASSOCIATION
A PILOT STUDY OF THE MOTIVATIONS AND PROBLEMS OF MIDDLE AGED
HOMEMAKERS IN LOWER SOCIO-ECONOMIC GROUPS IN SEEKING
EMPLOYMENT. /ASPIRATIONS/
JEWISH VACATION ASSOCIATION, INC, PROJECT ON MIDDLE AGE.
NEW YORK. MAR 1962.

WJOHNGG65884 JOHNSON GG
THE CHANGING STATUS OF THE SOUTHERN WOMAN.
/WORK-WOMAN-ROLE/
THE SOUTH IN CONTINUITY AND CHANGE. ED BY JOHN C MCKINNEY
AND EDGAR T THOMPSON. DUKE UNIVERSITY PRESS. DURHAM,
NORTH CAROLINA. 1965. PP 418-436.

WJONECX64009 MARY GIBS JONES COLLEGE
THE ROLE OF THE EDUCATED WOMAN. /WORK-WOMAN-ROLE/
MARY GIBS JONES COLLEGE. PROCEEDINGS OF A SYMPOSIUM. RICE
UNIVERSITY. HOUSTON, TEXAS. JAN 29-30 1963. PUBLISHED BY
RICE UNIVERSITY. HOUSTON, TEXAS. 1964.

WJOUROI62883 JOURNAL OF INDUSTRIAL RELS
SOME FACTORS WHICH DETERMINE THE DISTRIBUTION OF THE FEMALE
WORK-FORCE. /LABOR-FORCE/
JOURNAL OF INDUSTRIAL RELATIONS, VOL 4, OCT 1962.
PP 108-119.

WKAUFDX66886 KAUFFMAN D   *CITIZENS FOR FARM LABOR
STATEMENT, PUBLIC HEARING, WOMEN IN PUBLIC AND PRIVATE
EMPLOYMENT, CALIFORNIA. /EMPLOYMENT-CONDITIONS
MIGRANT-WORKERS/
CALIFORNIA ADVISORY COMMISSION ON THE STATUS OF WOMEN, STUDY
COMMITTEE NO 1, ON PUBLIC AND PRIVATE EMPLOYMENT. HEARINGS.
SACRAMENTO, CALIFORNIA. AP 29 1966. PP 255-296.

WKEENBC62887 KEENEY BC
WOMEN PROFESSORS AT BROWN. /OCCUPATIONS/
PEMBROKE ALUMNA, VOL 27, OCT 1962.

WKELLET66888 KELLEY ET
TESTIMONY, PUBLIC HEARING, WOMEN IN PUBLIC AND PRIVATE
EMPLOYMENT, CALIFORNIA. /EMPLOYMENT-CONDITIONS/
CALIFORNIA ADVISORY COMMISSION ON THE STATUS OF WOMEN, STUDY
COMMITTEE NO 1, ON PUBLIC AND PRIVATE EMPLOYMENT. HEARINGS.
SACRAMENTO, CALIFORNIA. AP 28 1966. PP 54-71.

WKENOBX65225 KENDLER B
AMERICAN WOMEN WHO WORK.
MICHIGAN MANPOWER QUARTERLY REVIEW, VOL 1, NO 2, SECOND
QUARTER 1965. PP 18-25.

WKENNKX64891 KENNISTON K   KENNISTON E
AN AMERICAN ANACHRONISM, THE IMAGE OF WOMEN AND WORK.
/WORK-WOMAN-ROLE/
AMERICAN SCHOLAR, VOL 33, SUMMER 1964. PP 355-375.

WKENNVX66890 KENNEDY V   *CAL RETAILERS ASSOCIATION
STATEMENT, PUBLIC HEARING, WOMEN IN PUBLIC AND PRIVATE
EMPLOYMENT, CALIFORNIA. /EMPLOYMENT-CONDITIONS/
CALIFORNIA ADVISORY COMMISSION ON THE STATUS OF WOMEN, STUDY
COMMITTEE NO 1, ON PUBLIC AND PRIVATE EMPLOYMENT. HEARINGS.
SACRAMENTO, CALIFORNIA. AP 29 1966. PP 268-275.

WKERNKK65892 KERN KK
HIGH SCHOOL FRESHMAN AND SENIORS VIEW THE ROLE OF WOMEN IN
MODERN SOCIETY. /WORK-FAMILY-CONFLICT/
THE BULLETIN ON FAMILY DEVELOPMENT, VOL 5, 1965. PP 9-13.

WKEYSMD64894 KEYSERLING MD   *US DEPARTMENT OF LABOR
DAY CARE IN A CHANGING ECONOMY. /EMPLOYMENT-CONDITIONS/
MARYLAND COMMITTEE ON GROUP DAY CARE OF CHILDREN. SPEECH.
BALTIMORE, MARYLAND. MAY 19 1964. PUBLISHED BY US
DEPARTMENT OF LABOR, WOMEN-S BUREAU. GPO. WASHINGTON, DC.
1964.

WKEYSMD64898 KEYSERLING MD   *US DEPARTMENT OF LABOR
NEW HORIZONS FOR WOMEN. /WORK-WOMAN-ROLE/
NATIONAL HOME DEMONSTRATION AGENTS ASSOCIATION. SPEECH.
WASHINGTON, DC. NOV 15 1964.

WKEYSMD64899 KEYSERLING MD   *US DEPARTMENT OF LABOR
NEW OPPORTUNITIES AND NEW RESPONSIBILITIES FOR WOMEN.
/WORK-WOMAN-ROLE/
SWEET BRIAR COLLEGE. CONVOCATION ADDRESS. SWEET BRIAR,
VIRGINIA. SEPT 17 1964.

WKEYSMD64900 KEYSERLING MD   *US DEPARTMENT OF LABOR
RESEARCH AND YOUR JOB. /TECHNOLOGICAL-CHANGE/
NATIONAL FEDERATION OF BUSINESS AND PROFESSIONAL WOMEN-S
CLUBS, INC. SPEECH. DETROIT, MICHIGAN. JULY 18 1964.

WKEYSMD65021 KEYSERLING MD
WOMEN JOURNALISTS AND TODAY-S WORLD. /OCCUPATIONS/
THE MATRIX, AP 1965.

WKEYSMD65644 KEYSERLING MD
TRENDS IN WOMEN-S EMPLOYMENT.
THE AMERICAN CHILD. VOL 47, NO 3, MAY 1965. PP 19-23.

WKEYSMD65893 KEYSERLING MD   *US DEPARTMENT OF LABOR
CHANGING REALITIES IN WOMEN-S LIVES. /WORK-WOMAN-ROLE/
MID-ATLANTIC CONFERENCE ON COUNSELING GIRLS IN THE 1960-S.
ADDRESS. PHILADELPHIA, PENNSYLVANIA. DEC 2 1965.

WKEYSMD65895 KEYSERLING MD   *US DEPARTMENT OF LABOR
FACING THE FACTS ABOUT WOMEN-S LIVES TODAY.
/WORK-WOMAN-ROLE/
MIDWEST REGIONAL PILOT CONFERENCE, NEW APPROACHES TO
COUNSELING GIRLS IN THE 1960-S. SPEECH. UNIVERSITY OF
CHICAGO. CHICAGO, ILLINOIS. FEB 26 1965. PUBLISHED BY US
DEPARTMENT OF LABOR, WOMEN-S BUREAU. GPO. WASHINGTON, DC.
1965.

WKEYSMD65897 KEYSERLING MD   *US DEPARTMENT OF LABOR
THE NATION-S WORKING MOTHERS AND THE NEED FOR DAY CARE.
ADDRESS. /EMPLOYMENT-CONDITIONS/
NATIONAL CONFERENCE ON DAY CARE SERVICES. ADDRESS.
WASHINGTON, DC. MAY 14 1965.

WKEYSMD66896 KEYSERLING MD
GOALS -- A WAY TO FULLER UTILIZATION.
UNIVERSITY OF SOUTHERN CALIFORNIA EXTENSION. EXPLODING THE
MYTHS. EXPANDING EMPLOYMENT OPPORTUNITIES FOR CAREER WOMEN.
CONFERENCE. SPEECH. LOS ANGELES, CALIFORNIA. DEC 3 1966.

WKEYSMD66901 KEYSERLING MD   *US DEPARTMENT OF LABOR
WOMANPOWER NEEDED.
AMERICAN PERSONNEL AND GUIDANCE ASSOCIATION, CONVENTION.
SPEECH. WASHINGTON, DC. AP 4 1966.

WKIBRAK58902 KIBRICK AK
DROP-OUTS FROM SCHOOLS OF NURSING. THE EFFECT OF SELF- AND
ROLE PERCEPTION.
HARVARD UNIVERSITY. UNPUBLISHED EDD THESIS. CAMBRIDGE,
MASSACHUSETTS. 1958.

WKILLJR65903 KILLIAN JR
ENHANCING THE ROLE OF WOMEN IN SCIENCE, ENGINEERING, AND
THE SOCIAL SCIENCES. /OCCUPATIONS/
WOMEN AND THE SCIENTIFIC PROFESSIONS. ED BY JACQUELINE A
MATTFELD AND CARL G VAN AKEN. MIT PRESS. CAMBRIDGE,
MASSACHUSETTS. 1965. PP 128-138.

WKINGAG56905 KING AG
NOT TOO LITTLE OR TOO LATE. /WORK-WOMAN-ROLE/
VASSAR ALUMNAE MAGAZINE, FEB 1956.

WKINGAG63904 KING AG
CAREER OPPORTUNITIES FOR WOMEN IN BUSINESS. /OCCUPATIONS/
E P DUTTON AND CO. NEW YORK. 1963.

WKINGCR66906 KING CR
VOCATIONAL TRAINING OF THE OLDER WOMAN.
NATIONAL CONFERENCE ON MANPOWER TRAINING AND THE OLDER
WORKER. BACKGROUND PAPER. WASHINGTON, DC. NATIONAL COUNCIL
ON THE AGING. 1966. 10 PP.

WKITTRE60313 KITTREDGE RE
INVESTIGATION OF DIFFERENCES IN OCCUPATIONAL PREFERENCES,
STEREOTYPIC THINKING, AND PSYCHOLOGICAL NEEDS AMONG
UNDERGRADUATE WOMEN STUDENTS IN SELECTED CURRICULAR AREAS.
/ASPIRATIONS/
MICHIGAN STATE UNIVERSITY, PHD DISSERTATION. LANSING,
MICHIGAN. 1960.

WKIUCFX62909 KLUCKHOHN F
THE AMERICAN WOMAN-S ROLE. /WORK-WOMAN-ROLE/
JOURNAL OF ASSOCIATION OF AMERICAN UNIVERSITY WOMEN,
VOL 55. MAY 1962.

WKLEIVX65908 KLEIN V   *OECD
WOMEN WORKERS. WORKING HOURS AND SERVICES.
ORGANIZATION FOR ECONOMIC CO-OPERATION AND DEVELOPMENT.
PARIS, FRANCE. 1965. 100 PP.

WKNIGRX61910 KNIGHT R
THAT GIRL IN THE OFFICE. /OCCUPATIONS/
SATURDAY EVENING POST, AP 29 1961. PP 28-29, 89-90.

WKNIGTF66911 KNIGHT TF   *CAL MANUFACTURERS ASSN
STATEMENT, PUBLIC HEARING, WOMEN IN PUBLIC AND PRIVATE
EMPLOYMENT, CALIFORNIA. /EMPLOYMENT-CONDITIONS/
CALIFORNIA ADVISORY COMMISSION ON THE STATUS OF WOMEN,
STUDY COMMITTEE NO 1, ON PUBLIC AND PRIVATE EMPLOYMENT.
HEARINGS. SACRAMENTO, CALIFORNIA. AP 29 1966. PP 256-266.

WKNILNO60034 KNILSEN NO   WEISS EJ
*OREGON BUREAU OF LABOR
THE SELF-SUPPORTING WOMAN IN OREGON.
OREGON STATE BUREAU OF LABOR. PORTLAND, OREGON. 1960.

WKOMAMX62912 KOMAROVSKY M
THE HOMEMAKER AND THE WORKING WIFE. /WORK-FAMILY-CONFLICT/
BLUE-COLLAR MARRIAGE. RANDOM HOUSE. NEW YORK. 1962.
PP 49-81.

WKONOGX66913 KONOPKA G
THE IMPACT OF CULTURAL CHANGE ON WOMEN-S POSITION.
/BLUE-COLLAR ASPIRATIONS/
THE ADOLESCENT GIRL IN CONFLICT. PRENTICE HALL. ENGLEWOOD
CLIFFS, NEW JERSEY. 1966. PP 70-86.

WKORBJX63435 KORBEL J
FEMALE LABOR-FORCE MOBILITY AND ITS SIMULATION.
HUMAN RESOURCES IN THE URBAN ECONOMY. ED BY MARK PERLMAN.
JOHNS HOPKINS PRESS. BALTIMORE, MARYLAND. 1963. PP 55-74.

WKOSAJX64915 KOSA J   OOKER RE
THE FEMALE PHYSICIAN IN PUBLIC HEALTH. CONFLICT AND
RECONCILIATION OF THE SEX AND PROFESSIONAL ROLES.
/OCCUPATIONS/
SOCIOLOGY AND SOCIAL RESEARCH, VOL 49. 1964. PP 294-305.

WKRECHS65381 KRECH HS
THE IDENTITY OF MODERN WOMAN. /WORK-WOMAN-ROLE/
THE NATION, VOL 201, SEPT 20 1965. PP 125-128.

WKREPJX64916 KREPS J
AUTOMATION AND EMPLOYMENT. /TECHNOLOGICAL-CHANGE/
HOLT, RINEHART, AND WINSTON, INC. NEW YORK. 1964.

WKRUGDH60917 KRUGER DH
PROFESSIONAL STANDARDS AND ECONOMIC-STATUS OF NURSES IN THE
UNITED STATES.
INTERNATIONAL NURSING REVIEW, VOL 7. DEC 1960. PP 43-48.

WKRUGDH64918 KRUGER DH
WOMEN AT WORK. /LABOR-FORCE/
BUSINESS TOPICS, VOL 12, SPRING 1964. PP 21-37.

WKRUGDH64997 KRUGER DH
WOMEN AT WORK.
THE PERSONNEL ADMINISTRATOR, VOL 9, JULY-AUG 1964. PP 7-15.

WKRUSMX58920 KRUSE M
THE SHORTAGE OF NURSES AND CONDITIONS OF WORK IN NURSING.
/OCCUPATIONS/
INTERNATIONAL LABOUR REVIEW, VOL 78, 1958. PP 476-503.

WKUNDRB65919 KUNDSIN RB
WHY NOBODY WANTS WOMEN IN SCIENCE. /OCCUPATIONS/
SCIENCE REPORT, VOL 58, OCT 1965. PP 60-65.

WKYRKHX56921 KYRK H
ECONOMIC ROLE OF WOMEN 45-65. /WORK-WOMAN-ROLE/
POTENTIALITIES OF WOMEN IN THE MIDDLE YEARS. ED BY
IRMA GROSS. MICHIGAN STATE UNIVERSITY PRESS. LANSING,
MICHIGAN. 1956.

WLAJEHC59922 LAJEWSKI HC   *US DEPT OF HEALTH ED WELFARE
WORKING MOTHERS AND THEIR ARRANGEMENTS FOR CARE OF THEIR
CHILDREN. /EMPLOYMENT-CONDITIONS/
US DEPARTMENT OF HEALTH, EDUCATION AND WELFARE, SOCIAL
SECURITY BULLETIN, AUG 1959. PP 8-13.

WLAURMW61923 LAURENCE MW
SOURCES OF SATISFACTION IN THE LIVES OF WORKING WOMEN.
JOURNAL OF GERONTOLOGY, 1961. PP 163-167.

WLEINMX64925 LEINER M
CHANGES IN SELECTED PERSONALITY CHARACTERISTICS AND
PERSISTENCE IN THE CAREER CHOICES OF WOMEN ASSOCIATED
WITH A FOUR YEAR COLLEGE EDUCATION AT ONE OF THE COLLEGES
OF THE CITY UNIVERSITY OF NEW-YORK. /ASPIRATIONS/
NEW YORK UNIVERSITY. PHD DISSERTATION. NEW YORK. 1964.

WLEITSF61926 LEITER SF   *US DEPARTMENT OF LABOR
LIFE INSURANCE SELLING AS A CAREER FOR WOMEN. /OCCUPATIONS/
US DEPARTMENT OF LABOR, BUREAU OF LABOR STATISTICS,
OCCUPATIONAL OUTLOOK QUARTERLY, VOL 5, NO 1, FEB 1961.
PP 18-23.

WLEOPAK59927 LEOPOLD AK
TODAY-S WOMEN COLLEGE GRADUATES. /WORK-WOMEN-ROLE/
PERSONNEL AND GUIDANCE JOURNAL, VOL 38, 1959-1960.
PP 280-284.

WLESECE58928 LESER CEV
TRENDS IN WOMEN-S WORK PARTICIPATION.
POPULATION STUDIES VOL 12, 1958-1959. PP 100-110.

WLEVIHS56929 LEVIN HS
OFFICE WORK AND AUTOMATION. /TECHNOLOGICAL-CHANGE/
WILEY. NEW YORK. 1956. 203 PP.

WLEVISA63039 LEVITAN SA   *UPJOHN INST EMPLOY RESEARCH
VOCATIONAL EDUCATION AND FEDERAL POLICY.
W E UPJOHN INSTITUTE FOR EMPLOYMENT RESEARCH, PUBLIC POLICY
INFORMATION BULLETIN. KALAMAZOO, MICHIGAN- MAY 1963.

WLEWIAB65930 LEWIS AB   BOBROFF E
FROM KITCHEN TO CAREER. /WORK-FAMILY-CONFLICT/
BOBBS-MERRILL. INDIANOPOLIS, INDIANA. 1565.

WLEWIEC65931 LEWIS EC
COUNSELORS AND GIRLS. /COUNSELING/
JOURNAL OF COUNSELING PSYCHOLOGY, VOL 12, NO 2, 1965.
PP 159-166.

WLEWIND57932 LEWIS ND
WOMEN AND MODERN SCIENCE. /OCCUPATIONS/
JOURNAL OF ASSOCIATION OF AMERICAN UNIVERSITY WOMEN, VOL 51,
OCT 1957. PP 18-20.

WLICHMW59933 LICHLITER M
LIBERAL ARTS WOMEN GRADUATES, CLASS OF 1958.
/WORK-WOMEN-ROLE/
NATIONAL VOCATIONAL GUIDANCE ASSOCIATION, WOMEN-S SECTION.
ST CHARLES, MISSOURI. 1959. 9 PP.

WLIFTRJ65935 LIFTON RJ ED
THE WOMAN IN AMERICA. /WORK-WOMEN-ROLE/
HOUGHTON MIFFLIN. BOSTON, MASSACHUSETTS. 1965.

WLINDFX63108 LINDEN F   *NATL INDUSTRIAL CONF BOARD
WORKING WIVES.
NATIONAL INDUSTRIAL CONFERENCE BOARD, BUSINESS MANAGEMENT
RECORD. OCT 1963. PP 38-40.

WLINDFX66117 LINDEN F   *NATL INDUSTRIAL CONF BOARD
THE WORKING-WIFE HOUSEHOLD. PARTS 1 AND 2.
NATIONAL INDUSTRIAL CONFERENCE BOARD, CONFERENCE BOARD
RECORD, NOV, DEC 1966. PP 30-32, 49-51.

WLIPSOX64936 LIPSTREU O
PROBLEM AREAS IN TRAINING FOR AUTOMATED WORK.
/TECHNOLOGICAL-CHANGE/
TRAINING DIRECTORS JOURNAL, VOL 18, NO 11, NOV 1964.
PP 12-15.

WLLOYBJ62633 LLOYD BJ
WOMANPOWER -- KEY TO MANAGEMENT MANPOWER SHORTAGE.
PERSONNEL JOURNAL, VOL 41, NO 4, AP 1962. PP 180-182.

WLLOYBJ64937 LLOYD BJ ED
A CONFERENCE TO ENLIST THE PARTICIPATION OF 50 INSTITUTIONS
OF HIGHER EDUCATION IN SPECIFIC R AND D PROGRAMS TO
PREPARE WOMEN FOR PRODUCTIVE EMPLOYMENT.
CARNEGIE INSTITUTE OF TECHNOLOGY, MARGARET MORRISON
CARNEGIE COLLEGE. PITTSBURGH, PENNSYLVANIA. 1964. 94 PP.

WLLOYBJ66938 LLOYD BJ
A QUESTIONNAIRE PORTRAIT OF THE FRESHMAN COED. AFTER COLLEGE
WHAT. /ASPIRATIONS/
JOURNAL OF THE NATIONAL ASSOCIATION OF WOMAN DEANS AND
COUNSELORS. VOL 29, NO 4, SUMMER 1966. PP 159-162.

WLLOYEX56941 LLOYD-JONES E
WOMEN-S STATUS -- WOMEN TODAY AND THEIR EDUCATION.
NATIONAL ASSOCIATION OF WOMEN DEANS AND COUNSELORS, ANNUAL
MEETING. SPEECH. CINCINNATI, OHIO. MARCH 24 1956.

WLLOYMX66940 LLOYD M
TESTIMONY, PUBLIC HEARING, WOMEN IN PUBLIC AND PRIVATE
EMPLOYMENT, CALIFORNIA. /FEP MIGRANT-WORKERS
EMPLOYMENT-CONDITIONS/
CALIFORNIA ADVISORY COMMISSION ON THE STATUS OF WOMEN,
STUDY COMMITTEE NO 1, ON PUBLIC AND PRIVATE EMPLOYMENT.
HEARINGS. SACRAMENTO, CALIFORNIA. MAR 31-AP 1 1966.
PP 137-146.

WLORIRK66942 LORING RK
A SURVEY OF SPECIAL EDUCATIONAL PROGRAMS FOR ADULT WOMEN IN
UNIVERSITY EXTENSION DIVISIONS AND EVENING COLLEGES AS OF
SPRING 1965.
UNIVERSITY OF SOUTHERN CALIFORNIA. MA IN EDUCATION ESSAY.
LOS ANGELES, CALIFORNIA. WINTER 1966.

WLOWEDX66943 LOWE D   *RETAIL CLERKS UNION
TESTIMONY, PUBLIC HEARING, WOMEN IN PUBLIC AND PRIVATE
EMPLOYMENT, CALIFORNIA. /FEP EMPLOYMENT CONDITIONS/
CALIFORNIA ADVISORY COMMISSION ON THE STATUS OF WOMEN,
STUDY COMMITTEE NO 1, ON PUBLIC AND PRIVATE EMPLOYMENT.
HEARINGS. SACRAMENTO, CALIFORNIA, AP 28 1966. PP 47-54.

WMACCEE58949 MACCOBY EE
CHILDREN AND WORKING MOTHERS.
CHILDREN, VOL 5, 1958. PP 83-89.

WMACKJW66950 MACKLE JW   *AEROJET GENERAL CORPORATION
  TESTIMONY, PUBLIC HEARING, WOMEN IN PUBLIC AND PRIVATE
    EMPLOYMENT, CALIFORNIA. /EMPLOYMENT-CONDITIONS/
  CALIFORNIA ADVISORY COMMISSION ON THE STATUS OF WOMEN,
  STUDY COMMITTEE NO 1, ON PUBLIC AND PRIVATE EMPLOYMENT.
  HEARINGS. SACRAMENTO, CALIFORNIA. FEB 24-25 1966. VOL 2,
  PP 98-104.

WMAGOTM66779 MAGOON TM   GOLANN SE
  NONTRADITIONALLY TRAINED WOMEN AS MENTAL HEALTH
    COUNSELORS/PSYCHOTHERAPISTS.
  PERSONNEL AND GUIDANCE JOURNAL, AP 1966. PP 788-793.

WMAHOTA61951 MAHONEY TA
  FACTORS DETERMINING THE LABOR-FORCE PARTICIPATION OF
    MARRIED WOMEN.
  INDUSTRIAL AND LABOR RELATIONS REVIEW, VOL 14, NO 4, 1961.
  PP 564-577.

WMAHRAH65953 MAHRER AH
  WOMEN AS EXECUTIVES AND MANAGERS. /OCCUPATIONS/
  MANAGEMENT, VOL 18, NO 2. NOV-DEC 1965. PP 8-15.

WMARCMR60C80 MARCUS MR
  WOMEN IN THE LABOR-FORCE.
  SOCIAL CASEWORK, VOL 41, JUNE 1960. PP 298-302.

WMARMJX66954 MARMOR J
  WOMAN AT WORK -- A STUDY IN PREJUDICE. /DISCRIMINATION/
  EXPLODING THE MYTHS. EXPANDING EMPLOYMENT OPPORTUNITIES FOR
  CAREER WOMEN. UNIVERSITY OF SOUTHERN CALIFORNIA. EXTENSION,
  CONFERENCE. SPEECH. LOS ANGELES, CALIFORNIA. DEC 3 1966.

WMARRAF61955 MARRIAGE AND FAMILY LIVING
  WOMEN AND WORK.
  MARRIAGE AND FAMILY LIVING, VOL 23, NOV 1961. PP 325-387,
  SPECIAL SECTION.

WMARSEM62956 MARSHALL EM
  WOMEN ARE TRAINING FOR BUSINESS. /OCCUPATIONS/
  MANAGEMENT, NOV-DEC 1962. PP 55-59.

WMARTHM63957 MARTSTON HM
  RUTGERS -- THE STATE UNIVERSITY, FORD FOUNDATION PROGRAM
    FOR THE RETRAINING IN MATHEMATICS OF COLLEGE GRADUATE
    WOMEN. /TRAINING/
  EDUCATION AND A WOMAN-S LIFE. ED BY LAWRENCE E DENNIS.
  AMERICAN COUNCIL ON EDUCATION. WASHINGTON, DC. 1963.
  PP 101-104.

WMASOVC62958 MASON VC
  WOMEN IN EDUCATION. /OCCUPATIONS/
  AMERICAN WOMEN. THE CHANGING IMAGE. ED BY BEVERLY B CASSARA.
  BEACON PRESS. BOSTON, MASSACHUSETTS. 1962. PP 116-123.

WMATHJP66959 MATHER JP
  AND ANGELS WALK WHERE ONLY MALES TREAD. THE EMERGENCE OF
    WOMANPOWER. /MANPOWER/
  THE CHALLENGE TO WOMEN. ED BY SEYMOUR M FARBER AND ROGER H
  WILSON. BASIC BOOKS, INC. NEW YORK. 1966. PP 101-110.

WMATTEX60961 MATTHEWS E
  MARRIAGE AND CAREER CONFLICTS IN GIRLS AND YOUNG WOMEN.
    /WORK-FAMILY-CONFLICT/
  HARVARD, GRADUATE SCHOOL OF EDUCATION. PHD DISSERTATION.
  CAMBRIDGE, MASSACHUSETTS. 1960.

WMATTEX63960 MATTHEWS E
  THE COUNSELOR AND GIRLS CAREER DEVELOPMENT. /COUNSELING/
  AMERICAN PERSONNEL AND GUIDANCE ASSOCIATION, ANNUAL
  CONVENTION. PAPER. AP 10 1963.

WMATTEX64962 MATTHEWS E   TIEDEMAN DV
  ATTITUDES TOWARD CAREER AND MARRIAGE AND THE DEVELOPMENT OF
    LIFE STYLES IN YOUNG WOMEN. /WORK-FAMILY-CONFLICT/
  JOURNAL OF COUNSELING PSYCHOLOGY, VOL 11, NO 4, WINTER 1964.
  PP 375-384.

WMATFJA65963 MATTFELD JA ED   VAN AKEN CG ED
  WOMEN AND THE SCIENTIFIC PROFESSIONS. THE MIT SYMPOSIUM
    ON AMERICAN WOMEN IN SCIENCE AND ENGINEERING.
    /OCCUPATIONS/
  MASSACHUSETTS INSTITUTE OF TECHNOLOGY. CAMBRIDGE,
  MASSACHUSETTS. 1965. 245 PP.

WMAULFX61065 MAULE F
  EXECUTIVE CAREERS FOR WOMEN. /OCCUPATIONS/
  HARPER AND BROTHERS. NEW YORK. 1961.

WMAYXEE59964 MAY EE   CORCORAN SP
  FRESHMEN INTERVIEW WORKING WIVES.
  JOURNAL OF HOME ECONOMICS, VOL 51, NO 6. JUNE 1959.
  PP 464-466.

WMCINMC61945 MCINTOSH MC   *ALUMNAE ADVISORY CENTER INC
  THE TEACHER COMES INTO HER OWN. /WORK-FAMILY-CONFLICT/
  FUTURES FOR COLLEGE WOMEN IN NEW YORK. ALUMNAE ADVISORY
  CENTER, INC. NEW YORK. 1961.

WMCKARC58946 MCKAY RC
  WOMAN-S CENTURY OF PROGRESS. IS IT TO END IN REGRESSION.
    /WORK-WOMAN-ROLE/
  SMITH ALUMNAE QUARTERLY, FALL 1958.

WMCLALX66947 MCLAIN L
  TESTIMONY, PUBLIC HEARING, WOMEN IN PUBLIC AND PRIVATE
    EMPLOYMENT, CALIFORNIA. /OCCUPATIONS
    EMPLOYMENT-CONDITIONS/
  CALIFORNIA ADVISORY COMMISSION ON THE STATUS OF WOMEN,
  STUDY COMMITTEE NO 1, ON PUBLIC AND PRIVATE EMPLOYMENT.
  HEARINGS. SACRAMENTO, CALIFORNIA. AP 28 1966. PP 118-125.

WMEADLX63967 MEADOW L   EDELSON RB
  AGE AND MARITAL-STATUS AND THEIR RELATIONSHIP TO SUCCESS IN
    PRACTICAL NURSING. /OCCUPATIONS/
  NURSING OUTLOOK, VOL 11, AP 1963. PP 289-290.

WMEADMX65966 MEAD M ED   KAPLAN FB ED
  *PRES-S COMM ON STATUS WOMEN
  AMERICAN WOMEN /WORK-WOMEN-ROLE/
  SCRIBNER-S. NEW YORK. 1965. 276 PP.

WMELSRC63968 MELSON RC
  KNOWLEDGE AND INTERESTS CONCERNING SIXTEEN OCCUPATIONS AMONG
    ELEMENTARY AND SECONDARY SCHOOL STUDENTS. /ASPIRATIONS/
  EDUCATION AND PSYCHOLOGICAL MEASUREMENT. 1963. PP 741-754.

WMENGVX66969 MENGELKOCH V
  TESTIMONY, PUBLIC HEARING, WOMEN IN PUBLIC AND PRIVATE

EMPLOYMENT, CALIFORNIA.
    /BLUE-COLLAR EMPLOYMENT-CONDITIONS/
  CALIFORNIA ADVISORY COMMISSION ON THE STATUS OF WOMEN,
  STUDY COMMITTEE NO 1, ON PUBLIC AND PRIVATE EMPLOYMENT.
  HEARINGS. SACRAMENTO, CALIFORNIA. MAR 31-AP 1 1966.
  PP 125-137.

WMEREJL60970 MEREDITH JL   *US DEPARTMENT OF LABOR
  PART-TIME JOB OPPORTUNITIES FOR WOMEN.
  US DEPARTMENT OF LABOR, BUREAU OF LABOR STATISTICS,
  OCCUPATIONAL OUTLOOK QUARTERLY, VOL 4, NO 1, FEB 1960.
  PP 21-22.

WMERIFH55971 MERING FH
  PROFESSIONAL AND NON-PROFESSIONAL WOMEN AS MOTHERS.
  JOURNAL OF SOCIAL PSYCHOLOGY, VOL 42, AUG 1955. PP 21-34.

WMERRMH63972 MERRY MH
  PILOT PROJECTS FOR CONTINUING EDUCATION FOR WOMEN.
  EDUCATION AND A WOMAN-S LIFE. ED BY LAWRENCE E DENNIS.
  AMERICAN COUNCIL ON EDUCATION. WASHINGTON, DC. 1963.
  PP 92-123.

WMETRLI63973 METROPOLITAN LIFE INSURANCE
  MOTHERS AT WORK.
  METROPOLITAN LIFE INSURANCE CO. NEW YORK. 1963.

WMEYEAE58974 MEYER AE
  WORK AND MARRIAGE. /WORK-FAMILY-CONFLICT/
  BARNARD COLLEGE VOCATIONAL CONFERENCE, ADDRESS. DEC 1958.
  BARNARD COLLEGE. NEW YORK. 1958.

WMEYEMB61975 MEYER MB   *US DEPARTMENT OF LABOR
  JOBS AND TRAINING FOR WOMEN TECHNICIANS. /TRAINING/
  US DEPARTMENT OF LABOR, BUREAU OF LABOR STATISTICS,
  OCCUPATIONAL OUTLOOK QUARTERLY, VOL 5, NO 4, DEC 1961.
  PP 9-14.

WMICOLA64976 MICHIGAN DEPARTMENT OF LABOR MICH EMPLOYMENT SECURITY COMM
  NORTHERN MICHIGAN UNIVERSITY   US DEPARTMENT OF LABOR
  CONFERENCE ON WOMEN IN THE UPPER PENINSULA ECONOMY. REPORT.
    /MICHIGAN/
  US DEPARTMENT OF LABOR, WOMEN-S BUREAU. GPO. WASHINGTON, DC.
  21 PP. 1964.

WMIDDAR65190 MID ATLANTIC REGIONAL CONF
  COUNSELING GIRLS TOWARD NEW PERSPECTIVES.
  MIDDLE ATLANTIC REGIONAL PILOT CONFERENCE REPORT.
  PHILADELPHIA, PENNSYLVANIA. DEC 2-4 1965. PUBLISHED BY
  US DEPARTMENT OF LABOR, WOMEN-S BUREAU. GPO. WASHINGTON, DC.
  1966.

WMIDWRP65209 MIDWEST REGIONAL PILOT CONF *US DEPARTMENT OF LABOR
  NEW APPROACHES TO COUNSELING GIRLS IN THE 1960-S.
  MIDWEST REGIONAL PILOT CONFERENCE. REPORT. UNIVERSITY OF
  CHICAGO CENTER FOR CONTINUING EDUCATION. CHICAGO, ILLINOIS.
  FEB 26-27 1965. 1965.

WMILLJJ66979 MILLER JJ   *AG PRODUCERS LABOR COMMITTEE
  STATEMENT, PUBLIC HEARING, WOMEN IN PUBLIC AND PRIVATE
    EMPLOYMENT, CALIFORNIA. /FEP EMPLOYMENT-CONDITIONS
    MIGRANT-WORKERS/
  CALIFORNIA ADVISORY COMMISSION ON THE STATUS OF WOMEN,
  STUDY COMMITTEE NO 1, ON PUBLIC AND PRIVATE EMPLOYMENT.
  HEARINGS. SACRAMENTO, CALIFORNIA. MAR 31-AP 1 1966.
  PP 87-92.

WMILLKL66980 MILLER KL   HIRD B
  *HUNT FOODS AND INDUSTRIES
  TESTIMONY, PUBLIC HEARING, WOMEN IN PUBLIC AND PRIVATE
    EMPLOYMENT, CALIFORNIA. /EMPLOYMENT-CONDITIONS/
  CALIFORNIA ADVISORY COMMISSION ON THE STATUS OF WOMEN,
  STUDY COMMITTEE NO 1, ON PUBLIC AND PRIVATE EMPLOYMENT.
  HEARINGS. SACRAMENTO, CALIFORNIA. MAR 31-AP 1 1966.
  PP 20-32.

WMILLMM61981 MILLER MM
  WOMEN IN UNIVERSITY TEACHING. /OCCUPATIONS/
  JOURNAL OF AMERICAN ASSOCIATION OF UNIVERSITY WOMEN, VOL 54,
  MAR 1961.

WMILLRX61983 MILLIKEN R
  POST-HIGH SCHOOL PLANS FOR SENIOR GIRLS IN RELATION TO
    SCHOLASTIC APTITUDE. /ASPIRATIONS/
  VOCATIONAL GUIDANCE QUARTERLY, VOL 10, AUTUMN 1961.
  PP 49-52.

WMILLRX66982 MILLER R   AVERY L
  BIRD C   MARCUS C
  RIGDALE L
  EMERGING OPPORTUNITIES FOR QUALIFIED WOMEN. /OCCUPATIONS/
  EXPLODING THE MYTHS. EXPANDING EMPLOYMENT OPPORTUNITIES FOR
  CAREER WOMEN. UNIVERSITY OF SOUTHERN CALIFORNIA. EXTENSION,
  CONFERENCE ROUND TABLE. DEC 3 1966.

WMINCJX60985 MINCER J
  LABOR SUPPLY, FAMILY INCOME, AND CONSUMPTION.
  AMERICAN ECONOMIC REVIEW, MAY 1960.

WMINCJX62984 MINCER J   *NATL BUREAU OF EC RESEARCH
  LABOR-FORCE PARTICIPATION OF MARRIED WOMEN. A STUDY OF LABOR
    SUPPLY.
  ASPECTS OF LABOR ECONOMICS, A CONFERENCE OF THE
  UNIVERSITIES. PRINCETON UNIVERSITY PRESS. PRINCETON,
  NEW JERSEY. 1962.

WMITCED57986 MITCHELL ED
  INTEREST PROFILES OF UNIVERSITY WOMEN. /ASPIRATIONS/
  VOCATIONAL GUIDANCE QUARTERLY, VOL 6, WINTER 1957-1958.
  PP 85-89.

WMONSKJ63987 MONSOUR KJ
  EDUCATION AND A WOMAN-S LIFE.
  EDUCATION AND A WOMAN-S LIFE. ED BY LAWRENCE E DENNIS.
  AMERICAN COUNCIL ON EDUCATION. WASHINGTON, DC. 1963.
  PP 9-28.

WMORAMX66995 MORAN M   *HRCME UNION
  TESTIMONY, PUBLIC HEARING, WOMEN IN PUBLIC AND PRIVATE
    EMPLOYMENT, CALIFORNIA. /EMPLOYMENT-CONDITIONS/
  CALIFORNIA ADVISORY COMMISSION ON THE STATUS OF WOMEN,
  STUDY COMMITTEE NO 1, ON PUBLIC AND PRIVATE EMPLOYMENT.
  HEARINGS. SACRAMENTO, CALIFORNIA. MARCH 31-AP 1 1966.
  PP 196-199.

WMORGDD62996 MORGAN DD
  PERCEPTIONS OF ROLE CONFLICTS AND SELF CONFLICTS AMONG
    CAREER AND NON-CAREER COLLEGE EDUCATED WOMEN.
    /WORK-FAMILY-CONFLICT/
  COLUMBIA UNIVERSITY, TEACHERS COLLEGE. PHD DISSERTATION.

NEW YORK. 1962.

WMORGJX65997 MORGAN J
TIME, WORK, AND WELFARE.
PATTERNS OF MARKET BEHAVIOR. ESSAYS IN HONOR OF PHILIP TAFT.
ED BY MICHAEL BRENNEN. BROWN UNIVERSITY PRESS. PROVIDENCE,
RHODE ISLAND. 1965.

WMORRMM66998 MORRIS MM
RAISING THE STATUS OF HOUSEHOLD EMPLOYMENT.
/HOUSEHOLD-WORKERS/
JOURNAL OF HOME ECONOMICS, VOL 58, NO 9, NOV 1966.

WMOSBWB57999 MOSBACHER WB
WOMEN GRADUATES OF COOPERATIVE WORK-STUDY PROGRAMS ON THE
COLLEGE LEVEL. /SKILLS/
PERSONNEL AND GUIDANCE JOURNAL, VOL 35, 1957. PP 508-511.

WMOSEEX65000 MOSES E
NURSING-S ECONOMIC PLIGHT. /ECONOMIC-STATUS/
AMERICAN JOURNAL OF NURSING, JAN 1965.

WMOTHWA66001 MOTHERS WORKING ALONE
TESTIMONY, PUBLIC HEARING, WOMEN IN PUBLIC AND PRIVATE
EMPLOYMENT, CALIFORNIA.
CALIFORNIA ADVISORY COMMISSION ON THE STATUS OF WOMEN,
STUDY COMMITTEE NO 1, ON PUBLIC AND PRIVATE EMPLOYMENT.
HEARINGS. SACRAMENTO, CALIFORNIA. AP 28 1966. PP 80-102.

WMOTZAB61002 MOTZ AB
ROLES OF THE MARRIED WOMAN IN SCIENCE. /OCCUPATIONS/
MARRIAGE AND FAMILY LIVING, VOL 23, NOV 1961. PP 374-376.

WMOUNHS64003 MOUNT HS
MOTHERS IN THE LABOR-FORCE.
BROWN UNIVERSITY. PHD DISSERTATION. PROVIDENCE, RHODE
ISLAND. 1964.

WMUELEL66004 MUELLER EL
WOMEN IN THE LABOR-MARKET.
NEW PATTERNS OF EMPLOYMENT. CENTER FOR CONTINUING EDUCATION
OF WOMEN. UNIVERSITY OF MICHIGAN. ANN ARBOR, MICHIGAN.
OCT 1966. PP 5-27.

WMULLLC60005 MULLER LC   MULLER OG
NEW HORIZONS FOR COLLEGE WOMEN. /WORK-WOMEN-ROLE/
PUBLIC AFFAIRS PRESS. WASHINGTON, DC. 1960.

WMULVMC61080 MULVEY MC
PSYCHOLOGICAL AND SOCIOLOGICAL FACTORS IN PREDICTION OF
CAREER PATTERNS OF WOMEN. /ASPIRATIONS/
HARVARD UNIVERSITY, GRADUATE SCHOOL OF EDUCATION. PHD
DISSERTATION. CAMBRIDGE, MASSACHUSETTS. 1961.

WMULVMC63006 MULVEY MC
PSYCHOLOGICAL AND SOCIOLOGICAL FACTORS IN PREDICTION OF
CAREER PATTERNS FOR WOMEN. /ASPIRATIONS/
GENETIC PSYCHOLOGY MONOGRAPHS, VOL 68, 1963. PP 309-386.

WMUNTEE56007 MUNTZ EE
WOMEN-S CHANGING ROLE IN THE US EMPLOYMENT MARKET.
INTERNATIONAL LABOUR REVIEW, VOL 74, 1956. PP 415-436.

WMURPMC60009 MURPHY MC
CAREERS FOR WOMEN IN BIOLOGICAL SCIENCES. /OCCUPATIONS/
US DEPARTMENT OF LABOR, BUREAU OF LABOR STATISTICS.
OCCUPATIONAL OUTLOOK QUARTERLY, VOL 4, NO 3, SEPT 1960.
PP 26-32.

WMURRPX65010 MURRAY P   EASTWOOD M
JANE CROW AND THE LAW. SEX DISCRIMINATION AND TITLE-VII.
GEORGE WASHINGTON LAW REVIEW, VOL 34. 1965. PP 232-256.

WMYERGC64011 MYERS GC
LABOR-FORCE PARTICIPATION OF SUBURBAN MOTHERS.
MARRIAGE AND FAMILY LIVING, VOL 26, 1964. PP 306-311.

WMYRDAX56012 MYRDAL A   KLEIN V
WOMEN-S TWO ROLES. /WORK-FAMILY-CONFLICT/
HUMANITIES PRESS. NEW YORK. 1956.

WMYRIRX66013 MYRICK R   *CAL DEPT OF SOCIAL WELFARE
TESTIMONY, PUBLIC HEARING, WOMEN IN PUBLIC AND PRIVATE
EMPLOYMENT, CALIFORNIA. /EMPLOYMENT-CONDITIONS/
CALIFORNIA ADVISORY COMMISSION ON THE STATUS OF WOMEN, STUDY
COMMITTEE NO 1, ON PUBLIC AND PRIVATE EMPLOYMENT. HEARINGS.
SACRAMENTO, CALIFORNIA. AP 29 1966. PP 201-217.

WNATLCH66014 NATL COMT ON HOUSEHOLD EMPLOY
A NATIONAL INQUIRY OF PRIVATE HOUSEHOLD-EMPLOYEES AND
EMPLOYERS.
NATIONAL COMMITTEE ON HOUSEHOLD EMPLOYMENT. WASHINGTON, DC.
JULY 1966. 50 PP.

WNATLCH66015 NATL COMT ON HOUSEHOLD EMPLOY
THESE ARE THE FACTS. /HOUSEHOLD-WORKERS/
NATIONAL COMMITTEE ON HOUSEHOLD EMPLOYMENT. WASHINGTON, DC.
1966.

WNATLCO65016 NATL CC OF ADMV WOMEN IN ED
WANTED. MORE WOMEN IN EDUCATIONAL LEADERSHIP. /OCCUPATIONS/
NATIONAL EDUCATION ASSOCIATION. WASHINGTON, DC. 1965.

WNATLCP61018 NATL CC OF WOMEN OF THE US
UPDATING TRAINING FOR THE RETURNING NURSE, SOCIAL WORKER
AND TEACHER.
NATIONAL COUNCIL OF WOMEN OF THE UNITED STATES, ALL DAY
WORKSHOP. NEW YORK. FEB 1961. MIMEOGRAPHED BY NATIONAL
COUNCIL OF WOMEN OF THE UNITED STATES. NEW YORK. 1961.
19 PP.

WNATLEA64019 NATIONAL EDUCATION ASSN   CATALYST IN EDUCATION
TEACHING. OPPORTUNITIES FOR WOMEN COLLEGE GRADUATES.
NATIONAL EDUCATION ASSOCIATION, NATIONAL COMMISSION ON
TEACHER EDUCATION AND PROFESSIONAL STANDARDS. WASHINGTON,
DC. 1964.

WNATLMC57020 NATL MANPOWER COUNCIL
WOMANPOWER.
COLUMBIA UNIVERSITY PRESS. NEW YORK. 1957.

WNATLMC57021 NATL MANPOWER COUNCIL
WORK IN THE LIVES OF MARRIED WOMEN.
COLUMBIA UNIVERSITY PRESS. NEW YORK. 1957.

WNATLSA65023 NATL SECRETARIES ASSN
NSA-S PROFESSIONAL STATUS SURVEY, 1964. /ECONOMIC-STATUS/
NATIONAL SECRETARIES ASSOCIATION. KANSAS CITY, MISSOURI.
1965.

WNATLSF61022 NATL SCIENCE FOUNDATION
WOMEN IN SCIENTIFIC CAREERS. /OCCUPATIONS/
NATIONAL SCIENCE FOUNDATION. WASHINGTON, DC. 1961. 13 PP.

WNEUBMX66024 NEUBERGER M
THE MEANING OF EQUALITY.
EXPLODING THE MYTHS. EXPANDING EMPLOYMENT OPPORTUNITIES FOR
CAREER WOMEN. UNIVERSITY OF SOUTHERN CALIFORNIA, EXTENSION.
CONFERENCE. ADDRESS. LOS ANGELES, CALIFORNIA. DEC 3 1966.

WNEUGBL59025 NEUGARTEN BL
WOMEN-S CHANGING ROLES THROUGH THE LIFE CYCLE.
JOURNAL OF THE NATIONAL ASSOCIATION OF WOMEN DEANS AND
COUNSELORS, VOL 23-24, OCT 1959-JUNE 1961. PP 163-170.

WNEUMRR63026 NEUMAN RR
WHEN WILL THE EDUCATIONAL NEEDS OF WOMEN BE MET. SOME
QUESTIONS FOR THE COUNSELOR.
JOURNAL OF COUNSELING PSYCHOLOGY, VOL 10, 1963. P 378-383.

WNEWCMX59027 NEWCOMER M
A CENTURY OF HIGHER EDUCATION FOR AMERICAN WOMEN.
HARPER AND BROTHERS. NEW YORK. 1959.

WNEWCMX64028 NEWCOMER M
WOMEN-S EDUCATION. FACTS, FINDINGS, AND APPARENT TRENDS.
JOURNAL OF THE NATIONAL ASSOCIATION OF WOMEN DEANS AND
COUNSELORS, VOL 24, NO 1, OCT 1964. PP 35-40.

WNEWSXX66029 NEWSWEEK
WHAT EDUCATED WOMEN WANT. /ASPIRATIONS/
NEWSWEEK, JUNE 13 1966. PP 68-75.

WNEWYGW64799 NY GOVRS COMT ED EMP WOMEN
NEW-YORK WOMEN. A REPORT AND RECOMMENDATIONS FROM THE
NEW-YORK GOVERNOR-S COMMITTEE ON THE EDUCATION AND
EMPLOYMENT OF WOMEN.
NEW YORK GOVERNOR-S COMMITTEE ON THE EDUCATION AND
EMPLOYMENT OF WOMEN. ALBANY, NEW YORK. DEC 1964. 96 PP.

WNICOHG64032 NICOL HG
REPORT ON UNDERGRADUATE COUNSELING AND CONTINUING EDUCATION
AND GUIDANCE FOR MATURE WOMAN.
CATALYST IN EDUCATION. LEWISTON, MAINE. MULTILITHOGRAPH.
1964. 11 PP.

WNIEMJX58033 NIEMEYER J
CAREERS AFTER FORTY. /WORK-FAMILY-CONFLICT/
JOURNAL OF THE AMERICAN ASSOCIATION OF UNIVERSITY WOMEN,
VOL 51, MAR 1958.

WNOBLJL59C35 NOBLE JL   DAVID OC
SUMMARY OF CURRENT RESEARCH ON WOMEN-S ROLES.
JOURNAL OF THE NATIONAL ASSOCIATION OF WOMEN DEANS AND
COUNSELORS. JAN 1959.

WNORRLW56036 NORRIS LW
ROLE OF WOMEN IN AMERICAN ECONOMIC LIFE.
ASSOCIATION OF AMERICAN COLLEGES BULLETIN, VOL 42, MAR 1956.
PP 51-60.

WNORTHR64037 NORTHRUP HR
EQUAL-OPPORTUNITY AND EQUAL-PAY.
MANAGEMENT OF PERSONNEL QUARTERLY, VOL 3, NO 3, FALL 1964.
PP 17-26.

WNYEXFI63038 NYE FI
PERSONAL SATISFACTIONS. /WORK-WOMAN-ROLE/
THE EMPLOYED MOTHER IN AMERICA. ED BY F IVAN NYE AND
LOIS W HOFFMAN. RAND MCNALLY. CHICAGO, ILLINOIS. 1963.
PP 320-330.

WNYEXFI63039 NYE FI   HOFFMAN LW
THE SOCIO-CULTURAL SETTING.
THE EMPLOYED MOTHER IN AMERICA. ED BY IVAN NYE AND LOIS W
HOFFMAN. RAND MCNALLY. CHICAGO, ILLINOIS. 1963. PP 3-17.

WNYEXFI63040 NYE FI   HOFFMAN LW
THE EMPLOYED MOTHER IN AMERICA.
RAND MCNALLY. CHICAGO, ILLINOIS. 1963.

WNYUYUG66031 NYU GRAD SCHOOL OF SOC WORK
SOCIAL WORK DEGREE PROGRESS REPORT. /TRAINING/
NEW YORK UNIVERSITY, GRADUATE SCHOOL OF SOCIAL WORK.
NEW YORK. 1966.

WODIOGS61042 ODIORNE GS   HANN AS
*UNIV OF MICH BUREAU IND RELS
EFFECTIVE COLLEGE RECRUITING. /TECHNOLOGICAL-CHANGE/
UNIVERSITY OF MICHIGAN, BUREAU OF INDUSTRIAL RELATIONS,
REPORT 13. ANN ARBOR, MICHIGAN. 1961.

WONEIBP65043 O NEILL BP
CAREERS FOR WOMEN AFTER MARRIAGE AND CHILDREN.
/WORK-FAMILY-CONFLICT/
MACMILLAN. NEW YORK. 1965. 401 PP.

WOPPEVK66096 OPPENHEIMER VK
THE FEMALE LABOR-FORCE IN THE UNITED STATES. FACTORS
GOVERNING ITS GROWTH AND CHANGING COMPOSITION.
UNIVERSITY OF CALIFORNIA. PHD DISSERTATION. BERKELEY,
CALIFORNIA. 1966.

WOPPEVK66289 OPPENHEIMER VK
THE INTERACTION OF DEMAND AND SUPPLY AND ITS EFFECT ON THE
FEMALE LABOR-FORCE IN THE UNITED STATES.
POPULATION ASSOCIATION OF AMERICA, 1966 MEETINGS. PAPER.

WORGAEC64045 OECD   US DEPARTMENT OF LABOR
CANADIAN DEPARTMENT OF LABOR
MANPOWER IMPLICATIONS OF AUTOMATION.
US DEPARTMENT OF LABOR. WASHINGTON, DC. DEC 8-10 1964.

WPALMGX66047 PALMQUIST G   *WOMEN-S ADVSY COMM TO FEPC
TESTIMONY, PUBLIC HEARING, WOMEN IN PUBLIC AND PRIVATE
EMPLOYMENT, CALIFORNIA. /EMPLOYMENT-CONDITIONS/
CALIFORNIA ADVISORY COMMISSION ON THE STATUS OF WOMEN, STUDY
COMMITTEE NO 1, ON PUBLIC AND PRIVATE EMPLOYMENT. HEARINGS.
SACRAMENTO, CALIFORNIA. MAR 31-AP 1 1966. PP 227-229.

WPARKRX66049 PARK R
REALITIES. EDUCATIONAL, ECONOMIC, LEGAL AND PERSONAL NEEDS
OF CAREER WOMEN.
EXPLODING THE MYTHS. EXPANDING EMPLOYMENT OPPORTUNITIES FOR
CAREER WOMEN. UNIVERSITY OF SOUTHERN CALIFORNIA EXTENSION,
CONFERENCE. SPEECH. LOS ANGELES, CALIFORNIA. DEC 3 1966.

WPARRJB61051 PARRISH JB
PROFESSIONAL WOMANPOWER AS A NATIONAL RESOURCE.
QUARTERLY REVIEW OF ECONOMICS OF BUSINESS, FEB 1961.

PP 54-63.

wPARRJB62283   PARRISH JB
               TOP LEVEL TRAINING CF WOMEN IN THE UNITED STATES, 1900-60.
               JOURNAL OF NATIONAL ASSOCIATION OF WOMEN DEANS AND
               COUNSELORS. JAN 1962.

WPARRJB65C50   PARRISH JB
               EMPLOYMENT OF WOMEN CHEMISTS IN INDUSTRIAL LABORATORIES.
               /OCCUPATIONS/
               SCIENCE, VOL 148, AP 30 1965. PP 657-658.

WPASCWX58178   PASCHELL W   WILLIS DF
               *US DEPARTMENT OF LABOR
               AUTOMATION AND EMPLOYMENT OPPORTUNITIES FOR OFFICE WORKERS.
               THE EFFECT OF ELECTRONIC COMPUTERS ON EMPLOYMENT OF
               CLERICAL WORKERS, WITH A SPECIAL REPORT ON PROGRAMMERS.
               US DEPARTMENT OF LABOR, BUREAU OF LABOR STATISTICS. GPO.
               WASHINGTION, DC. 1958. 14 PP.

WPEEVMX66052   PEEVEY M   *AFL-CIO
               TESTIMONY, PUBLIC HEARING, WOMEN IN PUBLIC AND PRIVATE
               EMPLOYMENT, CALIFCRNIA.
               /FEP EMPLOYMENT-CONDITIONS MIGRANT-WORKERS/
               CALIFORNIA ADVISORY COMMISSION ON THE STATUS OF WOMEN, STUDY
               COMMITTEE NO 1, ON PUBLIC AND PRIVATE EMPLOYMENT. HEARINGS.
               SACRAMENTO, CALIFORNIA. AP 28 1966. PP 30-47.

WPERLEX63100   PERLOFF E
               WHAT THE INDUSTRIAL PSYCHOLOGIST MUST KNOW ABOUT TODAY-S
               AND TOMORROW-S WOMAN.
               AMERICAN PSYCHOLOGICAL ASSOCIATION, MEETINGS. PAPER AT
               SYMPOSIUM. SEPT 1963. 10 PP.

WPETEEX62057   PETERSON E
               TRAINING. KEY TO EMPLOYMENT.
               AMERICAN VOCATIONAL JOURNAL, VOL 37, AP 1962. PP 14-15.

WPETEEX63053   PETERSON E
               THE IMPACT OF EDUCATION.
               UNIVERSITY OF CALIFORNIA, SCHOOL OF MEDICINE, SYMPOSIUM ON
               MAN AND CIVILIZATION. THE POTENTIAL OF WOMEN. SPEECH.
               SAN FRANCISCO, CALIFORNIA. JAN 26 1963.

WPETEEX63054   PETERSON E
               NEEDS AND OPPORTUNITIES IN OUR SOCIETY FOR THE EDUCATED
               WOMAN.
               EDUCATION AND A WOMAN-S LIFE. ED BY LAWRENCE E DENNIS.
               AMERICAN COUNCIL ON EDUCATION. WASHINGTON, DC. 1963.
               PP 51-71.

WPETEEX64056   PETERSON E
               STATUS OF WOMEN IN THE UNITED STATES.
               INTERNATIONAL LABOUR REVIEW, VOL 89, MAY 1964. PP 447-460.

WPETEEX64058   PETERSON E
               WORKING WOMEN.
               DAEDALUS, VCL 93, SPRING 1964. PP 671-699.

WPETEEX65055   PETERSON E
               OUTLOOK FOR WOMEN.
               AMERICAN ASSOCIATION OF SCHOOL ADMINISTRATORS. SPEECH.
               ATLANTIC CITY, NEW JERSEY. FEB 15 1965.

WPETEJX59059   PETERSON J
               EMPLOYMENT EFFECTS OF STATE MINIMUM WAGES FOR WOMEN.
               INDUSTRIAL AND LABOR RELATIONS REVIEW, VOL 12, NO 3,
               AP 1959. PP 406-422.

WPINEMX58061   PINES M   WEINBERGER DC
               SHOULD WOMEN BE TRAINED IN THE SCIENCES. /OCCUPATIONS/
               BARNARD ALUMNAE MAGIZINE. VOL 47, NO 3, 1958. PP 2-7.

WPINSAM63062   PINS AM   *COUNCIL ON SOCIAL WORK ED
               WHO CHOOSES SOCIAL WORK, WHEN AND WHY. /OCCUPATIONS/
               COUNCIL ON SOCIAL WORK EDUCATION. NEW YORK. 1963. 212 PP.

WPOLIEJ59454   POLINSKY EJ
               SOME IMPLICATIONS OF THE EMPLOYMENT PATTERNS OF WOMEN UNDER
               SOCIAL-SECURITY.
               AMERICAN UNIVERSITY. PHD DISSERTATION. WASHINGTON, DC. 1959.

WPOLIEJ65285   POLINSKY EJ   *US DEPT OF HEALTH ED WELFARE
               WOMEN HOUSEHOLD WORKERS COVERED BY OLD AGE, SURVIVORS, AND
               DISABILITY INSURANCE.
               US DEPARTMENT OF HEALTH, EDUCATION AND WELFARE, SOCIAL
               SECURITY BULLETIN, JULY 1965.

WPOLLLA65063   POLLARD LA
               WOMEN ON COLLEGE AND UNIVERSITY FACULTIES. A HISTORICAL
               SURVEY AND A STUDY OF THEIR PRESENT ACADEMIC STATUS.
               /OCCUPATIONS/
               UNIVERSITY OF GEORGIA. EDD DISSERTATION. ATHENS, GEORGIA.
               1965.

WPRESCO63064   PRES-S COMM ON STATUS WOMEN
               AMERICAN WOMEN. /WORK-WOMAN-ROLE/
               PRESIDENT-S COMMISSION ON THE STATUS OF WOMEN. GPO.
               WASHINGTON, DC. 1963.

WPRESCO63065   PRES-S COMM ON STATUS WOMEN
               REPORT OF THE COMMITTEE ON CIVIL AND POLITICAL RIGHTS.
               PRESIDENT-S COMMISSION ON THE STATUS OF WOMEN. GPO.
               WASHINGTON, DC. OCT 1963. 83 PP.

WPRESCO63C66   PRES-S COMM ON STATUS WOMEN
               REPORT OF THE COMMITTEE ON EDUCATION.
               /EQUAL-OPPORTUNITY COUNSELING/
               PRESIDENT-S COMMISSION ON THE STATUS OF WOMEN. GPO.
               WASHINGTON, DC. OCT 1963. 71 PP.

WPRESCO63067   PRES-S COMM ON STATUS WOMEN
               REPORT OF THE COMMITTEE ON FEDERAL EMPLOYMENT.
               PRESIDENT-S COMMISSION ON THE STATUS OF WOMEN. OCT 1963.
               195 PP.

WPRESCO63068   PRES-S COMM ON STATUS WOMEN
               REPORT OF THE COMMITTEE ON PRIVATE EMPLOYMENT, 1963.
               PRESIDENT-S COMMISSION ON THE STATUS OF WOMEN. GPO.
               WASHINGTON, DC. 1963.

WPRESCO63069   PRES-S COMM ON STATUS WOMEN
               REPORT OF THE COMMITTEE ON PROTECTIVE LABOR LEGISLATION,
               1963.
               PRESIDENT-S COMMISSION ON THE STATUS OF WOMEN. GPO.
               WASHINGTON, DC. 1963.

WPRESCO63070   PRES-S COMM ON STATUS WOMEN
               REPORT OF THE COMMITTEE ON SOCIAL INSURANCE AND TAXES, 1963.
               PRESIDENT-S COMMISSION ON THE STATUS OF WOMEN. GPO.

WPRESCO63993   PRES-S COMM ON STATUS WOMEN
               REPORT OF PRESIDENT-S COMMISSION ON STATUS OF WOMEN.
               US DEPARTMENT OF LABOR, MONTHLY LABOR REVIEW, VOL 86, NO 10,
               OCT 1963. PP 1166-1170.

WPUNKHH61C71   PUNKE HH
               SEX AND EQUAL-OPPORTUNITY IN HIGHER EDUCATION.
               NATIONAL ASSOCIATION OF SECONDARY SCHOOL PRINCIPALS
               BULLETIN, VOL 45, NOV 1961. PP 121-128.

WQUINFX62992   QUINN F   THOMAS JL
               WOMEN AT WORK. 1. THE FACTS AND WHY WOMEN WORK. 2. THE
               SIGNIFICANCE.
               SOCIAL ORDER, VOL 12, FEB 1962. PP 65-76.

WRADCCX56072   RADCLIFFE COLLEGE
               GRADUATE EDUCATION FOR WOMEN. THE RADCLIFFE PHD.
               HARVARD UNIVERSITY PRESS. CAMBRIDGE, MASSACHUSETTS. 1956.

WRAMSGV63104   RAMSEY GV   SMITH BK
               MOORE BM
               WOMEN VIEW THEIR WORKING WORLD.
               UNIVERSITY OF TEXAS, HOGG FOUNDATION FOR MENTAL HEALTH.
               AUSTIN, TEXAS. 1963. 47 PP.

WRAMSGV63132   RAMSEY GV
               SOME ATTITUDES AND OPINIONS OF EMPLOYED WOMEN.
               JOURNAL OF THE NATIONAL ASSOCIATION OF WCMEN DEANS AND
               COUNSELORS, VOL 26, NO 3, AP 1963. PP 30-36.

WRANDKS65073   RANDOLPH KS
               MATURE WOMEN IN DOCTORAL PROGRAMS. /OCCUPATIONS/
               INDIANA UNIVERSITY. EDD DISSERTATION. BLOOMINGTON, INDIANA.
               1965.

WRASKBL59074   RASKIN BL
               THE UNTAPPED RESOURCE... /OCCUPATIONS/
               GOUCHER COLLEGE BULLETIN, SERIES 11, NO 3, JAN 1959.

WRAUSEX61076   RAUSHENBUSH E
               UNFINISHED BUSINESS. CONTINUING EDUCATION FOR WOMEN.
               THE EDUCATIONAL RECORD, VOL 42, OCT 1961. PP 267-268.

WRAUSEX62075   RAUSHENBUSH E
               SECOND CHANCE. NEW EDUCATION FOR WOMEN.
               HARPERS, OCT 1962. PP 147-151.

WRAVIMJ57C77   RAVITZ MJ
               OCCUPATIONAL VALUES AND OCCUPATIONAL SELECTION.
               NURSING RESEARCH, VOL 6, 1957. PP 35-40.

WREEVNX63C78   REEVES N
               CURIOUS QUEST FOR WCMANPOWER.
               THE NATION, AUG 24 1963. PP 89-91.

WRIESDX56079   RIESMAN D
               SOME CONTINUITIES AND DISCONTINUITIES IN THE EDUCATION OF
               WOMEN. /WORK-FAMILY-CONFLICT/
               BENNINGTON COLLEGE. JOHN DEWEY MEMORIAL LECTURE. BENNINGTON,
               VERMONT. 1956. 28 PP.

WRIESDX58080   RIESMAN D
               WOMEN. THEIR ORBITS AND THEIR EDUCATION.
               /WORK-FAMILY-CONFLICT/
               JOURNAL OF AMERICAN ASSOCIATION OF UNIVERSITY WOMEN, VOL 51,
               JAN 1958. PP 77-81.

WRILEEX66081   RILEY E   *GLASS BOTTLE BLOWERS UNION
               TESTIMONY, PUBLIC HEARING, WOMEN IN PUBLIC AND PRIVATE
               EMPLOYMENT, CALIFORNIA. /EMPLOYMENT-CONDITIONS/
               CALIFORNIA ADVISORY COMMISSION ON THE STATUS OF WOMEN, STUDY
               COMMITTEE NO 1, ON PUBLIC AND PRIVATE EMPLOYMENT. HEARINGS.
               SACRAMENTO, CALIFORNIA. MAR 31-AP 1 1966. PP 187-196.

WRILESB61287   RILEY SB
               NEW SOURCES OF COLLEGE TEACHERS. /OCCUPATIONS/
               JOURNAL OF AMERICAN ASSOCIATION OF UNIVERSITY WOMEN, VOL 54,
               MAR 1961.

WRIOCMJ65082   RIOCH MJ
               IMPLICATIONS OF TWO PILOT PROJECTS IN TRAINING MATURE WOMEN
               AS COUNSELORS.
               AMERICAN PSYCHOLOGICAL ASSOCIATION MEETINGS, SYMPOSIUM.
               CHICAGO, ILLINOIS. SEPT 1965. MIMEOGRAPHED.

WROBISS63C83   ROBIN SS
               A COMPARISON OF THE MALE-FEMALE ROLES IN ENGINEERING.
               /OCCUPATION/
               PURDUE UNIVERSITY. UNPUBLISHED PHD DISSERTATION. LAFAYETTE,
               INDIANA. 1963.

WRODMHX65C84   RODMAN H
               MARRIAGE, FAMILY, AND SOCIETY. A READER.
               /WORK-FAMILY-CONFLICT/
               RANDOM HOUSE. NEW YORK. 1965.

WROEXAV64086   ROE AV
               CLIMBING A CAREER PYRAMID -- IN SKIRTS. /OCCUPATIONS/
               STEELWAYS, VOL 20, NOV 1964. PP 16-19.

WROEXAX56085   ROE A
               PSYCHOLOGY OF OCCUPATIONS.
               WILEY. NEW YORK. 1956.

WROEXAX66455   ROE A
               WOMEN IN SCIENCE. /OCCUPATIONS/
               PERSONNEL AND GUIDANCE JOURNAL, VOL 54, 1966. PP 784-787.

WROSECX62087   ROSENFELD C   *US DEPARTMENT OF LABOR
               THE EMPLOYMENT OF STUDENTS, OCTOBER 1961.
               US DEPARTMENT OF LABOR, MONTHLY LABOR REVIEW, VOL 85, NO 2,
               JUNE 1962. 18 PP.

WROSECX65088   ROSENFELD C   PERRELLA VC
               *US DEPARTMENT OF LABOR
               WHY WOMEN START AND STOP WORKING. A STUDY IN MOBILITY.
               US DEPARTMENT OF LABOR, MONTHLY LABOR REVIEW, VOL 88, NO 9,
               SEPT 1965. PP 1077-1082.

WROSERX58089   ROSETT R
               WORKING WIVES. AN ECONOMETRIC STUDY.
               STUDIES IN HOUSEHOLD ECONOMIC BEHAVIOR. ED BY THOMAS F
               DERNBERG ET AL. YALE UNIVERSITY PRESS. NEW HAVEN,
               CONNECTICUT. 1958. PP 51-100.

WROSSASN0133   ROSSI AS   *U CHI NATL OPINION RES CENT
               THE ROOTS OF AMBIVALENCE IN AMERICAN WOMEN.
               /WORK-FAMILY-CONFLICT/

UNIVERSITY OF CHICAGO, NATIONAL OPINION RESEARCH CENTER,
COMMITTEE ON HUMAN DEVELOPMENT. UNPUBLISHED. 34 PP.

WROSSAS64093   ROSSI AS
A GOOD WOMAN IS HARD TO FIND. /WORK-FAMILY-CONFLICT/
TRANS-ACTION, VOL 2, NO 1, NOV-DEC 1964. PP 20-23.

WROSSAS64132   ROSSI AS
EQUALITY BETWEEN THE SEXES. AN IMMODEST PROPOSAL.
/WORK-WOMEN-ROLE/
DAEDELUS, VOL 93, SPRING 1964. PP 607-652.

WROSSAS65091   ROSSI AS
BARRIERS TO THE CAREER CHOICE OF ENGINEERING, MEDICINE, OR
SCIENCE AMONG AMERICAN WOMEN. /OCCUPATIONS/
WOMEN AND THE SCIENTIFIC PROFESSIONS. ED BY JACQUELINE A
MATTFELD AND CAROL G VAN AKEN. MIT PRESS. CAMBRIDGE,
MASSACHUSETTS. 1965. PP 51-127.

WROSSAS65092   ROSSI AS
THE CASE AGAINST FULL-TIME MOTHERHOOD. /EMPLOYMENT/
REDBOOK MAGAZINE, VOL 51, MAR 1965. PP 129-131.

WROSSAS65094   ROSSI AS
WOMEN IN SCIENCE. WHY SO FEW. /OCCUPATIONS/
SCIENCE, VOL 148, NO 3674, MAY 28 1965. PP 1196-1202.

WROSSAS66090   ROSSI AS
AMBIVALENCE IN AMERICAN WOMEN. /WORK-FAMILY-CONFLICT/
ADULT EDUCATION ASSOCIATION, ANNUAL CONVENTION. PAPER.
CHICAGO, ILLINOIS. NOV 1966.

WROSSJE65770   ROSSMAN JE   CAMPBELL DP
WHY COLLEGE-TRAINED MOTHERS WORK.
PERSONNEL AND GUIDANCE JOURNAL, JUNE 1965. PP 986-992.

WROWEFB64095   ROWE FB   *SOUTHERN REGIONAL ED BOARD
CHARACTERISTICS OF WOMEN-S COLLEGE STUDENTS.
SOUTHERN REGIONAL EDUCATION BOARD. ATLANTA, GEORGIA. 1964.
55 PP.

WRUSHEM57096   RUSHER EM
A STUDY OF WOMEN IN OFFICE MANAGEMENT POSITIONS WITH
IMPLICATIONS FOR BUSINESS EDUCATION. /OCCUPATIONS/
OHIO STATE UNIVERSITY. UNPUBLISHED PHD DISSERTATION.
COLUMBUS, OHIO. 1957.

WRUSSRD62135   RUSSELL RD
EXPERIENCES OF NEGRO HIGH SCHOOL GIRLS WITH DOMESTIC
PLACEMENT AGENCIES. /HOUSEHOLD-WORKERS/
JOURNAL OF NEGRO EDUCATION, VOL 31, SPRING 1962. PP 172-176.

WRUTGMR64097   RUTGERS MATH RETRAINING PROG
MATHEMATICS RETRAINING PROGRAM. NOTES AND COMMENTS, APRIL
1964, 1965, 1966. /TRAINING/
RUTGERS -- THE STATE UNIVERSITY. NEW BRUNSWICK, NEW JERSEY.
AP 1964, 1965, 1966. 4, 4 AND 6 PP RESPECTIVELY.

WRUTGMR66098   RUTGERS MATH RETRAINING PROG
REPORT -- 1965-66 -- RETRAINING PROGRAM IN MATHEMATICS AND
SCIENCE FOR COLLEGE GRADUATE WOMEN.
RUTGERS -- THE STATE UNIVERSITY. NEW BRUNSWICK, NEW JERSEY.
1966. 7 PP.

WSAMPJX65099   SAMPSON J   BAGLEY LP
ANDERSON H   *CATALYST IN EDUCATION
*MAINE STATE DEPT OF ED
PART-TIME ASSIGNMENT OF WOMEN IN TEACHING. /OCCUPATIONS/
MAINE STATE DEPARTMENT OF EDUCATION, AND CATALYST IN
EDUCATION. AUGUSTA, MAINE. 1965. 119 PP.

WSANBHX64100   SANBORN H
PAY DIFFERENCES BETWEEN MEN AND WOMEN. /DISCRIMINATION/
INDUSTRIAL AND LABOR RELATIONS REVIEW, VOL 17, NO 4,
JULY 1964. PP 534-550.

WSANFNX57102   SANFORD N
IS COLLEGE EDUCATION WASTED ON WOMEN.
LADIES HOME JOURNAL, VOL 74, NO 5, MAY 1957. PP 78-79, 198.

WSANFNX62101   SANFORD N ED
THE AMERICAN COLLEGE. /WOMAN-WORK-ROLE/
JOHN WILEY AND SONS. NEW YORK. 1962. 1084 PP.

WSCHLVX63103   SCHLETZER V
UNIVERSITY OF MINNESOTA -- THE MINNESOTA PLAN. /EDUCATION/
EDUCATION AND A WOMAN-S LIFE. ED BY LAWRENCE E DENNIS.
AMERICAN COUNCIL ON EDUCATION. WASHINGTON, DC. 1963.
PP 120-122.

WSCHNWF63140   SCHNITZLER WF
A NEW WORLD FOR WORKING WOMEN.
AMERICAN FEDERATIONIST, VOL 70, AUG 1963. PP 18-22.

WSCHRDX62105   SCHREIBER D
SCHOOL DROPOUTS. THE FEMALE SPECIES.
NATIONAL ASSOCIATION OF WOMEN DEANS AND COUNSELORS JOURNAL,
VOL 25, JUNE 1962. PP 175-181.

WSCHRPX66104   SCHRADE P   *UAW UNION
TESTIMONY, PUBLIC HEARING, WOMEN IN PUBLIC AND PRIVATE
EMPLOYMENT, CALIFORNIA. /FEP EMPLOYMENT-CONDITIONS/
CALIFORNIA ADVISORY COMMISSION ON THE STATUS OF WOMEN, STUDY
COMMITTEE NO 1, ON PUBLIC AND PRIVATE EMPLOYMENT. HEARINGS.
SACRAMENTO, CALIFORNIA. MAR 31-AP 1 1966. PP 2-19.

WSCHWJX60108   SCHWARTZ J   *ALUMNAE ADVISORY CENTER INC
SECOND CAREER. /WORK-FAMILY-CONFLICT NEW-YORK/
FUTURES FOR COLLEGE WOMEN IN NEW YORK. ALUMNAE ADVISORY
CENTER, INC. NEW YORK. 1960.

WSCHWJX62106   SCHWARTZ J   *ALUMNAE ADVISORY CENTER INC
THE CHANGING ROLE OF COLLEGE WOMEN. A BIBLIOGRAPHY.
/WORK-WOMAN-ROLE/
ALUMNAE ADVISORY CENTER, INC. NEW YORK. 1962. 4 PP.

WSCHWJX64107   SCHWARTZ J   *ALUMNAE ADVISORY CENTER INC
PART-TIME EMPLOYMENT.
ALUMNAE ADVISORY CENTER, INC. NEW YORK. 1964.

WSCOFNE60109   SCOFIELD NE
SOME CHANGING ROLES OF WOMEN IN SUBURBIA. A SOCIAL
ANTHROPOLOGICAL CASE STUDY. /WORK-FAMILY-CONFLICT/
TRANSACTIONS OF THE NEW YORK ACADEMY OF SCIENCES. SERIES 2,
VOL 22, NO 6, AP 1960. PP 450-457.

WSENDVL61298   SENDERS VL
MINNESOTA PLAN FOR WOMEN-S CONTINUING EDUCATION. A PROGRESS
REPORT.
EDUCATIONAL RECORD, OCT 1961.

WSENDVL64110   SENDERS VL
EDUCATING TOMORROW-S WOMEN.
CHANGING PATTERNS IN EDUCATION BEYOND HIGH SCHOOL,
SYMPOSIUM. PAPER. BOULDER, COLORADO. AUG 8 1964. DITTOED BY
NEW ENGLAND BOARD OF HIGHER EDUCATION. WINCHESTER,
MASSACHUSETTS. 1964. 13 PP.

WSENDVL64111   SENDERS VL
WOMEN MATHEMATICIANS IN INDUSTRY. /OCCUPATIONS/
JOURNAL OF AMERICAN ASSOCIATION OF UNIVERSITY WOMEN,
MAR 1964. PP 114-118.

WSEXTPC62299   SEXTON PC
SPEAKING FOR THE WORKING CLASS WIFE. /BLUE-COLLAR/
HARPERS MAGAZINE, OCT 1962.

WSHEAHX66112   SHEAN H   SNIDER J
MCNETT T   *ASSN MACHINISTS AEROSPACE WS
TESTIMONY, PUBLIC HEARING, WOMEN IN PUBLIC AND PRIVATE
EMPLOYMENT, CALIFORNIA. /EMPLOYMENT-CONDITIONS/
CALIFORNIA ADVISORY COMMISSION ON THE STATUS OF WOMEN, STUDY
COMMITTEE NO 1, ON PUBLIC AND PRIVATE EMPLOYMENT. HEARINGS.
SACRAMENTO, CALIFORNIA. MAR 31-AP 1 1966. PP 57-80.

WSHOSRX56113   SHOSTECK R   *B-NAI B-RITH VOCAT SERV BUR
FIVE THOUSAND WOMEN COLLEGE GRADUATES REPORT.
B-NAI B-RITH VOCATIONAL SERVICE BUREAU. WASHINGTON, DC.
1956. 52 PP.

WSIEGAX63572   SIEGEL A   CURTIS E
FAMILIAL CORRELATES OF ORIENTATION TOWARD FUTURE EMPLOYMENT
AMONG COLLEGE WOMEN. /ASPIRATIONS/
JOURNAL OF EDUCATIONAL PSYCHOLOGY, VOL 54, 1963.

WSIMPAX66114   SIMPSON A
COUNSELING GIRLS IN THE SIXTIES.
AMERICAN PERSONNEL AND GUIDANCE ASSOCIATION, ANNUAL
CONVENTION. PAPER. WASHINGTON, DC. AP 4 1966.

WSIMPRL61115   SIMPSON RL   SIMPSON IH
OCCUPATIONAL CHOICE AMONG CAREER ORIENTED COLLEGE WOMEN.
/ASPIRATIONS/
MARRIAGE AND FAMILY LIVING, VOL 23, NOV 1961. PP 377-383.

WSLOCWL56116   SLOCUM WL   EMPEY LT
*WASH S INST AG EXPMT STATION
OCCUPATIONAL PLANNING BY YOUNG WOMEN, A STUDY OF
OCCUPATIONAL EXPERIENCES, ASPIRATIONS, ATTITUDES, AND
PLANS OF COLLEGE AND HIGH SCHOOL GIRLS.
WASHINGTON STATE COLLEGE, INSTITUTE OF AGRICULTURAL
SCIENCES, EXPERIMENT STATION. PULLMAN, WASHINGTON. AUG 1956.
33 PP.

WSLOTCT58117   SLOTE CT
WOMEN EXECUTIVES. FACT AND FANCY. /OCCUPATIONS/
DUN-S REVIEW AND MODERN INDUSTRY, DEC 1958.

WSMITCLN0118   SMITH COLLEGE LIBRARY
MATERIALS COLLECTION ON WOMEN.
SMITH COLLEGE LIBRARY, SOPHIA SMITH COLLECTION. NORTHAMPTON,
MASSACHUSETTS. ND.

WSMITCX63119   SMITH C
RADCLIFFE INSTITUTE FOR INDEPENDENT STUDY. /TRAINING/
EDUCATION AND A WOMAN-S LIFE. ED BY LAWRENCE E DENNIS.
AMERICAN COUNCIL ON EDUCATION. WASHINGTON, DC. 1963.
PP 111-115.

WSMITGM59122   SMITH GM   *RUTGERS INST MNGMT LAB RELS
OFFICE AUTOMATION AND WHITE-COLLAR EMPLOYMENT.
RUTGERS -- THE STATE UNIVERSITY, INSTITUTE OF MANAGEMENT AND
LABOR RELATIONS, BULLETIN 6. NEW BRUNSWICK, NEW JERSEY.
1959.

WSMITGM60120   SMITH GM   *RUTGERS INST MNGMT LAB RELS
THE CHANGING WOMAN WORKER. A STUDY OF THE FEMALE LABOR-FORCE
IN NEW-JERSEY AND IN THE NATION FROM 1940 TO 1958.
RUTGERS -- THE STATE UNIVERSITY, INSTITUTE OF MANAGEMENT AND
LABOR RELATIONS, BULLETIN NO 7, NEW BRUNSWICK, NEW JERSEY.
1960. 23 PP.

WSMITGM64121   SMITH GM   *RUTGERS INST MNGMT LAB RELS
HELP WANTED -- FEMALE. A STUDY OF DEMAND AND SUPPLY IN A
LOCAL JOB MARKET FOR WOMEN. /MANPOWER/
RUTGERS -- THE STATE UNIVERSITY, INSTITUTE OF MANAGEMENT
AND LABOR RELATIONS. NEW BRUNSWICK, NEW JERSEY. 1964. 99 PP.

WSMITWH66123   SMITH WH   *CAL CONF OF EMPLOYERS ASSNS
TESTIMONY, PUBLIC HEARING, WOMEN IN PUBLIC AND PRIVATE
EMPLOYMENT, CALIFORNIA. /FEP EMPLOYMENT-CONDITIONS
DISCRIMINATION/
CALIFORNIA ADVISORY COMMISSION ON THE STATUS OF WOMEN, STUDY
COMMITTEE NO 1, ON PUBLIC AND PRIVATE EMPLOYMENT. HEARINGS.
SACRAMENTO, CALIFORNIA. AP 29 1966. PP 243-252.

WSMUTRW59148   SMUT RW
WOMEN AND WORK IN AMERICA.
COLUMBIA UNIVERSITY PRESS. NEW YORK. 1959.

WSMUTRW60124   SMUTS RW
THE FEMALE LABOR-FORCE. A CASE STUDY IN THE INTERPRETATION
OF HISTORICAL STATISTICS.
JOURNAL OF AMERICAN STATISTICAL ASSOCIATION, VOL 55,
MAR 1960. PP 71-79.

WSOBOMB60125   SOBOL MB
CORRELATES OF PRESENT AND FUTURE WORK STATUS OF MARRIED
WOMEN.
UNIVERSITY OF MICHIGAN. UNPUBLISHED PHD DISSERTATION.
ANN ARBOR, MICHIGAN. 1960.

WSOBOMG63126   SOBOL MG
COMMITMENT TO WORK. /ASPIRATIONS/
THE EMPLOYED MOTHER IN AMERICA. ED BY F IVAN NYE AND LOIS W
HOFFMAN. RAND MCNALLY. CHICAGO, ILLINOIS. 1963. PP 40-66.

WSOCIOW62127   SOCIETY OF WOMEN ENGINEERS
WOMEN IN PROFESSIONAL ENGINEERING. /OCCUPATIONS/
SOCIETY OF WOMEN ENGINEERS, PROCEEDINGS OF THE PITTSBURGH
CONFERENCE. NEW YORK. 1962.

WSOLODX64128   SOLOMON D ED   *UNIV OF CHICAGO CFSOLEFA
THE CONTINUING LEARNER. /EDUCATION/
UNIVERSITY OF CHICAGO, CENTER FOR THE STUDY OF LIBERAL
EDUCATION FOR ADULTS. CHICAGO, ILLINOIS. 1964. 95 PP.

WSPENNX66129   SPENCER M   *LOS ANGELES AFL
TESTIMONY, PUBLIC HEARING, WOMEN IN PUBLIC AND PRIVATE
EMPLOYMENT, CALIFORNIA. /FEP EMPLOYMENT-CONDITIONS

DISCRIMINATION MIGRANT-WORKERS/
CALIFORNIA ADVISORY COMMISSION ON THE STATUS OF WOMEN, STUDY
COMMITTEE NO 1, ON PUBLIC AND PRIVATE EMPLOYMENT. HEARINGS.
SACRAMENTO, CALIFORNIA. MAR 31-AP 1 1966. PP 168-186.

WSPIRES60301 SPIRO ES
WOMEN IN INDUSTRY -- PATTERNS OF WOMEN-S WORK AND
   OCCUPATIONAL HEALTH AND SAFETY. /OCCUPATIONS/
AMERICAN JOURNAL OF PUBLIC HEALTH, SEPT 1960.

WSTATUI63131 STATE U IOWA BUR LABOR MNGMT
REPORT OF CONFERENCE ON EMPLOYMENT PROBLEMS OF WORKING
   WOMEN.
STATE UNIVERSITY OF IOWA, BUREAU OF LABOR AND MANAGEMENT,
CONFERENCE SERIAL NO 8. IOWA CITY, IOWA. MAY 10-11 1963.

WSTEIAX59137 STEINMANN A
WOMEN-S ATTITUDES TOWARD CAREERS.
VOCATIONAL GUIDANCE QUARTERLY, VOL 8, NO 1, AUTUMN 1959.
PP 15-18

WSTEIAX61136 STEINMANN A
THE VOCATIONAL ROLES OF OLDER MARRIED WOMEN.
   /WORK-WOMAN-ROLE/
JOURNAL OF SOCIAL PSYCHOLOGY, VOL 54, JUNE 1961, PP 93-101.

WSTEIAX63135 STEINMANN A
CONCEPT OF THE FEMININE ROLE. /WORK-WOMAN-ROLE/
INTERAMERICAN CONGRESS OF PSYCHOLOGY. SYMPOSIUM ON
INTERCULTURAL RESEARCH, PAPER. MAR DEL PLATA, ARGENTINA.
AP 3 1963.

WSTEIER62134 STEINBERG ER
WHAT ABOUT WOMANPOWER IN THE SPACE AGE.
SPACE DIGEST, AUG 1962. PP 56-58.

WSTEIER62153 STEINBERG ER   *EXECUTIVE OFFICE OF US PRES
*UNIVERSITY OF PITTSBURGH   *SOCIETY OF WOMEN ENGINEERS
WOMEN IN TECHNOLOGY. /OCCUPATIONS/
CONFERENCE ON WOMEN IN PROFESSIONAL ENGINEERING. PAPER.
UNIVERSITY OF PITTSBURGH. PITTSBURGH, PENNSYLVANIA.
AP 23-24 1962.

WSTEIER65133 STEINBERG ER
A NEW LIFE PATTERN FOR THE COLLEGE-EDUCATED WOMAN.
   /WORK-FAMILY-CONFLICT/
THE ELEUSIS OF CHI OMEGA, SEPT 1965. PP 535-540.

WSTEIRL61226 STEIN RL   *US DEPARTMENT OF LABOR
MARRIED WOMEN AND THE LEVEL OF UNEMPLOYMENT.
US DEPARTMENT OF LABOR, MONTHLY LABOR REVIEW, VOL 84, 1961.
PP 869-870.

WSTEPCM60139 STEPHENSON CM
THE MARRIED FEMALE SCHOOL TEACHER. A CONTINUED STUDY.
   /WORK-FAMILY-CONFLICT/
MARRIAGE AND FAMILY LIVING, VOL 22, NO 1, FEB 1960.
PP 69-70.

WSTEPRX66138 STEPHENS R   *CAL STATE PERSONNEL BOARD
TESTIMONY, PUBLIC HEARING, WOMEN IN PUBLIC AND PRIVATE
   EMPLOYMENT, CALIFORNIA. /LABOR-MARKET/
CALIFORNIA ADVISORY COMMISSION ON THE STATUS OF WOMEN,
STUDY COMMITTEE NO 1, ON PUBLIC AND PRIVATE EMPLOYMENT.
HEARINGS. SACRAMENTO, CALIFORNIA. FEB 24-25 1966. VOL 2,
PP 104-119.

WSTERAX66140 STERLING A   *CAL FEPC COMMISSIONER
TESTIMONY, PUBLIC HEARING, WOMEN IN PUBLIC AND PRIVATE
   EMPLOYMENT, CALIFORNIA. /FEPC/
CALIFORNIA ADVISORY COMMISSION ON THE STATUS OF WOMEN, STUDY
COMMITTEE NO 1, ON PUBLIC AND PRIVATE EMPLOYMENT. HEARINGS.
SACRAMENTO, CALIFORNIA. FEB 24-25 1966. VOL 1, PP 55-61.

WSTICGX56141 STICE G   MOLLENKOPF WG
TORGERSON WS
BACKGROUND FACTORS AND COLLEGE GOING PLANS AMONG HIGH
   APTITUDE PUBLIC HIGH SCHOOL SENIORS. /ASPIRATIONS/
EDUCATIONAL TESTING SERVICE. PRINCETON, NEW JERSEY.
AUG 1956. 117 PP.

WSTIEJX57142 STIEBER J
AUTOMATION AND THE WHITE-COLLAR WORKER.
PERSONNEL JOURNAL, NOV-DEC 1957. PP 8-17.

WSTOCFT59143 STOCKTON FT   *U KANSAS CENT RESEARCH BUS
SALARIED WOMEN IN UPPER LEVEL POSITIONS IN KANSAS BUSINESS
   FIRMS.
UNIVERSITY OF KANSAS, LAWRENCE CENTER FOR RESEARCH IN
BUSINESS. LAWRENCE, KANSAS. 1959. 38 PP.

WSUJAWW58144 SUJANENE WW   HOYT GC
ARE WOMEN WORKERS UNPREDICTABLE.
SUPERVISORY MANAGEMENT, VOL 3, JAN 1958. PP 12-16.

WSWERSX64145 SWERDLOFF S   *US DEPARTMENT OF LABOR
JOB OPPORTUNITIES FOR WOMEN COLLEGE GRADUATES.
US DEPARTMENT OF LABOR, MONTHLY LABOR REVIEW, VOL 87, NO 4,
AP 1964. PP 396-400.

WSWERSX64767 SWERDLOFF S   *US DEPARTMENT OF LABOR
ROOM AT THE TOP FOR COLLEGE WOMEN.
US DEPARTMENT OF LABOR, OCCUPATIONAL OUTLOOK QUARTERLY,
VOL 8, NO 2, MAY 1964. 5 PP.

WSWOPMR63146 SWOPE MR
HIGH SCHOOL GUIDANCE COUNSELOR-S PERCEPTIONS OF SELECTED
   CAREERS FOR WOMEN COLLEGE GRADUATES.
COLUMBIA UNIVERSITY. PHD DISSERTATION. NEW YORK. 1963.

WTACKAL66147 TACKMAN AL
PART-TIME PROGRAM FOR PROFESSIONALLY TRAINED WOMEN.
   /TRAINING/
NEW PATTERNS OF EMPLOYMENT. UNIVERSITY OF MICHIGAN, CENTER
FOR CONTINUING EDUCATION OF WOMEN. ANN ARBOR, MICHIGAN.
OCT 1966. PP 28-37.

WTELLAX65714 TELLA A
LABOR-FORCE SENSITIVITY TO EMPLOYMENT BY AGE, SEX.
INDUSTRIAL RELATIONS, VOL 4, FEB 1965. PP 69-83.

WTERLRX64148 TERLIN R
SPEECH ABOUT JOB OPPORTUNITIES FOR GIRLS BEFORE THE MARYLAND
   STATE PERSONNEL AND GUIDANCE ASSOCIATION.
MARYLAND STATE PERSONNEL AND GUIDANCE ASSOCIATION.
ANNAPOLIS, MARYLAND. MAY 2 1964.

WTHOMDX66151 THOMPSON D   *COMMUNICATIONS WORKERS UNION
TESTIMONY, PUBLIC HEARING, WOMEN IN PUBLIC AND PRIVATE
   EMPLOYMENT, CALIFORNIA. /EMPLOYMENT-CONDITIONS/

CALIFORNIA ADVISORY COMMISSION ON THE STATUS OF WOMEN,
STUDY COMMITTEE NO 1, ON PUBLIC AND PRIVATE EMPLOYMENT.
HEARINGS. SACRAMENTO, CALIFORNIA. MAR 31-AP 1 1966.
PP 202-212.

WTHOMGX66149 THOMAS G   *YWCA
TESTIMONY, PUBLIC HEARING, WOMEN IN PUBLIC AND PRIVATE
   EMPLOYMENT, CALIFORNIA. /EMPLOYMENT-CONDITIONS
   DISCRIMINATION/
CALIFORNIA ADVISORY COMMISSION ON THE STATUS OF WOMEN, STUDY
COMMITTEE NO 1, ON PUBLIC AND PRIVATE EMPLOYMENT. HEARINGS.
SACRAMENTO, CALIFORNIA. AP 29 1966. PP 252-255.

WTHOMJL56380 THOMAS JL
ROLE OF WOMEN. /WORK-WOMAN-ROLE/
COMMONWEAL, VOL 64, NO 7, MAY 18 1956. PP 171-174.

WTHOMMH63152 THOMPSON MH   *UCLA GRAD SCHOOL OF BUS ADM
TODAY-S BUSINESS WOMAN. HER CHARACTERISTICS, HER NEED FOR
   FURTHER EDUCATION, HER FUTURE IN MANAGEMENT.
   /OCCUPATIONS/
UNIVERSITY OF SOUTHERN CALIFORNIA, GRADUATE SCHOOL OF
BUSINESS ADMINISTRATION. LOS ANGELES, CALIFORNIA.
MIMEOGRAPHED. FEB 12 1963. 63 PP.

WTIEDDV58154 TIEDEMAN DV   C-HARA RP
MATHEWS E   *HARVARD GRAD SCHOOL OF ED
POSITION CHOICES AND CAREERS. ELEMENTS OF A THEORY.
   /ASPIRATIONS/
HARVARD, GRADUATE SCHOOL OF EDUCATION, HARVARD STUDIES IN
CAREER DEVELOPMENT NO 8. CAMBRIDGE, MASSACHUSETTS. 1958.

WTIEDDV59153 TIEDEMAN DV
CAREER DEVELOPMENT OF WOMEN. SOME PROPOSITIONS.
THE EDUCATION OF WOMEN -- SIGNS FOR THE FUTURE. ED BY
OPAL D DAVID. AMERICAN COUNCIL ON EDUCATION. WASHINGTON, DC.
1959. PP 64-68.

WTIMEXX61155 TIME
ONE WOMAN, TWO LIVES. /WORK-FAMILY-CONFLICT/
TIME, VOL 78, NOV 3 1961. PP 68-73.

WTINKAH64156 TINKER AH
UNIVERSITY PROGRAMS OF CONTINUING EDUCATION FOR THE ADULT
   WOMAN.
UNIVERSITY OF CHICAGO, DEPARTMENT OF EDUCATION. MA ESSAY.
CHICAGO, ILLINOIS. 1964. 93 PP.

WTORPWG62157 TORPEY WG
THE ROLE OF WOMEN IN PROFESSIONAL ENGINEERING.
   /OCCUPATIONS/
JOURNAL OF ENGINEERING EDUCATION, VOL 52, NO 10, JUNE 1962.
PP 656-658.

WTORREP62158 TORRANCE EP
GUIDING CREATIVE TALENT. /WORK-WOMAN-ROLE/
PRENTICE-HALL. ENGLEWOOD CLIFFS, NEW JERSEY. 1962. 287 PP.

WTOTAJV65159 TOTARO JV ED
WOMEN IN COLLEGE AND UNIVERSITY TEACHING. /OCCUPATIONS/
UNIVERSITY OF WISCONSIN, JOHNSON FOUNDATION. SYMPOSIUM ON
STAFF NEEDS AND OPPORTUNITIES IN HIGHER EDUCATION.
RACINE, WISCONSIN. AUG 10 1963. 54 PP. 1965.

WTURNMB64160 TURNER MB   *UCLA INSTITUTE OF IND RELS
WOMEN AND WORK.
UNIVERSITY OF SOUTHERN CALIFORNIA, INSTITUTE OF INDUSTRIAL
RELATIONS. LOS ANGELES, CALIFORNIA. 1964.

WTURNRH64162 TURNER RH
SOME ASPECTS OF WOMEN-S AMBITIONS.
AMERICAN JOURNAL OF SOCIOLOGY, VOL 70, NO 3, NOV 1964.
PP 271-285.

WTURNRH66161 TURNER RH
IS IT VIVA LA DIFFERENCE. /ASPIRATIONS/
EXPLODING THE MYTHS. EXPANDING EMPLOYMENT OPPORTUNITIES FOR
CAREER WOMEN. UNIVERSITY OF SOUTHERN CALIFORNIA EXTENSION.
CONFERENCE. SPEECH BEFORE. LOS ANGELES, CALIFORNIA. DEC 3
1966.

WUAWXCC66163 UAW CONSTITUTIONAL CONVENTION
WOMEN IN THE UAW. /EEO/
20TH UAW CONSTITUTIONAL CONVENTION. RESOLUTION. LONG BEACH,
CALIFORNIA. MAY 16-21 1966. 4 PP.

WUAWXWD65165 UAW WOMEN-S DEPARTMENT
WISCONSIN FAIR-EMPLOYMENT-PRACTICES DIVISION INQUIRY INTO
   THE CONFLICTS BETWEEN STATE PROTECTIVE LABOR LEGISLATION
   AND STATE AND FEDERAL LAWS PROHIBITING DISCRIMINATION
   BASED ON SEX. /EMPLOYMENT-CONDITIONS/
UAW WOMEN-S DEPARTMENT. DETROIT, MICHIGAN. 1965. 6 PP.

WUAWXWD66164 UAW WOMEN-S DEPARTMENT
STATEMENT ON WEIGHT LIFTING, HOURS, SENIORITY LAWS AND
   WOMEN. /EMPLOYMENT-CONDITIONS/
UAW WOMEN-S DEPARTMENT. DETROIT, MICHIGAN. 1966. 3 PP.

WUHLXGX66200 UHL G
SEX AND THE CIVIL-RIGHTS-ACT. /LEGISLATION/
INDUSTRIAL UNION DEPARTMENT OF THE AFL-CIO, IUD AGENDA,
VOL 2, NO 12, DEC 1966. PP 26-28.

WUNESCO64166 UNESCO
ACCESS OF GIRLS AND WOMEN TO EDUCATION IN RURAL AREAS. A
   COMPARATIVE STUDY.
UNESCO, EDUCATIONAL STUDIES AND DOCUMENTS NO 51. PARIS,
FRANCE. 1964. 62 PP.

WUSBURC59169 US BUREAU OF THE CENSUS
FAMILY CHARACTERISTICS OF WORKING WIVES.
US DEPARTMENT OF COMMERCE. BUREAU OF THE CENSUS, CURRENT
POPULATION REPORTS, SERIES P-50, NO 81, 1959.

WUSCISC61167 US CIVIL SERVICE COMMISSION
FEDERAL CAREERS FOR WOMEN.
US CIVIL SERVICE COMMISSION. GPO. WASHINGTON, DC. JAN 1961.
12 PP.

WUSCISC62168 US CIVIL SERVICE COMMISSION
OCCUPATIONS AND SALARIES OF WOMEN IN THE FEDERAL SERVICE.
US CIVIL SERVICE COMMISSION, PAMPHLET 62. GPO. WASHINGTON,
DC. FEB 1962.

WUSCISC66483 US CIVIL SERVICE COMMISSION *US IDEPTL COMT STATUS WOMEN
FEDERAL EMPLOYMENT OF WOMEN.
US CIVIL SERVICE COMMISSION. PREPARED FOR THE US
INTERDEPARTMENTAL COMMITTEE ON THE STATUS OF WOMEN. GPO.
WASHINGTON, DC. 1966. 22 PP.

WUSDHEW59171 US DEPT OF HEALTH EC WELFARE
CHILD CARE ARRANGEMENTS OF FULLTIME WORKING MOTHERS.
/EMPLOYMENT-CONDITIONS/
US DEPARTMENT OF HEALTH, EDUCATION AND WELFARE, CHILDREN-S
BUREAU, PUBLICATION NO 378. GPO. WASHINGTON, DC. 1959.

WUSDHEW60175 US DEPT OF HEALTH EC WELFARE
TRADE AND INDUSTRIAL EDUCATION FOR GIRLS AND WOMEN. A
DIRECTORY OF TRAINING PROGRAMS.
US DEPARTMENT OF HEALTH, EDUCATION AND WELFARE, OFFICE OF
EDUCATION, BULLETIN OE-84002. GPO. WASHINGTON, DC. 1960.

WUSDHEW61174 US DEPT OF HEALTH EC WELFARE
MANAGEMENT PROBLEMS OF HOMEMAKERS EMPLOYED OUTSIDE THE HOME.
/WORK-FAMILY-CONFLICT/
US DEPARTMENT OF HEALTH, EDUCATION AND WELFARE, OFFICE OF
EDUCATION, BULLETIN OE-83009. GPO. WASHINGTON, DC. 1961.

WUSDHEW65170 US DEPT OF HEALTH EC WELFARE
THE HEALTH OF WOMEN WHO WORK.
US DEPARTMENT OF HEALTH, EDUCATION AND WELFARE. GPO.
WASHINGTON, DC. 1965.

WUSDHEW65172 US DEPT OF HEALTH EC WELFARE
CHILD CARE ARRANGEMENTS OF THE NATION-S WORKING MOTHERS.
A PRELIMINARY REPORT.
US DEPARTMENT OF HEALTH, EDUCATION AND WELFARE, CHILDREN-S
BUREAU. GPO. WASHINGTON, DC. 1965.

WUSDHEW66173 US DEPT OF HEALTH EC WELFARE
CRITERIA FOR ASSESSING FEASIBILITY OF MOTHERS EMPLOYMENT
AND ADEQUACY OF CHILD CARE PLANS.
US DEPARTMENT OF HEALTH, EDUCATION AND WELFARE, CHILDREN-S
BUREAU. GPO. WASHINGTON, DC. AP 1966. 12 PP.

WUSDHEW66177 US DEPT OF HEALTH EC WELFARE
HEALTH MANPOWER SOURCE BOOK. SECTION 2. NURSING PERSONNEL.
US DEPARTMENT OF HEALTH, EDUCATION AND WELFARE, PUBLIC
HEALTH SERVICE, DIVISION OF NURSING. REVISED EDITION.
JAN 1966. 113 PP.

WUSDLABND191 US DEPARTMENT OF LABOR
DIGEST OF STATE LEGISLATION OF SPECIAL INTEREST TO WOMEN
WORKERS.
US DEPARTMENT OF LABOR, WOMEN-S BUREAU. GPO. WASHINGTON, DC.
ANNUAL.

WUSDLABND219 US DEPARTMENT OF LABOR
SUMMARY OF STATE LABOR LAWS FOR WOMEN.
US DEPARTMENT OF LABOR, WOMEN-S BUREAU. GPO. WASHINGTON, DC.
ANNUAL.

WUSDLABND224 US DEPARTMENT OF LABOR
UNIONS AND THE CHANGING STATUS OF WOMEN WORKERS.
US DEPARTMENT OF LABOR, WOMEN-S BUREAU. CONFERENCE. REPORT.
RUTGERS -- THE STATE UNIVERSITY. NEW BRUNSWICK, NEW JERSEY.
OCT 16 1964. TO BE PUBLISHED BY US DEPARTMENT OF LABOR. GPO.
WASHINGTON, DC.

WUSDLAB56989 US DEPARTMENT OF LABOR
EMPLOYMENT AND CHARACTERISTICS OF WOMEN ENGINEERS.
/OCCUPATIONS/
US DEPARTMENT OF LABOR, MONTHLY LABOR REVIEW, VOL 79, NO 5,
MAY 1956. PP 551-554.

WUSDLAB56990 US DEPARTMENT OF LABOR
EMPLOYMENT OF JUNE 1955 WOMEN COLLEGE GRADUATES.
US DEPARTMENT OF LABOR, MONTHLY LABOR REVIEW, VOL 79, NO 9,
SEPT 1956. PP 1057-1061.

WUSDLAB57198 US DEPARTMENT OF LABOR
GOVERNMENT CAREERS FOR WOMEN -- A STUDY.
US DEPARTMENT OF LABOR, WOMEN-S BUREAU. GPO. WASHINGTON, DC.
1957.

WUSDLAB57988 US DEPARTMENT OF LABOR
EARNINGS IN THE WOMEN-S AND MISSES COAT AND SUIT INDUSTRY.
US DEPARTMENT OF LABOR, MONTHLY LABOR REVIEW, VOL 80, NO 1,
NOV 1957. PP 1343-1347.

WUSDLAB57992 US DEPARTMENT OF LABOR
OCCUPATIONS AND SALARIES OF WOMEN FEDERAL EMPLOYEES.
US DEPARTMENT OF LABOR, MONTHLY LABOR REVIEW, VOL 80, NO 8,
AUG 1957. PP 955-959.

WUSDLAB59194 US DEPARTMENT OF LABOR
FIRST JOBS OF COLLEGE WOMEN -- REPORT ON WOMEN GRADUATES,
CLASS OF 1957.
US DEPARTMENT OF LABOR, WOMEN-S BUREAU, BULLETIN 260. GPO.
WASHINGTON, DC. 1959.

WUSDLAB60221 US DEPARTMENT OF LABOR
TRAINING OPPORTUNITIES FOR WOMEN AND GIRLS.
US DEPARTMENT OF LABOR, WOMEN-S BUREAU, BULLETIN 274. GPO.
WASHINGTON, DC. 1960.

WUSDLAB60206 US DEPARTMENT OF LABOR
MATERNITY BENEFIT PROVISIONS FOR EMPLOYED WOMEN.
/EMPLOYMENT-CONDITIONS/
US DEPARTMENT OF LABOR, WOMEN-S BUREAU, BULLETIN 272. GPO.
WASHINGTON, DC. 1960.

WUSDLAB60213 US DEPARTMENT OF LABOR
PART-TIME EMPLOYMENT FOR WOMEN.
US DEPARTMENT OF LABOR, WOMEN-S BUREAU, BULLETIN 273. GPO.
WASHINGTON, DC. 1960.

WUSDLAB61211 US DEPARTMENT OF LABOR
NURSES AND OTHER HOSPITAL PERSONNEL -- THEIR EARNINGS AND
EMPLOYMENT-CONDITIONS.
US DEPARTMENT OF LABOR, WOMEN-S BUREAU, PAMPHLET 6. GPO.
WASHINGTON, DC. 1961.

WUSDLAB62041 US DEPARTMENT OF LABOR
GREAT STRIDES MADE IN JOBS FOR WOMEN IN FEDERAL SERVICE.
US DEPARTMENT OF LABOR, BUREAU OF LABOR STATISTICS,
OCCUPATIONAL OUTLOOK QUARTERLY, VOL 6, NO 3, SEPT 1962.
PP 20-25.

WUSDLAB62189 US DEPARTMENT OF LABOR
EMPLOYMENT PROBLEMS OF WOMEN.
CONNECTICUT VALLEY CONFERENCE. MOUNT HOLYOKE COLLEGE.
SOUTH HADLEY, MASSACHUSETTS. MAR 16-17 1962. PUBLISHED BY US
DEPARTMENT OF LABOR, WOMEN-S BUREAU. GPO. WASHINGTON, DC.
1962.

WUSDLAB62193 US DEPARTMENT OF LABOR
FIFTEEN YEARS AFTER COLLEGE -- A STUDY OF ALUMNAE OF THE
CLASS OF 1945.
US DEPARTMENT OF LABOR, WOMEN-S BUREAU, BULLETIN 283. GPO.

WASHINGTON, DC. 1962.

WUSDLAB62241 US DEPARTMENT OF LABOR
WOMEN WORKERS IN 1960. GEOGRAPHICAL DIFFERENCES.
US DEPARTMENT OF LABOR, WOMEN-S BUREAU, BULLETIN 284. GPO.
WASHINGTON, DC. 1962.

WUSDLAB62253 US DEPARTMENT OF LABOR
THE CHANGING ROLE OF WOMEN IN OUR CHANGING SOCIETY.
US DEPARTMENT OF LABOR, WOMEN-S BUREAU. CONFERENCE.
UNIVERSITY OF UTAH. SALT LAKE CITY, UTAH. SEPT 7-8 1962.

WUSDLAB63226 US DEPARTMENT OF LABOR
WHAT-S NEW ABOUT WOMEN WORKERS.
US DEPARTMENT OF LABOR, WOMEN-S BUREAU. LEAFLET 18. GPO.
WASHINGTON, DC. REVISED 1963.

WUSDLAB63229 US DEPARTMENT OF LABOR
WHY CONTINUING EDUCATION PROGRAMS FOR WOMEN.
US DEPARTMENT OF LABOR, WOMEN-S BUREAU. GPO. WASHINGTON, DC.
DEC 1963.

WUSDLAB63239 US DEPARTMENT OF LABOR
WOMEN TELEPHONE WORKERS AND CHANGING TECHNOLOGY.
US DEPARTMENT OF LABOR, WOMEN-S BUREAU, BULLETIN 286. GPO.
WASHINGTON, DC. 1963.

WUSDLAB63243 US DEPARTMENT OF LABOR   US BUREAU APPRENTICESHIP TRNG
EVERYBODY-S TALKING ABOUT TRAINED WORKERS FOR THE FUTURE.
US DEPARTMENT OF LABOR, WOMEN-S BUREAU, AND US BUREAU OF
APPRENTICESHIP AND TRAINING. GPO. WASHINGTON, DC. 1963.

WUSDLAB63991 US DEPARTMENT OF LABOR
EQUAL-PAY-ACT OF 1963.
US DEPARTMENT OF LABOR, MONTHLY LABOR REVIEW, VOL 86, NO 7,
JULY 1963. PP 947.

WUSDLAB64179 US DEPARTMENT OF LABOR
OCCUPATIONAL TRAINING OF WOMEN UNDER THE
MANPOWER-DEVELOPMENT-AND-TRAINING-ACT.
US DEPARTMENT OF LABOR, OFFICE OF MANPOWER, AUTOMATION, AND
TRAINING, MANPOWER EVALUATION REPORT NO 3. GPO. WASHINGTON,
DC. JULY 1964. 19 PP.

WUSDLAB64183 US DEPARTMENT OF LABOR
ACTION FOR EQUAL-PAY.
US DEPARTMENT OF LABOR, WOMEN-S BUREAU. GPO. WASHINGTON, DC.
1964.

WUSDLAB64188 US DEPARTMENT OF LABOR
CLERICAL OCCUPATIONS FOR WOMEN -- TODAY AND TOMORROW.
/OCCUPATIONS/
US DEPARTMENT OF LABOR, WOMEN-S BUREAU, BULLETIN 289. GPO.
WASHINGTON, DC. 1964.

WUSDLAB64199 US DEPARTMENT OF LABOR
GOVERNORS COMMISSIONS ON THE STATUS OF WOMEN.
US DEPARTMENT OF LABOR, WOMEN-S BUREAU, LEAFLET 38. GPO.
WASHINGTON, DC. REVISED OCT 1964.

WUSDLAB64202 US DEPARTMENT OF LABOR
JOB HORIZONS FOR COLLEGE WOMEN IN THE 1960-S.
US DEPARTMENT OF LABOR, WOMEN-S BUREAU, BULLETIN 288. GPO.
WASHINGTON, DC. 1964.

WUSDLAB64204 US DEPARTMENT OF LABOR
LABOR-FORCE PARTICIPATION RATES AND PERCENT DISTRIBUTION OF
MOTHERS WITH HUSBAND PRESENT.
US DEPARTMENT OF LABOR, WOMEN-S BUREAU. GPO. WASHINGTON, DC.
MAR 1964.

WUSDLAB64212 US DEPARTMENT OF LABOR
PRIVATE-HOUSEHOLD EMPLOYMENT -- SUMMARY OF FIRST AND SECOND
CONSULTATIONS. /HOUSEHOLD-WORKERS/
US DEPARTMENT OF LABOR, WOMEN-S BUREAU. GPO. WASHINGTON, DC.
JUNE 1964 AND FEB 1965.

WUSDLAB64218 US DEPARTMENT OF LABOR
SUGGESTED LANGUAGE FOR A STATE ACT TO ABOLISH DISCRIMINATORY
WAGE RATES BASED ON SEX.
US DEPARTMENT OF LABOR, WOMEN-S BUREAU. GPO. WASHINGTON, DC.
DEC 1964.

WUSDLAB64227 US DEPARTMENT OF LABOR
WHAT THE EQUAL-PAY PRINCIPLE MEANS TO WOMEN.
US DEPARTMENT OF LABOR, WOMEN-S BUREAU. GPO. WASHINGTON, DC.
REVISED 1964.

WUSDLAB64228 US DEPARTMENT OF LABOR
WHO ARE THE DISADVANTAGED GIRLS 16-21 YEARS OLD.
US DEPARTMENT OF LABOR, WOMEN-S BUREAU. GPO. WASHINGTON, DC.
1964.

WUSDLAB64237 US DEPARTMENT OF LABOR
WOMEN IN POVERTY.
US DEPARTMENT OF LABOR, WOMEN-S BUREAU. GPO. WASHINGTON, DC.
1964.

WUSDLAB64240 US DEPARTMENT OF LABOR
WOMEN WORKERS IN MICHIGAN, 1960.
US DEPARTMENT OF LABOR, WOMEN-S BUREAU. GPO. WASHINGTON, DC.
REVISED 1964. 14 PP.

WUSDLAB64242 US DEPARTMENT OF LABOR
WORLD OF WORK CONFERENCE ON CAREER AND JOB OPPORTUNITIES,
WASHINGTON, DC. JULY 1962.
US DEPARTMENT OF LABOR, WOMEN-S BUREAU. GPO. WASHINGTON, DC.
1964.

WUSDLAB65196 US DEPARTMENT OF LABOR
FUTURE JOBS FOR HIGH SCHOOL GIRLS.
US DEPARTMENT OF LABOR, WOMEN-S BUREAU, PAMPHLET 7. GPO.
WASHINGTON, DC. REVISED 1965. 67 PP.

WUSDLAB65220 US DEPARTMENT OF LABOR
TO IMPROVE THE STATUS OF PRIVATE HOUSEHOLD WORK.
/HOUSEHOLD-WORKERS/
US DEPARTMENT OF LABOR, WOMEN-S BUREAU. GPO. WASHINGTON, DC.
MAR 1965.

WUSDLAB65222 US DEPARTMENT OF LABOR
TRENDS IN EDUCATIONAL-ATTAINMENT OF WOMEN.
US DEPARTMENT OF LABOR, WOMEN-S BUREAU. GPO. WASHINGTON, DC.
JAN 1965.

WUSDLAB65225 US DEPARTMENT OF LABOR
WHAT ABOUT WOMEN-S ABSENTEEISM AND LABOR TURNOVER.
US DEPARTMENT OF LABOR, WOMEN-S BUREAU. GPO. WASHINGTON, DC.
AUG 1965. 7 PP.

WUSDLAB65232 US DEPARTMENT OF LABOR
WISCONSIN GOVERNOR-S CONFERENCE ON THE CHANGING STATUS OF
WOMEN, JAN 31-FEB 1 1964.
US DEPARTMENT OF LABOR, WOMEN-S BUREAU. GPO. WASHINGTON, DC.
1965.

WUSDLAB65233 US DEPARTMENT OF LABOR
WOMAN-S DESTINY -- CHOICE OR CHANCE. REPORT OF CONFERENCE AT
THE UNIVERSITY OF WASHINGTON, NOVEMBER 21-22, 1963.
US DEPARTMENT OF LABOR, WOMEN-S BUREAU. GPO. WASHINGTON, DC.
1965.

WUSDLAB65234 US DEPARTMENT OF LABOR
WOMEN AND THE EQUAL-EMPLOYMENT PROVISIONS OF THE
CIVIL-RIGHTS-ACT.
US DEPARTMENT OF LABOR, WOMEN-S BUREAU. GPO. WASHINGTON, DC.
JULY 1965.

WUSDLAB66805 US DEPARTMENT OF LABOR
WHO ARE THE WORKING MOTHERS.
US DEPARTMENT OF LABOR, WOMEN-S BUREAU, LEAFLET 37. GPO.
WASHINGTON, DC. 1966.

WUSDLAB66K05 US DEPARTMENT OF LABOR
LAWS ON SEX DISCRIMINATION IN EMPLOYMENT.
US DEPARTMENT OF LABOR, WOMEN-S BUREAU. GPO. WASHINGTON, DC.
MAY 1 1966. 10 PP.

WUSDLAB66185 US DEPARTMENT OF LABOR
COLLEGE WOMEN SEVEN YEARS AFTER GRADUATION -- RESURVEY OF
WOMEN GRADUATES CLASS OF 1957.
US DEPARTMENT OF LABOR, WOMEN-S BUREAU, BULLETIN 292. GPO.
WASHINGTON, DC. 1966.

WUSDLAB66195 US DEPARTMENT OF LABOR
FRINGE BENEFIT PROVISIONS FROM STATE MINIMUM WAGE LAWS AND
ORDERS, SEPTEMBER 1, 1966. /EMPLOYMENT-CONDITIONS/
US DEPARTMENT OF LABOR, WOMEN-S BUREAU. GPO. WASHINGTON, DC.
1966. 112 PP.

WUSDLAB66197 US DEPARTMENT OF LABOR
GETTING THE FACTS ON EQUAL-PAY.
US DEPARTMENT OF LABOR, WOMEN-S BUREAU. GPO. WASHINGTON, DC.
JAN 1966. 3 PP.

WUSDLAB66200 US DEPARTMENT OF LABOR
1965 HANDBOOK ON WOMEN WORKERS.
US DEPARTMENT OF LABOR, WOMEN-S BUREAU, BULLETIN 290.
WASHINGTON, DC. 1966. BIENNIAL.

WUSDLAB66201 US DEPARTMENT OF LABOR
BIBLIOGRAPHY ON AMERICAN WOMEN WORKERS.
1965 HANDBOOK ON WOMEN WORKERS. US DEPARTMENT OF LABOR,
WOMEN-S BUREAU, REPRINT. GPO. WASHINGTON, DC. 1966.

WUSDLAB66217 US DEPARTMENT OF LABOR
SHORTAGE OR SURPLUS. AN ASSESSMENT OF BOSTON WOMANPOWER IN
INDUSTRY, GOVERNMENT, AND RESEARCH. JUNE 7-8, 1963.
/MASSACHUSETTS/
US DEPARTMENT OF LABOR, WOMEN-S BUREAU. GPO. WASHINGTON, DC.
1966.

WUSDLAB66223 US DEPARTMENT OF LABOR
UNDERUTILIZATION OF WOMEN WORKERS.
US DEPARTMENT OF LABOR, WOMEN-S BUREAU. GPO. WASHINGTON, DC.
OCT 1966. 27 PP.

WUSDLAB66230 US DEPARTMENT OF LABOR
WHY STATE EQUAL-PAY LAWS.
US DEPARTMENT OF LABOR, WOMEN-S BUREAU. GPO. WASHINGTON, DC.
JUNE 1966. 4 PP.

WUSDLAB66231 US DEPARTMENT OF LABOR
WHY WOMEN WORK.
US DEPARTMENT OF LABOR, WOMEN-S BUREAU. GPO. WASHINGTON, DC.
AUG 1966. 3 PP.

WUSDLAB66236 US DEPARTMENT OF LABOR
WOMEN-S EARNINGS IN LOW-INCOME FAMILIES.
US DEPARTMENT OF LABOR, WOMEN-S BUREAU. GPO. WASHINGTON, DC.
REVISED, AP 1966.

WUSDLAB66238 US DEPARTMENT OF LABOR
WOMEN PRIVATE HOUSEHOLD-WORKERS FACT SHEET.
US DEPARTMENT OF LABOR, WOMEN-S BUREAU. GPO. WASHINGTON, DC.
FEB 1966. 6 PP.

WUSDLAB66638 US DEPARTMENT OF LABOR
BACKGROUND FACTS ON WOMEN WORKERS IN THE UNITED STATES.
US DEPARTMENT OF LABOR, WOMEN-S BUREAU. WASHINGTON, DC.
MAY 1966. 16 PP.

WUSDLAB67806 US DEPARTMENT OF LABOR
TRENDS IN EDUCATIONAL-ATTAINMENT OF WOMEN.
US DEPARTMENT OF LABOR, WOMEN-S BUREAU. WASHINGTON, DC.
JAN 1967. 19 PP.

WUSEERH63215 USEEM RH
THE FUROR OVER WOMEN-S EDUCATION.
UNIVERSITY COLLEGE QUARTERLY, VOL 8, NO 4, 1963.

WUSEERH64255 USEEM RH
CHANGING CULTURAL CONCEPTS IN WOMEN-S LIVES.
/WORK-WOMAN-ROLE/
JOURNAL OF NATIONAL ASSOCIATION OF WOMEN DEANS AND
COUNSELORS, VOL 24, NO 1, OCT 1964. PP 29-34.

WUSHOUR62020 US HOUSE OF REPRESENTATIVES
EQUAL-PAY FOR EQUAL WORK.
US HOUSE OF REPRESENTATIVES, COMMITTEE ON EDUCATION AND
LABOR, HEARINGS. MAR-AP 1962.

WUSINCS65860 US IDEPTL COMT STATUS WOMEN
REPORT ON PROGRESS IN 1965 ON THE STATUS OF WOMEN.
/EDUCATION EMPLOYMENT-CONDITIONS/
US INTERDEPARTMENTAL COMMITTEE AND CITIZENS ADVISORY COUNCIL
ON THE STATUS OF WOMEN. SECOND ANNUAL REPORT.
WASHINGTON, DC. DEC 31 1965. 65 PP.

WUSNEWR64244 US NEWS AND WORLD REPORT
EQUAL-PAY FOR WOMEN. ITS EFFECT.
US NEWS AND WORLD REPORT, VOL 56, JUNE 14 1964. PP 91-92.

WUSNEWR65246 US NEWS AND WORLD REPORT
THE OFFICIAL WORD ON JOB RIGHTS FOR WOMEN.
US NEWS AND WORLD REPORT, VOL 59, NOV 22 1965. PP 90-91.

WUSNEWR66245 US NEWS AND WORLD REPORT
HOW WOMEN-S ROLE IN US IS CHANGING.
US NEWS AND WORLD REPORT, MAY 30 1966. PP 58-60.

WUSSMBA62248 US SMALL BUSINESS ADM
MANAGING WOMEN EMPLOYEES IN SMALL BUSINESS.
US SMALL BUSINESS ADMINISTRATION, SMALL MARKETERS AIDS
NO 75. WASHINGTON, DC. JAN 1962.

WUVCAEB66250 U OF CAL EXTENSION BERKELEY
PROFESSIONAL OPPORTUNITIES FOR WOMEN, PROCEEDINGS.
UNIVERSITY OF CALIFORNIA EXTENSION. BERKELEY, CALIFORNIA.
1966.

WUVCAEC66249 UCLA EXTENSION CONFERENCE
EXPLODING THE MYTHS. EXPANDING EMPLOYMENT OPPORTUNITIES FOR
CAREER WOMEN.
UNIVERSITY OF SOUTHERN CALIFORNIA EXTENSION CONFERENCE.
LOS ANGELES, CALIFORNIA. DEC 3 1966.

WUVCHCF61686 UNIV OF CHICAGO CFSOLEFA
CONTINUING EDUCATION FOR WOMEN.
CONTINUING EDUCATION FOR ADULTS. UNIVERSITY OF CHICAGO,
CENTER FOR THE STUDY OF LIBERAL EDUCATION FOR ADULTS.
CHICAGO, ILLINOIS. SEPT 1961.

WUVMICC65251 UM CENT FOR CONTNG ED WOMEN
OPPORTUNITIES FOR WOMEN THROUGH EDUCATION.
UNIVERSITY OF MICHIGAN, CENTER FOR CONTINUING EDUCATION OF
WOMEN, PROCEEDINGS OF THE CONFERENCE-WORKSHOP. ANN ARBOR,
MICHIGAN. MAR 16 1965. NOV 1965.

WUVMICC66685 UM CENT FOR CONT ED FOR WOMEN
NEW PATTERNS OF EMPLOYMENT.
UNIVERSITY OF MICHIGAN, CENTER FOR CONTINUING EDUCATION OF
WOMEN. ANN ARBOR, MICHIGAN, OCT 1966. 143 PP.

WUVUTXX66254 UNIVERSITY OF UTAH
3RD ANNUAL WOMEN-S CONFERENCE, PROCEEDINGS.
UNIVERSITY OF UTAH. SALT LAKE CITY, UTAH. MAR 19-20 1966.

WVAILLX66256 VAIL L   *CAL S CC OF RETAIL CLERKS
STATEMENT, PUBLIC HEARING, WOMEN IN PUBLIC AND PRIVATE
EMPLOYMENT, CALIFORNIA. /FEP EMPLOYMENT-CONDITIONS
DISCRIMINATION/
CALIFORNIA ADVISORY COMMISSION ON THE STATUS OF WOMEN, STUDY
COMMITTEE NO 1, ON PUBLIC AND PRIVATE EMPLOYMENT. HEARINGS.
SACRAMENTO, CALIFORNIA. AP 29 1966. PP 276-284.

WVETTLX64257 VETTER L   LEWIS EC
SOME CORRELATES OF HOMEMAKING VS CAREER PREFERENCE AMONG
COLLEGE HOME ECONOMICS STUDENTS. /WORK-FAMILY-CONFLICT/
PERSONNEL AND GUIDANCE JOURNAL, VOL 42, FEB 1964.
PP 593-598.

WVITAIX63218 VITAL ISSUES
FULL PARTNERSHIP FOR WOMEN -- WHAT STILL NEEDS TO BE DONE.
VITAL ISSUES, NOV 1963.

WWAGMMX66761 WAGMAN M
INTEREST AND VALUES OF CAREER AND HOME MAKING ORIENTED
WOMEN.
PERSONNEL AND GUIDANCE JOURNAL, AP 1966. PP 794-801.

WWALDSX65017 WALDMAN S
A LOOK AT THE OTHER WOMAN. /RACE DISCRIMINATION/
NATIONAL COUNCIL OF JEWISH WOMEN, COUNCIL PLATFORM, VOL 9,
NO 6, JUNE 1965. 5 PP.

WWALSCM57266 WALSH CM
THE CASE OF THE BATTLE-AXES. /EMPLOYMENT/
UNIVERSITY OF CALIFORNIA, BERKELEY. MBA THESIS. MAY 1957.
BERKELEY, CALIFORNIA. 98 PP. TYPESCRIPT.

WWALTDE62314 WALT DE
THE MOTIVATION FOR WOMEN TO WORK IN HIGH LEVEL PROFESSIONAL
POSITIONS.
THE AMERICAN UNIVERSITY, PHD DISSERTATION. WASHINGTON, DC.
1962. 197 PP.

WWARNCF61220 WARNATH CF
IS DISCRIMINATION AGAINST TALENTED WOMEN NECESSARY.
VOCATIONAL GUIDANCE QUARTERLY, VOL 9, 1961. PP 179 FF.

WWARNWL62993 WARNER WL   VAN RIPER PP
MARTIN NH   COLLINS OF
WOMEN EXECUTIVES IN THE FEDERAL-GOVERNMENT. /OCCUPATIONS/
PUBLIC PERSONNEL REVIEW, VOL 23, OCT 1962. PP 227-234.

WWARRPA59222 WARREN PA
VOCATIONAL INTERESTS AND OCCUPATIONAL ADJUSTMENT OF COLLEGE
WOMEN.
JOURNAL OF COUNSELING PSYCHOLOGY, VOL 6, 1959. PP 140-147.

WWASHBB65667 WASHINGTON BB
WOMEN IN POVERTY.
AMERICAN CHILD, VOL 47, NO 3, MAY 1965. PP 5-7.

WWEBBJR66226 WEBB JR   *SOCIETY OF WOMEN ENGINEERS
STATISTICS ON WOMEN PROFESSIONAL ENGINEERS. /OCCUPATIONS/
SOCIETY OF WOMEN ENGINEERS. NEW YORK. DEC 1966. 4 PP.

WWEBEJX66258 WEBER J   *CHILDREN-S CENTERS PROGRAM
TESTIMONY, PUBLIC HEARING, WOMEN IN PUBLIC AND PRIVATE
EMPLOYMENT, CALIFORNIA. /EMPLOYMENT-CONDITIONS
MIGRANT-WORKERS/
CALIFORNIA ADVISORY COMMISSION ON THE STATUS OF WOMEN, STUDY
COMMITTEE NO 1, ON PUBLIC AND PRIVATE EMPLOYMENT. HEARINGS.
SACRAMENTO, CALIFORNIA. AP 28 1960. PP 9-30, 297-298.

WWEINVX61259 WEINGARTEN V   *CHILD STUDY ASSN OF AMERICA
THE MOTHER WHO WORKS OUTSIDE THE HOUSE.
CHILD STUDY ASSOCIATION OF AMERICA. NEW YORK. 1961.

WWEITHX59260 WEITZ H   COLNER RM
RELATIONSHIP BETWEEN THE EDUCATIONAL GOALS AND THE ACADEMIC
PERFORMANCE OF WOMEN. A CONFIRMATION.
EDUCATIONAL AND PSYCHOLOGICAL MEASUREMENT, VOL 19, NO 3,
AUTUMN 1959. PP 373-380.

WWELCFJ60227 WELCH FJ
THE EVOLVING LOW-INCOME PROBLEM IN AGRICULTURE.
/ECONOMIC-STATUS/
AMERICAN ECONOMIC REVIEW, MAY 1960. PP 231-241.

WWELLJA60262 WELLS JA   *US DEPARTMENT OF LABOR
TRAINING WOMEN AND GIRLS FOR WORK.
US DEPARTMENT OF LABOR, BUREAU OF LABOR STATISTICS,
OCCUPATIONAL OUTLOOK QUARTERLY, VOL 4, NO 4, DEC 1960.
PP 9-16.

WWELLJA63263 WELLS JA
WOMEN AND GIRLS IN THE LABOR-MARKET TODAY AND TOMORROW.

NATIONAL CONFERENCE ON SOCIAL WELFARE. SPEECH. CLEVELAND, OHIO. MAY 21 1963.

WWELLMW61261 WELL MW
AN ANALYSIS OF FACTORS INFLUENCING MARRIED WOMEN-S ACTUAL OR PLANNED WORK PARTICIPATION.
AMERICAN SOCIOLOGICAL REVIEW, VOL 26, NO 1, FEB 1961. PP 91-96.

WWESTEM62265 WESTERVELT EM
WOMANPOWER -- WANTON WASTE OR WISHFUL THINKING.
VOCATIONAL GUIDANCE QUARTERLY, VOL 10, NO 2, 1962. PP 78-84.

WWESTEM65210 WESTERVELT EM   *US DEPARTMENT OF LABOR
COUNSELING TODAY-S GIRLS FOR TOMORROW-S WOMANHOOD.
NEW APPROACHES TO COUNSELING GIRLS IN THE 1960-S. MIDWEST REGIONAL PILOT CONFERENCE. REPORT. UNIVERSITY OF CHICAGO CENTER FOR CONTINUING EDUCATION. CHICAGO, ILLINOIS. FEB 26-27 1965. PP 11-33.

WWESTRC62214 WESTERN REGIONAL CONFERENCE   *US DEPARTMENT OF LABOR
PROBLEMS AND PROSPECTS OF WORKING WOMEN.
WESTERN REGIONAL CONFERENCE. REPORT. SEPT 1961. PUBLISHED BY US DEPARTMENT OF LABOR, WOMEN-S BUREAU. GPO. WASHINGTON, DC. 1962.

WWHITMS64266 WHITE MS   *RADCLIFFE INST INDPT STUDY
THE NEXT STEP -- A GUIDE TO PART-TIME OPPORTUNITIES IN GREATER BOSTON FOR THE EDUCATED WOMAN. /MASSACHUSETTS/
RADCLIFFE INSTITUTE FOR INDEPENDENT STUDY. CAMBRIDGE, MASSACHUSETTS. 1964.

WWIGNTX65267 WIGNEY T
THE EDUCATION OF WOMEN AND GIRLS IN A CHANGING SOCIETY. A SELECTED BIBLIOGRAPHY WITH ANNOTATIONS.
UNIVERSITY OF TORONTO, DEPARTMENT OF EDUCATIONAL RESEARCH. TORONTO, CANADA. 1965.

WWILCRX60268 WILCOCK R
WOMEN IN THE AMERICAN LABOR-FORCE. EMPLOYMENT AND UNEMPLOYMENT.
US SENATE, SPECIAL COMMITTEE ON UNEMPLOYMENT PROBLEMS. HEARINGS. 86TH CONGRESS, 2ND SESSION. GPO. WASHINGTON, DC. 1960.

WWILLJJ66269 WILLIAMS JJ
THE WOMEN PHYSICIANS DILEMMA. /OCCUPATIONS/
JOURNAL OF SOCIAL ISSUES, VOL 6, NO 3, 1950. PP 38-44. ALSO IN PROFESSIONALIZATION. ED BY HOWARD M VOLLMER AND DONALD L MILLS. PRENTICE-HALL. ENGLEWOOD CLIFFS, NEW JERSEY. 1966.

WWINTEX61270 WINTER E
A WOMAN-S GUIDE TO EARNING A GOOD LIVING.
SIMON AND SCHUSTER. NEW YORK. 1961.

WWIRTWW62181 WIRTZ WW   *US DEPARTMENT OF LABOR
WOMEN IN FEDERAL SERVICE, 1939-59.
US DEPARTMENT OF LABOR. GPO. WASHINGTON, DC. 1962. 21 PP.

WWIRTWW63271 WIRTZ WW   *US DEPARTMENT OF LABOR
CHANGING PROFILE OF THE NATION-S WORK-FORCE.
US DEPARTMENT OF LABOR, BUREAU OF LABOR STATISTICS. OCCUPATIONAL OUTLOOK QUARTERLY, VOL 7, NO 1, FEB 1963. PP 3-6.

WWISKGC65272 WIS GOVRS COMM STATUS OF WOME
WISCONSIN WOMEN. REPORT OF THE WISCONSIN GOVERNOR-S COMMISSION ON THE STATUS OF WOMEN.
WISCONSIN GOVERNOR-S COMMISSION ON THE STATUS OF WOMEN. MADISON, WISCONSIN. 1965. 44 PP.

WWOMEEA65275 WOMEN-S EDL AND IND UNION
PARTNERSHIP TEACHING PROGRAM. PROGRESS REPORT -- JAN-OCT 1965. SECTION I. /TRAINING/
WOMEN-S EDUCATIONAL AND INDUSTRIAL UNION. BOSTON, MASSACHUSETTS. 1965. 9 PP.

WWOMEIX66273 WOMEN INC   HILL H
WILSON B   *UNION PULP AND PAPER WORKERS
TESTIMONY, PUBLIC HEARING, WOMEN IN PUBLIC AND PRIVATE EMPLOYMENT, CALIFORNIA. /FEP EMPLOYMENT-CONDITIONS MIGRANT-WORKERS/
CALIFORNIA ADVISORY COMMISSION ON THE STATUS OF WOMEN, STUDY COMMITTEE NO 1, ON PUBLIC AND PRIVATE EMPLOYMENT. HEARINGS. SACRAMENTO, CALIFORNIA. AP 28 1966. PP 114-118.

WWOODWX66276 WOODS W   *PACIFIC TELEGRAPH TELEPHONE
TESTIMONY, PUBLIC HEARING, WOMEN IN PUBLIC AND PRIVATE EMPLOYMENT, CALIFORNIA. /EMPLOYMENT-CONDITIONS/
CALIFORNIA ADVISORY COMMISSION ON THE STATUS OF WOMEN, STUDY COMMITTEE NO 1, ON PUBLIC AND PRIVATE EMPLOYMENT. HEARINGS. SACRAMENTO, CALIFORNIA. AP 28 1966. PP 2-9.

WWORTNB60245 WORTHY NB
PART-TIME WORKING MOTHERS -- A CASE-STUDY.
MANAGEMENT RECORD, SEPT 1960.

WWRIGKW66277 WRIGHT KW
SUPPLY OF MEDICAL WOMEN IN THE UNITED STATES. /OCCUPATIONS/
MEDICAL WOMEN-S INTERNATIONAL ASSOCIATION, 10TH CONGRESS. SPEECH. ROCHESTER, NEW YORK. JULY 9-15 1966.

WWULSJH66278 WULSIN JH
ADMISSION OF WOMEN TO MEDICAL SCHOOL.
JOURNAL OF THE AMERICAN MEDICAL WOMEN-S ASSOCIATION, VOL 21, NO 8, AUG 1966. PP 674-676.

WYETTDX66246 YETT D
THE NURSING SHORTAGE AND THE NURSE TRAINING ACT OF 1964. /MANPOWER/
INDUSTRIAL AND LABOR RELATIONS REVIEW, JAN 1966.

WYOUNLM61279 YOUNG LM
THE AMERICAN WOMAN AT MIDCENTURY. /WORK-WOMAN-ROLE/
THE AMERICAN REVIEW, VOL 11, DEC 1961. PP 121-138.

WYWCAXX63078 YWCA
WOMEN TODAY. TRENDS AND ISSUES IN THE UNITED STATES. /WORK-WOMAN-ROLE/
YOUNG WOMEN-S CHRISTIAN ASSOCIATION OF THE USA. NEW YORK. 1963. 34 PP.

WYWCAXX66079 YWCA
TO FULFILL THESE RIGHTS. SUMMARY REPORT OF PRE-WHITE-HOUSE CONFERENCES.
YOUNG WOMEN-S CHRISTIAN ASSOCIATION OF THE USA. NEW YORK. 1966. 124 PP.

WZAPJMW56280 ZAPOLEON MW
THE COLLEGE GIRL LOOKS AHEAD TO HER CAREER OPPORTUNITIES.

HARPER AND BROTHERS. NEW YORK. 1956.

WZAPJMW59281 ZAPOLEON MW
COLLEGE WOMEN AND EMPLOYMENT.
THE EDUCATION OF WOMEN -- SIGNS FOR THE FUTURE. ED BY OPAL D DAVID. AMERICAN COUNCIL ON EDUCATION. WASHINGTON, DC. 1959.

WZAPJMW61282 ZAPOLEON MW
OCCUPATIONAL PLANNING FOR WOMEN.
HARPER AND BROTHERS. NEW YORK. 1961.

WZAPJMW64283 ZAPOLEON MW
WOMEN-S WORK. FACTS, FINDINGS, AND APPARENT TRENDS.
JOURNAL OF NATIONAL ASSOCIATION OF WOMEN DEANS AND COUNSELORS, VOL 24, NO 1, OCT 1964. PP 40-46.

WZISSCX62284 ZISSIS C
THE RELATIONSHIP OF SELECTED VARIABLES TO CAREER-MARRIAGE PLANS OF UNIVERSITY FRESHMAN WOMEN. /WORK-FAMILY-CONFLICT/
UNIVERSITY OF MICHIGAN, DEPARTMENT OF EDUCATION. PHD DISSERTATION. ANN ARBOR, MICHIGAN. 1962.

WZISSCX64285 ZISSIS C
A STUDY OF THE LIFE PLANNING OF 550 FRESHMEN WOMEN AT PURDUE UNIVERSITY. /WORK-FAMILY-CONFLICT/
JOURNAL OF THE NATIONAL ASSOCIATION OF WOMEN DEANS AND COUNSELORS, VOL 18, 1964. PP 153-159.

Author Index

BOWLBY R GBEDEMX64448
BOWLES GK GBOWLGK56433
GBOWEWG65749
WBOWEWGND652
GBOWLGK57415
GBOWLGK58397
GBOWLGK65424
GBOWLGK65432
GBOWLGK65434
GBOWLGK66414
GBOWLGK66430
GBOWLGK67920
GMAIEFH60417
GSKRARL57315
BOWMAN GW GBOWMGW61466
GBOWMGW63467
GBOWMGW64468
WBOWMGW56653
BOWMAN L PBOWALX62889
BOWMAN M NANDEAX53022
BOXLEY RF GBOXLRF65418
BOYD I NVALIPX56281
BOYD WM NBOYDWM46252
BOYER RO NBOYERO55105
BRADBURY WC NBRADWC53106
BRADEN C NBRADCX57107
BRADLEY ME GBRADME64797
BRADLEY P ED GBRADPX64247
BRADSHAW BS GBOWLGK66430
BRADY DS GBRADDS65679
BRAESTRUP P PBRAEPX58782
BRAGG EW NBRAGEW63312
BRAM J PBRAMJX62783
PBRAMJX63784
BRANDEIS E GBRANEX63796
BRANDWEIN S GBRANSX63876
BRAVERMAN H GBRAVHX59471
JBRAVHX58707
BRAY DW NGINZEX53415
BRAZAEL BR GBRAZBR51472
BRAZEAL BR NBRAZBR46108
BRAZER H GMORGJN62032
BRAZZIEL WF NBRAZWF58111
NBRAZWF60109
NBRAZWF60112
NBRAZWF64285
NBRAZWF64318
NBRAZWF64496
NBRAZWF66110
BREITMAN G NBREIGX52113
BREYTSPRAAK CH WBREYCH64654
BRIELAND D WBRIEDX61655
BRIGGS VM NMARSRX66327
NMARSRX67118
BRIGGS WA GBRIGWA62473
BRIGHAM YOUNG UNIVERSITY
IBRIGYUND442
BRIMMER AF GBRIMAF66475
NBRIMAF64891
NBRIMAF65890
NBRIMAF66114
NBRIMAF66661
BRIMMER AF ED NWOLFDP64338
BRINK W NBRINWX64116
BRITTIN N NBRITNX54892
BRODY DA GEDELHX63658
BRONSON CA NBRONCA51337
BRONZEN Y GBRONYX57921
BROOKS AD NBROOAD62117
BROOKS DJ WBROODJ64656
BROOKS JC ED NWAYNCM64295
BROOKS LB GBROOLB64795
BROOKS T NBROOTX62122
NBROOTX66631
BROOKS TR NBROOTR61119
NBROOTR61120
NBROOTR61121
NBROOTR63118
BROOM L NBROOLX65123
NBROOLX65124
OBROOLX55708
BROWN A NBROWAX58893
NBROWAX60125
WBROWAX66657
BROWN B NDEUTMX64268
BROWN DR WBROWDR62658
BROWN FJ GBROWFJ55476
BROWN FJ ED GBROWFJ45477
BROWN H NBROWHX63894
BROWN MC NBROWMC55126
BROWN MM NMARSCP65738
BROWN RG NBROWRG65895
BROWN WH NMANNCP53737
BROWNE VJ NBROWVJ54127
BROWNING HL MBROWHL64286
MBROWHL64368
BRUNER D NBRUNDX60128
BRYANT CD WBRYACD57659
BRYANT ES WBRYAE561660
BRYCE H GMILLSM64071
BRYENTON GL GBRYEGL65896
BRYSON WO NBRYSWO43129
BUCKINGHAM W GBUCKWX62875
BUCKLEY LF GBUCKLF
GBUCKLF63479
NBUCKLF61130
BUFFALO LAW REVIEW
GBUFFLR64484
BUFFMIRE D WBUFFDX66661
BUGGS JA NBUGGJA66111
BULLOCK HA NBULLHA50132
NBULLHA51133
BULLOCK P CBULLPX66136
GBULLPX60897
GBULLPX61523
GBULLPX62488
GBULLPX63489
GBULLPX66486
MBULLPX64369
NBULLPXND134
NBULLPX65138
NBULLPX65483
NBULLPX66135
NBULLPX66898
BUNKE HC NBUNKHC65122
BUNKER R IBUNKRX59899
BUNTING MI WBUNTMI61662
WBUNTMI61664
WBUNTMI61900
WBUNTMI65663

BURCH TA GBURCTA62408
NTAYLCC58411
BURCHINAL LG GBURCLE65490
WBURCLG61665
BUREAU OF NATIONAL AFFAIRS
GBURENAND495
GBURENA61498
GBURENA63946
GBURENA64497
GBURENA65494
GBUREON64492
GBUREON65491
GBUREON66493
NBURENA57315
BUREAU SOC SCIENCE RESEARCH
GBURESS57499
BURGESS ME NBURGME65140
BURK CJ MWHITNX60517
BURMA JH CBURMJH60287
CBURMJH60371
GBURMJH51500
MBURMJH61370
MJORGJM60422
BURNS H NBURNHX63902
BUSINESS MANAGEMENT
NBUSIMX64142
BUSINESS WEEK GBUSIWX61502
GBUSIWX62505
GBUSIWX65502
NBUSIWX54161
NBUSIWX51164
NBUSIWX54879
NBUSIWX56160
NBUSIWX56882
NBUSIWX58165
NBUSIWX58880
NBUSIWX60147
NBUSIWX60152
NBUSIWX60155
NBUSIWX60157
NBUSIWX60162
NBUSIWX61144
NBUSIWX61145
NBUSIWX61158
NBUSIWX62153
NBUSIWX62159
NBUSIWX63148
NBUSIWX63149
NBUSIWX63154
NBUSIWX64143
NBUSIWX64297
NBUSIWX64298
NBUSIWX64887
NBUSIWX65150
NBUSIWX65151
WBUSIWX61666
WBUSIWX62668
WBUSIWX63667
WBUSIWX63669
BUSTARD JL GBUSTJL49507
BUTCHER GT GBUTCG763508
BUTLER CP GBURCTA62408
CABRERA YA MCABRYA63373
MCABRYA65372
CAGLE LT NCAGLLT66904
CAHN E GCAHNEX66905
CAIN GG WCAINGG64671
WCAINGG66672
CAL ADVSY COMM INDIAN AFFAIRS
ICALACI66542
CAL ADVSY COMM STATUS WOMEN
WCALACW62675
WCALACW62676
WCALACW66674
WCALACW66677
CAL ASSEMBLY INTERIM COMT IR
GCALAIW64510
MCALAIC64374
CAL ASSEMBLY INTERIM COMT WM
GCALAIW64510
CAL ATTORNEY GENERALS OFFICE
GCALAGO60511
GCALAGO63512
CAL COMM MANPOWER AUTOM TECH
GCALCMA65515
CAL CONF ON APPRENTICESHIP
GCALCNA60516
CAL DEPT OF INDUSTRIAL RELS
CCALDIR63710
CCALDIR66168
GCALDIR60522
GCALDIR60527
GCALDIR63523
GCALDIR63526
ICALDIR65541
MCALDIR62376
MCALDIR64377
MCALDIR64379
NCALDIR63167
CAL DIV LABOR STATS RESEARCH
WCALIDL64678
CAL NEWSPAPER PUBLISHERS
CCALOGB65171
CAL OFFICE OF THE GOVENOR
GCALOGB63546
CAL OFFICE OF THE GOVERNOR
CCALOGB65171
CAL PUBLIC PERSONNEL ASSN
GCALPPA65547
CAL STATE PERSONNEL BOARD
CCALOGB65171
GCALSPB65551
GCALSPB65552
GCALFPB66173
CAL VOCATIONAL REHAB SERVICE
GCALVRS60553
CALDEN G NHOKAJE60559
CALDWELL WF GCALDWF65069
CALEF WC NCALEWC56069
CALIF DEPT OF INDUSTRIAL RELS
WCALDIR66268
WCALDIR66267

WCALDIR67269
CALIFORNIA BOARD OF EDUCATION
GCALBOE64513
CALIFORNIA DEPT OF EDUCATION
WCALDED60445
CALIFORNIA DEPT OF EMPLOYMENT
CCALDEM66166
CCALDEM66906
GCALDEM67907
GCALDEM63520
GCALDEM64521
GCALDEM65517
GCALDEM66518
GCALFEPND531
CALIFORNIA FEPC GCALFEPND537
GCALFEPND541
GCALFEP61533
GCALFEP63539
GCALFEP64536
GCALFEP65529
GCALFEP65542
GCALFEP66528
GCALFEP66532
GCALFEP66540
NCALFEP66169
CALIFORNIA LABOR FEDERATION
GCALLF X59544
GCALLF X64545
CALIFORNIA SES NCALFES63172
CALIFORNIA STATE EMPLOYEE
GCALSEM64548
CALIFORNIA STATE LIBRARY
GCALSLIND549
CALIFORNIA STATE SENATE
MCALSSE63380
CALIVER A NCALIAX49174
CALLAHAN KR NCARLEL64182
CALLOWAY E NCALLEX64175
CALUKINS DD IMILLFC64590
CALVERT R GCALVRX63555
CALVET IJ NCALVIJ63176
CAMPBELL AK NCAMPAKND177
CAMPBELL D WROSSJE65770
CAMPBELL EQ NCAMPEQ61909
CAMPBELL F NCAMPFX54178
CAMPBELL J GCAMPJX64093
CAMPBELL JT NCAMPJT65179
NCAMPJT66010
CAMPBELL RR NCAMPRR60180
CANADIAN DEPARTMENT OF LABOR
WORGAEC64045
CAPLAN N NCAPLNX66013
CAPLOVITZ D GCAPLDX63310
CAPLOW T WCAPLTX58679
CARDONA LA PCARDLA67874
CAREY JB NCAREJB58181
CARL EL NCARLEL64182
CARLISLE J NCARLJX65593
CARLTON RC PCARLRC59785
CARNEGIE ME CCARNME62183
WCARNME64910
CARNEGIE CORP OF NY QUARTERLY
WCARNCO62680
CARPER L NCARPLX66184
CARR H GCARRHX66558
CARROLL MS WCARRMS62681
CARTER B NCARTBX65999
CARTER EA GCARTEA56559
CARTER R GCARTRX65560
CASSARA BB ED WCASSBB62682
CASSEL FH NCASSFH66185
CASSELL FH GCASSFH63562
GCASSFH66561
GCASSFH66565
GCASSFH66744
CASTANO C PCASTCX58786
CATALYST WCATAXX64683
CATALYST IN EDUCATION
WNATLEA64019
CATHOLIC DIGEST NCATHDX57186
CAUDILL HM NCAUDHM62911
CAUDILL W OCAUDWX61711
CAVAN RS WCAVARS57684
CAYTON HR NCAYTHR51187
CC OF FEDERATED ORGANIZATIONS
NCOUNF063929
CC OF STATE GOVTS WEST OFFICE
MCOUNSH60386
CHALMERS FK GCHALFK48563
CHALMERS WE WCHALWE62189
WCHALWE64912
WCHALWE65188
CHANCE NA ICHANNA65943
CHANDLER HD WCHANHD66687
CHANGING TIMES NCHANTX63190
CHANSKY NM GCHANNM66803
CHANSKY NN NCHANNN65191
CHAPIN AA NCHAPAA66192
CHAPIN P NROSEBX59080
CHAPLIN D WCHAPDX64193
CHAPMAN EJ NCHAPEJ49351
CHASE ET NCHASET63195
NCHASET64196
CHASON W NCHASWX58194
CHATTANOOGA CC COOP ACTION
NCHATCC62197
CHAVEZ C MVALDLX66512
CHECKIS LD NCHECDX64890
CHEIN I NCHEIIX49198
CHEMICAL WEEK NCHEMWX61199
NCHEMWX63200
CHENKIN A JCHENAX61712
JCHENAX62713
CHI MAYORS COMT COM WELFARE
GCHICMC56566
CHICAGO BOYS CLUBS
GCHICBC65319
CHICAGO COMM ON HUMAN RELS
GCHICHR59565
GCHICHR62568
NCHICCO60201
CHICAGO REGIONAL CONFERENCE
WCHICRC62689
CHICAGO URBAN LEAGUE
NCHICULND203
NCHICUL58202
CHICAGO YOUTH CENTERS
GCHICBC65319

CHICK CA NCHICGA47914
NCHICCA53204
CHILDERS RR NCHILRR57205
CHILMAN C GCHILCX64571
GCHILCX64922
CHRISTENSEN DE NCHRIDE58206
CHRISTENSEN H WCHRIHX56690
CHURCH R GCHURRX55572
CHURN B NMCQURX60730
CIKINS WI NCIKIWI66207
CLAGUE E GCLAGEX64625
GCLAGEX65794
CLAPP RF WCLAPRF66112
CLARK JP NCLARJP62209
NCLARJP63208
CLARK KB GCLARKB60574
GCLARKB66915
NCLARKB59210
NCLARKB63214
NCLARKB64307
NCLARKB65211
NCLARKB65213
NCLARKB67212
CLARK KB ED NPARSTX66976
CLARK TD NCLARTD61055
CLARKE JH NCLARJH64309
CLAYTON FL WCLAYFL62691
CLAYTON HR NDRAKSC45291
CLEARY TA GCLEATA66924
NCLEATA66923
CLEAVES MP GCLEAMP66130
CLEMENTS HM WCLEMHM63381
CLEVELAND URBAN LEAGUE
NCLEVUL64916
CLIFT VA NCLIFVA66227
CLIFT VA ED NCLIFVA62215
CLIFTON FG WCLIFFG66692
CLINCHY R GCLINRX61577
CLOWARD R GCLOWRX66525
CLYMER E WCLYMEX59693
COBB CW GCOBBCW46578
COBB WM NCOBBWM48217
NCOBBWM58216
COCKFIELD HW NCOCKHW65218
COGLEY NJOHNXX63336
COHEN AK NCOHEAK63219
COHEN EE NCOHEEE63220
COHEN FS GCOHEFS46579
COHEN H CCOHEHX65917
COHEN NE GCOHENE65664
COHEN R NCOHERXND221
COHEN R GMORGJN62032
COHEN WJ GCOHEWJ64925
COLBERG MR GCOLBMR63994
GCOLBMR65793
COLE B CCOLEBX67918
COLE CG WCOLECG56694
COLE E GCOLEEX66131
COLE MW GCOLESG54580
COLE SG GCOLESG54580
COLEMAN C WCOLEC X69695
COLEMAN JS NCOLEJS66223
COLES R GCOLERX66133
COLLIER J ICOLLJX56544
COLLINS H NCOLLHX65491
COLLINS HA GSMITEA56140
COLLINS M WCOLLNX66696
COLLINS OF WWARNWL62993
COLLVER A WCOLLAX62697
COLNER RM WWEITHX59260
COLOMBOTOS J WCOLOJX63698
COLORADO LEGISLATIVE COUNCIL
MCOLOLC60382
MCOLOLC62383
COLORADO STATE DEPT OF ED
GCOLOSD59919
MCOLOSD61384
COLUMBIA LAW REVIEW
NCOLULR52226
NCOLULR57224
NCOLULR65225
COLUMBIA MISSOURIAN
WCOLUMX64699
WCOLUMX64700
COLUMBUS URBAN LEAGUE
NCOLUUL59227
COMM CC GTR NEW YORK
GCOMMCC64210
COMMENTARY NCOMMXX59228
NCOMMXX64467
COMMERCE CLEARING HOUSE
GCOMMCH64588
GCOMMCH64590
GCOMMCH65589
COMMITTEE FOR FULL EMPLOYMENT
GCOMIEF64592
COMMONWEAL NCOMMXX65229
WCOMMXX63701
COMMUNITY CONF ON EMPLOYMENT
NCOMUGE60230
COMPTON D WCOMPBX66702
COMT FOR ECONOMIC DEVELOPMENT
GCOMIED65591
CONANT JB NCONAJB61920
CONF AUTOMATION PUB WELFARE
GCONFAP63545
CONFERENCE ON EC PROGRESS
GCONFOE62873
GCONFOE66872
CONGRESSIONAL DIGEST
GCONGDX45596
GCONGDX50597
GCONGDX64594
GCONGDX66356
CONNOR C NCONNCX66232
CONNORS SISTER MAUREEN
NCONNSM65471
CONRAD E NCONREX47233
CONSUMERS LEAGUE OF NEW YORK
GCONSLO59926
CONWAY JE GCONWJE64599
GNEWYSB64104
CONWAY JT GCONWJT65496
CONYERS JE WCONYJE61704
WCONYJE63703
COOK FS WCOOKFS66705
COOK SW NCOOKSW57234
COOK W WCOOKWX60252
COOKSEY FC GCOOKFC86600
COOMBS LM ICOOMLM62646

COONEY RB GCOONRB64871
NCOONRB66927
COOPER J NCOOPJX64294
COOPER JE NCOOPJE56235
COOPER S GCOOPSX59928
GCOOPSX60601
GCOOPSX60603
GCOOPSX62602
GCOOPSX64743
GCOOPSX66604
CORCORAN SP WMAYXEE59964
CORDTZ D NCORDDX66030
CORMACK ML WCORMML67706
CORNELL UNIVERSITY
CPROJAX66237
CORT JC GCORTJC57372
CORWIN RG WCORWRG61707
COTHRAN ML MCOTHML66385
COTTON DW WCOTTDW65708
COUNCIL OF ECONOMIC ADVISORS
GCOUNEAND239
GCOUNEA62205
GCOUNEA66204
COUNCIL OF MEXICAN-AM AFFAIRS
MCOUNMA62930
COUNCIL OF STATE GOVERNMENTS
GCOUNSG58932
GCOUNSG60931
COUNTRYMAN V GCOUNVX64608
GCOUNVX65610
COUNTRYMAN V ED GCOUNVX65609
COUSENS FR GCOUSFR61612
GCOUSFR62613
GCOUSFR66478
NCOUSFR58611
COWHIG JD GCOWHJD59430
GCOWHJD60423
GCOWHJD61427
GCOWHJD63420
GCOWHJD63421
GCOWHJD64419
GCOWHJD64615
GCOWHJD64616
GCOWHJD65425
GCOWHJD65614
GCOWHJD65933
GMAITST60436
COX A GCOXXAX57617
COX OC NCOXXOC41934
NCOXXOC53935
COX T GCOXXTX63618
CRAIG CE GCRAICE65619
GCRAICE66620
NCRAICE65240
CRAIG L ED WFLAGJJ63130
CREAMER D GCREADX61621
CROFT ES NCROFES66242
CROMER R NCROMRX63243
CROMIEN F NCROMFX61121
CRONHEIM DH WCRONDH56709
CROSS KP WCROSKP63710
CROSSMAN ER GCROSER66148
CROWE GB NLERANL59404
NLERANL60403
CRYSTAL D JCRYSDX58714
CULBERSON GW GFINEMX64681
CULHANE MM GCULHMM65651
CULPAN P WCULPPX61382
CUMMING G WCUMMGX66711
CUMMINGS LD GCUMMLD65623
CUNNINGGIM M NCUNNMX56579
CUNNINGHAM GE NCUNNGE58244
CUNNINGHAM JT PCUNNJT57793
CURRAN RO GCURRRO60889
CURTIS E WSIEGAX63572
CUSSLER M WCUSSMX58712
CUTHBERT MV NCUTHMV49936
CUTLER JH WCUTLJH61713
CUTRIGHT P NCUTRPX65245
D-AMICO L NDAMILX64127
DAEDALUS NDAEDXX65246
WDAEDXX64714
DAILEY CA GDAILCA66926
DALTON M NDALTMX51247
DALY VR GDALYVR66625
DANIEL WG NDANIWG62248
NDANIWG63249
DANIEL WG ED NDANIWG63250
DANIELS R ODANIRX61716
ODANIRX66084
DANIELSON WF GBIANJC67590
DANZIG D NDANZDX64468
DARTMOUTH COLLEGE
NDARTCX64309
DARTNELL CORPORATION
GDARTCX47626
DAVID H GDAVIHX65629
JDAVIHX58717
WDAVIHX60715
WDAVIHX60941
DAVID LM NDAVILM64942
DAVID M GDAVIMX64870
GMORGJN62032
DAVID OD WDAVIOD59716
WNOBLJL59035
DAVID OD ED WDAVIOD57044
WDAVIOD59937
DAVIDOFF I WDAVIIX60717
DAVIDS RC IDAVIRC62546
DAVIE MR NDAVIMR49252
DAVIES JH NDAVIJH55253
DAVIS A GDAVIAX63132
NDAVIAX45938
NDAVIAX46254
DAVIS C WDAVICX63718
WDAVICX65719
WDAVICX65720
DAVIS E WDAVIEX64721
DAVIS F WDAVIFX66722
WDAVIFX66723
DAVIS FG WDAVIFG42260
DAVIS G NDAVIJA45259
DAVIS HW MDAVIHW66387
DAVIS IF GDAVIIF58939
DAVIS JA GDAVIJA46628
NDAVIJA42255
NDAVIJA45259
NDAVIJA46257
NDAVIJA46258
NDAVIJA52256
WDAVIJA64724
DAVIS JP NDAVIJP66260
DAVIS K GDAVIKX65663
DAVIS MP WDOLAEF60951
DAVIS NF NDAVINF60312
DAVIS WG GDAVIWG65629
DAY LH WDAYXLH57725
WDAYXLH61726
DC COMMRS COUNCIL ON HUM RELS
GDISTCC66642
DE COLON PP PDECOPP59794
DE NUEFVILLE R NCONNCX66232
DE SHAZO EA GDESHEA66633
DE VOS G OCAUDWX61711
DEAN JP GDEANJP55630
DEAN LR GDEANLR54944
DECKER PM NDECKPM60261
DECTER M CDECTMX61376
DEFENSE SUPPLY AGENCY
GDEFESA64631
DEGLER CN WDEGLCN64727
DEHOYOS A MDEHOAX61388
DELANO PJ WDELAPJ60224
DELAWARE COMT MIGRATORY LABOR
GDELACM58945
DELAWARE SES GDELASE59946
DELMET DT GDELMDT66147
DEMEMT AL WDEMEAL63728
DEMERATH NJ NMCCOWM58062
DEMERATH NJ ED NVANCRB54283
DEMSETZ H GDEMSHX65869
DENISON EF NDENIEF62262
DENNIS LB IDENNLB66547
DENNIS LE WDENNLE63729
DENNY GH GDENNGHND632
DENTON JH NDENTJH64263
DERBIGNY IA NDERBIA46251
DERNBERG T GDERNTX64947
DERNBURG T NDERNTX66264
DES MOINES COMM ON HUM RIGHTS
GDESMCH65635
NDESMCH65265
DESPAIN CW IDESPCW65548
DETROIT COMM COMMUNITY RELS
GDETRCC63638
GDETRCC63948
GDETRCC66639
NDETRCC63267
DEUTSCH M NBLOORX63096
NDEUTMX64268
DEUTSCH MP GDEUTMP56641
GDEUTMP60640
DEUTSCHER I WDEUTIX56730
WDEUTIX57369
WHUGHEC58851
DEVEREUX G WDEVEGX62731
DEWEY D NDEWEDX52270
NDEWEDX55269
NDEWEDX62271
DIAMOND DE NDIAMDE64272
NDIAMDE65273
DIAMOND L WFOXXDJ61767
DIAZ E PDIAZEX61795
DIBROG J WDIBRJX66732
DICKERSON BE MDICKBE65389
DILLINGHAM HC NDILLHCND274
DILLINGHAM WP NDILLWP58275
DIX L GDIXALX46643
DIXON R GDIXORX63644
DIZARD JE NDIZAJE66015
DOAR LE GDOARLE66645
NDOARLE66276
DOBBINS DA NDOBBDA58277
DODD AE NDODDAE45949
DODD EM GDODDEM45646
DODDY HH NDODDHH55950
NDODDHH63278
DODSON DW GDODSDW62647
DOERINGER PB GDOERPB67115
NDOERPB66279
NDOERPB66280
DOLAN EF WDOLAEF56734
WDOLAEF57735
WDOLAEF60951
WDOLAEF63952
WDOLAEF64736
WDOLAEF66733
DOLE AA WDOLEAA64737
DOLL PA WDOLLPA65738
DOLLARD J NDOLLJX49281
DOMESICK SR GMANNRD66937
DONAHUE C GDONACX64648
DONCHIAN D PDONCDX59796
DORAIS M WDORAMX66739
DORIOT GF NDORIGF64282
DORMAN M NDORMMX64953
DORNBUSCH SM CDORNSM56284
NDORNSM56283
DORSEY NW NCHALWE62189
DOUCKER P IDOUCPX63549
DOUGLAS AM WDOUGAM61740
DOUGLAS GV IDOUGGV60550
DOUGLAS JH NDOUGJH64285
NDOUGJH66286
DOUGLAS M GDOUGMX60650
DOUGLASS JH GDOUGJH61649
DOUTY A WDOUTAX62741
DOUVAN E WDOUVEX57742
DOYLE W NDOYLWX62287
DOZIER EP IDOZIEP57077
DRAKE SC NDRAKSC45291
NDRAKSC57290
NDRAKSC63288
NDRAKSC65289
DREGER RM NDREGRM60292
NDREGRM65293
DREW CR NDREWCR50294
DREWS EM WDREWEM61743
DREXEL INST OF TECHNOLOGY
NDREXIT64295
DRIVER HE IDRIVHE57954
DROEGE RC GDVORBJ65656
DU BOIS WE NDUBOWE41298
DUBOIS WEB NDUBOWE43297
NDUBOWE48299
DUCOFF LJ GDUCOLJ57955
MSKRARL62494
DUFFIELD LC MDUFFLC66390
DUFFY J GDUFFJX44522
DUGAN RD GDUGARD66651
DULLES FR NDULLFR49301
DUMMET CO NDUMMCO59302
DUMOND AL NDUMOAL45303
DUMONT RV IWAXXML64683
DUN-S REVIEW AND MOD INDUSTRY
NDUNSRA63310
DUNCAN B NDUNCBX65304
NDUNCOD55307
NDUNCOD57306
DUNCAN OD GDUNCOD63652
NDUNCOD55307
NDUNCOD57306
NDUNCOD59305
DUNKELBERGER J NDUNKJX64300
DUNKELBERGER JE GDUNKJE64653
DUNLOP JT ED GDUNLJT62698
DUNN DD GDUNNDD63654
DUNN ES NDUNNES62308
NDUNNES62309
DUNNE GH GDUNNGH64927
DUNNIGAN AA GDUNNAA62655
DUSCHA J NDUSCJX63311
DVORAK BJ GDVORBJ65650
GDVORBJ65656
DWORKIS MB PDWORMB57797
DWYER RJ NDWYERJ53312
NDWYERJ57956
DYKMAN RA WDYKMRA57745
DYSON RB GDYSORB65657
DYSON ED GDYSORB65657
E HARLEM YOUTH EMPLOY SERVICE
PEASTHY64799
EAGLE M PEAGLMX59303
EAGLESON OW CEAGLOW45313
EAST HARLEM PROJECT
PEASTHP61798
EASTWOOD M WMURRPX65010
EATHERLY BJ NEATHBJ64314
EBOINE A NEBOIAX60315
EBONY NEBONXX59318
NEBONXX63316
NEBONXX64317
ECKARD EW NECKAEW55319
ECKERT RE WECKERE59746
ECKSTEIN O NECKSOX66957
EDDY ED WEDDYED63747
EDELSBERG H GEDELHX63658
NEDELHX66320
EDELSON RB WMEADLX63967
EDMONDSON MS NEDMOMS65321
EDMUNDS ER GEDMUER44495
EDUCATIONAL TESTING SERVICE
GEDUCTS57959
NEDUCTS64322
EDWARDS GF NEDWAGF59324
NEDWAGF64323
NEDWAGF64326
EDWARDS GL NEDWAGL47325
EDWARDS RM NEDWARM61327
EDWARDS VA NEDWAVA42328
EELLS WC NEELLWC55329
EGGAN FR IEGGAFR66552
EHRLE RA GEHRLRA65791
EICHER CK IEICHCK60553
EICHNER AS NGINZEX64414
ELIZABETHTOWN COLLEGE
PELIZCX66031
ELLICKSON K WELLIKX63748
ELLIS DB. GFUCHRS66702
ELLIS GH NELLIGH59330
ELLIS MB IELLIMB57554
ELLMAN M WELLMMX65749
ELLSWORTH JS NELLSJS52331
ELMAN RM PELMARM66677
ELSON A GELSOAX47661
ELTON E CELTOEX63332
ELWARD E GELWAEX58662
EMBRY CB IEMBRCB56555
EMPEY LT WEMPELT58751
WSLOCWL56116
EMPLOYMENT AND EARNINGS
WEMPLAE59752
ENGLISH WH NENGLWH57333
ENION RA NHOMAHL63564
ENNEIS WH GENNEWH67928
EPPLEY MA PELIZCX66031
EPPS E NGURIPX66468
EPPS EG NEPPSEG64336
NEPPSEG65334
NEPPSEG66335
NMONTJB58809
EPSTEIN BR JEPSTBRND719
JEPSTBR58718
EPSTEIN LA NEPSTLA63337
EPSTEIN S WBERRJX63641
ERICKSON RW NERICRW46339
ERIKSON E NERIKEX64338
ERLICH L WCLYMEX59693
ERNST RC IERNSRC59556
EVANS JC NEVANJC43258
NEVANJC56340
EVANS RI GEVANRI62669
EVANS S WEVANSX66753
EWERS JC IEWERJC58557
IEWERJC60816
EYDE LD WEYDELD62754
WEYDELD67223
FACTORY MNGMT AND MAINTENANCE
GFACTMA56670
FACTS ON FILE NFACTOF64341
FAGGET HL NFAGGHL55255
FALCOME NS NFALCNS45342
FALL AG NFALLAG63343
FALTERMAYER EK GFALTEK64031
GFALTEK65032
FANTACI A GFANTAX64671
FARBER SM ED WFARBSM63756
WFARBSM66755
FARMER BM GTOLLGS67974
FARRELL GR NFARRGR65344
FAULKNER HU NFAULHU57345
FAVA SF WFAVASF60757
FAY M WFAYXMX66758
FEARN R GFEARRXND929
FEDERAL BAR JOURNAL
GFEDEBJ62672
FEDERAL REGISTER GFEDERX64673
FEDERAL RESERVE BANK BOSTON
GFEDERB62930
FEDERMAN P NSIEGAI59718
FEERY AB MFEERAB62392
FEILD JG GFEILJG62675
GFEILJG64676
GFEILJG65677
NFEILJG63346
FEIN R NFEINRX65347
NFEINRX65348
NFEINRX66349
FEINBERG B WFEINBX66760
FELDMAN H NFELDHX42351
FELDMAN JA NFELDJA61350
FENTON WN IFENTWN61620
FERGUSON CC GFERGCC64679
FERGUSON ML NFERGML49961
FERGUSON RH GFERGRH65012
FERMAN I GFERMIX60680
FERMAN LA GHABEWX63615
NAIKEMX66865
NFERMLA64353
NFERMLA65352
NFERMLA66790
FERNBACH FL GFERNFL65662
FEY HE IFEYXHE59558
FICHTER JH NFICHJH59464
NFICHJH64867
NFICHJH66789
FIELD B WFIELBX64762
FIELD JC WFIELJC61763
FILIPSKI JE NFILIJE66354
FINE M GFINEMX64681
FINE M ED JFINEMXND720
FINEBERG SA GFINESA49962
FINEGAN TA GBOWEWG65469
WBOWEWGND652
FINLEY O NFINLOX63355
FINLEY OE NFINLOE60356
FIRKEL E WFIRKEX63764
FISH CR IFISHCR66559
FISH L IFISHLX60560
FISHER BR IAMESDW59525
FISHER DA GMAITST59429
FISHMAN L ED GFISHLX66682
FISK UNIV RACE RELS INSTITUTE
GFISKUR51684
FISK UNIVERSITY NFISKUX44357
FITZGERALD K IFITZKXND440
FITZGERALD LE WFITZLE63963
FITZHUGH NH ED NFITZNH63358
FITZPATRICK JP PFITZJP55802
PFITZJP59801
FITZPATRICK R WGROPGL59805
FLACKS R GFLACRX64964
FLAGLER JJ ED WFLAGJJ63130
FLEISCHER BM PFLEIBM61804
PFLEIBM63437
PFLEIBM63803
FLEISCHMAN H GFLEIHX57686
GFLEIHX60685
GFLEIHX65106
NFLEIHX58361
NFLEIHX59359
NFLEIHX59360
FLEMING GJ NHAASFJ46548
FLEMING H NLOTHDX56710
FLEMING HC GFLEMHC63363
NFLEMHC66362
FLEMING JG GFLEMJG46688
GFLEMJG50687
FLINCHER C GFLINCX65120
FLORIDA COUNCIL ON HUMAN RELS
NFLORCO62366
FLORIDA HEALTH NOTES
GFLORHN60689
FLORIDA MANPOWER PROJECT
WFLORMP66326
FLORIDA STATE BOARD HEALTH
GFLORBH59690
FOGEL W CFOGEWX66367
MFOGEWX65393
OFOGEWX66721
FOLEY AS GFOLEAS52692
FOLEY EP NFOLEEP66369
FOLK H GRAABEX64120
FOLSOM FM GFOLSFM54693
FOLSOM MB GFOLSMB64109
FONER PS NFONEPS47370
FONG SLM OFONGSL65722
FOOD EMPLOYERS COUNCIL INC
GFOODECND694
FOOTE J WFOOTJX66765
FORBES J CFORBJX60561
FORD JA GFORDJA63695
GFORDJA65450
FORD FOUNDATION NFORDFX66133
FOREMAN C NFORECX51371
FORM WH ED GNOSOSX62336
FORMAN PB NFORMPB55372
FORSTER A JEPSTBRND719
JEPSTBR58718
JFORSAX63723
FORTUNE GFORTXX40459
GFORTXX50696
GFORTXX54047
GFORTXX59045
MFORTXX59374
NFORTUN45052
NFORTXX42541
NFORTXX43050
NFORTXX49054
NFORTXX55051
NFORTXX56881
NFORTXX57373
FOSTER D WEVANSX66753
FOSTER WZ NFOSTWZ53375
FOWLER G GBENEDX65434
FOWLER GH WFOWLGH65766
FOX DJ WFOXXDJ61767
FOX WM GFOXXWM65697
FRAENKEL OK GFRAEOK60697
FRAKELTON F CFRAKFX66375
FRANKE WH CWILCRC63322
FRANKLIN JH NFRANJH56060
FRANKLIN WH NFRANWH66698
FRAZIER EF NFRAZEF47384
NFRAZEF48379
NFRAZEF50382
NFRAZEF57371
NFRAZEF57378
NFRAZEF57381
NFRAZEF57966

FRAZIER EF ED   NFRAZEF58376
FRAZIER EF ED   NFRAZEF64380
FRAZIER FE   NFRAZEF51578
FRED EB   NBERNEH46077
FREDRICKSON C   WFREDCX61769
FREEDMAN M   GFREEMX60699
FREEDMAN MB   WFREEMB65770
FREEDMAN MK   GBENJJG65006
   GFREEMK64005
FREEDMAN R   NFREERX50967
FREEMAN M
FREIMAN DJ   NHODGRWND355
FRENCH RL   NFRENRL65385
FRENCH WL   GFRENWL66101
FREUND PA   GFREUPA64700
FREYMAN M   NFREYMX66386
FRIEDLAND LL   GFRIELL62701
FRIEND RE   CFRIERE63805
   GFRIERE62431
   GMAITST61383
   GMAITST61384
   MFRIERE63394
FRIERSON M   NFRIERX65387
FRUMKIN RM   NFRUMRM58388
FUCHS EF   WFUCHEF63772
FUCHS RS   GFUCHRS66702
FUERST JS   GFUERJS65703
FUGAL GR   GFUGAGR64704
FUGUITT G   NLEWISX66693
FULLER SB   NFULLSB63390
FULLER V   GFULLVX67931
   MFULLVX56396
FUND FOR THE REPUBLIC INC
   IFUNDFT61562
FUNDLER BL   GPRESSB58126
FURFEY PH   GFURFPH62705
FURNAS JC   GFURNJC52706
FUSFELD DR   NFUSFDR66014
GABEL L   WGABELX66773
GAINES RS   GGAINRL48341
GALARZA E   MGALAEX56400
   MGALAEX66397
GALLAGHER BG   JGALLBG58724
GALLARDO L   MGALLLX62399
GALLAWAY LE   GGALLLE65932
   NGALLLE65391
   NGALLLE66392
   NGALLLE67393
GANS HJ   GGANSHJ65696
GARAI J   GBARNRX62423
GARBIN AP   NGARBAP65394
GARCIA A   PGARCAX58806
GARDEN STATE COOPERATIVE ASSN
   PGARDSC58807
GARDNER BB   GGARDBB57774
GARDNER H   NGARDHX63395
GARFINKEL H   NGARFHX59396
GARFINKLE SH   WGARFSH57180
   WGARFSH57774
GASS GZ   GPEIMSC66139
   WGASSGZ59775
GAVETT EE   MMCELRC65385
GEIGER P   WGEIGPX66776
GEISEL P   NGEISPX62397
GENERAL CABLE CORPORATION
   GGENECC49713
GENERAL ELECTRIC   NGENEEX64398
GENTRY L   WGENTLX60790
GEORGETOWN LAW JOURNAL
   GGEORLJ65714
GEORGIA COUNCIL ON HUMAN RELS
   NGEORCH64399
GERNES AC   PGERNAC56808
GERSH G   NGERSGX65082
GERSHENFELD WJ   NGERSWJ65634
GERSHENSON M   WGERSMX66777
GESCHWENDER JA   NGESCJA64400
GETTELL RG   WGETTRG57778
GETTY HT   IGETTHT58563
   IGETTHT63564
GHISELLI EE   GGHISEE66788
GIANOPULOS A   WGIANAX57779
GIBBS JP   NGIBBJP65401
GIBSON H   GGIBSHX54969
   NGIBSHX54402
GILBERT E   NSAENGX50101
GILBERT R   WGILBRX66780
GILBRAITH KM   GREUSLA60391
   GREUSLA62388
GILBRETH LM   WGILBLM62782
   WGILBLM65781
GILDERSLEEVE GN   WGILDGN59783
GILL LJ   MGILLLJ62401
GILMAN HJ   GGILMHJ63636
   GGILMHJ63716
   GGILMHJ65717
GILMER BV   WGILMBV63970
GILMORE H   CGILMHX44403
   NWILSLX43327
GILMORE NR   MGILMNR62402
GILPATRICK EG   GGILPEG66632
GINSBURG GJ   GGINSGJ61718
GINZBERG E   GGINZEX64972
   NGINZEX51410
   NGINZEX53415
   NGINZEX56409
   NGINZEX58605
   NGINZEX59406
   NGINZEX60404
   NGINZEX60413
   NGINZEX61407
   NGINZEX61411
   NGINZEX64428
   NGINZEX64414
   NGINZEX66412
   NGINZEX66416
   NGINZEX66971
   NGINZEX67417
   WGINZEX62786
   WGINZEX58784
   WGINZEX66785
GINZBERG E ED   CGINZEX60720
GIOVANNINI PC   NGIOVPC64279
GIRARD RA   GGIRARA64721
GISSEN I   NGISSIX65418
GIST NP   NBENNWS64574
   NGISTNP63419
GITLOW AL ED   GGITLAL66134
GITTLER JB   GGITTJB56973

GIVEN JN   WGIVEJN60787
GIVENS RA   GGIVERA65695
GLASGOW RB   GMOOREJ64386
GLAZER N   JGLAZNX60726
   JGLAZNX63725
   NGLAZNX63420
   PGLAZNX58211
   PGLAZNX63909
GLAZIER W   GGLAZWX62866
GLENN EM   WGLENEM66788
GLENN HM   WGLENHM59789
GLENN ND   NBROOLX65123
   NBROOLX65124
   NGLENND62422
   NGLENND63421
   NGLENND63423
   NGLENND64424
   NGLENND65425
   NGLENND65676
GLENNON JR   GALBRLE63368
GLICK CE   GGLICCE47722
GLICK LB   MGLICLB66694
GLICK R   WGLICRX65791
GOFF RM   GGOFFRM54366
GOLANN SE   WMAGOTM66779
GOLDBERG A   GGOLDAX58974
   GGOLDAX62865
GOLDBERG GS   GGOLDGS66360
GOLDBERG MH   GGOLDMH64724
GOLDBERG ML   CGOLDML63426
GOLDBERG N   JGOLDNX62727
GOLDEN H   GGOLDHX58975
GOLDEN J   NGOLDJX65427
GOLDFINGER N   NGOLDNX66428
GOLDKIND V   CGOLDVX60494
GOLDMAN FH   NGOLDFH63430
   WGOLDFH65792
GOLDMAN FH ED   NGOLDFH63429
GOLDMAN MR   WGOLDMR63793
GOLDNER W   MGOLDNX59403
GOLDSBORO SM   NGOLDSM48350
GOLDSMITH SF   GGOLDSF62725
GOLDSTEIN N   CGOLDXX60374
GOLDSTEIN B   GROSORG66258
   WGOLDBX64794
GOLDSTEIN H   GGOLDHX63787
   GGOLDHX66931
GOLDSTEIN MS   NGOLDMS63431
GOLDSTON J   NKATZIX58638
GOLIGHTLY CL   NGOLICL45432
GOLUB F   GGOLUFX55812
GOLUB FT   GGOLUFT56811
GOMBERG W   NLIPSSM62043
GOMBERG W ED   GSHOSAB65685
GONZALEZ HB   MGONZHB63404
GOOD P   NGOODPX66433
GOODE B   NDOYLWX62287
GOODWIN RC   GGOODRC64622
   GGOODRC65726
GOOGE J   NGOOGGX48434
GORDON D   NGORDDX65976
GORDON J   NGORDJX65435
GORDON JB   GJAFFAJ66820
GORDON JE   GGORDJEND975
   GGORDJE65135
   GGORDJE66281
GORDON MM   CGORDMM63977
   NGORDMM64729
GORDON MS   CGORDMS63727
   GGORDMS63723
   GGORDMS65661
   GGORDMS65728
GORDON NS   GSAENGX48273
GORDON RA   GGORDRA64526
   GGORDRA64731
   GGORDRA64735
   GGORDRA65675
GOTSCH JW   PGOTSJW66808
GOULD HM   NGOULHM48436
GOULD J   GGOULJX63732
GOULD WB   NGOULWB64889
   NGOULWB65437
   NGOULWB67864
GOURLAY JC   NGOURJC65438
GOVERS COMM STATUS OF WOMEN
   WGOVECS65798
GOVRS COMMS STATUS OF WOMEN
   WGOVECS66215
GRAF MF   IGRAFMF66565
GRAGG WL   NGRAGWL49978
GRAHAM C   NGRAHCX65439
GRAHAM JC   OGRAHJC57728
GRAND RAPIDS HUMAN RELS COMM
   GGRANRH66733
GRANGER LB   GGRANLB57979
   NGRANLB40980
   NGRANLB41442
   NGRANLB41443
   NGRANLB42440
   NGRANLB58596
   NGRANLB62441
GRANT LJ   WGRANLJ63800
GRAVES RP   MGRAVRP60405
GRAVES TD   IGRAVTDND438
   IGRAVTD64566
   IGRAVTD65567
   IGRAVTD66146
   MGRAVTD67214
GRAVES WB   GGRAVWB48734
   GGRAVWB51735
GRAY CJ   GGRAYCJ51736
GRAY H   WGRAYHX62801
GRAY L   PGRAYLX63027
   PGRAYLX63813
GRAY SW   CGRAYSW47445
   NGRAYSW44446
GREBLER L   WGREBLX66406
GREEN GC   NGREEGC63447
GREEN M   NGREEMX48448
GREENBAUM C   NKATZIX63640
GREENBERG J   GGREEJX59981
GREENBERG L   GGREELX66614
   GGREELX64739
GREENBLUM S   GGREEJX53738
GREENFIELD M   NGREEMX63449
GREENHUT M   NGREEMX64450
GREENLEIGH ASSOCIATES INC
   GGREEAI64479
   GGREEAI65472
   GGREEAI65474
   GGREEAI65480
GREENSPAN H   GGREEHX66627
GREENWALD W   GGREEWX61741
GREER S   NGREESX53453
   NGREESX59451
   NGREESX61452
GREGORY G   GGREGGX61071
   GGREGGX62070
GREGORY P   PGREGPX61857
GREYSON SA   WBOWMGM65653
GRIER E   GGRIEGX64743
GRIER ES   NGRIEES57457
   NGRIEES57503
   NGRIEES58455
   NGRIEES58456
   NGRIEES58458
   NGRIEES63454
   NGRIEGXND982
   NGRIEGX66459
   NGRIEGX64743
GRIER G   NGRIEES57457
   NGRIEES57503
   NGRIEES58455
   NGRIEES58458
   NGRIEGXND982
   NGRIEGX66459
GRIGG C   GKILLLX62853
GRIGG CM   GMIDDRX59573
GRIGSBY SE   NKILLLX64652
   NKILLLX66511
   NYOUMEG65390
GRIMES AP   NGRIMAP64983
GRISHAM G   MGRISGXND408
GROB G   NGROBGX60640
GROOM P   GGROOPX64745
GROPPER JL   WGROPGL59805
GROSS IH ED   WGROSIH56806
GROSS JA   NGROSJA62461
GROSSACK M   NGROSMM57462
GROSSMAN SB   WGROSSB59807
GROVES HE   GGROVHE61744
GRUENBERG SM   MGRUESM57984
GRUMBACH O   WGRUMDX61379
GUBA EG   NGUBAEG59463
GUERNSEY EW   GGUERWX63746
GUERRA I   MGUERIX59409
GUERTIN C   MGUERCX62410
GUHA ME   NGUHAME65464
GUILLORY BM   NGUILBM60465
GUION RM   GGUIORM65693
   GGUIORM66747
GULICK J   IFENTWN61620
   IGULIJX60568
GUNDLACK RH   NGUNDRH50466
GUPTA RC   WGUPTRC66808
   WGUPTRC66809
GURALNICK L   GGURALX62748
GURIN G   GKAHNRL64733
GURIN MG   WGURIMG63810
GURIN P   NGURIPX66352
   NGURIPX66668
GURSSLIN OR   GGURSOR64749
GUSCOTT KI   NGUSCKI63469
GUZMAN JP ED   NGUZMJP47470
GUZMAN R   MGUZMRX65411
   MGUZMRX66412

HAAS FJ   NHAASFJ46548
HAAS TH   ICOLLJX56544
HABBE S   GHABBSX65112
   NHABBSX64473
   NHABBSX65474
   NHABBSX65472
   NHABBSX66472
HABER S   WHABESX58811
   GBECKJX65430
HABER W   GHABEWX54750
   GHABEWX64649
HACKER A   NHACKAX63475
HACKER HM   WHACKHM61812
HADLEY JN   IHADLJN57569
HAGAN JJ   GHAGAJJ63751
HAGAN WT   IHAGAWT61570
HAGER DJ   GHAGEDJ57752
HAGOOD MJ   GDUCOLJ57955
HALE R   GHALERX51754
HALE WH   NHALEWH52476
HALFTER IT   WHALFIT61814
   WHALFIT62813
HALL DE   NHALLDE53477
HALL W   NHALLWX42259
HALL WJ   NHALLWJ63815
HALLER GD   NHALLGD57987
HALLOWELL AI   IHALLAI63571
HAMANSKY LS   IHAMALS57985
HAMEL HR   GBOGAFA64460
HAMELETT ML   NHIMEJX62072
HAMILTON CH   GHAMICH65757
   NHAMICH59986
   NHAMICH64479
HAMILTON H   GSUVAEM65345
HAMILTON HC   NMAYOSC63762
HAMMEL HR   GHAMMHR66145
HAMMER CH   WFUCHEF63767
HAMMER R   PHAMMRX64153
HAMMETT I   GLONDJX54908
HAMMILL K   WHAMMKX56817
HAMMOND B   ISHEPMX64446
HAND H   WHANDHX57818
HANDLIN O   CHANDOX57758
HANEY GE   GHANEGE64004
HANN AS   WODIOGS61042
HANNAH H   GHANNJA61988
HANNETT F   WHANNFX58819
HANSL EB   WHANSEB62802
HANSON DE   WHANSDE64821
HANSON RC   MSIMMOG64491
HAPGOOD H   JHAPGHX65989
HARBISON FH   GBOWEWG65749
   GHARBFH64741
   GHARBFH65660
HARBISON FH ED   GHARBFH66476
HARDING J   NHARDJX52482
HARE N   NHARENX62483
   NHARENX65484
HARGRETT AJ   NHARGAJ65990
HARLEM YOUTH OPPORS UNLTD
   NHARLYO64485
HARLESTON BW   NHARLBW65486
HARMSWORTH HC   IHARMHC61572
HARPER RM   NHARPRM60487
HARPER S   WHARPPX62822
HARRINGTON M   GHARRMX63099
   GHARRMX64759
   GHARRMX64935
   GHARRMX65597
   GHARRMX65659
   GHARRMX66136
   GHARRMX66212
   NHARRMX61490
   NHARRMX65488
   NHARRMX67489
   NHARRMX62823
HARRINGTON TW   WHARRTW65824
HARRIS CV   NHARRCV65491
HARRIS EE   NHARREE66786
HARRIS H   NBACKSX59040
HARRIS L   NBRINWX64116
HARRIS NC   WHARRNC64825
HARRISON E   WHARREX64827
   WHARREX65826
HARRISON EC   NHARREC53493
   NHARREC59492
   NHARREC63367
HARRISON IE   NHARRIE66991
HARRISON LJ   NHARRLJ62494
HARRISON WR   GHARRWRND760
HART JW   NHARTJW64495
   NHARTJW64496
HART VS   IHARTVS63573
HARTE TJ   GFURFPH62705
HARTLEY RE   WHARTRE60828
   WHARTRE61829
   WHARTRE62830
HARTMAN P   GHARTPX58763
   GHARTPX62762
   JHARTPX58730
   JHARTPX63729
HARVARD BUSINESS SCHOOL
   JHARVBS65731
HARVARD LAW REVIEW
   NHARVLR40497
   NHARVLR49498
   NHARVLR62499
   NHARVLR64500
HASTE WH   NHASTWH42466
HATCHETT JF   NHATCJF66648
HATHAWAY DE   GHATHDE67936
   GPERKBX66150
HAUGHTON J   PHAUGJX60814
HAUSER PM   GHAUSPM54764
   NHAUSPM65501
   NHAUSPM66992
HAVEL J   WJAHOMX55879
HAVIGHURST RJ   IHAVIRJ57574
   WHAVIRJ65833
HAWAII DEPT LABOR IND RELS
   GHAWADL64766
   GHAWADL64767
HAWKES ALR   WHAWKAL60834
HAWLEY LT   NHAWLLT55502
HAYDEN RG   MHAYDRG66114
HAYES LJW   NHAYELJ42504
HAYES M   NHAYEMX62506
HAZLITT H   GHAZLHX66523
HEALAS DV   GHEALDV65646
   GHEALDV65647
HEALD H   NHEALHX64306
HEALY AK   WHEALAK63835
HEALY W   WHEALWX66836
HEATH RW   GBIANJC67590
HEBERLE R   NHEBERX46508
   NHEBERX56507
HECHINGER FM   NHECHFX64509
HECKSCHER A   GHECKAX64937
HEDGES JN   WHEDGJN64994
HEER DM   GHEERDM63769
HEIGHT DI   GCHALFX48563
HEIST P   WHEISPX59838
   WHEISPX61841
   WHEISPX62837
   WHEISPX62839
   WHEISPX63840
HELFGOTT BH   PHELFBH59481
HELFGOTT RB   PHELFRB57815
HELLER CS   MHELLCS63414
   MHELLCS64413
   MHELLCS65415
   MHELLCS66416
HELPER CW   GHELPCW63501
HEMPHILL IW   NGOLICL45432
HENDERSON EW   NHENDEW43510
HENDERSON G   NHENDGX67214
   NSCHWMX64110
HENDERSON J   GHENDJM64142
HENDERSON VW   NHENDVW60512
   NHENDVW60516
   NHENDVW61511
   NHENDVW62513
   NHENDVW63514
   NHENDVW66213
   NHENDVW67517
   NLONGHH62706
HENDRIX WE   GHENDWE59422
   GSOUTJH59325
HENNING JF   GHENNJF63278
   GHENNJF63770
HENTOFF N   NHENTNX64518
   NHENTNX65026
HERBERG W   NHERBWX53519
HERLING AK   GHERLAK64771
HERMAN H   GHERMHX64938
HERNANDEZ-ALVAREZ J   PHERNJX59816
HERRING NM   GHERRNM64772
HERSON PF   NHERSPF65520
HERZFELD NK   WHERZNK60377
HERZOG E   NHERZEX63522

HESLET MR GHESLMR63773
NHERZEX66521
WHERZEX64123
HESS RD NHESSRD64523
HETZEL R IHETZTX58575
HETZEL T IHETZTX58575
HEWER VH WHEWEVH64482
HEWES A WHEWEAX62863
HICKEY R GHICKRX66774
HICKS RA NHICKRA66740
HIESTAND D NGINZEX66416
NGINZEX67417
HIESTAND DL CHIESDL64775
HIGBE J GHIGBJX55995
HIGBEE J GHIGBJX67143
HIGHSAW RB ED GHIGHRB65056
HILL FG NHILLFG46524
HILL H GHILLH66691
NDOYLWX62287
NHILLH57533
NHILLH58531
NHILLH58996
NHILLH59529
NHILLH59530
NHILLH59534
NHILLH59543
NHILLH60525
NHILLH60532
NHILLH60542
NHILLH62526
NHILLH62528
NHILLH62535
NHILLH62537
NHILLH62539
NHILLH62547
NHILLH63527
NHILLH63548
NHILLH64550
NHILLH64997
NHILLH65536
NHILLH65540
NHILLH65541
NHILLH65545
NHILLH65549
NHILLH66538
NHILLH66544
NHILLH66546
NLIPSSM62043
WHILLH66844
WWOMEIX66273
HILL H ED NROSSAM67086
HILL M NLEWIHX56073
HILL MC NHILLMC43551
HILL SE GNORGPH64091
HILLIARD CA GBIANJC67590
HILLMAN B WHILLBX62845
HILTON TL GCLEATA66924
HIMES J NHIMEJX61071
NHIMEJX62072
HIMES JS NHIMEJS49553
NHIMEJS51552
NHIMEJS62998
NHIMEJS64554
HIMMELFARB M ED JFINEMXND0720
HINE R GZOOKDX64596
HIRABAYASHI J IHIRAJXND444
HIRD B WMILLKL66980
HIRSCH FI GHIRSFI64776
HOBART CW CHOBACW63555
HODGE P NHODGRW65556
HODGE RW GDUNCOD63652
NHODGRWND355
NHODGRW65556
HODGEN E NHODGEN62557
HODGES EN NCOHEAK63219
HODGES HM
HOFFMAN GL WHOFFGL61846
HOFFMAN H NHOFFHX65558
HOFFMAN LW WHOFFLW63847
WNYEXFI63039
WNYEXFI63040
HOGREFE R NHARDJX52482
HOKANSON JE NHOKAJE60559
HOLDEN A NVALIPX56281
HOLLAND J NHOLLJX65305
HOLLAND JH GHOLLJH58778
NHOLLJH58561
NHOLLJH65560
HOLLAND S MHOLLSX56417
HOLLAND SS GHOLLSS65124
NWETZJR66114
HOLLEMAN JR GHOLLJR61999
HOLLOWAY RG NHOLLRG59562
HOLLUM WE NHOLLWE61418
HOLMES A NHOLMAX66563
HOMAN HL NHOMAHL63564
HOOS IR WHOOSIR60000
WHOOSIR61848
HOPE J GHOPEJX64485
GHOPEJX49781
GHOPEJX51782
GHOPEJX51783
GHOPEJX61002
GHOPEJX61780
NHOPEJX52571
NHOPEJX53567
NHOPEJX53574
NHOPEJX54566
NHOPEJX55572
NHOPEJX56570
NHOPEJX56575
NHOPEJX60569
NHOPEJX60573
NHOPEJX63568
NHOPEJX63576
HORTON R NHORTRX64291
HOSLEY EM WHOSLEM64540
HOUSE EW GKAUFJJ67940
GKAUFJJ67963
HOUSTON L NHOUSLX65577
HOWARD UNIV GRAD SCH DIV SSC
NHOWAUG44579
HOWDEN E GBABOIX58606
GHOWDEX65785
NBABOIX58893
HOWE I NHOWEIX49581
HOWE RW NHOWERW56442
HOYER HC MHOYEHC64419
HOYT DP WHOYTDP58850
HOYT GC WSUJAWW58144
HUDDLE FP GHUDDFP46786

HUDSON B GSIMPDX64312
HUDSON JC GBEALCL64423
HUDSON JP GHABEWX63615
HUGHES EC GHUGHEC59787
NHUGHEC46584
NHUGHEC46586
NHUGHEC63585
WHUGHEC58851
HUGHES EJ NHUGHE J56583
HUGHES HM WHUGHEC58851
HUGHES WH NHUGHWH48587
HUMAN ORGANIZATION
IHUMAOX61820
HUMMEL DL GBRIGWA62473
HUMPHREY HH GHUMPHH64739
GHUMPHH65788
GHUMPHH66003
IHUMPHH66003
HUND JM NYOUNHB64346
HUNT DE GHUNTOE66939
HUNTER G ED NHUNTGX65588
HUNTINGTON EH WHUNTEH62271
HUNTON H GHUNTHX63789
HURST RL NHURSRL56253
HURT WR IHURTWR66576
HUSON CF NHUSOCF66328
HUTCHINS G CHUTCGX52589
HUTCHINSON J NHUTCJXND590
HUYCH EE GHUYCEE65790
HYMAN HH NHYMAHH56591
HYMEN B NBAROHX66055
IFFERT RE WIFFERE57854
IGA M OIGAXMX57732
ILL GOVR-S COMT ON UNEMPLOY
GILLIDI62004
ILL STATE CHAMBER OF COMMERCE
GILLISC56803
ILLICH I PILLIIX56818
ILLINOIS BUR EMPLOY SECURITY
WILLIBE64330
ILLINOIS COMM ON HUMAN RELS
GILLICH55792
GILLICH56794
GILLICH57793
GILLICH61791
ILLINOIS DEPARTMENT OF LABOR
GILLIDI62004
ILLINOIS FEPC GILLIFEND795
ILLINOIS GOVRS COMT UNEMPLOY
GILLIGC62799
GILLIGC63798
ILLINOIS INTERRACIAL COMM
GILLIIR48801
ILLINOIS LEGISLATIVE COUNCIL
GILLILC57802
IMMACULATE SISTER MARY
MIMMASM57420
IMSE TP PIMSETP62820
INDIANA CIVIL RIGHTS COMM
GINOICRND804
GINDICR61806
INDUSTRIAL BULLETIN
GINDUBX51811
GINDUBX57812
WINDUBX63857
WINDUBX65858
INDUSTRIAL RELATIONS PANEL
NINDURP66593
INDUSTRIAL RELS RESEARCH ASSN
GINDURR59814
GINDURR61813
INGERMAN S NSTRAGX65182
INGLE DJ NINGLDJ64067
INGRAM L WINGRLX66859
INST OF PUBLIC ADMINISTRATION
CINSTOP66034
INSTITUTE OF LIFE INSURANCE
GKALICB66012
INTERNATIONAL LABOUR CONF
GINTELC58817
INTERNATIONAL LABOUR OFFICE
WINTELO60862
INTERNATIONAL LABOUR REVIEW
WINTELR56871
WINTELR57867
WINTELR58864
WINTELR58869
WINTELR60870
WINTELR61868
WINTELR62865
WINTELR64866
INTERNATL CITY MANAGERS ASSN
GINTECM63816
INTERNATL LABOUR ORGANIZATION
WINTELO64863
INTL ASSN PERSONNEL WOMEN
WINTEAP58861
IOWA GOVRS COMM STATUS WOMEN
WIOWAGC64796
WIOWAGC64797
IOWA LAW REVIEW WIOWALR65102
IRISH LD WIRISLD62874
ISAACSON LE WISAALE57875
ISAMBERT-JAMUTI V
WISAMVX62876
IVES LM GIVESLM52819
JACKSON EG NJACKEG57070
JACKSON J NJACKJX51595
NJACKJX66641
JACKSON PW NGUBAEG59463
JACKSON TA NJACKTA66597
JACKSONVILLE CC SOC AGENCIES
NJACKCC46598
JACOB PE WJACOPE57877
JACOBOWSKY N WFOXXDJ61767
JACOBS P GJACOPX66527
GJACOPX63601
NJACOPX63602
NJACOPX67599
JAFFE AH WJAFFAH56878
JAFFE AJ GFIFTAJ66890
JAFFE LL GGIRARA64721
JAHODA M WJAHOMX55879
JAMES JH GHAGAJJ63751
JAMESON SM CJAMIRW46003
JANSSEN PA NJANSPA66603
JAVITS JK NJAVIJK60006
JEFFREY A GJEFFAX63822
JELTZ MM GJELTMM64823

JENKINS H NJENKHX47605
JENKINS MD NJENKMD48607
NJENKMD48608
NJENKMD50606
JENSEN JJ GJENSJJ66785
JEWISH EMPLOY AND VOCAT SERV
NJEWIEA64609
JEWISH EMPLOY VOCAT SERVICE
GJEWIEV65568
JEWISH LABOR COMMITTEE
GJEWILCND824
JEWISH VACATION ASSOCIATION
WJEWIVA61880
WJEWIV62881
WJEWIV62882
WJEWIV62883
JOHNPOLL BK NDOYLWX62287
JOHNS HOPKINS UNIVERSITY
NJOHNHU63735
JOHNSON NJOHNXX63336
JOHNSON CS NJOHNCS41611
NJOHNCS42544
NJOHNCS42550
NJOHNCS43008
NJOHNCS43617
NJOHNCS44612
NJOHNCS44615
NJOHNCS47007
NJOHNCS49613
NJOHNCS49616
NJOHNCS54614
JOHNSON GG WJOHNGG65884
JOHNSON GW GJOHNGW50825
JOHNSON HG NJOHNHG65826
JOHNSON JG NJOHNJG60618
JOHNSON MW GJOHNMW65827
JOHNSON RA NJOHNRA44620
NJOHNRA57619
JOHNSON T NJOHNTX65621
JOHNSTON DF GCOOPSX64743
JOHNSTON HL GLINDJR66603
JOHNSTON OF GCOOPSX66604
JONES AM NJONEAM65622
JONES BA NJONEBA66884
JONES BM MJONEBM62421
JONES ER NJONEER48343
JONES JA NJONEJAND738
JONES JE NJONEJE51883
JONES LB MJONELB65318
JONES LW NJONELW60010
JONES LW ED NJONELW50623
JONES M GJONEMX64829
JORGENSON J CBURMJH60371
JORGENSON JM MJORGJM60422
NJORGJM62624
JOSEPH A ITHOMLX65632
JOURNAL OF INDUSTRIAL RELS
WJOUROI62883
JOURNAL OF NEGRO EDUCATION
NJOURNE63626
NJOURNE65625
NJOURNE66627
JOURNAL OF NEGRO MEDICAL ASSN
NJOURNM52628
JOURNAL OF SOCIAL ISSUES.
NJOUROS53891
KAHL JA GKAHLJA57831
KAHN RL GKAHNRL64733
KAHN SD GKAHNSD65011
KAHN T NKAHNTX64629
KAIN JF NKAINJF64631
NKAINJF64630
KALISH CB GKALICB66012
KAMII CK CKAMICKND632
KAMMHOLZ T GKAMMTX65832
KAMOMHOLZ TC NKAMOTCND633
KANE NO GKANERD66863
KANSAS CITY COMM ON HUM RELS
GKANCIC62840
KANSAS CITY URBAN LEAGUE
NKANCIU40634
KAPLAN FB ED WMEADMX65966
KAPLAN J NKAPLJX66645
KAPP L NKAPPLX63635
KARRAKER CH NKARRCHND636
KART W GKARTWX67215
KARTER T NORSHMX61961
KASUN M CKASUMX59013
KATZ D NGURIPX66352
KATZ I NEPPSEG64336
NKATZIX58638
NKATZIX60639
NKATZIX63640
NKATZIX64637
KAUFER SF GKAUFSF64841
KAUFFMAN D WKAUFDX66886
KAUFMAN JJ GKAUFJJ67940
GKAUFJJ67963
KAUFMANN ET GKAUFET58014
KAYE C WDOUVEX57742
KEENAN V GKEENVX52015
KEENEY BC WKEENBC62887
KELLEY ET WKELLET66888
KELLEY KP NKELLKP66641
KELLOGG PL NKELLPL66734
KELLY TA NWOFFBM55333
KELLY WH IKELLWH57076
IKELLWH65877
IKELLWH67579
KEMPTON M NKEMPMX65293
KENDLER B WKENDBX65225
KENNEDEY TH NKENNTH54273
KENNEDY CE WHOYTDP58850
KENNEDY JF GKENNJF63842
GKENNJF63016
KENNEDY RD NKENNRF66017
KENNEDY V NKENNVX66890
KENNEDY VD NKENNVD63642
KENNISTON E WKENNKX64891
KENNISTON K WKENNKX64891
KENRICK SM WGRIFAM65803
KENTUCKY COMM ON HUMAN RIGHTS
GKENTHN60844
NKENTCH66643
KEPHART WM NKEPHWM54543

KERCKHOFF AC IKERCAC59018
KERN KK WBERRJX66642
WKERNKK65892
KERNS JH NKERNJH50644
NKERNJH51897
NKERNJH57645
KERR WA GKEENVX52015
KERR DM CDORNSM56284
KERSHAW JA GKERSJA66733
GKERSJA66941
KESSELMAN LC GKESSLC48847
GKESSLC56846
KESSLER MA GKESSMA63848
NKESSMA63019
KETCHAM WA GKETCWA65849
GKETCWA66942
KEYSERLING LH GKEYSLH64862
GKEYSLH64943
KEYSERLING MD CKEYSMD65646
WKEYSMD64894
WKEYSMD64898
WKEYSMD64899
WKEYSMD64900
WKEYSMD65021
WKEYSMD65644
WKEYSMD65893
WKEYSMD65895
WKEYSMD66896
WKEYSMD66901
KHEEL TW GKHEETW62852
GKHEETW63850
GKHEETW64851
KIBRICK AK WKIBRAK58902
KIEHL R NKIEHRX58647
NKIEHRX58648
NKIEHRX64333
KIFER A NKIFEAX64649
KILGALLON JJ GGREEHX66627
KILLIAN JR WKILLJR65903
KILLIAN L GKILLLX62853
KILLIAN LM NKILLLM52650
NKILLLM64652
NKILLLM65651
KILLINGSWORTH CC GKILLCC63755
GKILLCC66800
NKILLCC67653
KILLINGSWORTH CC ED GKILLCC62861
KIMMEL PR GKIMMPR66137
KINCH J GROSETXND250
KING AG WKINGAG56905
WKINGAG63904
KING CR WKINGCR66906
KING HC NYOUMEG65390
KING ML NKINGML62144
NKINGML64022
KING RL GKINGRL60854
KINZER RH NKINZRH50654
KIRSTEIN GC GKIRSGC64860
KISSINGER B GWALLPX66539
KITAGAWA D OKITADX65734
KITSUSE JI OBROOLX55708
KITTREDGE RE WKITTRE60313
KLEIN B AND CO IKLEIBA67899
KLEIN V WKLEIVX65908
KLEINER RJ NKLEIRJ62655
NPARKSX64973
KLINEBERG O JKLINOX58735
NKLINOX63657
KLINEBERG O ED NKLINOX44656
KLUCKHOHN F WKIUCFX62909
KNIGHT OB NKNIGOB65035
KNIGHT R GBENEDX65434
WKNIGRX61910
KNIGHT TF WKNIGTF66911
KNILSEN NO WKNILNO60034
KNOWLTON CS MKNOWCS61424
MKNOWCS66423
KOHLER MC GKOHLMC62855
KOHN ML GKOHNML56145
KOHRS EV GMETZJH65119
KOLKO G GKOLKGX62690
KOMAROVSKY M WKOMAMX62912
KONOPKA G WKONOGX66913
KONVITZ MR GKONVMR47856
GKONVMR61477
KOOS EL GKOOSEL57691
KOPP RW GKOPPRW65858
KORBEL J WKORBJX63435
KORNHAUSER WA NKORNWA50660
NKORNWA52661
NKORNWA53659
KOSA J WKOSAJX64915
KOSS JD PKOSSJD65822
KOSSORIS MD GBOKXDX64737
KOTHE CA ED GKOTHCA65732
KOVAL M GVOGAAS62074
KOVARSKY I GKOVAIX58026
GKOVAIX58860
GKOVAIX63025
NKOVAIX64663
NKOVAIX65024
KRAMER JR JKRAWJR61736
KRASS BM CPETEOL64988
KRASS E CSHANLW63122
KRASS EM CSHANLW64486
KRASSOWSKI W MKRASWX63425
KRAUT AI GKAHNRL64733
KRECH HS WGRUESM57984
WKRECHS65381
KREPS J WKREPJX64916
KRISLOV S NKRISSX67143
NKRISSX67665
KRONER JL GKRONJL65861
KRUEGER AO GKRUEAO63862
NKRUEAO63666
KRUG RE GKRUGRE64946
GKRUGRE66863
NKRUGRE64731
KRUGER DH GHABEWX64649
GKRUGHND865
GKRUGHD65628
GKRUGHD66864
IKRUGDH67811
NKRUGDH61667
WKRUGDH60917
WKRUGDH64918

Entry	Code(s)
	GMICFEA57979
MICHIGAN FEPC	GMICFEP60980 / GMICFEP61982 / GMICFEP61983 / GMICFEP63981 / NNICFEP58778 / NMICFEP63777
MICHIGAN LAW REVIEW	NMICLRX66068
MID ATLANTIC REGIONAL CONF	WMIDDAR65190
MIDDLETON R	GMIDDRX59573
MIDWEST REGIONAL PILOT CONF	WMIDOWRP65209
MIHLON LF	NMIHLLF62779
MILLER AS	GMILLAS55985 / NMILLAS57069
MILLER EW ED	NMILLEW66129
MILLER FC	IMILLFC64590
MILLER GW	GMILLGW64986 / NMILLGW64070
MILLER HH	NMILLHH60780
MILLER HP	GMILLHP55988 / GMILLHP63987 / GMILLHP64853 / GMILLHP65656 / GMILLHP65952 / GMILLHP66778 / NMILLHP62781 / NMILLHP63785 / NMILLHP64784 / NMILLHP65782 / NMILLHP65783 / NMILLHP66630
MILLER HP ED	GMILLHP66989
MILLER JA	GCOUSFR66478
MILLER JE	NMILLJE48250
MILLER JJ	WMILLJJ66979
MILLER JN	NMILLJN66787
MILLER KL	WMILLKL66980
MILLER KS	NDREGRM60292 / NDREGRM65293
MILLER L	NMILLLX63788
MILLER MM	WMILLMM61981
MILLER R	GMILLRX66020 / GMILLRX66021 / WMILLRX66982
MILLER SM	GMILLSM62354 / GMILLSM62570 / GMILLSM64071 / GMILLSM64727 / GMILLSM65953 / NMILLSM65789 / NMILLSM65790
MILLET GJ	NMILLGJ65791
MILLIKEN R	WMILLRX61983
MILLS AU	GRODOAL64241
MILLS DL	NVOLLHM66287
MILWAUKEE COMM ON COM RELS	NMILWCC63792
MILWAUKEE URBAN LEAGUE.	NMILWUL48793
MINARD RD	NNINARD52794
MINCER J	WMINCJX60985 / WMINCJX62984
MINDLIN A	NMINDAX66795
MINER JB	NMINEJB57796
MING WM	GCOUNVX65610
MINIKINS BC	NMINIBC65797
MINN GOVRS INTER-RACIAL COMM	NMINNGI45798 / NMINNGI49799
MINN STATE COMM AGAINST DISCR	GMINNSCND010
MINNEAPOLIS COM WELFARE CC	IMINLWC56545
MINNEAPOLIS MAYORS HUM RELS	GMINLMH65002
MINNESOTA LAW REVIEW	NMINNLR58800
MINNIS MS	IMINNMS63218
MINSKY H	GMINSHX65655
MINSKY J	GMINSJX65012
MIRENGOFF W	GMIREWX57499
MIRES M	GMIREMX59013
MISSOURI COMM ON HUM RIGHTS	GMISSCH63022 / NMISSCH60802 / NMISSCH64801
MISTER M	GFEILJG65677
MITCHAM JA	GMITCJA52016
MITCHEL JP	NMITCJP64295
MITCHELL B	GMITCBX57017
MITCHELL ED	WMITCED57986
MITCHELL HE	WGIANAX57779
MITCHELL HR	GMITCHR66018
MITCHELL JP	GMITCJP59954 / GMITCJP64277
MITCHELL LE	NMITCLE57804
MITTELBACH FG	MMITTFG66444
MITTLEBACH FG	CMITTFG66777
MITTLEBACH FG	MMITTFG66442
MOBILIZATION FOR YOUTH	CMOBIFY66024 / NMOBIFY62263 / PMOBIFYND024
MOBILIZATION FOR YOUTH INC	GMOBIFY65025
MODERN INDUSTRY	NMODEIX45805
MOED M	GMOEDMX66852
MOHR FT	NMOHRFT54806
MOLINAR RL	NMOLIRL66807
MOLLENKOPF WG	WSTICGX56141
MONDALE W	IMONDWX66591
MONISON A	NMONIAX65808
MONSERRAT J	PMONSJX57828
MONSOUR KJ	WMONSKJ63987
MONTAGUE JB	NMONTJB58809
MONTEZ P	NMONTPX60443
MONTROSS H	PMONTHX60830
MONTROSS HK	PMONTHK65829
MOONEY JD	GMOONJD66726
MOONEY JD ED	GHARBFH66448
MOORE BM	WRAMSGV63104
MOORE DG	GGARDBB55707
MOORE EJ	GMOOREJ64030 / GMOOREJ64386
MOORE J	MGUZMRX65411
MOORE JW	MMOORJW66444
MOORE PL	NMOORPL54079
MORAIS HM	NBOYERO55105
MORALES D	MMORADX63445
MORAN M	WMORAMX66995
MORGAN CA	GMORGCA57031
MORGAN DD	WMORGDD62996
MORGAN GD	NMORGGD62849
MORGAN J	NMORGJX62850 / WMORGJX65997
MORGAN JN	GMORGJN62032
MORGAN P	CSHANLW66123
MORGAN S	NMORGSX59851
MORRILL RL	NMORRRL65852
MORRIS LB	NEDWARM61327
MORRIS MM	WMORRMM66998
MORROW JJ	NMORRJJ57853 / NMORRJJ57854
MOSBACHER WB	WMOSBWB57999
MOSES E	WMOSEEX65000
MOSKOS CC	NMOSKCC66855
MOSS JA	NMOSSJA60857 / NMOSSJA61858 / NMOSSJA62856
MOTHERAL JR	GMOTHJR54405
MOTHERS WORKING ALONE	WMOTHWA66001
MOTLEY AW	GMOTLAW53033
MOTLEY CB	NMOTLCB66859
MOTZ AB	WMOTZAB61002
MOUNT HS	WMOUNHS64003
MOYNIHAN DP	JGLAZNX63725 / NGLAZNX63420 / NMOYNDP65860 / NMOYNDP65861 / NMOYNDP65862 / NMOYNDP65863
MUELLER E	NMUELEX66864
MUELLER EL	WMUELEL66004
MUELLER WR	NMUELWR45865
MULFORD RH	GMULFRH66116
MULLER LC	WMULLLC60005
MULLER OG	WMULLOG60005
MULVEY MC	WMULVMC63006
MUNOZ RF	MMUNORF57446
MUNTZ EE	WMUNTEE56007
MURPHY MC	WMURPMC60009
MURPHY RJ ED	NMURPRJ66866
MURRAY P	WMURRPX65010
MURRAY P ED	GMURRPX50034
MURRAY PM	NMURRPM55867
MUSE B	NMUSEBX64868 / NMUSEBX64869
MUSEUM OF THE PLAINS INDIANS	IMUSEPI57593
MYERS CA	GHARBFH64741
MYERS GC	WMYERGC64011
MYRDAL A	WMYRDAX56012
MYRDAL G	GMYRDGX63035 / WMYRDGX64851 / WMYRDGX64955 / NMYRDGX44870 / NMYRDGX48871
MYRICK R	WMYRIRX66013
N CAROLINA GOOD NEIGHBOR CC	GNORTCG64121
N CAROLINA S BRD PUB WELFARE	CNORTCS59934
NAACP	GAMERJC53388
NAACP NATL LEGAL COMMITTEE	GNAACNL45036
NACHMANN B	WGURIMG63810
NAIRO	GNATLAI49038 / NNATLAI55872
NAIRO COMM ON MANPOWER	GNATLAM60037
NALL F	MNALLFX59447
NAM CB	GCOWHJD61427
NAPIER A	INAPIAX58594
NASH P	INASHPX62595 / INASHPX62596 / INASHPX64134 / INASHPX64597
NATION	NNATIXX52873
NATIONAL CATHOLIC WELFARE CON	MNATLCBND082
NATIONAL CC OF CHURCHES	GNATLCRND046
NATIONAL EDUCATION ASSN	GNATLEA56047 / GNATLEA62126 / GNATLEA64019
NATIONAL JEWISH MONTHLY	JNATIJM63748
NATIONAL MANPOWER COUNCIL	GNATLMC54876
NATIONAL MEDICAL FELLOWSHIPS	NNATLMF52877 / NNATLMF62878
NATIONAL NEGRO CONGRESS	NNATLNC45879
NATIONAL PLANNING ASSN	NNATLPA55881
NATIONAL SHARECROPPERS FUND	NNATLSFND882 / NNATLSF61883
NATIONAL URBAN LEAGUE	GNATLULND085 / GNATLUL65084 / NNATLUL44900 / NNATLUL45896 / NNATLUL46891 / NNATLUL46894 / NNATLUL47904 / NNATLUL48903 / NNATLUL49895 / NNATLUL55901 / NNATLUL60899 / NNATLUL61885 / NNATLUL61898 / NNATLUL62083 / NNATLUL62886 / NNATLUL64887 / NNATLUL64890 / NNATLUL64892 / NNATLUL65884 / NNATLUL65889 / NNATLUL66888
NATL BUREAU OF EC RESEARCH	GNATLBE66611
NATL CATH CC SPANISH-SPEAKING	MNATLCA63081
NATL CC FOR A PERMANENT FEPC	GNATLCS45045
NATL CC OF ADMV WOMEN IN ED	WNATLCO65016
NATL CC OF WOMEN OF THE US	WNATLCP61018
NATL COM RELS ADVISORY CC	GNATLCJ48040
NATL COMM TECH AUTOM EC PRGR	GNATLCO66897 / GNATLCO66898 / GNATLCT66602 / GNATLCT66848 / GNATLCT66849 / GNATLCT66850
NATL COMT CHILDREN YOUTH	GNATLCC61039
NATL COMT ON HOUSEHOLD EMPLOY	WNATLCH66014 / WNATLCH66015
NATL CONF CHRISTIANS AND JEWS	GNATLCL49042 / GNATLCL54041
NATL CONF ON SOCIAL WELFARE	GNATLCN55044
NATL FEDN CONSTL LIBERTIES	GNATLFC46048
NATL INDUSTRIAL CONF BOARD	GNATLIC65593 / NNATLIC43921 / NNATLIC64231 / NNATLIC65874
NATL LABOR RELATIONS BOARD	NNATILR58875
NATL LABOR SERVICE	GNATLLS55051 / GNATLLS57049 / GNATLLS63050
NATL MANPOWER COUNCIL	GNATLMC55052 / GNATLMC66956
NATL OPINION RESEARCH CENTER	NNATLOR66880
NATL SCIENCE FOUNDATION	NNATLSF61022
NATL SECRETARIES ASSN	WNATLSA65023
NATL SHARECROPPERS FUND	GNATLSF57299
NAVAJO TRIBE PR AND INFO DEPT	INAVATP64598
NAVILLE P	GNAVIPX57007
NEAL EE	NNEALEE50905
NEBRASKA LAW REVIEW	GNEBRLR62086
NEBRASKA LEGISLATIVE COUNCIL	NNEBRLC51906
NEISSER EG	GNEISEG63054
NELSON E	WNELSEX66020
NELSON HJ	NCALEWC56069
NELSON RJ	GNELSRJ52055
NETTING RM ED	INETTRM60599
NEUBECK G	WHEWEVH64482
NEUBERGER M	WNEUBMX66024
NEUGARTEN BL	WNEUGBL59025
NEUMAN RR	WNEUMRR63026
NEW JERSEY COMM CIVIL RIGHTS	GNEWJDE64059
NEW JERSEY DEPT OF EDUCATION	GNEWJDE51060
NEW JERSEY SES	PNEWJSE63831
NEW POLITICS	NNEWXPX62910
NEW UNIVERSITY THOUGHT	NNEWXUT63088
NEW YORK BAR ASSOCIATION	GNEWYCB53069
NEW YORK CHAMBER OF COMMERCE	GNEWYCA64068
NEW YORK CITY BOARD OF ED	PNEWYCC56834 / PNEWYCC58833 / PNEWYCC64832
NEW YORK CITY DEPT OF WELFARE	PNEWYDW60835
NEW YORK LAW FORUM	GNEWYLF60075
NEW YORK LAW JOURNAL	GNEWXYL51100
NEW YORK STATE	GNEWYSX63087
NEW YORK URBAN LEAGUE	CPROJAX66237
NEWCOMB MR	GNEWCMR66163
NEWCOMB WW	INEWCWW56600
NEWCOMER M	WNEWCMX59027 / WNEWCMX64028
NEWMAN OK	NNEWMDK60957 / NNEWMDK65908 / NNEWMDK65909
NEWSWEEK	NNEWSXX63912 / NNEWSXX66911 / NNEWSXX64913 / NNEWSXX66029
NEWSYEAR EDS	NFACTOF64341
NEWTON IG	NNEWTIG62915
NICHOLLS WH	NNICHWH60322
NICHOLS L	NNICHLX54920
NICHOLS RC	WASTIAW64620
NICHOLSON LE	NNICHLE52922
NICOL HG	WNICOHG64032
NIEMEYER J	WNIEMJX58033
NIXON RA	GNIXORA66847
NIXON RM	GNIXORM56117
NJ DEPT LABOR AND INDUSTRY	CNEWJDL61907
NOBBE CE	CSCHMCF65107
NOBLE JL	CNOBLJL54924 / CNOBLJL55925 / CNOBLJL66923 / WNOBLJL59035
NOLAND EW	NNOLAEW49928 / NNOLAEW53926 / NNOLAEW65927
NORGREN PH	GNORGPH62120 / GNORGPH64091 / GNORGPH64119 / NNORGPH40930 / NNORGPH59932 / NNORGPH62931 / NNORGPH67929
NORMAN A	MNORMAX56448
NORRIS LW	WNORRLW56036
NORSWORTHY DR	NSIMPRL65140
NORTH RD	NNORTRD56935
NORTHERN MICHIGAN UNIVERSITY	WHICDLA64976
NORTHRUP HR	GBLOOGF65885 / GNORTHR47123 / GNORTHR52122 / NBLOOGF50095 / NNORTHR43941 / NNORTHR43942 / NNORTHR44943 / NNORTHR44944 / NNORTHR45946 / NNORTHR45948 / NNORTHR46947 / NNORTHR46945 / NNORTHR47939 / NNORTHR49936 / NNORTHR49940 / NNORTHR64937 / NNORTHR67938 / WNORTHR64037
NORTHRUP HR ED	NNORTHR65949
NORTHWESTERN UNIV LAW REVIEW	GNORTUL65672
NORTHWOOD LK	NNORTLK65950
NORTON MT	GNORTMT45124
NOSOW S ED	GNOSOSX62336
NOTRE DAME LAWYER	GNORTDL64093
NUTTALL RL	NNUTTRL46951
NY GOVRS COMT ED EMP WOMEN	WNEWYGW64799
NY STATE COMM AGAINST DISCR	GNEWYSAND084 / GNEWYSA47107 / GNEWYSA48078 / GNEWYSA52102 / GNEWYSA54077 / GNEWYSA57086 / GNEWYSA58076 / GNEWYSA58079 / GNEWYSA58081 / GNEWYSA58082 / GNEWYSA58089 / GNEWYSA58101 / GNEWYSA59083 / GNEWYSA60919 / NNEWYSA58836 / PNEWYSA58837
NY STATE DEPARTMENT OF LABOR	GNEWYSE58109 / GNEWYSE60108 / GNEWYSE60110 / PNEWYSE57840 / PNEWYSE60839
NY STATE DIVISION FOR YOUTH	CNEWYSD62090
NYBROTEN N	IHARMHC61572
NYBROTEN N ED	INYBRNX64603
NYC COMM ON HUMAN RIGHTS	CNEWYCO64916 / CNEWYCO64917 / PEASTHP61798
NYC DEPT COMMERCE PUB EVENTS	PNEWYDC56817
NYE FI	WNYEXFI63038 / WNYEXFI63039 / WNYEXFI63040
NYS COMM FOR HUMAN RIGHTS	GNEWYSBND106 / GNEWYSB62103 / GNEWYSB63105 / GNEWYSB64104 / PNEWYCO62838
NYS DIRECTOR INDIAN SERVICE	INEWYSF56601
NYS IDEPTL COMM FARM AND FOOD	GNEWYSJND113 / GNEWYSJ63112
NYS IDEPTL COMT INDIAN AFFAIR	INEWYSI64602
NYS JOINT LEGV COMT MIG LAB	GNEWYSLND115
NYU CENT STUDY UNEMP YOUTH	GNEWYUC66116
NYU GRAD SCHOOL OF SOC WORK	WNYUYUG66031
O NEILL BP	WONEIBP65043
O SHAUGHNESSY JB	NOSHAJB54964
O SHEA	NOSHEJX65965
O-CONNER WB	NOCONWB41094
O-DELL JH	NODELJH64953
O-HARA RP	WTIEDDV58154
OAK VV	NOAKXVV49952
OATES JF	GOATEJF64542
ODIORNE GS	WODIOGS61042
OECD	WORGAEC64045
OHIO CIVIL RIGHTS COMMISSION	GOHIOCR62132 / GOHIOCR64129 / GOHIOCR65125 / GOHIOCR66126 / GOHIOCR66127 / GOHIOCR66128 / NOHIOCR66605
OHIO GOVRS COMM CIVIL RIGHTS	GOHIOGC62095
OKUN A	GOKUNAX65133
OLANSKY H	NOLANHX43954
OLESEN VL	WDAVIFX66723
OLIVER LW	NOLIVLW56955
OLIVER W	GOLIVWX60134
OOKER RE	WKOSAJX64915
OPINION RESEARCH CORPORATION	NOPINRC51959

NOPINRC56956
NOPINRC63958
NOPINRC64957
OPPENHEIM DB NROBESO66961
OPPENHEIMER VK WOPPEVK66096
WOPPEVK66289
OREGON BUREAU OF LABOR
GOREGBLND135
GOREGBLND138
GOREGBLND139
ORGANISATION EC COOP DEVEL
GORGAEC64776
ORNATI AO GORNAOA67138
ORNATI OA GORNAOA64140
GORNAOA64958
GORNAOA66320
ORSHANSKY M GORSHMX63141
GORSHMX65142
GORSHMX65144
GORSHMX65959
GORSHMX66280
GORSHMX66282
GORSHMX66642
NORSHMX61961
NORSHMX64960
ORTIQUE CF NORTICF56962
ORTIZ M MORTIMX62449
ORTIZ R PORTIRX62841
OSBORNE EM CCARNME62183
OSBORNE GR NOSBOGR62460
OSBORNE HW GBERTAL59393
GPRICPH58395
OSBURN DD NOSBUDD66963
OTTLEY R NOTTLRX45966
OVERVIEW NOVERX61967
OWENS JA NOWENJA61968
OXLEY LA NOXLELA40969
PA GOVRS COMM IND RACE RELS
GPENNGC53159
PA STATE EMPLOYMENT SERVICE
GPENNSE65641
PADFIELD H MPADFHX65450
PADILLA E PPADIEX58842
PAGE D NPAGEDX66970
PAGE DA GPAGEDA64775
PALEY HA CPALEHA63098
PALLONE NJ NPALLNJ65332
PALMER EN GPALMEN47145
NPALMEN47971
PALMORE E GPALMFX63671
PALMORE ER NPALMER55972
PALMQUIST G WPALMGX66047
PAREDES A MPAREAX63451
PARENTON VJ NPELLRJ62981
PARIGI SF MPARISF64452
PARK R WPARKRX66049
PARKER S NPARKSX64973
PARKINSON R NPARKRX48974
PARRISH CH NPARRCH63975
PARRISH JA GPARRJA66147
PARRISH JB WPARRJB61051
WPARRJB62283
WPARRJB65050
PARSONS T ED NPARSTX66976
PASCHELL W WPASCWX58178
PASLEY RS GPASLRS57148
PASSOW HA ED GPASSHA63724
PATE JE NPATEJE43977
PATTEN MB NNORGPH59932
PATTEN TH NPATTTH63978
PATTERSON B NPATTBX64979
PAUL I PPAULIX55843
PEARL A GPEARAX65099
NPEARAX64980
PEARLIN LI GGREEJX53738
PEARSON HG GPEARHG66149
PEATTE LR ED INETTRM60599
PEDDER W GPEDDWX64150
PEEVEY M WPEEVMX66052
PEIMER SC GPEIMSC66139
PEITHMANN IM IPEITIM59284
IPEITIM64604
PELLEGRIN RJ NPELLRJ62981
PENALOSA F MPENAFX63453
PENNSYLVANIA ECONOMY LEAGUE
GPENNEL62502
PENNSYLVANIA FEPC
GPENNFE58153
PENNSYLVANIA HUMAN RELS COMM
GPENNHRND164
GPENNHRND165
GPENNHR62162
GPENNHR63166
GPENNHR65163
GPENNHR65167
PERKINS B GPERKBX66150
PERLMAN M ED GPERLMX63169
PERLO V NPERLVX52983
NPERLVX53982
PERLOFF E WPERLEX63100
PERRELLA VC GPERRVC64168
GPERRVC66774
WROSECX65088
PERRY J GPERRJX63170
NAMOSWE63021
NPERRJX64984
NPERRJX64985
PERRY P NPERRPX54987
PERSONNEL POLICIES FORUM
NPERSPF65562
PETERSON AS WGRIFAM65803
PETERSON CL CPETECL64988
CPETECX65989
MPETECL64454
PETERSON E WPETEEX62057
WPETEEX63053
WPETEEX63054
WPETEEX64056
WPETEEX64058
WPETEEX65055
PETERSON J WPETEJX59059
PETTIGREW TF NPETTTFND990
NPETTTF63063
NPETTTF64991
NPETTTF64992
PFAUTZ HW NPFAUHW63993
PFEIFFER DG MPFEIDG63456
PHILADELPHIA BRD OF EDUCATION
GPHILBE64172
PHILADELPHIA COMM HUMAN RELS

GPHILCH60181
GPHILCH61176
GPHILCH62178
GPHILCH62180
GPHILCH64179
GPHILCH65177
NPHILCH62995
PPITTCH64844
PHILIPSON M GPHILMX62616
PHILLIPS EW GPHILEW65773
PHILLIPS WB NPHILWB59996
PHILLIPS WM NPHILWM57997
PIERCE JA NPIERJA47998
PIERSEL WG NPIERWG41999
PIERSON GK NPIERGK61457
PIERSON JH GPIERJH64846
PIKER J NPIKEJX67101
PILCH J JPILCJX64749
PINES M WPINEMX58061
PINKNEY A CPINKAX63458
PINS AM WPINSAM63062
PITTS EW ED NWAYNCM64295
PITTS MAYOR-S COMM HUM RELS
NPITTMC65002
PITTSBURGH LEGAL JOURNAL
NPITTLJ65001
PIVEN FF GCLOWRX66525
PLAUT RL NPLAURL57003
PLOTKIN L NCLARKB63214
NPLOTLX59064
POLGAR S IPOLGSX60605
POLINSKY EJ WPOLIEJ59454
WPOLIEJ65285
POLISAR E GPOLIEX65102
NPOLIEX64219
NPOLIEX66004
POLK A NJOHNCS47007
POLLARD FM NPOLLFM64005
POLLARD LA WPOLLLA65063
POLLIT D NPOLLDX63006
POLLOCK S NPOLLSX66723
POPULATION REFERENCE BUREAU
NPOPURB58008
NPOPURB63007
PORTER RP CPORTRP43103
POTOMAC INSTITUTE INC.
GPOTOII65188
POTTS G GPOTTGX65189
POWELL EC NPOWEEC61009
POWELL EH NWILLSM64232
POWERS T GPOWETX64190
PRENTICE-HALL INC
GPRENHI64104
PRES COMT GOVT CONTRACT COMPL
GPRESCG53117
PRES COMT GOVT EMPLOY POLICY
GPRESCP55197
GPRESCP55198
GPRESCP55199
GPRESCP56193
GPRESCP57194
GPRESCP58195
GPRESCP59196
GPRESCP59201
GPRESCP60200
NPRESCP57017
NPRESCP60016
PRES-S COMM GOVT CONTRACTS
GPRESCH56191
PRES-S COMM ON STATUS WOMEN
WPRESCO63064
WPRESCO63065
WPRESCO63066
WPRESCO63067
WPRESCO63068
WPRESCO63069
WPRESCO63070
WPRESCO63993
PRES-S COMT CIVIL RIGHTS
GPRESCC47192
PRES-S COMT GOVT CONTRACTS
GPRESCH54120
GPRESCH55124
GPRESCH57122
GPRESCH58119
GPRESCH58121
GPRESCH60123
PRES-S COMT LABOR-MANAGE POL
GPRESCL64772
PRES-S TASK FORCE ON MANPOWER
GPRESTM64316
PRESIDENT-S COMMITTEE ON EEO
GPRESCO62105
GPRESCD62108
GPRESCD62109
GPRESCD63110
GPRESCD63115
GPRESCD64111
GPRESCD64112
GPRESCD64113
GPRESCD64114
GPRESCD64116
GPRESCD65107
NPRESCD61013
NPRESCD62011
NPRESCD62012
NPRESCD62014
NPRESCD63010
PRESIDENT-S COMT ON EEO
GPRESCD64106
PRESL COMT EQTY TRTMT OPPOR
NPRESCE50015
PRESSER HB NPRESHB62125
PRESSLER SB GPRESSB58126
PRICE DO NPRICDO48019
NPRICDO65018
PRICE JA IPRICJA65607
IPRICJA67606
IPRICJA67608
PRICE PH GPRICPH58395
PRICE WS GPRICWS65688
PRINCETON UNIV IND RELS SECT
NPRINUI54020
PROCTOR SD NPROCSD66021
PROGRESSIVE. NPROGXX62059
PROJECT ADVANCE CPROJAX66237
PROMINSKI HJ NPROMHJ59127
PROTHRO JW NMATTDR62758
PRUDENCE SISTER MARY
MVALDLX66512

PUBLISHERS WEEKLY
GPUBLWX63207
PUCKAT W JPUCKWX65750
PUEBLO REGIONAL PLANNING COMM
GPUEBRP65459
PUERTO RICAN FORUM
CPROJAX66237
PUERTO RICO DEPT OF LABOR
PPUERRDND788
PPUERRDND791
PPUERRDND792
PPUERRD57789
PPUERRD58787
PPUERRD60790
PUNER M GRABKSX58213
PUNKE HH WPUNKHH61071
PURCELL F GPURCFX66208
PURCELL TV NPURCTV62023
NPURCTV64022
NPURCTV67123
PURDY JW GPURDJW66209
PURDY L NPURDLX54024
PURYEAR MJ GPURYMJ62210
PURYEAR MT NPURYMT63026
NPURYMT63027
NPURYMT63028
PUTNAM H MSANCGI59478
QUARLES B NQUARBX47257
QUINLAN PA GQUINPA65771
QUINN F IQUINFX60609
WQUINFX62992
QUINN RP GKAHNRL64733
RAAB E GRAABEX64120
RABEAU ES IWAGNCJ64681
RABINOWITZ D JRABIDX59751
RABKIN S GRABKSX58213
GRABKSX64211
RABOCK SH NRABOSH53029
RACHLIN C GRACHCXND212
GRACHCX66214
RACKOW F GRACKFX49215
RADCLIFFE COLLEGE
WRADCCX56072
RADIN N CRADINX65031
RADIN NL CKAMICKND632
RAINWATER L NRAINLX66032
NRAINLX66033
RAMSEY GV WRAMSGV63104
WRAMSGV63132
RAMSON LA NRAMSLA43128
RAND C PRANDCX58845
RANDALL CM NJENKMD48608
RANDOLPH AP NRANDAP40576
NRANDAP62036
NRANDAP63035
NRANDAP64034
RANDOLPH KS WRANDKS65073
RAPER A GRAPEAX46037
RAPPING LA GRAPPLA66216
RASKIN AH NRASKAH64038
RASKIN BL WRASKBL59074
RATCHFORD BU NECKAEW55319
RATLIFF Y MRATLYX60460
RAUH JL GRAUHJL57217
RAUSHENBUSH C PRAUSCX61846
RAUSHENBUSH E GRAUSEX62218
WBUNTMI61664
WRAUSEX61076
WRAUSEX62075
RAUSHENBUSH W GRAUSWX45583
RAVITZ MJ GRAVIMJ61219
WRAVIMJ57077
RAWLINGS CW NSCHALX64102
RAYACK E NLURIMX66712
NRAYAEX61040
READ FT GREADFT64220
REAGAN MD GREAGMD64845
RECORD CW NRECOCW48041
NRECOCW59042
NRECOCW63043
REDDICK LD NREDDLD53044
REDDING JS NREDDJS43546
REDMOND W GREDMWX64221
REED BA NREEDBA47045
REED ET NREEDET62046
REED M NDAMILX64127
REES A GREESAX65119
GREESAX66722
REEVES N WREEVNX63078
REHN G GREHNGX65654
REICH N JREICNX64752
REID ID NREIDID47362
REID IDA NREIDID43048
NREIDID56047
REIFEL B IREIFBX58610
REIN M GMILLSM65953
REISSMAN L NREISLX65049
REITZES DC NREITDC53050
REMERI GN PREMEGN58847
RENDER FW NRENDFW64274
RENDON G MRENDGX63461
RENNER RR MRENNRR57462
RESEARCH INSTITUTE OF AMERICA
GRESEIA64222
REUSS LA GREUSLA60391
GREUSLA62388
REUTHER WP GREUTWP60223
NRANDAP63035
REYES I MREYEIX57463
REYNOLDS B GWALLPX66539
RHODE ISLAND COMM AGST DISCR
GRHODICND232
NRHODIC64051
RHODE ISLAND URBAN LEAGUE
NRHODIUND052
RHYNE B GRHYNCS63234
RHYNE CS GRHYNCS63234
RICE JD NRICEJD41053
RICH JC NRICHJC62054
RICH M NRICHMX65055
RICHARDS E GMCDOEC53050
NRICHEX43056
RICHARDS TW NRICHTW56057
RICHARDS WW GCRAICE66620
RICHEY E GRICHEX66235
RICHMOND C NRICHCX64058
RICHMOND CITY MANAGER
GRICHCM63236
RICO L GRICOLX66237
RIDDICK WE NWILLCV65989

RIESMAN D WRIESDX56079
WRIESDX58080
RIESSMAN F GPEARAX65099
NRIESFX65060
NRIESFX66059
RIGDALE L WMILLRX66982
RIGHTS GRIGHXX59238
JRIGHXX57753
JRIGHXX57754
JRIGHXX59755
JRIGHXX63756
JRIGHXX64757
RILEY E WRILEEX66081
RILEY SB WRILESB61287
RING HH NRINGHH53061
RIOCH MJ WRIOCMJ65082
RITTER AL NRITTAL45062
RITTER ED ORITTXX65758
RIVKIN E JRIVIEX58325
ROACH JL GGURSOR64749
ROBERTS G NROBEGX61063
NROBEGX62064
ROBERTS HW NROBEHW53065
ROBERTS SO GROBESO63683
NROBESO57067
NROBESO65068
NROBESO66961
ROBERTSON PC GROBEPC64239
NCAMPRR60180
ROBIN SS WROBISS63083
ROBINSON J NROBIJX63069
ROBISON JB GROBIJB64240
ROBISON ML NROBIML47070
ROBSON RT GROBSRT66721
ROCHE JP GROCHJP63057
RODMAN H WRODMHX65084
RODOMSKI AL GRODOAL64241
RODRIQUEZ-CANO F
MRODRFX66464
ROE A WROEXAX56085
WROEXAX66455
ROE AV WROEXAV64086
ROHRER WC NLERANL60401
NROHRWC58400
RONKEN HO NRONKHO52129
RONY V NRONYVX65072
ROONEY JF MROONJF61465
ROOSEVELT FD GROOSFD66242
ROPER E GROPEEXND243
GROPEEX49245
GROPEEX63244
NROPEEX52073
RORTY J GRORTJX58246
NFLEIHX58361
ROSE AM CROSEAM64553
NROSEAM48319
NROSEAM50294
NROSEAM51075
NROSEAM58291
NROSEAM60295
NROSEAM64296
NROSEAM65289
ROSE AM ED GROSEAM65249
NROSEAM64290
NROSEAM65074
ROSE AW GROSEAW50288
NROSEAW51292
NROSEAW53293
ROSE CB ED GROSEAM65249
ROSE HM NROSEHM61076
ROSE JC WGRIFAM65803
ROSE PI GROSEPI64251
ROSE R NROSERX53077
NROSERX65130
ROSE T GROSETXND250
ROSEN BC GROSEBC59252
ROSEN HS GROSEHS66253
ROSEN SJ GROSESJ65255
GROSESJ66254
NROSESJ62079
NROSESJ67078
ROSENBERG B NROSEBX59080
ROSENBERG JM GROSEJM66008
ROSENFELD C GROSECX60257
WROSECX62087
WROSECX65088
ROSETT R WROSERX58089
ROSOFSKY RG GROSORG66258
ROSS A GGORDRA64526
ROSS AM GROSSAM66083
GROSSAM66084
NROSSAM63259
NROSSAM66081
NROSSAM67082
NROSSAM67085
ROSS AM ED GROSSAM65720
NROSSAM67086
ROSS I NROSSIX63087
ROSS J NROSSJX50088
ROSS L GROSSLX66557
ROSS M GROSSMX47261
GROSSMX47262
GROSSMX48260
ROSS MS GROSSMS66844
ROSSI AS WROSSASND133
WROSSAS64093
WROSSAS64132
WROSSAS65091
WROSSAS65092
WROSSAS65094
WROSSAS66090
ROSSMAN JE WBURCLG61665
WROSSJE65770
ROUCEK J GROUCJX55263
ROUCEK J ED GBROWFJ45477
ROUSSEVE R NROUSRX63310
ROUSSEVE RJ NROUSRJ62089
ROUTH FB GROUTFB64264
ROWAN CT NROWACT60090
ROWAN RL NROWARL65703
NROWARL67091
ROWAN RL ED NNORTHR65949
ROWE FB WROWEFB64095
ROY EP IROYXEP59611
ROY P IROYXPX61612
IROYXPX66613
ISTONCX62626
RUBEL AJ MRUBEAJ66466
MRUBEAJ66467
MRUBEAJ66468

US DEPARTMENT OF STATE
  GUSDSTA61507
  NJOHNC S49613
US DEPARTMENT OF THE ARMY
  GUSDARM56192
  GUSDARM62193
US DEPARTMENT OF THE INTERIOR
  IUSDINTND452
US DEPT OF HEALTH ED WELFARE
  CUSDHEWND855
  GUSDHEW63434
  GUSDHEW63505
  GUSDHEW63834
  GUSDHEW64764
  GUSDHEW65156
  GUSDHEW65435
  GUSDHEW65763
  GUSDHEW66002
  GUSDHEW66639
  GUSDHEW66711
  GUSDHEW66978
  IUSDHEW58196
  IUSDHEW60639
  IUSDHEW66813
  NUSDHEW58241
  WUSDHEW59171
  WUSDHEW60175
  WUSDHEW61174
  WUSDHEW65170
  WUSDHEW65172
  WUSDHEW66173
  WUSDHEW66177
US DEPT OF THE AIR FORCE
  GUSDAIR62189
US EEO COMMISSION
  GUSEEOC66509
  GUSEEOC66510
US FEDERAL EXECUTIVE COUNCIL
  GUSFEDE63513
US FEP COMMITTEE GUSFEPC45512
  GUSFEPC47511
US GENERAL SERVICES ADM
  NUSGE SA63266
US HOUSE OF REPRESENTATIVES
  CUSHOUR64346
  GUSHOUR61343
  GUSHOUR61345
  GUSHOUR61985
  GUSHOUR62340
  GUSHOUR62342
  GUSHOUR62344
  GUSHOUR63338
  GUSHOUR63341
  GUSHOUR65339
  GUSHOUR65824
  IUSHOUR59669
  IUSHOUR63670
  MUSHOUR58509
  MUSHOUR63984
  WUSHOUR62020
US HOUSE OF REPRESENTIVES
  GUSHOUR63337
US HOUSING AND HOME FINANCE
  GUSHHFX63321
US IDEPTL COMT CHILDREN YOUTH
  GUSINCC53514
US IDEPTL COMT STATUS WOMEN
  WUSINCS65860
US LIBRARY OF CONGRESS
  GUSLIBC64823
US NATL AERONAUTICS SPACE ADM
  NUSNAAS63267
US NEWS AND WORLD REPORT
  GUSNEWR56517
  GUSNEWR66518
  IUSNEWR62672
  IUSNEWR66671
  NUSNEWR51272
  NUSNEWR56208
  NUSNEWR57209
  NUSNEWR57274
  NUSNEWR58271
  NUSNEWR62268
  NUSNEWR63207
  NUSNEWR63269
  NUSNEWR64292

WUSDLAB62041
WUSDLAB62189
WUSDLAB62193
WUSDLAB62241
WUSDLAB62253
WUSDLAB63226
WUSDLAB63229
WUSDLAB63239
WUSDLAB63243
WUSDLAB63991
WUSDLAB64179
WUSDLAB64183
WUSDLAB64188
WUSDLAB64199
WUSDLAB64202
WUSDLAB64204
WUSDLAB64212
WUSDLAB64218
WUSDLAB64227
WUSDLAB64228
WUSDLAB64237
WUSDLAB64240
WUSDLAB64242
WUSDLAB65196
WUSDLAB65220
WUSDLAB65222
WUSDLAB65225
WUSDLAB65232
WUSDLAB65233
WUSDLAB65234
WUSDLAB66B05
WUSDLAB66K05
WUSDLAB66185
WUSDLAB66195
WUSDLAB66197
WUSDLAB66200
WUSDLAB66201
WUSDLAB66217
WUSDLAB66223
WUSDLAB66230
WUSDLAB66231
WUSDLAB66236
WUSDLAB66238
WUSDLAB66638
WUSDLAB67806

NUSNEWR66270
NUSNEWR66273
NUSNEWR66244
WUSNEWR65246
WUSNEWR66245
US OFFICE OF PRODUCTION MNGMT
  GUSOFPM42519
US PO DEPT ADVISORY BOARD
  GUSPODA63516
US SENATE
  GUSSENA52347
  GUSSENA52350
  GUSSENA54330
  GUSSENA54353
  GUSSENA59469
  GUSSENA60352
  GUSSENA63305
  GUSSENA63331
  GUSSENA63349
  GUSSENA63618
  GUSSENA63822
  GUSSENA64306
  GUSSENA64332
  GUSSENA64334
  GUSSENA64348
  GUSSENA64355
  GUSSENA66351
  IUSSENA56673
  IUSSENA59674
  NUSSENA52333
  NUSSENA54275
US SMALL BUSINESS ADM
  WUSSMBA62248
US VETERANS ADMINISTRATION
  GUSVETA59521
US WAR MANPOWER COMMISSION
  NUSWAMC44276
USEEM RH
  WUSEERH63215
  WUSEERH64255
UZELL O NUZELOX61278
VAAS FJ GVAASFJ66534
VAIL L WVAILLX66256
VALDEZ B MVALDBX64448
  MVALDBX64449
VALDEZ L MVALDLX66512
VALIEN P GMASUJX63064

VAN AKEN CG ED WMATTJA65963
VAN RIPER PP WWARNWL62993
VANCE RB NVANCRB45282
VANCE RB ED NVANCRB54283
VANDERZANDEN JW GVANDJW63535
VATTER HG ED GWILLRE65665
VELIE L NVELILX59216
VETTER L WBERRJX66642
VIA E GHOPEJX61002
VILES GL MFULLVX56396
VINCENT N GVINCNX66113
VIORST J NVIORJX65284
VIOT VH GVIOTVH66113
VIRGINIA LAW REVIEW
  NVIRGLR64017
  NVIRGLR64018
VITAL ISSUES WVITAIX63218
VOGAL AS GVOGAAS62074
VOGET FW ED IVOGEFW61677
VOGL AJ NVOGLAJ64286
VOGT EZ IVOGTEZ57678
  IVOGTEZ61679
VOLLMER HM NVOLLHM66287
W VIRGINIA HUMAN RIGHTS COMM
  NVIRGHR64318
WACHTEL DD NWACHDD65288
WACHTEL HM NWACHHMND289
WACHTEL WW GWACHWWND536
WADDELL J IWADDJX66680
WADDELL JO MWADDJO62513
WAGERLY CW NWAGECW57290
WAGMAN M GWAGMMX66761
WAGNER CJ IWAGNCJ64681
WAGNER JA MWAGNJA63514
WAGONER DW MWAGODW57515
WAKEFIELD D PWAKEDX59858
WALDMAN E GPERRVC66774
WALDMAN S GWALDSX65017
WALKER GH NLLOYRG54045
WALKER HJ NWALKHJ57291
WALKER JO NWALKJO46580
WALKER RW GWALKRW66538
WALLACE LM GWALLLM63520
WALLACE P GWALLPX66539
WALLACE PA NWALLPA66591
WALLS F GWALLFX61221
  NWALLFX61221
WALSH CM WWALSCM57266
WALSH JP GWALSJP64540
  GWALSJP64620
WALSH ME GFURFPH62705
WALT DE WWALTDE62314
WANDERER JJ MSIMMOG64491
WARD LB JWARDLB65769
WARD R GWARDRX62821
WARNATH CF WWARNCF61220
WARNER WL NWARNWL62292
  NWARNWL62993
WARREN D NWARRDX64314
WARREN PA WWARRPA59222
WARREN URBAN LEAGUE
  NWARRUL64986
WARRIOR C IWARRCX65668
WASHBURN WE ED IWASHWE66520
WASHINGTON BB WWASHBB65667
WASHINGTON LAW REVIEW
  GWASHLR64541
WATKINS DO GWATKDO66588
WATSON MM GWATSMMND544
WATTENBERG WW GWATTWW66223
WATTERS P NWATTPX64293
  NWATTPX64294
  NWATTPX66545
WAX ML IWAXXML64683
WAX RH IWAXXRH64683
  IWAXXRH61224
  IWAXXRH67812
WAYNICK CM ED NWAYNCM64295
WEATHERFORD MD NWEATMD54296

WEAVER NJOHNXX63336
WEAVER EK NWEAVEK44297
WEAVER RC GWEAVRC66707
  NWEAVRC42307
  NWEAVRC43225
  NWEAVRC43301
  NWEAVRC44300
  NWEAVRC44304
  NWEAVRC45302
  NWEAVRC46304
  NWEAVRC48303
  NWEAVRC50305
  NWEAVRC63298
  NWEAVRC64299
WEBB EB GWEBBEB65546
  MWEBBEB66516
WEBB JR WWEBBJR66226
WEBER AR GWEBEAR66760
WEBER J WWEBEJX66258
WEBSTER AN NNORGPH59932
WECKLER JE NWECKJE45308
WECKSTEIN RS GWECKRS62987
WEIL FDG NWEILFD47309
WEINBERG E GGREELX64614
WEINBERG JL CWEINJL64310
WEINBERGER DC WPINEMX58061
WEINER FR WDEVEGX62731
WEINGARTEN V WWEINVX61259
WEINTRAUB R GWEINRX59988
  NWEINRX59311
WEISBROD BA ED GWEISBA65666
WEISS A JWEISAX58770
WEISS AJ GWEISAJ47547
WEISS EJ WKNILNO60034
WEISS L GWEISLX62597
WEITZ H NWEITHX59260
WELCH FJ WWELCFJ60227
WELFARE COUNCIL OF DELAWARE
  GWELFCD56548
WELL MW WWELLMW61261
WELLES S JWELLSX60571
WELLINGTON H GWELLHX58550
  GWELLHX61549
WELLS JA WWELLJA60262
  WWELLJA63263
  NWELSEK65304
WELSCH EK NCLARJP62209
WENNINGER EP NCLARJP63208
WEPPNER RS IWEPPRS55684
  IWEPPRS55685
WESSON WH NWESSWH55314
WEST E NWESTEX66315
WEST J GWESTJX66551
WESTBERG DL GWESTDL65552
WESTCHESTER COUNTY URB LEAG
  NWESTCU55316
WESTERN ELECTRIC CO
  GWESTEC64553
WESTERN REGIONAL CONFERENCE
  NWESTRC62214
WESTERN RESERVE LAW REVIEW
  GWESTRL53019
WESTERVELT EM WWESTEM62265
  WWESTEM65210
WESTON AF GWESTAF61557
WESTON ZJ NWESTZJ66317
WETZEL JR NWETZJR66114
WHEELER JH NWHEEJH64230
WHITAKER N MWHITNX60517
WHITE CR NSUSSMB59192
WHITE MS WWHITMS64266
WHITE R IWHITRX59686
WHITE RM NWHITRM59319
WHITE W NWHITWX42465
WHITE WL NWHITWL66231
  NWHITWL66320
WHITE HOUSE CONFERENCE
  GWHITHC60559
  GWHITHC65558
WHITEHEAD MJ NWHITMJ48249
WHITEMAN M NBLOORX63096
WHITLOW EW NWHITTEW64321
WHITMAN WT GGREEMX64450
WHYTE DR GWHYTDR60407
WHYTE WH GWHYTWH54560
WICKERSHAM E GWICKEX63637
WICKERSHAM ED GWICKED63361
WIDICK BJ NHOWEIX49581
WIGGINS CH GWIGGCH65598
WIGNEY T WWIGNTX65267
WILBER GL NLERANL60403
WILCOCK R WWILCRX60268
WILCOCK RC CWILCRC63322
  GWILCRC57562
WILKERSIN DA NWILKDA42233
WILKINSON WHH NWILKWH41323
WILL RE ED GWILLRE65665
WILLETTE LB GWILLLB59565
WILLHELM SM NWILLSM64232
WILLIAMS DE MJORGJM60422
WILLIAMS JJ CWILLJJ58324
  WWILLJJ66269
WILLIAMS JS GCOUNVX65610
WILLIAMS MM NWILLMM50234
WILLIAMS RM GKOHNML56145
WILLIE CV NWILLCV65989
WILLIS DF WPASCWX58178
WILSON A GWILSAX45566
WILSON AB CWILSAB63325
  CWILSAB59568
  GWILSAB60567
WILSON B WWOMEIX66273
WILSON CE NWILSCE65326
WILSON HC IWILSHC61687
  IWILSHC64235
WILSON J NCROFES66242
WILSON L CGILMHX44403
  NWILSLX43327
WILSON R ED WFARBSM63756
WILSON RH ED WFARBSM66755
WINGO W MMINGWX66536
WINN F NNINNFX43554
WINTER E WWINTEX61270
WINTER EL GWINTEL66569
WINTERS SB NWINTSB64329
WINTRAUB RE GGREEWX61741
WIRTZ W NWIRTWX66236
WIRTZ WW GWIRTWW64572

GWIRTWW65571
GWIRTWW66570
NWIRTWW63330
WWIRTWW62181
WWIRTWW63271
WIS GOVRS COMM ON HUM RIGHTS
  NWISCGC59331
WIS GOVRS COMM STATUS OF WOME
  WWISXGC65272
WIS LEGV REFERENCE LIBRARY
  GWISCLR52573
WISC IND COMM EEO DIV
  GWISCIC66587
WISPE LG GWISPLG65141
WISSNER HW NWISSHW55332
WITHERSPOON J GWITHJX65575
WITTENLORN HW GWITTHW64576
WOFFORD BM NWOFFBM55333
WOFFORD H GWOFFHX62577
WOLF M WFEINBX66760
WOLFBEIN S GWOFLSX64759
WOLFBEIN SL GWOLFSL63578
  GWOLFSL64624
  NWOLFSL45335
  NWOLFSL47334
WOLFE DP NWOLFDP62336
  NWOLFDP65337
WOLFE DP ED NWOLFDP64338
WOLFE L IWILSHC61687
WOLL JA GWOLLJA64579
WOLL M GWOLLMX54580
WOLOZIN H GWOLOHX65990
WOMEN INC WWOMEIX66273
WOMEN-S EDL AND IND UNION
  WWOMEEA65275
WONG LJ OWONGLJ64771
WOOD CA NWOODCA45339
WOODS MJ GWOODMJ64581
  GWOODMJ64518
  MWOODMJ65446
  MWOODMJ64518
WOODS W WWOODWX66276
WOODWARD CV NWOODCV60061
WOOFTER TJ NWOOFTJ57340
WORKERS DEFENSE LEAGUE
  GWORKDL63582
  GWORKDL65584
WORLD OVER JWORLOX64773
WORONOFF I NWOROIX62341
WORTHY BN WBOWMGW65653
WORTHY NB WWORTNB60245
WORTMAN MS GWORTMS64586
  GWORTMS65585
  GWORTMS65681
WOYTINSKY WS NWOYTWS53343
WRIGHT D GWRIGDX65604
WRIGHT DE GKUVLWP65867
WRIGHT KW WWRIGKW66277
WRIGHT SJ NWRIGSJ63344
WU CT OWUXXCT58772
WULSIN JH WWULSJH66278
YABROFF S GYABRSX65588
YABROFF SM GYABRSM65587
YALE LAW JOURNAL JYALELJ64774
  JYALELJ63599
  NYALELJ64600
YANCEY JMY PELIZCX66031
YANCEY WL NRAINLX66033
YANGAS R PYANGRX61859
YETT D WYETTDX66246
YINGER JM CYINGJM56519
  GSIMPGE65314
  GYINGJM58590
  GYINGJM66589
  IDOZIEP57077
  NYINGJM63345
YMCA OF METROPOLITAN CHICAGO
  GCHICBC65319
YMCA YOUTH AND WORK PROJECT
  CYMCAYA66329
YONKERS CITY COMM HUM RIGHTS
  GYONKCC66592
YOUMANS EG NYOUMEG65390
YOUNG HB NYOUNHB63347
  NYOUNHB64346
YOUNG J JYOUNJX65775
YOUNG LM WYOUNLM61279
YOUNG LB CYOUNMB65636
YOUNG ME GYOUNME64593
YOUNG MNE NYOUNMN44348
YOUNG S GYOUNSX67144
YOUNG WM NYOUNWM63352
  NYOUNWM63356
  NYOUNWM63600
  NYOUNWM64299
  NYOUNWM64349
  NYOUNWM64350
  NYOUNWM64351
  NYOUNWM64353
  NYOUNWM65000
  NYOUNWM65354
  NYOUNWM66355
YOUNGDAHL JE NYOUNJE56357
YOUNT CE NYOUNCE45358
YWCA WYWCAXX63078
  WYWCAXX66079
ZAPOLEON MW WZAPOMW56280
  WZAPOMW59281
  WZAPOMW61282
  WZAPOMW64283
ZARCHIN MM JZARCMM64776
ZEISEL JS GZEISJS63704
ZEITZ L NZEITL X65359
ZEMAN M GZEMAMX55594
ZILLER RC GZILLRC59595
ZIMMER BG NZIMMBG62360
  NZIMMBG64247
ZIMMERMAN W IZIMMWX57248
ZISSIS C WZISSC X62284
  WZISSC X64285
ZOOK D GZOOKDX64596
ZURCHER LA MZURCLA65520
ZURCHER SL MZURCLA65520

Institutional Sponsors Index

ACLU
  GFRAEOK60697
ACTION FOR BOSTON COM DEVEL
  NEDWARM61327
ADAMS S CENT CULTURAL STUDIE
  MSAUNLX58480
AEROJET GENERAL CORPORATION
  WMACKJW66950
AFL-CIO
  GFLEIHX57686
  NRANDAP63035
  WPEEVMX66052
AG PRODUCERS LABOR COMMITTEE
  WMILLJJ66979
ALUMNAE ADVISORY CENTER INC
  WMCINMC61945
  WSCHWJX60108
  WSCHWJX62106
  WSCHWJX64107
AM ANTHROPOLOGICAL ASSN
  ISPINLS62622
AM COUNCIL ON RACE RELATIONS
  GNAACNL45036
  GUVCHCE50211
AM FRIENDS SERVICE COMMITTEE
  IQUINFX60609
AMALGAMATED CLOTHING WORKERS
  WBLOCHX66649
AMERICAN CC ON EDUCATION
  NJOHNCS41611
AMERICAN ALUMNI COUNCIL
  WFIELBX64762
AMERICAN CC ON EDUCATION
  GBROWFJ55476
  WDAVIOD57044
  WDAVIOD59937
  WJAHOMX55879
AMERICAN JEWISH COMMITTEE
  JDAVIHX58717
  JFINEMXND720
  JGALLBG58724
AMERICAN JEWISH COMMITTEE.
  GKAUFSF64841
AMERICAN MANAGEMENT ASSN
  NBLOOJW64093
  NGOURJC65438
  NSCHEGX64103
ANN ARBOR HUMAN RELS COMM
  NPIKEJX67101
ANTI-DEFAMATION LEAGUE
  GABRACX58361
  GBERNBI62447
  GBRAVHX59471
  GEDELHX63658
  GFEILJG62675
  GHARTPX58763
  GHARTPX62762
  GMARSBX62942
  GNIXORM56117
  GRABKSX58213
  GROOSFD66242
  GTUCKJN56363
  GTUMIMM57164
  GUVCHCE50211
  GWOFFHX62577
  JBELTNC58702
  JEPSTBR58718
  JHARTPX58730
  JSIMOBX58763
  JWEISAX58770
  NGISSIX65418
  NNORTRD56935
  NROSEAM50294
  NSUCHEA58189
  NTUMIMM53065
  PSENICX61308
ANTI-DEFAMATION LEAGUE.
  NPATTBX64979
APPLIED PSYCHOLOGICAL SERV
  NSIEGAI59718
ARIZONA COUNCIL OF CHURCHES
  CSKILTO66324
ASSN MACHINISTS AEROSPACE WS
  WSHEAHX66112
ASSN ON AM INDIAN AFFAIRS
  IMADILX56587
ASSN WEST PULP PAPER WORKERS
  WHILLHX66844
B-NAI B-RITH VOCAT SERV BUR
  JSHOSRJ57761
  WSHOSRX56113
BISHOPS COMT SPANISHSPEAKING
  MFEERAB62392
BKBNDRS BINDERY WOMENS UNION
  WDIBRJX66732
BROOKINGS INSTITUTION
  NFEINRX65348
BUREAU OF BUSINESS PRACTICE
  GBENGEJ65436
BUREAU OF NATIONAL AFFAIRS
  NPERSPF65562
BYU INST AM INDIAN STUDIES
  ITYLESL64634
CAL ADVSY COMT TO US CR COMM
  GBECKWL62432
CAL CC BUILD SERV EMPS UNION
  WHEALWX66836
CAL CONF OF EMPLOYERS ASSNS
  WSMITWH66123
CAL DEPARTMENT OF EMPLOYMENT
  CELTOEX63332
CAL DEPT INDUSTRIAL WELFARE
  WGERSMX66777
CAL DEPT OF EMPLOYMENT
  WINGRLX66859
CAL DEPT OF INDUSTRIAL RELS
  GWEBBEB65546
  MWEBBEB66516
CAL DEPT OF SOCIAL WELFARE
  WMYRIRX66013
CAL DIV INDUSTRIAL WELFARE
  WCLIFFG66692
CAL DIV OF VOCATIONAL REHAB
  WCUMMGX66711
CAL FED BUS PROF WOMEN CLUBS
  WGUPTRC66808
  WGUPTRC66809
CAL FEPC COMMISSIONER
  WSTERAX66140
CAL GOVRS ADVSY COMM HOUSING
  MMCMIOX62434
CAL MANUFACTURERS ASSN
  WKNIGTF66911
CAL MINORITY EMPLOYMENT PROG
  MWOODMJ65446
CAL NEWSPAPERS ASSOCIATION
  WDORAMX66739
CAL OFFICE OF THE GOVERNOR
  GBECKWL65433
CAL RETAILERS ASSOCIATION
  WKENNVX66890
CAL S CC OF RETAIL CLERKS
  WVAILLX66256
CAL STATE EMPLOYEES ASSN
  WGEIGPX66776
CAL STATE LABOR COMMISSIONER
  CARYWSX66621
CAL STATE PERSONNEL BOARD
  WSTEPRX66138
CALIF DEPT OF SOC WELFARE
  GRAABEX64120
CALIFORNIA DEPT OF EDUCATION
  GCALSLIND505
CALIFORNIA FEPC
  GFORDJA65450
  GRUSHJT66268
  GZOOKDX64596
CATALYST IN EDUCATION
  WSAMPJX65099
CC CIVIC UNITY SAN FRANCISCO
  GBABOIX58606
CC OF SOC PLANNING BERKELEY
  NKENNVD63642
CENTER FOR STUDY DEMO INSTS
  NJOHNXX63336
CENTER STUDY DEMO INSTS
  GMICADN62978
CHI ASSN COMMMRCE INDUSTRY
  GCOMIEF64592
CHILD STUDY ASSN OF AMERICA
  WWEINVX61259
CHILDREN-S CENTERS PROGRAM
  WWEBEJX66258
CHINATOWN-NBEACH DISTRICT CC
  OWONGLJ64771
CHINESE-AM CITIZENS ALLIANCE
  OLOWXHW64745
CITIZENS FOR FARM LABOR
  WKAUFDX66886
COLO INST OF BEHAVIORAL SCI
  MSIMMOG64491
COLO NAVAHO URBAN RLOCAT RES
  IGRAVTD64566
  IGRAVTD65567
  IWEPPRS65684
  IWEPPRS65685
COLORADO ANTI-DISCR COMM
  GDENNGHND632
COLORADO STATE DEPT OF ED
  GATKIJA61408
  MATKIJA61361
COLUMBIA U CONSER OF HR PROJ
  NGINZEX51410
  NGINZEX59406
  NGINZEX61411
COLUMBIA U INST OF HIGHER ED
  NMCGREJ65720
COMMON COUNCIL FOR AM UNITY
  NDAVIJA46258
COMMUNICATIONS WORKERS UNION
  WTHOMDX66151
COMT ON ECONOMIC DEVELOPMENT
  NDENIEF62262
CONGRESS OF RACIAL EQUALITY
  GRACHCXND212
  GROBIJB64240
CONN COMM ON CIVIL RIGHTS
  GROPEEXND243
  GSTETHG53598
  NSTEEHG54176
COOK COUNTY DEPT PUBLIC AID
  WBROODJ64656
CORE
  NCOUNFO63929
CORNELL NYS SCHOOL OF ILR
  GRACKFX49215
CORNELL SOCT APPLIED ANTHRO
  GDEUTMP60640
CORNELL UNIV NYS SCHOOL OFIR
  NSEIDJX50114
COUNCIL ON INDIAN AFFAIRS
  IAMERIN64087
COUNCIL ON SOCIAL WORK ED
  WPINSAM63062
CWBHMC SERVICE WORKERS UNION
  WBELAJX66634
E HARLEM YOUTH EMPLOY SERV
  PHAUGJX60814
  PYANGRX61859
EAST HARLEM PROJECT
  PBORODXND781
EDUCATIONAL TESTING SERVICE
  GCAMPJX64093
  GCLEATA66924
  GKRUGRE54946
  NBARRRS65056
  NBLANJW64917
  NCAMPJT65179
  NCAMPJT66010
  NCLEATA66923
  NHOLLJH65560
  NKRUGRE64731
  NLOCKHC65701
  NROBESO65068
  NROBESO66961
  NWHITEW64121
  WCOLECG56694
EEOC
  GANDEBR67589
  GENNEWH67928
  NWALLPA65
EXECUTIVE OFFICE OF US PRES
  WSTEIER62153
FISK U SOCIAL SCIENCE INST
  NHENDVW60516
FLORIDA A AND M UNIVERSITY
  WFLORMP66326
FLORIDA STATE BOARD HEALTH
  GKOOSEL57691
GLASS BOTTLE BLOWERS UNION
  WRILEEX66081
HARTFORD SEMINARY FOUNDATION
  PPAULIX55843
HARVARD CENT FOR RES CAREERS
  WBARURX66457

HARVARD GRAD SCHOOL OF ED
  WTIEDDV58154
HARYOU-ACT
  NHOUSLX65577
HELLER COMT RESEARCH SOC ECS
  WHUNTEH62271
HOSP AND INST WORKERS UNIONS
  WHEALWX66836
HOSPITAL EMPLOYEES UNION
  WGLENEM66788
HRCME UNION
  WMORAMX66995
HUNT FOODS AND INDUSTRIES
  WMILLKL66980
IDAHO U BUR BUS EC RESEARCH
  INYBRNX64603
ILGWU
  WFEINBX66760
ILL GOURS ADVSY COMM ON CIVR
  PGARCAX58806
INDUSTRIAL RELS COUNSELORS
  NNORGPH59932
INDUSTRIAL RELS RESEARCH ASS
  GHABEWX54750
JACKSON STATE COLLEGE
  CSELFHO66325
JEWISH FEDERATION
  JMASAGX59746
JEWISH LABOR COMMISSION
  GGOLDHX58975
JOHNS HOPKINS DEPT SOC RELS
  NLEVEBX63684
JTSAM INST RELIG SOC STUDENTS
  GROPEEX49245
  NMACIRM49731
KANSAS CITY COM STUDIES
  NGIBSHX54402
LA COUNTY COMM ON HUM RELS
  MALMAAS64357
LA COUNTY SUPT OF SCHOOLS
  MWHITNX60517
LA ECA WELFARE PLANNING CC
  MORTIMX62449
LANCASTER COUNTY CAP COMT
  PELIZCX66031
LAUNDRY DRY CLEANING UNION.
  WCHANHD66687
LEAGUE FOR IND DEMOCRACY
  NKAHNTX64629
LEAGUE OF CALIFORNIA CITIES
  GCURRRC60889
LONDON INST OF RACE RELS
  IMCNIDX61586
LOS ANGELES AFL
  WSPENNX66129
MACHINIST-S UNION
  WFOOTJX66765
MAINE STATE DEPT OF ED
  WSAMPJX65099
MISS AGL EXPERIMENT STATION
  WBRYAES61660
MISSOURI COMM ON HUM RIGHTS
  GMILLRX66020
  GMILLRX66021
  GROBEPC64239
  NCAMPRR60180
MISSOURI DEPT LABOR IR
  WBERRJX66642
MIT CENTER INTERNATL STUDIES
  ISHAWLC60617
MOBILIZATION FOR YOUTH
  GORNAOA64140
  NJACKJX64596
  NJONEJAND738
  PBRAMJX62783
  PBRAMJX63784
  PORTIRX62841
MOBILIZATION FOR YOUTH INC
  GBARRSX64130
  GDAVIAX63132
MORRIS COUNTY URBAN LEAGUE
  NKERNJH57645
N CAROLINA LEAG OF MUNICIP
  NSTEEDL46173
N CAROLINA MAYORS COPNG COMT
  NWAYNCM64295
N CAROLINA S BRD PUB WELFARE
  NLARKJR52672
NAACP
  NCOBBWM48217
  NHILLHX58531
  NHILLHX59534
  NHILLHX60542
  NHILLHX65549
  NHILLHX66538
  NMARSTX51754
  NMEANGX57763
NAIRO
  GSEGABD59294
NATIONAL COUNCIL OF CHURCHES
  CBLAIBX59366
NATIONAL EDUCATION SERVICE
  GBIENHX64111
NATIONAL LABOR SERVICE
  NFLEIHX58361
NATIONAL PLANNING ASSN
  NDEWEDX55269
  NECKAEW55319
  NHAWLLT55502
  NHOPEJX55572
  NWESSWH55314
  NWISSHW55332
NATIONAL URBAN LEAGUE
  GBRIMAF66435
  NFINLOE60356
  NGRANLB41442
  NHOLLJH58561
  NJOHNRA44620
  NKERNJH51897
  NORSHMX61961
  NPURYMT63026
  NPURYMT63028
  NTANNAX40199
  NTHOMPX43203
  NYOUNWM63600
NATL ASSN MANUFACTURERS
  GKOTHCA65732
  GLONGNE65121
NATL BUREAU OF EC RESEARCH
  GBECKGS64700
  GDUCOLJ57955
  GLEBESX60276
  GLONGCX58047
  GWILCRC57562

NATL COMT FOR CHILDREN YOUTH
  WMINCJX62984
  NBEEGJA63072
NATL CONF CHRISTIANS JEWS
  GROPEEX63244
NATL CONF CHRISTIANS-JEWS
  GBOWMGW63467
NATL CONSUMERS COMT RES ED
  GWILLLB59565
NATL INDUSTRIAL CONF BOARD
  GBACKJX64876
  GBAKESS65702
  GHABBSX65112
  GVIOTVH66113
  NBAMBJJ49050
  NHABBSX64473
  NHABBSX65471
  NHABBSX65474
  NHABBSX65472
  NOCONWB41094
  NYOUNWM65000
  WLINDFX63108
  WLINDFX66117
NATL INST MUNICIPAL LAW
  GRHYNC63234
NATL INST OF MENTAL HEALTH
  WHARTRE60828
NATL OPINION RESEARCH CENTER
  NFICHJH64867
  NHUSOCF66328
NATL SSF FOR NEGRO STUDENTS
  NCLARKB63214
  NPLAURL57003
NEGRO AM LAB CC ST LOUIS DIV
  NCALLEX64175
NEW HAVEN HUM RELS COUNCIL
  PDONCDX59796
NEW JERSEY DEPT OF EDUCATION
  GBOGITX54057
  GMEYESM56058
NEW YORK CITY YOUTH BOARD
  GVOGAAS62074
NEW YORK OFFICE OF THE MAYOR
  NGORDJX65435
NJ AGL EXPERIMENT STATION
  PAINERO59777
NJ DEPT LAW PUBLIC SAFETY
  NLEVIMJ66607
NY PUBLIC AFFAIRS COMMITTEE
  NNORTHR45948
NY STATE COMM AGAINST DISCR
  CABRACX59001
  GANTOAX59401
  GANTOAX60400
  GLANGGE59884
  GMARKPI57085
  NANTOAX59026
  NBACKSX59040
  NGRIEES57457
  NGRIEES57503
  NGRIEES58455
  NGRIEES58456
  NGRIEES58458
  NHILLHX60525
  NLANGGE59670
  NROSEBX59080
  PHELFBH59481
NYC CIVIL SERVICE COMM
  GGREGGX61071
  GGREGGX62070
NYC COMM ON HUMAN RIGHTS
  GLOWESH63921
  GWATKDO66588
  NCROMFX61121
NYS WAR CC COMM DISCR EMPLOY
  NDAVIJA42255
  NFALCNS45342
NYU CEN STUDY UNEMP YOUTH
  GCOLEEX66131
NYU CENT STUDY UNEMP YOUTH
  GBATTMX66131
  GKANERD66863
  GMARTJM66854
  GMOEDMX66852
  GNIXORA66847
  GPURCFX65208
  GSPAREV66839
NYU CENTER STUDY UNEMP YOUTH
  GBENNGX66877
OECD
  GGREELX64739
  GLEVILA64623
  PGRAYLX63813
  WKLEIVX65908
OEO
  MMACNBL67335
OHIO STATE U BUR BUS RES
  WEYDELD62754
OPPORS INDIZATION CENTER
  GANDEBXND391
OREGON BUREAU OF LABOR
  WKNILNO60034
PA CITIZENS COMT ON MIG LAB
  NKARRCHND636
PACIFIC TELEGRAPH TELEPHONE
  WWOODWX66276
PENNSYLVANIA HUM RELS COMM
  GSTRUJW63338
PHILA COMM HUMAN RELS
  NMCGOOJ66583
PHILADELPHIA COMM HUMAN RELS
  GBERNYX64448
  NKLEIRJ62655
  NSCHEGX61104
  PMETARX59826
POTOMAC INSTITUTE INC
  GSCHEGX66280
  GSILAJX63310
PRES-S COMM ON STATUS WOMEN
  WMEADMX65966
PRES-S COMMON STATUS WOMEN
  WDAVICX63718
PRES-S COMT GOVT CONTRACTS
  GGRANLB57979
PRESIDENT-S COMMITTEE ON EEO
  GTROURX62163
  MUSCISC63504
  NLONGHH62705
PRINCETON U EC DEPT IR SECT
  WBOWEWGND652
PRINCETON UNIV IND RELS SECT
  NNORGPH62931

PRINCETON UNIVERSITY
  GBOWEWG65464
PUERTO RICO DEPT OF LABOR
  PDECOPP59794
RADCLIFFE INST INDPT STUDY
  WWHITMS64266
RAND CORPORATION
  WHABESX58811
RESEARCH INTERGROUP RELS
  GSAENGX48273
RETAIL CLERKS UNION
  WLQWEDX66943
ROCKEFELLER FOUNDATION
  NDARTCX64309
RUTGERS INST MNGMT LAB RELS
  NINDURP66593
  PGOLUFT56811
  WSMITGM59122
  WSMITGM60120
  WSMITGM64121
RUTGERS U URBAN STUDIES CENT
  NFARRGR65344
SAN ANTONIO BISHOPS COMT
  MWAGNJA63514
SAN FRANCISCO CC CIVIC UNITY
  GROSETXND0250
SAN FRANCISCO MAYOR-S OFFICE
  GMITCJP64277
SCREEN EXTRAS GUILD OF LA
  WGILBRX66780
SMITHSONIAN INSTITUTION
  IFENTWN61620
SNCC
  NCOUNFO63929
SOCIAL SCI RESEARCH COUNCIL
  GMILLHP55988
SOCIETY OF WOMEN ENGINEERS
  WSTEIER62153
  WWEBBJR66226
SOUTHERN REGIONAL COUNCIL
  NHENDVW63515
  NHUGHWH48587
  NMOSSJA62856
  NMUSEBX64868
  NMUSEBX64869
  NPATTBX64979
  NWATTPX64293
  NWATTPX64294
SOUTHERN REGIONAL ED BOARD
  WROWEFB64095
ST LOUIS URBAN LEAGUE
  NSOBEIX54178
SYRACUSE U YOUTH DEVEL CENT
  GMILLSM64071
TENNESSEE CC ON HUMAN RELS
  NLONGHH62706
TEXAS AGL EXP STATION
  MMETZWH60439
  MSKRARL66492
  MUPHAWK66511
TEXAS AGL EXPERIMENT STATION
  GSKRARL57315
  GSOUTJH59325
TUSKEGEE INSTITUTE
  NJONELW50623
TWENTIETH CENTURY FUND
  GSOVEMI66326
U CAL BERKELEY INST IND RELS
  WHUNTEH62271
U CAL GIAMININ FOUNDATION
  MFULLVX56396
U CHI COM FAMILY STUDY CENT
  GSHRYHS64309
U CHI NATL OPINION RES CENT
  WROSSASND133
U COLO TRI-ETHNIC RES PROJ
  MGRAVTD67214
  MRENDGX63461
U HOUSTON CENT RES BUS ECS
  GLIEBEE65569
U KANSAS CENT RESEARCH BUS
  WSTOCFT59143
U OF ALA INTER-U CASE PROG
  NSHERFP59130
U OF CAL BERKELEY INST OF IR
  GGORDRA64526
  GGORDRA65513
  GJACOPX66527
U OF CAL BERKELY INST OF IR
  GGORDRA64525
U OF CAL BUREAU PUBLIC ADM
  GDUFFJX44522
U OF CHI COMMUNITY INVENTORY
  NDUNCOD57306
U OF COLORADO CENT LABOR ED
  GUPHOWH64528
U OF ILL INST LABOR IND RELS
  NCHALWE64912
  NCHALWE65188
U OF MICH INST SOC RESEARCH
  NEPPSEG65334
  NEPPSEG66335
U OF MICH-WAYNE STATE U ILIR
  GCOUSFR66478
  NFERMLA66790
  NWACHDD65288
U OF TEXAS BUR BUS RESEARCH
  MBROWHL64368
U PITT LEARNING R AND D CENT
  NCOHERXND221
U TEXAS INST LAT-AM STUDIES
  MSANCGI59478
UAW UNION
  WSCHRPX66104
UAW WOMEN-S DEPARTMENT
  WDAVICX63718
  WDAVICX65719
  WDAVICX65720
UCLA
  IPRICJA65607
UCLA GRAD SCHOOL OF BUS ADM
  MFOGEWX65320
  WTHOMMH63152
UCLA INSTITUTE OF IND RELS
  GBULLPX60897
  GBULLPX61523
  GBULLPX62488
  GBULLPX63489
  GBULLPX66486
  GGORDMS65728
  MSLOBMX64495
  NBULLPX65483
  NCARLJX65593
  WTURNMB64160

UCLA MEX-AM STUDY PROJ
  MGREBLX66406
UCLA MEXICAN-AM STUDY PROJ
  MMOORJW66444
UM ISR SURVEY RESEARCH CENT
  GKAHNRL64733
  NGURIPX66352
  NMUELEX66864
  WDOUVEX57742
UNESCO
  GBERGMX54442
  NBERGMX54076
UNION PULP AND PAPER WORKERS
  WWOMEI X66273
UNIV OF CHICAGO CFSOLEFA
  NGOLDFH63429
  NGOLDFH63430
  NHENDVW63514
  NPARRCH63975
  WSOLODX64128
UNIV OF MICH BUREAU IND RELS
  WODIOGS61042
UNIV OF MINN IND RELS CENTER
  GNELSRJ52055
UNIV OF NORTH CAROLINA IRSS
  IGULIJX60568
  NPRICOO65018
UNIV OF WIS URBAN PROGRAM
  CSHANLW63484
UNIVERSITY OF PITTSBURGH
  WSTEIER62153
UNIVERSITY OF TEXAS
  NMARSRX66327
UPJOHN INST EMPLOY RESEARCH
  GBECKJX65430
  GHABEWX63615
  GLEVISA63899
  GLEVISA64897
  GLEVISA65601
  GLEVISA66531
  GWICKED63561
  GWICKEX63637
  NSHEPHL66128
  NSHEPHL66129
  WLEVISA63039
UPR MANPOWER RESOURCES PROJ
  PGREGPX61857
US BUREAU OF THE CENSUS
  GBOWLGK65433
  GCOWHJD61427
  GMILLHP55988
  GMILLHP66778
US CHAMBER OF COMMERCE
  CBATCAB66879
  GCLARKB66915
  GLEVISA66038
  GSWANJC66155
  NGINZEX66971
  NHAUSPM66992
  NWHITWL66231
US COMM ON CIVIL RIGHTS
  CRUBIEBND848
  CSAMOJX63474
  MSAMOJX62473
  MSAMOJX64475
US CONFERENCE OF MAYORS
  GKENNJF63842
US DEPARTMENT OF LABOR
  NBEDEMS53071
US DEPARTMENT OF AGRICULTURE
  GBEALCL63426
  GBEALCL64423
  GBIRDAR64450
  GBOWLGK56433
  GBOWLGK65424
  GBOWLGK65432
  GBOWLGK65434
  GBOWLGK66430
  GBOXLRF65418
  GCOWHJD59430
  GCOWHJD60423
  GCOWHJD61427
  GCOWHJD63420
  GCOWHJD63421
  GCOWHJD64419
  GCOWHJD65435
  GFRIERE62431
  GHENDWE59422
  GMAIEFH60417
  GMAITST58428
  GMAITST59429
  GMAITST60436
  GMAITST61383
  GMAITST61384
  GMETZWH55426
  GMETZWH60440
  GMETZWH62504
  GMOOREJ64386
  GSHAREF59428
  GSHAREF60427
  GUSDAGR60425
  GWHYTDR60407
  MFRIERE63394
  MGRISGXND408
  MMCELRCH65805
  NBEALCL58064
US DEPARTMENT OF COMMERCE
  CUVCAIIND524
  NBRIMAF64891
  NBRIMAF66114
US DEPARTMENT OF INTERIOR
  IBLOQJA59538
  ICOOMLM62646
  INASHPX64134
  INASHPX64597
  IREIFBX58610
US DEPARTMENT OF LABOR
  CKEYSMD65646
  CSAINMD66320
  CSELFHO66325
  CSKILTO66324
  CWEINJL64310
  GACKLGX66608
  GALTEJX65369
  GARNSSX64404
  GBANCGX60418
  GBANYCA61420
  GBARRGJ51425
  GBEDEMX64448
  GBLUMAW61117
  GBOGAFA64460

GBOGAFA65750
GBOGAFA66138
GBOGAFA66918
GBOKXD64736
GBOKXD64737
GCARRHX66558
GCASSFH66561
GCHICBC65319
GCHURRX55572
GCLAGEX65794
GCONWJT65496
GCOOPSX59928
GCOOPSX60601
GCOOPSX60603
GCOOPSX62602
GCOOPSX66604
GCOWHJD65933
GCRAICE65619
GCRAICE66620
GCULHMM65651
GCUMMLD65623
GDALYVR66625
GDOARLE66645
GDOERPB67115
GDVORBJ65650
GFANTAX64671
GGOLDHX63787
GGORDRA65675
GGRAYCJ51736
GGREEHX66627
GGREELX64614
GGROOPX64745
GHAMEHR63755
GHAMEHR65756
GHAMMHR66145
GHELPCW63501
GHOLLSS65124
GJELTMM66823
GJOHNDF63828
GJOHNDF65784
GKALICB66012
GKESSMA63848
GKRUGDH65628
GLAFADP65782
GLESTRA66532
GLOCKHC66906
GLUDELE52923
GMACYJW66933
GMANOSP63855
GMARSJX66944
GMEREJL61995
GMEREJL63067
GMICADN64673
GMILLHP64853
GMIREWX57499
GMITCHR66018
GMITCJP65594
GMOTLAW53033
GPERRVC64168
GPERRVC66774
GPOTTGX65189
GQUINPA65771
GROSECX60257
GROSORG66258
GRUDDEN63027
GRUSSJL66269
GSABESX64271
GSABESX64272
GSALNEX65769
GSALTAF66534
GSCHIJX60283
GSCHIJX61294
GSCHIJX62285
GSCHIJX63282
GSCHIJX63286
GSHOSAL66530
GSHULGX66142
GSPITRS45332
GSTAMHX65768
GSTEIRL63838
GSTEIRL64336
GSTRIHE66669
GSULLLH66220
GSWERSX66533
GTAYLHC66967
GTHAMME59022
GTRAVHX63836
GWATSMMND544
GWISPLG65141
GWOODMJ64581
GZEISJS63704
IARCHMS61526
IBECKJX66536
IFISHCR66559
IGRAFMF66565
ILINDVX64581
ILINDVX66580
ISANDJN62615
MDUFFLC66390
MGALLLX62399
NAMOSWE64331
NANDEBE65023
NBARDHX64095
NBEAUAG66067
NBRAZWF64318
NCASSFH66185
NCHAPAA66192
NCLARKB65213
NCOCKHW65218
NCRAICE65240
NCROFES66242
NDAVILM64942
NDOARLE66276
NFILIJE66354
NFRANWH66698
NFREYMX66386
NHARRCV65491
NHAYEMX62506
NHENDEW43510
NHOLMAX66563
NHUSOCF66328
NMARSRX62749
NMARSRX65744
NMARSRX66327
NMATTEG66759
NMCENDX50721
NMCKIGB56725
NMINIBC65797
NMOYNDP65862

NNEWMDKND957
NNEWMDK65908
NNEWMDK65909
NOXLELA64969
NPAGEDX66970
NPALLNJ65332
NRICHCX64058
NRINGHH53061
NRITTAL45062
NROSSAM66081
NRUSSJL66096
NWESTZJ66317
NWETZJR66114
NWHITWL66320
NWILKWH41323
NWOLFSL45335
NWOLFSL47334
PCASTCX58786
PMONTHK59829
PMONTHX60830
PPUERRDND788
WARRORC66216
WCARRMS62681
WCHICRC62689
WCOMPBX66702
WELLIKX63748
WFLORMP66326
WGARFSH57180
WGARFSH57774
WGOVECS66215
WGRIFVE58804
WGROSSB59807
WHEDGJN64994
WHOFFGL61846
WJAFFAH56878
WKEYSMD64894
WKEYSMD64898
WKEYSMD64899
WKEYSMD64900
WKEYSMD65893
WKEYSMD65895
WKEYSMD65897
WKEYSMD66901
WLEITSF61926
WMEREJL60970
WMEYEMB61975
WMIDWRP65209
WPASCWX58178
WROSECX62087
WROSECX65088
WSTEIRL61226
WSWERSX64145
WSWERSX64767
WWELLJA60262
WWESTEM65210
WWESTRC62214
WWIRTWW62181
WWIRTWH63271
US DEPARTMENT OF LABOR.
  NEDELHX66320
  NKESSMA63019
US DEPT HEALTH ED WELFARE
  GPALMFX63671
  GRODOAL64241
US DEPT OF HEALTH ED WELFARE
  GBENJJG65006
  GBRADDS65679
  GBROOLB64795
  GCOWHJD65614
  GGURALX62748
  GHANEGE64004
  GHUYCEE65790
  GORSHMX63141
  GORSHMX65142
  GORSHMX65144
  GORSHMX66280
  GORSHMX66282
  GORSHMX66642
  GSCHOAL65122
  GSIFFHX64105
  GTITMRM65359
  IWAGNCJ64681
  MCLAPRF66112
  MHAYDRG66114
  NBATEWM66880
  NCALIAX49174
  NCOLEJS66223
  NDOUGJH64285
  NEPSTLA63337
  NGURIPX66352
  NHERZEX63522
  NLITTLW66697
  NORSHMX64960
  NSAMOTX65128
  WBARKAE65628
  WHERZEX64123
  WHOFFGL61846
  WIFFERE57854
  WLAJEHC59922
  WPOLIEJ65285
US EEO COMMISSION
  GWALLPX66539
  NOSBUDD66963
US EMPLOYMENT SERVICE
  NLEVILX62686
  NLEVILX64685
US FEP COMMITTEE
  NGOLICL45432
US IDEPTL COMT STATUS WOMEN
  WUSCISC66483
US LIBRARY OF CONGRESS
  GELWAEX58662
  GGRAVWB48734
  GGRAVWB51735
  GHESLMR63773
US LIBRARY OF CONGRESS LRS
  GBUTCGT63508
  GMITCJA52016
US OFFICE OF EC OPPORTUNITY
  GCAHNEX66905
US PUBLIC HEALTH SERVICE
  WHARTRE60828
US VETERANS ADMINISTRATION
  GWALLLM63520
VIRGINIA STATE COLLEGE
  NBRAZWF64285
  NBRAZWF64318
WAITRESS CAFETERIA WK UNION
  WGABELX66773
WASH AGL EXPERIMENT STATION

```
                IROYXPX61612
WASH CENT FOR METROP STUDIES
                NGRIEES63454
                NGRIEGXND982
                NLEWIHX61040
WASH S INST AG EXPMT STATION
                WSLOCWL56116
WASH STATE LEGISLATIVE CC
                GWALLFX61221
                NWALLFX61221
WASH UNIV DEPT OF IND RELS
                NSOBEIX54178
WELFARE CC METROPOLITAN CHI
                MIMMASM57420
                NFRAZEF57378
                PMONSJX57828
WESTERN ELECTRONIC MNFG ASSN
                WEVANSX66753
WICHITA URBAN LEAGUE
                NBANNWM65051
WIS GOVRS COMM OF HUM RIGHTS
                GRAUSEX62218
WOMANS DIV CHRISTIAN SERVICE
                GMURRPX50034
WOMEN-S ADVSY COMM TO FEPC
                WPALMGX66047
WORKERS DEFENSE LEAGUE
                GRAUSWX45583
YMCA            GBRADPX46247
YMCA VOCATL SERVICE CENTER
                CYMCAYA66329
YWCA            WTHOMGX66149
```

List of Keywords

ABC
ABILITY
ABOLISH
ABSENT
ABSENTEEISM
ABSORPTION
ABSTRACT
ABUNDANCE
ABUSES
ACADEMIC
ACCEPTANCE
ACCESS
ACCIDENTAL
ACCOMODATION
ACCOMODATIONS
ACCREDITED
ACCULTURATION
ACCULTURIZATION
ACCUSED
ACHIEVEMENT
ACHIEVEMENTS
ACHIEVING
ACT
ACTION
ACTIONS
ACTIVE
ACTIVITIES
ACTIVITY
ACTS
ADAPTATION
ADAPTATIONS
ADC
ADDICT
ADDRESS
ADDRESSES
ADEQUACY
ADJUDICATION
ADJUSTING
ADJUSTMENT
ADJUSTMENTS
ADL
ADMINISTRATION
ADMINISTRATIVE
ADMINISTRATORS
ADMISSION
ADOLESCENCE
ADOLESCENT
ADOLESCENTS
ADULT
ADULT-EDUCATION
ADULTS
ADVANCEMENT
ADVANCES
ADVENTURE
ADVISORS
ADVISORY
AFDC
AFFIRMATIVE
AFFIRMATIVE-ACTION
AFFIRMATIVE-ACTIONS
AFFLUENCE
AFL
AFL-CIO
AGE
AGED
AGENCIES
AGENCY
AGENCY-S
AGES
AGGREGATE
AGGRESSIVE
AGING
AGRICULTURAL
AGRICULTURE
AID
AID-TO-DEPENDENT-CHI
AIDING
AIDS
AIR
AIR-FORCE
AIRCRAFT
AIRLINE
AIRPLANE
AKRON
ALABAMA
ALBANY
ALBION
ALBUQUERQUE
ALCOHOL
ALCORN-COUNTY
ALIENATION
ALLEGED
ALLEGING
ALLIANCE
ALONE
ALUMNAE
AMBITION
AMBITIONS
AMBIVALENCE
AMENDED
AMENDMENT
AMENDMENTS
AMERICAN-INDIAN
AMERICAN-INDIANS
AMERICAN-JEWISH-COMM
AMERICANIZATION
AMERICANS
ANALYSIS
ANALYTICAL
ANCESTRY
ANGLO
ANGLO-AMERIANS
ANGLO-CAUCASIANS
ANGLOS
ANN-ARBOR
ANNOTATED
ANNOTATIONS
ANNUAL
ANOMIA
ANOMIE
ANSWER
ANSWERS
ANTECEDENTS
ANTHROPOLOGICAL
ANTHROPOLOGY
ANTI
ANTI-BIAS
ANTI-DISCRIMINATION
ANTI-DISCRIMINATORY
ANTI-JAPANESE

ANTI-LABOR
ANTI-NEPOTISM
ANTI-POVERTY
ANTIDISCRIMINATION
ANXIETY
APACHE
APPEALS
APPLICANT
APPLICANTS
APPLICATION
APPLIES
APPLY
APPOINTMENT
APPOINTMENTS
APPRAISAL
APPRENTICE
APPRENTICES
APPRENTICESHIP
APPRENTICESHIPS
APPROACH
APPROACHES
APTITUDE
APTITUDES
ARAPAHOE
AREA
AREA-REDEVELOPMENT-A
AREAS
ARIZONA
ARIZONA-S
ARKANSAS
ARMED
ARMY
ARRANGEMENTS
ARREST
ARROWHEAD
ARTS
ASPIRATION
ASPIRATIONS
ASSEMBLY
ASSESSING
ASSESSMENT
ASSETS
ASSIGNMENT
ASSIGNMENTS
ASSIMILATION
ASSIST
ASSISTANCE
ASSISTANTS
ASSISTED
ASSOCIATION
ASSOCIATIONS
ASTD
ATASCOSA-COUNTY
ATLANTA
ATLANTA-S
ATLANTIC
ATLANTIC-CITY
ATOMIC-ENERGY-COMMIS
ATTACKS
ATTAINMENT
ATTENDANCE
ATTENDING
ATTITUDE
ATTITUDES
ATTITUDINAL
ATTRIBUTES
AUDIT
AUSTIN
AUTHORITARIANISM
AUTHORITY
AUTO
AUTOMATED
AUTOMATING
AUTOMATION
AUTOMOBILE
AUTOMOBILE-WORKERS
AVAILABILITY
BACK-TO-WORK
BACKGROUND
BACKGROUNDS
BAILEYS
BAKING
BALANCED
BALTIMORE
BALTIMORE-S
BAN
BANK
BANK-OF-AMERICA
BANKING
BANKS
BAR
BARGAINING
BARRIER
BARRIERS
BARRIO
BASE
BASES
BASIC
BATON-ROUGE
BATTLE
BATTLE-AXES
BATTLEFRONT
BAY
BEET
BEHAVIOR
BELATED
BELT
BENEFIT
BENEFIT-COST
BENEFITS
BERKELEY
BI-RACIAL
BIAS
BIBLIOGRAPHY
BICULTURATION
BIDS
BIGOTRY
BILL
BILLS
BIOLOGICAL
BIOSCIENTISTS
BIRMINGHAM
BIRTH
BISHOP-S
BISMARK
BLACK
BLACKFEET
BLACKLAND
BLANK
BLIND

BLINDNESS
BLOCK
BLS
BLUE-COLLAR
BLUEPRINT
BNA
BOARD
BOILERMAKERS
BOOK
BOOM
BOOTSTRAP
BORDER
BOSS
BOSSES
BOSTON
BOURGEOISIE
BOYCOTT
BOYS
BRACERO
BRACEROS
BRACKETS
BRAVE
BREAKDOWN
BREAKTHROUGH
BREWERIES
BREWERY
BRIEF
BRIGHT
BRONX
BROOKLYN
BROOME-COUNTY
BROTHERHOOD
BROTHERS
BRUNSWICK
BUFFALO
BUILD
BUILDING
BULLETIN
BURDEN
BURDENS
BUREAU
BUREAU-OF-INDIAN-AFF
BUSINESS
BUSINESS-MAN
BUSINESSES
BUSINESSMAN
BUSINESSMEN
CALIFORNIA
CALIFORNIA-S
CALIFORNIANS
CALVERT
CAMDEN
CAMP
CAMPAIGN
CAMPAIGNS
CAMPS
CAMPUS
CANDIDATES
CANNING
CANTONESE
CANTONESE-AMERICAN
CAPABILITIES
CAPACITIES
CAPITAL
CAPITOL
CAR
CARDERS
CARE
CAREER
CAREER-MARRIAGE
CAREER-MOTIVATED
CAREER-SEEKING
CAREERS
CAROLINAS
CARRIERS
CASE
CASE-REPORTS
CASE-STUDIES
CASE-STUDY
CASES
CASEWORK
CASTE
CASUALTIES
CATALYST
CATEGORIES
CATTLE
CAUSES
CENSUS
CENSUSES
CENTER
CENTRAL
CENTURY
CERTIFICATIONS
CHALLENGE
CHALLENGES
CHALLENGING
CHAMPAIGN-URBANA
CHANCE
CHANCES
CHANGE
CHANGES
CHANGING
CHARACTER
CHARACTERISTICS
CHARGES
CHARLOTTE
CHARTS
CHATTANOOGA
CHAUVINISM
CHEMICAL
CHEMISTS
CHEROKEE
CHEROKEES
CHICAGO
CHILD
CHILD-REARING
CHILDBEARING
CHILDREN
CHILDREN-S
CHINA-TOWN
CHINATOWN-NORTH
CHINESE
CHIPPEWA
CHOICE
CHOICES
CHRONICLE
CIGAR
CINCINNATI
CINNCINATI
CIO

CITIES
CITIZENS
CITY
CITY-S
CIVIC
CIVIL
CIVIL-AERONAUTICS-BO
CIVIL-LIBERTIES
CIVIL-RIGHTS
CIVIL-RIGHTS-ACT
CIVIL-SERVICE
CIVILIAN
CLAIMANTS
CLAIMS
CLARK
CLASH
CLASS
CLASSES
CLASSIFICATION
CLASSROOM
CLAUSE
CLAUSES
CLEAR
CLERICAL
CLERKS
CLEVELAND
CLEVELAND-S
CLIENTS
CLINICS
CLOTHING
CO-ED
CO-WORKERS
COACHELLA-VALLEY
COAHOMA
COAL
COAST
COASTAL
CODE
COED
COLLAR
COLLECTION
COLLECTIONS
COLLECTIVE
COLLECTIVE-BARGAININ
COLLEGE
COLLEGE-EDUCATED
COLLEGE-TRAINED
COLLEGES
COLOR
COLORADO
COLORED
COLUMBIA
COLVILLE
COMBATING
COMMENT
COMMENTARY
COMMENTS
COMMERCE
COMMERCIAL
COMMISSION
COMMISSION-AGAINST-D
COMMISSION-ON-CIVIL-
COMMISSIONER
COMMISSIONS
COMMITMENT
COMMITTEE
COMMITTEES
COMMUNICATION
COMMUNICATIONS
COMMUNITIES
COMMUNITY
COMMUNITY-ACTION
COMPANIES
COMPANY
COMPANY-S
COMPARATIVE
COMPARED
COMPARISON
COMPARISONS
COMPENSATING
COMPENSATION
COMPENSATORY
COMPENSATORY-EDUCATI
COMPETENCE
COMPETING
COMPETITIVE
COMPETITORS
COMPILATION
COMPILED
COMPLAINT
COMPLAINTS
COMPLIANCE
COMPOSITE
COMPOSITION
COMPREHENSIVE
COMPROMISE
COMPTON
COMPULSION
COMPUTER
COMPUTERS
CONCENTRATION
CONCEPT
CONCEPTION
CONCEPTS
CONCEPTUAL
CONCERN
CONCERNS
CONCILIATION
CONCLUSIONS
CONDITION
CONDITIONS
CONFERENCE
CONFERENCES
CONFLICT
CONFLICTING
CONFLICTS
CONFRONTATION
CONFRONTING
CONGRESS
CONGRESS-OF-RACIAL-E
CONGRESSIONAL
CONNECTICUT
CONQUEST
CONSCIENCE
CONSCIENTIOUS
CONSCIOUSNESS
CONSEQUENCES
CONSOLIDATED
CONSTITUTION
CONSTITUTIONAL
CONSTRAINTS

CONSTRUCTION
CONSULTANTS
CONSULTATIONS
CONSUMER
CONSUMPTION
CONTACT
CONTEMPORARY
CONTEXT
CONTINUING
CONTINUITIES
CONTRACT
CONTRACTOR
CONTRACTORS
CONTRACTS
CONTRASTS
CONTRIBUTION
CONTRIBUTIONS
CONTROL
CONTROLS
CONTROVERSIAL
CONTROVERSIES
CONTROVERSY
CONVENTION
COOPERATION
COOPERATIVE
COOPERATIVES
COORDINATED
COORDINATION
CORPORATE
CORPORATION
CORPORATIONS
CORRECTIVE
CORRELATES
CORRELATIONS
COST
COST-BENEFIT
COSTS
COTTON
COTTON-PICKER
COUNCIL
COUNCILS
COUNSELING
COUNSELLING
COUNSELOR
COUNSELOR-S
COUNSELORS
COUNTIES
COUNTY
COURSE
COURSES
COURT
COURTS
COVERAGE
COVERED
CPA
CPI
CRAFT
CRAFTSMEN
CREATION
CREDIT
CREED
CREWS
CRIME
CRIMINALITY
CRISES
CRISIS
CRITERIA
CRITICAL
CRITICS
CROSS-CULTURAL
CROSSROADS
CROW
CULTURAL
CULTURAL-BACKGROUND
CULTURALLY
CULTURE
CULTURE-OF-POVERTY
CULTURES
CUMBERLANDS
CURRENT
CURRICULAR
CURRICULUM
CUSTOMER
CUSTOMERS
CYBERNATION
CYCLE
DAKOTA
DALLAS
DATA
DAY
DAY-CARE
DEBATE
DECADES
DECAY
DECERTIFIES
DECISION
DECISION-MAKING
DECISIONS
DECLARATION
DECLINE
DEFENSE
DEGREE
DELANO
DELAWARE
DELINQUENCY
DELINQUENT
DELTA
DEMAND
DEMOCRACY
DEMOCRACY-S
DEMOCRATIC
DEMOGRAPHIC
DEMOGRAPHY
DEMONSTRATION
DEMONSTRATIONAL
DENTAL
DENTIST
DENTISTS
DENVER
DEPARTMENT
DEPARTMENT-OF-DEFENS
DEPARTMENT-OF-THE-TR
DEPARTMENTAL
DEPARTMENTS
DEPENDENCY
DEPENDENT
DEPRESSED
DEPRIVATION
DEPRIVATIONS
DEPRIVED

DES-MOINES
DESCENT
DESEGREGATION
DESERT
DESIGN
DESIGNATION
DESIGNED
DETERMINANTS
DETERMINATION
DETERMINE
DETERMINING
DETRIBALIZATION
DETROIT
DETROIT-S
DEVELOPING
DEVELOPMENT
DEVELOPMENTAL
DEVELOPMENTS
DIAGNOSTIC
DIALECT
DIETICIANS
DIFFERENCES
DIFFERENT
DIFFERENTIAL
DIFFERENTIALS
DIFFERENTIATION
DIGEST
DILEMMA
DILEMMAS
DIMENSION
DIMENSIONS
DIRECTIONS
DIRECTIVES
DIRECTORY
DISABILITY
DISADVANTAGED
DISADVANTAGES
DISCONTINUITIES
DISCRIMINATING
DISCRIMINATION
DISCRIMINATORY
DISCUSSION
DISCUSSIONS
DISINTEGRATION
DISORGANIZATION
DISPLACED
DISPLACEMENT
DISPOSSESSED
DISPUTES
DISTANCE
DISTINGUISH
DISTRIBUTION
DISTRICT
DISTRICT-OF-COLUMBIA
DIVISION
DIVISION-OF-LABOR
DIVISIONS
DIXIE
DOCTORAL
DOCTORS
DOCTRINE
DOCUMENT
DOCUMENTARY
DOGMA
DOLLARS
DOMESTIC
DOMESTIC-SERVANTS
DOMESTIC-SERVICE
DREAM
DRIVE
DRIVER
DRIVES
DROP-OUT
DROP-OUTS
DROPOUT
DROPOUTS
DUE
DULUTH
DURHAM
DUTIES
DUTY
DYNAMICS
EARNING
EARNINGS
EAST
EAST-HARLEM
EAST-HARLEM-YOUTH-EM
EASTERN
ECOLOGICAL
ECONOMETRIC
ECONOMIC
ECONOMIC-GROWTH
ECONOMIC-OPPORTUNITY
ECONOMIC-STATUS
ECONOMIC-TRENDS
ECONOMICAL
ECONOMICALLY
ECONOMICS
ECONOMIST-S
ECONOMY
EDUCABILITY
EDUCATE
EDUCATED
EDUCATING
EDUCATION
EDUCATION-S
EDUCATIONAL
EDUCATIONAL-ATTAINME
EDUCATORS
EEO
EEOC
EFFECT
EFFECTIVENESS
EFFECTS
EGO
EISENHOWER
EL-PASO
ELAN
ELDERLY
ELECTRIC
ELECTRONIC
ELEMENTARY
ELIMINATE
ELIMINATED
ELIMINATING
ELIMINATION
ELITE
ELMIRA
EMANCIPATION
EMMITSBURG

EMPIRICAL
EMPLOYABILITY
EMPLOYABLE
EMPLOYED
EMPLOYEE
EMPLOYEES
EMPLOYER
EMPLOYERS
EMPLOYING
EMPLOYMENT
EMPLOYMENT-AGENCIES
EMPLOYMENT-AGENCY
EMPLOYMENT-CONDITION
EMPLOYMENT-EDUCATION
EMPLOYMENT-OPPORTUNI
EMPLOYMENT-PRACTICE-
EMPLOYMENT-PRACTICES
EMPLOYMENT-SELECTION
EMPLOYMENT-SERVICE
EMPLOYMENT-STATUS
EMPLOYMENT-TRENDS
ENCYCLOPEDIA
END
ENDS
ENFORCEMENT
ENGINEERING
ENGINEERS
ENGLISH
ENJOIN
ENROLLED
ENROLLEES
ENROLLMENT
ENTERING
ENTERPRISE
ENTREPRENEUR
ENTREPRENEURSHIP
ENTRY
ENVIRONMENT
ENVIRONMENTAL
EQUAL
EQUAL-ECONOMIC-OPPOR
EQUAL-EMPLOYMENT
EQUAL-EMPLOYMENT-ACT
EQUAL-EMPLOYMENT-OPP
EQUAL-EMPLOYMENT-POL
EQUAL-JOB-OPPORTUNIT
EQUAL-JOB-RIGHTS
EQUAL-OPPORTUNITIES
EQUAL-OPPORTUNITY
EQUAL-PAY
EQUAL-PAY-ACT
EQUAL-RIGHTS
EQUALITY
EQUALIZATION
ESSAY
ESSAYS
ESSEX-COUNTY
ESTABLISHMENT
ESTIMATED
ESTIMATES
ETHICS
ETHNIC
ETHNIC-GROUP
ETHNICALLY
ETHNICITY
ETHNICS
ETHNOMICS
EUGENE-SPRINGFIELD
EVALUATED
EVALUATING
EVALUATION
EVENTS
EVIDENCE
EVOLUTION
EX-MIGRANT
EXAMINATION
EXAMINATIONS
EXAMPLES
EXCERPTS
EXCHANGE
EXCLUSION
EXCLUSIONS
EXECUTIVE
EXECUTIVE-ORDER
EXECUTIVE-SUITE
EXECUTIVES
EXPANDED
EXPANDING
EXPANDS
EXPANSION
EXPECTATION
EXPECTATIONS
EXPECTED-CASES
EXPENDITURES
EXPENSES
EXPERIENCE
EXPERIENCED
EXPERIENCES
EXPERIMENT
EXPERIMENTAL
EXPLORATION
EXPLORATORY
EXPOSURE
EXTREMISM
FACETED
FACETS
FACILITATION
FACILITATIVE
FACILITIES
FACT
FACTOR
FACTORS
FACTORY
FACTS
FACULTIES
FACULTY
FAILURE
FAILURES
FAIR
FAIR-EMPLOYERS
FAIR-EMPLOYMENT
FAIR-EMPLOYMENT-PRAC
FALLACIES
FAMILIAL
FAMILIES
FAMILY
FAMILY-S
FARM
FARMER
FARMERS

FARMING
FARMS
FARMWORKER
FARMWORKERS
FATHER
FATHER-ABSENCE
FATHERS
FEDERAL
FEDERAL-AVIATION-AGE
FEDERAL-EMPLOYMENT
FEDERAL-GOVERNMENT
FEDERAL-SERVICE
FEDERAL-SERVICES
FEDERAL-STATE
FEDERALLY-ASSISTED
FEMALE
FEMALE-BASED
FEMALE-HEADED
FEMALES
FEMININE
FEP
FEPC
FEPC-S
FIELD
FIELDS
FIGHT
FIGHTING
FIGHTS
FILIPINO
FILIPINOS
FINANCIAL
FINDINGS
FIRED
FIRM
FIRMS
FISCAL
FLORIDA
FOLK
FOLKWAYS
FOLLOW-UP
FOLLOWUP
FOOD
FORCE
FORCED
FORCES
FORD
FORECASTS
FOREIGN
FORMAL
FORMS
FORT-BELKNAP
FORT-HALL
FORT-PECK
FORTUNE
FORUMS
FOUNDATION
FOUNDATIONS
FOX
FRANCHISE
FREEDOM
FRENCH
FRESHMAN
FRESHMEN
FRINGE
FRONTIER
FRONTIERS
FRUIT
FRUITLAND
FRUSTRATION
FULL
FULL-EMPLOYMENT
FULL-TIME
FULLTIME
FUNCTION
FUNDS
FUTURE
FUTURES
GAINFUL
GAINS
GALLUP
GAP
GARMENT
GAS
GATEKEEPERS
GENERATION
GENERATIONS
GEOGRAPHIC
GEOGRAPHICAL
GEOGRAPHY
GEORGIA
GHETTO
GHETTOS
GI
GIFTED
GIRL
GIRLS
GLASS
GOAL
GOAL-ORIENTATIONS
GOALS
GOMPERS
GOVERNMENT
GOVERNMENT-CONTRACTO
GOVERNMENT-SPONSORED
GOVERNMENTAL
GOVERNMENTS
GOVERNOR
GOVERNOR-S
GOVERNORS
GRADE
GRADS
GRADUATE
GRADUATED
GRADUATES
GRADUATING
GRADUATION
GRAND-RAPIDS
GRANTS
GRAPE
GREAT-SOCIETY
GRIEVANCE-PROCEDURES
GROUP
GROUPINGS
GROUPS
GROWERS
GROWING
GROWTH
GUARANTEED-INCOME
GUARD
GUIDANCE

GUIDE
GUIDELINES
GUIDES
GUIDING
GUILTY
HALE
HANDBOOK
HANDICAPPED
HARD-CORE
HARD-TO-EMPLOY
HARLEM
HARRIS-COUNTY
HARTFORD
HARVARD
HARVEST
HARVESTER
HARVESTERS
HATE
HAWAII
HAY-COUNTY
HEALING
HEALTH
HEALTH-STATUS
HEARING
HEARINGS
HERITAGE
HIDDEN
HIGH
HIGHER
HIGHEST
HIGHLIGHTS
HIGHWAY
HINDSIGHT
HIRE
HIRED
HIRING
HISTORICAL
HISTORY
HOLDING
HOME
HOMEMAKER
HOMEMAKERS
HOMEMAKING
HOMEMAKING-MOTIVATED
HOMEMAKING-ORIENTED
HOMES
HOPE
HOPES
HOPI
HORIZONS
HOSPITAL
HOSPITALS
HOTEL
HOTELS
HOUGH
HOURS
HOUSE
HOUSEHOLD
HOUSEHOLD-EMPLOYEES
HOUSEHOLD-WORKERS
HOUSEHOLDS
HOUSEWIFE
HOUSING
HOUSTON
HUDON-COUNTY
HUELGA
HUGE
HUGHES
HUI-CH-IAO
HUMAN
HUMAN-RELATIONS
HUMAN-RELATIONS-COMM
HUMAN-RESOURCE
HUMAN-RESOURCES
HUMAN-RIGHTS
HUNT
HUSBAND
HUSBAND-S
HYPOTHESES
HYPOTHESIS
IDAHO
IDENTIFICATION
IDENTIFICATIONS
IDENTITY
IDEOLOGY
ILGWU
ILLEGAL
ILLINOIS
IMAGE
IMAGES
IMAGINATION
IMBALANCE
IMBALANCES
IMMIGRANT
IMMIGRANTS
IMMIGRATION
IMMOKALEE
IMPACT
IMPLEMENTATION
IMPLEMENTING
IMPLICATIONS
IMPORTED
IMPROVE
IMPROVED
IMPROVEMENT
IMPROVES
IMPROVING
IMPUTATIONS
IN-MIGRANT
INACTIVE
INCENTIVES
INCIDENCE
INCOME
INCOME-DISTRIBUTION
INCOME-GUARANTEE
INCOME-MAINTENANCE
INCOMES
INCREASED
INCREASES
INCREASING
INDEX
INDIAN
INDIANA
INDIANAPOLIS
INDIANS
INDICATOR
INDICATORS
INDICES
INDIVIDUAL
INDIVIDUALITY

INDIVIDUALS
INDUSTRIAL
INDUSTRIAL-RELATIONS
INDUSTRIALIZATION
INDUSTRIES
INDUSTRY
INDUSTRY-S
INEQUALITIES
INEQUALITY
INFLATION
INFLUENCE
INFLUENCES
INFLUENCING
INFORMATION
INFRINGEMENT
INHIBIT
INHIBITIVE
INITIATIVE
INJUSTICE
INQUIRIES
INQUIRY
INSECURITY
INSIGHT
INSPECTION
INSTITUTE
INSTITUTIONAL
INSTITUTIONS
INSTRUCTION
INSURANCE
INSURED
INSURING
INTEGRATE
INTEGRATED
INTEGRATING
INTEGRATION
INTEGRATIONISTS
INTELLECTUAL
INTELLECTUALLY
INTELLIGENCE
INTER-AGENCY
INTER-GROUP
INTER-INDUSTRY
INTER-RACIAL
INTERACTION
INTERAGENCY
INTEREST
INTERESTS
INTERGROUP
INTERGROUP-RELATIONS
INTERIM
INTERINDUSTRY
INTERIOR
INTERMOUNTAIN
INTERNATIONAL
INTERNATIONAL-HARVES
INTERPERSONAL
INTERPRETATION
INTERPRETATIONS
INTERPRETING
INTERPRETIVE
INTERRACIAL
INTERRELATIONSHIPS
INTERSTATE
INTERVENTION
INTERVIEW
INTERVIEWS
INTRA-PLANT
INTRODUCTION
INVASIONS
INVENTORY
INVESTIGATION
INVESTIGATIONS
INVESTIGATIVE
INVESTING
INVESTOR-OWNED
IOWA
IRON
IRREGULARITIES
ISOLATED
ISOLATION
ISSUE
ISSUES
ITALIAN
ITINERANT
JACKSONVILLE
JAPANESE
JAPANESE-AMERICANS
JEOPARDY
JEW
JEWISH
JEWS
JICARILLA
JIM-CROW
JOB
JOB-APPLICANTS
JOB-CHOICE
JOB-CORPS
JOB-DEVELOPMENT
JOB-EQUALITY
JOB-HOLDERS
JOB-LESS
JOB-MARKET
JOB-MOBILITY
JOB-OPPORTUNITIES
JOB-RELATED
JOB-SEARCH
JOBHOLDERS
JOBLESS
JOBLESSNESS
JOBS
JOB-SEEKERS
JOBSITE
JOHNSON
JOURNALISTS
JOURNEY
JUNIOR
JURISDICTION
JUSTICE
JUVENILE
JUVENILE-DELINQUENCY
JUVENILES
KANSAS
KANSAS-CITY
KENNEDY
KENTUCKY
KERN
KERN-COUNTY
KEY
KINSHIP
KITCHEN

KLAMATH
KLAMATH-FALLS
KLINEBERG
KNOWLEDGE
KOREA
LABOR
LABOR-FORCE
LABOR-MANAGEMENT
LABOR-MARKET
LABOR-MARKETS
LABOR-MOBILITY
LABOR-MOVEMENT
LABOR-NEGRO
LABOR-RELATIONS
LABOR-S
LABOR-SUPPLY
LABORATORIES
LABORER
LABORERS
LABORFFECTS
LABORING
LABOUR-FORCE
LAKE-ARROWHEAD
LAND
LANGUAGE
LANSING
LAREDO
LATIN
LATIN-AMERICAN
LATIN-AMERICANS
LAUNDRY
LAW
LAW-SOCIOLOGY
LAWFUL
LAWFULNESS
LAWS
LAWYER
LAWYERS
LAYOFFS
LEADER-S
LEADERS
LEADERSHIP
LEADING
LEAGUE-OF-WOMEN-VOTE
LEARN
LEARNER
LEARNING
LEAVERS
LEFT
LEGACY
LEGAL
LEGAL-STATUS
LEGALITY
LEGISLATION
LEGISLATIVE
LEGISLATURE
LENGTH
LESSON
LESSONS
LEVEL
LEVELS
LIBERAL
LIBERALISM
LIBERALS
LIBERTIES
LIBERTY
LIBRARIANS
LIBRARIES
LIBRARY
LIFE
LIFE-STYLE
LIFETIME
LIFTING
LIMIT
LIMITATIONS
LIMITED
LIMITS
LINK
LIST
LITERACY
LITERATURE
LITIGATION
LITTLE-ROCK
LIVE
LIVES
LIVING
LOAN
LOANS
LOCAL
LOCALS
LOCATION
LOCKHEED
LOCKHEED-AIRCRAFT-CO
LONG-RANGE
LONG-TERM
LONGEVITY
LONGSHORE
LONGSHOREMEN
LOS-ANGELES
LOSS
LOST
LOUISIANA
LOUISVILLE
LOW
LOW-INCOME
LOW-INCOMES
LOW-SKILL
LOW-WAGE
LOWER
LOWER-BLUE-COLLAR
LOWER-CLASS
LOWER-CLASSES
LOWER-EAST-SIDE
LUISENO
MACHINE
MACHINES
MACON
MAINLAND
MAINSTREAM
MAJOR
MAJORS
MALADJUSTED
MALE
MALE-FEMALE
MALES
MAN
MAN-S
MANAGEMENT
MANAGEMENT-S
MANAGEMENTS

MANAGER-S
MANAGERIAL
MANAGERS
MANAGING
MANDATORY
MANHATTAN
MANIFESTO
MANPOWER
MANPOWER-DEVELOPMENT
MANUAL
MANUFACTURING
MAP
MARCH-ON-WASHINGTON-
MARGINAL
MARGINALITY
MARIETTA
MARITAL
MARITAL-STATUS
MARKET
MARKETPLACE
MARKETS
MARKOV
MARRIAGE
MARRIAGES
MARRIED
MARSHALL
MARTYRS
MARYLAND
MASSACHUSETTS
MATCHED
MATERIAL
MATERIALS
MATERNAL
MATERNITY
MATHEMATICIANS
MATHEMATICS
MATRIARCHY
MATRIX
MATURE
MAYOR
MCCONE
MCCONE-COMMISSION
MCCONE-REPORT
MDTA
MEANS
MEASUREMENT
MEASURES
MEASURING
MEAT-PACKING
MECHANICAL
MECHANICS
MECHANIZATION
MEDICAL
MEDICINE
MEETING
MEETINGS
MEMBERS
MEMBERSHIP
MEMORANDUM
MEMPHIS
MEN
MENOMINEE
MENTAL
MENTALITIES
MERCED-COUNTY
MERCHANDISE
MERCHANTS
MERIT
MERIT-EMPLOYMENT
MERITOCRACY
MERRILL-TRUST-FUND
MESQUAKIE
METHOD
METHODIST
METHODOLOGICAL
METHODOLOGY
METHODS
METROPOLIS
METROPOLITAN
MEXICAN
MEXICAN-AMERICAN
MEXICAN-AMERICANS
MEXICANS
MEXICO
MIAMI
MICHIGAN
MICHIGAN-S
MID-CENTURY
MID-CONTINENT
MID-SIXTIES
MIDCENTURY
MIDCONTINENT
MIDDLE
MIDDLE-CLASS
MIDDLESEX-COUNTY
MIDST
MIDWEST
MIGRANT
MIGRANT-LABOR
MIGRANT-LABOR--THE
MIGRANT-WORKER
MIGRANT-WORKERS
MIGRANTS
MIGRATION
MIGRATORY
MIGRATORY-LABOR
MILITANTS
MILITARY
MILWAUKEE
MINIMUM
MINNEAPOLIS
MINNESOTA
MINORITIES
MINORITY
MINORITY-GROUP
MINORITY-GROUPS
MINUTES
MIRANDA
MISSISSIPPI
MISSOURI
MISSOURI-BASIN
MIT
MIXED
MMPI
MOBILITY
MOBILIZATION
MOBILIZATION-FOR-YOU
MOBILIZING
MODEL
MODERN

MODIFICATION
MOHAWKS
MONEY
MONTANA
MONTGOMERY
MORALE
MORRIS
MORTALITY
MOTEL
MOTHER
MOTHER-S
MOTHERHOOD
MOTHERS
MOTIVATING
MOTIVATION
MOTIVATIONAL
MOTIVATIONS
MOTIVE
MOTOROLA
MOVEMENT
MOVEMENTS
MOYNIHAN
MOYNIHAN-REPORT
MULTIPLE
MULTIRACIAL
MUNICIPAL
MUNICIPAL-EMPLOYEES
MUSKEGON
MUTUAL
MYART
MYRDALIAN
MYTHS
NAACP
NARRAGANSETT
NASHVILLE
NATION
NATION-S
NATIONAL
NATIONAL-LABOR
NATIONAL-LABOR-RELAT
NATIONAL-SHARECROPPE
NATIONALITY
NATIONWIDE
NATIVITY
NATURALIZATION
NAVAHO
NAVAJO
NAVAJOES
NAVAJOS
NAVY
NEBRASKA
NECESSARY
NECESSITIES
NEED
NEEDED
NEEDLE
NEEDS
NEGLECTED
NEGRO
NEGRO-AMERICAN
NEGRO-AMERICANS
NEGRO-LABOR
NEGRO-OWNED
NEGRO-S
NEGRO-UNION
NEGRO-WHITE
NEGROES
NEIGHBOR
NEIGHBORHOOD
NEIGHBORHOOD-YOUTH-C
NEIGHBORHOODS
NEIGHBORS
NET
NETWORKS
NEVADA
NEW-ENGLAND
NEW-HAVEN
NEW-HAVEN-S
NEW-JERSEY
NEW-MEXICO
NEW-ORLEANS
NEW-ROCHELLE
NEW-YORK
NEW-YORK-CITY
NEW-YORK-S
NEW-YORKEW-YORK
NEWARK
NEWCOMER
NEWCOMERS
NEWS
NEWSPAPERS
NILES
NJ
NLRA
NLRB
NLRB-FEPC
NON-CAREER
NON-DISCRIMINATION
NON-ENGLISH
NON-FARM
NON-FRENCH
NON-INDIAN
NON-INTELLECTUAL
NON-PRACTITIONERS
NON-PROFESSIONAL
NON-SEGREGATION
NON-VERBAL
NON-WHITE
NON-WHITES
NONDISCRIMINATION
NONFARM
NONFEDERAL
NONMETROPOLITAN
NONTRADITIONALLY
NONWHITE
NONWHITE-WHITE
NONWHITES
NORFOLK
NORTH
NORTH-CAROLINA
NORTH-CENTRAL
NORTH-DAKOTA
NORTH-SOUTH
NORTHEAST
NORTHEASTERN
NORTHERN
NORTHERN-CHEYENNE
NORTHWEST
NOTE
NOTES

NOTICE
NSA-S
NULLIFICATION
NUMBER
NURSE
NURSES
NURSING
NURSING-S
NURSING-STUDENTS
NY
OAK
OAKLAND
OBJECTIVE
OBJECTIVES
OBLIGATIONS
OBSERVATIONS
OBSTACLES
OCCUPATION
OCCUPATION-PATTERNS
OCCUPATIONAL
OCCUPATIONAL-CHOICES
OCCUPATIONAL-DISTRIB
OCCUPATIONAL-MOBILIT
OCCUPATIONAL-PATTERN
OCCUPATIONAL-STATUS
OCCUPATIONAL-STRATIF
OCCUPATIONAL-STRUCTU
OCCUPATIONS
OFF-RESERVATION
OFFENDER
OFFICE
OFFICER
OFFICES
OFFICIAL
OFFICIALS
OHIO
OKLAHOMA
OKLAHOMA-CITY
OKTIBBEHA
OLD-TIMERS
OLDER
ON-JOB-TRAINING
ON-THE-JOB
OPEN-SHOP
OPENING
OPENINGS
OPERATION
OPERATIONS
OPERATOR
OPERATORS
OPINION
OPINIONS
OPPORTUNITIES
OPPORTUNITIES-INDUST
OPPORTUNITY
OPPORTUNTIES
ORDER
ORDERS
ORDINANCES
OREGON
ORGANIZATION
ORGANIZATIONAL
ORGANIZATIONS
ORGANIZE
ORGANIZED
ORGANIZING
ORIENTAL
ORIENTATION
ORIENTATIONS
ORIENTED
ORIGIN
ORIGINS
OURAY
OUT-OF-SCHOOL
OUTLAWING
OUTLAWS
OUTLOOK
OUTREACH
OVERVIEW
OWNERS
OWNERSHIP
OWYHEE
PACKINGHOUSE
PACT
PAIRED
PALOUSE
PANEL
PAPAGO
PAPER
PAPERS
PARADOX
PARENTAGE
PARENTAL
PARENTS
PARLEY
PARLIAMENTARY
PAROLE
PART-TIME
PARTIAL
PARTICIPANT
PARTICIPANTS
PARTICIPATION
PARTNERSHIP
PASADENA
PAST
PATIENT
PATRON-PEON
PATRONAGE
PATTERN
PATTERNING
PATTERNS
PAY
PAYS
PENINSULA
PENNSYLVANIA
PEONAGE
PERCEIVED
PERCENT
PERCENTAGE
PERCEPTION
PERCEPTIONS
PERFORM
PERFORMANCE
PERFORMING-ARTS
PERKINS
PERPETUATION
PERSISTENCE
PERSISTENT
PERSISTING
PERSONAL

PERSONALITY
PERSONNEL
PERSONS
PERSPECTIVE
PERSPECTIVES
PERSUADER
PERTH-AMBOY
PETROLEUM
PHD
PHENOMENON
PHILADELPHIA
PHILADELPHIA-S
PHILADELPHIANS
PHOENIX
PHYSICIAN
PHYSICIANS
PICKETING
PIEDMONT
PILOT
PITTSBURGH
PLACE
PLACEMENT
PLACEMENTS
PLACES
PLACING
PLAINS
PLAN
PLAN-FOR-PROGRESS
PLANNED
PLANNING
PLANS
PLANS-FOR-PROGRESS
PLANT
PLANTATION
PLANTATIONS
PLANTS
PLATFORM
PLIGHT
PLUMBERS
PLUMBING
PLURALISM
POCAHONTAS
POLEMIC
POLICE
POLICEMAN
POLICEMEN
POLICIES
POLICY
POLICY-MAKING
POLICY-RECOMMENDATIO
POLITICAL
POLITICS
POOR
POPULATION
POPULATIONS
PORTENT
PORTENTS
PORTERS
POSITION
POSITIONS
POSITIVE
POST
POST-HIGH
POST-PARENTAL
POST-WAR
POSTAL
POSTGRADUATE
POSTMASTER
POSTS
POSTWAR
POTAWATOMIE
POTENTIAL
POTENTIALITIES
POTENTIALS
POVERTY
POVERTY-DEPENDENCY
POWER
POWERLESSNESS
POWERS
PRACTICE
PRACTICES
PRACTITIONERS
PRE-COLLEGE
PRE-EMPLOYMENT
PRE-WHITE-HOUSE
PREDICTING
PREDICTION
PREDICTIONS
PREDICTOR
PREDICTORS
PREFERENCE
PREFERENCES
PREFERENTIAL-HIRING
PREFERENTIAL-TREATME
PREJUDICE
PRELIMINARY
PREPARATION
PREPARE
PREPARING
PRESCRIPTION
PRESIDENT
PRESIDENT-S
PRESIDENT-S-COMMITTE
PRESIDENTIAL
PRESIDENTS
PRESS
PRESSURE
PRESSURES
PRESTIGE
PREVENTION
PRICE
PRINCETON-MANPOWER-S
PRINCETON-S
PRINCIPAL
PRINCIPALS
PRINCIPLE
PRINCIPLES
PRISON
PRISON-ADMISSIONS
PRIVACY
PRIVATE
PRIVATE-HOUSEHOLD
PRIVILEGES
PROCEDURE
PROCEDURES
PROCEEDINGS
PROCESS
PROCESSES
PROCESSING
PROCLAMATION

PROCUREMENT
PRODUCTION
PRODUCTIONS
PRODUCTIVE
PRODUCTIVITY
PROFESSION
PROFESSIONAL
PROFESSIONALISM
PROFESSIONALLY
PROFESSIONS
PROFESSORS
PROFILE
PROFILES
PROGRAM
PROGRAMMERS
PROGRAMMES
PROGRAMS
PROGRESS
PROGRESS-REPORT
PROHIBIT
PROHIBITED
PROHIBITING
PROJECT
PROJECTED
PROJECTIONS
PROJECTS
PROMOTABILITY
PROMOTE
PROMOTING
PROMOTION
PROMOTIONS
PROPOSAL
PROPOSALS
PROPOSITIONS
PROSPECT
PROSPECTIVE
PROSPECTS
PROSPECTUS
PROSPERITY
PROSPEROUS
PROTECTING
PROTECTION
PROTECTIVE
PROTEST
PROVIDENCE
PROVISIONS
PSYCHIATRIC
PSYCHOLOGICAL
PSYCHOLOGIST
PSYCHOLOGISTS
PSYCHOLOGY
PSYCHOTHERAPISTS
PUBLIC
PUBLIC-EMPLOYMENT
PUBLIC-SERVICE
PUEBLO
PUERTO-RICAN
PUERTO-RICANS
PUERTO-RICO
PURDUE
PUSH-BUTTON
QED
QUALIFICATIONS
QUALIFIED
QUALITY
QUANTIFIED
QUANTITATIVE
QUEENS
QUERIES
QUESTIONING
QUESTIONNAIRE
QUESTIONS
QUOTAS
RACE
RACE-RELATIONS
RACES
RACIAL
RACIAL-RELATIONS
RACIALLY
RACISM
RADCLIFFE
RAILROAD
RAILROADS
RAILWAY
RAISING
RANK
RATE
RATES
RATIOS
RE-EVALUATION
RE-EXAMINED
RE-SURVEY
REACTION
REACTIONS
READER
READINGS
READJUSTMENTS
REALITIES
REALITY
REALIZING
REAPER
REAPPRAISAL
REAPPRAISED
REARING
REASONS
REBUILDING
RECESSION
RECIPIENTS
RECOMMENDATIONS
RECONCILIATION
RECONVERSION
RECORD
RECORDS
RECRUIT
RECRUITING
RECRUITMENT
REDEVELOPMENT
REDISTRIBUTION
REDRESS
REDUCE
REDUCTION
REEXAMINATION
REFERENCE
REFERENCES
REFERRAL
REFINING
REFORM
REFORMER-S
REGION
REGIONAL

REGIONS
REGISTRIES
REGRESSION
REGULATION
REGULATIONS
REHABILITATION
REJECTION
REJECTS
RELATED
RELATION
RELATIONS
RELATIONSHIP
RELATIONSHIPS
RELIABLE
RELIEF
RELIGION
RELIGIOUS
RELOCATED
RELOCATEES
RELOCATION
RELUCTANT
REMARKS
REMEDIES
REPLACEMENT
REPORT
REPORTING
REPORTS
REPRESENTATION
REPRINT
REQUIREMENTS
RESEARCH
RESERVATION
RESERVATIONS
RESIDENCE
RESIDENT
RESIDENTIAL
RESIDENTIAL-SEGREGAT
RESIDENTS
RESISTANCE
RESOLUTION
RESOURCE
RESOURCES
RESPONSE
RESPONSES
RESPONSIBILITIES
RESPONSIBILITY
RESTAURANT
RESTRAINTS
RESURVEY
RETAIL
RETAILING
RETARDATION
RETENTION
RETIREMENT
RETRAINING
RETREATISM
RETURNING
REVEALED
REVENUE
REVIEW
REVIEWS
REVOLT
REVOLUTION
REVOLUTIONS
RHODE-ISLAND
RIGHT
RIGHT-TO-WORK
RIGHT-TO-WORK-LAWS
RIGHTS
RIO-GRANDE
RIOT
RIOTS
ROCHESTER
ROCKY-BAY-S
ROCKY-MOUNTAIN
ROLE
ROLES
ROOTS
ROSEBUD
RUBBER
RULES
RULINGS
RURAL
RURAL-FARM
RURAL-URBAN
RUTGERS
SABBATH
SAFETY
SALARIED
SALARIES
SALARY
SALES
SALESMEN
SAL TONSTALL
SAMPLE
SAMPLES
SAN-ANTONIO
SAN-CARLOS
SAN-DIEGO
SAN-DIEGO-S
SAN-FRANCISCO
SAN-JUAN
SAN-MATEO
SANCTIONS
SANTA-CLARA
SATISFACTION
SATISFACTIONS
SAVANNAH
SAVINGS
SCHOLAR
SCHOLARS
SCHOLASTIC
SCHOOL
SCHOOL-DESEGREGATION
SCHOOL-DISTRICT
SCHOOL-S
SCHOOLING
SCHOOLS
SCIENCE
SCIENCES
SCIENTIFIC
SCIENTISTS
SEABOARD
SEARCH
SEARCHING
SEASONAL
SEATTLE
SEC
SECONDARY
SECRETARIAL

SECRETARIAL-STENOGRA
SECRETARY
SECRETARY-S
SECTARIANISM
SECURITY
SEGREGATED
SEGREGATION
SEGREGATIVE
SELECTING
SELECTION
SELECTIVE
SELECTIVITY
SELF-ANALYSIS
SELF-HELP
SELF-IDENTIFICATION
SELF-IMPOSED
SELF-SUPPORTING
SELF-SURVEY
SELLING
SEMINAR
SEMINARS
SEMINOLE
SEMINOLES
SENATE
SENIOR
SENIORITY
SENIORS
SEPARATISM
SERIES
SERVANT
SERVICE
SERVICEMAN
SERVICEMEN
SERVICES
SERVICING
SES
SEX
SEX-ROLE
SEXES
SHARECROPPERS
SHIFT
SHIFTS
SHIPBUILDING
SHOP
SHOPPING
SHOPS
SHORTAGE
SHORTAGES
SIMULATION
SINGLE
SIOUX
SITUATION
SITUATIONAL
SIZE
SKILL
SKILLED
SKILLED-TRADES
SKILLED-WORKERS
SKILLS
SKILLS-BANK
SKIRT
SLOGAN
SLUM
SLUMS
SMALL
SOCIAL
SOCIAL-CHANGE
SOCIAL-CLASS
SOCIAL-CLASSES
SOCIAL-DEPENDENCY
SOCIAL-MOBILITY
SOCIAL-PSYCHOLOGICAL
SOCIAL-ROLES
SOCIAL-SECURITY
SOCIAL-STATUS
SOCIAL-STRATIFICATIO
SOCIAL-STRUCTURE
SOCIAL-WELFARE
SOCIALIZATION
SOCIETY
SOCIO-CULTURAL
SOCIO-ECONOMIC
SOCIOECONOMIC
SOCIOLOGICAL
SOCIOLOGY
SOLDIER
SOLUTION
SOLUTIONS
SOLVING
SOURCE
SOURCES
SOUTH
SOUTH-CAROLINA
SOUTH-S
SOUTHEAST
SOUTHEASTERN
SOUTHERN
SOUTHWEST
SOUTHWESTERN
SPANIARD
SPANISH
SPANISH-AMERICAN
SPANISH-AMERICANS
SPANISH-NAME
SPANISH-SPEAKING
SPANISH-SURNAME
SPEAKING
SPECIAL
SPECIAL-TRAINING-UNI
SPECIFICATIONS
SPEECH
SPOKANE
SPONSORSHIP
ST-LOUIS
ST-PAUL
ST-PETERSBURG
STABILITY
STABILIZATION
STAFF
STANDARD
STANDARDS
STANDING-ROCK
STATE
STATE-COMMISSION-AGA
STATE-EMPLOYMENT-SER
STATE-PERSONNEL-BOAR
STATE-S
STATEMENT
STATEMENTS
STATEN-ISLAND

STATES	THEORETICAL	VERIFIED
STATEWIDE	THEORIES	VERTICAL
STATISTICAL	THEORY	VETERAN
STATISTICS	THREAT	VETERANS
STATUS	THRUWAY	VETERANS-ADMINISTRAT
STATUS-SYSTEM	TIME	VIEW
STATUTES	TITLE-VII	VIEWPOINT
STATUTORY	TOBACCO	VIEWS
STEEL	TOKENISM	VIOLENCE
STEELWORKERS	TOLERANCE	VIRGINIA
STEREOTYPIC	TOOL	VISIBILITY
STOCKBRIDGE	TOOLS	VISIBLE
STORE	TOP-MANAGEMENT	VOCATIONAL
STORES	TOTAL	VOCATIONAL-TECHNICAL
STORY	TOWN	VOCATIONAL-TRAINING
STRAINS	TRADE	VOCATIONS
STRANGERS	TRADES	VOLUNTARY
STRATEGIC	TRADITION	WAGE
STRATEGIES	TRAIN	WAGE-EARNER
STRATEGY	TRAINED	WAGES
STRATIFICATION	TRAINEES	WAR
STREAM	TRAINING	WAR-AGAINST-POVERTY
STREAMS	TRAINS	WAR-ON-POVERTY
STRIKE	TRAITS	WAR-TIME
STRUCTURAL	TRANSCRIPT	WARDS
STRUCTURE	TRANSCULTURATION	WARREN
STRUCTURES	TRANSFORMATION	WARTIME
STRUGGLE	TRANSIENT	WASHINGTON
STUDENT	TRANSITION	WASHINGTON-DC
STUDENTS	TRANSPORTATION	WASTE
STUDIES	TREATMENT	WASTED
STUDY	TREND	WATTS
STUDY-SKILLS	TRENDS	WDL
STYLE	TRI-ETHNIC	WEALTH
STYLES	TRIAL	WEAPON
SUB-COMMITTEE	TRIALS	WEAPONS
SUB-CONTRACTS	TRIBAL	WEIGHT
SUB-EMPLOYMENT	TRIBE	WELFARE
SUBCOMMITTEE	TRIBES	WEST
SUBCONTRACTORS	TROY	WEST-VIRGINIA
SUBCONTRACTS	TRUST	WESTCHESTER
SUBORDINATION	TRUTH	WESTERN
SUBPROFESSIONAL	TUITION-AND-FEE	WESTERN-ELECTRIC
SUBURB	TULSA	WESTERNERS
SUBURBAN	TURNOVER	WHITE
SUBURBIA	TUSKEGEE	WHITE-COLLAR
SUBURBS	TUSKEGEE-INSTITUTE	WHITE-HOUSE-CONFEREN
SUCCESS	TV	WHITE-NEGRO
SUCCESSION	TVA	WHITE-NON-WHITE
SUGAR	TWIN-CITIES	WHITE-NONWHITE
SUIT	TYPE	WHITES
SUITABILITY	TYPES	WICHITA
SUMMARY	TYPOLOGICAL	WIFE
SUMMATION	UAW	WIFE-S
SUPERSTITION	UAW-CIO-S	WIND-RIVER
SUPERVISING	UINTAH	WISCONSIN
SUPERVISION	UNCONSTITUTIONAL	WITCHCRAFT
SUPERVISOR	UNCONSTITUTIONALLY	WITHDRAWAL
SUPERVISORY	UNDER-ACHIEVEMENT	WIVES
SUPPLEMENT	UNDER-UTILIZATION	WOMAN
SUPPLEMENTAL	UNDERCLASS	WOMAN-S
SUPPLEMENTARY	UNDERDEVELOPED	WOMAN-WORK-ROLE
SUPPLY	UNDEREMPLOYMENT	WOMANHOOD
SUPPORT	UNDERGRADUATE	WOMANPOWER
SUPPORTIVE	UNDERPRIVILEGED	WOMEN
SUPREME-COURT	UNDERUTILIZATION	WOMEN-S
SURNAME	UNEARNED	WORK
SURPLUS	UNEDUCATED	WORK-FAMILY-CONFLICT
SURVEY	UNEMPLOYABILITY	WORK-FORCE
SURVEYS	UNEMPLOYABLE	WORK-PATTERN
SURVIVAL	UNEMPLOYABLES	WORK-RELATED
SURVIVE	UNEMPLOYED	WORK-SEEKERS
SURVIVORS	UNEMPLOYMENT	WORK-STUDY
SYMPOSIUM	UNEQUAL	WORK-WOMAN-ROLE
SYNDROME	UNFAIR	WORK-WOMEN-ROLE
SYRACUSE	UNINCORPORATED	WORKER
SYSTEM	UNION	WORKER-S
SYSTEMS	UNION-BUSTING	WORKERS
TABLES	UNION-S	WORKING
TABULATION	UNIONISM	WORKING-CLASS
TACTICS	UNIONISTS	WORKING-FORCE
TAFT-HARTLEY	UNIONIZATION	WORKING-MOTHERS
TAILORING	UNIONS	WORKING-WIFE
TALENT	UNITED	WORKMEN-S
TALENTED	UNITED-STATES	WORKSHOP
TALENTS	UNIVERSITIES	WORLD
TAMPA	UNIVERSITY	WORLD-S
TARGET	UNLAWFUL	WORLD-WAR
TASK	UNPUBLISHED	WORLD-WAR-II
TASKS	UNQUALIFIED	WORLD-WARS
TASTES	UNRECRUITABLE	WYOMING
TAXES	UNRELATED	YANKTON
TB	UNSELECTED	YEARBOOK
TEACHER	UNSKILLED	YMCA
TEACHER-S	UNTAPPED	YONKERS
TEACHERS	UNTESTABLES	YOUNG
TEACHING	UNUSED	YOUTH
TECHNICAL	UNWANTED	YOUTH-S
TECHNICIANS	UPDATING	YOUTHFUL
TECHNIQUE	UPGRADES	YOUTHS
TECHNIQUES	UPGRADING	
TECHNOLOGICAL	UPLIFT	
TECHNOLOGICAL-CHANGE	UPPER	
TECHNOLOGY	UPPER-LEVEL	
TEEN-AGE	URBAN	
TEENAGE	URBAN-LEAGUE	
TEENAGERS	URBAN-RENEWAL	
TELEPHONE	URBANISM	
TELEVISION	URBANIZATION	
TEMPORARY	URGED	
TENANT	US	
TENNESSEE	USA	
TENSION	USES	
TENSIONS	UTAH	
TENURE	UTE	
TERM	UTILITIES	
TERMINATION	UTILIZATION	
TEST	UTILIZING	
TESTIMONY	VACANCIES	
TESTING	VALID	
TESTS	VALIDATION	
TEXANS	VALIDITY	
TEXAS	VALUE	
TEXAS-S	VALUES	
TEXT	VARIABLE	
TEXTBOOK	VARIABLES	
TEXTILE	VARIATION	
TEXTS	VD	
THEME	VEGETABLE	
THEMES	VERBAL	

List of Suppressed Words

ABLE
ACCENT
ACCEPTED
ACCOMPANY
ACCOMPLISHMENTS
ACCURATE
ACQUIRING
ACROSS
ACTUAL
AD
ADAPTED
ADMINISTER
ADMINISTERED
ADMINISTERING
ADMIT
ADOPTED
ADVANCE
ADVICE
AFFAIRS
AFFECT
AFFECTED
AFFECTING
AFFECTS
AFIELD
AFTER
AGAINST
AHEAD
AIMS
ALL
ALTERNATIVE
ALTERNATIVES
AM
AMERICA
AMERICA-S
AMERICAN
AMID
AMONG
ANACHRONISM
ANATOMY
ANGELS
ANNIVERSARY
ANOTHER
ANSWERED
APPARENT
APPENDIX
APPLIED
APPROACHING
APPROPRIATE
APPROVED
APRIL
APRIL-MAY
ARE
ARGUING
ARMING
ARTHUR
ASCENT
ASKED
ASPECT
ASPECTS
ASSERTS
ASSOCIATED
ASSUMPTIONS
ASSURING
ATTACHED
ATTEMPTS
ATTEND
ATTRACTIVENESS
AUGUST
AUGUST-SEPTEMBER
AWARENESS
BACK
BACKS
BALL
BASED
BASIS
BE
BEACH
BECAUSE
BEFORE
BEHALF
BEHIND
BEING
ABOUT
ABROAD
BELIEVE
BELL
BENJAMIN
BEST
BETTER
BETWEEN
BEYOND
BIG
BILLION
BILLION-DOLLAR
BITE
BOTH
BREAK
BREAKING
BRICKS
BRIDGE
BRINGING
BRINGS
BROADENING
BROKEN
BROWN
BRUNT
BUCK
BUT
CALL
CALLS
CAN
CAN-T
CARRIED
CARRYING
CAT
CATCH
CENTURY-OF
CERTAIN
CHANGEOVER
CHARLIE
CHIEF
CHOOSES
CIRCLE
CLIMATE
CLIMBING
CLOSE
CLOSED
CLOSER
CLOSET
CLOSING

COAT
COMBAT
COME
COMES
COMING
COMMON
COMPLEMENT
COMPLETION
COMPLEX
CON
CONCERNING
CONDUCTED
CONFEDERATE
CONFIDENCE
CONFIRMATION
CONFRONTS
CONSIDERATIONS
CONSTRUCTIVE
CONTINENT
CONTINUED
CONTINUITY
CONTRASTIVE
CONTROLLING
CONVOCATION
COORDINATING
COSPONSORED
COUNTING
COURTED
COUSIN
COVERING
CRACKS
CREATE
CREATIVE
CRUCIBLE
CRUMBLING
CRYSTAL
CURIOUS
CUTRIGHT
D
DANIEL
DARK
DAYS
DC
DEAL
DEALING
DEATH
DEC
DECADE
DECEMBER
DECISIVE
DECLINED
DEEP
DEEPENING
DEFIANCE
DEFICIENCIES
DEFINING
DEFINITION
DENIAL
DENIED
DESCRIPTIVE
DESIRE
DESIRES
DESPAIR
DESTINY
DICE
DID
DIFFERENCE
DIFFICULTIES
DIGNITY
DIRECT
DIRECTLY
DISAGREEMENT
DISAPPEARING
DISCOVERY
DISGRACE
DISGUISED
DO
DOES
DOING
DON-T
DONE
DOOR
DOORWAY
DOUBLE
DOWN
DRIFT
DU
DUAL
DUBIOUS
DURING
DYNAMITE
DYSFUNCTION
EACH
EARLY
EDITED
EDITION
EDITORIAL
EDMUND
EFFECTING
EFFECTIVE
EFFORT
EFFORTS
EIGHT
EIGHTEEN
ELBOW
ELEMENTS
ELEVEN
ELSEWHERE
EMERGENCE
EMERGENCY
EMERGING
EMPHASIS
ENACTED
ENCOURAGE
ENCOURAGING
ENDURING
ENHANCING
ENLIST
ENOUGH
EPISODE
EPOCH
ERA
EROSION
ESTABLISHED
ESTABLISHING
ETC
EVENING
EVERY
EVERYBODY
EVERYBODY-S

EVERYONE-S
EVOLVING
EXCEPTIONAL
EXERCISE
EXPLANATION
EXPLODING
EXTENDED
EXTENSION
EXTENT
EXTRAVAGANT
FACE
FACES
FACING
FAIL
FAILED
FAILS
FAKING
FANCY
FANTASY
FAR
FAREWELL
FATE
FEASIBILITY
FEATURES
FEBRUARY
FEEL
FEELS
FEW
FICTION
FIFTEEN
FIFTH
FIGURES
FINAL
FIND
FINDING
FIRE
FIRST
FIVE
FIVE-CITY
FIVE-STATE
FIVE-YEAR
FO
FOCI
FOCUS
FOES
FOLLOW
FOOT
FORBIDDEN
FOREGO
FORESIGHT
FORGOTTEN
FORM
FORMER
FORTH
FORTRESS
FORTY
FOUND
FOUR
FOURTEENTH
FOURTH
FRAME
FRAMEWORK
FREE
FRIENDS
FRONT
FULFILL
FULLER
FUNCTIONAL
FUNCTIONING
FUNCTIONS
FUND
FURNISHING
FUROR
FURTHER
FUTILITY
G
GARDEN
GATES
GEARS
GENERAL
GET
GETS
GETTING
GILDED
GIVEN
GIVING
GLEANED
GLEN
GLIMPSES
GO
GOES
GOING
GOOD
GOVERNING
GRANTED
GRANTING
GRAPHIC
GRASS
GREAT
GREATER
GREATEST
GREEN
GROUND
GROW
HABIT
HALL
HAND
HANDLE
HANDLED
HARD
HARDEST
HARMS
HAS
HAUNTS
HAVE
HAVEN-T
HEADS
HEART
HELD
HELP
HELPFUL
HELPING
HELPS
HER
HERE
HERE-S
HEREIN
HIGHLY
HIS
HITS

HOAX
HOC
HOLDS
HONORABLE
HOT
HOW
HR
HUNDRED
HURT
I
IGNORED
II
III
IMMODEST
IMPERATIVE
IMPORTANCE
IMPORTANT
IMPRESSIVE
IMPROPER
INC
INCIDENT
INCLUDES
INCLUDING
INCORPORATED
INDEPENDENT
INEFFECTIVE
INFORMAL
INITIAL
INITIATES
INITIATING
INITIATION
INSIDE
INTEGRAL
INTERMINGLED
INTERNAL
INTERRUPTION
INTO
INTRODUCING
INTRODUCTORY
INVERTED
INVISIBLE
INVOLVE
INVOLVED
INVOLVING
IRONIES
IS
ISI
ISLAND
ISSUED
IT
IT-S
ITEM
ITEMS
ITS
ITSELF
IV
JAN
JAN-JUNE
JAN-OCT
JANE
JANUARY
JANUARY-FEBRUARY
JIM
JOIN
JOINT
JORDAN
JUAN
JULY
JULY-AUGUST
JULY-DEC
JULY-DECEMBER
JUNE
KEEP
KEEPING
KIND
KNELL
KNITTING
KNOCK
KNOW
KNOWING
L
LA
LAC
LADDER
LADY
LAKE
LARGE
LARGER
LAST
LATE
LATER
LATEST
LEAD
LEAVES
LEAVING
LENCHER
LET-S
LIFELINE
LIFTS
LIGHT
LIKE
LINE
LITTLE
LIVELIHOOD
LONG
LONGER
LOOK
LOOKING
LOOKS
LOT
LOWEST
MADE
MAINLY
MAINSPRINGS
MAKE
MAKING
MANEUVER
MANNER
MANY
MARCH
MASS
MASSIVE
MASTER
MATTER
MATTERS
MAY
MEANING
MEANINGFULNESS
MEET
MET

MID-DECADE
MIGHT
MIND
MISSES
MIXED-UP
MOMENT
MONTH
MONTHLY
MONTHS
MORE
MOST
MOVE
MOVES
MOVING
MUCH
MUST
MY
NAME
NATURAL
NATURE
NEW
NEWEST
NEXT
NIGHT
NINE
NINTH
NO
NOBODY
NON
NOT
NOTEBOOK
NOTORIOUS
NOVEMBER
NOW
NOWHERE
OBSERVANCE
OBSERVER
OBTAIN
OBTAINING
OCTOBER
ODYSSEY
OFFERED
OLD
ON-GOING
ONE
ONE-THIRD
ONLY
OPEN
OPENED
OPERATED
OPERATES
OPERATING
OPPOSES
OPTIMAL
OPTIMISTIC
OR
ORALLY
ORBITS
ORDEAL
OTHER
OTHERS
OUR
OUT
OUTCOMES
OUTSIDE
OVER
OVERCOME
OVERCOMING
OWN
PACE
PAGES
PARNASSUS
PART
PARTICULAR
PARTS
PASS
PEOPLE
PEOPLES
PERMANENT
PERMITS
PERSON
PETTICOATS
PHASE
PHYSICAL
PICTORIAL
PILGRIMS
PIPES
PLAIN
PLAY
PLEA
PLEDGE
PLEDGED
PLEDGES
PLENTY
POINTS
PORTRAIT
POSE
POSSIBILITIES
POSSIBLE
POSSIBLY
PRACTICAL
PRACTICES-COMMISSION
PRAIRIES
PREDOMINANTLY
PRESENCE
PRESENT
PRESENTATION
PRESENTED
PREVAILING
PREVENT
PRIMARY
PRINCIPALSHIP
PRIZE
PRO
PROBLEM
PROBLEMS
PROFITABLE
PROMISE
PROMISING
PRONENESS
PROPER
PROPORTION
PROPOSED
PROVIDE
PROVIDES
PROVIDING
PROVING
PUBLICLY
PUBLISHED
PUEDE

PUNISHMENT
PURPOSE
PURSUIT
PUSH
PUT
PUTTING
PYRAMID
Q
QUARTER
QUEST
QUESTION
QUESTS
QUIET
R
RADIUS
RALLY
RANGE
RAPID
RATIONAL
RE
READ
READING
READY
REAFFIRMED
REAL
REAR
RECEIVING
RECENT
RECOGNITION
RECOGNIZING
RECOUNTING
REFLECTED
REFLECTIONS
REGARD
REGARDING
REGARDLESS
RELATE
RELATES
RELATING
RELATIONS-BOARD
RELATIVE
RELAXED
RELEASING
RELEVANCE
RELEVANT
REMAIN
REMOVING
RENDERED
REPLY
REPRESENT
REQUIRED
REQUIRES
RESORT
RESPECT
RESTATEMENT
RESTRICTED
RESULTING
RESUMPTION
RETROSPECT
RETURN
REVISED
REVISITED
REWARDING
RICH
RICHEST
RIDDLES
RISE
RISING
ROOF
ROOM
ROUND
RUSHES
RUSTLE
S
SAID
SATURDAY
SAVAGE
SAY
SCALE
SCANDAL
SCENE
SCOPE
SCORE
SE
SECOND
SECTION
SECTIONS
SECURE
SECURING
SEE
SEEK
SEEKER-S
SEEKERS
SEEKING
SEEMED
SEIZES
SELECTED
SELF
SELF-
SENSITIVITY
SENTIMENTAL
SEPARATE
SEPT
SEPTEMBER
SERVE
SERVED
SERVING
SESSION
SET
SETTING
SETTLEMENT
SETTLES
SEVEN
SEVENTH
SHALL
SHAME
SHARE
SHARPER
SHEET
SHEETS
SHORT
SHOULD
SHOW
SHOWING
SHOWS
SIDE
SIDES
SIGHT
SIGHTS
SIGNED

SIGNIFICANCE
SIGNIFICANT
SIGNING
SIGNS
SILENT
SIMILARITIES
SINCE
SIX
SIXTEEN
SIXTH-GRADE
SIXTIES
SIXTY
SKELETON
SKI
SKIRTS
SLEEPING
SLOW
SMALLER
SO
SOMETHING
SPACE
SPAN
SPEAKS
SPECIES
SPECIFIC
SPECIFIED
SPECTER
SPECULATIVE
SPIRIT
SPONSORED
SPOT
SPRING
SPRING-SUMMER
SPURS
SQUARE
SQUEEZE
STAGES
STAND
STANDING
START
STARTED
STARTS
STEM
STEP
STEPCHILD
STEPS
STIFF
STILL
STITCH
STOP
STOPS
STORM
STORMY
STRAW
STRENGTHENING
STRESSED
STRICTLY
STRIDES
STUDIED
STYMIES
SUBJECT
SUBMITTED
SUBSEQUENT
SUBSTANCE
SUCCEED
SUCCESSFULLY
SUGGESTED
SUGGESTIONS
SUMMER
SUN
SUPERFLUOUS
SUPERIOR
SUPPORTED
SUPREME
SWALLOWS
SWIFT
TABLE
TACKLED
TACKLES
TAKE
TAKEN
TAKES
TALE
TALES
TALK
TALKING
TAPPING
TELL
TEN
TENDENCIES
TENTH
TERMS
THAN
THAT
THAT-S
THEIR
THEM
THEMSELVES
THEN
THERE
THESAURUS
THESE
THEY
THINKING
THINKS
THIRD
THIRTEEN
THIS
THORNTONS
THOUGH
THOUSAND
THREE
THROUGH
TIDE
TIGHTENING
TIN
TODAY
TODAY-S
TODAYS
TOMORROW
TOMORROW-S
TOMS
TOO
TOP
TOUGH
TOWARD
TOWARDS
TRACKS
TRACTION
TRAGIC

TRAIL
TRAPPED
TREAD
TREATIES
TRICKLING
TRIP
TROUBLES
TROUBLESOME
TURNING
TWENTY
TWENTY-FIRST
TWENTY-SEVEN
TWO
TWO-FIFTHS
U
ULTIMATE
UN-MET
UNCOMMON
UNDER
UNDERLYING
UNDERSTANDING
UNDOING
UNFINISHED
UNIFIED
UNIQUE
UNIT
UNITS
UNLIMITED
UNPLEASANT
UNPREDICTABLE
UNTOLD
UP
UPHELD
UPON
USE
VALLEY
VANGUARD
VANISHING
VARIOUS
VERSION
VERSUS
VICIOUS
VICTORY
VIDA
VIEWED
VIGOROUS
VIS-A-VIS
VISITING
VISITS
VITAL
VIVA
VOICE
VOICES
VOL
VOLS
VOLUME
VS
WAIT
WALK
WALLS
WANT
WANTED
WANTON
WANTS
WARRIOR
WAS
WAVERING
WAY
WAYS
WE
WEEDS
WEEK
WELL
WHAT
WHAT-S
WHEN
WHERE
WHICH
WHO
WHO-S
WHOLE
WHY
WIDENS
WIDER
WILL
WIN
WING
WINNING
WIPE
WISHFUL
WITHIN
WITHOLD
WITHOUT
WORD
WORDS
WORKS
WORSENED
WRU
X
YEAR
YEAR-END
YEAR-S
YEARS
YOU
YOUR

Appendices

APPENDIX A

ABBREVIATIONS USED IN THE DART

AAPSS	American Academy of Political and Social Science
AAUW	American Association of University Women
ABC	A Better Chance
ACLU	American Civil Liberties Union
ACTION	Allegheny Council to Improve Our Neighborhood
ADC	Aid to Dependent Children
ADL	Anti-Defamation League
ADM	Administration
ADMV	Administrative
ADVANCE	Advancement
ADVSY	Advisory
AFDC	Aid to Families of Dependent Children
AFFAIR	Affairs
AFL	American Federation of Labor
AF of L	American Federation of Labor
AG	Agriculture (agricultural)
AGL	Agricultural
AGST	Against
ALA	Alabama
AM	American
ANTHRO	Anthropology
ANTI-DISCR	Anti-discrimination
AP	April
ASN	Association
ASSN	Association
ASSNS	Associations
ASSOC	Associated
AUG	August
AUTOM	Automation
BEHL	Behavioral
BKBNDRS	Bookbinders
BLS	Bureau of Labor Statistics
BNA	Bureau of National Affairs, Inc.
BRD	Board
BUILD	Building
BUR	Bureau
BUS	Business
BYU	Brigham Young University

CAL	California
CAP	Community Action Program
CATH	Catholic
CC	Council
CCS	Councils, Center for the Continuation of Study
CENT	Center
CFSOLEFA	Center for the Study of Liberal Education for Adults
CHI	Chicago
CIO	Congress of Industrial Organizations
CIVR	Civil Rights
COFO	Council of Federated Organizations
COLO	Colorado
COM	Community
COMM	Commission
COMMRS	Commissioner's
COMMS	Commissioner's
COMPL	Compliance
COMT	Committee
COND	Conditioning
CONF	Conference
CONN	Connecticut
CONT	Continuing
CONTG	Continuing
CONSER	Conservation
CONSTL	Constitutional
COOP	Cooperative
COPNG	Cooperating
CORE	Congress of Racial Equality
CORP	Corporation
CR	Civil Rights
CRS	Community Relations Service
CWBHMC	Culinary Workers, Bartenders, Hotel, Motel, Club
DC	District of Columbia
DEC	December
DEMO	Democratic
DEMTC	Democratic
DEPT	Department
DEVEL	Development
DISCR	Discrimination
DIST	District
DIV	Division

E	East
EC	Economic
ECA	East Central Area
ECS	Economics
ED	Education, Editor, Edited, Edition
EDD	Doctor of Education
EDL	Educational
EEO	Equal Employment Opportunity
EEOC	Equal Employment Opportunity Commission
EMP	Employment
EMPLOY	Employment
EMPS	Employees
ETHN	Ethnology
EXPRMT	Experiment
EXP	Experiment
FEB	February
FED	Federal (federation)
FEDN	Federation
FEP	Fair Employment Practice(s)
FEPC	Fair Employment Practice(s) Commission
FF	Following
FNDTS	Foundations
FRAN	Francisco
FRC	Friendly Relations Committee
FT	For The
GOVR	Governor
GOVRS	Governor's, Governors
GOVT	Government
GPO	Government Printing Office
GRAD	Graduate
HARYOU-ACT	Harlem Youth Opportunities Unlimited - Associated Community Teams
HED	Higher Education
HOSP	Hospital
HR	Human Resources
HRC	Human Relations Commission
HRCME	Hotel, Restaurant, Cafeteria and Motel Employees
HUM	Human

IDEPTL	Interdepartmental
ILGWU	International Ladies Garment Workers Union
ILIR	Institute of Labor and Industrial Relations
ILL	Illinois
ILR	Industrial and Labor Relations
INC	Incorporated
IND	Industrial
INDIZATION	Industrialization
INDPT	Independent
INFO	Information
INST	Institute, Institutional
INSTN	Institution
INSTS	Institutions
INTERNATL	International
INTER-U	Inter-University
IR	Industrial Relations
I-R	Inter-Racial
IRSS	Institute for Research in Social Science
ISR	Institute of Social Research
IUD	Industrial Union Department
JAN	January
JTSAM	Jewish Theological Seminary of America
KAN	Kansas
KY	Kentucky
LA	Los Angeles
LAB	Labor
LABOR-MANAGE	Labor-Management
LAT-AM	Latin-American
LEAG	League
LEGV	Legislative
LRS	Legislative Reference Service
MA	Master of Arts
MAR	March
MD	Maryland
MDTA	Manpower Development and Training Act
METROP	Metropolitan
MEXICAN-AM	Mexican American
MICH	Michigan
MICH-WAYNE	Michigan-Wayne

MID	Middle
MIG	Migrant
MINN	Minnesota
MISS	Mississippi
MIT	Massachusetts Institute of Technology
MMPI	Minnesota Multi-Phasic Personality Inventory
MNFG	Manufacturing
MNGMT	Management
MOD	Modern
MS	Master of Science
MUNICIP	Municipalities
N	North
NAACP	National Association for the Advancement of Colored People
NAIRO	National Association of Intergroup Relations Officials
NAM	National Association of Manufacturers
NATL	National
NAWDC	National Association of Women Deans and Counselors
NBEACH	North Beach
NC	North Carolina
ND	No Date
NBRHOOD	Neighborhood
NJ	New Jersey
NLRB	National Labor Relations Board
NO	Number
NOV	November
NY	New York
NYC	New York City
NYS	New York State
NYU	New York University
OCT	October
OECD	Organisation for Economic Cooperation and Development
OEO	Office of Economic Opportunity
OETR	On Education, Training, and Research
OPPOR	Opportunity
OPPORS	Opportunities
P	Page
PA	Pennsylvania
PFP	Plans for Progress
PHD	Doctor of Philosophy

PHMED	Physical Medicine
PITT	Pittsburgh
PO	Post Office
POL	Policy, policies
PP	Pages
PR	Public Relations
PRES	President, President's
PRESL	Presidential
PRES-S	President's
PRGR	Progress
PROBS	Problems
PROF	Prefessional
PROG	Program
PROGR	Progress
PROJ	Project
PRTO	Puerto
PUB	Public
QED	Quod Erat Demonstrandum (Latin, which was to be demonstrated)
R-AND-D	Research and Development
RAR	Records and Research
REFRIG	Refrigeration
REHAB	Rehabilitation
RELIG	Religious
RELS	Relations
RES	Research
RIGHT	Rights
RLOCAT	Relocation
RLR	Rights, Liberties, and Responsibilities
RN	Registered Nurse
S	State
SAN FRAN	San Francisco
SANFRAN	San Francisco
SCH	School
SCI	Science
SECT	Section
SEPT	September
SERV	Service
SES	State Employment Service
SNCC	Student Non-Violent Coordinating Committee

SOC	Social
SOCT	Society
SPB	State Personnel Board
SPSSI	Society for the Psychological Study of Social Issues
SSC	Social Sciences
SSF	Scholarship Service and Fund
ST	Saint, Street
STE	State
STATS	Statistics
SUPT	Superintendent
SWESTERN	Southwestern
SYS	System
TECH	Technology
TRNG	Training
U	University
UAAW	United Auto Aerospace Workers
UAW	United Automobile Workers
UCLA	University of California at Los Angeles
UM	University of Michigan
UNEMP	Unemployed
UNEMPLOY	Unemployment
UNESCO	United Nations Educational, Scientific, and Cultural Organization
UNIV	University
UNLTD	Unlimited
UPR	University of Puerto Rico
US	United States
USC	Urban Studies Center
VOCAT	Vocational
VOCATL	Vocational
VOL	Volume
VS	Versus
WAITRESS	Waitresses
WASH	Washington
WDL	Worker's Defense League
WEST	Western
WIS	Wisconsin
WM	Ways and Means

WORK	Workers
WPA	Works Progress Administration
WRKRS	Workers
WRU	Western Reserve University
WS	Workers
YMCA	Young Men's Christian Association

APPENDIX B

COMMISSIONS OR OTHER AGENCIES ADMINISTERING

FAIR EMPLOYMENT PRACTICES ACTS*

State and local agencies which administer fair employment practices acts generally issue periodic employment surveys and reports in addition to their annual reports of agency activities. Annual reports of such agencies have not been included in this index; an attempt has been made, however, to index special reports and employment surveys as these were made available through agency cooperation. The following list of agencies is presented as an aid to those who may wish to seek further information.

STATE   LOCAL

ALASKA

    Anchorage

    Alaska Commission for Human Rights
    Reed Building, Room 24
    Anchorage, Alaska   99501

ARIZONA

    Phoenix   Phoenix

    Arizona Civil Rights Commission   Human Relations Commission
    1623 West Washington Street   332 West Washington Street
    Phoenix, Arizona   85007   Phoenix, Arizona   85003

                                                    Tucson

                                                  Commission on Human Relations
                                                  134 West Council Street
                                                  Tucson, Arizona   85701

* Compiled July 10, 1967, by the Equal Employment Opportunity Commission.

STATE	LOCAL

CALIFORNIA

San Francisco (Head)

California Fair Employment Practices
   Commission
455 Golden Gate Avenue
Post Office Box 603
San Francisco, California 94101

Berkeley

Human Relations and Welfare
   Commission
City Hall
Berkeley, California 94704

Los Angeles

Los Angeles County Commission on
   Human Relations
320 West Temple Street
Los Angeles, California 90012

Oakland

Alameda County Human Relations
   Commission
Alameda County Court House
1225 Fallon Street
Oakland, California 94512

Pasadena

Human Relations Commission
100 North Garfield Avenue
Pasadena, California 91101

Richmond

Human Relations Commission
City Hall
Richmond, California 94804

San Bernardino

Human Relations Commission
536 West Eleventh Street
San Bernardino, California 92405

STATE	LOCAL
CALIFORNIA	
	San Diego
	Citizens Interracial Committee of San Diego County, Inc.
	Room 609
	520 E Street
	San Diego, California 92101
	San Francisco
	Human Rights Commission of San Francisco
	1254 Market Street, Suite 305
	San Francisco, California 94102
	San Jose
	Human Relations Commission
	City Hall
	801 North First Street
	San Jose, California 95110
COLORADO	
Denver	Denver
Civil Rights Commission	Commission on Community Relations
306 State Services Building	206 West Side Annex Building
1525 Sherman Street	West Colfax at Kalamath
Denver, Colorado 80203	Denver, Colorado 80204
CONNECTICUT	
Hartford	Hartford
Connecticut Commission on Civil Rights	Commission on Human Rights
92 Farmington Avenue	550 Main Street
Hartford, Connecticut 06115	Hartford, Connecticut 06103
	New Haven
	Commission on Equal Opportunities
	147 Court Street
	New Haven, Connecticut 06510

CONNECTICUT

Stamford

Human Rights Commission
Town Hall, Atlantic Square
Stamford, Connecticut   06901

DELAWARE

Wilmington

Division Against Discrimination
Department of Labor and Industrial
    Relations
506 West Tenth Street
Wilmington, Delaware   19801

DISTRICT OF COLUMBIA

Commissioners' Council on Human
    Relations
Room 427, District Building
Washington, D. C.   20004

FLORIDA

Dade County (Miami)

Community Relations Board
1401-D Courthouse
Miami, Florida   33130

Tampa

Commission of Community Relations
Citizens' Building, Room 806
Tampa, Florida   33602

GEORGIA

Atlanta

Community Relations Commission
Atlanta, Georgia

HAWAII

Honolulu

Department of Labor and Industrial
   Relations
Enforcement Division
825 Mililani Street
Honolulu, Hawaii   96813

IDAHO

Boise

Department of Labor
Industrial Administration Building
317 Main Street
Boise, Idaho   83702

ILLINOIS

Chicago

Illinois Fair Employment Practices
   Commission
160 North La Salle Street
Chicago, Illinois   60601

Chicago

Commission on Human Relations
211 West Wacker Drive
Chicago, Illinois   60606

Evanston

Community Relations Committee
1806 Maple Avenue
Evanston, Illinois   60201

INDIANA

Indianapolis

Indiana Civil Rights Commission
1004 State Office Building
Indianapolis, Indiana   46204

East Chicago

Human Relations Commission
Room 16, City Hall
4525 Indianapolis Boulevard
East Chicago, Indiana   46312

Evansville

Mayor's Commission on Human
   Relations
City Hall
Evansville, Indiana   47708

STATE	LOCAL
INDIANA	
	<u>Fort Wayne</u>
	Mayor's Commission on Human Relations Room 306, City Hall 300 East Berry Street Fort Wayne, Indiana 46802
	<u>Gary</u>
	Human Relations Commission 401 Broadway, Room B1 Gary, Indiana 46402
	<u>Indianapolis</u>
	Commission on Human Relations City-County Building, Room 1742 Indianapolis, Indiana 46204
	<u>South Bend</u>
	Human Relations and Fair Employment Practices Commission 226 West Colfax Street South Bend, Indiana 46601
IOWA	
<u>Des Moines</u>	<u>Des Moines</u>
Civil Rights Commission State Capitol Building Des Moines, Iowa 50319	Commission on Human Rights and Discrimination Armory Building East First and Des Moines Streets Des Moines, Iowa 50309
	<u>Waterloo</u>
	Human Rights Commission City Hall Waterloo, Iowa 50704

STATE	LOCAL
KANSAS	
Topeka	Kansas City
Kansas Commission on Civil Rights State Office Building, Room 1155W Topeka, Kansas 66612	Human Relations Commission City Hall 805 North Sixth Street Kansas City, Kansas 66101
	Topeka
	Human Relations Commission City Building Topeka, Kansas 66601
	Wichita
	Human Relations Commission City Building Annex 104 South Main Wichita, Kansas 67202
KENTUCKY	
Frankfort	Lexington
Kentucky Commission on Human Rights 172 Capitol Annex Building Frankfort, Kentucky 40601	Commission on Human Rights City Hall Annex 227 North Upper Street Lexington, Kentucky 40507
Louisville	Louisville
Kentucky Commission on Human Rights 601 North Walnut Street Louisville, Kentucky 40202	Human Relations Commission 101 F Mayor's Suite, City Hall Louisville, Kentucky 40501
LOUISIANA	
Baton Rouge	
Commission on Human Relations, Rights, and Responsibilities Post Office Box 4095 Capitol Station Baton Rouge, Louisiana 70804	

<u>STATE</u>	<u>LOCAL</u>

MAINE

   <u>Augusta</u>

   Department of Labor and Industry
   State Office Building
   Augusta, Maine   04331

MARYLAND

<u>Baltimore</u>	<u>Baltimore</u>
Maryland Commission on Interracial Problems and Relations 301 West Preston Street Baltimore, Maryland 21201	Community Relations Commission 210 North Calvert Street Baltimore, Maryland 21202

MASSACHUSETTS

<u>Boston</u>	<u>Springfield</u>
Massachusetts Commission Against Discrimination 41 Tremont Street Boston, Massachusetts 02108	Office of Intergroup Relations Room 228, City Hall Springfield, Massachusetts 01101

MICHIGAN

<u>Detroit</u>	<u>Ann Arbor</u>
Michigan Civil Rights Commission 900 Cadillac Square Building Detroit, Michigan 48226	Human Relations Commission City Hall Ann Arbor, Michigan 48106
	<u>Detroit</u>
	Commission on Community Relations 1106 Water Board Building 735 Randolph Street Detroit, Michigan 48226
	<u>Flint</u>
	Human Relations Commission 1101 South Saginaw Street Flint, Michigan 48502

<u>STATE</u>	<u>LOCAL</u>

MICHIGAN

<u>Grand Rapids</u>

Human Relations Commission
City Hall Annex
303 Ionia Avenue, North
Grand Rapids, Michigan   49502

<u>Kalamazoo</u>

Community Relations Board
City Hall
Kalamazoo, Michigan   49003

<u>Lansing</u>

Human Relations Committee
Fourth Floor, City Hall
Lansing, Michigan   48933

<u>Saginaw</u>

Human Relations Commission
City Hall Annex
Saginaw, Michigan   48601

MINNESOTA

    <u>St. Paul</u>

Minnesota State Commission
   Against Discrimination
53 State Office Building
St. Paul, Minnesota   55101

<u>Minneapolis</u>

Fair Employment Practice
   Commission
250 South Fourth Street
Minneapolis, Minnesota   55401

<u>St. Paul</u>

Fair Employment Practices
   Commission
1745 City Hall
St. Paul, Minnesota   55102

MISSOURI

   Jefferson City

   Missouri Commission on Human
      Rights
   314 East High Street
   Box 1129
   Jefferson City, Missouri   65102

   Kansas City

   Commission on Human Relations
   Sixteenth Floor, City Hall
   Kansas City, Missouri   64106

   St. Louis

   Council on Human Relations
   Room 200
   Municipal Courts Building
   St. Louis, Missouri   63103

   University City

   Commission on Human Rights
   City Hall
   University City, Missouri   63130

MONTANA

   Helena

   Department of Labor and Industry
   418 Mitchell Building
   Helena, Montana   59601

NEBRASKA

   Lincoln

   Equal Employment Opportunity
      Commission
   State Capitol Building
   Lincoln, Nebraska   68509

   Omaha

   Human Relations Board
   Room 404, Interim City Hall
   Eighteenth and Dodge Streets
   Omaha, Nebraska   68102

NEVEDA

   Las Vegas

   Nevada Commission on Equal Rights
      of Citizens
   Nevada State Building
   215 Bonanza Road
   Las Vegas, Nevada   89101

<u>STATE</u>	<u>LOCAL</u>

NEW HAMPSHIRE

<u>Concord</u>

State Commission for Human Rights
State House
Concord, New Hampshire   03301

NEW JERSEY

<u>Trenton</u>

New Jersey Division on Civil Rights
Department of Law and Public Safety
52 West State Street
Trenton, New Jersey   08608

<u>Elizabeth</u>

Commission on Human Relations
316 Irvington Avenue
Elizabeth, New Jersey   07208

<u>Newark</u>

Human Rights Commission
Room 214, City Hall
Newark, New Jersey   07102

<u>Paterson</u>

Commission on Human Rights
City Hall Annex
Paterson, New Jersey   07505

<u>Plainfield</u>

Human Relations Commission
City Hall
Plainfield, New Jersey   07601

NEW MEXICO

<u>Santa Fe</u>

Fair Employment Practice Commission
137 East DeVargas Street
Santa Fe, New Mexico   87502

<u>Albuquerque</u>

Fair Employment Practices
   Commission
State Office Building
Fifth and Marquette
Albuquerque, New Mexico   87102

NEW YORK

New York City   Buffalo

New York State Commission for Human   Commission on Human Relations
   Rights   1502 City Hall
270 Broadway   Buffalo, New York   14201
New York, New York   10007

                                                 Elmira

                                                 Chemung County Commission on
                                                    Human Relations
                                                 Federation Building
                                                 Elmira, New York   14901

                                                 Hauppauge

                                                 Suffolk County Human Relations
                                                    Commission
                                                 Veterans Memorial Highway
                                                 Hauppauge, New York   11787

                                                 Mineola

                                                 Commission on Human Rights
                                                 County Executive Building
                                                 Room 214
                                                 One West Street
                                                 Mineola, New York   11501

                                                 Monroe County (Rochester)

                                                 Human Relations Commission
                                                 County Office Building, Suite 405
                                                 39 Main Street West
                                                 Rochester, New York   14614

                                                 Mount Vernon

                                                 Commission on Human Relations
                                                 City Hall, Room 105
                                                 Mount Vernon, New York   10551

STATE	LOCAL

STATE

LOCAL

NEW YORK

New Rochelle

Human Rights Commission
City Hall
New Rochelle, New York   10802

New York City

Commission on Human Rights
80 Lafayette Street
New York, New York   10013

Syracuse

Mayor's Commission on Human
  Rights
211 City Hall
Syracuse, New York   13202

Yonkers

Commission on Human Rights
Room 103, City Hall
Yonkers, New York   10701

NORTH CAROLINA

Raleigh

North Carolina Good Neighbor Council
Post Office Box 584
Raleigh, North Carolina   27602

Greensboro

Commission on Human Relations
338 North Elm Street, Room 219
Drawer W-2
Greensboro, North Carolina   27401

OHIO

Columbus

Ohio Civil Rights Commission
240 Parsons Avenue
Columbus, Ohio   43215

Canton

Fair Employment Practices
  Advisory Board
City Hall
200 Cleveland Avenue, S.W.
Canton, Ohio   44702

<u>STATE</u>	<u>LOCAL</u>

OHIO

<u>Cincinnati</u>

Human Relations Commission
Room 158, City Hall
Cincinnati, Ohio   45202

<u>Cleveland</u>

Community Relations Board
311 CTS Building
1404 East Ninth Street
Cleveland, Ohio   44114

<u>Columbus</u>

Community Relations Commission
City Hall
Columbus, Ohio   43216

<u>Dayton</u>

Human Relations Commission
11 West Monument Building
Dayton, Ohio   45202

<u>Toledo</u>

Board of Community Relations
565 Erie Street
Toledo, Ohio   43602

<u>Youngstown</u>

Mayor's Human Relations Commission
City Hall
Youngstown, Ohio   44501

OKLAHOMA

<u>Oklahoma City</u>

Oklahoma Human Rights Commission
Post Office Box 53004
Oklahoma City, Oklahoma   73105

<u>Oklahoma City</u>

Community Relations Commission
City Hall
331 West Main
Oklahoma City, Oklahoma   73102

STATE	LOCAL

STATE

OKLAHOMA

OREGON

Portland

Oregon Bureau of Labor
Civil Rights Division
1400 S. W. Fifth Avenue
Room 408, State Office Building
Portland, Oregon 97201

PENNSYLVANIA

Harrisburg

Pennsylvania Human Relations Commission
Department of Labor and Industry
1401 Labor and Industry Building
Harrisburg, Pennsylvania 17120

PUERTO RICO

Hato Rey

Department of Labor
414 Barbosa Avenue
Hato Rey, Puerto Rico 00919

LOCAL

Tulsa

Community Relations Commission
613 Kennedy Building
Tulsa, Oklahoma 74103

Erie

Human Relations Commission
508 Municipal Building
Erie, Pennsylvania 16501

Philadelphia

Commission on Human Relations
601 City Hall Annex
Philadelphia, Pennsylvania 19107

Pittsburgh

Commission on Human Relations
708 City-County Building
Pittsburgh, Pennsylvania 15219

STATE   LOCAL

RHODE ISLAND

   Providence   Providence

   Rhode Island Commission Against   Human Relations Commission
      Discrimination   87 Weybosset Street
   State House, Room 306   Rooms 320-321
   Providence, Rhode Island   02903   Providence, Rhode Island   02903

TENNESSEE

   Nashville

   Tennessee Commission on Human
      Relations
   C3-305 Cordell Hull Building
   Nashville, Tennessee   37219

UTAH

   Salt Lake City

   Utah Anti-Discrimination Division
   Industrial Commission
   State Capitol, Room 418
   Salt Lake City, Utah   84114

VERMONT

   Montpelier

   Department of Industrial Relations
   Montpelier, Vermont   05602

VIRGINIA

   Richmond (Private)

   Virginia Council on Human Relations
   178 Cary Street
   Richmond, Virginia   23219

STATE	LOCAL

WASHINGTON

Olympia

Washington State Board Against
   Discrimination
General Administration Building
Olympia, Washington 98501

Seattle

Seattle Human Rights Commission
305 Seattle Municipal Building
Seattle, Washington 98104

WEST VIRGINIA

Charleston

West Virginia Human Rights Commission
W-202 State Capitol Building
Charleston, West Virginia 25305

WISCONSIN

Milwaukee

Equal Opportunities Division
Wisconsin Industrial Commission
819 North Sixth Street
Milwaukee, Wisconsin 53203

Milwaukee

Commission on Community Relations
Room 701-K, City Hall
Milwaukee, Wisconsin 53201

APPENDIX C

ORGANIZATIONS CONCERNED WITH MINORITY GROUP EMPLOYMENT

The following selected list is presented as an aid to users who may wish to inquire directly about the availability of unpublished or limited circulation documents. It supplements information obtainable from bibliographical citations in cases where the latter are too incomplete for purposes of correspondence.

AFL-CIO
815 Sixteenth Street, N. W.
Washington, D. C.   20006

American Council on Education
1785 Massachusetts Avenue, N. W.
Washington, D. C.   20036

American Foundation on Automation and
    Employment, Inc.
280 Park Avenue
New York, New York   10017

American Friends Service Committee
169 North Fifteenth Street
Philadelphia, Pennsylvania   19102

American Jewish Committee
165 East Fifty-sixth Street
New York, New York   10022

American Jewish Congress
15 East Eighty-fourth Street
New York, New York   10028

Anti-Defamation League of B'nai B'rith
315 Lexington Avenue
New York, New York   10016

Bishop's Committee for Migrant Workers
1300 South Wabash Avenue
Chicago, Illinois   60605

Bishop's Committee for the Spanish
    Speaking
828 Fredericksburg Road
San Antonio, Texas   78201

Brookings Institution
1775 Massachusetts Avenue, N. W.
Washington, D. C.   20036

Bureau of National Affairs, Inc.
1231 Twenty-fourth Street, N. W.
Washington, D. C.   20037

California Advisory Commission on the
    Status of Women
Eleventh and L Building, Suite 1012
Sacramento, California   95814

Center for the Study of Democratic
    Institutions
Box 4068
Santa Barbara, California   93103

Chinese-American Citizens Alliance
1044 Stockton
San Francisco, California   94112

Committee for Economic Development
14 E and Constitution Avenue, N.W.
Washington, D. C.   20001

Conference on Economic Progress
1001 Connecticut Avenue, N.W.
Washington, D. C.   20036

Congress on Racial Equality
38 Park Row
New York, New York   10038

Council on Social Work Education
345 East Forty-sixth Street
New York, New York   10017

Educational Testing Service
Rosedale Road
Princeton, New Jersey   08540

Ford Foundation
477 Madison Avenue
New York, New York   10022

Fund for the Republic
136 East Fifty-seventh Street
New York, New York   10022

Greenleigh Associates, Inc.
355 Lexington Avenue
New York, New York   10017

Harlem Youth Opportunities Unlimited, Inc
2092 Seventh Avenue
New York, New York   10027

HARYOU-ACT, Inc.
2092 Seventh Avenue
New York, New York   10027

Information Retrieval System on the
   Disadvantaged
Yeshiva University
55 Fifth Avenue
New York, New York   10003

Jewish Labor Committee
25 East Seventy-eighth Street
New York, New York   10021

Jewish Vacation Association
31 Union Square West
New York, New York   10003

League for Industrial Democracy
112 East Nineteenth Street
New York, New York   10003

League of Women Voters of the
   United States
1026 Seventeenth Street, N.W.
Washington, D. C.   20006

Mobilization for Youth, Inc.
214 East Second Street
New York, New York   10009

National Association for the Advancement
   of Colored People
20 West Fortieth Street
New York, New York   10018

National Association of Intergroup
   Relations Officials
2027 Massachusetts Avenue, N.W.
Washington, D. C.   20036

National Association of Manufacturers
277 Park Avenue
New York, New York   10017

National Bureau of Economic
    Research, Inc.
261 Madison Avenue
New York, New York   10023

National Committee for Children
    and Youth
1145 Nineteenth Street, N. W.
Washington, D. C.   20036

National Committee on the Employment
    of Youth
145 East Thirty-second and Lexington
New York, New York   10016

National Community Relations Advisory
    Council
55 West Forty-second Street
New York, New York   10036

National Conference of Christians and
    Jews
43 West Fifty-seventh Street
New York, New York   10019

National Council for the Spanish-Speaking
San Antonio Project
5511 San Pedro
San Antonio, Texas   49373

National Education Association
1201 Sixteenth Street, N. W.
Washington, D. C.   20036

National Industrial Conference Board
845 Third Avenue
New York, New York   10022

National Labor Service
165 East Fifty-sixth Street
New York, New York   10022

National Opinion Research Center
6030 South Ellis Avenue
Chicago, Illinois   60637

National Planning Association
1424 Sixteenth Street, N. W.
Washington, D. C.   20036

National Scholarship Service and Fund
    for Negro Students
Six East Eighty-second Street
New York, New York   10028

National Sharecroppers Fund
112 East Nineteenth Street
New York, New York   10003

National Urban League
55 East Fifty-second Street
New York, New York   10022

Negro American Labor Council
217 West 125th Street
New York, New York   10027

Organisation for Economic Cooperation
    and Development
1750 Pennsylvania Avenue, N. W.
Washington, D. C.   20006

Population Reference Bureau
1755 Massachusetts Avenue, N.W.
Washington, D. C.   20036

Potomac Institute, Inc.
1501 Eighteenth Street, N.W.
Washington, D. C.   20036

Public Personnel Association
1313 East Sixtieth Street
Chicago, Illinois   60637

A. Philip Randolph Institute
217 West 125th Street
New York, New York   10027

Scientific Information Exchange
Smithsonian Institution
Washington, D. C.   20006

Southern Regional Council
Five Forsyth Street, N.W.
Atlanta, Georgia   30303

Taconic Foundation, Inc.
666 Fifth Avenue
New York, New York   10019

Twentieth Century Fund
41 East Seventieth Street
New York, New York   10024

United Nations Educational, Scientific
  and Cultural Organization
New York, New York   10017

U.S. Chamber of Commerce
1615 H Street, N.W.
Washington, D. C.   20006

U.S. Civil Service Commission
1900 E Street, N.W.
Washington, D. C.   20415

U.S. Commission on Civil Rights
801 Nineteenth Street, N.W.
Washington, D. C.   20425

U.S. Conference of Mayors
1707 H Street, N.W.
Washington, D. C.   20006

U.S. Department of Agriculture
Washington, D. C.   20250

U.S. Department of Commerce
Fourteenth and Constitution Avenue
Washington, D. C.   20230

U.S. Department of Health, Education,
  and Welfare
330 Independence Avenue, S. W.
Washington, D. C.   20003

U.S. Department of the Interior
Bureau of Indian Affairs
Washington, D. C.   20242

U.S. Department of Labor
Fourteenth and Constitution Avenue
Washington, D. C.   20210

University of Puerto Rico
Social Service Research Center
Rio Piedras, Puerto Rico   00923

W. E. Upjohn Institute for Employment
  Research
300 South Westhedge Avenue
Kalamazoo, Michigan   49007

W. E. Upjohn Institute for Employment
    Research
1101 Seventeenth Street, N.W.
Washington, D. C.   20036

Washington Center for Metropolitan
    Studies
1717 Massachusetts Avenue, N.W.
Washington, D. C.   20036

Workers Defense League
112 East Nineteenth Street
New York, New York   10003